VOLUME

ONE

The Heritage

of

VOLUME

ONE

GINN · AND · COMPANY

American Literature

Edited by

LYON N. RICHARDSON
Professor of English, Western Reserve University

GEORGE H. ORIANS
Professor of English, University of Toledo

HERBERT R. BROWN
Professor of English, Bowdoin College

BOSTON · NEW YORK · CHICAGO · ATLANTA · DALLAS · COLUMBUS · SAN FRANCISCO · TORONTO · LONDON

Preface

In the preparation of this anthology we have in no way considered that our function should supplant that of the teacher. We have chiefly endeavored to supply the best possible selections representative of the literary works of writers in the United States from the earliest days to the present. In doing this, we have consistently sought to reproduce the best texts, and in each case we have stated the specific text used. The guiding principle has been to reproduce complete works, and we have sought to avoid snippets; but on occasions it has seemed wise to choose sections from longer works of fiction, poetry, and didactic pieces when the passages represented the authors at their best and were substantially complete units.

We have tried to include a liberal number of selections from works of major authors which represent special literary qualities and characteristic, abiding ideas. Whenever possible, we have included selections illustrating the various literary phases of important writers from early life to late maturity.

We have not been iconoclastic. We have not shunned reprinting basic works. But we have aimed to keep this material within reasonable bounds, and to include a relatively high percentage of essays, poems, and fiction which mirror the national mind and give a fresh approach to the body of our literature. In this quest we have sought to represent the whole of the United States, not only in time but geographically, and also to include selections from some of the better but less popular writers, both of the past and of the present, whenever their work has seemed characteristic of some phase of our national life. We have also given special attention to a reconsideration of the works of our women authors.

Distinguished examples of literary criticism have been included for the several eras. In selecting these essays we have consistently sought to choose criticism pertaining to the authors represented in the anthology, to exhibit changing trends, and to draw chiefly from the critical studies of authors who themselves were poets or writers of fiction in their own right. We have deviated from this third rule only when important ideas in major movements were voiced best by persons who were critics rather than poets or novelists, as, for instance, Irving Babbitt and H. L. Mencken.

Our own editorial contributions, we trust, have been kept strictly within proper bounds, but we hope that we have not dodged any responsibility of service to teachers and students. The general introductions to the periods are short and do not encroach on the premises of teachers. The biographical sketches introduce the students to pertinent factors in the lives of the authors and point out certain qualities which readers may note while studying the selections. It has been our aim only to prepare students for the lectures or discussions of the classroom.

Considerable labor has gone into the headnotes accompanying most of the selections. In each of these we have tried to be specific and fully informative, and, wherever possible, to recreate the situation leading to the writing of the selection. It is our hope that classes will thus approach the selections with some enthusiasm and historical understanding.

We have indulged rather heavily in a chronological table and in bibliographical aids to students for the preparation of all sorts of special studies. The bibliographical selections were not casually made. Special bibliographies of some length accompany each biographical sketch, and the references include books and articles on matters both general and specific. For courses in American Civilization an annotated, general bibliography has been supplied, "American Life and Literature: Selected Readings in American Culture and Civilization," covering the fields of literature, history, economics, sociology, education, philosophy, religion, and the fine arts.

We trust that teachers may find in the selections ample latitude for the development of special interests. For the seventeenth century there are chronicles of history, travel, and adventure, as well as pictures of the Puritan world. The eighteenth century is represented by selections illustrating the religious and political ferment, the Revolution, early nationalism, and the rise of a national literature. The first seven decades of the nineteenth century are characterized by romanticism in the Middle States and the South, the romantic fulfillment in New England, and the crisis of the Civil War. Humor, folklore, and songs and ballads extend through the century. The literature of the later nineteenth century is rich in realistic delineations of life in the various regions of the nation, and it also presents contrasting pictures of life in America and Europe. Still more exciting, perhaps, is the literature of the twentieth century, with its renaissance of poetry, its changing fashions in wit and humor, its experiment in the theater, its divergent critical voices, its flowering of the humane tradition, and its floods of "realistic" writing turning to naturalism.

The editors desire to record their indebtedness to Professor DeLancey Ferguson. At the inception of the project he was Chairman of the Division of English and Chairman of the Graduate Committee on American Culture at Western Reserve University, and he gave his wide knowledge and discriminating judgment to the formation of policy. Although later, when he became Chairman of the Department of English of Brooklyn College, the pressure of professional duties compelled him to withdraw as an active editor, he generously permitted the present editors to draw upon certain of the preliminary sketches he had written, for which they are deeply grateful.

L. N. R.

G. H. O.

H. R. B.

Contents

The Seventeenth Century: The Colonial Record

INTRODUCTION · Page 2

CHRONICLES OF HISTORY, TRAVEL, AND ADVENTURE

THE PURITAN WORLD

The Eighteenth Century: Fashioning a National Culture

INTRODUCTION · Page 96

THE AMERICAN SCENE

THE REVOLUTION AND EARLY NATIONALISM

THE RISE OF A NATIONAL LITERATURE

INTRODUCTION · Page 346

THE ROMANTIC ERA IN THE MIDDLE STATES AND THE SOUTH

THE ROMANTIC FULFILLMENT AND THE CRISIS

The Heritage
of American Literature

VOLUME
ONE

INTRODUCTION

WHERE should an account of American literature begin—with New England, Texas, or Kansas? If adventure and exploration be the guide, the trail leads first to the manuscripts recounting the voyage of Eric the Red along the northeast coast of North America. It leads thence to Cabeza de Vaca's *Relación* (1542) of his explorations in Texas, New Mexico, and Arizona; it proceeds to the travels of De Soto from Florida to the Mississippi River, recounted by an unknown Portuguese, a "Gentleman of Elvas," and published in 1557; and it goes on to Coronado's march from Mexico to Kansas (1540–1542), set down by Pedro Casteñeda a score of years later, though not published until 1896.

After the Spaniards came the English, and London presses supplied glowing accounts of the New World. Thomas Hariot, the Oxford mathematician chosen by Sir Walter Raleigh to be the official narrator of his ill-fated expedition to Virginia, published in 1588 *A Briefe and True Report of the New Found Land of Virginia*, the most prized of Americana. John Smith, "Admirall of New England," in *A True Relation of Such Occurences and Accidents of Noate as Hath Hapned in Virginia Since the First Planting of That Collony* (1608), his *New Englands Trials* (1620), and *The Generall Historie of Virginia, New-England, and the Summer Isles* (1624) not only defended himself and

added romance to adventure but painted Virginia in detail as an earthly paradise and dwelt heavily on the excellence of New England as a land of economic opportunity. The Reverend Alexander Whitaker's *Good Newes from Virginia* (1613) carried on the optimistic story. John Hammond, returning to England after residing in the South for over twenty years, favored life in America above life in England in *Leah and Rachel, or the Two Fruitfull Sisters, Virginia and Maryland* (1656), and George Alsop, indentured servant, expressed similar views in *A Character of the Province of Maryland* (1666).

Narrators of early settlements in New England were also recording their experiences, and their views mixed physical hardship with religious fervor. Working with manuscript accounts by two Plymouth men (Governor William Bradford and Edward Winslow), George Morton in 1622 published in London *A Relation or Journall of the Beginning and Proceedings of the English Plantation Setled at Plimoth*; and Edward Johnson, in *A History of New England* (1654), asserted the success of the Massachusetts Bay colony to be directly due to God's hand and will.

During this period, too, the French were not idle. Soldier and explorer, Samuel de Champlain wrote of New England and Indians in *Les Voyages* (1613) and of New York State in later writings

(1627); and the "Jesuit Relations," a series of reports published in Paris between 1632 and 1673, contain minute accounts of life around the Great Lakes.

But it remains true that the Pilgrim and Puritan settlements, beginning in the third decade of the seventeenth century, supplied the largest heritage to early American literature. And this being so, American literature just missed being directly a part of the great movement known as the Renaissance. That significant age of learning and advancement came to flower in England during the reign of Queen Elizabeth. But by the time the main waves of colonization were beating upon our shores, the splendor of Elizabethan achievement was dimming somewhat, and in its place came the stormy controversies of the period of Charles I and Archbishop Laud. These disputes and arguments turned the purely classical efforts of former Cambridge scholars into long dissertations in the pattern of Ramus. Controversy begets controversy, and the atmosphere of English ecclesiasticism became more and more charged with unyielding conflict. The Puritans were out to reform, and because they could not reform the Established Church of England, they came to a land where a new and free beginning could be made. Their purpose was not, of course, the establishment of communities that should be asylums for all oppressed peoples, but rather communities of the elect, where their covenant with the Lord

could be lived up to. In the beginning these Puritans were merely Nonconformists, the Pilgrims being the first to break ties with the Anglican Church. By 1630 the proprietary period was closed. Massachusetts Bay was a corporate colony, the Puritan church was established, and soon every town had its independent congregation.

The writings of New Englanders in the seventeenth century were not extensive. This was not the result of any lack of intellectuality, but of the immense absorption of energy in the actual demands of planting colonies and making life bearable. As Samuel E. Morison pointed out, not Puritanism but provincialism was responsible for the limitation in literary output; and the four English groups in New England, Virginia, Bermuda, and Jamaica ranked precisely in this order in the volume and worth of literary product. Puritanism was a factor in only one of these New World colonies, and in that one, New England, there was greatest evidence of creative writing. Puritanism, instead of constituting a literary blight, was the actual cause of literary work.

Virginia was second to New England in productivity, but writers of the South were few in number. Conditions in Virginia during the seventeenth century did little to encourage literature. Settlers were busy developing plantations, settling grievances with Charles, stalemating overzealous royal governors, fighting rebellions among their leaders, and conducting border warfare with the Indians, not to mention combatting sickness and famine. They were not militantly engaged in a religious crusade. So their early writings in Virginia were scanty, and the subjects that engaged their pens were utilitarian. The few authors wrote because it seemed necessary to record and describe the experiences of the settlers for the benefit of prospective residents and for the delight and satisfaction of the curious Elizabethan adventurers. The euphuistic style found in Smith's travel books and the romantic description in Strachey's account of a shipwrecked expedition (1610) pleased the splendor-loving Englishmen. Later in the century a retrospective mood crept into various historical works; these books tend to be more individual, homely, even racy. But throughout the seventeenth century literary production remained occasional; not until the eighteenth century did the Southern writers clearly establish themselves on the American literary scene.

In the New England colonies conditions were more conducive to both writing and printing. From the start New England was better organized and better equipped with men and supplies; a printing press and types arrived in Cambridge in 1639. Moreover, the caliber of New England settlers ranked exceptionally high. There is perhaps nowhere in recorded history a more cultured group of wilderness colonists than those who landed on New England shores. In their lofty ambitions, their zeal for knowledge, their display of erudition there is much of the Renaissance spirit and learning. Governor Bradford, for example, was not only a judicious leader of noble character; he was also a man acquainted with several foreign languages and well versed in the classics, and for achievement he erected an ebenezer for the glory of England as well as of God. John Winthrop and others were university men of learning and distinction. Two generations later there was the theocratic leader, Cotton Mather, literally America's Man of the Renaissance. His writings show extreme displays of learning; his energy was indefatigable, and he wrote almost five hundred books and pamphlets. The Puritans believed in rigid training for all their clergy. They had enjoyed the best opportunities for a thorough education in England, for Oxford and Cambridge were flourishing institutions in the early seventeenth century, and the Puritan migrants aimed to promote this quality of learning even in the wilderness. Before the middle of the century, not only had Harvard College been founded, but free common and grammar schools had been set up in the towns of a hundred families or more. Further stress on the education and advancement of Puritan youths is evidenced by the Harvard charter of 1650, which decreed that students must have a thorough knowledge of the classics, the Bible, and medieval philosophy and art, as well as the Renaissance subjects. Men like Brewster, Bradford, Winthrop, and the Mathers brought their volumes of Cicero, Caesar, Homer, Virgil, Aesop, Demosthenes, Epictetus, Plutarch, Plautus, and others across the seas with them, and every returning boat carried orders for more books.

Another phase of Puritanism that influenced writing was the Puritan State or Commonwealth. Besides humanistic learning, the Puritan clergy needed a knowledge of law and government. Political ideals, they believed, had their origin in the Bible; thus church and state were one. Because of such theories as natural depravity, inner evil, and God's providence, Puritan leaders extended firm control over all their marshalled groups, congregations, towns, and communities. This commanding authority of the theocrats gave impetus to multitudinous writings, political or religious, disputatious or homiletic. During the first half-century in particular there was continual bickering between the Nonconformists and the established order of the Puritan theocracy. There were arguments on the social compact, on the church and state as one body, and on growing ideas of democratic government. Sharp criticism and abuse were found at home and abroad. Thorny treatises for the offense were written by Roger Williams, Thomas Hooker, John Wise and others like them; on the defense were Increase and Cotton Mather, John Cotton, John Winthrop, and Nathaniel Ward. In their race for effectiveness controversial writers borrowed from the English such mediums as would best fit their purpose: biting satire, colorful invective, political allegory, hard-hitting logic.

In their theological views the Puritans were the heirs of Calvinism. Though they represented in their doctrine a protest against Laud's autocracy, they themselves were autocratic, and particularly opposed at home to heady, speculative interpretation. Their internal enemies were all of this type. The quarrel with Anne Hutchinson, generally called the Antinomian Controversy, centered around her gatherings, in which she commented on doctrinal points and differed in the main from the orthodox Bostonian position. Her support of young Governor Harry Vane in opposition to the Winthrop party did not predispose the General Court in her favor. The Gortonists, though opponents of a slightly different stamp, substituted alleged vision for doctrine drawn from the two Testaments. Especially were the Puritans alarmed by the innumerable sects and sectarians who sprang up during the Commonwealth period in England when the pressure of orthodoxy was lightened. Frightened by the multiplicity of dissenting opinion, they sought to hold fast to the Bible not only as the final statute book but as the guide to their religious thinking. Small wonder that the Quakers, who looked for authority to their own inner light, and who refused to subscribe to the immigration laws of the colony, became objects of special fear and dread. Small wonder also that as late as 1678 the New England Synod could regard the mild treatment of the Quakers as one of the fancied causes of God's displeasure with the colonies.

Fortunately, throughout the seventeenth century the colonists saw the need for writing on things other than the vexing doctrinal issues. After all, new colonies were being established and old ones were growing during this entire period, and they wanted their settlements to look alluring to potential immigrants. Glowing accounts of the New World had appeared in the beginning of the century, but those across the ocean needed full assurance that here was the Utopia they had been looking for. Besides the early graphic records of John Smith and George Percy, there were pamphlets by John Hammond and Francis Higginson.

In addition to emigration tracts there are many journals of everyday happenings by those who had in mind no purpose beyond recording their observations and experiences for the pleasure of others. The American Pepys, Samuel Sewall, grew gossipy on the everyday happenings in this country lately settled; Clap in his *Memoirs* told of Indians and Antinomians, as well as of God and Satan; and several of the theologians corresponded with the Royal Society.

The more serious and ambitious writers even attempted complete historical records. There is Winthrop's *Journal*, a great embodiment of everything from church polity to the minutiae of daily living; there is Edward Johnson's prose epic, *The Wonder-Working Providence of Sions Saviour in New England*; and there is Mather's *Magnalia*, a Fuller-like tome giving information on all the Puritan leaders, a veritable History of the Worthies of New England. The aim of all these men was to record the actual events as they happened and to emphasize the important figures in this great American experiment. The reasons for such a display of serious effort in historiography were twofold: to preserve historical records and to record the full lives of the forefathers so that descendants might admire them and understand how badly they themselves had fallen away from original greatness. In many of the biographies writers went one step beyond idealizing; they wrote of the spiritual workings of the heart and mind, so that all who were concerned with their own plight might be aided in self-analysis.

In a world given over to theology the dominant literary forms are rightly the meditation and the sermon. Meditations during this period were much influenced by the Renaissance writers and Owen Felltham. The form generally followed reflected the didactic essay in its aphoristic statement, use of analogy, explication of text, and inevitable moral. Other meditations, like those of Anne Bradstreet, were what Bacon called "dispersed meditations." And the first sermon in New England, on "Self Love," by Robert Cushman, actually is an essay. But other writers of sermons imitated more or less the structural development used in England by Fuller and Taylor. The most striking feature of the sermon during this century is its use of type characters. The Puritans, however, did not use the concise form of Theophrastus. Cotton Mather, for example, knew the classical model, but since succinctness did not usually fit his purpose, he modified the pattern, allowing himself comfortable room for moralizing. The funeral sermon introduced a surviving medieval practice known as the *exemplum*, a sketch of a person who exemplified a particular type of character, or afforded a model for others to follow. King William's death gave Puritan preachers timely subject matter in the form of *exempla*. Cotton Mather made *exempla* of the lives of Michael Wigglesworth, William Phips, Thomas Shepard, and others; but these appeared in ecclesiastical history rather than in sermons.

In comparison with the early travel books and journals, the abundant writings of the theologians now seem curious, profound, crabbed. This has been explained partly by the stress on classical and medieval thought in the education of the Puritan divines, and partly by the fact that the colonial writers not only used forms borrowed from seventeenth-century England but employed the Stuart style as well. With few exceptions the heavy Jacobean manner was the mode of the day; the more learned the author the more elaborate the style. A glance through some of the works of Cotton Mather would reveal most of the characteristics of that once-popular prose style: appeal to authority, pagan or Christian; embellishment by quotations, the more foreign the better; a flourish of metaphor; the piling up of examples and anecdotes; the use of balanced and parallel sentences; lavish display of learning; and a fondness for general adornment. In certain respects Mather out-Burtoned Burton. His delineations of conceit and pun, and his unrolling of phrase after phrase and clause after clause are done with the conscious art of a scientific rhetorician.

In poetry the metaphysical style of Quarles, Herbert, and Vaughan was perhaps best used in New England by Edward Taylor, while Anne Bradstreet echoed the French Huguenot poet Du Bartas. A compound of clipped balladry and versified Calvinism appeared in Michael Wigglesworth's well-known *Day of Doom*, popular because it was highly terrifying. In general during this period the poetry was crude and made of homespun materials, but it was dressed in the artificial garb of earlier poets. When the use of conceits and anagrams went out of fashion, so did the poetry.

In this cursory review of forms and styles of seventeenth-century American literature, a few conclusions may be drawn. The early authors left no masterpieces, but they gave our literature a sound and well-rounded beginning. Influences were both bad and good, including both the crabbedness of the Calvinists and the high culture of the classicists. As the colonists grew farther apart from England in time and experience, they became more individualistic, tending toward an independence of spirit which flowered in the eighteenth century.

CHRONICLES OF HISTORY, TRAVEL, AND ADVENTURE

JOHN SMITH (1579?–1631)

HISTORY and legend have made a hero of John Smith, professional soldier and author of the first substantial literary work written on American soil. He had none of the aristocratic lineage popularly regarded as essential for Elizabethan heroes, but his energy, versatility, and resourcefulness made him leader of the Jamestown colony despite the lack of co-operation of certain highborn fellow colonists. His *True Relation of . . . Virginia* was written as a letter to England in an attempt to offset the unfavorable influence of Wingfield, cousin of the Earl of Southampton, who constantly disputed Smith's boisterous dominance in Virginia affairs.

According to his own story, Smith was born in Lincolnshire in 1579, went to sea at an early age, served as a soldier in France and the Low Countries, and spent ten years in dangerous adventures in Bucovina, Moldavia, Transylvania, Turkey, and elsewhere in the Near East. When he reached America with the Jamestown colonists at the age of twenty-seven, he already had behind him a long record of exploits, part genuine, part apocryphal. He returned to England in 1609, after a strenuous but short term as leader. Except for two voyages of discovery to New England in 1614 and 1615, he remained in England until his death in 1631.

Smith, like Sir Walter Raleigh, was an ardent colonist, and he wanted to convince the English of the promise of Virginia and New England. Too good a storyteller to be a reliable historian, he wrote of romantic adventures in the New World. Never reticent concerning his own exploits, he had a vivid imagination, a lively curiosity, and a pithy downrightness which makes his narratives good reading. His first book, *A True Relation of Such Occurences and Accidents of Noate as Hath Hapned in Virginia Since the First Planting of That Collony*, published in London in 1608, was written in Jamestown. *A Map of Virginia, with a Description of the Country* (1612), deals with affairs of the colony. The most important of his other books and travel narratives, written during his later residence in England, is *The Generall Historie of Virginia, New England, and the Summer Isles* (1624).

BIBLIOGRAPHY · Although there have been abridged versions of Smith's *The Generall Historie* (1624), the only full edition of Smith's works is that of Edward Arber, *Travels and Works of Captain John Smith* (1884), which was reprinted in two volumes in 1910 with a biographical and critical introduction by A. G. Bradley. J. G. Fletcher and L. C. Wroth edited *The True Travels, Adventures and Observations of Captain John Smith* in 1930. The numerous biographies include A. G. Bradley, *Captain John Smith* (1905), E. K. Chatterton, *Captain John Smith* (1927), J. G. Fletcher, *John Smith, Also Pocahontas* (1928), G. C. Hill, *Captain John Smith* (1858), T. S. Jenks, *Captain John Smith* (1904), C. Poindexter, *Captain John Smith and His Critics* (1893), V. Quinn, *Exciting Adventures of Captain John Smith* (1923), W. G. Simms, *Captain John Smith* (1846), and C. D. Warner, *Life and Writings of John Smith* (1881). Wilberforce Eames compiled *A Bibliography of Captain John Smith* in a limited edition issued in 1927 by the Bibliographical Society. Critical appraisals include an essay by Henry Adams, "Captain John Smith," in the *North American Review* (January, 1867), and a treatment by M. C. Tyler in *A History of American Literature During the Colonial Time* (revised edition, 1897).

The Generall Historie of Virginia

ALMOST ALL WRITERS of tracts and news-books concerning colonial emigration attempted to satisfy the intense curiosity about the habits and customs of the natives of North America in the early seventeenth century. The fullest of these accounts in the first twenty-five years of the century was that by Captain John Smith, *The Generall Historie of Virginia* (1624).

The Generall Historie contained the famous story of Pocahontas which has long been a cherished American legend, used by poets and loved by school children. But the dubious nature of the story itself and the history of its publication compel the student to question its truth. In the first edition of *A True Relation* (1608) Smith made no mention of the incident, although it is certainly dramatic enough to have merited inclusion if it had been a fact. Pocahontas visited England in 1616 where she became a popular figure. Always an opportunist, Smith would have been quick to see the advantage of associating his name in so romantic a fashion with that of the charming court favorite. He wrote the now familiar story in a letter to the queen, and included the incident in his *Generall Historie*, published in London in 1624. The story was graphically retold in John Davis, *Four Years of Travel in America . . .* (1804), and was amplified in E. B. Smith, *Story of Pocahontas and Captain John Smith* (1906). The fullest treatment of the theme in English fiction is David Garnett's *Pocahontas* (1933).

The text below follows Arber's edition of 1884; the *u*'s and *j*'s have been modernized.

THE SECOND BOOKE · *Of the Naturall Inhabitants of Virginia*

The land is not populous, for the men be few; their far greater number is of women and children. Within 60 myles of James Towne, there are about some 5000 people, but of able men fit for their warres scarce 1500. To nourish so many together they have yet no meanes, because they make so small a benefit of their land, be it never so fertile.

Six or seaven hundred have beene the most hath beene seene together, when they gathered themselves to have surprised mee at Pamaunkee, having but fifteene to withstand the worst of their fury. As small as the proportion of ground that hath yet beene discovered, is in comparison of that yet unknowne: The people differ very much in stature, especially in language, as before is expressed.

Some being very great as the Sasquesahanocks; others very little, as the Wighcocomocoes: but generally tall and straight, of a comely proportion, and of a colour browne when they are of any age, but they are borne white. Their hayre is generally blacke, but few have any beards. The men weare halfe their beards shaven, the other halfe long; for Barbers they use their women, who with two shels will grate away the hayre, of any fashion they please. The women [i. e., their hair] are cut in many fashions, agreeable to their yeares, but ever some part remaineth long.

They are very strong, of an able body and full of agilitie, able to endure to lie in the woods under a tree by the fire, in the worst of winter, or in the weedes and grasse, in Ambuscado in the Sommer.

They are inconstant in every thing, but what feare constraineth them to keepe. Craftie, timerous, quicke of apprehension, and very ingenuous. Some are of disposition fearefull, some bold, most cautelous, all Savage. Generally covetous of Copper, Beads, and such like trash. They are soone moved to anger, and so malicious, that they seldome forget an injury: they seldome steale one from another, least their conjurers should reveale it, and so they be pursued and punished. That they are thus feared is certaine, but that any can reveale their offences by conjuration I am doubtfull. Their women are carefull not to be suspected of dishonestie without the leave of their husbands.

Each houshold knoweth their owne lands, and gardens, and most live of their owne labours.

For their apparell, they are some time covered with the skinnes of wilde beasts, which in Winter are dressed with the hayre, but in Sommer without. The better sort use large mantels of Deare skins, not much differing in fashion from the Irish mantels. Some imbrodered with white beads, some with Copper, other painted after their manner. But the common sort have scarce to cover their nakednesse, but with grasse, the leaves of trees, or such like. We have seene some use mantels made of Turky feathers, so prettily wrought and woven with threads that nothing could be discerned but the feathers. That was exceeding warme and very handsome. But the women are always covered about their middles with a skin, and very shamefast to be seene bare.

They adorne themselves most with copper beads and paintings. Their women, some have their legs, hands, breasts, and face cunningly imbrodered with divers workes, as beasts, serpents, artificially wrought into their flesh with blacke spots. In each eare commonly they have 3 great holes, whereat they hang chaines, bracelets, or copper. Some of their men weare in those holes, a small greene and yellow coloured snake, neare halfe a yard in length, which crawling and lapping her selfe about his necke oftentimes familiarly would kisse his lips. Others weare a dead Rat tyed by the taile. Some on their heads weare the wing of a bird, or some large feather with a Rattell. Those Rattels are somewhat like the chape of a Rapier, but lesse, which they take from the taile of a snake. Many have the whole skinne of a Hawke or some strange foule, stuffed with the wings abroad. Others a broad peece of Copper, and some the hand of their enemy dryed. Their heads and shoulders are painted red with the roote Pocone brayed to powder, mixed with oyle, this they hold in sommer to preserve them from the heate, and in winter from the cold. Many other formes of paintings they use, but he is the most gallant that is the most monstrous to behold.

Their buildings and habitations are for the most part by the rivers, or not farre distant from some fresh spring. Their houses are built like our Arbors, of small young springs bowed and tyed, and so close covered with Mats, or the barkes of trees very handsomely, that notwithstanding either winde, raine, or weather, they are as warme as stooves, but very smoaky, yet at the toppe of the house there is a hole made for the smoake to goe into right over the fire.

Against the fire they lie on little hurdles of Reeds covered with a Mat, borne from the ground a foote and more by a hurdle of wood. On these round about the house they lie heads and points one by th'other against the fire, some covered with Mats, some with skins, and some starke naked lie on the ground, from 6 to 20 in a house.

Their houses are in the midst of their fields or gardens, which are small plots of ground. Some 20 acres, some 40. some 100. some 200. some more, some lesse. In some places from 2 to 50 of those houses together, or but a little separated by groves of trees. Neare their habitations is little small wood or old trees on the ground by reason of their burning of them for fire. So that a man may gallop a horse amongst these woods any way, but where the creekes or Rivers shall hinder.

Men, women, and children have their severall names according to the severall humors of their Parents. Their women (they say) are easily delivered of childe, yet doe they love children very dearely. To make them hardie, in the coldest mornings they wash them in the rivers, and by painting and oyntments so tanne their skinnes, that after a yeare or two, no weather will hurt them.

The men bestow their times in fishing, hunting, warres, and such man-like exercises, scorning to be seene in any woman-like exercise, which is the cause that the women be very painefull, and the men often idle. The women and children doe the rest of the worke. They make mats, baskets, pots, morters, pound their corne, make their bread, prepare their victuals, plant their corne, gather their corne, beare all kind of burdens, and such like.

Their fire they kindle presently by chafing a dry pointed sticke in a hole of a little square peece of wood, that firing it selfe, will so fire mosse, leaves, or any such like dry thing, that will quickly burne.

In March and Aprill they live much upon their fishing wires; and feed on fish, Turkies, and Squirrels. In May and June they plant their fields, and live most of Acornes, Walnuts, and fish. But to amend their dyet, some disperse themselves in small companies, and live upon fish, beasts, crabs, oysters, land Tortoises, strawberries, mulberries, and such like. In June, July, and August, they feed upon the rootes of Tocknough, berries, fish, and greene wheat.

It is strange to see how their bodies alter with their dyet, even as the deere and wilde beasts they seeme fat and leane, strong and weake. Powhatan their great King, and some others that are provident, rost their fish and flesh upon hurdles as before is expressed, and keepe it till scarce times.

For fishing, hunting, and warres they use much their bow and arrowes. They bring their bowes to the forme of ours by the scraping of a shell. Their arrowes are made, some of straight young sprigs, which they head with bone, some 2 or 3 ynches long. These they use to shoot at Squirrels on trees. Another sort of arrowes they use made of Reeds. These are peeced with wood, headed with splinters of christall, or some sharpe stone, the spurres of a Turkey, or the bill of some bird. For his knife he hath the splinter of a Reed to cut his

feathers in forme. With this knife also, he will joynt a Deere, or any beast, shape his shooes, buskins, mantels, &c. To make the noch of his arrow he hath the tooth of a Beaver, set in a sticke, wherewith he grateth it by degrees. His arrow head he quickly maketh with a little bone, which he ever weareth at his bracert, of any splint of a stone, or glasse in the forme of a heart, and these they glew to the end of their arrowes. With the sinewes of Deere, and the tops of Deeres hornes boyled to a jelly, they make a glew that will not dissolve in cold water.

For their warres also they use Targets that are round and made of the barkes of trees, and a sword of wood at their backes, but oftentimes they use for swords the horne of a Deere put through a peece of wood in forme of a Pickaxe. Some a long stone sharpned at both ends, used in the same manner. This they were wont to use also for hatchets, but now by trucking they have plentie of the same forme of yron. And those are their chiefe instruments and armes. . . .

THE THIRD BOOKE · [*Captain Smith's Captivity*]

. . . But our Comædies never endured long without a Tragedie; some idle exceptions being muttered against Captaine Smith, for not discovering the head of Chickahamania River, and [being] taxed by the Councell, to be too slow in so worthy an attempt. The next voyage hee proceeded so farre that with much labour by cutting of trees insunder he made his passage; but when his Barge could passe no farther, he left her in a broad bay out of danger of shot, commanding none should goe a shore till his returne: Himselfe with two English and two Salvages went up higher in a Canowe; but hee was not long absent, but his men went a shore, whose want of government gave both occasion and opportunity to the Salvages to surprise one George Cassen, whom they slew, and much failed not to have cut of [f] the boat and all the rest.

Smith, little dreaming of that accident, being got to the marshes at the rivers head, twentie myles in the desert, had his two men slaine (as is supposed) sleeping by the Canowe, whilst himselfe by fowling sought them victuall: who finding he was beset with 200 Salvages, two of them hee slew, still defending himselfe with the ayd of a Salvage his guid, whom he bound to his arm with his garters, and used him as a buckler, yet he was shot in his thigh a little and had many arrowes that stucke in this cloathes but no great hurt, till at last they tooke him prisoner.

When this newes came to James towne, much was their sorrow for his losse, fewe expecting what ensued.

Sixe or seven weekes [rather about the three weeks 16 Dec. 1607–8 to 8 Jan. 1608] those Barbarians kept him prisoner, many strange triumphes and conjurations they made of him, yet hee so demeaned himselfe amongst them, as he not onely diverted them from surprising the Fort, but procured his owne libertie, and got himselfe and his company such estimation amongst them, that those salvages admired him more than their owne Quiyouckosucks.

The manner how they used and delivered him, is as followeth. . . .

He [Smith] demanding for their Captaine, they shewed him Opechankanough, King of Pamaunkee, to whom he gave a round Ivory double compass Dyall. Much they marvailed at the playing of the Fly and Needle, which they could see so plainely, and yet not touch it, because of the glasse that covered them. But when he demonstrated by that Globe-like Jewell, the roundnesse of the earth, and skies, the spheare of the Sunne, Moone, and Starres, and how the Sunne did chase the night round about the world continually; the greatnesse of the Land and Sea, the diversitie of Nations, varietie of complexions, and how we were to them Antipodes, and many other such like matters, they all stood as amazed with admiration.

Notwithstanding, within an houre after they tyed him to a tree, and as many as could stand about him prepared to shoot him: but the King holding up the Compass in his hand, they all laid downe their Bowes and Arrowes, and in a triumphant manner led him to Orapaks, where he was after their manner kindly feasted, and well used.

Their order in conducting him was thus; Drawing themselves all in fyle, the King in the middest had all their peeces and Swords borne before him. Captaine Smith was led after him by three great Salvages, holding him fast by each arme: and on each side six went in fyle with their Arrowes nocked. But arriving at the Towne (which was but onely thirtie or fortie hunting houses made of Mats, which they remove as they please, as we our tents) all the women and children staring to behold him, the souldiers first all in fyle performed the forme of a Bissone so well as could be; and on each flanke, officers as Serjeants to see them keepe their orders. A good time they continued this exercise, and then cast themselves in a ring, dauncing in such severall Postures, and singing and yelling out such hellish notes and screeches; being strangely painted, every one his quiver of Arrowes, and at his backe a club; on his arme a Fox or an Otters skinne, or some such matter for his vambrace; their heads and shoulders painted red, with Oyle and Pocones mingled together, which Scarlet-like colour made an exceeding handsome shew; his Bow in his hand, and the skinne of a Bird with her wings abroad dryed, tyed on his head, a peece of copper, a white shell, a long feather, with a small rattle growing at the tayles of their snak[e]s tyed to it, or some such like toy. All this while Smith and the King stood in the middest guarded, as before is said: and after three dances they all departed. Smith they conducted to a long house, where thirtie or fortie tall fellowes did guard him; and ere long more bread and venison was brought him then would have served twentie men. I thinke his stomacke at that time was not very good; what he left they put in baskets and tyed over his head. About midnight they set the meate againe before him, all this time not one of them would eate a bit with him, till the next morning they brought him as much more; and then did they eate all the old, and reserved the new as they had done the other, which made him thinke they would fat him to eat him. Yet in this desperate estate to defend him from the cold, one Maocassater brought him his gowne, in requitall of some beades and toyes Smith had given him at his first arrivall in Virginia.

Two dayes after a man would have slaine him (but that the guard prevented it) for the death of his sonne, to whom they conducted him to recover the poore man then breathing his last. Smith told them that at James towne he had a water would doe it, if they would let him fetch it, but they would not permit that: but made all the preparations they could to assault James towne, craving his advice; and for recompence he should have life, libertie, land, and women. In part of a Table booke he writ his minde to them at the Fort, what was intended, how they should follow that direction to affright the messengers, and without fayle send him such things as he writ for. And an Inventory with them. The difficultie and danger, he told the Salvages, of the Mines, great gunnes, and other Engins exceedingly affrighted them, yet according to his request they went to James towne, in as bitter weather as could be of frost and snow, and within three dayes returned with an answer.

But when they came to Jame[s] towne, seeing men sally out as he had told them they would, they fled; yet in the night they came againe to the same place where he had told them they should receive an answer, and such things as he had promised them: which they found accordingly, and with which they returned with no small expedition, to the wonder of them all that heard it, that he could either divine, or the paper could speake.

Then they led him to the Youthtanunds, the Mattapanients, the Payankatanks, the Nantaughtacunds, and Onawmanients upon the rivers of Rapahanock, and Patawomek; over all those rivers, and backe againe by divers other severall Nations, to the Kings habitation at Pamaunkee, where they entertained him with most strange and fearefull Conjurations;

> As if neare led to hell,
> Amongst the Devils to dwell.

Not long after, early in a morning a great fire was made in a long house, and a mat spread on the one side, as on the other; on the one they caused him to sit, and all the guard went out of the house, and presently came skipping in a great grim fellow, all painted over with coale, mingled with oyle; and many Snakes and Wesels skins stuffed with mosse, and all their tayles tyed together, so as they met on the crowne of his head in a tassell; and round about the tassell was as a Coronet of feathers, the skins hanging round about his head, backe, and shoulders, and in a manner covered his face; with a hellish voyce, and a rattle in his hand. With most strange gestures and passions he began his invocation, and environed the fire with a circle of meale; which done, three more such like devils came rushing in with the like antique tricks, painted halfe blacke, halfe red: but all their eyes were painted white, and some red stroakes like Mutchato's, along their cheekes: round about him those fiends daunced a pretty while, and then came in three more as ugly as the rest; with red eyes, and white stroakes over their blacke faces, at last they all sat downe right against him; three of them on the one hand of the chiefe Priest, and three on the other. Then all with their rattles began a song, which ended, the chiefe Priest layd downe five wheat cornes: then strayning his armes and hands with such violence that he sweat, and his veynes swelled, he began a short Oration: at the conclusion they all gave a short groane; and then layd down three graines more. After that, began their song againe, and then another Oration, ever laying downe so many cornes as before, till they had twice incirculed the fire; that done, they tooke a bunch of little stickes prepared for that purpose, continuing still their devotion, and at the end of every song and Oration, they layd downe a sticke betwixt the divisions of Corne. Till night, neither he nor they did either eate or drinke; and then they feasted merrily, with the best provisions they could make. Three dayes they used this Ceremony; the meaning whereof they told him, was to know if he intended them well or no. The circle of meale signified their Country, the circles of corne the bounds of the Sea, and the stickes his Country. They imagined the world to be flat and round, like a trencher; and they in the middest.

After this they brought him a bagge of gunpowder, which they carefully preserved till the next spring, to plant as they did their corne; because they would be acquainted with the nature of that seede.

Opitchapam the Kings brother invited him to his house, where, with as many platters of bread, foule, and wild beasts, as did environ him, he bid him wellcome; but not any of them would eate a bit with him, but put up all the remainder in Baskets.

At his returne to Opechancanoughs, all the Kings women, and their children, flocked about him for their parts, as a due by Custome, to be merry with such fragments.

11

But his waking mind in hydeous dreames did oft see
    wondrous shapes,
Of bodies strange, and huge in growth, and of stupen-
    dious makes.

[Pocahontas Saves Smith's Life]

At last they brought him to Meronocomoco [5 Jan. 1608], where was Powhatan their Emperor. Here more than two hundred of those grim Courtiers stood wondering at him, as he had beene a monster; till Powhatan and his trayne had put themselves in their greatest braveries. Before a fire upon a seat like a bedsted, he sat covered with a great robe, made of Rarowcun skinnes, and all the tayles hanging by. On either hand did sit a young wench of 16 or 18 yeares, and along on each side the house, two rowes of men, and behind them as many women, with all their heads and shoulders painted red: many of their heads bedecked with the white downe of Birds; but every one with something: and a great chayne of white beads about their necks.

At his entrance before the King, all the people gave a great shout. The Queene of Appamatuck was appointed to bring him water to wash his hands, and another brought him a bunch of feathers, in stead of a Towell to dry them: having feasted him after their best barbarous manner they could, a long consultation was held, but the conclusion was, two great stones were brought before Powhatan: then as many as could layd hands on him, dragged him to them, and thereon laid his head, and being ready with their clubs, to beate out his braines, Pocahontas the Kings dearest daughter, when no intreaty could prevaile, got his head in her armes, and laid her owne upon his to save him from death: whereat the Emperour was contented he should live to make him hatchets, and her bells, beads, and copper; for they thought him as well of all occupations as themselves. For the King himselfe will make his owne robes, shooes, bowes, arrowes, pots; plant, hunt, or doe any thing so well as the rest.

They say he bore a pleasant shew,
But sure his heart was sad.
For who can pleasant be, and rest,
That lives in feare and dread:
And having life suspected, doth
It still suspected lead.

JOHN PORY (1579?–1635?)

THE TRAVEL writings of John Pory, English geographer, explorer, and colonist, stand beside those of Captain John Smith in this popular form of Renaissance literature. His lively, descriptive letters and his editing of Leo's *Geographical History of Africa* place him in a category with the indefatigable Richard Hakluyt, English collector of travel accounts, under whom he studied for three years.

After receiving the degree of Master of Arts at Cambridge in 1610, Pory spent seven years traveling in Europe and the Near East, Ireland, France, Savoy, Italy, and Turkey. His connection with America dates from 1619, when he embarked for Jamestown to serve as the first Secretary of State in the colony. His earlier experience in Parliament during the six years from 1605 to 1611 made him a valuable man in the deliberations of the first General Assembly in Virginia. Between sessions he busied himself with voyages of exploration: to Accomac, up the James River and North Bay, and to the South River. One of his travel reports was printed in Smith's *Generall Historie of Virginia*.

On a return trip to England Pory stopped at New Plymouth, and not only supplied the inhabitants with provisions but gained materials for his enthusiastic descriptive letters. In these he paralleled Smith's achievement in describing two areas of the New World. In 1623 he was a member of a board of inquiry to study conditions of the Virginia colony, and subsequently he served as a member of the Virginia commission. He returned to England permanently in 1625.

BIBLIOGRAPHY · No full-length biography of John Pory has been written, but a brief sketch can be found in the *Dictionary of National Biography*. Nor is there a collected edition of his letters. Fourteen of them were printed in *The Court and Times of James the First*, compiled by Thomas Birch and edited by R. F. Williams, London, 1848. Pory's official communications from Virginia (as secretary of the colony), and six of his letters to Sir Edwin Sandys were reprinted in *The Records of the Virginia Company of London*, edited by Susan Myra Kingsbury, Washington, 1933. His "Reporte of the Manner of Proceeding in the General Assembly

Convened at James City" was reprinted in both Kingsbury and in Lyon G. Tyler's *Narratives of Early Virginia*, New York, 1907. In 1918 *John Pory's Lost Description of Plymouth* was edited by Champlin Burrage. Pory's activities are mentioned in Edward Waterhouse, *A Declaration of the State of the Colony and . . . a Relation of the Barbarous Massacre*, London, 1622 (reprinted in *Records of the Virginia Company*, III, 541–579).

Letter to Sir Dudley Carleton

JOHN PORY's letters record not only practical details in the administration of colonial affairs, but also the enthusiastic comments of the new settler. They read like the *New England Plantation* (1630) of Francis Higginson, and like his work are colored with the zeal of one who has committed himself to a new venture and is striving to bring others to share his optimism. Thus he dilates on the glorious prospects of the Virginia colony, if English plows, grape vines, and cattle can be procured in sufficient quantities. Pory's concern for vineyards and the future of Virginia vintages reflected his love of convivial company. His comments on New England are in general equally enthusiastic and provide interesting data for a period in the history of the Plymouth colony very incompletely described in extant records. The text of the Virginia letters is that in Susan Myra Kingsbury's edition, *The Records of the Virginia Company in London* (1933). Spelling of the original has been kept except for superior letters and the antique *u's* and *v's*.

[*Prospects of Jamestown, Virginia*]

James Citty in Virginia, Sept. 30, 1619.

Right Honorable and my singular good Lorde,
Having mett with so fitt a messenger as this man of warre of Flushing, I could not but imparte with your lordship (to whom I am so everlastingly bounde) these poore fruites of our labours here; wherein though your lordship will espie many errours and imperfections, and matters of lowe esteeme; yet withal you will be contente to observe the very principle and rudiments of our Infant- 40 Commonwealth; which though nowe contemptible, your lordship may live to see a flourishing Estate; maugre both Spaniards and Indians. The occasion of this ships coming hither was an accidental consortship in the West Indies with the Tresurer an English man of warre also, licensed by a Commission from the Duke of Savoye to take Spaniards as lawfull prize. This ship the

10 Treasurer wente out of England in Aprill was twelvemoneth, about a moneth, I thinke, before any peace was concluded between the king of Spaine and that prince. Hither shee came to Captaine Argall, then governor of this Colony, being parte-owner of her. Hee more for love of gaine (the root of all evil) [. . .] then for any true love he bore to this Plantation, victualed and manned her anewe, and sente her with the same Commission to raunge the Indies. The evente whereof (we may misdoubte) will prove some attempte of the Spaniard upon us, either by waye of revenge, or by way of prevention; lest we might in time make this place sedem belli against the West Indies. But our Governor, being a soldier truly bred in that university of warre the lowe Countries, purposeth at a place or two upon the river fortifiable to provide for them, animating in the meane while this warlike people (then whom for their small number, 20 no prince can be served with better) by his example to prepare their courages.

Both those of our nation and the Indians also have this Torride sommer bene visited with great sickness and mortality; which our good God (his name be blessed for it) hath recompensed with a marvelous plenty, suche as hath not bene since our first coming into the land. For myselfe I was partly at land and partly at sea vexed with a Calenture of some 4. or 5. moneths. But (praised be God) 30 I am nowe as healthfull as ever I was in my life. Here (as your lordship cannot be ignorant) I am, for faulte of a better, Secretary of Estate, the first that ever was chosen and appointed by Commission from the Counsell and Company in England, under their handes and common seale. By my fees I must maintaine myselfe; which the Governor telles me, may this yeare amounte to a matter of 300 li sterling; whereof fifty I doe owe to himselfe, and I pray God the remainder may amounte to a hundred more. As yet I have gotten nothing, save onely (if I may speak it without boasting) a general reputation of integrity, for having spoken freely to all matters, according to my conscience; and as neare as I could discerne, done every man right.

As touching the quality of this country, three things there be which in fewe yeares may bring this Colony to perfection; the English plough, Vineyards, and Cattle. For the first, there be many grounds here cleared by the Indians to our handes, which being muche worne out, will beare no more of their corne, which requireth an extraordinary deale of sappe and substance to nourish it; but of our graine of all sortes it will beare great abundance. We had had this yeare a plentifull cropp of English wheat, tho the last harvest 1618. was onely shed upon the subble, and so selfe-sowne, without any other manurance. In July last so soon as we had reaped this selfe-sowen wheate, we sett Indian corne upon the same grounde, which is come up in great abundance; and so by this meanes we are to enjoye two crops in one yeare from off one and the same fielde. The greattest labour we have yet bestowed upon English wheate, hath bene upon newe broken up groundes, one ploughing onely and one harrowing, far shorte of the Tilthe used in Christendome, which when we shall have ability enough to performe, we shall produce miracles out of this earthe.

Vines here are in suche abundance, as where soever a man treads, they are ready to embrace his foote. I have tasted here of a great black grape as big as a Damascin, that hath a true Muscatell-taste; the vine whereof now spending itselfe even to the topps of high trees, if it were reduced into a vineyard, and there domesticated, would yeild incomparable fruite. The like or a better taste have I founde in a lesser sorte of black grapes. White grapes also of great excellency I have hearde to be in the country; but they are very rare, nor did I ever see or taste of them. For cattle, they do mightily increase here, both kine, hogges, and goates, and are much greater in stature, then the race of them first brought out of England. No lesse are our horses and mares likely to multiply, which proove of a delicate shape, and of as good spirite and metall.

All our riches for the present doe consiste in Tobacco, wherein one man by his owne labour hath in one yeare raised to himselfe to the value of 200 li sterling; and another by the meanes of six servants hath cleared at one crop a thousand pound English. These be true, yet indeed rare examples, yet possible to be done by others. Our principall wealth (I should have said) consisteth in servants: But they are chardgeable to be furnished with armes, apparell and bedding, and for their trans-

portation and casuall, both at sea, and for their first yeare commonly at lande also: But if they escape, they proove very hardy, and sound able men.

Nowe that your lordship may knowe, we are not the veriest beggers in the worlde, our Cowe-keeper here of James citty on Sundayes goes accowterd all in freshe flaming silkes; and a wife of one that in England had professed the black arte, not of a scholler, but of a collier of Croydon, weares her rough bever hatt with a faire perle hattband, and a silken suite thereto correspondent. But to leave the Populace, and to come higher; the Governour here, who at his first coming, besides a great deale of worth in his person, brought onely his sworde with him, was at his late being in London, together with his lady, out of his meer gettings here, able to disburse very near three thousand pounde to furnishe himselfe for his voiage. And once within seven yeares, I am persuaded (*absit invidia verbo*) that the Governors place here may be as proffitable as the lord Depuities of Ireland.

All this notwithstanding, I may say of myselfe, that when I was the last yeare with your lordship at Middleborough, *si mens non laeva fuisset*, I might have gone to the Hagh with you, and founde myselfe there nowe in far better company, which indeed is the soule of this life, and might have bene deeply ingrafted into your lordship's service, which since I have a thousand times affected in vaine. And therfore seing I have missed that singular happiness, I must for what remaines, depende upon Gods providence, who, my hope is, wilbe so merciful towards me, as once more before I dye, to vouchsafe me the sight of your countenance, wherein, I speak unfainedly, I shall enjoye as muche happines as in any other thing I can imagine in this worlde.

At my first coming hither the solitary uncouthnes of this place, compared with those partes of Christendome or Turky where I had bene; and likewise my being sequestred from all occurrents and passages which are so rife there, did not a little vexe me. And yet in these five moneths of my continuance here, there have come at one time or another eleven saile of ships into this river, but fraighted more with ignorance, then with any thero marchandize. At length being hardned to this custome of abstinence from curiosity, I am resolved wholly to minde my busines here, and

14

nexte after my penne, to have some good book alwayes in store, being in solitude the best and choicest company. Besides among these Christall rivers, and odoriferous woods I doe escape muche expense, envye, contempte, vanity, and vexation of minde. Yet Good my lorde, have a little compassion upon me, and be pleased to sende me what pampletts and relations of the Interim since I was with you, as your lordship shall thinke good, directing the same (if you please) in a boxe to Mr. Ralfe Yeardley, Apothecary (brother to Sir George Yeardley our governour) dwelling at the signe of the Hartychoke in great Woodstreet, to be sente to me by the first, together with his brothers thinges. This pacquett I delivered to one Marmaduke Rayner, an Englishman, who goes intertained as Pilott in this Flemishe man of warre. If he come to your lordship, as he hathe promised, he wilbe the fittest messenger. All possible happines I wishe to your lordship and to my most honoured lady, and though remote in place, yet neare in affection, doe reste

Your lordships ever most humbly at your commaunde.

Jo. Pory.

Letters to Sir Edwin Sandys

[*Vineyards and Virginia*]

Jan. 16, 1619/20

... Mr. Nicholas Leate the Marchant hath upon my knowledge or (I am sure) had a lardge vine of Corynth grapes at the house he formerly dwelt in, the garden whereof Containinge the same vine is parted but by a wall from the garden of the house where he nowe dwelleth. ... If you Could procure any slips of that, howe gainefull might they prove with in seven or eight yeares, heere beinge Heat enough both to ripen and to dry them? There belonge so many severall skills to the planting and dressinge of a vineyard and to the makinge and preservinge of wines, whereof our nation is ignorant, as needes must wee have Vignerons from forraine partes: And vineyards beinge once planted where such infinite store of caske may be provided, wee might for want of other commodities lade all the ships that come, with as rich wines as France or Spaine doth yeild. Sir George brought

hither some plants which doe prosper passinge well, but his Vigneron being a fretful old man is dead. And because Canary wine is the most durable in all voyages and Climates of anie, and so Consequently the most salable and proffitable; yet would doe passinge well, if wee could get store of plantes from thence, ... it would one day acquite the Cost to procure plantes of those wines * * * Italy and Greece, which do emulate the Nectar. Then this, no Country is more apt for that purpose; for in time of yeare you Can scarce walke three steps in any place unmanured, where some vine or other will not be ready to entangle your foote. But of this subject enough, whereof I have so lardgely dilated, not because I thirst after it; for I thank god, I drinke water here with as much (if not more) pleasure and contente, as I dranke wine in those partes.

[*When to Sail for Virginia*]

June 12, 1620

... The thinges which I will nowe propound to your Consideration are first: the season of the yeare which for mens health may be fyttest to arrive in this Country. Wee here are in our opinions absolutely for the leafefall and the winter havinge found the springe and sommer both fatall and unprofitable to newe Commers, and those other two seasons quite Contrary, ffor instance, in these three last mentioned ships the people this spring came in sickly and too late either by plantinge, settinge, howinge, clearinge ground, or buildinge, to doe any worke of importance. The second thinge considerable is the eleccion of your people; that as near as may be none but sound persons be sent hither, and those if it be possible tradesmen, husbandmen, and true labourers. The inconvenience of unsound bodies amonge sound and healthfull and of arrivinge in the springe, wee found in our voyadge by the Dyana both at sea, and after wee come on shore. And of this the Jonathan may be a sad president, who lost twenty five of your land people at sea, beside Mr. Rand the Master and three marriners, and some more of the passengers nowe dead on shore. A third matter of importance is the passage from England hither, upon the speedines whereof the health of our people, and many other Commodities doe mainely depende. Such a passage wee hope Mr. Elford Pylot of the

15

Swan hath found by the Course of the Sommer Ilands, those other passages by the West Indyes, and by the North beinge the two extreames of

that golden Medium which I hope will by proffitable use verify the sayinge *Medio tutissimus ibis. . . .*

THOMAS MORTON (?–1647?)

THROUGH his one book, *New English Canaan*, published in Amsterdam in 1637, Thomas Morton has become a symbolic figure in the one-sided struggle between jollity and gloom as they contended for mastery in seventeenth-century New England. He also survives in the pages of Bradford and Winthrop as a rakehell whose dissolute conduct affronted both the bodies and souls of the pious builders of the theocracy in Massachusetts Bay Colony. His cavalier revels at Merry Mount, described imaginatively by Hawthorne in "The Maypole of Merry Mount" and his traffic in firearms with the Indians made him anathema to the colonists at Plymouth.

Morton first came to America in 1622, and sailed back to England after a few months. Later he returned with the party led by Captain Wollaston and settled on Quincy Bay (now Quincy, Massachusetts). Here in 1627 at Merry Mount, Morton built a house and engaged in pleasure and profit. Both pursuits were obnoxious to the Separatists. Morton's activities as a trader involved the exchange of powder and muskets for furs, and his success not only deprived the Plymouth colonists of profitable trade on the Kennebec but endangered their lives. Morton's famous Maypole was cut down twice, once by a band led by Captain Miles Standish in 1628, and two years later by a posse under Governor Endecott. Morton was twice captured by the outraged Puritans: in 1628 he was sent back to England under criminal charges, and upon his return eighteen months later, he was again deported and put in jail at Exeter.

The *New English Canaan* (1637) presents Morton's side of the story. It may be compared with Hawthorne's allegorical treatment of the Maypole episode, and with the critical contemporary references in Bradford and Winthrop. Morton, who invariably appended "of Clifford's Inn, Gent." to his name, thought of himself as a champion of the Church of England against Puritan bigotry. When he received a cold welcome upon his return to Plymouth in 1643, he took refuge in Maine, and later in Rhode Island. After another encounter with the Massachusetts Bay Colony, which resulted in imprisonment again for a year, he was released because of public expense. He died at Agamenticus, District of Maine.

BIBLIOGRAPHY · The *New English Canaan* was edited, with a biographical introduction, by C. F. Adams, Jr., for the Prince Society in 1883. The selections reprinted in this anthology have been taken from Adams's edition, which is based upon the text of the first printing in 1637. In addition to the contemporary references in Bradford and Winthrop, useful biographical details may be found in the sketches in the *Dictionary of National Biography* and the *Dictionary of American Biography*. Morton's early life is recounted by C. E. Banks, "Thomas Morton of Merrymount," *Proceedings of the Massachusetts Historical Society*, LVIII (1924), 147–193. The charges against Morton presented to "the Counsell of New-England," appear in *Collections of the Massachusetts Historical Society* (First Series), III (1794), 62–64. C. F. Adams, Jr., *Three Episodes of Massachusetts History*, I (1892), is a popular biographical account of Morton.

New English Canaan

THE TITLE PAGE of the first edition indicates that the *New English Canaan* was printed in Amsterdam in 1637. Since the work was revised and added to as late as 1634, a copyright entry in the Stationers' Register in London for 1633 would seem to show that the copyright was granted on the basis of the title alone. The exceedingly temperamental punctuation and the numerous typographical errors in the edition of 1637 are probably due to the fact that the compositor was not acquainted with English. C. F. Adams, Jr., in the text which he prepared for the Prince Society edition (1883), corrected the punctuation and the many unmistakable errors of the first printing. The Adams text is reprinted here.

BOOK III · Chapter xiv · [*The Revels at Merry Mount*]

The inhabitants of Pasonagessit, (having translated the name of their habitation from that ancient salvage name to Ma-re Mount, and having resolved to have the new name confirmed for a memorial to after ages,) did devise amongst themselves to have it performed in a solemne manner, with revels and merriment after the old English custome; [they] prepared to sett up a Maypole upon the festival day of Philip and Jacob,[n] and therefore brewed a barrell of excellent beare and provided a case of bottles, to be spent, with other good cheare, for all commers of that day. And because they would have it in a compleat forme, they had prepared a song fitting to the time and present occasion. And upon Mayday they brought the Maypole to the place appointed, with drumes, gunnes, pistols and other fitting instruments, for that purpose; and there erected it with the help of salvages, that came thether of purpose to see the manner of our revels. A goodly pine tree of 80 foote long was reared up, with a peare of buckshorns nayled one somewhat neare the top of it; where it stood, as a faire sea marke for directions how to find out the way to mine Hoste of Ma-re Mount.

And because it should more fully appeare to what ende it was placed there, they had a poem in readiness made, which was fixed to the Maypole to shew the new name confirmed upon that plantation; which, allthough it were made according to the occurrents of the time, it, being enigmatically composed, pusselled the Seperatists most pittifully to expound it.... The setting up of this Maypole was a lamentable spectacle to the precise seperatists, that lived at new Plimmouth. They termed it an Idoll; yea, they called it the Calfe of Horeb, and stood at defiance with the place, naming it Mount Dagon; threatening to make it a woefull mount and not a merry mount....

There was likewise a merry song made, which, (to make their revells more fashionable,) was sung with a corus, every man bearing his part; which they performed in a daunce, hand in hand about the Maypole, whiles one of the compny sung and filled out the good liquor, like gammedes[n] and Jupiter:

THE SONGE

Drinke and be merry, merry, merry boyes;
Let all your delight be in the Hymens joyes;
Io to Hymen, now the day is come,
About the merry Maypole take a roome.

festival . . . Jacob: the first of May. gammedes: Ganymede, the Greek cupbearer to the gods.

Make greene garlons, bring bottles out 5
And fill sweet nectar freely about.
Uncover thy head and feare no harme,
For her's good liquor to keepe it warme.
Then drinke and be merry, &c.
Io to Hymen, &c. 10

Nectar is a thing assign'd
By the Deitie's owne minde
To cure the heart opprest with greife,
And of good liquors is the cheife.
Then drinke, &c. 15
Io to Hymen, &c.

Give to the mellancolly man
A cup or two of 't now and than;
This physick will soone revive his bloud,
And make him be of a merrier moode. 20
Then drinke, &c.
Io to Hymen, &c.

Give to the Nymphe that's free from scorne
No Irish stuff nor Scotch over worne.
Lasses in beaver coats come away, 25
Yee shall be welcome to us night and day.
To drinke and be merry &c.
Io to Hymen, &c.

This harmles mirth by yonge men, (that lived in hope to have wifes brought over to them, that they would save them a laboure to make a voyage to fetch any over,) was much distasted by the precise Seperatists, that keepe much a doe about the tyth of Muit and Cummin,[n] troubling their braines more than reason would require about things that are indifferent: and from that time sought occasion against my honest Hoste of Ma-re Mount, to overthrow his ondertakings and to destroy his plantation quite and cleane....

Chapter XV · [Morton's Arrest, Escape, and Capture]

The Seperatists, envying the prosperity and hope of the plantation at Ma-re Mount, (which they perceaved beganne to come forward, and to be in a good way for gaine in the beaver trade,) conspired together against mine Hoste especially, (who was the owner of that plantation,) and made

Muit and Cummin: mint and cummin, Matthew 23: 23. ". . . ye pay tithe mint and anise and cummin, and have omitted the weightier matters of the law, judgment, mercy, and faith."

up a party against him; and mustred up what aide they could, accounting of him as a great Monster.

Many threatening speeches were given out against his person and his habitation, which they divulged should be consumed with fire: And taking advantage of the time when his company, (which seemed little to regard theire threats,) were gone up into the Inlands to trade with the Salvages for beaver, they set upon my honest host at a place called Wessaguscus,[n] where, by accident, they found him. The inhabitants there were in good hope of the subvertion of the plantation at Mare Mount, (which they principally aymed at;) and the rather because mine hoste was a man that indeavoured to advaunce the dignity of the Church of England; which they, (on the contrary part,) would laboure to vilifie with uncivile termes: enveying against the sacred booke of common prayer, and mine host that used it in a laudable manner amongst his family, as a practise of piety.

There hee would be a meanes to bringe sacks to their mill, (such is the thirst after Beaver,) and helped the conspiratores to surprise mine host, (who was there all alone;) and they chardged him, (because they would seeme to have some reasonable cause against him to sett a glosse upon their mallice,) with criminall things; which indeede had beene by such a person, but was of their conspiracy; mine host demaunded of the conspirators who it was that was author of that information, that seemed to be their ground for what they now intended. And because they answered they would not tell him, hee as peremptorily replyed, that hee would not say whether he had, or he had not done as they had bin informed.

The answere made no matter, (as it seemed,) whether it had bin negatively or affirmatively made; for they had resolved what hee should suffer, because, (as they boasted,) they were now become the greater number: they had shaked off their shackles of servitude, and were become Masters, and masterles people.

It appeares they were like beares whelpes in former time, when mine hosts plantation was of as much strength as theirs, but now, (theirs being stronger,) they, (like overgrowne beares,) seemed monsterous. In breife, mine host must indure to

Wessaguscus: Weymouth.

be their prisoner untill they could contrive it so that they might send him for England, (as they said,) there to suffer according to the merrit of the fact which they intended to father upon him; supposing, (belike,) it would proove a hainous crime.

Much rejoycing was made that they had gotten their capitall enemy, (as they concluded him;) whome they purposed to hamper in such sort that hee should not be able to uphold his plantation at Ma-re Mount.

The Conspirators sported themselves at my honest host, that meant them no hurt, and were so jocund that they feasted their bodies, and fell to tippeling as if they had obtained a great prize; like the Trojans when they had the custody of Hippeus pinetree horse.[n]

Mine host fained greefe, and could not be perswaded either to eate or drinke; because hee knew emptines would be a meanes to make him as watchfull as the geese kept in the Roman Cappitall: whereon, the contrary part, the conspirators would be so drowsy that hee might have an opportunity to give them a slip, insteade of a tester. Six persons of the conspiracy were set to watch him at Wessaguscus: But hee kept waking; and in the dead of night, (one lying on the bed for further suerty,) up gets mine host and got to the second dore that hee was to passe, which, notwithstanding the lock, hee got open, and shut it after him with such violence that it affrighted some of the conspirators.

The word, which was given with an alarme, was, o he's gon, he's gon, what shall wee doe, he's gon! The rest, (halfe a sleepe,) start up in a maze, and like rames, ran theire heads one at another full butt in the darke.

Theire grande leader, Captaine Shrimp,[n] tooke on most furiously and tore his clothes for anger, to see the empty nest, and their bird gone.

The rest were eager to have torne theire haire from theire heads; but it was so short that it would give them no hold. Now Captaine Shrimp thought

Hippeus pinetree horse: the large wooden figure of a horse in which a number of Greek warriors were concealed. After the horse had been drawn within the walls of Troy by a ruse, the Greeks opened the gates to admit the army.
Shrimp: Myles Standish.

18

in the losse of this prize, (which hee accoumpted his Master peece,) all his honor would be lost for ever.

In the meane time mine Host was got home to Ma-re Mount through the woods, eight miles round about the head of the river Monatoquit that parted the two Plantations, finding his way by the helpe of the lightening, (for it thundred as hee went terribly;) and there hee preepared powther, three pounds dried, for his present imployement, and foure good gunnes for him and the two assistants left at his howse, with bullets of severall sizes, three hounderd or thereabouts, to be used if the conspirators should pursue him thether: and these two persons promised theire aides in the quarrell, and confirmed that promise with health in good rosa solis.

Now Captaine Shrimp, the first Captaine in the Land, (as hee supposed,) must doe some new act to repaire this losse, and, to vindicate his reputation, who had sustained blemish by this oversight, begins now to study, how to repaire or survive his honor: in this manner, callinge of Councell, they conclude.

Hee takes eight persons more to him, and, (like the nine Worthies of New Canaan,) they imbarque with preparation against Ma-re Mount, where this Monster of a man, as theire phrase was, had his denne; the whole number, had the rest not bin from home, being but seaven, would have given Captaine Shrimpe, (a quondam Drummer,) such a wellcome as would have made him wish for a Drume as bigg as Diogenes tubb, that hee might have crept into it out of sight.

Now the nine Worthies are approached, and mine Host prepared: having intelligence by a Salvage, that hastened in love from Wessaguscus to give him notice of their intent.

One of mine Hosts men prooved a craven: the other had prooved his wits to purchase a little valoure, before mine Host had observed his posture.[n]

The nine worthies comming before the Denne of this supposed Monster, (this seaven headed hydra, as they termed him,) and began, like Don Quixote, against the Windmill, to beate a parly, and to offer quarter, if mine Host would yeald; for they resolved to send him for England; and bad him lay by his armes.

posture: drunken demeanor.

But hee, (who was the Sonne of a Souldier,) having taken up armes in his just defence, replyed that hee would not lay by those armes, because they were so needefull at Sea, if hee should be sent over. Yet, to save the effusion of so much worty bloud, as would have issued out of the vaynes of these 9. worthies of New Canaan, if mine Host should have played upon them out at his port holes, (for they came within danger like a flocke of wild geese, as if they had bin tayled one to another, as colts to be sold at a faier,) mine Host was content to yeelde upon quarter; and did capitulate with them in what manner it should be for more certainety, because hee knew what Captaine Shrimpe was.

Hee expressed that no violence should be offered to his person, none to his goods, nor any of his Howshold: but that hee should have his armes, and what els was requisit for the voyage: which their Herald retornes, it was agreed upon, and should be performed.

But mine Host no sooner had set open the dore, and issued out, but instantly Captaine Shrimpe and the rest of the worties stepped to him, layd hold of his armes, and had him downe: and so eagerly was every man bent against him, (not regarding any agreement made with such a carnall man,) that they fell upon him as if they would have eaten him: some of them were so violent that they would have a slice with scabbert, and all for haste; untill an old Souldier, (of the Queenes, as the Proverbe is,) that was there by accident, clapt his gunne under the weapons, and sharply rebuked these worthies for their unworthy practises. So the matter was taken into more deliberate consideration.

Captaine Shrimpe, and the rest of the nine worthies, made themselves, (by this outragious riot,) Masters of mine Hoste of Ma-re Mount, and disposed of what hee had at his plantation.

This they knew, (in the eye of the Salvages,) would add to their glory, and diminish the reputation of mine honest Host; whome they practised to be ridd of upon any termes, as willingly as if hee had bin the very Hidra[n] of the time.

Hidra: Hydra, the many-headed snake, whose heads grew again as fast as they were cut off; finally slain by Hercules.

MARY ROWLANDSON (c. 1635–c. 1678)

Mary Rowlandson's *Narrative*, depicting her captivity by the Indians, is not only the first of a long line of "captivity stories," but one of the most graphic and dramatic of the colonial narratives of adventure. The avidity with which it was read perhaps accounts for the fact that no copy of the first edition, printed at Cambridge in 1682, has survived. At least thirty editions and reprints, including a London imprint within a few months of the first printing in America, attest its popularity. Its readers were drawn to the story as much by its compelling narrative interest and its terrifying detail as by the author's quiet and pious revelation of God's mercies. Her purpose was to write "a memorandum of Gods dealing with her."

Mary Rowlandson was the wife of the Reverend Joseph Rowlandson, the first minister of Lancaster, Massachusetts. When that frontier village was burned by Indians on February 10, 1675, during King Philip's War, her husband was absent from home. Carried away by the Indians, who took also her three surviving children, Mrs. Rowlandson remained a captive for eleven weeks. She was finally ransomed for £20 on May 2, 1676, after eight separate "removes" as her captors wandered about central Massachusetts and southern New Hampshire to escape the colonial forces. The youngest of Mrs. Rowlandson's children died early in the captivity from a wound, but the other two were released soon after their mother's ransom. In 1677 the Reverend Joseph Rowlandson accepted a pastoral call to Wethersfield, Connecticut, where he died a year later. His widow was voted an annual pension of £30, but there is no record of the date of her death. Mrs. Rowlandson's *Narrative* has been praised by Palfrey and other historians as a valuable account of Indian life; its real distinction, however, is to be found in its genuine narrative power and in its revelation of a religious faith which discovered abundant evidences of God's goodness in the midst of extreme adversity.

BIBLIOGRAPHY · The full title of the *Narrative* is *The Sovereignty and Goodness of God, Together with the Faithfulness of His Promises Displayed; Being a Narrative of the Captivity and Restauration of Mrs. Mary Rowlandson*. The best edition is the facsimile of the second edition (1682) edited, with a biography and bibliography, by H. S. Nourse and J. E. Thayer, and published at Cambridge in 1903. This facsimile was reprinted in 1930 without the bibliography. Available biographical material is summarized by Lewis Hanke in the *Dictionary of American Biography*. See also J. Nelson, "Mary Rowlandson's Narrative," *Americana*, XXVII (1933), 45–62; and H. S. Nourse, "Mrs. Mary Rowlandson's Removes," *Proceedings of the American Antiquarian Society* (New Series), XII (1897–1898), 401–409. For special studies of the form and importance of the captivity narratives, see P. D. Carleton, "The Indian Captivity," *American Literature*, XV (1943), 169–180, and R. H. Pearce, "The Significances of the Captivity Narrative," ibid. XIX (March, 1947), 1–20.

A Narrative of the Captivity

For a good many years the published accounts of "Indian captivities" have been popular collectors' items. Few of these narratives possess greater power than the revelation of pious humility in the straightforward story told by Mary Rowlandson, one of the chief documents of King Philip's war. The text is that of the facsimile of the second edition cited in the bibliography.

[*The Attack and the Beginning of the Captivity*]

On the tenth of February 1675, Came the Indians with great numbers upon Lancaster. Their first coming was about Sun-rising; hearing the noise of some Guns, we looked out; several houses were burning, and the Smoke ascending to Heaven. There were five persons taken in one house, the Father, and the Mother and a sucking Child they knockt on the head; the other two they took and carried away alive. Their were two others, who being out of their Garison upon some occasion, were set upon; one was knockt on the head, the other escaped. Another their was, who, running along, was shot and wounded, and fell down; he begged of them his life, promising them Money, (as they told me,) but they would not hearken to him, but knockt him in [the] head, and stript him naked, and split open his Bowels. Another, seeing many of the Indians about his Barn, ventured and went out, but was quickly shot down. There were three others belonging to the same Garison who were killed; the Indians getting up upon the roof of the Barn, had advantage to shoot down upon them over their Fortification. Thus these murtherous wretches went on, burning, and destroying before them.

At length they came and beset our own house,

and quickly it was the dolefullest day that ever mine eyes saw. The House stood upon the edge of a hill; some of the Indians got behind the hill, others into the Barn, and others behind any thing that could shelter them; from all which places they shot against the House, so that the Bullets seemed to fly like hail; and quickly they wounded one man among us, then another, and then a third. About two hours (according to my observation, in that amazing time) they had been about the house before they prevailed to fire it (which they did with Flax and Hemp, which they brought out of the Barn, and there being no defence about the House, only two Flankers at two opposite corners and one of them not finished) they fired it once and one ventured out and quenched it, but they quickly fired it again, and that took. Now is the dreadful hour come, that I have often heard of (in time of War, as it was the case of others) but now mine eyes see it. Some in our house were fighting for their lives, others wallowing in their blood, the House on fire over our heads, and the bloody Heathen ready to knock us on the head if we stirred out. Now might we hear Mothers & Children crying out for themselves, and one another, Lord what shall we do? Then I took my Children (and one of my sisters, hers) to go forth and leave the house: but as soon as we came to the dore and appeared, the Indians shot so thick that the bulletts rattled against the House, as if one had taken a handfull of stones and threw them, so that we were fain to give back. We had six stout Dogs belonging to our Garrison, but none of them would stir, though another time, if any Indian had come to the door, they were ready to fly upon him and tear him down. The Lord hereby would make us the more to acknowledge his hand, and to see that our help is alwayes in him. But out we must go, the fire increasing, and coming along behind us, roaring, and the Indians gaping before us with their Guns, Spears, and Hatchets to devour us. No sooner were we out of the House, but my Brother in Law (being before wounded, in defending the house, in or near the throat) fell down dead, wherat the Indians scornfully shouted and hallowed, and were presently upon him, stripping off his cloaths, the bulletts flying thick, one went through my side, and the same (as would seem)

through the bowels and hand of my dear Child in my arms. One of my elder Sisters Children, named William, had then his Leg broken, which the Indians perceiving, they knockt him on the head. Thus were we butchered by those merciless Heathen, standing amazed, with the blood running down to our heels. My eldest Sister being yet in the House, and seeing those wofull sights, the Infidels haling Mothers one way, and Children another, and some wallowing in their blood: and her elder Son telling her that her Son William was dead, and my self was wounded, she said, And, Lord let me dy with them; which was no sooner said, but she was struck with a Bullet, and fell down dead over the threshold. I hope she is reaping the fruit of her good labours, being faithfull to the service of God in her place. In her younger years she lay under much trouble upon spiritual accounts, till it pleased God to make that precious Scripture take hold of her heart, 2 Cor. 12, 9. And he said unto me my Grace is sufficient for thee. More than twenty years after I have heard her tell how sweet and comfortable that place was to her. But to return: The Indians laid hold of us, pulling me one way, and the Children another, and said, *Come go along with us;* I told them they would kill me: they answered, If I were willing to go along with them, they would not hurt me.

Oh, the dolefull sight that now was to behold at this House! Come, behold the works of the Lord, what disolations he has made in the Earth. Of thirty seven persons who were in this one House, none escaped either present death, or a bitter captivity, save only one, who might say as he: Job 1, 15. And I only am escaped alone to tell the News. There were twelve killed, some shot, some stab'd with their Spears, some knock't down with their Hatchets. When we are in prosperity, Oh the little that we think of such dreadfull sights, and to see our dear Friends, and Relations ly bleeding out their heart-blood upon the ground. There was one who was chopt into the head with a Hatchet, and stript naked, and yet was crawling up and down. It is a solemn sight to see so many Christians lying in their blood, some here, and some there, like a company of Sheep torn by wolves. All of them stript naked by a company of hell-hounds, roaring, singing, ranting and insulting, as if they would have torn our very hearts out; yet the Lord by his Almighty power preserved a number of us from death, for there were twenty-four of us taken alive and carried Captive.

I had often before this said, that if the Indians should come, I should chuse rather to be killed by them then taken alive, but when it came to the tryal my mind changed; their glittering weapons so daunted my spirit, that I chose rather to go along with those (as I may say) ravenous Bears, then that moment to end my dayes; and that I may the better declare what happened to me during that grievous Captivity I shall particularly speak of the severall Removes we had up and down the wilderness.

The First Remove

Now away we must go with those Barbarous Creatures, with our bodies wounded and bleeding, and our hearts no less than our bodies. About a mile we went that night, up upon a hill within sight of the Town where they intended to lodge. There was hard by a vacant house (deserted by the English before, for fear of the Indians). I asked them whether I might not lodge in the house that night to which they answered, What, will you love English men still? This was the dolefullest night that ever my eyes saw. Oh the roaring, and singing and danceing, and yelling of those black creatures in the night, which made the place a lively resemblance of hell. And as miserable was the wast that was there made, of Horses, Cattle, Sheep, Swine, Calves, Lambs, Roasting Pigs, and Fowl (which they had plundered in the Town) some roasting, some lying and burning, and some boyling to feed our merciless Enemies; who were joyful enough though we were disconsolate. To add to the dolefulness of the former day, and the dismalness of the present night: my thoughts ran upon my losses and sad bereaved condicion. All was gone, my Husband gone (at least separated from me, he being in the Bay;[n] and to add to my grief, the Indians told me they would kill him as he came homeward) my children gone, my Relations and Friends gone, our House and home and

all our comforts within door, and without, all was gone, (except my life) and I knew not but the next moment that might go too. There remained nothing to me but one poor wounded Babe, and it seemed at present worse than death that it was in such a pitiful condition, bespeaking Compassion, and I had no refreshing for it, nor suitable things to revive it. Little do many think what is the savageness and bruitishness of this barbarous Enemy; even those that seem to profess more than others among them, when the English have fallen into their hands.

Those even that were killed at Lancaster the summer before upon a Sabbath day, and the one that was afterward killed upon a week day, were slain and mangled in a barbarous manner, by one-ey'd John and Marlborough's Praying Indians, which Capt. Mosely brought to Boston, as the Indians told me.

The Second Remove

But now, the next morning, I must turn my back upon the Town, and travel with them into the vast and desolate Wilderness, I knew not whither. It is not my tongue, or pen can express the sorrows of my heart, and bitterness of my spirit, that I had at this departure: but God was with me in a wonderfull manner, carrying me along, and bearing up my spirit, that it did not quite fail. One of the Indians carried my poor wounded Babe upon a horse; it went moaning all along, I shall dy, I shall dy. I went on foot after it, with sorrow that cannot be exprest. At length I took it off the horse, and carried it in my armes till my strength failed, and I fell down with it: then they set me upon a horse with my wounded Child in my lap, and there being no furniture upon the horse back, as we were going down a steep hill, we both fell over the horses head, at which they like inhumane creatures laught, and rejoyced to see it, though I thought we should there have ended our dayes, as overcome with so many difficulties. But the Lord renewed my strength still, and carried me along, that I might see more of his Power; yea, so much that I could never have thought of, had I not experienced it.

After this it quickly began to snow, and when night came on, they stopt: and now down I must

in the Bay: The Reverend Mr. Rowlandson, having been warned of the impending attack, was seeking assistance when the massacre occurred.

22

sit in the snow, by a little fire, and a few boughs behind me, with my sick Child in my lap; and calling much for water, being now (through the wound) fallen into a violent Fever. My own wound also growing so stiff, that I could scarce sit down or rise up; yet so it must be, that I must sit all this cold winter night upon the cold snowy ground, with my sick Child in my armes, looking that every hour would be the last of its life; and having no Christian friend near me, either to comfort or help me. Oh, I may see the wonderfull power of God, that my Spirit did not utterly sink under my affliction: still the Lord upheld me with his gracious and mercifull Spirit, and we were both alive to see the light of the next morning.

The Third Remove

The morning being come, they prepared to go on their way. One of the Indians got up upon a horse, and they set me up behind him, with my poor sick Babe in my lap. A very wearisome and tedious day I had of it; what with my own wound, and my Childs being so exceeding sick, and in a lamentable condition with her wound. It may be easily judged what a poor feeble condition we were in, there being not the least crumb of refreshing that came within either of our mouths, from Wednesday night to Saturday night, except only a little cold water. This day in the afternoon, about an hour by the Sun, we came to the place where they intended, viz. an Indian Town, called Wenimesset, norward of Quabeug. When we were come, Oh the number of Pagans (now merciless enemies) that were come about me, that I may say as David, Psal. 27. 13, I had fainted, unless I had believed &c. The next day was the Sabbath: I then remembered how carless I had been of Gods holy time, how many Sabbaths I had lost and mispent, and how evily I had walked in Gods sight; which lay so close unto my spirit, that it was easie for me to see how righteous it was with God to cut off the threed of my life, and cast me out of his presence forever. Yet the Lord still shewed mercy to me, and upheld me; and as he wounded me with one hand, so he healed me with the other. This day there came to me one Robert Pepper (a man belonging to Roxbury) who was taken in Captain Beers his fight, and had been now a con-

siderable time with the Indians; and up with them almost as far as Albany to see king Philip, as he told me, and was now very lately come into these parts. Hearing, I say, that I was in this Indian Town, he obtained leave to come and see me. He told me, he himself was wounded in the leg at Captain Beers his Fight; and was not able some time to go, but as they carried him, and as he took Oaken leafes and lain to his wound, and through the blessing of God he was able to travel again. Then I took Oaken leaves and laid to my side, and with the blessing of God it cured me also; yet before the cure was wrought, I may say, as it is in Psal. 38. 5, 6. My wounds stink and are corrupt, I am troubled, I am bound down greatly, I go mourning all the day long. I sat much alone with a poor wounded Child in my lap, which moaned night and day, having nothing to revive the body, or cheer the spirits of her, but in stead of that, sometimes one Indian would come and tell me one hour, that your Master will knock your Child in the head, and then a second, and then a third, your Master will quickly knock your Child in the head.

This was the comfort I had from them, miserable comforters are ye all, as he[n] said. Thus nine dayes I sat upon my knees, with my Babe in my lap, till my flesh was raw again; my Child being even ready to depart this sorrowfull world, they bade me carry it out to another Wigwam (I suppose because they would not be troubled with such spectacles), whither I went with a very heavy heart, and down I sat with the picture of death in my lap. About two houres in the night, my sweet Babe, like a Lambe departeth this life, on Feb. 18, 1675. It being about six yeares, and five months old. It was nine dayes from the first wounding, in this miserable condition, without any refreshing of one nature or other, except a little cold water. I cannot but take notice, how at another time I could not bear to be in the room where any dead person was, but now the case is changed; I must and could ly down by my dead Babe, side by side all the night after. I have thought since of the wonderfull goodness of God to me, in preserving me in the use of my reason and senses, in that distressed time, that I did not use wicked and

he: Job 16:2.

23

violent means to end my own miserable life. . . . I had one Child dead, another in the Wilderness, I knew not where, the third they would not let me come near to. Me (as he[n] said) have ye bereaved of my children, Joseph is not, and Simeon is not, and ye will take Benjamin also, all these things are against me. I could not sit still in this condition, but kept walking from one place to another. And as I was walking along, my heart was even overwhelm'd with the thoughts of my condition, and that I should have Children, and a Nation which I knew not ruled over them. Whereupon I earnestly entreated the Lord, that he would consider my low estate, and shew me a token for good, and if it were his blessed will, some sign and hope of some relief. And indeed quickly the Lord answered, in some measure, my poor prayers: for as I was going up and down mourning and lamenting my condition, my Son came to me, and asked me how I did; I had not seen him before, since the destruction of the Town, and I knew not where he was, till I was informed by himself, that he was amongst a smaller parcel of Indians, whose place was about six miles off; with tears in his eyes, he asked me whether his Sister Sarah was dead; and told me he had seen his Sister Mary; and prayed me, that I would not be troubled in reference to himself. . . .

The Eighth Remove

On the morrow morning we must go over the River, i. e. Connecticot, to meet with King Philip, two Cannoos full, they had carried over, the next Turn i myself was to go; but as my foot was on the Cannoo to step in, there was a sudden out-cry among them, and i must step back; and instead of going over the River, i must go four or five miles up the River farther Northward. Some of the indians ran one way, and some another. The cause of this rout was, as i thought, their espying some English Scouts, who were thereabout. In this travel up the River; about noon the Company made a stop, and sate down; some to eat, and others to rest them. As I sat amongst them, musing of things past, my Son Joseph unexpectedly came to me; we asked of each others welfare, bemoaning our dolefull condition, and the change that had

come upon uss. We had Husband and Father, and Children and Sisters, and Friends, and Relations, and House, and Home, and many Comforts of this Life: but now we may say, as Job, Naked came I out of my Mothers Womb, and naked shall I return: the Lord gave, and the Lord hath taken away, Blessed be the Name of the Lord.[n] . . . We travelled on till night; and in the morning, we must go over the River to Philip's Crew. When I was in the Cannoo, I could not but be amazed at the numerous crew of Pagans that were on the Bank on the other side. When I came ashore, they gathered all about me, I sitting alone in the midst: I observed they asked one another questions, and laughed, and rejoyced over their Gains and Victories. Then my heart began to fail: and I fell a weeping which was the first time to my remembrance, that I wept before them. Although I had met with much Affliction, and my heart was many times ready to break, yet could I not shed one tear in their sight: but rather had been all this while in a maze, and like one astonished: but now I may say as, Psal. 137. i. By the Rivers of Babylon, there we sate down: yea we wept when we remembered Zion. There one of them asked me, why I wept, I could hardly tell what to say: yet I answered, they would kill me. "No," said he, "none will hurt you." Then came one of them and gave me two spoonfulls of Meal to comfort me, and another gave me half a pint of Pease; which was more worth than many Bushels at another time. Then I went to see King Philip, he bade me come in and sit down, and asked me whether I would smoke it (a usual Complement now adayes amongst Saints and Sinners) but this no way suited me. For though I had formerly used Tobacco, yet I had left it ever since I was first taken. It seems to be a Bait, the Devil layes to make men loose their precious time. I remember with shame, how formerly, when I had taken two or three pipes, I was presently ready for another, such a bewitching thing it is: but I thank God, he has now given me power over it; surely there are many who may be better employed than to ly sucking a stinking Tobacco-pipe.

Now the Indians gather their Forces to go against North-Hampton: over-night one went about yelling and hooting to give notice of the

he: Genesis 42:36.

Naked came I . . .: Job 1:21.

24

design. Whereupon they fell to boyling of Ground-nuts, and parching of Corn (as many as had it) for their Provision: and in the morning away they went. During my abode in this place, Philip spake to me to make a shirt for his boy, which I did, for which he gave me a shilling; I offered the money to my master, but he bade me keep it: and with it I bought a piece of Horse flesh. After-wards he asked me to make a Cap for his boy, for which he invited me to Dinner. I went, and he gave me a Pancake, about as big as two fingers; it was made of parched wheat, beaten, and fryed in Bears grease, but I thought I never tasted pleas-anter meat in my life. There was a Squaw who spake to me to make a shirt for her Sannup, for which she gave me a piece of Bear. Another asked me to knit a pair of Stockins, for which she gave me a quart of Pease: I boyled my Pease and Bear together, and invited my master and mistress to dinner, but the proud Gossip, because I served them both in one Dish, would eat nothing, except one bit that he gave her upon the point of his knife. Hearing that my son was come to this place, I went to see him, and found him lying flat on the ground; I asked him how he could sleep so & he answered me, That he was not asleep, but at

Prayer; and lay so that they might not observe what he was doing. I pray God he may remember these things now he is returned in safety. At this Place (the Sun now getting higher) what with the beams and heat of the Sun, and the smoak of the Wigwams, I thought I should have been blind, I could scarce discern one Wigwam from another. There was one Mary Thurston of Medfield, who seeing how it was with me, lent me a Hat to wear: but as soon as I was gone, the Squaw who owned that Mary Thurston came running after me, and got it away again. Here was the Squaw that gave me one spoonfull of Meal. I put it in my Pocket to keep it safe: yet notwithstanding some body stole it, but put five Indian Corns in the room of it: which Corns were the greatest Provisions I had in my travel for one day.

The Indians returning from North-Hampton, brought with them some Horses, and Sheep, and other things which they had taken. I desired them, that they would carry me to Albany, upon one of those Horses, and sell me for Powder: for so they had sometimes discoursed. I was utterly hopeless of getting home on foot, the way that I came. I could hardly bear to think of the many weary steps I had taken, to come to this place. . . .

JOHN DUNTON (1659–1733)

ALTHOUGH John Dunton, a London bookseller, spent only eight months in Boston, his entertaining, fictional *Letters from New-England* belong to the literary and social record of the American scene. In 1685, when Monmouth's insurrection sent the book trade into a sharp decline, Dunton embarked for New England, partly to salvage some bad debts owed him there, and partly to dispose of overstocks of "practical" books which he deemed to be "very proper for that place." He landed in Boston in March, 1686, and the *Letters* were written during his sojourn there and in neighboring communities.

Dunton is known to literature chiefly through his *Athenian Mercury*, a phenomenally successful question-and-answer publication, issued weekly in London during the 1690's. His reputation is sustained also by a whimsical *Life and Errors* (1705) which drew upon his travels through ten kingdoms, but dwelt most in-timately upon life in Dublin, Holland, and New Eng-land. Besides his own adventures and observations, it

contains a long series of "characters" of contemporary printers, engravers, publishers, and authors ranging from divines to journalists.

Dunton began his vocation at the age of fourteen, with an apprenticeship to a bookseller, after his family despaired of his becoming the fourth in line of Dunton divines. He was married to Iris (Elizabeth) Annesley in 1682, with whom he lived happily until her death in 1697. A later marriage with the daughter of a rich widow seems to have turned out less fortunately. In 1688 he made a four-months' trip to Holland and toured up the Rhine. After his return in November of that year, he resumed the book trade, which engaged him without interruption for the next ten years. In 1690 he established the *Athenian Mercury*, the success of which saved him from financial worries for the next six years. The contents of the *Mercury* were ascribed to the Athenian Club, under which anonymous cloak Richard Sault, Dr. Norris, and Samuel Wesley turned out witty and serious essays. After 1708 Dunton

25

joined the Whig cause and, beginning with "Neck or Nothing," published some forty political tracts supporting the Hanoverian House. The death of his second wife, from whom he was separated, came in 1721. He died "in obscurity" in 1733.

BIBLIOGRAPHY · The only modern biography is that in the *Dictionary of National Biography*. Biographical details are to be found also in the Memoir affixed by John Bowyer Nichols to his 1818 edition of Dunton's *Life and Errors*, and some of Dunton's own passages appeared in Nichols's *Literary Anecdotes of the Eighteenth Century* (London, 1812–1815). There have been no reprints of any of Dunton's works. The Prince Society of Boston printed the *Letters from New-England* (1867) from a manuscript copy in the Bodleian Library. The *Letters* parallels a portion of his *Life and Errors*. The question of the dubious reliability of the *Letters* is discussed thoroughly in C. N. Greenough, "John Dunton's Letters from New England," *Publications of the Colonial Society of Massachusetts*, XIV (1913), 212–257, and in the same scholar's "John Dunton Again," *ibid.*, XXI (1920), 232–251.

Letters from New-England

CLOSELY RELATED to the periodical essay in the seventeenth century was the widely popular character sketch. Paralleling the general, conventionalized "character writing" as practiced by Overbury, Earle, Cleaveland, and Butler, the personal sketch, either expository or satiric, sometimes took a political turn, as in the verse "characters" of Dryden's *Absalom and Achitophel*, and sometimes an historical or descriptive turn, as in the studied passages of Clarendon's *History of the Rebellion*. Dunton's sketches of this order show a considerable diversity: some are illustrative of exemplary conduct, others are satirical or expository. The text is that of the Prince Society edition of 1867.

[Character of Mrs. Green and Other Females]

A Wife is the next Change that a Virgin can lawfully make, and draws many other Relations after it. Which Mrs. Green was sensible of; For I have heard her say, "That when she Married Mr. Green, she espous'd his Obligations also! and where-ever her Husband, either by Tyes of Nature or squeezing of Wax, owed either Money or Love, she esteem'd herself to be no less a Debtor." She knew her Marriage was an Adoption into his Family, and therefore paid to every Branch of it what their respective Stations requir'd. She is sensible that the Duty of her Place has several Aspects. First, As it relates to her Husbands Person, and next to his Relations, and thirdly to his Fortune. As to his Person, she well enough knew that the great Duty of a Wife is Love. Love was the reason that she marry'd him; for she knew, where Love is wanting, it is but the Carcase of a Marriage. It was her study therefore, to preserve this Flame of Love, that, like the Vestal Fire, it never might go out; and therefore she took care to guard it from all those things that might Extinguish it. Mrs. Green knew very well how fatal Jealousie had been to many; and therefore as she took care never to harbour it in her own breast, so she was nicely careful never to give her Husband the least umbrage for it. She knew, should she give way to Jealousie, she should not only lose her Ease, but run the hazard of parting also with somewhat of her Innocence; for Jealousie is very apt to muster up the Forces of our irascible part to abet its quarrel. Another Debt that Mrs. Green was sensible she ow'd, and was careful to pay to her Husband, was Fidelity. She knew that as she had espous'd his Interests, so she ought to be true to 'em, keep all his Secrets, inform him of his Dangers, and in a mild and gentle manner admonish him of his Faults. And this she knew (how ill soever many take it) is one of the most genuine Acts of Faithfulness; and to be wanting in it would be a Failure in her Duty. And she was sensible that, if she did not do it, she should be unfaithful to herself; as well knowing nothing does so much secure the Happiness of a Wife, as the Vertue and Piety of her Husband. But Matrimonial Fidelity has a special Relation to the Marriage-Bed; and in this Mrs. Green was so severely scrupulous, that she would never suffer any light Expressions or wanton Discourse in her Company; and this was so remarkable in her, that, there being an invitation of several Persons to a Gentleman's House in Boston, and some that were invited resolving to be very merry; one of the company made this an Objection "that Mrs. Green would be there, which would spoil their Mirth." To which another wild Spark in the Company replied, "It is but speaking two or three words of Bawdy, and she'll be gone presently."

Another thing that was very remarkable in Mrs. Green was her Obedience to her Husband;

to whose will she was so exactly observant, that he cou'd not be more ready to Command, than she was to obey; and when some of his Commands seem'd not to be so kind as she might have expected, she wou'd not only obey 'em, but wisely dissemble the Unkindness of them, as knowing where Men have not wholly put off humanity, there is a native Compassion to a meek sufferer. She was also extreamly tender of her Husbands Reputation, setting his Worth in the clearest Light, putting his Infirmities (for where is the Man that lives without 'em?) in the Shade. And as she was this way tender of his Reputation, so she was also in another respect more particularly relating to herself; for, knowing that the misbehaviour of the Wife reflects upon the Husband, she took care to abstain even from all appearance of evil, and resolved to be (what Caesar desir'd of his Wife) not only free from Fault, but from all suspicion of it.

But Mrs. Green was not only a Loving, a Faithful, and an Obedient Wife, but an Industrious Wife too; managing that part of his Business which he had deputed to her, with so much Application and Dexterity as if she had never come into the House; and yet so manag'd her House as if she had never gone into the Ware-house. The Emperour Augustus himself scarce wore anything but what was the Manufacture of his Wife, his Sister, his Daughter, or his Nieces. Should our gay English Ladies, those Lilies of our Fields, which neither sow nor spin, nor gather into Barns, be exempted from furnishing others, and only left to Cloath themselves, 'tis to be doubted they wou'd reverse Our Saviour's Parallel of Solomon's Glories, and no Beggar in all his Rags, wou'd be array'd like one of these.

But Mrs. Green follow'd the Example of Solomon's Vertuous Wife, who riseth while it is yet Night, giving Meat to her Household, and a Portion to her Maidens; and as she is a good Wife to her Husband, so she is also a good Mother to her Children, whom she brings up with that sweetness and Facility as is admirable, not keeping them at too great a distance, (as some do) thereby Discouraging their good Parts; nor by an Over-Fondness (a fault most Mothers are guilty of) betraying 'em into a thousand Inconveniences, which oftentimes proves fatal to 'em.

In brief, she takes care of their Education, and whatever else belongs to 'em; so that Mr. Green enjoys the comfort of his Children, without knowing anything of the trouble of 'em.

Nor is she less a Good Mistress than a good Mother; Treating her Servants with that Love and Gentleness as if she were their Mother; taking care both of their Souls and Bodies, and not letting them want any thing necessary for either. I one Day told her, That I believ'd she was an extraordinary Wife; but Mr. Green was so good a Man, she cou'd not well be otherwise. To which she answer'd "That she had so good a Husband, was her Mercy; but had her Husband been as bad a Man as any in the World, her Duty wou'd have been the same, and so she hop'd her Practice shou'd have been too." Which, as it is a great Truth, it wants to be more known and Practic'd.

The next is Dolly S—der, who us'd to come often to my Warehouse and would plague my man Palmer more than all my Customers besides: Her life is a perpetual Contradiction; and she is made up of "I will" and "I will not": "Palmer, Reach me that Book, yet let it alone too; but let me see't however; and yet 'tis no great matter neither;" was her constant Dialect in my Warehouse: She's very Fantastical, but cann't be call'd Irresolute; for an Irresolute Person is always beginning, and she never makes an End. She writes and blots out again, whilst the other deliberates what to write: I know two Negatives make an Affirmative, but what her I [Aye] and No together makes, I know not; nor what to make of it, but that she knows not what to make of it herself. Her head is just like a Squirrel's Cage, and her Mind the Squirrel that whirls it round: She never looks towards the End, but only the beginning of things: For she will call in all haste for one, and have nothing to say to him when he is come; and long, nay die, for some Toy or Trifle, and when she has got it, grows weary of it presently. None knows where to have her a moment, and whosoever would hit her thoughts, must shoot flying.

The next is Mrs. T——, whose Tongue was round like a Wheel, one spoke after another, for there's no End on't: She makes more noise and jangling than the Bells do on a Coronation-Day. It is some bodies happiness that she is yet unmarried, for she wou'd make a Husband wish that she were dumb, or he were deaf. You would wonder at her matter, to hear her talk; and admire at talk when you heard her matter; but considering both together, you'd wonder at neither, but conclude as one did of the Nightingale, That she's *Vox, et pretera nihil*, a voice and nothing else. To hear her always talking, one wou'd wonder how she holds out; but for that, her Tongue moves with as great facility, as leaves wag, when shaken by the Wind. She us'd to come to my Warehouse, not to buy Books, (for she talk'd so much, she had no time to read) but that others might hear her talk: so that (I'm apt to think) had she but the Faculty of Talking in her sleep, one might make the Perpetual Motion with her Tongue.

WILLIAM PENN (1644–1718)

THE PURITAN settlements in New England were made possible by a fusion of two qualities which have left a strong impress on the American character: practicality and idealism. The blend of these elements also played an important part in the establishment of the Quaker colony in Pennsylvania. Its aristocratic founder, William Penn, was eager to promote the material fortunes of the province, but he was no less loyal to the principles of Quakerism. His zeal is reflected in attitudes to religious tolerance and political democracy which contrast sharply with the prevailing points of view in the theocratic society in Massachusetts.

William Penn came under Puritan influence as a student at Christ Church, Oxford, from which he was expelled in 1662 for Nonconformist activities. His father, Admiral Sir William Penn, an Anglican, attempted to woo the young man from the principles of Independency by sending him on a continental tour, but this stratagem failed. A decisive influence in young Penn's liberalism was the persuasive preaching of the Quaker, Thomas Loe. By 1669 Penn had become an active and notably articulate Friend. His attack on the doctrine of the Trinity, *The Sandy Foundation Shaken* (1668), led to imprisonment in the Tower, where he wrote *No Cross No Crown* (1669). These works, along with tracts and pamphlets, contain the principles of religious, political, and economic liberalism which were destined to motivate the rest of his active life.

Although Penn's name is inevitably associated with Pennsylvania, his first interest in America was the Quaker settlement in New Jersey, of which he became a trustee as well as the chief author of its charter of liberties. In 1681 Penn was granted an immense tract of land north of Maryland in payment of an inherited claim originally owed by the Crown to Penn's father, in whose honor it was named. Settlers were attracted to the colony, which Penn called a "Holy Experiment,"

not only by his liberal *Frame of Government* (1682), but by generous terms of land tenure. The four years of Penn's residence in America (1682–1684, 1699–1701) are no adequate measure of his influence on the commonwealths in New Jersey, Delaware, and Pennsylvania. His honorable treatment of the Indians, his guarantees of the fundamental liberties of the individual, and the skill with which he tempered administrative efficiency with a concern for men's spirits are noble landmarks in the annals of American colonization.

BIBLIOGRAPHY · M. K. Spence, *William Penn: A Bibliography* (1932) lists most of the writings of Penn. There is no complete edition of his works, although a definitive edition has been in preparation by A. C. Myers since 1910. Of the four available collections, the most valuable is that of J. Besse, *A Collection of the Works of William Penn* (2 vols., 1726). A useful and readily available volume of representative selections is *The Peace of Europe: The Fruits of Solitude, and Other Writings* (1916) in Everyman's Library. Twentieth-century biographies and studies include: S. G. Fisher, *The True William Penn* (1900), J. W. Graham, *William Penn, Founder of Pennsylvania* (1917), M. R. Brailsford, *The Making of William Penn* (1930), Bonamy Dobree, *William Penn, Quaker and Pioneer* (1932), A. Pound, *The Penns of Pennsylvania and England* (1932), C. E. Vulliamy, *William Penn* (1934), W. I. Hull, *William Penn, A Topical Biography* (1937), E. C. O. Beatty, *William Penn as a Social Philosopher* (1939), and W. W. Comfort, *William Penn, 1644–1718: A Tercentenary Estimate* (1944). The sketches in the *Dictionary of National Biography* and the *Dictionary of American Biography* contain the most succinct accounts of Penn's European and American careers.

A Letter to the Indians

A DESIRE to establish cordial relations with the Indians is expressed by Penn in a noble letter which he addressed to the aborigines of Pennsylvania in 1681, before he left England on his first voyage to America. His subsequent dealings with the natives, especially his fair treaty with them, inspired Voltaire's tribute: *"C'est le seul traité entre ces peuples et les chrétiens qui n'ait point été juré et qui n'ait point été rompu."* In 1701 when Penn left his colony for the last time, he carried with him a document from a number of Indian chiefs testifying to his liberality and justice. His fair payment for their lands, the Indians declared, was an act "which no governor ever did before him." The text is that reprinted in Samuel Hazard, *Annals of Pennsylvania* (1850), 532–533.

To the Indians.

London, 18th of 8th month, 1681.

My friends—There is one great God and power that hath made the world and all things therein, to whom you and I, and all people owe their being and well-being, and to whom you and I must one day give an account for all that we do in this world; this great God hath written his law in our hearts, by which we are taught and commanded to love and help, and do good to one another, and not to do harm and mischief one to another. Now this great God hath been pleased to make me concerned in your parts of the world, and the king of the country where I live hath given unto me a great province, but I desire to enjoy it with your love and consent, that we may always live together as neighbors and friends, else what would the great God say to us, who hath made us not to devour and destroy one another, but live soberly and kindly together in the world? Now I would have you well observe, that I am very sensible of the unkindness and injustice that hath been too much exercised towards you by the people of these parts of the world, who sought themselves, and to make great advantages by you, rather than be examples of justice and goodness unto you, which I hear hath been matter of trouble to you, and caused great grudgings and animosities, sometimes to the shedding of blood, which hath made the God angry; but I am not such a man, as is well known in my own country; I have great love and regard towards you, and I desire to win and gain your love and friendship, by a kind, just, and peaceable life, and the people I send are of the same mind, and shall in all things behave themselves accordingly; and if in any thing shall offend you or your people,

you shall have a full and speedy satisfaction for the same, by an equal number of just men on both sides, that by no means you may have just occasion of being offended against them. I shall shortly come to you myself, at what time we may more largely and freely confer and discourse of these matters. In the mean time, I have sent my commissioners to treat with you about land, and a firm league of peace. Let me desire of you to be kind to them and the people, and receive these presents and tokens which I have sent to you, as a testimony of my good will to you, and my resolution to live justly, peaceably, and friendly with you.

I am your loving friend,

William Penn

Of the Natives or Aborigines

ALTHOUGH Penn wrote several accounts of the Indians in letters to his friends, the most complete exposition of his views is contained in a communication to the Free Society of Traders in London, dated August 16, 1683. This work, which was first published in 1683, also includes a "general description" of the natural resources of the province of Pennsylvania. The document was reprinted in *Old South Leaflets*, VII, No. 171 (undated), 377–392, upon which the following selection is based.

XI. The natives I shall consider in their persons, language, manners, religion, and government, with my sense of their original.[n] For their persons, they are generally tall, straight, well-built, and of singular proportion; they tread strong and clever, and mostly walk with a lofty chin: of complexion, black, but by design, as the gypsies in England. They grease themselves with bears-fat clarified; and using no defence against sun or weather, their skins must needs be swarthy. Their eye is little and black, not unlike a straight-looked Jew. The thick lip and flat nose, so frequent with the East-Indians and Blacks, are not common to them; for I have seen as comely European-like faces among them of both, as on your side of the sea; and truly an Italian complexion hath not much more of the white, and the noses of several of them have as much of the Roman.

original: origin.

29

XII. Their language is lofty, yet narrow; but, like the Hebrew, in signification full; like short-hand in writing, one word serveth in the place of three, and the rest are supplied by the under-standing of the hearer: imperfect in their tenses, wanting in their moods, participles, adverbs, conjunctions, interjections: I have made it my business to understand it, that I might not want an interpreter on any occasion: and I must say, that I know not a language spoken in Europe, that hath words of more sweetness or greatness, in accent or emphasis than theirs; for instance, *Octocockon, Rancocas, Oricton, Shak, Marian, Poquesien;* all which are names of places, and have a grandeur in them. Of words of sweetness, *anna,* is mother; *issimus,* a brother; *netcap,* friend; *usque oret,* very good; *pane,* bread; *metsa,* eat; *matta,* no; *batta,* to have; *payo,* to come; *Sepassen, Passijon,* the names of places; *Tamane, Secane, Menanse, Secatereus,* are the names of persons. If one ask them for anything they have not, they will answer, *Matta ne batta,* which to translate is, *Not I have,* instead of, *I have not.*

XIII. Of their customs and manners, there is much to be said; I will begin with children. So soon as they are born, they wash them in water, and while very young, and in cold weather to chuse, they plunge them in the rivers to harden and embolden them. Having wrapped them in a clout, they lay them on a straight thin board, a little more than the length and breadth of the child, and swaddle it fast upon the board to make it straight; wherefore all Indians have flat heads; and thus they carry them at their backs. The children will go very young, at nine months commonly; they wear only a small clout round their waste, till they are big; if boys, they go a fishing till ripe for the woods, which is about fifteen; then they hunt, and after having given some proofs of their manhood, by a good return of skins, they may marry, else it is a shame to think of a wife. The girls stay with their mothers, and help to hoe the ground, plant corn, and carry burthens; and they do well to use them to that young, which they must do when they are old; for the wives are the true servants of the husbands; otherwise the men are very affectionate to them.

XIV. When the young women are fit for marriage, they wear something on their heads for an advertisement, but so as their faces are hardly to be seen, but when they please. The age they marry at, if women, is about thirteen and fourteen; if men, seventeen and eighteen; they are rarely elder.

XV. Their houses are mats, or barks of trees, set on poles, in the fashion of an English barn, but out of the power of the winds, for they are hardly higher than a man; they lie on reeds or grass. In travel, they lodge in the woods about a great fire, with the mantle of duffils[n] they wear by day wrapped about them, and a few boughs stuck round about them.

XVI. Their diet is maize, or Indian corn, divers ways prepared; sometimes roasted in the ashes, sometimes beaten and boiled with water, which they call *homine;* they also make cakes, not unpleasant to eat. They have likewise several sorts of beans and pease, that are good nourishment; and the woods and rivers are their larder.

XVII. If an European comes to see them, or calls for lodging at their house, or wigwam, they give him the best place, and first cut. If they come to visit us, they salute us with an *itah,* which is as much as to say, Good be to you; and set them down, which is mostly on the ground, close to their heels, their legs upright; it may be they speak not a word, but observe all passages. If you give them anything to eat or drink, well, for they will not ask; and be it little or much, if it be with kindness, they are well pleased, else they go away sullen, but say nothing.

XVIII. They are great concealers of their own resentments, brought to it, I believe, by the revenge that hath been practised among them; in either of these, they are not exceeded by the Italians. A tragical instance fell out since I came into the country. A king's daughter thinking herself slighted by her husband, in suffering another woman to lie down between them, rose up, went out, plucked a root out of the ground, and ate it, upon which she immediately died; and for which,

duffils: duffle, a coarse cloth of wool.

last week, he made an offering to her kindred, for atonement, and liberty of marriage; as two others did to the kindred of their wives, that died a natural death. For till widowers have done so, they must not marry again. Some of the young women are said to take undue liberty before marriage, for a portion; but when married, chaste; when with child, they know their husbands no more, till delivered; and during their month, they touch no meat they eat but with a stick, lest they should 10 defile it; nor do their husbands frequent them, till that time be expired.

XIX. But in liberality they excel; nothing is too good for their friend; give them a fine gun, coat, or other thing, it may pass twenty hands before it sticks; light of heart, strong affections, but soon spent: the most merry creatures that live, feast and dance perpetually; they never have much, nor want much: wealth circulateth like the 20 blood, all parts partake; and though none shall want what another hath, yet exact observers of property. Some kings have sold, others presented me with several parcels of land; the pay or presents I made them, were not hoarded by the particular owners, but the neighboring kings and their clans being present when the goods were brought out, the parties chiefly concerned consulted what, and to whom they should give them. To every king then, by the hands of a person for that work 30 appointed, is a proportion sent, so sorted and folded, and with that gravity, that is admirable. Then that king subdivideth it in like manner among his dependents, they hardly leaving themselves an equal share with one of their subjects: and be it on such occasions as festivals, or at their common meals, the kings distribute, and to themselves last. They care for little, because they want but little, and the reason is, a little contents them. In this they are sufficiently revenged on us; if they are 40 ignorant of our pleasures, they are also free from our pains. They are not disquieted with bills of lading and exchange, nor perplexed with chancery-suits and exchequer reckonings. We sweat and toil to live; their pleasure feeds them; I mean their hunting, fishing, and fowling, and this table is spread everywhere: they eat twice a day, morning and evening; their seats and table are the ground.

Since the Europeans came into these parts, they are grown great lovers of strong liquors, rum especially; and for it exchange the richest of their skins and furs. If they are heated with liquors, they are restless till they have enough to sleep; that is their cry, Some more, and I will go to sleep; but, when drunk, one of the most wretched spectacles in the world.

XX. In sickness, impatient to be cured, and for it give anything, especially for their children, to whom they are extremely natural; they drink at those times a *teran*, or decoction of some roots in spring-water; and if they eat any flesh, it must be the female of any creature. If they die, they bury them with their apparel, be they man or woman, and the nearest of kin fling in something precious with them, as a token of their love. Their mourning is blacking of their faces, which they continue for a year. They are choice of the graves of their dead; for lest they should be lost by time, and fall to common use, they pick off the grass that grows upon them, and heap up the fallen earth with great care and exactness.

XXI. These poor people are under a dark night in things relating to religion, to be sure, the tradition of it; yet they believe a GOD and immortality, without the help of metaphysicks; for they say, "There is a great king who made them, who dwells in a glorious country to the southward of them; and that the souls of the good shall go thither, where they shall live again." Their worship consists of two parts, sacrifice and cantico. Their sacrifice is their first-fruits; the first and fattest buck they kill goeth to the fire, where he is all burnt, with a mournful ditty of him that performeth the ceremony, but with such mervellous fervency, and labour of body, that he will even sweat to a foam. The other part is their cantico, performed by round dances, sometimes words, sometimes songs, then shouts, two being in the middle that begin, and by singing, and drumming on a board, direct the chorus. Their postures in the dance are very antic, and differing, but all keep measure. This is done with equal earnestness and labour, but great appearance of joy. In the fall, when the corn cometh in, they begin to feast one another; there have been two great festivals

31

already, to which all come that will: I was at one myself; their entertainment was a green seat by a spring, under some shady trees, and twenty bucks, with hot cakes of new corn, both wheat and beans, which they make up in a square form, in the leaves of the stem, and bake them in the ashes; and after that they fall to a dance. But they that go must carry a small present in their money, it may be six-pence, which is made of the bone of a fish; the black is with them as gold, the white, silver; they 10 call it wampum.

XXII. The government is by kings, which they call *Sachama*, and those by succession, but always of the mother's side; for instance, the children of him that is now king, will not succeed, but his brother by the mother, or the children of his sister, whose sons (and after them the children of her daughters) will reign, for no woman inherits; the reason they render for this way of descent is, that their issue may not be spurious. 20

XXIII. Every king hath his council, and that consists of all the old and wise men of his nation, which perhaps is two hundred people; nothing of moment is undertaken, be it war, peace, selling of land or traffick, without advising with them; and, which is more, with the young men too. It is admirable to consider, how powerful the kings are, and yet how they move by the breath of their people. I have had occasion to be in council with 30 them upon treaties for land, and to adjust the terms of trade; their order is thus: the king sits in the middle of an half moon, and hath his council, the old and wise on each hand; behind them, or at a little distance, sit the younger fry, in the same figure. Having consulted and resolved their business, the king ordered one of them to speak to me; he stood up, came to me, and in the name of his king saluted me, then took me by the hand, and told me, "He was ordered by his king to speak to 40 me; and that now it was not he, but the king that spoke, because what he should say, was the king's mind." He first prayed me, "To excuse them that had not complied with me the last time; he feared there might be some fault in the interpreter, being neither Indian nor English; besides, it was the Indian custom to deliberate, and take up much time in council, before they resolve; and that if

the young people and owners of the land had been as ready as he, I had not met with so much delay." Having thus introduced his matter, he fell to the bounds of the land they had agreed to dispose of, and the price; which now is little and dear, that which would have brought twenty miles, not buying now two. During the time that this person spoke, not a man of them was observed to whisper or smile; the old grave, the young reverent in their deportment: they speak little, but fervently, and with elegance. I have never seen more natural sagacity, considering them without the help (I was going to say, the spoil) of tradition; and he will deserve the name of wise, that out-wits them in any treaty about a thing they understand. When the purchase was agreed, great promises passed between us of "kindness and good neighbourhood, and that the Indians and English must live in love, as long as the sun gave light." Which 20 done, another made a speech to the Indians, in the name of all the *sachamakers* or kings; first to tell them what was done; next, to charge and command them "To love the Christians, and particularly live in peace with me, and the people under my government: that many governors had been in the river, but that no governor had come himself to live and stay here before; and having now such an one that had treated them well, they should never do him or his any wrong." At every 30 sentence of which they shouted, and said, "Amen," in their way.

XXIV. The justice they have is pecuniary. In case of any wrong or evil fact, be it murther itself, they atone by feasts, and presents of their *wampum*, which is proportioned to the quality of the offence or person injured, or of the sex they are of: for in case they kill a woman, they pay double, and the reason they can render, is, "That she breedeth children, which men cannot do." It is rare that they fall out, if sober; and if drunk, they forgive it, saying, "It was the drink, and not the man, that abused them."

XXV. We have agreed, that in all differences between us, six of each side shall end the matter. Don't abuse them, but let them have justice, and you win them. The worst is, that they are the worse for the Christians, who have propagated their vices, and yielded them tradition for ill, and not for good things. But as low an ebb as these people are at, and as glorious as their own condition looks, the Christians have not outlived their sight, with all their pretensions to an higher manifestation. What good then might not a good people graft, where there is so distinct a knowledge left between good and evil? I beseech God to incline the hearts of all that come into these parts, to outlive the knowledge of the natives, by a fixed [10] obedience to their greater knowledge of the will of God; for it were miserable indeed for us to fall under the just censure of the poor Indian conscience, while we make profession of things so far transcending.

XXVI. For their original, I am ready to believe them of the Jewish race; I mean of the stock of the Ten Tribes,[n] and that for the following reasons; first, they were to go to a "land not planted or known," which, to be sure, Asia and Africa were, if not Europe; and He that intended that extraordinary judgment upon them, might make the passage not uneasy to them, as it is not impossible in itself, from the eastermosts parts of Asia, to the westermost of America. In the next place, I find them of like countenance, and their children of so lively a resemblance, that a man would think himself in Duke's-place or Bury-street in London, when he seeth them. But this is not all; they agree in rites, they reckon by moons; they offer their first-fruits, they have a kind of feast of tabernacles; they are said to lay their altar upon twelve stones; their mourning a year, customs of women, with many things that do not now occur. . . .

THE PURITAN WORLD

WILLIAM BRADFORD (1590–1657)

THE SON of a substantial Yorkshire family, William Bradford early in life became an orphan and was virtually adopted by William Brewster, the foremost Separatist of Scrooby, England. He joined the Separatists, accompanied them to Holland, sailed with them for America on the *Mayflower* in 1620, and became governor upon the death of John Carver the following year. Though he tried almost annually to withdraw from office, he held this post for thirty of the remaining thirty-five years of his life. Even in the free years he was chosen assistant. As governor, Bradford was astute, practical, efficient, and forward-looking. He kept his emotions well under control and aroused little personal opposition. He fought firmly for the colony of Plymouth against such enemies as Oldham, Morton, and others who sought to block the moves and to blacken the reputations of the founding fathers.

From the beginning, Bradford tried hard to meet the colonial obligations to the sponsoring adventurers in London, and to this end he sought to establish a fishing industry and to encourage trade in beaver pelts. Efforts to liquidate planter obligations led him, along with Brewster and seven other colonial leaders, to assume in 1627 the indebtedness of the colony in return for a monopoly of fishing and trading privileges. Loss of valuable cargoes to pirates, the "grosse miscarriages" of Allerton, the colony's agent, the waiving of the corn tax, and the appearance of formidable rivals for the Indian trade long delayed the final settlement, made only seven years before Bradford's death.

Of Plimoth Plantation is neither diary nor formal history; it is a private journal in which Bradford set down, without order, every detail that interested him in the life of the settlement. Thus at the same time a record of his life and of the community whose activities he led, it constitutes a primary source of information about the first New England colony. The difficulties of communal ownership, plagues, and low supplies, the vexations in formulating laws and establishing rules for the admission of strangers, and the troubles with the Pequod Indians in a war precipitated by Massachusetts Bay Colony were some of the problems that confronted this Plymouth leader. Bradford was zealous for the downfall of episcopacy in England as well as in America. He rejoiced at the success of Cromwell's

Ten Tribes: the Ten Tribes of Israel.

arms in the 1740's and opposed schismatics in the colony. He emerges from his journal as a courageous and resourceful leader. His prose is not eloquent or glowing, but his honest thought enables us to visualize a sturdy group of pioneers who survived the discouragements of pestilence, a hostile environment, and a non-idealistic opposition.

Plymouth had been founded in a barren section of the state. With the removal of numerous saints elsewhere, it had become almost a ghost town before the end of Bradford's life. But Bradford's own career was successful. He went to his death, as Cotton Mather remarked, "lamented by all the colonists of New England, as a common blessing, and father to them all."

BIBLIOGRAPHY · Forty-two years after *Of Plimoth Plantation* was first published in full in 1856, W. T. Davis edited the journal for the Original Narratives of Early American History series (1908). The best and most authoritative text is that edited by Worthington 10 C. Ford for the Massachusetts Historical Society in 1912. A convenient, modernized form was prepared for the press by H. Paget in 1929. Three brief accounts of his life have appeared: J. Shepard, *Governor William Bradford and His Son, Major William Bradford* (1900), A. H. Plumb, *William Bradford of Plymouth* (1920), and W. Walker, *Ten New England Leaders* (1901). Valuable criticism may be found in E. F. Bradford's "Conscious Art in Bradford's *History of Plymouth Plantation*," *The New England Quarterly*, I (April, 1928), and K. B. Murdock's chapter, "Colonial Historians" in John Macy's *American Writers on American Literature* (1931). 20

Of Plimoth Plantation

BRADFORD's journal was not printed until two centuries after his death. The manuscript, which had been used by Nathaniel Morton, Thomas Prince, and other early Massachusetts writers, was presumably carried to England by the British during the Revolution. In 1855 it was discovered in the library of the Bishop of London, at Fulham. The complete text was published 30 in the following year by the Massachusetts Historical Society, but the manuscript was not yielded to Massachusetts until 1897. Bradford's work was written between 1630 and 1650, and covers the years from 1620 to 1647. The most interesting section of the first Book is that supplying the motives for the migration to America. The selections here printed are from Book Two, in which Bradford methodically and movingly recorded the heroic struggles for survival on the part of the early settlers. His account of the settlement at Merry Mount may be compared with the nineteenth- 40 century literary treatment by Hawthorne in "The Maypole of Merry Mount." The text is that of the edition prepared by Charles Deane for the Massachusetts Historical Society in *Collections of the Massachusetts Historical Society* (Fourth Series), III (1856).

[*Early Days*]

The remainder of An°: 1620.

I shall a litle returne backe and begine with a combination made by them before they came ashore, being the first foundation of their governmente in this place; occasioned partly by the discontented & mutinous speeches that some of the strangers amongst them had let fall from them in the ship—That when they came a shore they would use their owne libertie; for none had power to command them, the patente they had being for Virginia, and not for New-england, which belonged to an other Government, with which the Virginia Company had nothing to doe. And partly that shuch an acte by them done (this their condition considered) might be as firme as any patent, and in some respects more sure.

The forme was as followeth.

In the name of God, Amen. We whose names are underwriten, the loyal subjects of our dread soveraigne Lord, King James, by the grace of God, of Great Britaine, Franc, & Ireland king, defender of the faith, &c., haveing undertaken, for the glorie of God, and advancemente of the Christian faith, and honour of our king & countrie, a voyage to plant the first colonie in the Northerne parts of Virginia, doe by these presents solemnly & mutualy in the presence of God, and one of another, covenant & combine our selves togeather into a civill body politick, for our better ordering & preservation & furtherance of the ends aforesaid; and by vertue hearof to enacte, constitute, and frame such just & equall lawes, ordinances, acts, constitutions, & offices, from time to time, as shall be thought most meet & convenient for the generall good of the Colonie, unto which we promise all due submission and obedience. In witnes wherof we have hereunder subscribed our names at Cap-Codd the 11. of November, in the year of the raigne of our soveraigne lord, King James, of England, France, & Ireland the eighteenth, and of Scotland the fiftie fourth. An°; Dom. 1620.

After this they chose, or rather confirmed, Mr. John Carver (a man godly & well approved amongst them) their Governour for that year. And after they had provided a place for their goods, or comone store, (which were long in unlading for want of boats, foulnes of winter weather, and sicknes of diverce,) and begune some small cottages for their habitation, as time would admitte they mette and consulted of lawes & orders, both for their civill & military Governmente, as the necessitie of their condition did require, still adding therunto as urgent occasion in severall times, and as cases did require.

In these hard & difficulte beginings they found some discontents & murmurings arise amongst some, and mutinous speeches & carriags in other; but they were soone quelled & overcome by the wisdome, patience, and just & equall carrage of things by the Govr and better part, wch clave faithfully togeather in the maine. But that which was most sadd & lamentable was, that in 2. or 3. moneths time halfe of their company dyed, espetialy in Jan: & February, being the depth of winter, and wanting houses & other comforts; being infected with the scurvie & other diseases, which this long voiage & their inacomodate condition had brought upon them; so as ther dyed some times 2. or 3. of a day, in the foresaid time; that of 100. & odd persons, scarce 50. remained. And of these in the time of most distres, ther was but 6. or 7. sound persons, who, to their great comendations be it spoken, spared no pains, night nor day, but with abundance of toyle and hazard of their owne health, fetched them woode, made them fires, drest them meat, made their beads, washed their lothsome cloaths, cloathed & uncloathed them; in a word, did all the homly & necessarie offices for them which dainty & quesie stomacks cannot endure to hear named; and all this willingly & cherfully, without any grudging in the least, shewing herein their true love unto their freinds & bretheren. A rare example & worthy to be remembred. Two of these 7. were Mr. William Brewster, ther reverend Elder, & Myles Standish, ther Captein & military comander, unto whom my selfe, & many others, were much beholden in our low & sicke condition. And yet the Lord so upheld these persons, as in this generall calamity they were not at all infected either with sicknes, or lamnes. And what I have said of these, I may say of many others who dyed in this generall vissitation, & others yet living, that whilst they had health, yea, or any strength continuing, they were not wanting to any that had need of them. And I doute not but their recompence is with the Lord.

But I may not hear pass by an other remarkable passage not to be forgotten. As this calamitie fell among the passengers that were to be left here to plant, and were hasted a shore and made to drinke water, that the sea-men might have the more bear, and one [which was the author him selfe] in his sicknes desiring but a small cann of beer, it was answered, that if he were their owne father he should have none; the disease begane to fall amongst them also, so as allmost halfe of their company dyed before they went away, and many of their officers and lustyest men, as the boatson, gunner, 3. quarter-maisters, the cooke, & others. At which the mr. was something strucken and sent to the sick a shore and tould the Govr he should send for beer for them that had need of it, though he drunke water homward bound. But now amongst his company ther was farr another kind of carriage in this miserie then amongst the passengers; for they that before had been boone conpanions in drinking & joyllity in the time of their health & wellfare, begane now to deserte one another in this calamitie, saing they would not hasard their lives for them, they should be infected by coming to help them in their cabins, and so, after they came to dye by it, would doe litle or nothing for them, but if they dyed let them dye. But shuch of the passengers as were yet abord shewed them what mercy they could, which made some of their harts relente, as the boatson (& some others), who was a prowd yonge man, and would often curse & scofe at the passengers; but when he grew weak, they had compassion on him and helped him; then he confessed he did not deserve it at their hands, he had abused them in word & deed. O! saith he, you, I now see, shew your love like Christians indeed one to another, but we let one another lye & dye like doggs. Another lay cursing his wife, saing if it had not ben for her he had never come this unlucky viage, and anone cursing his felows, saing he had done this & that, for some of them, he had spent so much, & so much, amongst them, and they were now weary of him, and did not help him, having need. Another gave his companion all he had, if he died, to help him in his weaknes; he went and got a litle spise & made him a mess of meat once or twise, and because he dyed not so soon as he expected, he went amongst his fellows & swore the rogue would cousen him, he would see him choaked before he made him any more meate; and yet the pore fellow dyed before morning.

All this while the Indians came skulking about them, and would sometimes show them selves aloofe of [f], but when any aproached near them, they would rune away. And once they stoale away their tools wher they had been at worke, & were gone to diner. But about the 16. of March a certaine Indian came bouldly amongst them, and spoke to them in broken English, which they could well understand, but marvelled at it. At length they understood by discourse with him, that he was not of these parts, but belonged to the eastrene parts, wher some English-ships came to fhish, with whom he was aquainted, & could name sundrie of them by their names, amongst whom he had gott his language. He became profitable to them in aquainting them with many things concerning the state of the cuntry in the east-parts wher he lived, which was afterwards profitable unto them; as also of the people hear, of their names, number, & strength; of their situation & distance from this place, and who was cheefe amongst them. His name was Samaset; he tould them also of another Indian whos name was Squanto, a native of this place, who had been in England & could speake better English then him selfe. Being, after some time of entertainmente & gifts, dismist, a while after he came againe, & 5. more with him, & they brought againe all the tooles that were stolen away before, and made way for the coming of their great Sachem, called Massasoyt; who, about 4. or 5. days after, came with the cheefe of his freinds & other attendance, with the aforesaid Squanto. With whom, after frendly entertainment, & some gifts given him, they made a peace with him (which hath now continued this 24. years). . . .

[Merry Mount]

Anno Dom: 1628. . . . Aboute some 3. or 4. years before this time, ther came over one Captaine Wolastone, (a man of pretie parts,) and with him 3. or 4. more of some eminencie, who brought with them a great many servants, with provissions & other impliments for to begine a plantation; and pitched them selves in a place within the Massachusets, which they called, after their Captains name, Mount-Wollaston. Amongst whom was one Mr. Morton, who, it should seeme, had some small adventure (of his owne or other mens) amongst them; but had litle respecte amongst them, and was sleghted by the meanest servants. Haveing continued ther some time, and not finding things to answer their expectations, nor profite to arise as they looked for, Captaine Wollaston takes a great part of the sarvants, and transports them to Virginia, wher he puts them of [f] at good rates, selling their time to other men; and writs back to one Mr. Rassdall, one of his cheefe partners, and accounted their marchant, to bring another parte of them to Verginia likewise, intending to put them of [f] there as he had done the rest. And he, with the consente of the said Rasdall, appoynted one Fitcher to be his Livetenante, and governe the remaines of the plantation, till he or Rasdall returned to take further order theraboute. But this Morton abovesaid, haveing more craft then honestie, (who had been a kind of petiefogger, of Furnefells Inne,) in the others absence, watches an oppertunitie, (commons being but hard amongst them,) and gott some strong drinck and other junkats, & made them a feast; and after they were merie, he begane to tell them, he would give them good counsell. You see (saith he) that many of your fellows are carried to Virginia; and if you stay till this Rasdall returne, you will also be carried away and sould for slaves with the rest. Therfore I would advise you to thruste out this Levetenant Fitcher; and I, having a parte in the plantation, will receive you as my partners and Consociats; so may you be free from service, and we will converse, trad, plante, & live togeather as equalls, & supporte & protecte one another, or to like effecte. This counsell was easily received; so they tooke oppertunitie, and thrust Levetenante Fitcher out a dores, and would suffer him to come no more amongst them, but forct him to seeke bread to eate, and other releefe from his neigbours, till he could gett passages for England. After this

36

they fell to great licenciousness, and led a dissolute life, powering out them selves into all profanenes. And Morton became lord of misrule, and maintained (as it were) a schoole of Athisme. And after they had gott some good into their hands, and gott much by trading with the Indeans, they spent it as vainly, in quaffing & drinking both wine & strong waters in great exsess, and, as some reported 10^{lis.} worth in a morning. They allso set up a May-pole, drinking and dancing aboute it many days togeather inviting the Indean women, for their consorts, dancing and frisking togither, (like so many fairies, or furies rather,) and worse practises. As if they had anew revived & celebrated the feasts of the Roman Goddes Flora, or the beasly practieses of the madd Bacchinalians. Morton likwise (to shew his poetrie) composed sundry rimes & verses, some tending to lasciviousnes, and others to the detraction & scandall of some persons, which he affixed to this idle or idoll May-polle. They chainged allso the name of their place, and in stead of calling it Mounte Wollaston, they call it Meriemounte, as if this joylity would have lasted ever. But this continued not long, for after Morton was sent for England, (as follows to be declared,) shortly after came over that worthy gentlman, Mr. John Indecott, who brought over a patent under the broad seall, for the governmente of the Massachusets, who visiting those parts caused that May-polle to be cutt downe, and rebuked them for their profannes, and admonished them to looke ther should be better walking; so they now, or others, changed the name of their place againe, and called it Mounte-Dagon.

Now to maintaine this riotous prodigallitie and profuse excess, Morton, thinking him selfe lawless, and hearing what gaine the French & fisher-men made by trading of peeces, powder, & shotte to the Indeans, he, as the head of this consortship, begane the practise of the same in these parts; and first he taught them how to use them, to charge, & discharg, and what proportion of powder to give the peece, according to the sise or bignes of the same; and what shotte to use for foule, and what for deare. And having thus instructed them, he imployed some of them to hunte & fowle for him, so as they became farr more active in that imploymente then any of the English, by reason of ther swiftnes of foote & nimblnes of body, being also quick-sighted, and by continuall exercise well knowing the hants of all sorts of game. So as when they saw the execution that a peece would doe, and the benefite that might come by the same, they became madd, as it were, after them, and would not stick to give any prise they could attaine too for them; accounting their bowes & arrowes but bables in comparison of them.

And here I may take occasion to bewaile the mischefe that this wicked man began in these parts, and which since base covetousnes prevailing in men that should know better, has now at length gott the upper hand, and made this thing commone, notwithstanding any laws to the contrary; so as the Indeans are full of peeces all over, both fouling peeces, muskets, pistols, &c. They have also their moulds to make shotte, of all sorts, as muskett bulletts, pistoll bullets, swane & gose shote, & of smaler sorts; yea, some have seen them have their scruplats to make scrupins them selves, when they wante them, with sundery other implements, wherwith they are ordinarily better fited & furnished then the English them selves. Yea, it is well knowne that they will have powder & shot, when the English want it, nor cannot gett it; and that in a time of warre or danger, as experience hath manifested, that when lead hath been scarce, and men for their owne defence would gladly have given a groat a li, which is dear enoughe, yet hath it bene bought up & sent to other places, and sould to shuch as trade it with the Indeans, at 12. pence the li.; and it is like they give 3. or 4. s. the pound, for they will have it at any rate. And these things have been done in the same times, when some of their neighbours & friends are daly killed by the Indeans, or are in deanger therof, and live but at the Indeans mercie. Yea, some (as they have aquainted them with all other things) have tould them how gunpowder is made, and all the materialls in it, and that they are to be had in their owne land; and I am confidente, could they attaine to make saltpeter, they would teach them to make powder. O, the horiblnes of this vilanie! how many both Dutch & English have been latly slaine by those Indeans, thus furnished; and no remedie provided, nay, the evill more increased, and the blood of their brethren sould for gaine, as

37

is to be feared; and in what danger all these colonies are in is too well known. Oh! that princes & parlements would take some timly order to prevente this mischeefe, and at length to suppress it, by some exemplerie punishmente upon some of these gaine thirstie murderers, (for they deserve no better title,) before their collonies in these parts be over throwne by these barbarous savages, thus armed with their owne weapons, by these evill instruments, and traytors to their neighbors and cuntrie. But I have forgott my selfe, and have been to longe in this digression; but now to returne. This Morton having thus taught them the use of peeces, he sould them all he could spare; and he and his consorts detirmined to send for many out of England, and had by some of the ships sente for above a score. The which being knowne, and his neighbours meeting the Indeans in the woods armed with guns in this sorte, it was a terrour unto them, who lived straglingly, and were of no strenght in any place. And other places (though more remote) saw this mischeefe would quictly spread over all, if not prevented. Besides, they saw they should keep no servants, for Morton would entertaine any, how vile soever, and all the scume of the countrie, or any discontents, would flock to him from all places, if this nest was not broken; and they should stand in more fear of their lives & goods (in short time) from this wicked & deboste crue, then from the salvages them selves.

So sundrie of the cheefe of the stragling plantations, meeting togither, agreed by mutuall consente to sollissite those of Plimoth (who were then of more strength then them all) to joyne with them, to prevente the further grouth of this mischeefe, and suppress Morton & his consortes before they grewe to further head and strength. Those that joyned in this acction (and after contributed to the charge of sending him for England) were from Pascataway, Namkeake, Winisimett, Weesagascusett, Natasco, and other places wher any English were seated. Those of Plimoth being thus sought too by their messengers & letters, and waying both their reasons, and the commone danger, were willing to afford them their help; though themselves had least cause of fear or hurte. So, to be short, they first resolved joyntly to write to him, and in a freindly & neigborly way to ad-

monish him to forbear these courses, & sent a messenger with their letters to bring his answer. But he was so highe as he scorned all advise, and asked who had to doe with him, he had and would trade peeces with the Indeans in dispite of all, with many other scurillous termes full of disdaine. They sente to him a second time, and bad him be better advised, and more temperate in his termes, for the countrie could not beare the injure he did; it was against their comone saftie, and against the king's proclamation. He answerd in high terms as before, and that the kings proclaimation was no law; demanding what penaltie was upon it. It was answered, more than he could bear, his majesties displeasure. But insolently he persisted, and said the king was dead and his displeasure with him, & many the like things; and threatened withall that if any came to molest him, let them looke to them selves, for he would prepare for them. Upon which they saw ther was no way but to take him by force; and having so farr proceeded, now to give over would make him farr more hautie & insolente. So they mutually resolved to proceed, and obtained of the Govr. of Plimoth to send Captaine Standish, & some other aide with him, to take Morton by force. The which accordingly was done; but they found him to stand stifly in his defence, having made fast his dors, armed his consorts, set diverse dishes of powder & bullets ready on the table; and if they had not been over armed with drinke, more hurt might have been done. They sommaned him to yeeld, but he kept his house, and they could gett nothing but scofes & scorns from him; but at length, fearing they would doe some violence to the house, he and some of his crue came out, but not to yeeld, but to shoote; but they were so steeld with drinke as their peeces were to heavie for them; him selfe with a carbine (over charged & allmost halfe fild with powder & shote, as was after found) had thought to have shot Captaine Standish; but he stept to him, & put by his peece, & tooke him. Neither was ther any hurte done to any of either side, save that one was so drunke that he rane his owne nose upon the pointe of a sword that one held before him as he entred the house; but he lost but a litle of his hott blood. Morton they brought away to Plimoth, wher he was kepte, till a ship went from the Ile of Shols for England, with which he was sente to the Counsell of New-England; and letters writen to give them information of his course & cariage; and also one was sent at their commone charge to informe their Ho [no]^{rs} more perticulerly, & to prosecute against them. But he foold of the messenger, after he was gone from hence, and though he wente for England, yet nothing was done to him, not so much as rebukte, for ought was heard; but returned the nexte year. Some of the worst of the company were disperst, and some of the more modest kepte the house till he should be heard from. But I have been too long aboute so unworthy a person, and bad a cause.

JOHN WINTHROP (1588-1649)

A GRADUATE of Trinity College, Cambridge, and member of the Inner Temple, London, John Winthrop was an able representative of the learned, influential class that constituted an important element of the religious band which embarked for Massachusetts Bay in 1630 and later shaped the character of New England. Winthrop's leadership was recognized during the formation of the Massachusetts Bay Company, and confirmed in 1629 by his election as governor. He was entrusted with the Royal Charter when in 1630 a fleet of six vessels carried the company of about seven hundred colonists to the New World, first to Salem and then to Shawmut Peninsula, afterward called Boston. Winthrop had the welfare of the community at heart, and neither he nor his colleagues had any desire to welcome ideas that might jeopardize the success of the experiment. When Anne Hutchinson, Samuel Gorton, and other Antinomians refused to submit to the legal system of a Biblical Commonwealth, they were summarily banished.

Winthrop, like Nathaniel Ward and other Puritans, drew a sharp line between liberty and license, delayed liberalizing changes in the charter, and opposed such democratic tendencies as might sweep aside the leadership of holy and learned counselors. He found no scriptural authority for democracy, accounting it the meanest and worst form of government; yet there is no evidence that he wished to govern arbitrarily. Although in Winthrop one encounters the rise of discipline as a Puritan regimen of life, he and his contemporaries do not display the provincial austerities of a later generation. His sternness of temper can be understood if one remembers the number of lives lost in the precarious early years of the colony. Necessity prompted strictness.

Winthrop's most famous work, his *Journal*, was kept with a fidelity testifying to his sense of the greatness of the enterprise which he and his associates were conducting. The record extends from 1630 to 1649, and furnished material for such Puritan historians as Prince, Morton, and Hubbard. The first two parts were not published until the 1790's; the third volume first appeared in the edition of 1825. The title usually given is the *History of New England*, although the material primarily covered is that of Massachusetts Bay. As a man of letters John Winthrop was far less gifted than William Bradford; as a governor, however, he was no less vital to the survival of the Massachusetts Bay Colony than Bradford was to the success of the Plymouth settlement. The histories written by both these men display not only the dangers besetting their idealistic enterprises, but also the qualities of leadership which successfully mastered them.

BIBLIOGRAPHY · Winthrop's *Journal*, like Bradford's *History*, remained in manuscript for many years. The best modern edition of the *Journal* is by J. K. Hosmer in 1908. Winthrop's letters are available in the *Collections of the Massachusetts Historical Society* (Fourth Series), VI and VII (1863-1864); Fifth Series, I (1871); the letters were reprinted in J. H. Twichell's *Some Old Puritan Love-Letters* (1893). The publication of the complete works of Winthrop by the Massachusetts Historical Society has been in progress over a period of years.

Biographies of Winthrop include R. C. Winthrop, *Life and Letters of John Winthrop* (1864), and J. H. Twichell, *John Winthrop, First Governor of Massachusetts Colony* (1891). The more important critical notices include S. Gray, "The Political Thought of John Winthrop," *New England Quarterly*, III (1930), 681-705; A. B. Hart, "John Winthrop, Commonwealth Builder," *Commonwealth History of Massachusetts* (1927); E. A. J. Johnson, "Economic Ideas of John Winthrop," *New England Quarterly*, III (1930), 235-250; A. Macphail, *Essays in Puritanism* (1905); S. E. Morison, *Builders of the Bay Colony* (1930); and M. C. Tyler, *History of American Literature, 1607-1678*, I (1878).

Letters of Margaret and John Winthrop

WHILE THE letters are not especially numerous, they have been preserved from the period of the Winthrops' courtship and from their married life in Old and New

England. Margaret Tyndal was Winthrop's third wife, and fourteen years his junior. They were married in 1618; Winthrop embarked for New England in 1630, and his wife joined him a year later. Many of the letters were written in great haste upon sudden notice of an available messenger. Only two elaborate letters have survived. One of these, Winthrop's special prenuptial epistle, has been included to make clear that the early Puritans were trained in the florid Elizabethan tradition, and that letter writers were sometimes as metaphysical as poets. The other letters are vocal with affection. Winthrop's charming note written in 1637, twenty years after his marriage, should dispel the myth of the sullen gloom of Puritan domestic life. The text is that of R. C. Winthrop, *Life and Letters of John Winthrop* (2 vols., 1864, 1867), although one of the letters has been collated with Winthrop's *History of New England*, edited by James Savage (1825).

To my best beloved Mrs Margaret Tyndall at Great Maplested, Essex.

Grace mercie & peace, &C:

My onely beloved Spouse, my most sweet freind, & faithfull companion of my pilgrimage, the happye & hopefull supplie (next Christ Jesus) of my greatest losses, I wishe thee a most plentifull increase of all true comfort in the love of Christ, wth a large & prosperous addition of whatsoever happynesse the sweet estate of holy wedlocke, in the kindest societye of a lovinge husbande, may afford thee. Beinge filled wth the ioye of thy love, & wantinge opportunitye of more familiar communion wth thee, wch my heart fervently desires, I am constrained to ease the burthen of my minde by this poore helpe of my scriblinge penne, beinge sufficiently assured that, although my presence is that wch thou desirest, yet in the want thereof, these lines shall not be unfruitfull of comfort unto thee. And now, my sweet Love, lett me a whyle solace my selfe in the remembrance of our love, of wch this springe tyme of o^r acquaintance can putt forthe as yet no more but the leaves & blossomes, whilest the fruit lyes wrapped up in the tender budde of hope; a little more patience will disclose this good fruit, & bringe it to some maturitye: let it be o^r care & labour to preserve these hopefull budds from the beasts of the fielde, & from frosts & other iniuryes of the ayre, least o^r fruit fall off

ere it be ripe, or lose ought in the beautye & pleasantnesse of it: Lett us pluck up suche nettles & thornes as would defraud o^r plants of their due nourishment; let us pruine off superfluous branches; let us not sticke at some labour in wateringe & manuringe them: — the plentye & goodnesse of o^r fruit shall recompense us abundantly: O^r trees are planted in a fruitfull soyle; the grounde, & patterne of o^r love, is not other but that betweene Christe & his deare spouse, of whom she speakes as she finds him, My welbeloved is mine & I am his: Love was their banquetting house, love was their wine, love was their ensigne; love was his invitinges, love was hir fayntinges; love was his apples, love was hir comforts; love was his embracinges, love was hir refreshinge: love made him see hir, love made hir seeke him: love made him wedde hir, love made hir followe him: love made him hir saviour, love makes hir his servant. Love bredd o^r fellowshippe, let love continue it, & love shall increase it, untill deathe dissolve it. The prime fruit of the Spirit is love; truethe of Spirit & true love: abounde wth the spirit, & abounde wth love: continue in the spirit and continue in love: Christ in his love so fill o^r hearts wth holy hunger and true appetite, to eate & drinke wth him & of him in this his sweet Love feast, wch we are now preparinge unto, that when o^r love feast shall come, Christ Jesus himself may come in unto us, & suppe wth us, & we wth him: so shall we be merrye indeed. (O my sweet Spouse) can we esteeme eache others love, as worthy the recompence of o^r best mutuall affections, & can we not discerne so muche of Christs exceedinge & undeserved love, as may cheerfully allure us to love him above all? He loved us & gave himselfe for us; & to helpe the weaknesse of the eyes & hande & mouthe of o^r faithe, wch must seeke him in heaven where he is, he offers himselfe to the eyes, hands & mouthe of o^r bodye, heere on earthe where he once was. The Lord increace o^r faithe. . . .

Thy husband by promise.

John Winthrop.

Groton, where I wish thee. Aprill 4. 1618.

My Sweet Wife,—The opportunitye of so fitt a messinger, & my deepe engagement of Affection

40

to thee, makes me write at this tyme though I hope to followe soone after. The Lorde o^r God hath ofte brought us togither wth comfort when we have been longe absent, & if it be good for us, he will doe so still. When I was in Irelande he brought us togither againe. When I was sicke heer at London, he restored us togither againe. How many dangers neere death hast thou been in thy selfe & yet the Lorde hath granted me to injoye thee still. If he did not watch over us, we need not goe over sea to seeke death or miserye; we should meet it at every steppe in everye jo^{r}nye: & is not he a God abroad as well as at home? Is not his power & providence the same in N:E: that it hath been in old E.? If o^r wayes please him he can commande deliverance & safetye in all places & can make the stones of the field, & the beasts, yea, the raginge seas & o^r verye enemies to be in leage wth us. But if we sinn ag^t him, he can rayse up evill ag^t vs out of o^r owne bowells, howses, estate, &c.

My good wife; trust in the Lorde, whom thou has found faithfull. He wilbe better to thee then any husband: & will restore thee thy husband wth advantage. But I must ende, wth all o^r salut. wth wch I have laden this bearer, that he may be the more kindly wellcome. so I kisse my sweet wife & blesse thee & all o^{rs} & rest. Thyne ever.

Feb: 14: 1629   *Jo: Winthrop*

Thou must be my valentine f^r none hath challenged me.

[Margaret Winthrop to Her Husband]

My Deare Husband,—I received thy sweet letter, and doe blesse God for all his mercyes to us, in the continuance of thy health and welfayre, and the rest of us heare. I am glad to heere you wil come home this weike, for I desire to enioy thy sweete presence as ofte as I can, before that longe partinge come wch I desyre the Lord to fit us for, and give me fayth and pacience to submite unto his will in all thinges wch he requires at my hands. I trust he wil sanctify it to me and give me a right use of it, that I may thearrby learn the more to depend upon him; when other comforters fayle me, I hope, he will supply by the comfort of his holy spirit in the assurance of his love in Jesus Christ our Lord and Savior. I see thy love to me and mine, my good Husband, is more then I can deserve, and thou art more willing to grant then I forward to desyre: the good Lord requit thee all thy kindnesse to me, but I will say no more of this till you come home. I beseech the Lord to send us a comforttable meetinge, and thus with my best love to thy selfe, my brother and sister Downinge, & all the rest of our frends, I desyre the Lord to send thee a good end of al thy troubles and inable thee to goe through them cherefully, as I trust he will not fayle thee, into whose hands I commit thee and rest

Thy faithful and obedyent wife,

[1630]   *Margaret Winthrope*

For Mrs. Winthrop at her house in Boston

Sweet Heart,—I was unwillingly hinderd from comminge to thee, nor am I like to see thee before the last daye of this weeke: therefore I shall want a band or 2: & cuffes. I pray thee also send me 6: or 7: leaves of Tobacco dried & powdred. Have care of thy selfe this colde weather, & speak to the folkes to keepe the goates well out of the Garden; & if my brother Peter hath not fetched away the sheep ramme, let them looke him up & give him meate, the green pease in the Garden &c are good for him: If any lettres be come for me send them by this bearer. I will trouble thee no further, the Lorde blesse & keepe thee my sweet wife & all o^r familye: & send us a comfortable meetinge, so I kisse thee & love thee ever & rest

Thy faithfull husband,

Jo: Winthrop

This 6th of the 9th, 1637.

Journal

THE FIRST two sections of Winthrop's *Journal*, preserved in manuscript by the elder branch of the Winthrop family, were transcribed by Governor Trumbull or his secretary; and after the Governor's death, they were printed from his copy in 1790. The last manuscript of the *Journal*, after its discovery in 1816 in the tower of the Old South Church in Boston, was carefully edited by the antiquarian, James Savage, and issued with the support of the Massachusetts Historical Society, as *The History of New England*, 2 vols. (1825).

41

The manuscript of the *Journal* had been in the possession of William Hubbard, who made it the basis of his work, *A General History of New England*, sometimes disposing the material in a different order, but never departing far from the original. Thomas Prince also used a portion of Winthrop's manuscript in the compilation of his *Chronological History of New England*.

Winthrop's *Journal*, which covers events from 1630 to 1649, is the fullest account of the settlement and early life of the largest of the New England colonies, Massachusetts Bay. As governor and deputy governor for a good many years, Winthrop was probably in the best position to chronicle the affairs of the colony. Like most annals of the period, the material is the basis for history, not history itself. The bizarre combination of great and insignificant matters is owing to the seventeenth-century concept of Providence, in which all matters both large and small were regarded as under divine watchfulness or as the expression of divine will and, therefore, all equally significant. Winthrop's account of the Puritan awareness of sin makes abundantly clear that daily life was often a tense and grim drama, and helps to explain the state of mind which later made possible the delusion of witchcraft.

The text is that of *The History of New England*, edited by James Savage (2 vols., 1825).

[*Selected Entries: 1630–1648*]

1630

Friday, [May] 21]. The wind still N. W.; little wind, and close weather. We stood S. W. with all our sails, but made little way, and at night it was a still calm.

A servant of one of our company had bargained with a child to sell him a box worth 3 d for three biscuits a day all the voyage, and had received about forty, and had sold them and many more to some other servants. We caused his hands to be tied to a bar, and hanged a basket with stones about his neck, and so he stood two hours.

Saturday, [June] 12]. About four in the morning we were near our port. We shot off two pieces of ordnance, and sent our skiff to Mr. Peirce his ship (which lay in the harbour, and had been there . . . days before.) About an hour after, Mr. Allerton came aboard us in a shallop as he was sailing to Pemaquid. As we stood towards the harbour, we saw another shallop coming to us; so we stood in to meet her, and passed through the narrow strait between Baker's Isle and Little Isle, and came to an anchor a little within the islands.

After Mr. Peirce came aboard us, and returned to fetch Mr. Endecott, who came to us about two of the clock, and with him Mr. Skelton and Capt. Levett. We that were of the assistants, and some other gentlemen, and some of the women, and our captain, returned with them to Nahumkeck, where we supped with a good venison pasty and good beer, and at night we returned to our ship, but some of the women stayed behind.

In the meantime most of our people went on shore upon the land of Cape Ann, which lay very near us, and gathered store of fine strawberries.

Thursday, 17]. We went to Massachusetts, to find out a place for our sitting down. We went up Mistick River about six miles.

September 30]. The wolves killed six calves at Salem, and they killed one wolf.

Thomas Morton adjudged to be imprisoned, till he were sent into England, and his house burnt down, for his many injuries offered to the Indians, and other misdemeanours. Capt. Brook, master of the *Gift*, refused to carry him. . . .

Finch of Watertown had his wigwam burnt and all his goods.

Billington executed at Plimouth for murdering one.

Mr. Philips, the minister of Watertown, and others, had their hay burnt.

The wolves killed some swine at Saugus. . . .

October 25]. . . . The governour, upon consideration of the inconveniences which had grown in England by drinking one to another, restrained it at his own table, and wished others to do the like, so as it grew, by little and little, to disuse. . . .

1631

March 16]. About noon the chimney of Mr. Sharp's house in Boston took fire, (the splinters being not clayed at the top,) and taking the thatch burnt it down, and the wind being N. W. drove the fire to Mr. Colburn's house, being . . . rods off, and burnt that down also, yet they saved most of their goods.

23.] Chickatabot came with his sannops and squaws, and presented the governour with a hogshead of Indian corn. After they had all dined, and had each a small cup of sack and beer, and the men tobacco, he sent away all his men and women, (though the governour would have stayed them, in regard of the rain and thunder.) Himself and one squaw and one sannop stayed all night, and, being in English clothes, the governour set him at his own table, where he behaved himself as soberly, &c. as an Englishman. The next day after dinner he returned home, the governour giving him cheese and peas and a mug and some other small things.

April 12]. At a court holden at Boston, (upon information to the governour, that they of Salem had called Mr. Williams to the office of a teacher,) a letter was written from the court to Mr. Endecott to this effect: That whereas Mr. Williams had refused to join with the congregation at Boston, because they would not make a publick declaration of their repentance for having communion with the churches of England, while they lived there; and, besides, had declared his opinion, that the magistrate might not punish the breach of the Sabbath, nor any other offense, as it was a breach of the first table; therefore, they marvelled they would choose him without advising with the council; and withal desiring him, that they would forbear to proceed till they had conferred about it.

April 17]. A General court at Boston. The former governour was chosen again, and all the freemen of the commons were sworn to this government. At noon, Cheeseborough's house was burnt down, all the people being present.

July 13]. Canonicus' son, the great sachem of Naraganset, came to the governour's house with John Sagamore. After they had dined, he gave the governour a skin, and the governour requited him with a fair pewter pot, which he took very thankfully, and stayed all night.

November 11]. We kept a day of thanksgiving at Boston.

February 7]. The governour, Mr. Nowell, Mr. Eliot, and others, went over Mistick River at Medford, and going N. and by E. among the rocks about two or three miles, they came to a very great pond, having in the midst an island of about one acre, and very thick with trees of pine and beech; and the pond had divers small rocks, standing up here and there in it, which they therefore called Spot Pond. They went all about it upon the ice. From thence (towards the N. W. about half a mile,) they came to the top of a very high rock, beneath which, (towards the N.) lies a goodly plain, part open land, and part woody, from whence there is a fair prospect, but it being then close and rainy, they could see but a small distance. This place they called Cheese Rock, because, when they went to eat somewhat, they had only cheese, (the governour's man forgetting, for haste, to put up some bread.)

1633

July 24.] A ship arrived from Weymouth, with about eighty passengers, and twelve kine, who sate down at Dorchester. They were twelve weeks coming, being forced into the Western Islands by a leak, where they stayed three weeks, and were very courteously used by the Portugals; but the extremity of the heat there, and the continual rain, brought sickness upon them, so as [many] died.

Much sickness at Plimouth, and above twenty died of pestilent fevers.

Sept. 4] The *Griffin*, a ship of three hundred tons, arrived. . . . She brought about two hundred passengers, having lost some four. . . . In this ship came Mr. Cotton, Mr. Hooker, and Mr. Stone, ministers, and Mr. Peirce, Mr. Haynes, (a gentleman of great estate,) Mr. Hoffe, and many other men of good estates. . . .

[*October*] *11*]. A fast at Newtown, where Mr. Hooker was chosen pastor, and Mr. Stone teacher, in such a manner as before at Boston.

The wolves continued to do much hurt among our cattle; and this month, by Mr. Grant, there came over four Irish greyhounds, which were sent to the governour by Mr. Downing, his brother-in-law. . . .

November]. A great mortality among the Indians. Chickatabot, the sagamore of Naponsett, died, and many of his people. The disease was the small pox. Some of them were cured by such means as they had from us; many of their children escaped, and were kept by the English. . . .

The scarcity of workmen had caused them to raise their wages to an excessive rate, so as a carpenter would have three shillings the day, a labourer two shillings and sixpence, &c.; and accordingly those who had commodities to sell advanced their prices sometime double to that they cost in England, so as it grew to a general complaint, which the court, taking knowledge of, as also of some further evils, which were springing out of the excessive rates of wages, they made an order, that carpenters, masons, &c. should take but two shillings the day, and labourers but eighteen pence, and that no commodity should be sold at above four pence in the shilling more than it cost for ready money in England; oil, wine &c. cheese, in regard of the hazard of bringing, &c. [excepted]. The evils which were springing &c. were, 1. Many spent much time idly, &c. because they could get as much in four days as would keep them a week. 2. They spent much in tobacco and strong waters, &c which was a great waste to the commonwealth, which, by reason of so many foreign commodities expended, could not have subsisted to this time, but that it was supplied by the cattle and corn, which were sold to new comers at very dear rates, viz. corn at six shillings the bushel, a cow at £20,—yea, some at £24, some £26,—a mare at £35, an ewe goat at 3 or 4 £; and yet many cattle were every year brought out of England, and some from Virginia. Soon after order was taken for prices of commodities, viz. not to exceed the rate of four pence in the shilling above the price in England, except cheese and liquors, &c.

The ministers in the bay and Sagus did meet, once a fortnight, at one of their houses by course, where some question of moment was debated.

Mr. Skelton, the pastor of Salem and Mr. Wil-

liams, who was removed from Plimouth thither, (but not in any office, though he exercised by way of prophecy,) took some exception against it, as fearing it might grow in time to a presbytery or superintendency, to the prejudice of the churches' liberties. But this fear was without cause; for they were all clear in that point, that no church or person can have power over another church; neither did they in their meetings exercise any such jurisdiction, &c. . . .

1636

November 17]. Two ships arrived here from London, and one a week before. They were full of passengers,—men, women, and children. One of them had been from London twenty-six weeks, and between land and land eighteen weeks; (the other two something less time;) their beer all spent and leaked out a month before their arrival, so as they were forced to stinking water (and that very little) mixt with sack or vinegar, and their other provisions very short and bad. Yet, through the great providence of the Lord, they came all safe on shore, and most of them sound, and well liking. They had continual tempests, and when they were near the shore, (being brought two or three days with a strong east wind,) the weather was so thick all that time, as they could not make land, and the seamen were in great perplexity, when on the sudden the fog cleared, so as they saw Cape Ann fair on their starboard bow, and presently grew thick again; yet by their compass they made their harbour. There were aboard that ship two godly ministers, Mr. Nathaniel Rogers and Mr. Partridge, and many good people in that and the other ships; and we had prayed earnestly for them; (for a small pinnace of thirty tons, which came out with them, and was come in three weeks before, brought us news of their coming.) In one of the other ships the passengers had but half a pint of drink for a day, fourteen days together; yet, through the Lord's mercy, did all well. One of the ships was overset in the night by a sudden gust, and lay so half an hour, yet righted of herself. . . .

November 20]. A general fast was kept in all the churches. The occasion was, the miserable state of the churches in Germany; the calamities upon our native country, the bishops making havock in the churches, putting down the faithful ministers, and advancing popish ceremonies and doctrines, the plague raging exceedingly, and famine and sword threatening them; the dangers of those at Connecticut, and of ourselves also, by the Indians; and the dissensions in our churches. . . .

1638

December 10]. The wind at N. E., there was so great a tempest of wind and snow all the night and the next day, as had not been since our time. Five men and youths perished between Mattapan and Dorchester, and a man and a woman between Boston and Roxbury. Anthony Dick, in a bark of thirty tons, cast away upon the head of Cape Cod. Three were starved to death with the cold; the other two got some fire and so lived there, by such food as they saved, seven weeks, till an Indian found them. &c. Two vessels bound for Quinipiack were cast away at Aquiday, but the people saved. Much other harm was done in staving of boats, &c. and by the great tides, which exceeded all before. This happened the days after a general fast, which occasioned some of our ministers to stir us up to seek the Lord better, because he seemed to discountenance the means of reconciliation. Whereupon the next general court, by advice of the elders, agreed to keep another day, and to seek further into the causes of such displeasure, &c.; which accordingly was performed.

1640

Mo. 5. 27]. Being the second day of the week, the Mary Rose, a ship of Bristol, of about 200 tons, her master one Capt. [blank] lying before Charlton, was blown in pieces with her own powder, being 21 barrels; wherein the judgment of God appeared, for the master and company were many of them profane scoffers at us, and at the ordinances of religion here; so as, our churches keeping a fast for our native country, &c. they kept aboard, at their common service, when all the rest of the masters came to our assemblies; likewise the Lord's day following; and a friend of his going aboard next day and asking him, why he came not on shore to our meetings, his answer was, that he had

a family of his own &c. and they had as good service aboard as we had on shore. Within two hours after this (being about dinner time) the powder took fire (no man knows how) and blew all up, viz. the captain and nine or ten of his men and some four or five strangers. There was a special providence that there were no more, for many principal men were going aboard at that time, and some were in a boat near the ship, and others were diverted by a sudden shower of rain, and others by other occasions. There was one man saved, being carried up in the scuttle, and so let fall in the same into the water, and being taken up by the ferry boat, near dead, he came to himself the next morning, but could not tell anything of the blowing up of the ship, or how he came there. The rest of the dead bodies were after found much bruised and broken. Some goods were saved, but the whole loss was estimated at £2,000. A 20s piece was found sticking in a chip, for there was above £300 in money in her, and 15 tons of lead, and 10 pieces of ordnance, which a year after were taken up, and the hull of the ship drawn ashore.

1645

3.14]. According to this agreement, presently after the lecture the magistrates and deputies took their places in the meeting house, and the people come together, and the deputy governour placing himself within the bar, as at the time of the hearing &c., the governour read the sentence of the court, without speaking any more, for the deputies had (by importunity) obtained a promise of silence from the magistrates. Then was the deputy governour [Winthrop] desired by the court to go up and take his place again upon the bench, which he did accordingly, and the court being about to arise, he desired leave for a little speech, which was to this effect.

I suppose something may be expected from me, upon this charge that has befallen me, which moves me to speak now to you; yet I intend not to intermeddle in the proceedings of the court, or with any of the persons concerned therein. Only I bless God, that I see an issue of this troublesome business. I also acknowledge the justice of the court, and, for mine own part, I am well satisfied, I was publickly charged, and I am publickly and legally acquitted, which is all I did expect or desire. And though this be sufficient for my justification before men, yet not so before the God, who hath seen so much amiss in my dispensations (and even in this affair) as calls me to be humble. For to be publickly and criminally charged in this court, is matter of humiliation, (and I desire to make a right use of it,) notwithstanding I be thus acquitted. If her father had spit in her face, (saith the Lord concerning Miriam,) should she not have been ashamed seven days? Shame had lien upon her, whatever the occasion had been. I am unwilling to stay you from your urgent affairs, yet give me leave (upon this special occasion) to speak a little more to this assembly. It may be of some good use, to inform and rectify the judgments of some of the people, and may prevent such distempers as have arisen amongst us. The great questions that have troubled the country, are about the authority of the magistrates and the liberty of the people. It is yourselves who have called us to this office, and being called by you, we have our authority from God, in way of an ordinance, such as hath the image of God eminently stamped upon it, the contempt and violation whereof hath been vindicated with examples of divine vengeance. I entreat you to consider, that when you choose magistrates, you take them from among yourselves, men subject to like passions as you are. Therefore when you see infirmities in us, you should reflect upon your own, and that would make you bear the more with us, and not be severe censurers of the failings of your magistrates, when you have continual experience of the like infirmities in yourselves and others. We account him a good servant, who breaks not his covenant. The covenant between you and us is the oath you have taken of us, which is to this purpose, that we shall govern you and judge your causes by the rules of God's laws and our own, according to our best skill. When you agree with a workman to build you a ship or house, &c., he undertakes as well for his skill as for his faithfulness, for it is his profession, and you pay him for both. But when you call one to be a magistrate, he doth not profess nor undertake to have sufficient skill for that office, nor can you furnish him with gifts, &c. therefore you must run the hazard of his skill and ability. But if he fail in

faithfulness, which by his oath he is bound unto, that he must answer for. If it fall out that the case be clear to common apprehension, and the rule clear, also, if he transgress here, the errour is not in the skill, but in the evil of the will: it must be required of him. But if the case be doubtful, or the rule doubtful, to men of such understanding and parts as your magistrates are, if your magistrates should err here, yourselves must bear it.

For the other point concerning liberty, I observe a great mistake in the country about that. There is a twofold liberty, natural (I mean as our nature is now corrupt) and civil or federal. The first is common to man with beasts and other creatures. By this, man, as he stands in relation to man simply, hath liberty to do what he lists; it is a liberty to evil as well as to good. This liberty is incompatible and inconsistent with authority, and cannot endure the least restraint of the most just authority. The exercise and maintaining of this liberty makes men grow more evil, and in time to be worse than brute beasts: omnes sumus licentia deteriores. This is that great enemy of truth and peace, that wild beasts, which all the ordinances of God are bent against, to restrain and subdue it. The other kind of liberty I call civil or federal, it may also be termed moral, in reference to the covenant between God and man, in the moral law, and the politic covenants and constitutions, amongst men themselves. This liberty is the proper end and object of authority, and cannot subsist without it; and it is a liberty to that only which is good, just, and honest. This liberty you are to stand for, with the hazard (not only of your goods, but) of your lives, if need be. Whatsoever crosseth this, is not authority, but a distemper thereof. This liberty is maintained and exercised in a way of subjection to authority; it is of the same kind of liberty wherewith Christ hath made us free. The woman's own choice makes such a man her husband; yet being so chosen, he is her lord, and she is to be subject to him, yet in a way of liberty, not of bondage; and a true wife accounts her subjection her honour and freedom, and would not think her condition safe and free, but in her subjection to her husband's authority. Such is the liberty of the church under the authority of Christ, her king and husband; his yoke is so easy and

46

sweet to her as a bride's ornaments; and if through frowardness or wantonness, &c. she shake it off, at any time, she is at no rest in her spirit, until she take it up again; and whether her lord smiles upon her, and embraceth her in his arms, or whether he frowns, or rebukes, or smites her, she apprehends the sweetness of his love in all, and is refreshed, supported and instructed by every such dispensation of his authority over her. On the other side, ye know who they are that complain of this yoke and say, let us break their bands, &c. we will not have this man to rule over us. Even so, brethren, it will be between you and your magistrates. If you stand for your natural corrupt liberties, and will do what is good in your own eyes, you will not endure the least weight of authority, but will murmur, and oppose, and be always striving to shake off that yoke; but if you will be satisfied to enjoy such civil and lawful liberties, such as Christ allows you, then will you quietly and cheerfully submit unto that authority which is set over you, in all the administrations of it, for your good. Wherein, if we fail at any time, we hope we shall be willing (by God's assistance) to hearken to good advice from any of you, or in any other way of God; so shall your liberties be preserved, in upholding the honour and power of authority amongst you.

2.13]. Mr. Hopkins, the governor of Hartford upon Connecticut, came to Boston, and brought his wife with him, (a godly young woman, and of special parts,) who was fallen into a sad infirmity, the loss of her understanding and reason, which had been growing upon her divers years, by occasion of her giving herself wholly to reading and writing, and had written many books. Her husband, being very loving and tender of her, was loath to grieve her; but he saw his error, when it was too late. For if she had attended her household affairs, and such things as belong to women, and not gone out of her way and calling to meddle in such things as are proper for men, whose minds are stronger, &c. she had kept her wits, and might have improved them usefully and honourably in the place God had set her. He brought her to Boston, and left her with her brother, one Mr. Yale, a merchant, to try what means might be had here for her. But no help could be had. . . .

15. (6)]. The synod met at Cambridge by adjournment from the (4) last. Mr. Allen of Dedham preached out of Acts 15, a very godly, learned, and particular handling of near all the doctrines and applications concerning that subject, with a clear discovery and refutation of such errors, objections and scruples as had been raised about it by some young heads in the country.

It fell out, about the midst of his sermon, there came a snake into the seat, where many of the elders sate behind the preacher. It came in at the door where people stood thick upon the stairs. Divers of the elders shifted from it, but Mr. Thomson, one of the elders of Braintree, (a man of much faith,) trode upon the head of it, and so held it with his foot and staff with a small pair of grains, until it was killed. This being so remarkable, and nothing falling out but by divine providence, it is out of doubt, the Lord discovered somewhat of his mind in it. The serpent is the devil; the synod, the representative of the churches of Christ in New England. The devil had formerly and lately attempted their disturbance and dissolution; but their faith in the seed of the woman overcame him and crushed his head.

The synod went on comfortably, and intended only the framing of a confession of faith, &c. and a form of church discipline (not entertaining any other business). For the first, they wholly agreed with that which the assembly in England had lately set forth. For the other, viz., for discipline, they drew it by itself, according to the general practice of our churches. So they ended in less than fourteen days.

This month, when our first harvest was near had in, the pigeons came again all over the country, but did no harm, (harvest being just in,) but proved a great blessing, it being incredible what multitudes of them were killed daily. It was ordinary for one man to kill eight or ten dozen in half a day, yea five or six dozen at one shoot, and some seven or eight. Thus the Lord showed us, that he could make the same creature, which formerly had been a great chastisement, now to become a great blessing.

About the midst of this summer, there arose a fly out of the ground, about the bigness of the top of a man's little finger, of brown colour. They filled the woods from Connecticut to Sudbury with a great noise, and eat up the young sprouts of the trees, but meddled not with the corn. They were also between Plymouth and Braintree, but came no further. If the Lord had not stopped them, they had spoiled all our orchards, for they did some few.

ROGER WILLIAMS (c. 1603–1683)

SEPARATIST, mystic, and liberal seeker after a better social order, Roger Williams has emerged as one of the superior figures of American colonial life. His magnanimity, his tolerance, and his demand for a democratic church in a democratic society offer a definite contrast to the harsh orthodoxy upheld by the Mathers. His stormy career also presents striking refutation of the easy assumption that Puritanism meant the same thing in all parts of New England at the same time. From his school and college days in England at Charterhouse and Cambridge, he seems to have inspired both a loyal following and an implacable opposition which testify equally to his attractive character and his uncompromising spirit. Williams was described by Cotton Mather as "the first rebel against the divine church-order established in the wilderness," and as a trouble-breeder whose "heresies" and fiery spirit threatened to set the whole country on fire.

After receiving his B.A. in 1627 from Pembroke, Williams remained at Cambridge for two years to prepare for the ministry. He married Mary Barnard, served briefly as chaplain to Sir Edwin Masham in Essex, and in 1631 landed in New England. Welcomed at first by Winthrop as "a godly minister," his separatist views led him to object to the church at Salem; and his impetuous agitation aroused the government into activity against him. He sent a treatise to the Governor and his assistants disputing their right to charter lands, and he spoke against the validity of the King's patent; he persuaded Endecott to slash the cross from the King's banner; he contended that unregenerate men could not take oaths; he opposed the union of the churches into a presbytery; he rebuked the settlers of Massachusetts Bay for their failure to sever their connections with the Established Church; and he scouted the notion that civil magistrates had the right to enforce religious matters.

Williams was not the only dissenter to annoy the magistracy; Richard Brown, John Wheelwright, Samuel Gorton, and other dissentient persons helped to keep controversial water hot. The machinery of orthodoxy was set in motion against him, and though Endecott and many in Salem supported him, Williams was ordered out of the jurisdiction in October, 1635.

He fled in 1636 "in the midst of a New England winter" to Narragansett Bay, where with a small band of followers he became the founder of Providence as an asylum "for persons distressed for conscience." In 1643 Williams sailed for England, where in March of the following year he secured a charter for the new colony. There, also, he saw through the press his *Key into the Language of America*. Returning to New England, he was able through his friendship with the Indians and his knowledge of their language to perform important services to the other colonies during Indian hostilities. After becoming a Baptist and helping to set up the first Baptist church in 1638, Williams finally became a Seeker. A Seeker he remained until his death in 1683, never relaxing his quest for the true relationship between the citizen and the state and between man and his Creator.

As the founder of a colony, Williams deserves an honored place along with Winthrop, Bradford, and Penn. Although more liberal than most governors, he opposed the fanaticism of the early Quakers; and like many another idealistic and zealous young man, he was sobered by administrative responsibilities. However, he never renounced his liberal principles, and today his fame rests upon his published works on freedom of conscience. The most famous of these, *The Bloudy Tenent of Persecution for the Cause of Conscience, discussed in a Conference between Truth and Peace* (1644), is an epitome of his views on religious toleration. Other documents illustrating Williams's irrepressible yearning for a freer world include *Queries of Highest Consideration* (1644), a plea urging Parliament to separate church and state, and *The Hireling Ministry None of Christ's* (1652). Williams's cumbersome and archaic style is in curious contrast to his advanced thinking, but in "A Letter to the Town of Providence" (1655) he achieved a clarity in harmony with the nobility of his thought.

BIBLIOGRAPHY · Williams's important writings were reprinted in the *Publications of the Narragansett Club* (1866–1874), from which edition the following selections are taken. Italics and obsolete abbreviations have been altered to conform to modern practice. Biographies include those of W. Gammel, *Roger Williams* (1844); R. Elton, *Life of Roger Williams* (1873); O. S. Strauss,

Roger Williams, the Pioneer of Religious Liberty (1894);
E. J. Carpenter, Roger Williams: a Study of the Life,
Times, and Character of a Political Pioneer (1909); E.
Easton, Roger Williams: Prophet and Pioneer (1930);
J. E. Ernst, Roger Williams, New England Firebrand
(1932); C. S. Longacre, Roger Williams (1939); S. H.
Brockunier, The Irrepressible Democrat, Roger Williams
(1940); J. Eaton, Lone Journey: Life of Roger Williams
(1944). Specialized and critical studies include those of
J. E. Ernst, The Political Thought of Roger Williams
(1929); G. A. Stead, "Roger Williams and the Massa-
chusetts Bay," New England Quarterly, VII (1934),
235–257; M. Freund, "Roger Williams, Apostle of Com-
plete Religious Liberty," Rhode Island Historical
Society Collections, XXVI (1933), 101–133; F. B.
Wiener, "Roger Williams's Contribution to Modern
Thought," ibid., XXVIII (1935), 1–20; H. B. Parkes,
"John Cotton and Roger Williams Debate Religious
Toleration," New England Quarterly, IV (1931), 735–
756; and A. B. Seidman, "Church and State in the
Early Years of the Massachusetts Bay Colony," ibid.
XVIII (1945), 211–233.

The Bloudy Tenent of Persecution

The Bloudy Tenent was one of five documents in a controversy between John Cotton and Roger Williams over
the principle of freedom of conscience. It was published while Williams was in England (after 1643), and
it was regarded as so subversive that Parliament ordered the common hangman to burn it. Williams contended that "the foundation of civil power lies in the
people," and that civil magistrates are sworn to uphold
the interests of all the people, not merely those of
church members. The whole work is a refutation of
Cotton and a committee of the New England clergy
in which he answers their arguments point by point,
Scriptural verse by Scriptural verse. The language is
archaic and somewhat ornate. The dialogue form employed was a popular rhetorical device in the Renaissance, used freely by Traherne, Erasmus, and others.
The title is partly explained in the following passage:

[it] may well bee called the bloudy tenent [because] so
directly contradicting the spirit and minde and practice of
the Prince of Peace; so deeply guilty of the blood of the
Soules compelled and forced to Hypocrisie in a spirituall and
soule rape; so deeply guilty of the blood of the Soules under
the Altar, persecuted in all ages for the cause of Conscience,
and so destructive to the civill peace and welfare of all Kingdomes, Countries, and Commonwealths.

[Selected Entries]

PREFACE . . . First, That the blood of so many
hundred thousand soules of Protestants and Pa-

pists, spilt in the Wars of present and former Ages,
for their respective Consciences, is not required
nor accepted by Jesus Christ the Prince of Peace.

Secondly, Pregnant Scriptures and Arguments
are throughout the Worke proposed against the
Doctrine of persecution for cause of Conscience.

Thirdly, Satisfactorie Answers are given to
Scriptures, and objections produced by Mr.
Calvin, Beza, Mr. Cotton, and the Ministers of the
New English Churches and others former and later,
tending to prove the Doctrine of persecution for
cause of Conscience.

Fourthly, The Doctrine of persecution for cause
of Conscience, is proved guilty of all the blood of
the Soules crying for vengeance under the Altar.

Fifthly, All Civill States with their Officers of
justice in their respective constitutions and administrations are proved essentially Civill, and
therefore not Judges, Governours or Defendours
of the Spirituall or Christian state and Worship.

Sixthly, It is the will and command of God,
that (since the coming of his Sonne the Lord
Jesus) a permission of the most Paganish, Jewish,
Turkish, or Antichristian consciences and worships, bee granted to all men in all Nations and
Countries; and they are onely to bee fought
against with that Sword which is only (in Soule
matters) able to conquer, to wit, the Sword of
God's Spirit, the Word of God.

Seventhly, The state of the Land of Israel, the
Kings and people thereof in Peace and War, is
proved figurative and ceremoniall, and no patterne
nor president for any Kingdome or civill state in
the world to follow.

Eighthly, God requireth not an uniformity of
Religion to be inacted and inforced in any civill
state; which inforced uniformity (sooner or later)
is the greatest occasion of civill Warre, ravishing of
conscience, persecution of Christ Jesus in his servants, and of the hypocrisie and destruction of
millions of souls.

Ninthly, In holding an inforced uniformity of
Religion in a civill state, wee must necessarily
disclaime our desires and hopes of the Jewes conversion to Christ.

Tenthly, An inforced uniformity of Religion
throughout a Nation or civill state, confounds the
Civill and Religious, denies the principles of

49

Christianity and civility, and that Jesus Christ is come in the Flesh.

Eleventhly, The permission of other consciences and worships than a state professeth, only can (according to God) procure a firme and lasting peace, (good assurance being taken according to the wisedome of the civill state for uniformity of civil obedience from all sorts.)

Twelfthly, lastly, true civility and Christianity may both flourish in a state or Kingdome, notwithstanding the permission of divers and countrary consciences, either of Jewe or Gentile.

IX. . . . Peace. It will here be said, Whence then ariseth civill dissentions and uproares about matters of Religion?

Truth. I answer: When a Kingdome or State, Towne or Family, lyes and lives in the guilt of a false God, false Christ, false worship: no wonder if sore eyes be troubled at the appearance of the light, be it never so sweet: No wonder if a body full of corrupt humours be troubled at strong (though wholesome) Physick? If persons sleepy and loving to sleepe be troubled at the noise of shrill (though silver) alarums: No wonder if Adonijah and all his company be amazed and troubled at the sound of the right Heyre[n] King Salomon, I King. I. If the Husbandmen were troubled when the Lord of the Vineyard sent servant after servant, and at last his onely Sonne, and they beat, and wounded, and kill'd even the Sonne himselfe, because they meant themselves to seize upon the inheritance, unto which they had no right, Matth. 21. 38. Hence all those tumults about the Apostles in the Acts, &c. whereas good eyes are not so troubled at light; vigilant and watchfull persons loyall and faithfull, are not so troubled at the true, no nor at a false Religion of Jew or Gentile.

Secondly, breach of civil peace may arise, when false and idolatrous practices are held forth, &c yet no breach of civil peace from the doctrine or practice, or the manner of holding forth, but from that wrong and preposterous way of suppressing, preventing, and extinquishing such doctrines or practices by weapons of wrath and blood, whips, stockes, imprisonment, banishment, death, &c. by which men commonly are persuaded to convert

Heyre: heir.

Heretickes, and to cast out uncleane spirits, which onely the finger of God can doe, that is the mighty power of the Spirit in the Word.

Hence the Towne is in an uproare, and the Country takes the Alarum to expell that fog or mist of Errour, Heresie, Blasphemy, (as is supposed) with Swords and Guns; whereas 'tis Light alone, even Light from the bright shining Sunne of Righteousnesse, which is able, in the soules and consciences of men to dispell and scatter such fogges and darknesse.

Hence the Sons of men, (as David speakes in another case, Psal. 39.) disquiet themselves in vaine, and unmercifully disquiet others, as (by the helpe of the Lord) in the sequell of this discourse shall more appeare.

XLV. Truth. . . . to batter downe Idolatry, false worship, heresie, schisme, blindnesse, hardnesse, out of the soule and spirit, it is vaine, improper, and unsutable to bring those weapons which are used by persecutors, stocks, whips, prisons, swords, gibbets, stakes, &c. (where these seem to prevaile with some Cities or Kingdomes, a stronger force sets up againe, what a weaker pull'd downe) but against these spirituall strong holds in the soules of men, Spirituall Artillery and weapons are proper, which are mighty through God to subdue and bring under the very thought to obedience, or else to binde fast the soule with chaines of darknesse, and locke it up in the prison of unbeleefe and hardnesse to eternity.

I observe that as civill weapons are improper in this businesse, and never able to effect ought in the soule: So (although they were proper, yet) they are unnecessary, for if as the Spirit here saith (and the Answerer grants) spirituall weapons in the hand of Church officers are able and ready to take vengeance on all disobedience, that is able and mighty, sufficient and ready for the Lord's worke either to save the soule, or to kill the soule of whomsoever, be the party or parties opposite, in which respect I may againe remember that speech of Job, How hast thou helped him that hath no power? Job 26.

Peace. Offer this (as Malachie once spake) to the Governours, the Kings of the Earth, when they besiege, beleagure, and assault great Cities,

Castles, Forts, &c. should any subject pretending his service bring store of pins, sticks, strawes, bulrushes, to beat and batter downe stone walls, mighty Bulwarkes, what might his expectation and reward be, but at least the censure of a man distract, beside himselfe? &c.

Truth. What shall we then conceive of His displeasure, (who is the chiefe or Prince of the Kings of the earth, and rides upon the Word of Truth and meeknesse, which is that white Horse, Rev. 6. and Rev. 19. with His holy witnesses the white Troopers upon white horses) when to His helpe and aid men bring and adde such unnecessary, improper and weake munition?

Will the Lord Jesus (did He ever in His owne Person practice, or did he appoint to) joyne to His Breastplate of Righteousnesse, the breastplate of iron and steele? to the Helmet of righteousnesse and salvation in Christ, an helmet and crest of iron, brasse, or steel, a target of wood to His shield of Faith? [to] His two edged sword comming forth of the mouth of Jesus, the materiall sword, the worke of Smiths and Cutlers? or a girdle of shooes leather to the girdle of truth, &c. Excellently fit and proper is that alarme and item, Psal. 2. Be wise therefore O ye Kings (especially those ten Horns, Rev. 17.) who under pretence of fighting for Christ Jesus give their power to the Beast against Him, and be warned ye Judges of the Earth: Kisse the Son, that is with subjection and affection, acknowledge Him only the King and Judge of soules (in that power bequeathed to His Ministers and Churches) lest if His wrath be kindled, yea but a little, then blessed are they that trust in Him.

LXXII. *Peace.* Brentius (whom you next quote, saith he) speaketh not to your cause. Wee willingly grant you, that man hath no power to make Lawes to binde conscience, but this hinders not, but men may see the Lawes of God observed which doe binde conscience.

Truth. I answer, In granting with Brentius that man hath not power to make Lawes to binde conscience, hee overthrowes such his tenent and practice as restraine men from their Worship, according to their Conscience and beleefe, and constraine them to such worships (though it bee out of a pretence that they are convinced) which their owne soules tell them they have no satisfaction nor faith in.

Secondly, whereas he affirmeth that men may make Lawes to see the Lawes of God observed.

I answer, as God needeth not the helpe of a materiall sword of steele to assist the sword of the Spirit in the affaires of conscience, so those men, those Magistrates, yea that Commonwealth which makes such Magistrates, must needs have power and authority from Christ Jesus to sit Judge and to determine in all the great controversies concerning doctrine, discipline, government, &c.

And then I aske, whether upon this ground it must not evidently follow, that

Either there is no lawfull Commonwealth nor civill State of men in the world, which is not qualified with this spirituall discerning: (and then also that the very Commonweale hath more light concerning the Church of Christ, than the Church it selfe.)

Or, that the Commonweale and Magistrates thereof must judge and punish as they are perswaded in their owne beleefe and conscience, (be their conscience Paganish, Turkish, or Antichristian) what is this but to confound Heaven and Earth together, and not onely to take away the being of Christianity out of the World, but to take away all civility, and the world out of the world, and to lay all upon heapes of confusion?

XCII. *Truth.* . . . . Here are divers considerable passages which I shall briefly examine, so far as concernes our controversie.

First, whereas they say, that the Civill Power may erect and establish what forme of civill Government may seeme in wisedome most meet, I acknowledge the proposition to be most true, both in it self, and also considered with the end of it, that a civill Government is an Ordinance of God, to conserve the civill peace of people, so farre as concernes their Bodies and Goods, as formerly hath beene said.

But from this Grant I infer, (as before hath been touched) that the Soveraigne, originall, and foundation of civill power lies in the people, (whom they must needs meane by the civill power distinct from the Government set up.) And if so, that a People may erect and establish what forme

51

of Government seemes to them most meete for their civill condition: It is evident that such Governments as are by them erected and established, have no more power, nor for no longer time, than the civill power or people consenting and agreeing shall betrust them with. This is cleere not only in Reason, but in the experience of all commonweales, where the people are not deprived of their naturall freedome by the power of Tyrants.

And if so, that the Magistrates receive their power of governing the Church, from the People; undeniably it followes, that a people, as a people, naturally considered (of what Nature or Nation soever in Europe, Asia, Africa or America) have fundamentally and originally, as men, a power to governe the Church, to see her doe her duty, to correct her, to redresse, reforme, establish &c. And if this be not to pull God and Christ, and Spirit out of Heaven, and subject them unto naturall, sinfull, inconstant men, and so consequently to Sathan himselfe, by whom all peoples naturally are guided, let Heaven and Earth judge.

Peace. It cannot by their owne Grant be denied, but that the wildest Indians in America ought (and in their kind and severall degress doe) to agree upon some formes of Government, some more civill, compact in Townes, &c some lesse. As also that their civill and earthly Governments be as lawfull and true as any Governments in the World, and therefore consequently their Governors are Keepers of the Church or both Tables, (if any Church of Christ should arise or be amongst them:) and therefore lastly, (if Christ have betrusted and charged the Civill Power with his Church) they must judge according to their Indian or American consciences, for other consciences it cannot be supposed they should have.

CXXXI. *Peace.* It is plausible, but not reasonable that God's people should (considering the drift of these positions) expect more liberty under a Christian than under a Heathen Magistrate: Have God's people more liberty to breake the command of a Christian than an Heathen governour? and so to set up Christ's Church and Ordinances after their owne conscience against his consent more than against the consent of an Heathen or unbeleeving Magistrate? what is become of all the great expectation what a Christian Magistrate may and ought to doe in establishing the Church, in reforming the Church, and in punishing the contrary? 'Tis true (say men) in Christ's time and in the time of the first Ministers and Churches there were no Christian Magistrates, and therefore in that case, it was in vaine for Christians to seeke unto the Heathen Magistrates to governe the Church, suppresse Hereticks, &c. but now we enjoy Christian Magistrates, &c.

Truth. All Reason and Religion would now expect more submission therefore (in matters concerning Christ) to a Christian Magistrate, than to a Pagan or Antichristian ruler! But (deare *Peace*) the day will discover, the fire will trie, 1 Cor. 3. what is but wood, hay, and stubble, though built (in men's upright intention) on that foundation Jesus Christ.

But (to winde up all) as it is most true that Magistracy in generall is of God (Rom. 13.) for the preservation of Mankinde in civill order and peace, (the World otherwise would bee like the Sea, wherein Men, like Fishes would hunt and devoure each other, and the greater devour the lesse:) So also it is true, that Magistracy in speciall for the severall kindes of it is of Man, 1. Pet. 2. 13. Now what kinde of Magistrate soever the people shall agree to set up, whether he receive Christianity before he be set in office, or whether he receive Christianity after, hee receives no more power of Magistracy, then a Magistrate that hath received no Christianity. For neither of them both can receive more, then the Commonweal, the Body of People and civill State, as men, communicate unto them, and betrust with them.

All lawfull Magistrates in the World, both before the comming of Christ Jesus, and since, (excepting those unparaleld typicall Magistrates of the Church of Israel) are but Derivatives and Agents immediately derived and employed as eyes and hands, serving for the good of the whole: Hence they have and can have no more Power, than fundamentally lies in the Bodies or Fountaines themselves, which Power, Might, or Authority, is not Religious, Christian, &c. but naturall, humane and civill.

And hence it is true, that a Christian Captaine, Christian Merchant, Physitian, Lawyer, Pilot,

Father, Master, and (so consequently) Magistrate, &c. is no more a Captaine, Merchant, Physitian, Lawyer, Pilot, Father, Master, Magistrate, &c. then a Captaine, Marchant, &c. of any other Conscience or Religion.

'Tis true, Christianity teacheth all these to act in their severall callings, to an higher ultimate end, from higher principles, in a more heavenly and spirituall manner, &c.

A Letter to the Town of Providence

THE LETTERS of Roger Williams, like those of John Winthrop, reveal the essential spirit of the man himself. Most of Williams's letters were written to his friends and furnish cheerful evidence of his genius for benign comradeship. Of the letters addressed to the public, the one reproduced here is a classic of American prose. It was written in 1655 to correct misinterpretations of Williams's advocacy of liberty of conscience.

[Providence, January 1654–1655]

That ever I should speak or write a tittle that tends to such an infinite liberty of conscience, is a mistake, and which I have ever disclaimed and abhorred. To prevent such mistakes, I shall at present only propose this case: There goes many a ship to sea, with many hundred souls in one ship, whose weal and woe is common, and is a true picture of a commonwealth, or a human combina- ³⁰ tion or society. It hath fallen out sometimes, that both papists and Protestants, Jews and Turks, may be embarked in one ship; upon which supposal I

affirm, that all the liberty of conscience, that ever I pleaded for, turns upon these two hinges—that none of the papists, Protestants, Jews, or Turks, be forced to come to the ship's prayers or worship, nor compelled from their own particular prayers or worship, if they practice any. I further add, that I never denied, that, notwithstanding this liberty, the commander of this ship ought to command the ship's course, yea, and also com-¹⁰ mand that justice, peace, and sobriety, be kept and practiced, both among the seamen and all the passengers. If any of the seamen refuse to perform their services, or passengers to pay their freight; if any refuse to help, in person or purse, towards the common charges or defence; if any refuse to obey the common laws and orders of the ship, concerning their common peace or preservation; if any shall mutiny and rise up against their commanders and officers; if any should preach or ²⁰ write that there ought to be no commanders or officers, because all are equal in Christ, therefore no masters nor officers, no laws nor orders, nor corrections nor punishments; — I say, I never denied, but in such cases, whatever is pretended, the commander or commanders may judge, resist, compel and punish such transgressors, according to their deserts and merits. This if seriously and honestly minded, may, if it so please the Father of lights, let in some light to such as willingly shut not ³⁰ their eyes.

I remain studious of your common peace and liberty.

Roger Williams

NATHANIEL WARD (1578?–1652)

NATHANIEL WARD, son of John Ward, a Puritan minister in Suffolk, came to America in 1634, after excommunication from the Church of England, to serve as pastor of the church at Ipswich, a settlement then known as Aggawam. Like many other Puritans who emigrated to America, Ward had attended Cambridge, where he received the degrees of B.A. (1599) and M.A. (1603) from Emmanuel College. Less common were Ward's legal training at Lincoln's Inn, to which he was admitted in 1607, and his nomination as a barrister in 1615. After practicing law for a few years, Ward spent some time in travel on the continent, and when he

entered the ministry in 1618, his first charge was that of chaplain to English residents at Elbing, Prussia. Later, in England, he was a vigorous preacher, holding curacies at St. James, Piccadilly, and Stonden Massey until Laud suspended him for nonconformity in 1633.

Ward's ill health compelled him to resign his New England pastorate in 1636 after a ministry of two years, but he remained in America until 1646. It is not surprising that his legal training should have led to his appointment by the General Court to draw up a code of laws for the colony, a formulation finally completed, adopted, and printed in 1641 as the *Body of*

Liberties. Except for minor alterations made by the General Court, Ward was the sole author of this code, important in American constitutional history.

But in the common mind Ward's name survives today because he wrote *The Simple Cobler of Aggawam* (1646), under the pseudonym of Theodore de la Guard.

This gusty and crotchety work bore the following title: *The Simple Cobler of Aggawam in America. Willing to help 'mend his Native Country, lamentably tattered, both in the upper-Leather and sole, with all the honest stiches he can take. And as willing never to bee paid for his work, by Old English wonted pay. It is his Trade to patch all the year long, gratis. Therefore I pray Gentlemen keep your purses.* Written in America, this book was published upon Ward's return to England in 1646, and the sale exhausted four editions in a year. It was a product of the years of sects and schisms, when the success of the New England experiment seemed jeopardized by a violent division of counsels. It was also the book of Ward's old age—the author was fifty-six when he came to America—and this may account for its minatory and scolding tone. The secret of its appeal, however, is its caustic wit, a quality which had won praise from Thomas Fuller and Cotton Mather in both old and New England. Expressed in a picturesque, Burtonian style, no more amusing book was written in America in the first half of the century. In later years Ward seems to have somewhat recovered his health; in June, 1647, he preached before the House of Commons. He received the living of Shenfield in Essex in 1648, where he died about four years later.

BIBLIOGRAPHY · A facsimile edition of *The Simple Cobler* was brought out by the Ipswich Historical Society in 1906. In 1937 the original was reproduced in Scholars' Facsimiles and Reprints series. A full-length biography, J. W. Dean, *A Memoir of the Rev. Nathaniel Ward* (1868), contains a bibliography. The best critical essay is that by S. E. Morison in *Builders of the Bay Colony* (1930).

The Simple Cobler of Aggawam

IN AN AGE which produced Antinomians, Gortonists, Anabaptists, Quakers, Fifth Monarchy Men, and other sects and parties, it is not surprising that Nathaniel Ward and his contemporaries, allowing their fears to overcome their liberalism, indulged in outcries against toleration. Their dread of special revelation was evoked by the wild outburst of strange opinions in the years after 1640. Ward's caustic *Simple Cobler* was mild in comparison with two English books whose contents are colorfully suggested by their titles: *Gangraena; or, a Catalogue and Discovery of Many of the Errors, Heresies, Blasphemies, and Pernicious Practices of the Sectaries of This Time. Vented and Acted in England in These Four Last Years;* and *Heresiography, or, a Description of the Heretics and Sectaries Sprung up in These Latter Times.* . . .

Ward's diatribe against women's fashions was a joint product of his age and his wit. But had he been inclined to treat the matter more seriously, he could have found ample justification in contemporary excesses. The General Court of Massachusetts Bay passed laws in 1634 against immodest fashions. In 1638 the Court admonished the people about "costliness of apparel and following new fashions," and pronounced the situation one of widespread disorder. Of this warning, Winthrop commented, little notice was taken. The work was first printed in 1646. A later edition, incorporating the author's additions, was fused with the edition published in Boston in 1713 for a revised version in 1843. The text is that of the version of David Pulsifer, published in Boston in 1843.

[Women's Fashions]

Should I not keepe promise in speaking a little to Womens fashions, they would take it unkindly: I was loath to pester better matter with such stuffe; I rather thought it meet to let them stand by themselves, like the *Quae Genus* in the Grammar, being Deficients, or Redundants, not to be brought under any Rule: I shall therefore make bold for this once, to borrow a little of their loose tongued Liberty, and mispend a word or two upon their long-wasted, but short-skirted patience: a little use of my stirrup will doe no harme. . . .

It is known more than enough, that I am neither Nigard, nor Cinick, to the due bravery of the true Gentry: if any man mislikes a bully mong drossock more than I, let him take her for his labour: I honour the woman that can honour herselfe with her attire: a good Text always deserves a fair Margent: I am not much offended if I see a trimme, far trimmer than she that wears it: in a word, whatever Christianity or Civility will allow, I can afford with *London* measure: but when I heare a nugiperous Gentledame inquire what dresse the Queen is in this week: what the nudiustertian fashion of the Court; I meane the very newest: with egge to be in it in all haste, what ever it be; I look at her as the very gizzard of a trifle, the product of a quarter of a cypher, the epitome of nothing, fitter to be kickt, if shee were of a kickable substance, than either honour'd or humour'd.

To speak moderately, I truly confesse, it is beyond the ken of my understanding to conceive, how those women should have any true grace, or valuable vertue, that have so little wit, as to disfigure themselves with such exotick garbes, as not only dismantles their native lovely lustre, but transclouts them into gant bar-geese, ill-shapen-shotten-shell-fish, Egyptian Hyeroglyphicks, or at the best into French flurts of the pastery, which a proper English woman should scorne with her heels: it is no marvell they weare drailes on the hinder part of their heads, having nothing as it seems in the fore-part, but a few Squirrils brains to help them frisk from [one] ill-favor'd fashion to another.

[Against Toleration]

Either I am in an Appoplexie, or that man is in a Lethargie, who doth not now sensibly feele God shaking the Heavens over his head, and the Earth under his feet: The Heavens so, as the Sun begins to turne into darknesse, the Moon into blood, the Starres to fall down to the ground; So that little Light of Comfort or Counsell is left to the sonnes of men: The Earth so, as the foundations are failing, the righteous scarce know where to finde rest, the Inhabitants stagger like drunken men: it is in a manner dissolved both in Religions and Relations: And no marvell; for, they have defiled it by transgressing the Laws, changing the Ordinances, and breaking the Everlasting Covenant. The Truths of God are the Pillars of the world, whereon States and Churches may stand quiet if they will; if they will not, He can easily shake them off into delusions, and distractions enough.

Sathan is now in his passions, hee feeles his passion approaching; hee loves to fish in royled waters. Though that Dragon cannot sting the vitals of the Elect mortally, yet that Beelzebub can fly-blow their Intellectuals miserably: The finer Religion grows, the finer hee spins his Cobwebs, hee will hold pace with Christ so long as his wits will serve him. Hee sees himselfe beaten out of grosse

Idolatries, Heresies, Ceremonies, where the Light breakes forth with power; he will therefore bestirre him to prevaricate Evangelicall Truths, and Ordinances, that if they will needs be walking, yet they shall *laborare varicibus*, and not keep their path: he will put them out of time and place; Assassinating for his Engineers, men of Paracelsian parts; well complexioned for honesty; for, such are fittest to Mountebanke his Chimistry into sicke Churches and weake Judgements.

Nor shall hee neede to stretch his strength overmuch in this worke: Too many men having not laid their foundation sure, nor ballasted their Spirits deepe with humility and feare, are prest enough of themselves to evaporate their owne apprehensions. Those that are acquainted with Story know, it hath ever been so in new Editions of Churches: Such as are least able, are most busie to pudder in the rubbish, and to raise dust in the eyes of more steady Repayrers. Civill Commotions make roome for uncivill practises: Religious mutations, for irreligious opinions: Change of Aire, discovers corrupt bodies: Reformation of Religion, unsound mindes. He that hath any well-faced phancy in his Crowne, and doth not vent it now, fears the pride of his owne heart will dub him dunce for ever. Such a one will trouble the whole *Israel* of God with his most untimely births, though he makes the bones of his vanity sticke up, to the view and griefe of all that are godly wise. The devill desires no better sport then to see light heads handle their heels, and fetch their carreers in a time, when the Roofe of Liberty stands open.

The next perplexed Question, with pious and ponderous men, will be: What should bee done for the healing of these comfortlesse exulcerations. I am the unablest adviser of a thousand, the unworthiest of ten thousand; yet I hope I may presume to assert what follows without just offence.

First, such as have given or taken any unfriendly reports of us *New-English*, should do well to recollect themselves. We have beene reputed a Colluvies of wild Opinionists, swarmed into a remote wildernes to find elbow-roome for our phanatick Doctrines and practises: I trust our diligence past, and constant sedulity against such persons and courses, will plead better things for us. I dare take upon me, to bee the Herauld of *New-*

England so farre, as to proclaime to the world, in the name of our Colony, that all Familists, Antinomians, Anabaptists, and other Enthusiasts, shall have free Liberty to keep away from us, and such as will come to be gone as fast as they can, the sooner the better.

Secondly, I dare averre, that God doth no where in his word tolerate Christian States, to give Tolerations to such adversaries of his Truth, if they have power in their hands to suppresse them.

Here is lately brought us an extract of a *Magna Charta*, so called, compiled between the Subplanters of a *West-Indian* Island; whereof the first Article of constipulation, firmely provides free stable-room and litter for all kinde of consciences, be they never so dirty or jadish; making it actionable, yea, treasonable, to disturbe any man in his Religion, or to discommend it, whatever it be. We are very sorry to see such professed profanenesse in English Professors, as industriously to lay their Religious Foundations on the ruine of true Religion; which strictly binds every conscience to contend earnestly for the Truth: to preserve unity of spirit, faith and Ordinances, to be all like-minded, of one accord; every man to take his brother into his Christian care: to stand fast with one spirit, with one mind, striving together for the faith of the Gospel: and by no meanes to permit Heresies or erroneous opinions: But God abhorring such loathsome beverages, hath in his righteous judgement blasted that enterprize, which might otherwise have prospered well, for ought I know; I presume their case is generally knowne ere this.

If the devill might have his free option, I beleeve he would ask nothing else, but liberty to enfranchize all false Religions, and to embondage the true; nor should he need: It is much to bee feared, that laxe Tolerations upon State pretences and planting necessities, will be the next subtle Stratagem he will spread, to distate the Truth of God and supplant the peace of the Churches. Tolerations in things tolerable, exquisitely drawn out by the lines of the Scripture, and pensill of the Spirit, are the sacred favours of Truth, the due latitudes of Love, the faire Compartiments of Christian fraternity: but irregular dispensations, dealt forth by the facilities of men, are the frontiers of errour, the redoubts of Schisme, the perillous irritaments of carnall and spirituall enmity.

My heart hath naturally detested foure things: The standing of the Apocrypha in the Bible; Forrainers dwelling in my Countrey, to crowd our native Subjects into the corners of the Earth; Alchymized coines; Tolerations of divers Religions, or of one Religion in segregant shapes: He that willingly assents to the last, if he examines his heart by day-light, his conscience will tell him, he is either an Atheist, or an Heretique, or an Hypocrite, or at best a captive to some lust: Poly-piety is the greatest impiety in the world. True Religion is *Ignis probationis*, which doth *congregare homogenea & segregare heterogenea*.

Not to tolerate things meerly indifferent to weak consciences, argues a conscience too strong: pressed uniformity in these, causes much disunity: To tolerate more than indifferents, is not to deale indifferently with God; He that doth it, takes his Scepter out of his hand, and bids him stand by. Who hath to doe to institute Religion but God. The power of all Religion and Ordinances, lies in their purity: their purity in their simplicity: then are mixtures pernicious. I lived in a City, where a Papist preached in one Church, a Lutheran in another, a Calvinist in a third; a Lutheran one part of the day, a Calvinist the other, in the same Pulpit: the Religion of that place was but motly and meagre, their affections Leopardlike.

If the whole Creature should conspire to doe the Creator a mischiefe, or offer him an insolency, it would be in nothing more, than in erecting untruths against his Truth, or by sophisticating his Truths with humane medleyes; the removing of some one iota in Scripture, may draw out all the life, and traverse all the Truth of the whole Bible: but to authorise an untruth, by a Toleration of State, is to build a Sconce against the walls of heaven, to batter God out of his Chaire: To tell a practicall lye, is a great sin, but yet transient; but to set up a Theoricall untruth, is to warrant every lye that lies from its root to the top of every branch it hath, which are not a few.

I would willingly hope that no Member of the Parliament hath skilfully ingratiated himselfe into the hearts of the House, that he might watch a time to midwife out some ungracious Toleration for his own turne, and for the sake of that, some others. I would also hope that a word of generall caution should not be particularly misapplied. I am the freer to suggest it, because I know not one man of that mind, my aime is generall, and I desire may be so accepted. Yet good Gentlemen, looke well about you, and remember how Tiberius plaid the Fox with the Senate of Rome, and how Fabius Maximus cropt his ears for his cunning.

That State is wise, that will improve all paines and patience rather to compose, then tolerate differences in Religion. There is no divine Truth, but hath much Celestial fire in it from the Spirit of Truth: nor no irreligious untruth, without its proportion of Antifire from the Spirit of Error to contradict it; the zeale of the one, the virulency of the other, must necessarily kindle Combustions. Fiery diseases seated in the spirit, embroile the whole frame of the body: others more externall and coole, are lesse dangerous. They which divide in Religion divide in God; they who divide in him, divide beyond *Genus Generalissimum*, where there is no reconciliation, without atonement; that is, without uniting in him, who is One, and in his Truth, which is also one.

Wise are those men who will be perswaded rather to live within the pale of Truth where they may bee quiet, than in the purlieu's, where they are sure to be hunted ever and anon, doe Authority what it can. Every singular Opinion, hath a singular opinion of itself; and he that holds it a singular opinion of himself, and a simple opinion of all contra-sentients: he that confutes them, must confute all three at once, or else he does nothing; which will not be done without more stir than the peace of the State or Church can endure. . . .

Concerning Tolerations I may further assert. . . .

He that is willing to tolerate any Religion, or discrepant way of Religion, besides his own, unlesse it be in matters meerly indifferent, either doubts of his own, or is not sincere in it.

He that is willing to tolerate any unsound Opinion, that his own may also be tolerated, though never so sound, will for a need hang Gods Bible at the Devils girdle.

Every Toleration of false Religions, or Opinions hath as many Errours and sins in it, as all the false Religions and Opinions it tolerates, and one sound one more.

That State that will give Liberty of Conscience in matters of Religion, must give Liberty of Conscience and Conversation in their Morall Laws, or else the Fiddle will be out of tune, and some of the strings cracke. . . .

The Body of Liberties (1641)

JOHN WINTHROP wrote on September 4, 1639: "The people had long desired a body of laws, and thought their condition very unsafe, while so much power rested in the discretion of magistrates. Divers attempts had been made at former courts, and the matter referred to some of the magistrates and some of the elders; but still it came to no effect; for, being committed to the care of many, whatsoever was done by some, was still disliked or neglected by others. At last it was referred to Mr. Cotton and Mr. Nathaniel Warde, etc., and each of them framed a model, which were presented to this general court, and by them committed to the governor and deputy and some others to consider of. . . ." In the main Ward's version was adopted. His part in the composition of *The Body of Liberties* was long obscured, partly because the original was not reprinted until 1890, and partly because John Cotton's codification of Leviticus (Moses' Judicials), issued in London in 1641, long passed as the original laws. This confusion obscured the genuine enlightenment of Ward and his generation—an enlightenment made apparent by a consideration of the liberties proclaimed in 1641, of which only sections 94 to 100 show close following of Leviticus, and then only because, for capital offenses, the formulators wanted warrant beyond their own judgments.

The free fruition of such liberties, Immunities and priveledges as humanity, Civility and Christianity call for as due to every man in his place and proportion without impeachment and Infringement hath ever been and ever will be the tranquillitie and Stabilitie of Churches and Commonwealths. And the deniall or deprivall thereof, the disturbance if not the ruine of both. We hould it therefore our dutie and safetie whilst we are about the further establishng of this Government to collect and express all such freedoms as for present we foresee may concern us, and our posterity after us, And to ratify them with our solemn consent.

We doe therefore this day religiously and unanimously decree and confirm these following Rites, liberties and privileges concerning our Churches and Civil State to be respectively impartially and inviolably enjoyed and observed throughout our Jurisdiction forever.

1. No man's life shall be taken away, no man's honour or good name shall be stained, no man's person shall be arrested, restrained, banished, dis- 10 membered, nor any ways punished, no man shall be deprived of his wife or children, no man's goods or estate shall be taken away from him, nor any way indammaged under coulor of law or Countenance of Authority unless it be by virtue or equitie of some expresse law of the Country warranting the same, established by a generall Court and sufficiently published, or in case of the defect of a law in any particular case, by the word of god. And in Capitall cases, or in cases concerning dis- 20 membering or banishment, according to that word to be judged by the Generall Court.

2. Every person within this Jurisdiction, whether Inhabitant or forreigner shall enjoy the same justice and law, that is generall for the plantation, which we constitute and execute one towards another without partiality or delay.

3. No man shall be urged to take any oath or 30 subscribe any articles, covenants or remonstrance,

of a publique and Civill nature, but such as the general Court hath considered, allowed, and required.

4. No man shall be punished for not appearing at or before any Civill Assembly Court, Councell, Magistrate, or Officer, nor for the omission of any office or service, if he shall be necessarily hindred by any apparent Act or providdence of God, which he could neither foresee nor avoid. Provided that this law shall not prejudice any person of his just cost or damage, in any civill Action.

5. No man shall be compelled to any publique worke or service unless the presse be grounded upon some act of the general Court, and have reasonable allowance therefore. . . .

9. No monopolies shall be granted or allowed amonsts us, but of such new Inventions that are profitable to the Countrie, and that for a short time. . . .

11. All persons which are of the age of 21 yeares, and of right understanding and memories, whether excommunicate or condemned shall have full power and libertie to make their wills and testaments, and other lawful alientations of their lands and estates, etc.

ANNE BRADSTREET (1612?–1672)

UNTIL THE discovery of the poems of Edward Taylor, Anne Bradstreet was regarded as the most noteworthy poet of seventeenth-century New England. She drew her inspiration largely from the religious poetry of her age, was influenced by the *Emblems* of Francis Quarles, and imitated the *Divine Semaine* of Guillaume Du Bartas as translated by Joshua Sylvester (1605). With Du Bartas as a guide, she quite naturally wrote of physics in the "Elements," of human nature in the "Humours" and "Ages" of man, and of natural philosophy in the "Seasons." For her rimed history of ancient Persia, Greece, Assyria, and Rome, "The Four Monarcheys," she paraphrased parts of Sir Walter Raleigh's *History of the World* (1614), supplementing his work with parts from the Bible, Plutarch, and Usher. Her "Contemplations," probably modeled on the "Spec-

tacles" in Sylvester's translation, and influenced by the poetry of Sidney and Spenser, is her best work, and remains currently alive; in these seven-line stanzas, using the materials and similes of nature, she revealed her own spiritual passion.

She was born in England, the daughter of Thomas Dudley, steward of the estate of the Puritan Earl of Lincoln. She was well reared: "When I was about seven . . . I had at one time eight tutors . . . in languages, music, dancing. . . ." When she was sixteen years of age she was married to Simon Bradstreet, and two years later they, with her parents, came to Massachusetts Bay with the Winthrop party. Both her father and her husband became Governors of the colony. Her poetry was composed under many handicaps. She had eight children "hatch'd in one nest," and many duties besides, in a period, as she said, when men considered a woman's hand better fitted to a needle than to a pen. But she wrote her poems, and a kinsman carried the manuscript to London, where it was published in 1650 under a title not of her own device: *The Tenth Muse Lately Sprung up in America. Or Severall Poems, Compiled with Great Variety of Wit and Learning. . . . By a Gentlewoman in Those Parts.* The second edition was printed in Boston, by John Foster, in 1678, with additions and corrections.

BIBLIOGRAPHY · The best edition, with biographical and critical comment, is that edited by J. H. Ellis, *The Works of Anne Bradstreet in Prose and Verse* (1867), from which the present text is taken. Ellis's book was reprinted in 1932. C. E. Norton, a descendant of the poet, wrote the introduction to a new edition based on that of 1867 but modernized as to spelling: *The Poems of Anne Bradstreet (1612–1672) Together with Her Prose Remains* (1897). For a close bibliographical study of her work see "The First Century of New England Verse," *Proceedings of the American Antiquarian Society,* LIII (1943), 219–508, an indispensable monograph for the study of all verse of the period. Biographical accounts are L. Caldwell, *An Account of Anne Bradstreet* (1898), and Helen Campbell, *Anne Bradstreet and Her Time* (1891). See also the article in the *Dictionary of American Biography* and S. E. Morison, *Builders of the Bay Colony* (1930).

To My Dear and Loving Husband

THIS POEM was first published in the second edition of *The Tenth Muse* (1678).

If ever two were one, then surely we.
If ever man were lov'd by wife, then thee;
If ever wife was happy in a man,
Compare with me ye women if you can.
I prize thy love more than whole Mines of gold, 5
Or all the riches that the East doth hold.
My love is such that Rivers cannot quench,
Nor ought but love from thee, give recompence.
Thy love is such I can no way repay,
The heavens reward thee manifold I pray. 10
Then while we live, in love lets so persever,
That when we live no more, we may live ever.

The Flesh and the Spirit

THE DEBATE was a pronounced medieval form, as in the famous *Owl and Nightingale,* and in this poem the medievalism in the puritanism of the poet is apparent. The poem has a close relationship to the other works of the author, for her forte is the personification of seasons, elements, or intellectual concepts, filled with comment appropriate to the symbolic pattern. For the Scriptural parallel the reader is referred to the eighth chapter of St. Paul's Epistle to the Romans.

Two sisters – The Flesh and The Spirit.

In secret place where once I stood
Close by the Banks of Lacrim flood
I heard two sisters reason on
Things that are past, and things to come;
One Flesh was call'd, who had her eye 5
On worldly wealth and vanity;
The other Spirit, who did rear
Her thoughts unto a higher sphere:
Sister, quoth Flesh, what liv'st thou on
Nothing but Meditation? 10
Doth Contemplation feed thee so
Regardlessly to let earth goe?
Can Speculation satisfy
Notion without Reality?
Dost dream of things beyond the Moon 15
And dost thou hope to dwell there soon?
Hast treasures there laid up in store
That all in th' world thou count'st but poor?
Art fancy sick, or turn'd a Sot
To catch at shadowes which are not? 20
Come, come, Ile shew unto thy sence,
Industry hath its recompence.
What canst desire, but thou maist see
True substance in variety?
Dost honour like? acquire the same, 25
As some to their immortal fame:
And trophyes to thy name erect
Which wearing time shall ne're deject.
For riches dost thou long full sore?
Behold enough of precious store. 30
Earth hath more silver, pearls and gold,
Than eyes can see, or hands can hold.
Affect's thou pleasure? take thy fill,
Earth hath enough of what you will.
Then let not goe, what thou maist find, 35
For things unknown, only in mind.
Spir. Be still thou unregenerate part,
Disturb no more my setled heart,
For I have vow'd, (and so will doe)
Thee as a foe, still to pursue. 40

And combate with thee will and must,
Untill I see thee laid in th' dust.
Sisters we are, ye[a] twins we be,
Yet deadly feud 'twixt thee and me;
For from one father are we not,   45
Thou by old Adam wast begot,
But my arise is from above,
Whence my dear father I do love.
Thou speakst me fair, but hatst me sore,
Thy flatt'ring shews Ile trust no more.   50
How oft thy slave, hast thou me made,
When I believ'd, what thou hast said,
And never had more cause of woe
Then when I did what thou bad'st doe.
Ile stop mine ears at these thy charms,   55
And count them for my deadly harms.
Thy sinfull pleasures I doe hate,
Thy riches are to me no bait,
Thine honours doe, nor will I love;
For my ambition lyes above.   60
My greatest honour it shall be
When I am victor over thee,
And triumph shall, with laurel head,
When thou my Captive shalt be led,
How I do live, thou need'st not scoff,   65
For I have meat thou know'st not off;
The hidden Manna I doe eat,
The word of life it is my meat.
My thoughts do yield me more content
Then can thy hours in pleasure spent.   70
Nor are they shadows which I catch,
Nor fancies vain at which I snatch,
But reach at things that are so high,
Beyond thy dull Capacity;
Eternal substance I do see,   75
With which inriched I would be:
Mine Eye doth pierce the heavens, and see
What is Invisible to thee.
My garments are not silk nor gold,
Nor such like trash which Earth doth hold,   80
But Royal Robes I shall have on,
More glorious then the glistring Sun;
My Crown not Diamonds, Pearls, and gold,
But such as Angels heads infold.
The City where I hope to dwell,   85
There's none on Earth can parallel;
The stately Walls both high and strong,

    85. City: Rev. 21: 10–27; and 22:1–5.

Are made of pretious Jasper stone;
The Gates of Pearl, both rich and clear,
And Angels are for Porters there;   90
The Streets thereof transparent gold,
Such as no Eye did e're behold,
A Chrystal River there doth run,
Which doth proceed from the Lambs Throne:
Of Life, there are the waters sure,   95
Which shall remain for ever pure,
Nor Sun, nor Moon, they have no need,
For glory doth from God proceed:
No Candle there, nor yet Torch light,
For there shall be no darksome night.   100
From sickness and infirmity,
For evermore they shall be free,
Nor withering age shall e're come there,
But beauty shall be bright and clear;
This City pure is not for thee,   105
For things unclean there shall not be:
If I of Heaven may have my fill,
Take thou the world, and all that will.

Contemplations

THOUGH there are obvious echoes of Du Bartas and
others in Anne Bradstreet, to some extent she composed poetry with her own eyes on the objects. The
New England landscape aroused her deep emotions,
some of which she expressed in her nature lyrics.
Especially is this fine enthusiasm apparent in "Contemplations." Like many another long poem, it is
broken into shorter poems, such as an ode to the
sun, a lay on antedeluvian days, an ode on man's immortality, and a nature idyl. All these are infused
with the moralizing strain characteristic of her age.
Lines 140 to 175 were partly inspired by the Merrimac
River.

1

Some time now past in the Autumnal Tide,
When Phœbus wanted but one hour to bed,
The trees all richly clad, yet void of pride,
Were gilded o'er by his rich golden head.
Their leaves & fruits seem'd painted, but was true 5
Of green, of red, of yellow, mixed hew,
Rapt were my sences at this delectable view.

2

I wist not what to wish, yet sure thought I,
If so much excellence abide below;

How excellent is he that dwells on high?   10
Whose power and beauty by his works we know.
Sure he is goodness, wisdome, glory, light,
That hath this under world so richly dight:
More Heaven then Earth was here no winter &
    no night.

3

Then on a stately Oak I cast mine Eye,   15
Whose russling top the Clouds seem'd to aspire;
How long since thou wast in thine Infancy?
Thy strength, and stature, more thy years admire,
Hath hundred winters past since thou wast born?
Or thousand since thou brakest thy shell of horn,
If so, all these as nought, Eternity doth scorn.   21

4

Then higher on the glistering Sun I gaz'd,
Whose beams was shaded by the leavie Tree,
The more I look'd, the more I grew amaz'd,
And softly said, what glory's like to thee?   25
Soul of this world, this Universes Eye,
No wonder, some made thee a Deity:
Had I not better known, (alas) the same had I.

5

Thou as a Bridegroom from thy Chamber rushes,
And as a strong man, joyes to run a race,   30
The morn doth usher thee, with smiles & blushes,
The Earth reflects her glances in thy face.
Birds, insects, Animals with Vegative,
Thy heart from death and dulness doth revive: 34
And in the darksome womb of fruitful nature dive.

6

Thy swift Annual, and diurnal Course,
Thy daily streight, and yearly oblique path,
Thy pleasing fervor, and thy scorching force,
All mortals here the feeling knowledg hath.
Thy presence makes it day, thy absence night,   40
Quaternal Seasons caused by thy might:
Hail Creature, full of sweetness, beauty & delight.

7

Art thou so full of glory, that no Eye
Hath strength, thy shining Rayes once to behold?
And is thy splendid Throne erect so high?   45
As to approach it, can no earthly mould.

How full of glory then must thy Creator be?
Who gave this bright light luster unto thee:
Admir'd, ador'd for ever, be that Majesty.

8

Silent alone, where none or saw, or heard,   50
In pathless paths I lead my wandring feet,
My humble Eyes to lofty Skyes I rear'd
To sing some Song, my mazed Muse thought
    meet.
My great Creator I would magnifie,
That nature had, thus decked liberally: 55
But Ah, and Ah, again, my imbecility!

9

I heard the merry grashopper then sing,
The black clad Cricket, bear a second part,
They kept one tune, and plaid on the same string,
Seeming to glory in their little Art.   60
Shall Creatures abject, thus their voices raise?
And in their kind resound their makers praise:
Whilst I as mute, can warble forth no higher layes.

10

When present times look back to Ages past,
And men in being fancy those are dead,   65
It makes things gone perpetually to last,
And calls back moneths and years that long since
    fled
It makes a man more aged in conceit,
Then was Methuselah, or's grand-sire great:
While of their persons & their acts his mind doth
    treat.   70

11

Sometimes in Eden fair, he seems to be,
Sees glorious Adam there made Lord of all,
Fancyes the Apple, dangle on the Tree,
That turn'd his Sovereign to a naked thral.
Who like a miscreant's driven from that place,   75
To get his bread with pain, and sweat of face:
A penalty impos'd on his backsliding Race.

12

Here sits our Grandame in retired place,
And in her lap, her bloody Cain new born,
The weeping Imp oft looks her in the face,   80
Bewails his unknown hap, and fate forlorn;

His Mother sighs, to think of Paradise,
And how she lost her bliss, to be more wise,
Believing him that was, and is, Father of lyes.

13

Here Cain and Abel come to sacrifice,   85
Fruits of the Earth, and Fatlings each do bring,
On Abels gift the fire descends from Skies,
But no such sign on false Cain's offering;
With sullen hateful looks he goes his wayes.
Hath thousand thoughts to end his brothers dayes,
Upon whose blood his future good he hopes to
    raise.   91

14

There Abel keeps his sheep, no ill he thinks,
His brother comes, then acts his fratricide,
The Virgin Earth, of blood her first draught
    drinks
But since that time she often hath been cloy'd;
The wretch with gastly face and dreadful mind, 96
Thinks each he sees will serve him in his kind,
Though none on Earth but kindred near then
    could he find.

15

Who fancyes not his looks now at the Barr,
His face like death, his heart with horror fraught,
Nor Male-factor ever felt like warr,   101
When deep dispair, with wish of life hath fought,
Branded with guilt, and crusht with treble woes,
A Vagabond to Land of *Nod* he goes.
A City builds, that wals might him secure from
    foes.   105

16

Who thinks not oft upon the Fathers ages
Their long descent, how nephews sons they saw,
The starry observations of those Sages,
And how their precepts to their sons were law,
How Adam sigh'd to see his Progeny,   110
Cloath'd all in his black sinfull Livery,
Who neither guilt, nor yet the punishment
    could fly.

17

Our Life compare we with their length of dayes
Who to the tenth of theirs doth now arrive?

And though thus short, we shorten many wayes, 115
Living so little while we are alive;
In eating, drinking, sleeping, vain delight
So unawares comes on perpetual night,
And puts all pleasures vain unto eternal flight.

18

When I behold the heavens as in their prime,   120
And then the earth (though old) stil clad in green,
The stones and trees, insensible of time,
Nor age nor wrinkle on their front are seen;
If winter come, and greeness then do fade,
A Spring returns, and they more youthfull made;
But Man grows old, lies down, remains where once
    he's laid.   126

19

By birth more noble then those creatures all,
Yet seems by nature and by custome curs'd,
No sooner born, but grief and care makes fall
That state obliterate he had at first: 130
Nor youth, nor strength, nor wisdom spring again
Nor habitations long their names retain,
But in oblivion to the final day remain.

20

Shall I then praise the heavens, the trees, the earth
Because their beauty and their strength last longer
Shall I wish there, or never to had birth,   136
Because they're bigger, & their bodyes stronger?
Nay, they shall darken, perish, fade and dye,
And when unmade, so ever shall they lye,
But man was made for endless immortality.   140

21

Under the cooling shadow of a stately Elm
Close sate I by a goodly Rivers side,
Where gliding streams the Rocks did overwhelm;
A lonely place, with pleasures dignifi'd.
I once that lov'd the shady woods so well,   145
Now thought the rivers did the trees excel,
And if the sun would ever shine, there would I
    dwell.

22

While on the stealing stream I fixt mine eye,
Which to the long'd for Ocean held its course,
I markt, nor crooks, nor rubs that there did lye 150
Could hinder ought, but still augment its force:

O happy Flood, quoth I, that holds thy race
Till thou arrive at thy beloved place,
Nor is it rocks or shoals that can obstruct thy pace.

23

Nor is't enough, that thou alone may'st slide, 155
But hundred brooks in thy cleer waves do meet,
So hand in hand along with thee they glide
To Thetis house, where all imbrace and greet:
Thou Emblem true, of what I count the best,
O could I lead my Rivolets to rest, 160
So may we press to that vast mansion, ever blest.

24

Ye Fish which in this liquid Region 'bide,
That for each season, have your habitation,
Now salt, now fresh where you think best to glide
To unknown coasts to give a visitation, 165
In Lakes and ponds, you leave your numerous fry,
So nature taught, and yet you know not why,
You watry folk that know not your felicity.

25

Look how the wantons frisk to tast the air,
Then to the colder bottome streight they dive,
Eftsoon to Neptun's glassie Hall repair 171
To see what trade they great ones there do drive,
Who forrage o're the spacious sea-green field,
And take the trembling prey before it yield,
Whose armour is their scales, their spreading fins
    their shield. 175

26

While musing thus with contemplation fed,
And thousand fancies buzzing in my brain,
The sweet-tongu'd Philomel percht ore my head,
And chanted forth a most melodious strain
Which rapt me so with wonder and delight, 180
I judg'd my hearing better then my sight,
And wisht me wings with her a while to take my
    flight.

must be a bird.
a nightingale
English bird.

27

O merry Bird (said I) that fears no snares,
That neither toyles nor hoards up in thy barn,
Feels no sad thoughts, nor cruciating cares 185
To gain more good, or shun what might thee harm

Thy cloaths ne're wear, thy meat is every where,
Thy bed a bough, thy drink the water cleer,
Reminds not what is past, nor whats to come
    dost fear.

28

The dawning morn with songs thou dost prevent,
Sets hundred notes unto thy feathered crew, 191
So each one tunes his pretty instrument,
And warbling out the old, begin anew,
And thus they pass their youth in summer season,
Then follow thee into a better Region, 195
Where winter's never felt by that sweet airy legion.

29

Man at the best a creature frail and vain,
In knowledg ignorant, in strength but weak,
Subject to sorrows, losses, sickness, pain,
Each storm his state, his mind, his body break, 200
From some of these he never finds cessation,
But day or night, within, without, vexation,
Troubles from foes, from friends, from dearest,
    near'st Relation.

30

And yet this sinfull creature, frail and vain,
This lump of wretchedness, of sin and sorrow,
This weather-beaten vessel wrackt with pain, 206
Joyes not in hope of an eternal morrow;
Nor all his losses, crosses and vexation,
In weight, in frequency and long duration
Can make him deeply groan for that divine
    Translation. 210

31

The Mariner that on smooth waves doth glide,
Sings merrily, and steers his Barque with ease,
As if he had command of wind and tide,
And now become great Master of the seas;
But suddenly a storm spoiles all the sport, 215
And makes him long for a more quiet port,
Which 'gainst all adverse winds may serve for fort.

32

So he that saileth in this world of pleasure,
Feeding on sweets, that never bit of th' sowre,
That's full of friends, of honour and of treasure, 220
Fond fool, he takes this earth ev'n for heav'ns
    bower.

But sad afflicton comes & makes him see
Here's neither honour, wealth, nor safety;
Only above is found all with security.

33

O Time the fatal wrack of mortal things,   225
That draws oblivions curtains over kings,
Their sumptuous monuments, men know them not,
Their names without a Record are forgot,
Their parts, their ports, their pomp's all laid in
    th' dust   10
Nor wit nor gold, nor buildings scape times rust;
But he whose name is grav'd in the white stone   231
Shall last and shine when all of these are gone.

Meditations

[*Selections*]

THE APHORISTIC tradition of the English copybooks,
of Bacon, Tuvil, and Osborne, continued through
much of the seventeenth century, sometimes in in-   20
tegrated form, as in Fuller or Felltham, sometimes
dispersed, as in Jonson, Selden, and Halifax. In this
tradition can be placed the following selections from
the occasional thoughts of Anne Bradstreet. They
were seventy-seven in all and were left, upon her
death, in a manuscript book for her children.

iii. Youth is the time of getting, middle age of
improving, and old age of spending; a negligent
youth is usually attended by an ignorant middle
age, and both by an empty old age. He that hath   30
nothing to feed on but vanity and lyes must needs
lye down in the Bed of sorrow.

iv. A ship that beares much saile, and little or
no ballast, is easily overset; and that man, whose
head hath great abilities, and his heart little or no
grace, is in danger of foundering.

vi. The finest bread hath the least bran; the
purest hony, the least wax; and the sincerest
Christian, the least self love.

xii. Authority without wisedome is like a heavy
axe without an edg, fitter to bruise then polish.

xliii. Fire hath its force abated by water, not
by wind; and anger must be alayed by cold words,
and not by blustering threats.

lv. We read of ten lepers that were Cleansed,
but of one that returned thanks: we are more
ready to receive mercys then we are to acknowledg
them: men can use great importunity when they
are in distresses, and shew great ingratitude after
their successes; but he that ordereth his conversation aright, will glorifie him that heard him in the
day of his trouble.

lxix. All the Comforts of this life may be compared to the gourd of Jonah, that notwithstanding
we take great delight for a season in them, and find
their shadow very comfortable, yet there is some
worm or other of discontent, of feare, or greife that
lyes at the root, which in great part withers the
pleasure which else we should take in them; and
well it is that we perceive a decay in their green-
nes, for were earthly comforts permanent, who
would look for heavenly?

lxxiii. A good name is as a precious oyntment,
and it is a great favour to have a good repute
among good men; yet it is not that which Com-
mends us to God, for by his ballance we must be
weighed, and by his Judgment we must be tryed,
and, as he passes the sentence, so shall we stand.

MICHAEL WIGGLESWORTH (1631-1705)

THE SEVENTEENTH century's poetic expression inclined
to elegy, epitaph, and meditation or versified sermon.
The last is well illustrated in the poems of Michael
Wigglesworth, whose *Day of Doom* provides concepts
of God's immutable judgments in a somewhat jingling
form. Firmly grounded in Biblical passages, the work

was highly popular in its own day. It was memorized
by children; it was freely quoted in the pulpit; it
was read for its piety and its edifying truths. Its
theology, sound Calvinism of the seventeenth century,
was so clearly and uncompromisingly expressed that it
gained wide circulation as a doctrinal aid. Though the
most popular of Wigglesworth's works, it was done
with less metrical skill than his other writings, for its

231. he . . . stone: Rev. 2:17.

harshly clipped lines and its trotting measure are manifestly unsuited to the theme.

In expressing the religious thought in his age, Wigglesworth wrote at least three other poems, doctrinally as orthodox as *The Day of Doom*, that possess more poetic merit. *God's Controversy with New England*, printed below, might be classified as an occasional poem. Another, *Vanity of Vanities*, appended to the third edition of *The Day of Doom*, bore the subtitle, "A Song of Emptiness to fill up the Empty Pages Following." A third, *Meat out of the Eater, or Meditations concerning the Necessity, End, and Usefulness of Afflictions unto God's Children*, presented the consolatory message usually associated with funerals. This poem, attempting to deduce spiritual wisdom from earthly affliction, voiced sentiments natural to one who all his life endured physical weakness. All four were written on sermon paper. As literature they reveal how, in a theological age, literary merit is not necessarily the ground upon which a reputation for a work is gained or perpetuated.

The main events of Wigglesworth's life may be summed up in a few sentences. He came with his parents to America at the age of seven, spent his remaining childhood in New Haven, studied divinity at Harvard, remained there as a tutor for three years, and in 1656 accepted a lifetime charge at Malden. Frail from youth, Wigglesworth always had more zest for work than strength for its performance. Cotton Mather referred to him as a "feeble, little shadow of a man." It is not surprising, therefore, that his health began to fail and he was forced to refrain from daily employment of his voice. At times he was unable for weeks to speak with any volume. This weakness, persisting through the years, had three consequences: he gave up his college tutorship; he made a seven months' trip to Bermuda in 1663 to improve his health, during which time he began the study of medicine which finally qualified him for the joint profession of spiritual and physical pilot; and he attempted to exert his pastoral influence by taking up the pen as a supplement to his rare appearances in the pulpit.

After 1686 his health seems to have improved, and he was called upon for extra efforts, including the giving of election sermons. He was thrice married, the third time at the age of sixty, and to these three marriages eight children were born, the last, Edward, becoming Hollis Professor at Harvard.

BIBLIOGRAPHY · *The Day of Doom: or A Poetical Description of the Great and Last Judgement* was issued in an edition of eighteen hundred copies in Cambridge in 1662. No copy of this first edition has been found, although the modernized reprint containing Wigglesworth's autobiographical essay, edited in 1867 by W. H. Burr and J. W. Dean, is readily available. The best recent reprint of *The Day of Doom* was designed by Bruce Rogers in 1929 and contains an excellent introduction by K. B. Murdock. *God's Controversy with New England*, composed in 1662, was first published in the *Proceedings of the Massachusetts Historical Society* (First Series), XII (1873), 83–93; and *Meat out of the Eater* (1669) was reprinted from the first edition in the *Yale University Library Gazette*, V (1931), 45–47. The most detailed biographical sketch is J. W. Dean, *Memoir of Rev. Michael Wigglesworth* (1871). Valuable material is included in: "Letters of Michael Wigglesworth to Increase Mather," *Collections of the Massachusetts Historical Society* (Fourth Series), VIII (1868), 645–647; M. B. Jones, "Notes for a Bibliography of Michael Wigglesworth's *Day of Doom* and *Meat out of the Eater*," *Proceedings of the American Antiquarian Society*, XXXIX (Part 1) (1929), 77–84; F. O. Matthiessen, "Wigglesworth, a Puritan Artist," *New England Quarterly*, I (1928), 491–504; and P. E. More, "Spirit and Poetry of Early New England," *Shelburne Essays* (Eleventh Series) (1921), 3–32.

The Day of Doom

A Postscript unto the Reader

THE AVIDITY with which *The Day of Doom* was read in 1662 may be measured by the fact that the first edition of eighteen hundred copies was disposed of in a year. If the title page of the Cambridge edition of 1701 is correct, there were at least four American editions in the seventeenth century. The poem was issued also in England in 1666 and 1673. It was reprinted six times in the eighteenth century, although Royall Tyler observed in his *Algerine Captive* (1797) that by the 1790's household libraries usually contained more diverting books than "some dreary somebody's day of Doom."

Students of early American literature have been diverted or bored by various treatments of Wigglesworth's poem, often cited as a sample of the harshness of Calvinistic thinking or as a robust example of what Puritan logic did to a sense of beauty. We are expected to conclude that the age was cantankerous, blind to beauty, and driven by an inexorable otherworldliness to a denial of ordinary human emotions.

All of this is pathetic to a student of human psychology, and it does injustice to a whole age and people. *The Day of Doom*, for all its consistent application of a text, contains no more of hell-fire than many a modern evangelistic sermon. As for the charge that the seventeenth century could write only doggerel, this is a judgment born only of ignorance and hasty generalization. Wigglesworth himself wrote better than the samples we are ordinarily given, and this meek, quiet little scholarly gentleman has a better claim to distinction than that stemming from the main body of his famous poem. Since we are concerned in Wigglesworth with a representative kind of poetry and not that which we read today for our pleasure and delight, we need ever to hold strongly to historical judgments.

If the principal section of the *Day of Doom* is primarily concerned with the theological concept of damnation, the Postscript furnishes the author's earnest concern for man's repentance. The text of the 1701 edition was made readily available in Kenneth B. Murdock's edition of 1929. Punctuation has been modernized.

... Perhaps thou harbourest such thoughts as these:

I hope I may enjoy my carnal ease
A little longer, and my self refresh
With those delights that gratifie the flesh,
And yet repent before it be too late,   5
And get into a comfortable state;
I hope I have yet many years to spend,
And time enough those matters to attend.
Presumptuous heart! Is God engag'd to give
A longer time to such as love to live   10
Like Rebels still, who think to stain his Glory
By wickedness, and after to be sory?
Unto thy lust shall he be made a drudge,
Who thee, and all ungodly men, shall judge?
Canst thou account sin sweet, and yet confess,   15
That first, or last, it ends in bitterness?
Is sin a thing that must procure thee sorrow?
And wouldst thou dally with't another morrow?
O foolish man, who lovest to enjoy
That which will thee distress, or else destroy!   20
What gained Sampson by his Delilah?
What gained David by his Bathsheba?
The one became a Slave, lost both his eyes,
And made them sport that were his Enemies;
The other penneth, as a certain token   25
Of Gods displeasure, that his bones were broken,
Besides the woes he after met withal,
To chasten him for that his grievous Fall:
His own Son Ammon using crafty wiles,
His Daughter Thamar wickedly defiles;   · 30

His second Son more beautiful than good,
His hands embreweth in his Brothers Blood:
And by and by aspiring to the Crown,
He strives to pull his gentle Father down:
With hellish rage, him fiercely persecuting,   35
And bruitishly his Concubines polluting.
Read whoso list, and ponder what he reads,
And he shall find small joy in evil deeds.
Moreover this consider, that the longer
Thou liv'st in sin, thy sin will grow the stronger,
And then it will an harder matter prove,   41
To leave those wicked haunts that thou dost love.
The Black-moor may as eas'ly change his skin,
As old transgressors leave their wonted sin.
And who can tell what may become of thee,   45
Or where thy Soul in one days time may be?
We see that Death ner old nor young men spares,
But one and other takes at unawares.
For in a moment, whil'st men Peace do cry,
Destruction seizeth on them suddenly.   50
Thou who this morning art a lively wight,
May'st be a Corps and damned Ghost ere night.
Oh, dream not then, that it will serve the turn,
Upon thy death bed for thy sins to mourn,
But think how many have been snatcht away,   55
And had no time for mercy once to pray.
It's just with God Repentance to deny
To such as put it off until they dy,
And late Repentance seldom proveth true,
Which if it fail, thou know'st what must ensue;   60
For after this short life is at an end,
What is amiss thou never canst amend.
Believe, O man, that to procrastinate,
And put it off until it be too late,
As 'tis thy sin, so is it Satans wile,   65
Whereby he doth great multitudes beguile.
How many thousands hath this strong delusion
Already brought to ruine and confusion,
Whose Souls are now reserv'd in Iron Chains,
Under thick darkness to eternal pains?   70
They thought of many years, as thou dost now,
But were deceived quite, and so may'st thou.
Oh, then my friend, while not away thy time,
Nor by rebellion aggravate thy Crime.
Oh put not off Repentance till to morrow,   75
Adventure not without Gods leave to borrow
Another day to spend upon thy lust,
Lest God (that is most holy, wise, and just)

Denounce in wrath, and to thy terrour say:
This night shall Devils fetch they Soul away.   80
Now seek the face of God with all thy heart;
Acknowledge unto him how vile thou art;
Tell him thy sins deserve eternal wrath,
And that it is a wonder that he hath
Permitted thee so long to draw thy breath,   85
Who might have cut thee off by sudden death,
And sent thy Soul into the lowest Pit,
From whence no price should ever ransom it,
And that he may most justly do it still
(Because thou hast deserv'd it) if he will.
Yet also tell him that, if he shall please,
He can forgive thy Sins, and thee release,
And that in Christ his Son he may be just,
And justifie all those that on him trust:
That though thy sins are of a crimson dy,   95
Yet Christ his Blood can cleanse thee thorowly.
Tell him, that he may make his glorious Name
More wonderful by covering thy shame;
That Mercy may be greatly magnify'd,
And Justice also fully satisfy'd,   100
If he shall please to own thee in his Son,
Who hath paid dear for Men's Redemption.
Tell him thou hast an unbelieving heart,
Which hindereth thee from coming for a part   104
In Christ: and that although his terrours aw thee,
Thou canst not come till he be pleas'd to draw thee.
Tell him thou know'st thine heart to be so bad,
And thy condition so exceeding sad,
That though Salvation may be had for nought
Thou canst not come and take, till thou be brought.
Oh beg of him to bow thy stubborn Will   111
To come to Christ, that he thy lusts may kill.
Look up to Christ for his attractive pow'r,
Which he exerteth in a needful hour;
Who saith, whenas I lifted up shall be,   115
Then will I draw all sorts of men to me.
O wait upon him with true diligence,
And trembling fear in every Ordinance;
Unto his call earnest attention give,
Whose voice makes deaf men hear, and dead men
    live.   120
Thus weep, and mourn, thus hearken, pray and
    wait,
Till he behold, and pitty thine estate,
Who is more ready to bestow his Grace,
Then thou the same art willing to imbrace;   124

Yea, he hath Might enough to bring thee home,
Though thou hast neither strength nor will to
    come.
If he delay to answer thy request,
Know that oft-times he doth it for the best:
Not with intent to drive us from his door,
But for to make us importune him more;   130
Or else to bring us duly to confess,
And be convinc'd of our unworthiness.
Oh, be not weary then, but persevere
To beg his Grace till he thy suit shall hear:
And leave him not, nor from his foot-stool go,   135
Till over thee Compassions skirt he throw.
Eternal Life will recompence thy pains,
If found at last, with everlasting gains.
For if the Lord be pleas'd to hear they cryes,
And to forgive thy great iniquities,   140
Thou wilt have cause for ever to admire,
And laud his Grace, that granted thy desire.
Then shalt thou find thy labour is not lost:
But that the good obtain'd surmounts the cost.
Nor shalt thou grieve for loss of sinful pleasures, 145
Exchang'd for heavenly joyes and lasting treasures.
The yoke of Christ, which once thou didst esteem
A tedious yoke, shall then most easie seem.
For why? The love of Christ shall thee constrain
To take delight in that which was thy pain;   150
The wayes of Wisdom shall be pleasant wayes,
And thou shalt chuse therein to spend thy dayes.
If once thy Soul be brought to such a pass,
O'bless the Lord, and magnifie his Grace.
Thou, that of late hadst reason to be sad,   155
May'st now rejoyce, and be exceeding glad,
For thy condition is as happy now,
As erst it was disconsolate and low;
Thou art become as rich as whilome poor,
As blessed now, as cursed heretofore;   160
For being cleansed with Christs precious Blood,
Thou hast an int'rest in the chiefest good:
Gods anger is towards thy Soul appeased,
And in his Christ he is with thee well pleased.
Yea, he doth look upon thee with a mild   165
And gracious aspect as upon his child;
He is become thy Father and thy Friend,
And will defend thee from the cursed Fiend.
Thou need'st not fear the roaring Lyon's rage,
Since God Almighty doth himself engage   170
To bear thy Soul in Everlasting Armes,

Above the reach of all destructive harms.
What ever here thy sufferings may be,
Yet from them all the Lord shall rescue thee.
He will preserve thee by his wond'rous might 175
Unto that rich Inheritance in light.
Oh, sing for joy, all ye regenerate,
Whom Christ hath brought into this blessed state!
O love the Lord, all ye his Saints, who hath
Redeemed you from everlasting wrath: 180
Who hath by dying made your Souls to live,
And what he dearly bought doth freely give:
Give up your selves to walk in all his wayes,
And study how to live unto his praise.
The time is short you have to serve him here: 185
The day of your deliv'rance draweth near.
Lift up your heads, ye upright ones in heart,
Who in Christ's purchase have obtain'd a part.
Behold, he rides upon a shining Cloud,
With Angels voice, and Trumpet sounding loud;
He comes to save his folk from all their foes, 191
And plague the men that Holiness oppose.
So come, Lord Jesus, quickly come we pray:
Yea come, and hasten our Redemption day.

Need not read

God's Controversy with New England

THE STUDENT of this piece needs to be familiar with
the Old Testament idea of a people's covenant with
the Lord. Dereliction in duty brings the wrath of
God upon them, and humiliation and repentance
stays His hand and restores a people to His favor.
Calamities are either the direct result of God's displeasure over a wayward generation or warnings of
more fearful distresses if repentance and amendment do
not speedily follow. The observations in Wigglesworth's poem were prompted by a serious drought in
1662. The text is from the March, 1871, *Proceedings of
the Massachusetts Historical Society*, where the poem
was first published.

*Written in the Time of the Great Drought Anno
1662* · [God Chides, Threatens, and Punishes
New England]

. . . .

"Are these the men that erst at my command
    Forsook their ancient seats and native soile,
To follow me into a desert land,
    Contemning all the travell and the toile,

Whose love was such to purest ordinances 5
    As made them set at nought their fair in-
        heritances?

"Are these the men that prized libèrtee
    To walk with God according to their light,
To be as good as he would have them bee,
    To serve and worship him with all their might, 10
Before the pleasures which a fruitfull field,
    And country flowing-full of all good things,
        could yield,

"Are these the folk whom from the brittish Iles,
    Through the stern billows of the watry main,
I safely led so many thousand miles, 15
    As if their journey had been through a plain?
Whom having from all enemies protected,
    And through so many deaths and dangers well
        directed,

"I brought and planted on the western shore,
    Where nought but bruits and salvage wights
        did swarm 20
(Untaught, untrain'd, untam'd by vertue's lore)
    That sought their blood, yet could not do them
        harm?
My fury's flaile them thresht, my fatall broom
    Did sweep them hence, to make my people
        elbow-room.

"Are these the men whose gates with peace I
    crown'd, 25
    To whom for bulwarks I salvation gave,
Whilst all things else with rattling tumults sound,
    And mortall frayes send thousands to the grave?
Whilst their own brethren bloody hands embrewed
    In brothers blood, and fields with carcases
        bestrewed? 30

"Is this the people blest with bounteous store,
    By land and sea full richly clad and fed,
Whom plenty's self stands waiting still before,
    And powreth out their cups well tempered?
For whose dear sake an howling wildernes 35
    I lately turned into a fruitful paradeis?

. . . .

"Are these the folk to whom I milked out
    And sweetnes stream'd from consolations brest;

68

Whose soules I fed and strengthened throughout
　　With finest spirituall food most finely drest?　40
On whom I rained living bred from Heaven
　　Withouten Errour's bane, or Superstition's
　　leaven?

"With whom I made a Covenant of peace,
　　And unto whom I did most firmly plight
My faithfulness, If whilst I live I cease　45
　　To be their Guide, their God, their full delight;
Since them with cords of love to me I drew,
　　Enwrapping in my grace such as should them
　　ensew.

"Are these the men, that now mine eyes behold,
　　Concerning whom I thought, and whilome spake,
First Heaven shall pass away together scrold,　51
　　Ere they my lawes and righteous wayes forsake,
Or that they slack to runn their heavenly race?
　　Are these the same? or are some others come in
　　place?

"If these be they, how is it that I find　55
　　In stead of holiness Carnality,
In stead of heavenly frames an Earthly mind,
　　For burning zeal luke-warm Indifferency,
For flaming love, key-cold Dead-heartedness,
　　For temperance (in meat, and drinke, and
　　cloaths) excess?　60

"Whence cometh it, that Pride, and Luxurie
　　Debate, Deceit, Contention, and Strife,
False-dealing, Covetousness, Hypocrisie
　　(With such like Crimes) amongst them are so
　　rife,
That one of them doth over-reach another?　65
　　And that an honest man can hardly trust his
　　Brother?

"How is it, that Security, and Sloth,
　　Amongst the best are Common to be found?
That grosser sins, in stead of Graces growth,
　　Amongst the many more and more abound?　70
I hate dissembling shews of Holiness.
　　Or practise as you talk, or never more profess.

"Judge not, vain world, that all are hypocrites
　　That do profess more hoilness then thou:

All foster not dissembling, guilefull sprites,　75
　　Nor love their lusts, though very many do.
Some sin through want of care and constant
　　watch,
　　Some with the sick converse, till they the sick-
　　ness catch.

"Some, that maintain a reall root of grace,
　　Are overgrown with many noysome weeds,　80
Whose heart, that those no longer may take place,
　　The benefit of due correction needs.
And such as these however gone astray
　　I shall by stripes reduce into a better way.

"Moreover some there be that still retain　85
　　Their anceient vigour and sincerity;
Whom both their own, and others sins, constrain
　　To sigh, and mourn, and weep, and wail, & cry;
And for their sakes I have forborn to powre
　　My wrath upon Revolters to this present houre.

"To praying Saints I always have respect,　91
　　And tender love, and pittifull regard:
Nor will I now in any wise neglect
　　Their love and faithfull service to reward;
Although I deal with others for their folly,　95
　　And turn their mirth to tears that have been
　　too jolly.

"For thinke not, O Backsliders, in your heart,
　　That I shall still your evill manners beare:
Your sinns me press as sheaves do load a cart,
　　And therefore I will plague you for this geare
Except you seriously, and soon, repent,　101
　　I'le not delay your pain and heavy punishment.
· · · · · · · · · ·
"But hear O Heavens! Let Earth amazed stand;
　　Ye Mountaines melt, and Hills come flowing
　　down:
Let horror seize upon both Sea and Land;　105
　　Let Natures self be cast into a stown.
I children nourisht, nurtur'd and upheld:
　　But they against a tender father have rebell'd.

"What could have been by me performed more?
　　Or wherein fell I short of your desire?　110
Had you but askt, I would have op't my store,
　　And given what lawful wishes could require.

For all this bounteous cost I lookt to see
  Heaven-reaching-hearts, & thoughts, Meekness,
    Humility.

"But lo, a sensuall Heart all void of grace,   115
  An Iron neck, a proud presumptuous Hand:
A self-conceited, stiff, stout, stubborn Race,
  That fears no threats, submitts to no command:
Self-will'd, perverse, such as can beare no yoke;
  A Generation even ripe for vengeance stroke. 120
. . . .

"What should I do with such a stiff-neckt race?
  How shall I ease me of such Foes as they?
What shall befall despizers of my Grace?
  I'le surely beare their candle-stick away,
And Lamps put out. Their glorious noon-day light
  I'le quickly turn into a dark Egyptian night. 126

"Oft have I charg'd you by my ministers
  To gird your selves with sack cloth, and repent.
Oft have I warnd you by my messengers;
  That so you might my wrathfull ire prevent: 130
But who among you hath this warning taken?
  Who hath his crooked wayes, & wicked works
    forsaken?
. . . .

"Now therefore hearken and encline your ear,
  In judgement I will henceforth with you plead;
And if by that you will not learn to fear,   135
  But still go on a sensuall life to lead:
I'le strike at once an All-Consuming stroke;
  Nor cries nor tears shall then my fierce intent
    revoke."

Thus ceast his Dreadful-threatning voice
  The High & lofty-One.   140
The Heavens stood still Appal'd thereat;
  The Earth beneath did groane:
Soon after I beheld and saw
  A mortall dart come flying:
I lookt again, & quickly saw   145
  Some fainting, others dying.
. . . .

One wave another followeth,
  And one disease begins
Before another cease, becaus
  We turn not from our sins.   150
We stopp our ear against reproof,

And hearken not to God:
God stops his ear against our prayer,
  And takes not off his rod.

Our fruitful seasons have been turnd   155
  Of late to barrenness,
Sometimes through great & parching drought,
  Sometimes through rain's excess.
Yea now the pastures & corn fields
  For want of rain do languish: 160
The cattell mourn, & hearts of men
  Are fill'd with fear & anguish.

The clouds are often gathered,
  As if we should have rain:
But for our great unworthiness   165
  Are scattered again.
We pray & fast, & make fair shewes,
  As if we meant to turn:
But whilst we turn not, God goes on
  Our field, & fruits to burn.   170

And Burnt are all things in such sort,
  That nothing now appears,
But what may wound our hearts with grief,
  And draw foorth floods of teares.
All things a famine do presage   175
  In that extremity,
As if both men, and also beasts,
  Should soon be done to dy.

This O New-England hast thou got
  By riot, & excess: 180
This hast thou brought upon thy self
  By pride & wantonness.
Thus must thy worldlyness be whipt
  They, that too much do crave,
Provoke the Lord to take away   185
  Such blessings as they have.

We have been also threatened
  With worser things then these:
And God can bring them on us still,
  To morrow if he please.   190
For if his mercy be abus'd,
  Which holpe us at our need
And mov'd his heart to pitty us,
  We shall be plagu'd indeed.

Beware, O sinful Land, beware; 195
  And do not think it strange
That sorer judgements are at hand,
  Unless thou quickly change.
Or God, or thou, must quickly change;
  Or else thou art undon: 200
Wrath cannot cease, if sin remain,
  Where judgement is begun.

Ah dear New England! dearest land to me;
  Which unto God hast hitherto been dear,
And mayst be still more dear than for- 205
    merlie,
  If to his voice thou wilt incline thine ear.

Consider wel & wisely what the rod,
  Wherewith thou art from yeer to yeer chastized,
Instructeth thee. Repent, & turn to God,
  Who will not have his nurture be despized. 210

Thou still hast in thee many praying saints,
  Of great account, and precious with the Lord,
Who dayly powre out unto him their plaints,
  And strive to please him both in deed & word.

Cheer on, sweet souls, my heart is with you all, 215
  And shall be with you, maugre Sathan's might:
And whereso'ere this body be a Thrall,
  Still in New-England shall be my delight.

ELEGIES AND EPITAPHS

WITH THE HIGH death rate in New England in the seventeenth century, human mortality held a much larger place in thinking than it does today, and meditations on the imminence of death were daily practice. It is not surprising, therefore, that the epitaph and the elegy should emerge as the freest poetic exercises of the century and the commonest of literary forms. These range from notices of the deaths of infants to eulogies of honored colonial dead. Printed verses were attached to hearses or hawked as broadsides. The poetic characteristics of these laments leave much to be desired, but are in accord with contemporary fashions. The metaphysical tendencies of the seventeenth century are apparent in the frequent anagrams, and colonial verse went through the various successive stages of baroque.

Closely allied to the personal elegy is the lament for the loss of towns. Many New England villages were decimated by Indian incursions in the Pequod and King Philip's Wars. Benjamin Tompson's poems, frequently called the first native poems printed in America, give the best seventeenth-century celebration of this theme. "Chelmsfords Fate" and "Rehoboths Fate" both appeared as laments in a supplement to his more famous poem, *New-Englands Crisis*.

BIBLIOGRAPHY · For long elegies of literary merit in the seventeenth century the reader may profitably examine certain poems: Urian Oakes, "Elegy upon . . . Thomas Shepard" (printed in Miller and Johnson, *The Puritans*, 641–50); John Cotton, "On . . . Thomas Hooker" (prefixed to Thomas Hooker, *A Survey of the Summe of Church-Discipline* (London, 1648); Benjamin Tompson, "The Grammarians Funeral" (printed in

Benjamin Tompson, His Poems (New York, 1924)); Nicholas Noyes, "An Elegy Upon . . . Joseph Green" (reprinted in the *Historical Collections of the Essex Institute*, VIII, 168–74); and Daniel Henchman, "Lamentations upon . . . Sir William Phips" (reprinted in Harold S. Jantz, "The First Century of New England Verse," in the *Proceedings of the American Antiquarian Society* for October, 1943).

Shorter pieces are to be found in the last part (years 1647 to 1668) of Nathaniel Morton's *New Englands Memoriall*, 1669 (reprinted, New York, 1937); Ola Winslow, Editor, *American Broadside Verse* (New Haven, 1930); *Harper's Literary Museum* (New York, 1927); and Kenneth B. Murdock, *Handkerchiefs from Paul* (Cambridge, 1927).

John Fiske: Two Anagrams on John Cotton

JOHN FISKE was pastor and schoolmaster at Salem, and later pastor at Wenham and Chelmsford. He composed six full-length elegies besides other anagrams and eulogistic pieces. In his anagrams he employed the same basic technique as that used by John Wilson.

Ad Matronam pientissimam spectatissimamque
Ipsius domini vixit Conthoralem dilectissimam
Sobolemque eique Charissimum.

John Cotton

1 Anagr · Thô onc', I not.

2 Anagr · I onc', thô not.

To 1st

Of me, Why doe you thus with dreary cryes
with sobbs, with Teares, with sighes with weeping
   eyes
Lament / your losse. In me / bewayle your lot?
Saying thô once I was; I now am not?
What I was once to you, and you, remind   5
You now will oft, and matter there youl' find
to aggravate that here, that breach is made
by Hand divine, with greife your selves to lade.

To 2d

But what thô I as now be not, who was
And what if I thus from you all doe passe   10
ner' to returne to this vayne world and state
that transitory is: mind it your Fate
And eeke remind that once I was, and blesse
that Hand that me you lent, yea and confesse
your portion greate that his rich grace in Mee   15
enricheth you, abids, tho ceast I bee.

                                          J:F

Thomas Dudley: Epitaph

THE FOLLOWING lines were found in the pocket of
Thomas Dudley (1576–1653) after his death. He was
Deputy Governor and Governor in Massachusetts.
They were reprinted in *Magnalia Christi Americana*,
I, 122–123. A variant version appeared in *Proceedings
of the Massachusetts Historical Society*, II (1835–1855),
221.

Dim eyes, deaf ears, cold stomach, shew
My dissolution is in view.
Eleven times seven near liv'd have I,
And now God calls, I willing die.
My shuttle's shot, my race is run,   5
My sun is set, my day is done.
My span is measur'd, tale is told,
My flower is faded, and grown old.
My dream is vanish'd, shadow's fled,
My soul with Christ, my body dead.   10
Farewel dear wife, children and friends,
Hate heresie, make blessed ends.
Bear poverty, live with good men;
So shall we live with joy agen.
Let men of God in courts and churches watch 15
O're such as do a *toleration* hatch,
Lest that ill egg bring forth a cockatrice,

To poison all with heresie and vice.
If men be left, and otherwise combine,
My *Epitaph's*, I Dy'd no libertine.   20

Edward Johnson: Wonder-Working Providence

The Lord Taketh Away

THE DEATH of many of the founding preachers was regarded by Edward Johnson as a warning from the Lord
to pursue more faithfully his good work, or he would
raise up another people to perform his behests. The
decline in leadership in the second generation and its
effect upon the church were probably his real reasons
for writing this lament. The poem appeared, along
with sixty-six others, in his *Wonder-Working Providence
of Sions Saviour* (London, 1654).

Oh thou, my soul, and every part in me
   Lament, the Lord his worthies from the earth
Takes to himself, and makes our earth to be
   A mourning place left destitute of mirth;
Are these the daies wherein that Beast shall fall? 5
Lord leave us means, though thou be all in all.

What courage was in Winthrope, it was thine;
   Shepheards sweet Sermons from thy blessing
      came,
Our heavenly Hooker thy grace did refine,
   And godly Burr receiv'd from thee his frame: 10
Philips didst thou indue with Scripture light,
And Huet had his arguings strong and right.

Grave Higginson his heavenly truths from thee,
   Maverick was made an able help to thine;
What Herver had thou gavest, for's people free;   15
   Follow Green full of grace, to work thou didst
      assign:
Godly Glover his rich gifts thou gavest,
Thus thou by means thy flocks from spoiling savest.

But Lord, why dost by death withdraw thy hand
   From us, these men and means are sever'd quite;
Stretch forth thy might, Lord Christ do thou
      command,   21
   Their doubled spirit on those left to light:
Forth of their graves call ten times ten again,
That thy dear flocks no damage may sustain.

Can I forget these means that thou hast used,   25
    To quicken up my drowsie drooping soul?
Lord I forget, and have the same abused,
    Which makes me now with grief their deaths
        condole,
And kiss thy rod, laid on with bowels tender,
By death of mine, makes me their death remember.

Lord, stay thy hand, thy Jacobs number's small,   31
    Powre out thy wrath on Antichrists proud
        Thrones;
Here [hear] thy poor flocks that on thee daily call,
    Bottle their tears, and pity their sad groans.
Where shall we go, Lord Christ? we turn to thee,
Heal our back-slidings, forward press shall we.   36

Not we, but all thy Saints the world throughout
    Shall on thee wait, thy wonders to behold;
Thou King of Saints, the Lord in battel stout
    Increase thy armies many thousand fold.   40
Oh Nations all, his anger seek to stay,
That doth create him armies every day.

Epitaph for Roger Harlackenden

THIS EPITAPH is one of several tributes to the ecclesiastical and lay leaders of New England in Johnson's *Wonder-Working Providence of Sions Saviour* (London, 1654). Such poems on New Englanders, whether eulogies or elegies, ranged from four to twenty-eight lines.

The tribute to Harlackenden is matched in expression and sympathy by those on John Eliot, Francis Higginson, Thomas Hooker, Thomas Shepard, Ezekiel Rogers, John Ward, John Davenport, and Peter Bulkeley.

    Harlackenden,
      Among these men
Of note Christ hath thee seated:
    In warlike way
      Christ thee aray   5
With zeal, and love well heated.
    As generall
      Belov'd of all
Christ Souldiers honour thee:
    In thy young yeares,   10
      Courage appeares,
And kinde benignity.

Short are thy days
    Spent in his praise,
Whose Church work thou must aid,   15
    His work shall bide,
    Silver tride,
But thine by death is staid.

Samuel Danforth: on William Tompson

SAMUEL DANFORTH was a fellow at Harvard College in 1642 and afterward pastor of the church at Roxbury, where he labored as colleague of John Eliot for twenty-four years. Danforth utilized his proficiency in rhyme for filling some of the pages of his Almanacs, of which copies for the years 1647, 1648, and 1649 (with their poems) survive. He wrote two anagrams on William Tompson, the first of which follows:

Anagram 1 · *lo, now i am past ill.*

Why wepe yea still for me, my Children dear?
    What Cause haue ye of sorow, grief or fear?
Lo, now all euill things are past and gone,
Terror, black Coller & strangullion;
My pains are Curd, no greif doth me anoy,   5
My sorrows all are turned in to joy.
No fiend of hell shall hence forth me asay,
My fears are heald, my teares are wipt away;
Gods reconciled face i now behould,
He that dispersd my darkness many fold;   10
In Abrams bosom now i swetely rest,
    Of perfect joy & hapiness posest.

John Wilson: Verses on Joseph Brisco

JOHN WILSON (1588?–1667) was a revered and beloved pastor in Boston. Educated at Cambridge, England, where he received the A.B. and A.M. degrees, he preached in a number of places before embarking for New England in 1630. It was as a versemaker that he gained his contemporary fame, though only a small portion of his poetry has come down to us. His versatility in versification is chiefly apparent in his anagrams, a poetical device much admired by seventeenth-century readers. Cotton Mather thus summarized his service to his contemporaries:

His Care to guide his Flock, and feed his Lambs,
By, Words, Works, Prayers, Psalms, Alms, and Anagrams:
Those Anagrams, in which he made to Start
Out of meer Nothings, by Creating Art,

Whole Words of Counsel; did to Motes unfold
Names, till they Lessons gave richer than Gold.

The following poem was printed as a broadside
shortly after Brisco's death in 1657. There are copies
at the Massachusetts Historical Society and the Huntington libraries. A facsimile reproduction appears in
S. A. Green's *Ten Fac-simile Reproductions Relating to
New England* (Boston, 1902).

A COPY OF VERSES · Made by that Reverend Man
  of God Mr. John Wilson, Pastor to the first
  Church in Boston; On the sudden Death of
  Mr. Joseph Brisco, Who was translated from
  Earth to Heaven Jan. 1. 1657.

> Not by a Fiery Chariot as Elisha was,
> But by the Water, which was the outward cause:
> And now at Rest with Christ his Saviour dear,
> Though he hath left his dear Relations here.

Joseph Briscoe ⎫
Job cries hopes ⎬ Anagram
               ⎭

There is no Job but cries to God and hopes,
And God his ear in Christ; to cries he opes,
Out of the deeps to him I cry'd and hop'd,
And unto me his gracious ear is op'd:
Doubt not of this ye that my death bewail,   5
What if it did so strangely me assail:
What if I was so soon in Waters drown'd,
And when I cry'd to men, no help I found:
There was a God in Heaven that heard my cry,
And lookt upon me with a gracious eye: 10
He that did pity Joseph in his grief,
Sent from above unto my soul relief:
He sent his Angels who did it conveigh
Into his Bosom, where poor Laz'rus lay:
Let none presume to censure my estate,   15
As Job his Friends did stumble at his Fate.
All things on Earth do fall alike to all,
To good Disciples, which on God that call;
To those that do Blaspheme his Holy Name,
And unto those that reverence the same: 20
He that from nature drew me unto Grace,
And look'd upon me with a Fathers face:
When in my blood upheld me to the last,
And now I do of joyes eternal tast.
Remember how Job's precious children Dy'd,   25
As also what the Prophet did Betide:

26. Prophet: Jonah.

What was the end of good Josiah's life,
And how it fared with Ezekiels Wife:
Remember what a Death it was that Christ
(Suffered for me) the Darling of the highest;   30
His Death of Deaths hath quite remov'd the sting,
No matter how or where the Lord doth bring
Us to our end, in Christ who live and die
And sure to live with Christ eternally.

Bacon's Epitaph Made by His Man

THERE WERE several poems written on the death of
Colonel Nathaniel Bacon, leader of Bacon's Rebellion
in Virginia (1676). Two survived and were printed in
the Burwell Papers in *Collections of the Massachusetts
Historical Society* (Second Series), I (1814), 58–60.
The more famous of these is the following anonymous
poem "drawne by the man that waited upon his person, it is said." The authorship is unknown.

Death why soe crewill! what no other way
To manifest thy spllene, but thus to slay
Our hopes of safety; liberty, our all
Which, through thy tyrany, with him must fall
To its late caoss? Had thy rigid force   5
Bin delt by retale, and not thus in gross
Grief had bin silent: Now wee must complaine
Since thou, in him, hast more then thousand slane
Whose lives and safetys did so much depend
On him there lif, with him their lives must end. 10
  If't be a sin to think Death brib'd can bee
Wee must be guilty; say twas bribery
Guided the fatall shaft. Verginias foes
To whom for secret crimes just vengeance owes
Disarved plagues, dreding their just disart   15
Corrupted Death by Parascellcian art
Him to destroy; whose well tried curage such,
There heartless harts, nor arms, nor strength could
    touch
  Who now must heale those wounds, or stop that
    blood
The Heathen made, and drew into a flood?   20
Who i'st must pleade our Cause? nor Trump nor
    Drum
Nor Deputations; these alass are dumb.
And Cannot speake. Our Arms (though near so
    strong)
Will want the aide of his Commanding tongue,

Which conquer'd more than Ceaser: He orethrew
Onely the outward frame; this could subdue   26
The ruged workes of nature. Soules repleate
With dull Child could, he'd annemate with heate
Drawne forth of reasons Lymbick. In a word
Marss and Minerva, both in him Concurd   30
For arts, for arms, whose pen and sword alike
As Catos did, may admireation strike
Into his foes; while they confess with all
It was their guilt stil'd him a Criminall.
Onely this differance does from truth proceed   35
They in the guilt, he in the name must bleed.
While none shall dare his obseques to sing
In desarv'd measures; untill time shall bring
Truth Crown'd with freedom, and from danger
    free
To sound his praises to posterity.   40
    Here let him rest; while wee this truth report
Hee's gone from hence unto a higher Court
To pleade his Cause where he by this doth know
Whether to Ceaser hee was friend, or foe.

Benjamin Tompson: New-Englands Crisis

BENJAMIN TOMPSON (1642–1714) is best known for
New-Englands Crisis (1676), a long poem on King
Philip's War. In the appendix of that poem he laments
the loss of certain towns, burned by Indian warriors in
that conflict.

Chelmsfords Fate

Ere famous Winthrops bones are laid to rest
The pagans Chelmsford with sad flames arrest,
Making an artifical day of night
By that plantations formidable light.
Here's midnight shrieks and Soul-amazing moanes,
Enough to melt the very marble stones: 6
Fire-brands and bullets, darts and deaths and
    wounds
Confusive outcryes every where resounds:
The natives shooting with the mixed cryes,
With all the crueltyes the foes devise   10
Might fill a volume, but I leave a space
For mercyes still successive in there place
No doubting but the foes have done their worst,
And shall by heaven suddenly be curst.

Rehoboths Fate

I once conjectur'd that those tygers hard
To reverend Newmans bones would have regard,
But were all SAINTS they met twere all one case,
They have no rev'rence to an Angels face:
But where they fix their griping lions paws   5
They rend without remorse or heed to laws.
Rehoboth here in common english, Rest
They ransack, Newmans Relicts to molest.
Here all the town is made a publick stage
Whereon these Nimrods act their monstrous rage.
All crueltyes which paper stain'd before   11
Are acted to the life here ore and ore.

Joseph Capen: a Funeral Elegy

Upon the Much to be Lamented Death and Most
    Deplorable Expiration of the Pious, Learned,
    Ingenious, and Eminently Usefull Servant of
    God Mr. John Foster Who Expired and Breathed
    out His Soul Quietly into the Arms of His
    Blessed Redeemer at Dorchester, Sept. 9th
    Anno Dom. 1681.   *Aetatis Anno 33*

JOHN FOSTER, pioneer printer of Boston, set up a press
in 1675. Two titles, both sermons of Increase Mather,
survive from that year. But he also printed material
of his own authorship, especially scientific papers.
Descriptive pieces on astronomy and brief essays upholding the Copernican system appeared in his Almanacs. The last lines of the following poem are
peculiarly appropriate for one of Foster's profession;
they are also interesting as anticipating Franklin's frequently quoted epitaph on himself, "Printer." The
elegy was printed from a manuscript copy in Thomas
C. Simonds's *History of South Boston* (1857). The
original broadside was advertised in William Brattle's
Almanac of 1682. Joseph Capen (1658–1725), author
of the poem, was pastor at Topsfield, Massachusetts.

Here lye the relict Fragments, which were took
Out of Consumtion's teeth, by Death the Cook
Voracious Apetite dost thus devour
Scarce ought hast left for worms t' live on an Hour
But Skin & Bones no bones thou mak'st of that   5
It is thy common trade t' eat all the fat.
Here lyes that earthly House, where once did dwell
That Soul that Scarce hath left its Parallel
For Sollid Judgment Piety & Parts

And peerless Skill in all the practick Arts 10
Which as the glittering Spheres, it passed by
Methinks, I saw it glance at Mercury;
Ascended now: 'bov Time & Tides 't abides,
Which Sometimes told the world, of Times and
    Tides,
Next to th' Third Heavens the Stars were his de-
    light, 15
Where's Contemplation dwelt both day and Night,
Soaring unceartainly but now at Shoar,
Whether Sol moves or Stands He Doubts no
    more.
He that despis'd the things the world admirrd,
As having Skill in rarer things acquired, 20
The heav'ns Interpreter doth disappear;
The Starre's translated to his proper Sphere.
What e're the World may think did Cause his
    death
Consumption 'twas not Cupid, Stopt his breath.
The Heav'ns which God's glory doe discover, 25
Have lost their constant Friend & instant Lover
Like Atlas, he help't bear up that rare Art
Astronomy; & always took his part:
Most happy Soul who didst not there Sit down
But didst make after an eternal Crown 30
Sage Archimede! Second Bezaleel
Oh how dost thou in Curious works excell!
Thine Art & Skill deserve to See the Press,
And be Composed in a Printer's dress.
Thy Name is worthy for to be enroll'd 35
In Printed Letters of the choicest Gold.
    Thy Death to five forefold Eclipses Sad,
A great one, unforetold doth Superad,
Successive to that Strange Æthereal Blaze,
Whereon thou didst so oft astonish'd gaze; 40
Which daily gives the world such fatal blows:
Still whats to come we dread; God only knows.
Thy Body which no activeness did lack
Now's laid aside like an old Almanack
But for the present only's out of date; 45
Twil have at length a far more active State.
    Yea, though with dust thy body Soiled be,
Yet at the Resurrection we Shall See
A fair Edition & of matchless worth,
Free from Errata, new in Heav'n set forth: 50
Tis but a word from God the Great Creatour,
It shall be done When he Saith Imprimatur.
                  Semoestus cecinit

John Saffin: New England Lamented

USE OF THE lamentation theme for social satire is apparent in "New England Lamented" by John Saffin
(1652–1710). Saffin wrote funeral pieces characteristic
of his age. Five of his long broadside elegies are not
extant; and some of his other verses were assigned,
until recently, to other authors. But his commonplace
book was preserved by the Rhode Island Historical
Society. Printed in 1928 (*John Saffin: his book,*
Caroline Hazard, ed., Harbor Press), it was called a
"collection of various matters of divinity, law, and
state affairs epitomized both in verse and prose."
From the last of the poems in this collection, written
in 1708, the following lines are taken:

First Part

If we Consider well our present Station
Great cause have we of Bitter Lamentation
For loe! all sorts of Persons much Complaine
But their bewayleings are allmost in vaine
The Inhabitants of Boston they complaine 5
For want of Trade Sufficient to mainetaine
Their familys: and divers lately Broken
Are of their poverty a certaine Token
Behold! New England how throughout the land
Thy Chiefest gainefull Trade is at a Stand 10
Thy Mercuries by whose Industrious Care
They brought into the Land both Money & ware
Even they begin to Sink, for want of Trade
Yet of the Publick Charge they most are made
To bear; which with their frequent loss at Sea
By Ship-wreck, Stormes, and by the Enemy 16
They'r much Disabl'd, and Discourag'd too
They know not where to send, nor what to doe
Their Ships lye by the walls, and none to tend them
Because for gaine, they know not where to send
    them. 20

The Countrey men Complaine and justly too
To pay their Rates they have so much Adoe
Nothing but money now, will serve the turn
They sell their Crops so low which makes them
    mourn
Brick without Straw is strictly now Requir'd 25
How money they should get is much Admir'd
Since when they sell their goods their Rates to pay
With Disappointments they are sent away
Sometimes with Scorn: at best with Disrespect
Shame and Reproach, and sometimes base Neglect

Yet Ner'theless Our Pomp and Gallantrie 31
In this poor land, did never Run so high
In publick State and Grandure

But woe, woe and Alas! the Female Traine
Doe make their Husbands scratch their heads in
    vaine 35
For they are grown to such a highth of Pride

That, Sodom-like, their sinfullness don't hid.
Come down proud Dames, garments of shame
    put on
Sitt in the Dust Daughters of Babilon
So here wee'll pause, and terminate our Song 40
Which toucheth not the Sober old nor young
But Idle Drones profuse and proud ones all
Publick or privet, whether great or small.

EDWARD TAYLOR (1645?-1729)

A FOUR-HUNDRED-PAGE manuscript volume which remained unpublished for more than two centuries contains the work of Edward Taylor, an orthodox Puritan minister, who is perhaps the foremost poet in colonial American literature. Unlike the verse of other Puritan poets, whose lines survive only because of their sincerity or historical importance, Taylor's poetry is of high literary value. It reflects the rapturous love of Christ in lines touched with vivid drama and imaginative power. In tenderness, delicacy, and intensity, the poems are unmatched in the entire literary record of New England Puritanism. Taylor's ardent absorption in the being of Christ suggests the transcendent contemplations of Jonathan Edwards. The poetry of Edward Taylor and the *Personal Narrative* of Edwards are likely to endure as the classic embodiment of Puritan aspiration in America.

Little is known about Edward Taylor's life. Born in Coventry or Sketchley, Leicestershire, he left England to complete his education and to avoid taking what to him would be the obnoxious oath of conformity required after the Restoration. A letter of introduction to Increase Mather insured a welcome for the refugee when he landed at Boston in July, 1668. Three years later he was graduated from Harvard, where he was the roommate and admired friend of Samuel Sewall. In the same year Taylor accepted a call to the church at Westfield, Massachusetts, which was to be the scene of his labors as pastor and physician for fifty-eight years. Taylor's lively sensibility and "quick passions" made him an effective preacher. Sewall recalled in 1729: "I have heard him preach a sermon at the Old South upon short warning which as the phrase in England is, might have been preached at Paul's Cross." Harvard made Taylor a Master of Arts in 1720. His obituary appeared in the *Boston News-Letter*, August 14, 1729.

The poetry of Taylor is almost entirely devotional. All of his enduring poems are comprised in two groups: "Gods Determinations" and "Sacramental Meditations." The theme of the first of these groups is that of the struggle between Christ and Satan for the prize of man's soul, reaching a climax in the redemption of man by the triumph of Mercy over Justice. "Gods Determinations" is written in a semi-dramatic form which suggests the influence of the morality play tradition; the chief distinction of the poem is in the exalted lyricism of its climax, a triumphant cry of religious ecstasy as the redeemed soul soars to meet its Saviour. Taylor's kinship with the English metaphysical poets is most apparent in the two hundred and seventeen poems entitled "Sacramental Meditations." Less even in quality, and lacking the variety of metrical patterns of "Gods Determinations," the "Meditations" glow with an ardent humility, and more than occasionally transmute his earnest devotion into poems of compelling intensity.

BIBLIOGRAPHY · The manuscript volume containing Taylor's poetry, along with other Taylor manuscripts, was presented to the Yale University Library in 1883. The poems were carefully edited by T. H. Johnson in *The Poetical Works of Edward Taylor* (New York, 1939). Johnson's edition has a biographical and critical introduction, and includes a list of the books in Taylor's library. The same editor wrote a succinct account of Taylor's life in the *Dictionary of American Biography*, XXI, 681–682 (Supplement One). Taylor's diary was printed in the *Proceedings of the Massachusetts Historical Society*, XVIII (1881), 4–18. Valuable articles on Taylor's poetry include W. C. Brown, "Edward Taylor: An American Metaphysical," *American Literature*, XVI (1944), 186–197. T. H. Johnson, "Edward Taylor: Puritan 'Sacred Poet,'" *New England Quarterly*, X (1937), 290–322; S. E. Lind, "Edward Taylor: A Revaluation," *New England Quarterly*, XXI (1948), 518–530; A. Warren, "Edward Taylor's Poetry: Colonial Baroque," *Kenyon Review*, III (1941), 355–371; W. T. Weathers, "Edward Taylor: Hellenistic Puritan," *American Literature*, XVIII (1946), 18–26; and N. Wright, "The Morality Tradition in the Poetry of Edward Taylor," *ibid.*, XVIII (1946), 1–17.

Gods Determinations

THE MATCHED POEMS that follow are drawn from a large section of Taylor's works entitled "Gods Determinations," in which the poet traces the soul's progress from sin to blessed communion in the Church of the Covenant. One stage of the combat between the elect and Satan is here presented with Christ's reply which encourages the souls in their tortuous struggle. The assault of Satan upon the soul is the substance of the first poem, and demonstrates how thoroughly men in the seventeenth century believed in the agency of a personal Devil seeking at all points to thwart the soul's salvation. A longer poem in the same section describes dramatically the sophistry of Satan, who employs spite, spleen, and gall in an attempt to lead man to dishonor God and to forfeit God's grace. The possible influences of the morality plays and of the Theocritan song contest upon the composition of "Gods Determinations" are suggested in two valuable articles by Nathalia Wright and W. T. Weathers which are cited in the bibliographical note.

The selections which follow are reprinted from *The Poetical Works of Edward Taylor* by permission of Princeton University Press.

The Souls Address to Christ against these Assaults

Thou Gracious Lord, Our Honour'd Generall,
  May't suite thy Pleasure never to impute
It our Presumption, when presume we shall,
  To line thy Noble Ears with our Greate suite?
  With ropes about our necks we come, and lie 5
  Before thy pleasure's Will and Clemency.

When we unto the height of Sin were grown,
  We sought thy Throne to overthrow; but were
In this our seeking Quickly overthrown:
  A Mass of Mercy in thy face shone cleare. 10
  We quarter had: though if we'de had our share,
  We had been quarter'd up as Rebells are.

Didst thou thy Grace on Treators arch expend?
  And force thy Favour on thy stubborn Foe?
And hast no Favour for a failing Friend, 15
  That in thy Quarrell trippeth with his toe?
  If thus it be, thy Foes Speed better far,
  Than do thy Friends, that go to fight thy War.

But is it as the Adversary said?
  Dost thou not hear his murdering Canons roare?

What Vollies fly? What Ambushments are laid? 21
  And still his stratagems grow more and more.
  Lord, fright this frightfull Enemy away.
  A Trip makes not a Traitor: Spare, we pray.

And if thou still suspect us, come and search: 25
  Pluck out our hearts and search them narrowly.
If Sin allow'd in any Corner learch,
  We beg a Pardon and a Remedy.
  Lord, Gybbit up such Rebells Arch, Who do
  Set ope the back doore to thy Cursed foe. 30

Christs Reply

I am a Captain to your Will;
  You found me Gracious, so shall still,
Whilst that my Will is your Design.
  If that you stick unto my Cause,
  Opposing whom oppose my Laws, 5
I am your own, and you are mine.

The weary Soule I will refresh,
  And Ease him of his heaviness.
Who'le slay a Friend? And save a Foe?
  Who in my War do take delight, 10
  Fight not for Prey, but Pray and Fight,
Although they slip, I'le mercy show.

Then Credit not your Enemy,
  Whose Chiefest daintie is a lie:
I will you comfort sweet extend. 15
  Behold I am a sun and shield,
  And a sharp sword to win the field:
I'le surely Crown you in the End.

His murdering Canons which do roare,
  And Engins though as many more, 20
Shoot onely aire: no Bullets fly.
  Unless you dare him with your Crest,
  And ope to him the naked breast,
Small Execution's done thereby.

To him that smiteth hip and thigh 25
  My foes as his: Walks warily,
I'le give him Grace: he'st give me praise.
  Let him whose foot doth hit a stone
  Through weakness, not rebellion,
Not faint, but think on former dayes. 30

The Joy of Church Fellowship rightly attended

In Heaven soaring up, I dropt an Eare
    On Earth: and oh! sweet Melody!
And listening, found it was the Saints who were
    Encoacht for Heaven that sang for Joy.
    For in Christs Coach they sweetly sing,   5
    As they to Glory ride therein.

Oh! joyous hearts! Enfir'de with holy Flame!
    Is speech thus tasseled with praise?
Will not your inward fire of Joy contain,
    That it in open flames doth blaze?   10
    For in Christ[s] Coach Saints sweetly sing,
    As they to Glory ride therein.

And if a string do slip by Chance, they soon
    Do screw it up again: whereby
They set it in a more melodious Tune   15
    And a Diviner Harmony.
    For in Christs Coach Saints sweetly sing,
    As they to Glory ride therein.

In all their Acts, publick and private, nay,
    And secret too, they praise impart.   20
But in their Acts Divine, and Worship, they
    With Hymns do offer up their Heart.
    Thus in Christs Coach they sweetly sing,
    As they to Glory ride therein.

Some few not in; and some whose Time and Place
    Block up this Coaches way, do goe   26
As Travellers afoot: and so do trace
    The Road that gives them right thereto;
    While in this Coach these sweetly sing,
    As they to Glory ride therein.   30

The Ebb and Flow

FIVE POEMS stand by themselves in the poetical works
of Taylor. Though not an integral part of either of his
two long series, they are all allegories or applications of
occasional matter to divine meditation. The following
poem, brief and emotional, shows the firm relationship
between syntactic structure and title that results from
close organization, aptness of thought, and clarity and
fluency of expression.

When first thou on me, Lord, wrough'st thy Sweet
    Print,
    My heart was made thy tinder box.

My 'ffections were thy tinder in't:
    Where fell thy Sparkes by drops.
Those holy Sparks of Heavenly fire that came   5
Did ever catch and often out would flame.

But now my Heart is made thy Censar trim,
    Full of thy golden Altars fire,
    To offer up Sweet Incense in
        Unto thyselfe intire: 10
I finde my tinder scarce thy sparks can feel
That drop out from thy Holy flint and Steel.

Hence doubts out bud for feare thy fire in mee
    'S a mocking Ignis Fatuus,
    Or lest thine Altars fire out bee,   15
        It's hid in ashes thus.
Yet when the bellows of thy Spirit blow
Away mine ashes, then thy fire doth glow.

Sacramental Meditations: The Experience

THE EXPERIENCE in this poem is that of mystic rapture,
intense as a flame. The exhilaration takes the poet
closer to the throne than the angels. Like many a
mystic he would like to remain in the realms of such
ineffable joy, but must, of course, be satisfied with the
intensity of an experience which momentarily, at least,
gives him a sense of identity with the great One, God, a
union with divine nature. Structurally the poem is
logical, tightly composed, and centers the aspiration,
as was common in Taylor's poems, in the poet's own
heart.

> The Song of Songs 1:3: Because of the savour of thy
> good ointments thy name is an ointment poured forth. . . .

Oh! that I always breath'd in such an aire,
    As I suckt in, feeding on Sweet Content!
Disht up unto my Soul ev'n in that pray're
    Pour'de out to God over last Sacrament.
    What Beam of Light wrapt up my Sight to finde
    Me neerer God than ere Came in my minde?   6

Most Strange it was! But yet more Strange that
    shine
    Which fill'd my Soul then to the brim to spy
My nature with thy Nature all Divine
    Together joynd in Him that's Thou, and I.   10

Flesh of my Flesh, Bone of my Bone: there's run
Thy Godhead, and my Manhood in thy Son.

Oh! that that Flame which thou didst on me Cast
    Might me enflame, and Lighten ery where.
Then Heaven to me would be less at last   15
    So much of heaven I should have while here.
      Oh! Sweet though Short! I'le not forget the
      same.
    My neerness, Lord, to thee did me Enflame.

I'le Claim my Right: Give place, ye Angells
    Bright.
    Ye further from the Godhead stande than I.   20
My Nature is your Lord; and doth Unite
    Better than Yours unto the Deity.
    Gods Throne is first and mine is next; to you
    Onely the place of Waiting-men is due.

Oh! that my Heart thy Golden Harp might bee   25
    Well tun'd by Glorious Grace, that e'ry string
Screw'd to the highest pitch, might unto thee
    All Praises wrapt in sweetest Musick bring.
    I praise thee, Lord, and better praise thee would
    If what I had, my heart might ever hold.   30

Meditation Six

IN MEDITATION SIX the poet aspires to greater assurance that he is one of God's elect. In the idea of the poem there is a considerable bridge between the sign of God's approval upon a soul and the lettering and mint marks upon a gold coin. This is clearly a metaphysical or fanciful feature of the poem, an aspect further apparent in the use of intentional ambiguity and of metrical roughness. The idea of money from ore to coin informs the poem. It gains clarity through the poem's clear division of thought: the first eight lines raise two queries and the last ten voice a petition.

Canticles 2:1: I am . . . the lily of the valleys.

Am I thy gold? Or purse, Lord, for thy Wealth;
    Whether in mine or mint refinde for thee?
Ime counted so, but count me o're thyselfe,
    Lest gold washt face, and brass in Heart I bee.
    I Feare my Touchstone touches when I try   5
    Mee, and my Counted Gold too overly.

Am I new minted by thy Stamp indeed?
    Mine Eyes are dim; I cannot clearly see.
Be thou my Spectacles that I may read
    Thine Image and Inscription stampt on mee.   10
    If thy bright Image do upon me stand,
    I am a Golden Angell in thy hand.

Lord, make my Soule thy Plate: thine Image
    bright
    Within the Circle of the same enfoile.
And on its brims in golden Letters write   15
    Thy Superscription in an Holy style.
    Then I shall be thy Money, thou my Hord:
    Let me thy Angell bee, bee thou my Lord.

Meditation Twenty-Eight

AGAIN WE have a poem in the full sweep of the metaphysical tradition, with emotion and bifurcated meaning. Superficially the poem has the structure of "a health." Not only is the application in this sense a somewhat jolting concept, but it leads immediately to other levels of feeling and thought which add intentionally to the complexity of the piece.

John 1:16: And of his fulness have all we received, and
    grace for grace

When I, Lord, send some Bits of Glory home,
    (For Lumps I lack) my Messenger, I finde,
Bewildred, lose his way, being alone:
    In my befogg'd Dark Phancy, Clouded minde,
    Thy Bits of Glory packt in Shreds of Praise   5
    My Messenger doth lose, losing his Wayes.

Lord, Cleare the Coast: and let thy sweet sun
    shine,
    That I may better speed a second time:
Oh! fill my Pipkin with thy Blood red Wine:
    I'l drinke thy Health: To pledge thee is no
    Crime.   10
    Although I but an Earthen Vessell bee,
    Convay some of thy Fulness into me.

Thou, thou my Lord, art full, top full of Grace,
    The Golden Sea of Grace: Whose springs
    thence come,
And Pretious Drills, boiling in ery place.   15
    Untap thy Cask, and let my Cup Catch some.

12. **Angell:** English coin showing Michael slaying
dragon.

Although it's in an Earthen Vessells Case,
Let it no Empty Vessell be of Grace.

Let thy Choice Caske shed, Lord, into my Cue   20
  A Drop of Juyce presst from thy Noble Vine.
My Bowl is but an Acorn Cup; I sue
  But for a Drop: this will not empty thine.
  Although I'me in an Earthen Vessells place,
  My Vessell make a Vessell, Lord, of Grace.

My Earthen Vessell make thy Font also: 25
  And let thy sea my Spring of Grace in't raise.
Spring up, oh Well! my Cup with Grace make flow.
  Thy Drops will on my Vessell ting thy Praise.
  I'l sing this Song, when I these Drops Embrace:
  My Vessell now's a Vessell of thy Grace.   30

Need not read this prose

[*A Love Letter of 1674*] .

THE DATE of this letter is not necessary to assign it to   20
the seventeenth century. Its provenance is amply indicated by its intense piety and especially by the tortured elaboration of its central figure of speech. The
pronounced metaphysical notes serve to give a unifying
character to Taylor's poetry and prose. The letter
was written by the Reverend Edward Taylor to Elizabeth Fitch, of Norwich, Connecticut, who became his
wife in 1675; it was published in a *Memoir* written for
the Taylor descendants in 1892.

              Westfield, 8th of 7th month, 1674.   30
My Dove:

  I send you not my heart, for that, I hope is sent
to heaven long since, and unless it hath awfully
deceived me, it hath not taken up its lodgings in
any one's bosom on this side of the royal city of
the great King, but yet most of it that is allowed
to be bestowed upon creature, doth solely and
singly fall to your share. So much my post pigeon
presents you with here in these lines. Look not,
I beseech you, upon it as one of love's hyperboles,   40
if I borrow the beams of some sparkling metaphor
to illustrate my respect unto thyself by, for you
having made my breast the cabinet of your affections as I yours mine, I know not how to offer a
fitter comparison to set out my love by, than to
compare it to a golden ball of fire, rolling up and
down my breast from which there flies now and

          19. **Cue:** beer.

then a spark like a glorious beam from the body of
the flaming sun, but I, alas, striving to catch these
sparks into a love-letter unto thyself, and to guide
it as with a sunbeam, find that by what time they
have fallen through my pen upon my paper, they
have lost their shine and look only like a little
smoke thereon instead of gilding it, wherefore
finding myself so much discouraged, I am ready
to begrudge my instrument, for though my love   10
within my breast is so large that my heart is not
sufficient to contain it, yet I can make it no more
room to ride in than to squeeze it up betwixt my
black ink and white paper, but know that it's the
coarsest part that's conversant there, for the
purest part's too fine to clothe in any Lingua
house-wifery to be expressed by words, and this
letter bears the coarsest part to you, yet the purest
is improved for you. But now my dear love, lest
my letter should be judged the lavish language of a
lover's pen, I shall endeavor to show that conjugal   20
love ought to exceed all other love:

  1st. It appears from that which it represents,
viz: the respect which is between Christ and his
Church (Ephesians V. 25) although it differs from
that in kind (for that is spiritual and this human),
and in a degree that is boundless and transcendent.

  2d. Because conjugal love is the ground of
conjugal union.

  3d. From the Christian duties which are incumbent on persons of this state, as not only a serv-   30
ing God together, a praying together, a joining together, in the ruling and instructing of their
families (which cannot be carried on as it should
be without a great degree of true love), a mutual
giving each other to each other, and a mutual encouraging each other in all states and grievances.
And how can this be when there is not love sur-
mounting all other love? It's with them therefore
for the most part, as with the strings of an instrument not tuned together, which when struck upon
make a harsh, jarring sound; but when the golden
wires of an instrument, equally drawn up and
rightly struck upon, tuned together, make sweet
music whose harmony doth enravish the ear, so
when the golden strings of pure affection are
strained up into right conjugal love, thus doth this
state harmonize to the comfort of each other and
the glory of God when sanctified. But though

81

conjugal love must exceed all other love, it must be kept within bounds too, for it must be subordinate to God's glory, the which that mine may be so, it having got you in my heart, doth offer my heart with you in it, as a more rich sacrifice unto God through Christ, and so it subscribeth me,

Your true love until death,

Edward Taylor.

SAMUEL SEWALL (1652–1730)

FOR A TIME after his graduation from Harvard in 1671 Samuel Sewall debated whether to become a minister or a merchant. His long indecision between the claims of the meeting house and the counting house, and his final choice of a mercantile career, illustrate the changes in New England which were transforming Puritans into Yankees. Sewall's *Diary*, kept conscientiously and without thought of publication from December 3, 1673, to October 13, 1729, contains the most intimate and revealing record of the social and intellectual climate of colonial New England.

Samuel Sewall came to America in 1661, resided for a number of years at Newbury, Massachusetts, a community founded by his father, and early struck root in Boston. Although he remained at Harvard to study theology and to act as tutor in 1673–1674, a sense of unworthiness and perhaps the ill success of his first ventures in the pulpit led him to devote his life to business. His success in combining piety with profit won for him an influential and distinguished position in the world of public affairs.

During the forty years after 1680 he held many offices. He became manager of the colony's printing press at Boston for three years after October, 1681, and was tax commissioner and deputy to the General Court in 1683. He was a member of the Council from 1684 to 1686, and in 1692 he became a judge of the Superior Court and a member of the special commission of Oyer and Terminer to try the witchcraft cases. He was made a captain of the Honorable Artillery Company in 1701 and a probate judge in 1715; and in 1718 he was named Chief Justice of Massachusetts, a position he held for ten years, relinquishing it only two years before his death. Sewall married Hannah Hull in 1675; she was the first of three wives who were to bear him fourteen children, only five of whom survived him.

Through all his public activity and amid the concerns of his many business ventures, Sewall maintained strict religious standards and regular pious devotions. Although he was notably prosperous and one of the first Bostonians to enjoy a large brick house, as a pious layman he was not only the father of a minister but never gave up his own early leanings toward the church. For an elder, in fact, he followed a regimen of life almost as thoroughly regulated as that of the ministers themselves; he indulged in frequent fasts, he read consistently in works of divinity, he reprehended undue displays of finery and frivolity, and he viewed with grave concern the religious problems of the day.

Only once did he depart from America after his arrival in 1661. That was in 1688, when he went to England for some months on business. But like Thoreau, who boasted he had traveled much in Concord, Sewall was a regular traveler on horseback and in coach in his own region. His goings and comings, duly recorded in the *Diary*, were so frequent that they must have baffled even the members of his own family.

Sewall published several formal works during his life, but these are cumbersome and angular with the exception of *The Selling of Joseph* (1700), the first antislavery tract in America, which he dashed off at white heat in June of that year. His fame today rests on a work not intended for the public, which was made available one hundred and fifty years after his death by the Massachusetts Historical Society. The *Diary* covers the period from 1673 to 1729 (excepting 1677–1685).

BIBLIOGRAPHY · *The Diary of Samuel Sewall* was published in the *Collections of the Massachusetts Historical Society* (Fifth Series), V, VI, and VII (1878–1882). An abridged one-volume version, edited by Mark Van Doren, appeared in 1927. Samuel Sewall's *Letter Book* also was issued by the Massachusetts Historical Society in its *Collections* (Sixth Series), I and II (1886–1888). Biographical accounts are fragmentary, but the *Diary* constitutes the best life of Sewall. Background material may be found in N. H. Chamberlin, *Samuel Sewall and the World He Lived In* (1897). Additional biographical material is contained in C. H. C. Howard, "Chief Justice Samuel Sewall," *Essex Institute Historical Collections*, XXXVII (1901), and in J. L. Sibley's twenty-page sketch in *Biographical Sketches of Graduates of Harvard University*, II (1881). Critical estimates include H. W. Lawrence, "Samuel Sewall, Revealer of Puritan New England," *South Atlantic Quarterly*, XXXIII (1934), and H. C. Lodge, *Studies in History* (1884).

Diary of Samuel Sewall

[Selected Entries, 1676–1707]

THE FOLLOWING excerpts from the *Diary* present an interesting profile of Samuel Sewall. They show that he took his public duties seriously, pursued them zealously, and yet was humble enough to confess his errors when his conscience smarted. Perhaps the most dramatic entry in the entire *Diary* is that which records his public penance for his share in the witchcraft trials. The selections reveal the activities of a man who had much business to attend to, but who was human enough to dodge unpleasantness and to relish a proper blending of strenuousness and leisure. They not only indicate that he was a prominent figure in the community, drilling with the militia company and sitting as a judge in the Court, but they also disclose his private enthusiasms and the minutiae of his existence with a frankness which has made the *Diary* a great personal document. The purchase of a penknife, a sermon by Cotton Mather, the planting of a tree, or the picking of raspberries alike receive the attention of this diarist. He also confided to his pages his annoyance at the appearance of a dancing-master in Boston and his disgust at the introduction of wigs. He spoke his mind sharply, but sometimes surprised those whom he chided with gifts of venison. Like Mather, Sewall was interested in eclipses and other unusual phenomena, which he and his generation regarded as providences of God, though not always intelligible.

Tragedy stalked all pioneer communities, and the death rate was high. While the brief entries do not reveal much of Sewall's emotion, he was deeply moved at the death of two wives and at the illnesses and death of nine of his children. He shared many another's grief as well, for he was a frequent pallbearer. On these occasions he received funeral gloves, and sometimes, if the estate of the deceased permitted, a mourning ring.

Although Sewall did not continue in the ministry, he never gave up his religious duties, never slackened his interest in truly spiritual problems, never shirked his responsibility in laying conviction upon his fellow citizens; and to the end of his life he regularly kept days of fasting in which he asked for personal direction and light. But the Samuel Sewall of the *Diary* is not only introspective; he is fearless, trustworthy, and concerned with civic problems. His was no ordinary combination of traits, and the world he lived in was interesting, as are all great periods of transition. Thus the most frequently reprinted section of the *Diary*, that in which Sewall described his vigorous courtship of Madam Winthrop, has not been included in this volume because it is not so typical as the entries which present the humdrum, day-dy-day industry and piety of a solid citizen of old Boston. These also afford a revealing insight into the life of a man who combined pious conduct and devout meditations with the necessary and wise activities of commercial enterprise.

The text is taken from the *Collections of the Massachusetts Historical Society*, cited in the bibliography.

Novem. 27, 1676, about 5M. Boston's greatest Fire brake forth at Mr. Moors, through the default of a Taylour Boy, who rising alone and early to work, fell asleep and let his Light fire the House, which gave fire to the next, so that about fifty Landlords were despoyled of their Housing. N. B. The House of the Man of God, Mr. Mather,[n] and Gods House were burnt with fire. Yet God mingled mercy, and sent a considerable rain, which gave check in great measure to the (otherwise) masterless flames: lasted all the time of the fire, though fair before and after. Mr. Mather saved his Books and other Goods.

Feb. 23, 1676. Mr. Torrey spake with my Father at Mrs. Norton's told him that he would fain have me preach, and not leave off my studies to follow Merchandize. Note. The evening before, Feb. 22, I resolved (if I could get an opportunity) to speak with Mr. Torrey, and ask his Counsel as to coming into Church, about my estate, and the temptations that made me to fear.—But he went home when I was at the Warehouse about Wood that The. Elkins brought.

March 30, 1677. I, together with Gilbert Cole, was admitted into Mr. Thacher's Church, making a Solem̃ covenant to take the L. Jehovah for our God, and to walk in Brotherly Love and watchfulness to Edification. Goodm. Cole first spake, then I, then the Relations of the Women were read: as we spake so were we admitted; then all-together covenanted. Prayer before, and after.

June 21, 1677. Just at the end of the Sermon (it made Mr. Allen break off the more abruptly) one Torrey, of Roxbury, gave a suddain and amazing cry which disturbed the whole Assembly.

Mr. Mather: Increase Mather.

It seems he had the falling sickness. Tis to be feared the Quaker disturbance and this are ominous.

July 8, 1677. New Meeting House [the third, or South] *Mane:*[n] In Sermon time there came in a female Quaker, in a Canvas Frock, her hair dishevelled and loose like a Periwigg, her face as black as ink, led by two other Quakers, and two other followed. It occasioned the greatest and most amazing uproar that I ever saw. Isaiah I. 12, 14.

Thursday, June 18 [1685]. A Quaker comes to the Governour and speaks of a Message he had which was to shew the great Calamities of Fire and Sword that would suddenly come on New-England. Would fain have spoken in the Meeting-house, but was prevented. Eliakim comes home this day, brings word that Capt. Henchman is coming away from Worcester with his Family.

Noyes this day of a French Pirat on the Coast, of 36 Guns.

Satterday, June 20th 1685. . . . Voted, the 16th of July to be observed as a Fast.

Satterday, P. M. Carried my wife to Dorchester to eat Cherries, Rasberries, chiefly to ride and take the Air: the Time my Wife and Mrs. Flint spent in the Orchard, I spent in Mr. Flint's Study, reading Calvin on the Psalms &. 45. 68. 24.

Thorsday, Nov[r]. *12.* Mr. Moodey preaches from Isa. 57. 1. Mr. Cobbet's Funeral Sermon; said also of Mr. Chauncy that he was a Man of Singular Worth. Said but 2 of the First Generation left.

After, the Ministers of this Town Come to the Court and complain against a Dancing Master who seeks to set up here and hath mixt Dances, and his time of Meeting is Lecture-Day; and 'tis reported he should say that by one Play he could teach more Divinity than Mr. Willard or the Old Testament. Mr. Moodey said 'twas not a time for N. E. to dance. Mr. Mather struck at the Root, speaking against mixt Dances. . . .

Nov[r]. *30.* [1685]. . . . At night viewed the Eclips, which in the total obscuration was ruddy; but

Mane: in the morning.

when began to receive some Light, the darkish ruddiness ceased. Horizon somewhat Hazy. Read in course the Eleventh of the Revelation.

Monday, Decemb[r]. *7th 1685.* About One in the Night my Wife is brought to Bed of a Son, of which Mother Hull brings me the first News: Mrs. Weeden Midwife.

Satterday, Dec[r]. *12, '85.* Father Wait buried: Magistrates and Ministers had Gloves. There heard of the Death of Capt. Hutchinson's Child by Convulsions, and so pass to the Funeral of little Samuel Hutchinson about Six weeks old, where also had a pair of Funeral Gloves.

Dec. 25. Friday. Carts come to Town and Shops open as is usual. Some somehow observe the day; but are vexed I believe that the Body of the People profane it, and blessed be God no Authority yet to compell them to keep it. A great Snow fell last night so this day and night very cold.

Satterday, June 5th [1686]. I rode to Newbury, to see my little Hull, and to keep out of the way of the Artillery Election, on which day eat Strawberries and Cream with Sister Longfellow at the Falls, visited Capt. Richard Dummer, rode to Salem, where lodged 2 nights for the sake of Mr. Noyes's Lecture, who preached excellently of Humility, from the woman's washing Christ's feet. Was invited by Mr. Higginson to Dinner, but could not stay. . . .

Friday, June 11. Waited on the Council, took the Oath of Allegiance, and rec'd my new Commission for Capt. Was before at a privat Fast at Deacon Allen's: so Capt. Hutchinson and I went about 5 aclock, and all the rest were sworn, Capt. Hutchinson at present refuses. I read the Oath myself holding the book in my Left hand, and holding up my Right Hand to Heaven.

Friday, June 18. My dear Son, Hull Sewall, dyes at Newbury about one aclock. . . .

Tuesday, January 18, 1686/7. Between two and three in the Afternoon, for near an hour together, was seen in a clear Skie such a Rainbow, Parelions and Circles as ware on January 2. 1684/5. In the night following falls a snow, not much. I was at the North-end when I first saw it. People were gazing at it from one end of the Town to tother.

Tuesday, July 26, 1687. About Nine aclock my dear Son Stephen Sewall expires, just after the Judges coming to Town; died in his Grandmother's Bed-Chamber in Nurse Hill's Arms. Had two Teeth cut, no Convulsions. Mr. Willard pray'd with him in the Morning, Mr. Moodey coming in when at Prayer.

Wednesday [September 14th, 1687]. See the Mill, get a Cut, visit Mrs. Rainer and her Daughter Broughton. Breakfast there. Ride into Swamp to see a Mast drawn of about 26 inches or 28; about two and thirty yoke of Oxen before, and about four yoke by the side of the Mast, between the fore and hinder wheels. 'Twas a very notable sight. Rode then to York, through very bad way, Jnº Broughton Pilot. Saw Mr. Sawyer's singular Saw-mill. Lodg'd at Cous. Dumer's with Mr. Martin. Rode to Wells on Thorsday 15th, to view the Records. Din'd at the Ordinary, (call'd at Mr. Wheelrights in the way.) Then I rode with Jnº Broughton to the Salmon-falls, got thether about 8; Lodg'd at Love's.

Sept. 17th [1688]. I speak to Mr. Gillam for a passage in his Ship. . . .

Wednesday, Oct. 3ᵈ. Have a day of Prayer at our House: One principal reason as to particular, about my going for England. Mr. Willard pray'd and preach'd excellently from Ps. 143. 10:, pray'd. Intermission. Mr. Allen pray'd, then Mr. Moodey, both very well, then 3ᵈ–7th verses of the 86th Ps., sung Cambridge Short Tune, which I set. Then had Govʳ. Bradstreet and his wife, Mr. Moodey and wife, Mr. Allin and Mr. Willard and wife, Cous. Dumer and wife, and Mrs. Clark her sister, Cousin Quinsey and wife, and Mrs. Scottow, should have reckon'd formerly Mother Hull and Self. . . .

Sabbath, Jan. 11th [1690]. At night the House of Joshua Gardener, at Muddy-River, is burnt,

and two of his Children; the Lord help us to repent that we do not likewise perish. 'Twas my turn to watch. I sent Eliakim; the north watch saw the light of the fire.

Tuesday, Jan. 26. 1691/2. News comes to Town by Robin Orchard, of Dolberry's being arrived at Cape Cod; Sir William Phips made Governour of the Province of New England. Foy (in whom went Mr. Lee) taken into France: Quelch and Bant also. Six weeks passage from Plimouth. This day almost at the same Time, news was brought of an Attack made by the Indians on York.

Sept. 18. [1695]. . . . This day Mr. Torrey and his wife, Mr. Willard and his wife, and Cous. Quinsey dine with us; 'tis the first time has been at our house with his new wife; was much pleas'd with our painted shutters; in pleasancy said he thought he had been got into Paradise. This day, Sept. 18, Mr. Cook enters the Lists with Col. Paige, and sues for Capt. Keyn's Farm again. Govʳ. Bradstreet arriv'd at Salem about 3 P.M.

Oct. 12. Jnº Cunable finishes the Stairs out of the wooden house to the top of the Brick House. Little Mary grows a little better after very sore illness.

[Petition put up by Mr. Sewall on the Fast Day]. Copy of the Bill I put up on the Fast day; giving it to Mr. Willard as he pass'd by, and standing up at the reading of it, and bowing when finished; in the Afternoon.

Samuel Sewall, sensible of the reiterated strokes of God upon himself and family; and being sensible, that as to the Guilt Contracted upon the opening of the late Comission of Oyer and Terminer at Salem (to which the order for this Day relates) he is, upon many accounts, more concerned than any that he knows of, Desires to take the Blame and shame of it, Asking pardon of men, And especially desiring prayers that God, who has an Unlimited Authority, would pardon that sin and all other his sins; personal and Relative: And according to his infinitive Benignity, and Sovereignty, Not Visit the sin of him, or of any other, upon himself or any of his, nor upon the Land:

But that He would powerfully defend him against all Temptations to Sin, for the future; and vouchsafe him the efficacious, saving Conduct of his Word and Spirit.

July, 15, 1698. Mr. Edward Taylor comes to our house from Westfield. Monday July 18. I walk'd with Mr. Edward Taylor upon Cotton Hill, thence to Becon Hill, the Pasture, along the Stone-wall: As came back, we sat down on the great Rock, and Mr. Taylor told me his courting his first wife, and Mr. Fitch his story of Mr. Dod's prayer to God to bring his Affection to close with a person pious, but hard-favoured. . . . This day John Ive, fishing in great Spie-pond, is arrested with mortal sickness which renders him in a manner speechless and senseless; dies next day; buried at Charlestown on the Wednesday. Was a very debauched, atheistical man. I was not at his Funeral. Had Gloves sent me, but the knowledge of his notoriously wicked life made me sick of going; and Mr. Mather, the president, came in just as I was ready to step out, and so I staid at home, and by that means lost a Ring: but hope had no loss. Follow thou Me, was I supose more complied with, than if I had left Mr. Mather's company to go to such a Funeral.

Second-day, Jany 23. 1698/9. I carry my two sons and three daughters in the Coach to Danford, the Turks head at Dorchester: eat sage Cheese, drunk Beer and Cider and came homeward. Call'd at Madam Dudley's, then visited Mr. Walter; told him there was all my stock, desired his Blessing of them; which he did.

Wednesday, June 21. A Pack of Cards are found strawed over my fore-yard, which tis supposed, some wight threw there to mock me, in spite of what I did at the Exchange Tavern last Satterday night.

Fifth-day, Novr the last. 1699. The Rain freezes upon the branches of the Trees to that thickness and weight, that great havock is thereby made of the Wood and Timber. Many young and strong Trees are broken off in the midst; and multitudes of Boughs rent off. Considerable hurt is done in Orchards. Two of our Apple-trees are broken down, Unkles Tree, two thirds of it, are broken down. Peach Trees at Mrs. Moodeys are almost all spoil'd. And my little Cedar almost quite mortified. Some think the Spoil that is made amounts to Thousands of pounds. How suddenly and with surprise can God destroy!

Fourth-day, June, 19, 1700. Mr. Jn° Eyre is entomed in the new burying place. Nine of his children are laid there to handsel the new Tomb: Bearers, Sewall, Addington, Townsend, Byfield, Dummer, Davis: Scarvs and Rings. Lt Govr and many of the Council there. Mr. Thomas Brattle led his mourning widowed Sister. When I parted, I pray'd God to be favourably present with her, and comfort her in the absence of so near and dear a Relation. Having been long and much dissatisfied with the Trade of fetching Negros from Guinea; at last I had a strong Inclination to Write something about it; but it wore off. At last reading Bayne, Ephes. about servants, who mentions Blackamoors; I began to be uneasy that I had so long neglected doing any thing. When I was thus thinking, in came Bro^r Belknap to shew me a Petition he intended to present to the Genl Court for freeing a Negro and his wife, who were unjustly held in Bondage. And there is a Motion by a Boston Committee to get a Law that all Importers of Negros shall pay 40s prhead, to discourage the bringing of them. And Mr. C. Mather resolves to publish a sheet to exhort Masters to labour their Conversion. Which makes me hope that I was call'd of God to Write this Apology for them; Let his Blessing accompany the same.

Friday, June, 18, 1703. My sons House was Raised at Muddy-River; The day very comfortable because dry, cloudy, windy, cool. I sent for Mr. Wigglesworth and his Wife from Deacon Barnard's in the Coach; to discourse with my Wife about her and Judith's Maladies. After they were sent back, being late in the Afternoon, I went alone in the Hackney-Coach to Roxbury, took Mr. Walter with me. By that Time got there, had just done their Work, and were going to Dinner in the new House. Mr. Walter crav'd a Blessing, Return'd Thanks. Many were there from Muddy-River, Dedham, Roxbury. I drove a Pin before Dinner. After Dinner sung the 127th Psal. and 8th v. 28th St. David's Tune, I set and read the Psalm. Brought home Madame Dudley and my Daughter. ,

Feria Sexta, Junij, 30, 1704. As the Governour sat at the Council-Table twas told him, Madam Paige was dead; He clap'd his hands, and quickly went out, and return'd not to the Chamber again; but ordered Mr. Secretary to prorogue the Court till the 16th of August, which Mr. Secretary did by going into the House of Deputies. After Dinner, about 3. p.m. I went to see the Execution. . . . Many were the people that saw upon Broughton's Hill. But when I came to see how the River was cover'd with People, I was amazed: Some say there were 100 Boats. 150 Boats and Canoes, saith Cousin Moody of York. He told them. Mr. Cotton Mather came with Capt. Quelch and six others for Execution from the Prison to Scarlet's Wharf, and from thence in the Boat to the place of Execution about the midway between Hanson's point and Broughton's Warehouse. Mr. Bridge was there also. When the scaffold was hoisted to a due height, the seven Malefactors went up; Mr. Mather pray'd for them standing upon the Boat. Ropes were all fasten'd to the Gallows (save King, who was Repriev'd) When the Scaffold was let to sink, there was such a Screech of the Women that my wife heard it sitting in our Entry next the Orchard, and was much surprised at it; yet the wind was souwest. Our house is a full mile from the place.

7ʳ 10th (1707). Midweek, sentenced a woman that whip'd a Man, to be whip'd; said a woman that had lost her Modesty, was like Salt that had lost its savor; good for nothing but to cast to the Dunghill: 7 or 8 join'd together, call'd the Man out of his Bed, guilefully praying him to shew them the way; then by help of a Negro youth, tore off his Cloaths and whip'd him with Rods; to chastise him for carrying it harshly to his wife. Got out of Town to Rehoboth.

Tuesday, Octʳ 28. 1707. The Fellows of Harvard College meet, and chuse Mr. Leverett President: He had eight votes, Dr. Increase Mather three, Mr. Cotton Mather, one, and Mr. Brattle of Cambridge, one. Mr. White did not vote, and Mr. Gibbs came when voting was over.

Second-day, Febʳ 9. 1707/8. . . . The apointment of a Judge for the Super. Court being to be made upon next Fifth day, Febr. 12, I pray'd God to Accept me in keeping a privat day of Prayer with Fasting for That and other Important Matters: I kept it upon the Third day Febr. 10. 1707/8 in the upper Chamber at the North-East end of the House, fastening the Shutters next the Street. . . . .

COTTON MATHER (1663-1728)

INCREASE MATHER has been called by his definitive biographer "the foremost American Puritan." To many devout Congregationalists of the late seventeenth and early eighteenth centuries, this eminence must also have seemed an appropriate label for his eldest son, Cotton Mather, the most famous divine of his generation. Inheriting his father's mantle as the chief spokesman of orthodoxy in a new age which was threatening the old theocracy, Cotton Mather found full scope for his enormous erudition and dynamic personality in the pulpit of the influential Second Church in Boston, in his pastoral duties, and in the composition of hundreds of theological books and pamphlets. What Cotton Mather wrote of his father is in part true of the son: "One adorned with Great Endowments of Knowledge, and Learning, and Prudence, which qualified him for Stations and Actions . . . A Great Man, and one employed in Great Services, as a Minister of the Gospel . . . and as a Writer of many Treatises, wherein the Talents both of the Scholar and of the Christian are laid out unto the best Advantage." Cotton Mather's activity was unending. He preached election and funeral sermons for important New Englanders; he admonished the youth and counseled the parents of Boston; he discoursed with criminals during their last hours; he offered consolation to the bereaved; he instructed young ministers, and he expounded theology to his parishioners. His published works are replete with erudition, exhortation, and elucidation.

For all his publishing activity and public service, Mather was not universally acclaimed by his fellow Bostonians. Certain of his traits of character, such as moodiness and testy partisanship, caused inroads on his popularity, and his overambitiousness sometimes stirred opposition. But for all this, he wielded power not only in religious but in state affairs. Cotton Mather led the merchants' revolt against the high-handed policies of Sir Edmund Andros; and when William Phips became provost marshal general at Boston and subsequently governor, he frequently turned for advice to the Mather household.

Although Cotton Mather did not attend the trials, he suffered some loss of prestige from the witchcraft delusion. His *Wonders of the Invisible World* (1693) is an account of a few of the prosecutions and a defense —written at the behest of the judges—of the verdicts. Like a majority of his contemporaries, he believed in supernatural creatures and image magic; but unlike many of them, he refused to sanction the use of spectral evidence. If such evidence had not been introduced into the court trials, and there relied upon, it is doubtful if any of the convictions could have been obtained. His *Wonders of the Invisible World*, despite its exposition of certain cases, had no influence on the trials, since all of the 112 persons in jail on charges of witchcraft when Mather's book was issued were later released. By 1700 Mather had recorded his conviction of the injustice of the Salem trials.

Like most divines of the age, Cotton Mather fought against any weakening of orthodoxy. His review of the past glories of the Puritan settlement, which he set down in his *Magnalia Christi Americana*, convinced him that the third generation was exhibiting a falling away from the pure godliness of the first. Mather opposed the current of popular thought for a time, but his was no unthinking opposition. He sought to show why good men should regard themselves as Temples of God, and he concerned himself with practical temporal matters as well. He stood for a religion of good works, as his *Essays to do Good* (1710), praised by Benjamin Franklin, makes clear. His admonishments to youth were practical directions in the art of living.

In outlook Cotton Mather was a forward-looking scientist as well as a thinker of his own age. A member of the Royal Society after 1713, he was interested in the latest philosophical and scientific theories; he published essays on earthquakes, and sent numerous items of *curiosa Americana* to the Society. Upon at least one occasion Mather's intellectual curiosity and fearlessness brought him physical danger. After he had per-

suaded Dr. Zabdiel Boylston to inoculate for smallpox, a measure vigorously opposed by contemporary medical opinion in Boston, his life was threatened and a grenade was thrown into his house. But he was not to be dissuaded from what he regarded as the truth. Though he never made a visit overseas, his wide scientific interests led to a correspondence with learned men in England and on the Continent.

A formative influence upon Cotton Mather was that of his family. Descended from Richard and Increase Mather, and on the maternal side from John Cotton, after whom he was named, he not only inherited the ambition but also the capacity to live up to his illustrious forebears. A precocious youth, he was ready for Harvard at the age of twelve, the youngest freshman in the history of the college. He could hardly remember a time when he was unable to speak Latin and Greek. Such literary "forcing" nurtured an enlarged youthful self-esteem and a tendency to correct the signs of Adam in the less godly of his contemporaries. He was graduated from Harvard at the age of fifteen, and proceeded to the A. M. in 1681. Four years later he became his father's assistant at the important Second Church, in which he came to have a proprietary interest, and an ever expanding sense of his own importance as God's vicar. He aspired to succeed his father as president of Harvard in 1701, but he failed to muster enough votes. He was thrice married, and outlived thirteen of his fifteen children; he died in 1728.

BIBLIOGRAPHY · Of the 444 known printed works of Cotton Mather, the most important is the *Magnalia Christi Americana: or the Ecclesiastical History of New England from its First Planting* (1702). Other items (letters, prefaces, postscripts, and the like, bringing the total number of his writings to 468) include *Parentator* (1724), a biography of his father, Increase Mather; *A Poem to the Memory of . . . Mr. Urian Oakes* (1682); *The Present State of New England* (1690); *Wonders of the Invisible World* (1693); *A Family Well-Ordered* (1699); *Reasonable Religion* (1700); *Some Few Remarks upon A Scandalous Book . . . By one Robert Calef* (1701); *A Faithful Man . . . Michael Wigglesworth* (1705); *Bonifacius* (1710), praised by Benjamin Franklin who knew it under its later title, *Essays to Do Good*; *The Christian Philosopher* (1721); *Sentiments on the Small Pox Inoculated* (1721); and *Manuductio ad Ministerium* (1726).

The definitive bibliography is the monumental *Cotton Mather: a Bibliography of His Works* (3 vols., 1940), compiled by T. J. Holmes. Barrett Wendell's *Cotton Mather* (1891, 1926) remains the best biography. Other valuable biographical material is contained in "The Mather Papers" in *Collections of the Massachusetts His-*

torical Society (Fourth Series), VIII (1868), and W. C. Ford's edition of the available sections of Mather's *Diary* in the same *Collections* (Eighth Series), VII–VIII (1921–1922). Readily available is K. B. Murdock's *Selections from Cotton Mather* (1926).

Important special studies include C. Deane, "The Light Shed upon Cotton Mather's *Magnalia* by His Diary," *Proceedings of the Massachusetts Historical Society*, VI (1862), 404–414; T. J. Holmes, "Cotton Mather and His Writings on Witchcraft," *Papers of the Bibliographical Society of America*, XVIII (1924), 31–59; T. Hornberger, "The Date, the Source, and the Significance of Cotton Mather's Interest in Science," *American Literature*, VI (1935), 413–420; G. L. Kittredge, "Cotton Mather's Election into the Royal Society," *Publications of the Colonial Society of Massachusetts*, XIV (1911–1913), 81–114, and the same authority's two articles in the *Proceedings of the American Antiquarian Society:* "Cotton Mather's Scientific Communications to the Royal Society," New Series, XXVI (1916), 18–57, and "Notes on Witchcraft," New Series, XVIII (1907), 148–212; H. C. Rice, "Cotton Mather Speaks to France: American Propaganda in the Age of Louis XIV," *New England Quarterly*, XVI (1943), 198–233; J. H. Tuttle, "The Libraries of the Mathers," *Proceedings of the American Antiquarian Society*, XX (1910), 269–356; and W. Walker, "The Services of the Mathers in New England Religious Developments," *Papers of the American Society of Church History*, V (1893), 61–85.

Ornaments for the Daughters of Zion

PUBLISHED in 1692, and written, as Mather announced on the title page, to direct the "Female-sex how to Express, the fear of God, in every *Age* and *State* of their life; and Obtain both *Temporal* and *Eternal* Blessedness. . . ." Admonition he also gave: "Go yee forth now array'd with such *Ornaments* as the *Apostles* have provided for you; Cloath your selves with the *Silk* of Piety, the *Satin* of Sanctity, the *Purple* of Modesty; so the Almighty God will be a *Lover* of you."

[*A Virtuous Woman*]

The Virtuous Woman counts the best Female Favour to be Deceitful, the best Female Beauty to be Vain.

By Favour is meant a Comely Presence, an Handsome Carriage, a Decent Gesture, a ready Wit agreeably expressing it self, with all other Graceful Motions, and whatsoever procures Favour for a Woman among her Neighbours. The Virtuous Woman is willing to have this Favour, so far as is consistent with Virtue; She counts it a Favour of God for one to be graced with it; But still she looks upon it as a Deceitful thing. She is careful, that She do not hereby Deceive her self into proud Imaginations, and into an Humour, Conceited of her self, or Contemptuous towards others. Careful she likewise is, lest hereby She Deceive Unwary men, into those Amours which bewitching looks and smiles do often betray the Children of men, especially those that are but Children of men, into.

By Beauty is meant, a good Proportion and Symmetry of the parts, and a skin well Varnished, or that which Chrysostom calls, A good mixture of Blood and Flegm shining through a good Skin; With all that Harmonious Air of the Countenance, which recommends it self, as a Beauty to the Eye of the Spectator. The Virtuous Woman is not unthankful for this Beauty, when the God of Nature has bestow'd any of it on her, and yet she counts it no Virtue for her to be very sensible of her being illustrated with such a Beauty. But still she looks upon it as a Vain thing. She reckons it so Vain, that she has no Assurance for the continuance of it; but that it is tempora & Morbi Ludibrium, as one of the Antients had descanted on it; a thing neither Age-proof, nor Ague-proof. She sees the Vanity in it, which is upon the quickly Withering Roses and Lillies of the Field; Such a Vanity as that Sick-beds or Sun-beams, or a thousand Casualties may soon destroy that Idol of the Amorites. And upon these thoughts a Virtuous Woman takes heed of becoming so Beautiful and Vain, as many Women are tempted by their favour and Beauty to become. . . .

Magnalia Christi Americana

AT ONCE the most formidable as well as the most famous of the 468 items which comprise the long list of the works of Cotton Mather, the *Magnalia Christi Americana* is the author's *magnum opus*. Published in two volumes in London in 1702, its seven books were designed to celebrate the triumph of Christ in the wilderness of the New World. In the development of this epic theme, Mather chronicled the "planting" of the colonies in New England, recounted the lives of the governors and the careers of the leading divines, compiled the history of Harvard College, and enumerated the "wonderful providences" illustrating how God had intervened to deliver his chosen people from their manifold afflictions and disturbances.

The many lives or sketches of the leaders of New England Congregationalism are often made memorable by Mather's use of illuminating anecdotes, vivid details, and highly individualized portraiture. Each biography buttresses Mather's main theme: the glory of God's pioneers in New England. The *Magnalia* is an historical source-book of first importance, and Nathaniel Hawthorne was only the most distinguished of the many writers who sought and found there treas- 10 ures for the inspiration of imaginative literature. Mather was at his best in biographical writing, but had shortcomings as a biographer, as were set forth by R. E. Watters in his study, "Biographical Technique in Cotton Mather's *Magnalia*," *William & Mary Quarterly*, II (1945), 154–163. The text of the following sections is that of the first American edition of the *Magnalia*, published in Hartford in 1820.

[William Bradford]

20

The leader of a people in a wilderness had need be a Moses; and if a Moses had not led the people of Plymouth Colony, when this worthy person was their governour, the people had never with so much unanimity and importunity still called him to lead them. Among many instances thereof, let this one piece of self-denial be told for a memorial of him, wheresoever this History shall be considered. The Patent of the Colony was taken in his name, running in these terms, To William 30 Bradford, his heirs, associates and assigns. But when the number of the freemen was much increased, and many new townships erected, the General Court there desired of Mr. Bradford, that he would make a surrender of the same into their hands, which he willingly and presently assented unto, and confirmed it according to their desire by his hand and seal, reserving no more for himself than was his proportion, with others, by agreement. But as he found the providence of heaven many 40 ways recompensing his many acts of self-denial, so he gave this testimony to the faithfulness of the divine promises; That he had forsaken friends, houses and lands for the sake of the gospel, and the Lord gave them him again. Here he prospered in his estate; and besides a worthy son which he had by a former wife, he had also two sons and a daughter by another, whom he married in this land.

He was a person for study as well as action; and hence, notwithstanding the difficulties through which he passed in his youth, he attained unto a notable skill in languages: the Dutch tongue was become almost as vernacular to him as the English; the French tongue he could also manage; the Latin and the Greek he had mastered; but the Hebrew he most of all studied, Because, he said, he would see with his own eyes the ancient oracles of God in their native beauty. He was also well skilled in History, in Antiquity, and in Philosophy; and for Theology he became so versed in it, that he was an irrefragable disputant against the errors, especially those of Anabaptism, which with trouble he saw rising in his colony; wherefore he wrote some significant things for the confutation of those errors. But the crown of all was his holy, prayerful, watchful and fruitful walk with God, wherein he was very exemplary.

[John Winthrop]

Let Greece boast of her patient Lycurgus, the lawgiver, by whom diligence, temperance, fortitude and wit were made the fashions of a therefore · long-lasting and renowned commonwealth: let Rome tell of her devout Numa, the lawgiver, by whom the most famous commonwealth saw peace triumphing over extinguished war, and cruel plunders; and murders giving place to the more mollifying exercises of his religion. Our New-England shall tell and boast of her WINTHROP, a lawgiver, as patient as Lycurgus, but not admitting any of his criminal disorders; as devout as Numa, but not liable to any of his heathenish madnesses; a governour in whom the excellencies of christianity made a most improving addition unto the virtues, wherein even without those he would have made a parallel for the great men of Greece, or of Rome, which the pen of a Plutarch has eternized.

A stock of heroes by right should afford nothing but what is heroical; and nothing but an extream degeneracy would make anything less to be expected from a stock of Winthrops. Mr. Adam Winthrop, the son of a worthy gentleman wearing the same name, was himself a worthy, a discreet, and a learned gentleman, particularly eminent for skill in the law, nor without remark for love to the gospel, under the reign of King

Henry VIII; and brother to a memorable favourer of the reformed religion in the days of Queen Mary, into whose hands the famous martyr Philpot committed his papers, which afterwards made no inconsiderable part of our martyr-books. . . .

. . . When the noble design of carrying a colony of chosen people into an American wilderness, was by some eminent persons undertaken, this eminent person [John] was, by the consent of all, chosen for the Moses, who must be the leader of so great an undertaking: and indeed nothing but a Mosaic spirit could have carried him through the temptations, to which either his farewel to his own land, or his travel in a strange land, must needs expose a gentleman of his education. Wherefore having sold a fair estate of six or seven hundred a year, he transported himself with the effects of it into New-England in the year 1630, where he spent it upon the service of a famous plantation founded and formed for the seat of the most reformed christianity: and continued there, conflicting with temptations of all sorts, as many years as the nodes of the moon take to dispatch a revolution. Those persons were never concerned in a new-plantation, who know not that the unavoidable difficulties of such a thing, will call for all the prudence and patience of a mortal man to encounter therewithal; and they must be very insensible of the influence, which the just wrath of heaven has permitted the devils to have upon this world, if they do not think that the difficulties of a new-plantation, devoted unto the evangelical worship of our Lord Jesus Christ, must be yet more than ordinary. How prudently, how patiently, and with how much resignation to our Lord Jesus Christ, our brave Winthrop waded through these difficulties, let posterity consider with admiration. And know, that as the picture of this their governour, was, after his death, hung up with honour in the state-house of his country, so the wisdom, courage, and holy zeal of his life, were an example well-worthy to be copied by all that shall succeed him in government. . . .

[Anne Bradstreet]

. . . If the rare learning of a daughter, was not the least of those bright things that adorned no less a Judge of England than Sir Thomas More;

it must now be said, that a Judge of New-England, namely, Thomas Dudley, Esq. had a daughter (besides other children) to be a crown unto him. Reader, America justly admires the learned women of the other hemisphere. She has heard of those that were tutoresses to the old professors of all philosophy: she hath heard of Hippatia, who formerly taught the liberal arts; and of Sarocchia, who more lately was very often the moderatrix in the disputations of the learned men of Rome: she has been told of the three Corinnaes, which equalled, if not excelled, the most celebrated poets of their time: she has been told of the Empress Endocia, who composed poetical paraphrases on divers parts of the Bible: and of Rosuida, who wrote the lives of holy men; and of Pamphilia, who wrote other histories unto the life: the writings of the most renowned Anna Maria Schurnian, have come over unto her. But she now prays, that into such catalogues of authoresses, as Beverovicius, Hottinger, and Voetius, have given unto the world, there may be a room now given unto Madam Ann Bradstreet, the daughter of our governour Dudley, and the consort of our governour Bradstreet, whose poems, divers times printed, have afforded a grateful entertainment unto the ingenious, and a monument for her memory beyond the stateliest marbles. . . .

Manuductio ad Ministerium

THIS BOOK of 170 pages, with subtitle "Directions for a Candidate of the Ministry," was published in Boston in 1726, two years before the author's death. Mather was an ardent advocate of the study of natural philosophy, mathematics, geography, and the ancient languages. But he did not encourage attention to logic, as he found it often employed against truth; and he held classical ethics to be usually a *Vile Thing*, full of "Mock Vertues," to be learned merely "to know what this *Paganism* is." His attitude on rhetoric, poetry, and style illustrates the point of view of the period. The book was reprinted by the Facsimile Text Society in 1938 under the excellent editorship of T. J. Holmes in K. B. Murdock. Italics have been removed.

[Rhetoric, Poetry, and Style]

But I will take this Opportunity to tell you, That there is no where to be found any such

Rhetoric, as there is in our Sacred Scriptures. Even a Pagan Longinus himself, will confess, The Sublime, shining in them. There can be nothing so Beautiful, or so Affectuous as the Figures every where used in them. They are Life. All meer Humane Flourishes are but Chaff to the Wheat that is there. Yea, they are an Hammer that breaks the Rocks to Pieces. In them the GOD of Glory Thunders, yea, does it very marvellously! There is in them that Voice of the Lord which is full of Majesty. . . . .

Poetry, whereof we have now even an Antediluvian Piece in our Hands, has from the Beginning been in such Request, that I must needs recommend unto you some Acquaintance with it. Though some have had a Soul so Unmusical, that they have decried all Verse, as being but a meer Playing and Fiddling upon Words; All Versifying, as if it were more Unnatural than if we should chuse Dancing instead of Walking; and Ryme, as if it were but a sort of Morisco Dancing with Bells: Yet I cannot wish you a Soul that shall be wholly Unpoetical. An Old Horace has left us an Art of Poetry, which you may do well to bestow a Perusal on. And besides your Lyrick Hours, I wish you may so far understand an Epic Poem, that the Beauties of an Homer and a Virgil may be discerned with you. As to the Moral Part of Homer, 'tis true, and let me not be counted a Zoilus for saying so, that by first exhibiting their Gods as no better than Rogues, he set open the Floodgates for a prodigious Inundation of Wickedness to break upon the Nations, and was one of the greatest Apostles the Devil ever had in this World. Among the rest that felt the Ill Impressions of this Universal Corrupter, (as Men of the best Sentiments have called him,) One was that overgrown Robber, of execrable Memory, whom we celebrate under the Name of Alexander the Great; who by his continual Admiring and Studying of his Iliad, and by following that false Model of Heroic Virtue set before him in his Achilles, became one of the worst of Men, and at length inflated with the Ridiculous Pride of being himself a Deity, exposed himself to all the Scorn that could belong unto a Lunatick. And hence, notwithstanding the Veneration which this Idol has had, yet Plato banishes him out of a Common-Wealth, the Welfare whereof he was concerned for. Nevertheless, Custom or Conscience obliges him to bear Testimonies unto many Points of Morality. And it is especially observable, That he commonly propounds Prayer to Heaven as a most necessary Preface unto all Important Enterprizes; and when the Action comes on too suddenly for a more extended Supplication, he yet will not let it come on without an Ejaculation; and he never speaks of any Supplication but he brings in a Gracious Answer to it. I have seen a Travesteering High-Flyer, not much to our Dishonour, Scoff at Homer for this; as making his Actors to be like those whom the English call Dissenters. But then, we are so much led into the Knowledge of Antiquities, by reading of this Poet, and into so many Parts of the Recondite Learning, that notwithstanding some little Nods in him, not a few Acute Pens besides the old Bishop of Thessalonica's, have got a Reputation by regaling us with Annotations upon him. Yea, Tho' One can't but smile at the Fancy of Croese, who tries with much Ostentation of Erudition, to show, That Homer has all along tendred us in a Disguise and Fable, the History of the Old Testament, yet many Illustrations of the sacred Scriptures, I find are to be fetched from him; who indeed had probably read what was Extant of them in his Days; Particularly, Our Eighteenth Psalm is what he has evidently imitated. Virgil too, who so much lived upon him, as well as after him, is unaccountably mad upon his Fate, which he makes to be he knows not what himself, but Superiour to Gods as well as to Men, and thro' his whole Composures he so asserts the Doctrine of this Nonsensical Power, as is plainly inconsistent with all Virtue. And what fatal Mischief did Fascinator do to the Roman Empire, when by Deifying one Great Emperor, he taught the Successors to claim the Adoration of Gods, while they were perpetrating the Crimes of Devils? I will not be a Carbilius upon him; nor will I say any thing, how little the Married State owes unto One who writes as if he were a Woman hater: Nor what his Blunders are about his poor-spirited and inconsistent Hero, for which many have taxed him. Nevertheless, 'tis observed, That the Pagans had no Rules of Manners, that were more Laudable and Regular than what are to be found in him.

And some have said, It is hardly possible seriously to Read his Works without being more disposed unto Goodness, as well as being agreeably entertained. Be sure, had Virgil writ before Plato, his Works had not been any of the Books prohibited. But then, This Poet also has abundance of Rare Antiquities for us: And such Things, as others besides a Servius, have imagined that they have instructed and obliged Mankind, by employing all their Days upon. Wherefore if his Aeneis, which tho' it were once near twenty times as big as he has left it, yet he has left it unfinished, may not appear so valuable to you, that you may think Twenty seven Verses of the Part that is the most finished in it, worth One and Twenty Hundred Pounds and odd Money, yet his Georgicks, which he put his last Hand unto, will furnish you with many things far from Despicable. But after all, when I said, I was willing that the Beauties of these Two Poets, might become Visible to your Visive Faculty in Poetry, I did not mean, that you should Judge nothing to be Admittable into an Epic Poem, which is not Authorised by their Example; but I perfectly concur with One who is inexpressibly more capable to be a Judge of such a Matter than I can be; That it is a false Critic who with a petulant Air, will insult Reason itself, if it presumes to oppose such Authority.

I proceed now to say, That if (under the Guidance of a Vida) you try your young Wings now and then to see what Flights you can make, at least for an Epigram, it may a little sharpen your Sense, and polish your Style, for more important Performances; For this Purpose you are now even overstock'd with Patterns, and——Poemata Passim. You may, like Nazianzen, all your Days, make a little Recreation of Poetry in the midst of your more painful Studies. Nevertheless, I cannot but advise you, Withod thy Throat from Thirst. Be not so set upon Poetry, as to be always poring on the Passionate and Measured Pages. Let not what should be Sauce rather than Food for you, Engross all your Application. Beware of a Boundless and Sickly Appetite, for the Reading of the Poems, which now the Rickety Nation swarms withal: And let not the Circaean Cup intoxicate you. But especially pre-

serve the Chastity of your Soul from the Dangers you may incur, by a Conversation with Muses that are no better than Harlots: Among which are others besides Ovid's Epistles, which for their Tendency to excite and foment Impure Flames, and cast Coals into your Bosom, deserve rather to be thrown into the Fire, than to be laid before the Eye which a Covenant should be made withal. Indeed, not meerly for the Impurities which they convey, but also on some other Accounts, the Powers of Darkness have a Library among us, whereof the Poets have been the most Numerous as well as the most Venomous Authors. Most of the Modern Plays, as well as the Romances and Novels and Fictions, which are a sort of Poems, do belong to the Catalogue of this cursed Library. The Plays, I say, in which there are so many Passages, that have a Tendency to overthrow all Piety, that one whose Name is Bedford, has extracted near Seven Thousand Instances of them, from the Plays chiefly of but Five Years preceeding; and says awfully upon them, They are National Sins, and therefore call for National Plagues; And if GOD should enter into Judgment all the Blood in the Nation would not be able to atone for them. How much do I wish that such Pestilences, and indeed all those worse than Egyptian Toads, (the Spawns of a Butler, & a Brown, and a Ward, and a Company whose Name is Legion!) might never crawl into your Chamber! The unclean Spirits that come like Frogs out of the Mouth of the Dragon, and of the Beast; which go forth unto the young People of the Earth, and expose them to be dealt withal as the Enemies of God, in the Battle of the Great Day of the Almighty. As for those wretched Scribbles of Madmen, My Son, Touch them not, Taste them not, Handle them not: Thou wilt perish in the using of them. They are, The Dragons whose Contagious Breath Peoples the dark Retreats of Death. To much better Purpose will an Excellent but an Envied Blackmore feast you, than those Vile Rapsodies (of that Vinum Daemonum) which you will find always leave a Taint upon your Mind, and among other ill Effects, will sensibly indispose you to converse with the Holy Oracles of God your Saviour.

But there is, what I may rather call a Parenthesis, than a Digression, which this may be not altogether an Improper Place for the introducing of.

[There has been a deal of a do about a Style; So much, that I must offer you my Sentiments upon it. There is a Way of Writing, wherein the Author endeavours, that the Reader may have Something to the Purpose in every Paragraph. There is not only a Vigour sensible in every Sentence, but the Paragraph is embellished with Profitable References, even to something beyond what is directly spoken. Formal and Painful Quotations are not studied; yet all that could be learnt from 'them is insinuated. The Writer pretends not unto Reading, yet he could not have writ as he does if he had not Read very much in his Time; and his Composures are not only a Cloth of Gold, but also stuck with as many Jewels, as the Gown of a Russian Embassador. This Way of Writing has been decried by many, and is at this Day more than ever so, for the same Reason, that in the old Story, the Grapes were decried, That they were not Ripe. A Lazy, Ignorant, Conceited Sett of Authors, would perswade the whole Tribe, to lay aside that Way of Writing, for the same Reason that one would have perswaded his Brethren to part with the Encumbrance of their Bushy Tails. But, however Fashion and Humour may prevail, they must not think that the Club at their Coffee-House is, All the World; but there will always be those, who will in this Case be governed by Indisputable Reason; And who will think that the real Excellency of a Book will never ly in saying of little; That the less one has for his Money in a Book, 'tis really the more Valuable for it; and that the less one is instructed in a Book, and the more of Superfluous Margin, and Superficial Harangue, and the less of Substantial Matter one has in it, the more 'tis to be accounted of. And if a more Massy Way of Writing be never so much disgusted at This Day, a Better Gust will come on, as will some other Thing, *quae jam Cecidere*. In the mean time, Nothing appears to me more Impertinent and Ridiculous than the Modern Way, (I cannot say, Rule; For they have None!) of Criticising. The Blades that set up for Criticks, I know not who constituted or commission'd 'em! —they appear to me, for the most part as Contemptible, as they are a Supercilious Generation. For indeed no Two of them have the same Style; and they are as intollerably Cross-grain'd and severe in their Censures upon one another, as they are upon the rest of Mankind. But while each of them, conceitedly enough, sets up for the Standard of Perfection, we are entirely at a Loss which Fire to follow. Nor can you easily find any one thing wherein they agree for their Style, except perhaps a perpetual Care to give us Jejune and Empty Pages, without such Touches of Erudition (to speak in the Style of an Ingenious Traveller) as may make the Discourses less Tedious, and more Enriching, to the Mind of him that peruses them. There is much Talk of a Florid Style, obtaining among the Pens, that are most in Vogue; but how often would it puzzle one, even with the best Glasses to find the Flowres! And if they were to be Chastized for it, it would be with as much of Justice, as Jerom was, for being a Ciceronian. After all, Every Man will have his own Style, which will distinguish him as much as his Gate: And if you can attain to that which I have newly described, but always writing so as to give an Easy Conveyance unto your idea's, I would not have you by any Scourging be driven out of your Gate, but if you must confess a Fault in it, make a Confession like that of the Lad, unto his Father while he was beating him for his Versifying.

However, since every Man will have his own Style, I would pray, that we may learn to treat one another with mutual Civilities, and Condescensions, and handsomely indulge one another in this, as Gentlemen do in other Matters.

I wonder what ails People, that they can't let Cicero write in the Style of Cicero, and Seneca write in the (much other!) Style of Seneca; and own that Both may please in their several Ways.— But I will freely tell you; what has made me consider the Humourists that set up for Criticks upon Style, as the most Unregardable Set of Mortals in the World, is This! Far more Illustrious Criticks than any of those to whom I am now bidding Defiance, and no less Men than your Erasmus's, and your Grotius's, have taxed the Greek Style of the New Testament, with I know not what Solaecisms and Barbarisms; And, how many learned Folks have Obsequiously run away with the Notion! Whereas 'tis an Ignorant and an Insolent Whimsey; which they have been guilty of. It may be (and particularly by an Ingenious Blackwal, it has been) Demonstrated, That the Gentlemen are mistaken in every one of their pretended Instances; All the Unquestionable Classicks, may be brought in, to convince them of their Mistakes. Those Glorious Oracles are as pure Greek as ever was written in the World; and so Correct, so Noble, so Sublime is their Style, that never any thing under the Cope of Heaven, but the Old Testament, has equall'd it.]

The Eighteenth

INTRODUCTION

THE EIGHTEENTH century was the great century of change, of revolution in religious, social, and governmental thinking, and of the fashioning of a national culture. It was the century of the people's attack on the established privileged orders—on law, on orthodoxy in religion, on government, on the solidified forms of the institutions of men. And it was the century of the reconstruction of institutions on new principles. As the decades advanced, Puritanism waned. Human interests veered to worldly affairs—to science, the laws of nature, and political justice. The discoveries of Newton suggested to deists—men like Paine and Jefferson—the principle of a world governed by universal, immutable principles. The study of natural laws came to be viewed as the study of God's way.

The influence of Lord Shaftesbury spread: if the universe and God were one, then the universe was a harmonious whole, "partial evil" was "universal good," and the path to perpetual improvement and human happiness lay in the search to understand the laws of nature and the nature of man.

The principles of John Locke, English philosopher, played into the hands of those seeking a more democratic order in the colonies. In a state of nature, Locke reasoned, man was independent. But to achieve the advantages inherent in a social structure, he had to surrender certain rights to government. Yet there resided in man certain inalienable rights no government could take away; and since government was created by the people, it derived its powers from the people. The people were superior to government, and no king could claim authority except through them. As the decades passed, the colonists increasingly adopted these principles as fundamental tenets, and the expanding commerce and trade made them yearn for equality as Englishmen—or for separation.

Theological Works

In New England the literary trend during the first quarter of the eighteenth century differed little from that of the seventeenth century, when most of the writing was done on sermon paper. These were the years of the prolific writings of the two stoutest defenders of theocracy, Increase and Cotton Mather. There had been much arguing to uphold Puritan authority in the seventeenth century, and during the eighteenth century doctrinal problems, to the spiritually inclined, became matters of life and death. Cotton Mather's great history of the Puritan world, the *Magnalia Christi Americana*, appeared in 1702, and his *Manuductio ad Ministerium*, a treatise to guide the studies of students of divinity, in 1726.

Century

FASHIONING A NATIONAL CULTURE

Yet it was during the decline of Puritanism that Jonathan Edwards flourished. He was the greatest of the Calvinists, though he was loath to claim specific attachment. His treatise, *A Careful and Strict Inquiry . . . of . . . Freedom of Will* (1754), which assured salvation only to "the elect" of God and refused salvation on the basis of man's own endeavor, together with his vigorous sermons exemplified by "The Eternity of Hell Torments," sharpened the New England conscience in the way of its past, but led ultimately to its refusal to accept his doctrines. Religion was pointing more toward Congregationalism in polity, as evidenced in John Wise's *A Vindication of the Government of New England Churches* (1717), and tending toward the Unitarianism visible in the writings of Charles Chauncy and Jonathan Mayhew.

The Drama

The eighteenth century witnessed the rise of the drama in the United States. In 1700 the population of New York was 5,000, of Boston 7,000, and of Philadelphia 10,000; Charleston was the fourth town of consequence. Still, there were theatric entertainments of sorts in Charleston and New York in the first decade of the eighteenth century, and in Williamsburg soon afterward; and theatres increased in number, as the population grew rapidly. The colonial inhabitants numbered 2,000,000 by 1775. For reasons of conscience, Boston lagged far behind in the theatre, but even here a theatre was opened for entertainments of various sorts in 1794.

The first performance of a play written in America probably was given in Charleston in 1703. Williamsburg could boast of a simple public hall with stage fittings in 1716, and in 1736 the students of the College of William and Mary produced Addison's *Cato*, from which tragedy the editors of schoolbooks frequently printed excerpts because of the play's lofty sentiments. Four years previously a playhouse had opened in New York.

The first company of players in the colonies was established in Philadelphia in 1749; and in 1767, four years after Thomas Godfrey's death, his poetic tragedy, *The Prince of Parthia*, was produced in his native city. This play, according to A. H. Quinn, was the first written in America to be produced in its native land by a professional company. The second play written by an American and produced in America by a professional company was Royall Tyler's prose comedy, *The Contrast*, played in New York in 1787; though it is based in part on Sheridan's *School for Scandal*, it introduced the character of the honest Yankee of native intelligence and sound worth in opposition to the deceits and fopperies of the gilded social class.

Throughout the century plays by English dramatists held the stage. In the winter of 1773–1774, for instance, fourteen plays by Shakespeare were produced in Charleston; and dramas by

Dryden, Otway, Congreve, Cibber, Addison, Farquhar, Goldsmith, Sheridan, and others were commonly played before and after the Revolution.

The wars of the eighteenth century, culminating in the Revolution, supplied native material written in dramatic form, though seldom was it produced on the stage. Selected titles indicate the trend. Major Robert Rogers, a native of Boston who had led a force of six hundred Rangers in the last of the French and Indian Wars, wrote the first tragedy of Indian life, *Ponteach*, published in London in 1766. Mercy Warren, sister of James Otis and wife of General Warren, who lost his life later at Bunker Hill, wrote a popular satire on the Royalists in Boston, *The Group*, published in 1775. Hugh Henry Brackenridge penned a blank-verse tragedy, *The Battle of Bunker's-Hill*, for production at Somerset Academy in Maryland, where he was a teacher; and later, in 1777, his second poetic tragedy, *The Death of General Montgomery*, was published. Reflecting travel in the American colonies, London, and North Africa, Susanna Haswell Rowson's first drama, *Slaves in Algiers*, was played in both Philadelphia and Baltimore in 1795.

The dominating force in the American theatre during the last decade of the eighteenth and first decade of the nineteenth centuries was William Dunlap, the famous playwright and producer in New York. His first play to be performed was *The Father; or, American Shandyism;* its appearance in New York in 1789 gave it the distinction of being the second comedy by a native American produced on the professional stage. A still better play, reflecting the Revolution, is his *André*, a tragedy in blank verse treating of the most famous incident of treachery in the Revolution. Dunlap's theatrical ventures were unfortunate, and he turned to his brushes as an artist to earn a meager living, but he remains in history as the distinguished entrepreneur of the stage in New York.

Travel and History

Books on travel, books explaining the "present state" of affairs, and historical accounts ran through the century. Sarah Kemble Knight's *Journal*, intimately describing her trip from Boston to New York in 1704, was exciting in an age when voyages by Bostonians to London were an everyday affair, whereas an overland journey to New York was a rare event. William Byrd, of Virginia, while supervising a surveying party along the North Carolina border in 1728, recorded his observations in a famous journal published as *The History of the Dividing Line* (1841), and his excursion into northern Virginia to explore the iron industry is set down in his *Progress to the Mines*.

The most delightful volumes of nature study are those by John and William Bartram, father and son. The father's *Observations* (1751) made while traveling from Pennsylvania to Lake Ontario is a vital book, and William's years of exploration produced two volumes of enduring worth, *Observations on the Creek and Cherokee Indians* (1789), and *Travels Through North and South Carolina, Georgia, East and West Florida* (1791). Chateaubriand, Coleridge, Rousseau, and Wordsworth drew on his work for their descriptions of the New World and its noble savages.

Especially enlightening, too, are John Woolman's notes made while his Quaker activities took him to colonies to the north, to western Pennsylvania, to Virginia, and finally to England. His antislavery observations, *Some Considerations on the Keeping of Negroes* (1754), his social tract, *A Plea for the Poor* (1763), later issued by the Fabian Society, and his general *Journal* (1774) are literary documents which the years have not dimmed.

Like Woolman, St. John de Crèvecoeur was a humanitarian opposed to the evils of slavery. Like Bartram, though with far less fidelity of observation, he loved the wilderness and fared well among the Indians. And in addition, he dreamed of America as an asylum from the religious dissensions, the class distinctions, the economic strait-jackets, the national hatreds, and the political autocracy of Europe. His *Letters from an American Farmer* (London, 1782) must be ranked with the best books of the century in America.

Men who were close to the historical scene sometimes wrote from their knowledge of events as well as from other sources. Explanatory, apologetic, biased, or objective, their accounts gave a sense of importance to the record which the colonists had made. Chief among these works are Robert Beverley's *History and Present State of Virginia* (1705), William Stith's *History of the First Discovery and Settlement of Virginia* (1747), Thomas Prince's *Chronological History of New England* (1736), Thomas Hutchinson's *History of the Province of Massachusetts Bay* (1767), and Thomas Jefferson's ever enlightening and philosophically refreshing *Notes on Virginia*, with comments on public affairs too intimate for publication at the time they were written.

Newspapers and Magazines

The beginning of newspapers and magazines awaited the eighteenth century. As a literary medium they were highly significant. The newspapers encouraged the writing of poetry and literary essays. They spread current news among the colonies, which previously had been nearer to England in thought and trade than to each other. They helped the colonies to recognize themselves as important governmental units with common aims and economic needs. Further, the papers were of immeasurable importance in stimulating the major political thinkers of the century, among them John Dickinson, Thomas Paine, and the authors of *The Federalist*, as well as the satirists in poetry, especially Freneau and the Connecticut Wits.

The Boston *News-Letter*, established in 1704, was the first paper to prosper, its predecessor, *Publick Occurrences*, having been strangled by colonial authorities after the first issue in 1690. Philadelphia's first newspaper was published in 1719, and New York's in 1725. Ten years later, the famous trial of Peter Zenger, newspaper publisher of New York, established a measure of freedom of the press against political censorship. By the time the Stamp Act came into force in 1765 there were forty-three newspapers in the colonies: ten in the South, thirteen in the Middle States, and twenty in New England. The number and importance of the journals mounted yearly.

The magazines of the century also stimulated literary work and reflected the interests of the age.

Among the editors were Thomas Prince, Jr. and Isaiah Thomas in Boston, William Livingston and Noah Webster in New York, and a whole group of Philadelphians, including Benjamin Franklin, Lewis Nicola, Provost William Smith, Thomas Paine, Hugh Henry Brackenridge, and Mathew Carey. The first two magazines in the colonies, *The American Magazine* and *The General Magazine*, both short-lived, appeared in 1741 in Philadelphia, and were published by Andrew Bradford and Benjamin Franklin, bitter competitors in the printing trade. The thirty-seven magazines from 1741 to 1789 recount the problems of King George's War, the French and Indian War, and the Revolution; they tell of the difficulties incident to extension of territory, security of trade lanes, the expansion of industry and commerce, treaties with the Indians, colonial fiscal and legislative disputes, the devising of state constitutions, the making of the Federal Constitution, and the division of political authority.

Literary artistry is found in the contributions of Jeremy Belknap, Philip Freneau, Francis Hopkinson, St. John de Crèvecoeur, Thomas Godfrey, Nathaniel Evans, William Ladd, John Trumbull, David Humphreys, Joel Barlow, Timothy and Theodore Dwight, Lemuel Hopkins, and many others. The Reverend Mather Byles, a man of wit and learning, was a contributor of occasional verse to Boston journals, which was collected in *Poems on Several Occasions* (1744), and he also was an early commentator on prose styles. Among the better early magazines were Prince's *Christian History* (1743–1745), *The American Magazine* (1743–1746) of Rogers and Fowle in Boston, Smith's *American Magazine* (1757–1758), Nicola's *American Magazine* (1769), Thomas's *Royal American Magazine* (1774–1775), Aitken's *Pennsylvania Magazine* (1775–1776), which was edited by Paine and Hopkinson, and Brackenridge's *United States Magazine* (1779). After the Revolution, Webster's *American Magazine* (1787–1788), *The Columbian Magazine* (1786–1790), and Carey's famous *American Museum* (1787–1792), the last a veritable museum or anthology of the writings of the period, set the tone that was later to flower in the larger cities during the nineteenth century. At the turn of the century Joseph Dennie, the "American

Addison," whose fame was soon to be superseded by that of Washington Irving, became the editor of *The Port Folio* (1802).

Political Essays

As the Revolution drew near, essays in political philosophy increased in number and cogency. Franklin, both in America and in England, tried until 1775 to preserve the Empire. But this greatest figure of the eighteenth century, original of mind, wise in the ways of man, and major contributor to science, to political philosophy, and to the world of letters, was powerless against the colonial attitude of Great Britain, and the mother country rebuked his efforts to make her the model empire.

Ineffective, too, was the pleading of the Philadelphia lawyer, John Dickinson, the moderate "Penman" of the Revolution, whose *Letters from a Farmer in Pennsylvania* (1767–1768), published in twenty-one of the colonial newspapers, ably presented the American point of view. But he was unwilling to sign the Declaration of Independence, and it remained for Tom Paine, in his *Common Sense* (1776) and the *Crisis* papers (1776–1783) to urge the colonies forward to separation and willingness to endure the trials of war. Thereafter, while Paine as a "Citizen of the World" was fighting for democracy along the course laid out later in *The Rights of Man* (1791), Alexander Hamilton, James Madison, and John Jay began to interpret the Constitution of the United States to the people, and to urge its adoption, through the *Federalist* papers (1787–1788).

Poetry

Poetry remained in its infancy during the earlier part of the century, but throve both during and after the period of the Revolution. Ebenezer Cook, an Englishman who spent some time in Maryland and Virginia, expressed his disgust of colonial life in a Hudibrastic satire, *The Sot-Weed Factor*, which may be translated as "The Tobacco Merchant," published in London in 1708. The light verse of Mather Byles, of Boston, gathered in *Poems on Several Occasions* (1744), the popular heroic couplets of Benjamin Church's *Choice*

(1756), and in the 1760's the romantic poetry of two friends, Thomas Godfrey and Nathaniel Evans of Philadelphia, represent the practice of polite writing for simple amusement and pleasure. The poets often leaned heavily on their English predecessors. In the earlier period the writers practiced exercises from the Latin, elegies, pastorals, heroic couplets, eclogues, and light verse forms. Later came blank verse, political satire, Miltonic octosyllabics, and romantic odes.

The Connecticut Wits as a group supplied the best verse of the century, though Philip Freneau remains chief among the poets. John Trumbull's *M'Fingal* (1776–1781) was the liveliest satire on the British occupation of Boston and on the war. It was copied extensively by the newspapers, and went through thirty editions during his lifetime. Timothy Dwight's *Conquest of Canaan* (1785), modeled on Vergil, Milton, and Pope, was an ambitious epic of 10,000 lines; in its allegorical structure, Dwight's contemporaries connected the Egyptians with Great Britain, the Israelites with the Colonists, and Joshua with Washington, but Dwight categorically denied the validity of the interpretation in a letter to Noah Webster, saying the poem was largely written before 1775. Dwight's mind was not original, but it was susceptible to the moods and styles of many English poets, and his long pastoral poem, *Greenfield Hill* (1794), and his mock epic on unorthodoxy, *The Triumph of Infidelity* (1788) continue the general tradition of English poetry. Joel Barlow was more original. His *Vision of Columbus* (1787) later expanded to become the long epic, *The Columbiad* (1807), while tiresome to readers of today, embodies the visions and the convictions of the Revolutionary days. David Humphreys, John Trumbull, Joel Barlow, and Lemuel Hopkins collaborated in writing the major mock epic against the Antifederalists, who were obstructing the establishment of a sound central government: *The Anarchiad, a Poem on the Reconstruction of Chaos and Substantial Night.*

Philip Freneau spanned three periods. Before the Revolution he and Brackenridge joined in writing *A Poem on the Rising Glory of America* (1772); during the war his satiric blasts against the English, his romantic poetry, and his *British*

Prison Ship (1781) raised him high among the poets of the Revolution. After the war his espousal of the French Republic and his further romantic poetry placed him indubitably first among the poets. His last volume appeared in 1815.

Fiction

Fiction came late in the eighteenth century. The works of such English authors as Defoe, Swift, Richardson, Fielding, Smollett, Johnson, Goldsmith, and Walpole were imported, especially in the Middle Colonies and the South; but native fiction did not spring into full life until after the Revolution. However, the period of the Revolution did introduce political allegories, the most famous being *A Pretty Story* (1774), by Francis Hopkinson, Philadelphian, who satirized the restrictive and dictatorial measures of England. In 1792 came a more ambitious attempt by Jeremy Belknap, in Massachusetts, who in *The Foresters* traced the fortunes of the colonists through the colonial wars, the Revolution, the formation of the Constitution and the early vicissitudes of the Republic.

Three other types of novels soon appeared: the sentimental tale of betrayal and domestic infidelity, the picaresque novel, and the Gothic romance. Among the first were William Hill Brown's *Power of Sympathy* (1789), Susanna Haswell Rowson's *Charlotte*—later *Charlotte Temple*—(1794), and Hannah Webster Foster's *Coquette* (1797), all based on domestic scandal, and all popular—especially *Charlotte Temple*, which kept presses occasionally busy deep into the nineteenth century.

The greatest single work of fiction of the century, however, was written in the picaresque vein by Hugh Henry Brackenridge, who had moved from Philadelphia to Pittsburgh to practice law. Educated in the classics, lover of the satire of Swift and of the tales of Cervantes, angered by popular defeat at the polls, he consoled himself by picturing the rude personal and civil life of western Pennsylvania and spending his fury on the pretensions of institutions in *Modern Chivalry*. It appeared in several parts between 1792 and 1815, and embodied new material as the author's course in life as lawyer, politician, newspaper owner and judge offered the incidents of experience to call forth his indignation, humor, and philosophy.

The reign of terror in fiction, exemplified by the Gothic romance, found its exponent in Charles Brockden Brown, of Philadelphia, the first literary man in the United States to attempt to earn his entire livelihood by writing fiction. In 1798 his *Wieland* was published, a story compounded of spontaneous combustion, religious fanaticism, ventriloquism, and murder. *Ormond* (1799) and *Arthur Mervyn* (1799–1800) are of interest for their delineation of the yellow-fever epidemics which had been rampant in New York and Philadelphia; and *Edgar Huntly* (1799) is a Gothic novel compounded of hair-raising dangers on the American frontier.

Recapitulation

The literature of the eighteenth century, born of reason and intellectual ferment, was at once humanistic and polemic. Confidence in the future glory of America was expressed in epic poetry and current dissatisfactions in the mock-epic form. The age excelled in prose, which came to a focus in the controversies leading to political independence, to the creation of a Federal union, and to the characteristics of the new nationalism. The fifty years after 1750 were a period of almost continual change. The clashes were imbedded in literature, both in the survival of contradictory concepts and in the spirit of compromise which resulted in political stability. At times many Americans were appalled by the excesses of the French sympathizers, and alarmed by the Shays's Rebellion and by evidences of religious infidelity. But time and the vitality of great ideas renewed their faith; and hope and optimism were characteristic of the era. When the century ended, the death of Washington called attention to the achievements of a great generation whose leaders had a genius for vigorous thinking and expression. They produced a political literature which for effectiveness, variety, and universality has strongly appealed to every succeeding generation.

THE AMERICAN SCENE

SARAH KEMBLE KNIGHT (1666–1727)

MADAM KNIGHT'S *Journal* is so illuminating and readable an account of provincial life in New England that when the document was first printed in 1825 its editor feared it would be mistaken for a piece of entertaining fiction. The unusual career of the author, Sarah Kemble Knight, makes it easy to understand why she was given the deferential title of *Madam* by her contemporaries. Her independence and resourcefulness are evident not only in her bold journey from Boston to New Haven and New York in 1704, but in the skill and shrewdness with which she conducted a number of business enterprises.

Sarah Kemble Knight was the daughter of a Charlestown shopkeeper, Thomas Kemble, who soon after 1666 moved to Boston. There she was reared and married Richard Knight, a ship captain and American agent of a London merchant. His prolonged absences from home threw her upon her own devices early in her married life; and when, about 1706, she was left a widow with one daughter, she found support by teaching school, keeping a shop, conducting a boarding-house, copying legal documents, and assisting in the settlement of estates. After the marriage of her daughter, who moved to Connecticut in 1714, Madam Knight lived in New London and Norwich until her death. In Connecticut she continued to engage in legal affairs; she also managed several farms, speculated successfully in Indian lands, and had accumulated an estate of £1800 at the time of her death in 1727. She is buried in New London.

Madam Knight was thirty-eight years of age when she set out on her trip to New York in 1704, not an easy undertaking for anyone, and an almost unheard-of venture for a lone "female." Before retiring each night, she recorded—very probably in shorthand— her observations of the day's travel. These notations, enlivened by an easygoing good humor and by the born traveler's instinct to be amused rather than made miserable by the vicissitudes of the road, constitute a precious record of the early American scene. For its engaging absorption in the externalities of her environment and for the detached amusement with which she regarded ordinary folk whom she encountered on her way, Madam Knight's *Journal* has a unique place among our literary and social records of the first part of the eighteenth century.

BIBLIOGRAPHY · The *Journal* was first published, with an introduction by Theodore Dwight, in *The Journals of Madam Knight and Reverend Buckingham*, in New York in 1825. Although Mrs. Knight's *Journal* has been reprinted frequently, the edition designed by Bruce Rogers and edited with a highly competent introduction by G. P. Winship in 1920 is the most attractive. The prefatory notes by Dwight and Winship, and the authoritative sketch by Sidney Gunn in the *Dictionary of American Biography*, X (1933), 468–469, contain the available biographical information.

Journal

WHEN Theodore Dwight prepared the first edition of the *Journal* in 1825, he used a manuscript "neatly copied into a small book." This document was made available to the first editor by an executor who administered the estate of Mrs. John Livingston, the author's only daughter. Whether the manuscript was in Mrs. Knight's own handwriting is not known; nor is it clear whether the published *Journal* constitutes all of the original manuscript, which seems to have been lost, except for a single leaf, before 1858. The text here is that of G. P. Winship's edition of the *Journal* (Boston, 1920).

[*A Trip from Boston to New York*]

Monday, Octb'r. the second, 1704. About three o'clock afternoon, I begun my Journey from Boston to New-Haven; being about two Hundred Mile. My Kinsman, Capt. Robert Luist, waited on me as farr as Dedham, where I was to meet the Western post.

I vissitted the Reverd. Mr. Belcher, the Minister of the town, and tarried there till evening, in hopes the post would come along. But he not coming, I resolved to go to Billingses where he used to lodg, being 12 miles further. But being ignorant of the way, Madam Belcher, seing no persuasions of her good spouses or hers could prevail with me to Lodg there that night, Very Kindly went wyth me to the Tavern, where I hoped to get my guide, And desired the Hostess to inquire of her guests whether any of them would go with mee. But they, being tyed by the Lipps to a pewter engine,[n] scarcely allowed themselves time to say. . . .

tyed . . . pewter engine: engaged in incessant drinking from pewter mugs.

Thus Jogging on with an easy pace, my Guide telling mee it was dangero's to Ride hard in the Night, (which his hors had the sence to avoid,) Hee entertained me with the Adventurs he had passed by late Rideing, and eminent Dangers he had escaped, so that, Remembering the Hero's in Parismus and the Knight of the Oracle, I didn't know but I had mett with a Prince disguis'd.

When we had Ridd about an how'r, wee come into a thick swamp, which, by Reason of a great fogg, very much startled mee, it being now very Dark. But nothing dismay'd John. Hee had encountered a thousand and a thousand such Swamps, having a Universall Knowledge in the woods; and readily Answered all my inquiries which were not a few.

In about an how'r, or something more, after we left the Swamp, we come to Billinges, where I was to Lodg. My Guide dismounted and very Complassantly help't me down and shewd the door, signing to me with his hand to Go in; which I Gladly did—But had not gone many steps into the Room, ere I was Interogated by a young Lady I understood afterwards was the Eldest daughter of the family, with these, or words to this purpose, (*viz.*): "Law for mee—what in the world brings You here at this time a night?—I never see a woman on the Rode so Dreadfull late, in all the days of my versall life. Who are You? Where are You going? I'me scar'd out of my witts"—with much now of the same Kind. I stood aghast, Prepareing to reply, when in comes my Guide—To him Madam turn'd, Roreing out: "Lawfull heart, John, is it You?—how de do! Where in the world are you going with this woman? Who is she?" John made no Answer, but sat down in the corner, fumbled out his black Junk,[n] and saluted that instead of Debb; she then turned agen to mee and fell anew into her silly questions, without asking mee to sitt down.

I told her shee treated me very Rudely, and I did not think it my duty to answer her unmannerly Questions. But to get ridd of them, I told her I come there to have the post's company with me tomorrow on my Journey, &c. Miss star'd awhile, drew a chair, bid me sitt, and then run upstairs and putts on two or three Rings, (or else I had not seen

Junk: pipe.

them before,) and returning, sett herself just before me, showing the way to Reding, that I might see her Ornaments, perhaps to gain the more respect. But her Granam's new Rung sow, had it appeared, would affected me as much. I paid honest John with money and dram according to contract, and Dismist him, and pray'd Miss to shew me where I must Lodg. Shee conducted me to a parlour in a little back Lento,[n] which was almost fill'd with the bedsted, which was so high that I was forced to climb on a chair to gitt up to the wretched bed that lay on it; on which having Stretcht my tired Limbs, and lay'd my head on a Sad-coloured pillow, I began to think on the transactions of the past day.

Tuesday, October the third, about 8 in the morning, I with the Post proceeded forward without observing anything remarkable; and about two, afternoon, arrived at the Post's second stage, where the western Post mett him and exchanged Letters. Here, having called for something to eat, the woman bro't in a twisted thing like a cable, but something whiter; and laying it on the bord, tugg'd for life to bring it into a capacity to spread; which having with great pains accomplished, she serv'd in a dish of Pork and Cabage, I suppose the remains of Dinner. The sause was of a deep Purple, which I thought was boil'd in her dye Kettle; the bread was Indian, and every thing on the Table service Agreeable to these. I, being hungry, gott a little down; but my stomach was soon cloy'd, and what cabbage I swallowed serv'd me for a Cudd the whole day after.

Having here discharged the Ordnary[n] for self and Guide, (as I understood was the custom,) About three, afternoon, went on with my Third Guide, who Rode very hard; and having crossed Providence Ferry, we come to a River which they generally Ride thro'. But I dare not venture; so the Post got a Ladd and Cannoo to carry me to tother side, and hee rid thro' and Led my hors. The Cannoo was very small and shallow, so that when we were in she seem'd redy to take in water, which greatly terrified mee, and caused me to be very circumspect, sitting with my hands fast on each side, my eyes stedy, not daring so much as to lodg

Lento: lean-to. **discharged the Ordnary:** paid the bill at the tavern.

103

my tongue a hair's breadth more on one side of my mouth than tother, nor so much as think on Lott's wife, for a wry thought would have oversett our wherey: But was soon put out of this pain, by feeling the Cannoo on shore, which I as soon almost saluted with me feet; and Rewarding my sculler, again mounted and made the best of our way forwards. The Rode here was very even and the day pleasant, it being now near Sunsett. But the Post told mee we had neer 14 miles to Ride 10 to the next Stage, (where we were to Lodg). I askt him of the rest of the Rode, foreseeing wee must travail in the night. Hee told mee there was a bad River we were to Ride thro', which was so very firce a hors could sometimes hardly stem it: But it was but narrow, and wee should soon be over. I cannot express the concern of mind this relation sett me in: no thoughts but those of the dang'ros River could entertain my Imagination, and they were as formidable as varios, still Torment- 20 ing me with blackest Ideas of my Approching fate—Sometimes seing my self drowning, other-whiles drowned, and at the best like a holy Sister just come out of a Spiritual Bath in dripping Garments.

Now was the Glorious Luminary, with his swift Coursers arrived at his Stage, leaving poor me with the rest of this part of the lower world in darkness, with which we were soon Surrounded. The only Glimering we now had was from the spangled 30 Skies, Whose Imperfect Reflections rendered very Object formidable. Each lifeless Trunk, with its shatter'd Limbs, appear'd an Armed Enymie; and every little stump like a Ravenous devourer. Nor could I so much as discern my Guide, when at any distance, which added to the terror.

Thus, absolutely lost in Thought, and dying with the very thoughts of drowning, I come up with the Post, who I did not see till even with his Hors: he told mee he stopt for mee; and wee 40 Rode on very deliberatly a few paces, when we entred a Thickett of Trees and Shrubbs, and I perceived by the Hors's going, we were on the descent of a Hill, which, as wee come neerer the bottom, 'twas totaly dark with the Trees that surrounded it. But I knew by the Going of the Hors wee had entred the water, which my Guide told mee was the hazzardos River he had told me off;

and hee, Riding up close to my Side, Bid me not fear—we should be over Imediatly. I now ralyed all the Courage I was mistriss of, knowing that I must either Venture my fate of drowning, or be left like the Children in the wood. So, as the Post bid me, I gave Reins to my Nagg; and sitting as Stedy as Just before in the Cannoo, in a few min-utes got safe to the other side, which hee told mee was the Narragansett country. . . .

Being come to Mr. Havens', I was very civilly Received, and courteously entertained, in a clean comfortable House; and the Good woman was very active in helping off my Riding clothes, and then ask't what I would eat. I told her I had some Chocolett, if shee would prepare it; which with the help of some Milk, and a little clean brass Kettle, she soon effected to my satisfaction. I then betook me to my Apartment, which was a little Room parted from the Kitchen by a single 20 bord partition; where, after I had noted the Oc-currances of the past day, I went to bed, which, tho' pretty hard, Yet neet and handsome. But I could get no sleep, because of the Clamor of some of the Town tope-ers in next Room, Who were entred into a strong debate concerning the Sig-nifycation of the name of their Country, (viz.) Narraganset. One said it was named so by the Indians, because there grew a Brier there, of a prodigious Highth and bigness, the like hardly 30 ever known, called by the Indians Narragansett; and quotes an Indian of so barberous a name for his Author, that I could not write it. His Antag-onist replyed no—It was from a Spring it had its name, which hee well knew where it was, which was extreem cold in summer, and as Hott as could be imagined in the winter, which was much re-sorted too by the natives, and by them called Narragansett, (Hott and Cold,) and that was the originall of their places name—with a thousand 40 Impertinances not worth notice, which He utter'd with such a Roreing voice and Thundering blows with the fist of wickedness on the Table, that it peirced my very head. I heartily fretted, and wish't 'um tongue-tyed; but with as little success as a friend of mine once, who was (as shee said) kept a whole night awake, on a Jorny, by a coun-try Left.[n] and a Sergent, Insigne[n] and a Deacon,

Left.: lieutenant. **Insigne:** ensign.

contriving how to bring a triangle into a Square. They kept calling for tother Gill, which they were swallowing, was some Intermission; But presently, like Oyle to fire, encreased the flame. I set my Candle on a Chest by the bedside, and setting up, fell to my old way of composing my Resentments, in the following manner:

I ask thy Aid, O Potent Rum!
To Charm these wrangling Topers Dum.
Thou hast their Giddy Brains possest—
The man confounded with the Beast—
And I, poor I, can get no rest.
Intoxicate them with thy fumes:
O still their Tongues till morning comes!

And I know not but my wishes took effect; for the dispute soon ended with 'tother Dram; and so Good night!

Saturday, Oct. 7th, we sett out early in the Morning, and being something unacquainted with the way, having ask't it of some wee mett, they told us wee must Ride a mile or two, and turne down a Lane on the Right hand; and by their Direction wee Rode on but not Yet comeing to the turning, we mett a Young fellow and ask't him how farr it was to the Lane which turn'd down towards Guilford. He said wee must Ride a little further, and turn down by the Corner of uncle Sams Lott. My Guide vented his Spleen at the Lubber; and we soon after came into the Rhode, and keeping still on, without any thing further Remarkabell, about two aclock afternoon we arrived at New Haven, where I was received with all Possible Respects and civility. . . .

They are Govern'd by the same Laws as wee in Boston, (or little differing,) thr'out this whole Colony of Connecticot, and much the same way of Church Government, and many of them good, Sociable people, and I hope Religious too: but a little too much Independant in their principalls, and, as I have been told, were formerly in their Zeal very Riggid in their Administrations towards such as their Lawes made Offenders, even to a harmless Kiss[n] or Innocent merriment among

10

20

30

40

Young People. Whipping being a frequent and counted an easy Punishment, about which as other Crimes, the Judges were absolute in their Sentences. They told mee a pleasant story about a pair of Justices in those parts, which I may not omit the relation of.

A negro Slave belonging to man in the Town, stole a hogs head from his master, and gave or sold it to an Indian, native of the place. The Indian sold it in the neighbourhood, and so the theft was found out. Thereupon the Heathen was Seized, and carried to the Justices House to be Examined. But his worship (it seems) was gone into the feild, with a Brother in office, to gather in his Pompions.[n] Whither the malefactor is hurried, And Complaint made, and satisfaction in the name of Justice demanded. Their Worships cann't proceed in form without a Bench: whereupon they Order one to be Imediately erected, which, for want of fitter materials, they made with pompions —which being finished, down setts their Worships, and the Malefactor call'd, and by the Senior Justice interrogated after the following manner: "You Indian, why did You steal from this man? You sho'dn't do so—it's a Grandy wicked thing to steal."

"Hol't, hol't," cryes the Justice Junior, "Brother, You speak negro to him. I'le ask him. You, sirrah, why did You steal this man's Hoggshead?"

"Hoggshead?" replys the Indian, "me no stomany."[n]

"No?" says his Worship; and, pulling off his hatt, patted his own head with his hand, says, "Tatapa—you; Tatapa—you; all one this. Hoggshead all one this."

"Hah!" says Netop, "now me stomany that." Whereupon the Company fell into a great Fitt of Laughter, even to Roreing. Silence is commanded, but to no effect: for they continued perfectly Shouting.

"Nay," says his worship, in an angry tone, "if it be so, *take mee off the Bench.*"

Their Diversions in this part of the Country are on Lecture days and Training days[n] mostly: on the former there is Riding from town to town.

Kiss: Madam Knight's father, Thomas Kemble, was said to have been put in the stocks as a punishment for kissing his wife on the Sabbath, after an absence of three years.

Pompions: pumpkins. **stomany:** understand. **Lecture days and Training days:** days set aside for religious lectures and for military drill.

105

And on training dayes the Youth divert themselves by Shooting at the Target, as they call it, (but it very much resembles a pillory,) where hee that hitts neerest the white has some yards of Red Ribbin presented him which being tied to his hattband, the two ends streeming down his back, he is Led away in Triumph, with great applause, as the winners of the Olympiack Games. They generally marry very young: the males oftener as I am told under twentie than above; they generally make public wedings, and have a way something singular (as they say) in some of them, *viz.* Just before Joyning hands, the Bridegroom quitts the place, who is soon followed by the Bridesmen, and as it were, dragg'd back to duty—being the reverse to the former practice among us, to steal the Bride.

There are great plenty of Oysters all along by the sea side, as farr as I Rode in the Collony, and those very good. And they Generally lived very well and comfortably in their famelies. But too Indulgent (especially the farmers) to their slaves: suffering too great familiarity from them, permitting them to sit at Table and eat with them, (as they say to save time,) and into the dish goes the black hoof as freely as the white hand. They told me that there was a farmer lived nere the Town where I lodgd who had some difference with his slave, concerning something the master had promised him and did not punctualy perform; which caused some hard words between them; but at length they put the matter to Arbitration and Bound themselves to stand to the award of such as they named—which done, the Arbitrators Having heard the Allegations of both parties, Order the master to pay 40^s to black face, and acknowledge his fault. And so the matter ended: the poor master very honestly standing to the award.

There are every where in the Towns as I passed, a Number of Indians the Natives of the Country, and are the most salvage of all the salvages of that kind that I had ever Seen: little or no care taken (as I heard upon enquiry) to make them otherwise. They have in some places Landes of their owne, and Govern'd by Law's of their own making;—they marry many wives and at pleasure put them away, and on the least dislike or fickle humour, on either side, saying *stand away* to one another is a sufficient Divorce. And indeed those uncomely *Stand aways*

are too much in Vougue among the English in this (Indulgent Colony) as their Records plentifully prove, and that on very trivial matters, of which some have been told me, but are not proper to be Related by a Female pen, tho some of that foolish sex have had too large a share in the story.

If the natives committ any crime on their own precincts among themselves, the English takes no Cognezens of. But if on the English ground, they are punishable by our Laws. They mourn for their Dead by blacking their faces, and cutting their hair, after an Awkerd and frightfull manner; But can't bear You should mention the names of their dead Relations to them: they trade most for Rum, for which they^d hazzard their very lives; and the English fit them Generally as well, by seasoning it plentifully with water.

They give the title of merchant to every trader; who Rate their Goods according to the time and spetia they pay in: viz. pay, mony, Pay as mony, and trusting. Pay is Grain, Pork, Beef, &c. at the prices sett by the General Court that Year; mony is pieces of Eight, Ryalls,^{n} or Boston or Bay shillings (as they call them,) or Good hard money, as sometimes silver coin is termed by them; also Wampom, vizt. Indian beads which serves for change. Pay as mony is provisions, as aforesaid one Third cheaper then as the Assembly or General Court sets it; and Trust as they and the merchant agree for time.

Now, when the buyer comes to ask for a commodity, sometimes before the merchant answers that he has it, he sais, "Is Your pay redy?" Perhaps the Chap reply's "Yes." "What do you pay in?" say's the merchant. The buyer having answered, then the price is set; as suppose he wants a sixpenny knife, in pay it is 12d—in pay as money eight pence, and hard money its own price, viz. 6d. It seems a very Intricate way of trade and what *Lex Mercatoria*^{n} had not thought of.

Being at a merchants house, in comes a tall country fellow, with his alfogeos^n full of Tobacco; for they seldom Loose their Cudd, but keep Chewing and Spitting as long as they'r eyes are open,—he advanc't to the middle of the Room, makes an Awkward Nodd, and spitting a Large deal of Aromatick

Ryalls: Spanish reals. **Lex Mercatoria:** the usual practice of merchants. **alfogeos:** cheeks.

Evident by some slaves in New England

Tincture, he gave a scrape with his shovel-like shoo, leaving a small shovel full of dirt on the floor, made a full stop, Hugging his own pretty Body with his hands under his arms, Stood staring rown'd him, like a Catt let out of a Baskett. At last, like the creature Balaam Rode on, he opened his mouth and said: "Have You any Ribinen for Hatbands to sell I pray?" The Questions and Answers about the pay being past, the Ribin is bro't and opened. Bumpkin Simpers cryes, "Its confounded Gay, I vow;" and beckning to the door, in comes Jone Tawdry, dropping about 50 curtsees, and stands by him: hee shows her the Ribin.

"Law You," sais shee, "its right Gent: do You take it, tis dreadfull pretty." Then she enquires, "Have You any hood silk, I pray?" which being brought and bought, "Have You any thred silk to sew it with?" says shee, which being accomodated with they Departed. They Generaly stand after they come in a great while speachless, and some-times dont say a word till they are askt what they want, which I impute to the Awe they stand in of the merchants, who they are constantly almost In-debted too; and must take what they bring with-out Liberty to choose for themselves; but they serve them as well, making the merchants stay long enough for their pay.

We may Observe here the great necessity and bennifitt both of Education and Conversation; for these people have as Large a portion of mother witt, and sometimes a Larger, than those who have bin brought up in Citties; but for want of em-provements, Render themselves almost Ridiculos, as above. I should be glad if they would leave such follies, and am sure all that Love Clean Houses (at least) would be glad on't too. . . .

Decr. 6th. . . . The Cittie of New York is a pleasant, well compacted place, situated on a Com-modius River which is a fine harbour for shipping. The Buildings Brick Generaly, very stately and high, though not altogether like ours in Boston. The Bricks in some of the Houses are of divers Coullers and laid in Checkers, being glazed look very agreeable. The inside of them are neat to admiration, the wooden work, for only the walls are plasterd, and the Sumers and Gist[n] are plained and kept very white scowr'd as so is all the parti-

tions if made of Bords. The fire places have no Jambs (as ours have) But the Backs run flush with the walls, and the Hearth is of Tyles and is as farr out into the Room at the Ends as before the fire, which is Generally Five foot in the Low'r rooms, and the peice over which the mantle tree should be is made as ours with Joyners work, and as I sup-pose is fasten'd to iron rodds inside. The House where the Vendue[n] was, had Chimney Corners like ours, and they and the hearths were laid with the finest tile that I ever see, and the stair cases laid all with white tile which is ever clean, and so are the walls of the Kitchen which had a Brick floor. They were making Great preparations to Receive their Govenor, Lord Cornbury from the Jerseys, and for that End raised the militia to Gard him on shore to the fort.

They are Generaly of the Church of England and have a New England Gentleman for their minister, and a very fine church set out with all Customary requisites. There are also a Dutch and Divers Conventicles as they call them, viz. Baptist, Quakers, &c. They are not strict in keep-ing the Sabbath as in Boston and other places where I had bin, But seem to deal with great exactness as farr as I see or Deall with. They are sociable to one another and Curteos and Civill to strangers and fare well in their houses. The English go very fasheonable in their dress. But the Dutch, es-pecially the middling sort, differ from our women, in their habitt go loose, were French muches[n] which are like a Capp and a head band in one, leaving their ears bare, which are sett out with Jewells of a large size and many in number. And their fingers hoop't with Rings, some with large stones in them of many Coullers as were their pendants in their ears, which You see very old women wear as well as Young.

They have Vendues very frequently and make their Earnings very well by them, for they treat with good Liquor Liberally, and Generally pay for't as well, by paying for that which they Bidd up Briskly for, after the sack has gone plentifully about, tho' sometimes good penny worths are got there. Their Diversions in the Winter is Riding Sleys about three or four Miles out of Town, where

Sumers and Gist: beams and joists.

Vendue: auction sale. **were French muches:** wear French caps.

107

they have Houses of entertainment at a place called the Bowery, and some go to friends Houses who handsomely treat them. Mr. Burroughs cary'd his spouse and Daughter and myself out to one Madame Dowes, a Gentlewoman that lived at a farm House, who gave us a handsome Entertainment of five or six Dishes and choice Beer and metheglin,[n] Cyder, &c. all which she said was the produce of her farm. I believe we mett 50 or 60 slays that day—they fly with great swiftness and some are so furious that they'le turn out of the path for none except a Loaden Cart. Nor do they spare for any diversion the place affords, and sociable to a degree, they'r Tables being as free to their Naybours as to themselves. . . I left New-York with no Little regrett. . . .

WILLIAM BYRD (1674–1744)

THE MONUMENT over Byrd's grave in the garden at Westover, his James River estate, describes this accomplished Virginia gentleman as a well-bred and polite companion who possessed a great elegance of taste and life. These qualities befit the most distinguished representative of the Virginia aristocracy, who was equally at home in the Raleigh Tavern in colonial Williamsburg and in the drawing rooms of Queen Anne's London. When his finished works—carefully preserved by his family as the *Westover Manuscripts*— were published in 1841, they proved that the first half of the eighteenth century in America, for all its deficiency in imaginative literature, did produce writing of graceful charm and amused tolerance. While he is remembered as a writer, Byrd never regarded himself as one; he published no work during a lifetime devoted to managing his property and living the life of a gentleman. Though the cultivation of the amenities was more difficult at Westover than in London, Byrd seems to have moved with urbanity as a princely figure among the planters and politicians of his native colony.

William Byrd was born, March 28, 1674, on the ample estate which his father, William Byrd I, had inherited from an uncle, Captain Stagg. There his father built Westover and began the collection of books later to become, through discriminating additions by the son, the best private library in the colonies. Byrd brought to the service of Virginia a legal education at the Middle Temple in London, and business training in Holland. Two of his five sojourns in England were for extended periods, 1697–1705 and 1715–1726, during which he became a cherished friend of Charles Boyle, Earl of Orrery, and enjoyed the companionship of Wycherley, Congreve, and Rowe. From these associations and his ardent admiration of the social and literary traditions of Augustan London, Byrd probably derived his Cavalier concept of literature as the exercise of leisure hours for the enjoyment of an intimate circle of friends.

As the heir to a large estate, Byrd was elected to the House of Burgesses in 1692, acted as agent of the Virginia Assembly in London, became receiver general of his Majesty's revenue in 1706, and from 1709 until his death in 1744 was an influential member of the King's Council. Despite his long residence in England and his friendship with nobility, Byrd had scant sympathy with autocratic exercise of authority. In the clash between Governor Spotswood and the planters, Byrd espoused the colonists' cause, and his exertions were at least partially responsible for the governor's removal and the restoration of constitutional government in Virginia. In 1743 Byrd's concern for the welfare of Virginia was recognized by his election as President of the Council.

Byrd's writings, sagacious, witty and satiric, were the result of his practical interests and his inveterate habit of keeping a journal. The basis of *The History of the Dividing Line* was a rough diary of thirty-two pages recounting his vivid impressions of the expedition by the boundary commission that ran the line between Virginia and North Carolina in 1728. A visit of inspection to some Virginia iron mines in 1732 was described in another journal entitled *A Progress to the Mines*, and a year later, in 1733, he capitalized his experiences during a trip to a tract of 20,000 acres in North Carolina in a witty and readable account, *A Journey to the Land of Eden*. In the twentieth century Byrd's "secret diary," originally kept in code, was discovered and edited. This highly interesting document offers a detailed and intimate account of his everyday life at home and abroad for three periods: 1709–1712, 1717–1721, and 1739–1741. Confident that his notations would be read by no eyes except his own, Byrd wrote without self-consciousness of his domestic infelicities, his amours, and his recreations in Williamsburg and London, in a way which reminds the reader that the diarist was a contemporary of Henry

metheglin: mead, a drink made with honey.

108

Fielding's Tom Jones. Byrd's diaries illuminate southern colonial life with an amplitude of revealing detail comparable to that contained in the personal records of Winthrop and Sewall in New England.

BIBLIOGRAPHY · *The Writings of Colonel William Byrd of Westover in Virginia*, edited by J. S. Bassett, is the standard but incomplete edition of Byrd's works. It should be supplemented by the text of the "Secret history of the Line" printed in W. K. Boyd's *William Byrd's Histories of the Dividing Line betwixt Virginia and North Carolina* (1929), and by the secret diaries, letters, and fugitive pieces published in L. B. Wright and M. Tinling, *The Secret Diary of William Byrd of Westover: 1709–1712* (1941) and M. H. Woodfin and M. Tinling, *Another Secret Diary of William Byrd of Westover: 1739–1741* (1942). *A Journey to the Land of Eden and Other Papers* was edited by M. Van Doren in 1928. Certain of Byrd's letters, *Letters Writ to Facetia by Varamour, 1703*, were privately printed in a limited edition in 1913. The first full-length biography is that of R. C. Beatty, *William Byrd of Westover* (1932). Valuable information is contained also in "Letters of William Byrd 2nd," *Virginia Magazine of History and Biography*, IX (October, 1901), and X (January, 1902); G. R. Lyle, "William Byrd, Book Collector," *American Book Collector*, V (1934), 163–165; J. R. Masterson, "William Byrd in Lubberland," *American Literature*, IX (1937), 153–170; M. H. Woodfin, "William Byrd and the Royal Society," *Virginia Magazine of History and Biography*, XL (1932), 23–34; and L. B. Wright, "A Shorthand Diary of William Byrd of Westover," *Huntington Library Quarterly*, II (1939), 489–496.

The History of the Dividing Line

The History of the Dividing Line is based upon a diary kept by Byrd in 1728 when he was one of the Virginia Commissioners charged with determining the boundary between Virginia and North Carolina. Though the diary itself was probably written for the practical purpose of inducing the Lords of Trade to provide adequate funds for the expenses of the expedition, the account was expanded and embellished for the amusement of the author and his friends. Byrd refused to allow the manuscript to be read until he had worked over his material to his own satisfaction: "The bashful bears hide their cubs until they have licked them into shape, nor am I too proud to follow the example of these modest animals." *The History* was not published in his lifetime, but the carefully written folio, bound in parchment, formed a part of the Westover Manuscripts which were preserved by the Byrd family and finally published in 1841.

The text is that of the Richmond, Virginia, Edition (1866). Excess contractions have been eliminated.

[Sketches of North Carolina and the Dismal Swamp]

[March] *10th* [1728]. The Sabbath happened very opportunely to give some ease to our jaded People, who rested religiously from every work, but that of cooking the Kettle. We observed very few corn-fields in our Walks, and those very small, which seemed the Stranger to us, because we could see no other Tokens of Husbandry or Improvement. But, upon further Inquiry, we were given to understand People only made Corn for themselves and not for their Stocks, which know very well how to get their own Living.

Both Cattle and Hogs ramble into the Neighbouring Marshes and Swamps, where they maintain themselves the whole Winter long, and are not fetched home till the Spring. Thus these Indolent Wretches, during one half of the Year, lose the Advantage of the Milk of their cattle, as well as their Dung, and many of the poor Creatures perish in the Mire, into the Bargain, by this ill Management.

Some, who pique themselves more upon Industry than their Neighbours, will, now and then, in compliment to their Cattle, cut down a Tree whose Limbs are loaden with the moss aforementioned. The trouble would be too great to Climb the Tree in order to gather this Provender, but the Shortest way (which in this Country is always counted the best) is to fell it, just like the lazy Indians, who do the same by such Trees as bear fruit, and so make one Harvest for all. By this bad Husbandry Milk is so Scarce, in the Winter Season, that were a Big-bellied woman to long for it, She would lose her Longing. And, in truth, I believe this is often the Case, and at the same time a very good reason why so many People in this Province are marked with a Custard Complexion. . . .

11. We ordered the Surveyors early to their Business, who were blessed with pretty dry Grounds for three Miles together. But they paid dear for it in the next two, consisting of one continued frightful Pocoson, which no Creatures but those of the amphibious kind ever had ventured into before.

This filthy Quagmire did in earnest put the Men's Courage to a Tryal, and though I cannot say it made them lose their Patience, yet they lost their Humour for Joking. They kept their Gravity like so many Spaniards, so that a Man might then have taken his Opportunity to plunge up to the Chin, without Danger of being laughed at. However, this unusual composure of countenance could not fairly be called complaining.

Their Day's-Work ended at the Mouth of Northern's Creek, which empties itself into Northwest River; though we chose to Quarter a little higher up the River, near Mossy Point. This we did for the Convenience of an Old house to Shelter our Persons and Baggage from the rain, which threated us hard. . . .

12. . . . we crossed the River before Noon, and advanced our Line three Miles. It was not possible to make more of it, by reason good Part of the way was either Marsh or Pocoson. The Line cut two or three Plantations, leaving Part of them in Virginia and part of them in Carolina. This was a Case that happened frequently, to the great Inconvenience of the Owners, who were therefore obliged to take out two Patents and Pay for a new Survey in each Government.

In the Evening we took up our Quarters in Mr. Ballance's Pasture, a little above the Bridge built over Northwest River. There we discharged the two Periaugas, which in truth had been very Serviceable in transporting us over the Many Waters in that Dirty and Difficult Part of our Business.

Our landlord had a tolerable good House and Clean Furniture, and yet we could not be tempted to lodge in it. We chose rather to lye in the open Field, for fear of growing too tender. A clear Sky, spangled with Stars, was our Canopy, which being the last thing we saw before we fell asleep, gave us Magnificent Dreams. The Truth of it is, we took so much pleasure in that natural kind of Lodging, that I think at the foot of the Account Mankind are great Losers by the Luxury of Feather-Beds and warm apartments.

The curiosity of beholding so new and withal so Sweet a Method of Encamping, brought one of the Senators of North Carolina to make us a Midnight Visit. But he was so very Clamorous in his Commendations of it, that the Centinel, not seeing his Quality, either through his habit or Behaviour, had like to have treated him roughly.

After excusing the Unseasonableness of his Visit, and letting us know he was a Parliament Man, he swore he was so taken with our Lodging, that he would set Fire to his House as soon as he got Home, and teach his Wife and Children to lie, like us, in the open field.

13. . . . Tis hardly credible how little the Bordering inhabitants were acquainted with this mighty Swamp, notwithstanding they had lived their whole lives within Smell of it. Yet, as great Strangers as they were to it, they pretended to be very exact in their Account of its Dimensions, and were positive it could not be above 7 or 8 Miles wide, but knew no more of the Matter than Stargazers know of the Distance of the Fixt Stars. At the Same time, they were Simple enough to amuse our Men with Idle Stories of the Lyons, Panthers and Alligators, they were like to encounter in that dreadful Place.

In short, we saw plainly there was no Intelligence of this Terra Incognita to be got, but from our own Experience. For that Reason it was resolved to make the requisite Dispositions to enter it next Morning. We allotted every one of the Surveyors for this painful Enterprise, with 12 Men to attend them. Fewer than that could not be employed in clearing the way, carrying the Chain, marking the Trees, and bearing the necessary Bedding and Provisions. Nor would the Commissioners themselves have Spared their Persons on this Occasion, but for fear of adding to the poor men's Burthen, while they were certain they could add nothing to their Resolution.

We quartered with our Friend and Fellow Traveller, William Wilkins, who had been our faithful Pilot to Coratuck, and lived about a mile from the Place where the Line ended. Every thing looked so very clean, and the Furniture so neat, that we were tempted to Lodge within Doors. But the Novelty of being shut up so close quite spoiled our rest, nor did we breathe so free by abundance, as when we lay in the open Air.

14. Before nine of the Clock this Morning, the Provisions, Bedding and other Necessaries, were made up into Packs for the Men to carry on their

Shoulders into the Dismal. They were victualled for 8 days at full Allowance, Nobody doubting but that would be abundantly Sufficient to carry them thro' that Inhospitable Place; nor Indeed was it possible for the Poor Fellows to Stagger under more. As it was, their Loads weighed from 60 to 70 Pounds, in just Proportion to the Strength of those who were to bear them.

Twould have been unconscionable to have Saddled them with Burthens heavier than that, when they were to lugg them thro' a filthy Bogg, which was hardly practicable with no Burthen at all. . . .

Altho' there was no need of Example to inflame Persons already so cheerful, yet to enter the People with better grace, the Author and two more of the Commissioners accompanied them half a Mile into the Dismal. The Skirts of it were thinly Planted with Dwarf Reeds and Gall-Bushes, but when we got into the Dismal itself, we found the Reeds grew there much taller and closer, and, to mend the matter was so interlaced with bamboe-briars, that there was no scuffling thro' them without the help of Pioneers. At the same time, we found the Ground moist and trembling under our feet like a Quagmire, insomuch that it was an easy Matter to run a Ten-Foot-Pole up to the Head in it, without exerting any uncommon Strength to do it.

Two of the Men, whose Burthens were the least cumbersome, had orders to march before, with their Tomahawks, and clear the way, in order to make an Opening for the Surveyors. By their Assistance we made a Shift to push the Line half a Mile in 3 Hours, and then reached a small piece of firm Land, about 100 Yards wide, Standing up above the rest like an Island. Here the people were glad to lay down their Loads and take a little refreshment, while the happy man, whose lot it was to carry the Jugg of Rum, began already, like Aesop's Bread-Carriers, to find it grow a good deal lighter.

After reposing about an Hour, the Commissioners recommended Vigour and Constancy to their Fellow-Travellers, by whom they were answered with 3 Cheerful Huzzas, in Token of Obedience. This Ceremony was no sooner over but they took up their Burthens and attended the Motion of the Surveyors, who, tho' they worked with all their might, could reach but one Mile farther, the same obstacles still attending them which they had met with in the Morning.

However small this distance may seem to such as are used to travel at their Ease, yet our Poor Men, who were obliged to work with an unwieldy Load at their Backs, had reason to think it a long way; Especially in a Bogg where they had no firm Footing, but every Step made a deep Impression, which was instantly filled with Water. At the same time they were labouring with their Hands to cut down the Reeds, which were Ten-feet high, their Legs were hampered with the Bryars. Besides, the Weather happened to be warm, and the tallness of the Reeds kept off every Friendly Breeze from coming to refresh them. And, indeed, it was a little provoking to hear the Wind whistling among the Branches of the White Cedars, which grew here and there amongst the Reeds, and at the same time not have the Comfort to feel the least Breath of it. . . .

15. The Surveyors pursued their work with all Diligence, but Still found the Soil of the Dismal so Spongy that the Water ouzed up into every footstep they took. To their Sorrow, too, they found the Reeds and Bryars more firmly interwoven than they did the day before. But the greatest Grievance was from large Cypresses, which the Wind had blown down and heaped upon one another. On the Limbs of most of them grew Sharp Snags, Pointing every way like so many Pikes, that required much Pains and Caution to avoid.

These Trees being Evergreens, and Shooting their Large Tops Very high, are easily overset by every Gust of Wind, because there is no firm Earth to Steddy their Roots. Thus many of them were laid prostrate to the great Encumbrance of the way. Such Variety of Difficulties made the Business go on heavily, insomuch that, from Morning till Night, the Line could advance no further than 1 Mile and 31 Poles. Never was Rum, that cordial of Life, found more necessary than it was in this Dirty Place. It did not only recruit the People's Spirits, now almost Jaded with Fatigue, but served to correct the Badness of the Water, and at the same time to resist the Malignity of the Air.

Whenever the Men wanted to drink, which was very often, they had nothing more to do but to make a Hole, and the Water bubbled up in a Moment. But it was far from being either clear or well tasted, and had besides a Physical Effect, from the Tincture it received from the Roots of the Shrubbs and Trees that grew in the Neighbourhood. . . .

16. The Line was this day carried one Mile and a half and sixteen Poles. The Soil continued soft 10 and Miry, but fuller of Trees, especially White cedars. Many of these too were thrown down and piled in Heaps, high enough for a good Muscovite Fortification. The worst of it was, the Poor Fellows began now to be troubled with Fluxes, occasioned by bad Water and moist Lodging: but chewing of Rhubarb kept that Malady within Bounds. . . . .

17. . . . Since the Surveyors had entered the Dismal, they had laid Eyes on no living Creature: 20 neither Bird nor Beast, Insect nor Reptile came in View. Doubtless, the Eternal Shade that broods over this mighty Bog, and hinders the sunbeams from blessing the Ground, makes it an uncomfortable Habitation for any thing that has life. Not so much as a Zealand Frog could endure so Aguish a Situation.

It had one Beauty, however, that delighted the Eye, though at the Expense of all the other Senses: the Moisture of the Soil preserves a con- 30 tinual Verdure, and makes every Plant an Evergreen, but at the same time the foul Damps ascend without ceasing, corrupt the Air, and render it unfit for Respiration. Not even a Turkey-Buzzard will venture to fly over it, no more than the Italian Vultures will over the filthy Lake Avernus, or the Birds in the Holy-Land, over the Salt Sea, where Sodom and Gomorrah formerly stood.

In these sad Circumstances, the kindest thing we could do for our Suffering Friends was to give 40 them a place in the Litany. Our Chaplain, for his Part, did his Office, and rubbed us up with a Seasonable Sermon. This was quite a new thing to our Brethren of North Carolina, who live in a climate where no clergyman can Breathe, any more than Spiders in Ireland. . . .

19. . . . We Ordered Several Men to Patrol on the Edge of the Dismal, both towards the North and towards the South, and to fire Guns at proper Distances. This they performed very punctually, but could hear nothing in return, nor gain any Sort of Intelligence. In the meantime whole Flocks of Women and Children flew hither to Stare at us, with as much curiosity as if we had lately Landed from Bantam or Morocco.

Some Borderers, too, had a great Mind to know where the Line would come out, being for the most part Apprehensive lest their Lands Should be taken into Virginia. In that case they must have submitted to some Sort of Order and Government; whereas, in North Carolina, every One does what seems best in his own Eyes. There were some good Women that brought their children to be Baptized, but brought no Capons along with them to make the Solemnity cheerful. In the meantime it was Strange that none came to be married in such a Multitude, if it had only been for the Novelty of having their Hands Joyned by one in Holy Orders. Yet so it was, that though our chaplain Christened above an Hundred, he did not marry so much as one Couple during the whole Expedition. But marriage is reckoned a Lay contract in Carolina, as I said before, and a Country Justice can tie the fatal Knot there, as fast as an Archbishop.

None of our Visitors could, however, tell us any News of the Surveyors, nor Indeed was it possible any of them should at that time, They being still laboring in the Midst of the Dismal. It seems they were able to carry the Line this Day no further than one mile and sixty-one Poles, and that whole distance was through a Miry cedar Bogg, where the ground trembled under their Feet most frightfully. In many places too their Passage was retarded by a great number of fallen Trees, that lay Horsing upon one Another.

Though many circumstances concurred to make this an unwholesome Situation, yet the Poor men had no time to be sick, nor can one conceive a more Calamitous Case than it would have been to be laid up in that uncomfortable Quagmire. Never were Patients more tractable, or willing to take Physic, than these honest Fellows; but it was from a Dread of laying their Bones in a Bogg that would soon spew them up again. That Consideration also put them upon more caution about their Lodging. They first covered the Ground with Square Pieces of Cypress bark, which now, in the Spring, they could easily Slip off the Tree for that purpose. On this they Spread their Bedding; but unhappily the Weight and Warmth of their Bodies made the Water rise up betwixt the Joints of the Bark, to their great Inconvenience. Thus they lay not only moist, but also exceedingly cold, because their Fires were continually going out. For no sooner was the Trash upon the Surface burnt away, but immediately the Fire was extinguished by the Moisture of the Soil, Insomuch that it was great part of the Centinel's business to rekindle it again in a Fresh Place, every Quarter of an Hour. Nor could they indeed do their duty better, because Cold was the only Enemy they had to Guard against in a miserable Morass, where nothing can inhabit. . . .

25. Surely there is no place in the World where the Inhabitants live with less Labour than in North Carolina. It approaches nearer to the Description of Lubberland than any other, by the great felicity of the Climate, the easiness of raising Provisions, and the Slothfulness of the People.

Indian Corn is of so great increase, that a little Pains will Subsist a very large Family with bread, and then they may have meat without any pains at all, by the Help of the Low Grounds, and the great Variety of Mast that grows on the Highland. The Men, for their Parts, just like the Indians, impose all the Work upon the poor Women. They make their Wives rise out of their Beds early in the Morning, at the same time that they lye and Snore, till the Sun has run one third of his course, and dispersed all the unwholesome Damps. Then, after Stretching and Yawning for half an Hour, they light their Pipes, and, under the Protection of a cloud of Smoak, venture out into the open Air; tho', if it happens to be never so little cold, they quickly return Shivering into the Chimney corner. When the Weather is mild, they stand leaning with both their arms upon the corn-field fence, and gravely consider whether they had best go and take a Small Heat at the Hough: but generally find reasons to put it off till another time. Thus they loiter away their Lives, like Solomon's Sluggard, with their Arms across, and at the Winding up of the Year Scarcely have Bread to Eat.

To speak the Truth, tis a thorough Aversion to Labor that makes People file off to North Carolina, where Plenty and a Warm Sun confirm them in their Disposition to Laziness for their whole Lives.

26. Since we were like to be confined to this place, till the People returned out of the Dismal, twas agreed that our Chaplain might Safely take a turn to Edenton, to preach the Gospel to the Infidels there, and Christen their Children. He was accompanied thither by Mr. Little, One of the Carolina Commissioners, who, to shew his regard for the Church, offered to treat Him on the Road with a Fricassee of Rum. They fry'd half a Dozen Rashers of very fat Bacon in a Pint of Rum, both which being disht up together, served the Company at once both for meat and Drink.

Most of the Rum they get in this Country comes from New England, and is so bad and unwholesome, that it is not improperly called "Kill-Devil." It is distilled there from forreign molosses, which, if Skilfully managed, yields near Gallon for Gallon. Their molosses comes from the same country, and has the name of "Long Sugar" in Carolina, I suppose from the Ropiness of it, and Serves all the purposes of Sugar, both in their Eating and Drinking.

When they entertain their Friends bountifully, they fail not to set before them a Capacious Bowl of Bombo, so called from the Admiral of that name. This is a Compound of Rum and Water in Equal Parts, made palatable with the said long Sugar. As good Humour begins to flow, and the Bowl to Ebb, they take Care to replenish it with Shear Rum, of which there always is a Reserve under the Table. But such Generous doings happen only when that Balsam of life is plenty; for they have often such Melancholy times, that neither Land-graves nor Cassicks can procure one drop for their Wives, when they ly in, or are troubled with the Colick or Vapours. Very few in this Country have the Industry to plant Orchards, which, in a Dearth of Rum, might supply them with much better Liquor.

The Truth is, there is one Inconvenience that easily discourages lazy People from making This improvement: very often, in Autumn, when the Apples begin to ripen, they are visited with

Numerous Flights of paraqueets, that bite all the Fruit to Pieces in a moment, for the sake of the Kernels. The Havock they make is Sometimes so great, that whole Orchards are laid waste in Spite of all the Noises that can be made, or Mawkins that can be dressed up, to fright 'em away. These Ravenous Birds visit North Carolina only during the warm Season, and so soon as the Cold begins to come on, retire back towards the Sun. They rarely Venture so far North as Virginia, except in a very hot Summer, when they visit the most Southern Parts of it. They are very Beautiful; but like some other pretty Creatures, are apt to be loud and mischievous. . . .

27. Most of the Houses in this Part of the Country are Log-houses, covered with Pine or Cypress Shingles, 3 feet long, and one broad. They are hung upon Laths with Peggs, and their doors too turn upon Wooden Hinges, and have wooden Locks to Secure them, so that the Building is finished without Nails or other Iron-Work. They also set up their Pales without any Nails at all, and indeed more Securely than those that are nailed. There are 3 Rails mortised into the Posts, the lowest of which serves as a Sill with a Groove in the Middle, big enough to receive the End of the Pales: the middle Part of the Pale rests against the Inside of the Next Rail, and the Top of it is brought forward to the outside of the uppermost. Such Wreathing of the Pales in and out makes them stand firm, and much harder to unfix than when nailed in the Ordinary way.

Within 3 or 4 Miles of Edenton, the Soil appears to be a little more fertile, tho' it is much cut with Slashes, which seem all to have a tendency towards the Dismal.

This Town is Situate on the North side of Albermarle Sound, which is there about 5 miles over. A Dirty Slash runs all along the Back of it, which in the Summer is a foul annoyance, and furnishes abundance of that Carolina plague, musquetas. There may be 40 or 50 Houses, most of them Small, and built without Expense. A Citizen here is counted Extravagant, if he has Ambition enough to aspire to a Brick-chimney. Justice herself is but indifferently Lodged, the Court-House having much the Air of a Common Tobacco-House. I believe this is the only Metropolis in the Christian or Mahometan World, where there is neither Church, Chappel, Mosque, Synagogue, or any other Place of Publick Worship of any Sect or Religion whatsoever.

What little Devotion there may happen to be is much more private than their vices. The People seem easy without a Minister, as long as they are exempted from paying Him. Sometimes the Society for propagating the Gospel has had the Charity to send over Missionaries to this Country; but unfortunately the Priest has been too Lewd for the people, or, which oftener happens, they too lewd for the Priest. For these Reasons these Reverend Gentlemen have always left their Flocks as arrant Heathen as they found them. Thus much however may be said for the Inhabitants of Edenton, that not a Soul has the least taint of Hypocrisy, or Superstition, acting very Frankly and aboveboard in all their Excesses.

Provisions here are extremely cheap, and extremely good, so that People may live plentifully at a triffleing expense. Nothing is dear but Law, Physick, and Strong Drink, which are all bad in their Kind, and the last they get with so much Difficulty, that they are never guilty of the Sin of Suffering it to Sour upon their Hands. Their Vanity generally lies not so much in having a handsome Dining-Room, as a Handsome House of Office: in this Kind of Structure they are really extravagant.

They are rarely guilty of Flattering or making any Court to their governors, but treat them with all the Excesses of Freedom and Familiarity. They are of Opinion their rulers would be apt to grow insolent, if they grew Rich, and for that reason take care to keep them poorer, and more dependent, if possible, than the Saints in New England used to do their Governors. They have very little coin, so they are forced to carry on their Home-Traffick with Paper-Money. This is the only Cash that will tarry in the Country, and for that reason the Discount goes on increasing between that and real Money, and will do so to the End of the Chapter. . . .

[October] 2d. So Soon as the Horses could be found, we hurried away the Surveyors, who advanced the line nine Miles and two hundred and fifty-four Poles. About three Miles from the Camp they crossed a large Creek, which the Indians

114

called Massamoni, Signifying, in their Language, Paint Creek, because of the great Quantity of Red ochre found in its banks. This in every Fresh tinges the Water just as the same Mineral did formerly, and to this day continues to tinge, the famous River Adonis, in Phoenicia, by which there hangs a celebrated Fable.

Three Miles beyond that we passed another Water with difficulty, called Yapatsco, or Beaver Creek. Those industrious Animals had dammed up the water so high, that we had much ado to get over. Tis hardly credible how much work of this kind they will do in the Space of one Night. They bite young Saplings into proper Lengths with their Fore-teeth, which are exceeding Strong and Sharp, and afterwards drag them to the Place where they intend to Stop the Water. Then they know how to join Timber and Earth together with so much Skill, that their Work is able to resist the most violent Flood that can happen. In this they are qualified to instruct their Betters, it being certain their dams will stand firm when the Strongest that are made by men will be carried down the Stream.

We observed very broad low Grounds upon this Creek, with a growth of large Trees, and all the other Signs of Fertility, but seemed subject to be everywhere overflowed in a fresh.

The certain way to catch these Sagacious Animals is thus: Squeeze all the Juice out of the large Pride of the Beaver, and six Drops out of the small Pride. Powder the inward Bark of Sassafras, and mix it with this Juice, then bait therewith a Steel Trap, and they will eagerly come to it, and be taken.

About three Miles and a half farther we came to the Banks of another creek, called, in the Saponi Language, Ohimpa-moni, Signifying Jumping Creek, from the frequent Jumping of Fish during the Spring Season.

Here we encamped, and by the time the Horses were hobbled, our Hunters brought us no less than a Brace and half of Deer, which made great Plenty, and consequently great content in our Quarters. Some of our People had Shot a great Wild Cat, which was that fatal moment making a comfortable Meal upon a Fox-Squirrel, and an Ambitious Sportsman of our Company claimed the merit of killing this monster after it was dead. The Wild-cat is as big again as any Household-Cat, and much the fiercest Inhabitant of the Woods. Whenever 'tis disabled, it will tear its own Flesh for madness. Although a Panther will run away from a Man, a Wild-cat will only make a Surly Retreat, now and then facing about, if he be too closely pursued; and will even pursue in his turn, if he observe the least Sign of Fear or even of caution in those that pretend to follow Him. The Flesh of this beast, as well as of the Panther, is as white as veal, and altogether as sweet and delicious.

3. We got to work early this Morning, and carried the line eight Miles and a hundred and sixty Poles. We forded Several Runs of Excellent Water, and afterwards traversed a large level of high land full of lofty Walnut, Poplar, and White Oak Trees, which are certain Proofs of a fruitful Soil. This level was near two Miles in length, and of an unknown breadth, quite out of Danger of being overflowed, which is a misfortune most of the Low Grounds are liable to in those Parts. As we marched along we saw many Buffalo-Tracks, and abundance of their Dung very Fresh, but could not have the pleasure of seeing them. They either Smelt us out, having that sense very Quick, or else were alarmed at the Noise that so many People must necessarily make in marching along. At the Sight of a Man they will Snort and Grunt, cock up their ridiculous Short Tails, and tear up the Ground with a Sort of Timorous Fury. These wild Cattle hardly ever range alone, but herd together like those that are tame. They are Seldom seen so far North as forty degrees of latitude, delighting much in canes and Reeds, which grow generally more Southerly.

We quartered on the Banks of a Creek that the Inhabitants call Tewahominy, or Tuskarooda creek, because one of that Nation had been killed thereabouts, and his Body thrown into the creek.

Our people had the Fortune to kill a Brace of does, one of which we presented to the Carolina Gentlemen, who were glad to partake of the Bounty of Providence, at the same time that they sneered at us for depending upon it. . . .

[November] 17. This being Sunday, we were Seasonably put in mind how much we were obliged to be thankfull for our happy return to the Inhabitants. Indeed, we had great reason to reflect with gratitude on the Signal Mercies we had received. First, that we had, day by day, been fed by the Bountifull hand of Providence in the desolate Wilderness, Insomuch that if any of our People wanted one Single Meal during the whole Expedition, it was entirely owing to their own imprudent Management.

Secondly, that not one Man of our whole Company had any Violent Distemper or bad Accident Befall him, from One End of the Line to the other. The very worst that happened was, that One of them gave himself a Smart cut on the Pan of his knee with a Tomahawk, which we had the good Fortune to cure in a Short time, without the help of a Surgeon. As for the Misadventures of Sticking in the Mire and falling into Rivers and Creeks, they were rather Subjects of Mirth than complaint, and served only to diversify our Travels with a little farcicall Variety. And, lastly, that many uncommon Incidents have concurred to prosper our Undertaking. We had not only a dry Spring before we went out, but the preceding Winter, and even a Year or two before, had been much drier than Ordinary. This made

not only the Dismal, but likewise most of the Sunken Grounds near the Sea-Side, just hard enough to bear us, which otherwise had been quite unpassable. And the whole time we were upon the Business, which was in all about Sixteen Weeks, we were never caught in the Rain except once, Nor was our Progress Interrupted by bad Weather above three or four days at most. Besides all this, we were Surprised by no Indian Enemy, but all of us brought our Scalps back Safe upon our Heads. This cruel Method of Scalping of Enemies is practiced by all the Savages in America, and perhaps is not the least proof of their Original from the Northern Inhabitants of Asia. Among the Ancient Scythians it was constantly used, who carried about these hairy Scalps as Trophies of Victory. They served them too as Towels at home, and Trappings for their Horses abroad. But these were not content with the Skin of their Enemies' Heads, but also made use of their Sculls for cups to drink out of upon high Festival days, & made greater Ostentation of them than if they had been made of Gold or the purest crystal. . . .

MATHER BYLES (1707-1788)

A GRANDSON of Increase Mather and a nephew of Cotton Mather, whose great library he inherited; a friend of Benjamin Franklin; a correspondent of Lansdowne, Watts, and Pope; a recipient of an honorary doctorate from Aberdeen; a sonorous and witty pulpit orator; author of two admired volumes of poetry and of a number of occasional poems—these facts explain why Mather Byles was regarded by his contemporaries as a major figure. He is remembered today, however, chiefly as an Augustan wit whose most characteristic work illustrates the influence of neoclassical standards in colonial New England.

Byles probably began writing verse during his college days at Harvard (1721-1725), where he encountered the "divine songs" of Dr. Watts and acquired a taste for Pope. A number of his religious, reflective, and occasional poems were published in the *New England Weekly Journal*, and a selection of his verse may have been issued as early as 1736. His poetry is contained in two extant volumes: *Poems on Several Occasions* (1744) and *Poems by Several Hands* (1745). In 1744 Byles foreswore further poetical endeavor and

bade "adieu to the airy Muse." No other colonial poet had so substantial a body of verse to offer to the public. Byles, however, owed his contemporary reputation to the general lack of good poetry in the second quarter of the eighteenth century rather than to any distinguished accomplishments of his own.

His impressive pulpit manner and his satirical wit kept Boston edified and amused until the Revolution, when his parishioners ousted him from his position as minister of the Hollis Street Congregational Church, in which he had been ordained in 1732. His Tory sympathies were notorious and led for a time to his imprisonment in his own home. Despite his affinities for Episcopalianism, Byles remained a Congregationalist, though his son Mather Byles, Jr., entered the Anglican priesthood. After the cessation of hostilities Byles lived quietly with his two daughters and died in Boston in 1788.

BIBLIOGRAPHY · The only biography is that of A. H. W. Eaton, *The Famous Mather Byles* (1914). See also *Dictionary of American Biography*, III, 381–382, for an excellent biographical sketch by K. B. Murdock. Some biographical details are contained in W. B. Sprague, *Annals of the American Pulpit*, I (1857), 376–382; and E. A. Duyckinck, *Cyclopaedia of American Literature*, I (1855), 116–120. Byles appears in the role of an incorrigible punster in W. Tudor, *Life of James Otis* (1823), and L. M. Child, *The Rebels* (1825). The Facsimile Text Society issued a convenient edition of *Poems on Several Occasions* (1940), with an informative introduction by C. L. Carlson. An account of Byles's library is given in J. H. Tuttle, "The Library of the Mathers," *Proceedings of the American Antiquarian Society* (New Series), XX (1911), 269–356. Byles's four letters to Pope are reproduced in Austin Warren, "To Mr. Pope: Letters from America," *PMLA*, XLVIII (1933), 61–73.

Criticism on Nonsense

BYLES WAS a frequent contributor to Boston periodicals such as the *New England Weekly Journal* and the *American Magazine and Historical Chronicle*. The following satirical essay appeared as the leading article in the latter magazine for January, 1745, from which this text is taken. The contribution, signed "L," was identified as the work of Byles by Lyon N. Richardson in *A History of Early American Magazines, 1741–1789* (1931). The *American Magazine*, in common with many of its contemporaries, was highly eclectic, and original material usually appeared alongside selections from Voltaire, Sterne, Richardson, and extracts from the *Spectator* and the *Grubstreet Journal*.

There have been innumerable Authors, from Aristotle's Rhetorick to Longinus's Treatise of the Sublime, and from thence down to the Compiler of our modern Horn-book, who have written Introductions to the Art of Polite Writing. Every one that can just distinguish his Twenty Four Letters sets up for a Judge of it; as all who are able to flourish a Goose's Quill, pretend to be Masters of that Secret. The noblest Productions have given Birth to many a supercillious Caveller; Criticks of all Sizes and Dimensions have nibled round the divinest Pages; and Ignorance and Conceit have endeavoured to shake down the most beautiful Structures, in order to build themselves a Reputation out of the Ruins. A superiour Genius, though he seems to kindle a wide Horizon of Light about him, and is admired by the understanding Part of Mankind, yet he must expect to be the Occasion of a great many Absurdities, with which the unknowing and envious will strive to satyrize him: As the

Sun scatters Day through a whole Frame of Worlds, but yet may, in some particular Spots, raise a Fog, or hatch a Nest of Vermin. To conclude, the Science of correct Writing having been a Subject exhausted by so many able Hands, and seeing all the Rabble of Scriblers are such indisputable Proficients in it; not to mention my own Incapacity for such an Undertaking; I shall not be so vain as to offer my Thoughts upon it: But I shall apply my Labours at this Time, to an Ornament of a contrary Nature, which is a Theme intirely New, Namely, The Art of writing Incorrectly.

This, I take it, is a Work that I am excellently well qualified for, and I doubt not but to convince the World that I am a perfect Master of my Subject. In the Prosecution of this useful Design, I shall show the Excellency of Incorrect Writing in general; I shall lay open the several Artifices, by which a Man of competent Abilities, may, with proper Application, attain to a tolerable Degree of Perfection in it; I shall produce pertinent Examples from Writers of undoubted Eminence in that improving Science: And in the last place, I may possibly address the World with a very pathetick Exhortation, to follow the Instructions which I shall give them, in order to accomplish themselves in the Art of Incorrect Writing. In short, I intend to entertain the Publick, with a regular Criticism upon Nonsense.

AUTHORS of this Kind may be divided into two Classes, generally known under the Denomination of the Bombastick and the Grubstreet. The latter of these Characters is easily attained, provided a Man can but keep himself from thinking, and yet so contrive Matters, as to let his Pen run along unmolested over a Sheet of White Paper, and drop a convenient Quantity of Words, at proper Intervals on it. A Person who is acquainted with this Secret, may, with great Facility and Composure of Mind, furnish himself with a comfortable Stock of Reputation, as often as he finds it requisite. This he might do, as without any Ruffle to his own Tranquility, so neither would it prove the least Disturbance to his Readers: For while he flow'd along with that unmeaning Softness, every one within the Warble of his Accents would undoubtedly dissolve away in a supine Indolence, and, (as a late Musical Author of this Species has very tenderly expressed it) be hush'd into lulling Dreams.

I shall, perhaps, dedicate some future Essay to the Incouragement of these worthy Gentlemen, but at this Time I intend to consider those my ingenious Fellow-Labourers, who deviate into the contrary Extream; I mean the Admirers of Bombast and Fustian.

THESE Writers, to avoid the Imputation of low and flat, blow up every Subject they take in Hand beyond its natural Dimensions; and nothing will please them that is not big and boisterous, wild and irregular. They wonderfully delight in Noise and Clamour; a Rattle of Words, and an Extravagance of Imagination, they look upon as the Perfection of Rhetorick; and are Transported beyond themselves, at the Tumult and Confusion that bellows through a Hurricane of Nonsense. In short, that which Men of this Turn applaud as the Masterpiece of good Writing, differs from the true Sublime, as a Boy's artificial Kite, wadling among the Clouds at the End of a Skein of Packthread, does from the natural Flight of an Eagle, towering with steddy Pinions up the Sky, and bearing full upon the Sun.

If this false Taste prevails amongst us, we shall quickly prove such a Generation of Blusterers, that our Country will resemble the Cave of *Æolus*, where the Winds make their general Rendezvous, and battel and clash together in an eternal Din and Uproar. For my own Part, I look upon it to be the Duty of every one, as far as in him lies, to lend his Assistance in banking out this Inundation of Sound, which, if it finds a clear Passage, will not fail to overwhelm us in a Deluge of Folly and Absurdity.

A friend of mine who writes in this exorbitant Style, Mr. Richard Stentor by Name, shall be the Hero of the present Essay. Mr. Stentor as to his exterior Figure, is one of the portliest Mortals that have flourished in our World, since Goliath overtop'd the Philistian Army. He is moderately speaking, Nine Foot high, and Four in Diameter. His Voice is not unlike the Roar and Rapidity of a Torrent foaming down a Mountain, and reverberated amongst the neighbouring Rocks. The Hurry of Vociferation with which he drives along in the Heat of an Argument, imitates the Thunder

of a Cart-load of Stones poured out upon a Pavement. He was educated in a Ship of War, and one would imagine he learnt the Notes of his Gamut, from the various Whistlings of a Tempest thro' the Rigging of his Vessel. I was once so unadvised as to offer my Dissent from one of his Opinions; but I had better have held my Tongue: He turned upon me, and Rung me such a Peal of Eloquence, that had I not made off with the greatest Precipitation, would have gone near to have stun'd, and made me deaf all my Days. Nay, I have cause to think my Hearing has been never the better for it to this Moment.

This is a short Description of his external Accomplishments; as to the Qualifications of his Mind, they will be best perceived, by a Transcript I shall here make, from an Oration he formerly composed in Praise of Beacon Hill. I must inform my Readers, that it was conceived as he stood upon the Summit of that little Mount, one Training-Day, when, as he has since owned to me, the Drums and Musquets assisted his Inspiration, and augmented and deepend the Rumbling of his Periods. It begins in the following Manner—

The gloriously-transcendent, and highly-exalted Precipice, from which the sonorous Accents of my Lungs resound with repeated Echoes, is so pompous, magnificent, illustrious, and loftily-towering, that, as I twirle around my Arm with the artful Flourish of an Orator, I seem to feel my Knucles rebound from the blew Vault of Heaven, which just arches over my Head. I stand upon an amazing Eminence that heaves itself up, on both sides steep and stupendous! high and horrendous! The spiry Teneriffe, the unshaken Atlas, or Olympus divine and celestial, when compared to this prodigious Mountain, sink to Sands, and dwindle to Atoms. It is deep-rooted in its ever-during Foundations, firm as the Earth, lasting as the Sun, immoveable as the Pillars of Nature! I behold from this awful and astonishing Scituation, the concave Expanse of uncreated Space, stretch itself above: and the Land and Ocean below, spreading an Infinitude of Extension all about me. But what daring Tropes and flaming Metaphores shall I select, O aspiring Beacon! to celebrate Thee with a suitable Grandeur, or exalt thee to a becoming Dignity? How does it shoot up its inconceivable Pinnacle into the superior Regions, and blend itself with the cerulian circum-ambient Æther! It mocks the fiercest Efforts of the most piercing Sight, to reach its impenetrable Sublimities. It looks down upon the diminish'd Spheres; the fixt Stars twinkle at an immeasurable Distance beneath it; while the Planets roll away, unperceived, in a vast, a fathomless Profound! . . .

By this little Quotation from Mr. Stentor's Panegyrick on Beacon Hill, my Reader will in some Measure be able to judge of his Manner of thinking, and expressing himself. It appears plainly that he heaps his Subject with improper and foreign Thoughts; that he strains those Thoughts into the most unnatural and ridiculous Distortions; and, last of all, that he clouds them with so many needless supernumerary Epithets, as to fling the whole Piece into this unaccountable Huddle of Impertinence and Inconsistency. Richard is mighty fond of great sounding Words, and, let his Topick be what it will, he has perpetual Recourse to them upon all Emergencies. He once took it in his Head to be in Love, and wrote a Poem to his Mistress on that delicate Passion: But instead of the gentle Flow of Harmony which any one would reasonably have expected, and which is indeed essential to Compositions of that Kind, his Numbers stalked along as sturdy and outragious as in any other of his Performances. I my self counted in Fifty Six Lines of it, three Celestials, eight Immortals, eleven Unboundeds, six Everlastings, four Eternities, and thirteen Infinites; Besides Bellowings, Ravings, Yellings, Horrors, Terribles, Rackets, Hubbubs, and Clutterings, without Number. But what pleased me the most of any of my Friend's Compositions, was, A Poetical Description of a Game at Push-pin. Sure, thought I, when I read the Title, there can be nothing very loud and impetuous upon so trivial a Matter as This. How I was surprized out of my mistake, my Reader will in some Measure conceive, when he understands that the first Distich of the Poem runs thus,

Rage, fire, and fury in my bosom roll,
And all the gods rush headlong on my soul.

He then proceeded to compare the Pins to two Comets, whose Heads, as he expressed it, en-lightned the boundless Desarts of the Skies with a bloody Glare, and threw behind them the ruddy Volumes of their tremendous Trains, into the tractless Wastes of Immensity. When the Pins met in the Progress of the Game, for a Similitude, he supposed the two Continents to be tossed from their Foundations, and encounted, with a direful Concussion, in the midst of the briny Atlantick: or rather, says he, as if two Systems of Worlds, Suns, Planets and all, should be hurled resistless one against another, and dash a horrible Chaos, from the general Ruins of Matter, and Wrecks of a whole Universe. He concluded the Poem with the following Lines, which I look upon to be the most finished Pattern of this Sort of Productions, that I have any where met with; whether I consider, the Uncouthness of the Language, the Ruggedness of the Style, or the Disproportion and Extravagance of the Images. Speaking of the Pins he says,

The Bars of Brass, harsh-crashing, loud resound,
And jarring discords rend th' astonish'd ground.
So when aloft dire hurricanes arise,
And with horrendous shatterings burst the skies,
Dread ghastly terrors drive along in crowds, 5
And hideous thunder howls amongst the clouds;
Eternal whirlwinds on the ocean roar,
Infinite earth-quakes rock the bounding shore.

I shall conclude these Remarks upon Bombast, with an Observation which I ought in Justice to make, in favour of those who fall into it; viz. That no Person can be a considerable Proficient this way, who has not a good Share of natural Powers and Abilities. Hence, when we see a Young Man delivering himself in this warm Manner, he is to be regarded as a good Genius run wild, for want of Cultivation from Study, and the Rules of Art: And it follows, that should such a juvenile Writer, take proper Methods to improve his Mind, in inuring himself to a close Way of Reasoning, and by conversing with the best Authors, however defective he might be in this Particular at first, he would in the End make a chaste and excellent Writer. Thus it happened to the immortal Virgil, whose divine Aeneid once shot itself into so great a Luxuriance, as to be near twenty Times as Large as it appears at this Day.

119

As his Imagination cooled by Years, and his Judgment ripened, and hasted on to Maturity, his Style dropped the false Glare of Ornaments, and shone with an equal Purity and Elegance; His Thoughts learned to proportion themselves to his Subject, and cast themselves into that exact Symmetry of Arrangement and Disposition, in which they now charm us; And, in a word, a new Beauty began to dawn in every Line of that exquisite Work which consecrates his deathless Fame to the Admiration of all Posterity.

L.

JONATHAN EDWARDS (1703-1758)

PURITANISM was an intellectual movement. Its clergymen, sharpened by hard study and doctrinal debate, were distinguished for scholarship as well as piety. Greatest of all the New England divines and philosophers was Jonathan Edwards, born in the twilight of the old theocracy, after the zeal of the first settlers had hardened into a rigid system. It was Edwards's destiny to recapture briefly for this later generation a full measure of the ecstasy of the early Puritans. To this task he brought a marvelously compelling power of spoken and written communication, a surpassingly lovely vision of the infinitude of God's beauty, and the finest and most subtle philosophic mind America had produced.

The great grandson of an Elizabethan clergyman whose widow came to America in 1640, and the grandson and son of New England ministers, Jonathan Edwards was born in 1703 in East Windsor, Connecticut. Tutored at home by parents of unusual intellectual stamina, young Edwards was able to enter Yale in 1716, before his thirteenth birthday. His precocious mind was further quickened in his sophomore year by reading Newton and Locke, the latter's *Essay on the Human Understanding* giving him more satisfaction "than the greedy miser finds when gathering up handfuls of silver and gold." At Yale he began recording his meticulous observations of the phenomena of the mind, notations which made him an expert in helping converts through the stages of redemption from profound self-abasement to ultimate regeneration. These "Notes on the Mind" also reveal his intuitive perception of divine excellence, inspiring him to lyrical fervor. Upon his graduation in 1720 Edwards studied theology in New Haven for two years, and—after a brief pastorate in New York—returned to Yale as a tutor in 1724. He resigned his appointment in 1726 to become the associate of Dr. Solomon Stoddard, minister of the church in Northampton.

The intensities of faith, depicted poetically in his spiritual autobiography, *A Personal Narrative*, written about 1740, and the rare mystical perceptions of Sarah Pierrepont, to whom he was married in 1727, led Edwards to assume that others possessed equal powers of spiritual awareness. This mistaken assumption and Edwards's insistence that church membership be limited to those who were able to testify to a personal experience of the transforming power of God's spirit led to a break with his congregation, and ultimately cost him his pulpit. Dr. Stoddard, following the milder test for membership sanctioned by the Massachusetts Synod in 1662, had admitted every parishioner who sought to lead a Christian life. After Dr. Stoddard's death in 1729, Edwards preached the doctrine of justification by faith with an eloquence heightened by his own conviction of the efficacy of saving grace and by his fear of the "Arminian heresy," which relied on moral sincerity alone. Drawn by the power of Edwards's sermons, some of the younger members of the congregation responded by organizing their own groups for prayer, and by the spring of 1734 conversions increased until at least thirty new converts each week professed the immediacy of the operation of God's spirit in their lives. The best statements of the phenomena of the revival, and of the psychology of the variety of religious experiences which induced this revival, are to be found in Edwards's *A Faithful Narrative of the Surprising Work of God . . .* (1737), *Some Thoughts Concerning the Present Revival of Religion in New England* (1742), and *A Treatise Concerning Religious Affections* (1746).

Although Edwards was fully aware of the excesses of emotionalism aroused by the revival, he attributed the excesses to the heightened feelings attendant upon inspiration, and refused to yield to the more conservative church members, who believed converts often lacked an intellectual basis for their testimony. Disagreements in the parish were further widened by irrelevant issues, such as Edwards's opposition to light reading, and the pastoral relation was finally ended in 1750. Fearing the divisive effects of forming a new church, Edwards accepted an appointment as minister to a small church at Stockbridge, where he also served as missionary to the Indians. Here he resumed his study of the human will, a project which had been interrupted by parish difficulties; and in 1754 he published the famous treatise, *A Careful . . . Inquiry into . . . Notions of that Freedom of Will . . .* , a logical justification of the Calvinistic dogmas of divine sovereignty and unconditional predestination. Known primarily as a preacher before 1754, Edwards now was recognized as the foremost philosophic champion of Calvinism. This new eminence led to his call to the presidency of the College of New Jersey (Princeton) in 1757. He died in March, 1758, a few months after his inauguration.

Edwards survives today in the popular mind as the foremost colonial preacher of hell-fire damnation and as the defender of a theology doomed to crumble in the liberal and secular age completely embodied by Benjamin Franklin. Yet of all the figures of the century, Franklin alone can match Edwards's distinction of prose and keenness of mind. The notoriety of *Sinners in the Hands of an Angry God* and the austere logic of the *Freedom of Will* have tended to obscure *A Personal Narrative*, the great spiritual autobiography on which Edwards's position as a man of letters largely rests. A precious document in the history of American idealism, this poetic record of spiritual rapture in the contemplation of God's beauty revealed in nature anticipates Wordsworth and Emerson. Whatever the debt owed by New England Transcendentalism to European literature, it has a strong kinship with the mysticism of Edwards.

BIBLIOGRAPHY · There are many editions of Edwards's writings. The earliest collection, issued in Leeds, London, and Philadelphia (1806–1811), was superseded by the "First American edition" edited in eight volumes by S. Austin, *The Works of President Edwards* (1808–1809). This edition, and the one edited in ten volumes by S. E. Dwight, *The Works of President Edwards* (1829, 1830), have been the basis of later collections. P. Miller edited *Images or Shadows of Divine Things* (1948). *Selected Sermons of Jonathan Edwards* (1904) was edited by H. N. Gardiner. The best volumes of selections are C. Van Doren, *Benjamin Franklin and Jonathan Edwards: Selections from their Writings* (1920), and C. H. Faust and T. H. Johnson, *Jonathan Edwards: Representative Selections* (1935). The latter collection contains an admirable bibliography. For a list of Edwards's separate works, see the bibliography in the *Cambridge History of American Literature*, I (1917), 426–432.

The most succinct account of Edwards's life is F. A. Christie's essay in the *Dictionary of American Biography*, VI (1931), 30–37. Perry Miller's *Jonathan Edwards* (1949) is indispensable. Earlier biographies include A. V.

G. Allen, *Jonathan Edwards* (1890), S. E. Dwight, *Life of President Edwards*, Vol. I of the *Works* (1829); H. B. Parkes, *Jonathan Edwards, the Fiery Puritan* (1930); and A. C. McGiffert, *Jonathan Edwards* (1932).

Illuminating chapters are contained in H. S. Canby, *Classic Americans* (1931); G. P. Fisher, *History of Christian Doctrine* (1896); F. H. Foster, *A Genetic History of the New England Theology* (1907); J. Haroutunian, *Piety versus Moralism: The Passing of the New England Theology* (1932); P. Miller, *Orthodoxy in Massachusetts, 1630–1650: A Genetic Study* (1933), and *The New England Mind* (1939); I. W. Riley, *American Philosophy: The Early Schools* (1907), and *American Thought from Puritanism to Pragmatism* (1923); H. W. Schneider, *The Puritan Mind* (1930); H. G. Townsend, *Philosophical Ideas in the United States* (1934); J. Tracy, *The Great Awakening: A History of the Revival of Religion in the Time of Edwards and Whitefield* (1841); and W. Walker, *A History of the Congregational Church in the United States* (1894), and *Ten New England Leaders* (1901).

Valuable specialized studies include E. H. Cady, "The Artistry of Jonathan Edwards," *New England Quarterly*, XXII (1949), 61–72; F. I. Carpenter, "The Radicalism of Jonathan Edwards," *New England Quarterly*, IV (1931), 629–644; W. H. Channing, "Jonathan Edwards and the Revivalists," *Christian Examiner*, XLIII (Fourth Series, VIII) (1847), 374–394; J. Dewitt, "Jonathan Edwards, a Study," *Princeton Theological Review*, II (1904), 88–109; F. B. Dexter, "On the Manuscripts of Jonathan Edwards," *Proceedings of the Massachusetts Historical Society* (Second Series), XV (1902), 2–16; G. P. Fisher, "The Value of Edwards for Today," *Congregationalist and Christian World*, LXXXVIII (1903), 469–472; J. Haroutunian, "Jonathan Edwards, a Study in Godliness," *Journal of Religion*, XI (1931), 400–419; T. Hornberger, "The Effect of the New Science upon the Thought of Jonathan Edwards," *American Literature*, IX (1937), 196–207; T. H. Johnson, "Jonathan Edwards and the 'Young Folks' Bible,'" *New England Quarterly*, V (1932), 37–54; and "Jonathan Edwards's Background of Reading," *Publications of the Colonial Society of Massachusetts*, XXVIII (1931), 193–222; H. M. Jones, "American Prose Style: 1700–1770," *Huntington Library Bulletin*, No. 6 (1934), 115–151; J. H. MacCracken, "The Sources of Jonathan Edwards's Idealism," *Philosophical Review*, XI (1902), 26–42; E. W. Miller, "The Great Awakening," *Princeton Theological Review*, II (1904), 545–562; P. Miller, "The Half-Way Covenant," *New England Quarterly*, VI (1933), 676–715; I. W. Riley, "The Real Jonathan Edwards," *Open Court*, XXII (1908), 705–715; G. L. Walker, "Jonathan Edwards and the Half-Way Covenant," *New Englander*, XLIII (1884), 601–614; and F. J. E. Woodbridge, "Jonathan Edwards," *Philosophical Review*, XIII (1904), 393–408.

A Divine and Supernatural Light

Immediately Imparted to The Soul By The Spirit of God, Shown to Be Both A Scriptural and Rational Doctrine.

THE VISION of divine beauty and the direct perception of divine ideas, powers possessed by the truly regenerate man, are traceable solely to a divine source. This idea, one of the central concepts of Edwards's *Treatise Concerning Religious Affections* (1746), was anticipated in the title and text of a sermon preached at Northampton in 1734. In this discourse, published by the parish, Edwards attempted to clarify the conditions under which divine illumination may be received. Although God may make use of man's reason and imagination, the truly spiritual light is a divine and superlative glory, an overwhelming sense of God's excellence, and a gift which God alone can bestow. Thus Edwards's mysticism in the late 1730's epistemologically served to support the Calvinist doctrine of divine sovereignty. The text is that of S. Austin, ed., *The Works of President Edwards* (1808–1809).

Matthew 16. 17. And Jesus answered and said unto him, Blessed art thou, Simon Barjona: for flesh and blood hath not revealed it unto thee, but my Father which is in heaven.

Doctrine · That there is such a thing as a Spiritual and Divine Light, immediately imparted to the soul by God, of a different nature from any that is obtained by natural means.

In what I say on this subject, at this time, I would,

I. Show what this divine light is.

II. How it is given immediately by God, and not obtained by natural means.

III. Show the truth of the doctrine.

And then conclude with a brief improvement.

I. I would show what this spiritual and divine light is. And in order to it, would show,

First, In a few things what it is not. And here,

1. Those convictions that natural men may have of their sin and misery, is not this spiritual and divine light. Men in a natural condition may have convictions of the guilt that lies upon them, and of the anger of God, and their danger of divine vengeance. Such convictions are from light or sensibleness of truth. That some sinners have a greater conviction of their guilt and misery than others, is because some have more light, or more of an apprehension of truth than others. And this light and conviction may be from the Spirit of God; the Spirit convinces men of sin: But yet nature is much more concerned in it than in the communication of that spiritual and divine light that is spoken of in the doctrine; it is from the Spirit of God only as assisting natural principles, and not as infusing any new principles. Common grace differs from special, in that it influences only by assisting of nature; and not by imparting grace, or bestowing any thing above nature. The light that is obtained is wholly natural, or of no superior kind to what mere nature attains to, though more of that kind be obtained than would be obtained if men were left wholly to themselves: or, in other words, common grace only assists the faculties of the soul to do that more fully which they do by nature, as natural conscience or reason will, by mere nature, make a man sensible of guilt, and will accuse and condemn him when he has done amiss. Conscience is a principle natural to men; and the work that it doth naturally, or of itself, is to give an apprehension of right and wrong, and to suggest to the mind the relation that there is between right and wrong, and a retribution. The Spirit of God, in those convictions which unregenerate men sometimes have, assists conscience to do this work in a further degree than it would do if they were left to themselves: he helps it against those things that tend to stupify it, and obstruct its exercise. But in the renewing and sanctifying work of the Holy Ghost, those things are wrought in the soul that are above nature, and of which there is nothing of the like kind in the soul by nature; and they are caused to exist in the soul habitually, and according to such a stated constitution or law that lays such a foundation for exercises in a continued course, as is called a principle of nature. Not only are remaining principles assisted to do their work more freely and fully, but those principles are restored that were utterly destroyed by the fall; and the mind thenceforward habitually exerts those acts that the dominion of sin had made it as wholly destitute of, as a dead body is of vital acts.

The Spirit of God acts in a very different manner in the one case, from what he doth in the other. He may indeed act upon the mind of a natural man, but he acts in the mind of a saint as an indwelling vital principle. He acts upon the mind of an unregenerate person as an extrinsic, occasional agent; for in acting upon them, he doth not unite himself to them; for notwithstanding all his influences that they may be the subjects of, they are still sensual, having not the Spirit. Jude 19. But he unites himself with the mind of a saint, takes him for his temple, actuates and influences him as a new supernatural principle of life and action. There is this difference, that the Spirit of God, in acting in the soul of a godly man, exerts and communicates himself there in his own proper nature. Holiness is the proper nature of the Spirit of God. The Holy Spirit operates in the minds of the godly, by uniting himself to them, and living in them, and exerting his own nature in the exercise of their faculties. The Spirit of God may act upon a creature, and yet not in acting communicate himself. The Spirit of God may act upon inanimate creatures; as, the Spirit moved upon the face of the waters, in the beginning of the creation; so the Spirit of God may act upon the minds of men many ways, and communicate himself no more than when he acts upon an inanimate creature. For instance, he may excite thoughts in them, may assist their natural reason and understanding, or may assist other natural principles, and this without any union with the soul, but may act, as it were, as upon an external object. But as he acts in his holy influences and spiritual operations, he acts in a way of peculiar communication of himself; so that the subject is thence denominated spiritual.

2. This spiritual and divine light does not consist in any impression made upon the imagination. It is no impression upon the mind, as though one saw any thing with the bodily eyes: it is no imagination or idea of an outward light or glory, or any beauty of form or countenance, or a visible lustre or brightness of any object. The imagination may be strongly impressed with such things; but this is not spiritual light. Indeed when the mind has a lively discovery of spiritual things, and is greatly affected by the power of divine light, it may, and probably very commonly doth, much affect the imagination; so that the impressions of an outward beauty or brightness may accompany those spiritual discoveries. But spiritual light is not that impression upon the imagination, but an exceeding different thing from it. Natural men may have lively impressions on their imaginations; and we cannot determine but the devil, who transforms himself into an angel of light, may cause imaginations of an outward beauty, or visible glory, and of sounds and speeches, and other such things; but these are things of a vastly inferior nature to spiritual light.

3. This spiritual light is not the suggesting of any new truths or propositions not contained in the word of God. This suggesting of new truths or doctrines to the mind, independent of any antecedent revelation of those propositions, either in word or writing, is inspiration; such as the prophets and apostles had, and such as some enthusiasts pretend to. But this spiritual light that I am speaking of, is quite a different thing from inspiration: it reveals no new doctrine, it suggests no new proposition to the mind, it teaches no new thing of God, or Christ, or another world, not taught in the Bible, but only gives a due apprehension of those things that are taught in the word of God.

4. It is not every affecting view that men have of the things of religion that is this spiritual and divine light. Men by mere principles of nature are capable of being affected with things that have a special relation to religion as well as other things. A person by mere nature, for instance, may be liable to be affected with the story of Jesus Christ, and the sufferings he underwent, as well as by any other tragical story: he may be the more affected with it from the interest he conceives mankind to have in it: yea, he may be affected with it without believing it; as well as a man may be affected with what he reads in a romance, or sees acted in a stage play. He may be affected with a lively and eloquent description of many pleasant things that attend the state of the blessed in heaven, as well as his imagination be entertained by a romantic description of the pleasantness of fairy

123

land, or the like. And that common belief of the truth of the things of religion, that persons may have from education or otherwise, may help forward their affection. We read in Scripture of many that were greatly affected with things of a religious nature, who yet are there represented as wholly graceless, and many of them very ill men. A person therefore may have affecting views of the things of religion, and yet be very destitute of spiritual light. Flesh and blood may be the author of this: one man may give another an affecting view of divine things with but common assistance: but God alone can give a spiritual discovery of them.

But I proceed to show,

Secondly, Positively what this spiritual and divine light is.

And it may be thus described: a true sense of the divine excellency of the things revealed in the word of God, and a conviction of the truth and reality of them thence arising.

This spiritual light primarily consists in the former of these, viz., a real sense and apprehension of the divine excellency of things revealed in the word of God. A spiritual and saving conviction of the truth and reality of these things, arises from such a sight of their divine excellency and glory; so that this conviction of their truth is an effect and natural consequence of this sight of their divine glory. There is therefore in this spiritual light,

1. A true sense of the divine and superlative excellency of the things of religion; a real sense of the excellency of God and Jesus Christ, and of the work of redemption, and the ways and works of God revealed in the gospel. There is a divine and superlative glory in these things; an excellency that is of a vastly higher kind, and more sublime in nature than in other things; a glory greatly distinguishing them from all that is earthly and temporal. He that is spiritually enlightened truly apprehends and sees it, or has a sense of it. He does not merely rationally believe that God is glorious, but he has a sense of the gloriousness of God in his heart. There is not only a rational belief that God is holy, and that holiness is a good

thing, but there is a sense of the loveliness of God's holiness. There is not only a speculatively judging that God is gracious, but a sense how amiable God is upon that account, or a sense of the beauty of this divine attribute.

There is a twofold understanding or knowledge of good that God has made the mind of man capable of. The first, that which is merely speculative and notional; as when a person only speculatively judges that any thing is, which, by the agreement of mankind, is called good or excellent, viz., that which is most to general advantage, and between which and a reward there is a suitableness, and the like. And the other is, that which consists in the sense of the heart: as when there is a sense of the beauty, amiableness, or sweetness of a thing; so that the heart is sensible of pleasure and delight in the presence of the idea of it. In the former is exercised merely the speculative faculty, or the understanding, strictly so called, or as spoken of in distinction from the will or disposition of the soul. In the latter, the will, or inclination, or heart, is mainly concerned.

Thus there is a difference between having an opinion, that God is holy and gracious, and having a sense of the loveliness and beauty of that holiness and grace. There is a difference between having a rational judgment that honey is sweet, and having a sense of its sweetness. A man may have the former, that knows not how honey tastes; but a man cannot have the latter unless he has an idea of the taste of honey in his mind. So there is a difference between believing that a person is beautiful, and having a sense of his beauty. The former may be obtained by hearsay, but the latter only by seeing the countenance. There is a wide difference between mere speculative rational judging any thing to be excellent, and having a sense of its sweetness and beauty. The former rests only in the head, speculation only is concerned in it; but the heart is concerned in the latter. When the heart is sensible of the beauty and amiableness of a thing, it necessarily feels pleasure in the apprehension. It is implied in a person's being heartily sensible of the loveliness of a thing, that the idea of it is sweet and pleasant to his soul; which is a far different thing from having a rational opinion that it is excellent.

2. There arises from this sense of divine excellency of things contained in the word of God, a conviction of the truth and reality of them; and that either directly or indirectly.

First, Indirectly, and that two ways.

1. As the prejudices that are in the heart, against the truth of divine things, are hereby removed; so that the mind becomes susceptive of the due force of rational arguments for their truth. The mind of man is naturally full of prejudices against the truth of divine things: it is full of enmity against the doctrines of the gospel; which is a disadvantage to those arguments that prove their truth, and causes them to lose their force upon the mind. But when a person has discovered to him the divine excellency of Christian doctrines, this destroys the enmity, removes those prejudices, and sanctifies the reason, and causes it to lie open to the force of arguments for their truth.

Hence was the different effect that Christ's miracles had to convince the disciples, from what they had to convince the Scribes and Pharisees. Not that they had a stronger reason, or had their reason more improved; but their reason was sanctified, and those blinding prejudices, that the Scribes and Pharisees were under, were removed by the sense they had of the excellency of Christ and his doctrine.

2. It not only removes the hindrances of reason, but positively helps reason. It makes even the speculative notions the more lively. It engages the attention of the mind, with the more fixedness and intenseness to that kind of objects; which causes it to have a clearer view of them, and enables it more clearly to see their mutual relations, and occasions it to take more notice of them. The ideas themselves that otherwise are dim and obscure, are by this means impressed with the greater strength, and have a light cast upon them; so that the mind can better judge of them. As he that beholds the objects on the face of the earth, when the light of the sun is cast upon them, is under greater advantage to discern them in their true forms and mutual relations, than he that sees them in a dim starlight or twilight.

The mind having a sensibleness of the excellency of divine objects, dwells upon them with delight; and the powers of the soul are more awakened and enlivened to employ themselves in the contemplation of them, and exert themselves more fully and much more to the purpose. The beauty and sweetness of the objects draws on the faculties, and draws forth their exercises: so that the reason itself is under far greater advantages for its proper and free exercises, and to attain its proper end, free of darkness and delusion. But,

Secondly. A true sense of the divine excellency of the things of God's word doth more directly and immediately convince of the truth of them; and that because the excellency of these things is so superlative. There is a beauty in them that is so divine and godlike, that is greatly and evidently distinguishing of them from things merely human, or that men are the inventors and authors of; a glory that is so high and great, that when clearly seen, commands assent to their divinity and reality. When there is an actual and lively discovery of this beauty and excellency, it will not allow of any such thought as that it is a human work, or the fruit of men's invention. This evidence that they that are spiritually enlightened have of the truth of the things of religion, is a kind of intuitive and immediate evidence. They believe the doctrines of God's word to be divine, because they see divinity in them; i.e., they see a divine, and transcendent, and most evidently distinguishing glory in them; such a glory as, if clearly seen, does not leave room to doubt of their being of God, and not of men.

Such a conviction of the truth of religion as this, arising, these ways, from a sense of the divine excellency of them, is that true spiritual conviction that there is in saving faith. And this original of it, is that by which it is most essentially distinguished from that common assent, which unregenerate men are capable of.

II. I proceed now to the second thing proposed, viz., to show how this light is immediately given by God, and not obtained by natural means. And here,

1. It is not intended that the natural faculties are not made use of in it. The natural faculties

125

are the subject of this light: and they are the subject in such a manner, that they are not merely passive, but active in it; the acts and exercises of man's understanding are concerned and made use of in it. God, in letting in this light into the soul, deals with man according to his nature, or as a rational creature; and makes use of his human faculties. But yet this light is not the less immediately from God for that; though the faculties are made use of, it is as the subject and not as the cause; and that acting of the faculties in it, is not the cause, but is either implied in the thing itself (in the light that is imparted) or is the consequence of it. As the use that we make of our eyes in beholding various objects, when the sun arises, is not the cause of the light that discovers those objects to us.

2. It is not intended that outward means have no concern in this affair. As I have observed already, it is not in this affair, as it is in inspiration, where new truths are suggested: for here is by this light only given a due apprehension of the same truths that are revealed in the word of God; and therefore it is not given without the word. The Gospel is made use of in this affair: this light is the light of the glorious gospel of Christ, 2 Cor. iv. 4. The gospel is as a glass, by which this light is conveyed to us, 1 Cor. xiii. 12. Now we see through a glass.—But,

3. When it is said that this light is given immediately by God, and not obtained by natural means, hereby is intended, that it is given by God without making use of any means that operate by their own power, or a natural force. God makes use of means; but it is not as mediate causes to produce this effect. There are not truly any second causes of it; but it is produced by God immediately. The word of God is no proper cause of this effect: it does not operate by any natural force in it. The word of God is only made use of to convey to the mind the subject matter of this saving instruction: and this indeed it doth convey to us by natural force or influence. It conveys to our minds these and those doctrines; it is the cause of the notion of them in our heads, but not of the sense of the divine excellency of them in our hearts.

Indeed a person cannot have spiritual light without the word. But that does not argue, that the word properly causes that light. The mind cannot see the excellency of any doctrine, unless that doctrine be first in the mind; but the seeing of the excellency of the doctrine may be immediately from the Spirit of God; though the conveying of the doctrine or proposition itself may be by the word. So that the notions that are the subject matter of this light, are conveyed to the mind by the word of God; but that due sense of the heart, wherein this light formally consists, is immediately by the Spirit of God. As for instance, that notion that there is a Christ, and that Christ is holy and gracious, is conveyed to the mind by the word of God: but the sense of the excellency of Christ by reason of that holiness and grace, is nevertheless immediately the work of the Holy Spirit.

Personal Narrative

BEFORE HE was twenty years old Edwards had formulated seventy Resolutions as reminders of his vow never to do anything "but what tends to the glory of God." He also kept continual watch over his spiritual progress in his Diary. In biographical and literary interest, however, these documents are far inferior to the *Personal Narrative* which Edwards wrote about 1743, during his pastorate at Northampton. This moving spiritual autobiography tells the story of Edwards's objections to the concept of God's absolute sovereignty and his final acquiescence in the doctrine as "exceedingly pleasant, bright, and sweet." It is a record of his intense absorption in the idea of God, his sense of the majesty and grace of God, and his burning desire to spend his eternity in divine communion. In power of utterance, in lyric expression of personal ecstasy, and in evocation of moods of rapture, the *Narrative* must be placed among the classics of the inner life. The text of the *Personal Narrative* is that of S. Austin, *The Works of President Edwards* (1808-1809).

I had a variety of concerns and exercises about my soul from my childhood; but I had two more remarkable seasons of awakening, before I met with that change by which I was brought to those new dispositions, and that new sense of things, that I have since had. The first time was when I was a boy, some years before I went to college, at a time of remarkable awakening in my father's congregation. I was then very much affected for many months, and concerned about the things of religion, and my soul's salvation; and was abundant in religious duties. I used to pray five times a day in secret, and to spend much time in religious talk with other boys; and used to meet with them to pray together. I experienced I know not what kind of delight in religion. My mind was much engaged in it, and had much self-righteous pleasure; and it was my delight to abound in religious duties. I with some of my schoolmates joined together, and built a booth in a swamp, in a very retired spot, for a place of prayer. And besides, I had particular secret places of my own in the woods, where I used to retire by myself; and was from time to time much affected. My affections seemed to be lively and easily moved, and I seemed to be in my element, when engaged in religious duties. And I am ready to think, many are deceived with such affections, and such a kind of delight as I then had in religion, and mistake it for grace.

But, in process of time, my convictions and affections wore off; and I entirely lost all those affections and delights and left off secret prayer, at least as to any constant preference of it; and returned like a dog to his vomit, and went on in the ways of sin. Indeed, I was at times very uneasy, especially towards the latter part of my time at college; when it pleased God, to seize me with a pleurisy; in which he brought me nigh to the grave, and shook me over the pit of hell. And yet, it was not long after my recovery, before I fell again into my old ways of sin. But God would not suffer me to go on with any quietness; I had great and violent inward struggles, till, after many conflicts with wicked inclinations, repeated resolutions, and bonds that I laid myself under by a kind of vows to God, I was brought wholly to break off all former wicked ways, and all ways of known outward sin; and to apply myself to seek salvation and practice many religious duties; but without that kind of affection and delight which I had formerly experienced. My concern now wrought more by inward struggles and conflicts and self-reflections. I made seeking my salvation the main

business of my life. But yet, it seems to me, I sought it after a miserable manner; which has made me sometimes since to question, whether ever it issued in that which was saving; being ready to doubt, whether such miserable seeking ever succeeded. I was indeed brought to seek salvation in a manner that I never was before; I felt a spirit to part with all things in the world, for an interest in Christ. My concern continued and prevailed, with many exercising thoughts and inward struggles; but yet it never seemed to be proper to express that concern by the name of terror.

From my childhood up, my mind had been full of objections against the doctrine of God's sovereignty, in choosing whom he would to eternal life, and rejecting whom he pleased; leaving them eternally to perish, and be everlastingly tormented in hell. It used to appear like a horrible doctrine to me. But I remember the time very well, when I seemed to be convinced, and fully satisfied, as to this sovereignty of God, and his justice in thus eternally disposing of men, according to his sovereign pleasure. But never could give an account, how, or by what means, I was thus convinced, not in the least imagining at the time, nor a long time after, that there was any extraordinary influence of God's Spirit in it; but only that now I saw further, and my reason apprehended the justice and reasonableness of it. However, my mind rested in it; and it put an end to all those cavils and objections. And there has been a wonderful alteration in my mind, with respect to the doctrine of God's sovereignty, from that day to this; so that I scarce ever have found so much as the rising of an objection against it, in the most absolute sense, in God shewing mercy to whom he will shew mercy, and hardening whom he will. God's absolute sovereignty and justice, with respect to salvation and damnation, is what my mind seems to rest assured of, as much as of any thing that I see with my eyes; at least it is so at times. But I have often, since that first conviction, had quite another kind of sense of God's sovereignty than I had then. I have often since had not only a conviction, but a delightful conviction. The doctrine has very often appeared exceedingly pleasant, bright, and sweet. Absolute sovereignty is what I love to ascribe to God. But my first conviction was not so.

The first instance that I remember of that sort of inward, sweet delight in God and divine things that I have lived much in since, was on reading those words, 1 Tim. i. 17. Now unto the King eternal, immortal, invisible, the only wise God, be honour and glory for ever and ever, Amen. As I read the words, there came into my soul, and was as it were diffused through it, a sense of the glory of the Divine Being; a new sense, quite different from any thing I ever experienced before. Never any [10] words of Scripture seemed to me as these words did. I thought with myself, how excellent a Being that was, and how happy I should be, if I might enjoy that God, and be rapt up to him in heaven, and be as it were swallowed up in him for ever! I kept saying, and as it were singing, over these words of scripture to myself; and went to pray to God that I might enjoy him, and prayed in a manner quite different from what I used to do; with a new sort of affection. But it never came into my [20] thought, that there was any thing spiritual, or of a saving nature in this.

From about that time, I began to have a new kind of apprehensions and ideas of Christ, and the work of redemption, and the glorious way of salvation by him. An inward, sweet sense of these things, at times, came into my heart; and my soul was led away in pleasant views and contemplations of them. And my mind was greatly engaged to spend my time in reading and meditating on Christ, [30] on the beauty and excellency of his person, and the lovely way of salvation by free grace in him. I found no books so delightful to me, as those that treated of these subjects. Those words Cant. ii. 1. used to be abundantly with me, I am the Rose of Sharon, and the Lily of the valleys. The words seemed to me, sweetly to represent the loveliness and beauty of Jesus Christ. The whole book of Canticles used to be pleasant to me, and I used to be much in reading it, about that time; and found, [40] from time to time, an inward sweetness, that would carry me away, in my contemplations. This I know not how to express otherwise, than by a calm, sweet abstraction of soul from all the concerns of this world; and sometimes a kind of vision, or fixed ideas and imaginations, of being alone in the mountains, or some solitary wilderness, far from all mankind, sweetly conversing with Christ, and

wrapt and swallowed up in God. The sense I had of divine things, would often of a sudden kindle up, as it were, a sweet burning in my heart; an ardour of soul, that I know not how to express.

Not long after I first began to experience these things, I gave an account to my father of some things that had passed in my mind. I was pretty much affected by the discourse we had together; and when the discourse was ended, I walked abroad alone, in a solitary place in my father's pasture, for contemplation. And as I was walking there, and looking upon the sky and clouds, there came into my mind so sweet a sense of the glorious majesty and grace of God, as I know not how to express. I seemed to see them both in a sweet conjunction; majesty and meekness joined together; it was a sweet, and gentle, and holy majesty; and also a majestic meekness; an awful sweetness; a high, and great, and holy gentleness.

After this my sense of divine things gradually increased, and became more and more lively, and had more of that inward sweetness. The appearance of every thing was altered; there seemed to be, as it were, a calm, sweet, cast, or appearance of divine glory, in almost every thing. God's excellency, his wisdom, his purity and love, seemed to appear in every thing; in the sun, moon, and stars; in the clouds and blue sky; in the grass, flowers, trees; in the water and all nature; which used greatly to [30] fix my mind. I often used to sit and view the moon for continuance; and in the day, spent much time in viewing the clouds and sky, to behold the sweet glory of God in these things; in the meantime, singing forth, with a low voice, my contemplations of the Creator and Redeemer. And scarce any thing, among all the works of nature, was so sweet to me as thunder and lightning; formerly, nothing had been so terrible to me. Before, I used to be uncommonly terrified with thunder, and to be struck [40] with terror when I saw a thunder-storm rising; but now, on the contrary, it rejoiced me. I felt God, if I may so speak, at the first appearance of a thunder-storm; and used to take the opportunity, at such times, to fix myself in order to view the clouds, and see the lightnings play, and hear the majestic and awful voice of God's thunder, which oftentimes was exceedingly entertaining, leading me to sweet contemplations of my great and

From this time on he is a mystic

The sense of divine things is the reality

glorious God. While thus engaged, it always seemed natural to me to sing, or chant forth my meditations; or, to speak my thoughts in soliloquies with a singing voice.

I felt then great satisfaction, as to my good state; but that did not content me. I had vehement longings of soul after God and Christ, and after more holiness, wherewith my heart seemed to be full, and ready to break; which often brought to my mind the words of the Psalmist, Psal. cxix. 28. My soul breaketh for the longing it hath. I often felt a mourning and lamenting in my heart, that I had not turned to God sooner, that I might have had more time to grow in grace. My mind was greatly fixed on divine things; almost perpetually in the contemplation of them. I spent most of my time in thinking of divine things, year after year; often walking alone in the woods, and solitary places, for meditation, soliloquy, and prayer, and converse with God; and it was always my manner, at such times, to sing forth my contemplations. I was almost constantly in ejaculatory prayer, wherever I was. Prayer seemed to be natural to me, as the breath by which the inward burnings of my heart had vent. The delights which I now felt in the things of religion, were of an exceedingly different kind from those before-mentioned, that I had when a boy; and what then I had no more notion of, than one born blind has of pleasant and beautiful colors. They were of a more inward, pure, soul-animating and refreshing nature. Those former delights never reached the heart; and did not arise from any sight of the divine excellency of the things of God; or any taste of the soul-satisfying and life-giving good there is in them.

My sense of divine things seemed gradually to increase, until I went to preach at New-York; which was about a year and a half after they began; and while I was there, I felt them, very sensibly, in a much higher degree, than I had done before. My longings after God and holiness were much increased. Pure and humble, holy and heavenly, Christianity appeared exceedingly amiable to me. I felt a burning desire to be, in every thing, a complete Christian; and conform to the blessed image of Christ; and that I might live, in all things, according to the pure, sweet and blessed rules of the gospel. I had an eager thirsting after progress in

these things; which put me upon pursuing and pressing after them. It was my continual strife day and night, and constant inquiry, how I should be more holy, and live more holily, and more becoming a child of God, and a disciple of Christ. I now sought an increase of grace and holiness, and a holy life, with much more earnestness, than ever I sought grace before I had it. I used to be continually examining myself, and studying and contriving for likely ways and means, how I should live holily, with far greater diligence and earnestness, than ever I pursued any thing in my life; but yet with too great a dependence on my own strength; which afterwards proved a great damage to me. My experience had not then taught me, as it has done since, my extreme feebleness and impotence, every manner of way; and the bottomless depths of secret corruption and deceit, there was in my heart. However, I went on with my eager pursuit after more holiness, and conformity to Christ.

The heaven I desired was a heaven of holiness; to be with God, and to spend my eternity in divine love, and holy communion with Christ. My mind was very much taken up with contemplations on heaven, and the enjoyments there; and living there in perfect holiness, humility and love: And it used at that time to appear a great part of the happiness of heaven, that there the saints could express their love to Christ. It appeared to me a great clog and burden, that what I felt within, I could not express as I desired. The inward ardour of my soul, seemed to be hindered and pent up, and could not freely flame out as it would. I used often to think, how in heaven this principle should freely and fully vent and express itself. Heaven appeared exceedingly delightful, as a world of love; and that all happiness consisted in living in pure, humble, heavenly, divine love.

I remember the thoughts I used then to have of holiness; and said sometimes to myself, "I do certainly know that I love holiness, such as the gospel prescribes." It appeared to me, that there was nothing in it but what was ravishingly lovely; the highest beauty and amiableness—a divine beauty; far purer than any thing here upon earth; and that every thing else was like mire and defilement, in comparison of it.

Holiness, as I then wrote down some of my contemplations on it, appeared to me to be of a sweet, pleasant, charming, serene, calm nature; which brought an inexpressible purity, brightness, peacefulness and ravishment to the soul. In other words, that it made the soul like a field or garden of God, with all manner of pleasant flowers; enjoying a sweet calm, and the gently vivifying beams of the sun. The soul of a true Christian, as I then wrote my meditations, appeared like such a little white flower as we see in the spring of the year; low and humble on the ground, opening its bosom to receive the pleasant beams of the sun's glory; rejoicing as it were in a calm rapture; diffusing around a sweet fragrancy; standing peacefully and lovingly, in the midst of other flowers round about; all in like manner opening their bosoms, to drink in the light of the sun. There was no part of creature-holiness, that I had so great a sense of its loveliness, as humility, brokenness of heart and poverty of spirit; and there was nothing that I so earnestly longed for. My heart panted after this, to lie low before God, as in the dust; that I might be nothing, and that God, might be ALL, that I might become as a little child.

While at New York, I was sometimes much affected with reflections on my past life, considering how late it was before I began to be truly religious; and how wickedly I had lived till then; and once so as to weep abundantly, and for a considerable time together.

On January 12, 1723, I made a solemn dedication of myself to God, and wrote it down; giving up myself, and all that I had to God; to be for the future in no respect my own; to act as one that had no right to himself, in any respect. And solemnly vowed, to take God for my whole portion and felicity; looking on nothing else as any part of my happiness, nor acting as if it were; and his law for the constant rule of my obedience; engaging to fight, with all my might, against the world, the flesh, and the devil, to the end of my life. But I have reason to be infinitely humbled, when I consider how much I have failed, of answering my obligation.

I had then abundance of sweet, religious conversation, in the family where I lived, with Mr. John Smith, and his pious mother. My heart was knit in affection to those in whom were appearances of true piety; and I could bear the thoughts of no other companions, but such as were holy, and the disciples of the blessed Jesus. I had great longings for the advancement of Christ's kingdom in the world; and my secret prayer used to be, in great part, taken up in praying for it. If I heard the least hint of any thing that happened, in any part of the world, that appeared, in some respect or other, to have a favourable aspect on the interests of Christ's kingdom, my soul eagerly catched at it; and it would much animate and refresh me. I used to be eager to read public news-letters, mainly for that end; to see if I could not find some news favourable to the interest of religion in the world.

I very frequently used to retire into a solitary place, on the banks of Hudson's River, at some distance from the city, for contemplation on divine things and secret converse with God: and had many sweet hours there. Sometimes Mr. Smith and I walked there together, to converse on the things of God; and our conversation used to turn much on the advancement of Christ's kingdom in the world, and the glorious things that God would accomplish for his church in the latter days. I had then, and at other times, the greatest delight in the holy scriptures, of any book whatsoever. Oftentimes in reading it, every word seemed to touch my heart. I felt a harmony between something in my heart, and those sweet and powerful words. I seemed often to see so much light exhibited by every sentence, and such a refreshing food communicated, that I could not get along in reading; often dwelling long on one sentence, to see the wonders contained in it; and yet almost every sentence seemed to be full of wonders.

I came away from New York in the month of April, 1723, and had a most bitter parting with Madam Smith and her son. My heart seemed to sink within me at leaving the family and city, where I had enjoyed so many sweet and pleasant days. I went from New York to Wethersfield, by water; and as I sailed away, I kept sight of the city as long as I could. However, that night, after this sorrowful parting, I was greatly comforted in God at Westchester, where we went ashore to lodge: and had a pleasant time of it all the voyage to Saybrook. It was sweet to me to think of meeting dear Christians in heaven, where we should never part more. At Saybrook we went ashore to lodge on Saturday, and there kept the Sabbath; where I had a sweet and refreshing season, walking alone in the fields.

After I came home to Windsor, I remained much in a like frame of mind, as when at New York; only sometimes I felt my heart ready to sink with the thoughts of my friends at New York. My support was in contemplations on the heavenly state; as I find in my Diary of May 1, 1723. It was a comfort to think of that state, where there is fulness of joy; where reigns heavenly, calm, and delightful love, without alloy; where there are continually the dearest expressions of this love; where is the enjoyment of the persons loved, without ever parting; where those persons who appear so lovely in this world, will really be inexpressibly more lovely and full of love to us. And how sweetly will the mutual lovers join together to sing the praises of God and the Lamb! How will it fill us with joy to think, that this enjoyment, these sweet exercises will never cease, but will last to all eternity! . . .

Since I came to this town [Northampton], I have often had sweet complacency in God, in views of his glorious perfections and the excellency of Jesus Christ. God has appeared to me a glorious and lovely being, chiefly on the account of his holiness. The holiness of God has always appeared to me the most lovely of all his attributes. The doctrines of God's absolute sovereignty, and free grace, in shewing mercy to whom he would shew mercy; and man's absolute dependance on the operations of God's Holy Spirit, have very often appeared to me as sweet and glorious doctrines. These doctrines have been much my delight. God's sovereignty has ever appeared to me, great part of his glory. It has often been my delight to approach God, and adore him as a sovereign God, and ask sovereign mercy of him.

I have loved the doctrines of the gospel; they have been to my soul like green pastures. The gospel has seemed to me the richest treasure; the treasure that I have most desired, and longed that it might dwell richly in me. The way of salvation by Christ has appeared, in a general way, glorious and excellent, most pleasant and most beautiful. It has often seemed to me, that it would in a great measure spoil heaven, to receive it in any other way. That text has often been affecting and delightful to me. Isa. xxxii. 2. A man shall be an hiding place from the wind, and a covert from the tempest, &c.

It has often appeared to me delightful, to be united to Christ; to have him for my head, and to be a member of his body; also to have Christ for my teacher and prophet. I very often think with sweetness, and longings, and pantings of soul, of being a little child, taking hold of Christ, to be led by him through the wilderness of this world. That text, Matth. xviii. 3, has often been sweet to me, except ye be converted and become as little children, &c. I love to think of coming to Christ, to receive salvation of him, poor in spirit, and quite empty of self, humbly exalting him alone; cut off entirely from my own root, in order to grow into, and out of Christ; to have God in Christ to be all in all; and to live by faith on the Son of God, a life of humble unfeigned confidence in him. . . .

I have sometimes had a sense of the excellent fulness of Christ, and his meetness and suitableness as a Saviour; whereby he has appeared to me, far above all, the chief of ten thousands. His blood and atonement have appeared sweet, and his righteousness sweet; which was always accompanied with ardency of spirit; and inward strugglings and breathings, and groanings that cannot be uttered, to be emptied of myself, and swallowed up in Christ.

Once, as I rode out into the woods for my health, in 1737, having alighted from my horse in a retired place, as my manner commonly has been, to walk for divine contemplation and prayer, I had a view that for me was extraordinary, of the glory of the Son of God, as Mediator between God and man, and his wonderful, great, full, pure and sweet grace and love, and meek and gentle condescension. This grace that appeared so calm and sweet, appeared also great above the heavens. The person of Christ appeared ineffably excellent with an excellency great enough to swallow up all thought and conception—which continued as near as I can judge, about an hour; which kept me the greater part of the time in a flood of tears, and weeping aloud. I felt an ardency of soul to be, what I know not otherwise how to express, emptied and annihilated; to lie in the dust, and to be full of Christ alone; to love him with a holy and pure love; to trust in him; to live upon him; to serve and follow him; and to be perfectly sanctified and made pure, with a divine and heavenly purity. I have, several other times, had views very much of the same nature, and which have had the same effects.

I have many times had a sense of the glory of the third person in the Trinity, in his office of Sanctifier; in his holy operations, communicating divine light and life to the soul. God, in the communications of his Holy Spirit, has appeared as an infinite fountain of divine glory and sweetness; being full, and sufficient to fill and satisfy the soul; pouring forth itself in sweet communications; like the sun in its glory, sweetly and pleasantly diffusing light and life. And I have sometimes had an affecting sense of the excellency of the word of God, as a word of life; as the light of life; a sweet, excellent, life-giving word; accompanied with a thirsting after that word, that it might dwell richly in my heart.

Often, since I lived in this town, I have had very affecting views of my own sinfulness and vileness; very frequently to such a degree as to hold me in a kind of loud weeping, sometimes for a considerable time together; so that I have often been forced to shut myself up. I have had a vastly greater sense of my own wickedness, and the badness of my own heart, than ever I had before my conversion. It has often appeared to me, that if God should mark iniquity against me, I should appear the very worst of all mankind; of all that have been, since the beginning of the world to this time; and that I should have by far the lowest place in hell. When others, that have come to talk with me about their soul concerns, have expressed the sense they have had of their own wickedness, by saying that it seemed to them, that they were as bad as the devil himself; I thought their expression seemed exceedingly faint and feeble, to represent my wickedness.

My wickedness, as I am in myself, has long appeared to me perfectly ineffable, and swallowing up all thought and imagination; like an infinite deluge, or mountains over my head. I know not how to express better what my sins appear to me to be, than by heaping infinite upon infinite, and multiplying infinite by infinite. Very often, for these many years, these expressions are in my mind, and in my mouth, "Infinite upon infinite—Infinite upon infinite!" When I look into my heart, and take a view of my wickedness, it looks like an abyss infinitely deeper than hell. And it appears to me, that were it not for free grace, exalted and raised up to the infinite height of all the fulness and glory of the great Jehovah, and the arm of his power and grace stretched forth in all the majesty of his power, and in all the glory of his sovereignty, I should appear sunk down in my sins below hell itself; far beyond the sight of every thing, but the eye of sovereign grace, that can pierce even down to such a depth. And yet, it seems to me, that my conviction of sin is exceeding small, and faint; it is enough to amaze me, that I have no more sense of my sin. I know certainly, that I have very little sense of my sinfulness. When I have had turns of weeping and crying for my sins, I thought I knew at the time, that my repentance was nothing to my sin.

I have greatly longed of late, for a broken heart, and to lie low before God; and, when I ask for humility, I cannot bear the thoughts of being no more humble than other Christians. It seems to me, that though their degrees of humility may be suitable for them, yet it would be a vile self-exaltation in me, not to be the lowest in humility of all mankind. Others speak of their longing to be "humbled to the dust;" that may be a proper expression for them, but I always think of myself, that I ought, and it is an expression that has long been natural for me to use in prayer, "to lie infinitely low before God." And it is affecting to think, how ignorant I was, when a young Christian, of the bottomless, infinite depths of wickedness, pride, hypocrisy and deceit, left in my heart.

I have a much greater sense of my universal, exceeding dependence on God's grace and strength, and mere good pleasure, of late, than I used formerly to have; and have experienced more of an abhorrence of my own righteousness. The very thought of any joy arising in me, on any consideration of my own amiableness, performances, or experiences, or any goodness of heart or life, is nauseous and detestable to me. And yet I am greatly afflicted with a proud and self-righteous spirit, much more sensibly than I used to be formerly. I see that serpent rising and putting forth its head continually, every where, all around me.

Though it seems to me, that, in some respects, I was a far better Christian, for two or three years after my first conversion, than I am now; and lived in a more constant delight and pleasure; yet, of late years, I have had a more full and constant sense of the absolute sovereignty of God, and a delight in that sovereignty; and have had more of a sense of the glory of Christ, as a Mediator revealed in the gospel. On one Saturday night, in particular, I had such a discovery of the excel- 20 lency of the gospel above all other doctrines, that

I could not but say to myself, "This is my chosen light, my chosen doctrine;" and of Christ, "This is my chosen Prophet." It appeared sweet, beyond all expression, to follow Christ, and to be taught, and enlightened, and instructed by him; to learn of him, and live to him. Another Saturday night, (January, 1739) I had such a sense, how sweet and blessed a thing it was to walk in the way of duty; to do that which was right and meet to be done, and agreeable to the holy mind of God; that it caused me to break forth into a kind of loud weeping, which held me some time, so that I was forced to shut myself up, and fasten the doors. I could not but, as it were, cry out, "How happy are they which do that which is right in the sight of God! They are blessed indeed, they are the happy ones!" I had, at the same time, a very affecting sense, how meet and suitable it was that God should govern the world, and order all things according to his own pleasure; and I rejoiced in it, that God reigned, and that his will was done.

JOHN WOOLMAN (1720–1772)

JOHN WOOLMAN, farm lad of New Jersey, was a tailor and merchant, but his real vocation was the ministry of love. His *Journal* (1774), which Whittier called "a classic of the inner life," is an important document in the history of American idealism. Its limpid prose provides the best introduction to the legacy of religious tolerance, humanitarianism, and mysticism bequeathed by the Quakers. It belongs on the shelf of American classics as one of the purest autobiographies in the English language.

Woolman was born at Northampton, New Jersey, in 1720. He began his career as a preacher at the age of 21, and spent the best years of his life as an itinerant minister, traveling through Massachusetts, Rhode Island, Connecticut, Pennsylvania, New Jersey, Virginia, Maryland, and the Carolinas, endeavoring with "sweet reasonableness" to show people the right way of life. Woolman was married to Sarah Ellis, August 18, 1749. She is mentioned but seldom in the *Journal* and the only reference to his family life is contained in the testimony of the Monthly-Meeting of Friends at Burlington, August, 1774: "He was a loving Husband, a tender Father, and very humane to every part of the Creation under his Care." Woolman's tender social conscience was especially manifested in his crusade

against slavery and in his zeal for inspiring ideals of brotherhood among the Indians. In 1772 Woolman felt "drawn" to England, where he spent several months visiting meetings of the Society of Friends. After a summer of work he journeyed to York, where he died of smallpox on the seventh of October, 1772.

In the record of American thought Woolman's *Journal* has two claims to remembrance: it shows the remarkable inner workings of Quaker doctrine and spiritual inner light as they led the author to contemplation and to right living; and it reveals a concern for social justice which challenged many forms of economic exploitation. An apostle of the brotherhood of man, Woolman proclaimed the ideal of individual worth and dignity as guides to conduct in social and economic life. Thus he sought unrelentingly to break down barriers between wealth and poverty, privilege and oppression. Uncompromising in the performance of what he regarded as his duty, he strove to establish equality among men, and to open the way for the operation of the Light, not so much in the narrow interests of individual salvation as of the liberation of the masses. On the other hand, the *Journal* is an intimate, private account of one person's striving to achieve the good life. As a record of an ardent Quaker, the book thus shows how energizing a force the doctrine of the Friends could be when it was allowed full and positive direction in an individual life. The *Journal* thus becomes not only a medium for the expression of Woolman's own Christian idealism, but also of Quaker religious views.

BIBLIOGRAPHY · The standard text of Woolman's *Journal* is *The Journals and Essays of John Woolman* (1922), edited by A. M. Gummere. The best nineteenth-century edition was issued by John Greenleaf Whittier in 1871. The *Journal* is conveniently available in the Everyman's Library (1910). Biographies of Woolman include W. T. Shore, *John Woolman: His Life and Our Times* (1913); A. Sharpless, *John Woolman, A Pioneer in Labor Reform* (1920); F. V. Morley, *The Tailor of Mount Holly: John Woolman* (1926); and J. P. Whitney, *John Woolman, American Quaker* (1942). M. C. Tyler's *Literary History of the American Revolution, 1763–1783* (1897) contains a valuable account of Woolman's life and work (II, 339–347). Other critical estimates include E. C. Wilson, "John Woolman: A Social Reformer of the Eighteenth Century," *Economic Review* (April, 1913); M. Kent, "John Woolman, Mystic and Reformer," *Hibbert Journal* (January, 1928); E. E. Taylor, *John Woolman, Craftsman Prophet* (1920).

Journal

JOHN WOOLMAN's *Journal* was not intended for publication, but it was written with great care in order to preserve an exact account of the author's spiritual enlightenment and his conduct as a practical mystic. Since its first printing in 1774 it has been reissued many times, appreciatively read, and widely praised as a colonial classic. Lamb, who confessed the *Journal* was the only American book he ever read twice, also admonished: "Get the writings of John Woolman by heart." Crabbe Robinson recorded in his journal: 'An illiterate tailor, he writes in a style of the most exquisite purity and grace. His moral qualities are transferred to his writings. Had he not been so very humble, he would have written a still better book; for, fearing to indulge in vanity, he conceals the events in which he was a great actor. His religion was love." Emerson declared, "I find more wisdom in these pages than in any other book written since the days of the Apostles." The text is that of the edition published in Philadelphia in 1775.

VIII. [*Ministry in Pennsylvania* 1761]

Having felt my mind drawn toward a visit to a few meetings in Pennsylvania, I was very desirous to be rightly instructed as to the time of seting off, and on the tenth day of the fifth month, 1761, being the first day of the week I went to Haddonfield meeting, concluding to seek for heavenly instruction, and come home or go on as I might then believe best for me; and there through the springing up of pure love, I felt encouragement and so crossed the river. In this visit I was at two quarterly and three monthly meetings, and in the love of truth, felt my way open to labour with some noted friends who kept negroes, and as I was favoured to keep the root, and endeavoured to discharge what I believed was required of me, I found inward peace therein from time to time, and thankfulness of heart to the Lord, who was graciously pleased to guide me.

In the eighth month, 1761, having felt drawings in my mind to visit friends in and about Shrewsbury; I went there, and was at their monthly-meeting and their first-day meeting and had a meeting at Squan and another at Squankum, and as way opened had conversation with some noted friends concerning their slaves, and I returned home in a thankful sense of the goodness of the Lord.

From a care I felt growing in me some years, I wrote Considerations on keeping Negroes, part second; which was printed this year, 1762. When the overseers of the press had done with it, they offered to get a number printed to be paid for, out of the yearly-meeting stock, and to be given away; but I being most easy to publish them at my own expense, and offering my reasons they appeared satisfied.

This stock is the contribution of the members of our religious society in general; amongst whom are many who keep negroes, and being inclined to continue them in slavery, are not likely to be satisfied with those books being spread amongst a people where many of the slaves are taught to read and especially not at their expense; and such often receiving them as a gift, conceal them. But as they who make a purchase, generally buy that which they have a mind for, I believed it best to sell them; expecting, by that means, they would more generaly be read with attention. Advertisements being signed by order of the overseers of the press, directed to be read in monthly-meetings of business within our yearly-meeting, informing where the books were, and that the price was no more than the cost of printing and binding them; many were taken of in our parts, some I sent to Virginia, some to New York, and some to Newport, to my acquaintance there, and some I kept, expecting to give part of them away, where there appear'd a prospect of service.

In my youth I was used to hard labour; and though I was midling healthy, yet my nature was not fited to endure so much as many others, that being often weary, I was prepared to sympathize with those whose circumstance in life, as free men, required constant labour to answer the demands of their creditors; and with others under oppression. In the uneasiness of body, which I have many times felt by too much labour, not as a forced but a voluntary opression, I have often been excited to think on the original cause of that opression, which is imposed on many in the world. And the latter part of the time wherein I laboured on the plantation, my heart, through the fresh visitations of heavenly love, being often tender; and my leisure time frequently spent in reading the life and doctrines of our blessed Redeemer, the account of the sufferings of martyrs, and the history of the first rise of our society, a belief was gradually setled in my mind, That if such who had great estates, generally lived in that humility and plainness which belongs to a christian life, and laid much easier rents and interests on their lands and monies, and thus led the way to a right use of things, so great a number of people might be employed in things useful, that labour both for men and other creatures would need to be no more than an agreeable employ. And divers branches of business, which serve chiefly to please the natural inclinations of our minds, and which at present, seems necessary to circulate that wealth which some gather might, in this way of pure wisdom, be discontinued. And as I have thus considered these things, a query at times, hath arisen: Do I, in all my proceedings, keep to that use of things which is agreeable to universal righteousness? And then there hath some degree of sadness, at times, come over me; for that I accustomed myself to some things, which ocasioned more labour than I believe divine wisdom intends for us.

From my early acquaintance with truth, I have often felt an inward distress, occasioned by the striving of a spirit in me, against the operation of the heavenly principle; and in this circumstance have been affected with a sense of my own wretchedness, and in a mourning condition felt earnest longing for that divine help, which brings the soul into true liberty and sometimes in this state, retireing into private places, the spirit of supplication hath been given me; and under a heavenly covering, have asked my gracious Father, to give me a heart in all things resigned to the direction of his wisdom, and in uttering language like this, the thoughts of my wearing hats and garments dyed with a dye injurious to them, has made lasting impressions on me.

In visiting people of note in the society who had slaves, and labouring with them in brotherly love on that account, I have seen and the sight has affected me, that a conformity to some customs, distinguishable from pure wisdom, has entangled many; and the desire of gain to support those customs, greatly opposed the work of truth. And sometimes when the prospect of the work before me has been such, that in bowedness of spirit I have been drawn into retired places, and besought the Lord with tears that he would take me wholly under his direction, and show me the way in which I ought to walk; it hath revived with strength of conviction, that if I would be his faithfull servant, I must in all things attend to his wisdom, and be teachable; and so cease from all customs contrary thereto, however used amongst religious people.

As he is the perfection of power, of wisdom, and of goodness; so I believe, he hath provided, that so much labour shall be necessary for men's support in this world, as would, being rightly divided, be a suitable employment of their time; and that we cannot go into superfluities, nor grasp after wealth in a way contrary to his wisdom, without having connection with some degree of oppression, and with that spirit which leads to self exaltation and strife, and which frequently brings calamities on countries, by parties contending about their claims.

Being thus fully convinced, and feeling an increasing desire to live in the spirit of peace; being often sorrowfully affected with thinking on the unquiet spirit in which wars are generally carried on, and with the miseries of many of my fellow-creatures engaged therein; some suddenly destroyed; some wounded, and after much pain remain crippled; some deprived of all their outward substance, and reduced to want; and some carried into captivity. Thinking often on these things, the use of hats and garments dyed with a dye hurtfull to them, and wearing more cloaths in summer than are usefull grew more uneasy to me; believing them to be customs which have not their foundation in pure wisdom. The apprehension of being singular from my beloved friends, was a strait upon me; and thus I remained in the use of some things contrary to my judgment.

And on the thirty-first day of the fifth month, 1761 I was taken ill of a fever; and after having it near a week, I was in great distress of body: and one day there was a cry raised in me, that I might understand the cause why I was afflicted, and improve under it; and my conformity to some customs, which I believed were not right, were brought to my remembrance; and in the continuation of the exercise, I felt all the powers in me yield themselves up into the hands of Him who gave me being; and was made thankfull, that he had taken hold of me by his chastisement: feeling the necessity of further purifying, there was now no desire in me for health, untill the design of my correction was answered; and thus I lay in abasement and brokenness of spirit, and as I felt a sinking down into a calm resignation, so I felt, as in an instant, an inward healing in my nature and from that time forward I grew better.

Though I was thus settled in mind in relation to hurtful dyes, I felt easy to wear my garments heretofore made; and so continued about nine months. Then I thought of getting a hat the natural colour of the fur; but the apprehension of being looked upon as one affecting singularity, felt uneasy to me: and here I had occasion to consider, that things though small in themselves, being clearly enjoined by divine authority as a duty, became great things to us; and I trusted that the Lord would support me in the trials that might attend singularity, while that singularity was only for his sake: on this account, I was under close exercise of mind in the time of our General Spring Meeting, 1762, greatly desiring to be rightly directed, when being deeply bowed in spirit before the Lord, I was made willing to submit to what I apprehended was required of me; and when I returned home, got a hat of the natural colour of the fur.

In attending meetings, this singularity was a trial upon me, and more especially at this time, white hats being used by some who were fond of following the changeable modes of dress; and as some friends, who knew not on what motives I wore it, carried shy of me, I felt my way for a time shut up in the exercise of the ministry: and in this condition my mind being turned toward my heavenly Father, with fervent cries that I might be preserved to walk before Him in the meekness of wisdom, my heart was often tender in meetings; and I felt an inward consolation, which to me was very precious under those difficulties.

I had several dyed garments fit for use, which, I believed it best to wear, till I had ocasion of new ones: and some friends were apprehensive, that my wearing such a hat savored of an affected singularity; and such who spake with me in a friendly way, I generally informed in a few words, that I believ'd my wearing it, was not in my own will. I had at times been sensible, that a superficial friendship had been dangerous to me; and many Friends now being uneasy with me, I had an inclination to acquaint some with the manner of my being led into these things; yet, upon a deeper thought, I was for a time most easy to omit it, believing the present dispensation was profitable, and trusting that if I kept my place, the Lord in his own time would open the hearts of friends toward me: since which, I have had cause to admire his goodness and loving-kindness, in leading about and instructing and opening and enlarging my heart in some of our meetings.

In the eleventh month of the year 1762, feeling an engagement of mind to visit some families in Mansfield: I joined my beloved friend Benjamin Jones, and we spent a few days together in that service. In the second month 1763, I joined in company with Elizabeth Smith and Mary Noble, on a visit to the families of friends at Ancocas;

136

in both which visits, through the baptizing power of truth, the sincere laborers were often comforted, and the hearts of Friends opened to receive us. And in the fourth month following I accompanied some Friends on a visit to the families of Friends in Mount-Holly, in which my mind was drawn into an inward awfullness, wherein strong desires were raised for the everlasting wellfare of my fellow-creatures; and through the kindness of our heavenly Father, our hearts were at times enlarged, and friends invited in the flowings of divine love to attend to that which would settle them on the sure foundation.

Having many years felt love in my heart towards the natives of this land, who dwell far back in the wilderness, whose ancestors were the owners and possessors of the land where we dwell, and who for a very small consideration Assigned their Inheritance to us, and being at Philadelphia in the eighth month, 1761, on a visit to some friends who had slaves, I fell in company with some of those natives, who lived on the east branch of the river Susquehannah at an Indian Town called Wehaloosing, two hundred miles from Philadelphia; and in conversation with them by an interpreter, as also by observations on their countenances and conduct, I believed some of them were measurably acquainted with that divine power which subjects the rough and froward will of the creature. And at times, I felt inward drawings toward a visit to that place of which I told none except my dear wife, until it came to some ripeness, and then in the winter, 1762, I laid it before friends at our monthly and quarterly and afterwards at our General spring meeting; and having the unity of friends, and being thoughtfull about an Indian pilot, there came a man and three women from a little beyond that town to Philadelphia on business: and I being informed thereof by letter, met them in Town in the fifth month, 1763; and after some conversation, finding they were sober people, I, by the concurrence of friends in that place, agreed to join with them as companions in their return, and on the seventh day of the sixth month following, we appointed to meet at Samuel Foulk's, at Richland in Bucks County. Now as this visit felt very weighty, and was performed at a time when traveling appeared perilous, so the dis-

pensations of Divine Providence, in preparing my mind for it, have been memorable; and I believe it good for me to give some hints thereof.

After I had given up to go, the thoughts of the journey were often attended with unusual sadness; in which times, my heart was frequently turned to the Lord with inward breathings for his heavenly support, that I might not fail to follow Him wheresoever He might lead me: and being at our youths meeting at Chesterfield, about a week before the time I expected to set off, was there led to speak on that prayer of our Redeemer to his Father: "I pray not that thou shouldest take them out of the world, but that thou shouldst keep them from the evil." And in attending to the pure openings of truth, had to mention what He elsewhere said to his Father, "I know that thou hearest me at all times." So that, as some of his followers kept their places, and as his prayer was granted, it followed necessarily that they were kept from evil, and as some of those met with great hardships and afflictions in this world, and at last suffered death by cruel men; it appears, that whatsoever befalls men while they live in pure obedience to God, as it certainly works for good, so it may not be considered an evil as it relates to them. As I spake on this Subject, my heart was much tendered, and great awfullness came over me; and then, on the first day of the next week, being at our own afternoon meeting, and my heart being enlarged in love, I was led to speak on the care and protection of the Lord over his people, and to make mention of that passage where a band of Assyrians endeavouring to take captive the prophet, were disappointed; and how the psalmist said, "the angel of the Lord encampeth round about them that fear him." And thus, in true love, and tenderness, I parted from friends, expecting the next morning to proceed on my journey; and being weary, went early to bed: and after I had been asleep a short time, I was awakened by a man calling at my door; and arising, was invited to meet some friends at a publick-house in our town, who came from Philadelphia so late that friends were generally gone to bed. These Friends informed me, that an express arrived the last morning from Pittsburgh, and brought news that the Indians had taken a fort from the English, westward, and slain and scalped English people in divers places, some near the said Pittsburgh; and that some elderly friends in Philadelphia, knowing the time of my expecting to set off, had conferred together, and thought good to inform me of these things, before I left home, that I might consider them, and proceed as I believed best; so I, going again to bed, told not my wife till morning. My heart was turned to the Lord for his heavenly instruction; and it was a humbling time to me. When I told my dear wife, she appeared to be deeply concerned about it; but in a few hours time, my mind became settled in a belief, that it was my duty to proceed on my journey; and she bore it with a good degree of resignation. In this conflict of spirit, there were great searchings of heart, and strong cries to the Lord, that no motion might be in the least degree attended to, but that of the pure Spirit of Truth.

The subjects before-mentioned, on which I had so lately spoke in publick, were now very fresh before me; and I was brought inwardly to commit myself to the Lord, to be disposed of as he Saw best. So I took leave of my family and neighbours, in much bowedness of spirit, and went to our monthly meeting at Burlington; and after taking leave of friends there, I crossed the river, accompanied by my friends Israel and John Pemberton; and parting the next morning with Israel, John bore me company to Samuel Foulks; where I met the before-mentioned Indians, and we were glad to see each other. Here my friend Benjamin Parvin met me, and proposed joining as a companion, we having passed some letters before on the subject; and now on his account I had a sharp trial, for as the journey appeared perilous, I thought if he went chiefly to bear me company, and we should be taken captive, my having been the means of drawing him into these difficulties, would add to my own afflictions: so I told him my mind freely, and let him know that I was resigned to go alone; but after all, if he really believed it to be his duty to go on, I believed his company would be very comfortable to me. It was indeed a time of deep exercise, and Benjamin appeared to be so fastened to the visit, that he could not be easy to leave me; so we went on accompanied by our friends John Pemberton and

William Lightfoot of Pikeland, and lodged at Bethlehem; and there parting with John, William and we went forward on the ninth day of the sixth month, and got lodging on the floor of a house about five miles from Fort Allen; here we parted with William, and at this place we met with an Indian trader, lately come from Wioming; and in conversation with him, I perceived that many white people do often sell rum to the Indians, which, I believe, is a great evil; first, they being thereby deprived of the use of their reason, and their spirits violently agitated, quarrels often arise which end in mischief; and the bitterness and resentments ocasioned hereby, are frequently of long continuance: again, their skins and furs, gotten thro' much fatigue and hard travels in hunting, with which they intended to buy cloathing, when they became intoxicated, they often sell at a low rate for more rum; and afterward, when they suffer for want of the necessaries of life, are angry with those who, for the sake of gain, took the advantage of their weakness: of this their chiefs have often complained, at their treaties with the English. Where cunning people pass counterfeits, and impose that on others which is only good for nothing, it is considered as a wickedness; but to sell that to people which we know does them harm, and which often works their ruin, for the sake of gain, manifests a hardened and corrupt heart; and it is an evil, which demands the care of all true lovers of virtue to suppress. And while my mind, this evening, was thus employed, I also remembered, that the people on the frontiers among whom this evil is too common, are often poor; who venture to the outside of a colony, that they may live more independent on such who are wealthy who often set high rents on their land: being then renewedly confirmed in a belief, that if all our inhabitants lived according to sound wisdom, labouring to promote universal love and righteousness, and ceased from every inordinate desire after wealth, and from all customs which are tinctured with luxury, the way would be easy for our inhabitants, though much more numerous than at present, to live comfortably on honest employments, without having that temptation they are often under of being drawn into schemes to make settlements on lands which have not been honestly purchased of the Indians, or of applying to that wicked practice of selling rum to them.

On the tenth day of the sixth month we set out early in the morning, and crossed the western branch of Delaware, called the Great Lehie, near fort Allen; the water being high, we went over in a canoe: here we met an Indian and had some friendly conversation with him and gave him some biscuit; and he having killed a deer, gave the Indians with us some of it: then after traveling some miles, we met several Indian men and women with a cow and horse, and some household goods, who were lately come from their dwelling at Wioming, and going to settle at another place; we made them some small presents, and some of them understanding English, I told them my motive in coming into their country; with which they appeared satisfied: and one of our guides talking a while with an antient woman concerning us, the poor old woman came to my companion and me, and took her leave of us with an appearance of sincere affection. So going on, we pitched our tent near the banks of the same river, having laboured hard in crossing some of those mountains, called the Blue Ridge; and by the roughness of the stones, and the cavities between them, and the steepness of the hills, it appeared dangerous: but we were preserved in safety, through the kindness of Him whose works in these mountainous deserts appeared awful; toward whom my heart was turned during this days travel.

Near our tent, on the sides of large trees peeled for that purpose, were various representations of men going to, and returning from the wars, and of some killed in battle. This being a path heretofore used by warriors; and as I walked about viewing those Indian histories, which were painted mostly in red but some in black, and thinking on the innumerable afflictions which the proud, fierce spirit produceth in the world; Thinking on the toils and fatigues of warriors, traveling over mountains and deserts, thinking on their miseries and distresses when wounded far from home by their enemies; and of their bruises and great weariness in chasing one another over the rocks and mountains; and of their restless, unquiet state of mind, who live in this spirit, and of the hatred which mutually grows up in the minds of the children of those nations engaged in war with each other: the desire to cherish the spirit of love and peace amongst these people, arose very fresh in me.

This was the first night that we lodged in the woods; and being wet with traveling in the rain, the ground, our tent, and the bushes which we purposed to lay under, our blankets also wet, all looked discouraging; but I believed that it was the Lord who had thus far brought me forward, and that he would dispose of me as He saw good, and therein I felt easy, so we kindled a fire, with our tent door open to it, and with some bushes next the ground, and then blankets, we made our bed, and lying down, got some sleep: and in the morning, feeling a little unwell, I went into the river; the water was cold, but soon after I felt fresh and well.

The eleventh day of the sixth month, the bushes being wet, we tarried in our tent till about eight o'clock; when going on, crossed a high mountain supposed to be upwards of four miles over; the steepness on the north side exceeding all the others: we also crossed two swamps; and it raining near night, we pitched our tent and lodged.

About noon, on our way, we were overtaken by one of the moravian brethren going to Wehaloosing, and an Indian man with him who could talk English; and we being together while our horses eat grass, had some friendly conversation; but they traveling faster than we, soon left us. This moravian, I understood, had spent some time this spring at Wehaloosing, and was by some of the Indians, invited to come again.

The twelfth day of the sixth month, and first of the week being a rainy day, we continued in our tent; and here I was led to think on the nature of the exercise which hath attended me: Love was the first motion, and then a concern arose to spend some time with the Indians, that I might feel and understand their life, and the spirit they live in, if happily I might receive some instruction from them, or they be in any degree helped forward by my following the leadings of truth amongst them: and as it pleased the Lord to make way for my going at a time when the troubles of war were increasing, and when, by reason of much wet weather, traveling was more difficult than usual at that season, I looked upon it as a more favourable oportunity to season my mind, and bring me into

139

a nearer sympathy with them: and as mine eye was to the great Father of mercies, humbly desiring to learn what his will was concerning me, I was made quiet and content.

Our guide's horse, though hoppled, went away in the night; and after finding our own, and searching some time for him, his footsteps were discovered in the path going back again, whereupon my kind companion went off in the rain, and after about seven hours returned with him: and here we lodged again, tying up our horses before we went to Bed, and loosing them to feed about break of day.

On the thirteenth day of the sixth month, the Sun appearing, we set forward; and as I rode over the barren hills, my meditations were on the alterations of the circumstances of the natives of this land since the coming in of the English. The lands near the sea, are conveniently situated for fishing; the lands near the rivers, where the tides flow, and some above, are in many places fertile, and not mountainous; while the runing of the tides, makes passing up and down easy with any kind of traffick. Those natives have in some places, for trifling considerations, sold their inheritance so favourably situated; and in other places, been driven back by superior force: so that, in many places, as their way of clothing themselves is now altered from what it was, and they far remote from us, have to pass over mountains, swamps, and barren deserts, where traveling is very troublesome, in bringing their furs and skins to trade with us.

By the extending of English settlements, and partly by English hunters, the wild beasts they chiefly depend on for a subsistence, are not so plenty as they were; and people too often, for the sake of gain, open a door for them to waste their skins and furs, in purchasing a liquor which tends to the ruin of them and their families.

My own will and desire being now very much broken, and my heart, with much earnestness, turned to the Lord, to whom alone I looked for help in the dangers before me, I had a prospect of the English along the coast, for upwards of nine hundred miles, where I have travelled; and the favourable situation of the English, and the difficulties attending the natives in many places, and the negroes, were open before me; and a weighty and heavenly care came over my mind,

and love filled my heart toward all mankind, in which I felt a strong engagement, that we might be obedient to the Lord while, in tender mercies, He is yet calling to us; and so attend to pure universal righteousness, as to give no just cause of offence to the Gentiles, who do not profess christianity, whether the blacks from Africa, or the native inhabitants of this continent: And here I was led into a close, laborious enquiry, whether I, as an individual, kept clear from all things which tended to stir up, or were connected with wars, either in this land or Africa; and my heart was deeply concerned, that in future I might in all things keep steadily to the pure truth, and live and walk in the plainness and simplicity of a sincere follower of Christ. And in this lonely journey, I did, this day, greatly bewail the spreading of a wrong spirit, believing that the prosperous conveniant situation of the English, requires a constant attention to divine love and wisdom to guide and support us in a way answerable to the will of that good, gracious, and almighty Being, who hath an equal regard to all mankind: And here, luxury and covetousness, with the numerous opressions, and other evils attending them, appeared very afflicting to me, and I felt in that which is immutable, that the seeds of great calamity and desolation are sown and growing fast on this continent: Nor have I words sufficient to set forth that longing I then felt, that we who are placed along the coast, and have tasted the love and goodness of God, might arise in his strength; and like faithful messengers, labour to check the growth of those seeds that they may not ripen to the ruin of our posterity.

We reached the Indian settlement at Wioming: and here we were told that an Indian runner had been at that place a day or two before us, and brought news of the Indians taking an English fort westward, and destroying the people, and that they were endeavouring to take another; and also, that another Indian runner came there about the middle of the night before we got there, who came from a town about ten miles above Wehaloosing, and brought news that some Indian warriors from distant parts, came to that town with two English scalps; and told the people that it was war with the English.

Our guides took us to the house of a very antient man; and soon after we had put in our baggage, there came a man from another Indian house some distance off; and I perceiving there was a man near the door, went out; and he having a tomahawk wrapped under his matchcoat out of sight, as I approached him, he took it in his hand; I, however, went forward, and speaking to him in a friendly way, perceived he understood some English: my companion then coming out, we had some talk with him concerning the nature of our visit in these parts; and then he going into the house with us, and talking with our guides, soon appeared friendly, and sat down and smoaked his pipe. Tho' his taking his hatchet in his hand at the instant I drew near to him, had a disagreeable appearance, I believe he had no other intent than to be in readiness in case any violence was offered to him.

Hearing the news brought by these Indian runners, and being told by the Indians where we lodged, that what Indians were about Wioming expected in a few days, to move to some larger towns, I thought that, to all outward appearance, it was dangerous travelling at this time; and after a hard day's journey, brought into a painfull exercise at night, in which I had to trace back, and view over the steps I had taken from my first moving in the visit; and tho' I had to bewail some weakness which at times had attended me, yet I could not find that I had ever given way to a wilfull disobedience; and then as I believed I had, under a sense of duty, come thus far, I was now earnest in spirit beseeching the Lord to shew me what I ought to do. In this great distress I grew jealous of myself, lest the desire of reputation, as a man firmly settled to persevere through dangers, or the fear of disgrace arising on my returning without performing the visit might have some place in me. Thus I lay full of thoughts, great part of the night, while my beloved companion lay and slept by me; till the Lord, my gracious Father, who saw the conflicts of my soul, was pleased to give quietness: then I was again strengthened to commit my life, and all things relating thereto, into his heavenly hands; and geting a little sleep toward day, when morning came we arose.

On the fourteenth day of the sixth month, we sought out and visited all the Indians hereabouts

that we could meet with; they being chiefly in one place, about a mile from where we lodged, in all perhaps twenty. Here I expressed the care I had on my mind for their good; and told them, that true love had made me willing thus to leave my family to come and see the Indians, and speak with them in their houses. Some of them appeared kind and friendly. So we took our leave of these Indians, and went up the river Susquehannah, about three miles, to the house of an Indian, called Jacob January, who had killed his hog; and the women were making store of bread, and preparing to move up the river. Here our pilots left their canoe when they came down in the spring, which, lying dry, was leaky; so that we, being detained some hours, had a good deal of friendly conversation with the family; and eating dinner with them, we made some small presents. Then putting our baggage in the canoe, some of them pushed slowly up the stream, and the rest of us rode our horses, and swimming them over a creek called Lahawahamunk, we pitched our tent a little above it, being a shower in the evening: and in a sense of God's goodness in helping me in my distress, sustained me under trials, and inclining my heart to trust in Him, I lay down in an humble bowed frame of mind and had a comfortable night's lodging.

On the fifteenth day of the sixth month, proceeded forward till the afternoon; and then a storm appearing, we met our canoe at an appointed place; and the rain continuing, we stayed all night, which was so heavy, that it beat through our tent and wet us and our baggage.

On the sixteenth day, we found on our way abundance of trees blown down with the storm yesterday; and had occasion reverently to consider the kind dealings of the Lord, who provided a safe place for us in the valley, while this storm continued. By the falling of abundance of trees across our path, we were much hindered, and in some swamps our way was so stopped, that we got throu—with extream difficulty.

I had this day often to consider myself as a sojourner in this world; and a belief in the all-sufficiency of God to support his people in their pilgrimage felt comfortable to me; and I was industriously employ'd to get to a state of perfect resignation.

We seldom saw our canoe but at appointed places by reason of the path going off from the river: and this afternoon, Job Chilaway, an Indian from Wehaloosing, who talks good English, and is acquainted with several people in and about Philadelphia, met our people on the river; and understanding where we expected to lodge, pushed back about six miles, and came to us after night; and in a while our own canoe came, it being hard work pushing up stream. Job told us, that an Indian came in haiste to their town yesterday, and told them, that three warriors, coming from some distance, lodged in a town above Wehaloosing a few nights past; and that these three men were going against the English at Juniatta. Job was going down the river to the province store at Shamokin. Though I was so far favoured with health as to continue travelling, yet through the various difficulties in our journey, and the different way of living from what I had been used to, I grew sick: and the news of these warriors being on their march so near us, and not knowing whether we might not fall in with them, it was a fresh trial of my faith, and though through the strength of divine love I had several times been enabled to commit myself to the divine disposal, I still found the want of my strength to be renewed, that I might persevere therein, and my cries for help were put up to the Lord, who, in great mercy gave me a resigned heart, in which I found quietness.

On the seventeenth day, parting from Job Chilaway, we went on, and reached Wehaloosing about the middle of the afternoon. The first Indian that we saw, was a woman of a modest countenance, with a Bible, who first spake to our guide; and then, with a harmonious voice, expressed her gladness at seeing us, having before heard of our coming: then, by the direction of our guide, we sat down on a log; and he went to the town, to tell the people we were come. My companion and I sitting thus together, in a deep inward stillness, the poor woman came and sat near us; and great awfulness coming over us, we rejoyced in a sense of God's love manifested to our poor souls. After a while, we heard a konkshell blow several times, and then came John Curtis, and another Indian man, who kindly invited us into a house near the town, where we found I suppose about sixty people, sitting in silence; and after sitting a short time, I stood up and in some tenderness of spirit acquainted them with the nature of my visit, and that a concern for their good had made me willing to come thus far to see them: all in a few short sentences, which some of them understanding interpreted to the others, and there appeared gladness amongst them. Then I shewed them my certificate, which was explained to them; and the moravian, who overtook us on the way, being now here, [bid] me wellcome.

On the eighteenth day, we rested ourselves this forenoon; and the Indians knowing that the moravian and I were of different religious societies, and as some of their people had encouraged him to come and stay awhile with them, were, I believe, concerned that no jarring or discord might be in their meetings: and they, I suppose, having conferred together, acquainted me, that the people, at my request, would, at any time, come together and hold meetings; and also told me, that they expected the moravian would speak in their settled meetings, which are commonly held morning and near evening. So I found liberty in my heart to speak to the moravian, and told him of the care I felt on my mind for the good of these people; and that I believed no ill effects would follow it, if I sometimes spake in their meetings when love engaged me thereto, without calling them together at times when they did not meet of course: whereupon he expresst his good-will toward my speaking at any time, all that I found in my heart to say: so near evening I was at their meeting, where the pure gospel love was felt, to the tendering some of our hearts, and the interpreters endeavouring to acquaint the people with what I said in short sentences, found some difficulty as none of them were quite perfect in the English and Delaware tongues; so they helped one another, and we laboured along, divine love attending: and afterwards feeling my mind covered with the spirit of prayer, I told the interpreters that I found it in my heart to pray to God, and believed if I prayed aright, he would hear me, and expressed my willingness for them to omit interpreting; so our meeting ended with a degree of divine love: and before the people went out, I observed Papunchang (the man who had been zealous in labouring for a reformation in that town being then very tender) spoke to one of the interpreters: and I was afterwards told that he said in substance as follows, "I Love to feel where words come from."

On the nineteenth day, and first of the week, this morning in the meeting the Indian who came up with the moravian, being also a member of that society, prayed; and then the moravian spake a short time to the people: and in the afternoon, they coming together, and my heart being filled with a heavenly care for their good, I spake to them awhile by interpreters; but none of them being perfect in the work, and I feeling the current of love run strong, told the interpreters that I believed some of the people would understand me, and I so proceeded: In which exercise, I believe the Holy Ghost wrought on some hearts to edification, where all the words were not understood. I looked upon it as a time of divine favor, and my heart was tendered and truly thankfull before the Lord; and after I sat down, one of the interpreters seemed spirited up to give the Indians the Substance of what I said.

Before our first meeting this morning, I was led to meditate on the manifold difficulties of these Indians, who, by the permission of the Six Nations, dwell in these parts; and a near sympathy with them was raised in me; and my heart being enlarged in the love of Christ, I thought that the affectionate care of a good man for his only brother in affliction, does not exceed what I then felt for that people.

I came to this place through much trouble; and though, through the mercies of God, I believed, that if I died in the journey it would be well with me; yet the thoughts of falling into the hands of Indian warriors, was in times of weakness, afflicting to me; and being of a tender constitution of body, the thoughts of captivity amongst them were, at times, grievous; as supposing, that they being strong and hardy, might demand service of me beyound what I could well bear; but the Lord alone was my keeper; and I believed, if I went into captivity, it would be for some good end; and thus, from time to time, my mind was centered in resignation, in which I always found quietness.

And now, this day, though I had the same dangerous wilderness between me and home, I was inwardly Joyfull that the Lord had strengthened me to come on this visit, and manifested a fatherly care over me in my poor lowly condition, when in mine own eyes I appear'd inferior to many amongst the Indians.

When the last mentioned meeting was ended, it being night, Papunchang went to bed; and one of the interpreters sitting by me, I observed Papunchang spoke with an harmonious voice, I suppose, a minute or two; and I asking the interpreter, was told, that "he was expressing his thankfullness to God for the favours he had received that day; and prayed that he would continue to favour him with that same, which he had experienced in that meeting." That though Papunchang had before agreed to receive the moravian, and to join with them, he still appeared kind and loving to us.

· · · · · · · · · · ·

The twenty-first day. This morning in meeting my heart was enlarged in pure love amongst them, and in short plain sentences expressed several things that rested upon me, which one of the interpreters gave the people pretty readily; and after which the meeting ended in supplication, and I had cause humbly to acknowledge the loving-kindness of the Lord toward us; and then I believed that a door remained open for the faithfull disciples of Jesus Christ, to labour amongst these people.

I now feeling my mind at liberty to return, took my leave of them in general, at the conclusion of what I said in meeting; and so we prepared to go homeward: but some of their most active men told us, that when we were ready to move, the people would choose to come and shake hands with us; which those who usually came to meeting did: and from a secret draught in my mind, I went amongst some who did not use to go to meetings, and took my leave of them also: and the moravian and his Indian interpreter, appeared respectful to us at parting. This town stands on the bank of Susquehannah, and consists, I believe, of about forty houses, mostly compact together; some about thirty feet long, and eighteen wide, some bigger, some less; mostly built of split plank, one end set in the ground and the other pinned to a plate, on which lay Rafters covered with bark. I understand a great flood last winter overflowed the chief part of the ground where the town Stands; and some were now about moving their houses to higher ground.

We expected only two Indians to be our company; but when we were ready to go we found many of them were going to Bethlehem with skins and furs, who chose to go in company with us: so they loaded two canoes, which they desired us to go in, telling us, that the waters were so raised with the rains that the horses should be taken by such who were better acquainted with the fording places; so we, with several Indians, went in the canoes, and others went on horses, there being seven besides ours. And we meeting with the Horsemen once on the way by appointment, and then near night, a little below a branch called Tankhannah, we lodged there; and some of the young men going out a little before dusk with their guns brought in a deer.

On the twenty-second day, through diligence, we reached Wioming before night, and understood the Indians were mostly gone from this place: here we went up a small creek into the woods with our canoes, and, pitching our tent, carried out our baggage; and before dark our horses came to us.

On the twenty-third day in the morning their horses were loaded, and we prepared our baggage and so set forward, being in all fourteen; and with diligent travelling were favoured to get near half way to Fort-Allen. The land on this road from Wioming to our frontier being mostly poor, and good grass scarce, they chose a piece of low ground to lodge on, as the best for grazeing; and I having sweat much in travelling, and being weary slept sound; I perceived in the night that I had taken cold, of which I was favoured to get better soon.

On the twenty-fourth day we passed Fort-Allen, and lodged near it in the woods. Having forded the westerly branch of Delaware three times, and thereby had a shorter way, and missed going over the top of the blue mountains, called the second ridge. In the second time fording, where the river cuts thro' the mountain, the waters being rapid and pretty deep, and my companion's

mare being a tall tractable animal, he sundry times drove her back thro' the river, and they loaded her with the burthens of some small horses, which they thought not sufficient to come through with their loads.

The troubles westward, and the difficulty for Indians to pass through our frontier, I apprehend was one reason why so many came; as expecting that our being in company, would prevent the outside inhabitants from being Surprised.

On the twenty-fifth day we reached Bethlehem, taking care on the way to keep foremost, and to acquaint people on and near the road who these Indians were: this we found very needful for the frontier inhabitants were often alarmed at the Report of English being killed by Indians westward.

Amongst our company were some who I did not remember to have seen at meeting, and some of these at first were very reserved; but we being several days together, and behaving friendly toward them, and making them suitable returns for the services they did us, they became more free and sociable.

On the twenty-sixth day and first of the week, having carefully endeavoured to settle all affairs with the Indians relative to our journey; we took leave of them, and I thought they generally parted with us affectionately; so we getting to Richland, had a very comfortable meeting amongst our friends: here I parted with my kind friend and companion Benjamin Parvin; and accompanied by my friend Samuel Foulks we rode to John Cadwallader's, from whence I reached home the next day, where I found my family middling well: and they and my friends all along appeared glad to see me return from a journey which they apprehended dangerous: but my mind, while I was out, had been employed in striving for a perfect resignation, I had so often been confirmed in a belief, that whatever the Lord might be pleased to allot for me, would work for good. I was careful lest I should admit any degree of selfishness in being glad overmuch, and laboured to improve by those trials in such a manner as my gracious Father and Protector intends for me. Between the English Inhabitants and Wehaloosing, we had only a narrow path, which in many places is much grown up with bushes, and interrupted by abundance of trees lying across it;

these, together with the mountains, swamps, and rough stones, make it a difficult road to travel; and the more so, for that rattle-snakes abound there, of which we killed four: that people who have never been in such places, have but an imperfect idea of them; but I was not only taught patience, but also made thankful to God, who thus led me about and instructed me, that I might have a quick and lively feeling of the afflictions of my fellow-creatures, whose situation in life is difficult.

MICHEL-GUILLAUME JEAN DE CRÈVECOEUR (1735–1813)

ALTHOUGH Crèvecoeur confessed, "There is something truly ridiculous in a farmer quitting his plough or his axe, and then flying to his pen," his *Letters from an American Farmer* (1782)—despite its romantic idealization of the simple life—possesses a sense of homely reality. In the twelfth letter, "Distresses of a Frontier Man," Crèvecoeur records poignantly his anguish when his Arcadian existence in the New World was disrupted by the struggle between the colonies and the crown. His more or less romantic and physiocratic interpretation of primitive nature in the *Letters*, which was read avidly by European romanticists, should be compared with his later vivid pictures of severe suffering on the frontier during the Revolution in *Sketches of Eighteenth Century America* (1925), printed from papers recovered in 1923. In no other writer is the humanitarian reaction to the ravages of war so apparent as in Crèvecoeur, and in no other is there so vivid a concept of the Revolution as a civil war.

Born Michel-Guillaume Jean de Crèvecoeur, January 31, 1735, near Caen in Normandy, Crèvecoeur is popularly known as J. Hector St. John, the name he assumed in 1765 when he became an American citizen in New York. In 1754 he sailed to Canada to serve as cartographer under Montcalm in the last of the French and Indian Wars. He seems to have covered much of what is now the Great Lakes region and the "Buckeye country," incorporating the information in a map of alleged French territory in 1758. After the end of hostilities in 1759 he made excursions along the Atlantic seaboard, and as merchandizer or surveyor traveled over much of Pennsylvania and New York. In 1769, four years after he became a naturalized citizen of New York, he married Mehitabel Tippet, of Yonkers, and settled down to the business of managing an estate. On his farm in Orange County, where his three children were born, he wrote the bucolic essays that impart so much fresh charm to his first book. The Revolution, however, broke in upon his retreat, destroyed his cherished dreams, and caught him in a vise between Tories and patriots; to neither group did he care to belong, although he had obvious aristocratic and loyalist leanings. He wanted only to be left alone, certainly an unrealistic ambition in wartime. Badgered and tormented by patriots, and subsequently imprisoned by the British, he returned to France via England. As soon as hostilities ceased, he returned to America, to find his home destroyed, his children missing, and his wife dead. He finally located his children, and remained in New York City as a French consul, occasionally writing articles on agriculture for American newspapers, distributing learned publications, and introducing in America such agricultural plants as alfalfa. In 1790 he left America for France and there, because of the French Revolution and continued ill health, he remained for his last twenty-three years.

One volume of Crèvecoeur's *Letters* was published in London in 1782 (American edition, 1792), and this London edition was sold by American booksellers. *Letters from an American Farmer*, dedicated to Abbé Raynal, is the most delightful and idyllic of his books. In it are fused interest in agriculture and observation of nature, expressed in a simple, dramatic, and somewhat sentimental style. Crèvecoeur's view of life was, in general, optimistic, when he was not plunged into tragic despair by the violence of war. The main purpose of the early essays seems to have been to present America in an attractive light to European readers. Because of their somewhat bitter tone, Crèvecoeur did not print in his first volume an equally bulky parcel of papers, which, in 1925 were printed as *Sketches of Eighteenth Century America*. These papers also reveal Crèvecoeur's humanitarianism more fully than his first work.

BIBLIOGRAPHY · There is no collected edition of Crèvecoeur. His *Letters from an American Farmer* is readily available in Everyman's Library, but the best edition is the 1904 reprint with a preface by W. P. Trent and an introduction by Ludwig Lewissohn. Other titles by Crèvecoeur are *Voyage dans la haute Pensylvanie et dans l'État de New-York* (1801), and *Sketches of Eighteenth Century America* (1925), recently discovered Crèvecoeur material, edited by H. L. Bourdin, R. H. Gabriel, and S. T. Williams. The only full biography is Julia Post Mitchell's *St. Jean de Crèvecoeur* (1916). The most careful study is H. C. Rice's *Le Cul-*

tivateur Américain (1933), which also contains useful bibliographical material. Other critical studies include H. L. Bourdin and S. T. Williams, "Crèvecoeur on the Susquehanna," *Yale Review* (April, 1925); Bourdin and Williams, "Unpublished Mss. of Crèvecoeur," *Studies in Philology* (July, 1925); J. B. Moore, "Crèvecoeur and Thoreau," *Papers of the Michigan Academy of Science, Art, and Letters* (1926); J. B. Moore, "The Rehabilitation of Crèvecoeur," *Sewanee Review* (April, 1927); and Robert de Crèvecoeur, *Saint Jean de Crèvecoeur: Sa Vie et Ses Ouvrages* (1883).

Letters from an American Farmer

III. *What Is an American?*

CRÈVECOEUR has been proclaimed the originator of the melting-pot myth. He regarded the air of freedom, ample subsistence, good will, and pride of ownership as the magic properties in the crucible which fused diverse European immigrants into new men, Americans. Although *Letters from an American Farmer* was first published in London in 1782, most of it was written before the Revolution, and its eloquent observations are chiefly applicable to the middle colonies and Nantucket in the mid-eighteenth century. But Crèvecoeur wandered more extensively over the American scene than from the Mohawk to the Susquehanna, as is indicated by the following outline of the contents: I. Introduction; II. On the Situation, Feelings, and Pleasures of an American Farmer; III. What is an American? IV. Description of the Island of Nantucket . . . ; V. Customary Education and Employment of the Inhabitants of Nantucket; VI. Description of the Island of Martha's Vineyard . . . ; VII. Manners and Customs at Nantucket; VIII. Peculiar Customs at Nantucket; IX. Description of Charles-Town . . . ; X. On Snakes and on the Humming Bird; XI. From Mr. Iw-n Al-Z, a Russian Gentleman, describing the Visit He Paid at my Request to Mr. John Bartram, the Celebrated Pennsylvania Botanist; XII. Distresses of a Frontier Man. The text is that of the edition published by Matthew Carey in Philadelphia in 1793.

I wish I could be acquainted with the feelings and thoughts which must agitate the heart and present themselves to the mind of an enlightened Englishman, when he first lands on this continent. He must greatly rejoice, that he lived at a time to see this fair country discovered and settled; he must necessarily feel a share of national pride, when he views the chain of settlements which em-

bellishes these extended shores. When he says to himself, this is the work of my countrymen, who, when convulsed by factions, afflicted by a variety of miseries and wants, restless and impatient, took refuge here. They brought along with them their national genius, to which they principally owe what liberty they enjoy, and what substance they possess. Here he sees the industry of his native country, displayed in a new manner, and traces in their works the embryos of all the arts, sciences, and ingenuity which flourish in Europe. Here he beholds fair cities, substantial villages, extensive fields, an immense country filled with decent houses, good roads, orchards, meadows, and bridges, where an hundred years ago all was wild, woody, and uncultivated!

What a train of pleasing ideas this fair spectacle must suggest! it is a prospect which must inspire a good citizen with the most heartfelt pleasure. The difficulty consists in the manner of viewing so extensive a scene. He is arrived on a new continent; a modern society offers itself to his contemplation, different from what he had hitherto seen. It is not composed, as in Europe, of great lords who possess everything, and of a herd of people who have nothing. Here are no aristocratical families, no courts, no kings, no bishops, no ecclesiastical dominion, no invisible power giving to a few a very visible one; no great manufacturers employing thousands, no great refinements of luxury. The rich and the poor are not so far removed from each other as they are in Europe.

Some few towns excepted, we are all tillers of the earth, from Nova Scotia to West Florida. We are a people of cultivators, scattered over an immense territory, communicating with each other by means of good roads and navigable rivers, united by the silken bands of mild government, all respecting the laws, without dreading their power, because they are equitable. We are all animated with the spirit of an industry which is unfettered, and unrestrained, because each person works for himself. If he travels through our rural districts, he views not the hostile castle, and the haughty mansion, contrasted with the clay-built hut and miserable cabin, where cattle and men help to keep each other warm, and dwell in meanness, smoke, and indigence. A pleasing uniformity of decent competence appears throughout our habitations. The meanest of our log-houses is a dry and comfortable habitation. Lawyer or merchant are the fairest titles our towns afford; that of a farmer is the only appellation of the rural inhabitants of our country. It must take some time ere he can reconcile himself to our dictionary, which is but short in words of dignity, and names of honour. There, on a Sunday, he sees a congregation of respectable farmers and their wives, all clad in neat homespun, well mounted, or riding in their own humble wagons. There is not among them an esquire, saving the unlettered magistrate. There he sees a parson as simple as his flock, a farmer who does not riot on the labor of others. We have no princes, for whom we toil, starve, and bleed: we are the most perfect society now existing in the world. Here man is free as he ought to be; nor is this pleasing equality so transitory as many others are. Many ages will not see the shores of our great lakes replenished with inland nations, nor the unknown bounds of North America entirely peopled. Who can tell how far it extends? Who can tell the millions of men whom it will feed and contain? for no European foot has as yet traveled half the extent of this mighty continent!

The next wish of this traveller will be to know whence came all these people? they are a mixture of English, Scotch, Irish, French, Dutch, Germans, and Swedes. From this promiscuous breed, that race now called Americans have arisen. The eastern provinces must indeed be excepted, as being the unmixed descendents of Englishmen. I have heard many wish that they had been more intermixed also: for my part, I am no wisher; and think it much better as it has happened. They exhibit a most conspicuous figure in this great and variegated picture; they too enter for a great share in the pleasing perspective displayed in these thirteen provinces. I know it is fashionable to reflect on them; but I respect them for what they have done; for the accuracy and wisdom with which they have settled their territory; for the decency of their manners; for their early love of letters; their ancient college, the first in this hemisphere; for their industry, which to me who am but a farmer, is the criterion of everything.

There never was a people, situated as they are, who, with so ungrateful a soil, have done more in so short a time. Do you think that the monarchical ingredients which are more prevalent in other governments, have purged them from all foul stains? Their histories assert the contrary.

In this great American asylum, the poor of Europe have by some means met together, and in consequence of various causes; to what purpose should they ask one another, what countrymen they are? Alas, two thirds of them had no country. Can a wretch who wanders about, who works and starves, whose life is a continual scene of sore affliction or pinching penury; can that man call England or any other kingdom his country? A country that had no bread for him, whose fields procured him no harvest, who met with nothing but the frowns of the rich, the severity of the laws, with jails and punishments; who owned not a single foot of the extensive surface of this planet? No! urged by a variety of motives, here they came. Every thing has tended to regenerate them; new laws, a new mode of living, a new social system; here they are become men: in Europe they were as so many useless plants, wanting vegetative mold, and refreshing showers; they withered, and were mowed down by want, hunger, and war; but now, by the power of transplantation, like all other plants, they have taken root and flourished! Formerly they were not numbered in any civil list of their country, except in those of the poor; here they rank as citizens. By what invisible power has this surprising metamorphosis been performed? By that of the laws and that of their industry. The laws, the indulgent laws, protect them as they arrive, stamping on them the symbol of adoption; they receive ample rewards for their labours; these accumulated rewards procure them lands; those lands confer on them the title of freemen; and to that title every benefit is affixed which men can possibly require. This is the great operation daily performed by our laws. From whence proceed these laws? From our government. Whence that government? It is derived from the original genius and strong desire of the people, ratified and confirmed by government. This is the great chain which links us all, this is the picture which every province exhibits, Nova Scotia excepted. There the crown has done all; either there were no people who had genius, or it was not much attended to: the consequence is, that the province is very thinly inhabited indeed; the power of the crown, in conjunction with the mosquitos has prevented men from settling there. Yet some part of it flourished once, and it contained a mild harmless set of people. But for the fault of a few leaders, the whole were banished. The greatest political error the crown ever committed in America, was to cut off men from a country which wanted nothing but men!

What attachment can a poor European emigrant have for a country where he had nothing? The knowledge of the language, the love of a few kindred as poor as himself, were the only cords that tied him: his country is now that which gives him land, bread, protection, and consequence: *Ubi panis ibi patria*, is the motto of all emigrants. What then is the American, this new man? He is either an European, or the descendant of an European; hence that strange mixture of blood, which you will find in no other country. I could point out to you a man whose grandfather was an Englishman, whose wife was Dutch, whose son married a French woman, and whose present four sons have now four wives of different nations. *He* is an American, who, leaving behind him all his ancient prejudices and manners, receives new ones from the new mode of life he has embraced, the new government he obeys, and the new rank he holds. He becomes an American by being received in the broad lap of our great *Alma Mater*.

Here individuals of all nations are melted into a new race of men, whose labors and posterity will one day cause great changes in the world. Americans are the western pilgrims, who are carrying along with them that great mass of arts, sciences, vigour, and industry, which began long since in the east; they will finish the great circle. The Americans were once scattered all over Europe; here they are incorporated into one of the finest systems of population which has ever appeared, and which will hereafter become distinct by the power of the different climates they inhabit. The American ought, therefore, to love this country much better than that wherein either he or his forefathers were born. Here the rewards of his industry follow with

equal steps the progress of his labour, his labour is founded on the basis of nature, *self-interest*; can it want a stronger allurement? Wives and children, who before in vain demanded of him a morsel of bread, now, fat and frolicsome, gladly help their father to clear those fields whence exuberant crops are to arise to feed and to clothe them all; without any part being claimed, either by a despotic prince, a rich abbot, or a mighty lord. Here religion demands but little of him; a small voluntary salary to the minister, and gratitude to God; can he refuse these? The American is a new man, who acts upon new principles; he must therefore entertain new ideas, and form new opinions. From involuntary idleness, servile dependence, penury, and useless labor, he has passed to toils of a very different nature, rewarded by ample subsistence. —This is an American.

British America is divided into many provinces, forming a large association, scattered along a coast 1500 miles [in] extent and about 200 wide. This society I would fain examine, at least such as it appears in the middle provinces; if it does not afford that variety of tinges and gradations which may be observed in Europe, we have colours peculiar to ourselves. For instance, it is natural to conceive that those who live near the sea, must be very different from those who live in the woods; the intermediate space will afford a separate and distinct class.

Men are like plants; the goodness and flavour of the fruit proceed from the peculiar soil and exposition in which they grow. We are nothing but what we derive from the air we breathe, the climate we inhabit, the government we obey, the system of religion we profess, and the nature of our employment. Here you will find but few crimes; these have acquired as yet no root among us. I wish I was able to trace all my ideas; if my ignorance prevents me from describing them properly, I hope I shall be able to delineate a few of the outlines, which are all I propose.

1. Those who live near the sea, feed more on fish than on flesh, and often encounter that boisterous element. This renders them more bold and enterprising; this leads them to neglect the confined occupations of the land. They see and converse with a variety of people; their intercourse with

mankind becomes extensive. The sea inspires them with a love of traffic, a desire of transporting produce from one place to another; leads them to a variety of resources, which supply the place of labour. Those who inhabit the middle settlements, by far the most numerous, must be very different; the simple cultivation of the earth purifies them; but the indulgences of the government, the soft remonstrances of religion, the rank of independent freeholders, must necessarily inspire them with sentiments, very little known in Europe among people of the same class. What do I say? Europe has no such class of men; the early knowledge they acquire, the early bargains they make, give them a great degree of sagacity. As freemen, they will be litigious; pride and obstinacy are often the cause of law suits; the nature of our laws and governments may be another. As citizens, it is easy to imagine, that they will carefully read the newspapers, enter into every political disquisition, freely blame or censure governors and others. As farmers, they will be careful and anxious to get as much as they can, because what they get is their own. As northern men, they will love the cheerful cup. As Christians, religion curbs them not in their opinions; the general indulgence leaves every one to think for himself in spiritual matters; the laws inspect our actions; our thoughts are left to God. Industry, good living, selfishness, litigiousness, country politics, the pride of freemen, religious indifference, are their characteristics.[3] If you recede still farther from the sea, you will come into more modern settlements; they exhibit the same strong lineaments, in a ruder appearance. Religion seems to have still less influence, and their manners are less improved.

Now we arrive near the great woods, near the last inhabited districts; there men seem to be placed still farther beyond the reach of government, which in some measure leaves them to themselves. How can it pervade every corner? as they were driven there by misfortunes, necessity of beginnings, desire of acquiring large tracts of land, idleness, frequent want of economy, ancient debts; the re-union of such people does not afford a very pleasing spectacle. When discord, want of unity and friendship—when either drunkenness or idleness prevail in such remote districts—contention,

inactivity, and wretchedness must ensue. There are not the same remedies to these evils as in a long established community. The few magistrates they have, are in general little better than the rest; they are often in a perfect state of war; that of man against man, sometimes decided by blows, sometimes by means of the law; that of man against every wild inhabitant of these venerable woods, of which they are come to dispossess them. There men appear to be no better than carnivorous animals of a superior rank, living on the flesh of wild animals when they can catch them, and when they are not able, they subsist on grain.

He who would wish to see America in its proper light, and have a true idea of its feeble beginnings and barbarous rudiments, must visit our extended line of frontiers where the last settlers dwell, and where he may see the first labours of settlement, the mode of clearing the earth, in all their different appearances; where men are wholly left dependent on their native tempers, and on the spur of uncertain industry, which often fails, when not sanctified by the efficacy of a few moral rules. There, remote from the power of example, and check of shame, many families exhibit the most hideous parts of our society. They are a kind of forlorn hope, preceding by ten or twelve years the most respectable army of veterans which come after them. In that space, prosperity will polish some, vice and the law will drive off the rest, who uniting again with others like themselves will recede still farther; making room for more industrious people, who will finish their improvements, convert the log-house into a convenient habitation, and rejoicing that the first heavy labours are finished, will change in a few years that hitherto barbarous country into a fine, fertile, well-regulated district.

Such is our progress, such is the march of the Europeans toward the interior parts of this continent. In all societies there are offcasts; this impure part serves as our precursors or pioneers; my father himself was one of that class; but he came upon honest principles, and was therefore one of the few who held fast; by good conduct and temperance, he transmitted to me his fair inheritance, when not above one in fourteen of his contemporaries had the same good fortune.

Forty years ago, this smiling country was thus

inhabited; it is now purged, a general decency of manners prevails throughout; and such has been the fate of our best countries.

Exclusive of those general characteristics, each province has its own, founded on the government, climate, mode of husbandry, customs, and peculiarity of circumstances. Europeans submit insensibly to these great powers, and become, in the course of a few generations, not only Americans in general, but either Pennsylvanians, Virginians, or provincials under some other name. Whoever traverses the continent, must easily observe those strong differences, which will grow more evident in time. The inhabitants of Canada, Massachusetts, the middle provinces, the southern ones will be as different as their climates; their only points of unity will be those of religion and language.

As I have endeavored to show you how Europeans become Americans; it may not be disagreeable to show you likewise how the various Christian sects introduced, wear out, and how religious indifference becomes prevalent. When any considerable number of a particular sect happen to dwell contiguous to each other, they immediately erect a temple, and there worship the divinity agreeably to their own peculiar ideas. Nobody disturbs them. If any new sect springs up in Europe, it may happen that many of its professors will come and settle in America. As they bring their zeal with them, they are at liberty to make proselytes if they can, and to build a meeting and to follow the dictates of their consciences; for neither the government nor any other power interferes. If they are peaceable subjects, and are industrious, what is it to their neighbors how and in what manner they think fit to address their prayers to the Supreme Being? But if the sectaries are not settled close together, if they are mixed with other denominations, their zeal will cool for want of fuel, and will be extinguished in a little time. Then the Americans become as to religion, what they are as to country, allied to all. In them, the name of Englishman, Frenchman, and European is lost: and in like manner, the strict modes of Christianity, as practiced in Europe, are lost also. This effect will extend itself still farther hereafter; and though this may appear to you as a strange idea, yet it is a very true one. I shall be able perhaps hereafter to explain

myself better; in the meanwhile, let the following example serve as my first justification.

Let us suppose you and I to be travelling; we observe that in this house, to the right, lives a Catholic, who prays to God as he has been taught, and believes in transubstantiation; he works and raises wheat, he has a large family of children, all hale and robust; his belief, his prayers offend nobody. About one mile farther on the same road, his next neighbor may be a good honest plodding German Lutheran, who addresses himself to the same God, the God of all, agreeably to the modes he has been educated in, and believes in consubstantiation; by so doing he scandalizes nobody; he also works in his fields, embellishes the earth, clears swamps, etc. What has the world to do with his Lutheran principles? He persecutes nobody, and nobody persecutes him: he visits his neighbors, and his neighbors visit him. Next to him lives a seceder, the most enthusiastic of all sectaries; his zeal is hot and fiery; but, separated as he is from others of the same complexion, he has no congregation of his own to resort to, where he might cabal and mingle religious pride with worldly obstinacy. He likewise raises good crops; his house is handsomely painted; his orchard is one of the fairest in the neighborhood. How does it concern the welfare of the country, or of the province at large, what this man's religious sentiments are? He is a good farmer; he is a sober, peaceable, good citizen: William Penn himself would not wish for more. This is the visible character; the invisible one is only guessed at, and is nobody's business. Next again lives a Low Dutchman, who implicitly believes the rules laid down by the synod of Dort. He conceives no other idea of a clergyman than that of an hired man; if he does his work well, he will pay him the stipulated sum; if not, he will dismiss him, and do without his sermons, and let his church be shut up for years. But notwithstanding this coarse idea, you will find his house and farm to be the neatest in all the country; and you will judge by his wagon and fat horses, that he thinks more of the affairs of this world than of those of the next. He is sober and laborious; therefore he is all he ought to be as to the affairs of this life; as for those of the next, he must trust to the great Creator.

150

Each of these people instruct their children as well as they can: but these instructions are feeble compared to those which are given to the youth of the poorest class in Europe. Their children will therefore grow up less zealous and more indifferent in matters of religion than their parents. The foolish vanity, or rather the fury of making proselytes, is unknown here; they have no time: the seasons call for all their attention; and thus in a few years, this mixed neighborhood will exhibit a strange religious medley, that will be neither pure Catholicism nor pure Calvinism. A very perceptible indifference even in the first generation, will become apparent; and it may happen, that the daughter of the Catholic will marry the son of the seceder, and settle by themselves at a distance from their parents. What religious education will they give their children? A very imperfect one. If there happens to be in the neighborhood any place of worship, we will suppose a Quaker's meeting; rather than not show their fine clothes, they will go to it; and some of them may perhaps attach themselves to that society. Others will remain in a perfect state of indifference; the children of these zealous parents will not be able to tell what their religious principles are, and their grandchildren still less. The neighborhood of a place of worship generally leads them to it; and the action of going thither, is the strongest evidence they can give of their attachment to any sect.

The Quakers are the only people who retain a fondness for their own mode of worship; for be they ever so far separated from each other, they hold a sort of communion with the society, and seldom depart from its rules, at least in this country.

Thus all sects are mixed as well as all nations; thus religious indifference is imperceptibly disseminated from one end of the continent to the other; which is at present one of the strongest characteristics of the Americans. Where this will reach, no one can tell; perhaps it may leave a vacuum, fit to receive other systems. Persecution, religious pride, the love of contradiction, are the food of what the world commonly calls religion. These motives have ceased here; zeal in Europe is confined; here it evaporates in the great distance it has to travel; there it is a grain of powder in-

closed; here it burns away in the open air, and consumes without effect.

But to return to our back settlers. I must tell you, that there is something in the proximity of the woods which is very singular. It is with men, as it is with the plants and animals that grow and live in the forests; they are entirely different from those that live in the plains. I will candidly tell you all my thoughts; but you are not to expect that I shall advance any reasons. By living in or near the woods, their actions are regulated by the wildness of the neighborhood. The deer often come to eat their grain, the wolves to destroy their sheep, the bears to kill their hogs, the foxes to catch their poultry. This surrounding hostility immediately puts the gun into their hands; they watch these animals, they kill some; and thus by defending their property, they soon become professed hunters; this is the progress; once hunters, farewell to the plough. The chase renders them ferocious, gloomy, and unsociable; a hunter wants no neighbors, he rather hates them, because he dreads the competition. In a little time their success in the woods makes them neglect their tillage. They trust to the natural fecundity of the earth, and therefore do little; carelessness in fencing, often exposes what little they sow, to destruction; they are not at home to watch; in order, therefore, to make up the deficiency, they go oftener to the woods. That new mode of life brings along with it a new set of manners, which I cannot easily describe. These new manners being grafted on the old stock, produce a strange sort of lawless profligacy, the impressions of which are indelible. The manners of the Indian natives are respectable, compared with this European medley. Their wives and children live in sloth and inactivity; and having no proper pursuits, you may judge what education the latter receive. Their tender minds have nothing else to contemplate but the example of their parents; like them they grow up a mongrel breed, half civilized, half savage, except nature stamps on them some constitutional propensities. That rich, that voluptuous sentiment is gone, which struck them so forcibly; the possession of their freeholds no longer conveys to their minds the same pleasure and pride. To all these reasons you must add their lonely situation; and

151

you cannot imagine what an effect on manners the great distances they live from each other has!

Consider one of the last settlements in its first view: of what is it composed? Europeans who have not that sufficient share of knowledge they ought to have, in order to prosper; people who have suddenly passed from oppression, dread of government, and fear of laws, into the unlimited freedom of the woods. This sudden change must have a very great effect on most men, and on that 10 class particularly. Eating of wild meat, whatever you may think, tends to alter their temper: though all the proof I can adduce, is, that I have seen it: and having no place of worship to resort to, what little society this might afford, is denied them. The Sunday meetings, exclusive of religious benefits, were the only social bonds that might have inspired them with some degree of emulation in neatness. Is it then surprising to see men thus situated, immersed in great and heavy labors, 20 degenerate a little? It is rather a wonder the effect is not more diffusive. The Moravians and the Quakers are the only instances in exception to what I have advanced. They never settle singly; it is a colony of the society which emigrates; they carry with them their forms, worship, rules, and decency; the others never begin so hard; they are always able to buy improvements, in which there is a great advantage; for by that time the country is recovered from its first barbarity. 30

Thus our bad people are those who are half cultivators and half hunters; and the worst of them are those who have degenerated altogether into the hunting state. As old ploughmen, and new men of the woods, as Europeans and new-made Indians, they contract the vices of both; they adopt the moroseness and ferocity of a native, without his mildness, or even his industry at home. If manners are not refined, at least they are rendered simple and inoffensive by tilling the earth; all 40 our wants are supplied by it; our time is divided between labor and rest, and none left for the commission of great misdeeds. As hunters, it is divided between the toil of the chase, the idleness of repose, or indulgence of inebriation. Hunting is but a licentious idle life; and if it does not always pervert good dispositions; yet, when it is united with bad luck, it leads to want: want stimulates that

propensity to rapacity and injustice, too natural to needy men, which is the fatal gradation. After this explanation of the effects which follow by living in the woods, shall we yet vainly flatter ourselves with the hope of converting the Indians? We should rather begin with converting our back-settlers; and now if I dare mention the name of religion, its sweet accents would be lost in the immensity of these woods. Men thus placed, are not fit either to receive or remember its mild instructions; they want temples and ministers; but as soon as men cease to remain at home, and begin to lead an erratic life, let them be either tawny or white, they cease to be its disciples.

Thus have I faintly and imperfectly endeavored to trace our society from the sea to our woods; yet you must not imagine that every person who moves back, acts upon the same principles, or falls into the same degeneracy. Many families 20 carry with them all their decency of conduct, purity of morals, and respect of religion; but these are scarce; the power of example is sometimes irresistible. Even among these back-settlers, their depravity is greater or less, according to what nation or province they belong. Were I to adduce proofs of this, I might be accused of partiality. If there happens to be some rich intervals, some fertile bottoms, in those remote districts, the people will there prefer tilling the land to hunting, 30 and will attach themselves to it; but even on these fertile spots, you may plainly perceive the inhabitants to acquire a great degree of rusticity and selfishness.

It is in consequence of this straggling situation, and the astonishing power it has on manners, that the back-settlers of both the Carolinas, Virginia, and many other parts, have been long a set of lawless people; it has been even dangerous to travel among them. Government can do nothing in so extensive a country; better it should wink at these irregularities, than that it should use means inconsistent with its usual mildness. Time will efface those stains: in proportion as the great body of population approaches them, they will reform, and become polished and subordinate. Whatever has been said of the four New England provinces, no such degeneracy of manners has ever tarnished their annals; their back-settlers have been kept

To here //

152

within the bounds of decency and government, by means of wise laws, and by the influence of religion.

What a detestable idea such people must have given to the natives of the Europeans! They trade with them; the worst of people are permitted to do that, which none but persons of the best characters should be employed in. They get drunk with them, and often defraud the Indians. Their avarice, removed from the eyes of their superiors, knows no bounds; and aided by a little superiority of knowledge, these traders deceive them, and even sometimes shed blood. Hence those shocking violations, those sudden devastations which have so often stained our frontiers, when hundreds of innocent people have been sacrificed for the crimes of a few. It was in consequence of such behavior, that the Indians took the hatchet against the Virginians in 1774. Thus are our first steps trod, thus are our first trees felled, in general, by the most vicious of our people; and thus the path is opened for the arrival of a second and better class, the true American freeholders; the most respectable set of people in this part of the world: respectable for their industry, their happy independence, the great share of freedom they possess, the good regulation of their families, and for extending the trade and the dominion of their country.

Europe contains hardly any other distinctions but lords and tenants; this fair country alone is settled by freeholders, the possessors of the soil they cultivate, members of the government they obey, and the framers of their own laws, by means of their representatives. This is a thought which you have taught me to cherish; our difference from Europe, far from diminishing, rather adds to our usefulness and consequence as men and subjects. Had our forefathers remained there, they would only have crowded it, and perhaps prolonged those convulsions which had shook it so long. Every industrious European who transports himself here, may be compared to a sprout growing at the foot of a great tree; it enjoys and draws but a little portion of sap; wrench it from the parent roots, transplant it, and it will become a tree bearing fruit also. Colonists are therefore entitled to the consideration due to the most useful subjects;

a hundred families barely existing in some parts of Scotland, will here in six years, cause an annual exportation of 10,000 bushels of wheat: 100 bushels being but a common quantity for an industrious family to sell, if they cultivate good land. It is here, then, that the idle may be employed, the useless become useful, and the poor become rich; but by riches I do not mean gold and silver; we have but little of those metals; I mean a better sort of wealth, cleared lands, cattle, good houses, good clothes, and an increase of people to enjoy them.

There is no wonder that this country has so many charms, and presents to Europeans so many temptations to remain in it. A traveller in Europe becomes a stranger as soon as he quits his own kingdom; but it is otherwise here. We know, properly speaking, no strangers; this is every person's country; the variety of our soils, situations, climates, governments, and produce, hath something which must please every body. No sooner does an European arrive, no matter of what condition, than his eyes are opened upon the fair prospect; he hears his language spoke, he retraces many of his own country manners, he perpetually hears the names of families and towns with which he is acquainted; he sees happiness and prosperity in all places disseminated; he meets with hospitality, kindness, and plenty everywhere; he beholds hardly any poor, he seldom hears of punishments and executions; and he wonders at the elegance of our towns, those miracles of industry and freedom. He cannot admire enough our rural districts, our convenient roads, good taverns, and our many accommodations; he involuntarily loves a country where everything is so lovely. When in England, he was a mere Englishman; here he stands on a larger portion of the globe, not less than its fourth part, and may see the productions of the north, in iron and naval stores; the provisions of Ireland, the grain of Egypt, the indigo, the rice of China. He does not find, as in Europe, a crowded society, where every place is over-stocked; he does not feel that perpetual collision of parties, that difficulty of beginning, that contention which oversets so many.

There is room for everybody in America: has he any particular talent, or industry? he exerts it in order to procure a livelihood, and it succeeds. Is he a merchant? the avenues of trade are infinite; is he eminent in any respect? he will be employed and respected. Does he love a country life? pleasant farms present themselves; he may purchase what he wants, and thereby become an American farmer. Is he a labourer, sober and industrious? he need not go many miles, nor receive many informations before he will be hired, well fed at the table of his employer, and paid four or five times more than he can get in Europe. Does he want uncultivated lands? thousands of acres present themselves, which he may purchase cheap. Whatever be his talents or inclinations, if they are moderate, he may satisfy them. I do not mean, that every one who comes will grow rich in a little time; no, but he may procure an easy, decent maintenance, by his industry. Instead of starving, he will be fed; instead of being idle, he will have employment; and these are riches enough for such men as come over here. The rich stay in Europe; it is only the middling and the poor that emigrate. Would you wish to travel in independent idleness, from north to south, you will find easy access, and the most cheerful reception at every house; society without ostentation, good cheer without pride, and every decent diversion which the country affords, with little expense. It is no wonder that the European who has lived here a few years, is desirous to remain; Europe with all its pomp, is not to be compared to this continent, for men of middle stations, or labourers.

An European, when he first arrives, seems limited in his intentions, as well as in his views; but he very suddenly alters his scale; two hundred miles formerly appeared a very great distance; it is now but a trifle; he no sooner breathes our air than he forms schemes, and embarks in designs he never would have thought of in his own country. There the plenitude of society confines many useful ideas, and often extinguishes the most laudable schemes which here ripen into maturity. Thus Europeans become Americans.

But how is this accomplished in that crowd of low, indigent people, who flock here every year from all parts of Europe? I will tell you; they no sooner arrive than they immediately feel the good effects of that plenty of provisions we possess: they fare on our best food, and they are kindly entertained; their talents, character, and peculiar industry are immediately enquired into; they find countrymen everywhere disseminated, let them come from whatever part of Europe.

Let me select one as an epitome of the rest; he is hired, he goes to work, and works moderately; instead of being employed by a haughty person, he finds himself with his equal, placed at the substantial table of the farmer, or else at an inferior one as good; his wages are high, his bed is not like that bed of sorrow on which he used to lie: if he behaves with propriety, and is faithful, he is caressed, and becomes, as it were, a member of the family. He begins to feel the effects of a sort of resurrection; hitherto he had not lived, but simply vegetated; he now feels himself a man, because he is treated as such; the laws of his own country had overlooked him in his insignificancy; the laws of this cover him with their mantle. Judge what an alteration there must arise in the mind and thoughts of this man; he begins to forget his former servitude and dependence; his heart involuntarily swells and glows; this first swell inspires him with those new thoughts which constitute an American. What love can he entertain for a country where his existence was a burden to him! if he is a generous good man, the love of this new adoptive parent, will sink deep into his heart. He looks around, and sees many a prosperous person, who but a few years before was as poor as himself. This encourages him much; he begins to form some little scheme, the first, alas, he ever formed in his life. If he is wise, he thus spends two or three years, in which time he acquires knowledge, the use of tools, the modes of working the lands, felling trees, etc. This prepares the foundation of a good name, the most useful acquisition he can make. He is encouraged; he has gained friends; he is advised and directed; he feels bold; he purchases some land; he gives all the money he has brought over, as well as what he has earned, and trusts to the God of harvests for the discharge of the rest. His good name procures him credit; he is now possessed of the deed, conveying to him and his posterity the fee simple, and absolute property of two hundred acres of land, situated on such a river. What an epoch in this man's life! He is become a freeholder, from perhaps a German boor—he is now an American, a Pennsylvanian. He is naturalized; his name is enrolled with those of the other citizens of the province. Instead of being a vagrant, he has a place of residence; he is called the inhabitant of such a county, or of such a district, and for the first time in his life counts for something; for hitherto he had been a cypher. I only repeat what I have heard many say, and no wonder their hearts should glow, and be agitated with a multitude of feelings, not easy to describe. From nothing to start into being; from a servant to the rank of a master; from being the slave of some despotic prince, to become a free man, invested with lands, to which every municipal blessing is annexed! What a change indeed! It is in consequence of that change, that he becomes an American.

This great metamorphosis has a double effect; it extinguishes all his European prejudices; he forgets that mechanism of subordination, that servility of disposition which poverty had taught him; and sometimes he is apt to forget too much, often passing from one extreme to the other. If he is a good man, he forms schemes of future prosperity; he proposes to educate his children better than he has been educated himself; he thinks of future modes of conduct, feels an ardour to labour he never felt before. Pride steps in, and leads him to everything that the laws do not forbid: he respects them; with a heartfelt gratitude he looks toward that government from whose wisdom all his new felicity is derived, and under whose wings and protection he now lives. These reflections constitute him the good man and the good subject.

Ye poor Europeans, ye, who sweat and work for the great—ye, who are obliged to give so many sheaves to the church, so many to your lords, so many to your government, and have hardly any left for yourselves—ye, who are held in less estimation than favourite hunters or useless lapdogs—ye, who only breathe the air of nature, because it cannot be withheld from you; it is here that ye can conceive the possibility of those feelings I have been describing; it is here the laws of naturalization invite every one to partake of our great labours and felicity, to till unrented, untaxed lands!

Many, corrupted beyond the power of amendment, have brought with them all their vices, and disregarding the advantages held to them, have gone on in their former career of iniquity, until they have been overtaken and punished by our laws. It is not every emigrant who succeeds; no, it is only the sober, the honest, and industrious: happy those, to whom this transition has served as a powerful spur to labour, to prosperity, and to the good establishment of children, born in the days of their poverty; and who had no other portion to expect, but the rags of their parents, had it not been for their happy emigration. Others again, have been led astray by this enchanting scene; their new pride, instead of leading them to the fields, has kept them in idleness; the idea of possessing lands is all that satisfies them—though surrounded with fertility, they have mouldered away their time in inactivity, misinformed husbandry, and ineffectual endeavours. How much wiser, in general, the honest Germans than almost all other Europeans; they hire themselves to some of their wealthy landsmen, and in that apprenticeship learn everything that is necessary. They attentively consider the prosperous industry of others, which imprints on their minds a strong desire of possessing the same advantages. This forcible idea never quits them; they launch forth, and by dint of sobriety, rigid parsimony, and the most persevering industry, they commonly succeed. Their astonishment at their first arrival from Germany is very great—it is to them a dream; the contrast must be powerful indeed; they observe their countrymen flourishing in every place; they travel through whole counties where not a word of English is spoken; and in the names and the language of the people, they retrace Germany. They have been an useful acquisition to this continent, and to Pennsylvania in particular; to them it owes some share of its prosperity; to their mechanical knowledge and patience, it owes the finest mills in all America, the best teams of horses, and many other advantages. The recollection of their former poverty and slavery never quits them as long as they live.

The Scotch and the Irish might have lived in their own country perhaps as poor; but enjoying more civil advantages, the effects of their new situation do not strike them so forcibly, nor has

155

it so lasting an effect. From whence the difference arises, I know not; but out of twelve families of emigrants of each country, generally seven Scotch will succeed, nine German, and four Irish. The Scotch are frugal and laborious; but their wives cannot work so hard as German women, who on the contrary, vie with their husbands, and often share with them the most severe toils of the field, which they understand better. They have therefore nothing to struggle against, but the common casualties of nature. The Irish do not prosper so well; they love to drink and to quarrel; they are litigious, and soon take to the gun, which is the ruin of everything; they seem, beside, to labour under a greater degree of ignorance in husbandry than the others; perhaps it is that their industry had less scope, and was less exercised at home. I have heard many relate, how the land was parceled out in that kingdom; their ancient conquest has been a great detriment to them, by over-setting their landed property. The lands, possessed by a few, are leased down *ad infinitum*; and the occupiers often pay five guineas an acre. The poor are worse lodged there than anywhere else in Europe; their potatoes, which are easily raised, are perhaps an inducement to laziness: their wages are too low, and their whisky too cheap.

There is no tracing observations of this kind, without making at the same time very great allowances; as there are every where to be found a great many exceptions. The Irish themselves, from different parts of that kingdom, are very different. It is difficult to account for this surprising locality; one would think, on so small an island all Irishmen must be alike; yet it is not so; they are different in their aptitude to, and in their love of labour.

The Scotch, on the contrary, are all industrious and saving; they want nothing more than a field to exert themselves in; and they are commonly sure of succeeding. The only difficulty they labor under is, that technical American knowledge, which requires some time to obtain; it is not easy for those who seldom saw a tree, to conceive how it is to be felled, cut up, and split into rails and posts.

As I am fond of seeing and talking of prosperous families, I intend to finish this letter by relating to you the history of an honest Scotch Hebridean, who came here in 1774, which will show you in epitome what the Scotch can do, wherever they have room for the exertion of their industry. Whenever I hear of any new settlement, I pay it a visit once or twice a year, on purpose to observe the different steps each settler takes, the gradual improvements, the different tempers of each family, on which their prosperity in a great nature depends; their different modifications of industry, their ingenuity, and contrivance; for being all poor, their life requires sagacity and prudence. In an evening I love to hear them tell their stories; they furnish me with new ideas. I sit still and listen to their ancient misfortunes, observing in many of them a strong degree of gratitude to God, and the government. Many a well-meant sermon have I preached to some of them. When I found laziness and inattention prevail, who could refrain from wishing well to these new countrymen, after having undergone so many fatigues? Who could withhold good advice? What a happy change it must be, to descend from the high, sterile, bleak lands of Scotland, where everything is barren and cold, to rest on some fertile farms in these middle provinces! Such a transition must have afforded the most pleasing satisfaction.

The following dialogue passed at an outsettlement, where I lately paid a visit:

Well, friend, how do you do now? I am come fifty odd miles on purpose to see you; how do you go on with your new cutting and slashing? Very well, good Sir; we learn the use of the axe bravely; we shall make it out; we have a belly full of victuals every day, our cows run about, and come home full of milk, our hogs get fat of themselves in the woods: Oh, this is a good country! God bless William Penn; we shall do very well by and by, if we keep our healths. Your log-house looks neat and light; where did you get these shingles? One of our neighbors is a New England man, and he showed us how to split them out of chestnut-trees. Now for a barn, but all in good time, here are fine trees to build it with. Who is to frame it? sure you don't understand that work yet? A countryman of ours, who has been in America these ten years, offers to wait for his money until the second crop is lodged in it. What did you give for your land? Thirty-five shillings per acre, payable in seven years. How many acres have you got? An hundred and

156

fifty. That is enough to begin with; is not your land pretty hard to clear? Yes, Sir, hard enough; but it would be harder still, if it were ready cleared, for then we should have no timber; and I love the woods much; the land is nothing without them. Have not you found out any bees yet? No, Sir; and if we had, we should not know what to do with them. I will tell you by and by. You are very kind. Farewell, honest man, God prosper you; whenever you travel toward——, inquire for J. S. He will entertain you kindly, provided you bring him good tidings from your family and farm.

In this manner I often visit them, and carefully examine their houses, their modes of ingenuity, their different ways; and make them all relate all they know, and describe all they feel. These are scenes which I believe you would willingly share with me. I well remember your philanthropic turn of mind. Is it not better to contemplate under these humble roofs, the rudiments of future wealth and population, than to behold the accumulated bundles of litigious papers in the office of a lawyer? To examine how the world is gradually settled, how the howling swamp is converted into a pleasing meadow, the rough ridge into a fine field; and to hear the cheerful whistling, the rural song, where there was no sound heard before, save the yell of the savage, the screech of the owl, or the hissing of the snake? Here an European, fatigued with luxuries, riches, and pleasures, may find a sweet relaxation in a series of interesting scenes, as affecting as they are new. England, which now contains so many domes, so many castles, was once like this, a place woody and marshy; its inhabitants, now the favourite nation for arts and commerce, were once painted like our neighbours. This country will flourish in its turn, and the same observations will be made which I have just delineated. Posterity will look back with avidity and pleasure, to trace, if possible, the era of this or that particular settlement. . . .

Agreeable to the account which several Scotchmen have given me of the north of Britain, of the Orkneys, and the Hebride Islands, they seem, on many accounts, to be unfit for the habitation of men; they appear to be calculated only for great sheep pastures. Who then can blame the inhabitants of these countries for transporting themselves hither? This great continent must in time absorb the poorest part of Europe; and this will happen in proportion as it becomes better known; and as war, taxation, oppression, and misery increase there. The Hebrides appear to be fit only for the residence of malefactors; and it would be much better to send felons there than either to Virginia or Maryland. What a strange compliment has our mother country paid to two of the finest provinces in America! She entertained in that respect very mistaken ideas; what was intended as a punishment, became the good fortune of several; many of those who were transported as felons, grew rich, and strangers to the stings of those wants that urged them to violations of the laws: they became industrious, exemplary, and useful citizens. The English government should have purchased the most northern and barren of those islands; it should have sent over to us the honest, primitive Hebrideans, settled them here on good lands, as a reward for their virtue and ancient poverty; and replaced them with a colony of her wicked sons. The severity of the climate, the inclemency of the seasons, the sterility of the soil, the tempestuousness of the sea, would have afflicted and punished enough. Could there be found a spot better adapted to retaliate the injury it had received by their crimes? Some of those islands might be considered as the hell of Great Britain, where all evil spirits should be sent. Two essential ends would have been answered by this simple operation. The good people, by emigration, would have been rendered happier; the bad ones would be placed where they ought to be. In a few years the dread of being sent to that wintry region would have a much stronger effect than that of transportation. This is no place of punishment; were I a poor, hopeless, breadless Englishman, and not restrained by the power of shame, I should be very thankful for the passage. It is of very little importance how, and in what manner an indigent man arrives; for if he is but sober, honest, and industrious, he has nothing more to ask of heaven. Let him go to work, he will have opportunities enough to earn a comfortable support, and even the means of procuring some land; which ought to be the utmost wish of every person who has health and hands to work. I knew a man who came to this country, in the literal sense of the expression, stark-naked. I think he was a Frenchman, and a sailor on board an English man-of-war. Being discontented, he had stripped himself and swam ashore; where, finding clothes and friends, he set tled afterwards at Maraneck, in the county of Chester, in the province of New York: he married and left a good farm to each of his sons. I knew another person, who was but twelve years old, when he was taken on the fron- 10 tiers of Canada, by the Indians; at his arrival at Albany he was purchased by a gentleman, who generously bound him apprentice to a tailor. He lived to the age of ninety, and left behind him a fine estate and a numerous family, all well settled; many of them I am acquainted with. Where is then the industrious European who ought to despair?

After a foreigner from any part of Europe is arrived, and become a citizen; let him devoutly listen to the voice of our great parent, which says 20 to him: "Welcome to my shores, distressed European; bless the hour in which thou didst see my verdant fields, my fair navigable rivers, and my green mountains!—If thou wilt work, I have bread for thee; if thou wilt be honest, sober and industrious, I have greater rewards to confer on thee—ease and independence. I will give thee fields to feed and clothe thee; a comfortable fireside to sit by, and tell thy children by what means thou hast prospered; and a decent bed to repose 30 on. I shall endow thee, beside, with the immunities of a freeman. If thou wilt carefully educate thy children, teach them gratitude to God, and reverence to that government, that philanthropic government, which has collected here so many men and made them happy. I will also provide for thy progeny: and to every good man this ought to be the most holy, the most powerful, the most earnest wish he can possibly form, as well as the most consolatory prospect when he dies. Go 40 thou, and work and till; thou shalt prosper, provided thou be just, grateful, and industrious."

Lettres d'un Cultivateur Américain

The Frontier Woman

THE PLIGHT of the frontiersman during the Revolution was grave indeed; even in those regions where the political issues seemed most remote, tragedy was common. In a moment, as Crèvecoeur declares, the pioneer might lose everything. The essay which follows is a protest against unnecessary cruelty and the enlistment of Indian tribes in the great conflict. It gains poignancy through the tragic events at Cherry Valley, New York, and Wyoming Valley, Pennsylvania. Wyoming has been the subject of three historical novels, and of poems by Thomas Campbell and Robert Southey. The essay first appeared in the fourth edition of *Lettres d'un Cultivateur Américain* (1787), from which this translation has been made.

What terrible destruction was caused by the army of General Burgoyne after its arrival in Ticonderoga despite the commander's personal humanity! Have you heard mention of the death of Miss MacRea? The day of the passage of the English army was the day she was to have wed an English officer. Fatal day! Her youth, her beauty, her delicate modesty, her simple appearance, at once elegant and natural, all contributed to render her singularly striking, and worthy of respect and admiration. She was meanwhile sacrificed, not to brutal jealousy but to a ferocious emulation of courage and fieriness.—Two savages, who had entered her house together, disputed a long time as to which of the two should present so beautiful a captive to General Burgoyne. Both were equally strong, equally determined to regard her as private prize. The combat ended only when one of them conceived the barbarous idea of destroying the object who had occasioned it. My feeble pen cannot describe an event so revolting! —Alas! what would you say, if you could have seen, as I, the havoc, the fires, the utter destruction which that army caused before its capitulation at Saratoga? You would quiver, I am sure of it.

I met accidentally not long since an ancient acquaintance of mine, who from the beginning of this war has been one of the fieriest of the torchbearers and one of the principal actors in these bloody scenes which for three years have desolated our frontiers: scenes which are rarely attended with any danger for the aggressors because everything is managed at night and by surprise.

"I am afraid," he told me, "that I shall not be permitted to die in peace, when my hour comes.

I can scarcely be alone without a thousand terrifying images presenting themselves to my imagination. Yet when I was employed upon these forays I felt no more concern than if I had been occupied in girdling so many useless trees. I am overwhelmed with involuntary reflections which afflict me and oppress me. I bear with me a weight of melancholy and sorrow that mounts from day to day. My heart! Oh, my heart! Sometimes it beats as if it were for the last time. And yet physically, I enjoy good health.

"One horrible secret, always present, accompanies me to my very bed—this bed where, before, I always enjoyed so peaceful a sleep.

"I hear daily the voices of the large number of children whom I have seen perishing on the border clinging to breasts which despair had dried up. I hear at every moment the curses, the imprecations of the desolated fathers; the sobs and groans of mothers whom I have seen reduced to such dire extremities that I dare not portray them for you.—These are some of the outstanding thoughts which agitate me and well up in my heart!

"Ah, that unfortunate young lady! Because she tried to escape after having been made prisoner, —I see her yet, stretched upon the ground, naked and sobbing, where I, I abandoned her to the birds of prey! Only one generous action did I engage in during the entire course of the war. To it I was impelled by I know not what motive. This action procured me the only balm which I can bring to my wounded heart.

"In the excursion of——, our party was composed of twenty-three, five white people and eighteen savages of the worst sort. We arrived at the forest's edge before the settlement clearing as the sun was setting. As we perceived no one in the fields, we concluded that the inhabitants, having finished their work, had retired to their houses, of which we counted eight. After we were divided into as many bands, we resolved to hide in the woods until deep night and all enter the houses upon a concerted signal. God forbid that I should drag out the lurid details of this butchery in which so much innocent blood was shed!

"I entered swiftly into the house that had fallen to my lot. The first object I behold was a woman neatly dressed and of peaceful and mild appearance, suckling two infants, and rocking at the same time a third. Scarcely had I entered when she arose and advanced toward me. 'I know your intention,' she said, 'Start with the small innocent ones, in order that they not languish and die from hunger when I am no more. Kill me as you killed my poor old father and my husband last April. I am weary of living.'—While uttering these words, she boldly removed, with her right hand, the handkerchief from her breast, whilst she still held her two infants with her left, and with noble courage she presented her bosom to me bare and throbbing. I was armed with a tomahawk, and at the very moment of the plunge, a sudden and involuntary compulsion constrained me. 'Brave woman, why should I kill you?' I told her. 'Your father's and husband's deaths are suffering enough!'

"'Strike,' she said, 'how dare you mention the name of the Lord? Your companions will soon be here, and this delay will only weaken my courage and prolong my misery. I hear them, the barbarians!—the butchers,—I hear them; I recognize the outcries of my poor cousin Susanne, in the next house! Ah, God, Universal Father, why hast Thou thus abandoned me?' She wept bitterly. Her appearance, her tears, and her courage disarmed me entirely. Transfixed, I stood like a statue, my hand still uplifted, and my eyes fixed on her. In this moment my heart swelled itself; I wept also, I who had not shed tears in many years before. 'No, brave and dear woman,' said I, 'I do not wish to kill you; I shall not touch even one hair of your head. Do these children belong to you?' 'Nature has given two of them to me, the mother of the third was killed in the month of April past, defending her husband, who was bedfast. The anguished cries of that poor child, left alone in its cradle between the bodies of its father and mother, whose blood stained the floor, forced me to go to its aid, as soon as the neighbors (who were hiding in the woods) had buried the bodies. I have nursed it ever since.'

"'And you have nursed it ever since! Live, generous woman, live! The present that I make to you of life becomes today the reward of your humanity in giving a part of the milk of your breast to this poor orphan!'

"The rest of the party soon joined me, carrying what little plunder they had collected. It cost me persistent and strenuous argument to make my barbarous companions consent that this poor woman should live. Her husband had been a rebel, and the women of the rebels deserved only to die. Her situation during this bloodthirsty debate was terrible. Her courage left her. She was seized with violent convulsions, but the touching spectacle of this prostrate woman, tossing on the floor, combined with the cries of the three children, enabled me finally to melt the hearts of my companions, to touch them with some ideas of compassion and humanity. Our orders were positive and we were supposed to destroy all. Read them and see if I can be justified before God and the world?" I read them, and raising my eyes toward heaven, that heaven where incomprehensible justice and mercy reside, I returned the paper to him. Thus ended our conversation.

It is thus that Great Britain treats us. Tell me (though you are English), is this the road that leads to conquest? We are victims sacrificed to her ambition, to her vengeance. It is the blood of our wives and of our children that they order spilled, to be finally mixed with the ashes of our homes. (A Mohawk[n] for this exploit crossed the sea and has been well received by the King, and received a commission of Captain, etc.) Our enemies often close in on the unfortunate victims, whom they surprise in their houses, and with ferocious and diabolical glee watch the fire that they have lighted and in the midst of which all will perish. Thus, in less than eighteen minutes I saw fourteen people perish in one of the largest dwellings of the neighborhood of——. I have myself helped to look for the bones of several inhabitants among the ruins of their homes, in order to cover them with earth. Sad and melancholy task!

[In a revision of his manuscript before his death, Crèvecoeur added at this point the following observations:]

Nor are these all the mischiefs caused by these devastations. Their effect is felt at a great distance, even where the danger is not so imminent, like a great storm on the ocean, which not only convulses

it and causes a great number of shipwrecks wherever its greatest violence bursts, but agitates the air so powerfully that it becomes dangerous to the mariners even at a great distance. The various accounts of these incursions have spread a general alarm far and near. The report of these dreadful transactions is even frequently magnified in the various relations of them which circulate through the country. It has set every one a-trembling; it has impressed every mind with the most terrific ideas. Consequently, rural improvements are neglected; the former cheerfulness and confidence are gone. The gloomy, treacherous silence of the neighboring woods prevents the husbandman from approaching them; everywhere we dread the fire of an invisible enemy from behind each tree. What mode of resistance, what means of security can be devised in so extensive a country? Who can guard every solitary house? He who has been toiling all day to earn subsistence for his family wants rest at night.

I have often persuaded many to retire into the more interior parts of the country,—so much easier is it to give advice than to follow it. Most of them are not able; others are attached to the soil, to their houses. Where shall we go, how shall we fare after leaving all our grain, all our cattle behind us? Some I have seen who, conscious of the integrity of their conduct, have flattered themselves with some marks of predilection; they seemed to comfort themselves with that idea. Poor souls! The same treacherous thoughts have often come into my head. They do not consider the spirit with which this species of war is conducted, and that we are all devoted to it.]

It is in consequence of these unheard-of cruelties that I have lost one of the best friends that I have ever had.[n] He possessed an ample fortune; he was a man of literary accomplishments; he was industrious, humane, and hospitable. He received a shot through the body in returning on horseback from visiting a neighbor. Scarcely had he fallen when these barbarians scalped him, clove his head, and left him in this horrible situation. Thus, a little later, he became a horrible spectacle to his wife, who was looking for him. Unfortunate woman! The tears that I have shed with her! They

Mohawk: Joseph Brandt [Author's note].

best friends . . . had: Mr. R. T. [Author's note].

have not been able to diminish the bitterness of this act. Neither reason nor religion has since had the least effect on her spirit. Her despair is without limit. She accuses Heaven of abandonment and injustice in allowing the innocent to fall with the guilty. In vain I have attempted to alleviate somewhat the traces of so cruel a scene.

She wants to hear nothing. "Whoever wishes to console me is my enemy," she responds. She pleases herself, on the contrary, by painting this deadly tragedy in the blackest colors and with the most somber energy. Death, for which she implores every moment the beneficent power, can alone erase the indelible and deeply traced impressions produced by the death of her husband.

Alas, neither our feebleness nor our insignificance, nor our lakes, nor our mountains, nor our rivers can afford us the least shelter. Our new enemies penetrate everywhere. Seldom do they leave behind them the slightest traces of the blooming settlements which they have pledged to destroy. If some degree of moderation had prevailed (moderation is useful, is necessary, even in a just war), a prodigious number of innocent families might have been spared whose blood has cemented a strong more implacable hatred of the Americans toward England. If clemency was banished from the more immediate seat of war, one would have retraced it with pleasure on the extremities. Some part of the great continent would have been saved from the general havoc. They would have observed with admiration the blessedness of its chastising hand, and as proof of its humanity, some thousands of families would have rested in peace in their dwellings.

If I have dwelled so long on these inferior calamities and neglected to treat the devastation of richer establishments and the reduction of whole villages to ashes, it is that the possessors of these long-established settlements have friends, connections, and a variety of resources which in some measure alleviate their calamities. But those of whom I have been speaking, those who trace the last furrows of our provinces, who cultivate the border lands of our most extended districts—when they are once ruined, they are ruined forever;— By every consideration they are deserving of your compassion and your pity.

Adieu,
St. John

WILLIAM BARTRAM (1739-1823)

MUCH OF the literature of exploration and travel was motivated by utilitarian interests. It answered the practical questions of pioneers who were concerned with the soil, climate, and natural resources of a new land. The distinction of William Bartram's *Travels* is of a different order. As a naturalist with a European reputation, Bartram wrote with the knowledge of a trained scientific observer; he also had the sensibilities of an artist and the temperament of a poet. These qualities were fused in a style which Carlyle declared "has a wondrous kind of flowering eloquence in it." Published in 1791, when the romantic movement was sweeping over Europe, the *Travels* was in exquisite harmony with the spirit of the times. Coleridge, Wordsworth, and Southey, who found inspiration in Bartram's fresh and exotic imagery, devoured the volume. It also provided Chateaubriand and other romantic writers with a picturesque American landscape, a glowing backdrop for Rousseau's noble savage.

The chief influence on the career of William Bartram was that of his distinguished father, John Bartram (1699–1777), in whose house, near Philadelphia, he was born in 1739. A member of the Royal Societies of London and Stockholm, a founder of the American Philosophical Society, the elder Bartram had established in 1728 the first botanical garden in America. The impressionable son, who showed an early proficiency in drawing, accompanied his father on his expeditions, met many of the eminent men who came to his father's house and garden, and shared John Bartram's zeal for natural science. In 1773, after a distasteful experience in business, William Bartram found himself in his true element when he struck out on a five-year journey of botanical exploration in East and West Florida, the basis of his famous *Travels through North and South Carolina, Georgia, East and West Florida* (1791). Upon his return to Philadelphia in 1778, Bartram continued the work of his father who had died a few months before, and carried on his own botanical and ornithological investigations. Ill health compelled him to decline the chair of botany at the University of Pennsylvania in 1782, and later to refuse

President Jefferson's offer of an appointment to the Lewis and Clark Expedition. Bartram died, in the midst of his labors, on July 22, 1823.

BIBLIOGRAPHY · The popularity of the *Travels*, first published in Philadelphia in 1791, is confirmed by two editions in England (1792, 1794), one in Dublin (1793), and other eighteenth-century imprints in Germany, Holland, and France. The most readily available is that edited by Mark Van Doren, *The Travels of William Bartram* (1928). An inclusive list of Bartram's writings is contained in "The Bartram Bibliography" compiled 10 by J. H. Barnhart in *Bartonia* (1931). The best biographies are N. B. Fagin, *William Bartram: Interpreter of the American Landscape* (1933) and E. Earnest, *John and William Bartram: Botanists and Explorers* (1940). Valuable special studies include J. L. Lowes's brilliant account of Bartram's influence on Wordsworth and Coleridge in *The Road to Xanadu* (1927); E. H. Coleridge, "Coleridge, Wordsworth, and the American Botanist William Bartram," *Transactions of the Royal Society of Literature* (Second Series), XXVII (1906), 69–92; and N. B. Fagin, "Bartram's *Travels*," *Modern Language Notes*, XLVI (1931), 288–291. 20

Travels

THE SELECTION from Part II, Chapter V, here printed has been taken from the first edition of the *Travels*, published in Philadelphia in 1791. London reprints followed in 1792 and 1794. By the latter year, Coleridge had read the enchanting volume, and his enthusiasm was shared by William and Dorothy Wordsworth. Coleridge was steeped in Bartram, as the entries 30 in his *Memorandum Book* bear eloquent witness. (See J. L. Lowes, *The Road to Xanadu* (1930), 5–31.) "Probably none of the books which Coleridge was reading during the gestation of 'The Ancient Mariner' left more lively images in his memory than Bartram's *Travels*," Lowes wrote. "The fascinating fifth chapter of Part II in particular had awakened him to all manner of poetic possibilities, and had prompted copious transcriptions in the Note Book. And these transcripts form, as it happens, a significant cluster."

[*The Battle of the Crocodiles*]

. . . The little lake, which is an expansion of the river, now appeared in view; on the east side are extensive marshes, and on the other, high forests and orange groves, and then a bay, lined with vast cypress swamps, both coasts gradually approaching each other, to the opening of the river again, which is in this place about three hundreds yards wide.

Evening now drawing on, I was anxious to reach some high bank of the river, where I intended to lodge; and agreeably to my wishes, I soon after discovered on the west shore a little promontory, at the turning of the river, contracting it here to about one hundred and fifty yards in width. This promontory is a peninsula, containing about three acres of high ground, and is one entire orange grove, with a few live oaks, magnolias and palms. . . . From this promontory, looking eastward across the river, I beheld a landscape of low country, unparalleled as I think; on the left is the east coast of the little lake, which I had just passed; and from the orange bluff at the lower end, the high forests begin, and increase in breadth from the shore of the lake, making a circular sweep to the right, and contain many hundred thousand acres of meadow; and this grand sweep of high forests encircles, as I apprehend, at least twenty miles of these green 20 fields, interspersed with hommocks or islets of evergreen trees, where the sovereign magnolia and lordly palm stand conspicuous. The islets are high shelly knolls, on the sides of creeks or branches of the river, which wind about and drain off the superabundant waters that cover these meadows during the winter season.

The evening was temperately cool and calm. The crocodiles began to roar and appear in uncommon numbers along the shores and in the river. I 30 fixed my camp in an open plain, near the utmost projection of the promontory, under the shelter of a large live oak, which stood on the highest part of the ground, and but a few yards from my boat. From this open, high situation, I had a free prospect of the river, which was a matter of no trivial consideration to me, having good reason to dread the subtle attacks of the alligators, who were crowding about my harbour. Having collected a good quantity of wood for the purpose of keeping up a light 40 and smoke during the night, I began to think of preparing my supper, when, upon examining my stores, I found but a scanty provision. I thereupon determined, as the most expeditious way of supplying my necessities, to take my bob and try for some trout. About one hundred yards above my harbour began a cove or bay of the river, out of which opened a large lagoon. The mouth or entrance from the river to it was narrow, but the waters soon after spread and formed a little lake, extending into the marshes: its entrance and shores within I observed to be verged with floating lawns of the pistia and nymphea and other aquatic plants; these I knew were excellent haunts for trout.

The verges and islets of the lagoon were elegantly embellished with flowering plants and shrubs; the laughing coots with wings half spread were tripping over the little coves and hiding themselves in the tufts of grass; young broods of the painted summer teal, skimming the still surface of the waters, and following the watchful parent unconscious of danger, were frequently surprised by the voracious trout; and he, in turn, as often by the subtle greedy alligator. Behold him rushing forth from the flags and reeds. His enormous body swells. His plaited tail brandished high, floats upon the lake. The waters like a cataract descend from his opening jaws. Clouds of smoke issue from his dilated nostrils. The earth trembles with his thunder. When immediately from the opposite coast of the lagoon, emerges from the deep his rival champion. They suddenly dart upon each other. The boiling surface of the lake marks their rapid course, and a terrific conflict commences. They now sink to the bottom folded together in horrid wreaths. The water becomes thick and discoloured. Again they rise, their jaws clap together, re-echoing through the deep surrounding forests. Again they sink, when the contest ends at the muddy bottom of the lake, and the vanquished makes a hazardous escape, hiding himself in the muddy turbulent waters and sedge on a distant shore. The proud victor exulting returns to the place of action. The shores and forests resound his dreadful roar, together with the triumphing shouts of the plaited tribes around, witnesses of the horrid combat.

My apprehensions were highly alarmed after being a spectator of so dreadful a battle. It was obvious that every delay would but tend to encrease my dangers and difficulties, as the sun was near setting, and the alligators gathered around my harbour from all quarters. From these considerations I concluded to be expeditious in my trip to the lagoon, in order to take some fish. Not thinking it prudent to take my fusee with me, lest I might lose it overboard in case of a battle, which I had every reason to dread before my return, I therefore furnished myself with a club for my defence, went on board, and penetrating the first line of those which surrounded my harbour, they gave way; but being pursued by several very large ones, I kept strictly on the watch, and paddled with all my might towards the entrance of the lagoon, hoping to be sheltered there from the multitude of my assailants; but ere I had half-way reached the place, I was attacked on all sides, several endeavouring to overset the canoe. My situation now became precarious to the last degree: two very large ones attacked me closely, at the same instant, rushing up with their heads and part of their bodies above the water, roaring terribly and belching floods of water over me. They struck their jaws together so close to my ears, as almost to stun me, and I expected every moment to be dragged out of the boat and instantly devoured. But I applied my weapons so effectually about me, though at random, that I was so successful as to beat them off a little; when, finding that they designed to renew the battle, I made for the shore, as the only means left me for my preservation; for, by keeping close to it, I should have my enemies on one side of me only, whereas I was before surrounded by them; and there was a probability, if pushed to the last extremity, of saving myself, by jumping out of the canoe on shore, as it is easy to outwalk them on land, although comparatively as swift as lightning in the water. I found this last expedient alone could fully answer my expectations, for as soon as I gained the shore, they drew off and kept aloof. . . . Returning to my camp, I found it undisturbed, and then continued on to the extreme point of the promontory, where I saw a scene, new and surprising, which at first threw my senses into such a tumult, that it was some time before I could comprehend what was the matter; however, I soon accounted for the prodigious assemblage of crocodiles at this place, which exceeded everything of the kind I had ever heard of.

How shall I express myself so as to convey an adequate idea of it, to the reader, and at the same time avoid raising suspicions of my veracity. Should I say, that the river (in this place) from shore to shore, and perhaps near half a mile above and below me, appeared to be one solid bank of fish, of various kinds, pushing through this narrow pass of St. Juan's into the little lake, on their return down the river, and that the alligators were in such incredible numbers, and so close together from shore to shore, that it would have been easy to have walked across on their heads, had the animals been harmless? What expressions can sufficiently declare the shocking scene that for some minutes continued, whilst this mighty army of fish were forcing the pass? During this attempt, thousands, I may say hundreds of thousands, of them were caught and swallowed by the devouring alligators. I have seen an alligator take up out of the water several great fish at a time, and just squeeze them betwixt his jaws, while the tails of the great trout flapped about his eyes and lips, ere he had swallowed them. The horrid noise of their closing jaws, their plunging amidst the broken banks of fish, and rising with their prey some feet upright above the water, the floods of water and blood rushing out of their mouths, and the clouds of vapour issuing from their wide nostrils, were truly frightful. This scene continued at intervals during the night, as the fish came to pass. After this sight, shocking and tremendous as it was, I found myself somewhat easier and more reconciled to my situation; being convinced that their extraordinary assemblage here was owing to this annual feast of fish; and that they were so well employed in their own element, that I had little occasion to fear their paying me a visit. . . .

The noise of the crocodiles kept me awake the greater part of the night; but when I arose in the morning, contrary to my expectations, there was perfect peace; very few of them to be seen, and those were asleep on the shore. Yet I was not able to suppress my fears and apprehensions of being attacked by them in future; and indeed yesterday's combat with them, notwithstanding I came off in a manner victorious, or at least made a safe retreat, had left sufficient impression on my mind to damp my courage; and it seemed too much for one of my strength, being alone in a very small boat, to encounter such collected danger. To pursue my voyage up the river, and be obliged every evening to pass such dangerous defiles, appeared to me as perilous as running the gauntlet betwixt two rows of Indians armed with knives and firebrands. I however resolved to continue my voyage one day longer, if I possibly could with safety, and then return down the river, should I find the like difficulties to oppose. Accordingly I got every thing on board, charged my gun, and set sail cautiously, along shore. As I passed by Battle lagoon, I began to tremble and keep a good look out; when suddenly a huge alligator rushed out of the reeds, and with a tremendous roar came up, and darted as swift as an arrow under my boat, emerging upright on my lee quarter, with open jaws, and belching water and smoke that fell upon me like rain in a hurricane. I laid soundly about his head with my club and beat him off; and after plunging and darting about my boat, he went off on a straight line through the water, seemingly with the rapidity of lightning, and entered the cape of the lagoon. I now employed my time to the very best advantage in paddling close along shore, but could not forbear looking now and then behind me, and presently perceived one of them coming up again. The water of the river hereabouts was shoal and very clear; the monster came up with the usual roar and menaces, and passed close by the side of my boat, when I could distinctly see a young brood of alligators, to the number of one hundred or more, following after her in a long train. They kept close together in a column without straggling off to the one side or the other; the young appeared to be of an equal size, about fifteen inches in length, almost black, with pale yellow transverse waved clouds or blotches, much like rattlesnakes in colour. I now lost sight of my enemy again.

Still keeping close along shore, on turning a point or projection of the river bank, at once I beheld a great number of hillocks or small pyramids, resembling hay-cocks, ranged like an encampment along the banks. They stood fifteen or twenty yards distant from the water, on a high marsh, about four feet perpendicular above the water. I knew them to be the nests of the crocodile, having had a description of them before; and now expected a furious and general attack, as I saw several large crocodiles swimming abreast of these buildings. These nests being so great a curiosity to me, I was determined at all events immediately to land and examine them. Accordingly, I ran my bark on shore at one of their landing-places, which was a sort of nick or little dock, from which ascended a sloping path or road up to the edge of the meadow, where their nests were; most of them were deserted, and the great thick whitish egg-shells lay broken and scattered upon the ground round about them.

The nests or hillocks are of the form of an obtuse cone, four feet high, and four or five feet in diameter at their bases; they are constructed with mud, grass, and herbage. At first they lay a floor of this kind of tempered mortar on the ground, upon which they deposit a layer of eggs, and upon this a stratum of mortar seven or eight inches in thickness, and then another layer of eggs, and in this manner one stratum upon another, nearly to the top. I believe they commonly lay from one to two hundred eggs in a nest: these are hatched, I suppose, by the heat of the sun; and perhaps the vegetable substances mixed with the earth, being acted upon by the sun, may cause a small degree of fermentation, and so increase the heat in those hillocks. The ground for several acres about these nests shewed evident marks of a continual resort of alligators; the grass was every where beaten down, hardly a blade or straw was left standing; whereas, all about, at a distance, it was five or six feet high, and as thick as it could grow together. The female, as I imagine, carefully watches her own nest of eggs until they are all hatched; or perhaps while she is attending her own brood, she takes under her care and protection as many as she can get at one time, either from her own particular nest or others: but certain it is, that the young are not left to shift for themselves; for I have had frequent opportunities of seeing the female alligator leading about the shores her train of young ones, just as a hen does her brood of chickens; and she is equally assiduous and courageous in defending the young, which are under her care, and providing for their subsistence; and when she is basking upon the warm banks, with her brood around her, you may hear the young ones continually whining and barking, like young puppies. I believe but a few of a brood live to the years of full growth and magnitude, as the old feed on the young as long as they can make prey of them. . . .

[Tropical Vegetation]

Having gratified my curiosity at this general breeding-place and nursery of crocodiles, I continued my voyage up the river without being greatly disturbed by them. In my way I observed islets or floating fields of the bright green Pistia, decorated with other amphibious plants, as Senecio Jacobea, Persicaria amphibia, Coreopsis bidens, Hydrocotyle fluitans, and many others of less note.

The swamps on the banks and islands of the river are generally three or four feet above the surface of the water, and very level; the timber large and growing thinly, more so than what is observed to be in the swamps below lake George; the black rich earth is covered with moderately tall, and very succulent tender grass, which when chewed is sweet and agreeable to the taste, somewhat like young sugar-cane: it is a jointed decumbent grass, sending out radiculæ at the joints into the earth, and so spreads itself, by creeping over its surface.

The large timber trees, which possess the low lands, are *Acer rubrum, Ac. negundo, Ac. glaucum, Ulmus sylvatica, Fraxinus excelsior, Frax. aquatica, Ulmus suberifer, Gleditsia monosperma, Gledit. triacanthus, Diospyros Virginica, Nyssa aquatica, Nyssa sylvatica, Juglans cinerea, Quercus dentata, Quercus phillos, Hopea tinctoria, Corypha palma, Morus rubra*, and many more. The palm grows on the edges of the banks, where they are raised higher than the adjacent level ground, by the accumulation of sand, river-shells, &c. I passed along several miles by those rich swamps: the channels of the river which encircle the several fertile islands I had passed, now uniting, formed one deep channel near three hundred yards over. The banks of the river on each side, began to rise and present shelly bluffs, adorned by beautiful Orange groves, Laurels and Live Oaks. And now appeared in sight, a tree that claimed my whole attention: it was the Carica papaya, both male and female, which were in flower; and the latter both in flower and fruit, some of which were ripe, as large, and of the form of a pear, and of a most charming appearance.

This admirable tree is certainly the most beautiful of any vegetable production I know of; the towering Laurel Magnolia, and exalted Palm, indeed exceed it in grandeur and magnificence, but not in elegance, delicacy, and gracefulness. It rises erect to the height of fifteen or twenty feet, with a perfectly straight tapering stem, which is smooth and polished, of a bright ash colour, resembling leaf silver, curiously inscribed with the footsteps of the fallen leaves; and these vestiges are placed in a very regular uniform imbricated order, which has a fine effect, as if the little column were elegantly carved all over. Its perfectly spherical top is formed of very large lobe-sinuate leaves, supported on very long footstalks; the lower leaves are the largest as well as their petioles the longest, and make a graceful sweep or flourish, like the long f or the branches of a sconce candlestick. The ripe and green fruit are placed round about the stem or trunk, from the lowermost leaves, where the ripe fruit are, and upwards almost to the top; the heart or inmost pithy part of the trunk is in a manner hollow, or at best consists of a very thin porous medullae or membranes. The tree very seldom branches or divides into limbs, I believe never unless the top is by accident broke off when very young: I saw one which had two tops or heads, the stem of which divided near the earth. It is always green, ornamented at the same time with flowers and fruit, which like figs come out singly from the trunk or stem. . . .

It is very pleasing to observe the banks of the river ornamented with hanging garlands, composed of varieties of climbing vegetables, both shrubs and plants, forming perpendicular green walls, with projecting jambs, pilasters, and deep apartments, twenty or thirty feet high, and completely covered with *Glycine frutescens, Glyc. apios, Vitis labrusca, Vitis vulpina, Rajana, Hedera quinquifolia, Hedera arborea, Eupatorium scandens, Bignonia crucigera*, and various species of Convolvulus, particularly an amazing tall climber of this genus, or perhaps an Ipomea. This has a very large white flower, as big as a small funnel; its tube is five or six inches in length, and not thicker than a pipe stem; the leaves are also very large, oblong and cordated, sometimes dentated or angled, near the insertion of the rootstalk; they are of a thin texture, and of a deep green colour. It is exceedingly curious to behold the Wild Squash climbing over the lofty limbs of the trees; its

yellow fruit, somewhat of the size and figure of a large orange, pendant from the extremities of the limbs over the water. . . .

The air continued sultry, and scarcely enough wind to flutter the leaves on the trees. The Eastern coast of the river now opens, and presents to view ample plains, consisting of grassy marshes and green meadows, and affords a prospect almost unlimited and extremely pleasing. The opposite shore exhibits a sublime contrast; a high bluff bearing magnificent forests of grand magnolia, glorious palms, fruitful orange groves, live oaks, bays and other trees. This grand elevation continues four or five hundred yards, describing a gentle curve on the river, ornamented by a sublime grove of palms, consisting of many hundreds of trees together; they entirely shade the ground under them. Above and below the bluff, the grounds gradually descend to the common level swamps on the river: at the back of this eminence open to view expansive green meadows or savannas, in which are to be seen glittering ponds of water, surrounded at a great distance by high open pine forests and hommocks, and islets of oaks and bays projecting into the savannas. After ranging about these solitary groves and peaceful shades, I reembarked and continued some miles up the river, between elevated banks of the swamps or low lands; when on the East shore, in a capacious cove or winding of the river, were pleasing floating fields of pistia; and in the bottom of this cove opened to view a large creek or branch of the river, which I knew to be the entrance to a beautiful lake, on the banks of which was the farm I was going to visit, and which I designed should be the last extent of my voyage up the river. . . .

My hospitable friend [Bartram's host at the farm], after supplying me with necessaries, prevailed on me to accept of the company and assistance of his purveyor, one day's voyage down the river, whom I was to set on shore at a certain bluff, upwards of twenty miles below, but not above one third that distance by land; he was to be out in the forests one day, on a hunt for turkeys.

The current of the river being here confined within its perpendicular banks, ran briskly down: we cheerfully descended the grand river St. Juan, enjoying enchanting prospects.

Before night we reached the destined port, at a spacious orange grove. Next morning we separated, and I proceeded down the river. The prospects on either hand are now pleasing, and I view them at leisure, and without toil or dread.

Induced by the beautiful appearance of the green meadows, which open to the Eastward, I determined not to pass this Elysium without a visit. Behold the loud, sonorous, watchful savanna cranes (*Grus pratensis*) with musical clangor, in detached squadrons. They spread their light elastic sail: at first they move from the earth heavy and slow; they labour and beat the dense air; they form the line with wide extended wings, tip to tip; they all rise and fall together as one bird; now they mount aloft, gradually wheeling about; each squadron performs its evolutions, encircling the expansive plains, observing each one its own orbit; then lowering sail, descend on the verge of some glittering lake; whilst other squadrons, ascending aloft in spiral circles, bound on interesting discoveries, wheel round and double the promontory, in the silver regions of the clouded skies, where, far from the scope of eye, they carefully observe the verdant meadows on the borders of the East Lake; then contract their plumes and descend to the earth, where, after resting awhile on some verdant eminence, near the flowery border of the lake, they, with dignified, yet slow, respectful steps, approach the kindred band, confer, and treat for habitation; the bounds and precincts being settled, they confederate and take possession. . . .

Having agreeably diverted away the intolerable heats of sultry noon in fruitful fragrant groves, with renewed vigor I again resume my sylvan pilgrimage. The afternoon and evening moderately warm, and exceeding pleasant views from the river and its varied shores. I passed by Battle lagoon and the bluff, without much opposition; but the crocodiles were already assembling in the pass. Before night I came to, at a charming orange grove bluff, on the East side of the little lake; and after fixing my camp on a high open situation, and collecting a plenty of dry wood for fuel, I had time to get some fine trout for supper, and joyfully return to my camp.

What a most beautiful creature is this fish before me! gliding to and fro, and figuring in the still clear waters, with his orient attendants and associates: the yellow bream or sun fish. It is about eight inches in length, nearly the shape of the trout, but rather larger in proportion over the shoulders and breast; the mouth large, and the branchiostega opens wide; the whole fish is of a pale gold (or burnished brass) colour, darker on the back and upper sides; the scales are of a proportionable size, regularly placed, and every where variably powdered with red, russet, silver, blue, and green specks, so laid on the scales as to appear like real dust or opaque bodies, each apparent particle being so projected by light and shade, and the various attitudes of the fish, as to deceive the sight; for in reality nothing can be of a more plain and polished surface than the scales and whole body of the fish. The fins are of an orange colour; and, like all the species of the bream, the ultimate angle of the branchiostega terminates by a little spatula, the extreme end of which represents a crescent of the finest ultramarine blue, encircled with silver and velvet black, like the eye in the feathers of a peacock's train. . . .

The orange grove is but narrow, betwixt the river banks and ancient Indian fields, where there are evident traces of the habitations of the ancients, surrounded with groves of live oak, laurel, magnolia, zanthoxylon, liquidambar, and others.

How harmonious and soothing is this native sylvan music now at still evening! inexpressibly tender are the responsive cooings of the innocent dove, in the fragrant zanthoxylon groves, and the variable and tuneful warblings of the nonpareil, with the more sprightly and elevated strains of the blue linnet and golden icterus: this is indeed harmony, even amidst the incessant croaking of the frogs: the shades of silent night are made more cheerful, with the shrill voice of the whip-poor-will and active mock-bird.

My situation high and airy: a brisk and cool breeze steadily and incessantly passing over the clear waters of the lake, and fluttering over me through the surrounding groves, wings its way to the moon-light savannas, while I repose on my sweet and healthy couch of the soft tillandsia usnea-adscites, and the latter gloomy and still hours of night pass rapidly away as it were in a moment. I arose, strengthened and cheerful, in the morning. Having some repairs to make in the tackle of my vessel, I paid my first attention to them; which being accomplished, my curiosity prompted me to penetrate the grove and view the illumined plains.

What a beautiful display of vegetation is here before me! seemingly unlimited in extent and variety: how the dew-drops twinkle and play upon the sight, trembling on the tips of the lucid, green savanna, sparkling as the gem that flames on the turban of the eastern prince. See the pearly tears rolling off the buds of the expanding Granadilla; behold the azure fields of cerulean Ixea! what can equal the rich golden flowers of the *Canna lutea*, which ornament the banks of yon serpentine rivulet, meandering over the meadows; the almost endless varieties of the gay Phlox, that

enamel the swelling green banks, associated with the purple Verbena corymbosa, Viola, pearly Gnaphalium, and silvery Perdicium? . . .

How glorious the powerful sun, minister of the Most High in the rule and government of this earth, leaves our hemisphere, retiring from our sight beyond the western forests! I behold with gratitude his departing smiles, tinging the fleecy
10 roseate clouds, now riding far away on the eastern horizon; behold they vanish from sight in the azure skies!

All now silent and peaceable, I suddenly fall asleep. At midnight I awake; when, raising my head erect, I find myself alone in the wilderness of Florida, on the shores of Lake George. Alone indeed, but under the care of the Almighty, and protected by the invisible hand of my guardian angel. . . .

THE REVOLUTION AND EARLY NATIONALISM

BENJAMIN FRANKLIN (1706-1790)

IT HAS BEEN remarked that of all men of the eighteenth century, Franklin would most quickly find himself at home if he were suddenly precipitated to earth today. He would discover in this present world many fruits from seeds his elder self had planted. He had given so much fundamental direction to educational and civic affairs, to science, and to statecraft, and he had caught so much wisdom in his writings, that in the world of today he would often be confronted by his own genius. In Philadelphia he was largely instrumental in establishing the Library Company (the first circulating library in America) in 1731, the American Philosophical Society in 1743, a city hospital in 1751, and the Academy for the Education of Youth (later the University of Pennsylvania) in 1751. His philanthropic benefactions to Boston and Philadelphia are still-living funds amounting to hundreds of thousands of dollars. He so discerned the nature of electricity as to apply the terms *positive* and *negative* and to do fundamental research on the condenser. He set forth the theory explaining why northeast storms in the United

States move against the wind, plotted major wind currents, and added to the knowledge concerning the Gulf Stream. He invented a stove to supplant the uneconomical fireplace, and a clock that would record hours, minutes, and seconds, yet had only three wheels and two pinions. He proved to himself the variability in heat absorption of various colors; he fashioned bifocal spectacles, and he devised a harmonica of thirty-seven glass hemispheres.

As clerk and subsequently member of the Pennsylvania Assembly from 1736 to 1764, he was a wise counselor, and as an executive he was an able deputy postmaster of Philadelphia and later of the Colonies from 1737 to 1774. In 1754, if his Plan of Union set forth at the Albany Convention had been accepted, England and her dissatisfied colonies would have had a framework of federation that might have solved much subsequent dissension. From 1757 to 1775, with only one break in 1762, he represented Pennsylvania and later most of the other colonies before the British Government and sketched the way of peaceful union that might have prevented war had his recommendations been followed. He had a part in the drawing up of the Declaration of Independence, and was one of the signers of the document, who would "hang together or hang separately." From 1776 to 1785 he was in France securing aid for the prosecution of the Revolutionary War and taking a major part in drafting the terms of peace. Back in the United States, he was chief among those who maintained that breadth of view and sanity of judgment which kept the Constitutional Convention from floundering on the rocks of permanent discord. And throughout his life he found time to write essays, treaties, and a book rich with the accumulated wisdom of his manifold activities.

An eminent scientist, a wise ambassador, a supreme philosopher of government, he bestrode two continents. As hardheaded John Adams wrote: "Franklin's reputation was more universal than that of Leibnitz or Newton, Frederick [the Great] or Voltaire; and his character more loved and esteemed than any or all of them. . . . His name was familiar to government and people, to kings, courtiers, nobility, clergy, and philosophers, as well as plebeians, to such a degree that there was scarcely a peasant or a citizen, *a valet de chambre*, coachman or footman, a lady's chambermaid or a scullion in a kitchen who was not familiar with it and who did not consider him a friend to human kind."

The classic account of Franklin's early life, his self-education and rise to success, as told in the famous *Autobiography*, still occupies a cherished place in the national imagination. He was born in Boston, January 17, 1706, the son of a tallow chandler and soapmaker and his second wife. He was the fifteenth child of his father, and the youngest son of the youngest son for five generations. At the age of twelve he was apprenticed to his half brother James, who was soon to found and publish the *New England Courant* (1721). By poring over a volume of Addison's *Spectator* and playing the "sedulous ape" by trying to complete the essays again, he increased his vocabulary and developed his style. The ensuing stages in his career are familiar pictures in the minds of most Americans. He is the runaway apprentice who at seventeen munches his penny roll on Market

Street in Philadelphia and gets a job as a printer. He is a young man stranded in London, unable to buy printing equipment because promised letters of credit were not forthcoming, and fortunate in being able to find employment at his trade. At twenty-four he is the sole owner of his printshop in Philadelphia, publisher and editor of the *Pennsylvania Gazette*, and husband of Deborah Read. As "Richard Saunders" in *Poor Richard's Almanac* from 1832 to 1857 he spreads his name and his collections of homespun aphorisms throughout the colonies, and his choice essay, Father Abraham's speech at the auction, in the last issue, is scattered over England and translated into French. As a citizen of Philadelphia he serves his city and state in many ways, identifying himself with the birth of humane institutions and with matters of state and colonial legislation. In 1748, at the age of forty-two, he retires from active business, operates through partnerships, and receives an assured income of at least two thousand pounds a year. Now he may devote himself to science and to the larger affairs of colonial and international importance. These and other achievements are told with ease and clarity in the *Autobiography*. But this unique self-portrait ends in 1757, the year of his leaving for England. Ahead of him lie thirty-three years of distinguished public service. Thirty-four years before, when he had fled from his half brother in Boston, Cotton Mather was still preaching and Jonathan Edwards was beginning his graduate study of theology. Now, as he leaves for England, he is well on his way to becoming the embodiment of the spirit of the Enlightenment, and in government to foreshadowing the future course of the United States.

Although his collected works occupy nine volumes in the A. H. Smyth edition, Franklin probably never thought of himself as a man of letters. Even his one book, the *Autobiography*, was done only as something that might be of service to his son. Charmingly written, clear and frank in its treatment of himself with relation to the world, it is the self-revelation of what Paul Elmer More called "the most alert and capacious intellect that ever concerned itself entirely with the present." The other works may be arranged in three groups: his scientific writings, his essays in

169

journals and pamphlets on social, practical, and political subjects, and his letters, literary hoaxes, and bagatelles.

Of his scientific writings, the records of his observations and experiments with electricity well reveal the temper of his mind. He made fundamental discoveries rather than simple adaptations of known principles. His letters to the Royal Society won Jeffrey's praise for their "amiable and inoffensive cheerfulness," and his exposition of the principles of electricity were admired by Sir Humphrey Davy as being equally readable by philosophers and laymen. Whether he was writing on the cause of smoky chimneys or on his "single fluid" theory of electricity, he wrote with incisive felicity.

His essays on social and political topics began with his anonymous contributions to the *New England Courant* in 1722, when in the guise of "Silence Dogood" he gaily observed and derided pedantry and the affectation of hoop skirts and formalized funeral elegies. His political essays, according to the nature of the subjects, are written with cool and detached irony, kindly cynicism, or biting satire. Among them the "Edict by the King of Prussia" (1773) and the "Rules by Which a Great Empire May Be Reduced to a Small One" (1773) are widely familiar to college students. Most accomplished in their gracefulness are the familiar essays and bagatelles written at Passy in the days of the American Revolution. The Philadelphia printer whose prudential maxims would have delighted Defoe and Richardson now devoted himself to the pleasant graces with a series of charming and fanciful trifles—enduring trivia— which amazed Abigail Adams as much as they captivated and diverted the guests of Madame Brillon and Madame Helvétius.

As a man of letters, his library was by far the largest in the colonies. All his writings were intended for specific occasions, his immediate concerns and pleasures. They live because they illumine life both in its peccadilloes and its greater reaches, to planes of detached wisdom on affairs of this world. He was not a mystic. But he could see clearly within the confines of reason and worldly experience, and he could bring both to bear in estimating the true value of things and ideas,

whether they be boyhood's whistles or the plans and schemes of men.

BIBLIOGRAPHY · The two standard editions are *The Complete Works of Benjamin Franklin* (10 vols., 1887–1888), edited by J. Bigelow; and *The Writings of Benjamin Franklin* (10 vols., 1905–1907), edited by A. H. Smyth. The latter work omits certain pieces which the editor felt reflected no credit on their author; both editions need to be supplemented by a number of available uncollected items. Valuable facsimiles of individual works include *The Life of Benjamin Franklin Written by Himself* (3 vols., 1875), edited by J. Bigelow; *Poor Richard's Almanack* [for 1733, 1749, 1756–58], with a foreword by P. Russell (1928); *A Dissertation on Liberty and Necessity, Pleasure and Pain* (1930), with a bibliographical note by L. C. Wroth; *Proposals Relating to the Education of Youth in Pennsylvania* (1931), with an introduction by W. Pepper; and *The General Magazine* [1741], with a bibliographical note by L. N. Richardson (1938). The best volumes of representative selections are *Benjamin Franklin* (1936), edited by F. L. Mott and C. E. Jorgenson, with an invaluable introduction and bibliography; and *Franklin and Edwards* (1920), edited by C. Van Doren. P. L. Ford's *Franklin Bibliography* (1889) needs to be supplemented by other sources for items after 1889.

The best biography is C. Van Doren, *Benjamin Franklin* (1938), which won the Pulitzer Prize of that year. J. Parton, *Life and Times of Benjamin Franklin* (2 vols., 1864), and A. H. Smyth, *Life of Franklin*, X, 141–510, of *The Writings of Benjamin Franklin* (1907), are the most notable early biographies. Other valuable biographical and critical studies include W. C. Bruce, *Benjamin Franklin Self-Revealed* (2 vols., 1917); V. W. Crane, *Benjamin Franklin: Englishman and American* (1936); B. Fay, *Franklin: The Apostle of Modern Times* (1929); P. L. Ford, *The Many-Sided Franklin* (1899); E. E. Hale and E. E. Hale, Jr., *Franklin in France* (2 vols., 1887–1888); J. T. Morse, *Benjamin Franklin* (1889); J. C. Oswald, *Benjamin Franklin, Printer* (1917); and J. H. Smythe, Jr., *The Amazing Benjamin Franklin* (1929). The most succinct and authoritative summary is the admirable fourteen-page sketch by C. Becker in the *Dictionary of American Biography*, VI, 585–598.

Valuable specialized studies include A. O. Aldridge, "Franklin's 'Shaftesburian' Dialogues not Franklin's," *American Literature*, XXI (1949), 151–159; W. G. Bleyer, *Main Currents in the History of American Journalism* (1927), Chapters I–II; V. W. Crane, "Certain Writings of Benjamin Franklin on the British Empire and the American Colonies," *Papers of the British Society*, XXVIII (1934), 1–27; I. B. Cohen, "Benjamin Franklin and Aeronautics," *Journal of the Franklin Institute*, CCXXXII (1941), 101–128, "Benjamin Franklin as Scientist and Citizen," *American Scholar*, XII (1943), 474–481, and "How Practical Was Benjamin Franklin's Science?" *Pennsyl-*

vania Magazine of History and Biography, LXIX (1945), 284–293; M. R. Eiselen, *Franklin's Political Theories* (1928); B. Fay, "Les Débuts de Franklin en France," *Revue de Paris* (Feb., 1931), 577–605; G. F. Horner, "Franklin's Do-Good Papers Re-examined," *Studies in Philology*, XXXVII (1940), 501–523; C. E. Jorgenson, "Benjamin Franklin and Rabelais," *Classical Journal*, XXIX (1934), 538–540, "The New Science in the Almanacs of Ames and Franklin," *New England Quarterly*, VIII (1935), 555–561, and "Sidelights on Benjamin Franklin's Principles of Rhetoric," *Revue Anglo-Américaine*, XI (1934), 209–223; L. S. Livingston, *Franklin and His Press at Passy* (1914); J. F. Ross, "The Character of Poor Richard: Its Source and Alteration," *PMLA*, LV (1940), 785–794; J. M. Stifler, *The Religion of Benjamin Franklin* (1925); A. Thaler, "Franklin and Fulke Greville," *PMLA*, LVI (1941), 1059–1064; C. Van Doren, "The Beginnings of the American Philosophical Society," *Proceedings of the American Philosophical Society*, LXXXVII (1943), 277–289; D. Wecter, "Burke, Franklin, and Samuel Petrie," *Huntington Library Quarterly*, IV (1941), 205–234; A. W. Wetzel, "Benjamin Franklin as an Economist," in *Johns Hopkins University Studies*, XIII (1895); and D. Williams, "More Light on Franklin's Religious Ideas," *American Historical Review*, XLIII (1938), 803–813.

Silence Dogood Papers

[*A Satire on Harvard College*]

OVER THE signature of Silence Dogood, represented as a widow with three children, Franklin at the age of fifteen contributed a series of letters to *The New-England Courant*, on which he worked as an apprentice to his half brother James. The following letter shows his early support of the leather-apron men—the men at the bench and the counter. He always identified himself as "printer." This is his first essay on education, published as number 4 of the Dogood Papers in the *Courant* for the week of May 7–14, 1722, from which this text is taken. It is the beginning of his long interest in education, which culminated in his essays and practical endeavors pertaining to the establishment of the University of Pennsylvania and the kind of curriculum it should adopt.

To the Author of the *New England Courant*

Sir,

Discoursing the other Day at Dinner with my Reverend Boarder, formerly mention'd, (whom for Distinction sake we will call by the Name of Clericus,) concerning the Education of Children, I ask'd his Advice about my young Son William, whether or no I had best bestow upon him Academical Learning, or (as our Phrase is) bring him up at our College: He perswaded me to do it by all Means, using many weighty Arguments with me, and answering all the Objections that I could form against it; telling me withal, that he did not doubt but the Lad would take his Learning very well, and not idle away his Time as too many there now-a-days do. These Words of Clericus gave me a Curiosity to inquire a little more strictly into the present Circumstances of that famous Seminary of Learning; but the Information which he gave me, was neither pleasant, nor such as I expected.

As soon as Dinner was over, I took a solitary Walk into my Orchard, still ruminating on Clericus's Discourse with much Consideration, until I came to my usual Place of Retirement under the Great Apple-Tree; where having seated my self, and carelessly laid my Head on a verdant Bank, I fell by Degrees into a soft and undisturbed Slumber. My waking Thoughts remained with me in my Sleep, and before I awak'd again, I dreamt the following Dream.

I fancy'd I was travelling over pleasant and delightful Fields and Meadows, and thro' many small Country Towns and Villages; and as I pass'd along, all Places resounded with the Fame of the Temple of Learning: Every Peasant, who had wherwithal, was preparing to send one of his Children at least to this famous Place; and in this Case most of them consulted their own Purses instead of their Childrens Capacities: So that I observed, a great many, yea, the most part of those who were travelling thither, were little better than Dunces and Blockheads. Alas! alas!

AT length I entered upon a spacious Plain, in the Midst of which was erected a large and stately Edifice: It was to this that a great Company of Youths from all Parts of the Country were going; so stepping in among the Crowd, I passed on with them, and presently arrived at the Gate.

The Passage was kept by two sturdy Porters named Riches and Poverty, and the latter obstinately refused to give Entrance to any who had not first gain'd the Favour of the former; so that I observed, many who came to the very Gate, were obliged to travel back again as ignorant as they came, for want of this necessary Qualification. However, as a Spectator I gain'd Admittance, and with the rest entered directly into the Temple.

IN the Middle of the great Hall stood a stately and magnificent Throne, which was ascended to by two high and difficult Steps. On the Top of it sat Learning in awful State; she was apparelled wholly in Black, and surrounded almost on every Side with innumerable Volumes in all Languages. She seem'd very busily employ'd in writing some- thing on half a Sheet of Paper, and upon Enquiry, I understood she was preparing a Paper call'd, *The New-England Courant*. On her Right Hand sat English, with a pleasant smiling Countenance, and handsomely attir'd; and on her left were seated several Antique Figures with their Faces vail'd. I was considerably puzzl'd to guess who they were, until one informed me, (who stood beside me,) that those Figures on her left Hand were Latin, Greek, Hebrew, &c. and that they were much reserv'd, and seldom or never unvail'd their Faces here, and then to few or none, tho' most of those who have in this Place acquir'd so much Learning as to distinguish them from English, pretended to an intimate Acquaintance with them. I then enquir'd of him, what could be the Reason why they continued vail'd, in this Place especially: He pointed to the Foot of the Throne, where I saw Idleness, attended with Ignorance, and these (he informed me) were they, who first vail'd them, and still kept them so.

Now I observed, that the whole Tribe who entered into the Temple with me, began to climb the Throne; but the Work proving troublesome and difficult to most of them, they withdrew their Hands from the Plow, and contented themselves to sit at the Foot, with Madam Idleness and her Maid Ignorance, until those who were assisted by Diligence and a docible Temper, had well-nigh got up the first Step: But the Time drawing nigh in which they could no way avoid ascending, they were fain to crave the Assistance of those who had got up before them, and who, for the Reward per- haps of a Pint of Milk, or a Piece of Plumb-Cake, lent the Lubbers a helping Hand, and sat them in the Eye of the World, upon a Level with them- selves.

The other Step being in the same Manner ascended, and the usual Ceremonies at an End, every Beetle-Scull seem'd well satisfy'd with his own Portion of Learning, tho' perhaps he was *e'en just* as ignorant as ever. And now the Time of their Departure being come, they march'd out of Doors to make Room for another Company, who waited for Entrance: And I, having seen all that was to be seen, quitted the Hall likewise, and went to make my Observations on those who were just gone out before me.

Some I perceiv'd took to Merchandizing, others to Travelling, some to one Thing, some to another, and some to Nothing; and many of them from henceforth, for want of Patrimony, liv'd as poor as Church Mice, being unable to dig, and asham'd to beg, and to live by their Wits it was impossible. But the most Part of the Crowd went along a large beaten Path, which led to a Temple at the further End of the Plain, call'd The Temple of Theology. The Business of those who were employ'd in this Temple being laborious and painful, I wonder'd exceedingly to see so many go towards it; but while I was pondering this Matter in my Mind, I spy'd Pecunia behind a Curtain, beckoning to them with her Hand, which Sight immediately satisfy'd me for whose Sake it was; that a great Part of them (I will not say all) travel'd that Road. In this Temple I saw nothing worth mentioning, except the ambitious and fraudulent Contrivances of Plagius, who (notwithstanding he had been severely reprehended for such Practices before) was diligently transcribing some eloquent Para- graphs out of Tillotson's Works, &c. to embellish his own.

Now I bethought my self in my Sleep, that it was Time to be at Home, and as I fancy'd I was travelling back thither, I reflected in my mind on the extream Folly of those Parents, who, blind to their Childrens Dulness, and insensible of the Solidity of their Skulls, because they think their Purses can afford it, will needs send them to the Temple of Learning, where, for want of a suitable Genius, they learn little more than how to carry themselves handsomely, and enter a Room gen- teely, (which might as well be acquir'd at Danc- ing-School,) and from whence they return, after Abundance of Trouble and Charge, as great Block- heads as ever, only more proud and self-conceited.

While I was in the midst of these unpleasant Reflections, Clericus (who with a Book in his Hand was walking under the Trees) accidently awak'd me; to him I related my Dream with all its Particulars, and he, without much Study, presently interpreted it, assuring me, That it was a lively Representation of Harvard College, Etcetera.

I remain, Sir,
Your Humble Servant
Silence Dogood.

Advice to a Young Tradesman

PUBLISHED in 1748, Franklin's advice purporting to come from "An Old Tradesman," had unusual authority, for in that year the author was able to retire from active business with one of the best incomes in the colonies. Franklin had kept his shop so well that it was able to keep him for the rest of his long life. The text is that of J. Bigelow, *The Complete Works*, II (1887).

To my Friend, A. B.:

As you have desired it of me, I write the following hints, which have been of service to me, and may, if observed, be so to you.

Remember that time is money. He that can earn ten shillings a day by his labor, and goes abroad, or sits idle, one half of that day, though he spends but sixpence during his diversion or idleness, ought not to reckon that the only expense; he has really spent, or rather thrown away, five shillings besides.

Remember that credit is money. If a man lets his money lie in my hands after it is due, he gives me the interest, or so much as I can make of it during that time. This amounts to a considerable sum where a man has good and large credit, and makes good use of it.

Remember that money is of the prolific, generating nature. Money can beget money, and its offspring can beget more, and so on. Five shillings turned is six, turned again it is seven and three-pence, and so on till it becomes an hundred pounds. The more there is of it, the more it produces every turning, so that the profits rise quicker and quicker. He that kills a breeding sow destroys all her offspring to the thousandth generation. He that murders a crown destroys all that it might have produced, even scores of pounds.

Remember that six pounds a year is but a groat a day. For this little sum (which may be daily wasted either in time or expense unperceived) a man of credit may, on his own security, have the constant possession and use of an hundred pounds. So much in stock, briskly turned by an industrious man, produces great advantage.

Remember this saying: The good paymaster is lord of another man's purse. He that is known to pay punctually and exactly to the time he promises, may at any time, and on any occasion, raise all the money his friends can spare. This is sometimes of great use. After industry and frugality, nothing contributes more to the raising of a young man in the world than punctuality and justice in all his dealings; therefore, never keep borrowed money an hour beyond the time you promised, lest a disappointment shut up your friend's purse for ever.

The most trifling actions that affect a man's credit are to be regarded. The sound of your hammer at five in the morning, or nine at night, heard by a creditor, makes him easy six months longer; but, if he sees you at a billiard-table, or hears your voice at a tavern when you should be at work, he sends for his money the next day; demands it, before he can receive it, in a lump.

It shows, besides, that you are mindful of what you owe; it makes you appear a careful as well as an honest man, and that still increases your credit.

Beware of thinking all your own that you possess, and of living accordingly. It is a mistake that many people who have credit fall into. To prevent this, keep an exact account for some time, both of your expenses and your income. If you take the pains at first to mention particulars, it will have this good effect: you will discover how wonderfully small, trifling expenses mount up to large sums, and will discern what might have been and may for the future be saved, without occasioning any great inconvenience.

In short, the way to wealth, if you desire it, is as plain as the way to market. It depends chiefly on two words, industry and frugality—that is, waste neither time nor money, but make the best use of both. Without industry and frugality nothing will do, and with them every thing. He that gets all he can honestly, and saves all he gets (necessary expenses excepted), will certainly become rich, if that Being who governs the world, to whom all should look for a blessing on their honest endeavours, doth not, in his wise providence, otherwise determine.

An Old Tradesman.

Proposals Relating to the Education of Youth in Pensilvania

Philadelphia: Printed in the year, MDCCXLIX.

As EARLY AS 1743 Franklin suggested to the Reverend Richard Peters the formation of an academy. In 1749 he published the *Proposals*, an elaborately documented pamphlet of 32 pages, in which he quoted from the educational theories of Locke and others. As a result [20] of Franklin's proposals, a Board of Trustees was organized, and on November 13, 1749, Franklin was elected president. The Academy was formally opened on January 7, 1751, with an address by the Reverend Mr. Peters, which Franklin later printed, appending thereto his own "Idea of the English School." The utilitarian Franklin had contemplated only an English School, but the richest member of the Board stood firmly for a Latin School also, and, to Franklin's disappointment, the latter's proposal was given precedence. With the coming of William Smith as provost in [30] 1754, Franklin found himself in growing opposition to the classical curriculum, and though he long remained a trustee, he resigned the presidency in 1756. For the steps by which the Academy ultimately became the University of Pennsylvania, see W. Pepper, "Benjamin Franklin: Founder of the University," *General Magazine and Historical Chronicle*, XL (1938), 318–324. The text of the *Proposal* follows the original of 1749, but omits the notes.

Advertisement to the Reader. It has long been [40] regretted as a Misfortune to the Youth of this Province, that we have no Academy, in which they might receive the Accomplishments of a regular Education.

The following Paper of Hints towards forming a Plan for that Purpose, is so far approv'd by some publick-spirited Gentlemen, to whom it has been privately communicated, that they have directed a Number of Copies to be made by the Press, and properly distributed, in order to obtain the Sentiments and Advice of Men of Learning, Understanding, and Experience in these Matters; and have determin'd to use their Interest and best Endeavours, to have the Scheme, when compleated, carried gradually into Execution; in which they have Reason to believe they shall have the hearty Concurrence and Assistance of many who [10] are Wellwishers to their Country.

Those who incline to favour the Design with their Advice, either as to the Parts of Learning to be taught, the Order of Study, the Method of Teaching, the Oeconomy of the School, or any other Matter of Importance to the Success of the Undertaking, are desired to communicate their Sentiments as soon as may be, by Letter directed to B. Franklin, Printer, in Philadelphia."

Proposals, Etc. The good Education of Youth [20] has been esteemed by wise Men in all Ages, as the surest Foundation of the Happiness both of private Families and of Common-wealths. Almost all Governments have therefore made it a principal Object of their Attention, to establish and endow with proper Revenues, such Seminaries of Learning, as might supply the succeeding Age with Men qualified to serve the Publick with Honour to themselves, and to their Country.

Many of the first Settlers of these Provinces [30] were Men who had received a good Education in Europe, and to their Wisdom and good Management we owe much of our present Prosperity. But their Hands were full, and they could not do all Things. The present Race are not thought to be generally of equal Ability: For though the American Youth are allow'd not to want Capacity; yet the best Capacities require Cultivation, it being truly with them, as with the best Ground, which unless well tilled and sowed with profitable [40] Seed, produces only ranker Weeds.

That we may obtain the Advantages arising from an Increase of Knowledge, and prevent as much as may be the mischievous Consequences that would attend a general Ignorance among us, the following Hints are offered towards forming a Plan for the Education of the Youth of Pennsylvania, viz.

It is propos'd,

THAT some Persons of Leisure and publick Spirit apply for a Charter, by which they may be incorporated, with Power to erect an Academy for the Education of Youth, to govern the same, provide Masters, make Rules, receive Donations, purchase Lands, etc. and to add to their Number, from Time to Time such other Persons as they shall judge suitable.

That the Members of the Corporation make it their Pleasure, and in some Degree their Business, to visit the Academy often, encourage and countenance the Youth, countenance and assist the Masters, and by all Means in their Power advance the Usefulness and Reputation of the Design; that they look on the Students as in some Sort their Children, treat them with Familiarity and Affection, and, when they have behav'd well, and gone through their Studies, and are to enter the World, zealously unite, and make all the Interest that can be made to establish them, whether in Business, Offices, Marriages, or any other Thing for their Advantage, preferably to all other Persons whatsoever even of equal Merit.

And if Men may, and frequently do, catch such a Taste for cultivating Flowers, for Planting, Grafting, Inoculating, and the like, as to despise all other Amusements for their Sake, why may not we expect they should acquire a Relish for that more useful Culture of young Minds. Thomson says,

> 'Tis Joy to see the human Blossoms blow,
> When infant Reason grows apace, and calls
> For the kind Hand of an assiduous Care;
> Delightful Task! to rear the tender Thought,
> To teach the young Idea how to shoot,
> To pour the fresh Instruction o'er the Mind,
> To breathe th' enliv'ning Spirit, and to fix
> The generous Purpose in the glowing Breast.

That a House be provided for the ACADEMY, if not in the Town, not many Miles from it; the Situation high and dry, and if it may be, not far from a River, having a Garden, Orchard, Meadow, and a Field or two.

That the House be furnished with a Library (if in the Country, if in the Town, the Town Libraries may serve) with Maps of all Countries, Globes, some mathematical Instruments, an Apparatus for Experiments in Natural Philosophy, and for Mechanics; Prints, of all Kinds, Prospects, Buildings, Machines, &c.

That the Rector be a Man of good Understanding, good Morals, diligent and patient, learn'd in the Languages and Sciences, and a correct pure Speaker and Writer of the English Tongue; to have such Tutors under him as shall be necessary.

That the boarding Scholars diet together, plainly, temperately, and frugally.

That to keep them in Health, and to strengthen and render active their Bodies, they be frequently exercis'd in Running, Leaping, Wrestling, and Swimming, &c.

That they have peculiar Habits to distinguish them from other Youth, if the Academy be in or near the Town; for this, among other Reasons, that their Behaviour may be the better observed.

As to their Studies, it would be well if they could be taught every Thing that is useful, and every Thing that is ornamental: But Art is long, and their Time is short. It is therefore propos'd that they learn those Things that are likely to be most useful and most ornamental. Regard being had to the several Professions for which they are intended.

All should be taught to write a fair Hand, and swift, as that is useful to All. And with it may be learnt something of Drawing, by Imitation of Prints, and some of the first Principles of Perspective.

Arithmetick, Accounts, and some of the first Principles of Geometry and Astronomy.

The English Language might be taught by Grammar; in which some of our best Writers, as Tillotson, Addison, Pope, Algernon Sidney, Cato's Letters, &c., should be Classicks: the Stiles principally to be cultivated, being the clear and the concise. Reading should also be taught, and pronouncing, properly, distinctly, emphatically; not with an even Tone, which under-does, nor a theatrical, which over-does Nature.

To form their Stile, they should be put on Writing Letters to each other, making Abstracts of what they read; or writing the same Things in their own Words; telling or writing Stories lately read, in their own Expressions. All to be revis'd and corrected by the Tutor, who should give his

Reasons, and explain the Force and Import of Words, &c.

To form their Pronunciation, they may be put on making Declamations, repeating Speeches, delivering Orations, &c. The Tutor assisting at the Rehearsals, teaching, advising, correcting their Accent, &c.

But if HISTORY be made a constant Part of their Reading, such as the Translations of the Greek and Roman Historians, and the modern Histories of ancient Greece and Rome, &c. may not almost all Kinds of useful Knowledge be that Way introduc'd to Advantage, and with Pleasure to the Student? As

Geography, by reading with Maps, and being required to point out the Places where the greatest Actions were done, to give their old and new Names, with the Bounds, Situation, Extent of the Countries concern'd, &c.

Chronology, by the Help of Helvicus or some other Writer of the Kind, who will enable them to tell when those Events happened; what Princes were Contemporaries, what States or famous Men flourish'd about that Time, &c. The several principal Epochas to be first well fix'd in their Memories.

Antient Customs, religious and civil, being frequently mentioned in History, will give Occasion for explaining them; in which the Prints of Medals, Basso-Relievo's, and antient Monuments will greatly assist.

Morality, by descanting and making continual Observations on the Causes of the Rise or Fall of any Man's Character, Fortune, Power, &c. mention'd in History; the Advantages of Temperance, Order, Frugality, Industry, Perseverance, &c. &c. Indeed the general natural Tendency of Reading good History, must be, to fix in the Minds of Youth deep Impressions of the Beauty and Usefulness of Virtue of all Kinds, Publick Spirit, Fortitude, &c.

History will show the wonderful Effects of Oratory, in governing, turning and leading great Bodies of Mankind, Armies, Cities, Nations. When the Minds of Youth are struck with Admiration at this, then is the Time to give them the Principles, of that Art, which they will study with Taste and Application. Then they may be made acquainted with the best Models among the Antients, their Beauties being particularly pointed out to them. Modern Political Oratory being chiefly performed by the Pen and Press, its Advantages over the Antient in some Respects are to be shown; as that its Effects are more extensive, more lasting, &c.

History will also afford frequent Opportunities of showing the Necessity of a Publick Religion from its Usefulness to the Publick; the Advantage of a Religious Character among private Persons; the Mischiefs of Superstition, &c. and the Excellency of the Christian Religion above all others antient or modern.

History will also give Occasion to expatiate on the Advantage of Civil Orders and Constitutions, how Men and their Properties are protected by joining in Societies and establishing Government; their Industry encouraged and rewarded, Arts invented, and Life made more comfortable: The Advantages of Liberty, Mischiefs of Licentiousness, Benefits arising from good Laws and a due Execution of Justice, &c. Thus may the first Principles of sound Politicks be fix'd in the Minds of Youth.

On Historical Occasions, Questions of Right and Wrong, Justice and Injustice, will naturally arise, and may be put to Youth, which they may debate in Conversation and in Writing. When they ardently desire Victory, for the Sake of the Praise attending it, they will begin to feel the Want, and be sensible of the Use of Logic, or the Art of Reasoning to discover Truth, and of Arguing to defend it, and convince Adversaries. This would be the Time to acquaint them with the Principles of that Art. *Grotius, Puffendorff*, and some other Writers of the same Kind, may be used on these Occasions to decide their Disputes. Publick Disputes warm the Imagination, whet the Industry, and strengthen the natural Abilities.

When Youth are told, that the Great Men whose Lives and Actions they read in History, spoke two of the best Languages that ever were, the most expressive, copious, beautiful; and that the finest Writings, the most correct Compositions, the most perfect Productions of human Wit and Wisdom, are in those Languages, which have endured Ages, and will endure while there are Men; that no Translation can do them Justice, or give the Pleasure found in Reading the Originals; that those Languages contain all Science; that one of them is become almost universal, being the Language of Learned Men in all Countries; that to understand them is a distinguishing Ornament, &c. they may be thereby made desirous of learning those Languages, and their Industry sharpen'd in the Acquisition of them. All intended for Divinity should be taught the Latin and Greek; for Physick, the Latin, Greek and French; for Law, the Latin and French; Merchants, the French, German, and Spanish: And though all should not be compell'd to learn Latin, Greek, or the modern foreign Languages; yet none that have an ardent Desire to learn them should be refused; their English, Arithmetick and other Studies absolutely necessary, being at the same Time not neglected.

If the new Universal History were also read, it would give a connected Idea of human Affairs, so far as it goes, which should be follow'd by the best modern Histories, particularly of our Mother Country; then of these Colonies; which should be accompanied with Observations on their Rise, Encrease, Use to Great-Britain, Encouragements, Discouragements, etc. the Means to make them flourish, secure their Liberties, &c.

With the History of Men, Times and Nations, should be read at proper Hours or Days, some of the best Histories of Nature, which would not only be delightful to Youth, and furnish them with Matter for their Letters, &c. as well as other History; but afterwards of great Use to them, whether they are Merchants, Handicrafts, or Divines; enabling the first the better to understand many Commodities, Drugs, &c; the second to improve his Trade or Handicraft by new Mixtures, Materials, &c., and the last to adorn his Discourses by beautiful Comparisons, and strengthen them by new Proofs of Divine Providence. The Conversation of all will be improved by it, as Occasions frequently occur of making Natural Observations, which are instructive, agreeable, and entertaining in almost all Companies. Natural History will also afford Opportunities of introducing many Observations, relating to the Preservation of Health, which may be afterwards of great Use. Arbuthnot on Air and Aliment, Sanctorius on Perspiration, Lemery on Foods, and some others, may now be read, and a very little Explanation will make them sufficiently intelligible to Youth.

While they are reading Natural History, might not a little Gardening, Planting, Grafting, Inoculating, etc., be taught and practised; and now and then Excursions made to the neighbouring Plantations of the best Farmers, their Methods observ'd and reason'd upon for the Information of Youth. The Improvement of Agriculture being useful to all, and Skill in it no Disparagement to any.

The History of Commerce, of the Invention of Arts, Rise of Manufactures, Progress of Trade, Change of its Seats, with the Reasons, Causes, &c., may also be made entertaining to Youth, and will be useful to all. And this, with the Accounts in other History of the prodigious Force and Effect of Engines and Machines used in War, will naturally introduce a Desire to be instructed in Mechanicks, and to be inform'd of the Principles of that Art by which weak Men perform such Wonders, Labour is sav'd, Manufactures expedited, &c. &c. This will be the Time to show them Prints of antient and modern Machines, to explain them, to let them be copied, and to give Lectures in Mechanical Philosophy.

With the whole should be constantly inculcated and cultivated, that Benignity of Mind, which shows itself in searching for and seizing every Opportunity to serve and to oblige; and is the Foundation of what is called Good Breeding; highly useful to the Possessor, and most agreeable to all.

The Idea of what is true Merit, should also be often presented to Youth, explain'd and impress'd on their Minds, as consisting in an Inclination join'd with an Ability to serve Mankind, one's Country, Friends and Family; which Ability is (with the Blessing of God) to be acquir'd or greatly encreas'd by true Learning; and should indeed be the great Aim and End of all Learning.

Poor Richard Improved

The Way to Wealth

FRANKLIN published his first *Almanack* in October, 1732 for the year 1733. It was issued as *Poor Richard, 1733. An Almanack. . .* By Richard Saunders, the *Poor Richard* springing from *Poor Robin*, a London

177

almanac, and Richard Saunders being the name of the editor of the English *Apollo Angelicanus*. In *Memoirs of the Life and Writings of Benjamin Franklin* (1818), by William T. Franklin, Franklin noted that he continued it "about twenty-five years. . . . I endeavored to make it both entertaining and useful, and it accordingly came to be in such demand that I reaped considerable profit from it; vending annually near ten thousand. . . . I . . . filled all the little spaces that occurred between the remarkable days in the Calendar, with proverbial sentences, chiefly such as inculcated industry and frugality, as the means of procuring wealth, and thereby securing virtue. . . . These proverbs, which contained the wisdom of many ages and nations, I assembled and formed into a connected discourse prefixed to the *Almanack* of 1757 [for the year 1758], as the harangue of a wise old man to the people attending an auction: the bringing all these scattered counsels thus into focus, enabled them to make greater impression." This "discourse" in *Poor Richard Improved*, commonly called "The Way to Wealth," was reprinted in newspapers generally throughout the colonies, issued separately in England, and circulated in two translations in France. The text here is from a facsimile of the *Almanack* of 1758.

Courteous Reader,

I have heard that nothing gives an Author so great Pleasure, as to find his Works respectfully quoted by other learned Authors. This Pleasure I have seldom enjoyed; for tho' I have been, if I may say it without Vanity, an eminent Author of Almanacks annually now a full Quarter of a Century, my Brother Authors in the same Way, for what Reason I know not, have ever been very sparing in their Applauses; and no other Author has taken the least Notice of me, so that did not my Writings produce me some solid Pudding, the great Deficiency of Praise would have quite discouraged me.

I concluded at length, that the People were the best Judges of my Merit; for they buy my Works; and besides, in my Rambles, where I am not personally known, I have frequently heard one or other of my Adages repeated, with, as Poor Richard says, at the End on't; this gave me some Satisfaction, as it showed not only that my Instructions were regarded, but discovered likewise some Respect for my Authority; and I own, that to encourage the Practice of remembering and repeating those wise Sentences, I have sometimes quoted myself with great Gravity.

Judge then how much I must have been gratified by an Incident I am going to relate to you. I stopt my Horse lately where a great Number of People were collected at a Vendue of Merchant Goods. The Hour of Sale not being come, they were conversing on the Badness of the Times, and one of the Company call'd to a plain clean old Man, with white Locks, Pray, Father Abraham, what think you of the Times? Won't these heavy Taxes quite ruin the Country? How shall we ever be able to pay them? What would you advise us to? ——Father Abraham stood up, and reply'd, If you'd have my Advice, I'll give it you in short, for a Word to the Wise is enough, and many Words won't fill a Bushel, as Poor Richard says. They join'd in desiring him to speak his Mind, and gathering round him, he proceeded as follows;

"Friends, says he, and Neighbours, the Taxes are indeed very heavy, and if those laid on by the Government were the only Ones we had to pay, we might more easily discharge them; but we have many others, and much more grievous to some of us. We are taxed twice as much by our Idleness, three times as much by our Pride, and four times as much by our Folly, and from these Taxes the Commissioners cannot ease or deliver us by allowing an Abatement. However let us hearken to good Advice, and something may be done for us; God helps them that help themselves, as Poor Richard says, in his Almanack of 1733.

It would be thought a hard Government that should tax its People one tenth Part of their Time, to be employed in its Service. But Idleness taxes many of us much more, if we reckon all that is spent in absolute Sloth, or doing of nothing, with that which is spent in idle Employments or Amusements, that amount to nothing. Sloth, by bringing on Diseases, absolutely shortens Life. Sloth, like Rust, consumes faster than Labour wears, while the used Key is always bright, as Poor Richard says. But dost thou love Life, then do not squander Time, for that's the Stuff Life is made of, as Poor Richard says.—How much more than is necessary do we spend in Sleep! forgetting that The sleeping Fox catches no Poultry, and that there will be sleeping enough in the Grave, as

Poor Richard says. If Time be of all Things the most precious, wasting Time must be, as Poor Richard says, the greatest Prodigality, since, as he elsewhere tells us, Lost Time is never found again; and what we call Time-enough, always proves little enough: Let us then up and be doing, and doing to the Purpose; so by Diligence shall we do more with less Perplexity. Sloth makes all Things difficult, but Industry all easy, as Poor Richard says; and He that riseth late, must trot all Day, and shall scarce overtake his Business at Night. While Laziness travels so slowly, that Poverty soon overtakes him, as we read in Poor Richard, who adds, Drive thy Business, let not that drive thee; and Early to Bed, and early to rise, makes a Man healthy, wealthy and wise.

So what signifies wishing and hoping for better Times. We may make these Times better if we bestir ourselves. Industry need not wish, as Poor Richard says, and He that lives upon Hope will die fasting. There are no Gains, without Pains; then Help Hands, for I have no Lands, or if I have, they are smartly taxed. And, as Poor Richard likewise observes, He that hath a Trade hath an Estate, and He that hath a Calling hath an Office of Profit and Honour; but then the Trade must be worked at, and the Calling well followed, or neither the Estate, nor the Office, will enable us to pay our Taxes.—If we are industrious we shall never starve; for, as Poor Richard says, At the working Man's House Hunger looks in, but dares not enter. Nor will the Bailiff or the Constable enter, for Industry pays Debts, while Despair encreaseth them, says Poor Richard.—What though you have found no Treasure, nor has any rich Relation left you a Legacy, Diligence is the Mother of Good-luck, as Poor Richard says, and God gives all Things to Industry. Then plough deep, while Sluggards sleep, and you shall have Corn to sell and to keep, says Poor Dick. Work while it is called To-day, for you know not how much you may be hindered To-morrow, which makes Poor Richard say, One To-day is worth two To-morrows; and farther, Have you somewhat to do To-morrow, do it To-day. If you were a Servant, would you not be ashamed that a good Master should catch you idle? Are you then your own Master, be ashamed to catch yourself idle, as Poor Dick says. When there is so much to be done for yourself, your Family, your Country, and your gracious King, be up by Peep of Day; Let not the Sun look down and say, Inglorious here he lies. Handle your Tools without Mittens; remember that the Cat in Gloves catches no Mice, as Poor Richard says. 'Tis true there is much to be done, and perhaps you are weak handed, but stick to it steadily, and you will see great Effects, for constant Dropping wears away Stones, and by Diligence and Patience the Mouse ate in two the Cable; and little Strokes fell great Oaks, as Poor Richard says in his Almanack, the Year I cannot just now remember.

Methinks I hear some of you say, Must a Man afford himself no Leisure?—I will tell thee, my Friend, what Poor Richard says, Employ thy Time well if thou meanest to gain Leisure; and since thou art not sure of a Minute, throw not away an Hour. Leisure, is Time for doing something useful; this Leisure the diligent Man will obtain, but the lazy Man never; so that, as Poor Richard says, a Life of Leisure and a Life of Laziness are two Things. Do you imagine that Sloth will afford you more Comfort than Labour? No, for as Poor Richard says, Trouble springs from Idleness, and grievous Toil from needless Ease. Many without Labour, would live by their Wits only, but they break for want of Stock. Whereas Industry gives Comfort, and Plenty, and Respect: Fly Pleasures, and they'll follow you. The diligent Spinner has a large Shift; and now I have a Sheep and a Cow, every Body bids me Good morrow; all which is well said by Poor Richard.

But with our Industry, we must likewise be steady, settled and careful, and oversee our own Affairs with our own Eyes, and not trust too much to others; for, as Poor Richard says,

I never saw an oft removed Tree,
Nor yet an oft removed Family,
That throve so well as those that settled be.

And again, Three Removes is as bad as a Fire; and again, Keep thy Shop, and thy Shop will keep thee; and again, If you would have your Business done, go; If not, send. And again,

He that by the Plough would thrive,
Himself must either hold or drive.

And again, The Eye of a Master will do more Work than both his Hands; and again, Want of Care does us more Damage than Want of Knowledge; and again, Not to oversee Workmen, is to leave them your Purse open. Trusting too much to others Care is the Ruin of many; for, as the Almanack says, In the Affairs of this World, Men are saved, not by Faith, but by the Want of it; but a Man's own Care is profitable; for, saith Poor Dick, Learning is to the Studious, and Riches to the Careful, as well as Power to the Bold, and Heaven to the Virtuous. And farther, If you would have a faithful Servant, and one that you like, serve yourself. And again, he adviseth to Circumspection and Care, even in the smallest Matters, because sometimes a little Neglect may breed great Mischief; adding, For want of a Nail the Shoe was lost; for want of a Shoe the Horse was lost; and for want of a Horse the Rider was lost, being overtaken and slain by the Enemy, all for want of Care about a Horse-shoe Nail.

So much for Industry, my Friends, and Attention to one's own Business; but to these we must add Frugality, if we would make our Industry more certainly successful. A Man may, if he knows not how to save as he gets, keep his Nose all his Life to the Grindstone, and die not worth a Groat at last. A fat Kitchen makes a lean Will, as Poor Richard says; and,

Many Estates are spent in the Getting,
Since Women for Tea forsook Spinning and Knitting,
And Men for Punch forsook Hewing and Splitting.

If you would be wealthy, says he, in another Almanack, think of Saving as well as of Getting: The Indies have not made Spain rich, because her Outgoes are greater than her Incomes. Away then with your expensive Follies, and you will not have so much Cause to complain of hard Times, heavy Taxes, and chargeable Families; for, as Poor Dick says,

Women and Wine, Game and Deceit,
Make the Wealth small, and the Wants great.

And farther, What maintains one Vice, would bring up two Children. You may think perhaps, That a little Tea, or a little Punch now and then, Diet a little more costly, Clothes a little finer, and a little Entertainment now and then, can be no great Matter; but remember what Poor Richard says, Many a Little makes a Mickle; and farther, Beware of little Expences; a small Leak will sink a great Ship; and again, Who Dainties love, shall Beggars prove; and moreover, Fools make Feasts, and wise Men eat them.

Here you are all got together at this Vendue of Fineries and Knicknacks. You call them Goods, but if you do not take Care, they will prove Evils to some of you. You expect they will be sold cheap, and perhaps they may for less than they cost; but if you have no Occasion for them, they must be dear to you. Remember what Poor Richard says, Buy what thou hast no Need of, and ere long thou shalt sell thy Necessaries. And again, At a great Pennyworth pause a while: He means, that perhaps the Cheapness is apparent only, and not real; or the Bargain, by straitning thee in thy Business, may do thee more Harm than Good. For in another Place he says, Many have been ruined by buying good Pennyworths. Again, Poor Richard says, 'Tis foolish to lay out Money in a Purchase of Repentance; and yet this Folly is practised every Day at Vendues, for want of minding the Almanack. Wise Men, as Poor Dick says, learn by others Harms, Fools scarcely by their own; but Felix quem faciunt aliena Pericula cautum. Many a one, for the Sake of Finery on the Back, have gone with a hungry Belly, and half starved their Families; Silks and Sattins, Scarlet and Velvets, as Poor Richard says, put out the Kitchen Fire. These are not the Necessaries of Life; they can scarcely be called the Conveniencies, and yet only because they look pretty, how many want to have them. The artificial Wants of Mankind thus become more numerous than the natural; and, as Poor Dick says, For one poor Person, there are an hundred indigent. By these, and other Extravagancies, the Genteel are reduced to Poverty, and forced to borrow of those whom they formerly despised, but who through Industry and Frugality have maintained their Standing; in which Case it appears plainly, that a Ploughman on his Legs is higher than a Gentleman on his Knees, as Poor Richard says. Perhaps they have had a small Estate left them which they knew not the Getting of; they think 'tis Day, and will never be Night; that a little to be spent out of so much, is not worth minding; (a Child and a Fool, as Poor Richard says, imagine Twenty Shillings and Twenty Years can never be spent) but, always taking out of, the Meal-tub, and never putting in, soon comes to the Bottom; then, as Poor Dick says, When the Well's dry, they know the Worth of Water. But this they might have known before, if they had taken his Advice; If you would know the Value of Money, go and try to borrow some; for, he that goes a borrowing goes a sorrowing; and indeed so does he that lends to such People, when he goes to get it in again.— Poor Dick farther advises, and says,

> Fond Pride of Dress is sure a very Curse;
> E'er Fancy you consult—consult your Purse.

And again, Pride is as loud a Beggar as Want, and a great deal more saucy. When you have bought one fine Thing you must buy ten more, that your Appearance may be all of a Piece; but Poor Dick says, 'Tis easier to suppress the first Desire, than to satisfy all that follow it. And 'tis as truly Folly for the Poor to ape the Rich, as for the Frog to swell, in order to equal the Ox.

> Great Estates may venture more,
> But little Boats should keep near Shore.

'Tis however a Folly soon punished; for Pride that dines on Vanity sups on Contempt, as Poor Richard says. And in another Place, Pride break-fasted with Plenty, dined with Poverty, and supped with Infamy. And after all, of what Use is this Pride of Appearance, for which so much is risked, so much is suffered? It cannot promote Health, or ease Pain; it makes no Increase of Merit in the Person, it creates Envy, it hastens Misfortune.

> What is a Butterfly? At best
> He's but a Caterpillar drest.
> The gaudy Fop's his Picture just,

as Poor Richard says.

But what Madness must it be to run in Debt for these Superfluities! We are offered, by the Terms of this Vendue, Six Months Credit; and that perhaps has induced some of us to attend it, because we cannot spare the ready Money, and hope now to be fine without it. But, ah, think

what you do when you run in Debt; You give to another, Power over your Liberty. If you cannot pay at the Time, you will be ashamed to see your Creditor; you will be in Fear when you speak to him; you will make poor pitiful sneaking Excuses, and by Degrees come to lose your Veracity, and sink into base downright lying; for, as Poor Richard says, The second Vice is Lying, the first is running in Debt. And again, to the same Purpose, Lying rides upon Debt's Back. Whereas a freeborn Englishman ought not to be ashamed or afraid to see or speak to any Man living. But Poverty often deprives a Man of all Spirit and Virtue: 'Tis hard for an empty Bag to stand upright, as Poor Richard truly says. What would you think of that Prince, or that Government, who should issue an Edict forbidding you to dress like a Gentleman or a Gentlewoman, on Pain of Imprisonment or Servitude? Would you not say, that you are free, have a Right to dress as you please, and that such an Edict would be a Breach of your Privileges, and such a Government tryannical? And yet you are about to put yourself under that Tyranny when you run in Debt for such Dress! Your Creditor has Authority at his Pleasure to deprive you of your Liberty, by confining you in Gaol for Life, or to sell you for a Servant, if you should not be able to pay him! When you have got your Bargain, you may, perhaps, think little of Payment; but Creditors, Poor Richard tells us, have better Memories than Debtors; and in another Place says, Creditors are a superstitious Sect, great Observers of set Days and Times. The Day comes round before you are aware, and the Demand is made before you are prepared to satisfy it. Or if you bear your Debt in Mind, the Term which at first seemed so long, will, as it lessens, appear extreamly short. Time will seem to have added Wings to his Heels as well as Shoulders. Those have a short Lent, saith Poor Richard, who owe Money to be paid at Easter. Then since, as he says, The Borrower is a Slave to the Lender, and the Debtor to the Creditor, disdain the Chain, preserve your Freedom; and maintain your Independency: Be industrious and free; be frugal and free. At present, perhaps, you may think yourself in thriving Circumstances, and that you can bear a little Extravagance without Injury; but,

> For Age and Want, save while you may;
> No Morning Sun lasts a whole Day,

as Poor Richard says,—Gain may be temporary and uncertain, but ever while you live, Expence is constant and certain; and 'tis easier to build two Chimnies than to keep one in Fuel, as Poor Richard says. So rather go to Bed supperless than rise in Debt.

> Get what you can, and what you get hold;
> 'Tis the Stone that will turn all your Lead into Gold,

as Poor Richard says. And when you have got the Philosopher's Stone, sure you will no longer complain of bad Times, or the Difficulty of paying Taxes.

This Doctrine, my Friends, is Reason and Wisdom; but after all, do not depend too much upon your own Industry, and Frugality, and Prudence, though excellent Things, for they may all 20 be blasted without the Blessing of Heaven; and therefore ask that Blessing humbly, and be not uncharitable to those that at present seem to want it, but comfort and help them. Remember Job suffered, and was afterwards prosperous.

And now to conclude, Experience keeps a dear School, but Fools will learn in no other, and scarce in that; for it is true, we may give Advice, but we cannot give Conduct, as Poor Richard says: However, remember this, They that won't 30 be counselled, can't be helped, as Poor Richard says: And farther, That if you will not hear Reason, she'll surely rap your Knuckles."

Thus the old Gentleman ended his Harangue. The People heard it, and approved the Doctrine, and immediately practised the contrary, just as if it had been a common Sermon; for the Vendue opened, and they began to buy extravagantly, notwithstanding all his Cautions, and their own Fear of Taxes.—I found the good Man had 40 thoroughly studied my Almanacks, and digested all I had dropt on those Topicks during the Course of Five-and-twenty Years. The frequent Mention he made of me must have tired any one else, but my Vanity was wonderfully delighted with it, though I was conscious that not a tenth Part of the Wisdom was my own which he ascribed to me, but rather the Gleanings I had made of

the Sense of all Ages and Nations. However, I resolved to be the better for the Echo of it; and though I had at first determined to buy Stuff for a new Coat, I went away resolved to wear my old One a little longer. Reader, if thou wilt do the same, thy Profit will be as great as mine.

> I am, as ever,
> Thine to serve thee,

July 7, 1757.   *Richard Saunders.*   10

Autobiography

[Striving for Moral Perfection]

FRANKLIN began writing his *Autobiography* in 1771 during his residence in England as colonial agent, carrying the account to 1731. The briefer second part he wrote while at Passy as minister to France. The third part, continuing the narrative to 1757, he began writing in August, 1788, after his return to Philadelphia. In 1789 he added a few pages. He died in 1790, leaving the story of his major years in politics untold in the *Autobiography*, but preserved in his many letters and miscellaneous writings. Manuscript copies of the first part of the *Autobiography* were sent to two or three friends in Europe, and one of these was probably used for *Mémoires de la vie privée de Benjamin Franklin*, Paris, 1791, a translation attributed to Dr. Jacques Gibelin. From this version a translation was made in English for the *Works* (1793). William Temple Franklin's edition in *Memoirs of the Life and Writings of Benjamin Franklin*, in three volumes, was published in London during 1817–1819. The edition of John Bigelow, *Autobiography of Benjamin Franklin*, Philadelphia, 1868, was the first based on Franklin's own copy and the first to contain all four parts. This text is that of Bigelow, *The Complete Works*, I (1887).

It was about this time I conceiv'd the bold and arduous project of arriving at moral perfection. I wish'd to live without committing any fault at any time; I would conquer all that either natural inclination, custom, or company might lead me into. As I knew, or thought I knew, what was right and wrong, I did not see why I might not always do the one and avoid the other. But I soon found I had undertaken a task of more difficulty than I had imagined. While my care was employ'd in guarding against one fault, I was often surprised by another; habit took the advantage of attention;

inclination was sometimes too strong for reason. I concluded, at length, that the mere speculative conviction that it was our interest to be completely virtuous, was not sufficient to prevent our slipping; and that the contrary habits must be broken, and good ones acquired and established, before we can have any dependence on a steady, uniform rectitude of conduct. For this purpose I therefore contrived the following method.

In the various enumerations of the moral virtues I had met with in my reading, I found the catalogue more or less numerous, as different writers included more or fewer ideas under the same name. Temperance, for example, was by some confined to eating and drinking, while by others it was extended to mean the moderating every other pleasure, appetite, inclination, or passion, bodily or mental, even to our avarice and ambition. I propos'd to myself, for the sake of clearness, to use rather more names, with fewer ideas annex'd to each, than a few names with more ideas; and I included under thirteen names of virtues all that at that time occurr'd to me as necessary or desirable, and annexed to each a short precept, which fully express'd the extent I gave to its meaning.

These names of virtues, with their precepts, were:

1. *Temperance.* Eat not to dullness; drink not to elevation.

2. *Silence.* Speak not but what may benefit others or yourself; avoid trifling conversation.

3. *Order.* Let all your things have their places; let each part of your business have its time.

4. *Resolution.* Resolve to perform what you ought; perform without fail what you resolve.

5. *Frugality.* Make no expense but to do good to others or yourself; *i. e.*, waste nothing.

6. *Industry.* Lose no time; be always employ'd in something useful; cut off all unnecessary actions.

7. *Sincerity.* Use no hurtful deceit; think innocently and justly, and, if you speak, speak accordingly.

8. *Justice.* Wrong none by doing injuries, or omitting the benefits that are your duty.

9. *Moderation.* Avoid extreams; forbear resenting injuries so much as you think they deserve.

10. *Cleanliness.* Tolerate no uncleanliness in body, cloaths, or habitation.

11. *Tranquillity.* Be not disturbed at trifles, or at accidents common or unavoidable.

12. *Chastity.* Rarely use venery but for health or offspring, never to dulness, weakness, or the injury of your own or another's peace or reputation.

13. *Humility.* Imitate Jesus and Socrates.

My intention being to acquire the habitude of all these virtues, I judg'd it would be well not to distract my attention by attempting the whole at once, but to fix it on one of them at a time; and, when I should be master of that, then to proceed to another, and so on, till I should have gone thro' the thirteen; and, as the previous acquisition of some might facilitate the acquisition of certain others, I arrang'd them with that view, as they stand above. Temperance first, as it tends to procure that coolness and clearness of head, which is so necessary where constant vigilance was to be kept up, and guard maintained against the unremitting attraction of ancient habits, and the force of perpetual temptations. This being acquir'd and establish'd, Silence would be more easy; and my desire being to gain knowledge at the same time that I improv'd in virtue, and considering that in conversation it was obtain'd rather by the use of the ears than of the tongue, and therefore wishing to break a habit I was getting into of prattling, punning, and joking, which only made me acceptable to trifling company, I gave Silence the second place. This and the next, Order, I expected would allow me more time for attending to my project and my studies. Resolution, once become habitual, would keep me firm in my endeavours to obtain all the subsequent virtues; Frugality and Industry freeing me from my remaining debt, and producing affluence and independence, would make more easy the practice of Sincerity and Justice, etc., etc. Conceiving then, that, agreeably to the advice of Pythagoras in his Golden Verses, daily examination would be necessary, I contrived the following method for conducting that examination.

I made a little book, in which I allotted a page for each of the virtues. I rul'd each page with red ink, so as to have seven columns, one for each day of the week, marking each column with a letter for the day. I cross'd these columns with thirteen red lines, marking the beginning of each line with the first letter of one of the virtues, on which line, and in its proper column, I might mark, by a little black spot, every fault I found upon examination to have been committed respecting that virtue upon that day.

Form of the Pages

TEMPERANCE.							
EAT NOT TO DULNESS. DRINK NOT TO ELEVATION.							
	S.	M.	T.	W.	T.	F.	S.
T.							
S.	*	*		*		*	
O.	* *	*	*	*		*	*	*
R.			*			*	
F.		*			*		
I.			*				
S.							
J.							
M.							
C.							
T.							
C.							
H.							

I determined to give a week's strict attention to each of the virtues successively. Thus, in the first week, my great guard was to avoid every the least offence against Temperance, leaving the other virtues to their ordinary chance, only marking every evening the faults of the day. Thus, if in the first week I could keep my first line, marked T, clear of spots, I suppos'd the habit of that virtue so much strengthen'd, and its opposite weaken'd, that I might venture extending my attention to include the next, and for the following week keep both lines clear of spots. Proceeding thus to the last, I could go thro' a course compleat

in thirteen weeks, and four courses in a year. And like him who, having a garden to weed, does not attempt to eradicate all the bad herbs at once, which would exceed his reach and his strength, but works on one of the beds at a time, and, having accomplish'd the first, proceeds to a second, so I should have, I hoped, the encouraging pleasure of seeing on my pages the progress I made in virtue, by clearing successively my lines of their spots, till in the end, by a number of courses, I should be happy in viewing a clean book, after a thirteen weeks' daily examination.

This my little book had for its motto these lines from Addison's Cato:

"Here will I hold. If there's a power above us
(And that there is, all nature cries aloud
Thro' all her works), He must delight in virtue;
And that which he delights in must be happy."

Another from Cicero,

"O vitæ Philosophia dux! O virtutum indagatrix expultrixque vitiorum! Unus dies, bene et ex praeceptis tuis actus, peccanti immortalitati est anteponendus."

Another from the Proverbs of Solomon, speaking of wisdom or virtue:

"Length of days is in her right hand, and in her left hand riches and honour. Her ways are ways of pleasantness, and all her paths are peace."—iii. 16, 17.

And conceiving God to be the fountain of wisdom, I thought it right and necessary to solicit his assistance for obtaining it; to this end I formed the following little prayer, which was prefix'd to my tables of examination, for daily use.

"O powerful Goodness! bountiful Father! merciful Guide! Increase in me that wisdom which discovers my truest interest. Strengthen my resolutions to perform what that wisdom dictates. Accept my kind offices to thy other children as the only return in my power for thy continual favours to me."

I used also sometimes a little prayer which I took from Thomson's Poems, viz.·

"Father of light and life, thou Good Supreme!
O teach me what is good; teach me Thyself!
Save me from folly, vanity, and vice,
From every low pursuit; and fill my soul
With knowledge, conscious peace, and virtue pure;
Sacred, substantial, never-fading bliss!"

The precept of *Order* requiring that *every part of my business should have its allotted time*, one page in my little book contain'd the following scheme of employment for the twenty-four hours of a natural day.

THE MORNING.

Question. What good shall I do this day?

| 5 6 7 | Rise, wash, and address *Powerful Goodness!* Contrive day's business, and take the resolution of the day; prosecute the present study, and breakfast. |
| 8 9 10 11 | Work. |

NOON.

| 12 1 | Read, or overlook my accounts, and dine. |
| 2 3 4 5 | Work. |

EVENING.

Question. What good have I done today?

6	Put things in their places. Supper.
7	Music or diversion, or conversation.
8	Examination of the day.
9	

NIGHT.

| 10 11 12 1 2 3 4 | Sleep. |

I enter'd upon the execution of this plan for self-examination, and continu'd it with occasional intermissions for some time. I was surpris'd to find myself so much fuller of faults than I had imagined; but I had the satisfaction of seeing them diminish. To avoid the trouble of renewing now and then my little book, which, by scraping out the marks on the paper of old faults to make room for new

ones in a new course, became full of holes, I transferr'd my tables and precepts to the ivory leaves of a memorandum book, on which the lines were drawn with red ink, that made a durable stain, and on those lines I mark'd my faults with a black-lead pencil, which marks I could easily wipe out with a wet sponge. After a while I went thro' one course only in a year, and afterward only one in several years, till at length I omitted them entirely, being employ'd in voyages and business abroad, with a multiplicity of affairs that interfered; but I always carried my little book with me.

My scheme of Order gave me the most trouble; and I found that, tho' it might be practicable where a man's business was such as to leave him the disposition of his time, that of a journeyman printer, for instance, it was not possible to be exactly observed by a master who must mix with the world and often receive people of business at their own hours. Order, too, with regard to places for things, papers, etc., I found extreamly difficult to acquire. I had not been early accustomed to it, and, having an exceeding good memory, I was not so sensible of the inconvenience attending want of method. This article, therefore cost me so much painful attention and my faults in it vexed me so much, and I made so little progress in amendment, and had such frequent relapses that I was almost ready to give up the attempt, and content myself with a faulty character in that respect, like the man who, in buying an ax of a smith, my neighbour, desired to have the whole of its surface as bright as the edge. The smith consented to grind it bright for him if he would turn the wheel; he turn'd while the smith press'd the broad face of the ax hard and heavily on the stone which made the turning of it very fatiguing. The man came every now and then from the wheel to see how the work went on and at length would take his ax as it was, without farther grinding. "No," said the smith, "turn on, turn on; we shall have it bright by-and-by; as yet, it is only speckled." "Yes," says the man, "but I think I like a speckled ax best." And I believe this may have been the case with many who, having, for want of some such means as I employ'd, found the difficulty of obtaining good and breaking bad habits in other points of vice and virtue, have given up the struggle, and concluded that "a speckled ax was best"; for something, that pretended to be reason, was every now and then suggesting to me that such extream nicety as I exacted of myself might be a kind of foppery in morals, which, if it were known, would make me ridiculous; that a perfect character might be attended with the inconvenience of being envied and hated; and that a benevolent man should allow a few faults in himself, to keep his friends in countenance.

In truth, I found myself incorrigible with respect to Order; and now I am grown old and my memory bad, I feel very sensibly the want of it. But, on the whole, tho' I never arrived at the perfection I had been so ambitious of obtaining, but fell far short of it, yet I was, by the endeavour, a better and a happier man than I otherwise should have been if I had not attempted it; as those who aim at perfect writing by imitating the engraved copies, tho' they never reach the wish'd-for excellence of those copies, their hand is mended by the endeavour, and is tolerable while it continues fair and legible.

It may be well my posterity should be informed that to this little artifice, with the blessing of God, their ancestor ow'd the constant felicity of his life, down to his 79th year in which this is written. What reverses may attend the remainder is in the hand of Providence; but, if they arrive, the reflection on past happiness enjoy'd ought to help his bearing them with more resignation. To Temperance he ascribes his long-continued health, and what is still left to him of a good constitution; to Industry and Frugality, the early easiness of his circumstances and acquisition of his fortune, with all that knowledge that enabled him to be a useful citizen, and obtained for him some degree of reputation among the learned; to Sincerity and Justice, the confidence of his country, and the honorable employs it conferred upon him; and to the joint influence of the whole mass of the virtues, even in the imperfect state he was able to acquire them, all that evenness of temper, and that cheerfulness in conversation, which makes his company still sought for and agreeable even to his younger acquaintance. I hope, therefore, that some of my descendants may follow the example and reap the benefit.

It will be remark'd that, tho' my scheme was not wholly without religion, there was in it no mark of any of the distinguishing tenets of any particular sect. I had purposely avoided them; for, being fully persuaded of the utility and excellency of my method, and that it might be serviceable to people in all religions, and intending some time or other to publish it, I would not have any thing in it that should prejudice any one, of any sect, against it. I purposed writing a little comment on each virtue, in which I would have shown the advantages of possessing it, and the mischiefs attending its opposite vice; and I should have called my book *The Art of Virtue*, because it would have shown the means and manner of obtaining virtue, which would have distinguished it from the mere exhortation to be good, that does not instruct and indicate the means, but is like the apostle's man of verbal charity, who only, without showing to the naked and hungry how or where they might get clothes or victuals, exhorted them to be fed and clothed.—James ii. 15, 16.

But it so happened that my intention of writing and publishing this comment was never fulfilled. I did, indeed, from time to time, put down short hints of the sentiments, reasonings, etc., to be made use of in it, some of which I have still by me; but the necessary close attention to private business in the earlier part of my life, and public business since, have occasioned my postponing it; for, it being connected in my mind with a great and extensive project that required the whole man to execute, and which an unforeseen succession of employs prevented my attending to, it has hitherto remain'd unfinish'd.

In this piece it was my design to explain and enforce this doctrine, that vicious actions are not hurtful because they are forbidden, but forbidden because they are hurtful, the nature of man alone considered; that it was, therefore, every one's interest to be virtuous who wish'd to be happy even in this world; and I should, from this circumstance (there being always in the world a number of rich merchants, nobility, states, and princes, who have need of honest instruments for the management of their affairs, and such being so rare), have endeavoured to convince young persons that no qualities were so likely to make a poor man's fortune as those of probity and integrity.

My list of virtues contain'd at first but twelve; but a Quaker friend having kindly informed me that I was generally thought proud; that my pride show'd itself frequently in conversation; that I was not content with being in the right when discussing any point, but was overbearing, and rather insolent, of which he convinc'd me by mentioning several instances; I determined endeavouring to cure myself, if I could, of this vice or folly among the rest, and I added Humility to 10 my list, giving an extensive meaning to the word.

I cannot boast of much success in acquiring the reality of this virtue, but I had a good deal with regard to the appearance of it. I made it a rule to forbear all direct contradiction to the sentiments of others, and all positive assertion of my own. I even forbid myself, agreeably to the old laws of our Junto, the use of every word or expression in the language that imported a fix'd opinion, such as certainly, undoubtedly, etc., and I adopted, 20 instead of them, I conceive, I apprehend, or I imagine a thing to be so or so; or it so appears to me at present. When another asserted something that I thought an error, I deny'd myself the pleasure of contradicting him abruptly, and of showing immediately some absurdity in his proposition; and in answering I began by observing that in certain cases or circumstances his opinion would be right, but in the present case there appear'd or seem'd to me some difference, etc. I 30 soon found the advantage of this change in my manner; the conversations I engag'd in went on more pleasantly. The modest way in which I propos'd my opinions procur'd them a readier reception and less contradiction; I had less mortification when I was found to be in the wrong, and I more easily prevail'd with others to give up their mistakes and join with me when I happened to be in the right.

And this mode, which I at first put on with some 40 violence to natural inclination, became at length so easy, and so habitual to me, that perhaps for these fifty years past no one has ever heard a dogmatical expression escape me. And to this habit (after my character of integrity) I think it principally owing that I had early so much weight with my fellow-citizens when I proposed new institutions, or alterations in the old, and so much influence in public councils when I became a member; for I was but a bad speaker, never eloquent, subject to much hesitation in my choice of words, hardly correct in language, and yet I generally carried my points.

In reality, there is, perhaps, no one of our natural passions so hard to subdue as pride. Disguise it, struggle with it, beat it down, stifle it, mortify it as much as one pleases, it is still alive, and will every now and then peep out and show itself; you will see it, perhaps, often in this history; for, even if I could conceive that I had compleatly overcome it, I should probably be proud of my humility.

Rules by Which a Great Empire May Be Reduced to a Small One

HOPING TO impress upon the Ministry and the King the unreasonableness of British policies toward the American colonies, Franklin as colonial representative or London agent composed two masterpieces of ironic hoax in the autumn of 1773. One, the *Rules*, appeared in the *Public Advertiser* in September. Rule by rule, he named the steps the Ministry had taken to alienate the colonies. Then, thinking that the King might be responsible for much in the nature of the policies, Franklin aimed at the throne with *An Edict by the King of Prussia*. At the home of Le Despenser, premier baron of England, Paul Whitehead, seeing the article, rushed, paper in hand, to a group which included Franklin, and excitedly began reading the piece. It produced anger and consternation until it was recognized as a hoax. Both articles were reprinted, widely read, and recognized as fair hits. The *Rules* were reprinted in the *Gentleman's Magazine* for September, and the *Edict* in the same magazine for October, 1773, which texts are here used.

An ancient Sage boasted, that, tho' he could not fiddle, he knew how to make a great city of a little one. The science that I, a modern simpleton, am about to communicate, is the very reverse.

I address myself to all ministers who have the management of extensive dominions, which from their very greatness are become troublesome to govern, because the multiplicity of their affairs leaves no time for fiddling.

I. In the first place, gentlemen, you are to consider, that a great empire, like a great cake, is most easily diminished at the edges. Turn your attention, therefore, first to your remotest provinces; that, as you get rid of them, the next may follow in order.

II. That the possibility of this separation may always exist, take special care the provinces are never incorporated with the mother country; that they do not enjoy the same common rights, the same privileges in commerce; and that they are governed by severer laws, all of your enacting, without allowing them any share in the choice of the legislators. By carefully making and preserving such distinctions, you will (to keep to my simile of the cake) act like a wise gingerbread baker, who, to facilitate a division, cuts his dough half through in those places where, when baked, he would have it broken to pieces.

III. These remote provinces have perhaps been acquired, purchased, or conquered, at the sole expence of the settlers or their ancestors, without the aid of the mother country. If this should happen to increase her strength by their growing numbers ready to join in her wars, her commerce by their growing demand for her manufactures, or her naval power by greater employment for her ships and seamen, they may probably suppose some merit in this, and that it entitles them to some favour; you are therefore to forget it all, or resent it, as if they had done you injury. If they happen to be zealous Whigs, friends of liberty, nurtured in revolution principles, remember all that to their prejudice, and resolve to punish it; for such principles, after a revolution is thoroughly established, are of no more use, they are even odious and abominable.

IV. However peaceably your colonies have submitted to your government, shewn their affection to your interests, and patiently borne their grievances, you are to suppose them always inclined to revolt, and treat them accordingly. Quarter troops among them, who by their insolence may provoke the rising of mobs, and by their bullets and bayonets suppress them. By this means, like the husband who uses his wife ill from suspicion, you may in time convert your suspicions into realities.

V. Remote provinces must have Governors, and Judges, to represent the Royal Person, and execute everywhere the delegated parts of his office and authority. You ministers know, that much of the strength of government depends on the opinion of the people; and much of that opinion on the choice of rulers placed immediately over them. If you send them wise and good men for governors, who study the interest of the colonists, and advance their prosperity, they will think their King wise and good, and that he wishes the welfare of his subjects. If you send them learned and upright men for Judges, they will think him a lover of justice. This may attach your provinces more to his government. You are, therefore, to be careful who you recommend for those offices.—If you can find prodigals who have ruined their fortunes, broken gamesters or stock-jobbers, these may do well as governors; for they will probably be rapacious, and provoke the people by their extortions. Wrangling proctors and pettifogging lawyers, too, are not amiss; for they will be for ever disputing and quarrelling with their little parliaments. If withal they should be ignorant, wrong-headed, and insolent, so much the better. Attornies clerks and Newgate solicitors will do for Chief-Justices, especially if they hold their places during your pleasure. And all will contribute to impress those ideas of your government that are proper for a people you would wish to renounce it.

VI. To confirm these impressions, and strike them deeper, whenever the injured come to the capital with complaints of mal-administration, oppression, or injustice, punish such suitors with long delay, enormous expence, and a final judgment in favour of the oppressor. This will have an admirable effect every way. The trouble of future complaints will be prevented, and Governors and Judges will be encouraged to farther acts of oppression and injustice; and thence the people may become more disaffected, *and at length desperate.*

VII. When such Governors have crammed their coffers, and made themselves so odious to the people that they can no longer remain among them in safety to their persons, recal and reward them with pensions. You may make them Baronets, too, if that respectable order should not think fit to resent it. All will contribute to encourage new governors in the same practices, and make the supreme government detestable.

VIII. If, when you are engaged in war, your colonies should vie in liberal aids of men and money against the common enemy, upon your simple requisition, and give far beyond their abilities, reflect, that a penny taken from them by your power is more honourable to you, than a pound presented by their benevolence. Despise therefore their voluntary grants, and resolve to harass them with novel taxes. They will probably complain to your parliaments, that they are taxed by a body in which they have no representative, and that this is contrary to common right. They will petition for redress. Let the Parliaments flout their claims, reject their petitions, refuse even to suffer the reading of them, and treat the petitioners with the utmost contempt. Nothing can have a better effect in producing the aliena- tion proposed; for though many can forgive in- juries, none ever forgave contempt.

IX. In laying these taxes, never regard the heavy burthens those remote people already undergo, in defending their own frontiers, supporting their own provincial governments, making new roads, building bridges, churches, and other public edifices, which in old countries have been done to your hands by your ancestors, but which occasion constant calls and demands on the purses of a new people. Forget the restraints you lay on their trade for your own benefit, and the advantage a monopoly of this trade gives your exacting mer- chants. Think nothing of the wealth those mer- chants and your manufacturers acquire by the colony commerce; their encreased ability thereby to pay taxes at home; their accumulating, in the price of their commodities, most of those taxes, and so levying them from their consuming cus- tomers; all this, and the employment and support

of thousands of your poor by the colonists, you are intirely to forget. But remember to make your arbitrary tax more grievous to your provinces, by public declarations importing that your power of taxing them has no limits; so that when you take from them without their consent one shilling in the pound, you have a clear right to the other nineteen. This will probably weaken every idea of security in their property, and convince them, that under such a government, they have nothing they can call their own; which can scarce fail of producing the happiest consequences!

X. Possibly, indeed, some of them might still comfort themselves, and say, 'Though we have no property, we have yet something left that is valuable; we have constitutional liberty, both of person and of conscience. This King, these Lords, and these Commons, who, it seems, are too re- mote from us to know us, and feel for us, cannot take from us our *Habeas Corpus* right, or our right of trial by a Jury of our neighbours; they cannot deprive us of the exercise of our religion, alter our ecclesiastical constitution, and compel us to be Papists, if they please, or Mahometans.' To an- nihilate this comfort, begin by laws to perplex their commerce with infinite regulations impossible to be remembered and observed; ordain seizures of their property for every failure; take away the trial of such property by Jury, and give it to arbitrary Judges of your own appointing, and of the lowest characters in the country, whose salaries and emoluments are to arise out of the duties or condemnations, and whose appointments are dur- ing pleasure. Then let there be a formal declara- tion of both Houses, that opposition to your edicts is treason; and that any person suspected of trea- son in the provinces may, according to some ob- solete law, be seized and sent to the metropolis of the empire for trial; and pass an act that those there charged with certain other offences shall be sent away in chains from their friends and country to be tried in the same manner for felony. Then erect a new Court of Inquisition among them, ac- companied by an armed force, with instructions to transport all such suspected persons, to be ruined by the expence if they bring over evidences to prove their innocence, or be found guilty and hanged if they cannot afford it. And, lest the people should think you cannot possibly go any farther, pass another solemn declaratory act, that 'King, Lords, and Commons had, hath, and of right ought to have, full power and authority to make statutes of sufficient force and validity to bind the unrepresented provinces in all cases whatsoever.' This will include spiritual with temporal; and, taken together, must operate wonderfully to your purpose, by convincing them, that they are at present under a power something like that spoken of in the scriptures, which cannot only kill their bodies, but damn their souls to all eternity, by compelling them, if it pleases, to worship the Devil.

XI. To make your taxes more odious, and more likely to procure resistance, send from the capital a board of officers to superintend the collection, composed of the most indiscreet, ill-bred, and insolent, you can find. Let these have large salaries out of the extorted revenue, and live in open grating luxury upon the sweat and blood of the industrious, whom they are to worry continually with groundless and expensive prosecutions before the above-mentioned arbitrary revenue Judges, all at the cost of the party prosecuted, tho' acquitted, because the King is to pay no costs.—Let these men, by your order, be exempted from all the common taxes and burthens of the province, though they and their property are protected by its laws. If any revenue officers are suspected of the least tenderness for the people, discard them. If others are justly complained of, protect and reward them. If any of the under officers behave so as to provoke the people to drub them, promote those to better offices: this will encourage others to procure for themselves such profitable drubbings, by multiplying and enlarging such provocations, and all will work towards the end you aim at.

XII. Another way to make your tax odious, is to misapply the produce of it. If it was originally appropriated for the defence of the provinces, the better support of government, and the administration of justice where it may be necessary, then apply none of it to that defence, but bestow it where

it is not necessary, in augmented salaries or pensions to every governor who has distinguished himself by his enmity to the people, and by calumniating them to their sovereign. This will make them pay it more unwillingly, and be more apt to quarrel with those that collect it, and those that imposed it, who will quarrel again with them, and all shall contribute to your main purpose of making them weary of your government.

XIII. If the people of any province have been accustomed to support their own Governors and Judges to satisfaction, you are to apprehend that such Governors and Judges may be thereby influenced to treat the people kindly, and to do them justice. This is another reason for applying part of that revenue in larger salaries to such Governors and Judges, given, as their commissions are, during your pleasure only, forbidding them to take any salaries from their provinces; that thus the people may no longer hope any kindness from their Governors, or (in Crown cases) any justice from their Judges. And as the money thus misapplied in one province is extorted from all, probably all will resent the misapplication.

XIV. If the parliaments of your provinces should dare to claim rights, or complain of your administration, order them to be harassed with repeated dissolutions. If the same men are continually returned by new elections, adjourn their meetings to some country village where they cannot be accommodated, and there keep them during pleasure; for this, you know, is your prerogative; and an excellent one it is, as you may manage it, to promote discontents among the people, diminish their respect, and increase their disaffection.

XV. Convert the brave honest officers of your navy into pimping tide-waiters and colony officers of the customs. Let those who, in time of war, fought gallantly in defence of the commerce of their countrymen, in peace be taught to prey upon it. Let them learn to be corrupted by great and real smugglers; but (to shew their diligence) scour with armed boats every bay, harbour, river, creek, cove, or nook, throughout the coast of your colonies; stop and detain every coaster, every

190

wood-boat, every fisherman, tumble their cargoes, and even their ballast, inside out, and upside down; and, if a penn'orth of pins is found un-entered, let the whole be seized and confiscated. Thus shall the trade of your colonists suffer more from their friends in time of peace, than it did from their enemies in war. Then let these boats crews land upon every farm in their way, rob the orchards, steal the pigs and the poultry, and insult the inhabitants. If the injured and exasperated farmers, unable to procure other justice, should attack the aggressors, drub them and burn their boats; you are to call this high treason and rebellion, order fleets and armies into their country, and threaten to carry all the offenders three thousand miles to be hanged, drawn, and quartered. O! this will work admirably!

XVI. If you are told of discontents in your colonies, never believe that they are general, or that you have given occasion for them; therefore, do not think of applying any remedy, or of changing any offensive measure. Redress no grievance, lest they should be encouraged to demand the redress of some other grievance. Grant no request that is just and reasonable, lest they should make another that is unreasonable. Take all your informations of the state of the colonies from your Governors and officers in enmity with them. Encourage and reward these leasing-makers; secrete their lying accusations, lest they should be confuted; but act upon them as the clearest evidence, and believe nothing you hear from the friends of the people: suppose all their complaints to be invented and promoted by a few factious demagogues, whom if you could catch and hang, all would be quiet. Catch and hang a few of them accordingly; and the blood of the Martyrs shall work miracles in favour of your purpose.

XVII. If you see rival nations rejoicing at the prospect of your disunion with your provinces, and endeavouring to promote it; if they translate, publish and applaud all the complaints of your discontented colonists, at the same time privately stimulating you to severer measures; let not that alarm or offend you. Why should it? since you all mean the same thing.

XVIII. If any colony should, at their own charge, erect a fortress to secure their port against the fleets of a foreign enemy, get your Governor to betray that fortress into your hands. Never think of paying what it cost the country, for that would look, at least, like some regard for justice; but turn it into a citadel to awe the inhabitants, and curb their commerce. If they should have lodged in such fortress the very arms they bought and used to aid you in your conquests, seize them all; it will provoke like ingratitude added to robbery. One admirable effect of these operations will be, to discourage every other colony from erecting such defences, and so your enemies may more easily invade them, to the great disgrace of your government, and, of course, the furtherance of your project.

XIX. Send armies into their country under pretence of protecting the inhabitants; but, instead of garrisoning the forts on their frontiers with those troops, to prevent incursions, demolish those forts, and order the troops into the heart of the country, that the savages may be encouraged to attack the frontiers, and that the troops may be protected by the inhabitants: this will seem to proceed from your ill-will or your ignorance, and contribute farther to produce and strengthen an opinion among them, that you are no longer fit to govern them.

XX. Lastly, invest the General of your army in the provinces with great and unconstitutional powers, and free him from the controul of even your own Civil Governors. Let him have troops enow under his command, with all the fortresses in his possession; and who knows but (like some provincial Generals in the Roman empire, and encouraged by the universal discontent you have produced) he may take it into his head to set up for himself. If he should, and you have carefully practised these few excellent rules of mine, take my word for it, all the provinces will immediately join him, and you will that day (if you have not done it sooner) get rid of the trouble of governing them, and all the plagues attending their commerce and connection, from thenceforth and for ever.

Q. E. D.

An Edict by the King of Prussia

Dantzick, Sept. 5, [1773].

We have long wondered here at the supineness of the English nation, under the Prussian impositions upon its trade entering our port. We did not, till lately, know the claims, ancient and modern, that hang over that nation, and therefore could not suspect that it might submit to those impositions from a sense of duty, or from 10 principles of equity. The following Edict, just made publick, may, if serious, throw some light upon this matter.

"Frederic, by the grace of God, King of Prussia, &c. &c. &c. to all present and to come, (*A tous presens et à venir.* Original.) Health. The peace now enjoyed throughout our dominions, having afforded us leisure to apply ourselves to the regulation of commerce, the improvement of our finances, and at the same time the easing our 20 domestic subjects in their taxes: For these causes, and other good considerations us thereunto moving, we hereby make known, that, after having deliberated these affairs in our council, present our dear brothers, and other great officers of the state, members of the same, we, of our certain knowledge, full power, and authority royal, have made and issued this present Edict, viz.

"Whereas it is well known to all the world, that the first German settlements made in the Island 30 of Britain were by colonies of people, subjects to our renowned ducal ancestors, and drawn from their dominions, under the conduct of Hengist, Horsa, Hella, Uffa, Cerdicus, Ida, and others; and that the said colonies have flourished under the protection of our august house, for ages past; have never been emancipated therefrom; and yet have hitherto yielded little profit to the same: And whereas we ourself have in the last war fought for and defended the said colonies, against the power 40 of France, and thereby enabled them to make conquests from the said power in America, for which we have not yet received adequate compensation: And whereas it is just and expedient that a revenue should be raised from the said colonies in Britain, towards our indemnification; and that those who are descendants of our ancient subjects, and thence still owe us due obedience, should contribute to

the replenishing of our royal coffers, as they must have done, had their ancestors remained in the territories now to us appertaining: We do therefore hereby ordain and command, That, from and after the date of these presents, there shall be levied, and paid to our officers of the customs, on all goods, wares, and merchandizes, and on all grain and other produce of the earth, exported from the said Island of Britain, and on all goods of whatever kind imported into the same, a duty of four and a half per cent ad valorem, for the use of us and our successors. And that the said duty may more effectually be collected, we do hereby ordain, that all ships or vessels bound from Great-Britain to any other part of the world, or from any other part of the world to Great-Britain, shall in their respective voyages touch at our port of Koningsberg, there to be unladen, searched, and charged with the said duties.

"And whereas there hath been from time to time discovered in the said island of Great-Britain, by our colonists there, many mines or beds of iron-stone; and sundry subjects of our ancient dominion, skilful in converting the said stone into metal, have in time past transported themselves thither, carrying with them and communicating that art; and the inhabitants of the said island, presuming that they had a natural right to make the best use they could of the natural productions of their country, for their own benefit, have not only built furnaces for smelting the said stone into iron, but have erected plating forges, slitting mills, and steel furnaces, for the more convenient manufacturing of the same, thereby endangering a diminution of the said manufacture in our ancient dominion; we do therefore hereby farther ordain, that, from and after the date hereof, no mill or other engine for slitting or rolling of iron, or any plating forge to work with a tilt-hammer, or any furnace for making steel, shall be erected or continued in the said island of Great-Britain: And the Lord-Lieutenant of every country in the said island is hereby commanded, on information of any such erection within his county, to order and by force to cause the same to be abated and destroyed, as he shall answer the neglect thereof to us at his peril. But we are nevertheless graciously pleased to permit the inhabitants of the said island to transport their iron into Prussia, there to be manufactured, and to them returned, they paying our Prussian subjects for the workmanship, with all the costs of commission, freight, and risk, coming and returning, any thing herein contained to the contrary notwithstanding.

"We do not, however, think fit to extend this our indulgence to the article of wool; but meaning to encourage not only manufacturing of woollen cloth, but also the raising of wool, in our ancient dominions; and to prevent both, as much as may be, in our said island, we do hereby absolutely forbid the transportation of wool from thence even to the mother country, Prussia: And that those islanders may be farther and more effectually restrained in making any advantage of their own wool, in the way of manufacture, we command that none shall be carried out of one county into another, nor shall any worsted, bay, or woolen-yarn, cloth, says, bays, kerseys, serges, frizes, druggets, cloth-serges, shalloons, or any other drapery stuffs, or woollen manufactures whatsoever, made up or mixed with wool in any of the said counties, be carried into any other county, or be water-borne even across the smallest river or creek, on penalty of forfeiture of the same, together with the boats, carriages, horses, &c. that shall be employed in removing them. Nevertheless, our loving subjects there are hereby permitted (if they think proper) to use all their wool as manure, for the improvement of their lands.

"And whereas the art and mystery of making hats hath arrived at great perfection in Prussia; and the making of hats by our remoter subjects ought to be as much as possible restrained: And forasmuch as the islanders before mentioned, being in possession of wool, beaver and other furs, have presumptuously conceived they had a right to make some advantage thereof, by manufacturing the same into hats, to the prejudice of our domestic manufacture: We do therefore hereby strictly command and ordain, that no hats or felts whatsoever, dyed or undyed, finished or unfinished, shall be loaded or put into or upon any vessel, cart, carriage, or horse, to be transported or conveyed out of one county in the said island into another county, or to any other place whatsoever, by any person or persons whatsoever; on pain of forfeit-

ing the same, with a penalty of five hundred pounds sterling for every offence. Nor shall any hatmaker, in any of the said counties, employ more than two apprentices, on penalty of five pounds sterling per month: we intending hereby that such hatmakers, being so restrained, both in the production and sale of their commodity, may find no advantage in continuing their business. But, lest the said islanders should suffer inconveniency by the want of hats, we are farther graciously pleased to permit them to send their beaver furs to Prussia; and we also permit hats made thereof to be exported from Prussia to Britain, the people thus favoured to pay all costs and charges of manufacturing, interest, commission to our merchants, insurance and freight going and returning, as in the case of iron.

"And lastly, being willing farther to favour our said colonies in Britain, we do hereby also ordain and command, that all the thieves, highway and street robbers, house-breakers, forgerers, murderers, s—d—tes, and villains of every denomination, who have forfeited their lives to the law in Prussia, but whom we, in our great clemency, do not think fit here to hang, shall be emptied out of our gaols into the said island of Great Britain, for the better peopling of that country.

"We flatter ourselves that these our royal regulations and commands will be thought just and reasonable by our much favoured colonists in England, the said regulations being copied from their own statutes of 10 & 11 Will. III. c. 10.–5 Geo. II. c. 22.–23 Geo. II. c. 29.–4 Geo. I. c. 11. and from other equitable laws made by their parliaments, or from instructions given by their Princes, or from resolutions of both Houses, entered into for the good government of their own colonies in Ireland and America.

"And all persons in the said island are hereby cautioned not to oppose in any wise the execution of this our Edict, or any part thereof, such opposition being high-treason, of which all who are suspected shall be transported in fetters from Britain to Prussia, there to be tried and executed according to the Prussian law.

"Such is our pleasure. "Given at Potsdam, this twenty-fifth day of the month of August, One thousand seven hundred and seventy-three, and in the thirty-third year of our reign.

"By the King, in his Council.

"*Rechtmaessig, Sec.*"

Some take this Edict to be merely one of the King's *Jeux d'Esprit*: others suppose it serious, and that he means a quarrel with England: but all here think the assertion it concludes with, "that these regulations are copied from acts of the English parliament respecting their colonies," a very injurious one; it being impossible to believe, that a people distinguished for their love of liberty, a nation so wise, so liberal in its sentiments, so just and equitable towards its neighbors, should, from mean and injudicious views of petty immediate profit, treat its own children in a manner so arbitrary and tyrannical!

The Ephemera: an Emblem of Human Life

IN A LETTER to William Carmichael, written at Passy, June 17, 1780, Franklin said: "Enclosed I send you the little piece ["The Ephemera"] you desire. . . . The person to whom it was addressed is Madame Brillon, a lady of most respectable character and pleasing conversation; mistress of an amiable family in this neighborhood, with which I spend an evening twice in every week. . . .

"The Moulin Joli is a little island in the Seine about two leagues hence, part of the country-seat of another friend, where we visit every summer, and spend a day in the pleasing society of the ingenious, learned, and very polite persons who inhabit it. At the time when the letter was written, all conversations at Paris were filled with disputes about the music of Gluck and Picini, a German and an Italian musician, who divided the town into violent parties. . . . The thought was partly taken from a little piece of some unknown writer [see "Human Vanity," in Franklin's *Pennsylvania Gazette*, December 4, 1735], which I met with fifty years since in a newspaper, and which the sight of the "Ephemera" brought to my recollection." (Bigelow, *The Complete Works*, VII, 1888.) "The Ephemera" was originally written in French, probably on September 20, 1778; Madame Brillon showed it to friends, and copies were made. Finally Franklin printed it at his press in Passy as the first of his bagatelles. The text is that of J. Bigelow, *The Complete Works*, VI (1888).

To Madame Brillon, of Passy.

You may remember, my dear friend, that when we lately spent that happy day in the delightful garden and sweet society of the Moulin Joly, I stopped a little in one of our walks, and staid some time behind the company. We had been shown numberless skeletons of a kind of little fly, called an ephemera, whose successive generations, we were told, were bred and expired within the day. I happened to see a living company of them on a leaf, who appeared to be engaged in conversation. You know I understand all the inferior animal tongues. My too great application to the study of them is the best excuse I can give for the little progress I have made in your charming language. I listened through curiosity to the discourse of these little creatures; but as they, in their national vivacity, spoke three or four together, I could make but little of their conversation. I found, however, by some broken expressions that I heard now and then, they were disputing warmly on the merit of two foreign musicians, one a *cousin*, the other a *moscheto*; in which dispute they spent their time, seemingly as regardless of the shortness of life as if they had been sure of living a month. Happy people! thought I, you live certainly under a wise, just, and mild government, since you have no public grievances to complain of, nor any subject of contention but the perfections and imperfections of foreign music. I turned my head from them to an old grey-headed one, who was single on another leaf, and talking to himself. Being amused with his soliloquy, I put it down in writing, in hopes it will likewise amuse her to whom I am so much indebted for the most pleasing of all amusements, her delicious company and heavenly harmony.

"It was," said he, "the opinion of learned philosophers of our race, who lived and flourished long before my time, that this vast world, the Moulin Joly, could not itself subsist more than eighteen hours; and I think there was some foundation for that opinion, since, by the apparent motion of the great luminary that gives life to all nature, and which in my time has evidently declined considerably towards the ocean at the end of our earth, it must then finish its course, be

194

extinguished in the waters that surround us, and leave the world in cold and darkness, necessarily producing universal death and destruction. I have lived seven of those hours, a great age, being no less than four hundred and twenty minutes of time. How very few of us continue so long! I have seen generations born, flourish, and expire. My present friends are the children and grandchildren of the friends of my youth, who are now, alas, no more! And I must soon follow them; for, by the course of nature, though still in health, I cannot expect to live above seven or eight minutes longer. What now avails all my toil and labor, in amassing honey-dew on this leaf, which I cannot live to enjoy! What the political struggles I have been engaged in for the good of my compatriot inhabitants of this bush, or my philosophical studies for the benefit of our race in general! for in politics what can laws do without morals? Our present race of ephemeræ will in a course of minutes become corrupt, like those of other and older bushes, and consequently as wretched. And in philosophy how small our progress! Alas! art is long, and life is short! My friends would comfort me with the idea of a name, they say, I shall leave behind me; and they tell me I have lived long enough to nature and to glory. But what will fame be to an ephemera who no longer exists? And what will become of all history in the eighteenth hour, when the world itself, even the whole Moulin Joly, shall come to its end, and be buried in universal ruin?"

To me, after all my eager pursuits, no solid pleasures now remain, but the reflection of a long life spent in meaning well, the sensible conversation of a few good lady ephemeræ, and now and then a kind smile and a tune from the ever amiable *Brillante.*

B. Franklin.

To Madame Helvétius

MADAME HELVÉTIUS (Anne Catherine de Ligniville d'Autricourt) was married in 1751 to Claude Adrien Helvétius, farmer general and French philosopher. After his death in 1771 she lived with her two daughters at Auteuil, near Passy, where she kept her salon. Just when Franklin proposed marriage, and how seriously, is not known; but she was resolved to remain faithful to the memory of her husband. The letter is commonly thought to have been written in 1778. No manuscript of this letter exists, nor any English version known to have been done by Franklin. He printed it twice as one of his bagatelles. See Carl Van Doren, *Benjamin Franklin*, pp. 646–53, 662. The text follows that of J. Bigelow, *The Complete Works*, VI (1888).

Mortified at the barbarous resolution pronounced by you so positively yesterday evening, that you would remain single the rest of your life as a compliment due to the memory of your husband, I retired to my chamber. Throwing myself upon my bed, I dreamt that I was dead, and was transported to the Elysian Fields.

I was asked whether I wished to see any persons in particular; to which I replied that I wished to see the philosophers. "There are two who live here at hand in this garden; they are good neighbors, and very friendly towards one another."—"Who are they?"—"Socrates and Helvétius."—"I esteem them both highly; but let me see Helvétius first, because I understand a little French, but not a word of Greek." I was conducted to him; he received me with much courtesy, having known me, he said, by character, some time past. He asked me a thousand questions relative to the war, the present state of religion, of liberty, of the government in France. "You do not inquire, then," said I, "after your dear friend, Madame Helvétius; yet she loves you exceedingly. I was in her company not more than an hour ago." "Ah," said he, "you make me recur to my past happiness, which ought to be forgotten in order to be happy here. For many years I could think of nothing but her, though at length I am consoled. I have taken another wife, the most like her that I could find; she is not indeed altogether so handsome, but she has a great fund of wit and good-sense, and her whole study is to please me. She is at this moment gone to fetch the best nectar and ambrosia to regale me; stay here awhile and you will see her." "I perceive," said I, "that your former friend is more faithful to you than you are to her; she has had several good offers, but has refused them all. I will confess to you that I loved her extremely; but she was cruel to me, and rejected me peremptorily for your sake."

"I pity you sincerely," said he, "for she is an excellent woman, handsome and amiable. But do not the Abbe de la R*** and the Abbe M**** visit her?"—"Certainly they do; not one of your friends has dropped her acquaintance."—"If you had gained the Abbe M**** with a bribe of good coffee and cream, perhaps you would have succeeded; for he is as deep a reasoner as Duns Scotus or St. Thomas; he arranges and methodizes his arguments in such a manner that they are almost irresistible. Or if by a fine edition of some old classic you had gained the Abbe de la R**** to speak against you, that would have been still better, as I always observed that when he recommended any thing to her, she had a great inclination to do directly the contrary." As he finished these words the new Madame Helvétius entered with the nectar, and I recognized her immediately as my former American friend, Mrs. Franklin! I reclaimed her, but she answered me coldly: "I was a good wife to you for forty-nine years and four months, nearly half a century; let that content you. I have formed a new connection here, which will last to eternity."

Indignant at this refusal of my Eurydice, I immediately resolved to quit those ungrateful shades, and return to this good world again, to behold the sun and you! Here I am; let us avenge ourselves!

The Whistle

DATED November 10, 1779, and sent to Madame Brillon, "The Whistle" was written in English and French, printed as a bagatelle in both versions. It was a result of conversations on getting the most out of mortal life. The text is that of J. Bigelow, *The Complete Works*, VI (1888).

To Madame Brillon.

I received my dear friend's two letters, one for Wednesday and one for Saturday. This is again Wednesday. I do not deserve one for to-day, because I have not answered the former. But, indolent as I am, and averse to writing, the fear of having no more of your pleasing epistles, if I do not contribute to the correspondence, obliges me to take up my pen; and as Mr. B. has kindly sent me word that he sets out to-morrow to see you, instead of spending this Wednesday evening, as I have done its namesakes, in your delightful company, I sit down to spend it in thinking of you, in writing to you, and in reading over and over again your letters.

I am charmed with your description of Paradise, and with your plan of living there; and I approve much of your conclusion, that, in the meantime, we should draw all the good we can from this world. In my opinion we might all draw more good from it than we do, and suffer less evil, if we would take care not to give too much for whistles. For to me it seems that most of the unhappy people we meet with are become so by neglect of that caution.

You ask what I mean? You love stories, and will excuse my telling one of myself.

When I was a child of seven years old, my friends, on a holiday, filled my pocket with coppers. I went directly to a shop where they sold toys for children; and being charmed with the sound of a whistle, that I met by the way in the hands of another boy, I voluntarily offered and gave all my money for one. I then came home, and went whistling all over the house, much pleased with my whistle, but disturbing all the family. My brothers, and sisters, and cousins, understanding the bargain I had made, told me I had given four times as much for it as it was worth; put me in mind what good things I might have bought with the rest of the money; and laughed at me so much for my folly, that I cried with vexation; and the reflection gave me more chagrin than the whistle gave me pleasure.

This however was afterwards of use to me, the impression continuing on my mind; so that often, when I was tempted to buy some unnecessary thing, I said to myself, Don't give too much for the whistle; and I saved my money.

As I grew up, came into the world, and observed the actions of men, I thought I met with many, very many, who gave too much for the whistle.

When I saw one too ambitious of court favour, sacrificing his time in attendance on levees, his repose, his liberty, his virtue, and perhaps his friends, to attain it, I have said to myself, This man gives too much for his whistle.

When I saw another fond of popularity, constantly employing himself in political bustles, neglecting his own affairs, and ruining them by that neglect, He pays, indeed, said I, too much for his whistle.

If I knew a miser, who gave up every kind of comfortable living, all the pleasure of doing good to others, all the esteem of his fellow-citizens, and the joys of benevolent friendship, for the sake of accumulating wealth, Poor man, said I, you pay too much for your whistle.

When I met with a man of pleasure, sacrificing 10 every laudable improvement of the mind, or of his fortune, to mere corporeal sensations, and ruining his health in their pursuit, Mistaken man, said I, you are providing pain for yourself, instead of pleasure; you give too much for your whistle.

If I see one fond of appearance, or fine clothes, fine houses, fine furniture, fine equipages, all above his fortune, for which he contracts debts, and ends his career in a prison, Alas! say I, he has paid dear, very dear, for his whistle. 20

When I see a beautiful, sweet-tempered girl married to an ill-natured brute of a husband, What a pity, say I, that she should pay so much for a whistle!

In short, I conceive that great part of the miseries of mankind are brought upon them by the false estimates they have made of the value of things, and by their giving too much for their whistles.

Yet I ought to have charity for these unhappy 30 people, when I consider that, with all this wisdom of which I am boasting, there are certain things in the world so tempting, for example, the apples of King John, which happily are not to be bought; for if they were put to sale by auction, I might very easily be led to ruin myself in the purchase, and find that I had once more given too much for the whistle.

Adieu, my dear friend, and believe me ever yours very sincerely and with unalterable affection, 40
B. Franklin.

Speech in the Convention, at the Conclusion of Its Deliberations

FRANKLIN's voice being weak, James Wilson read this remarkable speech for him on the final day of the Constitutional Convention, Monday, September 17, 1787.

Franklin then moved adoption of the Constitution. An octogenarian of active mind and sane humor, who was again to be elected president of Pennsylvania, Franklin gave great service to the Convention through his wise counsel and unusual powers as conciliator. The text is that of J. Bigelow, *The Complete Works*, IX (1888).

Mr. President:—I confess that I do not entirely approve of this Constitution at present; but, sir, I am not sure I shall never approve it; for, having lived long, I have experienced many instances of being obliged, by better information or fuller consideration, to change opinions even on important subjects, which I once thought right, but found to be otherwise. It is therefore that, the older I grow, the more apt I am to doubt my own judgment of others. Most men, indeed, as well as most sects in religion, think themselves in possession of all truth, and that wherever others differ from them, 20 it is so far error. Steele, a Protestant, in a dedication, tells the Pope that the only difference between our two churches in their opinions of the certainty of their doctrine is, the Romish Church is infallible, and the Church of England is never in the wrong. But though many private persons think almost as highly of their own infallibility as that of their sect, few express it so naturally as a certain French lady, who, in a little dispute with her sister, said: "But I meet with nobody but myself that is always in the right." "*Je ne trouve que moi qui aie toujours raison.*"

In these sentiments, sir, I agree to this Constitution, with all its faults—if they are such;— because I think a general government necessary for us, and there is no form of government but what may be a blessing to the people, if well administered; and I believe further, that this is likely to be well administered for a course of years, and can only end in despotism, as other forms have done before it, when the people shall become so corrupted as to need despotic government, being incapable of any other. I doubt, too, whether any other convention we can obtain, may be able to make a better Constitution; for, when you assemble a number of men, to have the advantage of their joint wisdom, you inevitably assemble with those men, all their prejudices, their passions, their errors of opinion, their local interests, and their selfish views. From such an assembly can a perfect production be expected? It therefore astonishes me, sir, to find this system approaching so near to perfection as it does; and I think it will astonish our enemies, who are waiting with confidence to hear that our counsels are confounded like those of the builders of Babel, and that our States are on the point of separation, only to meet hereafter for the purpose of cutting one another's throats. Thus I consent, sir, to this Constitution, 10 because I expect no better, and because I am not sure that it is not the best. The opinions I have had of its errors I sacrifice to the public good. I have never whispered a syllable of them abroad. Within these walls they were born, and here they shall die. If every one of us, in returning to our constituents, were to report the objections he has had to it, and endeavor to gain partisans in support of them, we might prevent its being generally received, and thereby lose all the 20 salutary effects and great advantages resulting naturally in our favor among foreign nations, as well as among ourselves, from our real or apparent unanimity. Much of the strength and efficiency of any government in procuring and securing happiness to the people, depends on opinion, on the general opinion, of the goodness of that government, as well as of the wisdom and integrity of its governors. I hope, therefore, for our own sakes, as a part of the people, and for the sake of our 30 posterity, that we shall act heartily and unanimously in recommending this Constitution, wherever our influence may extend, and turn our future thoughts and endeavors to the means of having it well administered.

On the whole, sir, I cannot help expressing a wish that every member of the convention who may still have objections to it would with me on this occasion doubt a little of his own infallibility, and, to make manifest our unanimity, put his 40 name to this instrument.

Letter to Lord Kames

[On Music]

LORD KAMES (Henry Home, 1696–1782), Edinburgh jurist, became one of Franklin's most valued friends and correspondents after the two met in 1759, when Franklin spent some time in Scotland. The text is that of J. Bigelow, *The Complete Works*, III (1887).

London, 2 June, 1765.

In my passage to America I read your excellent work, the Elements of Criticism, in which I found great entertainment. I only wished you had examined more fully the subject of Music, and demonstrated that the pleasure which artists feel in hearing much of that composed in the modern taste, is not the natural pleasure arising from melody or harmony of sounds, but of the same kind with the pleasure we feel on seeing the surprising feats of tumblers and rope-dancers, who execute difficult things. For my part I take this to be really the case, and suppose it is the reason why those who are unpractised in music, and therefore unacquainted with those difficulties, have little or no pleasure in hearing this music. Many pieces 20 of it are mere compositions of tricks. I have sometimes, at a concert, attended by a common audience, placed myself so as to see all their faces, and observed no signs of pleasure in them during the performance of a great part that was admired by the performers themselves; while a plain old Scotch tune, which they disdained, and could scarcely be prevailed on to play, gave manifest and general delight.

Give me leave, on this occasion, to extend a little 30 the sense of your position, that "melody, and harmony are separately agreeable, and in union delightful," and to give it as my opinion, that the reason why the Scotch tunes have lived so long, and will probably live forever (if they escape being stifled in modern affected ornament), is merely this, that they are really compositions of melody and harmony united, or rather that their melody is harmony. I mean the simple tunes sung by a single voice. As this will appear paradoxical, I 40 must explain my meaning. In common acceptation, indeed, only an agreeable succession of sounds is called melody, and only the coexistence of agreeable sounds, harmony. But, since the memory is capable of retaining for some moments a perfect idea of the pitch of a past sound, so as to compare with it the pitch of a succeeding sound, and judge truly of their agreement or disagreement, there may and does arise from thence a sense of harmony between the present and past sounds, equally pleasing with that between two present sounds.

Now the construction of the old Scotch tunes is this, that almost every succeeding emphatical note is a third, a fifth, an octave, or in short some note that is in concord with the preceding note. Thirds are chiefly used, which are very pleasing concords. I use the word emphatical to distinguish those notes which have a stress laid on them in singing the tune, from the lighter connecting notes, that serve merely, like grammar articles in common speech, to tack the whole together.

That we have a most perfect idea of a sound just past, I might appeal to all acquainted with music, who know how easy it is to repeat a sound in the same pitch with one just heard. In tuning an instrument, a good ear can as easily determine that two strings are in unison by sounding them separately, as by sounding them together; their disagreement is also as easily, I believe I may say more easily and better, distinguished, when sounded separately; for when sounded together, though you know by the beating that one is higher than the other, you cannot tell which it is. I have ascribed to memory the ability of comparing the pitch of a present tone with that of one past. But if there should be, as possibly there may be, something in the ear, similar to what we find in the eye, that ability would not be entirely owing to memory. Possibly the vibrations given to the auditory nerves by a particular sound may actually continue some time after the cause of those vibrations is past, and the agreement or disagreement of a subsequent sound become by comparison with them more discernible. For the impression made on the visual nerves by a luminous object will continue for twenty or thirty seconds. Sitting in a room, look earnestly at the middle of a window a little while when the day is bright, and then shut your eyes; the figure of the window will still remain in the eye, and so distinct that you may count the panes.

A remarkable circumstance attending this experiment is, that the impression of forms is better retained than that of colors; for after the eyes are shut, when you first discern the image of the window, the panes appear dark, and the cross bars of the sashes, with the window frames and walls,

appear white or bright; but, if you still add to the darkness in the eyes by covering them with your hand, the reverse instantly takes place, the panes appear luminous and the cross-bars dark. And by removing the hand they are again reversed. This I know not how to account for. Nor for the following: that, after looking long through green spectacles, the white paper of a book will on first taking them off appear to have a blush of red; and, after long looking through red glasses, a greenish cast; this seems to intimate a relation between green and red not yet explained.

Farther, when we consider by whom these ancient tunes were composed, and how they were first performed, we shall see that such harmonical succession of sounds was natural and even necessary in their construction. They were composed by the minstrels of those days to be played on the harp accompanied by the voice. The harp was strung with wire, which gives a sound of long continuance, and had no contrivance like that in the modern harpsichord, by which the sound of the preceding could be stopped, the moment a succeeding note began. To avoid actual discord, it was therefore necessary that the succeeding emphatic note should be a chord with the preceding, as their sounds must exist at the same time. Hence arose that beauty in those tunes that has so long pleased, and will please for ever, though men scarce know why. That they were originally composed for the harp, and of the most simple kind, I mean a harp without any half notes but those in the natural scale, and with no more than two octaves of strings, from C to C, I conjecture from another circumstance, which is, that not one of those tunes, really ancient, has a single artificial half note in it, and that in tunes where it was most convenient for the voice to use the middle notes of the harp, and place the key in F, there the B, which if used should be a B flat, is always omitted by passing over it with a third. The connoisseurs in modern music will say, I have no taste; but I cannot help adding, that I believe our ancestors, in hearing a good song, distinctly articulated, sung to one of those tunes, and accompanied by the harp, felt more real pleasure than is communicated by the generality of modern operas, exclusive of that arising from the scenery and dancing. Most tunes of late composition, not having this natural harmony united with their melody, have recourse to the artificial harmony of a bass, and other accompanying parts. This support, in my opinion, the old tunes do not need, and are rather confused than aided by it. Whoever has heard James Oswald play them on his violoncello, will be less inclined to dispute this with me. I have more than once seen tears of pleasure in the eyes of his auditors; and yet, I think, even his playing those tunes would please more, if he gave them less modern ornament.

I am, &c.,

B. Franklin

Letter to Joseph Priestley[n]

[On British Colonial Policy]

FRANKLIN was an indefatigable correspondent. Always observant of natural phenomena, sensitive to human concerns, analytical and curious of mind, he ranged broadly in his letters, especially in the fields of natural science and government. The text of the letter to Dr. Priestley is that of J. Bigelow, *The Complete Works*, V (1887).

Philadelphia, 7 July, 1775.

Dear Friend:—The Congress met at a time when all minds were so exasperated by the perfidy of General Gage,[n] and his attack on the country people, that propositions for attempting an accommodation were not much relished; and it has been with difficulty that we have carried another humble petition to the crown, to give Britain one more chance, one opportunity more, of recovering the friendship of the colonies; which, however, I think she has not sense enough to embrace, and so I conclude she has lost them forever.

She has begun to burn our seaport towns; secure, I suppose, that we shall never be able to return the outrage in kind. She may doubtless destroy them all; but, if she wishes to recover our commerce, are these the probable means? She must certainly be distracted; for no tradesman out of Bedlam ever thought of encreasing the number of his customers, by knocking them on the head; or of enabling them to pay their debts, by burning their houses. If she wishes to have us subjects, and that we should submit to her as our compound sovereign, she is now giving us such miserable specimens of her government, that we shall ever detest and avoid it, as a complication of robbery, murder, famine, fire, and pestilence.

You will have heard, before this reaches you, of the treacherous conduct of General Gage to the remaining people in Boston, in detaining their goods, after stipulating to let them go out with their effects, on pretence that merchants' goods were not effects; the defeat of a great body of his troops by the country people at Lexington; some other small advantages gained in skirmishes with their troops; and the action at Bunker's Hill, in which they were twice repulsed, and the third time gained a dear victory. Enough has happened one would think, to convince your ministers that the Americans will fight, and that this is a harder nut to crack than they imagined.

We have not yet applied to any foreign power for assistance, nor offered our commerce for their friendship. Perhaps we may never; yet it is natural to think of it, if we are pressed. We have now an army on the establishment, which still holds yours besieged. My time was never more fully employed. In the morning at six, I am at the Committee of Safety, appointed by the Assembly to put the province in a state of defence; which committee holds till near nine, when I am at the Congress, and that sits till after four in the afternoon. Both these bodies proceed with the greatest unanimity, and their meetings are well attended. It will scarce be credited in Britain, that men can be as diligent with us from zeal for the public good, as with you for thousands per annum. Such is the difference between uncorrupted new states, and corrupted old ones.

Great frugality and great industry are now become fashionable here. Gentlemen, who used to entertain with two or three courses, pride them-

Joseph Priestley: (1733–1804), English clergyman, chemist, and physicist, who supported the American and French Revolutions and, suffering disfavor at home, emigrated to Pennsylvania. **General Gage:** Thomas Gage (1721–1787), commander in chief of the British Army in America from 1763 to 1772, was sent back to Boston as governor after the Boston Tea Party of December, 1773. His enforcement of British policy led to the battle of Lexington, April 19, 1775.

selves now in treating with simple beef and pudding. By these means, and the stoppage of our consumptive trade with Britain, we shall be better able to pay our voluntary taxes for the support of our troops. Our savings in the article of trade amount to near five millions sterling per annum.

I shall communicate your letter to Mr. Winthrop[n] but the camp is at Cambridge, and he has as little leisure for philosophy as myself. Believe me ever, etc.,

B. Franklin.

Letter to Samuel Mather

[On Cotton Mather]

FRANKLIN heard both Increase and Cotton Mather preach in their famous Second Church in Boston. Their sermons, however, were less influential than Cotton Mather's *Essays to Do Good* (1710), which the young printer's apprentice read as an impressionable boy. Dr. Mather, sixty-one years of age at the time of the meeting described in the letter, had just succeeded his late father as pastor of the Second Church. The text is that of J. Bigelow, *The Complete Works*, VIII (1888).

Passy, 12 May, 1784.

Reverend Sir:—I received your kind letter, with your excellent advice to the people of the United States, which I read with great pleasure, and hope it will be duly regarded. Such writings, though they may be lightly passed over by many readers, yet, if they make a deep impression on one active mind in a hundred, the effects may be considerable. Permit me to mention one little instance, which, though it relates to myself, will not be quite uninteresting to you. When I was a boy, I met with a book, entitled "Essays to do Good," which I think was written by your father. It had been so little regarded by a former possessor, that several leaves of it were torn out; but the remainder gave me such a turn of thinking, as to have an influence on my conduct through life; for I have always set a greater value on the character of a doer of good, than on any other kind of reputation; and if I

Mr. Winthrop: John Winthrop (1714–1779), professor of Natural Philosophy at Harvard, and a correspondent of Franklin's on scientific and other matters.

have been, as you seem to think, a useful citizen, the public owes the advantage of it to that book.

You mention your being in your seventy-eighth year; I am in my seventy-ninth; we are grown old together. It is now more than sixty years since I left Boston, but I remember well both your father and grandfather, having heard them both in the pulpit, and seen them in their houses. The last time I saw your father was in the beginning of 1724, when I visited him after my first trip to Pennsylvania. He received me in his library, and on my taking leave showed me a shorter way out of the house, through a narrow passage, which was crossed by a beam over head. We were all talking as I withdrew, he accompanying me behind, and I turning partly towards him, when he said hastily, "Stoop, stoop!" I did not understand him, till I felt my head hit against the beam. He was a man that never missed any occasion of giving instruction, and upon this he said to me, "You are young, and have the world before you; stoop as you go through it, and will miss many hard thumps." This advice, thus beat into my head, has frequently been of use to me, and I often think of it when I see pride mortified and misfortunes brought upon people by their carrying their heads too high.

I long much to see my native place, and to lay my bones there. I left it in 1723; I visited it in 1733, 1743, 1753, and 1763. In 1773 I was in England; in 1775 I had a sight of it, but could not enter, it being in possession of the enemy. I did hope to have been there in 1783, but could not obtain my dismission from this employment here, and now I fear I shall never have that happiness. My best wishes however attend my dear country. *Esto perpetua.* It is now blest with an excellent constitution; may it last for ever!

This powerful monarchy continues its friendship for the United States. It is a friendship of the utmost importance to our security, and should be carefully cultivated. Britain has not yet well digested the loss of its dominion over us, and has still at times some flattering hopes of recovering it. Accidents may increase those hopes and encourage dangerous attempts. A breach between us and France would infallibly bring the English again upon our backs; and yet we have some wild heads among our countrymen who are endeavouring to weaken that connexion! Let us preserve our reputation by performing our engagements, our credit by fulfilling our contracts, and friends by gratitude and kindness; for we know not how soon we may again have occasion for all of them. With great and sincere esteem, I have the honour to be, etc.,

B. Franklin.

JOHN DICKINSON (1732–1808)

ALTHOUGH John Dickinson objected to the name of "rebel," and refused to sign the Declaration of Independence, he was one of the two members of Congress who took up arms against the Crown. With the exception of Thomas Paine, Dickinson was the most effective penman of the Revolution, and the most articulate and cultivated of those colonists who insisted upon their rights and liberties as subjects. His position was that of the lawyer who argued that the American colonists should enjoy rights equal to those of citizens in the mother country. Dickinson contended with legal acumen and disarming moderation that the measures which recently had been adopted in England with reference to the colonies were in violation of the fundamental principles of England's own law.

Trained in the office of a distinguished Philadelphia lawyer, Dickinson completed his legal studies at the Inns of Court in London. His naturally conservative temper prompted him to urge the colonists to seek to redress their wrongs by peaceable and orderly procedures. His utterances, contrasting coolly with the less temperate protests of violent partisans, are a fair measure of what an alert but judicial pleader might honestly and intelligently write in defense of the colonists' position. His outstanding contribution to the literary history of the Revolution was the series of twelve letters published anonymously in the *Pennsylvania Chronicle*, a Philadelphia newspaper, in 1767–1768, and widely reprinted in the colonial press. Before their appearance he had sat in the Pennsylvania legislature and had attended the Stamp Act Congress as a Pennsylvania delegate in 1765. Later, again entering the legislature, he drafted in 1771 the Petition to the King. For a short time in 1774 he was a member of the Continental Congress, and again of the Second Continental Congress in 1775. During the sessions of both assemblies he continued to strive for peaceable methods of settlement; but his authorship of a second Petition to the King alienated violent New England members. By 1776, although Dickinson still hoped for conciliation, the sentiment of the country went beyond him, especially when he cast his vote against the Declaration of Independence. His service as a private in the Battle of Brandywine testifies to his conviction that the defense of liberty by force of arms was a duty after methods of legal and constitutional redress had proved futile. For four years after 1775 his popularity was submerged by the radical temper of the times, but he subsequently gained a seat in Congress from Delaware, and was successively elected governor of Delaware and of Pennsylvania. He was an able member of the Constitutional Convention, his last major participation in government, although he remained active in public affairs until his death in Wilmington in 1808. Dickinson's political writings were printed in two volumes in 1801 and republished in 1814.

BIBLIOGRAPHY · The works of John Dickinson have been partially collected in P. L. Ford's *Writings of John Dickinson* (Vol. I, *Political Writings, 1764–1774*) issued in 1895 as Volume XIV of the *Memoirs of the Historical Society of Pennsylvania*. For Dickinson's "Letters of Fabius" (1788, 1797), see P. L. Ford (editor), *Pamphlets on the Constitution of the United States* (1888). See also *The Political Writings of John Dickinson* (2 vols., 1801, 1814). Biographical studies include C. J. Stillé, *The Life and Times of John Dickinson, 1732–1808* in Volume XIII of the *Memoirs of the Historical Society of Pennsylvania* (1891), and C. F. Himes, *The True John Dickinson* (1912), a pamphlet of thirty-two pages. For the most authoritative account of pamphleteering in the Revolution, see M. C. Tyler, *The Literary History of the American Revolution* (2 vols., 1897).

Letters from a Farmer in Pennsylvania

THE *Letters* were the most statesmanlike of the essay series produced by the controversies over the Stamp Act. They were widely reprinted, and their author was for at least five years the popular idol of all colonists who believed in the dignified assertion of their rights under the British constitution. Small wonder that the letters were issued in book form in 1768 as *Letters from a Farmer in Pennsylvania to the Inhabitants of the British Colonies*. First printed in Philadelphia, they appeared in four other editions in the same year in Boston, New York, and Philadelphia. The present text is taken from the Philadelphia edition of 1768.

III. [*The Need of Firm but Peaceable Measures*]

My dear Countrymen,

I rejoice to find that my two former letters to you, have been generally received with so much favour by such of you, whose sentiments I have had an opportunity of knowing. Could you look into my heart, you would instantly perceive a zealous attachment to your interests, and a lively resentment of every insult and injury offered to you, to be the only motives that have engaged me to address you.

I am no further concerned in anything affecting *America*, than any one of you; and when liberty leaves it, I can quit it much more conveniently than most of you: but while Divine Providence, that gave me existence in a land of freedom, permits my head to think, my lips to speak, and my hand to move, I shall so highly and gratefully value the blessing received, as to take care, that my silence and inactivity shall not give my implied assent to any act degrading my brethren and myself from the birthright, wherewith heaven itself "hath made us free."

Sorry I am to learn, that there are some few persons, who shake their heads with solemn motion, and pretend to wonder, what can be the meaning of these letters. "*Great Britain*," they say, "is too powerful to contend with; she is determined to oppress us; it is in vain to speak of right on one side, when there is power on the other; when we are strong enough to resist, we shall attempt it; but now we are not strong enough, and therefore we had better be quiet; it signifies nothing to convince us that our rights are invaded, when we cannot defend them; and if we should get into riots and tumults about the late act, it will only bring down heavier displeasure upon us."

What can such men design? What do their grave observations amount to, but this—"that these colonies, totally regardless of their liberties, should commit them, with humble resignation, to chance, time, and the tender mercies of ministers."

Are these men ignorant, that usurpations, which might have been successfully opposed at first, acquire strength by continuance, and thus become irresistible? Do they condemn the conduct of these colonies, concerning the Stamp-Act?

Or have they forgot its successful issue? Ought the colonies at that time, instead of acting as they did, to have trusted for relief, to the fortuitous events of futurity? If it is needless "to speak of rights" now, it was as needless then. If the behaviour of the colonies was prudent and glorious then, and successful too; it will be equally prudent and glorious to act in the same manner now, if our rights are equally invaded, and may be as successful. Therefore it becomes necessary to enquire, whether "our rights *are* invaded." To talk of "defending" them, as if they could be no otherwise "defended" than by arms, is as much out of the way, as if a man having a choice of several roads to reach his journey's end, should prefer the worst, for no other reason, but because it *is* the worst.

As to "riots and tumults," the gentlemen who are so apprehensive of them, are much mistaken, if they think, that grievances cannot be redressed without such assistance.

I will now tell the gentlemen, what is "the meaning of these letters." The meaning of them is, to convince the people of these colonies, that they are at this moment exposed to the most imminent dangers; and to persuade them immediately, vigorously, and unanimously, to exert themselves, in the most firm but most peaceable manner, for obtaining relief.

The cause of liberty is a cause of too much dignity, to be sullied by turbulence and tumult. It ought to be maintained in a manner suitable to her nature. Those who engage in it, should breathe a sedate, yet fervent spirit, animating them to actions of prudence, justice, modesty, bravery, humanity, and magnanimity.

To such a wonderful degree were the ancient Spartans, as brave and as free a people as ever existed, inspired by this happy temperature of soul, that rejecting even in their battles the use of trumpets, and other instruments for exciting heat and rage, they marched up to scenes of havock and horror, with the sound of flutes, to the tunes of which their steps kept pace—"exhibiting," as Plutarch says, "at once a terrible and delightful sight, and proceeding with a deliberate valour, full of hope and good assurance, as if some divinity had insensibly assisted them."

I hope, my dear countrymen, that you will, in every colony, be upon your guard against those, who may at any time endeavour to stir you up, under pretense of patriotism, to any measures disrespectful to our Sovereign and our mother country. Hot, rash, disorderly proceedings, injure the reputation of a people, as to wisdom, valour and virtue, without procuring them the least benefit. I pray God, that he may be pleased to inspire you and your posterity, to the latest ages, with a spirit, of which I have an idea, that I find a difficulty to express. To express in the best manner I can, I mean a spirit, that shall so guide you, that it will be impossible to determine, whether an American's character is most distinguishable for his loyalty to his Sovereign, his duty to his mother country, his love of freedom, or his affection for his native soil.

Every government, at some time or other, falls into wrong measures. These may proceed from mistake or passion. But every such measure does not dissolve the obligation between the governors and the governed. The mistake may be corrected; the passion may subside. It is the duty of the governed to endeavour to rectify the mistake, and appease the passion. They have not at first any other right, than to represent their grievances, and to pray for redress, unless an emergence is so pressing, as not to allow time for receiving an answer to their applications, which rarely happens. If their applications are disregarded, then that kind of opposition becomes justifiable, which can be made without breaking the laws, or disturbing the public peace. This consists in the prevention of the oppressors reaping advantage from their oppressions, and not in their punishment. For experience may teach them, what reason did not; and harsh methods cannot be proper, till milder ones have failed.

If at length it becomes undoubted, that an inveterate resolution is formed to annihilate the liberties of the governed, the English history affords frequent examples of resistance by force. What particular circumstances will in any future case justify such resistance, can never be ascertained, till they happen. Perhaps it may be allowable to say, generally, that it never can be justifiable, until the people are FULLY CONVINCED, that any further submission will be destructive to their happiness.

When the appeal is made to the sword, highly probable is it, that the punishment will exceed the offence; and the calamities attending on war out-weigh those preceding it. These considerations of justice and prudence will always have great influence with good and wise men.

To these reflections on this subject, it remains to be added, and ought forever to be remembered, that resistance in the case of colonies against their mother country, is extremely different from the resistance of a people against their prince. A nation may change their king, or race of kings, and, retaining their ancient form of government, be gainers by changing. Thus Great-Britain, under the illustrious house of Brunswick, a house that seems to flourish for the happiness of mankind, has found a felicity, unknown in the reigns of the Stuarts. But if once we are separated from our mother country, what new form of government shall we adopt, or when shall we find another Britain to supply our loss? Torn from the body, to which we are united by religion, liberty, laws, affections, relation, language and commerce, we must bleed at every vein.

In truth—the prosperity of these provinces is founded in their dependence on Great-Britain; and when she returns to "her old good humour, and old good nature," as Lord Clarendon expresses it, I hope they will always esteem it their duty and interest, as it most certainly will be, to promote her welfare by all the means in their power.

We cannot act with too much caution in our disputes. Anger produces anger; and differences, that might be accommodated by kind and respectful behaviour, may by imprudence be changed to an incurable rage. In quarrels between countries, as well as in those between individuals, when they have risen to a certain height, the first cause of dissension is no longer remembered, the minds of the parties being wholly engaged in recollecting and resenting the mutual expressions of their dislike. When feuds have reached that fatal point, all considerations of reason and equity vanish; and a blind fury governs, or rather confounds all things. A people no longer regards their interest, but the gratification of their wrath. The sway of the Cleons and Clodius's,[n] the designing and detestable flatterers of the prevailing passion, becomes confirmed. Wise and good men in vain oppose the storm, and may think themselves fortunate, if, endeavouring to preserve their ungrateful fellow citizens, they do not ruin themselves. Their prudence will be called baseness; their moderation will be called guilt; and if their virtue does not lead them to destruction, as that of many other great and excellent persons has done, they may survive to receive from their expiring country the mournful glory of her acknowledgement, that their counsels, if regarded, would have saved her.

The constitutional modes of obtaining relief, are those which I wish to see pursued on the present occasion; that is, by petitioning of our assemblies, or, where they are not permitted to meet, of the people, to the powers that can afford us relief.

We have an excellent prince, in whose good dispositions towards us we may confide. We have a generous, sensible, and humane nation, to whom we may apply. They may be deceived. They may, by artful men, be provoked to anger against us. I cannot believe they will be cruel or unjust; or that their anger will be implacable. Let us behave like dutiful children, who have received unmerited blows from a beloved parent. Let us complain to our parent; but let our complaints speak at the same time, the language of affliction and veneration.

If, however, it shall happen, by an unfortunate course of affairs, that our applications to his Majesty and the parliament for the redress, prove ineffectual, let us then take another step, by withholding from Great-Britain all the advantages she has been used to receive from us. Then let us try, if our ingenuity, industry, and frugality, will not give weight to our remonstrances. Let us all be united with one spirit in one cause. Let us invent —let us work—let us save—let us, continually, keep up our claim, and incessantly repeat our complaints,—but, above all, let us implore the protection of that infinite good and gracious

Being, "by whom kings reign, and princes decree justice."

"*Nil desperandum.*"

Nothing is to be despaired of.

A FARMER.

XI. [*The Wisdom of Opposing Each Wrong Singly*]

My dear Countrymen,

I have several times, in the course of these letters, mentioned the late act of parliament, as being the foundation of future measures injurious to these colonies; and the belief of this truth I wish to prevail, because I think it necessary to our safety.

A perpetual jealousy, respecting liberty, is absolutely requisite in all free states. The very texture of their constitution, in mixt governments, demands it. For the cautions with which power is distributed among the several orders, imply, that each has that share which is proper for the general welfare, and therefore, that any further imposition must be pernicious. Machiavel[n] employs a whole chapter in his discourses, to prove that a state, to be long lived, must be frequently corrected, and reduced to its first principles. But of all states that have existed, there never was any, in which this jealousy could be more proper than in these colonies. For the government here is not only mixt, but dependent, which circumstance occasions a peculiarity in its form, of a very delicate nature.

Two reasons induce me to desire, that this spirit of apprehension may be always kept up among us, in its utmost vigilance. The first is this—that as the happiness of these provinces indubitably consists in their connection with Great Britain, any separation between them is less likely to be occasioned by civil discords, if every disgusting measure is opposed singly, and while it is new. For in this manner of proceeding, every such measure is most likely to be rectified. On the other hand, oppressions and dissatisfactions being permitted to accumulate—if ever the governed throw off the load, they will do more. A people does not reform with moderation. The rights of the subject therefore cannot be too often considered, explained, or asserted; and whoever attempts to do this, shews himself, whatever may be the rash and peevish

Cleons and Clodius's: Cleon was a popular firebrand of Athens, and Clodius of Rome. Each plunged his country into calamities.

Machiavel: Machiavelli's *Discourses*, Book 3, Chapter 1.

reflections of pretended wisdom, and pretended duty, a friend to those who injudiciously exercise their power, as well as to them, over whom it is so exercised.

Had all the points of prerogative claimed by Charles the First been separately contested and settled in preceding reigns, his fate would in all probability have been very different; and the people would have been content with that liberty which is compatible with regal authority. But [10] he thought, it would be as dangerous for him to give up the powers which at any time had been by usurpation exercised by the crown, as those that were legally vested in it. This produced an equal excess on the part of the people. For when their passions were excited by multiplied grievances, they thought it would be as dangerous for them, to allow the powers that were legally vested in the crown, as those which at any time had been by usurpation exercised by it. Acts, that might by [20] themselves have been upon many considerations excused or extenuated, derived a contagious malignancy and odium from other acts, with which they were connected. They were not regarded according to the simple force of each, but as parts of a system of oppression. Everyone therefore, however small in itself, being alarming, is an additional evidence of tyrannical designs. It was in vain for prudent and moderate men to insist, that there was no necessity to abolish royalty. Nothing [30] less than the utter destruction of monarchy, could satisfy those who had suffered, and thought they had reason to believe, they always should suffer under it.

The consequences of these mutual distrusts are well known: but there is no other people mentioned in history, that I recollect, who have been so constantly watchful of their liberty, and so successful in their struggles for it, as the English. This consideration leads me to the second reason, [40] why I "desire that the spirit of apprehension may be always kept up among us in its utmost vigilance."

The first principles of government are to be looked for in human nature. Some of the best writers have asserted, and it seems with good reason, that "government is founded on opinion."

Custom undoubtedly has a mighty force in pro-ducing opinion, and reigns in nothing more arbitrarily than in public affairs. It gradually reconciles us to objects even of dread and detestation; and I cannot but think these lines of Mr. Pope, as applicable to vice in politics, as to vice in ethics.

> Vice is a monster of so horrid mien,
> As to be hated, needs but to be seen;
> Yet seen too oft, familiar with her face,
> We first endure, then pity, then embrace.

When an act injurious to freedom has been once done, and the people bear it, the repetition of it is most likely to meet with submission. For as the mischief of the one was found to be tolerable, they will hope that of the second will prove so too; and they will not regard the infamy of the last, because they are stained with that of the first.

Indeed nations, in general, are not apt to think until they feel; and therefore nations in general have lost their liberty: for as violations of the rights of the governed are commonly not only specious, but small at the beginning, they spread over the multitude in such a manner, as to touch individuals but slightly. Thus they are disregarded. The power or profit that arises from these violations, centering in few persons, is to them considerable. For this reason the governors having in view their particular purposes, successively preserve an uniformity of conduct for attaining them. They regularly increase the first injuries, till at length the inattentive people are compelled to perceive the heaviness of their burdens.—They begin to complain and enquire—but too late.—They find their oppressors so strengthened by success, and themselves so entangled in examples of express authority on the part of their rulers, and of tacit recognition on their own part, that they are quite confounded: for millions entertain no other idea of the legality of power, than that it is founded on the exercise of power. They voluntarily fasten their chains, by adopting a pusillanimous opinion, "that there will be too much danger in attempting a remedy,"—or another opinion no less fatal— "that the government has a right to treat them as it does." They then seek a wretched relief for their minds, by persuading themselves, that to yield their obedience is to discharge their duty. The deplorable poverty of spirit, that prostrates all the dignity bestowed by divine providence on our nature—of course succeeds.

From these reflections I conclude, that every free state should incessantly watch, and instantly take alarm on any addition being made to the power exercised over them. Innumerable instances might be produced to shew, from what slight beginnings the most extensive consequences have flowed; but I shall select two only from the history of England.

Henry the Seventh was the first monarch of that kingdom, who established a standing body of armed men. This was a band of fifty archers, called yeomen of the guard: and this institution, notwithstanding the smallness of the number, was to prevent discontent, "disguised under pretence of majesty and grandeur." In 1684 the standing forces were so much augmented, that Rapin says— "The King, in order to make his people fully sensible of their new slavery, affected to muster his troops, which amounted to 4,000 well armed and disciplined men." I think our army, at this time, consists of more than seventy regiments.

The method of taxing by excise was first introduced amidst the convulsions of civil wars. Extreme necessity was pretended for it, and its short continuance promised. After the restoration, an excise upon beer, ale and other liquors, was granted to the King, one half in fee, the other for life, as an equivalent for the court of wards. Upon James the Second's accession, the parliament gave him the first excise, with an additional duty on wine, tobacco, and some other things. Since the revolution it has been extended to salt, candles, leather, hides, hops, soap, paper, paste-board, mill-boards, scale-boards, vellum, parchment, starch, silks, calicoes, linens, stuffs, printed, stained, &c., wire, wrought plate, coffee, tea, chocolate, &c.

Thus a standing army and excise have, from the first slender origins, though always hated, always feared, always opposed, at length swelled up to their vast present bulk.

These facts are sufficient to support what I have said. 'Tis true that all the mischiefs apprehended by our ancestors from a standing army and excise, have not yet happened: but it does not follow from thence, that they will not happen. The inside of a house may catch fire, and the most valu-

able apartments be ruined, before the flames burst out. The question in these cases is not, what evil has actually attended particular measures—but, what evil, in the nature of things, is likely to attend them. Certain circumstances may for some time delay affects, that were reasonably expected, and that must ensue. There was a long period, after the Romans had prorogued the command to Q. Publius Philo, before that example destroyed their liberty. All our kings, from the revolution to the present reign, have been foreigners. Their ministers generally continued but a short time in authority; and they themselves were mild and virtuous princes.

A bold, ambitious prince, possessed of great abilities, firmly fixed in the throne by descent, served by ministers like himself, and rendered either venerable or terrible by the glory of his successes, may execute what his predecessors did not dare to attempt. Henry the Fourth tottered in his seat during his whole reign. Henry the Fifth drew the strength of the kingdom into France, to carry on his wars there, and left the Commons at home, protesting "that the people were not bound to serve out of the realm."

It is true, that a strong spirit of liberty subsists at present in Great Britain, but what reliance is to be placed in the temper of a people, when the prince is possessed of an unconstitutional power, our own history can sufficiently inform us. When Charles the Second had strengthened himself by the return of the garrison of Tangier, "England (says Rapin) saw on a sudden an amazing revolution; saw herself stripped of all her rights and privileges, excepting such as the king should vouchsafe to grant her; and what is more astonishing, the English themselves delivered up these very rights and privileges to Charles the Second, which they had so passionately, and, if I may say it, furiously defended against the designs of Charles the First." This happened only thirty-six years after this last prince had been beheaded.

Some persons are of opinion, that liberty is not violated, but by such open acts of force; but they seem to be greatly mistaken. I could mention a period within these forty years, when almost as great a change of disposition was produced by the secret measures of a long administration, as by

Charles's violence. Liberty, perhaps, is never exposed to so much danger, as when the people believe there is the least; for it may be subverted, and yet they not think so.

Public disgusting acts are seldom practised by the ambitious, at the beginning of their designs. Such conduct silences and discourages the weak, and the wicked, who would otherways have been their advocates or accomplices. It is of great consequence, to allow those, who, upon any account, are inclined to favour them, something specious to say in their defence. Their power may be fully established, though it would not be safe for them to do whatever they please. For there are things, which, at some times, even slaves will not bear. Julius Caesar and Oliver Cromwell did not dare to assume the title of king. The grand Seignior dares not lay a new tax. The king of France dares not be a Protestant. Certain popular points may be left untouched, and yet freedom be extinguished. The commonality of Venice imagine themselves free, because they are permitted to do what they ought not. But I quit a subject that would lead me too far from my purpose.

By the late act of parliament, taxes are to be levied upon us, for "defraying the charge of the administration of justice, the support of civil government—and the expenses of defending his Majesty's dominions in America."

If any man doubts what ought to be the conduct of these colonies on this occasion, I would ask him these questions.

Has not the parliament expressly avowed their intention of raising money from us for certain purposes? Is not this scheme popular in Great Britain? Will the taxes, imposed by the late act, answer those purposes? If it will, must it not take an immense sum from us? If it will not, is it to be expected, that the parliament will not fully execute their intention, when it is pleasing at home, and not opposed here? Must not this be done by imposing new taxes? Will not every addition, thus made to our taxes, be an addition to the power of the British legislature, by increasing the number of officers employed in the collection? Will not every additional tax therefore render it more difficult to abrogate any of them? When a branch of revenue is once established, does it not appear to many people invidious and undutiful, to attempt to abolish it? If taxes, sufficient to accomplish the intention of the parliament, are imposed by the parliament, what taxes will remain to be imposed by our assemblies? If no material taxes remain to be imposed by them, what must become of them, and the people they represent?

"If any person considers these things, and yet thinks our liberties are in no danger, I wonder at that person's security." [Demosthenes.]

One other argument is to be added, which, by itself, I hope, will be sufficient to convince the most incredulous man on this continent, that the late act of parliament is only designed to be a precedent, whereupon the future vassalage of these colonies may be established.

Every duty thereby laid on articles of British manufacture, is laid on some commodity, upon the exportation of which, from Great Britain, a drawback is payable. Those drawbacks, in most of the articles, are exactly double to the duties given by the late act. The parliament therefore might, in half a dozen lines, have raised much more money only by stopping the drawbacks in the hands of the officers at home, on exportation to these colonies, than by this solemn imposition of taxes upon us, to be collected here. Probably, the artful contrivers of this act formed it in this manner, in order to reserve to themselves, in case of any objections being made to it, this specious pretence—"That the drawbacks are gifts to the colonies; and that the act only lessens those gifts." But the truth is, that the drawbacks are intended for the encouragement and promotion of British manufactures and commerce, and are allowed on exportation to any foreign parts, as well as on exportation to these provinces. Besides, care has been taken to slide into the act, some articles on which there are no drawbacks. However, the whole duties laid by the late act on all the articles therein specified, are so small, that they will not amount to as much as the drawbacks which are allowed on part of them only. If, therefore, the sum to be obtained by the late act, has been the sole object in forming it, there would not have been any occasion for the "Commons of Great Britain to give and grant to his Majesty, rates and duties for raising a revenue in his Majesty's dominions in

America, for making a more certain and adequate provision for defraying the charges of the administration of justice, the support of civil government, and the expenses of defending the said dominions."—Nor would there have been any occasion for an expensive board of commissioners, and all the other new charges to which we are made liable.

Upon the whole, for my part, I regard the late act as an experiment made of our disposition. It is a bird sent over the waters, to discover whether the waves, that lately agitated this part of the world with such violence, are yet subsided. If this adventurer gets footing here, we shall quickly find it to be of the breed described by the poet—

"Infelix vates."

A direful foreteller of future calamities.

A Farmer.

FRANCIS HOPKINSON (1737-1791)

LAWYER, JUDGE, author of political allegories, poet, musician, composer, signer of the Declaration of Independence, and designer of the American flag, Francis Hopkinson was one of the active literary figures of the Revolutionary period. His satirical allegory of British colonial policy preceding the War, *A Pretty Story, Written in the Year of Our Lord 1774*, by Peter Grievous, Esq., went through three editions during the same year. It is one of the few fine allegories incident to the Revolutionary War, and has become a minor classic. Lyrics in the manner of Dryden, songs, satirical verse, burlesques, allegories, public letters—all are to be found in his collected works. Much of his work was published in the Philadelphia magazines.

Hopkinson was born in Philadelphia. In 1757 he received the first diploma issued by the College of Philadelphia. He thereafter studied law, became Collector of Customs at Salem, New Jersey, in 1763, and sailed for England three years later in an unsuccessful attempt to receive political favor at the hands of Lord North, a relative by marriage. In 1768 he married Anne Borden, daughter of the leading citizen of Bordentown, New Jersey, and shortly afterward engaged in the practice of law in that city. In 1774 he was appointed a member of the Governor's Council, and in 1776 he was elected to the Continental Congress. He was chairman of the Navy Board (1776-1778), Treasurer of Loans (1778-1781), Judge of Admiralty for Pennsylvania (1779-1789), and finally Federal judge for the eastern district of Pennsylvania until his death. During most of his public life he was a fairly regular contributor to magazines and newspapers.

BIBLIOGRAPHY · Before his death Hopkinson had collected nearly all his literary work in manuscript volumes which were published posthumously: *The Miscellaneous Essays and Occasional Writings of Francis Hopkinson, Esq.* (1792). The indispensable biography is G. E. Hastings, *The Life and Works of Francis Hopkinson* (1926).

See also O. G. T. Sonnek, *Francis Hopkinson, the First American Music-Composer* (1905, 1919). Among special studies are C. F. Arrowood, "Educational Themes in the Writings of Francis Hopkinson," *Peabody Journal of Education*, VI (1928), 145-160; G. E. Hastings, "Francis Hopkinson and the American Flag," *General Magazine and Historical Chronicle*, XLII (1939), 46-63; "Francis Hopkinson and the Flag," *Americana*, XXXIII (1939), 1-23; and "John Bull and His American Descendants," *American Literature*, I (1929), 40-68; L. Leary, "Francis Hopkinson, Jonathan Odell, and 'The Temple of Cloacina,'" *American Literature*, XV (1943), 183-191; and D. Wecter, "Francis Hopkinson and Benjamin Franklin," *American Literature*, XII (1940), 200-217.

A Pretty Story

THE TEXT is that of B. J. Lossing, who reproduced the original with a new title, *The Old Farm and the New Farm* (1857).

CHAPTER I

Once upon a Time, a great While ago, there lived a certain Nobleman,[n] who had long possessed a very valuable Farm,[n] and had a great Number of Children and Grandchildren.[n]

Besides the annual Profits of his Land, which were very considerable, he kept a large Shop of Goods; and being very successful in Trade, he became, in Process of Time, exceedingly rich and powerful; insomuch that all his Neighbours feared and respected him.

With Respect to the Management of his Family, it was thought he had adopted the most perfect Mode that could be devised; for he had been at the

Nobleman: King of Great Britain.   **Farm:** Britain.
Children and Grandchildren: subjects of the king.

Pains to examine the Œconomy of all his Neighbours, and had selected from their Plans all such Parts as appeared to be equitable and beneficial, and omitted those which from Experience were found to be inconvenient. Or rather, by blending their several Constitutions together he had so ingeniously counterbalanced the Evils of one Mode of Government with the Benefits of another, that the Advantages were richly enjoyed, and the Inconveniencies scarcely felt. In short, his Family was thought to be the best ordered of any in his Neighbourhood.

He never exercised any undue Authority over his Children or Servants; neither indeed could he oppress them if he was so disposed; for it was particularly covenanted in his Marriage Articles that he should not at any Time impose any Tasks or Hardships whatever upon his Children without the free Consent of his Wife.[n]

Now the Custom in his Family was this, that at the End of every seven Years his Marriage became of Course null and void; at which Time his Children and Grandchildren met together and chose another Wife for him, whom the old Gentleman was obliged to marry under the same Articles and Restrictions as before. If his late Wife had conducted herself, during her seven Year's Marriage, with Mildness, Discretion and Integrity, she was re-elected; if otherwise, deposed: By which Means the Children had always a great Interest in their Mother in Law; and through her, a reasonable Check upon their Father's Temper. For besides that he could do nothing material respecting his Children without her Approbation, she was sole Mistress of the Purse Strings; and gave him out, from Time to Time, such Sums of Money as she thought necessary for the Expences of his Family.

Being one Day in a very extraordinary good Humour, he gave his Children a Writing under his Hand and Seal, by which he released them from many Badges of Dependence, and confirmed to them several very important Privileges. The chief were the two following, viz. that none of his Children should be punished for any Offence, or supposed Offence, until his brethren had first declared him worthy of such Punishment; and

secondly, he gave fresh Assurances that he would impose no Hardships upon them without the Consent of their Mother in Law.

This Writing, on account of its singular Importance, was called The Great Paper.[n] After it was executed with the utmost solemnity, he caused his Chaplain to publish a dire *Anathema* against all who should attempt to violate the Articles of the *Great Paper*, in the Words following.

"In the Name of the Father, Son and Holy Ghost, Amen! Whereas our Lord and Master, to the Honour of God and for the common Profit of this Farm hath granted, for him and his Heirs forever, these Articles above written: I, his Chaplain and spiritual Pastor of all this Farm, do admonish the People of the Farm Once, Twice, and Thrice: Because that Shortness will not suffer so much Delay as to give Knowledge to the People of these Presents in Writing; I therefore enjoyn all Persons, of what Estate soever they be, that they and every of them, as much as in them is, shall uphold and maintain these Articles granted by our Lord and Master in all Points. And all those that in any Point do resist, or break, or in any Manner hereafter procure, counsel or any Ways assent to resist or break these Ordinances, or go about it by Word or Deed, openly or privately, by any Manner of Pretence or Colour: I the aforesaid Chaplain, by my Authority, do excommunicate and accurse, and from the Body of our Lord Jesus Christ, and from all the Company of Heaven, and from all the Sacraments of holy Church do sequester and exclude."

CHAPTER II

Now it came to pass that this Nobleman had, by some Means or other, obtained a Right to an immense Tract of wild uncultivated Country[n] at a vast Distance from his Mansion House. But he set little Store by this Acquisition, as it yielded him no Profit; nor was it likely to do so, being not only difficult of Access on Account of the Distance, but was also overrun with innumerable wild Beasts[n] very fierce and savage; so that it would be extremely dangerous to attempt taking Possession of it.

Wife: British Parliament.

The Great Paper: Magna Charta. **Country:** British lands in America. **Beasts:** Indians.

In Process of Time, however, some of his Children,[n] more stout and enterprising than the rest, requested Leave of their Father to go and settle on this distant Tract of Land. Leave was readily obtained; but before they set out certain Agreements were stipulated between them—the principal were—The old Gentleman, on his Part, engaged to protect and defend the Adventurers in their new Settlements; to assist them in chasing away the wild Beasts, and to extend to them all the Benefits of the Government under which they were born: Assuring them that although they should be removed so far from his Presence they should nevertheless be considered as the Children of his Family, and treated accordingly. At the same Time he gave each of them a Bond for the faithful performance of these Promises; in which, among other Things, it was covenanted that they should, each of them in their several Families, have a Liberty of making such Rules and Regulations for their own good Government as they should find convenient; provided these Rules and Regulations should not contradict or be inconsistent with the general standing Orders established in his Farm.

In Return for these Favours he insisted that they, on their Parts, should at all Times acknowledge him to be their Father; that they should not deal with their Neighbours without his Leave, but send to his Shop only for such Merchandize as they should want. But in Order to enable them to pay for such Goods as they should purchase, they were permitted to sell the Produce of their Lands to certain of his Neighbours.

These Preliminaries being duly adjusted, our Adventurers bid Adieu to the Comforts and Conveniences of their Father's House, and set off on their Journey—Many and great were the Difficulties they encountered on their Way: but many more and much greater had they to combat on their Arrival in the new Country. Here they found Nothing but wild Nature. Mountains overgrown with inaccessible Foliage, and Plains steeped in stagnated Waters. Their Ears are no longer attentive to the repeated Strokes of industrious Labour and the busy Hum of Men; instead of these, the roaring Tempest and incessant Howlings

Children: colonists.

of Beasts of Prey fill their minds with Horror and Dismay. The needful Comforts of Life are no longer in their Power—no friendly Roof to shelter them from inclement Skies; no Fortress to protect them from surrounding Dangers. Unaccustomed as they were to Hardships like these, some were cut off by Sickness and Disease, and others snatched away by the Hands of Barbarity. They began however, with great Perseverance, to clear the Land of encumbering Rubbish, and the Woods resound with the Strokes of Labour; they drain the Waters from the sedged Morass, and pour the Sun Beams on the reeking Soil; they are forced to exercise all the powers of Industry and Œconomy for bare Subsistence, and like their first Parent, when driven from Paradise, to earn their Bread with the Sweat of their Brows. In this Work they were frequently interrupted by the Incursions of the wild Beasts, against whom they defended themselves with heroic Prowess and Magnanimity.

After some Time, however, by Dint of indefatigable Perseverance, they found themselves comfortably settled in this new Farm; and had the delightful Prospect of vast Tracts of Land waving with luxuriant Harvests, and perfuming the Air with delicious Fruits, which before had been a dreary Wilderness, unfit for the Habitation of Men.

In the mean Time they kept up a constant Correspondence with their Father's Family, and at a great Expence provided Waggons, Horses and Drivers to bring from his Shop such Goods and Merchandize as they wanted, for which they paid out of the Produce of their Lands.

Chapter III

Now the new Settlers had adopted a Mode of Government in their several Families similar to that their Father had established in the old Farm; in taking a new Wife at the End of certain Periods of Time; which Wife was chosen for them by their Children, and without whose Consent they could do nothing material in the Conduct of their Affairs. Under these Circumstances they thrived exceedingly, and became very numerous; living in great Harmony amongst themselves, and in constitutional Obedience to their Father and his Wife.

Notwithstanding their successful Progress, however, they were frequently annoyed by the wild

211

Beasts, which were not yet expelled the Country; and were moreover troubled by some of their Neighbours, who wanted to drive them off the Land, and take Possession of it themselves.

To assist them in these Difficulties, and protect them from Danger, the old Nobleman sent over several of his Servants,[n] who with the Help of the new Settlers drove away their Enemies. But then he required that they should reimburse him for the Expence and Trouble he was at in their Behalf; this they did with great Cheerfulness, by applying from Time to Time to their respective Wives, who always commanded their Cash.

Thus did Matters go on for a considerable Time, to their mutual Happiness and Benefit. But now the Nobleman's Wife began to cast an avaricious Eye upon the new Settlers; saying to herself, if by the natural Consequence of their Intercourse with us my Wealth and Power are so much increased, how much more would they accumulate if I can persuade them that all they have belonged to us, and therefore I may at any Time demand from them such Part of their Earnings as I please. At the same Time she was fully sensible of the Promises and agreements her Husband had made when they left the old Farm, and of the Tenor and Purport of the Great Paper. She therefore thought it necessary to proceed with great Caution and Art, and endeavoured to gain her Point by imperceptible Steps.

In Order to [do] this, she first issued an Edict setting forth, That whereas the Tailors of her Family were greatly injured by the People of the new Farm, inasmuch as they presumed to make their own Clothes whereby the said Tailors were deprived of the Benefit of their Custom; it was therefore ordained that for the future the new Settlers should not be permitted to have amongst them any Shears or Scissars larger than a certain fixed size. In Consequence of this, our Adventurers were compelled to have their Clothes made by their Father's Tailors: But out of Regard to the old Gentleman, they patiently submitted to this Grievance.

Encouraged by this Success, she proceeded in her Plan. Observing that the new Settlers were very fond of a particular Kind of Cyder[n] which they purchased of a Neighbour, who was in Friend-

ship with their Father (the Apples proper for making this Cyder not growing on their own Farm) she published another Edict, obliging them to pay her a certain Stipend for every Barrel of Cyder used in their Families! To this likewise they submitted: Not yet seeing the Scope of her Designs against them.

After this Manner she proceeded, imposing Taxes upon them on various Pretences, and receiving the Fruits of their Industry with both Hands. Moreover, she persuaded her Husband to send amongst them from Time to Time a Number of the most lazy and useless of his Servants, under the specious Pretext of defending them in their Settlements, and of assisting to destroy the wild Beasts; but in Fact to rid his own House of their Company, not having Employment for them; and at the same Time to be a Watch and a Check upon the People of the new Farm.

It was likewise ordered that these Protectors, as they were called, should be supplied with Bread and Butter cut in a particular Form: But the Head of one of the Families refused to comply with this Order. He engaged to give the Guests thus forced upon him, Bread and Butter sufficient; but insisted that his Wife should have the liberty of cutting it in what shape she pleased.[n]

This put the old Nobleman into a violent Passion, insomuch that he had his Son's Wife put into Gaol for presuming to cut her Loaf otherwise than as had been directed.

CHAPTER IV

As the old Gentleman advanced in Years he began to neglect the Affairs of his Family, leaving them chiefly to the Management of his Steward.[n] Now the Steward had debauched his Wife, and by that Means gained an entire Ascendency over her. She no longer deliberated what would most benefit either the old Farm or the new; but said and did whatever the Steward pleased. Nay so much was she influenced by him that she could neither utter Ay or No but as he directed. For he had cunningly persuaded her that it was very fashionable for Women to wear Padlocks on their Lips, and that he

Servants: British troops. **Kind of Cyder:** rum.

shape she pleased: The Mutiny Act required colonists to quarter British troops. The Assembly of New York refused to comply in some respects. **Steward:** prime minister.

was sure they would become her exceedingly. He therefore fastened a Padlock to each Corner of her Mouth; when the one was open, she could only say Ay; and when the other was loosed, could only cry No. He took Care to keep the Keys of these Locks himself; so that her Will became entirely subject to his Power.

Now the old Lady and the Steward had set themselves against the People of the new Farm; and began to devise Ways and Means to impoverish and distress them.

They prevailed on the Nobleman to sign an Edict against the new Settlers, in which it was declared that it was their Duty as Children to pay something towards the supplying their Father's Table with Provisions, and to the supporting the Dignity of his Family; for that Purpose it was ordained that all their Spoons, Knives and Forks, Plates and Porringers, should be marked with a certain Mark;[n] by Officers appointed for that End; for which marking they were to pay a certain Stipend: And that they should not, under severe Penalties, presume to make use of any Spoon, Knife or Fork, Plate or Porringer, before it had been so marked, and the said Stipend paid to the Officer.

The Inhabitants of the new Farm began to see that their Father's Affections were alienated from them; and that their Mother was but a base Mother in Law debauched by their Enemy the Steward. They were thrown into great Confusion and Distress. They wrote the most supplicating Letters to the old Gentleman, in which they acknowledged him to be their Father in Terms of the greatest Respect and Affection—they recounted to him the Hardships and Difficulties they had suffered in settling his new Farm; and pointed out the great Addition of Wealth and Power his Family had acquired by the Improvement of that Wilderness; and showed him that all the Fruits of their Labours must in the natural Course of Things unite, in the long Run, in his Money Box. They also, in humble Terms, reminded him of his Promises and Engagements on their leaving Home, and of the Bonds he had given them; of the Solemnity and Importance of the Great Paper with the Curse annexed. They acknowledged that he ought to

Mark: Stamp tax.

be reimbursed the Expences he was at on their Account, and that it was their Duty to assist in supporting the Dignity of his Family. All this they declared they were ready and willing to do; but requested that they might do it agreeable to the Purport of the Great Paper, by applying to their several Wives for the Keys of their Money Boxes and furnishing him from thence; and not be subject to the Tyranny and Caprice of an avaricious Mother in Law, whom they had never chosen, and of a Steward who was their declared Enemy.

Some of these Letters were intercepted by the Steward; others were delivered to the old Gentleman, who was at the same Time persuaded to take no Notice of them; but, on the Contrary, to insist the more strenuously upon the Right his Wife claimed of marking their Spoons, Knives and Forks, Plates and Porringers.

The new Settlers, observing how Matters were conducted in their Father's Family became exceedingly distressed and mortified. They met together and agreed one and all that they would no longer submit to the arbitrary Impositions of their Mother in Law, and their Enemy the Steward. They determined to pay no Manner of Regard to the new Decree, considering it as a Violation of the Great Paper. But to go on and eat their Broth and Pudding as usual. The Cooks also and Butlers served up their Spoons, Knives and Forks, Plates and Porringers, without having them marked by the new Officers.

The Nobleman at length thought fit to reverse the Order which had been made respecting the Spoons, Knives and Forks, Plates and Porringers of the new Settlers. But he did this with a very ill Grace: For he, at the same Time avowed and declared that he and his Wife had a Right to mark all their Furniture, if they pleased, from the Silver Tankard down to the very Chamber Pots: That as he was their Father he had an absolute Controul over them, and that their Liberties, Lives and Properties were at the entire Disposal of him and his Wife:[n] That it was not fit that he who was allowed to be Omnipresent, Immortal, and incapable of Error, should be confined by the

Liberties . . . Wife: The Declaratory Act held that Parliament had power to "bind the colonies in all cases."

213

Shackles of the Great Paper; or obliged to fulfil the Bonds he had given them, which he averred he had a Right to cancel whenever he pleased.

His Wife also became intoxicated with Vanity. The Steward had told her that she was an omnipotent Goddess, and ought to be worshipped as such: That it was the Height of Impudence and Disobedience in the new Settlers to dispute her Authority, which, with Respect to them, was unlimited: That as they had removed from their Father's Family, they had forfeited all Pretensions to be considered as his Children, and lost the Privileges of the Great Paper: That, therefore, she might look on them only as Tenants at Will upon her Husband's Farm, and exact from them what Rent she pleased.

All this was perfectly agreeable to Madam, who admitted this new Doctrine in its full Sense.

The People of the new Farm however took little Notice of these pompous Declarations. They were glad the marking Decree was reversed, and were in Hopes that Things would gradually settle into their former Channel.

Chapter V

In the mean Time the new Settlers increased exceedingly, and as they increased, their Dealings at their Father's Shop were proportionably enlarged.

. It is true they suffered some Inconveniencies from the Protectors that had been sent amongst them, who became very troublesome in their Houses: They seduced their Daughters; introduced Riot and Intemperance into their Families, and derided and insulted the Orders and Regulations they had made for their own good Government. Moreover the old Nobleman had sent amongst them a great Number of Thieves, Ravishers and Murderers, who did a great deal of Mischief by practising those Crimes for which they had been banished the old Farm. But they bore these Grievances with as much Patience as could be expected; not choosing to trouble their aged Father with Complaints, unless in Cases of important Necessity.

Now the Steward continued to hate the new Settlers with exceeding great Hatred, and determined to renew his Attack upon their Peace and Happiness. He artfully insinuated to the old Gentleman and his foolish Wife, that it was very mean and unbecoming in them to receive the Contributions of the People of the new Farm, towards supporting the Dignity of his Family, through the Hands of their respective Wives: That upon this Footing it would be in their Power to refuse his Requisitions whenever they should be thought to be unreasonable, of which they would pretend to be Judges themselves; and that it was high Time they should be compelled to acknowledge his arbitrary Power, and his Wife's Omnipotence.

For this Purpose, another Decree was prepared and published, ordering that the new Settlers should pay a certain Stipend upon particular Goods, which they were not allowed to purchase any where but at their Father's Shop; and that this Stipend should not be deemed an Advance upon the original Price of the Goods, but be paid on their arrival at the new Farm, for the express Purpose of supporting the Dignity of the old Gentleman's Family, and of defraying the Expences he affected to afford them.

This new Decree gave our Adventurers the utmost Uneasiness. They saw that the Steward and their Mother in Law were determined to oppress and enslave them. They again met together and wrote to their Father, as before, the most humble and persuasive Letters; but to little Purpose: A deaf Ear was turned to all their Remonstrances; and their dutiful Requests treated with Contempt.

Finding this moderate and decent Conduct brought them no Relief, they had Recourse to another Expedient. They bound themselves in a solemn Engagement not to deal any more at their Father's Shop until this unconstitutional Decree should be reversed; which they declared to be a Violation of the Great Paper.

This Agreement was so strictly adhered to, that in a few Months the Clerks and Apprentices in the old Gentleman's Shop began to make a sad Outcry. They declared that their Master's Trade was declining exceedingly, and that his Wife and Steward would, by their mischievous Machinations, ruin the whole Farm: They forthwith sharpened their Pens and attacked the Steward, and even the old Lady herself with great Severity. Insomuch that it was thought proper to withdraw this Attempt likewise upon the Rights and Liberties of the new Settlers. One Part only of the new Decree remained unreversed—viz. the Tax upon Water Gruel.[n]

Now there were certain Men on the old Farm, who had obtained from the Nobleman an exclusive Right of selling Water Gruel. Vast Quantities of this Gruel were vended amongst the new Settlers; for it became very fashionable for them to use it in their Families in great Abundance. They did not however trouble themselves much about the Tax on Water Gruel: They were well pleased with the Reversal of the other Parts of the Decree, and considering Gruel as not absolutely necessary to the Comfort of Life, they were determined to endeavour to do without it, and by that Means avoid the remaining effects of the new Decree.

The Steward found his Designs once more frustrated; but was not discouraged by this Disappointment. He formed another Scheme so artfully contrived that he thought himself sure of Success. He sent for the Persons who had the sole Right of vending Water Gruel, and after reminding them of the Obligations they were under to the Nobleman and his Wife for their exclusive Privilege, he desired that they would send sundry Waggon Loads of Gruel to the new Farm, promising that the accustomed Duty which they paid for their exclusive Right should be taken off from all the Gruel they should send amongst the new Settlers: And that in Case their Cargoes should come to any Damage, he would take Care that the Loss should be repaired out of the old Gentleman's Coffers.

The Gruel Merchants[n] readily consented to this Proposal, knowing that if their Cargoes were sold, they would reap considerable Profits; and if they failed, the Steward was to make good the Damage. On the other hand the Steward concluded that the new Settlers could not resist purchasing the Gruel to which they had been so long accustomed; and if they did purchase it when subject to the Tax aforesaid, this would be an avowed Acknowledgment on their Parts that their Father and his Wife had a Right to break through the Tenor of the Great Paper, and to lay on them what Impositions they pleased, without the Consent of their respective Wives.

But the new Settlers were well aware of this Decoy. They saw clearly that the Gruel was not sent to accommodate, but to enslave them; and that if they suffered any Part of it to be sold amongst them, it would be deemed a Submission to the assumed Omnipotence of the Great Madam.

Chapter VI

On the Arrival of the Water Gruel, the People of the new Farm were again thrown into great Alarms and Confusions. Some of them would not suffer the Waggons to be unloaded at all, but sent them immediately back to the Gruel Merchants: Others permitted the Waggons to unload, but would not touch the hateful Commodity; so that it lay neglected about their Roads and Highways until it grew sour and spoiled. But one of the new Settlers, whose Name was Jack[n], either from a keener Sense of the Injuries attempted against him, or from the Necessity of his Situation, which was such that he could not send back the Gruel because of a Number of Mercenaries whom his Father had stationed before his House to watch and be a Check upon his Conduct: He, I say, being almost driven to Despair, fell to Work, and with great Zeal stove to Pieces the Casks of Gruel, which had been sent him, and utterly demolished the whole Cargoe.[n]

These Proceedings were soon known at the old Farm. Great and terrible was the Uproar there. The old Gentleman fell into great Wrath, declaring that his absent Children meant to throw off all Dependence upon him, and to become altogether disobedient. His Wife also tore the Padlocks from her Lips, and raved and stormed like a Billingsgate. The Steward lost all Patience and Moderation, swearing most prophanely that he would leave no Stone unturned 'till he had humbled the Settlers of the new Farm at his feet, and caused their Father to trample on their necks. Moreover the Gruel Merchants roared and bellowed for the Loss of their Gruel; and the Clerks and Apprentices were in the utmost Consternation lest the People of the new Farm should again

Water Gruel: tea.   **Gruel Merchants:** British East India Company.

Jack: Massachusetts.   **Cargoe:** Boston Tea Party, December 16, 1773.

agree to have no Dealings with their Father's Shop—Vengeance was immediately set on Foot, particularly against Jack. With him they determined to begin; hoping that by making an Example of him they should so terrify the other Families of the new Settlers, that they would all submit to the Designs of the Steward, and the Omnipotence of the old Lady.

A very large Padlock[n] was, accordingly, prepared to be fastened upon Jack's great gate; the Key of which was to be given to the old Gentleman; who was not to open it again until he had paid for the Gruel he had spilt, and resigned all Claim to the Privileges of the Great Paper: Nor then neither unless he thought fit. Secondly, a Decree was made to new model the Regulations and Œconomy of Jack's Family in such Manner that they might for the Future be more subject to the Will of the Steward. And, thirdly, a large Gallows was erected before the Mansion House in the old Farm, and an Order made that if any of Jack's Children or Servants should be suspected of Misbehaviour, they should not be convicted or acquitted by the Consent of their Brethren, agreeable to the Purport of the Great Paper, but be tied Neck and Heels and dragged to the Gallows at the Mansion House and there be hanged without Mercy.[n]

No sooner did tidings of this undue Severity reach the new Farm, but the People were almost ready to despair. They were altogether at a Loss how to act, or by what Means they should avert the Vengeance to which they were doomed: But the old Lady and Steward soon determined the Matter; for the Padlock was sent over, and without Ceremony fastened upon Jack's great Gate. They did not wait to know whether he would pay for the Gruel or not, or make the required Acknowledgments; nor give him the least Opportunity to make his Defence—The great Gate was locked, and the Key given to the old Nobleman, as had been determined.

Poor Jack found himself in a most deplorable Condition. The great Inlet to his Farm was entirely blocked up, so that he could neither carry out the Produce of his Land for Sale, nor receive from abroad the Necessaries for his Family.

But this was not all—His Father, along with the Padlock aforesaid, had sent an Overseer[n] to hector and domineer over him and his Family; and to endeavour to break his Spirit by exercising every possible Severity: For which Purpose he was attended by a great number of Mercenaries, and armed with more than common Authorities.

On his first arrival in Jack's Family he was received with considerable Respect, because he was the Delegate of their aged Father: For, notwithstanding all that had past, the People of the new Settlements loved and revered the old Gentleman with a truly filial Attachment; attributing his unkindness entirely to the Intrigues of their Enemy the Steward. But this fair Weather did not last long. The new Overseer took the first Opportunity of showing that he had no Intentions of living in Harmony and Friendship with the Family. Some of Jack's Domesticks had put on their Sunday Clothes, and attended the Overseer in the great Parlour, in Order to pay him their Compliments on his Arrival, and to request his Assistance in reconciling them to their Father: But he rudely stopped them short, in the Midst of their Speech; called them a Parcel of disobedient Scoundrels, and bid them go about their Business. So saying, he turned upon his Heel, and with great Contempt left the Room.

CHAPTER VII

Now Jack and his Family finding themselves oppressed, insulted and tyrannised over in the most cruel and arbitrary Manner, advised with their Brethren what Measures should be adopted to relieve them from their intolerable Grievances. Their Brethren, one and all, united in sympathising with their Afflictions; they advised them to bear their Sufferings with Fortitude for a Time, assuring them that they looked on the Punishments and Insults laid upon them with the same Indignation as if they had been inflicted on themselves, and that they would stand by and support them to the last. But, above all, earnestly recommended it to them to be firm and steady in the Cause of Liberty and Justice, and never acknowledge the Omnipo-

Padlock: bill to close the port of Boston, passed March 7, 1774. ... **without Mercy:** bill to conduct colonists charged with murder or treason to England for trial.

Overseer: General Gage.

tence of their Mother in Law; nor yield to the Machinations of their Enemy the Steward.

In the mean Time, lest Jack's Family should suffer for Want of Necessaries, their great Gate being fast locked, liberal and very generous Contributions were raised among the several Families of the new Settlements, for their present Relief. This seasonable Bounty was handed to Jack over the Garden Wall—All Access to the Front of his House being shut up. 10

Now the Overseer observed that the Children and Domesticks of Jack's Family had frequent Meetings and Consultations together: Sometimes in the Garret, and sometimes in the Stable: Understanding, likewise, that an Agreement not to deal in their Father's Shop, until their Grievances should be redressed, was much talked of amongst them, he wrote a thundering Prohibition, much like a Pope's Bull, which he caused to be pasted up in every Room in the House: In which he 20 declared and protested that these Meetings were treasonable, traiterous and rebellious; contrary to the Dignity of their Father, and inconsistent with the Omnipotence of their Mother in Law: Denouncing also terrible Punishments against any two of the Family who should from thenceforth be seen whispering together, and strictly forbidding the Domesticks to hold any more Meetings in the Garret or Stable.

These harsh and unconstitutional Proceedings 30 irritated Jack and the other inhabitants of the new Farm to such a Degree that . . .

Cætera desunt.[n]

Ode

[*For July 4, 1788*]

WRITTEN for the Grand Federal Procession in Philadelphia, on which occasion Hopkinson estimated 17,000 persons had assembled on Union Green, and about 5000 were in the line of floats, representing many organizations and trades. Hopkinson's poem was struck off a press mounted on the printer's float, and copies

Cætera desunt: the rest is lacking.

were tossed to the multitude. Ten states had recently adopted the Constitution, and a full account of the celebration appears in *The American Museum* for July, 1788, which text is used here.

Oh for a muse of fire! to mount the skies,
And to a list'ning world proclaim—
　　Behold! behold! an empire rise!
　　An era new, Time as he flies,
Hath enter'd in the book of Fame. 5
　　On Alleghany's tow'ring head
　　Echo shall stand—the tidings spread,
And o'er the lakes, and misty floods around,
An era new resound.

　　See! where Columbia sits alone, 10
　　And from her star-bespangled throne,
Beholds the gay procession move along,
And hears the trumpet, and the choral song—
　　She hears her sons rejoice—
　　Looks into future times, and sees 15
　　The num'rous blessings heav'n decrees,
And with HER plaudit, joins the gen'ral voice.

　　" 'Tis done! 'tis done! my sons," she cries,
　　"In war are valiant, and in council wise;
"Wisdom and valour shall my rights defend, 20
"And o'er my vast domain those rights extend;
"Science shall flourish—genius stretch her wing,
"In native strains Columbian muses sing;
"Wealth crown the arts, and justice clean her scales,
"Commerce her pond'rous anchor weigh, 25
　　"Wide spread her sails,
"And in far distant seas her flag display.

"My sons for freedom fought, nor fought in vain;
"But found a naked goddess was their gain:
"Good government alone can shew the maid, 30
"In robes, social happiness array'd."

　　Hail to this festival! all hail the day!
　　Columbia's standard on her roof display;
And let the people's motto ever be,
"United thus, and thus united, free." 35

217

PATRICK HENRY (1736-1799)

PATRICK HENRY bequeathed two fiery sentences to the American Scripture: "Caesar had his Brutus; Charles the First, his Cromwell; and George the Third—may profit by their example," and "I know not what course others may take; but as for me, give me liberty or give me death!" Upon the wings of these words, Henry has become a forensic folk hero in the popular imagination, but few Americans have read the speeches in which these emotional climaxes appear, or know much about the orator's contribution to the struggle for independence.

The frontier environment of Hanover County, Virginia, in which Patrick Henry was born in 1736, helps to account for his early sympathy with the democratic interests of the small farmers. He was also influenced by his reading of the Latin classics and by the eloquence of Samuel Davies, the great Virginia preacher, who settled in Hanover County in 1747. Henry turned to law after failing as a merchant and farmer, and was licensed to practice in 1760. Although he was better versed in the intricacies of human nature than in "Coke upon Littleton," he was conspicuously successful in handling 1,185 lawsuits in the first few years of his practice. His early career as a lawyer was crowned with popular success in 1763 when he challenged the right of the Crown to interfere with the provisions made by the Assembly to pay the clergy of the Established Church. After his election to the House of Burgesses in 1765, Henry represented the frontier region against the old tidewater aristocracy. During the Stamp Act agitation he introduced his "Virginia Resolves" in support of legislative independence, and urged the passage of his resolutions with his famous "Caesar had his Brutus" speech. His other celebrated utterance, "Give me liberty or give me death," he made in Richmond in March, 1775, in pleading for an act to put Virginia "into a posture of defense" against the British. Patrick Henry's public service included five terms as Governor of Virginia and participation in the first and second Continental Congresses, in which he proposed a declaration of independence; he later was an important factor in the adoption of the first ten amendments to the Federal Constitution. In 1795 President Washington offered Henry the appointment of Secretary of State, and in 1796, the position of Chief Justice, but both offers were declined. Failing health compelled his retirement to his plantation on the Staunton River, where he died on June 6, 1799.

BIBLIOGRAPHY · The text of Patrick Henry's great speeches is based upon the notes and impressions of William Wirt, who recreated the addresses after conversations with men who were present on the occasions, and upon the records of the House of Burgesses and minutes of the Virginia conventions. The first important biography is W. Wirt, *Sketches of the Life and Character of Patrick Henry* (1817). More fully documented biographies are M. C. Tyler, *Patrick Henry* (1887), in the American Statesmen Series, and W. W. Henry, *Patrick Henry: Life, Correspondence, and Speeches* (3 vols., 1891). Other important material is contained in J. Elliott, *The Debates, Resolutions, and Other Proceedings, in Convention, on the Adoption of the Federal Constitution*, II (1828); H. B. Grigsby, *The Virginia Convention of 1776* (1855); and W. E. Dodd, "Virginia Takes the Road to Revolution," in *The Spirit of '76* (1927), by C. Becker, J. M. Clark, and W. E. Dodd.

Speech in the Virginia Convention of Delegates

March 23, 1775

WHEN THE Virginia Convention of Delegates met in Richmond on March 20, 1775, the country was in an excited state of alarm. In January the assembly and provincial convention of Connecticut and Pennsylvania had ordered a muster of the militia; and in February the provincial congress of Massachusetts had urged speedy military preparations in defense of American liberty. On March 23 Patrick Henry spoke in support of his resolution that "this colony be immediately put into a posture of defense." No copy of the speech which contains Henry's most famous peroration is extant, and it is unlikely that the speech was ever written out. The text here reprinted is based upon the report published in William Wirt's life of Patrick Henry in 1817. Although Wirt had never seen Henry, he had conversations with men who were present at the convention. Moses Coit Tyler, Henry's most careful biographer, declared, "It is probably far more accurate and authentic than are most of the famous speeches attributed to public characters . . . before the art of reporting was brought to its present perfection."

No man thinks more highly than I do of the patriotism, as well as abilities, of the very worthy gentlemen who have just addressed the house. But different men often see the same subjects in different lights; and, therefore, I hope it will not be thought disrespectful to those gentlemen, if, entertaining as I do, opinions of a character very opposite to theirs, I shall speak forth my sentiments freely, and without reserve. This is no time for ceremony. The question before the house is one of awful moment to this country. For my own part, I consider it as nothing less than a question of freedom or slavery. And in proportion to the magnitude of the subject, ought to be the freedom of the debate. It is only in this way that we can hope to arrive at truth, and fulfil the great responsibility which we hold to God and our country. Should I keep back my opinions at such a time, through fear of giving offence, I should consider myself as guilty of treason towards my country, and of an act of disloyalty toward the majesty of Heaven, which I revere above all earthly kings.

Mr. President, it is natural to man to indulge in the illusions of hope. We are apt to shut our eyes against a painful truth and listen to the song of that syren, till she transforms us into beasts. Is this the part of wise men, engaged in a great and arduous struggle for liberty? Are we disposed to be of the number of those, who having eyes, see not, and having ears, hear not, the things which so nearly concern their temporal salvation? For my part, whatever anguish of spirit it may cost, I am willing to know the whole truth; to know the worst, and to provide for it.

I have but one lamp by which my feet are guided; and that is the lamp of experience. I know of no way of judging of the future but by the past. And judging by the past, I wish to know what there has been in the conduct of the British ministry for the last ten years, to justify those hopes with which gentlemen have been pleased to solace themselves and the house? Is it that insidious smile with which our petition has been lately received? Trust it not, sir; it will prove a snare to your feet. Suffer not yourselves to be betrayed with a kiss. Ask yourselves how this gracious reception of our petition comports with those warlike preparations which cover our waters and darken our land. Are fleets and armies necessary to a work of love and reconciliation? Have we shown ourselves so unwilling to be reconciled, that force must be called in to win back our love? Let us not deceive ourselves, sir. These are the implements of war and subjugation, the last arguments to which kings resort.

I ask gentlemen, sir, what means this martial array, if its purpose be not to force us to submission? Can gentlemen assign any other possible motive for it? Has Great Britain any enemy in this quarter of the world, to call for all this accumulation of navies and armies? No, sir, she has none. They are meant for us; they can be meant for no other. They are sent over to bind and rivet upon us those chains, which the British ministry have been so long forging. And what have we to oppose to them? Shall we try argument? Sir, we have been trying that for the last ten years. Have we any thing new to offer upon the subject? Nothing. We have held the subject up in every light of which it is capable; but it has been all in vain. Shall we resort to entreaty and humble supplication? What terms shall we find, which have not been already exhausted? Let us not, I beseech you, sir, deceive ourselves longer. Sir, we have done every thing that could be done, to avert the storm which is now coming on. We have petitioned, we have remonstrated, we have supplicated, we have prostrated ourselves before the throne, and have implored its interposition to arrest the tyrannical hands of the ministry and parliament. Our petitions have been slighted; our remonstrances have produced additional violence and insult; our supplications have been disregarded; and we have been spurned, with contempt, from the foot of the throne. In vain, after these things, may we indulge the fond hope of peace and reconciliation. There is no longer any room for hope. If we wish to be free, if we mean to preserve inviolate those inestimable privileges for which we have been so long contending, if we mean not basely to abandon the noble struggle in which we have been so long engaged, and which we have pledged ourselves never to abandon, until the glorious object of our contest shall be obtained, we must fight!—I repeat it, sir, we must fight!! An appeal to arms and to the God of Hosts is all that is left us!

They tell us, sir, that we are weak, unable to cope with so formidable an adversary. But when shall we be stronger? Will it be the next week or the next year? Will it be when we are totally disarmed, and when a British guard shall be stationed in every house? Shall we gather strength by irresolution and inaction? Shall we acquire the means of effectual resistance by lying supinely on our backs, and hugging the delusive phantom of hope, until our enemies shall have bound us hand and foot? Sir, we are not weak, if we make a proper use of those means which the God of nature hath placed in our power. Three millions of people, armed in the holy cause of liberty, and in such a country as that which we possess, are invincible by any force which our enemy can send against us. Besides, sir, we shall not fight our battles alone. There is a just God who presides over the destinies of nations, and who will raise up friends to fight our battles for us. The battle, sir, is not to the strong alone; it is to the vigilant, the active, the brave. Besides, sir, we have no election. If we were base enough to desire

it, it is now too late to retire from the contest. There is no retreat, but in submission and slavery! Our chains are forged. Their clanking may be heard on the plains of Boston! The war is inevitable— and let it come!! I repeat it, sir, let it come!!!

It is in vain, sir, to extenuate the matter. Gentlemen may cry, peace, peace—but there is no peace. The war is actually begun! The next gale that sweeps from the north will bring to our ears the clash of resounding arms! Our brethern are already in the field! Why stand we here idle? What is it that gentlemen wish? What would they have? Is life so dear, or peace so sweet, as to be purchased at the price of chains and slavery? Forbid it, Almighty God! I know not what course others may take; but as for me, give me liberty or give me death!

THOMAS PAINE (1737–1809)

JOEL BARLOW remarked in a letter written August 11, 1809, to a prospective biographer of Thomas Paine:

[If you should] give us Thomas Paine *complete*, in all his character, as one of the most benevolent and disinterested of mankind, endowed with the clearest perception, an uncommon share of original genius, and the greatest breadth of thought; if this piece of biography should analyze his literary labors and rank him as he ought to be ranked, among the brightest and undeviating luminaries of the age in which he lived, yet with a mind assailable by flattery, and receiving through that weak side a tincture of vanity which he was too proud to conceal; with a mind, though strong enough to bear him up and to rise elastic under the heaviest hand of oppression, yet unable to endure the contempt of his former friends and fellow-laborers, the rulers of the country that received his first and greatest services; a mind incapable of looking down with the serene compassion, as it ought, on the rude scoffs of their imitators, a new generation that knows him not; a mind that shrinks from their society, and unhappily seeks refuge in low company, or looks for consolation in the sordid, solitary bottle, . . . if you are disposed and prepared to write his life thus entire, to fill up the picture to which these hasty strokes of outline give but a rude sketch with great vacuities, your book may be a useful one for another age, but it will not be relished, nor scarcely tolerated, in this.

Paine, as a visiting acquaintance and as a literary friend, the only points of view from which I knew him, was one of the most instructive men I have ever known. He had a surprising memory and a brilliant fancy; his mind was a storehouse of facts and useful observations; he was full of lively

anecdote and ingenious, original, pertinent remarks upon almost every subject.

He was always charitable to the poor beyond his means, a sure protector and friend to all Americans in distress that he found in foreign countries. And he had frequent occasions to exert his influence in protecting them during the revolution in France. His writings will answer for his patriotism, and his entire devotion to what he conceived to be the best interest and happiness of mankind.

This portrait characterizes Paine in the days of his glory and the days of his neglect; it is a balanced estimate of the supreme propagandist of the American Revolution. Paine's *Common Sense* (1776) and *The Rights of Man* (1791–1792) made him the most forceful expositor in the late eighteenth century of the principles of representative government. His *Age of Reason* (1794–1795, 1807) places him high among the champions of the deistic theology, and reveals him as a powerful force in religious liberalism.

Paine's service to our country and to American ideas was not primarily in the novelty of his contentions. He got many of his ideas for *Common Sense* from Benjamin Rush, Samuel Adams, Richard Henry Lee, and David Rittenhouse, and many of his ideas for *The Age of Reason* from Thomas Young. His special contribution was his amazing skill in the art of persuasion. He created a demand for his works, not by the profundity of his ideas, but by saying what people needed and wanted to hear. A master in the use of telling epithets, Paine wrote with a sure instinct for such memorable phrases as "the ragged relic and the antiquated precedent, the monk and the monarch, will molder together," and "the summer soldier and the sunshine patriot." It was Paine who first used the words, "The United States of America." Lucidity, simplicity, and passion have rarely been so effectively united as in his fiery pamphlets.

Paine's religious training was that of a Quaker, a training which helps to account for the strong self-trust which he generally displayed. But self-confidence did not, early in his career, bring success. Paine had tried unsuccessfully a half-dozen trades and had reached middle life before he came to America in 1774. Almost as soon as he touched American soil his literary talents unfolded. To the *Pennsylvania Magazine*, which he served as editor for several months, he contributed humanitarian articles on slavery and politics. Then he became deeply interested in the controversy between the provinces and the mother country, and in 1776 came his most telling piece, *Common Sense*, urging separation from a feudalistic English government on both practical and theoretic grounds, voiced "in language as plain as A, B, C." During the Revolution he issued *The Crisis*, the sixteen numbers of which appeared at critical junctures of the struggle and had tonic effects on the national morale.

He went to France as aid in the mission of John Laurens (1781) with whom he returned the same year. He returned to Europe in 1787 to exhibit his iron bridge and to find an English manufacturer. While in England he moved in liberal circles and wrote *The Rights of Man* (two parts, 1791, 1792) originally prompted by a desire to answer Burke's *Reflections on the French Revolution*, but soon broadened into a general defense of the French cause. His direct and implied attacks on the vestiges of feudalism in England brought official condemnation of Part II. Paine found it safe to remain in France where he was residing at the moment of suppression. By the revolutionists Paine was welcomed as a comrade and made a member of the Convention. He became vocal in further political theory and criticism. But opposition to the extreme leftists brought imprisonment in 1793, and for ten months he languished in jail. Robespierre's death brought an end to the Reign of Terror, and shortly thereafter Monroe claimed Paine as an American citizen and secured his release. He was restored to his seat in the Convention and served until its adjournment in October, 1795. Until 1802 he resided in Paris, much of the time in acute financial distress.

The first three years after his release saw Paine busily engaged in writing such works as a *Dissertation on First-Principles of Government* (1795) and *Agrarian Justice* (1797). Early chapters of his ablest work, *The Age of Reason*, he had written in prison (Part I, 1794); the second part he completed for publication in 1796. In point of view it is a strongly deistic work, attacking superstition and elucidating the grounds for a rational religion. Paine's readiness to flout beliefs, his warfare with institutionalized powers, his disrespectful manner, and his occasional astonishing violence in utterance made him unpopular among religious groups and damaged his reputation with the public at large which had no knowledge of his actual writings. In America a rash of attacks by his Calvinistic-Federalistic contemporaries broke out in 1801. But despite the opposition Paine returned to the United States after the Peace of Amiens in 1802. He could not have gone to England, from which he had been expelled, though he had significant supporters there throughout the Napoleonic wars. But upon his return to New Rochelle and New York he was neglected by his former friends and everywhere damned and vilified. He died in obscurity in 1809 after failing to find solace in his last years in either unworthy companions or the bottle. But despite his somewhat inglorious end, Paine was a thinker greatly admired by radicals and true Jeffersonians of his own day, and in the last half century his real contribution to world thought has been fairly assessed.

Although he was born in England, Paine considered America "as the country of my heart and the place of my political and literary birth." "As far as I can judge of myself," he declared, "I believe I should never have been known to the world as an author on any subject whatever, had it not been for the affairs of America." When these affairs were at their most crucial stage, he brought the logic of John Locke and Baron von Pufendorf down to the level of practical political problems. In this achievement his early experience as lobbyist for his fellow excisemen (1772) and his consistent crusading in his magazine articles stood him in good stead. He soon displayed an almost thaumaturgic power of phrase-making, and he had the journalist's sense of dramatic timeliness. Thus it was that Paine influenced the Revolution itself and also the thought of men into whose hands the new government was to be entrusted. Even today it may not be generally enough recognized that, in his later writings, he was one of America's most fearless thinkers, with a mind free from traditionalism, superstition, and dogmatism. He had a deep and reverent awe of the Omnipotent, believed in the future life, and never opposed Christian morality;

yet it is one of the paradoxes of blundering humanity that Paine is still remembered in some circles by the inappropriate label of atheist.

BIBLIOGRAPHY · The standard scholarly text is that edited by Moncure D. Conway, *The Writings of Thomas Paine* (4 vols., 1894–1896). Some hitherto uncollected pieces are in William M. Van der Weyde's edition, *The Life and Works of Thomas Paine* (10 vols., 1925). For uncollected later letters see H. H. Clark's *Thomas Paine* (1944) which also contains the best critical study of its length (108 pages), treating of Paine's religious, ethical, political, economic, and humanitarian ideas. Complete enough for general purposes is P. S. Foner's two-volume edition, *The Complete Writings of Thomas Paine* (1945). Less complete, but carefully edited is A. W. Peach, *Selections from the Work of Thomas Paine* (1928).

M. D. Conway's *Life of Thomas Paine* (2 vols., 1892) remains the best biography. In general, biographical and critical studies are marred by excessive partisanship or antagonism, but see Hesketh Pearson, *Tom Paine, Friend of Mankind* (1936), and Frank Smith, *Thomas Paine, Liberator* (1938). For scholarly and interpretative studies see H. H. Clark, "Toward a Reinterpretation of Thomas Paine," *American Literature*, V (1933), 133–145; J. Dorfman, "The Economic Philosophy of Thomas Paine," *Political Science Quarterly*, LIII (1938), 372–386; and Howard Penniman, "Thomas Paine—Democrat," *American Political Science Review*, XXXVII (1943); P. Davidson, *Propaganda and the American Revolution, 1763–1783* (1941); E. P. Link, *Democratic-Republican Societies, 1790–1800* (1942); and R. L. Brunhouse, *The Counter-Revolution in Pennsylvania, 1776–1790* (1942).

Liberty Tree

THIS SONG was printed in the *Pennsylvania Magazine*, of which Paine was an editor, in July, 1775, and reprinted in the Pennsylvania *Evening Post* on September 16, 1775. It was one of the best songs inspired by the approaching Revolution.

In a chariot of light, from the regions of day,
  The Goddess of Liberty came,
Ten thousand celestials directed her way,
  And hither conducted the dame.
A fair budding branch from the gardens above, 5
  Where millions with millions agree,
She brought in her hand as a pledge of her love,
  And the plant she named Liberty Tree.

The celestial exotic stuck deep in the ground,
  Like a native it flourished and bore;   10

The fame of its fruit drew the nations around,
  To seek out this peaceable shore.
Unmindful of names or distinctions they came,
  For freemen like brothers agree;
With one spirit endued, they one friendship
    pursued,   15
  And their temple was Liberty Tree.

Beneath this fair tree, like the patriarchs of old,
  Their bread in contentment they ate,
Unvexed with the troubles of silver or gold,
  The cares of the grand and the great.   20
With timber and tar they Old England supplied,
  And supported her power on the sea:
Her battles they fought, without getting a groat,
  For the honour of Liberty Tree.

But hear, O ye swains, ('t is a tale most profane,)
  How all the tyrannical powers,   26
Kings, Commons, and Lords, are uniting amain
  To cut down this guardian of ours.
From the east to the west blow the trumpet to
    arms,
  Thro' the land let the sound of it flee: 30
Let the far and the near all unite with a cheer,
  In defence of our Liberty Tree.

Common Sense

Common Sense was published by Robert Bell, in Philadelphia, January 10, 1776. In his *Life of Thomas Paine* Conway quoted Paine's own words in explanation of the writing of the pamphlet:

In October, 1775, Dr. Franklin proposed giving me such materials as were in his hands towards completing a history of the present transactions, and seemed desirous of having the first volume out next spring. I had then formed the outlines of *Common Sense*, and had nearly finished the first part ("On the Origin and Design of Government in General, with Concise Remarks on the English Constitution"); and as I supposed the doctor's design in getting out a history was to open the new year with a new system, I expected to surprise him with a production on that subject much earlier than he thought of; and without informing him of what I was doing, got it ready for the press as fast as I conveniently could, and sent him the first pamphlet that was printed off.

Some of his Philadelphia contemporaries, Dr. Benjamin Rush, David Rittenhouse, Timothy Matlack, and Thomas Young may have furnished Paine with

222

some of the ideas for his pamphlet; but the style is certainly his own. For a historical account of the development of the spirit of independence, see Justin Winsor (editor), *A Narrative and Critical History of America*, Chapter III (1888).

The text is that of Moncure D. Conway (editor), *The Writings of Thomas Paine* (1894–1896).

Of Monarchy and Hereditary Succession

Mankind being originally equals in the order of creation, the equality could only be destroyed by some subsequent circumstance: the distinctions of rich and poor may in a great measure be accounted for, and that without having recourse to the harsh ill-sounding names of oppression and avarice. Oppression is often the consequence, but seldom or never the means of riches; and though avarice will preserve a man from being necessitously poor, it generally makes him too timorous to be wealthy.

But there is another and greater distinction for which no truly natural or religious reason can be assigned, and that is, the distinction of men into KINGS and SUBJECTS. Male and female are the distinctions of nature, good and bad the distinction of Heaven; but how a race of men came into the world so exalted above the rest, and distinguished like some new species, is worth enquiring into, and whether they are the means of happiness or of misery to mankind.

In the early ages of the world, according to the scripture chronology there were no kings; the consequence of which was, there were no wars: it is the pride of kings which throws mankind into confusion. Holland, without a king, hath enjoyed more peace for this last century than any of the monarchical governments in Europe. Antiquity favors the same remark; for the quiet and rural lives of the first Patriarchs have a happy something in them, which vanishes away when we come to the history of Jewish royalty.

Government by kings was first introduced into the world by the Heathens, from whom the children of Israel copied the custom. It was the most prosperous invention the Devil ever set on foot for the promotion of idolatry. The Heathens paid divine honours to their deceased kings, and the Christian World hath improved on the plan, by doing the same to their living ones. How impious is the title of sacred Majesty applied to a worm who in the midst of his splendor is crumbling into dust!

As the exalting one man so greatly above the rest cannot be justified on the equal rights of nature, so neither can it be defended on the authority of scripture; for the will of the Almighty, as declared by Gideon, and the prophet Samuel, expressly disapproves of the government by Kings. All anti-monarchical parts of scripture have been very smoothly glossed over in monarchical governments, but they undoubtedly merit the attention of countries which have their governments yet to form. Render unto Cæsar the things which are Caesar's is the scripture doctrine of courts, yet it is no support of monarchical government, for the Jews at that time were without a king, and in a state of vassalage to the Romans.

Near three thousand years passed away, from the Mosaic account of the creation before the Jews, under a national delusion, requested a king. Till then their form of government (except in extraordinary cases where the Almighty interposed) was a kind of Republic, administered by a judge and the elders of the tribe. Kings they had none, and it was held sinful to acknowledge any being under that title but the Lord of Hosts. And when a man seriously reflects on the idolatrous homage which is paid to the persons of kings, he need not wonder that the Almighty, ever jealous of his honour, should disapprove a form of government which so impiously invades the prerogative of Heaven.

Monarchy is ranked in scripture as one of the sins of the Jews, for which a curse in reserve is denounced against them. The history of that transaction is worth attending to.

The children of Israel being oppressed by the Midianites, Gideon marched against them with a small army, and victory, through the divine interposition, decided in his favor. The Jews, elate with success, and attributing it to the generalship of Gideon, proposed making him a king, saying, Rule thou over us, thou and thy son, and thy son's son. Here was temptation in its fullest extent; not a kingdom only, but an hereditary one; but Gideon in the piety of his soul replied, I will not rule over you, neither shall my son rule over you. THE LORD SHALL RULE OVER YOU. Words need not be more explicit; Gideon doth not decline the honour, but denieth their right to give it; neither doth he compliment them with invented declarations of his thanks, but in the positive style of a Prophet charges them with disaffection to their proper Sovereign, the King of Heaven.

About one hundred and thirty years after this, they fell again into the same error. The hankering which the Jews had for the idolatrous customs of the Heathens, is something exceedingly unaccountable; but so it was, that laying hold of the misconduct of Samuel's two sons, who were intrusted with some secular concerns, they came in an abrupt and clamorous manner to Samuel, saying, Behold thou art old, and thy sons walk not in thy ways, now make us a king to judge us like all the other nations. And here we cannot but observe that their motives were bad, viz., that they might be *like* unto other nations, *i.e.*, the Heathens, whereas their true glory lay in being as much *unlike* them as possible. But the thing displeased Samuel when they said, Give us a King to judge us; and Samuel prayed unto the Lord, and the Lord said unto Samuel, Harken unto the voice of the people in all that they say unto thee, for they have not rejected thee, but they have rejected me, THAT I SHOULD NOT REIGN OVER THEM. According to all the works which they have done since the day that I brought them up out of Egypt, even unto this day, wherewith they have forsaken me, and served other Gods: so do they also unto thee. Now therefore harken unto their voice, howbeit, protest solemnly unto them and show them the manner of the king that shall reign over them, *i.e.*, not of any particular king, but the general manner of the kings of the earth, whom Israel was so eagerly copying after. And notwithstanding the great distance of time and difference of manners, the character is still in fashion. And Samuel told all the words of the Lord unto the people, that asked of him a king. And he said, This shall be the manner of the King that shall reign over you. He will take your sons and appoint them for himself for his chariots, and to be his horsemen, and some shall run before his chariots (this description agrees with the present mode of impressing men) and he will appoint him captains over thousands and captains over fifties and will set them to ear his ground and to reap his harvest, and to make his instruments of war, and instruments of his chariots. And he will take your daughters to be confectionaries, and to be cooks and to be bakers (this describes the expense and luxury as well as the oppression of Kings) and he will take your fields and your vineyards, and your olive yards, even the best of them, and give them to his servants. And he will take the tenth of your seed, and of your vineyards, and give them to his officers and to his servants (by which we see that bribery, corruption, and favouritism, are the standing vices of Kings) and he will take the tenth of your men servants, and your maid servants, and your goodliest young men, and your asses, and put them to his work: and he will take the tenth of your sheep, and ye shall be his servants, and ye shall cry out in that day because of your king which ye shall have chosen, AND THE LORD WILL NOT HEAR YOU IN THAT DAY. This accounts for the continuation of Monarchy; neither do the characters of the few good kings which have lived since, either sanctify the title, or blot out the sinfulness of the origin; the high encomium given of David takes no notice of him officially as a king, but only as a Man after God's own heart. Nevertheless the people refused to obey the voice of Samuel, and they said, Nay, but we will have a king over us, that we may be like all the nations, and that our king may judge us, and go out before us and fight our battles. Samuel continued to reason with them but to no purpose; he set before them their ingratitude, but all would not avail; and seeing them fully bent on their folly, he cried out, I will call unto the Lord, and he shall send thunder and rain (which was then a punishment, being in the time of wheat harvest) that ye may perceive and see that your wickedness is great which ye have done in the sight of the Lord, IN ASKING YOU A KING. So Samuel called unto the Lord, and the Lord sent thunder and rain that day, and all the people greatly feared the Lord and Samuel. And all the people said unto Samuel, Pray for thy servants unto the Lord thy God that we die not, for WE HAVE ADDED UNTO OUR SINS THIS EVIL, TO ASK A KING. These portions of scripture are direct and positive. They admit of no equivocal construction. That the Almighty hath here entered his protest against monarchical government is true, or the scripture is false. And a man hath good reason to believe, that there is as much of kingcraft as priestcraft in withholding the scripture from the public in Popish countries. For monarchy in every instance is the Popery of government.

To the evil of monarchy we have added that of hereditary succession; and as the first is a degradation and lessening of ourselves, so the second, claimed as a matter of right, is an insult and imposition on posterity. For all men being originally equals, no one by birth could have a right to set up his own family in perpetual preference to all others forever, and though himself might deserve some decent degree of honours of his contemporaries, yet his descendants might be far too unworthy to inherit them. One of the strongest natural proofs of the folly of hereditary right of Kings, is that nature disapproves it, otherwise she would not so frequently turn it into ridicule, by giving mankind an ass for a lion.

Secondly, as no man at first could possess any other public honors than were bestowed upon him, so the givers of those honors could have no power to give away the right of posterity, and though they might say, "We choose you for our head," they could not, without manifest injustice to their children, say, "that your children and your children's children shall reign over ours for ever." Because such an unwise, unjust, unnatural compact might (perhaps) in the next succession put them under the government of a rogue or a fool. Most wise men in their private sentiments have ever treated hereditary right with contempt; yet it is one of those evils which when once established is not easily removed; many submit from fear, others from superstition, and the more powerful part shares with the king the plunder of the rest.

This is supposing the present race of kings in the world to have had an honorable origin: whereas it is more than probable, that, could we take off the dark covering of antiquity and trace them to their first rise, we should find the first of them nothing better than the principal ruffian of some restless gang, whose savage manners or preeminence in subtility obtained him the title of chief among plunderers; and who by increasing in power, and extending his depredations, overawed the quiet and defenceless to purchase their safety by frequent contributions. Yet his electors could have no idea of giving hereditary right to his descendants, because such a perpetual exclusion of themselves was incompatible with the free and unrestrained principles they professed to live by. Wherefore, hereditary succession in the early ages of monarchy could not take place as a matter of claim, but as something casual or complemental; but as few or no records were extant in those days, and traditionary history is stuffed with fables, it was very easy after the lapse of a few generations, to trump up some superstitious tale, conveniently timed, Mahomet-like, to cram hereditary right down the throats of the vulgar. Perhaps the disorders which threatened, or seemed to threaten, on the decease of a leader, and the choice of a new one (for elections among ruffians could not be very orderly) induced many at first to favor hereditary pretensions; by which means it happened, as it hath happened since, that what at first was submitted to as a convenience was afterwards claimed as a right.

England, since the conquest, hath known some few good monarchs, but groaned beneath a much larger number of bad ones: yet no man in his senses can say that their claim under William the Conqueror is a very honourable one. A French bastard, landing with an armed Banditti, and establishing himself king of England against the consent of the natives, is in plain terms a very paltry rascally original. It certainly hath no divinity in it. However, it is needless to spend much time in exposing the folly of hereditary right; if there are any so weak as to believe it, let them promiscuously worship the ass and the lion, and welcome. I shall neither copy their humility nor disturb their devotion.

Yet I should be glad to ask, how they suppose kings came at first? The question admits but of three answers, viz., either by lot, by election, or by usurpation. If the first king was taken by lot, it establishes a precedent for the next, which excludes hereditary succession. Saul was by lot, yet the succession was not hereditary, neither does it appear from that transaction that there was any intention it ever should. If the first king of any country was by election, that likewise establishes a precedent for the next; for to say, that the right of all future generations is taken away, by the act of the first electors, in their choice not only of a king, but of a family of kings forever, hath no parallel in or out of scripture but the doctrine of original sin, which supposes the free will of all men lost in Adam; and from such comparison, and it will admit of no other, hereditary succession can derive no glory. For as in Adam all sinned, and as in the first electors all men obeyed; as in the one all mankind were subjected to Satan, and in the other to sovereignty; as our innocence was lost in the first, and our authority in the last; and as both disable us from re-assuming some former state and privilege, it unanswerably follows that original sin and hereditary succession are parallels. Dishonourable rank! Inglorious connection! Yet the most subtile sophist cannot produce a juster simile.

As to usurpation, no man will be so hardy as to defend it; and that William the Conqueror was an usurper is a fact not to be contradicted. The plain truth is, that the antiquity of English monarchy will not bear looking into.

But it is not so much the absurdity as the evil of hereditary succession which concerns mankind. Did it ensure a race of good and wise men it would have the seal of divine authority, but as it opens a door to the foolish, the wicked, and the improper, it hath in it the nature of oppression. Men who look upon themselves born to reign, and others to obey, soon grow insolent. Selected from the rest of mankind, their minds are early poisoned by importance; and the world they act in differs so materially from the world at large, that they have but little opportunity of knowing its true interests, and when they succeed to the government are frequently the most ignorant and unfit of any throughout the dominions.

Another evil which attends hereditary succession is, that the throne is subject to be possessed by a minor at any age; all which time the regency acting under the cover of a king have every opportunity and inducement to betray their trust.

The same national misfortune happens when a king, worn out with age and infirmity, enters the last stage of human weakness. In both these cases the public becomes a prey of every miscreant who can tamper successfully with the follies either of age or infancy.

The most plausible plea which hath ever been offered in favor of hereditary succession is, that it preserves a nation from civil wars; and were this true, it would be weighty; whereas it is the most bare-faced falsity ever imposed upon mankind. The whole history of England disowns the fact. Thirty kings and two minors have reigned in that distracted kingdom since the conquest, in which time there have been (including the revolution) no less than eight civil wars and nineteen Rebellions. Wherefore, instead of making for peace, it makes against it, and destroys the very foundation it seems to stand on.

The contest for monarchy and succession, between the houses of York and Lancaster, laid England in a scene of blood for many years. Twelve pitched battles, besides skirmishes and sieges, were fought between Henry and Edward. Twice was Henry prisoner to Edward, who in his turn was prisoner to Henry. And so uncertain is the fate of war and the temper of a nation, when nothing but personal matters are the ground of a quarrel, that Henry was taken in triumph from a prison to a palace, and Edward obliged to fly from a palace to a foreign land; yet, as sudden transitions of temper are seldom lasting, Henry in his turn was driven from the throne, and Edward recalled to succeed him. The parliament always following the strongest side.

This contest began in the reign of Henry the Sixth, and was not entirely extinguished till Henry the Seventh, in whom the families were united. Including a period of sixty-seven years, viz., from 1422 to 1489.

In short, monarchy and succession have laid, not this or that kingdom only, but the world in blood and ashes. 'Tis a form of government which the word of God bears testimony against, and blood will attend it.

If we enquire into the business of a King, we shall find (and in some countries they have none) that after sauntering away their lives without pleasure to themselves or advantage to the nation, they withdraw from the scene, and leave their successors to tread the same useless and idle round. In absolute monarchies the whole weight of business, civil and military, lies on the King; the children of Israel in their request for a king urged this plea, "that he may judge us, and go out before us and fight our battles." But in countries where he is neither a judge nor a general, as in England, a man would be puzzled to know what *is* his business.

The nearer any government approaches to a republic, the less business there is for a king. It is somewhat difficult to find a proper name for the government of England. Sir William Meredith calls it a Republic; but in its present state it is unworthy of the name, because the corrupt influence of the Crown, by having all the places in its disposal, hath so effectually swallowed up the power, and eaten out the virtue of the House of Commons (the republican part in the constitution) that the government of England is nearly as monarchical as that of France or Spain. Men fall out with names without understanding them. For 'tis the republican and not the Monarchical part of the constitution of England which Englishmen glory in, viz., the liberty of choosing an House of Commons from out of their own body—and it is easy to see that when Republican virtue fails, slavery ensues. Why is the constitution of England sickly, but because monarchy hath poisoned the Republic; the crown hath engrossed the Commons?

In England a King hath little more to do than to make war and give away places; which, in plain terms, is to impoverish the nation and set it together by the ears. A pretty business indeed for a man to be allowed eight hundred thousand sterling a year for, and worshiped into the bargain! Of more worth is one honest man to society, and in the sight of God, than all the crowned ruffians that ever lived.

The Crisis

The American Crisis was a series of sixteen pamphlets published between December 19, 1776, and December 9, 1783. The first number, with its memorable opening sentence which still retains the power to stir the heart

like a trumpet, appeared the day before Washington had conceded, ". . . I think the game is pretty near up." In the next-to-the-last issue, on April 19, 1783, Paine could write triumphantly, "The times that tried men's souls are over—and the greatest and completest revolution the world ever knew, gloriously and happily accomplished." During the course of that struggle Paine's powerful words persuaded the wavering patriots that each British victory merely delayed the final triumph of the colonists. Even more than in *Common Sense* Paine displayed his journalistic sense of dramatic timing and his brilliance as a phrasemaker. *The Crisis* was read, at General Washington's orders, to the troops in camp and on the field. Number I of *The Crisis* was first printed in the *Pennsylvania Journal*, December 19, 1776.

The text is that of Moncure D. Conway (editor), *The Writings of Thomas Paine* (1894–1896).

I. *"These Are the Times that Try Men's Souls"*

These are the times that try men's souls. The summer soldier and the sunshine patriot will, in this crisis, shrink from the service of his country; but he that stands it *now*, deserves the love and thanks of man and woman. Tyranny, like hell, is not easily conquered; yet we have this consolation with us, that the harder the conflict, the more glorious the triumph. What we obtain too cheap, we esteem too lightly:—It is dearness only that gives every thing its value. Heaven knows how to put a proper price upon its goods; and it would be strange indeed if so celestial an article as FREEDOM should not be highly rated. Britain, with an army to enforce her tyranny, has declared that she has a right (*not only to* TAX) but "to BIND *us in all cases whatsoever*," and if being bound in that manner, is not slavery, then is there not such a thing as slavery upon earth. Even the expression is impious; for so unlimited a power can belong only to God.

Whether the independence of the continent was declared too soon, or delayed too long, I will not now enter into as an argument; my own simple opinion is, that had it been eight months earlier, it would have been much better. We did not make a proper use of last winter, neither could we, while we were in a dependent state. However, the fault, if it were one, was all our own; we have none to blame but ourselves. But no great deal is lost yet.

All that Howe has been doing for this month past, is rather a ravage than a conquest, which the spirit of the Jerseys, a year ago, would have quickly repulsed, and which time and a little resolution will soon recover.

I have as little superstition in me as any man living, but my secret opinion has ever been, and still is, that God Almighty will not give up a people to military destruction, or leave them unsupportedly to perish, who have so earnestly and so repeatedly sought to avoid the calamities of war, by every decent method which wisdom could invent. Neither have I so much of the infidel in me, as to suppose that He has relinquished the government of the world, and given us up to the care of devils; and as I do not, I cannot see on what grounds the king of Britain can look up to heaven for help against us: a common murderer, a highwayman, or a house-breaker, has as good a pretence as he.

'Tis surprising to see how rapidly a panic will sometimes run through a country. All nations and ages have been subject to them: Britain has trembled like an ague at the report of a French fleet of flat-bottomed boats; and in the fourteenth [fifteenth] century, the whole English army, after ravaging the kingdom of France, was driven back like men petrified with fear; and this brave exploit was performed by a few broken forces collected and headed by a woman, Joan of Arc. Would that heaven might inspire some Jersey maid to spirit up her countrymen, and save her fair fellow sufferers from ravage and ravishment! Yet panics, in some cases, have their uses; they produce as much good as hurt. Their duration is always short; the mind soon grows through them, and acquires a firmer habit than before. But their peculiar advantage is, that they are the touchstones of sincerity and hypocrisy, and bring things and men to light, which might otherwise have lain forever undiscovered. In fact, they have the same effect on secret traitors, which an imaginary apparition would have upon a private murderer. They sift out the hidden thoughts of man, and hold them up in public to the world. Many a disguised tory has lately shown his head, that shall penitentially solemnize with curses the day on which Howe arrived upon the Delaware.

As I was with the troops at Fort Lee, and marched with them to the edge of Pennsylvania, I am well acquainted with many circumstances, which those who live at a distance know but little or nothing of. Our situation there was exceedingly cramped, the place being a narrow neck of land between the North-River and the Hackensack. Our force was inconsiderable, being not one fourth so great as Howe could bring against us. We had no army at hand to have relieved the garrison, had we shut ourselves up and stood on our defence. Our ammunition, light artillery, and the best part of our stores, had been removed, on the apprehension that Howe would endeavor to penetrate the Jerseys, in which case Fort Lee could be of no use to us; for it must occur to every thinking man, whether in the army or not, that these kind of field forts are only for temporary purposes, and last in use no longer than the enemy directs his force against the particular object, which such forts are raised to defend. Such was our situation and condition at Fort Lee on the morning of the 20th of November, when an officer arrived with information that the enemy with 200 boats had landed about seven miles above: Major General [Nathaniel] Green, who commanded the garrison, immediately ordered them under arms, and sent express to General Washington at the town of Hackensack, distant by the way of the ferry—six miles. Our first object was to secure the bridge over the Hackensack, which laid up the river between the enemy and us, about six miles from us, and three from them. General Washington arrived in about three quarters of an hour, and marched at the head of the troops towards the bridge, which place I expected we should have a brush for; however, they did not choose to dispute it with us, and the greatest part of our troops went over the bridge, the rest over the ferry, except some which passed at a mill on a small creek, between the bridge and the ferry, and made their way through some marshy grounds up to the town of Hackensack, and there passed the river. We brought off as much baggage as the wagons could contain, the rest was lost. The simple object was to bring off the garrison, and march them on till they could be strengthened by the Jersey or Pennsylvania militia, so as to be enabled to make a stand. We staid four days at

Newark, collected our out-posts with some of the Jersey militia, and marched out twice to meet the enemy, on being informed that they were advancing, though our numbers were greatly inferior to theirs. Howe, in my little opinion, committed a great error in generalship in not throwing a body of forces off from Staten Island through Amboy, by which means he might have seized all our stores at Brunswick, and intercepted our march into Pennsylvania; but if we believe the power of hell to be limited, we must likewise believe that their agents are under some providential controul.

I shall not now attempt to give all the particulars of our retreat to the Delaware; suffice it for the present to say, that both officers and men, though greatly harassed and fatigued, frequently without rest, covering, or provision, the inevitable consequences of a long retreat, bore it with a manly and martial spirit. All their wishes centred in one, which was, that the country would turn out and help them to drive the enemy back. Voltaire has remarked that King William never appeared to full advantage but in difficulties and in action; the same remark may be made on General Washington, for the character fits him. There is a natural firmness in some minds which cannot be unlocked by trifles, but which, when unlocked, discovers a cabinet of fortitude; and I reckon it among those kind of public blessings, which we do not immediately see, that God hath blessed him with uninterrupted health, and given him a mind that can even flourish upon care.

I shall conclude this paper with some miscellaneous remarks on the state of our affairs; and shall begin with asking the following question, Why is it that the enemy have left the New-England provinces, and made these middle ones the seat of war? The answer is easy: New-England is not infested with tories, and we are. I have been tender in raising the cry against these men, and used numberless arguments to show them their danger, but it will not do to sacrifice a world either to their folly or their baseness. The period is now arrived, in which either they or we must change our sentiments, or one or both must fall. And what is a tory? Good God! what is he? I should not be afraid to go with a hundred whigs against a thousand tories, were they to attempt to get into arms. Every tory is a coward; for servile, slavish, self-interested fear is the foundation of toryism; and a man under such influence, though he may be cruel, never can be brave.

But, before the line of irrecoverable separation be drawn between us, let us reason the matter together: Your conduct is an invitation to the enemy, yet not one in a thousand of you has heart enough to join him. Howe is as much deceived by you as the American cause is injured by you. He expects you will all take up arms, and flock to his standard, with muskets on your shoulders. Your opinions are of no use to him, unless you support him personally, for 'tis soldiers, and not tories, that he wants.

I once felt all that kind of anger, which a man ought to feel, against the mean principles that are held by the tories: A noted one, who kept a tavern at Amboy, was standing at his door, with as pretty a child in his hand, about eight or nine years old, as I ever saw, and after speaking his mind as freely as he thought was prudent, finished with this unfatherly expression, "Well! give me peace in my day." Not a man lives on the continent but fully believes that a separation must some time or other finally take place, and a generous parent should have said, "If there must be trouble, let it be in my day, that my child may have peace;" and this single reflection, well applied, is sufficient to awaken every man to duty. Not a place upon earth might be so happy as America. Her situation is remote from all the wrangling world, and she has nothing to do but to trade with them. A man can distinguish himself between temper and principle, and I am as confident, as I am that God governs the world, that America will never be happy till she gets clear of foreign dominion. Wars, without ceasing, will break out till that period arrives, and the continent must in the end be conqueror; for though the flame of liberty may sometimes cease to shine, the coal can never expire.

America did not, nor does not want force; but she wanted a proper application of that force. Wisdom is not the purchase of a day, and it is no wonder that we should err at the first setting off. From an excess of tenderness, we were unwilling to raise an army, and trusted our cause to the temporary defence of a well-meaning militia. A summer's experience has now taught us better; yet with those troops, while they were collected, we were able to set bounds to the progress of the enemy, and, thank God! they are again assembling. I always considered militia as the best troops in the world for a sudden exertion, but they will not do for a long campaign. Howe, it is probable, will make an attempt on this city; should he fail on this side the Delaware, he is ruined. If he succeeds, our cause is not ruined. He stakes all on his side against a part on ours; admitting he succeeds, the consequence will be, that armies from both ends of the continent will march to assist their suffering friends in the middle states; for he cannot go everywhere, it is impossible. I consider Howe as the greatest enemy the tories have; he is bringing a war into their country, which, had it not been for him and partly for themselves, they had been clear of. Should he now be expelled, I wish with all the devotion of a Christian, that the names of whig and tory may never more be mentioned; but should the tories give him encouragement to come, or assistance if he come, I as sincerely wish that our next year's arms may expel them from the continent, and the Congress appropriate their possessions to the relief of those who have suffered in well-doing. A single successful battle next year will settle the whole. America could carry on a two years' war by the confiscation of the property of disaffected persons, and be made happy by their expulsion. Say not that this is revenge, call it rather the soft resentment of a suffering people, who, having no object in view but the good of all, have staked their own all upon a seemingly doubtful event. Yet it is folly to argue against determined hardness; eloquence may strike the ear, and the language of sorrow draw forth the tear of compassion, but nothing can reach the heart that is steeled with prejudice. *The Tories*

Quitting this class of men, I turn with the warm ardor of a friend to those who have nobly stood, and are yet determined to stand the matter out: I call not upon a few, but upon all: not on this state or that state, but on every state: up and help us; lay your shoulders to the wheel; better have too much force than too little, when so great an object is at stake. Let it be told to the future world, that in the depth of winter, when nothing but hope and virtue could survive, that the city and the country, alarmed at one common danger, came forth to meet and to repulse it. Say not that thousands are gone, turn out your tens of thousands; throw not the burden of the day upon Providence, but "show your faith by your works," that God may bless you. It matters not where you live, or what rank of life you hold, the evil or the blessing will reach you all. The far and the near, the home counties and the back, the rich and the poor, will suffer or rejoice alike. The heart that feels not now, is dead; the blood of his children will curse his cowardice, who shrinks back at a time when a little might have saved the whole, and made them happy. I love the man that can smile in trouble, that can gather strength from distress, and grow brave by reflection. 'Tis the business of little minds to shrink; but he whose heart is firm, and whose conscience approves his conduct, will pursue his principles unto death. My own line of reasoning is to myself as straight and clear as a ray of light. Not all the treasures of the world, so far as I believe, could have induced me to support an offensive war, for I think it murder; but if a thief breaks into my house, burns and destroys my property, and kills or threatens to kill me, or those that are in it, and to "bind me in all cases whatsoever" to his absolute will, am I to suffer it? What signifies it to me, whether he who does it is a king or a common man; my countryman or not my countryman; whether it be done by an individual villain, or an army of them? If we reason to the root of things we shall find no difference; neither can any just cause be assigned why we should punish in the one case and pardon in the other. Let them call me rebel, and welcome, I feel no concern from it; but I should suffer the misery of devils, were I to make a whore of my soul by swearing allegiance to one whose character is that of a sottish, stupid, stubborn, worthless, brutish man. I conceive likewise a horrid idea in receiving mercy from a being, who at the last day shall be shrieking to the rocks and mountains to cover him, and fleeing with terror from the orphan, the widow, and the slain of America.

There are cases which cannot be overdone by

language, and this is one. There are persons, too, who see not the full extent of the evil which threatens them; they solace themselves with hopes that the enemy, if he succeed, will be merciful. It is the madness of folly, to expect mercy from those who have refused to do justice; and even mercy, where conquest is the object, is only a trick of war; the cunning of the fox is as murderous as the violence of the wolf, and we ought to guard equally against both. Howe's first object is, partly by threats and partly by promises, to terrify or seduce the people to deliver up their arms and receive mercy. The ministry recommended the same plan to Gage, and this is what the tories call making their peace, "a peace which passeth all understanding" indeed! A peace which would be the immediate forerunner of a worse ruin than any we have yet thought of. Ye men of Pennsylvania, do reason upon these things! Were the back counties to give up their arms, they would fall an easy prey to the Indians, who are all armed: this perhaps is what some tories would not be sorry for. Were the home counties to deliver up their arms, they would be exposed to the resentment of the back counties, who would then have it in their power to chastise their defection at pleasure. And were any one state to give up its arms, that state must be garrisoned by all Howe's army of Britons and Hessians to preserve it from the anger of the rest. Mutual fear is the principal link in the chain of mutual love, and woe be to that state that breaks the compact. Howe is mercifully inviting you to barbarous destruction, and men must be either rogues or fools that will not see it. I dwell not upon the vapors of imagination; I bring reason to your ears, and, in language as plain as A, B, C, hold up truth to your eyes.

I thank *God* that I fear not. I see no real cause for fear. I know our situation well, and can see the way out of it. While our army was collected, Howe dared not risk a battle; and it is no credit to him that he decamped from the White Plains, and waited a mean opportunity to ravage the defenceless Jerseys; but it is great credit to us, that, with a handful of men, we sustained an orderly retreat for near an hundred miles, brought off our ammunition, all our field pieces, the greatest part of our stores, and had four rivers to pass.

None can say that our retreat was precipitate, for we were near three weeks in performing it, that the country might have time to come in. Twice we marched back to meet the enemy, and remained out till dark. The sign of fear was not seen in our camp, and had not some of the cowardly and disaffected inhabitants spread false alarms through the country, the Jerseys had never been ravaged. Once more we are again collected and collecting, our new army at both ends of the continent is recruiting fast, and we shall be able to open the next campaign with sixty thousand men, well armed and clothed. This is our situation, and who will may know it. By perseverance and fortitude we have the prospect of a glorious issue; by cowardice and submission, the sad choice of a variety of evils—a ravaged country—a depopulated city—habitations without safety, and slavery without hope—our homes turned into barracks and bawdy-houses for Hessians, and a future race to provide for, whose fathers we shall doubt of. Look on this picture and weep over it! and if there yet remains one thoughtless wretch who believes it not, let him suffer it unlamented.

Common Sense.

December 23, 1776.

The Rights of Man

MOST OF THE first part of *The Rights of Man* is a point-by-point refutation of Edmund Burke's *Reflections on the French Revolution* which had appeared on November 1, 1790, while Paine was living in England. His reply was handled fearfully by the first publisher who withdrew as agent at the threat of reprisals by the British government after only a few copies had been distributed. A second publisher, J. S. Jordan, issued the essay four months later. Part II appeared in February, 1792. After an inexpensive edition of Part I had been published in April, 1791, Paine was prosecuted and fled to France. In America also the work became a storm center. The most vigorous attack was by John Quincy Adams. For other American responses, see W. C. Ford's edition, *The Writings of J. Q. Adams*, I (1913–1917), 65–66.

The chapter printed below is not so much an answer to Burke as an exposition of Paine's theory of government. Concerning it, Paine remarks in his Preface to Part II:

When I began the chapter entitled the *Conclusion*, in the former part of *The Rights of Man*, published last year, it was my intention to have extended it to greater length; but in casting the whole matter in my mind which I wished to add, I found that I must either make the work too bulky or contract my plan too much. I therefore brought it to a close as soon as the subject would admit, and reserved what I had further to say to another opportunity.

The text is that of Moncure D. Conway (editor), *The Writings of Thomas Paine* (1894–96).

Conclusion

Reason and Ignorance, the opposite to each other, influence the great bulk of mankind. If either of these can be rendered sufficiently extensive in a country, the machinery of Government goes easily on. Reason obeys itself; and Ignorance submits to whatever is dictated to it.

The two modes of Government which prevail in the world, are, *first*, Government by election and representation: *secondly*, Government by hereditary succession. The former is generally known by the name of republic; the latter by that of monarchy and aristocracy.

Those two distinct and opposite forms, erect themselves on the two distinct and opposite bases of Reason and Ignorance.—As the exercise of Government requires talents and abilities, and as talents and abilities cannot have hereditary descent, it is evident that hereditary succession requires a belief from man to which his reason cannot subscribe, and which can only be established upon his ignorance; and the more ignorant any country is, the better it is fitted for this species of Government.

On the contrary, Government, in a well-constituted republic, requires no belief from man beyond what his reason can give. He sees the rationale of the whole system, its origin and its operation; and as it is best supported when best understood, the human faculties act with boldness, and acquire, under this form of government, a gigantic manliness.

As, therefore, each of those forms acts on a different base, the one moving freely by the aid of reason, the other by ignorance; we have next to consider, what it is that gives motion to that species of Government which is called Mixed Government, or, as it is sometimes ludicrously stiled, a Government of this, that, and t'other.

The moving power in this species of Government, is of necessity, Corruption. However imperfect election and representation may be in mixed Governments, they still give exercise to a greater portion of reason than is convenient to the hereditary Part; and therefore it becomes necessary to buy the reason up. A mixed Government is an imperfect everything, cementing and soldering the discordant parts together by corruption, to act as a whole. Mr. Burke appears highly disgusted that France, since she had resolved on a revolution, did not adopt what he calls "A British Constitution;" and the regretful manner in which he expresses himself on this occasion, implies a suspicion that the British Constitution needed something to keep its defects in countenance.

In mixed Governments there is no responsibility: the parts cover each other till responsibility is lost; and the corruption which moves the machine, contrives at the same time its own escape. When it is laid down as a maxim, that a King can do no wrong, it places him in a state of similar security with that of idiots and persons insane, and responsibility is out of the question with respect to himself. It then descends upon the Minister, who shelters himself under a majority in Parliament, which, by places, pensions, and corruption, he can always command; and that majority justifies itself by the same authority with which it protects the Minister. In this rotatory motion, responsibility is thrown off from the parts, and from the whole.

When there is Part in a Government which can do no wrong, it implies that it does nothing; and is only the machine of another power, by whose advice and direction it acts. What is supposed to be the King in the mixed Governments is the Cabinet; and as the Cabinet is always a part of the Parliament, and the members justifying in one character what they advise and act in another, a mixed Government becomes a continual enigma; entailing upon a country by the quantity of corruption necessary to solder the parts, the expence of supporting all the forms of government at once, and finally resolving itself into a Government by Committee; in which the advisers, the actors, the

232

approvers, the justifiers, the persons responsible, and the persons not responsible, are the same persons.

By this pantomimical contrivance, and change of scene and character, the parts help each other out in matters which neither of them singly would assume to act. When money is to be obtained, the mass of variety apparently dissolves, and a profusion of parliamentary praises passes between the parts. Each admires with astonishment, the wisdom, the liberality, and disinterestedness of the other: and all of them breathe a pitying sigh at the burdens of the Nation.

But in a well-constituted republic, nothing of this soldering, praising, and pitying, can take place; the representation being equal throughout the country, and compleat in itself, however it may be arranged into legislative and executive, they have all one and the same natural source. The parts are not foreigners to each other, like democracy, aristocracy, and monarchy. As there are no discordant distinctions, there is nothing to corrupt by compromise, nor confound by contrivance. Public measures appeal of themselves to the understanding of the Nation, and, resting on their own merits, disown any flattering applications to vanity. The continual whine of lamenting the burden of taxes, however successfully it may be practised in mixed Governments, is inconsistent with the sense and spirit of a republic. If taxes are necessary, they are of course advantageous; but if they require an apology, the apology itself implies an impeachment. Why, then, is man thus imposed upon, or why does he impose upon himself?

When men are spoken of as kings and subjects, or when Government is mentioned under the distinct and combined heads of monarchy, aristocracy, and democracy, what is it that reasoning man is to understand by the terms? If there really existed in the world two or more distinct and separate elements of human power, we should then see the several origins to which those terms would descriptively apply; but as there is but one species of man, there can be but one element of human power; and that element is man himself. Monarchy, aristocracy, and democracy, are but creatures of imagination; and a thousand such may be contrived as well as three.

From the Revolutions of America and France, and the symptoms that have appeared in other countries, it is evident that the opinion of the world is changing with respect to systems of Government, and that revolutions are not within the compass of political calculations. The progress of time and circumstances, which men assign to the accomplishment of great changes, is too mechanical to measure the force of the mind, and the rapidity of reflection, by which revolutions are generated: All the old governments have received a shock from those that already appear, and which were once more improbable, and are a greater subject of wonder, than a general revolution in Europe would be now.

When we survey the wretched condition of man, under the monarchical and hereditary systems of Government, dragged from his home by one power, or driven by another, and impoverished by taxes more than by enemies, it becomes evident that those systems are bad, and that a general revolution in the principle and construction of Governments is necessary.

What is government more than the management of the affairs of a Nation? It is not, and from its nature cannot be, the property of any particular man or family, but of the whole community, at whose expence it is supported; and though by force and contrivance it has been usurped into an inheritance, the usurpation cannot alter the right of things. Sovereignty, as a matter of right, appertains to the Nation only, and not to any individual; and a Nation has at all times an inherent indefeasible right to abolish any form of Government it finds inconvenient, and to establish such as accords with its interest, disposition and happiness. The romantic and barbarous distinction of men into Kings and subjects, though it may suit the condition of courtiers, cannot that of citizens; and is exploded by the principle upon which Governments are now founded. Every citizen is a member of the Sovereignty, and, as such, can acknowledge no personal subjection: and his obedience can be only to the laws.

When men think of what Government is, they must necessarily suppose it to possess a knowledge of all the objects and matters upon which its authority is to be exercised. In this view of Gov-

233

ernment, the Republican system, as established by America and France, operates to embrace the whole of a Nation; and the knowledge necessary to the interest of all the parts, is to be found in the centre, which the parts by representation form; but the old Governments are on a construction that excludes knowledge as well as happiness; Government by Monks, who knew nothing of the world beyond the walls of a Convent, is as consistent as government by Kings.

What were formerly called Revolutions, were little more than a change of persons, or an alteration of local circumstances. They rose and fell like things of course, and had nothing in their existence or their fate that could influence beyond the spot that produced them. But what we now see in the world, from the Revolutions of America and France, are a renovation of the natural order of things, a system of principles as universal as truth and the existence of man, and combining moral with political happiness and national prosperity.

"I. Men are born, and always continue, free and equal in respect of their rights. Civil distinctions, therefore, can be found only on public utility.

"II. The end of all political associations is the preservation of the natural and imprescriptible rights of man; and these rights are liberty, property, security, and resistance of oppression.

"III. The Nation is essentially the source of all sovereignty; nor can ANY INDIVIDUAL, or ANY BODY OF MEN, be entitled to any authority which is not expressly derived from it."

In these principles, there is nothing to throw a Nation into confusion by inflaming ambition. They are calculated to call forth wisdom and abilities, and to exercise them for the public good, and not for the emolument or aggrandisement of particular descriptions of men or families. Monarchical sovereignty, the enemy of mankind, and the source of misery, is abolished; and sovereignty itself is restored to its natural and original place, the Nation. Were this the case throughout Europe, the cause of wars would be taken away.

It is attributed to Henry the Fourth of France,

a man of enlarged and benevolent heart, that he proposed, about the year 1610, a plan for abolishing war in Europe. The plan consisted in constituting an European Congress, or as the French authors stile it, a Pacific Republic; by appointing delegates from the several Nations who were to act as a Court of arbitration in any disputes that might arise between nation and nation.

Had such a plan been adopted at the time it was proposed, the taxes of England and France, as two of the parties, would have been at least ten millions sterling annually to each Nation less than they were at the commencement of the French Revolution.

To conceive a cause why such a plan has not been adopted (and that instead of a Congress for the purpose of preventing war, it has been called only to terminate a war, after fruitless expence of several years) it will be necessary to consider the interest of Governments as a distinct interest to that of Nations.

Whatever is the cause of taxes to a Nation, becomes also the means of revenue to a Government. Every war terminates with an addition of taxes, and consequently with an addition of revenue; and in any event of war, in the manner they are now commenced and concluded, the power and interest of Governments are increased. War, therefore, from its productiveness, as it easily furnishes the pretence of necessity for taxes and appointments to places and offices, becomes a principal part of the system of old Governments; and to establish any mode to abolish war, however advantageous it might be to Nations, would be to take from such Government the most lucrative of its branches. The frivolous matters upon which war is made, shew the disposition and avidity of Governments to uphold the system of war, and betray the motives upon which they act.

Why are not Republics plunged into war, but because the nature of their Government does not admit of an interest distinct from that of the Nation? Even Holland, though an ill-constructed Republic, and with a commerce extending over the world, existed nearly a century without war: and the instant the form of Government was changed in France, the republican principles of peace and domestic prosperity and economy arose with the new Government; and the same consequences would follow the cause in other nations.

As war is the system of Government on the old construction, the animosity which Nations reciprocally entertain, is nothing more than what the policy of their Governments excites to keep up the spirit of the system. Each Government accuses the other of perfidy, intrigue, and ambition, as a means of heating the imagination of their respective Nations, and incensing them to hostilities. Man is not the enemy of man, but through the medium of a false system of Government. Instead, therefore, of exclaiming against the ambition of Kings, the exclamation should be directed against the principle of such Governments; and instead of seeking to reform the individual, the wisdom of a Nation should apply itself to reform the system.

Whether the forms and maxims of Governments which are still in practice, were adapted to the condition of the world at the period they were established, is not in this case the question. The older they are, the less correspondence can they have with the present state of things. Time, and change of circumstances and opinions, have the same progressive effect in rendering modes of Government obsolete as they have upon customs and manners.—Agriculture, commerce, manufacturers, and the tranquil arts, by which the prosperity of Nations is best promoted, require a different system of Government, and a different species of knowledge to direct its operations, than what might have been required in the former condition of the world.

As it is not difficult to perceive, from the enlightened state of mankind, that hereditary Governments are verging to their decline, and that Revolutions on the broad basis of national sovereignty and Government by representation, are making their way in Europe, it would be an act of wisdom to anticipate their approach, and produce Revolutions by reason and accommodation, rather than commit them to the issue of convulsions.

From what we now see, nothing of reform in the political world ought to be held improbable. It is an age of Revolutions, in which everything may be looked for. The intrigue of Courts, by which the system of war is kept up, may provoke a confederation of Nations to abolish it: and an European Congress to patronize the progress of free Government, and promote the civilisation of Nations with each other, is an event nearer in probability, than once were the revolutions and alliance of France and America.

The Age of Reason

The Age of Reason was published in two parts, 1794–1795. While writing the first part Paine was living in France, attached to the moderate Girondé group. The rise of the Reign of Terror led to his imprisonment in Luxembourg in December, 1793, which prevented his seeing the manuscript through the press. Eleven months later, with the fall of Robespierre, Paine was released.

Circumstances attending *The Age of Reason* are thus described by Paine in a letter to Samuel Adams dated January 1, 1803:

I have said . . . that it had long been my intention to publish my thoughts on Religion, but that I had reserved it to a later time of life. I have now to inform you why I wrote it and published it at the time I did.

In the first place, I saw my life in continual danger. My friends were falling as fast as the guillotine could cut their heads off. . . . I appeared to myself to be on my death-bed, for death was on every side of me, and I had no time to lose, . . . I had not finished the first part of that Work more than six hours before I was arrested and taken to prison. Joel Barlow was with me and knows the fact.

In the second place, the people of France were running headlong into Atheism, and I had the work translated and published in their own language to stop them in that career, and fix them to the first article (as I have said before) of every man's Creed who has any Creed at all, 'I believe in God.'

I. *The Author's Profession of Faith* [*Deism*]

It has been my intention, for several years past, to publish my thoughts upon religion; I am well aware of the difficulties that attend the subject, and from that consideration, had reserved it to a more advanced period of life. I intended it to be the last offering I should make to my fellow citizens of all nations, and that at a time when the purity of the motive that induced me to it could not admit of a question, even by those who might disapprove the work.

The circumstance that has now taken place in France, of the total abolition of the whole national order of priesthood, and of everything appertaining to compulsive systems of religion, and compulsive articles of faith, has not only precipitated my intention, but rendered a work of this kind exceedingly necessary, lest, in the general wreck of superstition, of false systems of government, and false theology, we lose sight of morality, of humanity, and of the theology that is true.

As several of my colleagues, and others of my fellow-citizens of France, have given me the example of making their voluntary and individual profession of faith, I also will make mine; and I do this with all that sincerity and frankness with which the mind of man communicates with itself.

I believe in one God, and no more; and I hope for happiness beyond this life.

I believe in the equality of man, and I believe that religious duties consist in doing justice, loving mercy, and endeavoring to make our fellow-creatures happy.

But, lest it should be supposed that I believe many other things in addition to these, I shall, in the progress of this work, declare the things I do not believe, and my reasons for not believing them.

I do not believe in the creed professed by the Jewish church, by the Roman church, by the Greek church, by the Turkish church, by the Protestant church, nor by any church that I know of. My own mind is my own church.

All national institutions of churches, whether Jewish, Christian, or Turkish, appear to me no other than human inventions set up to terrify and enslave mankind, and monopolize power and profit.

I do not mean by this declaration to condemn those who believe otherwise; they have the same right to their belief as I have to mine. But it is necessary to the happiness of man, that he be mentally faithful to himself. Infidelity does not consist in believing, or in disbelieving; it consists in professing to believe what he does not believe.

It is impossible to calculate the moral mischief, if I may so express it, that mental lying has produced in society. When a man has so far corrupted and prostituted the chastity of his mind, as to subscribe his professional belief to things he does not believe, he has prepared himself for the commission of every other crime. He takes up the trade of a priest for the sake of gain, and in order to qualify himself for that trade, he begins with a perjury. Can we conceive anything more destructive to morality than this?

Soon after I had published the pamphlet Common Sense, in America, I saw the exceeding probability that a revolution in the system of government would be followed by a revolution in the system of religion. The adulterous connection of church and state, wherever it had taken place, whether Jewish, Christian, or Turkish, had so effectually prohibited, by pains and penalties, every discussion upon established creeds, and upon first principles of religion, that until the system of government should be changed, those subjects could not be brought fairly and openly before the world; but that whenever this should be done, a revolution in the system of religion would follow. Human inventions and priest-craft would be detected; and man would return to the pure, unmixed, and unadulterated belief of one God, and no more.

IX. *In What the True Revelation Consists*

But some perhaps will say—Are we to have no word of God—no revelation?[n] I answer yes. There is a Word of God; there is a revelation.

THE WORD OF GOD IS THE CREATION WE BEHOLD: And it is in this word, which no human invention can counterfeit or alter, that God speaketh universally to man.

Human language is local and changeable, and is therefore incapable of being used as the means of unchangeable and universal information. The idea that God sent Jesus Christ to publish, as they say the glad tidings to all nations, from one end of the earth unto the other, is consistent only with the ignorance of those who know nothing of the extent of the world, and who believed, as those world-saviours believed, and continued to believe for several centuries, (and that in contradiction to the discoveries of philosophers and the experience of

revelation: At this point the French work has *Je réponds hardiment que nous ne sommes point condamnés à ce malheur*. "I boldly answer that we are not condemned to this misfortune."

236

navigators,) that the earth was flat like a trencher; and that a man might walk to the end of it.

But how was Jesus Christ to make anything known to all nations? He could speak but one language, which was Hebrew; and there are in the world several hundred languages. Scarcely any two nations speak the same language, or understand each other; and as to translations, every man who knows anything of languages, knows that it is impossible to translate from one language into another, not only without losing a great part of the original, but frequently of mistaking the sense; and besides all this, the art of printing was wholly unknown at the time Christ lived.

It is always necessary that the means that are to accomplish any end be equal to the accomplishment of that end, or the end cannot be accomplished. It is in this that the difference between finite and infinite power and wisdom discovers itself. Man frequently fails in accomplishing his end, from a natural inability of the power to the purpose; and frequently from the want of wisdom to apply power properly. But it is impossible for infinite power and wisdom to fail as man faileth. The means it useth are always equal to the end: but human language, more especially as there is not an universal language, is incapable of being used as an universal means of unchangeable and uniform information; and therefore it is not the means that God useth in manifesting himself universally to man.

It is only in the Creation that all our ideas and conceptions of a *word of God* can unite. The Creation speaketh an universal language, independently of human speech or human language, multiplied and various as they be. It is an ever existing original, which every man can read. It cannot be forged; it cannot be counterfeited; it cannot be lost; it cannot be altered; it cannot be suppressed. It does not depend upon the will of man whether it shall be published or not; it publishes itself from one end of the earth to the other. It preaches to all nations and to all worlds; and this word of God reveals to man all that is necessary for man to know of God.

Do we want to contemplate his power? We see it in the immensity of the creation. Do we want to contemplate his wisdom? We see it in the unchangeable order by which the incomprehensible Whole is governed. Do we want to contemplate his munificence? We see it in the abundance with which he fills the earth. Do we want to contemplate his mercy? We see it in his not withholding that abundance even from the unthankful. In fine, do we want to know what God is? Search not the book called the scripture, which any human hand might make, but the scripture called the Creation.

X. *Concerning God, and the Lights Cast on His Existence and Attributes by the Bible*

The only idea man can affix to the name of God, is that of a *first cause*, the cause of all things. And, incomprehensibly difficult as it is for a man to conceive what a first cause is, he arrives at the belief of it, from the tenfold greater difficulty of disbelieving it. It is difficult beyond description to conceive that space can have no end; but it is more difficult to conceive an end. It is difficult beyond the power of man to conceive an eternal duration of what we call time; but it is more impossible to conceive a time when there shall be no time.

In like manner of reasoning, everything we behold carries in itself the internal evidence that it did not make itself. Every man is an evidence to himself, that he did not make himself; neither could his father make himself, nor his grandfather, nor any of his race; neither could any tree, plant, or animal make itself; and it is the conviction arising from this evidence, that carries us on, as it were, by necessity, to the belief of a first cause eternally existing, of a nature totally different to any material existence we know of, and by the power of which all things exist; and this first cause, man calls God.

It is only by the exercise of reason, that man can discover God. Take away that reason, and he would be incapable of understanding anything; and in this case it would be just as consistent to read even the book called the Bible to a horse as to a man. How then is it that those people pretend to reject reason?

Almost the only parts in the book called the Bible, that convey to us any idea of God, are some chapters in Job, and the Nineteenth Psalm; I recollect no other. Those parts are true *deistical* compositions; for they treat of the *Deity* through his works. They take the book of Creation as the word of God; they refer to no other book; and all the inferences they make are drawn from that volume.

I insert in this place the Nineteenth Psalm, as paraphrased into English verse by Addison.[n] I recollect not the prose, and where I write this I have not the opportunity of seeing it:

> The spacious firmament on high,
> With all the blue ethereal sky,
> And spangled heavens, a shining frame,
> Their great original proclaim.
> The unwearied sun, from day to day,
> Does his Creator's power display,
> And publishes to every land
> The work of an Almighty hand.
> Soon as the evening shades prevail,
> The moon takes up the wondrous tale,
> And nightly to the list'ning earth
> Repeats the story of her birth;
> Whilst all the stars that round her burn,
> And all the planets, in their turn,
> Confirm the tidings as they roll,
> And spread the truth from pole to pole.
> What though in solemn silence all
> Move round this dark terrestrial ball;
> What though no real voice, nor sound,
> Amidst their radiant orbs be found,
> In reason's ear they all rejoice,
> And utter forth a glorious voice,
> Forever singing as they shine,
> The hand that made us is divine.

What more does man want to know, than that the hand or power that made these things is divine, is omnipotent? Let him believe this, with the force it is impossible to repel if he permits his reason to act, and his rule of moral life will follow of course.

The allusions in Job have all of them the same tendency with this Psalm; that of deducing or proving a truth that would be otherwise unknown, from truths already known.

I recollect not enough of the passages in Job to insert them correctly; but there is one that occurs to me that is applicable to the subject I am speaking upon. "Canst thou by searching find out God; canst thou find out the Almighty to perfection?"

I know not how the printers have pointed this passage, for I keep no Bible; but it contains two distinct questions that admit of distinct answers.

First, Canst thou by searching find out God? Yes. Because, in the first place, I know I did not make myself, and yet I have existence; and by searching into the nature of other things, I find that no other thing could make itself; and yet millions of other things exist; therefore it is, that I know, by positive conclusion resulting from this search, that there is a power superior to all those things, and that power is God.

Secondly, Canst thou find out the Almighty to perfection? No. Not only because the power and wisdom He has manifested in the structure of the Creation that I behold is to me incomprehensible; but because even this manifestation, great as it is, is probably but a small display of that immensity of power and wisdom, by which millions of other worlds, to me invisible by their distance, were created and continue to exist.

It is evident that both of these questions were put to the reason of the person to whom they are supposed to have been addressed; and it is only by admitting the first question to be answered affirmatively, that the second could follow. It would have been unnecessary, and even absurd, to have put a second question, more difficult than the first, if the first question had been answered negatively. The two questions have different objects; the first refers to the existence of God, the second to his attributes. Reason can discover the one, but it falls infinitely short in discovering the whole of the other. . . .

XV. *Advantages of the Existence of Many Worlds in Each Solar System*

It is an idea I have never lost sight of, that all our knowledge of science is derived from the revolutions (exhibited to our eye and from thence to our understanding) which those several planets or worlds of which our system is composed make in their circuit round the Sun.

Had then the quantity of matter which these six worlds contain been blended into one solitary globe, the consequence to us would have been, that

---

Addison: The French translator has substituted for this a version of the same psalm by Jean Baptiste Rousseau.

either no revolutionary motion would have existed, or not a sufficiency of it to give us the ideas and the knowledge of science we now have; and it is from the sciences that all the mechanical arts that contribute so much to our earthly felicity and comfort are derived.

As therefore the Creator made nothing in vain, so also must it be believed that he organized the structure of the universe in the most advantageous manner for the benefit of man; and as we see, and from experience feel, the benefits we derive from the structure of the universe, formed as it is, which benefits we should not have had the opportunity of enjoying if the structure, so far as relates to our system, had been a solitary globe, we can discover at least one reason why a plurality of worlds has been made, and that reason calls forth the devotional gratitude of man, as well as his admiration.

But it is not to us, the inhabitants of this globe, only, that the benefits arising from a plurality of worlds are limited. The inhabitants of each of the worlds of which our system is composed, enjoy the same opportunities of knowledge as we do. They behold the revolutionary motions of our earth, as we behold theirs. All the planets revolve in sight of each other; and, therefore, the same universal school of science presents itself to all.

Neither does the knowledge stop here. The system of worlds next to us exhibits, in its revolutions, the same principles and school of science, to the inhabitants of their system, as our system does to us, and in like manner throughout the immensity of space.

Our ideas, not only of the almightiness of the Creator, but of his wisdom and his beneficence, become enlarged in proportion as we contemplate the extent and the structure of the universe. The solitary[n] idea of a solitary world, rolling or at rest in the immense ocean of space, gives place to the cheerful idea of a society of worlds, so happily contrived as to administer, even by their motion, instruction to man.[n] We see our own earth filled with abundance; but we forget to consider how much of that abundance is owing to the scientific knowledge the vast machinery of the universe has unfolded.

Recapitulation

Having now extended the subject to a greater length than I first intended, I shall bring it to a close by abstracting a summary from the whole.

First, That the idea or belief of a word of God existing in print, or in writing, or in speech, is inconsistent in itself for the reasons already assigned. These reasons, among many others, are the want of an universal language; the mutability of language; the errors to which translations are subject; the possibility of totally suppressing such a word; the probability of altering it, or of fabricating the whole, and imposing it upon the world.

Secondly, That the Creation we behold is the real and ever existing word of God, in which we cannot be deceived. It proclaimeth his power, it demonstrates his wisdom, it manifests his goodness and beneficence.

Thirdly, That the moral duty of man consists in imitating the moral goodness and beneficence of God manifested in the creation towards all his creatures. That seeing as we daily do the goodness of God to all men, it is an example calling upon all men to practice the same towards each other; and, consequently, that every thing of persecution and revenge between man and man, and every thing of cruelty to animals, is a violation of moral duty.

I trouble not myself about the manner of future existence. I content myself with believing, even to positive conviction, that the power that gave me existence is able to continue it, in any form and manner he pleases, either with or without this body; and it appears more probable to me that I shall continue to exist hereafter than that I should have had existence, as I now have, before that existence began.

It is certain that, in one point, all nations of the earth and all religions agree. All believe in a God. The things in which they disagree are the redundancies annexed to that belief; and therefore, if ever an universal religion should prevail, it will not be believing any thing new, but in getting rid of redundancies, and believing as man believed

---

solitary: The French work has *triste*. man: The French work has *leur mouvement même est le premier éveil la première instruction de la raison dans l'homme.* "Their motion itself is the first awakening, the first instruction of the reason in man."

at first.[n] Adam, if ever there was such a man, was created a Deist; but in the mean time, let every man follow, as he has a right to do, the religion and worship he prefers.

THE FEDERALIST: ALEXANDER HAMILTON (1757-1804), JAMES MADISON (1751-1836), AND JOHN JAY (1745-1829)

The Federalist (1788) appeared a year after the production of the first successful American comedy and a year before the earliest native novel, yet in distinction it is far superior to the colonial achievement in imaginative literature. Its survival as a political classic indicates that eighteenth-century Americans were as mature in political experience as they were adolescent in esthetic interests. In the words of a modern editor, Edward Mead Earle, *The Federalist* "was the first and continues to be the most important discussion of federal government, for which the Constitution of the United States set a significant precedent. It was and still is a masterly analysis and interpretation of the Constitution and of the fundamental principles upon which the government of the United States was established."

When the new constitution was submitted to the conventions in the several states in 1787, its popular endorsement was by no means certain. This was especially true in the state of New York, where a determined and powerful opposition provoked a flurry of bristling tracts and newspaper articles on the defects and merits of the proposed instrument of government. In October, 1787, in the midst of the controversy, there arose the towering figure of "Publius," under whose name appeared a notable series of articles in the defense and interpretation of the Constitution. The chief architect of the project was Alexander Hamilton, a young and distinguished New York lawyer, who had been a member of the Constitutional Convention, and who was later to become Washington's brilliant Secretary of the Treasury. His collaborators in the enterprise were James Madison, later Secretary of State and President, who had made an invaluable contribution as a member of the Constitutional Convention, and John Jay, later Chief Justice, whose influence in New York was perhaps greater than that of either Hamilton or Madison. Of the eighty-five articles which make up *The Federalist*, Hamilton wrote more

than half, Madison about thirty, and Jay five. The authorship of about twelve of the individual numbers of *The Federalist* has been disputed, and cannot be ascribed conclusively to either Hamilton or Madison; others were the result of direct collaboration. Whether or not Hamilton, as the general editor of the series, did much revising is not known. The high excellence and remarkable coherence of the entire series indicate that all the writers observed a common editorial standard.

Although the *Federalist* was frankly utilitarian in its design to assure the adoption of the Constitution in the state of New York, its final importance does not rest upon its effect as a campaign document. Indeed, its influence in determining the ratification of the Constitution has been overemphasized. Ten states, one more than the number necessary to make the new government effective, already had approved the Constitution before New York, by a vote of 30 to 27, finally swung into line. The significance of the *Federalist* transcends the controversy which produced it. From the time of Chief Justice Marshall, who regarded it as a complete commentary on the Constitution, the *Federalist* has been considered as a source of constitutional law. It remains today a clear, vigorous, dignified, and at times noble statement of a perennial concern of republican government: how may the central government be made strong enough to secure the general welfare of society and, at the same time, respect the rights of the individuals and states which compose it?

BIBLIOGRAPHY · The best editions of *The Federalist* are those of P. L. Ford (1898), H. C. Lodge (1923), and E. M. Earle (1938). The most readily available of these is the Sesquicentennial Edition by Earle, which contains the texts of the call for the Federal Constitutional Convention, the Articles of Confederation, the Constitution, and its amendments. Other useful reprints and selections include those in Everyman's Library (n. d.), J. S. Bassett, *Selections from the Federalist* (1921), and E. G. Bourne, *The Federalist* (1937). For the controversy over the authorship of certain of the individual essays, see H. C. Lodge, *The Federalist* (1888), xxiii–xxxv; E. G. Bourne, "The Authorship of *The Federalist*," in *American Historical Review*, II (1897), 443–460, and the same authority's *Essays in Historical Criticism* (1901), Chapters II–III.

at first: "In the childhood of the world," according to the first (French) version; and the strict translation of the final sentence is: "Deism was the religion of Adam, supposing him not an imaginary being; but none the less must it be left to all men to follow, as is their right, the religion and worship they prefer."

The Federalist

ALL but eight of the eighty-five essays of the *Federalist* were first printed in the New York press between October, 1787, and May, 1788. The series was published in book form in the spring of 1788, the first edition appearing in two volumes: the first, on March 22, 1788, and the second, on May 28. Although the articles were still being printed in the New York newspapers when the second volume was issued, eight of the numbers (78 to 85 inclusive) were published for the first time in the second volume.

The work of all three of the authors of the *Federalist* is represented in the selections for this anthology. The text is that of the first edition, *The Federalist: A Collection of Essays written in Favour of the New Constitution, as Agreed upon by the Federal Convention, September 7, 1787* (New York, 1788).

I. [Hamilton: Introduction] · *Independent Journal*, October 27, 1787

After an unequivocal experience of the inefficiency of the subsisting federal government, you are called upon to deliberate on a new Constitution for the United States of America. The subject speaks its own importance; comprehending in its consequences nothing less than the existence of the Union, the safety and welfare of the parts of which it is composed, the fate of an empire in many respects the most interesting in the world. It has been frequently remarked that it seems to have been reserved to the people of this country, by their conduct and example, to decide the important question, whether societies of men are really capable or not of establishing good government from reflection and choice, or whether they are forever destined to depend for their political constitutions on accident and force. If there be any truth in the remark, the crisis at which we are arrived may with propriety be regarded as the era in which that decision is to be made; and a wrong election of the part we shall act may, in this view, deserve to be considered as the general misfortune of mankind.

This idea will add the inducements of philanthropy to those of patriotism, to heighten the solicitude which all considerate and good men must feel for the event. Happy will it be if our choice should be directed by a judicious estimate of our true interests, unperplexed and unbiased by considerations not connected with the public good. But this is a thing more ardently to be wished than seriously to be expected. The plan offered to our deliberations affects too many particular interests, innovates upon too many local institutions, not to involve in its discussion a variety of objects foreign to its merits, and of views, passions, and prejudices little favorable to the discovery of truth.

Among the most formidable of the obstacles which the new Constitution will have to encounter may readily be distinguished the obvious interest of a certain class of men in every State to resist all changes which may hazard a diminution of the power, emolument, and consequence of the offices they hold under the State establishment; and the perverted ambition of another class of men, who will either hope to aggrandize themselves by the confusions of their country, or will flatter themselves with fairer prospects of elevation from the subdivision of the empire into several partial confederacies than from its union under one government.

It is not, however, my design to dwell upon observations of this nature. I am well aware that it would be disingenuous to resolve indiscriminately the opposition of any set of men (merely because their situations might subject them to suspicion) into interested or ambitious views. Candor will oblige us to admit that even such men may be actuated by upright intentions; and it cannot be doubted that much of the opposition which has made its appearance, or may hereafter make its appearance, will spring from sources, blameless, at least, if not respectable—the honest errors of minds led astray by preconceived jealousies and fears. So numerous indeed and so powerful are the causes which serve to give a false bias to the judgment, that we, upon many occasions, see wise and good men on the wrong as well as on the right side of questions of the first magnitude to society. This circumstance, if duly attended to, would furnish a lesson of moderation to those who are ever so much persuaded of their being in the right in any controversy. And a further reason for caution, in this respect, might be drawn from the reflection that we are not always sure that those who advocate the truth are influenced by purer principles than their antagonists. Ambition, avarice, personal animosity, party opposition, and many other motives not more laudable than these, are apt to operate as well upon those who support as those who oppose the right side of a question. Were there not even these inducements to moderation, nothing could be more ill-judged than that intolerant spirit which has, at all times, characterized political parties. For in politics, as in religion, it is equally absurd to aim at making proselytes by fire and sword. Heresies in either can rarely be cured by persecution.

And yet, however just these sentiments will be allowed to be, we have already sufficient indications that it will happen in this as in all former cases of great national discussion. A torrent of angry and malignant passions will be let loose. To judge from the conduct of the opposite parties, we shall be led to conclude that they will mutually hope to evince the justness of their opinions, and to increase the number of their converts by the loudness of their declamations and the bitterness of their invectives. An enlightened zeal for the energy and efficiency of government will be stigmatized as the offspring of a temper fond of despotic power and hostile to the principles of liberty. And overscrupulous jealousy of danger to the rights of the people, which is more commonly the fault of the head than of the heart, will be represented as mere pretense and artifice, the stale bait for popularity at the expense of the public good. It will be forgotten, on the one hand, that jealousy is the usual concomitant of love, and that the noble enthusiasm of liberty is apt to be infected with a spirit of narrow and illiberal distrust. On the other hand, it will be equally forgotten that the vigor of government is essential to the security of liberty; that, in the contemplation of a sound and well-informed judgment, their interest can never be separated; and that a dangerous ambition more often lurks behind the specious mask of zeal for the rights of the people than under the forbidding appearance of zeal for the firmness and efficiency of government. History will teach us that the former has been found a much more certain road to the introduction of despotism than the latter, and that of those men who have overturned the liberties of republics, the greatest number have begun their career by paying an obsequious court to the people; commencing demagogues, and ending tyrants.

In the course of the preceding observations, I have had an eye, my fellow-citizens, to putting you upon your guard against all attempts, from whatever quarter, to influence your decision in a matter of the utmost moment to your welfare, by any impressions other than those which may result from the evidence of truth. You will, no doubt, at the same time have collected from the general scope of them, that they proceed from a source not unfriendly to the new Constitution. Yes, my countrymen, I own to you that, after having given it an attentive consideration, I am clearly of opinion it is your interest to adopt it. I am convinced that this is the safest course for your liberty, your dignity, and your happiness. I affect not reserves which I do not feel. I will not amuse you with an appearance of deliberation when I have decided. I frankly acknowledge to you my convictions, and I will freely lay before you the reasons on which they are founded. The consciousness of good intentions disdains ambiguity. I shall not, however, multiply professions on this head. My motives must remain in the depository of my own breast. My arguments will be open to all, and may be judged of by all. They shall at least be offered in a spirit which will not disgrace the cause of truth.

I propose, in a series of papers, to discuss the following interesting particulars:—The utility of the Union to your political prosperity—The insufficiency of the present Confederation to preserve that Union—The necessity of a government at least equally energetic with the one proposed, to the attainment of this object—The conformity of the proposed Constitution to the true principles of republican government—Its analogy to your own State constitution—and lastly, The additional security which its adoption will afford to the preservation of that species of government, to liberty, and to property.

In the progress of this discussion I shall endeavour to give a satisfactory answer to all the objections which shall have made their appearance, that may seem to have any claim to your attention.

It may perhaps be thought superfluous to offer

arguments to prove the utility of the Union, a point, no doubt, deeply engraved on the hearts of the great body of the people in every State, and one, which it may be imagined has no adversaries. But the fact is, that we already hear it whispered in the private circles of those who oppose the new constitution, that the Thirteen States are of too great extent for any general system, and that we must of necessity resort to separate confederacies of distinct portions of the whole.[n] This doctrine 10 will, in all probability, be gradually propagated, till it has votaries enough to countenance an open avowal of it. For nothing can be more evident, to those who are able to take an enlarged view of the subject, than the alternative of an adoption of the new constitution, or a dismemberment of the Union. It will therefore be of use to begin by examining the advantages of that Union, the certain evils and the probable dangers, to which every State will be exposed from its dissolution.—This 20 shall accordingly constitute the subject of my next address.

Publius

II. [Jay: Advantages of Union] · *Independent Journal*, October 31, 1787 · II. *Concerning Dangers from foreign Force and Influence*

When the people of America reflect that they are now called upon to decide a question, which, in its consequences, must prove one of the most 30 important, that ever engaged their attention, the propriety of their taking a very comprehensive, as well as a very serious view of it, will be evident.

Nothing is more certain than the indispensable necessity of government; and it is equally undeniable, that whenever and however it is instituted, the people must cede to it some of their natural rights, in order to vest it with requisite powers. It is well worthy of consideration therefore, whether it would conduce more to the in- 40 terest of the people of America, that they should, to all general purposes, be one nation, under one federal government, than that they should divide themselves into separate confederacies, and give to

separate . . . whole: the same idea, tracing the arguments to their consequences, is held out in several of the late publications against the new Constitution. (Hamilton's note)

the head of each, the same kind of powers which they are advised to place in one national government.

It has until lately been a received and uncontradicted opinion, that the prosperity of the people of America depended on their continuing firmly united, and the wishes, prayers and efforts of our best and wisest citizens have been constantly directed to that object. But politicians now appear, who insist that this opinion is erroneous, and that instead of looking for safety and happiness in union, we ought to seek it in a division of the states into distinct confederacies or sovereignties. However extraordinary this new doctrine may appear, it nevertheless has its advocates; and certain characters who were much opposed to it formerly, are at present of the number. Whatever may be the arguments or inducements, which have wrought this change in the sentiments and declarations of these gentlemen, it certainly would not be wise in the people at large to adopt these new political tenets without being fully convinced that they are founded in truth and sound Policy.

It has often given me pleasure to observe, that independent America was not composed of detached and distant territories, but that one connected, fertile, wide spreading country, was the portion of our western sons of liberty. Providence has in a particular manner blessed it with a variety of soils and productions, and watered it with innumerable streams, for the delight and accommodation of its inhabitants. A succession of navigable waters forms a kind of chain round its borders, as if to bind it together; while the most noble rivers in the world, running at convenient distances, present them with the highways for the easy communcation of friendly aids, and the mutual transportation and exchange of their various commodities.

With equal pleasure I have so often taken notice that Providence has been pleased to give this one connected country to one united people— a people descended from the same ancestors, speaking the same language, professing the same religion, attached to the same principles of government, very similar in their manners and customs, and who, by their joint counsels, arms, and efforts, fighting side by side throughout a long and bloody war, have nobly established general liberty and independence.

This country and this people seem to have been made for each other, and it appears as if it was the design of Providence that an inheritance so proper and convenient for a band of brethren united to each other by the strongest ties, should never be split into a number of unsocial, jealous, and alien sovereignties.

Similar sentiments have hitherto prevailed among all orders and denominations of men among us. To all general purposes we have uniformly been one people; each individual citizen everywhere enjoying the same national rights, privileges, and protection. As a nation we have made peace and war; as a nation we have formed alliances, and made treaties, and entered into various compacts and conventions with foreign states.

Strong sense of the value and blessings of union induced the people, at a very early period, to institute a federal government to preserve and perpetuate it. They formed it almost as soon as they had a political existence; nay, at a time when their habitations were in flames, when many of their citizens were bleeding, and when the progress of hostility and desolation left little room for those calm and mature inquiries and reflections which must ever precede the formation of a wise and well-balanced government for a free people. It is not to be wondered at that a government, instituted in times so inauspicious, should on experiment be found greatly deficient and inadequate to the purpose it was intended to answer.

This intelligent people perceived and regretted these defects. Still continuing no less attached to union than enamored of liberty, they observed the danger which immediately threatened the former and more remotely the latter; and being persuaded that ample security for both could only be found in a national government more wisely framed, they, as with one voice, convened the late convention at Philadelphia, to take that important subject under consideration.

This convention, composed of men who possessed the confidence of the people, and many of whom had become highly distinguished by their patriotism, virtue, and wisdom, in times which tried the mind and hearts of men, undertook the arduous task. In the mild season of peace, with minds unoccupied by other subjects, they passed many months in cool, uninterrupted, and daily consultation; and finally, without having been awed by power, or influenced by any passions except love for their country, they presented and recommended to the people the plan produced by their joint and very unanimous councils.

Admit, for so is the fact, that this plan is only recommended, not imposed, yet let it be remembered that it is neither recommended to blind approbation, nor to blind reprobation; but to that sedate and candid consideration which the magnitude and importance of the subject demand, and which it certainly ought to receive. But this (as was remarked in the foregoing number of this paper) is more to be wished than expected, that it may be so considered and examined. Experience on a former occasion teaches us not to be too sanguine in such hopes. It is not yet forgotten that well-grounded apprehensions of imminent danger induced the people of America to form the memorable Congress of 1774. That body recommended certain measures to their constituents, and the event proved their wisdom; yet it is fresh in our memories how soon the press began to teem with pamphlets and weekly papers against those very measures. Not only many of the officers of government, who obeyed the dictates of personal interest, but others, from a mistaken estimate of consequences, or the undue influence of former attachments, or whose ambition aimed at objects which did not correspond with the public good, were indefatigable in their efforts to persuade the people to reject the advice of that patriotic Congress. Many, indeed, were deceived and deluded, but the great majority of the people reasoned and decided judiciously; and happy they are in reflecting that they did so.

They considered that the Congress was composed of many wise and experienced men. That, being convened from different parts of the country, they brought with them and communicated to each other a variety of useful information. That in the course of the time they passed together in enquiring into and discussing the true interests of their country, they must have acquired a very accurate knowledge on that head.

That they were individually interested in the public liberty and prosperity, and therefore that it was not less their inclination, than their duty, to recommend only such measures, as after the most mature deliberation they really thought prudent and advisable.

These and similar considerations then induced the people to rely greatly on the judgment and integrity of the Congress; and they took their advice, notwithstanding the various arts and endeavours used to deter and dissuade them from it. But if the people at large had reason to confide in the men of that Congress, few of whom had then been fully tried or generally known, still greater reason have they now to respect the judgment and advice of the Convention, for it is well known that some of the most distinguished members of that Congress, who have been since tried and justly approved for patriotism and abilities, and who have grown old in acquiring political information, were also members of this Convention, and carried into it their accumulated knowledge and experience.

It is worthy of remark that not only the first, but every succeeding Congress, as well as the late Convention, have invariably joined with the people in thinking that the prosperity of America depended on its Union. To preserve and perpetuate it, was the great object of the people in forming that Convention, and it is also the great object of the plan which the Convention has advised them to adopt. With what propriety therefore, or for what good purposes, are attempts at this particular period, made by some men, to depreciate the importance of the Union? or why is it suggested that three or four confederacies would be better than one? I am persuaded in my own mind, that the people have always thought right on this subject, and that their universal and uniform attachment to the cause of the Union, rests on great and weighty reasons, which I shall endeavour to develope and explain in some ensuing papers. They who promote the idea of substituting a number of distinct confederacies in the room of the plan of the Convention, seem clearly to foresee that the rejection of it would put the continuance of the Union in the utmost jeopardy —that certainly would be the case, and I sincerely

wish that it may be as clearly foreseen by every good citizen, that whenever the dissolution of the Union arrives, America will have reason to exclaim in the words of the poet, "Farewell, a long farewell, to all my Greatness."

Publius

X. [Madison: Union a Safeguard against Internal Faction] · *New York Daily Advertiser*, November 22, 1787

Among the numerous advantages promised by a well constructed union, none deserves to be more accurately developed than its tendency to break and control the violence of faction. The friend of popular governments, never finds himself so much alarmed for their character and fate, as when he contemplates their propensity to this dangerous vice. He will not fail therefore to set a due value on any plan which, without violating the principles to which he is attached, provides a proper cure for it. The instability, injustice and confusion introduced into the public councils, have in truth been the mortal diseases under which popular governments have everywhere perished; as they continue to be the favorite and fruitful topics from which the adversaries to liberty derive their most specious declamations. The valuable improvements made by the American constitutions on the popular models, both ancient and modern, cannot certainly be too much admired; but it would be an unwarrantable partiality, to contend that they have as effectually obviated the danger on this side as was wished and expected. Complaints are everywhere heard from our most considerate and virtuous citizens, equally the friends of public and private faith, and of public and personal liberty; that our governments are too unstable; that the public good is disregarded in the conflicts of rival parties; and that measures are too often decided, not according to the rules of justice, and the rights of the minor party; but by the superior force of an interested and overbearing majority. However anxiously we may wish that these complaints had no foundation, the evidence of known facts will not permit us to deny that they are in some degree true. It will be found indeed, on a candid review of our situation, that some of the distresses under which we labor, have been erroneously charged on the operation of our governments; but it will be found at the same time, that other causes will not alone account for many of our heaviest misfortunes; and, particularly, for that prevailing and increasing distrust of public engagements, and alarm for private rights, which are echoed from one end of the continent to the other. These must be chiefly, if not wholly, effects of the unsteadiness and injustice, with which a factious spirit has tainted our public administration.

By a faction I understand a number of citizens, whether amounting to a majority or minority of the whole, who are united and actuated by some common impulse of passion, or of interest, adverse to the rights of other citizens, or to the permanent and aggregate interests of the community.

There are two methods of curing the mischiefs of faction: the one, by removing its causes; the other, by controlling its effects.

There are again two methods of removing the causes of faction: The one, by destroying the liberty which is essential to its existence; the other, by giving to every citizen the same opinions, the same passions, and the same interests.

It could never be more truly said than of the first remedy, that it is worse than the disease. Liberty is to faction, what air is to fire, an aliment without which it instantly expires. But it could not be a less folly to abolish liberty, which is essential to political life, because it nourishes faction, than it would be to wish the annihilation of air, which is essential to animal life, because it imparts to fire its destructive agency.

The second expedient is as impracticable as the first would be unwise. As long as the reason of man continues fallible, and he is at liberty to exercise it, different opinions will be formed. As long as the connection subsists between his reason and his self-love, his opinions and his passions will have a reciprocal influence on each other; and the former will be objects to which the latter will attach themselves. The diversity in the faculties of men, from which the rights of property originate, is not less an insuperable obstacle to a uniformity of interests. The protection of these faculties is the first object of government. From the protection of different and unequal faculties of acquiring property, the possession of different degrees and kinds of property immediately results; and from the influence of these on the sentiments and views of the respective proprietors ensues a division of the society into different interests and parties.

The latent causes of faction are thus sown in the nature of man; and we see them everywhere brought into different degrees of activity, according to the different circumstances of civil society. A zeal for different opinions concerning religion, concerning government and many other points, as well of speculation as of practice; an attachment to different leaders ambitiously contending for pre-eminence and power, or to persons of other descriptions whose fortunes have been interesting to the human passions, have, in turn, divided mankind into parties, inflamed them with mutual animosity, and rendered them much more disposed to vex and oppress each other, than to co-operate for their common good. So strong is this propensity of mankind to fall into mutual animosities, that where no substantial occasion presents itself, the most frivolous and fanciful distinctions have been sufficient to kindle their unfriendly passions and excite their most violent conflicts. But the most common and durable source of factions has been the various and unequal distribution of property. Those who hold and those who are without property have ever formed distinct interests in society. Those who are creditors and those who are debtors fall under a like discrimination. A landed interest, a manufacturing interest, a mercantile interest, a moneyed interest, with many lesser interests, grow up of necessity in civilized nations, and divide them into different classes, actuated by different sentiments and views. The regulation of these various and interfering interests forms the principal task of modern legislation, and involves the spirit of party and faction in the necessary and ordinary operations of the government.

No man is allowed to be a judge in his own cause; because his interest would certainly bias his judgment and, not improbably, corrupt his integrity. With equal, nay, with greater reason, a body of men are unfit to be both judges and parties at the same time; yet what are many of the most important acts of legislation, but so many judicial determinations, not indeed concerning the rights of single persons, but concerning the rights of large bodies of citizens? and what are the different classes of legislators, but advocates and parties to the causes which they determine? Is a law proposed concerning private debts?—it is a question to which the creditors are parties on one side, and the debtors on the other. Justice ought to hold the balance between them. Yet the parties are, and must be, themselves the judges; and the most numerous party, or, in other words, the most powerful faction, must be expected to prevail. Shall domestic manufactures be encouraged, and in what degree by restrictions on foreign manufactures? are questions which would be differently decided by the landed and the manufacturing classes, and probably by neither with a sole regard to justice and the public good. The apportionment of taxes on the various descriptions of property is an act which seems to require the most exact impartiality; yet there is, perhaps, no legislative act in which greater opportunity and temptation are given to a predominant party, to trample on the rules of justice. Every shilling with which they overburden the inferior number is a shilling saved to their own pockets.

It is in vain to say that enlightened statesmen will be able to adjust these clashing interests and render them all subservient to the public good. Enlightened statesmen will not always be at the helm; nor, in many cases, can such an adjustment be made at all, without taking into view indirect and remote considerations, which will rarely prevail over the immediate interest which one party may find in disregarding the rights of another or the good of the whole.

The inference to which we are brought is that the causes of faction cannot be removed, and that relief is only to be sought in the means of controlling its effects.

If a faction consists of less than a majority, relief is supplied by the republican principle, which enables the majority to defeat its sinister views by regular vote. It may clog the administration, it may convulse the society; but it will be unable to execute and mask its violence under the forms of the Constitution. When a majority is included in a faction, the form of popular government, on the other hand, enables it to sacrifice to its ruling passion or interest both the public good

and the rights of other citizens. To secure the public good, and private rights, against the danger of such a faction, and at the same time to preserve the spirit and the form of popular government, is then the great object to which our inquiries are directed. Let me add that it is the great *desideratum*, by which alone this form of government can be rescued from the opprobrium under which it has so long labored, and be recommended to the esteem and adoption of mankind.

By what means is this object attainable? Evidently by one of two only. Either the existence of the same passion or interest in a majority, at the same time, must be prevented; or the majority, having such coexistent passion or interest, must be rendered, by their number and local situation, unable to concert and carry into effect schemes of oppression. If the impulse and the opportunity be suffered to coincide, we well know that neither moral nor religious motives can be relied on as an adequate control. They are not found to be such on the injustice and violence of individuals, and lose their efficacy in proportion to the number combined together; that is, in proportion as their efficacy becomes needful.

From this view of the subject it may be concluded that a pure democracy, by which I mean a society consisting of a small number of citizens, who assemble and administer the government in person, can admit of no cure for the mischiefs of faction. A common passion or interest will, in almost every case, be felt by a majority of the whole; a communication and concert results from the form of government itself; and there is nothing to check the inducements to sacrifice the weaker party or an obnoxious individual. Hence it is that such democracies have ever been spectacles of turbulence and contention; have ever been found incompatible with personal security, or the rights of property, and have in general been as short in their lives as they have been violent in their deaths. Theoretic politicians, who have patronized this species of government, have erroneously supposed that by reducing mankind to a perfect equality in their political rights, they would at the same time be perfectly equalized and assimilated in their possessions, their opinions, and their passions.

A republic, by which I mean a government in

which the scheme of representation takes place, opens a different prospect, and promises the cure for which we are seeking. Let us examine the points in which it varies from pure democracy, and we shall comprehend both the nature of the cure and the efficacy which it must derive from the union.

The two great points of difference between a democracy and a republic are: First, the delegation of the government, in the latter, to a small number of citizens elected by the rest; secondly, the greater number of citizens, and greater sphere of country, over which the latter may be extended.

The effect of the first difference is, on the one hand, to refine and enlarge the public views, by passing them through the medium of a chosen body of citizens, whose wisdom may best discern the true interest of their country, and whose patriotism and love of justice will be least likely to sacrifice it to temporary or partial considerations. Under such a regulation, it may well happen that the public voice, pronounced by the representatives of the people, will be more consonant to the public good than if pronounced by the people themselves, convened for the purpose. On the other hand, the effect may be inverted. Men of factious tempers, of local prejudices, or of sinister designs, may by intrigue, by corruption, or by other means, first obtain the suffrages, and then betray the interests of the people. The question resulting is, whether small or extensive republics are most favorable to the election of proper guardians of the public weal; and it is clearly decided in favor of the latter by two obvious considerations.

In the first place, it is to be remarked that, however small the republic may be, the representatives must be raised to a certain number, in order to guard against the cabals of a few; and that, however large it may be, they must be limited to a certain number, in order to guard against the confusion of a multitude. Hence the number of representatives in the two cases not being in proportion to that of the constituents, and being proportionally greatest in the small republic, it follows, that if the proportion of fit characters be not less in the large than in the small republic, the former will present a greater option, and consequently a greater probability of a fit choice.

In the next place, as each representative will be chosen by a greater number of citizens in the large than in the small republic, it will be more difficult for unworthy candidates to practise with success the vicious arts, by which elections are too often carried; and the suffrages of the people being more free, will be more likely to centre on men who possess the most attractive merit, and the most diffusive and established characters.

It must be confessed, that in this, as in most other cases, there is a mean, on both sides of which inconveniences will be found to lie. By enlarging too much the number of electors, you render the representative too little acquainted with all their local circumstances and lesser interests; as by reducing it too much, you render him unduly attached to these, and too little fit to comprehend and pursue great and national objects. The federal constitution forms a happy combination in this respect; the great and aggregate interests being referred to the national, the local and particular to the state, legislatures.

The other point of difference is, the greater number of citizens and extent of territory which may be brought within the compass of republican, than of democratic government; and it is this circumstance principally which renders factious combinations less to be dreaded in the former, than in the latter. The smaller the society, the fewer probably will be the distinct parties and interests composing it; the fewer the distinct parties and interests, the more frequently will a majority be found of the same party; and the smaller the number of individuals composing a majority, and the smaller the compass within which they are placed, the more easily will they concert and execute their plans of oppression. Extend the sphere, and you take in a greater variety of parties and interests; you make it less probable that a majority of the whole will have a common motive to invade the rights of other citizens; or if such a common motive exists, it will be more difficult for all who feel it to discover their own strength, and to act in unison with each other. Besides other impediments, it may be remarked, that where there is a consciousness of unjust or dishonorable purposes, communication is always checked by distrust, in proportion to the number whose concurrence is necessary.

Hence it clearly appears, that the same advantage, which a republic has over a democracy, in controling the effects of faction, is enjoyed by a large over a small republic—is enjoyed by the union over the states composing it. Does this advantage consist in the substitution of representatives, whose enlightened views and virtuous sentiments render them superior to local prejudices, and to schemes of injustice? It will not be denied, that the representation of the union will be most likely 10 to possess these requisite endowments. Does it consist in the greater security afforded by a greater variety of parties, against the event of any one party being able to outnumber and oppress the rest? In an equal degree does the encreased variety of parties, comprised within the union, encrease this security. Does it, in fine, consist in the greater obstacles opposed to the concert and accomplishment of the secret wishes of an unjust and interested majority? Here, again, the extent of the 20 union gives it the most palpable advantage.

The influence of factious leaders may kindle a flame within their particular states, but will be unable to spread a general conflagration through the other states. A religious sect may degenerate into a political faction in a part of the confederacy; but the variety of sects dispersed over the entire face of it, must secure the national councils against any danger from that source: A rage for paper money, for an abolition of debts, for an equal division of property, or for any other improper and wicked project, will be less apt to pervade the whole body of the union, than a particular member of it; in the same proportion as such a malady is more likely to taint a particular county or district, than an entire state.

In the extent and proper structure of the union, therefore, we behold a republican remedy for the diseases most incident to republican government. And according to the degree of pleasure and pride, we feel in being republicans, ought to be our zeal in cherishing the spirit, and supporting the character of federalists.

Publius

THOMAS JEFFERSON (1743-1826)

WRITING was but one of the numerous interests of Thomas Jefferson, whose many-sided career rivals that of Benjamin Franklin. Yet in 1826, when he came to order his epitaph, he placed first his authorship of the Declaration of Independence. Jefferson was only thirty-three years old and extremely diffident in debate when he was chosen to draft the great document which is sure to be associated forever with his name. He probably owed his appointment to his colleagues' recognition of his "masterly pen." Again and again throughout an unusually long life devoted to public affairs, Jefferson's masterly pen continued to serve him as he strove to fulfill his vow of "eternal hostility against every form of tyranny over the mind of man." Of greater stature as a statesman than as a writer, Jefferson's ultimate distinction rests in his forward-looking democracy and liberalism. Dumas Malone declared that no other American "more deserves to be termed a major prophet, a supreme pioneer."

The pioneer instinct, which kept Jefferson in the forefront of his times, may have been in part a legacy from his father who lived on the western frontier of Virginia, where Thomas Jefferson was born in 1743. After his graduation from the College of William and Mary in 1762, Jefferson studied law under the noted teacher, George Wythe, and was admitted to the Virginia bar in 1767. He found court practice distasteful and soon abandoned it. The effects of his legal training, however, as well as his thorough mastery of Greek and Latin, can be seen in his notable state papers. Jefferson's public service was coextensive with the birth and early growth of the Republic itself. A list of his offices is a reminder of his contribution to American civilization: member of the House of Burgesses (1769–1775), member of the Virginia Convention (1775), member of the Continental Congress (1775–1776), member of the Virginia Legislature (1776–1779), Governor of Virginia (1779–1781), delegate to Congress (1783–1784), American minister plenipotentiary to France (1784–1789), Secretary of State (1790–1793), Vice-President of the United States (1797–1801), President of the United States (1801–1809).

Impressive as this list is, it does not present a full measure of Jefferson's influence on the American way of life. An impressive figure in the early days of the Republic, the proprietor of 10,000 acres of land and the owner of more than 100 slaves, Jefferson struck out against the idea of an artificial aristocracy, devoid of virtue or talents, founded solely upon wealth and birth. He abolished land-holding in fee tail; he helped to implement by legislation the divorce of religious opinion from civil rights; he established the first professorships of law and modern languages in America; he proposed, as early as 1784, a bill to forbid slavery in the Western territory; he was a persuasive and skillful diplomat; he was a diligent Secretary of State in a critical moment in foreign affairs; he formulated by both precept and practice the parliamentary procedure still used in the United States Senate; he set forth a comprehensive design of democratic education; not without grave misgivings, he helped to assure American expansion to the West; as the third President, he brought the government close to the people, confident of the integrity of the common man.

This recital fails to include many of Jefferson's interests: his absorption in the classics, science, and philosophy; his concern with the fine arts, such as architecture, music, and poetry; his gift for friendship, which flowered in his urbane and informative correspondence. Jefferson possessed "character" in the Emersonian sense of a reserved force, an inherent quality finer than anything which he said or accomplished. "He conquers because his arrival alters the face of affairs." At a formative period in our national life Jefferson embodied the democratic aspiration of his society.

BIBLIOGRAPHY · A definitive edition of the writings of Thomas Jefferson is under the general editorship of Julian Boyd. The best available edition is that by P. L. Ford, *The Writings of Thomas Jefferson* (10 vols., 1892–1899). More extensive in scope is the "Memorial Edition" edited by A. A. Lipscomb and A. E. Bergh (20 vols., 1903–1907). Other useful editions include those by T. J. Randolph (4 vols., 1892) and H. A. Washington (9 vols., 1853–1854). Valuable source material is contained in W. C. Ford's *Thomas Jefferson's Correspondence* (1916), and G. Chinard's *The Commonplace Book of Thomas Jefferson* (1926) and *The Literary Bible of Thomas Jefferson* (1928). The sharply divergent views held by Jefferson and Hamilton are represented in F. C. Prescott's *Alexander Hamilton and Thomas Jefferson: Selections* (1934). Good introductions to Jefferson's thought are to be found in J. T. Adams's *Jeffersonian Principles: Extracts from the Writings of Thomas Jefferson* (1928) and B. Mayo's *Jefferson Himself* (1942).

Dumas Malone's sketch in the *Dictionary of American Biography*, X, 17–35, is a trenchant summary of Jefferson's life. See also D. Malone, *Jefferson the Virginian* (1948). The best nineteenth-century biographies are H. S. Randall's *Life of Thomas Jefferson* (3 vols., 1858) and S. N. Randolph's *Domestic Life of Thomas Jefferson* (1871). Later biographies include G. Chinard's *Thomas Jefferson: The Apostle of Americanism* (1929), A. J. Nock's *Jefferson* (1926), and C. G. Bowers's *Jefferson in Power* (1936). Important special studies include C. A. Beard's *Economic Origins of Jeffersonian Democracy* (1915), Carl Becker's *Declaration of Independence* (1922), C. G. Bowers's *Jefferson and Hamilton* (1925), L. M. Sears's *Jefferson and the Embargo* (1927), and P. Wilstach's *Jefferson and Monticello* (1926). V. L. Parrington's *Main Currents in American Thought* (3 vols., 1927–1930) is a highly provocative history of American writing with a marked Jeffersonian bias.

The Unanimous Declaration of the Thirteen United States of America

ALTHOUGH this famous document is popularly known as "The Declaration of Independence," and is generally believed to have been signed on July 4, 1776, neither of these "facts" is strictly accurate. The official act by which the Continental Congress voted to separate from the mother country was a resolution passed on July 2; moreover, the title "Declaration of Independence" does not appear in any of the various copies of the document. As Carl Becker remarked, "the primary purpose of the Declaration was not to declare independence, but to proclaim to the world the reasons for declaring independence." One reason the task of drafting the document was given to Jefferson was that he could write effectively. For a discussion of the literary qualities of the Declaration, see Carl Becker, *The Declaration of Independence* (1922), 194–223.

When, in the Course of human events, it becomes necessary for one people to dissolve the political bands which have connected them with another, and to assume among the Powers of the earth, the separate and equal station to which the Laws of Nature and of Nature's God entitle them, a decent respect to the opinions of mankind requires that they should declare the causes which impel them to the separation.

10   We hold these truths to be self-evident, that all men are created equal, that they are endowed by their Creator with certain unalienable Rights, that among these are Life, Liberty and the pursuit of Happiness. That to secure these rights, Governments are instituted among Men, deriving their just powers from the consent of the governed. That whenever any Form of Government becomes destructive of these ends, it is the Right of the

People to alter or abolish it, and to institute new Government, laying its foundation on such principles and organizing its powers in such form as to them shall seem most likely to effect their Safety and Happiness. Prudence, indeed, will dictate that Governments long established should not be changed for light and transient causes; and accordingly all experience hath shown, that mankind are more disposed to suffer, while evils are sufferable, than to right themselves by abolishing the forms to which they are accustomed. But when a long train of abuses and usurpations, pursuing invariably the same Object, evinces a design to reduce them under absolute Despotism, it is their right, it is their duty, to throw off such Government, and to provide new Guards for their future security. Such has been the patient sufferance of these Colonies; and such is now the necessity which constrains them to alter their former Systems of Government. The history of the present King of Great Britain is a history of repeated injuries and usurpations, all having in direct object the establishment of an absolute Tyranny over these States. To prove this, let Facts be submitted to a candid world.

He has refused his Assent to Laws, the most wholesome and necessary for the public good.

He has forbidden his Governors to pass Laws of immediate and pressing importance, unless suspended in their operation till his Assent should be obtained; and when so suspended, he has utterly neglected to attend to them.

He has refused to pass other Laws for the accommodation of large districts of people, unless those people would relinquish the right of Representation in the Legislature, a right inestimable to them and formidable to tyrants only.

He has called together legislative bodies at places unusual, uncomfortable, and distant from the depository of their Public Records, for the sole purpose of fatiguing them into compliance with his measures.

He has dissolved Representative Houses repeatedly, for opposing with manly firmness his invasions on the rights of the people.

He has refused for a long time, after such dissolutions, to cause others to be elected; whereby the Legislative Powers, incapable of Annihilation, have returned to the People at large for their exercise; the State remaining in the mean time exposed to all the dangers of invasion from without, and convulsions within.

He has endeavoured to prevent the population of these States; for that purpose obstructing the Laws for Naturalization of Foreigners; refusing to pass others to encourage their migrations hither, and raising the conditions of new Appropriations of Lands.

He has obstructed the Administration of Justice by refusing his Assent to Laws for establishing Judiciary Powers.

He has made Judges dependent on his Will alone, for the tenure of their offices, and the amount and payment of their salaries.

He has erected a multitude of New Offices, and sent hither swarms of Officers to harass our People, and eat out their substance.

He has kept among us, in times of peace, Standing Armies without the Consent of our legislatures.

He has affected to render the Military independent of and superior to the Civil power.

He has combined with others to subject us to a jurisdiction foreign to our constitution, and unacknowledged by our laws; giving his Assent to their acts of pretended legislation:

For quartering large bodies of armed troops among us:

For protecting them, by a mock Trial, from Punishment for any Murders which they should commit on the Inhabitants of these States:

For cutting off our Trade with all parts of the world:

For imposing taxes on us without our Consent:

For depriving us in many cases, of the benefits of Trial by Jury:

For transporting us beyond Seas to be tried for pretended offences:

For abolishing the free System of English Laws in a neighbouring Province, establishing therein an Arbitrary government, and enlarging its Boundaries so as to render it at once an example and fit instrument for introducing the same absolute rule into these Colonies:

For taking away our Charters, abolishing our most valuable Laws, and altering fundamentally the Forms of our Governments:

For suspending our own Legislatures, and declaring themselves invested with Power to legislate for us in all cases whatsoever.

He has abdicated Government here, by declaring us out of his Protection and waging War against us.

He has plundered our seas, ravaged our Coasts, burnt our towns, and destroyed the lives of our people.

He is at this time transporting large armies of foreign mercenaries to compleat the works of death, desolation and tyranny, already begun with circumstances of Cruelty & perfidy scarcely paralleled in the most barbarous ages, and totally unworthy the Head of a civilized nation.

He has constrained our fellow Citizens taken Captive on the high Seas to bear Arms against their Country, to become the executioners of their friends and Brethren, or to fall themselves by their Hands.

He has excited domestic insurrections amongst us, and has endeavoured to bring on the inhabitants of our frontiers, the merciless Indian Savages, whose known rule of warfare, is an undistinguished destruction of all ages, sexes, and conditions.

In every stage of these Oppressions We have Petitioned for Redress in the most humble terms: Our repeated Petitions have been answered only by repeated injury. A Prince, whose character is thus marked by every act which may define a Tyrant, is unfit to be the ruler of a free People.

Nor have We been wanting in attentions to our British brethren. We have warned them from time to time of attempts by their legislature to extend an unwarrantable jurisdiction over us. We have reminded them of the circumstances of our emigration and settlement here. We have appealed to their native justice and magnanimity, and we have conjured them by the ties of our common kindred to disavow these usurpations, which would inevitably interrupt our connections and correspondence. They too have been deaf to the voice of justice and of consanguinity. We must, therefore, acquiesce in the necessity, which denounces our Separation, and hold them, as we hold the rest of mankind, Enemies in War, in Peace Friends.

We, therefore, the Representatives of the United States of America, in General Congress, Assembled,

appealing to the Supreme Judge of the world for the rectitude of our intentions, do, in the Name and by Authority of the good People of these Colonies, solemnly publish and declare, That these United Colonies are, and of Right ought to be Free and Independent States; that they are Absolved from all Allegiance to the British Crown, and that all political connection between them and the State of Great Britain, is and ought to be totally dissolved; and that as Free and Independent States, they have full Power to levy War, conclude Peace, contract Alliances, establish Commerce, and to do all other Acts and Things which Independent States may of right do. And for the support of this Declaration, with a firm reliance on the Protection of divine Providence, we mutually pledge to each other our Lives, our Fortunes and our sacred Honor.

Notes on the State of Virginia

[Religious Tolerance]

JEFFERSON collected and arranged his notes on his native state in response to an appeal for information by the Marquis de Barbé-Marbois, Secretary of the French Legation at Philadelphia in 1781. The *Notes* was prepared for the press in 1781 and 1782 at Monticello, and printed in Paris in 1784. In addition to data about the resources of the state, the treatise contains animated discussions about slavery, religious freedom, and popular education.

The first settlers in this country were emigrants from England, of the English church, just at a point of time when it was flushed with complete victory over the religious of all other persuasions. Possessed, as they became, of the powers of making, administering and executing the laws, they shewed equal intolerance in this country with their Presbyterian brethren, who had emigrated to the northern government. The poor Quakers were flying from persecution in England. They cast their eyes on these new countries as asylums of civil and religious freedom; but they found them free only for the reigning sect. Several acts of the Virginia assembly of 1659, 1662, and 1693, had made it penal in parents to refuse to have their children baptized; had prohibited the unlawful assembling of Quakers; had made it penal for any master of a vessel to bring a Quaker into the state; had ordered those already here, and such as should come thereafter, to be imprisoned till they should abjure the country; provided a milder punishment for their first and second return, but death for their third; had inhibited all persons from suffering their meetings in or near their houses, entertaining them individually, or disposing of books which supported their tenets. If no capital execu-[10]tion took place here, as it did in New-England, it was not owing to the moderation of the church, or spirit of the legislature, as may be inferred from the law itself; but to historical circumstances which have not been handed down to us. The Anglicans retained full possession of the country about a century. Other opinions began then to creep in, and the great care of the government to support their own church, having begotten an equal degree of indolence in its clergy, two thirds of the people [20] had become dissenters at the commencement of the present revolution. The laws indeed were still oppressive on them, but the spirit of the one party had subsided into moderation, and of the other had risen to a degree of determination which commanded respect.

The present state of our laws on the subject of religion is this. The convention of May 1776, in their declaration of rights, declared it to be a truth, and a natural right, that the exercise of [30] religion should be free; but when they proceeded to form on that declaration the ordinance of government, instead of taking up every principle declared in the bill of rights, and guarding it by legislative sanction, they passed over that which asserted our religious rights, leaving them as they found them. The same convention, however, when they met as a member of the general assembly in October 1776, repealed all acts of parliament which had rendered criminal the maintaining any opin-[40]ions in matters of religion, the forbearing to repair to church, and the exercising any mode of worship; and suspended the laws giving salaries to the clergy, which suspension was made perpetual in October 1779. Statutory oppressions in religion being thus wiped away, we remain at present under those only imposed by the common law, or by our own acts of assembly. At the common law, heresy was a capital offence, punishable by burning. Its definition was left to the ecclesiastical judges, before whom the conviction was, till the statute of the I El. C. I. circumscribed it, by declaring that nothing should be deemed heresy but what had been so determined by authority of the canonical scriptures, or by one of the four first general councils, or by some other council having for the grounds of their declaration the express and plain words of the scriptures. Heresy, thus circumscribed, being an offence at the common law, our act of assembly of October 1777, c. 17 gives cognizance of it to the general court, by declaring that the jurisdiction of that court shall be general in all matters at the common law. The execution is by the writ *De hæretico comburendo*. By our own act of assembly of 1705, c. 30, if a person brought up in the Christian religion denies the being of a God, or the Trinity, or asserts there are more Gods than one, or denies the Christian religion to be true, or the scriptures to be of divine authority, he is punishable on the first offence by incapacity to hold any office or employment ecclesiastical, civil, or military; on the second by disability to sue, to take any gift or legacy, to be guardian, executor or administrator, and by three years imprisonment, without bail. A father's right to the custody of his own children being founded in law on his right of guardianship, this being taken away, they may of course be severed from him and put, by the authority of a court, into more orthodox hands. This is a summary view of that religious slavery under which a people have been willing to remain who have lavished their lives and fortunes for the establishment of their civil freedom. The error seems not sufficiently eradicated, that the operations of the mind, as well as the acts of the body, are subject to the coercion of the laws. But our rulers can have authority over such natural rights, only as we have submitted to them. The rights of conscience we never submitted, we could not submit. We are answerable for them to our God. The legitimate powers of government extend to such acts only as are injurious to others. But it does me no injury for my neighbor to say there are twenty gods, or no god. It neither picks my pocket nor breaks my leg. If it be said his testimony in a court of justice cannot be relied on, reject it then, and be the stigma on him. Constraint may make him worse by making him a hypocrite, but it will never make him a truer man. It may fix him obstinately in his errors, but will not cure them. Reason and free inquiry are the only effectual agents against error. Give a loose to them, they will support the true religion by bringing every false one to their tribunal, to the test of their investigation. They are the natural enemies of error, and of error only. Had not the Roman government permitted free inquiry, Christianity could never have been introduced. Had not free inquiry been indulged, at the era of the reformation, the corruptions of Christianity could not have been purged away. If it be restrained now, the present corruptions will be protected, and new ones encouraged. Was the government to prescribe to us our medicine and diet, our bodies would be in such keeping as our souls are now. Thus in France the emetic was once forbidden as a medicine, and the potatoe as an article of food. Government is just as infallible, too, when it fixes systems in physics. Galileo was sent to the inquisition for affirming that the earth was a sphere; the government had declared it to be as flat as a trencher, and Galileo was obliged to abjure his error. This error however at length prevailed, the earth became a globe, and Descartes declared it was whirled round its axis by a vortex. The government in which he lived was wise enough to see that this was no question of civil jurisdiction, or we should all have been involved by authority in vortices. In fact the vortices have been exploded, and the Newtonian principle of gravitation is now more firmly established, on the basis of reason, than it would be were the government to step in and to make it an article of necessary faith. Reason and experiment have been indulged, and error has fled before them. It is error alone which needs the support of government. Truth can stand by itself. Subject opinion to coercion: whom will you make your inquisitors? Fallible men; men governed by bad passions, by private as well as public reasons. And why subject it to coercion? To produce uniformity. But is uniformity of opinion desireable? No more than of face and stature. Introduce the bed of Procrustes then, and as there

is danger that the large men may beat the small, make us all of a size, by lopping the former and stretching the latter. Difference of opinion is advantageous in religion. The several sects perform the office of a Censor morum over each other. Is uniformity attainable? Millions of innocent men, women and children, since the introduction of Christianity, have been burnt, tortured, fined, imprisoned: yet we have not advanced one inch towards uniformity. What has been the effect of coercion? To make one half the world fools, and the other half hypocrites. To support roguery and error all over the earth. Let us reflect that it is inhabited by a thousand millions of people. That these profess probably a thousand different systems of religion. That ours is but one of that thousand. That if there be but one right, and ours that one, we should wish to see the 999 wandering sects gathered into the fold of truth. But against such a majority we cannot effect this by force. Reason and persuasion are the only practicable instruments. To make way for these, free inquiry must be indulged; and how can we wish others to indulge it while we refuse it ourselves. But every state, says an inquisitor, has established some religion. "No two, say I, have established the same." Is this a proof of the infallibility of establishments? Our sister states of Pennsylvania and New York, however, have long subsisted without any establishment at all. The experiment was new and doubtful when they made it. It has answered beyond conception. They flourish infinitely. Religion is well supported; of various kinds indeed, but all good enough; all sufficient to preserve peace and order: or if a sect arises whose tenets would subvert morals, good sense has fair play, and reasons and laughs it out of doors, without suffering the state to be troubled with it. They do not hang more malefactors than we do. They are not more disturbed with religious dissentions. On the contrary, their harmony is unparallelled, and can be ascribed to nothing but their unbounded tolerance, because there is no other circumstance in which they differ from every nation on earth. They have made the happy discovery, that the way to silence religious disputes, is to take no notice of them. Let us too give this experiment fair play, and get rid, while we may, of those tyrannical laws. It is true we are as yet secured against them by the spirit of the times. I doubt whether the people of this country would suffer an execution for heresy, or a three years imprisonment for not comprehending the mysteries of the trinity. But is the spirit of the people an infallible, a permanent reliance? Is it government? Is this the kind of protection we receive in return for the rights we give up? Besides, the spirit of the times may alter, will alter. Our rulers will become corrupt, our people careless. A single zealot may commence persecuter, and better men be his victims. It can never be too often repeated, that the time for fixing every essential right on a legal basis is while our rulers are honest, and ourselves united. From the conclusion of this war we shall be going down hill. It will not then be necessary to resort every moment to the people for support. They will be forgotten therefore, and their rights disregarded. They will forget themselves, but in the sole faculty of making money, and will never think of uniting to effect a due respect for their rights. The shackles, therefore, which shall not be knocked off at the conclusion of this war, will remain on us long, will be made heavier and heavier, till our rights shall revive or expire in a convulsion.

[*Against Dictatorships*]

THE PROPOSALS of 1776 and 1781 in the Virginia legislature to establish a dictator over Virginia arose during the stress of war. By 1781 the British had overrun much of eastern Virginia, and the state legislature had repaired to Staunton, where George Nichols made the second proposal; not seeing the essential absurdity in his proposal, he suggested, to assure no misuse of power, that George Washington be asked to serve. The following essay is the closing section of Jefferson's chapter dealing with the defects of the constitution of the State of Virginia.

In enumerating the defects of the [state] constitution, it would be wrong to count among them what is only the error of particular persons. In December 1776, our circumstances being much distressed, it was proposed in the house of delegates to create a dictator, invested with every power legislative, executive, and judiciary, civil and military, of life and of death, over our persons and over our properties; and in June 1781, again under calamity, the same proposition was repeated, and wanted a few votes only of being passed.—One who entered into this contest from a pure love of liberty, and a sense of injured rights, who determined to make every sacrifice, and to meet every danger, for the re-establishment of those rights on a firm basis, who did not mean to expend his blood and substance for the wretched purpose of changing this master for that, but to place the powers of governing him in a plurality of hands of his own choice, so that the corrupt will of no one man might in future oppress him, must stand confounded and dismayed when he is told, that a considerable portion of that plurality had meditated the surrender of them into a single hand, and, in lieu of a limited monarch, to deliver him over to a despotic one! How must he find his efforts and sacrifices abused and baffled, if he may still, by a single vote, be laid prostrate at the feet of one man! In God's name, from whence have they derived this power? Is it from our ancient laws? None such can be produced. Is it from any principle in our new constitution expressed or implied? Every lineament of that expressed or implied, is in full opposition to it. Its fundamental principle is, that the state shall be governed as a commonwealth. It provides a republican organization, proscribes under the name of prerogative the exercise of all powers undefined by the laws; places on this basis the whole system of our laws; and by consolidating them together, chooses that they shall be left to stand or fall together, never providing for any circumstances, nor admitting that such could arise, wherein either should be suspended; no, not for a moment. Our ancient laws expressly declare, that those who are but delegates themselves shall not delegate to others powers which require judgment and integrity in their exercise. Or was this proposition moved on a supposed right in the movers, of abandoning their posts in a moment of distress? The same laws forbid the abandonment of that post, even on ordinary occasions; and much more a transfer of their powers into other hands and other forms, without consulting the people. They never admit the idea that these, like sheep or cattle, may be given from hand to hand without an appeal to their own will.—Was it from the neces-

255

sity of the case? Necessities which dissolve a government, do not convey its authority to an oligarchy or a monarchy. They throw back, into the hands of the people, the powers they had delegated, and leave them as individuals to shift for themselves. A leader may offer, but not impose himself, nor be imposed on them. Much less can their necks be submitted to his sword, their breath be held at his will or caprice. The necessity which should operate these tremendous effects should at least be palpable and irresistible. Yet in both instances, where it was feared, or pretended with us, it was belied by the event. It was belied, too, by the preceding experience of our sister states, several of whom had grappled through greater difficulties without abandoning their forms of government. When the proposition was first made, Massachusetts had found even the government of committees sufficient to carry them through an invasion. But we at the time of that proposition, were under no invasion. When the second was made, there had been added to this example those of Rhode Island, New York, New Jersey, and Pennsylvania, in all of which the republican form had been found equal to the task of carrying them through the severest trials. In this state alone did there exist so little virtue, that fear was to be fixed in the hearts of the people, and to become the motive of their exertions, and the principle of their government? The very thought alone was treason against the people; was treason against mankind in general; as rivetting forever the chains which bow down their necks by giving to their oppressors a proof, which they would have trumpeted through the universe, of the imbecility of republican government, in times of pressing danger, to shield them from harm. Those who assume the right of giving away the reins of government in any case, must be sure that the herd, whom they hand on to the rods and hatchet of the dictator, will lay their necks on the block when he shall nod to them. But if our assemblies supposed such a resignation in the people, I hope they mistook their character. I am of opinion, that the government, instead of being braced and invigorated for greater exertions under their difficulties, would have been thrown back upon the bungling machinery of county committees for administration, till a convention could have

been called, and its wheels again set into regular motion. What a cruel moment was this for creating such an embarrassment, for putting to the proof the attachment of our countrymen to republican government! Those who meant well, of the advocates for this measure, (and most of them meant well, for I know them personally, had been their fellow-laborers in the common cause, and had often proved the purity of their principles), had been seduced in their judgment by the example of an ancient republic, whose constitution and circumstances were fundamentally different. They had sought this precedent in the history of Rome, where alone it was to be found, and where at length, too, it had proved fatal. They had taken it from a republic rent by the most bitter factions and tumults, where the government was of a heavy-handed unfeeling aristocracy, over a people ferocious, and rendered desperate by poverty and wretchedness; tumults which could not be allayed under the most trying circumstances, but by the omnipotent hand of a single despot. Their constitution, therefore, allowed a temporary tyrant to be erected, under the name of a Dictator; and that temporary tyrant, after a few examples, became perpetual. They misapplied this precedent to a people mild in their dispositions, patient under their trial, united for the public liberty, and affectionate to their leaders. But if from the constitution of the Roman government there resulted to their Senate a power of submitting all their rights to the will of one man, does it follow that the assembly of Virginia have the same authority? What clause in our constitution has substituted that of Rome, by way of residuary provision, for all cases not otherwise provided for? Or if they may step ad libitum into any other form of government for precedents to rule us by, for what oppression may not a precedent be found in this world of the *bellum omnium in omnia*? Searching for the foundations of this proposition, I can find none which may pretend a color of right or reason, but the defect before developed, that there being no barrier between the legislative, executive, and judiciary departments, the legislature may seize the whole: that having seized it, and possessing a right to fix their own quorum, they may reduce that quorum to one, whom they may call a chairman, speaker, dictator, or by any other name they please.—Our situation is indeed perilous, and I hope my countrymen will be sensible of it, and will apply, at a proper season, the proper remedy; which is a convention to fix the constitution, to amend its defects, to bind up the several branches of government by certain laws, which, when they transgress, their acts shall become nullities; to render unnecessary an appeal to the people, or in other words a rebellion, on every infraction of their rights, 10 on the peril that their acquiescence shall be construed into an intention to surrender those rights.

First Inaugural Address

JEFFERSON was the first President inaugurated in Washington. His address was delivered on March 4, 1801, in the incompleted Capitol. The address was designed to conciliate his more moderate opponents.

Friends and Fellow-Citizens: Called upon to 20 undertake the duties of the first executive office of our country, I avail myself of the presence of that portion of my fellow-citizens which is here assembled to express my grateful thanks for the favor with which they have been pleased to look towards me, to declare a sincere consciousness that the task is above my talents, and that I approach it with those anxious and awful presentiments which the greatness of the charge and the weakness of my powers so justly inspire. A rising nation 30 spread over a wide and fruitful land, traversing all the seas with the rich productions of their industry, engaged in commerce with nations who feel power and forget right, advancing rapidly to destinies beyond the reach of mortal eye—when I contemplate these transcendent objects, and see the honor, the happiness, and the hopes of this beloved country committed to the issue and the auspices of this day, I shrink from the contemplation and humble myself before the magnitude of the undertaking. 40

Utterly, indeed, should I despair, did not the presence of many whom I here see remind me that in the other high authorities provided by our constitution I shall find resources of wisdom, of virtue, and of zeal on which to rely under all difficulties. To you then, gentlemen, who are charged with the sovereign functions of legislation, and to those associated with you, I look with encouragement for that guidance and support which may enable us to steer with safety the vessel in which we are all embarked, amidst the conflicting elements of a troubled sea.

During the contest of opinion through which we have passed, the animation of discussions and of exertions has sometimes worn an aspect which might impose on strangers unused to think freely and to speak and to write what they think. But this being now decided by the voice of the nation, announced according to the rules of the Constitution, all will, of course, arrange themselves under the will of the law and unite in common efforts for the common good. All too will bear in mind this sacred principle, that, though the will of the majority is in all cases to prevail, that will, to be rightful, must be reasonable; that the minority possess their equal rights, which equal laws must protect, and to violate would be oppression. Let us then, fellow-citizens, unite with one heart and one mind; let us restore to social intercourse that harmony and affection without which liberty, and even life itself, are but dreary things. And let us reflect that, having banished from our land that religious intolerance under which mankind so long bled and suffered, we have yet gained little if we countenance a political intolerance as despotic, as wicked, and capable of as bitter and bloody persecutions. During the throes and convulsions of the 30 ancient world,[n] during the agonizing spasms of infuriated man, seeking through blood and slaughter his long-lost liberty, it was not wonderful that the agitation of the billows should reach even this distant and peaceful shore; that this should be more felt and feared by some and less by others; and should divide opinions as to measures of safety. But every difference of opinion is not a difference of principle. We have called by different names brethren of the same principle. We are all Republicans; we are all Federalists. If there be any 40 among us who would wish to dissolve this Union, or to change its republican form, let them stand undisturbed as monuments of the safety with which error of opinion may be tolerated where reason is left free to combat it. I know, indeed, that some honest men have feared that a republican government cannot be strong; that this Govern-

throes . . . world: The French Revolution.

257

ment is not strong enough. But would the honest patriot, in the full tide of successful experiment, abandon a government which has so far kept us free and firm, on the theoretic and visionary fear that this Government, the world's best hope, may by possibility want energy to preserve itself? I trust not. I believe this, on the contrary, the strongest government on earth. I believe it the only one where every man, at the call of the law, would fly to the standard of the law; would meet invasions of the public order as his own personal concern. Sometimes it is said that man cannot be trusted with the government of himself. Can he, then, be trusted with the government of others? Or have we found angels in the form of kings to govern him? Let history answer this question.

Let us, then, pursue with courage and confidence our own federal and republican principles, our attachment to union and representative government. Kindly separated by nature and a wide ocean from the exterminating havoc of one quarter of the globe; too high-minded to endure the degradations of the others; possessing a chosen country, with room enough for our descendants to the hundredth and thousandth generation; entertaining a due sense of our equal right to the use of our own faculties, to the acquisitions of our own industry, to honor and confidence from our fellow-citizens, resulting not from birth, but from our actions and their sense of them; enlightened by a benign religion, professed indeed and practiced in various forms yet all of them inculcating honesty, truth, temperance, gratitude, and the love of man, acknowledging and adoring an overruling Providence, which by all its dispensations proves that it delights in the happiness of man here and his greater happiness hereafter—with all these blessings, what more is necessary to make us a happy and a prosperous people? Still one thing more, fellow-citizens—a wise and frugal Government, which shall restrain men from injuring one another, shall leave them otherwise free to regulate their own pursuits of industry and improvement, and shall not take from the mouth of labor the bread it has earned. This is the sum of good government, and this is necessary to close the circle of our felicities.

About to enter, fellow-citizens, on the exercise of duties which comprehend everything dear and valuable to you, it is proper you should understand what I deem the essential principles of our Government, and consequently those which ought to shape its Administration. I will compress them within the narrowest compass they will bear, stating the general principle, but not all its limitations. Equal and exact justice to all men, of whatever state or persuasion, religious or political; peace, commerce, and honest friendship with all nations, entangling alliances with none; the support of the State governments in all their rights, as the most competent administrations for our domestic concerns and the surest bulwarks against antirepublican tendencies; the preservation of the General Government in its whole constitutional vigor, as the sheet anchor of our peace at home and safety abroad; a jealous care of the right of election by the people—a mild and safe corrective of abuses which are lopped by the sword of revolution where peaceable remedies are unprovided; absolute acquiescence in the decisions of the majority, the vital principle of republics, from which is no appeal but to force, the vital principle and immediate parent of despotism; a well-disciplined militia, our best reliance in peace and for the first moments of war, till regulars may relieve them; the supremacy of the civil over the military authority; economy in the public expense, that labor may be lightly burthened; the honest payment of our debts and sacred preservation of the public faith; encouragement of agriculture, and of commerce as its handmaid; the diffusion of information and arraignment of all abuses at the bar of the public reason; freedom of religion; freedom of the press, and freedom of person under the protection of the habeas corpus, and trial by juries impartially selected. These principles form the bright constellation which has gone before us and guided our steps through an age of revolution and reformation. The wisdom of our sages and blood of our heroes have been devoted to their attainment. They should be the creed of our political faith, the text of civic instruction, the touchstone by which to try the services of those we trust; and should we wander from them in moments of error or of alarm, let us hasten to retrace our steps and to regain the road which alone leads to peace, liberty, and safety.

I repair, then, fellow-citizens, to the post you have assigned me. With experience enough in subordinate offices to have seen the difficulties of this the greatest of all, I have learnt to expect that it will rarely fall to the lot of imperfect man to retire from this station with the reputation and the favor which bring him into it. Without pretensions to that high confidence you reposed in our first and greatest revolutionary character, whose preeminent services had entitled him to the first place in his country's love and had destined for him the fairest page in the volume of faithful history, I ask so much confidence only as may give firmness and effect to the legal administration of your affairs. I shall often go wrong through defect of judgment. When right, I shall often be thought wrong by those whose positions will not command a view of the whole ground. I ask your indulgence for my own errors, which will never be intentional, and your support against the errors of others who may condemn what they would not, if seen in all its parts. The approbation implied by your suffrage is a great consolation to me for the past; and my future solicitude will be to retain the good opinion of those who have bestowed it in advance, to conciliate that of others by doing them all the good in my power, and to be instrumental to the happiness and freedom of all.

Relying then on the patronage of your goodwill, I advance with obedience to the work, ready to retire from it whenever you become sensible how much better choice it is in your power to make. And may that Infinite Power which rules the destinies of the universe lead our councils to what is best, and give them a favorable issue for your peace and prosperity.

Second Inaugural Address

JEFFERSON was sixty-two years old when he delivered his second inaugural on March 4, 1805. His remarks on the freedom of the press are significant in the light of the newspaper calumnies which were visited upon him during his first term in office.

[Freedom of the Press]

. . . During the course of this administration, and in order to disturb it, the artillery of the press has been levelled against us, charged with whatever its licentiousness could devise or dare. These abuses of an institution so important to freedom and science, are deeply to be regretted, inasmuch as they tend to lessen its usefulness, and to sap its safety; they might, indeed, have been corrected by the wholesome punishments reserved and provided by the laws of the several States against falsehood and defamation; but public duties more urgent press on the time of public servants, and the offenders have therefore been left to find their punishment in the public indignation.

Nor was it uninteresting to the world, that an experiment should be fairly and fully made, whether freedom of discussion, unaided by power, is not sufficient for the propagation and protection of truth—whether a government, conducting itself in the true spirit of its constitution, with zeal and purity, and doing no act which it should be unwilling the whole world should witness, can be written down by falsehood and defamation. The experiment has been tried; you have witnessed the scene; our fellow citizens have looked on, cool and collected, they saw the latent source from which these outrages proceeded; they gathered around these public functionaries, and when the constitution called them to the decision by the suffrage, they pronounced their verdict, honorable to those who had served them, and consolatory to the friend of man, who believes he may be intrusted with his own affairs.

No inference is here intended, that the laws, provided by the State against false and defamatory publications, should not be enforced. He who has time, renders a service to public morals and public tranquility, in reforming these abuses by the salutary coercions of the law, but the experiment is noted, to prove that, since truth and reason have maintained their ground against false opinions in league with false facts, the press, confined to truth, needs no other legal restraint; the public judgment will correct false reasonings and opinions, on a full hearing of all parties; and no other definite line can be drawn between the inestimable liberty of the press and its demoralizing licentiousness. If there be still improprieties which this rule would not restrain, its supplement must be sought in the censorship of public opinion. . . .

Letter to Mrs. John Adams

[Relationship with Mr. and Mrs. Adams]

Washington, June 13, 1804.

Dear Madam, The affectionate sentiments which you have had the goodness to express in your letter of May 20, towards my dear departed daughter, have awakened in me sensibilities natural to the occasion, & recalled your kindnesses to her, which I shall ever remember with gratitude & friendship. I can assure you with truth, they had made an indelible impression on her mind, and that to the last, on our meetings after long separations, whether I had heard lately of you, and how you did, were among the earliest of her inquiries. In giving you this assurance I perform a sacred duty for her, & at the same time, am thankful for the occasion furnished me, of expressing my regret that circumstances should have arisen, which have seemed to draw a line of separation between us. The friendship with which you honored me has ever been valued, and fully reciprocated; & altho' events have been passing which might be trying to some minds, I never believed yours to be of that kind, nor felt that my own was. Neither my estimate of your character, nor the esteem founded in that, have ever been lessened for a single moment, although doubts whether it would be acceptable may have forbidden manifestations of it.

Mr. Adams's friendship & mine began at an earlier date. It accompanied us thro' long & important scenes. The different conclusions we had drawn from our political reading & reflections, were not permitted to lessen mutual esteem; each party being conscious they were the result of an honest conviction in the other. Like differences of opinion existing among our fellow citizens, attached them to one or the other of us, and produced a rivalship in their minds which did not exist in ours. We never stood in one another's way; for if either had been withdrawn at any time, his favorers would not have gone over to the other, but would have sought for some one of homogeneous opinions. This consideration was sufficient to keep down all jealousy between us, & to guard our friendship from any disturbance by sentiments of rivalship; and I can say with truth, that one act of Mr. Adams's life, and one only, ever gave me a moment's personal displeasure. I did consider his last appointments to office as personally unkind. They were from among my most ardent political enemies, from whom no faithful co-operation could ever be expected; and laid me under the embarrassment of acting thro' men whose views were to defeat mine, or to encounter the odium of putting others in their places. It seemed but common justice to leave a successor free to act by instruments of his own choice. If my respect for him did not permit me to ascribe the whole blame to the influence of others, it left something for friendship to forgive, and after brooding over it for some little time, and not always resisting the expression of it, I forgave it cordially, and returned to the same state of esteem & respect for him which had so long subsisted. Having come into life a little later than Mr. Adams, his career has preceded mine, as mine is followed by some other; and it will probably be closed at the same distance after him which time originally placed between us. I maintain for him, & shall carry into private life, an uniform & high measure of respect and good will and for yourself a sincere attachment.

I have thus, my dear Madam, opened myself to you without reserve, which I have long wished an opportunity of doing; and without knowing how it will be received, I feel relief from being unbosomed. And I have now only to entreat your forgiveness for this transition from a subject of domestic affliction, to one which seems of a different aspect. But tho connected with political events, it has been viewed by me most strongly in its unfortunate bearings on my private friendships. The injury these have sustained has been a heavy price for what has never given me equal pleasure. That you may both be favored with health, tranquillity and long life, is the prayer of one who tenders you the assurance of his highest consideration and esteem.

Letter to John Adams

[A Natural Aristocracy of Intelligence]

October 28, 1813

. . . I agree with you that there is a natural aristocracy among men. The grounds of this are virtue and talents. Formerly, bodily powers gave place among the *aristoi*. But, since the invention of gunpowder has armed the weak as well as the strong with missile death, bodily strength, like beauty, good humor, politeness, and other accomplishments, has become but an auxiliary ground for distinction. There is also an artificial aristocracy, founded on wealth and birth, without either virtue or talents; for with these it would belong to the first class. The natural aristocracy I consider as the most precious gift of nature, for the instruction, the trusts, and government of society. And, indeed, it would have been inconsistent in creation to have formed man for the social state, and not to have provided virtue and wisdom enough to manage the concerns of society. May we not even say that that form of government is the best which provides the most effectually for a pure selection of these natural *aristoi* into the offices of government? The artificial aristocracy is a mischievous ingredient in government, and provision should be made to prevent its ascendancy. On the question what is the best provision, you and I differ; but we differ as rational friends, using the free exercise of our own reason, and mutually indulging its errors. You think it best to put the pseudo *aristoi* into a separate chamber of legislation, where they may be hindered from doing mischief by their co-ordinate branches, and where, also, they may be a protection to wealth against the agrarian and plundering enterprises of the majority of the people. I think that to give them power in order to prevent them from doing mischief is arming them for it, and increasing instead of remedying the evil. For, if the co-ordinate branches can arrest their action, so may they that of the co-ordinates. Mischief may be done negatively as well as positively. Of this a cabal in the Senate of the United States has furnished many proofs. Nor do I believe them necessary to protect the wealthy, because enough of these will find their way into every branch of the legislation to protect themselves. From fifteen to twenty legislatures of our own, in action for thirty years past, have proved that no fears of an equalization of property are to be apprehended from them. I think the best remedy is exactly that provided by all our constitutions, to leave to the citizens the free election and separation of the *aristoi* from the

pseudo *aristoi*, of the wheat from the chaff. In general they will elect the really good and wise. In some instances, wealth may corrupt, and birth blind them; but not in sufficient degree to endanger the society.

It is probable that our difference of opinion may, in some measure, be produced by a difference of character in those among whom we live. From what I have seen of Massachusetts and Connecticut myself, and still more from what I have heard, and the character given of the former by yourself, who know them so much better, there seems to be in those two States a traditionary reverence for certain families, which has rendered the offices of the government nearly hereditary in those families. I presume that from an early period of your history members of those families, happening to possess virtue and talents, have honestly exercised them for the good of the people and by their services have endeared their names to them. In coupling Connecticut with you, I mean it politically only, not morally. For having made the Bible the common law of their land, they seem to have modeled their morality on the story of Jacob and Laban. But, although this hereditary succession to office with you may, in some degree, be founded in real family merit, yet in a much higher degree it has proceeded from your strict alliance of Church and State. These families are canonized in the eyes of the people on common principles: "you tickle me, and I will tickle you." In Virginia we have nothing of this. Our clergy, before the revolution, having been secured against rivalship by fixed salaries, did not give themselves the trouble of acquiring influence over the people. Of wealth there were great accumulations in particular families, handed down from generation to generation, under the English law of entails. But the only object of ambition for the wealthy was a seat in the King's Council. All their court, then, was paid to the crown and its creatures; and they philippized in all collisions between the King and the people. Hence they were unpopular, and that unpopularity continues attached to their names. A Randolph, a Carter, or a Burwell must have great personal superiority over a common competitor to be elected by the people even at this day. At the first session of our legislature after the Declaration of Independence, we passed a law abolishing entails. And this was followed by one abolishing the privilege of primogeniture and dividing the lands of intestates equally among all their children or other representatives. These laws, drawn by myself, laid the ax to the foot of pseudo aristocracy. And had another which I prepared been adopted by the legislature, our work would have been complete. It was a bill for the more general diffusion of learning. This proposed to divide every county into wards of five or six miles square, like your townships; to establish in each ward a free school for reading, writing, and common arithmetic; to provide for the annual selection of the best subjects from these schools, who might receive, at the public expense, a higher degree of education at a district school; and from these district schools to select a certain number of the most promising subjects, to be completed at an university, where all the useful sciences should be taught. Worth and genius would thus have been sought out from every condition of life and completely prepared by education for defeating the competition of wealth and birth for public trusts. My proposition had, for a further object, to impart to these wards those portions of self-government for which they are best qualified, by confiding to them the care of their poor, their roads, police, elections, the nomination of jurors, administration of justice in small cases, elementary exercises of militia; in short, to have made them little republics, with a warden at the head of each, for all those concerns which, being under their eye, they would better manage than the larger republics of the county or State. A general call of ward meetings by their wardens on the same day through the State would at any time produce the genuine sense of the people on any required point and would enable the State to act in mass, as your people have so often done, and with so much effect, by their town meetings. The law for religious freedom, which made a part of this system, having put down the aristocracy of the clergy and restored to the citizen the freedom of the mind, and those of entails and descents nurturing an equality of condition among them, this on education would have raised the mass of the people to the high ground of moral respectability necessary

to their own safety and to orderly government, and would have completed the great object of qualifying them to select the veritable *aristoi* for the trusts of government, to the exclusion of the pseudalists. . . .

Although this law has not yet been acted on but in a small and inefficient degree, it is still considered as before the legislature, with other bills of the revised code, not yet taken up, and I have great hope that some patriotic spirit will, at a favorable moment, call it up, and make it the keystone of the arch of our government.

With respect to aristocracy, we should further consider that before the establishment of the American States nothing was known to history but the man of the old world, crowded within limits either small or overcharged, and steeped in the vices which that situation generates. A government adapted to such men would be one thing: but a very different one, that for men of these States. Here everyone may have land to labor for himself, if he chooses; or, preferring the exercise of any other industry, may exact for it such compensation as not only to afford a comfortable subsistence, but wherewith to provide for a cessation from labor in old age. Everyone, by his property, or by his satisfactory situation, is interested in the support of law and order. And such men may safely and advantageously reserve to themselves a wholesome control over their public affairs and a degree of freedom which, in the hands of the *canaille* of the cities of Europe, would be instantly perverted to the demolition and destruction of everything public and private. The history of the last twenty-five years of France, and of the last forty years in America, nay of its last two hundred years, proves the truth of both parts of this observation.

But even in Europe a change has sensibly taken place in the mind of man. Science had liberated the ideas of those who read and reflect, and the American example had kindled feelings of right in the people. An insurrection has consequently begun, of science, talents, and courage, against rank and birth, which have fallen into contempt. It has failed in its first effort because the mobs of the cities, the instrument used for its accomplishment, debased by ignorance, poverty, and vice, could not be restrained to rational action. But the world will recover from the panic of this first catastrophe. Science is progressive, and talents and enterprise on the alert. Resort may be had to the people of the country, a more governable power from their principles and subordination; and rank, and birth, and tinsel aristocracy will finally shrink into insignificance, even there. This, however, we have no right to meddle with. It suffices for us if the moral and physical condition of our own citizens qualifies them to select the able and good for the direction of their government, with a recurrence of elections at such short periods as will enable them to displace an unfaithful servant before the mischief he meditates may be irremediable.

I have thus stated my opinion on a point on which we differ, not with a view to controversy, for we are both too old to change opinions which are the result of a long life of inquiry and reflection; but on the suggestions of a former letter of yours, that we ought not to die before we have explained ourselves to each other. We acted in perfect harmony through a long and perilous contest for our liberty and independence. A constitution has been acquired, which, though neither of us thinks perfect, yet both consider as competent to render our fellow-citizens the happiest and the securest on whom the sun has ever shone. If we do not think exactly alike as to its imperfections, it matters little to our country, which, after devoting to it long lives of disinterested labor, we have delivered over to our successors in life, who will be able to take care of it and of themselves. . . .

Letter to Dr. Walter Jones

[*Character of George Washington*]

FROM *The Writings of Thomas Jefferson*, Andrew A. Lipscomb, Editor in Chief, and Albert Ellery Bergh, Managing Editor, issued under the auspices of The Thomas Jefferson Memorial Association.

Monticello, January 2, 1814.

Dear Sir,—Your favor of November the 25th reached this place December the 21st, having been near a month on the way. How this could happen I know not, as we have two mails a week both from Fredericksburg and Richmond. It found me just returned from a long journey and absence, during which so much business had accumulated, commanding the first attentions, that another week has been added to the delay.

I deplore, with you, the putrid state into which our newspapers have passed, and the malignity, the vulgarity, and mendacious spirit of those who write for them; and I enclose you a recent sample, the production of a New England judge, as a proof of the abyss of degradation into which we are fallen. These ordures are rapidly depraving the public taste, and lessening its relish for sound food. As vehicles of information, and a curb on our functionaries, they have rendered themselves useless, by forfeiting all title to belief. That this has, in a great degree, been produced by the violence and malignity of party spirit, I agree with you; and I have read with great pleasure the paper you enclosed me on that subject, which I now return. It is at the same time a perfect model of the style of discussion which candor and decency should observe, of the tone which renders difference of opinion even amiable, and a succinct, correct, and dispassionate history of the origin and progress of party among us. . . .

You say that in taking General Washington on your shoulders, to bear him harmless through the federal coalition, you encounter a perilous topic. I do not think so. You have given the genuine history of the course of his mind through the trying scenes in which it was engaged, and of the seductions by which it was deceived, but not depraved. I think I knew General Washington intimately and thoroughly; and were I called on to delineate his character, it should be in terms like these.

His mind was great and powerful, without being of the very first order; his penetration strong, though not so acute as that of a Newton, Bacon, or Locke; and as far as he saw, no judgment was ever sounder. It was slow in operation, being little aided by invention or imagination, but sure in conclusion. Hence the common remark of his officers, of the advantage he derived from councils of war, where hearing all suggestions, he selected whatever was best; and certainly no general ever planned his battles more judiciously. But if deranged during the course of the action, if any member of his plan was dislocated by sudden circumstances, he was slow in re-adjustment. The consequence was, that he often failed in the field, and rarely against an enemy in station, as at Boston and York. He was incapable of fear, meeting personal dangers with the calmest unconcern. Perhaps the strongest feature in his character was prudence, never acting until every circumstance, every consideration, was maturely weighed; refraining if he saw a doubt, but, when once decided, going through with his purpose, whatever obstacles opposed. His integrity was most pure, his justice the most inflexible I have ever known, no motives of interest or consanguinity, of friendship or hatred, being able to bias his decision. He was, indeed, in every sense of the words, a wise, a good, and a great man. His temper was naturally irritable and high toned; but reflection and resolution had obtained a firm and habitial ascendency over it. If ever, however, it broke its bonds, he was most tremendous in his wrath. In his expenses he was honorable, but exact; liberal in contributions to whatever promised utility; but frowning and unyielding on all visionary projects, and all unworthy calls on his charity. His heart was not warm in its affections; but he exactly calculated every man's value, and gave him a solid esteem proportioned to it. His person, you know, was fine, his stature exactly what one would wish, his deportment easy, erect, and noble; the best horseman of his age, and the most graceful figure that could be seen on horseback. Although in the circle of his friends, where he might be unreserved with safety, he took a free share in conversation, his colloquial talents were not above mediocrity, possessing neither copiousness of ideas nor fluency of words. In public, when called on for a sudden opinion, he was unready, short, and embarrassed. Yet he wrote readily, rather diffusely, in an easy and correct style. This he had acquired by conversation with the world, for his education was merely reading, writing, and common arithmetic, to which he added surveying at a later day. His time was employed in action chiefly, reading little, and that only in agriculture and English history. His correspondence became necessarily extensive, and, with journalizing his agricultural proceedings, occupied most of his leisure hours within doors.

On the whole, his character was, in its mass, perfect, in nothing bad, in few points indifferent; and it may truly be said, that never did nature and fortune combine more perfectly to make a man great, and to place him in the same constellation with whatever worthies have merited from man an everlasting remembrance. For his was the singular destiny and merit of leading the armies of his country successfully through an arduous war, for the establishment of its independence; of conducting its councils through the birth of a government, new in its forms and principles, until it had settled down into a quiet and orderly train; and of scrupulously obeying the laws through the whole of his career, civil and military, of which the history of the world furnishes no other example.

How, then, can it be perilous for you to take such a man on your shoulders? I am satisfied the great body of republicans think of him as I do. We were, indeed, dissatisfied with him on his ratification of the British treaty. But this was short lived. We knew his honesty, the wiles with which he was encompassed, and that age had already begun to relax the firmness of his purposes; and I am convinced he is more deeply seated in the love and gratitude of the republicans, than in the Pharisaical homage of the federal monarchists. For he was no monarchist from preference of his judgment. The soundness of that gave him correct views of the rights of man, and his severe justice devoted him to them. He has often declared to me that he considered our new Constitution as an experiment on the practicability of republican government, and with what dose of liberty man could be trusted for his own good; that he was determined the experiment should have a fair trial, and would lose the last drop of his blood in support of it. And these declarations he repeated to me the oftener and more pointedly, because he knew my suspicions of Colonel Hamilton's views, and probably had heard from him the same declarations which I had, to wit, "that the British constitution, with its unequal representation, corruption, and other existing abuses, was the most perfect government which had ever been established on earth, and that a reformation of those abuses would make it an impracticable government." I do believe that General Washington had not a firm confidence in the durability of our government. He was naturally distrustful of men, and inclined to gloomy apprehensions; and I was ever persuaded that a belief that we must at length end in something like a British constitution, had some weight in his adoption of the ceremonies of levees, birthdays, pompous meetings with Congress, and other forms of the same character, calculated to prepare us gradually for a change which he believed possible, and to let it come on with as little shock as might be to the public mind.

These are my opinions of General Washington, which I would vouch at the judgment seat of God, having been formed on an acquaintance of thirty years. I served with him in the Virginia legislature from 1769 to the Revolutionary war, and again, a short time in Congress, until he left us to take command of the army. During the war and after it we corresponded occasionally, and in the four years of my continuance in the office of Secretary of State, our intercourse was daily, confidential, and cordial. After I retired from that office, great and malignant pains were taken by our federal monarchists, and not entirely without effect, to make him view me as a theorist, holding French principles of government, which would lead infallibly to licentiousness and anarchy. And to this he listened the more easily, from my known disapprobation of the British treaty. I never saw him afterwards, or these malignant insinuations should have been dissipated before his just judgment, as mists before the sun. I felt on his death, with my countrymen, that "verily a great man hath fallen this day in Israel."

More time and recollection would enable me to add many other traits of his character; but why add them to you who knew him well? And I cannot justify to myself a longer detention of your paper.
Vale, proprieque tuum, me esse tibi persuadeas.

Letter to Edward Coles

[*On Slavery*]

August 25, 1814

. . . I had always hoped that the younger generation receiving their early impressions after the flame of liberty had been kindled in every breast, and had become as it were the vital spirit of every American, that the generous temperament of youth, analogous to the motion of their blood, and above the suggestions of avarice, would have sympathized with oppression, and found their love of liberty beyond their own share in it. But my intercourse with them, since my return has not been sufficient to ascertain that they have made towards this point the progress I had hoped. . . . Yet the hour of emancipation is advancing, in the march of time. It will come; and whether brought on by the generous energy of our own minds; or by the bloody process of St. Domingo, excited and conducted by the power of our present enemy, if once stationed permanently within our Country, and offering asylum and arms to the oppressed, is a leaf in our history not yet turned over. As to the method by which this difficult work is to be effected, if permitted to be done by ourselves, I have seen no proposition so expedient on the whole, as that of emancipation of those born after a given day, and of their education and expatriation after a given age. This would give time for a gradual extinction of that species of labor and substitution of another, and lessen the severity of the shock which an operation so fundamental cannot fail to produce. For men probably of any color, but of this color we know, brought from their infancy without necessity for thought or forecast, are by their habits rendered as incapable as children of taking care of themselves, and are extinguished promptly wherever industry is necessary for raising young. In the mean time they are pests in society by their idleness, and the depredations to which this leads them. . . . My opinion has ever been that, until more can be done for them, we should endeavor, with those whom fortune has thrown on our hands, to feed and clothe them well, protect them from ill usage, require such reasonable labor only as is performed voluntarily by freemen, and be led by no repugnancies to abdicate them, and our duties to them. The laws do not permit us to turn them loose, if that were for their good: and to commute them for other property is to commit them to those whose usage of them we cannot control.

Letter
to Doctor Thomas Humphreys

[*On Slavery*]

Monticello, February 8, 1817.

Dear Sir,—Your favor of January 2d did not come to my hands until the 5th instant. I concur entirely in your leading principles of gradual emancipation, of establishment on the coast of Africa, and the patronage of our nation until the emigrants shall be able to protect themselves. The subordinate details might be easily arranged. But the bare proposition of purchase by the United States generally, would excite infinite indignation in all the States alone which hold them; and the difficult question will be how to lessen this so as to reconcile our fellow citizens to it. Personally I am ready and desirous to make any sacrifice which shall ensure their gradual but complete retirement from the State, and effectually, at the same time, establish them elsewhere in freedom and safety. But I have not perceived the growth of this disposition in the rising generation, of which I once had sanguine hopes. No symptoms inform me that it will take place in my day. I leave it, therefore, to time, and not at all without hope that the day will come, equally desirable and welcome to us as to them. Perhaps the proposition now on the carpet at Washington to provide an establishment on the coast of Africa for voluntary emigrations of people of color, may be the corner stone of this future edifice. Praying for its completion as early as may most promote the good of all, I salute you with great esteem and respect.

JOHN TRUMBULL (1750–1831)

JOHN TRUMBULL was probably the most literary among the group of youthful college poets in the mid-1770's who turned from academic verses to the cause of independence. Earnest, high-minded, yet moderate in temper, he rendered valiant service to the Revolutionary cause with his *M'Fingal* (1776–1782). The first two cantos of this effective satire were published separately in 1775–1776, and in their ridicule of the Tory position proved of distinct value as propaganda. No sustained literary effort of the period so successfully combined political satire, sharp eighteenth-century wit, and shrewd observation. Although the author had a pronounced Whig bias, his partisanship did not prevent him from maintaining an Olympian view of the clashing arguments, nor keep him from burlesquing the absurdities of both sides in the town-meeting debate. If not violently partisan, Trumbull's poem was sharply satirical, and so full of quotable phrases that it had a wider popularity than any other Revolutionary poem. The last two cantos were not published until 1782. Trumbull's precociousness enabled him to write much meritorious work before *M'Fingal*, but in later life he made little effort to add to an already assured reputation.

Trumbull passed the Yale entrance examinations at the age of seven, entered college at thirteen, and was graduated four years later in 1767. He remained in New Haven as a graduate student for three years, and served as a tutor for two. During these years he did much to relieve the highly-starched Yale curriculum which neglected the study of English letters, and contributed two series of controversial essays to Boston and New Haven papers; he also penned elegies, experimented with octosyllabic verse, and tried his hand at other meters. A product of his tutorship was his famous mock-heroic piece, *The Progress of Dullness* (1772–1773). In this satire on college education, his crusade for the teaching of rhetoric and modern languages found effective utterance. Modeled upon Samuel Butler's *Hudibras*, the work is an attack upon the inconsequential, lazy, and inept student to whom college life was a mark of ambition but not of achievement, and whose subsequent life showed little of its influence and none of its amenities. One other work, an *Elegy for the Times* (1774), elicited enthusiasm among critics.

Trumbull studied law in the office of John Adams, in Boston, remaining there until Adams went to Philadelphia to sit with the Continental Congress. He later practiced at New Haven and Hartford (after 1790), entered wholeheartedly into his political career, and abandoned almost wholly any further poetical aspirations. He did join with other residents of Hartford in 1786–1787 in the composition of *The Anarchiad*, but this was his last flourish in verse. For many years he was a Justice of the Supreme Court of Connecticut. At seventy-five years of age he removed to Detroit to live with a daughter, and there in 1831 he died.

BIBLIOGRAPHY · *The Poetical Works of John Trumbull*, edited by the poet himself, and published in two volumes at Hartford in 1820, contains most of the poems.

The 1820 edition is most readily available in the reprint by the Andiron Club of New York, *The Colonnade*, XIV (1922), 289–538. V. L. Parrington's *Connecticut Wits* (1926) includes *The Progress of Dullness* and *M'Fingal*, with an informative introduction. Alexander Cowie's *John Trumbull, Connecticut Wit* (1936) is the best biography. A later study of the famous coterie to which Trumbull belonged is Leon Howard's *Connecticut Wits* (1943). Other pertinent studies include J. H. Trumbull, *The Origin of M'Fingal* (1868); H. A. Beers, *The Connecticut Wits and Other Essays* (1920); L. Grey, "John Adams and John Trumbull in the 'Boston Cycle,'" *New England Quarterly*, IV (1931), 509–514; A. Cowie, "John Trumbull as Revolutionist," *American Literature*, III (1931), 287–295; and A. Cowie, "John Trumbull as a Critic of Poetry," *New England Quarterly*, XI (1938), 773–793.

M'Fingal

ONE CRITIC of Trumbull charged the patriotic Americans of 1776 with reading *M'Fingal* for "its humorous account of Loyalist misadventures rather than for its poetry." Trumbull undoubtedly appealed to his readers' sense of humor, but the original first canto of *M'Fingal* (1776) contained few Tory mishaps and was primarily concerned with a burlesque of Tory arguments and motives. Cantos III and IV, which were completed in 1782, had more wit and greater literary finish. While the poem unquestionably lost something by its increased bulk, the author was able to change the work, in expanded form, from a mock-heroic satire to a mock-epic. Readers will find Homeric similes and other travesties of the epic style of Homer and Milton. The text is taken from the 1820 edition.

CANTO III · *The Liberty Pole*

Now warm with ministerial ire,
Fierce sallied forth our loyal 'Squire,
And on his striding steps attends
His desperate clan of Tory friends.
When sudden met his wrathful eye   5
A pole ascending through the sky,
Which numerous throngs of whiggish race
Were raising in the market-place.
Not higher school-boy's kites aspire,
Or royal mast, or country spire;   10
Like spears at Brobdignagian tilting,
Or Satan's walking-staff in Milton.
And on its top, the flag unfurl'd
Waved triumph o'er the gazing world,
Inscribed with inconsistent types   15
Of Liberty and thirteen stripes.

Beneath, the crowd without delay
The dedication-rites essay,
And gladly pay, in antient fashion,
The ceremonies of libation;   20
While briskly to each patriot lip
Walks eager round the inspiring flip:
Delicious draught! whose powers inherit
The quintessence of public spirit;
Which whoso tastes, perceives his mind   25
To nobler politics refined;
Or roused to martial controversy,
As from transforming cups of Circe;
Or warm'd with Homer's nectar'd liquor,
That fill'd the veins of gods with ichor.   30
At hand for new supplies in store,
The tavern opes its friendly door,
Whence to and fro the waiters run,
Like bucket-men at fires in town.
Then with three shouts that tore the sky,   35
'Tis consecrate to Liberty.
To guard it from th' attacks of Tories,
A grand Committee cull'd of four is;
Who foremost on the patriot spot,
Had brought the flip, and paid the shot.   40
    By this, M'FINGAL with his train
Advanced upon th' adjacent plain,
And full with loyalty possest,
Pour'd forth the zeal, that fired his breast.
    "What mad-brain'd rebel gave commission,   45
To raise this May-pole of sedition?
Like Babel, rear'd by bawling throngs,
With like confusion too of tongues,
To point at heaven and summon down
The thunders of the British crown?   50
Say, will this paltry Pole secure
Your forfeit heads from Gage's power?
Attack'd by heroes brave and crafty,
Is this to stand your ark of safety;
Or driven by Scottish laird and laddie,   55
Think ye to rest beneath its shadow?
When bombs, like fiery serpents, fly,
And balls rush hissing through the sky,
Will this vile Pole, devote to freedom,
Save like the Jewish pole in Edom;   60
Or like the brazen snake of Moses,
Cure your crackt skulls and batter'd noses?
    "Ye dupes to every factious rogue
And tavern-prating demagogue,

Whose tongue but rings, with sound more full, 65
On th' empty drumhead of his scull;
Behold you not what noisy fools
Use you, worse simpletons, for tools?
For Liberty, in your own by-sense,
Is but for crimes a patent license, 70
To break of law th' Egyptian yoke,
And throw the world in common stock;
Reduce all grievances and ills
To Magna Charta of your wills;
Establish cheats and frauds and nonsense, 75
Framed to the model of your conscience;
Cry justice down, as out of fashion,
And fix its scale of depreciation;
Defy all creditors to trouble ye,
And keep new years of Jewish jubilee; 80
Drive judges out, like Aaron's calves,
By jurisdiction of white staves,
And make the bar and bench and steeple
Submit t' our Sovereign Lord, The People;
By plunder rise to power and glory, 85
And brand all property, as Tory;
Expose all wares to lawful seizures
By mobbers or monopolizers;
Break heads and windows and the peace,
For your own interest and increase; 90
Dispute and pray and fight and groan
For public good, and mean your own;
Prevent the law by fierce attacks
From quitting scores upon your backs;
Lay your old dread, the gallows, low, 95
And seize the stocks, your ancient foe,
And turn them to convenient engines
To wreak your patriotic vengeance;
While all, your rights who understand,
Confess them in their owner's hand; 100
And when by clamours and confusions,
Your freedom's grown a public nuisance,
Cry 'Liberty,' with powerful yearning,
As he does 'Fire!' whose house is burning;
Though he already has much more 105
Than he can find occasion for.
While every clown, that tills the plains,
Though bankrupt in estate and brains,
By this new light transform'd to traitor,
Forsakes his plough to turn dictator, 110
Starts an haranguing chief of Whigs,
And drags you by the ears, like pigs.

All bluster, arm'd with factious licence,
New-born at once to politicians.
Each leather-apron'd dunce, grown wise, 115
Presents his forward face t' advise,
And tatter'd legislators meet,
From every workshop through the street.
His goose the tailor finds new use in,
To patch and turn the Constitution; 120
The blacksmith comes with sledge and grate
To iron-bind the wheels of state;
The quack forbears his patients' souse,
To purge the Council and the House;
The tinker quits his moulds and doxies, 125
To cast assembly-men and proxies.
From dunghills deep of blackest hue,
Your dirt-bred patriots spring to view,
To wealth and power and honors rise,
Like new-wing'd maggots changed to flies, 130
And fluttering round in high parade,
Strut in the robe, or gay cockade.
See Arnold quits, for ways more certain,
His bankrupt-perj'ries for his fortune,
Brews rum no longer in his store, 135
Jockey and skipper now no more,
Forsakes his warehouses and docks,
And writs of slander for the pox;
And cleansed by patriotism from shame,
Grows General of the foremost name. 140
For in this ferment of the stream
The dregs have work'd up to the brim,
And by the rule of topsy-turvies,
The scum stands foaming on the surface.
You've caused your pyramid t' ascend, 145
And set it on the little end.
Like Hudibras, your empire's made,
Whose crupper had o'ertopp'd his head.
You've push'd and turn'd the whole world up-
Side down, and got yourselves at top, 150
While all the great ones of your state
Are crush'd beneath the popular weight;
Nor can you boast, this present hour,
The shadow of the form of power.
For what's your Congress or its end? 155
A power, t' advise and recommend;
To call forth troops, adjust your quotas—
And yet no soul is bound to notice;
To pawn your faith to th' utmost limit,
But cannot bind you to redeem it; 160

268

And when in want no more in them lies,
Than begging from your State-Assemblies;
Can utter oracles of dread,
Like friar Bacon's brazen head,
But when a faction dares dispute 'em,   165
Has ne'er an arm to execute 'em:
As tho' you chose supreme dictators,
And put them under conservators.
You've but pursued the self-same way
With Shakespeare's Trinc'lo in the play;   170
'You shall be Viceroys here, 'tis true,
But we'll be Viceroys over you.'
What wild confusion hence must ensue?
Tho' common danger yet cements you:
So some wreck'd vessel, all in shatters,   175
Is held up by surrounding waters,
But stranded, when the pressure ceases,
Falls by its rottenness to pieces.
And fall it must! if wars were ended,
You'll ne'er have sense enough to mend it: 180
But creeping on, by low intrigues,
Like vermin of a thousand legs,
'Twill find as short a life assign'd,
As all things else of reptile kind.
Your Commonwealth's a common harlot,   185
The property of every varlet;
Which now in taste, and full employ,
All sorts admire, as all enjoy:
But soon a batter'd strumpet grown,
You'll curse and drum her out of town.   190
Such is the government you chose;
For this you bade the world be foes;
For this, so mark'd for dissolution,
You scorn the British Constitution,
That constitution form'd by sages,   195
The wonder of all modern ages;
Which owns no failure in reality,
Except corruption and venality;
And merely proves the adage just,
That best things spoil'd corrupt to worst: 200
So man supreme in earthly station,
And mighty lord of this creation,
When once his corse is dead as herring,
Becomes the most offensive carrion,
And sooner breeds the plague, 'tis found,   205
Than all beasts rotting on the ground.
Yet with republics to dismay us,
You've call'd up Anarchy from chaos,

With all the followers of her school,
Uproar and Rage and wild Misrule: 210
For whom this rout of Whigs distracted,
And ravings dire of every crack'd head;
These new-cast legislative engines
Of County-meetings and Conventions;
Committees vile of correspondence,   215
And mobs, whose tricks have almost undone 's:
While reason fails to check your course,
And Loyalty's kick'd out of doors,
And Folly, like inviting landlord,
Hoists on your poles her royal standard;   220
While the king's friends, in doleful dumps,
Have worn their courage to the stumps,
And leaving George in sad disaster,
Most sinfully deny their master.
What furies raged when you, in sea,   225
In shape of Indians, drown'd the tea;
When your gay sparks, fatigued to watch it,
Assumed the moggison and hatchet,
With wampum'd blankets hid their laces,   229
And like their sweethearts, primed their faces:
While not a red-coat dared oppose,
And scarce a Tory show'd his nose;
While Hutchinson, for sure retreat,
Manœuvred to his country seat,
And thence affrighted, in the suds,   235
Stole off bareheaded through the woods.
  "Have you not roused your mobs to join,
And make Mandamus-men resign,
Call'd forth each duffil-drest curmudgeon,
With dirty trowsers and white bludgeon,   240
Forced all our Councils through the land,
To yield their necks at your command;
While paleness marks their late disgraces,
Through all their rueful length of faces?
  "Have you not caused as woeful work   245
In our good city of New-York,
When all the rabble, well cockaded,
In triumph through the streets paraded,
And mobb'd the Tories, scared their spouses,
And ransack'd all the custom-houses;   250
Made such a tumult, bluster, jarring,
That mid the clash of tempests warring,
Smith's weather-cock, in veers forlorn,
Could hardly tell which way to turn?
Burn'd effigies of higher powers,   255
Contrived in planetary hours;

269

As witches with clay-images
Destroy or torture whom they please:
Till fired with rage, th' ungrateful club
Spared not your best friend, Beelzebub,   260
O'erlook'd his favors, and forgot
The reverence due his cloven foot,
And in the selfsame furnace frying,
Stew'd him, and North and Bute and Tryon?
Did you not, in as vile and shallow way,   265
Fright our poor Philadelphian, Galloway,
Your Congress, when the loyal ribald
Belied, berated and bescribbled?
What ropes and halters did you send,
Terrific emblems of his end,   270
Till, least he'd hang in more than effigy,
Fled in a fog the trembling refugee?
Now rising in progression fatal,
Have you not ventured to give battle?
When Treason chaced our heroes troubled,   275
With rusty gun, and leathern doublet;
Turn'd all stone-walls and groves and bushes,
To batteries arm'd with blunderbusses;
And with deep wounds, that fate portend,
Gaul'd many a Briton's latter end;   280
Drove them to Boston, as in jail,
Confined without mainprize or bail.
Were not these deeds enough betimes,
To heap the measure of your crimes:
But in this loyal town and dwelling,   285
Yoú raise these ensigns of rebellion?
'Tis done! fair Mercy shuts her door;
And Vengeance now shall sleep no more.
Rise then, my friends, in terror rise,
And sweep this scandal from the skies.   290
You'll see their Dagon, though well jointed,
Will shrink before the Lord's anointed;
And like old Jericho's proud wall,
Before our ram's horns prostrate fall."
This said, our 'Squire, yet undismay'd,   295
Call'd forth the Constable to aid,
And bade him read, in nearer station,
The Riot-act and Proclamation.
He swift, advancing to the ring,
Began, "Our Sovereign Lord, the King"—   300
When thousand clam'rous tongues he hears,
And clubs and stones assail his ears.
To fly was vain; to fight was idle;
By foes encompass'd in the middle,

His hope, in stratagems, he found,   305
And fell right craftily to ground;
Then crept to seek an hiding place,
'Twas all he could, beneath a brace;
Where soon the conq'ring crew espied him,
And where he lurk'd, they caught and tied him.
At once with resolution fatal,   311
Both Whigs and Tories rush'd to battle.
Instead of weapons, either band
Seized on such arms as came to hand.
And as famed Ovid paints th' adventures   315
Of wrangling Lapithæ and Centaurs,
Who at their feast, by Bacchus led,
Threw bottles at each other's head;
And these arms failing in their scuffles,
Attack'd with andirons, tongs and shovels: 320
So clubs and billets, staves and stones
Met fierce, encountering every sconce,
And cover'd o'er with knobs and pains
Each void receptacle for brains;
Their clamours rend the skies around,   325
The hills rebellow to the sound;
And many a groan increas'd the din
From batter'd nose and broken shin.
M'FINGAL, rising at the word,
Drew forth his old militia-sword;   330
Thrice cried "King George," as erst in distress,
Knights of romance invoked a mistress;
And brandishing the blade in air,
Struck terror through th' opposing war.
The Whigs, unsafe within the wind   335
Of such commotion, shrunk behind.
With whirling steel around address'd,
Fierce through their thickest throng he press'd,
(Who roll'd on either side in arch,
Like Red Sea waves in Israel's march)   340
And like a meteor rushing through,
Struck on their Pole a vengeful blow.
Around, the Whigs, of clubs and stones
Discharged whole vollies, in platoons,
That o'er in whistling fury fly;   345
But not a foe dares venture nigh.
And now perhaps with glory crown'd
Our 'Squire had fell'd the pole to ground,
Had not some Pow'r, a Whig at heart,
Descended down and took their part;   350
(Whether 'twere Pallas, Mars or Iris,
'Tis scarce worth while to make inquiries)

Who at the nick of time alarming,
Assumed the solemn form of Chairman,
Address'd a Whig, in every scene   355
The stoutest wrestler on the green,
And pointed where the spade was found,
Late used to set their pole in ground,
And urged, with equal arms and might,
To dare our 'Squire to single fight.   360
The Whig thus arm'd, untaught to yield,
Advanced tremendous to the field:
Nor did M'FINGAL shun the foe,
But stood to brave the desp'rate blow;
While all the party gazed, suspended   365
To see the deadly combat ended;
And Jove in equal balance weigh'd
The sword against the brandish'd spade,
He weigh'd; but lighter than a dream,
The sword flew up, and kick'd the beam.   370
Our 'Squire on tiptoe rising fair
Lifts high a noble stroke in air,
Which hung not, but like dreadful engines,
Descended on his foe in vengeance.
But ah! in danger, with dishonor   375
The sword perfidious fails its owner;
That sword, which oft had stood its ground,
By huge trainbands encircled round;
And on the bench, with blade right loyal,
Had won the day at many a trial,   380
Of stones and clubs had braved th' alarms,
Shrunk from these new Vulcanian arms.
The spade so temper'd from the sledge,
Nor keen nor solid harm'd its edge,
Now met it, from his arm of might,   385
Descending with steep force to smite;
The blade snapp'd short—and from his hand,
With rust embrown'd the glittering sand.
Swift turn'd M'FINGAL at the view,   *Satire*
And call'd to aid th' attendant crew,   390
In vain; the Tories all had run,   *Tories*
When scarce the fight was well begun;   *always*
Their setting wigs he saw decreas'd   *pictured*
Far in th' horizon tow'rd the west.   *as*
Amazed he view'd the shameful sight,   395
And saw no refuge, but a flight: *cowards*
But age unwieldy check'd his pace,
Though fear had wing'd his flying race;
For not a trifling prize at stake;
No less than great M'FINGAL's back.   400

With legs and arms he work'd his course,
Like rider that outgoes his horse,
And labor'd hard to get away, as
Old Satan struggling on through chaos;
'Till looking back, he spied in rear   405
The spade-arm'd chief advanced too near:
Then stopp'd and seized a stone, that lay
An ancient landmark near the way;
Nor shall we as old bards have done,
Affirm it weigh'd an hundred ton;   410
But such a stone, as at a shift
A modern might suffice to lift,
Since men, to credit their enigmas,
Are dwindled down to dwarfs and pigmies,
And giants exiled with their cronies   415
To Brobdignags and Patagonias.
But while our Hero turn'd him round,   *Very*
And tugg'd to raise it from the ground,   *humorous*
The fatal spade discharged a blow
Tremendous on his rear below: 420
His bent knee fail'd, and void of strength
Stretch'd on the ground his manly length.
Like ancient oak o'erturn'd, he lay,
Or tower to tempests fall'n a prey,
Or mountain sunk with all his pines,   425
Or flow'r the plow to dust consigns,
And more things else—but all men know 'em,
If slightly versed in epic poem.
At once the crew, at this dread crisis,
Fall on, and bind him, ere he rises;   430
And with loud shouts and joyful soul,
Conduct him prisoner to the pole.
When now the mob in lucky hour
Had got their en'mies in their power,
They first proceed, by grave command,   435
To take the Constable in hand.
Then from the pole's sublimest top   *Constable*
The active crew let down the rope,
At once its other end in haste bind,
And make it fast upon his waistband;   440
Till like the earth, as stretch'd on tenter,
He hung self-balanced on his centre.
Then upwards, all hands hoisting sail,   *Yells for*
They swung him, like a keg of ale,
Till to the pinnacle in height   445
He vaulted, like balloon or kite.   *mercy.*
As Socrates of old at first did
To aid philosophy get hoisted,

271

And found his thoughts flow strangely clear,
Swung in a basket in mid air: 450
Our culprit thus, in purer sky,
With like advantage raised his eye,
And looking forth in prospect wide,
His Tory errors clearly spied,
And from his elevated station,   455
With bawling voice began addressing.

   "Good Gentlemen and friends and kin,
For heaven's sake hear, if not for mine!
I here renounce the Pope, the Turks,
The King, the Devil and all their works;   460
And will, set me but once at ease,
Turn Whig or Christian, what you please;
And always mind your rules so justly,
Should I live long as old Methus'lah,
I'll never join in British rage,   465
Nor help Lord North, nor Gen'ral Gage;
Nor lift my gun in future fights,
Nor take away your Charter-rights;
Nor overcome your new-raised levies,
Destroy your towns, nor burn your navies;   470
Nor cut your poles down while I've breath,
Though raised more thick than hatchel-teeth:
But leave King George and all his elves
To do their conq'ring work themselves."

   This said, they lower'd him down in state,   475
Spread at all points, like falling cat;
But took a vote first on the question,
That they'd accept this full confession,
And to their fellowship and favor,
Restore him on his good behaviour.   480

   Not so our 'Squire submits to rule,
But stood, heroic as a mule.
"You'll find it all in vain, quoth he,
To play your rebel tricks on me.
All punishments, the world can render,   485
Serve only to provoke th' offender;
The will gains strength from treatment horrid,
As hides grow harder when they're curried.
With good opinion of the law;
No man e'er felt the halter draw,   490
Or held in method orthodox
His love of justice, in the stocks;
Or fail'd to lose by sheriff's shears
At once his loyalty and ears.
Have you made Murray look less big,   495
Or smoked old Williams to a Whig?

Did our mobb'd Ol'ver quit his station,
Or heed his vows of resignation?
Has Rivington, in dread of stripes,
Ceased lying since you stole his types?   500
And can you think my faith will alter,
By tarring, whipping or the halter?
I'll stand the worst; for recompense
I trust King George and Providence.
And when with conquest gain'd I come,   505
Array'd in law and terror home,
Ye'll rue this inauspicious morn,
And curse the day, when ye were born,
In Job's high style of imprecations,
With all his plagues, without his patience."   510

   Meanwhile beside the pole, the guard
A bench of Justice had prepared,
Where sitting round in awful sort
The grand Committee hold their Court;
While all the crew, in silent awe,   515
Wait from their lips the lore of law.
Few moments with deliberation
They hold the solemn consultation;
When soon in judgment all agree,
And Clerk proclaims the dread decree;   520
"That 'Squire M'FINGAL having grown
The vilest Tory in the town,
And now in full examination
Convicted by his own confession,
Finding no tokens of repentance,   525
This Court proceeds to render sentence:
That first the Mob a slip-knot single
Tie round the neck of said M'FINGAL,
And in due form do tar him next,
And feather, as the law directs;   530
Then through the town attendant ride him
In cart with Constable beside him,
And having held him up to shame,
Bring to the pole, from whence he came."

   Forthwith the crowd proceed to deck   535
With halter'd noose M'FINGAL's neck,
While he in peril of his soul
Stood tied half-hanging to the pole;
Then lifting high the ponderous jar,
Pour'd o'er his head the smoking tar.   540
With less profusion once was spread
Oil on the Jewish monarch's head,
That down his beard and vestments ran,
And cover'd all his outward man.

272

As when (so Claudian sings) the Gods 545
And earth-born Giants fell at odds,
The stout Enceladus in malice
Tore mountains up to throw at Pallas;
And while he held them o'er his head,
The river, from their fountains fed, 550
Pour'd down his back its copious tide,
And wore its channels in his hide:
So from the high-raised urn the torrents
Spread down his side their various currents;
His flowing wig, as next the brim, 555
First met and drank the sable stream; *Homeric*
Adown his visage stern and grave
Roll'd and adhered the viscid wave;
With arms depending as he stood,
Each cuff capacious holds the flood; 560
From nose and chin's remotest end,
The tarry icicles descend;
Till all o'erspread, with colors gay,
He glitter'd to the western ray,
Like sleet-bound trees in wintry skies, 565
Or Lapland idol carved in ice.
And now the feather-bag display'd
Is waved in triumph o'er his head,
And clouds him o'er with feathers missive,
And down, upon the tar, adhesive: 570
Not Maia's son, with wings for ears,
Such plumage round his visage wears;
Nor Milton's six-wing'd angel gathers
Such superfluity of feathers.
Now all complete appears our 'Squire, 575
Like Gorgon or Chimæra dire;
Nor more could boast on Plato's plan
To rank among the race of man,
Or prove his claim to human nature,
As a two-legg'd, unfeather'd creature. 580
   Then on the fatal cart, in state
They raised our grand Duumvirate.
And as at Rome a like committee,
Who found an owl within their city,
With solemn rites and grave processions 585
At every shrine perform'd lustrations;
And least infection might take place
From such grim fowl with feather'd face,
All Rome attends him through the street
In triumph to his country seat: 590
With like devotion all the choir
Paraded round our awful 'Squire;

In front the martial music comes
Of horns and fiddles, fifes and drums,
With jingling sound of carriage bells, 595
And treble creak of rusted wheels.
Behind, the croud, in lengthen'd row
With proud procession, closed the show.
And at fit periods every throat
Combined in universal shout; 600
And hail'd great Liberty in chorus,
Or bawl'd 'confusion to the Tories.'
Not louder storm the welkin braves
From clamors of conflicting waves;
Less dire in Lybian wilds the noise 605
When rav'ning lions lift their voice;
Or triumphs at town-meetings made,
On passing votes to regulate trade.
   Thus having borne them round the town,
Last at the pole they set them down; 610
And to the tavern take their way
To end in mirth the festal day.
   And now the Mob, dispersed and gone,
Left 'Squire and Constable alone.
The constable with rueful face 615
Lean'd sad and solemn o'er a brace;
And fast beside him, cheek by jowl
Stuck 'Squire M'FINGAL 'gainst the pole,
Glued by the tar t' his rear applied,
Like barnacle on vessel's side. 620
But though his body lack'd physician,
His spirit was in worse condition.
He found his fears of whips and ropes
By many a drachm outweigh'd his hopes.
As men in jail without mainprize 625
View every thing with other eyes,
And all goes wrong in church and state,
Seen through perspective of the grate:
So now M'FINGAL'S Second-sight
Beheld all things in gloomier light; 630
His visual nerve, well purged with tar,
Saw all the coming scenes of war.
As his prophetic soul grew stronger,
He found he could hold in no longer.
First from the pole, as fierce he shook, 635
His wig from pitchy durance broke,
His mouth unglued, his feathers flutter'd,
His tarr'd skirts crack'd, and thus he utter'd. *Squire*
   "Ah, Mr. Constable, in vain *M'Fingal's*
We strive 'gainst wind and tide and rain! 640 *prophecy*

273

Behold my doom! this feathery omen
Portends what dismal times are coming.
Now future scenes, before my eyes,
And second-sighted forms arise.
I hear a voice, that calls away,   645
And cries 'The Whigs will win the day.'
My beck'ning Genius gives command,
And bids me fly the fatal land;
Where changing name and constitution,
Rebellion turns to Revolution,   650
While Loyalty, oppress'd, in tears,

Stands trembling for its neck and ears.
    "Go, summon all our brethren, greeting,
To muster at our usual meeting;
There my prophetic voice shall warn 'em   655
Of all things future that concern 'em,
And scenes disclose on which, my friend,
Their conduct and their lives depend.
There I—but first 'tis more of use,
From this vile pole to set me loose;   660
Then go with cautious steps and steady,
While I steer home and make all ready."

JOEL BARLOW (1754–1812)

OUT OF A group of four or five intensely conservative Connecticut Wits, Joel Barlow was the only one to turn from rigid Federalism to democratic principles. Barlow's apostasy must have seemed complete to his onetime Connecticut associates when he defended the French Revolution and aided Thomas Paine in bringing out *The Age of Reason.* The key to this defection from the heavy dogmatism and orthodoxy of Connecticut Federalism is to be found in Barlow's eighteen years of residence abroad (1787–1805), during which he met some of the leading thinkers of Europe, including Condorcet, Holbach, and Volney, and became a citizen of the world. His cosmopolitanism was signalized by the fact that when he returned to America, it was to Washington rather than to the parochial capital of Connecticut that he turned for his residence.

When he reached maturity, Barlow became a crusader for rational, democratic thought. He shared Paine's conviction that the French Revolution was an extension of the American war for independence, and a second stage in the overthrow of the monarchical society of Europe. Seeking the complete destruction of feudalism, he began his attack by proclaiming that the power of the state should be exerted for the benefit of all, not merely for a privileged class. Inspired by the French perfectionists, he wrote incisively for the equality of men in rights and privileges, and derided all government founded solely upon legal precedent and static thinking.

Born in Redding, Connecticut, in 1754, Barlow was graduated from Yale in 1778, and after two years of graduate study he became, in 1780, chaplain of the Fourth Massachusetts Brigade. Seven years later, after a term of storekeeping, teaching, editing, and reading law, he contributed to "The Anarchiad" satiric blasts at democratic liberalism and agrarian eco-

nomics published serially in the *New-Haven Gazette, and Connecticut Magazine.* In the same year he published his philosophical, narrative, and descriptive poem, *The Vision of Columbus,* which he had finished early in 1783. The profound change in Barlow's views resulting from his experiences abroad called for alterations in the interpretative parts of the poem. The changes were heralded by a new title, *The Columbiad,* when the expanded epic was published in 1807.

In 1788 Barlow became the European agent of the Scioto Land Company, whose schemes he was not especially successful in promoting. Before leaving Hartford he had read Price's *Observations* and other stirring volumes which had helped to prepare him for his sympathetic association with those firebrands of revolutionary thought, Tom Paine, Horne Tooke, and the French *literati.* With his marked receptivity to new ideas, Barlow was soon not only absorbing all the radicalism of the French Revolution, but busy expounding its ideas and assailing its enemies. A true son of Enlightenment, he found scope for his argumentative genius in such works as *Letters to the National Convention in France* (1792), *Advice to the Privileged Orders* (1792), and a lively, slashing poem, *The Conspiracy of Kings* (1792). His literary defense of the cause brought him French citizenship and an entry into provincial politics at Savoy, where he went to forward his candidacy for membership in the Convention. While there, a chance taste of porridge, and the nostalgia it induced, inspired his witty, short mock-epic, *The Hasty Pudding* (1793). For a time after 1795 he was an important public servant, bargaining with his native patience and tenacity for the release of American prisoners in the Barbary states, and bringing Algeria, Tripoli, and Tunis into line with firm treaties. When the long negotiations were ended,

274

Barlow returned to America, and in two years he had *The Columbiad* in print. But his world citizenship did not confer the privilege of retirement. In 1811 he was commissioned to conclude a trade treaty with Napoleon. Finally, after months of delay, Napoleon designated Vilna as a meeting place for negotiations. Thither Barlow posted, but before a meeting could be effected, the French army had begun its wild flight from Moscow, and its commander was retreating much too rapidly for parleying. After exposure in subzero weather, Barlow died in Poland near the typhus-ridden city of Cracow.

BIBLIOGRAPHY · There is no collected edition of Barlow's works. The original writings were published as follows: *The Vision of Columbus* (1787); *Advice to the Privileged Orders* (1792–93); *The Hasty Pudding* (1796); *The Columbiad* (1807). The first and for a long time the only biography was Charles B. Todd's *Life and Letters of Joel Barlow* (1886), from which the anniversary poems are printed. Other studies include M. R. Adams, "Joel Barlow, Political Romanticist," *American Literature*, IX (1937), 113–152; Leon Howard, in *The Connecticut Wits* (1943); A. B. Hulbert, in *The Records and Original Proceedings of the Ohio Company* (1917), and "The Methods and Operations of the Scioto Group of Speculators," *Mississippi Valley Historical Review*, I (1915), 502–515; V. C. Miller, *Joel Barlow: Revolutionist, 1791–1792* (1932); V. L. Parrington, *Connecticut Wits* (1926); M. C. Tyler, in *Three Men of Letters* (1895); and T. A. Zunder, *The Early Days of Joel Barlow, a Connecticut Wit* (1934).

The Vision of Columbus

patriotic vein

THE POLITICAL independence of the United States of America in 1776 afforded a transcendent theme for orator and poet. To create a literature worthy of the greatness of America's political achievement became the first duty of all literary nationalists. Alert to this responsibility was Freneau, with his "Pictures of Columbus" and his "American Village." Timothy Dwight and David Humphreys also responded poetically to the engrossing theme of the grandeur and potentialities of the Federal Republic. Too often the aspiring poets confused the magnificence of their subject with the amplitude of their powers in their zeal to become the Homer or Vergil of America. Barlow's *Vision of Columbus*, completed in 1783, published in 1787, was enlarged and revised twenty years later as *The Columbiad*.

Barlow's purpose is apparent from the concluding section of his introduction:

The Author, at first, formed an idea of attempting a regular Epic Poem, on the discovery of America. But on examining the nature of that event, he found that the most brilliant subjects incident to such a plan would arise from the consequences of the discovery, and must be represented in vision. Indeed to have made it a patriotic Poem, by extending the subject to the settlement and revolutions of North America and their probable effect upon the future progress of society at large, would have protracted the vision to such a degree as to render it disproportionate to the rest of the work. To avoid an absurdity of this kind, which he supposed the critics would not pardon, he rejected the idea of a regular Epic form, and has confined his plan to the train of events which might be represented to the hero in vision. This form he considers as the best that the nature of the subject would admit; and the regularity of the parts will appear by observing, that there is a single poetical design constantly kept in view, which is to gratify and soothe the desponding mind of the hero: It being the greatest possible reward of his services, and the only one that his situation would permit him to enjoy, to convince him that his labours had not been bestowed in vain, and that he was the author of such extensive happiness to the human race.

Book VII (Book VIII in *The Columbiad*) fits admirably into this plan, for it singles out some of the signs of progress in American society. The verse paragraph beginning with line 23, imitative of Shenstone's "Elegy to the Winds," was written originally as separate lines on the death of the poet's brother Samuel. Sections from another piece—*A Poem Spoken at the Public Commencement* (1781)—were incorporated in Books VII and IX. The text is that of the original edition of 1787.

BOOK VII · *Argument. Hymn to Peace. Progress of Arts in America. Fur-trade. Fisheries. Productions and Commerce. Education. Philosophical inventions. Painting. Poetry.*

Hail sacred Peace, who claim'st thy bright abode,
Mid circling saints that grace the throne of God.
Before his arm, around the shapeless earth,
Stretch'd the wide heavens and gave to nature birth;
Ere morning stars his glowing chambers hung, 5
Or songs of gladness woke an angel's tongue,
Veil'd in the brightness of the Almighty's mind,
In blest repose thy placid form reclined;
Borne through the heavens with his creating voice,
Thy presence bade the unfolding worlds rejoice, 10
Gave to seraphic harps their sounding lays,
Their joys to angels, and to men their praise.

From scenes of blood, these beauteous shores that stain,
From gasping friends that press the sanguine plain,
From fields, long taught in vain thy flight to mourn, 15
I rise, delightful Power, and greet thy glad return.
Too long the groans of death, and battle's bray
Have rung discordant through the unpleasing lay:
Let pity's tear its balmy fragrance shed,
O'er heroes' wounds and patriot warriors dead; 20
Accept, departed Shades, these grateful sighs,
Your fond attendants to the approving skies.

   And thou, my earliest friend, my Brother dear,
Thy fall untimely wakes the tender tear.
In youthful sports, in toils, in blood allied, 25
My kind companion and my hopeful guide,
When Heaven's sad summons, from our infant eyes
Had call'd our last, loved parent to the skies.
Tho' young in arms, and still obscure thy name,
Thy bosom panted for the deeds of fame, 30
Beneath Montgomery's eye, when, by thy steel,
In northern wilds, the lurking savage fell.
Yet, hapless youth! when thy great leader bled,
Thro' the same wound thy parting spirit fled.

   But now the untuneful trump shall grate no more, 35
Ye silver streams, no longer swell with gore;
Bear from your beauteous banks the crimson stain,
With yon retiring navies to the main.
While other views, unfolding on my eyes,
And happier themes bid bolder numbers rise: 40
Bring, bounteous Peace, in thy celestial throng,
Life to my soul, and rapture to my song;
Give me to trace, with pure unclouded ray,
The arts and virtues that attend thy sway; 44
To see thy blissful charms, that here descend,
Through distant realms and endless years extend.

   To cast new glories o'er the changing clime,
The Seraph now reversed the flight of time;
Roll'd back the years, that led their course before,
And stretch'd immense the wild uncultured shore;
The paths of peaceful science raised to view, 51
And show'd the ascending crowds that useful arts pursue.
As o'er the canvass, when the master's mind,
Glows with a future landscape, well design'd,

While gardens, vales, and streets and structures rise, 55
A new creation to his kindling eyes;
He smiles o'er all; and, in delightful strife,
The pencil moves, and calls the whole to life.
So, while the great Columbus stood sublime, 59
And saw wild nature clothe the trackless clime;
The green banks heave, the winding currents pour,
The bays and harbours cleave the yielding shore,
The champaigns spread, the solemn groves arise,
And the rough mountains lengthen round the skies,
Through all the scene, he traced with skillful ken
The unform'd seats and future walks of men; 66
Mark'd where the fields should bloom, and streamers play,
And towns and empires claim their peaceful sway;
When, sudden waken'd by the Angel's hand,
They rose in pomp around the cultured land. 70

   In western wilds, where still the natives tread,
From sea to sea an inland commerce spread;
O'er the dim streams and thro' the gloomy grove,
The trading bands their cumberous burdens move;
Where furs and skins, and all the exhaustless store
Of midland realms descended to the shore. 76

   Where summer's suns, along the northern coast,
With feeble force dissolve the chains of frost,
Prolific waves the scaly nations trace,
And tempt the toils of man's laborious race. 80
Though rich Peruvian strands, beneath the tide,
Their rocks of pearl and sparkling pebbles hide;
Lured by the gaudy prize, the adventurous train
Plunge the dark deep and brave the surging main;
Whole realms of slaves the dangerous labours dare,
To stud a sceptre or emblaze a star: 86
Yet wealthier stores these genial tides display,
And busy throngs with nobler spoils repay.
The hero saw the hardy hosts advance,
Cast the long line and aim the barbed lance; 90
Load the deep floating barks, and bear abroad
To each far clime the life-sustaining food;
While growing swarms by nature's hand supplied,
People the shoals and fill the exhaustless tide.

   Where southern streams thro' broad savannahs bend, 95
The rice-clad vales their verdant rounds extend;
Tobago's plant its leaf expanding yields,
The maize luxuriant clothes a thousand fields;
Steeds, herds and flocks o'er northern regions rove,

Embrown the hill and wanton thro' the grove;
The wood-lands wide their sturdy honours bend,
The pines, the live-oaks to the shores descend; 102
Along the strand unnumber'd keels arise,
The huge hulls heave, and masts ascend the skies;
Launch'd in the deep, o'er eastern waves they fly,
Feed every isle and distant lands supply.　　106

　　Silent he gazed; when thus the guardian Power—
These works of peace awhile adorn the shore;
But other joys and deeds of lasting praise　　109
Shall crown their labours and thy rapture raise,
Each orient realm, the former pride of earth,
Where men and science drew their ancient birth,
Shall soon behold, on this enlighten'd coast,
Their fame transcended and their glory lost.
That train of arts, that graced mankind before, 115
Warm'd the glad sage or taught the Muse to soar,
Here with superior sway their progress trace,
And aid the triumphs of thy filial race;
While rising crouds, with genius unconfined,　119
Through deep inventions lead the astonish'd mind,
Wide o'er the world their name unrivall'd raise,
And bind their temples with immortal bays.

　　In youthful minds to wake the ardent flame,
To nurse the arts, and point the paths of fame,
Behold their liberal sires, with guardian care,　125
Thro' all the realms their seats of science rear.
Great without pomp the modest mansions rise;
Harvard and Yale and Princeton greet the skies;
Penn's ample walls o'er Del'ware's margin bend,
On James's bank the royal spires ascend,　　130
Thy turrets, York, Columbia's walks command,
Bosom'd in groves, see growing Dartmouth stand;
While, o'er the realm reflecting solar fires,
On yon tall hill Rhode-Island's seat aspires.

　　O'er all the shore, with sails and cities gay, 135
And where rude hamlets stretch their inland sway,
With humbler walls unnumber'd schools arise,
And youths unnumber'd seize the solid prize.
In no blest land has Science rear'd her fane,
And fix'd so firm her wide-extended reign;　140
Each rustic here, that turns the furrow'd soil,
The maid, the youth, that ply mechanic toil,
In freedom nurst, in useful arts inured,
Know their just claims, and see their rights
　　secured.
　　And lo, descending from the seats of art,　145
The growing throngs for active scenes depart;

In various garbs they tread the welcome land,
Swords at their side or sceptres in their hand,
With healing powers bid dire diseases cease,
Or sound the tidings of eternal peace.　　150

　　In no blest land has fair Religion shone,
And fix'd so firm her everlasting throne.
Where, o'er the realms those spacious temples
　　shine,
Frequent and full the throng'd assemblies join;
There, fired with virtue's animating flame,　155
The sacred task unnumber'd sages claim;
The task, for angels great; in early youth,
To lead whole nations in the walks of truth,
Shed the bright beams of knowledge on the mind,
For social compact harmonize mankind,　　160
To life, to happiness, to joys above,
The soften'd soul with ardent zeal to move;
For this the voice of Heaven, in early years,
Tuned the glad songs of life-inspiring seers,
For this consenting seraphs leave the skies,　165
The God compassionates, the Saviour dies.

　　Tho' different faiths their various orders show,
That seem discordant to the train below;
Yet one blest cause, one universal flame,
Wakes all their joys and centres every aim;　170
They tread the same bright steps, and smoothe the
　　road,
Lights of the world and messengers of God.
So the galaxy broad o'er heaven displays
Of various stars the same unbounded blaze;
Where great and small their mingling rays unite,
And earth and skies repay the friendly light.　176

　　While thus the hero view'd the sacred band,
Moved by one voice and guided by one hand,
He saw the heavens unfold, a form descend,
Down the dim skies his arm of light extend,　180
From God's own altar lift a living coal,
Touch their glad lips and brighten every soul;
Then, with accordant voice and heavenly tongue,
O'er the wide clime these welcome accents rung.

　　Ye darkling race of poor distrest mankind,　185
For bliss still groping and to virtue blind,
Hear from on high th' Almighty's voice descend;
Ye heavens, be silent, and thou earth, attend.
I reign the Lord of life; I fill the round,
Where stars and skies and angels know their bound;
Before all years, beyond all thought I live,　191
Light, form and motion, time and space I give;

Touch'd by this hand, all worlds within me roll,
Mine eye their splendor and my breath their soul.
Earth, with her lands and seas, my power proclaims,
There moves my spirit, there descend my flames;
Graced with the semblance of the Maker's mind,
Rose from the darksome dust the reasoning kind,
With powers of thought to trace the eternal Cause,
That all his works to one great system draws, 200
View the full chain of love, the all-ruling plan,
That binds the God, the angel and the man,
That gives all hearts to feel, all minds to know
The bliss of harmony, of strife the woe.
This heaven of concord, who of mortal strain 205
Shall dare oppose—he lifts his arm in vain;
The avenging universe shall on him roll
The intended wrong, and whelm his guilty soul.
Then lend your audience; hear, ye sons of earth,
Rise into life, behold the promised birth; 210
From pain to joy, from guilt to glory rise,
Be babes on earth, be seraphs in the skies.
Lo, to the cries of grief mild mercy bends,
Stern vengeance softens and the God descends,
The atoning God, the pardoning grace to seal, 215
The dead to quicken and the sick to heal.
See from his sacred side the life-blood flow,
Hear in his groans unutterable woe;
While, fixt in one strong pang, the all-suffering
    Mind
Bears and bewails the tortures of mankind. 220
But lo, the ascending pomp! around him move
His rising saints, the first-born sons of love;
View the glad throng, the glorious triumph join,
His paths pursue and in his splendor shine;
Purged from your stains in his atoning blood, 225
Assume his spotless robes and reign beside your
    God.
    Thus heard the hero—while his roving view
Traced other crouds that liberal arts pursue;
When thus the Seraph—Lo, a favourite band,
The torch of science flaming in their hand! 230
Thro' nature's range their ardent souls aspire,
Or wake to life the canvass and the lyre.
Fixt in sublimest thought, behold them rise,
Superior worlds unfolding to their eyes;
Heaven in their view unveils the eternal plan, 235
And gives new guidance to the paths of man.
    See on yon darkening height bold Franklin tread,
Heaven's awful thunders rolling o'er his head;

Convolving clouds the billowy skies deform, 239
And forky flames emblaze the blackening storm.
See the descending streams around him burn,
Glance on his rod and with his guidance turn;
He bids conflicting heavens their blasts expire,
Curbs the fierce blaze and holds the imprison'd fire.
No more, when folding storms the vault o'er-
    spread, 245
The livid glare shall strike thy race with dread;
Nor towers nor temples, shuddering with the sound,
Sink in the flames and spread destruction round.
His daring toils, the threatening blast that wait,
Shall teach mankind to ward the bolts of fate;
The pointed steel o'er-top the ascending spire, 251
And lead o'er trembling walls the harmless fire;
In his glad fame while distant worlds rejoice,
Far as the lightnings shine or thunders raise their
    voice.
    See the sage Rittenhouse, with ardent eye, 255
Lift the long tube and pierce the starry sky;
Clear in his view the circling systems roll,
And broader splendors gild the central pole.
He marks what laws the eccentric wanderers bind,
Copies creation in his forming mind, 260
And bids, beneath his hand, in semblance rise,
With mimic orbs, the labours of the skies.
There wondering crouds with raptured eye behold
The spangled heavens their mystic maze unfold;
While each glad sage his splendid hall shall grace,
With all the spheres that cleave the etherial space.
    To guide the sailor in his wandering way, 267
See Godfrey's toils reverse the beams of day.
His lifted quadrant to the eye displays
From adverse skies the counteracting rays; 270
And marks, as devious sails bewilder'd roll,
Each nice gradation from the stedfast pole.
    See, West with glowing life the canvass warms;
His sovereign hand creates impassion'd forms,
Spurns the cold critic rules, to seize the heart,
And boldly bursts the former bounds of Art. 276
No more her powers to ancient scenes confined,
He opes her liberal aid to all mankind;
She calls to life each patriot, chief or sage,
Garb'd in the dress and drapery of his age; 280
Again bold Regulus to death returns,
Again her falling Wolfe Britannia mourns;
Warriors in arms to frowning combat move,
And youths and virgins melt the soul to love;

Grief, rage and fear beneath his pencil start,   285
Roll the wild eye and pour the flowing heart;
While slumbering heroes wait his wakening call,
And distant ages fill the storied wall.

With rival force, see Copley's pencil trace
The air of action and the charms of face;   290
Fair in his tints unfold the scenes of state,
The Senate listens and the peers debate;
Pale consternation every heart appalls,
In act to speak, while death-struck Chatham falls.
His strong, deep shades a bold expression give,
Raised into light the starting figures live: 296
With polish'd pride the finish'd features boast,
The master's art in nature's softness lost.

Fired with the martial toils, that bathed in gore
His brave companions on his native shore   300
Trumbull with daring hand the scene recalls,
He shades with night Quebec's beleagur'd walls,
Mid flashing flames, that round the turrets rise,
Blind carnage raves and great Montgomery dies.
On Charlestown's height, thro' floods of rolling fire,
Brave Warren falls, and sullen hosts retire;   306
While other plains of death, that gloom the skies,
And chiefs immortal o'er his canvass rise.

See rural seats of innocence and ease,
High tufted towers and walks of waving trees,   310
The white waves dashing on the craggy shores,
Meandering streams and meads of spangled flowers,
Where nature's sons their wild excursions lead,
In just design, from Taylor's pencil spread.

Stewart and Brown the moving portrait raise,
Each rival stroke the force of life conveys;   316
See circling Beauties round their tablets stand,
And rise immortal from their plastic hand;
Each breathing form preserves its wonted grace,
And all the soul stands speaking in the face.   320

Two kindred arts the swelling statue heave,
Wake the dead wax and teach the stone to live.
While the bold chissel claims the rugged strife,
To rouse the sceptred marble into life;
While Latian shrines their figured patriots boast,
And gods and heroes croud each orient coast,   326
See Wright's fair hands the livlier fire controul,
In waxen forms she breathes the impass'd soul:
The pencil'd tint o'er moulded substance glows,
And different powers the unrivall'd art compose.

To equal fame ascends thy tuneful throng,   331
The boast of genius and the pride of song;

Warm'd with the scenes that grace their various
    clime,
Their lays shall triumph o'er the lapse of time.
    With keen-eyed glance thro' nature's walks to
        pierce,   335
With all the powers and every charm of verse,
Each science opening in his ample mind,
His fancy glowing and his taste refined,
See Trumbull lead the train. His skillful hand
Hurls the keen darts of Satire thro' the land;   340
Pride, knavery, dullness, feel his mortal stings
And listening virtue triumphs while he sings;
Proud Albion's sons, victorious now no more,
In guilt retiring from the wasted shore,
Strive their curst cruelties to hide in vain—   345
The world shall learn them from his deathless strain.

On glory's wing to raise the ravish'd soul,
Beyond the bounds of earth's benighted pole,
For daring Dwight the Epic Muse sublime
Hails her new empire on the western clime.   350
Fired with the themes by seers seraphic sung,
Heaven in his eye, and rapture on his tongue,
His voice divine revives the promised land,
The Heaven-taught Leader and the chosen band.
In Hanniel's fate, proud faction finds her doom,
Ai's midnight flames light nations to her tomb,
In visions bright supernal joys are given,   357
And all the dread futurities of heaven.

While freedom's cause his patriot bosom warms,
In counsel sage, nor inexpert in arms,   360
See Humphreys glorious from the field retire,
Sheathe the glad sword and string the sounding
    lyre;
That lyre which, erst, in hours of dark despair,
Roused the sad realms to urge the unfinish'd war.
O'er fallen friends, with all the strength of woe,
His heart-felt sighs in moving numbers flow;   366
His country's wrongs, her duties, dangers, praise,
Fire his full soul and animate his lays;
Immortal Washington with joy shall own
So fond a favourite and so great a son.   370

Advice to the Privileged Orders

BARLOW resided for a year in 1788–1789 in France,
where he moved among such revolutionists as Lagrange,
Laplace, Garat, Volney, and Thouin, whose combined
influence contributed much toward turning him away

from the staunch Federalism of his native Connecticut. After he removed to London, he associated with Paine, Price, Priestley, and Tooke, whose influence is to be found on every page of his *Advice to the Privileged Orders*, published February 11, 1792, eleven months after Paine's *Rights of Man, Part I*. It was suppressed by Pitt's cabinet, and Barlow was forced to seek haven in France. John Adams voiced the outraged feelings of many conservatives and of all Barlow's former Connecticut associates when he declared that Tom Paine himself was "not a more worthless fellow" than Joel Barlow. In the *Advice* Barlow assailed the feudal system with its kings and lords, the church, and the military system as devices for preservation of despotic government; and in the realms of jurisprudence and public revenue he offered what he believed to be principles of democratic administration. His radicalism is further illustrated in his *Conspiracy of Kings* and *Letter to the National Convention*, two more products of a year of feverish writing. But after his defeat in the election at Savoy, France, in February, 1793, he forsook political activities and devoted himself to business. The text is that of the English edition of 1792.

[*The United States and Aristotle's Politics*]

Whether men are born to govern, or to obey, or to enjoy equal liberty, depends not on the original capacity of the mind, but on the instinct of analogy, or the habit of thinking. When children of the same family are taught to believe in the unconquerable distinctions of birth among themselves, they are completely fitted for a feudal government; because their minds are familiarised with all the gradations and degradations that such a government requires. The birthright of domineering is not more readily claimed on the one hand, than it is acknowledged on the other; and the Jamaica planter is not more habitually convinced that an European is superior to an African, than he is that a Lord is better than himself.

This subject deserves to be placed in a light in which no writer, as far as I know, has yet considered it. When a person was repeating to Fontenelle the common adage, Habit is the second nature, the philosopher replied, And do me the favour to tell me which is the first. When we assert that nature has established inequalities among men, and has thus given to some the right of governing others, or when we maintain the contrary of this

position, we should be careful to define what sort of nature we mean, whether the first or second nature; or whether we mean that there is but one. A mere savage, Colocolo for instance, would decide the question of equality by a trial of bodily strength, designating the man that could lift the heaviest beam to be the legislator; and unless all men could lift the same beam, they could not be equal in their rights. Aristotle would give the preference to him that excelled in mental capacity. Ulysses would make the decision upon a compound ratio of both. But there appears to me another step in this ladder, and that the habit of thinking is the only safe and universal criterion to which, in practice, the question can be referred. Indeed, when interest is laid aside, it is the only one to which, in civilized ages, it ever is referred. We never submit to a King, because he is stronger than we in bodily force, nor because he is superior in understanding or in information; but because we believe him born to govern, or at least, because a majority of the society believes it.

This habit of thinking has so much of nature in it, it is so undistinguishable from the indelible marks of the man, that it is a perfectly safe foundation for any system that we may choose to build upon it; indeed it is the only foundation, for it is the only point of contact by which men communicate as moral associates. As a practical position therefore, and as relating to almost all places and almost all times, in which the experiment has yet been made, Aristotle was as right in teaching, That some are born to command, and others to be commanded, as the National Assembly was in declaring, That men are born and always continue free and equal in respect to their rights. The latter is as apparently false in the diet of Ratisbon, as the former is in the hall of the Jacobins.

Abstractly considered, there can be no doubt of the unchangeable truth of the assembly's declaration; and they have taken the right method to make it a practical truth, by publishing it to the world for discussion. A general belief that it is a truth, makes it at once practical, confirms it in one nation, and extends it to others.

A due attention to the astonishing effects that are wrought in the world by the habit of thinking, will serve many valuable purposes. I cannot therefore dismiss the subject as soon as I intended; but will mention one or two influences of these effects, and leave the reflection of the reader to make application to a thousand others.

First, It is evident that all arbitrary systems in the world are founded and supported on this second nature of man, in counteraction of the first. Systems which distort and crush and subjugate every thing that we can suppose original and characteristic in man, as an undistorted being. It sustains the most absurd and abominable theories of religion, and honors them with as many martyrs as it does those that are the most peaceful and beneficent.

But secondly, we find for our consolation, that it will likewise support systems of equal liberty and national happiness. In the United States of America, the science of liberty is universally understood, felt, and practised, as much by the simple as the wise, the weak as the strong. Their deeprooted and inveterate habit of thinking is, that all men are equal in their rights, that it is impossible to make them otherwise; and this being their undisturbed belief, they have no conception how any man in his senses can entertain any other. This point once settled, every thing is settled. Many operations, which in Europe have been considered as incredible tales or dangerous experiments, are but the infallible consequences of this great principle. The first of these operations is the business of election, which with that people is carried on with as much gravity as their daily labour. There is no jealousy on the occasion, nothing lucrative in office; any man in society may attain to any place in the government, and may exercise its functions. They believe that there is nothing more difficult in the management of the affairs of a nation than the affairs of a family, that it only requires more hands. They believe that it is the juggle of keeping up impositions to blind the eyes of the vulgar, that constitutes the intricacy of state. Banish the mysticism of inequality, and you banish almost all the evils attendant on human nature.

The people, being habituated to the election of all kinds of officers, the magnitude of the office makes no difficulty in the case. The president of the United States, who has more power while in office than some of the kings of Europe, is chosen with as little commotion as a churchwarden. There is a public service to be performed, and the people say who shall do it. The servant feels honoured with the confidence reposed in him, and generally expresses his gratitude by a faithful performance.

Another of these operations is making every citizen a soldier, and every soldier a citizen; not only permitting every man to arm, but obliging him to arm. This fact, told in Europe previous to the French revolution, would have gained little credit; or at least it would have been regarded as a mark of an uncivilized people, extremely dangerous to a well ordered society. Men who build systems on an inversion of nature are obliged to invert every thing that is to make part of that system. It is because the people are civilized that they are safely armed. It is an effect of their conscious dignity, as citizens enjoying equal rights, that they wish not to invade the rights of others. The danger (where there is any) from armed citizens is only to the government, not to the society; and as long as they have nothing to revenge in the government (which they cannot have while it is in their own hands), there are many advantages in their being accustomed to the use of arms, and no possible disadvantage.

Power, habitually in the hands of a whole community, loses all the ordinary associated ideas of power. The exercise of power is a relative term; it supposes an opposition,—something to operate upon. We perceive no exertion of power in the motion of the planetary system, but a very strong one in the movement of a whirlwind; it is because we see obstructions to the latter, but none to the former. Where the government is not in the hands of the people, there you find opposition, you perceive two contending interests, and get an idea of the exercise of power; and whether this power be in the hands of the government or of the people, or whether it change from side to side, it is always to be dreaded. But the word *people*, in America, has a different meaning from what it has in Europe. It there means the whole community and comprehends every human creature; here it means something else, more difficult to define.

Another consequence of the habitual idea of equality is the facility of changing the structure of their government, whenever and as often as the society shall think there is any thing in it to amend. As Mr. Burke has written no "reflections on the revolution" in America, the people there have never yet been told that they have no right "to frame a government for themselves"; they have therefore done much in this business without ever affixing to it the idea of "sacrilege" or "usurpation," or any other term of rant to be found in that gentleman's vocabulary.

Within a few years the fifteen states have not only framed each its own state-constitution and two successive federal constitutions, but since the settlement of the present general government in the year 1789, three of the states, Pennsylvania, South-Carolina, and Georgia, have totally new modeled their own. And all this is done without the least confusion, the operation being scarcely known beyond the limits of the state where it is performed. Thus they are in the habit of "choos- 20 ing their own governors," of "cashiering them for misconduct," of "framing a government for themselves," and all those abominable things, the mere naming of which, in Mr. Burke's opinion, has polluted the pulpit in the Old Jewry.

But it is said, These things will do very well for America where the people are less numerous, less indigent, and better instructed; but they will not apply to Europe. This objection deserves a reply, not because it is solid, but because it is fashionable. 30 It may be answered, that some parts of Spain, much of Poland, and almost the whole of Russia, are less peopled than the settled country in the United States; that poverty and ignorance are effects of slavery rather than its causes; but the best answer to be given is the example of France. To the event of that revolution I will trust the argument. Let the people have time to become thoroughly and soberly grounded in the doctrine of equality, and there is no danger of oppression either from govern- 40 ment or from anarchy. Very little instruction is necessary to teach a man his rights; and there is no person of common intellect, in the most ignorant corner of Europe, but receives lessons enough, if they were of the proper kind. For writing and reading are not indispensable to the object; it is thinking right which makes them act right. Every child is taught to repeat about fifty Latin prayers,

which set up the Pope, the Bishop, and the King, as the trinity of his adoration; he is taught that the powers that be are ordained of God, and therefore the soldier quartered in the parish has a right to cut his throat. Half this instruction, upon opposite principles, would go a great way; in that case, nature would be assisted, while here [in Europe] she is counteracted. Engrave it on the heart of a man, that all men are equal in rights, and that the gov- 10 ernment is their own, and then persuade him to sell his crucifix and buy a musquet,—and you have made him a good citizen.

Another consequence of a settled belief in the equality of rights is that under this belief there is no danger from anarchy. This word has likewise acquired a different meaning in America from what we read of it in books. In Europe it means confusion, attended with mobs and carnage, where the innocent perish with the guilty. But [it] is very dif- 20 ferent where a country is used to a representative government, though it should have an interval of no government at all. Where the people at large feel and know that they can do everything by themselves personally, they really do nothing by themselves personally. In the heat of the American revolution, when the people in some states were for a long time without the least shadow of law or government, they always acted by committees and representation. This they must call anarchy, 30 for they know no other.

These are materials for the formation of governments, which need not be dreaded, though disjointed and laid asunder to make some repairs. They are deep-rooted habits of thinking, which almost change the moral nature of man; they are principles as much unknown to the ancient republics as to the modern monarchies of Europe.

We must not therefore rely upon systems drawn from the experimental reasonings of 40 Aristotle, when we find them contradicted by what we feel to be the eternal truth of nature, and see them brought to the test of our own experience. Aristotle was certainly a great politician; and Claudius Ptolemy was a great geographer; but the latter has said not a word of America, the largest quarter of the globe; nor the former, of representative republics, the resource of afflicted humanity.

... Among the component parts of government, that, whose operation is the most direct on the moral habit of life, is the Administration of Justice. In this every person has a peculiar isolated interest, which is almost detached from the common sympathies of society. It is this which operates with a singular concentrated energy, collecting the whole force of the state from the community at large, and bringing it to act upon a single individual, affecting his life, reputation, or property; so that the governing power may say with peculiar propriety to the minister of justice, *divide et impera;* for, in case of oppression, the victim's cries will be too feeble to excite opposition; his cause having nothing in common with that of the citizens at large. If, therefore, we would obtain an idea of the condition of men on any given portion of the earth, we must pay a particular attention to their judiciary system, not in its form and theory, but in its spirit and practice. It may be said in general of this part of the civil polity of a nation, that, as it is a stream flowing from the common fountain of the government, and must be tinged with whatever impurities are found in the source from whence it descends, the only hope of cleaning the stream is by purifying the fountain. ...

It is generally understood, that the object of government, in this part of its administration, is merely to restrain the vices of men. But there is another object prior to this: an office more sacred, and equally indispensible, is to prevent their vices, —to correct them in their origin, or eradicate them totally from the adolescent mind. The latter is performed by instruction, the former by coercion; the one is the tender duty of a father, the other, the unrelenting drudgery of a master; but both are the business of government, and ought to be made concurrent branches of the system of jurisprudence.

The absurd and abominable doctrine, that private vices are public benefits, it is hoped will be blotted from the memory of man, expunged from the catalogue of human follies, with the systems of government which gave it birth. The ground of this insulting doctrine is, that advantage may be taken of the extravagant foibles of individuals to increase the revenues of the state; as if the chief end of society were, to steal money for the government's purse! to be squandered by the governors, to render them more insolent in their oppressions! it is humiliating, to answer such arguments as these; where we must lay open the most degrading retreats of prostituted logic, to discover the positions on which they are founded. But Orders and Privileges will lead to any thing: once teach a man, that some are born to command and others to be commanded; and after that, there is no camel too big for him to swallow.

This idea of the objects to be kept in view by the system of Justice, involving in it the business of prevention as well as of restriction, leads us to some observations on the particular subject of criminal jurisprudence. Every society, considered in itself as a moral and physical entity, has the undoubted faculty of self-preservation. It is an independent being; and, towards other beings in like circumstances of independence, it has a right to use this faculty of defending itself, without previous notice to the party; or without the observance of any duty, but that of abstaining from offensive operations. But when it acts towards the members of its own family, towards those dependent and defenceless beings that make part of itself, the *right* of coercion is preceded by the *duty* of instruction. It may be safely pronounced, that a State has no right to punish a man, to whom it has given no previous instruction; and consequently, any person has a right to do any action, unless he has been informed that it has an evil tendency. It is true, that, as relative to particular cases, the having given this information is a thing that the society must sometimes presume, and is not always obliged to prove. But these cases are rare, and ought never to form a general rule. This presumption has, however, passed into a general rule, and is adopted as universal practice. With what justice or propriety it is so adopted, a very little reflection will enable us to decide.

The great outlines of morality are extremely simple and easy to be understood; they may be said to be written on the heart of a man antecedent to his associating with his fellow-creatures. As a self-dependent being he is self-instructed; and as

283

long as he should remain a simple child of nature, he would receive from nature all the lessons necessary to his condition. He would be a complete moral agent; and should he violate the rights of another independent man like himself, he would sin against sufficient light, to merit any punishment that the offended party might inflict upon him. But Society opens upon us a new field of contemplation; it furnishes man with another class of rights, and imposes upon him an additional system of duties; it enlarges the sphere of his moral agency, and makes him a kind of artificial being, propelling and propelled by new dependencies, in which nature can no longer serve him as a guide. Being removed from her rudimental school, and entered in the college of society, he is called to encounter problems which the elementary tables of his heart will not always enable him to solve. Society then ought to be consistent with herself in her own institutions; if she sketches the lines of his duty with a variable pencil, too slight for his natural perception, she should lend him her optical glasses to discern them; if she takes the ferule in one hand, she is bound to use the fescue with the other.

We must observe farther,—that though Society itself be a state of nature, as relative to the nation at large,—though it be a state to which mankind naturally recur to satisfy their wants and increase the sum of their happiness,—though all its laws and regulations may be perfectly reasonable, and calculated to promote the good of the whole,—yet, with regard to an individual member, his having consented to these laws, or even chosen to live in the society, is but a fiction; and a rigid discipline, founded on a fiction, is surely hard upon its object. In general it may be said, that a man comes into society by birth; he neither consents nor dissents respecting his relative condition; he first opens his eyes on that state of human affairs in which the interests of his moral associates are infinitely complicated; with these his duties are so blended and intermingled, that nature can give him but little assistance in finding them out. His morality itself must be arbitrary; it must be varied at every moment, to comprehend some local and positive regulation; his science is to begin where that of preceding ages has ended; his alpha is their omega;

and he is called upon to act by instinct what they have but learnt to do from the experience of all mankind. Natural reason may teach me not to strike my neighbour without a cause; but it will never forbid my sending a sack of wool from England, or printing the French constitution in Spain. These are positive prohibitions, which nature has not written in her book; she has therefore never taught them to her children. The same may be said of all regulations that arise from the social compact.

It is a truth, I believe, not to be called in question, that every man is born with an imprescriptible claim to a portion of the elements; which portion is termed his birth-right. Society may vary this right, as to its form, but never can destroy it in substance. She has no control over the man, till he is born; and the right being born with him, and being necessary to his existence, she can no more annihilate the one than the other, though she has the power of new-modelling both. But on coming into the world, he finds that the ground which nature has promised him is taken up, and in the occupancy of others; society has changed the form of his birth-right; the general stock of elements, from which the lives of men are to be supported, has undergone a new modification; and his portion among the rest. He is told that he cannot claim it in its present form, as an independent inheritance; that he must draw on the stock of society, instead of the stock of nature; that he is banished from the mother and must cleave to the nurse. In this unexpected occurrence he is unprepared to act; but knowledge is a part of the stock of society; and an indispensable part to be allotted in the portion of the claimant is instruction relative to the new arrangement of natural right. To withhold this instruction therefore would be, not merely the omission of a duty, but the commission of a crime; and society in this case would sin against the man, before the man could sin against society. . . .

No nation is yet so numerous, nor any country so populous, as it is capable of becoming. Europe, taken together, would support at least five times its present number, even on its present system of cultivation; and how many times this increased population may be multiplied by new discoveries in the infinite science of subsistence, no man will

284

pretend to calculate. This of itself is sufficient to prove, that society at present has the means of rendering all its members happy in every respect, except the removal of bodily disease. The common stock of the community appears abundantly sufficient for this purpose. By common stock, I would not be understood to mean the goods exclusively appropriated to individuals. Exclusive property is not only consistent with good order among men, but it is conceived by some to be necessary to the existence of society. But the common stock of which I speak consists, first, in knowledge, or the improvement which men have made in the means of acquiring a support; and secondly, in the contributions which it is necessary should be collected from individuals, and applied to the maintenance of tranquillity in the State. The property exclusively belonging to individuals can only be the surplusage remaining in their hands, after deducting what is necessary to the real wants of society. Society is the first proprietor; as she is the original cause of the appropriation of wealth, and its indispensable guardian in the hands of the individual.

Society then is bound, in the first place, to distribute knowledge to every person according to his wants, to enable him to be useful and happy; so far as to dispose him to take an active interest in the welfare of the State. Secondly, where the faculties of the individual are naturally defective, so that he remains unable to provide for himself, she is bound still to support and render him happy. It is her duty in all cases to induce every human creature, by rational motives, to place his happiness in the tranquillity of the public, and in the security of individual peace and property. But thirdly, in cases where these precautions shall fail of their effect, she is driven indeed to the last extremity,—she is to use the rod of correction. These instances would doubtless be rare; and if we could suppose a long continuance of wise administration, such as a well organized government would ensure to every nation in the world, we may almost persuade ourselves to believe that the necessity for punishment would be reduced to nothing.

Proceeding however on the supposition of the existence of crimes, it must still remain an object of legislative wisdom, to discriminate between their different classes, and apply to each its proper remedy, in the quantity and mode of punishment. It is no part of my subject to enter into this inquiry, any farther than simply to observe, that it is the characteristic of arbitrary governments, to be jealous of their power. And, as jealousy is, of all human passions, the most vindictive and the least rational, these governments seek the revenge of injuries in the most absurd and tremendous punishments that their fury can invent. As far as any rule can be discovered in their gradation of punishments, it appears to be this, That the severity of the penalty is in proportion to the injustice of the law. The reason of this is simple,—the laws which counteract nature the most, are the most likely to be violated. . . .

All governments that lay any claim to respectability or justice, have proscribed the idea of *ex-post-facto* laws, or laws made after the performance of an action, constituting that action a crime, and punishing a party for a thing that was innocent at the time of its being done. Such laws would be so flagrant a violation of natural right, that in the French and several of the American State Constitutions they are solemnly interdicted in their Declarations of Rights. This proscription is likewise considered as a fundamental article of English liberty, and almost the only one that has not been habitually violated, within the present century. But let us resort to reason and justice, and ask what is the difference between a violation of this article and the observance of that tremendous maxim of jurisprudence, common to all the nations above mentioned, *ignorantia legis neminem excusat?*

Most of the laws of society are positive regulations, not taught by nature. Indeed, such only are applicable to the subject now in question. For *ignorantia legis* can have reference only to laws arising out of society, in which our natural feelings have no concern; and where a man is ignorant of such a law, he is in the same situation as if the law did not exist. To read it to him from the tribunal, where he stands arraigned for the breach of it, is to him precisely the same thing as it would be to originate it at the time by the same tribunal, for the express purpose of his condemnation. The law till then, as relative to him, is not in being. He is therefore in the same predicament that the society

285

in general would be, under the operation of an *ex-post-facto* law.* Hence we ought to conclude that, as it seems difficult for a government to dispense with the maxim above-mentioned, a free people ought, in their declaration of rights, to provide for universal public instruction. If they neglect to do this, and mean to avoid the absurdity of a self-destroying policy, by adhering to a system of justice which would preserve a dignity and inspire a confidence worthy the name of liberty, they 10 ought to reject the maxim altogether; and insert in their declaration of rights, that instruction alone can constitute a duty; and that laws can enforce no obedience, but where they are explained.

It is truly hard and sufficiently to be regretted that any part of society should be obliged to yield obedience to laws, to which they have not literally and personally consented. Such, however, is the state of things; it is necessary that a majority should govern. If it be an evil to obey a law to 20 which we have not consented, it is at least a necessary evil; but to compel a compliance with orders which are unknown, is carrying injustice beyond the bounds of necessity; it is absurd, and even impossible. Laws in this case may be avenged, but cannot be obeyed; they may inspire terror, but can never command respect.

Advice to a Raven in Russia

THIS POEM was first printed by Olmstead in the *Erie Chronicle* for October 10, 1843. It expresses Barlow's bitter disillusionment when, as minister to France, he was trying to negotiate with Napoleon amidst suffering, carnage, and desolation. The following text is from E. A. and G. L. Duyckinck, *Cyclopaedia of American Literature* (1856) who introduced the poem with this

*What shocking ideas of morals those governments must have inculcated, which first invented that exemption in penal statutes, called *the benefit of clergy!* To be able to write and read, was at that time an evidence of an uncommon degree of knowledge. Out of respect to learning (as it is presumed) it was therefore enacted, that any person convicted of a felony should be pardoned, on showing that he could write his name. As this talent was then chiefly confined to the clerks, or clergy, this circumstance gave name to the law. The language of the exemption is simply this, that those persons only *who know the law* are at liberty to violate it. There is indeed much reason for a distinction; but it should have been the other way.

(Barlow's note)

note: "His last poem is a withering expression of his sentiment toward Napoleon. It was dictated by Barlow, in December, 1812, while lying on his bed, to his secretary, Thomas Barlow, about midnight, only a night or two before the van of the French army, which had been defeated by the burning of Moscow, entered Wilna on their retreat, the same month in which he died. It was copied in diplomatic characters and sent to Mrs. Barlow in Paris, but it never reached her. The original poem written in Wilna is now in the possession of the Rev. Lemuel G. Olmstead, who has placed a copy at our disposal. The paper has, in watermark, a head of Napoleon, and the words, '*Napoleon Empereur des Francais et Roi D'Italie.*' "

December, 1812

Black fool, why winter here? These frozen skies,
Worn by your wings and deafened by your cries,
Should warn you hence, where milder suns invite,
And Day alternates with his mother Night.
You fear, perhaps your food will fail you there—
Your human carnage, that delicious fare, 6
That lured you hither, following still your friend,
The great Napoleon, to the world's bleak end.
You fear, because the southern climes pour'd forth
Their clustering nations to infest the north, 10
Bavarians, Austrians, those who Drink the Po,
And those who skirt the Tuscan seas below,
With all Germania, Neustria, Belgia, Gaul,
Doom'd here to wade through slaughter to their fall.
You fear he left behind no wars to feed 15
His feather'd cannibals and nurse the breed.
Fear not, my screamer, call your greedy train,
Sweep over Europe, hurry back to Spain—
You'll find his legions there, the valiant crew
Please best their master when they toil for you. 20
Abundant there they spread the country o'er,
And taint the breeze with every nation's gore—
Iberian, Russian, British, widely strown,
But still more wide and copious flows their own.
Go where you will; Calabria, Malta, Greece, 25
Egypt and Syria still his fame increase.
Domingo's fattened isle and India's plains
Glow deep with purple drawn from Gallic veins.
No Raven's wing can stretch the flight so far
As the torn bandrols of Napoleon's war. 30
Choose then your climate, fix your best abode—
He'll make you deserts and he'll bring you blood.

How could you fear a dearth? Have not mankind,
Though slain by millions, millions left behind?
Has not conscription still the power to wield   35
Her annual falchion o'er the human field?
A faithful harvester! or if a man
Escape that gleaner, shall he 'scape the ban?
The triple ban, that, like the hound of hell,
Gripes with three joles to hold his victim well.   40
Fear nothing, then! hatch fast your ravenous brood,
Teach them to cry to Buonaparte for food.
They'll be, like you, of all his suppliant train,
The only class that never cries in vain!
For see what mutual benefits you lend—   45
The surest way to fix the mutual friend—
While on his slaughtered troops your tribes are fed,
You cleanse his camp and carry off his dead.
Imperial Scavenger, but now, you know,
Your work is vain amid these hills of snow.   50
His tentless troops are marbled through with frost,
And change to crystal when the breath is lost.
Mere trunks of ice, tho limb'd like human frames
And lately warmed with life's endearing flames,
They cannot taint the air, the world infest,   55
Nor can you tear one fibre from their breast.
No! from their visual sockets as they lie,
With beak and claws you cannot pluck an eye—
The frozen orb, preserving still its form,
Defies your talons as it braves the storm,   60
But stands and stares to God as if to know,
In what curst hands he leaves his world below!
Fly then, or starve, though all the dreadful road
From Minsk to Moscow with their bodies strow'd
May count some myriads, yet they can't suffice
To feed you more beneath these dreadful skies.   66
Go back, and winter in the wilds of Spain;
Feast there awhile, and in the next campaign
Rejoin your master, for you'll find him then,
With his new millions of the race of men,   70
Clothed in his thunders, all his flags unfurl'd,
Raging and storming o'er a prostrate world.
War after war his hungry soul requires;
State after state shall sink beneath his fires.
Yet other Spains in victim smoke shall rise.   75
And other Moscows suffocate the skies.
Each land lie reeking with its people slain
And not a stream run bloodless to the main.
Till men resume their souls, and dare to shed
Earth's total vengeance on the monster's head!   80

287

Anniversary Poems

Todd quoted one of Barlow's contemporaries as saying: "The affection of Mr. Barlow for his lovely wife was unusually strong, and on her part it was fully reciprocated. . . . In their darkest days—and some of them were very dark—Barlow ever found light and encouragement at home in the smiles, sympathy, and counsel of his prudent, faithful wife. No matter how black and portentous the cloud that brooded over them might be, she always contrived to give it a silver lining, and his subsequent success in life he always attributed more to her influence over him than to anything else." Barlow himself penned a letter to his wife, while he was absent in Algiers in mortal danger from the plague, to be delivered only in the event of his death, in which he wrote: "I have no other value for my own life than as a means of continuing conjugal union with the best of women—the wife of my soul—my first, my last, my only love." And when he was forty-five, he wrote with a lover's ardor: "Never did two souls love as we have loved." The text is that in C. B. Todd, *Life and Letters of Joel Barlow* (1886).

1793

Blest Hymen, hail that memorable day
    Whose twelfth return my constant bosom warms,
Whose morning rose with promised pleasure gay,
    Whose faithful evening gave me Delia's charms—

Those charms that still, with ever new delight,   5
    Assuage and feed the flames of young desire,
Whose magic powers can temper and unite
    The husband's friendship with the lover's fire.

Say, gentle god, if e'er thy torch before
    Illum'ed the altar for so pure a pair?   10
If e'er approached thy consecrated bower
    A swain so grateful, so divine a fair?

Love, the delusive Power who often flies
    Submissive souls that yield to thy decree,
Charmed with our lasting flame approves the ties,
    Folds his white wings, and shares his throne
        with thee.   16

United Sovereigns! hear my fervent prayer,
    Extend through life your undivided sway,
In love and union bless your suppliant pair
    With many a sweet return of this delightful
    day.   20

My foolish rhymes on wedding days
    I thought would make you vain,
Or Love would sicken of his lays
    And ask them back again.

But little prospect now appears   5
    That aught our souls can sever,
Since after Hymen's twenty years
    I love you more than ever.

1802

If seven long years of laboring life
    Old Jacob served to gain a wife

She doubtless must have been the best,
The rarest beauty of the East—
For sure the sire of Jews had strove   5
To have his pennyworth even in love.
But thrice seven suns have passed the line
Since I have laboring been for mine,
And I'm expert at bargains too—
A Yankee blade, though not a Jew—   10
Which proves, unless I judge amiss,
My wife is thrice as good as his.
One thing I certainly can tell,
I always love her thrice as well.

10 years ago anthologies might not have included Taylor.

Considered first real American poet.

PHILIP FRENEAU (1752–1832)

PHILIP FRENEAU has often been called America's "first important writer in verse," "America's first romanticist," and "the poet of the American and French Revolutions." Such a series of "firsts" must not create the impression that all his work is even in merit or sustained in power. He lacked self-criticism; many of his annoyingly offhand poems contain much dross, and he rarely maintained himself for long on his highest poetic level. Yet he contributed enough solid work and possessed sufficient versatility to secure for himself an important place in American poetry; and his role of fiery crusader in prose for the principles of Jeffersonian and French democracy brought him additional fame. During most of his stormy career, Freneau was a political hornet stinging the Federalists into violent retort. For a full generation after American independence, he fought continuously for the rights of the common man and attacked every vestige of rank and caste. Jefferson credited his editorials in the *National Gazette* with saving our constitution, "which was galloping fast into monarchy."

Valuable as were Freneau's services to politics, it was not originally to the role of political protagonist that he felt called. As an undergraduate at Princeton, possessing a rich romantic imagination and a love of sensuous natural beauty, he dreamed of writing a great epic of the new world. But time moved on while he dreamed, and at twenty he found himself in a world divided by political conflict. Reluctantly in the mid-seventies he relinquished romantic dreams for the themes of war. It was his lament that "an age employed in edging steel" could no "poetic raptures feel." His turning alternately from active participation in the armed conflict to romantic escapes from it made his

work a diverse product, an incongruous compound of snarling satire and romantic lyricism. The pathos and frustration of Freneau's career induced Lewis Leary to append the subtitle "Study of Literary Failure" to his biography of the poet.

Freneau was the grandson of a successful importer who had settled in New York in 1707 and made heavy investments in land. The poet's father, Pierre, was early a man of some wealth, but before Philip Freneau entered college, the family estate had dwindled to a farm at Freehold, New Jersey, which became the poet's home. After his graduation in 1771 from Princeton, where he was a classmate of Hugh Henry Brackenridge and James Madison, and an interval as a teacher on Long Island, he turned to writing satires upon the British. Although Freneau later claimed service aboard American privateers from 1775 to 1778, his voyages to Bermuda and the West Indies were hardly belligerent in character, and resulted in considerable non-Revolutionary verse. After 1778 he enlisted as a private in the New Jersey militia, and, in addition, made several voyages as a blockade-runner. In 1777 and 1778 he wrote poems to encourage naval enlistment and to celebrate American triumphs on the sea. In May, 1780, while braving the British blockade on the *Aurora*, Freneau was captured and for six weeks was imprisoned. The brutal treatment accorded him inspired *The British Prison-Ship*, perhaps the bitterest hymn of hate to be penned in America. From 1781 to 1784, he was in Philadelphia editing the *Freeman's Journal*, and vigorously supporting the cause of independence by counteracting the Tory *Royal Gazette* in New York. To the *Freeman's Journal* he contributed the first version of his "Philosopher of the Forest" essays and his poem "To the Memory of the Brave Americans," which Sir Walter Scott was to pronounce "as fine a thing as there is of the kind in the language." After an interval spent in South Carolina to regain his shattered health in 1785, Freneau for the rest of the decade captained merchant vessels in the coastwise trade. He used his leisure for the writing of such romantic verse as "The Wild Honey Suckle" and "The Indian Student," and for the publication of his first collected edition, *The Poems of Philip Freneau* (1786) and the *Miscellaneous Works* (1788), containing his essays and additional poems.

After his marriage to Eleanor Forman and his retirement from the sea in 1789, Freneau was busy at his old trade of journalist, editing five journals in the next decade. Chief of these was *The National Gazette* (1791–1793), at Philadelphia, which Jefferson hoped would rally liberal opinion. Lashing out at Hamiltonianism as a threat to the democratic principles established by the Revolution, Freneau provoked Washington's slur, "that rascal Freneau," and aroused such antagonism that the reviews of his poetry became political counterblasts. The first quarter of the nineteenth century he spent on his New Jersey farm; meanwhile he issued a new edition of his poems in 1809, dedicated to "Revolutionary Republicans," and another in 1815, containing his stirring war ballads of 1812. After several years of mounting cares and financial difficulties, during which time he was all but forgotten, death came in 1832 from the effects of exposure during a snowstorm. After his death his reputation mounted. For a long time his poems of the Revolution were the basis for his fame, chiefly because the editions of 1861 and 1865 were merely reprints of his Revolutionary verse. It was not until the majority of his pieces were brought together in a three-volume edition (1902–1907) by Fred Lewis Pattee that Freneau's full stature as a poet of nature and humanity was finally established.

BIBLIOGRAPHY · The standard edition is *The Poems of Philip Freneau: Poet of the American Revolution* (3 vols., 1902–1907, Princeton University Press), edited by F. L. Pattee, from which most of the present text is taken. Five editions of Freneau's poetry were published during his lifetime: *The Poems* (1786), *The Miscellaneous Works* (1788), *Poems Written between the Years 1768 & 1794* (1795), *Poems Written and Published during the American Revolutionary War* (2 vols., 1809), and *A Collection of Poems on American Affairs . . .* (1815). Modern texts are H. H. Clark, *Poems of Freneau* (1929), and the Scholars' Facsimiles and Reprints edition, *Letters on Various Interesting and Important Subjects* (1943); C. F. Heartman, *Unpublished Freneauana* (1918); and L.

Leary, *The Last Poems of Philip Freneau* (1945). Bibliographical material is available in Vol. III of Pattee's edition; in L. Leary, *That Rascal Freneau* (1941); and in V. H. Palsits, *A Bibliography of the Separate and Collected Works of Philip Freneau*.

The first substantial biography is that of F. L. Pattee in Vol. I (pp. xiii–cxii) of *The Poems*; a later study is the valuable *That Rascal Freneau* (1941) by L. Leary. See also the discerning critical essay by H. H. Clark in *Poems of Freneau* (1929), pp. xiii–lx. Other valuable studies include J. M. Beatty, "Churchill and Freneau," *American Literature*, II (1930), 121–130; H. H. Clark, "The Literary Influences of Philip Freneau," *Studies in Philology*, XXII (1925), 1–33, and "What Made Freneau the Father of American Prose?" *Transactions of the Wisconsin Academy of Sciences, Arts, and Letters*, XXV (1930), 39–50; S. E. Forman, "The Political Activities of Philip Freneau," *Johns Hopkins University Studies in History and Political Science*, Series XX (1902); P. M. Marsh, "Philip Freneau and His Circle," *Pennsylvania Magazine of History and Biography*, LXIII (1939), 37–59, and "Was Freneau a Fighter?" *Proceedings of the New Jersey Historical Society*, LVI (1938), 211–218; F. L. Pattee, *Sidelights on American Literature* (1922), 250–292; and F. Smith, "Philip Freneau and *The Time-Piece and Literary Companion*," *American Literature*, IV (1932), 270–287.

The Beauties of Santa Cruz

FRENEAU anticipated Burns in his sensitivity and humanitarianism. On one occasion he put a thieving dog ashore on a Georgian island rather than shoot him, and his response to human suffering was even keener. Impressed with the hard lot of the common man, he was especially concerned with the problems of slavery. He pilloried a Jamaica sugar-planter for his cruelty to his slaves, and though the sentiment in the following lines (verses 70 to 78) is milder, he condemns the wickedness and cupidity of the slave trade. This poem was originally published in the *United States Magazine*, edited by Freneau's friend, Hugh Henry Brackenridge, in Philadelphia, in February, 1779.

[*Slave* versus *Free Labor*]

On yonder steepy hill, fresh harvests rise,
Where the dark tribe from Afric's sun-burnt plain
Oft o'er the ocean turn their wishful eyes
To isles remote high looming o'er the main,

And view soft seats of ease and fancied rest,   5
Their native groves new painted on the eye,

289

Where no proud misers their gay hours molest,
No lordly despots pass unsocial by.

See yonder slave that slowly bends this way,
With years, and pain, and ceaseless toil opprest, 10
Though no complaining words his woes betray,
The eye dejected proves the heart distrest.

Perhaps in chains he left his native shore,
Perhaps he left a helpless offspring there,
Perhaps a wife, that he must see no more, 15
Perhaps a father, who his love did share.

Curs'd be the ship that brought him o'er the main,
And curs'd the hands who from his country tore,
May she be stranded, ne'er to float again,
May they be shipwreck'd on some hostile shore—

O gold accurst, of every ill the spring, 21
For thee compassion flies the darken'd mind,
Reason's plain dictates no conviction bring,
And passion only sways all human kind.

O gold accurst! for thee we madly run 25
With murderous hearts across the briny flood,
Seek foreign climes beneath a foreign sun,
And there exult to shed a brother's blood.

But thou, who own'st this sugar-bearing soil, 29
To whom no good the great First Cause denies,
Let freeborn hands attend thy sultry toil,
And fairer harvests to thy view shall rise.

The teeming earth shall mightier stores disclose
Than ever struck thy longing eyes before,
And late content shall shed a soft repose, 35
Repose, so long a stranger at thy door.

The Northern Soldier

THE POEM, written in November, 1775, appeared as
the first song of Damon in the pastoral poem, *Mars
and Hymen*, and was used again as the song of the second
peasant in the fragment of a Revolutionary drama,
The Spy (1780). In 1786, under the title *Female Frailty*,
it was restored to pastoral setting in the 184-line dialogue of Damon, Lucinda, and Thyrsis. The third
stanza, however, did not appear either in 1775 or 1786.
The present title was affixed in the edition of 1795,
and this was the first appearance of the poem as a
separate lyric. At the same time the opening lines were
much improved.

Ours not to sleep in shady bowers,
    When frosts are chilling all the plain,
And nights are cold and long the hours
    To check the ardor of the swain,
    Who parting from his cheerful fire 5
        All comforts doth forego,
            And here and there
            And everywhere
        Pursues the prowling foe.

But we must sleep in frost and snows, 10
    No season shuts up our campaign;
Hard as the oaks, we dare oppose
    The autumn's or the winter's reign.
    Alike to us the winds that blow
        In summer's season gay, 15
            Or those that rave
            On Hudson's wave
        And drift his ice away.

For Liberty, celestial maid,
    With joy all hardships we endure. 20
In her blest smiles we are repaid,
    In her protection are secure.
    Then rise superior to the foe,
        Ye freeborn souls of fire;
            Respect these arms, 25
            'Tis freedom warms,
        To noble deeds aspire.

Winter and death may change the scene,
    The cold may freeze, the ball may kill,
And dire misfortunes intervene; 30
    But freedom shall be potent still
    To drive these Britons from our shore,
        Who, cruel and unkind,
            With slavish chain
            Attempt in vain 35
        Our freeborn limbs to bind.

To the Memory of the Brave Americans

Under General Greene, in South Carolina, who
fell in action of September 8, 1781

THIS POEM was first published in the *Freeman's Journal*
for November 21, 1781. *The Poems* of 1786 indicates
that Freneau substituted "standards" for "genius" in
line 21, and "Phoebus" for "sunshine" in the last line.

Eutaw Springs has been flooded over by the Santee
and Cooper Rivers Project, but a memorial still stands

on high ground to mark the spot where the men of General Greene attacked the British force led by Colonel Alexander Stuart. The next to the last stanza refers to the fact that Greene, in pursuing the British too closely, came upon a body of troops intrenched in a brick house and other ramparts, and there lost the greater part of the men killed or wounded in the battle. Bancroft stated that in the two engagements "the Americans lost in killed, wounded, and missing, five hundred and fifty-four men."

At Eutaw Springs the valiant died;
    Their limbs with dust are covered o'er—
Weep on, ye springs, your tearful tide;
    How many heroes are no more!

If in this wreck of ruin, they   5
    Can yet be thought to claim a tear,
O smite your gentle breast, and say
    The friends of freedom slumber here!

Thou, who shalt trace this bloody plain,
    If goodness rules thy generous breast,   10
Sigh for the wasted rural reign;
    Sigh for the shepherds, sunk to rest!

Stranger, their humble graves adorn;
    You too may fall, and ask a tear;
'Tis not the beauty of the morn   15
    That proves the evening shall be clear.—

They saw their injured country's woe;
    The flaming town, the wasted field;
Then rushed to meet the insulting foe;
    They took the spear—but left the shield.   20

Led by thy conquering genius, Greene,
    The Britons they compelled to fly:
None distant viewed the fatal plain,
    None grieved, in such a cause to die—

But, like the Parthian, famed of old,   25
    Who, flying, still their arrows threw,

20. They . . . shield: Sir Walter Scott paid Freneau the compliment of borrowing the line in *Marmion*: "And snatched the spear—but left the shield."

These routed Britons, full as bold,
    Retreated, and retreating slew.

Now rest in peace, our patriot band;
    Though far from nature's limits thrown,   30
We trust they find a happier land,
    A brighter sunshine of their own.

The British Prison-Ship

FRENEAU was captured in 1780 aboard the privateer *Aurora*, and with other captives was thrown into a prison ship at New York. Canto I tells of the ship's proceeding from Cape Henlopen and being captured by the British frigate *Iris*. Canto II describes the horrors aboard the prison ship *Scorpion*, where sickness, famine, brutality, and death torment the three hundred prisoners. From this "train of endless woes" the author was transferred to the loathsome hospital ship, *Hunter*, where the agonies were worse. Almost as soon as he was released, he hurled all the violent and bitter invectives that hate could prompt. The poem was first published in Philadelphia in 1781.

CANTO III · *The Hospital Prison-Ship*

Now tow'rd the Hunter's gloomy sides we came,
A slaughter-house, yet hospital in name;
For none came there (to pass through all degrees)
'Till half consum'd, and dying with disease;—
But when too near with labouring oars we ply'd,
The Mate with curses drove us from the side;   6
That wretch who, banish'd from the navy crew,
Grown old in blood, did here his trade renew;
His serpent's tongue, when on his charge let loose,
Utter'd reproaches, scandal, and abuse,   10
Gave all to hell who dar'd his king disown,
And swore mankind were made for George alone:
Ten thousand times, to irritate our woe,
He wished us foundered in the gulph below;
Ten thousand times he brandished high his stick,
And swore as often that we were not sick—   16
And yet so pale!—that we were thought by some
A freight of ghosts from Death's dominions come—
But calmed at length—for who can always rage,
Or the fierce war of endless passion wage,   20
He pointed to the stairs that led below
To damps, disease, and varied shapes of woe—
Down to the gloom I took my pensive way,
Along the decks the dying captives lay;

Some struck with madness, some with scurvy
    pain'd, 25
But still of putrid fevers most complain'd!
On the hard floors these wasted objects laid,
There toss'd and tumbled in the dismal shade,
There no soft voice their bitter fate bemoan'd,
And Death strode stately, while the victims
    groan'd; 30
Of leaky decks I heard them long complain,
Drown'd as they were in deluges of rain,
Deny'd the comforts of a dying bed,
And not a pillow to support the head—
How could they else but pine, and grieve, and sigh,
Detest a wretched life—and wish to die? 36
    Scarce had I mingled with this dismal band
When a thin spectre seiz'd me by the hand—
"And art thou come, (death heavy on his eyes)
"And art thou come to these abodes," he cries; 40
"Why didst thou leave the Scorpion's dark retreat,
"And hither haste a surer death to meet?
"Why didst thou leave thy damp infected cell?
"If that was purgatory, this is hell—
"We, too, grown weary of that horrid shade, 45
"Petitioned early for the doctor's aid;
"His aid denied, more deadly symptoms came,
"Weak, and yet weaker, glow'd the vital flame;
"And when disease had worn us down so low
"That few could tell if we were ghosts or no, 50
"And all asserted, death would be our fate—
"Then to the doctor we were sent—too late.
"Here wastes away Autolycus the brave,
"Here young Orestes finds a wat'ry grave,
"Here gay Alcander, gay, alas! no more, 55
"Dies far sequester'd from his native shore;
"He late, perhaps, too eager for the fray,
"Chac'd the vile Briton o'er the wat'ry way
" 'Till fortune jealous, bade her clouds appear,
"Turn'd hostile to his fame, and brought him here.
    "Thus do our warriors, thus our heroes fall, 61
"Imprison'd here, base ruin meets them all,
"Or, sent afar to Britain's barbarous shore,
"There die neglected, and return no more:
"Ah! rest in peace, poor, injur'd, parted shade, 65
"By cruel hands in death's dark weeds array'd,
"But happier climes, where suns unclouded shine,
"Light undisturb'd, and endless peace are thine."—
    From Brookland groves a Hessian doctor came,
Not great his skill, nor greater much his fame; 70

Fair Science never call'd the wretch her son,
And Art disdain'd the stupid man to own;—
Can you admire that Science was so coy,
Or Art refus'd his genius to employ!—
Do men with brutes an equal dullness share, 75
Or cuts yon' grovelling mole the midway air?
In polar worlds can Eden's blossoms blow?
Do trees of God in barren desarts grow?
Are loaded vines to Etna's summit known,
Or swells the peach beneath the torrid zone?— 80
Yet still he doom'd his genius to the rack,
And, as you may suppose, was own'd a quack.
    He on his charge the healing work begun
With antimonial mixtures, by the tun,
Ten minutes was the time he deigned to stay, 85
The time of grace allotted once a day—
He drencht us well with bitter draughts, 'tis true,
Nostrums from hell, and cortex from Peru—
Some with his pills he sent to Pluto's reign,
And some he blister'd with his flies of Spain; 90
His cream of Tartar walk'd its deadly round,
Till the lean patient at the potion frown'd,
And swore that hemlock, death, or what you will,
Were nonsense to the drugs that stuff'd his bill.—
On those refusing he bestow'd a kick, 95
Or menac'd vengeance with his walking stick;
Here uncontroul'd he exercis'd his trade,
And grew experienced by the deaths he made;
By frequent blows we from his cane endur'd
He kill'd at least as many as he cur'd; 100
On our lost comrades built his future fame,
And scatter'd fate, where'er his footsteps came.
    Some did not seem obedient to his will,
And swore he mingled poison with his pill,
But I acquit him by a fair confession, 105
He was no Englishman—he was a Hessian—
Although a dunce, he had some sense of sin,
Or else the Lord knows where we now had been;
Perhaps in that far country sent to range 109
Where never prisoner meets with an exchange—
Then had we all been banish'd out of time
Nor I return'd to plague the world with rhyme.
    Fool though he was, yet candour must confess
Not chief Physician was this dog of Hesse— 114
One master o'er the murdering tribe was plac'd,
By him the rest were honour'd or disgrac'd;—
Once, and but once, by some strange fortune led
He came to see the dying and the dead—

He came—but anger so deform'd his eye,
And such a faulchion glitter'd on his thigh,   120
And such a gloom his visage darken'd o'er,
And two such pistols in his hands he bore!
That, by the gods!—with such a load of steel
He came, we thought, to murder, not to heal—
Hell in his heart, and mischief in his head,   125
He gloom'd destruction, and had smote us dead,
Had he so dar'd—but fate with-held his hand—
He came—blasphem'd—and turn'd again to land.

From this poor vessel, and her sickly crew
An English ruffian all his titles drew,   130
Captain, esquire, commander, too, in chief,
And hence he gain'd his bread, and hence his beef,
But, sir, you might have search'd creation round
Ere such another miscreant could be found—
Though unprovok'd, an angry face he bore,   135
We stood astonish'd at the oaths he swore;
He swore, till every prisoner stood aghast,
And thought him Satan in a brimstone blast;
He wish'd us banish'd from the public light,
He wish'd us shrouded in perpetual night!   140
That were he king, no mercy would he show,
But drive all rebels to the world below;
That if we scoundrels did not scrub the decks
His staff should break our damn'd rebellious necks;
He swore, besides, that if the ship took fire   145
We too should in the pitchy flame expire;
And meant it so—this tyrant, I engage,
Had lost his breath to gratify his rage.—

If where he walk'd a captive carcase lay,
Still dreadful was the language of the day—   150
He call'd us dogs, and would have us'd us so,
But vengeance check'd the meditated blow,
The vengeance from our injur'd nation due
To him, and all the base unmanly crew.

Such food they sent, to make complete our woes,
It look'd like carrion torn from hungry crows,   156
Such vermin vile on every joint were seen,
So black, corrupted, mortified, and lean
That once we try'd to move our flinty chief,
And thus address'd him, holding up the beef: 160
"See, captain, see! what rotten bones we pick,
"What kills the healthy cannot cure the sick:
"Not dogs on such by Christian men are fed,
"And, see, good master, see, what lousy bread!"
"Your meat or bread (this man of flint replied)
"Is not my care to manage or provide—   166

"But this, damn'd rebel dogs, I'd have you know,
"That better than you merit we bestow;
"Out of my sight!"—nor more he deign'd to say,
But whisk'd about, and frowning, strode away.

Each day, at least three carcases we bore,   171
And scratch'd them graves along the sandy shore;
By feeble hands the shallow graves were made,
No stone memorial o'er the corpses laid;
In barren sands, and far from home, they lie,   175
No friend to shed a tear, when passing by;
O'er the mean tombs insulting Britons tread,
Spurn at the sand, and curse the rebel dead.

When to your arms these fatal islands fall,
(For first or last they must be conquer'd all)   180
Americans! to rites sepulchral just,
With gentlest footstep press this kindred dust,
And o'er the tombs, if tombs can then be found,
Place the green turf, and plant the myrtle round.

Barney's Invitation

THIS POEM appeared in the 1786 and 1809 editions of
Freneau's poetry. In the earlier book the song bore the
title "The Sailor's Invitation." The *Hyder Ali* was
purchased and outfitted by a group of private citizens
in Philadelphia in an effort to capture the *General
Monk*, a British vessel whose depredations were threatening the American cause. The *Hyder Ali* was named
in honor of a prince of Mysore, India, whose defeat of
the British in 1767 and whose later alliance with the
French made him a popular figure in America.

Come all ye lads who know no fear,
To wealth and honour with me steer
In the *Hyder Ali* privateer,
    Commanded by brave Barney.

She's new and true, and tight and sound,   5
Well rigged aloft, and all well found—
Come away and be with laurel crowned,
    Away—and leave your lasses.

Accept our terms without delay,
And make your fortunes while you may,   10
Such offers are not every day
    In the power of the jolly sailor.

Success and fame attend the brave,
But death the coward and the slave,

Who fears to plow the Atlantic wave, 15
    To seek the bold invaders.

Come, then, and take a cruising bout,
Our ship sails well, there is no doubt,
She has been tried both in and out,
    And answers expectation. 20

Let no proud foes whom Europe bore,
Distress our trade, insult our shore—
Teach them to know their reign is o'er,
    Bold Philadelphia sailors!

We'll teach them how to sail so near, 25
Or to venture on the Delaware,
When we in warlike trim appear
    And cruise without Henlopen.

Who cannot wounds and battle dare
Shall never clasp the blooming fair; 30
The brave alone their charms should share,
    The brave are their protectors.

With hand and heart united all,
Prepared to conquer or to fall,
Attend, my lads, to honour's call, 35
    Embark in our *Hyder Ali.*

From an Eastern prince she takes her name,
Who, smit with Freedom's sacred flame,
Usurping Britons brought to shame,
    His country's wrongs avenging; 40

See, on her stern the waving stars—
Inured to blood, inured to wars,
Come, enter quick, my jolly tars,
    To scourge these warlike Britons.

Here's grog enough—then drink a bout, 45
I know your hearts are firm and stout;
American blood will never give out,
    And often we have proved it.

Though stormy oceans round us roll,
We'll keep a firm undaunted soul, 50
Befriended by the cheering bowl,
    Sworn foes to melancholy:

While timorous landsmen lurk on shore,
'Tis ours to go where cannons roar—
On a coasting cruise we'll go once more, 55
    Despisers of all danger;

And Fortune still, who crowns the brave,
Shall guard us over the gloomy wave
A fearful heart betrays a knave—
    Success to the *Hyder Ali.* 60

Song[n]

On Captain Barney's Victory over the ship *General Monk*

FRENEAU prefaced this poem upon its first appearance in the *Freeman's Journal* for May 8, 1782, with the following letter from "Rusticus":

Mr. Bailey:

    Reading Capt. Barney's late gallant exploit [April 26, 1782] in your and other newspapers, I could not restrain myself from scribbling the few following stanzas relative to that affair and descriptive not of what was really said or done in the most minute particulars but of what might be supposed to have passed in similar circumstances.

                        Yours,
                        Rusticus

Dover, April 26, 1782

O'er the waste of waters cruising,
    Long the *General Monk* had reigned;
All subduing, all reducing,
    None her lawless rage restrained:
Many a brave and hearty fellow 5
    Yielding to this warlike foe,
When her guns began to bellow
    Struck his humbled colours low.

But grown bold with long successes,
    Leaving the wide watery way, 10
She, a stranger to distresses,
    Came to cruise within Cape May:
"Now we soon (said captain Rogers)
    Shall their men of commerce meet;
In our hold we'll have them lodgers, 15
    We shall capture half their fleet.

"Lo! I see their van appearing—
    Back our topsails to the mast—

Song: to the tune of the *Tempest* or *Hoosier's Ghost.*

They toward us full are steering
  With a gentle western blast: 20
I've a list of all their cargoes,
  All their guns, and all their men:
I am sure these modern Argos
  Can't escape us one in ten:

"Yonder comes the *Charming Sally*   25
  Sailing with the *General Greene*—
First we'll fight the *Hyder Ali*,
  Taking her is taking them:
She intends to give us battle,
  Bearing down with all her sail—   30
Now, boys, let our cannon rattle!
  To take her we cannot fail.

"Our eighteen guns, each a nine pounder,
  Soon shall terrify this foe;
We shall maul her, we shall wound her,   35
  Bringing rebel colours low."—
While he thus anticipated
  Conquests that he could not gain,
He in the Cape May channel waited
  For the ship that caused his pain.   40

Captain Barney then preparing,
  Thus addressed his gallant crew—
"Now, brave lads, be bold and daring,
  Let your hearts be firm and true;
This is a proud English cruiser,   45
  Roving up and down the main,
We must fight her—must reduce her,
  Though our decks be strewed with slain.

"Let who will be the survivor,
  We must conquer or must die,   50
We must take her up the river,
  Whate'er comes of you or I:
Though she shews most formidable
  With her eighteen pointed nines,
And her quarters clad in sable,   55
  Let us baulk her proud designs.

"With four nine pounders, and twelve sixes
  We will face that daring band;
Let no dangers damp your courage,
  Nothing can the brave withstand.   60
Fighting for your country's honour,
  Now to gallant deeds aspire;

Helmsman, bear us down upon her,
  Gunner, give the word to fire!"

Then yard arm and yard arm meeting,   65
  Strait began the dismal fray,
Cannon mouths, each other greeting,
  Belched their smoky flames away:
Soon the langrage, grape and chain shot,
  That from Barney's cannons flew,   70
Swept the *Monk*, and cleared each round top,
  Killed and wounded half her crew.

Captain Rogers strove to rally
  But they from their quarters fled,
While the roaring *Hyder Ali*   75
  Covered o'er his decks with dead.
When from their tops their dead men tumbled,
  And the streams of blood did flow,
Then their proudest hopes were humbled
  By their brave inferior foe.   80

All aghast, and all confounded,
  They beheld their champions fall,
And their captain, sorely wounded,
  Bade them quick for quarters call.
Then the *Monk's* proud flag descended,   85
  And her cannon ceased to roar;
By her crew no more defended,
  She confessed the contest o'er.

Come, brave boys, and fill your glasses,
  You have humbled one proud foe,   90
No brave action this surpasses,
  Fame shall tell the nations so—
Thus be Britain's woes completed,
  Thus abridged her cruel reign,
'Til she ever, thus defeated,   95
  Yields the sceptre of the main.

The Hurricane

THIS POEM first appeared in the *Freeman's Journal* for
April 13, 1785, where it carried the title, "Verses,
made at Sea, in a Heavy Gale." Freneau's own note
indicates that the storm occurred "near the east end of
Jamaica, July 30, 1784." When the poem was reprinted in the issue of the same journal for August 20,
1788, the following note was appended: "*In that violent
hurricane at Jamaica, on the night of the 30th of July,*

295

1784, in which, no more than eight, out of 150 sail of vessels, in the ports of Kingston and Port-Royal, were saved, capt. Freneau was at sea, and arrived at Kingston next morning, a mere wreck. On that occasion, the following beautiful lines . . . were penned." "The Hurricane" was reprinted in Samuel Kettell's *Specimens of American Poetry* (1829).

Happy the man who, safe on shore,
Now trims, at home, his evening fire;
Unmoved, he hears the tempests roar,
That on the tufted groves expire:
Alas! on us they doubly fall,   5
Our feeble barque must bear them all.

Now to their haunts the birds retreat,
The squirrel seeks his hollow tree,
Wolves in their shaded caverns meet,
All, all are blest but wretched we—   10
Foredoomed a stranger to repose,
No rest the unsettled ocean knows.

While o'er the dark abyss we roam,
Perhaps, with last departing gleam,
We saw the sun descend in gloom,   15
No more to see his morning beam;
But buried low, by far too deep,
On coral beds, unpitied, sleep!

But what a strange, uncoasted strand
Is that, where fate permits no day—   20
No charts have we to mark that land,
No compass to direct that way—
What Pilot shall explore that realm,
What new Columbus take the helm!

While death and darkness both surround,   25
And tempests rage with lawless power,
Of friendship's voice I hear no sound,
No comfort in this dreadful hour—
What friendship can in tempests be,
What comfort on this raging sea?   30

The barque, accustomed to obey,
No more the trembling pilots guide:
Alone she gropes her trackless way,
While mountains burst on either side—
Thus, skill and science both must fall;   35
And ruin is the lot of all.

The Wild Honey Suckle

THE DECIDUOUS, common wild honeysuckle is found in the eastern half of the United States, but its blossoms have a pinkish cast. The flower Freneau had in mind was probably the white swamp honeysuckle, which grows in damp, shady places in the Eastern and Southern states, and has a marked fragrance. Pattee drew from Chapman's *Southern Flora* the information that this honeysuckle (*azalea viscosum*) "flowers in the latitude of Charleston in July and August." The poem first appeared in the *Columbian Herald* for July 6, 1786, and was reprinted in the *Freeman's Journal* for August 2; it was collected in *Miscellaneous Works* (1788), and in *Poems* (1809). "The Wild Honey Suckle" is not, as has frequently been contended, a pure nature lyric, but a symbolic poem on the transiency of all earthly things.

Fair flower, that dost so comely grow,
Hid in this silent, dull retreat,
Untouched thy honied blossoms blow,
Unseen thy little branches greet:
No roving foot shall crush thee here,   5
No busy hand provoke a tear.

By Nature's self in white arrayed,
She bade thee shun the vulgar eye,
And planted here the guardian shade,
And sent soft waters murmuring by;   10
Thus quietly thy summer goes,
Thy days declining to repose.

Smit with those charms, that must decay,
I grieve to see your future doom;
They died—nor were those flowers more gay,   15
The flowers that did in Eden bloom;
Unpitying frosts, and Autumn's power
Shall leave no vestige of this flower.

From morning suns and evening dews
At first thy little being came: 20
If nothing once, you nothing lose,
For when you die you are the same;
The space between, is but an hour,
The frail duration of a flower.

The Indian Burying Ground

THIS POEM was first printed in the *American Museum* for November, 1787, and collected in the edition of 1788 in which it bore the title "Lines Occasioned by a

Visit to an old Indian Burying Ground." Freneau affixed the following note to the poem: "The North American Indians bury their dead in a sitting posture; decorating the corpse with wampum, the images of birds, quadrupeds, etc.: And (if that of a warrior) with bows, arrows, tomahawks, and other military weapons." In lines 17 to 20 the poet inserted an injunction, typical of epitaphs.

In spite of all the learned have said,
  I still my old opinion keep;
The posture, that we give the dead,
  Points out the soul's eternal sleep.

Not so the ancients of these lands—   5
  The Indian, when from life released,
Again is seated with his friends,
  And shares again the joyous feast.

His imaged birds, and painted bowl,
  And venison, for a journey dressed,   10
Bespeak the nature of the soul,
  Activity, that knows no rest.

His bow, for action ready bent,
  And arrows, with a head of stone,
Can only mean that life is spent,   15
  And not the old ideas gone.

Thou, stranger, that shalt come this way,
  No fraud upon the dead commit—
Observe the swelling turf, and say
  They do not lie, but here they sit.   20

Here still a lofty rock remains,
  On which the curious eye may trace
(Now wasted, half, by wearing rains)
  The fancies of a ruder race.

Here still an aged elm aspires,   25
  Beneath whose far-projecting shade
(And which the shepherd still admires)
  The children of the forest played!

There oft a restless Indian queen
  (Pale Shebah, with her braided hair)   30
And many a barbarous form is seen
  To chide the man that lingers there.

By midnight moons, o'er moistening dews;
  In habit for the chase arrayed,
The hunter still the deer pursues,   35
  The hunter and the deer, a shade!

And long shall timorous fancy see
  The painted chief, and pointed spear,
And Reason's self shall bow the knee
  To shadows and delusions here.   40

On Retirement

THE THEME of this poem was widely current in the eighteenth century because of the vogue of Horace. The sentiment about Horace's Sabine Farm and the joys of retirement can readily be traced in Abraham Cowley's "A Vote" in *Plantarum, Libr.* IV. See also Cowley's essay "Of Myself," and "The Country," a paraphrase of Horace. John Pomfret's "Choice" (1700) and Benjamin Church's "Choice" (1758) illustrate the same theme. Freneau's poem was written in 1775, though it probably was a revision of a college exercise.

(By Hezekiah Salem)

A hermit's house beside a stream,
  With forests planted round,
Whatever it to you may seem
More real happiness I deem
  Than if I were a monarch crown'd.   5

A cottage I could call my own,
  Remote from domes of care;
A little garden walled with stone,
The wall with ivy overgrown,
  A limpid fountain near,   10

Would more substantial joys afford,
  More real bliss impart
Than all the wealth that misers hoard,
Than vanquish'd worlds, or worlds restored—
  Mere cankers of the heart!   15

Vain, foolish man! how vast thy pride,
  How little can your wants supply!—
'Tis surely wrong to grasp so wide—
You act as if you only had
  To vanquish—not to die!   20

The Pictures of Columbus

FRENEAU'S interest in Columbus goes back to his undergraduate days at Princeton, where he dreamed of writing an epic of the New World. "The Pictures of Columbus" was written in 1774, prior to his arrival in New York. The poem was first published in *Miscellaneous Works* (1788).

PICTURE XVII · *Columbus in Chains*

During his third voyage, while in San Domingo, such unjust
representations were made of his conduct to the Court of
Spain, that a new admiral, Bovadilla, was appointed to
supersede him, who sent Columbus home in chains.
(Freneau's note)

Are these the honours they reserve for me,
Chains for the man that gave new worlds to
    Spain!
Rest here, my swelling heart!—O kings, O queens,
Patrons of monsters, and their progeny,
Authors of wrong, and slaves to fortune merely! 5
Why was I seated by my prince's side,
Honour'd, caress'd like some first peer of Spain?
Was it that I might fall most suddenly
From honour's summit to the sink of scandal!
'Tis done, 'tis done!—what madness is ambition!
What is there in that little breath of men,   11
Which they call Fame, that should induce the
    brave
To forfeit ease and that domestic bliss
Which is the lot of happy ignorance,
Less glorious aims, and dull humility?—   15
Whoe'er thou art that shalt aspire to honour,
And on the strength and vigour of the mind
Vainly depending, court a monarch's favour,
Pointing the way to vast extended empire;
First count your pay to be ingratitude,   20
Then chains and prisons, and disgrace like mine!
Each wretched pilot now shall spread his sails,
And treading in my footsteps, hail new worlds,
Which, but for me, had still been empty visions.

PICTURE XVIII · *Columbus at Valladolid*

After he found himself in disgrace with the Court of Spain,
he retired to Valladolid, a town of Old Castile, where he
died, it is said, more of a broken heart than any other
disease, on the 20th of May, 1506. (Freneau's note)

1

How sweet is sleep, when gain'd by length of toil!
    No dreams disturb the slumbers of the dead—
To snatch existence from this scanty soil,
    Were these the hopes deceitful fancy bred;
And were her painted pageants nothing more   5
Than this life's phantoms by delusion led?

2

The winds blow high: one other world remains;
    Once more without a guide I find the way;
In the dark tomb to slumber with my chains—
    Prais'd by no poet on my funeral day,   10
Nor even allow'd one dearly purchas'd claim—
My new found world not honour'd with my name.

3

Yet, in this joyless gloom while I repose,
    Some comfort will attend my pensive shade,
When memory paints, and golden fancy shows   15
    My toils rewarded, and my woes repaid;
When empires rise where lonely forests grew,
Where Freedom shall her generous plans pursue.

4

To shadowy forms, and ghosts and sleepy things,
    Columbus, now with dauntless heart repair;   20
You liv'd to find new worlds for thankless kings,
    Write this upon my tomb—yes—tell it there—
Tell of those chains that sullied all my glory—
Not mine, but their's—ah, tell the shameful story.

Epistle to Peter Pindar, Esq.

PETER PINDAR was the pen name of the late eighteenth-century English satirist, John Wolcot. During a brief period before 1790 Freneau imitated Pindar's manner in four or five poems; moreover, because of his humorous but satiric manner, Freneau was frequently called the Peter Pindar of America.

The poem first appeared in the New York *Daily Advertiser* for March 15, 1790. It refers to Wolcot's satiric matter and especially to his long poem, *The Lousiad*, which pillories George III. It was this target, as Freneau suggests, that partly endeared Wolcot to American readers. For a contemporary criticism of Peter Pindar see *The Port Folio*, I, 410 (1801).

Peter, methinks you are the happiest wight
That ever dealt in ink, or sharpen'd quill.
'Tis yours on every rank of fools to write—
Some prompt with pity, some with laughter kill;
  On scullions or on dukes you run your rigs,   5
  And value George no more than Whitbread's pigs.

From morn to night, thro' London's busy streets,
New subjects for your pen in crowds are seen,
At church, in taverns, balls, or birth-day treats,
Sir Joseph Banks, or England's breeding queen; 10
  How happy you, whom fortune has decreed
  Each character to hit—where all will read.

We, too, have had your monarch by the nose,
And pull'd the richest jewel from his crown—
Half Europe's kings are fools, the story goes,   15
Mere simpletons, and ideots of renown,
  Proud, in their frantic fits, man's blood to spill—
  'Tis time they all were travelling down the hill.

But, Peter, quit your dukes and little lords,
Young princes full of blood and scant of brains—
Our rebel coast some similes affords,   21
And many a subject for your pen contains
  Preserv'd as fuel for your comic rhymes,
  (Like Egypt's gods) to give to future times.

Ode

This ode was sung in Philadelphia on June 1, 1793, at a banquet in honor of Citizen Genêt. The reference to the rights of man suggests not only Condorcet and Rousseau, but more particularly Thomas Paine, whose *Rights of Man* (1791–1792) was an indignant reply to Burke's *Reflections on the Revolution in France* (1790). See Bernard Fay's *Revolutionary Spirit in France and America* (1927) for the historical background of the Ode. The poem was published in the *Poems* of 1809.

  God save the Rights of Man!
  Give us a heart to scan
  Blessings so dear:

6. George: George III. **Whitbread's pigs:** A disparaging reference to Samuel Whitbread (1758–1815), a wealthy brewer, whose stormy career in the House of Commons made him a target for satirists.
10. Sir Joseph Banks: (1743–1820), a botanist and president of the Royal Society. His strong-willed demeanor in office provoked complaints by some of the members.

Let them be spread around
Wherever man is found,   5
And with the welcome sound
Ravish his ear.

Let us with France agree,
And bid the world be free,
While tyrants fall!   10
Let the rude savage host
Of their vast numbers boast—
Freedom's almighty trust
Laughs at them all!

Though hosts of slaves conspire   15
To quench fair Gallia's fire,
Still shall they fail:
Though traitors round her rise,
Leagu'd with her enemies,
To war each patriot flies,   20
And will prevail.

No more is valour's flame
Devoted to a name,
Taught to adore—
Soldiers of Liberty   25
Disdain to bow the knee,
But teach Equality
To every shore.

The world at last will join
To aid thy grand design,   30
Dear Liberty!
To Russia's frozen lands
The generous flame expands:
On Afric's burning sands
Shall man be free!   35

In this our western world
Be Freedom's flag unfurl'd
Through all its shores!
May no destructive blast
Our heaven of joy o'ercast,   40
May Freedom's fabric last
While time endures.

If e'er her cause require!—
Should tyrants e'er aspire
To aim their stroke,   45

May no proud despot daunt—
Should he his standard plant,
Freedom will never want
Her hearts of oak!

The Republican Genius of Europe

IN THE following lines Freneau contended that the French Revolution was kindled in America. The poem is grounded in opposition to kings and in the promotion of the rights of man. S. E. Forman, writing of Freneau's liberalism, declared: "The editor of the *National Gazette* [Freneau] was the schoolmaster who drilled Jeffersonian or French democracy into the minds—willing or unwilling—of the American people." The poem appeared in the *Jersey Chronicle*, May 23, 1795. It was almost completely rewritten in Freneau's 1815 edition.

Emperors and kings! in vain you strive
  Your torments to conceal—
The age is come that shakes your thrones,
Tramples in dust despotic crowns,
  And bids the sceptre fail.   5

In western worlds the flame began:
  From thence to France it flew—
Through Europe, now, it takes its way,
Beams an insufferable day,
  And lays all tyrants low.   10

Genius of France! pursue the chace
  Till Reason's laws restore
Man to be Man, in every clime;—
That Being, active, great, sublime
  Debased in dust no more.   15

In dreadful pomp he takes his way
  O'er ruin'd crowns, demolish'd thrones—
    Pale tyrants shrink before his blaze—
Round him terrific lightnings play—
  With eyes of fire, he looks them through,   20
  Crushes the vile despotic crew,
    And Pride in ruin lays.

On a Honey Bee Drinking from a Glass of Wine and Drowned Therein

THIS POEM is among the sprightliest of Freneau's lighter poems which include "A Jug of Rum," "A Glass of Tea," and "To a Caty-Did." Modeled on Thomas Gray's "On the Death of a Favorite Cat," the poem, nevertheless, has elements of the lyricism that mark Freneau's best work. It was published in the edition of 1809.

Thou, born to sip the lake or spring,
Or quaff the waters of the stream,
Why hither come, on vagrant wing?—
Does Bacchus tempting seem—
Did he, for you, this glass prepare?—   5
Will I admit you to a share?

Did storms harass or foes perplex,
Did wasps or king-birds bring dismay—
Did wars distress, or labors vex,
Or did you miss your way?—   10
A better seat you could not take
Than on the margin of this lake.

Welcome!—I hail you to my glass:
All welcome, here, you find;
Here, let the cloud of trouble pass,   15
Here, be all care resigned.—
This fluid never fails to please,
And drown the griefs of men or bees.

What forced you here, we cannot know,
And you will scarcely tell—   20
But cheery we would have you go
And bid a glad farewell:
On lighter wings we bid you fly,
Your dart will now all foes defy.

Yet take not, oh! too deep a drink,   25
And in this ocean die;
Here bigger bees than you might sink,
Even bees full six feet high.
Like Pharaoh, then, you would be said
To perish in a sea of red.   30

Do as you please, your will is mine;
Enjoy it without fear—
And your grave will be this glass of wine,
Your epitaph—a tear—
Go, take your seat in Charon's boat,   35
We'll tell the hive, you died afloat.

On the Uniformity and Perfection of Nature

CENTRAL in the poem is the deistic concept of one God in the universe, whose power and will are expressed in all-reasonable and immutable laws. In a system thus logical, Freneau can imagine no interruption to the perfect ordering of natural laws by private petitions asking for special dispensation. The poem was first published in 1815.

On one fix'd point all nature moves,
Nor deviates from the track she loves;
Her system, drawn from reason's source,
She scorns to change her wonted course.

Could she descend from that great plan   5
To work unusual things for man,
To suit the insect of an hour—
This would betray a want of power,

Unsettled in its first design
And erring, when it did combine   10
The parts that form the vast machine,
The figures sketch'd on nature's scene.

Perfections of the great first cause
Submit to no contracted laws,
But all-sufficient, all-supreme,   15
Include no trivial views in them.

Who looks through nature with an eye
That would the scheme of heaven descry,
Observes her constant, still the same,
In all her laws, through all her frame.   20

No imperfection can be found
In all that is, above, around,—
All, nature made, in reason's sight
Is order all and all is right.

On the Religion of Nature

AS A DEIST Freneau believed in the harmonious laws of nature, a Newtonian concept. The universal light of nature serves as man's guide; thus religion is heralded as one of the gifts of nature. These views tended to deny the concepts of total depravity and to free man from the "tyranny" of theological systems. Further illustration of Freneau's religious views may be found in his poem "On a Book Called *Unitarian Theology*" (1786). "On the Religion of Nature" was published in the edition of 1815.

The power that gives with liberal hand
The blessings man enjoys, while here,
And scatters through a smiling land
The abundant products of the year;
That power of nature, ever bless'd,   5
Bestow'd religion with the rest.

Born with ourselves, her early sway
Inclines the tender mind to take
The path of right, fair virtue's way
Its own felicity to make.   10
This universally extends
And leads to no mysterious ends.

Religion, such as nature taught,
With all divine perfection suits;
Had all mankind this system sought   15
Sophists would cease their vain disputes,
And from this source would nations know
All that can make their heaven below.

This deals not curses on mankind,
Or dooms them to perpetual grief,   20
If from its aid no joys they find,
It damns them not for unbelief;
Upon a more exalted plan
Creatress nature dealt with man—

Joy to the day, when all agree   25
On such grand systems to proceed,
From fraud, design, and error free,
And which to truth and goodness lead:
Then persecution will retreat
And man's religion be complete.   30

The Pilgrim

VI. [Man's Mortality]

THIS ESSAY first appeared in the *Freeman's Journal* for December 26, 1781. In the first number of the essay series, *The Pilgrim*, No. 1, Freneau complained of the general preoccupation with political or local topics to the sad neglect of "morality and refined sentiment." Among the observations which he offered in correction of this defect were the following reflections on solitude and self-knowledge. The theme was highly popular in eighteenth-century literature. The text is that of the *Freeman's Journal.*

... Retirement has a thousand charms, advantages and amusements, which the generality of people have not the slightest idea of. Those who hurry to towns with a design to pass away time more agreeably there than in the country, may indeed find their ends answered, but the perpetual amusements and avocations of a citizen's life are enemies to the future peace of the mind, as they prevent men from looking into themselves, by which neglect they commonly live and die strangers to that self knowledge which it ought to be their constant study and greatest ambition to acquire. Such can hardly endure their own existence unless perpetually engaged in the hurry of business, enquiring after new events, busied in new pursuits and taken up with a multitude of novelties. When such persons are compelled to be alone, how wretched are they, how discontented; how heavily the hours drag on, 'till some new interview, some interesting piece of news, some favourite companion, or darling diversion dispels the horrors of solitude, and restores them again to the follies of life, which unhappily without those follies would be to them a burden.

Have not the oracles of truth told us, does not reason inform us, that the days of darkness shall be many? What misery then must those men endure when that thin partition is thrown down, that fine thread broken, that curtain drawn which divides us from the world unseen; when they must depart into those regions of immateriality where so many generations of men have gone before them, and where the disembodied spirit must be wretched indeed, unless in this life inured and habituated to those sentiments of virtue, upon which the soul must in some sense subsist, and which must constitute the ground work of her felicity through everlasting ages.

Every rational man, let his business or station in life be what it may, should, in my way of thinking, at least once a year withdraw himself from the numerous connections and allurements that are apt to give us too great a fondness for life; he should then take time to reflect, as a rational being ought to do, and consider well the end of his being. For life is not valuable, unless as a season of preparation for that which shall be more permanent; letting this consideration aside, it is weakness, vanity, and misery itself, as well as the occasion of innumerable evils to all around us. Yes; the life of man is supported by death and anguish: by blood and ruin the human race subsists. Even I, for whom the ox never bled, nor the lamb surrendered up his little life, even I have too often been compelled, with a heavy heart, a downcast eye, and a trembling hand, to pluck unripe fruits from the tender bough, and to deprive the roots of the earth of their principle of life, before they were swelled to a state of maturity. But death is often found in the very means of life; this apple or this root may possess, (at least for me) the seeds of destruction; it may be in surrounding inanimate substances, in this rock, in yonder aged oak, that now, decayed, threatens to fall, and carry all before it; it may fall, and in a moment, in one unguarded moment, you are gone! But, to exhibit the frailty of life in the most striking view, consider, are not all mankind at least one third part of their time clasped in the arms of death himself? Tell me, thou anxious worldling, what is sleep? The mother of death and the mother of sleep was one; they are brothers, and have an intimate connection; they are twin brothers; behold the striking resemblance! Look at a man in a sound sleep!—it came violently upon him, and forcibly subdued all opposition; he is now at an immense distance from the material world and converses with beings of an incorporeal nature. Was he a few moments ago powerful, or wise, or valiant; had he the eye of majesty, did he tread armies beneath his feet, or did he receive tribute from a thousand isles? Alas, he is nothing now! and were he but to continue what he is, would be forever as effectually dead to the duties of this life, as if laid in his grave, and his soul departed to its unchangeable destiny. Sleep was given thee, O man, not only as a relief to thy miseries. but a memento of thy mortality.

The Miscellaneous Works of Philip Freneau

II. Essays, Tales, and Poems · *Robert Slender's Idea of a Visit to a Modern Great Man*

The Miscellaneous Works of Philip Freneau (1788), from which the text is taken, contained a variety of essays on humorous, social, and literary topics. Freneau as a staunch democrat hating rank, pomposity, and egotism, was quick to advance equalitarian principles whether under his own name or under that of Robert Slender, his pen name.

From my earliest childhood I ever entertained a secret disgust for great men, and had even a sincere hatred to big men, till accident discovered to me that the terms were not always synonymous.

I owe this ridiculous prejudice to one David Doomsday, the constable of the village in which I was born, who was long reckoned the greatest man in those parts; one branch of his business having been to whip petty criminals, and put disorderly persons in the stocks.

Since I have arrived at maturer age, I have not seen much reason to alter my opinion in regard to the generality of the great men of the vulgar.

When we pay a visit to one of these great men, the first thing or idea that particularly strikes us, is the great man's tacit confession of his own real littleness by the magnitude of his buildings.—An everlasting solitude reigns in the front of his dwelling; his doors are forever shut, over whose inhospitable threshold the repeated voice of a surly knocker can with much ado procure an admittance.—No honest house dog advances to the marble steps to welcome the friendless stranger to a participation of the pleasures within; a snarling cur is only seen at a distance, within a gate, betraying himself, from his behaviour, to be as much a puppy as his master. Every thing wears the appearance of sordid selfishness, and every thing informs you that the tawdry daughters of equipage, and the strutting sons of fortune, are only welcome here.

But supposing we should be so happy as to make them hear us. The great man himself does not deign to advance to the door to receive you. A waiting man, or a pimp, or a sycophant, or a dependant, or a private secretary is sent, at the summons of the knocker, to be informed what you want, or to know who you are. If you are, apparently, of no great consequence, he keeps the lowermost of the two doors shut to, cautiously pulls the other scarcely half open, and then holds parley with you.

Now, may he suffer all the tortures of Tantalus, who first contrived this inhospitable sort of doors.

The fellow tells you a thousand lies, or makes a thousand lying excuses, rather than let you in. At last, by collecting the resolution and impudence of a devil, you intimidate him. He then unbolts the lower door, with a very ill will, and in you step.—The ceiling returns a hollow sound, like that of a vault.—The floor is of mahogany, lately rubbed over with wax. In spite of all your care, your shoes have soiled it, and you may of consequence assure yourself that the lady of the house, at least, is your enemy forever.

That is not the worst of it neither; a mahogany floor rubbed over several times with wax never fails to assume a devilish slippery quality. Your shoes or boots being hard and unpliant, your foothold deceives you, and you tumble along at full length upon the floor.

The whole house is instantly alarmed. The lap dog runs out in a rage to seize you by the throat—and it is with some difficulty that you are able at last to disengage yourself, and recover your legs.

The porter then walks slowly on before you through a long dreary entry, and at the same time treads so lightly that you can scarcely hear him at all. At length you arrive at the back parlour, or at the dining room, or at the study.—The great man nods with his head.

You look all around, and are amazed that the furniture is for show only and not for use. The bottoms or seats of the great man's chairs are of wrought damask, or red velvet.—Heaven forbid, cry you, that my weather beaten posteriors should come into contact with these curious and ingenious devices!—The weather is very cold.—You immediately conclude that the great man must be of a very warm constitution, inasmuch as his whole fire place and hearth are scarcely of the dimensions of a country chaffing-dish!—But, he certainly deems himself a very great man, nevertheless, for yonder hang a couple of pier glasses each full

303

eight feet in length. His size must certainly be in proportion thereto.

He is at breakfast—instead of asking you to sit down and partake with him, he, in a surly tone, and with a heavy countenance, demands your business in that place?—

No sooner have you made an effort to speak, or force out half a dozen words, than he catches up a newspaper and reads something to his wife.

You make another effort, but by the time you have articulated ten words more, in comes one of his clerks with a pen sticking behind his ear, and a long piece of writing in his hands.

They fall to examining of it, and in all appearance the examination will be tedious enough.—You find yourself agreeably deceived, however, as they finish in something less than two hours.

The clerk then walks off, and you renew your applications.—Fifteen words and an half are now uttered on your part—when a loud rap is heard at the door. "A loud rap at the door [sayeth Jacob Bœhman] always betokeneth importance in him that rappeth."—Away runs the house dog, lap dog, and footman.—The footman instantly returns with word, that "the lieutenant governor has urgent business with the great man, and must speak with him in less than ten minutes!"

Now, very likely, all this is nothing more than a villainous contrivance to get rid of you; but how are you to know that, Mr. Shovelshoes!

The very mention and idea of the lieutenant-governor strikes you dumb.—The great man desires you to call on him at some other time, a week or two hence, as he is very busy at present on other matters.

You either make no reply, or your remonstrances avail nothing.—In vain you tell him that you have travelled two hundred miles on foot, on purpose to settle this business—In vain do you put him in mind that you have but twenty shillings in your pocket, and cannot of course remain above three days longer in the city!—He is deaf to all this—you are conducted into the street a short way through a back door—the door is slammed after you, and you walk sullenly away, fretting and swearing, and wishing all great men to the devil.

The above is a true idea of a plebeian visit to a modern great man—*expereo crede Roberto.*

Tomo Cheeki[1]

IN THE COLUMNS of the *Jersey Chronicle* for 1795, and reissued in *The Time-Piece and Literary Companion* (1798) Freneau printed a series of fourteen essays entitled "Tomo Cheeki, the Creek Indian in Philadelphia." For the "amusement and information of the curious," he followed the old device of having an outlander comment upon the manners and morals of civilized society. This practice began with Montesquieu, continued with Goldsmith in *The Citizen of the World,* and is illustrated in the nineteenth century in the work of Scott and Lockhart. The convention enabled authors to satirize their own age without having to accept responsibility for personal comment. Freneau's Indian, a lover of nature and retirement, sees in late eighteenth-century America artificiality, lust for wealth, and misery. The text is that of first printing in the *Jersey Chronicle.*

X. The Creek Indian in Philadelphia

The more I consider the condition of the white men, the more fixed becomes my opinion, that instead of gaining, they have lost much by subjecting themselves to what they call the laws and regulations of civilized societies.

Endless wants are the natural cause of endless cares. It is these cares that make their lives a burthen, and force so many to rid themselves voluntarily of existence. They are the wisest lawgivers who have so contrived their community as, after teaching the people to be virtuous, to impose the fewest wants possible upon them.

But, among the white men of the east, the more a nation or tribe is bowed down, the better for those who govern.

These white men have enslaved almost the whole creation of living things, in order that they, in their turn, might become the slaves of all. They have multiplied wants till it is no longer possible to gratify them. They have persuaded each other that the mere luxuries of life are the absolute necessaries; and endless labour, pain, and watchfulness are the consequences.

There is a little leaf, chopped fine and dried, that is brought hither over the salt ocean in immense quantities from the very farthest ends of

[1]Courtesy of The New-York Historical Society, New York.

304

the earth—it is dry, tasteless, or at best insipid; but is daily used in abundance at their tables here, from the highest big captain to the poorest artisan or labourer. Without this, life would be deemed insupportable; and the females, in particular, would consider existence as no longer worth enjoying were they not twice a day to treat themselves profusely with a red liquor boiled from this foreign leaf.

How many great canoes must be built, and rigged, and furnished with sails before it can be brought to them. What labour, and sweat, and deadly diseases must be suffered! How many storms, combats, disasters, terrors, deaths, and disappointments experienced!

But, of itself, this leaf is held in small estimation. Thousands of canoes must be again built and employed in passing to and from the sultry islands of the south, to bring back a sweet substance to make the taste of the leaf pleasant to the palate, which is otherwise hot and bitter, grievous and ungrateful to the stomach.

Millions, again, groan under an intolerable slavery who are employed in producing this sweet substance from the burning soil that lies under another sun. How great a part of the race of white and black men are therefore rendered miserable, or perish in supplying the people of these shores with only this one sort of idle gratification of a false appetite!

Why are men so prodigiously multiplied only to become wretched, and of short and feverish duration!

Look at the labourer of the land. He rises long before the sun to attend his cattle. He waters the soil with the sweat of his brow, and is ready to faint with grief when he considers that but a little of all this labour is for himself. He enjoys but a scanty pittance of unsavory food, is compelled to struggle with incessant wants, and quenches his thirst at the fountain of tears!

If he has any happiness at all, it is centered in some one object only. When sickness or the accidents of life render him unfit for labour, there remain to him nothing but uneasiness of mind, the weak nerve, and the voice of sorrow. He is constantly encompassed with jails, laws, government, society. He has been taught to be in pain for the

future; and the tormentors of this world have taken care that he shall not enjoy the present. He is in want and penury amidst the amplest feast that Nature could set before him; and he is the perfect slave of error, passion, and prejudice.

Love itself has become degraded by the confusion arising from these invasions of the benign Law of Nature.—How comes it that love, as things go here, is directed only by sordid interest; and why is a link in that chain of amity which is thought to extend throughout the universe, broken, by one half of the human species (and that by far the most amiable and virtuous) being forbidden to declare their passion on equal terms with the object of their love.

Are the happiness and content of the people the great blessing intended by all laws?—Instead then, of contriving thousands of wants, why is it not the first care of the legislators to diminish these wants to a very few in number?—Let the head men begin with showing the simple people that they may be satisfied with three or four enjoyments, and the people will soon follow in their path. It is the example of the great chiefs and big men that must govern the conduct of the laborious people to make them happy.

The multiplication of wants has debased the spirit of man. Instead of being the lords of this beautiful creation, they have become slaves to each other, as well as to the inferior orders of beings.

Cast your eye on that huge and glittering machine, drawn by six horses. I see three fellows, called footmen, stationed behind it, gorgeously attired indeed, but slaves in whatever light I behold them. Some great idol is within the machine, and is rolled along with much rattling noise, meditating upon—mischief!—Another mounted on high, armed with a long whip, conducts the splendid chariot, appearing to govern the horses and direct their path. By his fierce countenance I would take him for a big captain, at least;—but he is nothing—he has not even the strength of a grasshopper—he has no will of his own, but is actuated merely by the wink and the nod of the great idol within!

But I am out of all patience when I reflect on the debased mind of my landlord's hostler; the man that attends the horses of travellers.—Yes!

305

I would smite him with my staff, and drive him before me to the Indian country, to be instructed how to become *a man*, did not the laws of the white men protect him from my just and terrible indignation!

Beyond all doubt, he came into this world with a soul capable of attaining the ideas of a man. But he is no other than a horse!—He is not even a horse: for what is base and servile in both natures being in him mingled, he is neither one nor the other. His days and his nights are spent in the rubbing down, currying and combing the horses of travellers, in giving them drink, in supplying them with herbage, and cleaning away their filth.

Why do the big-chiefs here hold long talks on the dignity of man, when such a wretch of their own species and colour is encouraged to live among them.

THE RISE OF A NATIONAL LITERATURE

TIMOTHY DWIGHT (1752–1817)

THE ESTABLISHED order in Connecticut had a doughty champion in Timothy Dwight, whose activities as theologian, educator, writer, orator, and publicist made him virtually the "moral legislator" of New England. Dwight was the grandson of Jonathan Edwards, but his career as the defender of eighteenth-century orthodoxy more nearly resembles that of Increase Mather. Dwight's works bristle with attacks on all forms of infidelity. Possessing an impressive stock of erudition, and impelled by a boundless aspiration for reputation and influence, he spent his undeniably great powers of mind in waging a losing battle against the forces of change. Today he is remembered chiefly as the embodiment of the religious, political, social, and literary points of view held by the Connecticut Wits.

Dwight's youth was distinguished by a precocity remarkable even for the eighteenth century. He was born in Northampton in 1752 where, as Moses Tyler remarked, he had begun to receive regular instruction in books almost as soon as he was able to speak. His mastery of the alphabet in a single lesson, his ability to read the Bible before his fourth birthday, his eagerness for study while his schoolmates were at play—these phenomena help not only to account for his admission to Yale at the age of thirteen, but also to explain why he was already familiar with many of the Greek and Latin authors prescribed during his first two years at college. Dwight was graduated with highest honors in 1769, and after an interval spent as a grammar-school teacher he returned to Yale as tutor in 1771. Here his enthusiasm for belles-lettres resulted in a broadening of the curriculum, and ultimately led to the formation of the coterie known as the Connecticut Wits, a notably articulate and ambitious literary group which played an important part in the cultivation of a taste for literature in the young republic. His duties at Yale were interrupted by his war service as a chaplain in the Continental Army. Of his patriotic songs and sermons, by far the most popular was "Columbia, Columbia, to Glory Arise." After his ordination in 1783 Dwight accepted a call to the Congregational Church at Greenfield Hill, Connecticut, where his reputation as a theologian, writer, and educator spread far beyond the limits of his parish. He established a highly successful coeducational school; he published his grandiose epic *The Conquest of Canaan* (1785) and his no less patriotic, but much more readable poem *Greenfield Hill* (1794); and he lashed out at the infidelity of deists such as Paine and Barlow, and at the tenets of democrats such as Jefferson in a series of vigorous sermons, addresses, and satires. In 1795 his efforts in behalf of religious and political fundamentalism were crowned by his election to the presidency of Yale.

The duties of his new office must have satisfied even Dwight's ambition for leadership. In addition to the responsibilities of the presidency, Dwight taught rhetoric, logic, metaphysics, and theology; he found time to fill the college pulpit and to serve as a "supply" pastor in many churches; he set forth his doctrinal views in a series of sermons published in five volumes as *Theology Explained and Defended* (1818–1819), and during college vacations he traveled extensively, collecting the voluminous notes for his *Travels in New England and New York*, a four-volume work which appeared posthumously in 1821–1822. A mine of information, this miscellany is the most readable of his writings. Dwight's dominance as a leader and the impressiveness of his personality led his admiring associates to compare him to St. Paul, though without the support of his majestic presence his writings today seem parochial and labored. No one, however, has been disposed to challenge Timothy Dwight's position as a great college president whose leadership extended far beyond his classes. It was not an accident that Federalism and Calvinism found a hospitable refuge in Connecticut long after their disintegration in other states.

BIBLIOGRAPHY · C. E. Cuningham's *Timothy Dwight, 1752–1817: A Biography* (1942) is a full-length life study. Early biographies include B. Silliman, *A Sketch of the Life and Character of President Dwight* (1817), and S. E. Dwight, "Memoir," published in *Theology Defined and Explained* (1818–1819). There is an especially valuable account of Dwight in Leon Howard, *The Connecticut Wits* (1943), 79–111, 342–401. Other useful sketches are those by F. B. Dexter, *Biographical Sketches of Graduates of Yale College*, III (1903); V. L. Parrington, *The Connecticut Wits* (1926), xxxix–xliii; H. E. Starr, *Dictionary of American Biography*, V, 573–577; and M. C. Tyler, *Three Men of Letters* (1895), 71–127. Special studies include F. B. Dexter, "Student Life at Yale under President Dwight," *Proceedings of the American Antiquarian Society* (New Series), XXVII (Oct., 1917); A. W. Griswold, "Three Puritans on Prosperity," *New England Quarterly*, VII (1934), 475–493; L. Leary, "The Author of *The Triumph of Infidelity*," *New England Quarterly*, XX (1947), 377–385; and T. A. Zunder, "Noah Webster and the Conquest of Canaan," *American Literature*, I (1929), 200–202.

Greenfield Hill

DWIGHT BEGAN his ministry in the Congregational church at Greenfield Hill, Connecticut, in 1783. There, four years later, he started writing *Greenfield Hill*, a poem in seven parts, written "to contribute to the innocent amusement of his country men, and to their improvement in manners, and in economical, political, and moral sentiments." Although Denham's *Cooper's Hill* suggested the plan of the work, and Pope, Gay, Thomson, Goldsmith, and other English poets were consciously and slavishly imitated, Dwight wrote to persuade Americans that their native land possessed scenes and themes superior to those of the Old World. Viewing the surrounding countryside from "a beautiful and pleasant eminence" in his parish, the poet celebrated the blessings of the American way of life. On every side he found the conditions of competence, equality, decency, and freedom as the solid foundations for the future greatness of the American Republic.

Oliver Goldsmith's *Deserted Village* provided the model for "The Flourishing Village." The text is that of the first edition, *Greenfield Hill: A Poem*, published in New York in 1794.

PART II · *The Flourishing Village*

Fair Verna! loveliest village of the west;
Of every joy, and every charm, posses'd;
How pleas'd amid thy varied walks I rove,
Sweet, cheerful walks of innocence, and love,
And o'er thy smiling prospects cast my eyes,   5
And see the seats of peace, and pleasure, rise,
And hear the voice of Industry resound,
And mark the smile of Competence, around!
Hail, happy village! O'er thy cheerful lawns,
With earliest beauty, spring delighted dawns;   10
The northward sun begins his vernal smile;
The spring-bird carols o'er the cressy rill:
The shower, that patters in the ruffled stream,
The ploughboy's voice, that chides the lingering team,
The bee, industrious, with his busy song,   15
The woodman's axe, the distant groves among,
The waggon, rattling down the rugged steep,
The light wind, lulling every care to sleep,
All these, with mingled music, from below,
Deceive intruding sorrow, as I go.   20

How pleas'd, fond Recollection, with a smile,
Surveys the varied round of wintery toil!
How pleas'd, amid the flowers, that scent the plain,
Recalls the vanish'd frost, and sleeted rain;
The chilling damp, the ice-endangering street,   25
And treacherous earth that slump'd beneath the feet.

Yet even stern winter's glooms could joy inspire:
Then social circles grac'd the nutwood fire;
The axe resounded, at the sunny door;
The swain, industrious, trimm'd his flaxen store;
Or thresh'd, with vigorous flail, the bounding wheat,   31
His poultry round him pilfering for their meat;
Or slid his firewood on the creaking snow;
Or bore his produce to the main below;
Or o'er his rich returns exulting laugh'd;   35
Or pledg'd the healthful orchard's sparkling draught:
While, on his board, for friends and neighbours spread,
The turkey smoak'd, his busy housewife fed;
And Hospitality look'd smiling round,
And Leisure told his tale, with gleeful sound.   40

307

Then too, the rough road hid beneath the sleigh,
The distant friend despis'd a length of way,
And join'd the warm embrace, and mingling smile,
And told of all his bliss, and all his toil; 44
And, many a month elaps'd, was pleased to view
How well the houshold far'd, the children grew;
While tales of sympathy deceiv'd the hour,
And Sleep, amus'd, resign'd his wonted power.

Yes! let the proud despise, the rich deride,
These humble joys, to Competence allied: 50
To me, they bloom, all fragrant to my heart,
Nor ask the pomp of wealth, nor gloss of art.
And as a bird, in prison long confin'd,
Springs from his open'd cage, and mounts the wind,

decries
pomp.

Thro' fields of flowers, and fragrance, gaily flies,
Or re-assumed his birth-right, in the skies: 56
Unprison'd thus from artificial joys,
Where pomp fatigues, and fussful fashion cloys,
The soul, reviving, loves to wander free
Thro' native scenes of sweet simplicity; 60
Thro' Peace' low vale, where Pleasure lingers long,
And every songster tunes his sweetest song,
And Zephyr hastes, to breathe his first perfume,
And Autumn stays, to drop his latest bloom:
'Till grown mature, and gathering strength to
      roam, 65
She lifts her lengthen'd wings, and seeks her home.

But now the wintery glooms are vanish'd all;

Winter
gone

The lingering drift behind the shady wall;
The dark-brown spots, that patch'd the snowy
      field;
The surly frost, that every bud conceal'd; 70
The russet veil, the way with slime o'erspread,
And all the saddening scenes of March are fled.

Sweet-smiling village! loveliest of the hills!
How green thy groves! How pure thy glassy rills!
With what new joy, I walk thy verdant streets! 75
How often pause, to breathe thy gale of sweets;
To mark thy well-built walls! thy budding fields!
And every charm, that rural nature yields;
And every joy, to Competence allied,
And every good, that Virtue gains from Pride! 80

No griping landlord here alarms the door,
To halve, for rent, the poor man's little store.

No haughty owner drives the humble swain
To some far refuge from his dread domain;
Nor wastes, upon his robe of useless pride, 85
The wealth, which shivering thousands want beside:
Nor in one palace sinks a hundred cots;
Nor in one manor drowns a thousand lots;
Nor, on one table, spread for death and pain,
Devours what would a village well sustain. 90

Competence

O Competence, thou bless'd by Heaven's decree,
How well exchang'd is empty pride for thee!
Oft to thy cot my feet delighted turn,
To meet thy chearful smile, at peep of morn;
To join thy toils, that bid the earth look gay; 95
To mark thy sports, that hail the eve of May;
To see thy ruddy children, at thy board,
And share thy temperate meal, and frugal hoard;
And every joy, by winning prattlers giv'n,
And every earnest of a future Heaven. 100

There the poor wanderer finds a table spread,
The fireside welcome, and the peaceful bed.
The needy neighbour, oft by wealth denied,
There finds the little needs of life supplied;
The horse, that bears to mill the hard-earn'd
      grain; 105
The day's work given, to reap the ripen'd plain;
The useful team, to house the precious food,
And all the offices of real good.

There too, divine Religion is a guest,
And all the Virtues join the daily feast. 110
Kind Hospitality attends the door,
To welcome in the stranger and the poor;
Sweet Charity, still blushing as she goes;
And Patience smiling at her train of woes;
And meek-eyed Innocence, and Truth refin'd, 115
And Fortitude, of bold, but gentle mind.

Thou pay'st the tax, the rich man will not pay;
Thou feed'st the poor, the rich man drives away.
Thy sons, for freedom, hazard limbs, and life, 119
While pride applauds, but shuns the manly strife:
Thou prop'st religion's cause, the world around,
And shew'st thy faith in works, and not in sound.

Virtue
not
sour

Say, child of passion! while, with idiot stare,
Thou seest proud grandeur wheel her sunny car;

While kings, and nobles, roll bespangled by,   125
And the tall palace lessens in the sky;
Say, while with pomp thy giddy brain runs round,
What joys, like these, in splendour can be found?
Ah, yonder turn thy wealth-inchanted eyes,
Where that poor, friendless wretch expiring lies!
Hear his sad partner shriek, beside his bed,   131
And call down curses on her landlord's head,
Who drove, from yon small cot, her household
    sweet,
To pine with want, and perish in the street.
See the pale tradesman toil, the livelong day,   135
To deck imperious lords, who never pay!
Who waste, at dice, their boundless breadth of soil,
But grudge the scanty meed of honest toil.
See hounds and horses riot on the store,
By HEAVEN created for the hapless poor!   140
See half a realm one tryant scarce sustain,
While meagre thousands round him glean the plain!
See, for his mistress' robe, a village sold,
Whose matrons shrink from nakedness and cold!
See too the Farmer prowl around the shed,   145
To rob the starving household of their bread;
And seize, with cruel fangs, the helpess swain,
While wives, and daughters, plead, and weep, in
    vain;
Or yield to infamy themselves, to save
Their sire from prison, famine, and the grave.   150

There too foul luxury taints the putrid mind,
And slavery there imbrutes the reasoning kind:
There humble worth, in damps of deep despair,
Is bound by poverty's eternal bar:
No motives bright the etherial aim impart,   155
Nor one fair ray of hope allures the heart.

But, O, sweet Competence! how chang'd the
    scene,
Where thy soft footsteps lightly print the green!
Where Freedom walks erect, with manly port,
And all the blessings to his side resort,   160
In every hamlet, Learning builds her schools,
And beggars' children gain her arts, and rules;
And mild Simplicity o'er manners reigns,
And blameless morals Purity sustains.

From thee the rich enjoyments round me spring,
Where every farmer reigns a little king;   166

Where all to comfort, none to danger, rise;
Where pride finds few, but nature all supplies;
Where peace and sweet civility are seen,
And meek good-neighbourhood endears the green.
Here every class (if classes those we call,   171
Where one extended class embraces all,
All mingling, as the rainbow's beauty blends,
Unknown where every hue begins or ends)
Each following, each, with uninvidious strife,   175
Wears every feature of improving life.
Each gains from other comeliness of dress,
And learns, with gentle mien to win and bless,
With welcome mild the stranger to receive,
And with plain, pleasing decency to live.   180
Refinement hence even humblest life improves;
Not the loose fair, that form and frippery loves;
But she, whose mansion is the gentle mind,
In thought, and action, virtuously refin'd.   184
Hence, wives and husbands act a lovelier part,
More just the conduct, and more kind the heart;
Hence brother, sister, parent, child, and friend,
The harmony of life more sweetly blend;
Hence labour brightens every rural scene;
Hence cheerful plenty lives along the green;   190
Still Prudence eyes her hoard, with watchful care,
And robes of thrift and neatness, all things wear.

But hark! what voice so gaily fills the wind?
Of care oblivious, whose that laughing mind?
'Tis yon poor black, who ceases now his song,   195
And whistling, drives the cumbrous wain along.
He never, dragg'd, with groans, the galling chain;
Nor hung, suspended, on th' infernal crane;
No dim, white spots deform his face, or hand,
Memorials hellish of the marking brand!   200
No seams of pincers, scars of scalding oil;
No waste of famine, and no wear of toil.
But kindly fed, and clad, and treated, he
Slides on, thro' life, with more than common glee.
For here mild manners good to all impart,   205
And stamp with infamy th' unfeeling heart;
Here law, from vengeful rage, the slave defends,
And here the gospel peace on earth extends.

He toils, 'tis true; but shares his master's toil;
With him, he feeds the herd, and trims the soil;
Helps to sustain the house, with clothes, and food,
And takes his portion of the common good: 212

309

Lost liberty his sole, peculiar ill,
And fix'd submission to another's will.
Ill, ah, how great! without the cheering sun,   215
The world is chang'd to one wide, frigid zone;
The mind, a chill'd exotic, cannot grow,
Nor leaf with vigour, nor with promise blow;
Pale, sickly, shrunk, it strives in vain to rise,
Scarce lives, while living, and untimely dies.   220

See fresh to life the Afric infant spring,
And plume its powers, and spread its little wing!
Firm is its frame, and vigorous is its mind,
Too young to think, and yet to misery blind.
But soon he sees himself to slavery born;   225
Soon meets the voice of power, the eye of scorn;
Sighs for the blessings of his peers, in vain;
Condition'd as a brute, tho' form'd a man.
Around he casts his fond, instinctive eyes,
And sees no good, to fill his wishes, rise: 230
(No motive warms, with animating beam,
Nor praise, nor property, nor kind esteem,
Bless'd independence, on his native ground,
Nor sweet equality with those around;)
Himself, and his, another's shrinks to find,   235
Levell'd below the lot of human kind.
Thus, shut from honour's paths, he turns to shame,
And filches the small good, he cannot claim.
To sour, and stupid, sinks his active mind;
Finds joys in drink, he cannot elsewhere find;   240
Rule disobeys; of half his labour cheats;
In some safe cot, the pilfer'd turkey eats;
Rides hard, by night, the steed, his art purloins;
Serene from conscience' bar himself essoins;
Sees from himself his sole redress must flow,   245
And makes revenge the balsam of his woe.

Thus slavery's blast bids sense and virtue die;
Thus lower'd to dust the sons of Afric lie.
Hence sages grave, to lunar systems given,
Shall ask, why two-legg'd brutes were made by
    Heaven;   250
.   .   .   .
All hail, thou western world! by heaven design'd
Th' example bright, to renovate mankind.
Soon shall thy sons across the mainland roam;
And claim, on far Pacific shores, their home;
Their rule, religion, manners, arts, convey,   255
And spread their freedom to the Asian sea.

Where erst six thousand suns have roll'd the year
O'er plains of slaughter, and o'er wilds of fear,
Towns, cities, fanes, shall lift their towery pride;
The village bloom, on every streamlet's side;   260
Proud Commerce' mole the western surges lave;
The long, white spire lie imag'd on the wave;
O'er morn's pellucid main expand their sails,
And the starr'd ensign court Korean gales.   264
Then nobler thoughts shall savage trains inform;
Then barbarous passions cease the heart to storm:
No more the captive circling flames devour;
Through the war path the Indian creep no more;
No midnight scout the slumbering village fire;
Nor the scalp'd infant stain his gasping sire: 270
But peace and truth, illumine the twilight mind,
The gospel's sunshine, and the purpose kind.
Where marshes teem'd with death, shall meads un-
    fold;
Untrodden cliffs resign their stores of gold;
The dance refin'd on Albion's margin move,   275
And her lone bowers rehearse the tale of love.
Where slept perennial night, shall science rise,
And new-born Oxfords cheer the evening skies;
Miltonic strains the Mexic hills prolong,
And Louis murmurs to Sicilian song.   280

Then to new climes the bliss shall trace its way,
And Tartar desarts hail the rising day;
From the long torpor startled China wake;
Her chains of misery rous'd Peruvia break;
Man link to man; with bosom bosom twine;   285
And one great bond the house of Adam join;
The sacred promise full completion know,
And peace, and piety, the world o'erflow.

[*A Female Worthy*]

Beyond that hillock, topp'd with scatter'd trees,
That meet, with freshest green, the hastening
    breeze,
There, where the glassy brook reflects the day,
Nor weeds, nor sedges, choke its crystal way,
Where budding willows feel the earliest spring,   5
And wonted red-breasts safely nest, and sing,
A female Worthy lives; and all the poor
Can point the way to her sequester'd door.

She, unseduc'd by dress and idle shew,
The forms, and rules, of fashion never knew;   10

310

Nor glittering in the ball, her form display'd;
Nor yet can tell a diamond, from a spade.
Far other objects claim'd her steady care;
The morning chapter, and the nightly prayer;
The frequent visit to the poor man's shed;   15
The wakeful nursing, at the sick man's bed;
Each day, to rise, before the early sun;
Each day, to see her daily duty done;
To cheer the partner of her household cares,   19
And mould her children, from their earliest years.

Small is her house; but fill'd with stores of good;
Good, earn'd with toil, and with delight bestow'd.
In the clean cellar, rang'd in order neat,
Gay-smiling Plenty boasts her casks of meat,   24
Points, to small eyes, the bins where apples glow,
And marks her cyder-butts, in stately row.
Her granary, fill'd with harvest's various pride,
Still sees the poor man's bushel laid aside;
Here swells the flaxen, there the fleecy store,   29
And the long wood-pile mocks the winter's power:
White are the swine; the poultry plump and large;
For every creature thrives, beneath her charge.

Plenteous, and plain, the furniture is seen;
All form'd for use, and all as silver clean.
On the clean dresser, pewter shines arow;   35
The clean-scower'd bowls are trimly set below;
While the wash'd coverlet, and linen white,
Assure the traveller a refreshing night.

Oft have I seen, and oft still hope to see,
This friend, this parent to the poor and me,   40
Tho' bent with years, and toil, and care, and woe,
Age lightly silver'd on her furrow'd brow,
Her frame still useful, and her mind still young,
Her judgment vigorous, and her memory strong,
Serene her spirits, and her temper sweet,   45
And pleas'd the youthful circle still to meet,
Cheerful, the long-accustom'd talk pursue,
Prevent the rust of age, and life renew;
To church, still pleas'd, and able still, to come, 49
And shame the lounging youth, who sleep at home.

Such are her toils, has been the bright reward;
For Heaven will always toils like these regard.
Safe, on her love, her truth and wisdom tried,
Her husband's heart, thro' lengthened life, relied;

From little, daily saw his wealth increase,   55
His neighbours love him, and his household bless;
In peace and plenty liv'd, and died resign'd,
And, dying, left six thousand pounds behind.
Her children, train'd to usefulness alone,
Still love the hand, which led them kindly on,   60
With pious duty, own her wise behest,
And, every day, rise up, and call her bless'd.

Travels in New-England and New-York

In September, 1796, a year after his election to the Yale presidency, Dwight began the course of travels during his vacations which he continued until 1815. A regard for his health was the least of the motives which sent him on his excursions. More compelling reasons were his eagerness to collect and to set forth information about the material and human resources of his beloved New England, and his desire to correct false impressions spread by ignorant or malicious foreign reporters. "Every new misrepresentation," Dwight declared, "made me more solicitous to carry it [his *Travels*] into execution." Dwight extended his itinerary to include New York, "as a considerable majority of its inhabitants are derived from New-England." The four huge volumes of the *Travels*, published posthumously in 1821–1822, testify to the author's insatiable intellectual curiosity which embraced the geography, institutions, resources, manners, and morals of the inhabitants of the region. Although the work was composed in the form of letters to "an English gentleman," Dwight failed to impart to his observations any illusion of the easy circumstantiality and informality of genuine letters. The text of the selections here reprinted is that of the first edition, *Travels in New-England and New-York* (4 vols., 1821–1822).

[Witchcraft]

From the year 1645, when the first suspicion of witchcraft in New England began at Springfield, several persons were accused of this crime. Of those who were accused, four (to wit, one at Charlestown, one at Dorchester, one at Cambridge, and one at Boston,) were executed. For almost thirty years afterwards, the subject seems to have slept in tolerable quiet. But in the year 1687, or 1688, four of the children of John Goodwin, a

311

respectable inhabitant of Boston, united in accusing a poor Irish woman of bewitching them. The accusation was unhappily regarded with an attention, which it very ill deserved. Not only did the citizens of the neighbourhood treat the subject as a thing of consequence; but a number of the Clergy held a day of fasting and prayer on the occasion at the house of Mr. Goodwin. This unhappy measure gave the affair a solemn aspect at once. . . .

The truth, as every intelligent, and candid, man will acknowledge, is: the existence of witchcraft had never been taken up by the human mind as a subject of investigation. This capital point had been uniformly omitted: and every enquirer, instead of examining whether there was any such thing as witchcraft, directed all his efforts to determine what were its causes, characteristics, proofs, limits, and effects. Where such was the nature of discussions, formed by Statesmen, Judges, Lawyers, and Divines; the only proper question concerning this subject must, it is obvious, be naturally and universally forgotten.

Near the close of February, 1692, two girls, about eleven years of age; (a daughter and a niece of Mr. Paris, minister of Danvers, then Salem-village;) and two other girls in the neighbourhood, began, as the children of Mr. Goodwin had done before, to act in a peculiar and unaccountable manner; creeping for example into holes, and under chairs, using many unnatural gestures, and uttering many ridiculous observations, equally destitute of sense and sobriety. This behaviour excited the attention of the neighbourhood. Several Physicians were consulted; all of whom, except one, declared themselves unable to assign a cause for these singular affections of the children. This man, more ignorant, or more superstitious, than his companions, confessed his suspicion, that the children were bewitched. The declaration appears to have been decisive. . . .

In the meantime fasts were multiplied. Several public ones were kept by the inhabitants of the village; and, finally, a general fast was holden throughout the Colony. By these successive solemnities the subject acquired a consideration literally sacred; and alarmed, and engrossed, the minds of the whole community. Magistrates,

and Clergymen, gave to it the weight of their belief, and their reputation; led their fellow-citizens into a labyrinth of error, and iniquity; and stained the character of their Country, in the eye of all succeeding generations. Had Mr. Paris, instead of listening to the complaints of the children in his family, and holding days of fasting, and prayer, on so preposterous an occasion, corrected them severely; had the physician, mentioned above, instead of pronouncing them bewitched, administered to them a strong dose of Ipecacuanha; had the magistrates, who received the accusations, and examined the accused, dismissed both, and ordered the accusers to prison, or finally, had the Judges of the Superior Court directed the first indictment to be quashed, and sent the prisoners home; the evil, in either of these stages, might undoubtedly have been stopped. But, unhappily all these were efforts of reason, which lay beyond the spirit of the times. . . .

[*New England Taverns*]

Your countrymen [the English] so often laugh at the fact, that Inns in New England are kept by persons, whose titles indicate them to be men of some consequence. . . . An Innkeeper in Great Britain, if I have not been misinformed, has usually no other respectability in the eyes of his countrymen, beside what he derives from his property, his civil manners, and his exact attention to the wishes of his guests. The fact is otherwise in New England. Our ancestors considered an Inn as a place, where corruption would naturally arise, and might easily spread; as a place, where travellers must trust themselves, their horses, baggage, and money; where women, as well as men, must at times lodge, might need humane and delicate offices, and might be subjected to disagreeable exposures. To provide for safety and comfort, and against danger and mischief, in all these cases, they took particular pains in their laws, and administrations, to prevent Inns from being kept by vicious, unprincipled, worthless men. Every Innkeeper in Connecticut must be recommended by the Selectmen, and Civil Authority, Constable and Grand Jurors of the town, in which he resides; and then licensed at the discretion of the Court of Common Pleas. Substantially in the same manner is the business regulated in Massachusetts and New Hampshire. In consequence of this system, men of no small personal respectability have ever kept Inns in this country. Here the contempt, with which Englishmen regard this subject, is not experienced, and is unknown. . . . A course of observation has convinced me, that our Ancestors were directed in their views concerning it by wisdom only. Unhappily, we have departed from their system, in instances sufficiently numerous to shew, but too plainly, our own folly. A great part of the New-England Innkeepers, however, and their families, treat a decent stranger, who behaves civilly to them, in such a manner, as to shew him plainly, that they feel an interest in his happiness; and, if he is sick or unhappy, will cheerfully contribute every thing in their power to his relief. . . .

[*Perfection in a State of Nature*]

You have, here, an account [of the degradation of the Indians] of that very state of society, which is preferred, and extolled by Godwin,[n] as the perfection of man. Here the human race, as nearly as possible, are without the restraint of law, morals, or religion. At the same time they are free in the fullest sense. No private individual possesses, or exercises, any power to control their conduct; and the Government of Connecticut, either from despair of doing them any good, or from the unwillingness of its magistrates to execute law among these people, seems, in a manner which I cannot justify, to have resigned them to the dictates of their own passions and appetites. Flagrant breaches of law would undoubtedly be punished in them as in others. At least, such as respected property, life, or limb. But few or no exertions have for a long time been made to restrain their commission of inferiour crimes; and to these crimes alone do they appear at present to have any strong propensity; i.e., as they estimate crimes; for lewdness seems not to be considered by them as criminal. Ordinarily, they do just what they please.

Promiscuous concubinage also, Godwin's great and favourite step towards perfection, they practice in the most unlimited manner. Nor are they less perfectly possessed of his other two essential ingredients in the constitution of his happy society. Why then are they not perfect and happy?

There are two great reasons to be assigned as an answer to this question, both of which have escaped this hoodwinked philosopher. The first is, that human depravity, or, in other words, sin, has no tendency to make a happy society; but, among all intelligent beings, will always render the social state unhappy, in exact proportion to the degree in which it exists. The other is, that labour is the only source of those enjoyments, which make up what Godwin calls happiness, and, that without the dominion of law, which alone secures to man the benefit of his efforts, no human being will labour. Godwin, and his associates, feel as if themselves should be happier if they were freed from the restraints which I have mentioned; not mistrusting, that without them, others, enjoying the same licentiousness of disposition, and the same impunity in indulging it, would plunder them of liberty, property, and life. Equally are they insensible, that without the perfection of law none would labour, and no part of those enjoyments, on which they riot, be brought into existence. Without law, religion, and morals, they might, indeed, be fornicators, and adulterers, thieves and assassins; but they would be beggars and vagabonds. The very wickedness which prompted Godwin to write his books, and which he has poured out upon almost every page with a portentous turpitude, would render all around him as hostile to him, as he is to religion, morals, and government; and make whatever he thought his own rights the tennis-ball of injustice and cruelty. In addition to all this . . . population instead of being increased would rapidly decay. These Indians have continually declined in their numbers, notwithstanding their decrease has been checked by their cohabitation with the blacks. Where the fruits of no man's labour are secured; where no man has acknowledged children to labour for; where, according to the wish of Godwin, every child is without a known father, and possessed of a casual

Godwin: William Godwin (1756–1836), English philosopher and novelist, whose *Political Justice* (1793) influenced Shelley and other romantic poets. He believed that laws and institutions were not necessary for harmonious and rational living.

313

instead of a family name, no man will labour. . . . What a pity it is, that Godwin, and all who relish his doctrines, should not obtain the privilege of sharing in the dignity and happiness, enjoyed in this state of human perfection!

[Yankee Enterprise]

A person who has extensively seen the efforts of the New-England people in colonizing new countries, cannot fail of being forcibly struck by 10 their enterprise, industry, and perseverance. In Maine, in New-Hampshire, in Vermont, in Massachusetts, and in New-York, I have passed the dwellings of several hundred thousand of these people, erected on grounds, which in 1760 were an absolute wilderness. A large part of these tracts they have already converted into fruitful fields; covered it with productive farms; surrounded it with enclosures; planted on it orchards; and beautified it with comfortable, and in many places with 20 handsome, houses. Considerable tracts I have traced through their whole progress from a desert to a garden; and have literally beheld the wilderness blossom as the rose.

There are minds, to whom little else than romantic adventures, splendid villas and palaces, the pomp of courts, the progress of armies, the glory of victories, and other magnificent displays of wealth and power, can give even a transient pleasure. To me there is something far more de- 30 lightful in contemplating the diffusion of enterprise and industry over an immense forest; where no oppression gives birth to the efforts of man; no sufferings have preceded the splendour; and no sacrifice of life, or even of comfort, is necessary to the existence of the triumph. The process is, here, all voluntary and free. In its several stages the forest is converted into a cultivated country; and lands literally useless, are made to yield sustenance, and convenience, to mankind. Poverty 40 is here commuted for competence, and competence for wealth. Towns and villages, in vast multitudes, rise up in the retreats of bears, and wolves; and churches assemble for the worship of God the numerous inhabitants, to whom He has given so goodly a heritage. Schools also, and colleges, enlighten, here, the young mind with the rudiments, and in many instances with the higher

attainments, of knowledge. Thus rational and virtuous man sees his race multiplying beyond all customary calculation, in the midst of blessings, equally and universally diffused, and obtained without fraud, without oppression, and without blood.

[New-England Women]

. . . The women of New-England are generally well, and often elegantly, formed. Their features have usually a good degree of regularity, are comely, and frequently handsome. Their complexion, like that of the men, is not so generally fair as that of the Irish, British, and other European women in the North, but very sensibly fairer than that of the French women; and a vast number of them have complexions inferiour to none in the world. In great numbers they have fine eyes; both blue and black; and generally possess that bloom, which health inimitably suffuses over a beautiful countenance. But regular features united with the most delicate complexion, cannot form beauty. This charming attribute, so coveted by one sex, and so fascinating to the other, is, as an eminent poet of your country has said,

an air divine,
Through which the mind's all gentle graces shine;
They, like the sun, irradiate all between;
And the face charms, because the soul is seen.

In this respect the women of New-England, to a great extent, triumph. Their minds, often possessing a fine share of intelligence, are remarkably distinguished by amiable dispositions. A gentle and affectionate temper, ornamented with sprightliness, and gilded with serenity, may be fairly considered as being extensively their proper character. They are said, by some of your countrymen, to be too feminine; and are certainly less masculine than most of their sex, who have visited these States from England or the European continent. To us, this is a delightful part of their character.

Their manners are in entire symmetry with their minds and faces. An universal sweetness and gentleness, blended with sprightly energy, is their most predominant characteristic. There is nothing languid in their deportment, and rarely any thing affected. They are affable, obliging, and

314

cheerful; while they are at the same time grave, discreet, and very rarely betrayed into any impropriety.

Very many of them are distinguished for moral excellence; are unaffectedly pious, humble, benevolent, patient, and self-denying. In this illustrious sphere of distinction, they put our own sex to shame. Were the church of Christ stripped of her female communicants, she would lose many of her brightest ornaments, and, I fear, two thirds of her whole family.

In perfect accordance with this representation, the women of New-England perform, in an exemplary manner, the various duties of life. They are almost universally industrious, economical, attentive to their families, and diligent in the education and government of their children. They are, to a great extent, excellent wives, mothers, and daughters. Few countries, it is believed, present, in proportion to the number of their inhabitants, so many instances of domestic good order, peace, and happiness.

The employments of the women of New-England are wholly domestic. The business, which is abroad, is all performed by men, even in the humblest spheres of life. That of the house is usually left entirely to the direction of the women, and is certainly managed by them with skill and propriety. Domestic concerns admit of improvement, and even of science; and it must, I believe, be acknowledged, that we might learn in this particular several useful things from you. Our economy is less systematical, and less perfect, than yours; and our activity sometimes less skilfully directed. I am apprehensive, however, that we approach nearer to you in the house, than either in the shop or the field. The houses, in this country are, with their furniture, almost all kept in good order; and a general neatness prevails, even among those who are in humble circumstances. Indeed a great part of the women in this country exert quite as much industry as is consistent with the preservation of health.[n]

There is another employment, in which I think they merit high encomiums. This is the diffusion of beneficence among the suffering. In

this they far excel the other sex, and discover more skill, more patience, more activity, and universally more excellence.

From these observations you will easily perceive that the female sex hold here an honourable station in society, and have an important influence upon its concerns. The first place at the table, in the family, in the social circle, and in every other situation where they are found, is given to them of course. On all occasions, they are treated with marked attention and respect; and the man, who behaves rudely or insolently to a woman, is considered as hardly meriting the name.

I have already given you a summary account of the manner in which young misses are educated in this country. They are all sent early to school; where they are taught to spell, and read, and write. From parochial schools, many of them are transferred to boarding-schools and academies. Here they learn to understand arithmetic, which indeed is usually taught them in parochial schools, and study English grammar, geography, history to some extent, criticism, and composition. In a few instances they are taught moral science, and in some ascend to higher branches of mathematics, the Latin and French languages. To these are added embroidery, drawing, and music.

On this subject I feel bound to observe, that we are in my own opinion seriously defective. Efforts of a higher nature than any which we make, are due to their daughters, from all persons who are possessed of wealth. The great doctrines of physical and moral science are as intelligible by the mind of a female, as by that of a male; and, were they made somewhat less technical, and stripped so far of some of their unnecessary accompaniments as to wear in a greater degree the aspect of common sense, might be introduced with advantage into every female academy where the instructor was competent to teach them. It is evidently high time that women should be considered less as pretty, and more as rational, and immortal beings; and that so far as the circumstances of parents will permit, their minds should be early led to the attainment of solid sense and sound wisdom. The instructions, which are, or ought to be, given by mothers, are of more importance to the well-being of children, than any which are, or can be given

Indeed . . . health: See on this subject at large, the remarks on Lambert. (Dwight's note)

315

by fathers. To give these instructions, they ought, as far as may be, to be thoroughly qualified, even if we were to act on selfish principles only. Such a design, extensively reduced to practice, would in any country change the whole state of society; and raise it to a dignity of which it is otherwise incapable.

The disposition to provide a superiour education for female children, is in this country widely diffused, and continually increasing. No regular scheme, however, has been formed on this subject, within my knowledge; and I have hitherto met with no books, which treat the sciences last specified, in a manner satisfactory either to my views or to my wishes. It is earnestly to be hoped, that ere long both these defects may be supplied; and that the women of this country, who, so far as they possess advantages, appear in no respect to be behind the other sex either in capacity or disposition to improve, may no longer be precluded from the best education by the negligence of men.

It is said, and I suspect with truth, that the American women lose their beauty and the brilliancy of youth at an earlier period of life than in England. A great part of them are slender. Multitudes lose their teeth at an untimely date; and many of them part with their bloom before they are thirty years of age. The causes of these disadvantages belong to the province of the learned among physicians. I may be permitted, however, to observe, that among them abstemiousness, which here is very general in that sex, and often excessive, probably has its share. The want of sufficient exercise abroad, has a still more malignant influence. Sedentariness seems regularly to be considered as intimately connected with the gentility of the female character. Walking is very little practised; and riding on horse-back, notwithstanding it exhibits the female figure to so much advantage, is almost out of the question. Until there is a material change in these respects, the women of New-England must be satisfied to yield their health, and youth, and bloom, and beauty, as an untimely sacrifice to the Moloch of fashion. The teeth of children, their mothers might preserve. Nothing more would be necessary than to compel them to commence life with vigourous exercise, and continue it; to avoid hot drinks, particularly, by requiring their children to eat milk, or thoroughly to dilute with it their tea and coffee; and to make their teeth cold by agitating cold water in the mouth five times a day; that is, once in the morning, once in the evening, and once after each meal. Could we learn wisdom from the Asiatics, and habituate ourselves to regular bathing; and follow that of our ancestors, by permitting children when at school to play during the session half an hour in the morning, and half an hour in the afternoon, encouraging those of both sexes to vigourous activity; the work of preserving health would in a great measure be accomplished.

To the character, which I have given of the women of New-England, there are unquestionably many exceptions. We have homely women, we have ignorant women, we have silly women, we have coarse women, and we have vicious women. At the same time we have no reason, in these particulars, to dread a comparison with other countries. In the most fashionable life we have frivolous women, who, having nothing to do, or choosing to do nothing of a useful nature, find time hangs heavily on them. To relieve themselves from the ennui, flowing of course from the want of regular and useful engagements, women of this description crowd to the theatre, the assembly-room, the card-table, routs, and squeezes; flutter from door to door on ceremonious visits, and from shop to shop to purchase what they do not want, and to look at what they do not intend to purchase; hurry to watering places, to recover health which they have not lost; and hurry back again in pursuit of pleasure which they cannot find. Happily, the number of these is not very great, even in our cities.

I am, Sir, yours, &c.

[The Notch of the White Mountains]

The Notch of the White Mountains is a phrase, appropriated to a very narrow defile, extending two miles in length between two huge cliffs, apparently rent asunder by some vast convulsion of nature. This convulsion was, in my own view, unquestionably that of the deluge. . . . When we entered the Notch we were struck with the wild and solemn appearance of everything before us. The scale, on which all the objects in view were formed, was the scale of grandeur only. The rocks, rude and ragged in a manner rarely paralleled, were fashioned, and piled on each other, by a hand, operating only in the boldest and most irregular manner. As we advanced, these appearances increased rapidly. Huge masses of granite, of every abrupt form, and hoary with a moss which seemed the product of ages, recalling to the mind the "*Saxum Vetustum*" of Virgil speedily rose to a mountainous height. Before us, the view widened fast to the South-East. Behind us, it closed almost instantaneously; and presented nothing to the eye, but an impassable barrier of mountains.

About half a mile from the entrance of the chasm, we saw in full view the most beautiful cascade, perhaps, in the world. It issued from a mountain on the right, about eight hundred feet above the subjacent valley, and at the distance of about two miles from us. The stream ran over a series of rocks, almost perpendicular, with the course so little broken, as to preserve the appearance of a uniform current, and yet so far disturbed, as to be perfectly white. The sun shone with the clearest splendour from a station in the heavens, the most advantageous to our prospect; and the cascade glittered down the vast steep, like a stream of burnished silver.

At the distance of three quarters of a mile from the entrance, we passed a brook, known in this region by the name of the Flume; from the strong resemblance to that object, exhibited by the channel, which it has worn for a considerable length in a bed of rocks; the sides being perpendicular to the bottom. . . . The stream fell from a height of 240 or 250 feet over three precipices: the second receding a small distance from the front of the first, and the third from that of the second. Down the first and second, it fell in a single current; and down the third in three, which united their streams at the bottom in a fine basin, formed by the hand of nature in the rocks, immediately beneath us. It is impossible for a brook of this size to be modelled into more diversified, or more delightful, forms; or for a cascade to descend over precipices more happily fitted to finish its beauty. The cliffs, together with a level at their foot, furnished a considerable opening, surrounded by the forest. The sun-beams, penetrating through the trees, painted here a great variety of fine images of light, and edged an equally numerous, and diversified, collection of shadows; both dancing on the waters, and alternately silvering and obscuring their course. Purer water was never seen. Exclusively of its murmurs, the world around us was solemn and silent. Every thing assumed the character of enchantment; and, had I been educated in the Grecian mythology, I should scarcely have been surprised to find an assemblage of Dryads, Naiads, and Oreades, sporting on the little plain below our feet. . . .

HUGH HENRY BRACKENRIDGE (1748-1816)

ORATOR, politician, jurist, editor, poet, and satirical novelist, H. H. Brackenridge is chiefly memorable today for his vivid pictures of democratic life in the early days of the republic. In the early seventeen-nineties— a full generation before the political triumph of Jacksonianism—Brackenridge was studying the ways of frontier democrats, with their forthrightness, crudity, and ignorance. Although a democrat himself, Brackenridge was trained in the school of Lucian and Cervantes, of Rabelais, Samuel Butler, and Swift; and he had the education, detachment, and understanding that enabled him to present the principles and fallacies which underlay the pioneer philosophy. From the Whisky Rebellion in 1793-1794 to the War of 1812, which was essentially a western war, he studied and satirized the American scene. His relation to American democracy is therefore distinct: Jefferson expounded its principles; Freneau defended them against the staunch Federalists; Brackenridge depicted democratic practices with sympathy and penetration.

Brackenridge, who was born in Scotland in 1748, came to this country at the age of five with his moneyless parents. They settled in York County, Pennsylvania, where they lived the hard life of pioneers. By diligence and labor, and with the encouragement of his mother, Henry managed to get what education the community afforded. At fifteen he taught school, and saved enough money, after five years, to enter Princeton in 1767. He was graduated in 1771, in the same class as his friends James Madison and Philip Freneau.

His undergraduate skill in composition and forensics is shown in the commencement poem, "The Rising Glory of America," which he wrote in collaboration with Freneau. After graduation he taught school for three years, earned a master's degree in theology in 1776, served for two years as a chaplain in the Revolution, and then gave up the ministry because of his liberal theological interpretations. Thereafter he followed two paths, the law as a career and a means of livelihood, and literature as a beloved avocation.

In January, 1779, he issued the first number of the *United States Magazine*, which he edited for a year, and published many youthful satires. The only enduring products of this venture are some of Freneau's poems. In 1781 he went to the frontier town of Pittsburgh to practice law. Here, five years later, he helped to found the first newspaper in Pittsburgh, the *Gazette* (1786), and was a frequent contributor to its columns. In the crucial years of 1787–1788 he worked zealously in support of the new Federal Constitution. Six years later he was struggling to soften the lacerated feelings aroused by the Whisky Rebellion, described in his *Incidents of the Insurrection* (1795). In 1799 he was made a justice of the Supreme Court of Pennsylvania, an appointment which he held until his death in 1816.

Brackenridge was an aristocratic democrat whose devotion to the principles of democracy did not blind him to the weaknesses and abuses in contemporary democratic life. An astute political and literary leader, he poured most of his ideas on democracy into the one work on which his fame rests, *Modern Chivalry*, a satirical, picaresque novel. While Brackenridge was tolerant in his views of western democracy and understood its unquestioned excellencies, his shrewdly satiric comment upon frontier leveling reveals that he was not a blind worshipper of demos. In no other work before Fenimore Cooper is there so clear and so vigorous a view of the dangers of irresponsible equalitarianism and the limitations of democratic machinery. The aggressiveness of selfish ambition parading as political wisdom he reprobated on every hand. As life's incongruities and the conflicts of his own life burned robustly in his mind, he added episode after episode to the narrative, piling satire upon satire in realistic dialogue. Brackenridge completed half of *Modern Chivalry* before the turn of the century. His writings after 1804 are primarily devoted to a defense of law and judges against militant attacks by Pennsylvania extremists. He was active in preserving the wisdom of the English common law for the American courts by the publication of *Law Miscellanies* in 1814. Earlier, in 1806, he collected a volume of his journalistic writings, and he compiled meanwhile his dispersed meditations for the last section of *Modern Chivalry* (1815). Brackenridge was a successful lawyer, but better known, despite some unpopularity resulting from the asperity of his pen, as an effective propagandist and as an honest and sturdy citizen. *Modern Chivalry* survives today as the most readable of eighteenth-century American novels.

BIBLIOGRAPHY · There has been no collected edition of Brackenridge's work. His *Battle of Bunker's Hill* (1776) was reissued in M. J. Moses, *Representative American Plays* (1918). *Modern Chivalry* (1792–1815) was reissued in its entirety, with an excellent critical introduction by Claude Newlin, in the American Fiction Series (1937). The only full biography is Claude Newlin's *The Life and Writings of Hugh Henry Brackenridge* (1932). C. F. Heartman compiled a *Bibliography of the Writings of Hugh Henry Brackenridge* in 1917. Other biographical and critical studies include H. M. Brackenridge, *Memoir*, printed in the 1846, and 1856 abridgements of *Modern Chivalry*; and M. I. Eakin, "Hugh Henry Brackenridge, Lawyer," *Western Pennsylvania Historical Magazine* (July, 1927).

Modern Chivalry

Since *Modern Chivalry* appeared in sections over a period of twenty-three years (1792–1815), and represents the author's judgments upon contemporary events, it obviously lacks the kind of unity that can be summarized in a brief introductory note. Brackenridge's attitudes to the French Revolution, to the Whisky Insurrection, to Jefferson, and to the press, and his opinions upon many nonpolitical topics were introduced as their timeliness stirred him. The Pittsburgh of his day was a trading center with a rough-and-tumble life, and democracy was lacking in refinement and in orderly procedure. To this community he brought the classical standards of an educated man insistent upon intellectual poise and suspended judgment.

His decision to indulge in general satire he set forth as follows:

We have often been asked for a key to this work. Every man of sense has the key in his own pocket. His own feelings; his own experience is the key. It is astonishing, with what avidity, we look for the application of satire which is general, and never had a prototype. But the fact is, that, in this work, the picture is taken from human nature, generally, and has no individual in view. It was never meant as a satire upon men; but upon things. An easy way, to slur sentiments, under the guise of allegory; which could not otherwise make their way to the ears of the curious. Can any man, suppose, upon reflection, that if ridicule was intended upon real persons, it would be conveyed in so bungling a manner that people would be at a loss to know, who was meant? That is not the way we fix our fools' caps.

Brackenridge suggested the model for his work in the conclusion to Part II, Volume II, though he disclaimed any intention of slavishly following any predecessor:

Comparing great things with small, we have written this book in the manners of certain of the ancients; that is, with a *dramatic cast*. The book of Job is amongst the earliest of all compositions, and after an introduction containing the history of his misfortunes, and malady, introduces the speakers in three different characters, and names, each sustaining his opinion; and giving the author an opportunity to canvass the subject he had in view, the ways of Providence, and to give lessons of humility and resignation to man.

The Socratic schools, and amongst these, have distinguished themselves chiefly, Plato in his dialogues, and Zenophon, in his Symposium, or Banquet.

It has been followed by the Romans; of whom Cicero in his book treating of the qualifications of an orator, or, as we commonly stile it, *de oratore*, is the happiest instance.

Sir Thomas More introduces his Utopia, in this manner. But the most complete model of such structure of writing, is a posthumous work of David Hume, his "Religion of Nature."

The vehicle which I have chosen of supposed travels, and conversations, affords great scope, and much freedom, and furnishes an opportunity to enliven with incident. Doubtless it is of the same nature, with many things in the novel way, written by philosophic men, who chose that form of writing, for the purpose merely of conveying sentiments, which in a didactic work, under the head of tract or dissertation, could not so easily gain attention, or procure readers.

But the characters which we have introduced, are many of them low. That gives the greater relief to the mind.

> The eye withdraws itself, to rest,
> Upon the green of folly's breast.

Shakespeare has his Bardolph, Nym, and Pistol, and the dialogue of these is a relief to the drama of the principal personages. It is so in nature; and why should it not be so represented in the images of her works. We have the sage and the fool, interspersed in society, and the fool gives occasion for the wise man to make his reflections. So in our book.

[A Frontier Campaign]

THE TEXT is that of the first edition of *Modern Chivalry*, Book I, Chapter III, published in 1792 in Philadelphia. This biting satire arose from Brackenridge's own humiliating defeat when running for political office.

The captain rising early next morning, and setting out on his way, had now arrived at a place where a number of people were convened, for the purpose of electing persons to represent them in the legislature of the state. There was a weaver who was a candidate for this appointment, and seemed to have a good deal of interest among the people. But another, who was a man of education, was his competitor. Relying on some talent of speaking which he thought he possessed, he addressed the multitude.

Said he, Fellow Citizens, I pretend not to any great abilities; but am conscious to myself that I have the best good will to serve you. But it is very astonishing to me, that this weaver should conceive himself qualified for the trust. For though my acquirements are not great, yet his are still less. The mechanical business which he pursues, must necessarily take up so much of his time, that he cannot apply himself to political studies. I should therefore think it would be more answerable to your dignity, and conducive to your interest, to be represented by a man at least of some letters, than by an illiterate handicraftsman like this. It will be more honourable for himself, to remain at his loom and knot threads, than to come forward in a legislative capacity: because, in the one case, he is in the sphere where God and nature has placed him; in the other, he is like a fish out of water, and must struggle for breath in a new element.

Is it possible he can understand the affairs of government, whose mind has been concentered to the small object of weaving webs; to the price by yard, the grist of the thread, and such like matters as concern a manufacturer of cloths? The feet of him who weaves, are more occupied than the head, or at least as much; and therefore the whole man must be, at least, but in half accustomed to exercise his mental powers. For these reasons, all other things set aside, the chance is in my favour, with respect to information. However, you will decide, and give your suffrages to him or to me, as you shall judge expedient.

The Captain hearing these observations, and looking at the weaver, could not help advancing, and undertaking to subjoin something in support of what had been just said. Said he, I have no prejudice against a weaver more than another man.

Nor do I know any harm in the trade; save that from the sedentary life in a damp place, there is usually a paleness of the countenance: but this is a physical, not a moral evil. Such usually occupy subterranean apartments; not for the purpose, like Demosthenes, of shaving their heads, and writing over eight times the history of Thucydides, and perfecting a stile of oratory; but rather to keep the thread moist; or because this is considered but as an inglorious sort of trade, and is frequently thrust away into cellars, and damp outhouses, which are not occupied for a better use.

But to rise from the cellar to the senate house, would be an unnatural hoist. To come from counting threads, and adjusting them to the splits of a reed, to regulate the finances of a government, would be preposterous; there being no congruity in the case. There is no analogy between knotting threads and framing laws. It would be a reversion of the order of things. Not that a manufacturer of linen or woolen, or other stuff, is an inferior character, but a different one, from that which ought to be employed in affairs of state. It is unnecessary to enlarge on this subject; for you must all be convinced of the truth and propriety of what I say. But if you will give me leave to take the manufacturer aside a little, I think I can explain to him my ideas on the subject; and very probably prevail with him to withdraw his pretensions. The people seeming to acquiesce, and beckoning to the weaver, they drew aside, and the Captain addressed him in the following words:

Mr. Traddle, said he, for that was the name of the manufacturer, I have not the smallest idea of wounding your sensibility; but it would seem to me, it would be more your interest to pursue your occupation, than to launch out into that of which you have no knowledge. When you go to the senate house, the application to you will not be to warp a web; but to make laws for the commonwealth. Now, suppose that the making these laws, requires a knowledge of commerce, or of the interests of agriculture, or those principles upon which the different manufactures depend, what service could you render? It is possible you might think justly enough; but could you speak? You are not in the habit of public speaking. You are not furnished with those commonplace ideas, with

which even very ignorant men can pass for knowing something. There is nothing makes a man so ridiculous as to attempt what is above his sphere. You are no tumbler for instance; yet should you give out that you vault upon a man's back; or turn head over heels, like the wheels of a cart; the stiffness of your joints would encumber you; and you would fall upon your backside to the ground. Such a squash as that would do you damage. The getting up to ride on the state is an unsafe thing to those who are not accustomed to such horsemanship. It is a disagreeable thing for a man to be laughed at, and there is no way of keeping ones self from it but by avoiding all affectation.

While they were thus discoursing, a bustle had taken place among the croud. Teague hearing so much about elections, and serving the government, took it into his head, that he could be a legislator himself. The thing was not displeasing to the people, who seemed to favour his pretensions; owing, in some degree, to there being several of his countrymen among the croud; but more especially to the fluctuation of the popular mind, and a disposition to what is new and ignoble. For though the weaver was not the most elevated object of choice, yet he was still preferable to this tatter-demalion, who was but a menial servant, and had so much of what is called the brogue on his tongue, as to fall far short of an elegant speaker.

The Captain coming up, and finding what was on the carpet, was greatly chagrined at not having been able to give the multitude a better idea of the importance of a legislative trust; alarmed also, from an apprehension of the loss of his servant. Under these impressions he resumed his address to the multitude. Said he, This is making the matter still worse, gentlemen: this servant of mine is but a bog-trotter; who can scarcely speak the dialect in which your laws ought to be written; but certainly has never read a single treatise on any political subject; for the truth is, he cannot read at all. The young people of the lower class, in Ireland, have seldom the advantage of a good education; especially the descendants of the ancient Irish, who have most of them a great assurance of countenance, but little information, or literature. This young man, whose family name is Oregan, has been my servant for several years. And, except a too great fondness for women, which now and then brings him into scrapes, he has demeaned himself in a manner tolerable enough. But he is totally ignorant of the great principles of legislation; and more especially, the particular interests of the government. A free government is a noble possession to a people: and this freedom consists in an equal right to make laws, and to have the benefit of the laws when made. Though doubtless, in such a government, the lowest citizen may become chief magistrate; yet it is sufficient to possess the right; not absolutely necessary to exercise it. Or even if you should think proper, now and then, to shew your privilege, and exert, in a signal manner, the democratic prerogative, yet is it not descending too low to filch away from me a hireling, which I cannot well spare, to serve your purposes. You are surely carrying the matter too far, in thinking to make a senator of this hostler; to take him away from an employment to which he has been bred, and put him to another, to which he has served no apprenticeship: to set those hands which have been lately employed in currying my horse, to the draughting bills, and preparing business for the house.

The people were tenacious of their choice, and insisted on giving Teague their suffrages; and by the frown upon their brows, seemed to indicate resentment at what has been said; as indirectly charging them with want of judgment; or calling in question their privilege to do what they thought proper. It is a very strange thing, said one of them, who was a speaker for the rest, that after having conquered Burgoyne and Cornwallis, and got a government of our own, we cannot put in it whom we please. This young man be your servant, or another man's servant; but if we chuse to make him a delegate, what is that to you. He may not be yet skilled in the matter, but there is a good day a-coming. We will impower him; and it is better to trust a plain man like him, than one of your high flyers, that will make laws to suit their own purposes.

Said the Captain, I had much rather you would send the weaver, though I thought that improper, than to invade my household, and thus detract from me the very person that I have about me to brush my boots, and clean my spurs. The pro-

locutor of the people gave him to understand that his surmises were useless, for the people had determined on the choice, and Teague they would have for a representative.

Finding it answered no end to expostulate with the multitude, he requested to speak a word with Teague by himself. Stepping aside, he said to him, composing his voice, and addressing him in a soft manner: Teague, you are quite wrong in this matter they have put into your head. Do you know what it is to be a member of a deliberate body? What qualifications are necessary? Do you understand any thing of geography? If a question should be, to make a law to dig a canal in some part of the state, can you describe the bearing of the mountains, and the course of the rivers? Or if commerce is to be pushed to some new quarter, by the force of regulations, are you competent to decide in such a case? There will be questions of law, and astronomy on the carpet. How you must gape and stare like a fool, when you come to be asked your opinion on these subjects? Are you acquainted with the abstract principles of finance; ... with the ways and means of raising the revenue; providing for the discharge of the public debts, and all other things which respect the economy of the government? Even if you had knowledge, have you a facility of speaking? I would suppose you would have too much pride to go to the house just to say, Ay, or No. This is not the fault of your nature, but of your education; having been accustomed to dig turf in your early years, rather than instructing yourself in the classics, or common school books.

When a man becomes a member of a public body, he is like a raccoon, or other beast that climbs up the fork of a tree; the boys pushing at him with pitch-forks, or throwing stones, or shooting at him with an arrow, the dogs barking in the mean time. One will find fault with your not speaking; another with your speaking, if you speak at all. They will have you in the news papers, and ridicule you as a perfect beast. There is what they call the caricatura; that is, representing you with a dog's head, or a cat's claw. As you have a red head, they will very probably make a fox of you, or a sorrel horse, or a brindled cow, or the like. It is the devil in hell to be exposed to the squibs

321

and crackers of the gazette wits and publications. You know no more about these matters than a goose; and yet you would undertake rashly, without advice, to enter on the office; nay, contrary to advice. For I would not for a thousand guineas, though I have not the half of it to spare, that the breed of the Oregans should come to this; bringing on them a worse stain than stealing sheep; to which they are addicted. You have nothing but your character, Teague, in a new country to depend upon. Let it never be said, that you quitted an honest livelihood, the taking care of my horse, to follow the new fangled whims of the times, and to be a statesman.

Teague was moved chiefly with the last part of the address, and consented to give up the object.

The Captain, glad of this, took him back to the people, and announced his disposition to decline the honour which they had intended him.

Teague acknowledged that he had changed his mind, and was willing to remain in a private station.

The people did not seem well pleased with the Captain; but as nothing more could be said about the matter, they turned their attention to the weaver, and gave him their suffrages.

[*Reflections on the French Revolution*]

THE TEXT is that of the edition of *Modern Chivalry*, Volume I, Part II, Chapter III, published in 1807 in Carlisle.

I never had a doubt with the Captain, but that the bulk of the Jacobins in France meant well; even Marat and Robespierre considered themselves as denouncing, and trucidating only the enemies of the republic. What a delightful trait of virtue discovers itself in the behavior of Peregrine, the brother of Robespierre, and proves that he thought his brother innocent. "I am innocent; and my brother is as innocent as I am." Doubtless they were both innocent. Innocent of what? Why; of meaning ill. "The time shall come, when they that kill you, shall think they are doing God service." Peregrine, led the column with his drawn sword in his hand, that entered and re-took Toulon. He threw himself into the denunciation. This ought to be a lesson to all republicans to have charity, for those that differ in opinion. Tiberius,

and Caius Gracchus at Rome meant well; Agis, and Cleomines at Sparta, the same; but they attempted a reform, well, in vision and imagination; but beyond what was practicable or expedient. They fell victims to the not distinguishing the times; the advanced state of society, which did not comport with the original simplicity of institutions.

Marat the journalist and Robespierre were pushed gradually to blood; by the principle, which governed them, of taking it for granted that all who thought differently upon a subject were traitors; and that a majority of vote was the criterion of being right. The mountain, the bulk of the national assembly, could not but be in their opinion, infallible. The eternal mountain at whose foot every one was disposed to place himself; the mountain on whose top were "thunders and lightnings, and a thick cloud;" but not a natural mountain of the earth, collecting refreshing showers, and from which descended streams. It was a mountain pregnant with subterranean fire. It burst, and exists a volcano to this day. So much for the majority of a public body, being always right; and so much for a journalist meaning well, and yet destroying the republic. It is a truth in nature, and a maxim in philosophy "that from whence our greatest good springs, our greatest evils arise." A journalist of spirit is a desideratum in a revolution. But when the new island, or continent is thrown up from the bottom of the ocean; and the subterranean gas dissipated, why seek for a convulsion? But rather leave nature to renew herself with forests, and rivers, and perennial springs. But that activity which was useful in the first effort, is unwilling to be checked in the further employment; and under the idea of a progressing reform, turns upon the establishment which it has produced, and intending good, does harm. The men are denounced that mean as well as the journalist, and perhaps understand the game better than himself though they differ in judgment on the move. In a revolution, every man thinks he has done all. He knows only, or chiefly, what he has done himself. Hence he is intolerant of the opinions of others, because he is ignorant of the services which are a proof of patriotism; and of the interest which is a pledge of fidelity. Fresh hands especially, are apt to over-do the matter, as I have seen at the building of a cabbin in the western country. A strong man takes hold of the end of a log, and he lifts faster than the other. From the unskilfulness and inequality of his exertions, accidents happen. Prudent people do not like rash hands. States have been best built up, by the wise as well as the honest.

There are men that we dislike in office. All men approved Marius, says the historian Sallust, when he began to proscribe, now and then, a bad man; but they did not foresee what soon happened, that he did not stop short, but went on to proscribe the good. It is better to bear an individual mischief, than a public inconvenience. This is a maxim of the common law. That is, it is better to endure an evil in a particular case, than to violate a general principle. There ought to be constitutional ground, and a just cause to remove the obnoxious. It will not do even in Ireland, to hang a man for stealing cloth, because he is a bad weaver.

Where parties exist in a republic, that party will predominate eventually which pursues justice. A democratic party, will find its only security in this. "If these things are done in the green tree, what shall be done in the dry." If democracy is not just, what shall we expect from aristocracy, where the pride of purse, and pride of family, raises the head; swells the port; produces the strut, and all the undervaluing which the few have for the many? Aristocracy, which claims by hereditary right, the honours and emoluments of the commonwealth. Who does not dislike the presumption of the purse proud, and the pride of connections? And it is for that reason that I wish my fellow democrats, "my brethren according to the flesh," to do right; to shew their majesty, the nobility of their nature, by their discrimination, and their sense of justice. For I am a democrat, if having no cousin, and no funds; and only to rely on my personal services, can make me one. And I believe this is a pretty good pledge for democracy in any man. Unless indeed, he should become a tool to those that have cousins and funds; and this he will not do if he has pride. He might be made a despot, but this can only be by the peoples destroying the essence of liberty, by pushing it to licentiousness. A despot is a spectre which

rises chiefly from the marsh of licentiousness. It was the jacobins made Bonaparte what he now is.

[On Judges and Laws]

THE TEXT is that of the edition of *Modern Chivalry*, Volume I, Part II, Chapter XII, published in 1808 in Philadelphia.

Having turned his back on the hospital, (the Captain saw) there was a concourse of people; the cry was a new code of laws.

A *new* code, said a grave man, Is not the *old*, the result of experience, a gradual accession of rules and regulations in society? Begin again, and you would come to the same result at last. But to form laws from abstract comprehension, fitted to all exigencies, is not within the compass of the powers of man. It is sufficient if he can form a schedule or plan of government; this is the outline; the interior gyrations, must be made up from repeated experiments.

The words *new* code, were mistaken by some amongst the crowd, for *no* code.

No code, was repeated through the multitude.

What, no laws at all, said the grave man?

No laws, was the outcry immediately, and every vociferous person wishing to hear himself speak, and every timid person, afraid of being suspected of incivicism, began to call out, no laws.

That will never do, said the grave man, it were better to have no judges than to have no laws, or at least as bad. For how can men judge but by laws. Arbitrary discretion is a blind guide.

The words no judges, had been heard more distinctly than the rest, and supposing it to be a substitute for no laws, voices came from every corner in support of the amendment. I support the amendment; I agree to the substitute, no judges, no judges.

The clamor became general, down with the judges.

This puts me in mind, said the Captain, of the sermons of the Lay Preacher. I should have no objection to an amendment of the law, or to new judges; but no laws, no judges, is more than I had expected to have heard in an assembly of republicans.

A person standing by was struck with the good

323

sense and moderation of this remark, and stepping forward, made his harangue.

I will not say, said he, that I am for no judges; but this I will say, that new judges is a desideratum in the body politic. The greater part that we have are grown gray, and are as blind as bats: they cannot see without spectacles. I am for new judges.

You talk of judges, said the grave man, as if it was as easy to make a judge of law as to make a bird-cage, or a rat-trap.

What, said a merry fellow, shall we have new shoes, new pantaloons, and new every thing; and shall we not have new judges? We shall never do any good with the present set of judges on the bench.

It was carried that there should be new judges. But having disposed of the old, it became a question whom they should elect for new. The bog-trotter was proposed for one, having had his name up before in the matter of the newspaper. 20

What, my waiter, said the Captain? Yes, your waiter, said a wag, or a fool, I do not know which.

You astonish me, said the Captain. My waiter a judge of the courts. He will make sad work on a bench of justice. He will put down all law. He will silence all lawyers. He will have no law: no books; no cases; all plain sailing with him. Every man his own lawyer, state his own cases, and speak for himself. No Hooks and Crooks; no Hawkins; no Bacons; or Blackstones; or Whitestones; no 30 Strange cases; no law of evidence. Every man sworn and tell what he knows, whether he has seen it, or heard it, at second, or at first hand: interest or no interest; all the same; let the jury believe what they think proper; and the judge state the law from his thumbs ends without books.

This is madness, and here I have more trouble on my hands with this bog-trotter, than I have ever had before. It is a more delicate matter to see him placed on the seat of justice, to administer the 40 laws, than to be in the Senate House, and assist to make them. For in that case he would be but a component member of a great body, and his errors, might be lost in the wisdom of the other members. But in the capacity of judge he is sole, or with but a few, and it is an easier matter to frame a single law than to expound and apply a thousand.

Gentlemen, said he, addressing himself to the

multitude, you will ruin your administration. You will bring disgrace upon it. The people will not feel your error at once; but they will feel it by and bye, and will depose you who have been the most active in this cavalcade. That is, they will withdraw from you their confidence. The abuse of power leads to the loss of it. No party in a government, can exist long, but by moderation and wisdom. The duration of power, will always be 10 in proportion to the discreet use of it. I am shocked at your indiscretion. Have not some of you read Don Quixotte? In the capacity of judge, Sancho Panza made some shrewd decisions; or rather Cervantes made them for him; for, I doubt much whether Sancho ever made one of them. But who is there of you, will make decisions for Teague? I doubt much whether he would take advice, or let any one judge in his behalf. Besides that of a judge is not a ministerial office, and cannot legally 20 be exercised by deputy. You will make pretty work of it with Teague for a judge. It may be according to the light of nature; but not according to the law of nature that he will judge. At least, not according to the law of nations: for no nation under heaven ever had such a judge. Not even in the most unenlightened times. If he had a knowledge even of the old Brehon law, in his native country, it might be some help. But in matters of meum and tuum he has a certain wrong headed- 30 ness that hinders him from ever seeing right. He thinks always on the one side; that is on his own side. But what he would do between suitors, I am not so clear, but I take it he would be a partial judge. The man has no principle of honour or honesty. He would be an unjust judge.

Will not the commission make him a judge, exclaimed one of the multitude.

But will it make him capable of judging, said the Captain?

Why not? said a boisterous man. What else 40 qualifies or makes fit? Can the most sensible man, or the most learned person, judge without a commission?

Doubtless that is the authority, said the Captain. But still the capacity.

Capacity! Said a man, with a bit out of the one side of the membrane of his nose, snivelling in his speech; capacity! Give me the commission, and

I will shew you the capacity. Let me see who will dare to question my capacity.

Such a burlesque, said the blind lawyer, tends naturally to the overthrow of justice. For able and conscientious men will withdraw from a degraded station. Intrigue, worse than, perhaps, the arm of flesh itself, will come to be employed in the management of causes. Security of person, property, and reputation, the great end of civil institutions, will be rendered precarious. The security of them depends upon fixed and known rules, as well as the application of them. It is not an easy matter to attain a knowledge of these rules. The laws of a single game at school, or of such as employ manhood, in an hour of amusement, is a thing of labour to acquire. The law parliamentary; or rules of a legislative body, is not learnt in a day. And yet without a knowledge of it, there is a want of order, as well as dispatch in business. The laws of municipal regulation in a community, laws of external structure, and internal police, are not attainable with the celerity of a moment's warning. But when we come to the rules of property, the laws of tenure and of contract, a field opens, that startles the imagination. Even the study of years, makes but a sciolist. But, you will say, lay aside rules. Let all decisions spring from the dictates of common sense applyed to the particular case before the judge. But the mere arbitrary sense of right and wrong, is an unsafe standard of justice. A free government, is a government of laws. A Cadi or a Mufti are tolerable only in despotic countries. You are destroying your republic by undermining the independence, and respectability of your judiciary. It is that branch of the government, on which liberty most essentially depends.

The multitude seemed to be but little moved by these observations, which made it necessary for the Captain to try what could be done with the bog-trotter himself, to dissuade him from accepting the appointment. Accordingly, taking him aside, he spoke to him as follows:

Teague, said he, will there be no end of your presumption? I take it to be a great error of education in our schools, and colleges, that ambition is encouraged by the distribution of honours, in consideration of progress in letters; that one shall be declared the first scholar in languages, another in mathematics. It is sufficient that the fact be so without announcing it. The self-love of the student will find it out himself, without information, and his fellows will be ready to acknowledge it, provided that it is not arrogated, or a demand made that it be formally acknowledged. For this takes away the friendship of others, and corrupts the moral feelings of the successful competitor himself. Ambition springs up, that accursed root which poisons the world. Now, you cannot lay your ambition to the charge of schools or colleges: for, you have never been at any seminary whatever, as far as I understand, if I may guess from your want of attainments in academic studies; and yet notwithstanding you have never been in the way of the distinction of grades, and prizes, and literary honours; you have discovered an ambition of a full grown size, even at this early period of your life. It must be a bad nature that has generated this preposterous aiming and stretching at promotion. A wise man will weigh, what he undertakes; what his shoulders can bear, and what they cannot. He will consider whether the office is fit for him, or whether he is fit for the office. He will reflect that the shade is oftentimes the most desirable situation. Do you see that bird upon the tree there? It builds its nest with care, and endeavours to render it convenient. But does it build it on the topmost bough, exposed to the sun, and the heavy rain; or rather does it not choose an inferior branch in the thickest of the umbrage? Take a lesson from the fowls of heaven, and the brutes of the field. It is not the elevation of place, but the conveniency of accommodation that governs them. Ambition is an accursed germ of evil in the human mind. It is equally destructive of the happiness of the possessor and of that of others. You a republican, and yet destitute of republican virtue, the basis of which I take to be humility and self-denial. Were I the master of an academy, the first, and continual lesson would be, to attain science, and be learned; but as to seeming so, to consider it as of no account. Science would discover itself. The possessing knowledge would be its own reward. The concealment of all self-knowledge of this advantage, not only constitutes the decent and the becoming in life, but lays the foundation of emolument in the good will of others. It may be pardonable in early age to have pride in the advantage of bodily form; but we call in question the modesty of a youth, male or female, who seems to set an inordinate value on a limb or a feature. How much less tolerable, the pride of mental superiority. But of all things under heaven the most contemptible, and the least sufferable, is that of incompetency to a trust, and the aspiring to a place, for which the candidate is not qualified; or, even if qualified, against modesty, and the claims of others. It brings a man to be the subject of a laugh, and ridicule. Do you know that the making you a judge, was but a farce, in the manner that Sancho Panza was advanced to a government. You have read the Don Quixotte of Cervento, I presume. But what do I say; you read Don Quixotte! You have read nothing; and yet you would be a judge. Ambition, I tell you is an evil. You have read of Julius Caesar, in the Roman History. Again I forget myself. You have read nothing. But I may tell you of him. What was the purple to him compared with losing the affections of his countrymen? Though, by the bye, there is some reason to think that it was neck or nothing with him, and that self-preservation made it necessary to usurp the empire, things having come to that state at Rome, that if he did not usurp, another would. But a good republican, and a virtuous man, would rather fall, than save his life, at the expence of the rights of others. But it slips my memory that I am talking to a bog-trotter. There is no making a silk purse out of a sow's ear. Suppose you were made a judge; in this hurly burly of the public mind, would your standing be secure, even with the most perfect competency for the place? You would not stand two throws of a weaver's shuttle. Your chair, under you, would be like an old piece of furniture bought at a vendue, put together for sale; the glueing gone, and the joints broken. It would fall before it had felt half your weight, and leave you, with your backside upon the floor. New judges to-day, and the public mind would have desired new judges to-morrow. Consider the physical consequence of being broken from the bench. Take my word it is not a common breaking this; it will affect your frame at every change of the weather. It will make an almanac of your whole

system. It will make your joints ache. It will be worse than a sprain in the ancle; or a rheumatism in the limbs; or a sciatica in the small of the back. It will give you a cholic every new moon, and take away your sleep at midnight. It will give you the jaundice; and hurt your complexion. Your eyes will become yellow, and your cheeks green. You will lose your appetite; and not be able to eat, even when you can get it. Why man, it will blister your feet, and break your shins. It will bring you to death's door, before you have lived half your days.

By de holy poker, said Teague, I will be no judge, if dat is de way of it. Dey may judge for demselves; I will be no judge. De devil a judge will I be; I would sooner dig turf or be a horse-jockey at fairs in Ireland, dan be a judge on dose terms; so dey may make whom dey please a judge for me.

The Captain was satisfied, finding that his expostulation, and remonstrance had had the desired effect.

[Frontier Indian Warfare]

THE TEXT is that of the edition of *Modern Chivalry*, Book IV, Chapter VIII, published in 1815 in Richmond.

A considerable traffic had been carried on for some time between the bulwark of the Christian religion, and the savages of North America, bordering on this new settlement. The traders of the bulwark, carried out bibles, and in return, received scalps.—What use spiritual, or temporal, these savages could make of bibles, is immaterial, as it is not the use of a thing that always gives it a value. Certain it is, that little use could be made of a bible by these people in the way of reading it. Nor if they did read it, could they understand it, without commentators to build up orthodox systems of faith, with the various points in controversy, between the catholic and protestant churches; much less those doctrines which distinguish the Calvinist [sic], Arminian, Socinian, and other creeds. But as to the use of scalps with the bulwark, it could not be difficult to comprehend, if the use of a skin dressed in the hair be understood; which, I take it, is the case with almost all that manufacture gloves, or muffs, for the ladies in any country. Children's Scalps, and the scalps of young females, were in request particularly for these purposes; and hence it was that the savages made their inroads into the settlement, attacking whole families for the sake of these; and as it was not uncommon to meet with some resistance on the part of the relations; and the young men even went so far as to shoot some of these depredators in taking off the scalps, and war [10] ensued. The savages after having made a pretty good hunt, as the phrase is, and taken scalp-peltry, retreated usually in great haste; inasmuch as they were liable to be pursued, and brought to an account for this outrage; as well as for the purpose of recovering property, which they were not always scrupulous of carrying with them, and not paying for according to value.

Pursuing some of these, a party had gone out from the settlement, amongst whom was Teague. [20]

The bog-trotter reflecting with himself that the savages were not likely to be overtaken, and so no great danger of fighting in the case, did not greatly hesitate to be one; inasmuch as if they should overtake these freebooters, there was such a thing as running from them, as well as after them. But after a few hours march, coming upon a trail of these, which appeared to have crossed from the settlement, in a transverse direction, the word Indians was given; which Teague no sooner hearing, [30] than he began to retrace his steps with some alacrity—It was on a ridge or bend of a hill; the Indians crossing the hill, had gone into the valley, and come round again nearly to the place where the whites had ascended it. It happened therefore very naturally, that the Indians and the bog-trotter, though neither meaning it, had fallen in with each other; the bog-trotter on the flank of the Indians. It had been for the sake of water to boil their kettles, that these savages had gone down [40] to the valley, and encamped the night before. Being now on their way to regain their direction, it happened that they came into the rear of the party pursuing them. The bog-trotter had by this time accelerated his speed considerably, and the declivity of the hill was such that he found it impossible to arrest himself, being under the impetus of the projectile motion which he had acquired;

and seeing nothing before him but death from the tomahawk of at least sixty Indians, and nevertheless being unable to stop his career, no more than could a stone projected from the precipice, he raised the tremendous shout of desperation; which the savages mistaking for the outcry of onset, as it is customary with them when they are sure of victory, to raise the war-whoop; magnifying the shout, by their imaginations into that of a large party overtaking them, they threw away their packs and scalps, and made their way towards the Indian country; not doubting but that the whole settlement was in pursuit of them.

When the party of the whites came up to the brow of the hill, and saw the bog-trotter in possession of the ground and the booty, they took it for granted, that singly, and alone, he had discomfitted the Indians. It was a devil of an engagement, said he; by de holy fader, I must have shot at least a hundred of dem; but de fun o' de world was to see de spalpeens carrying off de wounded on deir backs like de tiefs in Ireland dat stale shape. Tiefs of de world, why did you stay so long back and not come up to de engagement? Looking for Indians before o' your face. Spalpeens, if I had had two or tree good tight boys along wid me, when I came up wid dem, I could have kilt de whole, or made dem prisoners. Bad luck to d' ye, if it wasn't for de shame o' de ting upon de country, I would have a court martial upon de matter; but as to de packs and de booty, it is all my own. I had taken dem before you come up; and devil a hand had you in de victory.

This was not dissented to, and the matter was accommodated, on its being agreed that nothing more should be said about the court martial.

Though upon a small scale, this was thought a very brilliant affair of the bog-trotter. A sword was offered him, and there was a talk of making him a major general. In a republican government, the honest souls of the people are lavish of their gratitude; though they sometimes mistake the merit, or demerit of services.—And how can it otherwise be when the people cannot themselves be all present to see what is done; nor, if they were present, and could see, are the bulk capable of judging in what cases success is to be attributed to design or to execution; and indeed where the design and execution may have been all that human foresight and resolution could promise or perform, yet the event may have been unfortunate. Fortune de grace, applied to an individual, may be applied to measures.—There is a fatality in some cases that baffles the wisest councils, and the most heroic enterprize; and again a kind of magic, or something like a charm that turns to account what in nature and the ordinary course, ought to have produced nothing but disappointment, and the reverse of what has come to pass. Old generals are not always the most successful, because they are afraid of accident and leave too little to chance, while the know nothing, fear nothing, has oftentimes been the secret of fortunate adventure. . . .

Teague was spoken of as a major general, when he ought to have been dismissed the service, could the truth have been ascertained. But appearances were in his favour; for who could think that but for the most desperate courage, he would have attacked sixty or an hundred Indians: fifty or sixty, at least, it was said? For, the prisoners rescued, spoke of there being that number. These prisoners, chiefly consisting of individuals half dead, were incapable of distinguishing the circumstance of the bog-trotter, being precipitated upon their captors by an involuntary centripetal force; or the yell of despair from that of desperate resolution. And as their gratitude was lively for their deliverance, they yielded to no cold examination of the manner in which it was brought about. As for Teague, like Achilles, he claimed every thing for himself;—

Nihil non arrogat armis.

Though but of the grade of a corporal when he went out, he now thought himself entitled to be made general O'Regan. He had, at this time, certain it is, the perfect confidence of the people, who were clamorous for his appointment, and indeed he might be said to be forced upon the Governor.

Teague, said the governor, in my presence you know that you are no such kill devil as the people take you to be. This affair of yours was but matter of accident; and instead of being promoted, you ought to have been broke for it. Were you not actually running away, when you fell in with the Indians? Love your soul, now, said the bog-trotter, that is always the way wid your honour to make noting of de greatest battle dat was ever fought since the days of Chevalry, as dey call it, or Phelim O'Neal one of my own progenitors who kilt a score of men wid his crooked iron; and dey were noting de wiser for it. How could I get down to de bottom o' de hill, if I hadn't jumped upon dese Indians, when I saw dem, and de party of militia dat were after me, but so far behind; had dey come up in time, de devil burn an Indian dat would have escaped, or gone to deir own country, bad luck to dem. Give me a tight little bit od an army, wid me, and if I dont take de whole o' dem widin tree months at fardest, den you may say, I am not Teague O'Regan. My life for it, I will give a good account o' dem.

I thought it of little consequence, said the Governor, to countenance your ambition, Teague, in being a candidate for the legislature, or in being made a judge. The one or the other of these being a province in which property only is concerned; unless, indeed, in the case of a judge, in whose way, it may come sometimes to hang a person, though a jury must be accessary to it. But it is of more moment, to put a brigade or two of lives at a time, in the power of an incompetent person. It is not your inexperience that I so must distrust; for I am well aware, that as the good constitution of a patient often saves the credit of the physician, so the bravery of troops may gain a battle, which the want of skill in the commander had put in jeopardy. But it is your natural judgment that I distrust. I have never been able to discover in you, comprehension of mind that would seem to me to fit you for a general. I have no doubt of your being capable of being made, in due time, a good parade officer; attentive to the minutiae of dress, or movement of the body; or to wear the hat on a corner of the head; or to give words of command, such as face, march, halt, wheel, &c. in a broken sort of way, with the brogue on your tongue; but in all requisite comparing, and contriving, and reasoning, I have not a perfect confidence in your capacity. But as the people will have it so, in republican governments it cannot be avoided. Nor indeed in a monarchical government does it always follow, that the ablest men are appointed to offices. For favour, and family interest, will raise, and sometimes support, the unworthy. But take notice that you have not got a great reputation, and much will be expected of you. The smallest disappointment in the expectation of the people, will trundle you down as fast as your fears precipitated you from that hill, above the Indians, where you got a victory, or at least a pretty good booty. You think that you will be able always to stay in the rear, and send your men on before you. On the contrary, it will behoove you sometimes to reconnoitre; and in that case, you will be under the necessity of exposing yourself to sharp-shooters, and batteries. A cannon ball may take your head off, though at the distance of a mile or two. The post of danger is not always a private station. Charles the twelfth of Sweden was shot through the head with a musket ball. General Moreau was but reconnoitering when he had both legs shot off, or shot through, as he sat on his horse. This thing called grape-shot, is a disagreeable kind of article, coming about the head and ears, like flakes in a snow-storm. You may escape perhaps, with a few bullets in your belly, or groin; or with a shoulder taken off, or hip shot away; or if a skilful operator is at hand to take off an arm, it does not always follow that a man dies, though when the brains are out, there are very few that survive it. The smoke and fire of musketry and big guns, and the hurly burly of men pushing bayonets, is nothing to the war-whoop of Indians taking off scalps; which, I take it, you would not mind much, being a little used to think about it.

Here, O'Regan put his hand to his head as if feeling whether the scalp was yet on.

By de holy faders, said he, if dis is de way of being in one of dese battles, it is a better commission to be bog-trotting wid your honor. Keep d' your papers, and give it to some fool dat will take it. I prefer de having a good warm scalp upon my head, dan all de commissions in de nation; and my legs and my arms to my body, and my body to my legs, and arms. For having been so long friends, why should dey be parted, having been so long togeder, slaping in one bed, and eating at one table. Dere, is de paper; tell de people much good may it do dem. Some one dat has less wit may take it. I have occasion for all de brains dat I have in my own scull. Dose dat have dem to spare, may set up shop, and sell dem for a commission, I have done wid it.

The Governor being thus relieved from his embarrassment, by the resignation of the bog-trotter, took back the commission. It was a sufficient apology with him to the people, that General O'Regan, for reasons best known to himself, had thought proper to decline the appointment of Major General. . . .

O'Regan was no more fit for a general than my horse; but as I have said, it was not from his want of information and experience in military affairs; but from the actual want of sense in the man. And great credit is due to the Governor, for managing matters so, as by an address to his fear, to make it his own act to decline the honour; when, not to have appointed him in the first instance, or to have superseded him afterwards, would have been a thing so unpopular, that it would have shaken his own standing to have attempted it. There is nothing so difficult as to manage the public mind. It must be done by the lever, or the screw, or other mechanical power; to speak figuratively, and not by direct force.

NOAH WEBSTER (1758–1843)

It is one of the curious ironies of our literary history that the compiler of a famous "blue-backed" spelling book which sold almost one hundred million copies, and the editor of *An American Dictionary of the English Language* (1828), the most notable monument of scholarship produced by the young Republic, should occasionally be confused today in the popular mind with *Daniel* Webster. The great *Dictionary*, moreover,

was only one of Noah Webster's many achievements which reveal an omnicompetence and a versatility rivalled only by the many-sided career of his friend Benjamin Franklin.

In an essay series published in 1791 Noah Webster assumed the guise of "The Prompter," one who watches the actor "and with a moderate voice corrects him when wrong." Although Webster's voice at times was more strident than moderate, the role of prompter remained his most characteristic one throughout a long and vigorous lifetime. From classroom and public lecture platform, in the columns of newspapers and magazines, in pamphlets and books, and even in the definitions in his *Dictionary*, Noah Webster continued to prompt his countrymen to achieve their destiny as citizens of a strong and united nation.

Webster was born October 15, 1758, the son of a farmer at West Hartford, Connecticut. He was graduated from Yale in 1778 where, along with his classmate Joel Barlow, he profited from the curriculum which had been liberalized by the zeal of Timothy Dwight and John Trumbull. After his graduation he taught school, read law, and was admitted to the Connecticut bar in 1781. While teaching in 1780, he began his lifelong interest in education by writing four essays excoriating the niggardly support given to public instruction. The most famous of his pioneer textbooks was the *American Spelling Book* (1788) which enjoyed more than fifty printings before 1800, and was enormously influential in effecting a uniform American spelling. The speller was joined with a grammar and reader, issued as the *Grammatical Institute of the English Language* (1783–1785).

Webster's services to the cause of cultural independence from Great Britain and to nationalism took many forms. In his *Sketches of American Policy* (1785) he advocated giving Congress "the sole right of conducting the general affairs of the continent" as the only way to achieve the dignity and union of the country. His intense nationalism is reflected also in *Dissertations on the English Language* (1789), dedicated to Franklin, in which he proposed a distinctively American language as "necessary and unavoidable," and discussed reformations in spelling which had attracted Franklin's interest. Also nationalistic was his *Compendious Dictionary of the English Language* (1806), a forerunner of the monumental *American Dictionary of the English Language* (1828), containing a vocabulary of 70,000 words, 12,000 more than the total in Todd's edition of Dr. Johnson's lexicon.

Of Webster's essays and fugitive writings, the series issued in 1791 as *The Prompter* are the most graceful, and won praise from Joseph Dennie: "If there be any merits in the short essays of 'The Lay Preacher,' consider the author as your debtor." To Webster's achievements must be added his contribution to journalism as editor of the *American Magazine* (1787–1788), especially distinguished among early periodicals for its department of literary criticism, and his editorship of the *American Minerva* (1793). Webster also brought out the first American Revised Version of the Bible (1833).

Concerned with the morality as well as the orthography of the Republic, Webster continued his striving for cultural nationalism until his death in 1843 in his eighty-fifth year. Two of his sentences may serve as appropriate epitaphs: "If my name is a terror to evildoers, mention it." And "I know no party, but that of my country."

Dissertations on the English Language

WHILE TRAVELING among the colonies from Richmond, Virginia, to Portsmouth, New Hampshire, to urge the enactment of a uniform copyright law and to secure copyrights to his own textbooks, Webster spent the summer of 1785 in Baltimore. Here he delivered five lectures on the English language. The Baltimore lectures and the conversations on spelling reform with Benjamin Franklin in 1786, when he spent ten months in Philadelphia, were developed into the *Dissertations on the English Language*, published in Boston in 1789. Webster's stout Federalism is revealed in his desire for a uniform and distinctive national language, free to develop in its own way. His "Essay on the Necessity, Advantages and Practicability of Reforming the Mode of Spelling," which was appended to the *Dissertations*, shows the influence of Franklin, to whom he dedicated his book, though he did not go to the extremes Franklin advocated. The text of this selection is that of the Boston edition of 1789.

BIBLIOGRAPHY · There is no complete edition of Webster's writings. The best biography is H. R. Warfel's *Noah Webster: Schoolmaster to America* (1936). Other biographies include H. E. Scudder, *Noah Webster* (1881), and E. C. Shoemaker, *Noah Webster: Pioneer of Learning* (1936). Webster's diary and many of his most important letters have been carefully edited by Emily E. F. Skeel in E. E. F. Ford's compilation, *Notes on the Life of Noah Webster* (2 vols., 1912).

[A National Language]

A regular study of language has, in all civilized countries, formed a part of a liberal education. The Greeks, Romans, Italians and French successively improved their native tongues, taught them in Academies at home, and rendered them entertaining and useful to the foreign student.

The English tongue, tho later in its progress towards perfection, has attained to a considerable degree of purity, strength and elegance, and been employed, by an active and scientific nation, to record almost all the events and discoveries of ancient and modern times.

This language is the inheritance which the Americans have received from their British parents. To cultivate and adorn it, is a task reserved for men who shall understand the connection between language and logic, and form an adequate idea of the influence which a uniformity of speech may have on national attachments.

It will be readily admitted that the pleasures of reading and conversing, the advantage of accuracy in business, the necessity of clearness and precision in communicating ideas, require us to be able to speak and write our own tongue with ease and correctness. But there are more important reasons, why the language of this country should be reduced to such fixed principles, as may give its pronunciation and construction all the certainty and uniformity which any living tongue is capable of receiving.

The United States were settled by emigrants from different parts of Europe. But their descendants mostly speak the same tongue; and the intercourse among the learned of the different States, which the revolution has begun, and an American Court will perpetuate, must gradually destroy the differences of dialect which our ancestors brought from their native countries. This approximation of dialects will be certain; but without the operation of other causes than an intercourse at Court, it will be slow and partial. The body of the people, governed by habit, will still retain their respective peculiarities of speaking; and for want of schools and proper books, fall into many inaccuracies, which, incorporating with the language of the state where they live, may imperceptibly corrupt the national language. Nothing but the establishment of schools and some uniformity in the use of books, can annihilate differences in speaking and preserve the purity of the American tongue. A sameness of pronunciation is of considerable consequence in a political view; for provincial accents are disagreeable to strangers and sometimes have an unhappy effect upon social affections. All men have local attachments, which lead them to believe their own practice to be the least exceptionable. Pride and prejudice incline

men to treat the practice of their neighbors with some degree of contempt. Thus small differences in pronunciation at first excite ridicule—a habit of laughing at the singularities of strangers is followed by disrespect—and without respect friendship is a name, and social intercourse a mere ceremony.

These remarks hold equally true, with respect to individuals, to small societies and to large communities. Small causes, such as a nick-name, or a vulgar tone in speaking, have actually created a dissocial spirit between the inhabitants of the different states, which is often discoverable in private business and public deliberations. Our political harmony is therefore concerned in a uniformity of language.

As an independent nation, our honor requires us to have a system of our own, in language as well as government. Great Britain, whose children we are, and whose language we speak, should no longer be our standard; for the taste of her writers is already corrupted, and her language on the decline. But if it were not so, she is at too great a distance to be our model, and to instruct us in the principles of our own tongue.

It must be considered further, that the English is the common root or stock from which our national language will be derived. All others will gradually waste away—and within a century and a half, North America will be peopled with a hundred millions of men, all speaking the same language. Place this idea in comparison with the present and possible future bounds of the language in Europe—consider the Eastern Continent as inhabited by nations, whose knowledge and intercourse are embarrassed by differences of language; then anticipate the period when the people of one quarter of the world, will be able to associate and converse together like children of the same family. Compare this prospect, which is not visionary, with the state of the English language in Europe, almost confined to an Island and to a few millions of people; then let reason and reputation decide, how far America should be dependent on a transatlantic nation, for her standard and improvements in language.

Let me add, that whatever predilection the Americans may have for their native European tongues, and particularly the British descendants for the English, yet several circumstances render a future separation of the American tongue from the English, necessary and unavoidable. The vicinity of the European nations, with the uninterrupted communication in peace, and the changes of dominion in war, are gradually assimilating their respective languages. The English with others is suffering continual alterations. America, placed at a distance from those nations, will feel, in a much less degree, the influence of the assimilating causes; at the same time, numerous local causes, such as a new country, new associations of people, new combinations of ideas in arts and science, and some intercourse with tribes wholly unknown in Europe, will introduce new words into the American tongue. These causes will produce, in a course of time, a language in North America, as different from the future language of England, as the modern Dutch, Danish and Swedish are from the German, or from one another: Like remote branches of a tree springing from the same stock; or rays of light, shot from the same center, and diverging from each other, in proportion to their distance from the point of separation.

Whether the inhabitants of America can be brought to a perfect uniformity in the pronunciation of words, it is not easy to predict; but it is certain that no attempt of the kind has been made, and an experiment begun and pursued on the right principles, is the only way to decide the question. Schools in Great Britain have gone far towards demolishing local dialects—commerce has also had its influence—and in America these causes, operating more generally, must have a proportional effect.

In many parts of America, people at present attempt to copy the English phrases and pronunciation—an attempt that is favored by their habits, their prepossessions and the intercourse between the two countries. This attempt has, within the period of a few years, produced a multitude of changes in these particulars, especially among the leading classes of people. These changes make a difference between the language of the higher and common ranks; and indeed between the same ranks in different states; as the rage for copying the English, does not prevail equally in every part of North America.

But besides the reasons already assigned to prove this imitation absurd, there is a difficulty attending it, which will defeat the end proposed by its advocates; which is, that the English themselves have no standard of pronunciation, nor can they ever have one on the plan they propose. The Authors, who have attempted to give us a standard, make the practice of the court and stage in London the sole criterion of propriety in speaking. An attempt to establish a standard on this foundation is both unjust and idle. It is unjust, because it is abridging the nation of its rights: The general practice of a nation is the rule of propriety, and this practice should at least be consulted in so important a matter, as that of making laws for speaking. While all men are upon a footing and no singularities are accounted vulgar or ridiculous, every man enjoys perfect liberty. But when a particular set of men, in exalted stations, undertake to say, "we are the standards of propriety and elegance, and if all men do not conform to our practice, they shall be accounted vulgar and ignorant," they take a very great liberty with the rules of the language and the rights of civility.

But an attempt to fix a standard on the practice of any particular class of people is highly absurd: As a friend of mine once observed, it is like fixing a light house on a floating island. It is an attempt to fix that which is in itself variable; at least it must be variable so long as it is supposed that a local practice has no standard but a local practice; that is, no standard but itself. While this doctrine is believed, it will be impossible for a nation to follow as fast as the standard changes—for if the gentlemen at court constitute a standard, they are above it themselves, and their practice must shift with their passions and their whims.

But this is not all. If the practice of a few men in the capital is to be the standard, a knowledge of this must be communicated to the whole nation. Who shall do this? An able compiler perhaps attempts to give this practice in a dictionary; but it is probable that the pronunciation, even at court, or on the stage, is not uniform. The compiler therefore must follow his particular friends and patrons; in which case he is sure to be opposed and the authority of his standard called in question; or he must give two pronunciations as the standard, which leaves the student in the same uncertainty as it found him. Both these events have actually taken place in England, with respect to the most approved standards; and of course no one is universally followed.

Besides, if language must vary, like fashions, at the caprice of a court, we must have our standard dictionaries republished, with the fashionable pronunciation, at least once in five years; otherwise a gentleman in the country will become intolerably vulgar, by not being in a situation to adopt the fashion of the day. The new editions of them will supersede the old, and we shall have our pronunciation to re-learn, with the polite alterations, which are generally corruptions.

Such are the consequences of attempting to make a local practice the standard of language in a nation. The attempt must keep the language in perpetual fluctuation, and the learner in uncertainty.

If a standard therefore cannot be fixed on local and variable custom, on what shall it be fixed? If the most eminent speakers are not to direct our practice, where shall we look for a guide? The answer is extremely easy; the rules of the language itself, and the general practice of the nation, constitute propriety in speaking. If we examine the structure of any language, we shall find a certain principle of analogy running through the whole. We shall find in English that similar combinations of letters have usually the same pronunciation; and that words, having the same terminating syllable, generally have the accent at the same distance from the termination. These principles of analogy were not the result of design—they must have been the effect of accident, or that tendency which all men feel toward uniformity. But the principles, when established, are productive of great convenience, and become an authority superior to the arbitrary decisions of any man or class of men. There is one exception only to this remark: When a deviation from analogy has become the universal practice of a nation, it then takes [the] place of all rules and becomes the standard of propriety.

The two points therefore, which I conceive to be the basis of a standard in speaking, are these; universal undisputed practice, and the principle of analogy. Universal practice is generally, perhaps always, a rule of propriety; and in disputed points where people differ in opinion and practice, analogy should always decide the controversy.

These are authorities to which all men will submit—they are superior to the opinions and caprices of the great, and to the negligence and ignorance of the multitude. The authority of individuals is always liable to be called in question—but the unanimous consent of a nation, and a fixed principle interwoven with the very construction of a language, coeval and coextensive with it, are like the common laws of a land, or the immutable rules of morality, the propriety of which every man, however refractory, is forced to acknowledge, and to which most men will readily submit. Fashion is usually the child of caprice and the being of a day; principles of propriety are founded in the very nature of things, and remain unmoved and unchanged, amidst all the fluctuations of human affairs and the revolutions of time.

It must be confessed that languages are changing, from age to age, in proportion to improvements in science. Words, as Horace observes, are like leaves of trees; the old ones are dropping off and new ones growing. These changes are the necessary consequence of changes in customs, the introduction of new arts, and new ideas in the sciences. Still the body of a language and its general rules remain for ages the same, and the new words usually conform to these rules; otherwise they stand as exceptions, which are not to overthrow the principle of analogy already established. . . .

Altho stile, or the choice of words and manner of arranging them, may be necessarily liable to change, yet it does not follow that pronunciation and orthography cannot be rendered in a great measure permanent. An orthography, in which there would be a perfect correspondence between the spelling and pronunciation, would go very far towards effecting this desirable object. The Greek language suffered little or no change in these particulars, for about a thousand years; and the Roman was in a great degree fixed for several centuries.

Rapid changes of language proceed from violent causes; but these causes cannot be supposed to exist in North America. It is contrary to all rational calculation, that the United States will ever be conquered by any one nation, speaking a different language from that of the country. Removed from the danger of corruption by conquest, our language can change only with the slow operation of the causes beforementioned and the progress of arts and sciences, unless the folly of imitating our parent country should continue to govern us, and lead us into endless innovation. This folly however will lose its influence gradually, as our particular habits of respect for that country shall 10 wear away, and our *amor patriae* acquire strength and inspire us with a suitable respect for our own national character.

We have therefore the fairest opportunity of establishing a national language, and of giving it uniformity and perspicuity, in North America, that ever presented itself to mankind. Now is the time to begin the plan. The minds of the Americans are roused by the events of a revolution; the necessity of organizing the political body and of forming constitutions of government that shall secure freedom and property, has called all the faculties of the mind into exertion; and the danger of losing the benefits of independence, has disposed every man to embrace any scheme that shall tend, in its future operation, to reconcile the people of America to each other, and weaken the prejudices which oppose a cordial union. . . .

CHARLES BROCKDEN BROWN (1771–1810)

THE CAREER of Charles Brockden Brown is coextensive with the apologetic beginnings and final triumph of the early American novel. At the time of his birth in 1771 in Philadelphia, the colonies had failed to produce any native fiction, and moralists regarded even Samuel Richardson's didactic novels with grave misgivings. A generation later Brown's own novels were to be found on the shelves of popular lending libraries, along with other "Gothic romances" and "sentimental tales" for which there was an increasing number of avid readers. Historically Brown is important as our first native professional novelist; of more significance are his pioneer explorations of strange psychological behavior which quite possibly influenced the work of Poe and Hawthorne.

Brown's parents were Quakers who sent him to the Friends' Latin School in 1781, where he remained for five years, studying Latin and Greek, and reading with an intellectual curiosity which impressed his teachers. An early interest in native themes led him to plan, in his sixteenth year, ambitious epics on the discovery of America and the adventures of Pizarro and Cortes. Although Brown began to study law in 1787, he still yearned, like Irving and Longfellow in the early nineteenth century, for eminence in literature. More congenial than discussions of Blackstone were the activities of the Belles Lettres Club, of which Brown was the leading spirit. Some of the essays which he wrote for the Club were published as "The Rhapsodist" in the *Columbian Magazine* in 1789. Brown seemed ready for a successful legal career when, in 1793, he resolved to earn his living as a writer. His decision was strengthened by his friendship with Dr. Elihu

Hubbard Smith (1771–1798), one of the minor Connecticut Wits, who had come to Philadelphia for graduate study in medicine. Brown found further encouragement in New York, where Dr. Smith was a member of "The Friendly Club," a literary coterie which included William Dunlap, dramatist and historian of the theatre. A welcome visitor to this circle from 1794 to 1798, Brown finally moved to New York, and there in the cosmopolitan city he was stimulated to write the novels for which he is remembered. He later returned to Philadelphia.

Most memorable of his works are those novels written under the impact of Godwin's *Caleb Williams* (1794), a philosophic, humanitarian romance which confirmed many of the liberal ideas that Brown had encountered in French Revolutionary writers and in Godwin's *Political Justice* (1793). Like Godwin, Brown hoped to appeal to reflective readers by substituting credible psychological terrors for the puerile, skeleton-rattling supernaturalism of popular Gothic romances. He also catered to the literary patriotism of his countrymen by placing his scenes in Pennsylvania and New York, and by using American characters and such native material as Indian hostility, perils of the wilderness, and visitations of yellow fever in Philadelphia and New York. A perfectionist who believed in the transforming power of environment and education, Brown designed his novels to illustrate "the moral condition of man," but he sought to hold the interest of his readers by the use of sensational devices. His strongest novel, *Wieland* (1798), employs religious mania, ventriloquism, and a spectacular death by "spontaneous combustion"; *Edgar Huntly* (1799) contains sleep-walking episodes; and *Ormond* (1799) and *Arthur Mervyn* (1799–1800) utilize sickening details of a dreadful pestilence to heighten mental and spiritual horror.

Although these novels provide a welcome contrast to the popular, sentimental tales of seduction written by the American imitators of Samuel Richardson, Brown did not entirely escape their influence. *Wieland* was written in "epistolary" form and exploits the interest in the seduction motif. *Clara Howard* (1801) and *Jane Talbot* (1801), Brown's last novels, are cumbersomely constructed love stories in an artificial and stilted style. Brown returned to Philadelphia in 1801, where he spent his remaining years (1801–1810) in business and editorial hack work. He died of tuberculosis at the age of 39. Despite his failure to live up to the high promise of his precocious youth, his professional efforts to establish a national literature and his mastery in revealing character under the stress of intense emotion entitle him to a secure, though minor, place in American literature.

BIBLIOGRAPHY · *The Novels of Charles B. Brown* (6 vols.) was edited by David McKay (1887). Other collected editions were published in Boston in 1827, and in Philadelphia in 1857. *Wieland* is readily available in F. L. Pattee's edition in the American Authors Series (1926); *Edgar Huntley* (1928), edited by D. L. Clark, and *Ormond* (1937), edited by E. Marchand, contain informative introductions and useful bibliographies. *Alcuin* (Part I) was reproduced in a facsimile edition at New Haven in 1935. *The Rhapsodist*, containing Brown's first efforts as "a story-telling moralist," published in *The Universal Asylum, and Columbian Magazine* (August–November, 1789), was edited by H. R. Warfel and issued by Scholars' Facsimiles & Reprints (1943).

Warfel's biography of Brown is standard. William Dunlap's *Life of Charles Brockden Brown* (1815), the original source of biographical information, is inaccurate. D. L. Clark's *Charles Brockden Brown: a Critical Biography* (1923) contains new material, but is incomplete. Carl Van Doren's sketch in the *Dictionary of American Biography*, III, 107–110, is the best summary. Interesting biographical and critical material is included in W. B. Blake, "Brockden Brown and the Novel," *Sewanee Review*, XVIII (1910), 431–443; D. L. Clark, "Brockden Brown and the Rights of Women," *University of Texas Bulletin*, No. 2212 (1922), and "Brockden Brown's First Attempt at Journalism," *University of Texas Studies in English*, VII (1927), 155–174; T. McDowell, "Scott on Cooper and Brockden Brown," *Modern Language Notes*, XLV (1930), 18–20; A. R. Marble, *Heralds of American Literature* (1907), 279–318; E. Marchand, "The Literary Opinions of Charles Brockden Brown," *Studies in Philology*, XXXI (1934), 541–566; M. Morris, "Charles Brockden Brown and the American Indian," *American Literature*, XVIII (1946), 244–247; F. C. Prescott, " 'Wieland' and 'Frankenstein,' " *American Literature*, II (1930), 172–173; E. Sickels, "Shelley and Charles Brockden Brown," *PMLA*, XLV (1930), 1116–1128; M. T. Solve, "Shelley and the Novels of Brown," in *The Fred Newton Scott Anniversary Papers* (1929), 141–156; C. Van Doren, "Early American Realism," *Nation*, XCIX (1914), 577–578, and "Minor Tales of Brockden Brown," *Nation*, C (1915), 46–47); and M. S. Vilas, *C. B. Brown: a Study of Early American Fiction* (1904).

Arthur Mervyn

XV. [The Ravages of Yellow Fever]

BROWN had avoided the plague in Philadelphia in 1793, but he saw it at first hand in 1798 in New York, while staying at the home of his friend, Dr. Elihu Smith. Here he witnessed the illness and death of a Dr. Scandella, whom Smith had taken into his care, and in *Arthur Mervyn* Brown transferred this experience to Philadelphia.

. . . In proportion as I drew near the city, the tokens of its calamitous condition became more apparent. Every farm-house was filled with supernumerary tenants; fugitives from home; and haunting the skirts of the road, eager to detain every passenger with inquiries after news. The passengers were numerous; for the tide of emigration was by no means exhausted. Some were on foot, bearing in their countenances the tokens of their recent terror, and filled with mournful reflections on the forlornness of their state. Few had secured to themselves an asylum; some were without the means of paying for victuals or lodging for the coming night; others, who were not thus destitute, yet knew not whither to apply for entertainment, every house being already overstocked with inhabitants, or barring its inhospitable doors at their approach.

Families of weeping mothers, and dismayed children, attended with a few pieces of indispensable furniture, were carried in vehicles of every form. The parent or husband had perished; and the price of some moveable, or the pittance handed forth by public charity, had been expended to purchase the means of retiring from this theatre of disasters; though uncertain and hopeless of accommodation in the neighboring districts.

Between these and the fugitives whom curiosity had led to the road, dialogues frequently took place, to which I was suffered to listen. From every mouth the tale of sorrow was repeated with new aggravations. Pictures of their own distress, or of that of their neighbors, were exhibited in all the hues which imagination can annex to pestilence and poverty.

My preconceptions of the evil now appeared to have fallen short of the truth. The dangers into which I was rushing, seemed more numerous and imminent than I had previously imagined. I wavered not in my purpose. A panic crept to my heart, which more vehement exertions were necessary to subdue or control. . . . The sun had nearly set before I reached the precincts of the city. I pursued the track which I had formerly taken, and entered High Street after nightfall. Instead of equipages and a throng of passengers, the voice of levity and glee, which I had formerly observed, and which the mildness of the season would, at other times, have produced, I found nothing but a dreary solitude.

The market-place, and each side of this magnificent avenue were illuminated, as before, by lamps; but between the verge of Schuylkill and the heart of the city, I met not more than a dozen figures; and these were ghost-like, wrapt in cloaks, from behind which they cast upon me glances of wonder and suspicion; and, as I approached, changed their course, to avoid touching me. Their clothes were sprinkled with vinegar; and their nostrils defended from contagion by some powerful perfume.

I cast a look upon the houses, which I recollected to have formerly been, at this hour, brilliant with lights, resounding with lively voices, and thronged with busy faces. Now they were closed, above and below; dark, and without tokens of being inhabited. From the upper windows of some, a gleam sometimes fell upon the pavement I was traversing, and shewed that their tenants had not fled, but were secluded or disabled.

These tokens were new, and awakened all my panics. Death seemed to hover over this scene, and I dreaded that the floating pestilence had already lighted on my frame. I had scarcely overcome these tremors, when I approached a house, the door of which was opened, and before which stood a vehicle, which I presently recognized to be a hearse.

The driver was seated on it. I stood still to mark his visage, and to observe the course which he proposed to take. Presently a coffin, borne by two men, issued from the house. The driver was a negro, but his companions were white. Their features were marked by ferocious indifference to danger or pity. One of them as he assisted in thrusting the coffin into the cavity provided for it, said, "I'll be damned if I think the poor dog was quite dead. It wasn't the fever that ailed him, but the sight of the girl and her mother on the floor. I wonder how they all got into that room. What carried them there?"

The other surlily muttered, "Their legs to be sure."

"But what should they hug together in one room for?"

"To save us trouble, to be sure."

"And I thank them with all my heart; but damn it, it wasn't right to put him in his coffin before the breath was fairly gone. I thought the last look he gave me, told me to stay a few minutes."

"Pshaw! He could not live. The sooner dead the better for him; as well as for us. Did you mark how he eyed us, when we carried away his wife and daughter? I never cried in my life, since I was knee-high, but curse me if I ever felt in better tune for the business than just then."

"Hey!" continued he, looking up, and observing me standing a few paces distant, and listening to their discourse, "What's wanted? Any body dead?"

I stayed not to answer or parley, but hurried forward. My joints trembled, and cold drops stood on my forehead. I was ashamed of my own infirmity; and by vigorous efforts of my reason, regained some degree of composure. The evening had now advanced, and it behooved me to procure accommodation at some of the inns.

These were easily distinguishable by their signs, but many were without inhabitants. At length, I lighted upon one, the hall of which was open, and the windows lifted. After knocking for some time, a young girl appeared, with many marks of distress. In answer to my question, she answered that both her parents were sick, and that they could receive no one. I inquired, in vain, for any other tavern at which strangers might be accommodated. She knew of none such; and left me, on some one's calling to her from above, in the midst of my embarrassment. After a moment's pause, I returned, discomforted and perplexed, to the street.

I proceeded, in a considerable degree, at random. At length I reached a spacious building in Fourth-street, which the sign-post shewed me to be an inn. I knocked loudly and often at the door. At length a female opened the window of the second story, and in a tone of peevishness demanded what I wanted? I told her that I wanted lodging.

"Go hunt for it somewhere else," said she; "you'll find none here." I began to expostulate; but she shut the window with quickness, and left me to my own reflections. . . .

I immediately directed my steps toward the habitation of Thetford. Carriages bearing the dead were frequently discovered. A few passengers likewise occurred, whose hasty and perturbed steps, denoted their participation in the common distress. The house, of which I was in quest, quickly appeared. Light from an upper window indicated that it was still inhabited.

I paused a moment to reflect in what manner it became me to proceed. To ascertain the existence and condition of Wallace was the purpose of my journey. He had inhabited this house; and whether he remained in it, was now to be known. I felt repugnance to enter, since my safety might, by entering, be unawares and uselessly endangered. Most of the neighboring houses were apparently deserted. In some there were various tokens of people being within. Might I not inquire, at one of these, respecting the condition of Thetford's family? Yet why should I disturb them by inquiries so impertinent, at this unseasonable hour? To knock at Thetford's door, and put my questions to him who should obey the signal, was the obvious method.

I knocked dubiously and lightly. No one came. I knocked again, and more loudly; I likewise drew the bell. I distinctly heard its distant peals. If any were within, my signal could not fail to be noticed. I paused, and listened, but neither voice nor footsteps could be heard. The light, though obscured by window curtains, which seemed to be drawn close, was still perceptible.

I ruminated on the causes that might hinder my summons from being obeyed. I figured to myself nothing but the helplessness of disease, or the insensibility of death. These images only urged me to persist in endeavoring to gain admission. Without weighing the consequences of my act, I involuntarily lifted the latch. The door yielded to my hand, and I put my feet within the passage.

Once more I paused. The passage was of considerable extent, and at the end of it I perceived light as from a lamp or candle. This impelled me to go forward, till I reached the foot of a staircase. A candle stood upon the lowest step.

This was new proof that the house was not deserted. I struck my heel against the floor with some violence; but this, like my former signals, was unnoticed. Having proceeded thus far, it would have been absurd to retire with my purpose uneffected. . . .

I mounted the stair. As I approached the door of which I was in search, a vapor, infectious and deadly, assailed my senses. It resembled nothing of which I had ever before been sensible. Many odors had been met with, even since my arrival in the city, less supportable than this. I seemed not so much to smell as to taste the element that now encompassed me. I felt as if I had inhaled a poisonous and subtle fluid, whose power instantly bereft my stomach of all vigor. Some fatal influence appeared to seize upon my vitals; and the work of corrosion and decomposition to be hastily begun.

For a moment, I doubted whether imagination had not some share in producing my sensation; but I had not been previously panic struck; and even now I attended to my own sensations without mental discomposure. That I had imbibed this disease was not to be questioned. So far the chances in my behavior were annihilated. The lot of sickness was drawn.

Whether my case would be lenient or malignant; whether I should recover or perish, was to be left to the decision of the future. This incident, instead of appalling me, tended rather to invigorate my courage. The danger which I feared had come. I might enter with indifference, on this theatre of pestilence. I might execute without faltering, the duties that my circumstances might create. My state was no longer hazardous; and my destiny would be totally uninfluenced by my future conduct.

The pang with which I was first seized, and the momentary inclination to vomit, which it produced, presently subsided. My wholesome feelings, indeed, did not revisit me, but strength to proceed was restored to me. The effluvia became more sensible as I approached the door of the chamber. The door was ajar; and the light within was perceived. My belief, that those within were dead, was presently confuted by a sound, which I first supposed to be that of steps moving quickly and timorously across the floor. This ceased, and was succeeded by sounds of different, but inexplicable import.

Having entered the apartment, I saw a candle on the hearth. A table was covered with vials and other apparatus of a sick chamber. A bed stood on one side, the curtain of which was dropped at the foot, so as to conceal any one within. I fixed my eyes upon this object. There were sufficient tokens that some one lay upon the bed. Breath, drawn at long intervals; mutterings scarcely audible; and a tremulous motion in the bedstead, were fearful and intelligible indications.

If my heart faltered, it must not be supposed that my trepidations arose from any selfish considerations. Wallace only, the object of my search, was present to my fancy. . . . My fancy readily depicted the progress and completion of this tragedy. Wallace was the first of the family on whom this pestilence had seized. Thetford had fled from his habitation. Perhaps, as a father and husband, to shun the danger attending his stay, was the injunction of his duty. It was questionless the conduct which selfish regards would dictate. Wallace was left to perish alone; or, perhaps, which indeed was a supposition somewhat justified by appearances, he had been left to the tendence of mercenary wretches; by whom, at this desperate moment he had been abandoned.

I was not mindless of the possibility that these forebodings, specious as they were, might be false.

The dying person might be some other than Wallace. The whispers of my hope were, indeed, faint; but they, at least, prompted me to snatch a look at the expiring man. For this purpose, I advanced and thrust my head within the curtain.

Chapter XVI · [*Concluded*]

The features of one whom I had seen so transiently as Wallace, may be imagined to be not easily recognised, especially when those features were tremulous and deathful. Here, however, the differences were too conspicuous to mislead me. I beheld one in whom I could recollect none that bore resemblance. Though ghastly and livid, the traces of intelligence and beauty were undefaced. . . . His extremities were already cold. A vapor, noisome and contagious, hovered over him. The flutterings of his pulse had ceased. His existence was about to close amidst convulsion and pangs.

I withdrew my gaze from this object, and walked to a table. I was nearly unconscious of my movements. My thoughts were occupied with contemplations of the train of horrors and disasters that pursue the race of man. My musings were quickly interrupted by the sight of a small cabinet, the hinges of which were broken and the lid half raised. In the present state of my thoughts, I was prone to suspect the worst. Here were traces of pillage. Some casual or mercenary attendant, had not only contributed to hasten the death of the patient, but had rifled his property and fled.

This suspicion would, perhaps, have yielded to mature reflections, if I had been suffered to reflect. A moment scarcely elapsed, when some appearance in the mirror, which hung over the table, called my attention. It was a human figure; nothing could be briefer than the glance that I fixed upon this apparition, yet there was room enough for the vague conception to suggest itself, that the dying man had started from his bed and was approaching me. This belief was, at the same instant, confuted, by the survey of his form and garb. One eye, a scar upon his cheek, a tawny skin, a form grotesquely misproportioned, brawny as Hercules, and habited in livery, composed, as it were, the parts of one view.

To perceive, to fear, and to confront this apparition were blended into one sentiment. I

338

turned towards him with the swiftness of lightning, but my speed was useless to my safety. A blow upon my temple was succeeded by an utter oblivion of thought and of feeling. I sunk upon the floor prostrate and senseless.

My insensibility might be mistaken by observers for death, yet some part of this interval was haunted by a fearful dream. I conceived myself lying on the brink of a pit, whose bottom the eye could not reach. My hands and legs were fettered, so as to disable me from resisting two grim and gigantic figures, who stooped to lift me from the earth. Their purpose methought was to cast me into this abyss. My terrors were unspeakable, and I struggled with such force, that my bonds snapped and I found myself at liberty. At this moment my senses returned and I opened my eyes. . . .

I looked up with eagerness. Beside me I discovered three figures, whose character or office were explained by a coffin of pine boards which lay upon the floor. One stood with hammer and nails in his hand, as ready to replace and fasten the lid of the coffin, as soon as its burthen should be received.

I attempted to rise from the floor, but my head was dizzy and my sight confused. Perceiving me revive, one of the men, assisted me to regain my feet. The mist and confusion presently vanished, so as to allow me to stand unsupported and to move. I once more gazed at my attendants, and recognized the three men, whom I had met in High-street, and whose conversation I have mentioned that I overheard. I looked again upon the coffin. A wavering recollection of the incidents that led me hither and of the stunning blow which I had received, occurred to me. I saw into what error appearances had misled these men, and shuddered to reflect, by what hairbreadth means I had escaped being buried alive. . . .

JOSEPH DENNIE (1768-1812)

Acclaimed by his contemporary Timothy Dwight as "the Addison of America," Joseph Dennie likened his own essays in the *Port Folio* to those appearing in English periodicals such as the *Looker-on*, the *Observer*, and the *World*. Throughout his life Dennie stood as an important arbiter of taste, inflexibly defending the principles of neoclassicism before his readers. While his critical position was at times untenable, there is no doubt of the honesty of his convictions and of the salutary effect upon his literary followers of his aggressive devotion to rigid standards. He is remembered also for the political principles which he expounded at the turn of the century while editor of *The Gazette of the United States*. A staunch Federalist, he was suspicious of the ways of Democrats, and desired a kind of intellectual aristocracy to direct and restrain the impulsive and unpredictable actions of common men.

Joseph Dennie was born in Boston in 1768 of loyalist stock. After the outbreak of hostilities in 1775 the family removed to the village of Lexington, where the young son had opportunity to browse without serious interruption in his father's library. This isolation and Dennie's feeble health intensified his love of letters and inclined him to a way of life remote from that of his mercantile ancestry. At Harvard he excelled in literature, although he was a desultory student. His criticism of fustiness and mediocrity in collegiate instruction was rewarded by rustication for the last term of his senior year. For five years after his graduation in 1790 he studied and practiced law in Charlestown, New Hampshire, where he also wrote his "Farrago" essays, in part contributed to *The Eagle or Dartmouth Centinel*, at Hanover, New Hampshire. He made contributions to the *Federal Orrery* at Boston, and for a few weeks in 1795 he edited the Boston *Tablet*. His experience as a substitute minister late in 1795 suggested what turned out to be his most important series of essays, *The Lay Preacher*. Until 1799 he continued the practice of law and essay-writing at Walpole, New Hampshire, where he gained a national audience as editor of the *Farmer's Museum*. In the column entitled "From the Shop of Colon and Spondee" he was associated with Royall Tyler, Thomas Fessenden, Jeremiah Mason, and others. The financial troubles of the *Museum* and the eager solicitation of Federalist leaders sent him to Philadelphia in 1799 to take over heavy duties on the *Gazette of the United States*. Here he thundered at democratic delusions and factionalism, and entered cheerfully into the abuse of Jefferson and Paine. In 1801, after the removal of the national government to Washington, he remained in Philadelphia and edited the weekly *Port Folio* until his death.

339

Dennie's later years were saddened by inadequate financial returns from his writing, and by his failure to bring out a complete edition of his essay series; yet his disappointment must have been softened by his pleasure in the jovial meetings of the literary Tuesday Club, some of whose members contributed to the *Port Folio*. These friendly collaborators included John Blair Linn, Samuel Ewing, Joseph Hopkinson, Horace Binney, Thomas James, John Ewing Hall, and others. Through the *Port Folio*, easily the most distinguished periodical of the time, Dennie strove to infuse the love of polite letters into his countrymen, to elevate their manners, and to refine their taste. While assailing a bit too testily the ignorance and provinciality of his countrymen, and while extolling British writers as exemplars of excellence, Dennie kept up a running fire upon democratic standards of conduct and upon the activities of the Jefferson administration. He was easily spurred to attacks upon American parochial self-assertiveness, calling pure democracy sinister, unworkable, and contemptible. Despite his failing health which caused a year-by-year decrease of his own original compositions, Dennie managed to supply about one fourth of the "American Lounger" essays and a considerable bulk of "An Author's Evenings." Active or inactive, right or wrong, Dennie was one of those positive literary figures who are famous both for the friends and for the enemies they make. An irritating but valuable corrective to national and literary bumptiousness, Dennie served to remind his contemporaries of the existence of such qualities as grace, poise, and decorum.

BIBLIOGRAPHY · No complete edition of Dennie's works exists. A partial collection of "The Lay Preacher" essays was brought out in 1796 at Walpole, New Hampshire, and another selection of the essays, edited by John E. Hall, was published in Philadelphia in 1817, five years after Dennie's death. These two collections, edited by Milton Ellis, were issued as *The Lay Preacher* in Scholars' Facsimiles & Reprints (1943). This edition reprints sixty-six of the one hundred and seventeen essays. The twenty-five items of the *Farrago* and Dennie's share of the papers in "An Author's Evenings," "The American Lounger," and "The Saunterer," remain uncollected. The standard biography is by Milton Ellis, *Joseph Dennie and His Circle* (1915). Biographical material may be found in W. W. Clapp, *Joseph Dennie* (1880); A. R. Marble, *Heralds of American Literature* (1907); A. P. Peabody, "The Farmer's Weekly Museum," in *The Report of the Council of the American Antiquarian Society* (October 23, 1889); and A. H. Smyth, *Philadelphia Magazines and Their Contributors* (1892).

The Letters of Dennie, edited by L. G. Pedder, was issued as Bulletin No. 36 in the University of Maine

Studies (Second Series, 1936). The text of the essays reprinted in this volume is from the files of the *Port Folio*, in each case the last printing supervised by Dennie himself.

An Author's Evenings

The Conversation of Authors

THE FOLLOWING essay is not in one of the series written exclusively by Dennie, but its style and subject matter make his authorship quite probable. Moreover, it was published shortly after Dennie printed the following note in the first volume of the *Port Folio*: "When the Editor and a literary friend first projected the scheme of writing miscellaneous essays in conjunction, the prose was generally understood to be the province of the Editor, and the poetry that of his associate." This division of editorial labor was not a rigid one, but it was fairly well maintained. There is not much evidence that Tyler assisted Dennie in the first and second volume of the *Port Folio*. Of the series in which this essay appeared Dennie remarked in the first number of the *Port Folio*: "In the course of these little essays, a style desultory and broken will perpetually occur. The author's plan will resemble that of Aulus Gellius in his *Noctes Atticae*. A plenty of curious or valuable extracts will be given from the works of others and these will be followed up by incidental remark, or easy and obvious criticism." The text is taken from the *Port Folio*, II, 231 (1802).

Nothing is more common than the disappointment felt and expressed by those who are eager to be introduced to an Author.

Expectation having been highly raised, it is almost certain it will be mocked. He, whose writings have pleased, disgusts us by his talk, and men are astonished to find him, who is so correct in his pages, so careless in his life. The admirer of a fine stile is vexed that an author should descend to common topics and ordinary phrases. The moralist grieves that anything issues from the author's mouth but the proverbs of Solomon. Some are chagrined that he is sullen, and others are offended by his loquacity.

The ladies do not find him so handsome as was expected, and the coxcombs discover that he is unfashionably dressed! On the difference between an author's talents in his closet and in company, let us hear a sensible writer:

I have seen men remarkably lively and well informed in conversation appear to great disadvantage on committing their thoughts to paper; and others who write learnedly, elegantly, politely, and acutely, so dull and apparently so weak in conversation, as to be considered as unpleasant and uninstructive companions. I have observed this so often, as to be led to think, what may appear paradoxical, that a genius for writing and a genius for talking are different in their nature.

It appears to me that superficial men talk most fluently, and, in mixed companies, most agreeably. They are usually gay and cheerful, for their spirits are not exhausted by deep thought, nor drawn from things before them by absence. But gaiety and cheerfulness give them, in the convivial hour, a grace which the profound scholar, who utters his thoughts with gravity and hesitation, can seldom display.

A man of a superficial mind and little genius has no diffidence arising from those delicacies and sensibilities which often cruelly distress men of real ability. What he thinks, or has read, or heard, he utters with the confidence of an oracle: ignorant of objections, and fearless of mistake. His confidence gives him credit. The company is always disposed to listen with attention when any man speaks with the assurance of undoubting conviction. Attention gives him additional spirits, and he begins to claim the greatest share of conversation as his right, and at length, overpowers with volubility and emphasis the silent or gentle diffidence of modest merit.

Ignorant and superficial admirers, finding a voluble speaker just calculated for the meridian of their understandings, are highly delighted with him as a companion, and cry him up as a prodigy of parts and abilities.

Their voices uniting in his favour, procure him, perhaps, some professional, or official employment, in which composition may be necessary. He writes, and the wonder is no more. How are the mighty fallen! *Quantum mutatus!*

Applauded by a few, he ventures to publish. A fatal venture! For he, who appeared in conversation a giant, becomes, when approached in the closet, a pigmy or a Lilliputian.

I wish to prevent the hasty formation of the idea of a man's intellectual talents or genius solely from his pleasantness or vivacity as a companion. Constant experience proves it to be a fallacious criterion. Men of great thoughts, solid judgment, and well digested learning are able indeed to speak to great advantage on great occasions; but they are not sufficiently interested in trifling, or ordinary company; and without pride, or any intention to slight, naturally retreat from nonsense or levity to the pleasant indulgence of their own contemplations; therefore, they say but little in such company, and that little often from civility rather than because they are struck with what passes, or impelled to speak by the interesting nature of the question, or the manner in which it is discussed. In the meantime, a feather will tickle and excite a fool.

It is wrong therefore, I conclude, to form a decisive opinion of a man's professional abilities, from what appears in common conversation. The only true criterion is the exercise of those abilities in some act of his profession. I judge of the companion in company, but of the lawyer's abilities at the bar or from his written opinion; of the clergyman's from the pulpit or the press; of the physician's from the repeated success of his actual practice; judge of the merchant from his punctuality and payments from his behaviour on the mart, and not from his volubility at the coffee-house.

It is an erroneous judgment, which is often formed of children, as well as men, when those are supposed to have the best parts, who talk most. Excessive garrulity is certainly incompatible with solid thinking, and is the mark of that volatile and superficial turn, which, dwelling upon the surfaces of things, never penetrates deeply enough to make any valuable discoveries. But, as no rule is without exceptions, some great thinkers, it must be confessed, have also been great talkers. . . .

The Lay Preacher

On Gothic Romance

THE RANGE of the *Lay Preacher* essays was great. Many of the papers dealt with characters from the Old and New Testaments, but these were the logical result of Dennie's efforts to live up to his title. Others pilloried human eccentricities and excesses as bodied forth in type characters. Most of the essays were social satires, in which vices, both gross and venial, were the targets. When Dennie wrote the following essay on Gothic romances in 1803, proprietors of Philadelphia's popular lending libraries were complaining that their patrons could be satisfied with nothing less than "blue blazes," subterranean vaults, bloody daggers, and supernatural chills and fevers. To this first article of his series on the vogue of Gothic fiction, published in the *Port Folio*, July 9, 1803, from which this text is taken, he prefaced the following note:

> In the series of these little papers, it was thought useful to mingle Literary with moral topics, and, sometimes, to associate the candid Critic with the earnest Mentor. A fashionable and favorite species of Romance, from the magical pen of one of the most illustrious of her tribe, led the author of the ensuing Essay into a speculation, which, should the readers of the *Port Folio* have patience to peruse, will reward him for his efforts to *praise* the Genius and Style of Mrs. Radcliffe, and to *blame* the choice of some of those topics, which cause melancholy man to consider too curiously. . . . With the decent freedom that he assumes in no uncandid analysis, may he hope that neither this ingenious Lady, nor her partizans, will be offended. . . .

"They were partly vexed with monstrous apparitions—
Or a terrible sound of stones cast down—or a roaring
voice of most savage wild beasts, or a rebounding echo
from the hollow mountains: these things made them
swoon for fear."

The Son of Sirach, in his admirable book of Wisdom, applies the above to "timorous wickedness," to those, who are haunted by the terrors of a guilty conscience, and who, on the nightly couch, sleep only to be more broad awake to images of horror. From these topics a very solemn speculation might be raised, but on a subject so tremendous, serious, and awful, it is not fit that a *Lay Preacher* should expatiate. To describe the woes of guilt, and the terrors of futurity, and to start warning and consolatory topics, is the appropriate task of the legitimate clergyman. I shall not enter this hallowed ground. I confine myself to moral, economical, literary, or political subjects; and to essay sublimer themes comports neither with my plan, nor with my sense of propriety. Into the golden harvest of the Church let the legal labourers "thrust in the sickle." I only "glean, and gather among the sheaves."

Upon these principles, I shall apply my text to a familiar and literary topic, and suppose, for example, that the readers of the modern Romance are "vexed with monstrous apparitions, and with the rebounding echo from the hollow mountains." I have not, for some time, devoted a sermon to literature, and I think that in the course of describing and criticising a certain class of fashionable writings, I can suggest a few hints, moral, practical and salutary.

I believe it is Dr. Johnson, who remarks of some of the popular tales of an early age, that a Knight, a Damsel, and a Hermit, composed all their personages, and a shipwreck and a forest all their machinery. Romances thus rudely written, and compiled from such meagre materials, were at length derided by the observers, and the developers of human nature. Fielding, and after him the respectable train of Richardson, Smollett, and Burney, laughed at witches and woods, led their reader into social throngs, and introduced him, not to magicians, but to men, acting from the ordinary impulses of humanity. An innkeeper was found to be a much more amusing, as well as more natural character, than a Griffin. Women of sensibility and taste excited our admiration and love more than Urganda the sage, or Queen Pintiquiniestra. Commodore Trunion was discovered to be a heartier fellow than Don Belianis of Greece, and Grandison, Andrews, Jones, and Pickle, much finer gentlemen than Sir Launcelot of the Lake, or Florismarte of Hyrcania. Fielding's landladies proved more agreeable dragons than those of chivalry, and in the useful narrative of the life of Cecilia or of Camilla, more interesting description was found, than of a burning lake, a submarine palace, a giant, or a goblin.

But a style of writing, claiming close affinity with the rude romance of the twelfth century, has been lately introduced; and great names and debauched taste have given currency to the marvellous, the terrific, and the gloomy. Lord Orford, more generally known, perhaps, by the familiar name of Horace Walpole, was among the first of those, who, in the full blaze of the 18th century, chose to excite from the shades of Gothic superstition the dreary phantoms of the cave and cloister. His Castle of Otranto, and his tragedy, the Mysterious Mother, revived the exploded fondness for chivalric personages, improbable adventures, horrid incidents, and unnatural characters. He was followed by certain German writers, and by a Lady, the plots of whose novels I am half inclined to forgive, from my admiration of the purity and grace of her language, and her descriptions of natural scenery, which she ever beholds with the eye of a painter. But the example of Mrs. Radcliffe has seduced a tribe of minor authors, and old castles, sheeted ghosts, gliding light, and dank dungeons, described with intolerable prolixity, nauseate the judicious reader. All parts of Europe have been ransacked for 'old wive's fables,' respecting the wars of barons, the seclusion of beauty, the drugged bowl, and the bloody dagger. We have 'Haunted Caverns' and 'Haunted Palaces.' We have 'Mysteries Elucidated,' and mysteries not elucidated, together with mysteries so mysterious, that they never can be elucidated. Nay, a wretched imitator of Mrs. Radcliffe, one Mr. John Fox, has published a thing with the title of the 'Mysterious Pregnancy,' which must certainly be one of the most merry mysteries, within the memory of man. In London you may have a Sorcerer for half a crown, and his wand into the bargain. A Monk is as familiar in a bookseller's shop as a critic or a lounger; one may easily shake hands with an Enchanter, and if you wish to be acquainted with Danish, Saxon or Norman nobles, you may find them in every street. They all live in castles; and whether you ask for Edwy or Ethelred, or Robert and Adela, you will discover that they are all most agreeably in fear of their lives, and are well provided with chains, bread and water, rusty swords, poison, and other conveniences.

In works thus constructed, you may discover yet more to ridicule, or to reprehend. Wearisome sameness pervades the whole. A gallery, an unexplored chamber, a cottage on the shore, a cloister among the mountains, a distressed lady, and a few drops of blood, these are the scanty materials of the modern novelist. Their personages are useless, because they are not like other men and women. The good and the evil beings in romance have no more resemblance to humanity, than SHAKESPEARE'S fairies, or Caliban the monster. Adeline and Emily St. Aubert do not look like the pretty women of our acquaintance. These heroines are more sensitive, and more 'vexed with apparitions,' than other females. Under such woes human nature would not merely totter, but fall. On the other hand, the characters of Schedoni and Spalatro exceed, in malignancy, all the fiends with which MILTON has peopled his Hell. It is my delight and solace to disbelieve that Man is so desperately wicked. I know that malicious Monks, and revengeful Italians exist; but they do not appear in such horrid forms as in the romances of Radcliffe. She has embodied phantoms. In visions of the night, when deep sleep falls on others, she has seen, through the coloured glass of her telescope of fancy, a world of her own. It is not like our world. It is like the city of Shim Sham, all is moonshine and vapour.

The subject swells under my hands, and I cannot confine it within the narrow limits of a single sermon. Next week, I shall pursue my remarks and reflexions: till then, gentle reader, adieu; and may you nod sagaciously, rather than sleep profoundly, over what I have thus far imperfectly written.

On the Pleasures of Study

DENNIE devoted a section entitled "Literary Intelligence," in the first issue of the *Port Folio*, January 3, 1801, to an explanation of his literary models and his purpose in writing *The Lay Preacher*:

As the title appears ludicrous to some, and obscure to others; as many start at the word *Preacher*, and many sneer at a *Layman* tampering with theology, it is proper to state that the work in question is not a volume of sermons. It is a series of essays, modelled after the designs of Addison, and the harmless and playful levity of Oliver Goldsmith. The mottoes are copied from the oriental writings; but they are either a moral lesson, an economical precept, or a biographical picture. The topics, to which they are prefixed, are didactic, descriptive, or airy, as the gravity, or the humour of the hour prompted. On the fenced, and walled, and hallowed ground of religion, the author has never presumed to trench, nor carelessly, nor wantonly approach the confines of the regular clergy. . . .

The following essay appeared in the *Port Folio* for January 23, 1808.

Blessed is he that readeth.—*Rev.* i. I.

Whenever I reflect upon my habitual attachment to books, I feel a new glow or gratitude towards that Power who gave me a mind thus disposed, and to those liberal friends who have allowed the utmost latitude of indulgence to my propensity. Had I been born on a barbarous shore, denied the glorious privileges of education and interdicted an approach to the rich provinces of literature, I should have been the most miserable of mankind. With a temperament of sensibility, with the nerves of a valetudinarian, with an ardent thirst for knowledge and very scanty means for its acquisition, with a mind often clouded with care and depressed by dejection, I should have resembled the shrinking vegetable of irritableness, and like the mimosa of the gardens, have been doomed to be at once stupid and sensitive. The courses of nature and fortune having taken a different direction, parental benignity having furnished me with the keys, and discipline and habit having conducted me through the portico of education, I have ever found, whether walking in the vestibule of science, or meditating in the groves of philosophy, or hearkening to historians and poets, or rambling with Rabelais, such excellent companions that life has been beguiled of more than half its irksomeness. In sickness, in sorrow, in the most doleful days of dejection, or in the most gloomy seasons in the calendar, study is the sweetest solace and the surest refuge, particularly when my reading is directed to that immortal book whence the theme of this essay is taken. In an hour of adversity, when I have caught up this precious volume, I have found instantly the balm of Gilead and the medicine for the mind. The darkness of despair has been succeeded by the brightest rays of cheerfulness, and in place of grim phantoms I have found comfort, peace, and serenity.

I hope that this style of speaking occasionally in the first person will be forgiven, even by the most fastidious reader, when he adverts to the custom of my predecessors. A periodical writer can hardly avoid this sort of egotism, and it is surely very harmless when its employer muffles himself in the mantle of concealment and in the guise, whether of a shrewd Spectator or a simple Lay Preacher, walks unobtrusively abroad. Mr. Addison and Monsieur Montaigne perpetually indulge this habit; and on a very careful inspection of many editions of their essays, I have always found, by certain infallible marks, that those speculations had been most diligently perused which abound in little sketches of the manners, humours, and habits of their authors. We are naturally curious thus to peep through the keyhole of a study, to see a writer in his elbow-chair, and to listen to his story with the fondness and familiarity of friendship. Anonymous authors have a prescription from Parnassus to paint themselves; and when by a Tatler, a Spectator, or a Connoisseur, nothing but good colours and modest tinting is employed, men look with mingled curiosity and complacency at the picture. In a speculation on the blessings derived from a studious temper, if a miniature of a lover of books is introduced, provided it be a tolerable resemblance and viewed in a proper light, it will, by an easy association, lead the observer to reflect more intensely upon the value of literature.

The utility and delight of a taste for books are as demonstrable as any axiom of the severest science. The most prosperous fortune is often harassed by various vexations. The sturdiest son of strength is sometimes the victim of disease. Melancholy will sometimes involve the merriest in her shade, and the fairest month of the year will have its cloudy days. In these dreary seasons, from which no man may hope to escape, sensual delights will fill scarcely a nook in the gloomy void of the troubled time. "Brief as the lightning in the collied night," this sort of pleasure may flash before the giddy eyes, but then merely for a moment, and the twinkling radiance is still surrounded with the murkiest gloom. Eating, drinking, and sleeping; the song and the dance, the tabret and viol, the hurry of dissipation, the agitation of play—these resources, however husbanded, are inadequate to the claims of life. On the other hand, the studious and contemplative man has always a scheme of wisdom by which he can either endure or forget the sorrows of the heaviest day. Though he may be cursed with care, yet he is surely blessed when he readeth. Study is the *dulce lenimen laborum* of the Sabine bard. It is sorrow's sweet assuager. By the aid of a book he can transport himself to the vale of Tempe or the gardens of Armida. He may visit Pliny at his villa, or Pope at Twickenham. He may meet Plato on the banks of Illyssus, or Petrarch among the groves of Avignon. He may make philosophical experiments with Bacon, or enjoy the eloquence of Bolingbroke. He may speculate with Addison, moralize with Johnson, read tragedies and comedies with Shakspeare, and be raptured by the rhetoric of Burke.

In many of the old romances we are gravely informed that the unfortunate knight in the dungeon of some giant, or fascinated by some witch or enchanter, while he sees nothing but hideousness and horror before him, if haply a fairy or some other benignant being impart a talisman of wondrous virtue, on a sudden our disconsolate prisoner finds himself in a magnificent palace or a beautiful garden, in the bower of beauty or in the arms of love. This wild fable, which abounds in the legends of knight-errantry, has always appeared to me very finely to shadow out the enchantment of study. A book produces a delightful abstraction from the cares and sorrows of this world. They may press upon us, but when we are engrossed by study we do not acutely feel them. Nay, by the magic illusion of a fascinating author we are transported from the couch of anguish or the gripe of indigence to Milton's paradise or the elysium of Virgil.

INTRODUCTION

AMERICAN LITERATURE came of age during the first half of the nineteenth century. The period began in a conservative reaction to the excesses of the French Revolution, which retarded the acceptance of innovations in form and ideas. A starched classicism was still dominant, and the opening years of the era were characterized by a polite enthusiasm for the heroic couplet and the Addisonian essay. By the middle of the century it had passed through the urbane period of the metropolitan Knickerbockers and had achieved greatness in the flowering of noble prose and poetry, romantic in style but close to realities in thought and understanding. It closed with the "barbaric yawps" of Walt Whitman, whose reputation as a major author awaited another generation —a generation which would set his "yawps" to inspiring music. Whitman has therefore been reserved for Volume II.

Neoclassicism, the prevailing mode in English literature during the Napoleonic wars, declined slowly in the young Republic. Such English instructional poems as Samuel Rogers's *Pleasures of Memory* (1792) and Thomas Campbell's *Pleasures of Hope* (1799) were widely read. The most popular poet in America at the turn of the century was Robert Treat Paine, a Bostonian whose *Ruling Passion* (1797) was not only a measure of the survival of the style of Alexander Pope, but evidence that American authors were accepted in so far as they followed the fashionable didactic trends. The essayists of the age, like Joseph Dennie, "The American Addison," modeled their works strictly upon the *Spectator* and the writings of the genial Goldsmith, both in form and in their choice of subjects. Also in keeping with the age was the keen interest in wit and satire. The essays in the *Salmagundi Papers* (1807–1808), by the Irving brothers and James Kirke Paulding, were humorous attempts to castigate the foibles of the New Yorkers. Thomas Fessenden's *Pills, Poetical, Political and Philosophical* (1809) was a venomous attack on political and literary objectives. Irving's *History of New York* (1809), with its eighteenth-century mock-heroic spirit, satirized the administration of Jefferson and burlesqued the old Dutch traditions of New York City. In form it followed clearly in the vein of Jonathan Swift. Even as late as 1819, the *Croaker Papers* of Fitz-Greene Halleck and Joseph Rodman Drake were written to divert Gothamites, to hit off the foibles of social climbers, and to mock contemporary politics and events. Not until after 1820 was a pronouncedly new spirit perceptible, though Halleck's *Fanny* (1819), a satiric poem in the style of *Don Juan*, had demonstrated the influence of Byron in America and prepared the way for the romanticism of James Percival, Nathaniel Parker Willis, and Richard Henry Dana.

Century

THROUGH THE CIVIL WAR

The Spirit of Nationalism

Literary America thus remained eighteenth century in temper until after 1815, but the decline of neoclassical forms and techniques was soon hastened by the rising spirit of a national pride which demanded distinctive expression. Although the call for a native American literature was common in the decades after the Treaty of Paris (1783), it assumed giant proportions after the War of 1812. As early as the 1790's Royall Tyler, dramatist and novelist, and Noah Webster, nationalistic essayist and lexicographer, had called for an American language, an American epic, and an American literary achievement that would be a unique force among the nations of the world. Such patriotic agitation was part of the spirit of independence which led to the declaration that America should produce something to justify her new position in the family of nations, and also to the feeling that her literature should serve to safeguard her political experiment. Thus it was that Tyler insisted that American writers ought to cling to ordinary American life and avoid foreign manners based upon the caste system of Europe.

The nationalism that arose in the second decade of the nineteenth century was part of a Western World movement resulting from the breakup of Napoleon's empire, a movement which gave rise to regional pride in almost every European country. In America nationalism expressed itself in demands for a literature in keeping with the establishment of republican institutions. Moved by a desire to exalt the glory of America, authors turned to celebrate republicanism and manifest their delight in native subjects. A particular phase of the movement was the prompt refutation which American writers, speakers, and editors made to the strictures of Tory critics, especially to the attacks of the English *Quarterly Review*, and to the famous taunt of Sydney Smith in the *Edinburgh Review* in 1820: "In the four quarters of the globe, who reads an American book?"

In the earliest decades of the nineteenth century the desire for a native literature led to a search of our national past for material that could be treated in the Gothic tradition of Horace Walpole, in the autobiographical method of Daniel Defoe, or in the Oriental fashion of Lord Byron. At the turn of the century Charles Brockden Brown patriotically discarded "puerile superstition and exploded manners, Gothic castles and chimeras" and used in his fiction "incidents of Indian hostility and the perils of the wilderness" as materials more suitable for an American novelist. A few years later Irving and Cooper found distinctive American traits in the characters of the Dutch and the Indians.

By 1819 the feeling for nationalism had grown so great that everywhere the call sounded to celebrate American scenery, American seasons, and American heroes of the sea, frontier, and Revolution. Nativism, however, was no longer the cry.

It was enough if the writing proved interesting; it was enough if American subjects were cast in molds popular in England so that the American achievement might be properly measured and English approval the more readily assured. American writers like John Neal, Washington Allston, and Robert Sands made ready use of all forms that the English poets were making popular in an attempt to prove American alertness to the latest literary fashions. Irving's cosmopolitanism helped to win acclaim for *The Sketch Book* (1819–1820) on both sides of the Atlantic, while Fenimore Cooper's fiction won an audience by free employment of red men and mildly historical material.

Although Cooper enjoyed depicting the majesty of the American landscape in the grand manner, he thought that the display of a democratic spirit and the promulgation of "distinctive political opinions," rather than the glorification of native scenery, was the secret of true nationality in literature. Others, like William Cullen Bryant, offended by the literary chauvinists, stoutly refused to applaud a book merely because it was written by an American upon a native subject. Still others held that America as a subject ought to have a claim upon Americans as Americans, a sentiment voiced by Emerson in his characteristic antitraditional spirit: "Why should these words, Athenian, Roman, Asia, and England, so tingle in the ear? Where the heart is, there the muses, there the gods sojourn and not in any geography of fame. Massachusetts, Connecticut River and Boston Bay you think paltry places, and the ear loves names of foreign and classic topography. But here we are; and, if we tarry a little, we may come to learn that here is best."

The Knickerbockers

About 1820 there appeared on the scene an important group of New York authors whom history has designated "The Knickerbockers," chiefly after the pseudonym "Diedrich Knickerbocker" used by Washington Irving for his first important work, *A History of New York*. Though this new literary school claimed many lesser writers, such as James Kirke Paulding, Joseph Rodman Drake, and Fitz-Greene Halleck, it is best represented by the works of its three leaders, Washington Irving, James Fenimore Cooper, and William Cullen Bryant. Partly because of Irving's priority in activity, and partly because of the abundance and popularity of his writings, Irving became the central figure among the Knickerbockers. The enthusiastic reception of one book, *The Sketch Book of Geoffrey Crayon, Gent.*, established Irving's reputation and led to imitation in many circles. However, none of the rivals—Lewis Gaylord Clark, Richard Henry Dana, Sr., and Nathaniel Parker Willis—equaled Irving in the *genre* of the literary sketch, and his "Rip Van Winkle" and "The Legend of Sleepy Hollow" still remain classics in the literature of the short story.

Irving's success came in 1820; the next year William Cullen Bryant's first volume, *Poems* (1821), appeared and established his reputation as a distinguished American poet. Bryant captured the mood of the day with his echoes of the English "graveyard school," his celebration of the theme of the transiency of all things, and his appreciation of the beauty of his native environment. But he had also notes of distinction: the Wordsworthian dignity in blank verse, the sense of the healing power of nature, and visions of the grandeur and vastness of the country. "It is his proper praise," wrote Emerson, "that he first and he only made known to mankind our northern landscape." Bryant supplanted these themes in such poems as "The Lapse of Time" and "The Antiquity of Freedom" with the glorification of the national democratic ideal, of a government dedicated to the principles of freedom and justice.

The greatest novelist in the Knickerbocker group was James Fenimore Cooper, whose works probably have been more extensively read than those by any other American author. With *The Spy* (1821) he achieved instantaneous success; in it he applied the antiquarian methods of Scott to the subject of the American Revolution, proving that the methods of historical romance were as adaptable to America as they were to Europe. Two years later, when Cooper produced *The Pioneers*, the first of the Leatherstocking Tales, and *The Pilot*, the first of his sea stories, he entered the provinces of his greatest achievements. In each of these series he used backgrounds well known to him, the wilderness and the sea, and on these materials his place in literature rests. Cooper's most popular theme was the receding frontier with its colorful Indian warriors, a subject properly antiquarian, romantic, and distinctively American.

Cooper's novels not only established him as the first great American romancer, but they also reveal him as a shrewd and doughty critic of American society in its formative years between 1820 and the Civil War. Possessed of a more critical mind than that of his genial contemporary, the "easily pleased" Washington Irving, Cooper addressed himself to interpreting and criticizing the democratic form of government. He was a patrician-democrat of much the same stamp as Hugh Henry Brackenridge a generation earlier, and he advocated a brand of democracy that puzzled and irritated many of his countrymen. In the "era of the common man," they disliked his denunciation of the leveling-down tendencies in Jacksonian America. Like Brackenridge, Cooper feared that the majority would fall prey to demagogues, and that they would fail to discriminate between public opinion and law. He envisioned a social system combining the advantages of democratic liberty and the virtues of the old aristocratic order of landed gentlemen to which he was allied by birth and marriage.

Like the Knickerbockers, Herman Melville also came from New York City, but he was a lone figure of the mid-century and belonged to no particular group. In the temper of Hawthorne, Melville was a novelist more interested in the motives and fate of men than in the externalities of life. Though transcendental in his concern for the metaphysical and his passionate probing "into the essence of things . . . that which is beneath the seeming," he rejected the transcendental optimism toward nature and the general benevolence of the universe. Rather, the evil in the world became the center for Melville's writing: the abuses in the American navy and merchant marine, tyranny aboard whaling vessels, the rascality of French and English traders, and the blighting effects of white man's civilization upon a South Sea paradise. Contemplation of evil in so many realms led to demands for justice, as in *White-Jacket* (1850), to queries about the genesis of evil, as in the post-

humous *Billy Budd* (1924), to an indictment of life's realities, political, ecclesiastical, and social, as in *Mardi* (1849). Preoccupation with these problems gave a philosophical cast to his works which record his spiritual daring in seeking answers to those giant riddles of the universe: providence, foreknowledge, will, and fate. His masterpiece, *Moby Dick* (1851), is a notable achievement of original power in world literature.

Unitarianism and Transcendentalism

Unitarianism at first was primarily a New England movement. Like the older Trinitarian group, the Unitarians followed the Congregational form of church organization. From the time of the first avowedly Unitarian Church, King's Chapel of Boston, in 1785, the trend toward rational religion grew rapidly. In 1805, when an acknowledged Unitarian, the Reverend Henry Ware, captured the influential Hollis Professorship of Divinity at Harvard, the way to theological infiltration was opened, despite the establishment within three years of the conservative Andover Theological Seminary to offset this triumph of the liberals. Important events in the movement were William Ellery Channing's sermon at the ordination of the Reverend Jared Sparks in Baltimore in 1819, the meeting of the Berry Street Conference of Ministers in 1820, and the organization, in 1825, of the American Unitarian Association.

The liberal rationalism of this Unitarian movement, the inheritor of the surviving deism, weakened Calvinistic religious orthodoxy, especially by its opposition to the doctrines of inherited guilt and eternal punishment. Its influence, however, was fairly restricted to the East. West of the Appalachians (with the exception of an area around Cincinnati), the democratic sects of Methodists and Baptists not only rejected a rigorous predestination but expressed their equalitarianism through revival services. Unitarianism, except for the followers of Channing, had become a tepid, negative doctrine, without a strongly emotional appeal, but it had clung to the miracles and the concept of the divine origin of the Scriptures. The transcendentalists, who began as Unitarians, finally rejected not only the historical concepts of

Biblical interpretation, but denied the efficacy of understanding as compared with intuitive sources of knowledge. They found a fundamental defect in right-wing Unitarianism: it neglected the poetic side of man's nature. Emerson voiced their objection when he declared that every man is a poet. Each individual, according to the transcendentalists, received inspiration directly from the oversoul or universal nature, and each individual was, in a kind of Plotinian scheme, connected with the soul of the universe. Thus transcendentalism was at once religious and philosophical. Although it had no "organization" or consistent body of doctrine, it attracted so many social and political reformers and thinkers, such as Theodore Parker and George Ripley, that it was popularly regarded as a "movement." In this character it fostered the Brook Farm Association, sponsored a magazine, *The Dial* (1840–1844), sent lecturers, especially Parker and Emerson, upon Lyceum circuits, and prompted many books and magazine articles.

American transcendentalism, a current in the broad stream of nineteenth-century humanitarian and romantic thought, had more than one source, including the mystical aspects of Jonathan Edwards's Puritanism, with its faith in divine light "immediately imparted to the soul by the spirit of God." The central idea of transcendentalism went back to Immanuel Kant, German metaphysician, who contended that there were sources of knowledge, by him denominated *transcendental* forms, which (contrary to the sensationalism of John Locke) had not been acquired through the senses, and that these sources, these intuitions of the mind or "untaught sallies of the soul," have a validity greater than the integrated knowledge gained from the senses. These ideas, of which a belief in the infallibility of intuition is perhaps the most fundamental, came from a variety of sources besides Kant. The French eclectic school of Victor Cousin was one, but he, Collard, and their associates were primarily interpreters of German idealism. The same was true of the two main English sources of idealistic concepts: Coleridge, in *Aids to Reflection* (1925), and Carlyle, in *Sartor Resartus* (1833–1834); they became convenient transmitters of German thought. Emerson, Thoreau, and Parker gained ideas from Plato, from the mysteries of the

Oriental scriptures, and from the Swedish mystic, Emanuel Swedenborg. But they were heirs of Unitarian rationalism as well, and in the background of Unitarianism there was the Shaftesburian teaching about nature and humanitarianism and the universe as the reflection of the mind of God.

The importance of the transcendental movement is not in the central figures who comprised it, George Ripley, Orestes Brownson, and Bronson Alcott, but rather in those fearless and individual thinkers, Emerson and Thoreau, whose literary significance is the chief reason for referring to it at all. If it is true that the movement may conveniently be found in the journals and writings of these two men, it is also true that it is not the typical phases that are reflected there. Emerson's statement of the transcendental position is best found in his *Nature* (1836), which was a kind of *vade mecum* of the transcendentalists. Thoreau called himself a mystic and a transcendentalist, and his *Walden* (1854) has been proclaimed a treatise in transcendental economics.

Reform Movements

Unitarianism gave considerable comfort to leaders of reform movements, for the high estimate of human nature resulting from Unitarian concepts instigated beliefs in the perfectibility of man and his environment. Though the Unitarians lost their fervid interest in theological doctrines, they did not at the same time experience a weakening of their moral sense; and many of them, too emotional for flaccid intellectual exercise, turned to reform movements as an outlet for energy formerly used in fighting creeds. Moreover, a sound moral and logical reason for humanitarian impulses is inherent in the emphasis of all religious groups— Calvinistic, Unitarian, and Quaker—on the Fatherhood of God, a doctrine which prompted a belief in the brotherhood of man. Of even greater significance, however, were such material factors as the depression of 1837 (a financial panic that caused acute distress and was ended only by the Mexican War), the flurry of canal construction, and the mania accompanying the gold rush. These events led to much public clamor for more liberal land policies, more internal improvements, currency reforms, and a host of other programs. 4.

The woman's rights movement began when such crusaders as Lucretia Mott and Elizabeth Cady Stanton became indignant at being denied admission, because of their sex, to the antislavery convention in London in 1840. An abler though scarcely calmer protagonist for equal rights was the intellectual Margaret Fuller who, in *Woman in the Nineteenth Century* (1845), sought to elevate the position of women to the plane of democratic equality enjoyed by men. The movement for legal, political, and industrial equality made much greater strides, however, in the latter half of the century. *Womens' rights,*

Another reform movement well started by 1845 was the organized effort for temperance. The American Society for the Promotion of Temperance was formed in 1826, and international co-operation began in 1851 with the Order of Good Templars in Utica, New York. Shortly thereafter, a novel by Timothy Shay Arthur, *Ten Nights in a Barroom, and What I Saw There* (1854), made its author the teetotalers' prose laureate and did more for the cause than any of the thousands of temperance tracts of the day. J. B. Gough began lecturing for temperance in 1842 and secured pledge-signers by the thousands on his numerous tours. Other men of prominence who lent their public support to the movement before the Civil War *vs,* included Lyman Beecher, William Lloyd Garrison, William Ellery Channing, and Elihu Burritt, "the learned blacksmith." The latter two did not limit their efforts to one cause, and labored more ardently to arouse public opinion against war than against spiritous liquors. *Temperance* *war*

More portentous in scope and effect was the antislavery movement. As early as 1833 slaves in the British West Indies had been freed, but the increasing importance of slave labor in expanding cotton production, especially in Alabama and Mississippi, put a temporary end to a strong Southern movement for abolition. The south-westward migration, the invention of the cotton gin, and the opening of new lands for exploitation were the principal factors in fixing Negro slavery upon the South. The militant crusade for emancipation had its real beginning with William Lloyd

Garrison's *Liberator* (1831), a paper that continued for thirty-five years as a blatant mouthpiece of the abolitionists. Though there was considerable *anti-slavery* sentiment against extending slave territory (slavery had been kept out of the Northwest Territory by the Ordinance of 1787, and out of other states north of 36° 30' by the Missouri Compromise in 1820), there was little general public interest in the abolition movement as such until the 1850's. Many people realized that abolition did not constitute a solution to the Negro problem, and they were not attracted to the character of the agitators, who were too frequently intemperate in language and fanatic in their approach to solutions. The vituperative attacks of men like Garrison made many enemies in the North and even divided the ranks of the Anti-Slavery Society. Other than the bigoted abolitionists, men of talent and culture, such as Wendell Phillips, Theodore Parker, and Henry Ward Beecher, devoted much time to writing and making speeches for the cause. For a time, crusaders were denied space on Lyceum programs, and their demands for the use of pulpits and platforms caused serious controversies and schisms. The Liberty party, as a minority group, was the entering wedge which defeated the Whigs in 1844. In 1848 and 1852, abolitionists and free-soilers joined in the Free-Soil party, and in 1856 the new Republican party became the rallying organization for the antislavery forces. The enactment of the Fugitive Slave Law in 1850 drew the lines between North and South much more sharply. When this was followed by the Burns case in Boston, the Dred Scott decision, the spectacle of "bloody Kansas," and John Brown's raid at Harper's Ferry, both North and South were aroused to fever heat. Finally, the uncompromising temper of the abolitionists made any solution but war impossible.

Of particular importance among the literary *Whittier* leaders in this movement were John Greenleaf *&* Whittier and James Russell Lowell. Influenced *Lowell* by Robert Burns's feeling for democratic fellowship, and imbued with the Quaker doctrines of brotherhood of man, Whittier was an avowed believer in reform. He served the antislavery campaign by participating in conventions and by being its spokesman in newspapers and magazines.

In such poems as "Massachusetts to Virginia" he argued that the dignity of man was incompatible with slavery, and in "Laus Deo" he applauded the ultimate success of the antislavery program. Lowell, the younger of the two leaders, had a pronounced faith in human nature and a sympathetic attitude toward social problems. Though he was interested chiefly in expressing his romantic ideas in poetic form, he also wrote as a critic of current enthusiasms, and in such works as *The Biglow Papers* (1846, 1867), and in his contributions to *The Anti-Slavery Standard*, he decried the extension of slavery and adopted the humanitarian beliefs of his wife, Maria White Lowell, an ardent abolitionist.

Apart from Lowell, the writers of Cambridge had little sympathy with reform movements. Even Emerson, at Concord, was dubious about the reform activities of some of his followers, and remarked when queried about his unwillingness to join the communal experiment at Brook Farm: "Shall I raise siege to this hen-coop which is myself to lay siege to the towers of Babylon?" Nathaniel Hawthorne, who spent seven months at Brook Farm, could not stand the kind of defeatists attracted to such communities nor the brand of reformers he came in contact with at West Roxbury. For the rest of his life Hawthorne associated reform with blind and intransigent single-mindedness. In "The Hall of Fantasy" (1843), he characterized reformers as those who had "got possession of some crystal fragment of truth, the brightness of which so dazzled them that they could see nothing else in the wide universe."

New England Renaissance

Literary florescence in New England came after 1830 with the emergence of a school of writers whose works made the period a "golden age" in American letters. Universal Calvinism in New England had passed; the strict authority of Puritan dogma had been undermined by new doctrines and fresh influences. Rationalism, mysticism, individualism, and humanitarianism were stimulating the New England mind; the areas of Concord, Cambridge, and Boston were developing into fields for experiment, reform, and humanism.

The creative impulse in the section which had seemed to be suffering from atrophy since the time of Jonathan Edwards now flowered in a notable revival of letters and leadership.

James Russell Lowell, scholar, poet, critic, essayist, editor, orator, and diplomat, was a vigorous representative of this golden age. He began his varied and distinguished career as a writer of sonnets and humanitarian pieces, but soon he was penning *The Vision of Sir Launfal* (1848), a contribution to the romantic revival of the past, and writing the effective, controversial verse of *The Biglow Papers*, in which he transformed the Yankee dialect into a literary medium. *A Fable for Critics* (1848) and *Conversations on Some of the Old Poets* (1846) indicated clearly Lowell's capacity as a critic, and prepared the way for his editorship of the *Atlantic Monthly* (1857–1861) and the *North American Review* (1864–1872). Lowell's later efforts were spent in making public addresses and writing odes and critical essays, achievements which exhibit the author as one nourished on European culture, humanistic and cosmopolitan in spirit, and sympathetic and penetrating in his interpretations.

Another staunch New Englander was Oliver Wendell Holmes, who contributed to the fields of both literature and medicine. Boston's favorite wit, he was probably America's foremost poet in the tradition of *vers de société* which the English poets Matthew Prior, Frederick Locker-Sampson, and W. S. Gilbert made famous. He was also a scientific literary man, busy destroying nineteenth-century illusions. He was not, as he has been accused of being, a flogger of dead horses. His reflections upon the impact of science on theological dogma, his trenchant diatribes against the nostrum mania, and his contributions to medicine are now properly appreciated. In his war on the surviving tenets of Calvinism he was as interesting in his way as Emerson in his flank attacks through transcendentalism, and like Emerson, he belonged to the tradition of the essay in his famous series which began with *The Autocrat of the Breakfast-Table* (1857), and concluded with *Over the Tea-Cups* (1888).

Of all the New Englanders, the poet who made the greatest impression upon his generation was

Henry Wadsworth Longfellow, who was perhaps the most widely read poet in English in the century. His popularity and fame at home and abroad won him the honor of being the first American to be memorialized by a bust in the Poets' Corner of Westminster Abbey. Longfellow's poems have been praised for their lyric beauty, for their vivid imagery, and for their fine craftsmanship, especially in the sonnets; but today, though these qualities are recognized, his work is often criticized for its facile didacticism. Longfellow was the true romanticist in his general disregard of contemporary subjects and his strong preference for the remote in time and place, though occasionally his treatment of the domestic and homely is an exception to this detachment. His travels in Europe and his study of foreign literature undoubtedly influenced his handling of American themes, and his numerous translations of European works gave him a facility for blending form and substance without diffusion. These translations also illustrated Longfellow's attempt to bring home to Americans the vast treasures of lyric and narrative from the European storehouse. His purpose was to raise the knowledge of his fellow Americans to the level of European achievement; through his poetry the walls of his classroom in the Harvard Yard were extended to include all America. He went on, however, to celebrate characteristically native materials in such works as *Evangeline* (1847) and *Hiawatha* (1855), but he did not participate in the bewildering ideas and problems of the day as did Lowell and Holmes. He made no contributions to current thought nor proffered any stirring innovations.

Longfellow, Lowell, and Holmes represent the ideal among the educated Bostonians of their day. They all won contemporary fame, and in posthumous Riverside, Household, and Cambridge editions they continued to influence succeeding generations. Along with these renowned authors should be remembered that group of Boston historians who have preserved for us much of the New England tradition, retaining a sense of the human and the dramatic in all their writings. Taking a page from the historical romances of the day, men like Francis Parkman, John Lothrop Motley, and William Hickling Prescott showed that the past

was not a matter of state papers and protocols, but the time and record of living men. Whatever the field they selected—Mexico, Peru, or the Netherlands—these historians emphasized the importance of republicanism as a form of government, or, like George Bancroft, asserted the success of an achieved democracy, triumphant in its functioning, its wars, and in its symbols of freedom.

Just outside Boston, in historic Salem, lived the greatest American artist of Puritan ancestry, Nathaniel Hawthorne. His literary career, unlike those of his fellow New Englanders, was almost solely introspective and analytical. He retained strongly the ethical sense of his Puritan progenitors, but he recoiled from the rigors of the Puritan conscience, and applied its temper, not to reform or to contemplation of eternal torments, but rather to the artistic conscience of the artist and to the psychological study of evil. Hawthorne protested against the seeming negation of life to be found in the Calvinistic creed. With his main interest in the colonial past, and with his mind absorbed in the effects of evil, he was in a sense a product of his own Puritan background, yet he remained an antagonist of Puritan excesses.

Hawthorne's residence in the Old Manse for four years after his marriage did not make him a member of the Concord group of transcendentalists led by Emerson and Thoreau. Hawthorne was like them in his serious brooding over life, but he differed from them in almost every other way, from his employment of fiction as a literary medium to his distrust of science as the key to an optimistic future. He did employ, it has been contended, Emerson's concept of compensation, and he did live from April to November, 1841, at Brook Farm (though it left him unchanged), but otherwise he avoided isms and intimate social relationships.

Ralph Waldo Emerson and Henry David Thoreau were the distinguished authors of Concord who had real affinity of thought and outlook. Both were students of Oriental literature; both were professed transcendentalists; both were lovers of nature. Though Emerson was a poor camper-out, he did see enough of the outdoors for the purposes of his prose and poetry; Thoreau was constantly afield, peering, recording, winning intimacy with nature, and penetrating her secrets to seek a solution to the problem of life. Nature could produce for him his longed-for transports of mystical experience. Emerson, in a larger way, based most of his idealistic conceptions upon both the external and mystical senses of nature. He never walked as much nor looked as sharply as Thoreau, and only rarely was he seriously interested in anything less than spiritual meanings. He exhibited curiosity about science but regarded it, in the main, as a commodity, a field of knowledge which supplied him with illustrations and a store of ethical and spiritual implications. Thoreau took for his own the realm of natural science, but he did not have the equipment of an academic scientist, though he did count the annual rings of felled trees. His primary concern was with living creatures, with ecological combinations poetically viewed. He was, in short, exactly what he called himself: "a mystic, a transcendentalist, and a natural philosopher to boot."

The South

Literature in the South emerged as a vigorous movement shortly after the rise of the Knickerbockers. The lyric tradition, under the stimulus of Byron, had come to expression in the poetry of Richard Henry Wilde and Edward Coote Pinkney, and the essay had found illustration in the genial pages of William Wirt. Soon came the more important Southern contributions of John Pendleton Kennedy, which reflected both the sketch and historical romance as practiced by Irving and Scott. In *Swallow Barn* (1832), the first of his plantation novels, Kennedy developed a new romantic tradition, that of the life of the Virginia gentry. And with *Horse-Shoe Robinson* (1835) and *Rob of the Bowl* (1838) he moved into the full current of historical romance. Kennedy was instrumental, as a prominent Baltimore attorney and man of letters, in advancing Poe to a post on the *Southern Literary Messenger*, in Richmond, the leading journal of the South. But his claim to literary remembrance is clearly more valid than that based simply on his kindness to Poe, and Kennedy deserves to be remembered as one of the most graceful of American novelists.

Charleston was the largest literary center in the South both before and after 1840. Here the *Southern Review* (1828–1832) was published during its short life, and here the *Southern Quarterly Review* (1842–1857) flourished for a time. Here, too, a small group of Charleston authors issued the successive numbers of *Russell's Magazine* in the late fifties. Here the youthful Paul Hamilton Hayne brought out his poems, and literary discussion thrived. The mentor of the group was William Gilmore Simms, master of both historical and "blood pudding" romance. Indian tales, such as *The Yemassee* (1835) and *The Cassique of Kiawah* (1859), vied with historical romance as evidence of his genius. In the latter genre might be cited *The Partisan* (1835), *Mellichampe* (1836), *Katharine Walton* (1851), *The Forayers* (1855), *Eutaw* (1856), and *Woodcraft* (1854). Simms dispersed his creative energy in all types of literary activity —biography, verse, criticism, editing, history— and, of course, became involved in the sharp sectionalism which preceded the Civil War. Patterning his fiction after that of Cooper and Scott, he used much local material.

Most distinguished of the Southern writers was Edgar Allan Poe, a genius in poetry, short story, and criticism. Considered historically, his greatest contributions have been to the short story. Poe, despite an addiction to German romance in his early burlesques, finally brought to the story the elements of suspense and economy of detail that we recognize as attributes of a genre. True, he borrowed freely from the devices of the tales of terror, but his main emphasis was upon the malign rather than Gothic claptrap, and his best efforts stemmed from mystery, conscience, insanity, or remorse. It was his consistency of detail, carefully ordered events, and rational presentation that gave his stories their enduring appeal. The short story, as a form, of course, did not actually arrive until the time of Poe and Hawthorne, for in Irving and Bryant the demarcation between sketch and tale was not sharply drawn. They retained the "envelope" structure for their tales whose leisurely movement and interlarded reflections achieved mood rather than climax. Poe with his practice of cumulative effects soon put an end to the prominence of such unclassified writing.

Oratory

A prominent literary form on the American scene before 1860 was the oration, for speech rather than the printed word was still the primary agency in molding public opinion. The hundred years from 1760 to 1860 have been called the Golden Age of American oratory, and the last fifty years of this span produced the nation's most famous speakers and the country's greatest outpouring of oratorical literature. Many of the finest speeches have not been preserved from the earlier period, especially from the Revolutionary days, and the same is true of the nineteenth century prior to 1820. Important pages of the addresses of Fisher Ames, leading spokesman of New England Federalism, have survived, however, and non-theological passages from speeches by Reverend Joseph Buckminster have found their way into print. But for appreciation of genius print was never enough. Oratory was an oral art and needed the magnetic personality of the speaker, the sound of his persuasive voice, and his spontaneity, as well as the air of expectancy and even of forwardness upon the part of the audience. Every great oration was a collaboration between an intense, eager audience and an impressive, inspired, and sometimes transported speaker. And every speech of merit mounted to a figurative, rhythmic peroration which was looked forward to as its chief adornment.

After 1820 a new group of orators appeared, men with striking and impassioned utterance whose names will long be associated with the history of their period. Chief among these was Daniel Webster, whose eloquence, national spirit, learning, and splendid rhetoric remain the basis of his substantial reputation. Webster's comprehensiveness, logic, and sincerity mark him as greater than the lesser men of his era who attained the Presidency. He came close to the full height of eloquence for the age. In his later years, in what has been called his mature style, there was more of the straight exposition of thought, of rising above lucid statement and argument into vigorous and scintillating, fiery and breathless transport.

Less imaginative and poetic than Webster, Henry Clay, the protectionist from Kentucky,

always moved in his speeches on a practical level of performance. In the South John C. Calhoun, sincere student of economics and philosophy, and a skilled dialectician, indulged in no rhetorical flights. He aimed only at lucidity, and wrote in a style at once close and analytical. Appearing thus in simple address, and advancing with clarity of utterance marked with dignity and care, Calhoun deserves to be known as a writer and orator rather than as a politician.

Most of the contemporaries of these men, including Edward Everett, do not deserve the neglect that has been their lot merely because they employed oratory rather than the essay as a literary form. The greatly admired oratory of their time is too figurative, too full of purple passages to return to popular favor. Its affinity for measure and harmony, its kinship with poetry, and its love of the florid belong to an age of chivalry and of purely oral communication, not to an age of journalism.

The West

Shortly after the Revolution curiosity developed about the great Western country, especially that portion of it that lay beyond Appalachia and the settlements in the new states of Ohio and Kentucky. There had been a limited curiosity about the area at an earlier date, but few travelers ventured to explore the distant regions at a time when life was forfeit for intrusion into Indian territory. It was not until after the Indian Wars of 1782 and 1794 that any considerable number of Americans considered removing beyond the Alleghenies or west from Lake Ontario. And it was not until after the War of 1812 that settlers poured into major portions of the old Northwest Territory. At that time, descriptions of the beauty of the natural scenery, the fertility of the soil, and the majesty of the forests, which lured settlers westward, were usually oral accounts.

Before 1810 only isolated journals of Western exploration had been printed. But once the area became the center of enterprise to citizens of the older states, reports of it from various sources appeared. President Jefferson was responsible for two of the important volumes of the period. He instigated expeditions for the exploration of the sources of the Missouri, the Mississippi, and the Red rivers. The records of Pike's explorations of the Mississippi as far as Cass Lake and his travels to the headwaters of the Arkansas and the South Platte rivers were published in 1810. The results of the exploration of the Missouri and the Columbia were made belatedly available by the publication in 1814 of the papers of the Lewis and Clark expedition.

Darby's *Louisiana*, Nuttall's *Travels in Arkansas*, Beck's *Gazetteer of Illinois and Missouri*, while written primarily to assess the mineral and botanical wealth of the Mississippi Valley, nevertheless contributed to the love for the picturesque which William Bartram and Jeremy Belknap had awakened. Then came the expeditions to the Yellowstone River and the Upper Lakes and the sources of St. Peter's River. The first and last were under the leadership of Colonel Long; the second was led by Governor Cass.

A member of the Cass expedition was Henry Rowe Schoolcraft, who conducted another journey in 1832 to the sources of the Mississippi, proclaimed by him as Itasca Lake. Schoolcraft's literary interests resulted in several descriptive volumes, but especially in a volume of folklore about the Algonquin Indians that provided valuable source material for Longfellow's *Hiawatha*. The most interesting volume of the West in the earlier period was Timothy Flint's *Recollections of Ten Years in the West* (1826), which was praised for the author's fine balance of moral, intellectual, and literary qualities. The work portrays manners, keenly observed, but it is not blind to the beauty of the Allegheny hills, the picturesqueness of the Western river boatmen, and the cycloramic changes of beauty along the Mississippi and Red rivers. Flint's and Schoolcraft's descriptions were the forerunners of numerous romantic descriptions of the West. Succeeding volumes included John Frémont's *Fort Laramie and the Front Range of the Colorado Rockies* (1845), Parkman's famous *Oregon Trail* (1849), Lewis Garrad's *Wah-to-Yah, and the Taos Trail* (1850), Bayard Taylor's *Eldorado* (1850), Horace Greeley's *Overland Journey* (1860), and many others.

The literature of the West after the Civil War was a young literature of wonder, discovery, and expansion. The surrender at Appomattox Courthouse not only released soldiers for home but sent the land-hungry westward. Artists, geologists, naturalists, explorers, all contributed to the continental vision of wonder and magnificence, and at the same time wrote of the wild life of the Indian, the trapper, the hunter, and the surveyor. Before 1860 Americans had read the frontier pictures of Washington Irving, Albert Pike, Rufus Sage, T. D. Bonner, George Ruxton, and Kit Carson. After the war they read reports of Albert Richardson, A. K. McClure, and William F. Reynolds. The best literary explorer of the Colorado was John Wesley Powell, who followed the tributaries of the Colorado and the Colorado itself through the Grand Canyon; later, as administrator of the Geological Survey of the Federal government, he formulated policies of forestation, reclamation, and conservation which, if heeded, would have prevented the dust bowls of the 1920's.

Jacksonianism

The election of Andrew Jackson to the Presidency in 1828 proved a political triumph for the West and an important step in the further democratization of America. The ordinary man of the backwoods as well as the small businessman heralded Jackson as his hero, and the movement of broadening the base of democratic suffrage and privilege proceeded rapidly during Jackson's administration and that of his successor, Martin Van Buren. If reforms had been retarded from 1794 to 1828, it was because the excesses of the French Revolution had frightened the conservatives and aroused fears in some liberal circles. Now under the banner of Jackson, the evolution of democracy continued: state constitutions were revised, many of the barriers to office-holding were removed, and qualifications for suffrage liberalized.

New Englanders did not accommodate themselves easily to so sweeping a change, especially since their favorite son, John Quincy Adams, had been defeated by Jackson. Jackson's rise shocked Yankee writers into dismay over democracy. They echoed, as did Carlyle and Tocqueville, fears that democratic slogans and theories could never induce the populace to select for leaders those best able to lead. This was a problem that Brackenridge and Cooper worried over too, and one that has dogged the steps of every democratic thinker since their day. But Emerson, less despairing than his fellow New Englanders, could see in this upswing of the West a more aggressive America, determined to wipe out Old World traditions, and with them some of the empty forms of Old World society and imitative and sycophantic attitudes.

Jacksonianism was a purely native force which brought democracy home to all Americans. The celebration of the lowly had been an eighteenth-century romantic concept, and many of the democratic pieces of Longfellow, Whittier, and others stemmed from a literary tradition. But it is scarcely accurate to speak of democracy in America as initiated by the English tradition of Burns and Wordsworth. Two centuries of representative government stood behind the Federal Union, and what was social revolution in 1776 became, under Jacksonianism, simply a further remove from aristocracy toward popular rule. Jacksonianism was not so much a deepening of an eighteenth-century tradition as an onsweep of a flood which left slight traces of overseas influences. Democracy in America was entirely too large for the little literary receptacles into which some critics have tried to pour it. Ralph Gabriel, in discussing American democratic thought, satisfactorily traced its growth by emphasizing the individualism of the western pioneer and the typically free life of the American farmer, thus substituting pictures of reality for the abstract terms which can mean almost anything, and for arguments about concepts which are decorative pennants in the vast parade of humanity.

The Triumph of the Novel

Between 1800 and 1860 there was a revolutionary change in attitude toward the novel. When the period opened, fiction was generally condemned, either as a parcel of lies unworthy of serious attention or as a thing of absurdity likely to warp the characters of those addicted to reading it. This hostility was partly a result of a hesitancy to accept any comparatively new literary form, and partly a result of Puritan prejudice against imaginative writing not closely connected with fact or moral truth. But it was even more a protest against the sentimental excesses of the tale of sensibility on one hand and the absurdity of the Gothic romance on the other. When historical fiction emerged, much of the erstwhile opposition vanished. Cooper and John Esten Cooke could be read.

Not until the general ebullition of emotion, one of the marks of the romantic revolution, did women appear in any numbers as creators of imaginative literature. The sentimental novel at the turn of the century had been firmly gripped by the hands of women: Susanna Rowson, Sally Sayward Wood, Hannah Foster, and others found the tale of sensibility an inviting medium for their emotional outpourings. Substantially the same thing happened in the mid-nineteenth century. Before 1850, women had contributed freely to ladies' magazines, but had made comparatively few worthy contributions to the field of the novel. Catharine Maria Sedgwick, the most talented of the early women novelists, had gladdened a feminine world with her domestic fiction, and a few other writers merit recognition: Lydia Maria Child, Caroline Kirkland, and Margaret Fuller. But after 1850 the floodgates were opened.

The first phenomenal success was that of Susan Warner, whose tearful *The Wide, Wide World* (1850) recounted the experiences of a young orphan. Even greater success was reserved for Harriet Beecher Stowe's *Uncle Tom's Cabin* (1852), which sold more than two hundred and fifty thousand copies in one year, was translated into many foreign languages, and overwhelmed its author with international honors. A few women had discovered the kind of sentiment that could cause epic sensations in an emotionally wrought age, but scores of them put pens to paper endeavoring to capture the rising tide of sentiment for sentiment's sake. On the best-seller lists were such New England names as Caroline Lee Hentz, Ann Sophia Stephens, Sarah Josepha Hale, Maria Cummins, and Mary Jane Holmes. Popular, too, were Harriet Prescott Spofford, Louisa May Alcott, and Louise Chandler Moulton. Outside

New England were the well-known Mrs. E. D. E. N. Southworth and Augusta Jane Wilson. Little wonder that Hawthorne and Melville, serious metaphysical novelists, despaired of making any headway against such disturbing petticoat competition. This flood of feminine fiction was ephemeral, many of the novels being outgrowths of current emotional upheavals or attempts to out-sentimentalize even the eighteenth-century sentimentalists.

The Civil War

American life and literature were profoundly affected by the Civil War. It cut down many a potential author. It cut across the lives of those whose careers began in the eighteen-fifties, men like Hayne, Timrod, and Simms in the South, and De Forest, Taylor, and Aldrich in the North. In the heavy losses of men, especially among the impulsive, hotheaded youths who formed the early volunteer corps, the most idealistic wing of America's younger generation was destroyed, and the way prepared for the materialism, scepticism, and the eminently practical genius of the men who followed. In creating a shortage of labor, it speeded the adoption of machinery on farms and in towns, and opened the way for a literature first descriptive and then critical of industrialism.

Reconstruction, which followed the war and must be regarded as part of it, ushered in conditions as unpropitious for literary inspiration as ever prevailed in America's rawest pioneer days. The comparison is not inapt, for whole sections of the country had to be rebuilt; and, where the material face of the land was not affected, there were domestic tragedies that could not be forgotten, severed ties that could not be rewoven, and emotional scars that would not heal.

The Civil War exerted an influence on literature from the beginning, though many of the best works inspired by it came one or two generations after its close. For the decade of the war itself, 1860–1870, the total output may be summarized in a sentence: several collections of camp and marching songs, the speeches of Abraham Lincoln, the wartime pieces of Walt Whitman and Henry Timrod, and the novels of

John W. De Forest and Sidney Lanier constituted the response of the abler literary men to the internecine struggle.

Out of the song bag of the war era many pieces survived, gathered up in paper-backed "songsters," in magazines, or in compilations of historic ballads. The material of the songs was sometimes merely an incident, as in "Little Giffen," or "Sheridan's Ride" or "The Picket-Guard." Sometimes the military ardor was poured out in a vigorous and marked rhythmic pattern, as in "Dixie," "Marching Through Georgia," "John Brown's Body," "Battle Hymn of the Republic," "Three Hundred Thousand More," "The Battle Cry of Freedom," and "Stonewall Jackson's Way." Other songs contained sentimental notes, as "Tramp, Tramp, Tramp," and "Tenting on the Old Camp Ground," and occasionally, as in James Randall's "Maryland, My Maryland," the chivalric spirit was expressed in lines that encouraged the Southron to move to battle as the medieval knight moved to his tourney.

In Randall's lyric the literary manner is apparent and the poem serves as a transition to the Southern war poets, whose merits and promise call for special comment. Foremost among them was Henry Timrod, of literary Charleston, the best Southern poet in the interval between Poe and Lanier. Though his prewar verses were conventional, he gained in both force and spirit after 1860; and "Ethnogenesis," an ode to the proposed Southern nation, and his "Ode to the Confederate Dead at Magnolia Cemetery" showed Southern literary culture at its best. His "A Cry to Arms," and "Carolina," his most beautiful poem, clearly demonstrate his lyrical abilities.

Paul Hamilton Hayne, another gifted young man of Charleston, leader of its literary circle, and editor of *Russell's Magazine*, had his brightest hopes blighted by the outbreak of the war. Physically too frail to participate in the actual fighting, Hayne served for a time as a Confederate General's aide, intermittently writing such spirited pieces as appeared later in Simms's *War Poetry of the South*. At the close of the conflict, destitute of all possessions, he retreated to the Georgia pines where he quietly wrote the poems of his *Legends and Lyrics* (1872) and *The Mountain of the Lovers*

(1875). Though a lesser poet than Timrod, he occasionally revealed an easy eloquence and a lyrical beauty that distinguished him in the South as the "last literary cavalier." Sidney Lanier, whose participation in the war left him with a consumption-wracked body, was able to bear up until he had written masterpieces such as "The Revenge of Hamish," "Sunrise," and "The Marshes of Glynn," in the poetic-musical style in which he excelled. Shortly after the war, in 1867, he wrote a novel, *Tiger Lilies* (1867), which not only reprehended the tragedy of the conflict, but in its use of dialect and interpretation of mountaineer character anticipated the fuller Southern regionalism of Mary Noaillex Murfree (Charles Egbert Craddock) and George Washington Cable.

During the war another kind of Southern literary talent was exhibited, mostly in response to Northern satirical thrusts. Charles Henry Smith, alias "Bill Arp," revealed the persistence of the funny-man tradition. Smith's legal career had been interrupted by the war, but now and then in the midst of his wartime activities, he printed a series of letters addressed to Abe Linkhorn by a Middle-Georgia "cracker" whose remarks, though pointed, are without malice. His bulldog spirit, his animated reactions, and his homespun sentiments constituted his appeal. Employing direct accusations for palpable hits, Bill Arp represented the best satiric spirit of the South during the war and after, and his satire was always well directed, shrewd, and effective. Late in the conflict and during the Reconstruction era his tone became one of genial philosophizing, and sometimes he contrived aphorisms in the vein of other respected contemporary humorists.

In the North some stirring battle pieces were written by Thomas Buchanan Read, Julia Ward Howe, George Henry Boker, Theodore O'Hara, Francis Miles Finch, and others. Whittier's work as propagandist was over before the war broke out, but the conflict and its termination stirred him to such pieces as "Barbara Frietchie" and "Laus Deo." The war was the occasion of Lincoln's most eloquent addresses and papers, including his First and Second Inaugural and the Gettysburg Address. His speeches were models, not only in penetration and sympathy but in tact and phrasing.

THE ROMANTIC ERA IN THE MIDDLE STATES AND THE SOUTH

WASHINGTON IRVING (1783–1859)

OF THE MANY plausible labels which have been used to describe the mind and art of Washington Irving, *genial* is the one which comes closest to the core of his work. Suavity, charm, elegance, urbanity, ease, and grace—all these qualities were his in varying measures—but *genial* hits home. Merely to mention the name of Irving is to summon up a heart-warming vignette of the author in his later years, surrounded by a host of adoring nieces, basking in popular favor at Sunnyside on the Hudson. To recall his work is to invoke once more the genial warmth of the tone which casts its spell over the pages of *The Sketch Book* and *The Alhambra*. Geniality not only characterizes the charming suavity of Irving's style, a literary manner which won for America its first transatlantic triumph in belles-lettres, but it also provides an important clue to his philosophy. "I have always had the opinion," he confided in *Bracebridge Hall*, "that much good might be done by keeping mankind in good humor with one another." Irving fulfilled this modest mission.

Van Wyck Brooks described the era before the advent of Whitman and Twain as "The World of Washington Irving." Yet Irving was destined to conquer more worlds than one: the world of New Amsterdam and his own New York, the world of England and the Continent, and finally, the new world of the American West. After writing successful volumes about each of these spheres, he yielded New York to later and lesser authors, he relinquished Spanish-American history to Prescott, the West to Parkman and Mark Twain, and ended his career by tracing the life of George Washington in a biography which anticipates many of the impressionistic methods of the followers of Lytton Strachey.

Washington Irving was born in pleasure-loving New York in 1783. He took a comfortable advantage of his family's concern for his frail health by dreaming and idling while his brothers carried on their father's hardware business. Finding the sights and sounds of the growing metropolis more attractive than the austere house of his Scottish Presbyterian father, young Irving soon became a familiar figure along the New York water front and the banks of the Hudson and at the John Street playhouse, where he indulged his passion for the theatre. The shelves of the New York Society Library also offered a pleasant escape, and he read lazily, but with "a harvesting eye," in the works of Shakespeare, Addison, Goldsmith, and others. Before his fifteenth birthday, when he began his casual study of law, he had already written a play, scribbled some verse, and penned many sketches. His fragile health provided an excuse for a trip to Europe from 1804 to 1806, where he gratified his taste for "antiquities and associations." Back in New York, he was admitted to the bar in 1806—somewhat to the astonishment of his friends—but he found the books in his friend Henry Brevoort's library more to his taste than Blackstone, and soon was the prime spirit of a mildly bibulous and thoroughly gay association of kindred spirits known as "The Nine Worthies." These associates, who included, in addition to three of Irving's brothers, Henry Brevoort and J. K. Paulding, tossed off twenty numbers of a periodical essay series, *Salmagundi* (1807–1808), designed "to instruct the young, reform the old, correct the town, and castigate the age." These accomplished flippancies gave Irving a taste of literary success and the impetus for his next venture, *A History of New York* (1809), under the pen name of Diedrich Knickerbocker. It was originally intended as a burlesque of Dr. Samuel Mitchell's *Picture of New York* (1807), but was expanded to become a comic chronicle of Dutch Manhattan. Meanwhile, the death of Irving's fiancée, Matilda Hoffman, in 1809, tinged with sadness the triumphant reception of the *History*. For the next five years the author lived aimlessly, edited the *Analectic Magazine* in Philadelphia, and served desultorily as "social agent" for his brothers' firm, in which he had become a partner in 1810.

The next seventeen years were the most important in Irving's career as a man of letters. In 1815 he sailed for England to assist his brother Peter in the Liverpool office of the family business, but when the enterprise ended in bankruptcy in 1818, Irving finally determined to turn his pleasant avocation of authorship into a profession. His resources were his notebooks bulging with the impressions of a romantic traveler in England and on the Continent, where it had been his delight "to loiter about the ruined castle—to meditate on the falling tower." His chief asset was his style, in which he fused his reading and travels. He enveloped his sketches in a mood of gentle melancholy intensified by memories of the death of Matilda Hoffman and the desperate state of his family's business affairs. An instant success at home and abroad, *The Sketch Book of Geoffrey Crayon, Gent.* (1819–1820) determined his career. With the praise of Scott, Byron, Lockhart, and Hazlitt ringing in his ears, he followed the formula of *The Sketch Book* in the more diffuse and slightly less popular *Bracebridge Hall* (1822), and then, at the suggestion of Scott, crossed the Rhine to exploit the comparatively unworked vein of German folklore and literature in *Tales of a Traveler* (1824). In quest of fresh materials, Irving next visited Spain where he produced his *History of the Life and Voyages of Columbus* (1828), *The Conquest of Granada* (1829), and *The Alhambra* (1832), the last recapturing the exquisite harmony between style and subject matter which had distinguished the best of his essays in *The Sketch Book*.

Welcomed back to New York in 1832 as the leading American man of letters, Irving attempted to meet the popular demand for a book on a native subject by visiting the West. His journey resulted in *A Tour of the Prairies* (1835), but at fifty-two Irving was too old to respond fully to an environment lacking the accretions of tradition and history which he cherished in Europe. Irving's association with John Jacob Astor led to the publication of *Astoria* (1836) and *The Adventures of Captain Bonneville* (1837). The skill which Irving had gained while working over the voluminous sources of his *History of the Life and Voyages of Columbus* served him in writing a story of the fur trade, but one must go to Mark Twain for an authentic account of the American frontier. Irving's embarrassment at having written himself out was relieved by an appointment as Minister to Spain, where he served with distinction from 1842 to 1846. The biographical writings of his last years, including an eminently readable life of his master, *The Life of Oliver Goldsmith* (1849), were crowned by his five-volume *Life of George Washington* (1859). He completed the last volume shortly before his death at Sunnyside, November 28, 1859.

Irving's best work ended with *The Alhambra* in 1832. Historically he marks a transition from the eighteenth-century manner of Addison and Goldsmith to the nineteenth-century taste in the legendary and the Gothic. From Scott's *Waverley* novels he learned the retrospective view of life which his genius enabled him to make his own. In Irving's achievement, American literature needed no justification as a handmaiden to morality and politics. In a utilitarian age he threw a veil of glamor over the Hudson River as well as the Harz Mountains. His preference for the sketch and tale led to a discovery of new materials for short fiction. By blending Old World legends with American folklore and native settings in "Rip Van Winkle" and "The Legend of Sleepy Hollow," he made his readers aware that "there is a constant activity of thought and nicety of execution required in writings of this kind, more than the world appears to imagine." His legacy to American literature was mature craftsmanship and the assurance that the graces of urbanity, ease, and charm might indeed be qualities of American art.

BIBLIOGRAPHY · The standard text is that of the Author's Uniform Revised Edition, *The Works of Washington Irving* (21 vols., 1860–1861). The same text is used in the more available *Works of Washington Irving* (12 vols., 1881). Writings not to be found in the *Works* include *Journals of Washington Irving* (1919), edited by W. P. Trent and G. S. Hellman; *Journal of Washington Irving, 1828, and Miscellaneous Notes on Moorish Legend and History* (1936), edited by S. T. Williams; *Notes and Journal of Travel in Europe, 1804–1805* (1921), edited by W. P. Trent; *Notes while Preparing Sketch Book &c. 1817* (1927), edited by S. T. Williams; *Tour in Scotland, 1817, and Other Manuscript Notes by Washington Irving* (1927), edited by S. T. Williams; *Washington Irving Diary: Spain 1828–1829* (1927), edited by C. Penney; *Washington Irving on the Prairie; or, A Narrative of a Tour of the Southwest in the Year 1832* (1937), edited by S. T. Williams and B. D. Simison; and *The Western Journals of Washington Irving* (1936), edited by J. F. McDermott.

Among many separate editions of Irving's works are a few carefully edited ones: *Knickerbocker's History of New York*, edited (1919) by E. Greenlaw, edited (1927) by S. T. Williams and T. McDowell; *Letters of Jonathan Oldstyle*, edited (1941), by S. T. Williams; and *Washington Irving: Representative Selections*, edited (1934) by H. A. Pochmann, containing an admirable introduction and useful bibliography. The best bibliography is S. T. Williams and M. A. Sage, *A Bibliography of the Writings of Washington Irving* (1936).

The definitive life is that by S. T. Williams, *Washington Irving* (2 vols., 1935). Basic for all later biographies is P. M. Irving's *Life and Letters of Washington Irving, by His Nephew* (4 vols., 1862–1864). Other biographies include C. Adams, *Memoir of Washington Irving* (1870); G. S. Hellman, *Washington Irving, Esquire: Ambassador at Large from the New World to the Old* (1925); D. J. Hill, *Washington Irving* (1879); F. H. Underwood, *Washington Irving* (1890); and C. D. Warner, *Wash-*

ington Irving (1881). The important correspondence between Irving and Henry Brevoort was edited by G. S. Hellman in *Letters of Henry Brevoort . . .* (1918), and *Letters of Washington Irving to Henry Brevoort* (1918).

Among the many biographical and critical studies are S. Axson, "Washington Irving and the Knickerbocker Group," *Rice Institute Pamphlet*, XX (1933), 178–195; E. Boll, "Charles Dickens and Washington Irving," *Modern Language Quarterly*, V (1944), 453–467; H. W. Boynton, "Irving," in J. Macy (editor), *American Writers on American Literature* (1931); W. B. Cairns, *British Criticisms on American Writings, 1815–1833* (1922); H. S. Canby, *Classic Americans* (1931), 67–96; E. A. Duyckinck, *Irvingiana: A Memorial of Washington Irving . . .* (1860); E. A. Greenlaw, "A Comedy in Politics," *Texas Review* (April, 1916); L. M. Hoffman, "Irving's Use of Spanish Sources in *The Conquest of Granada*," *Hispania*, XXVIII (1945), 483–498; C. G. Laird, "Tragedy and Irony in *Knickerbocker's History*," *American Literature*, XII (1940), 157–172; E. E. Leisy, "Irving and the Genteel Tradition," *Southwest Review*, XXI (1936), 223–227; G. D. Morris, *Washington Irving's Fiction in the Light of French Criticism*, in *Indiana University Studies*, No. 30 (1916); W. C. D. Pacey, "Washington Irving and Charles Dickens," *American Literature*, XVI (1945), 332–339; H. A. Pochmann, "Irving's German Sources in *The Sketch Book*," *Studies in Philology*, XXVII (1930), 477–507; and "Irving's German Tour and Its Influence on His Tales," *PMLA*, XLV (1930), 1150–1187; I. T. Richards, "John Neal's Gleanings in Irvingiana," *American Literature*, VIII (1936), 170–179; J. A. Russell, "Irving: Recorder of Indian Life," *Journal of American History* (1931), 185–195; M. R. Small, "A Possible Ancestor of Diedrich Knickerbocker," *American Literature*, II (1930), 21–24; F. P. Smith, "Washington Irving, the Fosters, and Some Poetry," *American Literature*, IX (1937), 228–232; C. Webster, "Irving's Expurgations of the 1809 *History of New York*," *American Literature*, III (1932), 293–295; and S. T. Williams, "Washington Irving and Andrew Jackson," *Yale University Library Gazette*, XIX (1945), 67–69.

A History of New York . . . by Diedrich Knickerbocker

KNICKERBOCKER'S *History of New York* was introduced to the public through a famous literary hoax. The appearance of the book was preceded on October 26, 1809, by an advertisement in the *New York Evening Post*, soliciting information about the whereabouts of "a small elderly gentleman" named Knickerbocker. In the issue for November 6, "A Traveler" wrote that a person answering to the description of Knickerbocker was seen by the side of the road "a little above Kingsbridge." Finally, on November 16, the landlord of Knickerbocker's place of lodging announced his intention of disposing of a "very curious kind of a written book" in order to defray the hotel bills of the missing tenant. Thus heralded, the book itself appeared on December 6, 1809, being published simultaneously in New York, Philadelphia, Boston, Baltimore, and Charleston.

A History of New York from the Beginning of the World to the End of the Dutch Dynasty was written in the spirit of burlesque and inspired by such models as Cervantes, Ariosto, Swift, Fielding, and Arbuthnot. Scott recognized Irving's indebtedness to Swift, but he also noted a strain of sensibility suggesting the influence of Sterne. Along with materials wholly fictitious, Irving included some true incidents based upon antiquarian research. Despite the excesses and distortions, the history is, if we ignore certain errors and rollicking nonsense, in a broad sense authentic. The text used in this volume is that of the Hudson Edition of 1884.

[*Of the Renowned Wouter Van Twiller*] · Book III· *In Which Is Recorded the Golden Reign of Wouter Van Twiller* · Chapter I · *Of the Renowned Wouter Van Twiller, His Unparalleled Virtues— as Likewise His Unutterable Wisdom in the Law Case of Wandle Schoonhoven and Barent Bleecker —and the Great Admiration of the Public Thereat*

Grievous and very much to be commiserated is the task of the feeling historian, who writes the history of his native land. If it fall to his lot to be the recorder of calamity or crime, the mournful page is watered with his tears; nor can he recall the most prosperous and blissful era, without a melancholy sigh at the reflection that it has passed away forever! I know not whether it be owing to an immoderate love for the simplicity of former times, or to that certain tenderness of heart incident to all sentimental historians; but I candidly confess that I cannot look back on the happier days of our city, which I now describe, without great dejection of spirit. With faltering hand do I withdraw the curtain of oblivion, that veils the modest merit of our venerable ancestors, and as their figures rise to my mental vision, humble myself before their mighty shades.

Such are my feelings when I revisit the family mansion of the Knickerbockers, and spend a lonely hour in the chamber where hang the portraits of my forefathers, shrouded in dust, like the forms they represent. With pious reverence do I gaze on the countenances of those renowned burghers, who have preceded me in the steady march of existence,—whose sober and temperate blood now meanders through my veins, flowing slower and slower in its feeble conduits, until its current shall soon be stopped forever!

These, I say to myself, are but frail memorials of the mighty men who flourished in the days of the patriarchs; but who, alas, have long since mouldered in that tomb towards which my steps are insensibly and irresistibly hastening! As I pace the darkened chamber and lose myself in melancholy musings, the shadowy images around me almost seem to steal once more into existence,— their countenances to assume the animation of life,—their eyes to pursue me in every movement! Carried away by the delusions of fancy, I almost imagine myself surrounded by the shades of the departed, and holding sweet converse with the worthies of antiquity! Ah, hapless Diedrich! born in a degenerate age, abandoned to the buffetings of fortune,—a stranger and a weary pilgrim in thy native land,—blest with no weeping wife, nor family of helpless children, but doomed to wander neglected through those crowded streets, and elbowed by foreign upstarts from those fair abodes where once thine ancestors held sovereign empire!

Let me not, however, lose the historian in the man, nor suffer the doting recollections of age to overcome me, while dwelling with fond garrulity on the virtuous days of the patriarchs,—on those sweet days of simplicity and ease, which never more will dawn on the lovely island of Mannahata.

These melancholy reflections have been forced from me by the growing wealth and importance of New Amsterdam, which, I plainly perceive, are to involve it in all kinds of perils and disasters. Already, as I observed at the close of my last book, they had awakened the attention of the mother-country. The usual mark of protection shown by mother-countries to wealthy colonies was forthwith manifested; a governor being sent out to rule over the province and squeeze out of it as much revenue as possible. The arrival of a governor of course put an end to the protectorate of Oloffe the Dreamer. He appears, however, to have dreamt to some purpose during his sway, as we find him afterwards living as a patroon on a great landed estate on the banks of the Hudson; having virtually forfeited all right to his ancient appellation of Kortlandt or Lackland.

It was in the year of our Lord 1629 that Mynheer Wouter Van Twiller was appointed governor 10 of the province of Nieuw Nederlands, under the commission and control of their High Mightinesses the Lords States General and the United Netherlands, and the privileged West India Company.

This renowned old gentleman arrived at New Amsterdam in the merry month of June, the sweetest month in all the year; when dan Apollo seems to dance up the transparent firmament,— when the robin, the thrush, and a thousand other wanton songsters, make the woods to resound with 20 amorous ditties, and the luxurious little boblincon revels among the clover-blossoms of the meadows, —all which happy coincidence persuaded the old dames of New Amsterdam, who were skilled in the art of foretelling events, that this was to be a happy and prosperous administration.

The renowned Wouter (or Walter) Van Twiller was descended from a long line of Dutch burgomasters, who had successively dozed away their lives, and grown fat upon the bench of magistracy 30 in Rotterdam; and who had comported themselves with such singular wisdom and propriety, that they were never either heard or talked of,— which, next to being universally applauded, should be the object of ambition of all magistrates and rulers. There are two opposite ways by which some men make a figure in the world: one, by talking faster than they think, and the other, by holding their tongues and not thinking at all. By the first many a smatterer acquires the reputation 40 of a man of quick parts; by the other many a dunderpate, like the owl, the stupidest of birds, comes to be considered the very type of wisdom. This, by the way, is a casual remark, which I would not for the universe have it thought I apply to Governor Van Twiller. It is true he was a man shut up within himself, like an oyster, and rarely spoke except in monosyllables; but then it was allowed he

seldom said a foolish thing. So invincible was this gravity that he was never known to laugh or even to smile through the whole course of a long and prosperous life. Nay if a joke were uttered in his presence, that set light-minded hearers in a roar, it was observed to throw him into a state of perplexity. Sometimes he would deign to inquire into the matter, and when, after much explanation, the joke was made as plain as a pike-staff, he would continue to smoke his pipe in silence, and at length, knocking out the ashes, would exclaim, "Well! I see nothing in all that to laugh about."

With all his reflective habits, he never made up his mind on a subject. His adherents accounted for this by the astonishing magnitude of his ideas. He conceived every subject on so grand a scale that he had not room in his head to turn it over and examine both sides of it. Certain it is, that, if any matter were propounded to him on which 20 ordinary mortals would rashly determine at first glance, he would put on a vague, mysterious look, shake his capacious head, smoke some time in profound silence, and at length observe, that "he had his doubts about the matter"; which gained him the reputation of a man slow of belief, and not easily imposed upon. What is more, it gained him a lasting name: for to this habit of the mind has been attributed his surname of Twiller; which is said to be a corruption of the original Twijfler, or, in 30 plain English, Doubter.

The person of this illustrious old gentleman was formed and proportioned, as though it had been moulded by the hands of some cunning Dutch statuary, as a model of majesty and lordly grandeur. He was exactly five feet six inches in height, and six feet five inches in circumference. His head was a perfect sphere, and of such stupendous dimensions, that Dame Nature with all her sex's ingenuity, would have been puzzled to construct a neck capable of supporting it; wherefore she wisely declined the attempt, and settled it firmly on the top of his backbone, just between the shoulders. His body was oblong and particularly capacious at bottom; which was wisely ordered by Providence, seeing that he was a man of sedentary habits, and very averse to the idle labor of walking. His legs were short, but sturdy in proportion to the weight they had to sustain; so that when erect he had not

363

a little the appearance of a beer barrel on skids. His face, that infallible index of the mind, presented a vast expanse, unfurrowed by any of those lines and angles which disfigure the human countenance with what is termed expression. Two small gray eyes twinkled feebly in the midst, like two stars of lesser magnitude in a hazy firmament; and his full-fed cheeks, which seemed to have taken toll of every thing that went into his mouth, were curiously mottled and streaked with dusky red, like a spitzenberg apple.

His habits were as regular as his person. He daily took his four stated meals, appropriating exactly an hour to each; he smoked and doubted eight hours, and he slept the remaining twelve of the four-and-twenty. Such was the renowned Wouter Van Twiller,—a true philosopher, for his mind was either elevated above, or tranquilly settled below, the cares and perplexities of this world. He had lived in it for years, without feeling the least curiosity to know whether the sun revolved round it, or it round the sun; and he had watched, for at least half a century, the smoke curling from his pipe to the ceiling, without once troubling his head with any of those numerous theories by which a philosopher would have perplexed his brain, in accounting for its rising above the surrounding atmosphere.

In his council he presided with great state and solemnity. He sat in a huge chair of solid oak, hewn in the celebrated forest of the Hague, fabricated by an experienced timmerman of Amsterdam, and curiously carved about the arms and feet, into exact imitations of gigantic eagle's claws. Instead of a sceptre he swayed a long Turkish pipe, wrought with jasmin and amber, which had been presented to a stadtholder of Holland, at the conclusion of a treaty with one of the petty Barbary powers. In this stately chair would he sit, and this magnificent pipe would he smoke, shaking his right knee with a constant motion, and fixing his eye for hours together upon a little print of Amsterdam, which hung in a black frame against the opposite wall of the council-chamber. Nay, it has even been said, that when any deliberation of extraordinary length and intricacy was on the carpet, the renowned Wouter would shut his eyes for full two hours at a time, that he might not be disturbed by external

objects; and at such times the internal commotion of his mind was evinced by certain regular guttural sounds, which his admirers declared were merely the noise of conflict, made by his contending doubts and opinions.

It is with infinite difficulty I have been enabled to collect these biographical anecdotes of the great man under consideration. The facts respecting him were so scattered and vague, and divers of them so questionable in point of authenticity, that I have had to give up the search after many, and decline the admission of still more, which would have tended to heighten the coloring of his portrait.

I have been the more anxious to delineate fully the person and habits of Wouter Van Twiller, from the consideration that he was not only the first, but also the best governor that ever presided over this ancient and respectable province; and so tranquil and benevolent was his reign, that I do not find throughout the whole of it, a single instance of any offender being brought to punishment,—a most indubitable sign of a merciful governor, and a case unparalleled, excepting in the reign of the illustrious King Log, from whom, it is hinted, the renowned Van Twiller was a lineal descendant.

The very outset of the career of this excellent magistrate was distinguished by an example of legal acumen, that gave flattering presage of a wise and equitable administration. The morning after he had been installed in office, and at the moment that he was making his breakfast from a prodigious earthen dish, filled with milk and Indian pudding, he was interrupted by the appearance of Wandle Schoonhoven, a very important old burgher of New Amsterdam, who complained bitterly of one Barent Bleecker, inasmuch as he refused to come to a settlement of accounts, seeing that there was a heavy balance in favor of the said Wandle. Governor Van Twiller, as I have already observed, was a man of few words; he was likewise a mortal enemy to multiplying writings—or being disturbed at his breakfast. Having listened attentively to the statement of Wandle Schoonhoven, giving an occasional grunt, as he shovelled a spoonful of Indian pudding into his mouth,—either as a sign that he relished the dish, or comprehended the story,—he called unto him his constable, and pulling out of his breeches pocket a huge jack-knife, despatched it after the defendant as a summons, accompanied by his tobacco-box as a warrant.

This summary process was as effectual in those simple days as was the seal ring of the great Haroun Alraschid among the true believers. The two parties being confronted before him, each produced a book of accounts, written in a language and character that would have puzzled any but a High-Dutch commentator, or a learned decipherer of Egyptian obelisks. The sage Wouter took them one after the other, and having poised them in his hands, and attentively counted over the number of leaves, fell straightway into a very great doubt, and smoked for half an hour without saying a word; at length, laying his finger beside his nose, and shutting his eyes for a moment, with the air of a man who has just caught a subtle idea by the tail, he slowly took his pipe from his mouth, puffed forth a column of tobacco smoke, and with marvellous gravity and solemnity pronounced—that having carefully counted over the leaves and weighed the books, it was found, that one was just as thick and as heavy as the other—therefore it was the final opinion of the court that the accounts were equally balanced—therefore Wandle should give Barent a receipt, and Barent should give Wandle a receipt—and the constable should pay the costs.

This decision being straightway made known diffused general joy throughout New Amsterdam, for the people immediately perceived that they had a very wise and equitable magistrate to rule over them. But its happiest effect was, that not another lawsuit took place throughout the whole of his administration—and the office of constable fell into such decay, that there was not one of those losel scouts known in the province for many years. I am the more particular in dwelling on this transaction, not only because I deem it one of the most sage and righteous judgments on record, and well worthy the attention of modern magistrates; but because it was a miraculous event in the history of the renowned Wouter—being the only time he was ever known to come to a decision in the whole course of his life.

[The Golden Age] · Chapter IV · Containing Further Particulars of the Golden Age, and What Constituted a Fine Lady and Gentleman in the Days of Walter the Doubter

IN THIS dulcet period of my history, when the beauteous island of Manna-hata presented a scene, the very counterpart of those glowing pictures drawn of the golden reign of Saturn, there was, as I have before observed, a happy ignorance, an honest simplicity prevalent among its inhabitants, which, were I even able to depict, would be but little understood by the degenerate age for which I am doomed to write. Even the female sex, those arch innovators upon the tranquillity, the honesty, and gray-beard customs of society, seemed for a while to conduct themselves with incredible sobriety and comeliness.

Their hair, untortured by the abominations of art, was scrupulously pomatumed back from their foreheads with a candle, and covered with a little cap of quilted calico, which fitted exactly to their heads. Their petticoats of linsey-woolsey were striped with a variety of gorgeous dyes,—though I must confess these gallant garments were rather short, scarce reaching below the knee; but then they made up in the number, which generally equalled that of the gentlemen's small clothes; and what is still more praiseworthy, they were all of their own manufacture,—of which circumstance, as may well be supposed, they were not a little vain.

These were the honest days in which every woman staid at home, read the Bible, and wore pockets,—ay, and that too of a goodly size, fashioned with patchwork into many curious devices, and ostentatiously worn on the outside. These, in fact, were convenient receptacles, where all good housewives carefully stored away such things as they wished to have at hand; by which means they often came to be incredibly crammed; and I remember there was a story current when I was a boy, that the lady of Wouter Van Twiller once had occasion to empty her right pocket in search of a wooden ladle, when the contents filled a couple of corn baskets, and the utensil was discovered lying among some rubbish in one corner,—but we must not give too much faith to all these stories, the anecdotes of those remote periods being very subject to exaggeration.

Besides these notable pockets, they likewise wore scissors and pincushions suspended from their girdles by red ribands, or among the more opulent and showy classes, by brass, and even silver chains, indubitable tokens of thrifty housewives and industrious spinsters. I cannot say much in vindication of the shortness of the petticoats; it doubtless was introduced for the purpose of giving the stockings a chance to be seen, which were generally of blue worsted with magnificent red clocks, —or perhaps to display a well-turned ankle, and a neat, though serviceable foot, set off by a high-heeled leathern shoe, with a large and splendid silver buckle. Thus we find that the gentle sex in all ages have shown the same disposition to infringe a little upon the laws of decorum, in order to betray a lurking beauty, or gratify an innocent love of finery.

From the sketch here given, it will be seen that our good grandmothers differed considerably in their ideas of a fine figure from their scantily dressed descendants of the present day. A fine lady, in those times, waddled under more clothes, even on a fair summer's day, than would have clad the whole bevy of a modern ballroom. Nor were they the less admired by the gentlemen in consequence thereof. On the contrary, the greatness of a lover's passion seemed to increase in proportion to the magnitude of its object,—and a voluminous damsel, arrayed in a dozen of petticoats, was declared by a Low Dutch sonneteer of the province to be radiant as a sunflower, and luxuriant as a full-blown cabbage. Certain it is, that in those days the heart of a lover could not contain more than one lady at a time; whereas the heart of a modern gallant has often room enough to accommodate half a dozen. The reason of which I conclude to be, that either the hearts of the gentlemen have grown larger, or the persons of the ladies smaller,—this, however, is a question for physiologists to determine.

But there was a secret charm in these petticoats, which, no doubt, entered into the consideration of the prudent gallants. The wardrobe of a lady was in those days her only fortune; and she who had a good stock of petticoats and stockings, was as absolutely an heiress as is a Kamtchatka damsel with a store of bear skins, or a Lapland belle with a plenty of reindeer. The ladies, therefore, were very anxious to display these powerful attractions to the greatest advantage; and the best rooms in the house, instead of being adorned with caricatures of dame Nature, in water-colors and needlework, were always hung round with abundance of homespun garments, the manufacture and the property of the females,—a piece of laudable ostentation that still prevails among the heiresses of our Dutch villages.

The gentlemen, in fact, who figured in the circles of the gay world in these ancient times, corresponded, in most particulars, with the beauteous damsels whose smiles they were ambitious to deserve. True it is, their merits would make but a very inconsiderable impression upon the heart of a modern fair; they neither drove their curricles nor sported their tandems, for as yet those gaudy vehicles were not even dreamt of—neither did they distinguish themselves by their brilliancy at the table, and their consequent rencontres with watchmen, for our forefathers were of too pacific a disposition to need those guardians of the night, every soul throughout the town being sound asleep before nine o'clock. Neither did they establish their claims to gentility at the expense of their tailors,—for as yet those offenders against the pockets of society, and the tranquillity of all aspiring young gentlemen, were unknown in New Amsterdam; every good housewife made the clothes of her husband and family, and even the goede vrouw of Van Twiller himself thought it no disparagement to cut out her husband's linsey-woolsey galligaskins.

Not but what there were some two or three youngsters who manifested the first dawning of what is called fire and spirit; who held all labor in contempt; skulked about docks and market places; loitered in the sunshine; squandered what little money they could procure at hustle-cap and chuck-farthing; swore, boxed, fought cocks, and raced their neighbor's horses; in short, who promised to be the wonder, the talk, and abomination of the town, had not their stylish career been unfortunately cut short by an affair of honor with a whipping-post.

Far other, however, was the truly fashionable gentleman of those days—his dress, which served for both morning and evening, street and drawing-room, was a linsey-woolsey coat, made, perhaps, by the fair hands of the mistress of his affections, and gallantly bedecked with abundance of large brass buttons—half a score of breeches heightened the proportions of his figure—his shoes were decorated by enormous copper buckles; a low-crowned broad-brimmed hat overshadowed his burly visage, and his hair dangled down his back in a prodigious queue of eelskin.

Thus equipped, he would manfully sally forth with pipe in mouth to besiege some fair damsel's obdurate heart,—not such a pipe, good reader, as that which Acis did sweetly tune in praise of his Galatea, but one of true Delft manufacture, and furnished with a charge of fragrant tobacco. With this would he resolutely set himself down before the fortress, and rarely failed, in the process of time, to smoke the fair enemy into a surrender, upon honorable terms.

Such was the happy reign of Wouter Van Twiller, celebrated in many a long forgotten song as the real golden age, the rest being nothing but counterfeit copper-washed coin. In that delightful period, a sweet and holy calm reigned over the whole province. The burgomaster smoked his pipe in peace; the substantial solace of his domestic cares, after her daily toils were done, sat soberly at the door, with her arms crossed over her apron of snowy white, without being insulted by ribald street-walkers or vagabond boys,—those unlucky urchins, who do so infest our streets, displaying under the roses of youth the thorns and briers of iniquity. Then it was that the lover with ten breeches, and the damsel with petticoats of half a score, indulged in all the innocent endearments of virtuous love without fear and without reproach; for what had their virtue to fear, which was defended by a shield of good linsey-woolseys, equal at least to the seven bull-hides of the invincible Ajax?

Ah blissful and never to be forgotten age! when everything was better than it has ever been since, or ever will be again,—when Buttermilk Channel was quite dry at low water,—when the shad in the Hudson were all salmon,—and when the moon shone with a pure and resplendent whiteness, instead of that melancholy yellow light which is the consequence of her sickening at the abominations she every night witnesses in this degenerate city!

Happy would it have been for New Amsterdam could it always have existed in this state of blissful ignorance and lowly simplicity; but alas! the days of childhood are too sweet to last! Cities, like men, grow out of them in time, and are doomed alike to grow into the bustle, the cares, and miseries of the world. Let no man congratulate himself, when he beholds the child of his bosom or the city of his birth increasing in magnitude and importance,—let the history of his own life teach him the dangers of the one, and this excellent little history of Manna-hata convince him of the calamities of the other.

[*Peter Stuyvesant*] · Book V · *Containing the First Part of the Reign of Peter Stuyvesant, and His Troubles with the Amphictyonic Council* · Chapter I · *In which the Death of a Great Man is Shown to Be No Very Inconsolable Matter of Sorrow—and How Peter Stuyvesant Acquired a Great Name from the Uncommon Strength of His Head*

To a profound philosopher like myself, who am apt to see clear through a subject, where the penetration of ordinary people extends but halfway, there is no fact more simple and manifest than that the death of a great man is a matter of very little importance. Much as we may think of ourselves, and much as we may excite the empty plaudits of the million, it is certain that the greatest among us do actually fill but an exceeding small space in the world; and it is equally certain, that even that small space is quickly supplied when we leave it vacant. "Of what consequence is it," said Pliny, "that individuals appear, or make their exit? the world is a theatre whose scenes and actors are continually changing." Never did philosopher speak more correctly; and I only wonder that so wise a remark could have existed so many ages, and mankind not have laid it more to heart. Sage follows on in the footsteps of sage; one hero just steps out of his triumphal car, to make way for the hero who comes after him;

and of the proudest monarch it is merely said that, "he slept with his fathers, and his successor reigned in his stead."

The world, to tell the private truth, cares but little for their loss, and if left to itself would soon forget to grieve; and though a nation has often been figuratively drowned in tears on the death of a great man, yet it is ten to one if an individual tear has been shed on the occasion, excepting from the forlorn pen of some hungry author. It is the historian,—the biographer, and the poet, who have the whole burden of grief to sustain, who —kind souls!—like undertakers in England, act the part of chief mourners,—who inflate a nation with sighs it never heaved, and deluge it with tears it never dreamt of shedding. Thus, while the patriotic author is weeping and howling, in prose, in blank verse, and in rhyme, and collecting the drops of public sorrow into his volume, as into a lachrymal vase, it is more than probable his fellow-citizens are eating and drinking, fiddling and dancing, as utterly ignorant of the bitter lamentations made in their name, as are those men of straw, John Doe and Richard Roe, of the plaintiffs for whom they are generously pleased to become sureties.

The most glorious hero that ever desolated nations might have mouldered into oblivion among the rubbish of his own monument, did not some historian take him into favor, and benevolently transmit his name to posterity; and much as the valiant William Kieft worried, and bustled, and turmoiled, while he had the destinies of a whole colony in his hand, I question seriously whether he will not be obliged to this authentic history for all his future celebrity.

His exit occasioned no convulsion in the city of New Amsterdam nor its vicinity: the earth trembled not, neither did any stars shoot from their spheres; the heavens were not shrouded in black, as poets would fain persuade us they have been, on the death of a hero; the rocks (hard-hearted varlets!) melted not into tears, nor did the trees hang their heads in silent sorrow; and as to the sun, he lay a-bed the next night just as long, and showed as jolly a face when he rose, as he ever did on the same day of the month in any year, either before or since. The good people of New Amster-

dam, one and all, declared that he had been a very busy, active, bustling little governor; that he was "the father of his country"; that he was "the noblest work of God"; that "he was a man, take him for all in all, they ne'er should look upon his like again"; together with sundry other civil and affectionate speeches regularly said on the death of all great men: after which they smoked their pipes, thought no more about him, and Peter Stuyvesant succeeded to his station.

Peter Stuyvesant was the last, and, like the renowned Wouter Van Twiller, the best of our ancient Dutch governors. Wouter having surpassed all who preceded him, and Pieter or Piet, as he was sociably called by the old Dutch burghers, who were ever prone to familiarize names, having never been equalled by any successor. He was in fact the very man fitted by nature to retrieve the desperate fortunes of her beloved province, had not the fates, those most potent and unrelenting of all ancient spinsters, destined them to inextricable confusion.

To say merely that he was a hero would be doing him great injustice: he was in truth a combination of heroes; for he was of a sturdy, rawboned make like Ajax Telamon, with a pair of round shoulders that Hercules would have given his hide for (meaning his lion's hide) when he undertook to ease old Atlas of his load. He was, moreover, as Plutarch describes Coriolanus, not only terrible for the force of his arm, but likewise of his voice, which sounded as though it came out of a barrel; and, like the self-same warrior, he possessed a sovereign contempt for the sovereign people, and an iron aspect, which was enough of itself to make the very bowels of his adversaries quake with terror and dismay. All this martial excellency of appearance was inexpressibly heightened by an accidental advantage, with which I am surprised that neither Homer nor Virgil has graced any of their heroes. This was nothing less than a wooden leg, which was the only prize he had gained in bravely fighting the battles of his country, but of which he was so proud, that he was often heard to declare he valued it more than all his other limbs put together; indeed so highly did he esteem it, that he had it gallantly enchased and relieved with silver devices, which caused it to be related in divers histories and legends that he wore a silver leg.[n]

Like that choleric warrior Achilles, he was somewhat subject to extempore bursts of passion, which was rather unpleasant to his favorites and attendants, whose perceptions he was apt to quicken, after the manner of his illustrious imitator, Peter the Great, by anointing their shoulders with his walking-staff.

Though I cannot find that he had read Plato, or Aristotle, or Hobbes, or Bacon, or Algernon Sidney, or Tom Paine, yet did he sometimes manifest a shrewdness and sagacity in his measures, that one would hardly expect from a man who did not know Greek, and had never studied the ancients. True it is, and I confess it with sorrow, that he had an unreasonable aversion to experiments, and was fond of governing his province after the simplest manner; but then he contrived to keep it in better order than did the erudite Kieft, though he had all the philosophers, ancient and modern, to assist and perplex him. I must likewise own that he made but very few laws, but then again he took care that those few were rigidly and impartially enforced; and I do not know but justice on the whole was as well administered as if there had been volumes of sage acts and statutes yearly made, and daily neglected and forgotten.

He was, in fact, the very reverse of his predecessors, being neither tranquil and inert, like Walter the Doubter, nor restless and fidgeting, like William the Testy,—but a man, or rather a governor, of such uncommon activity and decision of mind, that he never sought nor accepted the advice of others; depending bravely upon his single head as would a hero of yore upon his single arm, to carry him through all difficulties and dangers. To tell the simple truth he wanted nothing more to complete him as a statesman than to think always right, for no one can say but that he always acted as he thought. He was never a man to flinch when he found himself in a scrape; but to dash forward through thick and thin, trusting, by hook or by crook, to make all things straight in the end. In a word, he possessed in an eminent degree that great quality in a statesman, called perseverance

---

silver leg: See the histories of Masters **Josselyn and Blome.** (Irving's note.)

by the polite, but nicknamed obstinacy by the vulgar. A wonderful salve for official blunders; since he who perseveres in error without flinching, gets the credit of boldness and consistency, while he who wavers in seeking to do what is right gets stigmatized as a trimmer. This much is certain; and it is a maxim well worthy the attention of all legislators, great and small, who stand shaking in the wind, irresolute which way to steer, that a ruler who follows his own will pleases himself, while he who seeks to satisfy the wishes and whims of others runs great risk of pleasing nobody. There is nothing too like putting down one's foot resolutely, when in doubt; and letting things take their course. The clock that stands still points right twice in the four and twenty hours: while others may keep going continually and be continually going wrong.

Nor did this magnanimous quality escape the discernment of the good people of Nieuw Nederlands; on the contrary, so much were they struck with the independent will and vigorous resolution displayed on all occasions by their new governor, that they universally called him Hard-Koppig Piet; or Peter the Headstrong,—a great compliment to the strength of his understanding.

If, from all that I have said, thou dost not gather, worthy reader, that Peter Stuyvesant was a tough, sturdy, valiant, weather-beaten, mettlesome, obstinate, leathern-sided, lion-hearted, generous-spirited old governor, either I have written to but little purpose, or thou art very dull at drawing conclusions.

This most excellent governor commenced his administration on the 29th of May, 1647,—a remarkably stormy day, distinguished in all the almanacs of the time which have come down to us by the name of Windy Friday. As he was very jealous of his personal and official dignity, he was inaugurated into office with great ceremony,— the goodly oaken chair of the renowned Wouter Van Twiller being carefully preserved for such occasions, in like manner as the chair and stone were reverentially preserved at Schone, in Scotland, for the coronation of the Caledonian monarchs.

I must not omit to mention, that the tempestuous state of the elements, together with its being that unlucky day of the week termed "hanging-day," did not fail to excite much grave speculation and divers very reasonable apprehensions among the more ancient and enlightened inhabitants; and several of the sager sex, who were reputed to be not a little skilled in the mysteries of astrology and fortune-telling, did declare outright that they were omens of a disastrous administration;—an event that came to be lamentably verified, and which proves, beyond dispute, the wisdom of attending to those preternatural intimations fur- 10 nished by dreams and visions, the flying of birds, falling of stones, and cackling of geese, on which the sages and rulers of ancient times placed such reliance—or to those shootings of stars, eclipses of the moon, howlings of dogs, and flarings of candles, carefully noted and interpreted by the oracular sybils of our day,—who, in my humble opinion, are the legitimate inheritors and preservers of the ancient science of divination. This much is certain, that Governor Stuyvesant succeeded to 20 the chair of state at a turbulent period; when foes thronged and threatened from without; when anarchy and stiff-necked opposition reigned rampant within; when the authority of their High Mightinesses the Lords States-General, though supported by economy, and defended by speeches, protests and proclamations, yet tottered to its very centre; and when the great city of New Amsterdam, though fortified by flag-staffs, trumpeters, and windmills, seemed, like some fair lady of easy 30 virtue, to lie open to attack, and ready to yield to the first invader.

The Sketch Book

The Author's Account of Himself

THE FOLLOWING essay formed the first part of No. 1 of *The Sketch Book*, a series of thirty-six sketches issued at irregular intervals from May 15, 1819, to September 40 13, 1820. The first number was finished by February, 1819. The motives which led Irving to undertake his tour are set forth charmingly in the introductory essay. *The Sketch Book* set the fashion, but unfortunately not the artistic level, of a flood of travel books by Americans in the first half of the nineteenth century, to which Mark Twain's *Innocents Abroad* (1869) was a hilarious corrective. The text is that of the author's revised Geoffrey Crayon Edition (1880).

'I am of this mind with Homer, that as the snaile that crept out of her shel was turned eftsoons into a toad, and thereby was forced to make a stoole to sit on; so the traveller that stragleth from his owne country is in a short time transformed into so monstrous a shape, that he is faine to alter his mansion with his manners, and to live where he can, not where he would.' (Lyly's *Euphues*.)

I was always fond of visiting new scenes, and 10 observing strange characters and manners. Even when a mere child I began my travels, and made many tours of discovery into foreign parts and unknown regions of my native city, to the frequent alarm of my parents, and the emolument of the town-crier. As I grew into boyhood, I extended the range of my observations. My holiday afternoons were spent in rambles about the surrounding country. I made myself familiar with all its places famous in history or fable. I knew every 20 spot where a murder or robbery had been committed, or a ghost seen. I visited the neighboring villages, and added greatly to my stock of knowledge, by noting their habits and customs, and conversing with their sages and great men. I even journeyed one long summer's day to the summit of the most distant hill, whence I stretched my eye over many a mile of terra incognita, and was astonished to find how vast a globe I inhabited.

This rambling propensity strengthened with 30 my years. Books of voyages and travels became my passion, and in devouring their contents, I neglected the regular exercises of the school. How wistfully would I wander about the pier-heads in fine weather, and watch the parting ships, bound to distant climes—with what longing eyes would I gaze after their lessening sails, and waft myself in imagination to the ends of the earth!

Further reading and thinking, though they brought this vague inclination into more reason- 40 able bounds, only served to make it more decided. I visited various parts of my own country; and had I been merely a lover of fine scenery, I should have felt little desire to seek elsewhere its gratification; for on no country have the charms of nature been more prodigally lavished. Her mighty lakes, like oceans of liquid silver; her mountains, with their bright aerial tints; her valleys, teeming with wild fertility; her tremendous cataracts, thundering in their solitudes; her boundless plains, waving with spontaneous verdure; her broad deep rivers, rolling in solemn silence to the ocean; her trackless forests, where vegetation puts forth all its magnificence; her skies, kindling with the magic of summer clouds and glorious sunshine;—no, never need an American look beyond his own country for the sublime and beautiful of natural scenery.

But Europe held forth the charms of storied and poetical association. There were to be seen the masterpieces of art, the refinements of highly-cultivated society, the quaint peculiarities of ancient and local custom. My native country was full of youthful promise: Europe was rich in the accumulated treasures of age. Her very ruins told the history of times gone by, and every mouldering stone was a chronicle. I longed to wander over the scenes of renowned achievement—to tread, as it were, in the footsteps of antiquity—to loiter about the ruined castle—to meditate on the falling tower—to escape, in short, from the commonplace realities of the present, and lose myself among the shadowy grandeurs of the past.

I had, beside all this, an earnest desire to see the great men of the earth. We have, it is true, our great men in America: not a city but has an ample share of them. I have mingled among them in my time, and been almost withered by the shade into which they cast me; for there is nothing so baleful to a small man as the shade of a great one, particularly the great man of a city. But I was anxious to see the great men of Europe; for I had read in the works of the various philosophers, that all animals degenerated in America, and man among the number. A great man of Europe, thought I, must therefore be as superior to a great man of America, as a peak of the Alps to a highland of the Hudson; and in this idea I was confirmed, by observing the comparative importance and swelling magnitude of many English travellers among us, who, I was assured, were very little people in their own country. I will visit this land of wonders, thought I, and see the gigantic race from which I am degenerated.

It has been either my good or evil lot to have my roving passion gratified. I have wandered through different countries, and witnessed many of the shifting scenes of life. I cannot say that I have studied them with the eye of a philosopher; but rather with the sauntering gaze with which humble lovers of the picturesque stroll from the window of one print-shop to another; caught sometimes by the delineations of beauty, sometimes by the distortions of caricature, and sometimes by the loveliness of landscape. As it is the fashion for modern tourists to travel pencil in hand, and bring home their port-folios filled with sketches, I am disposed to get up a few for the entertainment of my friends. When, however, I look over the hints and memorandums I have taken down for the purpose, my heart almost fails me at finding how my idle humor has led me aside from the great objects studied by every regular traveller who would make a book. I fear I shall give equal disappointment with an unlucky landscape painter, who had travelled on the continent, but, following the bent of his vagrant inclination, had sketched in nooks, and corners, and by-places. His sketch-book was accordingly crowded with cottages, and landscapes, and obscure ruins; but he had neglected to paint St. Peter's, or the Coliseum; the cascade of Terni, or the bay of Naples; and had not a single glacier or volcano in his whole collection.

Rip Van Winkle

THIS FAMOUS story, the most popular of all Irving's writings, appeared in the last part of the first number of *The Sketch Book* in 1819. Irving was led to the theme by Sir Walter Scott's suggestion that he study German folklore. The supernatural sleep motif was derived from Irving's reading of volumes of German legends by Otmar, Laun, and others; the story itself may have been inspired by such Scottish superstitions as those of Thomas the Rhymer. Irving was not the first to attempt to localize Old World material in America. Charles Brockden Brown had sought earlier to bring the Gothicism of Radcliff and Godwin to Pennsylvania and New York, but some of the ingredients were not very adaptable, and the success that attended his efforts was less than that of Irving. A dramatization of the story in 1865 provided Joseph Jefferson with the most famous role of his career of seventy-one years on the stage. The text is that of the author's revised Geoffrey Crayon Edition (1880).

371

[The following Tale was found among the papers of the late Diedrich Knickerbocker, an old gentleman of New York, who was very curious in the Dutch history of the province, and the manners of the descendants from its primitive settlers. His historical researches, however, did not lie so much among books as among men; for the former are lamentably scanty on his favorite topics, whereas he found the old burghers, and still more their wives, rich in that legendary lore so invaluable to true history. Whenever, therefore, he happened upon a genuine Dutch family, snugly shut up in its low-roofed farmhouse, under a spreading sycamore, he looked upon it as a little clasped volume of black-letter, and studied it with the zeal of a book-worm.

The result of all these researches was a history of the province during the reign of the Dutch governors, which he published some years since. There have been various opinions as to the literary character of his work, and, to tell the truth, it is not a whit better than it should be. Its chief merit is its scrupulous accuracy, which indeed was a little questioned, on its first appearance, but has since been completely established; and it is now admitted into all historical collections, as a book of unquestionable authority.

The old gentleman died shortly after the publication of his work, and now that he is dead and gone, it cannot do much harm to his memory to say, that his time might have been much better employed in weightier labors. He, however, was apt to ride his hobby his own way; and though it did now and then kick up the dust a little in the eyes of his neighbors, and grieve the spirit of some friends, for whom he felt the truest deference and affection; yet his errors and follies are remembered "more in sorrow than in anger," and it begins to be suspected, that he never intended to injure or offend. But however his memory may be appreciated by critics, it is still held dear by many folk whose good opinion is well worth having, particularly by certain biscuit-bakers, who have gone so far as to imprint his likeness on their New-year cakes, and have thus given him a chance for immortality, almost equal to the being stamped on a Waterloo medal or a Queen Anne's farthing.]

By Woden, God of Saxons,
From whence comes Wensday, that is Wodensday,
Truth is a thing that ever I will keep
Unto thylke day in which I creep into
My sepulchre——

                                        Cartwright.

Whoever has made a voyage up the Hudson must remember the Kaatskill mountains. They are a dismembered branch of the great Appalachian family, and are seen away to the west of the river, swelling up to a noble height, and lording it over the surrounding country. Every change of season, every change of weather, indeed, every hour of the day, produces some change in the magical hues and shapes of these mountains, and they are regarded by all the good wives, far and near, as perfect barometers. When the weather is fair and settled, they are clothed in blue and purple, and print their bold outlines on the clear evening sky; but sometimes, when the rest of the landscape is cloudless, they will gather a hood of gray vapors about their summits, which, in the last rays of the setting sun, will glow and light up like a crown of glory.

At the foot of these fairy mountains, the voyager may have descried the light smoke curling up from a village, whose shingle-roofs gleam among the trees, just where the blue tints of the upland melt away into the fresh green of the nearer landscape. It is a little village, of great antiquity, having been founded by some of the Dutch colonists, in the early times of the province, just about the beginning of the government of the good Peter Stuyvesant (may he rest in peace!) and there were some of the houses of the original settlers standing within a few years, built of small yellow bricks brought from Holland, having latticed windows and gable fronts, surmounted with weathercocks.

In that same village, and in one of these very houses (which, to tell the precise truth, was sadly time-worn and weather-beaten), there lived many years since, while the country was yet a province of Great Britain, a simple good-natured fellow, of the name of Rip Van Winkle. He was a descendant of the Van Winkles who figured so gallantly in the chivalrous days of Peter Stuyvesant, and accompanied him to the siege of Fort Christina. He inherited, however, but little of the martial character of his ancestors. I have observed that he was a simple good-natured man; he was, moreover, a kind neighbor, and an obedient henpecked husband. Indeed, to the latter circumstance might be owing that meekness of spirit which gained him such universal popularity; for those men are most apt to be obsequious and conciliating abroad, who are under the discipline of shrews at home. Their tempers, doubtless, are rendered pliant and malleable in the fiery furnace of domestic tribulation, and a curtain lecture is worth all the sermons in the world for teaching the virtues of patience and long-suffering. A termagant wife may, therefore, in some respects, be considered a tolerable blessing; and if so, Rip Van Winkle was thrice blessed.

Certain it is, that he was a great favorite among all the good wives of the village, who, as usual with the amiable sex, took his part in all family squabbles; and never failed, whenever they talked those matters over in their evening gossipings, to lay all the blame on Dame Van Winkle. The children of the village, too, would shout with joy whenever he approached. He assisted at their sports, made their playthings, taught them to fly kites and shoot marbles, and told them long stories of ghosts, witches, and Indians. Whenever he went dodging about the village, he was surrounded by a troop of them, hanging on his skirts, clambering on his back, and playing a thousand tricks on him with impunity; and not a dog would bark at him throughout the neighbourhood.

The great error in Rip's composition was an insuperable aversion to all kinds of profitable labor. It could not be from the want of assiduity or perseverance; for he would sit on a wet rock, with a rod as long and heavy as a Tartar's lance, and fish all day without a murmur, even though he should not be encouraged by a single nibble. He would carry a fowling-piece on his shoulder for hours together, trudging through woods and swamps, and up hill and down dale, to shoot a few squirrels or wild pigeons. He would never refuse to assist a neighbour even in the roughest toil, and was a foremost man at all country frolics for husking Indian corn, or building stone-fences; the women of the village, too, used to employ him to run their errands, and to do such little odd jobs as their less obliging husbands would not do for them. In a word, Rip was ready to attend to anybody's business but his own; but as to doing family duty, and keeping his farm in order, he found it impossible.

In fact, he declared it was of no use to work on his farm; it was the most pestilent little piece of ground in the whole country; everything about it went wrong, and would go wrong, in spite of him. His fences were continually falling to pieces; his cow would either go astray, or get among the cabbages; weeds were sure to grow quicker in his fields than anywhere else; the rain always made a point of setting in just as he had some out-door work to do; so that though his patrimonial estate had dwindled away under his management, acre by acre, until there was little more left than a mere patch of Indian corn and potatoes, yet it was the worst conditioned farm in the neighborhood.

His children, too, were as ragged and wild as if they belonged to nobody. His son Rip, an urchin begotten in his own likeness, promised to inherit the habits, with the old clothes of his father. He was generally seen trooping like a colt at his mother's heels, equipped in a pair of his father's cast-off galligaskins, which he had much ado to hold up with one hand, as a fine lady does her train in bad weather.

Rip Van Winkle, however, was one of those happy mortals, of foolish, well-oiled dispositions, who take the world easy, eat white bread or brown, whichever can be got with least thought or trouble, and would rather starve on a penny than work for a pound. If left to himself, he would have whistled life away in perfect contentment; but his wife kept continually dinning in his ears about his idleness, his carelessness, and the ruin he was bringing on his family. Morning, noon, and night, her tongue was incessantly going, and everything he said or did was sure to produce a torrent of household eloquence. Rip had but one way of replying to all lectures of the kind, and that, by frequent use, had grown into a habit. He shrugged his shoulders, shook his head, cast up his eyes, but said nothing. This, however, always provoked a fresh volley from his wife; so that he was fain to draw off his forces, and take to the outside of the house—the only side which, in truth, belongs to a hen-pecked husband.

Rip's sole domestic adherent was his dog Wolf, who was as much hen-pecked as his master; for Dame Van Winkle regarded them as companions in idleness, and even looked upon Wolf with an evil eye, as the cause of his master's going so often astray. True it is, in all points of spirit befitting an honorable dog, he was as courageous an animal as ever scoured the woods—but what courage can withstand the ever-during and all-besetting terrors of a woman's tongue? The moment Wolf entered the house his crest fell, his tail drooped to the ground or curled between his legs, he sneaked about with a gallows air, casting many a side-long glance at Dame Van Winkle, and at the least flourish of a broomstick or ladle, he would fly to the door with yelping precipitation.

Times grew worse and worse with Rip Van Winkle as years of matrimony rolled on; a tart temper never mellows with age, and a sharp tongue is the only edged tool that grows keener with constant use. For a long while he used to console himself, when driven from home, by frequenting a kind of perpetual club of the sages, philosophers, and other idle personages of the village; which held its sessions on a bench before a small inn, designated by a rubicund portrait of His Majesty George the Third. Here they used to sit in the shade through a long lazy summer's day, talking listlessly over village gossip, or telling endless sleepy stories about nothing. But it would have been worth any statesman's money to have heard the profound discussions that sometimes took place, when by chance an old newspaper fell into their hands from some passing traveller. How solemnly they would listen to the contents, as drawled out by Derrick Van Bummel, the schoolmaster, a dapper learned little man, who was not to be daunted by the most gigantic word in the dictionary; and how sagely they would deliberate upon public events some months after they had taken place.

The opinions of this junto were completely controlled by Nicholas Vedder, a patriarch of the village, and landlord of the inn, at the door of which he took his seat from morning till night, just moving sufficiently to avoid the sun and keep in the shade of a large tree; so that the neighbours could tell the hour by his movements as accurately as by a sundial. It is true he was rarely heard to speak, but smoked his pipe incessantly. His adherents, however (for every great man has his adherents), perfectly understood him, and knew how to gather his opinions. When anything that was read or related displeased him, he was observed to smoke his pipe vehemently, and to send forth short, frequent, and angry puffs; but when pleased he would inhale the smoke slowly and tranquilly, and emit it in light and placid clouds; and sometimes, taking the pipe from his mouth, and letting the fragrant vapor curl about his nose, would gravely nod his head in token of perfect approbation.

From even this stronghold the unlucky Rip was at length routed by his termagant wife, who would suddenly break in upon the tranquillity of the assemblage and call the members all to naught; nor was that august personage, Nicholas Vedder himself, sacred from the daring tongue of this terrible virago, who charged him outright with encouraging her husband in habits of idleness.

Poor Rip was at last reduced almost to despair; and his only alternative, to escape from the labor of the farm and clamor of his wife, was to take gun in hand and stroll away into the woods. Here he would sometimes seat himself at the foot of a tree, and share the contents of his wallet with Wolf, with whom he sympathized as a fellow-sufferer in persecution. "Poor Wolf," he would say, "thy mistress leads thee a dog's life of it; but never mind, my lad, whilst I live thou shalt never want a friend to stand by thee!" Wolf would wag his tail, look wistfully in his master's face, and if dogs can feel pity, I verily believe he reciprocated the sentiment with all his heart.

In a long ramble of the kind on a fine autumnal day, Rip had unconsciously scrambled to one of the highest parts of the Kaatskill mountains. He was after his favorite sport of squirrel-shooting, and the still solitudes had echoed and re-echoed with the reports of his gun. Panting and fatigued, he threw himself, late in the afternoon, on a green knoll, covered with mountain herbage, that crowned the brow of a precipice. From an opening between the trees he could overlook all the lower country for many a mile of rich woodland. He saw at a distance the lordly Hudson, far, far below him, moving on its silent but majestic course, with the reflection of a purple cloud, or the sail of a lagging bark, here and there sleeping on its glassy bosom, and at last losing itself in the blue highlands.

On the other side he looked down into a deep mountain glen, wild, lonely, and shagged, the bottom filled with fragments from the impending cliffs, and scarcely lighted by the reflected rays of the setting sun. For some time Rip lay musing on this scene; evening was gradually advancing; the mountains began to throw their long blue shadows over the valleys; he saw that it would be dark long before he could reach the village, and he heaved a heavy sigh when he thought of encountering the terrors of Dame Van Winkle.

As he was about to descend, he heard a voice from a distance, hallooing, "Rip Van Winkle! Rip Van Winkle!" He looked round, but could see nothing but a crow winging its solitary flight across the mountain. He thought his fancy must have deceived him, and turned again to descend, when he heard the same cry ring through the still evening air: "Rip Van Winkle! Rip Van Winkle!" —at the same time Wolf bristled up his back, and, giving a loud growl, skulked to his master's side, looking fearfully down into the glen. Rip now felt a vague apprehension stealing over him; he looked anxiously in the same direction, and perceived a strange figure slowly toiling up the rocks, and bending under the weight of something he carried on his back. He was surprised to see any human being in this lonely and unfrequented place; but supposing it to be some one of the neighbourhood in need of his assistance, he hastened down to yield it.

On nearer approach he was still more surprised at the singularity of the stranger's appearance. He was a short, square-built old fellow, with thick bushy hair and a grizzled beard. His dress was of the antique Dutch fashion—a cloth jerkin strapped round the waist—several pair of breeches, the outer one of ample volume, decorated with rows of buttons down the sides, and bunches at the knees. He bore on his shoulder a stout keg, that seemed full of liquor, and made signs for Rip to approach and assist him with the load. Though rather shy and distrustful of this new acquaintance, Rip complied with his usual alacrity; and mutually relieving each other, they clambered up a narrow gully, apparently the dry bed of a mountain torrent. As they ascended, Rip every now and then heard long rolling peals, like distant thunder, that seemed to issue out of a deep ravine, or rather cleft, between lofty rocks, toward which their rugged path conducted. He paused for an instant, but supposing it to be the muttering of one of those transient thunder-showers which often take place in mountain heights, he proceeded. Passing through the ravine, they came to a hollow, like a small amphitheatre, surrounded by perpendicular precipices, over the brinks of which impending trees shot their branches, so that you only caught glimpses of the azure sky and the bright evening cloud. During the whole time Rip and his companion had labored on in silence; for though the former marvelled greatly what could be the object of carrying a keg of liquor up this wild mountain, yet there was something strange and incomprehensible about the unknown, that inspired awe and checked familiarity.

On entering the amphitheatre, new objects of wonder presented themselves. On a level spot in the centre was a company of odd-looking personages playing at nine-pins. They were dressed in a quaint outlandish fashion; some wore short doublets, others jerkins, with long knives in their belts, and most of them had enormous breeches, of similar style with that of the guide's. Their visages, too, were peculiar: one had a large head, broad face, and small piggish eyes; the face of another seemed to consist entirely of nose, and was surmounted by a white sugar-loaf hat, set off with a little red cock's tail. They all had beards, of various shapes and colors. There was one who seemed to be the commander. He was a stout old gentleman, with a weather-beaten countenance; he wore a laced doublet, broad belt and hanger, high-crowned hat and feather, red stockings, and high-heeled shoes, with roses in them. The whole group reminded Rip of the figures in an old Flemish painting, in the parlor of Dominie Van Shaick, the village parson, and which had been brought over from Holland at the time of the settlement.

What seemed particularly odd to Rip was, that though these folks were evidently amusing themselves, yet they maintained the gravest faces, the most mysterious silence, and were, withal, the most melancholy party of pleasure he had ever witnessed. Nothing interrupted the stillness of the scene but the noise of the balls, which, whenever they were rolled, echoed along the mountains like rumbling peals of thunder.

As Rip and his companion approached them, they suddenly desisted from their play, and stared at him with such fixed, statue-like gaze, and such strange, uncouth, lack-lustre countenances, that his heart turned within him, and his knees smote together. His companion now emptied the contents of the keg into large flagons, and made signs to him to wait upon the company. He obeyed with 10 fear and trembling; they quaffed the liquor in profound silence, and then returned to the game.

By degrees Rip's awe and apprehension subsided. He even ventured, when no eye was fixed upon him, to taste the beverage, which he found had much of the flavor of excellent Hollands. He was naturally a thirsty soul, and was soon tempted to repeat the draught. One taste provoked another; and he reiterated his visits to the flagon so often, that at length his senses were overpowered, 20 his eyes swam in his head, his head gradually declined, and he fell into a deep sleep.

On waking, he found himself on the green knoll whence he had first seen the old man of the glen. He rubbed his eyes—it was a bright sunny morning. The birds were hopping and twittering among the bushes, and the eagle was wheeling aloft, and breasting the pure mountain breeze. "Surely," thought Rip, "I have not slept here all night." He recalled the occurrences before he fell 30 asleep. The strange man with a keg of liquor—the mountain ravine—the wild retreat among the rocks—the woe-begone party at nine-pins—the flagon—"Oh! that flagon! that wicked flagon!" thought Rip—"what excuse shall I make to Dame Van Winkle!"

He looked round for his gun, but in place of the clean well-oiled fowling-piece, he found an old firelock lying by him, the barrel incrusted with rust, the lock falling off, and the stock worm- 40 eaten. He now suspected that the grave roysters of the mountain had put a trick upon him, and, having dosed him with liquor, had robbed him of his gun. Wolf, too, had disappeared, but he might have strayed away after a squirrel or partridge. He whistled after him and shouted his name, but all in vain; the echoes repeated his whistle and shout, but no dog was to be seen.

He determined to revisit the scene of the last evening's gambol, and, if he met with any of the party, to demand his dog and gun. As he rose to walk, he found himself stiff in the joints, and wanting in his usual activity. "These mountain beds do not agree with me," thought Rip, "and if this frolic should lay me up with a fit of the rheumatism, I shall have a blessed time with Dame Van Winkle." With some difficulty he got down into the glen: he found the gully up which he and his companion had ascended the preceding evening; but, to his astonishment a mountain stream was now foaming down it, leaping from rock to rock, and filling the glen with babbling murmurs. He, however, made shift to scramble up its sides, working his toilsome way through thickets of birch, sassafras, and witch-hazel, and sometimes tripped up or entangled by the wild grape-vines that twisted their coils or tendrils from tree to tree, and spread a kind of network in his path.

At length he reached to where the ravine had opened through the cliffs to the amphitheatre; but no traces of such opening remained. The rocks presented a high impenetrable wall, over which the torrent came tumbling in a sheet of feathery foam, and fell into a broad deep basin, black from the shadows of the surrounding forest. Here, then, poor Rip was brought to a stand. He again called and whistled after his dog; he was only answered by the cawing of a flock of idle crows, sporting high in air about a dry tree that overhung a sunny precipice; and who, secure in their elevation, seemed to look down and scoff at the poor man's perplexities. What was to be done?—the morning was passing away, and Rip felt famished for want of his breakfast. He grieved to give up his dog and his gun; he dreaded to meet his wife; but it would not do to starve among the mountains. He shook his head, shouldered the rusty firelock, and, with a heart full of trouble and anxiety, turned his steps homeward.

As he approached the village he met a number of people, but none whom he knew, which somewhat surprised him, for he had thought himself acquainted with everyone in the country round. Their dress, too, was of a different fashion from that to which he was accustomed. They all stared at him with equal marks of surprise, and whenever they cast their eyes upon him, invariably stroked their chins. The constant recurrence of this gesture induced Rip, involuntarily, to do the same, when, to his astonishment, he found his beard had grown a foot long!

He had now entered the skirts of the village. A troop of strange children ran at his heels, hooting after him, and pointing at his gray beard. The dogs, too, not one of which he recognized for an old acquaintance, barked at him as he passed. The very village was altered; it was larger and more populous. There were rows of houses which he had never seen before, and those which had been his familiar haunts had disappeared. Strange names were over the doors—strange faces at the windows—everything was strange. His mind now misgave him; he began to doubt whether both he and the world around him were not bewitched. Surely this was his native village, which he had left but the day before. There stood the Kaatskill mountains—there ran the silver Hudson at a distance—there was every hill and dale precisely as it had always been—Rip was sorely perplexed—"That flagon last night," thought he, "has addled my poor head sadly!"

It was with some difficulty that he found the way to his own house, which he approached with silent awe, expecting every moment to hear the shrill voice of Dame Van Winkle. He found the house gone to decay—the roof fallen in, the windows shattered, and the doors off the hinges. A half-starved dog that looked like Wolf was skulking about it. Rip called him by name, but the cur snarled, showed his teeth, and passed on. This was an unkind cut indeed—"My very dog," sighed poor Rip, "has forgotten me!"

He entered the house, which, to tell the truth, Dame Van Winkle had always kept in neat order. It was empty, forlorn, and apparently abandoned. The desolateness overcame all his connubial fears— he called loudly for his wife and children—the lonely chambers rang for a moment with his voice, and then all again was silence.

He now hurried forth, and hastened to his old resort, the village inn—but it too was gone. A large rickety wooden building stood in its place, with great gaping windows, some of them broken and mended with old hats and petticoats, and over the door was painted, "The Union Hotel, by Jonathan Doolittle." Instead of the great tree that used to shelter the quiet little Dutch inn of yore, there was now reared a tall naked pole, with something on the top that looked like a red nightcap, and from it was fluttering a flag, on which was a singular assemblage of stars and stripes—all this was strange and incomprehensible. He recognized on the sign, however, the ruby face of King George, under which he had smoked so many a peaceful pipe; but even this was singularly metamorphosed. The red coat was changed for one of blue and buff, a sword was held in the hand instead of a sceptre, the head was decorated with a cocked hat, and underneath was painted in large characters, GENERAL WASHINGTON.

There was, as usual, a crowd of folks about the door, but none that Rip recollected. The very character of the people seemed changed. There was a busy, bustling, disputatious tone about it, instead of the accustomed phlegm and drowsy tranquillity. He looked in vain for the sage Nicholas Vedder, with his broad face, double chin, and fair long pipe, uttering clouds of tobacco-smoke instead of idle speeches; or Van Bummel, the schoolmaster, doling forth the contents of an ancient newspaper. In place of these, a lean, bilious-looking fellow, with his pockets full of hand-bills, was haranguing vehemently about rights of citizens—elections—members of Congress—liberty—Bunker's Hill—heroes of seventy-six—and other words, which were a perfect Babylonish jargon to the bewildered Van Winkle.

The appearance of Rip, with his long grizzled beard, his rusty fowling-piece, his uncouth dress, and an army of women and children at his heels, soon attracted the attention of the tavern politicians. They crowded round him, eyeing him from head to foot with great curiosity. The orator bustled up to him, and, drawing him partly aside, inquired "on which side he voted?" Rip stared in vacant stupidity. Another short but busy little fellow pulled him by the arm, and, rising on tiptoe, inquired in his ear, "Whether he was Federal or Democrat?" Rip was equally at a loss to comprehend the question; when a knowing, self-important old gentleman, in a sharp cocked hat, made his way through the crowd, putting them to the right and left with his elbows as he passed, and planting himself before Van Winkle, with one arm akimbo, the other resting on his cane, his keen eyes and sharp hat penetrating, as it were, into his very soul, demanded in an austere tone, "What brought him to the election with a gun on his shoulder, and a mob at his heels, and whether he meant to breed a riot in the village?"—"Alas! gentlemen," cried Rip, somewhat dismayed, "I am a poor quiet man, a native of the place, and a loyal subject of the king, God bless him!"

Here a general shout burst from the bystanders—"A tory! a tory! a spy! a refugee! hustle him! away with him!" It was with great difficulty that the self-important man in the cocked hat restored order; and, having assumed a tenfold austerity of brow, demanded again of the unknown culprit, what he came there for, and whom he was seeking? The poor man humbly assured him that he meant no harm, but merely came there in search of some of his neighbors, who used to keep about the tavern.

"Well—who are they?—name them."

Rip bethought himself a moment, and inquired, "Where's Nicholas Vedder?"

There was a silence for a little while, when an old man replied, in a thin piping voice, "Nicholas Vedder! why, he is dead and gone these eighteen years! There was a wooden tombstone in the churchyard that used to tell all about him, but that's rotten and gone too."

"Where's Brom Dutcher?"

"Oh, he went off to the army in the beginning of the war; some say he was killed at the storming of Stony Point—others say he was drowned in a squall at the foot of Antony's Nose. I don't know —he never came back again."

"Where's Van Bummel, the schoolmaster?"

"He went off to the wars too, was a great militia general, and is now in Congress."

Rip's heart died away at hearing of these sad changes in his home and friends, and finding himself thus alone in the world. Every answer puzzled him too, by treating of such enormous lapses of time, and of matters which he could not understand: war—Congress—Stony Point;—he had no courage to ask after any more friends, but cried out in despair, "Does nobody here know Rip Van Winkle?"

"Oh, Rip Van Winkle!" exclaimed two or three, "Oh, to be sure! that's Rip Van Winkle yonder, leaning against the tree."

Rip looked, and beheld a precise counterpart of himself, as he went up the mountain: apparently as lazy, and certainly as ragged. The poor fellow was now completely confounded. He doubted his own identity, and whether he was himself or another man. In the midst of his bewilderment, the man in the cocked hat demanded who he was, and what was his name?

"God knows," exclaimed he, at his wits' end; "I'm not myself—I'm somebody else—that's me yonder—no—that's somebody else got into my shoes—I was myself last night, but I fell asleep on the mountain, and they've changed my gun, and everything's changed, and I'm changed, and I can't tell what's my name, or who I am!"

The bystanders began now to look at each other, nod, wink significantly, and tap their fingers against their foreheads. There was a whisper, also, about securing the gun, and keeping the old fellow from doing mischief, at the very suggestion of which the self-important man in the cocked hat retired with some precipitation. At this critical moment a fresh comely woman pressed through the throng to get a peep at the gray-bearded man. She had a chubby child in her arms, which, frightened at his looks, began to cry. "Hush, Rip," cried she, "hush, you little fool; the old man won't hurt you." The name of the child, the air of the mother, the tone of her voice, all awakened a train of recollections in his mind.

"What is your name, my good woman?" asked he.

"Judith Gardenier."

"And your father's name?"

"Ah, poor man, Rip Van Winkle was his name, but it's twenty years since he went away from home with his gun, and never has been heard of since—his dog came home without him; but whether he shot himself, or was carried away by the Indians, nobody can tell. I was then but a little girl."

Rip had but one question more to ask; but he put it with a faltering voice:

"Where's your mother?"

"Oh, she too had died but a short time since;

she broke a blood-vessel in a fit of passion at a New-England pedler."

There was a drop of comfort, at least, in this intelligence. The honest man could contain himself no longer. He caught his daughter and her child in his arms. "I am your father!" cried he— "Young Rip Van Winkle once—old Rip Van Winkle now!—Does nobody know poor Rip Van Winkle?"

All stood amazed, until an old woman, tottering out from among the crowd, put her hand to her brow, and peering under it in his face for a moment, exclaimed, "Sure enough! it is Rip Van Winkle—it is himself! Welcome home again, old neighbor—Why, where have you been these twenty long years?"

Rip's story was soon told, for the whole twenty years had been to him but as one night. The neighbors stared when they heard it; some were seen to wink at each other, and put their tongues in their cheeks: and the self-important man in the cocked hat, who, when the alarm was over, had returned to the field, screwed down the corners of his mouth, and shook his head—upon which there was a general shaking of the head throughout the assemblage.

It was determined, however, to take the opinion of old Peter Vanderdonk, who was seen slowly advancing up the road. He was a descendant of the historian of that name, who wrote one of the earliest accounts of the province. Peter was the most ancient inhabitant of the village, and well versed in all the wonderful events and traditions of the neighborhood. He recollected Rip at once, and corroborated his story in the most satisfactory manner. He assured the company that it was a fact, handed down from his ancestor the historian, that the Kaatskill mountains had always been haunted by strange beings. That it was affirmed that the great Hendrick Hudson, the first discoverer of the river and country, kept a kind of vigil there every twenty years, with his crew of the *Half-moon*; being permitted in this way to revisit the scenes of his enterprise, and keep a guardian eye upon the river, and the great city called by his name. That his father had once seen them in their old Dutch dresses playing at nine-pins in a hollow of the mountain; and that he himself had heard, one summer afternoon, the sound of their balls, like distant peals of thunder.

To make a long story short, the company broke up, and returned to the more important concerns of the election. Rip's daughter took him home to live with her; she had a snug, well-furnished house, and a stout cheery farmer for a husband, whom Rip recollected for one of the urchins that used to climb upon his back. As to Rip's son and heir, who was the ditto of himself, seen leaning against the tree, he was employed to work on the farm; but evinced an hereditary disposition to attend to anything else but his business.

Rip now resumed his old walks and habits; he soon found many of his former cronies, though all rather the worse for the wear and tear of time; and preferred making friends among the rising generation, with whom he soon grew into great favor.

Having nothing to do at home, and being arrived at that happy age when a man can be idle with impunity, he took his place once more on the bench at the inn door, and was reverenced as one of the patriarchs of the village, and a chronicle of the old times "before the war." It was some time before he could get into the regular track of gossip, or could be made to comprehend the strange events that had taken place during his torpor. How that there had been a revolutionary war—that the country had thrown off the yoke of old England—and that, instead of being a subject of his Majesty George the Third, he was now a free citizen of the United States. Rip, in fact, was no politician; the changes of states and empires made but little impression on him; but there was one species of despotism under which he had long groaned, and that was—petticoat government. Happily that was at an end; he had got his neck out of the yoke of matrimony, and could go in and out whenever he pleased, without dreading the tyranny of Dame Van Winkle. Whenever her name was mentioned, however, he shook his head, shrugged his shoulders, and cast up his eyes; which might pass either for an expression of resignation to his fate, or joy at his deliverance.

He used to tell his story to every stranger that arrived at Mr. Doolittle's hotel. He was observed at first to vary on some points every time he told it, which was, doubtless, owing to his having so recently awaked. It at last settled down precisely to the tale I have related, and not a man, woman, or child in the neighborhood, but knew it by heart. Some always pretended to doubt the reality of it, and insisted that Rip had been out of his head, and that this was one point on which he always remained flighty. The old Dutch inhabitants, however, almost universally gave it full credit. Even to this day they never hear a thunderstorm of a summer afternoon about the Kaatskill, but they say Hendrick Hudson and his crew are at their game of nine-pins; and it is a common wish of all henpecked husbands in the neighborhood, when life hangs heavy on their hands, that they might have a quieting draught out of Rip Van Winkle's flagon.

NOTE.—The foregoing Tale, one would suspect, had been suggested to Mr. Knickerbocker by a little German superstition about the Emperor Frederick *der* *Rothbart*, and the Kypphaüser mountain: the subjoined note, however, which he had appended to the tale, shows that it is an absolute fact, narrated with his usual fidelity:

"The story of Rip Van Winkle may seem incredible to many, but nevertheless I give it my full belief, for I know the vicinity of our old Dutch settlements to have been very subject to marvellous events and appearances. Indeed, I have heard many stranger stories than this, in the villages along the Hudson, all of which were too well authenticated to admit of a doubt. I have even talked with Rip Van Winkle myself, who, when last I saw him, was a very venerable old man, and so perfectly rational and consistent on every other point, that I think no conscientious person could refuse to take this into the bargain; nay, I have seen a certificate on the subject taken before a country justice, and signed with a cross, in the justice's own handwriting. The story, therefore, is beyond the possibility of doubt. D. K."

POSTSCRIPT.—The following are travelling notes from a memorandum-book of Mr. Knickerbocker:

The Kaatsberg, or Catskill Mountains, have always been a region full of fable. The Indians considered them the abode of spirits, who influenced the weather, spreading sunshine or clouds over the landscape, and sending good or bad hunting seasons. They were ruled by an old squaw spirit, said to be their mother. She dwelt on the highest peak of the Catskills, and had charge of the doors of day and night, to open and shut them at the proper hour. She hung up the new moons in the skies, and cut up the old ones into stars. In times of drought, if properly propitiated, she would spin light summer clouds out of cobwebs and morning dew, and send them off from the crest of the mountain, flake after flake, like flakes of carded cotton, to float in the air: until, dissolved by the heat of the sun, they would fall in gentle showers, causing the grass to spring, the fruits to ripen, and the corn to grow an inch an hour. If displeased, however, she would brew up clouds black as ink, sitting in the midst of them like a bottle-bellied spider in the midst of its web; and when these clouds broke, woe betide the valleys!

In old times, say the Indian traditions, there was a kind of Manitou or Spirit, who kept about the wildest recesses of the Catskill Mountains, and took a mischievous pleasure in wreaking all kinds of evils and vexations upon the red men. Sometimes he would assume the form of a bear, a panther, or a deer, lead the bewildered hunter a weary chase through tangled forests and among ragged rocks; and then spring off with a loud ho! ho! leaving him aghast on the brink of a beetling precipice or raging torrent.

The favorite abode of this Manitou is still shown. It is a great rock or cliff on the loneliest part of the mountains, and, from the flowering vines which clamber about it, and the wild flowers which abound in its neighborhood, is known by the name of the Garden Rock. Near the foot of it is a small lake, the haunt of the solitary bittern, with water-snakes basking in the sun on the leaves of the pond-lilies, which lie on the surface. This place was held in great awe by the Indians, insomuch that the boldest hunter would not pursue his game within its precincts. Once upon a time, however, a hunter who had lost his way, penetrated to the Garden Rock, where he beheld a number of gourds placed in the crotches of trees. One of these he seized and made off with, but in the hurry of his retreat he let it fall among the rocks, when a great stream gushed forth, which washed him away and swept him down precipices, where he was dashed to pieces, and the stream made its way to the Hudson, and continues to flow to the present day, being the identical stream known by the name of the Kaaterskill.

Legend of the Moor's Legacy

IRVING PRODUCED several volumes descriptive of Moorish civilization and culture, of which the last, *The Alhambra*, was primarily a collection of tales.

This work represents a culmination of the romantic tendencies in Irving which had begun with *The Sketch Book*, and had been intensified by residence in England, France, and Germany. Irving arrived in Spain in 1826. The brilliant lights and shadows of the Iberian peninsula were peculiarly congenial to the author's sunny nature and he remained there for three years, living for the most part in Madrid as a member of the official family of the American consul, Rich. In 1829, Irving lived for several months in the Alhambra before the restoration of that medieval palace of the Moorish kings. In the first essay of *The Alhambra*, from which this story is taken, he thus describes his romantic abode:

> To the traveler imbued with a feeling for the historical and poetical, so inseparably intertwined in the annals of romantic Spain, the Alhambra is as much an object of devotion as is the Caaba to all true Moslems. How many legends and traditions, true and fabulous,—how many songs and ballads, Arabian and Spanish, of love and war and chivalry, are associated with this Oriental pile! It was the royal abode of the Moorish kings, where, surrounded with the splendors and refinements of Asiatic luxury, they held dominion over what they vaunted as a terrestrial paradise, and made their last stand for empire in Spain. The royal palace forms but a part of a fortress, the walls of which, studded with towers, stretch irregularly round the whole crest of a hill, a spur of the Sierra Nevada or Snowy Mountains, and overlook the city; externally it is a rude congregation of towers and battlements, with no regularity of plan nor grace of architecture, and giving little promise of the grace and beauty which prevail within.

> In the time of the Moors the fortress was capable of containing within its outward precincts an army of forty thousand men, and served occasionally as a stronghold of the sovereigns against their rebellious subjects. After the kingdom had passed into the hands of the Christians, the Alhambra continued to be a royal demesne, and was occasionally inhabited by the Castilian monarchs. . . . The last residents were Philip V and his beautiful queen, Elizabetta of Parma, early in the eighteenth century.

Irving's complete absorption in romance is happily illustrated by the "Legend of the Moor's Legacy." The text is that of the author's revised Geoffrey Crayon Edition (1880).

Just within the fortress of the Alhambra, in front of the royal palace, is a broad open esplanade, called the Place or Square of the Cisterns, (la plaza de los algibes,) so called from being undermined by reservoirs of water, hidden from sight, and which have existed from the time of the Moors. At one corner of this esplanade is a Moorish well, cut through the living rock to a great depth, the water of which is cold as ice and clear as crystal. The wells made by the Moors are always in repute, for it is well known what pains they took to penetrate to the purest and sweetest springs and fountains. The one of which we now speak is famous throughout Granada, insomuch that the water-carriers, some bearing great water-jars on their shoulders, others driving asses before them, laden with earthen vessels, are ascending and descending the steep woody avenues of the Alhambra from early dawn until a late hour of the night.

Fountains and wells, ever since the scriptural days, have been noted gossiping places in hot climates; and at the well in question there is a kind of perpetual club kept up during the livelong day, by the invalids, old women, and other curious, do-nothing folk of the fortress, who sit here on the stone benches, under an awning spread over the well to shelter the toll-gatherer from the sun, and dawdle over the gossip of the fortress, and question every water-carrier that arrives about the news of the city, and make long comments on everything they hear and see. Not an hour of the day but loitering housewives and idle maid-servants may be seen, lingering with pitcher on head or in hand, to hear the last of the endless tattle of these worthies.

Among the water-carriers who once resorted to this well, there was a sturdy, strong-backed, bandy-legged little fellow, named Pedro Gil, but called Peregil for shortness. Being a water-carrier, he was a Gallego, or native of Gallicia, of course. Nature seems to have formed races of men, as she has of animals, for different kinds of drudgery. In France the shoeblacks are all Savoyards, the porters of hotels all Swiss, and in the days of hoops and hair-powder in England, no man could give the regular swing to a sedan-chair but a bogtrotting Irishman. So in Spain the carriers of water and bearers of burdens are all sturdy little natives of Gallicia. No man says, "Get me a porter," but, "Call a Gallego."

To return from this digression, Peregil the Gallego had begun business with merely a great earthen jar which he carried upon his shoulder; by degrees he rose in the world, and was enabled to purchase an assistant of a correspondent class of animals, being a stout shaggy-haired donkey.

On each side of this his long-eared aid-de-camp, in a kind of pannier, were slung his water-jars covered with fig-leaves to protect them from the sun. There was not a more industrious water-carrier in all Granada, nor one more merry withal. The streets rang with his cheerful voice as he trudged after his donkey, singing forth the usual summer note that resounds through the Spanish towns: *"Quien quiere agua—agua mas fria que la nieve?—* Who wants water—water colder than snow? Who wants water from the well of the Alhambra, cold as ice and clear as crystal?" When he served a customer with a sparkling glass, it was always with a pleasant word that caused a smile; and if, perchance, it was a comely dame or dimpling damsel, it was always with a sly leer and a compliment to her beauty that was irresistible. Thus Peregil the Gallego was noted throughout all Granada for being one of the civilest, pleasantest, and happiest of mortals. Yet it is not he who sings loudest and jokes most that has the lightest heart. Under all this air of merriment, honest Peregil had his cares and troubles. He had a large family of ragged children to support, who were hungry and clamorous as a nest of young swallows, and beset him with their outcries for food whenever he came home of an evening. He had a helpmate, too, who was anything but a help to him. She had been a village beauty before marriage, noted for her skill in dancing the bolero and rattling the castanets; and she still retained her early propensities, spending the hard earnings of honest Peregil in frippery, and laying the very donkey under requisition for junketing parties into the country on Sundays, and saints' days, and those innumerable holidays which are rather more numerous in Spain than the days of the week. With all this she was a little of a slattern, something more of a lie-a-bed, and, above all, a gossip of the first water; neglecting house, household, and everything else, to loiter slipshod in the houses of her gossip neighbors.

He, however, who tempers the wind to the shorn lamb, accommodates the yoke of matrimony to the submissive neck. Peregil bore all the heavy dispensations of wife and children with as meek a spirit as his donkey bore the water-jars; and, however he might shake his ears in private, never ventured to question the household virtues of his slattern spouse.

He loved his children, too, even as an owl loves its owlets, seeing in them his own image multiplied and perpetuated; for they were a sturdy, long-backed, bandy-legged little brood. The great pleasure of honest Peregil was, whenever he could afford himself a scanty holiday and had a handful of maravedis to spare, to take the whole litter forth with him, some in his arms, some tugging at his skirts, and some trudging at his heels, and to treat them to a gambol among the orchards of the Vega, while his wife was dancing with her holiday friends in the Angosturas of the Darro.

It was a late hour one summer night, and most of the water-carriers had desisted from their toils. The day had been uncommonly sultry; the night was one of those delicious moonlights which tempt the inhabitants of southern climes to indemnify themselves for the heat and inaction of the day, by lingering in the open air, and enjoying its tempered sweetness until after midnight. Customers for water were therefore still abroad. Peregil, like a considerate, painstaking father, thought of his hungry children. "One more journey to the well," said he to himself, "to earn a Sunday's puchero for the little ones." So saying, he trudged manfully up the steep avenue of the Alhambra, singing as he went, and now and then bestowing a hearty thwack with a cudgel on the flanks of his donkey, either by way of cadence to the song, or refreshment to the animal; for dry blows serve in lieu for provender in Spain for all beasts of burden.

When arrived at the well, he found it deserted by every one except a solitary stranger in Moorish garb, seated on the stone bench in the moonlight. Peregil paused at first and regarded him with surprise, not unmixed with awe, but the Moor feebly beckoned him to approach.

"I am faint and ill," said he; "aid me to return to the city, and I will pay thee double what thou couldst gain by thy jars of water."

The honest heart of the little water-carrier was touched with compassion at the appeal of the stranger. "God forbid," said he, "that I should ask fee or reward for doing a common act of humanity."

He accordingly helped the Moor on his donkey, and set off slowly for Granada, the poor Moslem being so weak that it was necessary to hold him on the animal to keep him from falling to the earth.

When they entered the city, the water-carrier demanded whither he should conduct him. "Alas!" said the Moor, faintly, "I have neither home nor habitation; I am a stranger in the land. Suffer me to lay my head this night beneath thy roof, and thou shall be amply repaid."

Honest Peregil thus saw himself unexpectedly saddled with an infidel guest, but he was too humane to refuse a night's shelter to a fellow being in so forlorn a plight; so he conducted the Moor to his dwelling. The children, who had sallied forth open-mouthed as usual on hearing the tramp of the donkey, ran back with affright when they beheld the turbaned stranger, and hid themselves behind their mother. The latter stepped forth intrepidly, like a ruffling hen before her brood when a vagrant dog approaches.

"What infidel companion," cried she, "is this you have brought home at this late hour, to draw upon us the eyes of the inquisition?"

"Be quiet, wife," replied the Gallego, "here is a poor sick stranger, without friend or home: wouldst thou turn him forth to perish in the streets?"

The wife would still have remonstrated, for though she lived in a hovel, she was a furious stickler for the credit of her house; the little water-carrier, however, for once was stiff-necked, and refused to bend beneath the yoke. He assisted the poor Moslem to alight, and spread a mat and a sheep-skin for him, on the ground, in the coolest part of the house; being the only kind of bed that his poverty afforded.

In a little while the Moor was seized with violent convulsions, which defied all the ministering skill of the simple water-carrier. The eye of the poor patient acknowledged his kindness. During an interval of his fits he called him to his side, and addressing him in a low voice; "My end," said he, "I fear is at hand. If I die, I bequeath you this box as a reward for your charity;" so saying, he opened his albornoz, or cloak, and showed a small box of sandal-wood, strapped round his body.

"God grant, my friend," replied the worthy little Gallego, "that you may live many years to enjoy your treasure, whatever it may be."

The Moor shook his head; he laid his hand upon the box, and would have said something more concerning it, but his convulsions returned with increased violence, and in a little while he expired.

The water-carrier's wife was now as one distracted. "This comes," said she, "of your foolish good nature, always running into scrapes to oblige others. What will become of us when this corpse is found in our house? We shall be sent to prison as murderers; and if we escape with our lives, shall be ruined by notaries and alguazils."

Poor Peregil was in equal tribulation, and almost repented himself of having done a good deed. At length a thought struck him. "It is not yet day," said he; "I can convey the dead body out of the city and bury it in the sands on the banks of the Xenil. No one saw the Moor enter our dwelling, and no one will know anything of his death." So said, so done. The wife aided him; they rolled the body of the unfortunate Moslem in the mat on which he had expired, laid it across the ass, and Peregil set out with it for the banks of the river.

As ill luck would have it, there lived opposite to the water-carrier a barber named Pedrillo Pedrugo, one of the most prying, tattling, mischief-making of his gossip tribe. He was a weasel-faced, spider-legged varlet, supple and insinuating; the famous Barber of Seville could not surpass him for his universal knowledge of the affairs of others, and he had no more power of retention than a sieve. It was said that he slept with but one eye at a time, and kept one ear uncovered, so that, even in his sleep, he might see and hear all that was going on. Certain it is, he was a sort of scandalous chronicle for the quidnuncs of Granada, and had more customers than all the rest of his fraternity.

This meddlesome barber heard Peregil arrive at an unusual hour of night, and the exclamations of his wife and children. His head was instantly popped out of a little window which served him as a look-out, and he saw his neighbor assist a man in a Moorish garb into his dwelling. This was so strange an occurrence, that Pedrillo Pedrugo slept not a wink that night. Every five minutes he was at his loophole, watching the lights that gleamed through the chinks of his neighbor's door, and before daylight he beheld Peregil sally forth with his donkey unusually laden.

The inquisitive barber was in a fidget; he slipped on his clothes, and, stealing forth silently, followed the water-carrier at a distance, until he saw him dig a hole in the sandy bank of the Xenil, and bury something that had the appearance of a dead body.

The barber hied him home, and fidgeted about his shop, setting everything upside down, until sunrise. He then took a basin under his arm, and sallied forth to the house of his daily customer the Alcalde.

The Alcalde was just risen. Pedrillo Pedrugo seated him in a chair, threw a napkin round his neck, put a basin of hot water under his chin, and began to mollify his beard with his fingers.

"Strange doings!" said Pedrugo, who played barber and newsmonger at the same time,—"Strange doings!—Robbery, and murder, and burial all in one night!"

"Hey!—how!—what is that you say?" cried the Alcalde.

"I say," replied the barber, rubbing a piece of soap over the nose and mouth of the dignitary, for a Spanish barber disdains to employ a brush; "I say that Peregil the Gallego has robbed and murdered a Moorish Mussulman, and buried him, this blessed night. *Maldita sea la noche;*—accursed be the night for the same!"

"But how do you know all this?" demanded the Alcalde.

"Be patient, Señor, and you shall hear all about it," replied Pedrillo, taking him by the nose and sliding a razor over his cheek. He then recounted all that he had seen, going through both operations at the same time, shaving his beard, washing his chin, and wiping him dry with a dirty napkin, while he was robbing, murdering, and burying the Moslem.

Now it so happened that this Alcalde was one of the most overbearing, and at the same time most gripping and corrupt curmudgeons in all Granada. It could not be denied, however, that he set a high value upon justice, for he sold it at its weight in gold. He presumed the case in point to be one of murder and robbery; doubtless there must be rich spoil; how was it to be secured into the legitimate hands of the law? for as to merely entrapping the delinquent—that would be feeding the gallows; but entrapping the booty—that would be enriching the judge, and such, according to his creed,

was the great end of justice. So thinking, he summoned to his presence his trustiest alguazil—a gaunt, hungry-looking varlet, clad, according to the custom of his order, in the ancient Spanish garb, a broad black beaver, turned up at the sides; a quaint ruff; a small black cloak dangling from his shoulders; rusty black underclothes that set off his spare wiry frame, while in his hand he bore a slender white wand, the dreaded insignia of his office. Such was the legal bloodhound of the ancient Spanish breed, that he put upon the traces of the unlucky water-carrier, and such was his speed and certainty, that he was upon the haunches of poor Peregil before he had returned to his dwelling, and brought both him and his donkey before the dispenser of justice.

The Alcalde bent upon him one of his most terrific frowns. "Hark ye, culprit!" roared he, in a voice that made the knees of the little Gallego smite together,—"Hark ye, culprit! there is no need of denying thy guilt, everything is known to me. A gallows is the proper reward for the crime thou hast committed, but I am merciful, and readily listen to reason. The man that has been murdered in thy house was a Moor, an infidel, the enemy of our faith. It was doubtless in a fit of religious zeal that thou hast slain him. I will be indulgent, therefore; render up the property of which thou hast robbed him, and we will hush the matter up."

The poor water-carrier called upon all the saints to witness his innocence; alas! not one of them appeared; and if they had, the Alcalde would have disbelieved the whole kalendar. The water-carrier related the whole story of the dying Moor with the straightforward simplicity of truth, but it was all in vain. "Wilt thou persist in saying," demanded the judge, "that this Moslem had neither gold nor jewels, which were the object of thy cupidity?"

"As I hope to be saved, your worship," replied the water-carrier, "he had nothing but a small box of sandal-wood, which he bequeathed to me in reward for my services."

"A box of sandal-wood! a box of sandal-wood!" exclaimed the Alcalde, his eyes sparkling at the idea of precious jewels, "and where is this box? where have you concealed it?"

"An' it please your grace," replied the water-carrier, "it is in one of the panniers of my mule, and heartily at the service of your worship."

He had hardly spoken the words, when the keen alguazil darted off and reappeared in an instant with the mysterious box of sandal-wood. The Alcalde opened it with an eager and trembling hand; all pressed forward to gaze upon the treasure it was expected to contain; when, to their disappointment, nothing appeared within but a parchment scroll, covered with Arabic characters, and an end of a waxen taper.

When there is nothing to be gained by the conviction of a prisoner, justice, even in Spain, is apt to be impartial. The Alcalde, having recovered from his disappointment, and found there was really no booty in the case, now listened dispassionately to the explanation of the water-carrier, which was corroborated by the testimony of his wife. Being convinced, therefore, of his innocence, he discharged him from arrest; nay more, he permitted him to carry off the Moor's legacy, the box of sandal-wood and its contents, as the well-merited reward of his humanity; but he retained his donkey in payment of cost and charges.

Behold the unfortunate little Gallego reduced once more to the necessity of being his own water-carrier, and trudging up to the well of the Alhambra with a great earthen jar upon his shoulder. As he toiled up the hill in the heat of a summer noon his usual good-humor forsook him. "Dog of an Alcalde!" would he cry, "to rob a poor man of the means of his subsistence, of the best friend he had in the world!" And then at the remembrance of the beloved companion of his labors, all the kindness of his nature would break forth. "Ah, donkey of my heart!" would he exclaim, resting his burden on a stone, and wiping the sweat from his brow—"Ah, donkey of my heart! I warrant me thou thinkest of thy old master! I warrant me thou missest the water-jars—poor beast!"

To add to his afflictions, his wife received him, on his return home, with whimperings and repinings; she had clearly the vantage-ground of him, having warned him not to commit the egregious act of hospitality which had brought on him all these misfortunes; and like a knowing woman, she took every occasion to throw her superior

sagacity in his teeth. If ever her children lacked food, or needed a new garment, she would answer with a sneer, "Go to your father—he is heir to king Chico of the Alhambra: ask him to help you out of the Moor's strong box."

Was ever poor mortal so soundly punished, for having done a good action? The unlucky Peregil was grieved in flesh and spirit, but still he bore meekly with the railings of his spouse. At length, one evening, when, after a hot day's toil, she taunted him in the usual manner, he lost all patience. He did not venture to retort upon her, but his eye rested upon the box of sandal-wood, which lay on a shelf with lid half open, as if laughing in mockery of his vexation. Seizing it up he dashed it with indignation to the floor. "Unlucky was the day that I ever set eyes on thee," he cried, "or sheltered thy master beneath my roof!"

As the box struck the floor, the lid flew wide open, and the parchment scroll rolled forth. Peregil sat regarding the scroll for some time in moody silence. At length rallying his ideas, "Who knows," thought he, "but this writing may be of some importance, as the Moor seems to have guarded it with such care?" Picking it up therefore, he put it in his bosom, and the next morning, as he was crying water through the streets, he stopped at the shop of a Moor, a native of Tangiers, who sold trinkets and perfumery in the Zacatin, and asked him to explain the contents.

The Moor read the scroll attentively, then stroked his beard and smiled. "This manuscript," said he, "is a form of incantation for the recovery of hidden treasure that is under the power of enchantment. It is said to have such virtue that the strongest bolts and bars, nay the adamantine rock itself, will yield before it."

"Bah!" cried the little Gallego, "what is all that to me? I am no enchanter, and know nothing of buried treasure." So saying, he shouldered his water-jar, left the scroll in the hands of the Moor, and trudged forward on his daily rounds.

That evening, however, as he rested himself about twilight at the well of the Alhambra, he found a number of gossips assembled at the place, and their conversation, as is not unusual at that shadowy hour, turned upon old tales and traditions of a supernatural nature. Being all poor as rats,

385

they dwelt with peculiar fondness upon the popular theme of enchanted riches left by the Moors in various parts of the Alhambra. Above all, they concurred in the belief that there were great treasures buried deep in the earth under the tower of the seven floors.

These stories made an unusual impression on the mind of honest Peregil, and they sank deeper and deeper into his thoughts as he returned alone down the darkling avenues. "If, after all, there should be treasure hid beneath that tower; and if the scroll I left with the Moor should enable me to get at it!" In the sudden ecstasy of the thought he had well nigh let fall his water-jar.

That night he tumbled and tossed, and could scarcely get a wink of sleep for the thoughts that were bewildering his brain. Bright and early he repaired to the shop of the Moor, and told him all that was passing in his mind. "You can read Arabic," said he; "suppose we go together to the tower, and try the effect of the charm; if it fails, we are no worse off than before; but if it succeeds, we will share equally all the treasure we may discover."

"Hold," replied the Moslem, "this writing is not sufficient of itself; it must be read at midnight, by the light of a taper singularly compounded and prepared, the ingredients of which are not within my reach. Without such taper the scroll is of no avail."

"Say no more!" cried the little Gallego. "I have such a taper at hand, and will bring it here in a moment." So saying he hastened home, and soon returned with the end of a yellow wax taper that he had found in the box of sandal-wood. The Moor felt it, and smelt to it. "Here are rare and costly perfumes," said he, "combined with this yellow wax. This is the kind of taper specified in the scroll. While this burns, the strongest walls and most secret caverns will remain open; woe to him, however, who lingers within until it be extinguished. He will remain enchanted with the treasure."

It was now agreed between them to try the charm that very night. At a late hour, therefore, when nothing was stirring but bats and owls, they ascended the woody hill of the Alhambra, and approached that awful tower, shrouded by trees and rendered formidable by so many traditionary tales.

By the light of a lantern they groped their way through bushes, and over fallen stones, to the door of a vault beneath the tower. With fear and trembling they descended a flight of steps cut into the rock. It led to an empty chamber, damp and drear, from which another flight of steps led to a deeper vault. In this way they descended four several flights, leading into as many vaults, one below the other, but the floor of the fourth was solid; and though, according to tradition, there remained three vaults still below, it was said to be impossible to penetrate further, the residue being shut up by strong enchantment. The air of this vault was damp and chilly, and had an earthy smell, and the light scarce cast forth any rays. They paused here for a time, in breathless suspense, until they faintly heard the clock of the watch-tower strike midnight; upon this they lit the waxen taper, which diffused an odor of myrrh and frankincense and storax.

The Moor began to read in a hurried voice. He had scarce finished, when, there was a noise as of subterraneous thunder. The earth shook, and the floor yawning open, disclosed a flight of steps. Trembling with awe, they descended, and by the light of the lantern found themselves in another vault, covered with Arabic inscriptions. In the centre stood a great chest, secured with seven bands of steel, at each end of which sat an enchanted Moor in armour, but motionless as a statue, being controlled by the power of the incantation. Before the chest were several jars filled with gold and silver and precious stones. In the largest of these they thrust their arms up to the elbow, and at every dip hauled forth handfuls of broad yellow pieces of Moorish gold, or bracelets and ornaments of the same precious metal, while occasionally a necklace of oriental pearl would stick to their fingers. Still they trembled and breathed short while cramming their pockets with the spoils; and cast many a fearful glance at the two enchanted Moors, who sat grim and motionless, glaring upon them with unwinking eyes. At length, struck with a sudden panic at some fancied noise, they both rushed up the staircase, tumbled over one another into the upper apartment, overturned and extinguished the waxen taper, and the pavement again closed with a thundering sound.

Filled with dismay, they did not pause until they had groped their way out of the tower, and beheld the stars shining through the trees. Then seating themselves upon the grass, they divided the spoil, determining to content themselves for the present with this mere skimming of the jars, but to return on some future night and drain them to the bottom. To make sure of each other's good faith, also, they divided the talismans between them, one retaining the scroll and the other the taper; this done, they set off with light hearts and well-lined pockets for Granada.

As they wended their way down the hill, the shrewd Moor whispered a word of counsel in the ear of the simple little water-carrier.

"Friend Peregil," said he, "all this affair must be kept a profound secret until we have secured the treasure, and conveyed it out of harm's way. If a whisper of it gets to the ear of the Alcalde, we are undone!"

"Certainly!" replied the Gallego, "nothing can be more true."

"Friend Peregil," said the Moor, "you are a discreet man, and I make no doubt can keep a secret; but you have a wife."

"She shall not know a word of it," replied the little water-carrier, sturdily.

"Enough," said the Moor, "I depend upon thy discretion and thy promise."

Never was promise more positive and sincere; but alas! what man can keep a secret from his wife? Certainly not such a one as Peregil the water-carrier, who was one of the most loving and tractable of husbands. On his return home he found his wife moping in a corner.

"Mighty well," cried she, as he entered, "you've come at last, after rambling about until this hour of the night. I wonder you have not brought home another Moor as a house-mate." Then bursting into tears, she began to wring her hands and smite her breast. "Unhappy woman that I am!" exclaimed she, "what will become of me? My house stripped and plundered by lawyers and alguazils; my husband a do-no-good, that no longer brings home bread for his family, but goes rambling about day and night, with infidel Moors! O my children! my children! what will become of us? We shall all have to beg in the streets!"

Honest Peregil was so moved by the distress of his spouse, that he could not help whimpering also. His heart was as full as his pocket, and not to be restrained. Thrusting his hand into the latter he hauled forth three or four broad gold pieces, and slipped them into her bosom. The poor woman stared with astonishment, and could not understand the meaning of this golden shower. Before she could recover her surprise, the little Gallego drew forth a chain of gold and dangled it before her, capering with exultation, his mouth distended from ear to ear.

"Holy Virgin protect us!" exclaimed the wife. "What hast thou been doing, Peregil? Surely thou hast not been committing murder and robbery!"

The idea scarce entered the brain of the poor woman, than it became a certainty with her. She saw a prison and a gallows in the distance, and a little bandy-legged Gallego dangling pendant from it; and, overcome by the horrors conjured up by her imagination, fell into violent hysterics.

What could the poor man do? He had no other means of pacifying his wife, and dispelling the phantoms of her fancy, than by relating the whole story of his good fortune. This, however, he did not do until he had exacted from her the most solemn promise to keep it a profound secret from every living being.

To describe her joy would be impossible. She flung her arms round the neck of her husband, and almost strangled him with her caresses. "Now, wife," exclaimed the little man with honest exultation, "what say you now to the Moor's legacy? Henceforth never abuse me for helping a fellow-creature in distress."

The honest Gallego retired to his sheep-skin mat, and slept as soundly as if on a bed of down. Not so his wife; she emptied the whole contents of his pockets upon the mat, and sat counting gold pieces of Arabic coin, trying on necklaces and earrings, and fancying the figure she should one day make when permitted to enjoy her riches.

On the following morning the honest Gallego took a broad golden coin, and repaired with it to a jeweller's shop in the Zacatin to offer it for sale, pretending to have found it among the ruins of the Alhambra. The jeweller saw that it had an Arabic inscription, and was of the purest gold; he offered, however, but a third of its value, with which the water-carrier was perfectly content. Peregil now bought new clothes for his little flock, and all kinds of toys, together with ample provisions for a hearty meal, and returning to his dwelling, set all his children dancing around him, while he capered in the midst, the happiest of fathers.

The wife of the water-carrier kept her promise of secrecy with surprising strictness. For a whole day and a half she went about with a look of mystery and a heart swelling almost to bursting, yet she held her peace, though surrounded by her gossips. It is true she could not help giving herself a few airs, apologized for her ragged dress, and talked of ordering a new basquina all trimmed with gold lace and bugles, and a new lace mantilla. She threw out hints of her husband's intention of leaving off his trade of water-carrying, as it did not altogether agree with his health. In fact she thought they should all retire to the country for the summer, that the children might have the benefit of the mountain air, for there was no living in the city in this sultry season.

The neighbors stared at each other, and thought the poor woman had lost her wits; and her airs and graces and elegant pretensions were the theme of universal scoffing and merriment among her friends, the moment her back was turned.

If she restrained herself abroad, however, she indemnified herself at home, and putting a string of rich oriental pearls round her neck, Moorish bracelets on her arms, an aigrette of diamonds on her head, sailed backwards and forwards in her slattern rags about the room, now and then stopping to admire herself in a broken mirror. Nay, in the impulse of her simple vanity, she could not resist, on one occasion, showing herself at the window to enjoy the effect of her finery on the passers-by.

As the fates would have it, Pedrillo Pedrugo, the meddlesome barber, was at this moment sitting idly in his shop on the opposite side of the street, when his ever-watchful eye caught the sparkle of a diamond. In an instant he was at his loop-hole, reconnoitring the slattern spouse of the water-carrier, decorated with the splendor of an eastern bride. No sooner had he taken an accurate inventory of her ornaments, than he posted off with all speed to the Alcalde. In a little while the hungry alguazil was again on the scent, and before the day was over the unfortunate Peregil was again dragged into the presence of the judge.

"How is this, villain!" cried the Alcalde, in a furious voice. "You told me that the infidel who died in your house left nothing behind but an empty coffer, and now I hear of your wife flaunting in her rags decked out with pearls and diamonds. Wretch that thou art! prepare to render up the spoils of thy miserable victim, and to swing on the gallows that is already tired of waiting for thee."

The terrified water-carrier fell on his knees, and made a full relation of the marvellous manner in which he had gained his wealth. The Alcalde, the alguazil, and the inquisitive barber listened with greedy ears to this Arabian tale of enchanted treasure. The alguazil was despatched to bring the Moor who had assisted in the incantation. The Moslem entered half frightened out of his wits at finding himself in the hands of the harpies of the law. When he beheld the water-carrier standing with sheepish looks and downcast countenance, he comprehended the whole matter. "Miserable animal," said he, as he passed near him, "did I not warn thee against babbling to thy wife?"

The story of the Moor coincided exactly with that of his colleague; but the Alcalde affected to be slow of belief, and threw out menaces of imprisonment and rigorous investigation.

"Softly, good Señor Alcalde," said the Mussulman, who by this time had recovered his usual shrewdness and self-possession. "Let us not mar fortune's favors in the scramble for them. Nobody knows anything of this matter but ourselves; let us keep the secret. There is wealth enough in the cave to enrich us all. Promise a fair division, and all shall be produced; refuse, and the cave shall remain forever closed."

The Alcalde consulted apart with the alguazil. The latter was an old fox in his profession. "Promise anything," said he, "until you get possession of the treasure. You may then seize upon the whole, and if he and his accomplice dare to murmur, threaten them with the faggot and the stake as infidels and sorcerers."

The Alcalde relished the advice. Smoothing his brow and turning to the Moor, "This is a strange story," said he, "and may be true, but I must have ocular proof of it. This very night you must repeat the incantation in my presence. If there be really such treasure, we will share it amicably between us, and say nothing further of the matter; if ye have deceived me, expect no mercy at my hands. In the meantime you must remain in custody."

The Moor and the water-carrier cheerfully agreed to these conditions, satisfied that the event would prove the truth of their words.

Towards midnight the Alcalde sallied forth secretly, attended by the alguazil and the meddlesome barber, all strongly armed. They conducted the Moor and the water-carrier as prisoners, and were provided with the stout donkey of the latter to bear off the expected treasure. They arrived at the tower without being observed, and tying the donkey to a fig-tree, descended into the fourth vault of the tower.

The scroll was produced, the yellow waxen taper lighted, and the Moor read the form of incantation. The earth trembled as before, and the pavement opened with a thundering sound, disclosing the narrow flight of steps. The Alcalde, the alguazil, and the barber were struck aghast, and could not summon courage to descend. The Moor and the water-carrier entered the lower vault and found the two Moors seated as before, silent and motionless. They removed two of the great jars, filled with golden coin and precious stones. The water-carrier bore them up one by one upon his shoulders, but though a strong-backed little man, and accustomed to carry burdens, he staggered beneath their weight, and found, when slung on each side of his donkey, they were as much as the animal could bear.

"Let us be content for the present," said the Moor; "here is as much treasure as we can carry off without being perceived, and enough to make us all wealthy to our heart's desire."

"Is there more treasure remaining behind?" demanded the Alcalde.

"The greatest prize of all," said the Moor, "a huge coffer, bound with bands of steel, and filled with pearls and precious stones."

"Let us have up the coffer by all means," cried the grasping Alcalde.

"I will descend for no more," said the Moor, doggedly; "enough is enough for a reasonable man—more is superfluous."

"And I," said the water-carrier, "will bring up no further burden to break the back of my poor donkey."

Finding commands, threats, and entreaties equally vain, the Alcalde turned to his two adherents. "Aid me," said he, "to bring up the coffer, and its contents shall be divided between us." So saying, he descended the steps, followed with trembling reluctance, by the alguazil and the barber.

No sooner did the Moor behold them fairly earthed than he extinguished the yellow taper: the pavement closed with its usual crash, and the three worthies remained buried in its womb.

He then hastened up the different flights of steps, nor stopped until in the open air. The little water-carrier followed him as fast as his short legs would permit.

"What hast thou done?" cried Peregil, as soon as he could recover breath. "The Alcalde and the other two are shut up in the vault!"

"It is the will of Allah!" said the Moor, devoutly.

"And will you not release them?" demanded the Gallego.

"Allah forbid!" replied the Moor, smoothing his beard. "It is written in the book of fate that they shall remain enchanted until some future adventurer arrive to break the charm. The will of God be done!" So saying, he hurled the end of the waxen taper far among the gloomy thickets of the glen.

There was now no remedy; so the Moor and the water-carrier proceeded with the richly laden donkey towards the city, nor could honest Peregil refrain from hugging and kissing his long-eared fellow-laborer, thus restored to him from the clutches of the law; and, in fact, it is doubtful which gave the simple-hearted little man most joy at the moment, the gaining of the treasure or the recovery of the donkey.

The two partners in good luck divided their spoil amicably and fairly, except that the Moor, who had a little taste for trinketry, made out to get into his heap the most of the pearls and precious stones and other baubles, but then he always gave the water-carrier in lieu magnificent jewels of massy gold, four times the size, with which the latter was heartily content. They took care not to linger within reach of accidents, but made off to enjoy their wealth undisturbed in other countries. The Moor returned to Africa, to his native city of Tangiers, and the Gallego, with his wife, his children, and his donkey, made the best of his way to Portugal. Here, under the admonition and tuition of his wife, he became a personage of some consequence, for she made the worthy little man array his long body and short legs in doublet and hose, with a feather in his hat and a sword by his side, and laying aside his familiar appellation of Peregil, assume the more sonorous title of Don Pedro Gil; his progeny grew up a thriving and merry-hearted, though short and bandy-legged generation, while the Señora Gil, befringed, belaced, and betasselled from her head to her heels, with glittering rings on every finger, became a model of slattern fashion and finery.

As to the Alcalde, and his adjuncts, they remained shut up under the great tower of the seven floors, and there they remain spellbound at the present day. Whenever there shall be a lack in Spain of pimping barbers, sharking alguazils, and corrupt Alcaldes, they may be sought after; but if they have to wait until such time for their deliverance, there is danger of their enchantment enduring until doomsday.

Monday *what does he talk about? pick out*

[*A Tour on the Prairies*]

FIVE JOURNALS remain of those kept by Irving on his trip west from Cincinnati in 1832. These were published by the Bibliophile Society in 1919, but not all the material was new because Irving had used the journals as the basis of his *Tour on the Prairies* (1835). The following passage from Journal III should be compared with the account of the Osage camp which is reprinted herewith from the author's revised edition of 1865:

Chief cook of Osage villages—a great dignitary—combining grand chamberlain, minister of state, master of ceremonies and town crier—has under-cooks. He tastes broth &c. When strangers arrive he goes about the village and makes proclamation—great white man, great chief arrived—warriors turn out and prepare to receive him properly. Chief of lodge prepared for reception—mats placed, etc.

[The Osage Camp]

In the morning early, (Oct. 12,) the two Creeks who had been sent express by the commander of Fort Gibson, to stop the company of rangers, arrived at our encampment on their return. They had left the company encamped about fifty miles distant, in a fine place on the Arkansas, abounding in game, where they intended to await our arrival. This news spread animation throughout our party, and we set out on our march, at sunrise, with renewed spirit.

In mounting our steeds, the young Osage attempted to throw a blanket upon his wild horse. The fine, sensitive animal took fright, reared and recoiled. The attitudes of the wild horse and the almost naked savage would have formed studies for a painter or a statuary.

I often pleased myself, in the course of our march, with noticing the appearance of the young Count and his newly enlisted follower, as they rode before me. Never was preux chevalier better suited with an esquire. The Count was well mounted, and, as I have before observed, was a bold and graceful rider. He was fond, too, of caracoling his horse, and dashing about in the buoyancy of youthful spirits. His dress was a gay Indian hunting-frock, of dressed deer-skin, setting well to the shape, dyed of a beautiful purple, and fancifully embroidered with silks of various colors; as if it had been the work of some Indian beauty, to decorate a favorite chief. With this he wore leathern pantaloons and moccasins, a foraging-cap, and a double-barrelled gun slung by a bandoleer athwart his back: so that he was quite a picturesque figure as he managed gracefully his spirited steed.

The young Osage would ride close behind him on his wild and beautifully mottled horse, which was decorated with crimson tufts of hair. He rode, with his finely shaped head and bust naked; his blanket being girt round his waist. He carried his rifle in one hand, and managed his horse with the other, and seemed ready to dash off at a moment's warning, with his youthful leader, on any madcap foray or scamper. The Count, with the sanguine anticipations of youth, promised himself many hardy adventures and exploits in company with his youthful "brave," when we should get among the buffaloes, in the Pawnee hunting-grounds.

After riding some distance, we crossed a narrow, deep stream, upon a solid bridge, the remains of an old beaver dam; the industrious community 10 which had constructed it had all been destroyed. Above us, a streaming flight of wild geese, high in air, and making a vociferous noise, gave note of the waning year.

About half-past ten o'clock we made a halt in a forest, where there was abundance of pea-vine. Here we turned the horses loose to graze. A fire was made, water procured from an adjacent spring, and in a short time our little Frenchman, Tonish, had a pot of coffee prepared for our refreshment. 20 While partaking of it, we were joined by an old Osage, one of a small hunting party who had recently passed this way. He was in search of his horse, which had wandered away, or been stolen. Our half-breed, Beatte, made a wry face on hearing of Osage hunters in this direction. "Until we pass those hunters," said he, "we shall see no buffaloes. They frighten away everything like a prairie on fire."

The morning repast being over, the party 30 amused themselves in various ways. Some shot with their rifles at mark, others lay asleep half buried in the deep bed of foliage, with their heads resting on their saddles; others gossiped round the fire at the foot of a tree, which sent up wreaths of blue smoke among the branches. The horses banqueted luxuriously on the pea-vines, and some lay down and rolled amongst them.

We were overshadowed by lofty trees, with straight, smooth trunks, like stately columns; and 40 as the glancing rays of the sun shone through the transparent leaves, tinted with the many-colored hues of autumn, I was reminded of the effect of sunshine among the stained windows and clustering columns of a Gothic cathedral. Indeed there is a grandeur and solemnity in our spacious forests of the West, that awaken in me the same feeling I have experienced in those vast and venerable

piles, and the sound of the wind sweeping through them supplies occasionally the deep breathings of the organ.

About noon the bugle sounded to horse, and we were again on the march, hoping to arrive at the encampment of the rangers before night; as the old Osage had assured us it was not above ten or twelve miles distant. In our course through a forest, we passed by a lonely pool, covered with the most magnificent water-lilies I have ever beheld; among which swam several wood-ducks, one of the most beautiful of water-fowl, remarkable for the gracefulness and brilliancy of its plumage.

After proceeding some distance farther, we came down upon the banks of the Arkansas, at a place where tracks of numerous horses, all entering the water, showed where a party of Osage hunters had recently crossed the river on their way to the buffalo range. After letting our horses drink in the 20 river, we continued along its bank for a space, and then across prairies, where we saw a distant smoke, which we hoped might proceed from the encampment of the rangers. Following what we supposed to be their trail, we came to a meadow in which were a number of horses grazing; they were not, however, the horses of the troop. A little farther on, we reached a straggling Osage village, on the banks of the Arkansas. Our arrival created quite a sensation. A number of old men came forward and 30 shook hands with us all severally; while the women and children huddled together in groups, staring at us wildly, chattering and laughing among themselves. We found that all the young men of the village had departed on a hunting expedition, leaving the women and children and old men behind. Here the Commissioner made a speech from on horseback; informing his hearers of the purport of his mission, to promote a general peace among the tribes of the West, and urging them to 40 lay aside all warlike and bloodthirsty notions, and not to make any wanton attacks upon the Pawnees. This speech being interpreted by Beatte, seemed to have a most pacifying effect upon the multitude, who promised faithfully that, as far as in them lay, the peace should not be disturbed; and indeed their age and sex gave some reason to trust that they would keep their word.

Still hoping to reach the camp of the rangers

before nightfall, we pushed on until twilight, when we were obliged to halt on the borders of a ravine. The rangers bivouacked under trees, at the bottom of the dell, while we pitched our tent on a rocky knoll near a running stream. The night came on dark and overcast, with flying clouds, and much appearance of rain. The fires of the rangers burnt brightly in the dell, and threw strong masses of light upon the robber-looking groups that were cooking, eating, and drinking around them. To add to the wildness of the scene, several Osage Indians, visitors from the village we had passed, were mingled among the men. Three of them came and seated themselves by our fire. They watched everything that was going on round them in silence, and looked like figures of monumental bronze. We gave them food, and, what they most relished, coffee; for the Indians partake in the universal fondness for this beverage, which pervades the West. When they had made their supper, they stretched themselves side by side before the fire, and began a low nasal chant, drumming with their hands upon their breasts by way of accompaniment. Their chant seemed to consist of regular staves, every one terminating, not in a melodious cadence, but in the abrupt interjection huh! uttered almost like a hiccup. This chant, we were told by our interpreter, Beatte, related to ourselves, our appearance, our treatment of them, and all that they knew of our plans. In one part they spoke of the young Count, whose animated character and eagerness for Indian enterprise had struck their fancy, and they indulged in some waggery about him and the young Indian beauties, that produced great merriment among our half-breeds.

This mode of improvising is common throughout the savage tribes; and in this way, with a few simple inflections of the voice, they chant all their exploits in war and hunting, and occasionally indulge in a vein of comic humor and dry satire, to which the Indians appear to me much more prone than is generally imagined.

In fact, the Indians that I have had an opportunity of seeing in real life are quite different from those described in poetry. They are by no means the stoics that they are represented: taciturn, unbending, without a tear or a smile. Taciturn they are, it is true, when in company with white men, whose good-will they distrust, and whose language they do not understand; but the white man is equally taciturn under like circumstances. When the Indians are among themselves, however, there cannot be greater gossips. Half their time is taken up in talking over their adventures in war and hunting, and in telling whimsical stories. They are great mimics and buffoons, also, and entertain themselves excessively at the expense of the whites with whom they have associated, and who have supposed them impressed with profound respect for their grandeur and dignity. They are curious observers, noting everything in silence, but with a keen and watchful eye; occasionally exchanging a glance or a grunt with each other, when anything particularly strikes them; but reserving all comments until they are alone. Then it is that they give full scope to criticism, satire, mimicry, and mirth.

In the course of my journey along the frontier I have had repeated opportunities of noticing their excitability and boisterous merriment at their games; and have occasionally noticed a group of Osages sitting round a fire until a late hour at night, engaged in the most animated and lively conversation; and at times making the woods resound with peals of laughter. As to tears, they have them in abundance, both real and affected; at times they make a merit of them. No one weeps more bitterly or profusely at the death of a relative or friend; and they have stated times when they repair to howl and lament at their graves. I have heard doleful wailings at daybreak in the neighboring Indian villages, made by some of the inhabitants, who go out at that hour into the fields to mourn and weep for the dead; at such times, I am told, the tears will stream down their cheeks in torrents.

As far as I can judge, the Indian of poetical fiction is, like the shepherd of pastoral romance, a mere personification of imaginary attributes.

The nasal chant of our Osage guests gradually died away; they covered their heads with their blankets and fell fast asleep, and in a little while all was silent, excepting the pattering of scattered rain-drops upon our tent.

In the morning our Indian visitors breakfasted with us, but the young Osage who was to act as esquire to the Count in his knight-errantry on the prairies, was nowhere to be found. His wild horse, too, was missing, and, after many conjectures, we came to the conclusion that he had taken "Indian leave" of us in the night. We afterwards ascertained that he had been persuaded so to do by the Osages we had recently met with; who had represented to him the perils that would attend him in an expedition to the Pawnee hunting-grounds, where he might fall into the hands of the implacable enemies of his tribe; and, what was scarcely less to be apprehended, the annoyances to which he would be subjected from the capricious and overbearing conduct of the white men; who, as I have witnessed in my own short experience, are prone to treat the poor Indians as little better than brute animals. Indeed, he had had a specimen of it himself in the narrow escape he made from the infliction of "Lynch's law," by the hard-winking worthy of the frontier, for the flagitious crime of finding a stray horse.

The disappearance of the youth was generally regretted by our party, for we had all taken a great fancy to him from his handsome, frank, and manly appearance, and the easy grace of his deportment. He was indeed a native-born gentleman. By none, however, was he so much lamented as by the young Count, who thus suddenly found himself deprived of his esquire. I regretted the departure of the Osage for his own sake, for we should have cherished him throughout the expedition, and I am convinced, from the munificent spirit of his patron, he would have returned to his tribe laden with wealth of beads and trinkets and Indian blankets.

[A Republic of Prairie-dogs]

In returning from our expedition . . . I learned that a burrow, or village, as it is termed, of prairie-dogs had been discovered on the level summit of a hill, about a mile from the camp. Having heard much of the habits and peculiarities of these little animals, I determined to pay a visit to the community. The prairie-dog is, in fact, one of the curiosities of the Far West, about which travellers delight to tell marvelous tales, endowing him at times with something of the politic and social habits of a rational being, and giving him systems of civil government and domestic economy almost equal to what they used to bestow upon the beaver.

The prairie-dog is an animal of the coney kind, and about the size of a rabbit. He is of a sprightly mercurial nature: quick, sensitive, and somewhat petulant. He is very gregarious, living in large communities, sometimes of several acres in extent, where innumerable little heaps of earth show the entrances to the subterranean cells of the inhabitants, and the well beaten tracks, like lanes and streets, show their mobility and restlessness. According to the accounts given of them, they would seem to be continually full of sport, business, and public affairs; whisking about hither and thither, as if on gossiping visits to each other's houses, or congregating in the cool of the evening, or after a shower, and gambolling together in the open air. Sometimes, especially when the moon shines, they pass half the night in revelry, barking or yelping with short, quick, yet weak tones, like those of very young puppies. While in the height of their playfulness and clamor, however, should there be the least alarm, they all vanish into their cells in an instant, and the village remains blank and silent. In case they are hard pressed by their pursuers, without any hope of escape, they will assume a pugnacious air, and a most whimsical look of impotent wrath and defiance.

The prairie-dogs are not permitted to remain sole and undisturbed inhabitants of their own homes. Owls and rattlesnakes are said to take up their abodes with them; but whether as invited guests or unwelcome intruders, is a matter of controversy. The owls are of a peculiar kind, and would seem to partake of the character of the hawk; for they are taller and more erect on their legs, more alert in their looks and rapid in their flight than ordinary owls, and do not confine their excursions to the night, but sally forth in the broad day.

Some say that they only inhabit cells which the prairie-dogs have deserted, and suffered to go to ruin, in consequence of the death in them of some relative; for they would make out this little animal to be endowed with keen sensibilities, that will not permit it to remain in the dwelling where it has witnessed the death of a friend. Other fanciful speculators represent the owl as a kind of housekeeper to the prairie-dog; and, from having a

393

note very similar, insinuate that it acts, in a manner, as family preceptor, and teaches the young litter to bark.

As to the rattlesnake, nothing satisfactory has been ascertained of the part he plays in this most interesting household, though he is considered as little better than a sycophant and sharper, that winds himself into the concerns of the honest, credulous little dog, and takes him in most sadly. Certain it is, if he acts as toad-eater, he occasionally solaces himself with more than the usual perquisites of his order, as he is now and then detected with one of the younger members of the family in his maw.

Such are a few of the particulars that I could gather about the domestic economy of this little inhabitant of the prairies, who, with his pigmy republic, appears to be a subject of much whimsical speculation and burlesque remarks, among the hunters of the Far West.

It was towards evening that I set out with a companion, to visit the village in question. Unluckily, it had been invaded in the course of the day by some of the rangers, who had shot two or three of its inhabitants, and thrown the whole sensitive community in confusion. As we approached, we could perceive numbers of the inhabitants seated at the entrances of their cells, while sentinels seemed to have been posted on the outskirts, to keep a look-out. At sight of us, the picket guards scampered in and gave the alarm; whereupon every inhabitant gave a short yelp, or bark, and dived into his hole, his heels twinkling in the air as if he had thrown a somerset.

We traversed the whole village, or republic, which covered an area of about thirty acres; but not a whisker of an inhabitant was to be seen. We probed their cells as far as the ramrods of our rifles would reach, but could unearth neither dog,

nor owl, nor rattlesnake. Moving quietly to a little distance, we lay down upon the ground and watched for a long time, silent and motionless. By-and-by a cautious old burgher would slowly put forth the end of his nose, but instantly draw it in again. Another, at a greater distance, would emerge entirely; but, catching a glance of us, would throw a somerset, and plunge back again into his hole. At length, some who resided on the opposite side of the village, taking courage from the continued stillness, would steal forth, and hurry off to a distant hole, the residence possibly of some family connection, or gossiping friend, about whose safety they were solicitous, or with whom they wished to compare notes about the late occurrences.

Others, still more bold, assembled in little knots, in the streets and public places, as if to discuss the recent outrages offered to the commonwealth, and the atrocious murders of their fellow-burghers.

We rose from the ground and moved forward, to take a nearer view of these public proceedings, when, yelp! yelp! yelp!—there was a shrill alarm passed from mouth to mouth; the meetings suddenly dispersed; feet twinkled in the air in every direction; and in an instant all had vanished into the earth.

The dusk of evening put an end to our observations, but the train of whimsical comparisons produced in my brain by the moral attributes which I had heard given these little politic animals, still continued after my return to camp; and late in the night, as I lay awake after all the camp was asleep, and heard, in the stillness of the hour, a faint clamor of shrill voices from the distant village, I could not help picturing to myself the inhabitants gathered together in noisy assemblage, and windy debate, to devise plans for the public safety, and to vindicate the invaded rights and insulted dignity of the republic.

JAMES FENIMORE COOPER (1789–1851)

JAMES FENIMORE COOPER was born in 1789, the year of the publication of Sarah Wentworth Morton's *The Power of Sympathy*, a feverish compound of seduction, suicide, and sensibility. During Cooper's youth and young manhood Americans were reading the didactic and sentimental tales of the "handkerchief school"

which constitute the apologetic beginnings of American fiction. As late as 1818 John Bristed complained in the *North American Review*, "Of native novels we have no great stock, and none good. . . . There is, to be sure, some traditional romance about the Indians; but a novel describing these miserable barbarians, their squaws and papooses, would not be very interesting to the present race of American readers." Yet within three years the same periodical hailed Cooper's *The Spy* (1821) as the harbinger of great native historical novels. Within the next decade the appearance of *The Pioneers* (1823), *The Pilot* (1824), *The Last of the Mohicans* (1826), and *The Prairie* (1827) revealed the emergence of a novelist who could transmute the American experience on the ocean, along the frontier, and in the forests into a national epic of compelling power.

Although Cooper was almost immediately labeled "the American Scott" by the same facile critics who had dubbed Bryant "the American Wordsworth," no more staunch an American ever set pen to paper. His novels are heavily freighted with the distinctive American political principles which he believed to be the only source of true nationalism in literature. A patrician-democrat, preferring democracy to any other system, yet keenly aware of its pitfalls, Cooper boldly faced the problems inherent in the formative stages of American society. His strictures on the abuses in American life denied him the personal popularity enjoyed by the "easily pleased" Washington Irving, and warped the critical appraisals of such novels as *The Pathfinder* (1840) and *The Deerslayer* (1841). Moreover, Cooper's hasty methods of composition and his lack of concern for the "art" of the novel have made him a vulnerable target for later critics. Despite all this, even in an age whose sophisticates pretend to yawn over historical fiction, the splendid panoramas and the breathless narrative interest of Cooper's novels still retain their hold upon the final arbiter of literary reputation, "the common reader."

Cooper was born in Burlington, New Jersey, but his impressionable early years were spent at Cooperstown, New York, where his father was the proprietor of a large estate. Here the future novelist encountered at first hand a brawling frontier democracy and the baronial ideals of the landed gentry, a juxtaposition packed with implications for students of his fiction. The Federalist prejudices which young Cooper learned from his father, Judge William Cooper, were intensified by the precepts of his English tutor who prepared him for Yale. Cooper was not dismayed in 1806 when a prank in his junior year ended his college career. Later he enjoyed bestowing a Yale degree upon one of the least agreeable of his characters, although in *The Crater* (1847) he paid his alma mater a generous compliment. Following his dismissal from Yale he was articled to the captain of the *Sterling*, a merchant vessel, and in 1808 was admitted to the United States Navy as a midshipman. He resigned in

1811 to marry Susan De Lancey, daughter of a Tory family possessing extensive land holdings near Mamaroneck, New York. Cooper treated his Tory characters in *The Spy* with unusual liberality and understanding.

The story of the impulse which prompted Cooper's first novel is a familiar one. With characteristic bluntness Cooper boasted that he could write a better novel than the one being read aloud at the family fireside, and he tried to make good his boast with a persistence which was equally characteristic. The resulting manuscript was published anonymously in 1820 as *Precaution*, a run-of-the-mill, lending-library novel of manners in a style sufficiently genteel to suggest that Mrs. Cooper may have had a hand in its composition. Confident that he could write passably, Cooper next turned to an American theme in a setting which he knew intimately, Westchester County. *The Spy* (1821), a spirited story of the heroic services of Harvey Birch in the Revolution, captured the popular imagination at home and abroad. It contains many of the ingredients of Cooper's later work, especially his use of the pursuit-and-escape formula, and the artful preparation for climactic scenes. In 1823 with the publication of *The Pioneers* and *The Pilot*, Cooper widened his theater to include the frontier and the sea, and by the creation of Natty Bumppo he added a character to the gallery of immortals in world fiction.

An honorary M.A. from Columbia in 1824 capped the triumph of his three successes, and Cooper enjoyed his role as founder and leading spirit of a literary coterie, the Bread and Cheese Club, in New York City, where he had taken up residence in 1822. Cooper's reputation was further enhanced by *The Last of the Mohicans* (1826), the most popular of the Leatherstocking Tales, which introduced his most memorable Indian characters, and also by *The Prairie* (1827), in which Natty Bumppo's life story is brought to an eloquent close. From 1826 to 1833 Cooper and his family lived in Europe. Unlike Irving and Longfellow, who were content to accept uncritically the romantic legends of the Old World, Cooper studied social and political conditions, and objected to the worship of feudal traditions which Scott's wizardry had transfigured. Meanwhile, Cooper added to his lengthening shelf of novels with the publication of *The Red Rover* (1828), *The Wept of the Wish-ton-Wish* (1829), *The Water Witch* (1831), *The Heidenmauer* (1832), and *The Headsman* (1833). The last three of these novels illustrate his conviction that the American heritage of political and religious freedom is in itself sufficient to impart a distinctive national character to our literature.

For almost a decade following Cooper's return to

the United States in 1833 his work provoked an unprecedented flood of personal recrimination. A foretaste of this abuse had greeted his *Notions of the Americans* in 1828, which was caught in a crossfire of criticism from both sides of the Atlantic. In *A Letter to His Countrymen* (1834) and *The American Democrat* (1838), as well as in his novels *Homeward Bound* (1838) and *Home as Found* (1838), which were no less critical of the vulgarity, materialism, and narrowness of American society, Cooper irritated and puzzled his readers. Even *The Pathfinder* (1840) and *The Deerslayer* (1841) were attacked by the incensed Whig press. Of his later novels, *Satanstoe* (1845) is by far the best, with its appealing love story, its richly textured social background, its dramatic episodes of the attack on Ticonderoga, and the exciting rescue of Anneke Mordaunt from the break in the Hudson River ice dam. In *The Chainbearer* (1845) and *The Red Skins* (1846), forming with *Satanstoe* a chronicle of the Littlepage family; and in *The Crater* (1848) and *The Ways of the Hour* (1850), Cooper was not so successful in blending social criticism with his characters and narratives.

As the creator of the first substantial achievement in American fiction, Cooper's historical place is clear. He brought the masculine virtues of beef and iron to a form of writing which had been largely devoted to the perfumed evasions of genteel females. Despite the justice of Lowell's criticism of Cooper's women as creatures "sappy as maples and flat as a prairie," and notwithstanding his highly-starched diction and his supremely forgettable conventional heroes and heroines, Cooper's novels possess an abundance of vitalizing energy. His chief appeal is to reader rather than to critic, and readers continue to respond to his narrative power, to his skill in evoking suspense, to the fertility of his invention, and to his force of imagination, which fashioned a prose epic of the march of the pioneers across the American continent. Now that almost a century has elapsed since Cooper's death, few readers are disposed to question the essential fairness of Melville's reasoned judgment that the author of the Leatherstocking Tales "possessed not the slightest weakness but those which are only noticeable as the almost infallible indices of pervading greatness. He was a great, robust-souled man, all of whose merits are not yet fully appreciated."

BIBLIOGRAPHY · There is no definitive, carefully edited text of Cooper's complete writings. Usually available are *J. Fenimore Cooper's Works* (32 vols., 1884–1892), supervised by the novelist's daughter, Susan F. Cooper; and *The Works of James Fenimore Cooper* (33 vols., 1895–1900). A number of the popular items, edited and containing useful interpretative introductions, include *The Deerslayer*, edited by G. Paine (1927); *The Last of the Mohicans*, edited by F. L. Pattee (1927); *The Pathfinder*, edited by R. A. Sharp (1926); *The Prairie*, edited by H. Hansen (1940); *The Spy*, edited by T. McDowell (1931). Valuable editions of nonfictional works include *The American Democrat*, edited by H. L. Mencken (1931); *Gleanings in Europe*, edited by R. E. Spiller (2 vols., 1928–1930); and *New York*, edited by D. R. Fox (1930). R. E. Spiller's *James Fenimore Cooper: Representative Selections* (1933) contains a penetrating prefatory essay and an admirable selective bibliography.

The first substantial biography is T. R. Lounsbury, *James Fenimore Cooper* (1883). Later interpretations are H. W. Boynton, *James Fenimore Cooper* (1931) and James Grossman, *James Fenimore Cooper* (1949); see also William Cullen Bryant, "Discourse on the Life, Character, and Genius of James Fenimore Cooper," *Memorial of James Fenimore Cooper* (1852). Full-length studies of special aspects of Cooper include M. Clavel, *Fenimore Cooper and His Critics . . .* (1938); E. R. Outland, *The "Effingham Libels" on Cooper* in *Wisconsin Studies in Language and Literature* (1929); R. E. Spiller, *James Fenimore Cooper: Critic of His Times* (1931); and D. Waples, *The Whig Myth of James Fenimore Cooper* (1938). The standard bibliography is that compiled by R. E. Spiller and P. C. Blackburn, *A Descriptive Bibliography of the Writings of James Fenimore Cooper* (1934).

Additional biographical information is contained in N. F. Adkins, "James Fenimore Cooper and The Bread and Cheese Club," *Modern Language Notes*, XLVII (1932), 71–79; R. Birdsall, *The Story of Cooperstown* (1917); *The Correspondence of James Fenimore Cooper*, edited by J. F. Cooper, the novelist's grandson; S. F. Cooper, "A Glance Backward," and "A Second Glance Backward," *Atlantic Monthly*, LIX (1887), 199–206, LX (1887), 474–486; R. E. Spiller, "Fenimore Cooper and Lafayette: the Finance Controversy of 1831–1832," *American Literature*, III (1931), 28–44, and "Fenimore Cooper and Lafayette: Friends of Polish Freedom, 1830–1832," *American Literature*, VII (1935), 56–75; and D. Waples, "A Letter from James Fenimore Cooper," *New England Quarterly*, III (1930), 123–132.

Important critical studies include R. H. Ballinger, "Origins of James Fenimore Cooper's *The Two Admirals*," *American Literature*, XX (1948), 20–30; P. A. Barba, "Cooper in Germany" in *Indiana University Bulletin*, XII (1914); W. C. Brownell, *American Prose Masters* (1909), 3–60; H. S. Canby, *Classic Americans* (1931), 97–142; S. L. Clemens, "Fenimore Cooper's Literary Offenses," *North American Review*, CLXI (1895), 1–12, and "Fenimore Cooper's Further Literary Offenses," *New England Quarterly*, XIX (1946), 291–301; J. Conrad, *Notes on Life and Letters* (1921), 53–57; E. P. Dargan, "Balzac and Cooper: *Les Chouans*," *Modern Philology*, XIII (1915), 193–213; J. D. Ferguson, *American Literature* in Spain (1916), 32–54; E. Goggio, "Cooper's *Bravo* in Italy," *Romanic Review*, XX (1929), 220–230; E. E. Hale, Jr., "American Scenery in Cooper's Novels," *Sewanee Review*, XVIII (1910), 317–332; W. D. Howells, *Heroines of Fiction*, I (1901), 102–112; A. Keiser, *The Indian in American Literature* (1933), 101–143; E. E. Leisy, *The American Historical Novel Before 1860* . . . (1926); T. McDowell, "Scott on Cooper and Brockden Brown," *Modern Language Notes*, XLV (1930), 18–20, "James Fenimore Cooper as Self-Critic," *Studies in Philology*, XXVII (1930), 508–516, and "The Identity of Harvey Birch," *American Literature*, II (1930), 111–120; G. Paine, "Cooper and *The North American Review*," *Studies in Philology*, XXVIII (1931), 799–809, and "The Indians of the Leather-Stocking Tales," *Studies in Philology*, XXIII (1926), 16–39; L. Pound, "The Dialect of Cooper's Leather-Stocking," *American Speech*, II (1927), 479–488; H. H. Scudder, "Cooper's *The Crater*," *American Literature*, XIX (1947), 109–126; R. E. Spiller, "Fenimore Cooper's Defense of Slave-Owning America," *American Historical Review*, XXXV (1930), 575–582, and "Cooper's Notes on Language," *American Speech*, IV (1929), 294–300.

The American Democrat

IT IS one of the ironies of Cooper's career that he defended American democracy when he was abroad, and attacked it when he was at home. Published in 1838, *The American Democrat* is the most penetrating of his criticisms of democracy. "Cooper was probably the first American to write about Americans in a really frank spirit," declared H. L. Mencken, in his edition of the essay. "The fact has been pretty well forgotten by the college tutors who now boil Sophomores in the Leatherstocking Tales, but during his last ten or twelve years on earth it was what his countrymen chiefly remembered when they thought of him." The present text is that of the first edition in 1838.

An Aristocrat and a Democrat

We live in an age, when the words aristocrat and democrat are much used, without regard to the real significations. An aristocrat is one of a few, who possess the political power of a country; a democrat, one of the many. The words are also properly applied to those who entertain notions favorable to aristocratical, or democratical forms of government. Such persons are not, necessarily, either aristocrats, or democrats in fact, but merely so in opinion. Thus a member of a democratical government may have an aristocratical bias, and *vice versa*.

To call a man who has the habits and opinions of a gentleman, an aristocrat, from that fact alone, is an abuse of terms, and betrays ignorance of the true principles of government, as well as of the world. It must be an equivocal freedom, under which every one is not the master of his own innocent acts and associations, and he is a sneaking democrat, indeed, who will submit to be dictated to, in those habits over which neither law nor morality assumes a right of control.

Some men fancy that a democrat can only be one who seeks the level, social, mental and moral, of the majority, a rule that would at once exclude all men of refinement, education and taste from the class. These persons are enemies of democracy, as they at once render it impracticable. They are usually great sticklers for their own associations and habits, too, though unable to comprehend any of a nature that are superior. They are, in truth, aristocrats in principle, though assuming a contrary pretension; the ground work of all their feelings and arguments being self. Such is not the intention of liberty, whose aim is to leave every man to be the master of his own acts; denying hereditary honors, it is true, as unjust and unnecessary, but not denying the inevitable consequences of civilization.

The law of God is the only rule of conduct, in this, as in other matters. Each man should do as he would be done by. Were the question put to the greatest advocate of indiscriminate association, whether he would submit to have his company and habits dictated to him, he would be one of the first to resist the tyranny; for they, who are the most rigid in maintaining their own claims, in such matters, are usually the loudest in decrying those whom they fancy to be better off than themselves. Indeed, it may be taken as a rule in social intercourse, that he who is the most apt to question the pretensions of others, is the most conscious of the doubtful position he himself occupies; thus establishing the very claims he affects to deny, by letting his jealousy of it be seen. Manners, education and refinement, are positive things, and they bring with them innocent tastes which are productive of high enjoyments; and it is as unjust to deny their possessors their indulgence, as it would be to insist on the less fortunate's passing the time they would rather devote to athletic amusements, in listening to operas for which they have no relish, sung in a language they do not understand.

All that democracy means, is as equal a participation in rights as is practicable; and to pretend that social equality is a condition of popular institutions, is to assume that the latter are destructive of civilization, for, as nothing is more self-evident than the impossibility of raising all men to the highest standard of tastes and refinement, the alternative would be to reduce the entire community to the lowest. The whole embarrassment on this point exists in the difficulty of making men comprehend qualities they do not themselves possess. We can all perceive the difference between ourselves and our inferiors, but when it comes to a question of the difference between us and our superiors, we fail to appreciate merits of which we have no proper conceptions. In face of this obvious difficulty, there is the safe and just governing rule, already mentioned, or that of permitting every one to be the undisturbed judge of his own habits and associations, so long as they are innocent, and do not impair the rights of others to be equally judges for themselves. It follows, that social intercourse must regulate itself, independently of institutions, with the exception that the latter, while they withhold no natural, bestow no factitious advantages beyond those which are inseparable from the right of property, and general civilization.

In a democracy, men are just as free to aim at the highest attainable places in society, as to obtain the largest fortunes; and it would be clearly unworthy of all noble sentiment to say, that the grovelling competition for money shall alone be free, while that which enlists all the liberal acquirements and elevated sentiments of the race, is denied the democrat. Such an avowal would be at once, a declaration of the inferiority of the system, since nothing but ignorance and vulgarity could be its fruits.

The democratic gentleman must differ in many essential particulars, from the aristocratical gentleman, though in their ordinary habits and tastes they are virtually identical. Their principles vary; and, to a slight degree, their deportment accordingly. The democrat, recognizing the right of all to participate in power, will be more liberal in his general sentiments, a quality of superiority in itself; but, in conceding this much to his fellow man, he will proudly maintain his own independence of vulgar domination, as indispensable to his personal habits. The same principles and manliness that would induce him to depose a royal despot, would induce him to resist a vulgar tyrant.

There is no more capital, though more common error, than to suppose him an aristocrat who maintains his independence of habits; for democracy asserts the control of the majority, only, in matters of law, and not in matters of custom. The very object of the institution is the utmost practicable personal liberty, and to affirm the contrary, would be sacrificing the end to the means.

An aristocrat, therefore, is merely one who fortifies his exclusive privileges by positive institutions, and a democrat, one who is willing to admit of a free competition, in all things. To say, however, that the last supposes this competition will lead to nothing, is an assumption that means are employed without any reference to an end. He is the purest democrat who best maintains his rights, and no rights can be dearer to a man of cultivation, than exemptions from unseasonable invasions on his time, by the coarse-minded and ignorant.

On Liberty

Liberty, like equality, is a word more used than understood. Perfect and absolute liberty is as incompatible with the existence of society, as equality of condition. It is impracticable in a state of nature even, since, without the protection of the law, the strong would oppress and enslave the weak. We are then to understand by liberty, merely such a state of the social compact as permits the members of a community to lay no more restraints on themselves, than are required by their real necessities, and obvious interests. To this definition may be added, that it is a requisite of liberty, that the body of a nation should retain the power to modify its institutions, as circumstances shall require.

The natural disposition of all men being to enjoy a perfect freedom of action, it is a common error to suppose that the nation which possesses the mildest laws, or laws that impose the least personal restraints, is the freest. This opinion is untenable, since the power that concedes this freedom of action, can recall it. Unless it is lodged in the body of the community itself, there is, therefore, no pledge for the continuance of such a liberty. A familiar, supposititious case will render this truth more obvious.

A slave holder in Virginia is the master of two slaves: to one he grants his liberty, with the means to go to a town in a free state. The other accompanies his old associate clandestinely. In this town, they engage their services voluntarily, to a common master, who assigns to them equal shares in the same labor, paying them the same wages. In time, the master learns their situation, but, being an indulgent man, he allows the slave to retain his present situation. In all material things, these brothers are equal; they labor together, receive the same wages, and eat of the same food. Yet one is bond, and the other free, since it is in the power of the master, or of his heir, or of his assignee, at any time, to reclaim the services of the one who was not legally manumitted, and reduce him again to the condition of slavery. One of these brothers is the master of his own acts, while the other, though temporarily enjoying the same privileges, holds them subject to the will of a superior.

This is an all important distinction in the consideration of political liberty, since the circumstances of no two countries are precisely the same, and all municipal regulations ought to have direct reference to the actual condition of a community. It follows, that no country can properly be deemed free, unless the body of the nation possess, in the last resort, the legal power to frame its laws according to its wants. This power must also abide in the nation, or it becomes merely an historical fact, for he that was once free is not necessarily free always, any more than he that was once happy, is to consider himself happy in perpetuity.

This definition of liberty is new to the world, for a government founded on such principles is a novelty. Hitherto, a nation has been deemed free, whose people were possessed of a certain amount of franchises, without any reference to the general repository of power. Such a nation may not be absolutely enslaved, but it can scarcely be considered in possession of an affirmative political liberty, since it is not the master of its own fortunes.

Having settled what is the foundation of liberty,

it remains to be seen by what process a people can exercise this authority over themselves. The usual course is to refer all matters of choice to the decision of majorities. The common axiom of democracies, however, which says that "the majority must rule," is to be received with many limitations. Were the majority of a country to rule without restraint, it is probable as much injustice and oppression would follow, as are found under the dominion of one. It belongs to the nature of men to arrange themselves in parties, to lose sight of truth and justice in partizanship and prejudice, to mistake their own impulses for that which is proper, and to do wrong because they are indisposed to seek the right. Were it wise to trust power, unreservedly, to majorities, all fundamental and controlling laws would be unnecessary, since they might, as occasion required, emanate from the will of numbers. Constitutions would be useless.

The majority rules in prescribed cases, and in no other. It elects to office, it enacts ordinary laws, subject however to the restrictions of the constitution, and it decides most of the questions that arise in the primitive meetings of the people; questions that do not usually effect any of the principal interests of life.

The majority does not rule in settling fundamental laws, under the constitution; or when it does rule in such cases, it is with particular checks produced by time and new combinations; it does not pass judgment in trials at law, or under impeachment, and it is impotent in many matters touching vested rights. In the state of New York, the majority is impotent, in granting corporations, and in appropriating money for local purposes.

Though majorities often decide wrong, it is believed that they are less liable to do so than minorities. There can be no question that the educated and affluent classes of a country, are more capable of coming to wise and intelligent decisions in affairs of state, than the mass of a population. Their wealth and leisure afford them opportunities for observation and comparison, while their general information and greater knowledge of character, enable them to judge more accurately of men and measures. That these opportunities are not properly used, is owing to the unceasing desire of men to turn their advantages to their own particular

399

benefit, and to their passions. All history proves, when power is the sole possession of a few, that it is perverted to their sole advantage, the public suffering in order that their rulers may prosper. The same nature which imposes the necessity of governments at all, seems to point out the expediency of confiding its control, in the last resort, to the body of the nation, as the only lasting protection against gross abuses.

We do not adopt the popular polity because it is 10 perfect, but because it is less imperfect than any other. As man, by his nature, is liable to err, it is vain to expect an infallible whole that is composed of fallible parts. The government that emanates from a single will, supposing that will to be pure, enlightened, impartial, just and consistent, would be the best in the world, were it attainable for men. Such is the government of the universe, the result of which is perfect harmony. As no man is without spot in his justice, as no man has 20 infinite wisdom, or infinite mercy, we are driven to take refuge in the opposite extreme, or in a government of many.

It is common for the advocates of monarchy and aristocracy to deride the opinions of the mass, as no more than the impulses of ignorance and prejudices. While experience unhappily shows that this charge has too much truth, it also shows that the educated and few form no exemption to the common rule of humanity. The most intelli- 30 gent men of every country in which there is liberty of thought and action, yielding to their interests or their passions, are always found taking the opposite extremes of contested questions, thus triumphantly refuting an arrogant proposition, that of the exclusive fitness of the few to govern, by an unanswerable fact. The minority of a country is never known to agree, except in its efforts to reduce and oppress the majority. Were this not so, parties would be unknown in all countries but 40 democracies, whereas the factions of aristocracies have been among the fiercest and least governable of any recorded in history.

Although real political liberty can have but one character, that of a popular base, the world contains many modifications of governments that are, more or less, worthy to be termed free. In most of these states, however, the liberties of the mass, are

of the negative character of franchises, which franchises are not power of themselves, but merely an exemption from the abuses of power. Perhaps no state exists, in which the people, either by usage, or by direct concessions from the source of authority, do not possess some of these franchises; for, if there is no such thing, in practice, as perfect and absolute liberty, neither is there any such thing, in practice, as total and unmiti- 10 gated slavery. In the one case, nature has rendered man incapable of enjoying freedom without restraint, and in the other, incapable of submitting, entirely without resistance, to oppression. The harshest despots are compelled to acknowledge the immutable principles of eternal justice, affecting necessity and the love of right, for their most ruthless deeds.

England is a country in which the franchises of the subject are more than usually numerous. 20 Among the most conspicuous of these are the right of trial by jury, and that of the *habeas corpus*. Of the former it is unnecessary to speak, but as the latter is a phrase that may be unintelligible to many, it may be well to explain it.

The literal signification of *Habeas Corpus*[n] is, "thou may'st have the body." In arbitrary governments, it is much the usage to oppress men, under the pretence of justice, by causing them to be arrested on false, or trivial charges, and of sub- 30 jecting them to long and vexatious imprisonments, by protracting, or altogether evading the day of trial. The issue of a writ of *Habeas Corpus*, is an order to bring the accused before an impartial and independent judge, who examines into the charge, and who orders the prisoner to be set at liberty, unless there be sufficient legal ground for his detention.

This provision of the English law has been wisely retained in our system, for without some such regulation, it would be almost as easy to de- 40 tain a citizen unjustly, under a popular government, as to detain the subject of a monarchy; the difference in favor of the first, consisting only in the greater responsibility of its functionaries.

By comparing the privileges of the *Habeas Corpus*, where it exists alone, and as a franchise,

Habeas Corpus: "*Habeas*," second person singular, present tense, subjunctive mood, of the verb "*Habere*," to have; "*Corpus*," a noun, signifying "body." [Author's note.]

with those of the citizen who enjoys it merely as a provision of his own, against the abuses of ordinances that he had a voice in framing, we learn the essential difference between real liberty and franchises. The Englishman can appeal to a tribunal, against the abuse of an existing law, but if the law be not with him, he has no power to evade it, however unjust, or oppressive. The American has the same appeal against the abuse of a law, with the additional power to vote for its repeal, should the law itself be vicious. The one profits by a franchise to liberate his person only, submitting to his imprisonment however, if legality has been respected; while the other, in addition to this privilege, has a voice in getting rid of the obnoxious law, itself, and in preventing a recurrence of the wrong.

Some countries have the profession of possessing a government of the people, because an ancient dynasty has been set aside in a revolution, and a new one seated on the throne, either directed by the people, or by a combination that has been made to assume the character of a popular decision. Admitting that a people actually had an agency in framing such a system, and in naming their ruler, they cannot claim to be free, since they have parted with the power they did actually possess. No proposition can be clearer than that he who has given away a thing is no longer its master.

Of this nature is the present government of France. In that country the ancient dynasty has been set aside by a combination of leaders, through the agency of a few active spirits among the mass, and a prince put upon the throne, who is virtually invested with all the authority of his predecessor. Still, as the right of the last sovereign is clearly derived from a revolution, which has been made to assume the appearance of popular will, his government is termed a government of the people. This is a fallacy that can deceive no one of the smallest reflection. Such a system may be the best that France can now receive, but it is a mystification to call it by any other than its proper name. It is not a government of consultation, but one of pure force as respects a vast majority of Frenchmen.

A good deal of the same objection lies against the government of Great Britain, which, though freer in practice than that of France, is not based on a really free system. It may be said that both these governments are as free as comports with discretion, as indeed may be said of Turkey, since men get to be disqualified for the possession of any advantage in time; but such an admission is only an avowal of unfitness, and not a proof of enjoyment.

It is usual to maintain, that in democracies the tyranny of majorities is a greater evil than the oppression of minorities in narrow systems. Although this evil is exaggerated, since the laws being equal in their action it is not easy to oppress the few without oppressing all, it undeniably is the weak side of a popular government. To guard against this, we have framed constitutions, which point out the cases in which the majority shall decide, limiting their power, and bringing that they do possess within the circle of certain general and just principles. It will be elsewhere shown that it is a great mistake for the American citizen to take sides with the public, in doubtful cases affecting the rights of individuals, as this is the precise form in which oppression is the most likely to exhibit itself in a popular government.

Although it is true, that no genuine liberty can exist without being based on popular authority in the last resort, it is equally true that it can not exist when thus based, without many restraints on the power of the mass. These restraints are necessarily various and numerous. A familiar example will show their action. The majority of the people of a state might be in debt to its minority. Were the power of the former unrestrained, circumstances might arise in which they would declare depreciated bank notes a legal tender, and thus clear themselves of their liabilities, at the expense of their creditors. To prevent this, the constitution orders that nothing shall be made a legal tender but the precious metals, thus limiting the power of majorities in a way that the government is not limited in absolute monarchies, in which paper is often made to possess the value of gold and silver.

Liberty therefore may be defined to be a controlling authority that resides in the body of a nation, but so restrained as only to be exercised on certain general principles that shall do as little violence to natural justice, as is compatible with the peace and security of society.

"Your liberty ends where mine begins."

Satanstoe

THE POPULARITY of Cooper's narratives of breathless
adventure afloat and ashore has led readers to neglect
not only his trenchant criticism of American social
and political life but also his novels of manners. Of
these, *Satanstoe*, published in 1845, is the most interesting. The chapters printed herewith have been taken
from the edition of 1883.

Chapter XV · [*The Ice-Break on the Hudson*]

> "When lo! the voice of loud alarm
>   His inmost soul appals:
> What ho! Lord William, rise in haste!
>   The water saps thy walls!"
>
>   LORD WILLIAM.

The visit to Madam Schuyler occurred of a
Saturday evening; and the matter of our adventure in company with Jack and Moses, was to be
decided on the following Monday. When I rose 20
and looked out of my window on the Sunday
morning, however, there appeared but very little
prospect of its being effected that spring, inasmuch
as it rained heavily, and there was a fresh south
wind. We had reached the 21st of March, a period
of the year when a decided thaw was not only
ominous to the sleighing, but when it actually predicted a permanent breaking up of the winter.
The season had been late, and it was thought the
change could not be distant.   30

The rain and south wind continued all that
day, and torrents of water came rushing down the
short, steep streets, effectually washing away
everything like snow. Mr. Worden preached,
notwithstanding, and to a very respectable congregation. Dirck and myself attended; but Jason
preferred sitting out a double half-hour glass sermon in the Dutch church, delivered in a language
of which he understood very little, to lending his
countenance to the rites of the English service. 40
Both Anneke and Mary Wallace found their way
up the hill, going in a carriage; though I observed
that Herman Mordaunt was absent. Guert was
in the gallery, in which we also sat; but I could
not avoid remarking that neither of the young
ladies raised her eyes once, during the whole service, as high as our pews. Guert whispered something about this, as he hastened down stairs to

hand them to their carriage, when the congregation was dismissed, begging me, at the same time,
to be punctual to the appointment for the next
day. What he meant by this last remembrancer,
I did not understand; for the hills were beginning
to exhibit their bare breasts, and it was somewhat
surprising with what rapidity a rather unusual
amount of snow had disappeared. I had no opportunity to ask an explanation, as Guert was too
busy in placing the ladies in the carriage, and the   10
weather was not such as to admit of my remaining
a moment longer in the street than was indis-
pensably necessary.

A change occurred in the weather during the
night, the rain having ceased, though the atmosphere continued mild, and the wind was still
from the south. It was the commencement of the
spring; and, as I walked round to Guert Ten
Eyck's house, to meet him at breakfast, I observed
that several vehicles with wheels were already in   20
motion in the streets, and that divers persons appeared to be putting away their sleighs and sleds,
as things of no further use, until the next winter.
Our springs do not certainly come upon us as suddenly as some of which I have read, in the old
world; but when the snow and winter endure as
far into March as had been the case with that of
the year 1758, the change is often nearly magical.

"Here, then, is the spring opening," I said to
Dirck, as we walked along the well-washed streets;   30
"and, in a few weeks, we must be off to the bush.
Our business on the Patent must be got along with,
before the troops are put in motion, or we may
lose the opportunity of seeing a campaign."

With such expectations and feelings I entered
Guert's bachelor abode; and the first words I
uttered, were to sympathize in his supposed disappointment.

"It is a great pity you did not propose the drive
to the ladies for Saturday," I began; "for that was   40
not only a mild day, but the sleighing was excellent. As it is, you will have to postpone your triumph until next winter."

"I do not understand you!" cried Guert; "Jack
and Moses never were in better heart, or in better
condition. I think they are equal to going to
Kinderhook in two hours!"

"But who will furnish the roads with snow?

402

By looking out of the window, you will see that the streets are nearly bare."

"Streets and roads! Who cares for either, while we have the river? We often use the river here, weeks at a time, when the snow has left us. The ice has been remarkably even the whole of this winter, and, now the snow is off it, there will be no danger from the air-holes."

I confess I did not much like the notion of travelling twenty miles on the ice, but was far too 10 much of a man to offer any objections.

We breakfasted, and proceeded in a body to the residence of Herman Mordaunt. When the ladies first heard that we had come to claim the redemption of the half-promise given at Madam Schuyler's, their surprise was not less than mine had been, half an hour before, while their uneasiness was probably greater.

"Surely, Jack and Moses cannot exhibit all their noble qualities without snow!" exclaimed Anneke, 20 laughing, "Ten Eycks though they be!"

"We Albanians have the advantage of travelling on the ice, when the snow fails us," answered Guert. "Here is the river, near by, and never was the sleighing on it, better than at this moment."

"But, it has been many times safer, I should think. This looks very much like the breaking up of winter!"

"That is probable enough, and so much greater the reason why we should not delay, if you and 30 Miss Mary ever intend to learn what the blacks can do. It is for the honour of Holland that I desire it, else would I not presume so far. I feel every condescension of this sort, that I receive from you two ladies, in a way I cannot express; for no one knows, better than myself, how unworthy I am of your smallest notice."

This brought the signs of yielding, at once, into the mild countenance of Mary Wallace. Guert's self-humiliation never failed to do this. There 40 was so much obvious truth in his admission, so sincere a disposition to place himself, where nature and education, or a want of education had placed him, and most of all so profound a deference for the mental superiority of Mary herself, that the female heart found it impossible to resist. To my surprise, Guert's mistress, contrary to her habit in such things, was the first to join him, and to second

his proposal. Herman Mordaunt entering the room at this instant, the whole thing was referred to him, as in reason it ought to have been.

"I remember to have travelled on the Hudson, a few years since," returned Herman Mordaunt, "the entire distance between Albany and Sing-Sing, and a very good time we had of it; much better than had we gone by land, for there was little or no snow."

"Just our case now, Miss Anneke!" cried Guert. "Good sleighing on the river, but none on the land."

"Was that near the end of March, dear Papa?" asked Anneke, a little inquiringly.

"No, certainly not, for it was early in February. But the ice, at this moment, must be near eighteen inches thick, and strong enough to bear a load of hay."

"Yes, Masser Herman," observed Cato, a grey-headed black, who had never called his master by any other name, having known him from an infant; "yes, Masser Herman, a load do come over dis minute."

It appeared unreasonable to distrust the strength of the ice, after this proof to the contrary, and Anneke submitted. The party was arranged forthwith, and in the following manner:—The two ladies, Guert and myself, were to be drawn by the blacks, while Herman Mordaunt, Dirck, and any 30 one else they could enlist, were to follow in the New York sleigh. It was hoped that an elderly female connection, Mrs. Bogart, who resided at Albany, would consent to be of the party, as the plan was to visit and dine with another and a mutual connection of the Mordaunts, at Kinderhook. While the sleighs were getting ready, Herman Mordaunt walked round to the house of Mrs. Bogart, made his request, and was successful.

The clock in the tower of the English church struck ten, as both sleighs drove from Herman Mordaunt's door. There was literally no snow in the middle of the streets; but enough of it, mingled with ice, was still to be found nearer the houses, to enable us to get down to the ferry, the point where sleighs usually went upon the river. Here Herman Mordaunt, who was in advance, checked his horses, and turned to speak to Guert on the propriety of proceeding. The ice near the shore had evidently been moved, the river having risen a foot or two, in consequence of the wind and the thaw, and there was a sort of icy wave cast up near the land, over which it was indispensable to pass, in order to get fairly on the river. As the top of this ridge, or wave, was broken, it exposed a fissure that enabled us to see the thickness of the ice, and this Guert pointed out in proof of its strength. There was nothing unusual in a small movement of the covering of the river, which the current often produces; but, unless the vast fields below got in motion, it was impossible for those above materially to change their positions. Sleighs were passing, too, still bringing to town, hay from the flats on the eastern bank, and there was no longer any hesitation. Herman Mordaunt's sleigh passed slowly over the ridge, having a care to the legs of the horses, and ours followed in the same cautious manner, though the blacks jumped across the fissure in spite of their master's exertions.

Once on the river, however, Guert gave his blacks the whip and rein, and away we went like the wind. The smooth, icy surface of the Hudson was our road, the thaw having left very few traces of any track. The water had all passed beneath the ice, through cracks and fissures of one sort and another, leaving us an even, dry, surface to trot on. The wind was still southerly, though scarcely warm, while a bright sun contributed to render our excursion as gay to the eye, as it certainly was to our feelings. In a few minutes every trace of uneasiness had vanished. Away we went, the blacks doing full credit to their owner's boasts, seeming scarcely to touch the ice, from which their feet appeared to rebound with a sort of elastic force. Herman Mordaunt's bays followed on our heels, and the sleighs had passed over the well-known shoal of the Overslaugh, within the first twenty minutes after they touched the river.

Every northern American is familiar with the effect that the motion of a sleigh produces on the spirits, under favourable circumstances. Had our party been altogether composed of Albanians, there would probably have been no drawback on the enjoyment, for use would have prevented apprehension; but it required the few minutes I have mentioned to give Anneke and Mary Wallace full confidence in the ice. By the time we reached the Overslaugh, however, their fears had vanished; and Guert confirmed their sense of security, by telling them to listen to the sounds produced by his horses' hoofs, which certainly conveyed the impression of moving on a solid foundation.

Mary Wallace had never before been so gay in my presence, as she appeared to be that morning. Once, or twice, I fancied her eyes almost as bright as those of Anneke's, and certainly her laugh was as sweet and musical. Both the girls were full of spirits, and some little things occurred that gave me hopes Bulstrode had no reason to fancy himself as secure, as he sometimes seemed to be. A casual remark of Guert's had the effect to bring out some of Anneke's private sentiments on the subject; or, at least, so they appeared to be to me.

"I am surprised that Mr. Mordaunt forgot to invite Mr. Bulstrode to be one of our party, to-day," cried Guert, when we were below the Overslaugh. "The Major loves sleighing, and he would have filled the fourth seat, in the other sleigh, very agreeably. As for coming into this, that would be refused him, were he even a general!"

"Mr. Bulstrode is English," answered Anneke, with spirit, "and fancies American amusements beneath the tastes of one who has been presented at the Court of St. James."

"Well, Miss Anneke, I cannot say that I agree with you at all, in this opinion of Mr. Bulstrode," Guert returned, innocently. "It is true, he is English; that he fancies an advantage, as does Corny Littlepage, here; but we must make proper allowances for home-love and foreign-dislike."

" 'Corny Littlepage, here,' is only half English, and that half is colony-born and colony-bred," answered the laughing girl, "and he has loved a sleigh from the time when he first slid down hill—"

"Ah! Miss Anneke—let me entreat—"

"Oh! no allusion is intended to the Dutch church and its neighbourhood;—but, the sports of childhood are always dear to us, as are sometimes the discomforts. Habit and prejudice are sister hand-maidens; and I never see one of these gentlemen from home, taking extraordinary interest in any of our peculiarly colony usages, but I distrust an extra amount of complaisance, or a sort of enjoyment in which we do not strictly share."

"Is this altogether liberal to Bulstrode, Miss

Anneke," I ventured to put in; "he seems to like us, and I am sure he has good reason so to do. That he likes *some* of us, is too apparent to be concealed or denied."

"Mr. Bulstrode is a skilful actor, as all who saw his Cato must be aware," retorted the charming girl, compressing her pouting lips in a way that seemed to me to be inexpressibly pleasing; "and those who saw his Scrub must be equally convinced of the versatility of his talents. No, no; Major Bulstrode is better where he is, or will be to-day, at four o'clock—at the head of the mess of the ——th, instead of dining in a snug Dutch parlour, with my cousin, worthy Mrs. van der Heyden, at a dinner got up with colony hospitality, and colony good-will, and colony plainness. The entertainment we shall receive to-day, sweetened, as it will be, by the welcome which will come from the heart, can have no competitor in countries where a messenger must be sent two days before the visit, to ask permission to come, in order to escape cold looks and artificial surprise. I would prefer surprising my friends from the heart, instead of from the head."

Guert expressed his astonishment that any one should not always be glad and willing to receive his friends; and insisted on it, that no such inhospitable customs could exist. I knew, however, that society could not exist on the same terms, in old and in new countries—among a people that was pressed upon by numbers, and a people that had not yet felt the evils of a superabundant population. Americans are like dwellers in the country, who are always glad to see their friends; and I ventured to say something of the causes of these differences in habits.

Nothing occurred worthy of being dwelt on, in our ride to Kinderhook. Mrs. van der Heyden resided at a short distance from the river, and the blacks and the bays had some little difficulty in dragging us through the mud to her door. Once there, however, our welcome fully verified the theory of the colony habits, which had been talked over in our drive down. Anneke's worthy connection was not only glad to see her, as anybody might have been, but she would have been glad to receive as many as her house would hold. Few excuses were necessary, for we were all welcome.

The visit would retard her dinner an hour, as was frankly admitted—but that was nothing; and cakes and wine were set before us in the interval, did we feel hungry in consequence of a two hours' ride. Guert was desired to make free, and go to the stables to give his own orders. In a word, our reception was just that which every colonist has experienced, when he has gone unexpectedly to visit a friend, or a friend's friend. Our dinner was excellent, though not accompanied by much form. The wine was good; Mrs. van der Heyden's deceased husband having been a judge of what was desirable in that respect. Everybody was in good-humour; and our hostess insisted on giving us coffee before we took our departure.

"There will be a moon, cousin Herman," she said, "and the night will be both light and pleasant. Guert knows the road, which cannot well be missed, as it is the river; and if you quit me at eight, you will reach home in good season to go to rest. It is so seldom I see you, that I have a right to claim every minute you can spare. There remains much to be told concerning our old friends and mutual relatives."

When such words are accompanied by looks and acts that prove their sincerity, it is not easy to tear ourselves away from a pleasant house. We chatted on, laughed, listened to stories and colony anecdotes that carried us back to the last war, and heard a great many eulogiums on beaux and belles, that we young people had, all our lives, considered as respectable, elderly, common-place sort of persons.

At length the hour arrived when even Mrs. Bogart herself admitted we ought to part. Anneke and Mary were kissed, enveloped in their furs, and kissed again, and then we took our leave. As we left the house, I remarked that a clock in the passage struck eight. In a few minutes every one was placed, and the runners were striking fire from the flints of the bare ground. We had less difficulty in descending than in ascending the bank of the river, though there was no snow. It did not absolutely freeze, nor had it actually frozen since the commencement of the thaw, but the earth had stiffened since the disappearance of the sun. I was much rejoiced when the blacks sprang upon the ice, and whirled us away, on our return road, at a rate even exceeding the speed with which they had come down it in the morning. I thought it high time we should be in motion on our return; and in motion we were, if flying at the rate of eleven miles in the hour could thus be termed.

The light of the moon was not clear and bright, for there was a haze in the atmosphere, as is apt to occur in the mild weather of March; but there was enough to enable Guert to dash ahead with as great a velocity as was at all desirable. We were 10 all in high spirits; us two young men so much the more, because each of us fancied he had seen that day evidence of a tender interest existing in the heart of his mistress towards himself. Mary Wallace had managed, with a woman's tact, to make her suitor appear even respectable in female society, and had brought out in him many sentiments that denoted a generous disposition and a manly heart, if not a cultivated intellect; and Guert was getting confidence, and with it the means of giving his 20 capacity fairer play. As for Anneke, she now knew my aim, and I had some right to construe several little symptoms of feeling, that escaped her in the course of the day, favourably. I fancied that, gentle as it always was, her voice grew softer, and her smile sweeter and more winning, as she addressed herself to, or smiled on me; and she did just enough of both not to appear distant, and just little enough to appear conscious; at least such were the conjectures of one who I do not think 30 could be properly accused of too much confidence, and whose natural diffidence was much increased by the self-distrust of the purest love.

Away we went, Guert's complicated chimes of bells jingling their merry notes in a manner to be heard half a mile, the horses bearing hard on the bits, for they knew that their own stables lay at the end of their journey, and Herman Mordaunt's bays keeping so near us that, notwithstanding the noise we made with our own bells, the sounds of 40 his were constantly in our ears. An hour went swiftly by, and we had already passed Coejeman's, and had a hamlet that stretched along the strand, and which lay quite beneath the high bank of the river, in dim distant view. This place has since been known by the name of Monkey Town, and is a little remarkable as being the first cluster of houses on the shores of the Hudson after quitting

Albany. I dare say it has another name in law, but Guert gave it the appellation I have mentioned.

I have said that the night had a sombre, misty light, the moon wading across the heavens through a deep but thin ocean of vapour. We saw the shores plainly enough, and we saw the houses and trees, but it was difficult to distinguish smaller objects at any distance. In the course of the day twenty sleighs had been met or passed, but at that 10 hour everybody but ourselves appeared to have deserted the river. It was getting late for the simple habits of those who dwelt on its shores. When about half-way between the islands opposite to Coejeman's and the hamlet just named, Guert, who stood erect to drive, told us that some one who was out late, like themselves, was coming down. The horses of the strangers were in a very fast trot, and the sleigh was evidently inclining towards the west shore, as if those it held intended 20 to land at no great distance. As it passed, quite swiftly, a man's voice called out something on a high key, but our bells made so much noise that it was not easy to understand him. He spoke in Dutch, too, and none of our ears, those of Guert excepted, were sufficiently expert in that language to be particularly quick in comprehending what he said. The call passed unheeded, then, such things being quite frequent among the Dutch, who seldom passed each other on the highway without a greet- 30 ing of some sort or other. I was thinking of this practice, and of the points that distinguished our own habits from those of the people of this part of the colony, when sleigh-bells sounded quite near me, and turning my head, I saw Herman Mordaunt's bays galloping close to us, as if wishing to get alongside. At the next moment the object was effected, and Guert pulled up.

"Did you understand the man who passed down, Guert?" demanded Herman Mordaunt, 40 as soon as all noises ceased. "He called out to us, at the top of his voice, and would hardly do that without an object."

"These men seldom go home, after a visit to Albany, without filling their jugs," answered Guert drily; "what could he have to say, more than to wish us good-night?"

"I cannot tell, but Mrs. Bogart thought she understood something about 'Albany,' and 'the river.'"

"The ladies always fancy Albany is to sink into the river after a great thaw," answered Guert, good-humouredly; "but I can show either of them that the ice is sixteen inches thick, here where we stand."

Guert then gave me the reins, stepped out of the sleigh, went a short distance to a large crack that he had seen while speaking, and returned with a thumb placed on the handle of the whip, as a measure to show that his statement was true. The ice, at that spot, was certainly nearer eighteen than sixteen inches thick. Herman Mordaunt showed the measure to Mrs. Bogart, whose alarm was pacified by this positive proof. Neither Anneke nor Mary exhibited any fear; but, on the contrary, as the sleighs separated again, each had something pleasant, but feminine, to say at the expense of poor Mrs. Bogart's imagination.

I believe I was the only person in our own sleigh who felt any alarm, after the occurrence of this little incident. Why uneasiness beset *me*, I cannot precisely say. It must have been altogether on Anneke's account, and not in the least on my own. Such accidents as sleighs breaking through, on our New York lakes and rivers, happened almost every winter, and horses were often drowned; though it was seldom the consequences proved so serious to their owners. I recalled to mind the fragile nature of ice, the necessary effects of the great thaw and the heavy rains, remembering that frozen water might still retain most of its apparent thickness, after its consistency was greatly impaired. But, I could do nothing! If we landed, the roads were impassable for runners, almost for wheels, and another hour might carry the ladies, by means of the river, to their comfortable homes. That day, however, which, down to the moment of meeting the unknown sleigh, had been the very happiest of my life, was entirely changed in its aspect, and I no longer regarded it with any satisfaction. Had Anneke been at home, I could gladly have entered into a contract to pass a week on the river myself, as the condition of her safety. I thought but little of the others, to my shame be it said, though I cannot do myself the injustice to imagine, had Anneke been away, that I would have deserted even a horse, while there was a hope of saving him.

Away we went! Guert drove rapidly, but he drove with judgment, and it seemed as if his blacks knew what was expected of them. It was not long before we were trotting past the hamlet I have mentioned. It would seem that the bells of the two sleighs attracted the attention of the people on the shore, all of whom had not yet gone to bed; for the door of a house opened, and two men issued out of it, gazing at us as we trotted past at a pace that defied pursuit. These men also hallooed to us, in Dutch, and again Herman Mordaunt galloped up alongside, to speak to us.

"Did you understand these men?" he called out, for this time Guert did not see fit to stop his horses; "they, too, had something to tell us."

"These people always have something to tell an Albany sleigh, Mr. Mordaunt," answered Guert; "though it is not often that which it would do any good to hear."

"But Mrs. Bogart thinks they also had something to say about 'Albany,' and the 'river.' "

"I understand Dutch as well as excellent Mrs. Bogart," said Guert, a little drily; "and I heard nothing; while I fancy I understand the river better. This ice would bear a dozen loads of hay, in a close line."

This again satisfied Herman Mordaunt and the ladies, but it did not satisfy me. Our own bells made four times the noise of those of Herman Mordaunt; and it was very possible that one, who understood Dutch perfectly, might comprehend a call in that language, while seated in his own sleigh, when the same call could not be comprehended by the same person, while seated in Guert's. There was no pause, however; on we trotted; and another mile was passed, before any new occurrence attracted attention.

The laugh was again heard among us, for Mary Wallace consented to sing an air, that was rendered somewhat ludicrous by the accompaniment of the bells. This song, or verse or two, for the singer got no further on account of the interruption had drawn Guert's and my attention behind us, or away from the horses, when a whirling sound was heard, followed immediately by a loud shout. A sleigh passed within ten yards of us, going down, and the whirling sound was caused by its runners, while the shout came from a solitary man, who stood erect, waving his whip and calling to us in a loud voice, as long as he could be heard. This was but for a moment, however, as his horses were on the run; and the last we could see of the man, through the misty moon-light, he had turned his whip on his team, to urge it ahead still faster. In an instant, Herman Mordaunt was at our side, for the third time that night, and he called out to us somewhat authoritatively to stop.

"What can all this mean, Guert?" he asked. 10 "Three times have we had warnings about 'Albany' and the 'river.' I heard this man myself utter those two words, and cannot be mistaken."

"I dare say, sir, that you may have heard something of the sort," answered the still incredulous Guert; "for these chaps have generally some impertinence to utter, when they pass a team that is better than their own. These blacks of mine, Herman Mordaunt, awaken a good deal of envy, whenever I go out with them; and a Dutchman 20 will forgive you any other superiority, sooner than he will overlook your having the best team. That last man had a spur in his head, moreover, and is driving his cattle, at this moment, more like a spook than like a humane and rational being. I dare say he asked if we owned Albany and the river."

Guert's allusion to his horses occasioned a general laugh; and laughter is little favourable to cool reflection. We all looked out on the solemn and 30 silent night, cast our eyes along the wide and long reach of the river, in which we happened to be, and saw nothing but the calm of nature, rendered imposing by solitude and the stillness of the hour. Guert smilingly renewed his assurances that all was right, and moved on. Away we went! Guert evidently pressed his horses, as if desirous of being placed beyond this anxiety as soon as possible. The blacks flew, rather than trotted; and we were all beginning to submit to the exhilaration of so 40 rapid and easy a motion, when a sound which resembled that which one might suppose the simultaneous explosion of a thousand rifles would produce, was heard, and caused both drivers to pull up; the sleighs stopping quite near each other, and at the same instant! A slight exclamation escaped old Mrs. Bogart; but Anneke and Mary remained still as death.

"What means that sound, Guert?" inquired Herman Mordaunt; the concern he felt being betrayed by the very tone of his voice. "Something seems wrong!"

"Something is wrong," answered Guert, coolly, but very decidedly; "and it is something that must be seen to."

As this was said, Guert stepped out on the ice, which he struck a hard blow with the heel of his boot, as if to make certain of its solidity. A second report was heard, and it evidently came from behind us. Guert gazed intently down the river; then he laid his head close to the surface of the ice, and looked again. At the same time, three or four more of these startling reports followed each other in quick succession. Guert instantly rose to his feet.

"I understand it, now," he said, "and find I have been rather too confident. The ice, however, is safe and strong, and we have nothing to fear from its weakness. Perhaps it would be better to quit the river notwithstanding, though I am far from certain the better course will not be to push on."

"Let us know the danger at once, Mr. Ten Eyck," said Herman Mordaunt, "that we may decide for the best."

"Why, sir, I am afraid that the rains and the thaw together, have thrown so much water into the river, all at once, as it might be, as to have raised the ice and broken it loose, in spots, from the shores. When this happens above, before the ice has disappeared below, it sometimes causes dams to form, which heap up such a weight as to break the whole plain of ice far below it, and thus throw cakes over cakes until walls twenty or thirty feet high are formed. This has not happened yet, therefore there is no immediate danger; but by bending your heads low, you can see that such a break has just taken place about half a mile below us."

We did as Guert directed, and saw that a mound had arisen across the river nearer than the distance named by our companion, completely cutting off retreat by the way we had come. The bank on the west side of the Hudson was high at the point where we were, and looking intensely at it, I saw by the manner in which the trees disappeared, the more distant behind those that were nearer, that we were actually in motion! An involuntary exclamation caused the whole party to comprehend this startling fact at the same instant. We were certainly in motion, though very slowly, on the ice of that swollen river, in the quiet and solitude of a night in which the moon rather aided in making danger apparent than in assisting us to avoid it! What was to be done? It was necessary to decide, and that promptly and intelligently.

We waited for Herman Mordaunt to advise us, 10 but he referred the matter at once to Guert's greater experience.

"We cannot land here," answered the young man, "so long as the ice is in motion, and I think it better to push on. Every foot will bring us so much nearer to Albany, and we shall get among the islands a mile or two higher, where the chances of landing will be greatly increased. Besides, I have often crossed the river on a cake, for they frequently stop, and I have known even loaded 20 sleighs profit by them to get over the river. As yet there is nothing very alarming;—let us push on, and get nearer to the islands."

This, then, was done, though there was no longer heard the laugh or the song among us. I could see that Herman Mordaunt was uneasy about Anneke, though he could not bring her into his own sleigh, leaving Mary Wallace alone; neither could he abandon his respectable connection, Mrs. Bogart. Before we re-entered the 30 sleighs, I took an occasion to assure him that Anneke should be my especial care.

"God bless you, Corny, my dear boy," Herman Mordaunt answered, squeezing my hand with fervour. "God bless you, and enable you to protect her. I was about to ask you to change seats with me; but, on the whole, I think my child will be safer with you than she could be with me. We will await God's pleasure as accident has placed us." 40

"I will desert her only with life, Mr. Mordaunt. Be at ease on that subject."

"I know you will not—I am *sure* you will not, Littlepage; that affair of the lion is a pledge that you will not. Had Bulstrode come, we should have been strong enough to—but Guert is impatient to be off. God bless you, boy—God bless you. Do not neglect my child."

Guert was impatient, and no sooner was I in the sleigh than we were once more in rapid motion. I said a few words to encourage the girls, and then no sound of a human voice mingled with the gloomy scene.

Chapter XVI · [The Danger]

He started up, each limb convulsed
With agonizing fear,
He only heard the storm of night—
'T was music to his ear.

LORD WILLIAM.

Away we went! Guert's aim was the islands, which carried him nearer home, while it offered a place of retreat, in the event of the danger's becoming more serious. The fierce rapidity with which we now moved prevented all conversation, or even much reflection. The reports of the rending ice, however, became more and more frequent, first coming from above, and then from below. More than once it seemed as if the immense mass of weight that had evidently collected somewhere near the town of Albany, was about to pour down upon us in a flood—when the river would have been swept for miles, by a resistless torrent. Nevertheless, Guert held on his way; firstly, because he knew it would be impossible to get on either of the main shores, anywhere near the point where we happened to be; and secondly, because, having often seen similar dammings of the waters, he fancied we were still safe. That the distant reader may understand the precise character of the danger we ran, it may be well to give him some notion of the localities.

The banks of the Hudson are generally high and precipitous, and in some places they are mountainous. No flats worthy of being mentioned, occur, until Albany is approached; nor are those which lie south of that town, of any great extent, compared with the size of the stream. In this particular the Mohawk is a very different river, having extensive flats that, I have been told, resemble those of the Rhine, in miniature. As for the Hudson, it is generally esteemed in the colony as a very pleasing river; and I remember to have heard intelligent people from home, admit, that even the majestic Thames itself, is scarcely more worthy to

409

be visited, or that it better rewards the trouble and curiosity of the enlightened traveller.*

While there are flats on the shores of the Hudson, and of some extent, in the vicinity of Albany, the general formation of the adjacent country is preserved,—being high, bold, and in some quarters, more particularly to the northward and eastward, mountainous. Among these hills the stream meanders for sixty or eighty miles north of the town, receiving tributaries as it comes rushing down towards the sea. The character of the river changes entirely, a short distance above Albany; the tides flowing to that point, rendering it navigable, and easy of ascent in summer, all the way from the sea. Of the tributaries, the principal is the Mohawk, which runs a long distance towards the west—they tell me, for I have never visited these remote parts of the colony—among fertile plains, that are bounded north and south by precipitous highlands. Now, in the spring, when the vast quantities of snow, that frequently lie four feet deep in the forests, and among the mountains and valleys of the interior, are suddenly melted by the south winds and rains, freshets necessarily succeed, which have been known to do great injury. The flats of the Mohawk, they tell me, are annually overflown, and a moderate freshet is deemed a blessing; but, occasionally, a union of the causes I have mentioned, produces a species of deluge that has a very opposite character. Thus it is, that houses are swept away; and bridges from the smaller mountain streams, have been known to come floating past the wharves of Albany, holding

*This remark of Mr. Cornelius Littlepage's, may induce a smile in the reader. But, few persons of fifty can be found, who cannot recall the time, when it was a rare thing to imagine *anything* American, as good as its English counterpart. The American who could write a book—a real, live book—forty years since, was a sort of prodigy. It was the same with him who could paint any picture beyond a common portrait. The very fruits and natural productions of the country were esteemed, doubtingly; and he was a bold man who dared to extol even canvass-back ducks, in the year 1800! At the present day, the feeling is fast undergoing an organic change. It is now the fashion to *extol* everything American, and from submitting to a degree that was almost abject, to the feeling of colonial dependency, the country is filled, to-day, with the most profound provincial self-admiration. It is to be hoped that the next change will bring us to something like the truth.—EDITOR. [Cooper's note.]

their way towards the ocean. At such times the tides produce no counter-current; for it is a usual thing, in the early months of the spring, to have the stream pour downwards for weeks, the whole length of the river, and to find the water fresh even as low as New York.

Such was the general nature of the calamity we had been so unexpectedly made to encounter. The winter had been severe, and the snows unusually deep; and, as we drove furiously onward, I remembered to have heard my grandfather predict extraordinary freshets in the spring, from the character of the winter, as we had found it, even previously to my quitting home. The great thaw, and the heavy rains of the late storm, had produced the usual effect; and the waters thus let loose, among the distant, as well as the nearer hills, were now pouring down upon us in their collected might. In such cases, the first effect is, to loosen the ice from the shores; and, local causes forcing it to give way at particular points, a breaking up of its surface occurs, and dams are formed that set the stream back in floods upon all the adjacent low land, such as the flats in the vicinity of Albany.

We did not then know it, but, at the very moment Guert was thus urging his blacks to supernatural efforts—actually running them as if on a race-course—there was a long reach of the Hudson, opposite to, for a short distance below, and for a considerable distance above the town, which was quite clear of stationary ice. Vast cakes continued to come down, it is true, passing on to increase the dam that had formed below, near and on the Overslaugh, where it was buttressed by the islands, and rested on the bottom; but the whole of that firm field, on which we had first driven forth that morning, had disappeared! This we did not know at the time, or it might have changed the direction of Guert's movements; but I learned it afterwards, when placed in a situation to inquire into the causes of what had occurred.

Herman Mordaunt's bells, and the rumbling sound of his runners, were heard close behind us, as our own sleigh flew along the river at a rate that I firmly believe could not have been much less than that of twenty miles in the hour. As we were whirled northward, the reports made by the rending of the ice increased in frequency and force.

They really became appalling! Still, the girls continued silent, maintaining their self-command in a most admirable manner; though I doubt not that they felt, in the fullest extent, the true character of the awful circumstances in which we were placed. Such was the state of things, as Guert's blacks began sensibly to relax in their speed, for want of wind. They still galloped on, but it was no longer with the swiftness of the wind; and their master became sensible of the folly of hoping to reach the town ere the catastrophe should arrive. He reined in his panting horses, therefore, and was just falling into a trot, as a violent report was heard directly in our front. At the next instant the ice rose, positively, beneath our horses' hoofs, to the height of several feet, taking the form of the roof of a house. It was too late to retreat, and Guert shouting out "Jack"—"Moses," applied the whip, and the spirited animals actually went over the mound, leaping a crack three feet in width, and reaching the level ice beyond. All this was done, as it might be, in the twinkling of an eye. While the sleigh flew over this ridge, it was with difficulty I held the girls in their seats; though Guert stood nobly erect, like the pine that is too firmly rooted to yield to the tempest. No sooner was the danger passed, however, than he pulled up, and came to a dead halt.

We heard the bells of Herman Mordaunt's sleigh, on the other side of the barrier, but could see nothing. The broken cakes, pressed upon by millions of tons weight above, had risen fully ten feet, into an inclination that was nearly perpendicular; rendering crossing it next to impossible, even to one afoot. Then came Herman Mordaunt's voice, filled with paternal agony, and human grief, to increase the awe of that dreadful moment!

"Shore!—shore!—" he shouted, or rather yelled—"In the name of a righteous Providence, to the shore, Guert!"

The bells passed off towards the western bank, and the rumbling of the runners accompanied their sound. That was a breathless moment to us four. We heard the rending and grinding of the ice, on all sides of us; saw the broken barriers behind and in front; heard the jingling of Herman Mordaunt's bells, as it became more and more distant, and finally ceased; and felt as if we were cut off from the rest of our species. I do not think either of us felt any apprehension of breaking through; for use had so accustomed us to the field of the river, while the more appalling grounds of alarm were so evident, that no one thought of such a source of danger. Nor was there much, in truth, to apprehend from that cause. The thaw had not lasted long enough materially to diminish either the thickness or the tenacity of the common river ice; though it was found unequal to resisting the enormous pressure that bore upon it from above. It is probable that a cake of an acre's size would have upheld, not only ourselves, but our sleigh and horses, and carried us, like a raft, down the stream; had there been such a cake, free from stationary impediments. Even the girls now comprehended the danger, which was in a manner suspended over us,—as the impending wreath of snow menaces the fall of the avalanche. But, it was no moment for indecision or inaction.

Cut off, as we were, by an impassable barrier of ice, from the route taken by Herman Mordaunt, it was necessary to come to some resolution on our own course. We had the choice of endeavouring to pass to the western shore, on the upper side of the barrier, or of proceeding towards the nearest of several low islands which lay in the opposite direction. Guert determined on the last, walking his horses to the point of land, there being no apparent necessity for haste, while the animals greatly needed breath. As we went along, he explained to us that the fissure below cut us off from the only point where landing on the western shore could be practicable. At the same time, he put in practice a pious fraud, which had an excellent effect on the feelings and conduct of both the girls, throughout the remainder of the trying scenes of that fearful night; more especially on those of Anneke. He dwelt on the good fortune of Herman Mordaunt, in being on the right side of the barrier that separated the sleighs, in a way to induce those who did not penetrate his motive, to fancy the rest of the party was in a place of security, as the consequence of this accident. Thus did Anneke believe her father safe, and thus was she relieved from much agonizing doubt.

As soon as the sleigh came near the point of the island, Guert gave me the reins, and went ahead

411

to examine whether it were possible to land. He was absent fifteen minutes; returning to us only after he had made a thorough search into the condition of the island, as well as of that of the ice in its eastern channel. These were fifteen fearful minutes; the rending of the masses above, and the grinding of cake on cake, sounding like the roar of the ocean in a tempest. Notwithstanding all the awful accessories of this dreadful night, I could not but admire Guert's coolness of manner, and his admirable conduct. He was more than resolute; for he was cool, collected, and retained the use of all his faculties in perfection. As plausible as it might seem, to one less observant and clear-headed, to attempt escaping to the western shore, Guert had decided right in moving towards the island. The grinding of the ice, in another quarter, had apprised him that the water was forcing its way through, near the main land; and that escape would be nearly hopeless, on that side of the river. When he rejoined us, he called me to the heads of the horses, for a conference; first solemnly assuring our precious companions that there were no grounds for immediate apprehension. Mary Wallace anxiously asked him to repeat this to *her*, on the faith due from man to woman; and he did it; when I was permitted to join him without further opposition.

"Corny," said Guert, in a low tone, "Providence has punished me for my wicked wish of seeing Mary Wallace in the claws of lions; for all the savage beasts of the Old World, could hardly make our case more desperate than it now is. We must be cool, however, and preserve the girls, or die like men."

"Our fates are, and must be, the same. Do you devote yourself to Mary, and leave Anneke to me. But, why this language; surely, our case is by no means so desperate."

"It might not be so difficult for two active, vigorous young men to get ashore; but it would be different with females. The ice is in motion all around us; and the cakes are piling and grinding on each other in a most fearful manner. Were it light enough to see, we should do much better; but, as it is, I dare not trust Mary Wallace any distance from this island, at present. We may be compelled to pass the night here, and must make pro-

vision accordingly. You hear the ice grinding on the shore; a sign that everything is going down stream.—God send that the waters break through, ere long; though they may sweep all before them, when they do come. I fear me, Corny, that Herman Mordaunt and his party are lost!"

"Merciful Providence!—can it be as bad as that!—I rather hope they have reached the land."

"That is impossible, on the course they took. Even a man would be bewildered and swept away, in the torrent that is driving down under the west shore. It is that vent to the water, which saves us. But, no more words.—You now understand the extent of the danger, and will know what you are about. We must get our precious charge on the island, if possible, without further delay. Half an hour—nay, half a minute may bring down the torrent."

Guert took the direction of everything. Even while we had been talking, the ice had moved materially; and we found ourselves fifty feet further from the island than we had been. By causing the horses to advance, this distance was soon recovered; but it was found impossible to lead or drive them over the broken cakes with which the shore of the island now began to be lined. After one or two spirited and determined efforts, Guert gave the matter up, and asked me to help the ladies from the sleigh. Never did women behave better, than did these delicate and lovely girls, on an occasion so awfully trying. Without remonstrances, tears, exclamations or questions, both did as desired; and I cannot express the feeling of security I felt, when I had helped each over the broken and grinding border of white ice, that separated us from the shore. The night was far from cold; but the ground was now frozen sufficiently to prevent any unpleasant consequences from walking on what would otherwise have been a slimy, muddy alluvion; for the island was so very low, as often to be under water, when the river was particularly high. This, indeed, formed our danger, after we had reached it.

When I returned to Guert, I found him already drifted down some little distance; and this time we moved the sleigh so much above the point, as to be in less danger of getting out of sight of our precious wards. To my surprise, Guert was busy in stripping the harness from the horses, and Jack already stood only in his blinkers. Moses was soon reduced to the same state. I was wondering what was to be done next, when Guert drew each bridle from its animal, and gave a smart crack of his whip. The liberated horses started back with affright—snorted, reared, and, turning away, they went down the river, free as air, and almost as swift; the incessant and loud snapping of their master's whip, in no degree tending to diminish their speed. I asked the meaning of this.

"It would be cruel not to let the poor beasts make use of the strength and sagacity nature has given them to save their lives," answered Guert, straining his eyes after Moses, the horse that was behind, so long as his dark form could be distinguished, and leaning forward to listen to the blows of their hoofs, while the noises around us permitted them to be heard. "To us, they would only be an encumbrance, since they never could be forced over the cracks and caked ice in harness; nor would it be at all safe to follow them, if they could. The sleigh is light, and we are strong enough to shove it to land, when there is an opportunity; or, it may be left on the island."

Nothing could have served more effectually to convince me of the manner in which Guert regarded our situation, than to see him turn loose beasts which I knew he so highly prized. I mentioned this; and he answered me with a melancholy seriousness, that made the impression so much the stronger—

"It is possible they may get ashore, for nature has given a horse a keen instinct. They can swim, too, where you and I would drown. At all events, they are not fettered with harness, but have every chance it is in my power to give them. Should they land, any farmer would put them in his stable, and I should soon hear where they were to be found; if, indeed, I am living in the morning to make the inquiry."

"What is next to be done, Guert?" I asked, understanding at once both his feelings and his manner of reasoning.

"We must now run the sleigh on the island; after which it will be time to look after us, and to examine if it be possible to get the ladies on the main land."

Accordingly, Guert and I applied ourselves to the task, and had no great difficulty in dragging the sleigh over the cakes, grinding and in motion as they were. We pulled it as far as the tree beneath which Anneke and Mary stood; when the ladies got into it and took their seats, enveloped in the skins. The night was not cold for the season, and our companions were thickly clad, having tippets and muffs, still, the wolves' skins of Guert contributed to render them more comfortable. All apprehension of immediate danger now ceased, for a short time; nor do I think either of the females fancied they could run any more risk, beyond that of exposure to the night air, so long as they remained on *terra firma*. Such was not the case, however, as a very simple explanation will render apparent to the reader.

All the islands in this part of the Hudson are low, being rich, alluvial meadows, bordered by trees and bushes; most of the first being willows, sycamores, or nuts. The fertility of the soil had given to these trees rapid growths, and they were generally of some stature; though not one among them had that great size which ought to mark the body and branches of a venerable tenant of the forest. This fact, of itself, proved that no one tree of them all was very old; a circumstance that was certainly owing to the ravages of the annual freshets. I say annual; for though the freshet which now encompassed us, was far more serious than usual, each year brought something of the sort; and the islands were constantly increasing or diminishing under their action. To prevent the last, a thicket of trees was left at the head of each island, to form a sort of barricade against the inroads of the ice in the spring. So low was the face of the land, or meadow, however, that a rise of a very few feet in the river would be certain to bring it entirely under water. All this will be made more apparent by our own proceedings, after we had placed the ladies in the sleigh; and more especially, by the passing remarks of Guert while employed in his subsequent efforts.

No sooner did Guert Ten Eyck believe the ladies to be temporarily safe, than he proposed to me that we should take a closer look at the state of the river, in order to ascertain the most feasible means of getting on the main land. This was said aloud, and in a cheerful way, as if he no longer felt any apprehension, and, evidently to me, to encourage our companions. Anneke desired us to go, declaring that now she knew herself to be on dry land, all her own fears had vanished. We went accordingly, taking our first direction towards the head of the island.

A very few minutes sufficed to reach the limits of our narrow domain; and, as we approached them, Guert pointed out to me the mound of ice that was piling up behind it, as a most fearful symptom.

"There is our danger," he said, with emphasis, "and we must not trust to these trees. This freshet goes beyond any I ever saw on the river; and not a spring passes that we have not more or less of them. Do you not see, Corny, what saves us now?"

"We are on an island, and cannot be in much danger from the river while we stay here."

"Not so, my dear friend, not at all so. But, come with me and look for yourself."

I followed Guert, and did look for myself. We sprang upon the cakes of ice, which were piled quite thirty feet in height, on the head of the island, extending right and left, as far as our eyes could see, by that misty light. It was by no means difficult moving about on this massive pile, the movement in the cakes being slow, and frequently interrupted; but there was no concealing the true character of the danger. Had not the island, and the adjacent main interposed their obstacles, the ice would have continued to move bodily down the stream, cake shoving over cake, until the whole found vent in the wider space below, and floated off towards the ocean. Not only was our island there, however, but other islands lay near us, straitening the different channels or passages in such a way, as to compel the formation of an icy dam; and, on the strength of this dam rested all our security. Were it to be ruptured anywhere near us, we should inevitably be swept off in a body. Guert thought, however, as has been said already, that the waters had found narrow issues under the main land, both east and west of us; and should this prove to be true, there was a hope that the great calamity might be averted. In other words, if these floodgates sufficed, we might escape; otherwise the catastrophe was certain.

"I cannot excuse it to myself to remain here, without endeavouring to see what is the state of things nearer to the shore," said Guert, after we had viewed the fast accumulating mass of broken ice above us, as well as the light permitted, and we had talked over together the chances of safety, and the character of the danger. "Do you return to the ladies, Corny, and endeavour to keep up their spirits, while I cross this channel on our right, to the next island, and see what offers in that direction."

"I do not like the idea of your running all the risk alone; besides, something may occur to require the strength of two, instead of that of one, to overcome it."

"You can go with me as far as the next island, if you will, where we shall be able to ascertain at once whether it be ice or water that separates us from the eastern shore. If the first, you can return as fast as possible for the ladies, while I look for a place to cross. I do not like the appearance of this dam, to be honest with you; and have great fears for those who are now in the sleigh."

We were in the very act of moving away, when a loud, cracking noise, that arose within a few yards, alarmed us both; and running to the spot whence it proceeded, we saw that a large willow had snapped in two, like a pipe-stem, and that the whole barrier of ice was marching, slowly, but grandly, over the stump, crushing the fallen trunk and branches beneath its weight, as the slow-moving wheel of the loaded cart crushes the twig. Guert grasped my arm, and his fingers nearly entered the flesh, under his iron pressure.

"We must quit this spot—" he said firmly, "and at once. Let us go back to the sleigh."

I did not know Guert's intentions, but I saw it was time to act with decision. We moved swiftly down to the spot where we had left the sleigh; and the reader will judge of our horror, when we found it gone! The whole of the low point of the island where we had left it, was already covered with cakes of ice that were in motion, and which had doubtless swept off the sleigh during the few minutes that we had been absent! Looking around us, however, we saw an object on the river, a little distance below, that I fancied was the sleigh, and was about to rush after it, when a voice, filled with

414

alarm, took us in another direction. Mary Wallace came out from behind a tree, to which she had fled for safety, and seizing Guert's arm, implored him not to quit her again.

"Whither has Anneke gone?" I demanded, in an agony I cannot describe—"I see nothing of Anneke!"

"She would not quit the sleigh," answered Mary Wallace, almost panting for breath—"I implored —entreated her to follow me—said you *must* soon return; but she refused to quit the sleigh. Anneke is in the sleigh, if that can now be found."

I heard no more; but springing on the still moving cakes of ice, went leaping from cake to cake, until my sight showed me that, sure enough, the sleigh was on the bed of the river, over which it was in slow motion; forced downwards before the new coating of ice that was fast covering the original surface. At first I could see no one in the sleigh; but, on reaching it, I found Anneke buried in the skins. She was on her knees: the precious creature was asking succour from God!

I had a wild but sweet consolation in thus finding myself, as it might be, cut off from all the rest of my kind, in the midst of that scene of gloom and desolation, alone with Anneke Mordaunt. The moment I could make her conscious of my presence, she inquired after Mary Wallace, and was much relieved on learning that she was with Guert, and would not be left by him, for a single instant, again that night. Indeed, I saw their figures dimly, as they moved swiftly across the channel that divided the two islands, and disappear in that direction, among the bushes that lined the place to which they had gone.

"Let us follow," I said eagerly. "The crossing is yet easy, and we, too, may escape to the shore."

"Go you!" said Anneke, over whom a momentary physical torpor appeared to have passed. "Go you, Corny," she said; "a man may easily save himself; and you are an only child—the sole hope of your parents."

"Dearest, beloved Anneke!—why this indifference—this apathy on your own behalf? Are *you* not an only child, the sole hope of a widowed father?—do you forget *him?*"

"No, no, no!" exclaimed the dear girl, hurriedly. "Help me out of the sleigh, Corny: there,

I will go with you anywhere—any how—to the end of the world, to save my father from such anguish!"

From that moment the temporary imbecility of Anneke vanished, and I found her, for the remainder of the time we remained in jeopardy, quick to apprehend, and ready to second all my efforts. It was this passing submission to an imaginary doom, on the one hand, and the headlong effect of sudden fright on the other, which had separated the two girls, and which had been the means of dividing the whole party as described.

I scarcely know how to describe what followed. So intense was my apprehension on behalf of Anneke, that I can safely say, I did not think of my own fate, in the slightest degree, as disconnected from hers. The self-devoted reliance with which the dear girl seemed to place all her dependence on me, would, of itself, have produced this effect, had she not possessed my whole heart, as I was now so fully aware. Moments like those, make one alive to all the affections, and strip off every covering that habit or the dissembling of our manners is so apt to throw over the feelings. I believe I both spoke and acted towards Anneke, as one would cling to, or address the being dearest to him in the world, for the next few minutes; but, I can suppose the reader will naturally prefer learning what we did, under such circumstances, rather than what we said, or how we felt.

I repeat, it is not easy for me to describe what followed. I know we first rather ran, than walked, across the channel on which I had last seen the dim forms of Guert and Mary, and even crossed the island to its eastern side, in the hope of being able to reach the shore in that quarter. The attempt was useless, for we found the water running down over the ice like a race-way. Nothing could be seen of our late companions; and my loud and repeated calls to them were unanswered.

"Our case is hopeless, Cornelius," said Anneke; speaking with a forced calmness when she found retreat impossible in that direction. "Let us return to the sleigh, and submit to the will of God!"

"Beloved Anneke!—Think of your father, and summon your whole strength. The bed of the river is yet firm; we will cross it, and try the opposite shore."

Cross it we did, my delicate companion being as much sustained by my supporting arm, as by her own resolution, but we found the same obstacle to retreat interposing there also. The island above had turned the waters aside, until they found an outlet under each bank—shooting along their willowy shores, with the velocity of arrows. By this time, owing to our hurried movement, I found Anneke so far exhausted, that it was absolutely necessary to pause a minute to take breath. This pause was also necessary, in order to look about us, and to decide understandingly as to the course it was necessary now to pursue. This pause, brief as it was, moreover, contributed largely to the apparent horrors of our situation.

The grating, or grinding of the ice above us, cake upon cake, now sounded like the rushing of heavy winds, or the incessant roaring of a surf upon the sea-shore. The piles were becoming visible, by their height and their proximity, as the ragged barriers set slowly but steadily down upon us; and the whole river seemed to me to be in motion downwards. At this awful instant, when I began to think it was the will of Providence that Anneke and I were to perish together, a strange sound interrupted the fearful natural accessories of that frightful scene. I certainly heard the bells of a sleigh; at first they seemed distant and broken —then, nearer and incessant, attended by the rumbling of runners on the ice. I took off my cap and pressed my head, for I feared my brain was unsettled. There it came, however, more and more distinctly, until the trampling of horses' hoofs mingled in the noise.

"Can there be others as unhappy as ourselves!" exclaimed Anneke, forgetting her own fears in generous sympathy. "See, Littlepage!—see, *dear* Cornelius—yonder surely comes another sleigh!"

Come it did, like the tempest, or the whirlwind; passing within fifty feet of us. I knew it at a glance. It was the sleigh of Herman Mordaunt, empty; with the horses, maddened by terror, running wherever their fears impelled. As the sleigh passed, it was thrown on one side; then it was once more whirled up again; and it went out of sight, with the rumbling sound of the runners mingling with the jingling of bells and the tramp of hoofs.

At this instant a loud, distant cry from a human voice, was certainly heard. It seemed, to me, as if some one called my name; and Anneke said, she so understood it, too. The call, if call it was, came from the south, and from under the western shore. At the next moment, awful reports proceeded from the barrier above; and, passing an arm around the slender waist of my lovely companion, to support her, I began a rapid movement in the direction of that call. While attempting to reach the western shore, I had observed a high mound of broken ice, that was floating down; or rather, was pressed down on the smooth surface of the frozen river, in advance of the smaller cakes that came by in the current. It was increasing, in size, by accessions from these floating cakes, and threatened to form a new dam, at some narrow pass below, as soon as of sufficient size. It occurred to me we should be temporarily safe, could we reach that mound, for it rose so high as to be above danger from the water. Thither, then, I ran, almost carrying Anneke on my arm; our speed increased by the terrific sounds from the dam above us.

We reached the mound, and found the cakes so piled, as to be able to ascend them; though not without an effort. After getting up a layer or two, the broken mass became so irregular and ragged, as to render it necessary for me to mount first, and then to drag Anneke up after me. This I did, until exhausted; and we both seated ourselves on the edge of a cake, in order to recover our breath. While there, it struck me, that new sounds arose from the river; and, bending forward to examine, I saw that the water had forced its way through the dam above and was coming down upon us in a torrent.

Chapter XVII · [*The Rescue*]

My heart leaps up when I behold
  A rainbow in the sky:
So was it when my life began;
So is it now I am a man;
So be it when I shall grow old,
  Or let me die!
The child is father of the man;
  And I could wish my days to be
Bound each to each by natural piety.

WORDSWORTH

Five minutes longer on the ice of the main channel, and we should have been swept away.

Even as we still sat looking at the frightful force of the swift current, as well as the dim light of that clouded night would permit, I saw Guert Ten Eyck's sleigh whirl past us; and, only a minute later, Herman Mordaunt's followed; the poor, exhausted beasts struggling in the harness for freedom, that they might swim for their lives. Anneke heard the snorting of those wretched horses; but her unpractised eyes did not detect them, immersed, as they were, in the current; nor had she recognised the sleigh that whirled past us, as her father's. A little later, a fearful shriek came from one of the fettered beasts; such a heart-piercing cry as it is known the horse often gives. I said nothing on the subject, knowing that love for her father was one of the great incentives which had aroused my companion to exertion; and being unwilling to excite fears that were now latent.

Two or three minutes of rest were all that circumstances permitted. I could see that everything visible on the river, was in motion downwards; the piles of ice on which we were placed, as well as the cakes that glanced by us, in their quicker descent. Our own motion was slow, on account of the mass which doubtless pressed on the shoals of the west side of the river; as well as on account of the friction against the lateral fields of ice, and occasionally against the shore. Still, we were in motion; and I felt the necessity, on every account, of getting as soon as possible on the western verge of our floating island, in order to profit by any favourable occurrence that might offer.

Dear Anneke!—How admirably did she behave that fearful night! From the moment she regained her entire consciousness, after I found her praying in the bottom of the sleigh, down to that instant, she had been as little of an encumbrance to my own efforts, as was at all possible. Reasonable, resolute, compliant, and totally without any ill-timed exhibition of womanly apprehension, she had done all she was desired to do unhesitatingly, and with intelligence. In ascending that pile of ice, by no means an easy task under any circumstances, we had acted in perfect concert; every effort of mine being aided by one of her own, directed by my advice and greater experience.

"God has not deserted us, dearest Anneke," I said, now that my companion's strength appeared to have returned, "and we may yet hope to escape. I can anticipate the joy we shall bring to your father's heart, when he again takes you to his arms, safe and uninjured."

"Dear, dear father!—What agony he must now be suffering on my account.—Come, Corny, let us go to him at once, if it be possible."

As this was said, the precious girl arose, and adjusted her tippet in a way that should cause her no encumbrance; like one ready to set about the execution of a serious task with all her energies. The muff had been dropped on the river; for neither of us had any sensibility to cold. The night, however, was quite mild, for the season; and we probably should not have suffered, had our exertions been less violent. Anneke declared herself ready to proceed, and I commenced the difficult and delicate task of aiding her across an island composed of icy fragments, in order to reach its western margin. We were quite thirty feet in the air; and a fall into any of the numerous caverns, among which we had to proceed, might have been fatal; certainly would have crippled the sufferer. Then the surface of the ice was so smooth as to render walking on it an exceedingly delicate operation; more especially as the cakes lay at all manner of inclinations to the plane of the horizon. Fortunately, I wore buckskin moccasins over my boots; and their rough leather aided me greatly in maintaining my footing. Anneke, too, had socks of cloth; without which, I do not think, she could have possibly moved. By these aids, however, and by proceeding with the utmost caution, we had actually succeeded in attaining our object, when the floating mass shot into an eddy, and, turning slowly round, under this new influence, placed us on the outer side of the island again! Not a murmur escaped Anneke, at this disappointment; but, with a sweetness of temper that spoke volumes in favour of her natural disposition, and a resignation that told her training, she professed a readiness to renew her efforts. To this I would not consent, however; for I saw that the eddy was still whirling us about; and I thought it best to escape from its influence altogether, before we threw away our strength fruitlessly. Instead of re-crossing the pile, therefore, I told my fair companion that we would descend to a cake that lay level on the water, and which projected from the mass to such a distance, as to be close to the shore, should we again get near it. This descent was made, after some trouble, though I was compelled to receive Anneke entirely into my arms, in order to effect it. Effect it I did; placing the sweet girl safely at my side, on the outermost and lowest of all the cakes in our confused pile.

In some respects this change was for the better; while it did not improve our situation in others. It 10 placed both Anneke and myself behind a shelter, as respected the wind; which, though neither very strong nor very cold, had enough of March about it to render the change acceptable. It took my companion, too, from a position where motion was difficult, and often dangerous; leaving her on a level, even spot, where she could walk with ease and security, and keep the blood in motion by exercise. Then it put us both in the best possible situation to profit by any contact with that shore, along and 20 near which our island was now slowly moving.

There could no longer be any doubt of the state of the river in general. It had broken up; spring had come, like a thief in the night; and the ice below having given way, while the mass above had acquired too much power to be resisted, everything was set in motion; and, like the death of the strong man, the disruption of fields in themselves so thick and adhesive, had produced an agony surpassing the usual struggle of the seasons. Never- 30 theless, the downward motion had begun in earnest, and the centre of the river was running like a sluice, carrying away, in its current, those masses which had just before formed so menacing an obstacle above.

Luckily, our own pile was a little aside from the great downward rush. I have since thought, that it touched the bottom, which caused it to turn, as well as retarded its movement. Be this as it might, we still remained in a little bay, slowly turning in a 40 circle; and glad was I to see our low cake coming round again, in sight of the western shore. The moment now demanded decision; and I prepared Anneke to meet it. A large, low, level cake had driven up on the shore, and extended out so far as to promise that our own cake would touch it, in our evolutions. I knew that the ice, in general, had not broken in consequence of any weakness of

its own, but purely under the weight of the enormous pressure from above, and the mighty force of the current; and that we ran little, or no risk, in trusting our persons on the uttermost limits of any considerable fragment. A station was taken, accordingly, near a projection of the cake we were on; when we waited for the expected contact. At such moments, the slightest disappointment carried with it the force of the greatest circumstances. Several times did it appear, to us, that our island was on the point of touching the fastened cake, and as often did it incline aside; at no time coming nearer than within six or eight feet. This distance it would have been easy enough, for *me* to leap across, but, to Anneke, it was a barrier as impassable as the illimitable void. The sweet girl saw this; and, she acted like herself, under the circumstances. She took my hand, pressed it, and said earnestly, and with patient sweetness—

"You see how it is, Corny; I am not permitted to escape; but you can easily reach the shore. Go, then, and leave me in the hands of Providence. Go; I never can forget what you have already done; but it is useless to perish together!"

I have never doubted that Anneke was perfectly sincere in her wish that I should, at least, save my own life. The feeling with which she spoke; the despair that was coming over her; and the movement of our island, which, at that moment, gave signs of shooting away from the shore, altogether, roused me to a sudden, and certainly, to a very bold attempt. I tremble, even at this distance of time, as I write the particulars. A small cake of ice was floating in between us and that which lay firmly fastened to the shore. Its size was such as to allow it to pass between the two; though not without coming nearly, if not absolutely, in contact with one, if not with both. I observed all this; and, saying one word of encouragement to Anneke, I passed an arm around her waist—waited the proper moment—and sprang forward. It was necessary to make a short leap, with my precious burthen on my arm, in order to gain this floating bridge; but it was done, and successfully. Scarcely permitting Anneke's foot to touch this frail support, which was already sinking under our joint weight, I crossed it at two or three steps, and threw all my power into a last and desperate effort. I succeeded here, also; and fell, upon the firmer cake, with a heart filled with gratitude to God. The touch told me that we were safe; and, in the next instant, we reached the solid ground. Under such circumstances, one usually looks back to examine the danger he has just gone through. I did so; and saw that the floating cake of ice had already passed down, and was out of reach; while the mass that had been the means of saving us, was slowly following, under some new impulse, received from the furious currents of the river. But we were saved; and most devoutly did I thank my God, who had mercifully aided our escape from perils so imminent.

I was compelled to wait for Anneke, who fell upon her knees, and remained there quite a minute, before I could aid her in ascending the steep acclivity which formed the western bank of the Hudson, at this particular point. We reached the top, however, after a little delay, and pausing once or twice to take breath; when we first became really sensible of the true character of the scene from which we had been delivered. Dim as was the light, there was enough to enable us to overlook a considerable reach of the river, from that elevated stand. The Hudson resembled chaos rushing headlong between the banks. As for the cakes of ice—some darting past singly, and others piled as high as houses—of course, the stream was filled with such; but, a large, dark object was seen coming through that very channel, over which Anneke and I had stood, less than an hour before, sailing down the current with fearful rapidity. It was a house; of no great size, it is true, but large enough to present a singular object on the river. A bridge, of some size, followed; and a sloop, that had been borne away from the wharves of Albany, soon appeared in the strange assemblage, that was thus suddenly collected on this great artery of the colony.

But the hour was late; Anneke was yet to care for; it was necessary to seek a shelter. Still supporting my lovely companion, who now began to express her uneasiness on account of her father, and her other friends, I held the way inland; knowing that there was a high road parallel to the river, and at no great distance from it. We reached the highway, in the course of ten minutes, and turned our faces northward, as the direction which led towards Albany. We had not advanced far before I heard the voices of men, who were coming towards us; and glad was I to recognise that of Dirck Follock among the number. I called aloud, and was answered by a shout of exultation, which, as I afterwards discovered, spontaneously broke out of his mouth, when he recognised the form of Anneke. Dirck was powerfully agitated when we joined him; I had never, previously, seen anything like such a burst of feeling from him; and it was some time before I could address him.

"Of course, your whole party is safe?" I asked, a little doubtingly; for I had actually given up all who had been in Herman Mordaunt's sleigh for lost.

"Yes, thank God! all but the sleigh and horses. But where are Guert Ten Eyck and Miss Wallace?"

"Gone ashore on the other side of the river; we parted, and they took that direction, while we came hither." I said this to quiet Anneke's fears; but I had misgivings about their having got off the river at all. "But let me know the manner of your own escape."

Dirck then gave us a history of what had passed; the whole party turning back to accompany us, as soon as I told them that their errand—a search for the horses—was useless. The substance of what we heard was as follows:—In the first effort to reach the western shore, Herman Mordaunt had been met by the very obstacle which Guert had foreseen, and he turned south, hoping to find some spot at which to land, by going farther from the dam that had formed above. After repeated efforts, and having nearly lost his sleigh and the whole party, a point was reached at which Herman Mordaunt determined to get his female companion on shore, at every hazard. This was to be done only by crossing floating cakes of ice, in a current that was already running at the rate of four or five miles in the hour. Dirck was left in charge of the horses while the experiment was made; but seeing the adventurers in great danger, he flew to their assistance—when the whole party were immersed, though not in deep water. Left to themselves, and alarmed with the floundering in the river and the grinding of the cakes, Herman Mordaunt's bays went off in the confusion. Mrs. Bogart was assisted to the land, and was helped to reach the nearest dwelling—a comfortable farm-house, about a quarter of a mile beyond the point where we had met the party. There Mrs. Bogart had been placed in a warm bed, and the gentlemen were supplied with such dry clothes as the rustic wardrobe of these simple people could furnish. The change made, Dirck was on his way to ascertain what had become of the sleigh and horses, as has been mentioned.

On inquiry, I found that the spot where Anneke and myself had landed was quite three miles below the island on which Guert and I had drawn the sleigh. Nearly the whole of this distance had we floated with the pile of broken ice, in the short time we were on it; a proof of the furious rate at which the current was setting downward. No one had heard anything of Guert and Mary; but I encouraged my companion to believe that they were necessarily safe on the other shore. I certainly deemed this to be very questionable, but there was no use in anticipating evil.

On reaching the farm-house, Herman Mordaunt's delight and gratitude may more easily be imagined than described. He folded Anneke to his heart, and she wept like an infant on his bosom. Nor was I forgotten in this touching scene, but came in for a full share of notice.

"I want no details, noble young man—" I am professing to write the truth, and must be excused for relating such things as these, but—"I want no details, noble young man," said Herman Mordaunt, squeezing my hand, "to feel certain that, under God, I owe my child's life, for the second time, to you. I wish to Heaven!—but, no matter—it is now too late—some other way may and must offer. I scarce know what I say, Littlepage; but what I mean is, to express faintly, some small portion of the gratitude I feel, and to let you know how sensibly and deeply your services are felt and appreciated."

The reader may think it odd, that this incoherent, but pregnant speech, made little impression on me at the time, beyond the grateful conviction of having really rendered the greatest of all services to Anneke and her father; though I had better occasion to remember it afterwards.

It is unnecessary to dwell more particularly on the occurrences at the farm-house. The worthy people did what they could to make us comfortable, and we were all warm in bed, in the course of the next half-hour.

On the following morning a wagon was harnessed, and we left these simple countrymen and women—who refused everything like compensation, as a matter of course—and proceeded homeward. I have heard it said that we Americans are mercenary: it may be so, but not a man, probably, exists in the colonies, who would accept money for such assistance. We were two hours in reaching Albany, on wheels; and entered the place about ten, in a very different style from that in which we had quitted it the day before. As we drove along, the highway frequently led us to points that commanded views of the river, and we had so many opportunities of noting the effects of the freshet. Of ice, very little remained. Here and there a cake or a pile was seen still adhering to the shore, and occasionally fragments floated downwards; but, as a rule, the torrent had swept all before it. I particularly took notice of the island on which we had sought refuge. It was entirely under water, but its outlines were to be traced by the bushes which lined its low banks. Most of the trees on its upper end were cut down, and all that grew on it would unquestionably have gone, had not the dam given way as early as it did. A great number of trees had been broken down on all the islands; and large tops and heavy trunks were still floating in the current, that were lately tenants of the forest, and had been violently torn from their places.

We found all the lower part of Albany, too, under water. Boats were actually moving through the streets; a considerable portion of its inhabitants having no other means of communicating with their neighbours. A sloop of some size lay up on one of the lowest spots; and, as the water was already subsiding, it was said she would remain there until removed by the shipwrights. Nobody was drowned in the place; for it is not usual for the people of these colonies to remain in their beds, at such times, to await the appearance of the enemy in at their windows. We often read of such accidents destroying hundreds in the Old World; but, in the New, human life is of too much account to be unnecessarily thrown away, and so we make some efforts to preserve it.

As we drove into the street in which Herman Mordaunt lived, we heard a shout, and turning our heads, we saw Guert Ten Eyck waving his cap to us, with joy delineated in every feature of his handsome face. At the next moment he was at our side.

"Mr. Herman Mordaunt," he cried, shaking that gentleman most cordially by the hand, "I look upon you as one raised from the dead; you and my excellent neighbour, Mrs. Bogart, and Mr. Follock, here! How you got off the river is a mystery to me, for I well know that the water commonly breaks through first under the west shore. Corny and Miss Anneke—God bless you both! Mary Wallace is in terror lest ill news come from some of you; but I will run ahead and let her know the glad tidings. It is but five minutes since I left her, starting at every sound, lest it prove the foot of some ill-omened messenger."

Guert stopped to say no more. In a minute he was inside of Herman Mordaunt's house—in another Anneke and Mary Wallace were locked in each other's arms. After exchanging salutes, Mrs. Bogart was conveyed to her own residence, and there was a termination to that memorable expedition.

Guert had less to communicate, in the way of dangers and marvels, than I had anticipated. It seemed, that when he and Miss Wallace reached the inner margin of the last island, a large cake of ice had entered the strait, and got jammed; or rather, that it went through, forced by the tremendous pressure above; though not without losing large masses, as it came in contact with the shores, and grinding much of its material into powder, by the attrition. Guert's presence of mind and decision did him excellent service here. Without delaying an instant, the moment it was in his power, he led Mary on that cake, and crossed the narrow branch of the river, which alone separated him from the main land, on it, dry-shod. The water was beginning to find its way over this cake, as it usually did on all those that lay low, and which even stopped in their progress; but this did not offer any serious obstacles to persons who were so prompt. Safe themselves, our friends remained to see if we could

not be induced to join them; and the call we heard, was from Guert, who had actually re-crossed to the island, in the hope of meeting us, and directing us to a place of safety. Guert never said anything to me on the subject, himself; but I subsequently gathered from Mary Wallace's accounts, that the young man did not rejoin her without a good deal of hazard and difficulty, and after a long and fruitless search for his companions. Finding it useless to remain any longer on the river-side, Guert and his companion held their way towards Albany. About midnight they reached the ferry, opposite to the town; having walked quite six miles, filled with uneasiness on account of those who had been left behind. Guert was a man of decision, and he wisely determined it would be better to proceed, than to attempt waking up the inmates of any of the houses he passed. The river was now substantially free from ice, though running with great velocity. But, Guert was an expert oarsman; and, finding a skiff, he persuaded Mary Wallace to enter it; actually succeeding, by means of the eddies, in landing her within ten feet of the very spot where the hand-sled had deposited him and myself, only a few days before. From this point, there was no difficulty in walking home; and Miss Wallace actually slept in her own bed, that eventful night, if, indeed, she *could* sleep.

Such was the termination of this adventure; one that I have rightly termed memorable. In the end, Jack and Moses came in safe and sound; having probably swum ashore. They were found in the public road, only a short distance from the town, and were brought in to their master the same day. Every one who took any interest in horses—and what Dutchman does not?—knew Jack and Moses, and there was no difficulty in ascertaining to whom they belonged. What is singular, however, both sleighs were recovered; though at long intervals of time, and under very different circumstances. That of Guert, wolves' skins and all, actually went down the whole length of the river on the ice; passing out to sea through the Narrows. It must have gone by New York in the night, or doubtless it would have been picked up; while the difficulty of reaching it, was its protector on the descent, *above* the town. Once outside of the Narrows, it was thrown by the tide and winds upon the shore of Staten Island; where it was hauled to land, housed, and, properly advertised in our New York paper. Guert actually got tidings of it in time to receive it, skins and all, by one of the first sloops that ascended the Hudson that year; which was within a fortnight after the river had opened. The year 1758 was one of great activity, on account of the movements of the army, and no time was then unnecessarily lost.

The history of Herman Mordaunt's sleigh was very different. The poor bays must have drowned soon after we saw them floating past us in the torrent. Of course, life had no sooner left them, than they sank to the bottom of the river, carrying with them the sleigh to which they were still attached. In a few days the animals rose to the surface—as is usual with all swollen bodies—bringing up the sleigh again. In this condition, the wreck was overtaken by a downward bound sloop, the men of which saved the sleigh, harness, skins, foot-stoves, and such other articles as would not float away.

Our adventure made a good deal of noise in the circle of Albany; and I have reason to think that my own conduct was approved by those who heard of it. Bulstrode paid me an especial visit of thanks, the very day of my return, when the following conversation took place between us:—

"You seem fated, my dear Corny," the Major observed, after he had paid the usual compliments, "to be always serving me in the most material way, and I scarcely know how to express all I feel on the occasion. First, the lion, and now this affair of the river—but, that Guert will drown, or make away with the whole family before the summer is over, unless Mr. Mordaunt puts a stop to *his* interference."

"This accident was one that might have overtaken the oldest and most prudent man in Albany. The river seemed as solid as the street when we went on it; and another hour, even as it was, would have brought us all home, in entire safety."

"Ay, but that hour came near bringing death and desolation into the most charming family in the colony; and you have been the means of averting the heaviest part of the blow. I wish to Heaven, Littlepage, that you would consent to come into the army! Join us as a volunteer, the

moment we move, and I will write to Sir Harry to obtain a pair of colours for you. As soon as he hears that we are indebted to your coolness and courage for the life of Miss Mordaunt, he will move heaven and earth, to manifest his gratitude. The instant this good parent made up his mind to accept Miss Mordaunt as a daughter, he began to consider her as a child of his own."

"And Anneke—Miss Mordaunt, herself, Mr. Bulstrode—does she regard Sir Harry as a father?"

"Why, that must be coming by slow degrees, as a matter of course, you know. Women are slower than us men to admit such totally novel impressions; and I dare say Anneke fancies one father enough for her, just at this moment: though she sends very pleasant messages to Sir Harry, I can assure you, when in the humour! But, what makes you so grave, my good Corny?"

"Mr. Bulstrode, I conceive it no more than fair, to be as honest as yourself in this matter. You have told me that you are a suitor for Miss Mordaunt's hand; I will now own to you that I am your rival."

My companion heard this declaration with a quiet smile, and the most perfect good-nature.

"So you actually wish to become the husband of Anneke Mordaunt, yourself, my dear Corny, do you?" he said, so coolly, that I was at a loss to know of what sort of materials the man could be made.

"I do, Major Bulstrode—it is the first and last wish of my heart."

"Since you seem disposed to reciprocate my confidence you will not take offence if I ask you a question or two!"

"Certainly not, sir; your own frankness shall be a rule for my government."

"Have you ever let Miss Mordaunt know that such are your wishes?"

"I have, sir; and that in the plainest terms—such as cannot well be misunderstood."

"What! last night?—On that infernal ice!—While she thought her life was in your hands!"

"Nothing was said on the subject, last night, for we had other thoughts to occupy our minds."

"It would have been a most ungenerous thing to take advantage of a lady's fear—"

"Major Bulstrode!—I cannot submit—"

"Hush, my dear Corny," interrupted the other, holding out a hand in a most quiet and friendly manner; "there must be no misunderstanding between you and me. Men are never greater simpletons, than when they let the secret consciousness of their love of life push them into swaggering about their honour; when their honour has, in fact, nothing to do with the matter in hand. I shall not quarrel with you; and must beg you, in advance, to receive my apologies for any little indecorum into which I may be betrayed by surprise; as for great pieces of indecorum, I shall endeavour to avoid them."

"Enough has been said, Mr. Bulstrode; I am no wrangler, to quarrel with a shadow; and, I trust, not in the least, that most contemptible of all human beings, a social bully, to be on all occasions menacing the sword or the pistol. Such men usually *do* nothing, when matters come to a crisis. Even when they fight, they fight bunglingly, and innocently."

"You are right, Littlepage, and I honour your sentiments. I have remarked that the most expert swordsman with his tongue, and the deadest shot at a shingle, are commonly as innocent as lambs of the shedding of blood on the ground. They can sometimes screw themselves up to *meet* an adversary, but it exceeds their powers to use their weapons properly, when it comes to serious work. The swaggerer is ever a coward at heart, however well he may wear a mask for a time. But enough of this.—We understand each other, and are to remain friends, under all circumstances. May I question further?"

"Ask what you please, Bulstrode—I shall answer, or not, at my own discretion."

"Then, permit me to inquire, if Major Littlepage has authorized you to offer proper settlements?"

"I am authorized to offer nothing.—Nor is it usual for the husband to make settlements on his wife, in these colonies, further than what the law does for her, in favour of her own. The father, sometimes, has a care for the third generation. I should expect Herman Mordaunt to settle his estate on his daughter, and her rightful heirs, let her marry whom she may."

"Ay, that is a very American notion; and one on which Herman Mordaunt, who remembers his extraction, will be little likely to act. Well, Corny, we are rivals, as it would seem; but that is no reason we should not remain friends. We understand each other—though, perhaps, I ought to tell you all."

"I should be glad to know all, Mr. Bulstrode; and can meet my fate, I hope, like a man. Whatever it may cost me, if Anneke prefer another, her happiness will be dearer to me than my own."

"Yes, my dear fellow, we all say and think so at one-and-twenty; which is about your age, I believe. At two-and-twenty, we begin to see that our own happiness has an equal claim on us; and, at three-and-twenty, we even give it the preference. However, I will be just, if I am selfish. I have no reason to believe Anne Mordaunt does prefer me; though my *perhaps* is not altogether without a meaning, either."

"In which case, I may possibly be permitted to know to what it refers?"

"It refers to the father; and, I can tell you, my fine fellow, that fathers are of some account, in the arrangement of marriages between parties of any standing. Had not Sir Harry authorized my own proposals, where should I have been? Not a farthing of settlement could I have offered, while he remained Sir Harry; notwithstanding I had the prodigious advantage of the entail. I can tell you what it is, Corny; the existing power is always an important power since we all think more of the present time, than of the future. That is the reason so few of us get to Heaven. As for Herman Mordaunt, I deem it no more than fair to tell you, he is on my side, heart and hand. He likes my offers of settlement; he likes my family; he likes my rank, civil and military; and I am not altogether without the hope, that he likes me."

I made no direct answer, and the conversation soon changed. Bulstrode's declaration, however, caused me to remember both the speech and manner of Herman Mordaunt, when he thanked me for saving his daughter's life. I now began to reflect on it; and reflected on it much during the next few months. In the end, the reader will learn the effect it had on my happiness.

WILLIAM CULLEN BRYANT (1794-1878)

WHEN William Cullen Bryant died in 1878 at the age of eighty-four, his reputation was eclipsed by that of Longfellow, whose popularity was at its height. Yet Bryant was the first American to achieve enduring fame as a poet, just as Irving and Cooper were the first to win lasting distinction with their essays and novels. His experiments in prosody, and his trenchant critical essays on the nature and uses of poetry encouraged the rise of authentic native verse. His poems celebrating the beauty of the American landscape, refreshing in their concreteness, are rooted in an intimate knowledge of American birds, fruits, and flowers. Although his subjects extend to the prairies, which he visited in 1832, his poetic perceptions of the scenes and seasons of New England (especially his winter pieces), written before the poet moved to New York in 1825, are the most memorable. "It is his proper praise," wrote Emerson, "that he first and he only made known to mankind our northern landscape." Bryant's reputation has suffered from an uncritical acceptance of the conventional label, "our American Wordsworth," and by the popular but mistaken impression that his work is forbiddingly austere. Those who have been taught to regard his work as imitative and cold will be surprised to find in his best poems a profound emotional response to the sensuous appeal of nature's colors and sounds, and a lyric exultation in her beneficent healing powers. Nineteenth-century American poetry may be said to have come of age with the advent of Bryant.

The New England in which Bryant spent his formative years (1794-1825) profoundly influenced his work. The poet was born and reared amid the lovely Berkshire hills in Cummington, Massachusetts, in an atmosphere of Calvinism and Federalism. The orthodox theology cherished by the community was personified in the poet's grandfather, for whom young Bryant, at the age of ten, turned the Book of Job into couplets. Meanwhile, the poet's father, Dr. Peter Bryant, indoctrinated his son with the tenets of Federalism. Equally conservative were the prevailing neoclassical tastes which led Bryant to fashion his early verse on the pattern of Addison, Pope, and Johnson. His first published poem, *The Embargo*, issued at his father's expense in Boston in 1808, was written in heroic couplets. Perhaps the chief distinction of this youthful satire on Jeffersonian democracy, which the author later refused to include in his collected work, was that it induced Dr. Bryant to send his son to college.

Bryant was admitted to the sophomore class at Williams in 1810, but withdrew after seven months when the family finances did not permit him to transfer to Yale. For the next four years (1811-1815) he read law in Worthington and Bridgewater, and was admitted to the bar in August, 1815. Bryant's early passion for poetry was not dimmed by his poring over Blackstone. Although he practiced conscientiously in several Massachusetts towns, he found time for the study and composition of poetry; the influence of his reading in the English poets is reflected during this period in his abandonment of couplets for blank verse. His discovery of Burns, Cowper, White, Thomson—and most important of all, a few years later, of Wordsworth—deepened his love of nature which had been nurtured by the beauty of the Berkshires. The poetry of the "graveyard school" confirmed his interest in the theme of death, which had been intensified by his own frail health as a boy and by his early religious training.

A decisive factor in Bryant's career between 1816 and 1821 was the editorial encouragement of the *North American Review*. Dr. Bryant, zealous for his son's advancement, had submitted to the magazine manuscript copies of a number of poems, including the early version (probably composed in 1815) of "Thanatopsis." Their superiority to the quality of contemporary American poetry led Richard Henry Dana, Sr., to exclaim: "No one on this side of the Atlantic is capable of writing such verses." Later, the excellence of other contributions such as "The Yellow Violet" and "To a Waterfowl" compelled another editor, E. T. Channing, to remonstrate, "Unless you supply more, or set some other poet to work who will be worthy of your company, I fear our poetical department must be given up." With the prestige of the country's leading literary periodical behind him, Bryant published his first volume, *Poems* (1821), a landmark in the history of American poetry.

With the exception of the series of notable nature poems in the *United States Literary Gazette* in 1824-1825, and a few other pieces such as "The Prairies," first published in the *Knickerbocker Magazine* in 1833, Bryant's best poetry was in his first volume of forty-four pages. Here are the revised and expanded version of "Thanatopsis" and the impact upon his work of Wordsworth whose "lines caused a thousand springs to gush up at once in his heart." Here, too, are poems on the American Indian, and superb landscape pieces such as "The Inscription for the Entrance to a Wood,"

"To a Waterfowl," "Green River," and "A Walk at Sunset." Few poets have had their stature so fully established by their first book.

Bryant issued a second volume of his poetry in New York in 1832, arrangements for the London edition being made by Washington Irving; and he published later revisions and additions, as well as his translations of the *Iliad* (1870) and the *Odyssey* (1871–1872). His career, however, after 1825 when he left New England for New York belongs, in the main, to the history of American journalism. In 1827 he became assistant editor of the New York *Evening Post*, and two years later was made editor in chief, a position he held for forty-nine years. Under his direction the *Post* became a dignified journal of liberal opinion; alone among New York newspapers, it refused to join the popular cry against Fenimore Cooper. The core of Bryant's political philosophy is an abiding faith in the power of individual liberty. His editorials bear evidence of the distance he had traveled from the Federalist position of his youth. He espoused the principles of free trade, endorsed Andrew Jackson for the Presidency, attacked the Bank of the United States and speculation, advocated socially sound banking and currency regulations, led a movement for prison reforms, allied his paper with the new Republican party in 1856, and risked offending conservative opinion by championing the right of labor to bargain collectively and to strike. He broke with Webster over the Fugitive Slave Law, and after the Civil War he condemned the excesses of the Gilded Age.

Bryant's trenchant editorials distinguished for their clarity and directness are the most effective of his work in prose, although his critical essays, especially his "Lectures on Poetry," his travel essays, and his commemorative addresses are admirable. He survives today, however, as the first important American poet whose work transcends provincial standards.

BIBLIOGRAPHY · The best editions of Bryant's poetry are *The Poetical Works of William Cullen Bryant* (1876), which had the benefit of the author's own supervision; *The Poetical Works of William Cullen Bryant* (2 vols., 1882), containing additional poems, edited by Parke Godwin, and published as the third and fourth volume of Godwin, *The Life and Works of William Cullen Bryant* (6 vols., 1883–1884); and the Roslyn Edition, a one-volume collection. A readily available and useful one-volume edition is that edited by Tremaine McDowell, *William Cullen Bryant: Representative Selections* (1935), with an excellent critical introduction and an admirable bibliography supplementing that by H. C.

Sturges in the Roslyn Edition. Bryant's prose pieces and editorial writings have not been collected.

The standard biography is Parke Godwin, *A Biography of William Cullen Bryant, with Extracts from his Private Correspondence* (1883). See also John Bigelow, *William Cullen Bryant* (1890) in the American Men of Letters Series; and W. A. Bradley, *William Cullen Bryant* (1905) in the English Men of Letters Series; and G. W. Curtis, *The Life, Character, and Writings of William Cullen Bryant* (1879). These biographies should be supplemented by Allan Nevins, *The Evening Post: A Century of Journalism* (1922), and by the following specialized studies, especially those devoted to Bryant's formative years by Tremaine McDowell: C. I. Glicksberg, "Bryant and *The United States Review*," *New England Quarterly*, VII (1934), 687–701; "Bryant and the Sedgwick Family," *Americana*, XXXI (1937), 626–638; "William Cullen Bryant and Fanny Wright," *American Literature*, VI (1935), 427–432; W. D. Hoyt, "Some Unpublished Bryant Correspondence," *New York History*, XXI (1940), 63–70, 193–204; W. P. Hudson, "Archibald Alison and William Cullen Bryant," *American Literature*, XII (1940), 59–68; K. Huntress and F. W. Lorch, "Bryant and Illinois," *New England Quarterly*, XVI (1943), 634–647; Tremaine McDowell, "The Ancestry of William Cullen Bryant," *Americana*, XXII (1928), 408–420; "Bryant and *The North American Review*," *American Literature*, I (1929), 14–26; "Bryant's Practice in Composition and Revision," *PMLA*, LII (1937), 474–502; "Cullen Bryant at Williams College," *New England Quarterly*, I (1928), 443–466; "Cullen Bryant Prepares for College," *South Atlantic Quarterly*, XXX (1931), 125–133; "Edgar Allan Poe and William Cullen Bryant," *Philological Quarterly*, XVI (1937), 83–84; "The Juvenile Verse of William Cullen Bryant," *Studies in Philology*, XXVI (1929), 96–116; "William Cullen Bryant and Yale," *New England Quarterly*, III (1930), 706–716; J. C. Matthews, "Bryant's Knowledge of Dante," *Italica*, XVI (1939), 115–119; F. Smith, "Schoolcraft, Bryant, and Poetic Fame," *American Literature*, V (1933), 170–172; and J. T. Winterich, "Early American Books and Printing . . . Enter the Professional Author," *Publishers' Weekly* (May 19, 1934), CXXV, 1863–1866.

Valuable critical studies include G. W. Allen, *American Prosody* (1935), 27–55; E. J. Bailey, *Religious Thought in the Greater American Poets* (1922), 10–31; W. C. Bryant, II, "The Genesis of 'Thanatopsis,'" *New England Quarterly*, XXI (1948), 163–184; N. Foerster, *Nature in American Literature* (1923), 1–19; A. Kreymborg, *Our Singing Strength* (1929), 27–40; W. E. Leonard, "Bryant," *CHAL*, I, Ch. V, Pt. 1, 260–278; T. McDowell, *William Cullen Bryant: Representative Selections* (1935), xiii–lxviii; H. Monroe, "Aere Perennius," *Poetry*, VI (1915), 197–200, and *Dial*, LIX (1915), 314–315, 479–480; F. L. Pattee, *Side-Lights on American Literature* (1922), 293–326; W. L. Phelps, *Howells, James, Bryant,* and Other Essays (1924), 1–30; H. D. Sedgwick, Jr., "Bryant's Permanent Contribution to Literature," Atlantic Monthly, LXXIX (April, 1897), 539–549; E. C. Stedman, Poets of America (1885), 62–94; C. Van Doren, "The Growth of Thanatopsis," Nation (Oct. 7, 1915), CI, 432–433; and G. P. Voigt, The Religious and Ethical Elements in the Major American Poets (1925), 13–27.

Thanatopsis

BRYANT's biographers have invariably dated the first version of "Thanatopsis" during the summer or autumn of 1811, thus establishing the poet's artistic precocity. This early date, however, presents many difficulties for an understanding of Bryant's poetic development from 1811 to 1815. In a closely-reasoned analysis, "The Genesis of 'Thanatopsis' " in the New England Quarterly, XXI (1948), W. C. Bryant, II, argues convincingly that Bryant did not begin to compose the poem until the summer or autumn of 1815. If this later date is accepted, "Thanatopsis" was written at the end of a series of inferior poems which contain the genesis of Bryant's masterpiece.

The maturing of Bryant's poetic power is best revealed by a comparison of the original version of "Thanatopsis" printed in the North American Review, V (September, 1817), 338–340, with the revised text as it appeared in Poems (1821). The absence in both versions of the tenets of the Calvinism upon which young Bryant had been brought up, and especially the omission of any of the usual consolations of orthodox religion, indicate how thoroughly the Stoic tradition had modified the Christian elements in Bryant's thinking. The title means "view of death." The text is that of the first printing in the North American Review. The first four stanzas in iambic tetrameter, which were designed by Bryant as a separate poem on death, were mistaken by the editors as part of "Thanatopsis" and printed as below. In the 1821 version Bryant omitted these stanzas and substituted the lines which are now familiar to all lovers of American poetry.

Not that from life, and all its woes
The hand of death shall set me free;
Not that this head, shall then repose
In the low vale most peacefully.

Ah, when I touch time's farthest brink,   5
A kinder solace must attend;
It chills my very soul, to think
On that dread hour when life must end.

In vain the flatt'ring verse may breathe,
Of ease from pain, and rest from strife,   10
There is a sacred dread of death
Inwoven with the strings of life.

This bitter cup at first was given
When angry justice frown'd severe,
And 'tis th' eternal doom of heaven   15
That man must view the grave with fear.

———

Yet a few days, and thee,
The all-beholding sun, shall see no more,
In all his course; nor yet in the cold ground,
Where thy pale form was laid, with many tears, 20
Nor in th' embrace of ocean shall exist
Thy image. Earth, that nourished thee, shall claim
Thy growth, to be resolv'd to earth again;
And, lost each human trace, surrend'ring up
Thine individual being, shalt thou go   25
To mix forever with the elements,
To be a brother to th' insensible rock
And to the sluggish clod, which the rude swain
Turns with his share, and treads upon. The oak
Shall [s]end his roots abroad, and pierce thy mould.
Yet not to thy eternal resting place   31
Shalt thou retire alone—nor couldst thou wish
Couch more magnificent. Thou shalt lie down
With patriarchs of the infant world—with kings
The powerful of the earth—the wise, the good, 35
Fair forms, and hoary seers of ages past,
All in one mighty sepulchre.—The hills,
Rock-ribb'd and ancient as the sun,—the vales
Stretching in pensive quietness between;
The venerable woods—the floods that move   40
In majesty,—and the complaining brooks,
That wind among the meads, and make them green,
Are but the solemn decorations all,
Of the great tomb of man.—The golden sun,
The planets, all the infinite host of heaven   45
Are glowing on the sad abodes of death,
Through the still lapse of ages. All that tread
The globe are but a handful to the tribes
That slumber in its bosom.—Take the wings
Of morning—and the Borean desert pierce— 50

50. and the Borean desert pierce: penetrate the Arctic wastes. The 1821, 1832, and 1847 versions read "and the Barcan desert pierce"; Bryant shared the popular belief in the existence of a vast desert west of the Mississippi River.

Or lose thyself in the continuous woods
That veil Oregan, where he hears no sound
Save his own dashings—yet—the dead are there,
And millions in those solitudes, since first   54
The flight of years began, have laid them down
In their last sleep—the dead reign there alone.—
So shalt thou rest—and what if thou shalt fall
Unnoticed by the living—and no friend
Take note of thy departure? Thousands more
Will share thy destiny.—The tittering world   60
Dance to the grave. The busy brood of care
Plod on, and each one chases as before
His favourite phantom.—Yet all these shall leave
Their mirth and their employments, and shall come
And make their bed with thee!——   65

THE FAMILIAR version of Bryant's best-known poem
is the one which appeared for the first time in *Poems*
(1821). In addition to substituting lines 1–17 for the
first four quatrains which the editors of the *North
American Review* had mistakenly assumed were a part
of the poem, Bryant added sixteen lines at the end,
beginning with "As the long train" (line 66 of the
version printed below).

To him who in the love of Nature holds
Communion with her visible forms, she speaks
A various language; for his gayer hours
She has a voice of gladness, and a smile
And eloquence of beauty, and she glides   5
Into his darker musings, with a mild
And healing sympathy, that steals away
Their sharpness, ere he is aware. When thoughts
Of the last bitter hour come like a blight
Over thy spirit, and sad images   10
Of the stern agony, and shroud, and pall,
And breathless darkness, and the narrow house,
Make thee to shudder, and grow sick at heart;—
Go forth, under the open sky, and list
To Nature's teachings, while from all around— 15
Earth and her waters, and the depths of air—
Comes a still voice—
                    Yet a few days, and thee
The all-beholding sun shall see no more
In all his course; nor yet in the cold ground,
Where thy pale form was laid, with many tears, 20
Nor in the embrace of ocean, shall exist

52. **Oregan:** the Columbia River in the Oregon Territory.

Thy image. Earth, that nourished thee, shall claim
Thy growth, to be resolved to earth again,
And, lost each human trace, surrendering up
Thine individual being, shalt thou go   25
To mix for ever with the elements,
To be a brother to the insensible rock
And to the sluggish clod, which the rude swain
Turns with his share, and treads upon. The oak
Shall send his roots abroad, and pierce thy mould.

Yet not to thine eternal resting-place   31
Shalt thou retire alone, nor couldst thou wish
Couch more magnificent. Thou shalt lie down
With patriarchs of the infant world—with kings,
The powerful of the earth—the wise, the good, 35
Fair forms, and hoary seers of ages past,
All in one mighty sepulchre. The hills
Rock-ribbed and ancient as the sun,—the vales
Stretching in pensive quietness between;
The venerable woods—rivers that move   40
In majesty, and the complaining brooks
That make the meadows green; and, poured
    round all,
Old Ocean's gray and melancholy waste,—
Are but the solemn decorations all
Of the great tomb of man. The golden sun,   45
The planets, all the infinite host of heaven,
Are shining on the sad abodes of death,
Through the still lapse of ages. All that tread
The globe are but a handful to the tribes
That slumber in its bosom.—Take the wings 50
Of morning, pierce the Barcan wilderness,
Or lose thyself in the continuous woods
Where rolls the Oregon, and hears no sound,
Save his own dashings—yet the dead are there:
And millions in those solitudes, since first   55
The flight of years began, have laid them down
In their last sleep—the dead reign there alone.
So shalt thou rest, and what if thou withdraw
In silence from the living, and no friend
Take note of thy departure? All that breathe 60
Will share thy destiny. The gay will laugh
When thou art gone, the solemn brood of care
Plod on, and each one as before will chase
His favorite phantom; yet all these shall leave
Their mirth and their employments, and shall
    come   65
And make their bed with thee. As the long train

Of ages glide away, the sons of men,
The youth in life's green spring, and he who goes
In the full strength of years, matron and maid,
The speechless babe, and the gray-headed man— 70
Shall one by one be gathered to thy side
By those, who in their turn shall follow them.

So live that when thy summons comes to join
The innumerable caravan, which moves
To that mysterious realm, where each shall take 75
His chamber in the silent halls of death,
Thou go not, like the quarry-slave at night,
Scourged to his dungeon, but, sustained and
    soothed
By an unfaltering trust, approach thy grave,
Like one who wraps the drapery of his couch 80
About him, and lies down to pleasant dreams.

The Yellow Violet

THE CONCRETE details which distinguish the best of
Bryant's nature poetry derive from a specific knowledge
of American plants and flowers. Young Bryant was
introduced to the principles of botany by his father,
who prepared his own drugs and simples. "The Yellow
Violet," thought to have been written in 1814, betrays its early composition by its traces of neoclassical
"elegance" and formality. It first appeared in the
Poems of 1821, and is here reprinted from *Poems* (1832).

When beechen buds begin to swell,
    And woods the blue bird's warble know,
The yellow violet's modest bell
    Peeps from the last year's leaves below.

Ere russet fields their green resume,   5
    Sweet flower, I love, in forest bare,
To meet thee, when thy faint perfume
    Alone is in the virgin air.

Of all her train, the hands of Spring,
    First plant thee in the watery mould,   10
And I have seen thee blossoming
    Beside the snow-bank's edges cold.

Thy parent sun, who bade thee view
    Pale skies, and chilling moisture sip,
Has bathed thee in his own bright hue,   15
    And streaked with jet thy glowing lip.

Yet slight thy form, and low thy seat,
    And earthward bent thy gentle eye,
Unapt the passing view to meet,
    When loftier flowers are flaunting nigh.   20

Oft, in the sunless April day,
    Thy early smile has staid my walk,
But 'midst the gorgeous blooms of May,
    I passed thee on thy humble stalk.

So they, who climb to wealth, forget   25
    The friends in darker fortunes tried.
I copied them—but I regret
    That I should ape the ways of pride.

And when again the genial hour
    Awakes the painted tribes of light,   30
I'll not o'erlook the modest flower
    That made the woods of April bright.

Inscription for the Entrance to a Wood

BRYANT'S FAVORITE theme, the power of nature to
soothe the spirit of man, is well expressed in this poem.
Parke Godwin, the poet's biographer, noted that
the wood mentioned was at Cummington, "nearly in
front of the house now known as the Bryant Homestead." The lines were first printed as "A Fragment"
in the *North American Review* for September, 1817,
along with "Thanatopsis." When Bryant included
the poem in his first volume in 1821, he entitled it
"Inscription for the Entrance to a Wood," made
several changes in the text, and added the verses beginning

The cool wind,
That stirs the stream in play, shall come to thee . . .

The present text is that in *Poems* (1832).

Stranger, if thou hast learnt a truth which needs
No school of long experience, that the world
Is full of guilt and misery, and hast seen
Enough of all its sorrows, crimes, and cares,
To tire thee of it, enter this wild wood   5
And view the haunts of Nature. The calm shade
Shall bring a kindred calm, and the sweet breeze
That makes the green leaves dance, shall waft a
    balm
To thy sick heart. Thou wilt find nothing here
Of all that pained thee in the haunts of men   10

And made thee loathe thy life. The primal curse
Fell, it is true, upon the unsinning earth,
But not in vengeance. God hath yoked to guilt
Her pale tormentor, misery. Hence, these shades
Are still the abodes of gladness, the thick roof   15
Of green and stirring branches is alive
And musical with birds, that sing and sport
In wantonness of spirit; while below
The squirrel, with raised paws and form erect,
Chirps merrily. Throngs of insects in the shade   20
Try their thin wings and dance in the warm beam
That waked them into life. Even the green trees
Partake the deep contentment; as they bend
To the soft winds, the sun from the blue sky
Looks in and sheds a blessing on the scene.   25
Scarce less the cleft-born wild-flower seems to en-
    joy
Existence, than the winged plunderer
That sucks its sweets. The massy rocks themselves,
And the old and ponderous trunks of prostrate
    trees
That lead from knoll to knoll a causey rude   30
Or bridge the sunken brook, and their dark roots,
With all their earth upon them, twisting high,
Breathe fixed tranquility. The rivulet
Sends forth glad sounds and tripping o'er its bed
Of pebbly sands, or leaping down the rocks,   35
Seems, with continuous laughter, to rejoice
In its own being. Softly tread the marge,
Lest from her midway perch thou scare the wren
That dips her bill in water. The cool wind,
That stirs the stream in play, shall come to thee,   40
Like one that loves thee nor will let thee pass
Ungreeted, and shall give its light embrace.

To a Waterfowl

BRYANT WROTE that he felt "very forlorn and desolate"
as he walked from Cummington to Plainfield, Massachusetts, on December 15, 1815, in search of a
promising town in which to begin his career as a lawyer.
The sight of a solitary bird winging its way against
the horizon renewed his courage, and that night, at
the end of his journey, he wrote what Matthew Arnold
believed to be "the best short poem in the English
language." It was printed for the first time in the
North American Review, March, 1818, the text of which
is here reproduced.

Whither, 'midst falling dew,
While glow the heavens with the last steps of day,
Far, through their rosy depths, dost thou pursue
    Thy solitary way?

Vainly the fowler's eye   5
Might mark thy distant flight, to do thee wrong,
As, darkly painted on the crimson sky,
    Thy figure floats along.

Seek'st thou the plashy brink
Of weedy lake, or marge of river wide,   10
Or where the rocking billows rise and sink
    On the chafed ocean side?

There is a Power, whose care
Teaches thy way along that pathless coast,—
The desert and illimitable air,   15
    Lone wandering, but not lost.

All day thy wings have fann'd,
At that far height, the cold thin atmosphere;
Yet stoop not, weary, to the welcome land,
    Though the dark night is near.   20

And soon that toil shall end,
Soon shalt thou find a summer home, and rest,
And scream among thy fellows; reeds shall bend,
    Soon, o'er thy sheltered nest.

Thou'rt gone, the abyss of heaven   25
Hath swallowed up thy form, yet, on my heart
Deeply hath sunk the lesson thou hast given,
    And shall not soon depart.

He, who, from zone to zone,
Guides through the boundless sky thy certain
    flight,   30
In the long way that I must trace alone,
    Will lead my steps aright.

Green River

WHEN BRYANT moved to Great Barrington to study
and practice law, he found refreshment in excursions
up and down the valley of the Green River, a tributary

7. As . . . sky: Upon the objection of a friend, Bryant
later altered the third line of the second stanza to read "As
darkly seen against the crimson sky," but there is evidence
that the poet preferred the earlier phrase.

of the Housatonic, not far from the village. The poem was written in Great Barrington in 1819 and appeared first in R. H. Dana's *The Idle Man* (1821). Later in the same year it was collected in *Poems*. This text is that of *Poems* (1832).

When breezes are soft and skies are fair,
I steal an hour from study and care,
And hie me away to the woodland scene,
Where wanders the stream with waters of green;
As if the bright fringe of herbs on its brink,   5
Had given their stain to the wave they drink;
And they, whose meadows it murmurs through,
Have named the stream from its own fair hue.

Yet pure its waters—its shallows are bright
With colored pebbles and sparkles of light,   10
And clear the depths where its eddies play,
And dimples deepen and whirl away,
And the plane-tree's speckled arms o'ershoot
The swifter current that mines its root,
Through whose shifting leaves, as you walk the hill,
The quivering glimmer of sun and rill,   16
With a sudden flash on the eye is thrown,
Like the ray that streams from the diamond stone.
Oh, loveliest there the spring days come,
With blossoms, and birds, and wild-bees' hum;   20
The flowers of summer are fairest there,
And freshest the breath of the summer air;
And sweetest the golden autumn day
In silence and sunshine glides away.

Yet fair as thou art, thou shun'st to glide,   25
Beautiful stream! by the village side;
But windest away from haunts of men,
To quiet valley and shaded glen;
And forest, and meadow, and slope of hill,
Around thee, are lonely, lovely, and still.   30
Lonely—save when, by thy rippling tides,
From thicket to thicket the angler glides;
Or the simpler comes with basket and book,
For herbs of power on thy banks to look;
Or haply, some idle dreamer, like me,   35
To wander, and muse, and gaze on thee.
Still—save the chirp of birds that feed
On the river cherry and seedy reed,
And thy own mild music gushing out

33. **simpler:** one who gathers herbs.

With mellow murmur and fairy shout,   40
From dawn, to the blush of another day,
Like traveller singing along his way

That fairy music I never hear,
Nor gaze on those waters so green and clear,
And mark them winding away from sight,   45
Darkened with shade or flashing with light,
While o'er them the vine to its thicket clings,
And the zephyr stoops to freshen his wings,
But I wish that fate had left me free
To wander these quiet haunts with thee,   50
Till the eating cares of earth should depart,
And the peace of the scene pass into my heart;
And I envy thy stream, as it glides along,
Through its beautiful banks in a trance of song.   54

Though forced to drudge for the dregs of men,
And scrawl strange words with the barbarous pen,
And mingle among the jostling crowd,
Where the sons of strife are subtle and loud—
I often come to this quiet place,
To breathe the airs that ruffle thy face,   60
And gaze upon thee in silent dream,
For in thy lonely and lovely stream,
An image of that calm life appears,
That won my heart in my greener years.

A Winter Piece

This poem was written in 1820 at Great Barrington, Massachusetts, where Bryant did not allow his study and practice of law to prevent him from writing poetry and exploring the countryside in all seasons of the year. "A Winter Piece" was first printed in New York in R. H. Dana's journal, *The Idle Man*, in 1821. This text is that of *Poems* (1832).

The time has been that these wild solitudes,
Yet beautiful as wild—were trod by me
Oftener than now; and when the ills of life
Had chafed my spirit—when the unsteady pulse
Beat with strange flutterings—I would wander
   forth   5
And seek the woods. The sunshine on my path
Was to me as a friend. The swelling hills,
The quiet dells retiring far between,
With gentle invitation to explore
Their windings, were a calm society   10

That talked with me and soothed me. Then the
    chant
Of birds, and chime of brooks, and soft caress
Of the fresh sylvan air, made me forget
The thoughts that broke my peace, and I began
To gather simples by the fountain's brink,   15
And lose myself in day-dreams. While I stood
In nature's loneliness, I was with one
With whom I early grew familiar, one
Who never had a frown for me, whose voice
Never rebuked me for the hours I stole   20
From cares I loved not, but of which the world
Deems highest, to converse with her. When
    shrieked
The bleak November winds, and smote the woods,
And the brown fields were herbless, and the shades,
That met above the merry rivulet,   25
Were spoiled. I sought, I loved them still,—they
    seemed
Like old companions in adversity.
Still there was beauty in my walks; the brook,
Bordered with sparkling frost-work, was as gay
As with its fringe of summer flowers. Afar,   30
The village with its spires, the path of streams,
And dim receding valleys, hid before
By interposing trees, lay visible
Through the bare grove, and my familiar haunts
Seemed new to me. Nor was I slow to come   35
Among them, when the clouds, from their still
    skirts,
Had shaken down on earth the feathery snow,
And all was white. The pure keen air abroad,
Albeit it breathed no scent of herb, nor heard
Love call of bird nor merry hum of bee,   40
Was not the air of death. Bright mosses crept
Over the spotted trunks, and the close buds,
That lay along the boughs, instinct with life,
Patient, and waiting the soft breath of Spring,
Feared not the piercing spirit of the North.   45
The snow-bird twittered on the beechen bough,
And 'neath the hemlock, whose thick branches bent
Beneath its bright cold burden, and kept dry
A circle, on the earth, of withered leaves,
The partridge found a shelter. Through the snow
The rabbit sprang away. The lighter track   51
Of fox, and the racoon's broad path were there,
Crossing each other. From his hollow tree,
The squirrel was abroad, gathering the nuts

Just fallen, that asked the winter cold and sway   55
Of winter blast, to shake them from their hold.
    But winter has yet brighter scenes,—he boasts
Splendors beyond what gorgeous summer knows;
Or autumn, with his many fruits, and woods
All flushed with many hues. Come, when the
    rains   60
Have glazed the snow, and clothed the trees with
    ice;
While the slant sun of February pours
Into the bowers a flood of light. Approach!
The encrusted surface shall upbear thy steps,
And the broad arching portals of the grove   65
Welcome thy entering. Look! the massy trunks
Are cased in pure chrystal, each light spray,
Nodding and tinkling in the breath of heaven,
Is studded with its trembling water-drops,   69
That stream with rainbow radiance as they move.
But round the parent stem the long low boughs
Bend, in a glittering ring, and arbors hide
The grassy floor. Oh! you might deem the spot,
The spacious cavern of the virgin mine,
Deep in the womb of earth—where the gems
    grow,   75
And diamonds put forth radiant rods and bud
With amethyst and topaz—and the place
Lit up, most royally, with the pure beam
That dwells in them. Or haply the vast hall
Of fairy palace, that outlasts the night,   80
And fades not in the glory of the sun;—
Where chrystal columns send forth slender shafts
And crossing arches; and fantastic aisles
Wind from the sight in brightness, and are lost
Among the crowded pillars. Raise thine eye,— 85
Thou seest no cavern roof, no palace vault;
There the blue sky and the white drifting cloud
Look in. Again the wildered fancy dreams
Of spouting fountains, frozen as they rose,
And fixed, with all their branching jets, in air, 90
And all their sluices sealed. All, all is light;
Light without shade. But all shall pass away
With the next sun. From numberless vast trunks,
Loosened, the crashing ice shall make a sound
Like the far roar of rivers, and the eve   95
Shall close o'er the brown woods as it was wont.
    And it is pleasant, when the noisy streams
Are just set free, and milder suns melt off
The plashy snow, save only the firm drift

431

In the deep glen or the close shade of pines,— 100
'Tis pleasant to behold the wreaths of smoke
Roll up among the maples of the hill,
Where the shrill sound of youthful voices wakes
The shriller echo, as the clear pure lymph,
That from the wounded trees, in twinkling drops,
Falls, 'mid the golden brightness of the morn, 106
Is gathered in with brimming pails, and oft,
Wielded by sturdy hands, the stroke of axe
Makes the woods ring. Along the quiet air,
Come and float calmly off the soft light clouds, 110
Such as you see in summer, and the winds
Scarce stir the branches. Lodged in sunny cleft,
Where the cold breezes come not, bloom alone
The little wind-flower, whose just opened eye
Is blue as the spring heaven it gazes at— 115
Startling the loiterer in the naked groves
With unexpected beauty, for the time
Of blossoms and green leaves is yet afar.
And ere it comes, the encountering winds shall oft
Muster their wrath again, and rapid clouds 120
Shade heaven, and bounding on the frozen earth
Shall fall their volleyed stores, rounded like hail,
And white like snow, and the loud North again
Shall buffet the vexed forests in his rage.

Oh Fairest of the Rural Maids

Written in 1820, this poem was addressed to Frances
Fairchild, Bryant's future wife, a year before their
marriage. The poet's characteristic reticence may be
seen in the fact that "Oh Fairest of the Rural Maids"
is the only one of the love poems of this period to be
printed. It appeared first in the *Poems* of 1832, and
won Poe's praise as the best of all Bryant's verses.
The text: *Poems* (1832).

Nature's child

Oh fairest of the rural maids!
Thy birth was in the forest shades;
Green boughs, and glimpses of the sky,
Were all that met thy infant eye.

Thy sports, thy wanderings, when a child, 5
Were ever in the sylvan wild;
And all the beauty of the place
Is in thy heart and on thy face.

The twilight of the trees and rocks
Is in the light shade of thy locks; 10

Thy step is as the wind, that weaves
Its playful way among the leaves.

Same idea as Wordsworth

Thy eyes are springs, in whose serene
And silent waters heaven is seen;
Their lashes are the herbs that look 15
On their young figures in the brook.

The forest depths, by foot unprest,
Are not more sinless than thy breast;
The holy peace, that fills the air
Of those calm solitudes, is there. 20

nature is found. I make you lovely.

I Broke the Spell that Held Me Long

This poem expresses the debate in Bryant's mind while
he was practicing law at Great Barrington, Massachusetts, in 1824. Could he yield poetry for the
law? The following year he moved to New York
City to become editor of the *New York Review and
Athenaeum Magazine*. The poem was first published
in the *Atlantic Souvenir*, 1825.

I broke the spell that held me long,
The dear, dear witchery of song.
I said, the poet's idle lore
Shall waste my prime of years no more,
For Poetry, though heavenly born, 5
Consorts with poverty and scorn.

I broke the spell—nor deemed its power
Could fetter me another hour.
Ah, thoughtless! how could I forget
Its causes were around me yet? 10
For wheresoe'er I looked, the while,
Was Nature's everlasting smile.

Still came and lingered on my sight
Of flowers and streams the bloom and light,
And glory of the stars and sun;— 15
And these and poetry are one.
They, ere the world had held me long,
Recalled me to the love of song.

over to it

Forest Hymn

Outstanding

This poem, believed to have been written at Great
Barrington in 1825 shortly before Bryant left New
England for New York, was first printed in the

United States Literary Gazette for April 1, 1825, as
"A Hymn." In *Poems* (1832), the text here followed,
it was entitled "Forest Hymn."

The groves were God's first temples. Ere man
    learned
To hew the shaft, and lay the architrave,
And spread the roof above them,—ere he framed
The lofty vault, to gather and roll back
The sound of anthems; in the darkling wood, 5
Amidst the cool and silence, he knelt down
And offered to the Mightiest, solemn thanks
And supplication. For his simple heart
Might not resist the sacred influences,
Which, from the stilly twilight of the place, 10
And from the gray old trunks that high in heaven
Mingled their mossy boughs, and from the sound
Of the invisible breath that swayed at once
All their green tops, stole over him, and bowed
His spirit with the thought of boundless power 15
And inaccessible majesty. Ah, why
Should we, in the world's riper years, neglect
God's ancient sanctuaries, and adore
Only among the crowd, and under roofs
That our frail hands have raised. Let me, at least,
Here, in the shadow of this aged wood,   21
Offer one hymn—thrice happy, if it find
Acceptance in his ear.

                    Father, thy hand
Hath reared these venerable columns, thou
Didst weave this verdant roof. Thou didst look
    down   25
Upon the naked earth, and, forthwith, rose
All these fair ranks of trees. They, in thy sun,
Budded, and shook their green leaves in thy breeze,
And shot towards heaven. The century-living
    crow
Whose birth was in their tops, grew old and died 30
Among their branches, till, at last, they stood,
As now they stand, massive and tall and dark,
Fit shrine for humble worshipper to hold

    2. architrave: the entablature resting upon the capital
of a column in classical architecture. **16–19. Ah, why, etc.:**
A criticism in *Blackwood's Magazine* led Bryant to substitute the following verses for lines 16–19:

                          These dim vaults,
    These winding aisles, of human pomp or pride
    Report not.

Communion with his Maker. Here are seen
No traces of man's pomp or pride;—no silks   35
Rustle, nor jewels shine, nor envious eyes
Encounter; no fantastic carvings show
The boast of our vain race to change the form
Of thy fair works. But thou art here—thou fill'st
The solitude. Thou art in the soft winds   40
That run along the summit of these trees
In music;—thou art in the cooler breath,
That from the inmost darkness of the place,
Comes, scarcely felt;—the barky trunks, the
    ground,
The fresh moist ground, are all instinct with thee.
Here is continual worship;—nature, here,   46
In the tranquility that thou dost love,
Enjoys thy presence. Noiselessly, around,
From perch to perch, the solitary bird
Passes; and yon clear spring, that, 'midst its herbs,
Wells softly forth and visits the strong roots   51
Of half the mighty forest, tells no tale
Of all the good it does. Thou hast not left
Thyself without a witness, in these shades,
Of thy perfections. Grandeur, strength, and grace
Are here to speak of thee. This mighty oak—   56
By whose immoveable stem I stand and seem
Almost annihilated—not a prince,
In all that proud old world beyond the deep,
E'er wore his crown as loftily as he   60
Wears the green coronal of leaves with which
Thy hand has graced him. Nestled at his root
Is beauty, such as blooms not in the glare
Of the broad sun. That delicate forest flower,
With scented breath, and look so like a smile,   65
Seems, as it issues from the shapeless mould,
An emanation of the indwelling Life,
A visible token of the upholding Love,
That are the soul of this wide universe.

          My heart is awed within me, when I think   70
Of the great miracle that still goes on,
In silence, round me—the perpetual work
Of thy creation, finished, yet renewed
Forever. Written on thy works I read
The lesson of thy own eternity.   75
Lo! all grow old and die—but see, again,
How on the faltering footsteps of decay
Youth presses—ever gay and beautiful youth
In all its beautiful forms. These lofty trees

Wave not less proudly that their ancestors   80
Moulder beneath them. Oh, there is not lost
One of earth's charms: upon her bosom yet,
After the flight of untold centuries,
The freshness of her far beginning lies
And yet shall lie. Life mocks the idle hate   85
Of his arch enemy Death—yea—seats himself
Upon the sepulchre, and blooms and smiles,
And of the triumphs of his ghastly foe
Makes his own nourishment. For he came forth
From thine own bosom, and shall have no end.   90

There have been holy men who hid themselves
Deep in the woody wilderness, and gave
Their lives to thought and prayer, till they out-
     lived
The generation born with them, nor seemed
Less aged than the hoary trees and rocks   95
Around them;—and there have been holy men
Who deemed it were not well to pass life thus.
But let me often to these solitudes
Retire, and in thy presence reassure
My feeble virtue. Here its enemies,   100
The passions, at thy plainer footsteps shrink
And tremble and are still. Oh, God! when thou
Dost scare the world with tempests, set on fire
The heavens with falling thunderbolts, or fill,
With all the waters of the firmament,   105
The swift dark whirlwind that uproots the woods
And drowns the villages; when, at thy call,
Uprises the great deep and throws himself
Upon the continent and overwhelms
Its cities—who forgets not, at the sight   110
Of these tremendous tokens of thy power,
His pride, and lays his strifes and follies by?
Oh, from these sterner aspects of thy face
Spare me and mine, nor let us need the wrath
Of the mad unchained elements to teach   115
Who rules them. Be it ours to meditate
In these calm shades thy milder majesty,
And, to the beautiful order of thy works,
Learn to conform the order of our lives.

To a Mosquito

PUBLISHED in the *New York Review* for October, 1825, this poem was collected in the *Poems* of 1832, from which the present text is taken. Although Bryant is

sometimes charged with a lack of humor, this charge cannot survive a reading of "To a Mosquito" and "A Meditation on Rhode Island Coal."

Fair insect! that, with threadlike legs spread out,
     And blood-extracting bill and filmy wing,
Dost murmur, as thou slowly sail'st about,
     In pitiless ears full many a plaintive thing,
And tell how little our large veins should bleed, 5
Would we but yield them to thy bitter need.

Unwillingly, I own, and, what is worse,
     Full angrily men hearken to thy plaint,
Thou gettest many a brush, and many a curse,
     For saying thou art gaunt, and starved, and faint;
Even the old beggar, while he asks for food,   11
Would kill thee, hapless stranger, if he could.

I call thee stranger, for the town, I ween
     Has not the honor of so proud a birth,
Thou com'st from Jersey meadows, fresh and green,
     The offspring of the gods, though born on earth;
For Titan was thy sire, and fair was she   17
The ocean nymph that nursed thy infancy.

Beneath the rushes was thy cradle swung,
     And when, at length, thy gauzy wings grew
          strong,   20
Abroad to gentle airs their folds were flung,
     Rose in the sky and bore thee soft along;
The south wind breathed to waft thee on thy way
And danced and shone beneath the billowy bay.

And calm, afar, the city's spires arose,—   25
     Thence didst thou hear the distant hum of men,
And as its grateful odors met thy nose,
     Didst seem to smell thy native marsh again;
Fair lay its crowded streets, and at the sight
Thy tiny song grew shriller with delight.   30

At length thy pinions fluttered in Broadway—
     Ah, there were fairy steps, and white necks
          kissed
By wanton airs, and eyes whose killing ray
     Shone through the snowy veils like stars through
          mist;
And fresh as morn, on many a cheek and chin,   35
Bloomed the bright blood through the transparent
     skin.

434

Oh, these were sights to touch an anchorite!
    What! do I hear thy slender voice complain?
Thou wailest, when I talk of beauty's light,
    As if it brought the memory of pain: 40
Thou art a wayward being—well—come near,
And pour thy tale of sorrow in my ear.

What say'st thou—slanderer!—rouge makes thee
    sick?
    And China bloom at best is sorry food?
And Rowland's Kalydor, if laid on thick,   45
    Poisons the thirsty wretch that bores for blood?
Go! 'twas a just reward that met thy crime—
But shun the sacrilege another time.

That bloom was made to look at, not to touch,
    To worship, not approach, that radiant white:
And well might sudden vengeance light on such
    As dared like thee, most impiously, to bite;   52
Thou should'st have gazed at distance and admired,
Murmured thy adoration and retired.

Thou'rt welcome to the town—but why come here
    To bleed a brother poet, gaunt like thee,   56
Alas! the little blood I have is dear,
    And thin will be the banquet drawn from me.
Look round—the pale eyed sisters in my cell,   59
Thy old acquaintance, Song and Famine, dwell.

Try some plump alderman, and suck the blood
    Enriched by generous wine and costly meat;
On well-filled skins, sleek as thy native mud,
    Fix thy light pump and press thy freckled feet:
Go to the men for whom, in ocean's halls,   65
The oyster breeds, and the green turtle sprawls.

There corks are drawn, and the red vintage flows
    To fill the swelling veins for thee, and now
The ruddy cheek and now ruddier nose
    Shall tempt thee, as thou flittest round the brow;
And, when the hour of sleep its quiet brings,   71
No angry hand shall rise to brush thy wings.

The Prairies

Bryant crossed the Allegheny Mountains for the
first time in 1832 on a journey to visit his brothers'
plantation in Illinois. This poem, inspired by his first

45. Rowland's Kalydor: a cosmetic.

impression of the prairie country, appeared in the
Knickerbocker Magazine for December, 1833. A year
later it was included in the *Poems* (1834). The text
here used is that of Parke Godwin (ed.), *The Poetical
Works* (1883).

These are the gardens of the Desert, these
The unshorn fields, boundless and beautiful,
For which the speech of England has no name—
The Prairies. I behold them for the first,
And my heart swells, while the dilated sight   5
Takes in the encircling vastness. Lo! they stretch,
In airy undulations, far away,
As if the ocean, in his gentlest swell,
Stood still, with all his rounded billows fixed,
And motionless forever.—Motionless?—   10
No—they are all unchained again. The clouds
Sweep over with their shadows, and, beneath,
The surface rolls and fluctuates to the eye;
Dark hollows seem to glide along and chase
The sunny ridges. Breezes of the South!   15
Who toss the golden and the flame-like flowers,
And pass the prairie-hawk that, poised on high,
Flaps his broad wings, yet moves not—ye have
    played
Among the palms of Mexico and vines
Of Texas, and have crisped the limpid brooks   20
That from the mountains of Sonora glide
Into the calm Pacific—have ye fanned
A nobler or a lovelier scene than this?
Man hath no power in all this glorious work: 24
The hand that built the firmament hath heaved
And smoothed these verdant swells, and sown their
    slopes
With herbage, planted them with island groves,
And hedged them round with forests. Fitting floor
For this magnificent temple of the sky—
With flowers whose glory and whose multitude   30
Rival the constellations! The great heavens
Seem to stoop down upon the scene in love,—
A nearer vault, and of a tenderer blue,
Than that which bends above our eastern hills.

As o'er the verdant waste I guide my steed,   35
Among the high rank grass that sweeps his sides
The hollow beating of his footstep seems

3. no name: the word *prairie* was borrowed from the
French.   **21. Sonora:** a state in the northwest part of
Mexico.

A sacrilegious sound. I think of those
Upon whose rest he tramples. Are they here—
The dead of other days?—and did the dust   40
Of these fair solitudes once stir with life
And burn with passion? Let the mighty mounds
That overlook the rivers, or that rise
In the dim forest crowded with old oaks,
Answer. A race, that long has passed away,   45
Built them;—a disciplined and populous race
Heaped, with long toil, the earth, while yet the
     Greek
Was hewing the Pentelicus to forms
Of symmetry, and rearing on its rock
The glittering Parthenon. These ample fields   50
Nourished their harvests, here their herds were fed,
When haply by their stalls the bison lowed,
And bowed his manèd shoulder to the yoke.
All day this desert murmured with their toils,
Till twilight blushed, and lovers walked, and wooed
In a forgotten language, and old tunes,   56
From instruments of unremembered form,
Gave the soft winds a voice. The red man came—
The roaming hunter tribes, warlike and fierce,
And the mound-builders vanished from the earth.
The solitude of centuries untold   61
Has settled where they dwelt. The prairie-wolf
Hunts in their meadows, and his fresh-dug den
Yawns by my path. The gopher mines the ground
Where stood their swarming cities. All is gone;   65
All—save the piles of earth that hold their bones,
The platforms where they worshipped unknown
     gods,
The barriers which they builded from the soil
To keep the foe at bay—till o'er the walls
The wild beleaguerers broke, and, one by one,   70
The strongholds of the plain were forced, and
     heaped
With corpses. The brown vultures of the wood
Flocked to these vast uncovered sepulchres,
And sat unscared and silent at their feast.
Haply some solitary fugitive,   75
Lurking in the marsh and forest, till the sense

Of desolation and of fear became
Bitterer than death, yielded himself to die.
Man's better nature triumphed then. Kind words
Welcomed and soothed him; the rude conquerors
Seated the captive with their chiefs; he chose   81
A bride among the maidens, and at length
Seemed to forget—yet ne'er forgot—the wife
Of his first love, and her sweet little ones,
Butchered, amid their shrieks, with all his race.   85

   Thus change the forms of being. Thus arise
Races of living things, glorious in strength,
And perish, as the quickening breath of God
Fills them, or is withdrawn. The red man, too,
Has left the blooming wilds he ranged so long,   90
And, nearer to the Rocky Mountains, sought
A wilder hunting-ground. The beaver builds
No longer by these streams, but far away,
On waters whose blue surface ne'er gave back
The white man's face—among Missouri's springs,
And pools whose issues swell the Oregon—   96
He rears his little Venice. In these plains
The bison feeds no more. Twice twenty leagues
Beyond remotest smoke of hunter's camp,
Roams the majestic brute, in herds that shake   100
The earth with thundering steps—yet here I meet
His ancient footprints stamped beside the pool.

   Still this great solitude is quick with life.
Myriads of insects, gaudy as the flowers
They flutter over, gentle quadrupeds,   105
And birds, that scarce have learned the fear of man,
Are here, and sliding reptiles of the ground,
Startlingly beautiful. The graceful deer
Bounds to the wood at my approach. The bee,
A more adventurous colonist than man,   110
With whom he came across the eastern deep,
Fills the savannas with his murmurings,
And hides his sweets, as in the golden age,
Within the hollow oak. I listen long
To his domestic hum, and think I hear   115
The sound of that advancing multitude
Which soon shall fill these deserts. From the
     ground
Comes up the laugh of children, the soft voice
Of maidens, and the sweet and solemn hymn

   42. **mighty mounds:** Bryant noted that "The size and
extent of the mounds in the valley of the Mississippi indicate the existence, at a remote period, of a nation at once
populous and laborious. . . ." The poet mistook the Indian
mounds for the work of an ancient race of mound builders.

   48. **Pentelicus:** the quarries from which the marble was
taken for the Parthenon.

   96. **Oregon:** the Columbia River.   112. **savannas:**
treeless plains.

Of Sabbath worshippers. The low of herds   120
Blends with the rustling of the heavy grain
Over the dark brown furrows. All at once
A fresher wind sweeps by, and breaks my dream,
And I am in the wilderness alone.

last 2 lines I ask to present

To the Fringed Gentian

THIS POEM, written in 1829, appeared for the first   10
time in *Poems* (1832), the text here followed.

Thou blossom bright with autumn dew,
And colored with the heaven's own blue,
That openest, when the quiet light
Succeeds the keen and frosty night.

Thou comest not when violets lean   5
O'er wandering brooks and springs unseen,
Or columbines, in purple drest,
Nod o'er the ground bird's hidden nest.

Thou waitest late, and com'st alone,
When woods are bare and birds are flown,   10
And frosts and shortening days portend
The aged year is near its end.

Then doth thy sweet and quiet eye
Look through the fringes of the sky,
Blue—blue—as if that sky let fall   15
A flower from its cerulean wall.

I would that thus, when I shall see
The hour of death draw near to me,
Hope, blossoming within my heart,
May look to heaven as I depart.   20

Native Materials for American Fiction

ALTHOUGH BRYANT was far from being a chauvinist,
and warned that "writings are not to be applauded   40
merely because they are written by an American,"
he was confident that this country possessed the materials for the flowering of a rich and distinctive
imaginative literature. "If under these circumstances
our poetry should finally fail of rivalling that of
Europe," he told the Athenaeum Society in New
York in 1826, "it will be because Genius sits idle in
the midst of its treasures." Bryant was equally
sanguine with respect to the creation of American

novels. The following selection from a critical essay
on Catherine Sedgwick's *Redwood* (1824) was printed
in the *North American Review* for April, 1825. This
periodical had hailed the appearance of Cooper's
The Spy (1821), and Bryant shared its editors' hopes
for native fiction. The text is that of the first printing in the *North American Review*, XX (1825), 248 ff.

. . . On more than one occasion, we have already
given somewhat at large our opinion of the fertility
of our country, and its history, in the materials of   10
romance. If our reasonings needed any support
from successful examples of that kind of writing,
as a single fact is worth a volume of ingenious
theorising, we have had the triumph of seeing
them confirmed beyond all controversy, by the
works of a popular American author, who has
shown the literary world into what beautiful crea-
tions those materials may be wrought. In like
manner, we look upon the specimen before us as a
conclusive argument, that the writers of works of   20
fiction, of which the scene is laid in familiar and
domestic life, have a rich and varied field before
them in the United States. Indeed, the opinion
on this subject, which, till lately, prevailed pretty
extensively among us, that works of this kind,
descriptive of the manners of our countrymen,
could not succeed, never seemed to us to rest on a
very solid foundation. It was rather a sweeping
inference drawn from the fact, that no highly
meritorious work of the kind had appeared, and   30
the most satisfactory and comfortable way of accounting for this, was to assert, that no such
could be written. But it is not always safe to predict what a writer of genius will make of a given
subject. Twenty years ago, what possible conception could an English critic have had of the
admirable productions of Waverley, and of the
wonderful improvement his example has effected
in that kind of composition? Had the idea of one
of those captivating works, destined to take such   40
strong hold on all minds, been laid before him by
the future author, he would probably only have
wondered at his vanity.

There is nothing paradoxical in the opinion,
which maintains that all civilised countries, we
had almost said all countries whatever, furnish
matter for copies of real life, embodied in works of
fiction, which shall be of lasting and general in-

437

terest. Wherever there are human nature and society, there are subjects for the novelist. The passions and affections, virtue and vice, are of no country. Everywhere love comes to touch the hearts of the young, and everywhere scorn and jealousy, the obstacles of fortune and the prudence of the aged, are at hand to disturb the course of love. Everywhere there exists the desire of wealth, the love of power, and the wish to be admired, courage braving real dangers, and cowardice shrink-ing from imaginary ones, friendship and hatred, and all the train of motives and impulses, which affect the minds and influence the conduct of men. They not only exist everywhere, but they exist infinitely diversified and compounded, in various degrees of suppression and restraint, or fostered into unnatural growth and activity, modified by political institutions and laws, by national religions and subdivisions of those religions, by different degrees of refinement and civilisation, of poverty or of abundance, by arbitrary usages handed down from indefinite antiquity, and even by local situa-tion and climate. Nor is there a single one of all these innumerable modifications of human char-acter and human emotion which is not, in some degree, an object of curiosity and interest. Over all the world is human sagacity laying its plans, and chance and the malice of others are thwarting them, and fortune is raising up one man and throw-ing down another. In none of the places of human habitation are the accesses barred against joy or grief; the kindness of the good carries gladness into families, and the treachery of the false friend brings sorrow and ruin; in all countries are tears shed over the graves of the excellent, the brave, and the beautiful, and the oppressed breathe freer when the oppressor has gone to his account. Every-where has nature her features of grandeur and beauty, and these features receive a moral expres-sion from the remembrances of the past, and the interests of the present. On her face, as on an immense theatre, the passions and pursuits of men are performing the great drama of human exist-ence. At every moment, and in every corner of the world, these mighty and relentless agents are per-petually busy, under an infinity of forms and dis-guises, and the great representation goes on with that majestic continuity and uninterrupted regu-

larity, which mark all the courses of nature. Who then will undertake to say, that the hand of genius may not pencil off a few scenes, acted in our own vast country, and amidst our large population, that shall interest and delight the world?

It is a native writer only that must or can do this. It is he that must show how the infinite di-versities of human character are yet further varied, by causes that exist in our own country, exhibit our peculiar modes of thinking and action, and mark the effect of these upon individual fortunes and happiness. A foreigner is manifestly incompe-tent to the task; his observation would rest only upon the more general and obvious traits of our national character, a thousand delicate shades of manner would escape his notice, many interesting peculiarities would never come to his knowledge, and many more he would misapprehend. It is only on his native soil, that the author of such works can feel himself on safe and firm ground, that he can move confidently and fearlessly, and put forth the whole strength of his powers without risk of fail-ure. His delineations of character and action, if executed with ability, will have a raciness and fresh-ness about them, which will attest their fidelity, the secret charm, which belongs to truth and na-ture, and with which even the finest genius can-not invest a system of adscititious and imaginary manners. It is this quality, which recommends them powerfully to the sympathy and interest even of those, who are unacquainted with the original from which they are drawn, and make such pictures from such hands so delightful and captivating to the foreigner. By superadding, to the novelty of the manners described, the interest of a narrative, they create a sort of illusion, which places him in the midst of the country where the action of the piece is going on. He beholds the scenery of a distant land, hears its inhabitants conversing about their own concerns in their own dialect, finds himself in the bosom of its families, is made the depository of their secrets, and the observer of their fortunes, and becomes an inmate of their firesides without stirring from his own. Thus it is that American novels are eagerly read in Great Britain, and novels descriptive of English and Scottish manners as eagerly read in America.

It has been objected, that the habits of our

438

countrymen are too active and practical; that they are too universally and continually engrossed by the cares and occupations of business to have leisure for that intrigue, those plottings and counterplottings, which are necessary to give a sufficient degree of action and eventfulness to the novel of real life. It is said that we need for this purpose a class of men, whose condition in life places them above the necessity of active exertion, and who are driven to the practice of intrigue, because they have nothing else to do. It remains, however, to be proved that any considerable portion of this ingredient is necessary in the composition of a successful novel. To require that it should be made up of nothing better than the manœuvres of those, whose only employment is to glitter at places of public resort, to follow a perpetual round of amusements, and to form plans to outshine, thwart, and vex each other, is confining the writer to a narrow and most barren circle. It is requiring an undue proportion of heartlessness, selfishness, and vice in his pictures of society. It is compelling him to go out of the wholesome atmosphere of those classes, where the passions and affections have their most salutary and natural play, and employ his observations on that where they are the most perverted, sophisticated, and corrupt. But will it be seriously contended, that he can have no other resource but the rivalries and machinations of the idle, the frivolous, and the dissolute, to keep the reader from yawning over his pictures? Will it be urged that no striking and interesting incidents can come to pass without their miserable aid? If our country be not the country of intrigue, it is at least the country of enterprise; and nowhere are the great objects that worthily interest the passions, and call forth the exertions of men, pursued with more devotion and perseverance. The agency of chance too is not confined to the shores of Europe; our countrymen have not attained a sufficient degree of certainty in their calculations to exclude it from ours. It would really seem to us, that these two sources, along with that proportion of the blessed quality of intrigue, which even the least favorable view of our society will allow us, are abundantly fertile in interesting occurrences, for all the purposes of the novelist. Besides, it should be recollected, that it is not in any case the

dull diary of ordinary occupations, or amusements that forms the groundwork of his plot. On the contrary, it is some event, or at least a series of events, of unusual importance, standing out in strong relief from the rest of the biography of his principal characters, and to which the daily habits of their lives, whatever may be their rank or condition, are only a kind of accompaniment.

But the truth is, that the distinctions of rank, and the amusements of elegant idleness, are but the surface of society, and only so many splendid disguises put upon the reality of things. They are trappings which the writer of real genius, the anatomist of the human heart, strips away when he would exhibit his characters as they are, and engage our interest for them as beings of our own species. He reduces them to the same great level where distinctions of rank are nothing, and difference of character everything. It is here that James First, and Charles Second, and Louis Ninth, and Rob Roy, and Jeanie Deans, and Meg Merrilies are, by the author of the "Waverley Novels," made to meet. The monarch must come down from the dim elevation of his throne; he must lay aside the assumed and conventional manners of his station, and unbend and unbosom himself with his confidants, before that illustrious master will condescend to describe him. In the artificial sphere in which the great move, they are only puppets and pageants, but here they are men. A narrative, the scene of which is laid at the magnificent levees of princes, in the drawing-rooms of nobles, and the bright assemblies of fashion, may be a very pretty, showy sort of thing, and so may a story of the glittering dances and pranks of fairies. But we soon grow weary of all this, and ask for objects of sympathy and regard; for something, the recollection of which shall dwell on the heart, and to which it will love to recur; for something, in short, which is natural, the uneffaced traits of strength and weakness, of the tender and the comic, all which the pride of rank either removes from observation or obliterates.

If these things have any value, we hesitate not to say, that they are to be found abundantly in the characters of our countrymen, formed as they are under the influences of our free institutions, and shooting into a large and vigorous, though sometimes irregular, luxuriance. They exist most abundantly in our more ancient settlements, and amidst the more homogeneous races of our large population, where the causes that produce them have operated longest and with most activity. It is there that the human mind has learned best to enjoy our fortunate and equal institutions, and to profit by them. In the countries of Europe the laws chain men down to the condition in which they were born. This observation, of course, is not equally true of all those countries, but when they are brought into comparison with ours, it is in some degree applicable to them all. Men spring up and vegetate, and die, without thinking of passing from the sphere in which they find themselves, any more than the plants they cultivate think of removing from the places where they are rooted. It is the tendency of this rigid and melancholy destiny to contract and stint the intellectual faculties, to prevent the development of character, and to make the subjects of it timid, irresolute, and imbecile. With us, on the contrary, where the proudest honors in the state, and the highest deference in society, are set equally before all our citizens, a wholesome and quickening impulse is communicated to all parts of the social system. All are possessed with a spirit of ambition and a love of adventure, an intense competition calls forth and exalts the passions and faculties of men, their characters become strongly defined, their minds acquire a hardihood and an activity, which can be gained by no other discipline, and the community, throughout all its conditions, is full of bustle, and change, and action.

Whoever will take the pains to pursue this subject a little into its particulars, will be surprised at the infinite variety of forms of character, which spring up under the institutions of our country. Religion is admitted on all hands to be a mighty agent in moulding the human character; and, accordingly, with the perfect allowance and toleration of all religions, we see among us their innumerable and diverse influences upon the manners and temper of our people. Whatever may be his religious opinions, no one is restrained by fear of consequences from avowing them, but is left to nurse his peculiarities of doctrine into what importance he pleases. The Quaker is absolved from

submission to the laws in those particulars, which offend his conscience, the Moravian finds no barriers in the way of his work of proselytism and charity, the Roman Catholic is subjected to no penalty for pleasing himself with the magnificent ceremonial of his religion, and the Jew worships unmolested in his synagogue. In many parts of our country we see communities of that strange denomination, the Shakers, distinguished from their neighbors by a garb, a dialect, an architecture, a way of worship, of thinking, and of living, as different, as if they were in fact of a different origin, instead of being collected from the families around them. In other parts we see small neighborhoods of the Seventh Day Baptists, retaining the simplicity of manners and quaintness of language delivered down from their fathers. Here we find the austerities of puritanism preserved to this day, there the rites and doctrines of the Church of England are shown in their effect on the manners of the people, and yet in another part of the country springs up a new and numerous sect, who wash one another's feet, and profess to revive the primitive habits of the apostolic times.

It is in our country also, that these differences of character, which grow naturally out of geographical situation, are least tampered with and repressed by political regulations. The adventurous and roving natives of our seacoasts, and islands, are a different race of men from those who till the interior, and the hardy dwellers of our mountainous districts are not like the inhabitants of the rich plains, that skirt our mighty lakes and rivers. The manners of the northern states are said to be characterized by the keenness and importunity of their climate, and those of the southern to partake of the softness of theirs. In our cities you will see the polished manners of the European capitals, but pass into the more quiet and unvisited parts of the country, and you will find men whom you might take for the first planters of our colonies. The descendants of the Hollanders have not forgotten the traditions of their fathers, and the legends of Germany are still recited, and the ballads of Scotland still sung, in settlements whose inhabitants derive their origin from those countries. It is hardly possible that the rapid and continual growth and improvement of our country, a circumstance wonderfully exciting to the imagination and altogether unlike anything witnessed in other countries, should not have some influence in forming our national character. At all events, it is a most fertile source of incident. It does for us in a few short years, what, in Europe, is a work of centuries. The hardy and sagacious native of the eastern states, settles himself in the wilderness by the side of the emigrant from the British Isles; the pestilence of the marshes is [10] braved and overcome; the bear, and wolf, and catamount are chased from their haunts; and then you see cornfields, and roads, and towns springing up as if by enchantment. In the mean time pleasant Indian villages, situated on the skirts of their hunting grounds, with their beautiful green plats for dances and martial exercises, are taken into the bosom of our extending population, while new states are settled and cities founded far beyond them. Thus a great deal of history is crowded into [20] a brief space. Each little hamlet, in a few seasons, has more events and changes to tell of, than a European village can furnish in a course of ages.

But, if the writer of fictitious history does not find all the variety he wishes in the various kinds of our population, descended, in different parts of our country, from ancestors of different nations, and yet preserving innumerable and indubitable tokens of their origin, if the freedom with which every man is suffered to take his own way, in all [30] things not affecting the peace and good order of society, does not furnish him with a sufficient diversity of characters, employments, and modes of life, he has yet other resources. He may bring into his plots men, whose characters and manners were formed by the institutions and modes of society in the nations beyond the Atlantic, and he may describe them faithfully, as things which he has observed and studied. If he is not satisfied with indigenous virtue, he may take for the model [40] of his characters men of whom the old world is not worthy, and whom it has cast out of its bosom. If domestic villainy be not dark enough for his pictures, here are fugitives from the justice of Europe come to prowl in America. If the coxcombs of our own country are not sufficiently exquisite, affected, and absurd, here are plenty of silken fops from the capitals of foreign kingdoms. If he finds

himself in need of a class of men more stupid and degraded, than are to be found among the natives of the United States, here are crowds of the wretched peasantry of Great Britain and Germany, flying for refuge from intolerable suffering, in every vessel that comes to our shores. Hither also resort numbers of that order of men who, in foreign countries, are called the middling class, the most valuable part of the communities they leave, to enjoy a moderate affluence, where the abuses and exactions of a distempered system of government cannot reach them, to degrade them to the condition of peasantry. Our country is the asylum of the persecuted preachers of new religions, and the teachers of political doctrines, which Europe will not endure; a sanctuary for dethroned princes, and the consorts of slain emperors. When we consider all these innumerable differences of character, native and foreign, this infinite variety of pursuits and objects, this endless diversity of and change of fortunes, and behold them gathered and grouped into one vast assemblage in our own country, we shall feel little pride in the sagacity or the skill of that native author, who asks for a richer or wider field of observation. . . .

Editorials

As EDITOR of the *New York Evening Post* for half a century—from 1827 to 1878—Bryant was one of the most courageous and influential journalists in America. The two editorials printed below are typical examples of his liberalism. His defense of the right to strike, supporting the action of a group of tailors in New York, appeared June 13, 1836, and resulted in a partial boycott of the *Post* by irate businessmen. The action of a group of citizens of Cincinnati led to the editorial of August 8, 1836, defending freedom of speech. Texts are from files of the *Post*.

[*The Right to Strike*]

Sentence was passed on Saturday on the twenty "men who had determined not to work." The punishment selected, on due consideration, by the judge, was that officers appointed for the purpose should immediately demand from each of the delinquents a sum of money which was named in the sentence of the court. The amount demanded would not have fallen short of the savings of many years. Either the offenders had not parted with these savings, or their brother workmen raised the ransom money for them on the spot. The fine was paid over as required. All is now well; justice has been satisfied. But if the expenses of their families had anticipated the law, and left nothing in their hands, or if friends had not been ready to buy the freedom of their comrades, they would have been sent to prison, and there they would have staid, until their wives and children, besides earning their own bread, had saved enough to redeem the captives from their cells. Such has been their punishment. What was their offence? They had committed the crime of unanimously declining to go to work at the wages offered to them by their masters. They had said to one another, "Let us come out from the meanness and misery of our caste. Let us begin to do what every order more privileged and more honoured is doing every day. By the means which we believe to be the best let us raise ourselves and our families above the humbleness of our condition. We may be wrong, but we cannot help believing that we might do much if we were true brothers to each other, and would resolve not to sell the only thing which is our own, the cunning of our hands, for less than it is worth." What other things they may have done is nothing to the purpose: it was for this they were condemned; it is for this they are to endure the penalty of the law.

We call upon a candid and generous community to mark that the punishment inflicted upon these twenty "men who had determined not to work" is not directed against the offence of conspiring to prevent others by force from working at low wages, but expressly against the offence of settling by preconcert the compensation which they thought they were entitled to obtain. It is certainly superfluous to repeat, that this journal would be the very last to oppose a law levelled at any attempt to molest the labourer who chooses to work for less than the prices settled by the Union. We have said, and to cut off cavil, we say it now again, that a conspiracy to deter, by threats of violence, a fellow workman from arranging his own terms with his employers, is a conspiracy to commit a felony—a conspiracy which, being a crime against liberty, we should be the first to condemn—a

conspiracy which no strike should, for its own sake, countenance for a moment—a conspiracy already punishable by the statute, and far easier to reach than the one of which "the twenty" stood accused; but a conspiracy, we must add, that has not a single feature in common with the base and barbarous prohibition under which the offenders were indicted and condemned.

They were condemned because they had determined not to work for the wages that were offered them! Can any thing be imagined more abhorrent to every sentiment of generosity or justice, than the law which arms the rich with the legal right to fix, by assize, the wages of the poor? If this is not *slavery*, we have forgotten its definition. Strike the right of associating for the sale of labour from the privileges of a freeman, and you may as well at once bind him to a master, or ascribe him to the soil. If it be not in the colour of his skin, and in the poor franchise of naming his own terms in a contract for his work, what advantage has the labourer of the north over the bondman of the south? Punish by human laws a "determination not to work," make it penal by any other penalty than idleness inflicts, and it matters little whether the task-masters be one or many, an individual or an order, the hateful scheme of slavery will have gained a foothold in the land. And then the meanness of this law, which visits with its malice those who cling to it for protection, and shelters with all its fences those who are raised above its threats! A late solicitation for its aid against employers, is treated with derision and contempt, but the moment the "masters" invoked its intervention, it came down from its high place with most indecent haste, and has now discharged its fury upon the naked heads of wretches so forlorn, that their worst faults multiply their titles to a liberty which they must learn to win from livelier sensibilities than the barren benevolence of Wealth, or the tardy magnanimity of Power.

Since the above was written we have read the report of Judge Edwards's address on sentencing the journeymen. It will be found in another part of this paper. We see in this address an apparent disposition to mix up the question of combination which is a lawful act, with that of violence, which is allowed on all hands to be unlawful. We repeat—

that it was for the simple act of combining not to work under a certain rate of wages, and not for a disturbance of the peace, that the twenty journeymen were indicted, tried, convicted and punished. It was expressly so stated in Judge Edwards's charge to the jury which brought in the verdict of guilty; and whoever will look at the address made by him in pronouncing the sentence, will find that he still maintains and repeats, in various forms of expression, the doctrine that combinations to demand a fixed rate of wages are unlawful and punishable. This tyrannical doctrine we affirm to be a forced construction of the statute against conspiracies injurious to commerce—a construction which the makers of the law, we are sure, never contemplated. We are now told, however, that it will be insisted upon and enforced—let it be so—it is the very method by which either the courts of justice will be compelled to recede from their mistaken and arbitrary construction, or the legislature will interpose to declare that such is not the law. Carry it into effect impartially and without respect of persons, and there will not be people enough left without the penitentiaries to furnish subsistence to those who are confined within them.

"Self-created societies," says Judge Edwards, "are unknown to the constitution and laws, and will not be permitted to rear their crest and extend their baneful influence over any portion of the community." If there is any sense in this passage it means that self-created societies are unlawful, and must be put down by the courts. Down then with every literary, every religious, and every charitable association not incorporated! What nonsense is this! Self-created societies *are* known to the constitution and laws, for they are not prohibited, and the laws which allow them will, if justly administered, protect them. But suppose in charity that the reporter has put this absurdity into the mouth of Judge Edwards, and that he meant only those self-created societies which have an effect upon trade and commerce. Gather up then and sweep to the penitentiary all those who are confederated to carry on any business or trade in concert, by fixed rules, and see how many men you would leave at large in this city. The members of every partnership in the place will come under the penalties of the law, and not only these, but every person pursuing any occupation whatever, who governs himself by a mutual understanding with others that follow the same occupation. . . .

[*Abolitionist Press in Cincinnati*]

A meeting of the people of Cincinnati have proclaimed the right of silencing the expression of unpopular opinions by violence. We refer our readers to the proceedings of an anti-abolition meeting lately held in that city. They will be found in another part of this paper.

If the meeting had contented itself with declaring its disapprobation of the tenets of the abolitionists, we should have had nothing to say. They might have exhausted the resources of rhetorick and of language—they might have indulged in the very extravagance and wantonness of vehement condemnation, for aught we cared; they would still have been in the exercise of a right which the constitution and the laws secure to them. But when they go further, and declare that they have not only a right to condemn certain opinions in others, but the right to coerce those who hold them to silence, it is time to make an immediate and decided stand, and to meet the threat of coercion with defiance.

The Cincinnati meeting, in the concluding resolution offered by Wilson N. Brown, and adopted with the rest, declare in so many words that if they cannot put down the abolitionist press by fair means they will do it by foul; if they cannot silence it by remonstrance, they will silence it by violence; if they cannot persuade it to desist, they will stir up mobs against it, inflame them to madness, and turn their brutal rage against the dwellings, the property, the persons, the lives of the wretched abolitionists and their families. In announcing that they will put them down by force all this is included. Fire, robbery, bloodshed, are the common excesses of an enraged mob. There is no extreme of cruelty and destruction to which in the drunkenness and delirium of its fury it may not proceed. The commotions of the elements can as easily be appeased by appeals to the quality of mercy as these commotions of the human mind; the whirlwind and the lightning might as well be expected to pause and turn aside to spare the helpless and innocent, as an infuriated multitude.

443

If the abolitionists must be put down, and if the community are of that opinion, there is no necessity of violence to effect the object. The community may make a law declaring the discussion of slavery in a certain manner to be a crime, and imposing penalties. The law may then be put in force against the offenders, and their mouths may be gagged in due form, and with all the solemnities of justice.

What is the reason this is not done? The answer is ready. The community are for leaving the liberty of the press untrammelled—there is not a committee that can be raised in any of the state legislatures north of the Potomac who will report in favor of imposing penalties on those who declaim against slavery—there is not a legislature who would sanction such a report—and there is not a single free state the people of which would sustain a legislature in so doing. These are facts, and the advocates of mob law know them to be so.

Who then are the men that issue this invitation to silence the press by violence? Who but an insolent brawling minority, a few noisy fanatics who claim that their own opinions shall be the measure of freedom for the rest of the community, and who undertake to overawe a vast pacific majority by threats of wanton outrage and plunder? These men are for erecting an oligarchy of their own and riding rough shod over the people and the people's rights. They claim a right to repeal the laws established by the majority in favor of the freedom of the press. They make new laws of their own to which they require that the rest of the community shall submit, and in case of a refusal, they threaten to execute them by the ministry of a mob. There is no tyranny or oppression exercised in any part of the world more absolute or more frightful than that which they would establish.

So far as we are concerned we are determined that this despotism shall neither be submitted to nor encouraged. In whatever form it makes its appearance we shall raise our voice against it. We are resolved that the subject of slavery shall be as it ever has been, as free a subject of discussion and argument and declamation, as the difference between whiggism and democracy, or as the difference between the Arminians and the Calvinists. If the press chooses to be silent on the subject it shall be the silence of perfect free will, and not the silence of fear. We hold that this combination of the few to govern the many by the terror of illegal violence, is as wicked and indefensible as a conspiracy to rob on the highway. We hold it to be the duty of good citizens to protest against it whenever and wherever it shows itself, and to resist it if necessary to the death.

One piece of justice must be done to the South. Thousands there are of persons in that quarter of the country who disapprove, as heartily as any citizen of the North can do, the employment of violence against the presses or the preachers of the anti-slavery party. There are great numbers also, as we are well informed, who think that only harm could result from directing the penalties of the law against those who discuss the question of slavery. They are for leaving the mode of discussing this question solely to the calm and considerate good sense of the North, satisfied that the least show of a determination to abridge the liberty of speech in this matter is but throwing oil on the flames.

Discourse on the Life and Genius of Cooper

On February 25, 1852, five months after the death of Cooper, Bryant delivered this "Discourse" on the occasion of a "great public meeting" held in Metropolitan Hall, New York, Daniel Webster presiding, to raise money for a monument to Cooper. "A few hundred dollars were subscribed, and we thought we should have a monument, but there the matter ended. A few weeks since . . . the treasurer . . . paid over the money to the persons concerned in getting up the monument at Cooperstown" (Bryant to Richard Henry Dana, April 15, 1859, in Godwin, *A Biography*, II, 124). Bryant had met Cooper April 23, 1824, at a dinner party in New York, and the poet reported to his wife the next day that Cooper "engrossed the whole conversation, and seems a little giddy with the success his works have met with" (*ibid.*, I, 189). Thereafter the two men met each other on many occasions throughout Cooper's life, and though their temperaments were vastly different, they respected each other's opinions and craftsmanship. Bryant's "Discourse" was first published in *Memorial to James Fenimore Cooper*, 1852; it was reprinted by Godwin (ed.), *Prose Writings*, I, 1884, from which this text is taken.

. . . It happened to Cooper while he was abroad, as it not unfrequently happens to our countrymen, to hear the United States disadvantageously compared with Europe. He had himself been a close observer of things both here and in the old world, and was conscious of being able to refute the detractors of his country in regard to many points. He published in 1828, after he had been two years in Europe, a series of letters, entitled *Notions of the Americans, by a Travelling Bachelor*, in which he gave a favourable account of the working of our institutions, and vindicated his country from various flippant and ill-natured misrepresentations of foreigners. It is rather too measured in style, but is written from a mind full of the subject, and from a memory wonderfully stored with particulars. Although twenty-four years have elapsed since its publication, but little of the vindication has become obsolete.

Cooper loved his country and was proud of her history and her institutions, but it puzzles many that he should have appeared, at different times, as her eulogist and her censor. My friends, she is worthy both of praise and of blame, and Cooper was not the man to shrink from bestowing either at what seemed to him the proper time. He defended her from detractors abroad; he sought to save her from flatterers at home. I will not say that he was in as good-humor with his country when he wrote *Home as Found* as when he wrote his *Notions of the Americans*, but this I will say, that, whether he commended or censured, he did it in the sincerity of his heart, as a true American, and in the belief that it would do good. His *Notions of the Americans* were more likely to lessen than to increase his popularity in Europe, inasmuch as they were put forth without the slightest regard to European prejudices. . . .

In one of the controversies of that time, Cooper bore a distinguished part. The *Révue Britannique*, a periodical published in Paris, boldly affirmed the Government of the United States to be one of the most expensive in the world, and its people among the most heavily taxed of mankind. This assertion was supported with a certain show of proof, and the writer affected to have established the conclusion that a republic must necessarily be more expensive than a monarchy. The partisans of the court were

delighted with the reasoning of the article, and claimed a triumph over our ancient friend Lafayette, who, during forty years, had not ceased to hold up the government of the United States as the cheapest in the world. At the suggestion of Lafayette, Cooper replied to this attack upon his country, in a letter which was translated into French, and, together with another from General Bertrand, for many years a resident in America, was laid before the people of France.

These two letters provoked a shower of rejoinders, in which, according to Cooper, misstatements were mingled with scurrility. He commenced a series of letters on the question in dispute, which were published in the *National*, a daily sheet, and gave the first evidence of that extraordinary acuteness in controversy which was no less characteristic of his mind than the vigor of his imagination. The enemies of Lafayette pressed into service Mr. Leavitt Harris, of New Jersey, afterward our *chargé d'affaires* at the court of France, but Cooper replied to Mr. Harris, in the *National* of May 2, 1832, closing a discussion in which he had effectually silenced those who objected to our institutions on the score of economy. Of these letters, which would form an important chapter in political science, no entire copy, I have been told, is to be found in this country.

One of the consequences of earnest controversy is almost invariably personal ill-will. Cooper was told by one who held an official station under the French government, that the part he had taken in this dispute concerning taxation would neither be forgotten nor forgiven. The dislike he had incurred in that quarter was strengthened by his novel of *The Bravo*, published in the year 1831, while he was in the midst of his quarrel with the aristocratic party. In that work, of which he has himself justly said that it was thoroughly American in all that belonged to it, his object was to show how institutions, professedly created to prevent violence and wrong, become, when perverted from their natural destination, the instruments of injustice; and how, in every system which makes power the exclusive property of the strong, the weak are sure to be oppressed. The work is written with all the vigor and spirit of his best novels; the magnificent city of Venice, in which the scene of the story is laid, stands continually before the imagination; and from time to time the gorgeous ceremonies of the Venetian republic pass under our eyes, such as the marriage of the Doge with the Adriatic, and the contest of the gondolas for the prize of speed. The Bravo himself and several of the other characters are strongly conceived and distinguished, but the most remarkable of them all is the spirited and generous-hearted daughter of the jailer. . . .

Figaro, the wittiest of the French periodicals, and at that time on the liberal side, commended *The Bravo*; the journals on the side of the government censured it. *Figaro* afterward passed into the hands of the aristocratic party, and Cooper became the object of its attacks; he was not, however, a man to be driven from any purpose which he had formed, either by flattery or abuse, and both were tried with equal ill success. In 1832 he published his *Heidenmauer*, and in 1833 his *Headsman of Berne*, both with a political design similar to that of *The Bravo*, though neither of them takes the same high rank among his works.

In 1833, after a residence of seven years in different parts of Europe, but mostly in France, Cooper returned to his native country. The welcome which met him here was somewhat chilled by the effect of the attacks made upon him in France; and, remembering with what zeal, and at what sacrifice of the universal acceptance which his works would otherwise have met, he had maintained the cause of his country against the wits and orators of the court party in France, we cannot wonder that he should have felt this coldness as undeserved. He published, shortly after his arrival in this country, *A Letter to his Countrymen*, in which he complained of the censures cast upon him in the American newspapers, gave a history of the part he had taken in exposing the misstatements of the *Révue Britannique*, and warned his countrymen against the too common error of resorting, with a blind deference, to foreign authorities, often swayed by national or political prejudices, for our opinions of American authors. Going beyond this topic, he examined and reprehended the habit of applying to the interpretation of our own constitution maxims derived from the practice of other governments, particularly that of Great Britain. The importance of construing that instrument by its own principles he illustrated by considering several points in dispute between parties of the day, on which he gave very decided opinions.

The principal effect of this pamphlet, as it seemed to me, was to awaken in certain quarters a kind of resentment that a successful writer of fiction should presume to give lessons in politics. I meddle not here with the conclusions to which he arrived, though I must be allowed to say that they were stated and argued with great ability. In 1835 Cooper published *The Monikins*, a satirical work, partly with a political aim; and in the same year appeared *The American Democrat*, a view of the civil and social relations of the United States, discussing more gravely various topics touched upon in the former work, and pointing out in what respects he deemed the American people in their practice to have fallen short of the excellence of their institutions. . . .

In 1838 appeared *Homeward Bound* and *Home as Found*, two satirical novels, in which Cooper held up to ridicule a certain class of conductors of the newspaper press in America. These works had not the good fortune to become popular. Cooper did not, and, because he was too deeply in earnest, perhaps would not, infuse into his satirical works that gayety without which satire becomes wearisome. I believe, however, that if they had been written by any body else, they would have met with more favor; but the world knew that Cooper was able to give them something better, and would not be satisfied with any thing short of his best. Some childishly imagined that, because, in the two works I have just mentioned, a newspaper editor is introduced, in whose character almost every possible vice of his profession is made to find a place, Cooper intended an indiscriminate attack upon the whole body of writers for the newspaper press, forgetting that such a portraiture was a satire only on those to whom it bore a likeness. We have become less sensitive and more reasonable of late, and the monthly periodicals make sport for their readers of the follies and ignorance of the newspaper editors, without awakening the slightest resentment; but Cooper led the way in this sort of discipline, and I remember some in-

446

stances of towering indignation at his audacity expressed in the journals of that time. . . .

Scarce any thing in Cooper's life was so remarkable, or so strikingly illustrated his character, as his contest with the newspaper press. He engaged in it after provocations, many and long endured, and prosecuted it through years with great energy, perseverance, and practical dexterity, till he was left master of the field. In what I am about to say of it, I hope I shall not give offence to any one, as I shall speak without the slightest malevolence towards those with whom he waged this controversy. Over some of them, as over their renowned adversary, the grave has now closed. Yet where shall the truth be spoken, if not beside the grave?

I have already alluded to the principal causes which provoked the newspaper attacks upon Cooper. If he had never meddled with questions of government on either side of the Atlantic, and never satirized the newspaper press, I have little doubt that he would have been spared these attacks. I cannot, however, ascribe them all, or even the greater part of them, to personal malignity. One journal followed the example of another, with little reflection, I think, in most cases, till it became a sort of fashion, not merely to decry his works but to arraign his motives.

It is related that, in 1832, while he was at Paris, an article was shown him in an American newspaper, purporting to be a criticism on one of his works, but reflecting with much asperity on his personal character. "I care nothing," he is reported to have said, "for the criticism, but I am not indifferent to the slander. If these attacks on my character should be kept up five years after my return to America, I shall resort to the New York courts for protection." He gave the newspaper press of this state the full period of forbearance on which he had fixed, but, finding that forbearance seemed to encourage assault, he sought redress in the courts of law.

When these litigations were first begun, I recollect it seemed to me that Cooper had taken a step which would give him a great deal of trouble, and effect but little good. I said to myself—

"Alas! Leviathan is not so tamed!"

As he proceeded, however, I saw that he had understood the matter better than I. He put a hook into the nose of this huge monster, wallowing in his inky pool and bespattering the passers-by: he dragged him to the land and made him tractable. One suit followed another; one editor was sued, I think, half a dozen times; some of them found themselves under a second indictment before the first was tried. In vindicating himself to his readers against the charge of publishing one libel, the angry journalist often floundered into another. The occasions of these prosecutions seem to have been always carefully considered, for Cooper was almost uniformly successful in obtaining verdicts. In a letter of his, written in February, 1843, about five years, I think, from the commencement of the first prosecutions, he says: "I have beaten every man I have sued, who has not retracted his libels." . . .

In one of these suits, commenced against the late William L. Stone, of the *Commercial Advertiser*, and referred to the arbitration of three distinguished lawyers, he argued himself the question of the authenticity of his account of the battle of Lake Erie, which was the matter in dispute. I listened to his opening; it was clear, skillful, and persuasive, but his closing argument was said to be splendidly eloquent. "I have heard nothing like it," said a barrister to me, "since the days of Emmet."

Cooper behaved liberally towards his antagonists, so far as pecuniary damages were concerned, though some of them wholly escaped their payment by bankruptcy. After, I believe, about six years of litigation, the newspaper press gradually subsided into a pacific disposition towards its adversary, and the contest closed with the account of pecuniary profit and loss, so far as he was concerned, nearly balanced. The occasion of these suits was far from honorable to those who provoked them, but the result was, I had almost said, creditable to all parties; to him, as the courageous prosecutor, to the administration of justice in this country, and to the docility of the newspaper press, which he had disciplined into good manners. . . .

Of his failings I have said little; such as he had were obvious to all the world; they lay on the surface of his character; those who knew him least made the most account of them. With a character

447

so made up of positive qualities—a character so independent and uncompromising, and with a sensitiveness far more acute than he was willing to acknowledge, it is not surprising that occasions frequently arose to bring him sometimes into friendly collision, and sometimes into graver disagreements and misunderstandings with his fellow-men. For his infirmities, his friends found an ample counterpoise in the generous sincerity of his nature. He never thought of disguising his opinions, and he abhorred all disguise in others; he did not even deign to use that show of regard towards those of whom he did not think well, which the world tolerates, and almost demands. A manly expression of opinion, however different from his own, commanded his respect. Of his own works, he spoke with the same freedom as of the works of others; and never hesitated to express his judgment of a book for the reason that it was written by himself; yet he could bear with gentleness any dissent from the estimate he placed on his own writings. His character was like the bark of the cinnamon—a rough and astringent rind without, and an intense sweetness within. Those who penetrated below the surface found a genial temper, warm affections, and a heart with ample place for his friends, their pursuits, their good name, their welfare. They found him a philanthropist, though not precisely after the fashion of the day; a religious man, most devout where devotion is most apt to be a feeling rather than a custom, in the household circle; hospitable, and to the extent of his means, liberal-handed in acts of charity. They found also that, though in general he would as soon have thought of giving up an old friend as of giving up an opinion, he was not proof against testimony, and could part with a mistaken opinion as one parts with an old friend who has been proved faithless and unworthy. In short, Cooper was one of those who, to be loved, must be intimately known.

Of his literary character I have spoken largely in the narrative of his life, but there are yet one or two remarks which must be made to do it justice. In that way of writing in which he excelled, it seems to me that he united, in a pre-eminent degree, those qualities which enabled him to interest the largest number of readers. He wrote not for the fastidious, the over-refined, the morbidly delicate; for these find in his genius something too robust for their liking—something by which their sensibilities are too rudely shaken; but he wrote for mankind at large—for men and women in the ordinary healthful state of feeling—and in their admiration he found his reward. It is for this class that public libraries are obliged to provide themselves with an extraordinary number of copies of his works: the number in the Mercantile Library, in this city, I am told, is forty. Hence it is, that he has earned a fame wider, I think, than any author of modern times—wider, certainly, than any author of any age ever enjoyed in his lifetime. All his excellences are translatable—they pass readily into languages the least allied in their genius to that in which he wrote, and in them he touches the heart and kindles the imagination with the same power as in the original English.

Cooper was not wholly without humor; it is sometimes found lurking in the dialogue of Harvey Birch and of Leatherstocking; but it forms no considerable element in his works; and, if it did, it would have stood in the way of his universal popularity, since, of all qualities, it is the most difficult to transfuse into a foreign language. Nor did the effect he produced upon the reader depend on any grace of style which would escape a translator of ordinary skill. With his style, it is true, he took great pains, and in his earlier works, I am told, sometimes altered the proofs sent from the printer so largely that they might be said to be written over. Yet he attained no special felicity, variety, or compass of expression. His style, however, answered his purpose; it has defects, but it is manly and clear, and stamps on the mind of the reader the impression he desired to convey. I am not sure that some of the very defects of Cooper's novels do not add, by a certain force of contrast, to their power over the mind. He is long in getting at the interest of his narrative. The progress of the plot, at first, is like that of one of his own vessels of war, slowly, heavily, and even awkwardly working out of a harbor. We are impatient and weary, but when the vessel is once in the open sea, and feels the free breath of heaven in her full sheets, our delight and admiration are all the greater at the grace, the majesty, and power with which she

448

divides and bears down the waves, and pursues her course at will over the great waste of waters.

Such are the works so widely read and so universally admired in all the zones of the globe, and by men of every kindred and every tongue—works which have made of those who dwell in remote latitudes wanderers in our forests and observers of our manners, and have inspired them with an interest in our history. A gentleman who had returned from Europe just before the death of Cooper was asked what he found the people of the Continent doing. "They are all reading Cooper," he answered; "in the little kingdom of Holland, with its three millions of inhabitants, I looked into four different translations of Cooper in the language of the country." A traveler, who has seen much of the middle classes of Italy, lately said to me: "I found that all they knew of America, and that was not little, they had learned from Cooper's novels; from him they had learned the story of American liberty, and through him they had been introduced to our Washington; they had read his works till the shores of the Hudson, and the valleys of Westchester, and the banks of Otsego Lake, had become to them familiar ground." . . .

JOHN PENDLETON KENNEDY (1795-1870)

FRIEND AND admirer of Irving, with whom he has been too closely compared, John Pendleton Kennedy wrote of Maryland and the Carolinas in historical fiction, of plantation life in Virginia, and of the foibles of Jacksonian democracy. He gave closer attention to actual and typical events and persons than Irving was wont to do in his use of materials, and Kennedy's dialogue is closer to the spoken word. His first literary work, *The Red Book* (1818–1819) was to Baltimore what *Salmagundi* was to New York, and the model is apparent. Addisonian and Irvingesque, too, is Kennedy's *Swallow Barn; or, A Sojourn in the Old Dominion*, by "Mark Littleton" (1832, revised 1852), but with a difference in dialogue and idiom. The sunny descriptions of life on a Virginia plantation during the first quarter of the nineteenth century, the gaiety and companionableness of the characters illuminated by Kennedy's wit and kindly satire, and the twin threads of litigation and love which relate the forty-nine sketches, unite to place this book without peer as a local picture of its time and place. But Kennedy as "Littleton" forsook Irving in *Horse-Shoe Robinson; a Tale of the Tory Ascendancy* (1832, revised 1852), a novel of the Revolution in Virginia and the Carolinas featuring the Battle of King's Mountain. Among war novels it ranks with Cooper's *The Spy*, Simms's *The Partisan*, and S. Weir Mitchell's *Hugh Wynne, Free Quaker*. The background and action are treated with considerable regard for fact. The novel takes its name from Galbraith (alias Horse-Shoe) Robinson, a soldier in the war, whom Kennedy met one evening in 1819. *Rob of the Bowl: A Legend of St. Inigoes* is a distinctive Cavalier romance of the Protestant attempt in 1681 to overthrow Catholic Lord Baltimore. In approaching the story Kennedy wrote that he felt "a prompt sensibility to the fame of her Catholic founders, and though differing from them in his faith, cherishes a remembrance of their noble endeavors to establish religious freedom." In his last adventure in fiction, *Quodlibet* (1842), he challenged Jacksonian policies and pretensions with keen satire and humorous raillery.

Kennedy was born in Baltimore in 1795, the son of a prosperous Scotch merchant who had migrated from north Ireland and married into an English family in Virginia. He was graduated from Baltimore College in 1812, and, after light participation in the war, he studied law and entered into practice in 1816. The law was somewhat unsuited to Kennedy's genial nature and broad interests, and after he inherited a legacy from an uncle, he practiced as little as friends and associates would allow. In 1829 he married Elizabeth Gray, daughter of a wealthy cotton-mill owner of Baltimore. Kennedy's ample means, tolerance, and friendliness, and his interest in literature, education, and politics placed him among the first citizens of his city. He fostered the literary proclivities of those about him, and was one of the three judges who awarded Poe first prize for the "Ms. Found in a Bottle." He served as provost of the University of Maryland, president of the Board of Trustees of the Baltimore and Ohio Railway, and member of the Board of Trustees of Peabody Institute. Commercial connections expanded his sphere of acquaintanceship to Philadelphia, New York, Saratoga, and Newport. He grew nationally minded. In 1838, the year of *Rob of the Bowl*, he was elected to the national Congress to fill a vacancy; he failed of re-election at the close of the year, but was re-elected in 1840 and 1842. As a

449

Southern Whig he supported John Quincy Adams and opposed Jackson. In 1852, as Secretary of the Navy under Fillmore, he organized Matthew Perry's expedition to Japan. He opposed Secession, and at the close of the war voted for Grant. Interest in history, travel, politics, and public affairs led to his writing the *Memoirs of the Life of William Wirt* (1842), *The Border States* (1861), *Mr. Ambrose's Letters on the Rebellion* (1865), and the three volumes which appeared posthumously, *Political and Official Papers* (1872), *Occasional Addresses* (1872), and *At Home and Abroad: A Series of Essays: With a Journal in Europe in 1867–68* (1872). He died in Newport, Rhode Island, in 1870.

BIBLIOGRAPHY · During 1871–1872 *The Collected Works of John Pendleton Kennedy* were published in 10 volumes, the tenth being H. T. Tuckerman, *The Life of John Pendleton Kennedy*. There are excellent editions of *Swallow Barn* by J. B. Hubbell (1929) and of *Horse-Shoe Robinson* by E. E. Leisy (1937). In 1931 appeared E. M. Gwathmey, *John Pendleton Kennedy*. Articles include J. R. Moore, "Kennedy's *Horse-Shoe Robinson*: Fact or Fiction?" *American Literature*, IV (1932), 160–166, and J. E. Uhler, "Kennedy's Novels and His Posthumous Works," *American Literature*, III (1932), 471–479.

Swallow Barn

I, 2. *A Country Gentleman*

KENNEDY'S Meriwether may interestingly be compared with Irving's "The Village Politician" and "The Stout Gentleman" of *Bracebridge Hall*. Tuckerman, in his *Life of John Pendleton Kennedy*, pointed to Philip Pendleton, Kennedy's uncle, as the probable original of Frank Meriwether. The text is that of 1832.

The master of this lordly domain is Frank Meriwether. He is now in the meridian of life— somewhere about forty-five. Good cheer and an easy temper tell well upon him. The first has given him a comfortable, portly figure, and the latter a contemplative turn of mind, which inclines him to be lazy and philosophical.

He has some right to pride himself on his personal appearance, for he has a handsome face, with a dark blue eye and a fine intellectual brow. His head is growing scant of hair on the crown, which induces him to be somewhat particular in the management of his locks in that locality, and these are assuming a decided silvery hue.

It is pleasant to see him when he is going to ride to the Court House on business occasions. He is then apt to make his appearance in a coat of blue broadcloth, astonishingly glossy, and with an unusual amount of plaited ruffle strutting through the folds of a Marseilles waistcoat. A worshipful finish is given to this costume by a large straw hat, lined with green silk. There is a magisterial fulness in his garments which betokens condition in the world, and a heavy bunch of seals, suspended by a chain of gold, jingles as he moves, pronouncing him a man of superfluities.

It is considered rather extraordinary that he has never set up for Congress: but the truth is, he is an unambitious man, and has a great dislike to currying favor—as he calls it. And, besides, he is thoroughly convinced that there will always be men enough in Virginia willing to serve the people, and therefore does not see why he should trouble his head about it. Some years ago, however, there was really an impression that he meant to come out. By some sudden whim, he took it into his head to visit Washington during the session of Congress, and returned, after a fortnight, very seriously distempered with politics. He told curious anecdotes of certain secret intrigues which had been discovered in the affairs of the capital, gave a clear insight into the views of some deep-laid combinations, and became, all at once, painfully florid in his discourse, and dogmatical to a degree that made his wife stare. Fortunately, this orgasm soon subsided, and Frank relapsed into an indolent gentleman of the opposition; but it had the effect to give a much more decided cast to his studies, for he forthwith discarded the "Richmond Whig" from his newspaper subscription, and took to "The Enquirer," like a man who was not to be disturbed by doubts. And as it was morally impossible to believe all that was written on both sides, to prevent his mind from being abused, he from this time forward took a stand against the re-election of Mr. Adams to the Presidency, and resolved to give an implicit faith to all alleged facts which set against his administration. The consequence of this straightforward and confiding deportment was an unexpected complimentary notice of him by the Executive of the State. He was put into the commission of the peace, and having thus become a public man against his will,

450

his opinions were observed to undergo some essential changes. He now thinks that a good citizen ought neither to solicit nor decline office; that the magistracy of Virginia is the sturdiest pillar which supports the fabric of the Constitution; and that the people, "though in their opinions they may be mistaken, in their sentiments they are never wrong";—with some such other dogmas as, a few years ago, he did not hold in very good repute. In this temper, he has of late embarked on the millpond of county affairs, and notwithstanding his amiable character and his doctrinary republicanism, I am told he keeps the peace as if he commanded a garrison, and administers justice like a Cadi.

He has some claim to supremacy in this last department; for during three years he smoked segars in a lawyer's office in Richmond, which enabled him to obtain a bird's-eye view of Blackstone and the Revised Code. Besides this, he was a member of a Law Debating Society, which ate oysters once a week in a cellar; and he wore, in accordance with the usage of the most promising law students of that day, six cravats, one over the other, and yellow-topped boots, by which he was recognized as a blood of the metropolis. Having in this way qualified himself to assert and maintain his rights, he came to his estate, upon his arrival at age, a very model of landed gentlemen. Since that time his avocations have had a certain literary tincture; for having settled himself down as a married man, and got rid of his superfluous foppery, he rambled with wonderful assiduity through a wilderness of romances, poems, and dissertations, which are now collected in his library, and, with their battered blue covers, present a lively type of an army of continentals at the close of the war, or a hospital of invalids. These have all, at last, given way to the newspapers—a miscellaneous study very attractive and engrossing to country gentlemen. This line of study has rendered Meriwether a most perilous antagonist in the matter of legislative proceedings.

A landed proprietor, with a good house and a host of servants, is naturally a hospitable man. A guest is one of his daily wants. A friendly face is a necessary of life, without which the heart is apt to starve, or a luxury without which it grows parsimonious. Men who are isolated from society by distance, feel these wants by an instinct, and are grateful for the opportunity to relieve them. In Meriwether, the sentiment goes beyond this. It has, besides, something dialectic in it. His house is open to everybody, as freely almost as an inn. But to see him when he has had the good fortune to pick up an intelligent, educated gentleman,—and particularly one who listens well!—a respectable, assentatious stranger!—All the better if he has been in the Legislature, or better still, if in Congress. Such a person caught within the purlieus of Swallow Barn, may set down one week's entertainment as certain—inevitable, and as many more as he likes—the more the merrier. He will know something of the quality of Meriwether's rhetoric before he is gone.

Then again, it is very pleasant to see Frank's kind and considerate bearing towards his servants and dependents. His slaves appreciate this, and hold him in most affectionate reverence, and, therefore, are not only contented, but happy under his dominion.

Meriwether is not much of a traveller. He has never been in New England, and very seldom beyond the confines of Virginia. He makes now and then a winter excursion to Richmond, which, I rather think, he considers as the centre of civilization; and towards autumn, it is his custom to journey over the mountain to the Springs, which he is obliged to do to avoid the unhealthy season in the tide-water region. But the upper country is not much to his taste, and would not be endured by him if it were not for the crowds that resort there for the same reason which operates upon him; and I may add,—though he would not confess it—for the opportunity this concourse affords him for discussion of opinions.

He thinks lightly of the mercantile interest, and, in fact, undervalues the manners of the large cities generally. He believes that those who live in them are hollow-hearted and insincere, and wanting in that substantial intelligence and virtue, which he affirms to be characteristic of the country. He is an ardent admirer of the genius of Virginia, and is frequent in his commendation of a toast in which the state is compared to the mother of the Gracchi:—indeed, it is a familiar thing with him to speak of the aristocracy of talent as

451

only inferior to that of the landed interest,—the idea of a freeholder inferring to his mind a certain constitutional pre-eminence in all the virtues of citizenship, as a matter of course.

The solitary elevation of a country gentleman, well to do in the world, begets some magnificent notions. He becomes as infallible as the Pope; gradually acquires a habit of making long speeches; is apt to be impatient of contradiction, and is always very touchy on the point of honor. There is nothing more conclusive than a rich man's logic anywhere, but in the country, amongst his dependents, it flows with the smooth and unresisted course of a full stream irrigating a meadow, and depositing its mud in fertilizing luxuriance. Meriwether's sayings, about Swallow Barn, import absolute verity. But I have discovered that they are not so current out of his jurisdiction. Indeed, every now and then, we have quite obstinate discussions when some of the neighboring potentates, who stand in the same sphere with Frank, come to the house; for these worthies have opinions of their own, and nothing can be more dogged than the conflict between them. They sometimes fire away at each other with a most amiable and unconvincible hardihood for a whole evening, bandying interjections, and making bows, and saying shrewd things with all the courtesy imaginable. But for unextinguishable pertinacity in argument, and utter impregnability of belief, there is no disputant like your country-gentleman who reads the newspapers. When one of these discussions fairly gets under weigh, it never comes to an anchor again of its own accord;—it is either blown out so far to sea as to be given up for lost, or puts into port in distress for want of documents, —or is upset by a call for the bootjack and slippers—which is something like the previous question in Congress.

If my worthy cousin be somewhat over-argumentative as a politician, he restores the equilibrium of his character by a considerate coolness in religious matters. He piques himself upon being a high-churchman, but is not the most diligent frequenter of places of worship, and very seldom permits himself to get into a dispute upon points of faith. If Mr. Chub, the Presbyterian tutor in the family, ever succeeds in drawing him

into this field, as he occasionally has the address to do, Meriwether is sure to fly the course; he gets puzzled with scripture names, and makes some odd mistakes between Peter and Paul, and then generally turns the parson over to his wife, who, he says, has an astonishing memory.

He is somewhat distinguished as a breeder of blooded horses; and, ever since the celebrated race between Eclipse and Henry, has taken to this occupation with a renewed zeal, as a matter affecting the reputation of the state. It is delightful to hear him expatiate upon the value, importance, and patriotic bearing of this employment, and to listen to all his technical lore touching the mystery of horse-craft. He has some fine colts in training, which are committed to the care of a pragmatical old Negro, named Carey, who, in his reverence for the occupation, is the perfect shadow of his master. He and Frank hold grave and momentous consultations upon the affairs of the stable, in such a sagacious strain of equal debate, that it would puzzle a spectator to tell which was the leading member in the council. Carey thinks he knows a great deal more upon the subject than his master, and their frequent intercourse has begot a familiarity in the old Negro which is almost fatal to Meriwether's supremacy. The old man feels himself authorized to maintain his positions according to the freest parliamentary form, and sometimes with a violence of asseveration that compels his master to abandon his ground, purely out of faint-heartedness. Meriwether gets a little nettled by Carey's doggedness, but generally turns it off in a laugh. I was in the stable with him, a few mornings after my arrival, when he ventured to expostulate with the venerable groom upon a professional point, but the controversy terminated in its customary way. "Who sot you up, Master Frank, to tell me how to fodder that 'ere cretur, when I as good as nursed you on my knee?"

"Well, tie up your tongue, you old mastiff," replied Frank, as he walked out of the stable, "and cease growling, since you will have it your own way,"—and then, as we left the old man's presence, he added, with an affectionate chuckle—"a faithful old cur, too, that snaps at me out of pure honesty; he has not many years left, and it does no harm to humor him!"

452

II, 2. *Mike Brown*

STORIES OF encounters with the Devil have been common to literature through the ages, offering adventure, fantasy, and moral admonition. The basic plots, of course, are given local settings by the authors. In *Swallow Barn*, Ned Hazard and the author meet Hafen Blok by accident in the Goblin Swamp. Hafen came to this country as a Hessian soldier, and is now a ne'er-do-well living by trapping and by poaching on nearby farmyards. He condones his thievery by imagining himself ill-treated by the farmers, and he practices the principle that "Pick-up law is the cheapest law for a poor man." The author invites Hafen to Swallow Barn, where the Hessian relates the story of Mike Brown. It appears in the second chapter of the second volume of *Swallow Barn*. The following excerpt is from the edition of 1832, and carries Brown through his first encounter with the Devil.

Mike Brown was a blacksmith, who belonged to Harry Lee's light-horse, and shod almost all the 20 hoofs of the legion. He was a jolly, boisterous, red-faced fellow, with sandy hair, and light blue eyes so exceedingly blood-shot, that at a little distance off you could hardly tell that they were eyes at all. He had no leisure, during the Revolutionary War, to get them clarified; for what with the smoke of his furnace, and keeping late hours on patroles, and hard drinking, his time was filled to the entire disparagement of his complexion. He was a stark trooper, to whom no service came 30 amiss, whether at the anvil or in the field, having a decisive muscle for the management of a piece of hot iron, and an especial knack for a marauding bout; in which latter species of employment it was his luck to hold frequent velitations with the enemy, whereby he became notorious for picking up stragglers, cutting off baggage-wagons, and rifling rum-casks, and now and then, for easing a prisoner of his valuables. He could handle a broadsword as naturally as a sledge-hammer; and many 40 a time has Mike brandished his blade above his beaver, and made it glitter in the sun, with a true dragon flourish, whilst he gave the huzza to his companions as he headed an onset upon Tarleton's cavalry. . . .

Towards the close of the war, he served with Colonel Washington, and was promoted to the rank of sergeant for leading a party of the enemy into ambuscade: and, in addition to this honor, the colonel made him a present of a full suit of regimentals, in which, they say, Mike was a proper-looking fellow. His black leather cap, with a strip of bearskin over it, and a white buck-tail set on one side, gave a martial fierceness to his red flannel face. A shad-bellied blue bobtail coat, turned up with broad buff, and meeting at the pit of his stomach with a hook and eye, was well adapted to 10 show the breadth of his brawny chest, which was usually uncovered enough to reveal the shaggy mat of red hair that grew upon it. A buckskin belt, fastened round his waist with an immense brass buckle, sustained a sabre that rattled upon the ground when he walked. His yellow leather breeches were remarkable for the air of ostentatious foppery that they imparted to the vast hemisphere of his nether bulk; and, taken together with his ample horseman's boots, gave the richest 20 effect to his short and thick legs, that, thus appareled, might be said to be gorgeous specimens of the Egyptian column.

Such was the equipment of Sergeant Brown on all festival occasions; and he was said to be not a little proud of this reward of valor. On work days he exhibited an old pair of glazed, brown buckskin small-clothes, coarse woolen stockings, covered with spatterdashes made of untanned deer hide, and shoes garnished with immense 30 pewter buckles; though, as to the stockings, he did not always wear them. Hose or no hose, it was all the same to Mike! I am minute in mentioning the regimentals, because, for a long time after the war, Sergeant Mike was accustomed to indue himself in this identical suit on Sundays, and strut about with an air of a commander-in-chief.

Mike's skill in horseshoes rendered him very serviceable in the campaigns. On a damp morning, or over sandy roads, he could trail Tarleton like a hound. It was only for Mike to examine the prints upon the ground, and he could tell, with astonishing precision, whether the horses that had passed were of his own shoeing, how many were in company, how long they had gone by, and whether at a gallop, a trot, or a walk; whether they had halted, or had been driving cattle, and, in fact, almost as many particulars as might be read in a bulletin. Upon such occasions, when appearances were favorable, he had only to get a few of his dare-devils together, and Tarleton was sure to have some of Sergeant Brown's sauce in his pottage, before he had time to say grace over it.

Mike used always to commence these adventures by drinking the devil's health, as he called it; which was done, very devoutly, in a cup of rum seasoned with a cartridge of gun-powder, which, he said, was a charm against sword cuts and pistol shot. When his expedition was ended, he generally called his roll, marked down the names of the killed, wounded and missing by the scratch of his black thumb-nail, and then returned the dingy scroll into his pocket, with a knowing leer at the survivors, and the pithy apothegm, which he repeated with a sincere faith, "that the devil was good to his own." This familiarity with the "old gentleman," as Mike himself termed him, added to his trooper-like accomplishment of swearing till he made people's hair stand on end, begat a common belief in the corps that he was on very significant terms with his patron; and it was currently said, "that Mike Brown and the devil would one day be wearing each other's shirts."

When the war was over, the sergeant found himself a disbanded hero, in possession of more liberty than he knew what to do with; a sledge and shoeing hammer; an old pair of bellows; a cabinet of worn-out horseshoes; a leather apron; his Sunday regimentals in tolerable repair; and a raw-boned steed, somewhat spavined by service:—to say nothing of a light heart, and an arm as full of sinew as an ox's leg. Considering all which things, he concluded himself to be a well furnished and thriving person, and began to cast about him in what way he should best enjoy his laurels, and the ease the gods had made for him.

In his frequent ruminations over this momentous subject, he fell into some shrewd calculations upon the emolument and comfort which were likely to accrue from a judicious matrimonial partnership. There was at that time a thrifty, driving spinster, bearing the name of Mistress Ruth Saunders, who lived at the landing near Swallow Barn. This dame was now somewhat in the wane, and, together with her mother, occupied a little patch of ground on the river, upon which was erected a small one-storied frame house, the very tenement now in possession of Sandy Walker. Here her sire had, in his lifetime, kept a drinking tavern for the accommodation of the watermen who frequented the landing. The widow did not choose to relinquish a lucrative trade, and therefore kept up the house; whilst the principal cares of the hostelry fell upon the indefatigable and energetic Mistress Ruth, who, from all accounts, was signally endowed with the necessary qualifications which gave lustre to her calling.

Mike, being a free and easy, swaggering, sociable chap, and endowed with a remarkable instinct in finding out where the best liquors were to be had on the cheapest terms, had fallen insensibly into the habit of consorting with a certain set of idle, muddy-brained loiterers that made the widow Saunders' house their headquarters on Sunday afternoons, and as often on week days as they could find an excuse for getting together. And such had been Mike's habits of free entertainment in the army, that he acquired some celebrity for serving his comrades in the same manner that he had been used to treat the old Continental Congress; that is, he left them pretty generally to pay his scot.

By degrees, he began to be sensible to the slow invasion of the tender passion, which stole across his ferruginous bosom like a volume of dun smoke through a smithy. He hung about the bar-room with the languishing interest of a lover, and took upon himself sundry minute cares of the household, that excused some increase of familiarity. He laughed very loud whenever Mistress Ruth affected to be witty; and pounced, with his huge ponderous paws, upon the glasses, pitchers, or other implements that the lady fixed her eye upon, as needful in the occasions of her calling: not a little to the peril of the said articles of furniture:—for Mike's clutch was none of the gentlest, in his softest moods. In short, his assiduities soon made him master of the worshipful Mistress Ruth, her purse and person. She had seen the devil, according to the common computation, three times, and had been so much alarmed at his last visit that—the story goes—she swore an oath that she would marry his cousin-german, rather than be importuned by his further attentions. There is no knowing what a woman will do under such circumstances! I believe myself, that Mistress Ruth chose Sergeant Mike principally on account of his well known dare-devil qualities.

The dame whose worldly accomplishments and personal charms had dissolved the case-hardened heart of the redoubted blacksmith of the legion, was altogether worthy of her lord. A succession of agues had spun her out into a thread of some six feet long. A tide-water atmosphere had given her an ashen, dough face, sprinkled over with constella- 10 tions of freckles, and exhibiting features somewhat tart from daily crosses. Her thin, bluish lips had something of the bitterness of the crab, with the astringency of the persimmon. Her hair, which was jet-black, was plastered across her brow with the aid of a little tallow, in such a manner as to give it a rigid smoothness, that pretty accurately typified her temper on holiday occasions, and also aided, by its sleekness, in heightening the im- pression of a figure attenuated to the greatest 20 length consistent with the preservation of the bodily functions. A pair of glassy dark eyes, of which one looked rather obliquely out of its line, glared upon the world with a habitual dissatisfac- tion; and in short, take her for all and all, Mistress Ruth Saunders was a woman of a commanding temper, severe devotion to business, acute cir- cumspection, and paramount attraction for Mike Brown.

After the solemnization of the nuptials, Mike 30 took a lease of Mr. Tracy of the small tract of land bordering on the Goblin Swamp, which even at that day, was a very suspicious region, and the scene of many marvelous adventures. Of all places in the country, it seemed to have the greatest charm for Mike. He accordingly set up his habita- tion by the side of the old county road, that crossed the marsh by the causeway; and here he also opened his shop. Mistress Mike Brown resumed her former occupation, and sold spirits; whilst her 40 husband devoted his time to the pursuits of ag- riculture, the working of iron, and the uproarious delights of the bottle: whereto the managing Ruth also attached herself, and was sometimes as up- roarious as the sergeant.

In process of time they were surrounded by four or five imps, of either sex, whose red hair, squinting eyes, and gaunt and squat figures, showed

their legitimate descent. As they grew apace, they were to be seen hanging about the smithy bare- footed, half covered with rags, and with smutty faces looking wildly out of mops of hair, that radiated like the beams of the sun in the image of that luminary on a country sign.

The eldest boy was bred up to his father's trade; that is, he flirted a horse tail tied to a stick, all day long in summer, to keep the flies from the animals that were brought to be shod; at which sleepy employment Mike was wont to keep the youngster's attention alive by an occasional rap across the head, or an unpremediated application of his foot amongst the rags that graced the person of the heir-apparent. Upon this system of training, it is reported, there were many family differences betwixt Mike and his spouse, and some grievously disputed fields. But Mike's muscle was enough to settle any question. So that it is not wonderful that the suffering Ruth should sometimes have taken to flight, and had recourse to her tongue.

In this way, the spoiler Discord stealthily crept into the little Eden of the Browns; and from one flower-bed advanced to another, until he made himself master of the whole garden. Quarrels then became a domestic diversion; and travelers along the road could tell when the patriarch Mike was putting his household in order, by the sound of certain lusty thwacks which proceeded from the interior, and the frequent apparition of a young elf darting towards the shop, with one hand scratching his head, and the other holding up what seemed a pair of trowsers, but which, in real- ity, were Mike's old leather breeches. The cus- tomers at the shop, too, affirmed that it was a usual thing to hear Mistress Brown talking to herself, for two or three hours, in an amazingly shrill key, after Mike had gone to his anvil. And some persons went so far as to say, that in the dead hour of night, in the worst of weather, voices could be heard upon the wind, in the direction of Mike's dwelling, more than a mile off; one very high, and the other very gruff; and sometimes there was a third voice that shook the air like an earth- quake, and made the blood run cold at the sound of it.

From this it may be seen that Mike's house was not very comfortable to him; for he was, at bottom, a good-natured fellow who loved peace and quiet; or, at any rate, who did not like the clack of a woman, which, he said, "wore a man out like water on a drip-stone." To be sure, he did not care about noise, if it was of a jolly sort; but that he never found at home, and therefore, "as he took no pride in Ruth," to use his own phrase, upon Hafen's report, "he naturally took to roaming."

He was an open-hearted fellow, too, who liked to spend his money when he had it; but the provident Mistress Mike began to get the upper hand; and in nothing are the first encroachments of female despotism more decisively indicated than in the regulation of what is called the family economy. Ruth purloined Mike's breeches, robbed the pockets, and secured the treasure. She forestalled his debtors, and settled his accounts, paralyzed his credit, and, in short, did everything but publish her determination to pay no debts of his contracting. The stout dragoon quailed before these vexatious tactics. He could never have been taken by storm; but to turn the siege into a blockade, and to fret his soul with mouse-nibblings, it was enough to break the spirit of any man! Mike, however, covered himself with glory; for after being reduced to the last stage of vassalage, as happens sometimes with an oppressed nation, he resolved to be his own master again, (thanks to the lusty potations, or he never would have made so successful a rebellion!) and gave Mrs. Brown, on a memorable occasion, a tremendous beating, by which he regained the purse-strings, and spent where and when and as freely as suited his own entertainment.

There was one thing in which Mike showed the regularity and discipline of an old soldier. He was steady to it in the worst of times. No matter where his vagrant humors might lead him, to what distance, or at what hours, or how topsy-turvy he might have grown, he was always sure to make his way home before morning. From this cause he became a frequent traveler all over the country in all weathers, and at all times of night. Time or tide did not weigh a feather. "He would snap his fingers," said Hafen, "at the foggiest midnight, and swear he could walk the whole county blindfold." The fact was, Mike was a brave man, and feared

neither ghost nor devil,—and could hardly be said to be afraid even of his wife.

One winter night,—or rather one winter morning, for it was past midnight,—Mike was coming home from a carouse. The snow was lying about half-leg deep all over the fields; and there was a crust frozen upon it, that was barely strong enough to support his weight; at every step he took, it broke through with him, so that he floundered along sadly without a track; and there was a great rustling and creaking of his shoes as he walked. A sharp northwesterly wind whistled with that shrillness that showed the clearness of the atmosphere; and the moon was shining as bright as burnished silver, casting the black shadows of leafless trees like bold etchings, upon the driven snow. The stars were all glittering with that fine frosty lustre which makes the vault of heaven seem of the deepest blue; and except the rising and sinking notes of the wind, all was still, for it was cutting cold, and every living thing was mute in its midnight lair. Yet a lonely man might well fancy there were sentient beings abroad besides himself, for on such a night there are sounds in the breeze of human tones, like persons talking at a distance. At all events, Mike was at such a time on his way home; and as he crossed the trackless field that showed him his own habitation at a distance, being in the best possible humor with himself, and whistling away as loud as he could—not from fear, but from inward satisfaction—he all at once heard somebody whistling an entirely different tune close behind him. He stopped and looked around, but there was nothing but the moon and trees and shadows; so, nothing daunted, he stepped on again, whistling as before, when, to his great amazement, the other note was instantly resumed. He now halted a second time. Immediately all was still. Mike then whistled out a sort of flourish, by way of experiment. The other did the very same thing. Mike repeated this several times, and it was always answered quite near him.

"Who the devil are you!" exclaimed Mike, holding his hand up to his ear to catch the sound.

"Look behind you, and you will see," replied a harsh, screaming voice.

Mike turned suddenly round, and there he saw

on the snow the shadow of a thin, queer-looking man, in a very trig sort of a dress, mounted upon a horse, that, by the shadow, must have been a mere skeleton. These were moving at full speed, although there was no road for a horse to travel on either; but the shadow seemed to go over shrubs and trees and bushes, as smoothly as any shadow could travel; and Mike distinctly heard the striking of a horse's hoofs upon the snow at every bound; though he could see nothing of the real man or horse. Presently, as the sound of the feet died away, Mike heard a laugh from the voice in the direction of the swamp.

"Hollo!" cried Mike, "what's your hurry?" But there was no answer.

"Humph!" said Mike, as he stood stock still, with his hands in his breeches' pockets, and began to laugh. "That's a genius for you!" said he, with a kind of perplexed, drunken, half-humorous face.

As he found he was not likely to make much out of it, he walked on, and began to talk to himself, and after a while to whistle louder than ever. Whilst he was struggling forward in this way, he heard something like a cat-call down towards the swamp; and immediately there rushed past him the shadows of a pack of hounds, making every sort of yelping, and deep-mouthed cry. He could even hear the little chips of ice that were flung from their feet, whizzing along the crust of snow; but still he could see nothing but shadows; and the sounds grew fainter and fainter until they melted away in the bosom of the swamp.

Mike now stopped again, and folded his arms across his breast,—although he could not help tottering a little, for being rather top-heavy;— and, in this position, he fell gravely to considering. First, he looked all around him: then he took off his hat and ran his fingers through his hair, and after that he rubbed his eyes. "Tut," said he, "it's all a botheration! There's no drag in the world will lie upon this snow. That's some drunken vagabond that had better be in his bed."

"What's that you say, Mike Brown?" said the same harsh voice he had heard before, "you had better look out how you take any freedom with a gentleman of quality."

"Quality!" cried Mike, turning his head round as he spoke. "You and your quality had better be abed, like a sober man, than to be playing off your cantrips at this time of night."

Mike looked on the snow, and there was the shadow of the horse again, standing still, and the figure upon it had one arm set a-kimbo against his side. Mike could now observe, as the shadow turned, that he wore something like a hussar-jacket, for the shadow showed the short skirt strutting out behind, and under this was the shadow of a tail turned upwards, and thrown across his shoulder. His cap appeared to be a fantastical thing perched on the very top of his head; and below the ribs of the skeleton horse he could perceive the legs dangling with hoofs, one of which was cloven.

"Aha!" exclaimed Mike, "I begin to understand you, sir. You are no better than you should be; and I will not keep company with such a blackguard."

"Then, good night, Mike Brown!" said the voice, "you are an uncivil fellow, but I'll teach you manners the next time I meet you"; and thereupon the shadow moved off at a hard trot, rising up and down in his saddle, like a first-rate jockey.

"Good night!" replied Mike; and he made a low bow, taking off his hat, and scraping his foot, in a very polite fashion, through the snow.

After this, Mike pushed home pretty fast, for he was growing more sober, and his teeth began to chatter with cold. He had a way of thrusting aside a back-door bolt, and getting into the house without making a disturbance; and then, before he went to bed, he usually took a sleeping-draught from a stone jug which he kept in the cupboard. Mike went through this manual on the night in question, and was very soon afterwards stretched out upon his couch, where he set to snoring like a trumpeter.

He never could tell how long it was after he had got to bed that night, but it was before day, when he opened his eyes and saw, by the broad moonlight that was shining upon the floor through the window, a comical figure vaporing about the room. It had a thin, long face, of a dirty white hue, and a mouth that was drawn up at the corners with a smile. A pair of ram's horns seemed to be twisted above his brows, like ladies' curls; and his head was covered with hair that looked more like a bunch of thorns, with a stiff cue sticking straight out behind, and tied up with a large knot of red ribbons. His coat was black, herringboned across the breast with crimson, and bound round all the seams with the same color. It fitted as close to his body as the tailor could make it; and it had a rigid standing collar that seemed to lift up a pair of immense ears, which were thus projected outwards from the head. The coat was very short, and terminated in a diminutive skirt that partly rested upon a long, pliant tail, which was whisked about in constant motion. He wore tight crimson small clothes, bound with black; and silk stockings of black and red stripes, one of which terminated in a hoof instead of a human foot. As he walked about the room he made a great clatter, but particularly with the hoof, that clinked with the sound of loose iron. In his hand he carried a crimson cap with a large black tassel at the top of it.

Mike said that as soon as he saw this fellow in the room, he knew there was "something coming." He therefore drew his blanket well up around his shoulders, leaving his head out, that he might have an eye to what was going forward. In a little time the figure began to make bows to Mike from across the room. First, he bowed on one side, almost down to the floor, so as to throw his body into an acute angle; then, in the same fashion, on the other side, keeping his eyes all the time on Mike. He had, according to Mike's account, a strange swimming sort of motion, never still a moment in one place, and passing from spot to spot like something that floated. At one instant he brandished his arms and whisked his tail, and took one step forward, like a dancing master beginning to dance a gavot. In the next, he made a sweep, and retreated to his first position; where he erected his figure very stiffly, and strutted with pompous strides all round the room. All this while he was twisting his features into every sort of grimace. Then he shook himself like a merry-andrew, and sprang from the floor upwards, flinging about his arms and legs like a supple-jack, which being done, he laughed very loud, and winked his eye at Mike. Then he skipped on the top of a chest, and from that to a table, from the table to a chair, from the chair to the bed, and thence off, putting his foot upon Mike's breast as he passed, and pressing upon him so heavily, that for some moments Mike could

hardly breathe. After this, he danced a morrice dance close up to the bedside, and fetched a spring that brought him astride upon Mike's stomach; where he stooped down so as to bring his long nose almost to touch Mike's, and there he twisted his eyebrows and made faces at him for several minutes. From that position he flung a somerset backwards, as far as the room permitted.

All this time the foot with the loose iron clanked very loud. Mike was not in the least afraid; but he tried several times to speak without being able to utter a word. He was completely tongue-tied, nor could he move a limb to help himself, being, as he affirmed, under a spell. But there he lay, looking at all these strange capers, which appeared so odd to him, that if he had had the power he would have laughed outright.

At last the figure danced up to him, and stood still.

"I have the honor to address myself to Sergeant Brown the blacksmith?" said he, interrogatively, making a superlatively punctilious bow at the same time.

"The same," replied Mike, having in an instant recovered the power of speech.

"My name," said the figure, "is—," here he pronounced a terrible name of twenty syllables, that sounded something like water pouring out of a bottle, and which Mike never could repeat; "I am a full brother of Old Harry, and belong to the family of the Scratches. I have taken the liberty to call and make my respects this morning, because I want to be shod."

Thereupon he made another bow, and lifted up his right foot to let Mike see that the shoe was loose.

"No shoeing to be done at this time of night," said Mike.

"It does not want but two new nails," said the figure, "and the clinching of one old one."

"Blast the nail will you get till daylight!" replied Mike.

"I will thank you, Mr. Brown," said the figure, "if you will only take my hoof in your hand, and pull out the loose nail that makes such a rattling."

"I can't do that," answered Mike.

"Why not?"

"Because I am afraid of waking Ruthy."

"I'll answer for the consequences," said the other. "Mistress Brown knows me very well, and will never complain at your doing a good turn to one of my family."

"I'm sleepy," said Mike, "so, be about your business."

"Then, Mike Brown, I will waken you," cried the other, in a rage; "I told you I would teach you manners."

Saying these words he came close to Mike, and 10 seized his nose between the knuckles of the two first fingers of his right hand, and wrung it so hard that Mike roared aloud. Then, letting go his hold, he strutted away with a ludicrous short step, throwing his legs upwards as high as his head, and bringing them back nearly to the same spot on the floor, and, in this fashion, whistling all the time a slow march, he passed directly out of the window.

When Mike had sufficiently come to his senses, he found his gentle consort standing by his bedside, 20 with a blanket wrapt round her spare figure, calling him all sorts of hard names for disturbing her rest.

Her account of this matter, when she heard from the neighbors Mike's version of this marvelous visit from the devil, was that she did not know when he came into the house that night; nor did she see any thing of his strange visitor; although she was sure Old Nick must have been with him, and flung him into such an odd position as he was in; for he made a terrible, smothered sort of noise with his voice, which wakened her up, and there she found him stretched across the bed with his clothes on, and his head inclined backwards over the side, with both arms down towards the floor. She said, moreover, that he was a drunken brute, and she had a great mind to tweak his nose for him.

"And I will be bound she helped the old devil to do that very thing!" said Rip.

"I don't know how that was," replied Hafen, "but Mike's nose got bluer and bluer after that, and always looked very much bruised, which he said was upon account of the devil's fingers being hot and scorching him very much." . . .

WILLIAM GILMORE SIMMS (1806–1870)

THE LITERARY energy of William Gilmore Simms was expressed in the writing of at least eighty volumes, including twenty-eight long romances and seven volumes of short stories, nineteen volumes of verse, four volumes of reviews, three histories and a geography of South Carolina, several biographies, and two dramas. One so prolific could not always write well but he never lacked for original force and verve, and he revised his works whenever occasion permitted. As a poet Simms has been forgotten, but he lives as romancer of the frontier and of the Revolutionary War in the South. With *The Yemassee* (1835) and *The Partisan* (1835) he achieved in a single year his two most popular romances, the first a story of the war of the Yemassee Indians in South Carolina against the British in 1715, and the second a chronicle of the Revolutionary War in South Carolina from the fall of Charleston to the defeat of Gates.

The romance was Simms's ideal, and he saw himself somewhat in the Homeric tradition. "I have entitled this story a romance," he wrote of *The Yemassee*, "and not a novel. The reader will permit me to insist on the distinction. . . . Modern romance is the substitute which the people today offer for the ancient

epic. . . . It invests individuals with absorbing interest; . . . it requires the same unities of plan, of purpose, and harmony of parts, and it seeks for its adventures among the wild and wonderful." In 1853, before the War between the States had blighted Simms's moderate success, his friend Bryant wrote: "His novels have a wide circulation, and are admired for the fervor and rapidity of the narrative, their picturesque description, the energy with which they express the stronger emotions, and the force with which they portray local manners."

He excelled in spontaneous invention, and on occasion he blended history and romance to high advantage. The scene in which Occonestoga, the son of the Yemassee chief, having betrayed his tribe to the English, is tomahawked by his mother to save him from the Indian rites of ostracism and damnation both here and hereafter, is romance at its best, and more poetic than anything Cooper ever reached. In *The Partisan* he created one vital character, Porgy, a compound of Falstaff and the Carolina gentleman, who appears in all the other Revolutionary tales save *The Scout*. Throughout his work Simms infused his own generous and manly nature. That most of his volumes are now neglected or forgotten is due to his failure to see the pitfalls of romance into which he often fell headlong: downright sensationalism, sentimentalism, and insensibility to shades between black and white. He relied too often on one device of plot which he seldom lifted above melodrama—the pitting of Partisan and Tory, or frontier hero and villain, against one another in a struggle for a heroine or for life, or for both. He loved fact and history, and most of his romances are based on historical events; but too often these events lie surrounded by the fiction rather than being absorbed into it, and melodrama too often spoiled the finer qualities of romance. But when he held his wilder fancies in check, he wrote well.

Simms was born in 1806 to an undistinguished family in socially feudal Charleston, South Carolina. His native city never accorded him the respect that his fiction, his love of Charleston, and his labors in state history earned. While he was still a baby his mother died; and his father, failing in business and wholly disheartened, left Charleston, hoping to improve his fortunes in the Southwest. The boy was reared by his maternal grandmother amid limited circumstances. His formal schooling was unsatisfactory, and at fifteen he was apprenticed to a druggist. When eighteen, while making the first of three journeys to Mississippi to visit his father, he began to observe the rough life of the whites in the backwoods and the trading settlements, as well as life among the Creeks and Cherokees, and he gathered much material for his later frontier romances. But he would not exchange Western life for socially chilly Charleston. Returning home, he studied law, was married to Anna Giles in 1826, and in 1827 passed the bar and published his second and third volumes of verse. The practice of law was but a means to literature. In 1832 his wife died. He came North, met Bryant, and in New Haven wrote *Martin Faber* (1833), a crime story influenced by William Godwin's *Caleb Williams*. This was followed by *Guy Rivers* (1834), vigorous story of desperadoes, honest men, and love in the Georgia gold field setting of the 1820's. *The Yemassee* and *The Partisan* followed, and thereafter he was happiest when he returned to the Border and the war. In 1836 he married Chevillette Roach, daughter of the owner of "The Woodlands," a plantation between Charleston and Augusta. Thereafter for a quarter of a century he devoted himself chiefly to literature, spending the months from October to May on the plantation, and the summers in Charleston, with occasional visits to the North. As the Civil War approached he gave much time to defending the principles of the South, even going so far as to link slavery with divine decree. His home was twice burned during the war, the second time by Sherman's raiders. Poverty claimed him; domestic sorrows multiplied. His wife died in 1865, and when death came to him in 1870 he was survived by only five of his fourteen children.

A number of Simms's tales have been classified as Border romances though the word "frontier" more aptly characterizes them. They include, besides *The Yemassee*, an effective Indian tale, *The Cassique of Kiawah* (1859), and *The Wigwam and the Cabin* (1845), a collection of thirteen stories of Indian and settlement life, including "Grayling; or, Murder will Out," "The Lazy Crow," belonging to the fine family of Negro plantation stories, and the exotic "Jocasse: A Cherokee Legend." Of the other Border romances, *Richard Hurdis* (1838) and its sequel, *Border Beagles* (1840), retain some interest in spite of sensational treatment of passion and cunning, of villain and victim, because they treat of the outlaws led by the infamous John A. Murrell, organizer of banditry in Alabama and Mississippi. "The story is a genuine chronicle of the border region where the scene is laid," Simms wrote in *Richard Hurdis*; "I knew Stewart, the captor of Murrell, personally." *Beauchampe; or, The Kentucky Tragedy* (1842), and *Charlemont* (1856), an elaboration of the first part of the *Beauchampe* story, are exceedingly poor renderings of the famous "Kentucky Tragedy" of seduction and revenge.

Following *The Partisan*, two romances, *Mellichampe* (1836) and *Katharine Walton* (1851), continue the account of the Revolutionary War in South Carolina after the fall of Camden; they complete the trilogy Simms had planned to write, though the third is the actual sequel to *The Partisan*, and the second hardly belongs to the group. Four other novels are grouped with this trilogy. *The Kinsman* (1841), revised as *The Scout* (1854), opposes two half-brothers in love and war in a setting involving the Black Riders of the Congaree in the period of Greene's first victories. *The Sword and the Distaff* (1853), revised as *Woodcraft* (1854), has the advantages of less melodrama and of comedy in the character of Porgy at the close of the war. *The Forayers* (1855) recounts the retreat of the English from Nine-Six; its sequel, *Eutaw* (1856), describes the military operations ending in the battle giving title to the book.

Simms tried his hand also at Spanish material, but without success. *Pelayo: A Story of the Goth* (1838) and its sequel, *Count Julian* (1845), are Spanish in background; *The Damsel of Darien* (1839) is of the time of Balboa, and in *Vasconselos* (1853) he turned to Mexico.

BIBLIOGRAPHY · There is no complete edition of Simms's works, and many titles are unavailable. The Uniform Edition, *Works of William Gilmore Simms*, in 20 volumes, was published in New York during the years 1853 to 1866. The collected *Border Romances*, in 17 volumes, came out in 1859. A Chicago edition of the *Works*, in 17 volumes, was published in 1890. Volumes of the better-known books remain available. Alexander Cowie's edition of *The Yemassee* (1937) is excellent. William Peterfield Trent, *William Gilmore Simms* (1892), remains the standard critical biography, though later studies have corrected errors and added somewhat to the knowledge of the man and his work. See especially James G. Johnson, *Southern Fiction Prior to 1860* (1909), J. W. Hingham, "The Changing Loyalties of William Gilmore Simms," *Journal of Southern History*, IX (1943), 210–223; H. M. Jarrell, "Falstaff and Simms's Porgy," *American Literature*, III (1931), 204–213, and "Simms's Visits to the Southwest," *American Literature*, V (1933), 29–35; and J. A. Morris, "The Stories of William Gilmore Simms," *American Literature*, XIV (1942), 20–35. Simms's numerous contributions to periodicals, as well as his many books, have made the task of bibliography difficult; fortunately good work has been done. See A. S. Salley, Jr., "A Bibliography of William Gilmore Simms," *Publications of the Southern Historical Association*, I (1897), and "Additional Simms Bibliography," in the same journal, XI (1907); Oscar Wegelin, "William Gilmore Simms: A Short Sketch, with a Bibliography of His Separate Writings," *American Book Collector*, III (1933), 113–116, 149–151, 216–218, 284–286; and J. A. Morris's article mentioned above. Special studies include F. H. Deen, "A Comparison of Simms's *Richard Hurdis* with Its Sources," *Modern Language Notes*, LX (1945), 406–408, and "The Genesis of *Martin Faber* in *Caleb Williams*," *Modern Language Notes*, LIX (1944), 315–317; W. S. Hoole, "A Note on Simms's Visits to the Southwest," *American Literature*, VI (1934), 334–336; and R. I. McDavid, "*Ivanhoe* and Simms's *Vasconselos*," *Modern Language Notes*, LVI (1941), 294–297.

How Sharp Snaffles Got His Capital and His Wife

FIFTY-NINE short stories and tales have been definitely proved to belong to Simms. Among these, the subject, characters, and setting in the tale of Sharp Snaffles unite to make it one of his best. Simms was a born storyteller. The tall tale suited his romantic narrative gift admirably, yet held him away from the tearful sentimentality and the bloody, melodramatic encounters that mar many of his Border tales. The somewhat stilted aristocrats in his historical romances are absent from this story. Here, rather, he assembled a group of ordinary, resourceful men, lovers of forest and stream, speakers of a native idiom—types that give life to his Revolutionary romances. Further, they are sitting about the campfire fashioning their own entertainment from their own native wit. Some of Simms's happiest scenes are those he wrote for comic relief. With inconsequential deletions, the text of this story is taken from *Harper's Monthly Magazine*, where it appeared in October, 1870, four months after the death of the author.

I

The day's work was done, and a good day's work it was. We had bagged a couple of fine bucks and a fat doe; and now we lay camped at the foot of the "Balsam Range" of mountains in North Carolina, preparing for our supper. We were a right merry group of seven; four professional hunters, and three amateurs—myself among the latter. There were Jim Fisher, Aleck Wood, Sam or Sharp Snaffles, alias "Yaou," and Nathan Langford, alias the "Pious." . . .

Well, we had reached Saturday night. We had hunted day by day from the preceding Monday with considerable success—bagging some game daily, and camping nightly at the foot of the mountains. The season was a fine one. It was early winter, October, and the long ascent to the top of the mountains was through vast fields of green, the bushes still hanging heavy with their huckleberries.

From the summits we had looked over into Tennessee, Virginia, Georgia, North and South Carolina. In brief, to use the language of Natty Bumppo, we beheld "Creation." We had crossed the "Blue Ridge"; and the descending watercourses, no longer seeking the Atlantic, were now gushing headlong down the western slopes, and hurrying to lose themselves in the Gulf Stream and the Mississippi. . . .

Saturday night is devoted by the mountaineers engaged in a camp hunt, which sometimes contemplates a course of several weeks, to stories of their adventures—"long yarns"—chiefly relating to the objects of their chase, and the wild experiences of their professional life. The hunter who actually inclines to exaggeration is, at such a period, privileged to deal in all the extravagances of invention; nay, he is required to do so! To be literal, or confine himself to the bald and naked truth, is not only discreditable, but a finable offense! He is, in such a case, made to swallow a long, strong, and difficult potation! He can not be too extravagant in his incidents; but he is also required to exhibit a certain degree of art, in their use; and he thus frequently rises into a certain realm of fiction, the ingenuities of which are made to compensate for the exaggerations, as they do in the "Arabian Nights," and other Oriental ro- 10 mances.

This will suffice for explanation.

Nearly all our professional hunters assembled on the present occasion were tolerable *raconteurs*. They complimented Jim Fisher, by throwing the raw deer-skin over his shoulders; tying the antlers of the buck with a red handkerchief over his forehead; seating him on the biggest boulder which lay at hand; and sprinkling him with a stoup of whisky, they christened him "The Big Lie," for 20 the occasion. And in this character he complacently presided during the rest of the evening, till the company prepared for sleep, which was not till midnight. He was king of the feast.

It was the duty of the "Big Lie" to regulate proceedings, keep order, appoint the *raconteurs* severally, and admonish them when he found them foregoing their privileges, and narrating bald, naked, and uninteresting truth. They must deal in fiction. 30

Jim Fisher was seventy years old, and a veteran hunter, the most famous in all the country. He *looked* authority, and promptly began to assert it, which he did in a single word:

"Yaou!"

II

"Yaou" was the *nom de nique* of one of the hunters, whose proper name was Sam Snaffles, but who, from his special smartness, had obtained 40 the farther sobriquet of "*Sharp* Snaffles."

Columbus Mills whispered me that he was called "Yaou" from his frequent use of that word, which, in the Choctaw dialect, simply means "Yes." Snaffles had rambled considerably among the Choctaws, and picked up a variety of their words, which he was fond of using in preference to the vulgar English; and his common use of "Yaou,"

for the affirmative, had prompted the substitution of it for his own name. He answered to the name.

"Ay—yee, Yaou," was the response of Sam. "I was afeard, 'Big Lie,' that you'd be hitching me up the very first in your team."

"And what was you afeard of? You knows as well how to take up a crooked trail as the very best man among us; so you go ahead and spin your thread a'ter the best fashion."

"What shill it be?" asked Snaffles, as he mixed a calabash full of peach and honey, preparing evidently for a long yarn.

"Give 's the history of how you got your capital, Yaou!" was the cry from two or more.

"O Lawd! I've tell'd that so often, fellows, that I'm afeard you'll sleep on it; and then agin, I've tell'd it so often I've clean forgot how it goes. Somehow it changes a leetle every time I tells it."

"Never you mind! The Jedge never haird it, I reckon, for one; and I'm not sure that Columbus Mills ever did."

So the "Big Lie."

The "Jedge" was the *nom de guerre* which the hunters had conferred upon me; looking, no doubt, to my venerable aspect—for I had traveled considerably beyond my teens—and the general dignity of my bearing.

"Yaou," like other bashful beauties in oratory and singing, was disposed to hem and haw, and affect modesty and indifference, when he was brought up suddenly by the stern command of the "Big Lie," who cried out:

"Don't make yourself an etarnal fool, Sam Snaffles, by twisting your mouth out of shape, making all sorts of redickilous ixcuses. Open upon the trail at onst and give tongue, or, dern your digestion, but I'll fine you to hafe a gallon at a single swallow!" . . .

Thus adjured with a threat, Sam Snaffles swallowed his peach and honey at a gulp, hemmed thrice lustily, put himself into an attitude, and began as follows. I shall adopt his language as closely as possible; but it is not possible, in any degree, to convey any adequate idea of his manner, which was admirably appropriate to the subject matter. Indeed, the fellow was a born actor. . . .

"You see then, Jedge, it's about a dozen or fourteen years ago, when I was a young fellow without much beard on my chin, though I was full grown as I am now—strong as a horse, ef not quite so big as a buffalo. I was then jest a-beginning my 'prenticeship to the hunting business, and looking to sich persons as the 'Big Lie' thar to show me how to take the track of b'ar, buck, and painther." . . .

"Worm along, Yaou!"

"Well, Jedge, I warn't a-doing much among the bucks yit—jest for the reason that I was quite too eager in the scent a'ter a sartin doe! Now, Jedge, you never seed my wife—my Merry Ann, as I calls her; and ef you was to see her now—though she's prime grit yit—you would never believe that, of all the womankind in all these mountains, she was the very yaller flower of the forest; with the reddest rose cheeks you ever did see, and sich a mouth, and sich bright curly hair, and so tall, and so slender, and so all over beautiful! O Lawd! when I thinks of it and them times, I don't see how 'twas possible to think of buck-hunting when thar was sich a doe, with sich eyes shining me on!

"Well, Jedge, Merry Ann was the only da'ter of Jeff Hopson and Keziah Hopson, his wife, who was the da'ter of Squire Claypole, whose wife was Margery Clough, that lived down upon Pacolet River—"

"Look you, Yaou, ain't you gitting into them derned facts agin, eh?"

"I reckon I em, 'Big Lie!' Scuse me: I'll kiver the pegs direct-lie, one a'ter, t'other. Whar was I? Ah! Oh! Well, Jedge, poor hunter and poor man —jest, you see, a squatter on the side of a leetle bit of a mountain close on to Columbus Mills, at Mount Tryon, I was all the time on a hot trail a'ter Merry Ann Hopson. I went thar to see her a'most every night; and sometimes I carried a buck for the old people, and sometimes a doe-skin for the gal, and I do think, bad hunter as I then was, I pretty much kept the fambly in deer meat through the whole winter."

"Good for you, Yaou! You're a-coming to it! That's the only fair trail of a lie that you've struck yit!"

So the "Big Lie," from the chair.

"Glad to hyar you say so," was the answer. "I'll git on in time! Well, Jedge, though Jeff Hopson was glad enough to git my meat always, he didn't affection me, as I did his da'ter. He was a sharp, close, money-loving old fellow, who was always considerate of the main chaince; and the old lady, his wife, who hairdly dare say her soul was her own, she jest looked both ways, as I may say, for Sunday, never giving a fair look to me or my chainces, when his eyes were sot on her. But 'twa'n't so with my Merry Ann. She hed the eyes for me from the beginning, and soon she hed the feelings; and, you see, Jedge, we sometimes did git a chaince, when old Jeff was gone from home, to come to a sort of onderstanding about our feelings; and the long and the short of it was that Merry Ann confessed to me that she'd like nothing better than to be my wife. She liked no other man but me. Now, Jedge, a'ter that, what was a young fellow to do? That, I say, was the proper kind of incouragement. So I said, 'I'll ax your daddy.' Then she got scary, and said, 'Oh, don't; for somehow, Sam, I'm a-thinking daddy don't like you enough yit. Jest hold on a bit, and come often, and bring him venison, and try to make him laugh, which you kin do, you know, and a'ter a time you kin try him.' And so I did—or rather I didn't. I put off the axing. I come constant. I brought venison all the time, and b'ar meat a plenty, a'most three days in every week."

"That's it, Yaou. You're on trail. That's as derned a lie as you've tell'd yit; for all your hunting in them days, didn't git more meat than you could eat your one self."

"Thank you, 'Big Lie.' I hopes I'll come up in time to the right measure of the camp.

"Well, Jedge, this went on for a long time, a'most the whole winter, and spring, and summer, till the winter begun to come in agin. I carried 'em the venison, and Merry Ann meets me in the woods, and we hes sich a pleasant time when we meets on them little odd chainces that I gits hot as thunder to bring the business to a sweet honey finish.

"But Merry Ann keeps on scary, and she puts me off; ontil, one day, one a'ternoon, about sundown, she meets me in the woods, and she's all in a flusteration. And she ups and tells me how old John Grimstead, the old bachelor (a fellow about forty years old, and the dear gal not yet twenty), how he's a'ter her, and bekaise he's got a good fairm, and mules and horses, how her daddy's giving him the open mouth incouragement.

"Then I says to Merry Ann:

" 'You sees, I kain't put off no longer. I must out with it, and ax your daddy at onst.' And then her scary fit come on again, and she begs me not to—not jist yit. But I swears by all the Hokies that I won't put off another day; and so, as I haird the old man was in the house that very hour, I left Merry Ann in the woods, all in a trimbling, and I jist went ahead, determined to have the figure made straight, whether odd or even." . . .

IV

"Well, Jedge, as I tell you, I put a bold face on the business, though my hairt was gitting up into my throat, and I was almost a-gasping for my breath, when I was fairly in the big room, and standing up before the old Squire. He was a-setting in his big squar hide-bottom'd arm-chair, looking like a jedge upon the bench, jist about to send a poor fellow to the gallows. As he seed me come in, looking queer enough, I reckon, his mouth put on a sort of grin, which showed all his grinders, and he looked for all the world as ef he guessed the business I come about. But he said, good-natured enough:

" 'Well, Sam Snaffles, how goes it?'

"Says I:

" 'Pretty squar, considerin'. The winter's coming on fast, and I reckon the mountains will be full of meat before long.'

"Then says he, with another ugly grin, 'Ef 'twas your smoke-house that had it all, Sam Snaffles, 'stead of the mountains, 'twould be better for you, I reckon.'

" 'I 'grees with you,' says I. 'But I rether reckon I'll git my full shar' of it afore the spring of the leaf agin.'

" 'Well, Sam,' says he, 'I hopes, for your sake, 'twill be a big shar'. I'm afeard you're not the pusson to go for a big shar', Sam Snaffles. Seems to me you're too easy satisfied with a small shar'; sich as the fence-squarrel carries under his two airms, calkilating only on a small corn-crib in the chestnut-tree.'

" 'Don't you be afeard, Squaire. I'll come out right. My cabin sha'n't want for nothing that a strong man with a stout hairt kin git, with good working—enough and more for himself, and perhaps another pusson.'

" 'What other pusson?' says he, with another of his great grins, and showing of his grinders.

" 'Well,' says I, 'Squaire Hopson, that's jest what I come to talk to you about this blessed Friday night.'

"You see 'twas Friday!

" 'Well,' says he, 'go ahead, Sam Snaffles, and empty your brain-basket as soon as you kin, and I'll light my pipe while I'm a-hearing you.'

"So he lighted his pipe, and laid himself back in his chair, shet his eyes, and begin to puff like blazes.

"By this time my blood was beginning to bile in all my veins, for I seed that he was jest in the humor to tread on all my toes, and then ax a'ter my feelings. I said to myself:

" 'It's jest as well to git the worst at onst, and then thar'll be an eend of the oneasiness.' So I up and told him, in pretty soft, smooth sort of speechifying, as how I was mighty fond of Merry Ann, and she, I was a-thinking, of me; and that I jest come to ax ef I might hev Merry Ann for my wife.

"Then he opened his eyes wide, as ef he never ixpected to hear sich a proposal from me.

" 'What!' says he. 'You?'

" 'Jest so, Squaire,' says I. 'Ef it pleases you to believe me, and to consider it reasonable, the axing.'

"He sot quiet for a minit or more, then he gits up, knocks all the fire out of his pipe on the chimney, fills it, and lights it agin, and then comes straight up to me, whar I was a-setting on the chair in front of him, and without a word he takes the collar of my coat betwixt the thumb and forefinger of his left hand, and he says:

" 'Git up, Sam Snaffles. Git up, ef you please.'

"Well, I gits up, and he says:

" 'Hyar! Come! Hyar!'

"And with that he leads me right across the room to a big looking-glass that hung agin the partition wall, and thar he stops before the glass, facing it and holding me by the collar all the time. . . .

"Well, thar he hed me up, both on us standing in front of this glass, whar we could a'most see the whole of our full figgers, from head to foot.

"And when we hed stood thar for a minit or so, he says, quite solemn like:

" 'Look in the glass, Sam Snaffles.'

"So I looked.

" 'Well,' says I. 'I sees you, Squaire Hopson, and myself, Sam Snaffles.'

" 'Look good,' says he, 'obzarve well.'

" 'Well,' says I, 'I'm a-looking with all my eyes. I only sees what I tells you.'

" 'But you don't obzarve,' says he. 'Looking and seeing's one thing,' says he, 'but obzarving's another. Now obzarve.'

"By this time, Jedge, I was getting sort o' riled, for I could see that somehow he was jest a-trying to make me feel redickilous. So I says:

" 'Look you, Squaire Hopson, ef you thinks I never seed myself in a glass afore this, you're mighty mistaken. I've got my own glass at home, and though it's but a leetle sort of a small, mean consarn, it shows me as much of my own face and figger as I cares to see at any time. I never cares to look in it 'cept when I'm brushing, and combing, and clipping off the straggling beard when it's too long for my eating.'

" 'Very well,' says he; 'now obzarve! You sees your own figger, and your face, and your air obzarving as well as you know how. Now, Mr. Sam Snaffles—now that you've hed a fair look at yourself—jest now answer me, from your honest conscience, a'ter all you've seed, ef you honestly thinks you're the sort of pusson to hev my da'ter!'

"And with that he gin me a twist, and when I wheeled round he hed wheeled round too, and thar we stood, full facing one another.

"Lawd! how I was riled! But I answered, quick:

" 'And why not, I'd like to know, Squaire Hopson? I ain't the handsomest man in the world, but I'm not the ugliest; and folks don't generally consider me at all among the uglies. I'm as tall a man as you, and as stout and strong, and as good a man o' my inches as ever stepped in shoe-leather. And it's enough to tell you, Squaire, whatever *you* may think, that Merry Ann believes in me, and she's a way of thinking that I'm jest about the very pusson that ought to hev her.'

" 'Merry Ann's thinking,' says he, 'don't run all fours with her fayther's thinking. I axed you, Sam Snaffles, to obzarve yourself in the glass. I telled you that seeing warn't edzactly obzarving. You seed only the inches; you seed that you hed eyes and mouth and nose and the airms and legs of the man. But eyes and mouth and legs and airms don't make a man!'

" 'Oh, they don't!' says I.

" 'No, indeed,' says he. 'I seed that you hed all them; but then I seed thar was one thing that you hedn't got.'

" 'Jimini!' says I, mighty conflustered. 'What thing's a-wanting to me to make me a man?'

" 'Capital!' says he, and he lifted himself up and looked mighty grand.

" 'Capital!' says I; 'and what's that?'

" 'Thar air many kinds of capital,' says he. 'Money's capital, for it kin buy every thing. House and lands is capital; cattle and horses and sheep—when thar's enough on 'em—is capital. And as I obzarved you in the glass, Sam Snaffles, I seed that capital was the very thing that you wanted to make a man of you! Now I don't mean that any da'ter of mine shall marry a pusson that's not a perfect man. I obzarved you long ago, and seed whar you was wanting. I axed about you. I axed your horse.'

" 'Axed my horse!' says I, pretty nigh dumb-foundered.

" 'Yes, I axed your horse, and he said to me: "Look at me! I hain't got an ounce of spar' flesh on my bones. You kin count all my ribs. You kin lay the whole length of your airm betwixt any two on 'em, and it'll lie thar as snug as a black snake betweixt two poles of a log-house." Says he, "Sam's got no capital! He ain't got, any time, five bushels of corn in his crib; and he's such a monstrous feeder himself that he'll eat out four bushels, and think it mighty hard upon him to give *me* the other one." Thar, now, was your horse's testimony, Sam, agin you. Then I axed about your cabin, and your way of living. I was curious, and went to see you one day when I knowed you waur at home. You hed but one chair, which you gin me to set on, and you sot on the eend of a barrel for yourself. You gin me a rasher of bacon what hedn't a streak of fat in it. You hed a poor quarter of a poor doe hanging from the rafters—a poor beast that somebody hed disabled—'

" 'I shot it myself,' says I.

" 'Well, it was a-dying when you shot it; and all the hunters say you was a poor shooter at any thing. You cooked our dinner yourself, and the hoe-cake was all dough, not hafe done, and the meat was all done as tough as ef you had dried it for a month of Sundays in a Flurriday sun! Your cabin had but one room, and that you slept in and ate in; and the floor was six inches deep in dirt! Then, when I looked into your garden, I found seven stalks of long collards only, every one seven foot high, with all the leaves stript off it, as ef you wanted 'em for broth; till thar waur only three top leaves left on every stalk. You hedn't a stalk of corn growing, and when I scratched at your turnip-bed I found nothing bigger than a chestnut. Then, Sam, I begun to ask about your fairm, and I found that you was nothing but a squatter on land of Columbus Mills, who let you have an old nigger pole-house, and an acre or two of land. Says I to myself, says I, "This poor fellow's got no capital; and he hasn't the head to git capital"; and from that moment, Sam Snaffles, the more I obzarved you, the more sartin 'twas that you never could be a man, ef you waur to live a thousand years. You may think, in your vanity, that you air a man; but you ain't, and never will be, unless you kin find a way to git capital; and I loves my gal child too much to let her marry any pusson whom I don't altogether consider a man!' . . .

"I didn't stop for any more. I jest bolted, like a hot shot out of a shovel, and didn't know my own self, or whatever steps I tuk, tell I got into the thick and met Merry Ann coming towards me." . . .

V

"Well, Jedge, it was a hard meeting betwixt me and Merry Ann. The poor gal come to me in a sort of run, and hairdly drawing her breath, she cried out:

" 'Oh, Sam! What does he say?'

"What could I say? How tell her? I jest wrapped her up in my airms, and I cries out, making some violent remarks about the old Squire.

"Then she screamed, and I hed to squeeze her up, more close than ever, and kiss her, I reckon,

more than a dozen times, jest to keep her from gwine into historical fits. I telled her all, from beginning to eend. . . .

" 'Look at me,' says I, 'Merry Ann. Does I look like a man?'

" 'You're all the man I wants,' says she.

" 'That's enough,' says I. 'You shall see what I kin do, and what I will do! That's ef you air true to me.'

" 'I'll be true to you, Sam,' says she.

" 'And you won't think of nobody else?'

" 'Never,' says she.

" 'Well, you'll see what I kin do, and what I will do. You'll see that I em a man; and ef thar's capital to be got in all the country, by working and hunting, and fighting, ef that's needful, we shill hev it. Only you be true to me, Merry Ann.'

"And she throwed herself upon my buzzom, and cried out:

" 'I'll be true to you, Sam. I loves nobody in all the world so much as I loves you.'

" 'And you won't marry any other man, Merry Ann, no matter what your daddy says?'

" 'Never,' she says. . . .

"And so, after a million of squeezes and kisses, we parted; and she slipt along through the woods, the back way to the house, and I mounted my horse to go to my cabin. But, afore I mounted the beast, I gin him a dozen kicks in his ribs, jest for bearing his testimony agin me, and telling the old Squire that I hedn't 'capital' enough for a corn crib."

VI

"I was mightily let down, as you may think, by old Squire Hopson; but I was mightily lifted up by Merry Ann.

"But when I got to my cabin, and seed how mean every thing was there, and thought how true it was, all that old Squire Hopson had said, I felt overkim, and I said to myself, 'It's all true! How kin I bring that beautiful yaller flower of the forest to live in sich a mean cabin, and with sich poor accommydations? She that had every thing comforting and nice about her.' . . .

"I couldn't sleep all that night for the thinking, and obzarvations. That impudent talking of old

Hopson put me on a new track. I couldn't give up hunting. I knowed no other business, and I didn't hafe know that.

"Well, Jedge, as I said, I had a most miserable night of consideration and obzarvation and concatenation accordingly. . . . But I got to sleep at last. And I hed a dream. And I thought I seed the prettiest woman critter in the world, next to Merry Ann, standing close by my bedside; and, at first, I thought 'twas Merry Ann, and I was gwine to kiss her agin; but she drawed back and said:

"'Scuse me! I'm not Merry Ann; but I'm her friend and your friend; so don't you be down in the mouth, but keep a good hairt, and you'll hev help, and git the "capital" whar you don't look for it now. It's only needful that you be detarmined on good works and making a man of yourself.'

"A'ter that dream I slept like a top, woke at day-peep, took my rifle, called up my dog, mounted my horse, and put out for the laurel hollows. . . .

"Well, jest about sunset I come to a hollow of the hills that I hed never seed before; and in the middle of it was a great pond of water, what you call a lake; and it showed like so much purple glass in the sunset, and 'twas jest as smooth as the big looking-glass of Squaire Hopson's. Thar wa'n't a breath of wind stirring.

"I was mighty tired, so I eased down from the mar', tied up the bridle and check, and let her pick about, and laid myself down onder a tree, jest about twenty yards from the lake, and thought to rest myself ontil the moon riz, which I knowed would be about seven o'clock.

"I didn't mean to fall asleep, but I did it; and I reckon I must ha' slept a good hour, for when I woke the dark hed set in, and I could only see one or two bright stars hyar and thar, shooting out from the dark of the heavens. But, ef I seed nothing, I haird; and jest sich a sound and noise as I hed never haird before.

"Thar was a rushing and a roaring and a screaming and a plashing, in the air and in the water, as made you think the univarsal world was coming to an eend!

"All that set me up. I was waked up out of sleep and dreams, and my eyes opened to every thing that eye could see; and sich another sight I never seed before! I tell you, Jedge, ef there was one wild-goose settling down in that lake, thar was one hundred thousand of 'em! I couldn't see the eend of 'em. They come every minit, swarm a'ter swarm, in tens and twenties and fifties and hundreds; and sich a fuss as they did make! sich a gabbling, sich a splashing, sich a confusion, that I was fairly conflusterated; and I jest lay whar I was, a-watching 'em.

"You never seed beasts so happy! How they flapped their wings; how they gabbled to one another; how they swam hyar and thar, to the very middle of the lake and to the very edge of it, jest a fifty yards from whar I lay squat, never moving leg or arm! It was wonderful to see! I wondered how they could find room, for I reckon thar waur forty thousand on 'em, all scuffling in that leetle lake together!

"Well, as I watched 'em, I said to myself:

"'Now, if a fellow could only captivate all them wild-geese—fresh from Canniday, I reckon—what would they bring in the market at Spartanburg and Greenville? Walker, I knowed, would buy 'em up quick at fifty cents a head. Forty thousand geese at fifty cents a head. Thar was "capital!"' . . .

"What a haul 'twould be, if a man could only get 'em all in one net! Kiver 'em all at a fling!

"The idee worked like so much fire in my brain.

"How kin it be done?

"That was the question!

"'Kin it be done?' I axed myself.

"'It kin,' I said to myself; 'and I'm the very man to do it!' Then I begun to work away in the thinking. I thought over all the traps and nets and snares that I hed ever seen or haird of; and the leetle eends of the idee begun to come together in my head; and, watching all the time how the geese flopped and splashed and played and swum, I said to myself:

"'Oh! most beautiful critters! ef I don't make some "capital" out of you, then I'm not dezarving sich a beautiful yaller flower of the forest as my Merry Ann!' . . .

"So, in the morning, I went to work. I rode off to Spartanburg, and bought all the twine and cord and hafe the plow-lines in town; and I got a lot of great fishhooks, all to help make the tanglement parfect; and I got lead for sinkers, and I got corkwood for floaters; and I pushed for home jist as fast as my poor mar' could streak it.

"I was at work day and night, for nigh on to a week, making my net; and when 'twas done I borrowed a mule and cart from Columbus Mills, thar;—he'll tell you all about it—he kin make his affidavy to the truth of it.

"Well, off I driv with my great net, and got to the lake about noonday. I knowed 'twould take me some hours to make my fixings parfect, and git the net fairly stretched across the lake, and jest deep enough to do the tangling of every leg of the birds in the very midst of their swimming and snorting and splashing and cavorting! When I hed fixed it all fine, and jest as I wanted it, I brought the eends of my plow-lines up to where I was gwine to hide myself. This was onder a strong sapling, and my calkilation was when I hed got the beasts all hooked, forty thousand, more or less —and I could tell how that was from feeling on the line—why, then, I'd whip the line round the sapling, kitch it fast, and draw in my birds at my own ease, without axing much about their comfort. . . .

"Down they come, millions upon millions, till I was sartin thar waur already pretty nigh on to forty thousand in the lake. It waur always a nice calkilation of mine that the lake could hold fully forty thousand, though onst, when I went round to measure it, stepping it off, I was jubous whether it could hold over thirty-nine thousand; but, as I tuk the measure in hot weather and in a dry spell, I concluded that some of the water along the edges hed dried up, and 'twa'n't so full as when I made my first calkilation. So I hev stuck to that first calkilation ever since.

"Well, thar they waur, forty thousand, we'll say, with, it mout be, a few millions and hundreds over. And Lawd! how they played and splashed and screamed and dived! I calkilated on hooking a good many of them divers, in pertickilar, and so I watched and waited, ontil I thought I'd feel of my lines; and I begun, leetle by leetle, to haul in, when, Lawd love you, Jedge, sich a ripping and raging, and bouncing and flouncing, and flopping and splashing, and kicking and screaming, you never did hear in all your born days!

"By this I knowed that I hed captivated the captains of the host, and a pretty smart chaince, I reckoned, of the rigilar army, ef 'twa'n't edzactly forty thousand; for I calkilated that some few would get away—run off, jest as the cowards always does in the army, jest when the shooting and confusion begins; still, I reasonably calkilated on the main body of the regiments; and so, gitting more and more hot and eager, and pulling and hauling, I made one big mistake, and, instid of wrapping the eends of my lines around the sapling that was standing jest behind me, what does I do but wraps 'em round my own thigh— the right thigh, you see—and some of the loops waur hitched round my left arm at the same time!

"All this come of my hurry and ixcitement, for it was burning like a hot fever in my brain, and I didn't know when or how I hed tied myself up, ontil suddenly, with an all-fired scream, all together, them forty thousand geese rose like a great black cloud in the air, all tied up, rangled up— hooked about the legs, hooked about the gills, hooked and fast in some way in the beautiful leetle twistings of my net!

"Yes, Jedge, as I'm a living hunter to-night, hyar a-talking to you, they riz up all together, as ef they hed consulted upon it, like a mighty thunder-cloud, and off they went, screaming and flouncing, meaning, I reckon, to take the back track to Canniday, in spite of the freezing weather.

"Before I knowed whar I was, Jedge, I was twenty feet in the air, my right thigh up and my left arm, and the other thigh and arm a-dangling useless, and feeling every minit as ef they was gwine to drop off. . . .

"Oh, Jedge, jest consider my sitivation! It's sich a ricollection, Jedge, that I must rest and liquor, in order to rekiver the necessary strength to tell you what happened next."

VII

"Yes, Jedge," said Yaou, resuming his narrative, "jest stop whar you air, and consider my sitivation!

"Thar I was dangling, like a dead weight, at the tail of that all-fired cloud of wild-geese, head downward, and gwine, the Lawd knows whar!—to Canniday, or Jericho, or some other heathen territory beyond the Mississipp, and it mout be, over the great etarnal ocean! . . .

"And jest then I could see we waur a drawing nigh a great thunder-cloud. I could see the red tongues running out of its black jaws; and 'Lawd!' says I, 'ef these all-fired infarnal wild beasts of birds should carry me into that cloud to be burned to a coal, fried, and roasted, and biled alive by them tongues of red fire!'

"But the geese fought shy of the cloud though we passed mighty nigh on to it, and I could see one red streak of lightning run out of the cloud and give us chase for a full hafe a mile; but we waur too fast for it, and, in a tearing passion bekaise it couldn't ketch us, the red streak struck its horns into a great tree jest behind us, that we hed passed over, and tore it into flinders, in the twink of a musquito.

"But by this time I was beginning to feel quite stupid. I knowed that I waur fast gitting onsensible, and it did seem to me as ef my hour waur come, and I was gwine to die—and die by rope, and dangling in the air, a thousand miles from the airth!

"But jest then I was roused up. I felt something brush agin me; then my face was scratched; and, on a suddent, thar was a stop put to my travels by that conveyance. The geese had stopped flying, and waur in a mighty great conflusteration, flopping their wings, as well as they could, and screaming with all the tongues in their jaws. It was clar to me now that we hed run agin something that brought us all up with a short hitch.

"I was shook roughly agin the obstruction and I put out my right arm and cotched a hold of a long arm of an almighty big tree; then my legs waur cotched betwixt two other branches, and I rekivered myself, so as to set up a leetle and rest. The geese was a tumbling and flopping among the branches. The net was hooked hyar and thar; and the birds waur all about me, swinging and splurging, but onable to break loose and git away. . . .

" 'Hurrah!' I sings out. 'Hurrah, Merry Ann; we'll hev the "capital" now, I reckon!'

"And singing out, I drawed up my legs and shifted my body so as to find an easier seat in the crutch of the tree, which was an almighty big

chestnut oak, when, O Lawd! on a suddent the stump I hed been a-setting on give way onder me. 'Twas a rotten jint of the tree. It give way, Jedge, as I tell you, and down I went, my legs first and then my whole body—slipping down not on the outside, but into a great hollow of the tree, all the hairt of it being eat out by the rot; and afore I knowed whar I waur, I waur some twenty foot down, I reckon; and by the time I touched bottom, I was up to my neck in honey!

"It was an almighty big honey-tree, full of the sweet treacle; and the bees all gone and left it, I reckon, for a hundred years. And I in it up to my neck.

"I could smell it strong. I could taste it sweet. But I could see nothing." . . .

VIII

Yaou, after a great swallow of peach and honey, and a formidable groan after it, resumed his narrative as follows:

"Only think of me, Jedge, in my sitivation! Buried alive in the hollow of a mountain chestnut oak! Up to my neck in honey, with never no more an appetite to eat than ef it waur the very gall of bitterness that we reads of in the Holy Scripters!

"All dark, all silent as the grave; 'cept for the gabbling and the cackling of the wild-geese outside, that every now and then would make a great splurging and cavorting, trying to break away from their hitch, which was jist as fast fixed as my own. . . .

"Oh, Jedge, you couldn't jedge of my sitivation in that deep hollow, that cave, I may say, of mountain oak! My head waur jest above the honey, and ef I backed it to look up, my long ha'r at the back of the neck a'most stuck fast, so thick was the honey.

"But I couldn't help looking up. The hollow was a wide one at the top, and I could see when a star was passing over. Thar they shined, bright and beautiful, as ef they waur the very eyes of the angels; and, as I seed them come and go, looking smiling in upon me as they come, I cried out to 'em, one by one:

" 'Oh, sweet sperrits, blessed angels! ef so be thar's an angel sperrit, as they say, living in all

469

them stars, come down and extricate me from this fix; for, so fur as I kin see, I've got no chaince of help from mortal man or woman. Hairdly onst a year does a human come this way; and ef they did come, how would they know I'm hyar? How could I make them hyar me? O Lawd! O blessed, beautiful angels in them stars! O give me help! Help me out!' I knowed I prayed like a heathen sinner, but I prayed as well as I knowed how; and thar warn't a star passing over me that I didn't pray to, soon as I seed them shining over the opening of the hollow; and I prayed fast and faster as I seed them passing away and gitting out of sight.

"Well, Jedge, suddently, in the midst of my praying, and jest after one bright, big star hed gone over me without seeing my sitivation, I hed a fresh skeer.

"Suddent I haird a monstrous fluttering among my geese—my 'capital.' Then I haird a great scraping and scratching on the outside of the tree, and, suddent, as I looked up, the mouth of the hollow was shet up.

"All was dark. The stars and sky waur all gone. Something black kivered the hollow, and, in a minit a'ter, I haird something slipping down into the hollow right upon me.

"I could hairdly draw my breath. I begun to fear that I was to be siffocated alive; and as I haird the strange critter slipping down, I shoved out my hands and felt ha'r—coarse wool—and with one hand I cotched hold of the ha'ry leg of a beast, and with t'other hand I cotched hold of his tail.

" 'Twas a great b'ar, one of the biggest, come to git his honey. He knowed the tree, Jedge, you see, and ef any beast in the world loves honey, 'tis a b'ar beast. He'll go his death on honey, though the hounds are tearing at his very haunches. . . .

"Now, yer see, Jedge, thar was no chaince for him turning round upon me. He pretty much filled up the hollow. He knowed his way, and slipped down, eend foremost—the latter eend, you know. He could stand up on his hind-legs and eat all he wanted. Then, with his great sharp claws and his mighty muscle, he could work up, holding on to the sides of the tree, and git out a'most as easy as when he come down.

"Now, you see, ef he weighed five hundred pounds, and could climb like a cat, he could easy carry up a young fellow that hed no flesh to spar', and only weighed a hundred and twenty-five. So I laid my weight on him, eased him off as well as I could, but held on to tail and leg as ef all life and etarnity depended upon it.

"Now I reckon, Jedge, that b'ar was pretty much more skeered than I was. He couldn't turn in his shoes, and with something fastened to his ankles, and, as he thought, I reckon, some strange beast fastened to his tail, you never seed beast more eager to git away, and git upwards. He knowed the way, and stuck his claws in the rough sides of the hollow, hand over hand, jest as a sailor pulls a rope, and up we went. We hed, howsomdever, more than one slip back; but, Lawd bless you! I never let go. Up we went, I say, at last, and I stuck jest as close to his haunches as death sticks to a dead nigger. Up we went. I felt myself moving. My neck was out of the honey. My airms were free. I could feel the sticky thing slipping off from me, and a'ter a good quarter of an hour the b'ar was on the great mouth of the hollow; and as I felt that I let go his tail, still keeping fast hold of his leg, and with one hand I cotched hold of the outside rim of the hollow; I found it fast, held on to it; and jest then the b'ar sat squat on the very edge of the hollow, taking a sort of rest a'ter his labor.

"I don't know what 'twas, Jedge, that made me do it. I warn't a-thinking at all. I was only feeling and drawing a long breath. Jest then the b'ar sort o' looked round, as ef to see what varmint it was a-troubling him, when I gin him a mighty push, strong as I could, and he lost his balance and went over outside down cl'ar to the airth, and I could hyar his neck crack, almost as loud as a pistol." . . .

IX

"And thar I sot. So fur as I could see, Jedge, I was safe. I hed got out of the tie of the flying geese, and thar they all waur, spread before me, flopping now and then and trying to ixtricate themselves; but they couldn't come it! Thar they waur, captivated, and so much 'capital' for Sam Snaffles.

"And I hed got out of the lion's den; that is, I hed got out of the honey-tree, and warn't in no present danger of being buried alive agin. Thanks to the b'ar, and to the blessed, beautiful angel sperrits in the stars, that hed sent him thar seeking honey, to be my deliverance from my captivation! . . .

"Well, I calkilated.

"It was cold weather, freezing, and though I had good warm clothes on, I felt monstrous like sleeping, from the cold only, though perhaps the tire and the skeer together hed something to do with it. But I was afeard to sleep. I didn't know what would happen, and a man has never his right courage ontil daylight. I fou't agin sleep by keeping on my calkilation.

"Forty thousand wild-geese!

"Thar wa'n't forty thousand, edzactly—very far from it—but thar they waur, pretty thick; and for every goose I could git from forty to sixty cents in all the villages in South Carolina.

"Thar was 'capital'!

"Then thar waur the b'ar.

"Jedging from his strength in pulling me up, and from his size and fat in filling up that great hollow in the tree, I calkilated that he couldn't weigh less than five hundred pounds. His hide, I knowed, was worth twenty dollars. Then thar was the fat and tallow, and the biled marrow out of his bones, what they makes b'ars grease out of, to make chicken whiskers grow big enough for game-cocks. Then thar waur the meat, skinned, cleaned, and all; thar couldn't be much under four hundred and fifty pounds, and whether I sold him as fresh meat or cured, he'd bring me ten cents a pound at the least.

"Says I, 'Thar's capital!'

"'Then,' says I, 'thar's my honey-tree! I reckon thar's a matter of ten thousand gallons in this hyar same honey-tree; and if I kint git fifty to seventy cents a gallon for it thar's no alligators in Flurriday!'

"And I so calkilated through the night, fighting agin sleep, and thinking of my 'capital' and Merry Ann together. . . .

"But first I must tell you, Jedge, when I seed the first signs of daylight and looked around me, Lawd bless me, what should I see but old Tryon Mountain, with his great head lifting itself up in the east! And beyant I could see the house and fairm of Columbus Mills; and as I turned to look a leetle south of that, thar was my own poor leetle log-cabin standing quiet, but with never a smoke streaming out from the chimbley.

"'God bless them good angel sperrits,' I said, 'I ain't two miles from home!' Before I come down from the tree I knowed edzactly whar I waur. 'Twas only four miles off from the lake and whar I hitched the mule of Columbus Mills close by the cart. Thar, too, I hed left my rifle. Yit in my miserable fix, carried through the air by them wild-geese, I did think I hed gone a'most a thousand miles towards Canniday.

"Soon as I got down from the tree I pushed off at a trot to git the mule and cart. I was pretty sure of my b'ar and geese when I come back. The cart stood quiet enough. But the mule, having nothing to eat, was sharping her teeth upon a boulder, thinking she'd hev a bite or so before long.

"I hitched her up, brought her to my bee-tree, tumbled the b'ar into the cart, wrung the necks of all the geese that waur thar—many hed got away—and counted some twenty-seven hundred that I piled away atop of the b'ar."

"Twenty-seven hundred!" cried the "Big Lie" and all the hunters at a breath. "Twenty-seven hundred! Why, Yaou, whenever you telled of this thing before you always counted them at 3,150!"

"Well, ef I did, I reckon I was right. I was sartinly right then, it being all fresh in my 'membrance; and I'm not the man to go back agin his own words. No, fellows, I sticks to first words and first principles. I scorns to eat my own words. Ef I said 3,150, then 3,150 it waur, never a goose less. But you'll see how to 'count for all. I reckon 'twas only 2,700 I fotched to market. Thar was 200 I gin to Columbus Mills. Then thar was 200 more I carried to Merry Ann; and then thar waur 50 at least, I reckon, I kep for myself. Just you count up, Jedge, and you'll see how to squar' it on all sides. When I said 2,700 I only counted what I sold in the villages, every head of 'em at fifty cents a head; and a'ter putting the money in my pocket I felt all over that I hed the 'capital.'

"Well, Jedge, next about the b'ar. Sold the hide and tallow for a fine market-price; sold the meat, got ten cents a pound for it fresh—'twas most beautiful meat; biled down the bones for the marrow; melted down the grease; sold fourteen pounds of it to the barbers and apothecaries; got a dollar a pound for that; sold the hide for twenty dollars; and got the cash for every thing.

"Thar warn't a fambly in all Greenville and Spartanburg and Asheville that didn't git fresh, green wild-geese from me that season, at fifty cents a head, and glad to git, too; the cheapest fresh meat they could buy; and, I reckon, the finest. And all the people of them villages, ef they hed gone to heaven that week, in the flesh, would have carried nothing better than goose-flesh for the risurrection! Every body ate goose for a month, I reckon, as the weather was freezing cold all the time, and the beasts kept week after week, ontil they waur eaten. From the b'ar only I made a matter of full one hundred dollars. First, thar waur the hide, $20; then 450 pounds of meat, at 10 cents, was $45; then the grease, 14 pounds, $14; and the tallow, some $6 more; and the biled marrow, $11.

"Well, count up, Jedge; 2,700 wild-geese, at 50 cents, you sees, must be more than $1,350. I kin only say, that a'ter all the selling—and I driv at it day and night, with Columbus Mills's mule and cart, and went to every house in every street in all them villages. I hed a'most fifteen hundred dollars, safe stowed away onder the pillows of my bed, all in solid gould and silver.

"But I warn't done! Thar was my bee-tree. Don't you think I waur gwine to lose that honey! no, my darlint! I didn't beat the drum about nothing. I didn't let on to a soul what I was a-doing. They axed me about the wild-geese, but I sent 'em on a wild-goose chase; and 'twa'n't till I hed sold off all the b'ar meat and all the geese that I made ready to git at that honey. I reckon them bees must ha' been making that honey for a hundred years, and was then driv out by the b'ars.

"Columbus Mills will tell you; he axed me all about it; but, though he was always my good friend, I never even told it to him. But he lent me his mule and cart, good fellow as he is, and never said nothing more; and, quiet enough, without beat of drum, I bought up all the tight-bound barrels that ever brought whisky to Spartanburg and Greenville, whar they hes the taste for that article strong; and day by day I went off carrying as many barrels as the cart could hold and

the mule could draw. I tapped the old tree—which was one of the oldest and biggest chestnut oaks I ever did see—close to the bottom, and drawed off the beautiful treacle. I was more than sixteen days about it, and got something over two thousand gallons of the purest, sweetest, yellowest honey you ever did see. I could hairdly git barrels and jimmyjohns enough to hold it; and I sold it out at seventy cents a gallon, which was mighty cheap. So I got from the honey a matter of fourteen hundred dollars. . . .

"When I carried the mule and cart home to Columbus Mills I axed him about a sartin farm of one hundred and sixty acres that he hed to sell. It hed a good house on it. He selled it to me cheap. I paid him down, and put the titles in my pocket. 'Thar's capital!' says I.

"That waur a fixed thing for ever and ever. And when I hed moved everything from the old cabin to the new farm, Columbus let me hev a fine milch cow that gin eleven quarts a day, with a beautiful young caif. Jest about that time thar was a great sale of the furniter of the Ashmore family down at Spartanburg, and I remembered I hed no decent bedstead, or any thing rightly sarving for a young woman's chamber; so I went to the sale, and bought a fine strong mahogany bedstead, a dozen chairs, a chist of drawers, and some other things that ain't quite mentionable, Jedge, but all proper for a lady's chamber; and I soon hed the house fixed up ready for any thing. And up to this time I never let on to any body what I was a-thinking about or what I was a-doing, ontil I could stand up in my own doorway and look about me, and say to myself—this is my 'capital,' I reckon; and when I hed got all that I thought a needcessity to git, I took 'count of every thing.

"I spread the title-deeds of my fairm out on the table. I read 'em over three times to see ef 'twaur all right. Thar was my name several times in big letters, 'to hev and to hold.'

"Then I fixed the furniter. Then I brought out into the stable-yard the old mar'—you couldn't count her ribs *now*, and she was spry as ef she hed got a new conceit of herself.

"Then thar was my beautiful cow and caif, sealing fat, both on 'em, and sleek as a doe in autumn.

"Then thar waur a fine young mule that I

bought in Spartanburg; my cart, and a strong second-hand buggy, that could carry two pussons convenient of two different sexes. And I felt big, like a man of consequence and capital. . . .

"I hed a grand count of my money, Jedge. I hed it in a dozen or twenty little bags of leather—the gould—and the silver I hed in shot-bags. It took me a whole morning to count it up and git the figgers right. Then I stuffed it in my pockets, hyar and thar, every whar, wherever I could stow a bag; and the silver I stuffed away in my saddle-bags, and clapped it on the mar'.

"Then I mounted myself, and sot the mar's nose straight in a bee-line for the fairm of Squaire Hopson.

"I was a-gwine, you see, to supprise him with my 'capital'; but, fust, I meant to give him a mighty grand skeer.

"You see, when I was a-trading with Columbus Mills about the fairm and the cattle and other things, I ups and tells him about my courting of Merry Ann; and when I told him about Squaire Hopson's talk about 'capital,' he says:

"'The old skunk! What right hes he to be talking big so, when he kain't pay his own debts. He's been owing me three hundred and fifty dollars now gwine on three years, and I kain't git even the *intrust* out of him. I've got a mortgage on his fairm for the whole, and ef he won't let you hev his da'ter, jest you come to me, and I'll clap the screws to him in short order.'

"Says I, 'Columbus, won't you sell me that mortgage?'

"'You shill hev it for the face of the debt,' says he, 'not considerin' the intrust.'

"'It's a bargain,' says I; and I paid him down the money, and he signed the mortgage over to me for a vallyable consideration.

"I hed that beautiful paper in my breast pocket, and felt strong to face the Squaire in his own house, knowing how I could turn him out of it! And I mustn't forget to tell you how I got myself a new rig of clothing, with a mighty fine over-coat, and a new fur cap; and as I looked in the glass I felt my consequence all over at every for'a'd step I tuk; and I felt my inches growing with every pace of the mar' on the high-road to Merry Ann and her beautiful daddy!"

X

"Well, Jedge, before I quite got to the Squaire's farm, who should come out to meet me in the road but Merry Ann, her own self! She hed spied me, I reckon, as I crossed the bald ridge a quarter of a mile away. I do reckon the dear gal hed been looking out for me every day the whole eleven days in the week, counting in all the Sundays. In the mountains, you know, Jedge, that the weeks sometimes run to twelve, and even fourteen days, specially when we're on a long camp-hunt!

"Well, Merry Ann cried and laughed together, she was so tarnation glad to see me agin. Says she:

"'Oh, Sam! I'm so glad to see you! I was afeard you had clean gin me up. And thar's that fusty old bachelor Grimstead, he's a-coming here a'most every day; and daddy, he sw'ars that I shill marry him, and nobody else; and mammy, she's at me too, all the time, telling me how fine a fairm he's got, and what a nice carriage, and all that; and mammy says as how daddy'll be sure to beat me ef I don't hev him. But I kain't bear to look at him, the old griesly!'

"'Cuss him!' says I. 'Cuss him, Merry Ann!'

"And she did, but onder her breath—the old cuss.

"'Drot him!' says she; and she said louder, 'and drot me, too, Sam, ef I ever marries any body but you.'

"By this time I hed got down and gin her a long strong hug, and a'most twenty or a dozen kisses, and I says:

"'You sha'n't marry nobody but me, Merry Ann; and we'll hev the marriage this very night, ef you says so!'

"'Oh! psho, Sam! How you does talk!'

"'Ef I don't marry you to-night, Merry Ann, I'm a holy mortar, and a sinner not to be saved by any salting, though you puts the petre with the salt. I'm come for that very thing. Don't you see my new clothes?'

"'Well, you hev got a beautiful coat, Sam; all so blue, and with sich shiny buttons.'

"'Look at my waistcoat, Merry Ann! What do you think of that?'

"'Why, it's a most beautiful blue velvet!'

"'That's the very article,' says I. 'And see the breeches, Merry Ann; and the boots!'

" 'Well,' says she, 'I'm fair astonished, Sam! Why whar, Sam, did you find all the money for these fine things?'

" 'A beautiful young woman, a'most as beautiful as you, Merry Ann, come to me the very night of that day when your daddy driv me off with a flea in my ear. She come to me to my bed at midnight—'

" 'Oh, Sam! ain't you ashamed!'

" ' 'Twas in a dream, Merry Ann; and she tells me something to incourage me to go for'a'd, and I went for'a'd, bright and airly next morning, and I picked up three sarvants that hev been working for me ever sence.'

" 'What sarvants?' says she.

" 'One was a goose, one was a b'ar, and t'other was a bee!'

" 'Now you're a-fooling me, Sam.'

" 'You'll see! Only you git yourself ready, for, by the eternal Hokies, I marries you this very night, and takes you home to my fairm bright and airly to-morrow morning.'

" 'I do think, Sam, you must be downright crazy.'

" 'You'll see and believe! Do you go home and git yourself fixed up for the wedding. Old Parson Stovall lives only two miles from your daddy, and I'll hev him hyar by sundown. You'll see!'

" 'But ef I waur to b'lieve you, Sam—'

" 'I've got on my wedding-clothes o' purpose, Merry Ann.'

" 'But I hain't got no clothes fit for a gal to be married in,' says she.

" 'I'll marry you this very night, Merry Ann,' says I, 'though you hedn't a stitch of clothing at all!'

" 'Git out, you sassy Sam,' says she, slapping my face. Then I kissed her in her very mouth, and a'ter that we walked on together, I leading the mar'.

"Says she, as we neared the house, 'Sam, let me go before, or stay hyar in the thick, and you go in by yourself. Daddy's in the hall, smoking his pipe and reading the newspapers.'

" 'We'll walk in together,' says I, quite consekential.

"Says she, 'I'm so afeard.'

" 'Don't be you afeard, Merry Ann,' says I;

'you'll see that all will come out jest as I tells you. We'll be hitched to-night, ef Parson Stovall, or any other parson, kin be got to tie us up!'

"Says she, suddenly, 'Sam, you're a-walking lame, I'm a-thinking. What's the matter? Hev you hurt yourself any way?'

"Says I, 'It's only owning to my not balancing my accounts even in my pockets. You see I feel so much like flying in the air with the idee of marrying you to-night that I filled my pockets with rocks, jest to keep me down.'

" 'I do think, Sam, you're a leetle cracked in the upper story.'

" 'Well,' says I, 'ef so, the crack has let in a blessed chaince of the beautifulest sunlight! You'll see! Cracked, indeed! Ha, ha, ha! Wait till I've done with your daddy! I'm gwine to square accounts with him, and, I reckon, when I'm done with him, you'll guess that the crack's in his skull, and not in mine.' . . .

"Well, in I walked, and thar sat the old Squaire smoking his pipe and reading the newspaper. He looked at me through this specs over the newspaper, and when he seed who 'twas his mouth put on that same conceited sort of grin and smile that he ginerally hed when he spoke to me.

" 'Well,' says he, gruffly enough, 'it's you, Sam Snaffles, is it?' Then he seems to diskiver my new clothes and boots, and he sings out, 'Heigh! you're tip-toe fine to-day! What fool of a shop-keeper in Spartanburg have you tuk in this time, Sam?'

"Says I, cool enough, 'I'll answer all them iligant questions a'ter a while, Squaire; but would prefar to see to business fust.'

" 'Business!' says he; 'and what business kin you hev with me, I wants to know?'

" 'You shill know, Squaire, soon enough; and I only hopes it will be to your liking a'ter you l'arn it.'

"So I laid my saddle-bags down at my feet and tuk a chair quite at my ease; and I could see that he was all astare in wonderment at what he thought my sassiness. As I felt I had my hook in his gills, though he didn't know it yit, I felt in the humor to tickle him and play him as we does a trout.

"Says I, 'Squaire Hopson, you owes a sartin amount of money, say $350, with intrust on it for now three years, to Dr. Columbus Mills.'

"At this he squares round, looks me full in the face, and says:

" 'What the old Harry's that to you?'

"Says I, gwine on cool and straight, 'You gin him a mortgage on this fairm for security.'

" 'What's that to you?' says he.

" 'The mortgage is over-due by two years, Squaire,' says I.

" 'What the old Harry's all that to you, I say?' he fairly roared out.

" 'Well, nothing much, I reckon. The $350, with three years' intrust at seven per cent., making it now—I've calkelated it all without compounding—something over $425—well, Squaire, that's not much to you, I reckon, with your large capital. But it's something to me.'

" 'But I ask you again, Sir,' he says, 'what is all this to you?'

" 'Jist about what I tells you—say $425; and I've come hyar this morning, bright and airly, in hope you'll be able to square up and satisfy the mortgage. Hyar's the dockyment.'

"And I drawed the paper from my breast pocket.

" 'And you tell me that Dr. Mills sent you hyar,' says he, 'to collect this money?'

" 'No; I come myself on my own hook.'

" 'Well,' says he, 'you shill hev your answer at onst. Take that paper back to Dr. Mills and tell him that I'll take an airly opportunity to call and arrange the business with him. You hev your answer, Sir,' he says, quite grand, 'and the sooner you makes yourself scarce the better.'

" 'Much obleeged to you, Squaire, for your ceveelity,' says I; 'but I ain't quite satisfied with that answer. I've come for the money due on this paper, and must hev it, Squaire, or that will be what the lawyers call *four closures* upon it!'

" 'Enough! Tell Dr. Mills I will answer his demand in person.'

" 'You needn't trouble yourself, Squaire; for ef you'll jest look at the back of that paper, and read the 'signmeant, you'll see that you've got to settle with Sam Snaffles, and not with Columbus Mills!'

"Then he snatches up the dockyment, turns it over, and reads the rigilar 'signmeant, writ in Columbus Mills's own handwrite.

"Then the Squaire looks at me with a great stare, and he says, to himself like:

" 'It's a *bonny fodder* 'signmeant.'

" 'Yes,' says I, 'it's *bonny fodder*—rigilar in law —and the titles all made out complete to me, Sam Snaffles; signed, sealed, and delivered, as the lawyers says it.'

" 'And how the old Harry come you by this paper?' says he.

"I was gitting riled, and I was detarmined, this time, to gin my hook a pretty sharp jerk in his gills; so I says:

" 'What the old Harry's that to *you*, Squaire? Thar's but one question 'twixt us two—air you ready to pay that money down on the hub, at onst, to me, Sam Snaffles?'

" 'No, Sir, I am not.'

" 'How long a time will you ax from me, by way of marciful indulgence?'

" 'It must be some time yit,' says he, quite sulky; and then he goes on agin:

" 'I'd like to know how you come by that 'signmeant, Mr. Snaffles.'

"Mr. Snaffles! Ah! ha!

" 'I don't see any neecessity,' says I, 'for answering any questions. Thar's the dockyment to speak for itself. You see that Columbus Mills 'signs to me for full *con*sideration. That means I paid him!'

" 'And why did you buy this mortgage?'

" 'You might as well ax me how I come by the money to buy any thing,' says I.

" 'Well, I do ax you,' says he.

" 'And I answers you,' says I, 'in the very words from your own mouth, What the old Harry's that to you?'

" 'This is hardly 'spectful, Mr. Snaffles,' says he.

"Says I, ' 'Spectful gits only what 'spectful gives! Ef any man but you, Squaire, hed been so onrespectful in his talk to me as you hev been I'd ha' mashed his muzzle! But I don't wish to be onrespectful. All I axes is the civil answer. I wants to know when you kin pay this money?'

" 'I kain't say, Sir.'

" 'Well, you see, I thought as how you couldn't pay, spite of all your "capital," as you hedn't paid even the *intrust* on it for three years; and, to tell you the truth, I was in hopes you couldn't pay, as I am jest about to git married, you see—'

475

" 'Who the old Harry air you gwine to marry?' says he.

" 'What the old Harry's that to you?' says I, giving him as good as he sent. But I went on:

" 'You may be sure it's one of the woman kind. I don't hanker a'ter a wife with a beard; and I expects—God willing, weather permitting, and the parson being sober—to be married this very night!'

" 'To-night!' says he, not knowing well what to say.

" 'Yes; you see I've got my wedding-breeches on. I'm to be married to-night, and I wants to take my wife to her own fairm as soon as I kin. Now, you see, Squire, I all along set my hairt on this fairm of yourn, and I determined, ef ever I could git the "capital," to git hold of it; and that was the idee I hed when I bought the 'signmeant of the mortgage from Columbus Mills. So, you see, ef you kain't pay a'ter three years, you never kin pay, I reckon; and ef I don't git my money this day, why—I kain't help it—the lawyers will hev to see to the *four closures* to-morrow!'

" 'Great God, Sir!' says he, rising out of his chair, and crossing the room up and down, 'do you coolly propose to turn me and my family headlong out of my house?'

" 'Well now,' says I, 'Squire, that's not ed-zactly the way to put it. As I reads this docky-ment'—and I tuk up and put the mortgage in my pocket—'the house and fairm are mine by law. They onst was yourn; but it wants nothing now but the *four closures* to make 'em mine.'

" 'And would you force the sale of property worth $2000 and more for a miserable $400?'

" 'It must sell for what it'll bring, Squire; and I stands ready to buy it for my wife, you see ef it costs me twice as much as the mortgage.'

" 'Your wife!' says he; 'who the old Harry is she? You once pertended to have an affection for my da'ter.'

" 'So I hed; but you hedn't the proper affec-tion for your da'ter that I hed. You prefar'd money to her affections, and you driv me off to git "capital"! Well, I tuk your advice, and I've got the capital.'

" 'And whar the old Harry,' said he, 'did you git it?'

" 'Well, I made good tairms with the old devil for a hundred years, and he found me in the money.'

" 'It must hev been so,' said he. 'You waur not the man to git capital in any other way.'

"Then he goes on: 'But what becomes of your pertended affection for my da'ter?'

" 'Twa'n't pertended; but you throwed your-self betwixt us with all your force, and broke the gal's hairt, and broke mine, so far as you could; and as I couldn't live without company, I hed to look out for myself and find a wife as I could. I tell you, as I'm to be married tonight, and as I've swore a most etarnal oath to hev this fairm, you'll hev to raise the wind today, and square off with me, or the lawyers will be at you with the *four closures* to-morrow, bright and airly.'

" 'Dod dern you!' he cries out. 'Does you want to drive me mad!'

" 'By no manner of means,' says I, jest about as cool and quiet as a cowcumber. . . .

" 'Yes, you pertended to love my da'ter, and now you are pushing her father to desperation. Now ef you ever did love Merry Ann, honestly, raally, truly, and *bonny fodder*, you couldn't help loving her yit. And yit, hyar you're gwine to marry another woman, that, prehaps, you don't affection at all.'

" 'It's quite a sensible view you takes of the subject,' says I; 'the only pity is that you didn't take the same squint at it long ago, when I axed you to let me hev Merry Ann. Then you didn't valley her affections or mine. You hed no thought of nothing but the "capital" then, and the affec-tions might all go to Jericho, for what you keered! I'd ha' married Merry Ann, and she me, and we'd ha' got on for a spell in a log-cabin, for, though I was poor, I hed the genwine grit of a man, and would come to something, and we'd ha' got on; and yit, without any "capital" your own self, and kivered up with debt as with a winter over-coat, hyar, you waur positive that I shouldn't hev your da'ter, and you waur a-preparing to sell her hyar to an old sour-tempered bachelor, more than double her age. Dern the capital! A man's the best capital for any woman, ef so be he is a man. Bekaise, ef he be a man, he'll work out cl'ar, though he may hev a long straining for it through the sieve. Dern the capital! You've as good as sold that gal child to old Grimstead, jest from your love of money!'

" 'But she won't hev him,' says he.

" 'The wiser gal child,' says I. . . .

"The poor old Squaire fairly sweated; but he couldn't say much. He'd come up to me and say:

" 'Ef you only did love Merry Ann!'

" 'Oh,' says I, 'what's the use of your talking that? Ef you only hed ha' loved your own da'ter!' 10

"Then the old chap begun to cry, and as I seed that I jest kicked over my saddle-bags lying at my feet, and the silver Mexicans rolled out—a bushel on 'em, I reckon—and, O Lawd! how the old fellow jumped, staring with all his eyes at me and the dollars!

" 'It's money!' says he.

" 'Yes,' says I, 'jest a few hundreds of thousands of my "capital." ' I didn't stop at the figgers, you see. 20

"Then he turns to me and says, 'Sam Snaffles, you're a most wonderful man. You're a mystery to me. Whar, in the name of God, hev you been? and what hev you been doing? and whar did you git all this power of capital?'

"I jest laughed, and went to the door and called Merry Ann. She come mighty quick. I reckon she was watching and waiting.

"Says I, 'Merry Ann, that's money. Pick it up and put it back in the saddle-bags, ef you please.' 30

"Then says I, turning to the old man, 'Thar's that whole bushel of Mexicans, I reckon. Thar monstrous heavy. My old mar'—ax her about her ribs now!—she fairly squelched onder the weight of me and that money. And I'm pretty heavy loaded myself. I must lighten; with your leave, Squaire.'

"And I pulled out a leetle doeskin bag of gould half eagles from my right-hand pocket and poured them out upon the table; then I emptied my left- 40 hand pocket, then the side pockets of the coat, then the skairt pockets, and jist spread the shiners out upon the table.

"Merry Ann was fairly frightened, and run out of the room; then the old woman she come in, and as the old Squaire seed her, he tuk her by the shoulder and said:

" 'Jest you look at that thar.'

"And when she looked and seed, the poor old hypercritical scamp sinner turned round to me and flung her airms round my neck, and said:

" 'I always said you waur the only right man for Merry Ann.'

"The old spooney!

"Well, when I hed let 'em look enough, and wonder enough, I jest turned Merry Ann and her mother out of the room.

"The old Squaire, he waur a-setting down agin in his airm-chair, not edzactly knowing what to say or what to do, but watching all my motions, jest as sharp as a cat watches a mouse when she is hafe hungry. . . .

" 'Ah, Sam Snaffles, ef you ever did love my leetle Merry Ann, you would never marry any other woman.'

"Then you ought to ha' seed me. I felt myself sixteen feet high, and jest as solid as a chestnut oak. I walked up to the old man, and I tuk him quiet by the collar of his coat, with my thumb and forefinger, and I said:

" 'Git up, Squaire, for a bit.'

"And up he got.

"Then I marched him to the big glass agin the wall, and I said to him: 'Look, ef you please.'

"And he said, 'I'm looking.'

"And I said, 'What does you see?'

"He answered, 'I sees you and me.'

"I says, 'Look agin, and tell me what you obzarves.'

" 'Well,' says he, 'I obzarves.'

"And says I, 'What does your obzarving amount to? That's the how.'

"And says he, 'I sees a man alongside of me, as good-looking and handsome a young man as ever I seed in all my life.'

" 'Well,' says I, 'that's a correct obzarvation. But,' says I, 'what does you see of your own self?'

" 'Well, I kain't edzackly say.'

" 'Look good!' says I. 'Obzarve.'

"Says he, 'Don't ax me.'

" 'Now,' says I, 'that won't edzactly do. I tell you now, look good, and ax yourself ef you're the sawt of looking man that hes any right to be a feyther-in-law to a fine, young, handome-looking fellow like me, what's got the "capital"?'

"Then he laughed out at the humor of the

sitivation; and he says, 'Well, Sam Snaffles, you've got me dead this time. You're a different man from what I thought you. But, Sam, you'll confess, I reckon, that ef I hedn't sent you off with a flea in your ear when I hed you up afore the looking-glass, you'd never ha' gone to work to git in the "capital." '

" 'I don't know that, Squaire,' says I. 'Sarcumstances sarve to make a man take one road when he mout take another; but when you meets a man what has the hairt to love a woman strong as a lion, and to fight an inimy big as a buffalo, he's got the raal grit in him. You knowed I was young, and I was poor, and you knowed the business of a hunter is a mighty poor business ef the man ain't born to it. Well, I didn't do much at it jest bekaise my hairt was so full of Merry Ann; and you should ha' made a calkilation and allowed for that. But you poked your fun at me and riled me consumedly; but I was determined that you shouldn't break my hairt or the hairt of Merry Ann. Well, you hed your humors, and I've tried to take the change out of you. And now, ef you raally thinks, a'ter that obzarvation in the glass, that you kin make a respectable feyther-in-law to sich a fine-looking fellow as me, what's got the "capital," jest say the word, and we'll call Merry Ann in to bind the bargin. And you must talk out quick, for the wedding's to take place this very night. I've swore it by the etarnal Hokies.'

" 'To-night!' says he.

" 'Look at the "capital," ' says I; and I pinted to the gould on the table and the silver in the saddle-bags.

" 'But, Lawd love you, Sam,' says he, 'it's so suddent, and we kain't make the preparations in time.'

"Says I, 'Look at the "capital," Squaire, and dern the preparations!'

" 'But,' says he, 'we hain't time to ax the company.'

" 'Dern the company!' says I; 'I don't b'lieve in company the very night a man gits married. His new wife's company enough for him ef he's sensible.'

" 'But, Sam,' says he, 'it's not possible to git up a supper by to-night.'

"Says I, 'Look you, Squaire, the very last thing a man wants on his wedding night is supper.'

"Then he said something about the old woman, his wife.

"Says I, 'Jest you call her in and show her the "capital." '

"So he called in the old woman, and then in come Merry Ann, and thar was great hemmings and hawings; and the old woman she said:

" 'I've only got the one da'ter, Sam, and we must hev a big wedding! We must spread ourselves. We've got a smart chaince of friends and acquaintances, you see, and 'twon't be decent onless we axes them, and they won't like it! We must make a big show for the honor and 'spectability of the family.'

"Says I, 'Look you, old lady! I've swore a most tremendous oath, by the Holy Hokies, that Merry Ann and me air to be married this very night, and I kain't break sich an oath as that! Merry Ann,' says I, 'you wouldn't hev me break sich a tremendous oath as that?'

"And, all in a trimble, she says, 'Never, Sam! No!'

" 'You hyar that, old lady!' says I. 'We marries to-night, by the Holy Hokies! and we'll hev no company but old Parson Stovall, to make the hitch; and Merry Ann and me go off by sunrise to-morrow morning—you hyar?—to my own fairm, whar thar's a great deal of furniter fixing for her to do. A'ter that you kin advertise the whole county to come in, ef you please, and eat all the supper you kin spread! Now hurry up,' says I, 'and git as ready as you kin, for I'm gwine to ride over to Parson Stovall's this minit. I'll be back to dinner in hafe an hour. Merry Ann, you gether up that gould and silver, and lock it up. It's our "capital"! As for you, Squaire, thar's the mortgage on your fairm, which Merry Ann shill give you, to do as you please with it, as soon as the parson has done the hitch, and I kin call Merry Ann, Mrs. Snaffles—Madam Merry Ann Snaffles, and so forth, and aforesaid.'

" I laid down the law that time for all parties, and showed the old Squaire sich a picter of himself, and me standing aside him, looking seven foot high, at the least, that I jest worked the business 'cording to my own pleasure. When neither the daddy nor the mammy hed any thing more to say, I jumped on my mar' and rode over to old Parson Stovall.

478

"Says I, 'Parson, thar's to be a hitch tonight, and you're to see a'ter the right knot. You knows what I means. I wants you over at Squaire Hopson's. Me and Merry Ann, his da'ter, mean to hop the twig to-night, and you're to see that we hop squar', and that all's even, 'cording to the law, Moses, and the profits! I stand treat, Parson, and you won't be the worse for your riding. I pays in gould!'

"So he promised to come by dusk; and come he did. The old lady hed got some supper, and tried her best to do what she could at sich short notice. The venison ham was mighty fine, I reckon, for Parson Stovall played a great stick at it; and ef they hedn't cooked up four of my wild-geese, then the devil's an angel of light, and Sam Snaffles no better than a sinner! And thar was any quantity of jimmyjohns, peach and honey considered. Parson Stovall was a great feeder, and I begun to think he never would be done. But at last he wiped his mouth, swallowed his fifth cup of coffee, washed it down with a stiff dram of peach and honey, wiped his mouth agin, and pulled out his prayer-book, psalmody, and Holy Scrip—three volumes in all—and he hemmed three times, and begun to look out for the marriage text, but begun with giving out the 100th Psalm.

" 'With one consent, let's all unite—'

" 'No,' says I, 'Parson; not all! It's only Merry Ann and me what's to unite to-night!'

"Jest then, afore he could answer, who should pop in but old bachelor Grimstead! and he looked round 'bout him, specially upon me and the parson, as ef to say:

" 'What the old Harry's they doing hyar!'

"And I could see that the old Squaire was oneasy. But the blessed old Parson Stovall, he gin 'em no time for ixplanation or palaver; but he gits up, stands up squar', looks solemn as a meat-axe, and he says:

" 'Let the parties which I'm to bind together in the holy bonds of wedlock stand up before me!'

"And, Lawd bless you, as he says the words, what should that old skunk of a bachelor do, but he gits up, stately as an old buck in spring time, and he marches over to my Merry Ann! But I was too much and too spry for him. I puts in betwixt 'em, and I takes the old bachelor by his coat-collar,

10

20

30

40

'twixt my thumb and forefinger, and afore he knows whar he is, I marches him up to the big looking-glass, and I says:

" 'Look!'

" 'Well,' says he, 'what?'

" 'Look good,' says I.

" 'I'm looking,' says he. 'But what do you mean, Sir?'

" 'Says I, 'Obzarve! Do you see yourself? Obzarve!'

" 'I reckon I do,' says he.

" 'Then,' says I, 'ax yourself the question, ef you're the sawt of looking man to marry my Merry Ann.'

"Then the old Squaire burst out a-laughing. He couldn't help it.

" 'Capital!' says he.

" 'It's capital,' says I. 'But hyar we air, Parson. Put on the hitch, jest as quick as you kin clinch it; for thar's no telling how many slips thar may be 'twixt the cup and the lips when these hungry old bachelors air about.'

" 'Who gives away this young woman?' axes the parson; and the Squaire stands up and does the thing needful. I hed the ring ready, and before the parson had quite got through, old Grimstead vamoosed. . . .

"All that, Jedge, is jest thirteen years ago; and me and Merry Ann git on famously, and thar's no eend to the capital! Gould breeds like the cows, and it's only needful to squeeze the bags now and then to make Merry Ann happy as a tomtit. Thirteen years of married life, and look at me! You see for yourself, Jedge, that I'm not much the worse for wear; and I kin answer for Merry Ann, too, though, Jedge, we hev hed thirty-six children."

"What!" says I, "thirty-six children in thirteen years!"

The "Big Lie" roared aloud.

"Hurrah, Sharp! Go it! You're making it spread! That last shot will make the Jedge know that you're a right truthful sinner of a Saturday night, and in the 'Lying Camp.' "

"To be sure! You see, Merry Ann keeps on. But you've only got to do the ciphering for yourself. Here, now, Jedge, look at it. Count for yourself. First we had three gal children, you see. Very well! Put down three. Then we had

479

six boys, one every year for four years; and then, the fifth year, Merry Ann throwed deuce. Now put down the six boys a'ter the three galls, and ef that don't make thirty-six, thar's no snakes in all Flurriday!

"Now, men," says Sam, "let's liquor all round, and drink the health of Mrs. Merry Ann Snaffles and the thirty-six children, all alive and kicking; and glad to see you, Jedge, and the rest of the company. We're doing right well; but I hes, every now and then, to put my thumb and forefinger on the Squaire's collar, and show him his face in the big glass, and call on him for an obzarvation—for he's mighty fond of going shar's in my 'capital.' "

THE ROMANTIC FULFILLMENT AND THE CRISIS

EDGAR ALLAN POE (1809-1849)

It is a curious irony of literary history that Edgar Allan Poe should have been born in New England, and that the title page of his first book of poetry should carry the words, "By A Bostonian." The accident of birth was the only thing he had in common with the New England poets. Where they sought to edify, he strove to entertain; where they appealed to the intellectual and philosophical interests of their readers, he catered to man's capacity for beauty and strangeness. Emerson reflected the prevailing opinion held by the Boston and Concord writers when he dismissed Poe condescendingly as "the jingle man." Poe's career also contrasts sharply with the placid lives of his New England contemporaries, most of whom had other sources of income in addition to those from their writings. Within five years of the end of his pitifully short life, Poe could declare that he was a struggling journalist, facing poverty and a "thousand consequent contumelies" in a country "where, more than in any other region upon the face of the globe, to be poor is to be despised." Although Poe's imaginative work and his critical theory and practice were often drastically conditioned by the pressures and demands of a magazine-reading public, his best work rises above these limitations. No name is more closely associated with the development of the prose tale, and he is credited with inventing the modern detective story. Of all the poetry of American romanticism, Poe's lyrics are the most melodious in their evocation of moods of haunting melancholy and misty strangeness. Less popular abroad with ordinary readers than Longfellow, Poe continues to share with Whitman a leading position of influence among European writers and critics.

The chronology of Poe's life is a record of frustration and misfortune. He was born in Boston, January 19, 1809, the second son of the actors David and Elizabeth Arnold Poe. The future poet's adversities began a year later when the father disappeared soon after the birth of a third child. Mrs. Poe, a gifted English actress of charm and beauty, was only twenty-five when she died in Richmond, Virginia, December 8, 1811, after a gallant but losing struggle to support her family. Poe was four years of age when he was taken into the family of John Allan, a well-to-do Richmond merchant, where he was regarded as a member of the family, although he was never legally adopted. The Allans took Poe with them in 1815 when they went abroad for five years, and in 1817 entered him at Manor House School, at Stoke Newington, where he impressed his master as "a quick and clever boy." The influence of his three-year stay there is to be seen in the background of his story "William Wilson" (1839). References in other stories to mouldering tombs, ancient castles, and monuments of the past may also be due to the effect of his impressionable childhood years in England.

Upon the Allans' return to Richmond in 1820, young Poe's education was continued by private tutoring and attendance at Richmond Academy. Although he was ostensibly the foster son of an affluent Southern gentleman, the ambiguity of his relationship with John Allan became apparent between 1820 and 1826. In addition to temperamental differences, Poe was made aware of his dependence upon Allan's favor. The high-spirited boy also learned—probably as early as 1824—of the marital infidelity of his guardian. Another profound emotional shock was the death in 1824 of Jane Craig Stanard, the mother of a schoolmate, in whose sympathy Poe found solace. Years later he recalled his adoration of her as the inspiration of his stanzas "To Helen." His heightened need for understanding is revealed also in hints of other romantic attachments; before he left Richmond for the University of Virginia, he became engaged to Sarah Elmira Royster.

Poe was admitted to the University on February

14, 1826, entering the School of Ancient and Modern Languages. He achieved distinction in Latin and French, but the loose discipline prevailing in the recently established institution, the growing rift between Allan and Poe, and family opposition to his engagement with Miss Royster combined to increase Poe's instablity, and to account for his addiction to wine and gambling. His gaming debts—probably incurred by Poe's attempts to supplement the meager allowance sent by Allan—resulted in a withdrawal from the University in December, 1827, and a few months later, following further quarrels with Allan, in his leaving his guardian's house. The details of Poe's activities in the next few months are not entirely clear, but his trip to Boston in April may have been motivated by a desire to find a publisher for a manuscript of poems, and by the hope of encountering friends of his mother. When his first volume, *Tamerlane and Other Poems*, appeared in the early summer of 1827, the author was in uniform, having enlisted in the United States Army on May 26. A tour of duty at Fort Moultrie in the harbor of Charleston, South Carolina, provided the background for "The Gold Bug" (1839). After a military career which led to his promotion as regimental sergeant major, the highest noncommissioned rank, he resigned from the service in 1829. Poe's relations with his guardian were improved temporarily after the death of Mrs. Allan in 1829, and Allan supplied the funds for his protégé's admission to West Point in 1830. In the meantime, Poe published *Al Aaraaf, Tamerlane, and Other Poems* (1829), and looked forward to his life at the Military Academy at West Point as an opportunity for further writing. Disappointment of these hopes, coupled with the unwillingness of the authorities to allow credit for his training in the regular army, increased Poe's emotional instability; and when Allan's second marriage seemed to cut off any chances of reconciliation, Poe deliberately brought about his dismissal from West Point in February, 1831.

After his discharge Poe resided in Baltimore with a relative, Mrs. Maria Clemm, issued his third book, *Poems* (1831), and began the disheartening encounters with editors and publishers which were to continue for the remaining seventeen years of his life. The failure of his poetry to win much acclaim induced the author to turn to the short story, a form suited to periodical journalism in which he scored his first success by winning a prize for "The MS Found in a Bottle." In 1835 John Pendleton Kennedy assisted Poe to obtain a position with *The Southern Literary Messenger* in Richmond, Virginia. His editorial ability

was immediately reflected in every department of the magazine, especially in the book reviews, where his slashing criticism spurred the circulation but also incited animosities. An assured salary from the *Messenger* enabled Poe to marry Virginia Clemm, his cousin, on May 16, 1836, but he resigned his post in December when he felt he was not receiving a salary commensurate with his services. After an unsuccessful interlude in New York, Poe moved to Philadelphia in the summer of 1837, where his editorial appointments included brief connections with *Burton's Gentleman's Magazine*, and later with *Graham's Magazine* in 1841–1842. Twenty-five of his short stories were collected in *Tales of the Grotesque and Arabesque* (1840); the edition of 750 copies was not exhausted until after the author's death. After the failure of his desperate efforts to found a national magazine, Poe moved to New York in 1844, continuing his hack work, this time on Nathaniel Parker Willis's *New York Evening Mirror*. Here, as earlier in Philadelphia, his employers praised his contributions, but his appeal was too limited to justify a recompense of more than four or five dollars a page. To the indignities and worries caused by an income scarcely sufficient for subsistence must be added Poe's anguish occasioned by the suffering of his wife, Virginia, who was slowly dying of tuberculosis.

Poe's first popular fame as a poet came in 1845 with the publication of "The Raven" in the *Mirror*. Later in the same year he published a second collection of his stories, *Tales*, and *The Raven and Other Poems*. In 1846 the Poe family moved to a cottage in Fordham, where, in January of the following year, Virginia Poe died. Although Poe's drinking was not habitual, and was the result rather than the cause of his neuroticism, his intemperance increased after the death of his wife. His dependence on feminine sympathy also became more marked, and resulted in several somewhat febrile attachments. Finally, he became re-engaged to Sarah Elmira Royster, his boyhood sweetheart who had become a widow and was living in Richmond. On his way back to New York, Poe stopped in Baltimore, where he died on October 7, 1849; the circumstances of his death have never been satisfactorily explained. The frustrations which beset Poe did not end with his death. Rufus Griswold, his literary executor, was guilty of forgery and distortion in an account of the dead poet. Even the simple tombstone ordered by a cousin, Nelson Poe, was broken by an accident before it was placed at the grave.

The life of no American author, with the possible exception of that of Whitman or Melville, has attracted so much attention as that of Edgar Allan Poe. Popular interest in the man, however, has not obscured his position in our literature. By his precept and practice he enriched the art of the short narrative with the qualities of dramatic economy, lucidity of statement, intensity of mood, and carefulness of craftsmanship. He was the virtual founder of a school of fearless criticism, although his critical judgment was narrowly limited to those forms of which he was himself a master, the short narrative and lyric. As a poet his virtuosity as a prosodist sometimes exceeded his inspiration, as in "The Bells" and "The Raven." At his best, however, he stands with few peers among American lyrists by his perfect fusion of technical mastery with true poetic fire.

BIBLIOGRAPHY · The most satisfactory edition is *The Complete Works of Edgar Allan Poe* (17 vols., 1902), edited by J. A. Harrison. More easily available, but incomplete, is *The Works of Edgar Allan Poe* (10 vols., 1894–1895, 1914), edited by E. C. Stedman and G. E. Woodberry. The best editions of the poems are *The Complete Poems of Edgar Allan Poe* (1911), edited with notes and a bibliography by J. H. Whitty, and *The Poems of Edgar Allan Poe* (1917), edited by K. Campbell, containing indispensable notes. *The Complete Poems and Stories of Edgar Allan Poe* (2 vols., 1946) was edited with explanatory notes by A. H. Quinn, and bibliographical material by E. H. O'Neill. The best one-volume edition of the stories is K. Campbell, *Poe's Short Stories* (1927). An excellent one-volume book of selections is *Edgar Allan Poe: Representative Selections* (1935), edited by M. Alterton and H. Craig, with an introduction and bibliography. Extremely useful reprints of separate works of Poe are the following items published by the Facsimile Text Society: *Tamerlane and Other Poems*, reproduced in facsimile from the edition of 1827, with an introduction by T. O. Mabbott (1941); *Al Aaraaf, Tamerlane and Minor Poems*, reproduced from the edition of 1829, with a bibliographical note by T. O. Mabbott (1933); *Poems*, reproduced from the edition of 1831, with a note by K. Campbell (1936); and *The Raven and Other Poems*, reproduced from the edition of 1845, containing the author's corrections, edited by T. O. Mabbott (1942). John Ostrom (ed.), *The Letters of Edgar Allan Poe* (2 vols., 1948), is indispensable. Vol. XVI of *The Complete Works of Edgar Allan Poe*, edited by J. A. Harrison, contains a bibliography, which should be supplemented by C. F. Heartman and J. R. Canny, *A Bibliography of First Printings . . .* (1940), and J. W. Robertson, *A Bibliography . . .* (2 vols., 1934).

The most comprehensive biography is A. H. Quinn, *Edgar Allan Poe: A Critical Biography* (1941). N. B. Fagin, *The Histrionic Mr. Poe* (1949) is valuable. Exceedingly readable, but not wholly trustworthy is H. Allen, *Israfel: The Life and Times of Edgar Allan Poe* (2 vols., 1926; revised, 1934). The best of the earlier biographies

is G. E. Woodberry, *Edgar Allan Poe* (2 vols., 1909). Others include J. A. Harrison, *Life and Letters of Edgar Allan Poe* (2 vols., 1903); and U. Pope-Hennessey, *Edgar Allan Poe: A Critical Biography* (1934).

Among the more specialized biographical and critical studies are the following books and articles: M. Alterton, *Origins of Poe's Critical Theory* (1925); C. Baudelaire, "Edgar Poe, sa vie et ses œuvres," in *Nouvelles histoires-extraordinaires par Edgar Poe* (1856); W. C. Brownell, *American Prose Masters* (1909); C. P. Cambiaire, *The Influence of Edgar Allan Poe in France* (1927); K. Campbell, *The Mind of Poe and Other Studies* (1933), "The Poe-Griswold Controversy," *PMLA*, XXXIV (1919), 436–464, "Contemporary Opinion of Poe," *PMLA*, XXXVI (1921), 142–166, and "Poe's Knowledge of the Bible," *Studies in Philology*, XXVII (1930), 546–551; H. S. Canby, "Poe," in *Classic Americans* (1931), 263–307; C. Cestre, "Poe et Baudelaire," *Revue Anglo-Américaine*, XXI (1934), 322–330; P. Cobb, *The Influence of E. T. A. Hoffmann on the Tales of Edgar Allan Poe* (1908); N. Foerster, "Poe" in *American Criticism* (1928), 1–51; W. F. Friedman, "Edgar Allan Poe, Cryptographer," *American Literature*, VIII (1936), 266–280; E. Hungerford, "Poe and Phrenology," *American Literature*, II (1930), 209–231; D. R. Hutcherson, "Poe's Reputation in England and America, 1850–1909," *American Literature*, XIV (1942), 211–233; D. K. Jackson, *Poe and the "Southern Literary Messenger"* (1934); E. Lauvrière, *Le Génie Morbide d'Edgar Poe* (1935); L. Lemonnier, "L'influence d'Edgar Poe sur les conteurs français symbolistes et décadents," *Revue de littérature comparée*, XIII (1935), 102–133; J. R. Lowell, "Our Contributors, No. XVII, Edgar Allan Poe," *Graham's Magazine*, XXVII (1845), 49–53; T. O. Mabbott (editor), *Merlin, Baltimore, 1827, Together with Recollections of Edgar A. Poe by Lambert Wilmer* (1941); E. Marchand, "Poe as a Social Critic," *American Literature*, VI (1934), 28–43; P. E. More, "The Origins of Hawthorne and Poe," in *Shelburne Essays: First Series* (1904), 51–70; F. Stovall, "An Interpretation of Poe's 'Al Aaraaf,'" in *Texas University Studies in English*, IX (1929), 106–133; C. Ticknor, *Poe's Helen* (1916); C. Varner, "Notes on Poe's Use of Contemporary Materials in Certain of His Stories," *Journal of English and Germanic Philology*, XXXII (1933), 77–80; E. Wilson, "Poe as a Literary Critic," *Nation*, CLV (1941), 452–453; J. S. Wilson, "The Young Man Poe," *Virginia Quarterly Review*, II (1926), 238–253; and Y. Winters, "Edgar Allan Poe: A Crisis in the History of American Obscurantism," *American Literature*, VIII (1937), 379–401.

To Helen

"To Helen" appeared for the first time in the 1831 edition of the *Poems*. The present text is that of the revised version in *The Raven and Other Poems* (1845). The poem was inspired by Jane Stith Craig Stanard, the mother of Robert Stanard, a school friend of Poe in Richmond. In 1848 the author told Mrs. Sarah Whitman that the lines were written in his "passionate boyhood" to the "first, purely ideal love" of his soul.

Helen, thy beauty is to me
  Like those Nicéan barks of yore,
That gently, o'er a perfumed sea,
  The weary, way-worn wanderer bore
    To his own native shore.   5

On desperate seas long wont to roam,
  Thy hyacinth hair, thy classic face,
Thy Naiad airs have brought me home
  To the glory that was Greece,
    And the grandeur that was Rome.   10

Lo! in yon brilliant window-niche
  How statue-like I see thee stand,
The agate lamp within thy hand!
  Ah, Psyche, from the regions which
    Are Holy-Land!   15

The City in the Sea

THIS POEM first appeared under the title of "The Doomed City" in the volume of 1831; and thereafter in *The Southern Literary Messenger* (August, 1836) as "The City of Sin," and under the present title first in *The American Whig Review* (April, 1845) and *The Broadway Journal* (August 30, 1845). It underwent textual revision when republication permitted Poe to make improvements. For materials entering into this work of art, "one of the most original and imaginative" of Poe's poems, see Louise Pound, "On Poe's 'The City in the Sea,'" *American Literature*, VI (March, 1934). The text is that of 1845.

Lo! Death has reared himself a throne
In a strange city lying alone
Far down within the dim West,

2. **Nicéan:** The most plausible source of "Nicéan" is Catullus. See J. J. Jones, "Poe's 'Nicéan Barks,'" *American Literature*, II (1931), 433–438.

7. **hyacinth:** a Homeric appellation for hair, usually golden hair. In "Ligeia" Poe used "hyacinthine" to describe the heroine's raven-black tresses.

Where the good and the bad and the worst and the
    best
Have gone to their eternal rest.   5

There shrines and palaces and towers
(Time-eaten towers that tremble not!)
Resemble nothing that is ours.
Around, by lifting winds forgot,
Resignedly beneath the sky   10
The melancholy waters lie.

No rays from the holy heaven come down
On the long night-time of that town;
But light from out the lurid sea
Streams up the turrets silently—   15
Gleams up the pinnacles far and free—
Up domes—up spires—up kingly halls—
Up fanes—up Babylon-like walls—
Up shadowy long-forgotten bowers
Of sculptured ivy and stone flowers—   20
Up many and many a marvellous shrine
Whose wreathèd friezes intertwine
The viol, the violet, and the vine.

Resignedly beneath the sky
The melancholy waters lie.   25
So blend the turrets and shadows there
That all seem pendulous in air,
While from a proud tower in the town
Death looks gigantically down.

There open fanes and gaping graves   30
Yawn level with the luminous waves;
But not the riches there that lie
In each idol's diamond eye—
Not the gaily-jewelled dead
Tempt the waters from their bed;   35
For no ripples curl, alas!
Along that wilderness of glass—
No swellings tell that winds may be
Upon some far-off happier sea—
No heavings hint that winds have been   40
On seas less hideously serene.

But lo, a stir is in the air!
The wave—there is a movement there!
As if the towers had thrust aside,
In slightly sinking, the dull tide—   45

As if their tops had feebly given
A void within the filmy Heaven.
The waves have now a redder glow—
The hours are breathing faint and low—
And when, amid no earthly moans,   50
Down, down that town shall settle hence,
Hell, rising from a thousand thrones,
Shall do it reverence.

Israfel

"Israfel" was first printed in *Poems* (1831). The poem
also appeared in the *Southern Literary Messenger* for
August, 1836, the *Philadelphia Saturday Museum* for
March 4, 1843, and the *Broadway Journal* for July 26,
1845, before it was collected in *The Raven and Other
Poems* (1845). The present text is that of the edition
of 1845. "Israfel" is a triumphant illustration of
Poe's definition of poetry as "the rhythmical creation
of beauty." The last stanza contains a poignant comment upon the lack of harmony between the poet and
the America of the 1830's and 1840's.

In Heaven a spirit doth dwell
  "Whose heart-strings are a lute";
None sing so wildly well
As the angel Israfel,
And the giddy stars (so legends tell)   5
Ceasing their hymns, attend the spell
  Of his voice, all mute.

Tottering above
  In her highest noon,
  The enamoured moon   10
Blushes with love,
  While, to listen, the red levin
  (With the rapid Pleiads, even,
  Which were seven)
  Pauses in Heaven.   15

And they say (the starry choir
  And the other listening things)
That Israfeli's fire

4. **Israfel:** "And the angel Israfel, whose heart-strings
are a lute, and who has the sweetest voice of all God's
creatures."—*Koran* [Poe's footnote]. In *The Life of Edgar
Allan Poe*, I, 180n., G. E. Woodberry showed that the
quotation is not in the *Koran*, but is an adaptation of a
passage in the fourth section of Sale's "Preliminary Discourse" to his translation.

Is owing to that lyre
  By which he sits and sings—   20
The trembling living wire
  Of those unusual strings.

But the skies that angel trod,
  Where deep thoughts are a duty—
Where Love's a grown-up God—   25
  Where the Houri glances are
Imbued with all the beauty
  Which we worship in a star.

Therefore thou art not wrong,
  Israfeli, who despisest   30
An unimpassioned song;
To thee the laurels belong,
  Best bard, because the wisest!
Merrily live, and long!

The ecstasies above   35
  With thy burning measures suit—
Thy grief, thy joy, thy hate, thy love,
  With the fervour of thy lute—
  Well may the stars be mute!

Yes, Heaven is thine; but this   40
  Is a world of sweets and sours;
  Our flowers are merely—flowers,
And the shadow of thy perfect bliss
  Is the sunshine of ours.

If I could dwell   45
Where Israfel
  Hath dwelt, and he where I,
He might not sing so wildly well
  A mortal melody,
While a bolder note than this might swell   50
From my lyre within the sky.

Lenore

THE FIRST VERSION of "Lenore" appeared as "A
Paean" in twelve quatrains in *Poems* (1831). The
ballad stanzas were retained when the poem was reprinted in the *Southern Literary Messenger* for January,
1836, but in the *Pioneer* for February, 1843, where
the piece was entitled "Lenore," Poe used an irregular
stanzaic pattern. Further revisions resulted in the
long lines with internal rhymes in the form printed in

The Raven and Other Poems (1845), which is the basis of the present text. "Lenore" exemplifies Poe's conviction that sadness of tone is the highest manifestation of beauty. The last stanza also illustrates the author's belief that elegiac poetry should contain a triumphant note.

Ah, broken is the golden bowl! the spirit flown forever!
Let the bell toll!—a saintly soul floats on the Stygian river;
And, Guy De Vere, hast thou no tear?—weep now or never more!
See! on yon drear and rigid bier low lies thy love, Lenore!
Come! let the burial rite be read—the funeral song be sung!—   5
An anthem for the queenliest dead that ever died so young—
A dirge for her the doubly dead in that she died so young.

"Wretches! ye loved her for her wealth and hated her for her pride,
And when she fell in feeble health, ye blessed her—that she died!
How shall the ritual, then, be read—the requiem how be sung   10
By you—by yours, the evil eye,—by yours, the slanderous tongue
That did to death the innocence that died, and died so young?"

Peccavimus; but rave not thus! and let a Sabbath song
Go up to God so solemnly the dead may feel no wrong!
The sweet Lenore hath "gone before," with Hope, that flew beside,   15
Leaving thee wild for the dear child that should have been thy bride—
For her, the fair and debonair, that now so lowly lies,
The life upon her yellow hair but not within her eyes—
The life still there, upon her hair—the death upon her eyes.

13. Peccavimus: "We have sinned."

"Avaunt! to-night my heart is light. No dirge will I upraise,   20
But waft the angel on her flight with a Paean of old days!
Let no bell toll, then,—lest her soul, amid its hallowed mirth,
Should catch the note, as it doth float—up from the damnèd Earth!
To friends above, from fiends below, the indignant ghost is riven—
From Hell unto a high estate far up within the Heaven—   25
From grief and groan, to a golden throne, beside the King of Heaven."

To One in Paradise

THIS POEM was first printed as a part of Poe's story "The Visionary" in Godey's Lady's Book for January, 1834, and in the Southern Literary Messenger for July, 1835. Its first appearance as an independent poem occurred in Burton's Gentleman's Magazine for July, 1839, where it was entitled "To Ianthe in Heaven." It was also published as a separate poem in The Raven and Other Poems (1845). The present text is that of the 1845 edition.

Thou wast all that to me, love,
    For which my soul did pine—
A green isle in the sea, love,
    A fountain and a shrine,
All wreathed with fairy fruits and flowers,   5
    And all the flowers were mine.

Ah, dream too bright to last!
    Ah, starry Hope, that didst arise
But to be overcast!
    A voice from out the Future cries,   10
"On! on!"—but o'er the Past
    (Dim gulf!) my spirit hovering lies
Mute, motionless, aghast!

For, alas! alas! with me
    The light of Life is o'er!   15
No more—no more—no more—
    (Such language holds the solemn sea
To the sands upon the shore)
Shall bloom the thunder-blasted tree,
    Or the stricken eagle soar!   20

And all my days are trances,
  And all my nightly dreams
Are where thy dark eye glances,
  And where thy footstep gleams—
In what ethereal dances,   25
  By what eternal streams.

Dream-Land

"Dream-Land" was first published in *Graham's Magazine* for June, 1844; it was reprinted in the *Broadway
Journal* for June 28, and then collected in *The Raven
and Other Poems* (1845). Its chief significance in Poe's
poetic development is its anticipation of the style of
"The Raven" and "Ulalume." The present text is
that of the 1845 edition.

By a route obscure and lonely,
Haunted by ill angels only,
Where an Eidolon, named Night,
On a black throne reigns upright,
I have reached these lands but newly   5
From an ultimate dim Thule—
From a wild weird clime that lieth, sublime,
  Out of Space—out of Time.

Bottomless vales and boundless floods,
And chasms, and caves, and Titan woods,   10
With forms that no man can discover
For the dews that drip all over;
Mountains toppling evermore
Into seas without a shore;
Seas that restlessly aspire,   15
Surging, unto skies of fire;
Lakes that endlessly outspread
Their lone waters—lone and dead,—
Their still waters—still and chilly
With the snows of the lolling lily.   20

By the lakes that thus outspread
Their lone waters, lone and dead,—
Their sad waters, sad and chilly
With the snows of the lolling lily,—
By the mountains—near the river   25
Murmuring lowly, murmuring ever,—
By the grey woods,—by the swamp
Where the toad and the newt encamp,—
By the dismal tarns and pools

Where dwell the Ghouls,—   30
By each spot the most unholy—
In each nook most melancholy,—
There the traveller meets, aghast,
Sheeted Memories of the Past—
Shrouded forms that start and sigh   35
As they pass the wanderer by—
White-robed forms of friends long given,
In agony, to the Earth—and Heaven.

For the heart whose woes are legion
'Tis a peaceful, soothing region—   40
For the spirit that walks in shadow
'Tis—oh 'tis an Eldorado!
But the traveller, travelling through it,
May not—dare not openly view it;
Never its mysteries are exposed   45
To the weak human eye unclosed;
So wills its King, who hath forbid
The uplifting of the fringèd lid;
And thus the sad Soul that here passes
Beholds it but through darkened glasses.   50

By a route obscure and lonely,
Haunted by ill angels only,
Where an Eidolon, named Night,
On a black throne reigns upright,
I have wandered home but newly   55
From this ultimate dim Thule.

The Raven

Poe received only ten dollars for the manuscript of
"The Raven," his most famous poem. It appeared
in the New York *Evening Mirror* for January 29, 1845,
in advance of its publication in the February issue of
the *American Review*. The review of Dickens's *Barnaby
Rudge* in 1841, in which Poe suggested that the novelist
might have made more effective use of the bird's
prophetic croakings, indicates a very likely source.
For an account of his indebtedness to T. H. Chivers,
the Southern poet, see S. F. Damon's *Thomas
Holley Chivers: Friend of Poe* (1930), 198–219. Although it would be uncritical to accept literally Poe's
step-by-step account of the writing of "The Raven"
in "The Philosophy of Composition," the essay is a
revealing commentary on the quality of Poe's mind and
art. The text is that of *The Raven and Other Poems*
(1845), Lorimer Graham copy.

Once upon a midnight dreary, while I pondered,
  weak and weary,
Over many a quaint and curious volume of forgotten lore—
While I nodded, nearly napping, suddenly there
  came a tapping,
As of some one gently rapping, rapping at my
  chamber door.
" 'Tis some visitor," I muttered, "tapping at my
  chamber door—   5
    Only this and nothing more."

Ah, distinctly I remember it was in the bleak
  December;
And each separate dying ember wrought its
  ghost upon the floor.
Eagerly I wished the morrow;—vainly I had
  sought to borrow
From my books surcease of sorrow—sorrow for
  the lost Lenore—   10
For the rare and radiant maiden whom the angels
  name Lenore—
    Nameless here for evermore.

And the silken, sad, uncertain rustling of each
  purple curtain
Thrilled me—filled me with fantastic terrors never
  felt before;
So that now, to still the beating of my heart, I
  stood repeating   15
" 'Tis some visitor entreating entrance at my
  chamber door,
Some late visitor entreating entrance at my
  chamber door:
    This it is and nothing more."

Presently my soul grew stronger; hesitating then
  no longer,
"Sir," said I, "or Madam, truly your forgiveness
  I implore: 20
But the fact is I was napping, and so gently you
  came rapping,
And so faintly you came tapping, tapping at my
  chamber door,
That I scarce was sure I heard you"—here I
  opened wide the door:—
    Darkness there and nothing more.

Deep into that darkness peering, long I stood
  there wondering, fearing,   25
Doubting, dreaming dreams no mortal ever
  dared to dream before:
But the silence was unbroken, and the stillness
  gave no token,
And the only word there spoken was the whispered word, "Lenore?"
This I whispered, and an echo murmured back
  the word, "Lenore!"
    Merely this and nothing more.   30

Back into the chamber turning, all my soul within
  me burning,
Soon again I heard a tapping somewhat louder
  than before.
"Surely," said I, "surely that is something at my
  window lattice;
Let me see, then, what thereat is, and this mystery
  explore;
Let my heart be still a moment and this mystery
  explore;—   35
    'Tis the wind and nothing more!"

Open here I flung the shutter, when, with many a
  flirt and flutter,
In there stepped a stately Raven of the saintly
  days of yore;
Not the least obeisance made he; not a minute
  stopped or stayed he;
But, with mien of lord or lady, perched above my
  chamber door,   40
Perched upon a bust of Pallas just above my
  chamber door:
    Perched, and sat, and nothing more.

Then this ebony bird beguiling my sad fancy into
  smiling,
By the grave and stern decorum of the coun-
  tenance it wore,
"Though thy crest be shorn and shaven, thou,"
  I said, "art sure no craven,   45
Ghastly grim and ancient Raven wandering from
  the Nightly shore—

  41. Pallas: Athena, in Greek mythology, goddess of
wisdom.

Tell me what thy lordly name is on the Night's
Plutonian shore!"
Quoth the Raven, "Nevermore."

Much I marvelled this ungainly fowl to hear discourse so plainly,
Though its answer little meaning—little relevancy
bore;   50
For we cannot help agreeing that no living human
being
Ever yet was blessed with seeing bird above his
chamber door,
Bird or beast upon the sculptured bust above
his chamber door,
With such name as "Nevermore."

But the Raven, sitting lonely on the placid bust,
spoke only   55
That one word, as if his soul in that one word he did
outpour,
Nothing further then he uttered—not a feather
then he fluttered—
Till I scarcely more than muttered, "Other friends
have flown before—
On the morrow he will leave me, as my Hopes
have flown before."
Then the bird said, "Nevermore."   60

Startled at the stillness broken by reply so aptly
spoken,
"Doubtless," said I, "what it utters is its only stock
and store,
Caught from some unhappy master whom unmer-
ciful Disaster
Followed fast and followed faster till his songs one
burden bore—
Till the dirges of his Hope that melancholy burden
bore   65
Of 'Never—nevermore.' "

But the Raven still beguiling all my fancy into
smiling,
Straight I wheeled a cushioned seat in front of
bird and bust and door;
Then, upon the velvet sinking, I betook myself to
linking
Fancy unto fancy, thinking what this ominous
bird of yore,   70

What this grim, ungainly, ghastly, gaunt, and
ominous bird of yore
Meant in croaking "Nevermore."

This I sat engaged in guessing, but no syllable
expressing
To the fowl whose fiery eyes now burned into my
bosom's core;
This and more I sat divining, with my head at ease
reclining   75
On the cushion's velvet lining that the lamplight
gloated o'er,
But whose velvet violet lining with the lamplight
gloating o'er
She shall press, ah, nevermore!

Then, methought, the air grew denser, perfumed
from an unseen censer
Swung by seraphim whose foot-falls tinkled on the
tufted floor.   80
"Wretch," I cried, "thy God hath lent thee—
by these angels he hath sent thee
Respite—respite and nepenthe from thy memories
of Lenore!
Quaff, oh quaff this kind nepenthe, and forget
this lost Lenore!"
Quoth the Raven, "Nevermore."

"Prophet!" said I, "thing of evil! prophet still,
if bird or devil!—   85
Whether Tempter sent, or whether tempest tossed
thee here ashore,
Desolate yet all undaunted, on this desert land en-
chanted—
On this home by Horror haunted—tell me truly,
I implore—
Is there—is there balm in Gilead?—tell me—tell
me, I implore!"
Quoth the Raven, "Nevermore."   90

"Prophet!" said I, "thing of evil—prophet still,
if bird or devil!
By that Heaven that bends above us, by that
God we both adore,
Tell this soul with sorrow laden if, within the
distant Aidenn,

47. **Plutonian:** Pluto, in Greek mythology, the god of
the underworld.

89. **Gilead:** mountainous region east of the Jordan
(Joshua xii, 2).   **93. Aidenn:** Eden.

It shall clasp a sainted maiden whom the angels
    name Lenore—
Clasp a rare and radiant maiden whom the angels
    name Lenore!"   95
    Quoth the Raven, "Nevermore."

"Be that word our sign of parting, bird or fiend!"
    I shrieked, upstarting—
"Get thee back into the tempest and the Night's
    Plutonian shore!
Leave no black plume as a token of that lie thy
    soul hath spoken!
Leave my loneliness unbroken! quit the bust
    above my door!   100
Take thy beak from out my heart, and take thy
    form from off my door!"
    Quoth the Raven, "Nevermore."

And the Raven, never flitting, still is sitting, still
    is sitting
On the pallid bust of Pallas just above my chamber
    door;
And his eyes have all the seeming of a demon's
    that is dreaming,   105
And the lamp-light o'er him streaming throws
    his shadow on the floor:
And my soul from out that shadow that lies float-
    ing on the floor
    Shall be lifted—nevermore!

Ulalume

"Ulalume" was first published in the *American Whig
Review* for December, 1847, and was reprinted in the
Home Journal for January 1, 1848, the *Providence
Journal* for November 22, 1848, and in the *Literary
World* for March 3, 1849. Rufus Griswold included it
in *Poets and Poetry of America* (Tenth Edition, 1850).
The poem has been described as obscure by critics who
have confused indefiniteness with obscurity, and who
have forgotten that Poe employed vagueness as a means
to achieve the beauty which he believed to be the
true province of poetry. "Ulalume" has also been
cited as an example of Poe's technical virtuosity and
his lack of "heart" or human feeling and interest.
This view, however, fails to take into account the fact
that the poem was written after the death of Virginia
and records Poe's emotional conflicts and anguish.
The text is that of 1876.

The skies they were ashen and sober;
    The leaves they were crispèd and sere—
    The leaves they were withering and sere;
It was night in the lonesome October
    Of my most immemorial year;   5
It was hard by the dim lake of Auber,
    In the misty mid region of Weir—
It was down by the dank tarn of Auber,
    In the ghoul-haunted woodland of Weir.

Here once, through an alley Titanic   10
    Of cypress, I roamed with my Soul—
    Of cypress, with Psyche, my Soul.
These were days when my heart was volcanic
    As the scoriac rivers that roll—
    As the lavas that restlessly roll   15
Their sulphurous currents down Yaanek
    In the ultimate climes of the Pole—
That groan as they roll down Mount Yaanek
    In the realms of the Boreal Pole.

Our talk had been serious and sober,   20
    But our thoughts they were palsied and sere,
    Our memories were treacherous and sere—
For we knew not the month was October,
    And we marked not the night of the year,
    (Ah, night of all nights in the year!)   25
We noted not the dim lake of Auber—
    (Though once we had journeyed down here)
Remembered not the dank tarn of Auber,
    Nor the ghoul-haunted woodland of Weir.

And now, as the night was senescent   30
    And star-dials pointed to morn—
    As the star-dials hinted of morn—
At the end of our path a liquescent
    And nebulous lustre was born,
Out of which a miraculous crescent   35
    Arose, with a duplicate horn,
Astarte's bediamonded crescent
    Distinct with its duplicate horn.

And I said—"She is warmer than Dian:
    She rolls through an ether of sighs,   40

6. **Auber:** All place names in this poem are fictitious.
37. **Astarte:** in mythology the goddess of love, associated
with the moon, hence often represented by the symbol of
the crescent.   **39. Dian:** Diana, in mythology goddess of
the moon, protectress of the female sex.

She revels in a region of sighs:
She has seen that the tears are not dry on
  These cheeks, where the worm never dies,
And has come past the stars of the Lion
    To point us the path to the skies,   45
  To the Lethean peace of the skies:
Come up, in despite of the Lion,
  To shine on us with her bright eyes:
Come up through the lair of the Lion,
  With love in her luminous eyes."   50

But Psyche, uplifting her finger,
  Said—"Sadly this star I mistrust—
  Her pallor I strangely mistrust:—
Oh, hasten!—oh, let us not linger!
  Oh, fly!—let us fly!—for we must."   55
In terror she spoke, letting sink her
  Wings till they trailed in the dust—
In agony sobbed, letting sink her
  Plumes till they trailed in the dust—
  Till they sorrowfully trailed in the dust.   60

I replied—"This is nothing but dreaming:
  Let us on by this tremulous light!
  Let us bathe in this crystalline light!
Its Sibyllic splendor is beaming
  With hope and in beauty tonight: 65
  See, it flickers up the sky through the night!
Ah, we safely may trust to its gleaming,
  And be sure it will lead us aright—
We safely may trust to a gleaming
  That cannot but guide us aright,   70
  Since it flickers up to Heaven through the
    night."

Thus I pacified Psyche and kissed her,
  And tempted her out of her gloom—
  And conquered her scruples and gloom;
And we passed to the end of the vista,   75
  But were stopped by the door of a tomb,
  By the door of a legended tomb;
And I said—"What is written, sweet sister,
  On the door of this legended tomb?"
She replied—"Ulalume—Ulalume—   80
  'Tis the vault of thy lost Ulalume!"

44. **Lion:** Leo, a zodiacal constellation. **46 Lethean:**
Lethe in Greek mythology personified oblivion. **64.**
Sibyllic: prophetic, mysterious, rapturous.

Then my heart it grew ashen and sober
  As the leaves that were crispèd and sere,
  As the leaves that were withering and sere,
And I cried—"It was surely October   85
  On *this* very night of last year
  That I journeyed—I journeyed down here!—
  That I brought a dread burden down here—
  On this night of all nights in the year,
  Ah, what demon has tempted me here?   90
Well I know, now, this dim lake of Auber,
  This misty mid region of Weir:
Well I know, now, this dank tarn of Auber,
  This ghoul-haunted woodland of Weir.

The Bells

THIS POEM was first printed in *Sartain's Union Magazine*
for November, 1849, after having been in the editor's
hands for about a year. Along with "The Raven,"
"The Bells" has become a famous school piece. Its
popularity as an example of technical expertness in
the use of onomatopoeia and its lack of "moral and
intellectual truth" help to explain why Emerson referred to Poe as "the jingle man." The text is that
of 1876.

I

Hear the sledges with the bells—
    Silver bells!
What a world of merriment their melody foretells!
  How they tinkle, tinkle, tinkle,
    In the icy air of night!   5
  While the stars, that oversprinkle
  All the heavens, seem to twinkle
    With a crystalline delight;
  Keeping time, time, time,
  In a sort of Runic rhyme,   10
To the tintinnabulation that so musically wells
  From the bells, bells, bells, bells—
    Bells, bells, bells—
From the jingling and the tinkling of the bells.

II

Hear the mellow wedding bells—   15
    Golden bells!
What a world of happiness their harmony foretells!
  Through the balmy air of night
  How they ring out their delight!

10. **Runic:** pertaining to runes, old Finnish and Norse
poems.

490

From the molten-golden notes,   20
    And all in tune,
What a liquid ditty floats
To the turtledove that listens, while she gloats
    On the moon!
    Oh, from out the sounding cells,   25
What a gush of euphony voluminously wells!
    How it swells!
    How it dwells·
    On the Future! how it tells
    Of the rapture that impels   30
    To the swinging and the ringing
    Of the bells, bells, bells,
    Of the bells, bells, bells, bells,
    Bells, bells, bells—
To the rhyming and the chiming of the bells! 35

III

Hear the loud alarum bells—
    Brazen bells!
What a tale of terror, now, their turbulency tells!
In the startled ear of night
How they scream out their affright!   40
    Too much horrified to speak,
    They can only shriek, shriek,
    Out of tune,
In a clamorous appealing to the mercy of the fire,
In a mad expostulation with the deaf and frantic
    fire,   45
    Leaping higher, higher, higher,
    With a desperate desire,
    And a resolute endeavor
    Now—now to sit or never,
By the side of the pale-faced moon.   50
    Oh, the bells, bells, bells!
    What a tale their terror tells
    Of Despair!
How they clang, and clash, and roar!
What a horror they outpour   55
On the bosom of the palpitating air!
    Yet the ear it fully knows,
    By the twanging
    And the clanging,
    How the danger ebbs and flows;   60
Yet the ear distinctly tells,
    In the jangling
    And the wrangling,
How the danger sinks and swells,

By the sinking or the swelling in the anger of the
    bells—   65
    Of the bells—
Of the bells—
    Of the bells, bells, bells, bells,
    Bells, bells, bells—
In the clamor and the clangor of the bells!

IV

    Hear the tolling of the bells—   70
    Iron bells!
What a world of solemn thought their monody
    compels
    In the silence of the night
    How we shiver with affright
At the melancholy menace of their tone!   75
    For every sound that floats
    From the rust within their throats
    Is a groan.
    And the people—ah, the people—
    They that dwell up in the steeple,   80
    All alone,
    And who tolling, tolling, tolling
    In that muffled monotone,
    Feel a glory in so rolling
    On the human heart a stone—   85
    They are neither man nor woman—
    They are neither brute nor human—
    They are Ghouls:
    And their king it is who tolls;
    And he rolls, rolls, rolls,   90
    Rolls
    A pæan from the bells!
    And his merry bosom swells
    With the pæan of the bells!
    And he dances, and he yells;   95
    Keeping time, time, time,
    In a sort of Runic rhyme,
    To the pæan of the bells—
    Of the bells:
    Keeping time, time, time,   100
    In a sort of Runic rhyme,
    To the throbbing of the bells—
    Of the bells, bells, bells—
    To the sobbing of the bells;
    Keeping time, time, time,   105
    As he knells, knells, knells,

88. Ghouls: evil spirits, or ogres, who rob graves and
feed on dead bodies.

In a happy Runic rhyme,
    To the rolling of the bells—
        Of the bells, bells, bells:
            To the tolling of the bells,   110
        Of the bells, bells, bells, bells—
            Bells, bells, bells—
    To the moaning and the groaning of the bells.

Annabel Lee

THIS POEM was first published in the New York *Tribune*
for October 9, 1849, only two days after Poe's death
in Baltimore. It was reprinted in the *Southern Literary
Messenger* for November, 1849, and included in Griswold's *Poets and Poetry of America* (Tenth Edition,
1850). The poet's wife Virginia may have been the
inspiration of "Annabel Lee," but the theme of a
lover's lament for his dead mistress is a favorite one
in Poe's writings. In "The Philosophy of Composition"
he recorded his belief that the death of a beautiful
woman is the most poetic topic in the world, and
"equally is it beyond doubt that the lips best suited
for such a topic are those of a bereaved lover." The
text is that of 1876.

It was many and many a year ago,
    In a kingdom by the sea,
That a maiden there lived, whom you may know
    By the name of Annabel Lee;
And this maiden she lived with no other thought
    Than to love, and be loved by me.   6

She was a child and I was a child,
    In this kingdom by the sea;
But we loved with a love that was more than love—
    I and my Annabel Lee;   10
With a love that the wingèd seraphs of Heaven
    Coveted her and me.

And this was the reason that, long ago,
    In this kingdom by the sea,
A wind blew out of a cloud, chilling   15
    My beautiful Annabel Lee;
So that her highborn kinsmen came
    And bore her away from me,
To shut her up in a sepulcher
    In this kingdom by the sea.   20

The angels, not half so happy in heaven,
    Went envying her and me—

Yes!—that was the reason (as all men know,
    In this kingdom by the sea)
That the wind came out of the cloud by night,   25
    Chilling and killing my Annabel Lee.

But our love it was stronger by far than the love
    Of those who were older than we—
    Of many far wiser than we—
And neither the angels in Heaven above,   30
    Nor the demons down under the sea,
Can ever dissever my soul from the soul
    Of the beautiful Annabel Lee:

For the moon never beams without bringing me
        dreams
    Of the beautiful Annabel Lee;   35
And the stars never rise, but I feel the bright eyes
    Of the beautiful Annabel Lee;
And so, all the night-tide, I lie down by the side
Of my darling—my darling—my life and my
        bride,
    In her sepulcher there by the sea,   40
    In her tomb by the side of the sea.

Eldorado

"Eldorado" was first printed in the *Flag of Our Union*
for April 21, 1849, and was included in Griswold's
Poets and Poetry of America (Tenth Edition, 1850).
Although Poe's themes are commonly thought to have
little or no relation to the America of his own day,
many of his stories shrewdly exploit contemporary interests. "Eldorado" was written during the exciting
days of the gold rush, but Poe's gallant knight is in
search of human happiness, not material wealth. The
text is that of 1876.

        Gayly bedight,
        A gallant knight,
    In sunshine and in shadow,
        Had journeyed long,
        Singing a song,   5
    In search of Eldorado.

        But he grew old—
        This knight so bold—
    And o'er his heart a shadow

6. **Eldorado:** an undiscovered realm rich in gold, a land
of fabulous wealth.

492

Fell as he found   10
No spot of ground
That looked like Eldorado.

And, as his strength
Failed him at length,
He met a pilgrim shadow—   15
"Shadow," said he,
"Where can it be—
This land of Eldorado?"

"Over the Mountains
Of the Moon,   20
Down the Valley of the Shadow,
Ride, boldly ride,"
The shade replied,—
"If you seek for Eldorado!"

Ligeia *Monday*

Poe placed "Ligeia" first in the list of nine tales which
he assured James Russell Lowell represented his best
work. Two years later, in a letter to E. A. Duyckinck,
January 8, 1846, the author referred to the story as
"undoubtedly the best I have written." It appeared
for the first time in the *American Museum* for September, 1838, and was one of the twenty-five narratives
collected in *Tales of the Grotesque and Arabesque*
(1839). "Ligeia" is an "arabesque," a term used by
Poe to describe thirty-six of his stories, especially his
powerfully imaginative tales appealing to man's
faculty of wonder. Like certain other "arabesques,"
such as "The Masque of the Red Death" and "The
Pit and the Pendulum," "Ligeia" is concerned with
the theme of death. Poe's variations on this theme
may be studied with especial profit in "Berenice"
(1835), an earlier and less effective study of psychic
survival. The text is that of 1875.

I cannot, for my soul, remember how, when, or
even precisely where, I first became acquainted
with the Lady Ligeia. Long years have since
elapsed, and my memory is feeble through much
suffering. Or, perhaps, I cannot *now* bring these
points to mind, because, in truth, the character of
my beloved, her rare learning, her singular yet
placid cast of beauty, and the thrilling and en-
thralling eloquence of her low, musical language,
made their way into my heart by paces so steadily
and stealthily progressive that they have been unnoticed and unknown. Yet I believe that I met

her first and most frequently in some large, old,
decaying city near the Rhine. Of her family—I
have surely heard her speak —that it is of a remotely
ancient date cannot be doubted. Ligeia! Ligeia!
Buried in studies of a nature more than all else
adapted to deaden impressions of the outward
world, it is by that sweet word alone—by Ligeia—
that I bring before mine eyes in fancy the image of
her who is no more. And now, while I write, a
recollection flashes upon me that I have *never
known* the paternal name of her who was my friend
and my betrothed, and who became the partner
of my studies, and finally the wife of my bosom.
Was it a playful charge on the part of my Ligeia?
or was it a test of my strength of affection, that I
should institute no inquiries upon this point? or
was it rather a caprice of my own—a wildly romantic offering on the shrine of the most passionate
devotion? I but indistinctly recall the fact itself—
what wonder that I have utterly forgotten the
circumstances which originated or attended it?
And, indeed, if ever that spirit which is entitled
Romance—if ever she, the wan and the misty-
winged Ashtophet of idolatrous Egypt, presided,
as they tell, over marriages ill-omened, then most
surely she presided over mine.

There is one dear topic, however, on which my
memory fails me not. It is the *person* of Ligeia.
In stature she was tall, somewhat slender, and in
her latter days, even emaciated. I would in vain
attempt to portray the majesty, the quiet ease, of
her demeanor, or the incomprehensible lightness
and elasticity of her footfall. She came and departed as a shadow. I was never made aware of
her entrance into my closed study, save by the
dear music of her low sweet voice, as she placed her
marble hand upon my shoulder. In beauty of face
no maiden ever equalled her. It was the radiance
of an opium dream—an airy and spirit-lifting
vision more wildly divine than the fantasies which
hovered about the slumbering souls of the daughters of Delos.ⁿ Yet her features were not of that
regular mould which we have been falsely taught
to worship in the classical labors of the heathen.
"There is no exquisite beauty," says Bacon, Lord
Verulam, speaking truly of all the forms and *genera*
of beauty, "without some strangeness in the pro-

Delos: one of the Grecian islands.

493

portion." Yet, although I saw that the features of Ligeia were not of a classic regularity—although I perceived that her loveliness was indeed "exquisite," and felt that there was much of "strangeness" pervading it, yet I have tried in vain to detect the irregularity, and to trace home my own perception of "the strange." I examined the contour of the lofty and pale forehead—it was faultless—how cold indeed that word when applied to a majesty so divine!—the skin rivalling the purest ivory, the commanding extent and repose, the gentle prominence of the regions above the temples, and then the raven-black, the glossy, the luxuriant and naturally-curling tresses, setting forth the full force of the Homeric epithet, "hyacinthine!" I looked at the delicate outlines of the nose—and nowhere but in the graceful medallions of the Hebrews had I beheld a similar perfection. There were the same luxurious smoothness of surface, the same scarcely perceptible tendency to the aquiline, the same harmoniously curved nostrils speaking the free spirit. I regarded the sweet mouth. Here was indeed the triumph of all things heavenly—the magnificent turn of the short upper lip—the soft, voluptuous slumber of the under —the dimples which sported, and the color which spoke—the teeth glancing back, with a brilliancy almost startling, every ray of the holy light which fell upon them in her serene and placid, yet most exultingly radiant of all smiles. I scrutinized the formation of the chin—and here, too, I found the gentleness of breadth, the softness and the majesty, the fulness and the spirituality, of the Greek,—the contour which the god Apollo[n] revealed but in a dream, to Cleomenes,[n] the son of the Athenian. And then I peered into the large eyes of Ligeia.

For eyes we have no models in the remotely antique. It might have been, too, that in these eyes of my beloved lay the secret to which Lord Verulam alludes. They were, I must believe, far larger than the ordinary eyes of our own race. They were even far fuller than the fullest of the gazelle eyes of the tribe of the valley of Nourjahad.[n] Yet it was only at intervals—in moments of intense excitement—that this peculiarity became more than slightly noticeable in Ligeia. And at such moments was her beauty—in my heated fancy thus it appeared perhaps—the beauty of beings either above or apart from the earth—the beauty of the fabulous Houri[n] of the Turk. The hue of the orbs was the most brilliant of black, and, far over them, hung jetty lashes of great length. The brows, slightly irregular in outline, had the same hue. The "strangeness," however, which I found in the eyes, was of a nature distinct from the formation, or the color, or the brilliancy of the features, and must, after all, be referred to the expression. Ah, word of no meaning! behind whose vast latitude of mere sound we intrench our ignorance of so much of the spiritual. The expression of the eyes of Ligeia! How for long hours have I pondered upon it! How have I, through the whole of a midsummer night, struggled to fathom it! What was it—that something more profound than the well of Democritus[n]—which lay far within the pupils of my beloved? What was it? I was possessed with a passion to discover. Those eyes! those large, those shining, those divine orbs! they became to me twin stars of Leda,[n] and I to them devoutest of astrologers.

There is no point, among the many incomprehensible anomalies of the science of mind, more thrillingly exciting than the fact—never, I believe, noticed in the schools—that in our endeavors to recall to memory something long forgotten, we often find ourselves upon the very verge of remembrance without being able, in the end, to remember. And thus how frequently, in my intense scrutiny of Ligeia's eyes, have I felt approaching the full knowledge of their expression— felt it approaching—yet not quite be mine—and so at length entirely depart. And (strange, oh strangest mystery of all!) I found, in the commonest objects of the universe, a circle of analogies to that expression. I mean to say that, subsequently to the period when Ligeia's beauty passed into my spirit, there dwelling as in a shrine, I

Apollo: in Greek mythology, the god of youth, beauty, and music. **Cleomenes:** Greek sculptor of the third century, B.C. **Nourjahad:** see Frances Sheridan, *The History of Nourjahad* (1767), a novel.

Houri: nymph or beautiful woman in heaven, according to the Moslems. **Democritus:** (460–357? B.C.), Greek philosopher, who is reported to have said truth lies in a well. **Leda:** mother of Castor and Pollux, the two largest stars in the constellation Gemini.

derived, from many existences in the material world, a sentiment such as I felt always around, within me, by her large and luminous orbs. Yet not the more could I define that sentiment, or analyze, or even steadily view it. I recognized it, let me repeat, sometimes in the survey of a rapidly-growing vine—in the contemplation of a moth, a butterfly, a chrysalis, a stream of running water. I have felt it in the ocean; in the falling of a meteor. I have felt it in the glances of unusually aged people. And there are one or two stars in heaven—(one especially, a star of the sixth magnitude, double and changeable, to be found near the large star in Lyra) in a telescopic scrutiny of which I have been made aware of the feeling. I have been filled with it by certain sounds from stringed instruments, and not unfrequently by passages from books. Among innumerable other instances, I well remember something in a volume of Joseph Glanvill,[n] which (perhaps merely from its quaintness—who shall say?) never failed to inspire me with the sentiment: "And the will therein lieth, which dieth not. Who knoweth the mysteries of the will, with its vigor? For God is but a great will pervading all things by nature of its intentness. Man doth not yield him to the angels, nor unto death utterly, save only through the weakness of his feeble will."

Length of years, and subsequent reflection, have enabled me to trace, indeed, some remote connection between this passage in the English moralist and a portion of the character of Ligeia. An intensity in thought, action, or speech, was possibly, in her, a result or at least an index, of that gigantic volition which, during our long intercourse, failed to give other and more immediate evidence of its existence. Of all the women whom I have ever known, she, the outwardly calm, the ever-placid Ligeia, was the most violently a prey to the tumultuous vultures of stern passion. And of such passion I could form no estimate, save by the miraculous expansion of those eyes which at once so delighted and appalled me—by the almost magical melody, modulation, distinctness, and placidity of her very low voice—and by the fierce energy (rendered doubly effective by contrast with her

Joseph Glanvill: English divine and philosopher (1636–1680).

manner of utterance) of the words which she habitually uttered.

I have spoken of the learning of Ligeia: it was immense—such as I have never known in woman. In the classical tongues was she deeply proficient, and as far as my own acquaintance extended in regard to the modern dialects of Europe, I have never known her at fault. Indeed upon any theme of the most admired, because simply the most abstruse of the boasted erudition of the academy, have I ever found Ligeia at fault? How singularly—how thrillingly, this one point in the nature of my wife has forced itself, at this late period only, upon my attention! I said her knowledge was such as I have never known in woman—but where breathes the man who has traversed, and successfully, all the wide areas of moral, physical, and mathematical science? I saw not then what I now clearly perceive, that the acquisitions of Ligeia were gigantic, were astounding; yet I was sufficiently aware of her infinite supremacy to resign myself, with a child-like confidence, to her guidance through the chaotic world of metaphysical investigation at which I was most busily occupied during the earlier years of our marriage. With how vast a triumph—with how vivid a delight—with how much of all that is ethereal in hope—did I feel, as she bent over me in studies but little sought—but less known—that delicious vista by slow degrees expanding before me, down whose long, gorgeous, and all untrodden path, I might at length pass onward to the goal of a wisdom too divinely precious not to be forbidden!

How poignant, then, must have been the grief with which, after some years, I beheld my well-grounded expectations take wings to themselves and fly away! Without Ligeia I was but as a child groping benighted. Her presence, her readings alone, rendered vividly luminous the many mysteries of the transcendentalism in which we were immersed. Wanting the radiant lustre of her eyes, letters, lambent and golden, grew duller than Saturnian lead. And now those eyes shone less and less frequently upon the pages over which I pored. Ligeia grew ill. The wild eyes blazed with a too—too glorious effulgence; the pale fingers became of the transparent waxen hue of the grave—and the blue veins upon the lofty forehead swelled and sank impetuously with the tides of the most gentle emotion. I saw that she must die—and I struggled desperately in spirit with the grim Azrael.[n] And the struggles of the passionate wife were, to my astonishment, even more energetic than my own. There had been much in her stern nature to impress me with the belief that, to her, death would have come without its terrors; but not so. Words are impotent to convey any just idea of the fierceness of resistance with which she wrestled with the Shadow. I groaned in anguish at the pitiable spectacle. I would have soothed—I would have reasoned; but in the intensity of her wild desire for life—for life—*but* for life, solace and reason were alike the uttermost of folly. Yet not for an instant, amid the most convulsive writhings of her fierce spirit, was shaken the external placidity of her demeanor. Her voice grew more gentle—grew more low—yet I would not wish to dwell upon the wild meaning of the quietly-uttered words. My brain reeled as I hearkened, entranced, to a melody more than mortal—to assumptions and aspirations which mortality had never before known.

That she loved me I should not have doubted; and I might have been easily aware that, in a bosom such as hers, love would have reigned no ordinary passion. But in death only, was I fully impressed with the strength of her affection. For long hours, detaining my hand, would she pour out before me the overflowing of a heart whose more than passionate devotion amounted to idolatry. How had I deserved to be so blessed by such confessions?—how had I deserved to be so cursed with the removal of my beloved in the hour of her making them? But upon this subject I cannot bear to dilate. Let me say only, that in Ligeia's more than womanly abandonment to a love, alas! all unmerited, all unworthily bestowed, I at length recognized the principle of her longing, with so wildly earnest a desire, for the life which was now fleeing so rapidly away. It is this wild longing—it is this eager vehemence of desire for life—*but* for life—that I have no power to portray —no utterance capable of expressing.

At high noon of the night in which she departed,

Azrael: in Hebrew and Mohammedan theology, the angel of death.

beckoning me, peremptorily, to her side, she bade me repeat certain verses composed by herself not many days before. I obeyed her. They were these:

Lo! 'tis a gala night
  Within the lonesome latter years!
An angel throng, bewinged, bedight
  In veils, and drowned in tears,
Sit in a theatre, to see   5
  A play of hopes and fears,
While the orchestra breathes fitfully
  The music of the spheres.

Mimes, in the form of God on high,
  Mutter and mumble low,   10
And hither and thither fly;
  Mere puppets they, who come and go
At bidding of vast formless things
  That shift the scenery to and fro,
Flapping from out their condor wings   15
  Invisible Wo!

That motley drama!—oh, be sure
  It shall not be forgot!
With its Phantom chased for evermore,
  By a crowd that seize it not,   20
Through a circle that ever returneth in
  To the self-same spot;
And much of Madness, and more of Sin
  And horror, the soul of the plot!

But see, amid the mimic rout   25
  A crawling shape intrude!
A blood-red thing that writhes from out
  The scenic solitude!
It writhes!—it writhes!—with moral pangs
  The mimes become its food,   30
And seraphs sob at vermin fangs
  In human gore imbued.

Out—out are the lights—out all!
  And over each quivering form,
The curtain, a funeral pall,   35
  Comes down with the rush of a storm—
While the angels, all pallid and wan,
  Uprising, unveiling, affirm
That the play is the tragedy, "Man,"
  And its hero the Conqueror Worm.   40

"O God!" half shrieked Ligeia, leaping to her feet and extending her arms aloft with a spasmodic movement, as I made an end of these lines—"O God! O Divine Father!—shall these things be undeviatingly so?—shall this conqueror be not once conquered? Are we not part and parcel in Thee? Who—who knoweth the mysteries of the will with its vigor? Man doth not yield him to the angels, nor unto death utterly, save only through the weakness of his feeble will."

And now, as if exhausted with emotion, she suffered her white arms to fall, and returned solemnly to her bed of death. And as she breathed her last sighs, there came mingled with them a low murmur from her lips. I bent to them my ear and distinguished, again, the concluding words of the passage in Glanvill:—"Man doth not yield him to the angels, nor unto death utterly, save only through the weakness of his feeble will."

She died: and I, crushed into the very dust with sorrow, could no longer endure the lonely desolation of my dwelling in the dim and decaying city by the Rhine. I had no lack of what the world calls wealth—Ligeia had brought me far more, very far more, than ordinarily falls to the lot of mortals. After a few months, therefore, of weary and aimless wandering, I purchased, and put in some repair, an abbey, which I shall not name, in one of the wildest and least frequented portions of fair England. The gloomy and dreary grandeur of the building, the almost savage aspect of the domain, the many melancholy and time-honored memories connected with both, had much in unison with the feelings of utter abandonment which had driven me into that remote and unsocial region of the country. Yet although the external abbey, with its verdant decay hanging about it, suffered but little alteration, I gave way, with a child-like perversity, and perchance with a faint hope of alleviating my sorrows, to a display of more than regal magnificence within. For such follies, even in childhood, I had imbibed a taste, and now they came back to me as if in the dotage of grief. Alas, I feel how much even of incipient madness might have been discovered in the gorgeous and fantastic draperies, in the solemn carvings of Egypt, in the wild cornices and furniture, in the bedlam patterns of the carpets of tufted gold! I had become a bounden slave in the trammels of opium, and my labors and my orders had taken a coloring from my dreams. But these absurdities I must not pause to detail. Let me speak only of that one chamber,

ever accursed, whither, in a moment of mental alienation, I led from the altar as my bride—as the successor of the unforgotten Ligeia—the fair-haired and blue-eyed Lady Rowena Trevanion, of Tremaine.

There is no individual portion of the architecture and decoration of that bridal chamber which is not now visibly before me. Where were the souls of the haughty family of the bride, when, through thirst of gold, they permitted to pass the threshold of an apartment *so* bedecked, a maiden and a daughter so beloved? I have said, that I minutely remember the details of the chamber—yet I am sadly forgetful on topics of deep moment—and here there was no system, no keeping, in the fantastic display, to take hold upon the memory. The room lay in a high turret of the castellated abbey, was pentagonal in shape, and of capacious size. Occupying the whole southern face of the pentagon was the sole window—an immense sheet of unbroken glass from Venice—a single pane, and tinted of a leaden hue, so that the rays of either the sun or moon, passing through it, fell with a ghastly lustre on the objects within. Over the upper portion of this huge window, extended the trellis-work of an aged vine, which clambered up the massy walls of the turret. The ceiling, of gloomy-looking oak, was excessively lofty, vaulted, and elaborately fretted with the wildest and most grotesque specimens of a semi-Gothic, semi-Druidical device. From out the most central recess of this melancholy vaulting, depended, by a single chain of gold with long links, a huge censer of the same metal, Saracenic in pattern, and with many perforations so contrived that there writhed in and out of them, as if endued with a serpent vitality, a continual succession of parti-colored fires.

Some few ottomans and golden candelabra of Eastern figure, were in various stations about; and there was the couch, too—the bridal couch—of an Indian model, and low, and sculptured of solid ebony, with a canopy above. In each of the angles of the chamber stood on end a gigantic sarcophagus of black granite, from the tombs of the kings over against Luxor, with their aged lids full of immemorial sculpture. But in the draping of the apartment lay, alas! the chief fantasy of all. The lofty walls—gigantic in height—even un-proportionably so, were hung from summit to foot, in vast folds, with a heavy and massive-looking tapestry—tapestry of a material which was found alike as a carpet on the floor, as a covering for the ottomans and the ebony bed, as a canopy for the bed, and as the gorgeous volutes of the curtains which partially shaded the window. The material was the richest cloth of gold. It was spotted all over, at irregular intervals, with arabesque figures, about a foot in diameter, and wrought 10 upon the cloth in patterns of the most jetty black. But these figures partook of the true character of the arabesque only when regarded from a single point of view. By a contrivance now common, and indeed traceable to a very remote period of antiquity, they were made changeable in aspect. To one entering the room, they bore the appearance of simple monstrosities; but upon a farther advance, this appearance gradually departed; and, step by step, as the visiter moved his station in 20 the chamber, he saw himself surrounded by an endless succession of the ghastly forms which belong to the superstition of the Norman, or arise in the guilty slumbers of the monk. The phantasmagoric effect was vastly heightened by the artificial introduction of a strong continual current of wind behind the draperies—giving a hideous and uneasy animation to the whole.

In halls such as these—in a bridal chamber such as this—I passed, with the Lady of Tremaine, the 30 unhallowed hours of the first month of our marriage—passed them with but little disquietude. That my wife dreaded the fierce moodiness of my temper—that she shunned me, and loved me but little—I could not help perceiving; but it gave me rather pleasure than otherwise. I loathed her with a hatred belonging more to demon than to man. My memory flew back, (oh, with what intensity of regret!) to Ligeia, the beloved, the august, the beautiful, the entombed. I revelled in 40 recollections of her purity, of her wisdom, of her lofty, her ethereal nature, of her passionate, her idolatrous love. Now, then, did my spirit fully and freely burn with more than all the fires of her own. In the excitement of my opium dreams (for I was habitually fettered in the shackles of the drug), I would call aloud upon her name, during the silence of the night, or among the sheltered recesses of the glens by day, as if, through the wild eagerness, the solemn passion, the consuming ardor of my longing for the departed, I could restore her to the pathway she had abandoned—ah, *could* it be forever?—upon the earth.

About the commencement of the second month of the marriage, the Lady Rowena was attacked with sudden illness from which her recovery was slow. The fever which consumed her, rendered her nights uneasy; and, in her perturbed state of half-slumber, she spoke of sounds, and of motions, in and about the chamber of the turret, which I concluded had no origin save in the distemper of her fancy, or perhaps in the phantasmagoric influences of the chamber itself. She became at length convalescent—finally, well. Yet but a brief period elapsed, ere a second more violent disorder again threw her upon a bed of suffering; and from this attack her frame, at all times feeble, never altogether recovered. Her illnesses were, after this epoch, of alarming character, and of more alarming recurrence, defying alike the knowledge and the great exertions of her physicians. With the increase of the chronic disease, which had thus, apparently, taken too sure hold upon her constitution to be eradicated by human means, I could not fail to observe a similar increase in the nervous irritation of her temperament, and in her excitability by trivial causes of fear. She spoke again, and now more frequently and pertinaciously, of the slight sounds—and of the unusual motions among the tapestries, to which she had formerly alluded.

One night, near the closing in of September, she pressed this distressing subject with more than usual emphasis upon my attention. She had just awakened from an unquiet slumber, and I had been watching, with feelings half of anxiety, half of vague terror, the workings of her emaciated countenance. I sat by the side of her ebony bed, upon one of the ottomans of India. She partly arose, and spoke, in an earnest low whisper, of sounds which she then heard—but which I could not hear, of motions which she then saw, but which I could not perceive. The wind was rushing hurriedly behind the tapestries, and I wished to show her (what, let me confess it, I could not all believe) that those almost inarticulate breathings, and those very gentle variations of the figures upon the wall, were but the natural effects of that customary rushing of the wind. But a deadly pallor, overspreading her face, had proved to me that my exertions to reassure her would be fruitless. She appeared to be fainting, and no attendants were within call. I remembered where was deposited a decanter of light wine which had been ordered by her physicians, and hastened across the chamber to procure it. But, as I stepped beneath the light of the censer, two circumstances of a startling nature attracted my attention. I had felt that some palpable although invisible object had passed lightly by my person; and I saw that there lay upon the golden carpet, in the very middle of the rich lustre thrown from the censer, a shadow—a faint, indefinite shadow of angelic aspect—such as might be fancied for the shadow of a shade. But I was wild with the excitement of an immoderate dose of opium, and heeded these things but little, nor spoke of them to Rowena. Having found the wine, I recrossed the chamber, and poured out a gobletful, which I held to the lips of the fainting lady. She had now partially recovered, however, and took the vessel herself, while I sank upon an ottoman near me, with my eyes fastened upon her person. It was then that I became distinctly aware of a gentle foot-fall upon the carpet, and near the couch; and in a second thereafter, as Rowena was in the act of raising the wine to her lips, I saw, or may have dreamed that I saw, fall within the goblet, as if from some invisible spring in the atmosphere of the room, three or four large drops of a brilliant and ruby colored fluid. If this I saw—not so Rowena. She swallowed the wine unhesitatingly, and I forbore to speak to her of a circumstance which must, after all, I considered, have been but the suggestion of a vivid imagination, rendered morbidly active by the terror of the lady, by the opium, and by the hour.

Yet I cannot conceal it from my own perception that, immediately subsequent to the fall of the ruby-drops, a rapid change for the worst took place in the disorder of my wife; so that, on the third subsequent night, the hands of her menials prepared her for the tomb, and on the fourth, I sat alone, with her shrouded body, in that fantastic chamber which had received her as my bride.—

Wild visions, opium-engendered, flitted shadow-like before me. I gazed with unquiet eye upon the sarcophagi in the angles of the room, upon the varying figures of the drapery, and upon the writhing of the parti-colored fires in the censer overhead. My eyes then fell, as I called to mind the circumstances of a former night, to the spot beneath the glare of the censer where I had seen the faint traces of the shadow. It was there, however, no longer; and breathing with greater freedom, I turned my glances to the pallid and rigid figure upon the bed. Then rushed upon me a thousand memories of Ligeia—and then came back upon my heart, with the turbulent violence of a flood, the whole of that unutterable wo with which I had regarded her thus enshrouded. The night waned; and still, with a bosom full of bitter thoughts of the one only and supremely beloved, I remained gazing upon the body of Rowena.

It might have been midnight, or perhaps earlier, or later, for I had taken no note of time, when a sob, low, gentle, but very distinct, started me from my revery. I felt that it came from the bed of ebony—the bed of death. I listened in an agony of superstitious terror—but there was no repetition of the sound. I strained my vision to detect any motion in the corpse—but there was not the slightest perceptible. Yet I could not have been deceived. I had heard the noise, however faint, and my soul was awakened within me. I resolutely and perseveringly kept my attention riveted upon the body. Many minutes elapsed before any circumstance occurred tending to throw light upon the mystery. At length it became evident that a slight, a very feeble, and barely noticeable tinge of color had flushed up within the cheeks, and along the sunken small veins of the eyelids. Through a species of unutterable horror and awe, for which the language of mortality has no sufficiently energetic expression, I felt my heart cease to beat, my limbs grow rigid where I sat. Yet a sense of duty finally operated to restore my self-possession. I could no longer doubt that we had been precipitate in our preparations—that Rowena still lived. It was necessary that some immediate exertion be made; yet the turret was altogether apart from the portion of the abbey tenanted by the servants—there were none within call—I had no means of summoning them to my aid without leaving the room for many minutes—and this I could not venture to do. I therefore struggled alone in my endeavors to call back the spirit still hovering. In a short period it was certain, however, that a relapse had taken place; the color disappeared from both eyelid and cheek, leaving a wanness even more than that of marble; the lips became doubly shrivelled and pinched up in the ghastly expression of death; a repulsive clamminess and coldness overspread rapidly the surface of the body; and all the usual rigorous stiffness immediately supervened. I fell back with a shudder upon the couch from which I had been so startlingly aroused, and again gave myself up to passionate waking visions of Ligeia.

An hour thus elapsed when, (could it be possible?) I was a second time aware of some vague sound issuing from the region of the bed. I listened—in extremity of horror. The sound came again—it was a sigh. Rushing to the corpse, I saw—distinctly saw—a tremor upon the lips. In a minute afterward they relaxed, disclosing a bright line of the pearly teeth. Amazement now struggled in my bosom with the profound awe which had hitherto reigned there alone. I felt that my vision grew dim, that my reason wandered; and it was only by a violent effort that I at length succeeded in nerving myself to the task which duty thus once more had pointed out. There was now a partial glow upon the forehead and upon the cheek and throat; a perceptible warmth pervaded the whole frame; there was even a slight pulsation at the heart. The lady lived; and with redoubled ardor I betook myself to the task of restoration. I chafed and bathed the temples and the hands, and used every exertion which experience, and no little medical reading, could suggest. But in vain. Suddenly, the color fled, the pulsation ceased, the lips resumed the expression of the dead, and, in an instant afterward, the whole body took upon itself the icy chilliness, the livid hue, the intense rigidity, the sunken outline, and all the loathsome peculiarities of that which has been, for many days, a tenant of the tomb.

And again I sunk into visions of Ligeia—and again, (what marvel that I shudder while I write?) again there reached my ears a low sob from the region of the ebony bed. But why shall I minutely detail the unspeakable horrors of that night? Why shall I pause to relate how, time after time, until near the period of the gray dawn, this hideous drama of revivification was repeated; how each terrific relapse was only into a sterner and apparently more irredeemable death; how each agony wore the aspect of a struggle with some invisible foe; and how each struggle was succeeded by I know not what of wild change in the personal appearance of the corpse? Let me hurry to a conclusion.

The greater part of the fearful night had worn away, and she who had been dead once again stirred—and now more vigorously than hitherto, although arousing from a dissolution more appalling in its utter hopelessness than any. I had long ceased to struggle or to move, and remained sitting rigidly upon the ottoman, a helpless prey to a whirl of violent emotions, of which extreme awe was perhaps the least terrible, the least consuming. The corpse, I repeat, stirred, and now more vigorously than before. The hues of life flushed up with unwonted energy into the countenance—the limbs relaxed—and, save that the eyelids were yet pressed heavily together, and that the bandages and draperies of the grave still imparted their charnel character to the figure, I might have dreamed that Rowena had indeed shaken off, utterly, the fetters of Death. But if this idea was not, even then, altogether adopted, I could at least doubt no longer, when, arising from the bed, tottering, with feeble steps, with closed eyes, and with the manner of one bewildered in a dream, the thing that was enshrouded advanced boldly and palpably into the middle of the apartment.

I trembled not—I stirred not—for a crowd of unutterable fancies connected with the air, the stature, the demeanor of the figure, rushing hurriedly through my brain, had paralyzed—had chilled me into stone. I stirred not—but gazed upon the apparition. There was a mad disorder in my thoughts—a tumult unappeasable. Could it, indeed, be the living Rowena who confronted me? Could it indeed be Rowena at all—the fair-haired, the blue-eyed Lady Rowena Trevanion of Tremaine? Why, why, should I doubt it? The bandage lay heavily about the mouth—but then might it not be the mouth of the breathing Lady of Tremaine. And the cheeks—there were the roses as in her noon of life—yes, these might indeed be the fair cheeks of the living Lady of Tremaine. And the chin, with its dimples, as in health, might it not be hers?—but had she then grown taller since her malady? What inexpressible madness seized me with that thought? One bound, and I had reached her feet! Shrinking from my touch, she let fall from her head, unloosened, the ghastly cerements which had confined it, and there streamed forth, into the rushing atmosphere of the chamber, huge masses of long and dishevelled hair; it was blacker than the raven wings of the midnight! And now slowly opened the eyes of the figure which stood before me. "Here then, at least," I shrieked aloud, "can I never—can I never be mistaken—these are the full, and the black, and the wild eyes—of my lost love—of the Lady—of the Lady Ligeia."

The Purloined Letter

Poe considered "The Purloined Letter" the best of his detective stories, or "tales of ratiocination." Its first American appearance was in *The Gift*, a literary annual, for 1845. When the story was printed abroad in *Chambers' Edinburgh Journal*, for November, 1844, the original version was somewhat abridged. When Poe collected it for inclusion in the *Tales* (1845), he reprinted the tale as it appeared in *The Gift*. The text is that of 1876.

At Paris, just after dark one gusty evening in the autumn of 18—, I was enjoying the twofold luxury of meditation and a meerschaum, in company with my friend C. Auguste Dupin, in his little back library, or book-closet, *au troisième*, No. 33 *Rue Dunôt, Faubourg St. Germain.* For one hour at least we had maintained a profound silence; while each, to any casual observer, might have seemed intently and exclusively occupied with the curling eddies of smoke that oppressed the atmosphere of the chamber. For myself, however, I was mentally discussing certain topics which had formed matter for conversation between us at an earlier period of the evening; I mean the affair of the Rue Morgue, and the mystery attend-

ing the murder of Marie Rogêt. I looked upon it, therefore, as something of a coincidence, when the door of our apartment was thrown open and admitted our old acquaintance, Monsieur G.——, the Prefect of the Parisian police.

We gave him a hearty welcome; for there was nearly half as much of the entertaining as of the contemptible about the man, and we had not seen him for several years. We had been sitting in the dark, and Dupin now arose for the purpose of lighting a lamp, but sat down again, without doing so, upon G——'s saying that he had called to consult us, or rather to ask the opinion of my friend, about some official business which had occasioned a great deal of trouble.

"If it is any point requiring reflection," observed Dupin, as he forebore to enkindle the wick, "we shall examine it to better purpose in the dark."

"That is another of your odd notions," said the Prefect, who had a fashion of calling everything "odd" that was beyond his comprehension, and thus lived amid an absolute legion of "oddities."

"Very true," said Dupin, as he supplied his visitor with a pipe, and rolled toward him a comfortable chair.

"And what is the difficulty now?" I asked. "Nothing more in the assassination way, I hope?"

"Oh, no; nothing of that nature. The fact is, the business is *very* simple indeed, and I make no doubt that we can manage it sufficiently well ourselves; but then I thought Dupin would like to hear the details of it, because it is so excessively odd."

"Simple and odd," said Dupin.

"Why, yes; and not exactly that, either. The fact is, we have all been a good deal puzzled because the affair *is* so simple, and yet baffles us altogether."

"Perhaps it is the very simplicity of the thing which puts you at fault," said my friend.

"What nonsense you do talk!" replied the Prefect, laughing heartily.

"Perhaps the mystery is a little too plain," said Dupin.

"Oh, good heavens! who ever heard of such an idea?"

"A little too self-evident."

501

"Ha! ha! ha! ha! ha! ha!—ho! ho! ho!" roared our visitor, profoundly amused, "oh, Dupin, you will be the death of me yet!"

"And what, after all, *is* the matter on hand?" I asked.

"Why, I will tell you," replied the Prefect, as he gave a long, steady, and contemplative puff, and settled himself in his chair. "I will tell you in a few words; but, before I begin, let me caution you that this is an affair demanding the greatest secrecy, and that I should most probably lose the position I now hold, were it known that I confided it to any one."

"Proceed," said I.

"Or not, "said Dupin.

"Well, then; I have received personal information, from a very high quarter, that a certain document of the last importance has been purloined from the royal apartments. The individual who purloined it is known; this beyond a doubt; he was seen to take it. It is known, also, that it still remains in his possession."

"How is this known?" asked Dupin.

"It is clearly inferred," replied the Prefect, "from the nature of the document, and from the non-appearance of certain results which would at once arise from its passing out of the robber's possession;—that is to say, from his employing it as he must design in the end to employ it."

"Be a little more explicit," I said.

"Well, I may venture so far as to say that the paper gives its holder a certain power in a certain quarter where such power is immensely valuable." The Prefect was fond of the cant of diplomacy.

"Still I do not quite understand," said Dupin.

"No? Well; the disclosure of the document to a third person, who shall be nameless, would bring in question the honor of a personage of the most exalted station; and this fact gives the holder of the document an ascendancy over the illustrious personage whose honor and peace are so jeopardized."

"But this ascendancy," I interposed, "would depend upon the robber's knowledge of the loser's knowledge of the robber. Who would dare—"

"The thief," said G——, "is the Minister D——, who dares all things, those unbecoming as well as those becoming a man. The method of

the theft was not less ingenious than bold. The document in question—a letter, to be frank—had been received by the personage robbed while alone in the royal *boudoir*. During its perusal she was suddenly interrupted by the entrance of the other exalted personage from whom especially it was her wish to conceal it. After a hurried and vain endeavor to thrust it in a drawer, she was forced to place it, open as it was, upon a table. The address, however, was uppermost, and, the contents thus unexposed, the letter escaped notice. At this juncture enters the Minister D——. His lynx eye immediately perceives the paper, recognizes the handwriting of the address, observes the confusion of the personage addressed, and fathoms her secret. After some business transactions, hurried through in his ordinary manner, he produces a letter somewhat similar to the one in question, opens it, pretends to read it, and then places it in close juxtaposition to the other. Again he converses, for some fifteen minutes, upon the public affairs. At length, in taking leave, he takes also from the table the letter to which he had no claim. Its rightful owner saw, but, of course, dared not call attention to the act, in the presence of the third personage who stood at her elbow. The minister decamped; leaving his own letter—one of no importance—upon the table."

"Here, then," said Dupin to me, "you have precisely what you demand to make the ascendancy complete—the robber's knowledge of the loser's knowledge of the robber."

"Yes," replied the Prefect; "and the power thus attained has, for some months past, been wielded, for political purposes, to a very dangerous extent. The personage robbed is more thoroughly convinced, every day, of the necessity of reclaiming her letter. But this, of course, cannot be done openly. In fine, driven to despair, she has committed the matter to me."

"Than whom," said Dupin, amid a perfect whirlwind of smoke, "no more sagacious agent could, I suppose, be desired, or even imagined."

"You flatter me," replied the Prefect; "but it is possible that some such opinion may have been entertained."

"It is clear," said I, "as you observe, that the letter is still in the possession of the Minister;

502

since it is this possession, and not any employment of the letter, which bestows the power. With the employment the power departs."

"True," said G——; "and upon this conviction I proceeded. My first care was to make thorough search of the Minister's hotel; and here my chief embarrassment lay in the necessity of searching without his knowledge. Beyond all things, I have been warned of the danger which would result from giving him reason to suspect our design."

"But," said I, "you are quite *au fait* in these investigations. The Parisian police have done this thing often before."

"Oh, yes; and for this reason I did not despair. The habits of the minister gave me, too, a great advantage. He is frequently absent from home all night. His servants are by no means numerous. They sleep at a distance from their master's apartment, and, being chiefly Neapolitans, are readily made drunk. I have keys, as you know, with which I can open any chamber or cabinet in Paris. For three months a night has not passed during the greater part of which I have not been engaged, personally, in ransacking the D—— Hotel. My honor is interested, and, to mention a great secret, the reward is enormous. So I did not abandon the search until I had become fully satisfied that the thief is a more astute man than myself. I fancy that I have investigated every nook and corner of the premises in which it is possible that the paper can be concealed."

"But is it not possible," I suggested, "that although the letter may be in the possession of the minister, as it unquestionably is, he may have concealed it elsewhere than upon his own premises?"

"This is barely possible," said Dupin. "The present peculiar condition of affairs at court, and especially of those intrigues in which D—— is known to be involved, would render the instant availability of the document—its susceptibility of being produced at a moment's notice—a point of nearly equal importance with its possession."

"Its susceptibility of being produced?" said I.

"That is to say, of being destroyed," said Dupin.

"True," I observed; "the paper is clearly then upon the premises. As for its being upon the person of the minister, we may consider that as out of the question."

"Entirely," said the Prefect. "He has been twice waylaid, as if by footpads, and his person rigidly searched under my own inspection."

"You might have spared yourself this trouble," said Dupin. "D——, I presume, is not altogether a fool, and, if not, must have anticipated these waylayings, as a matter of course."

"Not altogether a fool," said G——, "but then he is a poet, which I take to be only one remove from a fool."

"True," said Dupin, after a long and thoughtful whiff from his meerschaum, "although I have been guilty of certain doggerel myself."

"Suppose you detail," said I, "the particulars of your search."

"Why the fact is, we took our time, and we searched everywhere. I have had long experience in these affairs. I took the entire building, room by room, devoting the nights of a whole week to each. We examined, first, the furniture of each apartment. We opened every possible drawer; and I presume you know that, to a properly trained police-agent, such a thing as a secret drawer is impossible. Any man is a dolt who permits a 'secret' drawer to escape him in a search of this kind. The thing is so plain. There is a certain amount of bulk—of space—to be accounted for in every cabinet. Then we have accurate rules. The fiftieth part of a line could not escape us. After the cabinets we took the chairs. The cushions we probed with the fine long needles you have seen me employ. From the tables we removed the tops."

"Why so?"

"Sometimes the top of a table, or other similarly arranged piece of furniture, is removed by the person wishing to conceal an article; then the leg is excavated, the article deposited within the cavity, and the top replaced. The bottoms and tops of bedposts are employed in the same way."

"But could not the cavity be detected by sounding?" I asked.

"By no means, if, when the article is deposited, a sufficient wadding of cotton be placed around it. Besides, in our case, we were obliged to proceed without noise."

"But you could not have removed—you could not have taken to pieces all articles of furniture in which it would have been possible to make a deposit in the manner you mention. A letter may be compressed into a thin spiral roll, not differing much in shape or bulk from a large knitting-needle, and in this form it might be inserted into the rung of a chair, for example. You did not take to pieces all the chairs?"

"Certainly not; but we did better—we examined the rungs of every chair in the hotel, and, indeed, the jointings of every description of furniture, by the aid of a most powerful microscope. Had there been any traces of recent disturbance we should not have failed to detect it instantly. A single grain of gimlet-dust, for example, would have been as obvious as an apple. Any disorder in the gluing—any unusual gaping in the joints—would have sufficed to insure detection."

"I presume you looked to the mirrors, between the boards and the plates, and you probed the beds and the bedclothes, as well as the curtains and carpets."

"That of course; and when we had absolutely completed every particle of the furniture in this way, then we examined the house itself. We divided its entire surface into compartments, which we numbered, so that none might be missed; then we scrutinized each individual square inch throughout the premises, including the two houses immediately adjoining, with the microscope, as before."

"The two houses adjoining!" I exclaimed; "you must have had a great deal of trouble."

"We had; but the reward offered is prodigious."

"You include the grounds about the houses?"

"All the grounds are paved with brick. They gave us comparatively little trouble. We examined the moss between the bricks, and found it undisturbed."

"You looked among D——'s papers, of course, and into the books of the library?"

"Certainly; we opened every package and parcel; we not only opened every book, but we turned over every leaf in each volume, not contenting ourselves with a mere shake, according to the fashion of some of our police officers. We also measured the thickness of every book-cover, with the most accurate admeasurement, and applied to each the most jealous scrutiny of the microscope.

Had any of the bindings been recently meddled with, it would have been utterly impossible that the fact should have escaped observation. Some five or six volumes, just from the hands of the binder, we carefully probed, longitudinally, with the needles."

"You explored the floors beneath the carpets?"

"Beyond doubt. We removed every carpet, and examined the boards with the microscope."

"And the paper on the walls?"

"Yes."

"You looked into the cellars?"

"We did."

"Then," I said, "you have been making a miscalculation, and the letter is *not* upon the premises, as you suppose."

"I fear you are right there," said the Prefect. "And now, Dupin, what would you advise me to do?"

"To make a thorough re-search of the premises."

"That is absolutely needless," replied G——. "I am not more sure that I breathe than I am that the letter is not at the Hotel."

"I have no better advice to give you," said Dupin. "You have, of course, an accurate description of the letter?"

"Oh yes!" And here the Prefect, producing a memorandum-book, proceeded to read aloud a minute account of the internal, and especially of the external, appearance of the missing document. Soon after finishing the perusal of this description, he took his departure, more entirely depressed in spirits than I had ever known the good gentleman before.

In about a month afterward he paid us another visit, and found us occupied very nearly as before. He took a pipe and a chair and entered into some ordinary conversation. At length I said,—

"Well, but G——, what of the purloined letter? I presume you have at last made up your mind that there is no such thing as overreaching the Minister?"

"Confound him, say I—yes; I made the re-examination, however, as Dupin suggested—but it was all labor lost, as I knew it would be."

"How much was the reward offered, did you say?" asked Dupin.

"Why, a very great deal—a *very* liberal reward

—I don't like to say how much, precisely; but one thing I *will* say, that I wouldn't mind giving my individual check for fifty thousand francs to any one who could obtain me that letter. The fact is, it is becoming of more and more importance every day; and the reward has been lately doubled. If it were trebled, however, I could do no more than I have done."

"Why, yes," said Dupin, drawlingly, between the whiffs of his meerschaum, "I really—think, G——, you have not exerted yourself—to the utmost in this matter. You might—do a little more, I think, eh?"

"How?—in what way?"

"Why"—puff, puff—"you might"—puff, puff—"employ counsel in the matter, eh"—puff, puff, puff. "Do you remember the story they tell of Abernethy?"

"No: hang Abernethy!"

"To be sure! Hang him and welcome. But, once upon a time, a certain miser conceived the design of spunging upon this Abernethy for a medical opinion. Getting up, for this purpose, an ordinary conversation in a private company, he insinuated his case to the physician as that of an imaginary individual.

"'We will suppose,' said the miser, 'that his symptoms are such and such; now, doctor, what would you have directed him to take?'

"'Take!' said Abernethy. 'Why, take advice, to be sure.'"

"But," said the Prefect, a little discomposed, "*I* am perfectly willing to take advice, and to pay for it. I would really give fifty thousand francs to any one who would aid me in the matter."

"In that case," replied Dupin, opening a drawer, and producing a check-book, "you may as well fill me up a check for the amount mentioned. When you have signed it, I will hand you the letter."

I was astounded. The Prefect appeared absolutely thunderstricken. For some minutes he remained speechless and motionless, looking incredulously at my friend with open mouth, and eyes that seemed starting from their sockets; then, apparently recovering himself in some measure, he seized a pen, and after several pauses and vacant stares, finally filled up and signed a check for fifty thousand francs, and handed it across the table to Dupin. The latter examined it carefully and deposited it in his pocketbook; then, unlocking an *escritoire*, took thence a letter and gave it to the Prefect. This functionary grasped it in a perfect agony of joy, opened it with a trembling hand, cast a rapid glance at its contents, and then, scrambling and struggling to the door, rushed at length unceremoniously from the room and from the house, without having uttered a syllable since Dupin had requested him to fill up the check.

When he had gone, my friend entered into some explanation.

"The Parisian police," he said, "are exceedingly able in their way. They are persevering, ingenious, cunning, and thoroughly versed in the knowledge which their duties seem chiefly to demand. Thus, when G—— detailed to us his mode of searching the premises at the Hotel D——, I felt entire confidence in his having made a satisfactory investigation—so far as his labors extended."

"So far as his labors extended?" said I.

"Yes," said Dupin. "The measures adopted were not only the best of their kind, but carried out to absolute perfection. Had the letter been deposited within the range of their search, these fellows would, beyond a question, have found it."

I merely laughed—but he seemed quite serious in all that he said.

"The measures, then," he continued, "were good in their kind, and well executed; their defect lay in their being inapplicable to the case and to the man. A certain set of highly ingenious resources are, with the Prefect, a sort of Procrustean bed, to which he forcibly adapts his designs. But he perpetually errs by being too deep or too shallow, for the matter in hand; and many a schoolboy is a better reasoner than he. I knew one about eight years of age, whose success at guessing in the game of 'even and odd' attracted universal admiration. This game is simple, and is played with marbles. One player holds in his hand a number of these toys, and demands of another whether that number is even or odd. If the guess is right, the guesser wins one; if wrong, he loses one. The boy to whom I allude won all the marbles of the school. Of course he had some principle of guessing; and this lay in mere observation and admeasurement of the astuteness of his opponents. For example, an arrant simpleton is his opponent, and, holding up his closed hand, asks, 'Are they even or odd?' Our schoolboy replies, 'Odd,' and loses; but upon the second trial he wins, for he then says to himself, 'The simpleton had them even upon the first trial, and his amount of cunning is just sufficient to make him have them odd upon the second; I will therefore guess odd'—he guesses odd, and wins. Now, with a simpleton a degree above the first, he would have reasoned thus: 'This fellow finds that in the first instance I guessed odd, and, in the second, he will propose to himself, upon the first impulse, a simple variation from even to odd, as did the first simpleton; but then a second thought will suggest that this is too simple a variation, and finally he will decide upon putting it even as before. I will therefore guess even,—he guesses even, and wins. Now this mode of reasoning in the schoolboy, whom his fellows termed 'Lucky,'—what, in its last analysis, is it?"

"It is merely," I said, "an identification of the reasoner's intellect with that of his opponent."

"It is," said Dupin; "and, upon inquiring of the boy by what means he effected the thorough identification in which his success consisted, I received answer as follows: 'When I wish to find out how wise, or how stupid, or how good, or how wicked is any one, or what are his thoughts at the moment, I fashion the expression of my face, as accurately as possible, in accordance with the expression of his, and then wait to see what thoughts or sentiments arise in my mind or heart, as if to match or correspond with the expression.' This response of the schoolboy lies at the bottom of all the spurious profundity which has been attributed to Rochefoucault, to La Bougive, to Machiavelli, and to Campanella."

"And the identification," I said, "of the reasoner's intellect with that of his opponent, depends, if I understand you aright, upon the accuracy with which the opponent's intellect is admeasured."

"For its practical value it depends upon this," replied Dupin; "and the Prefect and his cohort fail so frequently, first, by default of this identification, and, secondly, by ill-admeasurement, or rather through non-admeasurement, of the intellect with which they are engaged. They consider only their own ideas of ingenuity; and, in searching for anything hidden, advert only to the modes in which *they* would have hidden it. They are right in this much—that their own ingenuity is a faithful representative of that of the mass: but when the cunning of the individual felon is diverse in character from their own, the felon foils them of course. This always happens when it is above their own, and very usually when it is below. They have no variation of principle in their investigations; at best, when urged by some unusual emergency—by some extraordinary reward—they extend or exaggerate their old modes of practice, without touching their principles. What, for example, in this case of D——, has been done to vary the principle of action? What is all this boring, and probing, and sounding, and scrutinizing with the microscope, and dividing the surface of the building into registered square inches—what is it all but an exaggeration of the application of the one principle or set of principles of search, which are based upon the one set of notions regarding human ingenuity, to which the Prefect, in the long routine of his duty, has been accustomed? Do you not see he had taken it for granted that all men proceed to conceal a letter,—not exactly in a gimlet-hole bored in a chair-leg,—but, at least, in some out-of-the-way hole or corner suggested by the same tenor of thought which would urge a man to secrete a letter in a gimlet-hole bored in a chair-leg? And do you not see also, that such *recherché* nooks for concealment are adapted only for ordinary occasions, and would be adopted only by ordinary intellects; for, in all cases of concealment, a disposal of the article concealed—a disposal of it in this *recherché* manner—is, in the very first instance, presumable and presumed; and thus its discovery depends, not at all upon the acumen, but altogether upon the mere care, patience, and determination of the seekers; and where the case is of importance—or, what amounts to the same thing in the policial eyes, when the reward is of magnitude—the qualities in question have never been known to fail. You will now understand what I meant in suggesting that, had the purloined letter been hidden anywhere within the limits of the Prefect's examination—in other words, had the principle of its concealment been comprehended within the principles of the Prefect—its discovery would have been a matter altogether beyond question. This functionary, however, has been thoroughly mystified; and the remote source of his defeat lies in the supposition that the Minister is a fool, because he has acquired renown as a poet. All fools are poets; this the Prefect feels; and he is merely guilty of a *non distributio medii* in thence inferring that all poets are fools. . . .

"I mean to say," continued Dupin, ". . . that if the Minister had been no more than a mathematician, the Prefect would have been under no necessity of giving me this check. I knew him, however, as both mathematician and poet, and my measures were adapted to his capacity, with reference to the circumstances by which he was surrounded. I knew him as a courtier, too, and as a bold *intriguant*. Such a man, I considered, could not fail to be aware of the ordinary policial modes of action. He could not have failed to anticipate—and events have proved that he did not fail to anticipate—the waylayings to which he was subjected. He must have foreseen, I reflected, the secret investigations of his premises. His frequent absences from home at night, which were hailed by the Prefect as certain aids to his success, I regarded only as ruses, to afford opportunity for thorough search to the police, and thus the sooner to impress them with the conviction to which G——, in fact, did finally arrive—the conviction that the letter was not upon the premises. I felt, also, that the whole train of thought, which I was at some pains in detailing to you just now, concerning the invariable principle of policial action in searches for articles concealed—I felt that this whole train of thought would necessarily pass through the mind of the Minister. It would imperatively lead him to despise all the ordinary nooks of concealment. He could not, I reflected, be so weak as not to see that the most intricate and remote recess of his hotel would be as open as his commonest closets to the eyes, to the probes, to the gimlets, and to the microscopes of the Prefect. I saw, in fine, that he would be driven, as a matter of course, to simplicity, if not deliberately induced to it as a matter of choice. You will remember, perhaps, how desperately the Prefect laughed when I suggested, upon our first interview,

that it was just possible this mystery troubled him so much on account of its being so very self-evident."

"Yes," said I, "I remember his merriment well. I really thought he would have fallen into convulsions."

"The material world," continued Dupin, "abounds with very strict analogies to the immaterial; and thus some color of truth has been given to the rhetorical dogma, that metaphor, or simile, may be made to strengthen an argument, as well as to embellish a description. The principle of the *vis inertiae*, for example, seems to be identical in physics and metaphysics. It is not more true in the former, that a large body is with more difficulty set in motion than a smaller one, and that its subsequent *momentum* is commensurate with this difficulty, than it is, in the latter, that intellects of the vaster capacity, while more forcible, more constant, and more eventful in their movements than those of inferior grade, are yet the less readily moved, and more embarrassed and full of hesitation in the first few steps of their progress. Again: have you ever noticed which of the street signs, over the shop doors, are the most attractive of attention?"

"I have never given the matter a thought," I said.

"There is a game of puzzles," he resumed, "which is played upon a map. One party playing requires another to find a given word—the name of town, river, state or empire—any word, in short, upon the motley and perplexed surface of the chart. A novice in the game generally seeks to embarrass his opponents by giving them the most minutely lettered names; but the adept selects such words as stretch, in large characters, from one end of the chart to the other. These, like the over-largely lettered signs and placards of the street, escape observation by dint of being excessively obvious; and here the physical oversight is precisely analogous with the moral inapprehension by which the intellect suffers to pass unnoticed those considerations which are too obtrusively and too palpably self-evident. But this is a point, it appears, somewhat above or beneath the understanding of the Prefect. He never once thought it probable, or possible, that the

Minister had deposited the letter immediately beneath the nose of the whole world, by way of best preventing any portion of that world from perceiving it.

"But the more I reflected upon the daring, dashing, and discriminating ingenuity of D——; upon the fact that the document must always have been at hand, if he intended to use it to good purpose; and upon the decisive evidence, obtained by the Prefect, that it was not hidden within the limits of that dignitary's ordinary search—the more satisfied I became that, to conceal this letter, the Minister had resorted to the comprehensive and sagacious expedient of not attempting to conceal it.

"Full of these ideas, I prepared myself with a pair of green spectacles, and called one fine morning, quite by accident, at the Ministerial hotel. I found D—— at home, yawning, lounging, and dawdling, as usual, and pretending to be in the last extremity of *ennui*. He is, perhaps, the most really energetic human being now alive—but that is only when nobody sees him.

"To be even with him, I complained of my weak eyes, and lamented the necessity of the spectacles, under cover of which I cautiously and thoroughly surveyed the whole apartment, while seemingly intent only upon the conversation of my host.

"I paid especial attention to a large writing-table near which he sat, and upon which lay confusedly, some miscellaneous letters and other papers, with one or two musical instruments and a few books. Here, however, after a long and very deliberate scrutiny, I saw nothing to excite particular suspicion.

"At length my eyes, in going the circuit of the room, fell upon a trumpery filigree card-rack of pasteboard, that hung dangling by a dirty blue ribbon, from a little brass knob just beneath the middle of the mantel-piece. In this rack, which had three or four compartments, were five or six soiled cards and a solitary letter. This last was much soiled and crumpled. It was torn nearly in two, across the middle—as if a design, in the first instance, to tear it entirely up as worthless had been altered, or stayed, in the second. It had a large black seal, bearing the D—— cipher very conspicuously, and was addressed, in a diminutive female hand, to D——, the Minister, himself.

It was thrust carelessly, and even, as it seemed, contemptuously, into one of the uppermost divisions of the rack.

"No sooner had I glanced at this letter, than I concluded it to be that of which I was in search. To be sure, it was, to all appearance, radically different from the one of which the Prefect had read us so minute a description. Here the seal was large and black, with the D—— cipher; there it was small and red, with the ducal arms of the S—— family. Here, the address, to the Minister, was diminutive and feminine; there the superscription, to a certain royal personage, was markedly bold and decided; the size alone formed a point of correspondence. But, then, the radicalness of these differences, which was excessive; the dirt; the soiled and torn condition of the paper, so inconsistent with the true methodical habits of D——, and so consistent of a design to delude the beholder into an idea of the worthlessness of the document; these things, together with the hyperobtrusive situation of this document, full in the view of every visitor, and thus exactly in accordance with the conclusions to which I had previously arrived; these things, I say, were strongly corroborative of suspicion, in one who came with the intention to suspect.

"I protracted my visit as long as possible, and, while I maintained a most animated discussion with the Minister upon a topic which I knew well had never failed to interest and excite him, I kept my attention riveted upon the letter. In this examination, I committed to memory its external appearance and arrangement in the rack; and also fell, at length, upon a discovery which set at rest whatever trivial doubt I might have entertained. In scrutinizing the edges of the paper, I observed them to be more chafed than seemed necessary. They presented the broken appearance which is manifested when a stiff paper, having been once folded and pressed with a folder, is refolded in a reversed direction, in the same creases or edges which formed the original fold. This discovery was sufficient. It was clear to me that the letter had been turned, as a glove, inside out, re-directed and re-sealed. I bade the Minister good morning, and took my departure at once, leaving a gold snuff-box upon the table.

"The next morning I called for the snuff-box, when we resumed, quite eagerly, the conversation of the preceding day. While thus engaged, however, a loud report, as if of a pistol, was heard immediately beneath the windows of the hotel, and was succeeded by a series of fearful screams, and the shoutings of a terrified mob. D—— rushed to a casement, threw it open, and looked out. In the meantime, I stepped to the card-rack, took the letter, put it in my pocket, and replaced it by a facsimile (so far as regards externals), which I had carefully prepared at my lodgings—imitating the D—— cipher, very readily, by means of a seal formed of bread.

"The disturbance in the street had been occasioned by the frantic behavior of a man with a musket. He had fired it among a crowd of women and children. It proved, however, to have been without ball, and the fellow was suffered to go his way as a lunatic or a drunkard. When he had gone, D—— came from the window, whither I had followed him immediately upon securing the object in view. Soon afterward I bade him farewell. The pretended lunatic was a man in my own pay."

"But what purpose had you," I asked, "in replacing the letter by a facsimile? Would it not have been better, at the first visit, to have seized it openly and departed?"

"D——," replied Dupin, "is a desperate man and a man of nerve. His hotel, too, is not without attendants devoted to his interests. Had I made the wild attempt you suggest, I might never have left the Ministerial presence alive. The good people of Paris might have heard of me no more. But I had an object apart from these considerations. You know my political prepossessions. In this matter I act as a partisan of the lady concerned. For eighteen months the Minister has had her in his power. She has now him in hers—since, being unaware that the letter is not in his possession, he will proceed with his exactions as if it was. Thus will he inevitably commit himself, at once, to his political destruction. His downfall, too, will not be more precipitate than awkward. It is all very well to talk about the *facilis descensus Averni*; but in all kinds of climbing, as Catalani said of singing, it is far more easy to get up than to come down. In the present instance I have no sympathy —at least no pity—for him who descends. He is that *monstrum horrendum*, an unprincipled man of genius. I confess, however, that I should like very well to know the precise character of his thoughts, when, being defied by her whom the Prefect terms 'a certain personage,' he is reduced to opening the letter I left for him in the card-rack."

"How? Did you put anything particular in it?"

"Why—it did not seem altogether right to leave the interior blank—that would have been insulting. D——, at Vienna once, did me an evil turn, which I told him, quite good-humoredly, that I should remember. So, as I knew he would feel some curiosity in regard to the identity of the person who had outwitted him, I thought it a pity not to give him a clew. He is well acquainted with my MS., and I just copied into the middle of the blank sheet the words:

" '——*Un dessein si funeste,*
S'il n'est digne d'Atrée, este digne de Thyeste.'[n]

They are to be found in Crébillon's *Atrée*."

The Masque of the Red Death

THIS STORY was printed in *Graham's Magazine* for May, 1842, and appeared later in the *Broadway Journal* for July 19, 1845. It was not included among the twelve narratives selected for the *Tales* of 1845. In describing some of the details of the "Red Death," Poe may have relied upon his recollection of the epidemic of cholera in Baltimore in 1831. "The Masque of the Red Death" possesses "the immense force derivable from *totality*," which the author considered the chief advantage of the short story. Its atmospheric effect rivals that achieved in "The Fall of the House of Usher." The text is that of 1876.

The "Red Death" had long devastated the country. No pestilence had ever been so fatal, or so hideous. Blood was its Avator[n] and its sale— the redness and the horror of blood. There were sharp pains, and sudden dizziness, and then profuse bleeding at the pores, with dissolution. The scarlet

"Un . . . Thyeste": "A plot so sinister, if not worthy of Atreus, is worthy of Thyestes." **Avator**: avatar; descent into incarnate life, incarnation.

stains upon the body and especially upon the face of the victim, were the pest ban which shut him out from the aid and from the sympathy of his fellowmen. And the whole seizure, progress and termination of the disease, were the incidents of half an hour.

But the Prince Prospero was happy and dauntless and sagacious. When his dominions were half depopulated, he summoned to his presence a thousand hale and light-hearted friends from among the knights and dames of his court, and with these retired to the deep seclusion of one of his castellated abbeys. This was an extensive and magnificent structure, the creation of the prince's own eccentric yet august taste. A strong and lofty wall girdled it in. This wall had gates of iron. The courtiers, having entered, brought furnaces and massy hammers and welded the bolts. They resolved to leave means neither of ingress or egress to the sudden impulses of despair or of frenzy from within. The abbey was amply provisioned. With such precautions the courtiers might bid defiance to contagion. The external world could take care of itself. In the meantime it was folly to grieve, or to think. The prince had provided all the appliances of pleasure. There were buffoons, there were improvisatori, there were ballet-dancers, there were musicians, there was Beauty, there was wine. All these and security were within. Without was the "Red Death."

It was toward the close of the fifth or sixth month of his seclusion, and while the pestilence raged most furiously abroad, that the Prince Prospero entertained his thousand friends at a masked ball of the most unusual magnificence.

It was a voluptuous scene, that masquerade. But first let me tell of the rooms in which it was held. There were seven—an imperial suite. In many palaces, however, such suites form a long and straight vista, while the folding doors slide back nearly to the walls on either hand, so that the view of the whole extent is scarcely impeded. Here the case was very different; as might have been expected from the duke's love of the bizarre. The apartments were so irregularly disposed that the vision embraced but little more than one at a time. There was a sharp turn at every twenty or thirty yards, and at each turn a novel effect. To the right and left, in the middle of each wall, a tall and narrow Gothic window looked out upon a closed corridor which pursued the windings of the suite. These windows were of stained glass whose color varied in accordance with the prevailing hue of the decorations of the chamber into which it opened. That at the eastern extremity was hung, for example, in blue—and vividly blue were its windows. The second chamber was purple in its ornaments and tapestries, and here the panes were purple. The third was green throughout, and so were the casements. The fourth was furnished and lighted with orange—the fifth with white—the sixth with violet. The seventh apartment was closely shrouded in black velvet tapestries that hung all over the ceiling and down the walls, falling in heavy folds upon a carpet of the same material and hue. But in this chamber only, the color of the windows failed to correspond with the decorations. The panes here were scarlet—a deep blood color. Now in no one of the seven apartments was there any lamp or candelabrum, amid the profusion of golden ornaments that lay scattered to and fro or depended from the roof. There was no light of any kind emanating from lamp or candle within the suite of chambers. But in the corridors that followed the suite, there stood, opposite to each window, a heavy tripod, bearing a brazier of fire that projected its rays through the tinted glass and so glaringly illumined the room. And thus were produced a multitude of gaudy and fantastic appearances. But in the western or black chamber the effect of the firelight that streamed upon the dark hangings through the blood-tinted panes, was ghastly in the extreme, and produced so wild a look upon the countenances of those who entered, that there were few of the company bold enough to set foot within its precincts at all.

It was in this apartment, also, that there stood against the western wall, a gigantic clock of ebony. Its pendulum swung to and fro with a dull, heavy, monotonous clang; and when the minute-hand made the circuit of the face, and the hour was to be stricken, there came from the brazen lungs of the clock a sound which was clear and loud and deep and exceedingly musical, but of so peculiar a note and emphasis that, at each lapse of an hour, the musicians of the orchestra were constrained to pause, momentarily, in their performance, to hearken to the sound; and thus the waltzers perforce ceased their evolutions; and there was a brief disconcert of the whole gay company; and, while the chimes of the clock yet rang, it was observed that the giddiest grew pale, and the more aged and sedate passed their hands over their brows as if in confused revery or meditation. But when the echoes had fully ceased, a light laughter at once pervaded the assembly; the musicians looked at each other and smiled as if at their own nervousness and folly, and made whispering vows, each to the other, that the next chiming of the clock should produce in them no similar emotion; and then, after the lapse of sixty minutes (which embrace three thousand and six hundred seconds of the Time that flies), there came yet another chiming of the clock, and then were the same disconcert and tremulousness and meditation as before.

But, in spite of these things, it was a gay and magnificent revel. The tastes of the duke were peculiar. He had a fine eye for colors and effects. He disregarded the *decora* of mere fashion. His plans were bold and fiery, and his conceptions glowed with barbaric lustre. There are some who would have thought him mad. His followers felt that he was not. It was necessary to hear and see and touch him to be sure that he was not.

He had directed, in great part, the movable embellishments of the seven chambers, upon occasion of this great *fête;* and it was his own guiding taste which had given character to the masqueraders. Be sure they were grotesque. There was much glare and glitter and piquancy and phantasm —much of what has been since seen in "Hernani."[n] There were arabesque figures with unsuited limbs and appointments. There were delirious fancies such as the madman fashions. There was much of the beautiful, much of the wanton, much of the bizarre, something of the terrible, and not a little of that which might have excited disgust. To and fro in the seven chambers there stalked, in fact, a multitude of dreams. And these—the dreams— writhed in and about, taking hue from the rooms, and causing the wild music of the orchestra to seem

"**Hernani**": a drama by Victor Hugo (1802–1885), French novelist, poet, and dramatist.

as the echo of their steps. And, anon, there strikes the ebony clock which stands in the hall of the velvet. And then, for a moment, all is still, and all is silent save the voice of the clock. The dreams are stiff-frozen as they stand. But the echoes of the chime die away—they have endured but an instant—and a light, half-subdued laughter floats after them as they depart. And now again the music swells, and the dreams live, and writhe to and fro more merrily than ever, taking hue from the many tinted windows through which stream the rays from the tripods. But to the chamber which lies most westwardly of the seven, there are now none of the maskers who venture; for the night is waning away; and there flows a ruddier light through the blood-colored panes; and the blackness of the sable drapery appalls; and to him whose foot falls upon the sable carpet, there comes from the near clock of ebony a muffled peal more solemnly emphatic than any which reaches their ears who indulge in the more remote gayeties of the other apartments.

But these other apartments were densely crowded, and in them beat feverishly the heart of life. And the revel went whirlingly on, until at length there commenced the sounding of midnight upon the clock. And then the music ceased, as I have told; and the evolutions of the waltzers were quieted; and there was an uneasy cessation of all things as before. But now there were twelve strokes to be sounded by the bell of the clock; and thus it happened, perhaps, that more of thought crept, with more of time, into the meditations of the thoughtful among those who revelled. And thus, too, it happened, perhaps, that before the last echoes of the last chime had utterly sunk into silence, there were many individuals in the crowd who had found leisure to become aware of the presence of a masked figure which had arrested the attention of no single individual before. And the rumor of this new presence having spread itself whisperingly around, there arose at length from the whole company, a buzz, or murmur, expressive of disapprobation and surprise—then, finally, of terror, of horror, and of disgust.

In an assembly of phantasms such as I have painted, it may well be supposed that no ordinary appearance could have excited such sensation. In truth the masquerade license of the night was nearly unlimited; but the figure in question had out-Heroded Herod, and gone beyond the bounds of even the prince's indefinite decorum. There are chords in the hearts of the most reckless which cannot be touched without emotion. Even with the utterly lost, to whom life and death are equally jests, there are matters of which no jest can be made. The whole company, indeed, seemed now deeply to feel that in the costume and bearing of 10 the stranger neither wit nor propriety existed. The figure was tall and gaunt, and shrouded from head to foot in the habiliments of the grave. The mask which concealed the visage was made so nearly to resemble the countenance of a stiffened corpse that the closest scrutiny must have had difficulty in detecting the cheat. And yet all this might have been endured, if not approved, by the mad revellers around. But the mummer had gone so far as to assume the type of the Red Death. 20 His vesture was dabbled in blood—and his broad brow, with all the features of the face, was besprinkled with the scarlet horror.

When the eyes of Prince Prospero fell upon this spectral image (which with a slow and solemn movement, as if more fully to sustain its *rôle*, stalked to and fro among the waltzers) he was seen to be convulsed, in the first moment, with a strong shudder either of terror or distaste; but, in the next, his brow reddened with rage. 30

"Who dares?" he demanded hoarsely of the courtiers who stood near him—"who dares insult us with this blasphemous mockery? Seize him and unmask him—that we may know whom we have to hang at sunrise, from the battlements!"

It was in the eastern or blue chamber in which stood the Prince Prospero as he uttered these words. They rang throughout the seven rooms loudly and clearly—for the prince was a bold and robust man, and the music had become hushed at 40 the waving of his hand.

It was in the blue room where stood the prince, with a group of pale courtiers by his side. At first, as he spoke, there was a slight rushing movement of this group in the direction of the intruder, who at the moment was also near at hand, and now, with deliberate and stately step, made closer approach to the speaker. But from a certain nameless awe with which the mad assumptions of the mummer had inspired the whole party, there were found none who put forth hand to seize him; so that, unimpeded, he passed within a yard of the prince's person; and, while the vast assembly, as if with one impulse, shrank from the centres of the rooms to the walls, he made his way uninterruptedly, but with the same solemn and measured step which had distinguished him from the first, through the blue chamber to the purple—through the purple to the green—through the green to the orange—through this again to the white—and even thence to the violet, ere a decided movement had been made to arrest him. It was then, however, that the Prince Prospero, maddening with rage and the shame of his own momentary cowardice, rushed hurriedly through the six chambers, while none 20 followed him on account of a deadly terror that had seized upon all. He bore aloft a drawn dagger, and had approached, in rapid impetuosity, to within three or four feet of the retreating figure, when the latter, having attained the extremity of the velvet apartment, turned suddenly and confronted his pursuer. There was a sharp cry—and the dagger dropped gleaming upon the sable carpet, upon which, instantly afterwards, fell prostrate in death the Prince Prospero. Then, summoning the wild courage of despair, a throng of the 30 revellers at once threw themselves into the black apartment, and, seizing the mummer, whose tall figure stood erect and motionless within the shadow of the ebony clock, gasped in unutterable horror at finding the grave-cerements and corpse-like mask which they handled with so violent a rudeness, untenanted by any tangible form.

And now was acknowledged the presence of the Red Death. He had come like a thief in the night. And one by one dropped the revellers in the blood-40 bedewed halls of their revel, and died each in the despairing posture of his fall. And the life of the ebony clock went out with that of the last of the gay. And the flames of the tripods expired. And Darkness and Decay and the Red Death held illimitable dominion over all.

The Cask of Amontillado

THIS STORY is a brilliant illustration of how Poe's practice as a writer of short narratives was in close accord with his precepts as a critic. In his famous review of Hawthorne's *Twice-Told Tales* in *Graham's Magazine*, for May, 1842, Poe wrote: "In the whole composition there should be no word written of which the tendency, direct or indirect, is not to the one pre-established design." No critic has been disposed to deny that in "The Cask of Amontillado" Poe achieved a masterpiece of dramatic irony. It appeared for the first time in *Godey's Lady's Book*, for November, 1846, and was included in the *Works of the Late Edgar Allan Poe* (1850), edited by Rufus Griswold. The text is that of the edition of 1876.

The thousand injuries of Fortunato I had borne as I best could; but when he ventured upon insult, I vowed revenge. You, who so well know the nature of my soul, will not suppose, however, that I gave utterance to a threat. At length I would be avenged; this was a point definitely settled—but the very definiteness with which it was resolved precluded the idea of risk. I must not only punish, but punish with impunity. A wrong is unredressed when retribution overtakes its redresser. It is equally unredressed when the avenger fails to make himself felt as such to him who has done the wrong.

It must be understood that neither by word nor deed had I given Fortunato cause to doubt my good will. I continued, as was my wont, to smile in his face, and he did not perceive that my smile now was at the thought of his immolation.

He had a weak point—this Fortunato—although in other regards he was a man to be respected and even feared. He prided himself on his connoisseurship in wine. Few Italians have the true virtuoso spirit. For the most part their enthusiasm is adopted to suit the time and opportunity—to practice imposture upon the British and Austrian millionaires. In painting and gemmary, Fortunato, like his countrymen, was a quack—but in the matter of old wines he was sincere. In this respect I did not differ from him materially: I was skilful in the Italian vintages myself, and bought largely whenever I could.

It was about dusk, one evening during the supreme madness of the carnival season, that I encountered my friend. He accosted me with excessive warmth, for he had been drinking much. The man wore motley. He had on a tight-fitting parti-striped dress, and his head was surmounted by the conical cap and bells. I was so pleased to see him that I thought I should never have done wringing his hand.

I said to him—"My dear Fortunato, you are luckily met. How remarkably well you are looking today! But I have received a pipe of what passes for Amontillado,[n] and I have my doubts."

"How?" said he. "Amontillado? A pipe? Impossible! And in the middle of the carnival!"

"I have my doubts," I replied; "and I was silly enough to pay the full Amontillado price without consulting you in the matter. You were not to be found, and I was fearful of losing a bargain."

"Amontillado!"

"I have my doubts."

"Amontillado!"

"And I must satisfy them."

"Amontillado!"

"As you are engaged, I am on my way to Luchesi. If any one has a critical turn, it is he. He will tell me!—"

"Luchesi cannot tell Amontillado from Sherry."

"And yet some fools will have it that his taste is a match for your own."

"Come, let us go."

"Whither?"

"To your vaults."

"My friend, no; I will not impose upon your good nature. I perceive you have an engagement. Luchesi—"

"I have no engagement;—come."

"My friend, no. It is not the engagement, but the severe cold with which I perceive you are afflicted. The vaults are insufferably damp. They are incrusted with nitre."

"Let us go, nevertheless. The cold is merely nothing. Amontillado! You have been imposed upon. And as for Luchesi, he cannot distinguish Sherry from Amontillado."

Thus speaking, Fortunato possessed himself of my arm. Putting on a mask of black silk, and drawing a *roquelaire*[n] closely about my person, I suffered him to hurry me to my palazzo.

Amontillado: a Spanish wine.   *roquelaire:* a cloak.

513

There were no attendants at home; they had absconded to make merry in honor of the time. I had told them that I should not return until the morning, and had given them explicit orders not to stir from the house. These orders were sufficient, I well knew, to insure their immediate disappearance, one and all, as soon as my back was turned.

I took from their sconces two flambeaus, and giving one to Fortunato, bowed him through several suites of rooms to the archway that led into [10] the vaults. I passed down a long and winding staircase, requesting him to be cautious as he followed. We came at length to the foot of the descent, and stood together on the damp ground of the catacombs of the Montresors.

The gait of my friend was unsteady, and the bells upon his cap jingled as he strode.

"The pipe," said he.

"It is farther on," said I; "but observe the white web-work which gleams from these cavern [20] walls."

He turned towards me, and looked into my eyes with two filmy orbs that distilled the rheum of intoxication.

"Nitre?" he asked at length.

"Nitre," I replied. "How long have you had that cough?"

"Ugh! ugh! ugh!—ugh! ugh! ugh!—ugh! ugh! ugh!—ugh! ugh! ugh!—ugh! ugh! ugh!"

My poor friend found it impossible to reply [30] for many minutes.

"It is nothing," he said, at last.

"Come," I said, with decision, "we will go back; your health is precious. You are rich, respected, admired, beloved; you are happy, as once I was. You are a man to be missed. For me it is no matter. We will go back; you will be ill, and I cannot be responsible. Besides, there is Luchesi—"

"Enough," he said; "the cough is a mere nothing; it will not kill me. I shall not die of a [40] cough."

"True—true," I replied; "and, indeed, I had no intention of alarming you unnecessarily—but you should use all proper caution. A draught of this Medoc will defend us from the damps."

Here I knocked off the neck of a bottle which I drew from a long row of its fellows that lay upon the mold.

"Drink," I said, presenting him the wine.

He raised it to his lips with a leer. He paused and nodded to me familiarly, while his bells jingled.

"I drink," he said, "to the buried that repose around us."

"And I to your long life."

He again took my arm, and we proceeded.

"These vaults," he said, "are extensive."

"The Montresors," I replied, "were a great and numerous family."

"I forget your arms."

"A huge human foot d'or,[n] in a field azure; the foot crushes a serpent rampant whose fangs are embedded in the heel."

"And the motto?"

"*Nemo me impune lacessit*."[n]

"Good!" he said.

The wine sparkled in his eyes and the bells jingled. My own fancy grew warm with the Medoc. We had passed through walls of piled bones, with casks and puncheons intermingling, into the inmost recesses of the catacombs. I paused again, and this time I made bold to seize Fortunato by an arm above the elbow.

"The nitre!" I said; "see, it increases. It hangs like moss upon the vaults. We are below the river's bed. The drops of moisture trickle among the bones. Come, we will go back ere it is too late. [30] Your cough—"

"It is nothing," he said; "let us go on. But first, another draught of the Medoc."

I broke and reached him a flagon of De Grâve. He emptied it at a breath. His eyes flashed with a fierce light. He laughed and threw the bottle upwards with a gesticulation I did not understand.

I looked at him in surprise. He repeated the movement—a grotesque one.

"You do not comprehend?" he said.

"Not I," I replied.

"Then you are not of the brotherhood."

"How?"

"You are not of the masons."

"Yes, yes," I said, "yes, yes."

"You? Impossible! A mason?"

"A mason," I replied.

d'or: of gold. **"*Nemo . . . lacessit*"**: "No one attacks me with impunity."

514

"A sign," he said.

"It is this," I answered, producing a trowel from beneath the folds of my *roquelaire*.

"You jest," he exclaimed, recoiling a few paces. "But let us proceed to the Amontillado."

"Be it so," I said, replacing the tool beneath the cloak, and again offering him my arm. He leaned upon it heavily. We continued our route in search of the Amontillado. We passed through a range of low arches, descended, passed on, and, descending again, arrived at a deep crypt, in which the foulness of the air caused our flambeaus rather to glow than flame.

At the most remote end of the crypt there appeared another less spacious. Its walls had been lined with human remains, piled to the vault overhead, in the fashion of the great catacombs of Paris. Three sides of this interior crypt were still ornamented in this manner. From the fourth the bones had been thrown down, and lay promiscuously upon the earth, forming at one point a mound of some size. Within the wall thus exposed by the displacing of the bones, we perceived a still interior recess, in depth about four feet, in width three, in height six or seven. It seemed to have been constructed for no especial use within itself, but formed merely the interval between two of the colossal supports of the roof of the catacombs, and was backed by one of their circumscribing walls of solid granite.

It was in vain that Fortunato, uplifting his dull torch, endeavored to pry into the depth of the recess. Its termination the feeble light did not enable us to see.

"Proceed," I said; "herein is the Amontillado. As for Luchesi—"

"He is an ignoramus," interrupted my friend, as he stepped unsteadily forward, while I followed immediately at his heels. In an instant he had reached the extremity of the niche, and finding his progress arrested by the rock, stood stupidly bewildered. A moment more and I had fettered him to the granite. In its surface were two iron staples, distant from each other about two feet, horizontally. From one of these depended a short chain, from the other a padlock. Throwing the links about his waist, it was but the work of a few seconds to secure it. He was too much as-

tounded to resist. Withdrawing the key, I stepped back from the recess.

"Pass your hand," I said, "over the wall; you cannot help feeling the nitre. Indeed it is very damp. Once more let me implore you to return. No? Then I must positively leave you. But I must first render you all the little attentions in my power."

"The Amontillado!" ejaculated my friend, not yet recovered from his astonishment.

"True," I replied; "the Amontillado."

As I said these words I busied myself among the pile of bones of which I have before spoken. Throwing them aside, I soon uncovered a quantity of building stone and mortar. With these materials and with the aid of my trowel, I began vigorously to wall up the entrance of the niche.

I had scarcely laid the first tier of the masonry when I discovered that the intoxication of Fortunato had in a great measure worn off. The earliest indication I had of this was a low moaning cry from the depth of the recess. It was not the cry of a drunken man. There was then a long and obstinate silence. I laid the second tier, and the third, and the fourth; and then I heard the furious vibrations of the chain. The noise lasted for several minutes, during which, that I might hearken to it with the more satisfaction, I ceased my labors and sat down upon the bones. When at last the clanking subsided, I resumed the trowel, and finished without interruption the fifth, the sixth, and the seventh tier. The wall was now nearly upon a level with my breast. I again paused, and holding the flambeaus over the mason work, threw a few feeble rays upon the figure within.

A succession of loud and shrill screams, bursting suddenly from the throat of the chained form, seemed to thrust me violently back. For a brief moment I hesitated—I trembled. Unsheathing my rapier, I began to grope with it about the recess; but the thought of an instant reassured me. I placed my hand upon the solid fabric of the catacombs and felt satisfied. I reapproached the wall. I replied to the yells of him who clamored. I re-echoed—I aided—I surpassed them in volume and in strength. I did this, and the clamorer grew still.

It was now midnight, and my task was drawing to a close. I had completed the eighth, the ninth, and the tenth tier. I had finished a portion of the last and the eleventh; there remained but a single stone to be fitted and plastered in. I struggled with its weight; I placed it partially in its destined position. But now there came from out the niche a low laugh that erected the hairs upon my head. It was succeeded by a sad voice, which I had difficulty in recognizing as that of the noble Fortunato. The voice said—

"Ha! ha! ha!—he! he! he!—a very good joke indeed—an excellent jest. We will have many a rich laugh about it at the palazzo—he! he! he!—over our wine—he! he! he!"

"The Amontillado!" I said.

"He! he! he!—he! he! he!—yes, the Amontillado. But is it not getting late? Will not they be awaiting us at the palazzo,—the Lady Fortunato and the rest? Let us be gone."

"Yes," I said, "let us be gone."

"For the love of God, Montresor!"

"Yes," I said, "for the love of God!"

But to these words I hearkened in vain for a reply. I grew impatient. I called aloud—

"Fortunato!"

No answer. I called again—

"Fortunato!"

No answer still. I thrust a torch through the remaining aperture and let it fall within. There came forth in return only a jingling of the bells. My heart grew sick—on account of the dampness of the catacombs. I hastened to make an end of my labor. I forced the last stone into its position; I plastered it up. Against the new masonry I re-erected the old rampart of bones. For the half of a century no mortal has disturbed them. *In pace requiescat.*"

Hawthorne's Twice-Told Tales

POE'S REVIEWS bulk large in his collected writings, and he was perhaps better known in his own day as a critic than as poet or narrative writer. The most celebrated of his criticisms of the work of his contemporaries is his review of the second edition of Hawthorne's *Twice-Told Tales* in *Graham's Magazine* for April and May, 1842. His formula for the short story with its insistence upon "totality" as a requisite

In pace requiescat: May he rest in peace.

has been enormously influential, although it allows little room for the development of complex characters. The text is that of the 1876 edition of *The Works of Edgar Allan Poe*, which is a modification of the original.

. . . The pieces in the volumes entitled "Twice-Told Tales," are now in their third republication, and, of course, are thrice-told. Moreover, they are by no means all tales, either in the ordinary or in the legitimate understanding of the term. Many of them are pure essays; for example, "Sights from a Steeple," "Sunday at Home," "Little Annie's Ramble," "A Rill from the Town-Pump," "The Toll-Gatherer's Day," "The Haunted Mind," "The Sister Years," "Snow-Flakes," "Night Sketches," and "Foot-Prints on the Sea-Shore." I mention these matters chiefly on account of their discrepancy with that marked precision and finish by which the body of the work is distinguished.

Of the Essays just named, I must be content to speak in brief. They are each and all beautiful, without being characterized by the polish and adaptation so visible in the tales proper. A painter would at once note their leading or predominant feature, and style it repose. There is no attempt at effect. All is quiet, thoughtful, subdued. Yet this repose may exist simultaneously with high originality of thought; and Mr. Hawthorne has demonstrated the fact. At every turn we meet with novel combinations; yet these combinations never surpass the limits of the quiet. We are soothed as we read; and withal is a calm astonishment that ideas so apparently obvious have never occurred or been presented to us before. Herein our author differs materially from Lamb or Hunt or Hazlitt—who, with vivid originality of manner and expression, have less of the true novelty of thought than is generally supposed, and whose originality, at best, has an uneasy and meretricious quaintness, replete with startling effects unfounded in nature, and inducing trains of reflection which lead to no satisfactory result. The Essays of Hawthorne have much of the character of Irving, with more of originality, and less of finish; while, compared with the Spectator, they have a vast superiority at all points. The Spectator, Mr. Irving, and Hawthorne have in common that tranquil and subdued manner which I have chosen to denominate *repose*; but, in the case of the two former, this repose is attained rather by the absence of novel combination, or of originality, than otherwise, and consists chiefly in the calm, quiet, unostentatious expression of commonplace thoughts, in an unambitious, unadulterated Saxon. In them, by strong effort, we are made to conceive the absence of all. In the essays before me the absence of effort is too obvious to be mistaken, and a a strong under-current of suggestion runs continuously beneath the upper stream of the tranquil thesis. In short, these effusions of Mr. Hawthorne are the product of a truly imaginative intellect, restrained, and in some measure repressed, by fastidiousness of taste, by constitutional melancholy, and by indolence.

But it is of his tales that I desire principally to speak. The tale proper, in my opinion, affords unquestionably the fairest field for the exercise of the loftiest talent, which can be afforded by the wide domains of mere prose. Were I bidden to say how the highest genius could be most advantageously employed for the best display of its own powers, I should answer, without hesitation—in the composition of a rhymed poem, not to exceed in length what might be perused in an hour. Within this limit alone can the highest order of true poetry exist. I need only here say, upon this topic, that, in almost all classes of composition, the unity of effect or impression is a point of the greatest importance. It is clear, moreover, that this unity cannot be thoroughly preserved in productions whose perusal cannot be completed at one sitting. We may continue the reading of a prose composition, from the very nature of prose itself, much longer than we can persevere, to any good purpose, in the perusal of a poem. This latter, if truly fulfilling the demands of the poetic sentiment, induces an exaltation of the soul which cannot be long sustained. All high excitements are necessarily transient. Thus a long poem is a paradox. And, without unity of impression, the deepest effects cannot be brought about. Epics were the offspring of an imperfect sense of Art, and their reign is no more. A poem *too* brief may produce a vivid, but never an intense or enduring impression. Without a certain continuity of effort—without a certain duration or repetition of purpose—the soul

is never deeply moved. There must be the dropping of the water upon the rock. De Béranger has wrought brilliant things—pungent and spirit stirring—but, like all immassive bodies, they lack momentum, and thus fail to satisfy the Poetic Sentiment. They sparkle and excite, but, from want of continuity, fail deeply to impress. Extreme brevity will degenerate into epigrammatism; but the sin of extreme length is even more unpardonable. *In medio tutissimus ibis.*"

Were I called upon, however, to designate that class of composition which, next to such a poem as I have suggested, should best fulfil the demands of high genius—should offer it the most advantageous field of exertion—I should unhesitatingly speak of the prose tale, as Mr. Hawthorne has here exemplified it. I allude to the short prose narrative, requiring from a half-hour to one or two hours in its perusal. The ordinary novel is objectionable, from its length, for reasons already stated in substance. As it cannot be read at one sitting, it deprives itself, of course, of the immense force derivable from totality. Worldly interests intervening during the pauses of perusal, modify, annul, or counteract, in a greater or less degree, the impressions of the book. But simple cessation in reading would, of itself, be sufficient to destroy the true unity. In the brief tale, however, the author is enabled to carry out the fulness of his intention, be it what it may. During the hour of perusal the soul of the reader is at the writer's control. There are no external or extrinsic influences—resulting from weariness or interruption.

A skilful literary artist has constructed a tale. If wise, he has not fashioned his thoughts to accommodate his incidents; but having conceived, with deliberate care, a certain unique or single effect to be wrought out, he then invents such incidents—he then combines such events as may best aid him in establishing this preconceived effect. If his very initial sentence tend not to the outbringing of this effect, then he has failed in his first step. In the whole composition there should be no word written, of which the tendency, direct or indirect, is not to be the one pre-established design. And by such means, with such care and

In . . . ibis: You will be safest in adopting a middle course.

skill, a picture is at length painted which leaves in the mind of him who contemplates it with a kindred art, a sense of the fullest satisfaction. The idea of the tale has been presented unblemished, because undisturbed; and this is an end unattainable by the novel. Undue brevity is just as exceptionable here as in the poem; but undue length is yet more to be avoided.

We have said that the tale has a point of superiority even over the poem. In fact, while the rhythm of this latter is an essential aid in the development of the poem's highest idea—the idea of the Beautiful—the artificialities of this rhythm are an inseparable bar to the development of all points of thought or expression which have their basis in Truth. But Truth is often, and in very great degree, the aim of the tale. Some of the finest tales are tales of ratiocination. Thus the field of this species of composition, if not in so elevated a region on the mountain of Mind, is a table-land of far vaster extent than the domain of the mere poem. Its products are never so rich, but infinitely more numerous, and more appreciable by the mass of mankind. The writer of the prose tale, in short, may bring to his theme a vast variety of modes or inflections of thought and expression—(the ratiocinative, for example, the sarcastic or the humorous) which are not only antagonistical to the nature of the poem, but absolutely forbidden by one of its most peculiar and indispensable adjuncts; we allude, of course, to rhythm. It may be added, here, *par parenthèse*, that the author who aims at the purely beautiful in a prose tale is laboring at a great disadvantage. For Beauty can be better treated in the poem. Not so with terror, or passion, or horror, or a multitude of such other points. And here it will be seen how full of prejudice are the usual animadversions against those tales of effect, many fine examples of which were found in the earlier numbers of Blackwood. The impressions produced were wrought in a legitimate sphere of action, and constituted a legitimate although sometimes an exaggerated interest. They were relished by every man of genius: although there were found many men of genius who condemned them without just ground. The true critic will but demand that the design intended be accomplished, to the

fullest extent, by the means most advantageously applicable.

We have very few American tales of real merit—we may say, indeed, none, with the exception of "The Tales of a Traveller" of Washington Irving, and these "Twice-Told Tales" of Mr. Hawthorne. Some of the pieces of Mr. John Neal abound in vigor and originality; but in general, his compositions of this class are excessively diffuse, extravagant, and indicative of an imperfect sentiment of Art. Articles at random are, now and then, met with in our periodicals which might be advantageously compared with the best effusions of the British magazines; but, upon the whole, we are far behind our progenitors in this department of literature.

Of Mr. Hawthorne's Tales we would say, emphatically, that they belong to the highest region of Art—an Art subservient to genius of a very lofty order. We had supposed, with good reason for so supposing, that he had been thrust into his present position by one of the impudent *cliques* which beset our literature, and whose pretensions it is our full purpose to expose at the earliest opportunity; but we have been most agreeably mistaken. We know of few compositions which the critic can more honestly commend than these "Twice-Told Tales." As Americans, we feel proud of the book.

Mr. Hawthorne's distinctive trait is invention, creation, imagination, originality—a trait which, in the literature of fiction, is positively worth all the rest. But the nature of the originality, so far as regards its manifestation in letters, is but imperfectly understood. The inventive or original mind as frequently displays itself in novelty of tone as in novelty of matter. Mr. Hawthorne is original in all points.

It would be a matter of some difficulty to designate the best of these tales; we repeat that, without exception, they are beautiful. "Wakefield" is remarkable for the skill with which an old idea—a well-known incident—is worked up or discussed. A man of whims conceives the purpose of quitting his wife and residing *incognito*, for twenty years in her immediate neighborhood. Something of this kind actually happened in London. The force of Mr. Hawthorne's tale lies in the analysis of the motives which must or might have impelled the husband to such folly, in the first instance, with the possible causes of his perseverance. Upon this thesis a sketch of singular power has been constructed. "The Wedding Knell" is full of the boldest imagination—an imagination fully controlled by taste. The most captious critic could find no flaw in this production. "The Minister's Black Veil" is a masterly composition of which the sole defect is that to the rabble its exquisite skill will be *caviare*. The obvious meaning of this article will be found to smother its insinuated one. The moral put into the mouth of the dying minister will be supposed to convey the true import of the narrative; and that a crime of dark dye (having reference to the "young lady") has been committed, is a point which only minds congenial with that of the author will perceive. "Mr. Higginbotham's Catastrophe" is vividly original and managed most dexterously. "Dr. Heidegger's Experiment" is exceedingly well imagined, and executed with surpassing ability. The artist breathes in every line of it. "The White Old Maid" is objectionable, even more than the "Minister's Black Veil," on the score of its mysticism. Even with the thoughtful and analytic, there will be much trouble in penetrating its entire import.

"The Hollow of the Three Hills" we would quote in full, had we space;—not as evincing higher talent than any of the other pieces, but as affording an excellent example of the author's peculiar ability. The subject is commonplace. A witch subjects the Distant and the Past to the view of a mourner. It has been the fashion to describe, in such cases, a mirror in which the images of the absent appear; or a cloud of smoke is made to arise, and thence the figures are gradually unfolded. Mr. Hawthorne has wonderfully heightened his effect by making the ear, in place of the eye, the medium by which the fantasy is conveyed. The head of the mourner is enveloped in the cloak of the witch, and within its magic folds there arise sounds which have an all-sufficient intelligence. Throughout this article, also, the artist is conspicuous—not more in positive than in negative merits. Not only is all done that should be done, but (what perhaps is an end with more difficulty attained) there is nothing done which

should not be. Every word tells, and there is not a word which does not tell.

In "Howe's Masquerade" we observe something which resembles a plagiarism—but which may be a very flattering coincidence of thought. We quote the passage in question.

With a dark flush of wrath upon his brow they saw the general *draw his sword* and *advance to meet* the figure *in the cloak* before the latter had stepped one pace upon the floor. "*Villian, unmuffle yourself,*" cried he, "you pass no farther!" The figure, without blenching a hair's breadth from the sword which was pointed at his breast, made a solemn pause, and *lowered the cape of the cloak* from his face, yet not sufficiently for the spectators to catch a glimpse of it. But Sir William Howe had evidently seen enough. The sternness of his countenance gave place to a look of wild amazement, if not horror, while he recoiled several steps from the figure, *and let fall his sword* upon the floor.—See vol: 2, p. 20.

The idea here is, that the figure in the cloak is the phantom or reduplication of Sir William Howe; but in an article called "William Wilson," one of the "Tales of the Grotesque and Arabesque," we have not only the same idea, but the same idea similarly presented in several respects. We quote two paragraphs, which our readers may compare with what has been already given. We have italicized, above, the immediate particulars of resemblance.

The brief moment in which I averted my eyes had been sufficient to produce, apparently, a material change in the arrangement at the upper or farther end of the room. A large mirror, it appeared to me, now stood where none had been perceptible before; and as I stepped up to it in extremity of terror, mine own image, but with features all pale and dabbled in blood, *advanced* with a feeble and tottering gait to meet me. Thus it appeared I say, but was not. It was Wilson, who then stood before me in the agonies of dissolution. Not a line in all the marked and singular lineaments of that face which was not even identically mine own. *His mask and cloak lay where he had thrown them, upon the floor.* Vol. 2, p. 57.

Here, it will be observed that, not only are the two general conceptions identical, but there are various points of similarity. In each case the figure seen is the wraith or duplication of the beholder. In each case the scene is a masquerade. In each case the figure is cloaked. In each, there is a quarrel—that is to say, angry words pass between the parties. In each the beholder is enraged. In each the cloak and sword fall upon the floor. The "villain, unmuffle yourself," of Mr. H. is precisely paralleled by a passage at page 56, of "William Wilson."

I must hasten to conclude this paper with a summary of Mr. Hawthorne's merits and demerits. 10

He is peculiar and not original—unless in those detailed fancies and detached thoughts which his want of general originality will deprive of the appreciation due to them, in preventing them from ever reaching the public eye. He is infinitely too fond of allegory, and can never hope for popularity so long as he persists in it. This he will not do, for allegory is at war with the whole tone of his nature, which disports itself never so well as when escaping from the mysticism of his Goodman 20 Browns and White Old Maids into the hearty, genial, but still Indian-summer sunshine of his Wakefields and Little Annie's Rambles. Indeed, his spirit of "metaphor run-mad" is clearly imbibed from the phalanx and phalanstery atmosphere in which he has been so long struggling for breath. He has not half the material for the exclusiveness of authorship that he possesses for its universality. He has the purest style, the finest taste, the most available scholarship, the most 30 delicate humor, the most touching pathos, the most radiant imagination, the most consummate ingenuity; and with these varied good qualities he has done well as a mystic. But is there any one of these qualities which should prevent his doing doubly as well in a career of honest, upright, sensible, prehensible and comprehensible things? Let him mend his pen, get a bottle of visible ink, come out from the Old Manse, cut Mr. Alcott, hang (if possible) the editor of "The Dial," and 40 throw out of the window to the pigs all his odd numbers of "The North American Review."

The Poetic Principle

POE wrote "The Poetic Principle" as a lecture in 1848, and probably revised it in the year of his death. It did not appear in print until August 31, 1850, when it was published in the *Home Journal*. The essay thus became Poe's last testament of his poetic faith, a reaffirmation of his conviction that the true function of poetry is "the rhythmical creation of beauty." In his earlier attacks on "the heresy of the didactic," Poe had seemed to imply that moral and intellectual truth were not the proper concerns of poetry. In his last important critical article, however, the author makes clear that he has not limited the end of art merely to pleasure. His only condition is that "the lessons of Truth" be introduced aesthetically. The text is that of the edition of 1876.

In speaking of the Poetic Principle, I have no design to be either thorough or profound. While discussing, very much at random, the essentiality of what we call Poetry, my principal purpose will be to cite for consideration some few of those minor English or American poems which best suit my own taste, or which, upon my own fancy, have left the most definite impression. By "minor poems" I mean, of course, poems of little length. And here, in the beginning, permit me to say a few words in regard to a somewhat peculiar principle, which, whether rightfully or wrongfully, has always had its influence in my own critical estimate of the poem. I hold that a long poem does not exist. I maintain that the phrase, "a long poem," is simply a flat contradiction in terms.

I need scarcely observe that a poem deserves its title only inasmuch as it excites, by elevating the soul. The value of the poem is in the ratio of this elevating excitement. But all excitements are, through a psychal necessity, transient. That degree of excitement which would entitle a poem to be so called at all, cannot be sustained throughout a composition of any great length. After the lapse of half an hour, at the very utmost, it flags—fails—a revulsion ensues—and then the poem is, in effect, and in fact, no longer such.

There are, no doubt, many who have found difficulty in reconciling the critical dictum that the "Paradise Lost" is to be devoutly admired throughout, with the absolute impossibility of maintaining for it, during perusal, the amount of enthusiasm which that critical dictum would demand. This great work, in fact, is to be regarded as poetical only when, losing sight of that vital requisite in all works of Art, Unity, we view it

Wet

Read with great care

merely as a series of minor poems. If, to preserve its Unity—its totality of effect or impression—we read it (as would be necessary) at a single sitting, the result is but a constant alternation of excitement and depression. After a passage of what we feel to be true poetry, there follows, inevitably, a passage of platitude which no critical pre-judgment can force us to admire; but if, upon completing the work, we read it again, omitting the first book —that is to say, commencing with the second—we shall be surprised at now finding that admirable which we before condemned—that damnable which we had previously so much admired. It follows from all this that the ultimate, aggregate, or absolute effect of even the best epic under the sun, is a nullity: and this is precisely the fact.

In regard to the Iliad, we have, if not positive proof, at least very good reason, for believing it intended as a series of lyrics; but, granting the epic intention, I can say only that the work is based in an imperfect sense of Art. The modern epic is, of the supposititious ancient model, but an inconsiderate and blindfold imitation. But the day of these artistic anomalies is over. If, at any time, any very long poem were popular in reality, which I doubt, it is at least clear that no very long poem will ever be popular again.

That the extent of a poetical work is, *ceteris paribus*,[n] the measure of its merit, seems undoubtedly, when we thus state it, a proposition sufficiently absurd—yet we are indebted for it to the Quarterly Reviews. Surely there can be nothing in mere size, abstractly considered—there can be nothing in mere bulk, so far as a volume is concerned, which has so continuously elicited admiration from these saturnine pamphlets! A mountain, to be sure, by the mere sentiment of physical magnitude which it conveys, does impress us with a sense of the sublime—but no man is impressed after *this* fashion by the material grandeur of even "The Columbiad." Even the Quarterlies have not instructed us to be so impressed by it. As yet, they have not insisted on our estimating Lamartine[n] by the cubic foot, or Pollok[n] by the pound —but what else are we to infer from their con-

tinued prating about "sustained effort"? If, by "sustained effort," any little gentleman has accomplished an epic, let us frankly commend him for the effort—if this indeed be a thing commendable—but let us forbear praising the epic on the effort's account. It is to be hoped that common sense, in the time to come, will prefer deciding upon a work of Art, rather by the impression it makes—by the effect it produces—than by the time it took to impress the effect, or by the amount of "sustained effort" which had been found necessary in effecting the impression. The fact is, that perseverance is one thing and genius quite another—nor can all the Quarterlies in Christendom confound them. By-and-by, this proposition, with many which I have just been urging, will be received as self-evident. In the meantime, by being generally condemned as falsities, they will not be essentially damaged as truths.

On the other hand, it is clear that a poem may be improperly brief. Undue brevity degenerates into mere epigrammatism. A very short poem, while now and then producing a brilliant or vivid, never produces a profound or enduring effect. There must be the steady pressing down of the stamp upon the wax. De Béranger[n] has wrought innumerable things, pungent and spirit-stirring; but in general they have been too imponderous to stamp themselves deeply into the public attention, and thus, as so many feathers of fancy, have been blown aloft only to be whistled down the wind.

A remarkable instance of the effect of undue brevity in depressing a poem—in keeping it out of the popular view—is afforded by the following exquisite little Serenade:

> I arise from dreams of thee
> In the first sweet sleep of night,
> When the winds are breathing low,
> And the stars are shining bright;
> I arise from dreams of thee,   5
> And a spirit in my feet
> Has led me—who knows how?—
> To thy chamber-window, sweet!
>
> The wandering airs, they faint
> On the dark, the silent stream—   10

---

ceteris paribus: other things being equal. **Lamartine:** Alphonse de Lamartine (1790–1821), French romantic poet. **Pollok:** Robert Pollok (1798–1827), English poet.

De Béranger: Pierre de Béranger (1780–1857), French lyric poet.

The champak odors fail
    Like sweet thoughts in a dream;
The nightingale's complaint,
    It dies upon her heart,
As I must die on thine,   15
    O, beloved as thou art!

O, lift me from the grass!
    I die, I faint, I fail!
Let thy love in kisses rain
    On my lips and eyelids pale.   20
My cheek is cold and white, alas!
    My heart beats loud and fast:
Oh! press it close to thine again,
    Where it will break at last!

Very few perhaps are familiar with these lines—
yet no less a poet than Shelley is their author.
Their warm, yet delicate and ethereal imagination
will be appreciated by all—but by none so thoroughly as by him who has himself arisen from
sweet dreams of one beloved, to bathe in the aromatic air of a southern midsummer night.

One of the finest poems by Willis[n]—the very   10
best in my opinion which he has ever written—
has, no doubt, through this same defect of undue
brevity, been kept back from its proper position,
not less in the critical than in the popular view.

The shadows lay along Broadway,
    'Twas near the twilight-tide—
And slowly there a lady fair
    Was walking in her pride.
Alone walk'd she; but, viewlessly,   5
    Walk'd spirits at her side.   20

Peace charm'd the street beneath her feet,
    And Honour charm'd the air;
And all astir looked kind on her,
    And call'd her good and fair—   10
For all God ever gave to her
    She kept with chary care.

She kept with care her beauties rare
    From lovers warm and true—
For her heart was cold to all but gold,   15 30
    And the rich came not to woo—
But honour'd well are charms to sell,
    If priests the selling do.

Willis: Nathaniel P. Willis (1806–1867), American poet
and editor of New York City, highly popular in the forties.

Now walking there was one more fair—
    A slight girl, lily-pale;   20
And she had unseen company
    To make the spirit quail—
'Twixt Want and Scorn she walk'd forlorn,
    And nothing could avail.

No mercy now can clear her brow   25
    For this world's peace to pray;
For, as love's wild prayer dissolved in air,
    Her woman's heart gave way!—
But the sin forgiven by Christ in Heaven
    By man is cursed alway!   30

In this composition we find it difficult to recognize the Willis who has written so many mere
"verses of society." The lines are not only richly
ideal, but full of energy; while they breathe an
earnestness—an evident sincerity of sentiment—
for which we look in vain throughout all the other
works of this author.

While the epic mania—while the idea that, to
merit in poetry, prolixity is indispensable—has
for some years past been gradually dying out of the
public mind by mere dint of its own absurdity—
we find it succeeded by a heresy too palpably false
to be long tolerated, but one which, in the brief
period it has already endured, may be said to have
accomplished more in the corruption of our
Poetical Literature than all its other enemies combined. I allude to the heresy of The Didactic. It
has been assumed, tacitly and avowedly, directly
and indirectly, that the ultimate object of all
Poetry is Truth. Every poem, it is said, should
inculcate a moral; and by this moral is the poetical
merit of the work to be adjudged. We Americans
especially have patronized this happy idea; and
we Bostonians, very especially, have developed it in
full. We have taken it into our heads that to write
a poem simply for the poem's sake, and to acknowledge such to have been our design, would be to
confess ourselves radically wanting in the true
Poetic dignity and force:—but the simple fact is,
that would we but permit ourselves to look into
our own souls, we should immediately there discover that under the sun there neither exists nor
can exist any work more thoroughly dignified—
more supremely noble than this very poem—this
poem *per se*, this poem which is a poem and nothing

more—this poem written solely for the poem's sake.

With as deep a reverence for the True as ever inspired the bosom of man, I would nevertheless limit, in some measure, its modes of inculcation. I would limit to enforce them. I would not enfeeble them by dissipation. The demands of Truth are severe. She has no sympathy with the myrtles. All *that* which is so indispensable in Song is precisely all that with which she has nothing whatever to do. It is but making her a flaunting paradox to wreathe her in gems and flowers. In enforcing a truth, we need severity rather than efflorescence of language. We must be simple, precise, terse. We must be cool, calm, unimpassioned. In a word, we must be in that mood which, as nearly as possible, is the exact converse of the poetical. *He* must be blind indeed who does not perceive the radical and chasmal differences between the truthful and the poetical modes of inculcation. He must be theory-mad beyond redemption who, in spite of these differences, shall still persist in attempting to reconcile the obstinate oils and waters of Poetry and Truth.

Dividing the world of mind into its three most immediately obvious distinctions, we have the Pure Intellect, Taste, and the Moral Sense. I place Taste in the middle, because it is just this position which, in the mind, it occupies. It holds intimate relations with either extreme; but from the Moral Sense is separated by so faint a difference that Aristotle has not hesitated to place some of its operations among the virtues themselves. Nevertheless, we find the offices of the trio marked with a sufficient distinction. Just as the Intellect concerns itself with Truth, so Taste informs us of the Beautiful while the Moral Sense is regardful of Duty. Of this latter, while Conscience teaches the obligation, and Reason the expediency, Taste contents herself with displaying the charms:— waging war upon Vice solely on the ground of her deformity, her disproportion, her animosity to the fitting, to the appropriate, to the harmonious, in a word, to Beauty.

An immortal instinct, deep within the spirit of man, is thus plainly a sense of the Beautiful. This it is which administers to his delight in the manifold forms, and sounds, and odors, and sentiments, amid which he exists. And just as the lily is repeated in the lake, or the eyes of Amaryllis in the mirror, so is the mere oral or written repetition of these forms, and sounds, and colors, and odors, and sentiments, a duplicate source of delight. But this mere repetition is not poetry. He who shall simply sing, with however glowing enthusiasm, or with however vivid a truth of description, of the sights, and sounds, and odors, and colors, and sentiments, which greet him in common with all mankind—he, I say, has yet failed to prove his divine title. There is still a something in the distance which he has been unable to attain. We have still a thirst unquenchable, to allay which he has not shown us the crystal springs. This thirst belongs to the immortality of Man. It is at once a consequence and an indication of his perennial existence. It is the desire of the moth for the star. It is no mere appreciation of the Beauty before us —but a wild effort to reach the Beauty above. Inspired by an ecstatic prescience of the glories beyond the grave, we struggle by multiform combinations among the things and thoughts of Time, to attain a portion of that Loveliness whose very elements, perhaps, appertain to eternity alone. And thus when by Poetry—or when by Music, the most entrancing of the Poetic moods—we find ourselves melted into tears—we weep then—not as the Abbate Gravina[n] supposes—through excess of pleasure, but through a certain, petulant, impatient sorrow at our inability to grasp now, wholly, here on earth, at once and forever, those divine and rapturous joys, of which through the poem or through the music, we attain to but brief and indeterminate glimpses.

The struggle to apprehend the supernal Loveliness—this struggle, on the part of souls fittingly constituted—has given to the world all that which it (the world) has ever been enabled at once to understand and to feel as poetic.

The Poetic Sentiment, of course, may develop itself in various modes—in Painting, in Sculpture, in Architecture, in the Dance—very especially in Music—and very peculiarly, and with a wide field, in the composition of the Landscape Garden. Our present theme, however, has regard only to its manifestation in words. And here let me speak

Gravina: Giovanni Gravina (1664–1718), Italian critic.

briefly on the topic of rhythm. Contenting myself with the certainty that Music, in its various modes of metre, rhythm, and rhyme, is of so vast a moment in Poetry as never to be wisely rejected—is so vitally important an adjunct that he is simply silly who declines its assistance, I will not now pause to maintain its absolute essentiality. It is in Music, perhaps, that the soul most nearly attains the great end for which, when inspired by the Poetic Sentiment, it struggles—the creation of supernal Beauty. It may be, indeed, that here this sublime end is, now and then, attained in fact. We are often made to feel, with a shivering delight, that from an earthly harp are stricken notes which cannot have been unfamiliar to the angels. And thus there can be little doubt that in the union of Poetry with Music in its popular sense, we shall find the widest field for the Poetic development. The old Bards and Minnesingers had advantages which we do not posesss—and Thomas Moore,[n] singing his own songs, was, in the most legitimate manner, perfecting them as poems.

To recapitulate, then:—I would define, in brief, the Poetry of Words as The Rhythmical Creation of Beauty. Its sole arbiter is Taste. With the Intellect or with the Conscience, it has only collateral relations. Unless incidentally, it has no concern whatever either with Duty or with Truth.

A few words, however, in explanation. That pleasure which is at once the most pure, the most elevating, and the most intense, is derived, I maintain, from the contemplation of the Beautiful. In the contemplation of Beauty we alone find it possible to attain that pleasurable elevation, or excitement, of the soul, which we recognize as the Poetic Sentiment, and which is so easily distinguished from Truth, which is the satisfaction of the Reason, or from Passion, which is the excitement of the heart. I make Beauty, therefore—using the word as inclusive of the sublime—I make Beauty the province of the poem, simply because it is an obvious rule of Art that effects should be made to spring as directly as possible from their causes:—no one as yet having been weak enough to deny that the peculiar elevation in question is at least most readily attainable in the poem. It by no

Thomas Moore: English poet (1779–1852).

means follows, however, that the incitements of Passion, or the precepts of Duty, or even the lessons of Truth, may not be introduced into a poem, and with advantage; for they may subserve, incidentally, in various ways, the general purposes of the work:—but the true artist will always contrive to tone them down in proper subjection to that Beauty which is the atmosphere and the real essence of the poem.

I cannot better introduce the few poems which I shall present for your consideration, than by the citation of the Proem to Mr. Longfellow's "Waif":

> The day is done, and the darkness
>   Falls from the wings of Night,
> As a feather is wafted downward
>   From an eagle in his flight.
>
> I see the lights of the village   5
>   Gleam through the rain and the mist,
> And a feeling of sadness comes o'er me,
>   That my soul cannot resist;
>
> A feeling of sadness and longing,
>   That is not akin to pain,   10
> And resembles sorrow only
>   As the mist resembles the rain.
>
> Come, read to me some poem,
>   Some simple and heartfelt lay,
> That shall soothe this restless feeling,   15
>   And banish the thoughts of day.
>
> Not from the grand old masters,
>   Not from the bards sublime,
> Whose distant footsteps echo
>   Through the corridors of Time.   20
>
> For, like strains of martial music,
>   Their mighty thoughts suggest
> Life's endless toil and endeavor;
>   And to-night I long for rest.
>
> Read from some humbler poet,   25
>   Whose songs gushed from his heart,
> As showers from the clouds of summer,
>   Or tears from the eyelids start;
>
> Who through long days of labor,
>   And nights devoid of ease,   30
> Still heard in his soul the music
>   Of wonderful melodies.

Such songs have power to quiet
    The restless pulse of care,
And come like the benediction   35
    That follows after prayer.

Then read from the treasured volume
    The poem of thy choice,
And lend to the rhyme of the poet   40
    The beauty of thy voice.

And the night shall be filled with music,
    And the cares, that infest the day,
Shall fold their tents, like the Arabs,
    And as silently steal away.

With no great range of imagination, these lines have been justly admired for their delicacy of expression. Some of the images are very effective. Nothing can be better than

    ——The bards sublime,
    Whose distant footsteps echo
        Down the corridors of Time.

The idea of the last quatrain is also very effective. The poem, on the whole, however, is chiefly to be admired for the graceful *insouciance* of its metre, so 10 well in accordance with the character of the sentiments, and especially for the *ease* of the general manner. This "ease" or naturalness, in a literary style, it has long been the fashion to regard as ease in appearance alone—as a point of really difficult attainment. But not so:—a natural manner is difficult only to him who should never meddle with it—to the unnatural. It is but the result of writing with the understanding, or with the instinct, that the *tone*, in composition, should always 20 be that which the mass of mankind would adopt—and must perpetually vary, of course, with the occasion. The author who, after the fashion of "The North American Review," should be, upon all occasions, merely "quiet," must necessarily upon many occasions be simply silly, or stupid; and has no more right to be considered "easy" or "natural" than a Cockney exquisite, or than the sleeping Beauty in the wax-works.

Among the minor poems of Bryant, none has so 30 much impressed me as the one which he entitles "June." I quote only a portion of it:

There, through the long, long summer hours,
    The golden light should lie,

And thick young herbs and groups of flowers
    Stand in their beauty by.
The oriole should build and tell   5
    His love-tale, close beside my cell;
        The idle butterfly
Should rest him there, and there be heard
The housewife-bee and humming bird.

And what, if cheerful shouts, at noon 10
    Come, from the village sent,
Or songs of maids, beneath the moon,
    With fairy laughter blent?
And what if, in the evening light,
Betrothed lovers walk in sight   15
    Of my low monument?
I would the lovely scene around
Might know no sadder sight nor sound.

I know, I know I should not see
    The season's glorious show,   20
Nor would its brightness shine for me,
    Nor its wild music flow;
But if, around my place of sleep,
The friends I love should come to weep,
    They might not haste to go.   25
Soft airs, and song, and light, and bloom
Should keep them lingering by my tomb.

These to their soften'd hearts should bear
    The thought of what has been,
And speak of one who cannot share   30
    The gladness of the scene;
Whose part in all the pomp that fills
The circuit of the summer hills,
    Is—that his grave is green;
And deeply would their hearts rejoice   35
To hear again his living voice.

The rhythmical flow, here, is even voluptuous—nothing could be more melodious. The poem has always affected me in a remarkable manner. The intense melancholy which seems to well up, perforce, to the surface of all the poet's cheerful sayings about his grave, we find thrilling us to the soul—while there is the truest poetic elevation in the thrill. The impression left is one of a pleasurable sadness. And if, in the remaining compositions which I shall introduce to you, there be more or less of a similar tone always apparent, let me remind you that (how or why we know not) this certain taint of sadness is inseparably connected with all the higher manifestations of true Beauty. It is, nevertheless,

> A feeling of sadness and longing,
>> That is not akin to pain,
> And resembles sorrow only
>> As the mist resembles the rain.

The taint of which I speak is clearly perceptible even in a poem so full of brilliancy and spirit as the "Health" of Edward Coate Pinckney.[n]   10

> I fill this cup to one made up
>> Of loveliness alone,
> A woman, of her gentle sex
>> The seeming paragon;
> To whom the better elements   5
>> And kindly stars have given
> A form so fair, that, like the air,
>> 'Tis less of earth than heaven.

> Her every tone is music's own,
>> Like those of morning birds,   10
> And something more than melody
>> Dwells ever in her words;
> The coinage of her heart are they,
>> And from her lips each flows
> As one may see the burden'd bee   15
>> Forth issue from the rose.

> Affections are as thoughts to her,
>> The measures of her hours;
> Her feelings have the fragrancy,
>> The freshness of young flowers;   20
> And lovely passions, changing oft,
>> So fill her, she appears
> The image of themselves by turns,—
>> The idol of past years!

> Of her bright face one glance will trace   25
>> A picture on the brain,
> And of her voice in echoing hearts
>> A sound must long remain;
> But memory, such as mine of her,
>> So very much endears,   30
> When death is nigh my latest sigh
>> Will not be life's, but hers.

> I fill this cup to one made up
>> Of loveliness alone,
> A woman, of her gentle sex   35
>> The seeming paragon—

Edward Coate Pinckney: American poet (1802–1828).

> Her health! and would on earth there stood
>> Some more of such a frame,
> That life might be all poetry,
>> And weariness a name.   40

It was the misfortune of Mr. Pinckney to have been born too far south. Had he been a New Englander, it is probable that he would have been ranked as the first of American lyrists, by that magnanimous cabal which has so long controlled the destinies of American Letters, in conducting the thing called "The North American Review." The poem just cited is especially beautiful; but the poetic elevation which it induces, we must refer chiefly to our sympathy in the poet's enthusiasm. We pardon his hyperboles for the evident earnestness with which they are uttered.

It was by no means my design, however, to expatiate upon the merits of what I should read you. These will necessarily speak for themselves. Boccalini,[n] in his "Advertisements from Parnassus," tells us that Zoilus[n] once presented Apollo a very caustic criticism upon a very admirable book:— whereupon the god asked him for the beauties of the work. He replied that he only busied himself about the errors. On hearing this, Apollo, handing him a sack of unwinnowed wheat, bade him pick out all the chaff for his reward.

Now this fable answers very well as a hit at the critics—but I am by no means sure that the god was in the right. I am by no means certain that the true limits of the critical duty are not grossly misunderstood. Excellence, in a poem especially, may be considered in the light of an axiom, which need only be properly put, to become self-evident. It is not excellence if it require to be demonstrated as such:—and thus, to point out too particularly the merits of a work of Art, is to admit that they are not merits altogether.

Among the "Melodies" of Thomas Moore is one whose distinguished character as a poem proper, seems to have been singularly left out of view. I allude to his lines beginning—"Come, rest in this bosom." The intense energy of their expression is not surpassed by anything in Byron. There are two of the lines in which a sentiment is conveyed

Boccalini: Trajan Boccalini (1556–1613).   **Zoilus:** Greek critic of the fourth century, B.C., noted for his vitriolic pen.

that embodies the all in all of the divine passion of love—a sentiment which, perhaps, has found its echo in more, and in more passionate, human hearts than any other single sentiment ever embodied in words:

Come, rest in this bosom, my own stricken deer,
Though the herd have fled from thee, thy home is still
    here;
Here still is the smile, that no cloud can o'ercast,
And a heart and a hand all thy own to the last.

Oh! what was love made for, if 'tis not the same   5
Through joy and through torment, through glory and
    shame?
I know not, I ask not, if guilt's in that heart,
I but know that I love thee, whatever thou art.

Thou hast call'd me thy Angel in moments of bliss,
And thy Angel I'll be, 'mid the horrors of this,—   10
Through the furnace, unshrinking, thy steps to pursue,
And shield thee, and save thee,—or perish there too!

It has been the fashion, of late days, to deny Moore Imagination, while granting him Fancy—a distinction originating with Coleridge—than whom no man more fully comprehended the great powers of Moore. The fact is, that the fancy of this poet so far predominates over all his other faculties, and over the fancy of all other men, as to have induced, very naturally, the idea that he is fanciful only. But never was there a greater mistake. Never was a grosser wrong done the fame of a true poet. In the compass of the English language I can call to mind no poem more profoundly—more weirdly imaginative, in the best sense, than the lines commencing—"I would I were by that dim lake"—which are the composition of Thomas Moore. I regret that I am unable to remember them.

One of the noblest—and, speaking of Fancy, one of the most singularly fanciful of modern poets, was Thomas Hood.[n] His "Fair Ines" had always, for me, an inexpressible charm:

    O saw ye not fair Ines?
      She's gone into the West,
    To dazzle when the sun is down,
      And rob the world of rest:

Thomas Hood: English poet (1799–1845).

    She took our daylight with her,   5
      The smiles that we love best,
    With morning blushes on her cheek,
      And pearls upon her breast.

    O turn again, fair Ines,
      Before the fall of night,   10
    For fear the moon should shine alone,
      And stars unrivall'd bright;
    And blessed will the lover be
      That walks beneath their light,
    And breathes the love against thy cheek   15
      I dare not even write!

    Would I had been, fair Ines,
      That gallant cavalier,
    Who rode so gaily by thy side,
      And whisper'd thee so near!   20
    Were there no bonny dames at home,
      Or no true lovers here,
    That he should cross the seas to win
      The dearest of the dear?

    I saw thee, lovely Ines,   25
      Descend along the shore,
    With bands of noble gentlemen,
      And banners wav'd before;
    And gentle youth and maidens gay,
      And snowy plumes they wore;   30
    It would have been a beauteous dream,
      —If it had been no more!

    Alas, alas, fair Ines,
      She went away with song,
    With Music waiting on her steps,   35
      And shoutings of the throng;
    But some were sad, and felt no mirth,
      But only Music's wrong,
    In sounds that sang Farewell, Farewell,
      To her you've loved so long.   40

    Farewell, farewell, fair Ines,
      That vessel never bore
    So fair a lady on its deck,
      Nor danced so light before,—   45
    Alas for pleasure on the sea,
      And sorrow on the shore!
    The smile that blest one lover's heart
      Has broken many more!

"The Haunted House," by the same author, is one of the truest poems ever written—*one of the truest*—one of the most unexceptionable—one of the most thoroughly artistic, both in its theme and in its execution. It is, moreover, powerfully ideal—imaginative. I regret that its length renders it unsuitable for the purposes of this Lecture. In place of it, permit me to offer the universally appreciated "Bridge of Sighs."

One more Unfortunate,
Weary of breath,
Rashly importunate,
Gone to her death!

Take her up tenderly,   5
Lift her with care;—
Fashion'd so slenderly,
Young, and so fair!

Look at her garments
Clinging like cerements;   10
Whilst the wave constantly
Drips from her clothing;
Take her up instantly,
Loving, not loathing.—

Touch her not scornfully;   15
Think of her mournfully,
Gently and humanly;
Not of the stains of her,
All that remains of her
Now, is pure womanly.   20

Make no deep scrutiny
Into her mutiny
Rash and undutiful;
Past all dishonor,
Death has left on her   25
Only the beautiful.

Still, for all slips of hers,
One of Eve's family—
Wipe those poor lips of hers
Oozing so clammily,   30
Loop up her tresses
Escaped from the comb,
Her fair auburn tresses;
Whilst wonderment guesses
Where was her home?   35

Who was her father?
Who was her mother?
Had she a sister?
Had she a brother?
Or was there a dearer one   40

Still, and a nearer one
Yet, than all other?

Alas! for the rarity
Of Christian charity
Under the sun!   45
Oh! it was pitiful!
Near a whole city full,
Home she had none.

Sisterly, brotherly,
Fatherly, motherly   50
Feelings had changed:
Love, by harsh evidence,
Thrown from its eminence
Even God's providence
Seeming estranged.   55

Where the lamps quiver
So far in the river,
With many a light
From window and casement,
From garret to basement,   60
She stood, with amazement,
Houseless by night.

The bleak wind of March
Made her tremble and shiver;
But not the dark arch,   65
Or the black flowing river;
Mad from life's history,
Glad to death's mystery,
Swift to be hurl'd—
Anywhere, anywhere   70
Out of the world!

In she plunged boldly,
No matter how coldly
The rough river ran,—
Over the brink of it,   75
Picture it,—think of it,
Dissolute Man!
Lave in it, drink of it
Then, if you can!

Take her up tenderly,   80
Lift her with care;
Fashion'd so slenderly,
Young, and so fair!
Ere her limbs frigidly
Stiffen too rigidly,   85
Decently,—kindly,—

528

Smooth, and compose them;
And her eyes, close them,
Staring so blindly!

Dreadfully staring   90
Through muddy impurity,
As when with the daring
Last look of despairing
Fixed on futurity.

Perishing gloomily,   95
Spurred by contumely,
Cold inhumanity,
Burning insanity,
Into her rest,—
Cross her hands humbly,   100
As if praying dumbly,
Over her breast!
Owning her weakness,
Her evil behavior,
And leaving, with meekness,   105
Her sins to her Savior!

The vigor of this poem is no less remarkable
than its pathos. The versification, although carrying the fanciful to the very verge of the fantastic,
is nevertheless admirably adapted to the wild insanity which is the thesis of the poem.

Among the minor poems of Lord Byron is one[n]
which has never received from the critics the
praise which it undoubtedly deserves:

Though the day of my destiny's over,
    And the star of my fate hath declined,
Thy soft heart refused to discover
    The faults which so many could find;
Though thy soul with my grief was acquainted,   5
    It shrunk not to share it with me,
And the love which my spirit hath painted
    It never hath found but in thee.

Then when nature around me is smiling,
    The last smile which answers to mine,   10
I do not believe it beguiling,
    Because it reminds me of thine;
And when winds are at war with the ocean,
    As the breasts I believed in with me,
If their billows excite an emotion,   15
    It is that they bear me from thee.

Though the rock of my last hope is shivered,
    And its fragments are sunk in the wave,

one: "Stanzas to Augusta."

Though I feel that my soul is delivered
    To pain—it shall not be its slave.   20
There is many a pang to pursue me:
    They may crush, but they shall not contemn—
They may torture, but shall not subdue me—
    'Tis of thee that I think—not of them.

Though human, thou didst not deceive me,   25
    Though woman, thou didst not forsake,
Though loved, thou forborest to grieve me,
    Though slandered, thou never couldst shake,—
Though trusted, thou didst not disclaim me,
    Though parted, it was not to fly,   30
Though watchful, 'twas not to defame me,
    Nor mute, that the world might belie.

Yet I blame not the world, nor despise it,
    Nor the war of the many with one—
If my soul was not fitted to prize it,   35
    'Twas folly not sooner to shun:
And if dearly that error hath cost me,
    And more than I once could foresee,
I have found that whatever it lost me,
    It could not deprive me of thee.   40

From the wreck of the past, which hath perished,
    Thus much I at least may recall,
It hath taught me that which I most cherished,
    Deserved to be dearest of all:
In the desert a fountain is springing,   45
    In the wide waste there still is a tree,
And a bird in the solitude singing,
    Which speaks to my spirit of thee.

Although the rhythm here is one of the most difficult, the versification could scarcely be improved.
No nobler theme ever engaged the pen of poet.
It is the soul-elevating idea, that no man can consider himself entitled to complain of Fate while,
in his adversity, he still retains the unwavering
love of woman.

From Alfred Tennyson—although in perfect
sincerity I regard him as the noblest poet that ever
lived—I have left myself time to cite only a very
brief specimen. I call him, and think him the
noblest of poets—not because the impressions he
produces are, at all times, the most profound—not
because the poetical excitement which he induces
is, at all times, the most intense—but because it is,
at all times, the most ethereal—in other words, the
most elevating and most pure. No poet is so little

of the earth, earthy. What I am about to read is from his last long poem, "The Princess":

Tears, idle tears, I know not what they mean,
Tears from the depth of some divine despair
Rise in the heart, and gather to the eyes,
In looking on the happy Autumn-fields,
And thinking of the days that are no more.   5

Fresh as the first beam glittering on a sail,
That brings our friends up from the underworld,
Sad as the last which reddens over one
That sinks with all we love below the verge;
So sad, so fresh, the days that are no more.   10

Ah, sad and strange as in dark summer dawns
The earliest pipe of half-awaken'd birds
To dying ears, when unto dying eyes
The casement slowly grows a glimmering square;
So sad, so strange, the days that are no more.   15

Dear as remember'd kisses after death,
And sweet as those by hopeless fancy feign'd
On lips that are for others; deep as love,
Deep as first love, and wild with all regret;
O Death in Life, the days that are no more.   20

Thus, although in a very cursory and imperfect manner, I have endeavoured to convey to you my conception of the Poetic Principle. It has been my purpose to suggest that, while this Principle itself is strictly and simply the Human Aspiration for Supernal Beauty, the manifestation of the Principle is always found in an elevating excitement of the Soul—quite independent of that passion which is the intoxication of the Heart—or of that Truth which is the satisfaction of the Reason. For in regard to Passion, alas! its tendency is to degrade, rather than to elevate the Soul. Love, on the contrary—Love—the true, the divine Eros[n]—the Uranian,[n] as distinguished from the Dionaean[n] Venus—is unquestionably the purest and truest of all poetical themes. And in regard to Truth—if, to be sure, through the attainment of a truth, we are led to perceive a harmony where none was apparent before, we experience, at once, the true poetical effect—but this effect is referable to the harmony alone, and not in the least degree to the truth which merely served to render the harmony manifest.

We shall reach, however, more immediately a distinct conception of what the true Poetry is, by mere reference to a few of the simple elements which induce in the Poet himself the true poetical effect. He recognizes the ambrosia which nourishes his soul, in the bright orbs that shine in Heaven—in the volutes of the flower—in the clustering of low shrubberies—in the waving of the grain-fields—in the slanting of tall, Eastern trees—in the blue distance of mountains—in the grouping of clouds—in the twinkling of half-hidden brooks —in the gleaming of silver rivers—in the repose of sequestered lakes—in the star-mirroring depths of lonely wells. He perceives it in the songs of birds—in the harp of Aeolus[n]—in the sighing of the night-wind—in the repining voice of the forest—in the surf that complains to the shore—in the fresh breath of the woods—in the scent of the violet—in the voluptuous perfume of the hyacinth—in the suggestive odor that comes to him, at eventide, from far-distant, undiscovered islands, over dim oceans, illimitable and unexplored. He owns it in all noble thoughts—in all unworldly motives—in all holy impulses—in all chivalrous, generous, and self-sacrificing deeds. He feels it in the beauty of woman—in the grace of her step—in the lustre of her eye—in the melody of her voice—in her soft laughter—in her sigh—in the harmony of the rustling of her robes. He deeply feels it in her winning endearments—in her burning enthusiasms—in her gentle charities—in her meek and devotional endurances—but above all—ah, far above all—he kneels to it—he worships it in the faith, in the purity, in the strength, in the altogether divine majesty—of her love.

Let me conclude—by the recitation of yet another brief poem—one very different in character from any that I have before quoted. It is by Motherwell,[n] and is called "The Song of the Cavalier." With our modern and altogether rational ideas of the absurdity and impiety of warfare, we are not precisely in that frame of mind best adapted to sympathize with the sentiments,

Eros: in Greek mythology, the god of love. **Uranian:** heavenly. **Dionaean:** Dionaea, a name of Aphrodite, goddess of physical love and beauty.

Aeolus: in Greek mythology, god of the winds. **Motherwell:** William Motherwell (1797–1829), Scottish poet.

and thus to appreciate the real excellence of the poem. To do this fully we must identify ourselves in fancy with the soul of the old cavalier.

> Then mounte! then mounte, brave gallants, all,
>> And don your helmes amaine:
> Deathe's couriers, Fame and Honor, call
>> Us to the field againe.

> No shrewish teares shall fill our eye
>> When the sword-hilt's in our hand,—
> Heart-whole we'll part, and no whit sighe
>> For the fayrest of the land;
> Let piping swaine, and craven wight,
>> Thus weepe and puling crye,
> Our business is like men to fight,
>> And hero-like to die!

NATHANIEL HAWTHORNE (1804–1864)

HAWTHORNE came, remarked Paul Elmer More, "just when the moral ideas of New England were passing from the conscience to the imagination," in which shift "lies the very source of Hawthorne's art." In this development of an effective belletristic culture Hawthorne holds a firm place as a psychological interpreter of New England's past, and especially of the Puritan conscience. He was drawn to this subject by the stimulus of Walter Scott's antiquarian novels, by the general rage for legendary materials, by the haunting influence of his Puritan ancestors, and by an abiding interest in the deeper recesses of man's nature. Most of the major crises of the colonial period are found reflected somewhere in his works, and many colonial types of character provide the groundwork for his original tales. The free and easy use by American publishers of major English novels unprotected by copyright in the United States kept Hawthorne and many of his contemporaries from writing long fiction, and consequently for almost a quarter of a century he devoted himself to the form of the tale. It was the proper medium for the message he had to convey, as he shifted slowly from the legendary to the allegorical; and he excelled in it, as his European contemporaries Hoffmann and Gogol also did. His handling of historical and analytic material in his sketches, tales, and novels revealed fairly consistently the touch and the emotion of the master artist. His devotion to his craft was as deep and sincere as that of Irving and Poe; but unlike Irving, whose workmanship often surpassed his ideas, Hawthorne's artistry was fully employed by the complex demands of his tragic themes. And unlike Poe— despite an element of sombre intensity common to both authors—Hawthorne comprehended high seriousness of theme and a profound tragic vision.

Though Hawthorne's career is divided into two periods, a long one of tales and sketches and a shorter one of romances, in either medium he was writing essentially experimental case studies of a semiethical cast. It was the brooding quality of these studies that led to the labeling of Hawthorne as the recorder of the moral law. Puritanism is there, Henry James declared, "in the very quality of his vision, in the tone of the picture, in a certain coldness and exclusiveness of treatment." Moral aberration was the truly brooding subject of most of his studies. He traced the ramifications of evil, not so much as a moralist drawing lessons, but as a thoughtful, sometimes satirical, yet always objective observer, exploring with fascination the twistings of the human mind when afflicted with guilt, remorse, or ambition. Hawthorne recorded such mental states, verging on the pathological, in "Ethan Brand," "Roger Malvin's Burial," "Rappaccini's Daughter," "The Minister's Black Veil," and other tales.

The mark of sin and guilt is more dominant in his work than it is in other writers of his age because he was trying to deal with essentially psychological problems in the only language then available for their treatment, an ethical one. Puritanism for him was not an echo from the past, nor a current restrictive force, but a stimulus to creative art—and a religious conviction, the operations of which he might record. His literary contribution lay not in breadth, therefore, but in depth. Hawthorne analytically presented the mysterious workings of the human heart in all their profundity, especially when, for perversity or pride, the individual severed himself from life or his contemporaries. This last aspect of his work so impressed one biographer that he sought to explain all his fiction as a study of the factors which lead to a coldness of heart or of intellect. This is somewhat an oversimplification of Hawthorne's outlook, but it does serve to underscore certain features of his art. Fairly free from the didacticism of the pulpit, Hawthorne was nevertheless not above pointing out morals and using symbols. This is probably a mark of his integrity, his seriousness about his art and the business of living. He was always concerned with analyzing the motives of his characters, with probing their consciences and finding signs of larger meaning in the fluxful patterns of human life.

The isolation which marked half of Hawthorne's life was well calculated to produce the brooding, reflective, and analytic substance of his writing. It was not the kind of life that one might have expected from the descendant of a robust line of sea captains, but it served admirably to give to American fiction a singularly refined and delicate art. He was born in Salem, Massachusetts, in 1804. In this declining seaport town the young Hawthorne encountered many evidences of the past in which his ancestors had played an important part. His father's death, when Hawthorne was only four, enforced upon the family a state of genteel poverty. Upon this tragic event the mother went into partial seclusion. Such retirement threw shadows about the growing boy and fostered meditative habits. These tendencies were heightened by a foot injury at nine which not only forced him to withdraw from playground activities but turned him from the companionship of young and active friends to romantic reading. After recovering from this injury he spent many months in secluded Raymond, Maine, where at the home of an uncle he became a detached observer of frontier life. He took full advantage, however, of the opportunity for outdoor sports, especially fishing and skating.

Hawthorne returned to Salem to prepare for college, and then, in 1821, entered Bowdoin, where he was a classmate of Abbott, Longfellow, Decatur, and Horatio Bridge. He formed an intimate friendship with Bridge, and also with Franklin Pierce of the Class of 1824. In 1837 Bridge subsidized the publication of *Twice-Told Tales*, and Pierce, when President of the United States, appointed Hawthorne to a lucrative position abroad. During his undergraduate days Hawthorne indulged to some extent in the usual college dissipations, but he devoted most of his efforts to creative writing. Probably during the last two years he composed "Seven Tales of My Native Land," never published in book form. After graduation he returned to Salem to settle into the sedentary occupation of a man of letters. In 1828 he published anonymously *Fanshawe*, revelatory of Hawthorne's own expanding ambition and touching romantically upon Bowdoin college scenes. He later tried to destroy all copies. Hawthorne was so detached from life during these attic years that his stories had in consequence what he later characterized as a shadowy aspect: "they were born in the shade." For their substance he relied heavily upon his imagination. He contributed to the annuals and magazines, but such appearances won for him little reputation or profit. Without applause from friends or family, he devoted himself silently, faithfully to the discouraging business of the writer's craft.

But he did not create all his sketches from the world of fancy, and biographers have tended to overemphasize the seclusion of those twelve years in Salem. Through free passes on his uncle's stagecoach line he made numerous summer excursions to interesting areas of New England, during which periods, as he said, he "enjoyed as much of life as other people do in the whole year's round." Products of such excursions were "The Great Carbuncle," "Chippings with a Chisel," "The Canterbury Pilgrims," and probably "Sketches from Memory."

In 1836 he spent a half year in editorial hack work, and in 1837 brought out the first collection of his stories. While moderately praised by Longfellow and others, *Twice-Told Tales* aroused no general attention and furnished scant income. Slight financial return rewarded him also for his numerous contributions to the early volumes of *The Democratic Review*. But not for a moment did Hawthorne compromise his principles of art to win a reading public.

By 1838, when he became engaged to Sophia Peabody, of Salem, Hawthorne had emerged from his seclusion. An appointment as weigher and gauger at the Boston customhouse (1839–1840) brought rude contact with the world, and "the ungenial way of life" entailed by his duties left him little time for writing. The savings of these years enabled him to marry shortly afterwards, but his plan in 1840 to retire to utopian Brook Farm to humanize himself and to write as a "gentleman farmer" was abandoned after a few months. He protested in his journal at being compelled to spend "many days of blessed sunshine" on a manure pile, and in *The Blithedale Romance* (1852) he diagnosed the venture as another instance of attempting to overreach natural law and to accelerate the coming of the millennium. Failing to recover $524 of his original Brook Farm investment of $1000, Hawthorne accepted an arrangement whereby he was permitted to live for a time rent-free at the Old Manse in Concord. Here he took his bride in 1842, and here they lived in what he described as "the calm summer of my heart and mind." That same year he issued the second series of *Twice-Told Tales*. Despite Poe's favorable review of the volume, a reading public addicted to Sarah Josepha Hale, N. P. Willis, and Caroline L. Hentz was not likely to delight in Hawthorne's fragile stories, and for years he remained in financial need. At least partial relief came in the three years after 1846 when he held the political post of surveyor of the Port of Salem. Additional financial relief came from his stories for children, brought out in such volumes as *Grandfather's Chair* and *Famous Old People*.

Never satisfied with his tales, in 1849 Hawthorne launched upon a career as novelist, and he produced in the ensuing five-year period three great works which earned him such fame as he was to enjoy among his contemporaries. Classics in our literature today, these novels of the mid-century are sensitive, refined, brooding narratives, products of an unusually aloof, disciplined, mature, intellectual spirit. Hawthorne insisted to the end upon calling them romances, as this term freed him from too much insistence upon reality, though personally Hawthorne admired the Trollope-like fidelity to detail which he eschewed in his own work, pronouncing it folly "to insist on creating a semblance of a world out of airy matter." But create it he did, despite "daily life pressing so intrusively" upon him. *The Scarlet Letter*, the first of these great novels—which James pronounced "beautiful, admirable, extraordinary,"—was the work by which Hawthorne became known abroad. *The House of the Seven Gables* appeared the next year; it was both the most American and the most realistic of his works, though its realism was light, vague, and indefinable. *The Blithedale Romance*, written in West Newton, was not an actual transcript of Hawthorne's life at West Roxbury, but it does give a penetrating record of the Brook Farm Association.

A campaign life of his classmate, Franklin Pierce, brought Hawthorne an appointment as consul at Liverpool, 1853-1857. While resident there he wrote his English notebooks and made the excursions which afforded their substance. After the consulship he spent three years in England and Italy. Hawthorne's concept of romance made Rome the logical center for the action of *The Marble Faun* (1860), and his combination of tourist background and absorption with the effect of sin upon Donatello's soul left little space for less intellectual or moral passions. After 1860 Hawthorne resided in America, considerably exhausted and unable to bring to completion any of his four partial romances: *The Dolliver Romance*, *The Ancestral Footprint*, *Septimus Felton*, and *Dr. Grimshawe's Secret*. He died in 1864.

Hawthorne's concern with evil in his works made them incomprehensible to certain transcendentalists who were impressed with the beneficence of nature and ignored many genuine earthly or spiritual troubles. This same concern with evil gave an interpretive cast to his writing. He seized upon allegory as a serviceable method of probing to the reality which lies beneath the outward seeming. Such allegory with its attendant symbolism proved to be, in Hawthorne, a source of weakness as well as strength. His novels lack the solid specifications of the external world which some readers always expect, and too often his symbols bulk larger than his objects. Yet his masterpiece, *The Scarlet Letter*, and such stories as "Young Goodman Brown" and "Ethan Brand" achieved a perfect fusion of theme and symbol. James praised *The Scarlet Letter* as "full of the moral presence of the race that invented Hester's penance." Herman Melville's own preoccupation with man's fate enabled him to state, with peculiar authority, the secret of Hawthorne's power: "it appeals to that Calvinistic sense of Innate Depravity and Original Sin, from whose visitations, in some shape or other, no deeply thinking man is wholly free."

BIBLIOGRAPHY · *The Complete Works of Nathaniel Hawthorne* (12 vols., 1883), with introductory notes by G. P. Lathrop, is the authorized and standard edition. It was preceded by the Illustrated Library Edition (12 vols., 1871–1876), the Little Classic Edition (23 vols., 1875–1876), the Fireside Edition (12 vols., 1879), and the Globe Edition (6 vols., 1880). Good later editions include the Wayside Edition (24 vols., 1884) and the New Wayside Edition (13 vols., 1902). Some doubt still persists about the authenticity of *Hawthorne's First Diary* (1897), edited by S. T. Pickard. Editions of letters include *Love Letters of Nathaniel Hawthorne, 1839–41 and 1841–63* (2 vols., 1907), edited by R. Field, and *Letters of Hawthorne to William D. Ticknor, 1851–1864* (2 vols., 1910), issued privately by the Carteret Book Club. Many of the letters in the latter volume were printed in abridged form in C. Ticknor, *Hawthorne and His Publisher* (1913). A selection from the Journals, *The Heart of Hawthorne's Journals*, was made in 1929 by N. Arvin. Indispensable for students of Hawthorne are R. Stewart (editor), *The American Notebooks* (1932), and *The English Notebooks* (1941).

The best of the earlier biographies is G. E. Woodberry, *Nathaniel Hawthorne* (1902), but Julian Hawthorne, *Nathaniel Hawthorne and His Wife* (2 vols., 1884), remains an indispensable source book. Henry James, *Nathaniel Hawthorne* (1879) is a discerning study. Later biographical studies include N. Arvin, *Hawthorne* (1929); H. Gorman, *Hawthorne: A Study in Solitude* (1927); L. Morris, *The Rebellious Puritan: Portrait of Mr. Hawthorne* (1927); and R. Stewart, *Nathaniel Hawthorne* (1948). N. E. Browne, *A Bibliography of Nathaniel Hawthorne* (1905) should be supplemented by the excellent selective list in A. Warren, *Nathaniel Hawthorne: Representative Selections* (1934), and L. Leary (editor), *Articles on American Literature . . .* (1947). Mark Van Doren, *Nathaniel Hawthorne* (1949) is full of literary understanding and excellent in its appraisal. An extraordinarily large amount of material relevant to Hawthorne, his associates, his period, and his works comes to life in Robert Cantwell, *Nathaniel Hawthorne; The American Years* (1948), one of the best books.

More specialized biographical and critical studies include H. A. Beers, "Fifty Years of Hawthorne," in *Four Americans* (1919), 33–57; H. Bridge, *Personal Recollections of Nathaniel Hawthorne* (1893); E. K. Brown, "Hawthorne, Melville, and 'Ethan Brand,'" *American Literature*, III (1931), 72–75: W. C. Brownell, "Hawthorne," in *American Prose Masters* (1909), 63–130; E. L. Chandler, "Hawthorne's *Spectator*," *New England Quarterly*, IV (1931), 289–330; L. Dhaleine, *N. Hawthorne, sa Vie et son Œuvre* (1905); N. F. Doubleday, "Hawthorne's Hester and Feminism," *PMLA*, LIV (1939), 825–828; R. H. Fogle, "Ambiguity and Clarity in Hawthorne's 'Young Goodman Brown,'" *New England Quarterly*, XVIII (1945), 448–465, and "An Ambiguity of Sin or Sorrow," *New England Quarterly*, XXI (1948), 342–349; J. C. Gerber, "Form and Content in *The Scarlet Letter*," *New England Quarterly*, XVII (1944), 25–55; C. E. Goodspeed, "Nathaniel Hawthorne and the Museum of the East India Marine Society," *American Neptune*, V (1945), 266–272; T. M. Griffiths, *Maine Sources in* "*The House of the Seven Gables*" (1945); L. S. Hall, *Hawthorne: Critic of Society* (1944); J. Hawthorne, "The Making of *The Scarlet Letter*," *Bookman*, LXXIV (1931), 401–411; M. Hawthorne, "Nathaniel Hawthorne at Bowdoin," *New England Quarterly*, XIII (1940), 246–279, and "Parental and Family Influences on Hawthorne," *Essex Institute Historical Collections*, LXXVI (1940), 1–13; H. Hayford, "Hawthorne, Melville, and the Sea," *New England Quarterly*, XIX (1946), 435–452; J. Lundblad, *Nathaniel Hawthorne and the Tradition of Gothic Romance*, Vol. IV of *Essays and Studies on American Language and Literature* (Upsala, 1946); G. H. Orians, "Scott and Hawthorne's *Fanshawe*," *New England Quarterly*, XI (1938), 388–394; and "The Sources and Themes of Hawthorne's 'The Gentle Boy,'" *New England Quarterly*, XIV (1941), 664–678; R. H. Pearce, "Hawthorne and the Twilight of Romance," *Yale Review*, XXXVII (1948), 487–506; P. Rahv, "The Dark Lady of Salem," *Partisan Review*, VIII (1941), 362–381; A. L. Reed, "Self-Portraiture in the Works of Nathaniel Hawthorne," *Studies in Philology*, XXIII (1926), 40–54; A. E. Schönbach, "Beiträge zur Charakteristik Nathaniel Hawthornes," *Englische Studien*, VII (1884), 239–303; L. Schubert, *Hawthorne, the Artist: Fine-Art Devices in Fiction* (1944); R. Stewart, "Hawthorne and the Civil War," *Studies in Philology*, XXXIV (1937), 91–106, and "Hawthorne and *The Faerie Queen*," *Philological Quarterly*, XII (1933), 196–206; A. Turner, *Hawthorne as Editor* (1941); Y. Winters, "Maule's Curse: Hawthorne and the Problem of Allegory," *American Review*, IX (1937), 339–361.

The Maypole of Merry Mount

THERE IS an admirable foundation for a philosophic romance in the curious history of the early settlement of Mount Wollaston, or Merry Mount. In the slight sketch here attempted the facts, recorded on the grave pages of our New England annalists, have wrought themselves, almost spontaneously, into a sort of allegory. The masques, mummeries, and festive customs, described in the text, are in accordance with the manners of the age. Authority on these points may be found in Strutt's Book of English Sports and Pastimes. [Author's note]

"The Maypole of Merry Mount" is the fifth story of *Twice-Told Tales* (1837). For a historical account of the Merry Mount affair see William Bradford, "Merry Mount," from *Of Plimoth Plantation*, reprinted in this anthology and for a study of the sources of the story see G. H. Orians, "Hawthorne and 'The Maypole of Merry-Mount,'" *Modern Language Notes*, L (1938), 159–167. The Hawthorne text is that of the authorized edition of 1883.

Bright were the days at Merry Mount, when the Maypole was the banner staff of that gay colony! They who reared it, should their banner be triumphant, were to pour sunshine over New England's rugged hills, and scatter flower seeds throughout the soil. Jollity and gloom were contending for an empire. Midsummer eve had come, bringing deep verdure to the forest, and roses in her lap, of a more vivid hue than the tender buds of Spring. But May, or her mirthful spirit, dwelt all the year round at Merry Mount, sporting with the Summer months, and revelling with Autumn, and basking in the glow of Winter's fireside. Through a world of toil and care she flitted with a dreamlike smile, and came hither to find a home among the lightsome hearts of Merry Mount.

Never had the Maypole been so gayly decked as at sunset on midsummer eve. This venerated emblem was a pine-tree, which had preserved the slender grace of youth, while it equalled the loftiest height of the old wood monarchs. From its top streamed a silken banner, colored like the rainbow. Down nearly to the ground the pole was dressed with birchen boughs, and others of the liveliest green, and some with silvery leaves, fastened by ribbons that fluttered in fantastic knots of twenty different colors, but no sad ones. Garden flowers, and blossoms of the wilderness, laughed gladly forth amid the verdure, so fresh and dewy that they must have grown by magic on that happy pine-tree. Where this green and flowery splendor terminated, the shaft of the Maypole was stained with the seven brilliant hues of the banner at its

534

top. On the lowest green bough hung an abundant wreath of roses, some that had been gathered in the sunniest spots of the forest, and others, of still richer blush, which the colonists had reared from English seed. O, people of the Golden Age, the chief of your husbandry was to raise flowers!

But what was the wild throng that stood hand in hand about the Maypole? It could not be that the fauns and nymphs, when driven from their classic groves and homes of ancient fable, had sought refuge, as all the persecuted did, in the fresh woods of the West. These were Gothic monsters, though perhaps of Grecian ancestry. On the shoulders of a comely youth uprose the head and branching antlers of a stag; a second, human in all other points, had the grim visage of a wolf; a third, still with the trunk and limbs of a mortal man, showed the beard and horns of a venerable he-goat. There was the likeness of a bear erect, brute in all but his hind legs, which were adorned with pink silk stockings. And here again, almost as wondrous, stood a real bear of the dark forest, lending each of his fore paws to the grasp of a human hand, and as ready for the dance as any in that circle. His inferior nature rose half way, to meet his companions as they stooped. Other faces wore the similitude of man or woman, but distorted or extravagant, with red noses pendulous before their mouths, which seemed of awful depth, and stretched from ear to ear in an eternal fit of laughter. Here might be seen the Salvage Man, well known in heraldry, hairy as a baboon, and girdled with green leaves. By his side, a noble figure, but still a counterfeit, appeared an Indian hunter, with feathery crest and wampum belt. Many of this strange company wore foolscaps, and had little bells appended to their garments, tinkling with a silvery sound, responsive to the inaudible music of their gleesome spirits. Some youths and maidens were of soberer garb, yet well maintained their places in the irregular throng by the expression of wild revelry upon their features. Such were the colonists of Merry Mount, as they stood in the broad smile of sunset round their venerated Maypole.

Had a wanderer, bewildered in the melancholy forest, heard their mirth, and stolen a half-affrighted glance, he might have fancied them the crew of Comus, some already transformed to brutes, some midway between man and beast, and the others rioting in the flow of tipsy jollity that foreran the change. But a band of Puritans, who watched the scene, invisible themselves, compared the masques to those devils and ruined souls with whom their superstition peopled the black wilderness.

Within the ring of monsters appeared the two airiest forms that had ever trodden on any more solid footing than a purple and golden cloud. One was a youth in glistening apparel, with a scarf of the rainbow pattern crosswise on his breast. His right hand held a gilded staff, the ensign of high dignity among the revellers, and his left grasped the slender fingers of a fair maiden, not less gayly decorated than himself. Bright roses glowed in contrast with the dark and glossy curls of each, and were scattered round their feet, or had sprung up spontaneously there. Behind this lightsome couple, so close to the Maypole that its boughs shaded his jovial face, stood the figure of an English priest, canonically dressed, yet decked with flowers, in heathen fashion, and wearing a chaplet of the native vine leaves. By the riot of his rolling eye, and the pagan decorations of his holy garb, he seemed the wildest monster there, and the very Comus of the crew.

"Votaries of the Maypole," cried the flower-decked priest, "merrily, all day long, have the woods echoed to your mirth. But be this your merriest hour, my hearts! Lo here stand the Lord and Lady of the May, whom I, a clerk of Oxford, and high priest of Merry Mount, am presently to join in holy matrimony. Up with your nimble spirits, ye morris-dancers, green men, and glee maidens, bears and wolves, and horned gentlemen! Come; a chorus now, rich with the old mirth of Merry England, and the wilder glee of this fresh forest; and then a dance, to show the youthful pair what life is made of, and how airily they should go through it! All ye that love the Maypole, lend your voices to the nuptial song of the Lord and Lady of the May!

This wedlock was more serious than most affairs of Merry Mount, where jest and delusion, trick and fantasy, kept up a continual carnival. The Lord and Lady of the May, though their titles must be laid down at sunset, were really and truly to be partners for the dance of life, beginning the measure that same bright eve. The wreath of roses, that hung from the lowest green bough of the Maypole, had been twined for them, and would be thrown over both their heads, in symbol of their flowery union. When the priest had spoken, therefore a riotous uproar burst from the rout of monstrous figures.

"Begin you the stave, reverend Sir," cried they all; "and never did the woods ring to such a merry peal as we of the Maypole shall send up!"

Immediately a prelude of pipe, cithern, and viol, touched with practiced minstrelsy, began to play from a neighboring thicket, in such a mirthful cadence that the boughs of the Maypole quivered to the sound. But the May Lord, he of the gilded staff, chancing to look into his Lady's eyes, was wonder struck at the almost pensive glance that met his own.

"Edith, sweet Lady of the May," whispered he reproachfully, "is yon wreath of roses a garland to hang above our graves, that you look so sad? O, Edith, this is our golden time! Tarnish it not by any pensive shadow of the mind; for it may be that nothing of futurity will be brighter than the mere remembrance of what is now passing."

"That was the very thought that saddened me! How came it in your mind too?" said Edith, in a still lower tone than he, for it was high treason to be sad at Merry Mount. "Therefore do I sigh amid this festive music. And besides, dear Edgar, I struggle as with a dream, and fancy that these shapes of our jovial friends are visionary, and their mirth unreal, and that we are no true Lord and Lady of the May. What is the mystery in my heart?"

Just then, as if a spell had loosened them, down came a little shower of withering rose leaves from the Maypole. Alas, for the young lovers! No sooner had their hearts glowed with real passion than they were sensible of something vague and unsubstantial in their former pleasures, and felt a dreary presentiment of inevitable change. From the moment that they truly loved, they had subjected themselves to earth's doom of care and sorrow, and troubled joy, and had no more a home at Merry Mount. That was Edith's mystery. Now leave we the priest to marry them, and the

masquers to sport round the Maypole, till the last sunbeam be withdrawn from its summit, and the shadows of the forest mingle gloomily in the dance. Meanwhile, we may discover who these gay people were.

Two hundred years ago, and more, the old world and its inhabitants became mutually weary of each other. Men voyaged by thousands to the West: some to barter glass beads, and such like jewels, for the furs of the Indian hunter; some to conquer virgin empires; and one stern band to pray. But none of these motives had much weight with the colonists of Merry Mount. Their leaders were men who had sported so long with life that when Thought and Wisdom came, even these unwelcome guests were led astray by the crowd of vanities which they should have put to flight. Erring Thought and perverted Wisdom were made to put on masques and play the fool. The men of whom we speak, after losing the heart's fresh gayety, imagined a wild philosophy of pleasure, and came hither to act out their latest daydream. They gathered followers from all that giddy tribe whose whole life is like the festal days of soberer men. In their train were minstrels, not unknown in London streets; wandering players, whose theatres had been the halls of noblemen; mummers, rope-dancers, and mountebanks, who would long be missed at wakes, church ales, and fairs; in a word, mirth makers of every sort, such as abounded in that age, but now began to be discountenanced by the rapid growth of Puritanism. Light had their footsteps been on land, and as lightly they came across the sea. Many had been maddened by their previous troubles into a gay despair; others were as madly gay in the flush of youth, like the May Lord and his Lady; but whatever might be the quality of their mirth, old and young were gay at Merry Mount. The young deemed themselves happy. The elder spirits, if they knew that mirth was but the counterfeit of happiness, yet followed the false shadow wilfully, because at least her garments glittered brightest. Sworn triflers of a lifetime, they would not venture among the sober truths of life not even to be truly blest.

All the hereditary pastimes of Old England were transplanted hither. The King of Christmas was duly crowned, and the Lord of Misrule bore potent sway. On the Eve of St. John, they felled whole acres of the forest to make bonfires, and danced by the blaze all night, crowned with garlands, and throwing flowers into the flame. At harvest time, though their crop was of the smallest, they made an image with the sheaves of Indian corn, and wreathed it with autumnal garlands, and bore it home triumphantly. But what chiefly characterized the colonists of Merry Mount was their veneration for the Maypole. It has made their true history a poet's tale. Spring decked the hallowed emblem with young blossoms and fresh green boughs; Summer brought roses of the deepest blush and the perfected foliage of the forest; Autumn enriched it with that red and yellow gorgeousness which converts each wild-wood leaf into a painted flower; and Winter silvered it with sleet, and hung it round with icicles, till it flashed in the cold sunshine, itself a frozen sunbeam. Thus each alternate season did homage to the Maypole and paid it a tribute of its own richest splendor. Its votaries danced round it, once, at least, in every month; sometimes they called it their religion, or their altar; but always, it was the banner staff of Merry Mount.

Unfortunately, there were men in the new world of a sterner faith than these Maypole worshippers. Not far from Merry Mount was a settlement of Puritans, most dismal wretches, who said their prayers before daylight, and then wrought in the forest or the cornfield till evening made it prayer time again. Their weapons were always at hand to shoot down the straggling savage. When they met in conclave, it was never to keep up the old English mirth, but to hear sermons three hours long, or to proclaim bounties on the heads of wolves and the scalps of Indians. Their festivals were fast days, and their chief pastime the singing of psalms. Woe to the youth or maiden who did but dream of a dance! The selectman nodded to the constable; and there sat the light-heeled reprobate in the stocks; or if he danced, it was round the whipping-post, which might be termed the Puritan Maypole.

A party of these grim Puritans, toiling through the difficult woods, each with a horseload of iron armor to burden his footsteps, would sometimes draw near the sunny precincts of Merry Mount. There were the silken colonists, sporting round their Maypole; perhaps teaching a bear to dance, or striving to communicate their mirth to the grave Indian; or masquerading in the skins of deer and wolves, which they had hunted for that especial purpose. Often, the whole colony were playing at blindman's bluff, magistrates and all, with their eyes bandaged, except a single scapegoat, whom the blinded sinners pursued by the tinkling of the bells at his garments. Once, it is said, they were seen following a flower-decked corpse, with merriment and festive music, to his grave. But did the dead man laugh? In their quietest times, they sang ballads and told tales, for the edification of their pious visitors; or perplexed them with juggling tricks; or grinned at them through horse collars; and when sport itself grew wearisome, they made game of their own stupidity, and began a yawning match. At the very least of these enormities, the men of iron shook their heads and frowned so darkly that the revellers looked up, imagining that a momentary cloud had overcast the sunshine, which was to be perpetual there. On the other hand, the Puritans affirmed that, when a psalm was pealing from their place of worship, the echo which the forest sent them back seemed often like the chorus of a jolly catch, closing with a roar of laughter. Who but the fiend, and his bond slaves, the crew of Merry Mount, had thus disturbed them? In due time, a feud arose, stern and bitter on one side, and as serious on the other as anything could be among such light spirits as had sworn allegiance to the Maypole. The future complexion of New England was involved in this important quarrel. Should the grizzly saints establish their jurisdiction over the gay sinners, then would their spirits darken all the clime, and make it a land of clouded visages, of hard toil, of sermon and psalm forever. But should the banner staff of Merry Mount be fortunate, sunshine would break upon the hills, and flowers would beautify the forest, and late posterity do homage to the Maypole.

After these authentic passages from history, we return to the nuptials of the Lord and Lady of the May. Alas! we have delayed too long and must darken our tale too suddenly. As we glance again at the Maypole, a solitary sunbeam is fading from the summit and leaves only a faint, golden tinge blended with the hues of the rainbow banner. Even that dim light is now withdrawn, relinquishing the whole domain of Merry Mount to the evening gloom, which has rushed so instantaneously from the black surrounding woods. But some of these black shadows have rushed forth in human shape.

Yes, with the setting sun, the last day of mirth had passed from Merry Mount. The ring of gay masquers was disordered and broken; the stag lowered his antlers in dismay; the wolf grew weaker than a lamb; the bells of the morris-dancers tinkled with tremulous affright. The Puritans had played a characteristic part in the Maypole mummeries. Their darksome figures were intermixed with the wild shapes of their foes, and made the scene a picture of the moment, when waking thoughts start up amid the scattered fantasies of a dream. The leader of the hostile party stood in the center of the circle, while the rout of monsters cowered around him, like evil spirits in the presence of a dread magician. No fantastic foolery could look him in the face. So stern was the energy of his aspect, that the whole man, visage, frame, and soul, seemed wrought of iron, gifted with life and thought, yet all of one substance with his head-piece and breastplate. It was the Puritan of Puritans: it was Endicott himself!

"Stand off, priest of Baal!" said he, with a grim frown, and laying no reverent hand upon the surplice. "I know thee, Blackstone![n] Thou art the man who couldst not abide the rule even of thine own corrupted church, and hast come hither to preach iniquity, and to give example of it in thy life. But now shall it be seen that the Lord hath sanctified this wilderness for his peculiar people. Woe unto them that would defile it! And first, for this flower-decked abomination, the altar of thy worship!"

And with his keen sword Endicott assaulted the hallowed Maypole. Nor long did it resist his arm.

Blackstone: Did Governor Endicott speak less positively, we should suspect a mistake here. The Rev. Mr. Blackstone, though an eccentric, is not known to have been an immoral man. We rather doubt his identity with the priest of Merry Mount. [Author's note]

It groaned with a dismal sound; it showered leaves and rosebuds upon the remorseless enthusiast; and finally, with all its green boughs and ribbons and flowers, symbolic of departed pleasures, down fell the banner staff of Merry Mount. As it sank, tradition says, the evening sky grew darker, and the woods threw forth a more sombre shadow.

"There," cried Endicott, looking triumphantly on his work, "there lies the only Maypole in New England! The thought is strong within me that, by its fall, is shadowed forth the fate of light and idle mirth makers, amongst us and our posterity. Amen, saith John Endicott."

"Amen!" echoed his followers.

But the votaries of the Maypole gave one groan for their idol. At the sound, the Puritan leader glanced at the crew of Comus, each a figure of broad mirth, yet, at this moment, strangely expressive of sorrow and dismay.

"Valiant captain," quoth Peter Palfrey, the Ancient of the band, "what order shall be taken with the prisoners?"

"I thought not to repent me of cutting down a Maypole," replied Endicott, "yet now I could find in my heart to plant it again, and give each of these bestial pagans one other dance round their idol. It would have served rarely for a whipping-post!"

"But there are pine-trees enow," suggested the lieutenant.

"True, good Ancient," said the leader. "Wherefore, bind the heathen crew, and bestow on them a small matter of stripes apiece, as earnest of our future justice. Set some of the rogues in the stocks to rest themselves, so soon as Providence shall bring us to one of our own well-ordered settlements, where such accommodations may be found. Further penalites, such as branding and cropping of ears, shall be thought of hereafter."

"How many stripes for the priest?" inquired Ancient Palfrey.

"None as yet," answered Endicott, bending his iron frown upon the culprit. "It must be for the Great and General Court to determine, whether stripes and long imprisonment, and other grievous penalty, may atone for his transgressions. Let him look to himself! For such as violate our civil order, it may be permitted us to show mercy. But woe to the wretch that troubleth our religion!"

"And this dancing bear," resumed the officer. "Must he share the stripes of his fellows?"

"Shoot him through the head!" said the energetic Puritan. "I suspect witchcraft in the beast."

"Here be a couple of shining ones," continued Peter Palfrey, pointing his weapon at the Lord and Lady of the May. "They seem to be of high station among these misdoers. Methinks their dignity will not be fitted with less than a double share of stripes."

Endicott rested on his sword, and closely surveyed the dress and aspect of the hapless pair. There they stood, pale, downcast, and apprehensive. Yet there was an air of mutual support, and of pure affection, seeking aid and giving it, that showed them to be man and wife, with the sanction of a priest upon their love. The youth, in the peril of the moment, had dropped his gilded staff, and thrown his arm about the Lady of the May, who leaned against his breast, too lightly to burden him, but with weight enough to express that their destinies were linked together, for good or evil. They looked first at each other and then into the grim captain's face. There they stood, in the first hour of wedlock, while the idle pleasures of which their companions were the emblems, had given place to the sternest cares of life, personified by the dark Puritans. But never had their youthful beauty seemed so pure and high as when its glow was chastened by adversity.

"Youth," said Endicott, "ye stand in an evil case thou and thy maiden wife. Make ready presently, for I am minded that ye shall both have a token to remember your wedding day!"

"Stern man," cried the May Lord, "how can I move thee? Were the means at hand, I would resist to the death. Being powerless, I entreat! Do with me as thou wilt, but let Edith go untouched!"

"Not so," replied the immitigable zealot. "We are not wont to show an idle courtesy to that sex, which requireth the stricter discipline. What sayest thou, maid? Shall thy silken bridegroom suffer thy share of the penalty, besides his own?"

"Be it death," said Edith, "and lay it all on me!"

Truly, as Endicott had said, the poor lovers stood in a woful case. Their foes were triumphant, their friends captive and abased, their home desolate, the benighted wilderness around them, and a rigorous destiny, in the shape of the Puritan leader, their only guide. Yet the deepening twilight could not altogether conceal that the iron man was softened; he smiled at the fair spectacle of early love; he almost sighed for the inevitable blight of early hopes.

"The troubles of life have come hastily on this young couple," observed Endicott. "We will see how they comport themselves under their present trials ere we burden them with greater. If, among the spoil, there be any garments of a more decent fashion, let them be put upon this May Lord and his Lady, instead of their glistening vanities. Look to it, some of you."

"And shall not the youth's hair be cut?" asked Peter Palfrey, looking with abhorrence at the lovelock and long glossy curls of the young man.

"Crop it forthwith, and that in the true pumpkinshell fashion," answered the captain. "Then bring them along with us, but more gently than their fellows. There be qualities in the youth, which may make him valiant to fight, and sober to toil, and pious to pray; and in the maiden, that may fit her to become a mother in our Israel, bringing up babes in better nurture than her own hath been. Nor think ye, young ones, that they are the happiest, even in our lifetime of a moment, who misspend it in dancing round a Maypole!"

And Endicott, the severest Puritan of all who laid the rock foundation of New England, lifted the wreath of roses from the ruin of the Maypole, and threw it, with his own gauntleted hand, over the heads of the Lord and Lady of the May. It was a deed of prophecy. As the moral gloom of the world overpowers all systematic gayety, even so was their home of wild mirth made desolate amid the sad forest. They returned to it no more. But as their flowery garland was wreathed of the brightest roses that had grown there, so, in the tie that united them, were intertwined all the purest and best of their early joys. They went heavenward, supporting each other along the difficult path which it was their lot to tread, and never wasted one regretful thought on the vanities of Merry Mount.

Dr. Heidegger's Experiment

THIS STORY appeared as "The Fountain of Youth" when it was printed in the *Knickerbocker Magazine*, January, 1837, and in the Salem *Gazette* in March of the same year. It was reprinted in *Twice-Told Tales* (1837) under its present title. The idea of an elixir of life is a recurrent theme in Hawthorne's fiction. He may have been impressed by the treatment of the evils of earthly immortality in his early reading of Jonathan Swift's *Gulliver's Travels*, but it is probable that William Godwin's *St. Leon*, which Hawthorne read before entering Bowdoin, stimulated his interest in the subject. An entry in his notebook in 1836 is only one of many references to the engrossing theme: "Curious to imagine what murmurings and discontent would be excited, if any of the so-called calamities of human beings were to be abolished,—as, for instance, death." The elixir of life appears in "A Virtuoso's Collection" (1842) and in "The Birthmark" (1843), as well as in the unfinished romances *Septimius Felton*, *The Dolliver Romance* and *Dr. Grimshawe's Secret*. For an interesting suggestion about the inception of the story, see L. Hasting, "An Origin for 'Dr. Heidegger's Experiment,'" *American Literature*, IX (1938), 403–410. The text is that of the edition of 1883.

That very singular man, old Dr. Heidegger, once invited four venerable friends to meet him in his study. There were three white-bearded gentlemen, Mr. Medbourne, Colonel Killigrew, and Mr. Gascoigne, and a withered gentlewoman, whose name was the Widow Wycherly. They were all melancholy old creatures, who had been unfortunate in life, and whose greatest misfortune it was that they were not long ago in their graves. Mr. Medbourne, in the vigor of his age, had been a prosperous merchant, but had lost his all by a frantic speculation, and was now little better than a mendicant. Colonel Killigrew had wasted his best years, and his health and substance, in the pursuit of sinful pleasures, which had given birth to a brood of pains, such as the gout, and divers other torments of soul and body. Mr. Gascoigne was a ruined politician, a man of evil fame, or at least had been so till time had buried him from the knowledge of the present generation, and made him obscure instead of infamous. As for the Widow Wycherly, tradition tells us that she was a great beauty in her day; but, for a long while past, she

had lived in deep seclusion, on account of certain scandalous stories which had prejudiced the gentry of the town against her. It is a circumstance worth mentioning that each of these three old gentlemen, Mr. Medbourne, Colonel Killigrew, and Mr. Gascoigne, were early lovers of the Widow Wycherly, and had once been on the point of cutting each other's throats for her sake. And, before proceeding further, I will merely hint that Dr. Heidegger and all his four guests were sometimes thought to be a little beside themselves,—as is not unfrequently the case with old people, when worried either by present troubles or woful recollections.

"My dear old friends," said Dr. Heidegger, motioning them to be seated, "I am desirous of your assistance in one of those little experiments with which I amuse myself here in my study."

If all stories were true, Dr. Heidegger's study must have been a very curious place. It was a dim, old-fashioned chamber, festooned with cobwebs, and besprinkled with antique dust. Around the walls stood several oaken bookcases, the lower shelves of which were filled with rows of gigantic folios and black-letter quartos, and the upper with little parchment-covered duodecimos. Over the central bookcase was a bronze bust of Hippocrates, with which, according to some authorities, Dr. Heidegger was accustomed to hold consultations in all difficult cases of his practice. In the obscurest corner of the room stood a tall and narrow oaken closet, with its door ajar, within which doubtfully appeared a skeleton. Between two of the bookcases hung a looking-glass, presenting its high and dusty plate within a tarnished gilt frame. Among many wonderful stories related of this mirror, it was fabled that the spirits of all the doctor's deceased patients dwelt within its verge, and would stare him in the face whenever he looked thitherward. The opposite side of the chamber was ornamented with the full-length portrait of a young lady, arrayed in the faded magnificence of silk, satin, and brocade, and with a visage as faded as her dress. Above half a century ago, Dr. Heidegger had been on the point of marriage with this young lady; but, being affected with some slight disorder, she had swallowed one of her lover's prescriptions, and died on the bridal evening. The greatest curiosity of the study remains to be mentioned; it was a ponderous folio volume, bound in black leather, with massive silver clasps. There were no letters on the back, and nobody could tell the title of the book. But it was well known to be a book of magic; and once, when a chambermaid had lifted it, merely to brush away the dust, the skeleton had rattled in its closet, the picture of the young lady had stepped one foot upon the floor, and several ghastly faces had peeped forth from the mirror; while the brazen head of Hippocrates frowned, and said,—"Forbear!"

Such was Dr. Heidegger's study. On the summer afternoon of our tale a small round table, as black as ebony, stood in the centre of the room, sustaining a cut-glass vase of beautiful form and elaborate workmanship. The sunshine came through the window, between the heavy festoons of two faded damask curtains, and fell directly across this vase; so that a mild splendor was reflected from it on the ashen visages of the five old people who sat around. Four champagne glasses were also on the table.

"My dear old friends," repeated Dr. Heidegger, "may I reckon on your aid in performing an exceedingly curious experiment?"

Now Dr. Heidegger was a very strange old gentleman, whose eccentricity had become the nucleus for a thousand fantastic stories. Some of these fables, to my shame be it spoken, might possibly be traced back to mine own veracious self; and if any passages of the present tale should startle the reader's faith, I must be content to bear the stigma of a fictionmonger.

When the doctor's four guests heard him talk of his proposed experiment, they anticipated nothing more wonderful than the murder of a mouse in an air pump, or the examination of a cobweb by the microscope, or some similar nonsense, with which he was constantly in the habit of pestering his intimates. But without waiting for a reply, Dr. Heidegger hobbled across the chamber, and returned with the same ponderous folio, bound in black leather, which common report affirmed to be a book of magic. Undoing the silver clasps, he opened the volume, and took from among its black-letter pages a rose, or what was once a rose, though now the green leaves and crimson petals

had assumed one brownish hue, and the ancient flower seemed ready to crumble to dust in the doctor's hands.

"This rose," said Dr. Heidegger, with a sigh, "this same withered and crumbling flower, blossomed five and fifty years ago. It was given me by Sylvia Ward, whose portrait hangs yonder; and I meant to wear it in my bosom at our wedding. Five and fifty years it has been treasured between the leaves of this old volume. Now, would you deem it possible that this rose of half a century could ever bloom again?"

"Nonsense!" said the Widow Wycherly, with a peevish toss of her head. "You might as well ask whether an old woman's wrinkled face could ever bloom again."

"See!" answered Dr. Heidegger.

He uncovered the vase, and threw the faded rose into the water which it contained. At first, it lay lightly on the surface of the fluid, appearing to imbibe none of its moisture. Soon, however, a singular change began to be visible. The crushed and dried petals stirred, and assumed a deepening tinge of crimson, as if the flower were reviving from a deathlike slumber; the slender stalk and twigs of foliage became green; and there was the rose of half a century, looking as fresh as when Sylvia Ward had first given it to her lover. It was scarcely full blown; for some of its delicate red leaves curled modestly around its moist bosom, within which two or three dewdrops were sparkling.

"That is certainly a very pretty deception," said the doctor's friends; carelessly, however, for they had witnessed greater miracles at a conjurer's show; "pray how was it effected?"

"Did you never hear of the 'Fountain of Youth,'" asked Dr. Heidegger, "which Ponce De Leon, the Spanish adventurer, went in search of two or three centuries ago?"

"But did Ponce De Leon ever find it?" said the Widow Wycherly.

"No," answered Dr. Heidegger, "for he never sought it in the right place. The famous Fountain of Youth, if I am rightly informed, is situated in the southern part of the Floridian peninsula, not far from Lake Macaco. Its source is overshadowed by several gigantic magnolias, which, though numberless centuries old, have been kept as fresh as violets by the virtues of this wonderful water. An acquaintance of mine, knowing my curiosity in such matters, has sent me what you see in the vase."

"Ahem!" said Colonel Killigrew, who believed not a word of the doctor's story; "and what may be the effect of this fluid on the human frame?"

"You shall judge for yourself, my dear colonel," replied Dr. Heidegger; "and all of you, my respected friends, are welcome to so much of this admirable fluid as may restore to you the bloom of youth. For my own part, having had much trouble in growing old, I am in no hurry to grow young again. With your permission, therefore, I will merely watch the progress of the experiment."

While he spoke, Dr. Heidegger had been filling the four champagne glasses with the water of the Fountain of Youth. It was apparently impregnated with an effervescent gas, for little bubbles were continually ascending from the depths of the glasses, and bursting in silvery spray at the surface. As the liquor diffused a pleasant perfume, the old people doubted not that it possessed cordial and comfortable properties; and though utter skeptics as to its rejuvenescent power, they were inclined to swallow it at once. But Dr. Heidegger besought them to stay a moment.

"Before you drink, my respectable old friends," said he, "it would be well that, with the experience of a lifetime to direct you, you should draw up a few general rules for your guidance, in passing a second time through the perils of youth. Think what a sin and a shame it would be, if, with your peculiar advantages, you should not become patterns of virtue and wisdom to all the young people of the age!"

The doctor's four venerable friends made him no answer, except by a feeble and tremulous laugh; so very ridiculous was the idea that, knowing how closely repentance treads behind the steps of error, they should ever go astray again.

"Drink, then," said the doctor, bowing: "I rejoice that I have so well selected the subjects of my experiment."

With palsied hands, they raised the glasses to their lips. The liquor, if it really possessed such virtues as Dr. Heidegger imputed to it, could not have been bestowed on four human beings who needed it more wofully. They looked as if they had never known what youth or pleasure was, but had been the offspring of Nature's dotage, and always the gray, decrepit, sapless, miserable creatures, who now sat stooping round the doctor's table, without life enough in their souls or bodies to be animated even by the prospect of growing young again. They drank off the water, and replaced their glasses on the table.

Assuredly there was an almost immediate improvement in the aspect of the party, not unlike what might have been produced by a glass of generous wine, together with a sudden glow of cheerful sunshine brightening over all their visages at once. There was a healthful suffusion on their cheeks, instead of the ashen hue that had made them look so corpse-like. They gazed at one another, and fancied that some magic power had really begun to smooth away the deep and sad inscriptions which Father Time had been so long engraving on their brows. The Widow Wycherly adjusted her cap, for she felt almost like a woman again.

"Give us more of this wondrous water!" cried they, eagerly. "We are younger—but we are still too old! Quick—give us more!"

"Patience, patience!" quoth Dr. Heidegger, who sat watching the experiment with philosophic coolness. "You have been a long time growing old. Surely, you might be content to grow young in half an hour! But the water is at your service."

Again he filled their glasses with the liquor of youth, enough of which still remained in the vase to turn half the old people in the city to the age of their own grandchildren. While the bubbles were yet sparkling on the brim, the doctor's four guests snatched their glasses from the table, and swallowed the contents at a single gulp. Was it delusion? Even while the draught was passing down their throats, it seemed to have wrought a change on their whole systems. Their eyes grew clear and bright; a dark shade deepened among their silvery locks, they sat around the table, three gentlemen of middle age, and a woman, hardly beyond her buxom prime.

"My dear widow, you are charming!" cried

Colonel Killigrew, whose eyes had been fixed upon her face, while the shadows of age were flitting from it like darkness from the crimson daybreak.

The fair widow knew, of old, that Colonel Killigrew's compliments were not always measured by sober truth; so she started up and ran to the mirror, still dreading that the ugly visage of an old woman would meet her gaze. Meanwhile, the three gentlemen behaved in such a manner as proved that the water of the Fountain of Youth possessed some intoxicating qualities; unless, indeed, their exhilaration of spirits were merely a lightsome dizziness caused by the sudden removal of the weight of years. Mr. Gascoigne's mind seemed to run on political topics, but whether relating to the past, present, or future, could not easily be determined, since the same ideas and phrases have been in vogue these fifty years. Now he rattled forth full-throated sentences about patriotism, national glory, and the people's right; now he muttered some perilous stuff or other, in a sly and doubtful whisper, so cautiously that even his own conscience could scarcely catch the secret; and now, again, he spoke in measured accents, and a deeply deferential tone, as if a royal ear were listening to his well-turned periods. Colonel Killigrew all this time had been trolling forth a jolly bottle-song, and ringing his glass in symphony with the chorus, while his eyes wandered towards the buxom figure of the Widow Wycherly. On the other side of the table, Mr. Medbourne was involved in a calculation of dollars and cents, with which was strangely intermingled a project for supplying the East Indies with ice, by harnessing a team of whales to the polar icebergs.

As for the Widow Wycherly, she stood before the mirror curtsying and simpering to her own image, and greeting it as the friend whom she loved better than all the world beside. She thrust her face close to the glass, to see whether some long-remembered wrinkle or crow's foot had indeed vanished. She examined whether the snow had so entirely melted from her hair, that the venerable cap could be safely thrown aside. At last, turning briskly away, she came with a sort of dancing step to the table.

"My dear old doctor," cried she, "pray favor me with another glass!"

"Certainly, my dear madam, certainly!" replied the complaisant doctor; "see! I have already filled the glasses."

There, in fact, stood the four glasses, brimful of this wonderful water, the delicate spray of which, as it effervesced from the surface, resembled the tremulous glitter of diamonds. It was now so nearly sunset that the chamber had grown duskier than ever; but a mild and moonlike splendor gleamed from within the vase, and rested alike on the four guests, and on the doctor's venerable figure. He sat in a high-backed, elaborately-carved oaken armchair, with a gray dignity of aspect that might have well befitted that very Father Time, whose power had never been disputed, save by this fortunate company. Even while quaffing the third draught of the Fountain of Youth, they were almost awed by the expression of his mysterious visage.

But, the next moment, the exhilarating gush of young life shot through their veins. They were now in the happy prime of youth. Age, with its miserable train of cares, and sorrows, and diseases, was remembered only as the trouble of a dream from which they had joyously awoke. The fresh gloss of the soul, so early lost, and without which the world's successive scenes had been but a gallery of faded pictures, again threw its enchantment over all their prospects. They felt like new-created beings in a new-created universe.

"We are young! We are young!" they cried exultingly.

Youth, like the extremity of age, had effaced the strongly-marked characteristics of middle life, and mutually assimilated them all. They were a group of merry youngsters, almost maddened with the exuberant frolicsomeness of their years. The most singular effect of their gayety was an impulse to mock the infirmity and decrepitude of which they had so lately been the victims. They laughed loudly at their old-fashioned attire, the wide-skirted coats and flapped waistcoats of the young men, and the ancient cap and gown of the blooming girl. One limped across the floor like a gouty grandfather; one set a pair of spectacles astride of his nose, and pretended to pore over the black-letter pages of the book of magic; a third seated himself in an arm-chair, and strove to imitate the venerable dignity of Dr. Heidegger. Then all shouted mirthfully, and leaped about the room. The Widow Wycherly—if so fresh a damsel could be called a widow—tripped up to the doctor's chair, with a mischievous merriment in her rosy face.

"Doctor, you dear old soul," cried she, "get up and dance with me!" And then the four young people laughed louder than ever, to think what a queer figure the poor old doctor would cut.

"Pray excuse me," answered the doctor quietly. "I am old and rheumatic, and my dancing days were over long ago. But either of these gay young gentlemen will be glad of so pretty a partner."

"Dance with me, Clara!" cried Colonel Killi-grew.

"No, no, I will be her partner!" shouted Mr. Gascoigne.

"She promised me her hand, fifty years ago!" exclaimed Mr. Medbourne.

They all gathered round her. One caught both her hands in his passionate grasp—another threw his arm about her waist—the third buried his hand among the glossy curls that clustered beneath the widow's cap. Blushing, panting, struggling, chiding, laughing, her warm breath fanning each of their faces by turns, she strove to disengage herself, yet still remained in their triple embrace. Never was there a livelier picture of youthful rivalship, with bewitching beauty for the prize. Yet, by a strange deception, owing to the duskiness of the chamber, and the antique dresses which they still wore, the tall mirror is said to have reflected the figures of the three old, gray, withered grandsires, ridiculously contending for the skinny ugliness of a shriveled grandam.

But they were young: their burning passions proved them so. Inflamed to madness by the coquetry of the girl-widow, who neither granted nor quite withheld her favors, the three rivals began to interchange threatening glances. Still keeping hold of the fair prize, they grappled fiercely at one another's throats. As they struggled to and fro, the table was overturned, and the vase dashed into a thousand fragments. The precious Water of Youth flowed in a bright stream across the floor, moistening the wings of a butterfly, which, grown old in the decline of summer, had alighted there to die. The insect fluttered lightly through the chamber, and settled on the snowy head of Dr. Heidegger.

"Come, come, gentlemen!—come, Madame Wycherly," exclaimed the doctor, "I really must protest against this riot."

They stood still and shivered; for it seemed as if gray Time were calling them back from their sunny youth, far down into the chill and darksome vale of years. They looked at old Dr. Heidegger, who sat in his carved arm-chair, holding the rose of half a century, which he had rescued from among the fragments of the shattered vase. At the motion of his hand, the four rioters resumed their seats; the more readily, because their violent exertions had wearied them, youthful though they were.

"My poor Sylvia's rose!" ejaculated Dr. Heidegger, holding it in the light of the sunset clouds; "it appears to be fading again."

And so it was. Even while the party were looking at it, the flower continued to shrivel up, till it became as dry and fragile as when the doctor had first thrown it into the vase. He shook off the few drops of moisture which clung to its petals.

"I love it as well thus as in its dewy freshness," observed he, pressing the withered rose to his withered lips. While he spoke, the butterfly fluttered down from the doctor's snowy head, and fell upon the floor.

His guests shivered again. A strange chilliness, whether of the body or spirit they could not tell, was creeping gradually over them all. They gazed at one another, and fancied that each fleeting moment snatched away a charm, and left a deepening furrow where none had been before. Was it an illusion? Had the changes of a lifetime been crowded into so brief a space, and were they now four aged people, sitting with their old friend, Dr. Heidegger?

"Are we grown old again, so soon?" cried they, dolefully.

In truth they had. The Water of Youth possessed merely a virtue more transient than that of wine. The delirium which it created had effervesced away. Yes! they were old again. With a shuddering impulse, that showed her a woman still, the widow clasped her skinny hands before her face, and wished that the coffin lid were over it, since it could be no longer beautiful.

"Yes, friends, ye are old again," said Dr. Heidegger, "and lo! the Water of Youth is all lavished on the ground. Well—I bemoan it not; for if the fountain gushed at my very doorstep, I would not stoop to bathe my lips in it—no, though its delirium were for years instead of moments. Such is the lesson ye have taught me!"

But the doctor's four friends had taught no such lesson to themselves. They resolved forthwith to make a pilgrimage to Florida, and quaff 10 at morning, noon, and night, from the Fountain of Youth.

Lady Eleanore's Mantle

"Lady Eleanore's Mantle" first appeared in the *Democratic Review*, December, 1838, and was collected in *Twice-Told Tales, Second Series* (1842). It is the third tale in "Legends of the Province House," a group within *Twice-Told Tales*. An entry in the *American Notebooks* for 1841 contains a germ of the tale: "To 20 symbolize moral or spiritual disease by disease of the body;—thus, when a person committed any sin, it might cause a sore to appear on the body;—this to be wrought out." The text is that of the edition of 1883.

Mine excellent friend, the landlord of the Province House, was pleased, the other evening, to invite Mr. Tiffany and myself to an oyster supper. This slight mark of respect and gratitude, as he handsomely observed, was far less than the in- 30 genious tale-teller, and I, the humble note-taker of his narratives, had fairly earned, by the public notice which our joint lucubrations had attracted to his establishment. Many a cigar had been smoked within his premises—many a glass of wine, or more potent aqua vitæ, had been quaffed— many a dinner had been eaten by curious strangers, who, save for the fortunate conjunction of Mr. Tiffany and me, would never have ventured through that darksome avenue which gives access 40 to the historic precincts of the Province House. In short, if any credit be due to the courteous assurances of Mr. Thomas Waite, we had brought his forgotten mansion almost as effectually into public view as if we had thrown down the vulgar range of shoe shops and dry good stores which hides its aristocratic front from Washington Street. It may be unadvisable, however, to speak too loudly of the increased custom of the house, lest Mr. Waite should find it difficult to renew the lease on so favourable terms as heretofore.

Being thus welcomed as benefactors, neither Mr. Tiffany nor myself felt any scruple in doing full justice to the good things that were set before us. If the feast were less magnificent than those same panelled walls had witnessed in a by-gone century,—if mine host presided with somewhat less of state than might have befitted a successor of the royal Governors,—if the guests made a less imposing show than the bewigged and powdered and embroidered dignitaries, who erst banqueted at the gubernatorial table, and now sleep, within their armorial tombs on Copp's Hill, or round King's Chapel,—yet never, I may boldly say, did a more comfortable little party assemble in the Province House, from Queen Anne's days to the Revolution. The occasion was rendered more interesting by the presence of a venerable personage, whose own actual reminiscences went back to the epoch of Gage and Howe, and even supplied him with a doubtful anecdote or two of Hutchinson. He was one of that small, and now all but extinguished, class, whose attachment to royalty, and to the colonial institutions and customs that were connected with it, had never yielded to the democratic heresies of after times. The young queen of Britain has not a more loyal subject in her realm —perhaps not one who would kneel before her throne with such reverential love—as this old grandsire, whose head has whitened beneath the mild sway of the Republic, which still, in his mellower moments, he terms a usurpation. Yet prejudices so obstinate have not made him an ungentle or impracticable companion. If the truth must be told, the life of the aged loyalist has been of such a scrambling and unsettled character,—he has had so little choice of friends and been so often destitute of any,—that I doubt whether he would refuse a cup of kindness with either Oliver Cromwell or John Hancock,—to say nothing of any democrat now upon the stage. In another paper of this series I may perhaps give the reader a closer glimpse of his portrait.

Our host, in due season, uncorked a bottle of Madeira, of such exquisite perfume and admirable flavor, that he surely must have discovered it in an ancient bin, down deep beneath the deepest cellar, where some jolly old butler stored away the Governor's choicest wine, and forgot to reveal the secret on his death-bed. Peace to his red-nosed ghost, and a libation to his memory! This precious liquor was imbibed by Mr. Tiffany with peculiar zest; and after sipping the third glass, it was his pleasure to give us one of the oddest legends which he had yet raked from the storehouse where he keeps such matters. With some suitable adornments from my own fancy, it ran pretty much as follows:

Not long after Colonel Shute had assumed the government of Massachusetts Bay, now nearly a hundred and twenty years ago, a young lady of rank and fortune arrived from England, to claim his protection as her guardian. He was her distant relative, but the nearest who had survived the gradual extinction of her family; so that no more eligible shelter could be found for the rich and high-born Lady Eleanore Rochcliffe than within the Province House of a transatlantic colony. The consort of Governor Shute, moreover, had been as a mother to her childhood, and was now anxious to receive her, in the hope that a beautiful young woman would be exposed to infinitely less peril from the primitive society of New England than amid the artifices and corruptions of a court. If either the Governor or his lady had especially consulted their own comfort, they would probably have sought to devolve the responsibility on other hands; since, with some noble and splendid traits of character, Lady Eleanore was remarkable for a harsh, unyielding pride, a haughty consciousness of her hereditary and personal advantages which made her almost incapable of control. Judging from many traditionary anecdotes, this peculiar temper was hardly less than a monomania; or, if the acts which it inspired were those of a sane person, it seemed due from Providence that pride so sinful should be followed by as severe a retribution. That tinge of the marvellous, which is thrown over so many of these half-forgotten legends, has probably imparted an additional wildness to the strange story of Lady Eleanore Rochcliffe.

The ship in which she came passenger had arrived at Newport, whence Lady Eleanore was conveyed to Boston in the Governor's coach, attended by a small escort of gentlemen on horseback. The ponderous equipage, with its four black horses, attracted much notice as it rumbled through Cornhill, surrounded by the prancing steeds of half a dozen cavaliers, with swords dangling to their stirrups and pistols at their holsters. Through the large glass windows of the coach, as it rolled along, the people could discern the figure of Lady Eleanore, strangely combining an almost queenly stateliness with the grace and beauty of a maiden in her teens. A singular tale had gone abroad among the ladies of the province, that their fair rival was indebted for much of the irresistible charm of her appearance to a certain article of dress—an embroidered mantle —which had been wrought by the most skilful artist in London, and possessed even magical properties of adornment. On the present occasion, however, she owed nothing to the witchery of dress, being clad in a riding habit of velvet, which would have appeared stiff and ungraceful on any other form.

The coachman reined in his four black steeds, and the whole cavalcade came to a pause in front of the contorted iron balustrade that fenced the Province House from the public street. It was an awkward coincidence that the bell of the Old South was just then tolling for a funeral; so that, instead of a gladsome peal with which it was customary to announce the arrival of distinguished strangers, Lady Eleanore Rochcliffe was ushered by a doleful clang, as if calamity had come embodied in her beautiful person.

"A very great disrespect!" exclaimed Captain Langford, an English officer, who had recently brought despatches to Governor Shute. "The funeral should have been deferred, lest Lady Eleanore's spirits be affected by such a dismal welcome."

"With your pardon, sir," replied Doctor Clarke, a physician, and a famous champion of the popular party, "whatever the heralds may pretend, a dead beggar must have precedence of a living queen. King Death confers high privileges."

These remarks were interchanged while the speakers waited a passage through the crowd, which had gathered on each side of the gateway, leaving an open avenue to the portal of the Province House. A black slave in livery now leaped from behind the coach, and threw open the door; while at the same moment, Governor Shute descended the flight of steps from his mansion, to assist Lady Eleanore in alighting. But the Governor's stately approach was anticipated in a manner that excited general astonishment. A pale young man, with his black hair all in disorder, rushed from the throng, and prostrated himself beside the coach, thus offering his person as a footstool for Lady Eleanore Rochcliffe to tread upon. She held back an instant, yet with an expression as if doubting whether the young man were worthy to bear the weight of her footstep, rather than dissatisfied to receive such awful reverence from a fellow-mortal.

"Up, sir," said the Governor, sternly, at the same time lifting his cane over the intruder. "What means the Bedlamite by this freak?"

"Nay," answered Lady Eleanore playfully, but with more scorn than pity in her tone, "your Excellency shall not strike him. When men seek only to be trampled upon, it were a pity to deny them a favor so easily granted—and so well deserved!"

Then, though as lightly as a sunbeam on a cloud, she placed her foot upon the cowering form, and extended her hand to meet that of the Governor. There was a brief interval, during which Lady Eleanore retained this attitude; and never, surely, was there an apter emblem of aristocracy and hereditary pride trampling on human sympathies and the kindred of nature, than these two figures presented at that moment. Yet the spectators were so smitten with her beauty, and so essential did pride seem to the existence of such a creature, that they gave a simultaneous exclamation of applause.

"Who is this insolent young fellow?" inquired Captain Langford, who still remained beside Doctor Clarke. "If he be in his senses, his impertinence demands the bastinado. If mad, Lady Eleanore should be secured from further inconvenience, by his confinement."

"His name is Jervase Helwyse," answered the doctor; "a youth of no birth or fortune, or other advantages, save the mind and soul that nature gave him; and being secretary to our colonial agent in London, it was his misfortune to meet this Lady Eleanore Rochcliffe. He loved her— and her scorn has driven him mad."

"He was mad so to aspire," observed the English officer.

"It may be so," said Doctor Clarke, frowning as he spoke. "But I tell you, sir, I could well-nigh doubt the justice of the Heaven above us if no signal humiliation overtake this lady, who now treads so haughtily into yonder mansion. She seeks to place herself above the sympathies of our common nature, which envelops all human souls. See, if that nature do not assert its claim over her in some mode that shall bring her level with the lowest!"

"Never!" cried Captain Langford indignantly; "neither in life, nor when they lay her with her ancestors."

Not many days afterwards the Governor gave a ball in honor of Lady Eleanore Rochcliffe. The principal gentry of the colony received invitations, which were distributed to their residences, far and near, by messengers on horseback, bearing missives sealed with all the formality of official dispatches. In obedience to the summons, there was a general gathering of rank, wealth, and beauty; and the wide door of the Province House had seldom given admittance to more numerous and honorable guests than on the evening of Lady Eleanore's ball. Without much extravagance of eulogy, the spectacle might even be termed splendid; for, according to the fashion of the times, the ladies shone in rich silks and satins, outspread over wide projecting hoops; and the gentlemen glittered in gold embroidery, laid unsparingly upon the purple, or scarlet, or sky-blue velvet, which was the material of their coats and waistcoats. The latter article of dress was of great importance, since it enveloped the wearer's body nearly to the knees, and was perhaps bedizened with the amount of his whole year's income, in golden flowers and foliage. The altered taste of the present day—a taste symbolic of a deep change in the whole system of society—would look upon almost any of those gorgeous figures as ridiculous; although that evening the guests sought their reflections in the pier-glasses, and rejoiced to catch their own glitter amid the glittering crowd. What a pity that one of the stately mirrors has not preserved a picture of the scene, which, by the very traits that were so transitory, might have taught us much that would be worth knowing and remembering!

Would, at least, that either painter or mirror could convey to us some faint idea of a garment, already noticed in this legend,—the Lady Eleanore's embroidered mantle,—which the gossips whispered was invested with magic properties, so as to lend a new and untried grace to her figure each time that she put it on! Idle fancy as it is, this mysterious mantle has thrown an awe around my image of her, partly from its fabled virtues, and partly because it was the handiwork of a dying woman, and, perchance, owed the fantastic grace of its conception to the delirium of approaching death.

After the ceremonial greetings had been paid, Lady Eleanore Rochcliffe stood apart from the mob of guests, insulating herself within a small and distinguished circle, to whom she accorded a more cordial favor than to the general throng. The waxen torches threw their radiance vividly over the scene, bringing out its brilliant points in strong relief; but she gazed carelessly, and with now and then an expression of weariness or scorn, tempered with such feminine grace that her auditors scarcely perceived the moral deformity of which it was the utterance. She beheld the spectacle not with vulgar ridicule, as disdaining to be pleased with the provincial mockery of a court festival, but with the deeper scorn of one whose spirit held itself too high to participate in the enjoyment of other human souls. Whether or no the recollections of those who saw her that evening were influenced by the strange events with which she was subsequently connected, so it was that her figure ever after recurred to them as marked by something wild and unnatural,—although, at the time, the general whisper was of her exceeding beauty, and of the indescribable charm which her mantle threw around her. Some close observers, indeed, detected a feverish flush and alternate paleness of countenance, with a corresponding flow and revulsion of spirits, and once or twice, a painful and helpless betrayal of lassitude as if she were on the point of sinking to the ground. Then, with a nervous shudder, she seemed to arouse her energies and threw some bright and playful yet half-wicked sarcasm into the conversation. There was so strange a characteristic in her manners and sentiments that it astonished every right-minded listener; till looking in her face, a lurking and incomprehensible glance and smile perplexed them with doubts both as to her seriousness and sanity. Gradually, Lady Eleanore Rochcliffe's circle grew smaller, till only four gentlemen remained in it. These were Captain Langford, the English officer before mentioned; a Virginian planter, who had come to Massachusetts on some political errand; a young Episcopal clergyman, the grandson of a British earl; and, lastly, the private secretary of Governor Shute, whose obsequiousness had won a sort of tolerance from Lady Eleanore.

At different periods of the evening the liveried servants of the Province House passed among the guests, bearing huge trays of refreshment and French and Spanish wines. Lady Eleanore Rochcliffe, who refused to wet her beautiful lips even with a bubble of Champagne, had sunk back into a large damask chair, apparently overwearied either with the excitement of the scene or its tedium; and while, for an instant, she was unconscious of voices, laughter, and music, a young man stole forward, and knelt down at her feet. He bore a salver in his hand, on which was a chased silver goblet, filled to the brim with wine, which he offered as reverentially as to a crowned queen, or rather with the awful devotion of a priest doing sacrifice to his idol. Conscious that some one touched her robe, Lady Eleanore started, and unclosed her eyes upon the pale, wild features and dishevelled hair of Jervase Helwyse.

"Why do you haunt me thus?" said she, in a languid tone, but with a kindlier feeling than she ordinarily permitted herself to express. "They tell me that I have done you harm."

"Heaven knows if that be so," replied the young man, solemnly. "But, Lady Eleanore, in requital of that harm, if such there be, and for your own earthly and heavenly welfare, I pray you to take one sip of this holy wine, and then to pass the goblet round among the guests. And this shall be a symbol that you have not sought to withdraw yourself from the chain of human sympathies—which whoso would shake off must keep company with fallen angels."

"Where has this mad fellow stolen that sacramental vessel?" exclaimed the Episcopal clergyman.

This question drew the notice of the guests to the silver cup, which was recognised as appertaining to the communion plate of the Old South Church; and, for aught that could be known, it was brimming over with the consecrated wine.

"Perhaps it is poisoned," half whispered the Governor's secretary.

"Pour it down the villain's throat!" cried the Virginian, fiercely.

"Turn him out of the house!" cried Captain Langford, seizing Jervase Helwyse so roughly by the shoulder that the sacramental cup was overturned, and its contents sprinkled upon Lady Eleanore's mantle. "Whether knave, fool, or Bedlamite, it is intolerable that the fellow should go at large."

"Pray, gentlemen, do my poor admirer no harm," said Lady Eleanore, with a faint and weary smile. "Take him out of my sight, if such be your pleasure; for I can find in my heart to do nothing but laugh at him; whereas, in all decency and conscience, it would become me to weep for the mischief I have wrought!"

But while the bystanders were attempting to lead away the unfortunate young man, he broke from them, and with a wild, impassioned earnestness, offered a new and equally strange petition to Lady Eleanore. It was no other than that she should throw off the mantle, which, while he pressed the silver cup of wine upon her, she had drawn more closely around her form, so as almost to shroud herself within it.

"Cast it from you!" exclaimed Jervase Helwyse, clasping his hands in an agony of entreaty. "It may not yet be too late! Give the accursed garment to the flames!"

But Lady Eleanore, with a laugh of scorn, drew the rich folds of the embroidered mantle over her head, in such a fashion as to give a completely new aspect to her beautiful face, which—half hidden, half revealed—seemed to belong to some being of mysterious character and purposes.

"Farewell, Jervase Helwyse!" said she. "Keep my image in your remembrance, as you behold it now."

"Alas, lady!" he replied, in a tone no longer wild, but sad as a funeral bell. "We must meet shortly, when your face may wear another aspect—and that shall be the image that must abide within me."

He made no more resistance to the violent efforts of the gentlemen and servants, who almost dragged him out of the apartment, and dismissed him roughly from the iron gate of the Province House. Captain Langford, who had been very active in this affair, was returning to the presence of Lady Eleanore Rochcliffe, when he encountered the physician, Doctor Clarke, with whom he had held some casual talk on the day of her arrival. The Doctor stood apart, separated from Lady Eleanore by the width of the room, but eying her with such keen sagacity that Captain Langford involuntarily gave him credit for the discovery of some deep secret.

"You appear to be smitten, after all, with the charms of this queenly maiden," said he, hoping thus to draw forth the physician's hidden knowledge.

"God forbid!" answered Doctor Clarke, with a grave smile; "and if you be wise you will put up the same prayer for yourself. Woe to those who shall be smitten by this beautiful Lady Eleanore! But yonder stands the Governor—and I have a word or two for his private ear. Good night!"

He accordingly advanced to Governor Shute, and addressed him in so low a tone that none of the bystanders could catch a word of what he said, although the sudden change of his Excellency's hitherto cheerful visage betokened that the communication could be of no agreeable import. A very few moments afterwards it was announced to the guests that an unforeseen circumstance rendered it necessary to put a premature close to the festival.

The ball at the Province House supplied a topic of conversation for the colonial metropolis for some days after its occurrence, and might still longer have been the general theme, only that a subject of all-engrossing interest thrust it, for a time, from the public recollection. This was the appearance of a dreadful epidemic, which, in that age and long before and afterwards, was wont to slay its hundreds and thousands on both sides of the Atlantic. On the occasion of which we speak it was distinguished by a peculiar virulence, insomuch that it has left its traces—its pit-marks, to use an appropriate figure—on the history of the country, the affairs of which were thrown into confusion by its ravages. At first, unlike its ordinary course, the disease seemed to confine itself to the higher circles of society, selecting its victims from among the proud, the well-born, and the wealthy, entering unabashed into stately chambers, and lying down with the slumberers in silken beds. Some of the most distinguished guests of the Province House—even those whom the haughty Lady Eleanore Rochcliffe had deemed not unworthy of her favor—were stricken by this fatal scourge. It was noticed, with an ungenerous bitterness of feeling, that the four gentlemen—the Virginian, the British officer, the young clergyman, and the Governor's secretary—who had been her most devoted attendants on the evening of the ball, were the foremost on whom the plague stroke fell. But the disease, pursuing its onward progress, soon ceased to be exclusively a prerogative of aristocracy. Its red brand was no longer conferred like a noble's star, or an order of knighthood. It threaded its way through the narrow and crooked streets, and entered the low, mean, darksome dwellings, and laid its hand of death upon the artisans and labouring classes of the town. It compelled rich and poor to feel themselves brethren then; and stalking to and fro across the Three Hills, with a fierceness which made it almost a new pestilence, there was that mighty conqueror—that scourge and horror of our forefathers—the Small-Pox!

We cannot estimate the affright which this plague inspired of yore, by contemplating it as the fangless monster of the present day. We must remember, rather, with what awe we watched the gigantic footsteps of the Asiatic cholera striding from shore to shore of the Atlantic, and marching like destiny upon cities far remote which flight had already half depopulated. There is no other fear so horrible and unhumanising as that which makes man dread to breathe Heaven's vital air lest it be poison, or to grasp the hand of a brother or friend lest the gripe of the pestilence should clutch him. Such was the dismay that now followed in the track of the disease, or ran before it throughout the town. Graves were hastily dug, and the pestilential relics as hastily covered, because the dead were enemies of the living, and strove to draw them headlong, as it were, into their own dismal pit. The public councils were suspended, as if mortal wisdom might relinquish its devices now that an unearthly usurper had found his way into the ruler's mansion. Had an enemy's fleet been hovering on the coast, or his armies trampling on our soil, the people would probably have committed their defence to that same direful conqueror who had wrought their own calamity, and would permit no interference with his sway. This conqueror had a symbol of his triumphs. It was a blood-red flag, that fluttered in the tainted air over the door of every dwelling into which the Small-Pox had entered.

Such a banner was long since waving over the portal of the Province House; for thence, as was proved by tracking its footsteps back, had all this dreadful mischief issued. It had been traced back to a lady's luxurious chamber—to the proudest of the proud—to her that was so delicate, and hardly owned herself of earthly mould—to the haughty one who took her stand above human sympathies—to Lady Eleanore! There remained no room for doubt that the contagion had lurked in that gorgeous mantle which threw so strange a grace around her at the festival. Its fantastic splendor had been conceived in the delirious brain of a woman on her death-bed, and was the last toil of her stiffening fingers, which had interwoven fate and misery with its golden threads. This dark tale, whispered at first, was now bruited far and wide. The people raved against the Lady Eleanore, and cried out that her pride and scorn had evoked a fiend, and that, between them both, this monstrous evil had been born. At times, their rage and despair took the semblance of grinning mirth; and whenever the red flag of the pestilence was hoisted over another, and yet another door, they clapped their hands and shouted through the streets, in bitter mockery: "Behold a new triumph for the Lady Eleanore!"

One day, in the midst of these dismal times, a wild figure approached the portal of the Province House, and folding his arms, stood contemplating the scarlet banner, which a passing breeze shook fitfully, as if to fling abroad the contagion that it typified. At length, climbing one of the pillars by means of the iron balustrade, he took down the flag and entered the mansion, waving it above his head. At the foot of the staircase he met the Governor, booted and spurred, with his cloak drawn around him, evidently on the point of setting forth upon a journey.

"Wretched lunatic, what do you seek here?" exclaimed Shute, extending his cane to guard himself from contact. "There is nothing here but Death. Back—or you will meet him!"

"Death will not touch me, the banner-bearer of the pestilence!" cried Jervase Helwyse, shaking the red flag aloft: "Death and the Pestilence, who wears the aspect of the Lady Eleanore, will walk through the streets tonight, and I must march before them with this banner!"

"Why do I waste words on the fellow?" muttered the governor, drawing his cloak across his mouth. "What matters his miserable life, when none of us are sure of twelve hours' breath? On, fool, to your own destruction!"

He made way for Jervase Helwyse, who immediately ascended the staircase, but on the first landing-place, was arrested by the firm grasp of a hand upon his shoulder. Looking fiercely up, with a madman's impulse to struggle with and rend asunder his opponent, he found himself powerless beneath a calm, stern eye, which possessed the mysterious property of quelling frenzy at its height. The person whom he had now encountered was the physician, Doctor Clarke, the duties of whose sad profession had led him to the Province House, where he was an unfrequent guest in more prosperous times.

"Young man, what is your purpose?" demanded he.

"I seek the Lady Eleanore," answered Jervase Helwyse, submissively.

"All have fled from her," said the physician. "Why do you seek her now? I tell you, youth, her nurse fell death-stricken on the threshold of that fatal chamber. Know ye not, that never came such a curse to our shores as this lovely Lady Eleanore?—that her breath has filled the air with poison?—that she has shaken pestilence and death upon the land from the folds of her accursed mantle?"

"Let me look upon her!" rejoined the mad youth, more wildly. "Let me behold her, in her awful beauty, clad in the regal garments of the pestilence! She and Death sit on a throne together. Let me kneel down before them!"

"Poor youth!" said Doctor Clarke; and, moved by a deep sense of human weakness, a smile of caustic humour curled his lip even then. "Wilt thou still worship the destroyer and surround her image with fantasies the more magnificent the more evil she has wrought? Thus man doth ever to his tyrants! Approach, then! Madness, as I have noted, has that good efficacy, that it will guard you from contagion—and perchance its own cure may be found in yonder chamber."

Ascending another flight of stairs, he threw open a door and signed to Jervase Helwyse that he should enter. The poor lunatic, it seems probable, had cherished a delusion that his haughty mistress sat in state, unharmed herself by the pestilential influence, which, as by enchantment, she scattered round about her. He dreamed, no doubt, that her beauty was not dimmed, but brightened into superhuman splendor. With such anticipations, he stole reverentially to the door at which the physician stood, but paused upon the threshold, gazing fearfully into the gloom of the darkened chamber.

"Where is the Lady Eleanore?" whispered he.

"Call her," replied the physician.

"Lady Eleanore!—Princess!—Queen of Death!" cried Jervase Helwyse, advancing three steps into the chamber. "She is not here! There, on yonder table, I behold the sparkle of a diamond which once she wore upon her bosom. There"—and he shuddered—"there hangs her mantle, on which a dead woman embroidered a spell of dreadful potency. But where is the Lady Eleanore?"

Something stirred within the silken curtains of a canopied bed; and a low moan was uttered, which, listening intently, Jervase Helwyse began to distinguish as a woman's voice, complaining dolefully of thirst. He fancied, even, that he recognised its tones.

"My throat!—my throat is scorched," murmured the voice. "A drop of water!"

"What thing art thou?" said the brain-stricken youth, drawing near the bed and tearing asunder its curtains. "Whose voice hast thou stolen for thy murmurs and miserable petitions, as if Lady Eleanore could be conscious of mortal infirmity? Fie! Heap of diseased mortality, why lurkest thou in my lady's chamber?"

"O, Jervase Helwyse," said the voice—and as it spoke the figure contorted itself, struggling to hide its blasted face—"look not now on the woman you once loved! The curse of Heaven hath stricken me, because I would not call man my brother, nor woman sister. I wrapt myself in PRIDE as in a MANTLE, and scorned the sympathies of nature; and therefore has nature made this wretched body the medium of a dreadful sympathy. You are avenged —they are all avenged—Nature is avenged—for I am Eleanore Rochcliffe!"

The malice of his mental disease, the bitterness lurking at the bottom of his heart, mad as he was, for a blighted and ruined life, and love that had been paid with cruel scorn, awoke within the breast of Jervase Helwyse. He shook his finger at the wretched girl, and the chamber echoed, the curtains of the bed were shaken, with his outburst of insane merriment.

"Another triumph for the Lady Eleanore!" he cried. "All have been her victims! Who so worthy to be the final victim as herself?"

Impelled by some new fantasy of his crazed intellect, he snatched the fatal mantle and rushed from the chamber and the house. That night a procession passed by torch-light, through the streets, bearing in the midst the figure of a woman enveloped with a richly embroidered mantle; while in advance stalked Jervase Helwyse, waving the red flag of the pestilence. Arriving opposite the Province House, the mob burned the effigy, and a strong wind came and swept away the ashes. It was said that, from that very hour, the pestilence abated, as if its sway had some mysterious connection, from the first plague-stroke to the last, with Lady Eleanore's mantle. A remarkable uncertainty broods over that unhappy lady's fate. There is a belief, however, that in a certain chamber of this mansion a female form may sometimes be duskily discerned, shrinking into the darkest corner and muffling her face within an embroidered mantle. Supposing the legend true, can this be other than the once proud Lady Eleanore?

Mine host and the old loyalist and I bestowed no little warmth of applause upon this narrative, in which we had all been deeply interested; for the reader can scarcely conceive how unspeakably the effect of such a tale is heightened when, as in the present case, we may repose perfect confidence in the veracity of him who tells it. For my own part, knowing how scrupulous is Mr. Tiffany to settle the foundation of his facts, I could not have believed him one whit the more faithfully had he professed himself an eye-witness of the doings and sufferings of poor Lady Eleanore. Some sceptics, it is true, might demand documentary evidence, or even require him to produce the embroidered mantle, forgetting that—Heaven be praised—it was consumed to ashes. But now the old loyalist, whose blood was warmed by the good cheer, began to talk, in his turn, about the traditions of the Province House, and hinted that he, if it were agreeable, might add a few reminiscences to our legendary stock. Mr. Tiffany, having no cause to dread a rival, immediately besought him to favor us with a specimen; my own entreaties, of course, were urged to the same effect; and our venerable guest, well pleased to find willing auditors, awaited only the return of Mr. Thomas Waite, who had been summoned forth to provide accommodation for several new arrivals. Perchance the public—but be this as its own caprice and ours shall settle the matter—may read the result in another Tale of the Province House.

The Shaker Bridal

THIS STORY was first published in The Token in 1838, and collected in Twice-Told Tales: Second Series (1842). In 1833, two years after he had visited the Shaker village at Canterbury, New Hampshire, Hawthorne wrote "The Canterbury Pilgrims," depicting how a pair of lovers, after spending their childhood in the celibate community, sought their destiny of love in the outside world. The lovers were not dissuaded from their decision by the arguments of world-weary pilgrims on their way to join the community. Hawthorne believed in vital experience; he rejected withdrawal and retreat. In "The Shaker Bridal" he suggests that the frustration of fundamental instincts and emotions inevitably leads to tragedy. The text is that of the edition of 1883.

One day, in the sick chamber of Father Ephraim, who had been forty years the presiding elder over the Shaker settlement at Goshen, there was an assemblage of several of the chief men of the sect. Individuals had come from the rich establishment at Lebanon, from Canterbury, Harvard, and Alfred, and from all the other localities where this strange people have fertilized the rugged hills of New England by their systematic industry. An elder was likewise there who had made a pilgrimage of a thousand miles from a village of the faithful in Kentucky, to visit his spiritual kindred, the children of the sainted Mother Ann. He had partaken of the homely abundance of their tables, had quaffed the far-famed Shaker cider, and had joined in the sacred dance, every step of which is believed to alienate the enthusiast from earth, and bear him onward to heavenly purity and bliss. His brethren of the north had now courteously invited him to be present on an occasion, when the concurrence of every eminent member of their community was peculiarly desirable.

The venerable Father Ephraim sat in his easy chair, not only hoary headed and infirm with age, but worn down by a lingering disease, which, it was evident, would very soon transfer his patriarchal staff to other hands. At his footstool stood a man and woman, both clad in the Shaker garb.

"My brethren," said Father Ephraim to the surrounding elders, feebly exerting himself to utter these few words, "here are the son and daughter to whom I would commit the trust of which Providence is about to lighten my weary shoulders. Read their faces, I pray you, and say whether the inward movement of the spirit hath guided my choice aright."

Accordingly, each elder looked at the two candidates with a most scrutinizing gaze. The man, whose name was Adam Colburn, had a face sunburnt with labor in the fields, yet intelligent, thoughtful, and traced with cares enough for a whole lifetime, though he had barely reached middle age. There was something severe in his aspect, and a rigidity throughout his person, characteristics that caused him generally to be taken for a school-master; which vocation, in fact, he had formerly exercised for several years. The woman,

Martha Pierson, was somewhat above thirty, thin and pale, as a Shaker sister almost invariably is, and not entirely free from that corpse-like appearance which the garb of the sisterhood is so well calculated to impart.

"This pair are still in the summer of their years," observed the elder from Harvard, a shrewd old man. "I would like better to see the hoar-frost of autumn on their heads. Methinks, also, they will be exposed to peculiar temptations, on account of the carnal desires which have heretofore subsisted between them."

"Nay, brother," said the elder from Canterbury, "the hoar-frost and the black-frost hath done its work on Brother Adam and Sister Martha, even as we sometimes discern its traces in our cornfields, while they are yet green. And why should we question the wisdom of our venerable Father's purpose, although this pair, in their early youth, have loved one another as the world's people love? Are there not many brethren and sisters among us, who have lived long together in wedlock, yet, adopting our faith, find their hearts purified from all but spiritual affection?"

Whether or no the early loves of Adam and Martha had rendered it inexpedient that they should now preside together over a Shaker village, it was certainly most singular that such should be the final result of many warm and tender hopes. Children of neighboring families, their affection was older even than their school-days; it seemed an innate principle, interfused among all their sentiments and feelings, and not so much a distinct remembrance, as connected with their whole volume of remembrances. But, just as they reached a proper age for their union, misfortunes had fallen heavily on both, and made it necessary that they should resort to personal labor for a bare subsistence. Even under these circumstances, Martha Pierson would probably have consented to unite her fate with Adam Colburn's, and, secure of the bliss of mutual love, would patiently have awaited the less important gifts of fortune. But Adam, being of a calm and cautious character, was loth to relinquish the advantages which a single man possesses for raising himself in the world. Year after year, therefore, their marriage had been deferred.

Adam Colburn had followed many vocations,

had travelled far, and seen much of the world and of life. Martha had earned her bread sometimes as a seamstress, sometimes as help to a farmer's wife, sometimes as school-mistress of the village children, sometimes as a nurse or watcher of the sick, thus acquiring a varied experience, the ultimate use of which she little anticipated. But nothing had gone prosperously with either of the lovers; at no subsequent moment would matrimony have been so prudent a measure as when they had first parted, in the opening bloom of life, to seek a better fortune. Still they had held fast their mutual faith. Martha might have been the wife of a man who sat among the senators of his native state, and Adam could have won the hand, as he had unintentionally won the heart, of a rich and comely widow. But neither of them desired good fortune save to share it with the other.

At length that calm despair which occurs only in a strong and somewhat stubborn character, and yields to no second spring of hope, settled down on the spirit of Adam Colburn. He sought an interview with Martha, and proposed that they should join the Society of Shakers. The converts of this sect are oftener driven within its hospitable gates by worldly misfortune than drawn thither by fanaticism, and are received without inquisition as to their motives. Martha, faithful still, had placed her hand in that of her lover and accompanied him to the Shaker village. Here the natural capacity of each, cultivated and strengthened by the difficulties of their previous lives, had soon gained them an important rank in the Society, whose members are generally below the ordinary standard of intelligence. Their faith and feelings had, in some degree, become assimilated to those of their fellow-worshippers. Adam Colburn gradually acquired reputation, not only in the management of the temporal affairs of the Society, but as a clear and efficient preacher of their doctrines. Martha was not less distinguished in the duties proper to her sex. Finally, when the infirmities of Father Ephraim had admonished him to seek a successor in his patriarchal office, he thought of Adam and Martha, and proposed to renew, in their persons, the primitive form of Shaker government as established by Mother Ann. They were to be the Father and Mother of the village. The simple

ceremony which would constitute them such, was now to be performed.

"Son Adam and daughter Martha," said the venerable Father Ephraim, fixing his aged eyes piercingly upon them, "if ye can conscientiously undertake this charge, speak, that the brethren may not doubt of your fitness."

"Father," replied Adam, speaking with the calmness of his character, "I came to your village a disappointed man, weary of the world, worn out with continual trouble, seeking only a security against evil fortune, as I had no hope of good. Even my wishes of worldly success were almost dead within me. I came hither as a man might come to a tomb, willing to lie down in its gloom and coldness, for the sake of its peace and quiet. There was but one earthly affection in my breast, and it had grown calmer since my youth; so that I was satisfied to bring Martha to be my sister, in our new abode. We are brother and sister; nor would I have it otherwise. And in this peaceful village I have found all that I hope for,—all that I desire. I will strive, with my best strength, for the spiritual and temporal good of our community. My conscience is not doubtful in this matter. I am ready to receive the trust."

"Thou hast spoken well, son Adam," said the father. "God will bless thee in the office which I am about to resign."

"But our sister!" observed the elder from Harvard, "Hath she not likewise a gift to declare her sentiments?"

Martha started, and moved her lips, as if she would have made a formal reply to this appeal. But, had she attempted it, perhaps the old recollections, the long-repressed feelings of childhood, youth, and womanhood, might have gushed from her heart, in words that it would have been profanation to utter there.

"Adam has spoken," said she hurriedly; "his sentiments are likewise mine."

But while speaking these few words, Martha grew so pale that she looked fitter to be laid in her coffin than to stand in the presence of Father Ephraim and the elders; she shuddered, also, as if there were something awful or horrible in her situation and destiny. It required, indeed, a more than feminine strength of nerve, to sustain the fixed observance of men so exalted and famous throughout the sect as these were. They had overcome their natural sympathy with human frailties and affections. One, when he joined the Society, had brought with him his wife and children, but never, from that hour, had spoken a fond word to the former, or taken his best-loved child upon his knee. Another, whose family refused to follow him, had been enabled—such was his gift of holy fortitude—to leave them to the mercy of the world. The youngest of the elders, a man of about fifty, had been bred from infancy in a Shaker village, and was said never to have clasped a woman's hand in his own, and to have no conception of a closer tie than the cold fraternal one of the sect. Old Father Ephraim was the most awful character of all. In his youth he had been a dissolute libertine, but was converted by Mother Ann herself, and had partaken of the wild fanaticism of the early Shakers. Tradition whispered, at the firesides of the village, that Mother Ann had been compelled to sear his heart of flesh with a red-hot iron before it could be purified from earthly passions.

However that might be, poor Martha had a woman's heart, and a tender one, and it quailed within her, as she looked round at those strange old men, and from them to the calm features of Adam Colburn. But, perceiving that the elders eyed her doubtfully, she gasped for breath, and again spoke.

"With what strength is left me by my many troubles," said she, "I am ready to undertake this charge, and to do my best in it."

"My children, join your hands," said Father Ephraim.

They did so. The elders stood up around, and the Father feebly raised himself to a more erect position, but continued sitting in his great chair.

"I have bidden you to join your hands," said he, "not in earthly affection, for ye have cast off its chains forever; but as brother and sister in spiritual love, and helpers of one another in your allotted task. Teach unto others the faith which ye have received. Open wide your gates,—I deliver you the keys thereof,—open them wide to all who will give up the iniquities of the world, and come hither to lead lives of purity and peace. Receive the weary ones, who have known the vanity of earth,—receive the little children, that they may never learn that miserable lesson. And a blessing be upon your labors; so that the time may hasten on, when the mission of Mother Ann shall have wrought its full effect,—when children shall no more be born and die, and the last survivor of mortal race, some old and weary man like me, shall see the sun go down, nevermore to rise on a world of sin and sorrow!"

The aged Father sank back exhausted, and the surrounding elders deemed, with good reason, that the hour was come when the new heads of the village must enter on their patriarchal duties. In their attention to Father Ephraim, their eyes were turned from Martha Pierson, who grew paler and paler, unnoticed even by Adam Colburn. He, indeed, had withdrawn his hand from hers, and folded his arms with a sense of satisfied ambition. But paler and paler grew Martha by his side, till, like a corpse in its burial clothes, she sank down at the feet of her early lover; for, after many trials firmly borne, her heart could endure the weight of its desolate agony no longer.

Young Goodman Brown

"Young Goodman Brown" first appeared in the *New England Magazine* for April, 1835, and was collected in *Mosses from an Old Manse* (1846). The author does not state whether young Brown's dreadful witch-meeting was an actual experience or a dream. For an admirable analysis of Hawthorne's use of ambiguity as a narrative device, see R. H. Fogle's "Ambiguity and Clarity in Hawthorne's 'Young Goodman Brown,'" *New England Quarterly*, XVIII (1945), 448–465. The text is that of the edition of 1883.

Young Goodman Brown came forth at sunset into the street at Salem village; but put his head back, after crossing the threshold, to exchange a parting kiss with his young wife. And Faith, as the wife was aptly named, thrust her own pretty head into the street, letting the wind play with the pink ribbons of her cap while she called to Goodman Brown.

"Dearest heart," whispered she, softly and rather sadly, when her lips were close to his ear, "prithee put off your journey until sunrise and sleep in your own bed to-night. A lone woman is troubled with such dreams and such thoughts that she's afeard of herself sometimes. Pray tarry with me this night, dear husband, of all nights in the year."

"My love and my Faith," replied young Goodman Brown, "of all nights in the year, this one night must I tarry away from thee. My journey, as thou callest it, forth and back again, must needs be done 'twixt now and sunrise. What, my sweet, pretty wife, dost thou doubt me already, and we 10 but three months married?"

"Then God bless you!" said Faith, with the pink ribbons; "and may you find all well when you come back."

"Amen!" cried Goodman Brown. "Say thy prayers, dear Faith, and go to bed at dusk, and no harm will come to thee."

So they parted; and the young man pursued his way until, being about to turn the corner by the meeting-house, he looked back and saw the head of 20 Faith still peeping after him with a melancholy air, in spite of her pink ribbons.

"Poor little Faith!" thought he, for his heart smote him, "What a wretch am I to leave her on such an errand! She talks of dreams, too. Methought as she spoke there was trouble in her face, as if a dream had warned her what work is to be done to-night. But no, no; 't would kill her to think it. Well, she's a blessed angel on earth; and after this one night I'll cling to her skirts and follow 30 her to heaven."

With this excellent resolve for the future, Goodman Brown felt himself justified in making more haste on his present evil purpose. He had taken a dreary road, darkened by all the gloomiest trees of the forest, which barely stood aside to let the narrow path creep through, and closed immediately behind. It was all as lonely as could be; and there is this peculiarity in such a solitude, that the traveller knows not who may be concealed by the in- 40 numerable trunks and the thick boughs overhead; so that with lonely footsteps he may yet be passing through an unseen multitude.

"There may be a devilish Indian behind every tree," said Goodman Brown to himself; and he glanced fearfully behind him as he added, "What if the devil himself should be at my very elbow!"

His head being turned back, he passed a crook

of the road, and, looking forward again, beheld the figure of a man, in grave and decent attire, seated at the foot of an old tree. He arose at Goodman Brown's approach and walked onward side by side with him.

"You are late, Goodman Brown," said he. "The clock of the Old South was striking as I came through Boston, and that is full fifteen minutes agone."

"Faith kept me back a while," replied the young man, with a tremor in his voice, caused by the sudden appearance of his companion, though not wholly unexpected.

It was now deep dusk in the forest, and deepest in that part of it where these two were journeying. As nearly as could be discerned, the second traveller was about fifty years old, apparently in the same rank of life as Goodman Brown, and bearing a considerable resemblance to him, though perhaps more in expression than features. Still they might have been taken for father and son. And yet, though the elder person was as simply clad as the younger, and as simple in manner too, he had an indescribable air of one who knew the world, and who would not have felt abashed at the governor's dinner table or in King William's court, were it possible that his affairs should call him thither. But the only thing about him that could be fixed upon as remarkable was his staff, which bore the likeness of a great black snake, so curiously wrought that it might almost be seen to twist and wriggle itself like a living serpent. This, of course, must have been an ocular deception, assisted by the uncertain light.

"Come, Goodman Brown," cried his fellow-traveller, "this is a dull pace for the beginning of a journey. Take my staff, if you are so soon weary."

"Friend," said the other, exchanging his slow pace for a full stop, "having kept covenant by 40 meeting thee here, it is my purpose now to return whence I came. I have scruples touching the matter thou wot'st of."

"Sayest thou so?" replied he of the serpent, smiling apart. "Let us walk on, nevertheless, reasoning as we go; and if I convince thee not thou shalt turn back. We are but a little way in the forest yet."

"Too far! too far!" exclaimed the goodman,

unconsciously resuming his walk. "My father never went into the woods on such an errand, nor his father before him. We have been a race of honest men and good Christians since the days of the martyrs; and shall I be the first of the name of Brown that ever took this path and kept"—

"Such company, thou wouldst say," observed the elder person, interpreting his pause. "Well said, Goodman Brown! I have been as well acquainted with your family as with ever a one among the Puritans; and that's no trifle to say. I helped your grandfather, the constable, when he lashed the Quaker woman so smartly through the streets of Salem; and it was I that brought your father a pitch-pine knot, kindled at my own hearth, to set fire to an Indian village, in King Philip's war. They were my good friends, both; and many a pleasant walk have we had along this path, and returned merrily after midnight. I would fain be friends with you for their sake."

"If it be as thou sayest," replied Goodman Brown, "I marvel they never spoke of these matters; or, verily, I marvel not, seeing that the least rumor of the sort would have driven them from New England. We are a people of prayer, and good works to boot, and abide no such wickedness."

"Wickedness or not," said the traveller with the twisted staff, "I have a very general acquaintance here in New England. The deacons of many a church have drunk the communion wine with me; the selectmen of divers towns make me their chairman; and a majority of the Great and General Court are firm supporters of my interest. The governor and I, too—But these are state secrets."

"Can this be so?" cried Goodman Brown, with a stare of amazement at his undisturbed companion. "Howbeit, I have nothing to do with the governor and council; they have their own ways, and are no rule for a simple husbandman like me. But, were I to go on with thee, how should I meet the eye of that good old man, our minister, at Salem village? Oh, his voice would make me tremble both Sabbath day and lecture day."

Thus far the elder traveller had listened with due gravity; but now burst into a fit of irrepressible mirth, shaking himself so violently that his snake-like staff actually seemed to wriggle in sympathy.

"Ha! ha! ha!" shouted he again and again; then composing himself, "Well, go on, Goodman Brown, go on; but, prithee, don't kill me with laughing."

"Well, then, to end the matter at once," said Goodman Brown, considerably nettled, "there is my wife, Faith. It would break her dear little heart; and I'd rather break my own."

"Nay, if that be the case," answered the other, "e'en go thy ways, Goodman Brown. I would not for twenty old women like the one hobbling before us that Faith should come to any harm."

As he spoke he pointed his staff at a female figure on the path, in whom Goodman Brown recognized a very pious and exemplary dame, who had taught him his catechism in youth, and was still his moral and spiritual adviser, jointly with the minister and Deacon Gookin.

"A marvel, truly, that Goody Cloyse should be so far in the wilderness at nightfall," said he. "But with your leave, friend, I shall take a cut through the woods until we have left this Christian woman behind. Being a stranger to you, she might ask whom I was consorting with and whither I was going."

"Be it so," said his fellow-traveller. "Betake you to the woods, and let me keep the path."

Accordingly the young man turned aside, but took care to watch his companion, who advanced softly along the road until he had come within a staff's length of the old dame. She, meanwhile, was making the best of her way, with singular speed for so aged a woman, and mumbling some indistinct words—a prayer, doubtless—as she went. The traveller put forth his staff and touched her withered neck with what seemed the serpent's tail.

"The devil!" screamed the pious old lady.

"Then Goody Cloyse knows her old friend?" observed the traveller, confronting her and leaning on his writhing stick.

"Ah, forsooth, and is it your worship indeed?" cried the good dame. "Yea, truly is it, and in the very image of my old gossip, Goodman Brown, the grandfather of the silly fellow that now is. But—would your worship believe it?—my broomstick hath strangely disappeared, stolen, as I suspect, by that unhanged witch, Goody Cory, and that, too, when I was all anointed with the juice of smallage, and cinquefoil, and wolf's bane"—

"Mingled with fine wheat and the fat of a new-born babe," said the shape of old Goodman Brown.

"Ah, your worship knows the recipe," cried the old lady, cackling aloud. "So, as I was saying, being all ready for the meeting, and no horse to ride on, I made up my mind to foot it; for they tell me there is a nice young man to be taken into communion to-night. But now your good worship will lend me your arm, and we shall be there in a twinkling."

"That can hardly be," answered her friend. "I may not spare you my arm, Goody Cloyse; but here is my staff, if you will."

So saying, he threw it down at her feet, where, perhaps, it assumed life, being one of the rods which its owner had formerly lent to the Egyptian magi. Of this fact, however, Goodman Brown could not take cognizance. He had cast up his eyes in astonishment, and, looking down again, beheld neither Goody Cloyse nor the serpentine staff, but his fellow-traveller alone, who waited for him as calmly as if nothing had happened.

"That old woman taught me my catechism," said the young man; and there was a world of meaning in this simple comment.

They continued to walk onward, while the elder traveller exhorted his companion to make good speed and persevere in the path, discoursing so aptly that his arguments seemed rather to spring up in the bosom of his auditor than to be suggested by himself. As they went, he plucked a branch of maple to serve for a walking stick, and began to strip it of the twigs and little boughs, which were wet with evening dew. The moment his fingers touched them they became strangely withered and dried up as with a week's sunshine. Thus the pair proceeded, at a good free pace, until suddenly, in a gloomy hollow of the road, Goodman Brown sat himself down on the stump of a tree and refused to go any farther.

"Friend," said he, stubbornly, "my mind is made up. Not another step will I budge on this errand. What if a wretched old woman do choose to go to the devil when I thought she was going to heaven: is that any reason why I should quit my dear Faith and go after her?"

"You will think better of this by and by," said his acquaintance, composedly. "Sit here and rest yourself a while; and when you feel like moving again, there is my staff to help you along."

Without more words, he threw his companion the maple stick, and was as speedily out of sight as if he had vanished into the gloom. The young man sat a few moments by the roadside, applauding himself greatly, and thinking with how clear a conscience he should meet the minister in his morning walk, nor shrink from the eye of good old Deacon Gookin. And what calm sleep would be his that very night, which was to have been spent so wickedly, but so purely and sweetly now, in the arms of Faith! Amidst these pleasant and praiseworthy meditations, Goodman Brown heard the tramp of horses along the road, and deemed it advisable to conceal himself within the verge of the forest, conscious of the guilty purpose that had brought him thither, though now so happily turned from it.

On came the hoof tramps and the voices of the riders, two grave old voices, conversing soberly as they drew near. These mingled sounds appeared to pass along the road, within a few yards of the young man's hiding-place; but, owing doubtless to the depth of the gloom at that particular spot, neither the travellers nor their steeds were visible. Though their figures brushed the small boughs by the wayside, it could not be seen that they intercepted, even for a moment, the faint gleam from the strip of bright sky athwart which they must have passed. Goodman Brown alternately crouched and stood on tiptoe, pulling aside the branches and thrusting forth his head as far as he durst without discerning so much as a shadow. It vexed him the more, because he could have sworn, were such a thing possible, that he recognized the voices of the minister and Deacon Gookin jogging along quietly, as they were wont to do, when bound to some ordination or ecclesiastical council. While yet within hearing, one of the riders stopped to pluck a switch.

"Of the two, reverend sir," said the voice like the deacon's, "I had rather miss an ordination dinner than to-night's meeting. They tell me that some of our community are to be here from Falmouth and beyond, and others from Connecticut and Rhode Island, besides several of the Indian powwows, who, after their fashion, know almost as much deviltry as the best of us. Moreover, there is a goodly young woman to be taken into communion."

"Mighty well, Deacon Gookin!" replied the solemn old tones of the minister. "Spur up, or we shall be late. Nothing can be done, you know, until I get on the ground."

The hoofs clattered again; and the voices, talking so strangely in the empty air, passed on through the forest, where no church had ever been gathered or solitary Christian prayed. Whither, then, could these holy men be journeying so deep into the heathen wilderness? Young Goodman Brown caught hold of a tree for support, being ready to sink down on the ground, faint and overburdened, with the heavy sickness of his heart. He looked up to the sky, doubting whether there really was a heaven above him. Yet there was the blue arch, and the stars brightening in it.

"With heaven above and Faith below, I will yet stand firm against the devil!" cried Goodman Brown.

While he still gazed upward into the deep arch of the firmament and had lifted his hands to pray, a cloud, though no wind was stirring, hurried across the zenith and hid the brightening stars. The blue sky was still visible, except directly overhead, where this black mass of cloud was sweeping swiftly northward. Aloft in the air, as if from the depths of the cloud, came a confused and doubtful sound of voices. Once the listener fancied that he could distinguish the accents of townspeople of his own, men and women, both pious and ungodly, many of whom he had met at the communion table, and had seen others rioting at the tavern. The next moment, so indistinct were the sounds, he doubted whether he had heard aught but the murmur of the old forest, whispering without a wind. Then came a stronger swell of those familiar tones, heard daily in the sunshine at Salem village, but never until now from a cloud of night. There was one voice, of a young woman, uttering lamentations, yet with an uncertain sorrow, and entreating for some favor, which, perhaps, it would grieve her to obtain; and all the unseen multitude, both saints and sinners, seemed to encourage her onward.

"Faith!" shouted Goodman Brown, in a voice of agony and desperation; and the echoes of the forest mocked him, crying, "Faith! Faith!" as if bewildered wretches were seeking her all through the wilderness.

The cry of grief, rage, and terror was yet piercing the night, when the unhappy husband held his breath for a response. There was a scream, drowned immediately in a louder murmur of voices, fading into far-off laughter, as the dark cloud swept away, leaving the clear and silent sky above Goodman Brown. But something fluttered lightly down through the air and caught on the branch of a tree. The young man seized it, and beheld a pink ribbon.

"My Faith is gone!" cried he, after one stupefied moment. "There is no good on earth; and sin is but a name. Come, devil; for to thee is this world given."

And, maddened with despair, so that he laughed loud and long, did Goodman Brown grasp his staff and set forth again, at such a rate that he seemed to fly along the forest path rather than to walk or run. The road grew wilder and drearier and more faintly traced, and vanished at length, leaving him in the heart of the dark wilderness, still rushing onward with the instinct that guides mortal man to evil. The whole forest was peopled with frightful sounds—the creaking of the trees, the howling of wild beasts, and the yell of Indians; while sometimes the wind tolled like a distant church bell, and sometimes gave a broad roar around the traveller, as if all Nature were laughing him to scorn. But he was himself the chief horror of the scene, and shrank not from its other horrors.

"Ha! ha! ha!" roared Goodman Brown when the wind laughed at him. "Let us hear which will laugh loudest. Think not to frighten me with your deviltry. Come witch, come wizard, come Indian powwow, come devil himself, and here comes Goodman Brown. You may as well fear him as he fear you."

In truth, all through the haunted forest there could be nothing more frightful than the figure of Goodman Brown. On he flew among the black pines, brandishing his staff with frenzied gestures, now giving vent to an inspiration of horrid blasphemy, and now shouting forth such laughter as set all the echoes of the forest laughing like demons around him. The fiend in his own shape is less hideous than when he rages in the breast of man. Thus sped the demoniac on his course, until, quivering among the trees, he saw a red light before him, as when the felled trunks and branches of a clearing have been set on fire, and throw up their lurid blaze against the sky, at the hour of midnight. He paused, in a lull of the tempest that had driven him onward, and heard the swell of what seemed a hymn, rolling solemnly from a distance with the weight of many voices. He knew the tune; it was a familiar one in the choir of the village meeting-house. The verse died heavily away, and was lengthened by a chorus, not of human voices, but of all the sounds of the benighted wilderness pealing in awful harmony together. Goodman Brown cried out, and his cry was lost to his own ear by its unison with the cry of the desert.

In the interval of silence he stole forward until the light glared full upon his eyes. At one extremity of an open space, hemmed in by the dark wall of the forest, arose a rock, bearing some rude, natural resemblance either to an altar or a pulpit, and surrounded by four blazing pines, their tops aflame, their stems untouched, like candles at an evening meeting. The mass of foliage that had overgrown the summit of the rock was all on fire, blazing high into the night and fitfully illuminating the whole field. Each pendent twig and leafy festoon was in a blaze. As the red light arose and fell, a numerous congregation alternately shone forth, then disappeared in shadow, and again grew, as it were, out of the darkness, peopling the heart of the solitary woods at once.

"A grave and dark-clad company," quoth Goodman Brown.

In truth they were such. Among them, quivering to and fro between gloom and splendor, appeared faces that would be seen next day at the council board of the province, and others which, Sabbath after Sabbath, looked devoutly heavenward, and benignantly over the crowded pews, from the holiest pulpits in the land. Some affirm that the lady of the governor was there. At least there were high dames well known to her, and wives of honored husbands, and widows, a great multitude, and ancient maidens, all of excellent repute, and fair young girls, who trembled lest their mothers should espy them. Either the sudden gleams of light flashing over the obscure field bedazzled Goodman Brown, or he recognized a score of the church members of Salem village famous for their especial sanctity. Good old Deacon Gookin had arrived, and waited at the skirts of that venerable saint, his revered pastor. But, irreverently consorting with these grave, reputable, and pious people, these elders of the church, these chaste dames and dewy virgins, there were men of dissolute lives and women of spotted fame, wretches given over to all mean and filthy vice, and suspected even of horrid crimes. It was strange to see that the good shrank not from the wicked, nor were the sinners abashed by the saints. Scattered also among their pale-faced enemies were the Indian priests, or powwows, who had often scared their native forest with more hideous incantations than any known to English witchcraft.

"But where is Faith?" thought Goodman Brown; and, as hope came into his heart, he trembled.

Another verse of the hymn arose, a slow and mournful strain, such as the pious love, but joined to words which expressed all that our nature can conceive of sin, and darkly hinted at far more. Unfathomable to mere mortals is the lore of fiends. Verse after verse was sung; and still the chorus of the desert swelled between like the deepest tone of a mighty organ; and with the final peal of that dreadful anthem there came a sound, as if the roaring wind, the rushing streams, the howling beasts, and every other voice of the unconcerted wilderness were mingling and according with the voice of guilty man in homage to the prince of all. The four blazing pines threw up a loftier flame, and obscurely discovered shapes and visages of horror on the smoke wreaths above the impious assembly. At the same moment the fire on the rock shot redly forth and formed a glowing arch above its base, where now appeared a figure. With reverence be it spoken, the figure bore no slight similitude, both in garb and manner, to some grave divine of the New England churches.

"Bring forth the converts!" cried a voice that echoed through the field and rolled into the forest.

At the word, Goodman Brown stepped forth from the shadow of the trees and approached the congregation, with whom he felt a loathful brotherhood by the sympathy of all that was wicked in his heart. He could have well-nigh sworn that the shape of his own dead father beckoned him to advance, looking downward from a smoke wreath, while a woman, with dim features of despair, threw out her hand to warn him back. Was it his mother? But he had no power to retreat one step, nor to resist, even in thought, when the minister and good old Deacon Gookin seized his arms and led him to the blazing rock. Thither came also the slender form of a veiled female, led between Goody Cloyse, that pious teacher of the catechism, and Martha Carrier, who had received the devil's promise to be queen of hell. A rampant hag was she. And there stood the proselytes beneath the canopy of fire.

"Welcome, my children," said the dark figure, "to the communion of your race. Ye have found thus young your nature and your destiny. My children, look behind you!"

They turned; and flashing forth, as it were, in a sheet of flame, the fiend worshippers were seen; the smile of welcome gleamed darkly on every visage.

"There," resumed the sable form, "are all whom ye have reverenced from youth. Ye deemed them holier than yourselves, and shrank from your own sin, contrasting it with their lives of righteousness and prayerful aspirations heavenward. Yet here are they all in my worshipping assembly. This night it shall be granted you to know their secret deeds: how hoary-bearded elders of the church have whispered wanton words to the young maids of their households; how many a woman, eager for widows' weeds, has given her husband a drink at bedtime and let him sleep his last sleep in her bosom; how beardless youths have made haste to inherit their fathers' wealth: and how fair damsels —blush not, sweet ones—have dug little graves in the garden, and bidden me, the sole guest, to an infant's funeral. By the sympathy of your human hearts for sin ye shall scent out all the places— whether in church, bedchamber, street, field, or forest—where crime has been committed, and shall exult to behold the whole earth one stain of guilt, one mighty blood spot. Far more than this. It shall be yours to penetrate, in every bosom, the deep mystery of sin, the fountain of all wicked arts, and which inexhaustibly supplies more evil impulses than human power—than my power at its utmost—can make manifest in deeds. And now, my children, look upon each other."

They did so; and, by the blaze of the hell-kindled torches, the wretched man beheld his Faith, and the wife her husband, trembling before that unhallowed altar.

"Lo, there ye stand, my children," said the figure, in a deep and solemn tone, almost sad with its despairing awfulness, as if his once angelic nature could yet mourn for our miserable race. "Depending upon one another's hearts, ye had still hoped that virtue were not all a dream. Now are ye undeceived. Evil is the nature of mankind. Evil must be your only happiness. Welcome again, my children, to the communion of your race."

"Welcome," repeated the fiend worshippers, in one cry of despair and triumph.

And there they stood, the only pair, as it seemed, who were yet hesitating on the verge of wickedness in this dark world. A basin was hollowed, naturally, in the rock. Did it contain water, reddened by the lurid light? or was it blood? or, perchance, a liquid flame? Herein did the shape of evil dip his hand and prepare to lay the mark of baptism upon their foreheads, that they might be partakers of the mystery of sin, more conscious of the secret guilt of others, both in deed and thought, than they could now be of their own. The husband cast one look at his pale wife, and Faith at him. What polluted wretches would the next glance show them to each other, shuddering alike at what they disclosed and what they saw!

"Faith! Faith!" cried the husband, "look up to heaven, and resist the wicked one."

Whether Faith obeyed he knew not. Hardly had he spoken when he found himself amid calm night and solitude, listening to a roar of the wind which died heavily away through the forest. He staggered against the rock, and felt it chill and damp; while a hanging twig, that had been all on fire, besprinkled his cheek with the coldest dew.

The next morning young Goodman Brown came slowly into the street of Salem village, staring around him like a bewildered man. The good old minister was taking a walk along the graveyard to get an appetite for breakfast and meditate his sermon, and bestowed a blessing, as he passed, on Goodman Brown. He shrank from the venerable saint as if to avoid an anathema. Old Deacon Gookin was at domestic worship, and the holy words of his prayer were heard through the open window. "What God doth the wizard pray to?" quoth Goodman Brown. Goody Cloyse, that excellent old Christian, stood in the early sunshine at her own lattice, catechizing a little girl who had 10 brought her a pint of morning's milk. Goodman Brown snatched away the child as from the grasp of the fiend himself. Turning the corner by the meeting-house, he spied the head of Faith, with the pink ribbons, gazing anxiously forth, and bursting into such joy at sight of him that she skipped along the street and almost kissed her husband before the whole village. But Goodman Brown looked sternly and sadly into her face, and passed on without a greeting. 20

Had Goodman Brown fallen asleep in the forest and only dreamed a wild dream of a witch-meeting?

Be it so if you will; but, alas! it was a dream of evil omen for young Goodman Brown. A stern, a sad, a darkly meditative, a distrustful, if not a desperate man did he become from the night of that fearful dream. On the Sabbath day, when the congregation were singing a holy psalm, he could not listen because an anthem of sin rushed loudly upon his ear and drowned all the blessed strain. 30 When the minister spoke from the pulpit with power and fervid eloquence, and, with his hand on the open Bible, of the sacred truths of our religion, and of saint-like lives and triumphant deaths, and of future bliss or misery unutterable, then did Goodman Brown turn pale, dreading lest the roof should thunder down upon the gray blasphemer and his hearers. Often, awaking suddenly at midnight, he shrank from the bosom of Faith; and at morning or eventide, when the family knelt down 40 at prayer, he scowled and muttered to himself, and gazed sternly at his wife, and turned away. And when he had lived long, and was borne to his grave a hoary corpse, followed by Faith, an aged woman, and children and grandchildren, a goodly procession, besides neighbors not a few, they carved no hopeful verse upon his tombstone, for his dying hour was gloom.

The Celestial Railroad

after Emerson

"The Celestial Railroad" was first published in the *Democratic Review* for May, 1843, and later collected in *Mosses from an Old Manse* (1846). It was written in 1843 when New England was heavily charged with what one transcendentalist called the "moral electricity" of reform. Brook Farm and Fruitlands were only the most spectacular of many communal experiments. Hydropathy, phrenology, mesmerism, and other yeasty isms had their enthusiastic followers who were hopefully seeking short cuts to the millennium. Hawthorne's deeply rooted antipathy to reform movements kept him from sharing the general optimism. His distrust of reformers is recorded in a number of his stories: *The Blithedale Romance*, "The Hall of Fantasy," "The Procession of Life," and "A Select Party," as well as in various entries in his notebooks. "No human effort, on a grand scale," he felt, "has ever yet resulted according to the purpose of its projectors." His profound sense of misery in the world and evil in man's nature did not permit him to accept the transcendentalists' attitude toward evil as merely a negative force. The text is that of the edition of 1883.

Not a great while ago, passing through the gate of dreams, I visited that region of the earth in which lies the famous City of Destruction. It interested me much to learn that by the public spirit of some of the inhabitants a railroad has recently been established between this populous and flourishing town and the Celestial City. Having a little time upon my hands, I resolved to gratify a liberal curiosity by making a trip thither. Accordingly, one fine morning after paying my bill at the hotel, and directing the porter to stow my luggage behind a coach, I took my seat in the vehicle and set out for the station-house. It was my good fortune to enjoy the company of a gentleman—one Mr. Smooth-it-away—who, though he had never actually visited the Celestial City, yet seemed as well acquainted with its laws, customs, policy, and statistics, as with those of the City of Destruction, of which he was a native townsman. Being, moreover, a director of the railroad corporation and one of its largest stockholders, he had it in his power to give me all desirable information respecting that praiseworthy enterprise.

Our coach rattled out of the city, and at a short

distance from its outskirts passed over a bridge of elegant construction, but somewhat too slight, as I imagined, to sustain any considerable weight. On both sides lay an extensive quagmire, which could not have been more disagreeable, either to sight or smell, had all the kennels of the earth emptied their pollution there.

"This," remarked Mr. Smooth-it-away, "is the famous Slough of Despond—a disgrace to all the neighborhood; and the greater that it might so easily be converted into firm ground."

"I have understood," said I, "that efforts have been made for that purpose from time immemorial. Bunyan mentions that above twenty thousand cartloads of wholesome instructions had been thrown in here without effect."

"Very probably! And what effect could be anticipated from such unsubstantial stuff?" cried Mr. Smooth-it-away. "You observe this convenient bridge. We obtained a sufficient foundation for it by throwing into the slough some editions of books of morality; volumes of French philosophy and German rationalism; tracts, sermons, and essays of modern clergymen; extracts from Plato, Confucius, and various Hindoo sages, together with a few ingenious commentaries upon texts of Scripture,—all of which by some scientific process, have been converted into a mass like granite. The whole bog might be filled up with similar matter."

It really seemed to me, however, that the bridge vibrated and heaved up and down in a very formidable manner; and, spite of Mr. Smooth-it-away's testimony to the solidity of its foundation, I should be loath to cross it in a crowded omnibus, especially if each passenger were encumbered with as heavy luggage as that gentleman and myself. Nevertheless we got over without accident, and soon found ourselves at the station-house. This very neat and spacious edifice is erected on the site of the little wicket gate, which formerly, as all old pilgrims will recollect, stood directly across the highway, and, by its inconvenient narrowness, was a great obstruction to the traveller of liberal mind and expansive stomach. The reader of John Bunyan will be glad to know that Christian's old friend Evangelist, who was accustomed to supply each pilgrim with a mystic roll, now presides at the ticket office. Some malicious persons it is true deny the identity of this reputable character with the Evangelist of old times, and even pretend to bring competent evidence of an imposture. Without involving myself in a dispute I shall merely observe that, so far as my experience goes, the square pieces of pasteboard now delivered to passengers are much more convenient and useful along the road than the antique roll of parchment. Whether they will be as readily received at the gate of the Celestial City I decline giving an opinion.

A large number of passengers were already at the station-house awaiting the departure of the cars. By the aspect and demeanor of these persons it was easy to judge that the feelings of the community had undergone a very favorable change in reference to the celestial pilgrimage. It would have done Bunyan's heart good to see it. Instead of a lonely and ragged man with a huge burden on his back, plodding along sorrowfully on foot while the whole city hooted after him, here were parties of the first gentry and most respectable people in the neighborhood setting forth towards the Celestial City as cheerfully as if the pilgrimage were merely a summer tour. Among the gentlemen were characters of deserved eminence—magistrates, politicians, and men of wealth, by whose example religion could not but be greatly recommended to their meaner brethren. In the ladies' apartment, too, I rejoiced to distinguish some of those flowers of fashionable society who are so well fitted to adorn the most elevated circles of the Celestial City. There was much pleasant conversation about the news of the day, topics of business and politics, or the lighter matters of amusement; while religion, though indubitably the main thing at heart, was thrown tastefully into the background. Even an infidel would have heard little or nothing to shock his sensibility.

One great convenience of the new method of going on pilgrimage I must not forget to mention. Our enormous burdens, instead of being carried on our shoulders as had been the custom of old, were all snugly deposited in the baggage car, and, as I was assured, would be delivered to their respective owners at the journey's end. Another thing, likewise, the benevolent reader will be delighted to understand. It may be remembered that there was an ancient feud between Prince Beelzebub and the keeper of the wicket gate, and that the adherents of the former distinguished personage were accustomed to shoot deadly arrows at honest pilgrims while knocking at the door. This dispute, much to the credit as well of the illustrious potentate above mentioned as of the worthy and enlightened directors of the railroad, has been pacifically arranged on the principle of mutual compromise. The prince's subjects are now pretty numerously employed about the station-house, some in taking care of the baggage, others in collecting fuel, feeding the engines, and such congenial occupations; and I can conscientiously affirm that persons more attentive to their business, more willing to accommodate, or more generally agreeable to the passengers, are not to be found on any railroad. Every good heart must surely exult at so satisfactory an arrangement of an immemorial difficulty.

"Where is Mr. Greatheart?" inquired I. "Beyond a doubt the directors have engaged that famous old champion to be chief conductor on the railroad?"

"Why, no," said Mr. Smooth-it-away, with a dry cough. "He was offered the situation of brakeman; but, to tell you the truth, our friend Greatheart has grown preposterously stiff and narrow in his old age. He has so often guided pilgrims over the road on foot that he considers it a sin to travel in any other fashion. Besides, the old fellow had entered so heartily into the ancient feud with Prince Beelzebub that he would have been perpetually at blows or ill language with some of the prince's subjects, and thus have embroiled us anew. So, on the whole, we were not sorry when honest Greatheart went off to the Celestial City in a huff and left us at liberty to choose a more suitable and accommodating man. Yonder comes the engineer of the train. You will probably recognize him at once."

The engine at this moment took its station in advance of the cars, looking, I must confess, much more like a sort of mechanical demon that would hurry us to the infernal regions than a laudable contrivance for smoothing our way to the Celestial City. On its top sat a personage almost enveloped in smoke and flame, which, not to startle the reader, appeared to gush from his own mouth and stomach as well as from the engine's brazen abdomen.

"Do my eyes deceive me?" cried I. "What on earth is this! A living creature? If so, he is own brother to the engine he rides upon!"

"Poh, poh, you are obtuse!" said Mr. Smooth-it-away, with a hearty laugh. "Don't you know Apollyon, Christian's old enemy, with whom he fought so fierce a battle in the Valley of Humiliation? He was the very fellow to manage the engine; and so we have reconciled him to the custom of going on pilgrimage, and engaged him as chief engineer."

"Bravo, bravo!" exclaimed I, with irrepressible enthusiasm; "this shows the liberality of the age; this proves, if anything can, that all musty prejudices are in a fair way to be obliterated. And how will Christian rejoice to hear of this happy transformation of his old antagonist! I promise myself great pleasure in informing him of it when we reach the Celestial City."

The passengers being all comfortably seated, we now rattled away merrily, accomplishing a greater distance in ten minutes than Christian probably trudged over in a day. It was laughable, while we glanced along, as it were, at the tail of a thunderbolt, to observe two dusty foot travellers in the old pilgrim guise, with cockle shell and staff, their mystic rolls of parchment in their hands and their intolerable burdens on their backs. The preposterous obstinacy of these honest people in persisting to groan and stumble along the difficult pathway rather than take advantage of modern improvements, excited great mirth among our wiser brotherhood. We greeted the two pilgrims with many pleasant gibes and a roar of laughter; whereupon they gazed at us with such woful and absurdly compassionate visages that our merriment grew tenfold more obstreperous. Apollyon also entered heartily into the fun, and contrived to flirt the smoke and flame of the engine, or of his own breath, into their faces, and envelop them in an atmosphere of scalding steam. These little practical jokes amused us mightily, and doubtless afforded the pilgrims the gratification of considering themselves martyrs.

At some distance from the railroad Mr. Smooth-it-away pointed to a large, antique edifice, which, he observed, was a tavern of long standing, and had formerly been a noted stopping-place for pilgrims. In Bunyan's road-book it is mentioned as the Interpreter's House.

"I have long had a curiosity to visit that old mansion," remarked I.

"It is not one of our stations, as you perceive," said my companion. "The keeper was violently opposed to the railroad; and well he might be, as the track left his house of entertainment on one side, and thus was pretty certain to deprive him of all his reputable customers. But the footpath still passes his door, and the old gentleman now and then receives a call from some simple traveller, and entertains him with fare as old-fashioned as himself."

Before our talk on this subject came to a conclusion we were rushing by the place where Christian's burden fell from his shoulders at the sight of the Cross. This served as a theme for Mr. Smooth-it-away, Mr. Live-for-the-world, Mr. Hide-sin-in-the-heart, Mr. Scaly-conscience, and a knot of gentlemen from the town of Shun-repentance, to descant upon the inestimable advantages resulting from the safety of our baggage. Myself, and all the passengers indeed, joined with great unanimity in this view of the matter; for our burdens were rich in many things esteemed precious throughout the world; and, especially, we each of us possessed a great variety of favorite Habits, which we trusted would not be out of fashion even in the polite circles of the Celestial City. It would have been a sad spectacle to see such an assortment of valuable articles tumbling into the sepulchre. Thus pleasantly conversing on the favorable circumstances of our position as compared with those of past pilgrims and of narrow-minded ones at the present day, we soon found ourselves at the foot of the Hill Difficulty. Through the very heart of this rocky mountain a tunnel has been constructed of most admirable architecture, with a lofty arch and a spacious double track; so that, unless the earth and rocks should chance to crumble down, it will remain an eternal monument of the builder's skill and enterprise. It is a great though incidental advantage that the materials from the heart of the Hill Difficulty have been employed in filling up the Valley of Humiliation, thus obviating the necessity of descending into that disagreeable and unwholesome hollow.

"This is a wonderful improvement, indeed," said I. "Yet I should have been glad of an opportunity to visit the Palace Beautiful and be introduced to the charming young ladies—Miss Prudence, Miss Piety, Miss Charity, and the rest—who have the kindness to entertain pilgrims there."

"Young ladies!" cried Mr. Smooth-it-away, as soon as he could speak for laughing. "And charming young ladies! Why, my dear fellow, they are old maids, every soul of them—prim, starched, dry, and angular; and not one of them, I will venture to say, has altered so much as the fashion of her gown since the days of Christian's pilgrimage."

"Ah, well," said I, much comforted, "then I can very readily dispense with their acquaintance."

The respectable Apollyon was now putting on the steam at a prodigious rate, anxious, perhaps, to get rid of the unpleasant reminiscences connected with the spot where he had so disastrously encountered Christian. Consulting Mr. Bunyan's road-book, I perceived that we must now be within a few miles of the Valley of the Shadow of Death, into which doleful region, at our present speed, we should plunge much sooner than seemed at all desirable. In truth, I expected nothing better than to find myself in the ditch on one side or the quag on the other; but on communicating my apprehensions to Mr. Smooth-it-away, he assured me that the difficulties of this passage, even in its worst condition, had been vastly exaggerated, and that, in its present state of improvement, I might consider myself as safe as on any railroad in Christendom.

Even while we were speaking the train shot into the entrance of this dreaded Valley. Though I plead guilty to some foolish palpitations of the heart during our headlong rush over the causeway here constructed, yet it were unjust to withhold the highest encomiums on the boldness of its original conception and the ingenuity of those who executed it. It was gratifying, likewise, to observe how much care had been taken to dispel the everlasting gloom and supply the defect of cheerful sunshine, not a ray of which has ever penetrated among these awful shadows. For this purpose, the inflammable gas which exudes plentifully from the soil is collected by means of pipes, and thence communicated to a quadruple row of lamps along the whole extent of the passage. Thus a radiance has been created even out of the fiery and sulphurous curse that rests forever upon the valley—a radiance hurtful, however, to the eyes, and somewhat bewildering, as I discovered by the changes which it wrought in the visages of my companions. In this respect, as compared with natural daylight, there is the same difference as between truth and falsehood; but if the reader have ever travelled through the dark Valley, he will have learned to be thankful for any light that he could get—if not from the sky above, then from the blasted soil beneath. Such was the red brilliancy of these lamps that they appeared to build walls of fire on both sides of the track, between which we held our course at lightning speed, while a reverberating thunder filled the Valley with its echoes. Had the engine run off the track,—a catastrophe, it is whispered, by no means unprecedented,—the bottomless pit, if there be any such place, would undoubtedly have received us. Just as some dismal fooleries of this nature had made my heart quake there came a tremendous shriek, careering along the valley as if a thousand devils had burst their lungs to utter it, but which proved to be merely the whistle of the engine on arriving at a stopping-place.

The spot where we had now paused is the same that our friend Bunyan—a truthful man, but infected with many fantastic notions—has designated, in terms plainer than I like to repeat, as the mouth of the infernal region. This, however, must be a mistake, inasmuch as Mr. Smooth-it-away, while we remained in the smoky and lurid cavern, took occasion to prove that Tophet has not even a metaphorical existence. The place, he assured us, is no other than the crater of a half-extinct volcano, in which the directors had caused forges to be set up for the manufacture of railroad iron. Hence, also, is obtained a plentiful supply of fuel for the use of the engines. Whoever had gazed into the dismal obscurity of the broad cavern mouth, whence ever and anon darted huge tongues of dusky flame, and had seen the strange, half-shaped monsters, and visions of faces horribly grotesque, into which the smoke seemed to wreathe

itself, and had heard the awful murmurs, and shrieks, and deep shuddering whispers of the blast, sometimes forming themselves into words almost articulate, would have seized upon Mr. Smooth-it-away's comfortable explanation as greedily as we did. The inhabitants of the cavern, moreover, were unlovely personages, dark, smoke-begrimed, generally deformed, with misshapen feet, and a glow of dusky redness in their eyes as if their hearts had caught fire and were blazing out of the upper windows. It struck me as a peculiarity that the laborers at the forge and those who brought fuel to the engine, when they began to draw short breath, positively emitted smoke from their mouth and nostrils.

Among the idlers about the train, most of whom were puffing cigars which they had lighted at the flame of the crater, I was perplexed to notice several who, to my certain knowledge, had heretofore set forth by railroad for the Celestial City. They looked dark, wild, and smoky, with a singular resemblance, indeed, to the native inhabitants, like whom, also, they had a disagreeable propensity to ill-natured gibes and sneers, the habit of which had wrought a settled contortion of their visages. Having been on speaking terms with one of these persons,—an indolent, good-for-nothing fellow, who went by the name of Take-it-easy,—I called him, and inquired what was his business there.

"Did you not start," said I, "for the Celestial City?"

"That's a fact," said Mr. Take-it-easy, carelessly puffing some smoke into my eyes. "But I heard such bad accounts that I never took pains to climb the hill on which the city stands. No business doing, no fun going on, nothing to drink, and no smoking allowed, and a thrumming of church music from morning till night. I would not stay in such a place if they offered me house room and living free."

"But, my good Mr. Take-it-easy," cried I, "why take up your residence here, of all places in the world?"

"Oh," said the loafer, with a grin, "it is very warm hereabouts, and I meet with plenty of old acquaintances, and altogether the place suits me. I hope to see you back again some day soon. A pleasant journey to you."

566

While he was speaking the bell of the engine rang, and we dashed away after dropping a few passengers, but receiving no new ones. Rattling onward through the Valley, we were dazzled with the fiercely gleaming gas lamps, as before. But sometimes, in the dark of intense brightness, grim faces, that bore the aspect and expression of individual sins, or evil passions, seemed to thrust themselves through the veil of light, glaring upon us, and stretching forth a great, dusky hand, as if to impede our progress. I almost thought that they were my own sins that appalled me there. These were freaks of imagination—nothing more, certainly—mere delusions, which I ought to be heartily ashamed of; but all through the Dark Valley I was tormented, and pestered, and dolefully bewildered with the same kind of waking dreams. The mephitic gases of that region intoxicate the brain. As the light of natural day, however, began to struggle with the glow of the lanterns, these vain imaginations lost their vividness, and finally vanished with the first ray of sunshine that greeted our escape from the Valley of the Shadow of Death. Ere we had gone a mile beyond it I could well-nigh have taken my oath that this whole gloomy passage was a dream.

At the end of the valley, as John Bunyan mentions, is a cavern, where, in his days, dwelt two cruel giants, Pope and Pagan, who had strown the ground about their residence with the bones of slaughtered pilgrims. These vile old troglodytes are no longer there; but into their deserted cave another terrible giant has thrust himself, and makes it his business to seize upon honest travellers and fatten them for his table with plentiful meals of smoke, mist, moonshine, raw potatoes, and sawdust. He is a German by birth, and is called Giant Transcendentalist; but as to his form, his features, his substance, and his nature generally, it is the chief peculiarity of this huge miscreant that neither he for himself, nor anybody for him, has ever been able to describe them. As we rushed by the cavern's mouth we caught a hasty glimpse of him, looking somewhat like an ill-proportioned figure, but considerably more like a heap of fog and duskiness. He shouted after us, but in so strange a phraseology that we knew not what he meant, nor whether to be encouraged or affrighted.

It was late in the day when the train thundered into the ancient city of Vanity, where Vanity Fair is still at the height of prosperity, and exhibits an epitome of whatever is brilliant, gay, and fascinating beneath the sun. As I purposed to make a considerable stay here, it gratified me to learn that there is no longer the want of harmony between the town's-people and pilgrims, which impelled the former to such lamentably mistaken measures as the persecution of Christian and the fiery martyrdom of Faithful. On the contrary, as the new railroad brings with it great trade and a constant influx of strangers, the lord of Vanity Fair is its chief patron, and the capitalists of the city are among the largest stockholders. Many passengers stop to take their pleasure or make their profit in the Fair, instead of going onward to the Celestial City. Indeed, such are the charms of the place that people often affirm it to be the true and only heaven; stoutly contending that there is no other, that those who seek further are mere dreamers, and that, if the fabled brightness of the Celestial City lay but a bare mile beyond the gates of Vanity, they would not be fools enough to go thither. Without subscribing to these perhaps exaggerated encomiums, I can truly say that my abode in the city was mainly agreeable, and my intercourse with the inhabitants productive of much amusement and instruction.

Being naturally of a serious turn, my attention was directed to the solid advantages derivable from a residence here, rather than to the effervescent pleasures which are the grand object with too many visitants. The Christian reader, if he have had no accounts of the city later than Bunyan's time, will be surprised to hear that almost every street has its church, and that the reverend clergy are nowhere held in higher respect than at Vanity Fair. And well do they deserve such honorable estimation; for the maxims of wisdom and virtue which fall from their lips come from as deep a spiritual source, and tend to as lofty a religious aim, as those of the sagest philosophers of old. In justification of this high praise I need only mention the names of the Rev. Mr. Shallow-deep, the Rev. Mr. Stumble-at-truth, that fine old clerical character the Rev. Mr. This-to-day, who expects shortly to resign his pulpit to the Rev. Mr. That-to-morrow; together with the Rev. Mr. Bewilderment, the Rev. Mr. Clog-the-spirit, and, last and greatest, the Rev. Dr. Wind-of-doctrine. The labors of these eminent divines are aided by those of innumerable lecturers, who diffuse such a various profundity, in all subjects of human or celestial science, that any man may acquire an omnigenous erudition without the trouble of even learning to read. Thus literature is etherealized by assuming for its medium the human voice; and knowledge, depositing all its heavier particles, except, doubtless, its gold, becomes exhaled into a sound, which forthwith steals into the ever-open ear of the community. These ingenious methods constitute a sort of machinery, by which thought and study are done to every person's hand without his putting himself to the slightest inconvenience in the matter. There is another species of machine for the wholesale manufacture of individual morality. This excellent result is effected by societies for all manner of virtuous purposes, with which a man has merely to connect himself, throwing, as it were, his quota of virtue into the common stock, and the president and directors will take care that the aggregate amount be well applied. All these, and other wonderful improvements in ethics, religion, and literature, being made plain to my comprehension by the ingenious Mr. Smooth-it-away, inspired me with a vast admiration of Vanity Fair.

It would fill a volume, in an age of pamphlets, were I to record all my observations in this great capital of human business and pleasure. There was an unlimited range of society—the powerful, the wise, the witty, and the famous in every walk of life; princes, presidents, poets, generals, artists, actors, and philanthropists,—all making their own market at the fair, and deeming no price too exorbitant for such commodities as hit their fancy. It was well worth one's while, even if he had no idea of buying or selling, to loiter through the bazaars and observe the various sorts of traffic that were going forward.

Some of the purchasers, I thought, made very foolish bargains. For instance, a young man having inherited a splendid fortune, laid out a considerable portion of it in the purchase of diseases, and finally spent all the rest for a heavy lot of repentance and a suit of rags. A very pretty girl bartered a heart as clear as crystal, and which seemed her most valuable possession, for another jewel of the same kind, but so worn and defaced as to be utterly worthless. In one shop there were a great many crowns of laurel and myrtle, which soldiers, authors, statesmen, and various other people pressed eagerly to buy; some purchased these paltry wreaths with their lives, others by a toilsome servitude of years, and many sacrificed whatever was most valuable, yet finally slunk away without the crown. There was a sort of stock or scrip, called Conscience, which seemed to be in great demand, and would purchase almost anything. Indeed, few rich commodities were to be obtained without paying a heavy sum in this particular stock, and a man's business was seldom very lucrative unless he knew precisely when and how to throw his hoard of conscience into the market. Yet as this stock was the only thing of permanent value, whoever parted with it was sure to find himself a loser in the long run. Several of the speculations were of a questionable character. Occasionally a member of Congress recruited his pocket by the sale of his constituents; and I was assured that public officers have often sold their country at very moderate prices. Thousands sold their happiness for a whim. Gilded chains were in great demand, and purchased with almost any sacrifice. In truth, those who desired, according to the old adage, to sell anything valuable for a song, might find customers all over the Fair; and there were innumerable messes of pottage, piping hot, for such as chose to buy them with their birthrights. A few articles, however, could not be found genuine at Vanity Fair. If a customer wished to renew his stock of youth the dealers offered him a set of false teeth and an auburn wig; if he demanded peace of mind, they recommended opium or a brandy bottle.

Tracts of land and golden mansions, situate in the Celestial City, were often exchanged, at very disadvantageous rates, for a few years' lease of small, dismal, inconvenient tenements in Vanity Fair. Prince Beelzebub himself took great interest in this sort of traffic, and sometimes condescended to meddle with smaller matters. I once had the pleasure to see him bargaining with a miser for his soul, which, after much ingenious skirmishing on both sides, his highness succeeded in obtaining at about the value of sixpence. The prince remarked with a smile, that he was a loser by the transaction.

Day after day, as I walked the streets of Vanity, my manners and deportment became more and more like those of the inhabitants. The place began to seem like home; the idea of pursuing my travels to the Celestial City was almost obliterated from my mind. I was reminded of it, however, by the sight of the same pair of simple pilgrims at whom we had laughed so heartily when Apollyon puffed smoke and steam into their faces at the commencement of our journey. There they stood amidst the densest bustle of Vanity; the dealers offering them their purple and fine linen and jewels, the men of wit and humor gibing at them, a pair of buxom ladies ogling them askance, while the benevolent Mr. Smooth-it-away whispered some of his wisdom at their elbows, and pointed to a newly-erected temple; but there were these worthy simpletons, making the scene look wild and monstrous, merely by their sturdy repudiation of all part in its business or pleasures.

One of them—his name was Stick-to-the-right—perceived in my face, I suppose, a species of sympathy and almost admiration, which, to my own great surprise, I could not help feeling for this pragmatic couple. It prompted him to address me.

"Sir," inquired he, with a sad, yet mild and kindly voice, "do you call yourself a pilgrim?"

"Yes," I replied, "my right to that appellation is indubitable. I am merely a sojourner here in Vanity Fair, being bound to the Celestial City by the new railroad."

"Alas, friend," rejoined Mr. Stick-to-the-right, "I do assure you, and beseech you to receive the truth of my words, that that whole concern is a bubble. You may travel on it all your lifetime, were you to live thousands of years, and yet never get beyond the limits of Vanity Fair. Yea, though you should deem yourself entering the gates of the blessed city, it will be nothing but a miserable delusion."

"The Lord of the Celestial City," began the other pilgrim, whose name was Mr. Foot-it-to-heaven, "has refused, and will ever refuse, to grant an act of incorporation for this railroad; and unless that be obtained, no passenger can ever hope to enter his dominions. Wherefore every man who buys a ticket must lay his account with losing the purchase money, which is the value of his own soul."

"Poh, nonsense!" said Mr. Smooth-it-away, taking my arm and leading me off, "these fellows ought to be indicted for a libel. If the law stood as it once did in Vanity Fair we should see them grinning through the iron bars of the prison window."

This incident made a considerable impression on my mind, and contributed with other circumstances to indispose me to a permanent residence in the city of Vanity; although, of course, I was not simple enough to give up my original plan of gliding along easily and commodiously by railroad. Still, I grew anxious to be gone. There was one strange thing that troubled me. Amid the occupations or amusements of the Fair, nothing was more common than for a person—whether at feast, theatre, or church, or trafficking for wealth and honors, or whatever he might be doing, and however unseasonable the interruption—suddenly to vanish like a soap bubble, and be never more seen of his fellows; and so accustomed were the latter to such little accidents that they went on with their business as quietly as if nothing had happened. But it was otherwise with me.

Finally, after a pretty long residence at the Fair, I resumed my journey towards the Celestial City, still with Mr. Smooth-it-away at my side. At a short distance beyond the suburbs of Vanity we passed the ancient silver mine, of which Demas was the first discoverer, and which is now wrought to great advantage, supplying nearly all the coined currency of the world. A little further onward was the spot where Lot's wife had stood forever under the semblance of a pillar of salt. Curious travellers have long since carried it away piecemeal. Had all regrets been punished as rigorously as this poor dame's were, my yearning for the relinquished delights of Vanity Fair might have produced a similar change in my own corporeal substance, and left me a warning to future pilgrims.

The next remarkable object was a large edifice, constructed of mossgrown stone, but in a modern and airy style of architecture. The engine came to a pause in its vicinity, with the usual tremendous shriek.

"This was formerly the castle of the redoubted giant Despair," observed Mr. Smooth-it-away; "but since his death Mr. Flimsy-faith has repaired it, and keeps an excellent house of entertainment here. It is one of our stopping-places."

"It seems but slightly put together," remarked I, looking at the frail yet ponderous walls. "I do not envy Mr. Flimsy-faith his habitation. Some day it will thunder down upon the heads of the occupants."

"We shall escape at all events," said Mr. Smooth-it-away, "for Apollyon is putting on the steam again."

The road now plunged into a gorge of the Delectable Mountains, and traversed the field where in former ages the blind men wandered and stumbled among the tombs. One of these ancient tombstones had been thrust across the track by some malicious person, and gave the train of cars a terrible jolt. Far up the rugged side of a mountain I perceived a rusty iron door, half overgrown with bushes and creeping plants, but with smoke issuing from its crevices.

"Is that," inquired I, "the very door in the hillside which the shepherds assured Christian was a by-way to hell?"

"That was a joke on the part of the shepherds," said Mr. Smooth-it-away, with a smile. "It is neither more nor less than the door of a cavern which they use as a smoke-house for the preparation of mutton hams."

My recollections of the journey are now, for a little space, dim and confused, inasmuch as a singular drowsiness here overcame me, owing to the fact that we were passing over the enchanted ground, the air of which encourages a disposition to sleep. I awoke, however, as soon as we crossed the borders of the pleasant land of Beulah. All the passengers were rubbing their eyes, comparing watches, and congratulating one another on the prospect of arriving so seasonably at the journey's end. The sweet breezes of this happy clime came refreshingly to our nostrils; we beheld the glimmering gush of silver fountains, overhung by trees of beautiful foliage and delicious fruit, which were propagated by grafts from the celestial gardens. Once, as we dashed onward like a hurricane, there was a flutter of wings and the bright appearance of an angel in the air, speeding forth on some heavenly mission. The engine now announced the close vicinity of the final station-house by one last and horrible scream, in which there seemed to be distinguishable every kind of wailing and woe, and bitter fierceness of wrath, all mixed up with the wild laughter of a devil or a madman. Throughout our journey, at every stopping-place, Apollyon had exercised his ingenuity in screwing the most abominable sounds out of the whistle of the steam-engine; but in this closing effort he outdid himself and created an infernal uproar, which, besides disturbing the peaceful inhabitants of Beulah, must have sent its discord even through the celestial gates.

While the horrid clamor was still ringing in our ears we heard an exulting strain, as if a thousand instruments of music, with height and depth and sweetness in their tones, at once tender and triumphant, were struck in unison, to greet the approach of some illustrious hero, who had fought the good fight and won a glorious victory, and was come to lay aside his battered arms forever. Looking to ascertain what might be the occasion of this glad harmony, I perceived, on alighting from the cars, that a multitude of shining ones had assembled on the other side of the river, to welcome two poor pilgrims, who were just emerging from its depths. They were the same whom Apollyon and ourselves had persecuted with taunts, and gibes, and scalding steam, at the commencement of our journey—the same whose unworldly aspect and impressive words had stirred my conscience amid the wild revellers of Vanity Fair.

"How amazingly well those men have got on," cried I to Mr. Smooth-it-away. "I wish we were secure of as good a reception."

"Never fear, never fear!" answered my friend. "Come, make haste; the ferry boat will be off directly, and in three minutes you will be on the other side of the river. No doubt you will find coaches to carry you up to the city gates."

A steam ferry boat, the last improvement on this important route, lay at the river side, puffing, snorting, and emitting all those other disagreeable utterances which betoken the departure to be immediate. I hurried on board with the rest of the passengers, most of whom were in great perturbation: some bawling out for their baggage; some tearing their hair and exclaiming that the boat would explode or sink; some already pale with the heaving of the stream; some gazing affrighted at the ugly aspect of the steersman; and some still dizzy with the slumberous influences of the Enchanted Ground. Looking back to the shore, I was amazed to discern Mr. Smooth-it-away waving his hand in token of farewell.

"Don't you go over to the Celestial City?" exclaimed I.

"Oh, no!" answered he with a queer smile, and that same disagreeable contortion of visage which I had remarked in the inhabitants of the Dark Valley. "Oh, no! I have come thus far only for the sake of your pleasant company. Good-by! We shall meet again."

And then did my excellent friend Mr. Smooth-it-away laugh outright, in the midst of which cachinnation a smoke-wreath issued from his mouth and nostrils, while a twinkle of lurid flame darted out of either eye, proving indubitably that his heart was all of a red blaze. The impudent fiend! To deny the existence of Tophet, when he felt its fiery tortures raging within his breast. I rushed to the side of the boat, intending to fling myself on shore; but the wheels, as they began their revolutions, threw a dash of spray over me so cold—so deadly cold, with the chill that will never leave those waters until Death be drowned in his own river—that with a shiver and a heartquake I awoke. Thank Heaven it was a Dream!

Ethan Brand

THIS STORY was literally a "twice-told tale" before it was collected in *The Snow Image* (1851). It first appeared in the *Boston Museum* for January, 1850, and was later reprinted in the *Dollar Magazine*, May, 1851. The theme was anticipated by two entries in the *American Notebooks* in 1844: "The search of an investigator for the Unpardonable Sin;—he at last finds it in his own heart and practice."—"The Unpardonable Sin might consist in a want of love and reverence for the Human Soul; in consequence of which, the investigator pried into its dark depths, not with a hope or purpose of making it better, but with a cold philosophical curiosity.... Would not this, in other words, be the separation of the intellect from the heart?"

For minor details, such as the diorama, the reader may consult the *American Notebooks*, especially in the scattered passages for the summer of 1838 when Hawthorne visited North Adams. The concept of a fiend that could be evoked from the fire of the furnace links the story with "The Devil in Manuscript." Hawthorne had encountered many stagecoach agents while traveling about New England in 1831 on his uncle's stagecoach lines. The contrast between Ethan and the three vulgar personages, and the sardonic laugh that stills mirth are characteristic of Hawthorne. The text is that of the edition of 1883.

Bartram the lime-burner, a rough, heavy-looking man, begrimed with charcoal, sat watching his kiln at nightfall, while his little son played at building houses with the scattered fragments of marble, when, on the hill-side below them, they heard a roar of laughter, not mirthful, but slow, and even solemn, like a wind shaking the boughs of the forest.

"Father, what is that?" asked the little boy, leaving his play, and pressing betwixt his father's knees.

"Oh, some drunken man, I suppose," answered the lime-burner; "some merry fellow from the bar-room in the village, who dared not laugh loud enough within doors lest he should blow the roof of the house off. So here he is, shaking his jolly sides at the foot of Graylock."

"But, father," said the child, more sensitive than the obtuse, middle-aged clown, "he does not laugh like a man that is glad. So the noise frightens me!"

"Don't be a fool, child!" cried his father, gruffly. "You will never make a man, I do believe; there is too much of your mother in you. I have known the rustling of a leaf startle you. Hark! Here comes the merry fellow now. You shall see that there is no harm in him."

Bartram and his little son, while they were talking thus, sat watching the same lime-kiln that had been the scene of Ethan Brand's solitary and meditative life, before he began his search for the Unpardonable Sin. Many years, as we have seen, had now elapsed, since that portentous night when the IDEA was first developed. The kiln, however, on the mountain-side, stood unimpaired, and was in nothing changed since he had thrown his dark thoughts into the intense glow of its furnace, and melted them, as it were, into the one thought that took possession of his life. It was a rude, round, tower-like structure about twenty feet high, heavily built of rough stones, and with a hillock of earth heaped about the larger part of its circumference; so that the blocks and fragments of marble might be drawn by cart-loads, and thrown in at the top. There was an opening at the bottom of the tower, like an oven-mouth, but large enough to admit a man in a stooping posture, and provided with a massive iron door. With the smoke and jets of flame issuing from the chinks and crevices of this door, which seemed to give admittance into the hill-side, it resembled nothing so much as the private entrance to the infernal regions, which the shepherds of the Delectable Mountains were accustomed to show to pilgrims.

There are many such lime-kilns in that tract of country, for the purpose of burning the white marble which composes a large part of the substance of the hills. Some of them, built years ago, and long deserted, with weeds growing in the vacant round of the interior, which is open to the sky, and grass and wild-flowers rooting themselves into the chinks of the stones, look already like relics of antiquity, and may yet be overspread with the lichens of centuries to come. Others, where the lime-burner still feeds his daily and night-long fire, afford points of interest to the wanderer among the hills, who seats himself on a log of wood or a fragment of marble, to hold a chat with the solitary man. It is a lonesome, and, when the character is inclined to thought, may be an intensely thoughtful occupation; as it proved in the case of Ethan Brand, who had mused to such strange purpose, in days gone by, while the fire in this very kiln was burning.

The man who now watched the fire was of a different order, and troubled himself with no thoughts save the very few that were requisite to his business. At frequent intervals, he flung back the clashing weight of the iron door, and, turning his face from the insufferable glare, thrust in huge logs of oak, or stirred the immense brands with a long pole. Within the furnace were seen the curling and riotous flames, and the burning marble, almost molten with the intensity of heat; while

without, the reflection of the fire quivered on the dark intricacy of the surrounding forest, and showed in the foreground a bright and ruddy little picture of the hut, the spring beside its door, the athletic and coal-begrimed figure of the lime-burner, and the half-frightened child, shrinking into the protection of his father's shadow. And when, again, the iron door was closed, then reappeared the tender light of the half-full moon, which vainly strove to trace out the indistinct shapes of the neighbouring mountains; and, in the upper sky, there was a flitting congregation of clouds, still faintly tinged with the rosy sunset, though thus far down into the valley the sunshine had vanished long and long ago.

The little boy now crept still closer to his father, as footsteps were heard ascending the hillside, and a human form thrust aside the bushes that clustered beneath the trees.

"Halloo! who is it?" cried the lime-burner, vexed at his son's timidity, yet half infected by it. "Come forward, and show yourself, like a man, or I'll fling this chunk of marble at your head!"

"You offer me a rough welcome," said a gloomy voice, as the unknown man drew nigh. "Yet I neither claim nor desire a kinder one, even at my own fireside."

To obtain a distincter view, Bartram threw open the iron door of the kiln, whence immediately issued a gush of fierce light, that smote full upon the stranger's face and figure. To a careless eye there appeared nothing very remarkable in his aspect, which was that of a man in a coarse, brown, country-made suit of clothes, tall and thin, with the staff and heavy shoes of a wayfarer. As he advanced, he fixed his eyes—which were very bright—intently upon the brightness of the furnace, as if he beheld, or expected to behold, some object worthy of note within it.

"Good evening, stranger," said the lime-burner; "whence come you, so late in the day?"

"I come from my search," answered the wayfarer; "for, at last, it is finished."

"Drunk!—or crazy!" muttered Bartram to himself. "I shall have trouble with the fellow. The sooner I drive him away, the better."

The little boy, all in a tremble, whispered to his father, and begged him to shut the door of the kiln, so that there might not be so much light; for that there was something in the man's face which he was afraid to look at, yet could not look away from. And, indeed, even the lime-burner's dull and torpid sense began to be impressed by an indescribable something in that thin, rugged, thoughtful visage, with the grizzled hair hanging wildly about it, and those deeply sunken eyes, which gleamed like fires within the entrance of a mysterious cavern. But, as he closed the door, the stranger turned towards him, and spoke in a quiet, familiar way, that made Bartram feel as if he were a sane and sensible man, after all.

"Your task draws to an end, I see," said he. "This marble has already been burning three days. A few hours more will convert the stone to lime."

"Why, who are you?" exclaimed the limeburner. "You seem as well acquainted with my business as I am myself."

"And well I may be," said the stranger; "for I followed the same craft many a long year, and here, too, on this very spot. But you are a new-comer in these parts. Did you never hear of Ethan Brand?"

"The man that went in search of the Unpardonable Sin?" asked Bartram, with a laugh.

"The same," answered the stranger. "He has found what he sought, and therefore he comes back again."

"What! then you are Ethan Brand himself?" cried the lime-burner, in amazement. "I am a new-comer here, as you say, and they call it eighteen years since you left the foot of Graylock. But, I can tell you, the good folks still talk about Ethan Brand, in the village yonder, and what a strange errand took him away from his limekiln. Well, and so you have found the Unpardonable Sin?"

"Even so!" said the stranger, calmly.

"If the question is a fair one," proceeded Bartram, "where might it be?"

Ethan Brand laid his finger on his own heart.

"Here!" replied he.

And then, without mirth in his countenance, but as if moved by an involuntary recognition of the infinite absurdity of seeking throughout the world for what was the closest of all things to himself, and looking into every heart, save his own, for what was hidden in no other breast, he broke

into a laugh of scorn. It was the same slow, heavy laugh, that had almost appalled the lime-burner when it heralded the wayfarer's approach.

The solitary mountain-side was made dismal by it. Laughter, when out of place, mistimed, or bursting forth from a disordered state of feeling, may be the most terrible modulation of the human voice. The laughter of one asleep, even if it be a little child,—the madman's laugh,—the wild, screaming laugh of a born idiot,—are sounds that we sometimes tremble to hear, and would always willingly forget. Poets have imagined no utterance of fiends or hobgoblins so fearfully appropriate as a laugh. And even the obtuse lime-burner felt his nerves shaken, as this strange man looked inward at his own heart, and burst into laughter that rolled away into the night, and was indistinctly reverberated among the hills.

"Joe," said he to his little son, "scamper down to the tavern in the village, and tell the jolly fellows there that Ethan Brand has come back, and that he has found the Unpardonable Sin!"

The boy darted away on his errand, to which Ethan Brand made no objection, nor seemed hardly to notice it. He sat on a log of wood, looking steadfastly at the iron door of the kiln. When the child was out of sight, and his swift and light footsteps ceased to be heard treading first on the fallen leaves and then on the rocky mountainpath, the lime-burner began to regret his departure. He felt that the little fellow's presence had been a barrier between his guest and himself, and that he must now deal, heart to heart, with a man who, on his own confession, had committed the one only crime for which Heaven could afford no mercy. That crime, in its indistinct blackness, seemed to overshadow him. The lime-burner's own sins rose up within him, and made his memory riotous with a throng of evil shapes that asserted their kindred with the Master Sin, whatever it might be, which it was within the scope of man's corrupted nature to conceive and cherish. They were all of one family; they went to and fro between his breast and Ethan Brand's, and carried dark greetings from one to the other.

Then Bartram remembered the stories which had grown traditionary in reference to this strange man, who had come upon him like a shadow of the night, and was making himself at home in his old place, after so long absence, that the dead people, dead and buried for years, would have had more right to be at home, in any familiar spot, than he. Ethan Brand, it was said, had conversed with Satan himself in the lurid blaze of this very kiln. The legend had been matter of mirth heretofore, but looked grisly now. According to this tale, before Ethan Brand departed on his search, he had been accustomed to evoke a fiend from the hot furnace 10 of the lime-kiln, night after night, in order to confer with him about the Unpardonable Sin; the man and the fiend each labouring to frame the image of some mode of guilt which could neither be atoned for nor forgiven. And, with the first gleam of light upon the mountain-top, the fiend crept in at the iron door, there to abide the intensest element of fire until again summoned forth to share in the dreadful task of extending man's possible guilt beyond the scope of Heaven's else 20 infinite mercy.

While the lime-burner was struggling with the horror of these thoughts, Ethan Brand rose from the log, and flung open the door of the kiln. The action was in such accordance with the idea in Bartram's mind, that he almost expected to see the Evil One issue forth, red-hot, from the raging furnace.

"Hold! hold!" cried he, with a tremulous attempt to laugh; for he was ashamed of his fears, 30 although they overmastered him. "Don't, for mercy's sake, bring out your Devil now!"

"Man!" sternly replied Ethan Brand, "what need have I of the Devil? I have left him behind me, on my track. It is with such half-way sinners as you that he busies himself. Fear not, because I open the door. I do but act by old custom, and am going to trim your fire, like a lime-burner, as I was once."

He stirred the vast coals, thrust in more wood, 40 and bent forward to gaze into the hollow prison-house of the fire, regardless of the fierce glow that reddened upon his face. The lime-burner sat watching him, and half suspected this strange guest of a purpose, if not to evoke a fiend, at least to plunge bodily into the flames, and thus vanish from the sight of man. Ethan Brand, however, drew quietly back, and closed the door of the kiln.

"I have looked," said he, "into many a human heart that was seven times hotter with sinful passions than yonder furnace is with fire. But I found not there what I sought. No, not the Unpardonable Sin!"

"What is the Unpardonable Sin?" asked the lime-burner; and then he shrank farther from his companion, trembling lest his question should be answered.

"It is a sin that grew within my own breast," replied Ethan Brand, standing erect, with a pride that distinguishes all enthusiasts of his stamp. "A sin that grew nowhere else! The sin of an intellect that triumphed over the sense of brotherhood with man and reverence for God, and sacrificed everything to its own mighty claims! The only sin that deserves a recompense of immortal agony! Freely, were it to do again, would I incur the guilt. Unshrinkingly I accept the retribution!"

"The man's head is turned," muttered the lime-burner to himself. "He may be a sinner like the rest of us,—nothing more likely,—but, I'll be sworn, he is a madman too."

Nevertheless, he felt uncomfortable at his situation, alone with Ethan Brand on the wild mountain-side, and was right glad to hear the rough murmur of tongues, and the footsteps of what seemed a pretty numerous party, stumbling over the stones and rustling through the underbrush. Soon appeared the whole lazy regiment that was wont to infest the village tavern, comprehending three or four individuals who had drunk flip beside the bar-room fire through all the winters, and smoked their pipes beneath the stoop through all the summers, since Ethan Brand's departure. Laughing boisterously, and mingling all their voices together in unceremonious talk, they now burst into the moonshine and narrow streaks of firelight that illuminated the open space before the lime-kiln. Bartram set the door ajar again, flooding the spot with light, that the whole company might get a fair view of Ethan Brand, and he of them.

There, among other old acquaintances, was a once ubiquitous man, now almost extinct, but whom we were formerly sure to encounter at the hotel of every thriving village throughout the country. It was the stage-agent. The present specimen of the genus was a wilted and smoke-dried man, wrinkled and red-nosed, in a smartly cut, brown, bobtailed coat, with brass buttons, who, for a length of time unknown, had kept his desk and corner in the bar-room, and was still puffing what seemed to be the same cigar that he had lighted twenty years before. He had great fame as a dry joker, though, perhaps, less on account of any intrinsic humour than from a certain flavour of brandy-toddy and tobacco-smoke, which impreg- nated all his ideas and expressions, as well as his person. Another well-remembered, though strangely altered, face was that of Lawyer Giles, as people still called him in courtesy; an elderly ragamuffin, in his soiled shirt-sleeves and tow-cloth trousers. This poor fellow had been an at-torney, in what he called his better days, a sharp practitioner, and in great vogue among the village litigants; but flip, and sling, and toddy, and cock-tails, imbibed at all hours, morning, noon, and night, had caused him to slide from intellectual to various kinds and degrees of bodily labour, till at last, to adopt his own phrase, he slid into a soap-vat. In other words, Giles was now a soap-boiler, in a small way. He had come to be but the fragment of a human being, a part of one foot having been chopped off by an axe, and an entire hand torn away by the devilish gripe of a steam-engine. Yet, though the corporeal hand was gone, a spiritual member remained; for, stretching forth the stump, Giles steadfastly averred that he felt an invisible thumb and fingers with as vivid a sensation as before the real ones were amputated. A maimed and miserable wretch he was; but one, neverthe-less, whom the world could not trample on, and had no right to scorn, either in this or any previous stage of his misfortunes, since he had still kept up the courage and spirit of a man, asked nothing in charity, and with his one hand—and that the left one—fought a stern battle against want and hostile circumstances.

Among the throng, too, came another personage, who, with certain points of similarity to Lawyer Giles, had many more of difference. It was the village doctor; a man of some fifty years, whom, at an earlier period of his life, we introduced as paying a professional visit to Ethan Brand during the latter's supposed insanity. He was now a pur-ple-visaged, rude, and brutal, yet half-gentlemanly figure, with something wild, ruined, and desperate in his talk, and in all the details of his gesture and manners. Brandy possessed this man like an evil spirit, and made him as surly and savage as a wild beast, and as miserable as a lost soul; but there was supposed to be in him such wonderful skill, such native gifts of healing, beyond any which medical science could impart, that society caught hold of him, and would not let him sink out of its reach. So, swaying to and fro upon his horse, and grum-bling thick accents at the bedside, he visited all the sick-chambers for miles about among the moun-tain towns, and sometimes raised a dying man, as it were, by miracle, or quite as often, no doubt, sent his patient to a grave that was dug many a year too soon. The doctor had an everlasting pipe in his mouth, and, as somebody said, in allusion to his habit of swearing, it was always alight with hell-fire.

These three worthies pressed forward, and greeted Ethan Brand each after his own fashion, earnestly inviting him to partake of the contents of a certain black bottle, in which, as they averred, he would find something far better worth seeking for than the Unpardonable Sin. No mind, which has wrought itself by intense and solitary medita-tion into a high state of enthusiasm, can endure the kind of contact with low and vulgar modes of thought and feeling to which Ethan Brand was now subjected. It made him doubt—and, strange to say, it was a painful doubt—whether he had indeed found the Unpardonable Sin, and found it within himself. The whole question on which he had exhausted life, and more than life, looked like a delusion.

"Leave me," he said bitterly, "ye brute beasts, that have made yourselves so, shrivelling up your souls with fiery liquors! I have done with you. Years and years ago, I groped into your hearts and found nothing there for my purpose. Get ye gone!"

"Why, you uncivil scoundrel," cried the fierce doctor, "is that the way you respond to the kind-ness of your best friends? Then let me tell you the truth. You have no more found the Unpardonable Sin than yonder boy Joe has. You are but a crazy fellow,—I told you so twenty years ago,—neither better nor worse than a crazy fellow, and the fit companion of old Humphrey, here!"

He pointed to an old man, shabbily dressed, with long white hair, thin visage, and unsteady eyes. For some years past this aged person had been wandering about among the hills, inquiring of all travellers whom he met for his daughter. The girl, it seemed, had gone off with a company of circus-performers, and occasionally tidings of her came to the village, and fine stories were told of her glittering appearance as she rode on horseback in the ring, or performed marvellous feats on the tight-rope.

The white-haired father now approached Ethan Brand, and gazed unsteadily into his face.

"They tell me you have been all over the earth," said he, wringing his hands with earnestness. "You must have seen my daughter, for she makes a grand figure in the world, and everybody goes to see her. Did she send any word to her old father, or say when she was coming back?"

Ethan Brand's eye quailed beneath the old man's. That daughter, from whom he so earnestly desired a word of greeting, was the Esther of our tale, the very girl whom, with such cold and remorseless purpose, Ethan Brand had made the subject of a psychological experiment, and wasted, absorbed, and perhaps annihilated her soul, in the process.

"Yes," murmured he, turning away from the hoary wanderer, "it is no delusion. There is an Unpardonable Sin!"

While these things were passing, a merry scene was going forward in the area of cheerful light, beside the spring and before the door of the hut. A number of the youth of the village, young men and girls, had hurried up the hill-side, impelled by curiosity to see Ethan Brand, the hero of so many a legend familiar to their childhood. Finding nothing, however, very remarkable in his aspect,— nothing but a sunburnt wayfarer, in plain garb and dusty shoes, who sat looking into the fire as if he fancied pictures among the coals,—these young people speedily grew tired of observing him. As it happened, there was other amusement at hand. An old German Jew travelling with a diorama on his back, was passing down the mountain-road towards the village just as the party turned aside from it, and, in hopes of eking out the profits of the day, the showman had kept them company to the lime-kiln.

"Come, old Dutchman," cried one of the young men, "let us see your pictures, if you can swear they are worth looking at!"

"Oh, yes, Captain," answered the Jew,— whether as a matter of courtesy or craft, he styled everybody Captain,—"I shall show you, indeed, some very superb pictures!"

So, placing his box in a proper position, he invited the young men and girls to look through the glass orifices of the machine, and proceeded to exhibit a series of the most outrageous scratchings and daubings, as specimens of the fine arts, that ever an itinerant showman had the face to impose upon his circle of spectators. The pictures were worn out, moreover, tattered, full of cracks and wrinkles, dingy with tobacco-smoke, and otherwise in a most pitiable condition. Some purported to be cities, public edifices, and ruined castles in Europe; others represented Napoleon's battles and Nelson's sea-fights; and in the midst of these would be seen a gigantic, brown, hairy hand,—which might have been mistaken for the Hand of Destiny, though, in truth, it was only the showman's,—pointing its forefinger to various scenes of the conflict, while its owner gave historical illustrations. When, with much merriment at its abominable deficiency of merit, the exhibition was concluded, the German bade little Joe put his head into the box. Viewed through the magnifying-glasses, the boy's round, rosy visage assumed the strangest imaginable aspect of an immense Titanic child, the mouth grinning broadly, and the eyes and every other feature overflowing with fun at the joke. Suddenly, however, that merry face turned pale, and its expression changed to horror, for this easily impressed and excitable child had become sensible that the eye of Ethan Brand was fixed upon him through the glass.

"You make the little man to be afraid, Captain," said the German Jew, turning up the dark and strong outline of his visage from his stooping posture. "But look again, and, by chance, I shall cause you to see somewhat that is very fine, upon my word!"

Ethan Brand gazed into the box for an instant,

and then starting back, looked fixedly at the German. What had he seen? Nothing, apparently; for a curious youth, who had peeped in almost at the same moment, beheld only a vacant space of canvas.

"I remember you now," muttered Ethan Brand to the showman.

"Ah, Captain," whispered the Jew of Nuremburg, with a dark smile, "I find it to be a heavy matter in my show-box,—this Unpardonable Sin! By my faith, Captain, it has wearied my shoulders, this long day, to carry it over the mountain."

"Peace," answered Ethan Brand, sternly, "or get thee into the furnace yonder!"

The Jew's exhibition had scarcely concluded, when a great, elderly dog—who seemed to be his own master, as no person in the company laid claim to him—saw fit to render himself the object of public notice. Hitherto, he had shown himself a very quiet, well-disposed old dog, going round from one to another, and, by way of being sociable, offering his rough head to be patted by any kindly hand that would take so much trouble. But now, all of a sudden, this grave and venerable quadruped, of his own mere motion, and without the slightest suggestion from anybody else, began to run round after his tail, which, to heighten the absurdity of the proceeding, was a great deal shorter than it should have been. Never was seen such headlong eagerness in pursuit of an object that could not possibly be attained; never was heard such a tremendous outbreak of growling, snarling, barking, and snapping,—as if one end of the ridiculous brute's body were at deadly and most unforgivable enmity with the other. Faster and faster, round about went the cur; and faster and still faster fled the unapproachable brevity of his tail; and louder and fiercer grew his yells of rage and animosity; until, utterly exhausted, and as far from the goal as ever, the foolish old dog ceased his performance as suddenly as he had begun it. The next moment he was as mild, quiet, sensible, and respectable in his deportment, as when he first scraped acquaintance with the company.

As may be supposed, the exhibition was greeted with universal laughter, clapping of hands, and shouts of encore, to which the canine performer responded by wagging all that there was to wag of his tail, but appeared totally unable to repeat his very successful effort to amuse the spectators.

Meanwhile, Ethan Brand had resumed his seat upon the log, and moved, it might be, by a perception of some remote analogy between his own case and that of this self-pursuing cur, he broke into the awful laugh, which, more than any other token, expressed the condition of his inward being. From that moment, the merriment of the party was at an end; they stood aghast, dreading lest the inauspicious sound should be reverberated around the horizon, and that mountain would thunder it to mountain, and so the horror be prolonged upon their ears. Then, whispering one to another that it was late,—that the moon was almost down,— that the August night was growing chill,—they hurried homewards, leaving the lime-burner and little Joe to deal as they might with their unwelcome guest. Save for these three human beings, the open space on the hill-side was a solitude, set in a vast gloom of forest. Beyond that darksome verge, the firelight glimmered on the stately trunks and almost black foliage of pines, intermixed with the lighter verdure of sapling oaks, maples, and poplars, while here and there lay the gigantic corpses of dead trees, decaying on the leaf-strewn soil. And it seemed to little Joe—a timorous and imaginative child—that the silent forest was holding its breath until some fearful thing should happen.

Ethan Brand thrust more wood into the fire, and closed the door of the kiln; then looking over his shoulder at the lime-burner and his son, he bade, rather than advised, them to retire to rest.

"For myself, I cannot sleep," said he. "I have matters that it concerns me to meditate upon. I will watch the fire, as I used to do in the old time."

"And call the Devil out of the furnace to keep you company, I suppose," muttered Bartram, who had been making intimate acquaintance with the black bottle above mentioned. "But watch, if you like, and call as many devils as you like! For my part, I shall be all the better for a snooze. Come, Joe!"

As the boy followed his father into the hut, he looked back at the wayfarer, and the tears came into his eyes, for his tender spirit had an intuition of the bleak and terrible loneliness in which this man had enveloped himself.

When they had gone, Ethan Brand sat listening to the crackling of the kindled wood, and looking at the little spirits of fire that issued through the chinks of the door. These trifles, however, once so familiar, had but the slightest hold of his attention, while deep within his mind he was reviewing the gradual but marvellous change that had been wrought upon him by the search to which he had devoted himself. He remembered how the night dew had fallen upon him,—how the dark forest had whispered to him,—how the stars had gleamed upon him,—a simple and loving man, watching his fire in the years gone by, and ever musing as it burned. He remembered with what tenderness, with what love and sympathy for mankind, and what pity for human guilt and woe, he had first begun to contemplate those ideas which afterwards became the inspiration of his life; with what reverence he had then looked into the heart of man, viewing it as a temple originally divine, and, however desecrated, still to be held sacred by a brother; with what awful fear he had deprecated the success of his pursuit, and prayed that the Unpardonable Sin might never be revealed to him. Then ensued that vast intellectual development, which, in its progress, disturbed the counterpoise between his mind and heart. The Idea that possessed his life had operated as a means of education; it had gone on cultivating his powers to the highest point of which they were susceptible; it had raised him from the level of an unlettered labourer to stand on a star-lit eminence, whither the philosophers of the earth, laden with the lore of universities, might vainly strive to clamber after him. So much for the intellect! But where was the heart? That, indeed, had withered,—had contracted,—had hardened,—had perished! It had ceased to partake of the universal throb. He had lost his hold of the magnetic chain of humanity. He was no longer a brother-man, opening the chambers or the dungeons of our common nature by the key of holy sympathy, which gave him a right to share in all its secrets; he was now a cold observer, looking on mankind as the subject of his experiment, and, at length, converting man and woman to be his puppets, and pulling the wires that moved them to such degrees of crime as were demanded for his study.

Thus Ethan Brand became a fiend. He began to be so from the moment that his moral nature had ceased to keep the pace of improvement with his intellect. And now, as his highest effort and inevitable development,—as the bright and gorgeous flower, and rich, delicious fruit of his life's labour,—he had produced the Unpardonable Sin!

"What more have I to seek? what more to achieve?" said Ethan Brand to himself. "My task is done, and well done!"

Starting from the log with a certain alacrity in his gait and ascending the hillock of earth that was raised against the stone circumference of the lime-kiln, he thus reached the top of the structure. It was a space of perhaps ten feet across, from edge to edge, presenting a view of the upper surface of the immense mass of broken marble with which the kiln was heaped. All these innumerable blocks and fragments of marble were red-hot and vividly on fire, sending up great spouts of blue flame, which quivered aloft and danced madly, as within a magic circle, and sank and rose again, with continual and multitudinous activity. As the lonely man bent forward over this terrible body of fire, the blasting heat smote up against his person with a breath that, it might be supposed, would have scorched and shrivelled him up in a moment.

Ethan Brand stood erect, and raised his arms on high. The blue flames played upon his face, and imparted the wild and ghastly light which alone could have suited its expression; it was that of a fiend on the verge of plunging into his gulf of intensest torment.

"O Mother Earth," cried he, "who art no more my Mother, and into whose bosom this frame shall never be resolved! O mankind, whose brotherhood I have cast off, and trampled thy great heart beneath my feet! O stars of heaven, that shone on me of old, as if to light me onward and upward! —farewell all, and forever. Come, deadly element of Fire,—henceforth my familiar friend! Embrace me, as I do thee!"

That night the sound of a fearful peal of laughter rolled heavily through the sleep of the lime-burner and his little son; dim shapes of horror and anguish haunted their dreams, and seemed still present in the rude hovel, when they opened their eyes to the daylight.

"Up, boy, up!" cried the lime-burner, staring about him. "Thank Heaven, the night is gone, at last; and rather than pass such another, I would watch my lime-kiln, wide awake, for a twelvemonth. This Ethan Brand, with his humbug of an Unpardonable Sin, has done me no such mighty favour, in taking my place!"

He issued from the hut, followed by little Joe, who kept fast hold of his father's hand. The early sunshine was already pouring its gold upon the mountain-tops, and though the valleys were still in shadow, they smiled cheerfully in the promise of the bright day that was hastening onward. The village, completely shut in by hills, which swelled away gently about it, looked as if it had rested peacefully in the hollow of the great hand of Providence. Every dwelling was distinctly visible; the little spires of the two churches pointed upwards, and caught a fore-glimmering of brightness from the sun-gilt skies upon their gilded weathercocks. The tavern was astir, and the figure of the old, smoke-dried stage-agent, cigar in mouth, was seen beneath the stoop. Old Graylock was glorified with a golden cloud upon his head. Scattered likewise over the breasts of the surrounding mountains, there were heaps of hoary mist, in fantastic shapes, some of them far down into the valley, others high up towards the summits, and still others, of the same family of mist or cloud, hovering in the gold radiance of the upper atmosphere. Stepping from one to another of the clouds that rested on the hills, and thence to the loftier brotherhood that sailed in air, it seemed almost as if a mortal man might thus ascend into the heavenly regions. Earth was so mingled with sky that it was a day-dream to look at it.

To supply that charm of the familiar and homely, which Nature so readily adopts into a scene like this, the stage-coach was rattling down the mountain-road, and the driver sounded his horn, while Echo caught up the notes, and intertwined them into a rich and varied and elaborate harmony, of which the original performer could lay claim to little share. The great hills played a concert among themselves, each contributing a strain of airy sweetness.

Little Joe's face brightened at once.

"Dear father," cried he, skipping cheerily to and fro, "that strange man is gone, and the sky and the mountains all seem glad of it!"

"Yes," growled the lime-burner, with an oath, "but he has let the fire go down, and no thanks to him if five hundred bushels of lime are not spoiled. If I catch the fellow hereabouts again, I shall feel like tossing him into the furnace!"

With his long pole in his hand, he ascended to the top of the kiln. After a moment's pause, he called to his son.

"Come up here, Joe!" said he.

So little Joe ran up the hillock, and stood by his father's side. The marble was all burnt into perfect, snow-white lime. But on its surface, in the midst of the circle,—snow-white too, and thoroughly converted into lime,—lay a human skeleton, in the attitude of a person who, after long toil, lies down to long repose. Within the ribs—strange to say—was the shape of a human heart.

"Was the fellow's heart made of marble?" cried Bartram, in some perplexity at this phenomenon. "At any rate, it is burnt into what looks like special good lime; and, taking all the bones together, my kiln is half a bushel the richer for him."

So saying, the rude lime-burner lifted his pole, and, letting it fall upon the skeleton, the relics of Ethan Brand were crumbled into fragments.

Preface to The House of the Seven Gables

WHEN HAWTHORNE WROTE that *The House of the Seven Gables* was "a Romance, having a great deal more to do with the clouds overhead than with any portion of the actual soil of the County of Essex," he doubtless had in mind the recriminations aroused by his prefatory essay on the Custom House at Salem in *The Scarlet Letter* (1850). His preference for the latitude afforded by the Romance, the privilege of mellowing the lights and deepening the shadows of his story, arose from his desire to depict those inner truths and deeper mysteries which often lie beneath surface reality. The text is from the edition of 1883.

When a writer calls his work a Romance, it need hardly be observed that he wishes to claim a certain latitude, both as to its fashion and material, which he would not have felt himself entitled to assume had he professed to be writing a Novel. The latter form of composition is presumed to aim at a very minute fidelity, not merely to the possible, but to the probable and ordinary course of man's experience. The former—while, as a work of art, it must rigidly subject itself to laws, and while it sins unpardonably so far as it may swerve aside from the truth of the human heart— has fairly a right to present that truth under circumstances, to a great extent, of the writer's own choosing or creation. If he think fit, also, he may so manage his atmospherical medium as to bring out or mellow the lights and deepen and enrich the shadows of the picture. He will be wise, no doubt, to make a very moderate use of the privileges here stated, and, especially, to mingle the Marvellous rather as a slight, delicate, and evanescent flavor, than as any portion of the actual substance of the dish offered to the public. He can hardly be said, however, to commit a literary crime even if he disregard this caution.

In the present work, the author has proposed to himself—but with what success, fortunately, it is not for him to judge—to keep undeviatingly within his immunities. The point of view in which this tale comes under the Romantic definition lies in the attempt to connect a bygone time with the very present that is flitting away from us. It is a legend prolonging itself, from an epoch now gray in the distance, down into our own broad daylight, and bringing along with it some of its legendary mist, which the reader, according to his pleasure, may either disregard, or allow it to float almost imperceptibly about the characters and events for the sake of a picturesque effect. The narrative, it may be, is woven of so humble a texture as to require this advantage, and, at the same time, to render it the more difficult of attainment.

Many writers lay very great stress upon some definite moral purpose, at which they profess to aim their works. Not to be deficient in this particular, the author has provided himself with a moral,—the truth, namely, that the wrong-doing of one generation lives into the successive ones, and divesting itself of every temporary advantage, becomes a pure and uncontrollable mischief; and he would feel it a singular gratification if this ro-

mance might effectually convince mankind—or, indeed, any one man—of the folly of tumbling down an avalanche of ill-gotten gold, or real estate, on the heads of an unfortunate posterity, thereby to maim and crush them, until the accumulated mass shall be scattered abroad in its original atoms. In good faith, however, he is not sufficiently imaginative to flatter himself with the slightest hope of this kind. When romances do really teach anything, or produce any effective operation, it is usually through a far more subtle process than the ostensible one. The author has considered it hardly worth his while, therefore, relentlessly to impale the story with its moral as with an iron rod,—or, rather, as by sticking a pin through a butterfly,—thus at once depriving it of life, and causing it to stiffen in an ungainly and unnatural attitude. A high truth, indeed, fairly, finely, and skilfully wrought out, brightening at every step, and crowning the final development of a work of fiction, may add an artistic glory, but is never any truer, and seldom any more evident, at the last page than at the first.

The reader may perhaps choose to assign an actual locality to the imaginary events of this narrative. If permitted by the historical connection,—which, though slight, was essential to his plan,—the author would very willingly have avoided anything of this nature. Not to speak of other objections, it exposes the romance to an inflexible and exceedingly dangerous species of criticism, by bringing his fancy-pictures almost into positive contact with the realities of the moment. It has been no part of his object, however, to describe local manners, nor in any way to meddle with the characteristics of a community for whom he cherishes a proper respect and a natural regard. He trusts not to be considered as unpardonably offending by laying out a street that infringes upon nobody's private rights, and appropriating a lot of land which had no visible owner, and building a house of materials long in use for constructing castles in the air. The personages of the tale—though they give themselves out to be of ancient stability and considerable prominence— are really of the author's own making, or, at all events, of his own mixing; their virtues can shed no lustre, nor their defects redound, in the remotest degree, to the discredit of the venerable town of which they profess to be inhabitants. He would be glad, therefore, if—especially in the quarter to which he alludes—the book may be read strictly as a Romance, having a great deal more to do with the clouds overhead than with any portion of the actual soil of the County of Essex.

Lenox, January 27, 1851.

Our Old Home

[*English Scenery*]

HUNDREDS OF BOOKS on travel and life in foreign lands were written in America during the nineteenth century. This example from *Our Old Home*, in the chapter "Recollections of a Gifted Woman," is indicative of Hawthorne's love of scenery. The book was first published in 1863, and attained to a third edition in 1864, from which this text is taken.

From Leamington to Stratford-on-Avon the distance is eight or nine miles, over a road that seemed to me most beautiful. Not that I can recall any memorable peculiarities; for the country, most of the way, is a succession of the gentlest swells and subsidences, affording wide and far glimpses of champaign scenery here and there, and sinking almost to a dead level as we draw near Stratford. Any landscape in New England, even the tamest, has a more striking outline, and besides, would have its blue eyes open in those lakelets that we encounter almost from mile to mile at home, but of which the Old Country is utterly destitute; or it would smile in our faces through the medium of the wayside brooks that vanish under a low stone arch on one side of the road, and sparkle out again on the other. Neither of these pretty features is often to be found in an English scene. The charm of the latter consists in the rich verdure of the fields, in the stately wayside trees and carefully kept plantations of wood, and in the old and high cultivation that has humanized the very sods by mingling so much of man's toil and care among them. To an American there is a kind of sanctity even in an English turnip-field, when he thinks how long that small square of ground has been known and recognized as a possession, transmitted from father to son, trodden often by memorable feet, and utterly redeemed from savagery by old acquaintanceship with civilized eyes. The wildest things in England are more than half tame. The trees, for instance, whether in hedge-row, park, or what they call forest, have nothing wild about them. They are never ragged; there is a certain decorous restraint in the freest outspread of their branches, though they spread wider than any self-nurturing tree; they are tall, vigorous, bulky, with a look of age-long life, and a promise of more years to come, all of which will bring them into closer kindred with the race of man. Somebody or other has known them from the sapling upward; and if they endure long enough, they grow to be traditionally observed and honored, and connected with the fortunes of old families, till, like Tennyson's Talking Oak, they babble with a thousand leafy tongues to ears that can understand them.

An American tree, however, if it could grow in fair competition with an English one of similar species, would probably be the more picturesque object of the two. The Warwickshire elm has not so beautiful a shape as those that overhang our village street; and as for the redoubtable English oak, there is a certain John Bullism in its figure, a compact rotundity of foliage, a lack of irregular and various outline, that make it look wonderfully like a gigantic cauliflower. Its leaf, too, is much smaller than that of most varieties of American oak; nor do I mean to doubt that the latter, with free leave to grow, reverent care and cultivation, and immunity from the axe, would live out its centuries as sturdily as its English brother, and prove far the nobler and more majestic specimen of a tree at the end of them. Still, however one's Yankee patriotism may struggle against the admission, it must be owned that the trees and other objects of an English landscape take hold of the observer by numberless minute tendrils, as it were, which, look as closely as we choose, we never find in an American scene. The parasitic growth is so luxuriant, that the trunk of the tree, so gray and dry in our climate, is better worth observing than the boughs and foliage; a verdant mossiness coats it all over; so that it looks almost as green as the leaves; and often, moreover, the stately stem is clustered about, high upward, with creeping and twining shrubs, the ivy, and sometimes the mistletoe, close-clinging friends, nurtured by the moisture and never too fervid sunshine, and supporting themselves by the old tree's abundant strength. We call it a parasitical vegetation; but, if the phrase imply any reproach, it is unkind to bestow it on this beautiful affection and relationship which exist in England between one order of plants and another: the strong tree being always ready to give support to the trailing shrub, lift it to the sun, and feed it out of its own heart, if it 10 crave such food; and the shrub, on its part, repaying its foster-father with an ample luxuriance of beauty, and adding Corinthian grace to the tree's lofty strength. No bitter winter nips these tender little sympathies, no hot sun burns the life out of them; and therefore they outlast the longevity of the oak, and, if the woodman permitted, would bury it in a green grave, when all is over.

Should there be nothing else along the road to look at, an English hedge might well suffice to 20 occupy the eyes, and, to a depth beyond what he would suppose, the heart of an American. We often set out hedges in our own soil, but might as well set out figs or pineapples and expect to gather fruit of them. Something grows, to be sure, which we choose to call a hedge; but it lacks the dense, luxuriant variety of vegetation that is accumulated into the English original, in which a botanist would find a thousand shrubs and gracious herbs that the hedgemaker never thought of planting there. 30 Among them, growing wild, are many of the kindred blossoms of the very flowers which our pilgrim fathers brought from England, for the sake of their simple beauty and home-like associations, and which we have ever since been cultivating in gardens. There is not a softer trait to be found in the character of those stern men than that they should have been sensible of these flower-roots clinging among the fibres of their rugged hearts, and have felt the necessity of bringing them over 40 seas and making them hereditary in the new land, instead of trusting to what rarer beauty the wilderness might have in store for them.

Or, if the roadside has no hedge, the ugliest stone fence (such as, in America, would keep itself bare and unsympathizing till the end of time) is sure to be covered with the small handiwork of Nature; that careful mother lets nothing go naked there, and, if she cannot provide clothing, gives at least embroidery. No sooner is the fence built than she adopts and adorns it as a part of her original plan, treating the hard, uncomely construction as if it had all along been a favorite idea of her own. A little sprig of ivy may be seen creeping up the side of the low wall and clinging fast with its many feet to the rough surface; a tuft of grass roots itself between two of the stones, where a pinch or two of wayside dust has been moistened into nutritious soil for it; a small bunch of fern grows in another crevice; a deep, soft, verdant moss spreads itself along the top, and over all the available inequalities of the fence; and where nothing else will grow, lichens stick tenaciously to the bare stones, and variegate the monotonous gray with hues of yellow and red. Finally, a great deal of shrubbery clusters along the base of the stone wall, and takes away the hardness of its outline; and in due time, as the upshot of these apparently aimless or sportive touches, we recognize that the beneficent Creator of all things, working through his hand-maiden whom we call Nature, has deigned to mingle a charm of divine gracefulness even with so earthly an institution as a boundary fence. The clown who wrought at it little dreamed what fellow-laborer he had.

The English should send us photographs of portions of the trunks of trees, the tangled and various products of a hedge, and a square foot of an old wall. They can hardly send anything else so characteristic. Their artists, especially of the later school, sometimes toil to depict such subjects, but are apt to stiffen the lithe tendrils in the process. The poets succeed better, with Tennyson at their head, and often produce ravishing effects by dint of a tender minuteness of touch, to which the genius of the soil and climate artfully impels them: for, as regards grandeur, there are loftier scenes in many countries than the best that England can show; but, for the picturesqueness of the smallest object that lies under its gentle gloom and sunshine, there is no scenery like it anywhere. . . .

RALPH WALDO EMERSON (1803–1882)

"Be an opener of doors for such as come after thee." This counsel of Emerson's is abundantly fulfilled by his own writings, which open wide doors on much that is exciting and important in American thought. The passing of time has diminished the stature of many of his contemporaries, but Ralph Waldo Emerson still speaks with serene authority as one of the emancipators of the mind and spirit of man. He wrote in a period of acquisitive materialism when, as he put it in his *Ode* to Channing,

> Things are in the saddle,
> And ride mankind.

"This invasion of Nature by Trade," he noted in his Journal, "with its Money, its Credit, its Steam, its Railroads, threatens to upset the balance of man, and establish a new, universal Monarchy. . . ." Emerson, however, was not blind to the difference between "law for man" and "law for thing." For him, man was still king. Today, when a new mastery of "law for thing" is threatening to make modern man obsolete, Emerson's favorite doctrine of "the infinitude of the private man" sounds forth as a challenge and a prophecy.

Emerson was born in Boston on May 25, 1803, the descendant of a long line of ministers, an ancestry which Dr. Holmes was later to call "the Brahmin caste of New England," whose names are always on some college catalogue or other. Ralph Waldo was only seven years old when his father, the minister of the First Church, Boston, died in 1811. After four years at Boston Latin School (1813–1817), where he was remembered by a schoolmate as a "spiritual looking boy in blue nankeen," Emerson entered Harvard. He defrayed part of his college expenses by serving as a messenger for the president and by waiting on tables at the commons. In his junior year he began his lifelong habit of keeping a journal, and was graduated in 1821, the thirtieth in a class of fifty-nine members. For four years after his graduation (1821–1825), he taught school in Boston to help pay for the education of his brothers and to provide means for his own study at the Harvard Divinity School. He was licensed to preach, October 10, 1826, but ill health compelled him to spend the winter of 1826–1827 in South Carolina and Florida. After filling various pulpits in Cambridge and elsewhere, Emerson became associate pastor of the Second Church (Unitarian) of Boston in 1829, the year of his marriage to Ellen Tucker. In 1832 he resigned his pastorate because of his reluctance to administer the Lord's Supper. "It is my desire," he said in his farewell sermon, "in the office of a Christian minister, to do nothing which I cannot do with my whole heart." The anguish caused by his resignation and the profound shock of the loss of his wife, who died in 1831, undermined Emerson's health. He sailed for Europe in December, 1832.

Emerson's pilgrimage through Italy, France, and Great Britain differed sharply from the romantic tours made by Irving and Longfellow. He talked with Landor, Wordsworth, Coleridge, and Carlyle, absorbing ideas rather than atmosphere, and finding sanction for his own intuitions in German idealistic philosophy. His memorable visit with Carlyle began an inspiring friendship which bore fruit in a notable exchange of letters (1834–1872). Returning to Massachusetts in 1833, Emerson made his home in Concord in the following year, a town which his ancestors had helped to settle and the scene of the ministry of his grandfather who had built the Old Manse; in 1835 he married Lydia Jackson, and moved into the house which was to be his home for the rest of his life. He supplied various pulpits for several years, and welcomed the recently established Lyceum movement as an opportunity to make the nation his congregation. Emerson's fame as a speaker grew rapidly, especially after the delivery of his epochal Phi Beta Kappa address, "The American Scholar," at Cambridge, on August 31, 1837. Lecture fees from engagements in all sections of the country augmented the income he received from the estate of his first wife. The generous offers, he noted in his Journal, were tantamount to this: " 'I'll bet you fifty dollars a day that you will not leave your library, and wade and ride and run and suffer all manner of indignities and stand up for an hour each night reading in a hall'; and I answered, 'I'll bet I will.' "

The first appearance of Emerson as a lecturer preceded his emergence as an author, which was marked by the publication in Boston in 1836 of *Nature*, an essay largely made up of gleanings from his Journals and lecture notes. Although the ideas in *Nature* lack the clear articulation and grave eloquence which make memorable "The American Scholar," they established their author as the leader of the transcendental philosophy. Some of the ideas derive from the elder Channing and other thinkers in New England; Emerson also drew upon the idealism of Plato, the thought of the German philosophers of the eighteenth century, the writings of Wordsworth, Coleridge, Carlyle, and Swedenborg, and the mystical elements in the work of Jonathan Edwards.

Emerson's position as chief spokesman of the transcendentalists was confirmed by the publication of his *Essays, First Series* (1841), and *Essays, Second Series* (1844). Meanwhile, from 1842 to 1844, he edited *The Dial*, a quarterly designed to provide an avenue of expression for those who were drawn together by their belief in the infallibility of intuition. In the four years of its existence (1840–1844) *The Dial* introduced Thoreau to the reading public as essayist and poet, included some of Emerson's best poems (among them "The Sphinx" and "Ode to Beauty"), carried important articles by Margaret Fuller and Theodore Parker, and became the medium for ideas of the young idealists and reformers. In 1847 Emerson made a second visit to Europe and published *Poems*, his first volume of verse. Upon his return he continued his career as a lecturer, publishing some of his discourses in *Representative Men* (1850). His penetrating reflections on English life and character are contained in *English Traits* (1856). For other volumes, *The Conduct of Life* (1860), *Society and Solitude* (1870), and *Letters and Social Aims* (1876), he drew upon the materials of his lectures. Entries in the Journals after 1850 reveal a growing preoccupation with political issues. "The word *liberty* in the mouth of Mr. Webster," he wrote after the Seventh of March Speech in 1851, "sounds like the word *love* in the mouth of a courtezan." Of the "filthy" Fugitive Slave Law he exclaimed, "I will not obey it, by God." The poem, "Terminus," written in 1866, reveals the author's awareness of his declining intellectual powers. In 1872 he made his last trip abroad, returning in 1873 after a journey which carried him as far as the Nile. He died in Concord on April 27, 1882.

Emerson belongs among the greatest American writers. Hailed by Matthew Arnold as "the friend and aider of those who would live in the spirit," he is the embodiment of the idealism and the revolt against external authority (which stem from Jonathan Edwards) and the mystical strain in the Puritan heritage. As a seer and a mystic, and as the champion of "Man Thinking," Emerson has too often been represented as a bloodless symbol. We need Bliss Perry's illuminating reminder that Emerson's face was not only that of a seer, but also the face of a shrewd village Yankee. He was not a disembodied spirit without roots deep in the American soil. In his own day when public and private avarice made the air "thick and fat," Emerson fought stoutly for moral and spiritual values. He allied himself with the abolitionists, he denounced Webster's stand on the Fugitive Slave Law, and he opposed vigorously the complacency and mediocrity of the prevailing materialism of contemporary society.

Emerson's verbal artistry is now beginning to receive proper consideration. His mastery of the compact line, his instinct for the startling image, his refusal to dilute his meaning—H. W. Garrod has called Emerson an incomparable "word-catcher"—these elements in his work anticipate many constituents of the "new" poetry of the twentieth century. It must be conceded that Emerson's optimism and his insistence that goodness is the only reality seem unconvincing to many readers today. Yet Emerson still speaks with authority in his quest for spiritual perfection because he never lost sight of the individual whose self-liberation and self-mastery are essential for personal and social salvation. When Emerson wrote in his Journals, "He is my friend who makes me do what I can," he defined his relationship to countless readers in his time and ours by renewing their confidence in themselves in periods of stress, and by giving them direction and awakening their powers.

BIBLIOGRAPHY · The standard text is that of the Centenary Edition, *The Complete Works of Ralph Waldo Emerson* (12 vols., 1903–1921), with a biographical introduction and notes by Emerson's son, E. W. Emerson. Other texts include *Emerson's Complete Works*, issued as the Riverside Edition (12 vols., 1883–1893), edited by J. E. Cabot, and reprinted as the Standard Library Edition (1894). Volume IX (1884), Riverside Edition, printed the poems and is the text for the following poetical selections. The Centenary Edition was issued also as the Concord Edition (1904), and as the Autograph Centenary Edition (1905). E. W. Emerson and W. E. Forbes edited Emerson's *Journals* (10 vols., 1909–1914) from which Bliss Perry made a discriminating selection, *The Heart of Emerson's Journals* (1926). For other writings, see *The Uncollected Writings: Essays, Poems, Reviews, and Letters by Ralph Waldo Emerson*, edited by C. Bigelow (1912); and *Uncollected Lectures by Ralph Waldo Emerson* . . . , edited by C. L. F. Gohdes (1932). Certain hitherto unpublished discourses are contained in *Young Emerson Speaks*, edited by A. C. McGiffert (1938). Of Emerson's correspondence, more than two hundred letters appear in *The Correspondence of Thomas Carlyle and Ralph Waldo Emerson, 1834–1872*, edited by C. E. Norton (2 vols., 1888); *A Correspondence between John Sterling and Ralph Waldo Emerson*, edited by E. W. Emerson (1897); *Letters from Ralph Waldo Emerson to a Friend*, edited by C. E. Norton (1899); "Correspondence between Ralph Waldo Emerson and Herman Grimm," edited by F. W. Holls in *Atlantic Monthly*, XCI (1903), 467–479; *Records of a Lifelong Friendship*, edited by H. H. Furness (1910); and *Emerson-Clough Letters*, edited by H. F. Lowry and R. L. Rusk (1934). R. L. Rusk's monumental *Letters of Ralph Waldo Emerson* (6 vols., 1939) contain new letters and others that hitherto had been printed in fragmentary form. There are many books of selections, among which may be mentioned *The Complete Essays and Other Writings*, edited by B. Atkinson (1940); *Ralph Waldo Emerson: Representative Selections*, edited by F. I. Carpenter (1934); *The Heart of Emerson's Essays*, edited by B. Perry (1933); and *The Portable Emerson*, edited by M. Van Doren (1946). The bibliography compiled by G. W. Cooke, *A Bibliography of Ralph Waldo Emerson* (1908) needs to be supplemented by that of H. R. Steeves in the *Cambridge History of American Literature*, I (1917); and L. Leary, *Articles on American Literature*. . . . (1947), 49–57. G. S. Hubbell compiled a useful reference book, *A Concordance to the Poems . . .* (1932).

The definitive biography is that by R. L. Rusk, *The Life of Ralph Waldo Emerson* (1949). Valuable biographical studies include J. E. Cabot, *A Memoir of Ralph Waldo Emerson* (2 vols., 1887); G. W. Cooke, *Ralph Waldo Emerson* (1881); M. Dugard, *Ralph Waldo Emerson, sa Vie et son Œuvre* (1907); E. W. Emerson, *Emerson in Concord* (1888); O. W. Firkins, *Ralph Waldo Emerson* (1915); O. W. Holmes, *Ralph Waldo Emerson* (1885); A. Ireland, *Ralph Waldo Emerson* (1882); D. G. Haskins, *Ralph Waldo Emerson: His Maternal Ancestors* (1887); C. J. Woodbury, *Talks with Ralph Waldo Emerson* (1890); and G. E. Woodberry, *Ralph Waldo Emerson* (1907). The best of the later popular lives include Van Wyck Brooks, *The Life of Emerson* (1932); R. Michaud, *Emerson: the Enraptured Yankee* (1930); and P. Russell, *Emerson: the Wisest American* (1929).

The following critical studies are among those affording valuable intellectual and social backgrounds for a reading of Emerson: J. T. Adams, "Emerson Re-read," *Atlantic Monthly*, CXLVI (1930), 484–492; M. Arnold, *Discourses in America* (1885); C. Baker, "Emerson and Jones Very," *New England Quarterly*, VII (1934), 90–99; W. Blair and C. Faust, "Emerson's Literary Method," *Modern Philology*, XLII (1944), 79–95; W. Braswell, "Melville as a Critic of Emerson," *American Literature*, IX (1937), 317–334; S. G. Brown, "Emerson's Platonism," *New England Quarterly*, XVIII (1945), 325–345; W. C. Brownell, *American Prose Masters* (1909), 131–204; F. I. Carpenter, *Emerson and Asia* (1930); A. E. Christy, *The Orient in American Transcendentalism* (1932); H. H. Clark, "Emerson and Science," *Philological Quarterly*, X (1931), 225–260; H. S. Commager, "Tempest in a Boston Tea Cup," *New England Quarterly*, VI (1933), 651–675; R. P. Falk, "Emerson and Shakespeare," PMLA, LVI (1941), 523–543; N. Foerster, *Nature in American Literature* (1923); C. H. Foster, "Emerson as American Scripture," *New England Quarterly*, XVI (1943), 91–105; H. C. Goddard, *Studies in New England Transcendentalism* (1908); C. L. F. Gohdes, "Some Remarks on Emerson's Divinity School Address," *American Literature*, I (1929), 27–31; H. H. Hoeltje, "Emerson, Citizen of Concord," *American Literature*, XI (1940), 367–378, and *Sheltering Tree: A Story of the*

Friendship of Ralph Waldo Emerson and Bronson Alcott (1943); L. Hotson, "Emerson and the Swedenborgians," *Studies in Philology*, XXVII (1930), 517–545; H. Hummel, "Emerson and Nietzsche," *New England Quarterly*, XIX (1946), 63–84; A. C. Kern, "Emerson and Economics," *New England Quarterly*, XIII (1940), 678–696; K. A. McEwen, "Emerson's Rhymes," *American Literature*, XX (1948), 31–42; E. Marchand, "Emerson and the Frontier," *American Literature*, III (1931), 149–175; B. Perry, "Emerson's Most Famous Speech," *The Praise of Folly* (1923), 81–113; and *Emerson Today* (1931); R. Michaud, *L'Esthetique d'Emerson* (1927); L. N. Richardson, "What Rutherford B. Hayes Liked in Emerson," *American Literature*, XVII (1945), 22–32; F. B. Sanborn, ed., *The Genius and Character of Emerson* (1885); T. Scudder, 3rd, "A Chronological List of Emerson's Lectures on His British Tour of 1847–1848," PMLA, LI (1936), 243–248; F. T. Thompson, "Emerson and Carlyle," *Studies in Philology*, XXIV (1927), 438–453; "Emerson's Indebtedness to Coleridge," *Studies in Philology*, XXIII (1926), 44–76; and "Emerson's Theory and Practice of Poetry," PMLA, XLIII (1928), 1170–1184; F. B. Tolles, "Emerson and Quakerism," *American Literature*, X (1938), 142–165; H. R. Warfel, "Margaret Fuller and Ralph Waldo Emerson," PMLA, L (1935), 576–594; R. Wellek, "Emerson and German Philosophy," *New England Quarterly*, XVI (1943), 41–62; and J. D. Yohannan, "Emerson's Translations of Persian Poetry from German Sources," *American Literature*, XIV (1943), 407–420; and "The Influence of Persian Poetry on Emerson's Work," *American Literature*, XV (1943), 25–41.

Written in Naples, March, 1833

EMERSON's first wife, Ellen Tucker, died in 1831, and in 1832 he resigned his charge at the Second Church (Unitarian), Boston, on doctrinal grounds. Ill, and disturbed in mind, he determined to take a sea voyage to Italy in December, 1833, and left Boston harbor on Christmas day. Published first in *Poems* (1847).

We are what we are made; each following day
Is the Creator of our human mould
Not less than was the first; the all-wise God
Gilds a few points in every several life,
And as each flower upon the fresh hill-side,   5
And every colored petal of each flower,
Is sketched and dyed each with a new design,
Its spot of purple, and its streak of brown,
So each man's life shall have its proper lights,
And a few joys, a few peculiar charms,   10
For him round—in the melancholy hours
And reconcile him to the common days.

Not many men see beauty in the fogs
Of close low pine-woods in a river town;
Yet unto me not morn's magnificence,   15
Nor the red rainbow of a summer eve,
Nor Rome, nor joyful Paris, nor the halls
Of rich men blazing hospitable light,
Nor wit, nor eloquence,—no, nor even the song
Of any woman that is now alive,—   20
Hath such a soul, such divine influence,
Such resurrection of the happy past,
As is to me when I behold the morn
Ope in such low moist road-side, and beneath
Peep the blue violets out of the black loam,   25
Pathetic silent poets that sing to me
Thine elegy, sweet singer, sainted wife.

Concord Hymn

*Sung at the Completion of the Battle Monument,
April 19, 1836*

ON THE EVENING of April 18, 1775 General Gage dispatched about 700 British regulars from Boston to
Concord to seize provincial military stores. Paul Revere
and others spread the alarm. The next morning fights
occurred at Lexington, Concord, and along the line of
march back to Boston. During the day forty-nine
Americans were killed, and seventy-three British.
Emerson's "Hymn" was written to be sung at the
celebration of the completion of the monument com-
memorating the occasion, and was printed in sheet form
at Concord in 1837. It was reprinted in *Poems* (1847),
the title carrying the date April 19, 1836, as above;
in *May-Day and Other Pieces* (1867) and in *Poems* (1904)
the line reads, "Sung at the Completion of the Battle
Monument, July 4, 1837."

By the rude bridge that arched the flood,
    Their flag to April's breeze unfurled,
Here once the embattled farmers stood,
    And fired the shot heard round the world.

The foe long since in silence slept;   5
    Alike the conqueror silent sleeps;
And Time the ruined bridge has swept
    Down the dark stream which seaward creeps.

On this green bank, by this soft stream,
    We set to-day a votive stone;   10
That memory may their deed redeem,
    When, like our sires, our sons are gone.

Spirit, that made those heroes dare
    To die, and leave their children free,
Bid Time and Nature gently spare   15
    The shaft we raise to them and thee.

Each and All

FIRST PUBLISHED in the *Western Messenger*, February,
1839; first collected in *Poems* (1847). In an editorial
note to *Poems* (1904), 404, Edward W. Emerson
quoted a passage from Emerson's Journal, May 16,
1834, wherein Emerson noted that, attracted by their
luster, he often picked up shells along the seashore,
only to discover on arriving home that they had lost
their beauty. Thus he learned the theme expressed
in the poem—individual forms are only contributing
factors to the "perfect whole." For the red-cloaked
clown see *Journals*, III, 373, for November, 1834.

Little thinks, in the field, yon red-cloaked clown
Of thee from the hill-top looking down;
The heifer that lows in the upland farm,
Far-heard, lows not thine ear to charm;
The sexton, tolling his bell at noon,   5
Deems not that great Napoleon
Stops his horse, and lists with delight,
Whilst his files sweep round yon Alpine height;
Nor knowest thou what argument
Thy life to thy neighbor's creed has lent.   10
All are needed by each one;
Nothing is fair or good alone.
I thought the sparrow's note from heaven,
Singing at dawn on the alder bough;
I brought him home, in his nest, at even;   15
He sings the song, but it cheers not now,
For I did not bring home the river and sky;—
He sang to my ear,—they sang to my eye.
The delicate shells lay on the shore;
The bubbles of the latest wave   20
Fresh pearls to their enamel gave,
And the bellowing of the savage sea
Greeted their safe escape to me.
I wiped away the weeds and foam,
I fetched my sea-born treasures home;   25
But the poor, unsightly, noisome things
Had left their beauty on the shore
With the sun and the sand and the wild uproar.
The lover watched his graceful maid,
As 'mid the virgin train she strayed,   30

Nor knew her beauty's best attire
Was woven still by the snow-white choir.
At last she came to his hermitage,
Like the bird from the woodlands to the cage;—
The gay enchantment was undone,   35
A gentle wife, but fairy none.
Then I said, 'I covet truth;
Beauty is unripe childhood's cheat;
I leave it behind with the games of youth:'
As I spoke, beneath my feet   40
The ground-pine curled its pretty wreath,
Running over the club-moss burrs;
I inhaled the violet's breath;
Around me stood the oaks and firs;
Pine-cones and acorns lay on the ground;   45
Over me soared the eternal sky,
Full of light and of deity;
Again I saw, again I heard,
The rolling river, the morning bird;—
Beauty through my senses stole;   50
I yielded myself to the perfect whole.

Good-Bye

First published in the *Western Messenger* for April,
1839. In a letter to the editor, James Freeman Clarke,
Emerson said that he considered the verses, written
sixteen years previously, to be misanthropic beyond
his nature. Cabot dated the poem in April, 1824, when
Emerson was trying to conduct a finishing school for
young ladies at his mother's home in Boston, and was
already thinking in terms later developed in "Nature,"
"The American Scholar," "Self-Reliance," and "Society
and Solitude." First collected in *Poems* (1847).

Good-bye, proud world! I'm going home:
Thou art not my friend, and I'm not thine.
Long through thy weary crowds I roam;
A river-ark on the ocean brine,
Long I've been tossed like the driven foam;   5
But now, proud world! I'm going home.

Good-bye to Flattery's fawning face;
To Grandeur with his wise grimace;
To upstart Wealth's averted eye;
To supple Office, low and high;   10
To crowded halls, to court and street;
To frozen hearts and hasting feet;

To those who go, and those who come;
Good-bye, proud world! I'm going home.

I am going to my own hearth-stone,   15
Bosomed in yon green hills alone,—
A secret nook in a pleasant land,
Whose groves the frolic fairies planned;
Where arches green, the livelong day,
Echo the blackbird's roundelay,   20
And vulgar feet have never trod
A spot that is sacred to thought and God.

O, when I am safe in my sylvan home,
I tread on the pride of Greece and Rome;
And when I am stretched beneath the pines,   25
Where the evening star so holy shines,
I laugh at the lore and the pride of man,
At the sophist schools and the learned clan;
For what are they all, in their high conceit,
When man in the bush with God may meet?   30

The Rhodora: On Being Asked, Whence is the Flower?

This poem first appeared in the *Western Messenger* for
July, 1839, Emerson having sent it, along with "Good-
Bye," to James Freeman Clarke, who had requested
two poems. First collected in *Poems* (1847).

In May, when sea-winds pierced our solitudes,
I found the fresh Rhodora in the woods,
Spreading its leafless blooms in a damp nook,
To please the desert and the sluggish brook.
The purple petals, fallen in the pool,   5
Made the black water with their beauty gay;
Here might the red-bird come his plumes to cool,
And court the flower that cheapens his array.
Rhodora! if the sages ask thee why
This charm is wasted on the earth and sky,   10
Tell them, dear, that if eyes were made for
    seeing,
Then Beauty is its own excuse for being:
Why thou wert there, O rival of the rose!
I never thought to ask, I never knew:
But, in my simple ignorance, suppose   15
The self-same Power that brought me there
    brought you.

The Problem

E. W. EMERSON noted that this poem, written November 10, 1839, is better known and more frequently quoted than any other. In the *Journals*, August 28, 1838, Emerson expressed the dilemma: "I dislike to be a clergyman and refuse to be one. Yet how rich a music would be to me a holy clergyman in my town. It seems to me he cannot be a man, quite and whole; yet how plain is the need of one, and how high, yes, highest is the function."

I like a church; I like a cowl;
I love a prophet of the soul;
And on my heart monastic aisles
Fall like sweet strains, or pensive smiles:
Yet not for all his faith can see   5
Would I that cowlèd churchman be.

Why should the vest on him allure,
Which I could not on me endure?
Not from a vain or shallow thought
His awful Jove young Phidias brought;   10
Never from lips of cunning fell
The thrilling Delphic oracle;
Out from the heart of nature rolled
The burdens of the Bible old;
The litanies of nations came,   15
Like the volcano's tongue of flame,
Up from the burning core below,—
The canticles of love and woe:
The hand that rounded Peter's dome
And groined the aisles of Christian Rome   20
Wrought in a sad sincerity;
Himself from God he could not free;
He builded better than he knew;—
The conscious stone to beauty grew.

Know'st thou what wove yon woodbird's nest   25
Of leaves, and feathers from her breast?
Or how the fish outbuilt her shell,
Painting with morn each annual cell?
Or how the sacred pine-tree adds
To her old leaves new myriads?   30
Such and so grew these holy piles,
Whilst love and terror laid the tiles.
Earth proudly wears the Parthenon,
As the best gem upon her zone,
And Morning opes with haste her lids   35
To gaze upon the Pyramids;

O'er England's abbeys bends the sky,
As on its friends, with kindred eye;
For out of Thought's interior sphere
These wonders rose to upper air;   40
And Nature gladly gave them place,
Adopted them into her race,
And granted them an equal date
With Andes and with Ararat.

These temples grew as grows the grass;   45
Art might obey, but not surpass.
The Passive Master lent his hand
To the vast soul that o'er him planned;
And the same power that reared the shrine
Bestrode the tribes that knelt within.   50
Ever the fiery Pentecost
Girds with one flame the countless host,
Trances the heart through chanting choirs,
And through the priest the mind inspires.
The word unto the prophet spoken   55
Was writ on tables yet unbroken;
The word by seers or sibyls told,
In groves of oak, or fanes of gold,
Still floats upon the morning wind,
Still whispers to the willing mind.   60
One accent of the Holy Ghost
The heedless world hath never lost.
I know what say the fathers wise,—
The Book itself before me lies,
Old *Chrysostom*, best Augustine,   65
And he who blent both in his line,
The younger *Golden Lips* or mines,
Taylor, the Shakespeare of divines.
His words are music in my ear,
I see his cowlèd portrait dear;   70
And yet, for all his faith could see,
I would not the good bishop be.

Woodnotes, II

"Woodnotes" I and II were first published in the *Dial* for October, 1840, and October, 1841, respectively; first collected in *Poems* (1847). The white pine was Emerson's favorite tree, and the woods his favorite place for contemplation. He recorded in his Journal in January, 1841, that he had "scarce a day-dream" unassociated with the breath and shadows of the pines, and he considered for a time using "Forest Essays" as the title to his first series of essays, published in March of that year (see Edward W. Emerson, *Emerson in Concord*, pp. 63–64).

As sunbeams stream through liberal space
And nothing jostle or displace,
So waved the pine-tree through my thought
And fanned the dreams it never brought.

'Whether is better, the gift or the donor?   5
Come to me,'
Quoth the pine-tree,
'I am the giver of honor.
My garden is the cloven rock,
And my manure the snow;   10
And drifting sand-heaps feed my stock,
In summer's scorching glow.
He is great who can live by me.
The rough and bearded forester
Is better than the lord;   15
God fills the scrip and canister,
Sin piles the loaded board.
The lord is the peasant that was,
The peasant the lord that shall be;
The lord is hay, the peasant grass,   20
One dry, and one the living tree.
Who liveth by the ragged pine
Foundeth a heroic line;
Who liveth in the palace hall
Waneth fast and spendeth all.   25
He goes to my savage haunts,
With his chariot and his care;
My twilight realm he disenchants,
And finds his prison there.

'What prizes the town and the tower?   30
Only what the pine-tree yields;
Sinew that subdued the fields;
The wild-eyed boy, who in the woods
Chants his hymn to hills and floods,
Whom the city's poisoning spleen   35
Made not pale, or fat, or lean;
Whom the rain and the wind purgeth,
Whom the dawn and the day-star urgeth,
In whose cheek the rose-leaf blusheth,
In whose feet the lion rusheth,   40
Iron arms, and iron mould,
That know not fear, fatigue, or cold.
I give my rafters to his boat,
My billets to his boiler's throat,
And I will swim the ancient sea   45
To float my child to victory,
And grant to dwellers with the pine
Dominion o'er the palm and vine.
Who leaves the pine-tree, leaves his friend,
Unnerves his strength, invites his end.   50
Cut a bough from my parent stem,
And dip it in thy porcelain vase;
A little while each russet gem
Will swell and rise with wonted grace;
But when it seeks enlarged supplies,   55
The orphan of the forest dies.
Whoso walks in solitude
And inhabiteth the wood,
Choosing light, wave, rock, and bird,
Before the money-loving herd,   60
Into that forester shall pass,
From these companions, power and grace.
Clean shall he be, without, within,
From the old adhering sin,
All ill dissolving in the light   65
Of his triumphant piercing sight:
Not vain, sour, nor frivolous;
Not mad, athirst, nor garrulous;
Grave, chaste, contented, though retired,
And of all other men desired.   70
On him the light of star and moon
Shall fall with purer radiance down;
All constellations of the sky
Shed their virtue through his eye.
Him Nature giveth for defence   75
His formidable innocence;
The mounting sap, the shells, the sea,
All spheres, all stones, his helpers be;
He shall meet the speeding year,
Without wailing, without fear;   80
He shall be happy in his love,
Like to like shall joyful prove;
He shall be happy whilst he woos,
Muse-born, a daughter of the Muse.
But if with gold she bind her hair,   85
And deck her breast with diamond,
Take off thine eyes, thy heart forbear,
Though thou lie alone on the ground.

'Heed the old oracles,
Ponder my spells;   90

589

Song wakes in my pinnacles
When the wind swells.
Soundeth the prophetic wind,
The shadows shake on the rock behind,
And the countless leaves of the pine are strings 95
Tuned to the lay the wood-god sings.
     Hearken! Hearken!
If thou wouldst know the mystic song
Chanted when the sphere was young.
Aloft, abroad, the pæan swells; 100
O wise man! hear'st thou half it tells?
O wise man! hear'st thou the least part?
'Tis the chronicle of art.
To the open ear it sings
Sweet the genesis of things, 105
Of tendency through endless ages,
Of star-dust, and star-pilgrimages,
Of rounded worlds, of space and time,
Of the old flood's subsiding slime,
Of chemic matter, force and form, 110
Of poles and powers, cold, wet, and warm:
The rushing metamorphosis
Dissolving all that fixture is,
Melts things that be to things that seem,
And solid nature to a dream. 115
O, listen to the undersong,
The ever old, the ever young;
And, far within those cadent pauses,
The chorus of the ancient Causes!
Delights the dreadful Destiny 120
To fling his voice into the tree,
And shock thy weak ear with a note
Breathed from the everlasting throat.
In music he repeats the pang
Whence the fair flock of Nature sprang. 125
O mortal! thy ears are stones;
These echoes are laden with tones
Which only the pure can hear;
Thou canst not catch what they recite
Of Fate and Will, of Want and Right, 130
Of man to come, of human life,
Of Death and Fortune, Growth and Strife.'

  Once again the pine-tree sung:—
'Speak not thy speech my boughs among:
Put off thy years, wash in the breeze; 135
My hours are peaceful centuries.
Talk no more with feeble tongue;

No more the fool of space and time,
Come weave with mine a nobler rhyme.
Only thy Americans 140
Can read thy line, can meet thy glance,
But the runes that I rehearse
Understands the universe;
The least breath my boughs which tossed
Brings again the Pentecost; 145
To every soul resounding clear
In a voice of solemn cheer,—
"Am I not thine? Are not these thine?"
And they reply, "Forever mine!"
My branches speak Italian, 150
English, German, Basque, Castilian,
Mountain speech to Highlanders,
Ocean tongues to islanders,
To Fin and Lap and swart Malay,
To each his bosom-secret say. 155

  'Come learn with me the fatal song
Which knits the world in music strong,
Come lift thine eyes to lofty rhymes,
Of things with things, of times with times,
Primal chimes of sun and shade, 160
Of sound and echo, man and maid,
The land reflected in the flood,
Body with shadow still pursued.
For Nature beats in perfect tune,
And rounds with rhyme her every rune, 165
Whether she work in land or sea,
Or hide underground her alchemy.
Thou canst not wave thy staff in air,
Or dip thy paddle in the lake,
But it carves the bow of beauty there, 170
And the ripples in rhymes the oar forsake.
The wood is wiser far than thou;
The wood and wave each other know
Not unrelated, unaffied,
But to each thought and thing allied, 175
Is perfect Nature's every part,
Rooted in the mighty Heart.
But thou, poor child! unbound, unrhymed,
Whence camest thou, misplaced, mistimed,
Whence, O thou orphan and defrauded? 180
Is thy land peeled, thy realm marauded?
Who thee divorced, deceived and left?
Thee of thy faith who hath bereft,
And torn the ensigns from thy brow.

And sunk the immortal eye so low? 185
Thy cheek too white, thy form too slender,
Thy gait too slow, thy habits tender
For royal man;—they thee confess
An exile from the wilderness,—
The hills where health with health agrees, 190
And the wise soul expels disease.
Hark! in thy ear I will tell the sign
By which thy hurt thou may'st divine.
When thou shalt climb the mountain cliff,
Or see the wide shore from thy skiff, 195
To thee the horizon shall express
But emptiness on emptiness;
There lives no man of Nature's worth
In the circle of the earth;
And to thine eye the vast skies fall, 200
Dire and satirical,
On clucking hens and prating fools,
On thieves, on drudges, and on dolls.
And thou shalt say to the Most High,
"Godhead! all this astronomy, 205
And fate and practice and invention,
Strong art and beautiful pretension,
This radiant pomp of sun and star,
Throes that that were, and worlds that are,
Behold! were in vain and in vain;— 210
It cannot be,—I will look again.
Surely now will the curtain rise,
And earth's fit tenant me surprise;—
But the curtain doth not rise,
And Nature has miscarried wholly 215
Into failure, into folly."

'Alas! thine is the bankruptcy,
Blessed Nature so to see.
Come, lay thee in my soothing shade,
And heal the hurts which sin has made. 220
I see thee in the crowd alone;
I will be thy companion.
Quit thy friends as the dead in doom,
And build to them a final tomb;
Let the starred shade that nightly falls 225
Still celebrate their funerals,
And the bell of beetle and of bee
Knell their melodious memory.
Behind thee leave thy merchandise,
Thy churches and thy charities; 230
And leave thy peacock wit behind;

Enough for thee the primal mind
That flows in streams, that breathes in wind:
Leave all thy pedant lore apart;
God hid the whole world in thy heart. 235
Love shuns the sage, the child it crowns,
Gives all to them who all renounce.
The rain comes when the wind calls;
The river knows the way to the sea;
Without a pilot it runs and falls, 240
Blessing all lands with its charity;
The sea tosses and foams to find
Its way up to the cloud and wind;
The shadow sits close to the flying ball;
The date fails not on the palm-tree tall; 245
And thou,—go burn thy wormy pages,—
Shalt outsee seers, and outwit sages.
Oft didst thou thread the woods in vain
To find what bird had piped the strain;—
Seek not, and the little eremite 250
Flies gayly forth and sings in sight.

'Hearken once more!
I will tell thee the mundane lore.
Older am I than thy numbers wot,
Change I may, but I pass not. 255
Hitherto all things fast abide,
And anchored in the tempest ride.
Trenchant time behoves to hurry
All to yean and all to bury:
All the forms are fugitive, 260
But the substances survive.
Ever fresh the broad creation,
A divine improvisation,
From the heart of God proceeds,
A single will, a million deeds. 265
Once slept the world an egg of stone,
And pulse, and sound, and light was none;
And God said, "Throb!" and there was motion
And the vast mass became vast ocean.
Onward and on, the eternal Pan, 270
Who layeth the world's incessant plan,
Halteth never in one shape,
But forever doth escape,
Like wave or flame, into new forms
Of gem, and air, of plants, and worms. 275
I, that to-day am a pine,
Yesterday was a bundle of grass.
He is free and libertine,

Pouring of his power the wine
To every age, to every race; 280
Unto every race and age
He emptieth the beverage;
Unto each, and unto all,
Maker and original.
The world is the ring of his spells, 285
And the play of his miracles.
As he giveth to all to drink,
Thus or thus they are and think.
With one drop sheds form and feature;
With the next a special nature; 290
The third adds heat's indulgent spark;
The fourth gives light which eats the dark;
Into the fifth himself he flings,
And conscious Law is King of kings.
As the bee through the garden ranges, 295
From world to world the godhead changes;
As the sheep go feeding in the waste,
From form to form He maketh haste;
This vault which glows immense with light
Is the inn where he lodges for a night. 300
What recks such Traveller if the bowers
Which bloom and fade like meadow flowers
A bunch of fragrant lilies be,
Or the stars of eternity?
Alike to him the better, the worse,— 305
The glowing angel, the outcast corse.
Thou metest him by centuries,
And lo! he passes like the breeze;
Thou seek'st in globe and galaxy,
He hides in pure transparency; 310
Thou askest in fountains and in fires,
He is the essence that inquires.
He is the axis of the star;
He is the sparkle of the spar;
He is the heart of every creature; 315
He is the meaning of each feature;
And his mind is the sky,
Than all it holds more deep, more high.'

The Snow-Storm

FIRST PUBLISHED in the *Dial* for January, 1841; first
collected in *Poems* (1847). The poem contains two of
Emerson's most famous lines.

Announced by all the trumpets of the sky,
Arrives the snow, and, driving o'er the fields,
Seems nowhere to alight: the whited air
Hides hills and woods, the river, and the heaven,
And veils the farm-house at the garden's end, 5
The sled and traveller stopped, the courier's feet
Delayed, all friends shut out, the housemates sit
Around the radiant fireplace, enclosed
In a tumultuous privacy of storm.

Come see the north wind's masonry. 10
Out of an unseen quarry evermore
Furnished with tile, the fierce artificer
Curves his white bastions with projected roof
Round every windward stake, or tree, or door.
Speeding, the myriad-handed, his wild work 15
So fanciful, so savage, nought cares he
For number or proportion. Mockingly,
On coop or kennel he hangs Parian wreaths;
A swan-like form invests the hidden thorn;
Fills up the farmer's lane from wall to wall, 20
Maugre the farmer's sighs; and at the gate
A tapering turret overtops the work
And when his hours are numbered, and the world
Is all his own, retiring, as he were not,
Leaves, when the sun appears, astonished Art 25
To mimic in slow structures, stone by stone,
Built in an age, the mad wind's night-work,
The frolic architecture of the snow.

Bacchus

E. W. EMERSON (*Complete Works*, Centenary Edition,
IX, 443–5) refers to the chapter, "Idealism," in
Nature for the correlating conception of the inspiration
of Nature as a symbol of the universal oneness. F. I.
Carpenter (*Emerson and Asia*, pp. 169, 188–9) describes the relation of "Bacchus" to the works of the
Persian poet Hafiz, then being read by Emerson. This
poem is characteristic not only of Emerson's use of the
symbolical, but of his rise to highest ecstasy. Written,
1846; first published in *Poems*, 1847; reprinted from
the edition of 1884.

Bring me wine, but wine which never grew
In the belly of the grape,
Or grew on vine whose tap-roots, reaching through
Under the Andes to the Cape,
Suffer no savor of the earth to scape. 5

Let its grapes the morn salute
From a nocturnal root,

Which feels the acrid juice
Of Styx and Erebus;
And turns the woe of Night,   10
By its own craft, to a more rich delight.

We buy ashes for bread;
We buy diluted wine;
Give me of the true,—
Whose ample leaves and tendrils curled   15
Among the silver hills of heaven
Draw everlasting dew;
Wine of wine,
Blood of the world,
Form of forms, and mould of statures,   20
That I intoxicated,
And by the draught assimilated,
May float at pleasure through all natures;
The bird-language rightly spell,
And that which roses say so well.   25

Wine that is shed
Like the torrents of the sun
Up the horizon walls,
Or like the Atlantic streams, which run
When the South Sea calls.   30

Water and bread,
Food which needs no transmuting,
Rainbow-flowering, wisdom-fruiting,
Wine which is already man,
Food which teach and reason can.   35

Wine with Music is,—
Music and wine are one,—
That I, drinking this,
Shall hear far Chaos talk with me;
Kings unborn shall walk with me;   40
And the poor grass shall plot and plan
What it will do when it is man.
Quickened so, will I unlock
Every crypt of every rock.

I thank the joyful juice   45
For all I know;—
Winds of remembering
Of the ancient being blow,
And seeming-solid walls of use
Open and flow.   50

9. **Styx:** a river in Hades. **Erebus:** the gloomy nether-
world, or Hades.

Pour, Bacchus! the remembering wine;
Retrieve the loss of me and mine!
Vine for vine be antidote,
And the grape requite the lote!
Haste to cure the old despair,—   55
Reason in Nature's lotus drenched,
The memory of ages quenched;
Give them again to shine;
Let wine repair what this undid;
And where the infection slid,   60
A dazzling memory revive;
Refresh the faded tints,
Recut the aged prints,
And write my old adventures with the pen
Which on the first day drew,   65
Upon the tablets blue,
The dancing Pleiads and eternal men.

Hamatreya

THIS POEM was printed in *Poems* (1847). It is based
upon a passage from the *Vishnu Purana*, which Emerson
transcribed in his Journals in 1845. Emerson changed
the name "Maitreya" in his source to "Hamatreya."
In his essay "Plato; or, The Philosopher" he cited
the Hindu Scriptures for the highest expression of the
idea of fundamental unity, and quoted Krishna:
"Men contemplate distinctions, because they are
stupefied with ignorance. The words *I* and *mine*
constitute ignorance."

Bulkeley, Hunt, Willard, Hosmer, Meriam, Flint,
Possessed the land which rendered to their toil
Hay, corn, roots, hemp, flax, apples, wool and
   wood.
Each of these landlords walked amidst his farm,   4
Saying ' 'Tis mine, my children's and my name's:
How sweet the west-wind sounds in my own trees!
How graceful climb those shadows on my hill!
I fancy these pure waters and the flags
Know me, as does my dog: we sympathize;
And, I affirm, my actions smack of the soil.'   10

Where are these men? Asleep beneath their
   grounds;
And strangers, fond as they, their furrows plough.

  1. **Bulkeley . . . Flint:** The names in the first line are
those of settlers of Concord. See T. Scudder, *Concord:
American Town* (1947). 8. **flags:** the wild Iris common to
low places in Eastern United States.

Earth laughs in flowers, to see her boastful boys
Earth-proud, proud of the earth which is not
    theirs;
Who steer the plough, but cannot steer their feet
Clear of the grave.   16
They added ridge to valley, brook to pond,
And sighed for all that bounded their domain;
'This suits me for a pasture; that's my park;
We must have clay, lime, gravel, granite-ledge,
And misty lowland, where to go for peat.   21
The land is well,—lies fairly to the south.
'Tis good, when you have crossed the sea and back,
To find the sitfast acres where you left them.'
Ah! the hot owner sees not Death, who adds
Him to his land, a lump of mould the more.   26
Hear what the Earth says:—

Earth-Song

'Mine and yours;
Mine, not yours.
Earth endures;   30
Stars abide—
Shine down in the old sea;
Old are the shores;
But where are old men?
I who have seen much,   35
Such have I never seen.

'The lawyer's deed
Ran sure,
In tail,
To them, and to their heirs   40
Who shall succeed,
Without fail,
Forevermore.

'Here is the land,
Shaggy with wood,   45
With its old valley,
Mound and flood.
But the heritors?—
Fled like the flood's foam.
The lawyer, and the laws,   50
And the kingdom,
Clean swept herefrom.

'They called me theirs,
Who so controlled me;

Yet every one   55
Wished to stay, and is gone,
How am I theirs,
If they cannot hold me,
But I hold them?'

When I heard the Earth-song,   60
I was no longer brave;
My avarice cooled
Like lust in the chill of the grave.

Merlin

THE GERMINAL twenty-three unrhymed lines which later grew into the finished, rhymed "Merlin" are to be found in Emerson's Journal of 1845. They are reprinted in *Poems*, Centenary Edition (1904), p. 441, by the editor, Edward W. Emerson, who noted that his father, when young, was strongly moved by the *Morte d'Arthur*, the Ossianic tales, and the poems of the Cymrian bards. Merlin, bard, magician, prophet, tutor and counselor of King Arthur, is supposed to have flourished in Britain in the fifth century. Emerson made him the symbol of the poet, and, as in his other poems, the Concord sage strove "to smite the chords rudely and hard," the better to raise the poet to the stature of one who "modulates the king's affairs." He packed his lines with substance, often a thought to a line; and the lines are freighted with a wealth of original, spontaneous imagery—metaphors and symbols as personal as a mystic's vision. Paradox and surprise are met with everywhere. The image of the poet as "poet priest," as one who perceives the true depth of meaning in things, is often met with in Emerson's poems and essays. In "The Poet" (*Essays, Second Series*), the true poet—not the mere serenader—is the seer, the "true land-lord! sea-lord! air-lord!" to whom "the ideal shall be the real." "Merlin" was finished in the summer of 1846, and published first in *Poems* (1847).

I

Thy trivial harp will never please
Or fill my craving ear;
Its chords should ring as blows the breeze,
Free, peremptory, clear.
No jingling serenader's art,   5
Nor tinkle of piano strings,
Can make the wild blood start
In its mystic springs.

The kingly bard
Must smite the chords rudely and hard,   10
As with hammer or with mace;
That they may render back
Artful thunder, which conveys
Secrets of the solar track,
Sparks of the supersolar blaze.   15
Merlin's blows are strokes of fate,
Chiming with the forest tone,
When boughs buffet boughs in the wood;
Chiming with the gasp and moan
Of the ice-imprisoned flood;   20
With the pulse of manly hearts;
With the voice of orators;
With the din of city arts;
With the cannonades of wars;
With the marches of the brave;   25
And prayers of might from martyrs' cave.

Great is the art,
Great be the manners, of the bard.
He shall not his brain encumber
With the coil of rhythm and number;   30
But, leaving rule and pale forethought,
He shall aye climb
For his rhyme.
'Pass in, pass in,' the angels say,
'In to the upper doors,   35
Nor count compartments of the floors,
But mount to paradise
By the stairway of surprise.'

Blameless master of the games,
King of sport that never shames,   40
He shall daily joy dispense
Hid in song's sweet influence.
Forms more cheerly live and go,
What time the subtle mind
Sings aloud the tune whereto   45
Their pulses beat,
And march their feet,
And their members are combined.

By Sybarites beguiled,
He shall no task decline;   50
Merlin's mighty line
Extremes of nature reconciled,—
Bereaved a tyrant of his will,
And made the lion mild.

Songs can the tempest still,   55
Scattered on the stormy air,
Mould the year to fair increase,
And bring in poetic peace.

He shall not seek to weave,
In weak, unhappy times,   60
Efficacious rhymes;
Wait his returning strength.
Bird that from the nadir's floor
To the zenith's top can soar,—
The soaring orbit of the muse exceeds that jour-
    ney's length.   65
Nor profane affect to hit
Or compass that, by meddling wit,
Which only the propitious mind
Publishes when 't is inclined.
There are open hours   70
When the God's will sallies free,
And the dull idiot might see
The flowing fortunes of a thousand years;—
Sudden, at unawares,
Self-moved, fly-to the doors,   75
Nor sword of angels could reveal
What they conceal.

II

The rhyme of the poet
Modulates the king's affairs;
Balance-loving Nature
Made all things in pairs.
To every foot its antipode;   5
Each color with its counter glowed;
To every tone beat answering tones,
Higher or graver;
Flavor gladly blends with flavor;
Leaf answers leaf upon the bough;   10
And match the paired cotyledons.
Hands to hands, and feet to feet,
In one body grooms and brides;
Eldest rite, two married sides
In every mortal meet.   15
Light's far furnace shines,
Smelting balls and bars,
Forging double stars,
Glittering twins and trines.
The animals are sick with love,   20
Lovesick with rhyme;
Each with all propitious Time

Into chorus wove.
Like the dancers' ordered band,
Thoughts come also hand in hand;   25
In equal couples mated,
Or else alternated;
Adding by their mutual gage,
One to other, health and age.
Solitary fancies go   30
Short-lived wandering to and fro,
Most like to bachelors,
Or an ungiven maid,
Not ancestors,
With no posterity to make the lie afraid, 35
Or keep truth undecayed.
Perfect-paired as eagle's wings,
Justice is the rhyme of things;
Trade and counting use
The self-same tuneful muse;   40
And Nemesis,
Who with even matches odd.
Who athwart space redresses
The partial wrong,
Fills the just period.   45
And finishes the song.

Subtle rhymes, with ruin rife,
Murmur in the house of life,
Sung by the Sisters as they spin;
In perfect time and measure they   50
Build and unbuild our echoing clay.
As the two twilights of the day
Fold us music-drunken in.

Ode

Inscribed to W. H. Channing

WILLIAM HENRY CHANNING (1810–1884), friend of
Emerson and Unitarian clergyman, was an ardent
reformer, embracing Fourierism, socialism, abolition,
and other causes. Emerson's point of view is well expressed in his lecture, "New England Reformers,"
delivered March 3, 1844, and printed in *Essays, Second
Series.* He could not, he said, waste all his time in attacks; he recognized, too, that many reformers were
narrow and full of vanity, and that the current rampant
criticism against all manner of institutions was to no
avail unless the basic spirit of man be reformed—
"renovated." See also his *Journals,* VI, 494–5 and

VII, 192–3, 219–223, written in 1844 and 1846. But
increasingly he supported the abolitionists, and he
urged that the Fugitive Slave Law not be obeyed.
The "Ode" was first published in *Poems* (1847) and
reprinted in the Blue and Gold edition of 1865.

Though loath to grieve
The evil time's sole patriot,
I cannot leave
My honied thought
For the priest's cant,   5
Or statesman's rant.

If I refuse
My study for their politique,
Which at the best is trick,
The angry Muse   10
Puts confusion in my brain.

But who is he that prates
Of the culture of mankind,
Of better arts and life?
Go, blindworm, go,   15
Behold the famous States
Harrying Mexico
With rifle and with knife!

Or who, with accent bolder,
Dare praise the freedom-loving mountaineer? 20
I found by thee, O rushing Contoocook!
And in thy valleys, Agiochook!
The jackals of the negro-holder.

The God who made New Hampshire
Taunted the lofty land   25
With little men;—
Small bat and wren
House in the oak:—
If earth-fire cleave
The upheaved land, and bury the folk,   30
The southern crocodile would grieve.
Virtue palters; Right is hence;
Freedom praised, but hid;
Funeral eloquence
Rattles the coffin-lid.   35

17. Harrying Mexico: War against Mexico was declared
on May 13, 1846.   **21. Contoocook:** a river in New Hampshire.   **22. Agiochook:** an Indian name for the White
Mountains.

What boots thy zeal,
O glowing friend,
That would indignant rend
The northland from the south?
Wherefore? to what good end? 40
Boston Bay and Bunker Hill
Would serve things still;—
Things are of the snake.

The horseman serves the horse,
The neatherd serves the neat, 45
The merchant serves the purse,
The eater serves his meat;
'Tis the day of the chattel,
Web to weave, and corn to grind;
Things are in the saddle, 50
And ride mankind.

There are two laws discrete,
Not reconciled,—
Law for man, and law for thing;
The last builds town and fleet, 55
But it runs wild,
And doth the man unking.

'Tis fit the forest fall,
The steep be graded,
The mountain tunnelled, 60
The sand shaded,
The orchard planted,
The glebe tilled,
The prairie granted,
The steamer built. 65

Let man serve law for man;
Live for friendship, live for love,
For truth's and harmony's behoof;
The state may follow how it can,
As Olympus follows Jove. 70

Yet do not I implore
The wrinkled shopman to my sounding woods,
Nor bid the unwilling senator
Ask votes of thrushes in the solitudes.
Every one to his chosen work;— 75
Foolish hands may mix and mar;
Wise and sure the issues are.
Round they roll till dark is light,
Sex to sex, and even to odd;—

The over-god 80
Who marries Right to Might,
Who peoples, unpeoples,—
He who exterminates
Races by stronger races,
Black by white faces,— 85
Knows to bring honey
Out of the lion;
Grafts gentlest scion
On pirate and Turk.

The Cossack eats Poland, 90
Like stolen fruit;
Her last noble is ruined,
Her last poet mute:
Straight, into double band
The victors divide; 95
Half for freedom strike and stand;—
The astonished Muse finds thousands at her side.

Thine Eyes Still Shined

FIRST PUBLISHED in *Poems* (1847). E. W. Emerson
noted in the Centenary Edition, IX, 436, that the
poem was probably related to Emerson's affection for
Ellen Tucker (his first wife) when, before or after their
marriage (1829), she was absent in the South.

Thine eyes still shined for me, though far
    I lonely roved the land or sea:
As I behold yon evening star,
    Which yet beholds not me.

This morn I climbed the misty hill 5
    And roamed the pastures through;
How danced thy form before my path
    Amidst the deep-eyed dew!

When the redbird spread his sable wing,
    And showed his side of flame; 10
When the rosebud ripened to the rose,
    In both I read thy name.

Threnody

EMERSON'S eldest child, Waldo, aged five years,
stricken with scarlet fever, died after four days of illness, January 27, 1842. In his Journal for January 30,
the father wrote most poignantly of his loss (Edward W.
Emerson and Waldo Emerson Forbes, editors, *Journals*,

VI, 150–53). On February 28, in a letter to Carlyle, he again referred to his "perfect little boy": "You can never sympathize with me; you can never know how much of me such a young child can take away" (Holmes, *Ralph Waldo Emerson*, pp. 177–8). The first part of the poem expresses the father's overwhelming grief; the second part, beginning with "The deep Heart answered," reflective in tone, was written nearly two years later. On January 30, 1844, in a letter to Margaret Fuller, he promised to try to respond to her request, "copy my rude dirges to my darling," and send them to her (see Cabot, *A Memoir*, II, 481–4). The elegy, one of the best in the language, first appeared in *Poems* (1847).

The South-wind brings
Life, sunshine and desire,
And on every mount and meadow
Breathes aromatic fire;
But over the dead he has no power,   5
The lost, the lost, he cannot restore;
And, looking over the hills, I mourn
The darling who shall not return.

I see my empty house,
I see my trees repair their boughs;   10
And he, the wondrous child,
Whose silver warble wild
Outvalued every pulsing sound
Within the air's cerulean round,—
The hyacinthine boy, for whom   15
Morn well might break and April bloom,——
The gracious boy, who did adorn
The world whereinto he was born,
And by his countenance repay
The favor of the loving Day,—   20
Has disappeared from the Day's eye;
Far and wide she cannot find him;
My hopes pursue, they cannot bind him.
Returned this day, the south-wind searches,
And finds young pines and budding birches;   25
But finds not the budding man;
Nature who lost, cannot remake him;
Fate let him fall, Fate can't retake him;
Nature, Fate, men, him seek in vain.

And whither now, my truant wise and sweet,   30
O, whither tend thy feet?
I had the right, few days ago,

Thy steps to watch, thy place to know:
How have I forfeited the right?
Hast thou forgot me in a new delight?   35
I hearken for thy household cheer,
O eloquent child!
Whose voice, an equal messenger,
Conveyed thy meaning mild.
What though the pains and joys   40
Whereof it spoke were toys
Fitting his age and ken,
Yet fairest dames and bearded men,
Who heard the sweet request,
So gentle, wise and grave,   45
Bended with joy to his behest,
And let the world's affairs go by,
A while to share his cordial game,
Or mend his wicker wagon-frame,
Still plotting how their hungry ear   50
That winsome voice again might hear;
For his lips could well pronounce
Words that were persuasions.

Gentlest guardians marked serene
His early hope, his liberal mien;   55
Took counsel from his guiding eyes
To make this wisdom earthly wise.
Ah, vainly do these eyes recall
The school-march, each day's festival,
When every morn my bosom glowed   60
To watch the convoy on the road;
The babe in willow wagon closed,
With rolling eyes and face composed;
With children forward and behind,
Like Cupids studiously inclined;   65
And he the chieftain paced beside,
The centre of the troop allied,
With sunny face of sweet repose,
To guard the babe from fancied foes.
The little captain innocent   70
Took the eye with him as he went;
Each village senior paused to scan
And speak the lovely caravan.
From the window I look out
To mark thy beautiful parade,   75
Stately marching in cap and coat
To some tune by fairies played;—
A music heard by thee alone
To works as noble led thee on.

Now Love and Pride, alas! in vain,   80
Up and down their glances strain.
The painted sled stands where it stood;
The kennel by the corded wood;
His gathered sticks to stanch the wall
Of the snow-tower, when snow should fall;   85
The ominous hole he dug in the sand,
And childhood's castles built or planned;
His daily haunts I well discern,—
The poultry-yard, the shed, the barn,—
And every inch of garden ground   90
Paced by the blessed feet around,
From the roadside to the brook
Whereinto he loved to look.
Step the meek fowls where erst they ranged;
The wintry garden lies unchanged;   95
The brook into the stream runs on;
But the deep-eyed boy is gone.

On that shaded day,
Dark with more clouds than tempests are,
When thou didst yield thy innocent breath   100
In birdlike heavings unto death,
Night came, and Nature had not thee;
I said, 'We are mates in misery.'
The morrow dawned with needless glow;
Each snowbird chirped, each fowl must crow;   105
Each tramper started; but the feet
Of the most beautiful and sweet
Of human youth had left the hill
And garden,—they were bound and still.
There's not a sparrow or a wren,   110
There's not a blade of autumn grain,
Which the four seasons do not tend
And tides of life and increase lend;
And every chick of every bird,
And weed and rock-moss is preferred.   115
O ostrich-like forgetfulness!
O loss of larger in the less!
Was there no star that could be sent,
No watcher in the firmament,
No angel from the countless host   120
That loiters round the crystal coast,
Could stoop to heal that only child,
Nature's sweet marvel undefiled,
And keep the blossom of the earth,
Which all her harvests were not worth?   125
Not mine,—I never called thee mine,

But Nature's heir,—if I repine,
And seeing rashly torn and moved
Not what I made, but what I loved,
Grow early old with grief that thou   130
Must to the wastes of Nature go,—
'Tis because a general hope
Was quenched, and all must doubt and grope.
For flattering planets seemed to say
This child should ills of ages stay,   135
By wondrous tongue, and guided pen,
Bring the flown Muses back to men.
Perchance not he but Nature ailed,
The world and not the infant failed.
It was not ripe yet to sustain   140
A genius of so fine a strain,
Who gazed upon the sun and moon
As if he came unto his own,
And, pregnant with his grander thought,
Brought the old order into doubt.   145
His beauty once their beauty tried;
They could not feed him, and he died,
And wandered backward as in scorn,
To wait an æon to be born.
Ill day which made this beauty waste,   150
Plight broken, this high face defaced!
Some went and came about the dead;
And some in books of solace read;
Some to their friends the tidings say;
Some went to write, some went to pray;   155
One tarried here, there hurried one;
But their heart abode with none.
Covetous death bereaved us all,
To aggrandize one funeral.
The eager fate which carried thee   160
Took the largest part of me:
For this losing is true dying;
This is lordly man's down-lying,
This his slow but sure reclining,
Star by star his world resigning.   165

O that child of paradise,
Boy who made dear his father's home,
In whose deep eyes
Men read the welfare of the times to come,
I am too much bereft.   170
The world dishonored thou hast left.
O truth's and nature's costly lie!
O trusted broken prophecy!

O richest fortune sourly crossed!
Born for the future, to the future lost!			175

The deep Heart answered, 'Weepest thou?
Worthier cause for passion wild
If I had not taken the child.
And deemest thou as those who pore,
With aged eyes, short way before,—			180
Think'st Beauty vanished from the coast
Of matter, and thy darling lost?
Taught he not thee—the man of eld,
Whose eyes within his eyes beheld
Heaven's numerous hierarchy span			185
The mystic gulf from God to man?
To be alone wilt thou begin
When worlds of lovers hem thee in?
To-morrow, when the masks shall fall
That dizen Nature's carnival,			190

'The pure shall see by their own will,
Which overflowing Love shall fill,
'Tis not within the force of fate
The fate-conjoined to separate.
But thou, my votary, weepest thou?			195
I gave thee sight—where is it now?
I taught thy heart beyond the reach
Of ritual, bible, or of speech;
Wrote in thy mind's transparent table,
As far as the incommunicable;			200
Taught thee each private sign to raise
Lit by the supersolar blaze.
Past utterance, and past belief,
And past the blasphemy of grief,
The mysteries of Nature's heart;			205
And though no Muse can these impart,
Throb thine with Nature's throbbing breast,
And all is clear from east to west.

'I came to thee as to a friend;
Dearest, to thee I did not send			210
Tutors, but a joyful eye,
Innocence that matched the sky,
Lovely locks, a form of wonder,
Laughter rich as woodland thunder,
That thou might'st entertain apart			215
The richest flowering of all art:
And, as the great all-loving Day
Through smallest chambers takes its way,
That thou might'st break thy daily bread

With prophet, savior and head;			220
That thou might'st cherish for thine own
The riches of sweet Mary's Son,
Boy-Rabbi, Israel's paragon.
And thoughtest thou such guest
Would in thy hall take up his rest?			225
Would rushing life forget her laws,
Fate's glowing revolution pause?
High omens ask diviner guess;
Not to be conned to tediousness.
And know my higher gifts unbind			230
The zone that girds the incarnate mind.
When the scanty shores are full
With Thought's perilous, whirling pool;
When frail Nature can no more,
Then the Spirit strikes the hour:			235
My servant Death, with solving rite,
Pours finite into infinite.
Wilt thou freeze love's tidal flow,
Whose streams through Nature circling go?
Nail the wild star to its track			240
On the half-climbed zodiac?
Light is light which radiates,
Blood is blood which circulates,
Life is life which generates,
And many-seeming life is one,—			245
Wilt thou transfix and make it none?
Its onward force too starkly pent
In figure, bone and lineament?
Wilt thou, uncalled, interrogate,
Talker! the unreplying Fate!			250
Nor see the genius of the whole
Ascendant in the private soul,
Beckon it when to go and come,
Self-announced its hour of doom?
Fair the soul's recess and shrine,			255
Magic-built to last a season;
Masterpiece of love benign,
Fairer that expansive reason
Whose omen 'tis, and sign.
Wilt thou not ope thy heart to know			260
What rainbows teach, and sunsets show?
Verdict which accumulates
From lengthening scroll of human fates,
Voice of earth to earth returned,
Prayers of saints that inly burned,—			265
Saying, *What is excellent,*
As God lives, is permanent;

Hearts are dust, hearts' loves remain;
Heart's love will meet thee again.
Revere the Maker; fetch thine eye   270
Up to his style, and manners of the sky.
Not of adamant and gold
Built he heaven stark and cold;
No, but a nest of bending reeds,
Flowering grass and scented weeds;   275
Or like a traveller's fleeing tent,
Or bow above the tempest bent;
Built of tears and sacred flames,
And virtue reaching to its aims;
Built of furtherance and pursuing,   280
Not of spent deeds, but of doing.
Silent rushes the swift Lord
Through ruined systems still restored,
Broadsowing, bleak and void to bless,
Plants with worlds the wilderness;   285
Waters with tears of ancient sorrow
Apples of Eden ripe to-morrow.
House and tenant go to ground,
Lost in God, in Godhead found.'

Uriel

First published in *Poems* (1847). The lapse and fate of Uriel (Archangel of the Sun in *Paradise Lost*) in Emerson's poem becomes symbolic of his own religious experience. "A sad self-knowledge, withering, fell" on Emerson likewise, following the challenging principles in his "Address Delivered before the Senior Class in Divinity College," Harvard University, July 15, 1838. Shortly before this address, he had written in his diary of the "ugliness and unprofitableness of theology and churches at this day" (Cabot, *A Memoir*, I, 300). The "Address," touching on this theme, was not well received by many of the clergy; a lively controversy arose in which Emerson took no part. Like Uriel, he "withdrew . . . into his cloud" but remained serene in his reliance on personal inspiration and the commitments he had made (Holmes, *Ralph Waldo Emerson*, letters to Rev. Henry Ware, pp. 124–7), and confident that his message had, in its truth, power to disturb the ministers. See Edward W. Emerson's note, *Complete Writings* (1904), Centenary Edition, IX, 408–09.

It fell in the ancient periods
  Which the brooding soul surveys,

Or ever the wild Time coined itself
  Into calendar months and days.
This was the lapse of Uriel,   5
  Which in Paradise befell.
Once, among the Pleiads walking,
Seyd overheard the young gods talking;
And the treason, too long pent,
To his ears was evident.   10
The young deities discussed
Laws of form, and metre just,
Orb, quintessence, and sunbeams,
What subsisteth, and what seems.
One, with low tones that decide,   15
And doubt and reverend use defied,
With a look that solved the sphere,
And stirred the devils everywhere,
Gave his sentiment divine
Against the being of a line.   20
'Line in nature is not found;
Unit and universe are round;
In vain produced, all rays return;
Evil will bless, and ice will burn.'
As Uriel spoke with piercing eye,   25
A shudder ran around the sky;
The stern old war-gods shook their heads,
The seraphs frowned from myrtle-beds;
Seemed to the holy festival
The rash word boded ill to all;   30
The balance-beam of Fate was bent;
The bounds of good and ill were rent;
Strong Hades could not keep his own,
But all slid to confusion.

A sad self-knowledge, withering, fell   35
On the beauty of Uriel;
In heaven once eminent, the god
Withdrew, that hour, into his cloud;
Whether doomed to long gyration
In the sea of generation,   40
Or by knowledge grown too bright
To hit the nerve of feebler sight.
Straightway, a forgetting wind
Stole over the celestial kind,
And their lips the secret kept,   45
If in ashes the fire-seed slept.

31. The balance-beam of Fate: the sign of the Scales in the Zodiac.   **33. Hades:** the Greek god of the underworld.

But now and then, truth-speaking things
Shamed the angels' veiling wings;
And, shrilling from the solar course,
Or from fruit of chemic force,   50
Procession of a soul in matter,
Or the speeding change of water,
Or out of the good of evil born,
Came Uriel's voice of cherub scorn,
And a blush tinged the upper sky,   55
And the gods shook, they knew not why.

Mithridates

MITHRIDATES VI, king of Pontus (120–63 B.C.),
ascended the throne when eleven years of age. He is
said to have surmounted intrigues against his life by
accustoming himself to poisons and by taking anti-
dotes. The poem, first published in *Poems* (1847),
may be interestingly compared with one of the same
title by A. E. Housman.

I cannot spare water or wine,
  Tobacco-leaf, or poppy, or rose;
From the earth-poles to the line,
  All between that works or grows,
Every thing is kin of mine.   5

Give me agates for my meat;
Give me cantharids to eat;
From air and ocean bring me foods,
From all zones and latitudes;—

From all natures, sharp and slimy,   10
  Salt and basalt, wild and tame:
Tree and lichen, ape, sea-lion,
  Bird, and reptile, be my game.

Ivy for my fillet band;
Blinding dog-wood in my hand;   15
Hemlock for my sherbet cull me,
And the prussic juice to lull me;
Swing me in the upas boughs,
Vampyre-fanned, when I carouse.

Too long shut in strait and few,   20
Thinly dieted on dew,
I will use the world, and sift it,
To a thousand humors shift it,
As you spin a cherry.
O doleful ghosts, and goblins merry!   25
O all you virtues, methods, mights,

Means, appliances, delights,
Reputed wrongs and braggart rights,
Smug routine, and things allowed,
Minorities, things under cloud!   30
Hither! take me, use me, fill me,
Vein and artery, though ye kill me!

Brahma

THIS POEM first appeared in the *Atlantic Monthly*
for November, 1857, and was first collected in *May-Day
and Other Pieces* (1867). Emerson's awareness of the
perplexity it has caused countless "ordinary readers"
may be found in his remark to his daughter: "If you
tell them to say Jehovah instead of Brahma, they
will not feel any perplexity." The concept of the
unity of life—common to Hindu philosophy—of
which "Brahma" is the best expression in the English
language, is discussed by F. I. Carpenter in "Immortality in India," in *American Literature*, I (1929), 233–
242. The sources of "Brahma" include the *Vishnu
Purana*, the *Bhagavat Gita*, and the *Katha-Upanishad*.
For a further study of the origins of the poem, see the
Concord Edition, IX, 464–467. See also Emerson's
essay, "Immortality" in which he wrote: "Brahma
the supreme, whoever knows him obtains whatever
he wishes. The soul is not born; it does not die;
it was not produced from anyone. Nor was any produced from it. Unborn, eternal, it is not slain,
subtler than what is subtle, greater than what is
great. . . ."

If the red slayer think he slays,
  Or if the slain think he is slain,
They know not well the subtle ways
  I keep, and pass, and turn again.

Far or forgot to me is near;   5
  Shadow and sunlight are the same;
The vanished gods to me appear;
  And one to me are shame and fame.

They reckon ill who leave me out;
  When me they fly, I am the wings;   10
I am the doubter and the doubt,
  And I the hymn the Brahmin sings.

The strong gods pine for my abode,
  And pine in vain the sacred Seven;
But thou, meek lover of the good!   15
  Find me, and turn thy back on heaven.

Days

This poem was written in 1851, when Emerson was forty-eight years of age, and first printed in *The Atlantic Monthly* for November, 1857. A notation in his Journals in 1831 reveals that the germ of the poem existed twenty years before it achieved final form. In 1847 Emerson stated the "idea" of the poem in prose: "The days come and go like muffled and veiled figures sent from a distant friendly party, but they say nothing, and if we do not use the gifts they bring, they carry them as silently away." Emerson himself believed "Days" to be his best poem; its compact beauty has led countless readers to concur. For an admirable criticism of "Days" see E. S. Oliver's "Emerson's 'Days' " in the *New England Quarterly*, XIX (1946), 518–523.

Daughters of Time, the hypocritic Days,
Muffled and dumb like barefoot dervishes,
And marching single in an endless file,
Bring diadems and fagots in their hands.
To each they offer gifts after his will,   5
Bread, kingdoms, stars, and sky that holds them all.
I, in my pleachèd garden, watched the pomp,
Forgot my morning wishes, hastily
Took a few herbs and apples, and the Day
Turned and departed silent. I, too late,   10
Under her solemn fillet saw the scorn.

Terminus

First published in *The Atlantic Monthly* for January, 1867; collected in *May-Day and Other Pieces* (1867). In Roman mythology Terminus is the god of boundaries and frontiers. The poem was in manuscript form in 1866, when Emerson was aged 63.

It is time to be old,
To take in sail:—
The god of bounds,
Who sets to seas a shore,
Came to me in his fatal rounds,   5
And said: 'No more!
No farther shoot
Thy broad ambitious branches, and thy root.
Fancy departs: no more invent;
Contract thy firmament   10
To compass of a tent.

There's not enough for this and that,
Make thy option which of two;
Economize the failing river,
Not the less revere the Giver,   15
Leave the many and hold the few.
Timely wise accept the terms,
Soften the fall with wary foot;
A little while
Still plan and smile,   20
And,—fault of novel germs,—
Mature the unfallen fruit.
Curse, if thou wilt, thy sires,
Bad husbands of their fires,
Who, when they gave thee breath,   25
Failed to bequeath
The needful sinew stark as once,
The Baresark marrow to thy bones,
But left a legacy of ebbing veins,
Inconstant heat and nerveless reins,—   30
Amid the Muses, left thee deaf and dumb,
Amid the gladiators, halt and numb.'

As the bird trims her to the gale,
I trim myself to the storm of time,
I man the rudder, reef the sail,   35
Obey the voice at eve obeyed at prime:
'Lowly faithful, banish fear,
Right onward drive unharmed;
The port, well worth the cruise, is near,
And every wave is charmed.'   40

Nature

Nature, a small book of ninety-five pages, was published anonymously in Boston in 1836. Except for paper pamphlets, it was Emerson's first book. Although Thomas Wentworth Higginson reported a slow sale, twelve years being required to dispose of 500 copies, the essay was read by persons of importance and provoked a good deal of contemporary opinion. Emerson made a few revisions when the piece was reprinted in *Nature, Addresses, and Lectures* (1849). A facsimile of the first edition, edited with an introduction by K. W. Cameron, was issued by Scholars' Facsimiles & Reprints in 1940. The text given here is that of the first edition.

The title page of *Nature* carries a quotation from Plotinus, the Neoplatonist: "Nature is but an image or limitation of wisdom, the last thing of the soul;

nature being a thing which doth only do, but not know." Emerson found a congenial philosophy in Neoplatonism, an approach to pantheism, or at least the conviction that nature is the material counterpart of the Divine Spirit. The Neoplatonic elements in the essay probably emanated from Emerson's interpretations of Samuel Taylor Coleridge. *Nature* embodies many of the leading ideas of Emerson's later work. In the essay the author first discussed the *uses* of Nature, classifying them in four categories, "Commodity," "Beauty," "Language," and "Discipline," the third of which, with the two introductory sections, is here reprinted from the first edition. Three other sections follow: "Idealism," which "sees the world in God," and raises the question "whether nature outwardly exists"; "Spirit," from which point of view the world becomes the "expositor of the divine mind"; and "Prospects," which arrives at the conclusion, "What we are, that only can we see. . . . Build therefore your own world."

Introduction

Our age is retrospective. It builds the sepulchres of the fathers. It writes biographies, histories, and criticism. The foregoing generations beheld God and nature face to face; we, through their eyes. Why should not we also enjoy an original relation to the universe? Why should not we have a poetry and philosophy of insight and not of tradition, and a religion by revelation to us, and not the history of theirs? Embosomed for a season in nature, whose floods of life stream around and through us, and invite us, by the powers they supply, to action proportioned to nature, why should we grope among the dry bones of the past, or put the living generation into masquerade out of its faded wardrobe? The sun shines to-day also. There is more wool and flax in the fields. There are new lands, new men, new thoughts. Let us demand our own works and laws and worship.

Undoubtedly we have no questions to ask which are unanswerable. We must trust the perfection of the creation so far, as to believe that whatever curiosity the order of things has awakened in our minds, the order of things can satisfy. Everyman's condition is a solution in hieroglyphic to those inquiries he would put. He acts it as life, before he apprehends it as truth. In like manner, nature is already, in its forms and tendencies, describing

its own design. Let us interrogate the great apparition, that shines so peacefully around us. Let us inquire, to what end is nature?

All science has one aim, namely, to find a theory of nature. We have theories of races and of functions, but scarcely yet a remote approximation to an idea of creation. We are now so far from the road to truth, that religious teachers dispute and hate each other, and speculative men are esteemed unsound and frivolous. But to a sound judgment, the most abstract truth is the most practical. Whenever a true theory appears, it will be its own evidence. Its test is, that it will explain all phenomena. Now many are thought not only unexplained but inexplicable; as language, sleep, dreams, beasts, sex.

Philosophically considered, the universe is composed of Nature and the Soul. Strictly speaking, therefore, all that is separate from us, all which Philosophy distinguishes as the NOT ME, that is, both nature and art, all other men and my own body, must be ranked under this name, NATURE. In enumerating the values of nature and casting up their sum, I shall use the word in both senses; —in its common and in its philosophical import. In inquiries so general as our present one, the inaccuracy is not material; no confusion of thought will occur. Nature, in the common sense, refers to essences unchanged by man; space, the air, the river, the leaf. Art is applied to the mixture of his will with the same things, as in a house, a canal, a statue, a picture. But his operations taken together are so insignificant, a little chipping, baking, patching, and washing, that in an impression so grand as that of the world on the human mind, they do not vary the result.

I. *Nature*

To go into solitude, a man needs to retire as much from his chamber as from society. I am not solitary whilst I read and write, though nobody is with me. But if a man would be alone, let him look at the stars. The rays that come from those heavenly worlds, will separate between him and vulgar things. One might think the atmosphere was made transparent with this design, to give man, in the heavenly bodies, the perpetual presence of the sublime. Seen in the streets of cities, how

604

great they are! If the stars should appear one night in a thousand years, how would men believe and adore; and preserve for many generations the remembrance of the city of God which had been shown! But every night come out these preachers of beauty, and light the universe with their admonishing smile.

The stars awaken a certain reverence, because though always present, they are always inaccessible; but all natural objects make a kindred impression, when the mind is open to their influence. Nature never wears a mean appearance. Neither does the wisest man extort all her secret, and lose his curiosity by finding out all her perfection. Nature never became a toy to a wise spirit. The flowers, the animals, the mountains, reflected all the wisdom of his best hour, as much as they had delighted the simplicity of his childhood.

When we speak of nature in this manner, we have a distinct but most poetical sense in the mind. We mean the integrity of impression made by manifold natural objects. It is this which distinguishes the stick of timber of the wood-cutter, from the tree of the poet. The charming landscape which I saw this morning, is indubitably made up of some twenty or thirty farms. Miller owns this field, Locke that, and Manning the woodland beyond. But none of them owns the landscape. There is a property in the horizon which no man has but he whose eye can integrate all the parts, that is, the poet. This is the best part of these men's farms, yet to this their land-deeds give no title.

To speak truly, few adult persons can see nature. Most persons do not see the sun. At least they have a very superficial seeing The sun illuminates only the eye of the man, but shines into the eye and the heart of the child. The lover of nature is he whose inward and outward senses are still truly adjusted to each other; who has retained the spirit of infancy even into the era of manhood. His intercourse with heaven and earth, becomes part of his daily food. In the presence of nature, a wild delight runs through the man, in spite of real sorrows. Nature says,—he is my creature, and maugre all his impertinent griefs, he shall be glad with me. Not the sun or the summer alone, but every hour and season yields its tribute of delight; for every hour and change corresponds to and authorizes a different state of the mind, from breathless noon to grimmest midnight. Nature is a setting that fits equally well a comic or a mourning piece. In good health, the air is a cordial of incredible virtue. Crossing a bare common, in snow puddles, at twilight, under a clouded sky, without having in my thoughts any occurrence of special good fortune, I have enjoyed a perfect exhilaration. Almost I fear to think how glad I am. In the woods too, a man casts off his years, as the snake his slough, and at what period soever of life, is always a child. In the woods, is perpetual youth. Within these plantations of God, a decorum and sanctity reign, a perennial festival is dressed, and the guest sees not how he should tire of them in a thousand years. In the woods, we return to reason and faith. There I feel that nothing can befall me in life,—no disgrace, no calamity, (leaving me my eyes,) which nature cannot repair. Standing on the bare ground,—my head bathed by the blithe air, and uplifted into infinite space,—all mean egotism vanishes. I become a transparent eye-ball. I am nothing. I see all. The currents of the Universal Being circulate through me; I am part or particle of God. The name of the nearest friend sounds then foreign and accidental. To be brothers, to be acquaintances—master or servant, is then a trifle and a disturbance. I am the lover of uncontained and immortal beauty. In the wilderness, I find something more dear and connate than in streets or villages. In the tranquil landscape, and especially in the distant line of the horizon, man beholds somewhat as beautiful as his own nature.

The greatest delight which the fields and woods minister, is the suggestion of an occult relation between man and the vegetable. I am not alone and unacknowledged. They nod to me and I to them. The waving of the boughs in the storm, is new to me and old. It takes me by surprise, and yet is not unknown. Its effect is like that of a higher thought or a better emotion coming over me, when I deemed I was thinking justly or doing right.

Yet it is certain that the power to produce this delight, does not reside in nature, but in man, or in a harmony of both. It is necessary to use these pleasures with great temperance. For, nature is not always tricked in holiday attire, but the same scene which yesterday breathed perfume and glittered as for the frolic of the nymphs, is overspread with melancholy today. Nature always wears the colors of the spirit. To a man laboring under calamity, the heat of his own fire hath sadness in it. Then, there is a kind of contempt of the landscape felt by him who has just lost by death a dear friend. The sky is less grand as it shuts down over less worth in the population.

IV. *Language*

A third use which Nature subserves to man is that of language. Nature is the vehicle of thought, and in a simple, double, and threefold degree.

1. Words are signs of natural facts.

2. Particular natural facts are symbols of particular facts.

3. Nature is the symbol of spirit.

1. *Words are signs of natural facts.* The use of natural history is to give us aid in supernatural history. The use of the outer creation is to give us language for the beings and changes of the inward creation. Every word which is used to express a moral or intellectual fact, if traced to its root, is found to be borrowed from some material appearance. *Right* originally means *straight; wrong* means *twisted.* *Spirit* primarily means *wind; transgression,* the crossing of a *line; supercilious,* the *raising of the eye-brow.* We say the *heart* to express emotion, the *head* to denote thought; and *thought* and *emotion* are, in their turn, words borrowed from sensible things, and now appropriated to spiritual nature. Most of the process by which this transformation is made, is hidden from us in the remote time when language was framed; but the same tendency may be daily observed in children. Children and savages use only nouns or names of things, which they continually convert into verbs, and apply to analogous mental acts.

2. But this origin of all words that convey a spiritual import,—so conspicuous a fact in the history of language,—is our least debt to nature. It is not words only that are emblematic; it is things which are emblematic. Every natural fact is a symbol of some spiritual fact. Every appearance in nature corresponds to some state of the mind, and that state of the mind can only be described

by presenting that natural appearance as its picture. An enraged man is a lion, a cunning man is a fox, a firm man is a rock, a learned man is a torch. A lamb is innocence; a snake is subtle spite; flowers express to us the delicate affections. Light and darkness are our familiar expression for knowledge and ignorance; and heat for love. Visible distance behind and before us, is respectively our image of memory and hope.

Who looks upon a river in a meditative hour, and is not reminded of the flux of all things? Throw a stone into the stream, and the circles that propagate themselves are the beautiful type of all influence. Man is conscious of a universal soul within or behind his individual life, wherein, as in a firmament, the natures of Justice, Truth, Love, Freedom, arise and shine. This universal soul, he calls Reason: it is not mine or thine or his, but we are its; we are its property and men. And the blue sky in which the private earth is buried, the sky with its eternal calm, and full of everlasting orbs, is the type of Reason. That which intellectually considered, we call Reason, considered in relation to nature, we call Spirit. Spirit is the Creator. Spirit hath life in itself. And man in all ages and countries, embodies it in his language, as the FATHER.

It is easily seen that there is nothing lucky or capricious in these analogies, but that they are constant, and pervade nature. These are not the dreams of a few poets, here and there, but man is an analogist, and studies relations in all objects. He is placed in the centre of beings, and a ray of relation passes from every other being to him. And neither can man be understood without these objects, nor these objects without man. All the facts in natural history taken by themselves, have no value, but are barren like a single sex. But marry it to human history, and it is full of life. Whole floras, all Linnæus's[n] and Buffon's[n] volumes, are dry catalogues of facts; but the most trivial of these facts, the habit of a plant, the organs, or work, or noise of an insect, applied to the illustration of a fact in intellectual philosophy,

Linnæus: Carolus Linnæus, Latin form for Carl von Linne (1707–1778), Swedish botanist, father of the modern classification of botanical terms. **Buffon:** Georges Louis Leclerc, Comte de Buffon (1707–1788), French naturalist.

or, in any way associated to human nature, affects us in the most lively and agreeable manner. The seed of a plant,—to what affecting analogies in the nature of man, is that little fruit made use of, in all discourse, up to the voice of Paul, who calls the human corpse a seed,—"It is sown a natural body; it is raised a spiritual body." The motion of the earth round its axis, and round the sun, makes the day, and the year. These are certain amounts of brute light and heat. But is there no intent of an analogy between man's life and the seasons? And do the seasons gain no grandeur or pathos from that analogy? The instincts of the ant are very unimportant considered as the ant's; but the moment a ray of relation is seen to extend from it to man, and the little drudge is seen to be a monitor, a little body with a mighty heart, then all its habits, even that said to be recently observed, that it never sleeps, become sublime.

Because of this radical correspondence between visible things and human thoughts, savages, who have only what is necessary, converse in figures. As we go back in history, language becomes more picturesque, until its infancy, when it is all poetry; or, all spiritual facts are represented by natural symbols. The same symbols are found to make the original elements of all languages. It has more-over been observed, that the idioms of all languages approach each other in passages of the greatest eloquence and power. And as this is the first language, so it is the last. This immediate dependence of language upon nature, this conversion of an outward phenomenon into a type of somewhat in human life, never loses its power to affect us. It is this which gives that piquancy to the conversation of a strong-natured farmer or back-woodsman, which all men relish.

Thus is nature an interpreter, by whose means man converses with his fellowmen. A man's power to connect his thought with its proper symbol, and so to utter it, depends on the simplicity of his character, that is, upon his love of truth and his desire to communicate it without loss. The corruption of man is followed by the corruption of language. When simplicity of character and the sovereignty of ideas is broken up by the prevalence of secondary desires, the desire of riches, the desire of pleasure, the desire of power, the desire of

praise,—and duplicity and falsehood take place of simplicity and truth, the power over nature as an interpreter of the will, is in a degree lost; new imagery ceases to be created, and old words are perverted to stand for things which are not; a paper currency is employed when there is no bullion in the vaults. In due time, the fraud is manifest, and words lose all power to stimulate the understanding or the affections. Hundreds of writers may be found in every long-civilized nation who for a short time believe, and make others believe, that they see and utter truths, who do not of themselves clothe one thought in its natural garment, but who feed unconsciously upon the language created by the primary writers of the country, those, namely, who hold primarily on nature.

But wise men pierce this rotten diction and fasten words again to visible things; so that picturesque language is at once a commanding certificate that he who employs it, is a man in alliance with truth and God. The moment our discourse rises above the ground line of familiar facts, and is inflamed with passion or exalted by thought, it clothes itself in images. A man conversing in earnest, if he watch his intellectual processes, will find that always a material image, more or less luminous, arises in his mind, cotemporaneous with every thought, which furnishes the vestment of the thought. Hence, good writing and brilliant discourse are perpetual allegories. This imagery is spontaneous. It is the blending of experience with the present action of the mind. It is proper creation. It is the working of the Original Cause through the instruments he has already made.

These facts may suggest the advantage which the country-life possesses, for a powerful mind, over the artificial and curtailed life of cities. We know more from nature than we can at will communicate. Its light flows into the mind evermore, and we forget its presence. The poet, the orator, bred in the woods, whose senses have been nourished by their fair and appeasing changes, year after year, without design and without heed,— shall not lose their lesson altogether, in the roar of cities or the broil of politics. Long hereafter, amidst agitation and terror in national councils,— in the hour of revolution,—these solemn images shall reappear in their morning lustre, as fit symbols and words of the thoughts which the passing events shall awaken. At the call of a noble sentiment, again the woods wave, the pines murmur, the river rolls and shines, and the cattle low upon the mountains, as he saw and heard them in his infancy. And with these forms, the spells of persuasion, the keys of power are put into his hands.

3. We are thus assisted by natural objects in the expression of particular meanings. But how great a language to convey such pepper-corn informations! Did it need such noble races of creatures, this profusion of forms, this host of orbs in heaven, to furnish man with the dictionary and grammar of his municipal speech? Whilst we use this grand cipher to expedite the affairs of our pot and kettle, we feel that we have not yet put it to its use, neither are we able. We are like travellers using the cinders of a volcano to roast their eggs. Whilst we see that it always stands ready to clothe what we would say, we cannot avoid the question, whether the characters are not significant of themselves. Have mountains, and waves, and skies, no significance but what we consciously give them, when we employ them as emblems of our thoughts? The world is emblematic. Parts of speech are metaphors because the whole of nature is a metaphor of the human mind. The laws of moral nature answer to those of matter as face to face in a glass. "The visible world and the relation of its parts, is the dial plate of the invisible." The axioms of physics translate the laws of ethics. Thus, "the whole is greater than its part;" "reaction is equal to action;" "the smallest weight may be made to lift the greatest, the difference of weight being compensated by time;" and many the like propositions, which have an ethical as well as physical sense. These propositions have a much more extensive and universal sense when applied to human life, than when confined to technical use.

In like manner, the memorable words of history, and the proverbs of nations, consist usually of a natural fact, selected as a picture or parable of a moral truth. Thus: A rolling stone gathers no moss; A bird in the hand is worth two in the bush; A cripple in the right way, will beat a racer in the wrong; Make hay whilst the sun shines; 'Tis hard to carry a full cup even; Vinegar is the son of wine; The last ounce broke the camel's back; Long-lived trees make roots first;—and the like. In their primary sense these are trivial facts, but we repeat them for the value of their analogical import. What is true of proverbs, is true of all fables, parables, and allegories.

This relation between the mind and matter is not fancied by some poet, but stands in the will of God, and so is free to be known by all men. It appears to men, or it does not appear. When in fortunate hours we ponder this miracle, the wise man doubts, if, at all other times, he is not blind and deaf;

——Can these things be,
And overcome us like a summer's cloud,
Without our special wonder?

for the universe becomes transparent, and the light of higher laws than its own, shines through it. It is the standing problem which has exercised the wonder and the study of every fine genius since the world began; from the era of the Egyptians and the Brahmins, to that of Pythagoras,[n] of Plato,[n] of Bacon,[n] of Leibnitz,[n] of Swedenborg.[n] There sits the Sphinx at the road-side, and from age to age, as each prophet comes by, he tries his fortune at reading her riddle. There seems to be a necessity in spirit to manifest itself in material forms; and day and night, river and storm, beast and bird, acid and alkali, pre-exist in necessary Ideas in the mind of God, and are what they are by virtue of preceding affections, in the world of spirit. A Fact is the end or last issue of spirit. The visible creation is the terminus or the circumference of the invisible world. "Material objects," said a French philosopher, "are necessarily kinds of *scoriæ* of the substantial thoughts of the Creator, which must always preserve an exact

Pythagoras: Greek philosopher of the sixth century B.C., who thought that earthly life was merely a preparation for life hereafter. **Plato:** (427?–347 B.C.), Greek philosopher, student of Socrates and recorder of his philosophy. Founder of the academy. **Bacon:** Francis Bacon (1561–1626), English philosopher, whose *Novum Organum* introduced the inductive method of interpreting nature. **Leibnitz:** Gottfried Wilhelm von Leibnitz (1646–1716), German philosopher and mathematician, whose *Théodicé* presented an optimistic philosophy. **Swedenborg:** Emanuel Swedenborg (1688–1772), Swedish scientist and philosopher, who devoted the latter part of his life to theology.

relation to their first origin; in other words, visible nature must have a spiritual and moral side."

This doctrine is abstruse, and though the images of "garment," "scoriæ," "mirror," etc., may stimulate the fancy, we must summon the aid of subtler and more vital expositors to make it plain. "Every scripture is to be interpreted by the same spirit which gave it forth,"—is the fundamental law of criticism. A life in harmony with nature, the love of truth and of virtue, will purge the eyes to understand her text. By degrees we may come to know the primitive sense of the permanent objects of nature, so that the world shall be to us an open book, and every form significant of its hidden life and final cause.

A new interest surprises us, whilst, under the view now suggested, we contemplate the fearful extent and multitude of objects; since "every object rightly seen, unlocks a new faculty of the soul." That which was unconscious truth, becomes, when interpreted and defined in an object, a part of the domain of knowledge,—a new amount to the magazine of power.

The American Scholar

THIS ELECTRIC UTTERANCE, which Oliver Wendell Holmes called "our intellectual Declaration of Independence," is Emerson's most famous speech. It was delivered on August 31, 1837, before the "president and gentlemen" of the Phi Beta Kappa Society of Harvard College, who assembled in the meetinghouse of the First Parish, opposite the college yard. Emerson was thirty-four years old as he faced the dignified convocation of scholars, and he packed his address with the convictions which he had been pondering since his return from Europe in 1833. Although his words made the academic conservatives in the audience shudder, just as twelve months later he was to startle his hearers at the Divinity School, he received an eager response from the more youthful members of the assembly. Oliver Wendell Holmes reported that "the young men went out from it as if a prophet had been proclaiming to them, 'Thus saith the Lord!'" To them Emerson's eloquent call for a native literature, no longer to be "fed on the sere remains of foreign harvests," sounded forth as the trumpet of a prophecy.

For a delightful account of the effect of the speech upon the older and more conservative members of the audience as well as the youthful liberals, see Bliss Perry's "Emerson's Most Famous Speech," in *The Praise of Folly and Other Papers* (1923), pp. 81–113. This address of Emerson was issued as a pamphlet in 1837, and reprinted in 1838. In England it was published in 1844 as *Man Thinking*. It was collected in the first series of the *Essays*. The text is that of the New and Revised Edition of 1883.

Mr. President and Gentlemen, I greet you on the recommencement of our literary year. Our anniversary is one of hope, and, perhaps, not enough of labor. We do not meet for games of strength or skill, for the recitation of histories, tragedies, and odes, like the ancient Greeks; for parliaments of love and poesy, like the Troubadours; nor for the advancement of science, like our contemporaries in the British and European capitals. Thus far, our holiday has been simply a friendly sign of the survival of the love of letters amongst a people too busy to give to letters any more. As such it is precious as the sign of an indestructible instinct. Perhaps the time is already come when it ought to be, and will be, something else; when the sluggard intellect of this continent will look from under its iron lids and fill the postponed expectation of the world with something better than the exertions of mechanical skill. Our day of dependence, our long apprenticeship to the learning of other lands, draws to a close. The millions that around us are rushing into life, cannot always be fed on the sere remains of foreign harvests. Events, actions arise, that must be sung, that will sing themselves. Who can doubt that poetry will revive and lead in a new age, as the star in the constellation Harp, which now flames in our zenith, astronomers announce, shall one day be the polestar for a thousand years?

In this hope I accept the topic which not only usage but the nature of our association seem to prescribe to this day,—the AMERICAN SCHOLAR. Year by year we come up hither to read one more chapter of his biography. Let us inquire what light new days and events have thrown on his character and his hopes.

It is one of those fables which out of an unknown antiquity convey an unlooked-for wisdom, that the gods, in the beginning, divided Man into men, that he might be more helpful to himself;

just as the hand was divided into fingers, the better to answer its end.

The old fable covers a doctrine ever new and sublime; that there is One Man,—present to all particular men only partially, or through one faculty; and that you must take the whole society to find the whole man. Man is not a farmer, or a professor, or an engineer, but he is all. Man is priest, and scholar, and statesman, and producer, and soldier. In the divided or social state these functions are parcelled out to individuals, each of whom aims to do his stint of the joint work, whilst each other performs his. The fable implies that the individual, to possess himself, must sometimes return from his own labor to embrace all the other laborers. But, unfortunately, this original unit, this fountain of power, has been so distributed to multitudes, has been so minutely subdivided and peddled out, that it is spilled into drops, and cannot be gathered. The state of society is one in which the members have suffered amputation from the trunk, and strut about so many walking monsters,—a good finger, a neck, a stomach, an elbow, but never a man.

Man is thus metamorphosed into a thing, into many things. The planter, who is Man sent out into the field to gather food, is seldom cheered by any idea of the true dignity of his ministry. He sees his bushel and his cart, and nothing beyond, and sinks into the farmer, instead of Man on the farm. The tradesman scarcely ever gives an ideal worth to his work, but is ridden by the routine of his craft, and the soul is subject to dollars. The priest becomes a form; the attorney a statutebook; the mechanic a machine; the sailor a rope of the ship.

In this distribution of functions the scholar is the delegated intellect. In the right state he is Man Thinking. In the degenerate state, when the victim of society, he tends to become a mere thinker, or still worse, the parrot of other men's thinking.

In this view of him, as Man Thinking, the theory of his office is contained. Him Nature solicits with all her placid, all her monitory pictures; him the past instructs; him the future invites. Is not indeed every man a student, and do not all things exist for the student's behoof?

And, finally, is not the true scholar the only true master? But the old oracle said, "All things have two handles: beware of the wrong one." In life, too often, the scholar errs with mankind and forfeits his privilege. Let us see him in his school, and consider him in reference to the main influences he receives.

"nature"

I. The first in time and the first in importance of the influences upon the mind is that of nature. Every day, the sun; and, after the sunset, Night and her stars. Ever the winds blow; ever the grass grows. Every day, men and women, conversing, beholding and beholden. The scholar is he of all men whom this spectacle most engages. He must settle its value in his mind. What is nature to him? There is never a beginning, there is never an end, to the inexplicable continuity of this web of God, but always circular power returning into itself. Therein it resembles his own spirit, whose beginning, whose ending, he never can find,—so entire, so boundless. Far too as her splendors shine, system on system shooting like rays, upward, downward, without centre, without circumference,—in the mass and in the particle. Nature hastens to render account of herself to the mind. Classification begins. To the young mind every thing is individual, stands by itself. By and by, it finds how to join two things and see in them one nature; then three, then three thousand; and so, tyrannized over by its own unifying instinct, it goes on tying things together, diminishing anomalies, discovering roots running under ground whereby contrary and remote things cohere and flower out from one stem. It presently learns that since the dawn of history there has been a constant accumulation and classifying of facts. But what is classification but the perceiving that these objects are not chaotic, and are not foreign, but have a law which is also a law of the human mind? The astronomer discovers that geometry, a pure abstraction of the human mind, is the measure of planetary motion. The chemist finds proportions and intelligible method throughout matter; and science is nothing but the finding of analogy, identity, in the most remote parts. The ambitious soul sits down before each refractory fact; one after another reduces all strange constitutions, all new powers, to their class and their law, and goes on forever to animate the last fibre of organization, the outskirts of nature, by insight.

Thus to him, to this school-boy under the bending dome of day, is suggested that he and it proceed from one root; one is leaf and one is flower; relation, sympathy, stirring in every vein. And what is that root? Is not that the soul of his soul? A thought too bold; a dream too wild. Yet when this spiritual light shall have revealed the law of more earthly natures,—when he has learned to worship the soul, and to see that the natural philosophy that now is, is only the first gropings of its gigantic hand, he shall look forward to an ever expanding knowledge as to a becoming creator. He shall see that nature is the opposite of the soul, answering to it part for part. One is seal and one is print. Its beauty is the beauty of his own mind. Its laws are the laws of his own mind. Nature then becomes to him the measure of his attainments. So much of nature as he is ignorant of, so much of his own mind does he not yet possess. And, in fine, the ancient precept, "Know thyself," and the modern precept, "Study nature," become at last one maxim.

"Books"

II. The next great influence into the spirit of the scholar is the mind of the Past,—in whatever form, whether of literature, of art, of institutions, that mind is inscribed. Books are the best type of the influence of the past, and perhaps we shall get at the truth,—learn the amount of this influence more conveniently,—by considering their value alone.

The theory of books is noble. The scholar of the first age received into him the world around; brooded thereon; gave it the new arrangement of his own mind, and uttered it again. It came into him life; it went out from him truth. It came to him short-lived actions; it went out from him immortal thoughts. It came to him business; it went from him poetry. It was dead fact; now, it is quick thought. It can stand, and it can go. It now endures, it now flies, it now inspires. Precisely in proportion to the depth of mind from which it issued, so high does it soar, so long does it sing.

Or, I might say, it depends on how far the process had gone, of transmuting life into truth. In proportion to the completeness of the distillation, so will the purity and imperishableness of the product be. But none is quite perfect. As no air-pump can by any means make a perfect vacuum, so neither can any artist entirely exclude the conventional, the local, the perishable from his book, or write a book of pure thought, that shall be as efficient, in all respects, to a remote posterity, as to contemporaries, or rather to the second age. Each age, it is found, must write its own books; or rather, each generation for the next succeeding. The books of an older period will not fit this.

Yet hence arises a grave mischief. The sacredness which attaches to the act of creation, the act of thought, is transferred to the record. The poet chanting was felt to be a divine man: henceforth the chant is divine also. The writer was a just and wise spirit: henceforward it is settled the book is perfect; as love of the hero corrupts into worship of his statue. Instantly the book becomes noxious: the guide is a tyrant. The sluggish and perverted mind of the multitude, slow to open to the incursions of Reason, having once so opened, having once received this book, stands upon it, and makes an outcry if it is disparaged. Colleges are built on it. Books are written on it by thinkers, not by Man Thinking; by men of talent, that is, who start wrong, who set out from accepted dogmas, not from their own sight of principles. Meek young men grow up in libraries, believing it their duty to accept the views which Cicero, which Locke, which Bacon, have given; forgetful that Cicero, Locke, and Bacon were only young men in libraries when they wrote these books.

Hence, instead of Man Thinking, we have the bookworm. Hence the book-learned class, who value books, as such; not as related to nature and the human constitution, but as making a sort of Third Estate with the world and the soul. Hence the restorers of readings, the emendators, the bibliomaniacs of all degrees.

Books are the best of things, well used; abused, among the worst. What is the right use? What is the one end which all means go to effect? They are for nothing but to inspire. I had better never see a book than to be warped by its attraction clean out of my own orbit, and made a satellite instead of a system. The one thing in the world, of value, is the active soul. This every man is entitled to; this every man contains within him, although in almost all men obstructed, and as yet unborn. The soul active sees absolute truth and utters truth, or creates. In this action it is genius; not the privilege of here and there a favorite, but the sound estate of every man. In its essence it is progressive. The book, the college, the school of art, the institution of any kind, stop with some past utterance of genius. This is good, say they,—let us hold by this. They pin me down. They look backward and not forward. But genius looks forward: the eyes of man are set in his forehead, not in his hindhead: man hopes: genius creates. Whatever talents may be, if the man create not, the pure efflux of the Deity is not his;—cinders and smoke there may be, but not yet flame. There are creative manners, there are creative actions, and creative words; manners, actions, words, that is, indicative of no custom or authority, but springing spontaneous from the mind's own sense of good and fair.

On the other part, instead of being its own seer, let it receive from another mind its truth, though it were in torrents of light, without periods of solitude, inquest, and self-recovery, and a fatal disservice is done. Genius is always sufficiently the enemy of genius by over-influence. The literature of every nation bears me witness. The English dramatic poets have Shakspearized now for two hundred years.

Undoubtedly there is a right way of reading, so it be sternly subordinated. Man Thinking must not be subdued by his instruments. Books are for the scholar's idle times. When he can read God directly, the hour is too precious to be wasted in other men's transcripts of their readings. But when the intervals of darkness come, as come they must,—when the sun is hid and the stars withdraw their shining,—we repair to the lamps which were kindled by their ray, to guide our steps to the East again, where the dawn is. We hear, that we may speak. The Arabian proverb says, "A fig tree, looking on a fig tree, becometh fruitful."

It is remarkable, the character of the pleasure we derive from the best books. They impress us with the conviction that one nature wrote and the same reads. We read the verses of one of the great English poets, of Chaucer, of Marvell, of Dryden, with the most modern joy,—with a pleasure, I mean, which is in great part caused by the abstraction of all time from their verses. There is some awe mixed with the joy of our surprise, when this poet, who lived in some past world, two or three hundred years ago, says that which lies close to my own soul, that which I also had well-nigh thought and said. But for the evidence thence afforded to the philosophical doctrine of the identity of all minds, we should suppose some pre-established harmony, some foresight of souls that were to be, and some preparation of stores for their future wants, like the fact observed in insects, who lay up food before death for the young grub they shall never see.

I would not be hurried by any love of system, by any exaggeration of instincts, to underrate the Book. We all know, that as the human body can be nourished on any food, though it were boiled grass and the broth of shoes, so the human mind can be fed by any knowledge. And great and heroic men have existed who had almost no other information than by the printed page. I only would say that it needs a strong head to bear that diet. One must be an inventor to read well. As the proverb says, "He that would bring home the wealth of the Indies, must carry out the wealth of the Indies." There is then creative reading as well as creative writing. When the mind is braced by labor and invention, the page of whatever book we read becomes luminous with manifold allusion. Every sentence is doubly significant, and the sense of our author is as broad as the world. We then see, what is always true, that as the seer's hour of vision is short and rare among heavy days and months, so is its record, perchance, the least part of his volume. The discerning will read, in his Plato or Shakspeare, only that least part,—only the authentic utterances of the oracle;—all the rest he rejects, were it never so many times Plato's and Shakspeare's.

Of course there is a portion of reading quite indispensable to a wise man. History and exact science he must learn by laborious reading. Colleges, in like manner, have their indispensable office,—to teach elements. But they can only highly serve us when they aim not to drill, but to create; when they gather from far every ray of various genius to their hospitable halls, and by the concentrated fires, set the hearts of their youth on flame. Thought and knowledge are natures in which apparatus and pretension avail nothing. Gowns and pecuniary foundations, though of towns of gold, can never countervail the least sentence or syllable of wit. Forget this, and our American colleges will recede in their public importance, whilst they grow richer every year.

"action" of scholar

III. There goes in the world a notion that the scholar should be a recluse, a valetudinarian,—as unfit for any handiwork or public labor as a penknife for an axe. The so-called "practical men" sneer at speculative men, as if, because they speculate or *see*, they could do nothing. I have heard it said that the clergy,—who are always, more universally than any other class, the scholars of their day,—are addressed as women; that the rough, spontaneous conversation of men they do not hear, but only a mincing and diluted speech. They are often virtually disfranchised; and indeed there are advocates for their celibacy. As far as this is true of the studious classes, it is not just and wise. Action is with the scholar subordinate, but it is essential. Without it he is not yet man. Without it thought can never ripen into truth. Whilst the world hangs before the eye as a cloud of beauty, we cannot even see its beauty. Inaction is cowardice, but there can be no scholar without the heroic mind. The preamble of thought, the transition through which it passes from the unconscious to the conscious, is action. Only so much do I know, as I have lived. Instantly we know whose words are loaded with life, and whose not.

The world,—this shadow of the soul, or other me,—lies wide around. Its attractions are the keys which unlock my thoughts and make me acquainted with myself. I run eagerly into this resounding tumult. I grasp the hands of those next me, and take my place in the ring to suffer and to work, taught by an instinct that so shall the dumb abyss be vocal with speech. I pierce its order; I dissipate its fear; I dispose of it within the circuit of my expanding life. So much only of life as I know by experience, so much of the wilderness have I vanquished and planted, or so far have I extended my being, my dominion. I do not see how any man can afford, for the sake of his nerves and his nap, to spare any action in which he can partake. It is pearls and rubies to his discourse. Drudgery, calamity, exasperation, want, are instructors in eloquence and wisdom. The true scholar grudges every opportunity of action past by, as a loss of power.

It is the raw material out of which the intellect moulds her splendid products. A strange process too, this by which experience is converted into thought, as a mulberry leaf is converted into satin. The manufacture goes forward at all hours.

The actions and events of our childhood and youth are now matters of calmest observation. They lie like fair pictures in the air. Not so with our recent actions,—with the business which we now have in hand. On this we are quite unable to speculate. Our affections as yet circulate through it. We no more feel or know it than we feel the feet, or the hand, or the brain of our body. The new deed is yet a part of life,—remains for a time immersed in our unconscious life. In some contemplative hour it detaches itself from the life like a ripe fruit, to become a thought of the mind. Instantly it is raised, transfigured; the corruptible has put on incorruption. Henceforth it is an object of beauty, however base its origin and neighborhood. Observe too the impossibility of antedating this act. In its grub state, it cannot fly, it cannot shine, it is a dull grub. But suddenly, without observation, the selfsame thing unfurls beautiful wings, and is an angel of wisdom. So is there no fact, no event, in our private history, which shall not, sooner or later, lose its adhesive, inert form, and astonish us by soaring from our body into the empyrean. Cradle and infancy, school and playground, the fear of boys, and dogs, and ferules, the love of little maids and berries, and many another fact that once filled the whole sky, are gone already; friend and relative, profession and party, town and country, nation and world, must also soar and sing.

Of course, he who has put forth his total strength in fit actions has the richest return of wisdom. I will not shut myself out of this globe of action, and transplant an oak into a flower-pot, there to hunger and pine; nor trust the revenue of some single faculty, and exhaust one vein of thought, much like those Savoyards, who, getting their livelihood by carving shepherds, shepherdesses, and smoking Dutchmen, for all Europe, went out one day to the mountain to find stock, and discovered that they had whittled up the last of their pine-trees. Authors we have, in numbers, who have written out their vein, and who, moved by a commendable prudence, sail for Greece or Palestine, follow the trapper into the prairie, or ramble round Algiers, to replenish their merchantable stock.

If it were only for a vocabulary, the scholar would be covetous of action. Life is our dictionary. Years are well spent in country labors; in town; in the insight into trades and manufactures; in frank intercourse with many men and women; in science; in art; to the one end of mastering in all their facts a language by which to illustrate and embody our perceptions. I learn immediately from any speaker how much he has already lived, through the poverty or the splendor of his speech. Life lies behind us as the quarry from whence we get tiles and copestones for the masonry of to-day. This is the way to learn grammar. Colleges and books only copy the language which the field and the work-yard made.

But the final value of action, like that of books, and better than books, is that it is a resource. That great principle of Undulation in nature, that shows itself in the inspiring and expiring of the breath; in desire and satiety; in the ebb and flow of the sea; in day and night; in heat and cold; and, as yet more deeply ingrained in every atom and every fluid, is known to us under the name of Polarity,—these "fits of easy transmission and reflection," as Newton called them, are the law of nature because they are the law of spirit.

The mind now thinks, now acts, and each fit reproduces the other. When the artist has exhausted his materials, when the fancy no longer paints, when thoughts are no longer apprehended and books are a weariness,—he has always the resource to live. Character is higher than intellect. Thinking is the function. Living is the functionary. The stream retreats to its source. A great soul will be strong to live, as well as strong to

think. Does he lack organ or medium to impart his truth? He can still fall back on this elemental force of living them. This is a total act. Thinking is a partial act. Let the grandeur of justice shine in his affairs. Let the beauty of affection cheer his lowly roof. Those "far from fame," who dwell and act with him, will feel the force of his constitution in the doings and passages of the day better than it can be measured by any public and designed display. Time shall teach him that the scholar loses no hour which the man lives. Herein he unfolds the sacred germ of his instinct, screened from influence. What is lost in seemliness is gained in strength. Not out of those on whom systems of education have exhausted their culture, comes the helpful giant to destroy the old or to build the new, but out of unhandselled savage nature; out of terrible Druids and Berserkers come at last Alfred and Shakspeare.

I hear therefore with joy whatever is beginning to be said of the dignity and necessity of labor to every citizen. There is virtue yet in the hoe and the spade, for learned as well as for unlearned hands. And labor is everywhere welcome; always we are invited to work; only be this limitation observed, that a man shall not for the sake of wider activity sacrifice any opinion to the popular judgments and modes of action.

"Duties" of scholar.

I have now spoken of the education of the scholar by nature, by books, and by action. It remains to say somewhat of his duties.

They are such as become Man Thinking. They may all be comprised in self-trust. The office of the scholar is to cheer, to raise, and to guide men by showing them facts amidst appearances. He plies the slow, unhonored, and unpaid task of observation. Flamsteed and Herschel, in their glazed observatories, may catalogue the stars with the praise of all men, and the results being splendid and useful, honor is sure. But he, in his private observatory, cataloguing obscure and nebulous stars of the human mind, which as yet no man has thought of as such,—watching days and months sometimes for a few facts; correcting still his old records;—must relinquish display and immediate fame. In the long period of his preparation he must betray often an ignorance and shiftlessness in popular arts, incurring the disdain of the able who shoulder him aside. Long he must stammer in his speech; often forego the living for the dead. Worse yet, he must accept,—how often!—poverty and solitude. For the ease and pleasure of treading the old road, accepting the fashions, the education, the religion of society, he takes the cross of making his own, and, of course, the self-accusation, the faint heart, the frequent uncertainty and loss of time, which are the nettles and tangling vines in the way of the self-relying and self-directed; and the state of virtual hostility in which he seems to stand to society, and especially to educated society. For all this loss and scorn, what offset? He is to find consolation in exercising the highest functions of human nature. He is one who raises himself from private considerations and breathes and lives on public and illustrious thoughts. He is the world's eye. He is the world's heart. He is to resist the vulgar prosperity that retrogrades ever to barbarism, by preserving and communicating heroic sentiments, noble biographies, melodious verse, and the conclusions of history. Whatsoever oracles the human heart, in all emergencies, in all solemn hours, has uttered as its commentary on the world of actions,—these he shall receive and impart. And whatsoever new verdict Reason from her inviolable seat pronounces on the passing men and events of to-day,—this he shall hear and promulgate.

These being his functions, it becomes him to feel all confidence in himself, and to defer never to the popular cry. He and he only knows the world. The world of any moment is the merest appearance. Some great decorum, some fetish of a government, some ephemeral trade, or war, or man, is cried up by half mankind and cried down by the other half, as if all depended on this particular up or down. The odds are that the whole question is not worth the poorest thought which the scholar has lost in listening to the controversy. Let him not quit his belief that a popgun is a popgun, though the ancient and honorable of the earth affirm it to be the crack of doom. In silence, in steadiness, in severe abstraction, let him hold by himself; add observation to observation, patient of neglect, patient of reproach, and bide his own time,—happy enough if he can satisfy

himself alone that this day he has seen something truly. Success treads on every right step. For the instinct is sure, that prompts him to tell his brother what he thinks. He then learns that in going down into the secrets of his own mind he has descended into the secrets of all minds. He learns that he who has mastered any law in his private thoughts, is master to that extent of all men whose language he speaks, and of all into whose language his own can be translated. The poet, in utter solitude remembering his spontaneous thoughts and recording them, is found to have recorded that which men in crowded cities find true for them also. The orator distrusts at first the fitness of his frank confessions, his want of knowledge of the persons he addresses, until he finds that he is the complement of his hearers;—that they drink his words because he fulfils for them their own nature; the deeper he dives into his privatest, secretest presentiment, to his wonder he finds this *feeling that something will happen* is the most acceptable, most public, and universally true. The people delight in it; the better part of every man feels, This is my music; this myself.

In self-trust all the virtues are comprehended. Free should the scholar be,—free and brave. Free even to the definition of freedom, "without any hindrance that does not arise out of his own constitution." Brave; for fear is a thing which a scholar by his very function puts behind him. Fear always springs from ignorance. It is a shame to him if his tranquillity, amid dangerous times, arise from the presumption that like children and women his is a protected class; or if he seek a temporary peace by the diversion of his thoughts from politics or vexed questions, hiding his head like an ostrich in the flowering bushes, peeping into microscopes, and turning rhymes, as a boy whistles to keep his courage up. So is the danger a danger still; so is the fear worse. Manlike let him turn and face it. Let him look into its eye and search its nature, inspect its origin,—see the whelping of this lion,—which lies no great way back; he will then find in himself a perfect comprehension of its nature and extent; he will have made his hands meet on the other side, and can henceforth defy it and pass on superior. The world is his who can see through its pretension. What deafness, what stone-blind custom, what

overgrown error you behold is there only by sufferance,—by your sufferance. See it to be a lie,
and you have already dealt it its mortal blow.

Yes, we are the cowed,—we the trustless. It is a
mischievous notion that we are come late into nature; that the world was finished a long time ago.
As the world was plastic and fluid in the hands of
God, so it is ever to so much of his attributes as we
bring to it. To ignorance and sin, it is flint. They
adapt themselves to it as they may; but in propor- 10
tion as a man has any thing in him divine, the
firmament flows before him and takes his signet
and form. Not he is great who can alter matter, but
he who can alter my state of mind. They are the
kings of the world who give the color of their
present thought to all nature and all art, and
persuade men by the cheerful serenity of their
carrying the matter, that this thing which they do
is the apple which the ages have desired to pluck,
now at last ripe, and inviting nations to the 20
harvest. The great man makes the great thing.
Wherever Macdonald sits, there is the head of the
table. Linnæus makes botany the most alluring
of studies, and wins it from the farmer and the
herb-woman; Davy, chemistry; and Cuvier,
fossils. The day is always his who works in it with
serenity and great aims. The unstable estimates
of men crowd to him whose mind is filled with a
truth, as the heaped waves of the Atlantic follow
the moon. 30

For this self-trust, the reason is deeper than
can be fathomed,—darker than can be enlightened.
I might not carry with me the feeling of my audience in stating my own belief. But I have already shown the ground of my hope, in adverting
to the doctrine that man is one. I believe man has
been wronged; he has wronged himself. He has
almost lost the light that can lead him back to his
prerogatives. Men are become of no account.
Men in history, men in the world of to-day, are 40
bugs, are spawn, and are called "the mass" and
"the herd." In a century, in a millennium, one
or two men; that is to say, one or two approxima-
tions to the right state of every man. All the rest
behold in the hero or the poet their own green and
crude being,—ripened; yes, and are content to
be less, so that may attain to its full stature. What
a testimony, full of grandeur, full of pity, is borne

to the demands of his own nature, by the poor
clansman, the poor partisan, who rejoices in the
glory of his chief. The poor and the low find
some amends to their immense moral capacity, for
their acquiescence in a political and social inferiority. They are content to be brushed like flies
from the path of a great person, so that justice
shall be done by him to that common nature
which it is the dearest desire of all to see enlarged
and glorified. They sun themselves in the great 10
man's light, and feel it to be their own element.
They cast the dignity of man from their downtrod
selves upon the shoulders of a hero, and will perish
to add one drop of blood to make that great heart
beat, those giant sinews combat and conquer. He
lives for us, and we live in him.

Men such as they are, very naturally seek
money or power; and power because it is as good
as money,—the "spoils," so called, "of office."
And why not? for they aspire to the highest, and 20
this, in their sleep-walking, they dream is highest.
Wake them and they shall quit the false good and
leap to the true, and leave governments to clerks
and desks. This revolution is to be wrought by the
gradual domestication of the idea of Culture.
The main enterprise of the world for splendor, for
extent, is the upbuilding of a man. Here are the
materials strewn along the ground. The private
life of one man shall be a more illustrious monarchy,
more formidable to its enemy, more sweet and 30
serene in its influence to its friend, than any kingdom in history. For a man, rightly viewed, comprehendeth the particular natures of all men.
Each philosopher, each bard, each actor has only
done for me, as by a delegate, what one day I can
do for myself. The books which once we valued
more than the apple of the eye, we have quite exhausted. What is that but saying that we have
come up with the point of view which the universal
mind took through the eyes of one scribe; we have 40
been that man, and have passed on. First, one,
then another, we drain all cisterns, and waxing
greater by all these supplies, we crave a better and
more abundant food. The man has never lived that
can feed us ever. The human mind cannot be
enshrined in a person who shall set a barrier on any
one side to this unbounded, unboundable empire.
It is one central fire, which, flaming now out of

the lips of Etna, lightens the capes of Sicily, and now out of the throat of Vesuvius, illuminates the towers and vineyards of Naples. It is one light which beams out of a thousand stars. It is one soul which animates all men.

But I have dwelt perhaps tediously upon this abstraction of the Scholar. I ought not to delay longer to add what I have to say of nearer reference to the time and to this country.

Historically, there is thought to be a difference in the ideas which predominate over successive epochs, and there are data for marking the genius of the Classic, of the Romantic, and now of the Reflective or Philosophical age. With the views I have intimated of the oneness or the identity of the mind through all individuals, I do not much dwell on these differences. In fact, I believe each individual passes through all three. The boy is a Greek; the youth, romantic; the adult, reflective. I deny not, however, that a revolution in the leading idea may be distinctly enough traced.

Our age is bewailed as the age of Introversion. Must that needs be evil? We, it seems, are critical; we are embarrassed with second thoughts; we cannot enjoy anything for hankering to know whereof the pleasure consists; we are lined with eyes; we see with our feet; the time is infected with Hamlet's unhappiness,—

Sicklied o'er with the pale cast of thought.

It is so bad then? Sight is the last thing to be pitied. Would we be blind? Do we fear lest we should outsee nature and God, and drink truth dry? I look upon the discontent of the literary class as a mere announcement of the fact that they find themselves not in the state of mind of their fathers, and regret the coming state as untried; as a boy dreads the water before he has learned that he can swim. If there is any period one would desire to be born in, is it not the age of Revolution; when the old and the new stand side by side and admit of being compared; when the energies of all men are searched by fear and by hope; when the historic glories of the old can be compensated by the rich possibilities of the new era? This time, like all times, is a very good one, if we but know what to do with it.

I read with some joy of the auspicious signs of the coming days, as they glimmer already through poetry and art, through philosophy and science, through church and state.

One of these signs is the fact that the same movement which effected the elevation of what was called the lowest class in the state, assumed in literature a very marked and as benign an aspect. Instead of the sublime and beautiful, the near, the low, the common, was explored and poetized. That which had been negligently trodden under foot by those who were harnessing and provisioning themselves for long journeys into far countries, is suddenly found to be richer than all foreign parts. The literature of the poor, the feelings of the child, the philosophy of the street, the meaning of household life, are the topics of the time. It is a great stride. It is a sign,—is it not?—of new vigor when the extremities are made active, when currents of warm life run into the hands and the feet. I ask not for the great, the remote, the romantic; what is doing in Italy or Arabia; what is Greek art, or Provençal minstrelsy; I embrace the common, I explore and sit at the feet of the familiar, the low. Give me insight into to-day, and you may have the antique and future worlds. What would we really know the meaning of? The meal in the firkin; the milk in the pan; the ballad in the street; the news of the boat; the glance of the eye; the form and the gait of the body;—show me the ultimate reason of these matters; show me the sublime presence of the highest spiritual cause lurking, as always it does lurk, in these suburbs and extremities of nature; let me see every trifle bristling with the polarity that ranges it instantly on an eternal law; and the shop, the plough, and the ledger referred to the like cause by which light undulates and poets sing;—and the world lies no longer a dull miscellany and lumber-room, but has form and order; there is no trifle, there is no puzzle, but one design unites and animates the farthest pinnacle and the lowest trench.

This idea has inspired the genius of Goldsmith, Burns, Cowper, and, in a newer time, of Goethe, Wordsworth, and Carlyle. This idea they have differently followed and with various success. In contrast with their writing, the style of Pope, of Johnson, of Gibbon, looks cold and pedantic.

This writing is blood-warm. Man is surprised to find that things near are not less beautiful and wondrous than things remote. The near explains the far. The drop is a small ocean. A man is related to all nature. This perception of the worth of the vulgar is fruitful in discoveries. Goethe, in this very thing the most modern of the moderns, has shown us as none ever did, the genius of the ancients.

There is one man of genius who has done much 10 for this philosophy of life, whose literary value has never yet been rightly estimated;—I mean Emanuel Swedenborg. The most imaginative of men, yet writing with the precision of a mathematician, he endeavored to engraft a purely philosophical Ethics on the popular Christianity of his time. Such an attempt of course must have difficulty which no genius could surmount. But he saw and showed the connection between nature and the affections of the soul. He pierced the emblematic 20 or spiritual character of the visible, audible, tangible world. Especially did his shade-loving muse hover over and interpret the lower parts of nature; he showed the mysterious bond that allies moral evil to the foul material forms, and has given in epical parables a theory of insanity, of beasts, of unclean and fearful things. *individuality*

Another sign of our times, also marked by an analogous political movement, is the new importance given to the single person. Every thing that 30 tends to insulate the individual,—to surround him with barriers of natural respect, so that each man shall feel the world is his, and man shall treat with man as a sovereign state with a sovereign state,— tends to true union as well as greatness. "I learned," said the melancholy Pestalozzi, "that no man in God's wide earth is either willing or able to help any other man." Help must come from the bosom alone. The scholar is that man who must take up into himself all the ability of the time, all the con- 40 tributions of the past, all the hopes of the future. He must be an university of knowledges. If there be one lesson more than another which should pierce his ear, it is, The world is nothing, the man is all; in yourself is the law of all nature, and you know not yet how a globule of sap ascends; in yourself slumbers the whole of Reason; it is for you to know all; it is for you to dare all. Mr.

President and Gentlemen, this confidence in the unsearched might of man belongs, by all motives, by all prophecy, by all preparation, to the American Scholar. We have listened too long to the courtly muses of Europe. The spirit of the American freeman is already suspected to be timid, imitative, tame. Public and private avarice make the air we breathe thick and fat. The scholar is decent, indolent, complaisant. See already the tragic consequence. The mind of this country, taught to aim at low objects, eats upon itself. There is no work for any but the decorous and the complaisant. Young men of the fairest promise, who begin life upon our shores, inflated by the mountain winds, shined upon by all the stars of God, find the earth below not in unison with these, but are hindered from action by the disgust which the principles on which business is managed inspire, and turn drudges, or die of disgust, some of them 20 suicides. What is the remedy? They did not yet see, and thousands of young men as hopeful now crowding to the barriers for the career do not yet see, that if the single man plant himself indomitably on his instincts, and there abide, the huge world will come round to him. Patience,—patience; with the shades of all the good and great for company; and for solace the perspective of your own infinite life; and for work the study and the communication of principles, the making those instincts prevalent, the conversion of the world. 30 Is it not the chief disgrace in the world, not to be an unit;—not to be reckoned one character;— not to yield that peculiar fruit which each man was created to bear, but to be reckoned in the gross, in the hundred, or the thousand, of the party, the section, to which we belong; and our opinion predicted geographically, as the north, or the south? Not so, brothers and friends,—please God, ours shall not be so. We will walk on our 40 own feet; we will work with our own hands; we will speak our own minds. The study of letters shall be no longer a name for pity, for doubt, and for sensual indulgence. The dread of man and the love of man shall be a wall of defence and a wreath of joy around all. A nation of men will for the first time exist, because each believes himself inspired by the Divine Soul which also inspires all men.

Self-Reliance

EMERSON remarked of his Journals, "This Book is my Savings Bank." Of the many ideas drawn from notes in his diary for further development in his essays, none is more central in his teaching than that of the need for men to rely on themselves. In writing "Self-Reliance," Emerson used notes in his Journals extending back as far as 1832; he also drew upon the lectures in his courses on "The Philosophy of History" (1836–1837) and "Human Life" (1838–1839). The essay was first published in 1841 in *Essays, First Series.* The text is that of the edition of 1883.

I read the other day some verses written by an eminent painter which were original and not conventional. The soul always hears an admonition in such lines, let the subject be what it may. The sentiment they instil is of more value than any thought they may contain. To believe your own thought, to believe that what is true for you in your private heart is true for all men,—that is genius. Speak your latent conviction, and it shall be the universal sense; for the inmost in due time becomes the outmost, and our first thought is rendered back to us by the trumpets of the Last Judgment. Familiar as the voice of the mind is to each, the highest merit we ascribe to Moses, Plato and Milton is that they set at naught books and traditions, and spoke not what men, but what they thought. A man should learn to detect and watch that gleam of light which flashes across his mind from within, more than the luster of the firmament of bards and sages. Yet he dismisses without notice his thought, because it is his. In every work of genius we recognize our own rejected thoughts; they come back to us with a certain alienated majesty. Great works of art have no more affecting lesson for us than this. They teach us to abide by our spontaneous impression with good-humored inflexibility then most when the whole cry of voices is on the other side. Else tomorrow a stranger will say with masterly good sense precisely what we have thought and felt all the time, and we shall be forced to take with shame our own opinion from another.

There is a time in every man's education when he arrives at the conviction that envy is ignorance; that imitation is suicide; that he must take himself for better for worse as his portion; that though the wide universe is full of good, no kernel of nourishing corn can come to him but through his toil bestowed on that plot of ground which is given to him to till. The power which resides in him is new in nature, and none but he knows what that is which he can do, nor does he know until he has tried. Not for nothing one face, one character, one fact, makes much impression on him, and another none. This sculpture in the memory is not without preëstablished harmony. The eye was placed where one ray should fall, that it might testify of that particular ray. We but half express ourselves, and are ashamed of that divine idea which each of us represents. It may be safely intrusted as proportionate and of good issues, so it be faithfully imparted, but God will not have his work made manifest by cowards. A man is relieved and gay when he has put his heart into his work and done his best; but what he has said or done otherwise shall give him no peace. It is a deliverance which does not deliver. In the attempt his genius deserts him; no muse befriends; no invention, no hope.

Trust thyself: every heart vibrates to that iron string. Accept the place the divine providence has found for you, the society of your contemporaries, the connection of events. Great men have always done so, and confided themselves childlike to the genius of their age, betraying their perception that the absolutely trustworthy was seated at their heart, working through their hands, predominating in all their being. And we are now men, and must accept in the highest mind the same transcendent destiny; and not minors and invalids in a protected corner, not cowards fleeing before a revolution, but guides, redeemers and benefactors, obeying the Almighty effort and advancing on Chaos and the Dark.

What pretty oracles nature yields us on this text in the face and behavior of children, babes, and even brutes! That divided and rebel mind, that distrust of a sentiment because our arithmetic has computed the strength and means opposed to our purpose, these have not. Their mind being whole, their eye is as yet unconquered, and when we look in their faces we are disconcerted. Infancy conforms to nobody; all conform to it; so that one babe commonly makes four or five out of the adults who prattle and play to it. So God has armed youth and puberty and manhood no less with its own piquancy and charm, and made it enviable and gracious and its claims not to be put by, if it will stand by itself. Do not think the youth has no force, because he cannot speak to you and me. Hark! in the next room his voice is sufficiently clear and emphatic. It seems he knows how to speak to his contemporaries. Bashful or bold then, he will know how to make us seniors very unnecessary.

The nonchalance of boys who are sure of a dinner, and would disdain as much as a lord to do or say aught to conciliate one, is the healthy attitude of human nature. A boy is in the parlor what the pit is in the playhouse; independent, irresponsible, looking out from his corner on such people and facts as pass by, he tries and sentences them on their merits, in the swift, summary way of boys, as good, bad, interesting, silly, eloquent, troublesome. He cumbers himself never about consequences, about interests; he gives an independent, genuine verdict. You must court him; he does not court you. But the man is as it were clapped into jail by his consciousness. As soon as he has once acted or spoken with *éclat* he is a committed person, watched by the sympathy or the hatred of hundreds, whose affections must now enter into his account. There is no Lethe[n] for this. Ah, that he could pass again into his neutrality! Who can thus avoid all pledges and, having observed, observe again from the same unaffected, unbiased, unbribable, unaffrighted innocence,— must always be formidable. He would utter opinions on all passing affairs, which being seen to be not private but necessary, would sink like darts into the ear of men and put them in fear.

These are the voices which we hear in solitude, but they grow faint and inaudible as we enter into the world. Society everywhere is in conspiracy against the manhood of every one of its members. Society is a joint-stock company, in which the members agree, for the better securing of his bread to each shareholder, to surrender the liberty and culture of the eater. The virtue in most request is conformity. Self-reliance is its aversion. It loves not realities and creators, but names and customs.

Whoso would be a man, must be a nonconformist. He who would gather immortal palms must not be hindered by the name of goodness, but must explore if it be goodness. Nothing is at last sacred but the integrity of your own mind. Absolve you to yourself, and you shall have the suffrage of the world. I remember an answer which when quite young I was prompted to make to a valued adviser who was wont to importune me with the dear old doctrines of the church. On my saying, "What have I to do with the sacredness of traditions, if I live wholly from within?" my friend suggested,—"But these impulses may be from below, not from above." I replied, "They do not seem to me to be such; but if I am the Devil's child, I will live then from the Devil." No law can be sacred to me but that of my nature. Good and bad are but names very readily transferable to that or this; the only right is what is after my constitution; the only wrong what is against it. A man is to carry himself in the presence of all opposition as if everything were titular and ephemeral but he. I am ashamed to think how easily we capitulate to badges and names, to large societies and dead institutions. Every decent and well-spoken individual affects and sways me more than is right. I ought to go upright and vital, and speak the rude truth in all ways. If malice and vanity wear the coat of philanthropy, shall that pass? If an angry bigot assumes this bountiful cause of Abolition, and comes to me with his last news from Barbadoes,[n] why should I not say to him, "Go love thy infant; love thy woodchopper; be good-natured and modest; have that grace; and never varnish your hard, uncharitable ambition with this incredible tenderness for black folk a thousand miles off. Thy love afar is spite at home." Rough and graceless would be such greeting, but truth is handsomer than the affectation of love. Your goodness must have some edge to it,—else it is none. The doctrine of hatred must be preached, as the counteraction of the doctrine of love, when that pules and whines. I shun father and mother and wife and brother when

Lethe: a river in Hades, whose water, if drunk, caused forgetfulness.

Barbadoes: in British West Indies, where slavery had recently been abolished.

my genius calls me. I would write on the lintels of the door-post, Whim. I hope it is somewhat better than whim at last, but we cannot spend the day in explanation. Expect me not to show cause why I seek or why I exclude company. Then again, do not tell me, as a good man did to-day, of my obligation to put all poor men in good situations. Are they my poor? I tell thee, thou foolish philanthropist, that I grudge the dollar, the dime, the cent I give to such men as do not belong to me and to whom I do not belong. There is a class of persons to whom by all spiritual affinity I am bought and sold; for them I will go to prison if need be; but your miscellaneous popular charities; the education at college of fools; the building of meeting-houses to the vain end to which many now stand; alms to sots, and the thousand-fold Relief Societies; —though I confess with shame I sometimes succumb and give the dollar, it is a wicked dollar, which by and by I shall have the manhood to withhold.

Virtues are, in the popular estimate, rather the exception than the rule. There is the man and his virtues. Men do what is called a good action, as some piece of courage or charity, much as they would pay a fine in expiation of daily non-appearance on parade. Their works are done as an apology or extenuation of their living in the world, —as invalids and the insane pay a high board. Their virtues are penances. I do not wish to expiate, but to live. My life is for itself and not for a spectacle. I much prefer that it should be of a lower strain, so it be genuine and equal, than that it should be glittering and unsteady. I wish it to be sound and sweet, and not to need diet and bleeding. I ask primary evidence that you are a man, and refuse this appeal from the man to his actions. I know that for myself it makes no difference whether I do or forbear those actions which are reckoned excellent. I cannot consent to pay for a privilege where I have intrinsic right. Few and mean as my gifts may be, I actually am, and do not need for my own assurance or the assurance of my fellows any secondary testimony.

What I must do is all that concerns me, not what the people think. This rule, equally arduous in actual and in intellectual life, may serve for the whole distinction between greatness and meanness. It is the harder because you will always find those who think they know what is your duty better than you know it. It is easy in the world to live after the world's opinion; it is easy in solitude to live after our own; but the great man is he who in the midst of the crowd keeps with perfect sweetness the independence of solitude.

The objection to conforming to usages that have become dead to you is that it scatters your force. It loses your time and blurs the impression of your character. If you maintain a dead church, contribute to a dead Bible-society, vote with a great party either for the government or against it, spread your table like base housekeepers,—under all these screens I have difficulty to detect the precise man you are: and of course so much force is withdrawn from all your proper life. But do your work, and I shall know you. Do your work, and you shall reinforce yourself. A man must consider what a blindman's-buff is this game of conformity. If I know your sect I anticipate your argument. I hear a preacher announce for his text and topic the expediency of one of the institutions of his church. Do I not know beforehand that not possibly can he say a new and spontaneous word? Do I not know that with all this ostentation of examining the grounds of the institution he will do no such thing? Do I not know that he is pledged to himself not to look but at one side, the permitted side, not as a man, but as a parish minister? He is a retained attorney, and these airs of the bench are the emptiest affectation. Well, most men have bound their eyes with one or another handkerchief, and attached themselves to some one of these communities of opinion. This conformity makes them not false in a few particulars, authors of a few lies, but false in all particulars. Their every truth is not quite true. Their two is not the real two, their four not the real four; so that every word they say chagrins us and we know not where to begin to set them right. Meantime nature is not slow to equip us in the prison-uniform of the party to which we adhere. We come to wear one cut of face and figure, and acquire by degrees the gentlest asinine expression. There is a mortifying experience in particular, which does not fail to wreak itself also in the general history; I mean the "foolish face of praise," the forced smile which we put on in company where we do not feel at ease, in

621

answer to conversation which does not interest us. The muscles, not spontaneously moved but moved by a low usurping wilfulness, grow tight about the outline of the face, with the most disagreeable sensation.

For nonconformity the world whips you with its displeasure. And therefore a man must know how to estimate a sour face. The by-standers look askance on him in the public street or in the friend's parlor. If this aversion had its origin in contempt 10 and resistance like his own he might well go home with a sad countenance; but the sour faces of the multitude, like their sweet faces, have no deep cause, but are put on and off as the wind blows and a newspaper directs. Yet is the discontent of the multitude more formidable than that of the senate and the college. It is easy enough for a firm man who knows the world to brook the rage of the cultivated classes. Their rage is decorous and prudent, for they are timid, as being very 20 vulnerable themselves. But when to their feminine rage the indignation of the people is added, when the ignorant and the poor are aroused, when the unintelligent brute force that lies at the bottom of society is made to growl and mow, it needs the habit of magnanimity and religion to treat it god-like as a trifle of no concernment.

The other terror that scares us from self-trust is our consistency; a reverence for our past act or word because the eyes of others have no other 30 data for computing our orbit than our past acts, and we are loth to disappoint them.

But why should you keep your head over your shoulder? Why drag about this corpse of your memory, lest you contradict somewhat you have stated in this or that public place? Suppose you should contradict yourself; what then? It seems to be a rule of wisdom never to rely on your memory alone, scarcely even in acts of pure memory, but to bring the past for judgment into the 40 thousand-eyed present, and live ever in a new day. In your metaphysics you have denied personality to the Deity, yet when the devout motions of the soul come, yield to them heart and life, though they should clothe God with shape and color. Leave your theory, as Joseph[n] his coat in the hand of the harlot, and flee.

Joseph: See Genesis 39:13.

A foolish consistency is the hobgoblin of little minds, adored by little statesmen and philosophers and divines. With consistency a great soul has simply nothing to do. He may as well concern himself with his shadow on the wall. Speak what you think now in hard words and tomorrow speak what tomorrow thinks in hard words again, though it contradict everything you said to-day.—'Ah, so you shall be sure to be misunderstood.'—Is it so bad then to be misunderstood? Pythagoras was misunderstood, and Socrates, and Jesus, and Luther, and Copernicus, and Galileo, and Newton, and every pure and wise spirit that ever took flesh. To be great is to be misunderstood.

I suppose no man can violate his nature. All the sallies of his will are rounded in by the law of his being, as the inequalities of Andes and Himmaleh are insignificant in the curve of the sphere. Nor does it matter how you gage and try him. A character is like an acrostic or Alexandrian stanza,[n]—read it forward, backward, or across, it still spells the same thing. In this pleasing contrite wood-life which God allows me, let me record day by day my honest thought without prospect or retrospect, and, I cannot doubt, it will be found symmetrical, though I mean it not and see it not. My book should smell of pines and resound with the hum of insects. The swallow over my window should interweave that thread or straw he carries in his bill into my web also. We pass for what we are. Character teaches above our wills. Men imagine that they communicate their virtue or vice only by overt actions, and do not see that virtue or vice emit a breath every moment.

There will be an agreement in whatever variety of actions, so they be each honest and natural in their hour. For of one will, the actions will be harmonious, however unlike they seem. These varieties are lost sight of at a little distance, at a little height of thought. One tendency unites them all. The voyage of the best ship is a zigzag line of a hundred tacks. See the line from a sufficient distance, and it straightens itself to the average tendency. Your genuine action will explain itself and will explain your other genuine actions. Your conformity explains nothing. Act singly, and what you have already done singly will

Alexandrian stanza: Emerson means a palindrome.

justify you now. Greatness appeals to the future. If I can be firm enough to-day to do right and scorn eyes, I must have done so much right before as to defend me now. Be it how it will, do right now. Always scorn appearances and you always may. The force of character is cumulative. All the foregone days of virtue work their health into this. What makes the majesty of the heroes of the senate and the field, which so fills the imagination? The consciousness of a train of great days and victories behind. They shed a united light on the advancing actor. He is attended as by a visible escort of angels. That is it which throws thunder into Chatham's[n] voice, and dignity into Washington's port, and America into Adams's eye. Honor is venerable to us because it is no ephemera. It is always ancient virtue. We worship it to-day because it is not of to-day. We love it and pay it homage because it is not a trap for our love and homage, but is self-dependent, self-derived, and therefore of an old immaculate pedigree, even if shown in a young person.

I hope in these days we have heard the last of conformity and consistency. Let the words be gazetted and ridiculous henceforward. Instead of the gong for dinner, let us hear a whistle from the Spartan fife. Let us never bow and apologize more. A great man is coming to eat at my house. I do not wish to please him; I wish that he would wish to please me. I will stand here for humanity, and though I would make it kind, I would make it true. Let us affront and reprimand the smooth mediocrity and squalid contentment of the times, and hurl in the face of custom and trade and office, the fact which is the upshot of all history, that there is a great responsible Thinker and Actor working wherever a man works; that a true man belongs to no other time or place, but is the center of things. Where he is there is nature. He measures you and all men and all events. Ordinarily, everybody in society reminds us of somewhat else, or of some other person. Character, reality, reminds you of nothing else; it takes place of the whole creation. The man must be so much that he must make all circumstances indifferent. Every true man is a cause, a country, and an age; requires

infinite spaces and numbers and time fully to accomplish his design;—and posterity seem to follow his steps as a train of clients. A man Cæsar is born, and for ages after we have a Roman Empire. Christ is born, and millions of minds so grow and cleave to his genius that he is confounded with virtue and the possible of man. An institution is the lengthened shadow of one man; as, Monachism,[n] of the Hermit Antony[n]; the Reformation, of Luther[n]; Quakerism, of Fox[n]; Methodism, of Wesley[n]; Abolition, of Clarkson.[n] Scipio,[n] Milton called "the height of Rome"; and all history resolves itself very easily into the biography of a few stout and earnest persons.

Let a man then know his worth, and keep things under his feet. Let him not peep or steal, or skulk up and down with the air of a charity-boy, a bastard, or an interloper in the world which exists for him. But the man in the street, finding no worth in himself which corresponds to the force which built a tower or sculptured a marble god, feels poor when he looks on these. To him a palace, a statue, or a costly book have an alien and forbidding air, much like a gay equipage, and seem to say like that, 'Who are you, Sir?' Yet they all are his, suitors for his notice, petitioners to his faculties that they will come out and take possession. The picture waits for my verdict; it is not to command me, but I am to settle its claims to praise. That popular fable of the sot who was picked up dead-drunk in the street, carried to the duke's house, washed and dressed and laid in the duke's bed, and, on his waking, treated with all obsequious ceremony like the duke, and assured that he had been insane, owes its popularity to the fact that it symbolizes so well the state of man who is in the world a sort of sot, but now and then wakes up, exercises his reason and finds himself a true prince.

Our reading is mendicant and sycophantic. In history our imagination plays us false. Kingdom and lordship, power and estate, are a gaudier

Monachism: monasticism.   **Hermit Antony:** Saint Anthony (c. 250–350), Christian monk who withdrew to a life of solitude on a mountain by the Nile.   **Luther:** Martin Luther (1483–1546).   **Fox:** George Fox (1624–1691). **Wesley:** John Wesley (1703–1791).   **Clarkson:** Thomas Clarkson (1760–1846), English abolitionist.   **Scipio:** Scipio Africanus (237–183 B.C.), Roman general who defeated Hannibal, mentioned in *Paradise Lost*, IX, line 210.

Chatham: William Pitt, Earl of Chatham (1708–1788), English statesman and orator.

vocabulary than private John and Edward in a small house and common day's work; but the things of life are the same to both; the sum total of both is the same. Why all this deference to Alfred[n] and Scanderbeg[n] and Gustavus[n]? Suppose they were virtuous; did they wear out virtue? As great a stake depends on your private act to-day as followed their public and renowned steps. When private men shall act with original views, the luster will be transferred from the actions of kings to those of gentlemen.

The world has been instructed by its kings, who have so magnetized the eyes of nations. It has been taught by this colossal symbol the mutual reverence that is due from man to man. The joyful loyalty with which men have everywhere suffered the king, the noble, or the great proprietor to walk among them by law of his own, make his own scale of men and things and reverse theirs, pay for benefits not with money but with honor, and represent the law in his person, was the hieroglyphic by which they obscurely signified their consciousness of their own right and comeliness, the right of every man.

The magnetism which all original action exerts is explained when we inquire the reason of self-trust. Who is the Trustee? What is the aboriginal Self, on which a universal reliance may be grounded? What is the nature and power of that science-baffling star, without parallax, without calculable elements, which shoots a ray of beauty even into trivial and impure actions, if the least mark of independence appear? The inquiry leads us to that source, at once the essence of genius, of virtue, and of life, which we call Spontaneity or Instinct. We denote this primary wisdom as Intuition, whilst all later teachings are tuitions. In that deep force, the last fact behind which analysis cannot go, all things find their common origin. For the sense of being which in calm hours rises, we know not how, in the soul, is not diverse from things,

Alfred: Alfred the Great (849–899), King of the West Saxons, recognized as the sovereign of all England. **Scanderbeg:** George Castriota (1403?–1468), Albanian national hero, leader against the Turks: known as Scanderbeg from Turkish form of name, Iskender Beg. **Gustavus:** Gustavus II (1594–1632), Swedish king who won vic ories against the Holy Roman Empire; perhaps the reference is to Gustavus Vasa (1496–1560).

from space, from light, from time, from man, but one with them and proceeds obviously from the same source whence their life and being also proceed. We first share the life by which things exist and afterwards see them as appearances in nature and forget that we have shared their cause. Here is the fountain of action and of thought. Here are the lungs of that inspiration which giveth man wisdom and which cannot be denied without impiety and atheism. We lie in the lap of immense intelligence, which makes us receivers of its truth and organs of its activity. When we discern justice, when we discern truth, we do nothing of ourselves, but allow a passage to its beams. If we ask whence this comes, if we seek to pry into the soul that causes, all philosophy is at fault. Its presence or its absence is all we can affirm. Every man discriminates between the voluntary acts of his mind and his involuntary perceptions, and knows that to his involuntary perceptions a perfect faith is due. He may err in the expression of them, but he knows that these things are so, like day and night, not to be disputed. My wilful actions and acquisitions are but roving;—the idlest reverie, the faintest native emotion, command my curiosity and respect. Thoughtless people contradict as readily the statement of perceptions as of opinions, or rather much more readily; for they do not distinguish between perception and notion. They fancy that I choose to see this or that thing. But perception is not whimsical, but fatal. If I see a trait, my children will see it after me, and in course of time all mankind,—although it may chance that no one has seen it before me. For my perception of it is as much a fact as the sun.

The relations of the soul to the divine spirit are so pure that it is profane to seek to interpose helps. It must be that when God speaketh he should communicate, not one thing, but all things; should fill the world with his voice; should scatter forth light, nature, time, souls, from the center of the present thought; and new date and new create the whole. Whenever a mind is simple and receives a divine wisdom, old things pass away,—means, teachers, texts, temples fall; it lives now, and absorbs past and future into the present hour. All things are made sacred by relation to it,—one as much as another. All things are dissolved to their center by their cause, and in the universal miracle petty and particular miracles disappear. If therefore a man claims to know and speak of God and carries you backward to the phraseology of some old molded nation in another country, in another world, believe him not. Is the acorn better than the oak which is its fullness and completion? Is the parent better than the child into whom he has cast his ripened being? Whence then this worship of the past? The centuries are conspirators against the sanity and authority of the soul. Time and space are but physiological colors which the eye makes, but the soul is light: where it is, is day; where it was, is night; and history is an impertinence and an injury if it be anything more than a cheerful apologue or parable of my being and becoming.

Man is timid and apologetic; he is no longer upright; he dares not say 'I think,' 'I am,' but quotes some saint or sage. He is ashamed before the blade of grass or the blowing rose. These roses under my window make no reference to former roses or to better ones; they are for what they are; they exist with God to-day. There is no time to them. There is simply the rose; it is perfect in every moment of its existence. Before a leaf-bud has burst, its whole life acts; in the full-blown flower there is no more; in the leafless root there is no less. Its nature is satisfied and it satisfies nature in all moments alike. But man postpones or remembers; he does not live in the present, but with reverted eye laments the past, or, heedless of the riches that surround him, stands on tiptoe to foresee the future. He cannot be happy and strong until he too lives with nature in the present, above time.

This should be plain enough. Yet see what strong intellects dare not yet hear God himself unless he speak the phraseology of I know not what David, or Jeremiah, or Paul. We shall not always set so great a price on a few texts, on a few lives. We are like children who repeat by rote the sentences of grandames and tutors, and, as they grow older, of the men of talents and character they chance to see,—painfully recollecting the exact words they spoke; afterwards, when they come into the point of view which those had who uttered these sayings, they understand them and are willing to let the words go; for at any time they can use words as good when occasion comes. If we live truly, we shall see truly. It is as easy for the strong man to be strong, as it is for the weak to be weak. When we have new perception, we shall gladly disburden the memory of its hoarded treasures as old rubbish. When a man lives with God, his voice shall be as sweet as the murmur of the brook and the rustle of the corn.

And now at last the highest truth on this subject remains unsaid; probably cannot be said; for all that we say is the far-off remembering of the intuition. That thought by what I can now nearest approach to say it, is this. When good is near you, when you have life in yourself, it is not by any known or accustomed way; you shall not discern the footprints of any other; you shall not see the face of man; you shall not hear any name; —the way, the thought, the good, shall be wholly strange and new. It shall exclude example and experience. You take the way from man, not to man. All persons that ever existed are its forgotten ministers. Fear and hope are alike beneath it. There is somewhat low even in hope. In the hour of vision there is nothing that can be called gratitude, nor properly joy. The soul raised over passion beholds identity and eternal causation, perceives the self-existence of Truth and Right, and calms itself with knowing that all things go well. Vast spaces of nature, the Atlantic Ocean, the South Sea; long intervals of time, years, centuries, are of no account. This which I think and feel underlay every former state of life and circumstances, as it does underlie my present, and what is called life and what is called death.

Life only avails, not the having lived. Power ceases in the instant of repose; it resides in the moment of transition from a past to a new state, in the shooting of the gulf, in the darting to an aim. This one fact the world hates; that the soul becomes; for that forever degrades the past, turns all riches to poverty, all reputation to a shame, confounds the saint with the rogue, shoves Jesus and Judas equally aside. Why then do we prate of self-reliance? Inasmuch as the soul is present there will be power not confident but agent. To talk of reliance is a poor external way of speaking. Speak rather of that which relies because it works and is. Who has more obedience than I masters me, though he should not raise his finger. Round him I must revolve by the gravitation of spirits. We fancy it rhetoric when we speak of eminent virtue. We do not yet see that virtue is Height, and that a man or a company of men, plastic and permeable to principles, by the law of nature must overpower and ride all cities, nations, kings, rich men, poets, who are not.

This is the ultimate fact which we so quickly reach on this, as on every topic, the resolution of all in the ever-blessed ONE. Self-existence is the attribute of the Supreme Cause, and it constitutes the measure of good by the degree in which it enters into all lower forms. All things real are so by so much virtue as they contain. Commerce, husbandry, hunting, whaling, war, eloquence, personal weight, are somewhat, and engage my respect as examples of its presence and impure action. I see the same law working in nature for conservation and growth. Power is, in nature, the essential measure of right. Nature suffers nothing to remain in her kingdoms which cannot help itself. The genesis and maturation of a planet, its poise and orbit, the bended tree recovering itself from the strong wind, the vital resources of every animal and vegetable, are demonstrations of the self-sufficing and therefore self-relying soul.

Thus all concentrates: let us not rove; let us sit at home with the cause. Let us stun and astonish the intruding rabble of men and books and institutions by a simple declaration of the divine fact. Bid the invaders take the shoes from off their feet, for God is here within. Let our simplicity judge them, and our docility to our own law demonstrate the poverty of nature and fortune beside our native riches.

But now we are a mob. Man does not stand in awe of man, nor is his genius admonished to stay at home, to put itself in communication with the internal ocean, but it goes abroad to beg a cup of water of the urns of other men. We must go alone. I like the silent church before the service begins, better than any preaching. How far off, how cool, how chaste the persons look, begirt each one with a precinct or sanctuary! So let us always sit. Why should we assume the faults of our friend, or wife, or father, or child, because they sit around our

hearth, or are said to have the same blood? All men have my blood and I all men's. Not for that will I adopt their petulance or folly, even to the extent of being ashamed of it. But your isolation must not be mechanical, but spiritual, that is, must be elevation. At times the whole world seems to be in conspiracy to importune you with emphatic trifles. Friend, climate, child, sickness, fear, want, charity, all knock at once at thy closet door and say,—"Come out unto us." But keep thy state; come not into their confusion. The power men possess to annoy me I give them by a weak curiosity. No man can come near me but through my act. "What we love that we have, but by desire we bereave ourselves of the love."

If we cannot at once rise to the sanctities of obedience and faith, let us at least resist our temptations; let us enter into the state of war and wake Thor and Woden,[n] courage and constancy, in our Saxon breasts. This is to be done in our smooth times by speaking the truth. Check this lying hospitality and lying affection. Live no longer to the expectation of these deceived and deceiving people with whom we converse. Say to them, "O father, O mother, O wife, O brother, O friend, I have lived with you after appearances hitherto. Henceforward I am the truth's. Be it known unto you that henceforward I obey no law less than the eternal law. I will have no covenants but proximities. I shall endeavor to nourish my parents, to support my family, to be the chaste husband of one wife,—but these relations I must fill after a new and unprecedented way. I appeal from your customs. I must be myself. I cannot break myself any longer for you, or you. If you can love me for what I am, we shall be the happier. If you cannot, I will still seek to deserve that you should. I will not hide my tastes or aversions. I will so trust that what is deep is holy, that I will do strongly before the sun and moon whatever inly rejoices me and the heart appoints. If you are noble, I will love you; if you are not, I will not hurt you and myself by hypocritical attentions. If you are true, but not in the same truth with me, cleave to your

Thor and Woden: In Norse mythology Thor is the god of thunder and strength; Woden (the Scandinavian Odin) is greatest of the gods of Norse mythology, symbolizing "spirit" or "mind."

companions; I will seek my own. I do this not selfishly but humbly and truly. It is alike your interest, and mine, and all men's, however long we have dwelt in lies, to live in truth. Does this sound harsh to-day? You will soon love what is dictated by your nature as well as mine, and if we follow the truth it will bring us out safe at last." —But so may you give these friends pain. Yes, but I cannot sell my liberty and my power, to save their sensibility. Besides, all persons have their moments of reason, when they look out into the region of absolute truth; then will they justify me and do the same thing.

The populace think that your rejection of popular standards is a rejection of all standard, and mere antinomianism; and the bold sensualist will use the name of philosophy to gild his crimes. But the law of consciousness abides. There are two confessionals, in one or the other of which we must be shriven. You may fulfil your round of duties by clearing yourself in the direct or in the reflex way. Consider whether you have satisfied your relations to father, mother, cousin, neighbor, town, cat and dog—whether any of these can upbraid you. But I may also neglect this reflex standard and absolve me to myself. I have my own stern claims and perfect circle. It denies the name of duty to many offices that are called duties. But if I can discharge its debts it enables me to dispense with the popular code. If any one imagines that this law is lax, let him keep its commandment one day.

And truly it demands something godlike in him who has cast off the common motives of humanity and has ventured to trust himself for a taskmaster. High be his heart, faithful his will, clear his sight, that he may in good earnest be doctrine, society, law, to himself, that a simple purpose may be to him as strong as iron necessity is to others!

If any man consider the present aspects of what is called by distinction society, he will see the need of these ethics. The sinew and heart of man seem to be drawn out, and we are become timorous, desponding whimperers. We are afraid of truth, afraid of fortune, afraid of death, and afraid of each other. Our age yields no great and perfect persons. We want men and women who shall renovate life and our social state, but we see that most natures are insolvent, cannot satisfy their own wants, have an ambition out of all proportion to their practical force and do lean and beg day and night continually. Our housekeeping is mendicant, our arts, our occupations, our marriages, our religion we have not chosen, but society has chosen for us. We are parlor soldiers. We shun the rugged battle of fate, where strength is born.

If our young men miscarry in their first enterprises they lose all heart. If the young merchant fails, men say he is ruined. If the finest genius studies at one of our colleges and is not installed in an office within one year afterwards in the cities or suburbs of Boston or New York, it seems to his friends and to himself that he is right in being disheartened and in complaining the rest of his life. A sturdy lad from New Hampshire or Vermont, who in turn tries all the professions, who teams it, farms it, peddles, keeps a school, preaches, edits a newspaper, goes to Congress, buys a township, and so forth, in successive years, and always like a cat falls on his feet, is worth a hundred of these city dolls. He walks abreast with his days and feels no shame in not "studying a profession," for he does not postpone his life, but lives already. He has not one chance, but a hundred chances. Let a Stoic open the resources of man and tell men they are not leaning willows, but can and must detach themselves; that with the exercise of self-trust, new powers shall appear; that a man is the word made flesh, born to shed healing to the nations; that he should be ashamed of our compassion, and that the moment he acts from himself, tossing the laws, the books, idolatries and customs out of the window, we pity him no more but thank and revere him;—and that teacher shall restore the life of man to splendor and make his name dear to all history.

It is easy to see that a greater self-reliance must work a revolution in all the offices and relations of men; in their religion; in their education; in their pursuits; their modes of living; their association; in their property; in their speculative views.

1. In what prayers do men allow themselves! That which they call a holy office is not so much as brave and manly. Prayer looks abroad and asks for some foreign addition to come through some foreign virtue, and loses itself in endless mazes of

natural and supernatural, and mediatorial and miraculous. Prayer that craves a particular commodity, anything less than all good, is vicious. Prayer is the contemplation of the facts of life from the highest point of view. It is the soliloquy of a beholding and jubilant soul. It is the spirit of God pronouncing his works good. But prayer as a means to effect a private end is meanness and theft. It supposes dualism and not unity in nature and consciousness. As soon as the man is at one with God, he will not beg. He will then see prayer in all action. The prayer of the farmer kneeling in his field to weed it, the prayer of the rower kneeling with the stroke of his oar, are true prayers heard throughout nature, though for cheap ends. Caratach, in Fletcher's *Bonduca*,[n] when admonished to inquire the mind of the god Andate, replies,—

> His hidden meaning lies in our endeavors;
> Our valors are our best gods.

Another sort of false prayers are our regrets. Discontent is the want of self-reliance: it is infirmity of will. Regret calamities if you can thereby help the sufferer; if not, attend your own work and already the evil begins to be repaired. Our sympathy is just as base. We come to them who weep foolishly and sit down and cry for company, instead of imparting to them truth and health in rough electric shocks, putting them once more in communication with their own reason. The secret of fortune is joy in our hands. Welcome evermore to gods and men is the self-helping man. For him all doors are flung wide; him all tongues greet, all honors crown, all eyes follow with desire. Our love goes out to him and embraces him because he did not need it. We solicitously and apologetically caress and celebrate him because he held on his way and scorned our disapprobation. The gods love him because men hated him. "To the persevering mortal," said Zoroaster,[n] "the blessed Immortals are swift."

As men's prayers are a disease of the will, so are their creeds a disease of the intellect. They say with those foolish Israelites, "Let not God speak to us, lest we die. Speak thou, speak any man with us, and we will obey." Everywhere I am hindered of meeting God in my brother, because he has shut his own temple doors and recites fables merely of his brother's, or his brother's brother's God. Every new mind is a new classification. If it prove a mind of uncommon activity and power, a Locke,[n] a Lavoisier,[n] a Hutton,[n] a Bentham,[n] a Fourier,[n] it imposes its classification on other men, and lo! a new system! In proportion to the depth of the thought, and so to the number of the objects it touches and brings within reach of the pupil, is his complacency. But chiefly is this apparent in creeds and churches, which are also classifications of some powerful mind acting on the elemental thought of duty and man's relation to the Highest. Such is Calvinism, Quakerism, Swedenborgism. The pupil takes the same delight in subordinating everything to the new terminology as a girl who has just learned botany in seeing a new earth and new seasons thereby. It will happen for a time that the pupil will find his intellectual power has grown by the study of his master's mind. But in all unbalanced minds the classification is idolized, passes for the end and not for a speedily exhaustible means, so that the walls of the system blend to their eye in the remote horizon with the walls of the universe; the luminaries of heaven seem to them hung on the arch their master built. They cannot imagine how you aliens have any right to see,— how you can see; "It must be somehow that you stole the light from us." They do not yet perceive that light, unsystematic, indomitable, will break into any cabin, even into theirs. Let them chirp awhile and call it their own. If they are honest and

Fletcher's *Bonduca*: John Fletcher (1579–1625), English dramatist, collaborator with Beaumont, Massinger, and Shakespeare, but sole author of *Bonduca* and other plays. Emerson has altered slightly the quotation from Act III, Sc. i. **Zoroaster:** founder of national religion of Iranian people.

Locke: John Locke (1632–1704), father of English empiricism. **Lavoisier:** Antoine Laurent Lavoisier (1743–1794), French scientist, father of modern chemistry. **Hutton:** James Hutton (1726–1797), Scottish geologist, originator of the modern theory of the formation of the earth's crust. **Bentham:** Jeremy Bentham (1748–1832), expounder of utilitarianism—morality determined by "the greatest happiness to the greatest number." **Fourier:** François Marie Charles Fourier (1772–1837), French sociologist, advocator of phalansteries, or cooperative societies large enough to be self-sustaining.

628

do well, presently their neat new pinfold will be too strait and low, will crack, will lean, will rot and vanish, and the immortal light, all young and joyful, million-orbed, million-colored, will beam over the universe as on the first morning.

2. It is for want of self-culture that the superstition of Traveling, whose idols are Italy, England, Egypt, retains its fascination for all educated Americans. They who made England, Italy, or Greece venerable in the imagination, did so by sticking fast where they were, like an axis of the earth. In manly hours we feel that duty is our place. The soul is no traveler; the wise man stays at home, and when his necessities, his duties, on any occasion call him from his house, or into foreign lands, he is at home still and shall make men sensible by the expression of his countenance that he goes, the missionary of wisdom and virtue, and visits cities and men like a sovereign and not like an interloper or a valet.

I have no churlish objection to the circumnavigation of the globe for the purposes of art, of study, and benevolence, so that the man is first domesticated, or does not go abroad with the hope of finding somewhat greater than he knows. He who travels to be amused, or to get somewhat which he does not carry, travels away from himself, and grows old even in youth among old things. In Thebes, in Palmyra, his will and mind have become old and dilapidated as they. He carries ruins to ruins.

Travelling is a fool's paradise. Our first journeys discover to us the indifference of places. At home I dream that at Naples, at Rome, I can be intoxicated with beauty and lose my sadness. I pack my trunk, embrace my friends, embark on the sea and at last wake up in Naples, and there beside me is the stern fact, the sad self, unrelenting, identical, that I fled from. I seek the Vatican and the palaces. I affect to be intoxicated with sights and suggestions, but I am not intoxicated. My giant goes with me wherever I go.

3. But the rage of travelling is a symptom of a deeper unsoundness affecting the whole intellectual action. The intellect is vagabond, and our system of education fosters restlessness. Our minds travel when our bodies are forced to stay at home. We imitate; and what is imitation but the travelling of the mind? Our houses are built with foreign taste; our shelves are garnished with foreign ornaments; our opinions, our tastes, our faculties lean, and follow the Past and the Distant. The soul created the arts wherever they have flourished. It was in his own mind that the artist sought his model. It was an application of his own thought to the thing to be done and the conditions to be observed. And why need we copy the Doric or the Gothic model? Beauty, convenience, grandeur of thought and quaint expression are as near to us as to any, and if the American artist will study with hope and love the precise thing to be done by him, considering the climate, the soil, the length of the day, the wants of the people, the habit and form of the government, he will create a house in which all these will find themselves fitted, and taste and sentiment will be satisfied also.

Insist on yourself; never imitate. Your own gift you can present every moment with the cumulative force of a whole life's cultivation; but of the adopted talent of another you have only an extemporaneous half possession. That which each can do best, none but his Maker can teach him. No man yet knows what it is, nor can, till that person has exhibited it. Where is the master who could have taught Shakespeare? Where is the master who could have instructed Franklin, or Washington, or Bacon,[n] or Newton? Every great man is a unique. The Scipionism of Scipio is precisely that part he could not borrow. Shakespeare will never be made by the study of Shakespeare. Do that which is assigned you, and you cannot hope too much or dare too much. There is at this moment for you an utterance brave and grand as that of the colossal chisel of Phidias,[n] or trowel of the Egyptians, or the pen of Moses or Dante,[n] but different from all these. Not possibly will the soul, all rich, all eloquent, with thousand-cloven tongue, deign to repeat itself; but if you can hear what these patriarchs say, surely you can reply to them in the same pitch of voice; for the ear and the

Bacon: Francis Bacon (1561–1626), English philosopher whose *Novum Organum*, formulating the inductive method of arriving at knowledge was opposed to Aristotle's deductive method. **Phidias:** the greatest of Greek sculptors (498–432 B.C.), who made the sculptures of the Parthenon. **Dante:** Dante Alighieri (1265–1321), author of the *Divinia Commedia*.

tongue are two organs of one nature. Abide in the simple and noble regions of thy life, obey thy heart, and thou shalt reproduce the Foreworld again.

4. As our Religion, our Education, our Art look abroad, so does our spirit of society. All men plume themselves on the improvement of society, and no man improves.

Society never advances. It recedes as fast on one side as it gains on the other. It undergoes continual changes; it is barbarous, it is civilized, it is 10 Christianized, it is rich, it is scientific; but this change is not amelioration. For everything that is given something is taken. Society acquires new arts and loses old instincts. What a contrast between the well-clad, reading, writing, thinking American, with a watch, a pencil and a bill of exchange in his pocket, and the naked New Zealander, whose property is a club, a spear, a mat and an undivided twentieth of a shed to sleep under! But compare the health of the two men and you 20 shall see that the white man has lost his aboriginal strength. If the traveller tell us truly, strike the savage with a broadaxe and in a day or two the flesh shall unite and heal as if you struck the blow into soft pitch, and the same blow shall send the white to his grave.

The civilized man has built a coach, but has lost the use of his feet. He is supported on crutches, but lacks so much support of muscle. He has a fine Geneva watch, but he fails of the skill to tell the 30 hour by the sun. A Greenwich nautical almanac he has, and so being sure of the information when he wants it, the man in the street does not know a star in the sky. The solstice he does not observe; the equinox he knows as little; and the whole bright calendar of the year is without a dial in his mind. His note-books impair his memory; his libraries overload his wit; the insurance-office increases the number of accidents; and it may be a question whether machinery does not encumber; 40 whether we have not lost by refinement some energy, by a Christianity, entrenched in establishments and forms, some vigor of wild virtue. For every Stoic was a Stoic; but in Christendom where is the Christian?

There is no more deviation in the moral standard than in the standard of height or bulk. No greater men are now than ever were. A singular equality may be observed between the great men of the first and of the last ages; nor can all the science, art, religion, and philosophy of the nineteenth century avail to educate greater men than Plutarch's[n] heroes, three or four and twenty centuries ago. Not in time is the race progressive. Phocion,[n] Socrates,[n] Anaxagoras,[n] Diogenes,[n] are great men, but they leave no class. He who is really of their class will not be called by their name, but will be his own man, and in his turn the founder of a sect. The arts and inventions of each period are only its costume and do not invigorate men. The harm of the improved machinery may compensate its good. Hudson[n] and Behring[n] accomplished so much in their fishing-boats as to astonish Parry and Franklin,[n] whose equipment exhausted the resources of science and art. Galileo,[n] with an opera-glass, discovered a more splendid series of celestial phenomena than any one since. Columbus found the New World in an undecked boat. It is curious to see the periodical disuse and perishing of means and machinery which were introduced with loud laudation a few years or centuries before. The great genius returns to essential man. We reckoned the improvements of the art of war among the triumphs of science, and yet Napoleon conquered Europe by the bivouac, which consisted of falling back on naked valor and disencumbering it of all aids. The Emperor held it impossible to make a perfect army, says Las Casas,[n] "without abolishing our arms, magazines, commissaries and carriages, until, in imitation of the Roman custom, the soldier should receive his supply of corn, grind it in his hand-mill and bake his bread himself."

Plutarch: Greek biographer (46?–120? A.D.). **Phocion:** Athenian general and dictator (402?–317 B.C.). **Socrates:** Greek philosopher (470?–399 B.C.), whose idealistic doctrines are preserved in the writings of Plato. **Anaxagoras:** Greek philosopher (500?–428 B.C.), expounder of dualistic theory of universe. **Diogenes:** Greek philosopher and Cynic (412?–323 B.C.). **Hudson:** Henry Hudson (d. 1611), English discoverer of Hudson River. **Behring:** Vitus Behring or Bering (1680–1741), Danish discoverer of Bering Sea and Bering Strait. **Parry and Franklin:** Sir Edward Parry (1790–1855), and Sir John Franklin (1786–1847), English explorers of the Arctic. **Galileo:** Galileo Galilei (1564–1642), Italian astronomer denounced by religious authorities for supporting Copernican system. **Las Casas:** Comte Emmanuel Las Casas (1766–1842), French historian to whom Napoleon dedicated his memoirs while exiled on St. Helena.

Society is a wave. The wave moves onward, but the water of which it is composed does not. The same particle does not rise from the valley to the ridge. Its unity is only phenomenal. The persons who make up a nation to-day, next year die, and their experience dies with them.

And so the reliance on Property, including the reliance on governments which protect it, is the want of self-reliance. Men have looked away from themselves and at things so long that they have come to esteem the religious, learned and civil institutions as guards of property, and they deprecate assaults on these, because they feel them to be assaults on property. They measure their esteem of each other by what each has, and not by what each is. But a cultivated man becomes ashamed of his property, out of new respect for his nature. Especially he hates what he has if he see that it is accidental,—came to him by inheritance, or gift, or crime; then he feels that it is not having; it does not belong to him, has no root in him and merely lies there because no revolution or no robber takes it away. But that which a man is, does always by necessity acquire; and what the man acquires, is living property, which does not wait the beck of rulers, or mobs, or revolutions, or fire, or storm, or bankruptcies, but perpetually renews itself wherever the man breathes. "Thy lot or portion of life," said the Caliph Ali, "is seeking after thee; therefore be at rest from seeking after it." Our dependence on these foreign goods leads us to our slavish respect for numbers. The political parties meet in numerous conventions; the greater the concourse and with each new uproar of announcement, The delegation from Essex! The Democrats from New Hampshire! The Whigs of Maine! the young patriot feels himself stronger than before by a new thousand of eyes and arms. In like manner the reformers summon conventions and vote and resolve in multitude. Not so O friends! will the God deign to enter and inhabit you, but by a method precisely the reverse. It is only as a man puts off all foreign support and stands alone that I see him to be strong and to prevail. He is weaker by every recruit to his banner. Is not a man better than a town? Ask nothing of men, and, in the endless mutation, thou only firm column must presently appear the upholder of all

that surrounds thee. He who knows that power is inborn, that he is weak because he has looked for good out of him and elsewhere, and, so perceiving, throws himself unhesitatingly on his thought, instantly rights himself, stands in the erect position, commands his limbs, works miracles; just as a man who stands on his feet is stronger than a man who stands on his head.

So use all that is called Fortune. Most men gamble with her, and gain all, and lose all, as her wheel rolls. But do thou leave as unlawful these winnings, and deal with Cause and Effect, the chancellors of God. In the Will work and acquire, and thou hast chained the wheel of Chance, and shall sit hereafter out of fear from her rotations. A political victory, a rise of rents, the recovery of your sick or the return of your absent friend, or some other favorable event raises your spirits, and you think good days are preparing for you. Do not believe it. Nothing can bring you peace but yourself. Nothing can bring you peace but the triumph of principles.

The Over-Soul

This essay, which was developed from parts of several lectures given in 1836–1838, was printed in *Essays, First Series* (1841). F. I. Carpenter (*Emerson and Asia*, 75–81) has indicated the strong infusion in the essay of Neoplatonic thought, especially that of Plotinus; G. W. Cooke (*Ralph Waldo Emerson*, 307–316) has pointed out the influence of German idealistic philosophy as transmitted to the New England transcendentalists through the writings of Samuel Taylor Coleridge; A. E. Christy (*The Orient in American Transcendentalism*, 63–183) has discussed the similarities and distinctions between Emerson's Christianized concept of the Over-Soul and the concept in Oriental philosophy. See the Concord Edition, II, 426–428, for a list of sources of the ideas in the essay. The text is that of the edition of 1883.

There is a difference between one and another hour of life in their authority and subsequent effect. Our faith comes in moments; our vice is habitual. Yet there is a depth in those brief moments which constrains us to ascribe more reality to them than to all other experiences. For this reason the argument which is always forthcoming to silence those who conceive extraordinary hopes of man, namely the appeal to experience, is for ever invalid and vain. We give up the past to the objector, and yet we hope. He must explain this hope. We grant that human life is mean, but how did we find out that it was mean? What is the ground of this uneasiness of ours; of this old discontent? What is the universal sense of want and ignorance, but the fine innuendo by which the soul makes its enormous claim? Why do men feel that the natural history of man has never been written, but he is always leaving behind what you have said of him, and it becomes old, and books of metaphysics worthless? The philosophy of six thousand years has not searched the chambers and magazines of the soul. In its experiments there has always remained, in the last analysis, a residuum it could not resolve. Man is a stream whose source is hidden. Our being is descending into us from we know not whence. The most exact calculator has no prescience that somewhat incalculable may not balk the very next moment. I am constrained every moment to acknowledge a higher origin for events than the will I call mine.

As with events, so is it with thoughts. When I watch that flowing river, which, out of regions I see not, pours for a season its streams into me, I see that I am a pensioner; not a cause but a surprised spectator of this ethereal water; that I desire and look up and put myself in the attitude of reception, but from some alien energy the visions come.

The Supreme Critic on the errors of the past and the present, and the only prophet of that which must be, is that great nature in which we rest as the earth lies in the soft arms of the atmosphere; that Unity, that Over-Soul, within which every man's particular being is contained and made one with all other; that common heart of which all sincere conversation is the worship, to which all right action is submission; that overpowering reality which confutes our tricks and talents, and constrains every one to pass for what he is, and to speak from his character and not from his tongue, and which evermore tends to pass into our thought and hand and become wisdom and virtue and power and beauty. We live in succession, in division, in parts, in particles. Meantime within man is the soul of the whole; the wise silence; the universal

beauty, to which every part and particle is equally related; the eternal ONE. And this deep power in which we exist and whose beatitude is all accessible to us, is not only self-sufficing and perfect in every hour, but the act of seeing and the thing seen, the seer and the spectacle, the subject and the object, are one. We see the world piece by piece, as the sun, the moon, the animal, the tree; but the whole, of which these are the shining parts, is the soul. Only by the vision of that Wisdom can the horoscope of the ages be read, and by falling back on our better thoughts, by yielding to the spirit of prophecy which is innate in every man, we can know what it saith. Every man's words who speaks from that life must sound vain to those who do not dwell in the same thought on their own part. I dare not speak for it. My words do not carry its august sense; they fall short and cold. Only itself can inspire whom it will, and behold! their speech shall be lyrical, and sweet, and universal as the rising of the wind. Yet I desire, even by profane words, if I may not use sacred, to indicate the heaven of this deity and to report what hints I have collected of the transcendent simplicity and energy of the Highest Law.

If we consider what happens in conversation, in reveries, in remorse, in times of passion, in surprises, in the instructions of dreams, wherein often we see ourselves in masquerade,—the droll disguises only magnifying and enhancing a real element and forcing it on our distant notice,—we shall catch many hints that will broaden and lighten into knowledge of the secret of nature. All goes to show that the soul in man is not an organ, but animates and exercises all the organs; is not a function, like the power of memory, of calculation, of comparison, but uses these as hands and feet; is not a faculty, but a light; is not the intellect or the will, but the master of the intellect and the will; is the background of our being, in which they lie,—an immensity not possessed and that cannot be possessed. From within or from behind, a light shines through us upon things, and makes us aware that we are nothing, but the light is all. A man is the façade of a temple wherein all wisdom and all good abide. What we commonly call man, the eating, drinking, planting, counting man, does not, as we know him, represent himself, but misrepresents himself. Him we do not respect, but the soul, whose organ he is, would he let it appear through his action, would make our knees bend. When it breathes through his intellect, it is genius; when it breathes through his will, it is virtue; when it flows through his affection, it is love. And the blindness of the intellect begins when it would be something of itself. The weakness of the will begins when the individual would be something of himself. All reform aims in some one particular to let the soul have its way through us; in other words, to engage us to obey.

Of this pure nature every man is at some time sensible. Language cannot paint it with his colors. It is too subtle. It is undefinable, unmeasurable; but we know that it pervades and contains us. We know that all spiritual being is in man. A wise old proverb says, "God comes to see us without bell;" that is, as there is no screen or ceiling between our heads and the infinite heavens, so is there no bar or wall in the soul, where man, the effect, ceases, and God, the cause, begins. The walls are taken away. We lie open on one side to the deeps of spiritual nature, to the attributes of God. Justice we see and know, Love, Freedom, Power. These natures no man ever got above, but they tower over us, and most in the moment when our interests tempt us to wound them.

The sovereignty of this nature whereof we speak is made known by its independency of those limitations which circumscribe us on every hand. The soul circumscribes all things. As I have said, it contradicts all experience. In like manner it abolishes time and space. The influence of the senses has in most men overpowered the mind to that degree that the walls of time and space have come to look real and insurmountable; and to speak with levity of these limits is, in the world, the sign of insanity. Yet time and space are but inverse measures of the force of the soul. The spirit sports with time,—

Can crowd eternity into an hour,
Or stretch an hour to eternity.

We are often made to feel that there is another youth and age than that which is measured from the year of our natural birth. Some thoughts always find us young, and keep us so. Such a

thought is the love of the universal and eternal beauty. Every man parts from that contemplation with the feeling that it rather belongs to ages than to mortal life. The least activity of the intellectual powers redeems us in a degree from the conditions of time. In sickness, in languor, give us a strain of poetry or a profound sentence, and we are refreshed; or produce a volume of Plato or Shakspeare, or remind us of their names, and instantly we come into a feeling of longevity. See how the deep divine thought reduces centuries and millenniums, and makes itself present through all ages. Is the teaching of Christ less effective now than it was when first his mouth was opened? The emphasis of facts and persons in my thought has nothing to do with time. And so always the soul's scale is one, the scale of the senses and the understanding is another. Before the revelations of the soul, Time, Space, and Nature shrink away. In common speech we refer all things to time, as we habitually refer the immensely sundered stars to one concave sphere. And so we say that the Judgment is distant or near, that the Millennium approaches, that a day of certain political, moral, social reforms is at hand, and the like, when we mean that in the nature of things one of the facts we contemplate is external and fugitive, and the other is permanent and connate with the soul. The things we now esteem fixed shall, one by one, detach themselves like ripe fruit from our experience, and fall. The wind shall blow them none knows whither. The landscape, the figures, Boston, London, are facts as fugitive as any institution past, or any whiff of mist or smoke, and so is society, and so is the world. The soul looketh steadily forwards, creating a world before her, leaving worlds behind her. She has no dates, nor rites, nor persons, nor specialties, nor men. The soul knows only the soul; the web of events is the flowing robe in which she is clothed.

After its own law and not by arithmetic is the rate of its progress to be computed. The soul's advances are not made by gradation, such as can be represented by motion in a straight line, but rather by ascension of state, such as can be represented by metamorphosis,—from the egg to the worm, from the worm to the fly. The growths of genius are of a certain total character, that does not advance the elect individual first over John, then Adam, then Richard, and give to each the pain of discovered inferiority,—but by every throe of growth the man expands there where he works, passing, at each pulsation, classes, populations, of men. With each divine impulse the mind rends the thin rinds of the visible and finite, and comes out into eternity, and inspires and expires its air. It converses with truths that have always been spoken in the world, and becomes conscious of a closer sympathy with Zeno[n] and Arrian[n] than with persons in the house.

This is the law of moral and of mental gain. The simple rise as by specific levity not into a particular virtue, but into the region of all the virtues. They are in the spirit which contains them all. The soul requires purity, but purity is not it; requires justice, but justice is not that; requires beneficence, but is somewhat better; so that there is a kind of descent and accommodation felt when we leave speaking of moral nature to urge a virtue which it enjoins. To the well-born child all the virtues are natural, and not painfully acquired. Speak to his heart, and the man becomes suddenly virtuous.

Within the same sentiment is the germ of intellectual growth, which obeys the same law. Those who are capable of humility, of justice, of love, of aspiration, stand already on a platform that commands the sciences and arts, speech and poetry, action and grace. For whoso dwells in this moral beatitude already anticipates those special powers which men prize so highly. The lover has no talent, no skill, which passes for quite nothing with his enamored maiden, however little she may possess of related faculty; and the heart which abandons itself to the Supreme Mind finds itself related to all its works, and will travel a royal road to particular knowledges and powers. In ascending to this primary and aboriginal sentiment we have come from our remote station on the circumference instantaneously to the centre of the world, where, as in the closet of God, we see causes, and anticipate the universe, which is but a slow effect.

One mode of the divine teaching is the incarnation of the spirit in a form,—in forms, like my own. I live in society with persons who answer to thoughts in my own mind, or express a certain obedience to the great instincts to which I live. I see its presence to them. I am certified of a common nature; and these other souls, these separated selves, draw me as nothing else can. They stir in me the new emotions we call passion; of love, hatred, fear, admiration, pity; thence come conversation, competition, persuasion, cities, and war. Persons are supplementary to the primary teaching of the soul. In youth we are mad for persons. Childhood and youth see all the world in them. But the larger experience of man discovers the identical nature appearing through them all. Persons themselves acquaint us with the impersonal. In all conversation between two persons tacit reference is made, as to a third party, to a common nature. That third party or common nature is not social; it is impersonal; is God. And so in groups where debate is earnest, and especially on high questions, the company become aware that the thought rises to an equal level in all bosoms, that all have a spiritual property in what was said, as well as the sayer. They all become wiser than they were. It arches over them like a temple, this unity of thought in which every heart beats with nobler sense of power and duty, and thinks and acts with unusual solemnity. All are conscious of attaining to a higher self-possession. It shines for all. There is a certain wisdom of humanity which is common to the greatest men with the lowest, and which our ordinary education often labors to silence and obstruct. The mind is one, and the best minds, who love truth for its own sake, think much less of property in truth. They accept it thankfully everywhere, and do not label or stamp it with any man's name, for it is theirs long beforehand, and from eternity. The learned and the studious of thought have no monopoly of wisdom. Their violence of direction in some degree disqualifies them to think truly. We owe many valuable observations to people who are not very acute or profound, and who say the thing without effort which we want and have long been hunting in vain. The action of the soul is oftener in that which is felt and left unsaid than in that which is said in any conversation. It broods

Zeno: Greek philosopher (late fourth and early third centuries B.C.) who founded the Stoic school. **Arrian:** Greek historian and Stoic (second century A.D.), author of works on Epictetus.

over every society, and they unconsciously seek for it in each other. We know better than we do. We do not yet possess ourselves, and we know at the same time that we are much more. I feel the same truth how often in my trivial conversation with my neighbors, that somewhat higher in each of us overlooks this by-play, and Jove nods to Jove from behind each of us.

Men descend to meet. In their habitual and mean service to the world, for which they forsake their native nobleness, they resemble those Arabian sheiks who dwell in mean houses and affect an external poverty, to escape the rapacity of the Pacha, and reserve all their display of wealth for their interior and guarded retirements.

As it is present in all persons, so it is in every period of life. It is adult already in the infant man. In my dealing with my child, my Latin and Greek, my accomplishments and my money stead me nothing; but as much soul as I have avails. If I am wilful, he sets his will against mine, one for one, and leaves me, if I please, the degradation of beating him by my superiority of strength. But if I renounce my will and act for the soul, setting that up as umpire between us two, out of his young eyes looks the same soul; he reveres and loves with me.

The soul is the perceiver and revealer of truth. We know truth when we see it, let sceptic and scoffer say what they choose. Foolish people ask you, when you have spoken what they do not wish to hear, "How do you know it is truth, and not an error of your own?" We know truth when we see it, from opinion, as we know when we are awake that we are awake. It was a grand sentence of Emanuel Swedenborg,[n] which would alone indicate the greatness of that man's perception,— "It is no proof of a man's understanding to be able to affirm whatever he pleases; but to be able to discern that what is true is true, and that what is false is false,—this is the mark and character of intelligence." In the book I read, the good thought returns to me, as every truth will, the image of the whole soul. To the bad thought which I find in it, the same soul becomes a discerning, separating sword, and lops it away. We are wiser than we

know. If we will not interfere with our thought, but will act entirely, or see how the thing stands in God, we know the particular thing, and every thing, and every man. For the Maker of all things and all persons stands behind us and casts his dread omniscience through us over things.

But beyond this recognition of its own in particular passages of the individual's experience, it also reveals truth. And here we should seek to reinforce ourselves by its very presence, and to speak with a worthier, loftier strain of that advent. For the soul's communication of truth is the highest event in nature, since it then does not give somewhat from itself, but it gives itself, or passes into and becomes that man whom it enlightens; or in proportion to that truth he receives, it takes him to itself.

We distinguish the announcements of the soul, its manifestations of its own nature, by the term Revelation. These are always attended by the emotion of the sublime. For this communication is an influx of the Divine mind into our mind. It is an ebb of the individual rivulet before the flowing surges of the sea of life. Every distinct apprehension of this central commandment agitates men with awe and delight. A thrill passes through all men at the reception of new truth, or at the performance of a great action, which comes out of the heart of nature. In these communications the power to see is not separated from the will to do, but the insight proceeds from obedience, and the obedience proceeds from a joyful perception. Every moment when the individual feels himself invaded by it is memorable. By the necessity of our constitution a certain enthusiasm attends the individual's consciousness of that divine presence. The character and duration of this enthusiasm vary with the state of the individual, from an ecstasy and trance and prophetic inspiration,—which is its rarer appearance,—to the faintest glow of virtuous emotion, in which form it warms, like our household fires, all the families and associations of men, and make society possible. A certain tendency to insanity has always attended the opening of the religious sense in men, as if they had been "blasted with excess of light." The trances of Socrates,[n]

Emanuel Swedenborg: Swedish scientist and philosopher (1688–1772); his followers founded the New Jerusalem Church.

Socrates: Greek philosopher (470?–399 B.C.), teacher of Plato, and promulgator of idealistic philosophy. The divine voice spoke to him in his trances.

the "union" of Plotinus,[n] the vision of Porphyry,[n] the conversion of Paul,[n] the aurora of Behmen,[n] the convulsions of George Fox[n] and his Quakers, the illumination of Swedenborg, are of this kind. What was in the case of these remarkable persons a ravishment, has, in innumerable instances in common life, been exhibited in less striking manner. Everywhere the history of religion betrays a tendency to enthusiasm. The rapture of the Moravian[n] and Quietist[n]; the opening of the eternal sense of the Word, in the language of the New Jerusalem Church; the revival of the Calvinistic churches[n]; the experiences of the Methodists, are varying forms of that shudder of awe and delight with which the individual soul always mingles with the universal soul.

The nature of these revelations is the same; they are perceptions of the absolute law. They are solutions of the soul's own questions. They do not answer the questions which the understanding asks. The soul answers never by words, but by the thing itself that is inquired after.

Revelation is the disclosure of the soul. The popular notion of a revelation is that it is a telling of fortunes. In past oracles of the soul the understanding seeks to find answers to sensual questions, and undertakes to tell from God how long men shall exist, what their hands shall do and who shall be their company, adding names and dates and places. But we must pick no locks. We must check this low curiosity. An answer in words is delusive; it is really no answer to the questions you ask. Do not require a description of the countries towards which you sail. The description does not describe them to you, and to-morrow you arrive there and know them by inhabiting them. Men ask concerning the immortality of the soul, the employments of heaven, the state of the sinner, and so forth. They even dream that Jesus has left replies to precisely these interrogatories. Never a moment did that sublime spirit speak in their *patois*. To truth, justice, love, the attributes of the soul, the idea of immutableness is essentially associated. Jesus, living in these moral sentiments, heedless of sensual fortunes, heeding only the manifestations of these, never made the separation of the idea of duration from the essence of these attributes, nor uttered a syllable concerning the duration of the soul. It was left to his disciples to sever duration from the moral elements, and to teach the immortality of the soul as a doctrine, and maintain it by evidences. The moment the doctrine of the immortality is separately taught, man is already fallen. In the flowing of love, in the adoration of humility, there is no question of continuance. No inspired man ever asks this question or condescends to these evidences. For the soul is true to itself, and the man in whom it is shed abroad cannot wander from the present, which is infinite, to a future which would be finite.

These questions which we lust to ask about the future are a confession of sin. God has no answer for them. No answer in words can reply to a question of things. It is not in an arbitrary "decree of God," but in the nature of man, that a veil shuts down on the facts of to-morrow; for the soul will not have us read any other cipher than that of cause and effect. By this veil which curtains events it instructs the children of men to live in to-day. The only mode of obtaining an answer to these questions of the senses is to forego all low curiosity, and, accepting the tide of being which floats us into the secret of nature, work and live, work and live, and all unawares the advancing soul has built and forged for itself a new condition, and the question and the answer are one.

By the same fire, vital, consecrating, celestial, which burns until it shall dissolve all things into the waves and surges of an ocean of light, we see and know each other, and what spirit each is of.

Plotinus: Roman philosopher of Neoplatonic school (205?–270 A.D.), who held that the soul might rise in sublimity to final union with God. **Porphyry:** Greek scholar and follower of Plotinus (232?–304? A.D.). **the conversion of Paul:** see Acts ix:1–18. **Behmen:** Jakob Böhme Behmen (1575–1624), German mystic, the manuscript of whose *Aurora* was condemned as heretical. **George Fox:** English religious leader (1624–1691), founder of the Society of Friends. **Moravian:** one of the independent followers of John Huss (d. 1415), stressing purity of morals. **Quietist:** member of a seventeenth-century religious movement within the Church, holding to the doctrine of immediate inspiration and individual conscience. **Calvinistic churches:** named from John Calvin (1509–1564), French theologian, founder of a theocratic form of government at Geneva, Switzerland; preacher of the doctrine of predestination.

Who can tell the grounds of his knowledge of the character of the several individuals in his circle of friends? No man. Yet their acts and words do not disappoint him. In that man, though he knew no ill of him, he put no trust. In that other, though they had seldom met, authentic signs had yet passed, to signify that he might be trusted as one who had an interest in his own character. We know each other very well,—which of us has been just to himself and whether that which we 10 teach or behold is only an aspiration or is our honest effort also.

We are all discerners of spirits. That diagnosis lies aloft in our life or unconscious power. The intercourse of society, its trade, its religion, its friendships, its quarrels, is one wide judicial investigation of character. In full court, or in small committee, or confronted face to face, accuser and accused, men offer themselves to be judged. Against their will they exhibit those decisive trifles by which 20 character is read. But who judges? and what? Not our understanding. We do not read them by learning or craft. No; the wisdom of the wise man consists herein, that he does not judge them; he lets them judge themselves, and merely reads and records their own verdict.

By virtue of this inevitable nature, private will is overpowered, and, maugre our efforts or our imperfections, your genius will speak from you, and mine from me. That which we are, we shall 30 teach, not voluntarily but involuntarily. Thoughts come into our minds by avenues which we never left open, and thoughts go out of our minds through avenues which we never voluntarily opened. Character teaches over our head. The infallible index of true progress is found in the tone the man takes. Neither his age, nor his breeding, nor company, nor books, nor actions, nor talents, nor all together can hinder him from being deferential to a higher spirit than his own. If he have not found his home 40 in God, his manners, his forms of speech, the turn of his sentences, the build, shall I say, of all his opinions will involuntarily confess it, let him brave it out how he will. If he have found his centre, the Deity will shine through him, through all the disguises of ignorance, of ungenial temperament, of unfavorable circumstance. The tone of seeking is one, and the tone of having is another.

The great distinction between teachers sacred or literary,—between poets like Herbert,[n] and poets like Pope,[n]—between philosophers like Spinoza,[n] Kant[n] and Coleridge,[n] and philosophers like Locke,[n] Paley,[n] Mackintosh[n] and Stewart,[n]—between men of the world who are reckoned accomplished talkers, and here and there a fervent mystic, prophesying half insane under the infinitude of his thought,—is that one class speak from within, or from experience, as parties and possessors of the fact; and the other class from without, as spectators merely, or perhaps as acquainted with the fact on the evidence of third persons. It is of no use to preach to me from without. I can do that too easily myself. Jesus speaks always from within, and in a degree that transcends all others. In that is the miracle. I believe beforehand that it ought so to be. All men stand continually in the expectation of the appearance of such a teacher. But if a man do not speak from within the veil, where the word is one with that it tells of, let him lowly confess it.

The same Omniscience flows into the intellect and makes what we call genius. Much of the wisdom of the world is not wisdom, and the most illuminated class of men are no doubt superior to literary fame, and are not writers. Among the multitude of scholars and authors we feel no hallowing presence; we are sensible of a knack and skill rather than of inspiration; they have a light and know not whence it comes and call it their own; their talent is some exaggerated faculty, some overgrown member, so that their strength is a disease. In these instances the intellectual gifts do not make the impression of virtue, but almost of vice; and we feel that a man's talents stand in the

Herbert: George Herbert (1593–1633), English clergyman and metaphysical poet. **Pope:** Alexander Pope (1688–1744), English neoclassical and satiric poet. **Spinoza:** Baruch Spinoza (1632–1677), Dutch-Jewish philosopher, expounder of pantheism. **Kant:** Immanuel Kant (1724–1804), German transcendental philosopher and metaphysician. **Coleridge:** Samuel Taylor Coleridge (1772–1824), English poet and critic, interpreter of German transcendental idealism. **Locke:** John Locke (1632–1704), English philosopher, father of English empiricism. **Paley:** William Paley (1743–1805), English clergyman and utilitarian philosopher. **Mackintosh:** Sir James Mackintosh (1765–1832), Scottish philosopher and rationalist. **Stewart:** Dugald Stewart (1753–1828), Scottish philosopher and advocate of natural realism.

way of his advancement in truth. But genius is religious. It is a larger imbibing of the common heart. It is not anomalous, but more like and not less like other men. There is in all great poets a wisdom of humanity which is superior to any talents they exercise. The author, the wit, the partisan, the fine gentleman, does not take place of the man. Humanity shines in Homer, in Chaucer, in Spenser, in Shakspeare, in Milton. They are content with truth. They use the positive degree. They seem frigid and phlegmatic to those who have been spiced with the frantic passion and violent coloring of inferior but popular writers. For they are poets by the free course which they allow to the informing soul, which through their eyes beholds again and blesses the things which it hath made. The soul is superior to its knowledge, wiser than any of its works. The great poet makes us feel our own wealth, and then we think less of his compositions. His best communication to our mind is to teach us to despise all he has done. Shakspeare carries us to such a lofty strain of intelligent activity as to suggest a wealth which beggars his own; and we then feel that the splendid works which he has created, and which in other hours we extol as a sort of self-existent poetry, take no stronger hold of real nature than the shadow of a passing traveller on the rock. The inspiration which uttered itself in Hamlet and Lear could utter things as good from day to day forever. Why then should I make account of Hamlet and Lear, as if we had not the soul from which they fell as syllables from the tongue?

This energy does not descend into individual life on any other condition than entire possession. It comes to the lowly and simple; it comes to whomsoever will put off what is foreign and proud; it comes as insight; it comes as serenity and grandeur. When we see those whom it inhabits, we are apprised of new degrees of greatness. From that inspiration the man comes back with a changed tone. He does not talk with men with an eye to their opinion. He tries them. It requires of us to be plain and true. The vain traveller attempts to embellish his life by quoting my lord and the prince and the countess, who thus said or did to him. The ambitious vulgar show you their spoons and brooches and rings, and preserve their cards and compliments. The more cultivated, in their account of their own experience, cull out the pleasing, poetic circumstance,—the visit to Rome, the man of genius they saw, the brilliant friend they know; still further on perhaps the gorgeous landscape, the mountain lights, the mountain thoughts they enjoyed yesterday,—and so seek to throw a romantic color over their life. But the soul that ascends to worship the great God is plain and true; has no rose-color, no fine friends, no chivalry, no adventures; does not want admiration; dwells in the hour that now is, in the earnest experience of the common day,—by reason of the present moment and the mere trifle having become porous to thought and bibulous of the sea of light.

Converse with a mind that is grandly simple, and literature looks like word-catching. The simplest utterances are worthiest to be written, yet are they so cheap and so things of course, that in the infinite riches of the soul it is like gathering a few pebbles off the ground, or bottling a little air in a phial, when the whole earth and the whole atmosphere are ours. Nothing can pass there, or make you one of the circle, but the casting aside your trappings and dealing man to man in naked truth, plain confession and omniscient affirmation.

Souls such as these treat you as gods would, walk as gods in the earth, accepting without any admiration your wit, your bounty, your virtue even,—say rather your act of duty, for your virtue they own as their proper blood, royal as themselves, and over-royal, and the father of the gods. But what rebuke their plain fraternal bearing casts on the mutual flattery with which authors solace each other and wound themselves! These flatter not. I do not wonder that these men go to see Cromwell and Christina and Charles the Second and James the First and the Grand Turk. For they are, in their own elevation, the fellows of kings, and must feel the servile tone of conversation in the world. They must always be a godsend to princes, for they confront them, a king to a king, without ducking or concession, and give a high nature the refreshment and satisfaction of resistance, of plain humanity, of even companionship and of new ideas. They leave them wiser and superior men. Souls like these make us feel that sincerity is more excellent than flattery. Deal so plainly with man and woman as to constrain the utmost sincerity and destroy all hope of trifling with you. It is the highest compliment you can pay. Their "highest praising," said Milton, "is not flattery, and their plainest advice is a kind of praising."

Ineffable is the union of man and God in every act of the soul. The simplest person who in his integrity worships God, becomes God; yet forever and ever the influx of this better and universal self is new and unsearchable. It inspires awe and astonishment. How dear, how soothing to man, arises the idea of God, peopling the lonely place, effacing the scars of our mistakes and disappointments! When we have broken our god of tradition and ceased from our god of rhetoric, then may God fire the heart with his presence. It is the doubling of the heart itself, nay, the infinite enlargement of the heart with a power of growth to a new infinity on every side. It inspires in man an infallible trust. He has not the conviction, but the sight, that the best is the true, and may in that thought easily dismiss all particular uncertainties and fears, and adjourn to the sure revelation of time the solution of his private riddles. He is sure that his welfare is dear to the heart of being. In the presence of law to his mind he is overflowed with a reliance so universal that it sweeps away all cherished hopes and the most stable projects of mortal condition in its flood. He believes that he cannot escape from his good. The things that are really for thee gravitate to thee. You are running to seek your friend. Let your feet run, but your mind need not. If you do not find him, will you not acquiesce that it is best you should not find him? for there is a power, which, as it is in you, is in him also, and could therefore very well bring you together, if it were for the best. You are preparing with eagerness to go and render a service to which your talent and your taste invite you, the love of men and the hope of fame. Has it not occurred to you that you have no right to go, unless you are equally willing to be prevented from going? O, believe, as thou livest, that every sound that is spoken over the round world, which thou oughtest to hear, will vibrate on thine ear! Every proverb, every book, every byword that belongs to thee for aid or comfort, shall surely come home through open or winding passages. Every friend whom not thy fantastic will but the great and tender heart in thee craveth, shall lock thee in his embrace. And this because the heart in thee is the heart of all; not a valve, not a wall, not an intersection is there anywhere in nature, but one blood rolls uninterruptedly an endless circulation through all men, as the water of the globe is all one sea, and, truly seen, its tide is one.

Let man then learn the revelation of all nature and all thought to his heart; this, namely; that the Highest dwells with him; that the sources of nature are in his own mind, if the sentiment of duty is there. But if he would know what the great God speaketh, he must "go into his closet and shut the door," as Jesus said. God will not make himself manifest to cowards. He must greatly listen to himself, withdrawing himself from all the accents of other men's devotion. Even their prayers are hurtful to him, until he have made his own. Our religion vulgarly stands on numbers of believers. Whenever the appeal is made,—no matter how indirectly,—to numbers, proclamation is then and there made that religion is not. He that finds God a sweet enveloping thought to him never counts his company. When I sit in that presence, who shall dare to come in? When I rest in perfect humility, when I burn with pure love, what can Calvin or Swedenborg say?

It makes no difference whether the appeal is to numbers or to one. The faith that stands on authority is not faith. The reliance on authority measures the decline of religion, the withdrawal of the soul. The position men have given to Jesus, now for many centuries of history, is a position of authority. It characterizes themselves. It cannot alter the eternal facts. Great is the soul, and plain. It is no flatterer, it is no follower; it never appeals from itself. It believes in itself. Before the immense possibilities of man all mere experience, all past biography, however spotless and sainted, shrinks away. Before that heaven which our presentiments foreshow us, we cannot easily praise any form of life we have seen or read of. We not only affirm that we have few great men, but, absolutely speaking, that we have none; that we have no history, no record of any character or mode of living that entirely contents us. The saints and demigods whom history worships we are constrained to accept with a grain of allowance. Though in our lonely hours we draw a new strength out of their memory, yet, pressed on our attention, as they are by the thoughtless and customary, they fatigue and invade. The soul gives itself, alone, original and pure, to the Lonely, Original and Pure, who, on that condition, gladly inhabits, leads and speaks through it. Then is it glad, young and nimble. It is not wise, but it sees through all things. It is not called religious, but it is in- [10] nocent. It calls the light its own, and feels that the grass grows and the stone falls by a law inferior to, and dependent on, its nature. Behold, it saith, I am born into the great, the universal mind. I, the imperfect, adore my own Perfect. I am some- how receptive of the great soul, and thereby I do overlook the sun and the stars and feel them to be the fair accidents and effects which change and pass. More and more the surges of everlasting nature enter into me, and I become public and [20] human in my regards and actions. So come I to live in thoughts and act with energies which are immortal. Thus revering the soul, and learning, as the ancient said, that "its beauty is immense," man will come to see that the world is the perennial miracle which the soul worketh, and be less as- tonished at particular wonders; he will learn that there is no profane history; that all history is sacred; that the universe is represented in an atom, in a moment of time. He will weave no longer a [30] spotted life of shreds and patches, but he will live with a divine unity. He will cease from what is base and frivolous in his life and be content with all places and with any service he can render. He will calmly front the morrow in the negligency of that trust which carries God with it and so hath already the whole future in the bottom of the heart.

Politics

THIS ESSAY, developed from one of a series of lectures given in Boston in 1839–1840, was first published in *Essays, Second Series* (1844). For passages in the lecture omitted in the essay, see E. W. Emerson, editor, *Complete Works*, Centenary Edition, III, 334–344. The text is that of the edition of 1883.

In dealing with the State we ought to remember that its institutions are not aboriginal, though they existed before we were born; that they are not superior to the citizen; that every one of them was once the act of a single man; every law and usage was a man's expedient to meet a particular case; that they all are imitable, all alterable; we may make as good, we may make better. Society is an illusion to the young citizen. It lies before him in rigid repose, with certain names, men and institutions rooted like oak-trees to the centre, round which all arrange themselves the best they can. But the old statesman knows that society is fluid; there are no such roots and centres, but any particle may suddenly become the centre of the movement and compel the system to gyrate round it; as every man of strong will, like Pisistratus[n] or Cromwell,[n] does for a time, and every man of truth, like Plato[n] or Paul,[n] does forever. But politics rest on necessary foundations, and cannot be treated with levity. Republics abound in young [20] civilians who believe that the laws make the city, that grave modifications of the policy and modes of living and employments of the population, that commerce, education, and religion, may be voted in or out; and that any measure, though it were absurd, may be imposed on a people if only you can get sufficient voices to make it a law. But the wise know that foolish legislation is a rope of sand which perishes in the twisting; that the State must follow and not lead the character and progress of [30] the citizen; the strongest usurper is quickly got rid of; and they only who build on Ideas, build for eternity; and that the form of government which prevails is the expression of what cultivation exists in the population which permits it. The law is only a memorandum. We are superstitious, and esteem the statute somewhat: so much life as it has in the character of living men is its force. The statute stands there to say, Yesterday we agreed so and so, but how feel ye this article to-day? Our [40] statute is a currency which we stamp with our own portrait: it soon becomes unrecognizable, and in process of time will return to the mint. Nature is not democratic, nor limited-monarchical, but des-

Pisistratus: Athenian warrior and ruler (605?–527 B.C.). **Cromwell:** Oliver Cromwell (1599–1658), British general, Lord Protector of the Commonwealth, 1653–1658. **Plato:** Greek philosopher (427?–347 B.C.). **Paul:** the apostle, a convert to Christianity about 36 A.D.

potic, and will not be fooled or abated of any jot of her authority by the pertest of her sons; and as fast as the public mind is opened to more intelligence, the code is seen to be brute and stammering. It speaks not articulately, and must be made to. Meantime the education of the general mind never stops. The reveries of the true and simple are prophetic. What the tender poetic youth dreams, and prays, and paints to-day, but shuns the ridicule of saying aloud, shall presently be the resolutions of public bodies; then shall be carried as grievance and bill of rights through conflict and war, and then shall be triumphant law and establishment for a hundred years, until it gives place in turn to new prayers and pictures. The history of the State sketches in coarse outline the progress of thought, and follows at a distance the delicacy of culture and of aspiration.

The theory of politics which has possessed the mind of men, and which they have expressed the best they could in their laws and in their revolutions, considers persons and property as the two objects for whose protection government exists. Of persons, all have equal rights, in virtue of being identical in nature. This interest of course with its whole power demands a democracy. Whilst the rights of all as persons are equal, in virtue of their access to reason, their rights in property are very unequal. One man owns his clothes, and another owns a county. This accident, depending primarily on the skill and virtue of the parties, of which there is every degree, and secondarily on patrimony, falls unequally, and its rights of course are unequal. Personal rights, universally the same, demand a government framed on the ratio of the census; property demands a government framed on the ratio of owners and of owning. Laban,[n] who has flocks and herds, wishes them looked after by an officer on the frontiers, lest the Midianites shall drive them off; and pays a tax to that end. Jacob has no flocks or herds and no fear of the Midianites, and pays no tax to the officer. It seemed fit that Laban and Jacob should have equal rights to elect the officer who is to defend their persons, but that Laban and not Jacob should elect the officer who is to guard the sheep and cattle. And if question

Laban: the father of Leah and Rachel, and father-in-law of Jacob (Genesis: Chapters XXX and XXXI).

arise whether additional officers or watch-towers should be provided, must not Laban and Isaac,[n] and those who must sell part of their herds to buy protection for the rest, judge better of this, and with more right, than Jacob, who, because he is a youth and a traveller, eats their bread and not his own?

In the earliest society the proprietors made their own wealth, and so long as it comes to the owners in the direct way, no other opinion would arise in any equitable community than that property should make the law for property, and persons the law for persons.

But property passes through donation or inheritance to those who do not create it. Gift, in one case, makes it as really the new owner's, as labor made it the first owner's: in the other case, of patrimony, the law makes an ownership which will be valid in each man's view according to the estimate which he sets on the public tranquillity.

It was not however found easy to embody the readily admitted principle that property should make law for property, and persons for persons; since persons and property mixed themselves in every transaction. At last it seemed settled that the rightful distinction was that the proprietors should have more elective franchise than nonproprietors, on the Spartan principle of "calling that which is just, equal; not that which is equal, just."

That principle no longer looks so self-evident as it appeared in former times, partly because doubts have arisen whether too much weight had not been allowed in the laws to property, and such a structure given to our usages as allowed the rich to encroach on the poor, and to keep them poor; but mainly because there is an instinctive sense, however obscure and yet inarticulate, that the whole constitution of property, on its present tenures, is injurious, and its influence on persons deteriorating and degrading; that truly the only interest for the consideration of the State is persons; that property will always follow persons; that the highest end of government is the culture of men; and that if men can be educated, the institutions will share their improvement and the moral sentiment will write the law of the land.

Isaac: the father of Jacob.

If it be not easy to settle the equity of this question, the peril is less when we take note of our natural defences. We are kept by better guards than the vigilance of such magistrates as we commonly elect. Society always consists in greatest part of young and foolish persons. The old, who have seen through the hypocrisy of courts and statesmen, die and leave no wisdom to their sons. They believe their own newspaper, as their fathers did at their age. With such an ignorant and deceivable majority, States would soon run to ruin, but that there are limitations beyond which the folly and ambition of governors cannot go. Things have their laws, as well as men; and things refuse to be trifled with. Property will be protected. Corn will not grow unless it is planted and manured; but the farmer will not plant or hoe it unless the chances are a hundred to one that he will cut and harvest it. Under any forms, persons and property must and will have their just sway. They exert their power, as steadily as matter its attraction. Cover up a pound of earth never so cunningly, divide and subdivide it; melt it to liquid, convert it to gas; it will always weigh a pound; it will always attract and resist other matter by the full virtue of one pound weight:—and the attributes of a person, his wit and his moral energy, will exercise, under any law or extinguishing tyranny, their proper force,—if not overtly, then covertly; if not for the law, then against it; if not wholesomely, then poisonously; with right, or by might.

The boundaries of personal influence it is impossible to fix, as persons are organs of moral or supernatural force. Under the dominion of an idea which possesses the minds of multitudes, as civil freedom, or the religious sentiment, the powers of persons are no longer subjects of calculation. A nation of men unanimously bent on freedom or conquest can easily confound the arithmetic of statists, and achieve extravagant actions, out of all proportion to their means; as the Greeks, the Saracens, the Swiss, the Americans, and the French have done.

In like manner, to every particle of property belongs its own attraction. A cent is the representative of a certain quantity of corn or other commodity. Its value is in the necessities of the animal man. It is so much warmth, so much bread, so much water, so much land. The law may do what it will with the owner of property; its just power will still attach to the cent. The law may in a mad freak say that all shall have power except the owners of property; they shall have no vote. Nevertheless, by a higher law, the property will, year after year, write every statute that respects property. The non-proprietor will be the scribe of the proprietor. What the owners wish to do, the whole power of property will do, either through the law or else in defiance of it. Of course I speak of all the property, not merely of the great estates. When the rich are outvoted, as frequently happens, it is the joint treasury of the poor which exceeds their accumulations. Every man owns something, if it is only a cow, or a wheel-barrow, or his arms, and so has that property to dispose of.

The same necessity which secures the rights of persons and property against the malignity or folly of the magistrate, determines the form and methods of governing, which are proper to each nation and to its habit of thought, and nowise transferable to other states of society. In this country we are very vain of our political institutions, which are singular in this, that they sprung, within the memory of living men, from the character and condition of the people, which they still express with sufficient fidelity,—and we ostentatiously prefer them to any other in history. They are not better, but only fitter for us. We may be wise in asserting the advantage in modern times of the democratic form, but to other states of society, in which religion consecrated the monarchical, that and not this was expedient. Democracy is better for us because the religious sentiment of the present time accords better with it. Born democrats, we are nowise qualified to judge of monarchy, which, to our fathers living in the monarchical idea, was also relatively right. But our institutions, though in coincidence with the spirit of the age, have not any exemption from the practical defects which have discredited other forms. Every actual State is corrupt. Good men must not obey the laws too well. What satire on government can equal the severity of censure conveyed in the word *politic*, which now for ages has signified *cunning*, intimating that the State is a trick?

The same benign necessity and the same practical abuse appear in the parties, into which each State divides itself, of opponents and defenders of the administration of the government. Parties are also founded on instincts, and have better guides to their own humble aims than the sagacity of their leaders. They have nothing perverse in their origin, but rudely mark some real and lasting relation. We might as wisely reprove the east wind or the frost, as a political party, whose members, for the most part, could give no account of their position, but stand for the defense of those interests in which they find themselves. Our quarrel with them begins when they quit this deep natural ground at the bidding of some leader, and obeying personal considerations, throw themselves into the maintenance and defense of points nowise belonging to their system. A party is perpetually corrupted by personality. Whilst we absolve the association from dishonesty, we cannot extend the same charity to their leaders. They reap the rewards of the docility and zeal of the masses which they direct. Ordinarily our parties are parties of circumstance, and not of principle; as the planting interest in conflict with the commercial; the party of capitalists and that of operatives; parties which are identical in their moral character, and which can easily change ground with each other in the support of many of their measures. Parties of principle, as, religious sects, or the party of free-trade, of universal suffrage, of abolition of slavery, of abolition of capital punishment,—degenerate into personalities, or would inspire enthusiasm. The vice of our leading parties in this country (which may be cited as a fair specimen of these societies of opinion) is that they do not plant themselves on the deep and necessary grounds to which they are respectively entitled, but lash themselves to fury in the carrying of some local and momentary measure, nowise useful to the commonwealth. Of the two great parties which at this hour almost share the nation between them, I should say that one has the best cause, and the other contains the best men. The philosopher, the poet, or the religious man, will of course wish to cast his vote with the democrat, for free-trade, for wide suffrage, for the abolition of legal cruelties in the penal code, and for facilitating in every manner the access of the young and the poor to the sources of wealth

and power. But he can rarely accept the persons whom the so-called popular party propose to him as representatives of these liberalities. They have not at heart the ends which give to the name of democracy what hope and virtue are in it. The spirit of our American radicalism is destructive and aimless: it is not loving; it has no ulterior and divine ends, but is destructive only out of hatred and selfishness. On the other side, the conservative party, composed of the most moderate, able, and cultivated part of the population, is timid, and merely defensive of property. It vindicates no right, it aspires to no real good, it brands no crime, it proposes no generous policy, it does not build, nor write, nor cherish the arts, nor foster religion, nor establish schools, nor encourage science, nor emancipate the slave, nor befriend the poor, or the Indian, or the immigrant. From neither party, when in power, has the world any benefit to expect in science, art, or humanity, at all commensurate with the resources of the nation.

I do not for these defects despair of our republic. We are not at the mercy of any waves of chance. In the strife of ferocious parties, human nature always finds itself cherished; as the children of the convicts at Botany Bay are found to have as healthy a moral sentiment as other children. Citizens of feudal states are alarmed at our democratic institutions lapsing into anarchy, and the older and more cautious among ourselves are learning from Europeans to look with some terror at our turbulent freedom. It is said that in our license of construing the Constitution, and in the despotism of public opinion, we have no anchor; and one foreign observer thinks he has found the safeguard in the sanctity of Marriage among us; and another thinks he has found it in our Calvinism. Fisher Ames[n] expressed the popular security more wisely, when he compared a monarchy and a republic, saying, that a monarchy is a merchantman, which sails well, but will sometimes strike on a rock and go to the bottom; whilst a republic is a raft, which would never sink, but then your feet are always in water. No forms can have any dangerous importance, whilst we are befriended by the laws of things. It makes no difference how many

Fisher Ames: Boston statesman (1758–1808), U. S. Representative identified with the Federalist party.

tons weight of atmosphere presses on our heads, so long as the same pressure resists it within the lungs. Augment the mass a thousand fold, it cannot begin to crush us, as long as reaction is equal to action. The fact of two poles, of two forces, centripetal and centrifugal, is universal, and each force by its own activity develops the other. Wild liberty develops iron conscience. Want of liberty, by strengthening law and decorum, stupefies conscience. "Lynch-law" prevails only where there is greater hardihood and self-subsistency in the leaders. A mob cannot be a permanency: everybody's interest requires that it should not exist, and only justice satisfies all.

We must trust infinitely to the beneficent necessity which shines through all laws. Human nature expresses itself in them as characteristically as in statues, or songs, or railroads; and an abstract of the codes of nations would be a transcript of the common conscience. Governments have their origin in the moral identity of men. Reason for one is seen to be reason for another, and for every other. There is a middle measure which satisfies all parties, be they never so many or so resolute for their own. Every man finds a sanction for his simplest claims and deeds, in decisions of his own mind, which he calls Truth and Holiness. In these decisions all the citizens find a perfect agreement, and only in these; not in what is good to eat, good to wear, good use of time, or what amount of land or of public aid each is entitled to claim. This truth and justice men presently endeavor to make application of to the measuring of land, the apportionment of service, the protection of life and property. Their first endeavors, no doubt, are very awkward. Yet absolute right is the first governor; or, every government is an impure theocracy. The idea after which each community is aiming to make and mend its law, is the will of the wise man. The wise man it cannot find in nature, and it makes awkward but earnest efforts to secure his government by contrivance; as by causing the entire people to give their voices on every measure; or by a double choice to get the representation of the whole; or by a selection of the best citizens; or to secure the advantages of efficiency and internal peace by confiding the government to one, who may himself select his

agents. All forms of government symbolize an immortal government, common to all dynasties and independent of numbers, perfect where two men exist, perfect where there is only one man.

Every man's nature is a sufficient advertisement to him of the character of his fellows. My right and my wrong is their right and their wrong. Whilst I do what is fit for me, and abstain from what is unfit, my neighbor and I shall often agree in our means, and work together for a time to one end. But whenever I find my dominion over myself not sufficient for me, and undertake the direction of him also, I overstep the truth, and come into false relations to him. I may have so much more skill or strength than he that he cannot express adequately his sense of wrong, but it is a lie, and hurts like a lie both him and me. Love and nature cannot maintain the assumption; it must be executed by a practical lie, namely by force. This undertaking for another is the blunder which stands in colossal ugliness in the governments of the world. It is the same thing in numbers, as in a pair, only not quite so intelligible. I can see well enough a great difference between my setting myself down to a self-control, and my going to make somebody else act after my views; but when a quarter of the human race assume to tell me what I must do, I may be too much disturbed by the circumstances to see so clearly the absurdity of their command. Therefore all public ends look vague and quixotic beside private ones. For any laws but those which men make for themselves are laughable. If I put myself in the place of my child, and we stand in one thought and see that things are thus or thus, that perception is law for him and me. We are both there, both act. But if, without carrying him into the thought, I look over into his plot, and guessing how it is with him, ordain this or that, he will never obey me. This is the history of governments,—one man does something which is to bind another. A man who cannot be acquainted with me, taxes me; looking from afar at me ordains that a part of my labor shall go to this or that whimsical end,—not as I, but as he happens to fancy. Behold the consequence. Of all debts men are least willing to pay the taxes. What a satire is this on government! Everywhere they think they get their money's worth, except for these.

Hence the less government we have the better, —the fewer laws, and the less confided power. The antidote to this abuse of formal Government is the influence of private character, the growth of the Individual; the appearance of the principal to supersede the proxy; the appearance of the wise man, of whom the existing government is, it must be owned, but a shabby imitation. That which all things tend to educe; which freedom, cultivation, intercourse, revolutions, go to form and deliver, is character; that is the end of Nature, to reach unto this coronation of her king. To educate the wise man the State exists; and with the appearance of the wise man the State expires. The appearance of character makes the State unnecessary. The wise man is the State. He needs no army, fort, or navy,—he loves men too well; no bribe, or feast, or palace, to draw friends to him; no vantage ground, no favorable circumstance. He needs no library, for he has not done thinking; no church, for he is a prophet; no statute book, for he has the lawgiver; no money, for he is value; no road, for he is at home where he is; no experience, for the life of the creator shoots through him, and looks from his eyes. He has no personal friends, for he who has the spell to draw the prayer and piety of all men unto him needs not husband and educate a few to share with him a select and poetic life. His relation to men is angelic; his memory is myrrh to them; his presence, frankincense and flowers.

We think our civilization near its meridian, but we are yet only at the cock-crowing and the morning star. In our barbarous society the influence of character is in its infancy. As a political power, as the rightful lord who is to tumble all rulers from their chairs, its presence is hardly yet suspected. Malthus[n] and Ricardo[n] quite omit it; the Annual Register is silent; in the Conversations' Lexicon, it is not set down; the President's Message, the Queen's Speech, have not mentioned it; and yet it is never nothing. Every thought which genius and piety throw into the world, alters the world. The gladiators in the

Malthus: Thomas Robert Malthus (1766–1834), English economist, famous for his theory of population. **Ricardo:** David Ricardo (1772–1823), English economist, author of an important treatise on money.

lists of power feel, through all their frocks of force and simulation, the presence of worth. I think the very strife of trade and ambition are confession of this divinity; and successes in those fields are the poor amends, the fig-leaf with which the shamed soul attempts to hide its nakedness. I find the like unwilling homage in all quarters. It is because we know how much is due from us that we are impatient to show some petty talent as a substitute for worth. We are haunted by a conscience of this right to grandeur of character, and are false to it. But each of us has some talent, can do somewhat useful, or graceful, or formidable, or amusing, or lucrative. That we do, as an apology to others and to ourselves for not reaching the mark of a good and equal life. But it does not satisfy *us*, whilst we thrust it on the notice of our companions. It may throw dust in their eyes, but does not smooth our own brow, or give us the tranquillity of the strong when we walk abroad. We do penance as we go. Our talent is a sort of expiation, and we are constrained to reflect on our splendid moment with a certain humiliation, as somewhat too fine, and not as one act of many acts, a fair expression of our permanent energy. Most persons of ability meet in society with a kind of tacit appeal. Each seems to say, "I am not all here." Senators and presidents have climbed so high with pain enough, not because they think the place specially agreeable, but as an apology for real worth, and to vindicate their manhood in our eyes. This conspicuous chair is their compensation to themselves for being of a poor, cold, hard nature. They must do what they can. Like one class of forest animals, they have nothing but a prehensile tail; climb they must, or crawl. If a man found himself so rich-natured that he could enter into strict relations with the best persons and make life serene around him by the dignity and sweetness of his behavior, could he afford to circumvent the favor of the caucus and the press, and covet relations so hollow and pompous as those of a politician? Surely nobody would be a charlatan who could afford to be sincere.

The tendencies of the times favor the idea of self-government, and leave the individual, for all code, to the rewards and penalties of his own constitution; which work with more energy than we believe whilst we depend on artificial restraints. The movement in this direction has been very marked in modern history. Much has been blind and discreditable, but the nature of the revolution is not affected by the vices of the revolters; for this is a purely moral force. It was never adopted by any party in history, neither can be. It separates the individual from all party, and unites him at the same time to the race. It promises a recognition of higher rights than those of personal freedom, or the security of property. A man has a right to be employed, to be trusted, to be loved, to be revered. The power of love, as the basis of a State, has never been tried. We must not imagine that all things are lapsing into confusion if every tender protestant be not compelled to bear his part in certain social conventions; nor doubt that roads can be built, letters carried, and the fruit of labor secured, when the government of force is at an end. Are our methods now so excellent that all competition is hopeless? could not a nation of friends even devise better ways? On the other hand, let not the most conservative and timid fear anything from a premature surrender of the bayonet and the system of force. For, according to the order of nature, which is quite superior to our will, it stands thus: there will always be a government of force where men are selfish; and when they are pure enough to abjure the code of force they will be wise enough to see how these public ends of the post-office, of the highway, of commerce and the exchange of property, of museums and libraries, of institutions of art and science can be answered.

We live in a very low state of the world, and pay unwilling tribute to governments founded on force. There is not, among the most religious and instructed men of the most religious and civil nations, a reliance on the moral sentiment and a sufficient belief in the unity of things, to persuade them that society can be maintained without artificial restraints, as well as the solar system; or that the private citizen might be reasonable and a good neighbor, without the hint of a jail or a confiscation. What is strange too, there never was in any man sufficient faith in the power of rectitude to inspire him with the broad design of renovating the State on the principle of right and love. All those who have pretended this design have been partial reformers, and have admitted in some manner the supremacy of the bad State. I do not call to mind a single human being who has steadily denied the authority of the laws, on the simple ground of his own moral nature. Such designs, full of genius and full of faith as they are, are not entertained except avowedly as air-pictures. If the individual who exhibits them dare to think them practicable, he disgusts scholars and churchmen: and men of talent and women of superior sentiments cannot hide their contempt. Not the less does nature continue to fill the heart of youth with suggestions of this enthusiasm, and there are now men,—if indeed I can speak in the plural number,—more exactly, I will say, I have just been conversing with one man, to whom no weight of adverse experience will make it for a moment appear impossible that thousands of human beings might exercise towards each other the grandest and simplest sentiments, as well as a knot of friends, or a pair of lovers.

HENRY DAVID THOREAU (1817-1862)

THOREAU described himself as "a mystic, a transcendentalist, and a natural philosopher to boot." Biographers and critics have conferred other titles on him: the Bachelor of Nature, the Yankee Pan, the Poet-Naturalist, the Moralist of the Picturesque, the Economic Transcendentalist, and the Cosmic Yankee. Less complimentary epithets have been given, such as Robert Louis Stevenson's "the Concord skulker," Isaac Hecker's "a consecrated crank," and—most damaging of all—James Russell Lowell's labels of *poseur* and a second-rate Emerson. The variety of these characterizations affords a measure of Thoreau's many-sided appeal and his complexity. As Henry Seidel Canby remarked, "there are a half-dozen possible biographies of Thoreau, depending upon the point of view the biographer takes of his subject." The salient fact about Henry David Thoreau is that he has left a classic account of his practical efforts to live a life of dignity and integrity in an age of dominant materialism. His only "business" was to love wisdom.

Of the writers associated with Concord, Thoreau was the only native son. He was born on July 12, 1817, the son of a pencil maker, prepared for college at the village academy, and entered Harvard in 1833. Although he maintained a tranquil indifference to the conventional college honors, he attained an expert mastery of Greek, and spent long hours in the library reading the pre-Shakespeareans as well as the English poets of the seventeenth century; Emerson later introduced him to the sacred books of the East. A brief interlude of teaching at Canton, Massachusetts, in 1835, brought him into stimulating contact with Orestes Brownson, who plunged him into the exciting life of the mind. Thoreau was thus prepared for the profound influence of Emerson, whose Phi Beta Kappa address provided the intellectual shock at his graduation in 1837. Thoreau doubtless knew what to expect, for he had read his fellow townsman's *Nature* the year before.

After his graduation Thoreau returned to Concord to teach in the village school and later in a private academy conducted with his brother John. By 1838 Henry had begun to keep a Journal, to write poetry, and to lecture in the local lyceum. He now began his transforming association with Emerson, who found his young friend "a scholar and poet and as full of buds of promise as a young apple tree." The first number of *The Dial* for July, 1840, contained a poem by the twenty-three year old Thoreau, as well as his essay on Aulus Persius. Their fast-ripening friendship became a matter of almost daily contact when Thoreau lived at Emerson's house as a "general helper" from 1841 to 1843. Although Emerson could say at this time that Thoreau's thoughts "are my own originally drest," the younger of these "transcendental brothers" was too stout an individualist to slip easily into the role of uncritical disciple. Emerson confirmed Thoreau's intuitions and perceptions, but Thoreau believed that "To be a philosopher is not merely to have subtle thoughts. . . . It is to solve some of the problems of life, not only theoretically, but practically. . . ." The transcendentalists were urging self-reliance, freedom from the trammels of the past, and the following of one's inner convictions. Thoreau took positive action to sever himself from institutions he could not approve, and even to "resign" from those he had never joined. The transcendentalists and the Quakers taught the value of retirement and of communion with nature. Thoreau betook himself to Walden Pond, and for two years forsook society, even failing to provide visitors with a chair. "Thoreau," wrote Emerson, "gives me in flesh and blood . . . my own ethics."

Thoreau's residence at Walden from July 4, 1845, to September, 1847, was made famous in his best known book, *Walden*, which was not published until 1854. His essays and poems continued to appear in *The Dial* from 1840 to 1844, and a few other pieces found their way to the pages of the *Democratic Review* and *Graham's Magazine*; the latter periodical printed "Thomas Carlyle and his Works" in 1847. Thoreau underwrote the costs of publication of his first book, *A Week on the Concord and Merrimack Rivers* (1845). The volume was based upon an excursion with his brother John from August 31 to September 13, 1839. Of the edition of 1,000 copies, the author distributed 75, and the publisher sold 219. After Thoreau carried the remainder to his attic, he announced: "I have now a library of nearly nine hundred volumes, over seven hundred of which I wrote myself." The *Week*, originally planned as an autobiography, provided a framework for the distillation of Thoreau's reflections on his wide reading and for a far-ranging commentary on topics as diverse as canal boats and Homer. Thoreau's poetry here found an exquisite setting amid his matchless descriptions of nature. *Walden* (1854) was the only other of his books to appear during his lifetime. Meanwhile, his essay "Resistance to Civil Government" (later entitled *Essay on Civil Disobedience*) was published in *Aesthetic Papers* in 1849. Thoreau's preference for odd jobs as pencil maker, gardener, and surveyor gave him the necessary freedom for the travels which are recorded with such relish in his *Journals*. The accounts of his three trips to Maine in 1846, 1853, and 1857 form the basis for *The Maine Woods* (1864), issued two years after his death. His journey to Canada in 1850 with Ellery Channing resulted in the publication of "A Yankee in Canada" in *Putnam's Magazine* in 1853. Three of his four jaunts to Cape Cod furnished the material for "Cape Cod" in 1855, also issued in *Putnam's*. As early as 1855 Thoreau had spoken of his "months of feebleness," but it was not until December, 1860, that his malady was diagnosed as tuberculosis, the disease which had been fatal to his brother and father also. His last excursions in the spring and summer of the following year extended as far west as St. Paul in the vain hope of recovering his health. He died on May 6, 1862, in Concord.

To many of his contemporaries Thoreau seemed to be indeed a "consecrated crank" whose dramatic withdrawal to Walden Pond was a perverse attempt to prove that man could live as cheaply as a woodchuck. Emerson accused him of being content with leading a huckleberry party instead of engineering for all America. Lowell complained that Thoreau insisted in public on going back to flint and steel when there was a match box in his pocket. Yet Thoreau, of all the transcendentalists, today has the largest audience because he manfully confronted one of man's most persistent problems: How can an individual save his soul alive without becoming a slave to society or to the state? When he told the Brook Farmers, "It was better to keep bachelor's hall in hell than live in a boarding house in heaven," he gave a wry Yankee expression to the spirit of American individualism. To the growing complexity of life, he doggedly applied his formula of simplicity. And if his conduct seemed comic to his neighbors, Emerson's reminder that simplicity is always comic "in the double-dealing, quacking world," is a pertinent answer. Timeliness of message is not in itself sufficient to account for the major position Thoreau holds in our literature. Like Emerson, he was a powerful "word-catcher," the master of a style perfectly accommodated to his thoughts. Even Lowell was compelled to praise the "antique purity" of Thoreau's language. Thoreau's best work lives today because his wisdom is expressed in lean and sinewy sentences, barbed with wit, and illuminated by the perceptions of a poet. There are, as George Whicher conceded in his discerning centennial tribute to Thoreau, lapses into sentimentality, occasional descents to moral truisms, and a deficiency "on the side of heartiness." These defects, however, do not diminish Thoreau's total achievement. The remarkable impression he made on Tolstoi and Gandhi, as well as on generations of readers in America, was anticipated by Emerson in his tender eulogy: "His soul was made for the noblest society; he had in a short life exhausted the capabilities of the world; wherever there is knowledge, wherever there is virtue, wherever there is beauty, he will find a home."

BIBLIOGRAPHY · The two important editions of Thoreau's writings are *Collected Works* (20 vols., 1906), containing the manuscript insertions, and limited to 600 copies; and the Walden Edition (20 vols., 1906), issued without the manuscript insertions. *The Writings of Henry David Thoreau* (10 vols., 1894), published as the Riverside Edition, contains introductory notes by H. E. Scudder. *The Journal*, edited by B. Torrey, comprises volumes VII–XX of the Walden Edition. A short cut to the core of Thoreau's thinking is *The Heart of Thoreau's Journals*, edited by O. Shepard (1927). *Collected Poems of Henry Thoreau* was edited by C. Bode (1943). A judicious selection of Thoreau's writings is *Henry David Thoreau: Representative Selections*, edited by B. Crawford (1934). *A Bibliography of Henry David Thoreau*, compiled by F. H. Allen (1908), needs to

be supplemented by the selective lists made by H. Hartwick in W. F. Taylor, *A History of American Letters* (1936), and by L. Leary, *Articles on American Literature. . . .* (1947).

Excellent biographical and critical studies are H. S. Canby, *Thoreau* (1939), and J. W. Krutch, *Thoreau* (1949). Earlier biographical studies include B. Atkinson, *Henry D. Thoreau: the Cosmic Yankee* (1927); L. Bazalgette, *Henry Thoreau: Bachelor of Nature* (1924); W. E. Channing, *Thoreau: the Poet-Naturalist* (1873), revised and enlarged under the editorship of F. B. Sanborn (1902); E. W. Emerson, *Thoreau as Remembered by a Young Friend* (1917); R. L. Cook, *Passage to Walden* (1949); H. A. Page, *Thoreau: His Life and Aims* (1877); H. S. Salt, *The Life of Henry David Thoreau* (1890, rev. ed., 1896); F. B. Sanborn, *The Life of Henry David Thoreau, including Many Essays hitherto unpublished, and some Account of his Family and Friends* (1917), and *The Personality of Thoreau* (1901); and M. Van Doren, *Henry David Thoreau: a Critical Study* (1916).

Special biographical and critical studies include R. W. Adams, "Thoreau and Immortality," *Studies in Philology*, XXVI (1929), 58–66, "Thoreau's Literary Apprenticeship," *Studies in Philology*, XXIX (1932), 617–629, "Thoreau at Harvard," *New England Quarterly*, XIII (1940), 24–33, and "Thoreau's Sources for 'Resistance to Civil Government,'" *Studies in Philology*, XLII (1945), 640–653; F. H. Allen, "Thoreau's *Collected Poems*," *American Literature*, XVII (1945), 250–267; J. Burroughs, "Henry D. Thoreau," in *Indoor Studies* (1889), 1–42; C. Cestre, "Thoreau et Emerson," and "Thoreau et la Dialectique," *Revue Anglo-Américaine*, VII (1930), 215–230; A. Christy, "A Thoreau Fact Book," in *Colophon*, IV, Pt. 16 (March, 1934), and *The Orient in American Transcendentalism* (1932), 187–233; J. T. Flanagan, "Thoreau in Minnesota," *Minnesota History*, XVI (1935), 35–46; N. Foerster, "The Intellectual Heritage of Thoreau," *Texas Review*, II (1917), 192–212, "Thoreau as an Artist," *Sewanee Review*, XXIX (1921), 2–13, and "Thoreau," in *Nature in American Literature* (1923), 69–142; H. H. Hoeltje, "Thoreau as Lecturer," *New England Quarterly*, XIX (1946), 485–494; J. J. Kwiatt, "Thoreau's Philosophical Apprenticeship," *New England Quarterly*, XVIII (1945), 51–69; F. W. Lorch, "Thoreau and the Organic Principle in Poetry," *PMLA*, LIII (1938), 286–302; C. Manning, "Thoreau and Tolstoi," *New England Quarterly*, XVI (1938), 234–243; J. B. Moore, "Crèvecoeur and Thoreau," *Papers of the Michigan Academy of Science, Art, and Letters*, V (1926), 309–333, and "Thoreau Rejects Emerson," *American Literature*, IV (1932), 241–256; P. E. More, "A Hermit's Notes on Thoreau," in *Shelburn Essays: First Series* (1904), 1–21; L. Powys, "Thoreau: A Disparagement," *Bookman*, LXIX (1929), 163–165; T. M. Raysor, "The Love Story of Thoreau," *Studies in Philology*, XXIII (1926), 457–463; A. Rickett, "Thoreau," in *The Vagabond in Literature* (1906), 89–114; R. W. Robbins, *Discovery at Walden* (1947); E. M. Schuster, "Native American Anarchism," *Smith College Studies in History*, XVII (1931–1932), 5–202; R. L. Stevenson, "Henry David Thoreau: His Character and Opinions," *Cornhill Magazine*, XL (1880), 665–682; W. D. Templeman, "Thoreau: Moralist of the Picturesque," *PMLA*, XLVII (1932), 864–889; A. Warren, "Lowell on Thoreau," *Studies in Philology*, XXVII (1930), 442–461; and G. F. Whicher, *Walden Revisited* (1945).

My Prayer

THIS POEM was included in an unsigned article by Emerson under the title of "Prayers" in *The Dial* for July, 1842. It was reprinted in *A Yankee in Canada* (1866), and in *Poems of Nature* (1895). The text is that of its first appearance in *The Dial*.

Great God, I ask thee for no meaner pelf
Than that I may not disappoint myself,
That in my action I may soar as high,
As I can now discern with this clear eye.

And next in value, which thy kindness lends, 5
That I may greatly disappoint my friends,
Howe'er they think or hope that it may be,
They may not dream how thou'st distinguished me.

That my weak hand may equal my firm faith,
And my life practise more than my tongue saith; 10
That my low conduct may not show,
Nor my relenting lines,
That I thy purpose did not know,
Or overrated thy designs.

Smoke

"Smoke" and its companion piece, "Haze," were first printed under the general title "Orphics" in *The Dial* for April, 1843. "Smoke" was reprinted in *Walden* (1854), and later in *Poems of Nature* (1895). "Haze" was one of the poems imbedded in *A Week on the Concord and Merrimack Rivers* (1849), and later collected in *Poems of Nature*. The text is that of the printing in *The Dial*.

Light-winged smoke, Icarian bird,
Melting thy pinions in thy upward flight,

Smoke. 1. Icarian: from Icarus in Greek mythology. Escaping from the labyrinth in Crete, Icarus soared too close to the sun, which melted the wax in his artificial wings.

Lark without song, and messenger of dawn,
Circling above the hamlets as thy nest;
Or else, departing dream, and shadowy form 5
Of midnight vision, gathering up thy skirts;
By night star-veiling, and by day
Darkening the light and blotting out the sun;
Go thou my incense upward from this hearth,
And ask the Gods to pardon this clear flame. 10

Haze

Woof of the sun, ethereal gauze,
Woven of nature's richest stuffs,
Visible heat, air-water, and dry sea,
Last conquest of the eye;
Toil of the day displayed, sun-dust, 5
Aerial surf upon the shores of earth,
Ethereal estuary, frith of light,
Breakers of air, billows of heat,
Fine summer spray on inland seas;
Bird of the sun, transparent-winged, 10
Owlet of noon, soft-pinioned,
From heath or stubble rising without song;
Establish thy serenity o'er the fields.

Civil Disobedience

THIS ESSAY first appeared as "Resistance to Civil Government" in *Æsthetic Papers* (1849), edited by Elizabeth Peabody. It was reprinted in *A Yankee in Canada* (1866) under its present title. "Civil Disobedience" was prompted by the same opposition to the Mexican War and the increase of slave territory that inspired Lowell's *Biglow Papers*, although it was originally written as a lecture after Thoreau's famous night in jail for his refusal to pay his poll tax. Bronson Alcott, who also was jailed for his refusal to support a government which countenanced slavery, saluted "Civil Disobedience" enthusiastically: "This man is the independent of independents—is, indeed, the sole signer of the Declaration, and a Revolution in himself—a more than '76—having got beyond the signing to the doing it out fully." For an account of the influence of the essay on the formulation of passive resistance as a political weapon by Gandhi, see H. S. Salt, "Gandhi and Thoreau," *Nation and Athenaeum*, XLVI (1930), 728. The text is that of *A Yankee in Canada, with Anti-Slavery and Reform Papers* (1866).

7. frith: firth, a narrow arm of the sea.

I heartily accept the motto,—"That government is best which governs least" and I should like to see it acted up to more rapidly and systematically. Carried out, it finally amounts to this, which also I believe,— "That government is best which governs not at all" and when men are prepared for it, that will be the kind of government which they will have. Government is at best but an expedient; but most governments are usually, and all governments are sometimes, inexpedient. The objections which have been brought against a standing army, and they are many and weighty, and deserve to prevail, may also at last be brought against a standing government. The standing army is only an arm of the standing government. The government itself, which is only the mode which the people have chosen to execute their will, is equally liable to be abused and perverted before the people can act through it. Witness the present Mexican war, the work of comparatively a few individuals using the standing government as their tool; for, in the outset, the people would not have consented to this measure.

This American government,—what is it but a tradition, though a recent one, endeavoring to transmit itself unimpaired to posterity, but each instant losing some of its integrity? It has not the vitality and force of a single living man; for a single man can bend it to his will. It is a sort of wooden gun to the people themselves. But it is not the less necessary for this; for the people must have some complicated machinery or other, and hear its din, to satisfy that idea of government which they have. Governments show thus how successfully men can be imposed on, even impose on themselves, for their own advantage. It is excellent, we must all allow. Yet this government never of itself furthered any enterprise, but by the alacrity with which it got out of its way. *It* does not keep the country free. *It* does not settle the West. *It* does not educate. The character inherent in the American people has done all that has been accomplished; and it would have done somewhat more, if the government had not sometimes got in its way. For government is an expedient by which men would fain succeed in letting one another alone; and, as has been said, when it is most expedient, the governed are most let alone by it.

Trade and commerce, if they were not made of India-rubber, would never manage to bounce over the obstacles which legislators are continually putting in their way; and, if one were to judge these men wholly by the effects of their actions and not partly by their intentions, they would deserve to be classed and punished with those mischievous persons who put obstructions on the railroads.

But, to speak practically and as a citizen, unlike those who call themselves no-government men, I ask for, not at once no government, but at once a better government. Let every man make known what kind of government would command his respect, and that will be one step toward obtaining it.

After all, the practical reason why, when the power is once in the hands of the people, a majority are permitted, and for a long period continue, to rule is not because they are most likely to be in the right, nor because this seems fairest to the minority, but because they are physically the strongest. But a government in which the majority rule in all cases cannot be based on justice, even as far as men understand it. Can there not be a government in which majorities do not virtually decide right and wrong, but conscience?—in which majorities decide only those questions to which the rule of expediency is applicable? Must the citizen ever for a moment, or in the least degree, resign his conscience to the legislator? Why has every man a conscience, then? I think that we should be men first, and subjects afterward. It is not desirable to cultivate a respect for the law, so much as for the right. The only obligation which I have a right to assume, is to do at any time what I think right. It is truly enough said, that a corporation has no conscience; but a corporation of conscientious men is a corporation with a conscience. Law never made men a whit more just; and, by means of their respect for it, even the well-disposed are daily made the agents of injustice. A common and natural result of an undue respect for law is, that you may see a file of soldiers, colonel, captain, corporal, privates, powder-monkeys, and all, marching in admirable order over hill and dale to the wars, against their wills, ay, against their common sense and consciences, which makes it very steep marching indeed, and produces a palpitation of the heart. They have no doubt that it is a damnable business in which they are concerned; they are all peaceably inclined. Now, what are they? Men at all? or small movable forts and magazines, at the service of some unscrupulous man in power? Visit the Navy-Yard, and behold a marine, such a man as an American government can make, or such as it can make a man with its black arts,—a mere shadow and reminiscence of humanity, a man laid out alive and standing, and already, as one may say, buried under arms with funeral accompaniments, though it may be,

> Not a drum was heard, not a funeral note,
> As his corse to the rampart we hurried;
> Not a soldier discharged his farewell shot
> O'er the grave where our hero we buried.

The mass of men serve the state thus, not as men mainly, but as machines, with their bodies. They are the standing army, and the militia, jailers, constables, posse comitatus, &c. In most cases there is no free exercise whatever of the judgment or of the moral sense; but they put themselves on a level with wood and earth and stones; and wooden men can perhaps be manufactured that will serve the purpose as well. Such command no more respect than men of straw or a lump of dirt. They have the same sort of worth only as horses and dogs. Yet such as these even are commonly esteemed good citizens. Others,—as most legislators, politicians, lawyers, ministers, and office-holders,—serve the state chiefly with their heads; and, as they rarely make any moral distinctions, they are as likely to serve the Devil, without intending it, as God. A very few, as heroes, patriots, martyrs, reformers in the great sense, and men, serve the state with their consciences also, and so necessarily resist it for the most part; and they are commonly treated as enemies by it. A wise man will only be useful as a man, and will not submit to the "clay," and "stop a hole to keep the wind away," but leave that office to his dust at least:—

> I am too high-born to be propertied,
> To be a secondary at control,
> Or useful serving-man and instrument
> To any sovereign state throughout the world.

He who gives himself entirely to his fellowmen appears to them useless and selfish; but he who gives himself partially to them is pronounced a benefactor and philanthropist.

How does it become a man to behave toward this American government to-day? I answer, that he cannot without disgrace be associated with it. I cannot for an instant recognize that political organization as my government which is the slave's government also.

All men recognize the right of revolution; that is, the right to refuse allegiance to, and to resist, the government, when its tyranny or its inefficiency are great and unendurable. But almost all say that such is not the case now. But such was the case, they think, in the Revolution of '75. If one were to tell me that this was a bad government because it taxed certain foreign commodities brought to its ports, it is most probable that I should not make an ado about it, for I can do without them. All machines have their friction; and possibly this does enough good to counterbalance the evil. At any rate, it is a great evil to make a stir about it. But when the friction comes to have its machine, and oppression and robbery are organized, I say, let us not have such a machine any longer. In other words, when a sixth of the population of a nation which has undertaken to be the refuge of liberty are slaves, and a whole country is unjustly overrun and conquered by a foreign army, and subjected to military law, I think that it is not too soon for honest men to rebel and revolutionize. What makes this duty the more urgent is the fact that the country so overrun is not our own, but ours is the invading army.

Paley, a common authority with many on moral questions, in his chapter on the "Duty of Submission to Civil Government," resolves all civil obligation into expediency; and he proceeds to say, "that so long as the interest of the whole society requires it, that is, so long as the established government cannot be resisted or changed without public inconveniency, it is the will of God that the established government be obeyed, and no longer. . . . This principle being admitted, the justice of every particular case of resistance is reduced to a computation of the quantity of the danger and grievance on the one side, and of the probability and expense of redressing it on the other." Of this, he says, every man shall judge for himself. But

Paley appears never to have contemplated those cases to which the rule of expediency does not apply, in which a people, as well as an individual, must do justice, cost what it may. If I have unjustly wrested a plank from a drowning man, I must restore it to him though I drown myself. This, according to Paley, would be inconvenient. But he that would save his life, in such a case, shall lose it. This people must cease to hold slaves, and to make war on Mexico, though it cost them their existence as a people.

In their practice, nations agree with Paley; but does any one think that Massachusetts does exactly what is right at the present crisis?

A drab of state, a cloth-o'-silver slut,
To have her train borne up, and her soul trail in the
    dirt.

Practically speaking, the opponents to a reform in Massachusetts are not a hundred thousand politicians at the South, but a hundred thousand merchants and farmers here, who are more interested in commerce and agriculture than they are in humanity, and are not prepared to do justice to the slave and to Mexico, cost what it may. I quarrel not with far-off foes, but with those who, near at home, co-operate with, and do the bidding of, those far away, and without whom the latter would be harmless. We are accustomed to say, that the mass of men are unprepared; but improvement is slow, because the few are not materially wiser or better than the many. It is not so important that many should be as good as you, as that there be some absolute goodness somewhere; for that will leaven the whole lump. There are thousands who are in opinion opposed to slavery and to the war, who yet in effect do nothing to put an end to them; who, esteeming themselves children of Washington and Franklin, sit down with their hands in their pockets, and say that they know not what to do, and do nothing; who even postpone the question of freedom to the question of free-trade, and quietly read the prices-current along with the latest advices from Mexico, after dinner, and, it may be, fall asleep over them both. What is the price-current of an honest man and patriot to-day? They hesitate, and they regret, and sometimes they petition; but they do nothing

in earnest and with effect. They will wait, well disposed, for others to remedy the evil, that they may no longer have it to regret. At most, they give only a cheap vote, and a feeble countenance and God-speed, to the right, as it goes by them. There are nine hundred and ninety-nine patrons of virtue to one virtuous man. But it is easier to deal with the real possessor of a thing than with the temporary guardian of it.

All voting is a sort of gaming, like checkers or backgammon, with a slight moral tinge to it, a playing with right and wrong, with moral questions; and betting naturally accompanies it. The character of the voters is not staked. I cast my vote, perchance, as I think right; but I am not vitally concerned that that right should prevail. I am willing to leave it to the majority. Its obligation, therefore, never exceeds that of expediency. Even voting for the right is doing nothing for it. It is only expressing to men feebly your desire that it should prevail. A wise man will not leave the right to the mercy of chance nor wish it to prevail through the power of the majority. There is but little virtue in the action of masses of men. When the majority shall at length vote for the abolition of slavery, it will be because they are indifferent to slavery, or because there is but little slavery left to be abolished by their vote. They will then be the only slaves. Only his vote can hasten the abolition of slavery who asserts his own freedom by his vote.

I hear of a convention to be held at Baltimore, or elsewhere, for the selection of a candidate for the Presidency, made up chiefly of editors, and men who are politicians by profession; but I think, what is it to any independent, intelligent, and respectable man what decision they may come to? Shall we not have the advantage of his wisdom and honesty, nevertheless? Can we not count upon some independent votes? Are there not many individuals in the country who do not attend conventions? But no: I find that the respectable man, so called, has immediately drifted from his position, and despairs of his country, when his country has more reason to despair of him. He forthwith adopts one of the candidates thus selected as the only available one, thus proving that he is himself available for any purposes of the demagogue. His vote is of no more worth than that of any un-principled foreigner or hireling native, who may have been bought. O for a man who is a man, and, as my neighbor says, has a bone in his back which you cannot pass your hand through! Our statistics are at fault: the population has been returned too large. How many men are there to a square thousand miles in this country? Hardly one. Does not America offer any inducement for men to settle here? The American has dwindled into an Odd Fellow,—one who may be known by the de-velopment of his organ of gregariousness, and a manifest lack of intellect and cheerful self-reliance; whose first and chief concern, on coming into the world, is to see that the Almshouses are in good repair; and, before yet he has lawfully donned the virile garb, to collect a fund for the support of the widows and orphans that may be; who, in short, ventures to live only by the aid of the Mutual Insurance company, which has promised to bury him decently.

It is not a man's duty, as a matter of course, to devote himself to the eradication of any, even the most enormous wrong; he may still properly have other concerns to engage him; but it is his duty, at least, to wash his hands of it, and, if he gives it no thought longer, not to give it practically his support. If I devote myself to other pursuits and contemplations, I must first see, at least, that I do not pursue them sitting upon another man's shoulders. I must get off him first, that he may pursue his contemplations too. See what gross in-consistency is tolerated. I have heard some of my townsmen say, "I should like to have them order me out to help put down an insurrection of the slaves, or to march to Mexico;—see if I would go"; and yet these very men have each, directly by their allegiance, and so indirectly, at least, by their money, furnished a substitute. The soldier is ap-plauded who refuses to serve in an unjust war by those who do not refuse to sustain the unjust government which makes the war; is applauded by those whose own act and authority he disregards and sets at naught; as if the state were penitent to that degree that it hired one to scourge it while it sinned, but not to that degree that it left off sinning for a moment. Thus, under the name of Order and Civil Government, we are all made at

last to pay homage to and support our own mean-ness. After the first blush of sin comes its indiffer-ence; and from immoral it becomes, as it were, *un*moral, and not quite unnecessary to that life which we have made.

The broadest and most prevalent error requires the most disinterested virtue to sustain it. The slight reproach to which the virtue of patriotism is commonly liable, the noble are most likely to incur. Those who, while they disapprove of the character and measures of a government, yield to it their allegiance and support are undoubtedly its most conscientious supporters, and so frequently the most serious obstacles to reform. Some are peti-tioning the state to dissolve the Union, to disregard the requisitions of the President. Why do they not dissolve it themselves,—the union between themselves and the state,—and refuse to pay their quota into its treasury? Do not they stand in the same relation to the state that the state does to the Union? And have not the same reasons prevented the state from resisting the Union which have pre-vented them from resisting the state?

How can a man be satisfied to entertain an opinion merely, and enjoy it? Is there any en-joyment in it, if his opinion is that he is aggrieved? If you are cheated out of a single dollar by your neighbor, you do not rest satisfied with knowing that you are cheated, or with saying that you are cheated, or even with petitioning him to pay you your due; but you take effectual steps at once to obtain the full amount, and see that you are never cheated again. Action from principle, the percep-tion and the performance of right, changes things and relations; it is essentially revolutionary, and does not consist wholly with anything which was. It not only divides states and churches, it divides families; ay, it divides the individual, separating the diabolical in him from the divine.

Unjust laws exist: shall we be content to obey them, or shall we endeavor to amend them, and obey them until we have succeeded, or shall we transgress them at once? Men generally, under such a government as this, think that they ought to wait until they have persuaded the majority to alter them. They think that, if they should resist, the remedy would be worse than the evil. But it is the fault of the government itself that the

653

remedy *is* worse than the evil. *It* makes it worse. Why is it not more apt to anticipate and provide for reform? Why does it not cherish its wise minority? Why does it cry and resist before it is hurt? Why does it not encourage its citizens to be on the alert to point out its faults, and *do* better than it would have them? Why does it always crucify Christ, and excommunicate Copernicus and Luther, and pronounce Washington and Franklin rebels?

One would think, that a deliberate and practical denial of its authority was the only offense never contemplated by government; else, why has it not assigned its definite, its suitable and proportionate penalty? If a man who has no property refuses but once to earn nine shillings for the state, he is put in prison for a period unlimited by any law that I know, and determined only by the discretion of those who placed him there; but if he should steal ninety times nine shillings from the state, he is soon permitted to go at large again.

If the injustice is part of the necessary friction of the machine of government, let it go, let it go: perchance it will wear smooth,—certainly the machine will wear out. If the injustice has a spring, or a pulley, or a rope, or a crank, exclusively for itself, then perhaps you may consider whether the remedy will not be worse than the evil; but if it is of such a nature that it requires you to be the agent of injustice to another, then, I say, break the law. Let your life be a counter friction to stop the machine. What I have to do is to see, at any rate, that I do not lend myself to the wrong which I condemn.

As for adopting the ways which the State has provided for remedying the evil, I know not of such ways. They take too much time, and a man's life will be gone. I have other affairs to attend to. I came into this world, not chiefly to make this a good place to live in, but to live in it, be it good or bad. A man has not everything to do, but something; and because he cannot do everything, it is not necessary that he should do something wrong. It is not my business to be petitioning the Governor or the Legislature any more than it is theirs to petition me; and if they should not hear my petition, what should I do then? But in this case the state has provided no way: its very Constitution

is the evil. This may seem to be harsh and stubborn and unconciliatory; but it is to treat with the utmost kindness and consideration the only spirit that can appreciate or deserves it. So is all change for the better, like birth and death, which convulse the body.

I do not hesitate to say, that those who call themselves Abolitionists should at once effectually withdraw their support, both in person and property, from the government of Massachusetts, and not wait till they constitute a majority of one, before they suffer the right to prevail through them. I think that it is enough if they have God on their side, without waiting for that other one. Moreover, any man more right than his neighbors constitutes a majority of one already.

I meet this American government, or its representative, the state government, directly, and face to face, once a year—no more—in the person of its tax-gatherer; this is the only mode in which a man situated as I am necessarily meets it; and it then says distinctly, Recognize me; and the simplest, the most effectual, and, in the present posture of affairs, the indispensablest mode of treating with it on this head, of expressing your little satisfaction with and love for it is to deny it then. My civil neighbor, the tax-gatherer, is the very man I have to deal with,—for it is, after all, with men and not with parchment that I quarrel,—and he has voluntarily chosen to be an agent of the government. How shall he ever know well what he is and does as an officer of the government, or as a man, until he is obliged to consider whether he shall treat me, his neighbor, for whom he has respect, as a neighbor and well-disposed man, or as a maniac and disturber of the peace, and see if he can get over this obstruction to his neighborliness without a ruler and more impetuous thought or speech corresponding with his action. I know this well, that if one thousand, if one hundred, if ten men whom I could name,—if ten honest men only,—ay, if one HONEST man, in this State of Massachusetts, ceasing to hold slaves, were actually to withdraw from this copartnership, and be locked up in the county jail therefor, it would be the abolition of slavery in America. For it matters not how small the beginning may seem to be: what is once well done is done forever. But we love better to talk about it: that we say is our mission. Reform keeps many scores of newspapers in its service, but not one man. If my esteemed neighbor, the State's ambassador, who will devote his days to the settlement of the question of human rights in the Council Chamber, instead of being threatened with the prisons of Carolina, were to sit down the prisoner of Massachusetts, that State which is so anxious to foist the sin of slavery upon her sister, —though at present she can discover only an act of inhospitality to be the ground of a quarrel with her,—the Legislature would not wholly waive the subject the following winter.

Under a government which imprisons any unjustly, the true place for a just man is also a prison. The proper place to-day, the only place which Massachusetts has provided for her freer and less desponding spirits, is in her prisons, to be put out and locked out of the State by her own act, as they have already put themselves out by their principles. It is there that the fugitive slave, and the Mexican prisoner on parole, and the Indian come to plead the wrongs of his race should find them; on that separate, but more free and honorable ground, where the State places those who are not with her, but against her,—the only house in a slave State in which a free man can abide with honor. If any think that their influence would be lost there, and their voices no longer afflict the ear of the State, that they would not be as an enemy within its walls, they do not know by how much truth is stronger than error, nor how much more eloquently and effectively he can combat injustice who has experienced a little in his own person. Cast your whole vote, not a strip of paper merely, but your whole influence. A minority is powerless while it conforms to the majority; it is not even a minority then; but it is irresistible when it clogs by its whole weight. If the alternative is to keep all just men in prison, or give up war and slavery, the State will not hesitate which to choose. If a thousand men were not to pay their tax-bills this year, that would not be a violent and bloody measure, as it would be to pay them, and enable the State to commit violence and shed innocent blood. This is, in fact, the definition of a peaceable revolution, if any such is possible. If the tax-gatherer, or any other public officer, asks me, as

one has done, "But what shall I do?" my answer is, "If you really wish to do anything, resign your office." When the subject has refused allegiance, and the officer has resigned his office, then the revolution is accomplished. But even suppose blood should flow. Is there not a sort of blood shed when the conscience is wounded? Through this wound a man's real manhood and immortality flow out, and he bleeds to an everlasting death. I see this blood flowing now.

I have contemplated the imprisonment of the offender, rather than the seizure of his goods,— though both will serve the same purpose,—because they who assert the purest right, and consequently are most dangerous to a corrupt State, commonly have not spent much time in accumulating property. To such the State renders comparatively small service, and a slight tax is wont to appear exorbitant, particularly if they are obliged to earn it by special labor with their hands. If there were one who lived wholly without the use of money, the State itself would hesitate to demand it of him. But the rich man—not to make any invidious comparison—is always sold to the institution which makes him rich. Absolutely speaking, the more money, the less virtue; for money comes between a man and his objects, and obtains them for him; and it was certainly no great virtue to obtain it. It puts to rest many questions which he would otherwise be taxed to answer; while the only new question which it puts is the hard but superfluous one, how to spend it. Thus his moral ground is taken from under his feet. The opportunities of living are diminished in proportion as what are called the "means" are increased. The best thing a man can do for his culture when he is rich is to endeavor to carry out those schemes which he entertained when he was poor. Christ answered the Herodians according to their condition. "Show me the tribute-money," said he;— and one took a penny out of his pocket;—if you use money which has the image of Cæsar on it, and which he has made current and valuable, that is, if you are men of the State, and gladly enjoy the advantages of Cæsar's government, then pay him back some of his own when he demands it. "Render therefore to Cæsar that which is Cæsar's, and to God those things which are God's,"—leaving them no wiser than before as to which was which; for they did not wish to know.

When I converse with the freest of my neighbors, I perceive that, whatever they may say about the magnitude and seriousness of the question, and their regard for the public tranquillity, the long and the short of the matter is, that they cannot spare the protection of the existing government, and they dread the consequences to their property and families of disobedience to it. For my own part, I should not like to think that I rely on the protection of the State. But, if I deny the authority of the State when it presents its tax-bill, it will soon take and waste all my property, and so harass me and my children without end. This is hard. This makes it impossible for a man to live honestly, and at the same time comfortably, in outward respects. It will not be worth the while to accumulate property; that would be sure to go again. You must hire or squat somewhere, and raise but a small crop, and eat that soon. You must live within yourself, and depend upon yourself always tucked up and ready for a start, and not have many affairs. A man may grow rich in Turkey even, if he will be in all respects a good subject of the Turkish government. Confucius said: "If a state is governed by the principles of reason, poverty and misery are subjects of shame; if a state is not governed by the principles of reason, riches and honors are the subjects of shame." No: until I want the protection of Massachusetts to be extended to me in some distant Southern port, where my liberty is endangered, or until I am bent solely on building up an estate at home by peaceful enterprise, I can afford to refuse allegiance to Massachusetts, and her right to my property and life. It costs me less in every sense to incur the penalty of disobedience to the State than it would to obey. I should feel as if I were worth less in that case.

Some years ago, the State met me in behalf of the Church, and commanded me to pay a certain sum toward the support of a clergyman whose preaching my father attended, but never I myself. "Pay," it said, "or be locked up in the jail." I declined to pay. But, unfortunately, another man saw fit to pay it. I did not see why the schoolmaster should be taxed to support the priest, and not the priest the schoolmaster; for I was not the State's schoolmaster, but I supported myself by voluntary subscription. I did not see why the lyceum should not present its tax-bill, and have the State to back its demand, as well as the Church. However, at the request of the selectmen, I condescended to make some such statement as this in writing:—"Know all men by these presents, that I, Henry Thoreau, do not wish to be regarded as a member of any incorporated society which I have not joined." This I gave to the town clerk; and he has it. The State, having thus learned that I did not wish to be regarded as a member of that church, has never made a like demand on me since; though it said that it must adhere to its original presumption that time. If I had known how to name them, I should then have signed off in detail from all the societies which I never signed on to; but I did not know where to find a complete list.

I have paid no poll-tax for six years. I was put into a jail once on this account, for one night; and, as I stood considering the walls of solid stone, two or three feet thick, the door of wood and iron, a foot thick, and the iron grating which strained the light, I could not help being struck with the foolishness of that institution which treated me as if I were mere flesh and blood and bones, to be locked up. I wondered that it should have concluded at length that this was the best use it could put me to, and had never thought to avail itself of my services in some way. I saw that, if there was a wall of stone between me and my townsmen, there was a still more difficult one to climb or break through before they could get to be as free as I was. I did not for a moment feel confined, and the walls seemed a great waste of stone and mortar. I felt as if I alone of all my townsmen had paid my tax. They plainly did not know how to treat me, but behaved like persons who are underbred. In every threat and in every compliment there was a blunder; for they thought that my chief desire was to stand the other side of that stone wall. I could not but smile to see how industriously they locked the door on my meditations, which followed them out again without let or hindrance, and they were really all that was dangerous. As they could not reach me, they had resolved to punish my body; just as boys, if they cannot come at some person against whom they have a spite, will abuse his dog. I saw that the State was half-witted, that it was timid as a lone woman with her silver spoons, and that it did not know its friends from its foes, and I lost all my remaining respect for it, and pitied it.

Thus the State never intentionally confronts a man's sense, intellectual or moral, but only his body, his senses. It is not armed with superior wit or honesty, but with superior physical strength. I was not born to be forced. I will breathe after my own fashion. Let us see who is the strongest. What force has a multitude? They only can force me who obey a higher law than I. They force me to become like themselves. I do not hear of men being forced to live this way or that by masses of men. What sort of life were that to live? When I meet a government which says to me, "Your money or your life," why should I be in haste to give it my money? It may be in a great strait, and not know what to do: I cannot help that. It must help itself; do as I do. It is not worth the while to snivel about it. I am not responsible for the successful working of the machinery of society. I am not the son of the engineer. I perceive that, when an acorn and a chestnut fall side by side, the one does not remain inert to make way for the other, but both obey their own laws, and spring and grow and flourish as best they can, till one, perchance, overshadows and destroys the other. If a plant cannot live according to its nature, it dies; and so a man.

The night in prison was novel and interesting enough. The prisoners in their shirt-sleeves were enjoying a chat and the evening air in the doorway, when I entered. But the jailer said, "Come, boys, it is time to lock up;" and so they dispersed, and I heard the sound of their steps returning into the hollow apartments. My room-mate was introduced to me by the jailer as "a first-rate fellow and a clever man." When the door was locked, he showed me where to hang my hat, and how he managed matters there. The rooms were whitewashed once a month; and this one, at least, was the whitest, most simply furnished, and probably the neatest apartment in the town. He naturally wanted to know where I came from, and what brought me there; and, when I had told him, I asked him in my turn how he came there, pre-

suming him to be an honest man, of course; and, as the world goes, I believe he was. "Why," said he, "they accuse me of burning a barn; but I never did it." As near as I could discover, he had probably gone to bed in a barn when drunk, and smoked his pipe there; and so a barn was burnt. He had the reputation of being a clever man, had been there some three months waiting for his trial to come on, and would have to wait as much longer, but he was quite domesticated and contented, since he got his board for nothing, and thought that he was well treated.

He occupied one window, and I the other; and I saw that if one stayed there long, his principal business would be to look out the window. I had soon read all the tracts that were left there, and examined where former prisoners had broken out, and where a grate had been sawed off, and heard the history of the various occupants of that room; for I found that even here there was a history and a gossip which never circulated beyond the walls of the jail. Probably this is the only house in the town where verses are composed, which are afterward printed in a circular form, but not published. I was shown quite a long list of verses which were composed by some young men who had been detected in an attempt to escape, who avenged themselves by singing them.

I pumped my fellow-prisoner as dry as I could, for fear I should never see him again; but at length he showed me which was my bed, and left me to blow out the lamp.

It was like traveling into a far country, such as I had never expected to behold, to lie there for one night. It seemed to me that I never had heard the town-clock strike before, nor the evening sounds of the village; for we slept with the windows open, which were inside the grating. It was to see my native village in the light of the Middle Ages, and our Concord was turned into a Rhine stream, and visions of knights and castles passed before me. They were the voices of old burghers that I heard in the streets. I was an involuntary spectator and auditor of whatever was done and said in the kitchen of the adjacent village-inn,—a wholly new and rare experience to me. It was a closer view of my native town. I was fairly inside of it. I never had seen its institutions before.

This is one of its peculiar institutions; for it is a shire town. I began to comprehend what its inhabitants were about.

In the morning, our breakfasts were put through the hole in the door, in small oblong-square tin pans, made to fit, and holding a pint of chocolate, with brown bread, and an iron spoon. When they called for the vessels again, I was green enough to return what bread I had left; but my comrade seized it, and said that I should lay that up for lunch or dinner. Soon after he was let out to work at haying in a neighboring field, whither he went every day, and would not be back till noon; so he bade me good-day, saying that he doubted if he should see me again.

When I came out of prison,—for some one interfered, and paid that tax,—I did not perceive that great changes had taken place on the common, such as he observed who went in a youth and emerged a tottering and gray-headed man; and yet a change had to my eyes come over the scene,— the town, and State, and country,—greater than any that mere time could effect. I saw yet more distinctly the State in which I lived. I saw to what extent the people among whom I lived could be trusted as good neighbors and friends; that their friendship was for summer weather only; that they did not greatly propose to do right; that they were a distinct race from me by their prejudices and superstitions, as the Chinamen and Malays are; that in their sacrifices to humanity they ran no risks, not even to their property; that after all they were not so noble but they treated the thief as he had treated them, and hoped, by a certain outward observance and a few prayers, and by walking in a particular straight though useless path from time to time, to save their souls. This may be to judge my neighbors harshly; for I believe that many of them are not aware that they have such an institution as the jail in their village.

It was formerly the custom in our village, when a poor debtor came out of jail, for his acquaintances to salute him, looking through their fingers, which were crossed to represent the grating of a jail window, "How do ye do?" My neighbors did not thus salute me, but first looked at me, and then at one another, as if I had returned from a long journey. I was put into jail as I was going to the shoe-

maker's to get a shoe which was mended. When I was let out the next morning, I proceeded to finish my errand, and, having put on my mended shoe, joined a huckleberry party, who were impatient to put themselves under my conduct; and in half an hour,—for the horse was soon tackled,—was in the midst of a huckleberry field, on one of our highest hills, two miles off, and then the State was nowhere to be seen.

This is the whole history of "My Prisons."

I have never declined paying the highway tax, because I am as desirous of being a good neighbor as I am of being a bad subject; and as for supporting schools, I am doing my part to educate my fellow-countrymen now. It is for no particular item in the tax-bill that I refuse to pay it. I simply wish to refuse allegiance to the State, to withdraw and stand aloof from it effectually. I do not care to trace the course of my dollar, if I could, till it buys a man or a musket to shoot one with,— the dollar is innocent,—but I am concerned to trace the effects of my allegiance. In fact, I quietly declare war with the State, after my fashion, though I will still make what use and get what advantage of her I can, as is usual in such cases.

If others pay the tax which is demanded of me, from a sympathy with the State, they do but what they have already done in their own case, or rather they abet injustice to a greater extent than the State requires. If they pay the tax from a mistaken interest in the individual taxed, to save his property, or prevent his going to jail, it is because they have not considered wisely how far they let their private feelings interfere with the public good.

This, then, is my position at present. But one cannot be too much on his guard in such a case, lest his action be biased by obstinacy or an undue regard for the opinions of men. Let him see that he does only what belongs to himself and to the hour.

I think sometimes, Why, this people mean well, they are only ignorant; they would do better if they knew how: why give your neighbors this pain to treat you as they are not inclined to? But I think again, This is no reason why I should do as they do, or permit others to suffer much greater pain of a different kind. Again, I sometimes say to myself, When many millions of men, without heat, without ill will, without personal feeling of any kind, demand of you a few shillings only, without the possibility, such is their constitution, of retracting or altering their present demand, and without the possibility, on your side, of appeal to any other millions, why expose yourself to this overwhelming brute force? You do not resist cold and hunger, the winds and the waves, thus obstinately; you quietly submit to a thousand similar necessities. You do not put your head into the fire. But just in proportion as I regard this as not wholly a brute force, but partly a human force, and consider that I have relations to those millions as to so many millions of men, and not of mere brute or inanimate things, I see that appeal is possible, first and instantaneously, from them to the Maker of them, and, secondly, from them to themselves. But if I put my head deliberately into the fire, there is no appeal to fire or to the Maker of fire, and I have only myself to blame. If I could convince myself that I have any right to be satisfied with men as they are, and to treat them accordingly, and not according, in some respects, to my requisitions and expectations of what they and I ought to be, then, like a good Mussulman and fatalist, I should endeavor to be satisfied with things as they are, and say it is the will of God. And, above all, there is this difference between resisting this and a purely brute or natural force, that I can resist this with some effect; but I cannot expect, like Orpheus, to change the nature of the rocks and trees and beasts.

I do not wish to quarrel with any man or nation. I do not wish to split hairs, to make fine distinctions, or set myself up as better than my neighbors. I seek rather, I may say, even an excuse for conforming to the laws of the land. I am but too ready to conform to them. Indeed, I have reason to suspect myself on this head; and each year, as the tax-gatherer comes round, I find myself disposed to review the acts and position of the general and State governments, and the spirit of the people, to discover a pretext for conformity.

We must affect our country as our parents,
And if at any time we alienate

Our love or industry from doing it honor,
We must respect effects and teach the soul
Matter of conscience and religion,
And not desire of rule or benefit.

I believe that the State will soon be able to take all my work of this sort out of my hands, and then I shall be no better a patriot than my fellow-countrymen. Seen from a lower point of view the Constitution, with all its faults, is very good; the law and the courts are very respectable; even this State and this American government are, in many respects, very admirable, and rare things, to be thankful for, such as a great many have described them; but seen from a point of view a little higher, they are what I have described them; seen from a higher still, and the highest, who shall say what they are, or that they are worth looking at or thinking of at all?

However, the government does not concern me much, and I shall bestow the fewest possible thoughts on it. It is not many moments that I live under a government, even in this world. If a man is thought-free, fancy-free, imagination-free, that which is not never for a long time appearing to be to him, unwise rulers or reformers cannot fatally interrupt him.

I know that most men think differently from myself; but those whose lives are by profession devoted to the study of these or kindred subjects content me as little as any. Statesmen and legislators, standing so completely within the institution, never distinctly and nakedly behold it. They speak of moving society, but have no resting-place without it. They may be men of a certain experience and discrimination, and have no doubt invented ingenious and even useful systems, for which we sincerely thank them; but all their wit and usefulness lie within certain not very wide limits. They are wont to forget that the world is not governed by policy and expediency. Webster never goes behind government, and so cannot speak with authority about it. His words are wisdom to those legislators who contemplate no essential reform in the existing government; but for thinkers, and those who legislate for all time, he never once glances at the subject. I know of those whose serene and wise speculations on this theme would soon reveal the limits of his mind's range and hospitality. Yet, compared with the cheap professions of most reformers, and the still cheaper wisdom and eloquence of politicians in general, his are almost the only sensible and valuable words, and we thank Heaven for him. Comparatively, he is always strong, original, and, above all, practical. Still, his quality is not wisdom, but prudence. The lawyer's truth is not Truth, but consistency or a consistent expediency. Truth is always in harmony with herself, and is not concerned chiefly to reveal the justice that may consist with wrong-doing. He well deserves to be called, as he has been called, the Defender of the Constitution. There are really no blows to be given by him but defensive ones. He is not a leader, but a follower. His leaders are the men of '87. "I have never made an effort," he says, "and never propose to make an effort; I have never countenanced an effort, and never mean to countenance an effort, to disturb the arrangement as originally made, by which the various States came into the Union." Still thinking of the sanction which the Constitution gives to slavery, he says, "Because it was a part of the original compact,— let it stand." Notwithstanding his special acuteness and ability, he is unable to take a fact out of its merely political relations, and behold it as it lies absolutely to be disposed of by the intellect,— what, for instance, it behooves a man to do here in America to-day with regard to slavery,—but ventures, or is driven, to make some such desperate answer as the following, while professing to speak absolutely, and as a private man,—from which what new and singular code of social duties might be inferred? "The manner," says he, "in which the governments of those States where slavery exists are to regulate it is for their own consideration, under their responsibility to their constituents, to the general laws of propriety, humanity, and justice, and to God. Associations formed elsewhere, springing from a feeling of humanity, or any other cause, have nothing whatever to do with it. They have never received any encouragement from me, and they never will."[n]

They who know of no purer sources of truth, who have traced up its stream no higher, stand, and wisely stand, by the Bible and the Constitution, and drink at it there with reverence and humility; but they who behold where it comes trickling into this lake or that pool, gird up their loins once more, and continue their pilgrimage toward its fountain-head.

No man with a genius for legislation has appeared in America. They are rare in the history of the world. There are orators, politicians, and eloquent men, by the thousand; but the speaker has not yet opened his mouth to speak who is capable of settling the much-vexed questions of the day. We love eloquence for its own sake, and not for any truth which it may utter, or any heroism it may inspire. Our legislators have not yet learned the comparative value of free-trade and of freedom, of union, and of rectitude, to a nation. They have no genius or talent for comparatively humble questions of taxation and finance, commerce and manufactures and agriculture. If we were left solely to the wordy wit of legislators in Congress for our guidance, uncorrected by the seasonable experience and the effectual complaints of the people, America would not long retain her rank among the nations. For eighteen hundred years, though perchance I have no right to say it, the New Testament has been written; yet where is the legislator who has wisdom and practical talent enough to avail himself of the light which it sheds on the science of legislation?

The authority of government, even such as I am willing to submit to,—for I will cheerfully obey those who know and can do better than I, and in many things even those who neither know nor can do so well,—is still an impure one: to be strictly just, it must have the sanction and consent of the governed. It can have no pure right over my person and property but what I concede to it. The progress from an absolute to a limited monarchy, from a limited monarchy to a democracy, is a progress toward a true respect for the individual. Even the Chinese philosopher was wise enough to regard the individual as the basis of the empire. Is a democracy, such as we know it, the last improvement possible in government? Is it not possible to take a step further towards recognizing and organizing the rights of man? There will never be a really free and enlightened State until

These extracts have been inserted since the lecture was read. [Thoreau's Note.]

the State comes to recognize the individual as a higher and independent power, from which all its own power and authority are derived, and treats him accordingly. I please myself with imagining a State at last which can afford to be just to all men, and to treat the individual with respect as a neighbor; which even would not think it inconsistent with its own repose if a few were to live aloof from it, not meddling with it, nor embraced by it, who fulfilled all the duties of neighbors and fellow-men. A State which bore this kind of fruit, and suffered it to drop off as fast as it ripened, would prepare the way for a still more perfect and glorious State, which also I have imagined, but not yet anywhere seen.

Walden, or Life in the Woods

Walden (1854), one of the two books by Thoreau to appear during his lifetime, contains the core of the author's social gospel and records his experiences at Walden Pond between July 4, 1845, and September 6, 1847. Thoreau's original manuscript indicates that a large portion of the book was written about 1846. Other sections, however, were taken from his Journals from 1838 to 1854.

The contents of *Walden*, of which the following sections form a part, can be most quickly scanned from the titles to the various sections: Economy; Where I Lived, and What I Lived For; Reading; Sounds; Solitude; Visitors; The Bean-Field; The Village; The Ponds; Baker Farm; Higher Laws; Brute Neighbors; House-Warming; Former Inhabitants, and Winter Visitors; Winter Animals; The Pond in Winter; Spring; Conclusion.

Thoreau did not retire to his cabin in the surly garb of a Stoic because he was at odds with his fellow men or because he had grown weary of them. He had a book to write and he knew "that a man may pay too dearly for a livelihood." His was an experiment in reducing life to its lowest common denominator, to determine to what extent he could depend upon himself and upon nature instead of society or a trade. Thus with $68.76 and a bean patch, Thoreau sustained himself for two years and two months. *Walden* is Thoreau's masterpiece and it has had a steady growth in influence. During the 1930's when the gospel of retrenchment found an eager audience, Thoreau showed how at least one man might be independent of the demands of society, free of the urge to keep up

with the Joneses, and free to think and observe. Thoreau had no wish to urge others to adopt his way of life; every man, he knew, must settle his problems for himself. The text is that of the first edition of 1854.

II. *Where I Lived, and What I Lived For*

At a certain season of our life we are accustomed to consider every spot as the possible site of a house. I have thus surveyed the country on every side within a dozen miles of where I live. In imagination I have bought all the farms in succession, for all were to be bought, and I knew their price. I walked over each farmer's premises, tasted his wild apples, discoursed on husbandry with him, took his farm at his price, at any price, mortgaging it to him in my mind; even put a higher price on it,—took everything but a deed of it,—took his word for his deed, for I dearly love to talk,—cultivated it, and him too to some extent, I trust, and withdrew when I had enjoyed it long enough, leaving him to carry it on. This experience entitled me to be regarded as a sort of real-estate broker by my friends. Wherever I sat, there I might live, and the landscape radiated from me accordingly. What is a house but a *sedes*, a seat?—better if a country seat. I discovered many a site for a house not likely to be soon improved, which some might have thought too far from the village, but to my eyes the village was too far from it. Well, there I might live, I said; and there I did live, for an hour, a summer and a winter life; saw how I could let the years run off, buffet the winter through, and see the spring come in. The future inhabitants of this region, wherever they may place their houses, may be sure that they have been anticipated. An afternoon sufficed to lay out the land into orchard, woodlot, and pasture, and to decide what fine oaks or pines should be left to stand before the door, and whence each blasted tree could be seen to the best advantage; and then I let lie, fallow perchance, for a man is rich in proportion to the number of things which he can afford to let alone.

My imagination carried me so far that I even had the refusal of several farms,—the refusal was all I wanted,—but I never got my fingers burned by actual possession. The nearest that I came to actual possession was when I bought the Hollowell place, and had begun to sort my seeds, and collected materials with which to make a wheelbarrow to carry it on or off with; but before the owner gave me a deed of it, his wife—every man has such a wife—changed her mind and wished to keep it, and he offered me ten dollars to release him. Now, to speak the truth, I had but ten cents in the world, and it surpassed my arithmetic to tell, if I was that man who had ten cents, or who had a farm, or ten dollars, or all together. However, I let him keep the ten dollars and the farm too, for I had carried it far enough; or rather, to be generous, I sold him the farm for just what I gave for it, and, as he was not a rich man, made him a present of ten dollars, and still had my ten cents, and seeds, and materials for a wheelbarrow left. I found thus that I had been a rich man without any damage to my poverty. But I retained the landscape, and I have since annually carried off what it yielded without a wheelbarrow. With respect to land- 20 scapes,—

> I am monarch of all I *survey*,
> My right there is none to dispute.

I have frequently seen a poet withdraw, having enjoyed the most valuable part of a farm, while the crusty farmer supposed that he had got a few wild apples only. Why, the owner does not know it for many years when a poet has put his farm in rhyme, the most admirable kind of invisible fence, has 30 fairly impounded it, milked it, skimmed it, and got all the cream, and left the farmer only the skimmed milk.

The real attractions of the Hollowell farm, to me, were: its complete retirement, being about two miles from the village, half a mile from the nearest neighbor, and separated from the highway by a broad field; its bounding on the river, which the owner said protected it by its fogs from frosts in the spring, though that was nothing to me; the gray 40 color and ruinous state of the house and barn, and the dilapidated fences, which put such an interval between me and the last occupant; the hollow and lichen-covered apple trees, gnawed by rabbits, showing what kind of neighbors I should have; but above all, the recollection I had of it from my earliest voyages up the river, when the house was concealed behind a dense grove of red maples,

through which I heard the house-dog bark. I was in haste to buy it, before the proprietor finished getting out some rocks, cutting down the hollow apple trees, and grubbing up some young birches which had sprung up in the pasture, or, in short, had made any more of his improvements. To enjoy these advantages I was ready to carry it on; like Atlas, to take the world on my shoulders,—I never heard what compensation he received for that,—and do all those things which had no other motive or excuse but that I might pay for it and be unmolested in my possession of it; for I knew all the while that it would yield the most abundant crop of the kind I wanted if I could only afford to let it alone. But it turned out as I have said.

All that I could say, then, with respect to farming on a large scale (I have always cultivated a garden) was, that I had had my seeds ready. Many think that seeds improve with age. I have no doubt that time discriminates between the good and the bad; and when at last I shall plant, I shall be less likely to be disappointed. But I would say to my fellows, once for all, As long as possible live free and uncommitted. It makes but little difference whether you are committed to a farm or the county jail.

Old Cato, whose "De Re Rustica" is my "Cultivator," says, and the only translation I have seen makes sheer nonsense of the passage, "When you think of getting a farm, turn it thus in your mind, not to buy greedily; nor spare your pains to look at it, and do not think it enough to go round it once. The oftener you go there the more it will please you, if it is good." I think I shall not buy greedily, but go round and round it as long as I live, and be buried in it first, that it may please me the more at last.

The present was my next experiment of this kind, which I purpose to describe more at length; for convenience, putting the experience of two years into one. As I have said,[n] I do not propose to write an ode to dejection, but to brag as lustily as chanticleer in the morning, standing on his roost, if only to wake my neighbors up.

When first I took up my abode in the woods,

As I have said: The rest of this sentence was used as the motto on the title page of the first edition.

that is, began to spend my nights as well as days there, which, by accident, was on Independence day, or the fourth of July, 1845, my house was not finished for winter, but was merely a defense against the rain, without plastering or chimney, the walls being of rough, weather-stained boards, with wide chinks, which made it cool at night. The upright white hewn studs and freshly planed door and window casings gave it a clean and airy look, especially in the morning, when its timbers were saturated with dew, so that I fancied that by noon some sweet gum would exude from them. To my imagination it retained throughout the day more or less of this auroral character, reminding me of a certain house on a mountain which I had visited the year before. This was an airy and unplastered cabin, fit to entertain a travelling god, and where a goddess might trail her garments. The winds which passed over my dwelling were such as sweep over the ridges of mountains, bearing the broken strains, or celestial parts only, of terrestrial music. The morning wind forever blows, the poem of creation is uninterrupted; but few are the ears that hear it. Olympus is but the outside of the earth every where.

The only house I had been the owner of before, if I except a boat, was a tent, which I used occasionally when making excursions in the summer, and this is still rolled up in my garret; but the boat, after passing from hand to hand, has gone down the stream of time. With this more substantial shelter about me, I had made some progress toward settling in the world. This frame, so slightly clad, was a sort of crystallization around me, and reacted on the builder. It was suggestive somewhat as a picture in outlines. I did not need to go outdoors to take the air, for the atmosphere within had lost none of its freshness. It was not so much within-doors as behind a door where I sat, even in the rainiest weather. The Harivansa[n] says, "An abode without birds is like a meat without seasoning." Such was not my abode, for I found myself suddenly neighbor to the birds; not by having imprisoned one, but having caged myself near them. I was not only nearer to some of those which commonly frequent the garden and the orchard, but to those wilder and more thrilling songsters of the

The Harivansa: a sacred Hindu poem (in Sanskrit).

forest which never, or rarely, serenade a villager,— the wood thrush, the veery, the scarlet tanager, the field-sparrow, the whippoorwill, and many others.

I was seated by the shore of a small pond, about a mile and a half south of the village of Concord and somewhat higher than it, in the midst of an extensive wood between that town and Lincoln, and about two miles south of that our only field known to fame, Concord Battle Ground; but I was so low in the woods that the opposite shore, half a mile off, like the rest, covered with wood, was my most distant horizon. For the first week, whenever I looked out on the pond it impressed me like a tarn high up on the side of a mountain, its bottom far above the surface of other lakes, and, as the sun arose, I saw it throwing off its nightly clothing of mist, and here and there, by degrees, its soft ripples or its smooth reflecting surface was revealed, while the mists, like ghosts, were stealthily withdrawing in every direction into the woods, as at the breaking up of some nocturnal conventicle. The very dew seemed to hang upon the trees later into the day than usual, as on the sides of mountains.

This small lake was of most value as a neighbor in the intervals of a gentle rainstorm in August, when, both air and water being perfectly still, but the sky overcast, mid-afternoon had all the serenity of evening, and the wood thrush sang around, and was heard from shore to shore. A lake like this is never smoother than at such a time; and the clear portion of the air above it being shallow and darkened by clouds, the water, full of light and reflections, becomes a lower heaven itself so much the more important. From a hill top near by, where the wood had been recently cut off, there was a pleasing vista southward across the pond, through a wide indentation in the hills which form the shore there, where their opposite sides sloping toward each other suggested a stream flowing out in that direction through a wooded valley, but stream there was none. That way I looked between and over the near green hills to some distant and higher ones in the horizon, tinged with blue. Indeed, by standing on tiptoe I could catch a glimpse of some of the peaks of the still bluer and more distant mountain ranges in the north-west, those true-blue coins from heaven's own mint, and also of some portion of the village.

663

But in other directions, even from this point, I could not see over or beyond the woods which surrounded me. It is well to have some water in your neighborhood, to give buoyancy to and float the earth. One value even of the smallest well is, that when you look into it you see that earth is not continent but insular. This is as important as that it keeps butter cool. When I looked across the pond from this peak toward the Sudbury meadows, which in time of flood I distinguished elevated perhaps by a mirage in their seething valley, like a coin in a basin, all the earth beyond the pond appeared like a thin crust insulated and floated even by this small sheet of intervening water, and I was reminded that this on which I dwelt was but dry land.

Though the view from my door was still more contracted, I did not feel crowded or confined in the least. There was pasture enough for my imagination. The low shrub-oak plateau to which the opposite shore arose, stretched away toward the prairies of the West and the steppes of Tartary, affording ample room for all the roving families of men. "There are none happy in the world but beings who enjoy freely a vast horizon,"—said Damodara,[n] when his herds required new and larger pastures.

Both place and time were changed, and I dwelt nearer to those parts of the universe and to those eras in history which had most attracted me. Where I lived was as far off as many a region viewed nightly by astronomers. We are wont to imagine rare and delectable places in some remote and more celestial corner of the system, behind the constellation of Cassiopeia's Chair, far from noise and disturbance. I discovered that my house actually had its site in such a withdrawn, but forever new and unprofaned, part of the universe. If it were worth the while to settle in those parts near to the Pleiades or the Hyades, to Aldebaran or Altair, then I was really there, or at an equal remoteness from the life which I had left behind, dwindled and twinkling with as fine a ray to my nearest neighbor, and to be seen only in moonless nights by him. Such was that part of creation where I had squatted;—

Damodara: another name for Krishna, a divinity in Hindu mythology.

There was a shepherd that did live,
  And held his thoughts as high
As were the mounts whereon his flocks
  Did hourly feed him by.

What should we think of the shepherd's life if his flocks always wandered to higher pastures than his thoughts?

Every morning was a cheerful invitation to make my life of equal simplicity, and I may say innocence, with Nature herself. I have been as sincere a worshiper of Aurora as the Greeks. I got up early and bathed in the pond; that was a religious exercise, and one of the best things which I did. They say that characters were engraven on the bathing tub of King Tching-thang to this effect: "Renew thyself completely each day; do it again, and again, and forever again." I can understand that. Morning brings back the heroic ages. I was as much affected by the faint hum of a mosquito making its invisible and unimaginable tour through my apartment at earliest dawn, when I was sitting with door and windows open, as I could be by any trumpet that ever sang of fame. It was Homer's requiem; itself an Iliad and Odyssey in the air, singing its own wrath and wanderings. There was something cosmical about it; a standing advertisement, till forbidden, of the everlasting vigor and fertility of the world. The morning, which is the most memorable season of the day, is the awakening hour. Then there is least somnolence in us; and for an hour, at least, some part of us awakes which slumbers all the rest of the day and night. Little is to be expected of that day, if it can be called a day, to which we are not awakened by our Genius, but by the mechanical nudgings of some servitor, are not awakened by our own newly acquired force and aspirations from within, accompanied by the undulations of celestial music, instead of factory bells, and a fragrance filling the air—to a higher life than we fell asleep from; and thus the darkness bear its fruit, and prove itself to be good, no less than the light. That man who does not believe that each day contains an earlier, more sacred, and auroral hour than he has yet profaned, has despaired of life, and is pursuing a descending and darkening way of life. After a partial cessation of his sensuous life, the soul of man, or its organs rather, are reinvigorated each day, and his Genius tries again what noble life it can make. All memorable events, I should say, transpire in morning time and in a morning atmosphere. The Vedas say, "All intelligences awake with the morning." Poetry and art, and the fairest and most memorable of the actions of men, date from such an hour. All poets and heroes, like Memnon, are the children of Aurora, and emit their music at sunrise. To him whose elastic and vigorous thought keeps pace with the sun, the day is a perpetual morning. It matters not what the clocks say or the attitudes and labors of men. Morning is when I am awake and there is a dawn in me. Moral reform is the effort to throw off sleep. Why is it that men give so poor an account of their day if they have not been slumbering? They are not such poor calculators. If they had not been overcome with drowsiness, they would have performed something. The millions are awake enough for physical labor; but only one in a million is awake enough for effective intellectual exertion, only one in a hundred millions to a poetic or divine life. To be awake is to be alive. I have never yet met a man who was quite awake. How could I have looked him in the face?

We must learn to reawaken and keep ourselves awake, not by mechanical aids, but by an infinite expectation of the dawn, which does not forsake us in our soundest sleep. I know of no more encouraging fact than the unquestionable ability of man to elevate his life by a conscious endeavor. It is something to be able to paint a particular picture, or to carve a statue, and so to make a few objects beautiful; but it is far more glorious to carve and paint the very atmosphere and medium through which we look, which morally we can do. To affect the quality of the day, that is the highest of arts. Every man is tasked to make his life, even in its details, worthy of the contemplation of his most elevated and critical hour. If we refused, or rather used up, such paltry information as we get, the oracles would distinctly inform us how this might be done.

I went to the woods because I wished to live deliberately, to front only the essential facts of life, and see if I could not learn what it had to teach, and not, when I came to die, discover that I had not lived. I did not wish to live what was not life, living is so dear; nor did I wish to practice resignation, unless it was quite necessary. I wanted to live deep and suck out all the marrow of life, to live so sturdily and Spartan-like as to put to rout all that was not life, to cut a broad swath and shave close, to drive life into a corner, and reduce it to its lowest terms, and, if it proved to be mean, why then to get the whole and genuine meanness of it, and publish its meanness to the world; or if it were sublime, to know it by experience, and be able to give a true account of it in my next excursion. For most men, it appears to me, are in a strange uncertainty about it, whether it is of the devil or of God, and have somewhat hastily concluded that it is the chief end of man here to "glorify God and enjoy him forever."

Still we live meanly, like ants; though the fable tells us that we were long ago changed into men; like pygmies we fight with cranes; it is error upon error, and clout upon clout, and our best virtue has for its occasion a superfluous and evitable wretchedness. Our life is frittered away by detail. An honest man has hardly need to count more than his ten fingers, or in extreme cases he may add his ten toes, and lump the rest. Simplicity, simplicity, simplicity! I say, let your affairs be as two or three, and not a hundred or a thousand; instead of a million count half a dozen, and keep your accounts on your thumb-nail. In the midst of this chopping sea of civilized life, such are the clouds and storms and quicksands and thousand-and-one items to be allowed for, that a man has to live, if he would not founder and go to the bottom and not make his port at all, by dead reckoning, and he must be a great calculator indeed who succeeds. Simplify, simplify. Instead of three meals a day, if it be necessary eat but one; instead of a hundred dishes, five; and reduce other things in proportion. Our life is like a German Confederacy, made up of petty states, with its boundary forever fluctuating, so that even a German cannot tell you how it is bounded at any moment. The nation itself, with all its so called internal improvements, which, by the way, are all external and superficial, is just such an unwieldy and overgrown establishment, cluttered with furniture and tripped up by its own traps, ruined by luxury and heedless expense, by want of calculation and a worthy aim, as the million households in the land; and the only cure for it as for them is in a rigid economy, a stern and more than Spartan simplicity of life and elevation of purpose. It lives too fast. Men think that it is essential that the Nation have commerce, and export ice, and talk through a telegraph, and ride thirty miles an hour, without a doubt, whether they do or not; but whether we should live like baboons or like men, is a little uncertain. If we do not get our sleepers, and forge rails, and devote days and nights to the work, but go to tinkering upon our lives to improve them, who will build railroads? And if railroads are not built, how shall we get to heaven in season? But if we stay at home and mind our business, who will want railroads? We do not ride on the railroad; it rides upon us. Did you ever think what those sleepers are that underlie the railroad? Each one is a man, an Irishman, or a Yankee man. The rails are laid on them, and they are covered with sand, and the cars run smoothly over them. They are sound sleepers, I assure you. And every few years a new lot is laid down and run over; so that, if some have the pleasure of riding on a rail, others have the misfortune to be ridden upon. And when they run over a man that is walking in his sleep, a supernumerary sleeper in the wrong position, and wake him up, they suddenly stop the cars, and make a hue and cry about it, as if this were an exception. I am glad to know that it takes a gang of men for every five miles to keep the sleepers down and level in their beds as it is, for this is a sign that they may sometimes get up again.

Why should we live with such hurry and waste of life? We are determined to be starved before we are hungry. Men say that a stitch in time saves nine, and so they take a thousand stitches to-day to save nine to-morrow. As for work, we haven't any of any consequence. We have the Saint Vitus' dance, and cannot possibly keep our heads still. If I should only give a few pulls at the parish bell-rope, as for a fire, that is, without setting the bell, there is hardly a man on his farm in the outskirts of Concord, notwithstanding that press of engagements which was his excuse so many times this morning, nor a boy, nor a woman, I might almost say, but would forsake all and follow that sound, not mainly to save property from the flames, but, if we will confess the truth, much more, see it burn, since burn it must, and we, be it known, did not set it on fire,—or to see it put out, and have a hand in it, if that is done as handsomely; yes, even if it were the parish church itself. Hardly a man takes a half-hour's nap after dinner, but when he wakes he holds up his head and asks, "What's the news?" as if the rest of mankind had stood his sentinels. Some give directions to be waked every half-hour, doubtless for no other purpose; and then, to pay for it, they tell what they have dreamed. After a night's sleep the news is as indispensable as the breakfast. "Pray tell me anything new that has happened to a man anywhere on this globe,"—and he reads it over his coffee and rolls, that a man has had his eyes gouged out this morning on the Wachito River; never dreaming the while that he lives in the dark unfathomed mammoth cave of this world, and has but the rudiment of an eye himself.

For my part, I could easily do without the post-office. I think that there are very few important communications made through it. To speak critically, I never received more than one or two letters in my life—I wrote this some years ago—that were worth the postage. The penny-post is, commonly, an institution through which you seriously offer a man that penny for his thoughts which is so often safely offered in jest. And I am sure that I never read any memorable news in a newspaper. If we read of one man robbed, or murdered, or killed by accident, or one house burned, or one vessel wrecked, or one steamboat blown up, or one cow run over on the Western Railroad, or one mad dog killed, or one lot of grasshoppers in the winter,—we never need read of another. One is enough. If you are acquainted with the principle, what do you care for a myriad instances and applications? To a philosopher all news, as it is called, is gossip, and they who edit and read it are old women over their tea. Yet not a few are greedy after this gossip. There was such a rush, as I hear, the other day at one of the offices to learn the foreign news by the last arrival, that several large squares of plate glass belonging to the establishment were broken by the pressure,—news which I seriously think a ready wit might write a twelvemonth or twelve years beforehand with sufficient accuracy. As for Spain, for instance, if you know how to throw in Don Carlos and the Infanta, and Don Pedro and Seville and Granada, from time to time in the right proportions,—they may have changed the names a little since I saw the papers,—and serve up a bull-fight when other entertainments fail, it will be true to the letter, and give us as good an idea of the exact state or ruin of things in Spain as the most succinct and lucid reports under this head in the newspapers: and as for England, almost the last significant scrap of news from that quarter was the revolution of 1649; and if you have learned the history of her crops for an average year, you never need attend to that thing again, unless your speculations are of a merely pecuniary character. If one may judge who rarely looks into the newspapers, nothing new does ever happen in foreign parts, a French revolution not excepted.

What news! how much more important to know what that is which was never old! "Kieou-he-yu (great dignitary of the state of Wei) sent a man to Khoung-tseu to know his news. Khoung-tseu caused the messenger to be seated near him, and questioned him in these terms: What is your master doing? The messenger answered with respect: My master desires to diminish the number of his faults, but he cannot come to the end of them. The messenger being gone, the philosopher remarked: What a worthy messenger! What a worthy messenger!" The preacher, instead of vexing the ears of drowsy farmers on their day of rest at the end of the week,—for Sunday is the fit conclusion of an ill-spent week, and not the fresh and brave beginning of a new one,—with this one other draggle-tail of a sermon, should shout with thundering voice,—"Pause! Avast! Why so seeming fast, but deadly slow?"

Shams and delusions are esteemed for soundest truths, while reality is fabulous. If men would steadily observe realities only, and not allow themselves to be deluded, life, to compare it with such things as we know, would be like a fairy tale and the Arabian Nights' Entertainments. If we respected only what is inevitable and has a right to be, music and poetry would resound along the streets. When we are unhurried and wise, we perceive that only great and worthy things have any permanent and absolute existence,—that petty fears and petty pleasures are but the shadow of the reality. This is always exhilarating and sublime. By closing the eyes and slumbering, and consenting to be deceived by shows, men establish and confirm their daily life of routine and habit every where, which still is built on purely illusory foundations. Children, who play life, discern its true law and relations more clearly than men, who fail to live it worthily, but who think that they are wiser by experience, that is, by failure. I have read in a Hindoo book, that "there was a king's son, who, being expelled in infancy from his native city, was brought up by a forester, and, growing up to maturity in that state, imagined himself to belong to the barbarous race with which he lived. One of his father's ministers having discovered him, revealed to him what he was, and the misconception of his character was removed, and he knew himself to be a prince. So soul," continues the Hindoo philosopher, "from the circumstances in which it is placed, mistakes its own character, until the truth is revealed to it by some holy teacher, and then it knows itself to be *Brahme*." I perceive that we inhabitants of New England live this mean life that we do because our vision does not penetrate the surface of things. We think that that is which appears to be. If a man should walk through this town and see only the reality, where, think you, would the "Mill-dam" go to? If he should give us an account of the realities he beheld there, we should not recognize the place in his description. Look at a meeting-house, or a court-house, or a jail, or a shop, or a dwelling-house, and say what that thing really is before a true gaze, and they would all go to pieces in your account of them. Men esteem truth remote, in the outskirts of the system, behind the farthest star, before Adam and after the last man. In eternity there is indeed something true and sublime. But all these times and places and occasions are now and here. God himself culminates in the present moment, and will never be more divine in the lapse of all the ages. And we are enabled to apprehend at all what is sublime and noble only by the perpetual instilling and drenching of the reality that surrounds us. The universe constantly and obediently answers to our conceptions; whether we travel fast or slow, the track is laid for us. Let us spend our lives in conceiving then. The poet or the artist never yet had so fair and noble a design but some of his posterity at least could accomplish it.

Let us spend one day as deliberately as Nature, and not be thrown off the track by every nutshell and mosquito's wing that falls on the rails. Let us 10 rise early and fast, or break fast, gently and without perturbation; let company come and let company go, let the bells ring and the children cry,— determined to make a day of it. Why should we knock under and go with the stream? Let us not be upset and overwhelmed in that terrible rapid and whirlpool called a dinner, situated in the meridian shallows. Weather this danger and you are safe, for the rest of the way is down hill. With unrelaxed nerves, with morning vigor, sail by it, 20 looking another way, tied to the mast like Ulysses. If the engine whistles, let it whistle till it is hoarse for its pains. If the bell rings, why should we run? We will consider what kind of music they are like. Let us settle ourselves, and work and wedge our feet downward through the mud and slush of opinion, and prejudice, and tradition, and delusion, and appearance, that alluvion which covers the globe, through Paris and London, through New York and Boston and Concord, through church 30 and state, through poetry and philosophy and religion, till we come to a hard bottom and rocks in place, which we can call reality, and say, This is, and no mistake; and then begin, having a *point d'appui*, below freshet and frost and fire, a place where you might found a wall or a state, or set a lamp-post safely, or perhaps a gauge, not a Nilometer, but a Realometer, that future ages might know how deep a freshet of shams and appearances had gathered from time to time. If you stand right 40 fronting and face to face to a fact, you will see the sun glimmer on both its surfaces, as if it were a cimeter,[n] and feel its sweet edge dividing you through the heart and marrow, and so you will happily conclude your mortal career. Be it life or death, we crave only reality. If we are really dying, let us hear the rattle in our throats and

cimeter: a scimitar.

feel cold in the extremities; if we are alive, let us go about our business.

Time is but the stream I go a-fishing in. I drink at it; but while I drink I see the sandy bottom and detect how shallow it is. Its thin current slides away, but eternity remains. I would drink deeper; fish in the sky, whose bottom is pebbly with stars. I cannot count one. I know not the first letter of the alphabet. I have always been regretting that I was not as wise as the day I was born. The intellect is a cleaver; it discerns and rifts its way into the secret of things. I do not wish to be any more busy with my hands than is necessary. My head is hands and feet. I feel all my best faculties concentrated in it. My instinct tells me that my head is an organ for burrowing, as some creatures use their snout and fore-paws, and with it I would mine and burrow my way through these hills. I think that the richest vein is somewhere hereabouts; so by the divining-rod and thin rising vapors I judge; and here I will begin to mine.

IV. *Sounds* To here following vacation

But while we are confined to books, though the most select and classic, and read only particular written languages, which are themselves but dialects and provincial, we are in danger of forgetting the language which all things and events speak without metaphor, which alone is copious and standard. Much is published, but little printed. The rays which stream through the shutter will be no longer remembered when the shutter is wholly removed. No method nor discipline can supersede the necessity of being forever on the alert. What is a course of history, or philosophy, or poetry, no matter how well selected, or the best society, or the most admirable routine of life, compared with the discipline of looking always at what is to be seen? Will you be a reader, a student merely, or a seer? Read your fate, see what is before you, and walk on into futurity.

I did not read books the first summer; I hoed beans. Nay, I often did better than this. There were times when I could not afford to sacrifice the bloom of the present moment to any work, whether of the head or hands. I love a broad margin to my life. Sometimes, in a summer morning, having taken my accustomed bath, I sat in my sunny doorway from sunrise till noon, rapt in a revery, amidst the pines and hickories and sumachs, in undisturbed solitude and stillness, while the birds sang around or flitted noiseless through the house, until by the sun falling in at my west window, or the noise of some traveler's wagon on the distant highway, I was reminded of the lapse of time. I grew in those seasons like corn in the night, and they were far better than any work of the hands would have been. They were not time subtracted from my life, but so much over and above my usual allowance. I realized what the Orientals mean by contemplation and the forsaking of works. For the most part, I minded not how the hours went. The day advanced as if to light some work of mine; it was morning, and lo, now it is evening, and nothing memorable is accomplished. Instead of singing like the birds, I silently smiled at my incessant good fortune. As the sparrow had its trill, sitting on the hickory before my door, so had I my chuckle or suppressed warble which he might hear out of my nest. My days were not days of the week, bearing the stamp of any heathen deity, nor were they minced into hours and fretted by the ticking of a clock; for I lived like the Puri Indians, of whom it is said that "for yesterday, to-day, and to-morrow they have only one word, and they express the variety of meaning by pointing backward for yesterday, forward for to-morrow, and overhead for the passing day." This was sheer idleness to my fellow-townsmen, no doubt; but if the birds and flowers had tried me by their standard, I should not have been found wanting. A man must find his occasions in himself, it is true. The natural day is very calm, and will hardly reprove his indolence.

I had this advantage, at least, in my mode of life, over those who were obliged to look abroad for amusement, to society and the theater, that my life itself was become my amusement and never ceased to be novel. It was a drama of many scenes and without an end. If we were always indeed getting our living, and regulating our lives according to the last and best mode we had learned, we should never be troubled with ennui. Follow your genius closely enough, and it will not fail to show you a fresh prospect every hour. Housework was a pleasant pastime. When my floor was dirty, I rose early, and, setting all my furniture out of doors on the grass, bed and bedstead making but one budget, dashed water on the floor, and sprinkled white sand from the pond on it, and then with a broom scrubbed it clean and white; and by the time the villagers had broken their fast the morning sun had dried my house sufficiently to allow me to move in again, and my meditations were almost uninterrupted. It was pleasant to see my whole household effects out on the grass, making a little pile like a gypsy's pack, and my three-legged table, from which I did not remove the books and pen and ink, standing amid the pines and hickories. They seemed glad to get out themselves, and as if unwilling to be brought in. I was sometimes tempted to stretch an awning over them and take my seat there. It was worth the while to see the sun shine on these things, and hear the free wind blow on them; so much more interesting most familiar objects look out of doors than in the house. A bird sits on the next bough, life-everlasting grows under the table, and blackberry vines run round its legs; pine cones, chestnut burs, and strawberry leaves are strewn about. It looked as if this was the way these forms came to be transferred to our furniture, to tables, chairs, and bedsteads,—because they once stood in their midst.

My house was on the side of a hill, immediately on the edge of the larger wood, in the midst of a young forest of pitch pines and hickories, and half a dozen rods from the pond, to which a narrow footpath led down the hill. In my front yard grew the strawberry, blackberry, and life-everlasting, johnswort and goldenrod, shrub-oaks and sand-cherry, blueberry and groundnut. Near the end of May, the sand-cherry (*cerasus pumila*) adorned the sides of the path with its delicate flowers arranged in umbels cylindrically about its short stems, which last, in the fall, weighed down with good-sized and handsome cherries, fell over in wreaths like rays on every side. I tasted them out of compliment to Nature, though they were scarcely palatable. The sumach (*rhus glabra*) grew luxuriantly about the house, pushing up through the embankment which I had made, and growing five or six feet the first season. Its broad pinnate tropical leaf was pleasant though strange to look on. The large buds, suddenly pushing out late in the spring from dry sticks which had seemed to be dead, developed themselves as by magic into graceful green and tender boughs, an inch in diameter; and sometimes, as I sat at my window, so heedlessly did they grow and tax their weak joints, I heard a fresh and tender bough suddenly fall like a fan to the ground, when there was not a breath of air stirring, broken off by its own weight. In August, the large masses of berries, which, when in flower, had attracted many wild 10 bees, gradually assumed their bright velvety crimson hue, and by their weight again bent down and broke the tender limbs.

As I sit at my window this summer afternoon, hawks are circling about my clearing; the tantivy of wild pigeons, flying by twos and threes athwart my view, or perching restless on the white pine boughs behind my house, gives a voice to the air; a fish hawk dimples the glassy surface of the pond 20 and brings up a fish; a mink steals out of the marsh before my door and seizes a frog by the shore; the sedge is bending under the weight of the reed-birds flitting hither and thither; and for the last half-hour I have heard the rattle of railroad cars, now dying away and then reviving like the beat of a partridge, conveying travelers from Boston to the country. For I did not live so out of the world as that boy, who, as I hear, was put out to a farmer in the east part of the town, but ere long ran away 30 and came home again, quite down at the heel and homesick. He had never seen such a dull and out-of-the-way place; the folks were all gone off; why, you couldn't even hear the whistle! I doubt if there is such a place in Massachusetts now:—

In truth, our village has become a butt
For one of those fleet railroad shafts, and o'er
Our peaceful plain its soothing sound is—Concord.

The Fitchburg Railroad touches the pond about 40 a hundred rods south of where I dwell. I usually go to the village along its causeway, and am, as it were, related to society by this link. The men on the freight trains, who go over the whole length of the road, bow to me as to an old acquaintance, they pass me so often, and apparently they take me for an employee; and so I am. I too would fain be a track-repairer somewhere in the orbit of the earth.

The whistle of the locomotive penetrates my woods summer and winter, sounding like the scream of a hawk sailing over some farmer's yard, informing me that many restless city merchants are arriving within the circle of the town, or adventurous country traders from the other side. As they come under one horizon, they shout their warning to get off the track to the other, heard sometimes through the circles of two towns. Here come your groceries, country; your rations, countrymen! Nor is there any man so independent on his farm that he can say them nay. And here's your pay for them! screams the countryman's whistle; timber like long battering-rams going twenty miles an hour against the city's walls, and chairs enough to seat all the weary and heavy laden that dwell within them. With such huge and lumbering civility the country hands a chair to the city. All the Indian huckleberry hills are stripped, all the cranberry meadows are raked into the city. Up comes the cotton, down goes the woven cloth; up comes the silk, down goes the woolen; up come the books, but down goes the wit that writes them.

When I meet the engine with its train of cars moving off with planetary motion,—or, rather, like a comet, for the beholder knows not if with that velocity and with that direction it will ever revisit this system, since its orbit does not look like a returning curve,—with its steam cloud like a banner streaming behind in golden and silver wreaths, like many a downy cloud which I have seen, high in the heavens, unfolding its masses to the light,—as if this traveling demigod, this cloud-compeller, would ere long take the sunset sky for the livery of his train; when I hear the iron horse make the hills echo with his snort like thunder, shaking the earth with his feet, and breathing fire and smoke from his nostrils (what kind of winged horse or fiery dragon they will put into the new Mythology I don't know,) it seems as if the earth had got a race now worthy to inhabit it. If all were as it seems, and men made the elements their servants for noble ends! If the cloud that hangs over the engine were the perspiration of heroic deeds, or as beneficent as that which floats over the farmer's fields, then the elements and Nature herself would cheerfully accompany men on their errands and be their escort.

670

I watch the passage of the morning cars with the same feeling that I do the rising of the sun, which is hardly more regular. Their train of clouds stretching far behind and rising higher and higher, going to heaven while the cars are going to Boston, conceals the sun for a minute and casts my distant field into the shade, a celestial train beside which the petty train of cars which hugs the earth is but the barb of the spear. The stabler of the iron horse was up early this winter morning by the light of the stars amid the mountains, to fodder and harness his steed. Fire, too, was awakened thus early to put the vital heat in him and get him off. If the enterprise were as innocent as it is early! If the snow lies deep, they strap on his snowshoes, and with the giant plough, plough a furrow from the mountains to the seaboard, in which the cars, like a following drill-barrow, sprinkle all the restless men and floating merchandise in the country for seed. All day the fire-steed flies over the country, stopping only that his master may rest, and I am awakened by his tramp and defiant snort at midnight, when in some remote glen in the woods he fronts the elements incased in ice and snow; and he will reach his stall only with the morning star, to start once more on his travels without rest or slumber. Or perchance, at evening, I hear him in his stable blowing off the superfluous energy of the day, that he may calm his nerves and cool his liver and brain for a few hours of iron slumber. If the enterprise were as heroic and commanding as it is protracted and unwearied!

Far through unfrequented woods on the confines of towns, where once only the hunter penetrated by day, in the darkest night dart these bright saloons without the knowledge of their inhabitants; this moment stopping at some brilliant station-house in town or city, where a social crowd is gathered, the next in the Dismal Swamp, scaring the owl and fox. The startings and arrivals of the cars are now the epochs in the village day. They go and come with such regularity and precision, and their whistle can be heard so far, that the farmers set their clocks by them, and thus one well conducted institution regulates a whole country. Have not men improved somewhat in punctuality since the railroad was invented? Do they not talk and think faster in the depot than they did in the stage-office? There is something electrifying in the atmosphere of the former place. I have been astonished at the miracles it has wrought; that some of my neighbors, who, I should have prophesied, once for all, would never get to Boston by so prompt a conveyance, are on hand when the bell rings. To do things "railroad fashion" is now the byword; and it is worth the while to be warned so often and so sincerely by any power to get off its track. There is no stopping to read the riot act, no firing over the heads of the mob, in this case. We have constructed a fate, an *Atropos*, that never turns aside. (Let that be the name of your engine.) Men are advertised that at a certain hour and minute these bolts will be shot toward particular points of the compass; yet it interferes with no man's business, and the children go to school on the other track. We live the steadier for it. We are all educated thus to be sons of Tell. The air is full of invisible bolts. Every path but your own is the path of fate. Keep on your own track, then.

What recommends commerce to me is its enterprise and bravery. It does not clasp its hands and pray to Jupiter. I see these men every day go about their business with more or less courage and content, doing more even than they suspect, and perchance better employed than they could have consciously devised. I am less affected by their heroism who stood up for half an hour in the front line at Buena Vista,[n] than by the steady and cheerful valor of the men who inhabit the snow-plough for their winter quarters; who have not merely the three-o'-clock-in-the-morning courage, which Bonaparte thought was the rarest, but whose courage does not go to rest so early, who go to sleep only when the storm sleeps or the sinews of their iron steed are frozen. On this morning of the Great Snow, perchance, which is still raging and chilling men's blood, I hear the muffled tone of their engine bell from out the fog bank of their chilled breath, which announces that the cars are coming, without long delay, notwithstanding the veto of a New England north-east snowstorm, and I behold the ploughmen covered with snow and rime, their heads peering above the mould-

Buena Vista: a battle in the Mexican War, February 22–23, 1847.

board which is turning down other than daisies and the nests of field-mice, like boulders of the Sierra Nevada, that occupy an outside place in the universe.

Commerce is unexpectedly confident and serene, alert, adventurous, and unwearied. It is very natural in its methods withal, far more so than many fantastic enterprises and sentimental experiments, and hence its singular success. I am refreshed and expanded when the freight train 10 rattles past me, and I smell the stores which go dispensing their odors all the way from Long Wharf to Lake Champlain, reminding me of foreign parts, of coral reefs, and Indian oceans, and tropical climes, and the extent of the globe. I feel more like a citizen of the world at the sight of the palm-leaf which will cover so many flaxen New England heads the next summer, the Manilla hemp and cocoa-nut husks, the old junk, gunny bags, scrap iron, and rusty nails. This car-load of 20 torn sails is more legible and interesting now than if they should be wrought into paper and printed books. Who can write so graphically the history of the storms they have weathered as these rents have done? They are proof-sheets which need no correction. Here goes lumber from the Maine woods, which did not go out to sea in the last freshet, risen four dollars on the thousand because of what did go out or was split up; pine, spruce, cedar,—first, second, third and fourth qualities, 30 so lately all of one quality, to wave over the bear, and moose, and caribou. Next rolls Thomaston lime, a prime lot, which will get far among the hills before it gets slacked. These rags in bales, of all hues and qualities, the lowest condition to which cotton and linen descend, the final result of dress,—of patterns which are now no longer cried up, unless it be in Milwaukee, as those splendid articles, English, French, or American prints, ginghams, muslins, etc., gathered from all 40 quarters both of fashion and poverty, going to become paper of one color or a few shades only, on which forsooth will be written tales of real life, high and low, and founded on fact! This closed car smells of salt fish, the strong New England and commercial scent, reminding me of the Grand Banks and the fisheries. Who has not seen a salt fish, thoroughly cured for this world, so that

nothing can spoil it, and putting the perseverance of the saints to the blush? with which you may sweep or pave the streets, and split your kindlings, and the teamster shelter himself and his lading against sun, wind, and rain behind it,—and the trader, as a Concord trader once did, hang it up by his door for a sign when he commences business, until at last his oldest customer cannot tell surely whether it be animal, vegetable, or mineral, and yet it shall be as pure as a snowflake, and if it be put into a pot and boiled, will come out an excellent dun fish for a Saturday's dinner. Next Spanish hides, with the tails still preserving their twist and the angle of elevation they had when the oxen that wore them were careering over the pampas of the Spanish main,—a type of all obstinacy, and evincing how almost hopeless and incurable are all constitutional vices. I confess, that practically speaking, when I have learned a man's real disposition, I have no hopes of changing it for the better or worse in this state of existence. As the Orientals say, "A cur's tail may be warmed, and pressed, and bound round with ligatures, and after a twelve years' labor bestowed upon it, still it will retain its natural form." The only effectual cure for such inveteracies as these tails exhibit is to make glue of them, which I believe is what is usually done with them, and then they will stay put and stick. Here is a hogs-head of molasses or of brandy directed to John Smith, Cuttingsville, Vermont, some trader among the Green Mountains, who imports for the farmers near his clearing, and now perchance stands over his bulk-head and thinks of the last arrivals on the coast, how they may affect the price for him, telling his customers this moment, as he has told them twenty times before this morning, that he expects some by the next train of prime quality. It is advertised in the Cuttingsville Times.

While these things go up other things come down. Warned by the whizzing sound, I look up from my book and see some tall pine, hewn on far northern hills, which has winged its way over the Green Mountains and the Connecticut, shot like an arrow through the township within ten minutes, and scarce another eye beholds it; going

to be the mast
Of some great ammiral.

And hark! here comes the cattle-train bearing the cattle of a thousand hills, sheepcots, stables, and cow-yards in the air, drovers with their sticks, and shepherd boys in the midst of their flocks, all but the mountain pastures, whirled along like leaves blown from the mountains by the September gales. The air is filled with the bleating of calves and sheep, and the hustling of oxen, as if a pastoral valley were going by. When the old bell-wether at the head rattles his bell, the mountains do indeed skip like rams and the little hills like lambs. A carload of drovers, too, in the midst, on a level with their droves now, their vocation gone, but still clinging to their useless sticks as their badge of office. But their dogs, where are they? It is a stampede to them; they are quite thrown out; they have lost the scent. Methinks I hear them barking behind the Peterboro' Hills, or panting up the western slope of the Green Mountains. They will not be in at the death. Their vocation, too, is gone. Their fidelity and sagacity are below par now. They will slink back to their kennels in disgrace, or perchance run wild and strike a league with the wolf and the fox. So is your pastoral life whirled past and away. But the bell rings, and I must get off the track and let the cars go by;—

> What's the railroad to me?
> I never go to see
> Where it ends.
> It fills a few hollows,
> And makes banks for the swallows,
> It sets the sand a-blowing,
> And the blackberries a-growing,

but I cross it like a cart-path in the woods. I will not have my eyes put out and my ears spoiled by its smoke and steam and hissing.

Now that the cars are gone by and all the restless world with them, and the fishes in the pond no longer feel their rumbling, I am more alone than ever. For the rest of the long afternoon, perhaps, my meditations are interrupted only by the faint rattle of a carriage or team along the distant highway.

Sometimes, on Sundays, I heard the bells, the Lincoln, Acton, Bedford, or Concord bell, when the wind was favorable, a faint, sweet, and, as it were, natural melody, worth importing into the wilderness. At a sufficient distance over the woods this sound acquires a certain vibratory hum, as if the pine needles in the horizon were the strings of a harp which it swept. All sound heard at the greatest possible distance produces one and the same effect, a vibration of the universal lyre, just as the intervening atmosphere makes a distant ridge of earth interesting to our eyes by the azure tint it imparts to it. There came to me in this case a melody which the air had strained, and which had conversed with every leaf and needle of the wood, that portion of the sound which the elements had taken up and modulated and echoed from vale to vale. The echo is, to some extent, an original sound, and therein is the magic and charm of it. It is not merely a repetition of what was worth repeating in the bell, but partly the voice of the wood; the same trivial words and notes sung by a wood-nymph.

At evening, the distant lowing of some cow in the horizon beyond the woods sounded sweet and melodious, and at first I would mistake it for the voices of certain minstrels by whom I was sometimes serenaded, who might be straying over hill and dale; but soon I was not unpleasantly disappointed when it was prolonged into the cheap and natural music of the cow. I do not mean to be satirical, but to express my appreciation of those youths' singing, when I state that I perceived clearly that it was akin to the music of the cow, and they were at length one articulation of Nature.

Regularly at half past seven, in one part of the summer, after the evening train had gone by, the whippoorwills chanted their vespers for half an hour, sitting on a stump by my door, or upon the ridgepole of the house. They would begin to sing almost with as much precision as a clock, within five minutes of a particular time, referred to the setting of the sun, every evening. I had a rare opportunity to become acquainted with their habits. Sometimes I heard four or five at once in different parts of the wood, by accident one a bar behind another, and so near me that I distinguished not only the cluck after each note, but often that singular buzzing sound like a fly in a spider's web, only proportionally louder. Sometimes one would circle round and round me in the woods a few feet distant as if tethered by a string, when probably I was near its eggs. They sang at intervals throughout the night, and were again as musical as ever just before and about dawn.

When other birds are still the screech owls take up the strain, like mourning women their ancient u-lu-lu. Their dismal scream is truly Ben Jonsonian. Wise midnight hags! It is no honest and blunt tu-whit tu-who of the poets, but, without jesting, a most solemn graveyard ditty, the mutual consolations of suicide lovers remembering the pangs and the delights of supernal love in the infernal groves. Yet I love to hear their wailing, their doleful responses, trilled along the woodside; reminding me sometimes of music and singing birds; as if it were the dark and tearful side of music, the regrets and sighs that would fain be sung. They are the spirits, the low spirits and melancholy forebodings, of fallen souls that once in human shape night-walked the earth and did the deeds of darkness, now expiating their sins with their wailing hymns or threnodies in the scenery of their transgressions. They give me a new sense of the variety and capacity of that nature which is our common dwelling. *Oh-o-o-o-o that I never had been bor-r-r-n!* sighs one on this side of the pond, and circles with the restlessness of despair to some new perch on the gray oaks. Then—*that I never had been bor-r-r-n!* echoes another on the farther side with tremulous sincerity, and—*bor-r-r-n!* comes faintly from far in the Lincoln woods.

I was also serenaded by a hooting owl. Near at hand you could fancy it the most melancholy sound in Nature, as if she meant by this to stereotype and make permanent in her choir the dying moans of a human being,—some poor weak relic of mortality who has left hope behind, and howls like an animal, yet with human sobs, on entering the dark valley, made more awful by a certain gurgling melodiousness,—I find myself beginning with the letters *gl* when I try to imitate it,—expressive of a mind which has reached the gelatinous, mildewy stage in the mortification of all healthy and courageous thought. It reminded me of ghouls and idiots and insane howlings. But now one answers from far woods in a strain made really melodious by distance,—*Hoo hoo hoo, hoorer hoo;* and indeed for the most part it suggested only pleasing associations, whether heard by day or night, summer or winter.

I rejoice that there are owls. Let them do the idiotic and maniacal hooting for men. It is a sound admirably suited to swamps and twilight woods which no day illustrates, suggesting a vast and undeveloped nature which men have not recognized. They represent the stark twilight and unsatisfied thoughts which all have. All day the sun has shone on the surface of some savage swamp, where the single spruce stands hung with usnea lichens, and small hawks circulate above, and the chickadee lisps amid the evergreens, and the partridge and rabbit skulk beneath; but now a more dismal and fitting day dawns, and a different race of creatures awakes to express the meaning of Nature there.

Late in the evening I heard the distant rumbling of wagons over bridges,—a sound heard farther than almost any other at night,—the baying of dogs, and sometimes again the lowing of some disconsolate cow in a distant barn-yard. In the meanwhile all the shore rang with the trump of bullfrogs, the sturdy spirits of ancient winebibbers and wassailers, still unrepentant, trying to sing a catch in their Stygian lake,—if the Walden nymphs will pardon the comparison, for though there are almost no weeds, there are frogs there,—who would fain keep up the hilarious rules of their old festal tables, though their voices have waxed hoarse and solemnly grave, mocking at mirth, and the wine has lost its flavor, and become only liquor to distend their paunches, and sweet intoxication never comes to drown the memory of the past, but mere saturation and waterloggedness and distention. The most aldermanic, with his chin upon a heartleaf, which serves for a napkin to his drooling chaps, under this northern shore quaffs a deep draught of the once scorned water, and passes round the cup with the ejaculation *tr-r-r-oonk, tr-r-r-oonk, tr-r-r-oonk!* and straightway comes over the water from some distant cove the same password repeated, where the next in seniority and girth has gulped down to his mark; and when this observance has made the circuit of the shores, then ejaculates the master of ceremonies, with satisfaction, *tr-r-r-oonk!* and each in his turn repeats the same down to the least distended, leakiest, and flabbiest paunched, that there be no mistake; and then the bowl goes round again and again, until the sun disperses the morning mist, and only the patriarch is not under the pond, but vainly bellowing *troonk* from time to time, and pausing for a reply.

I am not sure that I ever heard the sound of cock-crowing from my clearing, and I thought that it might be worth the while to keep a cockerel for his music merely, as a singing bird. The note of this once wild Indian pheasant is certainly the most remarkable of any bird's, and if they could be naturalized without being domesticated, it would soon become the most famous sound in our woods, surpassing the clangor of the goose and the hooting of the owl; and then imagine the cackling of the hens to fill the pauses when their lords' clarions rested! No wonder that man added this bird to his tame stock,—to say nothing of the eggs and drumsticks. To walk in a winter morning in a wood where these birds abounded, their native woods, and hear the wild cockerels crow on the trees, clear and shrill for miles over the resounding earth, drowning the feebler notes of other birds,—think of it! It would put nations on the alert. Who would not be early to rise, and rise earlier and earlier every successive day of his life, till he became unspeakably healthy, wealthy, and wise? This foreign bird's note is celebrated by the poets of all countries along with the notes of their native songsters. All climates agree with brave Chanticleer. He is more indigenous even than the natives. His health is ever good, his lungs are sound, his spirits never flag. Even the sailor on the Atlantic and Pacific is awakened by his voice; but its shrill sound never roused me from my slumbers. I kept neither dog, cat, cow, pig, nor hens, so that you would have said there was a deficiency of domestic sounds; neither the churn, nor the spinning-wheel, nor even the singing of the kettle, nor the hissing of the urn, nor children crying, to comfort one. An old-fashioned man would have lost his senses or died of ennui before this. Not even rats in the wall, for they were starved out, or rather were never baited in,—only squirrels on the roof and under the floor, a whippoorwill on the ridgepole, a bluejay screaming beneath the window, a hare or woodchuck under the house, a screech-owl or a cat-owl behind it, a flock of wild geese or a laughing loon on the pond, and a fox to bark in the night. Not even a lark or an oriole, those mild plantation birds, ever visited my clearing. No cockerels to crow nor hens to cackle in the yard. No yard! but unfenced Nature reaching up to your very sills. A young forest growing up under your windows, and wild sumachs and blackberry vines breaking through into your cellar; sturdy pitch-pines rubbing and creaking against the shingles for want of room, their roots reaching quite under the house. Instead of a scuttle or a blind blown off in the gale,—a pine tree snapped off or torn up by the roots behind your house for fuel. Instead of no path to the front-yard gate in the Great Snow,—no gate—no front-yard,—and no path to the civilized world!

V. *Solitude*

This is a delicious evening, when the whole body is one sense, and imbibes delight through every pore. I go and come with a strange liberty in Nature, a part of herself. As I walk along the stony shore of the pond in my shirtsleeves, though it is cool as well as cloudy and windy, and I see nothing special to attract me, all the elements are unusually congenial to me. The bullfrogs trump to usher in the night, and the note of the whippoorwill is borne on the rippling wind from over the water. Sympathy with the fluttering alder and poplar leaves almost takes away my breath; yet, like the lake, my serenity is rippled but not ruffled. These small waves raised by the evening wind are as remote from storm as the smooth reflecting surface. Though it is now dark, the wind still blows and roars in the wood, the waves still dash, and some creatures lull the rest with their notes. The repose is never complete. The wildest animals do not repose, but seek their prey now; the fox, and skunk, and rabbit, now roam the fields and woods without fear. They are Nature's watchmen,—links which connect the days of animated life.

When I return to my house I find that visitors have been there and left their cards, either a bunch of flowers, or a wreath of evergreen, or a name in pencil on a yellow walnut leaf or a chip. They who come rarely to the woods take some little piece of the forest into their hands to play with by the way, which they leave, either intentionally or accidentally. One has peeled a willow wand, woven it into a ring, and dropped it on my table. I could always tell if visitors had called in my absence, either by the bended twigs or grass, or the print of their shoes, and generally of what sex or age or quality they were by some slight trace left, as a flower dropped, or a bunch of grass plucked and thrown away, even as far off as the railroad, half a mile distant, or by the lingering odor of a cigar or pipe. Nay, I was frequently notified of the passage of a traveler along the highway sixty rods off by the scent of his pipe.

There is commonly sufficient space about us. Our horizon is never quite at our elbows. The thick wood is not just at our door, nor the pond, but somewhat is always clearing, familiar and worn by us, appropriated and fenced in some way, and reclaimed from Nature. For what reason have I this vast range and circuit, some square miles of unfrequented forest, for my privacy, abandoned to me by men? My nearest neighbor is a mile distant, and no house is visible from any place but the hill-tops within half a mile of my own. I have my horizon bounded by woods all to myself; a distant view of the railroad where it touches the pond on the one hand, and of the fence which skirts the woodland road on the other. But for the most part it is as solitary where I live as on the prairies. It is as much Asia or Africa as New England. I have, as it were, my own sun and moon and stars, and a little world all to myself. At night there was never a traveler passed my house, or knocked at my door, more than if I were the first or last man; unless it were in the spring, when at long intervals some came from the village to fish for pouts,— they plainly fished much more in the Walden Pond of their own natures, and baited their hooks with darkness,—but they soon retreated, usually with light baskets, and left "the world to darkness and to me," and the black kernel of the night was never profaned by any human neighborhood. I believe that men are generally still a little afraid of the dark, though the witches are all hung, and Christianity and candles have been introduced.

Yet I experienced sometimes that the most sweet and tender, the most innocent and encouraging society may be found in any natural object, even for the poor misanthrope and most melancholy man. There can be no very black melancholy to him who lives in the midst of Nature and has his senses still. There was never yet such a storm but it was Æolian music to a healthy and innocent ear.

Nothing can rightly compel a simple and brave man to a vulgar sadness. While I enjoy the friendship of the seasons I trust that nothing can make life a burden to me. The gentle rain which waters my beans and keeps me in the house to-day is not drear and melancholy, but good for me too. Though it prevents my hoeing them, it is of far more worth than my hoeing. If it should continue so long as to cause the seeds to rot in the ground and destroy the potatoes in the low lands, it would still be good for the grass on the uplands, and, being good for the grass, it would be good for me. Sometimes, when I compare myself with other men, it seems as if I were more favored by the gods than they, beyond any deserts that I am conscious of; as if I had a warrant and surety at their hands which my fellows have not, and were especially guided and guarded. I do not flatter myself, but if it be possible they flatter me. I have never felt lonesome, or in the least oppressed by a sense of solitude, but once, and that was a few weeks after I came to the woods, when, for an hour, I doubted if the near neighborhood of man was not essential to a serene and healthy life. To be alone was something unpleasant. But I was at the same time conscious of a slight insanity in my mood, and seemed to foresee my recovery. In the midst of a gentle rain while these thoughts prevailed, I was suddenly sensible of such sweet and beneficent society in Nature, in the very pattering of the drops, and in every sound and sight around my house, an infinite and unaccountable friendliness all at once like an atmosphere sustaining me, as made the fancied advantages of human neighborhood insignificant, and I have never thought of them since. Every little pine needle expanded and swelled with sympathy and befriended me. I was so distinctly made aware of the presence of something kindred to me, even in scenes which we are accustomed to call wild and dreary, and also that the nearest of blood to me and humanest was not a person nor a villager, that I thought no place could ever be strange to me again.—

Mourning untimely consumes the sad;
Few are their days in the land of the living,
Beautiful daughter of Toscar.

Some of my pleasantest hours were during the long rainstorms in the spring or fall, which confined

676

me to the house for the afternoon as well as the forenoon, soothed by their ceaseless roar and pelting; when an early twilight ushered in a long evening in which many thoughts had time to take root and unfold themselves. In those driving northeast rains which tried the village houses so, when the maids stood ready with mop and pail in front entries to keep the deluge out, I sat behind my door in my little house, which was all entry, and thoroughly enjoyed its protection. In one heavy [10] thundershower the lightning struck a large pitch-pine across the pond, making a very conspicuous and perfectly regular spiral groove from top to bottom, an inch or more deep, and four or five inches wide, as you would groove a walking-stick. I passed it again the other day, and was struck with awe on looking up and beholding that mark, now more distinct than ever, where a terrific and resistless bolt came down out of the harmless sky eight years ago. Men frequently say to me, "I should [20] think you would feel lonesome down there, and want to be nearer to folks, rainy and snowy days and nights especially." I am tempted to reply to such,—This whole earth which we inhabit is but a point in space. How far apart, think you, dwell the two most distant inhabitants of yonder star, the breadth of whose disk cannot be appreciated by our instruments? Why should I feel lonely? is not our planet in the Milky Way? This which you put seems to me not to be the most important question. [30] What sort of space is that which separates a man from his fellows and makes him solitary? I have found that no exertion of the legs can bring two minds much nearer to one another. What do we want most to dwell near to? Not to many men surely, the depot, the post-office, the bar-room, the meeting-house, the school-house, the grocery, Beacon Hill, or the Five Points, where men most congregate, but to the perennial source of our life, whence in all our experience we have found that [40] to issue, as the willow stands near the water and sends out its roots in that direction. This will vary with different natures, but this is the place where a wise man will dig his cellar.... I one evening overtook one of my townsmen, who has accumulated what is called "a handsome property,"—though I never got a *fair* view of it,—on the Walden road, driving a pair of cattle to market, who inquired of

me how I could bring my mind to give up so many of the comforts of life. I answered that I was very sure I liked it passably well; I was not joking. And so I went home to my bed, and left him to pick his way through the darkness and the mud to Brighton,—or Bright-town,—which place he would reach some time in the morning.

Any prospect of awakening or coming to life to a dead man makes indifferent all times and places. The place where that may occur is always the same, and indescribably pleasant to all our senses. For the most part we allow only outlying and transient circumstances to make our occasions. They are, in fact, the cause of our distraction. Nearest to all things is that power which fashions their being. Next to us the grandest laws are continually being executed. Next to us is not the workman whom we have hired, with whom we love so well to talk, but the workman whose work we are.

"How vast and profound is the influence of the subtile powers of Heaven and of Earth!"

"We seek to perceive them, and we do not see them; we seek to hear them, and we do not hear them; identified with the substance of things, they cannot be separated from them."

"They cause that in all the universe men purify and sanctify their hearts, and clothe themselves in their holiday garments to offer sacrifices and oblations to their ancestors. It is an ocean of subtile intelligences. They are every where, above us, on our left, on our right; they environ us on all sides."

We are the subjects of an experiment which is not a little interesting to me. Can we not do without the society of our gossips a little while under these circumstances,—have our own thoughts to cheer us? Confucius says truly, "Virtue does not remain as an abandoned orphan; it must of necessity have neighbors."

With thinking we may be beside ourselves in a sane sense. By a conscious effort of the mind we can stand aloof from actions and their consequences; and all things, good and bad, go by us like a torrent. We are not wholly involved in Nature. I may be either the driftwood in the stream, or Indra[n] in the sky looking down on it. I may be affected by a theatrical exhibition; on the other hand, I may not be affected by an actual

Indra: a God of the air in Hindu mythology.

677

event which appears to concern me much more. I only know myself as a human entity; the scene, so to speak, of thoughts and affections; and am sensible of a certain doubleness by which I can stand as remote from myself as from another. However intense my experience, I am conscious of the presence and criticism of a part of me, which, as it were, is not a part of me, but spectator, sharing no experience, but taking note of it; and that is no more I than it is you. When the play, it may be the tragedy, of life is over, the spectator goes his way. It was a kind of fiction, a work of the imagination only, so far as he was concerned. This doubleness may easily make us poor neighbors and friends sometimes.

I find it wholesome to be alone the greater part of the time. To be in company, even with the best, is soon wearisome and dissipating. I love to be alone. I never found the companion that was so companionable as solitude. We are for the most part more lonely when we go abroad among men than when we stay in our chambers. A man thinking or working is always alone, let him be where he will. Solitude is not measured by the miles of space that intervene between a man and his fellows. The really diligent student in one of the crowded hives of Cambridge College is as solitary as a dervish in the desert. The farmer can work alone in the field or the woods all day, hoeing or chopping, and not feel lonesome, because he is employed; but when he comes home at night he cannot sit down in a room alone, at the mercy of his thoughts, but must be where he can "see the folks," and recreate, and, as he thinks, remunerate, himself for his day's solitude; and hence he wonders how the student can sit alone in the house all night and most of the day without ennui and "the blues"; but he does not realize that the student, though in the house, is still at work in his field, and chopping in his woods, as the farmer in his, and in turn seeks the same recreation and society that the latter does, though it may be a more condensed form of it.

Society is commonly too cheap. We meet at very short intervals, not having had time to acquire any new value for each other. We meet at meals three times a day, and give each other a new taste of that old musty cheese that we are. We have had to agree on a certain set of rules, called etiquette and politeness, to make this frequent meeting tolerable and that we need not come to open war. We meet at the post-office, and at the sociable, and about the fireside every night; we live thick and are in each other's way, and stumble over one another, and I think that we thus lose some respect for one another. Certainly less frequency would suffice for all important and hearty communications. Consider the girls in a factory,—never alone, hardly in their dreams. It would be better if there were but one inhabitant to a square mile, as where I live. The value of a man is not in his skin, that we should touch him.

I have heard of a man lost in the woods and dying of famine and exhaustion at the foot of a tree, whose loneliness was relieved by the grotesque visions with which, owing to bodily weakness, his diseased imagination surrounded him, and which he believed to be real. So also, owing to bodily and mental health and strength, we may be continually cheered by a like but more normal and natural society, and come to know that we are never alone.

I have a great deal of company in my house; especially in the morning, when nobody calls. Let me suggest a few comparisons, that some one may convey an idea of my situation. I am no more lonely than the loon in the pond that laughs so loud, or than Walden Pond itself. What company has that lonely lake, I pray? And yet it has not the blue devils, but the blue angels in it, in the azure tint of its waters. The sun is alone, except in thick weather, when there sometimes appear to be two, but one is a mock sun. God is alone,—but the devil, he is far from being alone; he sees a great deal of company; he is legion. I am no more lonely than a single mullein or dandelion in a pasture, or a bean leaf, or sorrel, or a horsefly, or a humble-bee. I am no more lonely than the Mill Brook, or a weathercock, or the north star, or the south wind, or an April shower, or a January thaw, or the first spider in a new house.

I have occasional visits in the long winter evenings, when the snow falls fast and the wind howls in the wood, from an old settler and original proprietor, who is reported to have dug Walden Pond, and stoned it, and fringed it with pine woods; who tells me stories of old time and of new eternity; and between us we manage to pass a cheerful evening with social mirth and pleasant views of things, even without apples or cider,—a most wise and humorous friend, whom I love much, who keeps himself more secret than ever did Goffe or Whalley;[n] and though he is thought to be dead, none can show where he is buried. An elderly dame, too, dwells in my neighborhood, invisible to most persons, in whose odorous herb garden I love to stroll sometimes, gathering simples and listening to her fables; for she has a genius of unequaled fertility, and her memory runs back farther than mythology, and she can tell me the original of every fable, and on what fact every one is founded, for the incidents occurred when she was young. A ruddy and lusty old dame, who delights in all weathers and seasons, and is likely to outlive all her children yet.

The indescribable innocence and beneficence of Nature,—of sun and wind and rain, of summer and winter,—such health, such cheer, they afford forever! and such sympathy have they ever with our race, that all Nature would be affected, and the sun's brightness fade, and the winds would sigh humanely, and the clouds rain tears, and the woods shed their leaves and put on mourning in midsummer, if any man should ever for a just cause grieve. Shall I not have intelligence with the earth? Am I not partly leaves and vegetable mold myself?

What is the pill which will keep us well, serene, contented? Not my or thy great-grandfather's, but our great-grandmother Nature's universal, vegetable, botanic medicines, by which she has kept herself young always, outlived so many old Parrs in her day, and fed her health with their decaying fatness. For my panacea, instead of one of those quack vials of a mixture dipped from Acheron and the Dead Sea, which come out of those long shallow black-schooner looking wagons which we sometimes see made to carry bottles, let me have a draught of undiluted morning air. Morning air! If men will not drink of this at the fountain-head of the day, why, then, we must even bottle up some and sell it in the shops, for the benefit of those who have lost their subscription ticket to morning time in this world. But remember, it will not keep quite till noonday even in the coolest cellar, but drive out the stopples long ere that and

Goffe or Whalley: regicides who hid in New England until their decease.

follow westward the steps of Aurora. I am no worshiper of Hygeia, who was the daughter of that old herb-doctor Æsculapius, and who is represented on monuments holding a serpent in one hand, and in the other a cup out of which the serpent sometimes drinks; but rather of Hebe, cup-bearer to Jupiter, who was the daughter of Juno and wild lettuce, and who had the power of restoring gods and men to the vigor of youth. She was probably the only thoroughly sound-conditioned, healthy, and robust young lady that ever walked the globe, and wherever she came it was spring.

XII. *Brute Neighbors*

. . . .

It is remarkable how many creatures live wild and free though secret in the woods, and still sustain themselves in the neighborhood of towns, suspected by hunters only. How retired the otter manages to live here! He grows to be four feet long, as big as a small boy, perhaps without any human being getting a glimpse of him. I formerly saw the raccoon in the woods behind where my house is built, and probably still heard their whinnering at night. Commonly I rested an hour or two in the shade at noon, after planting, and ate my lunch, and read a little by a spring which was the source of a swamp and of a brook, oozing from under Brister's Hill, half a mile from my field. The approach to this was through a succession of descending grassy hollows, full of young pitch-pines, into a larger wood about the swamp. There, in a very secluded and shaded spot, under a spreading white-pine, there was yet a clean firm sward to sit on. I had dug out the spring and made a well of clear gray water, where I could dip up a pailful without roiling it, and thither I went for this purpose almost every day in midsummer, when the pond was warmest. Thither too the wood-cock led her brood, to prove the mud for worms, flying but a foot above them down the bank, while they ran in a troop beneath; but at last, spying me, she would leave her young and circle round and round me, nearer and nearer till within four or five feet, pretending broken wings and legs, to attract my attention, and get off her young, who would already have taken up their march, with faint wiry peep, single file through the swamp, as she directed.

679

Or I heard the peep of the young when I could not see the parent bird. There too the turtle-doves sat over the spring, or fluttered from bough to bough of the soft white-pines over my head; or the red squirrel, coursing down the nearest bough, was particularly familiar and inquisitive. You only need sit still long enough in some attractive spot in the woods that all its inhabitants may exhibit themselves to you by turns.

I was witness to events of a less peaceful char- [10] acter. One day when I went out to my wood-pile, or rather my pile of stumps, I observed two large ants, the one red, the other much larger, nearly half an inch long, and black, fiercely contending with one another. Having once got hold they never let go, but struggled and wrestled and rolled on the chips incessantly. Looking farther, I was surprised to find that the chips were covered with such combatants, that it was not a *duellum*, but a *bellum*, a war between two races of ants, the red [20] always pitted against the black, and frequently two red ones to one black. The legions of these Myrmidons[n] covered all the hills and vales in my wood-yard, and the ground was already strewn with the dead and dying, both red and black. It was the only battle I have ever witnessed, the only battle-field I ever trod while the battle was raging; internecine war; the red republicans on the one hand, and the black imperialists on the other. On every side they were engaged in deadly combat, [30] yet without any noise that I could hear, and human soldiers never fought so resolutely. I watched a couple that were fast locked in each other's embraces, in a little sunny valley amid the chips, now at noon-day prepared to fight till the sun went down, or life went out. The smaller red champion had fastened himself like a vice to his adversary's front, and through all the tumblings on that field never for an instant ceased to gnaw at one of his feelers near the root, having already caused the [40] other to go by the board; while the stronger black one dashed him from side to side, and as I saw on looking nearer, had already divested him of several of his members. They fought with more pertinacity than bull-dogs. Neither manifested the least disposition to retreat. It was evident that their battle-cry was Conquer or die. In the mean

Myrmidons: the soldiers of Achilles in the Trojan War.

while there came along a single red ant on the hill-side of this valley, evidently full of excitement, who either had despatched his foe, or had not yet taken part in the battle; probably the latter, for he had lost none of his limbs; whose mother had charged him to return with his shield or upon it. Or perchance he was some Achilles, who had nourished his wrath apart, and had now come to avenge or rescue his Patroclus.[n] He saw this unequal combat from afar,—for the blacks were nearly twice the size of the red,—he drew near with rapid pace till he stood on his guard within half an inch of the combatants; then, watching his opportunity, he sprang upon the black warrior, and commenced his operations near the root of his right fore-leg, leaving the foe to select among his own members; and so there were three united for life, as if a new kind of attraction had been invented which put all other locks and cements to shame. I should not have wondered by this time to find that they had their respective musical bands stationed on some eminent chip, and playing their national airs the while, to excite the slow and cheer the dying combatants. I was myself excited somewhat even as if they had been men. The more you think of it, the less the difference. And certainly there is not the fight recorded in Concord history, at least, if in the history of America, that will bear a moment's comparison with this, whether for the numbers engaged in it, or for the patriotism and heroism displayed. For numbers and for carnage it was an Austerlitz or Dresden.[n] Concord Fight! Two killed on the patriots' side, and Luther Blanchard wounded! Why here every ant was a Buttrick,— "Fire! for God's sake fire!"—and thousands shared the fate of Davis and Hosmer.[n] There was not one hireling there. I have no doubt that it was a principle they fought for, as much as our ancestors, and not to avoid a three-penny tax on their tea; and the results of this battle will be as important and memorable to those whom it concerns as those of the battle of Bunker Hill at least.

Patroclus: the death of Patroclus caused Achilles to leave his tent and avenge the loss of his friend by slaying Hector. **Austerlitz or Dresden:** Battles of Austerlitz (1805) and Dresden (1813) were unusually bloody. **Davis and Hosmer:** residents of Concord who lost their lives in the skirmish with the British.

I took up the chip on which the three I have particularly described were struggling, carried it into my house, and placed it under a tumbler on my window-sill, in order to see the issue. Holding a microscope to the first-mentioned red ant, I saw that, though he was assiduously gnawing at the near fore-leg of his enemy, having severed his remaining feeler, his own breast was all torn away, exposing what vitals he had there to the jaws of the black warrior, whose breast-plate was apparently too thick for him to pierce; and the dark carbuncles of the sufferer's eyes shone with ferocity such as war only could excite. They struggled half an hour longer under the tumbler, and when I looked again the black soldier had severed the heads of his foes from their bodies, and the still living heads were hanging on either side of him like ghastly trophies at his saddlebow, still apparently as firmly fastened as ever, and he was endeavoring with feeble struggles, being without feelers and with only the remnant of a leg, and I know not how many other wounds, to divest himself of them; which at length, after half an hour more, he accomplished. I raised the glass, and he went off over the window-sill in that crippled state. Whether he finally survived that combat, and spent the remainder of his days in some Hotel des Invalides, I do not know; but I thought that his industry would not be worth much thereafter. I never learned which party was victorious, nor the cause of the war; but I felt for the rest of that day as if I had my feelings excited and harrowed by witnessing the struggle, the ferocity and carnage, of a human battle before my door.

Kirby and Spence tell us that the battles of ants have long been celebrated and the date of them recorded, though they say that Huber is the only modern author who appears to have witnessed them. "Aeneas Sylvius," say they, "after giving a very circumstantial account of one contested with great obstinacy by a great and small species on the trunk of a pear tree," adds that " 'This action was fought in the pontificate of Eugenius the Fourth, in the presence of Nicholas Pistoriensis, an eminent lawyer, who related tne whole history of the battle with the greatest fidelity.' A similar engagement between great and small ants is recorded by Olaus Magnus, in which the small ones, being victorious, are said to have buried the bodies of their own soldiers, but left those of their giant enemies a prey to the birds. This event happened previous to the expulsion of the tyrant Christiern the Second from Sweden." The battle which I witnessed took place in the Presidency of Polk, five years before the passage of Webster's Fugitive-Slave Bill. . . .

Walking

"Walking" was first printed in the *Atlantic Monthly* for June, 1862, less than a month after Thoreau's death, and was collected in *Excursions* (1863), from which this text is taken. Thoreau was an inveterate walker "to exercise both body and spirit." In *Walden*, he cautioned, "We do not ride upon the railroad; it rides upon us." A number of contemporary portraits represent the author while walking. The paper was given as a lecture before its publication.

I wish to speak a word for Nature, for absolute freedom and wildness, as contrasted with a freedom and culture merely civil,—to regard man as an inhabitant, or a part and parcel of Nature, rather than a member of society. I wish to make an extreme statement, if so I may make an emphatic one, for there are enough champions of civilization: the minister and the school-committee, and every one of you will take care of that.

I have met with but one or two persons in the course of my life who understood the art of Walking, that is, of taking walks,—who had a genius, so to speak, for *sauntering*: which word is beautifully derived "from idle people who roved about the country, in the Middle Ages, and asked charity, under pretense of going *à la Sainte Terre*," to the Holy Land, till the children exclaimed, "There goes a *Sainte-Terrer*," a Saunterer, a Holy-Lander. They who never go to the Holy Land in their walks, as they pretend, are indeed mere idlers and vagabonds; but they who do go there are saunterers in the good sense, such as I mean. Some, however, would derive the word from *sans terre*, without land or a home, which, therefore, in the good sense, will mean, having no particular home, but equally at home everywhere. For this is the secret of successful sauntering. He who sits still in a house all the time may be the greatest vagrant of all; but the saunterer, in the good sense, is no more vagrant than the meandering river, which is all the while sedulously seeking the shortest course to the sea. But I prefer the first, which, indeed, is the most probable derivation. For every walk is a sort of crusade, preached by some Peter the Hermit in us, to go forth and reconquer this Holy Land from the hands of the Infidels.

It is true, we are but faint-hearted crusaders, even the walkers, nowadays, who undertake no persevering, never-ending enterprises. Our expeditions are but tours, and come round again at evening to the old hearth-side from which we set out. Half the walk is but retracing our steps. We should go forth on the shortest walk, perchance, in the spirit of undying adventure, never to return, —prepared to send back our embalmed hearts only as relics to our desolate kingdoms. If you are ready to leave father and mother, and brother and sister, and wife and child and friends, and never see them again,—if you have paid your debts, and made your will, and settled all your affairs, and are a free man, then you are ready for a walk.

To come down to my own experience, my companion and I, for I sometimes have a companion, take pleasure in fancying ourselves knights of a new, or rather an old, order,—not Equestrians or Chevaliers, not Ritters or Riders, but Walkers, a still more ancient and honorable class, I trust. The chivalric and heroic spirit which once belonged to the Rider seems now to reside in, or perchance to have subsided into, the Walker,—not the Knight, but Walker Errant. He is a sort of fourth estate, outside of Church and State and People.

We have felt that we almost alone hereabouts practiced this noble art; though, to tell the truth, at least, if their own assertions are to be received, most of my townsmen would fain walk sometimes, as I do, but they cannot. No wealth can buy the requisite leisure, freedom, and independence which are the capital in this profession. It comes only by the grace of God. It requires a direct dispensation from Heaven to become a walker. You must be born into the family of the Walkers. *Ambulator nascitur, non fit.*[n] Some of my townsmen, it is true, can remember and have described to me

Ambulator . . . fit: "The walker is born, not made."

some walks which they took ten years ago, in which they were so blessed as to lose themselves for half an hour in the woods; but I know very well that they have confined themselves to the highway ever since, whatever pretensions they may make to belong to this select class. No doubt they were elevated for a moment as by the reminiscence of a previous state of existence, when even they were foresters and outlaws.

> When he came to grene wode,
>   In a mery mornynge,
> There he herde the notes small
>   Of byrdes mery syngynge.
>
> It is ferre gone, sayd Robyn,
>   That I was last here;
> Me lyste a lytell for to shote
>   At the donne dere.

I think that I cannot preserve my health and spirits, unless I spend four hours a day at least,— and it is commonly more than that,—sauntering through the woods and over the hills and fields, absolutely free from all worldly engagements. You may safely say, A penny for your thoughts, or a thousand pounds. When sometimes I am reminded that the mechanics and shopkeepers stay in their shops not only all the forenoon, but all the afternoon too, sitting with crossed legs, so many of them,—as if the legs were made to sit upon, and not to stand or walk upon,—I think that they deserve some credit for not having all committed suicide long ago.

I, who cannot stay in my chamber for a single day without acquiring some rust, and when sometimes I have stolen forth for a walk at the eleventh hour or four o'clock in the afternoon, too late to redeem the day, when the shades of night were already beginning to be mingled with the daylight, have felt as if I had committed some sin to be atoned for,—I confess that I am astonished at the power of endurance, to say nothing of the moral insensibility, of my neighbors who confine themselves to shops and offices the whole day for weeks and months, ay, and years almost together. I know not what manner of stuff they are of,— sitting there now at three o'clock in the afternoon, as if it were three o'clock in the morning. Bonaparte may talk of the three-o'clock-in-the-morning courage, but it is nothing to the courage which can sit down cheerfully at this hour in the afternoon over against one's self whom you have known all the morning, to starve out a garrison to whom you are bound by such strong ties of sympathy. I wonder that about this time, or say between four and five o'clock in the afternoon, too late for the morning papers and too early for the evening ones, there is not a general explosion heard up and down the street, scattering a legion of antiquated and house-bred notions and whims to the four winds for an airing,—and so the evil cures itself. . . .

The village is the place to which the roads tend, a sort of expansion of the highway, as a lake of a river. It is the body of which roads are the arms and legs,—a trivial or quadrivial place, the thoroughfare and ordinary of travelers. The word is from the Latin *villa* which together with *via*, a way, or more anciently *ved* and *vella*, Varro derives from *veho*, to carry, because the villa is the place to and from which things are carried. They who got their living by teaming were said *vellaturam facere*. Hence, too, the Latin word *vilis* and our vile; also *villain*. This suggests what kind of degeneracy villagers are liable to. They are way-worn by the travel that goes by and over them, without traveling themselves.

Some do not walk at all; others walk in the highways; a few walk across lots. Roads are made for horses and men of business. I do not travel in them much, comparatively, because I am not in a hurry to get to any tavern or grocery or livery-stable or depot to which they lead. I am a good horse to travel, but not from choice a roadster. The landscape-painter uses the figures of men to mark a road. He would not make that use of my figure. I walk out into a Nature such as the old prophets and poets, Menu, Moses, Homer, Chaucer, walked in. You may name it America, but it is not America; neither Americus Vespucius, nor Columbus, nor the rest were the discoverers of it. There is a truer account of it in mythology than in any history of America, so called, that I have seen. . . .

Some months ago I went to see a panorama of the Rhine. It was like a dream of the Middle Ages. I floated down its historic stream in something more than imagination, under bridges built by the Romans, and repaired by later heroes, past cities and castles whose very names were music to my eyes, and each of which was the subject of a legend. . . .

Soon after, I went to see a panorama of the Mississippi, and as I worked my way up the river in the light of to-day, and saw the steam-boats wooding up, counted the rising cities, gazed on the fresh ruins of Nauvoo, beheld the Indians moving west across the stream, and, as before I had looked up the Moselle now looked up the Ohio and the Missouri, and heard the legends of Dubuque and of Wenona's Cliff,—still thinking more of the future than of the past or present,—I saw that this was a Rhine stream of a different kind; that the foundations of castles were yet to be laid, and the famous bridges were yet to be thrown over the river; and I felt that this was the heroic age itself, though we know it not, for the hero is commonly the simplest and obscurest of men.

Hope and the future for me are not in lawns and cultivated fields, not in towns and cities, but in the impervious and quaking swamps. When, formerly, I have analyzed my partiality for some farm which I had contemplated purchasing, I have frequently found that I was attracted solely by a few square rods of impermeable and unfathomable bog,—a natural sink in one corner of it. That was the jewel which dazzled me. I derive more of my subsistence from the swamps which surround my native town than from the cultivated gardens in the village. There are no richer parterres to my eyes than the dense beds of dwarf andromeda (*Cassandra calyculata*) which cover these tender places on the earth's surface. Botany cannot go farther than tell me the names of the shrubs which grow there, —the high-blueberry, panicled andromeda, lamb-kill, azalea, and rhodora,—all standing in the quaking sphagnum. I often think that I should like to have my house front on this mass of dull red bushes, omitting other flower plots and borders, transplanted spruce and trim box, even gravelled walks,—to have this fertile spot under my windows, not a few imported barrow-fulls of soil only to cover the sand which was thrown out in digging the cellar. Why not put my house, my parlor, behind this plot, instead of behind that meagre assemblage of curiosities, that poor apology for a

Nature and Art, which I call my front-yard? It is an effort to clear up and make a decent appearance when the carpenter and mason have departed, though done as much for the passer-by as the dweller within. The most tasteful front-yard fence was never an agreeable object of study to me; the most elaborate ornaments, acorn-tops, or what not, soon wearied and disgusted me. Bring your sills up to the very edge of the swamp, then (though it may not be the best place for a dry cellar), so that there be no access on that side to citizens. Front-yards are not made to walk in, but, at most, through, and you could go in the back way.

Yes, though you may think me perverse, if it were proposed to me to dwell in the neighborhood of the most beautiful garden that ever human art contrived, or else of a Dismal Swamp, I should certainly decide for the swamp. How vain, then, have been all your labors, citizens, for me!

My spirits infallibly rise in proportion to the outward dreariness. Give me the ocean, the desert, or the wilderness! In the desert, pure air and solitude compensate for want of moisture and fertility. The traveler Burton says of it: "Your *morale* improves; you become frank and cordial, hospitable and single-minded. . . . In the desert, spirituous liquors excite only disgust. There is a keen enjoyment in a mere animal existence." They who have been traveling long on the steppes of Tartary say: "On reëntering cultivated lands, the agitation, perplexity, and turmoil of civilization oppressed and suffocated us; the air seemed to fail us, and we felt every moment as if about to die of asphyxia." When I would recreate myself, I seek the darkest wood, the thickest and most interminable and, to the citizen, most dismal swamp. I enter a swamp as a sacred place,—a *sanctum sanctorum*. There is the strength, the marrow of Nature. The wild-wood covers the virgin mould,—and the same soil is good for men and for trees. A man's health requires as many acres of meadow to his prospect as his farm does loads of muck. There are the strong meats on which he feeds. A town is saved, not more by the righteous men in it than by the woods and swamps that surround it. A township where one primitive forest waves above while another primitive forest rots below,—such a town is fitted to raise not only corn and potatoes, but poets and philosophers for the coming ages. In such a soil grew Homer and Confucius and the rest, and out of such a wilderness comes the Reformer eating locusts and wild honey.

To preserve wild animals implies generally the creation of a forest for them to dwell in or resort to. So it is with man. A hundred years ago they sold bark in our streets peeled from our own woods. In the very aspect of those primitive and rugged trees there was, methinks, a tanning principle which hardened and consolidated the fibres of men's thoughts. Ah! already I shudder for these comparatively degenerate days of my native village, when you cannot collect a load of bark of good thickness,—and we no longer produce tar and turpentine.

The civilized nations—Greece, Rome, England—have been sustained by the primitive forests which anciently rotted where they stand. They survive as long as the soil is not exhausted. Alas for human culture! little is to be expected of a nation, when the vegetable mould is exhausted, and it is compelled to make manure of the bones of its fathers. There the poet sustains himself merely by his own superfluous fat, and the philosopher comes down on his marrow-bones.

It is said to be the task of the American "to work the virgin soil," and that "agriculture here already assumes proportions unknown everywhere else." I think that the farmer displaces the Indian even because he redeems the meadow, and so makes himself stronger and in some respects more natural. I was surveying for a man the other day a single straight line one hundred and thirty-two rods long, through a swamp, at whose entrance might have been written the words which Dante read over the entrance to the infernal regions,—"Leave all hope, ye that enter,"—that is, of ever getting out again; where at one time I saw my employer actually up to his neck and swimming for his life in his property, though it was still winter. He had another similar swamp which I could not survey at all, because it was completely under water, and nevertheless, with regard to a third swamp, which I did *survey* from a distance, he remarked to me, true to his instincts, that he would not part with it for any consideration, on account of the mud which it contained. And that man intends to put a girdling ditch round the whole in the course of forty months, and so redeem it by the magic of his spade. I refer to him only as the type of a class.

The weapons with which we have gained our most important victories, which should be handed down as heirlooms from father to son, are not the sword and the lance, but the bush-whack, the turf-cutter, the spade, and the bog-hoe, rusted with the blood of many a meadow, and begrimed with the dust of many a hard-fought field. The very winds blew the Indian's corn-field into the meadow, and pointed out the way which he had not the skill to follow. He had no better implement with which to intrench himself in the land than a clamshell. But the farmer is armed with plough and spade.

In Literature it is only the wild that attracts us. Dulness is but another name for tameness. It is the uncivilized free and wild thinking in Hamlet and the Iliad, in all the Scriptures and Mythologies, not learned in the schools, that delights us. As the wild duck is more swift and beautiful than the tame, so is the wild—the mallard—thought, which 'mid falling dews wings its way above the fens. A truly good book is something as natural, and as unexpectedly and unaccountably fair and perfect, as a wild flower discovered on the prairies of the West or in the jungles of the East. Genius is a light which makes the darkness visible, like the lightning's flash, which perchance shatters the temple of knowledge itself,—and not a taper lighted at the hearthstone of the race, which pales before the light of common day.

English literature, from the days of the minstrels to the Lake Poets,—Chaucer and Spenser and Milton, and even Shakespeare, included,—breathes no quite fresh and, in this sense, wild strain. It is an essentially tame and civilized literature, reflecting Greece and Rome. Her wilderness is a greenwood, her wild man a Robin Hood. There is plenty of genial love of Nature, but not so much of Nature herself. Her chronicles inform us when her wild animals, but not when the wild man in her, became extinct.

The science of Humboldt[n] is one thing, poetry

Humboldt: Baron Friedrich Alexander von (1769–1859), German naturalist and traveler

is another thing. The poet to-day, notwithstanding all the discoveries of science, and the accumulated learning of mankind, enjoys no advantage over Homer. . . .

We hug the earth,—how rarely we mount! Methinks we might elevate ourselves a little more. We might climb a tree, at least. I found my account in climbing a tree once. It was a tall white pine, on the top of a hill; and though I got well pitched, I was well paid for it, for I discovered new mountains in the horizon which I had never seen before,—so much more of the earth and the heavens. I might have walked about the foot of the tree for three-score years and ten, and yet I certainly should never have seen them. But, above all, I discovered around me,—it was near the end of June,—on the ends of the topmost branches only, a few minute and delicate red cone-like blossoms, the fertile flower of the white pine looking heavenward. I carried straightway to the village the topmost spire, and showed it to stranger jurymen who walked the streets,—for it was court-week,—and to farmers and lumber-dealers and wood-choppers and hunters, and not one had ever seen the like before, but they wondered as at a star dropped down. Tell of ancient architects finishing their works on the tops of columns as perfectly as on the lower and more visible parts! Nature has from the first expanded the minute blossoms of the forest only toward the heavens, above men's heads and unobserved by them. We see only the flowers that are under our feet in the meadows. The pines have developed their delicate blossoms on the highest twigs of the wood every summer for ages, as well over the heads of Nature's red children as of her white ones; yet scarcely a farmer or hunter in the land has ever seen them. . . .

We had a remarkable sunset one day last November. I was walking in a meadow, the source of a small brook, when the sun at last, just before setting, after a cold gray day, reached a clear stratum in the horizon, and the softest, brightest morning sunlight fell on the dry grass and on the stems of the trees in the opposite horizon and on the leaves of the shrub-oaks on the hill-side, while our shadows stretched long over the meadow eastward, as if we were the only motes in its beams.

It was such a light as we could not have imagined a moment before, and the air also was so warm and serene that nothing was wanting to make a paradise of that meadow. When we reflected that this was not a solitary phenomenon, never to happen again, but that it would happen forever and ever an infinite number of evenings, and cheer and reassure the latest child that walked there, it was more glorious still.

The sun sets on some retired meadow, where no house is visible, with all the glory and splendor that it lavishes on cities, and perchance as it has never set before,—where there is but a solitary marsh-hawk to have his wings gilded by it, or only a musquash looks out from his cabin, and there is some little black-veined brook in the midst of the marsh, just beginning to meander, winding slowly round a decaying stump. We walked in so pure and bright a light, gilding the withered grass and leaves, so softly and serenely bright, I thought I had never bathed in such a golden flood, without a ripple or a murmur to it. The west side of every wood and rising ground gleamed like the boundary of Elysium, and the sun on our backs seemed like a gentle herdsman driving us home at evening.

So we saunter toward the Holy Land, till one day the sun shall shine more brightly than ever he has done, shall perchance shine into our minds and hearts, and light up our whole lives with a great awakening light, as warm and serene and golden as on a bank-side in autumn.

Life without Principle

"Life without Principle" first appeared in *The Atlantic Monthly* for October, 1863, a year and a half after Thoreau's death. It was reprinted in *A Yankee in Canada* (1866), from which this text is taken. Like many other writings of Thoreau, this essay was originally designed as a lecture. It bore the title "Getting a Living" when it was delivered at New Bedford, Massachusetts, in late December, 1854. The thought of "Life without Principle" is an independent statement of ideas similar to those in the Conclusion of *Walden*. Most of the ideas concentrated in the essay were drawn from entries in the Journals between 1850 and 1854.

At a lyceum, not long since, I felt that the lecturer had chosen a theme too foreign to himself, and so failed to interest me as much as he might have done. He described things not in or near to his heart, but toward his extremities and superficies. There was, in this sense, no truly central or centralizing thought in the lecture. I would have had him deal with his privatest experience, as the poet does. The greatest compliment that was ever paid me was when one asked me what I thought, and attended to my answer. I am surprised, as well as delighted, when this happens, it is such a rare use he would make of me, as if he were acquainted with the tool. Commonly, if men want anything of me, it is only to know how many acres I make of their land,—since I am a surveyor,—or, at most, what trivial news I have burdened myself with. They never will go to law for my meat; they prefer the shell. A man once came a considerable distance to ask me to lecture on Slavery; but on conversing with him, I found that he and his clique expected seven eighths of the lecture to be theirs, and only one eighth mine; so I declined. I take it for granted, when I am invited to lecture anywhere,—for I have had a little experience in that business,—that there is a desire to hear what I think on some subject, though I may be the greatest fool in the country,—and not that I should say pleasant things merely, or such as the audience will assent to; and I resolve, accordingly, that I will give them a strong dose of myself. They have sent for me, and engaged to pay for me, and I am determined that they shall have me, though I bore them beyond all precedent.

So now I would say something similar to you, my readers. Since you are my readers, and I have not been much of a traveller, I will not talk about people a thousand miles off, but come as near home as I can. As the time is short, I will leave out all the flattery, and retain all the criticism.

Let us consider the way in which we spend our lives.

This world is a place of business. What an infinite bustle! I am awaked almost every night by the panting of the locomotive. It interrupts my dreams. There is no sabbath. It would be glorious to see mankind at leisure for once. It is nothing but work, work, work. I cannot easily buy a blank-book to write thoughts in; they are commonly ruled for dollars and cents. An Irishman, seeing me making a minute in the fields, took it for granted that I was calculating my wages. If a man was tossed out of a window when an infant, and so made a cripple for life, or scared out of his wits by the Indians, it is regretted chiefly because he was thus incapacitated for—business! I think that there is nothing, not even crime, more opposed to poetry, to philosophy, ay, to life itself, than this incessant business. . . .

If a man walk in the woods for love of them half of each day, he is in danger of being regarded as a loafer; but if he spends his whole day as a speculator, shearing off those woods and making earth bald before her time, he is esteemed an industrious and enterprising citizen. As if a town had no interest in its forests but to cut them down!

Most men would feel insulted if it were proposed to employ them in throwing stones over a wall, and then in throwing them back, merely that they might earn their wages. But many are no more worthily employed now. For instance: just after sunrise, one summer morning, I noticed one of my neighbors walking beside his team, which was slowly drawing a heavy hewn stone swung under the axle, surrounded by an atmosphere of industry,—his day's work begun,—his brow commenced to sweat,—a reproach to all sluggards and idlers,—pausing abreast the shoulders of his oxen, and half turning round with a flourish of his merciful whip, while they gained their length on him. And I thought, Such is the labor which the American Congress exists to protect,—honest, manly toil,—honest as the day is long,—that makes his bread taste sweet, and keeps society sweet,—which all men respect and have consecrated; one of the sacred band, doing the needful but irksome drudgery. Indeed, I felt a slight reproach, because I observed this from a window, and was not abroad and stirring about a similar business. The day went by, and at evening I passed the yard of another neighbor, who keeps many servants and spends much money foolishly, while he adds nothing to the common stock, and there I saw the stone of the morning lying beside a whimsical structure intended to adorn this Lord Timothy Dexter's premises, and the dignity forthwith departed from the teamster's labor, in

my eyes. In my opinion, the sun was made to light worthier toil than this. I may add that his employer has since run off, in debt to a good part of the town, and, after passing through Chancery, has settled somewhere else, there to become once more a patron of the arts.

The ways by which you may get money almost without exception lead downward. To have done anything by which you earned money merely is to have been truly idle or worse. If the laborer gets no more than the wages which his employer pays him, he is cheated, he cheats himself. If you would get money as a writer or lecturer, you must be popular, which is to go down perpendicularly. Those services which the community will most readily pay for, it is most disagreeable to render. You are paid for being something less than a man. The State does not commonly reward a genius any more wisely. Even the poet-laureate would rather not have to celebrate the accidents of royalty. He must be bribed with a pipe of wine; and perhaps another poet is called away from his muse to gauge that very pipe. As for my own business, even that kind of surveying which I could do with most satisfaction my employers do not want. They would prefer that I should do my work coarsely and not too well, ay, not well enough. When I observe that there are different ways of surveying, my employer commonly asks which will give him the most land, not which is most correct. I once invented a rule for measuring cord-wood, and tried to introduce it in Boston; but the measurer there told me that the sellers did not wish to have their wood measured correctly,—that he was already too accurate for them, and therefore they commonly got their wood measured in Charlestown before crossing the bridge. . . .

It is remarkable that there are few men so well employed, so much to their minds, but that a little money or fame would commonly buy them off from their present pursuit. I see advertisements for active young men, as if activity were the whole of a young man's capital. Yet I have been surprised when one has with confidence proposed to me, a grown man, to embark in some enterprise of his, as if I had absolutely nothing to do, my life having been a complete failure hitherto. What a doubtful compliment this to pay me! As if he had met me halfway across the ocean beating up against the wind, but bound nowhere, and proposed to me to go along with him! If I did, what do you think the underwriters would say? No, no! I am not without employment at this stage of the voyage. To tell the truth, I saw an advertisement for able-bodied seamen, when I was a boy, sauntering in my native port, and as soon as I came of age I embarked.

The community has no bribe that will tempt a wise man. You may raise money enough to tunnel a mountain, but you cannot raise money enough to hire a man who is minding his own business. An efficient and valuable man does what he can, whether the community pay him for it or not. The inefficient offer their inefficiency to the highest bidder, and are forever expecting to be put into office. One would suppose that they were rarely disappointed.

Perhaps I am more than usually jealous with respect to my freedom. I feel that my connection with and obligation to society are still very slight and transient. Those slight labors which afford me a livelihood, and by which it is allowed that I am to some extent serviceable to my contemporaries, are as yet commonly a pleasure to me, and I am not often reminded that they are a necessity. So far I am successful. But I foresee that if my wants should be much increased, the labor required to supply them would become a drudgery. If I should sell both my forenoons and afternoons to society, as most appear to do, I am sure that for me there would be nothing left worth living for. I trust that I shall never thus sell my birthright for a mess of pottage. I wish to suggest that a man may be very industrious, and yet not spend his time well. There is no more fatal blunderer than he who consumes the greater part of his life getting his living. All great enterprises are self-supporting. The poet, for instance, must sustain his body by his poetry, as a steam planing-mill feeds its boilers with the shavings it makes. You must get your living by loving. But as it is said of the merchants that ninety-seven in a hundred fail, so the life of men generally, tried by this standard, is a failure, and bankruptcy may be surely prophesied.

Merely to come into the world the heir of a fortune is not to be born, but to be still-born, rather. To be supported by the charity of friends, or a government-pension,—provided you continue to breathe,—by whatever fine synonyms you describe these relations, is to go into the almshouse. On Sundays the poor debtor goes to church to take an account of stock, and finds, of course, that his outgoes have been greater than his income. In the Catholic Church, especially, they go into Chancery, make a clean confession, give up all, and think to start again. Thus men will lie on their backs, talking about the fall of man, and never make an effort to get up. . . .

The title wise is, for the most part, falsely applied. How can one be a wise man, if he does not know any better how to live than other men?—if he is only more cunning and intellectually subtle? Does Wisdom work in a treadmill? or does she teach how to succeed by her example? Is there any such thing as wisdom not applied to life? Is she merely the miller who grinds the finest logic? It is pertinent to ask if Plato got his living in a better way or more successfully than his contemporaries,—or did he succumb to the difficulties of life like other men? Did he seem to prevail over some of them merely by indifference, or by assuming grand airs? or find it easier to live, because his aunt remembered him in her will? The ways in which most men get their living, that is, live, are mere makeshifts, and a shirking of the real business of life,—chiefly because they do not know, but partly because they do not mean, any better.

The rush to California, for instance, and the attitude, not merely of merchants, but of philosophers and prophets, so called, in relation to it, reflect the greatest disgrace on mankind. That so many are ready to live by luck, and so get the means of commanding the labor of others less lucky, without contributing any value to society! And that is called enterprise! I know of no more startling development of the immorality of trade, and all the common modes of getting a living. The philosophy and poetry and religion of such a mankind are not worth the dust of a puff-ball. The hog that gets his living by rooting, stirring up the soil so, would be ashamed of such company. If I could command the wealth of all the worlds by lifting my finger, I would not pay such a price for it. Even Mahomet knew that God did not make this world in jest. It makes God to be a moneyed gentleman who scatters a handful of pennies in order to see mankind scramble for them. The world's raffle! A subsistence in the domains of Nature a thing to be raffled for! What a comment, what a satire, on our institutions! The conclusion will be, that mankind will hang itself upon a tree. And have all the precepts in all the Bibles taught men only this? and is the last and most admirable invention of the human race only an improved muck-rake? Is this the ground on which Orientals and Occidentals meet? Did God direct us so to get our living, digging where we never planted,—and He would, perchance, reward us with lumps of gold?

God gave the righteous man a certificate entitling him to food and raiment, but the unrighteous man found a *fac-simile* of the same in God's coffers, and appropriated it, and obtained food and raiment like the former. It is one of the most extensive systems of counterfeiting that the world has seen. I did not know that mankind were suffering for want of gold. I have seen a little of it. I know that it is very malleable, but not so malleable as wit. A grain of gold will gild a great surface, but not so much as a grain of wisdom.

The gold-digger in the ravines of the mountains is as much a gambler as his fellow in the saloons of San Francisco. What difference does it make whether you shake dirt or shake dice? If you win, society is the loser. The gold-digger is the enemy of the honest laborer, whatever checks and compensations there may be. It is not enough to tell me that you worked hard to get your gold. So does the Devil work hard. The way of transgressors may be hard in many respects. The humblest observer who goes to the mines sees and says that gold-digging is of the character of a lottery; the gold thus obtained is not the same thing with the wages of honest toil. But, practically, he forgets what he has seen, for he has seen only the fact, not the principle, and goes into trade there, that is, buys a ticket in what commonly proves another lottery, where the fact is not so obvious.

After reading Howitt's account of the Australian gold-diggings one evening, I had in my mind's eye,

all night, the numerous valleys, with their streams, all cut up with foul pits, from ten to one hundred feet deep, and half a dozen feet across, as close as they can be dug, and partly filled with water,—the locality to which men furiously rush to probe for their fortunes,—uncertain where they shall break ground,—not knowing but the gold is under their camp itself,—sometimes digging one hundred and sixty feet before they strike the vein, or then missing it by a foot,—turned into demons, and regardless of each others' rights, in their thirst for riches,—whole valleys, for thirty miles, suddenly honeycombed by the pits of the miners, so that even hundreds are drowned in them,—standing in water, and covered with mud and clay, they work night and day, dying of exposure and disease. Having read this, and partly forgotten it, I was thinking, accidentally, of my own unsatisfactory life, doing as others do; and with that vision of the diggings still before me, I asked myself why *I* might not be washing some gold daily, though it were only the finest particles,—why *I* might not sink a shaft down to the gold within me, and work that mine. *There* is a Ballarat, a Bendigo for you,—what though it were a sulky-gully? At any rate, I might pursue some path, however solitary and narrow and crooked, in which I could walk with love and reverence. Wherever a man separates from the multitude, and goes his own way in this mood, there indeed is a fork in the road, though ordinary travellers may see only a gap in the paling. His solitary path across-lots will turn out the *higher way* of the two.

Men rush to California and Australia as if the true gold were to be found in that direction; but that is to go to the very opposite extreme to where it lies. They go prospecting farther and farther away from the true lead, and are most unfortunate when they think themselves most successful. Is not our *native* soil auriferous? Does not a stream from the golden mountains flow through our native valley? and has not this for more than geologic ages been bringing down the shining particles and forming the nuggets for us? Yet, strange to tell, if a digger steal away, prospecting for this true gold, into the unexplored solitudes around us, there is no danger that any will dog his steps, and endeavor to supplant him.

He may claim and undermine the whole valley even, both the cultivated and the uncultivated portions, his whole life long in peace, for no one will ever dispute his claim. They will not mind his cradles or his toms. He is not confined to a claim twelve feet square, as at Ballarat, but may mine anywhere, and wash the whole wide world in his tom.

Howitt says of the man who found the great nugget which weighed twenty-eight pounds, at the Bendigo diggings in Australia: "He soon began to drink; got a horse, and rode all about, generally at full gallop, and, when he met people, called out to inquire if they knew who he was, and then kindly informed them that he was 'the bloody wretch that had found the nugget.' At last he rode full speed against a tree, and nearly knocked his brains out." I think, however, there was no danger of that, for he had already knocked his brains out against the nugget. Howitt adds, "He is a hopelessly ruined man." But he is a type of the class. They are all fast men. Hear some of the names of the places where they dig: "Jackass Flat,"—"Sheep's-Head Gully,"—"Murderer's Bar," etc. Is there no satire in these names? Let them carry their ill-gotten wealth where they will, I am thinking it will still be "Jackass Flat," if not "Murderer's Bar," where they live.

The last resource of our energy has been the robbing of graveyards on the Isthmus of Darien, an enterprise which appears to be but in its infancy; for, according to late accounts, an act has passed its second reading in the legislature of New Granada, regulating this kind of mining; and a correspondent of the Tribune writes: "In the dry season, when the weather will permit of the country being properly prospected, no doubt other rich *guacas* [that is, graveyards] will be found." To emigrants he says: "Do not come before December; take the Isthmus route in preference to the Boca del Toro one; bring no useless baggage, and do not cumber yourself with a tent; but a good pair of blankets will be necessary; a pick, shovel, and axe of good material will be almost all that is required": advice which might have been taken from the Burker's Guide. And he concludes with this line in italics and small capitals: "If you are doing well at home, stay there," which may fairly be inter-

preted to mean, "If you are getting a good living by robbing graveyards at home, stay there."

But why go to California for a text? She is the child of New England, bred at her own school and church.

It is remarkable that among all the preachers there are so few moral teachers. The prophets are employed in excusing the ways of men. Most reverend seniors, the *illuminati* of the age, tell me, with a gracious, reminiscent smile, betwixt an aspiration and a shudder, not to be too tender about these things,—to lump all that, that is, make a lump of gold of it. The highest advice I have heard on these subjects was groveling. The burden of it was, —It is not worth your while to undertake to reform the world in this particular. Do not ask how your bread is buttered; it will make you sick, if you do, —and the like. A man had better starve at once than lose his innocence in the process of getting his bread. If within the sophisticated man there is not an unsophisticated one, then he is but one of the Devil's angels. As we grow old, we live more coarsely, we relax a little in our disciplines, and, to some extent, cease to obey our finest instincts. But we should be fastidious to the extreme of sanity, disregarding the gibes of those who are more unfortunate than ourselves.

In our science and philosophy, even, there is commonly no true and absolute account of things. The spirit of sect and bigotry has planted its hoof amid the stars. You have only to discuss the problem, whether the stars are inhabited or not, in order to discover it. Why must we daub the heavens as well as the earth? It was an unfortunate discovery that Dr. Kane was a Mason, and that Sir John Franklin was another. But it was a more cruel suggestion that possibly that was the reason why the former went in search of the latter. There is not a popular magazine in this country that would dare to print a child's thought on important subjects without comment. It must be submitted to the D.D.'s. I would it were the chickadee-dees.

You come from attending the funeral of mankind to attend to a natural phenomenon. A little thought is sexton to all the world.

I hardly know an intellectual man, even, who is so broad and truly liberal that you can think aloud in his society. Most with whom you endeavor to talk soon come to a stand against some institution in which they appear to hold stock,—that is, some particular, not universal, way of viewing things. They will continually thrust their own low roof, with its narrow skylight, between you and the sky, when it is the unobstructed heavens you would view. Get out of the way with your cobwebs, wash your windows, I say! In some lyceums they tell me that they have voted to exclude the subject of religion. But how do I know what their religion is, and when I am near to or far from it? I have walked into such an arena and done my best to make a clean breast of what religion I have experienced, and the audience never suspected what I was about. The lecture was as harmless as moonshine to them. Whereas, if I had read to them the biography of the greatest scamps in history, they might have thought that I had written the lives of the deacons of their church. Ordinarily, the inquiry is, Where did you come from? or, Where are you going? That was a more pertinent question which I overheard one of my auditors put to another once,—"What does he lecture for?" It made me quake in my shoes.

To speak impartially, the best men that I know are not serene, a world in themselves. For the most part, they dwell in forms, and flatter and study effect only more finely than the rest. We select granite for the underpinning of our houses and barns; we build fences of stone; but we do not ourselves rest on an underpinning of granitic truth, the lowest primitive rock. Our sills are rotten. What stuff is the man made of who is not coexistent in our thought with the purest and subtilest truth? I often accuse my finest acquaintances of an immense frivolity; for, while there are manners and compliments we do not meet, we do not teach one another the lessons of honesty and sincerity that the brutes do, or of steadiness and solidity that the rocks do. The fault is commonly mutual, however; for we do not habitually demand any more of each other. . . .

Just so hollow and ineffectual, for the most part, is our ordinary conversation. Surface meets surface. When our life ceases to be inward and private, conversation degenerates into mere gossip. We rarely meet a man who can tell us any news which he has not read in a newspaper, or been told by his neighbor; and, for the most part, the only difference between us and our fellow is that he has seen the newspaper, or been out to tea, and we have not. In proportion as our inward life fails, we go more constantly and desperately to the post-office. You may depend on it, that the poor fellow who walks away with the greatest number of letters proud of his extensive correspondence has not heard from himself this long while.

I do not know but it is too much to read one newspaper a week. I have tried it recently, and for so long it seems to me that I have not dwelt in my native region. The sun, the clouds, the snow, the trees say not so much to me. You cannot serve two masters. It requires more than a day's devotion to know and to possess the wealth of a day.

We may well be ashamed to tell what things we have read or heard in our day. I do not know why my news should be so trivial,—considering what one's dreams and expectations are, why the developments should be so paltry. The news we hear, for the most part, is not news to our genius. It is the stalest repetition. You are often tempted to ask why such stress is laid on a particular experience which you have had,—that, after twenty-five years, you should meet Hobbins, Registrar of Deeds, again on the sidewalk. Have you not budged an inch, then? Such is the daily news. Its facts appear to float in the atmosphere, insignificant as the sporules of fungi, and impinge on some neglected *thallus*, or surface of our minds, which affords a basis for them, and hence a parasitic growth. We should wash ourselves clean of such news. Of what consequence, though our planet explode, if there is no character involved in the explosion? In health we have not the least curiosity about such events. We do not live for idle amusement. I would not run round a corner to see the world blow up.

All summer, and far into the autumn, perchance, you unconsciously went by the newspapers and the news, and now you find it was because the morning and the evening were full of news to you. Your walks were full of incidents. You attended, not to the affairs of Europe, but to your own affairs in Massachusetts fields. If you chance to live and move and have your being in that thin stratum in which the events that make the news transpire,—thinner than the paper on which it is printed,—

then these things will fill the world for you; but if you soar above or dive below that plane, you cannot remember nor be reminded of them. Really to see the sun rise or go down every day, so to relate ourselves to a universal fact, would preserve us sane forever. Nations! What are nations? Tartars, and Huns, and Chinamen! Like insects, they swarm. The historian strives in vain to make them memorable. It is for want of a man that there are so many men. It is individuals that populate the world. Any man thinking may say with the Spirit of Lodin,—

> I look down from my height on nations,
> And they become ashes before me;—
> Calm is my dwelling in the clouds;
> Pleasant are the great fields of my rest.

Pray, let us live without being drawn by dogs, Esquimaux-fashion, tearing over hill and dale, and biting each other's ears.

Not without a slight shudder at the danger, I often perceive how near I had come to admitting into my mind the details of some trivial affair,— the news of the street; and I am astonished to observe how willing men are to lumber their minds with such rubbish,—to permit idle rumors and incidents of the most insignificant kind to intrude on ground which should be sacred to thought. Shall the mind be a public arena, where the affairs of the street and the gossip of the tea-table chiefly are discussed? Or shall it be a quarter of heaven itself,— an hypæthral temple, consecrated to the service of the gods? I find it so difficult to dispose of the few facts which to me are significant, that I hesitate to burden my attention with those which are insignificant, which only a divine mind could illustrate. Such is, for the most part, the news in newspapers and conversation. It is important to preserve the mind's chastity in this respect. Think of admitting the details of a single case of the criminal court into our thoughts, to stalk profanely through their very *sanctum sanctorum* for an hour, ay, for many hours! to make a very bar-room of the mind's inmost apartment, as if for so long the dust of the street had occupied us,—the very street itself, with all its travel, its bustle, and filth, had passed through our thoughts' shrine! Would it not be an intellectual and moral suicide? When I have

been compelled to sit spectator and auditor in a courtroom for some hours, and have seen my neighbors, who were not compelled, stealing in from time to time, and tiptoeing about with washed hands and faces, it has appeared to my mind's eye, that, when they took off their hats, their ears suddenly expanded into vast hoppers for sound, between which even their narrow heads were crowded. Like the vanes of windmills, they caught the broad but shallow stream of sound, which, after a few titillating gyrations in their coggy brains, passed out the other side. I wondered if, when they got home, they were as careful to wash their ears as before their hands and faces. It has seemed to me, at such a time, that the auditors and the witnesses, the jury and the counsel, the judge and the criminal at the bar,—if I may presume him guilty before he is convicted,—were all equally criminal, and a thunderbolt might be expected to descend and consume them all together.

By all kinds of traps and signboards, threatening the extreme penalty of the divine law, exclude such trespassers from the only ground which can be sacred to you. It is so hard to forget what it is worse than useless to remember! If I am to be a thoroughfare, I prefer that it be of the mountain-brooks, the Parnassian streams, and not the town-sewers. There is inspiration, that gossip which comes to the ear of the attentive mind from the courts of heaven. There is the profane and stale revelation of the bar-room and the police court. The same ear is fitted to receive both communications. Only the character of the hearer determines to which it shall be open, and to which closed. I believe that the mind can be permanently profaned by the habit of attending to trivial things, so that all our thoughts shall be tinged with triviality. Our very intellect shall be macadamized, as it were,—its foundation broken into fragments for the wheels of travel to roll over; and if you would know what will make the most durable pavement, surpassing rolled stones, spruce blocks, and asphaltum, you have only to look into some of our minds which have been subjected to this treatment so long.

If we have thus desecrated ourselves,—as who has not?—the remedy will be by wariness and devotion to reconsecrate ourselves, and make once more a fane of the mind. We should treat our minds, that is, ourselves, as innocent and ingenuous children, whose guardians we are, and be careful what objects and what subjects we thrust on their attention. Read not the Times. Read the Eternities. Conventionalities are at length as bad as impurities. Even the facts of science may dust the mind by their dryness, unless they are in a sense effaced each morning, or rather rendered fertile by the dews of fresh and living truth. Knowledge does not come to us by details, but in flashes of light 10 from heaven. Yes, every thought that passes through the mind helps to wear and tear it, and to deepen the ruts, which, as in the streets of Pompeii, evince how much it has been used. How many things there are concerning which we might well deliberate whether we had better know them,— had better let their peddling-carts be driven, even at the slowest trot or walk, over that bridge of glorious span by which we trust to pass at last from the farthest brink of time to the nearest shore of 20 eternity! Have we no culture, no refinement,— but skill only to live coarsely and serve the Devil? —to acquire a little worldly wealth, or fame, or liberty, and make a false show with it, as if we were all husk and shell, with no tender and living kernel to us? Shall our institutions be like those chestnut-burs which contain abortive nuts, perfect only to prick the fingers?

America is said to be the arena on which the battle of freedom is to be fought; but surely it 30 cannot be freedom in a merely political sense that is meant. Even if we grant that the American has freed himself from a political tyrant, he is still the slave of an economical and moral tyrant. Now that the republic—the *respublica*—has been settled, it is time to look after the *res-privata*,—the private state,—to see, as the Roman senate charged its consuls, "*ne quid res-privata detrimenti caperet*," that the private state receive no detriment.

Do we call this the land of the free? What is it 40 to be free from King George and continue the slaves of King Prejudice? What is it to be born free and not to live free? What is the value of any political freedom, but as a means to moral freedom? Is it a freedom to be slaves, or a freedom to be free, of which we boast? We are a nation of politicians, concerned about the outmost defenses only of freedom. It is our children's children who

may perchance be really free. We tax ourselves unjustly. There is a part of us which is not represented. It is taxation without representation. We quarter troops, we quarter fools and cattle of all sorts upon ourselves. We quarter our gross bodies on our poor souls, till the former eat up all the latter's substance.

With respect to a true culture and manhood, we are essentially provincial still, not metropolitan, —mere Jonathans. We are provincial, because we do not find at home our standards; because we do not worship truth, but the reflection of truth; because we are warped and narrowed by an exclusive devotion to trade and commerce and manufactures and agriculture and the like, which are but means, and not the end.

So is the English Parliament provincial. Mere country-bumpkins, they betray themselves, when any more important question arises for them to settle, the Irish question, for instance,—the English question why did I not say? Their natures are subdued to what they work in. Their "good breeding" respects only secondary objects. The finest manners in the world are awkwardness and fatuity when contrasted with a finer intelligence. They appear but as the fashions of past days,— mere courtliness, knee-buckles and small-clothes, out of date. It is the vice, but not the excellence of manners, that they are continually being deserted by the character; they are cast-off clothes or shells, claiming the respect which belonged to the living creature. You are presented with the shells instead of the meat, and it is no excuse generally, that, in the case of some fishes, the shells are of more worth than the meat. The man who thrusts his manners upon me does as if he were to insist on introducing me to his cabinet of curiosities, when I wished to see himself. It was not in this sense that the poet Decker called Christ "the first true gentleman that ever breathed." I repeat that in this sense the most splendid court in Christendom is provincial, having authority to consult about Transalpine interests only, and not the affairs of Rome. A prætor or proconsul would suffice to settle the questions which absorb the attention of the English Parliament and the American Congress.

Government and legislation! these I thought were respectable professions. We have heard of heaven-born Numas, Lycurguses, and Solons, in the history of the world, whose names at least may stand for ideal legislators; but think of legislating to regulate the breeding of slaves, or the exportation of tobacco! What have divine legislators to do with the exportation or the importation of tobacco? what humane ones with the breeding of slaves? Suppose you were to submit the question to any son of God,—and has He no children in the nineteenth century? is it a family which is extinct? —in what condition would you get it again? What shall a State like Virginia say for itself at the last day, in which these have been the principal, the staple productions? What ground is there for patriotism in such a State? I derive my facts from statistical tables which the States themselves have published. . . .

Lieutenant Herndon, whom our Government sent to explore the Amazon, and, it is said, to extend the area of slavery, observed that there was wanting there "an industrious and active population, who know what the comforts of life are, and who have artificial wants to draw out the great resources of the country." But what are the "artificial wants" to be encouraged? Not the love of luxuries, like the tobacco and slaves of, I believe, his native Virginia, nor the ice and granite and other material wealth of our native New England; nor are "the great resources of a country" that fertility or barrenness of soil which produces these. The chief want, in every State that I have been into, was a high and earnest purpose in its inhabitants. This alone draws out "the great resources" of Nature, and at last taxes her beyond her resources; for man naturally dies out of her. When we want culture more than potatoes, and illumination more than sugar-plums, then the great resources of a world are taxed and drawn out, and the result, or staple production, is, not slaves, nor operatives, but men,—those rare fruits called heroes, saints, poets, philosophers, and redeemers.

In short, as a snow-drift is formed where there is a lull in the wind, so, one would say, where there is a lull of truth, an institution springs up. But the truth blows right on over it, nevertheless, and at length blows it down.

What is called politics is comparatively something so superficial and inhuman, that practically I have never fairly recognized that it concerns me at all. The newspapers, I perceive, devote some of their columns specially to politics or government without charge; and this, one would say, is all that saves it; but as I love literature and to some extent the truth also, I never read those columns at any rate. I do not wish to blunt my sense of right so much. I have not got to answer for having read a single President's Message. A strange age of the world this, when empires, kingdoms, and republics come a-begging to a private man's door, and utter their complaints at his elbow! I cannot take up a newspaper but I find that some wretched government or other, hard pushed, and on its last legs, is interceding with me, the reader, to vote for it,— more importunate than an Italian beggar; and if I have a mind to look at its certificate, made, perchance, by some benevolent merchant's clerk, or the skipper that brought it over, for it cannot speak a word of English itself, I shall probably read of the eruption of some Vesuvius, or the overflowing of some Po, true or forged, which brought it into this condition. I do not hesitate, in such a case, to suggest work, or the almshouse; or why not keep its castle in silence, as I do commonly? The poor President, what with preserving his popularity and doing his duty, is completely bewildered. The newspapers are the ruling power. Any other government is reduced to a few marines at Fort Independence. If a man neglects to read the Daily Times, government will go down on its knees to him, for this is the only treason in these days.

Those things which now most engage the attention of men, as politics and the daily routine, are, it is true, vital functions of human society, but should be unconsciously performed, like the corresponding functions of the physical body. They are *infra*-human, a kind of vegetation. I sometimes awake to a half-consciousness of them going on about me, as a man may become conscious of some of the processes of digestion in a morbid state, and so have the dyspepsia, as it is called. It is as if a thinker submitted himself to be rasped by the great gizzard of creation. Politics is, as it were, the gizzard of society, full of grit and gravel, and the two political parties are its two opposite halves,—sometimes split into quarters, it may be, which grind on each other. Not only individuals, but states, have thus a confirmed dyspepsia, which expresses itself, you can imagine by what sort of eloquence. Thus our life is not altogether a forgetting, but also, alas! to a great extent, a remembering, of that which we should never have been conscious of, certainly not in our waking hours. Why should we not meet, not always as dyspeptics, to tell our bad dreams, but sometimes as *eu*peptics, to congratulate each other on the ever-glorious morning? I do not make an exorbitant demand, surely.

HENRY WADSWORTH LONGFELLOW (1807–1882)

HENRY WADSWORTH LONGFELLOW was the most widely read poet in English in the nineteenth century. His books enjoyed almost uninterrupted sale in the years of the War between the States, bringing comfort to countless homes. In England ten thousand copies of *The Courtship of Miles Standish* were sold in London the first day of issue, and Hawthorne, when American consul at Liverpool, observed that no other poet enjoyed anything like Longfellow's vogue. The admiring Emperor of Brazil tried his hand at a translation. By 1900 Longfellow's works had been translated in greater or less degree into Bohemian, Danish, Dutch, French, German, Hungarian, Italian, Portuguese, Russian, and Spanish. And all this good fortune came to the man who among all the nineteenth-century poets, according to Holmes, had attained the most fully rounded life, "beginning early with large promise, equaling every anticipation in its maturity, fertile and beautiful to its close in the ripeness of its well-filled years."

He was a great romanticist in the romantic age of Europe and America. His essential nature was but strengthened by his years in Germany, France, and Italy. In his lifetime his name became a sign of perfection in lyric beauty, in balladry, in the sonnet, and in narrative verse. *Evangeline* was the flawless story of its period. The religious Indian myth of *Hiawatha*, based on Schoolcraft, though modified and Christianized, spread over the continents. *The Courtship of Miles Standish* was almost the sole picture of Puritan life to millions of people. *Tales of a Wayside Inn*, written with an eye on Chaucer, brought old stories of two continents, newly told, to countless hearthsides where they were read aloud.

He had little of the fighting spirit of Whittier and Lowell, little of Whitman's urge to project himself as a symbol, and he could not evoke the intellectual excitement of Emerson. The fratricidal Civil War and the industrial strife of the next decades did not change his outlook. But he had moral strength and poetic beauty. His inspiration came from books, his materials from the past. At his worst, he turned these materials into mere records detached from life, to be savored and romanticized; at his best, he recreated life.

In his sentimental, gentle didacticism he was the image of that Victorian complacency which irritated the new generation in revolt during the early years of the twentieth century. In a Unitarian world where all people are saved, and in a romantic world where affairs are ever growing better, he represented a benign contentment which disgusted the critics of the new century. Even Hawthorne, his classmate at Bowdoin, not without malice, had said that Longfellow always reminded him of a sunflower; and decades later Bliss Perry, consciously indulging his wit, remarked that criticizing Longfellow would be like "carrying a rifle into a national park." The poet's works were relegated to high schools; he became the "children's poet."

But in more recent years Longfellow's reputation has risen somewhat again. H. M. Jones's bold essay of praise in 1931 sent young scholars to revising their colorless notes and rereading the poetry. And it was true, they found, that lucidity, melody, gentleness, and gracious humanity characterize Longfellow's works, that *Miles Standish* is "one of the astonishing reconstructions of American poetry," and that *Evangeline* has all the colorings of the English landscape school of painting. They also found in him fine qualities of the Renaissance and of the nineteenth century; for he had translated Dante with felicity, though he had not caught all the fire, and his romanticism was akin to that of Goethe, Uhland, and Carlyle. Only a world careless of tradition would wish to drop Longfellow and, with him, the world as he saw it.

Longfellow was born at Portland, Maine, February 27, 1807. On his maternal side his ancestry traced back to John and Priscilla Alden of the *Mayflower*. His father was a prominent attorney who became a judge and member of Congress, and his extensive library introduced his son to such writers as Dante, Cowper, Thomson, and Macpherson. As a boy Longfellow imitated Irving's prose; his earliest published poem, "The Battle of Lovell's Pond," appeared in *The Portland Gazette* when he was thirteen years of age. Other poems were published during his years as a student at Bowdoin College, from where he confided to his father "I most eagerly aspire after future eminence in literature," an aim which aroused no sympathy in the practical judge. Upon his graduation in 1825, fourth in a class of thirty-nine, he was offered a professorship in modern languages on condition that he study abroad, and he persuaded his father, who was a trustee of Bowdoin, to let him travel in Europe. He sailed in May, 1826, and visited France, Spain, Italy, and England for over three years, acquiring Old World culture. Of special value was his meeting in Italy with George W. Greene, who became his intimate friend; without Longfellow's letters to Greene much of the inward life of the poet would be lost to biographic record. He returned to Maine in August, 1829, and soon took up his classes at Bowdoin.

But life at Brunswick was much too limited for the ambitious, traveled young teacher. On his return the authorities had wanted him to start as an instructor; he had been forced to fight to keep his promised rank as professor, and he had been required to accept added duties as librarian. His marriage in 1831 to Mary Potter, of Portland, brought him great happiness, but did not make him content to remain at Bowdoin. Restlessly he turned to the writing of textbooks, and to recapturing his European experiences in *Outre-Mer*, which appeared serially in *The New England Magazine* in 1831–1832 and was revised and published in book form in 1835. He sought appointment elsewhere. For a time he entertained hope of a position in New York; gladly he accepted an invitation in 1834 to the chair of modern languages shortly to be vacated by George Ticknor at Harvard. Again he sailed for Europe, with his wife, leaving for England in April, 1835. Tragedy lay ahead. When leaving Scandinavia for the Netherlands Mrs. Longfellow fell ill, and died in childbirth at Rotterdam on November 19. Longfellow continued his studies at Heidelberg. Later, in Switzerland, he met lovely, dark-eyed Frances Appleton and her sister, daughters of a wealthy Boston merchant. Longfellow was twenty-six, Frances nineteen; before his return to Harvard he had formed a strong regard for her.

He began teaching at Harvard in 1836. In 1839 two of his books were published. One, *Voices of the Night*, issued by John Owen at Cambridge, established Longfellow as a poet. The other, *Hyperion: A Romance*, nearly wrecked him emotionally. Miss Appleton had not yielded to his tempestuous love, and he had thought he might win her by this veiled romance wherein she was the heroine. The thin disguise misled no one, and nothing could have angered her more. "It is the end," he wrote distractedly. But persistence and his personality won after seven years, and in 1843 she be-

came his wife. Her father purchased Craigie House in Cambridge for them. Here their six children were born; here they lived happily, attended by servants, enjoying the amenities of life—even the luxuries.

Teaching at Harvard had gone on apace, and with it his volumes of poetry: *Ballads and Other Poems* (1841); *Poems on Slavery* (1842), written probably in Europe and on the way home; *The Belfry of Bruges and Other Poems* (December, 1845); *Evangeline: A Tale of Acadie* (1847); a prose tale, *Kavanaugh* (1849); *The Seaside and the Fireside* (1849); *The Golden Legend* (1851). Increasingly he came to dislike the classroom, and he resigned his chair in 1854 to give full attention to his poetry. Then came *The Song of Hiawatha* (1855), and *The Courtship of Miles Standish and Other Poems* (1858). In the midst of happiness his wife died in 1861 as the result of an accidental burn, and Longfellow never fully recovered from this loss. He set himself to the task of finishing his translation of *The Divine Comedy of Dante Alighieri* (1865–1869), with the critical assistance of his friend Charles Eliot Norton. Meanwhile he issued the first part of *Tales of a Wayside Inn* (1863) and made his last visit to Europe in 1868–1869. He wrote poetic drama as well as lyrical verse in his closing years. In 1872 he completed *Christus: A Mystery*, in which are collected *The Golden Legend* of 1851, *The New England Tragedies* of 1868, and *The Divine Tragedy* of 1871. In 1875 he published *The Masque of Pandora*. *Michael Angelo* was posthumously issued in 1883. In addition to these dramas he continued writing lyrics, in which form his powers never failed. *Kéramos and Other Poems* was published in 1878, *Ultima Thule* in 1880, and *In the Harbor: Ultima Thule—Part II* in 1882.

His death in 1882 brought many extended essays of appreciation, and he had so fully entered the hearts of the English people that a bust in his memory was placed in Westminster Abbey. He and Lowell are the only American men of letters thus honored.

BIBLIOGRAPHY · *The Poetical Works of Henry Wadsworth Longfellow, with Bibliographical and Critical Notes* (6 vols., 1886) is the text here used. The authorized biography was written by the poet's youngest brother, Samuel Longfellow, being the *Life of Henry Wadsworth Longfellow, with Extracts from His Journals and Correspondence* (3 vols., 1891). To both sets were added the prose works to comprise *The Works of Henry Wadsworth Longfellow* (14 vols., 1886–1891), which text is here used for the review of *Twice-Told Tales*. The best single volume of poetry is H. E. Scudder, ed., *The Complete Poetical Works of Henry Wadsworth Longfellow* (1893). See also F. Greenslet, ed., *The Sonnets of*

Henry Wadsworth Longfellow (1907), and R. W. Pettengill, ed., Longfellow's Boyhood Poems (1925). For bibliography see L. S. Livingstone, A Bibliography of the First Editions in Book Form of the Writings of Henry Wadsworth Longfellow (1908), H. H. Clark, in Major American Poets (1936), and Odell Shepard, ed., Henry Wadsworth Longfellow (1934). Other biographical volumes include G. R. Carpenter, Henry Wadsworth Longfellow (1901); H. S. Gorman, A Victorian American: Henry Wadsworth Longfellow (1926); J. T. Hatfield, New Light on Longfellow (1933), discussing life at Harvard, and German influence, and "The Longfellow-Freiligrath Correspondence," PMLA, XLVIII (1933), 1223–1293; H. Hawthorne, The Poet of Craigie House . . . (1936), for popular reading; T. W. Higginson (a fellow townsman), Henry Wadsworth Longfellow (1902); C. L. Johnson, Professor Longfellow at Harvard (1944), and "Longfellow's Beginnings in Foreign Languages," New England Quarterly, XX (1947), 317–329; C. E. Norton (a close personal friend), Henry Wadsworth Longfellow: A Sketch of His Life (1907); Lawrance Thompson, Young Longfellow, 1807–1843 (1938).

Among the better critical studies are G. W. Allen, in American Prosody (1935); W. C. Bronson's article in the Dictionary of American Biography (1933); W. Charvat, "Longfellow's Income from His Writings, 1840–1852," Papers of the Biographical Society of America, XXXVIII (1944), 9–21; G. R. Elliott, "Gentle Shades of Longfellow," Southwest Review, X (1925), 34–53; J. DeLancey Ferguson's chapter on Longfellow in American Literature in Spain (1916); Emilio Goggio, "The Sources of Longfellow's Michael Angelo," Romanic Review, XXV (1934), 314–324; C. L. F. Gohdes, "Check List of Volumes by Longfellow Published in the British Isles during the Nineteenth Century," Bulletin of Bibliography, XVII, Nos. 3–5 (1940–1941), 46, 67–69, 93–96; M. G. Hill, "Some of Longfellow's Sources for the Second Part of Evangeline," PMLA, XXXI (1916), 161–180; J. T. Krumpelmann, "Longfellow's 'Golden Legend' and the 'Armer Heinrich' Theme in Modern German Literature," Journal of English and Germanic Philology, XXX (1926), 173–192; O. W. Long, "Henry Wadsworth Longfellow," in Literary Pioneers (1935), 159–198; J. P. Pritchard, "The Horatian Influence Upon Longfellow," American Literature, IV (1932), 22–29; C. S. Sanborn and Stellanova Osborn, Schoolcraft—Longfellow—Hiawatha (1942); W. L. Schramm, "Hiawatha and Its Predecessors," Philological Quarterly, XI (1932), 321–343; S. Thompson, "The Indian Legend of Hiawatha," PMLA, XXXVII (1922), 128–140.

A Psalm of Life

THIS POEM was written on July 26, 1838, as noted in Longfellow's journals. He later wrote, "I kept it some time in manuscript, unwilling to show it to anyone,

it being a voice from my inmost heart at a time when I was rallying from the depression of disappointment" (Thompson, Young Longfellow, pp. 270, 229–30). The poet, aged 31, was living in Craigie House, Cambridge, and was completing his second year as Smith Professor at Harvard, where he was in charge of the modern-language courses and delivering lectures in belles-lettres. He was trying to rally from the disappointment suffered by Miss Frances Appleton's temporary rebuke to his profession of love, and he was swimming in two currents of emotional turmoil, both rising from his European trip of 1835–1836. One current, expressed in "A Psalm of Life," shows the influence of Goethe and proclaims Longfellow's determination to lift himself from his disappointment and engage in the active life of the present, letting "the dead Past bury its dead." The other current was filled with the melancholy "night thoughts" of Novalis in Voices of the Night, with thoughts of the death of Mary Potter Longfellow, his young wife, in Rotterdam in 1835, and with his love of Miss Appleton; this is expressed in other poems of the period, including "Hymn to the Night," emphasizing the urge of his soul toward peace, retirement, memories, and mixed "sounds of sorrow and delight" in the "haunted chambers of the Night."

"A Psalm of Life" is the best-known of his early didactic poems, and was highly regarded by Whittier and others. It was first published in the Knickerbocker, September, 1838.

> Tell me not, in mournful numbers,
>   Life is but an empty dream!—
> For the soul is dead that slumbers,
>   And things are not what they seem.
>
> Life is real! Life is earnest!   5
>   And the grave is not its goal;
> Dust thou art, to dust returnest,
>   Was not spoken of the soul.
>
> Not enjoyment, and not sorrow,
>   Is our destined end or way;   10
> But to act, that each to-morrow
>   Find us farther than to-day.
>
> Art is long, and Time is fleeting,
>   And our hearts, though stout and brave,
> Still, like muffled drums, are beating   15
>   Funeral marches to the grave.

In the world's broad field of battle,
In the bivouac of Life,
Be not like dumb, driven cattle!
Be a hero in the strife! 20

Trust no Future, howe'er pleasant!
Let the dead Past bury its dead!
Act,—act in the living Present!
Heart within, and God o'erhead!

Lives of great men all remind us 25
We can make our lives sublime,
And, departing, leave behind us
Footprints on the sands of time;

Footprints, that perhaps another,
Sailing o'er life's solemn main, 30
A forlorn and shipwrecked brother,
Seeing, shall take heart again.

Let us, then, be up and doing,
With a heart for any fate;
Still achieving, still pursuing, 35
Learn to labor and to wait.

Midnight Mass for the Dying Year

WRITTEN on September 17, 1839, this poem appeared in the *Knickerbocker* for October, 1839, as "The Fifth Psalm," and was collected in *Voices of the Night* (1839). In submitting the poem to Lewis Gaylord Clark, editor of the *Knickerbocker*, Longfellow called it the best poem he had ever written. In his review of *Voices of the Night* in *Burton's Gentleman's Magazine* for February, 1840, Edgar Allan Poe accused Longfellow of plagiarism, citing Tennyson's "The Death of the Old Year" as the prototype. Longfellow, in a letter to a friend, denied knowledge of the existence of the poem by Tennyson. He did, however, own a volume of Tennyson containing the poem in question. (Thompson, *Young Longfellow*, pp. 306–07, 416).

Yes, the Year is growing old,
And his eye is pale and bleared!
Death, with frosty hand and cold,
Plucks the old man by the beard,
Sorely, sorely! 5

The leaves are falling, falling,
Solemnly and slow;

Caw! caw! the rooks are calling,
It is a sound of woe,
A sound of woe! 10

Through woods and mountain passes
The winds, like anthems, roll;
They are chanting solemn masses,
Singing, "Pray for this poor soul,
Pray, pray!" 15

And the hooded clouds, like friars,
Tell their beads in drops of rain,
And patter their doleful prayers;
But their prayers are all in vain,
All in vain! 20

There he stands in the foul weather,
The foolish, fond Old Year,
Crowned with wild flowers and with heather,
Like weak, despised Lear,
A king, a king! 25

Then comes the summer-like day,
Bids the old man rejoice!
His joy! his last! Oh, the old man gray
Loveth that ever-soft voice,
Gentle and low. 30

To the crimson woods he saith,
To the voice gentle and low
Of the soft air, like a daughter's breath,
"Pray do not mock me so!
Do not laugh at me!" 35

And now the sweet day is dead;
Cold in his arms it lies;
No stain from its breath is spread
Over the glassy skies,
No mist or stain! 40

Then, too, the Old Year dieth,
And the forests utter a moan,
Like the voice of one who crieth
In the wilderness alone,
"Vex not his ghost!" 45

Then comes, with an awful roar,
Gathering and sounding on,
The storm-sound from Labrador,
The wind Euroclydon,
The storm-wind! 50

Howl! howl! and from the forest
  Sweep the red leaves away!
Would the sins that thou abhorrest,
  O soul! could thus decay,
    And be swept away!   55

For there shall come a mightier blast,
  There shall be a darker day;
And the stars, from heaven down-cast
  Like red leaves be swept away!
    Kyrie, eleyson!   60
    Christe, eleyson!

Hymn to the Night

THIS POEM, one of Longfellow's finest lyrics, has been set to music. Poe, Bryant, and others expressed high admiration for it. The Greek motto, from the *Iliad*, "The welcome, the thrice-prayed for," is incorporated in the last stanza. Longfellow noted in the Riverside Edition that the poem was composed in the summer of 1839, "while sitting at my chamber window, on one of the balmiest nights of the year." The poem was published in *Voices of the Night* (1839). Not over fifty copies of the first printing of 900 remained after a fortnight; Longfellow announced a third edition in a letter to his father dated December 10, 1840; by 1857 the American sale had climbed to 43,500 (Samuel Longfellow, *Life*, I, 352–53, 379; II, 329).

'Ασπασίη, τρίλλιστος—ILIAD

I heard the trailing garments of the Night
  Sweep through her marble halls!
I saw her sable skirts all fringed with light
  From the celestial walls!

I felt her presence, by its spell of might,   5
  Stoop o'er me from above;
The calm, majestic presence of the Night,
  As of the one I love.

I heard the sounds of sorrow and delight,
  The manifold, soft chimes,   10
That fill the haunted chambers of the Night,
  Like some old poet's rhymes.

60–61. Kyrie . . . eleyson: These two lines may be freely translated "Lord, have mercy on us! Christ, have mercy on us!"

From the cool cisterns of the midnight air
  My spirit drank repose;
The fountain of perpetual peace flows there,—   15
  From those deep cisterns flows.

O holy Night! from thee I learn to bear
  What man has borne before!
Thou layest thy finger on the lips of Care,
  And they complain no more.   20

Peace! Peace! Orestes-like I breathe this prayer!
  Descend with broad-winged flight,
The welcome, the thrice-prayed for, the most fair,
  The best-beloved Night!

Serenade

THIS "Serenade" is from Act I of *The Spanish Student*, a drama written in 1840, published in *Graham's Magazine*, September-November, 1842, and as a book in 1843.

Stars of the summer night!
  Far in yon azure deeps,
Hide, hide your golden light!
  She sleeps!
My lady sleeps!   5
  Sleeps!

Moon of the summer night!
  Far down yon western steeps,
Sink, sink in silver light!
  She sleeps!   10
My lady sleeps!
  Sleeps!

Wind of the summer night!
  Where yonder woodbine creeps,
Fold, fold thy pinions light!   15
  She sleeps!
My lady sleeps!
  Sleeps!

Dreams of the summer night!
  Tell her, her lover keeps   20
Watch! while in slumbers light
  She sleeps!
My lady sleeps!
  Sleeps!

The Wreck of the Hesperus

Park Benjamin sent Longfellow $25 for publication of this poem in *The New World*, saying in his letter of January 7, 1840, that it would appear "Saturday next" (Samuel Longfellow, *Life*, I, 355). In his journal entry of December 17, 1839, Longfellow commented on the news of horrible shipwrecks off the coast, with twenty bodies washed ashore near Gloucester: "There is a reef called Norman's Woe where many of these took place; among others the schooner Hesperus [not the actual name]. Also the Sea-flower on Black Rock. I must write a ballad upon this; also two others,—'The Skeleton in Armor,' and 'Sir Humphrey Gilbert' " (ibid. I, 348–349). On December 30, 1839, he wrote in his Journal: ". . . I sat till twelve o'clock by my fire, smoking, when suddenly it came to my mind to write the 'Ballad of the Schooner Hesperus'; which I accordingly did. Then I went to bed, but could not sleep. New thoughts were running in my mind, and I got up to add them to the ballad. It was three by the clock. I then went to bed and fell asleep. . . . It did not come into my mind by lines but by stanzas" (ibid. I, 350). The poem was first collected in *Ballads and Other Poems* (1841); by 1857 American editions of this volume totaled 40,740 copies (ibid. II, 329).

It was the schooner Hesperus,
  That sailed the wintry sea;
And the skipper had taken his little daughtèr,
  To bear him company.

Blue were her eyes as the fairy-flax,   5
  Her cheeks like the dawn of day,
And her bosom white as the hawthorn buds,
  That ope in the month of May.

The skipper he stood beside the helm,
  His pipe was in his mouth,   10
And he watched how the veering flaw did blow
  The smoke now West, now South.

Then up and spake an old Sailòr,
  Had sailed to the Spanish Main,
"I pray thee, put into yonder port,   15
  For I fear a hurricane.

"Last night, the moon had a golden ring,
  And to-night no moon we see!"
The skipper, he blew a whiff from his pipe,
  And a scornful laugh laughed he.   20

Colder and louder blew the wind,
  A gale from the Northeast,
The snow fell hissing in the brine,
  And the billows frothed like yeast.

Down came the storm, and smote amain   25
  The vessel in its strength;
She shuddered and paused, like a frighted steed,
  Then leaped her cable's length.

"Come hither! come hither! my little daughtèr,
  And do not tremble so;   30
For I can weather the roughest gale
  That ever wind did blow."

He wrapped her warm in his seaman's coat
  Against the stinging blast;
He cut a rope from a broken spar,   35
  And bound her to the mast.

"O father! I hear the church-bells ring,
  Oh say, what may it be?"
"'Tis a fog-bell on a rock-bound coast!"—
  And he steered for the open sea.   40

"O father! I hear the sound of guns,
  Oh say, what may it be?"
"Some ship in distress, that cannot live
  In such an angry sea!"

"O father! I see a gleaming light,   45
  Oh say, what may it be?"
But the father answered never a word,
  A frozen corpse was he.

Lashed to the helm, all stiff and stark,
  With his face turned to the skies,   50
The lantern gleamed through the gleaming snow
  On his fixed and glassy eyes.

Then the maiden clasped her hands and prayed
  That savèd she might be;
And she thought of Christ, who stilled the wave,   55
  On the Lake of Galilee.

And fast through the midnight dark and drear,
  Through the whistling sleet and snow,
Like a sheeted ghost, the vessel swept
  Tow'rds the reef of Norman's Woe.   60

And ever the fitful gusts between
  A sound came from the land;
It was the sound of the trampling surf
  On the rocks and the hard sea-sand.

The breakers were right beneath her bows,   65
  She drifted a dreary wreck,
And a whooping billow swept the crew
  Like icicles from her deck.

She struck where the white and fleecy waves
  Looked soft as carded wool,   70
But the cruel rocks, they gored her side
  Like the horns of an angry bull.

Her rattling shrouds, all sheathed in ice,
  With the masts went by the board;
Like a vessel of glass, she stove and sank,   75
  Ho! ho! the breakers roared!

At daybreak, on the bleak sea-beach,
  A fisherman stood aghast,
To see the form of a maiden fair,
  Lashed close to a drifting mast.   80

The salt sea was frozen on her breast,
  The salt tears in her eyes;
And he saw her hair, like the brown sea-weed,
  On the billows fall and rise.

Such was the wreck of the Hesperus,   85
  In the midnight and the snow!
Christ save us all from a death like this,
  On the reef of Norman's Woe!

Mezzo Cammin

THIS SONNET, though written at Boppard on the
Rhine in August, 1842, was first published by his
brother Samuel in the *Life* (1886), four years after
the poet's death. Longfellow was on a vacation in the
hope of improving both health and spirits. Highly
subjective, the poem probably refers to his mourning
the death of his first wife, and possibly also to his
distraction arising from the continued aloofness of
Miss Appleton. The title is taken from the first line
of Dante's *Inferno*: *Nel mezzo del cammin di nostra
vita*—"In the midway of the road of our life."

Half of my life is gone, and I have let
  The years slip from me and have not fulfilled

The aspiration of my youth, to build
  Some tower of song with lofty parapet.
Not indolence, nor pleasure, nor the fret   5
  Of restless passions that would not be stilled,
  But sorrow, and a care that almost killed,
Kept me from what I may accomplish yet;

Though, half-way up the hill, I see the Past
  Lying beneath me with its sounds and sights,—
  A city in the twilight dim and vast,   11
With smoking roofs, soft bells, and gleaming
    lights,—
  And hear above me on the autumnal blast
  The cataract of Death far thundering from the
    heights.

Nuremberg

ON SEPTEMBER 24, 1842, in a letter to his friend, the
young German poet Ferdinand Freiligrath, Longfellow wrote with rapture of his current visit in Nuremberg. On that day he saw "the best works of Albrecht
Dürer," and in Hans Sachs's old residence, now an
alehouse, he and a companion "drank a tankard of ale
to the memory of the poet, reading at the same time
from a volume of his works . . ." (Samuel Longfellow,
Life, I, 437). The poem was first published in *Graham's
Magazine*, June, 1844; collected in *The Belfry of
Bruges, and Other Poems.*

In the valley of the Pegnitz, where across broad
    meadow-lands
Rise the blue Franconian mountains, Nuremberg,
    the ancient, stands.

Quaint old town of toil and traffic, quaint old town
    of art and song,
Memories haunt thy pointed gables, like the rooks
    that round them throng:

Memories of the Middle Ages, when the emperors,
    rough and bold,   5
Had their dwelling in thy castle, time-defying,
    centuries old;

And thy brave and thrifty burghers boasted, in
    their uncouth rhyme,
That their great imperial city stretched its hand
    through every clime.

701

In the court-yard of the castle, bound with many
　an iron band,
Stands the mighty linden planted by Queen
　Cunigunde's hand;　　　　　　　　　　　10

On the square the oriel window, where in old heroic
　days
Sat the poet Melchior singing Kaiser Maximilian's
　praise.

Everywhere I see around me rise the wondrous
　world of Art:
Fountains wrought with richest sculpture standing
　in the common mart;

And above cathedral doorways saints and bishops
　carved in stone,　　　　　　　　　　　15
By a former age commissioned as apostles to our
　own.

In the church of sainted Sebald sleeps enshrined
　his holy dust,
And in bronze the Twelve Apostles guard from age
　to age their trust;

In the church of sainted Lawrence stands a pix of
　sculpture rare,
Like the foamy sheaf of fountains, rising through
　the painted air.　　　　　　　　　　　20

Here, when Art was still religion, with a simple,
　reverent heart,
Lived and labored Albrecht Dürer, the Evangelist
　of Art;

Hence in silence and in sorrow, toiling still with
　busy hand,
Like an emigrant he wandered, seeking for the
　Better Land.

Emigravit is the inscription on the tombstone where
　he lies;　　　　　　　　　　　25
Dead he is not, but departed,—for the artist never
　dies.

Fairer seems the ancient city, and the sunshine
　seems more fair,
That he once has trod its pavement, that he once
　has breathed its air!

Through these streets so broad and stately, these
　obscure and dismal lanes,
Walked of yore the Mastersingers, chanting rude
　poetic strains.　　　　　　　　　　　30

From remote and sunless suburbs came they to the
　friendly guild,
Building nests in Fame's great temple, as in spouts
　the swallows build.

As the weaver plied the shuttle, wove he too the
　mystic rhyme,
And the smith his iron measures hammered to the
　anvil's chime;

Thanking God, whose boundless wisdom makes the
　flowers of poesy bloom　　　　　　　　35
In the forge's dust and cinders, in the tissues of
　the loom.

Here Hans Sachs, the cobbler-poet, laureate of the
　gentle craft,
Wisest of the Twelve Wise Masters, in huge folios
　sang and laughed.

But his house is now an ale-house, with a nicely
　sanded floor,
And a garland in the window, and his face above
　the door;　　　　　　　　　　　40

Painted by some humble artist, as in Adam Pusch-
　man's song,
As the old man gray and dove-like, with his great
　beard white and long.

And at night the swart mechanic comes to drown
　his cark and care,
Quaffing ale from pewter tankards, in the master's
　antique chair.

Vanished is the ancient splendor, and before my
　dreamy eye　　　　　　　　　　　45
Wave these mingled shapes and figures, like a
　faded tapestry.

Not thy Councils, not thy Kaisers, win for thee the
　world's regard;
But thy painter, Albrecht Dürer, and Hans Sachs
　thy cobbler bard.

Thus, O Nuremberg, a wanderer from a region far
    away,
As he paced thy streets and court-yards, sang in
    thought his careless lay: 50

Gathering from the pavement's crevice, as a
    floweret of the soil,
The nobility of labor,—the long pedigree of toil.

The Day Is Done

PROEM to a volume of poems selected by Longfellow,
The Waif (1844).   *night poem*

The day is done, and the darkness
    Falls from the wings of Night,
As a feather is wafted downward
    From an eagle in his flight.

I see the lights of the village   5
    Gleam through the rain and the mist,
And a feeling of sadness comes o'er me
    That my soul cannot resist:

A feeling of sadness and longing,
    That is not akin to pain,   10
And resembles sorrow only
    As the mist resembles the rain.

Come, read to me some poem,
    Some simple and heartfelt lay,
That shall soothe this restless feeling,   15
    And banish the thoughts of day.

Not from the grand old masters,
    Not from the bards sublime,
Whose distant footsteps echo
    Through the corridors of Time.   20

For, like strains of martial music,
    Their mighty thoughts suggest
Life's endless toil and endeavor;
    And to-night I long for rest.

Read from some humbler poet,   25
    Whose songs gushed from his heart,
As showers from the clouds of summer,
    Or tears from the eyelids start;

Who, through long days of labor,
    And nights devoid of ease,   30
Still heard in his soul the music
    Of wonderful melodies.

Such songs have power to quiet
    The restless pulse of care,
And come like the benediction   35
    That follows after prayer.

Then read from the treasured volume
    The poem of thy choice,
And lend to the rhyme of the poet
    The beauty of thy voice.

And the night shall be filled with music,
    And the cares, that infest the day,
Shall fold their tents, like the Arabs,
    And as silently steal away.

The Arsenal at Springfield

ON HIS WEDDING JOURNEY in the summer of 1843
Longfellow passed through Springfield, Massachusetts,
and visited the United States arsenal there, in company
with Charles Sumner. "While Mr. Sumner was endeavoring," said Samuel Longfellow, "to impress
upon the attendant that the money expended upon
these weapons of war would have been much better
spent upon a great library, Mrs. Longfellow pleased
her husband by remarking how like an organ looked
the ranged and shining gun-barrels which covered the
walls from floor to ceiling, and suggesting what mournful music Death would bring from them. 'We grew
quite warlike against war,' she wrote, 'and I urged H.
to write a peace poem.'" The poem was written some
months later and published in *Graham's Magazine*,
April, 1844. Mr. Longfellow in writing of it to Mr.
Sumner noted, "On the back of my peace poem is a
paper called *The Battle-Grounds of America*. This
is the reverse of the medal."

This is the Arsenal. From floor to ceiling,
    Like a huge organ, rise the burnished arms;
But from their silent pipes no anthem pealing
    Startles the villages with strange alarms.

Ah! what a sound will rise, how wild and dreary,   5
    When the death-angel touches those swift keys!
What loud lament and dismal Miserere
    Will mingle with their awful symphonies!

I hear even now the infinite fierce chorus,
  The cries of agony, the endless groan,   10
Which, through the ages that have gone before us,
  In long reverberations reach our own.

On helm and harness rings the Saxon hammer,
  Through Cimbric forest roars the Norseman's
      song,
And loud, amid the universal clamor,   15
  O'er distant deserts sounds the Tartar gong.

I hear the Florentine, who from his palace
  Wheels out his battle-bell with dreadful din,
And Aztec priests upon their teocallis
  Beat the wild war-drums made of serpent's
      skin;   20

The tumult of each sacked and burning village;
  The shout that every prayer for mercy drowns;
The soldiers' revels in the midst of pillage;
  The wail of famine in beleaguered towns;

The bursting shell, the gateway wrenched asunder,
  The rattling musketry, the clashing blade;   26
And ever and anon, in tones of thunder
  The diapason of the cannonade.

Is it, O man, with such discordant noises,
  With such accursed instruments as these,   30
Thou drownest Nature's sweet and kindly voices,
  And jarrest the celestial harmonies?

Were half the power, that fills the world with
    terror,
  Were half the wealth bestowed on camps and
      courts,
Given to redeem the human mind from error,   35
  There were no need of arsenals or forts:

The warrior's name would be a name abhorred!
  And every nation, that should lift again
Its hand against a brother, on its forehead
  Would wear forevermore the curse of Cain!   40

Down the dark future, through long generations,
  The echoing sounds grow fainter and then cease;
And like a bell, with solemn, sweet vibrations,
  I hear once more the voice of Christ say, "Peace!"

Peace! and no longer from its brazen portals   45
  The blast of War's great organ shakes the skies!
But beautiful as songs of the immortals,
  The holy melodies of love arise.

The Evening Star

SAMUEL LONGFELLOW (*Life*, II, 24) refers to this poem
as being the "only 'love-poem' among Mr. Longfellow's
verses," and quotes from the poet's Journal: "[October]
30th [1845]. The Indian summer still in its glory.
Wrote the sonnet 'Hesperus' in the rustic seat of the
old apple-tree." Published in *The Belfry of Bruges, and
Other Poems* (1845).

Lo! in the painted oriel of the West,
  Whose panes the sunken sun incarnadines,
  Like a fair lady at her casement, shines
The evening star, the star of love and rest!
And then anon she doth herself divest   5
  Of all her radiant garments, and reclines
  Behind the sombre screen of yonder pines,
With slumber and soft dreams of love oppressed.
O my beloved, my sweet Hesperus!
  My morning and my evening star of love!   10
My best and gentlest lady! even thus,
As that fair planet in the sky above,
  Dost thou retire unto thy rest at night,
  And from thy darkened window fades the light.

The Song of Hiawatha

ON JUNE 5, 1854, Longfellow noted in his journal that
he was reading the Finnish epic *Kalevala* with "delight,"
and by the 22nd he had "at length hit upon a plan for a
poem on the American Indians," to be written so as
"to weave together their beautiful traditions as a
whole," using the form of the *Kalevala*. On the 28th
he expressed his preference for "Hiawatha" over "Man-
abozho," another name for the same hero (S. Longfellow, *Life*, II, 273). He set to work with zeal, and on
March 21, 1855, finished the poem. On November 10
he wrote: "Hiawatha published to-day, . . . more than
four thousnad out of the five of the first edition are
sold"; and by December an English publisher reported the sale of 11,800 in England (ibid. II, 292). In
the meantime, Lowell had been chosen as Longfellow's
successor to the Harvard professorship in modern
languages, and Longfellow was happy in his resignation
from a chair of which he had grown weary. The poem

continued to sell well. It was translated into several European languages, and as late as March, 1860, the American publisher was selling 2,000 copies yearly, though 50,000 had already been sold (ibid. II, 400). For the sensational success of the poem in England, see C. L. F. Gohdes, *American Literature in Nineteenth-Century England* (1944).

In a note to the poem Longfellow wrote, "This Indian Edda—if I may so call it—is founded on a tradition, prevalent among the North American Indians, of a personage of miraculous birth, who was sent among them to clear their rivers, forests, and fishing-grounds, and to teach them the arts of peace. . . . Mr. Schoolcraft gives an account of him in his *Algic Researches*, I, 134; and in his *History, Condition, and Prospects of the Indian Tribes of the United States*, Part III, 314, may be found the Iroquois form of the tradition. . . . The scene of the poem is among the Ojibways on the southern shore of Lake Superior, in the region between the Pictured Rocks and the Grand Sable."

In the poem Longfellow treats of the prophecy of the coming of Hiawatha, prophet and deliverer, his miraculous birth, his early valor, his gift of corn to the people, his building of the birch-bark canoe, his slaying of the king of fishes, his great duel with the magician Pearl-Feather, his wooing of Minnehaha and their marriage, his pursuit of Pau-Puk-Keewis the evildoer, his endurance of the famine and the death of Minnehaha, his meeting with the white man, and his departure to the Land of the Hereafter. The scenes have lent themselves to pageantry on a number of occasions; in 1900 the Ojibways invited the Longfellow family to a performance, saying the memory of their tribe would live forever through the poem (T. W. Higginson, *Henry Wadsworth Longfellow*, 318).

V · Hiawatha's Fasting

You shall hear how Hiawatha
Prayed and fasted in the forest,
Not for greater skill in hunting,
Not for greater craft in fishing,
Not for triumphs in the battle, 5
And renown among the warriors,
But for profit of the people,
For advantage of the nations.

First he built a lodge for fasting,
Built a wigwam in the forest, 10
By the shining Big-Sea-Water,
In the blithe and pleasant Spring-time,
In the Moon of Leaves he built it,

And, with dreams and visions many,
Seven whole days and nights he fasted. 15
On the first day of his fasting
Through the leafy woods he wandered;
Saw the deer start from the thicket,
Saw the rabbit in his burrow,
Heard the pheasant, Bena, drumming, 20
Heard the squirrel, Adjidaumo,
Rattling in his hoard of acorns,
Saw the pigeon, the Omeme,
Building nests among the pine-trees,
And in flocks the wild-goose, Wawa, 25
Flying to the fen-lands northward,
Whirring, wailing far above him.
"Master of Life!" he cried, desponding,
"Must our lives depend on these things?"
On the next day of his fasting 30
By the river's brink he wandered,
Through the Muskoday, the meadow,
Saw the wild rice, Mahnomonee,
Saw the blueberry, Meenahga,
And the strawberry, Odahmin, 35
And the gooseberry, Shahbomin,
And the grape-vine, the Bemahgut,
Trailing o'er the alder-branches,
Filling all the air with fragrance!
"Master of Life!" he cried, desponding, 40
"Must our lives depend on these things?"
On the third day of his fasting
By the lake he sat and pondered,
By the still, transparent water;
Saw the sturgeon, Nahma, leaping, 45
Scattering drops like beads of wampum,
Saw the yellow perch, the Sahwa,
Like a sunbeam in the water,
Saw the pike, the Maskenozha,
And the herring, Okahahwis, 50
And the Shawgashee, the craw-fish!
"Master of Life!" he cried, desponding,
"Must our lives depend on these things?"
On the fourth day of his fasting
In his lodge he lay exhausted; 55
From his couch of leaves and branches
Gazing with half-open eyelids,
Full of shadowy dreams and visions,
On the dizzy, swimming landscape,
On the gleaming of the water, 60
On the splendor of the sunset.

And he saw a youth approaching,
Dressed in garments green and yellow,
Coming through the purple twilight,
Through the splendor of the sunset;   65
Plumes of green bent o'er his forehead,
And his hair was soft and golden.

Standing at the open doorway,
Long he looked at Hiawatha,
Looked with pity and compassion   70
On his wasted form and features,
And, in accents like the sighing
Of the South-Wind in the tree-tops,
Said he, "O my Hiawatha!
All your prayers are heard in heaven,   75
For you pray not like the others;
Not for greater skill in hunting,
Not for greater craft in fishing,
Not for triumph in the battle,
Nor renown among the warriors,   80
But for profit of the people,
For advantage of the nations.

"From the Master of Life descending,
I, the friend of man, Mondamin,
Come to warn you and instruct you,   85
How by struggle and by labor
You shall gain what you have prayed for.
Rise up from your bed of branches,
Rise, O youth, and wrestle with me!"

Faint with famine, Hiawatha   90
Started from his bed of branches,
From the twilight of his wigwam
Forth into the flush of sunset
Came, and wrestled with Mondamin;
At his touch he felt new courage   95
Throbbing in his brain and bosom,
Felt new life and hope and vigor
Run through every nerve and fibre.

So they wrestled there together
In the glory of the sunset,   100
And the more they strove and struggled,
Stronger still grew Hiawatha;
Till the darkness fell around them,
And the heron, the Shuh-shuh-gah,
From her nest among the pine-trees,   105
Gave a cry of lamentation,
Gave a scream of pain and famine.

"'Tis enough!" then said Mondamin,
Smiling upon Hiawatha,

"But to-morrow, when the sun sets,   110
I will come again to try you."
And he vanished, and was seen not;
Whether sinking as the rain sinks,
Whether rising as the mists rise,
Hiawatha saw not, knew not,   115
Only saw that he had vanished,
Leaving him alone and fainting,
With the misty lake below him,
And the reeling stars above him.

On the morrow and the next day,   120
When the sun through heaven descending,
Like a red and burning cinder
From the hearth of the Great Spirit,
Fell into the western waters,
Came Mondamin for the trial,   125
For the strife with Hiawatha;
Came as silent as the dew comes,
From the empty air appearing,
Into empty air returning,
Taking shape when earth it touches,   130
But invisible to all men
In its coming and its going.

Thrice they wrestled there together
In the glory of the sunset,
Till the darkness fell around them,   135
Till the heron, the Shuh-shuh-gah,
From her nest among the pine-trees,
Uttered her loud cry of famine,
And Mondamin paused to listen.

Tall and beautiful he stood there,   140
In his garments green and yellow;
To and fro his plumes above him
Waved and nodded with his breathing,
And the sweat of the encounter
Stood like drops of dew upon him.   145

And he cried, "O Hiawatha!
Bravely have you wrestled with me,
Thrice have wrestled stoutly with me,
And the Master of Life, who sees us,
He will give to you the triumph!"   150

Then he smiled, and said: "To-morrow
Is the last day of your conflict,
Is the last day of your fasting.
You will conquer and o'ercome me;
Make a bed for me to lie in,   155
Where the rain may fall upon me,
Where the sun may come and warm me;

Strip these garments, green and yellow,
Strip this nodding plumage from me,
Lay me in the earth, and make it   160
Soft and loose and light above me.

    "Let no hand disturb my slumber,
Let no weed nor worm molest me,
Let not Kahgahgee, the raven,
Come to haunt me and molest me,   165
Only come yourself to watch me,
Till I wake, and start, and quicken,
Till I leap into the sunshine."

    And thus saying, he departed;
Peacefully slept Hiawatha,   170
But he heard the Wawonaissa,
Heard the whippoorwill complaining,
Perched upon his lonely wigwam;
Heard the rushing Sebowisha,
Heard the rivulet rippling near him,   175
Talking to the darksome forest;
Heard the sighing of the branches,
As they lifted and subsided
At the passing of the night-wind,
Heard them, as one hears in slumber   180
Far-off murmurs, dreamy whispers:
Peacefully slept Hiawatha.

    On the morrow came Nokomis,
On the seventh day of his fasting,
Came with food for Hiawatha,   185
Came imploring and bewailing,
Lest his hunger should o'ercome him,
Lest his fasting should be fatal.

    But he tasted not, and touched not,
Only said to her, "Nokomis,   190
Wait until the sun is setting,
Till the darkness falls around us,
Till the heron, the Shuh-shuh-gah,
Crying from the desolate marshes,
Tells us that the day is ended."   195

    Homeward weeping went Nokomis,
Sorrowing for her Hiawatha,
Fearing lest his strength should fail him,
Lest his fasting should be fatal.
He meanwhile sat weary waiting   200
For the coming of Mondamin,
Till the shadows, pointing eastward,
Lengthened over field and forest,
Till the sun dropped from the heaven,
Floating on the waters westward,   205

As a red leaf in the Autumn
Falls and floats upon the water,
Falls and sinks into its bosom.

    And behold! the young Mondamin,
With his soft and shining tresses,   210
With his garments green and yellow,
With his long and glossy plumage,
Stood and beckoned at the doorway.
And as one in slumber walking,
Pale and haggard, but undaunted,   215
From the wigwam Hiawatha
Came and wrestled with Mondamin.

    Round about him spun the landscape,
Sky and forest reeled together,
And his strong heart leaped within him,   220
As the sturgeon leaps and struggles
In a net to break its meshes.
Like a ring of fire around him
Blazed and flared the red horizon,
And a hundred suns seemed looking   225
At the combat of the wrestlers.

    Suddenly upon the greensward
All alone stood Hiawatha,
Panting with his wild exertion,
Palpitating with the struggle;   230
And before him breathless, lifeless,
Lay the youth, with hair dishevelled,
Plumage torn, and garments tattered,
Dead he lay there in the sunset.

    And victorious Hiawatha   235
Made the grave as he commanded,
Stripped the garments from Mondamin,
Stripped his tattered plumage from him,
Laid him in the earth, and made it
Soft and loose and light above him;   240
And the heron, the Shuh-shuh-gah,
From the melancholy moorlands,
Gave a cry of lamentation,
Gave a cry of pain and anguish!

    Homeward then went Hiawatha   245
To the lodge of old Nokomis,
And the seven days of his fasting
Were accomplished and completed.
But the place was not forgotten
Where he wrestled with Mondamin;   250
Nor forgotten nor neglected
Was the grave where lay Mondamin,
Sleeping in the rain and sunshine,

Where his scattered plumes and garments
Faded in the rain and sunshine. 255

    Day by day did Hiawatha
Go to wait and watch beside it;
Kept the dark mould soft above it,
Kept it clean from weeds and insects,
Drove away, with scoffs and shoutings, 260
Kahgahgee, the king of ravens.

    Till at length a small green feather
From the earth shot slowly upward,
Then another and another,
And before the Summer ended 265
Stood the maize in all its beauty,
With its shining robes about it,
And its long, soft, yellow tresses;
And in rapture Hiawatha
Cried aloud, "It is Mondamin! 270
Yes, the friend of man, Mondamin!"

    Then he called to old Nokomis
And Iagoo, the great boaster,
Showed them where the maize was growing,
Told them of his wondrous vision, 275
Of his wrestling and his triumph,
Of this new gift to the nations,
Which should be their food forever.

    And still later, when the Autumn
Changed the long, green leaves to yellow, 280
And the soft and juicy kernels
Grew like wampum hard and yellow,
Then the ripened ears he gathered,
Stripped the withered husks from off them,
As he once had stripped the wrestler, 285
Gave the first Feast of Mondamin,
And made known unto the people
This new gift of the Great Spirit.

My Lost Youth

LONGFELLOW was forty-eight years of age. "A day of
pain; cowering over the fire," he wrote on March 29,
1855. "At night as I lie in bed, a poem comes into my
mind,—a memory of Portland, my native town, the
city by the sea" (S. Longfellow, *Life*, II, 284). Two
lines from Dante's *Inferno* were in his mind:

> Sitteth the city wherein I was born
> Upon the seashore.

On the following day he wrote the poem, using as a
refrain two lines from a Lapland song:

A boy's will is the wind's will,
And the thoughts of youth are long, long thoughts.

J. T. Hatfield (*PMLA*, XLV, 1188–1192) noted that
the original sense of the lines implied "hesitating, uncertain," whereas Longfellow's lines suggest "out-
reaching visions and dreams." The poem was published
in *Putnam's Monthly* for August, 1855, and collected in
The Courtship of Miles Standish, and Other Poems (1858).

Often I think of the beautiful town
   That is seated by the sea;
Often in thought go up and down
The pleasant streets of that dear old town,
   And my youth comes back to me. 5
     And a verse of a Lapland song
     Is haunting my memory still:
     "A boy's will is the wind's will,
And the thoughts of youth are long, long thoughts."

I can see the shadowy lines of its trees, 10
   And catch, in sudden gleams,
The sheen of the far-surrounding seas,
And islands that were the Hesperides
   Of all my boyish dreams.
     And the burden of that old song, 15
     It murmurs and whispers still:
     "A boy's will is the wind's will,
And the thoughts of youth are long, long thoughts."

I remember the black wharves and the slips,
   And the sea-tides tossing free; 20
And Spanish sailors with bearded lips,
And the beauty and mystery of the ships,
   And the magic of the sea.
     And the voice of that wayward song
     Is singing and saying still: 25
     "A boy's will is the wind's will,
And the thoughts of youth are long, long thoughts."

I remember the bulwarks by the shore,
   And the fort upon the hill;
The sunrise gun, with its hollow roar, 30
The drum-beat repeated o'er and o'er,
   And the bugle wild and shrill.
     And the music of that old song
     Throbs in my memory still:
     "A boy's will is the wind's will, 35
And the thoughts of youth are long, long thoughts."

I remember the sea-fight far away,
  How it thundered o'er the tide!
And the dead captains, as they lay
In their graves, o'erlooking the tranquil bay   40
  Where they in battle died.
    And the sound of that mournful song
    Goes through me with a thrill:
    "A boy's will is the wind's will,
And the thoughts of youth are long, long thoughts."

I can see the breezy dome of groves,   46
  The shadows of Deering's Woods;
And the friendships old and the early loves
Come back with a Sabbath sound, as of doves
  In quiet neighborhoods.   50
    And the verse of that sweet old song,
    It flutters and murmurs still:
    "A boy's will is the wind's will,
And the thoughts of youth are long, long thoughts."

I remember the gleams and glooms that dart   55
  Across the school-boy's brain;
The song and the silence in the heart,
That in part are prophecies, and in part
  Are longings wild and vain.
    And the voice of that fitful song   60
    Sings on, and is never still:
    "A boy's will is the wind's will,
And the thoughts of youth are long, long thoughts."

There are things of which I may not speak;
  There are dreams that cannot die;   65
There are thoughts that make the strong heart
    weak,
And bring a pallor into the cheek,
  And a mist before the eye.
    And the words of that fatal song
    Come over me like a chill: 70
    "A boy's will is the wind's will,
And the thoughts of youth are long, long thoughts."

Strange to me now are the forms I meet
  When I visit the dear old town;
But the native air is pure and sweet,   75
And the trees that o'ershadow each well-known
    street,
  As they balance up and down,
    Are singing the beautiful song,
    Are sighing and whispering still:

"A boy's will is the wind's will,   80
And the thoughts of youth are long, long thoughts."

And Deering's Woods are fresh and fair,
  And with joy that is almost pain
My heart goes back to wander there,
And among the dreams of the days that were,   85
  I find my lost youth again.
    And the strange and beautiful song,
    The groves are repeating it still:
    "A boy's will is the wind's will,   89
And the thoughts of youth are long, long thoughts."

The Jewish Cemetery at Newport

THE POET wrote in his Journal for July 9, 1852: "Went
this morning into the Jewish burying-ground, with a
polite old gentleman who keeps the key. There are few
graves; nearly all are low tombstones of marble, with
Hebrew inscriptions, and a few words added in English
or Portuguese. At the foot of each, the letters S. A. G.
D. G. [*Su Alma Goce Divina Gloria.* May his soul enjoy divine glory.] It is a shady nook, at the corner of
two dusty, frequented streets, with an iron fence and
a granite gateway, erected at the expense of Mr. Touro,
of New Orleans." The poem was collected in *The
Courtship of Miles Standish, and Other Poems* (1858).

How strange it seems! These Hebrews in their
    graves,
  Close by the street of this fair seaport town,
Silent beside the never-silent waves,
  At rest in all this moving up and down!

The trees are white with dust, that o'er their sleep
  Wave their broad curtains in the south-wind's
    breath,   6
While underneath these leafy tents they keep
  The long, mysterious Exodus of Death.

The very names recorded here are strange,
  Of foreign accent, and of different climes;   10
Alvares and Rivera interchange
  With Abraham and Jacob of old times.

"Blessed be God! for he created Death!"
  The mourners said, "and Death is rest and
    peace;"
Then added, in the certainty of faith,   15
  "And giveth Life that nevermore shall cease."

Closed are the portals of their Synagogue,
  No Psalms of David now the silence break,
No Rabbi reads the ancient Decalogue
  In the grand dialect the Prophets spake.   20

Gone are the living, but the dead remain,
  And not neglected; for a hand unseen,
Scattering its bounty, like a summer rain,
  Still keeps their graves and their remembrance
    green.

How came they here? What burst of Christian
    hate,   25
  What persecution, merciless and blind,
Drove o'er the sea—that desert desolate—
  These Ishmaels and Hagars of mankind?

They lived in narrow streets and lanes obscure,
  Ghetto and Judenstrass, in mirk and mire;   30
Taught in the school of patience to endure
  The life of anguish and the death of fire.

All their lives long, with the unleavened bread
  And bitter herbs of exile and its fears,
The wasting famine of the heart they fed,   35
  And slaked its thirst with marah of their tears.

Anathema maranatha! was their cry
  That rang from town to town, from street to
    street;
At every gate the accursed Mordecai
  Was mocked and jeered, and spurned by Chris-
    tian feet.   40

Pride and humiliation hand in hand
  Walked with them through the world where'er
    they went;
Trampled and beaten were they as the sand,
  And yet unshaken as the continent.

For in the background figures vague and vast   45
  Of patriarchs and of prophets rose sublime,
And all the great traditions of the Past
  They saw reflected in the coming time.

And thus forever with reverted look
  The mystic volume of the world they read,   50
Spelling it backward, like a Hebrew book,
  Till life became a Legend of the Dead.

But ah! what once has been shall be no more!
  The groaning earth in travail and in pain
Brings forth its races, but does not restore,   55
  And the dead nations never rise again.

Sandalphon

On November 2, 1857, Longfellow noted, "Scherb read to me . . . from Corrodi's *Chiliasmus*,—of the great angel Sandalphon." He also marked passages in J. P. Stehelin's *The Traditions of the Jews* referring to Sandalphon, "who standeth on earth and reacheth with his head to the door of Heaven." He finished the poem January 18, 1858; it was published in *The Atlantic Monthly* in April, and was included in *The Courtship of Miles Standish, and Other Stories* volume of the same year. (See S. Longfellow, *Life*, II, 344, 351.)

Have you read in the Talmud of old,
In the Legends the Rabbins have told
  Of the limitless realms of the air,
Have you read it,—the marvellous story
Of Sandalphon, the Angel of Glory,   5
  Sandalphon, the Angel of Prayer?

How, erect, at the outermost gates
Of the City Celestial he waits,
  With his feet on the ladder of light,
That, crowded with angels unnumbered,   10
By Jacob was seen, as he slumbered
  Alone in the desert at night?

The Angels of Wind and of Fire
Chant only one hymn, and expire
  With the song's irresistible stress;   15
Expire in their rapture and wonder,
As harp-strings are broken asunder
  By music they throb to express.

But serene in the rapturous throng,
Unmoved by the rush of the song,   20
  With eyes unimpassioned and slow,
Among the dead angels, the deathless
Sandalphon stands listening breathless
  To sounds that ascend from below;—

From the spirits on earth that adore,   25
From the souls that entreat and implore
  In the fervor and passion of prayer;

710

From the hearts that are broken with losses,
And weary with dragging the crosses
   Too heavy for mortals to bear.   30

And he gathers the prayers as he stands,
And they change into flowers in his hands,
   Into garlands of purple and red;
And beneath the great arch of the portal,
Through the streets of the City Immortal   35
   Is wafted the fragrance they shed.

It is but a legend, I know,—
A fable, a phantom, a show,
   Of the ancient Rabbinical lore;
Yet the old mediæval tradition,   40
The beautiful, strange superstition,
   But haunts me and holds me the more.

When I look from my window at night,
And the welkin above is all white,
   All throbbing and panting with stars,   45
Among them majestic is standing
Sandalphon the angel, expanding
   His pinions in nebulous bars.

And the legend, I feel, is a part
Of the hunger and thirst of the heart,   50
   The frenzy and fire of the brain,
That grasps at the fruitage forbidden,
The golden pomegranates of Eden,
   To quiet its fever and pain.

Paul Revere's Ride

On January 1, 1798, Paul Revere wrote a letter describing the ride of April 18, 1775. For a reprint see *Proceedings of the Massachusetts Historical Society*, XVI (1879), 371–376; for historical background, see also Justin Winsor, ed., *The Memorial History of Boston*, III (1881), 101, and Esther Forbes, *Paul Revere . . .* (1942), 474–485. Samuel Longfellow stated that Longfellow might have seen Revere's letter.

In the evening, before Revere arrived at the home of Dr. Joseph Warren on summons, Warren had dispatched William Dawes to Lexington, but begged Revere to go also, spread the alarm, and inform John Hancock and Samuel Adams, who were in hiding at Lexington, of the movement of British soldiers and ships. Revere ordered the lanterns hung in accordance with previous agreement, but did not wait to see them. He was rowed to Charlestown and took horse. He ar-

rived at Lexington, but was intercepted on his way to Concord by British soldiers, who permitted him to return to Lexington, but kept his horse. Revere's friend mentioned in the poem was Richard Devens; but the Landlord, who is the narrator of this tale, was Longfellow's friend, Lyman Howe.

Longfellow began writing the poem April 19, 1860; it was published in January, 1861, in *The Atlantic Monthly*, and in 1863 became the first tale in the *Tales of a Wayside Inn*, "First Day," published November 25 in an edition of 15,000. The tales of the second day were published in 1872, and of the third day in 1874. In 1878 Longfellow recorded reading H. W. Holland's *"William Dawes, and his Ride with Paul Revere*, in which he convicts me of high historical crimes and misdemeanors" (S. Longfellow, *Life*, III, 292).

The Landlord's Tale

Listen, my children, and you shall hear
Of the midnight ride of Paul Revere,
On the eighteenth of April, in Seventy-five;
Hardly a man is now alive
Who remembers that famous day and year.   5

He said to his friend, "If the British march
By land or sea from the town to-night,
Hang a lantern aloft in the belfry arch
Of the North Church tower as a signal light,—
One, if by land, and two, if by sea;   10
And I on the opposite shore will be,
Ready to ride and spread the alarm
Through every Middlesex village and farm,
For the country folk to be up and to arm."

Then he said, "Good night!" and with muffled oar
Silently rowed to the Charlestown shore,   16
Just as the moon rose over the bay,
Where swinging wide at her moorings lay
The Somerset, British man-of-war;
A phantom ship, with each mast and spar   20
Across the moon like a prison bar,
And a huge black hulk, that was magnified
By its own reflection in the tide.

Meanwhile, his friend, through alley and street,
Wanders and watches with eager ears,   25
Till in the silence around him he hears
The muster of men at the barrack door,
The sound of arms, and the tramp of feet,
And the measured tread of the grenadiers,
Marching down to their boats on the shore.   30

Then he climbed the tower of the Old North
        Church,
By the wooden stairs, with stealthy tread,
To the belfry-chamber overhead,
And startled the pigeons from their perch
On the sombre rafters, that round him made   35
Masses and moving shapes of shade,—
By the trembling ladder, steep and tall,
To the highest window in the wall,
Where he paused to listen and look down
A moment on the roofs of the town,   40
And the moonlight flowing over all.

Beneath, in the churchyard, lay the dead,
In their night-encampment on the hill,
Wrapped in silence so deep and still
That he could hear, like a sentinel's tread,   45
The watchful night-wind, as it went
Creeping along from tent to tent,
And seeming to whisper, "All is well!"
A moment only he feels the spell
Of the place and the hour, and the secret dread   50
Of the lonely belfry and the dead;
For suddenly all his thoughts are bent
On a shadowy something far away,
Where the river widens to meet the bay,—
A line of black that bends and floats   55
On the rising tide, like a bridge of boats.

Meanwhile, impatient to mount and ride,
Booted and spurred, with a heavy stride
On the opposite shore walked Paul Revere.
Now he patted his horse's side,   60
Now gazed at the landscape far and near,
Then, impetuous, stamped the earth,
And turned and tightened his saddle-girth;
But mostly he watched with eager search
The belfry-tower of the Old North Church,   65
As it rose above the graves on the hill,
Lonely and spectral and sombre and still.
And lo! as he looks, on the belfry's height
A glimmer, and then a gleam of light!
He springs to the saddle, the bridle he turns,   70
But lingers and gazes, till full on his sight
A second lamp in the belfry burns!

A hurry of hoofs in a village street,
A shape in the moonlight, a bulk in the dark,
And beneath, from the pebbles, in passing, a spark

Struck out by a steed flying fearless and fleet: 76
That was all! And yet, through the gloom and the
        light,
The fate of a nation was riding that night;
And the spark struck out by that steed, in his
        flight,
Kindled the land into flame with its heat.   80

He has left the village and mounted the steep,
And beneath him, tranquil and broad and deep,
Is the Mystic, meeting the ocean tides;
And under the alders that skirt its edge,
Now soft on the sand, now loud on the ledge,   85
Is heard the tramp of his steed as he rides.

It was twelve by the village clock,
When he crossed the bridge into Medford town.
He heard the crowing of the cock,
And the barking of the farmer's dog,   90
And felt the damp of the river fog,
That rises after the sun goes down.

It was one by the village clock,
When he galloped into Lexington.
He saw the gilded weathercock   95
Swim in the moonlight as he passed,
And the meeting-house windows, blank and bare,
Gaze at him with a spectral glare,
As if they already stood aghast
At the bloody work they would look upon.   100

It was two by the village clock,
When he came to the bridge in Concord town.
He heard the bleating of the flock,
And the twitter of birds among the trees,
And felt the breath of the morning breeze   105
Blowing over the meadows brown.
And one was safe and asleep in his bed
Who at the bridge would be first to fall,
Who that day would be lying dead,
Pierced by a British musket-ball.   110

You know the rest. In the books you have read,
How the British Regulars fired and fled,—
How the farmers gave them ball for ball,
From behind each fence and farm-yard wall,
Chasing the red-coats down the lane,   115
Then crossing the fields to emerge again
Under the trees at the turn of the road,
And only pausing to fire and load.

So through the night rode Paul Revere;
And so through the night went his cry of alarm 120
To every Middlesex village and farm,—
A cry of defiance and not of fear,
A voice in the darkness, a knock at the door,
And a word that shall echo forevermore!
For, borne on the night-wind of the Past, 125
Through all our history, to the last,
In the hour of darkness and peril and need,
The people will waken and listen to hear
The hurrying hoof-beats of that steed,
And the midnight message of Paul Revere. 130

Hawthorne

HAWTHORNE AND LONGFELLOW were classmates at
Bowdoin, and throughout Hawthorne's life they occasionally dined together and corresponded, though
there was no deep friendship. To Longfellow, Hawthorne was "a strange owl," "a grand fellow . . . destined
to shine," "a man of strange, original fancies" (S. Longfellow, *Life*, I, 311, 345; II, 61). In 1837 Longfellow
wrote a review commending *Twice-Told Tales*; and
in 1847, on an occasion when Hawthorne, Longfellow,
and H. L. Conolly were dining together, Hawthorne
turned over for Longfellow's use the basic *Evangeline*
story, which Conolly had been urging Hawthorne to
write. Later Longfellow acknowledged Hawthorne's
congratulations upon the triumph of *Evangeline* by
writing: "This success I owe entirely to you, for being
willing to forego the pleasure of writing a prose tale
which many people would have taken for poetry, that
I might write a poem which many people take for
prose."

On June 23, 1864, exactly one month after Hawthorne's death, Longfellow sent the poem on Hawthorne to James T. Fields for publication in *The Atlantic
Monthly*, where it appeared in August under the title
"Concord."

May 23, 1864

How beautiful it was, that one bright day
    In the long week of rain!
Though all its splendor could not chase away
    The omnipresent pain.

The lovely town was white with apple-blooms, 5
    And the great elms o'erhead
Dark shadows wove on their aerial looms
    Shot through with golden thread.

Across the meadows, by the gray old manse,
    The historic river flowed: 10
I was as one who wanders in a trance,
    Unconscious of his road.

The faces of familiar friends seemed strange;
    Their voices I could hear,
And yet the words they uttered seemed to change
    Their meaning to my ear. 16

For the one face I looked for was not there,
    The one low voice was mute;
Only an unseen presence filled the air,
    And baffled my pursuit. 20

Now I look back, and meadow, manse, and stream
    Dimly my thought defines;
I only see—a dream within a dream—
    The hill-top hearsed with pines.

I only hear above his place of rest 25
    Their tender undertone,
The infinite longings of a troubled breast,
    The voice so like his own.

There in seclusion and remote from men
    The wizard hand lies cold, 30
Which at its topmost speed let fall the pen,
    And left the tale half told.

Ah! who shall lift that wand of magic power,
    And the lost clew regain?
The unfinished window in Aladdin's tower 35
    Unfinished must remain!

Divina Commedia

TWO SONNETS accompany each of the three divisions
of Longfellow's translation of Dante's *Divine Comedy*.
The first two, for the *Inferno*, were written in 1864; the
second two, for the *Purgatorio*, in 1865 and 1867; the
third two, for the *Paradiso*, in 1866. Three short translations from the *Divina Commedia* had appeared in
Voices of the Night (1839), and Longfellow had the year
before delivered at Harvard lectures on Dante. In
March, 1843, he began translating the *Divina Commedia*
with more serious intent, but soon laid the work aside,
not to resume it until 1853, when further progress was
made. After the death of his wife in 1861 he turned to
the labor in earnest, and finished the *Inferno* on April

16, 1863: "So the whole work is done, the *Purgatorio* and *Paradiso* having been finished before. . . . Now I must make some Notes. Meanwhile the Sudbury Tales [*Tales of a Wayside Inn*] are in press." In his Journal on May 7, 1864, he wrote, "In translating Dante, something must be relinquished. Shall it be the beautiful rhyme that blossoms all along the lines like a honeysuckle on a hedge? It must be, in order to retain something more precious than the rhyme; namely, fidelity, truth,—the life of the hedge itself." During 1864–1867 he was busy on the "Notes" and in seeing the volumes through the press—the first in 1865 for the six hundredth anniversary of the birth of Dante, and the second and third in 1867. (See S. Longfellow, *Life*, III, 21–22, 35, 52–53, 93.) The work remains one of the best translations in English.

The six sonnets also were collected in *Flower-de-Luce* (1867). "O poet saturnine" and "O star of morning and of liberty" are references to Dante.

I

Oft have I seen at some cathedral door
  A laborer, pausing in the dust and heat,
  Lay down his burden, and with reverent feet
  Enter, and cross himself, and on the floor
Kneel to repeat his paternoster o'er;   5
  Far off the noises of the world retreat;
  The loud vociferations of the street
  Become an undistinguishable roar.
So, as I enter here from day to day,
  And leave my burden at this minster gate,   10
  Kneeling in prayer, and not ashamed to pray,
The tumult of the time disconsolate
  To inarticulate murmurs dies away,
  While the eternal ages watch and wait.

II

How strange the sculptures that adorn these towers!
  This crowd of statues, in whose folded sleeves
  Birds build their nests; while canopied with leaves
  Parvis and portal bloom like trellised bowers,
And the vast minster seems a cross of flowers!   5
  But fiends and dragons on the gargoyled eaves
  Watch the dead Christ between the living thieves,
  And, underneath, the traitor Judas lowers!

I, 12. tumult of the time: the period of the Civil War, in which Longfellow's son Charles was wounded in 1863.

Ah! from what agonies of heart and brain,
  What exultations trampling on despair,   10
  What tenderness, what tears, what hate of wrong,
What passionate outcry of a soul in pain,
  Uprose this poem of the earth and air,
  This mediæval miracle of song!

III

I enter, and I see thee in the gloom
  Of the long aisles, O poet saturnine!
  And strive to make my steps keep pace with thine.
  The air is filled with some unknown perfume;
The congregation of the dead make room   5
  For thee to pass; the votive tapers shine;
  Like rooks that haunt Ravenna's groves of pine
  The hovering echoes fly from tomb to tomb.
From the confessionals I hear arise
  Rehearsals of forgotten tragedies,   10
  And lamentations from the crypts below;
And then a voice celestial that begins
  With the pathetic words, "Although your sins
  As scarlet be," and ends with "as the snow."

IV

With snow-white veil and garments as of flame,
  She stands before thee, who so long ago
  Filled thy young heart with passion and the woe
  From which thy song and all its splendors came;
And while with stern rebuke she speaks thy name,
  The ice about thy heart melts as the snow   6
  On mountain heights, and in swift overflow
  Comes gushing from thy lips in sobs of shame.
Thou makest full confession; and a gleam,
  As of the dawn on some dark forest cast,   10
  Seems on thy lifted forehead to increase;
Lethe and Eunoë—the remembered dream
  And the forgotten sorrow—bring at last
  That perfect pardon which is perfect peace.

V

I lift mine eyes, and all the windows blaze
  With forms of Saints and holy men who died,
  Here martyred and hereafter glorified;
  And the great Rose upon its leaves displays

III, 7. Ravenna: Dante's burial place.   **IV, 2. She:** Beatrice, immortalized by Dante.   **IV, 12. Lethe:** the river of forgetfulness.   **Eunoë:** the river of memory.

(handwritten: Beatrice & Dante go on to-gether)

Christ's Triumph, and the angelic roundelays, 5
  With splendor upon splendor multiplied;
  And Beatrice again at Dante's side
  No more rebukes, but smiles her words of praise.
And then the organ sounds, and unseen choirs
  Sing the old Latin hymns of peace and love 10
  And benedictions of the Holy Ghost;
  And the melodious bells among the spires
O'er all the house-tops and through heaven above
  Proclaim the elevation of the Host!

(handwritten: Flowers of rhyme)

VI

O star of morning and of liberty!
  O bringer of the light, whose splendor shines
  Above the darkness of the Apennines,
  Forerunner of the day that is to be!
The voices of the city and the sea, *(handwritten: World's poet)*
  The voices of the mountains and the pines,
  Repeat thy song, till the familiar lines
  Are footpaths for the thought of Italy!
Thy flame is blown abroad from all the heights,
  Through all the nations, and a sound is heard, 10
  As of a mighty wind, and men devout,
Strangers of Rome, and the new proselytes,
  In their own language hear thy wondrous word,
  And many are amazed and many doubt.

Milton

WRITTEN November 13, 1873; published in *The Masque of Pandora, and Other Poems* (1875).

I pace the sounding sea-beach and behold
  How the voluminous billows roll and run,
  Upheaving and subsiding, while the sun
  Shines through their sheeted emerald far un-
      rolled, 4
And the ninth wave, slow gathering fold by fold
  All its loose-flowing garments into one,
  Plunges upon the shore, and floods the dun
  Pale reach of sands, and changes them to gold.
So in majestic cadence rise and fall
  The mighty undulations of thy song, 10
  O sightless bard, England's Mæonides!
And ever and anon, high over all
  Uplifted, a ninth wave superb and strong,
  Floods all the soul with its melodious seas.

Milton. 11. Mæonides: the patronymic of Homer.

The Sound of the Sea

WRITTEN July 27, 1874; published in *The Masque of Pandora, and Other Poems.*

The sea awoke at midnight from its sleep,
  And round the pebbly beaches far and wide
  I heard the first wave of the rising tide
  Rush onward with uninterrupted sweep;
A voice out of the silence of the deep, 5
  A sound mysteriously multiplied
  As of a cataract from the mountain's side,
  Or roar of winds upon a wooded steep.
So comes to us at times, from the unknown
  And inaccessible solitudes of being, 10
  The rushing of the sea-tides of the soul;
And inspirations, that we deem our own,
  Are some divine foreshadowing and foreseeing
  Of things beyond our reason or control.

Morituri Salutamus

Poem for the Fiftieth Anniversary of the Class of 1825 in Bowdoin College

> *Tempora labuntur, tacitisque senescimus annis,*
>   *Et fugiunt freno non remorante dies.*[n]
>   OVID, *Fastorum*, Lib. VI.

LONGFELLOW finished writing "Morituri Salutamus"[n] November 24, 1874. It is one of his best poems, although he disliked writing for special occasions and shuddered at the approach of the day—July 7, 1875—when he read it on the fiftieth anniversary of his class at Bowdoin (S. Longfellow, *Life*, III, 238, 250). The poem was first published in *Harper's Monthly* for August, 1875; Longfellow received one thousand dollars for it. It was included in *The Masque of Pandora and Other Poems.*

"O Cæsar, we who are about to die
Salute you!" was the gladiators' cry
In the arena, standing face to face
With death and with the Roman populace.

O ye familiar scenes,—ye groves of pine, 5
That once were mine and are no longer mine,—

Tempora . . . dies: "Time slips by, and we become old with the silent years, and the days fly by with no bridle to delay them." **"Morituri Salutamus":** The title and the idea came from Longfellow's seeing Gerome's painting of the gladiators hailing Caesar as they entered the arena: "We who are about to die salute you."

715

Thou river, widening through the meadows green
To the vast sea, so near and yet unseen,—
Ye halls, in whose seclusion and repose
Phantoms of fame, like exhalations, rose   10
And vanished,—we who are about to die,
Salute you; earth and air and sea and sky,
And the Imperial Sun that scatters down
His sovereign splendors upon grove and town.

Ye do not answer us! ye do not hear!   15
We are forgotten; and in your austere
And calm indifference, ye little care
Whether we come or go, or whence or where.
What passing generations fill these halls,
What passing voices echo from these walls,   20
Ye heed not; we are only as the blast,
A moment heard, and then forever past.

Not so the teachers who in earlier days
Led our bewildered feet through learning's maze;
They answer us—alas! what have I said?   25
What greetings come there from the voiceless dead?
What salutation, welcome, or reply?
What pressure from the hands that lifeless lie?
They are no longer here; they all are gone
Into the land of shadows,—all save one.   30
Honor and reverence, and the good repute
That follows faithful service as its fruit,
Be unto him, whom living we salute.

The great Italian poet, when he made
His dreadful journey to the realms of shade,   35
Met there the old instructor of his youth,
And cried in tones of pity and of ruth:
"Oh, never from the memory of my heart
Your dear, paternal image shall depart,
Who while on earth, ere yet by death surprised,
Taught me how mortals are immortalized;   41
How grateful am I for that patient care
All my life long my language shall declare."

To-day we make the poet's words our own,
And utter them in plaintive undertone;   45
Nor to the living only be they said,
But to the other living called the dead,

30. all save one: refers to Professor Alpheus Spring
Packard (1798–1884), who was a member of the faculty at
Bowdoin for sixty-three years. **34. The great Italian poet:**
Dante, whose *Divina Commedia* Longfellow translated.

Whose dear, paternal images appear
Not wrapped in gloom, but robed in sunshine here;
Whose simple lives, complete and without flaw,
Were part and parcel of great Nature's law;   51
Who said not to their Lord, as if afraid,
"Here is thy talent in a napkin laid,"
But labored in their sphere, as men who live
In the delight that work alone can give.   55
Peace be to them; eternal peace and rest,
And the fulfilment of the great behest:
"Ye have been faithful over a few things,
Over ten cities shall ye reign as kings."

And ye who fill the places we once filled,   60
And follow in the furrows that we tilled,
Young men, whose generous hearts are beating
      high,
We who are old, and are about to die,
Salute you; hail you; take your hands in ours,
And crown you with our welcome as with flowers!

How beautiful is youth! how bright it gleams   66
With its illusions, aspirations, dreams!
Book of Beginnings, Story without End,
Each maid a heroine, and each man a friend!
Aladdin's Lamp, and Fortunatus' Purse,   70
That holds the treasures of the universe!
All possibilities are in its hands,
No danger daunts it, and no foe withstands;
In its sublime audacity of faith,
"Be thou removed!" it to the mountain saith,
And with ambitious feet, secure and proud,   76
Ascends the ladder leaning on the cloud!

As ancient Priam at the Scæan gate
Sat on the walls of Troy in regal state
With the old men, too old and weak to fight,   80
Chirping like grasshoppers in their delight
To see the embattled hosts, with spear and shield,
Of Trojans and Achaians in the field;
So from the snowy summits of our years
We see you in the plain, as each appears,   85
And question of you; asking, "Who is he
That towers above the others? Which may be
Atreides, Menelaus, Odysseus,
Ajax the great, or bold Idomeneus?"

Let him not boast who puts his armor on   90
As he who puts it off, the battle done.

716

Study yourselves; and most of all note well
Wherein kind Nature meant you to excel.
Not every blossom ripens into fruit;
Minerva, the inventress of the flute,   95
Flung it aside, when she her face surveyed
Distorted in a fountain as she played;
The unlucky Marsyas found it, and his fate
Was one to make the bravest hesitate.

Write on your doors the saying wise and old,   100
"Be bold! be bold!" and everywhere, "Be bold;
Be not too bold!" Yet better the excess
Than the defect; better the more than less;
Better like Hector in the field to die,
Than like a perfumed Paris turn and fly.   105

And now, my classmates; ye remaining few
That number not the half of those we knew,
Ye, against whose familiar names not yet
The fatal asterisk of death is set,
Ye I salute! The horologe of Time   110
Strikes the half-century with a solemn chime,
And summons us together once again,
The joy of meeting not unmixed with pain.

Where are the others? Voices from the deep
Caverns of darkness answer me: "They sleep!"
I name no names; instinctively I feel   116
Each at some well-remembered grave will kneel,
And from the inscription wipe the weeds and moss,
For every heart best knoweth its own loss.
I see their scattered gravestones gleaming white
Through the pale dusk of the impending night;
O'er all alike the impartial sunset throws   122
Its golden lilies mingled with the rose;
We give to each a tender thought, and pass
Out of the graveyards with their tangled grass,
Unto these scenes frequented by our feet   126
When we were young, and life was fresh and sweet.

What shall I say to you? What can I say
Better than silence is? When I survey
This throng of faces turned to meet my own,   130
Friendly and fair, and yet to me unknown,
Transformed the very landscape seems to be;
It is the same, yet not the same to me.
So many memories crowd upon my brain,
So many ghosts are in the wooded plain,   135
I fain would steal away, with noiseless tread,

As from a house where some one lieth dead.
I cannot go;—I pause;—I hesitate;
My feet reluctant linger at the gate;
As one who struggles in a troubled dream   140
To speak and cannot, to myself I seem.

Vanish the dream! Vanish the idle fears!
Vanish the rolling mists of fifty years!
Whatever time or space may intervene,
I will not be a stranger in this scene.   145
Here every doubt, all indecision, ends;
Hail, my companions, comrades, classmates, friends!

Ah me! the fifty years since last we met
Seem to me fifty folios bound and set   149
By Time, the great transcriber, on his shelves,
Wherein are written the histories of ourselves.
What tragedies, what comedies, are there;
What joy and grief, what rapture and despair!
What chronicles of triumph and defeat,
Of struggle, and temptation, and retreat!   155
What records of regrets, and doubts, and fears!
What pages blotted, blistered by our tears!
What lovely landscapes on the margin shine,
What sweet, angelic faces, what divine
And holy images of love and trust,   160
Undimmed by age, unsoiled by damp or dust!

Whose hand shall dare to open and explore
These volumes, closed and clasped forevermore?
Not mine. With reverential feet I pass;
I hear a voice that cries, "Alas! alas!   165
Whatever hath been written shall remain,
Nor be erased nor written o'er again;
The unwritten only still belongs to thee:
Take heed, and ponder well what that shall be."

As children frightened by a thunder-cloud   170
Are reassured if some one reads aloud
A tale of wonder, with enchantment fraught,
Or wild adventure, that diverts their thought,
Let me endeavor with a tale to chase
The gathering shadows of the time and place, 175
And banish what we all too deeply feel
Wholly to say, or wholly to conceal.

In mediæval Rome, I know not where,
There stood an image with its arm in air,
And on its lifted finger, shining clear,   180

A golden ring with the device, "Strike here!"
Greatly the people wondered, though none guessed
The meaning that these words but half expressed,
Until a learned clerk, who at noonday
With downcast eyes was passing on his way, 185
Paused, and observed the spot, and marked it well,
Whereon the shadow of the finger fell;
And, coming back at midnight, delved, and found
A secret stairway leading underground.
Down this he passed into a spacious hall, 190
Lit by a flaming jewel on the wall;
And opposite, in threatening attitude,
With bow and shaft a brazen statue stood.
Upon its forehead, like a coronet,
Were these mysterious words of menace set: 195
"That which I am, I am; my fatal aim
None can escape, not even yon luminous flame!"

Midway the hall was a fair table placed,
With cloth of gold, and golden cups enchased
With rubies, and the plates and knives were gold,
And gold the bread and viands manifold. 201
Around it, silent, motionless, and sad,
Were seated gallant knights in armor clad,
And ladies beautiful with plume and zone,
But they were stone, their hearts within were
  stone; 205
And the vast hall was filled in every part
With silent crowds, stony in face and heart.

Long at the scene, bewildered and amazed,
The trembling clerk in speechless wonder gazed;
Then from the table, by his greed made bold, 210
He seized a goblet and a knife of gold,
And suddenly from their seats the guests upsprang,
The vaulted ceiling with loud clamors rang,
The archer sped his arrow, at their call,
Shattering the lambent jewel on the wall, 215
And all was dark around and overhead;—
Stark on the floor the luckless clerk lay dead!

The writer of this legend then records
Its ghostly application in these words:
The image is the Adversary old, 220
Whose beckoning finger points to realms of gold;
Our lusts and passions are the downward stair
That leads the soul from a diviner air;
The archer, Death; the flaming jewel, Life;

Terrestrial goods, the goblet and the knife; 225
The knights and ladies, all whose flesh and bone
By avarice have been hardened into stone;
The clerk, the scholar whom the love of pelf
Tempts from his books and from his nobler self.

The scholar and the world! The endless strife, 230
The discord in the harmonies of life!
The love of learning, the sequestered nooks,
And all the sweet serenity of books;
The market-place, the eager love of gain,
Whose aim is vanity, and whose end is pain! 235

But why, you ask me, should this tale be told
To men grown old, or who are growing old?
It is too late! Ah, nothing is too late
Till the tired heart shall cease to palpitate.
Cato learned Greek at eighty; Sophocles 240
Wrote his grand Œdipus, and Simonides
Bore off the prize of verse from his compeers,
When each had numbered more than four-score
  years,
And Theophrastus, at fourscore and ten,
Had but begun his "Characters of Men." 245
Chaucer, at Woodstock with the nightingales,
At sixty wrote the Canterbury Tales;
Goethe at Weimar, toiling to the last,
Completed Faust when eighty years were past.
These are indeed exceptions; but they show 250
How far the gulf-stream of our youth may flow
Into the arctic regions of our lives,
Where little else than life itself survives.
As the barometer foretells the storm
While still the skies are clear, the weather warm,
So something in us, as old age draws near, 256
Betrays the pressure of the atmosphere.
The nimble mercury, ere we are aware,
Descends the elastic ladder of the air;
The telltale blood in artery and vein 260
Sinks from its higher levels in the brain;
Whatever poet, orator, or sage
May say of it, old age is still old age.
It is the waning, not the crescent moon;
The dusk of evening, not the blaze of noon; 265
It is not strength, but weakness; not desire,
But its surcease; not the fierce heat of fire,
The burning and consuming element,
But that of ashes and of embers spent,

718

In which some living sparks we still discern,   270
Enough to warm, but not enough to burn.

What then? Shall we sit idly down and say
The night hath come; it is no longer day?
The night hath not yet come; we are not quite
Cut off from labor by the failing light;   275
Something remains for us to do or dare;
Even the oldest tree some fruit may bear;
Not Œdipus Coloneus, or Greek Ode,
Or tales of pilgrims that one morning rode
Out of the gateway of the Tabard Inn,   280
But other something, would we but begin;
For age is opportunity no less
Than youth itself, though in another dress,
And as the evening twilight fades away
The sky is filled with stars, invisible by day.   285

A Dutch Picture

G. R. ELLIOTT in *The Cycle of Modern Poetry* (1929)
cites the third and sixth stanzas of "A Dutch Picture"
as anticipating the "neat glory" of the Imagists. Published in *Kéramos and Other Poems* (1878).

Simon Danz has come home again,
    From cruising about with his buccaneers;
He has singed the beard of the King of Spain,
And carried away the Dean of Jaen
    And sold him in Algiers.   5

In his house by the Maese, with its roof of tiles,
    And weathercocks flying aloft in air,
There are silver tankards of antique styles,
Plunder of convent and castle, and piles
    Of carpets rich and rare.   10

In his tulip-garden there by the town,
    Overlooking the sluggish stream,
With his Moorish cap and dressing-gown,
The old sea-captain, hale and brown,
    Walks in a waking dream.   15

A smile in his gray mustachio lurks
    Whenever he thinks of the King of.Spain,
And the listed tulips look like Turks,
And the silent gardener as he works
    Is changed to the Dean of Jaen.   20

4. **Jaen:** city in Andalusia, Spain.   6. **Maese:** Dutch
for Meuse.

The windmills on the outermost
    Verge of the landscape in the haze,
To him are towers on the Spanish coast,
With whiskered sentinels at their post,
    Though this is the river Maese.   25

But when the winter rains begin,
    He sits and smokes by the blazing brands,
And old seafaring men come in,
Goat-bearded, gray, and with double chin,
    And rings upon their hands.   30

They sit there in the shadow and shine
    Of the flickering fire of the winter night;
Figures in color and design
Like those by Rembrandt of the Rhine,
    Half darkness and half light.   35

And they talk of ventures lost or won,
    And their talk is ever and ever the same,
While they drink the red wine of Tarragon,
From the cellars of some Spanish Don,
    Or convent set on flame.   40

Restless at times with heavy strides
    He paces his parlor to and fro;
He is like a ship that at anchor rides,
And swings with the rising and falling tides,
    And tugs at her anchor-tow.   45

Voices mysterious far and near,
    Sound of the wind and sound of the sea,
Are calling and whispering in his ear,
"Simon Danz! Why stayest thou here?
    Come forth and follow me!"   50

So he thinks he shall take to the sea again
    For one more cruise with his buccaneers,
To singe the beard of the King of Spain,
And capture another Dean of Jaen
    And sell him in Algiers.   55

The Three Silences of Molinos

WRITTEN for the occasion of *The Atlantic Monthly*
dinner held at the Brunswick Hotel, December 17,
1877, in honor of the thirtieth anniversary of the magazine and Whittier's seventieth birthday. Miguel de
Molinos (1640–1697) was a Spanish theologian, whose
Spiritual Guide (1675) was condemned by the Inquisition. From the *Guide*: "By not speaking, not desiring,

not thinking, one arrives at the true and perfect mystical silence wherein God speaks with the soul . . ." (*Poetical Works*, III (1886), 303). Collected in *Kéramos and Other Poems* (1878).

To John Greenleaf Whittier

Three Silences there are: the first of speech,
  The second of desire, the third of thought;
  This is the lore a Spanish monk, distraught
  With dreams and visions, was the first to teach.
These Silences, commingling each with each,   5
  Made up the perfect Silence that he sought
  And prayed for, and wherein at times he caught
  Mysterious sounds from realms beyond our reach.
O thou, whose daily life anticipates
  The life to come, and in whose thought and word
  The spiritual world preponderates,   11
Hermit of Amesbury! thou too hast heard
  Voices and melodies from beyond the gates,
  And speakest only when thy soul is stirred!

The Tide Rises, the Tide Falls

WRITTEN in 1879; published in *Ultima Thule* (1880). Longfellow loved the seashore and often mentioned the tides. Three of his sonnets of 1874 treat of the shore.

The tide rises, the tide falls,
The twilight darkens, the curlew calls;
Along the sea-sands damp and brown
The traveler hastens toward the town,
  And the tide rises, the tide falls.   5

Darkness settles on roofs and walls,
But the sea, the sea in the darkness calls;
The little waves, with their soft, white hands,
Efface the footprints in the sands,
  And the tide rises, the tide falls.   10

The morning breaks; the steeds in their stalls
Stamp and neigh, as the hostler calls;
The day returns, but nevermore
Returns the traveler to the shore,
  And the tide rises, the tide falls.   15

The Cross of Snow

WRITTEN July 10, 1879. On July 9, 1861, while in the library with "her two little girls, engaged in sealing up some small packages of their curls which she had just

cut off," Frances Appleton Longfellow's dress caught fire, and the following morning she died of the burns received; her husband was unable to attend the funeral, being "confined . . . by the severe burns which he had himself received" (S. Longfellow, *Life*, II, 421). The poem was posthumously published in *Life*, II, 425–426.

In the long, sleepless watches of the night,
  A gentle face—the face of one long dead—
  Looks at me from the wall, where round its head
  The night-lamp casts a halo of pale light.
Here in this room she died; and soul more white   5
  Never through martyrdom of fire was led
  To its repose; nor can in books be read
  The legend of a life more benedight.
There is a mountain in the distant West
  That, sun-defying, in its deep ravines   10
  Displays a cross of snow upon its side.
Such is the cross I wear upon my breast
  These eighteen years, through all the changing scenes
  And seasons, changeless since the day she died.

Review of Twice-Told Tales

FIRST PUBLISHED in *The North American Review* for July, 1837; collected and condensed in *Works*, VII, from which this text is taken. Having sent a copy of *Twice-Told Tales* to Longfellow, Hawthorne wrote on June 4, 1837, that he had lacked the stimulus of public approbation as well as materials, "for I have seen so little of the world that I have nothing but thin air to concoct my stories of"; and on June 19 he expressed to Longfellow his "huge delight" in the latter's kind review (S. Longfellow, *Life*, II, 220, 264–266). After graduating from Bowdoin, Longfellow had spent two long periods of residence in Europe and was becoming used to the chair at Harvard lately vacated by Ticknor, while Hawthorne had retired to Salem, traveled little and not far, and was still unknown to all but a small circle, which included Samuel Goodrich, a Boston publisher, for whom he had done some literary hack work.

When a new star rises in the heavens, people gaze after it for a season with the naked eye, and with such telescopes as they can find. In the stream of thought which flows so peacefully deep and clear through the pages of this book, we see the

9. mountain: Holy Cross Mountain in Colorado.

bright reflection of a spiritual star, after which men will be fain to gaze "with the naked eye, and with the spy-glasses of criticism." This star is but newly risen, and erelong the observations of numerous star-gazers, perched upon armchairs and editors' tables, will inform the world of its magnitude and its place in the heaven of poetry, whether it be in the paw of the Great Bear, or on the forehead of Pegasus, or on the strings of the Lyre, or in the wing of the Eagle. My own observations are as follows.

To this little work let us say, as was said to Sidney's "Arcadia": "Live ever, sweet, sweet book! the simple image of his gentle wit, and the golden pillar of his noble courage; and ever notify unto the world that thy writer was the secretary of eloquence, the breath of the Muses, the honeybee of the daintiest flowers of wit and art." It comes from the hand of a man of genius. Everything about it has the freshness of morning and of May. These flowers and green leaves of poetry have not the dust of the highway upon them. They have been gathered fresh from the secret places of a peaceful and gentle heart. There flow deep waters, silent, calm, and cool; and the green trees look into them and "God's blue heaven."

This book, though in prose, is written nevertheless by a poet. He looks upon all things in the spirit of love, and with lively sympathies; for to him external form is but the representation of internal being, all things having a life, an end and aim. The true poet is a friendly man. He takes to his arms even cold and inanimate things, and rejoices in his heart, as did St. Francis of old, when he kissed his bride of snow. To his eye all things are beautiful and holy; all are objects of feeling and of song, from the great hierarchy of the silent, saint-like stars, that rule the night, down to the little flowers which are "stars in the firmament of the earth."

It is one of the attributes of the poetic mind to feel a universal sympathy with Nature, both in the material world and in the soul of man. It identifies itself likewise with every object of its sympathy, giving it new sensation and poetic life, whatever that object may be, whether man, bird, beast, flower, or star. As to the pure mind all things are pure, so to the poetic mind all things

are poetical. To such souls no age and no country can be utterly dull and prosaic. They make unto themselves their age and country, dwelling in the universal mind of man, and in the universal forms of things. Of such is the author of this book.

There are many who think that the ages of poetry and romance are gone by. They look upon the Present as a dull, unrhymed, and prosaic translation of a brilliant and poetic Past. Their dreams are of the days of eld; of the Dark Ages, the ages of Chivalry, and Bards, and Troubadours, and Minnesingers; and the times of which Milton says: "The villages also must have their visitors to inquire what lectures the bagpipe, and the rebeck reads even to the ballatry, and the gammuth of every municipal fiddler, for these are the countryman's Arcadia and his Monte Mayors."

We all love ancient ballads. Pleasantly to all ears sounds the voice of the people in song, swelling fitfully through the desolate chambers of the Past like the wind of evening among ruins. And yet this voice does not persuade us that the days of balladry were more poetic than our own. The spirit of the Past pleads for itself, and the spirit of the Present likewise. If poetry be an element of the human mind, and consequently in accordance with nature and truth, it would be strange indeed if, as the human mind advances, poetry should recede. The truth is, that, when we look back upon the Past, we see only its bright and poetic features. All that is dull, prosaic, and commonplace is lost in the shadowy distance. We see the moated castle on the hill, and,

Golden and red, above it
The clouds float gorgeously;

but we see not the valley below, where the patient bondman toils like a beast of burden. We see the tree-tops waving in the wind, and hear the merry birds singing under their green roofs; but we forget that at their roots there are swine feeding upon acorns. With the Present it is not so. We stand too near to see objects in a picturesque light. What to others, at a distance, is a bright and folded summer cloud, is to us, who are in it, a dismal, drizzling rain. Thus has it been since the world began. Ours is not the only Present which has seemed dull, commonplace, and prosaic.

The truth is, the heaven of poetry and romance still lies around us and within us. So long as truth is stranger than fiction, the elements of poetry and romance will not be wanting in common life. If, invisible ourselves, we could follow a single human being through a single day of his life, and know all his secret thoughts and hopes and anxieties, his prayers and tears and good resolves, his passionate delights and struggles against temptation,—all that excites, and all that soothes the heart of man, —we should have poetry enough to fill a volume. Nay, set the imagination free, like another bottle-imp, and bid it lift for you the roofs of the city, street by street, and after a single night's observation you may sit down and write poetry and romance for the rest of your life.

The Twice-Told Tales are so called from having been first published in various annuals and magazines, and now collected together and told a second time in a volume. And a very delightful volume they make;—one of those which excite in you a feeling of personal interest for the author, A calm, thoughtful face seems to be looking at you from every page, with now a pleasant smile, and now a shade of sadness stealing over its features. Sometimes, though not often, it glares wildly at you, with a strange and painful expression, as in the German romance, the bronze knocker of the Archivarius Lindhorst makes up faces at the Student Anselmus.

One of the prominent characteristics of these tales is, that they are national in their character. The author has chosen his themes among the traditions of New England, the dusty legends of "the good old Colony times, when we lived under a king." This is the right material for story. It seems as natural to make tales out of old, tumble-down traditions, as canes and snuff-boxes out of old steeples, or trees planted by great men. The dreary old Puritanical times begin to look romantic in the distance. Who would not like to have strolled through the city of Agamenticus, where a market was held every week, on Wednesday, and there were two annual fairs at St. James's and St. Paul's? Who would not like to have been present at the court of the worshipful Thomas Gorges, in those palmy days of the law when Tom Heard was fined five shillings for being drunk, and John Payne the same, "for swearing one oath"? Who would not like to have seen Thomas Taylor presented to the grand jury "for abusing Captain Raynes, being in authority, by thee-ing and thou-ing him"; and John Wardell likewise, for denying Cambridge College to be an ordinance of God; and people fined for winking at comely damsels in church; and others for being common sleepers there on the Lord's day? Truly, many quaint and quiet customs, many comic scenes and strange adventures, many wild and wondrous things, fit for humorous tale and soft, pathetic story, lie all about us here in New England. There is no tradition of the Rhine nor of the Black Forest which surpasses in beauty that of the Phantom Ship of New Haven. The Flying Dutchman of the Cape, and the Klabotermann of the Baltic, are nowise superior. The story of Peter Rugg, the man who could not find Boston, is as good as that told by Gervase of Tilbury, of a man who gave himself to the devils by an unfortunate imprecation, and was used by them as a wheelbarrow; and the Great Carbuncle of the White Mountains shines with no less splendor than that which illuminated the subterranean palace in Rome, as related by William of Malmesbury.

Another characteristic of this writer is the exceeding beauty of his style. It is as clear as running waters. Indeed, he uses words as mere stepping-stones, upon which, with a free and youthful bound, his spirit crosses and recrosses the bright and rushing stream of thought. Some writers of the present day have introduced a kind of Gothic architecture into their style. All is fantastic, vast, and wondrous in the outward form, and within is mysterious twilight, and the swelling sound of an organ, and a voice chanting hymns in Latin, which need a translation for many of the crowd. To this I do not object. Let the priest chant in what language he will, so long as he understands his own Mass-book. But if he wishes the world to listen and be edified, he will do well to choose a language that is generally understood.

JOHN GREENLEAF WHITTIER (1807–1892)

DURING the earlier part of his life Whittier was known as an editor, a balladist of New England lore, and a fiery Northern poet of the abolition movement. But increasingly he came to write on two abiding themes: common life in rural surroundings, and religious devotion. He caught the true human spirit of family life on the farm and of dignified labor at the tradesman's bench; and, lacking all venom, and with the inward consciousness of frailty, he wrote the devotional poems which have placed him among the great hymnologists. In balladry some of his narratives still keep alive stories of odd occurrences, small human dramas, and deeds of moral zeal from colonial times in New England to the years of the Civil War in Virginia and Kansas, but they were sometimes garbled in their facts and are now of lesser interest. The course of time has cooled the fire of "Massachusetts to Virginia" and over three hundred other antislavery poems; they are becoming museum pieces of passion spent. But other themes have remained. The countryside may still be found when sought. There are barefoot boys and swarming bees; there are families still living together in sixes and sevens instead of twos and threes, and men of great spirit and perspicacity working at their own small trades. More and more often are the hymns sung which Whittier wrote as simple poems, such as "The Brewing of Soma" and "Our Master."

As a poet of rural life Whittier continued the countryside tradition of Timothy Dwight and Robert Burns, and he anticipated the neighborliness of Robert Frost. He set about supplying America with "Yankee pastorals" by writing ballads of seacoast legends, singing of the joy of labor in shop and field, and recalling tenderly the simple life of village and farm. The household poems of both Longfellow and Whittier were read aloud at the hearthsides of the nation. Yet there is some distinction between them. The romantic narratives of Longfellow have wider appeal than the poetic tales of Whittier, always excepting "Snow-Bound." But while Longfellow wrote of historic moods in his narratives of the days of Christ, of Christian medieval life, and of harsh New England Christian tragedies, Whittier has become a part of the very hearts of thousands of Christian congregations in song.

John Greenleaf Whittier was born to a Quaker family on a farm near Haverhill, Massachusetts. His formal education was meager. His early reading, mostly of a religious cast, included the Bible, the lives of important Quakers, *Davideis*, and some of the poems of Gray, Cowper, and Burns. The publication of his poem "The Exile's Departure," sent by his sister Mary to *The Newburyport Free Press* in 1826, led to his meeting the abolitionist William Lloyd Garrison; and Abijah W. Thayer, editor of *The Haverhill* (later *Essex*) *Gazette*, published weekly other poems by Whittier. Garrison pleaded unsuccessfully with Whittier's father to allow the young poet further schooling, but Thayer's later similar plea was granted, and in 1827 Whittier began his twelve months' study at Haverhill Academy, broken by a few months of teaching.

Then began Whittier's long period as abolitionist, journalist, politician, and lobbyist. In 1829, through the help of Garrison and others, he became at the age of twenty-one the editor of *The American Manufacturer*, a pro-Clay paper in Boston, but he resigned this post after seven months to help his ailing father on the farm. In 1830 his father died. In the same year Whittier assisted in editing *The Essex Gazette* and then became editor of *The New England Weekly Review*, at Hartford, Connecticut, another paper which supported Clay. In 1831 his first book appeared, *Legends of New England*. Early in 1832 ill health caused him to resign his editorship. In the following year his first important abolitionist tract, *Justice and Expediency*, was published, and this pamphlet, soon republished in large quantities, brought him national recognition. He was elected to the Massachusetts legislature in 1835, and in the same year was mobbed at Concord, New Hampshire, for abolitionist activities. Through his political activities he forced Caleb Cushing, of Massachusetts, to take a stand against slavery in the elections of 1834, 1836, and 1838 for membership in the national House of Representatives. He again edited *The Essex Gazette* for several months in 1836, and in the same year sold the homestead and moved to Amesbury. From March, 1838, to February, 1840, he edited *The Pennsylvania Freeman*, an antislavery paper in Philadelphia, resigning because of ill health. Later he returned again to journalism, and from July, 1844, to March, 1845, edited the Liberty party's *Middlesex Standard*, at Lowell, Massachusetts. In 1846 he gathered some of his antislavery poems into *Voices of Freedom*. In the same year he became corresponding editor of *The National Era*, the famous antislavery paper in Washington, D. C., which published Harriet Beecher Stowe's *Uncle Tom's Cabin* in 1851–1852. Tall, swarthy, with piercingly dark eyes and the mind of a reformer intent on one goal, he devoted himself to abolition, opposed the Mexican War, and was one of the first to suggest the formation of the Republican party.

During these years he was thrice moved beyond friendship. In early manhood he fell violently in love with Mary Emerson Smith; she married another man, but one printed letter of Whittier's dated May 23, 1829, remains as testimony. In 1841 Lucy Hooper, a Brooklyn poet, died of tuberculosis. The intensity of her love for Whittier was made known to him after her death and this revelation prompted him to write a letter in which he confessed that "poverty, protracted illness, and our separate faiths," as well as his pledge of devotion to a single cause, had led him to crush every warmer feeling than that of a brother's love. Finally, while editing *The Pennsylvania Freeman*, he formed a friendship with the poet Elizabeth Lloyd; in 1853 she married Robert Howell but was left a widow in 1856, and she and Whittier resumed their friendship. Their attachment was broken by Whittier in 1859, when she attacked her own Quaker creed. He remained a bachelor. His mother died in 1858, and his family circle was soon further broken by the death of his sister Mary in 1860.

Whittier's volumes of poems came regularly from the press: *Lays of My Home, and Other Poems* (1843), *Songs of Labor, and Other Poems* (1850), a London edition of his *Poetical Works* (1850), *The Chapel of the Hermit, and Other Poems* (1853), and *The Panorama, and Other Poems* (1856). The establishment of *The Atlantic Monthly* in 1857 and the stimulus of Lowell's criticism as editor led Whittier, as a contributor, to scrutinize his poetry more carefully; some of his best poems, including "Snow-Bound," first appeared in this magazine. The books kept on coming: *In War Time and Other Poems* (1864), *Snow-Bound* (1866), *The Tent on the Beach* (1867), *Maud Muller* (1867), *Mabel Martin* (1876), *Among the Hills, and Other Poems* (1869), *Complete Poetical Works* in expanding editions of 1873, 1876, and 1884, *The Writings* (7 vols., 1888–1889), *At Sundown* (1890), and *The Works* (7 vols., 1892).

The close of the Civil War definitely brought an end to his social crusading. He was conservative in his economic philosophy, and opposed the railroad strikes of 1877. His literary work became less propagandistic. In 1876, aged 69, he moved to Danvers to live with relatives, but he maintained his legal residence at Amesbury, where he was buried in 1892.

BIBLIOGRAPHY · The standard edition, used for all selections in this book, is *The Writings of John Greenleaf Whittier* (7 vols., 1888–1889). The best one-volume edition of the poems is that of H. E. Scudder, ed., *The Complete Poetical Works* (1894). The official biography is S. T. Pickard's *Life and Letters of John Greenleaf Whittier* (2 vols., 1894). A. Mordell adds biographical and political materials in *Quaker Militant: John Greenleaf Whittier* (1933). Sociological and political emphasis characterizes W. Bennett's *Whittier: Bard of Freedom* (1941). For an intimate account of the social life of the antislavery circle in Philadelphia, see T. F. Currier's *Elizabeth Lloyd and the Whittiers* (1939). Currier's *A Bibliography of John Greenleaf Whittier* (1937) is definitive.

Special factors of importance are presented in E. H. Cady and H. H. Clark, eds., *Whittier on Writers and Writing: The Uncollected Critical Writings . . .* (1950); A. Christy, "Orientalism in New England: Whittier," *American Literature*, I (1930), 372–392, and "The Orientalism of Whittier," *American Literature*, V (1933), 247–257; Cora Dolbee, "Kansas and 'The Prairied West' of John G. Whittier," *Essex Institute Historical Collections*, LXXXI (1945), 307–347; Mrs. J. T. Fields, *Whittier: Notes of His Life and Friendships* (1893); C. I. Glicksberg, "Bryant and Whittier," *Essex Institute Historical Collections*, LXXII (1936), 111–116; M. J. Griswold, "American Quaker History in the Works of Whittier, Hawthorne, and Longfellow," *Americana*, XXXIV (1940), 220–263; T. W. Higginson, *John Greenleaf Whittier* (1902); E. F. Hoxie, "Harriet Livermore: Vixen and Devotee," *New England Quarterly*, XVII (1945), 39–50; S. T. Pickard, *Whittier as a Politician* (1900), and *Whittier-Land* (1904); F. M. Pray, *A Study of Whittier's Apprenticeship as a Poet* (1930); L. C. Schaedler, "Whittier's Attitude toward Puritanism," *New England Quarterly*, XXI (1948), 350–367; W. T. Scott, "Poetry in America: A New Consideration of Whittier's Verse," *New England Quarterly*, VII (1934), 258–275; M. H. Shackford, "Whittier and Some Cousins," *New England Quarterly*, XV (1942), 467–496; and B.–M. Stearns, "John Greenleaf Whittier: Editor," *New England Quarterly*, XIII (1940), 280–304.

Pennsylvania Hall

THIS POEM was read by Charles C. Burleigh on May 15, 1838, during the dedicatory ceremonies of Pennsylvania Hall, Philadelphia, built by an association of citizens interested in the abolition of slavery and the spread of civil liberties. The building housed the editorial office of *The Pennsylvania Freeman*, the abolition journal which Whittier was editing. Later Burleigh assumed the editorship. Dedicatory exercises began on May 14, and the Hall was opened to the public on the following day. On the evening of May 16, while a program was in progress within the Hall, a mob broke some windows; the next evening a mob of 15,000 burned the building to the ground. The poem was first printed in *The Liberator*, May 25, 1838, and appeared the same year as a pamphlet entitled *Address Read at the Opening of the Pennsylvania Hall, on The 15th of Fifth Month, 1838.*

Not with the splendors of the days of old,
The spoils of nations, and barbaric gold;
No weapons wrested from the fields of blood,
Where dark and stern the unyielding Roman stood,
And the proud eagles of his cohorts saw 5
A world, war-wasted, crouching to his law;
Nor blazoned car, nor banners floating gay,
Like those which swept along the Appian Way,
When, to the welcome of imperial Rome,
The victor warrior came in triumph home, 10
And trumpet peal, and shoutings wild and high,
Stirred the blue quiet of the Italian sky;
But calm and grateful, prayerful and sincere,
As Christian freemen only, gathering here,
We dedicate our fair and lofty Hall, 15
Pillar and arch, entablature and wall,
As Virtue's shrine, as Liberty's abode,
Sacred to Freedom, and to Freedom's God!
Far statelier Halls, 'neath brighter skies than these,
Stood darkly mirrored in the Ægean seas, 20
Pillar and shrine, and life-like statues seen,
Graceful and pure, the marble shafts between;
Where glorious Athens from her rocky hill
Saw Art and Beauty subject to her will;
And the chaste temple, and the classic grove, 25
The hall of sages, and the bowers of love,
Arch, fane, and column, graced the shores, and gave
Their shadows to the blue Saronic wave;
And statelier rose, on Tiber's winding side,
The Pantheon's dome, the Coliseum's pride, 30
The Capitol, whose arches backward flung
The deep, clear cadence of the Roman tongue,
Whence stern decrees, like words of fate, went forth
To the awed nations of a conquered earth,
Where the proud Cæsars in their glory came, 35
And Brutus lightened from his lips of flame!
Yet in the porches of Athena's halls,
And in the shadow of her stately walls,
Lurked the sad bondman, and his tears of woe
Wet the cold marble with unheeded flow; 40
And fetters clanked beneath the silver dome
Of the proud Pantheon of imperious Rome.
Oh, not for him, the chained and stricken slave,
By Tiber's shore, or blue Ægina's wave,
In the thronged forum, or the sages' seat, 45
The bold lip pleaded, and the warm heart beat;
No soul of sorrow melted at his pain,
No tear of pity rusted on his chain!

But this fair Hall to Truth and Freedom given,
Pledged to the Right before all Earth and Heaven,
A free arena for the strife of mind,
To caste, or sect, or color unconfined,
Shall thrill with echoes such as ne'er of old
From Roman hall or Grecian temple rolled;
Thoughts shall find utterance such as never yet
The Propylea or the Forum met.
Beneath its roof no gladiator's strife
Shall win applauses with the waste of life;
No lordly lictor urge the barbarous game,
No wanton Lais glory in her shame.
But here the tear of sympathy shall flow,
As the ear listens to the tale of woe;
Here in stern judgment of the oppressor's wrong
Shall strong rebukings thrill on Freedom's tongue,
No partial justice hold th' unequal scale,
No pride of caste a brother's rights assail,
No tyrant's mandates echo from this wall,
Holy to Freedom and the Rights of All!
But a fair field, where mind may close with mind,
Free as the sunshine and the chainless wind;
Where the high trust is fixed on Truth alone,
And bonds and fetters from the soul are thrown;
Where wealth, and rank, and worldly pomp, and might,
Yield to the presence of the Truth and Right.

And fitting is it that this Hall should stand
Where Pennsylvania's Founder led his band,
From thy blue waters, Delaware!—to press
The virgin verdure of the wilderness.
Here, where all Europe with amazement saw
The soul's high freedom trammeled by no law;
Here, where the fierce and war-like forest men
Gathered, in peace, around the home of Penn,
Awed by the weapons Love alone had given
Drawn from the holy armory of Heaven;
Where Nature's voice against the bondman's wrong
First found an earnest and indignant tongue;
Where Lay's bold message to the proud was borne;
And Keith's rebuke, and Franklin's manly scorn!
Fitting it is that here, where Freedom first
From her fair feet shook off the Old World's dust,
Spread her white pinions to our Western blast,
And her free tresses to our sunshine cast,
One Hall should rise redeemed from Slavery's ban,
One Temple sacred to the Rights of Man!

726

Oh! if the spirits of the parted come,   95
Visiting angels, to their olden home;
If the dead fathers of the land look forth
From their fair dwellings, to the things of earth,
Is it a dream, that with their eyes of love,
They gaze now on us from the bowers above?   100
Lay's ardent soul, and Benezet the mild,
Steadfast in faith, yet gentle as a child,
Meek-hearted Woolman, and that brother-band,
The sorrowing exiles from their "Father land,"
Leaving their homes in Krieshiem's bowers of vine,   105
And the blue beauty of their glorious Rhine,
To seek amidst our solemn depths of wood
Freedom from man, and holy peace with God;
Who first of all their testimonial gave
Against the oppressor, for the outcast slave,   110
Is it a dream that such as these look down,
And with their blessing our rejoicings crown?
Let us rejoice, that while the pulpit's door
Is barred against the pleaders for the poor;
While the Church, wrangling upon points of faith,   115
Forgets her bondmen suffering unto death;
While crafty Traffic and the lust of Gain
Unite to forge Oppression's triple chain,
One door is open, and one Temple free,
As a resting-place for hunted Liberty!   120
Where men may speak, unshackled and unawed,
High words of Truth, for Freedom and for God.
And when that truth its perfect work hath done,
And rich with blessings o'er our land hath gone;
When not a slave beneath his yoke shall pine,   125
From broad Potomac to the far Sabine:
When unto angel lips at last is given
The silver trump of Jubilee in Heaven;
And from Virginia's plains, Kentucky's shades,
And through the dim Floridian everglades,   130
Rises, to meet that angel-trumpet's sound,
The voice of millions from their chains unbound;
Then, though this Hall be crumbling in decay,
Its strong walls blending with the common clay,
Yet, round the ruins of its strength shall stand   135
The best and noblest of a ransomed land—
Pilgrims, like those who throng around the shrine
Of Mecca, or of holy Palestine!
A prouder glory shall that ruin own
Than that which lingers round the Parthenon.   140
Here shall the child of after years be taught

727

The works of Freedom which his fathers wrought;
Told of the trials of the present hour,
Our weary strife with prejudice and power;
How the high errand quickened woman's soul,   145
And touched her lip as with a living coal;
How Freedom's martyrs kept their lofty faith
True and unwavering, unto bonds and death;
The pencil's art shall sketch the ruined Hall,
The Muses' garland crown its aged wall,   150
And History's pen for after times record
Its consecration unto Freedom's God!

Massachusetts to Virginia

Of "Massachusetts to Virginia" Whittier wrote: "Written on reading an account of the proceedings of the citizens of Norfolk, Va., in reference to George Latimer, the alleged fugitive slave, who was seized in Boston without warrant at the request of James B. Grey, of Norfolk, claiming to be his master." The Chief Justice of Massachusetts refused Latimer a trial by jury. The case aroused nationwide excitement, and in Massachusetts conventions met in every county on January 2, 1843. Latimer's freedom was purchased for $400, but the conventions led to a petition to Congress, signed by over 62,000 names, "calling for such laws and proposed amendments to the Constitution," in Whittier's words, "as should relieve the Commonwealth from all further participation in the crime of oppression." Whittier's poem was read at the Essex County convention. It was first published anonymously by Garrison in *The Liberator*, Boston, January 27, 1843, and first collected in Whittier's *Lays of My Home, and Other Poems* (1843). It is perhaps the finest example of his poetry of propaganda.

The blast from Freedom's Northern hills, upon its Southern way,
Bears greeting to Virginia from Massachusetts Bay:
No word of haughty challenging, nor battle-bugle's peal,
Nor steady tread of marching files, nor clang of horsemen's steel.

No trains of deep-mouthed cannon along our highways go;   5
Around our silent arsenals untrodden lies the snow;
And to the land-breeze of our ports, upon their errands far,
A thousand sails of commerce swell, but none are spread for war.

We hear thy threats, Virginia! thy stormy words and high,
Swell harshly on the Southern winds which melt along our sky;   10
Yet, not one brown, hard hand foregoes its honest labor here,
No hewer of our mountain oaks suspends his axe in fear.

Wild are the waves which lash the reefs along St. George's bank;
Cold on the shore of Labrador the fog lies white and dank;
Through storm, and wave, and blinding mist, stout are the hearts which man   15
The fishing-smacks of Marblehead, the sea-boats of Cape Ann.

The cold north light and wintry sun glare on their icy forms,
Bent grimly o'er their straining lines or wrestling with the storms;
Free as the winds they drive before, rough as the waves they roam,
They laugh to scorn the slaver's threat against their rocky home.   20

728

What means the Old Dominion? Hath she forgot the day
When o'er her conquered valleys swept the Briton's steel array?
How side by side, with sons of hers, the Massachusetts men
Encountered Tarleton's charge of fire, and stout Cornwallis, then?

Forgets she how the Bay State, in answer to the call   25
Of her old House of Burgesses, spoke out from Faneuil Hall?
When, echoing back her Henry's cry, came pulsing on each breath
Of Northern winds the thrilling sounds of "Liberty or Death!"

What asks the Old Dominion? If now her sons have proved
False to their fathers' memory, false to the faith they loved;   30
If she can scoff at Freedom, and its great charter spurn,
Must we of Massachusetts from truth and duty turn?

We hunt your bondmen, flying from Slavery's hateful hell;
Our voices, at your bidding, take up the bloodhound's yell;
We gather, at your summons, above our fathers' graves,   35
From Freedom's holy altar-horns to tear your wretched slaves!

Thank God! not yet so vilely can Massachusetts bow;
The spirit of her early time is with her even now;
Dream not because her Pilgrim blood moves slow and calm and cool,
She thus can stoop her chainless neck, a sister's slave and tool!   40

All that a sister State should do, all that a free State may,
Heart, hand, and purse we proffer, as in our early day;
But that one dark loathsome burden ye must stagger with alone,
And reap the bitter harvest which ye yourselves have sown!

Hold, while ye may, your struggling slaves, and burden God's free air   45
With woman's shriek beneath the lash, and manhood's wild despair;
Cling closer to the "cleaving curse" that writes upon your plains
The blasting of Almighty wrath against a land of chains.

Still shame your gallant ancestry, the cavaliers of old,
By watching round the shambles where human flesh is sold;   50
Gloat o'er the new-born child, and count his market value, when
The maddened mother's cry of woe shall pierce the slaver's den!

Lower than plummet soundeth, sink the Virginian name;
Plant, if ye will, your fathers' graves with rankest weeds of shame;
Be, if ye will, the scandal of God's fair universe;   55
We wash our hands forever of your sin and shame and curse.

A voice from lips whereon the coal from Freedom's shrine hath been,
Thrilled, as but yesterday, the hearts of Berkshire's mountain men:
The echoes of that solemn voice are sadly lingering still
In all our sunny valleys, on every wind-swept hill.   60

729

And when the prowling man-thief came hunting for his prey
Beneath the very shadow of Bunker's shaft of gray,
How, through the free lips of the son, the father's warning spoke;
How, from its bonds of trade and sect, the Pilgrim city broke!

A hundred thousand right arms were lifted up on high,   65
A hundred thousand voices sent back their loud reply;
Through the thronged towns of Essex the startling summons rang,
And up from bench and loom and wheel her young mechanics sprang!

The voice of free, broad Middlesex, of thousands as of one,
The shaft of Bunker calling to that of Lexington;   70
From Norfolk's ancient villages; from Plymouth's rocky bound
To where Nantucket feels the arms of ocean close her round;

From rich and rural Worcester, where through the calm repose
Of cultured vales and fringing woods the gentle Nashua flows,
To where Wachuset's wintry blasts the mountain larches stir,   75
Swelled up to Heaven the thrilling cry of "God save Latimer!"

And sandy Barnstable rose up, wet with the salt sea spray;
And Bristol sent her answering shout down Narragansett Bay!
Along the broad Connecticut old Hampden felt the thrill,
And the cheer of Hampshire's woodmen swept down from Holyoke Hill.   80

The voice of Massachusetts! Of her free sons and daughters,
Deep calling unto deep aloud, the sound of many waters!
Against the burden of that voice what tyrant power shall stand?
No fetters in the Bay State! No slave upon her land!

Look to it well, Virginians! In calmness we have borne,   85
In answer to our faith and trust, your insult and your scorn;
You've spurned our kindest counsels, you've hunted for our lives;
And shaken round our hearths and homes your manacles and gyves!

We wage no war, we lift no arm, we fling no torch within
The fire-damps of the quaking mine beneath your soil of sin;   90
We leave ye with your bondmen, to wrestle, while ye can,
With the strong upward tendencies and God-like soul of man!

But for us and for our children, the vow which we have given
For freedom and humanity is registered in heaven;
No slave-hunt in our borders, no pirate on our strand!   95
No fetters in the Bay State—no slave upon our land!

To a Southern Statesman

"JOHN C. CALHOUN, who had strongly urged the extension of slave territory by the annexation of Texas, even if it should involve a war with England, was unwilling to promote the acquisition of Oregon, which would enlarge the Northern domain of freedom, and pleaded as an excuse the peril of foreign complications

730

which he had defied when the interests of slavery were involved." (Whittier's note, Riverside Edition, III, 1888–1889). First published in the *National Era*, Jan. 27, 1848, under title "To John C. Calhoun"; collected in *Poetical Works* (1857).

Is this thy voice whose treble notes of fear
Wail in the wind? And dost thou shake to hear,
Actæon-like, the bay of thine own hounds,
Spurning the leash, and leaping o'er their bounds?
Sore-baffled statesman! when thy eager hand, 5
With game afoot, unslipped the hungry pack,
To hunt down Freedom in her chosen land,
Hadst thou no fear, that, erelong, doubling back,
These dogs of thine might snuff on Slavery's track?
Where's now the boast, which even thy guarded
   tongue, 10
Cold, calm, and proud, in the teeth o' the Senate
   flung,
O'er the fulfilment of thy baleful plan,
Like Satan's triumph at the fall of man?
How stood'st thou then, thy feet on Freedom
   planting,
And pointing to the lurid heaven afar, 15
Whence all could see, through the south windows
   slanting,
Crimson as blood, the beams of that Lone Star!
The Fates are just; they give us but our own;
Nemesis ripens what our hands have sown.
There is an Eastern Story, not unknown, 20
Doubtless, to thee, of one whose magic skill
Called demons up his water-jars to fill;
Deftly and silently, they did his will,
But, when the task was done, kept pouring still.
In vain with spell and charm the wizard wrought,
Faster and faster were the buckets brought, 26
Higher and higher rose the flood around,
Till the fiends clapped their hands above their
   master drowned!
So, Carolinian, it may prove with thee,
For God still overrules man's schemes, and takes
Craftiness in its self-set snare, and makes 31
The wrath of man to praise Him. It may be,
That the roused spirits of Democracy
May leave to freer States the same wide door 34
Through which thy slave-cursed Texas entered in,
From out the blood and fire, the wrong and sin,
Of the stormed city and the ghastly plain,
Beat by hot hail, and wet with bloody rain,

The myriad-handed pioneer may pour, 39
And the wild West with the roused North combine
And heave the engineer of evil with his mine.

Proem

DATED "11th mo., 1847," this proem served as an introduction to Whittier's first collected *Poems* (1849), and to subsequent collected editions.

I love the old melodious lays
Which softly melt the ages through,
   The songs of Spenser's golden days,
   Arcadian Sidney's silvery phrase,
Sprinkling our noon of time with freshest morning
   dew. 5

Yet, vainly in my quiet hours
To breathe their marvellous notes I try;
   I feel them, as the leaves and flowers
   In silence feel the dewy showers,
And drink with glad, still lips the blessing of the
   sky. 10

   The rigor of a frozen clime,
The harshness of an untaught ear,
   The jarring words of one whose rhyme
   Beat often Labor's hurried time,
Or Duty's rugged march through storm and strife,
   are here. 15

   Of mystic beauty, dreamy grace,
No rounded art the lack supplies;
   Unskilled the subtle lines to trace,
   Or softer shades of Nature's face, 19
I view her common forms with unanointed eyes.

   Nor mine the seer-like power to show
The secrets of the heart and mind;
   To drop the plummet-line below
   Our common world of joy and woe, 24
A more intense despair or brighter hope to find.

   Yet here at least an earnest sense
Of human right and weal is shown;
   A hate of tyranny intense,
   And hearty in its vehemence, 29
As if my brother's pain and sorrow were my own.

731

O Freedom! if to me belong
Nor mighty Milton's gift divine,
   Nor Marvell's wit and graceful song,
   Still with a love as deep and strong
As theirs, I lay, like them, my best gifts on thy
      shrine!   35

The Poor Voter on Election Day

PUBLISHED FIRST in *The National Era*, December 23,
1852; collected in *The Chapel of the Hermits, and Other
Poems* (1853).

The proudest now is but my peer,
   The highest not more high;
To-day, of all the weary year,
   A king of men am I.
To-day, alike are great and small,   5
   The nameless and the known;
My palace is the people's hall,
   The ballot-box my throne!

Who serves to-day upon the list
   Beside the served shall stand;   10
Alike the brown and wrinkled fist,
   The gloved and dainty hand!
The rich is level with the poor,
   The weak is strong to-day;
And sleekest broadcloth counts no more   15
   Than homespun frock of gray.

To-day let pomp and vain pretence
   My stubborn right abide;
I set a plain man's common sense
   Against the pedant's pride.   20
To-day shall simple manhood try
   The strength of gold and land;
The wide world has not wealth to buy
   The power in my right hand!

While there's a grief to seek redress,   25
   Or balance to adjust,
Where weighs our living manhood less
   Than Mammon's vilest dust,—
While there's a right to need my vote,
   A wrong to sweep away,   30
Up! clouted knee and ragged coat!
   A man's a man to-day!

Ichabod

THIS POEM first appeared in *The National Era* for May 2,
1850, and was included in the second part of *Songs of
Labor*, published in the same year. It was also printed
in *National Lyrics* (1865), and in *Favorite Poems* (1877).
Almost forty years after the composition of the poem
Whittier appended a note from which the following
excerpt is taken: "This poem was the outcome of the
surprise and grief and forecast of evil consequences
which I felt on reading the seventh of March speech of
Daniel Webster in support of the 'compromise' and the
Fugitive Slave Bill. No partisan or personal enmity
dictated it. On the contrary my admiration of the
splendid personality and intellectual power of the great
Senator was never stronger than when I laid down his
speech, and, in one of the saddest moments of my life,
penned my protest. . . ."

So fallen! so lost! the light withdrawn
   Which once he wore!
The glory from his gray hairs gone
   Forevermore!

Revile him not, the Tempter hath   5
   A snare for all;
And pitying tears, not scorn and wrath,
   Befit his fall!

Oh, dumb be passion's stormy rage,
   When he who might   10
Have lighted up and led his age,
   Falls back in night.

Scorn! would the angels laugh, to mark
   A bright soul driven,
Fiend-goaded, down the endless dark,   15
   From hope and heaven!

Let not the land once proud of him
   Insult him now,
Nor brand with deeper shame his dim,
   Dishonored brow.   20

But let its humbled sons, instead,
   From sea to lake,
A long lament, as for the dead,
   In sadness make.

Ichabod: "And she named the child Ichabod, saying,
'The glory is departed from Israel.'" See 1 Samuel, 4:21.

732

Of all we loved and honored, naught   25
  Save power remains;
A fallen angel's pride of thought,
  Still strong in chains.

All else is gone; from those great eyes
  The soul has fled: 30
When faith is lost, when honor dies,
  The man is dead!

Then, pay the reverence of old days
  To his dead fame;
Walk backward, with averted gaze,   35
  And hide the shame!

First-Day Thoughts

FIRST PRINTED in *The Chapel of the Hermits, and Other Poems* (1853).

In calm and cool and silence, once again
  I find my old accustomed place among
  My brethren, where, perchance, no human
    tongue
  Shall utter words; where never hymn is sung,
  Nor deep-toned organ blown, nor censer swung,
Nor dim light falling through the pictured pane!
There, syllabled by silence, let me hear   7
The still small voice which reached the prophet's
    ear;
Read in my heart a still diviner law
Than Israel's leader on his tables saw!   10
There let me strive with each besetting sin,
  Recall my wandering fancies, and restrain
  The sore disquiet of a restless brain;
  And, as the path of duty is made plain,
May grace be given that I may walk therein,   15
  Not like the hireling, for his selfish gain,
With backward glances and reluctant tread,
Making a merit of his coward dread,
  But, cheerful, in the light around me thrown,
  Walking as one to pleasant service led;   20
  Doing God's will as if it were my own,
Yet trusting not in mine, but in His strength alone!

Maud Muller

As TO the genesis of the poem, Whittier recalled having long previously taken a journey with his sister along the Maine coast, and resting his horse under an apple tree near a brook. While there they engaged in conversation with a young girl who, blushing, was trying to hide her bare feet in the hay she was raking. The poem was first published in *The National Era*, December 28, 1854, and collected in *The Panorama, and Other Poems* (1856). Whittier did not think too well of this piece, but the public did. For an exposure of its basic sentimental fallacy, see Bret Harte's "Mrs. Judge Jenkins," in *East and West Poems* (1871).

Maud Muller on a summer's day,
Raked the meadow sweet with hay.

Beneath her torn hat glowed the wealth
Of simple beauty and rustic health.

Singing, she wrought, and her merry glee   5
The mock-bird echoed from his tree.

But when she glanced to the far-off town,
White from its hill-slope looking down,

The sweet song died, and a vague unrest
And a nameless longing filled her breast,—   10

A wish, that she hardly dared to own,
For something better than she had known.

The Judge rode slowly down the lane,
Smoothing his horse's chestnut mane.

He drew his bridle in the shade   15
Of the apple-trees, to greet the maid,

And asked a draught from the spring that flowed
Through the meadow across the road.

She stooped where the cool spring bubbled up,
And filled for him her small tin cup,   20

And blushed as she gave it, looking down
On her feet so bare, and her tattered gown.

"Thanks!" said the Judge; "a sweeter draught
From a fairer hand was never quaffed."

He spoke of the grass and flowers and trees,   25
Of the singing birds and the humming bees;

Then talked of the haying, and wondered whether
The cloud in the west would bring foul weather.

And Maud forgot her brier-torn gown
And her graceful ankles bare and brown;   30

And listened, while a pleased surprise
Looked from her long-lashed hazel eyes.

At last, like one who for delay
Seeks a vain excuse, he rode away.

Maud Muller looked and sighed: "Ah me!   35
That I the Judge's bride might be!

"He would dress me up in silks so fine,
And praise and toast me at his wine.

"My father should wear a broadcloth coat;
My brother should sail a painted boat.   40

"I'd dress my mother so grand and gay,
And the baby should have a new toy each day.

"And I'd feed the hungry and clothe the poor,
And all should bless me who left our door."

The Judge looked back as he climbed the hill,   45
And saw Maud Muller standing still.

"A form more fair, a face more sweet,
Ne'er hath it been my lot to meet.

"And her modest answer and graceful air
Show her wise and good as she is fair.   50

"Would she were mine, and I to-day,
Like her, a harvester of hay;

"No doubtful balance of rights and wrongs,
Nor weary lawyers with endless tongues,

"But low of cattle and song of birds,   55
And health and quiet and loving words."

But he thought of his sisters, proud and cold,
And his mother, vain of her rank and gold.

So, closing his heart, the Judge rode on,
And Maud was left in the field alone.   60

But the lawyers smiled that afternoon,
When he hummed in court an old love-tune;

And the young girl mused beside the well
Till the rain on the unraked clover fell.

He wedded a wife of richest dower,   65
Who lived for fashion, as he for power.

Yet oft, in his marble hearth's bright glow,
He watched a picture come and go;

And sweet Maud Muller's hazel eyes
Looked out in their innocent surprise.   70

Oft, when the wine in his glass was red,
He longed for the wayside well instead;

And closed his eyes on his garnished rooms
To dream of meadows and clover-blooms.

And the proud man sighed, with a secret pain,   75
"Ah, that I were free again!

"Free as when I rode that day,
Where the barefoot maiden raked her hay."

She wedded a man unlearned and poor,
And many children played round her door.   80

But care and sorrow, and childbirth pain,
Left their traces on heart and brain.

And oft, when the summer sun shone hot
On the new-mown hay in the meadow lot,

And she heard the little spring brook fall   85
Over the roadside, through the wall,

In the shade of the apple-tree again
She saw a rider draw his rein.

And, gazing down with timid grace,
She felt his pleased eyes read her face.   90

Sometimes her narrow kitchen walls
Stretched away into stately halls;

The weary wheel to a spinnet turned,
The tallow candle an astral burned,

And for him who sat by the chimney lug,   95
Dozing and grumbling o'er pipe and mug,

734

A manly form at her side she saw,
And joy was duty and love was law.

Then she took up her burden of life again,
Saying only, "It might have been."   100

Alas for maiden, alas for Judge,
For rich repiner and household drudge!

God pity them both! and pity us all,
Who vainly the dreams of youth recall.

For of all sad words of tongue or pen   105
The saddest are these: "It might have been!"

Ah, well! for us all some sweet hope lies
Deeply buried from human eyes;

And, in the hereafter, angels may
Roll the stone from its grave away!   110

Skipper Ireson's Ride

THIS WAS the second of Whittier's poems to appear in *The Atlantic Monthly* (December, 1857), then in its first year. He had heard the refrain from a schoolmate from Marblehead, and had begun writing the ballad in 1828, though he did not finish it until 1857. In a letter to James Russell Lowell, editor of *The Atlantic*, Whittier remarked that the incident had occurred in the previous century, and that the refrain was the song of the marching women. Lowell replied, saying that he was familiar with the story, and he suggested changes in the spelling of the words of the refrain to conform with Marblehead dialect. Whittier agreed to the changes in the lines set within quotation marks. Decades later the poet learned from Samuel Roads, Jr. (*History and Traditions of Marblehead* (1879)), that Captain Benjamin Ireson had been tarred and feathered in 1807, the year of Whittier's birth, and that the captain had not been responsible for abandoning the ship, but had been falsely accused by the crew for an act of their own commission. Whittier thanked Roads for bringing the truth to light. The ballad was first collected in *Home Ballads and Poems* (1860); it was set to music in 1925 by Alec Rowley.

Of all the rides since the birth of time,
Told in story or sung in rhyme,—
On Apuleius's Golden Ass,
Or one-eyed Calendar's horse of brass,

Witch astride of a human hack,   5
Islam's prophet on Al-Borák,—
The strangest ride that ever was sped
Was Ireson's, out from Marblehead!
     Old Floyd Ireson, for his hard heart
     Tarred and feathered and carried in a cart   10
          By the women of Marblehead!

Body of turkey, head of owl,
Wings a-droop like a rained-on fowl,
Feathered and ruffled in every part,
Skipper Ireson stood in the cart.   15
Scores of women, old and young,
Strong of muscle, and glib of tongue,
Pushed and pulled up the rocky lane,
Shouting and singing the shrill refrain:
     "Here's Flud Oirson, fur his horrd horrt,   20
     Torr'd an' futherr'd an' corr'd in a corrt
          By the women o' Morble'ead!"

Wrinkled scolds with hands on hips,
Girls in bloom of cheek and lips,
Wild-eyed, free-limbed, such as chase   25
Bacchus round some antique vase,
Brief of skirt, with ankles bare,
Loose of kerchief and loose of hair,
With conch-shells blowing and fish-horns' twang,
Over and over the Mænads sang: 30
     "Here's Flud Oirson, fur his horrd horrt,
     Torr'd an' futherr'd an' corr'd in a corrt
          By the women o' Morble'ead!"

Small pity for him!—He sailed away
From a leaking ship, in Chaleur Bay,—   35
Sailed away from a sinking wreck,
With his own town's-people on her deck!
"Lay by! lay by!" they called to him.
Back he answered, "Sink or swim!
Brag of your catch of fish again!"   40
And off he sailed through the fog and rain!
     Old Floyd Ireson, for his hard heart,
     Tarred and feathered and carried in a cart
          By the women of Marblehead.

Fathoms deep in dark Chaleur   45
That wreck shall lie forevermore.
Mother and sister, wife and maid,
Looked from the rocks of Marblehead

Over the moaning and rainy sea,—
Looked for the coming that might not be! 50
What did the winds and the sea-birds say
Of the cruel captain who sailed away?
    Old Floyd Ireson, for his hard heart,
    Tarred and feathered and carried in a cart
        By the women of Marblehead! 55

Through the street, on either side,
Up flew windows, doors swung wide;
Sharp-tongued spinsters, old wives gray,
Treble lent the fish-horn's bray;
Sea-worn grandsires, cripple-bound, 60
Hulks of old sailors run aground,
Shook head, and fist, and hat, and cane,
And cracked with curses the hoarse refrain:
    "Here's Flud Oirson, fur his horrd horrt,
    Torr'd an' futherr'd an' corr'd in a corrt 65
        By the women o' Morble'ead!"

Sweetly along the Salem road
Bloom of orchard and lilac showed.
Little the wicked skipper knew
Of the fields so green and the sky so blue. 70
Riding there in his sorry trim,
Like an Indian idol glum and grim,
Scarcely he seemed the sound to hear
Of voices shouting, far and near:
    "Here's Flud Oirson, fur his horrd horrt, 75
    Torr'd an' futherr'd an' corr'd in a corrt
        By the women o' Morble'ead!"

"Hear me, neighbors!" at last he cried,—
"What to me is this noisy ride?
What is the shame that clothes the skin 80
To the nameless horror that lives within?
Waking or sleeping, I see a wreck,
And hear a cry from a reeling deck!
Hate me and curse me—I only dread
The hand of God and the face of the dead!" 85
    Said old Floyd Ireson, for his hard heart,
    Tarred and feathered and carried in a cart
        By the women of Marblehead!

Then the wife of the skipper lost at sea
Said, "God has touched him! why should we?" 90
Said an old wife mourning her only son,
"Cut the rogue's tether and let him run!"
So with soft relentings and rude excuse,

Half scorn, half pity, they cut him loose,
And gave him a cloak to hide him in, 95
And left him alone with his shame and sin.
    Poor Floyd Ireson, for his hard heart,
    Tarred and feathered and carried in a cart
        By the women of Marblehead!

Telling the Bees

WHITTIER submitted this poem to Lowell, editor of
The Atlantic Monthly, February 16, 1858, under the
title "The Bees of Fernside." On February 22 he submitted some changes, mentioned that he had just been
elected a member of the Board of Overseers of Harvard
College, and humorously cautioned Lowell, as a Harvard professor, to pay attention to the new overseer's
request that Lowell give him a frank critical estimate
of the poem. Whittier thought very well of the
ballad, but he was not sure how others would regard it.
In his first letter to Lowell, Whittier remarked that
what the author thought to be "simplicity" might be
considered by others as merely "silliness" (Pickard,
Life). It has come to be regarded as one of his finest
ballads, unmarred by didacticism. The scene is
Whittier's birthplace, the Haverhill homestead, which
Whittier had left on moving to Amesbury a score of
years previously; the beehives, the path over Job's
Hill, the gap in the wall, the steppingstones in the
brook, and other items are precise descriptions of his
boyhood home. The story is imaginative. His sister
Mary was living, but his mother had recently died.
Whittier's note reads: "A remarkable custom, brought
from the Old Country, formerly prevailed in the rural
districts of New England. On the death of a member
of the family, the bees were at once informed of the
event, and their hives dressed in mourning. This
ceremony was supposed to be necessary to prevent the
swarms from leaving their hives and seeking a new
home." First appearance of the poem was in *The
Atlantic Monthly*, April, 1858; it was first collected in
Home Ballads and Poems (1860).

Here is the place; right over the hill
    Runs the path I took;
You can see the gap in the old wall still,
    And the stepping-stones in the shallow brook.

There is the house, with the gate red-barred, 5
    And the poplars tall;
And the barn's brown length, and the cattle-yard,
    And the white horns tossing above the wall.

736

There are the bee-hives ranged in the sun;
    And down by the brink   10
Of the brook are her poor flowers, weed o'er-run,
    Pansy and daffodil, rose and pink.

A year has gone, as the tortoise goes,
    Heavy and slow;
And the same rose blows, and the same sun glows, 15
    And the same brook sings of a year ago.

There's the same sweet clover-smell in the breeze;
    And the June sun warm
Tangles his wings of fire in the trees,
    Setting, as then, over Fernside farm.   20

I mind me how with a lover's care
    From my Sunday coat
I brushed off the burs, and smoothed my hair,
    And cooled at the brookside my brow and throat.

Since we parted, a month had passed,—   25
    To love, a year;
Down through the beeches I looked at last
    On the little red gate and the well-sweep near.

I can see it all now,—the slantwise rain
    Of light through the leaves,   30
The sundown's blaze on her window-pane,
    The bloom of her roses under the eaves.

Just the same as a month before,—
    The house and the trees,
The barn's brown gable, the vine by the door,—
    Nothing changed but the hives of bees.   36

Before them, under the garden wall,
    Forward and back,
Went drearily singing the chore-girl small,
    Draping each hive with a shred of black.   40

Trembling, I listened: the summer sun
    Had the chill of snow;
For I knew she was telling the bees of one
    Gone on the journey we all must go!

Then I said to myself, "My Mary weeps   45
    For the dead to-day:
Haply her blind old grandsire sleeps
    The fret and the pain of his age away."

But her dog whined low; on the doorway sill,
    With his cane to his chin,   50
The old man sat; and the chore-girl still
    Sung to the bees stealing out and in.

And the song she was singing ever since
    In my ear sounds on:—
"Stay at home, pretty bees, fly not hence!   55
    Mistress Mary is dead and gone!"

My Playmate

PICKARD STATES and Mordell affirms that the Mary of
this poem was Mary Emerson Smith, a distant relative
of Whittier's, a friend of his childhood days, a schoolmate at Haverhill Academy, and the girl commemo-
rated in his more personal poem "Memories." Mordell
presents evidence to support his thesis that Whittier
fell passionately in love with Miss Smith, and continued his advances while editing *The American Manufacturer* in Boston, though she rejected him. The uneven road of his love, according to Mordell, is responsible for a number of his early poems and prose
writings. She was not a Quaker, and Whittier's social
background and economic prospects did not impress
her. She later married a judge in Kentucky and became the mother of ten children. In her widowhood
Whittier and she met occasionally on her visits to New
England and maintained correspondence. After submitting the poem to Lowell, Whittier wrote three
letters to him during January and February, 1860, requesting changes (Pickard, *Life*). The present eighth
stanza was added; the stanza that was to follow it was
deleted; the present fifteenth stanza was substituted
for one that had been in this place, and a number of
alterations were made in the proof. The poem, in
manuscript, was entitled "Eleanor." Ramoth hill,
the pond (Kimball's), and Follymill woods are near
Whittier's Amesbury home. First publication was in
The Atlantic Monthly, May, 1860; it was collected in
Home Ballads and Poems (1860).

The pines were dark on Ramoth hill,
    Their song was soft and low;
The blossoms in the soft May wind
    Were falling like the snow.

The blossoms drifted at our feet,   5
    The orchard birds sang clear;
The sweetest and the saddest day
    It seemed of all the year.

For, more to me than birds or flowers,
 My playmate left her home 10
And took with her the laughing spring,
 The music and the bloom.

She kissed the lips of kith and kin,
 She laid her hand in mine:
What more could ask the bashful boy 15
 Who fed her father's kine?

She left us in the bloom of May:
 The constant years told o'er
Their seasons with as sweet May morns,
 But she came back no more. 20

I walk, with noiseless feet, the round
 Of uneventful years;
Still o'er and o'er I sow the spring
 And reap the autumn ears.

She lives where all the golden year 25
 Her summer roses blow;
The dusky children of the sun
 Before her come and go.

There haply with her jewelled hands
 She smooths her silken gown,— 30
No more the homespun lap wherein
 I shook the walnuts down.

The wild grapes wait us by the brook,
 The brown nuts on the hill,
And still the May-day flowers make sweet 35
 The woods of Follymill.

The lilies blossom in the pond,
 The bird builds in the tree,
The dark pines sing on Ramoth hill
 The slow song of the sea. 40

I wonder if she thinks of them,
 And how the old time seems,—
If ever the pines of Ramoth wood
 Are sounding in her dreams.

I see her face, I hear her voice: 45
 Does she remember mine?
And what to her is now the boy
 Who fed her father's kine?

What cares she that the orioles build
 For other eyes than ours,— 50
That other hands with nuts are filled,
 And other laps with flowers?

O playmate in the golden time!
 Our mossy seat is green,
Its fringing violets blossom yet, 55
 The old trees o'er it lean.

The winds so sweet with birch and fern
 A sweeter memory blow;
And there in spring the veeries sing
 The song of long ago. 60

And still the pines of Ramoth wood
 Are moaning like the sea,—
The moaning of the sea of change
 Between myself and thee!

Laus Deo[n]

THIS POEM was published in *The Independent*, New York, for February 9, 1865, and first collected in *National Lyrics* (1865). Whittier was in the Friends' meetinghouse at Amesbury when he heard the sound of the bells and cannon in celebration of the passage by Congress of the constitutional amendment abolishing slavery, January 31, 1865. He immediately began composing the poem, which "wrote itself, or rather sang itself, while the bells rang."

  It is done!
 Clang of bell and roar of gun
 Send the tidings up and down.
  How the belfries rock and reel!
  How the great guns, peal on peal, 5
 Fling the joy from town to town!

  Ring, O bells!
 Every stroke exulting tells
 Of the burial hour of crime.
  Loud and long, that all may hear, 10
  Ring for every listening ear
 Of Eternity and Time!

  Let us kneel:
 God's own voice is in that peal,
 And this spot is holy ground. 15

 Laus Deo: "Praise be to God."

Lord, forgive us! What are we,
That our eyes this glory see,
That our ears have heard the sound!

    For the Lord
On the whirlwind is abroad;   20
In the earthquake He has spoken;
He has smitten with His thunder
The iron walls asunder,
And the gates of brass are broken!

    Loud and long   25
Lift the old exulting song;
Sing with Miriam by the sea,
He has cast the mighty down;
Horse and rider sink and drown;
"He hath triumphed gloriously!"   30

    Did we dare,
In our agony of prayer,
Ask for more than He has done?
When was ever His right hand
Over any time or land   35
Stretched as now beneath the sun?

    How they pale,
Ancient myth and song and tale,
In this wonder of our days,
When the cruel rod of war   40
Blossoms white with righteous law,
And the wrath of man is praise!

    Blotted out!
All within and all about
Shall a fresher life begin;   45
Freer breathe the universe
As it rolls its heavy curse
On the dead and buried sin!

    It is done!
In the circuit of the sun   50
Shall the sound thereof go forth.
It shall bid the sad rejoice,
It shall give the dumb a voice,
It shall belt with joy the earth!

    Ring and swing,   55
Bells of joy! On morning's wing
Sound the song of praise abroad!

With a sound of broken chains
Tell the nations that He reigns,
Who alone is Lord and God!   60

The Eternal Goodness

THOUGH WHITTIER cared little for music beyond balladry, approximately 100 hymns are derived from 59 of his religious poems. (See Clifton E. Moore, "Whittier's Contribution to Hymnology," unpublished monograph, 1944, Western Reserve University Library.) Currier lists four renderings in sheet music of "The Eternal Goodness," and nine derivative hymns. It was first published in *The Independent*, March 16, 1865; was collected in *The Tent on the Beach, and Other Poems* (1867). The Riverside Edition contains 73 titles under "Religious Poems."

O friends! with whom my feet have trod
    The quiet aisles of prayer,
Glad witness to your zeal for God
    And love of man I bear.

I trace your lines of argument;   5
    Your logic linked and strong
I weigh as one who dreads dissent,
    And fears a doubt as wrong.

But still my human hands are weak
    To hold your iron creeds: 10
Against the words ye bid me speak
    My heart within me pleads.

Who fathoms the Eternal Thought?
    Who talks of scheme and plan?
The Lord is God! He needeth not   15
    The poor device of man.

I walk with bare, hushed feet the ground
    Ye tread with boldness shod;
I dare not fix with mete and bound
    The love and power of God.   20

Ye praise His justice; even such
    His pitying love I deem:
Ye seek a king; I fain would touch
    The robe that hath no seam.

Ye see the curse which overbroods   25
    A world of pain and loss;

739

I hear our Lord's beatitudes
 And prayer upon the cross.

More than your schoolmen teach, within
 Myself, alas! I know: 30
Too dark ye cannot paint the sin,
 Too small the merit show.

I bow my forehead to the dust,
 I veil mine eyes for shame,
And urge, in trembling self-distrust, 35
 A prayer without a claim.

I see the wrong that round me lies,
 I feel the guilt within;
I hear, with groan and travail-cries,
 The world confess its sin.   40

Yet, in the maddening maze of things,
 And tossed by storm and flood,
To one fixed trust my spirit clings;
 I know that God is good!

Not mine to look where cherubim 45
 And seraphs may not see,
But nothing can be good in Him
 Which evil is in me.

The wrong that pains my soul below
 I dare not throne above,   50
I know not of His hate,—I know
 His goodness and His love.

I dimly guess from blessings known
 Of greater out of sight,
And, with the chastened Psalmist, own 55
 His judgments too are right.

I long for household voices gone,
 For vanished smiles I long,
But God hath led my dear ones on,
 And He can do no wrong.   60

I know not what the future hath
 Of marvel or surprise,
Assured alone that life and death
 His mercy underlies.

And if my heart and flesh are weak 65
 To bear an untried pain,

The bruisèd reed He will not break,
 But strengthen and sustain.

No offering of my own I have,
 Nor works my faith to prove; 70
I can but give the gifts He gave,
 And plea His love for love.

And so beside the Silent Sea
 I wait the muffled oar;
No harm from Him can come to me 75
 On ocean or on shore.

I know not where His islands lift
 Their fronded palms in air;
I only know I cannot drift
 Beyond His love and care.   80

O brothers! if my faith is vain,
 If hopes like these betray,
Pray for me that my feet may gain
 The sure and safer way.

And Thou, O Lord! by whom are seen 85
 Thy creatures as they be,
Forgive me if too close I lean
 My human heart on Thee!

Snow-Bound

A Winter Idyll · To the memory of the household it describes, this poem is dedicated by the author

In August, 1865, Whittier mentioned to James T. Fields that he was writing "Snow-Bound," which he sent to the publisher on October 3. Later Whittier modified, added, and deleted lines in a half-dozen places. The greatest change occurred in lines 267 to 283, which originally read:

 She made for us the sunset shine
 Aslant the tall columnar pine;
 The river at her father's door
 Its rippled moanings whispered o'er;
 We heard the hawks at twilight play, 5
 The boat-horn on Piscataqua,
 The loon's weird laughter far away.
 So well she gleaned from earth and sky
 That harvest of the ear and eye,
 We almost felt the gusty air 10
 That swept her native wood-paths bare,

Heard the far thresher's rhythmic flail,
The flapping of the fisher's sail,
Or saw in sheltered cove and bay
The ducks' black squadron anchored lay,   15
Or heard the wild geese calling loud
Beneath the gray November cloud.

The poem first appeared as a booklet in February, 1866, and sold so well that Whittier's royalties on the first issue, which ran through numerous printings, amounted to $10,000. Currier (*A Bibliography*) listed twenty-one editions between 1860 and 1930, exclusive of four editions for the blind.

Whittier prefaced the following note:

"The inmates of the family at the Whittier homestead who are referred to in the poem were my father, mother, my brother and two sisters, and my uncle and aunt both unmarried. In addition, there was the district school-master who boarded with us. The 'not unfeared, half-welcome guest' was Harriet Livermore, daughter of Judge Livermore, of New Hampshire, a young woman of fine natural ability, enthusiastic, eccentric, with slight control over her violent temper, which sometimes made her religious profession doubtful. She was equally ready to exhort in school-house prayer-meetings and dance in a Washington ball-room, while her father was a member of Congress. She early embraced the doctrine of the Second Advent, and felt it her duty to proclaim the Lord's speedy coming. With this message she crossed the Atlantic and spent the greater part of a long life in traveling over Europe and Asia. . . .

"In my boyhood, in our lonely farm-house, we had scanty sources of information; few books and only a small weekly newspaper. Our only annual was the Almanac. Under such circumstances story-telling was a necessary resource in the long winter evenings. My father when a young man had traversed the wilderness to Canada, and could tell us of his adventures with Indians and wild beasts, and of his sojourn in the French villages. My uncle was ready with his record of hunting and fishing and, it must be confessed, with stories which he at least half believed, of witchcraft and apparitions. My mother, who was born in the Indian-haunted region of Somersworth, New Hampshire, between Dover and Portsmouth, told us of the inroads of the savages, and the narrow escape of her ancestors. She described strange people who lived on the Piscataqua and Cocheco, among whom was Bantam the sorcerer. I have in my possession the wizard's 'conjuring book,' which he solemnly opened when consulted. It is a copy of Cornelius Agrippa's *Magic* printed in 1651. . . ."

"As the Spirits of Darkness be stronger in the dark, so good Spirits which be Angels of Light, are augmented not only by the Divine light of the Sun, but also by our common VVood Fire: and as the Celestial Fire drives away dark spirits, so also this our Fire of VVood doth the same."
COR. AGRIPPA, *Occult Philosophy*, Book I. ch. v.

The sun that brief December day
Rose cheerless over hills of gray,
And, darkly circled, gave at noon
A sadder light than waning moon.
Slow tracing down the thickening sky   5
Its mute and ominous prophecy,
A portent seeming less than threat,
It sank from sight before it set.
A chill no coat, however stout,
Of homespun stuff could quite shut out,   10
A hard, dull bitterness of cold,
That checked, mid-vein, the circling race
Of life-blood in the sharpened face,
The coming of the snow-storm told.
The wind blew east; we heard the roar   15
Of Ocean on his wintry shore,
And felt the strong pulse throbbing there
Beat with low rhythm our inland air.

Meanwhile we did our nightly chores,—
Brought in the wood from out of doors,   20
Littered the stalls, and from the mows
Raked down the herd's grass for the cows:
Heard the horse whinnying for his corn;
And, sharply clashing horn on horn,
Impatient down the stanchion rows   25
The cattle shake their walnut bows;
While, peering from his early perch
Upon the scaffold's pole of birch,
The cock his crested helmet bent
And down his querulous challenge sent.   30

Unwarmed by any sunset light
The gray day darkened into night,
A night made hoary with the swarm,
And whirl-dance of the blinding storm,
As zigzag, wavering to and fro   35
Crossed and recrossed the wingèd snow:
And ere the early bedtime came
The white drift piled the window-frame,
And through the glass the clothes-line posts
Looked in like tall and sheeted ghosts.   40

So all night long the storm roared on:
The morning broke without a sun;
In tiny spherule traced with lines
Of Nature's geometric signs,
In starry flake, and pellicle,   45
All day the hoary meteor fell;

And, when the second morning shone,
We looked upon a world unknown,
On nothing we could call our own.
Around the glistening wonder bent   50
The blue walls of the firmament,
No cloud above, no earth below,—
A universe of sky and snow!
The old familiar sights of ours
Took marvellous shapes; strange domes and
    towers
Rose up where sty or corn-crib stood,   56
Or garden-wall, or belt of wood;
A smooth white mound the brush-pile showed,
A fenceless drift what once was road;
The bridle-post an old man sat   60
With loose-flung coat and high cocked hat;
The well-curb had a Chinese roof;
And even the long sweep, high aloof,
In its slant splendor, seemed to tell
Of Pisa's leaning miracle.   65

A prompt, decisive man, no breath
Our father wasted: "Boys, a path!"
Well pleased, (for when did farmer boy
Count such a summons less than joy?)
Our buskins on our feet we drew;   70
With mittened hands, and caps drawn low,
To guard our necks and ears from snow,
We cut the solid whiteness through.
And, where the drift was deepest, made
A tunnel walled and overlaid   75
With dazzling crystal: we had read
Of rare Aladdin's wondrous cave,
And to our own his name we gave,
With many a wish the luck were ours
To test his lamp's supernal powers.   80
We reached the barn with merry din,
And roused the prisoned brutes within.
The old horse thrust his long head out,
And grave with wonder gazed about;
The cock his lusty greeting said,   85
And forth his speckled harem led;
The oxen lashed their tails, and hooked,
And mild reproach of hunger looked;
The hornèd patriarch of the sheep,
Like Egypt's Amun roused from sleep,   90

    90. Amun: Ancient Egyptian god with the head of a
ram.

Shook his sage head with gesture mute,
And emphasized with stamp of foot.

All day the gusty north-wind bore
The loosening drift its breath before;
Low circling round its southern zone,   95
The sun through dazzling snow-mist shone.
No church-bell lent its Christian tone
To the savage air, no social smoke
Curled over woods of snow-hung oak.
A solitude made more intense   100
By dreary-voicèd elements,
The shrieking of the mindless wind,
The moaning tree-boughs swaying blind,
And on the glass the unmeaning beat
Of ghostly finger-tips of sleet.   105
Beyond the circle of our hearth
No welcome sound of toil or mirth
Unbound the spell, and testified
Of human life and thought outside.
We minded that the sharpest ear   110
The buried brooklet could not hear,
The music of whose liquid lip
Had been to us companionship,
And, in our lonely life, had grown
To have an almost human tone.   115

As night drew on, and, from the crest
Of wooded knolls that ridged the west,
The sun, a snow-blown traveller, sank
From sight beneath the smothering bank,
We piled, with care, our nightly stack   120
Of wood against the chimney-back,—
The oaken log, green, huge, and thick,
And on its top the stout back-stick;
The knotty forestick laid apart,
And filled between with curious art   125
The ragged brush; then, hovering near,
We watched the first red blaze appear,
Heard the sharp crackle, caught the gleam
On whitewashed wall and sagging beam,
Until the old, rude-furnished room   130
Burst, flower-like, into rosy bloom;
While radiant with a mimic flame
Outside the sparkling drift became,
And through the bare-boughed lilac-tree
Our own warm hearth seemed blazing free.   135
The crane and pendent trammels showed,
The Turks' heads on the andirons glowed;

While childish fancy, prompt to tell
The meaning of the miracle,
Whispered the old rhyme: *"Under the tree,* 140
When the fire outdoors burns merrily,
There the witches are making tea."

The moon above the eastern wood
Shone at its full; the hill-range stood
Transfigured in the silver flood, 145
Its blown snows flashing cold and keen,
Dead white, save where some sharp ravine
Took shadow, or the sombre green
Of hemlocks turned to pitchy black
Against the whiteness at their back. 150
For such a world and such a night
Most fitting that unwarming light,
Which only seemed where'er it fell
To make the coldness visible.

Shut in from all the world without, 155
We sat the clean-winged hearth about,
Content to let the north-wind roar
In baffled rage at pane and door,
While the red logs before us beat
The frost-line back with tropic heat; 160
And ever, when a louder blast
Shook beam and rafter as it passed,
The merrier up its roaring draught
The great throat of the chimney laughed;
The house-dog on his paws outspread 165
Laid to the fire his drowsy head,
The cat's dark silhouette on the wall
A couchant tiger's seemed to fall;
And, for the winter fireside meet,
Between the andirons' straddling feet, 170
The mug of cider simmered slow,
The apples sputtered in a row,
And, close at hand, the basket stood
With nuts from brown October's wood.

What matter how the night behaved? 175
What matter how the north-wind raved?
Blow high, blow low, not all its snow
Could quench our hearth-fire's ruddy glow.
O Time and Change!—with hair as gray
As was my sire's that winter day, 180
How strange it seems, with so much gone
Of life and love, to still live on!

Ah, brother! only I and thou
Are left of all that circle now,—
The dear home faces whereupon 185
That fitful firelight paled and shone.
Henceforward, listen as we will,
The voices of that hearth are still;
Look where we may, the wide earth o'er
Those lighted faces smile no more. 190
We tread the paths their feet have worn,
We sit beneath their orchard trees,
We hear, like them, the hum of bees
And rustle of the bladed corn;
We turn the pages that they read, 195
Their written words we linger o'er,
But in the sun they cast no shade,
No voice is heard, no sign is made,
No step is on the conscious floor!
Yet Love will dream, and Faith will trust, 200
(Since He who knows our need is just,)
That somehow, somewhere, meet we must.
Alas for him who never sees
The stars shine through his cypress-trees!
Who, hopeless, lays his dead away, 205
Nor looks to see the breaking day
Across the mournful marbles play!
Who hath not learned, in hours of faith,
The truth to flesh and sense unknown,
That Life is ever lord of Death, 210
And Love can never lose its own!

We sped the time with stories old,
Wrought puzzles out, and riddles told,
Or stammered from our school-book lore
"The chief of Gambia's golden shore." 215
How often since, when all the land
Was clay in Slavery's shaping hand,
As if a far-blown trumpet stirred
The languorous sin-sick air, I heard:
"Does not the voice of reason cry, 220
Claim the first right which Nature gave,
From the red scourge of bondage fly,
Nor deign to live a burdened slave!"
Our father rode again his ride
On Memphremagog's wooded side; 225

183. brother: Matthew Franklin Whittier (1812–1883) was the only other living member of the family when the poem was written. **224. father:** John Whittier (1760–1830) had made more than one trip through the wilderness into Canada.

Sat down again to moose and samp,
In trapper's hut and Indian camp;
Lived o'er the old idyllic ease
Beneath St. François' hemlock-trees;
Again for him the moonlight shone   230
On Norman cap and bodiced zone;
Again he heard the violin play
Which led the village dance away,
And mingled in its merry whirl
The grandam and the laughing girl.   235
Or, nearer home, our steps he led
Where Salisbury's level marshes spread
   Mile-wide as flies the laden bee;
Where merry mowers, hale and strong,
Swept, scythe on scythe, their swaths along   240
   The low green prairies of the sea.
We shared the fishing off Boar's Head,
   And round the rocky Isles of Shoals
   The hake-broil on the drift-wood coals;
The chowder on the sand-beach made,   245
Dipped by the hungry, steaming hot,
With spoons of clam-shell from the pot.
We heard the tales of witchcraft old,
And dream and sign and marvel told
To sleepy listeners as they lay   250
Stretched idly on the salted hay,
Adrift along the winding shores,
When favoring breezes deigned to blow
The square sail of the gundelow
And idle lay the useless oars.   255

Our mother, while she turned her wheel
Or run the new-knit stocking-heel,
Told how the Indian hordes came down
At midnight on Cocheco town,
And how her own great-uncle bore   260
His cruel scalp-mark to fourscore.
Recalling, in her fitting phrase,
   So rich and picturesque and free
   (The common unrhymed poetry
Of simple life and country ways,)   265

The story of her early days,—
She made us welcome to her home;
Old hearths grew wide to give us room;
We stole with her a frightened look
At the gray wizard's conjuring-book,   270
The fame whereof went far and wide
Through all the simple country-side;
We heard the hawks at twilight play,
The boat-horn on Piscataqua,
The loon's weird laughter far away;   275
We fished her little trout-brook, knew
What flowers in wood and meadow grew,
What sunny hillsides autumn-brown
She climbed to shake the ripe nuts down,
Saw where in sheltered cove and bay   280
The duck's black squadron anchored lay,
And heard the wild-geese calling loud
Beneath the gray November cloud.

Then, haply, with a look more grave,
And soberer tone, some tale she gave   285
From painful Sewel's ancient tome,
Beloved in every Quaker home,
Of faith fire-winged by martyrdom,
Or Chalkley's Journal, old and quaint,—
Gentlest of skippers, rare sea-saint!—   290
Who, when the dreary calms prevailed,
And water-butt and bread-cask failed,
And cruel, hungry eyes pursued
His portly presence, mad for food
With dark hints muttered under breath   295
Of casting lots for life or death,
Offered, if Heaven withheld supplies,
To be himself the sacrifice.
Then, suddenly, as if to save
The good man from his living grave,   300
A ripple on the water grew,
A school of porpoise flashed in view.
"Take, eat," he said, "and be content;
These fishes in my stead are sent

225. Memphremagog: a lake in Vermont and Canada.
237. Salisbury: near Haverhill in northeastern Massachusetts. **242. Boar's Head:** on the coast of New Hampshire.
243. Isles of Shoals: islands off the New Hampshire coast.
256. mother: Abigail Hussey Whittier (1781–1857) was
known for her dignity. **259. Cocheco:** scene of an Indian
massacre in southern New Hampshire.

274. Piscataqua: a river forming the lower boundary
between Maine and New Hampshire. **286. Sewel:** William
Sewel published his *History of the Origin and Progress of the
Society Called Quakers* in 1717. **289. Chalkley's Journal:**
The *Journal* of Thomas Chalkley (1675–1741), a Friends'
minister and master of a merchant ship, and an early settler
in Pennsylvania. A passage in the *Journal* (1747), referring
to hunger at sea, in which extremity Chalkley had offered
to give up his life without drawing lots, was quoted by
Whittier in a note.

By Him who gave the tangled ram 305
To spare the child of Abraham."

Our uncle, innocent of books,
Was rich in lore of fields and brooks,
The ancient teachers never dumb
Of Nature's unhoused lyceum. 310
In moons and tides and weather wise,
He read the clouds as prophecies,
And foul or fair could well divine,
By many an occult hint and sign,
Holding the cunning-warded keys 315
To all the woodcraft mysteries;
Himself to Nature's heart so near
That all her voices in his ear
Of beast or bird had meanings clear,
Like Apollonius of old, 320
Who knew the tales the sparrows told,
Or Hermes, who interpreted
What the sage cranes of Nilus said;
A simple, guileless, childlike man,
Content to live where life began; 325
Strong only on his native grounds,
The little world of sights and sounds,
Whose girdle was the parish bounds,
Whereof his fondly partial pride
The common features magnified, 330
As Surrey hills to mountains grew
In White of Selborne's loving view,—
He told how teal and loon he shot,
And how the eagle's eggs he got,
The feats on pond and river done, 335
The prodigies of rod and gun;
Till, warming with the tales he told,
Forgotten was the outside cold,
The bitter wind unheeded blew,
From ripening corn the pigeons flew, 340
The partridge drummed i' the wood, the mink
Went fishing down the river-brink.
In fields with bean or clover gay,
The woodchuck, like a hermit gray,
    Peered from the doorway of his cell; 345
The muskrat plied the mason's trade,
And tier by tier his mud-walls laid;

And from the shagbark overhead
    The grizzled squirrel dropped his shell.

Next, the dear aunt, whose smile of cheer 350
And voice in dreams I see and hear,—
The sweetest woman ever Fate
Perverse denied a household mate,
Who, lonely, homeless, not the less
Found peace in love's unselfishness, 355
And welcome wheresoe'er she went,
A calm and gracious element,
Whose presence seemed the sweet income
And womanly atmosphere of home,—
Called up her girlhood memories, 360
The huskings and the apple-bees,
The sleigh-rides and the summer sails,
Weaving through all the poor details
And homespun warp of circumstance
A golden woof-thread of romance. 365
For well she kept her genial mood
And simple faith of maidenhood;
Before her still a cloud-land lay,
The mirage loomed across her way;
The morning dew, that dried so soon 370
With others, glistened at her noon;
Through years of toil and soil and care,
From glossy tress to thin gray hair,
All unprofaned she held apart
The virgin fancies of the heart. 375
Be shame to him of woman born
Who had for such but thought of scorn.

There, too, our elder sister plied
Her evening task the stand beside;
A full, rich nature, free to trust, 380
Truthful and almost sternly just,
Impulsive, earnest, prompt to act,
And make her generous thought a fact,
Keeping with many a light disguise
The secret of self-sacrifice. 385
O heart sore-tried! thou hast the best
That Heaven itself could give thee,—rest,
Rest from all bitter thoughts and things!
    How many a poor one's blessing went
    With thee beneath the low green tent 390
Whose curtain never outward swings!

307. uncle: Moses Whittier (1762–1804) was an ardent
hunter and fisherman.   332. White of Selborne: Gilbert
White (1720–1793) was an English author famed for his
Natural History of Selborne (1789).

350. aunt: Mercy Hussey, more vivacious than her
sister, the poet's mother, died a spinster in 1846.   378. elder
sister: Mary Whittier Caldwell (1806–1860).

As one who held herself a part
Of all she saw, and let her heart
　　Against the household bosom lean,
Upon the motley-braided mat　　　　　　395
Our youngest and our dearest sat,
Lifting her large, sweet, asking eyes,
　　Now bathed within the unfading green
And holy peace of Paradise.
Oh, looking from some heavenly hill,　　400
　　Or from the shade of saintly palms,
　　Or silver reach of river calms,
Do those large eyes behold me still?
With me one little year ago:—
The chill weight of the winter snow　　405
　　For months upon her grave has lain;
And now, when summer south-winds blow
　　And brier and harebell bloom again,
I tread the pleasant paths we trod,
I see the violet-sprinkled sod　　　　　410
Whereon she leaned, too frail and weak
The hillside flowers she loved to seek,
Yet following me where'er I went
With dark eyes full of love's content.
The birds are glad; the brier-rose fills　415
The air with sweetness; all the hills
Stretch green to June's unclouded sky;
But still I wait with ear and eye
For something gone which should be nigh,
A loss in all familiar things,　　　　　420
In flower that blooms, and bird that sings.
And yet, dear heart! remembering thee,
　　Am I not richer than of old?
Safe in thy immortality,
　　What change can reach the wealth I hold?　425
　　What chance can mar the pearl and gold
Thy love hath left in trust with me?
And while in life's late afternoon,
　　Where cool and long the shadows grow,
I walk to meet the night that soon　　　430
　　Shall shape and shadow overflow,
I cannot feel that thou art far,
Since near at need the angels are;
And when the sunset gates unbar,
　　Shall I not see thee waiting stand,　　435
And, white against the evening star,
　　The welcome of thy beckoning hand?

396. youngest: Whittier's sister Elizabeth (1815–1864),
who made a home for her brother until her death.

Brisk wielder of the birch and rule,
The master of the district school
Held at the fire his favored place,　　　440
Its warm glow lit a laughing face
Fresh-hued and fair, where scarce appeared
The uncertain prophecy of beard.
He teased the mitten-blinded cat,
Played cross-pins on my uncle's hat,　　445
Sang songs, and told us what befalls
In classic Dartmouth's college halls.
Born the wild Northern hills among,
From whence his yeoman father wrung
By patient toil subsistence scant,　　　450
Not competence and yet not want,
He early gained the power to pay
His cheerful, self-reliant way;
Could doff at ease his scholar's gown
To peddle wares from town to town;　　455
Or through the long vacation's reach
In lonely lowland districts teach,
Where all the droll experience found
At stranger hearths in boarding round,
The moonlit skater's keen delight,　　　460
The sleigh-drive through the frosty night,
The rustic party, with its rough
Accompaniment of blind-man's-buff,
And whirling plate, and forfeits paid,
His winter task a pastime made.　　　465
Happy the snow-locked homes wherein
He tuned his merry violin,
Or played the athlete in the barn,
Or held the good dame's winding-yarn,
Or mirth-provoking versions told　　　470
Of classic legends rare and old,
Wherein the scenes of Greece and Rome
Had all the commonplace of home,
And little seemed at best the odds
'Twixt Yankee pedlers and old gods;　475
Where Pindus-born Arachthus took
The guise of any grist-mill brook,
And dread Olympus at his will
Became a huckleberry hill.

A careless boy that night he seemed;　480
　　But at his desk he had the look
And air of one who wisely schemed,

439. master: George Haskell. He was educated at
Dartmouth; died in 1876.

746

And hostage from the future took
In trainèd thought and lore of book.
Large-brained, clear-eyed, of such as he   485
Shall Freedom's young apostles be,
Who, following in War's bloody trail,
Shall every lingering wrong assail;
All chains from limb and spirit strike,
Uplift the black and white alike;   490
Scatter before their swift advance
The darkness and the ignorance,
The pride, the lust, the squalid sloth,
Which nurtured Treason's monstrous growth,
Made murder pastime, and the hell   495
Of prison-torture possible;
The cruel lie of caste refute,
Old forms remould, and substitute
For Slavery's lash the freeman's will,
For blind routine, wise-handed skill;   500
A school-house plant on every hill,
Stretching in radiate nerve-lines thence
The quick wires of intelligence;
Till North and South together brought
Shall own the same electric thought,   505
In peace a common flag salute,
And, side by side in labor's free
And unresentful rivalry,
Harvest the fields wherein they fought.

Another guest that winter night   510
Flashed back from lustrous eyes the light.
Unmarked by time, and yet not young,
The honeyed music of her tongue
And words of meekness scarcely told
A nature passionate and bold,   515
Strong, self-concentred, spurning guide,
Its milder features dwarfed beside
Her unbent will's majestic pride.
She sat among us, at the best,
A not unfeared, half-welcome guest,   520
Rebuking with her cultured phrase
Our homeliness of words and ways.
A certain pard-like, treacherous grace
Swayed the lithe limbs and dropped the lash,

510. Another guest: Harriet Livermore (1788–1867) was distressed by the reference in the poem. For a charming sketch of her interesting life, see Elizabeth Hoxie's "Harriet Livermore: 'Vixen and Devotee,'" in *The New England Quarterly*, XVIII (1945), 39–50.

Lent the white teeth their dazzling flash;   525
And under low brows, black with night,
Rayed out at times a dangerous light;
The sharp heat-lightnings of her face
Presaging ill to him whom Fate
Condemned to share her love or hate.   530
A woman tropical, intense
In thought and act, in soul and sense,
She blended in a like degree
The vixen and the devotee,
Revealing with each freak of feint   535
    The temper of Petruchio's Kate,
The raptures of Siena's saint.
Her tapering hand and rounded wrist
Had facile power to form a fist;
The warm, dark languish of her eyes   540
Was never safe from wrath's surprise.
Brows saintly calm and lips devout
Knew every change of scowl and pout;
And the sweet voice had notes more high
And shrill for social battle-cry.   545

Since then what old cathedral town
Has missed her pilgrim staff and gown,
What convent-gate has held its lock
Against the challenge of her knock!
Through Smyrna's plague-hushed thoroughfares,
Up sea-set Malta's rocky stairs,   551
Gray olive slopes of hills that hem
    Thy tombs and shrines, Jerusalem,
Or startling on her desert throne
The crazy Queen of Lebanon   555
With claims fantastic as her own,
Her tireless feet have held their way;
And still, unrestful, bowed, and gray,
She watches under Eastern skies,
    With hope each day renewed and fresh,   560
    The Lord's quick coming in the flesh,
Whereof she dreams and prophesies!

Where'er her troubled path may be,
    The Lord's sweet pity with her go!
The outward wayward life we see,   565
    The hidden springs we may not know.
Nor is it given us to discern
    What threads the fatal sisters spun,
    Through what ancestral years has run
The sorrow with the woman born,   570

What forged her cruel chain of moods,
What set her feet in solitudes,
   And held the love within her mute,
What mingled madness in the blood,
   A life-long discord and annoy,   575
   Water of tears with oil of joy,
And hid within the folded bud
   Perversities of flower and fruit.
It is not ours to separate
   The tangled skein of will and fate,   580
To show what metes and bounds should stand
Upon the soul's debatable land,
And between choice and Providence
Divide the circle of events;
But He who knows our frame is just,   585
Merciful and compassionate,
And full of sweet assurances
And hope for all the language is,
That He remembereth we are dust!

At last the great logs, crumbling low,   590
Sent out a dull and duller glow,
The bull's-eye watch that hung in view,
Ticking its weary circuit through,
Pointed with mutely warning sign
Its black hand to the hour of nine.   595
That sign the pleasant circle broke:
My uncle ceased his pipe to smoke,
Knocked from its bowl the refuse gray,
And laid it tenderly away,
Then roused himself to safely cover   600
The dull red brands with ashes over.
And while, with care, our mother laid
The work aside, her steps she stayed
One moment, seeking to express
Her grateful sense of happiness   605
For food and shelter, warmth and health,
And love's contentment more than wealth,
With simple wishes (not the weak,
Vain prayers which no fulfillment seek,
But such as warm the generous heart,   610
O'er-prompt to do with Heaven its part)
That none might lack, that bitter night,
For bread and clothing, warmth and light.

Within our beds awhile we heard
The wind that round the gables roared,   615
With now and then a ruder shock,
Which made our very bedsteads rock.

We heard the loosened clapboards tost,
The board-nails snapping in the frost;
And on us, through the unplastered wall,   620
Felt the light sifted snow-flakes fall.
But sleep stole on, as sleep will do
When hearts are light and life is new;
Faint and more faint the murmurs grew,
Till in the summer-land of dreams   625
They softened to the sound of streams,
Low stir of leaves, and dip of oars,
And lapsing waves on quiet shores.

Next morn we wakened with the shout
Of merry voices high and clear;   630
And saw the teamsters drawing near
To break the drifted highways out.
Down the long hillside treading slow
We saw the half-buried oxen go,
Shaking the snow from heads uptost,   635
Their straining nostrils white with frost.
Before our door the straggling train
Drew up, an added team to gain.
The elders threshed their hands a-cold,
   Passed, with the cider-mug, their jokes 640
   From lip to lip; the younger folks
Down the loose snow-banks, wrestling, rolled,
Then toiled again the cavalcade
   O'er windy hill, through clogged ravine,
   And woodland paths that wound between   645
Low drooping pine-boughs winter-weighed.
From every barn a team afoot,
At every house a new recruit,
Where, drawn by Nature's subtlest law
Haply the watchful young men saw   650
Sweet doorway pictures of the curls
And curious eyes of merry girls,
Lifting their hands in mock defence
Against the snow-ball's compliments,
And reading in each missive tost   655
The charm which Eden never lost.

We heard once more the sleigh-bells' sound;
   And, following where the teamsters led,
The wise old Doctor went his round,
Just pausing at our door to say,   660
In the brief autocratic way

659. **Doctor:** Dr. Elias Weld, of the neighboring settlement at Rocks Village.

Of one who, prompt at Duty's call,
Was free to urge her claim on all,
    That some poor neighbor sick abed
At night our mother's aid would need.   665
For, one in generous thought and deed,
    What mattered in the sufferer's sight
    The Quaker matron's inward light,
The Doctor's mail of Calvin's creed?
All hearts confess the saints elect   670
    Who, twain in faith, in love agree,
And melt not in an acid sect
    The Christian pearl of charity!

So days went on: a week had passed
Since the great world was heard from last.   675
The Almanac we studied o'er,
Read and reread our little store
Of books and pamphlets, scarce a score;
One harmless novel, mostly hid
From younger eyes, a book forbid,   680
And poetry, (or good or bad,
A single book was all we had,)
Where Ellwood's meek, drab-skirted Muse,
    A stranger to the heathen Nine,
    Sang, with a somewhat nasal whine,   685
The wars of David and the Jews.
At last the floundering carrier bore
The village paper to our door.
Lo! broadening outward as we read,
To warmer zones the horizon spread;   690
In panoramic length unrolled
We saw the marvel that it told.
Before us passed the painted Creeks,
    And daft McGregor on his raids
    In Costa Rica's everglades.   695
And up Taygetus winding slow
Rode Ypsilanti's Mainote Greeks,
A Turk's head at each saddle-bow!
Welcome to us its week-old news,
Its corner for the rustic Muse,   700
    Its monthly gauge of snow and rain,
Its record, mingling in a breath
The wedding bell and dirge of death;

683. **Ellwood:** Thomas Ellwood (1639–1713), English
Quaker, author of *Davideis* (1712). **697. Ypsilanti:** Prince
Aleksandros Ypsilanti (1792–1828), Greek general and patriot, who became a leader in 1820 in the struggle for Greek
independence.

Jest, anecdote, and love-lorn tale,
The latest culprit sent to jail;   705
Its hue and cry of stolen and lost,
Its vendue sales and goods at cost,
    And traffic calling loud for gain.
We felt the stir of hall and street,
The pulse of life that round us beat;   710
The chill embargo of the snow
Was melted in the genial glow;
Wide swung again our ice-locked door,
And all the world was ours once more!

Clasp, Angel of the backward look   715
    And folded wings of ashen gray
    And voice of echoes far away,
The brazen covers of thy book;
The weird palimpsest old and vast,
Wherein thou hid'st the spectral past;   720
Where, closely mingling, pale and glow
The characters of joy and woe;
The monographs of outlived years,
Or smile-illumed or dim with tears,
    Green hills of life that slope to death,   725
And haunts of home, whose vistaed trees
Shade off to mournful cypresses
    With the white amaranths underneath.
Even while I look, I can but heed
    The restless sands' incessant fall,   730
Importunate hours that hours succeed,
Each clamorous with its own sharp need,
    And duty keeping pace with all.
Shut down and clasp the heavy lids;
I hear again the voice that bids   735
The dreamer leave his dream midway
For larger hopes and graver fears:
Life greatens in these later years,
The century's aloe flowers to-day!

Yet, haply, in some lull of life,   740
Some Truce of God which breaks its strife,
The worldling's eyes shall gather dew,
    Dreaming in throngful city ways
Of winter joys his boyhood knew;
And dear and early friends—the few   745
Who yet remain—shall pause to view
    These Flemish pictures of old days;
Sit with me by the homestead hearth,
And stretch the hands of memory forth

749

To warm them at the wood-fire's blaze!   750
And thanks untraced to lips unknown
Shall greet me like the odors blown
From unseen meadows newly mown,
Or lilies floating in some pond,
Wood-fringed, the wayside gaze beyond;   755
The traveller owns the grateful sense
Of sweetness near, he knows not whence,
And, pausing, takes with forehead bare
The benediction of the air.

Abraham Davenport

"The famous Dark Day of New England, May19,1780,
was a physical puzzle for many years to our ancestors,
but its occurrence brought something more than
philosophical speculation into the minds of those who
passed through it. The incident of Colonel Abraham
Davenport's sturdy protest is a matter of history"
(Whittier's note). The poem is Whittier's "one notable
experiment in blank verse" (Bennett, *Whittier*, p. 294).
First published in *The Atlantic Monthly*, May, 1866;
first collected in *The Tent on the Beach, and Other
Poems* (1867).

In the old days (a custom laid aside
With breeches and cocked hats) the people sent
Their wisest men to make the public laws.
And so, from a brown homestead, where the Sound
Drinks the small tribute of the Mianas,   5
Waved over by the woods of Rippowams,
And hallowed by pure lives and tranquil deaths,
Stamford sent up to the councils of the State
Wisdom and grace in Abraham Davenport.

'Twas on a May-day of the far old year   10
Seventeen hundred eighty, that there fell
Over the bloom and sweet life of the Spring,
Over the fresh earth and the heaven of noon,
A horror of great darkness, like the night
In day of which the Norland sagas tell,—   15
The Twilight of the Gods. The low-hung sky
Was black with ominous clouds, save where its rim
Was fringed with a dull glow, like that which
    climbs
The crater's sides from the red hell below.
Birds ceased to sing, and all the barn-yard fowls
Roosted; the cattle at the pasture bars   21

Lowed, and looked homeward; bats on leathern
    wings
Flitted abroad; the sounds of labor died;
Men prayed, and women wept; all ears grew sharp
To hear the doom-blast of the trumpet shatter
The black sky, that the dreadful face of Christ   26
Might look from the rent clouds, not as He looked
A loving guest at Bethany, but stern
As Justice and inexorable Law.

Meanwhile in old State House, dim as ghosts,
Sat the lawgivers of Connecticut,   31
Trembling beneath their legislative robes.
"It is the Lord's Great Day! Let us adjourn,"
Some said; and then, as if with one accord,
All eyes were turned to Abraham Davenport.   35
He rose, slow cleaving with his steady voice
The intolerable hush. "This well may be
The Day of Judgment which the world awaits;
But be it so or not, I only know
My present duty, and my Lord's command   40
To occupy till He come. So at the post
Where He hath set me in His providence,
I choose, for one, to meet Him face to face,—
No faithless servant frightened from my task,
But ready when the Lord of the harvest calls;   45
And therefore, with all reverence, I would say,
Let God do His work, we will see to ours.
Bring in the candles." And they brought them in.

Then by the flaring lights the Speaker read,
Albeit with husky voice and shaking hands,   50
An act to amend an act to regulate
The shad and alewive fisheries. Whereupon
Wisely and well spake Abraham Davenport,
Straight to the question, with no figures of speech
Save the ten Arab signs, yet not without   55
The shrewd dry humor natural to the man:
His awe-struck colleagues listening all the while,
Between the pauses of his argument,
To hear the thunder of the wrath of God
Break from the hollow trumpet of the cloud.   60

And there he stands in memory to this day,
Erect, self-poised, a rugged face, half seen
Against the background of unnatural dark,
A witness to the ages as they pass,
That simple duty hath no place for fear.   65

Our Master

CURRIER (*A Bibliography*) lists two renderings of this poem in sheet-music form, and nine hymns derived from it. First published in *The Independent*, Nov. 1, 1866; collected in *The Tent on the Beach, and Other Poems* (1867).

I read the whole poem. It is filled with inspiring beauty & love

Immortal Love, forever full,
  Forever flowing free,
Forever shared, forever whole,
  A never-ebbing sea!

Our outward lips confess the name   5
  All other names above;
Love only knoweth whence it came
  And comprehendeth love.

Blow, winds of God, awake and blow
  The mists of earth away!   10
Shine out, O Light Divine, and show
  How wide and far we stray!

Hush every lip, close every book,
  The strife of tongues forbear;
Why forward reach, or backward look,   15
  For love that clasps like air?

We may not climb the heavenly steeps
  To bring the Lord Christ down:
In vain we search the lowest deeps,
  For Him no depths can drown.   20

Nor holy bread, nor blood of grape,
  The lineaments restore
Of Him we know in outward shape
  And in the flesh no more.

He cometh not a king to reign;   25
  The world's long hope is dim;
The weary centuries watch in vain
  The clouds of heaven for Him.

Death comes, life goes; the asking eye
  And ear are answerless;   30
The grave is dumb, the hollow sky
  Is sad with silentness.

The letter fails, and systems fall,
  And every symbol wanes;
The Spirit over-brooding all   35
  Eternal Love remains.

And not for signs in heaven above
  Or earth below they look.
Who know with John His smile of love,
  With Peter His rebuke.   40

In joy of inward peace, or sense
  Of sorrow over sin,
He is His own best evidence,
  His witness is within.

No fable old, nor mythic lore,   45
  Nor dream of bards and seers,
No dead fact stranded on the shore
  Of the oblivious years;—

But warm, sweet, tender, even yet
  A present help is He;   50
And faith has still its Olivet,
  And love its Galilee.

The healing of His seamless dress
  Is by our beds of pain;
We touch Him in life's throng and press,   55
  And we are whole again.

Through Him the first fond prayers are said
  Our lips of childhood frame,
The last low whispers of our dead
  Are burdened with His name.   60

Our Lord and Master of us all!
  Whate'er our name or sign,
We own Thy sway, we hear Thy call,
  We test our lives by Thine.

Thou judgest us; Thy purity   65
  Doth all our lusts condemn;
The love that draws us nearer Thee
  Is hot with wrath to them.

Our thoughts lie open to Thy sight;
  And, naked to Thy glance,   70
Our secret sins are in the light
  Of Thy pure countenance.

Thy healing pains, a keen distress
  Thy tender light shines in;
Thy sweetness is the bitterness,   75
  Thy grace the pang of sin.

Yet, weak and blinded though we be,
  Thou dost our service own;
We bring our varying gifts to Thee,
  And Thou rejectest none.   80

To Thee our full humanity,
  Its joys and pains, belong;
The wrong of man to man on Thee
  Inflicts a deeper wrong.

Who hates, hates Thee, who loves becomes   85
  Therein to Thee allied;
All sweet accords of hearts and homes
  In Thee are multiplied.

Deep strike Thy roots, O heavenly Vine,
  Within our earthly sod,   90
Most human and yet most divine,
  The flower of man and God!

O Love! O Life! Our faith and sight
  Thy presence maketh one
As through transfigured clouds of white   95
  We trace the noon-day sun.

So, to our mortal eyes subdued,
  Flesh-veiled, but not concealed,
We know in Thee the fatherhood
  And heart of God revealed.   100

We faintly hear, we dimly see,
  In differing phrase we pray;
But, dim or clear, we own in Thee
  The Light, the Truth, the Way!

The homage that we render Thee   105
  Is still our Father's own;
No jealous claim or rivalry
  Divides the Cross and Throne.

To do Thy will is more than praise,
  As words are less than deeds,   110
And simple trust can find Thy ways
  We miss with chart of creeds.

No pride of self Thy service hath,
  No place for me and mine;
Our human strength is weakness, death   115
  Our life, apart from Thine.

Apart from Thee all gain is loss,
  All labor vainly done;
The solemn shadow of Thy Cross
  Is better than the sun.   120

Alone, O Love ineffable!
  Thy saving name is given;
To turn aside from Thee is hell,
  To walk with Thee is heaven!

How vain, secure in all Thou art,   125
  Our noisy championship!
The sighing of the contrite heart
  Is more than flattering lip.

Not Thine the bigot's partial plea,
  Nor Thine the zealot's ban;   130
Thou well canst spare a love of Thee
  Which ends in hate of man.

Our Friend, our Brother, and our Lord,
  What may Thy service be?—
Nor name, nor form, nor ritual word,   135
  But simply following Thee.

We bring no ghastly holocaust,
  We pile no graven stone;
He serves Thee best who loveth most
  His brothers and Thy own.   140

Thy litanies, sweet offices
  Of love and gratitude;
Thy sacramental liturgies,
  The joy of doing good.

In vain shall waves of incense drift   145
  The vaulted nave around,
In vain the minster turret lift
  Its brazen weights of sound.

The heart must ring Thy Christmas bells,
  Thy inward altars raise;   150
Its faith and hope Thy canticles,
  And its obedience praise!

The Brewing of Soma

THIS POEM, first published in *The Atlantic Monthly* for
April, 1872, and collected the same year in *The Pennsylvania Pilgrim, and Other Poems*, contains Whittier's most
popular and beloved hymn, "Dear Lord and Father of
Mankind."

The fagots blazed, the caldron's smoke
  Up through the green wood curled;
"Bring honey from the hollow oak,
Bring milky sap," the brewers spoke,
  In the childhood of the world. 5

And brewed they well or brewed they ill,
  The priests thrust in their rods,
First tasted, and then drank their fill,
And shouted, with one voice and will,
  "Behold the drink of gods!" 10

They drank, and lo! in heart and brain
  A new, glad life began;
The gray of hair grew young again,
The sick man laughed away his pain,
  The cripple leaped and ran. 15

"Drink, mortals, what the gods have sent,
  Forget your long annoy."
So sang the priests. From tent to tent
The Soma's sacred madness went,
  A storm of drunken joy. 20

Then knew each rapt inebriate
  A winged and glorious birth,
Soared upward, with strange joy elate,
Beat, with dazed head, Varuna's gate,
  And, sobered, sank to earth. 25

The land with Soma's praises rang;
  On Gihon's banks of shade
Its hymns the dusky maidens sang;
In joy of life or mortal pang
  All men to Soma prayed. 30

The morning twilight of the race
  Sends down these matin psalms;
And still with wondering eyes we trace
The simple prayers to Soma's grace,
  That Vedic verse embalms. 35

As in that child-world's early year,
  Each after age has striven

By music, incense, vigils drear,
And trance, to bring the skies more near,
  Or lift men up to heaven! 40

Some fever of the blood and brain,
  Some self-exalting spell,
The scourger's keen delight of pain,
The Dervish dance, the Orphic strain,
  The wild-haired Bacchant's yell,— 45

The desert's hair-grown hermit sunk
  The saner brute below;
The naked Santon, Hashish-drunk,
The cloister madness of the monk,
  The fakir's torture-show! 50

And yet the past comes round again,
  And new doth old fulfil;
In sensual transports wild as vain
We brew in many a Christian fane
  The heathen Soma still! 55

Dear Lord and Father of mankind,
  Forgive our foolish ways!
Reclothe us in our rightful mind,
In purer lives Thy service find,
  In deeper reverence, praise. 60

[handwritten marginalia: Most beautiful Hymn.]

In simple trust like theirs who heard
  Beside the Syrian sea
The gracious calling of the Lord,
Let us, like them, without a word,
  Rise up and follow Thee. 65

O Sabbath rest by Galilee!
  O calm of hills above,
Where Jesus knelt to share with Thee
The silence of eternity
  Interpreted by love! 70

With that deep hush subduing all
  Our words and works that drown
The tender whisper of Thy call,
As noiseless let Thy blessings fall
  As fell Thy manna down. 75

Drop Thy still dews of quietness,
  Till all our strivings cease;
Take from our souls the strain and stress,
And let our ordered lives confess
  The beauty of Thy peace. 80

Breathe through the heats of our desire
    Thy coolness and Thy balm;
Let sense be dumb, let flesh retire;
Speak through the earthquake, wind, and fire,
    O still, small voice of calm!   85

The Bartholdi Statue

THE STATUE OF LIBERTY, designed by Frédéric Auguste Bartholdi (1834–1904), French sculptor, was dedicated in October, 1886. The poem appeared first in *The Independent*, October 28, 1886, and was collected in *Writings* (1888). Rochambeau (1725–1807) commanded the French forces at the siege of Yorktown, 1781.

The land, that, from the rule of kings,
    In freeing us, itself made free,
Our Old World Sister, to us brings
    Her sculptured Dream of Liberty:

Unlike the shapes on Egypt's sands   5
    Uplifted by the toil-worn slave,
On Freedom's soil with freemen's hands
    We rear the symbol free hands gave.

O France, the beautiful! to thee
    Once more a debt of love we owe: 10
In peace beneath thy Colors Three,
    We hail a later Rochambeau!

Rise, stately Symbol! holding forth
    Thy light and hope to all who sit
In chains and darkness! Belt the earth   15
    With watch-fires from thy torch uplit!

Reveal the primal mandate still
    Which Chaos heard and ceased to be,
Trace on mid-air th' Eternal Will
    In signs of fire: "Let man be free!"   20

Shine far, shine free, a guiding light
    To Reason's ways and Virtue's aim,
A lightning-flash the wretch to smite
    Who shields his license with thy name!

The Shoemakers

WHITTIER himself had learned the shoemaker's trade. He had a strong sense of the dignity of labor, and he took pride in craftsmanship. "The Shoemakers" was

first published in *The United States Magazine and Democratic Review* for July, 1845, and collected in *Songs of Labor, and Other Poems* (1850).

Ho! workers of the old time styled
    The Gentle Craft of Leather!
Young brothers of the ancient guild,
    Stand forth once more together!
Call out again your long array,   5
    In the olden merry manner!
Once more, on gay St. Crispin's day,
    Fling out your blazoned banner!

Rap, rap! upon the well-worn stone
    How falls the polished hammer!   10
Rap, rap! the measured sound has grown
    A quick and merry clamor.
Now shape the sole! now deftly curl
    The glossy vamp around it,
And bless the while the bright-eyed girl   15
    Whose gentle fingers bound it!

For you, along the Spanish main
    A hundred keels are ploughing;
For you, the Indian on the plain
    His lasso-coil is throwing;   20
For you, deep glens with hemlock dark
    The woodman's fire is lighting;
For you, upon the oak's gray bark,
    The woodman's axe is smiting.

For you, from Carolina's pine   25
    The rosin-gum is stealing;
For you, the dark-eyed Florentine
    Her silken skein is reeling;
For you, the dizzy goatherd roams
    His rugged Alpine ledges;   30
For you, round all her shepherd homes
    Bloom England's thorny hedges.

The foremost still, by day or night,
    On moated mound or heather,
Where'er the need of trampled right   35
    Brought toiling men together;
Where the free burghers from the wall
    Defied the mail-clad master,
Than yours at Freedom's trumpet-call,
    No craftsmen rallied faster.   40

7. **St. Crispin's day:** October 25. The Christian martyrs, Crispin and Crispinian, were put to death in the third century. Both were shoemakers.

Let foplings sneer, let fools deride,
　Ye heed no idle scorner;
Free hands and hearts are still your pride,
　And duty done, your honor.
Ye dare to trust, for honest fame,　　　　45
　The jury Time empanels,
And leave to truth each noble name
　Which glorifies your annals.

Thy songs, Hans Sachs, are living yet,
　In strong and hearty German;　　　　　50
And Bloomfield's lay, and Gifford's wit,
　And patriot fame of Sherman;
Still from his book, a mystic seer,
　The soul of Behmen teaches,
And England's priesthood shakes to hear　　55
　Of Fox's leathern breeches.

The foot is yours; where'er it falls,
　It treads your well-wrought leather,
On earthen floor, in marble halls,
　On carpet, or on heather.　　　　　　　60
Still there the sweetest charm is found
　Of matron grace or vestal's,
As Hebe's foot bore nectar round
　Among the old celestials!

Rap, rap!—your stout and bluff brogan,　　65
　With footsteps slow and weary,
May wander where the sky's blue span
　Shuts down upon the prairie.
On Beauty's foot your slippers glance,
　By Saratoga's fountains,　　　　　　　70
Or twinkle down the summer dance
　Beneath the Crystal Mountains!

The red brick to the mason's hand,
　The brown earth to the tiller's,
The shoe in yours shall wealth command,　　75
　Like fairy Cinderella's!

49. **Hans Sachs:** Sachs (1494–1576), a German poet and
Meistersinger, plied his craft as shoemaker in Nuremberg.
51. **Bloomfield's lay:** Robert Bloomfield (1766–1823), an
English poet, was apprenticed to "the gentle craft" of cob-
bling. **Gifford's wit:** William Gifford (1756–1826), a founder
of the English *Quarterly Review*, was once a shoemaker.
52. **Sherman:** Roger Sherman (1721–1793), a signer of the
Declaration of Independence, was a shoemaker in his youth.
54. **Behmen:** Jacob Behmen (Böhme), a German mystic
(1575–1624), was once a cobbler.　56. **Fox:** George Fox
(1624–1691), another famous cobbler, founded the Society
of Friends.　63. **Hebe's:** Hebe was cup bearer of the gods.

As they who shunned the household maid
　Beheld the crown upon her,
So all shall see your toil repaid
　With hearth and home and honor.　　　80

Then let the toast be freely quaffed,
　In water cool and brimming,—
"All honor to the good old Craft,
　Its merry men and women!"
Call out again your long array,　　　　　85
　In the old time's pleasant manner:
Once more, on gay St. Crispin's day,
　Fling out his blazoned banner!

Justice and Expediency

In 1833 the English Parliament abolished slavery
throughout British territory. In June of the same year
appeared Whittier's pamphlet, *Justice and Expediency;
or, Slavery Considered with a View to its Rightful and
Effectual Remedy, Abolition,* printed at Haverhill by
Whittier's friend, C. P. Thayer, in an edition of five
hundred copies, at the author's expense. Whittier was
twenty-five years of age and doing some editorial work
for the *Haverhill Gazette.* Arthur Tappan, an abolitionist of New York, paid for five thousand copies to be
distributed free, and another issue was advertised at
$25 per thousand (Bennett, *Whittier*). The pamphlet
established its author as a national figure in the abolition
movement. Whittier opposed the programs of the
Colonization Society and of the gradual emancipation-
ists as being ineffectual in an age of increasing slavery
in the United States, and as avoiding the issue of the
rights of man. He presented evidence to show that
socially and economically slavery was a curse to the
South. In December, 1833, the first antislavery convention was held at Philadelphia. The essay is collected in *Writings* (1888). The notes accompanying this
article are Whittier's.

. . . I come now to the only practicable, the
only just scheme of emancipation: Immediate
abolition of slavery; an immediate acknowledgment of the great truth, that man cannot hold
property in man; an immediate surrender of baneful prejudice to Christian love; an immediate
practical obedience to the command of Jesus
Christ: "Whatsoever ye would that men should
do unto you, do ye even so to them."

A correct understanding of what is meant by

immediate abolition must convince every candid mind that it is neither visionary nor dangerous; that it involves no disastrous consequences of bloodshed and desolation; but, on the contrary, that it is a safe, practicable, efficient remedy for the evils of the slave system.

The term immediate[n] is used in contrast with that of gradual. Earnestly as I wish it, I do not expect, no one expects, that the tremendous system of oppression can be instantaneously overthrown. The terrible and unrebukable indignation of a free people has not yet been sufficiently concentrated against it. The friends of abolition have not forgotten the peculiar organization of our confederacy, the delicate division of power between the states and the general government. They see the many obstacles in their pathway; but they know that public opinion can overcome them all. They ask no aid of physical coercion. They seek to obtain their object not with the weapons of violence and blood, but with those of reason and truth, prayer to God, and entreaty to man.

They seek to impress indelibly upon every human heart the true doctrines of the rights of man; to establish now and forever this great and fundamental truth of human liberty, that man cannot hold property in his brother; for they believe that the general admission of this truth will utterly destroy the system of slavery, based as that system is upon a denial or disregard of it. To make use of the clear exposition of an eminent advocate of immediate abolition,[n] our plan of emancipation is simply this: "To promulgate the true doctrine of human rights in high places and low places, and all places where there are human beings; to whisper it in chimney corners, and to proclaim it from the house-tops, yea, from the mountain-tops; to pour

it out like water from the pulpit and the press; to raise it up with all the food of the inner man, from infancy to gray hairs; to give 'line upon line, and precept upon precept,' till it forms one of the foundation principles and parts indestructible of the public soul. Let those who contemn this plan renounce, if they have not done it already, the gospel plan of converting the world; let them renounce every plan of moral reformation, and every plan whatsoever, which does not terminate in the gratification of their own animal natures.". . .

Far be it from me to cast new bitterness into the gall and wormwood waters of sectional prejudice. No; I desire peace, the peace of universal love, of catholic sympathy, the peace of a common interest, a common feeling, a common humanity. But so long as slavery is tolerated, no such peace can exist. Liberty and slavery cannot dwell in harmony together. There will be a perpetual "war in the members" of the political Mezentius between the living and the dead. God and man have placed between them an everlasting barrier, an eternal separation. No matter under what name or law or compact their union is attempted, the ordination of Providence has forbidden it, and it cannot stand. Peace! there can be no peace between justice and oppression, between robbery and righteousness, truth and falsehood, freedom and slavery.

The slave-holding states are not free. The name of liberty is there, but the spirit is wanting. They do not partake of its invaluable blessings. Wherever slavery exists to any considerable extent, with the exception of some recently settled portions of the country, and which have not yet felt in a great degree the baneful and deteriorating influences of slave labor, we hear at this moment the cry of suffering. We are told of grass-grown streets, of crumbling mansions, of beggared planters and barren plantations, of fear from without, of terror within. The once fertile fields are wasted and tenantless, for the curse of slavery, the improvidence of that labor whose hire has been kept back by fraud, has been there, poisoning the very earth beyond the reviving influence of the early and the latter rain. A moral mildew mingles with and blasts the economy of nature. It is as if the finger of the everlasting God had written upon the soil of the slave-holder the language of His displeasure.

immediate: Rev. Dr. Thomson, of Edinburgh, thus speaks of it: "Were I to treat the term gradual as some of our enemies have the term immediate, I could easily, by the help of a little quibbling, bring you to the conclusion that, as hitherto employed, it means that the abolition of slavery will never take place." "The meaning of the word as used by us is perfectly clear; it is to be considered and understood under the direction of common sense, and as modified and expounded by the statements with which it is associated." **advocate . . . abolition:** President Wright, of the Western Reserve College, Hudson, Ohio.

Let, then, the slave-holding states consult their present interest by beginning without delay the work of emancipation. If they fear not, and mock at the fiery indignation of Him, to whom vengeance belongeth, let temporal interest persuade them. They know, they must know, that the present state of things cannot long continue. Mind is the same everywhere, no matter what may be the complexion of the frame which it animates: there is a love of liberty which the scourge cannot eradicate, a hatred of oppression which centuries of degradation cannot extinguish. The slave will become conscious sooner or later of his brute strength, his physical superiority, and will exert it. His torch will be at the threshold and his knife at the throat of the planter. Horrible and indiscriminate will be his vengeance. Where, then, will be the pride, the beauty, and the chivalry of the South? The smoke of her torment will rise upward like a thick cloud visible over the whole earth.

Belie the Negro's powers: in headlong will,
Christian, thy brother thou shalt find him still.
Belie his virtues: since his wrongs began,
His follies and his crimes have stamped him man.[n]

Let the cause of insurrection be removed, then, as speedily as possible. Cease to oppress. "Let him that stole steal no more." Let the laborer have his hire. Bind him no longer by the cords of slavery, but with those of kindness and brotherly love. Watch over him for his good. Pray for him; instruct him; pour light into the darkness of his mind.

Let this be done, and the horrible fears which now haunt the slumbers of the slave-holder will depart. Conscience will take down its racks and gibbets, and his soul will be at peace. His lands will no longer disappoint his hopes. Free labor will renovate them.

Historical facts; the nature of the human mind; the demonstrated truths of political economy; the analysis of cause and effect, all concur in establishing:

1. That immediate abolition is a safe and just and peaceful remedy for the evils of the slave system.

2. That free labor, its necessary consequence, is more productive, and more advantageous to the planter than slave labor.

In proof of the first proposition it is only necessary to state the undeniable fact that immediate emancipation, whether by an individual or a community, has in no instance been attended with violence and disorder on the part of the emancipated; but that on the contrary it has promoted cheerfulness, industry, and laudable ambition in the place of sullen discontent, indolence, and despair. . . .

The present condition of Hayti may be judged of from the following well-authenticated facts: its population is more than 700,000, its resources ample, its prosperity and happiness general, its crimes few, its labor crowned with abundance, with no paupers save the decrepit and aged, its people hospitable, respectful, orderly, and contented."[n]

The manumitted slaves, who to the number of two thousand were settled in Nova Scotia by the British Government at the close of the Revolutionary War, "led a harmless life, and gained the character of an honest, industrious people from their white neighbors."[n] Of the free laborers of Trinidad we have the same report. At the Cape of Good Hope, three thousand Negroes received their freedom, and with scarce a single exception betook themselves to laborious employments.[n]

But we have yet stronger evidence. The total abolishment of slavery in the southern republics has proved beyond dispute the safety and utility of immediate abolition. The departed Bolivar indeed deserves his glorious title of Liberator, for he began his career of freedom by striking off the fetters of his own slaves, seven hundred in number.

In an official letter from the Mexican Envoy of the British Government, dated Mexico, March, 1826, and addressed to the Right Hon. George Canning, the superiority of free over slave labor is clearly demonstrated by the following facts:—

1. The sugar and coffee cultivation of Mexico is almost exclusively confined to the great valley of Ceurnavaca and Cauntala Amilpas.

Belie . . . man: Montgomery (James Montgomery (1771–1854), famed for humanitarian and religious verse).

. . . contented: C. Stewart, Capt. R. N. **. . . neighbors:** Clarkson. **. . . employments:** *Anti-Slavery Report* for 1832.

2. It is now carried on exclusively by the labor of free blacks.

3. It was formerly wholly sustained by the forced labor of slaves, purchased at $300 to $400 each.

4. Abolition in this section was effected not by governmental interference, not even from motives of humanity, but from an irresistible conviction on the part of the planters that their pecuniary interest demanded it.

5. The result has proved the entire correctness of this conviction; and the planters would now be as unwilling as the blacks themselves to return to the old system.

Let our Southern brethren imitate this example. It is in vain, in the face of facts like these, to talk of the necessity of maintaining the abominable system, operating as it does like a double curse upon planters and slaves. Heaven and earth deny its necessity. It is as necessary as other robberies, and no more. . . .

Let us look at this subject from another point of view. The large sum of money necessary for stocking a plantation with slaves has an inevitable tendency to place the agriculture of a slave-holding community exclusively in the hands of the wealthy, a tendency at war with practical republicanism and conflicting with the best maxims of political economy.

Two hundred slaves at $200 per head would cost in the outset $40,000. Compare this enormous outlay for the labor of a single plantation with the beautiful system of free labor as exhibited in New England, where every young laborer, with health and ordinary prudence, may acquire by his labor on the farms of others, in a few years, a farm of his own, and the stock necessary for its proper cultivation; where on a hard and unthankful soil independence and competence may be attained by all.

Free labor is perfectly in accordance with the spirit of our institutions; slave labor is a relic of a barbarous, despotic age. The one, like the firmament of heaven, is the equal diffusion of similar lights, manifest, harmonious, regular; the other is the fiery predominance of some disastrous star, hiding all lesser luminaries around it in one consuming glare.

Emancipation would reform this evil. The planter would no longer be under the necessity of a heavy expenditure for slaves. He would only pay a very moderate price for his labor; a price, indeed, far less than the cost of the maintenance of a promiscuous gang of slaves, which the present system requires.

In an old plantation of three hundred slaves, not more than one hundred effective laborers will be found. Children, the old and superannuated, the sick and decrepit, the idle and incorrigibly vicious, will be found to constitute two thirds of the whole number. The remaining third perform only about one third as much work as the same number of free laborers.

Now disburden the master of this heavy load of maintenance; let him employ free, able, industrious laborers only, those who feel conscious of a personal interest in the fruits of their labor, and who does not see that such a system would be vastly more safe and economical than the present? . . .

But it may be said that Virginia will ultimately liberate her slaves on condition of their colonization in Africa, peacefully if possible, forcibly if necessary.

Well, admitting that Virginia may be able and willing at some remote period to rid herself of the evil by commuting the punishment of her unoffending colored people from slavery to exile, will her fearful remedy apply to some of the other slaveholding states?

It is a fact, strongly insisted upon by our Southern brethren as a reason for the perpetuation of slavery, that their climate and peculiar agriculture will not admit of hard labor on the part of the whites; that amidst the fatal malaria of the rice plantations the white man is almost annually visited by the country fever; that few of the white overseers of these plantations reach the middle period of ordinary life; that the owners are compelled to fly from their estates as the hot season approaches, without being able to return until the first frosts have fallen. But we are told that the slaves remain there, at their work, mid-leg in putrid water, breathing the noisome atmosphere, loaded with contagion, and underneath the scorching fervor of a terrible sun; that they indeed suffer; but that their habits, constitutions, and their long practice enable them to labor, surrounded by such destructive influences, with comparative safety.

The conclusive answer, therefore, to those who in reality cherish the visionary hope of colonizing all the colored people of the United States in Africa or elsewhere, is this single, all-important fact: The labor of the blacks will not and cannot be dispensed with by the planter of the South.

To what remedy, then, can the friends of humanity betake themselves but to that of emancipation?

And nothing but a strong, unequivocal expression of public sentiment is needed to carry into effect this remedy, so far as the general government is concerned.

And when the voice of all the non-slave-holding states shall be heard on this question, a voice of expostulation, rebuke, entreaty—when the full light of truth shall break through the night of prejudice, and reveal all the foul abominations of slavery, will Delaware still cling to the curse which is wasting her moral strength, and still rivet the fetters upon her three or four thousand slaves?

Let Delaware begin the work, and Maryland and Virginia must follow; the example will be contagious; and the great object of universal emancipation will be attained.

Freemen, Christians, lovers of truth and justice! Why stand ye idle? Ours is a government of opinion, and slavery is interwoven with it. Change the current of opinion, and slavery will be swept away. Let the awful sovereignty of Heaven arise and pronounce judgment against the crying iniquity. Let each individual remember that upon himself rests a portion of that sovereignty; a part of the tremendous responsibility of its exercise. The burning, withering concentration of public opinion upon the slave system is alone needed for its total annihilation. God has given us the power to overthrow it; a power peaceful, yet mighty, benevolent, yet effectual, "awful without severity," a moral strength equal to the emergency. . . .

And when the stain on our own escutcheon shall be seen no more; when the Declaration of our Independence and the practice of our people shall agree; when truth shall be exalted among us; when love shall take the place of wrong; when all the baneful pride and prejudice of caste and color shall fall forever; when under one common sun of political liberty the slave-holding portions of our republic shall no longer sit, like the Egyptians of old, themselves mantled in thick darkness, while all around them is glowing with the blessed light of freedom and equality, then, and not till then, shall it go well for America!

Democracy and Slavery

FIRST PUBLISHED as "The Mission of Democracy" in *The National Era*, of which Whittier was corresponding editor, April 13, 1848, and collected in *Writings* (1888).

The great leader of American Democracy, Thomas Jefferson, was an ultra-abolitionist in theory, while from youth to age a slave-holder in practice. With a zeal which never abated, with a warmth which the frost of years could not chill, he urged the great truths, that each man should be the guardian of his own weal; that one man should never have absolute control over another. He maintained the entire equality of the race, the inherent right of self-ownership, the equal claim of all to a fair participation in the enactment of the laws by which they are governed.

He saw clearly that slavery, as it existed in the South and on his own plantation, was inconsistent with this doctrine. His early efforts for emancipation in Virginia failed of success; but he next turned his attention to the vast northwestern territory, and laid the foundation of that ordinance of 1787, which, like the flaming sword of the angel at the gates of Paradise, has effectually guarded that territory against the entrance of slavery. Nor did he stop here. He was the friend and admirer of the ultra-abolitionists of revolutionary France; he warmly urged his British friend, Dr. Price, to send his anti-slavery pamphlets into Virginia; he omitted no opportunity to protest against slavery as anti-democratic, unjust, and dangerous to the common welfare; and in his letter to the territorial governor of Illinois, written in old age, he bequeathed, in earnest and affecting language, the cause of Negro emancipation to the rising generation. "This enterprise," said he, "is for the young, for those who can carry it forward to its consummation. It shall have all my prayers, and these are the only weapons of an old man."

Such was Thomas Jefferson, the great founder of American Democracy, the advocate of the equality of human rights, irrespective of any conditions of birth, or climate, or color. His political doctrines, it is strange to say, found their earliest recipients and most zealous admirers in the slave states of the Union. The privileged class of slave-holders, whose rank and station "supersede the necessity of an order of nobility," became earnest advocates of equality among themselves—the democracy of an aristocracy. With the misery and degradation of servitude always before them, in the condition of their own slaves, an intense love of personal independence, and a haughty impatience of any control over their actions, prepared them to adopt the democratic idea, so far as it might be applied to their own order. Of that enlarged and generous democracy, the love, not of individual freedom alone, but of the rights and liberties of all men, the unselfish desire to give to others the privileges which all men value for themselves, we are constrained to believe the great body of Thomas Jefferson's slave-holding admirers had no adequate conception. They were just such democrats as the patricians of Rome and the aristocracy of Venice; lords over their own plantations, a sort of "holy alliance" of planters, admitting and defending each other's divine right of mastership.

Still, in Virginia, Maryland, and in other sections of the slave states, truer exponents and exemplifiers of the idea of democracy, as it existed in the mind of Jefferson, were not wanting. In the debate on the memorials presented to the first Congress of the United States, praying for the abolition of slavery, the voice of the Virginia delegation in that body was unanimous in deprecation of slavery as an evil, social, moral, and political. In the Virginia constitutional convention of 1829 there were men who had the wisdom to perceive and the firmness to declare that slavery was not only incompatible with the honor and prosperity of the state, but wholly indefensible on any grounds which could be consistently taken by a republican people. In the debate on the same subject in the legislature in 1832, universal and impartial democracy found utterance from eloquent lips. We might say as much of Kentucky, the child of Virginia. But it remains true that these were exceptions to the general rule. With the language of universal liberty on their lips, and moved by the most zealous spirit of democratic propagandism, the greater number of the slave-holders of the Union seem never to have understood the true meaning, or to have measured the length and breadth of that doctrine which they were the first to adopt, and of which they have claimed all along to be the peculiar and chosen advocates.

The Northern States were slow to adopt the Democratic creed. The oligarchy of New England, and the rich proprietors and landholders of the Middle States, turned with alarm and horror from the leveling doctrines urged upon them by the "liberty and equality" propagandists of the South. The doctrines of Virginia were quite as unpalatable to Massachusetts at the beginning of the present century as those of Massachusetts now are to the Old Dominion. Democracy interfered with old usages and time-honored institutions, and threatened to plough up the very foundations of the social fabric. It was zealously opposed by the representatives of New England in Congress and in the home legislatures; and in many pulpits hands were lifted to God in humble entreaty that the curse and bane of democracy, an offshoot of the rabid Jacobinism of revolutionary France, might not be permitted to take root and overshadow the goodly heritage of Puritanism. The alarmists of the South, in their most fervid pictures of the evils to be apprehended from the prevalence of anti-slavery doctrines in their midst, have drawn nothing more fearful than the visions of such

Prophets of war and harbingers of ill

as Fisher Ames in the forum and Parish in the desk, when contemplating the inroads of Jeffersonian democracy upon the politics, religion, and property of the North.

But great numbers of the free laborers of the Northern States, the mechanics and small farmers, took a very different view of the matter. The doctrines of Jefferson were received as their political gospel. It was in vain that federalism denounced with indignation the impertinent inconsistency of slave-holding interference in behalf of liberty in the free states. Come the doctrine from whom it might, the people felt it to be true. State after state revolted from the ranks of federalism, and enrolled itself on the side of democracy. The old order of things was broken up; equality before the law was established, religious tests and restrictions of the right of suffrage were abrogated. Take Massachusetts, for example. There the resistance to democratic principles was the most strenuous and longest continued. Yet, at this time, there is no state in the Union more thorough in its practical adoption of them. No property qualifications or religious tests prevail; all distinctions of sect, birth, or color, are repudiated, and suffrage is universal. The democracy, which in the South has only been held in a state of gaseous abstraction, hardened into concrete reality in the cold air of the North. The ideal became practical, for it had found lodgment among men who were accustomed to act out their convictions and test all their theories by actual experience.

While thus making a practical application of the new doctrine, the people of the free states could not but perceive the incongruity of democracy and slavery.

Selleck Osborn,[n] who narrowly escaped the honor of a Democratic martyr in Connecticut, denounced slave-holding, in common with other forms of oppression. Barlow,[n] fresh from communion with Gregoire, Brissot, and Robespierre, devoted to Negro slavery some of the most vigorous and truthful lines of his great poem. Eaton,[n] returning from his romantic achievements in Tunis for the deliverance of white slaves, improved the occasion to read a lecture to his countrymen on the inconsistency and guilt of holding blacks in servitude. In the Missouri struggle of 1819–20, the people of the free states, with a few ignoble exceptions, took issue with the South against the extension of slavery. Some ten years later, the present anti-slavery agitation commenced. It originated, beyond a question, in the democratic element. With the words of Jefferson on their lips, young, earnest, and enthusiastic men called

the attention of the community to the moral wrong and political reproach of slavery. In the name and spirit of democracy, the moral and political powers of the people were invoked to limit, discountenance, and put an end to a system so manifestly subversive of its foundation principles. It was a revival of the language of Jefferson and Page and Randolph, an echo of the voice of him who penned the Declaration of Independence and originated the ordinance of 1787.

Meanwhile the South had wellnigh forgotten the actual significance of the teachings of its early political prophets, and their renewal in the shape of abolitionism was, as might have been expected, strange and unwelcome. Pleasant enough it had been to hold up occasionally these democratic abstractions for the purpose of challenging the world's admiration and cheaply acquiring the character of lovers of liberty and equality. Frederick of Prussia, apostrophizing the shades of Cato and Brutus,

Vous de la liberté héros que je révère,

while in the full exercise of his despotic power, was quite as consistent as these democratic slaveowners, whose admiration of liberty increased in exact ratio with its distance from their own plantations. They had not calculated upon seeing their doctrine clothed with life and power, a practical reality, pressing for application to their slaves as well as to themselves. They had not taken into account the beautiful ordination of Providence, that no man can vindicate his own rights, without directly or impliedly including in that vindication the rights of all other men. The haughty and oppressive barons who wrung from their reluctant monarch the Great Charter at Runnymede, acting only for themselves and their class, little dreamed of the universal application which has since been made of their guaranty of rights and liberties. As little did the nobles of the parliament of Paris, when strengthening themselves by limiting the kingly prerogative, dream of the emancipation of their own serfs, by a revolution to which they were blindly giving the first impulse. God's truth is universal; it cannot be monopolized by selfishness.

Osborn: Selleck Osborn (*c.* 1782–*c.* 1826), journalist and poet.   **Barlow:** Joel Barlow (1754–1812). See biographical sketch on pages 274–275.   **Eaton:** William Eaton (1764–1811), consul to Tunis and "Navy Agent to the Barbary States."

OLIVER WENDELL HOLMES (1809–1894)

OLIVER WENDELL HOLMES brought to American litera-ture nineteenth-century thought clothed in the literary graces of the eighteenth century. He was a master in the use of neoclassic tints of wit, shafts of sense, precision of phrase, and tenderness of sentiment. Like Gold-smith, whose works he admired, he achieved distinction in both prose and poetry. By fortunate accident the birth of *The Atlantic Monthly* in 1857, which his friend Lowell founded and Holmes himself christened, saved his mature wit in essay form, even as Boswell saved much of Samuel Johnson's table talk.

Holmes was not in sympathy with many writers of literature in his own age in America and England. Not to his mind or taste were the dark moodiness of Haw-thorne, the rebelliousness of Thoreau, the mysticism in Emerson, and the militancy of Whittier. Uncongenial to him were Wordsworth's intimations of immortality, the flights of Shelley, and the poetry of those whom he termed the dreamy, "Hasheesh crazy lot," exemplified by Keats and Tennyson. In spirit he was the literary companion of Pope and Campbell, and the lover of Greek verse and Latin phrase. He loved, too, the good eighteenth-century sensibility of Mackenzie, or better still, of Sterne. *Tristram Shandy* and *The Autocrat of the Breakfast-Table* meet in Uncle Toby's fly and the Professor's alcohol lamp.

Holmes was not of the type of Edward Bellamy, Henry George, or the utopian William Dean Howells. To Holmes's way of thinking, culture resided in music and lecture halls, in museums of art and natural history, in clubs and selective social groups. Culture was to be fostered by philanthropy; and it was idle business to run away to Brook Farm, as certain of the transcendentalists did. Surely, thought Holmes, human beings, cities, and nations grow strong by inheritance and the accretion of virtues, by planned endeavor, by evolution, even as the chambered nautilus builds its shell; not by rash revolution and the operations of blind rage. He took no joy in the thought of new eras roughly born. What of the "perishing classes of Boston" which so worried Channing, and what of the slums, and the deadening grind of long hours at mill labor? Well, according to Holmes, the very laws of nature are selective, relentless. Men should be and are helpful to their fellow men. But certain well-bred horses will win the races, and biologi-cal inheritance is the law and snobbery of nature. Its only democracy lies in the occasional mutation from the humble majority, when "a series of felicitous crosses develops an improved strain of blood, and reaches its maximum perfection at last in the large un-combed youth who goes to college and startles the class leaders by striding past them all." By such reasoning, and with faith in a certain generosity among men, Holmes dismissed the problems of sociology, except in the realm of crime. Here he struck out fearlessly. As a biologist he was a determinist, and as a psychologist he held that much of the crime and sin in the world are the result of mental disease. He wrote three "medi-cated novels" to support his conviction that only the healthy in mind may be charged with full responsibili-ties of freedom of will. *Elsie Venner* (1861), *The Guard-ian Angel* (1867), and *A Mortal Antipathy* (1885) are all studies in mental abnormality, the first two stressing the effects of heredity and the last the force of early experience. As novels they are weak, but as studies in psychology they excite the interest of modern psychia-trists. By reason of his stand on mental disease, Holmes became a champion of penal reform. Then, too, belief in biological determinism led him to reject the deter-minism of Calvinist theology as unjust; and he forswore the religion of his father, a Calvinist minister, accepted Unitarianism, and rose to considerable poetic passion in denial of damnation in *The Poet of the Breakfast-Table*.

A lineal descendant of Anne Bradstreet, Holmes was born in Cambridge, Massachusetts. From Phillips Academy at Andover, Massachusetts, he entered Har-vard as a member of the class of 1829, which he made famous in verse. Following his graduation from Harvard in liberal arts he continued to study there. After a year at law he turned to medicine for two years, proceeded to Paris for advanced study in hospitals during 1833–1835, returned to Harvard in 1835, and received his medical degree in 1836. A volume of sprightly verse, his first *Poems*, published in the same year, won local commendation but did not advance him as a physician; perhaps it harmed him. He gave up literary work for twenty-one years, except for the *Poems* of 1846 and 1849, a course of lectures on English poets at the Lowell Institute in 1853, and other lectures. His distaste for the general practice of medicine was lightened by a professorship of anatomy at Dartmouth, where he went three months each year during 1838–1840, and he quit active practice when the professorship of anatomy and physiology at Harvard came to him in 1847, seven years after his marriage to Amelia Lee Jackson, daughter of a justice of the Supreme Court of Massachusetts. The even tenor of his life lasted at Harvard during the rest of his career. He was Dean of the School of Medicine, 1847–1853, and continued as a professor until 1882. He was the author of several medical treatises, one in particular, "The Contagious-ness of Puerperal Fever," noteworthy for the controversy it incited and the service it performed in helping to overcome the prevalence of the disease. But it was as a teacher that he made his greatest contribution to the medical profession. Short, nimble, his "face a convenience rather than an ornament," as he occasionally remarked, he was a Leyden jar of energy and wit.

When James Russell Lowell assumed editorship of the new *Atlantic* in 1857, he insisted that Holmes resume literary work. Twenty-six years previously Holmes had done two essays, "The Autocrat of the Breakfast-Table," for the *New England Magazine*; thinking again of them, he began his new *Atlantic* series under the same title and with the famous first clause, "I was just going to say, when I was interrupted. . . ." The *Autocrat* (1858) was followed by *The Professor at the Breakfast-Table* (1869), *The Poet at the Breakfast-Table* (1872), and *Over the Tea-Cups* (1891). In them he established himself as a champion of intellectual freedom and a foe of religious bigotry. In them, too, he wrote charmingly of his love of horses, trees, old books, microscopy, photography, electricity, psychology, and the hand stereoscope, with the invention of which he has been credited. In his Breakfast-Table series he was at his best. As a public lecturer he had discovered that to close with a poem was to be a success, and he continued this practice in his essays. He developed, too, in this series a new form of essay, establishing the central figure as the talker and expounder, and expanding the effect by noting the silent though varied responses of the other members of the table party. Along with the essays new books of poetry appeared: *Songs in Many Keys* (1862), *Songs of Many Seasons* (1875), *The Iron Gate, and Other Poems* (1880), and *Before the Curfew, and Other Poems* (1888), and two biographies, *Motley* (1878), and *Emerson* (1885).

In both prose and poetry Holmes was fanciful, humorous, deft, nobly serious, a master of *vers d'oc-casion*, of sense and sensibility. His perceptions were clinically sharp; he excelled in simile and metaphor and in wit achieved by well-turned phrase.

BIBLIOGRAPHY · The basic edition, used for this book, is *The Writings of Oliver Wendell Holmes*, Riverside Edition (14 vols., 1891), with notes by the author. The last three volumes contain the poems. In 1892 this edition was augmented by a new volume XI, being biographies of Ralph Waldo Emerson and John Lothrop Motley, and the poetry became volumes XII, XIII, XIV. In 1892 also appeared the Standard Library Edition from the Riverside plates, in 13 volumes, the poems being gathered in two instead of three volumes; to this edition were later added volumes XIV and XV, *Life and Letters of Oliver Wendell Holmes* (1896), by John T. Morse, Jr., authorized biographer. An important later biography is E. M. Tilton, *Amiable Autocrat* (1949). The best single volume of poems is H. E. Scudder, ed., *The Complete Poetical Works of Oliver Wendell Holmes*, Cambridge Edition (1895). For bibliography see G. B. Ives, *A Bibliography of Oliver Wendell Holmes* (1907) and S. I. Hayakawa and H. M. Jones, editors, *Oliver Wendell Holmes*, American Writers Series (1939), the latter also essential for its critical introduction. Holmes as psychologist has been treated by C. P. Oberndorf, *The Psychiatric Novels of Oliver Wendell Holmes* (1943; revised, enlarged, 1946). Theological studies include E. J. Bailey, in *Religious Thought in the Greater American Poets*; W. V. Gavigan, "The Doctor Looks at Religion: Dr. Holmes and the Church," in the *Catholic World*, CXXXVII (1933), 53–59; A. H. Strong, in *American Poets and Their Theology* (1916); and E. S. Turner, "The Autocrat's Theology: Unpublished Letters of Holmes," *Putnam's Magazine*, VI (1909), 662–667. Among other special studies are H. H. Clark, "Dr. Holmes: A Reinterpretation," *New England Quarterly*, XII (1939), 19–34; J. D. Ferguson, "The Unfamiliar Autocrat," *Colophon*, N. S., I (1936), 388–396; J. T. Flanagan, "Dr. Holmes Advises Young Ignatius Donnelly," *American Literature*, XIII (1941), 59–61; and R. Withington, "The Patriotism of the Autocrat," *Harvard Graduates Magazine* (1928), 523–532.

The Ballad of the Oysterman

FIRST PUBLISHED in the Boston *Amateur*, July 17, 1830; first collected in *Poems* (1836).

It was a tall young oysterman lived by the river-side,
His shop was just upon the bank, his boat was on the tide;
The daughter of a fisherman, that was so straight and slim,
Lived over on the other bank, right opposite to him.

It was the pensive oysterman that saw a lovely maid,
Upon a moonlight evening, a sitting in the shade;

He saw her wave her handkerchief, as much as if to say,
"I'm wide awake, young oysterman, and all the folks away."

Then up arose the oysterman, and to himself said he,
"I guess I'll leave the skiff at home, for fear that folks should see;   10
I read it in the story-book, that, for to kiss his dear,
Leander swam the Hellespont,—and I will swim this here."

And he has leaped into the waves, and crossed the shining stream,
And he has clambered up the bank, all in the moonlight gleam;
O there were kisses sweet as dew, and words as soft as rain,—   15
But they have heard her father's step, and in he leaps again!

Out spoke the ancient fisherman,—"O what was that, my daughter?"
" 'Twas nothing but a pebble, sir, I threw into the water."
"And what is that, pray tell me, love, that paddles off so fast?"
"It's nothing but a porpoise, sir, that's been a swimming past."   20

Out spoke the ancient fisherman,—"Now bring me my harpoon!
I'll get into my fishing-boat, and fix the fellow soon."
Down fell that pretty innocent, as falls a snow-white lamb,
Her hair drooped round her pallid cheeks, like seaweed on a clam.

Alas for those two loving ones! she waked not from her swound,   25
And he was taken with the cramp, and in the waves was drowned;
But Fate has metamorphosed them, in pity of their woe,
And now they keep an oyster-shop for mermaids down below.

The Last Leaf

THIS LYRIC is unique in its mingling of drollery and
sentiment. The character described is Major Thomas
Melville, grandfather of Herman Melville, an "Indian"
of the Boston Tea Party, and an officer in the Revolutionary War. First published in the Boston *Amateur*,
March 26, 1831; republished in several other journals
and first collected in *Poems* (1836).

I saw him once before,
As he passed by the door,
   And again
The pavement stones resound,
As he totters o'er the ground   5
   With his cane.

They say that in his prime,
Ere the pruning-knife of Time
   Cut him down,
Not a better man was found   10
By the Crier on his round
   Through the town.

But now he walks the streets,
And he looks at all he meets
   Sad and wan,   15
And he shakes his feeble head,
That it seems as if he said,
   "They are gone."

The mossy marbles rest
On the lips that he has prest   20
   In their bloom,
And the names he loved to hear
Have been carved for many a year
   On the tomb.

My grandmamma has said—   25
Poor old lady, she is dead
   Long ago—
That he had a Roman nose,
And his cheek was like a rose
   In the snow.   30

But now his nose is thin,
And it rests upon his chin

Like a staff,
And a crook is in his back,
And a melancholy crack   35
   In his laugh.

I know it is a sin
For me to sit and grin
   At him here;
But the old three-cornered hat,   40
And the breeches, and all that,
   Are so queer!

And if I should live to be
The last leaf upon the tree
   In the spring,   45
Let them smile, as I do now,
At the old forsaken bough
   Where I cling.

My Aunt

THIS POEM is typical of Holmes's mixture of humor,
sentiment, and tender ridicule. First published in *The
New England Magazine*, October, 1831; first collected
in *Poems* (1836).

My aunt! my dear unmarried aunt!
   Long years have o'er her flown;
Yet still she strains the aching clasp
   That binds her virgin zone;
I know it hurts her,—though she looks   5
   As cheerful as she can;
Her waist is ampler than her life,
   For life is but a span.

My aunt! my poor deluded aunt!
   Her hair is almost gray;   10
Why will she train that winter curl
   In such a spring-like way?
How can she lay her glasses down,
   And say she reads as well,
When, through a double convex lens,   15
   She just makes out to spell?

Her father—grandpapa! forgive
   This erring lip its smiles—
Vowed she should make the finest girl
   Within a hundred miles;   20
He sent her to a stylish school;
   'Twas in her thirteenth June;

And with her, as the rules required,
   "Two towels and a spoon."

They braced my aunt against a board,   25
   To make her straight and tall;
They laced her up, they starved her down,
   To make her light and small;
They pinched her feet, they singed her hair,
   They screwed it up with pins;—   30
O never mortal suffered more
   In penance for her sins.

So, when my precious aunt was done,
   My grandsire brought her back;
(By daylight, lest some rabid youth   35
   Might follow on the track);
"Ah!" said my grandsire, as he shook
   Some powder in his pan,
"What could this lovely creature do
   Against a desperate man!"   40

Alas! nor chariot, nor barouche,
   Nor bandit cavalcade,
Tore from the trembling father's arms
   His all-accomplished maid.
For her how happy had it been!   45
   And Heaven had spared to me
To see one sad, ungathered rose
   On my ancestral tree.

The Moral Bully

ORIGINALLY this poem was a part of the long poem
"Astræa: the Balance of Illusions," delivered at a
meeting of the Phi Beta Kappa Society at Yale in 1850,
and printed the same year as a pamphlet; published
among the extracts from "Astræa" in *Songs in Many
Keys* (1862), and as a separate poem in the Household
(1877) and later editions.

Yon whey-faced brother, who delights to wear
A weedy flux of ill-conditioned hair,
Seems of the sort that in a crowded place
One elbows freely into smallest space;
A timid creature, lax of knee and hip,   5
Whom small disturbance whitens round the lip;
One of those harmless spectacled machines,
The Holy-Week of Protestants convenes;
Whom school-boys question if their walk transcends
The last advices of maternal friends;   10

Whom John, obedient to his master's sign,
Conducts, laborious, up to ninety-nine,
While Peter, glistening with luxurious scorn,
Husks his white ivories like an ear of corn;
Dark in the brow and bilious in the cheek,   15
Whose yellowish linen flowers but once a week,
Conspicuous, annual, in their threadbare suits,
And the laced high-lows which they call their boots
Well mayst thou shun that dingy front severe,   19
But him, O stranger, him thou canst not fear!

Be slow to judge, and slower to despise,
Man of broad shoulders and heroic size!
The tiger, writhing from the boa's rings,
Drops at the fountain where the cobra stings.
In that lean phantom, whose extended glove   25
Points to the text of universal love,
Behold the master that can tame thee down
To crouch, the vassal of his Sunday frown;
His velvet throat against thy corded wrist,
His loosened tongue against thy doubled fist!   30

The MORAL BULLY, though he never swears,
Nor kicks intruders down his entry stairs,
Though meekness plants his backward-sloping hat,
And non-resistance ties his white cravat,   34
Though his black broadcloth glories to be seen
In the same plight with Shylock's gaberdine,
Hugs the same passion to his narrow breast
That heaves the cuirass on the trooper's chest,
Hears the same hell-hounds yelling in his rear   39
That chase from port the maddened buccaneer,
Feels the same comfort while his acrid words
Turn the sweet milk of kindness into curds,
Or with grim logic prove, beyond debate,
That all we love is worthiest of our hate,
As the scarred ruffian of the pirate's deck,   45
When his long swivel rakes the staggering wreck!

Heaven keep us all! Is every rascal clown
Whose arm is stronger free to knock us down?
Has every scarecrow, whose cachectic soul
Seems fresh from Bedlam, airing on parole,   50
Who, though he carries but a doubtful trace
Of angel visits on his hungry face,
From lack of marrow or the coins to pay,
Has dodged some vices in a shabby way,

The right to stick us with his cutthroat terms,   55
And bait his homilies with his brother worms?

Dorothy Q.

A Family *Portrait*

FIRST PUBLISHED in *The Atlantic Monthly*, January,
1871; first collected in *Songs of Many Seasons* (1875).
For the Riverside Edition (1891), Holmes wrote the
following note:

"I cannot tell the story of Dorothy Q. more simply
in prose than I have told it in verse, but I can add something to it.

"Dorothy Q. was the daughter of Judge Edmund
Quincy, and the niece of Josiah Quincy, junior, the
young patriot and orator who died just before the
American Revolution, of which he was one of the most
eloquent and effective promoters. . . .

"The canvas of the painting was so much decayed
that it had to be replaced by a new one, in doing which
the rapier thrust was of course filled up."

Grandmother's mother: her age, I guess,
Thirteen summers, or something less;
Girlish bust, but womanly air;
Smooth, square forehead with uprolled hair,
Lips that lover has never kissed;   5
Taper fingers and slender wrist;
Hanging sleeves of stiff brocade;
So they painted the little maid.

On her hand a parrot green
Sits unmoving and broods serene.   10
Hold up the canvas full in view,—
Look! there's a rent the light shines through,
Dark with a century's fringe of dust,—
That was a Red-Coat's rapier-thrust!
Such is the tale the lady old,   15
Dorothy's daughter's daughter, told.

Who the painter was none may tell,—
One whose best was not over well;
Hard and dry, it must be confessed,
Flat as a rose that has long been pressed;   20
Yet in her cheek the hues are bright,
Dainty colors of red and white,
And in her slender shape are seen
Hint and promise of stately mien.

766

Look not on her with eyes of scorn,— 25
Dorothy Q. was a lady born!
Ay! since the galloping Normans came,
England's annals have known her name;
And still to the three-hilled rebel town
Dear is that ancient name's renown, 30
For many a civic wreath they won,
The youthful sire and the gray-haired son.

O Damsel Dorothy! Dorothy Q.!
Strange is the gift that I owe to you;
Such a gift as never a king 35
Save to daughter or son might bring,—
All my tenure of heart and hand,
All my title to house and land;
Mother and sister and child and wife
And joy and sorrow and death and life! 40

What if a hundred years ago
Those close-shut lips had answered No,
When forth the tremulous question came
That cost the maiden her Norman name,
And under the folds that look so still 45
The bodice swelled with the bosom's thrill?
Should I be I, or would it be
One tenth another, to nine tenths me?

Soft is the breath of a maiden's YES:
Not the light gossamer stirs with less; 50
But never a cable that holds so fast
Through all the battles of wave and blast,
And never an echo of speech or song
That lives in the babbling air so long!
There were tones in the voice that whispered then
You may hear to-day in a hundred men. 56

O lady and lover, how faint and far
Your images hover,—and here we are,
Solid and stirring in flesh and bone,—
Edward's and Dorothy's—all their own,— 60
A goodly record for Time to show
Of a syllable spoken so long ago!—
Shall I bless you, Dorothy, or forgive
For the tender whisper that bade me live?

It shall be a blessing, my little maid! 65
I will heal the stab of the Red-Coat's blade,
And freshen the gold of the tarnished frame,
And gild with a rhyme your household name;

So you shall smile on us brave and bright
As first you greeted the morning's light, 70
And live untroubled by woes and fears
Through a second youth of a hundred years.

The Organ-blower

FIRST PUBLISHED in *Old and New* for January, 1872;
first collected in *Songs of Many Seasons* (1875).

Devoutest of my Sunday friends,
The patient Organ-blower bends;
I see his figure sink and rise,
(Forgive me, Heaven, my wandering eyes!)
A moment lost, the next half seen, 5
His head above the scanty screen,
Still measuring out his deep salaams
Through quavering hymns and panting psalms.

No priest that prays in gilded stole,
To save a rich man's mortgaged soul; 10
No sister, fresh from holy vows,
So humbly stoops, so meekly bows;
His large obeisance puts to shame
The proudest genuflecting dame,
Whose Easter bonnet low descends 15
With all the grace devotion lends.

O brother with the supple spine,
How much we owe those bows of thine!
Without thine arm to lend the breeze,
How vain the finger on the keys! 20
Though all unmatched the player's skill,
Those thousand throats were dumb and still:
Another's art may shape the tone,
The breath that fills it is thine own.

Six days the silent Memnon waits 25
Behind his temple's folded gates;
But when the seventh day's sunshine falls
Through rainbowed windows on the walls,
He breathes, he sings, he shouts, he fills
The quivering air with rapturous thrills; 30
The roof resounds, the pillars shake,
And all the slumbering echoes wake!

The Preacher from the Bible-text
With weary words my soul has vexed
(Some stranger, fumbling far astray 35
To find the lesson for the day);

He tells us truths too plainly true,
And reads the service all askew,—
Why, why the—mischief—can't he look
Beforehand in the service-book? 40

But thou, with decent mien and face,
Art always ready in thy place;
Thy strenuous blast, whate'er the tune,
As steady as the strong monsoon;
Thy only dread a leathery creak, 45
Or small residual extra squeak,
To send along the shadowy aisles
A sunlit wave of dimpled smiles.

Not all the preaching, O my friend,
Comes from the church's pulpit end! 50
Not all that bend the knee and bow
Yield service half so true as thou!
One simple task performed aright,
With slender skill, but all thy might,
Where honest labor does its best, 55
And leaves the player all the rest.

This many-diapasoned maze,
Through which the breath of being strays,
Whose music makes our earth divine,
Has work for mortal hands like mine. 60
My duty lies before me. Lo,
The lever there! Take hold and blow!
And He whose hand is on the keys
Will play the tune as He shall please.

Wind-Clouds and Star-Drifts

The Poet at the Breakfast-Table first appeared serially in
The Atlantic Monthly from January through December,
1872, and each installment from May through November
closed with a "Wind-Clouds and Star-Drifts" poem,
seven in all, written by the Young Astronomer. The
series was treated as a separate poetical work in the
Household (1877) and later editions of *The Poetical
Works of Oliver Wendell Holmes.* Of the seven poems,
I, III, and VII have been selected to indicate Holmes
at his best in serious verse, when his moral nature was
deeply stirred.

I. *Ambition*

Another clouded night; the stars are hid,
The orb that waits my search is hid with them.

Patience! Why grudge an hour, a month, a year,
To plant my ladder and to gain the round
That leads my footsteps to the heaven of fame, 5
Where waits the wreath my sleepless midnights
 won?
Not the stained laurel such as heroes wear
That withers when some stronger conqueror's heel
Treads down their shrivelling trophies in the dust;
But the fair garland whose undying green 10
Not time can change, nor wrath of gods or men!

With quickened heart-beats I shall hear the
 tongues
That speak my praise; but better far the sense
That in the unshaped ages, buried deep
In the dark mines of unaccomplished time 15
Yet to be stamped with morning's royal die
And coined in golden days,—in those dim years
I shall be reckoned with the undying dead,
My name emblazoned on the fiery arch,
Unfading till the stars themselves shall fade. 20
Then, as they call the roll of shining worlds,
Sages of race unborn in accents new
Shall count me with the Olympian ones of old,
Whose glories kindle through the midnight sky:
Here glows the God of Battles; this recalls 25
The Lord of Ocean, and yon far-off sphere
The Sire of Him who gave his ancient name
To the dim planet with the wondrous rings;
Here flames the Queen of Beauty's silver lamp,
And there the moon-girt orb of mighty Jove; 30
But this, unseen through all earth's æons past,
A youth who watched beneath the western star
Sought in the darkness, found, and showed to men;
Linked with his name thenceforth and evermore!
So shall that name be syllabled anew 35
In all the tongues of all the tribes of men:
I that have been through immemorial years
Dust in the dust of my forgotten time
Shall live in accents shaped of bloodwarm breath,
Yea, rise in mortal semblance, newly born 40
In shining stone, in undecaying bronze,
And stand on high, and look serenely down
On the new race that calls the earth its own.

Is this a cloud, that, blown athwart my soul,
Wears a false seeming of the pearly stain 45
Where worlds beyond the world their mingling rays

Blend in soft white,—a cloud that, born of earth,
Would cheat the soul that looks for light from
     heaven?
Must every coral-insect leave his sign
On each poor grain he lent to build the reef,   50
As Babel's builders stamped their sunburnt clay,
Or deem his patient service all in vain?
What if another sit beneath the shade
Of the broad elm I planted by the way,—
What if another heed the beacon light   55
I set upon the rock that wrecked my keel,—
Have I not done my task and served my kind?
Nay, rather act thy part, unnamed, unknown,
And let Fame blow her trumpet through the world
With noisy wind to swell a fool's renown,   60
Joined with some truth he stumbled blindly o'er,
Or coupled with some single shining deed
That in the great account of all his days
Will stand alone upon the bankrupt sheet
His pitying angel shows the clerk of Heaven.   65
The noblest service comes from nameless hands,
And the best servant does his work unseen.
Who found the seeds of fire and made them shoot,
Fed by his breath, in buds and flowers of flame?
Who forged in roaring flames the ponderous
     stone,   70
And shaped the moulded metal to his need?
Who gave the dragging car its rolling wheel,
And tamed the steed that whirls its circling round?
All these have left their work and not their
     names,—
Why should I murmur at a fate like theirs?   75
This is the heavenly light; the pearly stain
Was but a wind-cloud drifting o'er the stars!

III. *Sympathies*

The snows that glittered on the disk of Mars
Have melted, and the planet's fiery orb
Rolls in the crimson summer of its year;
But what to me the summer or the snow
Of worlds that throb with life in forms unknown,   5
If life indeed be theirs; I heed not these.
My heart is simply human; all my care
For them whose dust is fashioned like mine own;
These ache with cold and hunger, live in pain,
And shake with fear of worlds more full of woe;   10
There may be others worthier of my love,
But such I know not save through these I know.

There are two veils of language, hid beneath
Whose sheltering folds, we dare to be ourselves;
And not that other self which nods and smiles   15
And babbles in our name; the one is Prayer,
Lending its licensed freedom to the tongue
That tells our sorrows and our sins to Heaven;
The other, Verse, that throws its spangled web
Around our naked speech and makes it bold.   20
I, whose best prayer is silence; sitting dumb
In the great temple where I nightly serve
Him who is throned in light, have dared to claim
The poet's franchise, though I may not hope
To wear his garland; hear me while I tell   25
My story in such form as poets use,
But breathed in fitful whispers, as the wind
Sighs and then slumbers, wakes and sighs again.

Thou Vision, floating in the breathless air
Between me and the fairest of the stars,   30
I tell my lonely thoughts as unto thee.
Look not for marvels of the scholar's pen
In my rude measure; I can only show
A slender-margined, unillumined page,
And trust its meaning to the flattering eye   35
That reads it in the gracious light of love.
Ah, wouldst thou clothe thyself in breathing shape
And nestle at my side, my voice should lend
Whate'er my verse may lack of tender rhythm
To make thee listen.
                              I have stood entranced   40
When, with her fingers wandering o'er the keys,
The white enchantress with the golden hair
Breathed all her soul through some unvalued
     rhyme;
Some flower of song that long had lost its bloom;
Lo! its dead summer kindled as she sang!   45
The sweet contralto, like the ringdove's coo,
Thrilled it with brooding, fond, caressing tones,
And the pale minstrel's passion lived again,
Tearful and trembling as a dewy rose
The wind has shaken till it fills the air   50
With light and fragrance. Such the wondrous
     charm
A song can borrow when the bosom throbs
That lends it breath.
                              So from the poet's lips
His verse sounds doubly sweet, for none like him
Feels every cadence of its wave-like flow;   55

He lives the passion over, while he reads,
That shook him as he sang his lofty strain,
And pours his life through each resounding line,
As ocean, when the stormy winds are hushed,   59
Still rolls and thunders through his billowy caves.

VII. *Worship*

From my lone turret as I look around
O'er the green meadows to the ring of blue,
From slope, from summit, and from half-hid vale
The sky is stabbed with dagger-pointed spires,
Their gilded symbols whirling in the wind,   5
Their brazen tongues proclaiming to the world,
"Here truth is sold, the only genuine ware;
See that it has our trade-mark! You will buy
Poison instead of food across the way,
The lies of——" this or that, each several name   10
The standard's blazon and the battle-cry
Of some true-gospel faction, and again
The token of the Beast to all beside.
And grouped round each I see a huddling crowd
Alike in all things save the words they use;   15
In love, in longing, hate and fear the same.

Whom do we trust and serve? We speak of one
And bow to many; Athens still would find
The shrines of all she worshipped safe within
Our tall barbarian temples, and the thrones   20
That crowned Olympus mighty as of old.
The god of music rules the Sabbath choir;
The lyric muse must leave the sacred nine
To help us please the dilettante's ear;
Plutus limps homeward with us, as we leave   25
The portals of the temple where we knelt
And listened while the god of eloquence
(Hermes of ancient days, but now disguised
In sable vestments) with that other god
Somnus, the son of Erebus and Nox,   30
Fights in unequal contest for our souls;
The dreadful sovereign of the under world
Still shakes his sceptre at us, and we hear
The baying of the triple-throated hound;
Eros is young as ever, and as fair   35
The lovely Goddess born of ocean's foam.

These be thy gods, O Israel! Who is he,
The one ye name and tell us that ye serve,
Whom ye would call me from my lonely tower
To worship with the many-headed throng?   40

Is it the God that walked in Eden's grove
In the cool hour to seek our guilty sire?
The God who dealt with Abraham as the sons
Of that old patriarch deal with other men?
The jealous God of Moses, one who feels   45
An image as an insult, and is wroth
With him who made it and his child unborn?
The God who plagued his people for the sin
Of their adulterous king, beloved of him,—
The same who offers to a chosen few   50
The right to praise him in eternal song
While a vast shrieking world of endless woe
Blends its dread chorus with their rapturous hymn?
Is this the God ye mean, or is it he
Who heeds the sparrow's fall, whose loving heart
Is as the pitying father's to his child,   56
Whose lesson to his children is "Forgive,"
Whose plea for all, "They know not what they do"?

Grandmother's Story of Bunker-Hill Battle

THIS POEM was first printed in *Memorial, Bunker Hill* (1875), and later collected in the Household (1877) and other editions. Holmes remarked in the Riverside Edition (1891): "I have often been asked what steeple it was from which the little group I speak of looked upon the conflict. . . . Christ Church in Salem Street is the one I always think of, but I do not insist upon its claim."

As She Saw It from the Belfry

'Tis like stirring living embers when, at eighty, one remembers
All the achings and the quakings of "the times that tried men's souls";
When I talk of Whig and Tory, when I tell the Rebel story,
To you the words are ashes, but to me they're burning coals.

I had heard the muskets' rattle of the April running battle;   5
Lord Percy's hunted soldiers, I can see their red coats still;

2. "the times . . . souls": The quotation is a modification of the most famous sentence in Paine's *The Crisis*.
6. Percy's: Lord Percy commanded reinforcements sent to the assistance of the British retreating from Concord and Lexington, April 19, 1775.

770

But a deadly chill comes o'er me, as the day looms
    up before me,
When a thousand men lay bleeding on the slopes
    of Bunker's Hill.

'Twas a peaceful summer's morning, when the
    first thing gave us warning
Was the booming of the cannon from the river
    and the shore: 10
"Child," says grandma, "what's the matter, what
    is all this noise and clatter?
Have those scalping Indian devils come to murder
    us once more?"

Poor old soul! my sides were shaking in the midst
    of all my quaking,
To hear her talk of Indians when the guns began
    to roar:
She had seen the burning village, and the slaughter
    and the pillage,   15
When the Mohawks killed her father with their
    bullets through his door.

Then I said, "Now, dear old granny, don't you
    fret and worry any,
For I'll soon come back and tell you whether this
    is work or play;
There can't be mischief in it, so I won't be gone a
    minute"—
For a minute then I started. I was gone the live-
    long day.   20

No time for bodice-lacing or for looking-glass
    grimacing;
Down my hair went as I hurried, tumbling half-
    way to my heels;
God forbid your ever knowing, when there's
    blood around her flowing,
How the lonely, helpless daughter of a quiet
    household feels!

In the street I heard a thumping; and I knew it
    was the stumping   25
Of the Corporal, our old neighbor, on that wooden
    leg he wore,
With a knot of women round him,—it was lucky I
    had found him,
So I followed with the others, and the Corporal
    marched before.

They were making for the steeple,—the old soldier
    and his people;
The pigeons circled round us as we climbed the
    creaking stair,   30
Just across the narrow river—O, so close it made
    me shiver!—
Stood a fortress on the hill-top that but yesterday
    was bare.

Not slow our eyes to find it; well we knew who
    stood behind it,
Though the earthwork hid them from us, and the
    stubborn walls were dumb:
Here were sister, wife, and mother, looking wild
    upon each other,   35
And their lips were white with terror as they said,
    THE HOUR HAS COME!

The morning slowly wasted, not a morsel had we
    tasted,
And our heads were almost splitting with the
    cannons' deafening thrill,
When a figure tall and stately round the rampart
    strode sedately;
It was PRESCOTT, one since told me; he com-
    manded on the hill.   40

Every woman's heart grew bigger when we saw his
    manly figure,
With the banyan buckled round it, standing up so
    straight and tall;
Like a gentleman of leisure who is strolling out for
    pleasure,
Through the storm of shells and cannon-shot he
    walked around the wall.

At eleven the streets were swarming, for the red-
    coats' ranks were forming;   45
At noon in marching order they were moving to
    the piers;
How the bayonets gleamed and glistened, as we
    looked far down, and listened
To the trampling and the drum-beat of the belted
    grenadiers!

40. Prescott: Colonel William Prescott (1726–1795)
commanded the colonial forces on Breed's Hill, which he
had fortified instead of Bunker Hill because he believed
the former commanded Boston more effectively.

At length the men have started, with a cheer (it
    seemed faint-hearted),
In their scarlet regimentals, with their knapsacks
    on their backs,   50
And the reddening, rippling water, as after a sea-
    fight's slaughter,
Round the barges gliding onward blushed like
    blood along their tracks.

So they crossed to the other border, and again
    they formed in order;
And the boats came back for soldiers, came for
    soldiers, soldiers still:
The time seemed everlasting to us women faint and
    fasting,—   55
At last they're moving, marching, marching
    proudly up the hill.

We can see the bright steel glancing all along the
    lines advancing—
Now the front rank fires a volley—they have
    thrown away their shot;
For behind their earthwork lying, all the balls
    above them flying,
Our people need not hurry; so they wait and an-
    swer not.   60

Then the Corporal, our old cripple (he would
    swear sometimes and tipple),—
He had heard the bullets whistle (in the old French
    war) before,—
Calls out in words of jeering, just as if they all
    were hearing,—
And his wooden leg thumps fiercely on the dusty
    belfry floor:—

"Oh! fire away, ye villains, and earn King George's
    shillin's,   65
But ye'll waste a ton of powder afore a 'rebel' falls;
You may bang the dirt and welcome, they're as
    safe as Dan'l Malcolm
Ten foot beneath the gravestone that you've
    splintered with your balls!"

67. Dan'l Malcolm: Daniel Malcolm (1725–1769),
Boston sea captain, who in 1768 led the colonials in the
first armed clash with the British as a result of the importation revenue acts. Holmes stated in a note: "Malcolm's
gravestone, splintered by British bullets, may be seen in
the Copp's Hill burial-ground."

In the hush of expectation, in the awe and trepida-
    tion
Of the dread approaching moment, we are well-
    nigh breathless all;   70
Though the rotten bars are failing on the rickety
    belfry railing,
We are crowding up against them like the waves
    against a wall.

Just a glimpse (the air is clearer), they are nearer,
    —nearer,—nearer,
When a flash—a curling smoke-wreath—then a
    crash—the steeple shakes—
The deadly truce is ended; the tempest's shroud is
    rended;   75
Like a morning mist it gathered, like a thunder-
    cloud it breaks!

O the sight our eyes discover as the blue-black
    smoke blows over!
The red-coats stretched in windrows as a mower
    rakes his hay;
Here a scarlet heap is lying, there a headlong
    crowd is flying
Like a billow that has broken and is shivered into
    spray.   80

Then we cried, "The troops are routed! they are
    beat—it can't be doubted!
God be thanked, the fight is over!"—Ah! the
    grim old soldier's smile!
"Tell us, tell us why you look so?" (we could
    hardly speak, we shook so),—
"Are they beaten? *Are* they beaten? ARE they
    beaten?"—"Wait a while."

O the trembling and the terror! for too soon we
    saw our error: 85
They are baffled, not defeated; we have driven
    them back in vain;
And the columns that were scattered, round the
    colors that were tattered,
Toward the sullen silent fortress turn their belted
    breasts again.

All at once, as we are gazing, lo the roofs of
    Charlestown blazing!
They have fired the harmless village; in an hour
    it will be down!   90

The Lord in heaven confound them, rain his fire
  and brimstone round them,—
The robbing, murdering red-coats, that would
  burn a peaceful town!

They are marching, stern and solemn; we can see
  each massive column
As they near the naked earth-mound with the
  slanting walls so steep.
Have our soldiers got faint-hearted, and in noiseless haste departed?   95
Are they panic-struck and helpless? Are they
  palsied or asleep?

Now! the walls they're almost under! scarce a rod
  the foes asunder!
Not a firelock flashed against them! up the earthwork they will swarm!
But the words have scarce been spoken, when the
  ominous calm is broken,
And a bellowing crash has emptied all the vengeance of the storm!   100

So again, with murderous slaughter, pelted backwards to the water,
Fly Pigot's running heroes and the frightened
  braves of Howe;
And we shout, "At last they're done for, it's their
  barges they have run for:
They are beaten, beaten, beaten; and the battle's
  over now!"

And we looked, poor timid creatures, on the rough
  old soldier's features,   105
Our lips afraid to question, but he knew what we
  would ask:
"Not sure," he said; "keep quiet,—once more, I
  guess, they'll try it—
Here's damnation to the cut-throats!"——then he
  handed me his flask,

Saying, "Gal, you're looking shaky; have a drop
  of old Jamaiky;
I'm afeard there'll be more trouble afore the job is
  done";   110

102. **Pigot . . . Howe:** Colonel Pigot and General
William Howe were British officers.

So I took one scorching swallow; dreadful faint I
  felt and hollow,
Standing there from early morning when the firing
  was begun.

All through those hours of trial I had watched a
  calm clock dial,
As the hands kept creeping, creeping,—they were
  creeping round to four,
When the old man said, "They're forming with
  their bagonets fixed for storming: 115
It's the death-grip that's a coming,—they will try
  the works once more."

With brazen trumpets blaring, the flames behind
  them glaring,
The deadly wall before them, in close array they
  come;
Still onward, upward toiling, like a dragon's fold
  uncoiling,—
Like the rattlesnake's shrill warning the reverberating drum!   120

Over heaps all torn and gory—shall I tell the fearful story,
How they surged above the breastwork, as a sea
  breaks over a deck;
How, driven, yet scarce defeated, our worn-out
  men retreated,
With their powder-horns all emptied, like the
  swimmers from a wreck?

It has all been told and painted; as for me, they
  say I fainted,   125
And the wooden-legged old Corporal stumped with
  me down the stair:
When I woke from dreams affrighted the evening
  lamps were lighted,—
On the floor a youth was lying; his bleeding breast
  was bare.

And I heard through all the flurry, "Send for
  WARREN! hurry! hurry!
Tell him here's a soldier bleeding, and he'll come
  and dress his wound!"   130

129. **Warren:** Dr. Joseph Warren (1741–1775), who had
dispatched William Dawes and Paul Revere to Lexington
and Concord the night before, refused to take command
over General Putnam at Bunker Hill; Putnam sent him
to Breed's Hill, where he was killed by a British soldier.

Ah, we knew not till the morrow told its tale of
    death and sorrow,
How the starlight found him stiffened on the dark
    and bloody ground.

Who the youth was, what his name was, where the
    place from which he came was,
Who had brought him from the battle, and had
    left him at our door,
He could not speak to tell us; but 'twas one of
    our brave fellows,   135
As the homespun plainly showed us which the
    dying soldier wore.

For they all thought he was dying, as they gath-
    ered round him crying,—
And they said, "O, how they'll miss him!" and,
    "What will his mother do?"
Then, his eyelids just unclosing like a child's that
    has been dozing,
He faintly murmured, "Mother!"——and—I saw
    his eyes were blue.   140

"Why, grandma, how you're winking!"—Ah,
    my child, it sets me thinking
Of a story not like this one. Well, he somehow
    lived along;
So we came to know each other, and I nursed him
    like a—mother,
Till at last he stood before me, tall, and rosy-
    cheeked, and strong.

And we sometimes walked together in the pleasant
    summer weather,—   145
"Please to tell us what his name was?"—Just
    your own, my little dear,—
There's his picture Copley painted: we became
    so well acquainted,
That—in short, that's why I'm grandma, and you
    children all are here!

Welcome to the Nations

Philadelphia, July 4, 1876

WRITTEN for the Centennial Celebration of the
Declaration of Independence; first collected in *The
Poetical Works of Oliver Wendell Holmes* (1877).

    147. Copley: John Singleton Copley (1738–1815) was
Boston's celebrated portrait painter; he established himself in London in 1775, where he remained until his death.

Bright on the banners of lily and rose
    Lo! the last sun of our century sets!
Wreath the black cannon that scowled on our foes,
    All but her friendships the nation forgets!
    All but her friends and their welcome forgets! 5
These are around her; but where are her foes?
    Lo, while the sun of her century sets,
    Peace with her garlands of lily and rose!

Welcome! a shout like the war trumpet's swell
    Wakes the wild echoes that slumber around! 10
Welcome! it quivers from Liberty's bell;
    Welcome! the walls of her temple resound!
    Hark! the gray walls of her temple resound!
Fade the far voices o'er hillside and dell;
    Welcome! still whisper the echoes around; 15
    Welcome! still trembles on Liberty's bell!

Thrones of the continents! isles of the sea!
    Yours are the garlands of peace we entwine;
Welcome, once more, to the land of the free,
    Shadowed alike by the palm and the pine; 20
    Softly they murmur, the palm and the pine,
"Hushed is our strife, in the land of the free";
    Over your children their branches entwine,
    Thrones of the continents! isles of the sea!

The Autocrat of the Breakfast-Table

WHEN LOWELL agreed to become editor of *The Atlantic
Monthly* in 1857, he insisted that Holmes be a contributor. Thus he awakened Holmes "from a kind of
literary lethargy" ten years after the physician and
writer of occasional verse had settled down as Professor
and Dean of the Harvard Medical School. *The Autocrat of the Breakfast-Table* appeared serially in the first
twelve numbers of *The Atlantic* (November, 1857–
October, 1858). Holmes had published two essays under
the same title in *The New England Magazine* twenty-
five years previously (November, 1831–February,
1832), and he resuscitated the title for the new series.
When Holmes began *The Autocrat*, which was to place
him securely among the masters of the familiar essay,
he had no fully completed plan. For example, though
he at first thought he would arrange a marriage between the Schoolmistress and the Divinity Student,
she grew lovelier and livelier in his imagination, and
the Autocrat became the only man at the table worthy
of her. *The Autocrat* is a book that could have been
written only in New England, yet in its **provinciality**

it delighted two continents. Slightly altered in text, the series was published in book form in 1858, and ran through many editions in England as well as in the United States.

I

. . . .

—What if, instead of talking this morning, I should read you a copy of verses, with critical remarks by the author? Any of the company can retire that like.

Album Verses

When Eve had led her lord away,
   And Cain had killed his brother,
The stars and flowers, the poets say,
   Agreed with one another

To cheat the cunning tempter's art,   5
   And teach the race its duty,
By keeping on its wicked heart
   Their eyes of light and beauty.

A million sleepless lids, they say,
   Will be at least a warning;   10
And so the flowers would watch by day,
   The stars from eve to morning.

On hill and prairie, field and lawn,
   Their dewy eyes upturning,
The flowers still watch from reddening dawn   15
   Till western skies are burning.

Alas! each hour of daylight tells
   A tale of shame so crushing,
That some turn white as sea-bleached shells,
   And some are always blushing.   20

But when the patient stars look down
   On all their light discovers,
The traitor's smile, the murderer's frown,
   The lips of lying lovers,

They try to shut their saddening eyes,   25
   And in the vain endeavour
We see them twinkling in the skies,
   And so they wink forever.

What do *you* think of these verses, my friends? —Is that piece an impromptu? said my landlady's daughter. (Æt. 19 +. Tender-eyed blonde. Long ringlets. Cameo pin. Gold pencil-case on a chain. Locket. Bracelet. Album. Autograph-book.

Accordion. Reads Byron, Tupper,[n] and Sylvanus Cobb,[n] junior, while her mother makes the puddings. Says, "Yes?" when you tell her anything.) —*Oui et non, ma petite,*—Yes and no, my child. Five of the seven verses were written off-hand; the other two took a week,—that is, were hanging round the desk in a ragged, forlorn unrhymed condition as long as that. All poets will tell you just such stories. *C'est le* DERNIER *pas qui coute.*[n] Don't you know how hard it is for some people to get out of a room after their visit is really over? They want to be off, and you want to have them off, but they don't know how to manage it. One would think they had been built in your parlor or study, and were waiting to be launched. I have contrived a sort of ceremonial inclined plane for such visitors, which being lubricated with certain smooth phrases, I back them down, metaphorically speaking, stern-foremost, into their "native element," the great ocean of out-doors. Well, now, there are poems as hard to get rid of as these rural visitors. They come in glibly, use up all the serviceable rhymes, *day, ray, beauty, duty, skies, eyes, other, brother, mountain, fountain,* and the like; and so they go on until you think it is time for the wind-up, and the wind-up won't come on any terms. So they lie about until you get sick of the sight of them, and end by thrusting some cold scrap of a final couplet upon them, and turning them out of doors. I suspect a good many "impromptus" could tell just such a story as the above. —Here turning to our landlady, I used an illustration which pleased the company much at the time, and has since been highly commended. "Madam," I said, "you can pour three gills and three quarters of honey from that pint jug if it is full, in less than one minute; but, Madam, you could not empty that last quarter of a gill, though you were turned into a marble Hebe,[n] and held the vessel upside down for a thousand years."

One gets tired to death of the old, old rhymes, such as you see in that copy of verses,—which I

Tupper: Martin Farquhar Tupper (1810–1889) was the author of *Proverbial Philosophy* (1838–1842), a popular book of commonplace maxims. **Cobb:** Sylvanus Cobb, Jr. (1823–1887) was an American writer of melodramatic fiction. *C'est . . . coute:* "It is the last step that costs." **Hebe:** goddess in Greek mythology; she filled the cups of the gods with nectar.

don't mean to abuse, or to praise either. I always feel as if I were a cobbler, putting new top-leathers to an old pair of boot-soles and bodies, when I am fitting sentiments to these venerable jingles.

.   .   .   .   .   youth
.   .   .   .   .   morning
.   .   .   .   .   truth
.   .   .   .   .   warning.

Nine tenths of the "Juvenile Poems" written spring out of the above musical and suggestive coincidences.

"Yes?" said our landlady's daughter.

I did not address the following remark to her, and I trust, from her limited range of reading, she will never see it; I said it softly to my next neighbour.

When a young female wears a flat circular side-curl, gummed on each temple,—when she walks with a male, not arm in arm, but his arm against the back of hers,—and when she says "Yes?" with the note of interrogation, you are generally safe in asking her what wages she gets, and who the "feller" was you saw her with.

"What were you whispering?" said the daughter of the house, moistening her lips, as she spoke, in a very engaging manner.

"I was only laying down a principle of social diagnosis."

"Yes?"

III

When John and Thomas, for instance, are talking together, it is natural enough that among the six there should be more or less confusion and misapprehension.

[Our landlady turned pale;—no doubt she thought there was a screw loose in my intellects,— and that involved the probable loss of a boarder. A severe-looking person, who wears a Spanish cloak and a sad cheek, fluted by the passions of the melodrama, whom I understand to be the professional ruffian of the neighbouring theatre, alluded, with a certain lifting of the brow, drawing down of the corners of the mouth, and somewhat rasping *voce di petto*,[n] to Falstaff's nine men in

voce di petto: "throaty voice."

buckram. Everybody looked up; I believe the old gentleman opposite was afraid I should seize the carving-knife; at any rate, he slid it to one side, as it were carelessly.]

I think, I said, I can make it plain to Benjamin Franklin here, that there are at least six personalities distinctly to be recognized as taking part in that dialogue between John and Thomas.

[*Three Johns*]

1. The real John; known only to his Maker.
2. John's ideal John; never the real one, and often very unlike him.
3. Thomas's ideal John; never the real John, not John's John, but often very unlike either.

[*Three Thomases*]

1. The real Thomas.
2. Thomas's ideal Thomas.
3. John's ideal Thomas.

Only one of the three Johns is taxed; only one can be weighed on a platform-balance; but the other two are just as important in the conversation. Let us suppose the real John to be old, dull, and ill-looking. But as the Higher Powers have not conferred on men the gift of seeing themselves in the true light, John very possibly conceives himself to be youthful, witty, and fascinating, and talks from the point of view of this ideal. Thomas, again, believes him to be an artful rogue, we will say; therefore he *is*, so far as Thomas's attitude in the conversation is concerned, an artful rogue, though really simple and stupid. The same conditions apply to the three Thomases. It follows, that, until a man can be found who knows himself as his Maker knows him, or who sees himself as others see him, there must be at least six persons engaged in every dialogue between two. Of these, the least important, philosophically speaking, is the one that we have called the real person. No wonder two disputants often get angry, when there are six of them talking and listening all at the same time.

.   .   .   .

IV

Memory, imagination, old sentiments and associations, are more readily reached through the sense of SMELL *than by almost any other channel.*

Of course the particular odors which act upon

each person's susceptibilities differ.—O, yes! I will tell you some of mine. The smell of *phosphorus* is one of them. During a year or two of adolescence I used to be dabbling in chemistry a good deal, and as about that time I had my little aspirations and passions like another, some of these things got mixed up with each other: orange-colored fumes of nitrous acid, and visions as bright and transient; reddening litmus-paper, and blushing cheeks;— *eheu!*[n]

Soles occidere et redire possunt,[n]

but there is no reagent that will redden the faded roses of eighteen hundred and—spare them! But, as I was saying, phosphorus fires this train of associations in an instant; its luminous vapours with their penetrating odour throw me into a trance; it comes to me in a double sense "trailing clouds of glory." Only the confounded Vienna matches, *ohne phosphorgeruch,*[n] have worn my sensibilities a little.

Then there is the marigold. When I was of smallest dimensions, and wont to ride impacted between the knees of fond parental pair, we would sometimes cross the bridge to the next village-town and stop opposite a low, brown, "gambrel-roofed" cottage. Out of it would come one Sally, sister of its swarthy tenant, swarthy herself, shady-lipped, sad-voiced, and, bending over her flower-bed, would gather a "posy," as she called it, for the little boy. Sally lies in the churchyard with a slab of blue slate at her head, lichen-crusted, and leaning a little within the last few years. Cottage, garden-beds, posies, grenadier-like rows of seedling onions,—stateliest of vegetables,—all are gone, but the breath of a marigold brings them all back to me.

Perhaps the herb *everlasting*, the fragrant *immortelle* of our autumn fields, has the most suggestive odor to me of all those that set me dreaming. I can hardly describe the strange thoughts and emotions that come to me as I inhale the aroma of its pale, dry, rustling flowers. A something it has of sepulchral spicery, as if it had been brought from the core of some great pyramid, where it had lain on the breast of a mummied Pharaoh. Something, too, of immortality in the sad, faint sweet-

ness lingering so long in its lifeless petals. Yet this does not tell why it fills my eyes with tears and carries me in blissful thought to the banks of asphodel that border the River of Life.

—I should not have talked so much about these personal susceptibilities, if I had not a remark to make about them which I believe is a new one. It is this. There may be a physical reason for the strange connection between the sense of smell and the mind. The olfactory nerve,—so my friend, the Professor, tells me,—is the only one directly connected with the hemispheres of the brain, the parts in which, as we have every reason to believe, the intellectual processes are performed. To speak more truly, the olfactory "nerve" is not a nerve at all, he says, but a part of the brain, in intimate connection with its anterior lobes. Whether this anatomical arrangement is at the bottom of the facts I have mentioned, I will not decide, but it is curious enough to be worth remembering. Contrast the sense of taste, as a source of suggestive impressions, with that of smell. Now the Professor assures me that you will find the nerve of taste has no immediate connection with the brain proper, but only with the prolongation of the spinal cord.

[The old gentleman opposite did not pay much attention, I think, to this hypothesis of mine. But while I was speaking about the sense of smell he nestled about in his seat, and presently succeeded in getting out a large red bandanna handkerchief. Then he lurched a little to the other side, and after much tribulation at last extricated an ample round snuff-box. I looked as he opened it and felt for the wonted pugil. Moist rappee, and a Tonka-bean lying therein. I made the manual sign understood of all mankind that use the precious dust, and presently my brain, too, responded to the long unused stimulus.—O boys,—that were,—actual papas and possible grandpapas,—some of you with crowns like billiard-balls,—some in locks of sable silvered,[n] and some of silver sabled,—do you remember, as you doze over this, those after-dinners at the Trois Frères, when the Scotch-plaided snuff-box went round, and the dry Lundy-Foot tickled its way along into our happy sensoria? Then it was that the Chambertin[n] or the Clos Vougeot[n] came

eheu: "alas." *Soles . . . possunt:* "suns may set and come back again." *ohne phosphorgeruch:* "without phosphorous odor."

locks of sable silvered: *Hamlet,* I, Sc. ii. **Chambertin, Clos Vougeot:** wines.

in, slumbering in its straw cradle. And one among you,—do you remember how he would have a bit of ice always in his Burgundy, and sit tinkling it against the sides of the bubble-like glass, saying that he was hearing the cow-bells as he used to hear them, when the deep-breathing kine came home at twilight from the huckleberry pasture, in the old home a thousand leagues towards the sunset?]

Ah me! what strains and strophes of unwritten verse pulsate through my soul when I open a certain closet in the ancient house where I was born! On its shelves used to lie bundles of sweet-marjoram and pennyroyal and lavender and mint and catnip; there apples were stored until their seeds should grow black, which happy period there were sharp little milk-teeth always ready to anticipate; there peaches lay in the dark, thinking of the sunshine they had lost, until, like the hearts of saints that dream of heaven in their sorrow, they grew fragrant as the breath of angels. The odorous echo of a score of dead summers lingers yet in those dim recesses.

.　.　.　.　.　.　.　.　.　.　.　.　.

—I will thank you for that pie,—said the provoking young fellow whom I have named repeatedly. He looked at it for a moment, and put his hands to his eyes as if moved.—I was thinking, —he said indistinctly—

—How? What is't?—said our landlady.

—I was thinking—said he—who was king of England when this old pie was baked,—and it made me feel bad to think how long he must have been dead.

[Our landlady is a decent body, poor, and a widow, of course; *celà va sans dire.*[n] She told me her story once; it was as if a grain of corn that had been ground and bolted had tried to individualize itself by a special narrative. There was the wooing and the wedding,—the start in life,—the disappointment,—the children she had buried,—the struggle against fate,—the dismantling of life, first of its small luxuries, and then of its comforts,— the broken spirits,—the altered character of the one on whom she leaned,—and at last the death that came and drew the black curtain between her and all her earthly hopes.

celà va sans dire: "that goes without saying."

I never laughed at my landlady after she had told me her story, but I often cried,—not those pattering tears that run off the eaves upon our neighbors' grounds, the *stillicidium*[n] of self-conscious sentiment, but those which steal noiselessly through their conduits until they reach the cisterns lying round about the heart; those tears that we weep inwardly with unchanging features; —such I did shed for her often when the imps of the boarding-house Inferno tugged at her soul with their red-hot pincers.]

Young man,—I said—the pasty you speak lightly of is not old, but courtesy to those who labour to serve us, especially if they are of the weaker sex, is very old, and yet well worth retaining. May I recommend to you the following caution, as a guide, whenever you are dealing with a woman, or an artist, or a poet,—if you are handling an editor or politician, it is superfluous advice. I take it from the back of one of those little French toys which contain pasteboard figures moved by a small running stream of fine sand; Benjamin Franklin will translate it for you: *"Quoiqu'elle soit très solidement montée il faut ne pas* brutaliser *la machine."*[n] I will thank you for the pie, if you please. . . . *cruel humor,*

.　.　.　.　.　.　.　.　.　.　.　.

—Do you want an image of the human will, or the self-determining principle, as compared with its prearranged and impassable restrictions? A drop of water, imprisoned in a crystal; you may see such a one in any mineralogical collection. One little fluid particle in the crystalline prism of the solid universe!

—Weaken moral obligations?—No, not weaken but define them. When I preach that sermon I spoke of the other day, I shall have to lay down some principles not fully recognized in some of your text-books.

.　.　.　.　.　.　.　.　.　.　.　.

—I have a creed,—I replied; none better, and none shorter. It is told in two words,—the two first of the Paternoster. And when I say these words I mean them. And when I compared the human will to a drop in a crystal, and said I meant

stillicidium: "continually dropping tears." *"Quoiqu'elle . . . machine"*: "although it may be solidly set up, the machine must not be handled roughly."

to define moral obligations, and not weaken them, this was what I intended to express: that the fluent, self-determining power of human beings is a very strictly limited agency in the universe. The chief planes of its enclosing solid are, of course, organization, education, condition. Organization may reduce the power of the will to nothing, as in some idiots; and from this zero the scale mounts upwards by slight gradations. Education is only second to nature. Imagine all the infants born this year in Boston and Timbuctoo to change places! Condition does less, but "Give me neither poverty nor riches" was the prayer of Agur,[n] and with good reason.

· · · · · · · · · · · ·

So you will not think I mean to speak lightly of old friendships, because we cannot help instituting comparisons between our present and former selves by the aid of those who were what we were, but are not what we are. Nothing strikes one more, in the race of life, than to see how many give out in the first half of the course. "Commencement day" always reminds me of the start for the "Derby," when the beautiful high-bred three-year olds of the season are brought up for trial. That day is the start, and life is the race. Here we are at Cambridge, and a class is just "graduating." Poor Harry! he was to have been there too, but he has paid forfeit; step out here into the grass back of the church; ah! there it is:—

> *Hunc lapiden posuerunt*
> *socii mœrentes.*[n]

But this is the start, and here they are,—coats bright as silk, and manes as smooth as *eau lustrale*[n] can make them. Some of the best of the colts are pranced round, a few minutes each, to show their paces. What is that old gentleman crying about? and the old lady by him, and the three girls, what are they all covering their eyes for? Oh, that is their colt which has just been trotted up on the stage. Do they really think those little thin legs can do anything in such a slashing sweepstakes as is coming off in these next forty years? Oh, this terrible gift of second-sight that comes to some of

us when we begin to look through the silvered rings of the *arcus senilis!*[n]

Ten years gone. First turn in the race. A few broken down; two or three bolted. Several show in advance of the ruck. *Cassock,* a black colt, seems to be ahead of the rest; those black colts commonly get the start, I have noticed, of the others, in the first quarter. *Meteor* has pulled up.

Twenty years. Second corner turned. *Cassock* has dropped from the front, and *Judex,* an iron-gray, has the lead. But look! how they have thinned out! Down flat,—five,—six,—how many? They lie still enough! they will not get up again in this race, be very sure! And the rest of them, what a "tailing off"! Anybody can see who is going to win,—perhaps.

Thirty years. Third corner turned. *Dives,* bright sorrel, ridden by the fellow in a yellow jacket, begins to make play fast; is getting to be the favorite with many. But who is that other one that has been lengthening his stride from the first, and now shows close up to the front? Don't you remember the quiet brown colt *Asteroid,* with the star in his forehead? That is he; he is one of the sort that lasts; look out for him! The black "colt," as we used to call him, is in the background, taking it easily in a gentle trot. There is one they used to call *the Filly,* on account of a certain feminine air he had; well up, you see; the Filly is not to be despised, my boy!

Forty years. More dropping off,—but places much as before.

Fifty years. Race over. All that are on the course are coming in at a walk; no more running. Who is ahead? Ahead? What! and the winning-post a slab of white or gray stone standing out from that turf where there is no more jockeying or straining for victory! Well, the world marks their places in its betting-book; but be sure that these matter very little, if they have run as well as they knew how!

—Did I not say to you a little while ago that the universe swam in an ocean of similitudes and analogies? I will not quote Cowley, or Burns, or Wordsworth, just now, to show you what thoughts were suggested to them by the simplest natural

Agur: Proverbs 30:8. *Hunc . . . mœrentes:* "his grieving associates set up this stone." *eau lustrale:* a dressing fluid.

arcus senilis: a whitish ring on the border of the cornea in the eyes of old persons.

objects, such as a flower or a leaf; but I will read you a few lines, if you do not object, suggested by looking at a section of one of those chambered shells to which is given the name of Pearly Nautilus.[n] We need not trouble ourselves about the distinction between this and the Paper Nautilus, the *Argonauta* of the ancients. The name applied to both shows that each has long been compared to a ship, as you may see more fully in Webster's Dictionary, or the "Encyclopedia," to which he refers. If you will look into Roget's Bridgewater Treatise, you will find a figure of one of these shells, and a section of it. The last will show you the series of enlarging compartments successively dwelt in by the animal that inhabits the shell, which is built in a widening spiral. Can you find no lesson in this?

The Chambered Nautilus

This is the ship of pearl, which, poets feign,   20
   Sails the unshadowed main,—
   The venturous bark that flings
On the sweet summer wind its purpled wings
In gulfs enchanted, where the Siren sings,   5
   And coral reefs lie bare,
Where the cold sea-maids rise to sun their streaming hair.

Its web of living gauze no more unfurl;
   Wrecked is the ship of pearl!
   And every chambered cell,   10
Where its dim dreaming life was wont to dwell,
As the frail tenant shaped his growing shell,
   Before thee lies revealed,—
Its irised ceiling rent, its sunless crypt unsealed!

Year after year beheld the silent toil   15
   That spread his lustrous coil;
   Still, as the spiral grew,
He left the past year's dwelling for the new,
Stole with soft step its shining archway through,
   Built up its idle door,   20
Stretched in his last-found home, and knew the old no
   more.

Thanks for the heavenly message brought by thee,
   Child of the wandering sea,
   Cast from her lap, forlorn!
From thy dead lips a clearer note is born   25

Pearly Nautilus: The pearly nautilus and the paper nautilus are both, according to Holmes, associated with the fables referring to Physalia, or Portuguese man-of-war, as well as to the two molluscs.

Than ever Triton blew from wreathèd horn!
   While on mine ear it rings,
Through the deep caves of thought I hear a voice that
   sings:—

Build thee more stately mansions, O my soul,
   As the swift seasons roll!   30
   Leave thy low-vaulted past!
Let each new temple, nobler than the last,
Shut thee from heaven with a dome more vast,
   Till thou at length art free,   34
Leaving thine outgrown shell by life's unresting sea!

XI

. . . .

I am willing,—I said,—to exercise your ingenuity in a rational and contemplative manner. —No, I do not proscribe certain forms of philosophical speculation which involve an approach to the absurd or the ludicrous, such as you may find, for example, in the folio of the Reverend Father Thomas Sanchez,[n] in his famous Disputations, "De Sancto Matrimonio." I will therefore turn this levity of yours to profit by reading you a rhymed problem, wrought out by my friend the Professor.

The Deacon's Masterpiece
or, The Wonderful "One-Hoss Shay"
A Logical Story

Have you heard of the wonderful one-hoss-shay,
That was built in such a logical way
It ran a hundred years to a day,
And then, of a sudden, it—ah, but stay,
I'll tell you what happened without delay,   5
Scaring the parson into fits,
Frightening people out of their wits,—
Have you ever heard of that, I say?

Seventeen hundred and fifty-five.
Georgius Secundus was then alive,—   10
Snuffy old drone from the German hive;
That was the year when Lisbon-town
Saw the earth open and gulp her down,
And Braddock's army was done so brown,
Left without a scalp to its crown.   15
It was on the terrible Earthquake-day
That the Deacon finished the one-hoss shay.

Sanchez: Father Thomas Sanchez (1550–1610), a Spanish Jesuit theologian.

Now in building of chaises, I tell you what,
There is always *somewhere* a weakest spot,—
In hub, tire, felloe, in spring or thill,   20
In panel, or crossbar, or floor, or sill,
In screw, bolt, thoroughbrace,—lurking still,
Find it somewhere you must and will,—
Above or below, or within or without,—
And that's the reason, beyond a doubt,   25
A chaise *breaks down*, but doesn't *wear out*.

But the Deacon swore (as Deacons do,
With an "I dew vum," or an "I tell *yeou*")
He would build one shay to beat the taown
'n' the keounty 'n' all the kentry raoun';   30
It should be so built that it *couldn'* break daown:
—"Fur," said the Deacon, "'t's mighty plain
Thut the weakes' place mus' stan' the strain;
'n' the way t' fix it, uz I maintain
           Is only jest   35
T' make that place uz strong uz the rest."

So the Deacon inquired of the village folk
Where he could find the strongest oak,
That couldn't be split nor bent nor broke,—
That was for spokes and floor and sills;   40
He sent for lancewood to make the thills;
The crossbars were ash, from the straightest trees;
The panels of white-wood, that cuts like cheese,
But lasts like iron for things like these;
The hubs of logs from the "Settler's ellum,"—   45
Last of its timber,—they couldn't sell 'em,
Never an axe had seen their chips,
And the wedges flew from between their lips,
Their blunt ends frizzled like celery-tips;
Step and prop-iron, bolt and screw,   50
Spring, tire, axle, and linchpin too,
Steel of the finest, bright and blue;
Thoroughbrace, bison-skin, thick and wide;
Boot, top, dasher, from tough old hide
Found in the pit when the tanner died.   55
That was the way he "put her through."—
"There!" said the Deacon, "naow she'll dew!"

Do! I tell you, I rather guess
She was a wonder, and nothing less!
Colts grew horses, beards turned gray,   60
Deacon and deaconess dropped away,
Children and grandchildren—where were they?
But there stood the stout old one-hoss-shay
As fresh as on Lisbon-earthquake-day!

EIGHTEEN HUNDRED;—it came and found   65
The Deacon's Masterpiece strong and sound.

Eighteen hundred increased by ten;—
"Hahnsum kerridge" they called it then.
Eighteen hundred and twenty came;—
Running as usual; much the same.   70
Thirty and forty at last arrive,
And then come fifty, and FIFTY-FIVE.

Little of all we value here
Wakes on the morn of its hundredth year
Without both feeling and looking queer.   75
In fact, there's nothing that keeps its youth,
So far as I know, but a tree and truth.
(This is a moral that runs at large;
Take it.—You're welcome.—No extra charge.)

FIRST OF NOVEMBER,—the Earthquake-day.—   80
There are traces of age in the one-hoss-shay,
A general flavor of mild decay,
But nothing local, as one may say.
There couldn't be,—for the Deacon's art
Had made it so like in every part   85
That there wasn't a chance for one to start.
For the wheels were just as strong as the thills,
And the floor was just as strong as the sills,
And the panels just as strong as the floor,
And the whippletree neither less nor more,   90
And the back crossbar as strong as the fore,
And spring and axle and hub *encore*.
And yet, *as a whole*, it is past a doubt,
In another hour it will be *worn out*!

First of November, 'Fifty-five!   95
This morning the parson takes a drive.
Now, small boys, get out of the way!
Here comes the wonderful one-hoss shay,
Drawn by a rat-tailed, ewe-necked bay.
"Huddup!" said the parson.—Off went they.   100

The parson was working his Sunday's text,—
Had got to *fifthly*, and stopped perplexed
At what the—Moses—was coming next.
All at once the horse stood still,
Close by the meet'n'-house on the hill.   105
—First a shiver, and then a thrill,
Then something decidedly like a spill,—
And the parson was sitting upon a rock,
At half-past nine by the meet'n'-house clock,—
Just the hour of the Earthquake shock!   110
—What do you think the parson found,
When he got up and stared around?
The poor old chaise in a heap or mound,
As if it had been to the mill and ground!
You see, of course, if you're not a dunce,   115

781

How it went to pieces all at once,—
All at once and nothing first,—
Just as bubbles do when they burst.

End of the wonderful one-hoss-shay.
Logic is logic. That's all I say.   120

.   .   .   .

—I have lived by the sea-shore and by the mountains.—No, I am not going to say which is best. The one where your place is is the best for you. But this difference there is: you can domes-ticate mountains, but the sea is *feræ naturæ.*[n] You may have a hut, or know the owner of one, on the mountain-side; you see a light half-way up its ascent in the evening, and you know there is a home, and you might share it. You have noted certain trees, perhaps; you know the particular zone where the hemlocks look so black in October, when the maples and beeches have faded. All its reliefs and intaglios have electrotyped themselves in the medallions that hang round the walls of your memory's chamber.—The sea remembers nothing. It is feline. It licks your feet,—its huge flanks purr very pleasantly for you; but it will crack your bones and eat you, for all that, and wipe the crimsoned foam from its jaws as if noth-ing had happened. The mountains give their lost children berries and water; the sea mocks their thirst and lets them die. The mountains have a grand, stupid, lovable tranquillity; the sea has a fascinating, treacherous intelligence. The moun-tains lie about like huge ruminants, their broad backs awful to look upon, but safe to handle. The sea smooths its silver scales until you cannot see their joints,—but their shining is that of a snake's belly, after all.—In deeper suggestiveness I find as great a difference. The mountains dwarf man-kind and foreshorten the procession of its long generations. The sea drowns out humanity and time; it has no sympathy with either; for it be-longs to eternity, and of that it sings its monoto-nous song for ever and ever.

Yet I should love to have a little box by the seashore. I should love to gaze out on the wild feline element from a front window of my own, just as I should love to look on a caged panther, and see it stretch its shining length, and then curl over and

feræ naturæ: "of a wild nature."

lap its smooth sides, and by-and-by begin to lash itself into rage and show its white teeth and spring at its bars, and howl the cry of its mad, but, to me, harmless fury.—And then,—to look at it with that inward eye,—who does not love to shuffle off time and its concerns, at intervals,—to forget who is President and who is Governor, what race he belongs to, what language he speaks, which golden-headed nail of the firmament his particular planetary system is hung upon, and listen to the great liquid metronome as it beats its solemn measure, steadily swinging when the solo or duet of human life began, and to swing just as steadily after the human chorus has died out and man is a fossil on its shores?

.   .   .   .

—Should you like to hear what moderate wishes life brings one to at last? I used to be very am-bitious,—wasteful, extravagant, and luxurious in all my fancies. Read too much in the "Arabian Nights." Must have the lamp,—couldn't do with-out the ring. Exercise every morning on the brazen horse. Plump down into castles as full of milk-white princesses as a nest is of young sparrows. All love me dearly at once.—Charming idea of life, but too high-colored for the reality. I have out-grown all this; my tastes have become ex-ceedingly primitive,—almost, perhaps, ascetic. We carry happiness into our condition, but must not hope to find it there. I think you will be will-ing to hear some lines which embody the subdued and limited desires of my maturity.

Contentment

"Man wants but little here below."

Little I ask; *my* wants *are* few;
  I only wish a hut of stone,
(A *very plain* brown stone will do,)
    That I may call my own;—
And close at hand is such a one,   5
In yonder street that fronts the sun.

Plain food is quite enough for me;
  Three courses are as good as ten;—
If Nature can subsist on three,
    Thank Heaven for three. Amen!   10
I always thought cold victual nice;—
My *choice* would be vanilla-ice.

I care not much for gold or land;—
  Give me a mortgage here and there,—
Some good bank-stock,—some note of hand,   15
  Or trifling railroad share;—
I only ask that Fortune send
A *little* more than I shall spend.

Honors are silly toys, I know,
  And titles are but empty names;—   20
I would, *perhaps*, be Plenipo,—
  But only near St. James;—
I'm very sure I should not care
To fill our Gubernator's chair.

Jewels are baubles; 'tis a sin   25
  To care for such unfruitful things;—
One good-sized diamond in a pin,—
  Some, *not so large*, in rings,—
A ruby and a pearl, or so,
Will do for me;—I laugh at show.   30

My dame should dress in cheap attire;
  (Good, heavy silks are never dear;)—
I own perhaps I *might* desire
  Some shawls of true cashmere,—
Some marrowy crapes of China silk,   35
Like wrinkled skins on scalded milk.

I would not have the horse I drive
  So fast that folks must stop and stare:
An easy gait—two, forty-five—
  Suits me; I do not care;—   40
Perhaps, for just a *single spurt*,
Some seconds less would do no hurt.

Of pictures, I should like to own
  Titians and Raphaels three or four.—
I love so much their style and tone,—   45
  One Turner, and no more,—
(A landscape,—foreground golden dirt,—
The sunshine painted with a squirt.)—

Of books but few,—some fifty score
  For daily use, and bound for wear;   50
The rest upon an upper floor;—
  Some *little* luxury *there*
Of red morocco's gilded gleam,
And vellum rich as country cream.

Busts, cameos, gems,—such things as these,   55
  Which others often show for pride,
I value for their power to please,
  And selfish churls deride;—
One Stradivarius, I confess,
Two Meerschaums, I would fain possess.   60

Wealth's wasteful tricks I will not learn,
  Nor ape the glittering upstart fool;—
Shall not carved tables serve my turn,
  But *all* must be of buhl?
Give grasping pomp its double share,—   65
I ask but *one* recumbent chair.

Thus humble let me live and die,
  Nor long for Midas' golden touch,
If Heaven more generous gifts deny,
  I shall not miss them *much*,—   70
Too grateful for the blessing lent
Of simple tastes and mind content!

XII

. . . .

—When it became known among the boarders that two of their number had joined hands to walk down the long path of life side by side, there was, as you may suppose, no small sensation. I confess I pitied our landlady. It took her all of a suddin,—she said. Had not known that we was keepin' company, and never mistrusted anything partic'lar. Ma'am was right to better herself. Didn't look very rugged to take care of a femily,
10 but could get hired haälp, she calc'lated.—The great maternal instinct came crowding up in her soul just then, and her eyes wandered until they settled on her daughter.

—No, poor, dear woman,—that could not have been. But I am dropping one of my internal tears for you, with this pleasant smile on my face all the time.

The great mystery of God's providence is the permitted crushing out of flowering instincts.
20 Life is maintained by the respiration of oxygen and of sentiments. In the long catalogue of scientific cruelties there is hardly anything quite so painful to think of as that experiment of putting an animal under the bell of an air-pump and exhausting the air from it. [I never saw the accursed trick performed. *Laus Deo!*[n]] There comes a time when the souls of human beings, women, perhaps, more even than men, begin to faint for the atmosphere of the affections they were made
30 to breathe. Then it is that Society places its transparent bell-glass over the young woman who

Laus Deo: "praise be to God."

783

is to be the subject of one of its fatal experiments. The element by which only the heart lives is sucked out of her crystalline prison. Watch her through its transparent walls;—her bosom is heaving; but it is in a vacuum. Death is no riddle, compared to this. I remember a poor girl's story in the "Book of Martyrs." The "dry-pan and the gradual fire" were the images that frightened her most. How many have withered and wasted under as slow a torment in the walls of that larger In- 10 quisition which we call Civilization!

Yes, my surface-thought laughs at you, you foolish, plain, over-dressed, mincing, cheaply-organized, self-saturated young person, whoever you may be, now reading this,—little thinking you are what I describe, and in blissful unconsciousness that you are destined to the lingering asphyxia of soul which is the lot of such multitudes worthier than yourself. But it is only my surface-thought which laughs. For that great procession 20 of the UNLOVED, who not only wear the crown of thorns, but must hide it under the locks of brown or gray,—under the snowy cap, under the chilling turban,—hide it even from themselves,—perhaps never know they wear it, though it kills them, there is no depth of tenderness in my nature that Pity has not sounded. Somewhere,—somewhere,—love is in store for them,—the universe must not be allowed to fool them so cruelly. What infinite pathos in the small, half-unconscious artifices by 30 which unattractive young persons seek to recommend themselves to the favor of those towards whom our dear sisters, the unloved, like the rest, are impelled by their God-given instincts!

Read what the singing-women—one to ten thousand of the suffering women—tell us, and think of the griefs that die unspoken! Nature is in earnest when she makes a woman; and there are women enough lying in the next churchyard with very commonplace blue slate-stones at their head 40 and feet, for whom it was just as true that "all sounds of life assumed one tone of love," as for Letitia Landon,[n] of whom Elizabeth Browning said it; but she could give words to her grief, and they could not.—Will you hear a few stanzas of mine?

Letitia Landon: (1802–1839), English author of sentimental and romantic poems.

The Voiceless

We count the broken lyres that rest
  Where the sweet wailing singers slumber,—
But o'er their silent sister's breast
  The wild-flowers who will stoop to number?
A few can touch the magic string,   5
  And noisy Fame is proud to win them;—
Alas for those that never sing,
  But die with all their music in them!

Nay, grieve not for the dead alone   9
  Whose song has told their hearts' sad story,—
Weep for the voiceless, who have known
  The cross without the crown of glory!
Not where Leucadian breezes sweep
  O'er Sappho's memory-haunted billow,
But where the glistening night-dews weep   15
  On nameless sorrow's churchyard pillow.

O hearts that break and give no sign
  Save whitening lip and fading tresses,
Till Death pours out his longed-for wine[n]   19
  Slow-dropped from Misery's crushing presses,—
If singing breath or echoing chord
  To every hidden pang were given,
What endless melodies were poured,
  As sad as earth, as sweet as heaven!

I hope that our landlady's daughter is not so badly off, after all. That young man from another city, who made the remark which you remember about Boston State-house and Boston folks, has appeared at our table repeatedly of late, and has seemed to me rather attentive to this young lady. Only last evening I saw him leaning over her while she was playing the accordion,—indeed, I undertook to join them in a song, and got as far as "Come rest in this boo-oo," when, my voice getting tremulous, I turned off, as one steps out of a procession, and left the basso and soprano to finish it. I see no reason why this young woman should not be a very proper match for a man that laughs about Boston State-house. He can't be very particular.

Cinders from the Ashes

THIS RECORD from memory of Holmes's life at Phillips Academy, Andover, Massachusetts, which he left in 1825 to attend Harvard, was first published in *The Atlantic Monthly* for January, 1869, and collected in

longed-for wine: In the first edition of *The Autocrat* the phrase is "cordial wine."

Pages from an Old Volume of Life, Volume VIII of the Riverside Edition of the *Writings* (1891).

The personal revelations contained in my report of certain breakfast-table conversations were so charitably listened to and so good-naturedly interpreted, that I may be in danger of becoming over-communicative. Still, I should never have ventured to tell the trivial experiences here thrown together, were it not that my brief story is illuminated here and there by a glimpse of some shining figure that trod the same path with me for a time, or crossed it, leaving a momentary or lasting brightness in its track. . . .

After leaving the school of Dame Prentiss, best remembered by infantine loves, those pretty preludes of more serious passions; by the great forfeit-basket, filled with its miscellaneous waifs and deodands, and by the long willow stick by the aid of which the good old body, now stricken in years and unwieldy in person, could stimulate the sluggish faculties or check the mischievous sallies of the child most distant from her ample chair,— a school where I think my most noted schoolmate was the present Bishop of Delaware,—I became the pupil of Master William Biglow. This generation is not familiar with his title to renown, although he fills three columns and a half in Mr. Duyckinck's "Cyclopædia of American Literature." He was a humorist hardly robust enough for more than a brief local immortality. I am afraid we were an undistinguished set, for I do not remember anybody near a bishop in dignity graduating from our benches.

At about ten years of age I began going to what we always called the "Port School," because it was kept at Cambridgeport, a mile from the College. This suburb was at that time thinly inhabited, and, being much of it marshy and imperfectly reclaimed, had a dreary look as compared with the thriving College settlement. The tenants of the many beautiful mansions that have sprung up along Main Street, Harvard Street, and Broadway can hardly recall the time when, except the "Dana House" and the "Opposition House" and the "Clark House," these roads were almost all the way bordered by pastures until we reached the "stores" of Main Street, or were abreast of that forlorn "First Row" of Harvard Street. We called the boys of that locality "port-chucks." They called us "Cambridge-chucks," but we got along very well together in the main.

Among my schoolmates at the Port School was a young girl of singular loveliness. I once before referred to her as "the golden blonde," but did not trust myself to describe her charms. The day of her appearance in the school was almost as much a revelation to us boys as the appearance of Miranda was to Caliban. Her abounding natural curls were so full of sunshine, her skin was so delicately white, her smile and her voice were so all-subduing, that half our heads were turned. Her fascinations were everywhere confessed a few years afterwards; and when I last met her, though she said she was a grandmother, I questioned her statement, for her winning looks and ways would still have made her admired in any company.

Not far from the golden blonde were two small boys, one of them very small, perhaps the youngest boy in school, both ruddy, sturdy, quiet, reserved, sticking loyally by each other, the oldest, however, beginning to enter into social relations with us of somewhat maturer years. One of these two boys was destined to be widely known, first in literature, as author of one of the most popular books of its time and which is freighted for a long voyage; then as an eminent lawyer; a man who, if his countrymen are wise, will yet be prominent in the national councils. Richard Henry Dana, Junior, is the name he bore and bears; he found it famous, and will bequeath it a fresh renown.

Sitting on the girls' benches, conspicuous among the school-girls of unlettered origin by that look which rarely fails to betray hereditary and congenital culture, was a young person very nearly of my own age. She came with the reputation of being "smart," as we should have called it, clever as we say nowadays. This was Margaret Fuller, the only one among us who, like "Jean Paul," like "The Duke," like "Bettina," has slipped the cable of the more distinctive name to which she was anchored, and floats on the waves of speech as "Margaret." Her air to her schoolmates was marked by a certain stateliness and distance, as if she had other thoughts than theirs and was not of them. She was a great student and a great reader of what she used to call "náw-véls." I remember her so well as she appeared at school and later, that I regret that she had not been faithfully given to canvas or marble in the day of her best looks. None know her aspect who have not seen her living. Margaret, as I remember her at school and afterwards, was tall, fair complexioned, with a watery, aqua-marine lustre in her light eyes, which she used to make small, as one does who looks at the sunshine. A remarkable point about her was that long, flexible neck, arching and undulating in strange sinuous movements, which one who loved her would compare to those of a swan, and one who loved her not to those of the ophidian who tempted our common mother. Her talk was affluent, magisterial, *de haut en bas*, some would say euphuistic, but surpassing the talk of women in breadth and audacity. Her face kindled and reddened and dilated in every feature as she spoke, and, as I once saw her in a fine storm of indignation at the supposed ill-treatment of a relative, showed itself capable of something resembling what Milton calls the viraginian aspect.

Little incidents bear telling when they recall anything of such a celebrity as Margaret. I remember being greatly awed once, in our school-days, with the maturity of one of her expressions. Some themes were brought home from the school for examination by my father, among them one of hers. I took it up with a certain emulous interest (for I fancied at that day that I too had drawn a prize, say a five-dollar one, at least, in the great intellectual life-lottery) and read the first words.

"It is a trite remark," she began.

I stopped. Alas! I did not know what *trite* meant. How could I ever judge Margaret fairly after such a crushing discovery of her superiority? I doubt if I ever did; yet oh, how pleasant it would have been, at about the age, say, of three-score and ten, to rake over these ashes for cinders with her,—she in a snowy cap, and I in a decent peruke!

After being five years at the Port School, the time drew near when I was to enter college. It seemed advisable to give me a year of higher training, and for that end some public school was thought to offer advantages. Phillips Academy at Andover was well known to us. We had been up there, my father and myself, at anniversaries.

Some Boston boys of well-known and distinguished parentage had been scholars there very lately,—Master Edmund Quincy, Master Samuel Hurd Walley, Master Nathaniel Parker Willis,—all promising youth, who fulfilled their promise.

I do not believe there was any thought of getting a little respite of quiet by my temporary absence, but I have wondered that there was not. Exceptional boys of fourteen or fifteen make home a heaven, it is true; but I have suspected, late in life, that I was not one of the exceptional kind. I had tendencies in the direction of flageolets and octave flutes. I had a pistol and a gun, and popped at everything that stirred, pretty nearly, except the house-cat. Worse than this, I would buy a cigar and smoke it by instalments, putting it meantime in the barrel of my pistol, by a stroke of ingenuity which it gives me a grim pleasure to recall; for no maternal or other female eyes would explore the cavity of that dread implement in search of contraband commodities.

It was settled, then, that I should go to Phillips Academy, and preparations were made that I might join the school at the beginning of the autumn. . . .

It was a shallow, two-story white house before which we stopped, just at the entrance of the central village, the residence of a very worthy professor in the theological seminary,—learned, amiable, exemplary, but thought by certain experts to be a little questionable in the matter of homoousianism,[n] or some such doctrine. There was a great rock that showed its round back in the narrow front yard. It looked cold and hard; but it hinted firmness and indifference to the sentiments fast struggling to get uppermost in my youthful bosom; for I was not too old for home-sickness,—who is? The carriage and my fond companions had to leave me at last. I saw it go down the declivity that sloped southward, then climb the next ascent, then sink gradually until the window in the back of it disappeared like an eye that shuts, and leaves the world dark to some widowed heart.

Sea-sickness and home-sickness are hard to deal with by any remedy but time. Mine was not a

homoousianism: term adopted by Nicean Council to express the doctrine that the Son was of the same substance as the Father.

bad case, but it excited sympathy. There was an ancient, faded old lady in the house, very kindly, but very deaf, rustling about in dark autumnal foliage of silk or other murmurous fabric, somewhat given to snuff, but a very worthy gentlewoman of the poor-relation variety. She comforted me, I well remember, but not with apples, and stayed me, but not with flagons. She went in her benevolence, and, taking a blue and white soda-powder, mingled the same in water, and encouraged me to drink the result. It might be a specific for sea-sickness, but it was not for homesickness. The *fiz* was a mockery, and the saline refrigerant struck a colder chill to my despondent heart. I did not disgrace myself, however, and a few days cured me, as a week on the water often cures sea-sickness.

There was a sober-faced boy of minute dimensions in the house, who began to make some advances to me, and who, in spite of all the conditions surrounding him, turned out, on better acquaintance, to be one of the most amusing, free-spoken, mocking little imps I ever met in my life. My room-mate came later. He was the son of a clergyman in a neighboring town,—in fact I may remark that I knew a good many clergymen's sons at Andover. He and I went in harness together as well as most boys do, I suspect; and I have no grudge against him, except that once, when I was slightly indisposed, he administered to me,—with the best intentions, no doubt,—a dose of Indian pills, which effectually knocked me out of time, as Mr. Morrissey would say,—not quite into eternity, but so near it that I perfectly remember one of the good ladies told me (after I had come to my senses a little, and was just ready for a sip of cordial and a word of encouragement), with that delightful plainness of speech which so brings realities home to the imagination, that "I never should look any whiter when I was laid out as a corpse." After my room-mate and I had been separated twenty-five years, fate made us fellow-townsmen and acquaintances once more in Berkshire, and now again we are close literary neighbors; for I have just read a very pleasant article, signed by him, in the last number of the "Galaxy." Does it not sometimes seem as if we were all marching round and round in a circle, like the supernumeraries who constitute

the "army" of a theatre, and that each of us meets and is met by the same and only the same people, or their doubles, twice, thrice, or a little oftener, before the curtain drops and the "army" puts off its borrowed clothes?

The old Academy building had a dreary look, with its flat face, bare and uninteresting as our own "University Building" at Cambridge, since the piazza which relieved its monotony was taken away, and, to balance the ugliness thus produced, the hideous projection was added to "Harvard Hall." Two masters sat at the end of the great room,—the principal and his assistant. Two others presided in separate rooms,—one of them the late Rev. Samuel Horatio Stearns, an excellent and lovable man, who looked kindly on me, and for whom I always cherished a sincere regard,— a clergyman's son, too, which privilege I did not always find the warrant of signal virtues; but no matter about that here, and I have promised myself to be amiable.

On the side of the long room was a large clock-dial, bearing these words:—

YOUTH IS THE SEED-TIME OF LIFE

I had indulged in a prejudice, up to that hour, that youth was the budding time of life, and this clock-dial, perpetually twitting me with its seedy moral, always had a forbidding look to my vernal apprehension.

I was put into a seat with an older and much bigger boy, or youth, with a fuliginous complexion, a dilating and whitening nostril, and a singularly malignant scowl. Many years afterwards he committed an act of murderous violence, and ended by going to finish his days in a madhouse. His delight was to kick my shins with all his might, under the desk, not at all as an act of hostility, but as a gratifying and harmless pastime. Finding this, so far as I was concerned, equally devoid of pleasure and profit, I managed to get a seat by another boy, the son of a very distinguished divine. He was bright enough, and more select in his choice of recreations, at least during school hours, than my late homicidal neighbor. But the principal called me up presently, and cautioned me against him as a dangerous companion. Could it be so? If the son of that boy's father could not be trusted, what boy in Christendom could? It seemed like the story of the youth doomed to be slain by a lion before reaching a certain age, and whose fate found him out in the heart of the tower where his father had shut him up for safety. Here was I, in the very dove's nest of Puritan faith, and out of one of its eggs a serpent had been hatched and was trying to nestle in my bosom! I parted from him, however, none the worse for his companionship so far as I can remember. . . .

My especial intimate was a fine, rosy-faced boy, not quite so free of speech as myself, perhaps, but with qualities that promised a noble manhood, and ripened into it in due season. His name was Phineas Barnes, and, if he is inquired after in Portland or anywhere in the State of Maine, something will be heard to his advantage from any honest and intelligent citizen of that Commonwealth who answers the question. This was one of two or three friendships that lasted. There were other friends and classmates, one of them a natural humorist of the liveliest sort, who would have been quarantined in any Puritan port, his laugh was so potently contagious.

Of the noted men of Andover the one whom I remember best was Professor Moses Stuart. His house was nearly opposite the one in which I resided and I often met him and listened to him in the chapel of the Seminary. I have seen few more striking figures in my life than his, as I remember it. Tall, lean, with strong, bold features, a keen, scholarly, accipitrine nose, thin, expressive lips, great solemnity and impressiveness of voice and manner, he was my early model of a classic orator. His air was Roman, his neck long and bare like Cicero's, and his *toga*,—that is his broadcloth cloak,—was carried on his arm, whatever might have been the weather, with such a statue-like rigid grace that he might have been turned into marble as he stood, and looked noble by the side of the antiques of the Vatican. . . .

Dr. Woods looked his creed more decidedly, perhaps, than any of the Professors. He had the firm fibre of a theological athlete, and lived to be old without ever mellowing, I think, into a kind of half-heterodoxy, as old ministers of stern creed are said to do now and then,—just as old doctors grow to be sparing of the more exasperating drugs

in their later days. He had manipulated the mysteries of the Infinite so long and so exhaustively, that he would have seemed more at home among the mediæval schoolmen than amidst the working clergy of our own time. . . .

There were various distractions to make the time not passed in study a season of relief. One good lady, I was told, was in the habit of asking students to her house on Saturday afternoons and praying with and for them. Bodily exercise was not, however, entirely superseded by spiritual exercises, and a rudimentary form of base-ball and the heroic sport of foot-ball were followed with some spirit.

A slight immature boy finds his materials of thought and enjoyment in very shallow and simple sources. Yet a kind of romance gilds for me the sober tableland of that cold New England hill where I came in contact with a world so strange to me, and destined to leave such mingled and lasting impressions. I looked across the valley to the hillside where Methuen hung suspended, and dreamed of its wooded seclusion as a village paradise. I tripped lightly down the long northern slope with *facilis descensus* on my lips, and toiled up again, repeating *sed revocare gradum*. I wandered in the autumnal woods that crown the "Indian Ridge," much wondering at that vast embankment, which we young philosophers believed with the vulgar to be of aboriginal workmanship, not less curious, perhaps, since we call it an escar, and refer it to alluvial agencies. The little Shawshine was our swimming-school, and the great Merrimack, the right arm of four toiling cities, was within reach of a morning stroll. At home we had the small imp to make us laugh at his enormities, for he spared nothing in his talk, and was the drollest little living protest against the prevailing solemnities of the locality. It did not take much to please us, I suspect, and it is a blessing that this is apt to be so with young people. What else could have made us think it great sport to leave our warm beds in the middle of winter and "camp out,"— on the floor of our room,—with blankets disposed tent-wise, except the fact that to a boy a new discomfort in place of an old comfort is often a luxury.

More exciting occupation than any of these was to watch one of the preceptors to see if he would not drop dead while he was praying. He had a dream one night that he should, and looked upon it as a warning, and told it round very seriously, and asked the boys to come and visit him in turn, as one whom they were soon to lose. More than one boy kept his eye on him during his public devotions, possessed by the same feeling the man had who followed Van Amburgh about with the expectation, let us not say the hope, of seeing the lion bite his head off sooner or later. . . .

On the last day of August, 1867, not having been at Andover for many years, I took the cars at noon, and in an hour or a little more found myself at the station, just at the foot of the hill. My first pilgrimage was to the old elm, which I remembered so well as standing by the tavern, and of which they used to tell the story that it held, buried in it by growth, the iron rings put round it in the old time to keep the Indians from chopping it with their tomahawks. I then began the once familiar toil of ascending the long declivity. Academic villages seem to change very slowly. Once in a hundred years the library burns down with all its books. A new edifice or two may be put up, and a new library begun in the course of the same century; but these places are poor, for the most part, and cannot afford to pull down their old barracks.

These sentimental journeys to old haunts must be made alone. The story of them must be told succinctly. It is like the opium-smoker's showing you the pipe from which he has just inhaled elysian bliss, empty of the precious extract which has given him his dream. . . .

The ghost of a boy was at my side as I wandered among the places he knew so well. I went to the front of the house. There was the great rock showing its broad back in the front yard. "I used to crack nuts on that," whispered the small ghost. I looked in at the upper window in the farther part of the house. "I looked out of that on four long changing seasons," said the ghost. I should have liked to explore farther, but, while I was looking, one came into the small garden, or what used to be the garden, in front of the house, and I desisted from my investigation and went on my way. The apparition that put me and my little ghost to flight had a dressing-gown on its person and a gun

in its hand. I think it was the dressing-gown, and not the gun, which drove me off.

And now here is the shop, or store, that used to be Shipman's, after passing what I think used to be Jonathan Leavitt's bookbindery, and here is the back road that will lead me round by the old Academy building.

Could I believe my senses when I found that it was turned into a gymnasium, and heard the low thunder of ninepin balls, and the crash of tumbling pins from those precincts? The little ghost said, "Never! It cannot be." But it was. "Have they a billiard-room in the upper story?" I asked myself. "Do the theological professors take a hand at all-fours or poker on week-days, now and then, and read the secular columns of the 'Boston Recorder' on Sundays?" I was demoralized for the moment, it is plain; but now that I have recovered from the shock, I must say that the fact mentioned seems to show a great advance in common sense from the notions prevailing in my time.

I sauntered,—we, rather, my ghost and I,—until we came to a broken field where there was quarrying and digging going on,—our old base-ball ground, hard by the burial-place. There I paused; and if any thoughtful boy who loves to tread in the footsteps that another has sown with memories of the time when he was young shall follow my footsteps, I need not ask him to rest here awhile, for he will be enchained by the noble view before him. Far to the north and west the mountains of New Hampshire lifted their summits in a long encircling ridge of pale blue waves. The day was clear, and every mound and peak traced its outline with perfect definition against the sky. This was a sight which had more virtue and refreshment in it than any aspect of nature that I had looked upon, I am afraid I must say for years. I have been by the seaside now and then, but the sea is constantly busy with its own affairs, running here and there, listening to what the winds have to say and getting angry with them, always indifferent, often insolent, and ready to do a mischief to those who seek its companionship. But these still, serene, unchanging mountains,—Monadnock, Kearsarge,—what memories that name recalls!—and the others, the dateless Pyramids of New England, the eternal monuments of her ancient race, around which cluster the homes of so many of her bravest and hardiest children,—I can never look at them without feeling that, vast and remote and awful as they are, there is a kind of inward heat and muffled throb in their stony cores, that brings them into a vague sort of sympathy with human hearts. It is more than a year since I have looked on those blue mountains, and they "are to me as a feeling" now, and have been ever since. . . .

The sun was getting far past the meridian, and I sought a shelter under which to partake of the hermit fare I had brought with me. Following the slope of the hill northward behind the cemetery, I found a pleasant clump of trees grouped about some rocks, disposed so as to give a seat, a table, and a shade. I left my benediction on this pretty little natural caravansera, and a brief record on one of its white birches, hoping to visit it again on some sweet summer or autumn day.

Two scenes remained to look upon,—the Shaw- shine River and the Indian Ridge. The streamlet proved to have about the width with which it flowed through my memory. The young men and the boys were bathing in its shallow current, or dressing and undressing upon its banks as in the days of old; the same river, only the water changed; "The same boys, only the names and the accidents of local memory different," I whispered to my little ghost.

The Indian Ridge more than equalled what I expected of it. It is well worth a long ride to visit. The lofty wooded bank is a mile and a half in extent, with other ridges in its neighborhood, in general running nearly parallel with it, one of them still longer. These singular formations are supposed to have been built up by the eddies of conflicting currents scattering sand and gravel and stones as they swept over the continent. But I think they pleased me better when I was taught that the Indians built them; and while I thank Professor Hitchcock, I sometimes feel as if I should like to found a chair to teach the ignorance of what people do not want to know.

"Two tickets to Boston," I said to the man at the station.

But the little ghost whispered, "When you leave this place you leave me behind you."

"*One* ticket to Boston, if you please. Good by, little ghost."

I believe the boy-shadow still lingers around the well-remembered scenes I traversed on that day, and that, whenever I revisit them, I shall find him again as my companion.

Over the Tea-Cups

[Emerson and Whitman]

AFTER the first number of "this series of papers," as Holmes called *Over the Tea-Cups*, was published in *The Atlantic Monthly* in March, 1888, when the author was aged 78, "the course of events"—bereavement in the loss of wife and daughter—brought an interruption of nearly two years. The papers were resumed in January, 1890, when Holmes was 81, and continued through November. The following year they were published as a book, and Holmes was much gratified when 20,000 copies were sold in a few months, enjoying, as he said, not only the "pleasure of the *pocket*" but also the "pleasure of the *heart*," which was of "a better quality" (John T. Morse, *Life*, II, 89).

. . . Thomas Jefferson is commonly recognized as the first to proclaim before the world the political independence of America. It is not so generally agreed upon as to who was the first to announce the literary emancipation of our country.

One of Mr. Emerson's biographers has claimed that his Phi Beta Kappa Oration was our Declaration of Literary Independence. But Mr. Emerson did not cut himself loose from all the traditions of Old World scholarship. He spelled his words correctly, he constructed his sentences grammatically. He adhered to the slavish rules of propriety, and observed the reticences which a traditional delicacy has considered inviolable in decent society, European and Oriental alike. When he wrote poetry, he commonly selected subjects which seemed adapted to poetical treatment,—apparently thinking that all things were not equally calculated to inspire the true poet's genius. Once, indeed, he ventured to refer to "the meal in the firkin, the milk in the pan," but he chiefly restricted himself to subjects such as a fastidious conventionalism would approve as having a certain fitness for poetical treatment. He was not always so careful as he might have been in the rhythm and rhyme of his verse, but in the main he recognized the old established laws which have been accepted as regulating both. In short, with all his originality, he worked in Old World harness, and cannot be considered as the creator of a truly American, self-governed, self-centered, absolutely independent style of thinking and writing, knowing no law but its own sovereign will and pleasure.

A stronger claim might be urged for Mr. Whitman. He takes into his hospitable vocabulary words which no English dictionary recognizes as belonging to the language,—words which will be looked for in vain outside of his own pages. He accepts as poetical subjects all things alike, common and unclean, without discrimination, miscellaneous as the contents of the great sheet which Peter saw let down from heaven. He carries the principle of republicanism through the whole world of created objects. He will "thread a thread through [his] poems," he tells us, "that no one thing in the universe is inferior to another thing." No man has ever asserted the surpassing dignity and importance of the American citizen so boldly and freely as Mr. Whitman. He calls himself "teacher of the unquenchable creed, namely, egotism." He begins one of his chants, "I celebrate myself," but he takes us all in as partners in self-glorification. He believes in America as the new Eden. . . .

Letter to James Russell Lowell

[*War, Slavery, Temperance, Poverty, Reform*]

On October 14, 1846, a year before he became Professor and Dean of the Harvard Medical School, Holmes delivered "A Rhymed Lesson (Urania)," a poem of about 800 lines, before the Boston Mercantile Library Association. Soon afterward James Russell Lowell, a fiery journalist and social reformer who was doing installments of *The Biglow Papers* for the Boston *Courier*, rebuked Holmes for his conservative attitude, and specifically referred to the "Rhymed Lesson." Lowell may well have taken offense at Holmes's reference to those who were "fretful to change and rabid to discuss," who were "lean-cheeked maniacs of the tongue and pen!" Lowell's letter troubled Holmes deeply, and evoked this reply. The selection from John T. Morse, Jr., *Life and Letters of Oliver Wendell Holmes* (1896), is reprinted by permission of and arrangement with Houghton Mifflin Company, the authorized publishers.

Boston, November 29, 1846.

My Dear Sir,—I have read your letter, as I believe, in the same spirit as that in which it was written. There is nothing in its frankness which offends me; on the contrary, that is the very quality in it which makes it valuable and acceptable. I thank you for it, and shall endeavor to make a wholesome application of whatever truth and wisdom it contains.

And now let me be frank with you. If I have endeavored to look at myself from your point of view, to correct my observations by your quadrant, will you be equally patient with me while I defend and explain some of my own views in a very tedious manner?

And first, my defense against certain specific grounds of complaint which you have in a very mild and proper way urged upon me:—

I am not aware that I have arrayed myself against any of the "Causes" to which you refer, and I hardly know where to look for the "many shrewd rubs" you say I have given them. First, *War*. That old poem you refer to had a single passage in which I used expressions which I think I should be unwilling to use now. But its main object was to show that war is one of the most powerful stimulants in bringing out the power of the human intellect. Some years afterwards I wrote a Canadian war song, which my better feelings prompted me not to print. I own that I find in myself a growing hatred and disgust to this mode of settling national quarrels, and that in many points I sympathized with Mr. Sumner in his Fourth of July oration. But I cannot shut my eyes to the beauty of heroism and self-devotion which the battlefield has witnessed. I think our fathers were right in taking up arms to defend their liberties, and I have even now a mitigated and *quasi* kind of satisfaction in hearing of the courage and constancy of our countrymen in so poor a quarrel [Mexican War] as we are engaged in. I believe there is nothing in this last poem which would go farther than defending our revolutionary struggle, and certainly I have a right to claim some credit for not lugging in Major Ringgold and General Taylor. If, as you seem to think, silence in regard to any great question is affording an incidental aid to its antagonists, then I administered a rebuke to the war party in not alluding to our recent "glorious victories."

Secondly, *Slavery*. I plead guilty of a thoughtless verse delivered at the same time with my Φ B K poem, meant in the most perfect good nature for a harmless though a dull jest, and taken, to my great surprise, as a harsh and brutal expression of contempt: "The abolition men and maids," etc. Very certainly I should not write such a verse now, partly because this party has grown more powerful, perhaps, but partly also because I now know it would give offense to many good persons, whose motives and many of whose principles I hold in profound respect. I believe my positive offenses under this head stop at this period—1836 —with this one hardly-judged stanza.

Thirdly, *Temperance*. I have written songs occasionally for social meetings in which the pleasures of convivial excitement were, perhaps, too warmly drawn. Here is a verse from one:—

> The Grecian's mound, the Roman's urn,
>   Are silent when we call,
> Yet still the purple grapes return
>   To cluster on the wall;
> It was a bright Immortal's head
>   They circled with the vine,
> And o'er their best and bravest dead
>   They poured the dark red wine.

I think I may say that it was from conscientious motives, in part, at least, if not mainly, that I never published the little poem from which this is taken—though I had a fondness for it. This was written for the Porcellian Club, many years ago; but long since that I not only wrote but printed a song of a very different character for a temperance celebration in New York, thereby showing, what is true, that my sympathies, and in some humble measure my coöperation, were with the advocates of temperance. More than this, I took two hundred and fifty dollars instead of four hundred, rent, during the present year, for a store on Long Wharf, which I managed for my mother, rather than let it, like many of those about it, for a grocery, knowing that rum would be retailed from it. I mention this because it implies that I am not wholly insensible to the significance of this particular reform, and that, if needs be, I can make some little sacrifice for it.

Fourthly, *The claims of the poor*. I believe I have never treated them unkindly in any way. I am sure that I feel a deep interest in all well-directed efforts for improving their condition, and am ready to lend my cordial support to such practical measures as furnishing them with better dwellings, and similar movements.

Fifthly and lastly, *Reform* in general, and *reformers*. It is a mistake of yours to suppose me a thorough-going conservatist; and I think you cannot have found that in my writings which does not belong to my opinions and character. I am an out-and-out republican in politics, a firm believer in the omnipotence of truth, in the constant onward struggle of the race, in the growing influence and blessed agency of the great moral principles now at work in the midst of all the errors and excesses with which they are attended. In a little club of ten physicians I rather think I occupy the extreme left of the liberal side of the house. The idea of my belonging to the party that resists all change is an entire misconception. I may be lazy, or indifferent, or timid, but I am by no means one of those (such as a few of my friends) who are wedded for better for worse to the *status quo*, with an iron ring that Reason cannot get away unless it takes the finger with it.

But you refer to a certain passage in my last poem as implying that I treat it as a matter of choice which side of the great questions of the day one shall espouse. You then accuse me of ignoring the existence of conscience in the spiritual organization. On the strength of this you indulge in nearly a whole page of ironical amplifications. . . .

As to war, I am perfectly willing to condemn it as a barbarous custom, whenever I can do so with any particular efficiency and propriety. Probably, however, in the present state of my opinions I should not go far enough to satisfy you—certainly not to meet the views of Edmund Quincy. But I saw no particular necessity to introduce war before my peaceful assemblage at the Tremont Temple, very few of whom could tell gunpowder from onion seed.

As to slavery, there would have been still less fitness in introducing it. No doubt the audience would have applauded,—it would have been a popular thing to do. But I have in this place just two things to say: 1. Slavery is a dreadful business, but the people about me are not slaveholders and generally hate it pretty thoroughly already. 2. All the resources of language have been so liberally employed upon this subject—all the cloacæ of vituperative eloquence having of late years found their freest vent just upon this very point— that nothing is so flat and unprofitable as weakly flavored verses relating to it. Did you ever see a volume of lines—not by you or me—that illus- 10 trated this fact?

Once more, I believe that at present you and I cannot prevent the existence of slavery. But the catastrophe of disunion I believe we can prevent, and thus avert a future of war and bloodshed which is equally frightful to both of us in contemplation. Can you trust me that I really *believe* this, or do you confine all honest faith and intelligent judgment to those who think with you? *Mind this one thing,*—I give these as reasons why I did not 20 feel specially called upon to introduce the subject of slavery in preference to many others, but I am glad there are always eloquent men to keep the moral sense of the world alive on the subject. I thought disunion the most vital matter at present.

I gave many lessons in my late poem on the most serious subjects. They were on points that most interested me. Most of all, I enforced as well as I could, in a long series of connected passages, 30 the duty of religious charity. To vary my exercise, which was addressed to a young and somewhat mixed audience, I introduced many light passages, relating to trifling matters, every one of which was meant to convey some useful hint, if possible coupled with a pleasant thought. The consequence has been that one set of critics proscribe me for being serious and another for being gay,—you will take neither the one hand nor the other with a good grace, because I am not philo-melanic or miso- 40 polemic enough to meet your standard.

I supposed that you, and such as you, would feel that I had taught a lesson of love, and would thank me for it. I supposed that you would say I had tried in my humble way to adorn some of the scenes of this common life that surrounds us, with colors borrowed from the imagination and the feelings, and thank me for my effort. I supposed

you would recognize a glow of kindly feeling in every word of my poor lesson—even in its slight touches of satire, which were only aimed at the excesses of well-meaning people. I supposed you would thank me for laughing at that ridiculous phantom of the one poet that is to be, whose imaginary performances inferior persons are in the habit of appealing to, to prove that you and such as you are mere scribblers. I am sorry that I have failed in giving you pleasure because I have omitted two subjects on which you would have loved to hear my testimony.

If you have read as far as this, take courage, for I have almost done.

I listen to your suggestions with great respect. I mean to reflect upon them, and I hope to gain something from them. But I must say, with regard to art and the management of my own powers, I think I shall in the main follow my own judgment and taste rather than mould myself upon those of others.

I shall follow the bent of my natural thoughts, which grow more grave and tender, or will do so as years creep over me. I shall not be afraid of gayety more than of old, but I shall have more courage to be serious. Above all, I shall always be pleased rather to show what is beautiful in the life around me than to be pitching into giant vices, against which the acrid pulpit and the corrosive newspaper will always anticipate the gentle poet. Each of us has his theory of life, of art, of his own existence and relations. It is too much to ask of you to enter fully into mine, but be very well assured that it exists,—that it has its axioms, its intuitions, its connected beliefs as well as your own. Let me try to improve and please my fellow-men after my own fashion at present; when I come to your way of thinking (this may happen) I hope I shall be found worthy of a less qualified approbation than you have felt constrained to give me at this time.

The Autocrat—Oliver Wendell Holmes

Born 1809. Died October 7, 1894

THESE ANONYMOUS STANZAS appeared in *Punch, or the London Charivari* for the issue of October 20, 1894.

"The Last Leaf!" Can it be true,
We have turned it, and on *you*
   Friend of all?
That the years at last have power?
That life's foliage and its flower   5
   Fade and fall?

Was there one who ever took
From its shelf, by chance, a book
   Penned by you,
But was fast your friend, for life,   10
With *one* refuge from its strife
   Safe and true?

Even gentle Elia's self
Might be proud to share that shelf,
   Leaf to leaf,   15
With a soul of kindred sort,
Who could bind strong sense and sport
   In one sheaf.

From that Boston breakfast table
Wit and wisdom, fun and fable,   20
   Radiated
Through all English-speaking places.
When were Science and the Graces
   So well mated?

Of sweet singers the most sane,   25
Of keen wits the most humane,
   Wide yet clear,

Like the blue, above us bent;
Giving sense and sentiment
   Each its sphere;   30

With a manly breadth of soul,
And a fancy quaint and droll;
   Ripe and mellow:
With a virile power of "hit,"
Finished scholar, poet, wit,   35
   And good fellow!

Sturdy patriot, and yet
True world's citizen! Regret
   Dims our eyes
As we turn each well-thumbed leaf;   40
Yet a glory 'midst our grief
   Will arise.

Years your spirit could not tame,
And they will not dim your fame;
   England joys   45
In your songs all strength and ease,
And the "dreams" you "wrote to please
   Grey-haired boys." — *Sat. Clubs*

And of such were you not one?
Age chilled not your fire or fun.   50
   Heart alive
Makes a boy of a grey bard,
Though his years be—"by the card"—
   Eighty-five!

HERMAN MELVILLE (1819–1891)

THERE IS dramatic irony in the fact that Melville's great fight to escape skepticism so mystified and offended his own generation in America that he came finally to suffer neglect; yet it was this same search for philosophic affirmation—for some sign of justice in man's fate—that gave character to his literary achievements, played a part in his rise to posthumous fame in the twentieth century, and placed him among the greatest American writers. Adventuresome stories of life on the Pacific and the Atlantic oceans, mixed with criticism of white missionaries in Polynesia and of the treatment of sailors on the high seas, brought him early recognition as an author. Then began his spiritual quest, and his own generation lost interest. Belated fame came sixty years or more after he had practically abandoned prose.

Melville's lifelong search for the "Ultimate," for the answer to the ambiguities of good and evil as he found them in the world, are mirrored in *Mardi, and a Voyage Thither* (1849), *Moby Dick; or, The Whale* (1851), *Pierre; or, The Ambiguities* (1852), "Benito Cereno" (1855), and *Billy Budd, Foretopman* (written 1888–1891, published 1924). Naming the world Mardi, he mixed romance with the South Seas, philosophized on governments and institutions in fable, and, while "intent upon the essence of things," unhappily sailed beyond the island of Serenia, where Love was the law.

In *Moby Dick* he tried again. This novel may be enjoyed as a unique and powerful tale of life on a whaler when the industry was at its height, and it may be probed for its symbolism. Its great virtue lies in its adaptability to the special meanings which each reader may find according to his own light. Into this book Melville poured an immense amount of his store of knowledge of men, customs, philosophy, and the sea. Plato, Rabelais, Montaigne, Shakespeare, Hobbes, Sir Thomas Browne, Voltaire, Goethe, Emerson, and Hawthorne are but a partial list of those whose thought he compounded in the book. The verbal harmony of Browne, the astringent tone of Voltaire, and the soaring language of Shakespeare rise from the pages of *Moby Dick*; and there is something of Lear in Captain Ahab. Melville is Ishmael, but he also recognizes his kinship with Ahab, whose "quenchless feud" seemed Melville's too, and who threw away the moorings of knowledge—the quadrant and the compass—in going forth determined to slay the enemy of mankind. Yet Melville knew, too, that this enemy regarded man with indifference rather than hostility, and he knew the penalty of monomania as exemplified in Ahab: "God help thee, old man, thy thoughts have created a creature in thee"; and that this creature was feeding on its creator's heart. The materials and thought and emotion are not wholly fused in this novel, but the book is rich in high adventure, homily, rhapsody, imagery, splendor, terror, and horror.

Pierre is less powerful, more muddled. In this book, the world will have nothing to do with the virtues that Pierre, in his "Heaven-appointed duty," strives to practice. Still seeking, Melville had not found a formula explaining the world. He had come only to the conclusion that the most fervently sought answer to the ambiguities he wished to resolve would be greeted only by "Silence." Still, he was not resigned. On November 20, 1856, at Liverpool, Hawthorne recorded in his Journal a long visit with Melville, "who will never rest until he gets hold of some definite belief. . . . He can neither believe, nor be comfortable in unbelief. . . . He has a very high and noble nature, and is better worth immortality than most of us." Near the close of his life, however, Melville did attain an inward calm. There is higher tragedy in *Billy Budd* than in *Moby Dick* or *Pierre*, for Ahab is consumed of hate, and Pierre—in whom there is something of Hamlet—is addled. But Billy Budd, a normal young man, innocent before nature, can speak kindly of his immobile judge as he climbs to his death at the yard end, bathed in the "soft glory" of the sun shining through fleecy clouds. The unmanageable materials of *Moby Dick*, and its wild agony, are supplanted in *Billy Budd* by sound form and unity, and the content is reduced to its essence with art in control.

Herman Melville was born in New York City, August 1, 1819, of distinguished Dutch and Scottish ancestry. The family moved to Albany in 1830. Two years later his father died in bankruptcy. For three years Melville was a clerk in Albany. Aged seventeen, he crossed to Liverpool and back as a cabin boy on the merchantman *Highlander*. Between 1837 and 1841 little is known of him beyond certain records of school-teaching at East Albany. Then came the great decision. On January 3, 1841, he shipped from Fairhaven, Massachusetts, on the whaler *Acushnet*, "my Yale College and Harvard," and started on the adventures in the Pacific that supplied him with materials for his books. He deserted ship on the island of Nukahiva among the Marquesas, where he lived for some weeks with cannibals in the valley of Taipi. He escaped on a whaler to Tahiti. From there he shipped on another whaler that sailed in Japanese waters before coming to port at Honolulu. In August, 1843, he joined the naval service and came home on the frigate *United States*, being discharged in Boston on October 14, 1844, aged twenty-three years. *Typee: A Peep at Polynesian Life During a Four-Months' Residence* (1846), a narrative of his life in the Taipi valley mixed with some booklore and fancy, and *Omoo: A Narrative of Adventures in the South Seas* (1847), the sequel, were well received by critics, excepting those of the evangelical press, who took offense at Melville's attack on missionaries and others of the white race for disrupting a culture in some respects better in practice than their own.

Having established himself somewhat in the literary profession, he married Elizabeth Shaw, daughter of the Chief Justice of the Supreme Court of Massachusetts, and they set up their residence in New York City. He became a member of the literati of the city and had access to the 17,000 volumes in the library of his friend and mentor, Evert Duyckinck, editor of *The Literary World*. He was determined, he said, since his first two books were "received with incredulity," to write a romance. In this endeavor he was not successful; the philosophical implications of *Mardi* repelled his readers. But *Redburn: His First Voyage* (1849), based on the Liverpool voyage, was well received as an attack on the inhumane treatment of sailors as seen through a sailor boy's confessions and reminiscences. It was a philosophical study, too, in disillusionment, but the narrative of realistic details made it also a good sea story. *White-Jacket: or, The World in a Man-of-War* (1850) came next, a mixture of truth and fiction recounting the author's life on the frigate *United States*; it pleased the general readers, though it was attacked by naval authorities.

In the same year, 1850, while he was writing *Moby Dick*, Melville removed with his family to Pittsfield,

Massachusetts, and soon to Arrowhead farm. Hawthorne, Melville's senior by fifteen years, was enjoying the success of *The Scarlet Letter* and writing *The House of the Seven Gables* near Lenox, six miles distant, and the two men became friends.

Moby Dick and *Pierre* were written in intensity of spirit, and their poor reception was all the more discouraging because of the energy consumed. But Melville continued to write. He contributed to *Harper's* and *Putnam's*, and in an effort to plumb new sources retreated to the period of the Revolutionary War for *Israel Potter: His Fifty Years of Exile* (1855), a book of only ordinary worth. He collected a volume of good short stories, *The Piazza Tales* (1856), which included "Benito Cereno," and then again changed his scene. In *The Confidence-Man; His Masquerade* (1857) he gathered all sorts and conditions of men on a Mississippi steamboat: swindlers and planters, Negroes, French Jews, Indians, and Creoles, persons of different religious faiths and occupations, in a story that treats dismally of man's nature. When this book failed, Melville gave up prose. He took passage to Scotland and England, lectured unsuccessfully in the United States during 1857–1860, published a volume of poetry, *Battle-Pieces and Aspects of the War* (1866), and after efforts to secure political preferment, he was in the same year appointed District Inspector of Customs in New York. He retained the position until 1885. Three more volumes of verse were published: *Clarel; a Poem and Pilgrimage in the Holy Land* (1876), based on his travels of 1856–1857, *John Marr and Other Sailors, with Some Sea-Pieces* (1888), and *Timoleon, Etc.* (1891). He died September 28, 1891. His masterly *Billy Budd* was found among his papers, revised and completed; it was published in London in 1924 in the period of the renaissance of his work.

BIBLIOGRAPHY · *The Works of Herman Melville* (16 vols., Constable and Co., London, 1922–1924) is the standard edition. Under the general editorship of H. P. Vincent, Farrar Straus and Co., N. Y., is publishing the complete works of Herman Melville, carefully annotated, planned to extend to 14 volumes. H. A. Murray, ed., *Pierre; or, The Ambiguities* (1949), is excellent, as is W. Thorp, ed., *Moby Dick* (1947). R. M. Weaver collected *Shorter Novels of Herman Melville* (1928). M. Minnigerode, ed., *Some Personal Letters of Herman Melville and a Bibliography* (1922), contains some errors in transcription. H. Chapin, ed., *The Apple Tree and Other Sketches* (1922), prints hitherto uncollected contributions of Melville to *Harper's* and *Putnam's* magazines from 1850 to 1856. V. H. Paltsits, ed., *Family Correspondence of Herman Melville, 1830–1904* (1929), reprinted from *Bulletin of the New York Public Library,*

XXXIII, is excellently done. Of specific interest is R. M. Weaver, ed., *Journal Up the Straits, October 11, 1856–May 5, 1857* (1935).

The trends of scholarly interest in Melville's life and methods may be followed chronologically in R. M. Weaver, *Herman Melville, Mariner and Mystic* (1921), the first full-length biography, which later studies have corrected as to a number of its assumptions; J. Freeman, *Herman Melville* (1926); L. Mumford, *Herman Melville* (1929), correcting the romantic idea that Melville's powers were seriously impaired in later years; W. Thorp, ed., *Herman Melville* (1938), American Writers Series, an indispensable review of previous studies on Melville, correcting many errors, and by further research establishing a sound picture of the man; C. R. Anderson, *Melville in the South Seas* (1939), a carefully documented and valuable study; W. E. Sedgwick, *Herman Melville: The Tragedy of Mind* (1944), an excellent critique; H. P. Vincent, *The Trying-Out of Moby Dick* (1949); and N. Wright, *Melville's Use of the Bible* (1949).

Among the better special studies are W. S. Ament, "Bowdler and the Whale," *American Literature*, IV (1932), 39–46; C. R. Anderson, "A Reply to Herman Melville's *White-Jacket* by Rear-Admiral Thomas O. Selfridge, Sr.," *American Literature*, VII (1935), 123–144, also ed., *Journal of a Cruise to the Pacific Ocean, 1842–1844, in the Frigate* United States (1937), "Contemporary American Opinions of *Typee* and *Omoo*," *American Literature*, IX (1937), 1–25, "Melville's English Debut," *American Literature*, XI (1939), 23–38, and "The Genesis of *Billy Budd*," *American Literature*, XII (1940), 329–346; R. P. Blackmur, "The Craft of Herman Melville," *Virginia Quarterly Review*, XIV (1938), 266–282; W. Braswell, "Melville as a Critic of Emerson," *American Literature*, IX (1937), 317–334; V. W. Brooks, "Notes on Herman Melville," in *Emerson and Others* (1927), showing influence of Rabelais, Thomas Moore, Butler, Carlyle; E. K. Brown, "Hawthorne, Melville and 'Ethan Brand,'" *American Literature*, III (1931), 72–75; H. S. Canby, "Hawthorne and Melville," in *Classic Americans* (1931); W. Charvat, "Melville's Income," *American Literature*, XV (1943), 251–261; L. Concord, "Notes on Moby Dick," *Freeman*, V (1922), 559–562, 585–587; F. Feltenstein, "Melville's 'Benito Cereno,'" *American Literature*, XIX (1947), 245–255; R. S. Forsythe, "Herman Melville in the Marquesas," *Philological Quarterly*, XV (1936), 1–15, and "Herman Melville in Tahiti," *Philological Quarterly*, XVI (1937), 344–357; E. Foster, "Melville and Geology," *American Literature*, XVII (1945), 50–65; F. B. Freeman, *Melville's Billy Budd* (1948); G. C. Homans, "The Dark Angel: The Tragedy of Herman Melville," *New England Quarterly*, V (1932), 699–730; D. Jaffé, "Some Sources of Melville's *Mardi*," *American Literature*, IX (1937), 56–69; R. P. McCutcheon, "The Technique of Melville's *Israel Potter*," *South Atlantic Quarterly*, XXVII (1928), 161–174; L. S. Mansfield, "Glimpses of Herman Melville's Life in Pittsfield, 1850–1851," *American Literature*, IX (1937), 26–48; H. A. Myers, "Captain Ahab's Discovery: The Tragic Meaning of *Moby Dick*," *New England Quarterly*, XV (1942), 15–34; E. S. Oliver, "Cock-A-Doodle-Doo! Transcendental Hocus-Pocus," *New England Quarterly*, XXI (June, 1948), 204–216; C. Olson, "Lear and Moby Dick," *Twice a Year*, I (1938), 165–189; H. F. Pommer, "Herman Melville and the Wake of the *Essex*," *American Literature*, XX (1948), 290–304; J. M. Purcell, "Melville's Contribution to English," *PMLA*, LVI (1941), 797–808; H. H. Scudder, "Melville's *Benito Cereno* and Captain Delano's Voyages," *PMLA*, XLIII (1928), 502–532; M. M. Sealts, "Herman Melville's 'I and My Chimney,'" *American Literature*, XIII (1941), 142–154; R. Thomas, "Melville's Use of Some Sources in *The Encantadas*," *American Literature*, III (1932), 432–456; E. L. G. Watson, "Melville's *Pierre*," *New England Quarterly*, III (1930), 195–234, and "Melville's Testament of Acceptance," *New England Quarterly*, VI (1933), 319–327; and W. H. Wells, "*Moby Dick* and Rabelais," *Modern Language Notes*, XXXVIII (1923), 123.

Hawthorne and His Mosses

PUBLISHED in *The Literary World*, August 17 and 24, 1850, as written "By a Virginian spending July in Vermont." Actually, of course, Melville was not a Virginian, and he was living in Pittsfield, Massachusetts, on Arrowhead farm, not in Vermont. At the time of writing, Melville was separated from Hawthorne by a distance of only six miles, for Hawthorne was on a farm outside Lenox. They met for the first time several days later. Hawthorne had already greatly enjoyed Melville's books, and a close friendship developed between the two men. Willard Thorp, ed., *Herman Melville* (1938), p. 423, has reprinted a letter by Mrs. Hawthorne indicating that Hawthorne was reading a new book by Melville "on the new hay in the barn," at the time Melville was reading a book by Hawthorne in the Arrowhead barn.

A papered chamber in a fine old farm-house, a mile from any other dwelling, and dipped to the eaves in foliage—surrounded by mountains, old woods, and Indian ponds,—this, surely, is the place to write of Hawthorne. Some charm is in this northern air, for love and duty seem both impelling to the task. A man of a deep and noble nature has seized me in this seclusion. His wild, witch-voice rings through me; or, in softer cadences, I seem to hear it in the songs of the hill-side birds that sing in the larch trees at my window. . . .

It is curious how a man may travel along a country road, and yet miss the grandest or sweetest of prospects by reason of an intervening hedge, so like all other hedges, as in no way to hint of the wide landscape beyond. So has it been with me concerning the enchanting landscape in the soul of this Hawthorne, this most excellent Man of Mosses. His "Old Manse" has been written now four years, but I never read it till a day or two since. I had seen it in the book-stores—heard of it often—even had it recommended to me by a tasteful friend, as a rare, quiet book, perhaps too deserving of popularity to be popular. But there are so many books called "excellent," and so much unpopular merit, that amid the thick stir of other things, the hint of my tasteful friend was disregarded; and for four years the Mosses on the Old Manse never refreshed me with their perennial green. It may be, however, that all this while the book, likewise, was only improving in flavor and body. At any rate, it so chanced that this long procrastination eventuated in a happy result. At breakfast the other day, a mountain girl, a cousin of mine, who for the last two weeks has every morning helped me to strawberries and raspberries, which, like the roses and pearls in the fairy tale, seemed to fall into the saucer from those strawberry-beds, her cheeks—this delightful creature, this charming Cherry says to me—"I see you spend your mornings in the hay-mow; and yesterday I found there 'Dwight's Travels in New England.' Now I have something far better than that, something more congenial to our summer on these hills. Take these raspberries, and then I will give you some moss." "Moss!" said I. "Yes, and you must take it to the barn with you, and good-bye to 'Dwight.' "

With that she left me, and soon returned with a volume, verdantly bound, and garnished with a curious frontispiece in green; nothing less than a fragment of real moss, cunningly pressed to a fly-leaf. "Why, this," said I, spilling my raspberries, "this is the 'Mosses from an Old Manse.' " "Yes," said cousin Cherry, "yes, it is that flowery Hawthorne." "Hawthorne and Mosses," said I, "no more: it is morning: it is July in the country: and I am off for the barn."

Stretched on that new mown clover, the hillside breeze blowing over me through the wide barn-door, and soothed by the hum of the bees in the meadows around, how magically stole over me this Mossy Man! and how amply, how bountifully, did he redeem that delicious promise to his guests in the Old Manse, of whom it is written—"Others could give them pleasure, or amusement, or instruction—these could be picked up anywhere—but it was for me to give them rest. Rest, in a life of trouble! What better could be done for weary and world-worn spirits? What better could be done for anybody, who came within our magic circle, than to throw the spell of a magic spirit over him?" So all that day, half-buried in the new clover, I watched this Hawthorne's "Assyrian dawn, and Paphian sunset and moonrise, from the summit of our Eastern Hill."

The soft ravishments of the man spun me round about in a web of dreams, and when the book was closed, when the spell was over, this wizard "dismissed me with but misty reminiscences, as if I had been dreaming of him."

What a wild moonlight of contemplative humor bathes that Old Manse!—the rich and rare distilment of a spicy and slowly-oozing heart. No rollicking rudeness, no gross fun fed on fat dinners, and bred in the lees of wine,—but a humor so spiritually gentle, so high, so deep, and yet so richly relishable, that it were hardly inappropriate in an angel. It is the very religion of mirth; for nothing so human but it may be advanced to that. The orchard of the Old Manse seems the visible type of the fine mind that has described it—those twisted and contorted old trees, "that stretch out their crooked branches, and take such hold of the imagination, that we remember them as humorists and odd-fellows." And then, as surrounded by these grotesque forms, and hushed in the noon-day repose of this Hawthorne's spell, how aptly might the still fall of his ruddy thoughts into your soul be symbolized by "the thump of a great apple, in the stillest afternoon, falling without a breath of wind, from the mere necessity of perfect ripeness!" For no less ripe than ruddy are the apples of the thoughts and fancies in this sweet Man of Mosses—

Buds and Bird-voices—

What a delicious thing is that! "Will the world

ever be so decayed, that Spring may not renew its greenness?" And the "Fire-Worship." Was ever the hearth so glorified into an altar before? The mere title of that piece is better than any common work in fifty folio volumes. How exquisite is this:—"Nor did it lessen the charm of his soft, familiar courtesy and helpfulness, that the mighty spirit, were opportunity offered him, would run riot through the peaceful house, wrap its inmates in his terrible embrace, and leave nothing of them save their whitened bones. This possibility of mad destruction only made his domestic kindness the more beautiful and touching. It was so sweet of him, being endowed with such power, to dwell, day after day, and one long, lonesome night after another, on the dusky hearth, only now and then betraying his wild nature, by thrusting his red tongue out of the chimney-top! True, he had done much mischief in the world, and was pretty certain to do more, but his warm heart atoned for all; He was kindly to the race of man."

But he has still other apples, not quite so ruddy, though full as ripe;—apples, that have been left to wither on the tree, after the pleasant autumn gathering is past. The sketch of "The Old Apple-Dealer" is conceived in the subtlest spirit of sadness; he whose "subdued and nerveless boyhood prefigured his abortive prime, which, likewise, contained within itself the prophecy and image of his lean and torpid age." Such touches as are in this piece cannot proceed from any common heart. They argue such a depth of tenderness, such a boundless sympathy with all forms of being, such an omnipresent love, that we must needs say that this Hawthorne is here almost alone in his generation,—at least, in the artistic manifestation of these things. Still more. Such touches as these,—and many, very many similar ones, all through his chapters—furnish clues whereby we enter a little way into the intricate, profound heart where they originated. And we see that suffering, some time or other and in some shape or other,—this only can enable any man to depict it in others. All over him, Hawthorne's melancholy rests like an Indian-summer, which, though bathing a whole country in one softness, still reveals the distinctive hue of every towering hill and each far-winding vale. . . .

How profound, nay appalling, is the moral

798

evolved by the "Earth's Holocaust"; where—beginning with the hollow follies and affectations of the world,—all vanities and empty theories and forms are, one after another, and by an admirably graduated, growing comprehensiveness, thrown into the allegorical fire, till, at length, nothing is left but the all-engendering heart of man; which remaining still unconsumed, the great conflagration is naught.

Of a piece with this, is the "Intelligence Office," a wondrous symbolizing of the secret workings in men's souls. There are other sketches still more charged with ponderous import.

"The Christmas Banquet," and "The Bosom Serpent," would be fine subjects for a curious and elaborate analysis, touching the conjectural parts of the mind that produced them. For spite of all the Indian-summer sunlight on the hither side of Hawthorne's soul, the other side—like the dark half of the physical sphere—is shrouded in a blackness, ten times black. But this darkness but gives more effect to the ever-moving dawn, that for ever advances through it, and circumnavigates his world. Whether Hawthorne has simply availed himself of this mystical blackness as a means to the wondrous effects he makes it to produce in his lights and shades; or whether there really lurks in him, perhaps unknown to himself, a touch of Puritanic gloom,—this, I cannot altogether tell. Certain it is, however, that this great power of blackness in him derives its force from its appeals to that Calvinistic sense of Innate Depravity and Original Sin, from whose visitations, in some shape or other, no deeply thinking mind is always and wholly free. For, in certain moods, no man can weigh this world without throwing in something, somehow like Original Sin, to strike the uneven balance. At all events, perhaps no writer has ever wielded this terrific thought with greater terror than this same harmless Hawthorne. Still more: this black conceit pervades him through and through. You may be witched by his sunlight,—transported by the bright gildings in the skies he builds over you; but there is the blackness of darkness beyond; and even his bright gildings but fringe and play upon the edges of thunderclouds. In one word, the world is mistaken in this Nathaniel Hawthorne. He himself must often have smiled at its absurd misconception of him. He is immeasurably deeper than the plummet of the mere critic. For it is not the brain that can test such a man; it is only the heart. You cannot come to know greatness by inspecting it; there is no glimpse to be caught of it, except by intuition; you need not ring it, you but touch it, and you find it is gold.

Now, it is that blackness in Hawthorne, of which I have spoken, that so fixes and fascinates me. It may be, nevertheless, that it is too largely developed in him. Perhaps he does not give us a ray of his light for every shade of his dark. But however this may be, this blackness it is that furnishes the infinite obscure of his back-ground,—that back-ground, against which Shakspeare plays his grandest conceits, the things that have made for Shakspeare his loftiest but most circumscribed renown, as the profoundest of thinkers. For by philosophers Shakspeare is not adored as the great man of tragedy and comedy.—"Off with his head; so much for Buckingham!" This sort of rant, interlined by another hand, brings down the house,—those mistaken souls, who dream of Shakspeare as a mere man of Richard-the-Third humps and Macbeth daggers. But it is those deep far-away things in him; those occasional flashings-forth of the intuitive Truth in him; those short, quick probings at the very axis of reality;—these are the things that make Shakspeare, Shakspeare. Through the mouths of the dark characters of Hamlet, Timon, Lear, and Iago, he craftily says, or sometimes insinuates the things which we feel to be so terrifically true, that it were all but madness for any good man, in his own proper character, to utter, or even hint of them. Tormented into desperation, Lear, the frantic king, tears off the mask, and speaks the same madness of vital truth. But, as I before said, it is the least part of genius that attracts admiration. And so, much of the blind, unbridled admiration that has been heaped upon Shakspeare, has been lavished upon the least part of him. And few of his endless commentators and critics seem to have remembered, or even perceived, that the immediate products of a great mind are not so great as that undeveloped and sometimes undevelopable yet dimly-discernible greatness, to which those immediate products are but the infallible indices. In Shakspeare's tomb lies infinitely more than

Shakspeare ever wrote. And if I magnify Shak-speare, it is not so much for what he did do as for what he did not do, or refrained from doing. For in this world of lies, Truth is forced to fly like a scared white doe in the woodlands; and only by cunning glimpses will she reveal herself, as in Shakspeare and other masters of the great Art of Telling the Truth,—even though it be covertly and by snatches. . . .

It is true, that but few of them [American writers] as yet have evinced that decided original-ity which merits great praise. But that graceful writer,ⁿ who perhaps of all Americans has received the most plaudits from his own country for his productions,—that very popular and amiable writer, however good and self-reliant in many things, perhaps owes his chief reputation to the self-acknowledged imitation of a foreign model, and to the studied avoidance of all topics but smooth ones. But it is better to fail in originality, than to succeed in imitation. He who has never failed somewhere, that man cannot be great. Failure is the true test of greatness. And if it be said, that continual success is a proof that a man wisely knows his powers,—it is only to be added, that, in that case, he knows them to be small. Let us believe it, then, once for all, that there is no hope for us in these smooth, pleasing writers that know their powers. Without malice, but to speak the plain fact, they but furnish an appendix to Goldsmith, and other English authors. And we want no American Goldsmiths: nay, we want no American Miltons. It were the vilest thing you could say of a true American author, that he were an American Tompkins. Call him an American and have done, for you cannot say a nobler thing of him. But it is not meant that all American writers should studiously cleave to nationality in their writings; only this, no American writer should write like an Englishman or a Frenchman; let him write like a man, for then he will be sure to write like an American. Let us away with this leaven of literary flunkeyism towards England. If either must play the flunkey in this thing, let England do it, not us. While we are rapidly pre-paring for that political supremacy among the

graceful writer: Melville is probably referring to Washington Irving.

nations which prophetically awaits us at the close of the present century, in a literary point of view, we are deplorably unprepared for it; and we seem studious to remain so. Hitherto, reasons might have existed why this should be; but no good rea-son exists now. And all that is requisite to amend-ment in this matter, is simply this: that while fully acknowledging all excellence everywhere, we should refrain from unduly lauding foreign writers, and, at the same time, duly recognize the merito-rious writers that are our own;—those writers who breathe that unshackled, democratic spirit of Christianity in all things, which now takes the practical lead in this world, though at the same time led by ourselves—us Americans. Let us boldly contemn all imitation, though it comes to us graceful and fragrant as the morning; and foster all originality, though at first it be crabbed and ugly as our own pine knots. And if any of our authors fail, or seem to fail, then, in the words of my Carolina cousin, let us clap him on the shoulder, and back him against all Europe for his second round. The truth is, that in one point of view, this matter of a national literature has come to such a pass with us, that in some sense we must turn bullies, else the day is lost, or superiority so far beyond us, that we can hardly say it will ever be ours.

And now, my countrymen, as an excellent author of your own flesh and blood,—an unimitat-ing, and, perhaps, in his way, an inimitable man—whom better can I commend to you, in the first place, than Nathaniel Hawthorne? He is one of the new, and far better generation of your writers. The smell of your beeches and hemlocks is upon him; your own broad prairies are in his soul; and if you travel away inland into his deep and noble nature, you will hear the far roar of his Niagara. Give not over to future generations the glad duty of acknowledging him for what he is. Take that joy to yourself, in your own generation; and so shall he feel those grateful impulses on him, that may possibly prompt him to the full flower of some still greater achievement in your eyes. And by confessing him you thereby confess others; you brace the whole brotherhood. For genius, all over the world, stands hand in hand, and one shock of recognition runs the whole circle round.

In treating of Hawthorne, or rather of Hawthorne in his writings (for I never saw the man; and in the chances of a quiet plantation life, remote from his haunts, perhaps never shall); in treating of his works, I say, I have thus far omitted all mention of his "Twice Told Tales," and "Scarlet Letter." Both are excellent, but full of such manifold, strange, and diffusive beauties, that time would all but fail me to point the half of them out. But there are things in those two books, which, had they been written in England a century ago, Nathaniel Hawthorne had utterly displaced many of the bright names we now revere on authority. But I am content to leave Hawthorne to himself, and to the infallible finding of posterity; and however great may be the praise I have bestowed upon him, I feel that in so doing I have more served and honored myself, than him. For, at bottom, great excellence is praise enough to itself; but the feeling of a sincere and appreciative love and admiration towards it, this is relieved by utterance; and warm, honest praise, ever leaves a pleasant flavor in the mouth; and it is an honorable thing to confess to what is honorable in others. . . .

Twenty-four hours have elapsed since writing the foregoing. I have just returned from the hay-mow, charged more and more with love and admiration of Hawthorne. For I have just been gleaning through the Mosses, picking up many things here and there that had previously escaped me. And I found that but to glean after this man, is better than to be in at the harvest of others. To be frank (though, perhaps, rather foolish) notwithstanding what I wrote yesterday of these Mosses, I had not then culled them all; but had, nevertheless, been sufficiently sensible of the subtle essence in them, as to write as I did. To what infinite height of loving wonder and admiration I may yet be borne, when by repeatedly banqueting on these Mosses I shall have thoroughly incorporated their whole stuff into my being,—that, I cannot tell. But already I feel that this Hawthorne has dropped germinous seeds into my soul. He expands and deepens down, the more I contemplate him; and further and further, shoots his strong New England roots in the hot soil of my Southern soul.

By careful reference to the "Table of Contents," I now find that I have gone through all the sketches; but that when I yesterday wrote, I had not at all read two particular pieces, to which I now desire to call special attention,—"A Select Party," and "Young Goodman Brown." Here, be it said to all those whom this poor fugitive scrawl of mine may tempt to the perusal of the "Mosses," that they must on no account suffer themselves to be trifled with, disappointed, or deceived by the triviality of many of the titles to these sketches. For in more than one instance, the title utterly belies the piece. It is as if rustic demijohns containing the very best and costliest of Falernian and Tokay, were labelled "Cider," "Perry," and "Elder-berry wine." The truth seems to be, that like many other geniuses, this Man of Mosses takes great delight in hoodwinking the world,—at least, with respect to himself. . . . Besides, at the bottom of their natures, men like Hawthorne, in many things, deem the plaudits of the public such strong presumptive evidence of mediocrity in the object of them, that it would in some degree render them doubtful of their own powers, did they hear much and vociferous braying concerning them in the public pastures. True, I have been braying myself (if you please to be witty enough to have it so), but then I claim to be the first that has so brayed in this particular matter; and therefore, while pleading guilty to the charge, still claim all the merit due to originality.

But with whatever motive, playful or profound, Nathaniel Hawthorne has chosen to entitle his pieces in the manner he has, it is certain that some of them are directly calculated to deceive—egregiously deceive, the superficial skimmer of pages. To be downright and candid once more, let me cheerfully say, that two of these titles did dolefully dupe no less an eager-eyed reader than myself; and that, too, after I had been impressed with a sense of the great depth and breadth of this American man. "Who in the name of thunder" (as the country-people say in this neighborhood), "who in the name of thunder, would anticipate any marvel in a piece entitled 'Young Goodman Brown'?" You would of course suppose that it was a simple little tale, intended as a supplement to "Goody Two Shoes." Whereas, it is deep as Dante; nor can you finish it, without addressing the author in his own words—"It is yours to penetrate, in every bosom, the deep mystery of sin." And with Young Goodman, too, in allegorical pursuit of his Puritan wife, you cry out in your anguish:

'Faith!' shouted Goodman Brown, in a voice of agony and desperation; and the echoes of the forest mocked him, crying—'Faith! Faith!' as if bewildered wretches were seeking her all through the wilderness.

Now this same piece, entitled "Young Goodman Brown," is one of the two that I had not all read yesterday; and I allude to it now, because it is, in itself, such a strong positive illustration of that blackness in Hawthorne, which I had assumed from the mere occasional shadows of it, as revealed in several of the other sketches. But had I previously perused "Young Goodman Brown," I should have been at no pains to draw the conclusion, which I came to at a time when I was ignorant that the book contained one such direct and unqualified manifestation of it. . . .

Once more—for it is hard to be finite upon an infinite subject, and all subjects are infinite. By some people this entire scrawl of mine may be esteemed altogether unnecessary, inasmuch "as years ago" (they may say) "we found out the rich and rare stuff in this Hawthorne, whom you now parade forth, as if only yourself were the discoverer of this Portuguese diamond in our literature." But even granting all this—and adding to it, the assumption that the books of Hawthorne have sold by the five thousand,—what does that signify? They should be sold by the hundred thousand; and read by the million; and admired by every one who is capable of admiration.

Billy Budd, Foretopman[1]

What Befell Him in the Year of the Great Mutiny

MELVILLE began this great tragedy on Friday, November 16, 1888, started his revising on March 2, 1889, and finished his work April 19, 1891. He dedicated it to "Jack Chase, Englishman. Wherever that great heart may now be here on Earth or harbored in Paradise. Captain of the maintop in the year 1843 in the U.S. frigate 'United States.'" It completed the cycle of

[1]Reprinted by permission of the Harvard College Library.

great novels of pursuit of the "Ultimate," begun with *Mardi.* In the tragic fate of Billy Budd, there was no answer for Melville to the ambiguities of good and evil, though he could now accept injustice as the fate of man without the earlier turmoil of spirit. The tale is living evidence that in spite of the exhaustion of mind following *Pierre*, Melville's great powers were still fresh after almost forty years.

Billy Budd, Foretopman is an expansion and revision of a twelve-thousand-word short story, "Baby Budd, Sailor," which was found embedded in the manuscript pages of the novel now preserved in the Harvard University Library. Mr. F. Barron Freeman, the discoverer of the tale, has issued a careful transcription of the text of both the short story and the novel in *Melville's Billy Budd* (1948).

Preface

The year 1797, the year of this narrative, belongs to a period which, as every thinker now feels, involved a crisis for Christendom not exceeded in its undetermined momentousness at the time by any other era whereof there is record. The opening proposition made by the Spirit of that Age involved rectification of the Old World's hereditary wrongs. In France, to some extent, this was bloodily effected. But what then? Straightway the Revolution itself became a wrongdoer, one more oppressive than the kings. Under Napoleon it enthroned upstart kings, and initiated that prolonged agony of continual war whose final throe was Waterloo. During those years not the wisest could have foreseen that the outcome of all would be what to some thinkers apparently it has since turned out to be—a political advance along nearly the whole line for Europeans.

Now, as elsewhere hinted, it was something caught from the Revolutionary Spirit that at Spithead emboldened the man-of-war's men to rise against real abuses, long-standing ones, and afterwards at the Nore to make inordinate and aggressive demands—successful resistance to which was confirmed only when the ringleaders were hung for an admonitory spectacle to the anchored fleet. Yet in a way analogous to the operation of the Revolution at large—the Great Mutiny, though by Englishmen naturally deemed monstrous at the time, doubtless gave the first latent prompting to most important reforms in the British navy.

In the time before steamships, or then more frequently than now, a stroller along the docks of any considerable seaport would occasionally have his attention arrested by a group of bronzed marines, man-of-war's men or merchant-sailors in holiday attire ashore on liberty. In certain instances they would flank, or, like a bodyguard, quite surround some superior figure of their own class, moving along with them like Aldebaran among the lesser lights of his constellation. That signal object was the "Handsome Sailor" of the less prosaic time, alike of the military and merchant navies. With no perceptible trace of the vainglorious about him, rather with the off-hand unaffectedness of natural regality, he seemed to accept the spontaneous homage of his shipmates. A somewhat remarkable instance recurs to me. In Liverpool, now half a century ago I saw under the shadow of the great dingy street-wall of Prince's Dock (an obstruction long since removed) a common sailor, so intensely black that he must needs have been a native African of the unadulterated blood of Ham. A symmetric figure, much above the average in height. The two ends of a gay silk handkerchief thrown loose about the neck danced upon the displayed ebony in his chest; in his ears were big hoops of gold, and a Scotch Highland bonnet with a tartan band set off his shapely head.

It was a hot noon in July, and his face, lustrous with perspiration, beamed with barbaric good-humour. In jovial sallies right and left, his white teeth flashing into view, he rollicked along, the centre of a company of his shipmates. These were made up of such an assortment of tribes and complexions as would have well fitted them to be marched up by Anacharsis Cloots[n] before the bar of the first French Assembly as Representatives of the Human Race. At each spontaneous tribute rendered by the wayfarers to this black pagod of a fellow—the tribute of a pause and stare, and less frequent an exclamation—the motley retinue showed that they took that sort of pride in the evoker of it which the Assyrian priests doubtless showed for their grand sculptured Bull when the faithful prostrated themselves. To return—

If in some cases a bit of a nautical Murat[n] in setting forth his person ashore, the Handsome Sailor of the period in question evinced nothing of the dandified Billy-be-Damn—an amusing character all but extinct now, but occasionally to be encountered, and in a form yet more amusing than the original, at the tiller of the boats on the tempestuous Erie Canal or, more likely, vapouring in the groggeries along the towpath. Invariably a proficient in his perilous calling, he was also more or less of a mighty boxer or wrestler. It was strength and beauty. Tales of his prowess were recited. Ashore he was the champion; afloat the spokesman; on every suitable occasion always foremost. Close-reefing topsails in a gale, there he was—astride the weather yard-arm-end, foot in "stirrup," both hands tugging at the "ear-ring" as at a bridle, in very much the attitude of the young Alexander curbing the fiery Bucephalus. A superb figure, tossed up as by the horns of Taurus against the thunderous sky, cheerily ballooning to the strenuous file along the spar.

The moral nature was seldom out of keeping with the physical make. Indeed, except as toned by the former, the comeliness and power, always attractive in masculine perfection, hardly could have drawn the sort of homage the Handsome Sailor, in some examples, received from his less gifted associates.

Such a cynosure, at least in aspect, and something such too in nature, though with important variations made apparent as the story proceeds, was welkin-eyed Billy Budd, or Baby Budd—as more familiarly, under circumstances hereafter to be given, he at last came to be called—aged twenty-one, a foretopman of the fleet towards the close of the last decade of the eighteenth century. It was not very long prior to the time of the narration that follows, that he had entered the King's Service, having been impressed on the Narrow Seas from a homeward-bound English merchantman into a seventy-four outward-bound, H.M.S. *Indomitable*;

Cloots: To test the democratic theory, during the French Revolution Cloots presented a motley assembly of men of various nations before the National Assembly, claiming their right to attend its meetings.

Murat: Joachim Murat (1771–1815), Marshal of France, King of Naples.

which ship, as was not unusual in those hurried days, had been obliged to put to sea short of her proper complement of men. Plump upon Billy at first sight in the gangway the boarding officer, Lieutenant Ratcliffe, pounced, even before the merchantman's crew formally was mustered on the quarter-deck for his deliberate inspection. 'And him only he elected. For whether it was because the other men when ranged before him showed to ill advantage after Billy, or whether he had some scruples in view of the merchantman being rather short-handed; however it might be, the officer contented himself with his first spontaneous choice. To the surprise of the ship's company, though much to the Lieutenant's satisfaction, Billy made no demur. But indeed any demur would have been as idle as the protest of a goldfinch popped into a cage.

Noting this uncomplaining acquiescence, all but cheerful one might say, the shipmates turned a surprised glance of silent reproach at the sailor. The shipmaster was one of those worthy mortals found in every vocation,—even the humbler ones, —the sort of person whom everybody agrees in calling "a respectable man." And—nor so strange to report as it may appear to be—though a ploughman of the troubled waters, life-long contending with the intractable elements, there was nothing this honest soul at heart loved better than simple peace and quiet. For the rest, he was fifty or thereabouts, a little inclined to corpulence, a prepossessing face, unwhiskered, and of an agreeable colour—a rather full face, humanely intelligent in expression. On a fair day with a fair wind and all going well, a certain musical chime in his voice seemed to be the veritable unobstructed outcome of the innermost man. He had much prudence, much conscientiousness, and there were occasions when these virtues were the cause of overmuch disquietude in him. On a passage, so long as his craft was in any proximity to land, there was no sleep for Captain Graveling. He took to heart those serious responsibilities not so heavily borne by some shipmasters.

Now, while Billy Budd was down in the forecastle, getting his kit together, the *Indomitable's* Lieutenant—burly and bluff, no wise disconcerted by Captain Graveling's omitting to proffer the customary hospitalities on an occasion so unwelcome to him; an omission simply caused by preoccupation of thought—unceremoniously invited himself into the cabin, and also to a flask from the spirit locker, a receptacle which his experienced eye instantly discovered. In fact, he was one of those sea-dogs in whom all the hardship and peril of naval life in the great prolonged wars of his time never impaired the natural instinct for sensuous enjoyment. His duty he always faithfully did; but duty is sometimes a dry obligation, and he was for irrigating its aridity whensoever possible with a fertilizing decoction of strong waters. For the cabin's proprietor there was nothing left but to play the part of the enforced host with whatever grace and alacrity were practicable. As necessary adjuncts to the flask he silently placed tumbler and water-jug before the irrepressible guest. But excusing himself from partaking just then, he dismally watched the unembarrassed officer deliberately diluting his grog a little, then tossing it off in three swallows, pushing the empty tumbler away, yet not so far as to be beyond easy reach, at the same time settling himself in his seat and smacking his lips with high satisfaction, looking straight at the host.

These proceedings over, the Master broke the silence; and there lurked a rueful reproach in the tone of his voice: "Lieutenant, you are going to take my best man from me, the jewel of 'em."

"Yes, I know," rejoined the other, immediately drawing back the tumbler preliminary to a replenishing. "Yes, I know. Sorry."

"Beg pardon, but you don't understand, Lieutenant. See here now. Before I shipped that young fellow, my forecastle was a rat-pit of quarrels. It was black times, I tell you, aboard the '*Rights*' here. I was worried to that degree my pipe had no comfort for me. But Billy came; and it was like a Catholic priest striking peace in an Irish shindy. Not that he preached to them or said or did anything in particular; but a virtue went out of him, sugaring the sour ones. They took to him like hornets to treacle; all but the bluffer of the gang, the big shaggy chap with the fire-red whiskers. He, indeed, out of envy perhaps of the newcomer, and thinking such a 'sweet and pleasant fellow,' as he mockingly designated him to the others, could hardly have the spirit of a game-cock, must needs bestir himself in trying to get up an ugly row with him. Billy forebore with him and reasoned with him in a pleasant way—he is something like myself, Lieutenant, to whom aught like a quarrel is hateful—but nothing served. So, in the second dog-watch one day the Red-Whiskers, in the presence of the others, under pretence of showing Billy just whence a sirloin steak was cut—for the fellow had once been a butcher—insult- 10 ingly gave him a dig under the ribs. Quick as lightning Billy let fly his arm. I dare say he never meant to do quite as much as he did, but anyhow he gave the burly fool a terrible drubbing. It took about half a minute, I should think. And, Lord bless you, the lubber was astonished at the celerity. And will you believe it, Lieutenant, the Red-Whiskers now really loves Billy—loves him, or is the biggest hypocrite that ever I heard of. But they all love him. Some of 'em do his wash- 20 ing, darn old trousers for him; the carpenter is at odd times making a pretty little chest of drawers for him. Anybody will do anything for Billy Budd; and it's the happy family here. Now, Lieutenant, if that young fellow goes—I know how it will be aboard the 'Rights.' Not again very soon shall I, coming up from dinner, lean over the capstan smoking a quiet pipe—no, not very soon again, I think. Ay, Lieutenant, you are going to take away the jewel of 'em; you are going to take 30 away my peacemaker." And with that the good soul had really some ado in checking a rising sob.

"Well," answered the Lieutenant, who had listened with amused interest to all this, and now waxing merry with his tipple, "Well, blessed are the peacemakers, especially the fighting peace-makers! And such are the seventy-four beauties, some of which you see poking their noses out of the portholes of yonder warship lying-to there for me," pointing through the cabin window at the 40 *Indomitable*. "But courage! don't look so down-hearted, man. Why, I pledge you in advance the royal approbation. Rest assured that His Majesty will be delighted to know that in a time when his hard-tack is not sought for by sailors with such avidity as should be; a time also when some ship-masters privily resent the borrowing from them of a tar or two for the service; His Majesty, I say,

will be delighted to learn that one shipmaster, at least, cheerfully surrenders to the King the flower of his flock: a sailor who with equal loyalty makes no dissent.—But where's my beauty? Ah," looking through the cabin's open door. "Here he comes; and, by Jove—lugging along his chest—Apollo with his portmanteau! My man," stepping out to him, "you can't take that big box on board a warship. The boxes there are mostly shot-boxes. Put up your duds in a bag, lad. Boot and 10 saddle for the cavalryman, bag and hammock for the man-of-war's man."

The transfer from chest to bag was made. And, after seeing his man into the cutter, and then following him down, the Lieutenant pushed off from the *Rights-of-Man*. That was the merchant ship's name; though by her master and crew abbreviated in sailor fashion into the "*Rights*." The hard-headed Dundee owner was a staunch admirer of Thomas Paine, whose book in rejoinder to Burke's 20 arraignment of the French Revolution had then been published for some time and had gone every-where. In christening his vessel after the title of Paine's volume, the man of Dundee was some-thing like his contemporary shipowner, Stephen Girard of Philadelphia, whose sympathies alike with his native land and its liberal philosophies he evinced by naming his ships after Voltaire, Diderot, and so forth.

But now, when the boat swept under the mer- 30 chantman's stern, and officer and oarsmen were noting,—some bitterly and others with a grin,—the name emblazoned there; just then it was that the new recruit jumped up from the bow where the coxswain had directed him to sit, waving his hat to his silent shipmates sorrowfully looking over at him from the taffrail, and bade the lads a genial good-bye. Then making a salutation as to the ship herself, "And good-bye to you too, old *Rights-of-Man!*" 40

"Down, Sir," roared the Lieutenant, instantly assuming all the rigour of his rank, though with difficulty repressing a smile.

To be sure, Billy's action was a terrible breach of naval decorum. But in that decorum he had never been instructed; in consideration of which the Lieutenant would hardly have been so ener-getic in reproof but for the concluding farewell to the ship. This he rather took as meant to convey a covert sally on the new recruit's part—a sly slur at impressment in general, and that of himself in especial. And yet, more likely, if satire it was in effect, it was hardly so by intention, for Billy (though happily endowed with the gaiety of high health, youth and a free heart) was yet by no means of a satirical turn. The will to it and the sinister dexterity were alike wanting. To deal in double meaning and insinuations of any sort was quite foreign to his nature.

As to his enforced enlistment—that he seemed to take pretty much as he was wont to take any vicissitude of weather. Like the animals, though no philosopher, he was, without knowing it, practically a fatalist. And, it may be, that he rather liked this adventurous turn in his affairs which promised an opening into novel scenes and martial excitements.

Aboard the *Indomitable* our merchant-sailor was forthwith rated as an able seaman, and assigned to the starboard watch of the foretop. He was soon at home in the service, not at all disliked for his unpretentious good looks and his rather genial happy-go-lucky air. No merrier man in his mess; in marked contrast to certain other individuals included like himself among the impressed portions of the ship's company; for these when not actively employed were sometimes—and more particularly in the last dog-watch, when the drawing near of twilight induced revery—apt to fall into a saddish mood which in some partook of sullenness. But they were not so young as our foretopman, and no few of them must have known a hearth of some sort, others may have had wives and children left, too probably, in uncertain circumstances, and hardly any but must have acknowledged kith and kin; while for Billy, as will shortly be seen, his entire family was practically invested in himself.

Chapter II

Though our new-made foretopman was well received in the top and on the gun-decks, hardly here was he that cynosure he had previously been among those minor ship's companies of the merchant marine, with which companies only had he hitherto consorted.

He was young; and despite his all but fully developed frame, in aspect looked even younger than he really was. This was owing to a lingering adolescent expression in the as yet smooth face, all but feminine in purity of natural complexion, but where, thanks to his seagoing, the lily was quite suppressed and the rose had some ado visibly to flush through the tan.

To one essentially such a novice in the complexities of factitious life, the abrupt transition from his former and simpler sphere to the ampler and more knowing world of a great war-ship—this might well have abashed him had there been any conceit or vanity in his composition. Among her miscellaneous multitude, the *Indomitable* mustered several individuals who, however inferior in grade, were of no common natural stamp: sailors more signally susceptive of that air which continuous martial discipline and repeated presence in battle can in some degree impart even to the average man. As the "Handsome Sailor" Billy Budd's position aboard the seventy-four was something analogous to that of a rustic beauty transplanted from the provinces and brought into competition with the high-born dames of the court. But this change of circumstances he scarce noted. As little did he observe that something about him provoked an ambiguous smile in one or two harder faces among the bluejackets. Nor less unaware was he of the peculiar favourable effect his person and demeanour had upon the more intelligent gentlemen of the quarterdeck. Nor could this well have been otherwise. Cast in a mould peculiar to the finest physical examples of those Englishmen in whom the Saxon strain would seem not at all to partake of any Norman or other admixture, he showed in face that humane look of reposeful good nature which the Greek sculptor in some instances gave to his heroic strong man, Hercules. But this again was subtly modified by another and pervasive quality. The ear, small and shapely, the arch of the foot, the curve in mouth and nostril, even the indurated hand dyed to the orange-tawny of the toucan's bill, a hand telling of the halyards and tar-buckets; but, above all, something in the mobile expression, and every chance attitude and movement, something suggestive of a mother eminently favoured by Love and the Graces; all this strangely indicated a lineage in direct contradiction to his lot. The mysteriousness here became less mysterious through a matter of fact elicited when Billy at the capstan was being formally mustered into the service. Asked by the officer, a small, brisk little gentleman as it chanced, among other questions, his place of birth, he replied, "Please, Sir, I don't know."

"Don't know where you were born? Who was your father?"

"God knows, Sir." [10]

Struck by the straightforward simplicity of these replies, the officer next asked, "Do you know anything about your beginning?"

"No, Sir. But I have heard that I was found in a pretty silk-lined basket hanging one morning from the knocker of a good man's door in Bristol."

" 'Found,' say you? Well," throwing back his head and looking up and down the new recruit, "well, it turns out to have been a pretty good find. Hope they'll find some more like you, my man; [20] the fleet sadly needs them."

Yes, Billy Budd was a foundling, a presumable by-blow, and, evidently, no ignoble one. Noble descent was as evident in him as in a blood horse.

For the rest, with little or no sharpness of faculty or any trace of the wisdom of the serpent, nor yet quite a dove, he possessed that kind and degree of intelligence which goes along with the unconventional rectitude of a sound human creature —one to whom not as yet had been proffered the [30] questionable apple of knowledge. He was illiterate. He could not read, but he could sing, and like the illiterate nightingale was sometimes the composer of his own song.

Of self-consciousness he seemed to have little or none, or about as much as we may reasonably impute to a dog of St. Bernard's breed.

Habitually being with the elements, and knowing little more of the land than as a beach, or, rather, that portion of the terraqueous globe [40] providentially set apart for dance-houses, doxies and tapsters, in short what sailors call a "fiddlers' green," his simple nature remained unsophisticated by those moral obliquities which are not in every case incomparable with that manufacturable thing known as respectability. But are sailors, frequenters of fiddlers' greens, without vices? No; but less often than with landsmen do their vices,

so called, partake of crookedness of heart, seeming less to proceed from viciousness than from exuberance of vitality after long restraint, frank manifestations in accordance with natural law. By his original constitution aided by the co-operating influences of his lot, Billy in many respects was little more than a sort of upright barbarian, much such perhaps as Adam presumably might have been ere the urbane Serpent [10] wriggled himself into his company.

And here be it submitted that, apparently going to corroborate the doctrine of man's fall— a doctrine now popularly ignored—it is observable that where certain virtues pristine and unadulterate peculiarly characterize anybody in the external uniform of civilization, they will upon scrutiny seem not to be derived from custom or convention but rather to be out of keeping with these, as if indeed exceptionally transmitted from a period [20] prior to Cain's City and citified man. The character marked by such qualities has to an unvitiated taste an untampered-with flavour like that of berries, while the man thoroughly civilized, even in a fair specimen of the breed, has to the same moral palate a questionable smack as of a compounded wine. To any stray inheritor of these primitive qualities found, like Caspar Hauser,[n] wandering dazed in any Christian capital of our time, the poet's famous invocation, near two [30] thousand years ago, of the good rustic out of his latitude in the Rome of the Cæsars, still appropriately holds:—

> Faithful in word and thought,
> What has Thee, Fabian, to the city brought?

Though our Handsome Sailor had as much of masculine beauty as one can expect anywhere to see; nevertheless, like the beautiful woman in one of Hawthorne's minor tales, there was just one thing amiss in him. No visible blemish, indeed, as with the lady; no, but an occasional liability to a vocal defect. Though in the hour of elemental uproar or peril, he was everything that a sailor should be, yet under sudden provocation of strong heart-feeling his voice, otherwise singularly musical,

Hauser: Kaspar Hauser (1812?–1833), German foundling, discovered by police in Nuremberg in 1828. Stories of noble birth grew up around him.

as if expressive of the harmony within, was apt to develop an organic hesitancy,—in fact more or less of a stutter or even worse. In this particular Billy was a striking instance that the arch interpreter, the envious marplot of Eden, still has more or less to do with every human consignment to this planet of earth. In every case, one way or another, he is sure to slip in his little card, as much as to remind us—I too have a hand here.

The avowal of such an imperfection in the Handsome Sailor should be evidence not alone that he is not presented as conventional hero, but also that the story in which he is the main figure is no romance.

Chapter III

At the time of Billy Budd's arbitrary enlistment into the *Indomitable* that ship was on her way to join the Mediterranean fleet. No long time elapsed before the junction was effected. As one of that fleet the seventy-four participated in its movements: though at times on account of her superior sailing qualities, in the absence of frigates, despatched on separate duty as a scout—and at times on less temporary service. But with all this the story has little concernment, restricted as it is to the inner life of one particular ship and the career of an individual sailor.

It was the summer of 1797. In April of that year had occurred the commotion at Spithead, followed in May by a second and yet more serious outbreak in the fleet at the Nore. The latter is known, and without exaggeration in the epithet, as the Great Mutiny. It was indeed a demonstration more menacing to England than the contemporary manifestoes and conquering and proselyting armies of the French Directory.

To the Empire, the Nore Mutiny was what a strike in the fire-brigade would be to London threatened by general arson. In a crisis when the Kingdom might well have anticipated the famous signal that some years later published along the naval line of battle what it was that upon occasion England expected of Englishmen; *that* was the time when at the mast-heads of the three-deckers and seventy-fours moored in our own roadstead— a fleet, the right arm of a Power then all but the sole free conservative one of the Old World, the

blue-jackets, to be numbered by thousands, ran up with hurras the British colours with the union and cross wiped out; by that cancellation transmuting the flag of founded law and freedom defined, into the enemy's red meteor of unbridled and unbounded revolt. Reasonable discontent growing out of practical grievances in the fleet had been ignited into irrational combustion as by live cinders blown across the Channel from France in flames.

The event converted into irony for a time those spirited strains of Dibdin[n]—as a song-writer no mean auxiliary to the English Government—at this European conjuncture, strains celebrating, among other things, the patriotic devotion of the British tar:

And as for my life, 'tis the King's!

Such an episode in the Island's grand naval story her naval historians naturally abridge; one of them (G. P. R. James) candidly acknowledging that fain would he pass it over did not "impartiality forbid fastidiousness." And yet his mention is less a narration than a reference, having to do hardly at all with details. Nor are these readily to be found in the libraries. Like some other events in every age befalling states everywhere, including America, the Great Mutiny was of such character that national pride along with views of policy would fain shade it off into the historical background. Such events cannot be ignored, but there is a considerate way of historically treating them. If a well-constituted individual refrains from blazoning aught amiss or calamitous in his family, a nation in the like circumstance may without reproach be equally discreet.

Though after parleyings between Government and the ring-leaders, and concessions by the former as to some glaring abuses, the first uprising —that at Spithead—with difficulty was put down, or matters for a time pacified; yet at the Nore the unforeseen renewal of insurrection on a yet larger scale, and emphasized in the conferences that ensued by demands deemed by the authorities not only inadmissible but aggressively insolent, indicated, if the red flag did not sufficiently do so,

Dibdin: Charles Dibdin (1745–1814), British dramatist and song writer.

what was the spirit animating the men. Final suppression, however, there was, but only made possible perhaps by the unswerving loyalty of the marine corps, and a voluntary resumption of loyalty among influential sections of the crews. To some extent the Nore Mutiny may be regarded as analogous to the distempering irruption of contagious fever in a frame constitutionally sound, and which anon throws it off.

At all events, of these thousands of mutineers were some of the tars who not so very long afterwards—whether wholly prompted thereto by patriotism, or pugnacious instinct, or by both,—helped to win a coronet for Nelson at the Nile, and the naval crown of crowns for him at Trafalgar. To the mutineers those battles, and especially Trafalgar, were a plenary absolution; and a grand one; for all that goes to make up scenic naval display is heroic magnificence in arms. Those battles, especially Trafalgar, stand unmatched in human annals.

Chapter IV · *Concerning "The Greatest Sailor Since The World Began"*—Tennyson

In this matter of writing, resolve as one may to keep to the main road, some bypaths have an enticement not readily to be withstood. Beckoned by the genius of Nelson, I am going to err into such a bypath. If the reader will keep me company I shall be glad. At the least we can promise ourselves that pleasure which is wickedly said to be in sinning, for a literary sin the divergence will be.

Very likely it is no new remark that the inventions of our time have at last brought about a change in sea warfare in degree corresponding to the revolution in all warfare effected by the original introduction from China into Europe of gunpowder. The first European firearm, a clumsy contrivance, was, as is well known, scouted by no few of the knights as a base implement, good enough peradventure for weavers too craven to stand up crossing steel with steel in frank fight. But as ashore knightly valour, though shorn of its blazonry, did not cease with the knights, neither on the seas, though nowadays in encounters there a certain kind of displayed gallantry be fallen out of date as hardly applicable under changed circumstances, did the nobler qualities of such naval magnates as Don John of Austria, Doria, Van Tromp, Jean Bart, the long line of British admirals and the American Decaturs of 1812 become obsolete with their wooden walls.

Nevertheless, to anybody who can hold the Present at its worth without being inappreciative of the Past, it may be forgiven, if to such an one the solitary old hulk at Portsmouth, Nelson's *Victory*, seems to float there, not alone as the decaying monument of a fame incorruptible, but also as a poetic reproach, softened by its picturesqueness, to the *Monitors* and yet mightier hulls of the European ironsides. And this not altogether because such craft are unsightly, unavoidably lacking the symmetry and grand lines of the old battleships, but equally for other reasons.

There are some, perhaps, who while not altogether inaccessible to that poetic reproach just alluded to, may yet on behalf of the new order be disposed to parry it; and this to the extent of iconoclasm, if need be. For example, prompted by the sight of the star inserted in the *Victory's* deck designating the spot where the Great Sailor fell, these martial utilitarians may suggest considerations implying that Nelson's ornate publication of his person in battle was not only unnecessary, but not military, nay, savoured of foolhardiness and vanity. They may add, too, that at Trafalgar it was in effect nothing less than a challenge to death: and death came; and that but for his bravado the victorious admiral might possibly have survived the battle, and so, instead of having his sagacious dying injunction overruled by his immediate successor in command, he himself when the contest was decided might have brought his shattered fleet to anchor, a proceeding which might have averted the deplorable loss of life by shipwreck in the elemental tempest that followed the martial one.

Well, should we set aside the more disputable point whether for various reasons it was possible to anchor the fleet, then plausibly enough the Benthamites[n] of war may urge the above.

But it *might have been* is but boggy ground to build on. And certainly in foresight as to the

Benthamites: followers of Jeremy Bentham (1748–1832), British writer on jurisprudence, who advocated the social principle of "the greatest good for the greatest number."

larger issue of an encounter, and anxious preparation for it—buoying the deadly way and mapping it out, as at Copenhagen—few commanders have been so painstakingly circumspect as this reckless declarer of his person in fight.

Personal prudence, even when dictated by quite other than selfish considerations, is surely no special virtue in a military man; while an excessive love of glory, exercising to the uttermost the heartfelt sense of duty, is the first. If the name of *Wellington* is not so much a trumpet to the blood as the simpler name of *Nelson*, the reason for this may be inferred from the above. Alfred[n] in his funeral ode on the victor of Waterloo ventures not to call him the greatest soldier of all time, though in the same ode he invokes Nelson as "the greatest sailor since the world began."

At Trafalgar, Nelson, on the brink of opening the fight, sat down and wrote his last brief will and testament. If under the presentiment of the most magnificent of all victories, to be crowned by his own glorious death, a sort of priestly motive led him to dress his person in the jewelled vouchers of his own shining deeds; if thus to have adorned himself for the altar and the sacrifice were indeed vainglory, then affectation and fustian is each truly heroic line in the great epics and dramas, since in such lines the poet but embodies in verse those exaltations of sentiment that a nature like Nelson, the opportunity being given, vitalizes into acts.

Chapter V

The outbreak at the Nore was put down. But not every grievance was redressed. If the contractors, for example, were no longer permitted to ply some practices peculiar to their tribe everywhere, such as providing shoddy cloth, rations not sound, or false in the measure; not the less impressment, for one thing, went on. By custom sanctioned for centuries, and judicially maintained by a Lord Chancellor as late as Mansfield, that mode of manning the fleet, a mode now fallen into a sort of abeyance but never formally renounced, it was not practicable to give up in those years. Its abrogation would have crippled the indispensable fleet, one wholly under canvas, no steam-power, its

Alfred: Alfred Lord Tennyson's "Ode on the Death of the Duke of Wellington."

innumerable sails and thousands of cannon, everything, in short, worked by muscle alone; a fleet the more insatiate in demand for men, because then multiplying its ships of all grades against contingencies present and to come of the convulsed Continent.

Discontent foreran the Two Mutinies, and more or less it lurkingly survived them. Hence it was not unreasonable to apprehend some return of trouble, sporadic or general. One instance of such apprehensions: In the same year with this story, Nelson, then Vice-Admiral Sir Horatio, being with the fleet off the Spanish coast, was directed by the Admiral in command to shift his pennant from the *Captain* to the *Theseus*; and for this reason: that the latter ship having newly arrived in the station from home where it had taken part in the Great Mutiny, danger was apprehended from the temper of the men; and it was thought that an officer like Nelson was the one, not indeed to terrorize the crew into base subjection, but to win them by force of his mere presence back to an allegiance, if not as enthusiastic as his own, yet as true. So it was that for a time on more than one quarterdeck anxiety did exist. At sea precautionary vigilance was strained against relapse. At short notice an engagement might come on. When it did, the lieutenants assigned to batteries felt it incumbent on them in some instances to stand with drawn swords behind the men working the guns.

But on board the seventy-four in which Billy now swung his hammock, very little in the manner of the men and nothing obvious in the demeanour of the officers would have suggested to an ordinary observer that the Great Mutiny was a recent event. In their general bearing and conduct the commissioned officers of a war-ship naturally take their tone from the commander, that is if he has that ascendency of character that ought to be his.

Captain the Honourable Edward Fairfax Vere, to give his full title, was a bachelor of forty or thereabouts, a sailor of distinction, even in a time prolific of renowned seamen. Though allied to the higher nobility, his advancement had not been altogether owing to influences connected with that circumstance. He had seen much service, been in various engagements, always acquitting himself as an officer mindful of the welfare of his men, but never tolerating an infraction of discipline; thoroughly versed in the science of his profession, and intrepid to the verge of temerity, though never injudiciously so. For his gallantry in the West Indian waters as flag-lieutenant under Rodney[n] in that Admiral's crowning victory, over De Grasse, he was made a post-captain.

Ashore in the garb of a civilian, scarce any one would have taken him for a sailor, more especially that he never garnished unprofessional talk with nautical terms, and grave in his bearing, evinced little appreciation of mere humour. It was not out of keeping with these traits that on a passage when nothing demanded his paramount action, he was the most undemonstrative of men. Any landsman observing this gentleman not conspicuous by his stature and wearing no pronounced insignia, emerging from his retreat to the open deck, and noting the silent deference of the officers retiring to leeward, might have taken him for the King's guest, a civilian aboard the King's ship, some highly honourable discreet envoy on his way to an important post. But, in fact, this unobtrusiveness of demeanour may have proceeded from a certain unaffected modesty of manhood sometimes accompanying a resolute nature, a modesty evinced at all times not calling for pronounced action, and which shown in any rank of life suggests a virtue aristocratic in kind.

As with some others engaged in various departments of the world's more heroic activities, Captain Vere, though practical enough upon occasion, would at times betray a certain dreaminess of mood. Standing alone on the weather-side of the greater deck, one hand holding by the rigging, he would absently gaze off at the black sea. At the presentation to him then of some minor matter interrupting the current of his thoughts, he would show more or less irascibility; but instantly he would control it.

In the navy he was popularly known by the appellation—Starry Vere. How such a designation happened to fall upon one who, whatever his sturdy qualities, was without any brilliant ones, was in this wise: a favourite kinsman, Lord Denton, a

free-handed fellow, had been the first to meet and congratulate him upon his return to England from the West Indian cruise; and but the day previous turning over a copy of Andrew Marvell's poems had lighted, not for the first time, however, upon the lines entitled "Appleton House," the name of one of the seats of their common ancestor, a hero in the German wars of the seventeenth century, in which poem occur the lines,

> This 'tis to have been from the first
> In a domestic heaven nursed,
> Under the discipline severe
> Of Fairfax and the starry Vere.

And so, upon embracing his cousin fresh from Rodney's victory, wherein he had played so gallant a part, brimming over with just family pride in the sailor of their house, he exuberantly exclaimed, "Give ye joy, Ed; give ye joy, my starry Vere!" This got currency, and the novel prefix serving in familiar parlance readily to distinguish the *Indomitable's* Captain from another Vere, his senior, a distant relative, an officer of like rank in the navy, it remained permanently attached to the surname.

Chapter VI

In view of the part that the commander of the *Indomitable* plays in scenes shortly to follow, it may be well to fill out that sketch of him outlined in the previous chapter. Aside from his qualities as a sea-officer Captain Vere was an exceptional character. Unlike no few of England's renowned sailors, long and arduous service with signal devotion to it, had not resulted in absorbing and *salting* the entire man. He had a marked leaning towards everything intellectual. He loved books, never going to sea without a newly replenished library, compact but of the best. The isolated leisure, in some cases so wearisome, falling at intervals to commanders even during a war-cruise, never was tedious to Captain Vere. With nothing of that literary taste which less heeds the thing conveyed than the vehicle, his bias was towards those books to which every serious mind of superior order occupying any active post of authority in the world, naturally inclines; books treating of actual men and events, no matter of what era—history, biog-

---

Rodney: George B. Rodney (1719–1792), British admiral, who defeated François De Grasse (1723–1788), French admiral, off Santo Domingo in 1782.

raphy and unconventional writers, who, free from cant and convention, like Montaigne, honestly, and in the spirit of common sense, philosophize upon realities.

In this love of reading he found confirmation of his own more reserved thoughts—confirmation which he had vainly sought in social converse, so that as touching most fundamental topics, there had got to be established in him some positive convictions which he forefelt would abide in him essentially unmodified so long as his intelligent part remained unimpaired. In view of the humbled position in which his lot was cast, this was well for him. His settled convictions were as a dyke against those invading waters of novel opinion, social, political, and otherwise, which carried away as in a torrent no few minds in those days, minds by nature not inferior to his own. While other members of that aristocracy to which by birth he belonged were incensed at the innovators mainly because their theories were inimical to the privileged classes, Captain Vere disinterestedly opposed them because they seemed to him incapable of embodiment in lasting institutions, but at war with the peace of the world and the good of mankind.

With minds less stored than his and less earnest, some officers of his rank, with whom at times he would necessarily consort, found him lacking in the companionable quality, a dry and bookish gentleman as they deemed. Upon any chance withdrawal from their company one would be apt to say to another something like this: "Vere is a noble fellow, Starry Vere. 'Spite the gazettes, Sir Horatio is at bottom scarce a better seaman or fighter. But between you and me now, don't you think there is a queer streak of the pedantic running through him? Yes, like the King's yarn in a coil of navy-rope?"

Some apparent ground there was for this sort of confidential criticism; since not only did the Captain's discourse never fall into the jocosely familiar, but in illustrating any point touching the stirring personages and events of the time, he would cite some historic character or incident of antiquity with the same easy air that he would cite from the moderns. He seemed unmindful of the circumstance that to his bluff company such remote allusions, however pertinent they might really be, were altogether alien to men whose reading was mainly confined to the journals. But considerateness in such matters is not easy to natures constituted like Captain Vere's. Their honesty prescribes to them directness, sometimes far-reaching, like that of a migratory fowl that in its flight never heeds when it crosses a frontier.

Chapter VII

The lieutenants and other commissioned gentlemen forming Captain Vere's staff it is not necessary here to particularize nor needs it to make mention of any of the warrant-officers. But among the petty officers was one who, having much to do with the story, may as well be forthwith introduced. This portrait I essay, but shall never hit it.

This was John Claggart, the master-at-arms. But that sea-title may to landsmen seem somewhat equivocal. Originally, doubtless, that petty-officer's function was the instruction of the men in the use of arms, sword, or cutlass. But very long ago, owing to the advance in gunnery making hand-to-hand encounters less frequent—and giving to nitre and sulphur the pre-eminence over steel—that function ceased; the master-at-arms of a great war-ship becoming a sort of Chief of Police charged, among other matters, with the duty of preserving order on the populous lower gun-decks.

Claggart was a man of about five-and-thirty, somewhat spare and tall yet of no ill figure upon the whole. His hand was too small and shapely to have been accustomed to hard toil. The face was a notable one; the features, all except the chin, cleanly cut as those on a Greek medallion; yet the chin, beardless as Tecumseh's, had something of the strange protuberant heaviness in its make that recalled the prints of the Rev. Dr. Titus Oates, the historical deponent with the clerical drawl in the time of Charles II, and the fraud of the alleged Popish Plot. It served Claggart in his office that his eye could cast a tutoring glance. His brow was of the sort phrenologically associated with more than average intellect; silken jet curls partly clustering over it, making a foil to the pallor below, a pallor tinged with a faint shade of amber akin to the hue of time-tinted marbles of old.

This complexion singularly contrasting with the red or deeply bronzed visages of the sailors, and in part the result of his official seclusion from the sunlight, though it was not exactly displeasing, nevertheless seemed to hint of something defective or abnormal in the constitution and blood. But his general aspect and manner were so suggestive of an education and career incongruous with his naval function, that when not actively engaged in it he looked like a man of high quality, social and moral, who for reasons of his own was keeping incognito. Nothing was known of his former life. It might be that he was an Englishman; and yet there lurked a bit of accent in his speech suggesting that possibly he was not such by birth, but through naturalization in early childhood. Among certain grizzled sea-gossips of the gun-decks and forecastle went a rumour perdue that the master-at-arms was a chevalier who had volunteered into the King's navy by way of compounding for some mysterious swindle whereof he had been arraigned at the King's bench. The fact that nobody could substantiate this report was, of course, nothing against its secret currency. Such a rumour once started on the gun-decks in reference to almost any one below the rank of a commissioned officer would, during the period assigned to this narrative, have seemed not altogether wanting in credibility to the tarry old wiseacres of a man-of-war crew. And indeed a man of Claggart's accomplishments, without prior nautical experience, entering the navy at mature life, as he did, and necessarily allotted at the start to the lowest grade in it; a man, too, who never made allusion to his previous life ashore; these were circumstances which in the dearth of exact knowledge as to his true antecedents opened to the invidious a vague field for unfavourable surmise.

But the sailors' dog-watch gossip concerning him derived a vague plausibility from the fact that now, for some period, the British Navy could so little afford to be squeamish in the matter of keeping up the muster-rolls, that not only were press-gangs notoriously abroad both afloat and ashore, but there was little or no secret about another matter, namely, that the London police were at liberty to capture any able-bodied suspect, and any questionable fellow at large, and summarily ship him to the dock-yard or fleet. Furthermore, ever among voluntary enlistments, there were instances where the motive thereto partook neither of patriotic impulse nor yet of a random desire to experience a bit of sea-life and martial adventure. Insolvent debtors of minor grade, together with the promiscuous lame ducks of morality, found in the navy a convenient and secure refuge. Secure, because once enlisted aboard a King's ship, they were as much in sanctuary as the transgressor of the middle ages harbouring himself under the shadow of the altar. Such sanctioned irregularities, which for obvious reasons the Government would hardly think to parade at the time—and which consequently, and as affecting the least influential class of mankind, have all but dropped into oblivion—lend colour to something for the truth whereof I do not vouch, and hence have some scruple in stating; something I remember having seen in print, though the book I cannot recall; but the same thing was personally communicated to me now more than forty years ago by an old pensioner in a cocked hat, with whom I had a most interesting talk on the terrace at Greenwich, a Baltimore negro, a Trafalgar man. It was to this effect: In the case of a war-ship short of hands, whose speedy sailing was imperative, the deficient quota, in lack of any other way of making it good, would be eked out by drafts called direct from the jails. For reasons previously suggested it would not perhaps be very easy at the present day directly to prove or disprove the allegation. But allowed as a verity, how significant would it be of England's straits at the time, confronted by those wars which, like a flight of harpies, rose shrieking from the din and dust of the fallen Bastille. That era appears measurably clear to us who look back at it, and but read of it. But to the grandfathers of us greybeards, the thoughtful of them, the genius of it presented an aspect like that of Camoëns' "Spirit of the Cape," an eclipsing menace, mysterious and prodigious. Not America even was exempt from apprehension. At the height of Napoleon's unexampled conquests, there were Americans who had fought at Bunker Hill, who looked forward to the possibility that the Atlantic might prove no barrier against the ultimate schemes of this portentous upstart from the revo-

813

lutionary chaos, who seemed in act of fulfilling the judgment prefigured in the Apocalypse.

But the less credence was to be given to the gun-deck talk touching Claggart, seeing that no man holding his office in a man-of-war can ever hope to be popular with the crew. Besides, in derogatory comments upon any one against whom they have a grudge, or for any reason or no reason mislike, sailors are much like landsmen: they are apt to exaggerate or romance.

About as much was really known to the *Indomitable's* tars of the master-at-arms' career before entering the service as an astronomer knows about a comet's travels prior to its first observable appearance in the sky. The verdict of the sea-*quidnuncs* has been cited only by way of showing what sort of moral impression the man made upon rude uncultivated natures whose conceptions of human wickedness were necessarily of the narrowest, limited to ideas of vulgar rascality,—a thief among the swinging hammocks during a night-watch, or the man-brokers and land-sharks of the seaports.

It was no gossip, however, but fact, that though, as before hinted, Claggart upon his entrance into the navy was, as a novice, assigned to the least honourable section of a man-of-war's crew, embracing the drudges, he did not long remain there.

The superior capacity he immediately evinced, his constitutional sobriety, his ingratiating deference to superiors, together with a peculiar ferreting genius manifested on a singular occasion, all this capped by a certain austere patriotism, abruptly advanced him to the position of Master-at-arms.

Of this maritime Chief of Police the ship's-corporals, so called, were the immediate subordinates, and compliant ones; and this—as is to be noted in some business departments ashore—almost to a degree inconsistent with entire moral volition. His place put various converging wires of underground influence under the Chief's control, capable when astutely worked through his understrappers of operating to the mysterious discomfort, if nothing worse, of any of the sea-commonalty.

Chapter VIII

Life in the foretop well agreed with Billy Budd. There, when not actually engaged on the yards yet higher aloft, the topmen, who as such had been picked out for youth and activity, constituted an aerial club, lounging at ease against the smaller stun'sails rolled up into cushions, spinning yarns like the lazy gods, and frequently amused with what was going on in the busy world of the decks below. No wonder then that a young fellow of Billy's disposition was well content in such society. Giving no cause of offence to anybody, he was always alert at a call. So in the merchant service it had been with him. But now such punctiliousness in duty was shown that his top-mates would sometimes good-naturedly laugh at him for it. This heightened alacrity had its cause, namely, the impression made upon him by the first formal gangway-punishment he had ever witnessed, which befell the day following his impressment. It had been incurred by a little fellow, young, a novice, an after-guardsman absent from his assigned post when the ship was being put about, a dereliction resulting in a rather serious hitch to that manœuvre, one demanding instantaneous promptitude in letting go and making fast. When Billy saw the culprit's naked back under the scourge gridironed with red welts, and worse; when he marked the dire expression in the liberated man's face, as with his woolen shirt flung over him by the executioner, he rushed forward from the spot to bury himself in the crowd, Billy was horrified. He resolved that never through remissness would he make himself liable to such a visitation, or do or omit aught that might merit even verbal reproof. What then was his surprise and concern when ultimately he found himself getting into petty trouble occasionally about such matters as the stowage of his bag, or something amiss in his hammock, matters under the police oversight of the ship's-corporals of the lower decks, and which brought down on him a vague threat from one of them.

So heedful in all things as he was, how could this be? He could not understand it, and it more than vexed him. When he spoke to his young top-mates about it, they were either lightly incredulous, or found something comical in his unconcealed anxiety. "Is it your bag, Billy?" said one; "well, sew yourself up in it, Billy boy, and then you'll be sure to know if anybody meddles with it."

Now there was a veteran aboard who, because his years began to disqualify him for more active work, had been recently assigned duty as mainmast-man in his watch, looking to the gear belayed at the rail round about that great spar near the deck. At off-times the foretopman had picked up some acquaintance with him, and now in his trouble it occurred to him that he might be the sort of person to go to for wise council. He was an old Dansker long anglicized in the service, of few words, many wrinkles and some honourable scars. His wizened face, time-tinted and weather-stormed to the complexion of an antique parchment, was here and there peppered blue by the chance explosion of a gun-cartridge in action. He was an *Agamemnon*-man; some two years prior to the time of this story having served under Nelson, when but Sir Horatio, in that ship immortal in naval memory, and which, dismantled and in part broken up to her bare ribs, is seen a grand skeleton in Haydon's etching. As one of a boarding-party from the *Agamemnon* he had received a cut slantwise along one temple and cheek, leaving a long pale scar like a streak of dawn's light falling athwart the dark visage. It was on account of that scar and the affair in which it was known that he had received it, as well as from his blue-peppered complexion, that the Dansker went among the *Indomitable's* crew by the name of "Board-her-in-the-smoke."

Now the first time that his small weazel-eyes happened to light on Billy Budd, a certain grim internal merriment set all his ancient wrinkles into antic play. Was it that his eccentric unsentimental old sapience, primitive in its kind, saw, or thought it saw, something which in contrast with the war-ship's environment looked oddly incongruous in the Handsome Sailor? But after slyly studying him at intervals, the old Merlin's equivocal merriment was modified. For now when the twain would meet, it would start in his face a quizzing sort of look, but it would be but momentary, and sometimes replaced by an expression of speculative query as to what might eventually befall a nature like that, dropped into a world not without some man-traps and against whose subtleties simple courage lacking experience and address and without any touch of defensive ugliness, is of little avail; and where such innocence as man is capable of does yet, in a moral emergency, not always sharpen the faculties or enlighten the will.

However it was, the Dansker in his ascetic way rather took to Billy. Nor was this only because of a certain philosophic interest in such a character. There was another cause. While the old man's eccentricities, sometimes bordering on the ursine, repelled the juniors, Billy, undeterred thereby, would make advances, never passing the old *Agamemnon*-man without a salutation marked by that respect which is seldom lost on the aged, however crabbed at times, or whatever their station in life. There was a vein of dry humour, or what not, in the mast-man; and whether in freak of patriarchal irony touching Billy's youth and athletic frame, or for some other and more recondite reason, from the first in addressing him he always substituted Baby for Billy. The Dansker, in fact, being the originator of the name by which the foretopman eventually became known aboard ship.

Well then, in his mysterious little difficulty going in quest of the wrinkled one, Billy found him off duty in a dog-watch ruminating by himself, seated on a shot-box of the upper gun-deck, now and then surveying with a somewhat cynical regard certain of the more swaggering promenaders there. Billy recounted his trouble, again wondering how it all happened. The salt seer attentively listened, accompanying the foretopman's recitals with queer twitchings of his wrinkles and problematical little sparkles of his small ferret eyes. Making an end of his story, the foretopman asked, "And now, Dansker, do tell me what you think of it."

The old man, shoving up the front of his tarpaulin and deliberately rubbing the long slant scar at the point where it entered the thin hair, laconically said, "Baby Budd, *Jimmy Legs*" (meaning the master-at-arms) "is down on you."

"*Jimmy Legs!*" ejaculated Billy, his welkin eyes expanding. "What for? Why he calls me *the sweet and pleasant young fellow*, they tell me."

"Does he so?" grinned the grizzled one; then said, "Ay, Baby Lad, a sweet voice has *Jimmy Legs*."

"No, not always. But to me he has. I seldom pass him but there comes a pleasant word."

815

"And that's because he's down upon you, Baby Budd."

Such reiteration, along with the manner of it (incomprehensible to a novice), disturbed Billy almost as much as the mystery for which he had sought explanation. Something less unpleasingly oracular he tried to extract. But the old sea-Chiron, thinking perhaps that for the nonce he had sufficiently instructed his young Achilles, pursed his lips, gathered all his wrinkles together, and would commit himself to nothing further.

Years, and those experiences which befall certain shrewder men subordinated life-long to the will of superiors, all this had developed in the Dansker the pithy guarded cynicism that was his leading characteristic.

Chapter IX

The next day an incident served to confirm Billy Budd in his incredulity as to the Dansker's strange summing up of the case submitted.

The ship at noon going large before the wind was rolling on her course, and he, below at dinner and engaged in some sportful talk with the members of his mess, chanced in a sudden lurch to spill the entire contents of his soup-pan upon the new scrubbed deck. Claggart, the master-at-arms, official rattan in hand, happened to be passing along the battery, in a bay of which the mess was lodged, and the greasy liquid streamed just across his path. Stepping over it, he was proceeding on his way without comment, since the matter was nothing to take notice of under the circumstances, when he happened to observe who it was that had done the spilling. His countenance changed. Pausing, he was about to ejaculate something hasty at the sailor, but checked himself, and pointing down to the streaming soup, playfully tapped him from behind with his rattan, saying, in a low musical voice, peculiar to him at times, "Handsomely done, my lad! And handsome is as handsome did it, too!" and with that passed on. Not noted by Billy as not coming within his view was the involuntary smile, or rather grimace, that accompanied Claggart's equivocal words. Aridly it drew down the thin corners of his shapely mouth. But everybody taking his remark as meant for humorous, and at which therefore as coming from a superior

they were bound to laugh, "with counterfeited glee" acted accordingly; and Billy tickled, it may be, by the allusion to his being the handsome sailor, merrily joined in; then addressing his messmates exclaimed, "There now, who says that Jimmy Legs is down on me!"

"And who said he was, Beauty?" demanded one Donald with some surprise. Whereat the foretop-man looked a little foolish, recalling that it was only one person, Board-her-in-the-smoke, who had suggested what to him was the smoky idea that this master-at-arms was in any peculiar way hostile to him. Meantime that functionary resuming his path must have momentarily worn some expression less guarded than that of the bitter smile and, usurping the face from the heart, some distorting expression perhaps—for a drummer-boy, heedlessly frolicking along from the opposite direction, and chancing to come into light collision with his person was strangely disconcerted by his aspect. Nor was the impression lessened when the official, impulsively giving him a sharp cut with the rattan, vehemently exclaimed, "Look where you go!"

Chapter X

What was the matter with the master-at-arms? And, be the matter what it might, how could it have direct relation to Billy Budd, with whom prior to the affair of the spilled soup he had never come into any special contact, official or otherwise? What indeed could the trouble have to do with one so little inclined to give offence as the merchant-ship's *peacemaker*, even him who in Claggart's own phrase was "The sweet and pleasant young fellow"? Yes, why should *Jimmy Legs*, to borrow the Dansker's expression, be *down* on the Handsome Sailor?

But at heart and not for nothing, as the late chance encounter may indicate to the discerning, down on him, secretly down on him, he assuredly was.

Now to invent something touching the more private career of Claggart—something involving Billy Budd, of which something the latter should be wholly ignorant, some romantic incident implying that Claggart's knowledge of the young blue-jacket began at some period anterior to catching sight of him on board the seventy-four—all this, not so difficult to do, might avail in a more or less interesting way to account for whatever enigma may appear to lurk in the case. But, in fact, there was nothing of the sort. And yet the cause, necessarily to be assumed as the sole one assignable, is in its very realism as much charged with that prime element of Radcliffian romance, *the mysterious*, as any that the ingenuity of the author of the "Mysteries of Udolpho" could devise. For what can more partake of the mysterious than an antipathy spontaneous and profound such as is evoked in certain exceptional mortals by the mere aspect of some other mortal, however harmless he may be?—if not called forth by that very harmlessness itself.

Now there can exist no irritating juxtaposition of dissimilar personalities comparable to that which is possible aboard a great war-ship fully manned and at sea. There, every day, among all ranks, almost every man comes into more or less of contact with almost every other man. Wholly there to avoid even the sight of an aggravating object one must needs give it Jonah's toss, or jump overboard himself. Imagine how all this might eventually operate on some peculiar human creature the direct reverse of a saint?

But for the adequate comprehending of Claggart by a normal nature, these hints are insufficient. To pass from a normal nature to him one must cross "The deadly space between," and this is best done by indirection.

Long ago an honest scholar, my senior, said to me in reference to one who like himself is now no more, a man so unimpeachably respectable that against him nothing was ever openly said, though among the few something was whispered, "Yes X—— is a nut not to be cracked by the tap of a lady's fan. You are aware that I am the adherent of no organized religion, much less of any philosophy built into a system. Well, for all that, I think that to try and get into X——, enter his labyrinth and get out again, without a clue derived from some source other than what is known as *knowledge of the world*—that were hardly possible, at least for me."

"Why," said I, "X——, however singular a study to some, is yet human, and knowledge of the world assuredly implies the knowledge of human nature, and in most of its varieties."

"Yes, but a superficial knowledge of it, serving ordinary purposes. But for anything deeper, I am not certain whether to know the world and to know human nature be not two distinct branches of knowledge, which while they may co-exist in the same heart, yet either may exist with little or nothing of the other. Nay, in an average man of the world, his constant rubbing with it blunts that fine spiritual insight indispensable to the understanding of the essential in certain exceptional characters, whether evil ones or good. In a matter of some importance I have seen a girl wind an old lawyer about her little finger. Nor was it the dotage of senile love. Nothing of the sort. But he knew law better than he knew the girl's heart. Coke and Blackstone hardly shed so much light into obscure spiritual places as the Hebrew prophets. And who were they? Mostly recluses."

At the time my inexperience was such that I did not quite see the drift of all this. It may be that I see it now. And, indeed, if that lexicon which is based on Holy Writ were any longer popular, one might with less difficulty define and denominate certain phenomenal men. As it is, one must turn to some authority not liable to the charge of being tinctured with the Biblical element.

In a list of definitions included in the authentic translation of Plato, a list attributed to him, occurs this: "Natural Depravity: a depravity according to nature." A definition which though savouring of Calvinism by no means involves Calvin's dogma as to total mankind. Evidently its intent makes it applicable but to individuals. Not many are the examples of this depravity which the gallows and jail supply. At any rate, for notable instances,—since these have no vulgar alloy of the brute in them, but invariably are dominated by intellectuality,—one must go elsewhere. Civilization, especially if of the austerer sort, is auspicious to it. It folds itself in the mantle of respectability. It has its certain negative virtues serving as silent auxiliaries. It never allows wine to get within its guard. It is not going too far to say that it is without vices or small sins. There is a phenomenal pride in it that excludes them from anything. Never mercenary or avaricious. In short, the depravity here meant partakes nothing of the sordid or sensual. It is serious, but free from acerbity. Though no flatterer of mankind it never speaks ill of it.

But the thing which in eminent instances signalizes so exceptional a nature is this: though the man's even temper and discreet bearing would seem to intimate a mind peculiarly subject to the law of reason, not the less in his soul's recesses he would seem to riot in complete exemption from that law, having apparently little to do with reason further than to employ it as an ambidexter implement for effecting the irrational. That is to say: towards the accomplishment of an aim which in wantonness of malignity would seem to partake of the insane, he will direct a cool judgment sagacious and sound.

These men are true madmen, and of the most dangerous sort, for their lunacy is not continuous, but occasional; evoked by some special object; it is secretive and self-contained: so that when most active it is, to the average mind, not distinguished from sanity; and for the reason above suggested, that whatever its aims may be (and the aim is never disclosed) the method and the outward proceeding is always perfectly rational.

Now something such was Claggart, in whom was the mania of an evil nature, not engendered by vicious training or corrupting books or licentious living, but born with him and innate, in short, "a depravity according to nature."

Can it be this phenomenon, disowned or not acknowledged, that in some criminal cases puzzles the courts? For this cause have our juries at times not only to endure the prolonged contentions of lawyers with their fees, but also the yet more perplexing strife of the medical experts with theirs? And why leave it to them? Why not subpoena as well the clerical proficients? Their vocation bringing them into peculiar contact with so many human beings, and sometimes in their least guarded hour, in interviews very much more confidential than those of physician and patient; this would seem to qualify them to know something about those intricacies involved in the question of moral responsibility; whether in a given case, say, the crime proceeded from mania in the brain or rabies of the heart. As to any differences among themselves which clerical proficients might develop on the stand, these could hardly be greater than the direct contradictions exchanged between the remunerated medical experts.

Dark sayings are these, some will say. But why? It is because they somewhat savour of Holy Writ in its phrase "mysteries of iniquity."

The point of the story turning on the hidden nature of the master-at-arms has necessitated this chapter. With an added hint or two in connection with the incident at the mess, the resumed narrative must be left to vindicate as it may its own credibility.

Chapter XI · (*Pale Ire, Envy and Despair*)

That Claggart's figure was not amiss, and his face, save the chin, well moulded, has already been said. Of these favourable points he seemed not insensible, for he was not only neat but careful in his dress. But the form of Billy Budd was heroic; and if his face was without the intellectual look of the pallid Claggart's, not the less was it lit, like his, from within, though from a different source. The bonfire in his heart made luminous the rose-tan in his cheek.

In view of the marked contrast between the persons of the twain, it is more than probable that when the master-at-arms in the scene last given applied to the sailor the proverb *Handsome is as handsome does* he there let escape an ironic inkling, not caught by the young sailors who heard it, as to what it was that had first moved him against Billy, namely, his significant personal beauty.

Now envy and antipathy, passions irreconcilable in reason, nevertheless in fact may spring conjoined like Chang and Eng[n] in one birth. Is Envy then such a monster? Well, though many an arraigned mortal has in hopes of mitigated penalty pleaded guilty to horrible actions, did ever anybody seriously confess to envy? Something there is in it universally felt to be more shameful than even felonious crime. And not only does everybody disown it, but the better sort are inclined to incredulity when it is in earnest imputed to an intelligent man. But since its lodgment is in the heart, not the brain, no degree of intellect supplies a guarantee against it. But Claggart's was no

Chang and Eng: famed "Siamese Twins" (1811–1874).

vulgar form of the passion. Nor, as directed toward Billy Budd, did it partake of that streak of apprehensive jealousy which marred Saul's visage perturbedly brooding on the comely young David. Claggart's envy struck deeper. If askance he eyed the good looks, cheery health and frank enjoyment of young life in Billy Budd, it was because these happened to go along with a nature that, as Claggart magnetically felt, had in its simplicity never willed malice or experienced the reactionary bite of that serpent. To him, the spirit lodged within Billy and looking out from his welkin eyes as from windows—that ineffability it was which made the dimple in his dyed cheeks, suppled his joints, and dancing in his yellow curls made him pre-eminently the Handsome Sailor. One person excepted, the master-at-arms was perhaps the only man in the ship intellectually capable of adequately appreciating the moral phenomenon presented in Billy Budd, and the insight but intensified his passion, which, assuming various secret forms within him, at times assumed that of cynic disdain—disdain of innocence. To be nothing more than innocent! Yet in an æsthetic way he saw the charm of it, the courageous free-and-easy temper of it, and fain would have shared it, but he despaired of it.

With no power to annul the elemental evil in himself, though readily enough he could hide it; apprehending the good, but powerless to be it; a nature like Claggart's, surcharged with energy as such natures almost invariably are, what recourse is left to it but to recoil upon itself and like the scorpion for which the Creator alone is responsible, act out to the end the part allotted it.

Passion, and passion in its profoundest, is not a thing demanding a palatial stage whereon to play its part. Down among the groundlings, among the beggars and rakers of the garbage, profound passion is enacted. And the circumstances that provoke it, however trivial or mean, are no measure of its power. In the present instance the stage is a scrubbed gun-deck, and one of the external provocations a man-of-war's man's spilled soup.

Now when the master-at-arms noticed whence came that greasy fluid streaming before his feet, he must have taken it—to some extent wilfully perhaps—not for the mere accident it assuredly was, but for the sly escape of a spontaneous feeling on Billy's part more or less answering to the antipathy on his own. In effect a foolish demonstration he must have thought, and very harmless, like the futile kick of a heifer, which yet were the heifer a shod stallion would not be so harmless. Even so was it that into the gall of envy Claggart infused the vitriol of his contempt. But the incident confirmed to him certain tell-tale reports purveyed to his ear by *Squeak*, one of his more cunning corporals, a grizzled little man, so nicknamed by the sailors on account of his squeaky voice and sharp visage ferreting about the dark corners of the lower decks after interlopers, satirically suggesting to them the idea of a rat in a cellar.

Now his chief's employing him as an implicit tool in laying little traps for the worriment of the foretopman—for it was from the master-at-arms that the petty persecutions heretofore adverted to had proceeded—the corporal, having naturally enough concluded that his master could have no love for the sailor, made it his business, faithful understrapper that he was, to ferment the ill blood by perverting to his chief certain innocent frolics of the good-natured foretopman, besides inventing for his master sundry contumelious epithets he claimed to have overheard him let fall. The master-at-arms never suspected the veracity of these reports, more especially as to the epithets, for he well knew how secretly unpopular may become a master-at-arms—at least a master-at-arms of those days, zealous in his function—how the blue-jackets shot at him in private their raillery and wit; the nickname by which he goes among them (*Jimmy Legs*) implying under the form of merriment their cherished disrespect and dislike.

But in view of the greediness of hate for provocation, it hardly needed a purveyor to feed Claggart's passion. An uncommon prudence is habitual with the subtler depravity, for it has everything to hide. And in case of any merely suspected injury its secretiveness voluntarily cuts it off from enlightenment or disillusion; and not unreluctantly, action is taken upon surmise as upon certainty. And the retaliation is apt to be in monstrous disproportion to the supposed offence; for when in anybody was revenge in its exactions aught else but an inordinate usurer? But how with

Claggart's conscience? For though consciences are unlike as foreheads, every intelligence, not including the Scriptural devils who "believe and tremble," has one. But Claggart's conscience being but the lawyer to his will, made ogres of trifles, probably arguing that the motive imputed to Billy in spilling the soup just when he did, together with the epithets alleged—these, if nothing more, made a strong case against him; nay, justified animosity into a sort of retributive righteousness. The Pharisee is the Guy Fawkes prowling in the hid chambers underlying some natures like Claggart's. And they can really form no conception of an unreciprocated malice. Probably, the master-at-arms' clandestine persecutions of Billy were started to try the temper of the man; but they had not developed any quality in him that enmity could make official use of, or ever pervert into even plausible self-justification; so that the occurrence at the mess, petty if it were, was a welcome one to that peculiar conscience assigned to be the private mentor of Claggart; and for the rest, not improbably it put him upon new experiments.

Chapter XII

Not many days after the last incident narrated, something befell Billy Budd that more gravelled him than aught that had previously occurred.

It was a warm night for the latitude; and the foretopman, whose watch was at the time properly below, was dozing on the uppermost deck whither he had ascended from his hot hammock—one of hundreds suspended so closely wedged together over a lower gun-deck that there was little or no swing to them. He lay as in the shadow of a hillside stretched under the lee of the booms, a piled ridge of spare spars, and among which the ship's largest boat, the launch, was stowed. Alongside of three other slumberers from below, he lay near one end of the booms which approached from the foremast; his station aloft on duty as a foretopman being just over the deck station of the forecastlemen entitling him according to usage to make himself more or less at home in that neighbourhood.

Presently he was stirred into semi-consciousness by somebody, who must have previously sounded the sleep of the others, touching his shoulder, and then as the foretopman raised his head, breathing into his ear in a quick whisper, "Slip into the lee fore-chains, Billy; there is something in the wind—don't speak. Quick. I will meet you there;" and disappeared.

Now Billy—like sundry other essentially good-natured ones—had some of the weakness inseparable from essential good nature; and among these was a reluctance, almost an incapacity of plumply saying no to an abrupt proposition not obviously absurd, on the face of it, nor obviously unfriendly, nor iniquitous. And being of warm blood he had not the phlegm to negative any proposition by unresponsive inaction. Like his sense of fear, his apprehension as to aught outside of the honest and natural was seldom very quick. Besides, upon the present occasion, the drowse from his sleep still hung upon him.

However it was, he mechanically rose and, sleepily wondering what could be in the wind, betook himself to the designated place, a narrow platform, one of six, outside of the high bulwarks and screened by the great dead-eyes and multiple columned lanyards of the shrouds and back-stays; and, in a great war-ship of that time, of dimensions commensurate to the ample hull's magnitude; a tarry balcony, in short, overhanging the sea, and so secluded that one mariner of the *Indomitable*, a non-conformist old tar of serious turn, made it even in daytime his private oratory.

In this retired nook the stranger soon joined Billy Budd. There was no moon as yet; a haze obscured the star-light. He could not distinctly see the stranger's face. Yet from something in the outline and carriage, Billy took him to be, and correctly, one of the afterguard.

"Hist, Billy!" said the man, in the same quick cautionary whisper as before. "You were impressed, weren't you? Well, so was I;" and he paused as to mark the effect. But Billy, not knowing exactly what to make of this, said nothing. Then the other: "We are not the only impressed ones, Billy. There's a gang of us. Couldn't you—help—at a pinch?"

"What do you mean?" demanded Billy, here shaking off his drowse.

"Hist, hist!" the hurried whisper now growing husky, "see here;" and the man held up two small objects faintly twinkling in the night light. "See, they are yours, Bill, if you'll only—"

But Billy here broke in, and in his resentful eagerness to deliver himself his vocal infirmity somewhat intruded: "D-D-Damme, I don't know what you are d-driving at, or what you mean, but you had better g-g-go where you belong!" For the moment the fellow, as confounded, did not stir; and Billy, springing to his feet, said, "If you d-don't start, I'll t-t-toss you back over the r-rail!" There was no mistaking this, and the mysterious emissary decamped, disappearing in the direction of the mainmast in the shadow of the booms.

"Hallo, what's the matter?" here came growling from a forecastleman awakened from his deck-doze by Billy's raised voice. And as the foretop-man reappeared and was recognized by him: "Ah, *Beauty*, is it you? Well, something must have been the matter for you st-st-stuttered."

"Oh," rejoined Billy, now mastering the impediment; "I found an afterguardsman in our part of the ship here and I bid him be off where he belongs."

"And is that all you did about it, foretop-man?" gruffly demanded another, an irascible old fellow of brick-coloured visage and hair, and who was known to his associate forecastlemen as *Red Pepper*.

"Such sneaks I should like to marry to the gunner's daughter!" by that expression meaning that he would like to subject them to disciplinary castigation over a gun.

However, Billy's rendering of the matter satisfactorily accounted to these inquirers for the brief commotion, since of all the sections of a ship's company the forecastlemen, veterans for the most part, and bigoted in their sea-prejudices, are the most jealous in resenting territorial encroachments, especially on the part of any of the afterguard, of whom they have but a sorry opinion, chiefly landsmen, never going aloft except to reef or furl the mainsail, and in no wise competent to handle a marlingspike or turn in a *dead-eye*, say.

Chapter XIII

This incident sorely puzzled Billy Budd. It was an entirely new experience—the first time in his life that he had ever been personally approached in underhanded intriguing fashion. Prior to this encounter he had known nothing of the after-guardsman, the two men being stationed wide apart, one forward and aloft during his watch, the other on deck and aft.

What could it mean? And could they really be guineas, those two glittering objects the interloper had held up to his (Billy's) eyes? Where could the fellow get guineas? Why, even buttons, spare buttons, are not so plentiful at sea. The more he turned the matter over, the more he was nonplussed, and made uneasy and discomfited. In his disgustful recoil from an overture which, though he but ill comprehended, he instinctively knew must involve evil of some sort—Billy Budd was like a young horse fresh from the pasture suddenly inhaling a vile whiff from some chemical factory and by repeated snortings trying to get it out of his nostrils and lungs. This frame of mind barred all desire of holding further parley with the fellow, even were it but for the purpose of gaining some enlightenment as to his design in approaching him. And yet he was not without natural curiosity to see how such a visitor in the dark would look in broad day.

He espied him the following afternoon in his first dog-watch below, one of the smokers on that forward part of the upper gun-deck allotted to the pipe. He recognized him by his general cut and build, more than by his round freckled face and glassy eyes of pale blue, veiled with lashes all but white. And yet Billy was a bit uncertain whether indeed it were he—yonder chap about his own age, chatting and laughing in a free-hearted way, leaning against a gun,—a genial young fellow enough to look at, and something of a rattle-brain, to all appearance. Rather chubby, too, for a sailor, even an afterguardsman. In short the last man in the world—one would think—to be overburthened with thoughts, especially those perilous thoughts that must needs belong to a conspirator in any serious project, or even to the underling of such a conspirator.

Although Billy was not aware of it, the fellow, with one sidelong watchful glance had perceived Billy first, and then noting that Billy was looking at him, thereupon nodded a familiar sort of friendly recognition as to an old acquaintance, without interrupting the talk he was engaged in with the group of smokers. A day or two afterwards, chancing in the evening promenade on a gun-deck to pass Billy, he offered a flying word of good-fellowship, as it were, which by its unexpectedness, and equivocalness under the circumstances, so embarrassed Billy that he knew not how to respond to it, and let it go unnoticed.

Billy was now left more at a loss than before. The ineffectual speculations into which he was led were so disturbingly alien to him that he did his best to smother them. It never entered his mind that here was a matter, which, from its extreme questionableness, it was his duty as a loyal blue-jacket to report in the proper quarter. And, probably, had such a step been suggested to him, he would have been deterred from taking it by the thought—one of novice-magnanimity—that it would savour overmuch of the dirty work of a tell-tale. He kept the thing to himself. Yet upon one occasion he could not forbear a little disburthening himself to the old Dansker, tempted thereto perhaps by the influence of a balmy night when the ship lay becalmed; the twain, silent for the most part, sitting together on deck, their heads propped against the bulwarks. But it was only a partial and anonymous account that Billy gave—the unfounded scruples above referred to preventing full disclosure to anybody. Upon hearing Billy's version, the sage Dansker seemed to divine more than he was told; and after a little meditation, during which his wrinkles were pursed as into a point—quite effacing for the time that quizzing expression his face sometimes wore—answered: "Didn't I say so, Baby Budd?"

"Say what?" demanded Billy.

"Why, *Jimmy Legs* is *down* on you."

"And what," rejoined Billy in amazement, "has *Jimmy Legs* to do with that cracked afterguardsman?"

"Ho, it was an afterguardsman, then: a cat's-paw, only a cat's-paw!" And with that exclamation, which, whether it had reference to a light puff of air just then coming over the calm sea, or subtler relation to the afterguardsman, there is no telling. The old Merlin gave a twisting wrench with his black teeth at his plug of tobacco—vouchsafing no reply to Billy's impetuous question, though now repeated, for it was his wont to relapse into grim silence when interrogated in sceptical sort as to any of his sententious oracles, not always very clear ones, but rather partaking of that obscurity which invests most Delphic deliverances from any quarter.

Chapter XIV

Long experience had very likely brought this old man to that bitter prudence which never interferes in aught, and never gives advice.

Yes, despite the Dansker's pithy insistence as to the master-at-arms being at the bottom of these strange experiences of Billy on board the *Indomitable*, the young sailor was ready to ascribe them to almost anybody but the man who, to use Billy's own expression, "always had a pleasant word for him." This is to be wondered at. Yet not so much to be wondered at. In certain matters, some sailors even in mature life, remain unsophisticated enough. But a young seafarer of the disposition of our athletic foretopman is very much of a child-man. And yet a child's utter innocence is but its blank ignorance, and the innocence more or less wanes as intelligence waxes. But in Billy Budd intelligence, such as it was, had advanced, while yet his simple-mindedness remained for the most part unaffected. Experience is a teacher indeed; yet did Billy's years make his experience small. Besides, he had none of that intuitive knowledge of the bad which in natures not good, or incompletely so, foreruns experience, and therefore may pertain, as in some instances it too clearly does pertain, even to youth.

And what could Billy know of man except of man as a mere sailor? And the old-fashioned sailor, the veritable man-before-the-mast—the sailor from boyhood up—he, though indeed of the same species as a landsman, is in some respects singularly distinct from him. The sailor is frankness, the landsman is finesse. Life is not a game with the sailor, demanding the long head; no intricate game of chess where few moves are made in straight forwardness, and ends are attained by indirection; an oblique, tedious, barren game hardly worth that poor candle burnt out in playing it.

Yes, as a class, sailors are in character a juvenile race. Even their deviations are marked by juvenility. And this more especially holding true with the sailors of Billy's time. Then, too, certain things which apply to all sailors, do more pointedly operate here and there upon the junior one. Every sailor, too, is accustomed to obey orders without debating them; his life afloat is externally ruled for him; he is not brought into that promiscuous commerce with mankind where unobstructed free agency on equal terms—equal superficially, at least—soon teaches one that unless upon occasion he exercises a distrust keen in proportion to the fairness of the appearance, some foul turn may be served him. A ruled, undemonstrative distrustfulness is so habitual, not with business-men so much, as with men who know their kind in less shallow relations than business, namely certain men-of-the-world, that they come at last to employ it all but unconsciously; and some of them would very likely feel real surprise at being charged with it as one of their general characteristics.

Chapter XV

But after the little matter at the mess Billy Budd no more found himself in strange trouble at times about his hammock or his clothes-bag, or what not. While, as to that smile that occasionally sunned him, and the pleasant passing word: these were, if not more frequent, yet if anything more pronounced than before.

But for all that, there were certain other demonstrations now. When Claggart's unobserved glance happened to light on belted Billy rolling along the upper gun-deck in the leisure of the second dogwatch, exchanging passing broadsides of fun with other young promenaders in the crowd; that glance would follow the cheerful sea-Hyperion with a settled meditative and melancholy expression—his eyes strangely suffused with incipient feverish tears. Then would Claggart look like the man of sorrows. Yes, and sometimes the melancholy expression would have in it a touch of soft yearning, as if Claggart could even have loved Billy but for fate and ban. But this was an evanescence, and quickly repented of, as it were, by an immitigable look, pinching and shrivelling the visage into the momentary semblance of a wrinkled walnut. But sometimes, catching sight in advance of the foretopman coming in his direction, he would, upon their nearing, step aside a little to let him

pass, dwelling upon Billy for the moment with the glittering dental satire of a Guise. Yet, upon an abrupt unforeseen encounter, a red light would flash forth from his eye, like a spark from an anvil in a dusky smithy. That quick fierce light was a strange one, darted from orbs which in repose were of a colour nearest approaching a deeper violet, the softest of shades.

Though some of these caprices of the pit could not but be observed by their object, yet were they beyond the construing of such a nature. And the thews of Billy were hardly comparable with that sort of sensitive spiritual organization which in some cases instinctively conveys to ignorant innocence an admonition of the proximity of the malign. He thought the master-at-arms acted in a manner rather queer at times. That was all. But the occasional frank air and pleasant word went for what they purported to be—the young sailor never having heard as yet of the "too fair-spoken man."

Had the foretopman been conscious of having done or said anything to provoke the ill will of the official, it would have been different with him, and his sight might have been purged if not sharpened.

So was it with him in yet another matter. Two minor officers, the Armourer, and Captain of the Hold, with whom he had never exchanged a word, his position on the ship not bringing him into contact with them; these men now for the first began to cast upon Billy—when they chanced to encounter him—that peculiar glance which evidences that the man from whom it comes has been some way tampered with, and to the prejudice of him upon whom the glance lights. Never did it occur to Billy as a thing to be noted, or a thing suspicious—though he well knew the fact that the Armourer and Captain of the Hold, with the ship's yeoman, apothecary, and others of that grade, were by naval usage, mess-mates of the master-at-arms; men with ears convenient to his confidential tongue.

But the general popularity of our Handsome Sailor's manly forwardness upon occasion and his irresistible good nature, indicating no mental superiority tending to excite an invidious feeling; this good will on the part of most of his ship-mates made him the less to concern himself about such mute aspects toward him as those whereto allusion has just been made.

As to the afterguardsman, though Billy for reasons already given, necessarily saw little of him, yet when the two did happen to meet, invariably came the fellow's off-hand cheerful recognition, sometimes accompanied by a passing pleasant word or two. Whatever that equivocal young person's original design may really have been, or the design of which he might have been the deputy, certain it was from his manner upon these occasions, that he had wholly dropped it.

It was as if his precocity of crookedness (and every vulgar villain is precocious) had for once deceived him, and the man he had sought to entrap as a simpleton had, through his very simplicity, baffled him.

But shrewd ones may opine that it was hardly possible for Billy to refrain from going up to the afterguardsman and bluntly demanding to know his purpose in the initial interview, so abruptly closed in the fore-chains. Shrewd ones may also think it but natural in Billy to set about sounding some of the other impressed men of the ship in order to discover what basis, if any, there was for the emissary's obscure suggestions as to plotting disaffection aboard. The shrewd may so think. But something more, or rather, something else than mere shrewdness is perhaps needful for the due understanding of such a character as Billy Budd's.

As to Claggart, the monomania in the man—if that indeed it were—as involuntarily disclosed by starts in the manifestations detailed, yet in general covered over by his self-contained and rational demeanour; this, like a subterranean fire, was eating its way deeper and deeper in him. Something decisive must come of it.

Chapter XVI

After the mysterious interview in the fore-chains—the one so abruptly ended there by Billy—nothing especially germane to the story occurred until the events now about to be narrated.

Elsewhere it has been said that owing to the lack of frigates (of course better sailors than line-of-battle ships) in the English squadron up the Straits at that period, the *Indomitable* was oc-

casionally employed not only as an available substitute for a scout, but at times on detached service of more important kind. This was not alone because of her sailing qualities, not common in a ship of her rate, but quite as much, probably, that the character of her commander—it was thought —specially adapted him for any duty where, under unforeseen difficulties, a prompt initiative might have to be taken in some matter demanding knowledge and ability in addition to those qualities employed in good seamanship. It was on an expedition of the latter sort, a somewhat distant one, and when the *Indomitable* was almost at her furthest remove from the fleet, that in the latter part of an afternoon-watch she unexpectedly came in sight of a ship of the enemy. It proved to be a frigate. The latter—perceiving through the glass that the weight of men and metal would be heavily against her—invoking her light heels, crowded on sail to get away. After a chase urged almost against hope—and lasting until about the middle of the first dog-watch—she signally succeeded in effecting her escape.

Not long after the pursuit had been given up, and ere the excitement incident thereto had altogether waned away, the master-at-arms, ascending from his cavernous sphere, made his appearance (cap in hand) by the mainmast: respectfully awaiting the notice of Captain Vere—then solitary walking the weather-side of the quarter-deck—doubtless somewhat chafed at the failure of the pursuit. The spot where Claggart stood was the place allotted to the men of lesser grades when seeking some more particular interview either with the officer-of-the-deck or the Captain himself. But from the latter it was not often that a sailor or petty-officer of those days would seek a hearing; only some exceptional cause, would, according to established custom, have warranted that.

Presently, just as the Commander, absorbed in his reflections, was on the point of turning aft in his promenade, he became sensible of Claggart's presence, and saw the doffed cap held in deferential expectancy. Here be it said that Captain Vere's personal knowledge of this petty-officer had only begun at the time of the ship's last sailing from home, Claggart then for the first, in transfer from a ship detained for repairs, supplying on board the

Indomitable the place of a previous master-at-arms disabled and ashore.

No sooner did the Commander observe who it was that now so deferentially stood awaiting his notice, than a peculiar expression came over him. It was not unlike that which uncontrollably will flit across the countenance of one at unawares encountering a person, who, though known to him, indeed, has hardly been long enough known for thorough knowledge, but something in whose aspect nevertheless now, for the first time, provokes a vaguely repellent distaste. Coming to a stand and resuming much of his wonted official manner, save that a sort of impatience lurked in the intonation of the opening word, he said, "Well? what is it, master-at-arms?"

With the air of a subordinate grieved at the necessity of being a messenger of ill tidings, and while conscientiously determined to be frank, yet equally resolved upon shunning overstatement, Claggart at this invitation, or rather summons to disburthen, spoke up. What he said, conveyed in the language of no uneducated man, was to the effect following if not altogether in these words, namely, that during the chase and preparations for the possible encounter he had seen enough to convince him that at least one sailor aboard was a dangerous character in a ship mustering some who not only had taken a guilty part in the late serious trouble, but others also who, like the man in question, had entered His Majesty's service under another form than enlistment.

At this point Captain Vere, with some impatience, interrupted him:

"Be direct, man; say impressed men."

Claggart made a gesture of subservience and proceeded. Quite lately he (Claggart) had begun to suspect that some sort of movement prompted by the sailor in question was covertly going on, but he had not thought himself warranted in reporting the suspicion so long as it remained indistinct. But from what he had that afternoon observed in the man referred to, the suspicion of something clandestine going on had advanced to a point less removed from certainty. He deeply felt—he added—the serious responsibility assumed in making a report involving such possible consequences to the individual mainly concerned, besides tending to augment those natural anxieties which every naval commander must feel in view of the extraordinary outbreak so recent as those which, he sorrowfully said it, it needed not to name.

Now at the first broaching of the matter Captain Vere, taken by surprise, could not wholly dissemble his disquietude, but as Claggart went on, the former's aspect changed into restiveness under something in the testifier's manner in giving his testimony. However, he refrained from interrupting him. And Claggart, continuing, concluded with this:

"God forbid, your honour, that the *Indomitable's* should be the experience of the—"

"Never mind that!" here peremptorily broke in the superior, his face altering with anger instantly, divining the ship that the other was about to name, one in which the Nore Mutiny had assumed a singularly tragical character that for a time jeopardized the life of its Commander. Under the circumstances he was indignant at the purposed allusion. When the commissioned officers themselves were on all occasions very heedful how they referred to the recent events,—for a petty-officer unnecessarily to allude to them in the presence of his Captain, this struck him as a most immodest presumption. Besides, to his quick sense of self-respect, it even looked under the circumstances something like an attempt to alarm him. Nor at that was he without some surprise that one who, so far as he had hitherto come under his notice, had shown considerable tact in his function, should in this particular evince such lack of it.

But these thoughts and kindred dubious ones flitting across his mind were suddenly replaced by an intuitional surmise, which though as yet obscure in form, served practically to affect his reception of the ill tidings. Certain it is that, long versed in everything pertaining to the complicated gun-deck life (which like every other form of life has its secret mines and dubious side; the side popularly disclaimed), Captain Vere did not permit himself to be unduly disturbed by the general tenor of his subordinate's report. Furthermore, if in view of recent events prompt action should be taken at the first palpable sign of recurring insubordination —for all that, not judicious would it be, he thought, to keep the idea of lingering disaffection alive by undue forwardness in crediting an informer, even if his own subordinate, and charged with police surveillance of the crew. This feeling would not perhaps have so prevailed with him were it not that upon a prior occasion the patriotic zeal officially evinced by Claggart had somewhat irritated him as appearing rather supersensible and strained. Furthermore, something even in the official's self-possessed and somewhat ostentatious manner in making his specifications strangely reminded him of a bandsman, a perjured witness in a capital case before a court-martial ashore of which when a lieutenant he, Captain Vere, had been a member.

Now the peremptory check given to Claggart in the matter of the arrested allusion was quickly followed up by this: "You say that there is at least one dangerous man aboard. Name him."

"William Budd, a foretopman, your honour—"

"William Budd," repeated Captain Vere with unfeigned astonishment, "and mean you the man our Lieutenant Ratcliffe took from the merchant-man not very long ago—the young fellow who seems to be so popular with the men—Billy, the Handsome Sailor, as they call him?"

"The same, your honour; but for all his youth and good looks, a deep one. Not for nothing does he insinuate himself into the good will of his ship-mates, since at the least they will at a pinch say a good word for him at all hazards. Did Lieutenant Ratcliffe happen to tell your honour of that adroit fling of Budd's jumping up in the Cutter's bow under the merchantman's stern when he was being taken off? It is even masqued by that sort of good-humoured air that at heart he resents his impress-ment. You have but noted his fair cheek. A man-trap may be under his fine ruddy-tipped daisies."

Now the *Handsome Sailor*, as a signal figure among the crew, had naturally enough attracted the Captain's attention from the first. Though in general not very demonstrative to his officers, he had congratulated Lieutenant Ratcliffe upon his good fortune in lighting on such a fine specimen of the *genus homo* who, in the nude, might have posed for a statue of young Adam before the fall.

As to Billy's adieu to the ship *Rights-of-Man*, which the boarding lieutenant had indeed re-ported to him,—but in a deferential way—more as a good story than aught else,—Captain Vere, though mistakenly understanding it as a satiric sally, had but thought so much the better of the impressed man for it; as a military sailor, admiring the spirit that could take an arbitrary enlistment so merrily and sensibly. The foretopman's con-duct, too, so far as it had fallen under the Cap-tain's notice had confirmed the first happy augury, while the new recruit's qualities as a sailor-man seemed to be such that he had thought of recom-mending him to the executive officer for promo-tion to a place that would more frequently bring him under his own observation, namely, the cap-taincy of the mizzen-top, replacing there in the star-board watch a man not so young whom partly for that reason he deemed less fitted for the post. Be it parenthesized here that since the mizzen-topmen have not to handle such breadths of heavy canvas as the lower sailors on the main-mast and fore-mast, a young man if of the right stuff not only seems best adapted to duty there, but, in fact, is generally selected for the captaincy of that top, and the company under him are light hands, and often but striplings. In sum, Captain Vere had from the beginning deemed Billy Budd to be what in the naval parlance of the times was called a *"King's bargain,"* that is to say, for His Britannic Majesty's navy a capital investment at small out-lay or none at all.

After a brief pause—during which the reminis-cences above mentioned passed vividly through his mind—he weighed the import of Claggart's last suggestion, conveyed in the phrase, "pitfall under the clover," and the more he weighed it the less reliance he felt in the informer's good faith. Suddenly he turned upon him: "Do you come to me, master-at-arms, with so foggy a tale? As to Budd, cite me an act or spoken word of his confirmatory of what you here in general charge against him. Stay," drawing nearer to him, "heed what you speak. Just now and in a case like this, there is a yard-arm-end for the false-witness."

"Ah, your honour!" sighed Claggart, mildly shaking his shapely head as in sad deprecation of such unmerited severity of tone. Then bridling—erecting himself as in virtuous self-assertion, he circumstantially alleged certain words and acts which collectively, if credited, led to presump-tions mortally inculpating Budd, and for some of these averments, he added, substantiating proof was not far.

With gray eyes now impatient and distrustful, essaying to fathom to the bottom Claggart's calm violet ones, Captain Vere again heard him out; then for the moment stood ruminating. The mood he evinced, Claggart—himself for the time liberated from the other's scrutiny—steadily regarded with a look difficult to render,—a look curious of the operation of his tactics, a look such as might have been that of the spokesman of the envious children of Jacob deceptively imposing upon the troubled patriarch the blood-dyed coat of young Joseph.

Though something exceptional in the moral quality of Captain Vere made him, in earnest encounter with a fellow-man, a veritable touchstone of that man's essential nature, yet now as to Claggart and what was really going on in him his feeling partook less of intuitional conviction than of strong suspicion clogged by strange dubieties. The perplexity he evinced proceeded less from aught touching the man informed against—as Claggart doubtless opined—than from considerations how best to act in regard to the informer. At first, indeed, he was naturally for summoning that substantiation of his allegations which Claggart said was at hand. But such a proceeding would result in the matter at once getting abroad—which—in the present stage of it, he thought, might undesirably affect the ship's company. If Claggart was a false witness,—that closed the affair. And therefore, before trying the accusation, he would first practically test the accuser; and he thought this could be done in a quiet undemonstrative way.

The measure he determined upon involved a shifting of the scene—a transfer to a place less exposed to observation than the broad quarter-deck. For although the few gun-room officers there at the time had, in due observance of naval etiquette, withdrawn to leeward the moment Captain Vere had begun his promenade on the deck's weatherside; and though during the colloquy with Claggart they of course ventured not to diminish the distance; and though throughout the interview Captain Vere's voice was far from high, and Claggart's silvery and low; and the wind in the cord-

age and the wash of the sea helped the more to put them beyond ear-shot; nevertheless, the interview's continuance already had attracted observation from some topmen aloft, and other sailors in the waist or further forward.

Having now determined upon his measures, Captain Vere forthwith took action. Abruptly turning to Claggart he asked, "Master-at-arms, is it now Budd's watch aloft?"

"No, your honour." Whereupon — "Mr. Wilkes," summoning the nearest midshipman, "tell Albert to come to me." Albert was the Captain's hammock-boy, a sort of sea-valet in whose discretion and fidelity his master had much confidence. The lad appeared. "You know Budd the foretopman?"

"I do, Sir."

"Go find him. It is his watch off. Manage to tell him out of earshot that he is wanted aft. Contrive it that he speaks to nobody. Keep him in talk yourself. And not till you get well aft here, not till then, let him know that the place where he is wanted is my cabin. You understand? Go.— Master-at-arms, show yourself on the decks below, and when you think it time for Albert to be coming with his man, stand by quietly to follow the sailor in."

Chapter XVII

Now when the foretopman found himself closeted, as it were, in the cabin with the Captain and Claggart, he was surprised enough. But it was a surprise unaccompanied by apprehension or distrust. To an immature nature, essentially honest and humane, forewarning intimations of subtler danger from one's kind come tardily, if at all. The only thing that took shape in the young sailor's mind was this: "Yes, the Captain, I have always thought, looks kindly upon me. I wonder if he's going to make me his coxswain. I should like that. And maybe now he is going to ask the master-at-arms about me."

"Shut the door there, sentry," said the commander. "Stand without and let nobody come in. —Now, master-at-arms, tell this man to his face what you told of him to me;" and stood prepared to scrutinize the mutually confronting visages.

With the measured step and calm collected air

of an asylum physician approaching in the public hall some patient beginning to show indications of a coming paroxysm, Claggart deliberately advanced within short range of Billy, and mesmerically looking him in the eye, briefly recapitulated the accusation.

Not at first did Billy take it in. When he did the rose-tan of his cheek looked struck as by white leprosy. He stood like one impaled and gagged. Meanwhile the accuser's eyes, removing not as yet from the blue, dilated ones, underwent a phenomenal change, their wonted rich violet colour blurring into a muddy purple. Those lights of human intelligence losing human expression, gelidly protruding like the alien eyes of certain uncatalogued creatures of the deep.

The first mesmeric glance was one of surprised fascination; the last was the hungry lurch of the torpedo-fish.

"Speak, man!" said Captain Vere to the transfixed one, struck by his aspect even more than by Claggart's, "Speak! defend yourself." Which appeal caused but a strange, dumb gesturing and gurgling in Billy; amazement at such an accusation so suddenly sprung on inexperienced nonage; this, and it may be horror at the accuser, serving to bring out his lurking defect, and in this instance for the time intensifying it into a convulsed tongue-tie; while the intent head and entire form straining forward in an agony of ineffectual eagerness to obey the injunction to speak and defend himself, gave an expression to the face like that of a condemned vestal priestess in the moment of her being buried alive, and in the first struggle against suffocation.

Though at the time Captain Vere was quite ignorant of Billy's liability to vocal impediment, he now immediately divined it, since vividly Billy's aspect recalled to him that of a bright young schoolmate of his whom he had seen struck by much the same startling impotence in the act of eagerly rising in the class to be foremost in response to a testing question put to it by the master. Going close up to the young sailor, and laying a soothing hand on his shoulder, he said, "There is no hurry, my boy. Take your time, take your time." Contrary to the effect intended, these words, so fatherly in tone, doubtless touching

Billy's heart to the quick, prompted yet more violent efforts at utterance—efforts soon ending for the time in confirming the paralysis, and bringing to the face an expression which was as a crucifixion to behold. The next instant, quick as the flame from a discharged cannon at night—his right arm shot out and Claggart dropped to the deck. Whether intentionally, or but owing to the young athlete's superior height, the blow had taken effect full upon the forehead, so shapely and intellectual-looking a feature in the master-at-arms, so that the body fell over lengthwise, like a heavy plank tilted from erectness. A gasp or two and he lay motionless.

"Fated boy," breathed Captain Vere in a tone so low as to be almost a whisper, "what have you done! But here, help me."

The twain raised the felled one from the loins up into a sitting position. The spare form flexibly acquiesced, but inertly. It was like handling a dead snake. They lowered it back. Regaining erectness, Captain Vere with one hand covering his face stood to all appearance as impassive as to the object at his feet. Was he absorbed in taking in all the bearings of the event, and what was best not only now at once to be done, but also in the sequel? Slowly he uncovered his face; forthwith the effect was as if the moon, emerging from eclipse, should reappear with quite another aspect than that which had gone into hiding. The father in him, manifested towards Billy thus far in the scene, was replaced by the military disciplinarian. In his official tone he bade the foretopman retire to a state-room aft (pointing it out), and there remain till thence summoned. This order Billy in silence mechanically obeyed. Then, going to the cabin door where it opened on the quarter-deck, Captain Vere said to the sentry without, "Tell somebody to send Albert here." When the lad appeared his master so contrived it that he should not catch sight of the prone one. "Albert," he said to him, "tell the surgeon I wish to see him. You need not come back till called."

When the surgeon entered—a self-poised character of that grave sense and experience that hardly anything could take him aback—Captain Vere advanced to meet him, thus unconsciously interrupting his view of Claggart and interrupting the other's wonted ceremonious salutation, said, "Nay, tell me how it is with yonder man," directing his attention to the prostrate one.

The surgeon looked, and for all his self-command, somewhat started at the abrupt revelation. On Claggart's always pallid complexion, thick black blood was now oozing from mouth and ear. To the gazer's professional eyes it was unmistakably no living man that he saw.

"Is it so, then?" said Captain Vere intently 10 watching him. "I thought it. But verify it." Whereupon the customary tests confirmed the surgeon's first glance, who now looking up in unfeigned concern, cast a look of intense inquisitiveness upon his superior. But Captain Vere, with one hand to his brow, was standing motionless. Suddenly, catching the surgeon's arm convulsively, he exclaimed, pointing down to the body,—"It is the divine judgment of Ananias! Look!"

Disturbed by the excited manner he had never 20 before observed in the *Indomitable's* Captain, and as yet wholly ignorant of the affair, the prudent surgeon nevertheless held his peace, only again looking an earnest interrogation as to what it was that had resulted in such a tragedy.

But Captain Vere was now again motionless, standing absorbed in thought. Once again starting, he vehemently exclaimed—"Struck dead by an angel of God. Yet the angel must hang!"

At these interjections, incoherences to the 30 listener as yet unapprised of the antecedent events, the surgeon was profoundly discomfited. But now, as recollecting himself, Captain Vere in less harsh tone briefly related the circumstances leading up to the event.

"But come; we must despatch," he added, "help me to remove him (meaning the body) to yonder compartment"—designating one opposite where the foretopman remained immured. Anew disturbed by a request that, as implying a desire 40 for secrecy, seemed unaccountably strange to him, there was nothing for the subordinate to do but comply.

"Go now," said Captain Vere, with something of his wonted manner. "Go now. I shall presently call a drum-head court. Tell the lieutenants what has happened, and tell Mr. Morton"—meaning

Ananias: Ananias (Acts, 5) lied unto God, and fell dead.

the captain of marines. "And charge them to keep the matter to themselves."

Full of disquietude and misgivings, the surgeon left the cabin. Was Captain Vere suddenly affected in his mind, or was it but a transient excitement brought about by so strange and extraordinary a happening? As to the drum-head court, it struck the surgeon as impolitic, if nothing more. The thing to do, he thought, was to place Billy Budd in confinement, and in a way dictated by usage, and postpone further action in so extraordinary a case to such time as they should again join the squadron, and then transfer it to the Admiral. He recalled the unwonted agitation of Captain Vere and his exciting exclamations so at variance with his normal manner. Was he unhinged? But assuming that he was, it were not so susceptible of proof. What then could he do? No worse trying situation is conceivable than that of an officer subordinated under a Captain whom he suspects to be, not mad indeed, but yet not quite unaffected in his intellect. To argue his order to him would be insolence. To resist him would be mutiny. In obedience to Captain Vere he communicated to the lieutenants and captain of marines what had happened; saying nothing as to the Captain's state. They stared at him in surprise and concern. Like him they seemed to think that such a matter should be reported to the 30 Admiral.

Who in the rainbow can draw the line where the violet tint ends and the orange tint begins? Distinctly we see the difference of the colour, but where exactly does the first one visibly enter into the other? So with sanity and insanity. In pronounced cases there is no question about them. But in some cases, in various degrees supposedly less pronounced, to draw the line of demarkation few will undertake, though for a fee some professional experts will. There is nothing namable but that some men will undertake to do for pay. In other words, there are instances where it is next to impossible to determine whether a man is sane or beginning to be otherwise.

Whether Captain Vere, as the surgeon professionally surmised, was really the sudden victim of any degree of aberration, one must determine for himself by such light as this narrative may afford.

Chapter XVIII

The unhappy event which has been narrated could not have happened at a worse juncture. For it was close on the heel of the suppressed insurrections, an after-time very critical to naval authority, demanding from every English sea-commander two qualities not readily interfusable—prudence and rigour. Moreover, there was something crucial in the case.

In the jugglery of circumstances preceding and attending the event on board the *Indomitable* and in the light of that martial code whereby it was formally to be judged, innocence and guilt, personified in Claggart and Budd, in effect changed places.

In the legal view the apparent victim of the tragedy was he who had sought to victimize a man blameless; and the indisputable deed of the latter, navally regarded, constituted the most heinous of military crimes. Yet more. The essential right and wrong involved in the matter, the clearer that might be, so much the worse for the responsibility of a loyal sea-commander, inasmuch as he was authorized to determine the matter on that primitive legal basis.

Small wonder then that the *Indomitable's* Captain, though in general a man of rigid decision, felt that circumspectness not less than promptitude was necessary. Until he could decide upon his course, and in each detail; and not only so, but until the concluding measure was upon the point of being enacted, he deemed it advisable, in view of all the circumstances, to guard as much as possible against publicity. Here he may or may not have erred. Certain it is, however, that subsequently in the confidential talk of more than one or two gun-rooms and cabins he was not a little criticized by some officers, a fact imputed by his friends, and vehemently by his cousin Jack Denton, to professional jealousy of Starry Vere. Some imaginative ground for invidious comment there was. The maintenance of secrecy in the matter, the confining all knowledge of it for a time to the place where the homicide occurred—the quarter-deck cabin; in these particulars lurked some resemblance to the policy adopted in those tragedies of the palace which have occurred more than once

in the capital founded by Peter the Barbarian, great chiefly by his crimes.

The case was such that fain would the *Indomitable's* Captain have deferred taking any action whatever respecting it further than to keep the foretopman a close prisoner till the ship rejoined the squadron, and then submitting the matter to the judgment of his Admiral.

But a true military officer is, in one particular, like a true monk. Not with more of self-abnegation will the latter keep his vows of monastic obedience than the former his vows of allegiance to martial duty.

Feeling that unless quick action were taken on it, the deed of the foretopman, as soon as it should be known on the gun-decks, would tend to awaken any slumbering embers of the Nore among the crews—a sense of the urgency of the case overruled in Captain Vere all other considerations. But though a conscientious disciplinarian, he was no lover of authority for mere authority's sake. Very far was he from embracing opportunities for monopolizing to himself the perils of moral responsibility, none at least that could properly be referred to an official superior, or shared with him by his official equals or even subordinates. So thinking, he was glad it would not be at variance with usage to turn the matter over to a summary court of his own officers, reserving to himself, as the one on whom the ultimate accountability would rest, the right of maintaining a supervision of it, or formally or informally interposing at need. Accordingly a drum-head court was summarily convened, he electing the individuals composing it, the First Lieutenant, the Captain of Marines, and the Sailing Master.

In associating an officer of marines with the sea-lieutenants in a case having to do with a sailor, the Commander perhaps deviated from general custom. He was prompted thereto by the circumstances that he took that soldier to be a judicious person, thoughtful and not altogether incapable of gripping with a difficult case unprecedented in his prior experience. Yet even as to him he was not without some latent misgiving, for withal he was an extremely good-natured man, an enjoyer of his dinner, a sound sleeper, and inclined to obesity. The sort of man who, though he would always maintain his manhood in battle, might not prove altogether reliable in a moral dilemma involving aught of the tragic. As to the First Lieutenant and the Sailing Master, Captain Vere could not but be aware that though honest natures, of approved gallantry upon occasion, their intelligence was mostly confined to the matter of active seamanship, and the fighting demands of their profession. The court was held in the same cabin where the unfortunate affair had taken place. This cabin, the Commander's, embraced the entire area under the poop-deck. Aft, and on either side, was a small state-room—the one room temporarily a jail, and the other a dead-house—and a yet smaller compartment leaving a space between, expanding forward into a goodly oblong of length coinciding with the ship's beam. A sky-light of moderate dimension was overhead, and at each end of the oblong space were two sashed port-hole windows, easily convertible back into embrasures for short carronades.

All being quickly in readiness, Billy Budd was arraigned, Captain Vere necessarily appearing as the sole witness in the case, and as such temporarily sinking his rank, though singularly maintaining it in a matter apparently trivial, namely, that he testified from the ship's weather-side, with that object having caused the court to sit on the lee-side. Concisely he narrated all that had led up to the catastrophe, omitting nothing in Claggart's accusation and deposing as to the manner in which the prisoner had received it. At this testimony the three officers glanced with no little surprise at Billy Budd, the last man they would have suspected, either of mutinous design alleged by Claggart, or of the undeniable deed he himself had done. The First Lieutenant, taking judicial primacy and turning towards the prisoner, said, "Captain Vere has spoken. Is it or is it not as Captain Vere says?" In response came syllables not so much impeded in the utterance as might have been anticipated. They were these:

"Captain Vere tells the truth. It is just as Captain Vere says, but it is not as the master-at-arms said. I have eaten the King's bread and I am true to the King."

"I believe you, my man," said the witness, his voice indicating a suppressed emotion not otherwise betrayed.

"God will bless you for that, your honour!" not without stammering said Billy, and all but broke down. But immediately was recalled to self-control by another question, with which the same emotional difficulty of utterance came: "No, there was no malice between us. I never bore malice against the master-at-arms. I am sorry that he is dead. I did not mean to kill him. Could I have used my tongue I would not have struck him. But he foully lied to my face, and in the presence of my Captain, and I had to say something, and I could only say it with a blow. God help me!"

In the impulsive above-board manner of the frank one the court saw confirmed all that was implied in words which just previously had perplexed them, coming as they did from the testifier to the tragedy, and promptly following Billy's impassioned disclaimer of mutinous intent—Captain Vere's words, "I believe you, my man."

Next it was asked of him whether he knew of or suspected aught savouring of incipient trouble (meaning a mutiny, though the explicit term was avoided) going on in any section of the ship's company.

The reply lingered. This was naturally imputed by the court to the same vocal embarrassment which had retarded or obstructed previous answers. But in main it was otherwise here; the question immediately recalling to Billy's mind the interview with the after-guardsman in the fore-chains. But an innate repugnance to playing a part at all approaching that of an informer against one's own shipmates—the same erring sense of uninstructed honour which had stood in the way of his reporting the matter at the time; though as a loyal man-of-war's man it was incumbent on him and failure so to do, charged against him and proven, would have subjected him to the heaviest of penalties—this, with the blind feeling now his, that nothing really was being hatched, prevailed with him. When the answer came it was a negative.

"One question more," said the officer of marines now first speaking and with a troubled earnestness. "You tell us that what the master-at-arms said against you was a lie. Now why should he have so lied, so maliciously lied, since you declare there was no malice between you?"

At that question, unintentionally touching on a spiritual sphere wholly obscure to Billy's thoughts, he was nonplussed, evincing a confusion indeed that some observers, such as can be imagined, would have construed into involuntary evidence of hidden guilt. Nevertheless he strove some way to answer, but all at once relinquished the vain endeavour; at the same time turning an appealing glance towards Captain Vere as deeming him his best helper and friend. Captain Vere, who had been seated for a time, rose to his feet, addressing the interrogator. "The question you put to him comes naturally enough. But can he rightly answer it?—or anybody else? unless indeed it be he who lies within there," designating the compartment where lay the corpse. "But the prone one there will not rise to our summons. In effect though, as it seems to me, the point you make is hardly material. Quite aside from any conceivable motive actuating the master-at-arms, and irrespective of the provocation of the blow, a martial court must needs in the present case confine its attention to the blow's consequence, which consequence is to be deemed not otherwise than as the striker's deed!"

This utterance, the full significance of which it was not at all likely that Billy took in, nevertheless caused him to turn a wistful, interrogative look towards the speaker, a look in its dumb expressiveness not unlike that which a dog of generous breed might turn upon his master, seeking in his face some elucidation of a previous gesture ambiguous to the canine intelligence. Nor was the same utterance without marked effect upon the three officers, more especially the soldier. Couched in it seemed to them a meaning unanticipated, involving a prejudgment on the speaker's part. It served to augment a mental disturbance previously evident enough.

The soldier once more spoke, in a tone of suggestive dubiety addressing at once his associates and Captain Vere: "Nobody is present—none of the ship's company, I mean, who might shed lateral light, if any is to be had, upon what remains mysterious in this matter."

"That is thoughtfully put," said Captain Vere; "I see your drift. Ay, there is a mystery; but to use a Scriptural phrase, it is 'a mystery of iniquity,' a matter for only psychologic theologians to dis-

cuss. But what has a military court to do with it? Not to add that for us any possible investigation of it is cut off by the lasting tongue-tie of him in yonder," again designating the mortuary stateroom. "The prisoner's deed. With that alone we have to do."

To this, and particularly the closing reiteration, the marine soldier, knowing not how aptly to reply, sadly abstained from saying aught. The First Lieutenant, who at the outset had not unnaturally assumed primacy in the court, now overrulingly instructed by a glance from Captain Vere (a glance more effective than words), resumed that primacy. Turning to the prisoner: "Budd," he said, and scarce in equable tones, "Budd, if you have aught further to say for yourself, say it now."

Upon this the young sailor turned another quick glance towards Captain Vere; then, as taking a hint from that aspect, a hint confirming his own instinct that silence was now best, replied to the Lieutenant, "I have said all, Sir."

The marine—the same who had been the sentinel without the cabin-door at the time that the foretopman, followed by the master-at-arms, entered it—he, standing by the sailor throughout their judicial proceedings, was now directed to take him back to the after compartment originally assigned to the prisoner and his custodian. As the twain disappeared from view, the three officers, as partially liberated from some inward constraint associated with Billy's mere presence—simultaneously stirred in their seats. They exchanged looks of troubled indecision, yet feeling that decide they must, and without long delay; for Captain Vere was for the time sitting unconsciously with his back towards them, apparently in one of his absent fits, gazing out from a sashed port-hole to windward upon the monotonous blank of the twilight sea. But the court's silence continuing, broken only at moments by brief consultations in low earnest tones, this seemed to assure him and encourage him. Turning, he to-and-fro paced the cabin athwart; in the returning ascent to windward, climbing the slant deck in the ship's lee roll; without knowing it symbolizing thus in his action a mind resolute to surmount difficulties even if against primitive instincts strong as the wind and the sea. Presently he came to a stand before the three. After scanning their faces he stood less as mustering his thoughts for expression, than as one inly deliberating how best to put them to well-meaning men not intellectually mature—men with whom it was necessary to demonstrate certain principles that were axioms to himself. Similar impatience as to talking is perhaps one reason that deters some minds from addressing any popular assemblies; under which head is to be classed most legislatures in a Democracy.

When speak he did, something both in the substance of what he said and his manner of saying it, showed the influence of unshared studies modifying and tempering the practical training of an active career. This, along with his phraseology now and then, was suggestive of the grounds whereon rested that imputation of a certain pedantry socially alleged against him by certain naval men of wholly practical cast, captains who nevertheless would frankly concede that His Majesty's Navy mustered no more efficient officers of their grade than "*Starry Vere.*"

What he said was to this effect: "Hitherto I have been but the witness, little more; and I should hardly think now to take another tone, that of your coadjutor, for the time, did I not perceive in you—at the crisis too—a troubled hesitancy, proceeding, I doubt not, from the clashing of military duty with moral scruple—scruple vitalized by compassion. For the compassion, how can I otherwise than share it. But, mindful of paramount obligation, I strive against scruples that may tend to enervate decision. Not, gentlemen, that I hide from myself that the case is an exceptional one. Speculatively regarded, it well might be referred to a jury of casuists. But for us here, acting not as casuists or moralists, it is a case practical and under martial law practically to be dealt with.

"But your scruples: do they move as in a dusk? Challenge them. Make them advance and declare themselves. Come now: do they import something like this: If, mindless of palliating circumstances, we are bound to regard the death of the master-at-arms as the prisoner's deed, then does that deed constitute a capital crime whereof the penalty is a mortal one? But in natural justice is nothing but the prisoner's overt act to be considered? Now can we adjudge to summary and shameful death a fellow-creature innocent before God, and whom we feel to be so?—Does that state it aright? You sign sad assent. Well, I too feel that, the full force of that. It is Nature. But do these buttons that we wear attest that our allegiance is to Nature? No, to the King. Though the ocean, which is inviolate Nature primeval, though this be the element where we move and have our being as sailors, yet as the King's officers lies our duty in a sphere correspondingly natural? So little is that true, that in receiving our commissions we in the most important regards ceased to be natural free-agents. When war is declared, are we the commissioned fighters previously consulted? We fight at command. If our judgments approve the war, that is but coincidence. So in other particulars. So now, would it be so much we ourselves that would condemn as it would be martial law operating through us? For that law and the rigour of it, we are not responsible. Our vowed responsibility is in this: That however pitilessly that law may operate, we nevertheless adhere to it and administer it.

"But the exceptional in the matter moves the heart within you. Even so, too, is mine moved. But let not warm hearts betray heads that should be cool. Ashore in a criminal case will an upright judge allow himself when off the bench to be waylaid by some tender kinswoman of the accused seeking to touch him with her tearful plea? Well, the heart here is as that piteous woman. The heart is the feminine in man, and hard though it be, she must here be ruled out."

He paused, earnestly studying them for a moment; then resumed.

"But something in your aspect seems to urge that it is not solely that heart that moves in you, but also the conscience, the private conscience. Then, tell me whether or not, occupying the position we do, private conscience should not yield to that imperial one formulated in the code under which alone we officially proceed?"

Here the three men moved in their seats, less convinced than agitated by the course of an argument troubling but the more the spontaneous conflict within. Perceiving which, the speaker paused for a moment; then abruptly changing his tone, went on:

"To steady us a bit, let us recur to the facts.—In war-time at sea a man-of-war's man strikes his superior in grade, and the blow kills. Apart from its effect, the blow itself is, according to the Articles of War, a capital crime. Furthermore—"

"Ay, Sir," emotionally broke in the officer of marines, "in one sense it was. But surely Budd proposed neither mutiny nor homicide."

"Surely not, my good man. And before a court less arbitrary and more merciful than a martial one that plea would largely extenuate. At the Last Assizes it shall acquit. But how here? We proceed under the law of the Mutiny Act. In feature no child can resemble his father more than that Act resembles in spirit the thing from which it derives—War. In His Majesty's service—in this ship indeed—there are Englishmen forced to fight for the King against their will. Against their conscience, for aught we know. Though as their fellow-creatures some of us may appreciate their position, yet as Navy officers, what reck we of it? Still less recks the enemy. Our impressed men he would fain cut down in the same swath with our volunteers. As regards the enemy's naval conscripts, some of whom may even share our own abhorrence of the regicidal French Directory, it is the same on our side. War looks but to the frontage, the appearance. And the Mutiny Act, War's child, takes after the father. Budd's intent or non-intent is nothing to the purpose.

"But while, put to it by those anxieties in you which I cannot but respect, I only repeat myself—while thus strangely we prolong proceedings that should be summary, the enemy may be sighted and an engagement result. We must do; and one of two things must we do—condemn or let go."

"Can we not convict and yet mitigate the penalty?" asked the junior Lieutenant here speaking, and falteringly, for the first time.

"Lieutenant, were that clearly lawful for us under the circumstances, consider the consequences of such clemency. The people" (meaning the ship's company) "have native sense; most of them are familiar with our naval usage and tradition; and how would they take it? Even could you explain to them—which our official position forbids—they, long moulded by arbitrary discipline, have not that kind of intelligent responsiveness that might qualify them to comprehend and discriminate. No, to the people the foretopman's deed, however it be worded in the announcement, will be plain homicide committed in a flagrant act of mutiny. What penalty for that should follow, they know. But it does not follow. *Why?* they will ruminate. You know what sailors are. Will they not revert to the recent outbreak at the Nore? Ay, they know the well-founded alarm—the panic it struck throughout England. Your clement sentence they would account pusillanimous. They would think that we flinch, that we are afraid of them—afraid of practising a lawful rigour singularly demanded at this juncture lest it should provoke new troubles. What shame to us such a conjecture on their part, and how deadly to discipline. You see then whither, prompted by duty and the law, I steadfastly drive. But I beseech you, my friends, do not take me amiss. I feel as you do for this unfortunate boy. But did he know our hearts, I take him to be of that generous nature that he would feel even for us on whom in this military necessity so heavy a compulsion is laid."

With that, crossing the deck, he resumed his place by the sashed port-hole, tacitly leaving the three to come to a decision. On the cabin's opposite side the troubled court sat silent. Loyal lieges, plain and practical, though at bottom they dissented from some points Captain Vere had put to them, they were without the faculty, hardly had the inclination to gainsay one whom they felt to be an earnest man—one, too, not less their superior in mind than in naval rank. But it is not improbable that even such of his words as were not without influence over them, less came home to them than his closing appeal to their instinct as sea-officers, in the forethought he threw out as to the practical consequences to discipline (considering the unconfirmed tone of the fleet at the time)—should a man-of-war's man's violent killing at sea of a superior in grade be allowed to pass for aught else than a capital crime, demanding prompt infliction of the penalty.

Not unlikely they were brought to something more or less akin to that harassed frame of mind which in the year 1842 actuated the commander of the U.S. brig-of-war *Somers* to resolve (under the so-called Articles of War—Articles modelled upon the English Mutiny Act) to resolve upon the execution at sea of a midshipman and two petty-officers as mutineers designing the seizure of the brig. Which resolution was carried out, though in a time of peace and within not many days' sail of home. An act vindicated by a naval court of inquiry subsequently convened ashore—history, and here cited without comment. True, the circumstances on board the *Somers* were different 10 from those on board the *Indomitable*. But the urgency felt, well-warranted or otherwise, was much the same.

Says a writer whom few know, "Forty years after a battle it is easy for a non-combatant to reason about how it ought to have been fought. It is another thing personally and under fire to direct the fighting while involved in the obscuring smoke of it. Much so with respect to other emergencies involving considerations both practical 20 and moral, and when it is imperative promptly to act. The greater the fog, the more it imperils the steamer, and speed is put on though at the hazard of running somebody down. Little ween the snug card-players in the cabin of the responsibilities of the sleepless man on the bridge."

In brief, Billy Budd was formally convicted and sentenced to be hung at the yard-arm in the early morning-watch, it being now night. Otherwise, as is customary in such cases, the sentence 30 would forthwith have been carried out. In wartime on the field or in the fleet, a mortal punishment decreed by a drum-head court—on the field sometimes decreed by but a nod from the General —follows without a delay on the heel of conviction without appeal.

Chapter XIX

It was Captain Vere himself who, of his own motion, communicated the finding of the court 40 to the prisoner; for that purpose going to the compartment where he was in custody, and bidding the marine there to withdraw for the time.

Beyond the communication of the sentence, what took place at this interview was never known. But, in view of the character of the twain briefly closeted in that state-room, each radically sharing in the rarer qualities of one nature—so rare, in-deed, as to be all but incredible to average minds however much cultivated—some conjectures may be ventured.

It would have been in consonance with the spirit of our Captain Vere should he on this occasion have concealed nothing from the condemned one—should he indeed have frankly disclosed to him the part he himself had played in bringing about the decision, at the same time revealing his actuating motives. On Billy's side it is not improbable that such a confession would have been received in much the same spirit that prompted it. Not without a sort of joy indeed he might have appreciated the brave opinion of him implied in his Captain making such a confidant of him. Nor as to the sentence itself could he have been insensible that it was imparted to him as to one not afraid to die. Even more may have been. Captain Vere in the end may have developed the passion sometimes latent under an exterior stoical or indifferent. He was old enough to have been Billy's father. The austere devotee of military duty, letting himself melt back into what remains primeval in our formalized humanity, may in the end have caught Billy to heart, even as Abraham may have caught young Isaac on the brink of resolutely offering him up in obedience to the exacting behest. But there is no telling the sacrament— seldom if in any case revealed to the gadding world —wherever under circumstances at all akin to those here attempted to be set forth, two of great Nature's nobler order embrace. There is privacy at the time, inviolable to the survivor, and holy oblivion (the sequel to each diviner magnanimity) providentially covers all at last.

The first to encounter Captain Vere in the act of leaving the compartment was the senior Lieutenant. The face he beheld, for the moment one expressive of the agony of the strong, was to that officer, though a man of fifty, a startling revelation. That the condemned one suffered less than he who mainly had effected the condemnation, was apparently indicated by the former's exclamation in the scene soon perforce to be touched upon.

Of a series of incidents within a brief term rapidly following each other, the adequate narration may take up a term less brief, especially if explanation or comment here and there seem requisite to the better understanding of such incidents. Between the entrance into the cabin of him who never left it alive, and him who when he did leave it left it as one condemned to die; between this and the closeted interview just given, less than an hour and a half had elapsed. It was an interval long enough, however, to awaken speculations among no few of the ship's company as to what it was that could be detaining in the cabin the Master-at-arms and the sailor, for it was rumoured that both of them had been seen to enter it and neither of them had been seen to emerge. This rumour had got abroad upon the gun-decks and in the tops; the people of a great war-ship being in one respect like villagers, taking microscopic note of every untoward movement or non-movement going on. When therefore in weather not at all tempestuous all hands were called in the second dog-watch, a summons under such circumstances not usual in those hours, the crew were not wholly unprepared for some announcement extraordinary, one having connection, too, with the continued absence of the two men from their wonted haunts.

There was a moderate sea at the time; and the moon, newly risen and near to being at its full, silvered the white spar-deck wherever not blotted by the clear-cut shadows horizontally thrown of fixtures and moving men. On either side of the quarter-deck the marine guard under arms was drawn up; and Captain Vere, standing up in his place surrounded by all the ward-room officers, addressed his men. In so doing his manner showed neither more nor less than that properly pertaining to his supreme position aboard his own ship. In clear terms and concise he told them what had taken place in the cabin; and the master-at-arms was dead; that he who had killed him had been already tried by a summary court and condemned to death; and that the execution would take place in the early morning watch. The word *mutiny* was not named in what he said. He refrained, too, from making the occasion an opportunity for any preachment as to the maintenance of discipline, thinking, perhaps, that under existing circumstances in the navy the consequence of violating discipline should be made to speak for itself.

Their Captain's announcement was listened to

by the throng of standing sailors in a dumbness like that of a seated congregation of believers in Hell listening to the clergyman's announcement of his Calvinistic text.

At the close, however, a confused murmur went up. It began to wax all but instantly, then, at a sign, was pierced and suppressed by shrill whistles of the Boatswain and his mates piping "Down one watch."

To be prepared for burial Claggart's body was delivered to certain petty-officers of his mess. And here, not to clog the sequel with lateral matters, it may be added that at a suitable hour, the master-at-arms was committed to the sea with every funeral honour properly belonging to his naval grade.

In this proceeding, as in every public one growing out of the tragedy, strict adherence to usage was observed. Nor in any point could it have been at all deviated from, either with respect to Claggart or Billy Budd, without begetting undesirable speculations in the ship's company, the sailors, and more particularly the man-of-war's men, being of all men the greatest sticklers for usage.

For similar cause all communication between Captain Vere and the condemned one ended with the closeted interview already given, the latter being now surrendered to the ordinary routine preliminary to the end. This transfer under guard from the Captain's quarters was effected without unusual precautions—at least no visible ones.

If possible, not to let the men so much as surmise that their officers anticipate aught amiss from them is the tacit rule in a military ship. And the more that some sort of trouble should really be apprehended, the more do the officers keep that apprehension to themselves; though not the less unostentatious vigilance may be augmented.

In the present instance the sentry placed over the prisoner had strict orders to let no one have communication with him but the Chaplain. And certain unobtrusive measures were taken absolutely to insure this point.

Chapter XX

In a seventy-four of the old order the deck known as the upper gun-deck was the one covered

836

over by the spar-deck, which last, though not without its armament, was for the most part exposed to the weather. In general it was at all hours free from hammocks; those of the crew swinging on the lower gun-deck and berth-deck, the latter being not only a dormitory but also the place for the stowing of the sailors' bags, and on both sides lined with the large chests or movable pantries of the many messes of the men.

On the starboard side of the *Indomitable's* upper gun-deck, behold Billy Budd under sentry lying prone in irons in one of the bays formed by the regular spacing of the guns comprising the batteries on either side. All these pieces were of the heavier calibre of that period. Mounted on lumbering wooden carriages, they were hampered with cumbersome harness of breeching and strong sidetackles for running them out. Guns and carriages, together with the long rammers and shorter lintstocks lodged in loops overhead—all these, as customary, were painted black; and the heavy hempen breechings, tarred to the same tint, wore the like livery of the undertakers. In contrast with the funereal tone of these surrounding the prone sailor's exterior apparel, white jumper and white duck trousers, each more or less soiled, dimly glimmered in the obscure light of the bay like a patch of discoloured snow in early April lingering at some upland cave's black mouth. In effect he is already in his shroud or the garments that shall serve him in lieu of one. Over him, but scarce illuminating him, two battle-lanterns swing from two massive beams of the deck above. Fed with the oil supplied by the war-contractors (whose gains, honest or otherwise, are in every land an anticipated portion of the harvest of death), with flickering splashes of dirty yellow light they pollute the pale moonshine all but ineffectually struggling in obstructed flecks through the open ports from which the tompioned cannon protrude. Other lanterns at intervals serve but to bring out somewhat the obscurer bays which, like small confessionals or side-chapels in a cathedral, branch from the long, dim-vasted, broad aisle between the two batteries of that covered tier.

Such was the deck where now lay the Handsome Sailor. Through the rose-tan of his complexion, no pallor could have shown. It would have taken days of sequestration from the winds and the sun to have brought about the effacement of that young sea-bloom. But the skeleton in the cheekbone at the point of its angle was just beginning delicately to be defined under the warm-tinted skin. In fervid hearts self-contained some brief experiences devour our human tissue as secret fire in a ship's hold consumes cotton in the bale.

But now, lying between the two guns, as nipped in the vice of fate, Billy's agony, mainly proceeding from a generous young heart's virgin experience of the diabolical incarnate and effective in some men—the tension of that agony was over now. It survived not the something healing in the closeted interview with Captain Vere. Without movement, he lay as in a trance, that adolescent expression previously noted as his taking on something akin to the look of a slumbering child in the cradle when the warm hearth-glow of the still chamber of night plays on the dimples that at whiles mysteriously form in the cheek, silently coming and going there. For now and then in the gyved one's trance, a serene happy light born of some wandering reminiscence or dream would diffuse itself over his face, and then wane away only anew to return.

The Chaplain coming to see him and finding him thus, and perceiving no sign that he was conscious of his presence, attentively regarded him for a space, then slipping aside, withdrew for the time, peradventure feeling that even he, the minister of Christ, though receiving his stipend from wars, had no consolation to proffer which could result in a peace transcending that which he beheld. But in the small hours he came again. And the prisoner, now awake to his surroundings, noticed his approach, and civilly, all but cheerfully, welcomed him. But it was to little purpose that in the interview following the good man sought to bring Billy Budd to some Godly understanding that he must die, and at dawn. True, Billy himself freely referred to his death as a thing close at hand; but it was something in the way that children will refer to death in general, who yet among their other sports will play a funeral with hearse and mourners. Not that like children Billy was incapable of conceiving what death really is. No, but he was wholly without irrational fear of it, a fear more prevalent in highly civilized communities than those so-called barbarous ones which in all respects stand nearer to unadulterate Nature. And, as elsewhere said, a barbarian Billy radically was; as much so, for all the costume, as his countrymen the British captives, living trophies made to march in the Roman triumph of Germanicus. Quite as much so as those later barbarians, young men probably, and picked specimens among the earlier British converts to Christianity, at least nominally such, and taken to Rome (as to-day converts from lesser isles of the sea may be taken to London), of whom the Pope of that time, admiring the strangeness of their personal beauty—so unlike the Italian stamp, their clear, ruddy complexions and curled flaxen locks, exclaimed, "Angles" (meaning *English*, the modern derivative)—"Angles do you call them? And is it because they look so like *Angels?*" Had it been later in time one would think that the Pope had in mind Fra Angelico's seraphs, some of whom, plucking apples in gardens of Hesperides, have the faint rose-bud complexion of the more beautiful English girls.

Chapter XXI

If in vain the kind Chaplain sought to impress the young barbarian with ideas of death akin to those conveyed in the skull, dial and cross-bones on old tombstones; equally futile to all appearances were his efforts to bring home to him the thought of salvation and a Saviour. Billy listened, but less out of awe or reverence, perhaps, than from a certain natural politeness; doubtless at bottom regarding all that in much the same way which most mariners of his class take any discourse abstract or out of the common tone of the workaday world. And this sailor way of taking clerical discourse is not wholly unlike the way in which the pioneer of Christianity—full of transcendent miracles—was received long ago on tropic isles by any superior *savage* so called: a Tahitian say of Captain Cook's time or shortly after that time. Out of a natural courtesy he received but did not appreciate. It was like a gift placed in the palm of an out-stretched hand upon which the fingers do not close.

But the *Indomitable's* Chaplain was a discreet man possessing the good sense of a good heart. So he insisted not in his vocation here. At the instance of Captain Vere, a lieutenant had apprised him of pretty much of everything as to Billy; and since he felt that innocence was even a better thing than religion wherewith to go to judgment, he reluctantly withdrew; but in his emotion not without performing an act strange enough in an Englishman, and under the circumstances yet more so in any regular priest. Stooping over, he kissed on the fair cheek his fellow man, a felon in martial law, one who, though in the confines of death, he felt he could never convert to a dogma; nor for all that did he fear for his future.

Marvel not that, having been made acquainted with the young sailor's essential innocence, the worthy man lifted not a finger to avert the doom of such a martyr to martial discipline. So to do would not only have been as idle as invoking the desert, but would also have been an audacious transgression of the bounds of his function—one as exactly prescribed to him by military law as that of any other naval officer. Bluntly put, a chaplain is the minister of the Prince of Peace serving in the host of the God of War—Mars. As such, he is as incongruous as a musket would be on the altar at Christmas. Why then is he there? Because he indirectly subserves the purpose attested by the cannon; because, too, he lends the sanction of the religion of the meek to that which practically is the abrogation of everything but force.

Chapter XXII

The night so luminous on the spar-deck, but otherwise on the cavernous ones below—levels so very like the tiered galleries in a coal-mine—the luminous night passed away. Like the prophet in the chariot disappearing in heaven and dropping his mantle to Elisha, the withdrawing night transferred its pale robe to the peeping day. A meek shy light appeared in the East, where stretched a diaphanous fleece of white furrowed vapour. That light slowly waxed. Suddenly eight bells was struck aft, responded to by one louder metallic stroke from forward. It was four o'clock in the morning. Instantly the silver whistles were heard summoning all hands to witness punishment. Up through the great hatchway rimmed with racks of heavy shot, the watch below came pouring, overspreading with the watch already on deck the space between the mainmast and foremast, including that occupied by the capacious launch and the black booms tiered on either side of it—boat and booms making a summit of observation for the powder boys and younger tars. A different group comprising one watch of topmen leaned over the side of the rail of that sea-balcony, no small one in a seventy-four, looking down on the crowd below. Man or boy, none spake but in whisper, and few spake at all. Captain Vere—as before, the central figure among the assembled commissioned officers—stood nigh the break of the poop-deck, facing forward. Just below him on the quarter-deck the marines in full equipment were drawn up much as at the scene of the promulgated sentence.

At sea in the old time, the execution by halter of a military sailor was generally from the foreyard. In the present instance—for special reasons—the main-yard was assigned. Under an arm of that yard the prisoner was presently brought up, the Chaplain attending him. It was noted at the time, and remarked upon afterwards, that in this final scene the good man evinced little or nothing of the perfunctory. Brief speech indeed he had with the condemned one, but the genuine gospel was less on his tongue than in his aspect and manner towards him. The final preparations personal to the latter being speedily brought to an end by two boatswain's-mates, the consummation impended. Billy stood facing aft. At the penultimate moment, his words, his only ones, words wholly unobstructed in the utterance, were these—"God bless Captain Vere!" Syllables so unanticipated coming from one with the ignominious hemp about his neck—a conventional felon's benediction directed aft towards the quarters of honour; syllables, too, delivered in the clear melody of a singing-bird on the point of launching from the twig, had a phenomenal effect, not unenhanced by the rare personal beauty of the young sailor, spiritualized now through late experiences so poignantly profound.

Without volition, as it were, as if indeed the ship's populace were the vehicles of some vocal electric current, with one voice, from alow and aloft, came a resonant echo—"God bless Captain Vere!" And yet, at that instant, Billy alone

must have been in their hearts, even as he was in their eyes.

At the pronounced words and the spontaneous echo that voluminously rebounded them, Captain Vere, either through stoic self-control or a sort of momentary paralysis induced by emotional shock, stood erectly rigid as a musket in the ship-armour's rack.

The hull, deliberately recovering from the periodic roll to leeward, was just regaining an even keel—when the last signal, the preconcerted dumb one, was given. At the same moment it chanced that the vapoury fleece hanging low in the East, was shot through with a soft glory as of the fleece of the Lamb of God seen in mystical vision; and simultaneously therewith, watched by the wedged mass of upturned faces, Billy ascended; and ascending, took the full rose of the dawn.

In the pinioned figure, arrived at the yardend, to the wonder of all no motion was apparent save that created by the slow roll of the hull, in moderate weather so majestic in a great ship heavy-cannoned.

A Digression

When, some days afterwards, in reference to the singularity just mentioned, the Purser (a rather ruddy, rotund person, more accurate as an accountant than profound as a philosopher) said at mess to the Surgeon, "What testimony to the force lodged in will-power," the latter, spare and tall, one in whom a discreet causticity went along with a manner less genial than polite, replied, "Your pardon, Mr. Purser. In a hanging so scientifically conducted—and, under special orders, I myself directed how Budd's was to be effected—any movement following the completed suspension and originating in the body suspended, such movement indicates mechanical spasm in the muscular system. Hence the absence of that is no more attributable to will-power, as you call it, than to horse-power—begging your pardon."

"But this muscular spasm you speak of—is not that, in a degree, more or less invariable in these cases?"

"Assuredly so, Mr. Purser."

"How then, my good sir, do you account for its absence in this instance?"

"Mr. Purser, it is clear that your sense of the singularity in this matter equals not mine. You account for it by what you call will-power, a term not yet included in the lexicon of science. As for me, I do not with my present knowledge pretend to account for it at all. Even should one assume the hypothesis that, at the first touch of the halyards, the action of Budd's heart, intensified by extraordinary emotion at its climax, abruptly stopped—much like a watch when in carelessly winding it up you strain at the finish, thus snapping the spring—even under that hypothesis, how account for the phenomenon that followed?"

"You admit, then, that the absence of spasmodic movement was phenomenal?"

"It was phenomenal, Mr. Purser, in the sense that it was an appearance, the cause of which is not immediately to be assigned."

"But tell me, my dear sir," pertinaciously continued the other, "was the man's death effected by the halter, or was it a species of euthanasia?"

"*Euthanasia*, Mr. Purser, is something like your will-power; I doubt its authenticity as a scientific term—begging your pardon again. It is at once imaginative and metaphysical; in short, Greek. But," abruptly changing his tone, "there is a case in the sick-bay which I do not care to leave to my assistants. Begging your pardon, but excuse me." And rising from the mess he formally withdrew.

Chapter XXIII

The silence at the moment of execution, and for a moment or two continuing thereafter (but emphasized by the regular wash of the sea against the hull, or the flutter of a sail caused by the helmsman's eyes being tempted astray), this emphasized silence was gradually disturbed by a sound not easily to be here verbally rendered. Whoever has heard the freshet-wave of a torrent suddenly swelled by pouring showers in tropical mountains, showers not shared by the plain; whoever has heard the first muffled murmur of its sloping advance through precipitous woods, may form some conception of the sound now heard. The seeming remoteness of its source was because of its murmurous indistinctness, since it came from close by, even from the men massed on the ship's open deck. Being inarticulate, it was dubious in

significance further in that it seemed to indicate some capricious revulsion of thought or feeling such as mobs ashore are liable to—in the present instance possibly implying a sullen revocation on the men's part of their involuntary echoing of Billy's benediction. But ere the murmur had time to wax into clamour it was met by a strategic command, the more telling that it came with abrupt unexpectedness.

"Pipe down the starboard watch, Boatswain, and see that they go."

Shrill as the shriek of the sea-hawk the whistles of the Boatswain and his Mates pierced that ominous low sound, dissipating it; and yielding to the mechanism of discipline the throng was thinned by one half. For the remainder most of them were set to temporary employments connected with trimming the yards and so forth, business readily to be found upon occasion by any officer-of-the-deck.

Now each proceeding that follows a mortal sentence pronounced at sea by a drum-head court is characterized by a promptitude not perceptibly merging into hurry, though bordering that. The hammock, the one which had been Billy's bed when alive, having already been ballasted with shot and otherwise prepared to serve for his canvas coffin, the last offices of the sea-undertakers, the Sail-maker's Mates, were now speedily completed. When everything was in readiness, a second call for all hands, made necessary by the strategic movement before mentioned, was sounded: and now to witness burial.

The details of this closing formality it needs not to give. But when the tilted plank let slide its freight into the sea, a second strange human murmur was heard—blended now with another inarticulate sound proceeding from certain larger sea-fowl, whose attention having been attracted by the peculiar commotion in the water resulting from the heavy sloped dive of the shotted hammock into the sea, flew screaming to the spot. So near the hull did they come, that the stridor or bony creak of their gaunt double-jointed pinions was audible. As the ship under light airs passed on, leaving the burial spot astern, they still kept circling it low down with the moving shadow of their outstretched wings and the cracked requiem of their cries.

Upon sailors as superstitious as those of the age preceding ours—all men-of-war's men, too, who had just beheld the prodigy of repose in the form suspended in air and now foundering in the deeps; to such mariners the action of the sea-fowl, though dictated by a mere animal greed for prey, was big with no prosaic significance. An uncertain movement began among them, in which some encroachment was made. It was tolerated but for a moment. For suddenly the drum beat to quarters—which 10 familiar sound, happening at least twice every day, had upon the present occasion some signal peremptoriness in it. True martial discipline long continued superinduces in an average man a sort of impulse of docility, whose operation at the official tone of command much resembles in its promptitude the effect of an instinct.

The drum-beat dissolved the multitude, distributing most of them along the batteries of the two covered gun-decks. There, as wont, the gun 20 crews stood by their respective cannon erect and silent. In due course the First officer, sword under arm and standing in his place on the quarter-deck, formally received the successive reports of the sworded Lieutenants commanding the sections of batteries below; the last of which reports being made, the summed report he delivered with the customary salute to the Commander. All of this occupied time, which, in the present case, was the object of beating to quarters at an hour prior to 30 the customary one. That such variance from usage was authorized by an officer like Captain Vere (a martinet as some deemed him), was evidence of the necessity for unusual action implied in what he deemed to be temporarily the mood of his men. "With mankind," he would say, "forms, measured forms, are everything; and that is the import couched in the story of Orpheus, with his lyre, spell-binding the wild denizens of the woods." And this he once applied to the disruption of forms 40 going on across the Channel and the consequence thereof.

At this unwonted muster at quarters, all proceeded as at the regular hour. The band on the quarter-deck played a sacred air. After which the Chaplain went through with the customary morning service. That done, the drum beat the retreat, and toned by music and religious rites subserving the discipline and purpose of war, the men in their wonted, orderly manner dispersed to the places allotted them when not at the guns.

And now it was full day. The fleece of low-hanging vapour had vanished, licked up by the sun that late had so glorified it. And the circumambient air in the clearness of its serenity was like smooth white marble in the polished block not yet removed from the marble-dealer's yard.

Chapter XXIV

The symmetry of form attainable in pure fiction cannot so readily be achieved in a narration essentially having less to do with fable than with fact. Truth uncompromisingly told will always have its ragged edges; hence the conclusion of such a narration is apt to be less finished than an architectural finial.

How it fared with the Handsome Sailor during the year of the great mutiny has been faithfully given. But though properly the story ends with his life, something in way of a sequel will not be amiss. Three brief chapters will suffice.

In the general re-christening under the Directory of the craft originally forming the navy of the French Monarchy, the *St. Louis* line-of-battle ship was named the *Athéiste*. Such a name, like some other substituted ones in the Revolutionary fleet, while proclaiming the infidel audacity of the ruling power, was yet (though not so intended to be) the aptest name, if one consider it, ever given to a war-ship; far more so, indeed, than the *Devastation* or the *Eritus* (the Hell) and similar names bestowed upon fighting ships.

On the return passage to the full English fleet from the detached cruise during which occurred the events already recorded, the *Indomitable* fell in with the *Athéiste*. An engagement ensued; during which Captain Vere, in the act of putting his ship alongside the enemy with a view of throwing his boarders across the bulwarks, was hit by a musket-ball from a port-hole of the enemy's main cabin. More than disabled, he dropped to the deck and was carried below to the same cock-pit where some of his men already lay. The senior Lieutenant took command. Under him the enemy was finally captured, and though much crippled, was by rare good fortune successfully taken into

Gibraltar, an English fort not very distant from the scene of the fight. There Captain Vere with the rest of the wounded was put ashore. He lingered for some days, but the end came. Unhappily he was cut off too early for the Nile and Trafalgar. The spirit that, in spite of its philosophic austerity, may yet have indulged in the most secret of all passions—ambition—never attained to the fulness of fame.

Not long before death, while lying under the influence of that magical drug which, in soothing the physical frame, mysteriously operates on the subtler element in man, he was heard to murmur words inexplicable to his attendant—"Billy Budd, Billy Budd." That these were not the accents of remorse, would seem clear from what the attendant said to the *Indomitable's* senior officer of marines, who, as the most reluctant to condemn of the members of the drum-head court, too well knew (though here he kept the knowledge to himself) who Billy Budd was.

Chapter XXV

Some few weeks after the execution, among other matters under the main head of *News from the Mediterranean*, there appeared in one naval chronicle of the time, an authorized weekly publication, an account of the affair. It was doubtless for the most part written in good faith, though the medium, partly rumour, through which the facts must have reached the writer, served to deflect and in part to falsify them. The account was as follows:—

"On the tenth of the last month a deplorable occurrence took place on board *H.M.S. Indomitable*. John Claggart, the ship's master-at-arms, discovering that some sort of plot was incipient among an inferior section of the ship's company, and that the ring-leader was one William Budd, he, Claggart, in the act of arraigning the man before the Captain was vindictively stabbed to the heart by the suddenly drawn sheath-knife of Budd.

"The deed and the implement employed sufficiently suggest that, though mustered into the service under an English name, the assassin was no Englishman but one of those aliens adopting English cognomen whom the present extraordinary necessities of the Service have caused to be admitted into it in considerable numbers.

"The enormity of the crime and the extreme depravity of the criminal, appear the greater in view of the character of the victim—a middle-aged man, respectable and discreet, belonging to that minor official grade, the petty-officers, upon whom, as none know better than the commissioned gentlemen, the efficiency of His Majesty's navy so largely depends. His function was a responsible one—at once onerous and thankless—and his fidelity in it the greater because of his strong patriotic impulse. In this instance, as in so many other instances in these days, the character of the unfortunate man signally refutes, if refutation were needed, that peevish saying attributed to the late Dr. Johnson, that patriotism is the last refuge of a scoundrel.

"The criminal paid the penalty of his crime. The promptitude of the punishment has proved salutary. Nothing amiss is now apprehended aboard the *H.M.S. Indomitable*."

The above item, appearing in a publication now long ago superannuated and forgotten, is all that hitherto has stood in human record to attest what manner of men respectively were John Claggart and Billy Budd.

Chapter XXVI

Everything is for a season remarkable in navies. Any tangible object associated with some striking incident of the service is converted into a monument. The spar from which the foretopman was suspended was for some few years kept trace of by the bluejackets. Then knowledge followed it from ship to dock-yard, and again from dock-yard to ship, still pursuing it even when at last reduced to a mere dock-yard boom. To them a chip of it was as a piece of the Cross. Ignorant though they were of the real facts of the happening, and not thinking but that the penalty was unavoidably inflicted from the naval point of view, for all that they instinctively felt that Billy was a sort of man as incapable of mutiny as of wilful murder. They recalled the fresh young image of the Handsome Sailor, that face never deformed by a sneer or subtler vile freak of the heart within! This impression of him was doubtless deepened by the fact that he was gone, and in a measure mysteriously gone. On the gun-decks of the *Indomitable* the general estimate of his nature and its unconscious simplicity eventually found rude utterance from another foretopman, one of his own watch, gifted as some sailors are with an artless poetic temperament. Those tarry hands made some lines which, after circulating among the ship-board crew for a while, finally were rudely printed at Portsmouth as a ballad. The title given to it was the sailor's own:

Billy in the Darbies

Good of the Chaplain to enter Lone Bay
And down on his marrow-bones here and pray
For the likes just o' me, Billy Budd.—But look:
Through the port comes the moon-shine astray!
It tips the guard's cutlass and silvers this nook;
But 'twill die in the dawning of Billy's last day.
A jewel-block they'll make of me to-morrow,
Pendant pearl from the yard-arm-end
Like the ear-drop I gave to Bristol Molly—

O, 'tis me, not the sentence, they'll suspend.   10
Ay, Ay, all is up; and I must up too
Early in the morning, aloft from alow.
On an empty stomach, now, never it would do.
They'll give me a nibble—bit o' biscuit ere I go.   14
Sure, a messmate will reach me the last parting cup;
But, turning heads away from the hoist and the belay,
Heaven knows who will have the running of me up!
No pipe to those halyards.—But aren't it all sham?
A blur's in my eyes, it is dreaming that I am.
A hatchet to my hauser? all adrift to go?   20
The drum roll to grog, and Billy never know?
But Donald he has promised to stand by the plank;
So I'll shake a friendly hand ere I sink.
But—no! It is dead then I'll be, come to think.—
I remember Taff the Welshman when he sank,   25
And his cheek it was like the budding pink.
But me, they'll lash me in hammock, drop me deep,
Fathoms down, fathoms down, how I'll dream fast
    asleep.
I feel it stealing now. Sentry, are you there?
Just ease these darbies at the wrist,   30
And roll me over fair,
I am sleepy, and the oozy weeds about me twist.

JAMES RUSSELL LOWELL (1819-1891)

JAMES RUSSELL LOWELL's wide range of activities made him the most representative American man of letters in the last half of the nineteenth century. Others less versatile have become enduring symbols of greatness: Emerson's philosophic reach, Hawthorne's searching of the heart, Thoreau's iconoclasm, Melville's plumbing of the ambiguities of good and evil, Longfellow's narrative skill in poetry, Whittier's religious humility, Howells's work as critic and novelist in Realism, James's interest in the nature of the creative process in literature—all of these particular attributes give lasting force to Lowell's contemporaries. But Lowell was ardently involved in a greater number of contemporary affairs. He was poet, critic, essayist, professor, editor, public servant, and diplomat.

His early life was full of romanticism and reform, fraught with a great deal of travail when he could not seem to bring his talents into focus; but in 1848, when he was twenty-nine years of age, he achieved remarkable public recognition with three volumes of poetry. Lowell was born at "Elmwood," Cambridge, Massachusetts, February 22, 1819. His father was the pastor of the Unitarian West Church of Boston for over forty years. On the paternal side his grandfather was a judge,

and an uncle introduced cotton spinning into the United States and founded the city of Lowell. His ancestral line stretched back through a succession of ministers. On his mother's side he stemmed from Orkney Island stock, and from her he inherited his love of fancy and poetry. A preparatory education in the classics was followed by entrance to Harvard in 1834, where Thoreau was a sophomore and Longfellow would come the following year as Professor of Romance Languages. At Harvard, Lowell read everything, he said, "except the books prescribed by the faculty," and his undistinguished college career was brightened only in his senior year by his editorship of *Harvardiana* and his election to the honor of being class poet. He wrote the graduation poem, but was rusticated by the faculty for six weeks because of neglect of duties, and a friend was called on to read the poem. However, Lowell was allowed to return for graduation, and he received his diploma at the age of nineteen. Undecided as to his career, he attended the Harvard Law School. Graduating in 1840, he entered a law office and in the same year became engaged to Maria White, who was interested in poetry and the antislavery movement; financial problems prevented their marriage until December, 1844.

Lowell was unhappy in the law. Restive, he gave public addresses against slavery and for temperance; he contributed poetry to *Graham's Magazine* and published *A Year's Life and Other Poems* (1841), containing verses to Miss White and showing the influence of the romantics, especially Keats. In 1842 he gave up the pretense of practicing law. The following year he contributed articles to *The Pennsylvania Freeman*, an anti-slavery newspaper in Philadelphia, and with Robert Carter he began publishing *The Pioneer: A Literary and Critical Magazine*, which printed pieces by Poe, Hawthorne, and Whittier, but which died in three months through lack of financial support. In 1844 he published *Poems by James Russell Lowell*, and after his marriage in December the Lowells spent a winter in Philadelphia, where he contributed poetry to *Graham's Magazine* (it had paid him $30 a poem), and fortnightly articles to *The Pennsylvania Freeman* at $10 a month. In May, 1845, on their way home to Elmwood, the Lowells stayed a while in New York, where they visited at the home of Charles F. Briggs, editor of *The Broadway Journal*, and both Lowell and his wife contributed to the periodical. In 1845, too, Lowell published *Conversations with Some of the Old Poets*, chapters of which had appeared in *The Boston Miscellany*. In 1846 he commenced writing for *The Anti-Slavery Standard*, of New York, and, what is more important, he began *The Biglow Papers* in *The Boston Courier*.

Life in Philadelphia and New York had proved beneficial to Lowell; and, in Boston again, he worked to better purpose. The two years following his marriage had prepared him for his *annus mirabilis*, 1848, when *Poems by James Russell Lowell* (2 vols.), *The Vision of Sir Launfal*, *A Fable for Critics*, and *The Biglow Papers* (First Series) were published. Some of the *Poems* are still read; *A Fable for Critics* remains not only the most enjoyable group picture of Lowell's contemporaries but also a mine of sound criticism; *The Vision of Sir Launfal* is still a classic for secondary schools; and *The Biglow Papers* stands without challenge as the great satire of the Mexican War. Lowell had become a national figure as a man of letters. But his family life had been crossed with sorrow, and sorrow lay ahead. His daughter Blanche, born in 1845, died in 1847, the year of the birth of Mabel; Rose, born in 1849, died within a few months; Walter was born in 1850. The following year the family sailed for Europe, taking a goat on the voyage to supply milk for the children. When Walter died in Italy in 1852, the Lowells returned home. In 1853 Mrs. Lowell died. During the next two years Lowell wrote only sketches of his travels.

But a new life began in 1855, when he was appointed to the chair of Romance Languages and Belles-Lettres at Harvard, vacated by Longfellow. To prepare himself for this position he sailed in June for Europe and remained until August, 1856. The following year three important events filled his life. He began his work at Harvard, he established *The Atlantic Monthly* as a major factor in the encouragement of American literature, and he married Miss Frances Dunlap, who had been the governess of his daughter. The editorship of the *Atlantic* brought him $2,500 annually. In 1861 he resigned this post to James T. Fields, who was chosen to attract younger writers to the magazine. But Lowell retained his interest in the periodical, and in 1862 began contributing to it the poems which became *The Biglow Papers* (Second Series). He believed this series, treating of the Civil War, to be better than the first. Certainly the second lacks the exuberance of spirit of the first, but it contains more of tempered wisdom and of high and serious feeling.

Lowell's interest in public affairs did not abate during his years as a professor. In 1860 he was a delegate to the Republican convention, which nominated Lincoln for the Presidency. In 1864 he joined Charles Eliot Norton as coeditor of *The North American Review*, a magazine dedicated rather to social affairs than to literature. To it he contributed a number of political essays, including the highly important paper in January, 1864, supporting Abraham Lincoln's Administration at a time when it was being widely criticized. But he did not resign from belles-lettres. In 1865 he recited the most famous of his odes, the "Ode Recited at the Harvard Commemoration"; in 1866 *The Biglow Papers* (Second Series) was published as a book, with additions; the notable and acute essay "On a Certain Condescension in Foreigners" was printed in the *Atlantic* for January, 1869, and in the same year he issued another book of poems, *Under the Willows*. In 1870 he published *The Cathedral*, over which he labored more than on any other of his poems. Life at Harvard gave him subjects for two volumes of collections, *Among My Books* (1870), and *My Study Windows* (1871); a few years later, in 1875, he gathered a companion volume of essays, *Among My Books* (Second Series). His own work, as Norman Foerster has pointed out, was associated with "gusto and flashes of insight, the free play of feeling and intelligence"; yet Lowell was no impressionist in his critical studies. He held that literature is the ideal reflection of nature, that it must have form and be endowed with imagination, and that in its highest reaches, as exemplified by Dante, it must give our experiences universal significance. Foerster concluded in his *American Criticism* that Lowell was our

844 *What he says about poetry*

"most distinguished literary critic" of the nineteenth century.

Another major change in Lowell's life came in 1872, when he was fifty-eight years of age. In that year he resigned both his chair at Harvard and his editorship of *The North American Review*. He made an extended visit to Europe, received honorary degrees from Oxford (1873) and Cambridge (1874), and returned in 1875 to Elmwood and to Harvard. The last three of his distinguished odes were delivered in quick succession: the "Ode Read at the One Hundredth Anniversary of the Fight at Concord Bridge, 19th April, 1875," "Under the Old Elm, Poem Read at Cambridge on the Hundredth Anniversary of Washington's Taking Command of the American Army, 3d July, 1775," and "Ode for the Fourth of July, 1876." In their stately and restrained eloquence, Lowell's four odes are collectively without peer in our national letters. In 1876 he was not only a delegate to the Republican convention which nominated Hayes for the Presidency, but also he was a staunch elector in the Hayes-Tilden election dispute. Diplomatic service followed, first as Minister to Spain (1877–1880), and then to the Court of St. James's (1880–1885). In 1885 his wife died, and Lowell returned to Elmwood to write verse and to gather together his uncollected writings. From these labors emerged *Democracy and Other Addresses* (1887), *Literary and Political Addresses* (1888), and a volume of poems, *Heartsease and Rue* (1888). He died in the house of his birth August 12, 1891.

BIBLIOGRAPHY · The standard edition is the Riverside, *The Writings of James Russell Lowell* (11 vols., 1890–1892), used for the text in this book. C. E. Norton, ed., *Letters of James Russell Lowell* (2 vols., 1894, enlarged to 3 vols., 1904), and H. E. Scudder, *James Russell Lowell: A Biography* (2 vols., 1901) were added to the *Writings* to make the Elmwood Edition, *The Complete Writings of James Russell Lowell* (16 vols., 1904). In 1932 M. A. DeW. Howe edited *New Letters of James Russell Lowell*. The best single volume of the poetry is H. E. Scudder, ed., *The Complete Poetical Works of James Russell Lowell* (1897, 1917, 1924). For bibliography see G. W. Cooke, *A Bibliography of James Russell Lowell* (1906), and L. S. Livingston, *A Bibliography of First Editions in Book Form of the Writings of J. R. Lowell* (1914).

Other biographies include R. C. Beatty, *James Russell Lowell* (1942), which enjoys the advantages of later scholarship; G. W. Curtis, *James Russell Lowell: An Address* (1892); F. Greenslet, *James Russell Lowell: His Life and Work* (1905); E. E. Hale, *James Russell Lowell and His Friends* (1901); and F. H. Underwood, *James Russell Lowell: A Biographical Sketch* (1882), and *The Poet and the Man: Recollections and Appreciations of James Russell Lowell* (1893).

Valuable critical studies may be found in the following books and journals: G. W. Allen, *American Prosody* (1935), 244–270; H. V. Bail, "Harvard's Commemoration Day: July 21, 1865," *New England Quarterly*, XV (1942), 259–279, and "James Russell Lowell's Ode Recited at the Commemoration of the Living and Dead Soldiers of Harvard University, July 21, 1865," *Papers of the Bibliographical Society of America*, XXXVII (1943), 169–202; R. C. Beatty, "Lowell's Commonplace Books," *New England Quarterly*, XVIII (1945), 391–401; S. Bradley, "Lowell, Emerson, and the *Pioneer*," *American Literature*, XIX (1947), 231–244; W. C. Brownell, *American Prose Masters* (1909), 271–335; H. H. Clark, "Lowell's Criticism of Romantic Literature," *PMLA*, XLI (1926), 209–228; H. H. Clark and N. Foerster, eds., *James Russell Lowell*, American Writers Series (1947), ii–clxvi; E. H. Duncan, "Lowell's 'Battle of the Kettle and the Pot,'" *American Literature*, XV (1943), 127–138; N. Foerster, *Nature in American Literature* (1923), 143–175; W. D. Howells, *Literary Friends and Acquaintance* (1900), 212–250; W. G. Jenkins, "Lowell's Criteria of Political Values," *New England Quarterly*, VII (1934), 115–141; M. Killheffer, "A Comparison of the Dialect of 'The Biglow Papers' with the Dialect of Four Yankee Plays," *American Speech*, III (1928), 222–236; E. D. Mead, "Lowell's *Pioneer*," *New England Magazine*, n.s., V (1891), 235–258; J. P. Pritchard, "Lowell's Debt to Horace's *Ars Poetica*," *American Literature*, III (1931), 259–276; J. J. Reilly, *James Russell Lowell as Critic* (1915); E. C. Stedman, *Poets of America* (1885), 204–348; A. W. M. Voss, "The Evolution of Lowell's 'The Courtin','" *American Literature*, XV (1943), 42–50; and A. Warren, "Lowell on Thoreau," *Studies in Philology*, XXVII (1930), 442–462.

I Would Not Have This Perfect Love of Ours

LOWELL's first book, *A Year's Life* (1841), contains the sonnet "I Would Not Have This Perfect Love of Ours," inspired by Maria White, whom he had met in Watertown, Massachusetts, in 1839, and whom he married in 1844. Lowell had "just emerged from the darkest and unhappiest period" of his life, he told Longfellow (Scudder, *James Russell Lowell*, I, 97).

I would not have this perfect love of ours
Grow from a single root, a single stem,
Bearing no goodly fruit, but only flowers
That idly hide life's iron diadem:
It should grow alway like that Eastern tree   5
Whose limbs take root and spread forth constantly;

That love for one, from which there doth not
	spring
Wide love for all, is but a worthless thing.
Not in another world, as poets prate,
Dwell we apart above the tide of things,   10
High floating o'er earth's clouds on faery wings;
But our pure love doth ever elevate
Into a holy bond of brotherhood
All earthly things, making them pure and good.

To the Spirit of Keats

LOWELL's second volume, *Poems* (copyrighted 1844),
appeared in Boston late in 1843, and in London in 1844
where it was issued by three publishers. This volume
contains the sonnet to Keats (first printed in *Arc-
turus*, January, 1842), whose influence is evident in
much of Lowell's early work.

Great soul, thou sittest with me in my room,
Uplifting me with thy vast, quiet eyes,
On whose full orbs, with kindly lustre, lies
The twilight warmth of ruddy ember-gloom:
Thy clear, strong tones will oft bring sudden bloom
Of hope secure, to him who lonely cries,   6
Wrestling with the young poet's agonies,
Neglect and scorn, which seem a certain doom:
Yes! the few words which, like great thunderdrops,
Thy large heart down to earth shook doubtfully,
Thrilled by the inward lightning of its might,
Serene and pure, like gushing joy of light,   12
Shall track the eternal chords of Destiny,
After the moon-led pulse of ocean stops.

My Love, I Have No Fear that Thou Shouldst Die

THIS POEM was addressed to Miss Maria White, to
whom he became engaged in 1840; they were married
four years later. First published in *Poems* (1844).

My Love, I have no fear that thou shouldst die;
Albeit I ask no fairer life than this,
Whose numbering-clock is still thy gentle kiss,
While Time and Peace with hands enlockèd fly;
Yet care I not where in Eternity   5
We live and love, well knowing that there is
No backward step for those who feel the bliss
Of Faith as their most lofty yearnings high:

Love hath so purified my being's core,
Meseems I scarcely should be startled, even,   10
To find, some morn, that thou hadst gone before;
Since, with thy love, this knowledge too was given,
Which each calm day doth strengthen more and
	more,
That they who love are but one step from Heaven.

Stanzas on Freedom

SUNG at the antislavery picnic at Dedham, Massachusetts, on the anniversary of the West-Indian Emancipation, August 1, 1843. Collected in *Poems* (1844).

Men! whose boast it is that ye
Come of fathers brave and free,
If there breathe on earth a slave,
Are ye truly free and brave?
If ye do not feel the chain,   5
When it works a brother's pain,
Are ye not base slaves indeed,
Slaves unworthy to be freed?

Women! who shall one day bear
Sons to breathe New England air,   10
If ye hear, without a blush,
Deeds to make the roused blood rush
Like red lava through your veins,
For your sisters now in chains,—
Answer! are ye fit to be   15
Mothers of the brave and free?

Is true Freedom but to break
Fetters for our own dear sake,
And, with leathern hearts, forget
That we owe mankind a debt?   20
No! true freedom is to share
All the chains our brothers wear,
And, with heart and hand, to be
Earnest to make others free!

They are slaves who fear to speak   25
For the fallen and the weak;
They are slaves who will not choose
Hatred, scoffing, and abuse,
Rather than in silence shrink
From the truth they needs must think;   30
They are slaves who dare not be
In the right with two or three.

The Present Crisis

THE "crisis" was the imminent annexation of Texas as a slave state. Written in December, 1844, it was published in the Boston *Courier* December 11, 1845, and collected in 1848 in *Poems* (Second Series). See G. W. Cooke, *A Bibliography of James Russell Lowell.*

When a deed is done for Freedom, through the broad earth's aching breast
Runs a thrill of joy prophetic, trembling on from east to west,
And the slave, where'er he cowers, feels the soul within him climb
To the awful verge of manhood, as the energy sublime
Of a century bursts full-blossomed on the thorny stem of Time.   5

Through the walls of hut and palace shoots the instantaneous throe,
When the travail of the Ages wrings earth's systems to and fro;
At the birth of each new Era, with a recognizing start,
Nation wildly looks at nation, standing with mute lips apart,
And glad Truth's yet mightier man-child leaps beneath the Future's heart.   10

So the Evil's triumph sendeth, with a terror and a chill,
Under continent to continent, the sense of coming ill,
And the slave, where'er he cowers, feels his sympathies with God
In hot tear-drops ebbing earthward, to be drunk up by the sod,
Till a corpse crawls round unburied, delving in the nobler clod.   15

For mankind are one in spirit, and an instinct bears along,
Round the earth's electric circle, the swift flash of right or wrong;
Whether conscious or unconscious, yet Humanity's vast frame
Through its ocean-sundered fibres feels the gush of joy or shame;—
In the gain or loss of one race all the rest have equal claim.   20

Once to every man and nation comes the moment to decide,
In the strife of Truth with Falsehood, for the good or evil side;
Some great cause, God's new Messiah, offering each the bloom or blight,
Parts the goats upon the left hand, and the sheep upon the right,
And the choice goes by forever 'twixt that darkness and that light.   25

Hast thou chosen, O my people, on whose party thou shalt stand,
Ere the Doom from its worn sandals shakes the dust against our land?
Though the cause of Evil prosper, yet 'tis Truth alone is strong,
And, albeit she wander outcast now, I see around her throng
Troops of beautiful, tall angels, to enshield her from all wrong.   30

Backward look across the ages and the beacon-moments see,
That, like peaks of some sunk continent, jut through Oblivion's sea;
Not an ear in court or market for the low foreboding cry
Of those Crises, God's stern winnowers, from whose feet earth's chaff must fly;
Never shows the choice momentous till the judgment hath passed by.   35

Careless seems the great Avenger; history's pages but record
One death-grapple in the darkness 'twixt old systems and the Word;

Truth forever on the scaffold, Wrong forever on the throne,—
Yet that scaffold sways the future, and, behind the dim unknown,
Standeth God within the shadow, keeping watch above his own.   40

We see dimly in the Present what is small and what is great,
Slow of faith how weak an arm may turn the iron helm of fate,
But the soul is still oracular; amid the market's din,
List the ominous stern whisper from the Delphic cave within,—
"They enslave their children's children who make compromise with sin."   45

Slavery, the earth-born Cyclops, fellest of the giant brood,
Sons of brutish Force and Darkness, who have drenched the earth with blood,
Famished in his self-made desert, blinded by our purer day,
Gropes in yet unblasted regions for his miserable prey;—
Shall we guide his gory fingers where our helpless children play?   50

Then to side with Truth is noble when we share her wretched crust,
Ere her cause bring fame and profit, and 'tis prosperous to be just;
Then it is the brave man chooses, while the coward stands aside,
Doubting in his abject spirit, till his Lord is crucified,
And the multitude make virtue of the faith they had denied.   55

Count me o'er earth's chosen heroes,—they were souls that stood alone,
While the men they agonized for hurled the contumelious stone,
Stood serene, and down the future saw the golden beam incline
To the side of perfect justice, mastered by their faith divine,
By one man's plain truth to manhood and to God's supreme design.   60

By the light of burning heretics Christ's bleeding feet I track,
Toiling up new Calvaries ever with the cross that turns not back,
And these mounts of anguish number how each generation learned
One new word of that grand *Credo* which in prophet-hearts hath burned
Since the first man stood God-conquered with his face to heaven upturned.   65

For Humanity sweeps onward: where today the martyr stands,
On the morrow crouches Judas with the silver in his hands;
Far in front the cross stands ready and the crackling fagots burn,
While the hooting mob of yesterday in silent awe return
To glean up the scattered ashes into History's golden urn.   70

'Tis as easy to be heroes as to sit the idle slaves
Of a legendary virtue carved upon our fathers' graves,
Worshippers of light ancestral make the present light a crime;—
Was the Mayflower launched by cowards, steered by men behind their time?
Turn those tracks toward Past or Future, that make Plymouth Rock sublime?   75

They were men of present valor, stalwart old iconoclasts,
Unconvinced by axe or gibbet that all virtue was the Past's;
But we make their truth our falsehood, thinking that hath made us free,
Hoarding it in mouldy parchments, while our tender spirits flee
The rude grasp of that great Impulse which drove them across the sea.   80

848

They have rights who dare maintain them; we are traitors to our sires,
Smothering in their holy ashes Freedom's new-lit altar-fires;
Shall we make their creed our jailer? Shall we, in our haste to slay,
From the tombs of the old prophets steal the funeral lamps away
To light up the martyr-fagots round the prophets of to-day?   **85**

New occasions teach new duties; Time makes ancient good uncouth;
They must upward still, and onward, who would keep abreast of Truth;
Lo, before us gleam her camp-fires! we ourselves must Pilgrims be,
Launch our Mayflower, and steer boldly through the desperate winter sea,
Nor attempt the Future's portal with the Past's blood-rusted key.   **90**

A Fable for Critics [Selections]

In May, 1845, the Lowells had visited at the home of Charles F. Briggs, editor of *The Broadway Journal.* Probably in October, 1847, Lowell began *A Fable for Critics,* on which he sought Briggs's criticism and aid in finding a publisher. His letters to Briggs (Norton, ed., *Letters,* I) reveal that 600 lines were done by November 13 (when *Poems,* Second Series, was in press), that before March 26, 1848, he had sent Briggs half of the poem, and that by August 22 he had completed the manuscript. It was published as a book, without Lowell's name, late in October, and soon went into a second and corrected edition, though by November, 1849, the sale had not exceeded 3,000 copies. Lowell later regretted only one of the portraits, that of Bryant, to whom he felt he had done injustice.

In the Introduction, Apollo, tired of a dull visiting critic, sends him on an errand. E. A. Duyckinck, the New York publisher and anthologist, is then made to protest the unfairness of critics who find no merit in American writings. Rufus Griswold, editor of *The Poets and Poetry of America* (1842) and other anthologies, then shepherds in his flock, whom Apollo characterizes.

. . . .

"But stay, here comes Tityrus Griswold, and leads on
The flocks whom he first plucks alive, and then feeds on,—
A loud-cackling swarm, in whose feathers warm drest,
He goes for as perfect a—swan as the rest.

"There comes Emerson first, whose rich words, every one,   5
Are like gold nails in temples to hang trophies on,

Whose prose is grand verse, while his verse, the Lord knows,
Is some of it pr—No, 'tis not even prose;
I'm speaking of metres; some poems have welled
From those rare depths of soul that have ne'er been excelled;   10
They're not epics, but that doesn't matter a pin,
In creating, the only hard thing's to begin;
A grass-blade's no easier to make than an oak;
If you've once found the way, you've achieved the grand stroke;   14
In the worst of his poems are mines of rich matter,
But thrown in a heap with a crash and a clatter;
Now it is not one thing nor another alone
Makes a poem, but rather the general tone,
The something pervading, uniting the whole,
The before unconceived, unconceivable soul,   20
So that just in removing this trifle or that, you
Take away, as it were, a chief limb of the statue;
Roots, wood, bark, and leaves singly perfect may be,
But, clapt hodge-podge together, they don't make a tree.

"But, to come back to Emerson (whom, by the way,   25
I believe we left waiting),—his is, we may say,
A Greek head on right Yankee shoulders, whose range
Has Olympus for one pole, for t'other the Exchange;
He seems, to my thinking (although I'm afraid
The comparison must, long ere this, have been made),   30
A Plotinus-Montaigne, where the Egyptian's gold mist
And the Gascon's shrewd wit cheek-by-jowl coexist;

849

Phil & Esinyst.

All admire, and yet scarcely six converts he's got
To I don't (nor they either) exactly know what;
For though he builds glorious temples, 'tis odd
He leaves never a doorway to get in a god.   36
'Tis refreshing to old-fashioned people like me
To meet such a primitive Pagan as he,
In whose mind all creation is duly respected
As parts of himself—just a little projected;   40
And who's willing to worship the stars and the sun,
A convert to—nothing but Emerson.
So perfect a balance there is in his head,
That he talks of things sometimes as if they were
     dead;
Life, nature, love, God, and affairs of that sort,
He looks at as merely ideas; in short,   46
As if they were fossils stuck round in a cabinet,
Of such vast extent that our earth's a mere dab
     in it;
Composed just as he is inclined to conjecture her,
Namely, one part pure earth, ninety-nine parts
     pure lecturer;   50
You are filled with delight at his clear demon-
     stration,
Each figure, word, gesture, just fits the occasion,
With the quiet precision of science he'll sort 'em,
But you can't help suspecting the whole a *post
     mortem.*

     "There are persons, mole-blind to the soul's
          make and style,   55
Who insist on a likeness 'twixt him and Carlyle;
To compare him with Plato would be vastly fairer,
Carlyle's the more burly, but E. is the rarer;
He sees fewer objects, but clearlier, truelier,
If C.'s as original, E.'s more peculiar;   60
That he's more of a man you might say of the one,
Of the other he's more of an Emerson;
C.'s the Titan, as shaggy of mind as of limb,—
E. the clear-eyed Olympian, rapid and slim;
The one's two thirds Norseman, the other half
     Greek,   65
Where the one's most abounding, the other's to
     seek;
C.'s generals require to be seen in the mass,—
E.'s specialties gain if enlarged by the glass;
C. gives nature and God his own fits of the blues,
And rims common-sense things with mystical hues,—
E. sits in a mystery calm and intense,   71

And looks coolly around him with sharp common-
     sense;
C. shows you how every-day matters unite
With the dim transdiurnal recesses of night,—
While E., in a plain, preternatural way,   75
Makes mysteries matters of mere every day;
C. draws all his characters quite *à la* Fuseli,—
Not sketching their bundles of muscles and thews
     illy,
He paints with a brush so untamed and profuse
They seem nothing but bundles of muscles and
     thews;   80
E. is rather like Flaxman, lines strait and severe,
And a colorless outline, but full, round, and clear;—
To the men he thinks worthy he frankly accords
The design of a white marble statue in words.
C. labors to get at the centre, and then   85
Take a reckoning from there of his actions and men;
E. calmly assumes the said centre as granted,
And, given himself, has whatever is wanted.

     "He has imitators in scores, who omit
No part of the man but his wisdom and wit,—
Who go carefully o'er the sky-blue of his brain, 91
And when he has skimmed it once, skim it again;
If at all they resemble him, you may be sure it is
Because their shoals mirror his mists and obscurities,
As a mud-puddle seems deep as heaven for a
     minute,   95
While a cloud that floats o'er is reflected within it.
· · · · · · · · · · · ·

     "There is Bryant, as quiet, as cool, and as
          dignified,
As a smooth, silent iceberg, that never is ignified,
Save when by reflection 'tis kindled o' nights
With a semblance of flame by the chill Northern
     Lights.   100
He may rank (Griswold says so) first bard of your
     nation
(There's no doubt that he stands in supreme ice-
     olation),
Your topmost Parnassus he may set his heel on,
But no warm applauses come, peal following peal
     on,—

77. **Fuseli:** John Fuseli, eighteenth-century London
painter.   81. **Flaxman:** John Flaxman, eighteenth-century
English sculptor.   103. **Parnassus:** Mountain in Greece
sacred to Apollo and the Muses.

He's too smooth and too polished to hang any
    zeal on: 105
Unqualified merits, I'll grant, if you choose, he
    has 'em,
But he lacks the one merit of kindling enthusiasm;
If he stir you at all, it is just, on my soul,
Like being stirred up with the very North Pole.

    "He is very nice reading in summer, but *inter
Nos*, we don't want *extra* freezing in winter;   111
Take him up in the depth of July, my advice is,
When you feel an Egyptian devotion to ices.
But, deduct all you can, there's enough that's
    right good in him,
He has a true soul for field, river, and wood in him;
And his heart, in the midst of brick walls, or
    where'er it is,   116
Glows, softens, and thrills with the tenderest
    charities—
To you mortals that delve in this trade-ridden
    planet.
No, to old Berkshire's hills, with their limestone
    and granite.
If you're one who *in loco* (add *foco* here) *desipis*,
You will get of his outermost heart (as I guess)
    a piece;   121
But you'd get deeper down if you came as a prec-
    ipice,
And would break the last seal of its inwardest
    fountain,
If you only could palm yourself off for a mountain.
Mr. Quivis, or somebody quite as discerning,   125
Some scholar who's hourly expecting his learning,
Calls B. the American Wordsworth; but Words-
    worth
May be rated at more than your whole tuneful
    herd's worth.
No, don't be absurd, he's an excellent Bryant;
But, my friends, you'll endanger the life of your
    client,   130
By attempting to stretch him up into a giant:
If you choose to compare him, I think there are
    two per-
-sons fit for a parallel—Thomson and Cowper;
I don't mean exactly,—there's something of each,
There's T.'s love of nature, C.'s penchant to preach;

Just mix up their minds so that C.'s spice of
    craziness   136
Shall balance and neutralize T.'s turn for laziness,
And it gives you a brain cool, quite frictionless,
    quiet,
Whose internal police nips the buds of all riot,—
A brain like a permanent strait-jacket put on   140
The heart that strives vainly to burst off a button,—
A brain which, without being slow or mechanic,
Does more than a larger less drilled, more volcanic;
He's a Cowper condensed, with no craziness bitten,
And the advantage that Wordsworth before him
    had written.   145

    "But, my dear little bardlings, don't prick up
    your ears
Nor suppose I would rank you and Bryant as peers;
If I call him an iceberg, I don't mean to say
There is nothing in that which is grand in its way;
He is almost the one of your poets that knows
How much grace, strength, and dignity lie in
    Repose;   151
If he sometimes fall short, he is too wise to mar
His thought's modest fulness by going too far;
'Twould be well if your authors should all make
    a trial
Of what virtue there is in severe self-denial,   155
And measure their writings by Hesiod's staff,
Which teaches that all has less value than half.

    "There is Whittier, whose swelling and vehe-
    ment heart
Strains the strait-breasted drab of the Quaker apart,
And reveals the live Man, still supreme and erect,
Underneath the bemummying wrappers of sect;
There was ne'er a man born who had more of the
    swing   162
Of the true lyric bard and all that kind of thing;
And his failures arise (though he seem not to know
    it)
From the very same cause that has made him a
    poet,—   165
A fervor of mind which knows no separation
'Twixt simple excitement and pure inspiration,
As my Pythoness erst sometimes erred from not
    knowing

    120. loco . . . foco: pun on the "Locofocos" who sup-
ported President Van Buren's subtreasury bill.

    168. Pythoness: in Greek mythology the priestess who
gave the oracles of Apollo.

If 'twere I or mere wind through her tripod was
    blowing;
Let his mind once get head in its favorite direction
And the torrent of verse bursts the dams of re-
    flection,   171
While, borne with the rush of the metre along,
The poet may chance to go right or go wrong,
Content with the whirl and delirium of song;
Then his grammar's not always correct, nor his
    rhymes,   175
And he's prone to repeat his own lyrics sometimes,
Not his best, though, for those are struck off at
    white-heats
When the heart in his breast like a triphammer
    beats,
And can ne'er be repeated again any more
Than they could have been carefully plotted
    before: 180
Like old what's-his-name there at the battle of
    Hastings
(Who, however, gave more than mere rhyth-
    mical bastings),
Our Quaker leads off metaphorical fights
For reform and whatever they call human rights,
Both singing and striking in front of the war, 185
And hitting his foes with the mallet of Thor;
Anne haec, one exclaims, on beholding his knocks,
Vestis filii tui, O leather-clad Fox?
Can that be thy son, in the battle's mid din,
Preaching brotherly love and then driving it in
To the brain of the tough old Goliath of sin, 191
With the smoothest of pebbles from Castaly's
    spring
Impressed on his hard moral sense with a sling?

"All honor and praise to the right-hearted bard
Who was true to The Voice when such service
    was hard,   195
Who himself was so free he dared sing for the slave
When to look but a protest in silence was brave;
All honor and praise to the women and men
Who spoke out for the dumb and the down-
    trodden then!
It needs not to name them, already for each 200
I see History preparing the statue and niche;

They were harsh, but shall *you* be so shocked at
    hard words
Who have beaten your pruning-hooks up into
    swords,
Whose rewards and hurrahs men are surer to gain
By the reaping of men and of women than grain?
Why should *you* stand aghast at their fierce wordy
    war, if   206
You scalp one another for Bank or for Tariff?
Your calling them cut-throats and knaves all day
    long
Doesn't prove that the use of hard language is
    wrong;
While the World's heart beats quicker to think
    of such men   210
As signed Tyranny's doom with a bloody steel-
    pen,
While on Fourth-of-Julys beardless orators fright
    one
With hints at Harmodius and Aristogeiton,
You need not look shy at your sisters and brothers
Who stab with sharp words for the freedom of
    others;—   215
No, a wreath, twine a wreath for the loyal and true
Who, for sake of the many, dared stand with the
    few,
Not of blood-spattered laurel for enemies braved,
But of broad, peaceful oak-leaves for citizens saved!

  "There is Hawthorne, with genius so shrinking
    and rare   220
That you hardly at first see the strength that is
    there;
A frame so robust, with a nature so sweet,
So earnest, so graceful, so lithe and so fleet,
Is worth a descent from Olympus to meet;
'Tis as if a rough oak that for ages had stood, 225
With his gnarled bony branches like ribs of the
    wood,
Should bloom, after cycles of struggle and scathe,
With a single anemone trembly and rathe;
His strength is so tender, his wildness so meek,
That a suitable parallel sets one to seek,— 230
He's a John Bunyan Fouqué, a Puritan Tieck;

187–188. *Anne haec . . . Vestis filii tui*: Is this the
dress of thy son?   **188. Fox:** George Fox, seventeenth-
century Englishman, founder of the Society of Friends.

213. Harmodius and Aristogeiton: Athenian conspirators
against Hippias and Hipparchus.   **231. Fouqué:** Friedrich
Fouqué (1777–1843), German poet and romancer.   **Tieck:**
Ludwig Tieck (1773–1853), German poet and novelist.

When Nature was shaping him, clay was not granted
For making so full-sized a man as she wanted,
So, to fill out her model, a little she spared
From some finer-grained stuff for a woman pre-
    pared,   235
And she could not have hit a more excellent plan
For making him fully and perfectly man.

    "Here's Cooper, who's written six volumes to
    show
He's as good as a lord: well, let's grant that he's so;
If a person prefer that description of praise,   240
Why, a coronet's certainly cheaper than bays;
But he need take no pains to convince us he's not
(As his enemies say) the American Scott.
Choose any twelve men, and let C. read aloud
That one of his novels of which he's most proud, 245
And I'd lay any bet that, without ever quitting
Their box, they'd be all, to a man, for acquitting.
He has drawn you one character, though, that is
    new,
One wildflower he's plucked that is wet with the
    dew
Of this fresh Western world, and, the thing not to
    mince,   250
He has done naught but copy it ill ever since;
His Indians, with proper respect be it said,
Are just Natty Bumppo, daubed over with red,
And his very Long Toms are the same useful Nat,
Rigged up in duck pants and a sou'wester hat 255
(Though once in a Coffin, a good chance was found
To have slipped the old fellow away underground).
All his other men-figures are clothes upon sticks,
The *dernière chemise* of a man in a fix   259
(As a captain besieged, when his garrison's small,
Sets up caps upon poles to be seen o'er the wall);
And the women he draws from one model don't
    vary,
All sappy as maples and flat as a prairie.
When a character's wanted, he goes to the task
As a cooper would do in composing a cask;   265
He picks out the staves, of their qualities heedful,
Just hoops them together as tight as is needful,
And, if the best fortune should crown the attempt,
    he
Has made at the most something wooden and
    empty.

    259. dernière chemise: "last shirt."

"Don't suppose I would underrate Cooper's
    abilities;   270
If I thought you'd do that, I should feel very ill
    at ease;
The men who have given to *one* character life
And objective existence are not very rife;
You may number them all, both prose-writers and
    singers,
Without overrunning the bounds of your fingers,
And Natty won't go to oblivion quicker   276
Than Adams the parson or Primrose the vicar.

    "There is one thing in Cooper I like, too, and
    that is
That on manners he lectures his countrymen gratis;
Not precisely so either, because, for a rarity, 280
He is paid for his tickets in unpopularity.
Now he may overcharge his American pictures,
But you'll grant there's a good deal of truth in his
    strictures;
And I honor the man who is willing to sink   284
Half his present repute for the freedom to think,
And, when he has thought, be his cause strong or
    weak,
Will risk t'other half for the freedom to speak,
Caring naught for what vengeance the mob has in
    store,
Let that mob be the upper ten thousand or lower.

    "There comes Poe, with his raven, like Barnaby
    Rudge,   290
Three fifths of him genius and two fifths sheer
    fudge,
Who talks like a book of iambs and pentameters,
In a way to make people of common sense damn
    metres,
Who has written some things quite the best of
    their kind,
But the heart somehow seems all squeezed out by
    the mind,   295
Who—But hey-day! What's this? Messieurs
    Mathews and Poe,
You mustn't fling mud-balls at Longfellow so,

    277. Adams: character in Fielding's novel *Joseph Andrews.* **Primrose:** character in Goldsmith's *Vicar of Wakefield.* **290. Barnaby Rudge:** Barnaby Rudge, in Dickens's novel by the same name, owns a raven. **296. Mathews:** Cornelius Mathews, nineteenth-century New York critic, poet, and humorist.

Does it make a man worse that his character's such
As to make his friends love him (as you think) too
    much?
Why, there is not a bard at this moment alive 300
More willing than he that his fellows should thrive;
While you are abusing him thus, even now
He would help either one of you out of a slough;
You may say that he's smooth and all that till
    you're hoarse,
But remember that elegance also is force; 305
After polishing granite as much as you will,
The heart keeps its tough old persistency still;
Deduct all you can, *that* still keeps you at bay;
Why, he'll live till men weary of Collins and Gray.
I'm not over-fond of Greek metres in English, 310
To me rhyme's a gain, so it be not too jinglish,
And your modern hexameter verses are no more
Like Greek ones than sleek Mr. Pope is like Homer;
As the roar of the sea to the coo of a pigeon is,
So, compared to your moderns, sounds old Mele-
    sigenes; 315
I may be too partial, the reason, perhaps, o't is
That I've heard the old blind man recite his own
    rhapsodies,
And my ear with that music impregnate may be,
Like the poor exiled shell with the soul of the sea,
Or as one can't bear Strauss when his nature is
    cloven 320
To its deeps within deeps by the stroke of Bee-
    thoven;
But, set that aside, and 'tis truth that I speak,
Had Theocritus written in English, not Greek,
I believe that his exquisite sense would scarce
    change a line 324
In that rare, tender, virgin-like pastoral Evangeline.
That's not ancient nor modern, its place is apart
Where time has no sway, in the realm of pure Art,
'Tis a shrine of retreat from Earth's hubbub and
    strife
As quiet and chaste as the author's own life.

    "What! Irving? thrice welcome, warm heart
    and fine brain, 330
You bring back the happiest spirit from Spain,
And the gravest sweet humor, that ever were there
Since Cervantes met death in his gentle despair;

   315. Melesigenes: Homer.   **323. Theocritus:** Greek
pastoral poet, third century B.C.

Nay, don't be embarrassed, nor look so beseeching,
I sha'n't run directly against my own preaching,
And, having just laughed at their Raphaels and
    Dantes, 336
Go to setting you up beside matchless Cervantes;
But allow me to speak what I honestly feel,—
To a true poet-heart add the fun of Dick Steele,
Throw in all of Addison, *minus* the chill, 340
With the whole of that partnership's stock and
    good-will,
Mix well, and while stirring, hum o'er, as a spell,
The fine *old* English Gentleman, simmer it well,
Sweeten just to your own private liking, then
    strain,
That only the finest and clearest remain, 345
Let it stand out of doors till a soul it receives
From the warm lazy sun loitering down through
    green leaves,
And you'll find a choice nature, not wholly deserv-
    ing
A name either English or Yankee,—just Irving.

    "There's Holmes, who is matchless among you
    for wit; 350
A Leyden-jar always full-charged, from which flit
The electrical tingles of hit after hit;
In long poems 'tis painful sometimes, and invites
A thought of the way the new Telegraph writes,
Which pricks down its little sharp sentences spite-
    fully 355
As if you got more than you'd title to rightfully,
And you find yourself hoping its wild father
    Lightning
Would flame in for a second and give you a fright'-
    ning.
He has perfect sway of what *I* call a sham metre,
But many admire it, the English pentameter, 360
And Campbell, I think, wrote most commonly
    worse,
With less nerve, swing, and fire in the same kind
    of verse,
Nor e'er achieved aught in't so worthy of praise
As the tribute of Holmes to the grand *Marseillaise.*
You went crazy last year over Bulwer's New
    Timon;— 365
Why, if B., to the day of his dying, should rhyme
    on,
Heaping verses on verses and tomes upon tomes,

He could ne'er reach the best point and vigor of
   Holmes.
His are just the fine hands, too, to weave you a
   lyric
Full of fancy, fun, feeling, or spiced with satiric 370
In a measure so kindly you doubt if the toes
That are trodden upon are your own or your foes'.

   "There is Lowell, who's striving Parnassus to
   climb
With a whole bale of *isms* tied together with rhyme,
He might get on alone, spite of brambles and
   boulders,   375
But he can't with that bundle he has on his shoul-
   ders,
The top of the hill he will ne'er come nigh reaching
Till he learns the distinction 'twixt singing and
   preaching;
His lyre has some chords that would ring pretty well,
But he'd rather by half make a drum of the shell,
And rattle away till he's old as Methusalem,   381
At the head of a march to the last new Jerusalem."

. . . .

The Biglow Papers

LOWELL'S RISE to popular fame came rather unexpectedly from the First Series of *The Biglow Papers*,
objecting to the war with Mexico as a means of extending slavery. On June 16, 1846, Lowell had written to
Sydney Gay, editor of *The National Anti-Slavery
Standard*, of New York, saying that if he had any vocation, it was the writing of poetry, and that he intended
to send all his poems to the *Standard* except "such
arrows" as he thought better to "shoot" from the
Courier, edited by Joseph T. Buckingham, the only
paper in Boston that would print such propaganda.
The "arrows" became *The Biglow Papers*, which were
reprinted in the *Standard* and elsewhere. The series
continued through 1847 and into 1848; in May, 1848,
the *Standard* was first to publish "The Pious Editor's
Creed," and in September it first published the final
piece. All nine appeared in book form late in 1848,
shortly after *A Fable for Critics*.

   In the Introduction to the Second Series (1866)
Lowell described the origin of the First Series. Be- 10
lieving American letters had become effete and turgid,
he said he wished to be ranked with those who knew the
virtue of a sentence such as "The fire spread" as compared with "The conflagration extended its devastating

career." Biglow was created to express common sense
in New England, Parson Wilbur to represent the more
cautious element, and Birdofredum Sawin (whose last
name sprang both from the need for a rhyme for
"cawin,'" and from a desire to ridicule imperialism)
was brought in as clown. The Second Series, treating of the Civil War, began in the *Atlantic* for January, 1862, and ran irregularly through May, 1866.
Lowell had planned to rid himself of the garrulous
Wilbur as early as March, 1862, but did not do so
until the seventh number (*Atlantic*, February, 1863),
when the minister's death by apoplexy was announced. "The Courtin'" was originally written to
fill a blank page in the first edition of the First Series;
to this he added a conclusion in a later edition, and still
later revised the poem to its present state in the Second
Series, published in book form in 1867 with two numbers hitherto unprinted, the present VIII and IX.

MELIBŒUS-HIPPONAX.

THE

Biglow Papers,

EDITED,

WITH AN INTRODUCTION, NOTES,
GLOSSARY, AND COPIOUS INDEX,

BY

HOMER WILBUR, A. M.,

PASTOR OF THE FIRST CHURCH IN JAALAM, AND (PROSPECTIVE)
MEMBER OF MANY LITERARY, LEARNED, AND SCIENTIFIC
SOCIETIES,

(*for which see page 20.*)

The ploughman's whistle, or the trivial flute,
Finds more respect than great Apollo's lute.
      Quarles's Emblems, B. ii. E. 8.

Margaritas, munde porcine, calcâsti : en, siliquas accipe.
      Jac. Car. Fil. ad Pub. Leg. § 1.

Note to Title-page

IT WILL NOT have escaped the attentive eye, that
I have, on the title-page, omitted those honorary appendages to the editorial name which
not only add greatly to the value of every book,
but whet and exacerbate the appetite of the
reader. For not only does he surmise that an
honorary membership of literary and scientific
societies implies a certain amount of necessary
distinction on the part of the recipient of such
decorations, but he is willing to trust himself
more entirely to an author who writes under the
fearful responsibility of involving the reputation of such bodies as the *S. Archæol. Dahom.*
or the *Acad. Lit. et Scient. Kamtschat.* . . . .

Nevertheless, finding that, without descending to a smaller size of type than would have been compatible with the dignity of the several societies to be named, I could not compress my intended list within the limits of a single page, and thinking, moreover, that the act would carry with it an air of decorous modesty, I have chosen to take the reader aside, as it were, into my private closet, and there not only exhibit to him the diplomas which I already possess, but also to furnish him with a prophetic vision of those which I may, without undue presumption, hope for, as not beyond the reach of human ambition and attainment. And I am the rather induced to this from the fact that my name has been unaccountably dropped from the last triennial catalogue of our beloved *Alma Mater.* . . .

Introduction

WHEN, more than three years ago, my talented young parishioner, Mr. Biglow, came to me and submitted to my animadversions the first of his poems which he intended to commit to the more hazardous trial of a city newspaper, it never so much as entered my imagination to conceive that his productions would ever be gathered into a fair volume, and ushered into the august presence of the reading public by myself. So little are we shortsighted mortals able to predict the event! . . .

I was at first inclined to discourage Mr. Biglow's attempts, as knowing that the desire to poetize is one of the diseases naturally incident to adolescence, which, if the fitting remedies be not at once and with a bold hand applied, may become chronic, and render one, who might else have become in due time an ornament of the social circle, a painful object even to nearest friends and relatives. But thinking, on a further experience, that there was a germ of promise in 40 him which required only culture and the pulling up of weeds from about it, I thought it best to set before him the acknowledged examples of English composition in verse, and leave the rest to natural emulation. With this view, I accordingly lent him some volumes of Pope and Goldsmith, to the assiduous study of which he promised to devote his evenings. . . .

[FIRST SERIES] · I · *A Letter from Mr. Ezekiel Biglow of Jaalam to the Hon. Joseph T. Buckingham, editor of the Boston* Courier, *inclosing a poem of his son, Mr. Hosea Biglow*

JAYLEM, june 1846.

Mister Eddyter:—Our Hosea wuz down to Boston last week, and he see a cruetin Sarjunt a struttin round as popler as a hen with 1 chicking,
10 with 2 fellers a drummin and fifin arter him like all nater. the sarjunt he thout Hosea hed n't gut his i teeth cut cos he looked a kindo 's though he 'd jest com down, so he cal'lated to hook him in, but Hosy wood n't take none o' his sarse for all he hed much as 20 Rooster's tales stuck onto his hat and eenamost enuf brass a bobbin up and down on his shoulders and figureed onto his coat and trousis, let alone wut nater hed sot in his featers, to make a 6 pounder out on.
20 wal, Hosea he com home considerabal riled, and arter I 'd gone to bed I heern Him a thrashin round like a short-tailed Bull in fli-time. The old Woman ses she to me ses she, Zekle, ses she, our Hosee 's gut the chollery or suthin anuther ses she, don't you Bee skeered, ses I, he's oney amakin pottery[n] ses i, he's ollers on hand at that ere busynes like Da & martin, and shure enuf, cum mornin, Hosy he cum down stares full chizzle, hare on eend and cote tales flyin, and sot rite of to go reed his varses
30 to Parson Wilbur bein he haint aney grate shows o' book larnin himself, bimeby he cum back and sed the parson wuz dreffle tickled with 'em as i hoop you will Be, and said they wuz True grit.

Hosea ses taint hardly fair to call 'em hisn now, cos the parson kind o' slicked off sum o' the last varses, but he told Hosee he did n't want to put his ore in to tetch to the Rest on 'em, bein they wuz verry well As thay wuz, and then Hosy ses he sed suthin a nuther about Simplex Mundishes[n] or sum sech feller, but I guess Hosea kind o' did n't hear him, for I never hearn o' nobody o' that name in this villadge, and I 've lived here man and boy 76 year cum next tater diggin, and thair aint no wheres a kitting spryer 'n I be.

If you print 'em I wish you 'd jest let folks know

Aut insanit, aut versos facit.—H[omer] W[ilbur]. ["Either the man is insane or he is making verses."] **Simplex Mundishes:** *simplex munditiis,* "plain in duty."

who hosy's father is, cos my ant Keziah used to
say it 's nater to be curus ses she, she aint livin
though and he 's a likely kind o' lad.

Ezekiel Biglow.

Thrash away, you 'll *hev* to rattle
  On them kittle-drums o' yourn,—
'Taint a knowin' kind o' cattle
  Thet is ketched with mouldy corn;
Put in stiff, you fifer feller,   5
  Let folks see how spry you be,—
Guess you 'll toot till you are yeller
  'Fore you git ahold o' me!

Thet air flag 's a leetle rotten,
  Hope it aint your Sunday's best;—   10
Fact! it takes a sight o' cotton
  To stuff out a soger's chest:
Sence we farmers hev to pay fer 't,
  Ef you must wear humps like these,
S'posin' you should try salt hay fer 't, 15
  It would du ez slick ez grease.

'T would n't suit them Southun fellers,
  They're a dreffle graspin' set,
We must ollers blow the bellers
  Wen they want their irons het;   20
May be it 's all right ez preachin',
  But *my* narves it kind o' grates,
Wen I see the overreachin'
  O' them nigger-drivin' States.

Them thet rule us, them slave-traders,   25
  Haint they cut a thunderin' swarth
(Helped by Yankee renegaders),
  Thru the vartu o' the North!
We begin to think it 's nater
  To take sarse an' not be riled;—   30
Who 'd expect to see a tater
  All on eend at bein' biled?

Ez fer war, I call it murder,—
  There you hev it plain an' flat;
I don't want to go no furder   35
  Than my Testyment fer that;
God hez sed so plump an' fairly,
  It 's ez long ez it is broad,
An' you 've gut to git up airly
  Ef you want to take in God.   40

'Taint your eppyletts an' feathers
  Make the thing a grain more right;
'Taint afollerin' your bell-wethers
  Will excuse ye in His sight;
Ef you take a sword an' dror it,   45
  An' go stick a feller thru,
Guv'ment aint to answer for it,
  God 'll send the bill to you.

Wut 's the use o' meetin'-goin'
  Every Sabbath, wet or dry,   50
Ef it 's right to go amowin'
  Feller-men like oats an' rye?
I dunno but wut it 's pooty
  Trainin' round in bobtail coats,—
But it 's curus Christian dooty   55
  This 'ere cuttin' folks's throats.

They may talk o' Freedom's airy
  Tell they 're pupple in the face,—
It 's a grand gret cemetary
  Fer the barthrights of our race;   60
They jest want this Californy
  So 's to lug new slave-states in
To abuse ye, an' to scorn ye,
  An' to plunder ye like sin.

Aint it cute to see a Yankee   65
  Take sech everlastin' pains,
All to get the Devil's thankee
  Helpin' on 'em weld their chains?
Wy, it 's jest ez clear ez figgers,
  Clear ez one an' one make two,   70
Chaps thet make black slaves o' niggers
  Want to make wite slaves o' you.

Tell ye jest the eend I've come to
  Arter cipherin' plaguy smart,
An' it makes a handy sum, tu,   75
  Any gump could larn by heart;
Laborin' man an' laborin' woman
  Hev one glory an' one shame.
Ev'y thin' thet 's done inhuman
  Injers all on 'em the same.   80

'Taint by turnin' out to hack folks
  You 're agoin' to git your right,
Nor by lookin' down on black folks
  Coz you 're put upon by wite;

857

Slavery aint o' nary color,
  'Taint the hide thet makes it wus,
All it keers fer in a feller
  'S jest to make him fill its pus.

Want to tackle *me* in, du ye?
  I expect you 'll hev to wait; 90
Wen cold lead puts daylight thru ye
  You 'll begin to kal'late;
S'pose the crows wun't fall to pickin'
  All the carkiss from your bones,
Coz you helped to give a lickin' 95
  To them poor half-Spanish drones?

Jest go home an' ask our Nancy
  Wether I 'd be sech a goose
Ez to jine ye,—guess you 'd fancy
  The etarnal bung wuz loose! 100
She wants me fer home consumption,
  Let alone the hay's to mow,—
Ef you 're arter folks o' gumption,
  You 've a darned long row to hoe.

Take them editors thet 's crowin' 105
  Like a cockerel three months old,—
Don't ketch any on 'em goin',
  Though they *be* so blasted bold;
Aint they a prime lot o' fellers?
  'Fore they think on 't guess they 'll sprout 110
(Like a peach thet 's got the yellers),
  With the meanness bustin' out.

Wal, go 'long to help 'em stealin'
  Bigger pens to cram with slaves,
Help the men thet 's ollers dealin' 115
  Insults on your fathers' graves;
Help the strong to grind the feeble,
  Help the many agin the few,
Help the men thet call your people
  Witewashed slaves an' peddlin' crew! 120

Massachusetts, God forgive her,
  She 's akneelin' with the rest,
She, thet ough' to ha' clung ferever
  In her grand old eagle-nest;
She thet ough' to stand so fearless 125
  W'ile the wracks are round her hurled,
Holdin' up a beacon peerless
  To the oppressed of all the world!

Ha'n't they sold your colored seamen?
  Ha'n't they made your env'ys w'iz? 130
Wut 'll make ye act like freemen?
  Wut 'll git your dander riz?
Come, I'll tell ye wut I'm thinkin'
  Is our dooty in this fix,
They 'd ha' done 't ez quick ez winkin' 135
  In the days o' seventy-six.

Clang the bells in every steeple,
  Call all true men to disown
The tradoocers of our people,
  The enslavers o' their own; 140
Let our dear old Bay State proudly
  Put the trumpet to her mouth,
Let her ring this messidge loudly
  In the ears of all the South:—

"I 'll return ye good fer evil 145
  Much ez we frail mortils can,
But I wun't go help the Devil
  Makin' man the cus o' man;
Call me coward, call me traiter,
  Jest ez suits your mean idees,— 150
Here I stand a tyrant-hater,
  An' the friend o' God an' Peace!"

Ef I 'd *my* way I hed ruther
  We should go to work an' part,
They take one way, we take t' other, 155
  Guess it would n't break my heart;
Men hed ough' to put asunder
  Them thet God has noways jined;
An' I should n't gretly wonder
  Ef there 's thousands o' my mind. 160

VI · *The Pious Editor's Creed*

[At the special instance of Mr. Biglow, I preface the following satire with an extract from a sermon preached during the past summer, from Ezekiel xxxiv. 2: "Son of man, prophesy against the shepherds of Israel." Since the Sabbath on which this discourse was delivered, the editor of the "Jaalam Independent Blunderbuss" has unaccountably absented himself from our house of worship.

"I know of no so responsible position as that of the public journalist. The editor of our day bears the same relation to his time that the clerk bore to the age before the invention of printing. Indeed, the position which he holds is that which the clergyman should hold even now. But the clergyman chooses to walk off to the extreme edge of the world, and to throw such seed as he has clear over into that darkness which he calls the Next Life. . . .

"Meanwhile, see what a pulpit the editor mounts daily, sometimes with a congregation of fifty thousand within reach of his voice, and never so much as a nodder, even, among them! . . .

"Nevertheless, our editor will not come so far within even the shadow of Sinai as Mahomet did, but chooses rather to construe Moses by Joe Smith. He takes up the crook, not that the sheep may be fed, but that he may never want a warm woollen suit and a joint of mutton. For which reason I would derive the name *editor* not so much from *edo*, to publish, as from *edo*, to eat, that being the peculiar profession to which he esteems himself called. He blows up the flames of political discord for no other occasion than that he may thereby handily boil his own pot. I believe there are two thousand of these mutton-loving shepherds in the United States, and of these, how many have even the dimmest perception of their immense power, and the duties consequent thereon? Here and there, haply, one. Nine hundred and ninety-nine labor to impress upon the people the great principles of *Tweedledum*, and other nine hundred and ninety-nine preach with equal earnestness the gospel according to *Tweedledee*."—H. W.]

I du believe in Freedom's cause,
    Ez fur away ez Payris is;
I love to see her stick her claws
    In them infarnal Phayrisees;
It 's wal enough agin a king   5
    To dror resolves an' triggers,—
But libbaty 's a kind o' thing
    Thet don't agree with niggers.

I du believe the people want
    A tax on teas an' coffees,   10
Thet nothin' aint extravygunt,—
    Purvidin' I 'm in office;
Fer I hev loved my country sence
    My eye-teeth filled their sockets,
An' Uncle Sam I reverence,   15
    Partic'larly his pockets.

I du believe in *any* plan
    O' levyin' the texes,
Ez long ez, like a lumberman,
    I git jest wut I axes;   20
I go free-trade thru thick an' thin,
    Because it kind o' rouses
The folks to vote,—an' keeps us in
    Our quiet custom-houses.

I du believe it 's wise an' good   25
    To sen' out furrin missions,

Thet is, on sartin understood
    An' orthydox conditions;—
I mean nine thousan' dolls. per ann.,
    Nine thousan' more fer outfit,   30
An' me to recommend a man
    The place 'ould jest about fit.

I du believe in special ways
    O' prayin' an' convartin';
The bread comes back in many days,   35
    An' buttered, tu, fer sartin;
I mean in preyin' till one busts
    On wut the party chooses,
An' in convartin' public trusts
    To very privit uses.   40

I du believe hard coin the stuff
    Fer 'lectioneers to spout on;
The people's ollers soft enough
    To make hard money out on;
Dear Uncle Sam pervides fer his,   45
    An' gives a good-sized junk to all,—
I don't care *how* hard money is,
    Ez long ez mine 's paid punctooal.

I du believe with all my soul
    In the gret Press's freedom,   50
To pint the people to the goal
    An' in the traces lead 'em;
Palsied the arm thet forges yokes
    At my fat contracts squintin',
An' withered be the nose thet pokes   55
    Inter the gov'ment printin'!

I du believe thet I should give
    Wut 's his'n unto Cæsar,
Fer it 's by him I move an' live,
    Frum him my bread an' cheese air;   60
I du believe thet all o' me
    Doth bear his superscription,—
Will, conscience, honor, honesty,
    An' things o' thet description.

I du believe in prayer an' praise   65
    To him thet hez the grantin'
O' jobs,—in every thin' thet pays,
    But most of all in CANTIN';
This doth my cup with marcies fill,
    This lays all thought o' sin to rest,—   70

859

I *don't* believe in princerple,
  But oh, I *du* in interest.

I du believe in bein' this
  Or thet, ez it may happen
One way or 't other hendiest is   75
  To ketch the people nappin';
It aint by princerples nor men
  My preudunt course is steadied,—
I scent wich pays the best, an' then
  Go into it baldheaded.   80

I du believe thet holdin' slaves
  Comes nat'ral to a Presidunt,
Let 'lone the rowdedow it saves
  To hev a wal-broke precedunt;
Fer any office, small or gret,   85
  I could n't ax with no face
'uthout I 'd ben, thru dry an' wet,
  Th' unrizzest kind o' doughface.

I du believe wutever trash
  'll keep the people in blindness,—   90
Thet we the Mexicuns can thrash
  Right inter brotherly kindness,
Thet bombshells, grape, an' powder 'n' ball
  Air good-will's strongest magnets,
Thet peace, to make it stick at all,   95
  Must be druv in with bagnets.

In short, I firmly du believe
  In Humbug generally,
Fer it 's a thing thet I perceive
  To hev a solid vally;   100
This heth my faithful shepherd ben,
  In pasturs sweet heth led me,
An' this 'll keep the people green
  To feed ez they hev fed me.

[SECOND SERIES] · The Courtin'

God makes sech nights, all white an' still
  Fur 'z you can look or listen,
Moonshine an' snow on field an' hill,
  All silence an' all glisten.

Zekle crep' up quite unbeknown   5
  An' peeked in thru' the winder,
An' there sot Huldy all alone,
  'ith no one nigh to hender.

A fireplace filled the room's one side
  With half a cord o' wood in—   10
There war n't no stoves (tell comfort died)
  To bake ye to a puddin'.

The wa'nut logs shot sparkles out
  Towards the pootiest, bless her,
An' leetle flames danced all about   15
  The chiny on the dresser.

Agin the chimbley crook-necks hung,
  An' in amongst 'em rusted
The ole queen's-arm thet gran'ther Young
  Fetched back f'om Concord busted.   20

The very room, coz she was in,
  Seemed warm f'om floor to ceilin',
An' she looked full ez rosy agin
  Ez the apples she was peelin'.

'T was kin' o' kingdom-come to look   25
  On sech a blessed cretur,
A dog-rose blushin' to a brook
  Ain't modester nor sweeter.

He was six foot o' man, A 1,
  Clear grit an' human natur',   30
None could n't quicker pitch a ton
  Nor dror a furrer straighter.

He 'd sparked it with full twenty gals,
  Hed squired 'em, danced 'em, druv 'em,
Fust this one, an' then thet, by spells— 35
  All is, he could n't love 'em.

But long o' her his veins 'ould run
  All crinkly like curled maple,
The side she breshed felt full o' sun
  Ez a south slope in Ap'il.   40

She thought no v'ice hed sech a swing
  Ez hisn in the choir;
My! when he made Ole Hundred ring,
  She *knowed* the Lord was nigher.

An' she 'd blush scarlit, right in prayer, 45
  When her new meetin'-bunnet
Felt somehow thru' its crown a pair
  O' blue eyes sot upun it.

Thet night, I tell ye, she looked *some!*
  She seemed to 've gut a new soul,   50

For she felt sartin-sure he 'd come,
  Down to her very shoe-sole.

She heered a foot, an' knowed it tu,
  A-raspin' on the scraper,—
All ways to once her feelins flew   55
  Like sparks in burnt-up paper.

He kin' o' l'itered on the mat,
  Some doubtfle o' the sekle,
His heart kep' goin' pity-pat,
  But hern went pity Zekle.   60

An' yit she gin her cheer a jerk
  Ez though she wished him furder,
An' on her apples kep' to work,
  Parin' away like murder.

"You want to see my Pa, I s'pose?"   65
  "Wal . . . no . . . I come dasignin' "—
"To see my Ma? She 's sprinklin' clo'es
  Agin to-morrer's i'nin'."

To say why gals acts so or so,
  Or don't, 'ould be persumin';   70
Mebby to mean *yes* an' say *no*
  Comes nateral to women.

He stood a spell on one foot fust,
  Then stood a spell on t' other,
An' on which one he felt the wust   75
  He could n't ha' told ye nuther.

Says he, "I 'd better call agin;"
  Says she, "Think likely, Mister:"
Thet last word pricked him like a pin,
  An' . . . Wal, he up an' kist her.   80

When Ma bimeby upon 'em slips,
  Huldy sot pale ez ashes,
All kin' o' smily roun' the lips
  An' teary roun' the lashes.

For she was jes' the quiet kind   85
  Whose naturs never vary,
Like streams that keep a summer mind
  Snowhid in Jenooary.

The blood clost roun' her heart felt glued
  Too tight for all expressin',   90
Tell mother see how metters stood,
  An' gin 'em both her blessin'.

Then her red come back like the tide
  Down to the Bay o' Fundy,
An' all I know is they was cried   95
  In meetin' come nex' Sunday.

VI · *Sunthin' in the Pastoral Line*

To the Editors of *The Atlantic Monthly*

Jaalam, 17th May, 1862.

Gentlemen,—At the special request of Mr.
Biglow, I intended to inclose, together with his
own contribution, (into which, at my suggestion,
he has thrown a little more of pastoral sentiment
than usual,) some passages from my sermon on the
day of the National Fast, from the text, "Remember them that are in bonds, as bound with them,"
Heb. xiii. 3. But I have not leisure sufficient at
present for the copying of them, even were I al-   10
together satisfied with the production as it stands.
I should prefer, I confess, to contribute the entire
discourse to the pages of your respectable miscellany, if it should be found acceptable upon perusal,
especially as I find the difficulty in selection of
greater magnitude than I had anticipated. . . .

  With esteem and respect,
    Your obedient servant,
      Homer Wilbur.

Once git a smell o' musk into a draw,
An' it clings hold like precerdents in law:
Your gra'ma'am put it there,—when, goodness
    knows,—
To jes' this-worldify her Sunday-clo'es;
But the old chist wun't sarve her gran'son's wife,
(For, 'thout new funnitoor, wut good in life?) 6
An' so ole clawfoot, from the precinks dread
O' the spare chamber, slinks into the shed,
Where, dim with dust, it fust or last subsides
To holdin' seeds an' fifty things besides;   10
But better days stick fast in heart an' husk,
An' all you keep in 't gits a scent o' musk.

Jes' so with poets: wut they've airly read
Gits kind o' worked into their heart an' head,
So 's 't they can't seem to write but jest on sheers
With furrin countries or played-out ideers,   16
Nor hev a feelin', ef it doos n't smack
O' wut some critter chose to feel 'way back:

This makes 'em talk o' daisies, larks, an' things,
Ez though we 'd nothin' here that blows an' sings,—
(Why, I 'd give more for one live bobolink   21
Than a square mile o' larks in printer's ink,)—
This makes 'em think our fust o' May is May,
Which 't ain't, for all the almanicks can say.

O little city-gals, don't never go it   25
Blind on the word o' noospaper or poet!
They 're apt to puff, an' May-day seldom looks
Up in the country ez it doos in books;
They 're no more like than hornets'-nests an' hives,
Or printed sarmons be to holy lives.   30
I, with my trouses perched on cowhide boots,
Tuggin' my foundered feet out by the roots,
Hev seen ye come to fling on April's hearse
Your muslin nosegays from the milliner's,
Puzzlin' to find dry ground your queen to choose,
An' dance your throats sore in morocker shoes: 36
I 've seen ye an' felt proud, thet, come wut would,
Our Pilgrim stock wuz pethed with hardihood.
Pleasure doos make us Yankees kind o' winch,
Ez though 't wuz sunthin' paid for by the inch;
But yit we du contrive to worry thru,   41
Ef Dooty tells us thet the thing 's to du,
An' kerry a hollerday, ef we set out,
Ez stiddily ez though 't wuz a redoubt.

I, country-born an' bred, know where to find   45
Some blooms thet make the season suit the mind,
An' seem to metch the doubtin' bluebird's notes,—
Half-vent'rin' liverworts in furry coats,
Bloodroots, whose rolled-up leaves ef you oncurl,
Each on 'em 's cradle to a baby-pearl,—   50
But these are jes' Spring's pickets; sure ez sin,
The rebble frosts 'll try to drive 'em in;
For half our May 's so awfully like May n't,
't would rile a Shaker or an evrige saint;
Though I own up I like our back'ard springs   55
Thet kind o' haggle with their greens an' things,
An' when you 'most give up, 'uthout more words
Toss the fields full o' blossoms, leaves, an' birds;
Thet's Northun natur', slow an' apt to doubt,
But when it *doos* git stirred, ther' 's no gin-out!   60

Fust come the blackbirds clatt'rin' in tall trees,
An' settlin' things in windy Congresses,—
Queer politicians, though, for I 'll be skinned
Ef all on 'em don't head aginst the wind.

'fore long the trees begin to show belief,—   65
The maple crimsons to a coral-reef,
Then saffern swarms swing off from all the willers
So plump they look like yaller caterpillars,
Then gray hossches'nuts leetle hands unfold
Softer 'n a baby's be at three days old: 70
Thet 's robin-redbreast's almanick; he knows
Thet arter this ther' 's only blossom-snows;
So, choosin' out a handy crotch an' spouse,
He goes to plast'rin' his adobë house.   74

Then seems to come a hitch,—things lag behind,
Till some fine mornin' Spring makes up her mind,
An' ez, when snow-swelled rivers cresh their dams
Heaped-up with ice thet dovetails in an' jams,
A leak comes spirtin' thru some pine-hole cleft,
Grows stronger, fercer, tears out right an' left,   80
Then all the waters bow themselves an' come,
Suddin, in one gret slope o' shedderin' foam,
Jes' so our Spring gits everythin' in tune
An' gives one leap from Aperl into June:
Then all comes crowdin' in; afore you think,   85
Young oak-leaves mist the side-hill woods with
        pink;
The catbird in the laylock-bush is loud;
The orchards turn to heaps o' rosy cloud;
Red-cedars blossom tu, though few folks know it,
An' look all dipt in sunshine like a poet;   90
The lime-trees pile their solid stacks o' shade
An' drows'ly simmer with the bees' sweet trade;
In ellum-shrouds the flashin' hangbird clings
An' for the summer vy'ge his hammock slings;   94
All down the loose-walled lanes in archin' bowers
The barb'ry droops its strings o' golden flowers,
Whose shrinkin' hearts the school-gals love to try
With pins,—they 'll worry yourn so, boys, bimeby!
But I don't love your cat'logue style,—do you?—
Ez ef to sell off Natur' by vendoo;   100
One word with blood in 't 's twice ez good ez two:
'nuff sed, June's bridesman, poet o' the year,
Gladness on wings, the bobolink, is here;
Half-hid in tip-top apple-blooms he swings,
Or climbs aginst the breeze with quiverin' wings,
Or, givin' way to 't in a mock despair,   106
Runs down, a brook o' laughter, thru the air.

I ollus feel the sap start in my veins
In Spring, with curus heats an' prickly pains,

Thet drive me, when I git a chance, to walk   110
Off by myself to hev a privit talk
With a queer critter thet can't seem to 'gree
Along o' me like most folks,—Mister Me.
Ther' 's times when I'm unsoshle ez a stone,
An' sort o' suffercate to be alone,—   115
I 'm crowded jes' to think thet folks are nigh,
An' can't bear nothin' closer than the sky;
Now the wind 's full ez shifty in the mind
Ez wut it is ou'-doors, if I ain't blind,
An' sometimes, in the fairest sou'west weather,
My innard vane pints east for weeks together,   121
My natur' gits all goose-flesh, an' my sins
Come drizzlin' on my conscience sharp ez pins:
Wal, et sech times I jes' slip out o' sight
An' take it out in a fair stan'-up fight   125
With the one cuss I can't lay on the shelf,
The crook'dest stick in all the heap,—Myself.

'T wuz so las' Sabbath arter meetin'-time:
Findin' my feelin's would n't noways rhyme
With nobody's, but off the hendle flew   130
An' took things from an east-wind pint o' view,
I started off to lose me in the hills
Where the pines be, up back o' 'Siah's Mills:
Pines ef you 're blue, are the best friends I know,
They mope an' sigh an' sheer your feelin's so,—
They hesh the ground beneath so, tu, I swan,   136
You half-forgit you 've gut a body on.
Ther' 's a small school'us' there where four roads
    meet,
The door-steps hollered out by little feet,
An' side-posts carved with names whose owners
    grew   140
To gret men, some on 'em, an' deacons, tu;
't ain't used no longer, coz the town hez gut
A high-school, where they teach the Lord knows
    wut:
Three-story larnin' 's pop'lar now; I guess
We thriv' ez wal on jes' two stories less,   145
For it strikes me ther' 's sech a thing ez sinnin'
By overloadin' children's underpinnin':
Wal, here it wuz I larned my A B C,
An' it 's a kind o' favorite spot with me.

We 're curus critters: Now ain't jes' the minute
Thet ever fits us easy while we're in it;   151
Long ez 't wuz futur', 't would be perfect bliss,—

Soon ez it 's past, *thet* time 's wuth ten o' this;
An' yit there ain't a man thet need be told
Thet Now 's the only bird lays eggs o' gold.   155
A knee-high lad, I used to plot an' plan
An' think 't wuz life's cap-sheaf to be a man;
Now, gittin' gray, there 's nothin' I enjoy
Like dreamin' back along into a boy:
So the ole school'us' is a place I choose   160
Afore all others, ef I want to muse;
I set down where I used to set, an' git
My boyhood back, an' better things with it,—
Faith, Hope, an' sunthin', ef it is n't Cherrity,   164
It 's want o' guile, an' thet 's ez gret a rerrity,—
While Fancy's cushin', free to Prince and Clown,
Makes the hard bench ez soft ez milk-weed-down.

Now, 'fore I knowed, thet Sabbath arternoon
When I sot out to tramp myself in tune,
I found me in the school'us' on my seat,   170
Drummin' the march to No-wheres with my feet.
Thinkin' o' nothin', I 've heerd ole folks say
Is a hard kind o' dooty in its way:
It 's thinkin' everythin' you ever knew,
Or ever hearn, to make your feelin's blue.   175
I sot there tryin' thet on for a spell:
I thought o' the Rebellion, then o' Hell,
Which some folks tell ye now is jest a metterfor
(A the'ry, p'raps, it wun't *feel* none the better for);
I thought o' Reconstruction, wut we'd win   180
Patchin' our patent self-blow-up agin;
I thought ef this 'ere milkin' o' the wits,
So much a month, warn't givin' Natur' fits,—
Ef folks warn't druv, findin' their own milk fail,
To work the cow thet hez an iron tail,   185
An' ef idees 'thout ripenin' in the pan
Would send up cream to humor ary man:
From this to thet I let my worryin' creep,
Till finally I must ha' fell asleep.

Our lives in sleep are some like streams thet glide
'twixt flesh an' sperrit boundin' on each side,   191
Where both shores' shadders kind o' mix an'
    mingle
In sunthin' thet ain't jes' like either single;
An' when you cast off moorin's from To-day,
An' down towards To-morrer drift away,   195
The imiges thet tengle on the stream
Make a new upside-down'ard world o' dream:

Sometimes they seem like sunrise-streaks an'
    warnin's
O' wut 'll be in Heaven on Sabbath-mornin's,
An', mixed right in ez ef jest out o' spite,   200
Sunthin' thet says your supper ain't gone right.
I 'm gret on dreams, an' often when I wake,
I 've lived so much it makes my mem'ry ache,
An' can't skurce take a cat-nap in my cheer
'thout hevin' 'em, some good, some bad, all queer.

Now I wuz settin' where I 'd ben, it seemed, 206
An' ain't sure yit whether I r'ally dreamed,
Nor, ef I did, how long I might ha' slep',
When I hearn some un stompin' up the step,
An' lookin' round, ef two an' two make four, 210
I see a Pilgrim Father in the door.
He wore a steeple-hat, tall boots, an' spurs
With rowels to 'em big ez ches'nut-burrs,
An' his gret sword behind him sloped away
Long 'z a man's speech thet dunno wut to say.—
"Ef you name 's Biglow, an' your given-name 216
Hosee," sez he, "it 's arter you I came;
I 'm your gret-gran'ther multiplied by three."—
"My *wut?*" sez I.— "Your gret-gret-gret," sez he:
"You would n't ha' never ben here but for me.
Two hundred an' three year ago this May 221
The ship I come in sailed up Boston Bay;
I 'd been a cunnle in our Civil War,—
But wut on airth hev *you* gut up one for?
Coz we du things in England, 't ain't for you
To git a notion you can du 'em tu: 226
I 'm told you write in public prints: ef true,
It 's nateral you should know a thing or two."—
"Thet air 's an argymunt I can't endorse,—
't would prove, coz you wear spurs, you kep' a
    horse: 230
For brains," sez I, "wutever you may think,
Ain't boun' to cash the drafs o' pen-an'-ink,—
Though mos' folks write ez ef they hoped jes'
    quickenin'
The churn would argoo skim-milk into thickenin';
But skim-milk ain't a thing to change its view 235
O' wut it 's meant for more 'n a smoky flue.
But du pray tell me, 'fore we furder go,
How in all Natur' did you come to know
'bout our affairs," sez I, "in Kingdom-Come?"—
"Wal, I worked round at sperrit-rappin' some, 240
An' danced the tables till their legs wuz gone,

In hopes o' larnin' wut wuz goin' on,"
Sez he, "but mejums lie so like all-split
Thet I concluded it wuz best to quit.
But, come now, ef you wun't confess to knowin',
You 've some conjectures how the thing 's a-
    goin'."— 246
"Gran'ther," sez I, "a vane warn't never known
Nor asked to hev a jedgment of its own;
An' yit, ef 't ain't gut rusty in the jints,
It 's safe to trust its say on certin pints: 250
It knows the wind's opinions to a T,
An' the wind settles wut the weather'll be."
"I never thought a scion of our stock
Could grow the wood to make a weather-cock;
When I wuz younger 'n you, skurce more 'n a
    shaver, 255
No airthly wind," sez he, "could make me waver!"
(Ez he said this, he clinched his jaw an' forehead,
Hitchin' his belt to bring his sword-hilt forrard.)—
"Jes so it wuz with me," sez I, "I swow,
When *I* wuz younger 'n wut you see me now,— 260
Nothin' from Adam's fall to Huldy's bonnet,
Thet I warn't full-cocked with my jedgment on it;
But now I 'm gittin' on in life, I find
It 's a sight harder to make up my mind,—
Nor I don't often try tu, when events 265
Will du it for me free of all expense.
The moral question 's ollus plain enough,—
It 's jes' the human-natur' side thet 's tough;
Wut 's best to think may n't puzzle me nor you,—
The pinch comes in decidin' wut to *du*; 270
Ef you *read* History, all runs smooth ez grease,
Coz there the men ain't nothin' more 'n idees,—
But come to *make* it, ez we must to-day,
Th' idees hev arms an' legs an' stop the way:
It 's easy fixin' things in facts an' figgers,— 275
They can't resist, nor warn't brought up with nig-
    gers;
But come to try your the'ry on,—why, then
Your facts an' figgers change to ign'ant men
Actin' ez ugly—" —"Smite 'em hip an' thigh!"
Sez gran'ther, "and let every man-child die! 280
Oh for three weeks o' Crommle an' the Lord!
Up, Isr'el, to your tents an' grind the sword!"—
"Thet kind o' thing worked wal in ole Judee,
But you forgit how long it 's been A. D.;

281. Crommle: Oliver Cromwell (1599–1658), English
general, Lord Protector of the Commonwealth.

You think thet 's ellerkence,—I call it shoddy, 285
A thing," sez I, "wun't cover soul nor body;
I like the plain all-wool o' common-sense,
Thet warms ye now, an' will a twelve-month
    hence.
You took to follerin' where the Prophets beck-
    oned,
An', fust you knowed on, back come Charles the
    Second; 290
Now wut I want 's to hev all *we* gain stick,
An' not to start Millennium too quick;
We hain't to punish only, but to keep,
An' the cure 's gut to go a cent'ry deep."
"Wall, milk-an'-water ain't the best o' glue," 295
Sez he, "an' so you 'll find afore you 're thru;
Ef reshness venters sunthin', shilly-shally
Loses ez often wut 's ten times the vally.
Thet exe of ourn, when Charles's neck gut split,
Opened a gap thet ain't bridged over yit: 300
Slav'ry 's your Charles, the Lord hez gin the exe"—
"Our Charles," sez I, "hez gut eight million necks.
The hardest question ain't the black man's right,
The trouble is to 'mancipate the white;
One 's chained in body an' can be sot free, 305
But t' other 's chained in soul to an idee:
It 's a long job, but we shall worry thru it;
Ef bagnets fail, the spellin'-book must du it."
"Hosee," sez he, "I think you 're goin' to fail:
The rettlesnake ain't dangerous in the tail; 310
This 'ere rebellion 's nothing but the rettle,—
You 'll stomp on thet an' think you've won the
    bettle;
It 's Slavery thet 's the fangs an' thinkin' head,
An' ef you want selvation, cresh it dead,—
An' cresh it suddin, or you 'll larn by waitin' 315
Thet Chance wun't stop to listen to debatin'!"—
"God's truth!" sez I,—"an' ef *I* held the club,
An' knowed jes' where to strike,—but there 's the
    rub!"
"Strike soon," sez he, "or you 'll be deadly ailin',—
Folks thet 's afeared to fail are sure o' failin'; 320
God hates your sneakin' creturs thet believe
He 'll settle things they run away an' leave!"
He brought his foot down fercely, ez he spoke,
An' give me sech a startle thet I woke.

290. Charles the Second (1630–1685): son of Charles
the First, who in 1660 came to the throne of England after
the downfall of the Commonwealth.

Ode Recited at the Harvard Commemoration, July 21, 1865

IN LETTERS to Jane Norton, James B. Thayer, and
Richard Watson Gilder (Norton, ed., *Letters*, I, II)
Lowell wrote that he had been "hopelessly dumb" until
two days before the Commencement, when he began
to write with "vehement speed" night and day. The
thought in the eleventh strophe took him longer to
develop than all the others combined. The strophe to
Lincoln (VI) was added after the poem had been delivered; it contains some of the thoughts Lowell had
printed eighteen months earlier in an essay on Lincoln
in *The North American Review*. The poem appeared in
The Atlantic Monthly, September, 1865.

Six hundred of Harvard's 2,700 young men had
entered the armed forces. In their honor well over
1,200 persons had gathered for the commemoration
ceremonies. Among those on the program were Emerson, Holmes, Phillips Brooks, and Major-General
Meade.

In a letter to Thayer dated January 14, 1877, Lowell
expressed certain critical theories on structure. A
critic in *The Cornhill Magazine* had called the *Commemoration Ode* rather more akin to Cowley than to
Pindar. Lowell pointed out that all his odes had been
written for public recitation, and that entire regularity
would be monotonous to the ear. The rhymed heroic
was the least tedious, but even this needed the relief
of wit and change of verse form. Lowell first considered
mixing rhymed and blank verses, as in *Samson Agon-
istes*, and wrote some lines to test the effect. But
he found his ear was more attracted to an all-rhyme
scheme, with certain rhymes coming at longer intervals,
producing approximately the effect of mixed rhymed
and blank verses, with the added charm of "faint
reminiscence of consonance."

I

Weak-winged is song,
Nor aims at that clear-ethered height
Whither the brave deed climbs for light:
    We seem to do them wrong,
Bringing our robin's-leaf to deck their hearse 5
Who in warm life-blood wrote their nobler verse,
Our trivial song to honor those who come
With ears attuned to strenuous trump and drum,
And shaped in squadron-strophes their desire,
Live battle-odes whose lines were steel and fire:
    Yet sometimes feathered words are strong, 11

A gracious memory to buoy up and save
From Lethe's dreamless ooze, the common grave
    Of the unventurous throng.

II

To-day our Reverend Mother welcomes back   15
Her wisest Scholars, those who understood
The deeper teaching of her mystic tome,
   And offered their fresh lives to make it good:
      No lore of Greece or Rome,
No science peddling with the names of things,   20
Or reading stars to find inglorious fates,
      Can lift our life with wings
Far from Death's idle gulf that for the many waits,
      And lengthen out our dates
With that clear fame whose memory sings   25
In manly hearts to come, and nerves them and
      dilates:
Nor such thy teaching, Mother of us all!
      Not such the trumpet-call
      Of thy diviner mood,
      That could thy sons entice   30
From happy homes and toils, the fruitful nest
Of those half-virtues which the world calls best,
      Into War's tumult rude;
      But rather far that stern device
The sponsors chose that round thy cradle stood 35
   In the dim, unventured wood,
   The VERITAS that lurks beneath
   The letter's unprolific sheath,
   Life of whate'er makes life worth living,
Seed-grain of high emprise, immortal food,   40
   One heavenly thing whereof earth hath the
      giving.

III

Many loved Truth, and lavished life's best oil
   Amid the dust of books to find her,
Content at last, for guerdon of their toil,
   With the cast mantle she hath left behind her.
      Many in sad faith sought for her,   46
      Many with crossed hands sighed for her;
      But these, our brothers, fought for her;
      At life's dear peril wrought for her,
      So loved her that they died for her,   50
      Tasting the raptured fleetness
      Of her divine completeness:

37. Veritas: "Truth," Harvard motto.

      Their higher instinct knew
Those love her best who to themselves are true,
And what they dare to dream of, dare to do;   55
      They followed her and found her
      Where all may hope to find,
Not in the ashes of the burnt-out mind,
But beautiful, with danger's sweetness round her.
      Where faith made whole with deed   60
      Breathes its awakening breath
      Into the lifeless creed,
      They saw her plumed and mailed,
      With sweet, stern face unveiled,
And all-repaying eyes, look proud on them in
      death.   65

IV

Our slender life runs rippling by, and glides
   Into the silent hollow of the past;
      What is there that abides
   To make the next age better for the last?
      Is earth too poor to give us   70
   Something to live for here that shall outlive us?
      Some more substantial boon
Than such as flows and ebbs with Fortune's fickle
      moon?
      The little that we see
      From doubt is never free;   75
      The little that we do
      Is but half-nobly true;
      With our laborious hiving
What men call treasure, and the gods call dross,
   Life seems a jest of Fate's contriving,   80
   Only secure in every one's conniving,
A long account of nothings paid with loss,
Where we poor puppets, jerked by unseen wires,
   After our little hour of strut and rave,
With all our pasteboard passions and desires,   85
Loves, hates, ambitions, and immortal fires,
   Are tossed pell-mell together in the grave.
   But stay! no age was e'er degenerate,
   Unless men held it at too cheap a rate,
   For in our likeness still we shape our fate.   90
      Ah, there is something here
      Unfathomed by the cynic's sneer,
      Something that gives our feeble light
      A high immunity from Night,
      Something that leaps life's narrow bars   95
To claim its birthright with the hosts of heaven;

A seed of sunshine that can leaven
Our earthly dullness with the beams of stars,
   And glorify our clay
With light from fountains elder than the Day;
    A conscience more divine than we,   101
    A gladness fed with secret tears,
    A vexing, forward-reaching sense
    Of some more noble permanence;
    A light across the sea,   105
Which haunts the soul and will not let it be,
Still beaconing from the heights of undegenerate
    years.

V

   Whither leads the path
   To ampler fates that leads?
   Not down through flowery meads,   110
   To reap an aftermath
   Of youth's vainglorious weeds,
   But up the steep, amid the wrath
   And shock of deadly-hostile creeds,
   Where the world's best hope and stay   115
By battle's flashes gropes a desperate way,
And every turf the fierce foot clings to bleeds.
   Peace hath her not ignoble wreath,
   Ere yet the sharp, decisive word
Light the black lips of cannon, and the sword   120
   Dreams in its easeful sheath;
But some day the live coal behind the thought,
   Whether from Baäl's stone obscene,
   Or from the shrine serene
   Of God's pure altar brought,   125
Bursts up in flame; the war of tongue and pen
Learns with what deadly purpose it was fraught,
And, helpless in the fiery passion caught,
Shakes all the pillared state with shock of men:
Some day the soft Ideal that we wooed   130
Confronts us fiercely, foe-beset, pursued,
And cries reproachful: "Was it, then, my praise,
And not myself was loved? Prove now thy truth;
I claim of thee the promise of thy youth;
Give me thy life, or cower in empty phrase,   135
The victim of thy genius, not its mate!"
   Life may be given in many ways,
   And loyalty to Truth be sealed
As bravely in the closet as the field,

123. **Baäl's stone:** I Kings, 18; used in a ceremony to
determine the true God.

So bountiful is Fate;   140
   But then to stand beside her,
   When craven churls deride her,
To front a lie in arms and not to yield,
   This shows, methinks, God's plan
   And measure of a stalwart man,   145
   Limbed like the old heroic breeds,
   Who stands self-poised on manhood's solid
    earth,
   Not forced to frame excuses for his birth,
Fed from within with all the strength he needs.

VI

Such was he, our Martyr-Chief,   150
   Whom late the Nation he had led,
   With ashes on her head,
Wept with the passion of an angry grief:
Forgive me, if from present things I turn
To speak what in my heart will beat and burn,
And hang my wreath on his world-honored urn. 156
   Nature, they say, doth dote,
   And cannot make a man
   Save on some worn-out plan,
   Repeating us by rote: 160
For him her Old-World moulds aside she threw,
   And, choosing sweet clay from the breast
   Of the unexhausted West,
With stuff untainted shaped a hero new,
Wise, steadfast in the strength of God, and true. 165
   How beautiful to see
Once more a shepherd of mankind indeed,
Who loved his charge, but never loved to lead;
One whose meek flock the people joyed to be,
   Not lured by any cheat of birth,   170
   But by his clear-grained human worth,
And brave old wisdom of sincerity!
   They knew that outward grace is dust;
   They could not choose but trust
In that sure-footed mind's unfaltering skill,   175
   And supple-tempered will
That bent like perfect steel to spring again and
    thrust.
   His was no lonely mountain-peak of mind,
   Thrusting to thin air o'er our cloudy bars,
   A sea-mark now, now lost in vapors blind; 180
   Broad prairie rather, genial, level-lined,
   Fruitful and friendly for all human kind,

150. **Martyr-Chief:** Abraham Lincoln.

Yet also nigh to heaven and loved of loftiest stars.
    Nothing of Europe here,
Or, then, of Europe fronting mornward still, 185
    Ere any names of Serf and Peer
    Could Nature's equal scheme deface
    And thwart her genial will;
    Here was a type of the true elder race,
And one of Plutarch's men talked with us face to
    face. 190
    I praise him not; it were too late;
And some innative weakness there must be
In him who condescends to victory
Such as the Present gives, and cannot wait,
    Safe in himself as in a fate. 195
    So always firmly he:
    He knew to bide his time,
    And can his fame abide,
Still patient in his simple faith sublime,
    Till the wise years decide. 200
Great captains, with their guns and drums,
    Disturb our judgment for the hour,
    But at last silence comes;
These all are gone, and, standing like a tower,
    Our children shall behold his fame. 205
    The kindly-earnest, brave, foreseeing man,
Sagacious, patient, dreading praise, not blame,
    New birth of our new soil, the first American.

VII

Long as man's hope insatiate can discern
    Or only guess some more inspiring goal 210
    Outside of Self, enduring as the pole,
    Along whose course the flying axles burn
Of spirits bravely-pitched, earth's manlier brood;
    Long as below we cannot find
    The meed that stills the inexorable mind; 215
So long this faith to some ideal Good,
Under whatever mortal names it masks,
Freedom, Law, Country, this ethereal mood
That thanks the Fates for their severer tasks,
    Feeling its challenged pulses leap, 220
    While others skulk in subterfuges cheap,
And, set in Danger's van, has all the boon it asks,
    Shall win man's praise and woman's love,
    Shall be a wisdom that we set above
All other skills and gifts to culture dear, 225
    A virtue round whose forehead we inwreathe
    Laurels that with a living passion breathe

When other crowns grow, while we twine them,
    sear.
    What brings us thronging these high rites to pay,
And seal these hours the noblest of our year, 230
    Save that our brothers found this better way?

VIII

We sit here in the Promised Land
    That flows with Freedom's honey and milk;
    But 'twas they won it, sword in hand,
Making the nettle danger soft for us as silk. 235
    We welcome back our bravest and our best;—
    Ah me! not all! some come not with the rest,
Who went forth brave and bright as any here!
I strive to mix some gladness with my strain,
    But the sad strings complain, 240
    And will not please the ear:
I sweep them for a pæan, but they wane
    Again and yet again
Into a dirge, and die away, in pain.
In these brave ranks I only see the gaps, 245
Thinking of dear ones whom the dumb turf wraps,
Dark to the triumph which they died to gain:
    Fitlier may others greet the living,
    For me the past is unforgiving;
    I with uncovered head 250
    Salute the sacred dead,
Who went, and who return not.—Say not so!
'Tis not the grapes of Canaan that repay,
But the high faith that failed not by the way;
Virtue treads paths that end not in the grave; 255
No ban of endless night exiles the brave;
    And to the saner mind
We rather seem the dead that stayed behind.
Blow, trumpets, all your exultations blow!
For never shall their aureoled presence lack: 260
I see them muster in a gleaming row,
With ever-youthful brows that nobler show;
We find in our dull road their shining track;
    In every nobler mood
We feel the orient of their spirit glow, 265
Part of our life's unalterable good,
Of all our saintlier aspiration;
    They come transfigured back,
Secure from change in their high-hearted ways,

253. grapes of Canaan: Numbers, 13:20–27. The Israel-ites, investigating the riches of Canaan, returned with a bunch of grapes so large that it required two men to carry it.

Beautiful evermore, and with the rays   270
Of morn on their white Shields of Expectation!

IX

But is there hope to save
Even this ethereal essence from the grave?
What ever 'scaped Oblivion's subtle wrong
Save a few clarion names, or golden threads of
    song?   275
    Before my musing eye
    The mighty ones of old sweep by,
Disvoicèd now and insubstantial things,
As noisy once as we; poor ghosts of kings,
Shadows of empire wholly gone to dust,   280
And many races, nameless long ago,
To darkness driven by that imperious gust
Of ever-rushing Time that here doth blow:
O visionary world, condition strange,
Where naught abiding is but only Change,   285
Where the deep-bolted stars themselves still shift
    and range!
Shall we to more continuance make pretence?
Renown builds tombs; a life-estate is Wit;
    And, bit by bit,   289
The cunning years steal all from us but woe;
    Leaves are we, whose decays no harvest sow.
    But, when we vanish hence,
Shall they lie forceless in the dark below,
Save to make green their little length of sods,
Or deepen pansies for a year or two,   295
Who now to us are shining-sweet as gods?
Was dying all they had the skill to do?
That were not fruitless: but the Soul resents
Such short-lived service, as if blind events
Ruled without her, or earth could so endure;   300
She claims a more divine investiture
Of longer tenure than Fame's airy rents;
Whate'er she touches doth her nature share;
Her inspiration haunts the ennobled air,
    Gives eyes to mountains blind,   305
Ears to the deaf earth, voices to the wind,
And her clear trump sings succor everywhere
By lonely bivouacs to the wakeful mind;
For soul inherits all that soul could dare:
    Yea, Manhood hath a wider span   310
And larger privilege of life than man.
The single deed, the private sacrifice,
So radiant now through proudly-hidden tears,

Is covered up erelong from mortal eyes   314
With thoughtless drift of the deciduous years;
But that high privilege that makes all men peers,
That leap of heart whereby a people rise
    Up to a noble anger's height,
And, flamed on by the Fates, not shrink, but grow
    more bright,
    That swift validity in noble veins,   320
    Of choosing danger and disdaining shame,
    Of being set on flame
By the pure fire that flies all contact base,
But wraps its chosen with angelic might,
    These are imperishable gains,   325
Sure as the sun, medicinal as light,
These hold great futures in their lusty reins
And certify to earth a new imperial race.

X

    Who now shall sneer?
    Who dare again to say we trace   330
    Our lines to a plebeian race?
    Roundhead and Cavalier!
Dumb are those names erewhile in battle loud;
Dream-footed as the shadow of a cloud,
    They flit across the ear: 333
That is best blood that hath most iron in't,
To edge resolve with, pouring without stint
    For what makes manhood dear.
    Tell us not of Plantagenets,
Hapsburgs, and Guelfs, whose thin bloods crawl   340
Down from some victor in a border-brawl!
    How poor their outworn coronets,
Matched with one leaf of that plain civic wreath
Our brave for honor's blazon shall bequeath,
    Through whose desert a rescued Nation sets   345
Her heel on treason, and the trumpet hears
Shout victory, tingling Europe's sullen ears
    With vain resentments and more vain regrets!

XI

    Not in anger, not in pride,
    Pure from passion's mixture rude   350
    Ever to base earth allied,
    But with far-heard gratitude,
    Still with heart and voice renewed,
To heroes living and dear martyrs dead,
The strain should close that consecrates our brave.
    Lift the heart and lift the head!   356

Lofty be its mood and grave,
Not without a martial ring,
Not without a prouder tread
And a peal of exultation: 360
Little right has he to sing
Through whose heart in such an hour
Beats no march of conscious power,
Sweeps no tumult of elation!
'Tis no Man we celebrate,   365
By his country's victories great,
A hero half, and half the whim of Fate,
But the pith and marrow of a Nation
Drawing force from all her men,
Highest, humblest, weakest, all,   370
For her time of need, and then
Pulsing it again through them,
Till the basest can no longer cower,
Feeling his soul spring up divinely tall,
Touched but in passing by her mantle-hem.   375
Come back, then, noble pride, for 'tis her
    dower!
    How could poet ever tower,
    If his passions, hopes, and fears,
    If his triumphs and his tears,
    Kept not measure with his people?   380
Boom, cannon, boom to all the winds and waves!
Clash out, glad bells, from every rocking steeple!
Banners, advance with triumph, bend your staves!
    And from every mountain-peak
    Let beacon-fire to answering beacon speak, 385
    Katahdin tell Monadnock, Whiteface he,
And so leap on in light from sea to sea,
    Till the glad news be sent
    Across a kindling continent,
Making earth feel more firm and air breathe braver:
"Be proud! for she is saved, and all have helped to
    save her!   391
She that lifts up the manhood of the poor,
She of the open soul and open door,
With room about her hearth for all mankind!
The fire is dreadful in her eyes no more;   395
From her bold front the helm she doth un-
    bind,
Sends all her handmaid armies back to spin,
And bids her navies, that so lately hurled

386. *Katahdin, Whiteface:* Katahdin is a mountain
in Maine, Monadnock a mountain in New Hampshire,
Whiteface a mountain in New York.

Their crashing battle, hold their thunders in,
Swimming like birds of calm along the un-
    harmful shore.   400
No challenge sends she to the elder world,
That looked askance and hated; a light scorn
Plays o'er her mouth, as round her mighty
    knees
She calls her children back, and waits the morn
Of nobler day, enthroned between her subject
    seas."   405

XII

Bow down, dear Land, for thou hast found release!
    Thy God, in these distempered days,
    Hath taught thee the sure wisdom of His ways,
And through thine enemies hath wrought thy
    peace!
    Bow down in prayer and praise!   410
No poorest in thy borders but may now
Lift to the juster skies a man's enfranchised brow.
O Beautiful! my Country! ours once more!
Smoothing thy gold of war-dishevelled hair
O'er such sweet brows as never other wore,   415
    And letting thy set lips,
    Freed from wrath's pale eclipse,
The rosy edges of their smile lay bare,
What words divine of lover or of poet
Could tell our love and make thee know it,   420
Among the Nations bright beyond compare?
    What were our lives without thee?
    What all our lives to save thee?
    We reck not what we gave thee;
    We will not dare to doubt thee,   425
But ask whatever else, and we will dare!

To H. W. L.

On His Birthday, 27th February, 1867

ON THIS DAY Lowell sent Longfellow a letter and a corrected copy of these verses, which had appeared on the
same morning in the *Advertiser*. The poem was collected in *Under the Willows* (1868).

I need not praise the sweetness of his song,
    Where limpid verse to limpid verse succeeds
Smooth as our Charles, when, fearing lest he wrong
The new moon's mirrored skiff, he slides along,
    Full without noise, and whispers in his reeds. 5

With loving breath of all the winds his name
  Is blown about the world, but to his friends
A sweeter secret hides behind his fame,
And Love steals shyly through the loud acclaim
  To murmur a *God bless you!* and there ends. 10

As I muse backward up the checkered years
  Wherein so much was given, so much was lost,
Blessings in both kinds, such as cheapen tears,—
But hush! this is not for profaner ears;
  Let them drink molten pearls nor dream the
      cost. 15

Some suck up poison from a sorrow's core,
  As naught but nightshade grew upon earth's
      ground;
Love turned all his to heart's-ease, and the more
Fate tried his bastions, she but forced a door
  Leading to sweeter manhood and more sound.

Even as a wind-waved fountain's swaying shade 21
  Seems of mixed race, a gray wraith shot with sun,
So through his trial faith translucent rayed
Till darkness, half disnatured so, betrayed
  A heart of sunshine that would fain o'errun. 25

Surely if skill in song the shears may stay
  And of its purpose cheat the charmed abyss,
If our poor life be lengthened by a lay,
He shall not go, although his presence may,
  And the next age in praise shall double this. 30

Long days be his, and each as lusty-sweet
  As gracious natures find his song to be;
May Age steal on with softly-cadenced feet
Falling in music, as for him were meet 34
  Whose choicest verse is harsher-toned than he!

The Cathedral

WHILE STUDYING in France in 1855, Lowell made an
excursion to the famous Cathedral at Chartres. He
began writing the poem fourteen years later. In a
letter to C. E. Norton, September 6, 1869, he remarked
that no other poem had so engrossed him; for weeks
he had worked on it, until his wife "well-nigh grew
jealous" (Norton, *Letters*, II). The poem, somewhat
abbreviated, appeared in *The Atlantic Monthly* for
January, 1870, and at full length in the volume published for the Christmas trade of 1869, dated 1870. On

March 25, 1870, he thanked Leslie Stephen for his appreciation, and said he had no thought of satirizing the
English in some lines on two Englishmen (Norton,
Letters, II). He was not fully satisfied with the poem as
it appeared in 1869, though he had altered the title
from "A Day at Chartres," as in the *Atlantic*, to *The
Cathedral*. In subsequent editions he omitted the lines
on the Englishmen and added two passages—the seven
lines which follow "Wrought for good's sake," and the
twenty-four lines following "After these dizzy elations
of the mind." The omitted lines are set off in brackets
below:

The flies and I its only customers,
[Till by and by there came two Englishmen,
Who made me feel, in their engaging way,
I was a poacher on their self-preserve,
Intent constructively on lese-anglicism.
To them (in those old razor-ridden days)
My beard translated me to hostile French;
So they, desiring guidance in the town,
Half condescended to my baser sphere,
And, clubbing in one mess their lack of phrase,
Set their best man to grapple with the Gaul.
'Esker vous ate a nabitang?' he asked;
'I never ate one; are they good?' asked I;
Whereat they stared, then laughed, and we were friends,
The seas, the wars, the centuries interposed,
Abolished in the truce of common speech
And mutual comfort of the mother-tongue.
Like escaped convicts of Propriety,
They furtively partook the joys of men,
Glancing behind when buzzed some louder fly.]
Eluding these, I loitered through the town, . . .

Far through the memory shines a happy day,
Cloudless of care, down-shod to every sense,
And simply perfect from its own resource,
As to a bee the new campanula's
Illuminate seclusion swung in air. 5
Such days are not the prey of setting suns,
Nor ever blurred with mist of after-thought;
Like words made magical by poets dead,
Wherein the music of all meaning is
The sense hath garnered or the soul divined, 10
They mingle with our life's ethereal part,
Sweetening and gathering sweetness evermore,
By Beauty's franchise disenthralled of time.

I can recall, nay, they are present still,
Parts of myself, the perfume of my mind, 15
Days that seem farther off than Homer's now
Ere yet the child had loudened to the boy,

And I, recluse from playmates, found perforce
Companionship in things that not denied
Nor granted wholly; as is Nature's wont, 20
Who, safe in uncontaminate reserve,
Lets us mistake our longing for her love,
And mocks with various echo of ourselves.

These first sweet frauds upon our consciousness,
That blend the sensual with its imaged world, 25
These virginal cognitions, gifts of morn,
Ere life grow noisy, and slower-footed thought
Can overtake the rapture of the sense,
To thrust between ourselves and what we feel,
Have something in them secretly divine. 30
Vainly the eye, once schooled to serve the brain,
With pains deliberate studies to renew
The ideal vision: second-thoughts are prose;
For Beauty's acme hath a term as brief
As the wave's poise before it break in pearl. 35
Our own breath dims the mirror of the sense,
Looking too long and closely: at a flash
We snatch the essential grace of meaning out,
And that first passion beggars all behind,
Heirs of a tamer transport prepossessed. 40
Who, seeing once, has truly seen again
The gray vague of unsympathizing sea
That dragged his Fancy from her moorings back
To shores inhospitable of eldest time,
Till blank foreboding of earth-gendered power, 45
Pitiless seignories in the elements,
Omnipotences blind that darkling smite,
Misgave him, and repaganized the world?
Yet, by some subtler touch of sympathy,
These primal apprehensions, dimly stirred, 50
Perplex the eye with pictures from within.
This hath made poets dream of lives foregone
In worlds fantastical, more fair than ours;
So Memory cheats us, glimpsing half-revealed.
Even as I write she tries her wonted spell 55
In that continuous redbreast boding rain:
The bird I hear sings not from yonder elm;
But the flown ecstasy my childhood heard
Is vocal in my mind, renewed by him,
Haply made sweeter by the accumulate thrill 60
That threads my undivided life and steals
A pathos from the years and graves between.

I know not how it is with other men,
Whom I but guess, deciphering myself;

For me, once felt is so felt nevermore. 65
The fleeting relish at sensation's brim
Had in it the best ferment of the wine.
One spring I knew as never any since:
All night the surges of the warm southwest
Boomed intermittent through the shuddering
    elms, 70
And brought a morning from the Gulf adrift,
Omnipotent with sunshine, whose quick charm
Startled with crocuses the sullen turf
And wiled the bluebird to his whiff of song:
One summer hour abides, what time I perched, 75
Dappled with noonday, under simmering leaves,
And pulled the pulpy oxhearts, while aloof
An oriole clattered and the robins shrilled,
Denouncing me an alien and a thief:
One morn of autumn lords it o'er the rest, 80
When in the lane I watched the ash-leaves fall,
Balancing softly earthward without wind,
Or twirling with directer impulse down
On those fallen yesterday, now barbed with frost,
While I grew pensive with the pensive year: 85
And once I learned how marvellous winter was,
When past the fence-rails, downy-gray with rime,
I creaked adventurous o'er the spangled crust
That made familiar fields seem far and strange
As those stark wastes that whiten endlessly 90
In ghastly solitude about the pole,
And gleam relentless to the unsetting sun:
Instant the candid chambers of my brain
Were painted with these sovran images;
And later visions seem but copies pale 95
From those unfading frescos of the past,
Which I, young savage, in my age of flint,
Gazed at, and dimly felt a power in me
Parted from Nature by the joy in her
That doubtfully revealed me to myself. 100
Thenceforward I must stand outside the gate;
And paradise was paradise the more,
Known once and barred against satiety.

What we call Nature, all outside ourselves,
Is but our own conceit of what we see, 105
Our own reaction upon what we feel;
The world's a woman to our shifting mood,
Feeling with us, or making due pretence;
And therefore we the more persuade ourselves
To make all things our thought's confederates, 110

Conniving with us in whate'er we dream.
So when our Fancy seeks analogies,
Though she have hidden what she after finds,
She loves to cheat herself with feigned surprise.
I find my own complexion everywhere: 115
No rose, I doubt, was ever, like the first,
A marvel to the bush it dawned upon,
The rapture of its life made visible,
The mystery of its yearning realized,
As the first babe to the first woman born;   120
No falcon ever felt delight of wings
As when, an eyas, from the stolid cliff
Loosing himself, he followed his high heart
To swim on sunshine, masterless as wind;
And I believe the brown Earth takes delight   125
In the new snowdrop looking back at her,
To think that by some vernal alchemy
It could transmute her darkness into pearl;
What is the buxom peony after that,
With its coarse constancy of hoyden blush?   130
What the full summer to that wonder new?

But, if in nothing else, in us there is
A sense fastidious hardly reconciled
To the poor makeshifts of life's scenery,
Where the same slide must double all its parts, 135
Shoved in for Tarsus and hitched back for Tyre.
I blame not in the soul this daintiness,
Rasher of surfeit than a humming-bird,
In things indifferent by sense purveyed;
It argues her an immortality   140
And dateless incomes of experience,
This unthrift housekeeping that will not brook
A dish warmed-over at the feast of life,
And finds Twice stale, served with whatever sauce.
Nor matters much how it may go with me   145
Who dwell in Grub Street and am proud to drudge
Where men, my betters, wet their crust with tears:
Use can make sweet the peach's shady side,
That only by reflection tastes of sun.

But she, my Princess, who will sometimes deign
My garret to illumine till the walls,   151
Narrow and dingy, scrawled with hackneyed
     thought
(Poor Richard slowly elbowing Plato out),
Dilate and drape themselves with tapestries

136. **Tarsus, Tyre:** cities in Asia Minor.

Nausikaa might have stooped o'er, while, between,
Mirrors, effaced in their own clearness, send   156
Her only image on through deepening deeps
With endless repercussion of delight,—
Bringer of life, witching each sense to soul,
That sometimes almost gives me to believe   160
I might have been a poet, gives at least
A brain desaxonized, an ear that makes
Music where none is, and a keener pang
Of exquisite surmise outleaping thought,—
Her will I pamper in her luxury: 165
No crumpled rose-leaf of too careless choice
Shall bring a northern nightmare to her dreams,
Vexing with sense of exile; hers shall be
The invitiate firstlings of experience,
Vibrations felt but once and felt lifelong: 170
Oh, more than half-way turn that Grecian front
Upon me, while with self-rebuke I spell,
On the plain fillet that confines thy hair
In conscious bounds of seeming unconstraint,
The Naught in overplus, thy race's badge!   175

One feast for her I secretly designed
In that Old World so strangely beautiful
To us the disinherited of eld,—
A day at Chartres, with no soul beside
To roil with pedant prate my joy serene   180
And make the minster shy of confidence.
I went, and, with the Saxon's pious care,
First ordered dinner at the pea-green inn,
The flies and I its only customers.
Eluding these, I loitered through the town,   185
With hope to take my minster unawares
In its grave solitude of memory.
A pretty burgh, and such as Fancy loves
For bygone grandeurs, faintly rumorous now
Upon the mind's horizon, as of storm   190
Brooding its dreamy thunders far aloof,
That mingle with our mood, but not disturb.
Its once grim bulwarks, tamed to lovers' walks,
Look down unwatchful on the sliding Eure,
Whose listless leisure suits the quiet place,   195
Lisping among his shallows homelike sounds
At Concord and by Bankside heard before.
Chance led me to a public pleasure-ground,
Where I grew kindly with the merry groups,
And blessed the Frenchman for his simple art   200

194. **Eure:** river flowing into the Seine.

Of being domestic in the light of day.
His language has no word, we growl, for Home;
But he can find a fireside in the sun,
Play with his child, make love, and shriek his mind,
By throngs of strangers undisprivacied.   205
He makes his life a public gallery,
Nor feels himself till what he feels comes back
In manifold reflection from without;
While we, each pore alert with consciousness,
Hide our best selves as we had stolen them,   210
And each bystander a detective were,
Keen-eyed for every chink of undisguise.

So, musing o'er the problem which was best,—
A life wide-windowed, shining all abroad,
Or curtains drawn to shield from sight profane
The rites we pay to the mysterious I,—   216
With outward senses furloughed and head bowed
I followed some fine instinct in my feet,
Till, to unbend me from the loom of thought,
Looking up suddenly, I found mine eyes   220
Confronted with the minster's vast repose.
Silent and gray as forest-leaguered cliff
Left inland by the ocean's slow retreat,
That hears afar the breeze-borne rote and longs,
Remembering shocks of surf that clomb and fell,
Spume-sliding down the baffled decuman,   226
It rose before me, patiently remote
From the great tides of life it breasted once,
Hearing the noise of men as in a dream.
I stood before the triple northern port,   230
Where dedicated shapes of saints and kings,
Stern faces bleared with immemorial watch,
Looked down benignly grave and seemed to say,
Ye come and go incessant; we remain
Safe in the hallowed quiets of the past;   235
Be reverent, ye who flit and are forgot,
Of faith so nobly realized as this.
I seem to have heard it said by learnëd folk
Who drench you with æsthetics till you feel
As if all beauty were a ghastly bore,   240
The faucet to let loose a wash of words,
That Gothic is not Grecian, therefore worse;
But, being convinced by much experiment
How little inventiveness there is in man,
Grave copier of copies, I give thanks   245
For a new relish, careless to inquire
My pleasure's pedigree, if so it please,

Nobly, I mean, nor renegade to art.
The Grecian gluts me with its perfectness,
Unanswerable as Euclid, self-contained,   250
The one thing finished in this hasty world,
Forever finished, though the barbarous pit,
Fanatical on hearsay, stamp and shout
As if a miracle could be encored.
But ah! this other, this that never ends,   255
Still climbing, luring fancy still to climb,
As full of morals half-divined as life,
Graceful, grotesque, with ever new surprise
Of hazardous caprices sure to please,
Heavy as nightmare, airy-light as fern,   260
Imagination's very self in stone!
With one long sigh of infinite release
From pedantries past, present, or to come,
I looked, and owned myself a happy Goth.
Your blood is mine, ye architects of dream,   265
Builders of aspiration incomplete,
So more consummate, souls self-confident,
Who felt your own thought worthy of record
In monumental pomp! No Grecian drop
Rebukes these veins that leap with kindred thrill,
After long exile, to the mother-tongue.   271

Ovid in Pontus, puling for his Rome
Of men invirile and disnatured dames
That poison sucked from the Attic bloom decayed,
Shrank with a shudder from the blue-eyed race
Whose force rough-handed should renew the world,
And from the dregs of Romulus express   277
Such wine as Dante poured, or he who blew
Roland's vain blast, or sang the Campeador
In verse that clanks like armor in the charge,   280
Homeric juice, though brimmed in Odin's horn.
And they could build, if not the columned fane
That from the height gleamed seaward many-
    hued,
Something more friendly with their ruder skies:
The gray spire, molten now in driving mist,   285
Now lulled with the incommunicable blue;
The carvings touched to meanings new with snow,
Or commented with fleeting grace of shade;

  272. Ovid: Roman poet of the Augustan age. **279. Ro-**
land: hero of the *Chanson de Roland*, greatest champion
of the Charlemagne legends, killed at Roncesvalles, 778 A.D.
Campeador: "Champion," name of the Cid, Christian champion of the eleventh century in the Spanish wars against the
Moors.   **281. Odin:** chief of the Norse gods.

The statues, motley as man's memory,
Partial as that, so mixed of true and false,   290
History and legend meeting with a kiss
Across this bound-mark where their realms confine;
The painted windows, freaking gloom with glow,
Dusking the sunshine which they seem to cheer,
Meet symbol of the senses and the soul,   295
And the whole pile, grim with the Northman's
     thought
Of life and death, and doom, life's equal fee,—
These were before me: and I gazed abashed,
Child of an age that lectures, not creates,
Plastering our swallow-nests on the awful Past,
And twittering round the work of larger men,   301
As we had builded what we but deface.
Far up the great bells wallowed in delight,
Tossing their clangors o'er the heedless town,
To call the worshippers who never came,   305
Or women mostly, in loath twos and threes.
I entered, reverent of whatever shrine
Guards piety and solace for my kind
Or gives the soul a moment's truce of God,
And shared decorous in the ancient rite   310
My sterner fathers held idolatrous.
The service over, I was tranced in thought:
Solemn the deepening vaults, and most to me,
Fresh from the fragile realm of deal and paint,
Or brick mock-pious with a marble front;   315
Solemn the lift of high-embowered roof,
The clustered stems that spread in boughs dis-
     leaved,
Through which the organ blew a dream of storm,
Though not more potent to sublime with awe
And shut the heart up in tranquillity,   320
Than aisles to me familiar that o'erarch
The conscious silences of brooding woods,
Centurial shadows, cloisters of the elk:
Yet here was sense of undefined regret,
Irreparable loss, uncertain what: 325
Was all this grandeur but anachronism,
A shell divorced of its informing life,
Where the priest housed him like a hermit-crab,
An alien to that faith of elder days
That gathered round it this fair shape of stone?   330
Is old Religion but a spectre now,
Haunting the solitude of darkened minds,
Mocked out of memory by the sceptic day?
Is there no corner safe from peeping Doubt,

Since Gutenberg made thought cosmopolite   335
And stretched electric threads from mind to mind?
Nay, did Faith build this wonder? or did Fear,
That makes a fetish and misnames it God
(Blockish or metaphysic, matters not),
Contrive this coop to shut its tyrant in,   340
Appeased with playthings, that he might not harm?

I turned and saw a beldame on her knees;
With eyes astray, she told mechanic beads
Before some shrine of saintly womanhood,
Bribed intercessor with the far-off Judge: 345
Such my first thought, by kindlier soon rebuked,
Pleading for whatsoever touches life
With upward impulse: be He nowhere else,
God is in all that liberates and lifts,
In all that humbles, sweetens, and consoles: 350
Blessëd the natures shored on every side
With landmarks of hereditary thought!
Thrice happy they that wander not lifelong
Beyond near succor of the household faith,
The guarded fold that shelters, not confines!   355
Their steps find patience in familiar paths,
Printed with hope by loved feet gone before
Of parent, child, or lover, glorified
By simple magic of dividing Time.
My lids were moistened as the woman knelt,   360
And—was it will, or some vibration faint
Of sacred Nature, deeper than the will?—
My heart occultly felt itself in hers,
Through mutual intercession gently leagued.

Or was it not mere sympathy of brain?   365
A sweetness intellectually conceived
In simpler creeds to me impossible?
A juggle of that pity for ourselves
In others, which puts on such pretty masks
And snares self-love with bait of charity?   370
Something of all it might be, or of none:
Yet for a moment I was snatched away
And had the evidence of things not seen;
For one rapt moment; then it all came back,   374
This age that blots out life with question-marks,
This nineteenth century with its knife and glass
That make thought physical, and thrust far off
The Heaven, so neighborly with man of old,
To voids sparse-sown with alienated stars.

335. Gutenberg: Johannes Gutenberg (*c.* 1397–1468),
inventor of printing from movable types.

'Tis irrecoverable, that ancient faith,
Homely and wholesome, suited to the time,
With rod or candy for child-minded men:
No theologic tube, with lens on lens
Of syllogism transparent, brings it near,— 385
At best resolving some new nebula,
Or blurring some fixed-star of hope to mist.
Science was Faith once; Faith were Science now,
Would she but lay her bow and arrows by
And arm her with the weapons of the time.
Nothing that keeps thought out is safe from thought.
For there's no virgin-fort but self-respect, 391
And Truth defensive hath lost hold on God.
Shall we treat Him as if He were a child
That knew not His own purpose? nor dare trust
The Rock of Ages to their chemic tests, 395
Lest some day the all-sustaining base divine
Should fail from under us, dissolved in gas?
The armèd eye that with a glance discerns
In a dry blood-speck between ox and man,
Stares helpless at this miracle called life, 400
This shaping potency behind the egg,
This circulation swift of deity,
Where suns and systems inconspicuous float
As the poor blood-disks in our mortal veins.
Each age must worship its own thought of God, 405
More or less earthy, clarifying still
With subsidence continuous of the dregs;
Nor saint nor sage could fix immutably
The fluent image of the unstable Best, 409
Still changing in their very hands that wrought:
To-day's eternal truth To-morrow proved
Frail as frost-landscapes on a window-pane.
Meanwhile Thou smiledst, inaccessible,
At Thought's own substance made a cage for
        Thought,
        414
And Truth locked fast with her own master-key;
Nor didst Thou reck what image man might make
Of his own shadow on the flowing world;
The climbing instinct was enough for Thee.
Or wast Thou, then, an ebbing tide that left
Strewn with dead miracle those eldest shores, 420
For men to dry, and dryly lecture on,
Thyself thenceforth incapable of flood?
Idle who hopes with prophets to be snatched
By virtue in their mantles left below;
Shall the soul live on other men's report, 425
Herself a pleasing fable of herself?

Man cannot be God's outlaw if he would,
Nor so abscond him in the caves of sense
But Nature still shall search some crevice out
With messages of splendor from that Source 430
Which, dive he, soar he, baffles still and lures.
This life were brutish did we not sometimes
Have intimation clear of wider scope,
Hints of occasion infinite, to keep
The soul alert with noble discontent 435
And onward yearnings of unstilled desire;
Fruitless, except we now and then divined
A mystery of Purpose, gleaming through
The secular confusions of the world,
Whose will we darkly accomplish, doing ours. 440
No man can think nor in himself perceive,
Sometimes at waking, in the street sometimes,
Or on the hillside, always unforewarned,
A grace of being, finer than himself,
That beckons and is gone,—a larger life 445
Upon his own impinging, with swift glimpse
Of spacious circles luminous with mind,
To which the ethereal substance of his own
Seems but gross cloud to make that visible,
Touched to a sudden glory round the edge. 450
Who that hath known these visitations fleet
Would strive to make them trite and ritual?
I, that still pray at morning and at eve,
Loving those roots that feed us from the past,
And prizing more than Plato things I learned 455
At that best academe, a mother's knee,
Thrice in my life perhaps have truly prayed,
Thrice, stirred below my conscious self, have felt
That perfect disenthralment which is God;
Nor know I which to hold worst enemy, 460
Him who on speculation's windy waste
Would turn me loose, stript of the raiment warm
By Faith contrived against our nakedness,
Or him who, cruel-kind, would fain obscure,
With painted saints and paraphrase of God, 465
The soul's east-window of divine surprise.
Where others worship I but look and long;
For, though not recreant to my fathers' faith,
Its forms to me are weariness, and most
That drony vacuum of compulsory prayer, 470
Still pumping phrases for the Ineffable,
Though all the valves of memory gasp and wheeze.
Words that have drawn transcendent meanings up
From the best passion of all bygone time, 474

Steeped through with tears of triumph and remorse,
Sweet with all sainthood, cleansed in martyr-fires,
Can they, so consecrate and so inspired,
By repetition wane to vexing wind?
Alas! we cannot draw habitual breath
In the thin air of life's supremer heights,   480
We cannot make each meal a sacrament,
Nor with our tailors be disbodied souls,—
We men, too conscious of earth's comedy,
Who see two sides, with our posed selves debate,
And only for great stakes can be sublime!   485
Let us be thankful when, as I do here,
We can read Bethel on a pile of stones,
And, seeing where God *has* been, trust in Him.

Brave Peter Fischer there in Nuremberg,
Moulding Saint Sebald's miracles in bronze,   490
Put saint and stander-by in that quaint garb
Familiar to him in his daily walk,
Not doubting God could grant a miracle
Then and in Nuremberg, if so He would;
But never artist for three hundred years   495
Hath dared the contradiction ludicrous
Of supernatural in modern clothes.
Perhaps the deeper faith that is to come
Will see God rather in the strenuous doubt,
Than in the creed held as an infant's hand   500
Holds purposeless whatso is placed therein.

Say it is drift, not progress, none the less,
With the old sextant of the fathers' creed,
We shape our courses by new-risen stars,
And, still lip-loyal to what once was truth,   505
Smuggle new meanings under ancient names,
Unconscious perverts of the Jesuit, Time.
Change is the mask that all Continuance wears
To keep us youngsters harmlessly amused;
Meanwhile, some ailing or more watchful child,
Sitting apart, sees the old eyes gleam out,   511
Stern, and yet soft with humorous pity too.
Whilere, men burnt men for a doubtful point,
As if the mind were quenchable with fire,
And Faith danced round them with her war-paint
    on,   515
Devoutly savage as an Iroquois;
Now Calvin and Servetus at one board

Snuff in grave sympathy a milder roast,
And o'er their claret settle Comte unread.
Fagot and stake were desperately sincere: 520
Our cooler martyrdoms are done in types;
And flames that shine in controversial eyes
Burn out no brains but his who kindles them.
This is no age to get cathedrals built:
Did God, then, wait for one in Bethlehem?   525
Worst is not yet: lo, where his coming looms,
Of Earth's anarchic children latest born,
Democracy, a Titan who hath learned
To laugh at Jove's old-fashioned thunderbolts,—
Could he not also forge them, if he would?   530
He, better skilled, with solvents merciless,
Loosened in air and borne on every wind,
Saps unperceived: the calm Olympian height
Of ancient order feels its bases yield,
And pale gods glance for help to gods as pale.   535
What will be left of good or worshipful,
Of spiritual secrets, mysteries,
Of fair Religion's guarded heritage,
Heirlooms of soul, passed downward unprofaned
From eldest Ind? This Western giant coarse,   540
Scorning refinements which he lacks himself,
Loves not nor heeds the ancestral hierarchies,
Each rank dependent on the next above
In orderly gradation fixed as fate.
King by mere manhood, nor allowing aught   545
Of holier unction than the sweat of toil;
In his own strength sufficient; called to solve,
On the rough edges of society,
Problems long sacred to the choicer few,
And improvise what elsewhere men receive   550
As gifts of Deity; tough foundling reared
Where every man's his own Melchisedek,
How make him reverent of a King of kings?
Or Judge self-make, executor of laws
By him not first discussed and voted on?   555
For him no tree of knowledge is forbid,
Or sweeter if forbid. How save the ark,
Or holy of holies, unprofaned a day
From his unscrupulous curiosity
That handles everything as if to buy,   560
Tossing aside what fabrics delicate

517. **Servetus:** Michael Servetus (1509–1553), Spanish theologian who opposed the doctrine of the Trinity, was prosecuted by Calvin, and burned to death.

528. **Titan:** primeval deity, one who is gigantic.
552. **Melchisedek:** priest-king to whom even Abraham paid tithes; in the *Psalms*, a liberator; in *Hebrews*, a King of Righteousness and Peace.

Suit not the rough-and-tumble of his ways?
What hope for those fine-nerved humanities
That made earth gracious once with gentler arts,
Now the rude hands have caught the trick of
    thought   565
And claim an equal suffrage with the brain?

The born disciple of an elder time,
(To me sufficient, friendlier than the new,)
Who in my blood feel motions of the Past,
I thank benignant Nature most for this,—   570
A force of sympathy, or call it lack
Of character firm-planted, loosing me
From the pent chamber of habitual self
To dwell enlarged in alien modes of thought,
Haply distasteful, wholesomer for that,   575
And through imagination to possess,
As they were mine, the lives of other men.
This growth original of virgin soil,
By fascination felt in opposites,
Pleases and shocks, entices and perturbs.   580
In this brown-fisted rough, this shirt-sleeved
    Cid,
This backwoods Charlemagne of empires new,
Whose blundering heel instinctively finds out
The goutier foot of speechless dignities,   584
Who, meeting Cæsar's self, would slap his back,
Call him "Old Horse," and challenge to a drink,
My lungs draw braver air, my breast dilates
With ampler manhood, and I front both worlds,
Of sense and spirit, as my natural fiefs,
To shape and then reshape them as I will.   590
It was the first man's charter; why not mine?
How forfeit? when deposed in other hands?

Thou shudder'st, Ovid? Dost in him forebode
A new avatar of the large-limbed Goth,
To break, or seem to break, tradition's clew, 595
And chase to dreamland back thy gods dethroned?
I think man's soul dwells nearer to the east,
Nearer to morning's fountains than the sun;
Herself the source whence all tradition sprang,
Herself at once both labyrinth and clew.   600
The miracle fades out of history,
But faith and wonder and the primal earth
Are born into the world with every child.
Shall this self-maker with the prying eyes,

582. **Charlemagne:** king of the Franks, crowned Emperor
of the West by Leo III in 800, died at Aix-la-Chapelle.

This creature disenchanted of respect   605
By the New World's new fiend, Publicity,
Whose testing thumb leaves everywhere its smutch,
Not one day feel within himself the need
Of loyalty to better than himself,   609
That shall ennoble him with the upward look?
Shall he not catch the Voice that wanders earth,
With spiritual summons, dreamed or heard,
As sometimes, just ere sleep seals up the sense,
We hear our mother call from deeps of Time,
And, waking, find it vision,—none the less   615
The benediction bides, old skies return,
And that unreal thing, preëminent,
Makes air and dream of all we see and feel?
Shall he divine no strength unmade of votes,
Inward, impregnable, found soon as sought,   620
Not cognizable of sense, o'er sense supreme?
Else were he desolate as none before.
His holy places may not be of stone,
Nor made with hands, yet fairer far than aught
By artist feigned or pious ardor reared,   625
Fit altars for who guards inviolate
God's chosen seat, the sacred form of man.
Doubtless his church will be no hospital
For superannuate forms and mumping shams,
No parlor where men issue policies   630
Of life-assurance on the Eternal Mind,
Nor his religion but an ambulance
To fetch life's wounded and malingerers in,
Scorned by the strong; yet he, unconscious heir
To the influence sweet of Athens and of Rome,
And old Judæa's gift of secret fire,   636
Spite of himself shall surely learn to know
And worship some ideal of himself,
Some divine thing, large-hearted, brotherly,
Not nice in trifles, a soft creditor,   640
Pleased with his world, and hating only cant.
And, if his Church be doubtful, it is sure
That, in a world, made for whatever else,
Not made for mere enjoyment, in a world
Of toil but half-requited, or, at best,   645
Paid in some futile currency of breath,
A world of incompleteness, sorrow swift
And consolation laggard, whatsoe'er
The form of building or the creed professed,
The Cross, bold type of shame to homage turned,
Of an unfinished life that sways the world,   651
Shall tower as sovereign emblem over all.

878

The kobold Thought moves with us when we shift
Our dwelling to escape him; perched aloft
On the first load of household-stuff he went;   655
For, where the mind goes, goes old furniture.
I, who to Chartres came to feed my eye
And give to Fancy one clear holiday,
Scarce saw the minster for the thoughts it stirred
Buzzing o'er past and future with vain quest.
Here once there stood a homely wooden church,
Which slow devotion nobly changed for this   662
That echoes vaguely to my modern steps.
By suffrage universal it was built,
As practised then, for all the country came   665
From far as Rouen, to give votes for God,
Each vote a block of stone securely laid
Obedient to the master's deep-mused plan.
Will what our ballots rear, responsible
To no grave forethought, stand so long as this?
Delight like this the eye of after days   671
Brightening with pride that here, at least, were men
Who meant and did the noblest thing they knew?
Can our religion cope with deeds like this?
We, too, build Gothic contract-shams, because
Our deacons have discovered that it pays,   676
And pews sell better under vaulted roofs
Of plaster painted like an Indian squaw.
Shall not that Western Goth, of whom we spoke,
So fiercely practical, so keen of eye,   680
Find out, some day, that nothing pays but God,
Served whether on the smoke-shut battle-field,
In work obscure done honestly, or vote
For truth unpopular, or faith maintained
To ruinous convictions, or good deeds   685
Wrought for good's sake, mindless of heaven, or
    hell?
Shall he not learn that all prosperity,
Whose bases stretch not deeper than the sense,
Is but a trick of this world's atmosphere,
A desert-born mirage of spire and dome,   690
Or find too late, the Past's long lesson missed,
That dust the prophets shake from off their feet
Grows heavy to drag down both tower and wall?
I know not; but, sustained by sure belief
That man still rises level with the height   695
Of noblest opportunities, or makes
Such, if the time supply not, I can wait.
I gaze round on the windows, pride of France,
Each the bright gift of some mechanic guild

Who loved their city and thought gold well spent
To make her beautiful with piety;   701
I pause, transfigured by some stripe of bloom,
And my mind throngs with shining auguries,
Circle on circle, bright as seraphim,
With golden trumpets, silent, that await   705
The signal to blow news of good to men.

Then the revulsion came that always comes
After these dizzy elations of the mind:
And with a passionate pang of doubt I cried,
"O mountain-born, sweet with snow-filtered air
From uncontaminate wells of ether drawn   711
And never-broken secrecies of sky,
Freedom, with anguish won, misprized till lost,
They keep thee not who from thy sacred eyes
Catch the consuming lust of sensual good   715
And the brute's license of unfettered will.
Far from the popular shout and venal breath
Of Cleon blowing the mob's baser mind
To bubbles of wind-piloted conceit,
Thou shrinkest, gathering up thy skirts, to hide
In fortresses of solitary thought   721
And private virtue strong in self-restraint.
Must we too forfeit thee misunderstood,
Content with names, nor inly wise to know
That best things perish of their own excess,   725
And quality o'er-driven becomes defect?
Nay, is it thou indeed that we have glimpsed,
Or rather such illusion as of old
Through Athens glided menadlike and Rome,
A shape of vapor, mother of vain dreams   730
And mutinous traditions, specious plea
Of the glaived tyrant and long-memoried priest?"

I walked forth saddened; for all thought is sad,
And leaves a bitterish savor in the brain,
Tonic, it may be, not delectable,   735
And turned, reluctant, for a parting look
At those old weather-pitted images
Of bygone struggle, now so sternly calm.
About their shoulders sparrows had built nests,
And fluttered, chirping, from gray perch to perch,
Now on a mitre poising, now a crown,   741
Irreverently happy. While I thought
How confident they were, what careless hearts
Flew on those lightsome wings and shared the sun,

    718. Cleon: Athenian demagogue, satirized by Aris-
tophanes.

A larger shadow crossed; and looking up,   745
I saw where, nesting in the hoary towers,
The sparrow-hawk slid forth on noiseless air,
With sidelong head that watched the joy below,
Grim Norman baron o'er this clan of Kelts.
Enduring Nature, force conservative,   750
Indifferent to our noisy whims! Men prate
Of all heads to an equal grade cashiered
On level with the dullest, and expect
(Sick of no worse distemper than themselves)
A wondrous cure-all in equality;   755
They reason that To-morrow must be wise
Because To-day was not, nor Yesterday,
As if good days were shapen of themselves,
Not of the very lifeblood of men's souls;
Meanwhile, long-suffering, imperturbable,   760
Thou quietly complet'st thy syllogism,
And from the premise sparrow here below
Draw'st sure conclusion of the hawk above,
Pleased with the soft-billed songster, pleased no less
With the fierce beak of natures aquiline.   765

Thou beautiful Old Time, now hid away
In the Past's valley of Avilion,
Haply, like Arthur, till thy wound be healed,
Then to reclaim the sword and crown again!
Thrice beautiful to us; perchance less fair   770
To who possessed thee, as a mountain seems
To dwellers round its bases but a heap
Of barren obstacle that lairs the storm
And the avalanche's silent bolt holds back
Leashed with a hair,—meanwhile some far-off
        clown,   775
Hereditary delver of the plain,
Sees it an unmoved vision of repose,
Nest of the morning, and conjectures there
The dance of streams to idle shepherds' pipes,
And fairer habitations softly hung   780
On breezy slopes, or hid in valleys cool,
For happier men. No mortal ever dreams
That the scant isthmus he encamps upon
Between two oceans, one, the Stormy, passed,
And one, the Peaceful, yet to venture on,   785
Has been that future whereto prophets yearned
For the fulfilment of Earth's cheated hope,
Shall be that past which nerveless poets moan

767. **Avilion:** in Celtic mythology, the land of the blessed.
768. **Arthur:** legendary sixth-century king of Britain.

As the lost opportunity of song.
O Power, more near my life than life itself   790
(Or what seems life to us in sense immured),
Even as the roots, shut in the darksome earth,
Share in the tree-top's joyance, and conceive
Of sunshine and wide air and wingëd things
By sympathy of nature, so do I   795
Have evidence of Thee so far above,
Yet in and of me! Rather Thou the root
Invisibly sustaining, hid in light,
Not darkness, or in darkness made by us.
If sometimes I must hear good men debate   800
Of other witness of Thyself than Thou,
As if there needed any help of ours
To nurse Thy flickering life, that else must cease,
Blown out, as 't were a candle, by men's breath,
My soul shall not be taken in their snare,   805
To change her inward surety for their doubt
Muffled from sight in formal robes of proof:
While she can only feel herself through Thee,
I fear not Thy withdrawal; more I fear,
Seeing, to know Thee not, hoodwinked with dreams
Of signs and wonders, while, unnoticed, Thou,   811
Walking Thy garden still, commun'st with men,
Missed in the commonplace of miracle.

An Ode for the Fourth of July, 1876

LOWELL wrote this ode near the close of Grant's second
Administration, when the nation was in the midst of
political and social unrest. The South had not fully
escaped from the chains of Reconstruction; Western
silver men were in conflict with Eastern financiers; the
panic of 1873 was followed by an increasing number of
commercial failures, rising to nearly 9,000 in 1876. The
President, personally honest, was surrounded by the
kind of political corruptionists whom Mark Twain and
Charles D. Warner described in *The Gilded Age*. Our
first great industrial conflict, the "Great Strike" of
1877, would come the next year. Even Walt Whitman
in 1871 had written, "Society in these States is
cankered, crude, superstitious, and rotten" (*Democratic
Vistas*). All of this and more lay in Lowell's mind as he
now wrote:

> Murmur of many voices in the air
> Denounces us degenerate,

and he was actively engaged in the public weal. He had
just returned from Cincinnati, where he was a delegate
to the national convention nominating Hayes, and he

believed reform in civil service would follow. His faith in democracy, though tempered by experience, remained firm:

> The land to Human Nature dear
> Shall not be unbeloved by Thee.

The ode was first published in *The Atlantic Monthly*, December, 1876, and collected in *Three Memorial Poems* (1877).

PART ONE

1

Entranced I saw a vision in the cloud
That loitered dreaming in yon sunset sky,
Full of fair shapes, half creatures of the eye,
Half chance-evoked by the wind's fantasy
In golden mist, an ever-shifting crowd: 5
There, 'mid unreal forms that came and went
In air-spun robes, of evanescent dye,
A woman's semblance shone preëminent;
Not armed like Pallas, not like Hera proud,
But, as on household diligence intent,   10
Beside her visionary wheel she bent
Like Aretë or Bertha, nor than they
Less queenly in her port: about her knee
Glad children clustered confident in play:
Placid her pose, the calm of energy;   15
And over her broad brow in many a round
(That loosened would have gilt her garment's hem),
Succinct, as toil prescribes, the hair was wound
In lustrous coils, a natural diadem.
The cloud changed shape, obsequious to the whim
Of some transmuting influence felt in me,   21
And, looking now, a wolf I seemed to see
Limned in that vapor, gaunt and hunger-bold,
Threatening her charge: resolve in every limb,
Erect she flamed in mail of sun-wove gold,   25
Penthesilea's self for battle dight;
One arm uplifted braced a flickering spear,
And one her adamantine shield made light;
Her face, helm-shadowed, grew a thing to fear,
And her fierce eyes, by danger challenged, took   30
Her trident-sceptred mother's dauntless look.
"I know thee now, O goddess-born!" I cried,
And turned with loftier brow and firmer stride;
For in that spectral cloud-work I had seen

9. Pallas: Greek goddess of wisdom. **Hera:** Greek queen of heaven. **12. Aretë:** daughter of Aristippus, famed for her careful education of her son. **Bertha:** mother of Charles the Great. **26. Penthesilea:** Queen of the Amazons.

Her image, bodied forth by love and pride,   35
The fearless, the benign, the mother-eyed,
The fairer world's toil-consecrated queen.

2

What shape by exile dreamed elates the mind
Like hers whose hand, a fortress of the poor,
No blood in vengeance spilt, though lawful, stains?
Who never turned a suppliant from her door?   41
Whose conquests are the gains of all mankind?
To-day her thanks shall fly on every wind,
Unstinted, unrebuked, from shore to shore,
One love, one hope, and not a doubt behind!   45
Cannon to cannon shall repeat her praise,
Banner to banner flap it forth in flame;
Her children shall rise up to bless her name,
And wish her harmless length of days,
The mighty mother of a mighty brood,   50
Blessed in all tongues and dear to every blood,
The beautiful, the strong, and, best of all, the good!

3

Seven years long was the bow
Of battle bent, and the heightening
Storm-heaps convulsed with the throe   55
Of their uncontainable lightning;
Seven years long heard the sea
Crash of navies and wave-borne thunder;
Then drifted the cloud-rack a-lee,
And new stars were seen, a world's wonder;   60
Each by her sisters made bright,
All binding all to their stations,
Cluster of manifold light
Startling the old constellations:
Men looked up and grew pale: 65
Was it a comet or star,
Omen of blessing or bale,
Hung o'er the ocean afar?

4

Stormy the day of her birth:
Was she not born of the strong,   70
She, the last ripeness of earth,
Beautiful, prophesied long?
Stormy the days of her prime:
Hers are the pulses that beat
Higher for perils sublime,   75
Making them fawn at her feet.

Was she not born of the strong?
Was she not born of the wise?
Daring and counsel belong
Of right to her confident eyes: 80
Human and motherly they,
Careless of station or race:
Hearken! her children to-day
Shout for the joy of her face.

PART TWO

1

No praises of the past are hers,   85
No fanes by hallowing time caressed,
No broken arch that ministers
To Time's sad instinct in the breast:
She has not gathered from the years
Grandeur of tragedies and tears,   90
Nor from long leisure the unrest
That finds repose in forms of classic grace:
These may delight the coming race
Who haply shall not count it to our crime
That we who fain would sing are here before our
    time.   95
She also hath her monuments;
Not such as stand decrepitly resigned
To ruin-mark the path of dead events
That left no seed of better days behind,
The tourist's pensioners that show their scars   100
And maunder of forgotten wars;
She builds not on the ground, but in the mind,
Her open-hearted palaces
For larger-thoughted men with heaven and earth at
    ease:
Her march the plump mow marks, the sleepless
    wheel,   105
The golden sheaf, the self-swayed commonweal;
The happy homesteads hid in orchard trees
Whose sacrificial smokes through peaceful air
Rise lost in heaven, the household's silent prayer;
What architect hath bettered these?   110
With softened eye the westward traveller sees
A thousand miles of neighbors side by side,
Holding by toil-won titles fresh from God
The lands no serf or seigneur ever trod,
With manhood latent in the very sod,   115
Where the long billow of the wheatfield's tide
Flows to the sky across the prairie wide,

A sweeter vision than the castled Rhine,
Kindly with thoughts of Ruth and Bible-days
    benign.

2

O ancient commonwealths, that we revere   120
Haply because we could not know you near,
Your deeds like statues down the aisles of Time
Shine peerless in memorial calm sublime,
And Athens is a trumpet still, and Rome;
Yet which of your achievements is not foam   125
Weighed with this one of hers (below you far
In fame, and born beneath a milder star),
That to Earth's orphans, far as curves the dome
Of death-deaf sky, the bounteous West means
    home,
With dear precedency of natural ties   130
That stretch from roof to roof and make men
    gently wise?
And if the nobler passions wane,
Distorted to base use, if the near goal
Of insubstantial gain
Tempt from the proper race-course of the soul   135
That crowns their patient breath
Whose feet, song-sandalled, are too fleet for Death,
Yet may she claim one privilege urbane
And haply first upon the civic roll,
That none can breathe her air nor grow humane.   140

3

Oh, better far the briefest hour
Of Athens self-consumed, whose plastic power
Hid Beauty safe from Death in words or stone;
Of Rome, fair quarry where those eagles crowd
Whose fulgurous vans about the world had blown
Triumphant storm and seeds of polity;   146
Of Venice, fading o'er her shipless sea,
Last iridescence of a sunset cloud;
Than this inert prosperity,
This bovine comfort in the sense alone!   150
Yet art came slowly even to such as those,
Whom no past genius cheated of their own
With prudence of o'ermastering precedent;
Petal by petal spreads the perfect rose,
Secure of the divine event;   155
And only children rend the bud half-blown
To forestall Nature in her calm intent:
Time hath a quiver full of purposes

Which miss not of their aim, to us unknown,
And brings about the impossible with ease: 160
Haply for us the ideal dawn shall break
From where in legend-tinted line
The peaks of Hellas drink the morning's wine,
To tremble on our lids with mystic sign
Till the drowsed ichor in our veins awake   165
And set our pulse in tune with moods divine:
Long the day lingered in its sea-fringed nest,
Then touched the Tuscan hills with golden lance
And paused; then on to Spain and France
The splendor flew, and Albion's misty crest: 170
Shall Ocean bar him from his destined West?
Or are we, then, arrived too late,
Doomed with the rest to grope disconsolate,
Foreclosed of Beauty by our modern date?

PART THREE
1

Poets, as their heads grow gray,   175
Look from too far behind the eyes,
Too long-experienced to be wise
In guileless youth's diviner way;
Life sings not now, but prophesies;
Time's shadows they no more behold,   180
But, under them, the riddle old
That mocks, bewilders, and defies:
In childhood's face the seed of shame,
In the green tree an ambushed flame,
In Phosphor a vaunt-guard of Night,   185
They, though against their will, divine,
And dread the care-dispelling wine
Stored from the Muse's vintage bright,
By age imbued with second-sight.
From Faith's own eyelids there peeps out,   190
Even as they look, the leer of doubt;
The festal wreath their fancy loads
With care that whispers and forebodes:
Nor this our triumph-day can blunt
     Megæra's goads.

2

Murmur of many voices in the air   195
Denounces us degenerate,
Unfaithful guardians of a noble fate,
And prompts indifference or despair:

Is this the country that we dreamed in youth,
Where wisdom and not numbers should have
     weight,   200
Seed-field of simpler manners, braver truth,
Where shams should cease to dominate
In household, church, and state?
Is this Atlantis? This the unpoisoned soil,
Sea-whelmed for ages and recovered late,   205
Where parasitic greed no more should coil
Round Freedom's stem to bend awry and blight
What grew so fair, sole plant of love and light?
Who sit where once in crowned seclusion sate
The long-proved athletes of debate   210
Trained from their youth, as none thinks needful
     now?
Is this debating club where boys dispute,
And wrangle o'er their stolen fruit,
The Senate, erewhile cloister of the few,
Where Clay once flashed and Webster's cloudy
     brow   215
Brooded those bolts of thought that all the horizon
     knew?

3

Oh, as this pensive moonlight blurs my pines,
Here while I sit and meditate these lines,
To gray-green dreams of what they are by day,
So would some light, not reason's sharp-edged ray,
Trance me in moonshine as before the flight   221
Of years had won me this unwelcome right
To see things as they are, or shall be soon,
In the frank prose of undissembling noon!

4

Back to my breast, ungrateful sigh!   225
Whoever fails, whoever errs,
The penalty be ours, not hers!
The present still seems vulgar, seen too nigh;
The golden age is still the age that's past:
I ask no drowsy opiate   230
To dull my vision of that only state
Founded on faith in man, and therefore sure to last.
For, O my country, touched by thee,
The gray hairs gather back their gold;
Thy thought sets all my pulses free;   235
The heart refuses to be old;

185. Phosphor: the morning star. **194. Megæra:** one
of the three Furies who punished men for crimes.

204. Atlantis: mythical island northwest of Africa, supposed to have sunk into the Atlantic.

The love is all that I can see.
Not to thy natal-day belong
Time's prudent doubt or age's wrong,
But gifts of gratitude and song: 240
Unsummoned crowd the thankful words,
As sap in spring-time floods the tree,
Foreboding the return of birds,
For all that thou hast been to me!

Part Four

1

Flawless his heart and tempered to the core   245
Who, beckoned by the forward-leaning wave,
First left behind him the firm-footed shore,
And, urged by every nerve of sail and oar,
Steered for the Unknown which gods to mortals
          gave,
Of thought and action the mysterious door,   250
Bugbear of fools, a summons to the brave:
Strength found he in the unsympathizing sun,
And strange stars from beneath the horizon won,
And the dumb ocean pitilessly grave:
High-hearted surely he;   255
But bolder they who first off-cast
Their moorings from the habitable Past
And ventured chartless on the sea
Of storm-engendering Liberty:
For all earth's width of waters is a span,   260
And their convulsed existence mere repose,
Matched with the unstable heart of man,
Shoreless in wants, mist-girt in all it knows,
Open to every wind of sect or clan,
And sudden-passionate in ebbs and flows.   265

2

They steered by stars the elder shipmen knew,
And laid their courses where the currents draw
Of ancient wisdom channelled deep in law,
The undaunted few
Who changed the Old World for the New,   270
And more devoutly prized
Than all perfection theorized
The more imperfect that had roots and grew.
They founded deep and well,
Those danger-chosen chiefs of men   275
Who still believed in Heaven and Hell,
Nor hoped to find a spell,
In some fine flourish of a pen,

To make a better man
Than long-considering Nature will or can,   280
Secure against his own mistakes,
Content with what life gives or takes,
And acting still on some fore-ordered plan,
A cog of iron in an iron wheel,
Too nicely poised to think or feel,   285
Dumb motor in a clock-like commonweal.
They wasted not their brain in schemes
Of what man might be in some bubble-sphere,
As if he must be other than he seems
Because he was not what he should be here,   290
Postponing Time's slow proof to petulant dreams:
Yet herein they were great
Beyond the incredulous lawgivers of yore,
And wiser than the wisdom of the shelf,
That they conceived a deeper-rooted state,   295
Of hardier growth, alive from rind to core,
By making man sole sponsor of himself.

3

God of our fathers, Thou who wast,
Art, and shalt be when those eye-wise who flout
Thy secret presence shall be lost   300
In the great light that dazzles them to doubt,
We, sprung from loins of stalwart men
Whose strength was in their trust
That Thou wouldst make thy dwelling in their dust
And walk with those a fellow-citizen   305
Who build a city of the just,
We, who believe Life's bases rest
Beyond the probe of chemic test,
Still, like our fathers, feel Thee near,
Sure that, while lasts the immutable decree,   310
The land to Human Nature dear
Shall not be unbeloved of Thee.

Emerson the Lecturer

THIS ESSAY first appeared in *The Nation* for November 12, 1868, extended from Lowell's review of Emerson's *The Conduct of Life* in *The Atlantic Monthly* for February, 1861, and collected in *My Study Windows* (1871). Lowell had known Emerson personally in 1838, when Lowell had been rusticated from Harvard for neglect of duties and placed under the charge of the Reverend Barzillai Frost at Concord. When Lowell established *The Atlantic Monthly* in 1857, Emerson became one of the most valued contributors.

It is a singular fact, that Mr. Emerson is the most steadily attractive lecturer in America. Into that somewhat cold-waterish region adventurers of the sensational kind come down now and then with a splash, to become disregarded King Logs[n] before the next season. But Mr. Emerson always draws. A lecturer now for something like a third of a century, one of the pioneers of the lecturing system, the charm of his voice, his manner, and his matter has never lost its power over his earlier hearers, and continually winds new ones in its enchanting meshes. What they do not fully understand they take on trust, and listen, saying to themselves, as the old poet of Sir Philip Sidney,—

"A sweet, attractive, kind of grace,
    A full assurance given by looks,
Continual comfort in a face,
    The lineaments of gospel books."

We call it a singular fact, because we Yankees are thought to be fond of the spread-eagle style, and nothing can be more remote from that than his. We are reckoned a practical folk, who would rather hear about a new air-tight stove than about Plato; yet our favorite teacher's practicality is not in the least of the Poor Richard variety. If he have any Buncombe constituency, it is that unrealized commonwealth of philosophers which Plotinus proposed to establish; and if he were to make an almanac, his directions to farmers would be something like this: "OCTOBER: *Indian Summer;* now is the time to get in your early Vedas." What, then, is his secret? Is it not that he out-Yankees us all? that his range includes us all? that he is equally at home with the potato-disease and original sin, with pegging shoes and the Over-soul? that, as we try all trades, so has he tried all cultures? and above all, that his mysticism gives us a counterpoise to our super-practicality?

There is no man living to whom, as a writer, so many of us feel and thankfully acknowledge so great an indebtedness for ennobling impulses,— none whom so many cannot abide. What does he mean? ask these last. Where is his system? What is the use of it all? What the deuce have we to do

with Brahma? I do not propose to write an essay on Emerson at this time. I will only say that one may find grandeur and consolation in a starlit night without caring to ask what it means, save grandeur and consolation; one may like Montaigne, as some ten generations before us have done, without thinking him so systematic as some more eminently tedious (or shall we say tediously eminent?) authors; one may think roses as good in their way as cabbages, though the latter would make a better show in the witness-box, if cross-examined as to their usefulness; and as for Brahma, why he can take care of himself, and won't bite us at any rate.

The bother with Mr. Emerson is, that, though he writes in prose, he is essentially a poet. If you undertake to paraphrase what he says, and to reduce it to words of one syllable for infant minds, you will make as sad work of it as the good monk with his analysis of Homer in the "Epistolæ Obscurorum Virorum."[n] We look upon him as one of the few men of genius whom our age has produced, and there needs no better proof of it than his masculine faculty of fecundating other minds. Search for his eloquence in his books and you will perchance miss it, but meanwhile you will find that it has kindled all your thoughts. For choice and pith of language he belongs to a better age than ours, and might rub shoulders with Fuller and Browne,—though he does use that abominable word *reliable.* His eye for a fine, telling phrase that will carry true is like that of a backwoodsman for a rifle; and he will dredge you up a choice word from the mud of Cotton Mather himself. A diction at once so rich and so homely as his I know not where to match in these days of writing by the page; it is like homespun cloth-of-gold. The many cannot miss his meaning, and only the few can find it. It is the open secret of all true genius. It is wholesome to angle in those profound pools, though one be rewarded with nothing more than the leap of a fish that flashes his freckled side in the sun and as suddenly absconds in the dark and dreamy waters again. There is keen excitement, though there be no ponderable acquisition. If we carry nothing home in our baskets, there is ample gain in dilated lungs and stimulated blood. What

King Logs: Aesop relates that Jupiter, on petition from the frogs that he send them a king, threw them a log which they duly respected until they discovered it was a log.

"Epistolæ . . . Virorum": *Letters of Obscure Men.*

885

does he mean, quotha? He means inspiring hints, a divining-rod to your deeper nature. No doubt, Emerson, like all original men, has his peculiar audience, and yet I know none that can hold a promiscuous crowd in pleased attention so long as he. As in all original men, there is something for every palate. "Would you know," says Goethe, "the ripest cherries? Ask the boys and the blackbirds."

The announcement that such a pleasure as a new course of lectures by him is coming, to people as old as I am, is something like those forebodings of spring that prepare us every year for a familiar novelty, none the less novel, when it arrives, because it is familiar. We know perfectly well what we are to expect from Mr. Emerson, and yet what he says always penetrates and stirs us, as is apt to be the case with genius, in a very unlooked-for fashion. Perhaps genius is one of the few things which we gladly allow to repeat itself,—one of the few that multiply rather than weaken the force of their impression by iteration? Perhaps some of us hear more than the mere words, are moved by something deeper than the thoughts? If it be so, we are quite right, for it is thirty years and more of "plain living and high thinking" that speak to us in this altogether unique lay-preacher. We have shared in the beneficence of this varied culture, this fearless impartiality in criticism and speculation, this masculine sincerity, this sweetness of nature which rather stimulates than cloys, for a generation long. If ever there was a standing testimonial to the cumulative power and value of Character (and we need it sadly in these days), we have it in this gracious and dignified presence. What an antiseptic is a pure life! At sixty-five (or two years beyond his grand climacteric, as he would prefer to call it) he has that privilege of soul which abolishes the calendar, and presents him to us always the unwasted contemporary of his own prime. I do not know if he seem old to his younger hearers, but we who have known him so long wonder at the tenacity with which he maintains himself even in the outposts of youth. I suppose it is not the Emerson of 1868 to whom we listen. For us the whole life of the man is distilled in the clear drop of every sentence, and behind each word we divine the force of a noble character, the weight of a large capital of thinking and being. We do not go to hear what Emerson says so much as to hear Emerson. Not that we perceive any falling-off in anything that ever was essential to the charm of Mr. Emerson's peculiar style of thought or phrase. The first lecture, to be sure, was more disjointed even than common. It was as if, after vainly trying to get his paragraphs into sequence and order, he had at last tried the desperate expedient of shuffling them. It was chaos come again, but it was a chaos full of shooting-stars, a jumble of creative forces. The second lecture, on "Criticism and Poetry," was quite up to the level of old times, full of that power of strangely-subtle association whose indirect approaches startle the mind into almost painful attention, of those flashes of mutual understanding between speaker and hearer that are gone ere one can say it lightens. The vice of Emerson's criticism seems to be, that while no man is so sensitive to what is poetical, few men are less sensible than he of what makes a poem. He values the solid meaning of thought above the subtler meaning of style. He would prefer Donne,[n] I suspect, to Spenser,[n] and sometimes mistakes the queer for the original.

To be young is surely the best, if the most precarious, gift of life; yet there are some of us who would hardly consent to be young again, if it were at the cost of our recollection of Mr. Emerson's first lectures during the consulate of Van Buren. We used to walk in from the country to the Masonic Temple (I think it was), through the crisp winter night, and listen to that thrilling voice of his, so charged with subtle meaning and subtle music, as shipwrecked men on a raft to the hail of a ship that came with unhoped-for food and rescue. Cynics might say what they liked. Did our own imaginations transfigure dry remainder-biscuit into ambrosia? At any rate, he brought us life, which, on the whole, is no bad thing. Was it all transcendentalism? magic-lantern pictures on mist? As you will. Those, then, were just what we wanted. But it was not so. The delight and the benefit were that he put us in communication with

Donne: John Donne (1573–1631), English metaphysical poet whose verse is full of "hard thought." **Spenser:** Edmund Spenser (1552?–1599), English poet of sheer rhythmical beauty; "the poet's poet."

a larger style of thought, sharpened our wits with a more pungent phrase, gave us ravishing glimpses of an ideal under the dry husk of our New England; made us conscious of the supreme and everlasting originality of whatever bit of soul might be in any of us; freed us, in short, from the stocks of prose in which we had sat so long that we had grown well-nigh contented in our cramps. And who that saw the audience will ever forget it, where every one still capable of fire, or longing to renew in himself the half-forgotten sense of it, was gathered? Those faces, young and old, agleam with pale intellectual light, eager with pleased attention, flash upon me once more from the deep recesses of the years with an exquisite pathos. Ah, beautiful young eyes, brimming with love and hope, wholly vanished now in that other world we call the Past, or peering doubtfully through the pensive gloaming of memory, your light impoverishes these cheaper days! I hear again that rustle of sensation, as they turned to exchange glances over some pithier thought, some keener flash of that humor which always played about the horizon of his mind like heat-lightning, and it seems now like the sad whisper of the autumn leaves that are whirling around me. But would my picture be complete if I forgot that ample and vegete countenance of Mr. R—— of W——, — how, from its regular post at the corner of the front bench, it turned in ruddy triumph to the profaner audience as if he were the inexplicably appointed fugleman of appreciation? I was reminded of him by those hearty cherubs in Titian's Assumption that look at you as who should say, "Did you ever see a Madonna like that? Did you ever behold one hundred and fifty pounds of womanhood mount heavenward before like a rocket?"

To some of us that long-past experience remains as the most marvellous and fruitful we have ever had. Emerson awakened us, saved us from the body of this death. It is the sound of the trumpet that the young soul longs for, careless what breath may fill it. Sidney[n] heard it in the ballad of "Chevy Chase," and we in Emerson. Nor did it blow retreat, but called to us with assurance of victory. Did they say he was disconnected? So were the stars, that seemed larger to our eyes, still keen with that excitement, as we walked homeward with prouder stride over the creaking snow. And were they not knit together by a higher logic than our mere sense could master? Were we enthusiasts? I hope and believe we were, and am thankful to the man who made us worth something for once in our lives. If asked what was left? what we carried home? we should not have been careful for an answer. It would have been enough if we had said that something beautiful had passed that way. Or we might have asked in return what one brought away from a symphony of Beethoven? Enough that he had set that ferment of wholesome discontent at work in us. There is one, at least, of those old hearers, so many of whom are now in the fruition of that intellectual beauty of which Emerson gave them both the desire and the foretaste, who will always love to repeat:—

Che in la mente m' è fitta, ed or m' accuora
La cara e buona immagine paterna
Di voi, quando nel mondo ad ora ad ora
M'insegnavaste come l' uom s' eterna.[n]

I am unconsciously thinking, as I write, of the third lecture of the present course, in which Mr. Emerson gave some delightful reminiscences of the intellectual influences in whose movement he had shared. It was like hearing Goethe read some passages of the "Wahrheit aus seinem Leben."[n] Not that there was not a little *Dichtung*,[n] too, here and there, as the lecturer built up so lofty a pedestal under certain figures as to lift them into a prominence of obscurity, and seem to masthead them there. Everybody was asking his neighbor who this or that recondite great man was, in the faint hope that somebody might once have heard of him. There are those who call Mr. Emerson cold. Let them revise their judgment in presence of this loyalty of his that can keep warm for half

Che in la mente . . . s' eterna:

"For in my mind is fixed, and touches now
    My heart, the dear and good paternal image
    Of you, when in the world from hour to hour
You taught me how a man becomes eternal."
Dante, *Inferno*, XV, lines 82–85,
                                    as translated by Longfellow.

"Wahrheit . . . Leben": "Truth from His Life." **Dichtung:** "poetry."

Sidney: Sir Philip Sidney (1554–1586), English statesman, poet, and critic.

887

a century, that never forgets a friendship, or fails to pay even a fancied obligation to the uttermost farthing. This substantiation of shadows was but incidental, and pleasantly characteristic of the man to those who know and love him. The greater part of the lecture was devoted to reminiscences of things substantial in themselves. He spoke of Everett,[n] fresh from Greece and Germany; of Channing[n]; of the translations of Margaret Fuller,[n] Ripley,[n] and Dwight[n]; of the *Dial* and Brook Farm. To what he said of the latter an undertone of good-humored irony gave special zest. But what every one of his hearers felt was that the protagonist in the drama was left out. The lecturer was no Æneas to babble the *quorum magna pars fui*,[n] and, as one of his listeners, I cannot help wishing to say how each of them was commenting the story as it went along, and filling up the necessary gaps in it from his own private store of memories. His younger hearers could not know how much they owed to the benign impersonality, the quiet scorn of everything ignoble, the never-sated hunger of self-culture, that were personified in the man before them. But the older knew how much the country's intellectual emancipation was due to the stimulus of his teaching and example, how constantly he had kept burning the beacon of an ideal life above our lower region of turmoil. To him more than to all other causes together did the young martyrs of our civil war owe the sustaining strength of thoughtful heroism that is so touching in every record of their lives. Those who are grateful to Mr. Emerson, as many of us are, for what they feel to be most valuable in their culture, or perhaps I should say their impulse, are grateful not so much for any direct teachings of his as for that inspiring lift which only genius can give, and without which all doctrine is chaff.

Everett: Edward Everett (1794–1865), of Boston, Unitarian minister, professor of Greek at Harvard, later U. S. Congressman and Governor of Massachusetts. **Channing:** William Ellery Channing (1818–1901), Concord, Mass., author, whose poetry was the subject of an essay by Emerson in *The Dial*. **Fuller:** Margaret Fuller (1810–1850), author, translator, member of Brook Farm, editor of *The Dial*. **Ripley:** George Ripley (1802–1880), Unitarian minister, author of philosophical works. **Dwight:** John Sullivan Dwight, Unitarian minister, Boston, member of the Transcendental Club. **quorum . . . fui:** "of which things I was a great part."

This was something like the *caret* which some of us older boys wished to fill up on the margin of the master's lecture. Few men have been so much to so many, and through so large a range of aptitudes and temperaments, and this simply because all of us value manhood beyond any or all other qualities of character. We may suspect in him, here and there, a certain thinness and vagueness of quality, but let the waters go over him as they list, this masculine fibre of his will keep its lively color and its toughness of texture. I have heard some great speakers and some accomplished orators, but never any that so moved and persuaded men as he. There is a kind of undertow in that rich baritone of his that sweeps our minds from their foothold into deeper waters with a drift we cannot and would not resist. And how artfully (for Emerson is a long-studied artist in these things) does the deliberate utterance, that seems waiting for the fit word, appear to admit us partners in the labor of thought and make us feel as if the glance of humor were a sudden suggestion, as if the perfect phrase lying written there on the desk were as unexpected to him as to us! In that closely filed speech of his at the Burns centenary dinner, every word seemed to have just dropped down to him from the clouds. He looked far away over the heads of his hearers, with a vague kind of expectation, as into some private heaven of invention, and the winged period came at last obedient to his spell. "My dainty Ariel!"[n] he seemed murmuring to himself as he cast down his eyes as if in deprecation of the frenzy of approval and caught another sentence from the Sibylline leaves that lay before him, ambushed behind a dish of fruit and seen only by nearest neighbors. Every sentence brought down the house, as I never saw one brought down before,—and it is not so easy to hit Scotsmen with a sentiment that has no hint of native brogue in it. I watched, for it was an interesting study, how the quick sympathy ran flashing from face to face down the long tables, like an electric spark thrilling as it went, and then exploded in a thunder of plaudits. I watched till tables and faces vanished, for I, too, found myself caught up in the common enthusiasm, and my ex-

"My dainty Ariel!": Prospero to Ariel, in Shakespeare's *Tempest*, V, i.

cited fancy set me under the *bema* listening to him who fulmined over Greece. I can never help applying to him what Ben Jonson said of Bacon: "There happened in my time one noble speaker, who was full of gravity in his speaking. His language was nobly censorious. No man ever spake more neatly, more pressly, more weightily, or suffered less emptiness, less idleness, in what he uttered. No member of his speech but consisted of his own graces. His hearers could not cough, or look aside from him, without loss. He commanded where he spoke." Those who heard him while their natures were yet plastic, and their mental nerves trembled under the slightest breath of divine air, will never cease to feel and say:—

Was never eye did see that face,
Was never ear did hear that tongue,
Was never mind did mind his grace,
That ever thought the travail long;
But eyes, and ears, and every thought,
Were with his sweet perfections caught.

Democracy

Lowell was sixty-five years of age, and in his fifth year as Ambassador to the Court of St. James's, when he delivered this address October 6, 1884, at Birmingham, England, on the occasion of his inauguration to the presidency of the Birmingham and Midland Institute. Though at the time he did not highly regard this address, it has come to be considered one of his best. He was personally one of the best-liked of American ambassadors. His support of American democracy in comparison with British and Continental governments required courage as well as faith in British fair-mindedness. "Democracy" was published immediately upon its delivery, and first collected in *Democracy and Other Addresses* (1886).

He must be a born leader or misleader of men, or must have been sent into the world unfurnished with that modulating and restraining balance-wheel which we call a sense of humor, who, in old age, has as strong a confidence in his opinions and in the necessity of bringing the universe into conformity with them as he had in youth. In a world the very condition of whose being is that it should be in a perpetual flux, where all seems mirage, and the one abiding thing is the effort to distinguish realities from appearances, the elderly

man must be indeed of a singularly tough and valid fibre who is certain that he has any clarified residuum of experience, any assured verdict of reflection, that deserves to be called an opinion, or who, even if he had, feels that he is justified in holding mankind by the button while he is expounding it. And in a world of daily—nay, almost hourly—journalism, where every clever man, every man who thinks himself clever, or whom anybody else thinks clever, is called upon to deliver his judgment point-blank and at the word of command on every conceivable subject of human thought, or, on what sometimes seems to him very much the same thing, on every inconceivable display of human want of thought, there is such a spendthrift waste of all those commonplaces which furnish the permitted staple of public discourse that there is little chance of beguiling a new tune out of the one-stringed instrument on which we have been thrumming so long. In this desperate necessity one is often tempted to think that, if all the words of the dictionary were tumbled down in a heap and then all those fortuitous juxtapositions and combinations that made tolerable sense were picked out and pieced together, we might find among them some poignant suggestions toward novelty of thought or expression. But, alas! it is only the great poets who seem to have this unsolicited profusion of unexpected and incalculable phrase, this infinite variety of topic. For everybody else everything has been said before, and said over again after. He who has read his Aristotle will be apt to think that observation has on most points of general applicability said its last word, and he who has mounted the tower of Plato to look abroad from it will never hope to climb another with so lofty a vantage of speculation. Where it is so simple if not so easy a thing to hold one's peace, why add to the general confusion of tongues? There is something disheartening, too, in being expected to fill up not less than a certain measure of time, as if the mind were an hour-glass, that need only be shaken and set on one end or the other, as the case may be, to run its allotted sixty minutes with decorous exactitude. I recollect being once told by the late eminent naturalist, Agassiz,[n] that when he was to

Agassiz: Louis Agassiz (1807–1873), Harvard professor, friend of Lowell; see Lowell's "Ode to Agassiz."

deliver his first lecture as professor (at Zürich, I believe) he had grave doubts of his ability to occupy the prescribed three quarters of an hour. He was speaking without notes, and glancing anxiously from time to time at the watch that lay before him on the desk. "When I had spoken a half hour," he said, "I had told them everything I knew in the world, everything! Then I began to repeat myself," he added, roguishly, "and I have done nothing else ever since." Beneath the humorous exaggeration of the story I seemed to see the face of a very serious and improving moral. And yet if one were to say only what he had to say and then stopped, his audience would feel defrauded of their honest measure. Let us take courage by the example of the French, whose exportation of Bordeaux wines increases as the area of their land in vineyards is diminished.

To me, somewhat hopelessly revolving these things, the undelayable year has rolled round, and I find myself called upon to say something in this place, where so many wiser men have spoken before me. Precluded, in my quality of national guest, by motives of taste and discretion, from dealing with any question of immediate and domestic concern, it seemed to me wisest, or at any rate most prudent, to choose a topic of comparatively abstract interest, and to ask your indulgence for a few somewhat generalized remarks on a matter concerning which I had some experimental knowledge, derived from the use of such eyes and ears as Nature had been pleased to endow me withal, and such report as I had been able to win from them. The subject which most readily suggested itself was the spirit and the working of those conceptions of life and polity which are lumped together, whether for reproach or commendation, under the name of Democracy. By temperament and education of a conservative turn, I saw the last years of that quaint Arcadia which French travellers saw with delighted amazement a century ago, and have watched the change (to me a sad one) from an agricultural to a proletary population. The testimony of Balaam should carry some conviction. I have grown to manhood and am now growing old with the growth of this system of government in my native land, have watched its advances, or what some would call its encroach-

ments, gradual and irresistible as those of a glacier, have been an ear-witness to the forebodings of wise and good and timid men, and have lived to see those forebodings belied by the course of events, which is apt to show itself humorously careless of the reputation of prophets. I recollect hearing a sagacious old gentleman say in 1840 that the doing away with the property qualification for suffrage twenty years before had been the ruin of the State of Massachusetts; that it had put public credit and private estate alike at the mercy of demagogues. I lived to see that Commonwealth twenty odd years later paying the interest on her bonds in gold, though it cost her sometimes nearly three for one to keep her faith, and that while suffering an unparalleled drain of men and treasure in helping to sustain the unity and self-respect of the nation.

If universal suffrage has worked ill in our larger cities, as it certainly has, this has been mainly because the hands that wielded it were untrained to its use. There the election of a majority of the trustees of the public money is controlled by the most ignorant and vicious of a population which has come to us from abroad, wholly unpracticed in self-government and incapable of assimilation by American habits and methods. But the finances of our towns, where the native tradition is still dominant and whose affairs are discussed and settled in a public assembly of the people, have been in general honestly and prudently administered. Even in manufacturing towns, where a majority of the voters live by their daily wages, it is not so often the recklessness as the moderation of public expenditure that surprises an old-fashioned observer. "The beggar is in the saddle at last," cries Proverbial Wisdom. "Why, in the name of all former experience, doesn't he ride to the Devil?" Because in the very act of mounting he ceased to be a beggar and became part owner of the piece of property he bestrides. The last thing we need be anxious about is property. It always has friends or the means of making them. If riches have wings to fly away from their owner, they have wings also to escape danger.

I hear America sometimes playfully accused of sending you all your storms, and am in the habit of parrying the charge by alleging that we are enabled to do this because, in virtue of our protective system, we can afford to make better bad weather than anybody else. And what wiser use could we make of it than to export it in return for the paupers which some European countries are good enough to send over to us who have not attained to the same skill in the manufacture of them? But bad weather is not the worst thing that is laid at our door. A French gentleman, not long ago, forgetting Burke's monition[n] of how unwise it is to draw an indictment against a whole people, has charged us with the responsibility of whatever he finds disagreeable in the morals or manners of his countrymen. If M. Zola[n] or some other competent witness would only go into the box and tell us what those morals and manners were before our example corrupted them! But I confess that I find little to interest and less to edify me in these international bandyings of "You're another."

I shall address myself to a single point only in the long list of offences of which we are more or less gravely accused, because that really includes all the rest. It is that we are infecting the Old World with what seems to be thought the entirely new disease of Democracy. It is generally people who are in what are called easy circumstances who can afford the leisure to treat themselves to a handsome complaint, and these experience an immediate alleviation when once they have found a sonorous Greek name to abuse it by. There is something consolatory also, something flattering to their sense of personal dignity, and to that conceit of singularity which is the natural recoil from our uneasy consciousness of being commonplace, in thinking ourselves victims of a malady by which no one had ever suffered before. Accordingly they find it simpler to class under one comprehensive heading whatever they find offensive to their nerves, their tastes, their interests, or what they suppose to be their opinions, and christen it Democracy, much as physicians label every obscure disease gout, or as cross-grained fellows lay their ill-temper to the weather. But is it really a new ailment, and, if it be, is America answerable for it? Even if she

were, would it account for the phylloxera, and hoof-and-mouth disease, and bad harvests, and bad English, and the German bands, and the Boers, and all the other discomforts with which these later days have vexed the souls of them that go in chariots? Yet I have seen the evil example of Democracy in America cited as the source and origin of things quite as heterogeneous and quite as little connected with it by any sequence of cause and effect. Surely this ferment is nothing new. It has been at work for centuries, and we are more conscious of it only because in this age of publicity, where the newspapers offer a rostrum to whoever has a grievance, or fancies that he has, the bubbles and scum thrown up by it are more noticeable on the surface than in those dumb ages when there was a cover of silence and suppression on the cauldron. Bernardo Navagero,[n] speaking of the Provinces of Lower Austria in 1546, tells us that "in them there are five sorts of persons, Clergy, Barons, Nobles, Burghers, and Peasants. Of these last no account is made, because they have no voice in the Diet."

Nor was it among the people that subversive or mistaken doctrines had their rise. A Father of the Church said that property was theft many centuries before Proudhon[n] was born. Bourdaloue[n] reaffirmed it. Montesquieu[n] was the inventor of national workshops, and of the theory that the State owed every man a living. Nay, was not the Church herself the first organized Democracy? A few centuries ago the chief end of man was to keep his soul alive, and then the little kernel of leaven that sets the gases at work was religious, and produced the Reformation. Even in that, far-sighted persons like the Emperor Charles V[n] saw the germ of political and social revolution. Now that the chief end of man seems to have become the keeping of the body alive, and as comfortably alive as possible, the leaven also has become wholly political and social. But there

monition: Edmund Burke (1729–1797) gave the "monition" in *Speech on Conciliation with America* (1775). Zola: Émile Zola (1840–1902), French novelist of the school of naturalism.

Bernardo Navagero: (1507–1565), Venetian cardinal and diplomat, whose *Relazione* was first published in the nineteenth century. Proudhon: Pierre J. Proudhon (1809–1865), French socialist. Bourdaloue: Louis Bourdaloue (1632–1704), Jesuit, famous for his sermons. Montesquieu: Charles Louis de Secondat (1689–1755), French judge and philosopher, and advocate of liberalism. Charles V: (1500–1558), Emperor of the Holy Roman Empire.

had also been social upheavals before the Reformation and contemporaneously with it, especially among men of Teutonic race. The Reformation gave outlet and direction to an unrest already existing. Formerly the immense majority of men —our brothers—knew only their sufferings, their wants, and their desires. They are beginning now to know their opportunity and their power. All persons who see deeper than their plates are rather inclined to thank God for it than to bewail it, for the sores of Lazarus have a poison in them against which Dives[n] has no antidote.

There can be no doubt that the spectacle of a great and prosperous Democracy on the other side of the Atlantic must react powerfully on the aspirations and political theories of men in the Old World who do not find things to their mind; but, whether for good or evil, it should not be overlooked that the acorn from which it sprang was ripened on the British oak. Every successive swarm that has gone out from this *officina gentium*[n] has, when left to its own instincts—may I not call them hereditary instincts?—assumed a more or less thoroughly democratic form. This would seem to show, what I believe to be the fact, that the British Constitution, under whatever disguises of prudence or decorum, is essentially democratic. England, indeed, may be called a monarchy with democratic tendencies, the United States a democracy with conservative instincts. People are continually saying that America is in the air, and I am glad to think it is, since this means only that a clearer conception of human claims and human duties is beginning to be prevalent. The discontent with the existing order of things, however, pervaded the atmosphere wherever the conditions were favorable, long before Columbus, seeking the back door of Asia, found himself knocking at the front door of America. I say wherever the conditions were favorable, for it is certain that the germs of disease do not stick or find a prosperous field for their development and noxious activity unless where the simplest sanitary precautions have been neglected. "For this effect defective comes by cause," as Polonius[n]

said long ago. It is only by instigation of the wrongs of men that what are called the Rights of Man become turbulent and dangerous. It is then only that they syllogize unwelcome truths. It is not the insurrections of ignorance that are dangerous, but the revolts of intelligence:—

> The wicked and the weak rebel in vain,
> Slaves by their own compulsion.[n]

Had the governing classes in France during the last century paid as much heed to their proper business as to their pleasures or manners, the guillotine need never have severed that spinal-marrow of orderly and secular tradition through which in a normally constituted state the brain sympathizes with the extremities and sends will and impulsion thither. It is only when the reasonable and practicable are denied that men demand the unreasonable and impracticable; only when the possible is made difficult that they fancy the impossible to be easy. Fairy tales are made out of the dreams of the poor. No; the sentiment which lies at the root of democracy is nothing new. I am speaking always of a sentiment, a spirit, and not of a form of government; for this was but the outgrowth of the other and not its cause. This sentiment is merely an expression of the natural wish of people to have a hand, if need be a controlling hand, in the management of their own affairs. What is new is that they are more and more gaining that control, and learning more and more how to be worthy of it. What we used to call the tendency or drift—what we are being taught to call more wisely the evolution of things— has for some time been setting steadily in this direction. There is no good in arguing with the inevitable. The only argument available with an east wind is to put on your overcoat. And in this case, also, the prudent will prepare themselves to encounter what they cannot prevent. Some people advise us to put on the brakes, as if the movement of which we are conscious were that of a railway train running down an incline. But a metaphor is no argument, though it be sometimes the gunpowder to drive one home and imbed it in the memory. Our disquiet comes of what nurses and

Dives: Luke, 16:19, "a certain rich man." *officina gentium*: "laboratory of nations." **Polonius**: see Shakespeare's *Hamlet*, II, ii.

The wicked . . . compulsion: Samuel Taylor Coleridge, "France: An Ode."

other experienced persons call growing-pains, and need not seriously alarm us. They are what every generation before us—certainly every generation since the invention of printing—has gone through with more or less good fortune. To the door of every generation there comes a knocking, and unless the household, like the Thane of Cawdor and his wife, have been doing some deed without a name, they need not shudder. It turns out at worst to be a poor relation who wishes to come in out of the cold. The porter always grumbles and is slow to open. "Who's there, in the name of Beelzebub?"[n] he mutters. Not a change for the better in our human housekeeping has ever taken place that wise and good men have not opposed it,—have not prophesied with the alderman that the world would wake up to find its throat cut in consequence of it. The world, on the contrary, wakes up, rubs its eyes, yawns, stretches itself, and goes about its business as if nothing had happened. Suppression of the slave trade, abolition of slavery, trade unions,—at all of these excellent people shook their heads despondingly, and murmured "Ichabod."[n] But the trade unions are now debating instead of conspiring, and we all read their discussions with comfort and hope, sure that they are learning the business of citizenship and the difficulties of practical legislation.

One of the most curious of these frenzies of exclusion was that against the emancipation of the Jews. All share in the government of the world was denied for centuries to perhaps the ablest, certainly the most tenacious, race that had ever lived in it—the race to whom we owed our religion and the purest spiritual stimulus and consolation to be found in all literature—a race in which ability seems as natural and hereditary as the curve of their noses, and whose blood, furtively mingling with the bluest bloods in Europe, has quickened them with its own indomitable impulsion. We drove them into a corner, but they had their revenge, as the wronged are always sure to have it sooner or later. They made their corner the counter and banking-house of the world, and thence they rule it and us with the ignobler sceptre of finance. Your grandfathers mobbed Priestley[n] only that you might set up his statue and make Birmingham the headquarters of English Unitarianism. We hear it said sometimes that this is an age of transition, as if that made matters clearer; but can any one point us to an age that was not? If he could, he would show us an age of stagnation. The question for us, as it has been for all before us, is to make the transition gradual and easy, to see that our points are right so that the train may not come to grief. For we should remember that nothing is more natural for people whose education has been neglected than to spell evolution with an initial "r." A great man struggling with the storms of fate has been called a sublime spectacle; but surely a great man wrestling with these new forces that have come into the world, mastering them and controlling them to beneficent ends, would be a yet sublimer. Here is not a danger, and if there were it would be only a better school of manhood, a nobler scope for ambition. I have hinted that what people are afraid of in democracy is less the thing itself than what they conceive to be its necessary adjuncts and consequences. It is supposed to reduce all mankind to a dead level of mediocrity in character and culture, to vulgarize men's conceptions of life, and therefore their code of morals, manners, and conduct—to endanger the rights of property and possession. But I believe that the real gravamen of the charges lies in the habit it has of making itself generally disagreeable by asking the Powers that Be at the most inconvenient moment whether they are the powers that ought to be. If the powers that be are in a condition to give a satisfactory answer to this inevitable question, they need feel in no way discomfited by it.

Few people take the trouble of trying to find out what democracy really is. Yet this would be a great help, for it is our lawless and uncertain thoughts, it is the indefiniteness of our impressions, that fill darkness, whether mental or physical, with spectres and hobgoblins. Democracy is nothing more than an experiment in government, more likely to succeed in a new soil, but likely to be tried in all soils, which must stand or fall on its

"Who's there . . . Beelzebub?": Shakespeare's *Macbeth*, II, iii.   "Ichabod": See 1 Samuel, 4:21.

Priestley: Joseph Priestley (1733–1804), English chemist, theologian, and liberal, who moved to Pennsylvania in 1794, three years after his house was burned by a mob.

893

own merits as others have done before it. For there is no trick of perpetual motion in politics any more than in mechanics. President Lincoln defined democracy to be "the government of the people by the people for the people." This is a sufficiently compact statement of it as a political arrangement. Theodore Parker[n] said that "Democracy meant not 'I'm as good as you are,' but 'You're as good as I am.'" And this is the ethical conception of it, necessary as a complement of the other; a conception which, could it be made actual and practical, would easily solve all the riddles that the old sphinx of political and social economy who sits by the roadside has been proposing to mankind from the beginning, and which mankind have shown such a singular talent for answering wrongly. In this sense Christ was the first true democrat that ever breathed, as the old dramatist Dekker[n] said he was the first true gentleman. The characters may be easily doubled, so strong is the likeness between them. A beautiful and profound parable of the Persian poet Jellaladeen[n] tells us that "One knocked at the Beloved's door, and a voice asked from within 'Who is there?' and he answered 'It is I.' Then the voice said, 'This house will not hold me and thee'; and the door was not opened. Then went the lover into the desert and fasted and prayed in solitude, and after a year he returned and knocked again at the door; and again the voice asked 'Who is there?' and he said 'It is thyself'; and the door was opened to him." But that is idealism, you will say, and this is an only too practical world. I grant it; but I am one of those who believe that the real will never find an irremovable basis till it rests on the ideal. It used to be thought that a democracy was possible only in a small territory, and this is doubtless true of a democracy strictly defined, for in such all the citizens decide directly upon every question of public concern in a general assembly. An example still survives in the tiny Swiss canton of Appenzell. But this immediate intervention of the people in their own affairs is not of the essence of democracy;

it is not necessary, nor indeed, in most cases, practicable. Democracies to which Mr. Lincoln's definition would fairly enough apply have existed, and now exist, in which, though the supreme authority reside in the people, yet they can act only indirectly on the national policy. This generation has seen democracy with an imperial figurehead,[n] and in all that have ever existed the body politic has never embraced all the inhabitants included within its territory: the right to share in the direction of affairs has been confined to citizens, and citizenship has been further restricted by various limitations, sometimes of property, sometimes of nativity, and always of age and sex.

The framers of the American Constitution were far from wishing or intending to found a democracy in the strict sense of the word, though, as was inevitable, every expansion of the scheme of government they elaborated has been in a democratical direction. But this has been generally the slow result of growth, and not the sudden innovation of theory; in fact, they had a profound disbelief in theory, and knew better than to commit the folly of breaking with the past. They were not seduced by the French fallacy that a new system of government could be ordered like a new suit of clothes. They would as soon have thought of ordering a new suit of flesh and skin. It is only on the roaring loom of time that the stuff is woven for such a vesture of their thought and experience as they were meditating. They recognized fully the value of tradition and habit as the great allies of permanence and stability. They all had that distaste for innovation which belonged to their race, and many of them a distrust of human nature derived from their creed. The day of sentiment was over, and no dithyrambic affirmations or finedrawn analyses of the Rights of Man would serve their present turn. This was a practical question, and they addressed themselves to it as men of knowledge and judgment should. Their problem was how to adapt English principles and precedents to the new conditions of American life, and they solved it with singular discretion. They put as many obstacles as they could contrive, not in the way of the people's will, but of their whim. With few exceptions they probably admitted the

Theodore Parker: (1810–1860), outstanding Unitarian of Boston, abolitionist, social reformer; paid particular attention to the plight of the poor in the city. **Dekker:** Thomas Dekker (*c*. 1570–*c*. 1641), English dramatist. **Jelladeen:** (*c*. 1200–1272), mystic poet.

imperial figurehead: Napoleon III (1808–1873).

logic of the then accepted syllogism,—democracy, anarchy, despotism. But this formula was framed upon the experience of small cities shut up to stew within their narrow walls, where the number of citizens made but an inconsiderable fraction of the inhabitants, where every passion was reverberated from house to house and from man to man with gathering rumor till every impulse became gregarious and therefore inconsiderate, and every popular assembly needed but an infusion of eloquent sophistry to turn it into a mob, all the more dangerous because sanctified with the formality of law.

Fortunately their case was wholly different. They were to legislate for a widely scattered population and for States already practised in the discipline of a partial independence. They had an unequalled opportunity and enormous advantages. The material they had to work upon was already democratical by instinct and habitude. It was tempered to their hands by more than a century's schooling in self-government. They had but to give permanent and conservative form to a ductile mass. In giving impulse and direction to their new institutions, especially in supplying them with checks and balances, they had a great help and safeguard in their federal organization. The different, sometimes conflicting, interests and social systems of the several States made existence as a Union and coalescence into a nation conditional on a constant practice of moderation and compromise. The very elements of disintegration were the best guides in political training. Their children learned the lesson of compromise only too well, and it was the application of it to a question of fundamental morals that cost us our civil war. We learned once for all that compromise makes a good umbrella but a poor roof; that it is a temporary expedient, often wise in party politics, almost sure to be unwise in statesmanship.

Has not the trial of democracy in America proved, on the whole, successful? If it had not, would the Old World be vexed with any fears of its proving contagious? This trial would have been less severe could it have been made with a people homogeneous in race, language, and traditions, whereas the United States have been called on to absorb and assimilate enormous masses of foreign population, heterogeneous in all these respects, and drawn mainly from that class which might fairly say that the world was not their friend, nor the world's law. The previous condition too often justified the traditional Irishman, who, landing in New York and asked what his politics were, inquired if there was a Government there, and on being told that there was, retorted, "Thin I'm agin it!" We have taken from Europe the poorest, the most ignorant, the most turbulent of her people, and have made them over into good citizens, who have added to our wealth, and who are ready to die in defence of a country and of institutions which they know to be worth dying for. The exceptions have been (and they are lamentable exceptions) where these hordes of ignorance and poverty have coagulated in great cities. But the social system is yet to seek which has not to look the same terrible wolf in the eyes. On the other hand, at this very moment Irish peasants are buying up the worn-out farms of Massachusetts, and making them productive again by the same virtues of industry and thrift that once made them profitable to the English ancestors of the men who are deserting them. To have achieved even these prosaic results (if you choose to call them so), and that out of materials the most discordant,—I might say the most recalcitrant,—argues a certain beneficent virtue in the system that could do it, and is not to be accounted for by mere luck. Carlyle said scornfully that America meant only roast turkey every day for everybody. He forgot that States, as Bacon said of wars, go on their bellies. As for the security of property, it should be tolerably well secured in a country where every other man hopes to be rich, even though the only property qualification be the ownership of two hands that add to the general wealth. Is it not the best security for anything to interest the largest possible number of persons in its preservation and the smallest in its division? In point of fact, far-seeing men count the increasing power of wealth and its combinations as one of the chief dangers with which the institutions of the United States are threatened in the not distant future. The right of individual property is no doubt the very cornerstone of civilization as hitherto understood, but I am a little impatient of being told that property is entitled to exceptional consideration because it bears all burdens of the State. It bears those, indeed, which can most easily be borne, but poverty pays with its person the chief expenses of war, pestilence, and famine. Wealth should not forget this, for poverty is beginning to think of it now and then. Let me not be misunderstood. I see as clearly as any man possibly can, and rate as highly, the value of wealth, and of hereditary wealth, as the security of refinement, the feeder of all those arts that ennoble and beautify life, and as making a country worth living in. Many an ancestral hall here in England has been a nursery of that culture which has been of example and benefit to all. Old gold has a civilizing virtue which new gold must grow old to be capable of secreting.

I should not think of coming before you to defend or to criticise any form of government. All have their virtues, all their defects, and all have illustrated one period or another in the history of the race, with signal services to humanity and culture. There is not one that could stand a cynical cross-examination by an experienced criminal lawyer, except that of a perfectly wise and perfectly good despot, such as the world has never seen, except in that white-haired king of Browning's, who

> Lived long ago
> In the morning of the world,
> When Earth was nearer Heaven than now.

The English race, if they did not invent government by discussion, have at least carried it nearest to perfection in practice. It seems a very safe and reasonable contrivance for occupying the attention of the country, and is certainly a better way of settling questions than by push of pike. Yet, if one should ask it why it should not rather be called government by gabble," it would have to fumble in its pocket a good while before it found the change for a convincing reply. As matters stand, too, it is beginning to be doubtful whether Parliament and Congress sit at Westminster and Washington or in the editors' rooms of the leading journals, so thoroughly is everything debated before the authorized and responsible debaters get on their legs. And what shall we say of government by a majority of voices? To a person who in

government by gabble: Carlyle's reference to Parliament as the National Palaver in *Past and Present* was obviously in Lowell's mind.

the last century would have called himself an Impartial Observer, a numerical preponderance seems, on the whole, as clumsy a way of arriving at truth as could well be devised, but experience has apparently shown it to be a convenient arrangement for determining what may be expedient or advisable or practicable at any given moment. Truth, after all, wears a different face to everybody, and it would be too tedious to wait till all were agreed. She is said to lie at the bottom of a well, for the very reason, perhaps, that whoever looks down in search of her sees his own image at the bottom, and is persuaded not only that he has seen the goddess, but that she is far better-looking than he had imagined.

The arguments against universal suffrage are equally unanswerable. "What," we exclaim, "shall Tom, Dick, and Harry have as much weight in the scale as I?" Of course, nothing could be more absurd. And yet universal suffrage has not been the instrument of greater unwisdom than contrivances of a more select description. Assemblies could be mentioned composed entirely of Masters of Arts and Doctors in Divinity which have sometimes shown traces of human passion or prejudice in their votes. Have the Serene Highnesses and Enlightened Classes carried on the business of Mankind so well, then, that there is no use in trying a less costly method? The democratic theory is that those Constitutions are likely to prove steadiest which have the broadest base, that the right to vote makes a safety-valve of every voter, and that the best way of teaching a man how to vote is to give him the chance of practice. For the question is no longer the academic one, "Is it wise to give every man the ballot?" but rather the practical one, "Is it prudent to deprive whole classes of it any longer?" It may be conjectured that it is cheaper in the long run to lift men up than to hold them down, and that the ballot in their hands is less dangerous to society than a sense of wrong in their heads. At any rate this is the dilemma to which the drift of opinion has been for some time sweeping us, and in politics a dilemma is a more unmanageable thing to hold by the horns than a wolf by the ears. It is said that the right of suffrage is not valued when it is indiscriminately bestowed, and there may be some truth in this, for

I have observed that what men prize most is a privilege, even if it be that of chief mourner at a funeral. But is there not danger that it will be valued at more than its worth if denied, and that some illegitimate way will be sought to make up for the want of it? Men who have a voice in public affairs are at once affiliated with one or other of the great parties between which society is divided, merge their individual hopes and opinions in its safer, because more generalized, hopes and opinions, are disciplined by its tactics, and acquire, to a certain degree, the orderly qualities of an army. They no longer belong to a class, but to a body corporate. Of one thing, at least, we may be certain, that, under whatever method of helping things to go wrong man's wit can contrive, those who have the divine right to govern will be found to govern in the end, and that the highest privilege to which the majority of mankind can aspire is that of being governed by those wiser than they. Universal suffrage has in the United States sometimes been made the instrument of inconsiderate changes, under the notion of reform, and this from a misconception of the true meaning of popular government. One of these has been the substitution in many of the States of popular election for official selection in the choice of judges. The same system applied to military officers was the source of much evil during our civil war, and, I believe, had to be abandoned. But it has been also true that on all great questions of national policy a reserve of prudence and discretion has been brought out at the critical moment to turn the scale in favor of a wiser decision. An appeal to the reason of the people has never been known to fail in the long run. It is, perhaps, true that, by effacing the principle of passive obedience, democracy, ill understood, has slackened the spring of that ductility to discipline which is essential to "the unity and married calm of States." But I feel assured that experience and necessity will cure this evil, as they have shown their power to cure others. And under what frame of policy have evils ever been remedied till they became intolerable, and shook men out of their indolent indifference through their fears?

We are told that the inevitable result of democracy is to sap the foundations of personal independence, to weaken the principle of authority, to lessen the respect due to eminence, whether in station, virtue, or genius. If these things were so, society could not hold together. Perhaps the best forcing-house of robust individuality would be where public opinion is inclined to be most overbearing, as he must be of heroic temper who should walk along Piccadilly at the height of the season in a soft hat. As for authority, it is one of the symptoms of the time that the religious reverence for it is declining everywhere, but this is due partly to the fact that state-craft is no longer looked upon as a mystery, but as a business, and partly to the decay of superstition, by which I mean the habit of respecting what we are told to respect rather than what is respectable in itself. There is more rough and tumble in the American democracy than is altogether agreeable to people of sensitive nerves and refined habits, and the people take their political duties lightly and laughingly, as is, perhaps, neither unnatural nor unbecoming in a young giant. Democracies can no more jump away from their own shadows than the rest of us can. They no doubt sometimes make mistakes and pay honor to men who do not deserve it. But they do this because they believe them worthy of it, and though it be true that the idol is the measure of the worshipper, yet the worship has in it the germ of a nobler religion. But is it democracies alone that fall into these errors? I, who have seen it proposed to erect a statue to Hudson[n], the railway king, and have heard Louis Napoleon hailed as the saviour of society by men who certainly had no democratic associations or leanings, am not ready to think so. But democracies have likewise their finer instincts. I have also seen the wisest statesman and most pregnant speaker of our generation, a man of humble birth and ungainly manners, of little culture beyond what his own genius supplied, become more absolute in power than any monarch of modern times through the reverence of his countrymen for his honesty, his wisdom, his sincerity, his faith in God and man, and the nobly humane simplicity of his character. And I remember another whom popular respect enveloped as with a halo, the least vulgar of men, the most austerely genial, and the most independent of opinion.

Hudson: George Hudson (1800–1871), English promoter of railroads.

Wherever he went he never met a stranger, but everywhere neighbors and friends proud of him as their ornament and decoration. Institutions which could bear and breed such men as Lincoln and Emerson had surely some energy for good. No, amid all the fruitless turmoil and miscarriage of the world, if there be one thing steadfast and of favorable omen, one thing to make optimism distrust its own obscure distrust, it is the rooted instinct in men to admire what is better and more beautiful than themselves. The touchstone of political and social institutions is their ability to supply them with worthy objects of this sentiment, which is the very tap-root of civilization and progress. There would seem to be no readier way of feeding it with the elements of growth and vigor than such an organization of society as will enable men to respect themselves, and so to justify them in respecting others.

Such a result is quite possible under other conditions than those of an avowedly democratical Constitution. For I take it that the real essence of democracy was fairly enough defined by the First Napoleon when he said that the French Revolution meant "la carrière ouverte aux talents"[n]— a clear pathway for merit of whatever kind. I should be inclined to paraphrase this by calling democracy that form of society, no matter what its political classification, in which every man had a chance and knew that he had it. If a man can climb, and feels himself encouraged to climb, from a coalpit to the highest position for which he is fitted, he can well afford to be indifferent what name is given to the government under which he lives. The Bailli of Mirabeau, uncle of the more famous tribune of that name, wrote in 1771: "The English are, in my opinion, a hundred times more agitated and more unfortunate than the very Algerines themselves, because they do not know and will not know till the destruction of their over-swollen power, which I believe very near, whether they are monarchy, aristocracy, or democracy, and wish to play the part of all three." England has not been obliging enough to fulfil the Bailli's prophecy, and perhaps it was this very carelessness about the name, and concern about the substance of popular government, this skill in getting the best out of things as they are, in utilizing all the motives which influence men, and in giving one direction to many impulses, that has been a principal factor of her greatness and power. Perhaps it is fortunate to have an unwritten Constitution, for men are prone to be tinkering the work of their own hands, whereas they are more willing to let time and circumstance mend or modify what time and circumstance have made. All free governments, whatever their name, are in reality governments by public opinion, and it is on the quality of this public opinion that their prosperity depends. It is, therefore, their first duty to purify the element from which they draw the breath of life. With the growth of democracy grows also the fear, if not the danger, that this atmosphere may be corrupted with poisonous exhalations from lower and more malarious levels, and the question of sanitation becomes more instant and pressing. Democracy in its best sense is merely the letting in of light and air. Lord Sherbrooke,[n] with his usual epigrammatic terseness, bids you educate your future rulers. But would this alone be a sufficient safeguard? To educate the intelligence is to enlarge the horizon of its desires and wants. And it is well that this should be so. But the enterprise must go deeper and prepare the way for satisfying those desires and wants in so far as they are legitimate. What is really ominous of danger to the existing order of things is not democracy (which, properly understood, is a conservative force), but the Socialism which may find a fulcrum in it. If we cannot equalize conditions and fortunes any more than we can equalize the brains of men—and a very sagacious person has said that "where two men ride on a horse one must ride behind"—we can yet, perhaps, do something to correct those methods and influences that lead to enormous inequalities, and to prevent their growing more enormous. It is all very well to pooh-pooh Mr. George[n] and to prove him mistaken in his political economy. I do not believe that land should be divided because the quantity of it is limited by nature. Of what may this not be said? A fortiori,[n] we might on the same principle

Lord Sherbrooke: English statesman (1811–1892). **George:** Henry George (1839–1897), American advocate of the "single tax." **A fortiori:** "with stronger reason."

"la carrière . . . talents": "a chance for those of talent."

insist on a division of human wit, for I have observed that the quantity of this has been even more inconveniently limited. Mr. George himself has an inequitably large share of it. But he is right in his impelling motive; right, also, I am convinced, in insisting that humanity makes a part, by far the most important part, of political economy; and in thinking man to be of more concern and more convincing than the longest column of figures in the world. For unless you include human nature in your addition, your total is sure to be wrong and your deductions from it fallacious. Communism means barbarism, but Socialism means, or wishes to mean, co-operation and community of interests, sympathy, the giving to the hands not so large a share as to the brains, but a larger share than hitherto in the wealth they must combine to produce—means, in short, the practical application of Christianity to life, and has in it the secret of an orderly and benign reconstruction. State Socialism would cut off the very roots in personal character—self-help, forethought, and frugality—which nourish and sustain the trunk and branches of every vigorous Commonwealth.

I do not believe in violent changes, nor do I expect them. Things in possession have a very firm grip. One of the strongest cements of society is the conviction of mankind that the state of things into which they are born is a part of the order of the universe, as natural, let us say, as that the sun should go round the earth. It is a conviction that they will not surrender except on compulsion, and a wise society should look to it that this compulsion be not put upon them. For the individual man there is no radical cure, outside of human nature itself, for the evils to which human nature is heir. The rule will always hold good that you must

Be your own palace or the world's your gaol.

But for artificial evils, for evils that spring from want of thought, thought must find a remedy somewhere. There has been no period of time in which wealth has been more sensible of its duties than now. It builds hospitals, it establishes missions among the poor, it endows schools. It is one of the advantages of accumulated wealth, and of the leisure it renders possible, that people have

time to think of the wants and sorrows of their fellows. But all these remedies are partial and palliative merely. It is as if we should apply plasters to a single pustule of the small-pox with a view of driving out the disease. The true way is to discover and to extirpate the germs. As society is now constituted these are in the air it breathes, in the water it drinks, in things that seem, and which it has always believed, to be the most innocent and healthful. The evil elements it neglects corrupt these in their springs and pollute them in their courses. Let us be of good cheer, however, remembering that the misfortunes hardest to bear are those which never come. The world has outlived much, and will outlive a great deal more, and men have contrived to be happy in it. It has shown the strength of its constitution in nothing more than in surviving the quack medicines it has tried. In the scales of the destinies brawn will never weigh so much as brain. Our healing is not in the storm or in the whirlwind, it is not in monarchies, or aristocracies, or democracies, but will be revealed by the still small voice that speaks to the conscience and the heart, prompting us to a wider and wiser humanity.

The Progress of the World

THIS ESSAY was written as an introduction to *The World's Progress*, published by Gately and O'Gorman (Boston, 1886).

. . . In casting the figure of the World's future, many new elements, many disturbing forces, must be taken into account. First of all is Democracy, which, within the memory of men yet living, has assumed almost the privilege of a Law of Nature, and seems to be making constant advances towards universal dominion. Its ideal is to substitute the interest of the many for that of the few as the test of what is wise in polity and administration, and the opinion of the many for that of the few as the rule of conduct in public affairs. That the interest of the many is the object of whatever social organization man has hitherto been able to effect seems unquestionable; whether their opinions are so safe a guide as the opinions of the few, and whether it will ever be possible, or wise if possible, to sub.

stitute the one for the other in the hegemony of the World, is a question still open for debate. Whether there was ever such a thing as a Social Contract or not, as has been somewhat otiosely discussed, this, at least, is certain,—that the basis of all Society is the putting of the force of all at the disposal of all, by means of some arrangement assented to by all, for the protection of all, and this under certain prescribed forms. This has always been, consciously or unconsciously, the object for which men have striven, and which they have more or less clumsily accomplished. The State—some established Order of Things, under whatever name—has always been, and must always be, the supremely important thing; because in it the interests of all are invested, by it the duties of all imposed and exacted. In point of fact, though it be often strangely overlooked, the claim to any selfish hereditary privilege because you are born a man is as absurd as the same claim because you are born a noble. In a last analysis, there is but one natural right; and that is the right of superior force. This primary right, having been found unworkable in practice, has been deposited, for the convenience of all, with the State, from which, as the maker, guardian, and executor of Law, and as a common fund for the use of all, the rights of each are derived, and man thus made as free as he can be without harm to his neighbor. It was this surrender of private jurisdiction which made civilization possible, and keeps it so. The abrogation of the right of private war has done more to secure the rights of man, properly understood,—and, consequently, for his well-being,—than all the theories spun from the brain of the most subtle speculator, who, finding himself cramped by the actual conditions of life, fancies it as easy to make a better world than God intended, as it has been proved difficult to keep in running order the world that man has made out of his fragmentary conception of the divine thought. The great peril of democracy is, that the assertion of private right should be pushed to the obscuring of the superior obligation of public duty.

The pluralizing of his single person, by the Editor of the Newspaper, of the offices once divided among the Church, the University, and the Courts of Law, is one of the most striking phenomena of modern times in democratized countries, and is calculated to inspire thoughtful men with some distrust. Such pretension to omniscience and to the functions it involves has not been seen since the days of Voltaire, and even he never aspired to anything beyond the privilege of issuing his own private notes and not the bonds on which the credit of the Universe depends. The Church, the University, and the Courts taught at least under the guidance of some extrinsic standard of Authority, or of Experience, or of Tradition, but what may be the outcome of a world edited subjectively every morning is matter of alarming conjecture. Anonymousness also evades responsibility. But it is encouraging to note that the higher type of editor is coming every day to a fuller sense of the meaning of his many-sided calling, and that the newspaper itself is really beginning to furnish an instructive epitome of contemporary culture in all its branches, which, if it cannot supply the place of more thorough and special training, may inspire in some an appetite for it, and prevent others from suffering, so much as they otherwise might, by the want of it. Moreover, the power to influence public opinion is cumulative, gathering slowly but surely to the abler and more scrupulous conductors of the press, and it is observable that Wisdom generally comes to stay, while Error is apt to be but a transitory lodger.

Another very serious factor in the problem of the future is Socialism. This, it is true, is no novel phenomenon. Its theory, at least, must have been dimly conceived by the first man who had little and wanted more, and who found Society guilty of the shortcomings whose cause may have been mainly in himself. Nay, there is dynamite enough in the New Testament, if illegitimately applied, to blow all our existing institutions to atoms. All well-meaning and humane men sympathize with the aims of Lasalle and Karl Marx. All thoughtful men see well-founded and insuperable difficulties in the way of their accomplishment. But the socialism of the closet is a very different thing from that of hordes of unthinking men to whom universal suffrage may give the power of unmaking Order by making Laws. Our federal system gives us a safeguard, however, that is wanting in more centralized governments. Should one State choose to make the experiment of mending its watch by taking out the mainspring, the others can meanwhile look on and take warning by the result. We have already observed a movement towards the introduction of socialistic theories into both State and National legislation, though, if History teach anything, it teaches that the true function of Government is the prevention and remedy of evils so far only as these depend on causes within the reach of law, and that it has lost any proper conception of its duty when it becomes a distributor of alms. Timid people dread the insurrection of Bone and Sinew without seeing that unwise concessions to their unreasoned demands, which include the right to revive private war, will lead inevitably to the revolt of Brain, with consequences far more disastrous to the liberties so painfully won in all the ages during which man has been visible to us. When men formed their first Society, they instinctively recognized, in the Priest, the Lawgiver, or the Great Captain, the supreme fact that Intellect is the divinely appointed lieutenant of God in the government of this World, and in the ordering of man's place in it and of his relations towards it. This viceroy may be deposed, as during the drunkenness of the French Revolution, but out of the very crime will arise the Avenger.

It has seemed to some, and those not the least wise of their generation, that the advance of Science on which we so much plume ourselves was no unmixed good, and that this seemingly gracious benefactress perhaps took away with one hand as much as she gave with the other. We are not yet in a position to compute the results of its influence in modifying human thought and action. That it may be great none doubt who are capable of forming a judgment; and, if long life were for any reason a desirable thing, I can conceive of none more valid than that it might be prolonged till some of these results could be classed and tabulated. I cannot share their fears who are made unhappy by the foreboding that Science is in some unexplained way to take from us our sense of spiritual things. What she may do is to forbid our vulgarizing them by materialistic conceptions of their nature; and in this she will be serving the best interests of Truth and of mankind also. For it is Man's highest distinction and safeguard that he cannot if he would rest satisfied till he have pushed to its full circumference whatever fragmentary arc of truth he has been able to trace with the compasses of his mind. Give to Science her undisputed prerogative in the realm of matter, and she must become, whether she will or no, the tributary of Faith. . . . Whatever else Science may accomplish, she will never contrive to make all men equally tall in body or mind. By labor-saving expedients she may multiply every man's hands by fifty, but she can never find a substitute for the planning and directing head; nor, though she abolish space and time, can she endow electricity and vibration with the higher functions of soul. The more she makes one lobe of the brain Aristotelian, so much more will the other intrigue for an invitation to the banquet of Plato. Theology will find out in good time that there is no atheism at once so stupid and so harmful as the fancying God to be afraid of any knowledge with which He has enabled Man to equip himself. Should the doctrines of Natural Selection, Survival of the Fittest, and Heredity be accepted as Laws of Nature, they must profoundly modify the thought of man and, consequently, their action. But we should remember that it is the privilege and distinction of man to mitigate natural laws, and to make them his partners if he cannot make them his servants. Human nature is too expansive a force to be safely bottled up in any scientific formula, however incontrovertible.

I should be glad to speculate also on the effect of the tendency of population towards great cities; no new thing, but intensified as never before by increased and increasing ease of locomutation. The evil is intensified by the fact that this migration is recruited much more largely from the helpless than from the energetic class of the rural population; and it is not only an evil but a danger where, as with us, suffrage has no precautionary limits. If no remedy be possible, a palliative should be sought in whatever will make the country more entertaining; as in village libraries that may turn solitude into society, and in a more thorough and intelligent teaching of natural history in our public schools. The ploughman who is also a naturalist runs his furrow through the most interesting museum in the world. To discuss the cohesive or disruptive forces of Race and of Nationality might tempt me still to linger, but I have kept the reader quite long enough from the book itself. I have barely touched on several points on which it has roused or quickened thought. So far as the material prosperity of mankind is concerned, the

review is by no means discomforting, and as I am one of those who believe that only when the bodily appetites of man are satisfied, does he become first conscious of a spiritual hunger and thirst that demand quite other food to appease them, so we may say, with some confidence, *sicut patribus erit Deus nobis.*[n]

ABRAHAM LINCOLN (1809–1865)

WILLIAM DEAN HOWELLS's "campaign biography" of Abraham Lincoln has long gathered dust on library shelves. But Lincoln's own short sketch sent to J. W. Fell on December 20, 1859, in response to a request for biographical information to use in the political campaign, has been reprinted innumerable times. "There is not much of it," Lincoln wrote, "for the reason, I suppose, that there is not much of me. If anything be made out of it, I wish it to be modest, and not to go beyond the material." The sketch, in the text of Nicolay and Hay, follows.

[*Autobiography*]

I was born February 12, 1809, in Hardin County, Kentucky. My parents were both born in Virginia, of undistinguished families—second families, perhaps I should say. My mother, who died in my tenth year, was of a family of the name of Hanks, some of whom now reside in Adams, and others in Macon County, Illinois. My paternal grandfather, Abraham Lincoln, emigrated from Rockingham County, Virginia, to Kentucky about 1781 or 1782, where a year or two later he was killed by the Indians, not in battle, but by stealth, when he was laboring to open a farm in the forest. His ancestors, who were Quakers, went to Virginia from Berks County, Pennsylvania. An effort to identify them with the New England family of the same name ended in nothing more definite than a similarity of Christian names in both families, such as Enoch, Levi, Mordecai, Solomon, Abraham, and the like.

My father, at the death of his father, was but six years of age, and he grew up literally without education. He removed from Kentucky to what is now Spencer County, Indiana, in my eighth year. We reached our new home about the time the state came into the Union. It was a wild region, with many bears and other wild animals still in the woods. There I grew up. There were some schools, so called, but no qualification was ever required of a teacher beyond "readin', writin', and cipherin'," to the rule of three. If a straggler supposed to understand Latin happened to sojourn in the neighborhood, he was looked upon as a wizard. There was absolutely nothing to excite ambition for education. Of course, when I came of age I did not know much. Still, somehow, I could read, write, and cipher to the rule of three, but that was all. I have not been to

school since. The little advance I now have upon this store of education, I have picked up from time to time under the pressure of necessity.

I was raised to farm work, which I continued till I was twenty-two. At twenty-one I came to Illinois, Macon County. Then I got to New Salem, at that time in Sangamon, now in Menard County, where I remained a year as a sort of clerk in a store. Then came the Black Hawk War; and I was elected a captain of volunteers, a success which gave me more pleasure than any I have had since. I went the campaign, was elated, ran for the legislature the same year (1832), and was beaten—the only time I ever have been beaten by the people. The next and three succeeding biennial elections I was elected to the legislature. I was not a candidate afterward. During this legislative period I had studied law, and removed to Springfield to practice it. In 1846 I was once elected to the lower House of Congress. Was not a candidate for re-election. From 1849 to 1854, both inclusive, practiced law more assiduously than ever before. Always a Whig in politics; and generally on the Whig electoral tickets, making active canvasses. I was losing interest in politics when the repeal of the Missouri Compromise aroused me again. What I have done since then is pretty well known.

If any personal description of me is thought desirable, it may be said I am, in height, six feet four inches, nearly; lean in flesh, weighing on an average one hundred and eighty pounds; dark complexion, with coarse black hair and gray eyes. No other marks or brands recollected.

In 1858 the Lincoln-Douglas debates extended his reputation far beyond the boundaries of Illinois by reason of his conservative attitude toward antislavery and his advocacy of popular sovereignty. His reputation in the East was further heightened by his famous address at Cooper Institute, New York, February 27, 1860, showing that the acts of the thirty-nine "founding fathers" who signed the Constitution gave overwhelming proof that they would assert the right of the Federal government to forbid slavery in the Federal territories. In 1860 he was nominated for the Presidency on the third

sicut . . . nobis: "As with our fathers, God will be with us."

ballot at the Republican Convention, and won the election. After four strenuous years he was re-elected in 1864. On the evening of April 14, 1865, he was shot by John Wilkes Booth, and died the following morning. He escaped both the crudities of frontier literary expression and the magniloquence of his contemporaries educated in the classics. He was a master of direct expression. The depth of his feeling and sincerity of mind joined with his restraint, modesty, and poetic sense of rhythm to make several of his addresses enduring literature.

BIBLIOGRAPHY · The best edition of Lincoln's writings is J. G. Nicolay and John Hay, ed., *Complete Works of Abraham Lincoln* (12 vols., 1905). See also P. M. Angle, ed., *New Letters and Papers of Lincoln* (1930) and G. A. Tracy, ed., *Uncollected Letters of Abraham Lincoln* (1930). Two basic biographies by men who knew Lincoln are J. G. Nicolay and John Hay, *Abraham Lincoln: A History* (10 vols., 1886–1890) and W. H. Herndon and J. W. Weik, *Abraham Lincoln* (2 vols., 1888). P. M. Angle has edited the latter biography as *Herndon's Lincoln: the True Story of a Great Life* (1930); see also E. Hertz, *The Hidden Lincoln from the Letters and Papers of William H. Herndon* (1938). Most readable is Carl Sandburg, *Abraham Lincoln: the Prairie Years* (2 vols., 1936) and *Abraham Lincoln: the War Years* (4 vols., 1936–1939). There are innumerable studies. Among the volumes are W. Baringer, *Lincoln's Rise to Power* (1937), A. J. Beveridge, *Abraham Lincoln, 1809–1858* (4 vols., 1928), T. Dennett, *Lincoln and the Civil War in the Diaries and Letters of John Hay* (1939), and B. J. Hendrick, *Lincoln's War Cabinet* (1946). Among special articles are R. P. Basler, "Abraham Lincoln's Rhetoric," *American Literature*, XI (1939), 167–182; M. F. Berry, "Lincoln—The Speaker," *Quarterly Journal of Speech*, XVII (1931), 25–40, 177–190; J. W. Fesler, "Lincoln's Gettysburg Address," *Indiana Magazine of History*, XL (1944), 209–226; L. H. Warren, "Herndon's Contribution to Lincoln Mythology," *Indiana Magazine of History*, XLI (1945), 221–244; E. J. Wesson, "Lincoln Bibliography—Its Present Status and Needs," *Papers of the Bibliographical Society of America*, XXXIV (1940), 327–348; and P. S. Whitcomb, "Lincoln's 'Gettysburg Address,'" *Tyler's Quarterly Historical and General Magazine*, XII (1931), 221–235.

First Inaugural Address

March 4, 1861

WHEN LINCOLN left Springfield on February 11, 1861, for Washington, seven states had seceded and formed a Confederacy. Anxiety ran high as to the President-elect's personal safety. He entered Washington under cover of secrecy and took residence at Willard's hotel. On the day of the Inaugural sharpshooters were stationed at the ends of the Capitol windows, and General Winfield Scott, with troops and cannon, stood ready against possible riot. The address in Lincoln's pocket was a plea for union. William Henry Seward, who was to be Secretary of State, had read it carefully. Suggesting greater emphasis on conciliation at the close, he wrote a final paragraph which Lincoln reworked. The changes are a clear example of Lincoln's mastery of style, rising from his mood and thought. Seward's paragraph read: "I close. We are not, we must not be, aliens or enemies, but fellow-countrymen and brethren. Although passion has strained our bonds of affection too hardly, they must not, I am sure they will not, be broken. The mystic chords which, proceeding from so many battle fields and so many patriot graves, pass through all the hearts and all the hearths in this broad continent of ours, will yet again harmonize in their ancient music when breathed upon by the guardian angel of the nation." The text here is from the *Complete Works of Abraham Lincoln*, edited by Nicolay and Hay.

Fellow-citizens of the United States: In compliance with a custom as old as the government itself, I appear before you to address you briefly, and to take in your presence the oath prescribed by the Constitution of the United States to be taken by the President "before he enters on the execution of his office."

I do not consider it necessary at present for me to discuss those matters of administration about which there is no special anxiety or excitement.

Apprehension seems to exist among the people of the Southern States that by the accession of a Republican administration their property and their peace and personal security are to be endangered. There has never been any reasonable cause for such apprehension. Indeed, the most ample evidence to the contrary has all the while existed and been open to their inspection. It is found in nearly all the published speeches of him who now addresses you. I do but quote from one of those speeches when I declare that "I have no purpose, directly or indirectly, to interfere with the institution of slavery in the States where it exists. I believe I have no lawful right to do so, and I have no inclination to do so." Those who nominated and elected me did so with full knowledge that I had made this and many similar declarations, and had never recanted them. And, more than this, they placed in the platform for my acceptance, and as a law to themselves and to me, the clear and emphatic resolution which I now read:

Resolved, That the maintenance inviolate of the rights of the States, and especially the right of each State to order and control its own domestic institutions according to its own judgment exclusively, is essential to that balance of power on which the perfection and endurance of our political fabric depend, and we denounce the lawless invasion by armed force of the soil of any State or Territory, no matter under what pretext, as among the gravest of crimes.

I now reiterate these sentiments; and, in doing so, I only press upon the public attention the most conclusive evidence of which the case is susceptible, that the property, peace, and security of no section are to be in any wise endangered by the now incoming administration. I add, too, that all the protection which, consistently with the Constitution and the laws, can be given, will be cheerfully given to all the States when lawfully demanded, for whatever cause—as cheerfully to one section as to another.

There is much controversy about the delivering up of fugitives from service or labor. The clause I now read is as plainly written in the Constitution as any other of its provisions:

No person held to service or labor in one State, under the laws thereof, escaping into another, shall in consequence of any law or regulation therein be discharged from such service or labor, but shall be delivered up on claim of the party to whom such service or labor may be due.

It is scarcely questioned that this provision was intended by those who made it for the reclaiming of what we call fugitive slaves; and the intention of the lawgiver is the law. All members of Congress swear their support to the whole Constitution—to this provision as much as to any other. To the proposition, then, that slaves whose cases come within the terms of this clause "shall be delivered up," their oaths are unanimous. Now, if they would make the effort in good temper, could they not with nearly equal unanimity frame and pass a law by means of which to keep good that unanimous oath?

There is some difference of opinion whether this clause should be enforced by national or by State authority; but surely that difference is not a very material one. If the slave is to be surrendered, it can be of but little consequence to him or to others by which authority it is done. And should any one in any case be content that his oath shall go unkept on a merely unsubstantial controversy as to how it shall be kept?

Again, in any law upon this subject, ought not all the safeguards of liberty known in civilized and humane jurisprudence to be introduced, so that a free man be not, in any case, surrendered as a slave? And might it not be well at the same time to provide by law for the enforcement of that clause in the Constitution which guarantees that "the citizen of each State shall be entitled to all privileges and immunities of citizens in the several States"?

I take the official oath to-day with no mental reservations, and with no purpose to construe the Constitution or laws by any hypercritical rules. And while I do not choose now to specify particular acts of Congress as proper to be enforced, I do suggest that it will be much safer for all, both in official and private stations, to conform to and abide by all those acts which stand unrepealed, than to violate any of them, trusting to find impunity in having them held to be unconstitutional.

It is seventy-two years since the first inauguration of a President under our National Constitution. During that period fifteen different and greatly distinguished citizens have, in succession, administered the executive branch of the government. They have conducted it through many perils, and generally with great success. Yet, with all this scope of precedent, I now enter upon the same task for the brief constitutional term of four years under great and peculiar difficulty. A disruption of the Federal Union, heretofore only menaced, is now formidably attempted.

I hold that, in contemplation of universal law and of the Constitution, the Union of these States is perpetual. Perpetuity is implied, if not expressed, in the fundamental law of all national governments. It is safe to assert that no government proper ever had a provision in its organic law for its own termination. Continue to execute all the express provisions of our National Constitution, and the Union will endure forever—it being impossible to destroy it except by some action not provided for in the instrument itself.

Again, if the United States be not a government proper, but an association of States in the nature of contract merely, can it, as a contract, be peaceably unmade by less than all the parties who made it? One party to a contract may violate it—break it, so to speak; but does it not require all to lawfully rescind it?

Descending from these general principles, we find the proposition that, in legal contemplation the Union is perpetual confirmed by the history of the Union itself. The Union is much older than the Constitution. It was formed, in fact, by the Articles of Association in 1774. It was matured and continued by the Declaration of Independence in 1776. It was further matured, and the faith of all the then thirteen States expressly plighted and engaged that it should be perpetual, by the Articles of Confederation in 1778. And, finally, in 1787 one of the declared objects for ordaining and establishing the Constitution was "to form a more perfect Union."

But if the destruction of the Union by one or by a part only of the States be lawfully possible, the Union is less perfect than before the Constitution, having lost the vital element of perpetuity.

It follows from these views that no State upon its own mere motion can lawfully get out of the Union; that resolves and ordinances to that effect are legally void; and that acts of violence, within any State or States, against the authority of the United States, are insurrectionary or revolutionary, according to circumstances.

I therefore consider that, in view of the Constitution and the laws, the Union is unbroken; and to the extent of my ability I shall take care, as the Constitution itself expressly enjoins upon me, that the laws of the Union be faithfully executed in all the States. Doing this I deem to be only a simple duty on my part; and I shall perform it so far as practicable, unless my rightful masters, the American people, shall withhold the requisite means, or in some authoritative manner

direct the contrary. I trust this will not be regarded as a menace, but only as the declared purpose of the Union that it will constitutionally defend and maintain itself.

In doing this there needs to be no bloodshed or violence; and there shall be none, unless it be forced upon the national authority. The power confided to me will be used to hold, occupy, and possess the property and places belonging to the government, and to collect the duties and imposts; but beyond what may be necessary for these objects, there will be no invasion, no using of force against or among the people anywhere. Where hostility to the United States, in any interior locality, shall be so great and universal as to prevent competent resident citizens from holding the Federal offices, there will be no attempt to force obnoxious strangers among the people for that object. While the strict legal right may exist in the government to enforce the exercise of these offices, the attempt to do so would be so irritating, and so nearly impracticable withal, that I deem it better to forego for the time the uses of such offices.

The mails, unless repelled, will continue to be furnished in all parts of the Union. So far as possible, the people everywhere shall have that sense of perfect security which is most favorable to calm thought and reflection. The course here indicated will be followed unless current events and experience shall show a modification or change to be proper, and in every case and exigency my best discretion will be exercised according to circumstances actually existing, and with a view and a hope of a peaceful solution of the national troubles and the restoration of fraternal sympathies and affections.

That there are persons in one section or another who seek to destroy the Union at all events, and are glad of any pretext to do it, I will neither affirm nor deny; but if there be such, I need address no word to them. To those, however, who really love the Union may I not speak?

Before entering upon so grave a matter as the destruction of our national fabric, with all its benefits, its memories, and its hopes, would it not be wise to ascertain precisely why we do it? Will you hazard so desperate a step while there is any possibility that any portion of the ills you fly from have no real existence? Will you, while the certain ills you fly to are greater than all the real ones you fly from—will you risk the commission of so fearful a mistake?

All profess to be content in the Union if all constitutional rights can be maintained. Is it true, then, that any right, plainly written in the Constitution, has been denied? I think not. Happily the human mind is so constituted that no party can reach to the audacity of doing this. Think, if you can, of a single instance in which a plainly written provision of the Constitution has ever been denied. If by the mere force of numbers a majority should deprive a minority of any clearly written constitutional right, it might, in a moral point of view, justify revolution—certainly would if such a right were a vital one. But such is not our case. All the vital rights of minorities and of individuals are so plainly assured to them by affirmations and negations, guarantees and prohibitions, in the Constitution, that controversies never arise concerning them. But no organic law can ever be framed with a provision specifically applicable to every question which may occur in practical administration. No foresight can anticipate, nor any document of reasonable length contain, express provisions for all possible questions. Shall fugitives from labor be surrendered by national or by State authority? The Constitution does not expressly say. *May* Congress prohibit slavery in the Territories? The Constitution does not expressly say. *Must* Congress protect slavery in the Territories? The Constitution does not expressly say.

From questions of this class spring all our constitutional controversies, and we divide upon them into majorities and minorities. If the minority will not acquiesce, the majority must, or the government must cease. There is no other alternative; for continuing the government is acquiescence on one side or the other.

If a minority in such case will secede rather than acquiesce, they make a precedent which in turn will divide and ruin them; for a minority of their own will secede from them whenever a majority refuses to be controlled by such minority. For instance, why may not any portion of a new confederacy a year or two hence arbitrarily secede again, precisely as portions of the present Union now claim to secede from it? All who cherish disunion sentiments are now being educated to the exact temper of doing this.

Is there such perfect identity of interests among the States to compose a new Union, as to produce harmony only, and prevent renewed secession?

Plainly, the central idea of secession is the essence of anarchy. A majority held in restraint by constitutional checks and limitations, and always changing easily with deliberate changes of popular opinions and sentiments, is the only true sovereign of a free people. Whoever rejects it does, of necessity, fly to anarchy or to despotism. Unanimity is impossible; the rule of a minority, as a permanent arrangement, is wholly inadmissible; so that, rejecting the majority principle, anarchy or despotism in some form is all that is left.

I do not forget the position, assumed by some, that constitutional questions are to be decided by the Supreme Court; nor do I deny that such decisions must be binding, in any case, upon the parties to a suit, as to the object of that suit, while they are also entitled to very high respect and consideration in all parallel cases by all other departments of the government. And while it is obviously possible that such decision may be erroneous in any given case, still the evil effect following it, being limited to that particular case, with the chance that it may be overruled and never become a precedent for other cases, can better be borne than could the evils of a different practice. At the same time, the candid citizen must confess that if the policy of the government, upon vital questions affecting the whole people, is to be irrevocably fixed by decisions of the Supreme Court, the instant they are made, in ordinary litigation between parties in personal actions, the people will have ceased to be their own rulers, having to that extent practically resigned their government into the hands of that eminent tribunal. Nor is there in this view any assault upon the court or the judges. It is a duty from which they may not shrink to decide cases properly brought before them, and it is no fault of theirs if others seek to turn their decisions to political purposes.

One section of our country believes slavery is right, and ought to be extended, while the other believes it is wrong, and ought not to be extended. This is the only substantial dispute. The fugitive-slave clause of the Constitution, and the law for the suppression of the foreign slave-trade, are each as well enforced, perhaps, as any law can ever be in a community where the moral sense of the people imperfectly supports the law itself. The great body of the people abide by the dry legal obligation in both cases, and a few break over in each. This, I think, cannot be perfectly cured; and it would be worse in both cases after the separation of the sections than before. The foreign slave-trade, now imperfectly suppressed, would be ultimately revived, without restriction, in one section, while fugitive slaves, now only partially surrendered, would not be surrendered at all by the other.

Physically speaking, we cannot separate. We cannot remove our respective sections from each other, nor build an impassable wall between them. A husband and wife may be divorced, and go out of the presence and beyond the reach of each other; but the different parts of our country cannot do this. They cannot but remain face to face, and intercourse, either amicable or hostile, must continue between them. Is it possible, then, to make that intercourse more advantageous or more satisfactory after separation than before? Can aliens make treaties easier than friends can make laws? Can treaties be more faithfully enforced between aliens than laws can among friends? Suppose you go to war, you cannot fight always; and when, after much loss on both sides, and no gain on either, you cease fighting, the identical old questions as to terms of intercourse are again upon you.

This country, with its institutions, belongs to the people who inhabit it. Whenever they shall grow weary of the existing government, they can exercise their constitutional right of amending it, or their revolutionary right to dismember or overthrow it. I cannot be ignorant of the fact that many worthy and patriotic citizens are desirous of having the National Constitution amended. While I make no recommendation of amendments, I fully recognize the rightful authority of the people over the whole subject, to be exercised in either of the modes prescribed in the instrument itself; and I should, under existing circumstances, favor rather than oppose a fair opportunity being afforded the people to act upon it. I will venture to add that to me the convention mode seems preferable, in that it allows amendments to originate with the people themselves, instead of only permitting them to take or reject propositions originated by others not especially chosen for the purpose, and which might not be precisely such as they would wish to either accept or refuse. I understand a proposed amendment to the Constitution—which amendment, however, I have not seen—has passed Congress, to the effect that the Federal Government shall never interfere with the domestic institutions of the States, including that of persons held to service. To avoid misconstruction of what I have said, I depart from my purpose not to speak of particular amendments so far as to say that, holding such a provision to now be implied constitutional law, I have no objection to its being made express and irrevocable.

The chief magistrate derives all his authority from the people, and they have conferred none upon him to fix terms for the separation of the States. The people themselves can do this also if they choose; but the executive, as such, has nothing to do with it. His duty is to administer the present government, as it came to his hands, and to transmit it, unimpaired by him, to his successor.

Why should there not be a patient confidence in the ultimate justice of the people? Is there any better or equal hope in the world? In our present differences is either party without faith of being in the right? If the Almighty Ruler of Nations, with his eternal truth and justice, be on your side of the North, or on yours of the South, that truth and that justice will surely prevail by the judgment of this great tribunal of the American people.

By the frame of the government under which we live, this same people have wisely given their public servants but little power for mischief; and have, with equal wisdom, provided for the return of that little to their own hands at very short intervals. While the people retain their virtue and vigilance, no administration, by any extreme of wickedness or folly, can very seriously injure the government in the short space of four years.

My countrymen, one and all, think calmly and well upon this whole subject. Nothing valuable can be lost by taking time. If there be an object to hurry any of you in hot haste to a step which you would never take deliberately, that object will be frustrated by taking time; but no good object can be frustrated by it. Such of you as are now dissatisfied, still have the old Constitution unimpaired, and, on the sensitive point, the laws of your own framing under it; while the new administration will have no immediate power, if it would, to change either. If it were admitted that you who are dissatisfied hold the right side in the dispute, there still is no single good reason for precipitate action. Intelligence, patriotism, Christianity, and a firm reliance on Him who has never yet forsaken this favored land, are still competent to adjust in the best way all our present difficulty.

In your hands, my dissatisfied fellow-countrymen, and not in mine, is the momentous issue of civil war. The government will not assail you. You can have no conflict without being yourselves the aggressors. You have no oath registered in heaven to destroy the government, while I shall have the most solemn one to "preserve, protect, and defend it."

I am loath to close. We are not enemies, but friends. We must not be enemies. Though passion may have strained, it must not break our bonds of affection. The mystic chords of memory, stretching from every battle-field and patriot grave to every living heart and hearthstone all over this broad land, will yet swell the chorus of the Union when again touched, as surely they will be, by the better angels of our nature.

Letter to Horace Greeley

HORACE GREELEY, owner and editor of the New York *Tribune*, attacked Lincoln in an editorial, "The Prayer of 20,000,000," published August 19, 1862, finding him "strangely remiss" in enforcement of laws and asserting that the Northern soldiers seemed more interested in upholding slavery than in putting down the rebellion. The following letter is Lincoln's reply of August 22. Greeley was unaware that exactly a month before the appearance of the editorial—July 22—Lincoln had read a draft of the Emancipation Proclamation to his Cabinet, and that Seward had counseled postponement until success of Northern arms would assure some degree of enforcement. The Proclamation was published September 24, 1862.

Executive Mansion, Washington,
August 22, 1862.

Hon. Horace Greeley.

Dear Sir: I have just read yours of the 19th, addressed to myself through the New York "Tribune." If there be in it any statements or assumptions of fact which I may know to be erroneous, I do not, now and here, controvert them. If there be in it any inferences which I may believe to be falsely drawn, I do not, now and here, argue against them. If there be perceptible in it an impatient and dictatorial tone, I waive it in deference to an old friend whose heart I have always supposed to be right.

As to the policy I "seem to be pursuing," as you say, I have not meant to leave any one in doubt.

I would save the Union. I would save it the shortest way under the Constitution. The sooner the national authority can be restored, the nearer the Union will be "the Union as it was." If there be those who would not save the Union unless they could at the same time save slavery, I do not agree with them. If there be those who would not save the Union unless they could at the same time destroy slavery, I do not agree with them. My paramount object in this struggle is to save the Union, and is not either to save or to destroy slavery. If I could save the Union without freeing any slave, I would do it; and if I could save it by freeing all the slaves, I would do it; and if I could save it by freeing some and leaving others alone, I would also do that. What I do about slavery and the colored race, I do because I believe it helps to save the Union; and what I forbear, I forbear because I do not believe it would help to save the Union. I shall do less whenever I shall believe what I am doing hurts the cause, and I shall do more whenever I shall believe doing more will help the cause. I shall try to correct errors when shown to be errors, and I shall adopt new views so fast as they shall appear to be true views.

I have here stated my purpose according to my view of official duty; and I intend no modification of my oft-expressed personal wish that all men everywhere could be free.

Yours,

A. Lincoln.

The Gettysburg Address

November 19, 1863

THE DEDICATION CEREMONY at Gettysburg, Pennsylvania, was delayed from October 13, 1863, to Thursday, November 19, at the request of the principal orator, Edward Everett, so that he might have more time to prepare his address. Lincoln arrived in the town on the evening of the 18th, and was entertained at the Wills home. That evening he called on Seward, but what Seward may or may not have suggested regarding Lincoln's manuscript is not known. The next day Everett spoke eloquently for two hours; Lincoln followed, reading his ten sentences from two pages of manuscript for five minutes. On November 20, Everett wrote to Lincoln: "I should be glad if I could flatter myself that I came as near to the central idea of the occasion in two hours as you did in two minutes." The following revision will indicate Lincoln's fine sense of literary form. An earlier draft read: "This we may, in all propriety do"; it was altered to the familiar sentence: "It is altogether fitting and proper that we should do this." The text here is from the *Complete Works of Abraham Lincoln*, edited by Nicolay and Hay.

Fourscore and seven years ago our fathers brought forth on this continent a new nation, conceived in liberty, and dedicated to the proposition that all men are created equal.

Now we are engaged in a great civil war, testing whether that nation, or any nation so conceived and so dedicated, can long endure. We are met on a great battle-field of that war. We have come to dedicate a portion of that field as a final resting-place for those who here gave their lives that that nation might live. It is altogether fitting and proper that we should do this.

But, in a larger sense, we cannot dedicate—we cannot consecrate—we cannot hallow—this ground. The brave men, living and dead, who struggled here, have consecrated it far above our poor power to add or detract. The world will little note nor long remember what we say here, but it can never forget what they did here. It is for us, the living, rather, to be dedicated here to the unfinished work which they who fought here have thus far so nobly advanced. It is rather for us to be here dedicated to the great task remaining before us—that from these honored dead we take increased devotion to that cause for which they gave the last full measure of devotion; that we here highly resolve that these dead shall not have died in vain; that this nation, under God, shall have a new birth of freedom; and that government of the people, by the people, for the people, shall not perish from the earth.

Letter to Mrs. Bixby

IN SEPTEMBER, 1864, Lincoln received a request from Governor Andrew, of Massachusetts, requesting that Lincoln write a letter of condolence to Mrs. Lydia Bixby, of Boston, a widow whose five sons had all been killed in action. The facts were certified to Lincoln by the War Department in October. In the letter, the President thought of Mrs. Bixby as the symbol of all mothers who had lost sons in the war. The letter was first published in the *Transcript* and the *Advertiser*, of Boston, the day following Thanksgiving.

Executive Mansion, Washington,
November 21, 1864.

Mrs. Bixby,
Boston, Massachusetts.

Dear Madam: I have been shown in the files of the War Department a statement of the Adjutant-General of Massachusetts that you are the mother of five sons who have died gloriously on the field of battle. I feel how weak and fruitless must be any words of mine which should attempt to beguile you from the grief of a loss so overwhelming. But I cannot refrain from tendering to you the consolation that may be found in the thanks of the Republic they died to save. I pray that your heavenly Father may assuage the anguish of your bereavement, and leave you only the cherished memory of the loved and lost, and the solemn pride that must be yours to have laid so costly a sacrifice upon the altar of freedom.

Yours very sincerely and respectfully,

Abraham Lincoln.

Second Inaugural Address

March 4, 1865

A LIGHT RAIN was falling as the people gathered for the Second Inaugural ceremonies. The sections of the great Capitol dome, which had been lying on the ground at the First Inaugural, were now in place, a fitting symbol of the year which was to mark the close of the conflict. Though the end of the "great scourge of war" lay ahead, Lincoln was already thinking of more difficult responsibilities, "to bind up the nation's wounds," to achieve "a just and lasting peace." The text here is from the *Complete Works of Abraham Lincoln*, edited by Nicolay and Hay.

Fellow-countrymen: At this second appearing to take the oath of the presidential office, there is less occasion for an extended address than there was at the first. Then a statement, somewhat in detail, of a course to be pursued, seemed fitting and proper. Now, at the expiration of four years, during which public declarations have been constantly called forth on every point and phase of the great contest which still absorbs the attention and engrosses the energies of the nation, little that is new could be presented. The progress of our arms, upon which all else chiefly depends, is as well known to the public as to myself; and it is, I trust, reasonably satisfactory and encouraging to all. With high hope for the future, no prediction in regard to it is ventured.

On the occasion corresponding to this four years ago, all thoughts were anxiously directed to an impending civil war. All dreaded it—all sought to avert it. While the inaugural address was being delivered from this place, devoted altogether to saving the Union without war, insurgent agents were in the city seeking to destroy it without war—seeking to dissolve the Union, and divide effects, by negotiation. Both parties deprecated war; but one of them would make war rather than let the nation survive; and the other would accept war rather than let it perish. And the war came.

One-eighth of the whole population were colored slaves, not distributed generally over the Union, but localized in the Southern part of it. These slaves constituted a peculiar and powerful interest. All knew that this interest was, somehow, the cause of the war. To strengthen, perpetuate, and extend this interest was the object for which the insurgents would rend the Union, even by war; while the government claimed no right to do more than to restrict the territorial enlargement of it.

Neither party expected for the war the magnitude or the duration which it has already attained. Neither anticipated that the cause of the conflict might cease with, or even before, the conflict itself should cease. Each looked for an easier triumph, and a result less fundamental and astounding. Both read the same Bible, and pray to the same God; and each invokes his aid against the other. It may seem strange that any men should dare to ask a just God's assistance in wringing their bread from the sweat of other men's faces; but let us judge not, that we be not judged. The prayers of both could not be answered—that of neither has been answered fully.

The Almighty has his own purposes. "Woe unto the world because of offenses! for it must needs be that offenses come; but woe to that man by whom the offense cometh." If we shall suppose that American slavery is one of those offenses which, in the providence of God, must needs come, but which, having continued through his appointed time, he now wills to remove, and that he gives to both North and South this terrible war, as the woe due to those by whom the offense came, shall we discern therein any departure from those divine attributes which the believers in a living God always ascribe to him? Fondly do we hope—fervently do we pray—that this mighty scourge of war may speedily pass away. Yet, if God wills that it continue until all the wealth piled by the bondman's two hundred and fifty years of unrequited toil shall be sunk, and until every drop of blood drawn with the lash shall be paid by another drawn with the sword, as was said three thousand years ago, so still it must be said, "The judgments of the Lord are true and righteous altogether."

With malice toward none; with charity for all; with firmness in the right, as God gives us to see the right, let us strive on to finish the work we are in; to bind up the nation's wounds; to care for him who shall have borne the battle, and for his widow, and his orphan—to do all which may achieve and cherish a just and lasting peace among ourselves, and with all nations.

HENRY TIMROD (1828–1867)

THE CIVIL WAR hastened the development of Henry Timrod from a writer of graceful amatory and sentimental verse to a true lyrist who won Whittier's praise for "the true fire within." Timrod's early poetry, much of which is conventional and imitative, reveals the vision and yearning but not the achievement of full poetic power. His most memorable poems, "The Cotton Boll," "Spring," "The Unknown Dead," and the tender memorial "Ode," were all inspired by the war. It was the war and its aftermath, however, which also contributed to the causes of his broken last years and early death. Although he lived long enough to see his dream of a victorious and generous South shattered by defeat, the dream itself, as Professor Jay Hubbell suggests, was born of "that mood of exalted devotion which characterized the Confederacy at its best."

Timrod was born in Charleston, South Carolina, on December 8, 1828. He attended the Coates School in Charleston, where he began his lifelong friendship with Paul Hamilton Hayne, a fellow poet who later brought out a collected edition of Timrod's poems. In 1845 Timrod entered the University of Georgia, but he withdrew after a year and a half because of his frail health and poverty. After a brief term as reader of law in the Charleston office of James Petigru, Timrod became a private tutor in planters' families in the Carolinas. In 1849 he began contributing poems to *The Southern Literary Messenger*. Later in the next decade he sent much of his prose and verse to *Russell's Magazine*, founded in 1857 and edited by Hayne. *Poems*, the only volume of Timrod's verse to appear during his lifetime, was published in Boston by Ticknor and Fields in 1860. Timrod enlisted in the Confederate Army in December, 1861, but his precarious health caused by incipient tuberculosis prevented him from serving more than eight or nine months. Following his discharge he found an editorial position on *The Charleston Mercury*, which provided only the barest means of support. His next appointment, the associate editorship of *The South Carolinian*, published at Columbia, ended when the state capital was burned in the wake of Sherman's march to the sea. The pitiful record of Timrod's last years bears out his earlier prophecy that he was one of those people who "never by any chance win a single gift from Fortune." Cut off by the war from Northern publishers, in failing health, saddened by the death of his only son, and grieved by his inability to provide adequately for his wife and sister, Timrod died on October 7, 1867.

The spirited Civil War songs of Timrod won for him the title of "The Laureate of the Confederacy." Yet this phrase is too narrow to do the poet complete justice. In his *Last Years of Henry Timrod*, Professor Hubbell remarks justly, "Timrod was not a secessionist and he was not interested in filling his poems with local color or in exploiting Southern themes. He was singularly free from Southern literary provincialism; and, like Poe, he wanted to write poetry that would be adjudged great by international standards. As it happened, the coming of the Civil War greatly stimulated his poetic development, and his best poems grew out of that conflict. If he had been given twenty years more to live, however, I think his war poems would bulk no larger in his collected poems than do Whitman's war poems in *Leaves of Grass*."

BIBLIOGRAPHY · Paul Hamilton Hayne issued *The Poems of Henry Timrod* (1873), with a brief biographical sketch. This volume constitutes the text for the following selections. A few additional poems are contained in the Memorial Edition, *Poems of Henry Timrod* (1899). The number of poems hitherto collected were more than doubled by the publication of G. A. Cardwell, Jr., *The Uncollected Poems of Henry Timrod* (1942). Letters and a number of formerly uncollected prose pieces are included in J. B. Hubbell, *The Last Years of Henry Timrod: 1864–1867* (1941). *The Essays of Henry Timrod* (1942), edited by E. W. Parks, is important for the poet's literary criticism.

Additional biographical and critical information is contained in G. A. Cardwell, Jr., "The Date of Henry Timrod's Birth," *American Literature*, VII (1935), 207–208; and "William Henry Timrod, the Charleston Volunteers, and the Defense of St. Augustine," *North Carolina Historical Review*, XVIII (1941), 27–37; W. Fidler, "Henry Timrod: Poet of the Confederacy," *Southern Literary Messenger*, II (1940), 527–532; E. W. Parks, "Timrod's College Days," *American Literature*, VIII (1936), 294–296; R. Taylor, "Henry Timrod's Ancestor, Hannah Caesar," *American Literature*, IX (1938), 419–430; H. T. Thompson, *Henry Timrod: Laureate of the Confederacy* (1928); G. P. Voigt, "Timrod's Essays in Literary Criticism," *American Literature*, VI (1934), 163–167; and G. A. Wauchope, *Henry Timrod: Man and Poet* (1915).

In his memoir of the poet Paul Hamilton Hayne wrote, "Timrod looked up to Wordsworth as his poetic guide and mentor." One of the effects of Wordsworth's influence, especially upon the early poetry, is to be seen in Timrod's devotion to the form of the sonnet. See Timrod's essay, "The Character and Scope of the Sonnet" in *Russell's Magazine*, I (1857), 156–159; the article is reprinted in Edd Winfield Parks, *The Essays of Henry Timrod* (1942). In *Segments of Southern Thought* (1938) Professor Parks cites the following sonnets as evidence of Timrod's maturing power.

I Know Not Why

I know not why, but all this weary day,
Suggested by no definite grief or pain,
Sad fancies have been flitting through my brain;
Now it has been a vessel losing way,
Rounding a stormy headland; now a gray   5
Dull waste of clouds above a wintry main;
And then, a banner, drooping in the rain,
And meadows beaten into bloody clay.
Strolling at random with this shadowy woe
At heart, I chanced to wander hither! Lo!   10
A league of desolate marsh-land, with its lush,
Hot grasses in a noisome, tide-left bed,
And faint, warm airs, that rustle in the hush,
Like whispers round the body of the dead!

Most Men Know Love but as a Part of Life

Most men know love but as a part of life;   15
They hide it in some corner of the breast,
Even from themselves; and only when they rest
In the brief pauses of that daily strife,
Wherewith the world might else be not so rife,
They draw it forth (as one draws forth a toy   20
To soothe some ardent, kiss-exacting boy)
And hold it up to sister, child, or wife.
Ah me! why may not love and life be one?
Why walk we thus alone, when by our side,
Love, like a visible God, might be our guide?   25
How would the marts grow noble! and the street,
Worn like a dungeon-floor by weary feet,
Seem then a golden court-way of the Sun!

The Cotton Boll

"The Cotton Boll" appeared in *The Charleston Mercury*, September 3, 1861.

While I recline
At ease beneath
This immemorial pine,
Small sphere!

(By dusky fingers brought this morning here   5
And shown with boastful smiles),
I turn thy cloven sheath,
Through which the soft white fibers peer,
That, with their gossamer bands,
Unite, like love, the sea-divided lands,   10
And slowly, thread by thread,
Draw forth the folded strands,
Than which the trembling line,
By whose frail help yon startled spider fled
Down the tall spear-grass from his swinging bed, 15
Is scarce more fine;
And as the tangled skein
Unravels in my hands,
Betwixt me and the noonday light,
A veil seems lifted, and for miles and miles   20
The landscape broadens on my sight,
As, in the little boll, there lurked a spell
Like that which, in the ocean shell,
With mystic sound,
Breaks down the narrow walls that hem us round,
And turns some city lane   26
Into the restless main,
With all his capes and isles!

Yonder bird,
Which floats, as if at rest,   30
In those blue tracts above the thunder, where
No vapors cloud the stainless air,
And never sound is heard,
Unless at such rare time
When, from the City of the Blest,   35
Rings down some golden chime,
Sees not from his high place
So vast a cirque of summer space
As widens round me in one mighty field,
Which, rimmed by seas and sands,   40
Doth hail its earliest daylight in the beams
Of gray Atlantic dawns;
And, broad as realms made up of many lands,
Is lost afar
Behind the crimson hills and purple lawns   45
Of sunset, among plains which roll their streams
Against the Evening Star!

And lo!
To the remotest point of sight,
Although I gaze upon no waste of snow,   50
The endless field is white;

And the whole landscape glows,
For many a shining league away,
With such accumulated light
As Polar lands would flash beneath a tropic day! 55
Nor lack there (for the vision grows,
And the small charm within my hands—
More potent even than the fabled one,
Which oped whatever golden mystery
Lay hid in fairy wood or magic vale, 60
The curious ointment of the Arabian tale—
Beyond all mortal sense
Doth stretch my sight's horizon, and I see,
Beneath its simple influence,
As if with Uriel's crown, 65
I stood in some great temple of the Sun,
And looked, as Uriel, down!)
Nor lack there pastures rich and fields all green
With all the common gifts of God,
For temperate airs and torrid sheen 70
Weave Edens of the sod;
Through lands which look one sea of billowy gold
Broad rivers wind their devious ways;
A hundred isles in their embraces fold
A hundred luminous bays; 75
And through yon purple haze
Vast mountains lift their plumed peaks cloud-
      crowned;
And, save where up their sides the plowman creeps,
An unhewn forest girds them grandly round,
In whose dark shades a future navy sleeps! 80
Ye Stars, which, though unseen, yet with me gaze
Upon this loveliest fragment of the earth!
Thou Sun, that kindlest all thy gentlest rays
Above it, as to light a favorite hearth!
Ye Clouds, that in your temples in the West 85
See nothing brighter than its humblest flowers!
And you, ye Winds, that on the ocean's breast
Are kissed to coolness ere ye reach its bowers!
Bear witness with me in my song of praise,
And tell the world that, since the world began, 90
No fairer land hath fired a poet's lays,
Or given a home to man!

But these are charms already widely blown!
His be the meed whose pencil's trace
Hath touched our very swamps with grace, 95
And round whose tuneful way
All Southern laurels bloom;

The Poet of "The Woodlands," unto whom
Alike are known 99
The flute's low breathing and the trumpet's tone,
And the soft west wind's sighs;
But who shall utter all the debt,
O land wherein all powers are met
That bind a people's heart,
The world doth owe thee at this day, 105
And which it never can repay,
Yet scarcely deigns to own!
Where sleeps the poet who shall fitly sing
The source wherefrom doth spring
That mighty commerce which, confined 110
To the mean channels of no selfish mart,
Goes out to every shore
Of this broad earth, and throngs the sea with ships
That bear no thunders; hushes hungry lips
In alien lands; 115
Joins with a delicate web remotest strands;
And gladdening rich and poor,
Doth gild Parisian domes,
Or feed the cottage-smoke of English homes,
And only bounds its blessings by mankind!
In offices like these, thy mission lies, 121
My Country! and it shall not end
As long as rain shall fall and Heaven bend
In blue above thee; though thy foes be hard
And cruel their weapons, it shall guard 125
Thy hearth-stones as a bulwark; make thee great
In white and bloodless state;
And haply, as the years increase—
Still working through its humbler reach 129
With that large wisdom which the ages teach—
Revive the half-dead dream of universal peace!
As men who labor in that mine
Of Cornwall, hollowed out beneath the bed
Of ocean, when a storm rolls overhead,
Hear the dull booming of the world of brine 135
Above them, and a mighty muffled roar
Of winds and waters, yet toil calmly on,
And split the rock, and pile the massive ore,
Or carve a niche, or shape the archèd roof;
So I, as calmly, weave my woof 140
Of song, chanting the days to come,
Unsilenced, though the quiet summer air
Stirs with the bruit of battles, and each dawn
Wakes from its starry silence to the hum
Of many gathering armies. Still, 145

913

In that we sometimes hear,
Upon the Northern winds, the voice of woe
Not wholly drowned in triumph, though I know
The end must crown us, and a few brief years
Dry all our tears,   150
I may not sing too gladly. To Thy Will
Resigned, O Lord! we cannot all forget
That there is much even Victory must regret.
And, therefore, not too long
From the great burthen of our country's wrong
Delay our just release!   156
And, if it may be, save
These sacred fields of peace
From stain of patriot or of hostile blood!
Oh, help us, Lord! to roll the crimson flood
Back on its course, and while our banners wing 161
Northward, strike with us! till the Goth shall cling
To his own blasted altar-stones, and crave
Mercy; and we shall grant it, and dictate
The lenient future of his fate   165
There, where some rotting ships and crumbling
    quays
Shall one day mark the Port which ruled the
    Western seas.

Charleston

This poem was printed in *The Charleston Mercury*,
December 13, 1862.

Calm as that second summer which precedes
    The first fall of the snow,
In the broad sunlight of heroic deeds
    The City bides the foe.

As yet, behind their ramparts stern and proud,   5
    Her bolted thunders sleep—
Dark Sumter like a battlemented cloud
    Looms o'er the solemn deep.

No Calpe frowns from lofty cliff or scar
    To guard the holy strand;   10
But Moultrie holds in leash her dogs of war
    Above the level sand.

And down the dunes a thousand guns lie couched
    Unseen beside the flood,
Like tigers in some Orient jungle crouched,   15
    That wait and watch for blood.

    9. Calpe: less-familiar name for Gibraltar.

Meanwhile, through streets still echoing with
    trade,
    Walk grave and thoughtful men
Whose hands may one day wield the patriot's
    blade
    As lightly as the pen.   20

And maidens with such eyes as would grow dim
    Over a bleeding hound
Seem each one to have caught the strength of him
    Whose sword she sadly bound.

Thus girt without and garrisoned at home,   25
    Day patient following day,
Old Charleston looks from roof and spire and dome
    Across her tranquil bay.

Ships, through a hundred foes, from Saxon lands
    And spicy Indian ports   30
Bring Saxon steel and iron to her hands
    And Summer to her courts.

But still, along yon dim Atlantic line
    The only hostile smoke
Creeps like a harmless mist above the brine   35
    From some frail, floating oak.

Shall the Spring dawn, and she, still clad in smiles
    And with an unscathed brow,
Rest in the strong arms of her palm-crowned isles
    As fair and free as now?   40

We know not: in the temple of the Fates
    God has inscribed her doom;
And, all untroubled in her faith, she waits
    The triumph or the tomb.

The Unknown Dead

This poem was first printed in *The Southern Illustrated
News*, July 4, 1863.

The rain is plashing on my sill,
But all the winds of Heaven are still;
And so it falls with that dull sound
Which thrills us in the church-yard ground,
When the first spadeful drops like lead   5
Upon the coffin of the dead.
Beyond my streaming window-pane,
I cannot see the neighboring vane,

Yet from its old familiar tower
The bell comes, muffled, through the shower. 10
What strange and unsuspected link
Of feeling touched, has made me think—
While with a vacant soul and eye
I watch that gray and stony sky—
Of nameless graves on battle-plains 15
Washed by a single winter's rains,
Where, some beneath Virginian hills,
And some by green Atlantic rills,
Some by the waters of the West,
A myriad unknown heroes rest. 20
Ah! not the chiefs, who, dying, see
Their flags in front of victory,
Or, at their life-blood's noble cost
Pay for a battle nobly lost,
Claim from their monumental beds 25
The bitterest tears a nation sheds.
Beneath yon lonely mound—the spot
By all save some fond few forgot—
Lie the true martyrs of the fight
Which strikes for freedom and for right. 30
Of them, their patriot zeal and pride,
The lofty faith that with them died,
No grateful page shall farther tell
Than that so many bravely fell;
And we can only dimly guess 35
What world of all this world's distress,
What utter woe, despair and dearth,
Their fate has brought to many a hearth.
Just such a sky as this should weep
Above them, always, where they sleep; 40
Yet, haply, at this very hour,
Their graves are like a lover's bower;
And Nature's self, with eyes unwet,
Oblivious of the crimson debt
To which she owes her April's grace, 45
Laughs gayly o'er their burial-place.

Ode

This poem, described by E. P. Whipple as "the noblest
poem ever written by a Southern poet," was sung at a
commemorative ceremony in the Magnolia Cemetery
in Charleston on June 16, 1866. It was published in the
Courier two days after the exercises. Professor Gilbert
Voigt discovered a hitherto unknown revised version
in the *Courier* for July 23, 1866. For an account of the
revisions, see G. P. Voigt, "New Light on Timrod's

'Memorial Ode,' " *American Literature*, IV (1933), 395–
396. The "Ode" was reprinted in Emerson's *Parnassus*
(1874).

Sleep sweetly in your humble graves,
    Sleep, martyrs of a fallen cause;
Though yet no marble column craves
    The pilgrim here to pause.

In seeds of laurel in the earth 5
    The blossom of your fame is blown,
And somewhere, waiting for its birth,
    The shaft is in the stone!

Meanwhile, behalf the tardy years
    Which keep in trust your storied tombs, 10
Behold! your sisters bring their tears,
    And these memorial blooms.

Small tributes! but your shades will smile
    More proudly on these wreaths to-day,
Than when some cannon-moulded pile 15
    Shall overlook this bay.

Stoop, angels, hither from the skies!
    There is no holier spot of ground
Than where defeated valor lies,
    By mourning beauty crowned! 20

A Theory of Poetry

The most comprehensive statement of Timrod's
poetic theory is set forth in this critical essay which was
read as a lecture at the Methodist Female College,
Columbia, South Carolina, in the winter of 1863–1864.
Especially notable is Timrod's vigorous and sound dissent from Poe's dogmatic assertions that a long poem is
"simply a flat contradiction in terms," and that beauty
is the sole province of poetry. "A Theory of Poetry"
was abridged in *The Independent*, LIII (1901), 712–716,
760–764, 830–833, and reprinted in *The Atlantic
Monthly*, XCVI (1905), 313–326, "from a copy of the
original manuscript." The present text is that of *The
Atlantic Monthly*. For a valuable commentary upon
the essay and a reproduction of the original manuscript,
see Edd Winfield Parks, *The Essays of Henry Timrod*
(1942).

There have been few poetical eras without their
peculiar theories of poetry. But no age was ever

so rich in poetical creeds as the first half of the present century. The expositions of some of these creeds are not without some value; one or two, indeed, though incomplete, are profound and philosophical, but the majority are utterly worthless. Every little poet "Spins, toiling out his own cocoon," and wrapping himself snugly in it, to the exclusion of others, hopes to go down thus warmly protected to posterity.

I shall pass most of these theories to consider only two, one of which I shall discuss at some length. The first is that definition of poetry which represents it simply as the expression in verse of thought, sentiment, or passion, and which measures the difference between the poet and versifier only by the depth, power, and vivacity of their several productions. This definition was ably advocated not long ago in a well-known Southern periodical by one of the most acute of Southern writers. It would not be difficult to prove its total inadequacy, but I do not think it necessary to do so, except so far as the truth of that inadequacy may be involved in the establishment of a theory altogether opposed to it. I am the less inclined to give it a minute examination because though the idea is an old one and in strict accordance with the common usage of the word poetry, it has never become popular, nor is it likely to become so, as it fails to satisfy even those who, displeased, they do not know why, and dimly conscious of the true faith, are yet unable to discover in their undefined emotions a logical refutation of the heresy. The genuine lovers of poetry feel that its essential characteristics underlie the various forms which it assumes, however dim and shadowy those characteristics may seem to them, and notwithstanding that they elude the search, like the jar of gold which is fabled to be buried at the foot of the rainbow.

The second theory which I desire to examine critically was propounded a number of years ago by the most exquisite poetical genius to which America has yet given birth.

Poe begins his disquisition with the dogma that a long poem does not exist; that the phrase "a long poem" is simply a flat contradiction in terms. . . .

I am disposed to think that the young lady who pores over the metrical novels of Scott till midnight and wakes up the next morning with her bright eyes dimmed and a little swollen, or the young poet who follows for the first time the steps of Dante and his guide down to the spiral abysses of his imaginary hell, could not be easily induced to assent to these assertions. The declaration made with such cool metaphysical dogmatism "that all excitements are, through a psychical necessity, transient," needs considerable qualification. All violent excitements are, indeed, transient; but that moderate and chastened excitement which accompanies the perusal of the noblest poetry, of such poetry as is characterized, not by a spasmodic vehemency and the short-lived power imparted by excessive passion but by a thoughtful sublimity and the matured and almost inexhaustible strength of a healthy intellect, may be sustained, and often is, during a much longer period than the space of thirty minutes. . . .

I affirm that he who takes up *Paradise Lost* in this spirit will lay it down at the completion of the first book, or—if, as is not unlikely, he should have been beguiled further—at the completion of the second book, not simply with an impression of satisfaction, but in a state of mind in which awe and delight are blended together in a deep though sober rapture. I say, too, that upon resuming the book at some future time, if he comes to it with the same reverential precautions, and not as one who must finish a book to-night simply because he began it yesterday, there will occur no such utter disconnection between his perusal of the first and his perusal of the second part of the poem as will produce an effect at all similar to that which is produced by the perusal of two distinct poems. I say that no hiatus of platitude, whether real or the result of mere jaded attention, is sufficient so to separate two parts of an artistically constructed poem, like *Paradise Lost*, as to disturb the general harmony of its effect. And the thoughtful reader, instead of sitting down to the study of the third book as to a new poem, brings with him all the impressions of his former reading to heighten the color and deepen the effect of that which is before him. The continuation of the poem seems all the more beautiful because he is familiar with the beginning, and necessarily so from the roundness and completeness of a structure the parts of which add alike to the strength and grace of the whole and of each other. . . .

What, then, is poetry? In the last century, if one had asked the question, one would have been answered readily enough; and the answer would have been the definition which I dismissed a little while ago as unworthy of minute examination. But the deeper philosophical criticism of the present century will not remain satisfied with such a surface view of poetry. Its aim is to penetrate to the essence, to analyze and comprehend those impressions and operations of the mind, acting upon and being acted upon by mental or physical phenomena, which when incarnated in language all recognize as the utterance of poetry and which affect us like the music of angels. That this is the aim of present criticism I need not attempt to show by quotation, since it looks out from the pages of the most popular writers of the day. Indeed, so very general has the feeling become that it is not of the forms of poetry that we need a description, that if you ask any man of common intelligence, who is not merely a creature of facts and figures, to define poetry, he will endeavor to convey to you his idea, vague, doubtless, and shadowy, of that which in his imagination constitutes its spirit. The poets who attempt to solve the question look rather into themselves than into the poems they have written. One, very characteristically, when his own poems are considered, defines it as "emotions recollected in tranquillity"; and another as "the best and happiest moments of the best and happiest minds." These definitions, if definitions they can be called, are unsatisfactory enough, but they indicate correctly the direction in which the distinctive principle of poetry is to be sought. . . .

It is then in the feelings awakened by certain moods of the mind, when we stand in the presence of Truth, Beauty, and Power, that I recognize what we all agree to call poetry. To analyze the nature of these feelings, inextricably tangled as they are with the different faculties of the mind, and especially with that great faculty which is the prime minister of poetry, imagination, is not absolutely necessary to the present purpose. . . .

Now there are two classes of poets differing essentially in their several characters.

The one class desires only to understand musically its own peculiar thoughts, feelings, sentiments, or passions, without regard to their truth or falsehood, their morality or want of morality, but in simple reference to their poetical effect. The other class, with more poetry at its command than the first, regards poetry simply as the minister, the highest minister indeed, but still only the minister, of Truth, and refuses to address itself to the sense of the beautiful alone. The former class is content simply to create beauty, and writes such poems as *The Raven* of Poe or *The Corsair* of Byron. The latter class aims to create beauty also, but it desires at the same time to mould this beauty into the shape of a temple dedicated to Truth. It is to this class that we owe the authorship of such poems as the *Paradise Lost* of Milton, the *Lines at Tintern Abbey* and the *Excursion* of Wordsworth, and the *In Memoriam* of Tennyson.

The former class can afford to write brief and faultless poems, because its end is a narrow one; the second class is forced to demand an ampler field, because it is influenced by a vaster purpose. . . .

It seems to me that I may strengthen still further my theory that truth as much as beauty is the source of poetry by reference to the works of a poet who always refused to separate them. When Poe speaks of the impossibility of "reconciling the obstinate oils and waters of poetry and truth," he is, unconsciously to himself, confounding truth with science and matter of fact. It is, of course, impossible to see poetry in the dry facts and details of business, or in the arguments and commonplaces of politicians, or in the fact that the three angles of any triangle are equal to two right angles. But there is poetry in the truths of the mind and heart, and in the truths that affect us in our daily relations with men, and even in the grand general truths of science, when they become familiar to us and help us to understand and appreciate the beauties of the universe. This is what Coleridge meant in part, when he said that poetry was "the blossom and the fragrance of all human knowledge, human thoughts, human passions, emotions, language"; and what Wordsworth meant, when he, not less eloquently, described it "as the breath and finer spirit of all knowledge, the impassioned expression which is in the countenance of all science. . . ."

I have been induced to undertake a refutation of Poe's theory, while attempting to establish another, not because I believe Poe's the one most prevalently adopted, but because I regard it as the one most artfully put and at the same time most likely to excite interest in an American audience. There is an admirably written essay prefixed to the second edition of the poems of Matthew Arnold, in which that poet endeavors to show that all the poets of the present century have been working 10 on mistaken principles, and that the ancients were the only true masters of the poetic art. A theory to the full as true as Poe's might also be drawn from the works of the Brownings, which would lead to the exclusion of Poe from the roll of great poets as surely as the theory of Poe leads to the exclusion of the Brownings. . . .

I am not protesting against an evil existing only in my imagination. I have known more than one young lover of poetry who read nothing but 20 Browning, and there are hundreds who have drowned all the poets of the past and present in the deep music of Tennyson. But is it not possible, with the whole wealth of literature at our command, to attain views broad enough to enable us to do justice to genius of every class and character? That certainly can be no true poetical creed that leads directly to the neglect of those masterpieces which, though wrought hundreds of thousands of years ago, still preserve the freshness of perennial youth. . . .

Oh! rest assured that there are no stereotyped forms of poetry. It is a vital power and may assume any guise and take any shape, at one time towering like an alp in the darkness, and at another sunning itself in the bell of a tulip or the cup of a lily; and until one shall have learned to recognize it in all its various developments he has no right to echo back the benison of Wordsworth,

> Blessings be on them and eternal praise,
> The poets, who on earth have made us heirs
> Of Truth and pure delight in heavenly lays.

PAUL HAMILTON HAYNE (1830–1886)

THE POETRY of Paul Hamilton Hayne has been so overshadowed by that of his friend, Henry Timrod, and of Sidney Lanier, whose genius he was among the first to recognize, that his services to Southern literature are likely to be forgotten. As editor of *Russell's Magazine* (1857–1860) he did much to promote letters in the South. His poems were published widely in such magazines as *The Atlantic Monthly* and *Scribner's*. Above all, he devoted his entire life to poetry, daring to depend upon it as the only source of his income. As Edwin Mims has remarked justly, "He is the representative of that small band of Southern writers who before the war bore aloft the torch of literature . . . and passed it on to Lanier on the awakening of the section to national consciousness." Hayne's slender fame will probably rest upon a few excellent sonnets and fragile lyrics. The best of these, especially his poems celebrating the loveliness of the Southern landscape, led many contemporary readers to acclaim him as "the laureate of the South."

Hayne was born in Charleston on the first of January, 1830, the son of Paul Hamilton Hayne, a lieutenant in the United States Navy, and the nephew of the distinguished Senator Robert Hayne. Graduating from Charleston College in 1850, Hayne read law, but found it distasteful and turned to journalism and poetry. He was a member of the spirited coterie of literary men who often met at the bookstore of John Russell, and who sponsored *Russell's Magazine* in 1857, with Hayne as coeditor After a promising beginning the venture was ended abruptly by the Civil War. In the decade preceding the outbreak of fighting Hayne had published three volumes of poetry: *Poems* (1855), *Sonnets and Other Poems* (1857), and *Avolio: A Legend of the Island of Cos* (1860). Unable to engage in active military service because of fragile health, he aided the Southern cause by writing many patriotic and martial songs. Hayne's family income was stopped by wartime conditions, and his home and library were burned in the bombardment of Charleston. Hayne never recovered from the tragedy of the war, although he survived until 1886, living at "Copse Hill," near Augusta, Georgia. The best of his later poetry was included in *Legends and Lyrics* (1872). In the following year he brought out a collection of the poetry of Henry Timrod, with a generous tribute to the genius of his lifelong friend. The period of Reconstruction only served to intensify Hayne's longing for happier days in antebellum Charleston. He is most appropriately remembered, in Maurice Thompson's phrase, as "the last literary cavalier."

BIBLIOGRAPHY · Six volumes of Hayne's poetry were published during the poet's lifetime: *Poems*

(1855), *Sonnets and Other Poems* (1857), *Avolio: A Legend of the Island of Cos* (1860), *Legends and Lyrics* (1872), *The Mountain of the Lovers* (1875), and *Poems of Paul Hamilton Hayne* (1882). The last volume, edited by M. J. Preston, is the most nearly complete, containing over four hundred of Hayne's pieces. Two hundred and twenty-nine of the poet's letters are in D. M. McKeithan, *A Collection of Hayne Letters* (1944). There is no full-length life of Hayne. Biographical and critical information is included in J. T. Brown, Jr., "Paul Hamilton Hayne," *Sewanee Review*, XIV (1906), 236–247; E. G. Bernard, "Northern Bryant and Southern Hayne," *Colophon*, New Series, I (1936), 536–540; W. H. Hayne, "Paul H. Hayne's Methods of Composition," *Lippincott's*, L (1892), 793–796; M. L. Griffin, "Whittier and Hayne: A Record of Friendship," *American Literature*, XIX (1947), 41–58; T. W. Higginson, "Paul Hamilton Hayne," *Chautauquan*, VII (1887), 228–232; D. M. McKeithan, "Paul Hamilton Hayne's Reputation in Augusta at the Time of His Death," *University of Texas Studies in English*, XVIII (1938), 163–173; and M. Thompson, "The Last Literary Cavalier," *Critic*, XXXVIII (1901), 352–354.

My Study

THIS SONNET was collected in *Avolio: A Legend of the Island of Cos* (1860). The present text is that of *Poems of Paul Hamilton Hayne* (1882).

This is my world! within these narrow walls,
I own a princely service; the hot care
And tumult of our frenzied life are here
But as a ghost, and echo; what befalls
In the far mart to me is less than naught;   5
I walk the fields of quiet Arcadies,
And wander by the brink of hoary seas,
Calmed to the tendance of untroubled thought:
Or if a livelier humor should enhance
The slow-timed pulse, 'tis not for present strife,
The sordid zeal with which our age is rife,   11
Its mammon conflicts crowned by fraud or chance,
But gleanings of the lost, heroic life,
Flashed through the gorgeous vistas of romance.

A Little While I Fain Would Linger Yet

THIS POEM first appeared in *Poems of Paul Hamilton Hayne* (1882), the basis of the present text.

A little while (my life is almost set!)
  I fain would pause along the downward way,
  Musing an hour in this sad sunset-ray,
While, Sweet! our eyes with tender tears are wet;
A little hour I fain would linger yet.   5

A little while I fain would linger yet,
  All for love's sake, for love that cannot tire;
  Though fervid youth be dead, with youth's desire,
And hope has faded to a vague regret,
A little while I fain would linger yet.   10

A little while I fain would linger here:
  Behold! who knows what strange, mysterious bars
  'Twixt souls that love, may rise in other stars?
Nor can love deem the face of death is fair;
A little while I still would linger here.   15

A little while I yearn to hold fast,
  Hand locked in hand, and loyal heart to heart;
  (O pitying Christ! whose woeful words, "We part!")
So ere the darkness fall, the light be past,
A little while I fain would hold thee fast.   20

A little while, when night and twilight meet;
Behind, our broken years; before, the deep
Weird wonder of the last unfathomed sleep.
A little while I still would clasp thee, Sweet;
A little while, when night and twilight meet.   25

A little while I fain would linger here;
Behold! who knows what soul-dividing bars
Earth's faithful loves may part in other stars?
Nor can love deem the face of death is fair:
A little while I still would linger here.   30

In Harbor

"In Harbor" first appeared in *Poems of Paul Hamilton
Hayne* (1882), from which this text is taken.

I think it is over, over,
  I think it is over at last,
Voices of foeman and lover,
The sweet and the bitter have passed:—
Life, like a tempest of ocean   5
Hath outblown its ultimate blast:
There's but a faint sobbing sea-ward
While the calm of the tide deepens lee-ward,
And behold! like the welcoming quiver
Of heart-pulses throbbed thro' the river,   10
  Those lights in the harbor at last,
  The heavenly harbor at last!

I feel it is over! over!
  For the winds and the waters surcease;
Ah!—few were the days of the rover   15
  That smiled in the beauty of peace!
And distant and dim was the omen
That hinted redress or release:—
From the ravage of life, and its riot
What marvel I yearn for the quiet   20
  Which bides in the harbor at last?
For the lights with their welcoming quiver
That through the sanctified river
  Which girdles the harbor at last,
  This heavenly harbor at last?   25

I *know* it is over, over,
  I know it is over at last!
Down sail! the sheathed anchor uncover,
For the stress of the voyage has passed:
Life, like a tempest of ocean   30
  Hath outbreathed its ultimate blast:

There's but a faint sobbing sea-ward,
While the calm of the tide deepens lee-ward;
And behold! like the welcoming quiver
Of heart-pulses throbbed thro' the river,   35
  Those lights in the harbor at last,
  The heavenly harbor at last!

The Mocking Bird

THE MOCKING BIRD has been as inevitable in Southern
poetry as the nightingale has been in English verse.
Compare Hayne's lines with those of Lanier, page 929,
below.

A golden pallor of voluptuous light
Filled the warm southern night:
The moon, clear orbed, above the sylvan scene
Moved like a stately queen,
So rife with conscious beauty all the while,   5
What could she do but smile
At her own perfect loveliness below,
Glassed in the tranquil flow
Of crystal fountains and unruffled streams?
Half lost in waking dreams,   10
As down the loneliest forest dell I strayed,
Lo! from a neighboring glade,
Flashed through the drifts of moonshine, swiftly
  came
A fairy shape of flame.
It rose in dazzling spirals overhead,   15
Whence to wild sweetness wed,
Poured marvellous melodies, silvery trill on trill;
The very leaves grew still
On the charmed trees to hearken; while for me,
Heart-trilled to ecstasy,   20
I followed—followed the bright shape that flew,
Still circling up the blue,

Till as a fountain that has reached its height,
Falls back in sprays of light
Slowly dissolved, so that enrapturing lay, 25
Divinely melts away

Through tremulous spaces to a music-mist,
Soon by the fitful breeze
  How gently kissed
Into remote and tender silences. 30

SIDNEY LANIER (1842–1881)

SIDNEY LANIER remains first among the "lost generation" of Southern poets—to which Timrod and Hayne belong—whose health and fortune were broken by the blight of the Civil War and the very tragic years that followed. He is the symbol of the dichotomy and the unity of poetry and music, to which he gave his life. His was a "shining presence," as Lowell wrote; he was a man of nobility and charm. He surmounted the gloom of Poe, his early idol, and did not fall into the provincial hate of Timrod toward the North. His symbol of the nation was expressed in "Corn," not in "The Cotton Boll." His allegiance was to the world of romanticism; he made the world of trade his enemy. His early novel, *Tiger-Lilies* (1867), laid in the locale of the Tennessee mountains, was written to express the concepts of beauty, love, art, music, and metaphysics; begun by Lanier at Fort Boykin during the Civil War, it reached beyond carnage and disease into the romantic world of Novalis and Jean Paul Richter, and became a companion piece to Longfellow's *Hyperion*. His limitations were the shoals of romanticism—overindulgence in sensory flights, lack of "regulative control."

Poet, musician, scholar, Lanier was born at Macon, Georgia, February 3, 1842, the son of a prominent lawyer. Music was his first love. At Oglethorpe University the concept of the relationship between science and art came to him when he thought of the flute both as an instrument and as sound. Graduating at the head of his class in 1860, he was soon plunged into active service in the War, was taken prisoner, and after four years returned home badly stricken with tuberculosis, only fifteen years of life remaining. "Pretty much the whole of life has been merely not dying," he wrote Bayard Taylor in 1875. The South was prostrate. Postwar trials as hotel clerk, teacher, and lawyer unhappy in his work were lightened chiefly by his "idyllic" marriage to Mary Day in 1867. Returning from Texas in 1873, where he had sought but not found health, he determined, against the wish of his father, to spend the rest of his days in music and poetry. His new life began at Baltimore, where in 1873 he joined the Peabody Orchestra as flutist, and in 1878 became a member of the faculty of Johns Hopkins University.

Not until the Baltimore years did he write his major poems and engage in scholarly studies. Then poems began appearing in such magazines as *Lippincott's*, *Harper's*, and *Scribner's*, and were collected in *Poems* (1877). To increase his income for his growing family he edited four juvenile books—the *Froissart* (1879), *King Arthur* (1880), *Mabinogion*, and the posthumous *Percy* (1882). *The Science of English Verse* (1880) broadened his reputation. A number of volumes were published after his death on September 7, 1881. His wife edited *Poems of Sidney Lanier* (1884, revised and enlarged 1891, 1916). His son, Henry W. Lanier, edited *Letters of Sidney Lanier* (1899), *Shakspere and His Forerunners* (2 vols., 1902), *Poem Outlines* (1908), and *Selections from Sidney Lanier* (1916). *The English Novel*, from lectures delivered at Johns Hopkins, appeared in 1883, *Music and Poetry* in 1898, and *Retrospects and Prospects* in 1899.

BIBLIOGRAPHY · The magnificent Centennial Edition of *Sidney Lanier* (10 vols., 1945), under the general editorship of C. R. Anderson, is definitive. Vol. I, *Poems and Outlines*, was edited by C. R. Anderson; Vol. II, *The Science of English Verse and Essays on Music*, by P. F. Baum; Vol. III, *Shakspere and His Forerunners*, by K. Malone; Vol. IV, *The English Novel and Essays on Literature*, by C. Gohdes and K. Malone; Vol. V, *Tiger-Lilies and Southern Prose*, by G. Greever; Vol. VI, *Florida and Miscellaneous Prose*, by Philip Graham; Vols. VII–X, *Letters*, by C. R. Anderson and A. H. Starke. The text used for this book is that of *Poems* (1884), the basic book edited by Lanier's wife.

The earliest standard study of Lanier's life is E. Mims, *Sidney Lanier* (1905); the exhaustive, definitive biography is A. H. Starke, *Sidney Lanier: A Biographical and Critical Study* (1933). See also G. H. Clarke, *Some Reminiscences and Early Letters of Sidney Lanier* (1907); L. Lorenz, *The Life of Sidney Lanier* (1935), E. W. Parks, ed., *Southern Poets*, American Writers Series (1936); R. Webb and E. R. Coulson, *Sidney Lanier, Poet and Prosodist* (1941). Among critical and biographical studies are F. W. Cady, "Writings of Sidney Lanier," *South Atlantic Quarterly*, XIII (1914), 156–173; P. Graham, "Sidney Lanier's Thought in Relation to That of His Age," *University of Chicago Abstract of Theses*, Humanistic Series, VI (1927–1928); H. E. Harman, "A Study of Lanier's 'The Symphony,' " *South Atlantic Quarterly*, XVII (1918), 32–39; J. S.

Mayfield, "Lanier in Lastekas," *Southwest Review*, XVII (1931), 20–38; and "Lanier's Trail in Texas," *Texas Monthly*, III (1929), 329–337; J. C. Ransom, "Hearts and Heads," *American Review*, II (1934), 554–571; J. A. Shackford, "Sidney Lanier as Southerner," *Sewanee Review*, XLVIII (1940), 157–173, 348–355, 480–493; J. S. Short, "Sidney Lanier, 'Familiar Citizen of the Town,'" *Maryland Historical Magazine*, XXXV (1940), 121–146; and N. Wright, "The East Tennessee Background of Sidney Lanier's *Tiger-Lilies*," *American Literature*, XIX (1947), 127–138.

Corn

LANIER had written "Corn" in 1874; Howells had refused the poem for *The Atlantic Monthly* (it was published in *Lippincott's Magazine*, February, 1875), and the torture of this refusal led Lanier to review his abilities and ambitions, and to decide, regardless of Howells's rejection, that his "business in life was to make poems" (Starke, *Sidney Lanier*, page 190).

Today the woods are trembling through and
    through
With shimmering forms, that flash before my view,
Then melt in green as dawn-stars melt in blue.
    The leaves that wave against my cheek caress
    Like women's hands; the embracing boughs
        express   5
    A subtlety of mighty tenderness;
The copse-depths into little noises start,
That sound anon like beatings of a heart,
Anon like talk 'twixt lips not far apart.   9
The beech dreams balm, as a dreamer hums a song;
    Through that vague wafture, expirations strong
    Throb from young hickories breathing deep
        and long
With stress and urgence bold of prisoned spring
    And ecstasy of burgeoning.
    Now, since the dew-plashed road of morn is dry,
    Forth venture odors of more quality   16
    And heavenlier giving. Like Jove's locks awry,
        Long muscadines
Rich-wreathe the spacious foreheads of great pines,
And breathe ambrosial passion from their vines.
    I pray with mosses, ferns and flowers shy   21
    That hide like gentle nuns from human eye
    To lift adoring perfumes to the sky.
I hear faint bridal-sighs of brown and green
Dying to silent hints of kisses keen   25
As far lights fringe into a pleasant sheen.

I start at fragmentary whispers, blown
From undertalks of leafy souls unknown,
Vague purports sweet, of inarticulate tone.

Dreaming of gods, men, nuns and brides, between
Old companies of oaks that inward lean   31
To join their radiant amplitudes of green
    I slowly move, with ranging looks that pass
    Up from the matted miracles of grass
Into yon veined complex of space,   35
Where sky and leafage interlace
    So close, the heaven of blue is seen
    Inwoven with a heaven of green.

I wander to the zigzag-cornered fence
Where sassafras, intrenched in brambles dense,
Contests with stolid vehemence   41
    The march of culture, setting limb and thorn
    As pikes against the army of the corn.

There, while I pause, my fieldward-faring eyes
Take harvests, where the stately corn-ranks rise
    Of inward dignities   46
And large benignities and insights wise,
    Graces and modest majesties.
Thus, without theft, I reap another's field;
Thus, without tilth, I house a wondrous yield, 50
And heap my heart with quintuple crops concealed.

Look, out of line one tall corn-captain stands
Advanced beyond the foremost of his bands,
    And waves his blades upon the very edge
    And hottest thicket of the battling hedge. 55
Thou lustrous stalk, that ne'er mayst walk nor talk,
    Still shalt thou type the poet-soul sublime
    That leads the vanward of his timid time
    And sings up cowards with commanding rhyme—

Soul calm, like thee, yet fain, like thee, to grow
By double increment, above, below;   61
    Soul homely, as thou art, yet rich in grace like
        thee,
    Teaching the yeomen selfless chivalry
    That moves in gentle curves of courtesy;
Soul filled like thy long veins with sweetness tense,
    By every godlike sense   66
Transmuted from the four wild elements.
    Drawn to high plans,
    Thou lift'st more stature than a mortal man's,

Yet ever piercest downward in the mould 70
  And keepest hold
 Upon the reverend and steadfast earth
  That gave thee birth;
 Yea, standest smiling in thy future grave, 75
  Serene and brave,
 With unremitting breath
 Inhaling life from death,
Thine epitaph writ fair in fruitage eloquent,
  Thyself thy monument.

   As poets should 80
Thou hast built up thy hardihood
With universal food,
  Drawn in select proportion fair
 From honest mould and vagabond air;
From darkness of the dreadful night, 85
  And joyful light;
 From antique ashes, whose departed flame
 In thee has finer life and longer fame;
From wounds and balms,
From storms and calms, 90
From potsherds and dry bones
  And ruin-stones.
Into thy vigorous substance thou hast wrought
Whate'er the hand of Circumstance hath brought;
  Yea, into cool solacing green hast spun 95
 White radiance hot from out the sun.
So thou dost mutually leaven
Strength of earth with grace of heaven;
  So thou dost marry new and old
 Into a one of higher mould; 100
 So thou dost reconcile the hot and cold,
  The dark and bright,
And many a heart-perplexing opposite:
  And so,
 Akin by blood to high and low, 105
Fitly thou playest out thy poet's part,
Richly expending thy much-bruisèd heart
 In equal care to nourish lord in hall
  Or beast in stall:
 Thou took'st from all that thou might'st give
  to all. 110

O steadfast dweller on the selfsame spot
Where thou wast born, that still repinest not—
Type of the home-fond heart, the happy lot!—
 Deeply thy mild content rebukes the land
 Whose flimsy homes, built on the shifting sand

Of trade, forever rise and fall 116
With alternation whimsical,
  Enduring scarce a day,
  Then swept away
By swift engulfments of incalculable tides 120
Whereon capricious Commerce rides.

Look, thou substantial spirit of content!
Across this little vale, thy continent,
 To where, beyond the mouldering mill,
 Yon old deserted Georgian hill 125
Bares to the sun his piteous aged crest
  And seamy breast,
 By restless-hearted children left to lie
 Untended there beneath the heedless sky,
 As barbarous folk expose their old to die. 130
Upon that generous-rounding side,
  With gullies scarified
 Where keen Neglect his lash hath plied,
Dwelt one I knew of old, who played at toil,
And gave to coquette Cotton soul and soil. 135
 Scorning the slow reward of patient grain,
 He sowed his heart with hopes of swifter gain,
 Then sat him down and waited for the rain.
He sailed in borrowed ships of usury—
A foolish Jason on a treacherous sea, 140
Seeking the Fleece and finding misery.
 Lulled by smooth-rippling loans, in idle trance
 He lay, content that unthrift Circumstance
 Should plow for him the stony field of Chance.
Yea, gathering crops whose worth no man might tell,
He staked his life on games of Buy-and-Sell, 146
And turned each field into a gambler's hell.
  Aye, as each year began,
  My farmer to the neighboring city ran;
Passed with a mournful anxious face 150
Into the banker's inner place;
Parleyed, excused, pleaded for longer grace;
 Railed at the drought, the worm, the rust, the
  grass;
 Protested ne'er again 'twould come to pass;
 With many an *oh* and *if* and *but alas* 155
Parried or swallowed searching questions rude,
And kissed the dust to soften Dives's mood.
At last, small loans by pledges great renewed,
 He issues smiling from the fatal door,
 And buys with lavish hand his yearly store 160
 Till his small borrowings will yield no more.

Aye, as each year declined,
With bitter heart and ever-brooding mind
He mourned his fate unkind.
   In dust, in rain, with might and main,   165
   He nursed his cotton, cursed his grain,
   Fretted for news that made him fret again,
Snatched at each telegram of Future Sale,
And thrilled with Bulls' or Bears' alternate wail—
In hope or fear alike forever pale.   170
   And thus from year to year, through hope and fear,
   With many a curse and many a secret tear,
   Striving in vain his cloud of debt to clear,
      At last
He woke to find his foolish dreaming past,   175
   And all his best-of-life the easy prey
   Of squandering scamps and quacks that lined
     his way
    With vile array,
From rascal statesman down to petty knave;
Himself, at best, for all his bragging brave,   180
A gamester's catspaw and a banker's slave.
   Then, worn and gray, and sick with deep unrest,
   He fled away into the oblivious West,
   Unmourned, unblest.

Old hill! old hill! thou gashed and hairy Lear
Whom the divine Cordelia of the year,   186
E'en pitying Spring, will vainly strive to cheer—
   King, that no subject man nor beast may own,
   Discrowned, undaughtered and alone—
Yet shall the great God turn thy fate,   190
And bring thee back into thy monarch state
   And majesty immaculate.
Lo, through hot waverings of the August morn,
   Thou givest from thy vasty sides forlorn
   Visions of golden treasuries of corn—   195
Ripe largesse lingering for some bolder heart
That manfully shall take thy part,
   And tend thee,
   And defend thee,
With antique sinew and with modern art.   200

The Symphony

THIS POEM presents Lanier's belief that trade, in power
during four hundred years, was despoiling religion,
politics, social life, literature, and music. For prose
statements of this theme, see his letters to P. H. Hayne,

April 17, 1872 (Starke, *Sidney Lanier*, pp. 195–196),
and to L. E. Bleckley, November, 1874 (ibid. p. 196).
Lanier told Gibson Peacock, March 24, 1875, that the
idea of "The Symphony" had four days previously
taken hold of him "like a real James River Ague," and
that he had been "in a mortal shake with the same, day
and night, ever since." *Lippincott's* paid Lanier $100
for the poem.

"O Trade! O Trade! would thou wert dead!
The Time needs heart—'tis tired of head:
We're all for love," the violins said.
"Of what avail the rigorous tale
Of bill for coin and box for bale?   5
Grant thee, O Trade! thine uttermost hope:
Level red gold with blue sky-slope,
And base it deep as devils grope:
When all's done, what hast thou won
Of the only sweet that's under the sun?   10
Ay, canst thou buy a single sigh
Of true love's least, least ecstasy?"
Then, with a bridegroom's heart-beats trembling,
All the mightier strings assembling
Ranged them on the violins' side   15
As when the bridegroom leads the bride,
And, heart in voice, together cried:
"Yea, what avail the endless tale
Of gain by cunning and plus by sale?
Look up the land, look down the land   20
The poor, the poor, the poor, they stand
Wedged by the pressing of Trade's hand
Against an inward-opening door
That pressure tightens evermore:
They sigh a monstrous foul-air sigh   25
For the outside leagues of liberty,
Where Art, sweet lark, translates the sky
Into a heavenly melody.
'Each day, all day' (these poor folks say),
'In the same old year-long, drear-long way,   30
We weave in the mills and heave in the kilns,
We sieve mine-meshes under the hills,
And thieve much gold from the Devil's bank tills,
To relieve, O God, what manner of ills?—
The beasts, they hunger, and eat, and die;   35
And so do we, and the world's a sty;
Hush, fellow-swine: why nuzzle and cry?
Swinehood hath no remedy
Say many men, and hasten by,
Clamping the nose and blinking the eye.   40

But who said once, in the lordly tone,
Man shall not live by bread alone
But all that cometh from the Throne?
    Hath God said so?
    But Trade saith *No:*   45
And the kilns and the curt-tongued mills say *Go!*
There's plenty that can, if you can't; we know.
Move out, if you think you're underpaid.
The poor are prolific; we're not afraid;
Trade is trade.' "   50
Thereat this passionate protesting
    Meekly changed, and softened till
It sank to sad requesting
    And suggesting sadder still:
    "And oh, if men might some time see   55
How piteous-false the poor decree
That trade no more than trade must be!
Does business mean, *Die, you—live, I?*
Then 'Trade is trade' but sings a lie:
'Tis only war grown miserly.   60
If business is battle, name it so:
War-crimes less will shame it so,
And widows less will blame it so.
Alas, for the poor to have some part
In yon sweet living lands of Art,   65
Makes problem not for head, but heart.
Vainly might Plato's brain revolve it:
Plainly the heart of a child could solve it."

And then, as when from words that seem but rude
We pass to silent pain that sits abroad   70
Back in our heart's great dark and solitude,
So sank the strings to gentle throbbing
Of long chords change-marked with sobbing—
Motherly sobbing, not distinctlier heard   74
Than half wing-openings of the sleeping bird,
Some dream of danger to her young hath stirred.

Then stirring and demurring ceased, and lo!
Every least ripple of the strings' song-flow
Died to a level with each level bow
And made a great chord tranquil-surfaced so,   80
As a brook beneath his curving bank doth go
To linger in the sacred dark and green
Where many boughs the still pool overlean
And many leaves make shadow with their sheen.
    But presently   85
A velvet flute-note fell down pleasantly

Upon the bosom of that harmony,
And sailed and sailed incessantly,
As if a petal from a wild-rose blown
Had fluttered down upon that pool of tone   90
And boatwise dropped o' the convex side
And floated down the glassy tide
And clarified and glorified
The solemn spaces where the shadows bide.
From the warm concave of that fluted note   95
Somewhat, half song, half odor, forth did float,
As if a rose might somehow be a throat:
"When Nature from her far-off glen
Flutes her soft messages to men,
The flute can say them o'er again;   100
Yea, Nature, singing sweet and lone,
Breathes through life's strident polyphone
The flute-voice in the world of tone.
    Sweet friends,
    Man's love ascends   105
To finer and diviner ends
Than man's mere thought e'er comprehends
    For I, e'en I,
    As here I lie,
A petal on a harmony,   110
Demand of Science whence and why
Man's tender pain, man's inward cry,
When he doth gaze on earth and sky?
I am not overbold:
    I hold   115
Full powers from Nature manifold.
I speak for each no-tonguèd tree
That, spring by spring, doth nobler be,
And dumbly and most wistfully
His mighty prayerful arms outspreads   120
Above men's oft-unheeding heads,
And his big blessing downward sheds.
I speak for all-shaped blooms and leaves,
Lichens on stones and moss on eaves,
Grasses and grains in ranks and sheaves;   125
Broad-fronded ferns and keen-leaved canes,
And briery mazes bounding lanes,
And marsh-plants, thirsty-cupped for rains,
And milky stems and sugary veins;
For every long-armed woman-vine   130
That round a piteous tree doth twine;
For passionate odors, and divine
Pistils, and petals crystalline;
All purities of shady springs,

All shynesses of film-winged things   135
That fly from tree-trunks and bark-rings;
All modesties of mountain-fawns
That leap to covert from wild lawns,
And tremble if the day but dawns;
All sparklings of small beady eyes   140
Of birds, and sidelong glances wise
Wherewith the jay hints tragedies;
All piquancies of prickly burs,
And smoothnesses of downs and furs
Of eiders and of minevers;   145
All limpid honeys that do lie
At stamen-bases, nor deny
The humming-birds' fine roguery,
Bee-thighs, nor any butterfly;
All gracious curves of slender wings,   150
Bark-mottlings, fibre-spiralings,
Fern-wavings and leaf-flickerings;
Each dial-marked leaf and flower-bell
Wherewith in every lonesome dell
Time to himself his hours doth tell;   155
All tree-sounds, rustlings of pine-cones,
Wind-sighings, doves' melodious moans,
And night's unearthly under-tones;
All placid lakes and waveless deeps,
All cool reposing mountain-steeps,   160
Vale-calms and tranquil lotos-sleeps;—
Yea, all fair forms, and sounds, and lights,
And warmths, and mysteries, and mights,
Of Nature's utmost depths and heights,
—These doth my timid tongue present,   165
Their mouthpiece and leal instrument
And servant, all love-eloquent.
I heard, when 'All for love' the violins cried:
So, Nature calls through all her system wide,
Give me thy love, O man, so long denied.   170
Much time is run, and man hath changed his ways,
Since Nature, in the antique fable-days,
Was hid from man's true love by proxy fays,
False fauns and rascal gods that stole her praise.   174
The nymphs, cold creatures of man's colder brain,
Chilled Nature's streams till man's warm heart was
    fain
Never to lave its love in them again.
Later, a sweet Voice *Love thy neighbor* said;
Then first the bounds of neighborhood outspread
Beyond all confines of old ethnic dread.   180
Vainly the Jew might wag his covenant head:

'*All men are neighbors,*' so the sweet Voice said.
So, when man's arms had circled all man's race,
The liberal compass of his warm embrace   184
Stretched bigger yet in the dark bounds of space;
With hands a-grope he felt smooth Nature's grace,
Drew her to breast and kissed her sweetheart face:
Yea man found neighbors in great hills and trees
And streams and clouds and suns and birds and bees,
And throbbed with neighbor-loves in loving these.
But oh, the poor! the poor! the poor!   191
That stand by the inward-opening door
Trade's hand doth tighten ever more,
And sigh their monstrous foul-air sigh
For the outside hills of liberty,   195
Where Nature spreads her wild blue sky
For Art to make into melody!
Thou Trade! thou king of the modern days!
    Change thy ways,
    Change thy ways;   200
Let the sweaty laborers file
    A little while,
    A little while,
Where Art and Nature sing and smile.
Trade! is thy heart all dead, all dead?   205
And hast thou nothing but a head?
I'm all for heart," the flute-voice said,
And into sudden silence fled,
Like as a blush that while 'tis red
Dies to a still, still white instead.   210

    Thereto a thrilling calm succeeds,
Till presently the silence breeds
A little breeze among the reeds
That seems to blow by sea-marsh weeds:
Then from the gentle stir and fret   215
Sings out the melting clarionet,
Like as a lady sings while yet
Her eyes with salty tears are wet.
"O Trade! O Trade!" the Lady said,
"I too will wish thee utterly dead   220
If all thy heart is in thy head.
For O my God! and O my God!
What shameful ways have women trod
At beckoning of Trade's golden rod!
Alas when sighs are traders' lies,   225
And heart's-ease eyes and violet eyes
    Are merchandise!
O purchased lips that kiss with pain!

O cheeks coin-spotted with smirch and stain!
O trafficked hearts that break in twain!   230
—And yet what wonder at my sisters' crime?
So hath Trade withered up Love's sinewy prime,
Men love not women as in olden time.
Ah, not in these cold merchantable days
Deem men their life an opal gray, where plays   235
The one red Sweet of gracious ladies'-praise.
Now, comes a suitor with sharp prying eye—
Says, *Here, you Lady, if you'll sell, I'll buy:*
Come, heart for heart—a trade? What! weeping? why?
Shame on such wooers' dapper mercery!   240
I would my lover kneeling at my feet
In humble manliness should cry, *O sweet!*
I know not if thy heart my heart will greet:
I ask not if thy love my love can meet:
Whate'er thy worshipful soft tongue shall say,   245
I'll kiss thine answer, be it yea or nay:
I do but know I love thee, and I pray
To be thy knight until my dying day.
Woe him that cunning trades in hearts contrives!
Base love good women to base loving drives.   250
If men loved larger, larger were our lives;
And wooed they nobler, won they nobler wives."

There thrust the bold straightforward horn
To battle for that lady lorn,
With heartsome voice of mellow scorn,   255
Like any knight in knighthood's morn.
   "Now comfort thee," said he,
      "Fair Lady.
For God shall right thy grievous wrong,
And man shall sing thee a true-love song,   260
Voiced in act his whole life long,
      Yea, all thy sweet life long,
         Fair Lady.
Where's he that craftily hath said,
The day of chivalry is dead?   265
I'll prove that lie upon his head,
      Or I will die instead,
         Fair Lady.
Is Honor gone into his grave?
Hath Faith become a caitiff knave,   270
And Selfhood turned into a slave
      To work in Mammon's cave,
         Fair Lady?
Will Truth's long blade ne'er gleam again?
Hath Giant Trade in dungeons slain   275

All great contempts of mean-got gain
   And hates of inward stain,
      Fair Lady?
For aye shall name and fame be sold,
And place be hugged for the sake of gold,   280
And smirch-robed Justice feebly scold
      At Crime all money-bold,
         Fair Lady?
Shall self-wrapt husbands aye forget
Kiss-pardons for the daily fret   285
Wherewith sweet wifely eyes are wet—
      Blind to lips kiss-wise set—
         Fair Lady?
Shall lovers higgle, heart for heart,
Till wooing grows a trading mart   290
Where much for little, and all for part,
      Make love a cheapening art,
         Fair Lady?
Shall woman scorch for a single sin
That her betrayer may revel in,   295
And she be burnt, and he but grin
      When that the flames begin,
         Fair Lady?
Shall ne'er prevail the woman's plea,
We maids would far, far whiter be   300
If that our eyes might sometimes see
      Men maids in purity,
         Fair Lady?
Shall Trade aye salve his conscience-aches
With jibes at Chivalry's old mistakes—   305
The wars that o'erhot knighthood makes
      For Christ's and ladies' sakes,
         Fair Lady?
Now by each knight that e'er hath prayed
To fight like a man and love like a maid,   310
Since Pembroke's life, as Pembroke's blade,
      I' the scabbard, death, was laid,
         Fair Lady,
I dare avouch my faith is bright
That God doth right and God hath might.   315
Nor time hath changed His hair to white,
      Nor His dear love to spite,
         Fair Lady.
I doubt no doubts: I strive, and shrive my clay,
And fight my fight in the patient modern way 320
For true love and for thee—ah me! and pray
      To be thy knight until my dying day,
         Fair Lady."

Made end that knightly horn, and spurred away
Into the thick of the melodious fray.   325

And then the hautboy played and smiled,
And sang like any large-eyed child,
Cool-hearted and all undefiled.
   "Huge Trade!" he said,
"Would thou wouldst lift me on thy head   330
And run where'er my finger led!
Once said a Man—and wise was He—
Never shalt thou the heavens see,
Save as a little child thou be."
Then o'er sea-lashings of commingling tunes,   335
The ancient wise bassoons,
    Like weird
    Gray-beard
Old harpers sitting on the high sea-dunes,
    Chanted runes: 340
"Bright-waved gain, gray-waved loss,
The sea of all doth lash and toss,
One wave forward and one across:
But now 'twas trough, now 'tis crest,
And worst doth foam and flash to best,   345
    And curst to blest.

Life! Life! thou sea-fugue, writ from east to
    west,
    Love, Love alone can pore
    On thy dissolving score
    Of harsh half-phrasings,   350
      Blotted ere writ,
    And double erasings
      Of chords most fit.
Yea, Love, sole music-master blest,
May read thy weltering palimpsest.   355
To follow Time's dying melodies through,
And never to lose the old in the new,
And ever to solve the discords true—
    Love alone can do.
And ever Love hears the poor-folks' crying,   360
And ever Love hears the women's sighing,
And ever sweet knighthood's death-defying,
And ever wise childhood's deep implying,
But never a trader's glozing and lying.

And yet shall Love himself be heard,   365
Though long deferred, though long deferred:
O'er the modern waste a dove hath whirred:
Music is Love in search of a word."

Song of the Chattahoochee

THIS is the most popular of Lanier's poems. Mrs. Lanier dated the composition as of 1877 and believed it appeared in *Scott's Magazine*, but that magazine had long ceased publication. F. V. N. Painter printed a version in *Poets of the South*, 1903, which Starke (*Sidney Lanier*, p. 291) believed might be earlier than the one published posthumously in *The Independent*, December 20, 1883. The Chattahoochee River flows from the Blue Ridge Mountains in Habersham County in northeast Georgia, and intersects Hall County in its course southward.

   Out of the hills of Habersham,
     Down the valleys of Hall,
I hurry amain to reach the plain,
Run the rapid and leap the fall,
Split at the rock and together again,   5
Accept my bed, or narrow or wide,
And flee from folly on every side
With a lover's pain to attain the plain
     Far from the hills of Habersham,
     Far from the valleys of Hall.   10

   All down the hills of Habersham,
     All through the valleys of Hall,
The rushes cried *Abide*, *abide*,
The willful waterweeds held me thrall,
The laving laurel turned my tide,   15
The ferns and the fondling grass said *Stay*,
The dewberry dipped for to work delay,
And the little reeds sighed *Abide*, *abide*,
    Here in the hills of Habersham,
    Here in the valleys of Hall.   20

   High o'er the hills of Habersham,
     Veiling the valleys of Hall,
The hickory told me manifold
Fair tales of shade, the poplar tall
Wrought me her shadowy self to hold,   25
The chestnut, the oak, the walnut, the pine,
Overleaning, with flickering meaning and sign,
Said, *Pass not, so cold, these manifold*
    Deep shades of the Hills of Habersham,
    These glades in the valleys of Hall.   30

   And oft in the hills of Habersham,
     And oft in the valleys of Hall,
The white quartz shone, and the smooth brook-stone
Did bar me of passage with friendly brawl,

And many a luminous jewel lone   35
—Crystals clear or a-cloud with mist,
Ruby, garnet and amethyst—
Made lures with the lights of streaming stone
    In the clefts of the hills of Habersham,
    In the beds of the valleys of Hall.   40

    But oh, not the hills of Habersham,
    And oh, not the valleys of Hall
Avail: I am fain for to water the plain.
Downward the voices of Duty call—
Downward, to toil and be mixed with the main, 45
The dry fields burn, and the mills are to turn,
And a myriad flowers mortally yearn,
And the lordly main from beyond the plain
    Calls o'er the hills of Habersham,
    Calls through the valleys of Hall.   50

The Mocking Bird

FIRST PUBLISHED in *The Galaxy*, August, 1877.

Superb and sole, upon a plumèd spray
    That o'er the general leafage boldly grew,
    He summ'd the woods in song; or typic drew
The watch of hungry hawks, the lone dismay
Of languid doves when long their lovers stray,   5
    And all birds' passion-plays that sprinkle dew
    At morn in brake or bosky avenue.
Whate'er birds did or dreamed, this bird could say.
Then down he shot, bounced airily along   9
    The sward, twitched in a grasshopper, made song
    Midflight, perched, prinked, and to his art again.
Sweet Science, this large riddle read me plain:
    How may the death of that dull insect be
    The life of yon trim Shakspere on the tree?

The Marshes of Glynn

THIS POEM describes the coastal marshes around Brunswick, Georgia. Written in Baltimore in 1878, it is the first and best of the four "Hymns of the Marshes." It was first published in *A Masque of Poets* (1879), edited by G. P. Lathrop.

Glooms of the live-oaks, beautiful-braided and woven
With intricate shades of the vines that myriad-cloven
    Clamber the forks of the multiform boughs,—
            Emerald twilights,—
            Virginal shy lights,   5
Wrought of the leaves to allure to the whisper of vows,
When lovers pace timidly down through the green colonnades
Of the dim sweet woods, of the dear dark woods,
    Of the heavenly woods and glades,
That run to the radiant marginal sand-beach within   10
        The wide sea-marshes of Glynn;—

Beautiful glooms, soft dusks in the noon-day fire,—
Wildwood privacies, closets of lone desire,
Chamber from chamber parted with wavering arras of leaves,—
Cells for the passionate pleasure of prayer to the soul that grieves,   15
Pure with a sense of the passing of saints through the wood,
Cool for the dutiful weighing of ill with good;—

O braided dusks of the oak and woven shades of the vine,
While the riotous noon-day sun of the June-day long did shine
Ye held me fast in your heart and I held you fast in mine;   20
But now when the noon is no more, and riot is rest,
And the sun is a-wait at the ponderous gate of the West,

929

And the slant yellow beam down the wood-aisle doth seem
Like a lane into heaven that leads from a dream,—
Ay, now, when my soul all day hath drunken the soul of the oak,   25
And my heart is at ease from men, and the wearisome sound of the stroke
   Of the scythe of time and the trowel of trade is low,
     And belief overmasters doubt, and I know that I know,
     And my spirit is grown to a lordly great compass within,
That the length and the breadth and the sweep of the marshes of Glynn   30
Will work me no fear like the fear they have wrought me of yore
When length was fatigue, and when breadth was but bitterness sore,
And when terror and shrinking and dreary unnamable pain
Drew over me out of the merciless miles of the plain,—

Oh, now, unafraid, I am fain to face   35
   The vast sweet visage of space.
To the edge of the wood I am drawn, I am drawn,
Where the gray beach glimmering runs, as a belt of the dawn,
   For a mete and a mark
     To the forest-dark:—   40
        So:
Affable live-oak, leaning low,—
Thus—with your favor—soft, with a reverent hand,
(Not lightly touching your person, Lord of the land!)
Bending your beauty aside, with a step I stand   45
On the firm-packed sand,
     Free
By a world of marsh that borders a world of sea.
   Sinuous southward and sinuous northward the shimmering band
    Of the sand-beach fastens the fringe of the marsh to the folds of the land. 50
Inward and outward to northward and southward the beach-lines linger and curl
As a silver-wrought garment that clings to and follows the firm sweet limbs of a girl.
Vanishing, swerving, evermore curving again into sight,
Softly the sand-beach wavers away to a dim gray looping of light.
And what if behind me to westward the wall of the woods stands high?   55
The world lies east: how ample, the marsh and the sea and the sky!
A league and a league of marsh-grass, waist-high, broad in the blade,
Green, and all of a height, and unflecked with a light or a shade,
Stretch leisurely off, in a pleasant plain,
To the terminal blue of the main.   60

Oh, what is abroad in the marsh and the terminal sea?
   Somehow my soul seems suddenly free
From the weighing of fate and the sad discussion of sin,
By the length and the breadth and the sweep of the marshes of Glynn.

Ye marshes, how candid and simple and nothing-withholding and free   65
Ye publish yourselves to the sky and offer yourselves to the sea!
Tolerant plains, that suffer the sea and the rains and the sun,
Ye spread and span like the catholic man who hath mightily won

God out of knowledge and good out of infinite pain
And sight out of blindness and purity out of a stain. 70

As the marsh-hen secretly builds on the watery sod,
Behold I will build me a nest on the greatness of God;
I will fly in the greatness of God as the marsh-hen flies
In the freedom that fills all the space 'twixt the marsh and the skies:
By so many roots as the marsh-grass sends in the sod 75
I will heartily lay me a-hold on the greatness of God:
Oh, like to the greatness of God is the greatness within
The range of the marshes, the liberal marshes of Glynn.

And the sea lends large, as the marsh: lo, out of his plenty the sea
Pours fast: full soon the time of the flood-tide must be: 80
Look how the grace of the sea doth go
About and about through the intricate channels that flow
        Here and there,
            Everywhere,
Till his waters have flooded the uttermost creeks and the low-lying lanes, 85
And the marsh is meshed with a million veins,
That like as with rosy and silvery essences flow
    In the rose-and-silver evening glow.
            Farewell, my lord Sun!
The creeks overflow: a thousand rivulets run 90
'Twixt the roots of the sod; the blades of the marsh-grass stir;
Passeth a hurrying sound of wings that westward whirr;
Passeth, and all is still; and the currents cease to run;
And the sea and the marsh are one.

How still the plains of the waters be! 95
The tide is in his ecstasy.
The tide is at his highest height:
        And it is night.

And now from the Vast of the Lord will the waters of sleep
Roll in on the souls of men, 100
But who will reveal to our waking ken
The forms that swim and the shapes that creep
        Under the waters of sleep?
And I would I could know what swimmeth below when the tide comes in
On the length and the breadth of the marvellous marshes of Glynn. 105

A Ballad of Trees and the Master

"The finest of Lanier's lyrics and probably the most perfect poem he ever wrote, it was composed at one sitting in 'fifteen or twenty minutes . . . just as we have it without erasure or correction. . . .' " (Charles R. Anderson, *Centenary Edition*, I, 365.) At one time it was incorporated as one of three songs in "Sunrise," but it was later removed. It was written about December 1, 1880, and published in *The Independent* on the 23d of the same month; Lanier received $15 for the poem.

Into the woods my Master went,
Clean forspent, forspent.
Into the woods my Master came,
Forspent with love and shame.
But the olives they were not blind to Him,   5
The little gray leaves were kind to Him:
The thorn-tree had a mind to Him
When into the woods He came.

Out of the woods my Master went,
And He was well content.   10
Out of the woods my Master came,
Content with death and shame.
When Death and Shame would woo Him last,
From under the trees they drew Him last:
'Twas on a tree they slew Him—last   15
When out of the woods He came.

How Love Looked for Hell

ORIGINALLY PUBLISHED in *The Century Magazine*,
March, 1884.

"To heal this heart of long-time pain
One day Prince Love for to travel was fain
  With Ministers Mind and Sense.
'Now what to thee most strange may be?'
Quoth Mind and Sense. 'All things above,   5
One curious thing I first would see—
  Hell,' quoth Love.

"Then Mind rode in and Sense rode out:
They searched the ways of man about.
  First frightfully groaneth Sense.   10
' 'Tis here, 'tis here,' and spurreth in fear
To the top of the hill that hangeth above
And plucketh the Prince: 'Come, come, 'tis here—'
  'Where?' quoth Love—

" 'Not far, not far,' said shivering Sense   15
As they rode on. 'A short way hence,
  —But seventy paces hence:
Look, King, dost see where suddenly
This road doth dip from the height above?
Cold blew a mouldy wind by me'   20
  ('Cold?' quoth Love)

" 'As I rode down, and the River was black,
And yon-side, lo! an endless wrack
  And rabble of souls,' sighed Sense,

'Their eyes upturned and begged and burned   25
In brimstone lakes, and a Hand above
Beat back the hands that upward yearned—'
  'Nay!' quoth Love—

" 'Yea, yea, sweet Prince; thyself shalt see,
Wilt thou but down this slope with me;   30
  'Tis palpable,' whispered Sense.
—At the foot of the hill a living rill
Shone, and the lilies shone white above;
'But now 'twas black, 'twas a river, this rill,'
  ('Black?' quoth Love)   35

" 'Ay, black, but lo! the lilies grow,
And yon-side where was woe, was woe,
  —Where the rabble of souls,' cried Sense,
'Did shrivel and turn and beg and burn,
Thrust back in the brimstone from above—   40
Is banked of violet, rose, and fern:'
  'How?' quoth Love:

" 'For lakes of pain, yon pleasant plain
Of woods and grass and yellow grain
  Doth ravish the soul and sense: 45
And never a sigh beneath the sky,
And folk that smile and gaze above—'
'But saw'st thou here, with thine own eye,
  Hell?' quoth Love.

" 'I saw true hell with mine own eye,   50
True hell, or light hath told a lie,
  True, verily,' quoth stout Sense.
Then Love rode round and searched the ground,
The caves below, the hills above;
'But I cannot find where thou hast found   55
  Hell,' quoth Love.

"There while they stood in a green wood
And marvelled still on Ill and Good,
  Came suddenly Minister Mind.
'In the heart of sin doth hell begin: 60
'Tis not below, 'tis not above,
It lieth within, it lieth within:'
  ('Where?' quoth Love)

" 'I saw a man sit by a corse;
Hell's in the murderer's breast: remorse!   65
  Thus clamored his mind to his mind:
Not fleshly dole is the sinner's goal,
Hell's not below, nor yet above,

'Tis fixed in the ever-damnèd soul—'
    'Fixed?' quoth Love—   70

" 'Fixed: follow me, would'st thou but see:
He weepeth under yon willow tree,
    Fast chained to the corse,' quoth Mind.
Full soon they passed, for they rode fast,
Where the piteous willow bent above.   75
'Now shall I see at last, at last,
    Hell,' quoth Love.

"There when they came Mind suffered shame:
'These be the same and not the same,'
    A-wondering whispered Mind.   80
Lo, face by face two spirits pace
Where the blissful willow waves above:
One saith: 'Do me a friendly grace—'
    ('Grace!' quoth Love)

" 'Read me two dreams that linger long,   85
Dim as returns of old-time song
    That flicker about the mind.
I dreamed (how deep in mortal sleep!)
I struck thee dead, then stood above,
With tears that none but dreamers weep;'   90
    'Dreams,' quoth Love;

" 'In dreams, again, I plucked a flower
That clung with pain and stung with power,
    Yea, nettled me, body and mind.'
' 'Twas the nettle of sin, 'twas medicine;   95
No need nor seed of it here Above;
In dreams of hate true loves begin.'
    'True,' quoth Love.

" 'Now strange,' quoth Sense, and 'Strange,'
    quoth Mind,
'We saw it, and yet 'tis hard to find,   100
    —But we saw it,' quoth Sense and Mind.
Stretched on the ground, beautiful-crowned
Of piteous willow that wreathed above,
'But I cannot find where ye have found
    Hell,' quoth Love."   105

The Science of English Verse

THIS BOOK was largely written in the summer of 1879.
The following autumn Lanier returned to his Peabody
Orchestra work and gave a series of lectures at Johns
Hopkins. With a copy of the volume to Bayard Taylor, Lanier sent a note expressing the hope the book
might be of interest "since, in finding physical principles of classification for all possible phenomena of
verse, it seems to place these phenomena in their true
relations,—for the first time, so far as I know" (Starke,
Sidney Lanier, p. 346).

I · *Investigation of Sound as Artistic Material*

Perhaps no one will find difficulty in accepting
the assertion that when formal poetry, or verse,—
two terms which will always be used here as convertible,—is repeated aloud, it impresses itself
upon the ear as verse only by means of certain
relations existing among its component words considered purely as sounds, without reference to their
associated ideas. If the least doubt upon this point
should be entertained, it may be dispelled by
observing that all ideas may be abolished out of a   10
poem without disturbing its effect upon the ear as
verse. This may be practically demonstrated by
the simple experiment of substituting for the words
of a formal poem any other words which preserve
the accentuation, alliteration, and rhyme, but which
convey no ideas to the mind,—words of some
foreign language not understood by the experi-
menter being the most effective for this purpose.
Upon repeating aloud the poem thus treated it
will be found that the verse-structure has not been   20
impaired. If, therefore, the ear accepts as perfect
verse a series of words from which ideas are wholly
absent,—that is to say, a series of sounds,—it is
clear that what we call "verse" is a set of specially
related sounds, at least in the case of a formal poem
repeated aloud.

But a much more sweeping proposition is true.
If we advance from the case of formal poetry repeated aloud to that of formal poetry silently
perused by the eye of a reader, a slight examination   30
will show the proposition good that here, as before,
verse is still a set of specially related sounds. For,
in this instance, the characters of print or writing
in which the words are embodied are simply signs
of sounds; and although originally received by the
eye, they are handed over to the ear, are interpreted by the auditory sense, and take their final
lodgement, not at all as conceptions of sight, but as
conceptions of hearing. The function of the eye

is now purely ministerial: it merely purveys for the ear. An analogous process is indicated in the Arabian saw which affirms that "that is the best description which makes the ear an eye." In general, the reader will do well to recall that each sense has not only what is ordinarily called its physical province, but also its corresponding imaginative province; the eye has its imagination, the ear its imagination; and when the term "imagination of the ear" is hereinafter used it must be understood to suggest those perceptions of sound which come to exist in the mind, not by virtue of actual vibratory impact upon the tympanum immediately preceding the perception, but by virtue of indirect causes (such as the characters of print and of writing) which in any way amount to practical equivalents of such impact. Now these signs convey, along with their corresponding sounds, the same relations between those sounds which are suggested to the ear when the sounds themselves fall upon the tympanum. It is therefore strictly true that, although the great majority of formal poems in modern times are perceived by the mind through the original agency of the eye, the relations indicated by the term "verse" are still relations between sounds.

Nor—to call the briefest attention to the only other case in which this fundamental proposition could seem at all doubtful—is this connection of verse with sound less essential when the formal poem is merely conceived in the thought of its author without ever reaching either visible or audible embodiment. For the formal poem is necessarily conceived in words, and in the imagination of the sounds (words) is necessarily involved the imagination of the relations between the sounds, that is, of verse.

In short, when we hear verse, we hear a set of relations between sounds; when we silently read verse, we see that which brings to us a set of relations between sounds; when we imagine verse, we imagine a set of relations between sounds.

Approached in this way, the proposition given below will probably not seem difficult of acceptance; indeed it is possible many will be surprised that the ideas leading to it have been dwelt upon so long. In point of fact, however, it is the very failure to recognize verse as in all respects a phenomenon of sound and to appreciate the necessary consequences thereof which has caused the non-existence of a science of formal poetry. Occasion will presently arise to show how this has happened, with some detail; meantime, we are now prepared to formulate a proposition which will serve as the basis of a science of verse.

The term "verse" denotes a set of specially related sounds.

It is clear that if we can now ascertain all the possible relations between sounds we will have discovered all the possible determinants of verse, and will have secured physical principles for the classification of all verse-effects from which there can be no appeal. This investigation can fortunately be carried on with the confidence attaching to the methods of physical science. For it involves mainly the observation of sensible appearances; and these are, furthermore, in the present instance not complex.

The study of verse must therefore begin with the study of sounds.

Sounds may be studied with reference to four and only four, particulars. We may observe—

(1) How long a sound lasts (*duration*);

(2) How loud a sound is (*intensity*);

(3) How shrill—that is, how high, as to bass or treble—a sound is (*pitch*);

and

(4) Of what sounds a given sound is composed—for, as in studying colors we find purple composed of red and violet, and the like, so many sounds have been found to be made up of other sounds (tone-color).

These differences in sounds, although really so distinct from each other as to be the origin of some of the most striking and widely-separated phenomena both in art and in our daily life, are so confused by most persons who have had no special occasion to examine them that there are no terms of ordinary use in which they can be expressed with scientific precision. The reader, however, will not only advance with ease, but will win a whole new world of possible delight, by acquiring at the outset such a familiarity with the sound-relations above termed duration, intensity, pitch, and tone-color, that the ear will immediately

934

and intelligently refer every sound heard to all those particulars and measure its relations to the preceding or suceeding sound in terms of them. The remarkable powers which the human ear possesses of making perfectly accurate comparisons of sound with sound in three of these particulars will presently be detailed. . . .

We have now reached a point where we can profitably inquire as to the precise differentiation between the two species of the art of sound—music and verse. We have found that the art of sound, in general, embraces phenomena of rhythm, of tune, and of tone-color. Many will be disposed to think that the second class of these phenomena just named—tune—is not found in verse, and that the absence of it should be one of the first differences to be noted as between music and verse. Tune is, however, quite as essential a constituent of verse as of music; and the disposition to believe otherwise is due only to the complete unconsciousness with which we come to use these tunes after the myriad repetitions of them which occur in all our daily intercourse by words. We will presently find, from numerous proofs and illustrations which are submitted in Part II., on the Tunes of Verse, that our modern speech is made up quite as much of tunes as of words, and that our ability to convey our thoughts depends upon the existence of a great number of curious melodies of speech which have somehow acquired form and significance. These "tunes" are not mere vague variations of pitch in successive words,—which would deserve the name of tune only in the most general sense of that term,—but they are perfectly definite and organized melodies of the speaking-voice, composed of exact variations of pitch so well marked as to be instantly recognized by every ear. If they were *not* thus recognized a large portion of the ideas which we now convey with ease would be wholly inexpressible. Reserving, then, all details upon this matter until their appropriate place under the head of the Tunes of Verse, in Part II. above cited, it will be sufficient here if the reader is asked to realize them in a practical way by first attempting to utter any significant sentences of prose or verse in an absolutely unchanging voice from beginning to end. This will be found quite difficult, and when successfully executed produces an impression of strangeness which all the more clearly illustrates how habitually and how unconsciously the tunes of speech are used. If, having uttered the sentences in a rigidly unvarying tone, the reader will then utter them in the tunes which we feel—by some inward perceptions too subtle for treatment here—to be appropriate to them, it will be easily seen that definite successions of tones are being used,—so definite that they are kept in mind for their appropriate occasions just as words are, and so regular in their organizations as to be in all respects worthy the name of "tunes," instead of the vague terms "intonation," or "inflection," which have so long concealed the real function of these wonderful melodies of the speaking-voice.

The art of verse, then, as well as the art of music,—the two species of the genus art of sound,—includes all the three great classes of phenomena summed up under the terms rhythm, tune, and tone-color. We will presently find many problems solved by the full recognition of this fact that there is absolutely no difference between the sound-relations used in music and those used in verse.

If this be true,—if the sound-relations of music and verse are the same,—we are necessarily forced to look for the difference between the two arts in the nature of the *sounds* themselves with which they deal. Here, indeed, the difference lies. Expressed, as far as possible, in popular terms, it is as follows:—

When those exact co-ordinations which the ear perceives as rhythm, tune, and tone-color, are suggested to the ear by a series of *musical sounds*, the result is. . . . . Music.
When those exact co-ordinations which the ear perceives as rhythm, tune, and tone-color, are suggested to the ear by a series of *spoken words*, the result is. . . . . Verse.

But it is necessary to attain a very much more philosophical view of the relation between "musical sounds" and "words" than is generally implied in the popular use of those terms; for a slight examination will show that words are themselves musical sounds. They are capable of the exactest co-ordination in respect of their duration, their pitch, and their tone-color; they are capable of as exact co-ordination in respect of their intensity (loudness or softness) as any other sounds; they give pleasure to the ear by their fall: in short, without here attempting a definition of musical sounds, it must be said that from a scientific point of view there is no incident of them which is not also an incident of words. For all purposes of verse, words are unquestionably musical sounds produced by a reed-instrument—the human voice. It must therefore be clearly understood by the reader that, in the above distinction between music and verse, what are called musical sounds are only one set out of the possible body of musical sounds; while what are called words are another set; that is, that "words" (in the sense of the above distinction) means simply one kind of musical sounds, and "musical sounds" means simply another kind. It is to be regretted that our language does not afford us more precise terms for these purposes. Music, although a very old art, has only recently been investigated by exact methods: the same may be said of poetry; and it is probably owing to this circumstance that we have no terms which embody precise relations between spoken words and musical tones. The terms "vocal" and "instrumental" are not satisfactory, because they hide one of the most important facts to be kept in view in all such

investigations as the present, namely, the purely instrumental character of the speaking-voice and of its tones (words). "Vocal" here *is* "instrumental." Let the reader always conceive, first, a general body of musical tones; then let the speaking-voice be conceived as an instrument consisting of a tube (the mouth, nose, and throat) and a pair of reeds (the vocal chords), which produces a certain set of these musical sounds. It is true that this certain set has received a special name, "words," because it has come to be used for a special purpose, namely, that of communicating ideas from man to man. It will assist the reader to a clearer conception of this matter, if the fact be called to mind that the selection of vocal sounds for the purpose of communicating ideas was not at all a necessary one. Other sets of musical sounds might have been selected for this purpose, those of whistles or flutes, for instance; or no sounds at all might have been used, and "words" might have been entirely eye-signs, as is actually the case with the deaf and dumb. In fine, when the term "words" is used as describing the peculiar set of sounds used in verse, the reader must understand it merely as a convenient method of singling out that specialized set of musical sounds made by the musical instrument called "the human speaking-voice." . . .

936

Chronology

LITERARY EVENTS	SOCIAL AND POLITICAL EVENTS
1603 Shakespeare, *Hamlet*, printed in First Quarto.	**1603** Death of Queen Elizabeth; accession of James I.
1605–1606 Shakespeare, *Macbeth* and *King Lear*.	**1606** Charters granted to the London Company and the Plymouth Company.
	1607 Jamestown founded, first successful English settlement in America.
	1607–1608 Separatists removed from Scrooby, England, to Amsterdam.
1608 John Smith, *A True Relation*, the first English book written in America.	**1608** Founding of Quebec by Champlain.
1611 Authorized version of the *Bible*.	
	1614 Dutch set up a trading post, New Amsterdam, on Manhattan Island.
1616 John Smith, *A Description of New England*, illustrative of propaganda used in urging colonization of America.	**1616** Death of Shakespeare.
	1619 Negro slavery allegedly introduced into Virginia. Representative government inaugurated in America when the Virginia legislative body first convened, July 30.
	1620 Settlement of the Plymouth Colony on the coast of Massachusetts. *Mayflower Compact* signed in Cape Cod Bay, November 11.
1622 William Bradford and Edward Winslow, *Mourt's Relation*, description of the Plymouth settlement.	
	1623 Governor Bradford of Plymouth Colony proclaimed a day of Thanksgiving celebrating abundant harvest.
1624 John Smith, *A Map of Virginia*.	
	1625 Death of James I; accession of Charles I.
	1626 Peter Minuit bought Manhattan Island from the Indians for $24 worth of trinkets.
	1627 Delaware settled by Finns and Swedes. Partnership between the London capitalists and the Pilgrims was dissolved when a group of colonial "Under-

LITERARY, SOCIAL, AND POLITICAL

LITERARY EVENTS	SOCIAL AND POLITICAL EVENTS
	takers," assuming the debts of the colony, agreed to pay £1800 in nine annual installments.
1630 Francis Higginson, *New England's Plantation*. John Winthrop began his *Journal*.	**1630** First large migration of the Puritans to Massachusetts Bay, led by John Winthrop. Boston established.
	1632 George Calvert, Lord Baltimore, granted charter to the Chesapeake Bay region. Acadia relinquished to France by England.
	1634 With the House of Deputies (representatives to the General Court) in Massachusetts Bay, the second house of representatives in America was created.
	1635 Boston Latin School founded.
1636 *New Englands First Fruits*, a propaganda tract by the promoters of New England to encourage emigration from England to Massachusetts Bay.	**1636** Harvard College founded. Roger Williams and five friends founded settlement at Providence, Rhode Island.
1637 Thomas Morton, *New English Canaan*.	**1637** Pequot War in Connecticut. The first synod of the New England churches. Antinomian controversy in Massachusetts; Anne Hutchinson banished.
1639 Stephen Daye founded in Cambridge the first press in the English colonies in America and published an almanac.	
1640 The Bay Psalm Book (actual title, *The Whole Booke of Psalmes*) first book printed in English colonies in America.	**1640** Population in all the colonies was 27,950. In New England, there were 21,200 people, 12,000 cattle, and 3000 sheep.
	1641 Body of Liberties adopted at Boston.
	1642 Civil War in England broke out. Harvard conferred nine A.B. degrees.
1644 Roger Williams, *The Bloudy Tenent of Persecution for Cause of Conscience*.	
1647 John Cotton, *The Bloody Tenent Washed*.... Nathaniel Ward, *The Simple Cobbler of Aggawam*.	
	1648 First full law code printed at Boston. Treaty of Westphalia concluded the Thirty Years' War, but prepared the way for commercial rivalry between England and the Netherlands.

939

LITERARY EVENTS	SOCIAL AND POLITICAL EVENTS
	1649 Charles I beheaded; Oliver Cromwell became Protector. House of Lords abolished.
1650 Anne Bradstreet, *The Tenth Muse Lately Sprung Up in America*.	1650 Colonial population estimated at 51,700.
	1651 First Navigation Act passed by Parliament to remove Dutch mercantile competition; goods from colonies to England were to be carried only in English ships.
1652 Roger Williams, *The Bloody Tenent Yet More Bloody; by Mr. Cotton's Endeavor to wash it White in the Blood of the Lamb*.	
1654 Edward Johnson, *The Wonder-Working Providence of Sion's Saviour*.	
	1655 New Sweden seized by the Dutch.
	1656 Persecution of Quakers in New England began.
	1658 Laws of Connecticut printed. Richard Cromwell became Protector.
	1660 Population, 84,800. Restoration of monarchy in England; accession of Charles II.
1662 Michael Wigglesworth, *The Day of Doom*.	1662 General Council of Churches in New England held at Boston. Act of Uniformity in England drove many dissenting clergymen to America. Royal Society of London chartered.
	1663 Charter granted Carolina.
	1664 Colonial and imperial interests led to attack upon New Amsterdam, with English success in August.
	1666 Great fire of London.
1667 John Milton, *Paradise Lost*, great English epic, first published.	1667 Treaty of Breda transferred possession of Dutch colonies in America to England.
	1668 Joliet explored portions of the Great Lakes region.
	1670 Settlement of Charleston, South Carolina.
	1672 "No taxation without representation" cry first raised in Massachusetts.
1674 First entries in Samuel Sewall's *Diary* (published 1878–1882).	
	1675–1676 King Philip's War; chaos on the frontier.
1676 Increase Mather, *Brief History of the Warr with the Indians*. Benjamin Tompson, *New England's Crisis*.	1676 Bacon's Rebellion in Virginia was successful, but Bacon's death ended the cause of reform.
1678 John Bunyan, *Pilgrim's Progress*, Part I, powerfully influential English Puritan masterpiece.	
1681 William Penn, *Some Account of the Province of Pensilvania in America*.	1679 New Hampshire made a separate royal province.
1682 Mary Rowlandson, *Captivity and Restoration*.	1682 Philadelphia founded as a Quaker city.
1684 Increase Mather, *An Essay for the Recording of Illustrious Providences*.	1684 Massachusetts charter forfeited to the Crown.
	1685 Death of Charles II; accession of James II. Revocation of the Edict of Nantes drove many Huguenots to America.
1687 Sir Isaac Newton, *Principia*, important treatise by the greatest English physicist of the age.	
	1688 The "Glorious Revolution" in England; James II escaped to France.
1689 John Locke, *Treatise of Civil Government*; strong in-	1689 William and Mary chosen King and Queen by Par-

LITERARY EVENTS	SOCIAL AND POLITICAL EVENTS
fluence on the political philosophy of the American revolutionists.	liament. King William's War with French occasioned by Louis XIV's championship of the deposed James.
1690 *The New England Primer*, first edition between 1687–1690. *Publick Occurrences*, Boston, first American newspaper, was suppressed after first number.	
	1691 Property, instead of church membership, made basis of suffrage by new Massachusetts charter.
	1692 Witchcraft trials at Salem.
1693 Cotton Mather, *Wonders of the Invisible World*.	1693 William and Mary College founded.
	1697 Peace of Ryswick, proclaimed in Boston, December 10, ended King William's War.
	1700 Population, 275,000.
	1701 Queen Anne's War (1701–1713). Detroit founded. Yale College founded.
1702 Cotton Mather, *Magnalia Christi Americana*.	
1704 Sarah Kemble Knight, *The Journal of Madame Knight*. First regular newspaper, *Boston News-Letter*, established.	
	1710 Population, 375,000.
	1714 Accession of George I.
	1718 New Orleans founded.
	1720 Population, 475,000.
1721 *New England Courant*, newspaper edited by James Franklin. Cotton Mather, *The Christian Philosopher*.	
1722 Benjamin Franklin, *The Dogood Papers*.	
	1727 Accession of George II.
	1729 Baltimore founded.
	1730 Population, 655,000.
1732 Franklin's almanac, *Poor Richard*.	
	1734 "Great Awakening" started in New England.
	1735 Zenger trial established principle of a free press.
1740 Samuel Richardson, *Pamela*, early influential English novel.	1740 Population, 889,000.
1741 *The General Magazine*, Benjamin Franklin, editor and publisher.	
	1744 King George's War (1744–1748).
	1749 The Ohio Company of Virginia given grant for land.
	1750 Population, 1,207,000.
1754 Jonathan Edwards, *Freedom of the Will*.	1754 French and Indian War (1754–1763).
1755 Samuel Johnson, *A Dictionary of the English Language*, published in England.	
1756 John Woolman, *Journal*.	
	1760 Population, 1,610,000. Accession of George III.
	1762 France secretly gave Louisiana to Spain.
	1763 Treaty of Paris gave Canada and Florida to Great Britain. Mason-Dixon survey was begun.
	1765 Stamp Act Congress.
	1766 Stamp Act repealed.
1768 John Dickinson, *Letters from a Farmer in Pennsylvania*.	1768 British troops sent to Boston.
	1770 Population, 2,200,000. Boston Massacre.
1772 Philip Freneau and Hugh Henry Brackenridge, *A Poem on the Rising Glory of America*.	

LITERARY EVENTS	SOCIAL AND POLITICAL EVENTS
1773 Franklin, *An Edict by the King of Prussia* and *Rules by Which a Great Empire May Be Reduced to a Small One*.	1773 Boston Tea Party.
1774 Francis Hopkinson, *A Pretty Story*.	1774 First Continental Congress met in Philadelphia.
1775 John Trumbull, *M'Fingal*. Edmund Burke, *Speech on Conciliation with America*.	1775 Revolutionary War: Battles of Lexington, Concord, and Bunker Hill. Second Continental Congress. George Washington, Commander-in-Chief of Continental Army.
1776 Thomas Paine, *Common Sense* and *The Crisis*.	1776 Declaration of Independence. San Francisco Mission founded.
	1777 Articles of Confederation submitted for ratification. Washington and army in winter quarters at Valley Forge.
1779 Brackenridge established *The United States Magazine*.	
	1780 Population, 2,781,000.
1781 Freneau, *The British Prison-Ship*.	1781 Cornwallis surrendered at Yorktown, Virginia.
1782 St. Jean de Crèvecoeur, *Letters from an American Farmer*.	
	1783 Treaty of Paris.
1785 Thomas Jefferson, *Notes on the State of Virginia*.	
1786 Freneau, *The Poems of Philip Freneau*.	1786 Shays's Rebellion.
1787 Joel Barlow, *The Vision of Columbus*.	1787 Constitutional Convention.
1788 Timothy Dwight, *The Triumph of Infidelity*.	1788 Constitution ratified by eleven states.
1789 Noah Webster, *Dissertations on the English Language*.	1789 George Washington, President (1789-1797). French Revolution began.
	1790 First official census; population, 4,000,000.
1791 Paine, *The Rights of Man*. William Bartram, *Travels . . . .*	
1792 Barlow, *Advice to the Privileged Orders in the Several States of Europe*. Brackenridge, *Modern Chivalry*.	
	1793 Eli Whitney invented the cotton gin.
1794 Paine, *The Age of Reason*. Susanna Rowson, *Charlotte Temple*.	
	1797 John Adams, President (1797-1801).
1798 Charles Brockden Brown, *Wieland*. Samuel Taylor Coleridge and William Wordsworth, *Lyrical Ballads*, herald of English romantic movement.	
1799 Brown, *Ormond, Arthur Mervyn, Edgar Huntly*.	
	1800 Population, 5,300,000. Congress met first time in Washington.
1801 *Port Folio* (1801-1827), edited by Joseph Dennie, 1801-1809.	1801 Thomas Jefferson, President (1801-1809).
	1803 Louisiana Purchase.
	1804-1806 Lewis and Clark Expedition.
1807 Barlow, *The Columbiad*. Washington Irving and others, *Salmagundi*.	1807 Embargo Act.
	1808 Foreign slave trade prohibited.
1809 Irving, *A History of New York*.	1809 James Madison, President (1809-1817).
	1811 *New Orleans*, first steamboat on western waters, built.
	1812 War of 1812 (1812-1815).
	1813 Perry's victory on Lake Erie.
1814 Francis Scott Key, *The Star-Spangled Banner*.	1814 White House burned by British. War ended by Treaty of Ghent.
1815 Freneau, *A Collection of Poems*.	1815 Battle of New Orleans.
1817 William Cullen Bryant, *Thanatopsis*.	1817 James Monroe, President (1817-1825).
1818 Bryant, *To a Waterfowl*.	

LITERARY EVENTS	SOCIAL AND POLITICAL EVENTS
1819 Irving, *The Sketch Book of Geoffrey Crayon, Gent.*	**1819** Florida purchased from Spain.
1820 James Fenimore Cooper, *Precaution.*	**1820** Population, 9,700,000. Missouri Compromise.
1821 Cooper, *The Spy.* Bryant, *Poems.*	
1823 Cooper, *The Pioneers, The Pilot.*	**1823** Monroe Doctrine.
	1825 John Quincy Adams, President (1825–1829). Erie Canal opened.
1826 Cooper, *The Last of the Mohicans.*	
1827 Edgar Allan Poe, *Tamerlane and Other Poems.* Cooper, *The Prairie.*	
1828 Noah Webster, *An American Dictionary of the English Language.*	**1828** Baltimore and Ohio Railroad was begun.
1829 Poe, *Al Aaraaf, Tamerlane and Minor Poems.* Irving, *Conquest of Granada.* Samuel Kettell, *Specimens of American Poetry, with Critical and Biographical Notices.*	**1829** Andrew Jackson, President (1829–1837).
1830 Oliver Wendell Holmes, "Old Ironsides." *Godey's Lady's Book* (1830–1898).	**1830** Population, 12,870,000. Mormon church organized by Joseph Smith.
1831 Poe, *Poems.* William Lloyd Garrison, *The Liberator* (1831–1865).	
1832 Bryant, *Poems.* John Pendleton Kennedy, *Swallow Barn.* Irving, *The Alhambra.*	**1832** Black Hawk War. President Jackson's Nullification Proclamation.
1833 Henry Wadsworth Longfellow, *Outre-Mer.* Poe, "Ms. Found in a Bottle." Seba Smith, *The Life and Writings of Major Jack Downing of Downingville.*	
1834 *The Southern Literary Messenger* (1834–1864).	**1834** Cyrus Hall McCormick patented the reaper.
1835 Augustus Baldwin Longstreet, *Georgia Scenes, Characters, Incidents.* William Gilmore Simms, *The Yemassee, The Partisan.* Irving, *A Tour on the Prairies.* Alexis de Tocqueville, *De la Démocratie en Amérique.*	**1835** Period of the antimonopolists or "Locofocos."
1836 Ralph Waldo Emerson, *Nature.* Beginning of transcendental movement in New England.	
1837 Nathaniel Hawthorne, *Twice-Told Tales.* Emerson, *The American Scholar.*	**1837** Martin Van Buren, President (1837–1841).
1838 Emerson, *An Address Delivered before the Senior Class in Divinity College, Cambridge.* Cooper, *The American Democrat.* John Greenleaf Whittier, *Poems.*	
1840 Richard Henry Dana, Jr., *Two Years Before the Mast.* Cooper, *The Pathfinder.* Poe, *Tales of the Grotesque and Arabesque.* *The Dial* (1840–1844).	**1840** Population, 17,100,000.
1841 Emerson, *Essays.* Cooper, *The Deerslayer.* James Russell Lowell, *A Year's Life.*	**1841** William Henry Harrison, President, 1841. John Tyler, President (1841–1845).
	1842 John Charles Frémont explored western land.
1843 Poe, *The Murders in the Rue Morgue.*	
1844 Emerson, *Essays.*	**1844** Morse developed the telegraph.
1845 Poe, *The Raven and Other Poems* and *Tales.* Sylvester Judd, *Margaret.* Johnson Jones Hooper, *Some Adventures of Captain Simon Suggs.* Cooper, *Satanstoe.*	**1845** James K. Polk, President (1845–1849). Texas annexed.
1846 Herman Melville, *Typee.* Hawthorne, *Mosses from an Old Manse.* Holmes, *Poems.*	**1846** War with Mexico (1846–1848). Oregon boundary determined. Wilmot Proviso. Elias Howe patented the sewing machine. First successful use of ether as an anesthetic.
1847 Longfellow, *Evangeline.* Melville, *Omoo.* Emerson, *Poems.*	**1847** Rotary printing press invented. Free-Soil party organized.

LITERARY EVENTS	SOCIAL AND POLITICAL EVENTS
1848 Lowell, *The Biglow Papers*, *A Fable for Critics*, and *The Vision of Sir Launfal*.	**1848** California gold rush.
1849 Francis Parkman, *The California and Oregon Trail*. Melville, *Mardi* and *Redburn*. Henry D. Thoreau, *A Week on the Concord and Merrimack Rivers*.	**1849** Zachary Taylor, President (1849–1850). Riots at the Astor Place Opera House in New York City against English actor William Macready.
1850 Hawthorne, *The Scarlet Letter*. Melville, *White-Jacket*. Whittier, *Songs of Labor and Other Poems*. Daniel Webster, "Seventh of March" speech.	**1850** Millard Fillmore, President (1850–1853). Population, 23,200,000. Compromise of 1850 admitted California as free state and Utah and New Mexico as territories, and tightened fugitive slave law.
1851 Melville, *Moby Dick*. Hawthorne, *The House of the Seven Gables*.	**1851** Great fire in San Francisco.
1852 Harriet B. Stowe, *Uncle Tom's Cabin*.	
1853 Joseph G. Baldwin, *The Flush Times of Alabama and Mississippi*.	**1853** Franklin Pierce, President (1853–1857). Japan opened ports. Gadsden purchase of territory from Mexico, added to Arizona and New Mexico.
1854 Thoreau, *Walden*.	**1854** Kansas-Nebraska Act gave these two territories popular choice as to question of slavery.
1855 Walt Whitman, *Leaves of Grass*. Longfellow, *The Song of Hiawatha*.	
	1856 Republican party organized nationally.
1857 *Atlantic Monthly* (1857–). *Harper's Weekly* (1857–1916).	**1857** James Buchanan, President (1857–1861). Dred Scott decision asserted Negroes could not be citizens, and neither Congress nor Territories could prohibit slavery in Territories. Financial panic.
1858 Longfellow, *The Courtship of Miles Standish*. Holmes, *The Autocrat of the Breakfast Table*.	**1858** Lincoln-Douglas debates. Atlantic cable.
	1859 John Brown's raid on Harpers Ferry.
1860 Hawthorne, *The Marble Faun*. Holmes, *The Professor at the Breakfast Table*. Henry Timrod, *Poems*.	**1860** Population, 31,500,000. South Carolina seceded from the Union.
1861 Holmes, *Elsie Venner*. Timrod, "Ethnogenesis."	**1861** Abraham Lincoln, President (1861–1865). Confederate States of America organized with Jefferson Davis as president. Confederates fired on Fort Sumter and began the Civil War. First Battle of Bull Run.
1862 Charles Farrar Browne, *Artemus Ward: His Book*.	**1862** Fight between the *Monitor* and the *Merrimac*. Battles of Shiloh, second Bull Run, Antietam, and Vicksburg.
1863 Longfellow, *Tales of a Wayside Inn*. Lincoln, "Gettysburg Address."	**1863** Battles of Chancellorsville and Gettysburg. Lincoln, "Emancipation Proclamation."
	1864 Union Army commanded by Ulysses S. Grant. Sherman's march to the sea.
1865 Whitman, *Drum Taps*. Lowell, *Commemoration Ode*.	**1865** Lee surrendered to Grant at Appomattox; Civil War ended. Lincoln assassinated. Andrew Johnson, President (1865–1869).
1866 Whittier, *Snow-Bound*.	**1866** Ku Klux Klan active.
1867 John De Forest, *Miss Ravenel's Conversion from Secession to Loyalty*. Longfellow, translation, *The Divine Comedy of Dante Alighieri* (1865–1867). Whittier, *The Tent on the Beach*. Lowell, *The Biglow Papers, Second Series*.	**1867** Alaska purchased from Russia. Karl Marx published *Das Kapital*.
1868 Bret Harte, *The Luck of Roaring Camp*. Louisa May Alcott, *Little Women* (1868–1869). *Lippincott's Magazine* (1868–1916). *Overland Monthly* (1868–1875, 1883–1933).	**1868** Fourteenth Amendment, guaranteeing citizenship to all persons born in the United States and equal protection under law. President Johnson impeached.

LITERARY EVENTS	SOCIAL AND POLITICAL EVENTS
1869 Mark Twain, *Innocents Abroad.* Harte, *Tennessee's Partner.*	**1869** Ulysses S. Grant, President (1869–1877). Fifteenth Amendment guaranteed right of suffrage in any state, unabridged by "race, color, or previous condition of servitude." "Black Friday," Wall Street gold panic.
1870 *Scribner's Monthly* (1870–1881).	**1870** Population, 38,900,000.
1871 Edward Eggleston, *The Hoosier Schoolmaster.* Whitman, *Democratic Vistas* and *Passage to India.*	**1871** Chicago fire.
1872 Mark Twain, *Roughing It.* Holmes, *Poet at the Breakfast Table.*	
1873 Mark Twain and Charles Dudley Warner, *The Gilded Age.* Timrod, *The Poems of Henry Timrod.*	**1873** Major financial panic.
1874 Eggleston, *The Circuit Rider.*	**1874** Women's Christian Temperance Union founded.
1875 Henry James, *A Passionate Pilgrim and Other Tales.*	
1876 Mark Twain, *The Adventures of Tom Sawyer.* James, *Roderick Hudson.*	**1876** Bell telephone patented. Centennial Exposition in Philadelphia.
1877 James, *The American.*	**1877** Rutherford B. Hayes, President (1877–1881). Reconstruction completed. Labor strikes.
1878 James, *Daisy Miller* and *The Europeans.* Sidney Lanier, "The Marshes of Glynn."	
1879 George Washington Cable, *Old Creole Days.* William Dean Howells, *The Lady of the Aroostook.*	**1879** Incandescent lamp invented by Edison.
1880 Henry Adams, *Democracy.* Cable, *The Grandissimes.* Lew Wallace, *Ben Hur.*	**1880** Population, 50,200,000.
1881 James, *Washington Square* and *The Portrait of a Lady.* Joel Chandler Harris, *Uncle Remus: His Songs and His Sayings. Century Illustrated Monthly Magazine* established.	**1881** James A. Garfield, President, 1881, was assassinated and Vice-President Chester A. Arthur became President (1881–1885). First official convention of Federation of Organized Trades, which became the American Federation of Labor in 1886.
1882 Mark Twain, *The Prince and the Pauper.* Whitman, *Specimen Days and Collect* (1882–1883). Howells, *A Modern Instance.*	**1882** Act passed prohibiting admission of Chinese laborers to the United States for ten years. Robert Koch, German bacteriologist, isolated tuberculosis germ.
1883 Mark Twain, *Life on the Mississippi.* Edgar Watson Howe, *The Story of a Country Town.* Harris, *Nights with Uncle Remus.*	**1883** Civil Service law prohibited assessments for partisan purposes on members of the civil service.
1884 Helen Hunt Jackson, *Ramona.* Francis Richard Stockton, *The Lady or the Tiger? and Other Stories.* Henry Adams, *Esther: A Novel. Poems of Sidney Lanier,* edited by Mrs. Lanier. Mark Twain, *Huckleberry Finn.*	**1884** Grover Cleveland elected President in campaign against James G. Blaine. "Mugwumps" was term used against prominent republicans who supported Cleveland. Steam turbine invented by Parsons.
1885 Howells, *The Rise of Silas Lapham.*	**1885** Grover Cleveland, President (1885–1889).
1886 James, *The Bostonians* and *The Princess Casamassima.* Howells, *Indian Summer.*	**1886** Statue of Liberty, gift of people of France to commemorate one hundred years of American independence, dedicated.
1887 Joseph Kirkland, *Zury: the Meanest Man in Spring County.*	**1887** Interstate Commerce Act provided a commission to supervise general regulations.
1888 Whitman, *November Boughs* and *Complete Poems and Prose of Walt Whitman, 1855–1888.* Lowell, *Political Essays* and *Heartsease and Rue.* Edward Bellamy, *Looking Backward: 2000–1887.*	**1888** At Richmond, Virginia, first electric surface street cars operated.
1889 Mark Twain, *A Connecticut Yankee in King Arthur's Court.*	**1889** Benjamin Harrison, President (1889–1893). Ten states adopted Australian (secret) ballot. Secretary of Agriculture became member of President's cabinet. Johnstown flood. Indian Territory (now Oklahoma) opened to settlers.

1890 Dickinson, *Poems by Emily Dickinson*. James, *The Tragic Muse*. Howells, *A Hazard of New Fortunes*.

1890 Population, 63,000,000. Sherman Antitrust law.

1891 Holmes, *Over the Tea Cups*. Hamlin Garland, *Main-Travelled Roads*. Howells, *Criticism and Fiction*.

1891 Ellis Island opened as immigrant station.

1893 Stephen Crane, *Maggie: A Girl of the Streets*.

1893 Grover Cleveland, President (1893–1897). World's Columbian Exposition in Chicago. Panic caused by great exportation of gold. Edison brought out kinetoscope, basically the motion-picture machine.

1894 Howells, *A Traveler from Altruria*.

1894 Unemployed formed Coxey's army and marched on Washington.

1895 Crane, *The Red Badge of Courage* and *The Black Riders and Other Lines*.

1895 Roentgen discovered the X ray. Supreme Court declared income tax law unconstitutional.

1896 Dickinson, *Poems by Emily Dickinson, Third Series*. Sarah Orne Jewett, *The Country of the Pointed Firs*. Harold Frederic, *The Damnation of Theron Ware*. Charles Monroe Sheldon, *In His Steps*.

1896 Klondike gold rush began.

1897 Edwin Arlington Robinson, *The Children of the Night*.

1897 William McKinley, President (1897–1901).

1898 James, *The Two Magics*, *The Turn of the Screw*, and *Covering End*.

1898 U.S.S. *Maine* sunk in Havana harbor, starting Spanish-American War. Peace Treaty signed at Paris. Philippines purchased for $20,000,000.

1899 James, *The Awkward Age*. Crane, *War Is Kind*.

1899 "Open door" policy in China.

1900 Theodore Dreiser, *Sister Carrie*. Ellen Glasgow, *The Voice of the People*. Jack London, *The Son of the Wolf*.

1900 Population, 76,000,000. Boxer uprising in China.

1901 Frank Norris, *The Octopus*.

1901 Transatlantic wireless.

1902 William James, *The Varieties of Religious Experience*. Owen Wister, *The Virginian*. Edith Wharton, *The Valley of Decision*.

1903 James, *The Ambassadors*. London, *The Call of the Wild*. Norris, *The Pit*.

1903 San Francisco–Manila cable. Wright brothers experiment with airplane at Kitty Hawk, N.C.

1904 Henry Adams, *Mont-Saint-Michel and Chartres*. London, *The Sea-Wolf*.

1904 Panama Canal begun.

1905 George Santayana, *The Life of Reason* (1905–1906). David Belasco, *The Girl of the Golden West*. Wharton, *The House of Mirth*.

1905 Industrial Workers of the World organized in Chicago.

1906 Upton Sinclair, *The Jungle*. O. Henry, *The Four Million*.

1906 Earthquake and fire at San Francisco. Pure Food and Drug Act passed.

1907 Adams, *The Education of Henry Adams: An Autobiography*. William James, *Pragmatism: A New Name for Some Old Ways of Thinking*.

1907 Financial panic.

1909 William V. Moody, *The Great Divide*.

1909 William Howard Taft, President (1909–1913). Robert Peary reached North Pole. Model-T Fords completed.

1910 John A. Lomax, *Cowboy Songs and Other Frontier Ballads*.

1910 Population, 92,000,000.

1911 Dreiser, *Jennie Gerhardt*. Wharton, *Ethan Frome*. Belasco, *The Return of Peter Grimm*.

1911 Supreme Court ordered Standard Oil and American Tobacco trusts dissolved.

1912 Amy Lowell, *A Dome of Many-Colored Glass*. Dreiser, *The Financier*. Robinson Jeffers, *Flagons and Apples*. *Poetry: A Magazine of Verse* established.

1912 Progressive party organized. *Titanic* sunk.

1913 Edward Sheldon, *Romance*. Glasgow, *Virginia*. Willa Cather, *O Pioneers*. Robert Frost, *A Boy's Will*. Vachel Lindsay, *General Booth Enters into Heaven and Other Poems*.

1913 Woodrow Wilson, President (1913–1921). Department of Labor established. Sixteenth Amendment gave Congress power to collect income tax. Seventeenth Amendment provided direct election of Senators. Federal Reserve Act passed.

LITERARY EVENTS	SOCIAL AND POLITICAL EVENTS
1914 Lindsay, *The Congo and Other Poems.* Frost, *North of Boston.* Amy Lowell, *Sword Blades and Poppy Seed.* Dreiser, *The Titan.*	**1914** Panama Canal opened. Federal Trade Commission created. Clayton Antitrust Act approved. Beginning of First World War. Battle of the Marne.
1915 Edgar Lee Masters, *Spoon River Anthology.* Cather, *The Song of the Lark.* Dreiser, *The Genius.*	**1915** *Lusitania* sunk. Dardanelles campaign lost by English. Einstein announced theory of relativity.
1916 Wharton, *Xingu and Other Stories.* Carl Sandburg, *Chicago Poems.* Frost, *Mountain Interval.* Mark Twain, *The Mysterious Stranger.* Robinson, *The Man Against the Sky.*	**1916** German failure at Verdun. Pancho Villa attacked Columbus, New Mexico. Major-General Pershing commanded American expedition into Mexico.
1917 Lindsay, *The Chinese Nightingale and Other Poems.* T. S. Eliot, *Prufrock and Other Observations.*	**1917** United States declared war against Germany. Bolshevists seized Russia.
1918 Cather, *My Ántonia.* Booth Tarkington, *The Magnificent Ambersons.*	**1918** Battles of Château-Thierry, Saint-Mihiel, and Argonne. President Wilson laid down Fourteen Points as basis for peace with Germany. Armistice signed. Peace Conference in Paris.
1919 Mencken, *Prejudices* (6 series, 1919–1927) and *The American Language* (First Edition). Joseph Hergesheimer, *Java Head.* Sherwood Anderson, *Winesburg, Ohio.* James Branch Cabell, *Jurgen* and *Beyond Life.*	**1919** Peace Conference adopted resolutions to create League of Nations. United States Senate adjourned in December without ratifying Treaty of Peace. American Legion organized in Paris.
1920 Francis Scott Fitzgerald, *This Side of Paradise.* Eugene O'Neill, *Beyond the Horizon.* Edna St. Vincent Millay, *A Few Figs from Thistles.* Eliot, *Poems.* Wharton, *The Age of Innocence.* Sinclair Lewis, *Main Street.*	**1920** Population, 105,700,000. Eighteenth Amendment (prohibition) ratified. Nineteenth Amendment (woman suffrage) ratified. League of Nations held first meeting.
1921 Elinor Wylie, *Nets to Catch the Wind.* John Dos Passos, *Three Soldiers.* O'Neill, *The Emperor Jones, Diff'rent,* and *The Straw.* Tarkington, *Alice Adams.*	**1921** Warren Gamaliel Harding, President (1921–1923). Peace treaty with Germany. Washington Conference on naval disarmament. Transcontinental airmail service in operation.
1922 Eliot, *The Waste Land.* Lewis, *Babbitt.* O'Neill, *The Hairy Ape, Anna Christie,* and *The First Man.* John Dewey, *Human Nature and Conduct.*	
1923 Cather, *A Lost Lady.* Wylie, *Black Armour.* Elmer Rice, *The Adding Machine.* Santayana, *Scepticism and Animal Faith.*	**1923** Calvin Coolidge, President (1923–1929). Teapot Dome scandal.
1924 Jeffers, *Tamar and Other Poems.* O'Neill, *All God's Chillun Got Wings.* Sidney Coe Howard, *They Knew What They Wanted.* Laurence Stallings and Maxwell Anderson, *What Price Glory?* Melville, *Billy Budd and Other Prose Pieces.*	**1924** Soldiers' bonus passed. Child Labor Amendment submitted for ratification. Americans made first airplane flight around the world. Progressive party organized under La Follette.
1925 Dos Passos, *Manhattan Transfer.* Dreiser, *An American Tragedy.* Lewis, *Arrowsmith.* Glasgow, *Barren Ground.* Fitzgerald, *The Great Gatsby.* Jeffers, *Roan Stallion.* O'Neill, *Desire Under the Elms.*	**1925** Bell laboratories invented telephotography. Millikan discovered cosmic rays.
1926 Ernest Hemingway, *The Sun Also Rises.* O'Neill, *The Great God Brown, The Fountain,* and *The Moon of the Caribbees and Other Plays.* Sidney Howard, *The Silver Cord.*	**1926** Radio telephonic transmission between London and New York. Amundsen-Ellsworth expedition, first flight across North Pole. Talking pictures exhibited to public.
1927 Robinson, *Tristram.* Cather, *Death Comes for the Archbishop.* Don Marquis, *archy and mehitabel.* Ole Rölvaag, *Giants in the Earth.* Thornton Wilder, *The Bridge of San Luis Rey.* Hemingway, *Men Without Women.* Santayana, *The Realm of Essence.*	**1927** Charles A. Lindbergh made nonstop solo flight from New York to Paris.

LITERARY EVENTS	SOCIAL AND POLITICAL EVENTS
1928 O'Neill, *Strange Interlude.* Archibald MacLeish, *The Hamlet of A. MacLeish.* Sinclair, *Boston.* Frost, *West-Running Brook.* Ezra Pound, *Selected Poems.*	**1928** U.S.S.R. began Five Year Plan.
1929 Hemingway, *A Farewell to Arms.* Thomas Wolfe, *Look Homeward, Angel.* Lewis, *Dodsworth.* William Faulkner, *The Sound and the Fury.* Elmer Rice, *Street Scene.* Glasgow, *They Stooped to Folly.*	**1929** Herbert Hoover, President (1929–1933). Briand–Kellogg Treaty became effective, with sixty-two nations renouncing war as an international policy. Great depression began with stock-market crash.
1930 Eliot, *Ash Wednesday.* MacLeish, *New Found Land.* Marc Connelly, *The Green Pastures.* Dos Passos, *The 42d Parallel.* Santayana, *The Realm of Matter.* Katherine Anne Porter, *Flowering Judas.*	**1930** Population, 123,000,000. Charles E. Hughes nominated Chief Justice of Supreme Court. Senate ratified London Naval Treaty. Work on Hoover Dam started.
1931 O'Neill, *Mourning Becomes Electra.* Cather, *Shadows on the Rock.* Edmund Wilson, *Axel's Castle.* Pearl Buck, *The Good Earth.* Faulkner, *Sanctuary.*	**1931** Sino-Japanese War began. Hoover's proposal for moratorium on international debts ratified.
1932 Erskine Caldwell, *Tobacco Road.* Glasgow, *The Sheltered Life.* MacLeish, *Conquistador.*	**1932** Special act of Congress created Reconstruction Finance Corporation to revive industry by restoring credit. Unemployed World War veterans marched to Washington, seeking economic relief.
1933 Gertrude Stein, *The Autobiography of Alice B. Toklas.* Hervey Allen, *Anthony Adverse.* O'Neill, *Ah, Wilderness!* Lewis, *Ann Vickers.*	**1933** Franklin Delano Roosevelt, President (1933–1945). New Deal inaugurated. U.S.S.R. recognized by the United States. Twentieth Amendment abolished the "lame duck" sessions of Congress. Twenty-first Amendment repealed Eighteenth Amendment. Bank holiday proclaimed. President signed Muscle Shoals–TVA bill. National Industrial Recovery Act signed.
1934 William Saroyan, *The Daring Young Man on the Flying Trapeze, and Other Stories.* Robert Sherwood, *The Petrified Forest.* James Farrell, *The Young Manhood of Studs Lonigan.*	**1934** Congress passed Philippine Independence Bill. Dust storms on plains east of Rockies.
1935 Lewis, *It Can't Happen Here.* Wolfe, *Of Time and the River.* John Steinbeck, *Tortilla Flat.* Clarence John Day, *Life with Father.* Maxwell Anderson, *Winterset.*	**1935** Works Relief and Social Security bills passed. Supreme Court declared N.R.A. unconstitutional. Income tax expanded.
1936 Dos Passos, *The Big Money.* Santayana, *The Last Puritan.* Frost, *A Further Range.* Margaret Mitchell, *Gone with the Wind.* Sandburg, *The People, Yes.* Steinbeck, *In Dubious Battle.*	**1936** Pan–American Peace Conference in Buenos Aires.
1937 Santayana, *The Realm of Truth.* John P. Marquand, *The Late George Apley.* Steinbeck, *Of Mice and Men,* and *The Red Pony.* Maxwell Anderson, *High Tor.* MacLeish, *The Fall of the City.*	**1937** Roosevelt signed United States Neutrality Act.
1938 Wilder, *Our Town.*	**1938** Wages and Hours bill passed. Eighth Pan–American Conference in Lima.
1939 Sherwood, *Abe Lincoln in Illinois.* Steinbeck, *The Grapes of Wrath.* Frost, *Collected Poems of Robert Frost.* Saroyan, *The Time of Your Life.* Wolfe, *The Web and the Rock.*	**1939** Neutrality Act amended by repealing the embargo on arms. Great Britain and France declared war on Germany.
1940 Santayana, *The Realm of Spirit.* MacLeish, *The Irresponsibles: A Declaration.* Hemingway, *For Whom the Bell Tolls.* Wolfe, *You Can't Go Home Again.* Sherwood, *There Shall Be No Night.*	**1940** Population, 131,700,000. Fifty overaged destroyers transferred to Great Britain in exchange for leases for naval bases on Atlantic coast. Selective Service Act passed.
1941 Marquand, *H. M. Pulham, Esquire.* MacLeish, *A Time to Speak: the Selected Prose of Archibald Mac-*	**1941** Lend-Lease bill passed to aid other democracies at war. Roosevelt and Churchill drew up Atlantic

LITERARY EVENTS	SOCIAL AND POLITICAL EVENTS
Leish. Glasgow, *In This Our Life*. Millay, *Collected Sonnets of Edna St. Vincent Millay*.	Charter outlining nature of the peace. Japan attacked Pearl Harbor. United States declared war on Japan, Germany, and Italy. Japan invaded Philippines.
1942 Wilder, *The Skin of Our Teeth*.	1942 Twenty-six United Nations pledged co-operative war effort. Philippines lost to Japan. Naval battles in the Pacific. American troops in North Africa.
1943 Rodgers and Hammerstein, *Oklahoma!* Santayana, *Persons and Places*.	1943 United States forces in Italy. Italian armistice. Teheran meeting of Roosevelt, Churchill, and Stalin.
1944 B. A. Botkin, ed., *A Treasury of American Folklore*.	1944 Bombing of Japan. Allies invaded Western Europe. United Nations planned at Dumbarton Oaks.
1945 Stephen Vincent Benét, *Western Star*. Frost, *A Masque of Reason*. Tennessee Williams, *The Glass Menagerie*. Richard Wright, *Black Boy*. Stein, *Wars I Have Seen*.	1945 United States forces retook Philippines. President Roosevelt died April 12. Harry S. Truman, President (1945–). German surrender signed in Berlin, May 9. United Nations Charter drawn at San Francisco. Atomic bombs dropped on Hiroshima and Nagasaki. Japanese surrender at Tokio, September 2.
1946 Robert Penn Warren, *All the King's Men*.	1946 Major labor strikes in several industries, including railroads. Civilian production, $150,000,000,000 yearly. League of Nations dissolved. United Nations Atomic Energy Commission convened for first time. Atomic-bomb tests at Bikini. Paris Peace Conference of twenty-one nations.
1947 Frost, *Masque of Mercy*. Lewis, *Kingsblood Royal*. *Notebooks of Henry James*.	1947 Marshall Plan for recovery of Europe proposed. Taft–Hartley bill in force.
1948 Ross Lockridge, Jr., *Raintree County*. Norman Mailler, *The Naked and the Dead*. Thomas Mann, *Dr. Faustus*. Thomas Heggen and Joshua Logan, *Mr. Roberts*. Sandburg, *Remembrance Rock*. Peter Viereck, *Terror and Decorum*. Eliot awarded Nobel Prize.	1948 Selective Service Act. Congress passed Economic Co-operation Act. President emphasized Civil Rights Program. Election of Harry S. Truman to the Presidency.
1949 Frost, *Complete Poems*. A. B. Guthrie, *The Way West*. Arthur Miller, *Death of a Salesman*.	1949 Communists seized China. West German Republic organized. End of war in Greece and Israel.
1950 Eliot, *The Cocktail Party*. Hemingway, *Across the River and into the Trees*. John Hersey, *The Wall*. Robert Nathan, *The Green Leaf*. Henry M. Robinson, *The Cardinal*. Deaths of Edgar Lee Masters, John Gould Fletcher, and Edna St. Vincent Millay. Faulkner awarded Nobel Prize.	1950 North Korean Communist invasion army driven from South Korea by forces of the United Nations. Chinese Communists invade North Korea and Tibet.

THE BIBLIOGRAPHIC RECORD

Bibliographies, General Reference Books, Handbooks, Periodicals

ADAMS, J. T., and COLEMAN, R. V. (General Editors). *Atlas of American History.* 1943. Supplements *Dictionary of American History.*

ADAMS, R. F. *Western Words: A Dictionary of the Range, Cow Camp and Trail.* 1944. Good guide.

American Economic Review. 1911–. Official journal of the American Economic Association. Five times yearly.

American Historical Review, The. Oct. 1895–. Quarterly.

American Newspapers: 1690–1820, History and Bibliography of. Edited by C. S. Brigham. 2 vols. 1947. Complete; repositories given.

American Newspapers: 1821–1936. Edited by W. Gregory. 1937. Complete; repositories given.

American Literature; A Journal of Literary History, Criticism, and Bibliography. 1929–. Quarterly. Official journal of the American Literature section of the Modern Language Association. Indispensable for "Research in Progress" and "Articles on American Literature Appearing in Current Periodicals."

American Political Science Review, The. 1906–. Bimonthly. Official publication of the American Political Science Association.

American Quarterly. 1949–. Essays in the culture of the United States, past and present.

American Sociological Review, The. 1936–. Bimonthly. Official publication of the American Sociological Association.

American Speech: A Quarterly of Linguistic Usage. 1925–.

Annual Magazine Subject Index. 1908–. American and English periodicals, with indispensable "Dramatic Index."

Art Index. 1929–. Cumulative author and subject index to a selected list of fine-arts periodicals and museum bulletins.

BEERS, H. P. *Bibliographies in American History: Guide to Materials for Research.* Rev. ed., 1942. Well organized.

BERRY, L. V., and VAN DEN BARK, M. *The American Thesaurus of Slang, with Supplement: A Complete Reference Book of Colloquial Speech.* 1947.

Bibliographic Index. A Cumulative Bibliography of Bibliographies. 1937–. Excellent.

BURKE, W. J., and HOWE, W. D. (Eds.). *American Authors and Books, 1640–1940.* 1943. Includes 15,000 entries.

COAN, O. W., and LILLARD, R. G. *America in Fiction: An Annotated List of Novels that Interpret Aspects of Life in the United States.* Rev. ed., 1945.

COX, E. G. *A Reference Guide to the Literature of Travel, Including Voyages, Geographical Descriptions, Adventures, Shipwrecks and Expeditions.* 2 vols. 1935–1938.

Cumulative Book Index. 1898–. Books published since 1898. The great source for books published in English.

Dictionary of American Biography. Edited by A. Johnson and D. Malone. 21 vols., including Index, 1928–1939; Supplement I, 1944. Auspices of the American Council of Learned Societies.

Dictionary of American English on Historical Principles. Edited by W. A. Craigie and J. R. Hulbert. 4 vols. 1938–1944. The great work in this field.

Dictionary of American History. Edited by J. T. Adams and R. V. Coleman. 6 vols. 1940. Excellent for ready reference.

Encyclopaedia of the Social Sciences. Edited by E. R. A. Seligman and A. Johnson. 15 vols. 1931–1935. Excellent for ready reference.

Essay and General Literature Index. 1900–. Index to many thousands of articles in thousands of "volumes of collections of essays and miscellaneous works."

SELECTED READINGS IN AMERICAN CULTURE

EVANS, C. *American Bibliography.* 12 vols. 1903–1934. Books printed in the United States, 1639–1799. For supplement see *The Huntington Library Bulletin*, No. 3 (1933), 1–95.

HART, J. D. *The Oxford Companion to American Literature.* Revised and enlarged. 1948. Indispensable for short biographies and bibliographies of American authors; summaries of American fiction, essays, poems, plays; definitions of literary schools, movements, and terms.

International Index to Periodicals. 1920–. Index of scholarly periodicals "devoted chiefly to the humanities and science"; supplements *Readers' Guide.*

JOHNSON, M. DE V. *Merle Johnson's American First Editions.* 4th ed. Revised and enlarged by Jacob Blanck. 1942. Lists 187 well-known authors.

Journal of Aesthetics and Art Criticism, The. 1941–. Quarterly. Sponsored by the American Society for Aesthetics.

KELLY, J. *The American Catalogue of Books . . . 1861–1871.* 2 vols. 1866–1871, reprinted 1928.

KUNITZ, S. J., and HAYCRAFT, H. (Eds.). *American Authors: 1600–1900.* 1938. Includes 1300 biographies, 400 portraits.

KUNITZ, S. J., and HAYCRAFT, H. (Eds.). *Twentieth Century Authors.* 1942. Includes 1850 biographies, 1700 portraits.

Language. 1925–. Quarterly. Official journal of the Linguistic Society of America.

LEARY, L. G. (Ed.). *Articles on American Literature Appearing in Current Periodicals, 1920–1945.* 1947. Indispensable.

MILLETT, F. B. *Contemporary American Authors: A Critical Survey and 219 Bio-bibliographies.* 1940. Excellent for ready reference.

Mississippi Valley Historical Review, The. June 1914–. Quarterly.

New England Quarterly, The: A Historical Review of New England Life and Letters. 1928–. The March issue contains an annual bibliography for New England.

New York Theatre Critics' Reviews. 1940–. Reprints reviews of dramatic criticism in New York newspapers.

Nineteenth Century Readers' Guide to Periodical Literature: 1890–1899; with Supplemental Indexing 1900–1922. 1944. Fifty-one British and American magazines.

Pacific Northwest Quarterly, The. 1906–.

Pacific Spectator, The. 1947–.

PMLA: Publications of the Modern Language Association of America. 1884–. Quarterly. Annual Supplement contains "American Bibliography" of articles appearing in many scholarly journals.

Quarterly Journal of Speech, The. 1915–. Official publication of the Speech Association of America (with title changes).

Readers' Guide to Periodical Literature. 1900–. Index to the more general magazines.

ROORBACH, O. A. *Bibliotheca Americana.* 4 vols. 1852–1861. American books published during the period 1820–1860.

ROSE, L. A. "A Bibliographical Survey of Economic and Political Writings, 1865–1900," *American Literature,* XV (1944), 381–410; augmented by "Supplement I" and "Supplement II," in mimeograph form, April 28 and October 1, 1944, Houghton, Michigan. Period covered, 1865 to 1900, with economic and utopian novels extending to 1917.

SABIN, J. *A Dictionary of Books Relating to America from its Discovery to the Present Time.* 29 vols. 1868–1936. Extensive bibliographical aid.

South Atlantic Quarterly, The. 1902–.

Southern Bibliography: Fiction, A. 1929–1938. Compiled by J. M. Agnew, 1939. Excludes novels of Southern writers not about the South and "titles commonly grouped as Love Stories, Mystery and Adventure Stories."

Southwest Review, The. 1915–.

SPARGO, J. W. *A Bibliographical Manual for Students of the English Language and Literature of England and the United States.* 1941.

STEWART, G. R. *Names on the Land: A Historical Account of Place-Naming in the United States.* 1945. Excellent for reference.

THOMPSON, R. *American Literary Annuals and Gift Books, 1825–1865.* 1936.

Union List of Serials in Libraries of the United States and Canada. Edited by W. Gregory. Second edition, edited by G. E. Malikoff. Supplement, 1943. Repositories given for all periodicals and serials.

United States Catalog. 10 vols. 1900–1928. Books published in the United States, 1899–1927.

WHITE, W. W. *Political Dictionary.* 1947. Definitions of terminologies in political science.

Who's Who in America. 1899–. Biennial.

WRIGHT, L. H. *American Fiction 1774–1850: A Contribution Toward a Bibliography.* Revised edition. 1948. Indispensable for scholars and collectors.

THE LITERARY RECORD

General Literary History and Criticism

American Writers Series. General editor, H. H. Clark. 1934–. Over 20 vols., usually of major authors, with extended biographies, bibliographies, and selections.

BLAIR, W. *Horse Sense in American Humor, from Benjamin Franklin to Ogden Nash.* 1942. American use of humor to illuminate truth.

BLAIR, W. *Native American Humor (1800–1900).* 1937. Sound criticism, good selections, extensive bibliography.

BOYNTON, P. H. *Literature and American Life.* 1936. Excellent large one-volume history.

BRAWLEY, B. *Early Negro American Writers: Selections, with Biographical and Critical Introductions.* 1935. An anthology.

BROOKS, VAN W. *America's Coming of Age.* 1915.

BROOKS, VAN W. *The Flowering of New England, 1815–1865.* 1936. First of a series of popular and valuable studies in American literature.

BROOKS, VAN W. *New England: Indian Summer, 1865–1915.* 1940.

BROOKS, VAN W. *The Times of Melville and Whitman.* 1947.

BROOKS, VAN W. *The World of Washington Irving.* 1944.

CALVERTON, V. F. *The Liberation of American Literature.* 1932. Marxian interpretation.

Cambridge History of American Literature. Edited by W. P. Trent, J. Erskine, S. P. Sherman, and C. Van Doren, 4 vols., 1917–1921. Bibliographies, I, II, IV. The major literary history of the period.

CANBY, H. S. *Classic Americans; A Study of Eminent American Writers from Irving to Whitman.* 1931. Sound criticism.

CHARVAT, W. *The Origins of American Critical Thought, 1810–1835.* 1936. A careful, sound study.

COFFIN, R. P. T. *New Poetry of New England: Frost and Robinson.* 1938.

Criticism in America, Its Functions and Status. I. Babbitt, Van W. Brooks, W. C. Brownell, E. Boyd, T. S. Eliot, H. L. Mencken, S. P. Sherman, J. E. Spingarn, G. E. Woodbury. 1924. First essay dates from 1910.

EASTMAN, M. *Enjoyment of Laughter.* 1936.

FLANAGAN, J. T. (Ed.). *America is West: An Anthology of Middlewestern Life and Literature.* 1945.

FOERSTER, N. *American Criticism: A Study in Literary Theory from Poe to the Present.* 1928. Original, thorough.

FOERSTER, N. *Nature in American Literature: Studies in the Modern View of Nature.* 1923. Sound.

FOERSTER, N. (Ed.). *The Reinterpretation of American Literature; Some Contributions toward the Understanding of its Historical Development.* 1928. Organized discussion by a group of scholars.

FOERSTER, N. *Toward Standards: A Study of the Present Critical Movement in American Letters.* 1930. "Survey of the development of humanistic principles in criticism."

GOHDES, C. L. F. *American Literature in Nineteenth-Century England.* 1944. Based on extensive research; a model.

GOHDES, C. L. F. *The Periodicals of American Transcendentalism.* 1931. Indispensable.

JACKSON, D. K. (Ed.). *The Contributors and Contributions to the Southern Literary Messenger (1834–1864).* 1936. Elaborate index.

KAZIN, A. *On Native Grounds: An Interpretation of Modern American Prose Literature.* 1942. Serious literary history from 1890–1940.

KRAPP, G. P. *The English Language in America.* 2 vols. 1925. Standard.

Library of Southern Literature, A. Edited by F. A. Alderman, J. C. Harris, and C. W. Kent. 16 vols. Supplement. 1908–1913.

Literary History of the United States. Edited by R. E. Spiller, W. Thorp, T. H. Johnson, and H. S. Canby. 3 vols. 1948. See Spiller, R. E.

MACY, J. *The Spirit of American Literature.* 1913. Original and stimulating.

MATTHIESSEN, F. O. *American Renaissance: Art and Expression in the Age of Emerson and Whitman.* 1941. Informative, stimulating.

MENCKEN, H. L. *The American Language; An Inquiry into the Development of English in the United States.* 1936. Supplements I, II, 1945, 1948. Indispensable, emphasizing the growth of the language, with thousands of examples.

MILLER, P. *The New England Mind: The Seventeenth Century.* 1939. A fundamental study.

MILLER, P., and JOHNSON, T. H. (Eds.). *The Puritans.* 1938. American Literature Series. Readings, with critical introductions.

MOTT, F. L. *American Journalism: A History of Newspapers in the United States through 250 Years, 1690 to 1940.* 1941. Standard, authoritative.

MOTT, F. L. *A History of American Magazines.* 1930. 3 vols. 1930, 1938. Indispensable for a study of American life and letters.

ORIANS, G. H. *A Short History of American Literature, Analyzed by Decades.* 1940.

OSWALD, J. C. *Printing in the Americas.* 1937. Short historical survey.

PARRINGTON, V. L. *Main Currents in American Thought; An Interpretation of American Literature from the Beginnings to 1920.* 3 vols. 1927, 1930. A major, vital, and stimulating study, with Jeffersonian bias.

PATTEE, F. L. *The Feminine Fifties.* 1940. Study of popular women writers.

PATTEE, F. L. *The First Century of American Literature, 1770–1870.* 1935. A standard history.

PATTEE, F. L. *A History of American Literature Since 1870.* 1915. A standard history.

PATTEE, F. L. *The New American Literature, 1890–1930.* 1930. A standard history.

POLLOCK, T. C. *The Nature of Literature: Its Relation to Science, Language, and Human Experience.* 1942. The language of science as distinct from the language of literature.

PRITCHARD, J. P. *Return to the Fountains: Some Classical Sources of American Criticism.* 1942. Influence of Aristotle and Horace. Major authors from Bryant to S. P. Sherman.

RANSOM, J. C. *The New Criticism.* 1941. Highly valuable.

RICHARDSON, L. N. *A History of Early American Magazines, 1741–1789.* 1931.

ROURKE, C. *American Humor: A Study of the National Character.* 1931. A scholarly study.

RUSK, R. L. *The Literature of the Middle Western Frontier.* 2 vols. 1925. Exhaustive scholarly study; much of the second volume is devoted to bibliography.

SHERMAN, S. P. *Americans.* 1922. Essays on Mencken, Franklin, Emerson, Hawthorne, Whitman, Miller, Sandburg, More, others.

SMITH, B. *Forces in American Criticism; A Study in the History of American Literary Thought.* 1939.

SPILLER, R. E., THORP, W., JOHNSON, T. H., CANBY, H. S. *Literary History of the United States.* 3 vols. 1948. A major historical and critical work, with chapters by a long list of contributors; the third volume is an excellent bibliography.

STEDMAN, E. C., and HUTCHINSON, E. M. (Eds.). *A Library of American Literature from Earliest Settlement to the Present Time.* 11 vols. New ed., 1894.

STOVALL, F. *American Idealism.* 1943. Critical study of many writers from Wigglesworth to Dos Passos.

TAYLOR, W. F. *A History of American Letters. With Bibliographies by Harry Hartwick.* 1936. American Literature Series. Short, sound; excellent bibliographical selections.

TRENT, W. P., and WELLS, B. W. (Eds.). *Colonial Prose and Poetry.* 3 vols. in 1. 1929.

TYLER, M. C. *A History of American Literature during the Colonial Period, 1607–1765.* 2 vols. 1897. Standard.

TYLER, M. C. *The Literary History of the American Revolution, 1763–1783.* 2 vols. 1897. Reissued in facsimile, 1941. Standard.

WALKER, F. *San Francisco's Literary Frontier.* 1939. Literary history on the Pacific coast from 1848–1875.

WARFEL, H. R., and ORIANS, G. H. (Eds.). *American Local-Color Stories.* 1941. Anthology of stories by 38 authors from James Hall to Zona Gale.

WARREN, A., and WELLEK, R. *The Theory of Literature.* 1949.

WILLIAMS, S. T. *The American Spirit in Letters.* 1926. From pioneer days to modern times. One of the Pageant of America series.

WILSON, E. *The Triple Thinkers.* Revised and enlarged. 1948.

WINSHIP, G. P. *The Cambridge Press, 1638–1692: A Reexamination of the Evidence Concerning the Bay Psalm Book and the Eliot Indian Bible as Well as Other Contemporary Books and People.* 1945. Definitive study.

WINTERS, Y. *Maule's Curse: Seven Studies in the History of American Obscurantism: Hawthorne, Cooper, Melville, Poe, Emerson, Jones Very, Emily Dickinson, and Henry James.* 1938. Exploratory.

ZABEL, M. D. (Ed.). *Literary Opinion in America; Essays Illustrating the Status, Methods, and Problems of Criticism in the United States since the War.* 1937. Fifty American critical essays.

Literary Types

DRAMA

CLARK, B. H. (General Editor). *America's Lost Plays.* 20 vols. 1940–1942. Hitherto unpublished; collected under auspices of the Dramatists' Guild of the Author's League of America.

COAD, O. S., and MIMS, E., JR. *The American Stage.* 1929. Illustrated survey. One of the Pageant of America series.

DUNLAP, W. *A History of the American Theater.* 2 vols. 1833. Standard, authoritative.

HALLINE, A. G. (Ed.). *American Plays.* 1935. Anthology of 17 plays from beginnings to contemporary times.

HARTMAN, J. G. *The Development of American Social Comedy from 1787–1936.* 1939. Comprehensive.

KRUTCH, J. W. *The American Drama Since 1918: An Informal History.* 1939. Summary and critical estimate of 75 plays.

MACMINN, G. R. *The Theatre of the Golden Era in California.* 1941. Exciting picture of the theater and audiences of the gold-rush days.

MOSES, M. J. (Ed.). *Representative Plays by American Dramatists.* 3 vols. 1918–1925. An anthology comprising plays by 30 dramatists dating from 1765 to contemporary times.

MOSES, M. J., and BROWN, J. M. (Eds.). *The American Theatre as Seen by Its Critics, 1752–1934*. 1934. Valuable storehouse.

ODELL, G. C. D. *Annals of the New York Stage*. 15 vols. 1927–1949. Definitive.

O'HARA, F. H. *Today in American Drama*. 1939. Social implications in drama between 1921–1935.

QUINN, A. H. *A History of American Drama, from the Beginning to the Civil War* (2d ed.). 1943. Standard.

QUINN, A. H. *A History of the American Drama from the Civil War to the Present Day*. 2 vols. 1927. Standard.

QUINN, A. H. (Ed.). *Representative American Plays* (6th ed., rev. and enl.). 1938. Standard anthology.

FICTION

BEACH, J. W. *American Fiction: 1920–1940*. 1941. Dos Passos, Hemingway, Faulkner, Wolfe, Caldwell, Farrell, Marquand, and Steinbeck.

BEACH, J. W. *The Twentieth Century Novel: Studies in Technique*. 1932. Scholarly criticism.

BOTKIN, B. A. (Ed.). *A Treasury of American Folklore; Stories, Ballads, and Traditions of the People*. 1944.

BOYNTON, P. H. *America in Contemporary Fiction*. 1940. Critical essays.

BROWN, H. R. *The Sentimental Novel in America: 1789–1860*. 1940. Fully documented history.

BURGUM, E. B. *The Novel and the World's Dilemma*. 1947. Of Proust, Joyce, Stein, Faulkner, Saroyan, Hemingway, Wolfe, and others.

COWIE, A. *The Rise of the American Novel*. 1948. Excellent historical study; elaborate treatment to 1890.

DUNLAP, G. A. *The City in the American Novel: 1789–1900*. 1934. Contemporary conditions in New York, Philadelphia, and Boston.

FLORY, C. R. *Economic Criticism in American Fiction, 1792–1900*. 1936.

GEISMAR, M. *Writers in Crisis: The American Novel between Two Wars*. 1942. Lardner, Hemingway, Dos Passos, Wolfe, Faulkner, and Steinbeck.

HACKETT, A. P. *Fifty Years of Best Sellers*. 1945.

HARTWICK, H. *The Foreground of American Fiction*. 1934. Analysis of current fiction.

HATCHER, H. *Creating the Modern American Novel*. 1935. Competent study from 1900 to the present.

HICKS, G. *The Great Tradition: An Interpretation of American Literature since the Civil War*. 1933 (rev. ed., 1935). Interpretation from a social point of view.

KNIGHT, G. C. *The Novel in English*. 1931. Survey of English and American fiction.

LEISY, E. E. *The American Historical Novel*. 1950. Novels grouped by historical epochs.

LOSHE, L. D. *The Early American Novel*. 1907. To 1830.

MASTERSON, J. R. *Tall Tales of Arkansaw*. 1943. A rich collection.

MEINE, F. J. (Ed.). *Tall Tales of the Southwest; An Anthology of Southern and Southwestern Humor, 1830–1860*. 1930.

MICHAUD, R. *The American Novel To-day: A Social and Psychological Study*. 1938. From Hawthorne to the present; emphasis on psychology.

MONROE, N. E. *The Novel and Society: A Critical Study of the Modern Novel*. 1941. Important criticism.

MOTT, F. L. *Golden Multitudes: The Story of Best Sellers in the United States*. 1947. From *The Day of Doom* to *Forever Amber*.

MULLER, H. J. *Modern Fiction: A Study of Values*. 1937. Major figures in modern English, American and European fiction.

PATTEE, F. L. *The Development of the American Short Story; An Historical Survey*. 1923. Scholarly criticism.

PEARSON, E. L. *Dime Novels; or, Following an Old Trail in Popular Literature*. 1929. Thorough, informal.

QUINN, A. H. *American Fiction: An Historical and Critical Survey*. 1936. Excellent historical study. Bibliography, pp. 725–772.

SNELL, G. *The Shapers of American Fiction: 1798–1947*. 1947. A critical study.

TAYLOR, W. F. *The Economic Novel in America*. 1942. Indispensable, elaborate study from 1870 forward.

VAN DOREN, C. *The American Novel: 1789–1939*. 1940. Excellent critical study. Bibliography, pp. 367–382.

WHITE, G. L., JR. *Scandinavian Themes in American Fiction*. 1937. Critical essays on Lewis, Cather, Rolvaag, Boyesen.

POETRY

ALLEN, G. W. *American Prosody*. 1935. Detailed analysis of works of major poets.

BROOKS, C. *Modern Poetry and the Tradition*. 1939. Critical essays on Eliot, MacLeish, and others.

GREGORY, H., and ZATURENSKA, M. *A History of American Poetry, 1900–1940*. 1946. Two poets estimate their contemporaries.

HENDERSON, D., KIERAN, J., and RICE, G. (Eds.). *Reveille: War Poems. By Members of Our Armed Forces*. 1943. Ideals and aspects of the Second World War.

IRISH, WYNOT R. *The Modern American Muse: A Complete Bibliography of American Verse, 1900–1925*. 1950.

JANTZ, H. S. *The First Century of New England Verse*. 1945. Indispensable; the major source.

STEDMAN, E. C. *Poets of America*. 1885. Criticism of nineteenth-century authors from the nineteenth-century point of view.

UNTERMEYER, L. (Ed.). *Modern American Poetry, a Critical Anthology*. 6th rev. ed., 1942.

WELLS, H. W. *The American Way of Poetry*. 1943. Highly valuable.

WILDER, A. N. *The Spiritual Aspects of the New Poetry*. 1940. Critical review of contemporary poetry.

THE SOCIAL RECORD
Economics and Sociology

BERNARD, L. L., and BERNARD, J. *Origins of American Sociology: The Social Science Movement in the United States.* 1943. A history.

CENTERS, R. *The Psychology of Social Classes: A Study of Class Consciousness.* 1949. Essential for reference.

CHURCHILL, H. S. *The City Is the People.* 1945. City planning, by a well-known architect.

DOLLARD, J. *Caste and Class in a Southern Town.* Rev. ed., 1949.

DORFMAN, J. *The Economic Mind in American Civilization, 1606–1865.* 2 vols. 1946. An extensive, detailed study. A third volume (1949) covers the period 1865–1918.

FAIRCHILD, H. P. *Immigration.* Rev. ed., 1928. Comprehensive treatment of immigration from colonial times.

FRAZIER, E. F. *The Negro in the United States.* 1949.

GAINES, F. P. *The Southern Plantation.* 1925.

GREER, T. H. *American Social Reform Movements: Their Pattern Since 1865.* 1949.

HACKER, L. M. *The Triumph of American Capitalism.* 1948.

HANEY, L. H. *History of Economic Thought; A Critical Account of the Origin and Development of the Economic Theories of the Leading Thinkers in the Leading Nations.* 3d ed., enl. 1936. Comprehensive.

HERRON, I. H. *The Small Town in American Literature.* 1939. A thorough survey.

KIRKLAND, E. C. *A History of American Economic Life.* 1932. Comprehensive.

KIRKLAND, E. C. *Men, Cities, and Transportation: A Study in New England History, 1820–1900.* 2 vols. 1948. Detailed and authoritative.

LEIGHTON, A. H. *Human Relations in a Changing World: Observations on the Use of the Social Sciences.* 1949. A guide for policymakers.

LYND, R. S., and LYND, H. M. *Middletown: A Study in Contemporary American Culture.* 1929. Middletown is the name given to a representative American town studied by field investigators. A valuable contribution.

LYND, R. S., and LYND, H. M. *Middletown in Transition: A Study in Cultural Conflict.* 1937. Sequel to *Middletown.*

McILWAINE, S. *The Southern Poor-White from Lubberland to Tobacco Road.* 1939. Social history of poor whites in literature.

MYRDAL, G. *An American Dilemma: The Negro Problem and Modern Democracy.* 1944. A sound contribution to social science.

O'CONNOR, M. J. L. *Origins of Academic Economics in the United States.* 1944. Intellectual history in the first half of the 19th century.

ODUM, H. W. *American Social Problems: An Introduction to the Study of the People, Their Dilemmas.* Rev. ed., 1945. Excellent.

SLICHTER, S. H. *The American Economy.* 1948. Scholarly analysis.

SMITH, H. N. *Virgin Land: The American West as Symbol and Myth.* 1950.

SUMNER, W. G. *Folkways; A Study of the Sociological Importance of Usages, Manners, Customs, Mores, and Morals.* Centennial ed., 1940. A classic.

WECTER, D. *The Saga of American Society; A Record of Social Aspiration, 1607–1937.* 1937. Valuable history of American society.

YOUNG, K. *Social Psychology.* 2d ed., 1944. First rate.

YOUNG, K. *Sociology: A Study of Society and Culture.* 1942.

ZIMMERMAN, C. C. *Outline of Cultural Rural Sociology.* 1948. Rev. and enl. ed. of author's *Outline of American Rural Sociology.*

Education, Philosophy and Religion

ANDERSON, P. R., and FISCH, M. H. *Philosophy in America from the Puritans to James.* 1939. Well-edited anthology of American philosophy, with introductory essays and biographical notes.

ATKINS, G. G., and FAGLEY, F. L. *History of American Congregationalism.* 1942. Competent.

BLAU, J. L. (Ed.). *American Philosophic Addresses, 1700–1900.* 1946. Companion volume to Schneider, H. W., *History of American Philosophy.* 1946.

CONNER, F. W. *Cosmic Optimism: A Study of the Interpretation of Evolution by American Poets from Emerson to Robinson.* 1949.

CUBBERLEY, E. P. *Public Education in the United States.* Rev. ed., 1934. Dominant history.

FAY, J. W. *American Psychology before William James.* 1939. Chief psychological theories from 1640 to 1890, with "Chronological Table of American Works and Foreign Sources."

FLEXNER, A. *Universities: American, English, German.* 1930. A good survey.

FOSTER, F. H. *The Modern Movement in American Theology: Sketches in the History of American Protestant Thought from the Civil War to the World War.* 1939. Able, interesting.

HALL, T. C. *The Religious Background of American Culture.* 1930. Scholarly history.

HOWE, M. A. DeW. *Classic Shades.* 1928. Timothy Dwight, Mary Lyon, Mark Hopkins, James McCosh, and Charles William Eliot.

JAMES, W. *Pragmatism: A New Name for Some Old Ways of Thinking.* 1907. The basic work.

MILLER, P. (Ed.). *The Transcendentalists.* 1950.

MORE, P. E. *A New England Group and Others.* 1921. Humanistic point of view.

MORISON, S. E. *Three Centuries of Harvard, 1636–1936.* 1936. Splendid history.

PERRY, R. B. *Philosophy of the Recent Past; An Outline*

of European and American Philosophy Since 1860. 1926. Clear, thorough.

POLLOCK, T. C., DeVANE, W. C., and SPILLER, R. E. *The English Language in American Education.* 1945. "American education in writing, reading, and speaking the mother tongue."

POST, A. *Popular Freethought in America, 1825–1850.* 1943. Primary attention to religious aspects of free thought.

RILEY, I. W. *American Thought from Puritanism to Pragmatism and Beyond.* 2d ed. 1923. Simplified history of philosophical thought.

ROGERS, A. K. *English and American Philosophy since 1800: A Critical Survey.* 1928.

ROWE, H. K. *The History of Religion in the United States.* 1924. Interpretive essays.

ROYCE, J. *The Philosophy of Loyalty.* 1908. A practical presentation.

SANTAYANA, G. *Character and Opinion in the United States, With Reminiscences of William James and Josiah Royce and Academic Life in America.* 1920. A major treatise.

SCHNEIDER, H. W. *History of American Philosophy.* 1946. A standard history.

SWEET, W. W. *The Story of Religions in America.* 1930. Systematic general survey.

TOWNSEND, H. G. *Philosophical Ideas in the United States.* 1934. Excellent survey from colonial times to John Dewey.

WIENER, P. P. *Evolution and the Founders of Pragmatism.* 1949.

Fine Arts

BECK, E. C. *Songs of the Michigan Lumberjacks.* 1942.

BOSWELL, P., JR. *Modern American Painting.* 1939. A survey, with 86 illustrations in full color.

BURROUGHS, A. *Limners and Likenesses: Three Centuries of American Painting.* 1936. Well-documented study.

CHAPPELL, L. W. (Ed.). *Folk-Songs of the Roanoke and the Albemarle.* 1939.

DOWNES, O., and SIEGMEISTER, E. (Eds.). *A Treasury of American Song.* 1940. Piano accompaniment.

ELSON, L. C. *The History of American Music.* 1925.

FLANDERS, H. H., and others (Eds.). *The New Green Mountain Songster: Traditional Folk Songs of Vermont.* 1939.

GARDNER, E. E., and CHICKERING, G. J. (Eds.). *Ballads and Songs of Southern Michigan.* 1939.

HAMLIN, T. F. *The American Spirit in Architecture.* 1926. Illustrated survey. One of the Pageant of America series.

HARTMANN, S. *A History of American Art.* 2 vols. Rev. ed., 1934. Standard.

HOWARD, J. T. *Our American Music: Three Hundred Years of It.* 3d ed., 1946. Accurate, concise.

HUGHES, L., and BONTEMPS, A. (Eds.). *The Poetry of the Negro: 1746–1949.* 1949.

ISHAM, S. *The History of American Painting.* 1927. New ed., with supplemental chapters by Royal Cortissoz. Solid criticism.

JACKSON, G. P. *White and Negro Spirituals: Their Life Span and Kinship.* 1943.

JOHNSON, J. W. (Ed.). *The Books of American Negro Spirituals, Including The Book of American Negro Spirituals and The Second Book of Negro Spirituals* by James Weldon Johnson and J. Rosamond Johnson. 1940. Excellent collection; words and music.

JORDAN, P. D., and KESSLER, L. *Songs of Yesterday, A Song Anthology of American Life.* 1941. American nineteenth-century songs, with words and music.

KIMBALL, S. F. *Domestic Architecture of the American Colonies and of the Early Republic.* 1922. Rich in history and biography.

KIMBALL, S. F., and EDGELL, G. H. *A History of Architecture.* 1918. Standard.

LaFOLLETTE, S. *Art in America from Colonial Times to the Present Day.* 1929. Standard treatise.

LARKIN, O. W. *Art and Life in America.* 1949. Indispensable.

LINSCOTT, E. H. (Ed.). *Folk Songs of Old New England.* 1939. Words and music.

LOMAX, J. A., and LOMAX, A. (Eds.). *American Ballads and Folk Songs.* 1934. Nearly 300 ballads and folk songs, some with music.

LOMAX, J. A., and LOMAX, A. (Eds.). *Our Singing Country: A Second Volume of American Ballads and Folk Songs.* 1941. Two hundred and fifty ballads and songs.

MATHER, F. J., JR., MOREY, C. R., and HENDERSON, W. J. *The American Spirit in Art.* 1927. Illustrated survey. One of the Pageant of America series.

MUMFORD, L. *The Brown Decades; A Study of the Arts in America, 1865–1895.* 1931. City planning, landscape architecture, painting.

MUMFORD, L. *Sticks and Stones: A Study of American Architecture and Civilization.* 1924. Sound, original.

MUNRO, T. *The Arts and Their Interrelations.* 1949. Authoritative.

POUND, L. (Ed.). *American Ballads and Songs.* 1922.

SONNECK, O. G. *Report on "The Star-Spangled Banner," "Hail Columbia," "America," "Yankee Doodle."* 1909. Definitive research study.

TAFT, L. *The History of American Sculpture.* Rev. ed. 1930. Standard.

TALLMADGE, T. E. *The Story of Architecture in America.* Rev. ed., 1936. Personal and popular history.

WHEELER, M. *Steamboatin' Days: Folk Songs of the River Packet Era.* 1944.

History: Intellectual and Social

ADAMS, J. T., and others (Eds.). *Album of American History.* 4 vols. 1944–1948. Pictures illustrating American history.

AMERICAN LAKES SERIES. Edited by M. M. Quaiffe. 1944–. Excellent social and economic history.

BEARD, M. R. *Woman as Force in History: A Study in Traditions and Realities.* 1946. Sound historical technique.

BECKER, C. L. *How New Will the Better World Be?* 1944. Essay on postwar reconstruction.

BESTOR, A. E., JR. *Backwoods Utopias: The Sectarian and Owenite Phases of Communitarian Socialism in America, 1663–1829.* 1950.

BILLINGTON, R. A. *Westward Expansion: A History of the American Frontier.* 1949.

BOAS, G. (Ed.). *Romanticism in America.* 1940. Papers by E. F. Goldman, E. P. Spencer, W. Nathan, R. P. Boas, O. E. Winslow, R. Gilman, A. Addison, L. Keefer, and G. Boas.

BRIDENBAUGH, C., and BRIDENBAUGH, J. *Rebels and Gentlemen: Philadelphia in the Age of Franklin.* 1942. Valuable history.

CARGILL, O. *Intellectual America: Ideas on the March.* 1941. An integrated, vigorous treatment of the evolution of ideas.

CHRONICLES OF AMERICA SERIES, THE. General Editor, A. Johnson. 50 vols. 1919. Authoritative, entertaining pageant from aboriginal times to 1919, done by able scholars.

CLARK, T. D. *The Rampaging Frontier: Manners and Humors of Pioneer Days in the South and the Middle West.* 1939. Sources are diaries, memoirs, travel books, legislative records, and humorous stories of frontier life in newspapers.

CLELAND, R. G. *From Wilderness to Empire: A History of California, 1542–1900.* 1944. Substantial.

COHEN, I. B. *Some Early Tools of American Science.* 1950.

COLLINGWOOD, R. G. *The Idea of History.* 1946. Critical and scholarly.

COMMAGER, H. S. *The American Mind: An Interpretation of American Thought and Character since the 1880's.* 1950. Excellent interpretation from a liberal point of view.

COMMAGER, H. S. *Documents in American History.* 5th revised edition. 1950. Standard.

CURTI, M. *The Growth of American Thought.* 1943. Comprehensive.

DE VOTO, B. A. *Across the Wide Missouri.* 1947. The mountain men and the fur trade.

DICK, E. N. *The Sod-House Frontier, 1854–1890; A Social History of the Northern Plains from the Creation of Kansas & Nebraska to the Admission of the Dakotas.* 1937.

EATON, C. *Freedom of Thought in the Old South.* 1940. Valuable study.

EKIRCH, A. A., JR. *The Idea of Progress in America, 1815–1860.* 1944. Significant.

FAUST, A. B. *The German Element in the United States, with Special Reference to Its Political, Moral, Social, and Educational Influence.* 2 vols. in 1. 1927.

FOSTER, R. A. *The School in American Literature.* 1930. Authoritative survey.

FRANKLIN, J. H. *From Slavery to Freedom: A History of American Negroes.* 1947. Comprehensive.

GABRIEL, R. H. *The Course of American Democratic Thought: An Intellectual History since 1815.* 1940. Significant.

GREENBIE, M. *American Saga: The History and Literature of the American Dream of a Better Life.* 1939. Records from colonial times to the present.

GREENSLET, F. *The Lowells and Their Seven Worlds.* 1946. History of New England through ten generations of the Lowell family.

HANSEN, M. L. *The Atlantic Migration, 1607–1860: A History of the Continuing Settlement of the United States.* 1940.

HATCHER, H. *The Western Reserve.* 1949.

HAVIGHURST, W. *Land of Promise: The Story of the Northwest Territory.* 1946. Entertaining and informative.

HISTORY OF AMERICAN LIFE, A. Edited by A. M. Schlesinger and D. R. Fox. 12 vols. 1927–1944. A series. Periods in American history treated by eminent authorities.

HOFSTADTER, R. *Social Darwinism in American Thought, 1860–1915.* 1944. Efforts to apply Darwinism to human society.

HORNBERGER, T. *Scientific Thought in American Colleges: 1638–1800.* 1945.

JONES, H. M. *American and French Culture, 1750–1848.* 1927. Comprehensive survey.

JONES, H. M. *Ideas in America.* 1944. Scholarly, challenging.

LASKI, H. J. *The American Democracy: A Commentary and an Interpretation.* 1948. Valuable.

LORWIN, L. L., and FLEXNER, J. A. *American Federation of Labor: History, Policies, and Prospects.* 1933. Impartial, painstaking research.

MADISON, C. A. *Critics & Crusaders: A Century of American Protest.* 1947. Sketches of fifteen dissenting Americans.

MURDOCK, K. B. *Literature and Theology in Colonial New England.* 1949.

NIEBUHR, R. *The Children of Light and the Children of Darkness; A Vindication of Democracy and a Critique of Its Traditional Defence.* 1944. Discussion of democratic theory.

PAGEANT OF AMERICA: A PICTORIAL HISTORY OF THE UNITED STATES, THE. Edited by R. H. Gabriel. 15 vols. 1925–1929. A series on exploration, settlement, politics, cultural institutions, architecture, letters, ideals, sports.

PARRINGTON, V. L., JR. *American Dreams: A Study of American Utopias.* 1947.

PERRY, R. B. *Puritanism and Democracy.* 1944. Strong, thought-provoking book.

RAESLY, E. L. *Portrait of New Netherland.* 1945. Fresh, interesting, sound.

RIVERS OF AMERICA, THE. Edited by C. L. Skinner and others. 1937–. A series. Excellent social and economic history.

ROOSEVELT, F. D. *The Public Papers and Addresses of Franklin D. Roosevelt.* Ed., Samuel I. Rosenman. 13 vols. 1938–1950.

THAYER, F. *Legal Control of the Press.* 1944. Excellent as a text and reference work.

TOCQUEVILLE, A. DE. *Democracy in America.* Edited by P. Bradley. 2 vols. 1945. Century-old book still relevant; of major significance.

TURNER, F. J. *The Frontier in American History.* 1928. Famous essays.

TURNER, F. J. *The United States, 1830–1850: The Nation and Its Sections.* 1935. Uncompleted at Turner's death. Continues his sectional philosophy.

VAIL, R. W. G. *The Old Frontier.* 1950. Excellent bibliography.

WEBB, W. P. *The Great Plains.* 1931. Effect of the Great Plains on the history of America.

WECTER, D. *The Age of the Great Depression, 1929–1941.* 1948.

WERTENBAKER, T. J. *The Golden Age of Colonial Culture.* 1942. Excellent study of mid-eighteenth-century colonial culture.

WILLISON, G. F. *Saints and Strangers: The Saga of the Pilgrims.* 1945. Thoroughly documented.

WISH, H. *Contemporary America: The National Scene since 1900.* 2d ed. 1948. Patterns of historical behavior; sound interpretation and integration.

WISH, H. *Society and Thought in Early America.* 1950. Companion volume to *Contemporary America,* equally sound.

WISSLER, C. *The American Indian; An Introduction to the Anthropology of the New World.* 3d ed. 1938. Standard.

WITTKE, C. *We Who Built America: The Saga of the Immigrant.* 1939. Comprehensive, interesting, invaluable.

WRIGHT, L. B. *The Atlantic Frontier: Colonial American Civilization, 1607–1763.* 1948.

WRIGHT, L. B. *The First Gentlemen of Virginia: Intellectual Qualities of the Early Colonial Ruling Class.* 1940. Admirable study.

History: Political

ADAMS, J. T. *The Founding of New England.* 1930. A good short history.

ANDREWS, C. M. *The Colonial Background of the American Revolution.* Rev. ed., 1931. Four admirable essays.

ANDREWS, C. M. *The Colonial Period of American History.* 4 vols. 1934–1938. Indispensable.

BAILEY, T. A. *A Diplomatic History of the American People.* 1940. Fascinating, authoritative text.

BEARD, C. A., and BEARD, M. R. *The Rise of American Civilization.* 4 vols. 1927–1942. The outstanding work emphasizing the economic interpretation.

BEMIS, S. F. *A Diplomatic History of the United States.* 1936. Comprehensive, scholarly, clear.

BOWERS, C. G. *Jefferson and Hamilton.* 1925. Vigorous, dramatic, pro-Jeffersonian.

BOWERS, C. G. *The Tragic Era: The Revolution after Lincoln.* 1929. Reconstruction interpreted favorably to Johnson's policies.

BRYCE, J. B. *The American Commonwealth.* Rev. ed. 2 vols. 1931–1933. Among the few great interpretations; by an Englishman.

BUCK, S. J. *The Agrarian Crusade.* 1920.

CHANNING, E. *A History of the United States.* 6 vols. 1905–1925. Outstanding among encyclopedic histories.

CORWIN, E. S. *The Twilight of the Supreme Court; A History of Our Constitutional Theory.* 1935. Thoughtful analysis.

FAULKNER, H. U. *American Political and Social History.* 5th ed., 1948. Excellent one-volume text.

FILLER, L. *Crusaders for American Liberalism.* 1939. History of the reform movement in the twentieth century.

FREEMAN, D. S. *George Washington*; Vols. I and II, *Young Washington.* 1949.

GOODRICH, L. M., and HAMBRO, E. *Charter of the United Nations: Commentary and Documents.* 1946. Excellent guide to the Charter.

HAINES, C. G. *The Role of the Supreme Court in American Government and Politics, 1789–1835.* 1944. Comprehensive.

HEINDEL, R. H. *The American Impact on Great Britain, 1898–1914: A Study of the United States in World History.* 1940. Important to students of American and English social history.

HICKS, J. D. *The Populist Revolt; A History of the Farmers' Alliance and the People's Party.* 1931. Scholarly history.

KNOX, D. W. *A History of the United States Navy.* 1936. Comprehensive.

LABAREE, L. W. *Conservatism in Early American History.* 1949.

MONTROSS, L. *The Reluctant Rebels: The Story of the Continental Congress, 1774–1789.* 1950.

MORISON, S. E., and COMMAGER, H. S. *The Growth of the American Republic.* 2 vols. 3d ed., 1942. Sound, well-written text.

MORRIS, L. *Postscript to Yesterday. America: The Last Fifty Years.* 2 vols. 1947–. Survey of American civilization since 1896.

NEVINS, A. *Ordeal of the Union.* 2 vols. 1947. Vol. 1, 1847–1852; Vol. 2, 1852–1857; Vol. 3 unpublished. Political and cultural interpretation; detailed and sound.

ODEGARD, P. H., and HELMS, E. A. *American Politics: A Study in Political Dynamics.* Rev. ed., 1948. Analysis of party politics.

PERKINS, D. *Hands Off; A History of the Monroe Doc-*

trine. 1941. Very readable condensation of the author's 3-volume study, *The Monroe Doctrine.*

RANDALL, J. G. *The Civil War and Reconstruction.* 1937. Good general history.

SCHLESINGER, A. M., JR. *The Age of Jackson.* 1945. Rise and significance of Jacksonian democracy.

SHOUP, E. L. *The Government of the American People.* 1946. Outstanding text; uses the functional approach.

STEPHENSON, G. M. *A History of American Immigration, 1820–1924.* 1926. Discusses influence of immigration upon the political development of America.

STEPHENSON, W. H., and COULTER, E. M. (Eds.). *A History of the South.* To be in 10 vols. 1947–. To be a history of the South from 1607 to the present. Vol. 10 in process of publication. Intended to be a definitive series.

VAN DOREN, C. *The Great Rehearsal: The Story of the Making and Ratifying of the Constitution of the United States.* 1948. Important addition to our history.

WARREN, C. *The Making of the Constitution.* 1928. Authoritative history.

WARREN, C. *The Supreme Court in United States History.* Rev. ed. 2 vols. 1937.

WATKINS, F. *The Political Tradition of the West.* 1948.

WHITE, L. D. *The Federalists.* 1948.

WINTHER, O. O. *The Great Northwest: A History.* 1947. Excellent survey.

WOOD, R. (Ed.). *The Pennsylvania Germans,* by Arthur D. Graeff, Walter M. Kollmorgen, and Clyde S. Stine. 1942.

WRIGHT, L. B. *The Atlantic Frontier: Colonial American Civilization, 1607–1763.* 1947. Readable study from a broad social, economic, and political point of view.

Index of Authors and Titles

963

Index of First Lines of Poems

Index of First Lines of Poems